THE HISTORY OF PARLIAMENT

THE HOUSE OF COMMONS 1558-1603

THE HISTORY OF PARLIAMENT

THE
HOUSE OF COMMONS
1558-1603

P. W. Hasler

III
MEMBERS
M–Z

PUBLISHED FOR THE HISTORY OF PARLIAMENT TRUST
BY HER MAJESTY'S STATIONERY OFFICE, LONDON
1981

Typeset by Computacomp (UK) Ltd
Fort William, Scotland
Printed in England for Her Majesty's Stationery Office by
Hobbs the Printers of Southampton
(1327) Dd290421 C20 8/81 G56-1323

Contributors

T.F.T.B.	T. F. T. Baker
K.B.	Kenneth Bartlett
S.T.B.	S. T. Bindoff
M.B.	Marjorie Blatcher
I.C.	Irene Cassidy
J.J.C.	J. J. Clarke
G.M.C.	G. M. Coles
P.C.	Patrick Collinson
A.D.	Alan Davidson
B.D.	Brian Dietz
A.H.D.	A. H. Dodd
P.S.E.	P. S. Edwards
J.P.F.	J. P. Ferris
N.M.F.	N. M. Fuidge
R.C.G.	R. C. Gabriel
J.J.G.	J. J. Goring
A.H.	Alan Harding
J.H.	Joan Hasler
P.W.H.	P. W. Hasler
A.D.K.H.	A. D. K. Hawkyard
J.C.H.	J. C. Henderson
P.H.	Patricia Hyde
W.J.J.	W. J. Jones
C.M.	Cecilia Meredith
H.M.	Helen Miller
A.M.M.	A. M. Mimardière
V.M.	Virginia Moseley
J.E.M.	J. E. Mousley
E.L.C.M.	E. L. C. Mullins
J.E.N.	J. E. Neale
M.N.	Mary Newhall
D.O.	Dorothy Owen
H.G.O.	H. G. Owen
M.A.P.	M. A. Phillips
M.R.P.	M. R. Pickering
M.I.R.	M. I. Redstone

A.B.R.   A. B. Rosen
A.G.R.S.   A. G. R. Smith
N.M.S.   N. M. Sutherland
R.J.W.S.   R. J. W. Swales
S.M.T.   S. M. Thorpe
R.V.   Roger Virgoe

Those articles to which no initials are appended are editorial redactions of drafts by Sir John Neale.

Abbreviations

lic.	licence
ld. lt.	lord lieutenant
m.	married
Mq.	Marquess
o.	only
PC	Privy Council
poss.	possibly
prob.	probably
rem.	removed
rest.	restored
ret.	retired
s.	son(s)
sec.	secretary
s.p.	*sine prole*
sis.	sister
suc.	succeeded
summ.	summoned
unm.	unmarried
v.p.	*vita parentis*
w.	wife
wid.	widow
yr.	younger
yst.	youngest

in the footnotes

Add.	Additional mss, British Library
APC	*Acts of the Privy Council*
Bath mss	Bath mss, Thynne Pprs.
BL	British Library
Bodl.	Bodleian Library, Oxford
Bull. IHR	*Bulletin, Institute of Historical Research*
CJ	*Commons Journals*
Collinson thesis	P. Collinson, 'The puritan classical movement in the reign of Elizabeth I' (London Univ. Ph.D. thesis, 1957)
Cott.	Cotton mss, British Library
CPR	*Calendar of Patent Rolls*
CSP Dom.	*Calendar of State Papers, Domestic*
CSP For.	*Calendar of State Papers, Foreign*
CSP Ire.	*Calendar of State Papers, Ireland*
CSP Scot.	*Calendar of State Papers, Scotland 1547–74* (4vv)
CSP Scot. ed Thorpe	*Calendar of State Papers, Scotland 1509–1603* (2vv)
CSP Span.	*Calendar of State Papers, Spain*
CSP Ven.	*Calendar of State Papers, Venice*
D'Ewes	*A Complete Journal of the ... Lords and ... Commons* collected by Sir Simonds D'Ewes (1682)

DKR	Deputy Keeper's Report
DNB	*Dictionary of National Biography*
DWB	*Dictionary of Welsh Biography*
Egerton	Egerton mss, British Library
EHR	*English Historical Review*
Fuidge thesis	N. M. Fuidge, 'The personnel of the House of Commons, 1563–7' (London Univ. M.A. thesis, 1950)
Gabriel thesis	R. C. Gabriel, 'Members of the House of Commons, 1586–7' (London Univ. M.A. thesis, 1954)
Harl.	Harleian mss, British Library
HL	Henry E. Huntington Library, San Marino, California
HMC	*Historical Manuscripts Commission*
Lansd.	Lansdowne mss, British Library
LJ	*Lords Journals*
Mort thesis	M. K. Mort, 'The personnel of the House of Commons in 1601' (London Univ. M.A. thesis, 1952)
Mousley thesis	J. E. Mousley, 'Sussex country gentry in the reign of Elizabeth' (London Univ. Ph.D. thesis, 1956)
N. and Q.	*Notes and Queries*
NLW	National Library of Wales
NRA	National Register of Archives
n.d.	no date
n.s.	new series
PCC	Prerogative Court of Canterbury
Petyt mss	Inner Temple, Petyt mss
Price thesis	M. G. Price, 'English borough representation, 1509–58' (Oxf. D.Phil. thesis, 1960)
PRO	Public Record Office
RO	Record Office
Roberts thesis	J. C. Roberts, 'The parliamentary representation of Devon and Dorset, 1559–1601' (London Univ. M.A. thesis, 1958)
Royal	Royal mss, British Library
Rylands	John Rylands Library, Manchester
Sloane	Sloane mss, British Library
Smith thesis	A. H. Smith, 'The Elizabethan gentry of Norfolk: office-holding and faction' (London Univ. Ph.D. thesis, 1959)
Stowe	Stowe mss, British Library
VCH	*Victoria County History*
Vis.	*Visitations*
UCNW	University College of North Wales

MEMBERS
M–Z

MACWILLIAM, Henry (c.1532–86), of Stambourne Hall, Essex and St. Martin-in-the-Fields, Mdx.

DORCHESTER	1571
LISKEARD	1572
APPLEBY	1584
CARLISLE	1586*

b. c.1532, 1st s. of Henry Macwilliam of Stambourne by his 2nd w. Ella or Elizabeth, da. and h. of Sir John Leyes. *m.* c.1558, Mary, da. and coh. of Richard Hill, wid. of Sir John Cheke†, 1s. 5da. *suc.* fa. 1539.
Keeper, Colchester castle Jan. 1559; gent. pens. by 1566; j.p. Essex from c.1569, Suff. from c.1580.[1]

'A gentleman of the court and of considerable quality', Macwilliam was said to have been of Irish extraction. Almost nothing is known of him before his marriage to the widowed Lady Cheke, a gentlewoman of Elizabeth's privy chamber. Two of her sons were in Cecil's household; and Cecil's first wife was Sir John Cheke's sister. Presumably it was Cecil's influence with the 2nd Earl of Bedford that brought about Macwilliam's return for Dorchester and Liskeard, but Macwilliam had a personal connexion at Dorchester, his sister Anne having married Arthur Stourton† of Overmoigne, some six miles from the borough. Macwilliam's patron at Appleby may have been Bedford's son-in-law, the Earl of Cumberland. Macwilliam would in any case have been known to Bedford through his 'especial good friend' Edmund Tremayne*, and he was one of Leicester's 22 noblemen and gentlemen who jousted before the Queen in November 1565 at the marriage of the Earl of Warwick to Bedford's daughter, Lady Anne Russell. His return for Carlisle, after Bedford's death, may have been due to its governor, Lord Scrope.[2]

Macwilliam was also on friendly terms with (Sir) Christopher Hatton I*. He witnessed a land settlement drawn up for Hatton in 1579, and there is ground for thinking that it was Hatton who had him appointed keeper of the Earl of Arundel in the Tower in April 1585. There was talk of replacing him in June but he was still at the Tower in April 1586, an early biographer of Arundel stating that 'almost a year or more' after the Earl's commitment to the Tower Macwilliam suggested to him that he might regain his freedom 'if he would but show so much conformity as to read [protestant] books'. Later in 1586 Hatton asked Macwilliam to examine Chidiock Tichbourne's wife Jane, one of the Babington conspirators.[3]

In addition to lands inherited from his father in Essex and Suffolk, Macwilliam had temporary possession of much of his wife's property. He was keeper of Colchester castle for life; in 1566 he, as gentleman pensioner, and his wife were granted 'for their service' the 31-year lease of lands in north Wales and Anglesey, and in the following year he received the lease of several duchy of Lancaster manors in Essex and Suffolk. Jointly with Robert Colshill* and two members of the Gorges family, he was granted in 1575 the office of writing and engrossing writs of subpoena in the court of Chancery. Custody of 'the house and mansion called St. James, Westminster' was granted to him and his wife in 1576, and in 1577 he and Colshill were granted the Queen's moiety of forfeitures for the unlawful transportation of corn.[4]

He died 27 Dec. 1586. His nuncupative will has no religious preamble. His duchy of Lancaster lands were to descend to his son Henry, who fought under Sir John Norris* in Brittany, and was killed in a duel in 1599, leaving no children. The other landed property went to his widow for life. The eldest of his five daughters married (Sir)

John Stanhope* and another Sir Christopher Hatton's cousin Edward Saunders and afterwards Goddard Pemberton*.[5]

[1] C142/61/67; Wright, *Essex*, i. 640; Morant, *Essex*, ii. 345, 357; *CPR*, 1558–60, p. 62; E. St. John Brooks, *Sir Christopher Hatton*, 52. [2] Strype, *Cheke*, 133–4; H. Nicolas, *Mems. Sir C. Hatton*, 207; Morant, ii. 357; *Vis. Dorset* (Harl. Soc. xx), 86. [3] Brooks, 256, 296, 389; Lansd. 45, f. 208 seq.; *Cath. Rec. Soc.* xxi. 117, 131, 316; *APC*, xiv. 56. [4] *CPR*, 1558–60, p. 62; 1563–6, p. 522; Lansd. 4, f. 143; Brooks, 52; Morant; Somerville, *Duchy*, i. 603; *CSP Dom.* Add. 1566–79, p. 486; PRO Index 16770 (18 Eliz.), f. 6. [5] PCC 26 Spencer; Copinger, *Suff. Manors*, i. 243; v. 258–9; Lansd. 78, ff. 138–9; *HMC Hatfield*, vi. 570; ix. 246; Rylands Eng. ms 311; Brooks, 69.

N.M.F.

MAINWARING, Sir Arthur (c.1525–90), of Ightfield, Salop.

SHROPSHIRE　　　　　　　　1559

b. c.1525, 1st. s. of Sir Richard Mainwaring by Dorothy, da. of Robert Corbet of Moreton Corbet, Salop. *educ.* G. Inn 1542. *m.* by 1557, Margaret, da. and coh. of Sir Randolph Mainwaring of Peover, Cheshire, 1s. George* 3da. Kntd. Oct. 1547. *suc.* fa. 1558.[1]

　　Capt. at Berwick Jan. 1558; j.p. Salop 1562, sheriff 1562–3, 1576–7, commr. musters by 1573, dep. lt. by 1587.[2]

Mainwaring was a considerable landowner, much of whose property lay outside Shropshire. The death of his father-in-law in September 1557 brought him extensive estates, from the Cheshire branch of his family, in Bradley, Stretton and elsewhere in that county, together with houses in the city of Chester. In Shropshire he owned the manor of Ightfield, a large house at Cotton, and land in Steele, Whitchurch and Whixall. Through his mother he was related to Sir Andrew Corbet, the other Shropshire knight of the shire in 1559.[3]

Soon after he came of age Mainwaring served at Berwick under John Dudley‡, Earl of Warwick, who knighted him there in October 1547. During the last year of Mary's reign he was in the north again for the Scottish campaign, in charge of 200 Shropshire men, and in May 1560 he took part in the attack on Leith.[4]

After this he settled in the 'rude and barbarous soil' of Shropshire, where he was an active official for nearly 30 years. The bishop of Chester classified him as favourable to the established church in 1564. Mainwaring was a deputy lieutenant at the time of the Armada, and in June 1588 sent a reprimand to officials of several hundreds in the county for not furnishing adequate information about arms and equipment. He died 2 Sept. 1590, having made his will that day, asking to be buried in Ightfield parish church. He left the greater part of his property to the executor and heir, George, who was then over 40. The only other members of the family mentioned were a daughter, Elizabeth, wife of Thomas Aston, her son Arthur, and Mainwaring's brother James of Cotton.[5]

[1] C142/124/188; E150/875/4; *Vis. Salop* (Harl. Soc. xxix), 348–9; *Vis. Cheshire* (Harl. Soc. xviii), 165; G. Ormerod, *Cheshire*, i. 482. [2] *APC*, vi. 244; Lansd. 56, f. 168 seq.; *HMC Foljambe*, 26. [3] C142/231/75; Ormerod. [4] *APC*, vi. 244; *CSP Scot.* 1547–63, p. 393. [5] *HMC 7th Rep.* 662; *Cam. Misc.* ix(3), p. 44; *Trans. Salop Arch. Soc.* (ser. 2), iii. 101, 104–5; PCC 49 Sainberbe; C142/231/75.

N.M.F.

MAINWARING, Edward (1577–1647), of Whitmore, Staffs.

NEWCASTLE-UNDER-LYME　　　　1601

b. 1577, 1st s. of Edward Mainwaring of Whitmore by Jane, da. of Matthew Craddock of Staffs. *educ.* Magdalen Hall, Oxf. 1594; M. Temple 1595. *m.* 1600, Sarah (*d.*1648), da. and coh. of John Stone, haberdasher, of Bow Churchyard, London, 2s. 1da. *suc.* fa. 1604.

　　Mayor, Newcastle-under-Lyme 1609, 1640, 1643; j.p. Staffs. 1615; sheriff 1645–6.

Whitmore was some four miles from Newcastle, for which borough Mainwaring was returned while still at the Middle Temple. He was a parliamentarian in the civil war, and died in 1647. The 1625 MP for Newcastle-under-Lyme was his son.

PCC 46 Dorset; J. C. Wedgwood, *Staffs. Parl. Hist.* (Wm. Salt Arch. Soc.), i.; *Vis. Staffs.* (Wm. Salt Arch. Soc. v. pt. 2), 207–8; *Wm. Salt Arch. Soc.* 1912, p. 287; T. Pape, *Newcastle-under-Lyme*, 50, 80, 268; *Committee at Stafford* (Staffs. Rec. Soc. ser. 4, i), 353.

J.J.C./J.P.F.

MAINWARING, George (bef. 1551–1628), of Ightfield, Salop.

SHROPSHIRE　　　　　　　　1572

b. bef. 1551, o.s. of Sir Arthur Mainwaring* by Margaret, da. and coh. of Sir Randolph Mainwaring of Peover, Cheshire. *educ.* Shrewsbury 1562; I. Temple 1565. *m.* Anne, da. of William More I* of Loseley, Surr., 4s. 1da. *suc.* fa. 1590. Kntd. c.1593.

　　J.p.q. Salop by 1593, custos rot. c.1593–6, dep. lt. by 1608; member, council in marches of Wales by 1617.

Mainwaring's wife came from a family high in Elizabeth's favour, so presumably his relative obscurity was self-imposed. Perhaps, like his father, he disliked travelling outside Shropshire; perhaps his health was poor. In May 1601 his brother-in-law (Sir) Thomas Egerton I* wrote to Sir Robert Cecil asking for the wardship of a son of 'George Mainwaring who is sickly'. Still, in James I's reign, when Ralph Eure*, 3rd Baron Eure was made president of the council in the marches of Wales, Mainwaring became one of his five deputy lieutenants in Shropshire, and later he was appointed a councillor in the marches. He died at Ightfield 5 May 1628, leaving no written will. Three witnesses testified that,

　　being visited with sickness, but of perfect and sound

memory, [he] did often and at several times since Michaelmas [1626] publish and declare his will and true meaning to be, that his eldest son Sir Arthur Mainwaring, knight, should have all his goods, chattels and estate whatsoever.

Sir Arthur, who was over 40 by the time he entered on his inheritance, was granted administration of the non-landed property in the month following his father's death. Sir George's inquisition post mortem, officially for Shropshire but listing also lands and houses in Cheshire and the city of Chester, was not taken until April 1631.

There was another George Mainwaring who held a minor Household post in the 1590s, travelled abroad with Sir Anthony Shirley, and died about 1612.

C142/231/75; *Vis. Salop* (Harl. Soc. xxix), 348–9; *Vis. Cheshire* (Harl. Soc. xviii), 165; *CSP Dom.* 1591–4, p. 144; SP14/33, f. 4; *Cal. Wynn Pprs.* 130; E351/1795, ff. 12v, 54; Sloane 105 passim; PCC 9 Capell; *HMC 7th Rep.* 662; *HMC Hatfield*, xi. 193; SP14/33, f. 4; PCC 58 Barrington; Wards 7/85/161.

N.M.F.

MALET, John (by 1520–70), of Woolleigh in Beaford, Devon.

PLYMOUTH　　　　　　　　1554 (Apr.)
BODMIN　　　　　　　　　1563

b. by 1520, 1st s. of Baldwin Malet (*d.* 1533) of St. Audries, Som. by his 2nd w. Anne, da. of Thomas Hatch of Woolleigh by Alice, da. of Sir John Bassett of Tehidy, Cornw. *educ.* I. Temple. *m.* Alice, da. of Anthony Monck of Great Potheridge, Devon, 4s. 4da.
　　Churchwarden, the Temple 1546–7; commr. relief, Devon 1550; j.p. by 1559; sheriff May–Nov. 1562, 1569–*d.*

Malet was a lawyer who had some connexion with the 2nd Earl of Bedford, who endeavoured to have him returned for Exeter in December 1562. Rebuffed here, he came in for Bodmin, where he had local connexions through his mother and sister, though Bedford probably obtained him the seat. Malet died 26 Oct. 1570 during his second shrievalty, before his account was rendered. His will was proved 14 Nov. It asks that he should be buried 'as becometh a Christian man without great pomp or cost of funerals'. Every poor man, woman or child who 'should happen to come' to the burial was to be given 2*d.* There were legacies to the prisoners in Exeter castle and elsewhere, to the poor of South Molton, Crediton and Torrington, where Malet owned land, and for the repair of his parish church. His son Malachias was the sole executor. The inquisition post mortem was taken in October 1571.

C142/55/38, 156/34; Vivian, *Vis. Devon*, 455; A. Malet, *Notices Malet Fam.* 49–57; *Som. Jnl.* xvi. 35–6; PCC 4 Hogen, 37 Lyon; E150/193/13.

A.D.K.H.

MALLARD, Thomas (*d.* 1614), of Hereford.

HEREFORD　　　　　　　　　1593

?s. of John Mallard, mayor of Hereford 1560, 1564, 1567, 1574. *m.* Alice, wid. of John Towers, 2s. 1da.
　　Mayor, Hereford 1591, alderman bef. 1614.

Mallard must have been a lawyer, though no record has been found of his admission to an inn of court. He lived and practised in Hereford, receiving fees from such companies as the cordwainers, and becoming prosperous enough to build himself a large town house. The sole reference to him found in the proceedings of the House of Commons is permission for him to depart, 21 Mar. 1593. In his will, dated 18 July and proved 12 Nov. 1614, he commended his soul 'into the hands of Almighty God ... trusting by the death and passion of Jesus Christ, to have remission and pardon' of his sins, and he divided his property between his wife and his sons, while his daughter, Mary Taylor, received only £5, Mallard 'desiring that by no means the same ... may be to the use of her most unthrifty husband'.

W. R. Williams, *Parl. Hist. Herefs.* 87; D'Ewes, 507; *Cam. Misc.* ix(3), p. 15; PCC 127 Lawe; J. Price, *Account of Hereford*, 258.

J.J.C.

MALLETT, Thomas (1546–80), of Enmore and Currypool, Som.

MINEHEAD　　　　　　　　　1571

b. 31 May 1546, 1st s. of Richard Mallett of Currypool by Elizabeth, da. of Sir Andrew Luttrell of Dunster Castle. *educ.* I. Temple 1560. *m.* by June 1566, Elizabeth, da. of Humphrey Colles†, half-sis. of John Colles*, Mallett's co-Member for Minehead, at least 2s. 2da. *suc.* fa. 1551.[1]
　　J.p. Som. by Sept. 1574,[2] sheriff 1576–7.

A ward of the lord chamberlain, Sir Thomas Darcy†, 1st Baron Darcy of Chiche, Mallett inherited large estates in Somerset, with property at Dewdon and South Molton in Devon, Wraxhall in Wiltshire, and Shirehampton and elsewhere in Gloucestershire. At the 1569 Somerset musters he was heavily assessed for the provision of armour, and in addition supplied three horses, two from Currypool park, where he was keeper. His return to the 1571 Parliament was no doubt due to his mother's relatives the Luttrells, who owned Dunster Castle near Minehead, and were patrons of the borough.[3]

Mallett's name occurs in only a few scattered references before his premature death. In November 1578 the Privy Council ordered him to help his step-father Sir George Speake* to settle a dispute involving a local attorney, Richard Cornish, and he was one of the three justices who in the following summer were asked to prevent the Taunton clothiers from disobeying the law by exploiting weavers and tuckers.[4]

Mallett died either 15 or 16 Oct. 1580. The will he made on his deathbed was proved 1 Feb. following. He left £1,000, plate and cattle, to his wife; 1,000 marks to each of his two daughters at their marriages or 18th birthdays; and £500, as well as lands in Gloucestershire and Somerset, to his younger son George. The heir, John, who was only about seven years old, was named as sole executor, with Sir George Speake, 'my brother John Colles' and two others as overseers. For some reason the taking of the inquisition post mortem was delayed for six years.[5]

[1] Wards 7/6/3, 27, 55; *Vis. Som.* ed. Weaver, 43, 45–6; PCC 4 Darcy, 24 Holney. [2] *Som. Rec. Soc.* li. 83. [3] *CPR*, 1550–3, p. 312; Wards 7/6/3, 27, 55; *Som. Rec. Soc.* xx. 248, 252. [4] *APC*, x. 406; xi. 126. [5] PCC 4 Darcy; C142/210/114, 214/233. The two inquisitions post mortem differ as to whether he died on 15 or 16 Oct. The will was drawn up on the first of these dates.

N.M.F.

MALLOCK, John (*d.* c. Jan. 1567), of Axmouth, Devon.

LYME REGIS 1553 (Oct.), 1554 (Apr.), 1554 (Nov.), 1559

s. of William Mallock of Axmouth by Agnes, da. of William Newbury of Stockland. *m.* (1) Matilda or Maud, da. of John Weston of Colyton, 2da.; (2) Elizabeth, da. of John Chaplyn of Taunton, Som., 3s. 1da.
Collector of customs, Poole 1553–60; alnager, Som. and Dorset by 1566.

Mallock leased property in Lyme and had other connexions with the borough sufficient to account for his repeated returns to Parliament. The only reference found to him in the known surviving records of the House of Commons is to leave of absence granted 18 Mar. 1559. His will, made 21 Dec. 1566, was proved by his son William on 28 Jan. 1567.

Vivian, *Vis. Devon*, 546; E122/122/9, 123/3; Lansd. 114, f. 125; Lyme Regis, fugitive pieces, 2, f. 16; *CJ*, i. 58; PCC 2 Stonard.

N.M.F.

MALLORY, John (*d.* 1619), of Hutton Park and Studley, Yorks.

THIRSK 1601
RIPON[1] 1604[2]

1st s. of Sir William Mallory* of Hutton Park and Studley by Ursula, da. of George Gale† of York. *educ.* L. Inn 1574. *m.* by 1578, Anne, da. of William, 2nd Baron Eure, 9s. 6da. *suc.* fa. Mar. 1603. Kntd. April 1603.[3]
J.p. Yorks. by 1597; commr. gaol delivery and j.p. Ripon and other liberties c. Sept. 1601; member, council in the north by 1603.[4]

During Elizabeth's reign Mallory was overshadowed by his father. Almost the only information found about his activities between his marriage and his return for Thirsk concerns the contested county election of 1597, when he supported Sir John Stanhope* and Sir Thomas Posthumous Hoby*, presumably leading the Mallory freeholders as heir of his father, who did not attend. He seems in his youth to have been a client of the Cecils: writing to Sir Robert in May 1603, complaining of rumours that Cecil was 'hardly conceived' against him, and insisting that he had 'more relied of your house than of any other of the nobility whomsoever'.[5]

The chief Mallory estate was only some 12 miles from Thirsk, and the family had considerable local influence, but Mallory may have owed his parliamentary election to the lord of the manor of Thirsk, the 6th Earl of Derby, whose 'high steward' he claimed to be in the course of the continuation of a quarrel which broke out at the end of Elizabeth's reign between the elder Mallory and Sir Stephen Proctor, a new justice of the peace in Yorkshire. On his father's death Mallory continued the dispute, complaining to the Earl of Salisbury in October 1605 about 'divers unkindnesses' between Proctor and others over Derby's property. Four years later the controversy was still not settled. Proctor, who claimed to have been appointed steward of Thirsk by Salisbury and Lady Derby, accused Mallory of attending the open fair in the town accompanied by 40 or 50 men, and turning out Proctor's deputy.[6]

Mallory died in 1619.[7]

[1] Browne Willis. [2] He sat on a committee, 30 Mar. 1604, *CJ*, i. 160. [3] *Vis. Yorks.* ed. Foster, 156–7; *Vis. Yorks.* (Harl. Soc. xvi), 196; Walbran, *Gen. and Biog. Mems. Lords of Studley in Yorks.* 11; *CSP Dom.* 1598–1601, p. 61. [4] *HMC Hatfield*, vii. 416; Reid, *Council of the North*, 496; C181/9. [5] A. Gooder, *Parl. Rep. Yorks.* ii. (Yorks. Arch. Soc. rec. ser. xcvi), 124; *HMC Hatfield*, xv. 82. [6] *HMC Hatfield*, xii. 161; xvii. 445; *CSP Dom.* 1603–10, pp. 494, 539; Reid, loc. cit. [7] C142/708/102.

N.M.S.

MALLORY, Sir William (*d.* 1603), of Hutton Park and Studley, Yorks.

YORKSHIRE 1584

2nd s. and h. of Sir William Mallory of Hutton Park and Studley by Jane, da. of Sir John Norton of Norton. *m.* Ursula, da. of George Gale† of York, at least 5s. inc. John* 4da. Kntd. by 1560.[1]
J.p. Yorks. (N. Riding) from 1559, (W. Riding) from 1561, (E. Riding) from 1583; member, council in the north from 1582; sheriff, Yorks. 1592–3; dep. lt. Yorks. (N. Riding) by 1596; high steward, Ripon from c.1570; member, high commission, province of York 1599.[2]

Mallory, related to Cardinal Allen through the Conyers family, had a recusant mother, wife, sister and brother. His heir was suspected of sheltering priests, and another son and two daughters became outright Catholics. Two other sons, however, became Anglican dignitaries: one archdeacon of Richmond and dean of Chester, another an ecclesiastical lawyer in Durham. Mallory himself was ostentatiously loyal. In 1560 he was one of the English captains 'as best served' under Lord Grey in Scotland, and was evidently knighted during the campaign. At the time of the northern rebellion, he was one of the first to inform the Earl of Sussex, lord president of the north, of the 'bruits' in Yorkshire, and also warned him to take heed for his own person. Mallory and 'divers other honest gentlemen' suddenly left their houses. As they would not have done this without great cause, their action served as a warning of impending trouble to those who were already on their guard. In 1569, when Queen Mary was moved from Bolton castle to Tutbury, it was suggested that she might stop at Mallory's house, one mile from Ripon. In 1570 Sussex recommended Mallory for the office of high steward because he had 'truly served the Queen, from the first suspicion of the rebellion', but it is not clear when he was actually appointed. Mallory's relative Sir William Ingleby was also recommended for reward, because together, Sussex informed the Queen, they had delivered him more intelligence than any other, and they were honest and loyal. If she rewarded them, they would be comforted, she would be truly served, and it would stop them from further suit.[3]

The 3rd Earl of Huntingdon, the next president of the council in the north, wrote to Walsingham in 1577 that Mallory was one of the four 'most fit' persons to be added to the council. His name was included in the commission of 1582. As knight of the shire for Yorkshire he would have been on the subsidy committee 24 Feb. 1585. He also took charge of the bill for the better observing of the Sabbath day (27 Nov. 1584), and was named to a conference with the Lords 15 Feb. 1585 concerning fraudulent conveyances.[4]

It was thought in 1581 that Sir William Mallory and Sir Robert Stapleton*, would be able, 'by their tenants, kinsfolk and friends', to furnish 200 horse, and in 1588 Huntingdon declared Mallory 'a very fit man' to lead 100 horse, 'being himself well furnished with horse and geldings'.[5]

In 1593 Mallory had a quarrel with Sir Edward Yorke, a matter which seems to have been connected with the murder of one of Mallory's sons by one of Yorke's servants. The parties evidently appealed to the Earl of Essex, whom Mallory went to see at Richmond. Yorke therefore wrote to Essex craving that he might not 'utterly be beggared', which was all Mallory's 'bloody and greedy mind doth thirst after'. The quarrel seems to have dragged on, since Mallory was summoned by the Privy Council in February 1596, upon which occasion the 'unkindness and difference' between him, his sons and Sir Edward Yorke were ended, to the satisfaction of all parties. The Privy Council was anxious that Mallory, a gentleman 'of good reputation and calling' should not suffer on account of their having sent for him. They therefore thought good to inform the council in the north and the archbishop of York that 'the cause of his sending for up grew upon no evil opinion had of him in any sort'.[6]

Mallory supported Sir Thomas Posthumous Hoby* and Sir John Stanhope* in the contested county election of 1597. In 1599 he was reported to be one of those on the council in the north who had become 'aged and weak and cannot conveniently attend any service'. In spite of this, he wrote to Cecil in August 1599 to offer his services to the Queen because it was reported in the north that foreign forces were to be employed against her. Again, in 1601, upon hearing of the 'conspiracies and wicked treasons intended against the sacred person of our most gracious Queen', he wrote to Cecil to offer his life and all he possessed. He expressed his willingness to repair to the court either privately or 'with such company as you, from her Highness, shall direct me'. Mallory was not, in fact, too aged or ill to make the journey from Yorkshire to Westminster, and he went to court in the summer of 1600, apparently hoping to obtain some reward for his past services. In January 1601 he wrote to Cecil of the 'gracious speeches' the Queen had made him at that time. But she was then so heavily charged with the cost of defence 'as she must for a time restrain her bountiful hand from rewarding her servants, giving me this comfort, that she would not be forgetful of the duty and service she had always found in me'. Mallory wished to know 'how her Majesty's disposition resteth at this time'. So far as is known he received no reward. In October 1602 Mallory again wrote to Cecil, this time to complain of Sir Stephen Proctor, who had brought a case against him in the Star Chamber, charging him with negligence in enforcing the religious laws, and with corruption in connexion with the musters. Mallory denied the charges and asked for satisfaction against Proctor. This was not 'for pride', but because he had been a justice of the peace for 44 years, was 'her Majesty's sworn servant', and had been on the council in the north for 20 years, 'in all which time my loyalty and service have been known'. He therefore desired justice in order to be 'enabled to serve her Majesty the better'. But the days of his service were already numbered, and he was buried on 22 Mar. 1603. His will, which is at York, was dated 15 June 1586. His wife Ursula and his son and heir John were the executors. He provided for his family but does not appear to have possessed extensive lands.[7]

[1] *Vis. Yorks.* (Harl. Soc. xvi), 195–6; *CSP Scot.* 1547–63, p. 438; Walbran, *Lords of Studley in Yorks.* 9. [2] *HMC Hatfield*, ix. 396; xii. 452–3; *CSP Dom.* Add. 1580–1625, p. 80; 1595–7, p. 167; 1598–1601, p. 61. [3] H. Aveling, 'W. Riding Recusants 1558–1790', *Procs. Leeds Phil. and Lit. Soc.* x(6); J. J. Cartwright, *Chapters in Yorks. Hist.* 68; *CSP Scot.* 1547–63, p. 438; 1563–9, p. 605; Gooder, *Parl. Rep. Yorks.* ii. 30; *CSP Dom.* Add. 1566–79, pp. 91, 92, 93, 181–2. [4] *CSP Dom.* Add. 1566–79, p. 516; 1580–1625, p. 80; D'Ewes, 333, 349; Lansd. 43, anon. jnl. f. 171. [5] *CSP Scot.* v. 585; *Cal. Border Pprs.* i. 324. [6] *HMC Hatfield*, iv. 285; xiv. 144; *APC*, xxv. 192, 261. [7] *HMC Hatfield*, vii. 416; ix. 242, 303; xi. 18, 76–7; xii. 452–3; Walbran, 9.

N.M.F.

MAN, Edward (c.1550–1622), of Poole, Dorset.[1]

POOLE	1589, 1593, 1604

b. c.1550. *m.* Eleanor, 2s. 4da.

Freeman, Poole 1585, mayor 1589–90, collector of revenues 1600–2.

The son of a Poole merchant, Man was himself granted the freedom of the borough in 1585, when he obtained dispensation from performing any office in the town for six years, and freedom after that from becoming water-bailiff or constable. Made mayor nevertheless in 1589, he began to keep a book of the staple in which were entered copies of all the documents to which the town seal was affixed. When he visited London in 1589 he was given a list of instructions, signed by Robert Gregory* and other townsmen, and addressed 'to our trusty and well beloved mayor', and £30 to spend (more could be spent by the advice of the recorder) 'praying [him] to be a good husband for the corporation'. He was asked 'to return as soon as conveniently' he could. It is not clear whether this journey was combined with that required for his attendance at the Parliament, or whether he made two visits to London in that year. Early in 1592 the corporation again sent him to London, once more with a 'remembrance'. He twice represented his borough in Parliament during the Elizabethan period.

Man died 22 Dec. 1622. Apart from his property in Poole, he owned houses at Weymouth and some lands at Frome Bellot. In his will, dated 15 Sept. 1622, he left bequests to his servants, to the church and poor of Poole, and to Nicholas Jeffreys, 'preacher of God's word' there, for a funeral sermon. He left his 'well-beloved wife' Eleanor the residue and appointed her executrix, with his 'cousins' Richard Swayne and Anthony Weekes overseers. The will mentions no children. Man asked to be buried at Poole, where his widow set up a memorial bearing the inscription:

This merchant Man purchased a jewel rare,
When to gain Christ (God man) he took great care.[2]

[1] This biography is based upon the Roberts thesis. [2] Hutchins, *Dorset*, i. 47, 31; Poole recs., bk. of the staple, audit bk.; *Som. and Dorset N. and Q.* vi. 171, 315; *Dorset Nat. Hist. and Arch. Soc. Procs.* liii. 82–3; PCC 7 Swann.

P.W.H.

MAN, John (*d.*1569), of Bolingbroke and Sutton St. James, Lincs.

MONTGOMERY BOROUGHS	1559

s. of John Man of Bolingbroke by Margaret, da. of William Dobbyn of Gedney. *m.* Audrey, da. of Richard Ogle of Pinchbeck, 2s. 2da.

J.p. Lincs. (Holland and Lindsey) 1559; duchy of Lancaster feodary, Lincs. from 1559; dep. receiver, honour of Bolingbroke 1560.

Of a number of contemporary namesakes, including a messenger and groom of the chamber and another courtier who served Henry VIII, Edward VI and Mary by examining fortifications and provisioning the army, the most likely to have been the MP was the Lincolnshire gentleman whose particulars appear above. Little enough is known of him. In 1554 he was described as citizen and grocer of London, and by 1559 he had returned to his native county to assume a place in the local administration of the duchy of Lancaster. He had few interests outside the county and his friends and relatives were members of local families. John Skinner of Thorpe by Wainfleet, whose deputy as receiver of the honour of Bolingbroke Man was, was a friend and overseer of Man's will, while Skinner's son Vincent – a future secretary to Lord Burghley – later married Man's widow. But through his wife's family, the Ogles of Pinchbeck, Man was connected with a wider circle. Audrey Man was the niece of Sir Anthony Cooke*, the father-in-law of Sir William Cecil, and it was probably to this relationship that Man owed his return to Parliament in 1559 through Edward Herbert I*, who at one time or another was associated with Cecil, the 2nd Earl of Bedford, and Sir Ambrose Cave*, Man's superior as chancellor of the duchy of Lancaster.

Man died in June 1569, a few weeks after making his will. He endowed his younger daughter, Frances, with land in Sutton St. Edmund and Sutton St. James, and made small bequests to two godsons, to his brother, to his brother-in-law Thomas Ogle, and to Adlard Welby, a connexion of his wife's who later became his daughter's father-in-law. The disposition of the lands must have been made earlier, for in the will his surviving son Richard received only a seal ring. Man appointed his wife, Audrey, sole executrix, bequeathing to her all his goods and chattels. The supervisors were John Skinner and Man's brother-in-law, Nicholas Ogle*. The will was proved in February 1570 by Vincent Skinner on behalf of the widow.

Lincs. Peds. (Harl. Soc. li), 630, 730–1; *Vis. Essex* (Harl. Soc. xiii), 39; *DWB*, 348; Read, *Cecil*, 179, 211, 234; *CPR*, 1553–4, pp. 36, 445; 1554–5, p. 109; 1563–6, p. 24; Somerville, *Duchy*, i. 580, 582; *CSP Dom.* Add. 1566–79, pp. 48–9; PCC 6 Lyon.

I.C.

MANNERS, George (c.1569–1623), of Haddon Hall, Derbys. and Uffington, Lincs.

NOTTINGHAM	1589
DERBYSHIRE	1593

b. c.1569, 1st s. of John Manners* of Haddon Hall by Dorothy, da. and coh. of Sir George Vernon, bro. of Roger II*. *educ.* Camb.[1]; I. Temple 1586. *m.* c.1593, Grace, da. of Sir Henry Pierrepont of Holme Pierrepont, Notts., 4s. 5da. Kntd. 23 Apr. 1603; *suc.* fa. June 1611.

J.p. Derbys. temp. Jas. I, custos rot. by 1617, dep. lt. by 1621.

An important influence on Manners during his early years was his uncle, Roger Manners I*, a younger brother of Henry, 2nd Earl of Rutland. When not at the university or the Inner Temple, the young man spent much of his time at his uncle's house at Uffington, where he studied reluctantly and rode willingly. 'God keep him from falling', his uncle commented on his horsemanship; as to his studies, he should

> learn to write better and ... rise earlier in a morning. For two hours' study in the morning is better than four in the afternoon.

His uncle's advice that George should marry the daughter of Sir Henry Darcy* was ignored in favour of the dowager Countess of Shrewsbury's candidate, her grand-daughter Grace Pierrepont.

Manners owed his return for Nottingham in 1589 and for Derbyshire in the next Parliament to family influence. The Manners had strong connexions with Nottingham, where they normally held the office of constable of the castle. Manners is not mentioned by name in the records of the House, but he may have attended two committees in 1593 concerning the subsidy (26 Feb.) and legal business (9 Mar.) to which he was appointed by virtue of his position as knight of the shire. By the end of Elizabeth's reign he had begun to participate in county administration, and with his father and others he proclaimed James's succession at Chesterfield, on 29 Mar. 1603. Three years later, when his father was seriously ill, George was recommended to succeed him as custos rotulorum. Sir John, however, survived until 1611, when his son inherited the extensive Derbyshire estates and property in Nottinghamshire. Manners himself died 23 Apr. 1623 and was buried in the same church, at Bakewell. An inventory of goods at his home at Haddon, taken on his death, showed a total value of £1,270 3s. 4d. Of his four sons, only the second, John, survived him, becoming in 1641 the 8th Earl of Rutland on the death of his cousin the 7th Earl.[2]

[1] Manners's presence at Cambridge, presumably at the university, is referred to in *HMC Rutland*, i. 282. This letter should probably be dated 1584/5. [2] J. C. Cox, *Notes on Derbys. Churches*, ii. 26–7; D'Ewes, 474, 496; *HMC Rutland*, i. passim; ii. 343; Lodge, *Illus.* iii(2), 189; PCC 82 Wood; C142/320/66, 401/128; *CP*, xi. 263.

B.D.

MANNERS, John (bef. 1535–1611), of Shelford, Notts. and Haddon Hall, Derbys.

NOTTINGHAMSHIRE 1559, 1563

b. bef. 1535, 2nd s. of Thomas, 1st Earl of Rutland, by his 2nd w. Eleanor, da. of Sir William Paston of Paston, Norf.; bro. of Roger I* and Sir Thomas*. *educ.* St. John's, Camb. 1549; I. Temple 1554. *m.* Dorothy, da. and coh. of Sir George Vernon† of Haddon, 2s. George* and Roger II* 1da. Kntd. 20 Apr. 1603.

J.p. Notts. from c.1559–c.74, 1583–c.92, Derbys. from c.1574, custos rot. from 1580, sheriff 1575–6, 1588–9, 1597–8, dep. lt. from 1585; c.j. Sherwood forest by 1591.[1]

During his early years Manners lived first with his family at Belvoir Castle, and later at Shelford. His Nottinghamshire estates were not large, but his social position was sufficient to ensure his election as knight of the shire. He was probably the Mr. Manners who was appointed to the succession committee 31 Oct. 1566 and the Mr. Manerie who was put in charge of the committee concerning armour 3 Dec. 1566. Manners made a fortunate marriage, and when his father-in-law's estates were divided between the coheirs, he and his wife came into most of the Derbyshire property, including Haddon Hall. Manners was living there by 1571, and for the remaining 40 years of his life was one of the most prominent, active and wealthy gentlemen of the county, though he never represented it in Parliament.[2]

Manners was supported in the county by his brother-in-law and close friend, George, 6th Earl of Shrewsbury, who appointed Manners a deputy when he became lord lieutenant of Derbyshire in 1585. The other deputy lieutenant was Sir John Zouche†. Manners, the Earl explained, was appointed 'for trusting', Zouche 'to please others'. When, in the following year, Zouche died and Shrewsbury's attention was distracted by illness and family feuds, Manners controlled the county administration. He acted as collector of the 1589 loan, for which he was excused his own payment. On Shrewsbury's death in 1590, Manners lost his pre-eminence, and his relations with Gilbert, the 7th Earl, who succeeded as lord lieutenant, were cooler, though the two men continued to work together.[3]

In the later years of his life Manners rarely left Haddon, 'almost out of the world, where I hear little and see less'. He controlled profitable lead mining operations which involved him in the usual friction over patents, and finally in lawsuits brought by Sir John Zouche, Richard Wennesley* and others. 'I fear your over-travail', his brother Roger wrote in 1590, 'and you fear my idleness ... Mend you the one, and by God's grace I will mend the other.' In 1599, illness and advancing age persuaded him to ask Shrewsbury to appoint more deputy lieutenants to share the burden of county administration.[4]

Manners died at Haddon on 4 June 1611 and was buried with his wife in Bakewell church, in the chapel where Sir George Vernon's tomb also lay. His will, drawn up in February 1609, made bequests to the poor, including £30 to provide six beds in the almshouses at Bakewell and an annuity of £22 to the governors and poor of St. John's hospital in the same village. Gifts of money and ornaments were made to his daughter, her husband and son, and to the Earl of Rutland. Whitwell manor, which he had acquired from the Whalley family in 1592, he bequeathed to his second son Roger, together with furniture and £500. Haddon went to the heir, George.[5]

[1] J. C. Cox, *Three Cents. Derbys. Annals*, i. 23; *HMC Rutland*, i. 120–3; ii. 294. [2] *CSP Dom.* 1547–80, pp. 440–1; *HMC Rutland*, i. 94; D'Ewes, 127; *CJ*, i. 79; J. C. Cox, *Notes on Derbys. Churches*, ii. 24–5. [3] Coll. of Arms, Talbot mss, transcribed by G. R. Batho, G, ff. 15–18, 78, 409; I, f. 1; *HMC Rutland*, i. 120 passim; E. Lodge, *Illus.* iii(2), 42 et passim; Cox, *Derbys. Annals*, i. 150 seq. [4] *HMC Rutland*, i. 118, 140, 209, 210, 287; M. B. Donald, *Eliz. Monopolies*, 154–5, 163, 170–4; Lansd. 31, f. 166 seq.; Lodge, iii (2), pp. 118, 138. [5] PCC 82 Wood; C142/320/66.

B.D.

MANNERS, Oliver (c.1581–1613), of Belvoir, Lincs. and Pillerton, Warws.

GRANTHAM 1601

b. c.1581, 4th s. of John, 4th Earl of Rutland, by Elizabeth, da. of Francis Charlton of Apley Castle, Salop. *educ.* Christ's, Camb. 1594–5; I. Temple 1598. *unm.* Kntd. 1603.

Jt. (with cos. Thomas Savage) clerk of Star Chamber in reversion 1604; King's carver 1604–5.

Manners was presumably returned for Grantham through the intervention of his great-uncle, Roger Manners I*, to whose custody the 5th Earl of Rutland, Oliver Manners's eldest brother, had been committed after his part in the Essex rebellion. As his two other brothers, George and Francis, were also in disgrace, Oliver was one of the few possible candidates from the Manners family. He was knighted and given a job by James I but on 10 Feb. 1606 Sir Edward Hoby wrote:

> Sir Oliver Manners is said to have been made privy to these late treasons [Gunpowder Plot], but utterly detesting the fact; and, having a little good nature, though very Popish, being the King's carver, would not reveal it, but sold his place and went over.

Manners had in fact been converted to Catholicism by the Jesuit John Gerard, and his departure for the Continent was with the King's permission. When his intimacy with the conspirators came to light, James ordered Rutland to withhold Manners's allowance, but in 1608 his licence to travel abroad was renewed. It was rumoured that year that he had become a Jesuit. Finally permitted to return home in 1610, Manners remained abroad, was ordained to the priesthood at Rome, 5 Apr. 1611, and returned to England in 1612, probably on hearing of the death of his eldest brother: on 11 Aug. Chamberlain reported that Manners had 'new come out of France'. He spent the last year of his life with his two surviving brothers, dying in London in late July or early August 1613. He was embalmed at Belvoir, and buried in Bosworth parish church with his ancestors.

CP, xi. 259 seq.; Collins, *Peerage*, 470 seq.; *HMC Rutland*, i. passim; ii. 352, 353; iv. passim; *HMC Hatfield*, xvi. 32; xvii. 499; xviii. 313;

CSP Dom. Add. 1580–1625, p. 468; 1603–10, pp. 60, 176, 260, 261, 429, 526, 610; 1611–18, pp. 83, 199; T. Birch, *Court and Times Jas. I.* 49–50; J. Gerard, *Autobiog. of an Elizabethan*, tr. Caraman, 185–7; PCC 100 Capell.

S.M.T.

MANNERS, Roger I (c.1536–1607), of Uffington, Lincs.

GRANTHAM 1563

b. c.1536, 3rd s. of Thomas Manners, 1st Earl of Rutland, by his 2nd w. Eleanor, da. of Sir William Paston of Paston, Norf.; bro. of John* and Sir Thomas*. *educ.* Corpus, Camb. 1550. *unm.*

Esquire of the body to Queen Mary and Queen Elizabeth; constable of Nottingham castle during the minority of 3rd Earl of Rutland Dec. 1563.

When Manners reached early manhood he was sent to sea under the Lord Admiral, whose good opinion he won. He promised to apply himself 'to the understanding of the marine causes and affairs', which he did for most of Mary's reign, probably taking part in the battle of St. Quentin. Doubtless through his mother, who was popular with Queen Mary, he obtained the post of esquire of the body, and when Elizabeth came to the throne he gave up the sea for the court, where he spent much of the rest of his life. At first, he was continually attendant on the Queen, but in 1583, in respect of his good services, the Queen relieved him of most of his duties, and permitted him to attend only when he wished, or at her express command.

Numerous letters from Manners to his family survive. As well as providing an intimate picture of court life during the reign, they give a detailed insight into his character. Never married – the endorsement 'concerning a match with Roger Manners's daughter', on a letter from Lord Morley, certainly misinterprets the contents – Manners was an affectionate brother and uncle. In many ways, despite his constant reiteration that he wished to be a countryman and 'follow the plough', he was a typical courtier: pliable, amusing, ready with tongue and pen, cynical and engagingly lazy; a keen sportsman, always ready to curtail a letter if called to the pleasure of the chase; an open handed host, ever anxious to entertain visitors in his 'poor cottage' at Uffington, where the hospitality dispensed was much remarked on.

In 1572, when suspected of having favoured the late Duke of Norfolk, he deplored 'popish idolatry', and it is apparent that his religious attitude depended entirely on his loyalty to the Crown. In 1603, when the Queen lay dying, he wrote to his brother John: 'I will not go about to make kings, nor seek to pull down any; only will obey such as be chosen and crowned'. In 1601, when his great-nephews, the 5th Earl of Rutland and the Earl's brothers, were involved in the Essex rising, he wished that they 'had never been born, than so horrible offence offend so gracious a sovereign to the overthrow of their house and name for ever, always before loyal'. His distress was such that the Queen sent Sir John Stanhope* to comfort him, and Robert Cecil wrote him letters of encouragement. It was doubtless as a token of the Queen's confidence in his loyalty that Rutland was finally committed to his custody – a responsibility of which Manners soon tired.

There is no reason to doubt that this 'old experimented courtier' was sincere when, summing up his knowledge for his niece, Bridget, on her entrance to the Queen's service, he advised:

> First and above all things ... forget not to use daily prayers to the Almighty God to endue you with his grace ... apply yourself wholly to the service of her Majesty, with all meekness, love and obedience, wherein you must be diligent, secret and faithful. To your elders and superiors [be] of reverent behaviour; to your equals and fellow servants, civil and courteous; to your inferiors ... be no meddler in the cause of others. [Let] your speech and endeavours ever bend to the good of all and to the hurt of none.

After sitting for the local borough of Grantham in 1563, Manners seems neither to have sought election to Parliament himself nor, in general, to have influenced his nephew the 5th Earl's patronage. However, in 1601 he may have played a part in the return of Oliver Manners at Grantham and did intervene to have Henry Capell II brought in at Boston, a borough which had never before returned a Rutland candidate. But at the time of this election, several members of the family, as well as the 5th Earl himself, were in disgrace, and it looks as though Manners was exercising the family patronage on their behalf.

Under James I Manners lived in retirement, either at Enfield or at his town house in the Savoy. He had done well out of royal bounty, and had augmented his portion as a younger son with several manors and chantry lands, as well as leases. These he settled in his last years on various of his nephews and great-nephews. The manor of Long Bennington went to the 5th Earl of Rutland, Fleet Fitzwaters and Holbeach and chantry property to his namesake Roger Manners II*, and Pillerton to Oliver Manners; other tithes, and rectories and leases were left to his nephew Charles's young sons. He also made careful arrangements that enough of his property should be in the hands of his executors for a sufficient time to yield sizeable dowries for some of his neices, on a scale with the dowry he had given one during his lifetime. Before his death he had also given generously to the building and upkeep of Corpus Christi, Cambridge. Manners died 11 Dec. 1607, and was buried in the tomb in Uffington church which he had long ago erected for himself and his younger brother, Oliver, who had died in 1563. His soul he bequeathed to the Trinity who in the person of Jesus Christ had redeemed him 'from the tyranny of the Devil, to be one of the society and elect company of heaven by the only merit of [his] dreadful passion'.

This biography is based on L. C. John, 'Roger Manners, Elizabethan Courtier', *HL Quarterly*, xii. 57–84; *HMC Rutland*, i, ii, iv. passim; *HMC Hatfield*, passim; Lodge, *Illus.* passim; PCC 95 Huddleston; Lansd. 15, f.178; 46, f. 124; 77, f. 71 seq.; 78, f. 24; 79, f. 150; 80, f. 2; 89, f. 33; 108, ff. 5, 7, 9; *APC*, xxxii. 340; *CSP Dom.* 1601–3, p. 89; C142/303/137, 146; 304/19; *CPR*, 1563–6, p. 45; Coll. of Arms, Talbot mss, transcribed by G. R. Batho.

S.M.T.

MANNERS, Roger II (c.1575–1632), of Whitwell, Derbys.

EAST RETFORD	1601

b. c.1575, 2nd s. of John Manners* and bro. of George*. *unm.* Kntd. 1615.
    Sheriff, Derbys. 1618–19, j.p. by 1618.

When the writs for the new Parliament were issued in September 1601, Roger, 5th Earl of Rutland, and two of his brothers were still in disgrace for their part in the abortive Essex rising, so leaving the way open for junior members of the family to be returned for boroughs where Rutland normally had influence. Manners received from his great-uncle and namesake the manors of Fleet Fitzwaters and Holbeach, Lincolnshire, and, from his father the manor of Whitwell, Derbyshire. He was thus endowed with a sufficient estate to take his place as a country gentleman. He died in 1632, asking to be buried in Whitwell church, with as 'small funeral pomp as may be, having respect to my birth and calling'.

Collins, *Peerage*, i. 469; PCC 103 Audley; C142/304/19, 523/70(2); *HMC Rutland*, i. passim; iv. 225; *CSP Dom.* 1629–31, pp. 522, 543, 544; 1631–3, p. 179.

S.M.T.

MANNERS, Sir Thomas (1537–91), of Nottingham Castle.

NOTTINGHAM	1572
NOTTINGHAMSHIRE	1584, 1586

b. 1537, 4th s. of Thomas Manners, 1st Earl of Rutland, by his 2nd w. Eleanor, da. of Sir William Paston of Paston, Norf.; bro. of John* and Roger I*. *educ.* St. John's, Camb. 1549 (impubes). *m.* 1571, Theodosia, da. of Sir Thomas Newton, at least 2s. 4da. Kntd. 1570.[1]
    J.p.q. Notts. by 1583 to at least 1587; constable, Nottingham castle and c.j. Sherwood forest 1588; steward of Mansfield.[2]

The career of Thomas Manners exhibits some of the qualities of action, adventure and loyal service which have been held to typify the age in which he lived. Known to his relatives as 'lusty' Manners, he rejected both country and court life – preferred by his brothers John and Roger – for the career of a soldier. Unfortunately he coupled his military fame with a disastrous inability to handle his own affairs.[3]

His family background was distinguished. His father had raised the family to the front rank of the nobility by his devotion to Henry VIII, and could also claim royal blood, inherited from Edward IV's sister. Thomas's brother, Henry, succeeded to the earldom of Rutland and two of his sisters were married to the Earls of Westmorland and Shrewsbury. Though only a fourth son, he possessed, therefore, advantages.[4]

Manners took to soldiering soon after he came down from Cambridge without a degree. There are constant references to his long and honourable service, but little is known in detail of his activities. One former comrade in arms wished that Sir Thomas could be a captain overseas again with 2,000 men and himself as his lieutenant, both unmarried. In the early years of Elizabeth's reign, he saw service in Ireland, for which he received an annuity of £30, but it is his part in the Scottish campaign of 1570 which is best documented. Together with Robert Constable* he commanded 500 men raised in London to join this punitive expedition against some of the border lords. He was present at the siege and destruction of Hamilton castle where the leader of the expedition, Sir William Drury, committed the Duchess of Chastelherault to his personal care. From there the army advanced to Edinburgh where, in anticipation of suspected treachery, Manners was sent forward with two bands of foot soldiers to seize one of the gates, a foray which he brought off skilfully. It was during this short campaign that he was knighted by the Earl of Sussex at Berwick.[5]

Ten years later he was appointed to serve in Ireland once more, with the command of 300 foot raised in London, but at the last moment – for what reason is not known – the Privy Council countermanded the order 'as the said Sir Thomas shall not be at this time employed'. In the critical year 1588 his services were called upon again, not only as leader of the militia of his own county, but in command of a thousand troops raised in Surrey to help resist Parma's expected invasion. The Rutland papers have occasional references to his service elsewhere in the intervening years, but no details are given.[6]

Though his family's principal residence was at Belvoir castle in Leicestershire, Manners came to be associated more with Nottinghamshire, to which he had moved by 1562. At one time he is found living at the White Friars in Nottingham, but by 1580 he was in residence at the castle. His brother Henry, 2nd Earl of Rutland, had been granted in Edward VI's reign the hereditary titles of constable of Nottingham castle and chief justice of Sherwood forest, and these were given to Sir Thomas in 1588 during the minority of the 5th Earl. He owned land in several parts of the county and his father had left him a manor at Hemingbrough just over the border in Yorkshire. The Queen showed her gratitude for his service by occasional grants of land. Thus he received property confiscated from the Northern rebels and, later, the reversion to St.

Sepulchre's chapel, York. He was also given a reversion of the lease of the manor of Frodsham, Cheshire, but this may have been an exchange only.[7]

His apparently friendly relations with the Nottingham authorities explain his return for the borough in 1572, while his family's local influence was obviously sufficient to gain him the county seat on two occasions. In the 1584 Parliament, Manners sat on two committees concerned with religious matters (27 Nov., 16 Dec.). The second of these was the important body which petitioned the Lords to support their plea for improvements in the qualifications of ministers of the Church. Though the committee was dominated by puritans there is nothing to suggest that Manners was of their persuasion – indeed the general pattern of his life makes it unlikely. On 24 Feb. 1585 he served on the subsidy committee. On 4 Nov. 1586 he was a member of the committee which pressed for the execution of Mary Queen of Scots; the following year he and his wife were among the official mourners at her funeral service in Peterborough cathedral. It is possible that he had some contact with Mary during her long imprisonment in the care of his brother-in-law, the Earl of Shrewsbury. As first knight for Nottinghamshire he was entitled to attend the subsidy committee on 22 Feb. 1587.[8]

Between his campaigns Manners lived on his Nottinghamshire estates. Three successive earls of Rutland died young, leaving in each case a youthful successor dependent on the experience of older members of the family. Thomas was one of those expected to fill this role – he even offered 'the carcase of a true gentleman most readily to be employed in your service' to one of them – but he proved an inept adviser, and the last years of his life were increasingly burdened by ill-health and debt. As early as 1558 the then Countess of Rutland helped to settle a bill for him, and as time passed it became increasingly apparent that, either through extravagance or incompetence, he was incapable of living within his income. Time after time his brothers rallied to his support, Roger on one occasion offering to sell his house at Lincoln to help him out of his difficulties. His nephew, the 4th Earl, also granted him an annuity. In 1570 his weakness might have got him into serious trouble. While on the Scottish expedition Manners and Price, his lieutenant, were charged with exacting money and armour from 'the poor men of Worcestershire' and the Privy Council told the Earl of Sussex to withhold part of Manners's wages until the money was repaid and to order him to return the armour. Shortly afterwards it appears that only the intervention of Rutland prevented him from being brought to court by Sir John Zouche. Finally he was outlawed for debt, probably at the very end of his life. He died, in disgrace, in London and was buried near his mother in St. Leonard's, Shoreditch, on 29 May 1591. An elaborate monument testified to the 'many valiant services performed by him for his prince and country ... witnessed by sundry great wounds he therein received'. The Queen and Rutland gave what help they could to his widow and children. In December they were granted 'all the goods forfeited to her Majesty by the outlawry of Sir Thomas'.[9]

[1] *HMC Rutland*, iv. 277; *DNB* (Manners, Thomas, 1st Earl); Nichols, *Leics.* ii. 67, table. [2] *Royal* 18, D.111, f. 52; *Lansd.* 737, f. 36; E163/14/8; *HMC Rutland*, i. 241, 293. [3] *HMC Rutland*, i. 145, 180–1, 207. [4] I. Eller, *Belvoir Castle*, 42–3. [5] *Al. Cant.* i(3), 135; Cooper, *Ath. Cant.* ii. 538; *HMC Rutland*, i. 101; *CPR*, 1560–3, p. 507; *CSP Dom.* 1547–80, p. 365; Add. 1566–79, pp. 252, 268, 308; Lansd. 22, f. 51; Holinshed, *Chron.* (1808) iv. 243–4, 248–52; *CSP Scot.* 1569–71, p. 173; *Churchyard's Chips*, ed. Chalmers, 118, 120, 136. [6] *APC*, xii. 216, 217, 226; *HMC Foljambe*, 45, 47. [7] *Nottingham Recs.* iv. 163; *HMC Rutland*, i. 123, 139, 214; *Notts. Presentment Bills 1587* (Thoroton Rec. Soc. xi), 27; *Testamenta Vetusta*, ii. 719–21; *HMC Hatfield*, ii. 143; *CPR*, 1563–6, p. 456; Lansd. 108, f. 3. [8] *Nottingham Recs.* iv. 141; *HMC Rutland*, i. 221; D'Ewes, 333, 340, 356, 394, 409. [9] *HMC Middleton*, 454–7; *HMC Var.* ii. 78; *HMC Rutland*, i. passim; Add. 12504; *APC*, vii. 358–9; *CSP Dom.* 1591–4, p. 136; Add. 1566–79, p. 268; H. Ellis, *St. Leonard's, Shoreditch*, 57–8; Coll. of Arms, Talbot mss, transcribed by G. R. Batho, H. ff. 295, 325.

M.R.P.

MANSELL, Sir Robert (c.1569–1656), of Pentney and Norwich, Norf. and Penrice, Glam.

KING'S LYNN	1601
CARMARTHENSHIRE	1604, 1614
GLAMORGANSHIRE	1624, 1625
LOSTWITHIEL	1626
GLAMORGANSHIRE	1628

b. c.1569, 4th s. of (Sir) Edward Mansell[†] of Margam, Glam. by Lady Jane Somerset, da. of Henry, 2nd Earl of Worcester; bro. of Sir Thomas*. *educ.* Brasenose, Oxf. 1587. *m.* (1) c.1593, Elizabeth, da. of (Sir) Nicholas Bacon[†], wid. of Francis Wyndham*, *s.p.*; (2) 1617, Anne, da. of Sir John Roper, *s.p.* Kntd. on Cadiz voyage 1596.[1]

J.p. Norf. from c.1592, rem. c.1600, rest. j.p.q. c.1601–26; v.-adm. Norf. and narrow seas c.1599; commr. musters, Norf. 1601; treasurer of navy 1604–18; v.-adm. England 1618.[2]

Mansell was a distinguished naval commander and administrator, who presumably owed his career to the patronage of his relative Lord Admiral Howard of Effingham, Earl of Nottingham. His connexion with Norfolk probably began with his first marriage. Justice Francis Wyndham, the first husband of Elizabeth Bacon, died without direct heirs, and Mansell, when he married the widow, was therefore able to settle on Wyndham's estate at Pentney, about eight miles from King's Lynn. He also leased a house in Chapel Fields, Norwich. In 1593 he became a justice of the peace but he was none the less considered a 'stranger' in the county until at least the end of Elizabeth's reign, and in spite of his connexion with the influential Bacon and Gawdy families, he failed to gain a county seat. His frequent visits to court in the late 1590s, and his absences abroad, for example on the Cadiz and Islands voyages, prevented his admission into the close circle of Norfolk landed families.

After becoming vice-admiral of Norfolk and the narrow seas, he was employed on active service fairly regularly, and during the last four years of Elizabeth's reign there are many references to him as a sailor. In 1599 he left Plymouth with victuals for Ireland, and took action against the rebels at Waterford. In October an official there wrote to the Earl of Essex that 'this honourable knight ... saved me and many gentlemen and our tenants a good portion of cattle and some towns unburnt'. In waters more directly in his sphere of office, he joined ships from the Netherlands in attacking Spanish galleys off Brittany: during 1602 he wrote many letters from the Downs or Dover to Cecil and Nottingham describing his preparations to resist the Spaniards. In September, when he was hourly expecting action, he wrote to the Lord Admiral, 'Howsoever my pen, through haste or swelling of the sea, may err, I beseech you to rest confident that my actions shall neither taste of shame nor indiscretion'.[3]

Discretion was not one of his strongest characteristics. Early in October 1600 a longstanding quarrel with the Heydon family culminated in a duel which brought him and his opponent, Sir John Heydon, before the Privy Council. Heydon came from an old and declining Norfolk family, associated with the Earl of Essex, while Mansell, the newcomer, was wealthy and high in court favour, particularly with his relative Lord High Admiral Nottingham, who had doubtless gained for him the coveted office of vice-admiral of Norfolk, earlier held by Heydon's father. The most likely explanation for the fight, which took place during the Michaelmas sessions, is that it was connected with the county petition against compounding for purveyance – a matter hotly debated among the justices of the peace. Mansell's relatives, the Bacons, were collecting signatures for the petition, while the Heydon brothers and their ally in the county, Sir Arthur Heveningham, wanted to continue composition. In his later examination, Mansell referred to 'articles' which he had forced Heydon to sign at the end of the fight. These 'articles' may have been the petition against composition: the Privy Council suspected that signatures had been 'solicited and laboured' by unjust methods. In the event, Heydon lost a hand and Mansell the use of his right arm, much of the use of his left, and one of his wounds 'rattled'. In a letter written perhaps a month after the duel, the weather was 'such an enemy' to his right arm that he dared not stir from the fireside. He had left Heydon lying on the ground and it was at first rumoured that both men were dead. By December they were threatening another 'outrage', Chief Justice Popham writing to Sir Robert Cecil on 31st that he feared violence during the coming quarter sessions, since the Heydon-Mansell feud had made an even wider breach in a county which was 'already too much wrought into faction'. Five days later, Popham banned weapons at the sessions. In January the Privy Council summoned both Mansell and

Heydon before them, and Mansell at least was put off the commission of the peace.[4]

To add to the disturbances in Norfolk, at the end of 1600 a parliamentary election was expected, and Sir Bassingbourne Gawdy, who had decided to stand for the senior seat, began to campaign for Mansell as the junior Member, 'we being determined to join, myself to have the first voice and he the second'. The Essex rebellion in February 1601 postponed the election, incidentally weakening the position of the Heydons in the county. Mansell, on the other hand, was active against the conspirators, leading a detachment 'on the waterside' of Essex house. But he was still unable to muster enough support for the county seat. As Nathaniel Bacon* wrote to Gawdy:

> He that is appointed by authority a keeper of the peace, and that by oath, should not be a breaker of the peace. And therefore his remove [from the commission is] very just, and this notwithstanding, for him to seek to have himself countenanced here below [by election to Parliament] when he is discountenanced above is not as it should be.

Sir Bassingbourne was apparently still paired with Mansell three days before the election in October, but finally the junior seat went to another member of the Gawdy family, and Mansell had to be content with a borough, being returned for King's Lynn four days after the county election. His position as vice-admiral and owner of Pentney was no doubt enough to secure his election without need of a patron. He sat on a committee in this Parliament concerned with the export of iron ordnance, 8 Dec. 1601. He showed his gratitude for Sir Bassingbourne's support in the county by asking Nottingham, who was expected to become lord lieutenant of Norfolk, to make Gawdy one of his deputies.[5]

During the reigns of James and Charles I, and for much of the interregnum, Mansell remained a leading sailor and naval administrator. After the death of his first wife he returned to Wales, where he achieved his ambition of becoming a knight of the shire. He died intestate in 1656, administration of the estate being granted to his widow.[6]

[1] *DNB*; A. H. Smith thesis, 21; *HMC Gawdy*, 70, 79. [2] A. H. Smith thesis, 21, 308–10, App. II; Gawdy mss in custody of Norf. Arch. Soc. at Norwich, ff. 20–1; *DNB*; *APC*, xxxi. 227; xxxii. 373. [3] A. H. Smith thesis, 21, 43; *HMC Gawdy*, 62, 71–2, 79; *CSP Dom.* 1595–7, p. 472; *HMC Hatfield*, vi. 368; ix. 110–11, 172, 365–6; x. 337; xi. 367; xii. 189, 267, 279, 332, 384, 389, 675. [4] A. H. Smith thesis, 318–22; Add. 27961, f. 36 et passim; *HMC Hatfield*, x. 432–3; *Chamberlain Letters* ed. McClure, i. 107, passim. [5] Neale, *Commons*, 57–60; A. H. Smith thesis, 43–4, 325–6; *HMC Bath*, v. 278; *HMC Gawdy*, 74; Add. 36989, f. 11; D'Ewes, 672. [6] PCC admon. act bk. 1656, f. 132v.

N.M.F.

MANSELL, Sir Thomas (c.1555–1631), of Margam, Glam.

GLAMORGANSHIRE   1597, 1604*, 1614

b. c.1555, 1st s. of (Sir) Edward Mansell[†] of Margam, and bro. of Sir Robert*. *m.* (1) 1582, at Chelsea, Mary, da. of Lewis Mordaunt*, 3rd Baron Mordaunt, 3s.; (2) Jane, da. of Thomas Pole of Bishop Hall, Mdx., wid. of John Fuller and John Bussey, 2da. *suc.* fa. 1585. Kntd. c.1591; *cr.* Bt. 1611.

J.p. Glam. from c.1583, q. from c.1592, sheriff 1593–4, 1603–4, 1622–3; commr. piracy 1586, dep. lt. 1595; dep. lt. Pemb. 1590; member, council in the marches of Wales 1601; chamberlain, S. Wales; steward, royal manor of Penkelly; steward, Swansea.[1]

Mansell was the heir of one of the wealthiest families in South Wales. They had settled in Gower during the reign of Edward I, but in the second half of the sixteenth century the nucleus of their estates was land that had once belonged to Margam abbey. There is no evidence that Mansell himself received any formal education, but he did travel abroad in his early twenties, writing to his father from Pisa in 1578. Once he had returned he married a daughter of the Bedfordshire peer, Lord Mordaunt, who brought with her a portion of £2,000, and subsequently he began to play a part in the affairs of his home county. Even before his father's death he was appointed to the commission of the peace. During Elizabeth's reign Mansell was a country gentleman rather than a courtier. In 1590 he was one of four appointed temporary deputy lieutenants in Pembrokeshire, the two permanent deputy lieutenants being continually absent from the county about their own affairs. The four chosen were to divide into pairs and reside for one month alternately in Milford Haven to see to its defences. In 1592 he was one of the Glamorganshire justices instructed to see that all members of the commission of the peace for the county had taken the requisite oaths. That he took his responsibilities seriously is shown in a letter to his cousin (Sir) Edward Stradling[†], written when he was about to set out for London:

> And because I would, as near as I can, do my endeavour to prevent that no inconvenience or disorder may happen in my neighbourhood during my absence, these are right heartily to pray you that you will take upon you the protection of my poor neighbours and friends in preventing that the rich shall not oppress the poor, and that the poor injure not the wealthy. In doing whereof you shall do a charitable deed, cause them to be bound unto you, and find me not only thankful, but also ready to be employed in case like by you or any of yours.[2]

Elected knight for Glamorganshire in 1597, Mansell was qualified to attend committees concerning enclosures (5 Nov.), the poor law (5 Nov.; named to the committee 22 Nov.), armour and weapons (8 Nov.), the penal laws (8 Nov.), monopolies (10 Nov.), the subsidy (15 Nov.) and the bridge at Newport (29 Nov.). In James I's reign he was more at court, purchased a baronetcy in 1611, and was placed third in precedence in the new order. In 1612 he was one of the six baronets who carried the canopy over the effigy of the prince at the funeral of Prince Henry. Mansell died 20 Dec. 1631. His will, which was proved by his son-in-law Sir John Stradling on 10 Mar. 1632, had been drawn up some time in 1631. He desired to be buried in the vault where his father, his mother, and his two wives were already interred.[3]

[1] C142/209/35; *Baronetage*, i. 4; Clark, *Limbus*, 495; E. P. Statham, *Hist. Fam. Maunsell*, ii(1) p. 1; Royal, 18 D.111, f. 104; Lansd. 737, f. 166; 111, f. 50; E163/14/8, f. 46; *APC*, xiv. 144; xix. 248, 287–8, 309, 335; xxv. 14–15, 18; P. H. Williams, *Council in Marches of Wales*, 352–3; W. S. K. Thomas, *Glam. Historian*, ed. S. Williams, i. 29. [2] *DWB*, 611; *HMC Hatfield*, ii. 173; Statham, 77; *APC*, xix. 248, 287–8, 309, 335; xxiii. 260; *Stradling Corresp.* ed. Traherne, 317–18. [3] D'Ewes, 552, 553, 555, 557, 561, 565; Statham, 1–2; Lansd. 111, f. 50; 152, f. 16 seq.; Nichols, *Progresses Jas. I*, ii. 498; C142/490/179; PCC 31 Audley.

A.M.M.

MANSFIELD, John (1558–c.1601), of Huttons Ambo, nr. Malton, Yorks.

BEVERLEY 1593

b. 1558, s. and h. of Lancelot Mansfield of Skirpenbeck by Anne, da. of Sir Ralph Eure[1]. *m.* (1) Mary Holborn of London; (2) Elizabeth; 1s. 3da.[1]
  J.p. Yorks. (N. Riding) from c.1597, q. from 1601.

Mansfield's father was a minor country gentleman who married a sister of the 2nd Lord Eure, a member of the council in the north. Mansfield himself became associated with the lord president of the council, the 3rd Earl of Huntingdon, being variously described as his servant or deputy and acting for him, for example, in disputes with the Mountjoys over copper and alum mines in Dorset. It was obviously these powerful figures in the council in the north who obtained Mansfield his parliamentary seat at Beverley in 1593. The burgesses for the Yorkshire boroughs were appointed to a cloth committee on 23 Mar. 1593, and to a committee concerning weirs (28 Mar.).[2]

Described as of London in 1582, when he was still in Huntingdon's service, Mansfield had settled at Huttons Ambo (Hutton-in-Derwent) by 1588. His house was not far from York and he apparently became acquainted with the archbishop. In 1597, when Mansfield offered himself for election at Scarborough, the archbishop recommended him to the bailiffs and burgesses, a recommendation reinforced by that of his prospective fellow burgess, Sir Thomas Posthumous Hoby, who secured the senior seat. But neither he nor the archbishop could prevail upon the borough authorities to accept Mansfield's nomination.[3]

Mansfield's will, which was undated, was proved in July 1601. His estate, which included mills at York and Stamford Bridge, was divided into six parts, two of which passed to the son and heir John, who was apprenticed to a

merchant. The remainder were shared between Mansfield's wife Elizabeth, and his three daughters.[4]

[1] *Misc. Gen. et Her.* (ser. 5), iii. 146; *Hist. Northumb.* (Northumb. Co. Hist. Comm.), xii. 496. [2] SP13/H.20, 21; *CSP Dom.* 1591–4, pp. 268–9; *CSP Dom.* Add. 1580–1625, p. 65; *APC*, xiii. 303–4, 359; D'Ewes, 507, 512. [3] SP13/H.20, 21; Scarborough Recs. bdle. C.I. [4] PCC 47 Woodhall.

B.D.

MANTELL, Matthew (bef. 1550–89), of Milton, Northants.; Monks Horton and Hythe, Kent.

BRACKLEY 1571, 1572

b. bef. 1550, 1st s. of Sir Walter Mantell (exec. 1554), of Horton, by Mary or Jane, da. of Sir James Hales of Canterbury. *educ.* I. Temple 1568 or 9. *m.* Lucrecia, da. of John Wake of Hartwell, Northants., 2s.[1]

Mantell, the eldest of four sons named in order after the evangelists, was born into a good family whose misfortunes began in 1541 when Mantell's uncle, the heir to the estates, was executed for the murder of a park-keeper. In 1554 Mantell's father and his cousin, Walter, were attainted and executed for their part in Wyatt's rebellion. Next, in the same year his maternal grandfather, Sir James Hales, committed suicide, and all his goods, chattels and leases went to the Crown, including those brought to him by his marriage with Margaret Wood, Mantell's paternal grandmother.[2]

Mantell was evidently brought up in his grandmother's household. While she lived, the family had still some means of support, for she retained the lands settled on her and the considerable estates she held in her own right as heir to her father, Oliver Wood. Her youngest son claimed that even in such circumstances his mother did not abate one whit of her 'great housekeeping', so Mantell no doubt lived in an environment of luxury and increasing debt.

In 1571 Elizabeth restored to him his father's property, including the reversion of Horton, but he was apparently never restored in blood. In the same year, at a time when he was living on his grandmother's estates in the county, but with the backing of no obvious patron, Mantell was twice returned to Parliament for Brackley, leaving no trace upon the records. He was one of the Kent gentlemen who petitioned the archbishop of Canterbury in 1584 for the reinstatement of their suspended puritan preachers, departing in anger when the archbishop was unmoved by their plea. In 1573 Mantell's grandmother died, whereupon he took possession of such lands as he could in the face of an opposing claim from his uncle Thomas Mantell, and in 1583 they were again at odds over manors at Milton and Collingtree seized as concealed lands. Finally Mantell took up residence at Hythe in Kent, where he died in 1589. In the briefest of wills he bequeathed all his goods to his wife. His male heirs continued to live at Monks Horton.[3]

[1] Add. 5521, f. 43; Berry, *Co. Genealogies, Kent*, 332; *Vis. Kent* (Harl. Soc. xlii), 87; *Assoc. Architectural Soc. Reps.* vi (1861–2), ped. between pp. 18–19. [2] Add. 5521, f. 43; Baker, *Northants.* i. 182, 183; *CPR*, 1560–3, p. 261; *DNB* (Hales, James). [3] *CPR*, 1569–72, p. 206; Add. 5521, ff. 17–18; Add. 27984, f. 5; *DNB* (Hales, James), where wife is wrongly identified; Hasted, *Kent*, viii. 60–1; Bridges, *Northants.* i. 350; Collinson thesis, 443–5; Lansd. 43, f. 7; PCC 74 Leicester.

S.M.T.

MANWOOD, John (by 1524–71), of Sandwich, Kent.

SANDWICH	1571

b. by 1524,[1] 1st s. of Thomas Manwood, draper of Sandwich, by Catherine, da. of John Galloway of Cley, Norf.; bro. of Roger*. *m.* (1) ?1545, Alice Jones of Sandwich, wid., 5s. 2da.; (2) ?1557, Agnes Arras of Faversham, wid., *s.p.*; (3) 1562, Katherine Brough or Brock, 2s. 4da. *suc.* fa. 1538.

Freeman, Sandwich 1545, common councilman 1546, auditor 1547–8 and many later years, searcher of woollen cloths 1552, keeper of chest 1552–5, jurat 1553, mayor 1555–6, 1559–60, brodhull rep. 1552, 1556, 1558, 1559, 1561, 1564, 1565, 1567, 1568, keeper of orphans 1557–67, bailiff to Gt. Yarmouth 1559, 1561, burgess of Shepway court 1559, foundation governor free grammar school 1563, sessor for levying men for defence 1564.[2]

Manwood owed his return for Sandwich to his family's standing, and in particular to his younger brother Roger, the town's recorder. Once before, in December 1557, the brothers had stood for election together, but John, though chosen by Sandwich, had been replaced by a nominee of the lord warden. In 1571 Roger Manwood wrote to the town on his brother's behalf, believing, according to his later statement, that the warden had given his consent. Finding that he was mistaken, and that Cobham had intended the second seat for John Vaughan, he deferred to Cobham, but the corporation maintained that they must have one resident freeman, 'sworn to our liberties', and in the end returned both Manwoods. The town books have an entry about the election: '5 March, John Manwood, jurat'. No other name is mentioned and no information about any parliamentary activity has been found, unless he and not Roger (who is probably meant) was the 'Mr. Manwood' who sat on the committee for griefs and petitions on 7 Apr. 1571. He probably died in the same year, soon after the end of the Parliament, though his will, made 15 June 1571, was not proved until April 1574. He left one third of his property to his wife, one third to his sons Thomas, Roger and John, and the remainder to his six 'natural children', i.e. those by his third wife. If anything in the will should be 'badly expressed', his brother was to have power to amend it. The executors were the widow and her stepsons Thomas and Roger.[3]

[1] Date of birth estimated from admission to freedom of Sandwich. [2] *Vis. Kent* (Harl. Soc. lxxv), 136; W. Boys, *Hist. Sandwich*, i. ped. opp. p. 246, 842; J. M. Cowper, *Regs. of St. Alphage, Canterbury*, 106; Sandwich old red bk. 1529–51, new red bk. 1568–81, little black bk. passim; Cinque Ports white bk. 248–62; *CPR*, 1560–3, p. 613. [3] Little black bk. ff. 122, 149; new red bk. 1568–81, f. 72; C3/123/85; O. Baker, *Hist. Sandwich and Richborough Castle*, 22; *APC*, vi. 199; *CJ*, i. 83; Canterbury prob. reg. A 42, ff. 185–6.

A.D.K.H./N.M.F.

MANWOOD, Peter (1571–1625), of Hackington, nr. Canterbury, Kent.

SANDWICH	1589, 1593, 1597, 1601
SALTASH	1604
KENT	1614
NEW ROMNEY	1621

b. 1571,[1] 1st s. of Roger Manwood* of Hackington by his 1st w. Dorothy, da. of John Theobald of Seal. *educ.* I. Temple Nov. 1583. *m.* Jan. 1588, Frances, da. of Sir George Hart of Lullingstone, at least 7s. 4da. *suc.* fa. 1592. Kntd. 1603.

J.p.q. Kent from c.1593, dep. lt. from 31 Dec. 1601, sheriff 1602–3; commr. Dover haven by 1591, grain 1596, musters by 1597.[2]

Member, Antiq. Soc. c.1591.

Manwood inherited his father's wealth but not his ambition, being content to remain at Hackington, rebuilt by his father, living the life of a country gentleman. He played a part in the administration of the county, and sat in Parliament, but preferred the company of writers and scholars. Camden spoke highly of him in his *Britannia*, and a letter survives from Manwood to Robert Cotton† asking for information about his library and, in particular, requesting the loan of a life of Henry VIII. The chapter house library at Canterbury preserves a copy which Manwood made of an ancient manuscript recording the claim of the Kings of England to the French crown. In a note, describing the state of the original, he lamented that 'the seams were partly consumed, and the letters dimmed and almost worn out by time, the devourer of all things'. His years spent at the Inner Temple, of which his father was a distinguished member, and the licence he was granted in 1598 to travel abroad 'for his increase in good knowledge and learning', provided a sound basis for his later academic pursuits. He in fact maintained a connexion with his old inn all his life, though he was never called to the bar. He served as steward of the Christmas feast five times between 1615 and 1623, and four of his sons were specially admitted.[3]

As well as the manors which Manwood inherited from his father, including Hackington, Chislet and Ash in Kent, and other lands in Essex, he leased land from the archbishop of Canterbury, made several purchases himself, and was granted by the Crown the manor of Raynehurst at Chalk, Kent. The family still owned houses in their home town of Sandwich, including two of the principal properties, known as the King's Lodging and the

Castle of Flint. Roger Manwood's bequests to his son were accompanied by the advice to 'keep a good house within the proportion of his living'. He felt it necessary to give both his wife and son lessons in household management, as they were 'but young and raw housekeepers'. Manwood also owned a London house in the parish of St. Bartholomew, Farringdon Without, valued at £40 for the purposes of a shipmoney assessment in 1596; he refused to contribute, stating that he had paid his subsidy elsewhere.[4]

It may be that Manwood's father had wished him to pursue a similar career to his own. He was sent to the Inner Temple as soon as possible, and, just before the 1586 election, when Peter was still only 15, his father wrote to the Sandwich corporation asking for him to be elected to Parliament. This they did not do, but at the next election he became the senior Sandwich MP at the age of 18, and continued to occupy the seat for the rest of this period. He was never paid for his services and his name does not appear in the records of the House, although as a Member for Sandwich he was appointed to committees concerning the explanation of statutes (28 Mar. 1593), brewers (3 Apr.), the Severn harbour (21 Nov. 1601) and the main business committee (23 Nov.).[5]

Manwood was made a deputy lieutenant at the special request of the 11th Lord Cobham, and when Sandwich wished to oblige Cobham as lord warden in 1601, they did so by returning Manwood at his suggestion. His connexion with the school his father founded continued, but by the early 1620s he was heavily in debt, and had to go abroad. After making an arrangement with his creditors he returned to England in time to serve as steward of the Inner Temple Christmas feast in 1623. He died in 1625. The family fortunes were revived by his son John, courtier and lieutenant of Dover castle, who sat for Sandwich in 1640.[6]

[1] Date of birth established from his being of age on his father's death and from the date of his parents' marriage: C142/244/112. [2] DNB; Vis. Kent (Harl. Soc. xlii), 144; Cal. I.T. Recs. i. 327; Nichols, Progresses Jas. I, i. 224 n; Hatfield ms 278; APC, xxvii. 109; xxxii. 450; Lansd. 66, ff. 27 seq.; CSP Dom. 1595–7, p. 224. [3] Archaeologia, i. p. xxi; Camden, Britannia (1607), p. 239; Lansd. 89, f. 185; HMC 9th Rep. pt. 1, p. 127; Cal. I.T. Recs. ii. 50, 74, 90, 97, 104, 109, 140; CSP Dom. 1598–1601, p. 132. [4] Hasted, Kent, ii. 49, 464, 469; vii. 313–14; ix. 46–7, 50, 207, 231, 240, 245; Arch. Cant. xvi. 60; xx. 268 n; xxvii. 84; xlv. 202; Lansd. 81, f. 83. [5] Sandwich year bks. 1582–1608, ff. 59, 101, 179, 234, 295; D'Ewes, 511, 514, 624, 647. [6] APC, xxv. 334; xxvii. 109, 298, 308; xxviii. 29; xxx. 436; 1618–19, pp. 339–40; HMC Hatfield, xv. 120, 121, 122, 123, 152–3, 172, 215; Lansd. 78, ff. 138 seq.; Nichols, i. 225 n; PRO Index 4208, p. 246; W. Boys, Sandwich, 203, 249–50; CSP Dom. 1623–5, p. 213; Chamberlain Letters ed. McClure, ii. 456; C142/451/108.

M.R.P.

MANWOOD, Roger (by 1532–92), of Hackington, nr. Canterbury, Kent, and 'St. Bartholomew's House', London.

HASTINGS	1555
SANDWICH	1558, 1559, 1563, 1571, 1572*

b. by 1532, 2nd s. of Thomas Manwood of Sandwich, Kent, and bro. of John*. educ. St. Peter's sch. Sandwich; I. Temple 1548, called. m. (1) settlement 30 May 1571, Dorothy (d. 1575), da. of John Theobald of Seal, Kent, wid. of John Croke† of London and of Christopher Allen of London, 3s. inc. Peter* 2da.; (2) Elizabeth, da. of John Coppinger of Allhallows, Kent, wid. of John Wilkins of Stoke, Kent, s.p. Kntd. 1578.[1]

Common serjeant, I. Temple 1552, bencher 1558, Lent reader 1565, serjeant-at-law 1567.

Recorder, Sandwich Apr. 1555–66; j.p.q. Kent 1561–d., Mdx. 1564–d., many other counties from 1573; commr. Rochester bridge 1561, 1568, 1571, 1574; steward or judge of Chancery and Admiralty cts. of Dover temp. Eliz.; steward of liberties to Archbishop Parker to 1572; puisne judge c.p. 14 Oct. 1572; circuit judge, western circuit by 1573–4, Oxford circuit by 1587; chief baron, Exchequer 17 Nov. 1578–d.; member, high commission 23 Apr. 1576; receiver of petitions, Parlts. of 1584, 1586, 1589.[2]

'A reverend judge of great and excellent knowledge of the law, and accompanied with a ready invention and good elocution' was the verdict of (Sir) Edward Coke*. Others regarded Manwood as a proud and cruel man who oppressed and deceived his neighbours, and who resorted to corruption and bribery to further his advance towards high legal office. Five hundred in Kent would rejoice at his death, wrote Richard Barrey*, lieutenant of Dover castle. Still, he is remembered in his native Sandwich and at Canterbury as a public benefactor, and he was generous in his treatment of his servants. He was granted the manor of St. Stephen's near Canterbury in 1563, and spent freely on the estate.

Manwood began his career as adviser to the Cinque Ports in general and to Sandwich in particular. By the 1570s and 1580s the Ports were clearly proud to retain their links with the now eminent judge. Despite an openly hostile attitude towards the lord warden, Manwood, for his part, remained ready to advise Sandwich and the other Ports, demonstrating in 1570, for example, that they were exempt from loans, aids and other similar contributions. He was not slow to tell them when a gift presented at the right time would find them useful friends. In 1573 his fee was made permanent, 'now as a gift ... for his worship's benevolence and good will heretofore shown to the Ports'.[3]

Apart from one committee concerning fraudulent conveyances on 5 Mar. 1563, nothing is known of Manwood's work in Parliament before 1571. However, something must have been expected from him, for an entry in the Rye chamberlain's accounts for 21 Nov. 1566 shows that a present of fish was sent to him 'to speak for the liberties of the ports in the Parliament house'. By 1571 he had been appointed serjeant-at-law. On 12 Apr. 1571 he spoke on the treasons bill, wishing to include slanderous words 'for whoso shall affirm her Highness to be an heretic doth doubtless wish her the pains of an heretic, that is to be burnt'. He could see no reason why Norton's proposal concerning the succession to the throne should not be added to the government's bill as the majority of the House desired. He was appointed to the committee on the treasons bill that day, and to a subsequent committee on 11 May. On 14 Apr. the House was discussing Carleton's bill against licences and dispensations granted by the archbishop of Canterbury. As one of the archbishop's legal advisers, Manwood was in a good position to judge the bill's merits. Speaking 'very judiciously and moderately' he urged the House to ascertain the nature of the abuses before any remedies were applied, 'for to conclude without knowledge and in a generality, it were over much absurd'. His committee work during this Parliament included returns (6 Apr.), church attendance (6 Apr.), griefs and petitions (7 Apr.), unspecified religious matters (10 Apr.), fraudulent conveyances (11 Apr.), the order of parliamentary business (21, 26 Apr.), vagabonds (23 Apr.), respite of homage (27 Apr.), priests disguised in serving-men's apparel (1 May), jeofails (12 May) and fugitives (25 May).

During the 1572 Parliament he was appointed to committees concerning Mary Queen of Scots on 12 May and 6 June, speaking on the subject on 7 June. He introduced a bill on 4 June to clarify a clause in the statute of fugitives enacted in the previous Parliament, and on 28 June he made a long and technical speech on the bill of jeofails. He was appointed to committees concerning grants by corporations (30 May), delays in judgments (24 June), and the continuation of statutes (26 June).[4]

The 1572 session proved to be Manwood's last in the Commons, though he served as a receiver of petitions in the Lords in 1584, 1586 and 1589. His knowledge of the law, his performances in the Commons and his influential acquaintances all played a part in his elevation to the bench. Archbishop Parker had been a close friend for a number of years, and there is some evidence that Sir Thomas Gresham was trying to find Manwood a suitable appointment. Ironically, he had written to Burghley only a month or two earlier, asking him not to make Manwood a judge as he was making more money as a serjeant. He won a reputation for severity towards religious extremists and traitors, and he took part in many of the major trials of the period, including the examination of Mary Stuart at Fotheringay in the autumn of 1586, and, after her death, the Star Chamber inquiry which accused William Davison* of 'misprision and contempt'. He was present at the trials of William Parry*, Anthony Babington and the Earl of Arundel, and the Star Chamber inquiry into Lord Vaux of Harrowden's suspected harbouring of the Jesuit, Campion.[5]

Many charges of bribery, corruption and oppression were levelled against Manwood in his lifetime. That he attempted to obtain the office of chief justice of the Queen's bench in May 1592 by offering Burghley 500 marks is certain: his letter still survives. It is almost as certain that he made a similar gesture ten years earlier to succeed Dyer as chief justice of the common pleas. When he was censured by the Queen for selling one of the offices in his gift, he replied that this was standard procedure, and his defence would probably have followed this line in the two instances just mentioned. But no other letters of this nature have been found concerning such high offices, and Recorder Fleetwood's reaction in 1582 suggests that such occurrences were rare:

There runneth a marvellous speech over all London that greater sums of money were offered (to whom I know not) than I may well write of by one of the Exchequer. If it were true, the party did not well: if it were not true, the first reporters were much to blame, to scandalise such an officer of her Majesty, by which means he is grown into a greater discredit than may be in a short time easily forgotten.

He reported that Burghley did all he could to keep the offender out of the office which he had tried to buy.[6]

The charges of corruption and oppression levelled against Manwood are extensive and varied. In some instances the surviving evidence is insufficient to form any conclusions about his conduct, but, due allowance being made for the inevitable distortions resulting from reliance on the evidence of victims of his activities, the stories are so many and so consistent that the verdict must go against him. Where he did try to offer an explanation, perhaps to Burghley or the Council, his manner was off-hand or offensive. The incident which nearly brought about his downfall illustrates his arrogance. The story, concerning a gold chain which Manwood was supposed to have illegally seized from a goldsmith named Underwood, is confused. The goldsmith complained to the Privy Council as early as 1586, but it was not until 1591 that the matter became serious. The Council wrote to Manwood accusing him of obtaining the chain by means of threatening speeches, after it had been 'bought lawfully in open market'. They called his conduct 'a very foul example and slanderous to the rest of your calling'. His letter of explanation to Burghley contained a postscript asking for a more lucrative office. The crisis came in April 1592 when Manwood, summoned by the Council to explain his conduct, sent them a contemptuous letter refusing to recognize their authority in the matter. The Council's response was more than he had bargained for. He was confined to his house in St. Bartholomew's and only obtained his release by writing a grovelling letter on 12 May and by signing a statement of submission in the Council's presence at Greenwich two days later. He apologized 'for my late faults committed in my foresaid writings'. Evidently the Council, as a body, had had enough of Manwood's behaviour and manner. The Queen's reaction to these events is not known. Though he did not lose his office, his death on 14 Dec. may have saved him from further humiliation.[7]

His will, completed two days previously, exhibits many of the characteristics which he displayed in his lifetime, but a hint of puritanism is to be found. Confident that he was 'one of the number of His elect', he asked to be buried at Hackington, 'without vain pomp'. Though no money was to be given to the 'vagrant and idle poor', he left instructions for the quiet distribution of £20 amongst the poor of Hackington and five adjoining parishes. There was an additional £40 to set the poor to work. He also ordered that a sermon should be preached at Hackington and at St. Mary's, Sandwich, every year for seven years, and that some mention was to be made of 'the frailty and vain delights of this world'. He made provision for his relatives, all of whom received a gold ring, giving £800 to the family of his dead brother John, 1,000 marks to his granddaughter, and sums of money or lands to his cousins at Sandwich. His second wife received large quantities of household goods, plate and jewellery, livestock, 500 marks in cash, and the leases of lands and other property in west Kent and London worth over £550 a year. His only surviving son and heir, Peter, was left the rest of the household goods and all the lands in east Kent and Canterbury. Manwood hoped that his son and widow would continue to share a household, 'if they could so like and agree together', spending the summers at Hackington and the winters in London. Peter was to have unlimited enjoyment of the property only if he lived five years beyond Queen Elizabeth's death without committing treason. The servants were generously treated, those who had served Manwood for more than seven years receiving annuities of up to £10. Others could stay at St. Stephen's for a year after his death while they looked, if they chose, for suitable posts elsewhere. A large proportion of the will is taken up with detailed accounts of Manwood's charitable foundations, amounting in all, as he carefully points out, to at least one tenth of his wealth. At Sandwich he founded, in 1563, the grammar school which still bears his name. The original grant was made with the help of other citizens of the port, of Archbishop Parker, and the dean and chapter of Canterbury, who provided a suitable site.

Manwood was buried beneath an elaborate monument which he had erected in his lifetime in Hackington church. An inquisition post mortem was taken 25 May 1595.[8]

[1] DNB; Vis. Kent (Harl. Soc. lxxv), 135; Foss, Judges, v. 516, 523; Add. 29759, ff. 26–7; Arch. Cant. xvii. 239 n. [2] Foss, v. 516–17; Cal. I.T. Recs. i. passim; Sandwich little black bk. 1552–67, f. 62; Cinque Ports white bk. ff. 250, 254, 255, 256, 260; Canterbury burmote bk. 1, ff. 146, 273; Strype, Parker, ii. 168; Foss, v. 407, 408; Egerton 2345, f. 45; APC, xv. 226; Strype, Grindal, 309–10. [3] Cinque Ports white bk. ff. 250, 252, 254; black bk. ff. 5, 17; Sandwich little black bk. f. 62; CSP Dom. 1547–80, pp. 384, 407; HMC 5th Rep. 569, 570; HMC 13th Rep. IV, 2, 3, 26, 29, 41. [4] CJ, i. 67, 76, 83, 84, 85, 86, 87, 89, 92, 95, 99, 101, 102, 103; D'Ewes 156, 158, 159, 160, 165, 167, 178, 179, 180, 183, 188, 206, 220, 222, 223, 224, 228, 229; Trinity, Dublin, anon. jnl. ff. 18–19, 22; Neale, Parlts. i. 210; Trinity, Dublin, Thos. Cromwell's jnl. ff. 49, 55, 68–9. [5] LJ, ii. 61, 113, 145; Strype, Parker, ii. 433, 434; iii. 337, 343; Foss, v. 517–19; CSP Dom. 1547–80, pp. 441, 566; Arch. Cant. xlv. 201; xlviii. 238; Strype, Grindal, 345–6; APC, viii. 402; Lansd. 68, f. 108; 155, f. 61; HMC 9th Rep. pt. 1, 168; HMC 11th Rep. VII, 163–5; Strype, Aylmer, 213; Whitgift, ii. 70; iii. 241; Annals, iii(1), p. 529; Howell, State Trials, i. 1095, 1114, 1128, 1167; Archaeologia, xxx. 102 seq. [6] SP12/246/16; Lansd. 71, f. 172; Foss, v. 520–1; Harl. 6995, f. 49; Strype, Annals, iii(1), pp. 199–200. [7] Foss, v. 521–2; Lansd. 50, f. 69; 71, ff. 9–13; APC, xix. 316, 358–9; xx. 95–6, 219–20; xxii. 449–51. [8] W. Boys, Sandwich, 199–244, 256–69; Hasted, Kent, iv. 81, 84; ix. 50–2; CPR, 1560–3, pp. 37, 613; Arch. Cant. xvii. 216–17, 239–40; Strype, Whitgift, i. 542–5; Foss, v. 519, 522; HMC 9th Rep. pt. 1, 159; Lansd. 6, f. 172; Strype, Parker, i. 273–6; C142/244/112.

M.R.P.

MARBURY, William (1524–81), of the Middle Temple, London, and ?of Girsby, Lincs.

NEWPORT IUXTA LAUNCESTON 1572

b. 1524, 1st s. of Robert Marbury of Burgh on Bain, Girsby, Lincs. by his w. Katherine. educ. ?Pembroke, Camb. 1544, M. Temple 1551, called by 1571. m. Agnes or Anne, da. of John Lenton of Old Wynkill, ?Staffs., 4s. 3da. suc. fa. 1545.

The Members of Parliament for the south-west of England in Elizabeth's reign included a large number of Middle Templars, probably because of the system of 'binding' new entrants at the Temple with existing lawyers there. This custom led to the formation of local or family groups at the inns of court, and when combined with local patronage, provided suitable MPs who presumably asked no fees, for small boroughs. It seems likely then, that the Newport Member was the William Marbury of the Middle Temple, who had possibly been admitted to Pembroke College in 1544. The identity of this man has not been definitely established, but he was probably the William Marbury of Lincolnshire who in his will bequeathed law books to his relatives. He had a long career at the Middle Temple, where he was admitted 'specially ... at the instance of Mr. Francis Barnades' in May 1551, and was still active in 1573. At that time the governing body decided that Mr. Marbury, one of the masters of the utter bar, should 'be admitted into any vacant chamber if no master of the bench or person called to the bench desire it'. His name appears from time to time in the records of his inn, for example as steward for Christmas 1570. In the following November he was fined ten marks for not giving the autumn reading.[1]

Apart from his legal career, little has been discovered about Marbury. He is mentioned only once in the known surviving records of the Commons, when he was appointed to the committee of the bill against excess of apparel, 10 Mar. 1576. It was possibly his son and namesake who entered Cecil's service and who went with the 2nd Earl of Essex on his 1597 voyage, being forced to return, 'much against his will', because there was 'such an antipathy between him and the sea, that it [was] vain for him to strive'.[2]

Marbury died in 1581, his will, drawn up in January of that year, being proved in the following November. He asked to be buried in the church or churchyard of the parish where he died, and left charitable bequests to various servants, with 20 marks to 'poor scholars of Oxford and Cambridge'. His youngest son Francis, who was to have all the books except the 'English and law' ones, was also bequeathed 20 nobles and a gold ring – a usual form of bequest in the will: Marbury noted that he had 'labelled' all the rings he meant to be given away. Two daughters, Mary and Katherine, received £200 each, and the widow was to have lands and houses at Burgh and Biscathorpe, Lincolnshire. The will also bequeathed to her a number of horses, sheep, pigs and a large amount of farm produce, with 'six loads of wood and two chalder of coals' annually. The household furnishings and plate listed include much silver, pewter and brass. There was an eldest son William, but he was probably dead by 1581. The manor of Girsby was to go to the second son, Edward, who was appointed sole executor.[3]

[1] Lincs. Peds. (Harl. Soc. li), 638; M.T. Adm. 19; M.T. Recs. i. 172, 182, 191. [2] CJ, i. 113; CSP Dom. 1595-7, pp. 464, 467, 468. [3] PCC 39 Darcy.

N.M.F.

MARCHE, Robert (aft.1522–63), of Rye, Suss.

RYE   1559

b. aft. 1522, 2nd s. of John Marche of Rye by his w. Joan. m. Agnes, at least 6s. 1da.
Chamberlain, Rye 1555, jurat by 1557, mayor 1561–2.

Marche was not of age when his father made his will in March 1543. He inherited some leasehold farms and cattle, and went on to buy further property in and just out-side Rye, including a slaughterhouse from the Rye corporation. In April 1560 Edward, Lord Windsor, whose family had received a crown grant of estates belonging to St. Bartholomew's hospital at Rye at the dissolution of the monasteries, sold a large part of them to a syndicate of four, including Marche. The partners divided the land among themselves, Marche's share being mainly in Rye, Peasmarsh and Udimore. Some of it he had resold before the end of 1561. His will and inquisition post mortem mention property in Playden and Iden, Sussex; Stone, Ivychurch, Romney Marsh and Wittersham, Kent; and houses in Rye, including one in 'Mr. Rucke's land', bought from Goddard White* of Winchelsea. He was paid £11 4s. 0d. for his services as Member of Parliament, at the

rate of 2s. a day for 112 days. He died 3 Feb. 1563, perhaps of the plague, which killed over 500 persons in Rye that year. The widow had presumably remarried by April 1566, when the wardship of his son and heir Simon was granted to George Chatfield and his wife Agnes. Simon died in 1584.

E. Suss. RO, Rye mss; PCC 15 Chayre, 24 Spert; Herts. RO; Halsey mss; C142/141/23; Egerton 2094, f. 191; Suss. Rec. Soc. iii. 29 seq.; CPR, 1558-60, p. 367; 1560-3, pp. 87, 136; 1563-6, p. 469; Suss. Arch. Colls. lxxxiii. 80; W. Holloway, Hist. Rye, 306.

N.M.F.

MARKHAM, Sir John (by 1486–1559), of Cotham, Notts.[1]

NOTTINGHAMSHIRE	1529
NOTTINGHAM	1539, ?1542, 1545
NOTTINGHAMSHIRE	1547, 1558, 1559

b. by 1486, s. of Sir John Markham of Cotham by Alice, da. of Sir William Skipwith of Ormsby, Lincs. m. (1) Anne, da. and h. of Sir George Neville, 2s.; (2) Margery, da. of Sir Ralph Longford, 1s. 3da.; (3) Anne (d. 12 Oct. 1554), da. and coh. of Sir John Strelley of Strelley, wid. of Richard Stanhope of Rampton, 2s. Thomas* and William† 3da. suc. fa. 1508. Kntd. 25 Sept. 1513.
Sheriff, Notts. and Derbys. 1518–19, 1526–7, 1534–5, 1538–9, 1545–6, Lincs. 1532–3; j.p. Notts. 1521, q. 1559. Chamberlain and receiver of court of general surveyors 1545; lt. of Tower of London 1549–Oct. 1551.[2]

Markham was the descendant of a family long established in Nottinghamshire. His father had fought beside Henry VII at the battle of Stoke and afterwards was much at court, while Markham himself served Henry VIII both as soldier and courtier, continuing a member of the royal household until the Duke of Somerset's fall, when he appears to have retired from court. As early as 1537 his old friend Archbishop Cranmer wrote, 'Sir John of long season hath unfeignedly favoured the truth of God's word', and later he was described by Edward Underhill as 'both wise and zealous in the Lord'. His daughter Isabella and his son Thomas entered the Princess Elizabeth's household at Hatfield during Mary's reign.[3]

Markham's local standing had already earned him election as knight of the shire before the accession of Elizabeth. It was to be expected that such a man, prominent in his own locality, a protestant and a friend of the protestant 2nd Earl of Rutland, would be elected to the crucial first Parliament of the new reign; and while Sir John sat for the county, his son sat for the city of Nottingham.[4]

Markham made his will in April 1559. Only the necessary minimum was left to his heir, Robert*, the son of his deceased eldest son John. A disposition was made of his movable property to the prejudice of Robert. The executors of the will were Markham's sons, Thomas and William, his friend Henry Needham, and his servant

Nicholas Blouston. They were to hold lands in East Markham and Tuxford for 20 years for the payment of debts and legacies. Among these was a bequest of £100 to Thomas Cranmer, son of the archbishop, 'for a due debt that I am bound in my conscience'. Markham appointed as supervisors (Sir) Gervase Clifton† and his cousin Ellis Markham†. The will was proved in October 1559.[5]

[1] This and the next two biographies are largely based upon C. R. Markham, *Markham Memorials*, vol. i and D. F. Markham, *Hist. Markham Fam.* [2] *Genealogist*, n.s. vii. 18; *Vis. Notts.* (Harl. Soc. iv), 24; *North Country Wills* (Surtees Soc. cxxi), 15–16; *LP Hen. VIII*, i(2), p. 1028; xx(2), p. 555; *CIPM Hen. VII*, iii. 325–6; *APC*, ii. 371; iii. 401. [3] Jenkyns, *Remains of Archbishop Cranmer*, i. 153–5, 224–5; *Narratives of the Reformation* (Cam. Soc. lxxvii), 173; I. Grimble, *Harington Fam.* 92. [4] *LP Hen. VIII*, xi. p. 223 et passim; xvii. p. 332. [5] PCC 50 Chaynay; *N. Country Wills* (Surtees Soc. cxxi), 15–16.

I.C.

MARKHAM, Robert (1536–1606), of Cotham, Notts.

NOTTINGHAMSHIRE	1571
GRANTHAM	1586
NOTTINGHAMSHIRE	1589

b. 1536, 1st s. of John Markham of Cotham by Catherine, da. of Sir Anthony Babington† of Dethick. *m.* (1) in 1562, Mary, da. of Francis Leck* of Sutton in the Dale, Derbys., 5s. 3da.; (2) in 1597, Jane, da. of William Burnell of Winkburn, *s.p. suc.* gd.-fa. 1559.

J.p. Notts. from 1564, sheriff 1571–2, 1583–4.[1]

Markham's father died when he was still young and his position in his early years was weakened by the dislike of his grandfather, who disinherited him as far as he could. The plate and furniture at Cotham, and all the houses and lands that were not entailed, went to his grandfather's sons by his third wife, and Markham had to refurnish Cotham when he inherited the estate. He was described as a 'favourer of religion' by the archbishop of York in 1564 and in April 1565 he was one of those whom the Privy Council asked to take special care in assessing the subsidy. His name occurs a number of times in the following years in connexion with local administration. He and Sir John Byron produced a list of Nottinghamshire recusants in 1577, with the value of their property, and in 1590 Markham was amongst the local justices to inquire into complaints of engrossing in Nottingham.[2]

Sir George Chaworth, Markham's cousin, was a relative and henchman of the 3rd Earl of Rutland, and Markham himself was a follower of the Earl. He owed his return to Parliament for Grantham to Rutland, who was granted both nominations by the borough in that year, and Rutland was no doubt behind his election for the county in 1571. Although Markham was still a follower of the Rutlands in 1588, when he was an assistant at the 4th Earl's funeral, during the long minority that followed he became a follower of the earls of Shrewsbury, and his third son Gervase became the champion of the Countess of

Shrewsbury. Before the election for the 1593 Parliament Robert Markham had the backing of the 7th Earl of Shrewsbury for one of the county seats, but he withdrew before the election and in the event never sat again. In the 1586 and 1589 Parliaments Markham was active. On 21 Nov. 1586 he asked for advice on dealing with the claim for wages made against the borough by his predecessor as MP for Grantham, Arthur Hall. He was named (2 Dec.) to the committee set up to deal with this. The following 10 Mar. he was on the committee of the bill about East Retford, and, 18 Mar., he was one of those appointed to attend the Queen to hear her thanks for the benevolence just granted. In 1589 he was appointed to committees dealing with returns (8 Feb.), purveyors (27 Feb.), Lincoln (11 Mar.), the debts of Thomas Hanford (18 Mar.) and glass making (19 Mar.). On 21 Mar. 1589 he introduced a motion 'on behalf of Mr. Aylmer'. As first knight for Nottinghamshire he was also entitled to attend the subsidy committee appointed on 11 Feb. 1589.[3]

Markham was frequently at court. Through his grandmother he was descended from the Beauforts, and was thus distantly related to the Queen. She called him 'Markham the Lion'. But his expenses at court forced him to sell the park at Maplebeck, Lincolnshire, and he was in debt at his death, intestate, on 20 Nov. 1606.[4]

[1] *Vis. Notts.* (Harl. Soc. iv), 24–5; Thoroton, *Notts.* 344; C66/998; Egerton 2345, f. 22v; Hatfield ms 278; SP13/case F/11, ff. 22v–5. [2] PCC 50 Chaynay; *Cam. Misc.* ix(3), p. 72; Lansd. 8, f. 80; *CSP Dom.* 1547–80, p. 563; *APC*, xx. 153. [3] *HMC Rutland*, i. 245, 306; D'Ewes, 404, 407, 414, 416, 430, 431, 440, 445, 447, 448, 451. [4] C2 Eliz./M7/20; C142/696/155.

A.M.M.

MARKHAM, Thomas (by 1523–1607), of Ollerton, Notts. and Kirby Bellars, Leics.

NOTTINGHAM	1553 (Oct.), 1559

b. by 1523, s. of Sir John Markham* by his 3rd w.; bro. of William. *m.* by 1565, Mary, da. and h. of Sir Rice Griffin of Braybrooke and Dingley, Northants., 7s. 4da. in addition to 7ch. *d. inf.*[1]

Gent. waiter to 2nd Earl of Rutland by 1549; bailiff, manor of Mansfield, Notts. Nov. 1550, Clipston, Notts. 1568; keeper, Lyndhurst and Normanswood within Sherwood forest Nov. 1550, Sherwood forest 1564; member, household of Princess Elizabeth by 1558; gent. pens. and standard bearer 1559–73 j.p.q. Notts. 1561–91; steward, lordship of Newark, Notts. 1568; sheriff, Notts. 1577–8; commr. to administer oath of supremacy 1592.[2]

Ollerton, Markham's main seat, came to him from his father, together with property at Elkesley and Bothamstall. He also owned Nottinghamshire estates, land at Chipping Warden, on the borders of Oxfordshire and Northamptonshire, and part of a former monastic estate in Leicestershire. Some details of his early career are given in the dedicatory epistle to the *Metamorphosis of Ajax*, written in 1596 by his nephew Sir John Harington. This describes him as

> Her Majesty's servant extraordinary. Why, was he once ordinary? Yea, that he was, ask all old Hatfield men, and ask them quickly too, for they be almost all gone.

At the time of Queen Mary's last illness Markham was commanding 300 foot soldiers at Berwick. Here he received a message from Thomas Parry* to the effect that Elizabeth wished him to repair to Brocket Hall 'with all convenient speed' leaving his men under trustworthy captains. He duly reported to Elizabeth, bringing with him a testimonial signed by his captains professing their readiness to adventure their lives in her service. The new Queen made him a gentleman pensioner and his sister Isabella (afterwards Sir John Harington's mother) a gentlewoman of her privy chamber, and the climate seemed set fair for Markham to enjoy a distinguished career at court.

Markham had already sat in the Commons under Queen Mary, voting against the government's religious measures in the Parliament of October 1553. He did not sit again until Elizabeth's first, when he was returned for Nottingham and his father for the county. He received promotion in the band of gentlemen pensioners in 1564, and valuable grants of land, but from the 1580s things began to go wrong. The trouble started with a bitter quarrel with the 3rd Earl of Rutland over the fees and profits Markham had taken as 'steward, keeper, warden and chief justice' of Sherwood forest during that nobleman's minority. In the end the Queen heard the opinion of the judges, but took the case into her own hands, so that 'her old servant' should enjoy his privileges and fees 'according to her free gift and meaning, which she is best able to expound'. The disputes continued, however, with successive earls, until at least 1597.[3]

In fact Markham was more country gentleman than courtier, and, according to Harington, resigned his job as standard bearer of the gentlemen pensioners because it demanded too much time at court. Perhaps there were other reasons: his epithet of 'Black Markham' referred as much to his stubborn character as to his swarthy countenance. Certainly most of the references found to him are concerned with local rather than national matters, though he was still recounting court gossip from Westminster in February 1590. From about this time, however, his position was undermined by the Catholicism of his wife, 'a great persuader of weak women to popery'. Again the Queen intervened, through the Privy Council, to bar recusancy proceedings against her, as Markham was 'one of her Majesty's ancient servants, and well known ... to be of good credit and reputation'. Though Markham himself conformed – in 1592 he was administering the oath of supremacy in Nottinghamshire – his sons did not,

and Markham wrote several letters to Burghley between 1592 and 1594 regretting the behaviour of, especially, Griffin, who finally was accused of treason. If he were guilty and deserved death, 'let him have it. My humble [?prayer] is that he may be clear yet'. Griffin was let off this time, and so he was again in the next reign, when he was implicated with his brother Thomas in the so-called 'Bye' plot.[4]

It was at this very period that Markham stood in the disputed Nottinghamshire election of 1593 in harness with Sir Thomas Stanhope. It is not clear why he wished to represent the county for the first time when aged over 70. Perhaps the very fact that his fortunes were at a low ebb encouraged him to make the effort to be at the centre of affairs once more. Or perhaps it was a matter of Nottinghamshire politics. While his nephew Robert Markham of Cotham was in Shrewsbury's camp, Thomas Markham's mother had once been married to a Stanhope. The contest came to nothing, Stanhope and Thomas Markham 'accompanied with none but their sons and servants' being shut out of the poll through the partiality of the sheriff.[5]

In 1597 Markham was ill, and three years later rumours of his death circulated. About 1601 he became senile. 'Old Markham dotes at home' wrote Harington some two years later, adding that his wife had 'cozened' him out of 8,000 marks. He was buried at Ollerton on 8 Mar. 1607 and administration of his property was granted at York on 30 Apr. following.[6]

[1] *Vis. Notts.* (Thoroton Soc. rec. ser. xiii), 21; *Vis. Notts.* (Harl. Soc. iv), 24; C. Brown, *Newark*, i. 41.[2] *HMC Rutland*, i. 294; iv. 363; *CPR*, 1549–51, p. 210; 1563–6, pp. 73–4; 1566–9, pp. 127, 323; *HMC Hatfield*, iv. 189; E407/1/6; LC2/4/3, pp. 95–6; *CSP Dom.* Add. 1566–79, p. 31. [3] PCC 50 Chaynay; E. Young, *Hist. Colston Bassett, Notts.* 39; Bodl. e Museo 17; *HMC Hatfield*, iv. 189; vii. 302; *CPR*, 1563–6, p. 73; 1566–9, pp. 69, 313; *CSP Dom.* Add. 1580–1625, p. 22. [4] *CSP For.* 1559–60, p. 600; 1560–1, p. 234; *APC*, x. 172, 246; xii. 357; xvi. 321, 364; xx. 242, 266; xxi. 187; xxii. 56, 63, 205; xxiii. 258; *Nottingham Recs.* iv. 141, 148; *HMC Hatfield*, iv. 113; v. 253; *CSP Dom.* 1591–4, pp. 25, 174; Strype, *Annals*, iv. 156–7; *HMC Shrewsbury and Talbot*, ii. 262, 331. [5] See NOTTINGHAMSHIRE. [6] *HMC Hatfield*, vii. 302; x. 328; xv. 98, 312; York admon. act bk. 1607.

N.M.F.

MARSHE, John (by 1516–79), of London and Sywell, Northants.

READING	1547
LONDON	1553 (Mar.), 1553 (Oct.), 1554 (Apr.)
OLD SARUM	1555
LONDON	1558, 1559, 1563, 1571, 1572*

b. by 1516, 1st s. of Walter Marshe, mercer of London, by his w. Eleanor. *educ.* L. Inn 1536, called 1545. *m.* 1543, Alice, da. and h. of William Gresham of Holt, Norf. and of London, at least 3s. 1da. *suc.* fa. Jan. 1540.[1]

Sewer of the chamber by 1543; steward, manor of Finsbury 1543; under-sheriff, Mdx. 1545–6; common serjeant, London 1547–63; under-sheriff 1563–4; surveyor, ct. of augmentations, Northants. by 1553; gov. Merchant Adventurers 1555, 1559–60, 1562–72; warden, Mercers' Co. 1558–9, 1565–6; receiver-gen. Exchequer, Salop and Worcs. 1559–74; constable, the Staple 1561; eccles. commr. 1572; pres. Spanish Company 1577; j.p. Mdx. 1547–54, from 1561, Northants. 1547–54, 1559–62.[2]

Marshe, a London merchant, had a parliamentary career that spanned three reigns. In Queen Mary's reign he both 'stood for the true religion', and opposed a major government bill in the House of Commons. Having upheld protestantism under Mary, it is natural to find him classified by the bishops in 1564 as a 'favourer' of the Elizabethan settlement.

He took an active part in his Elizabethan Parliaments. On 24 Feb. 1559 Marshe spoke in the House of Commons on behalf of his fellow London merchants who had been defrauded of goods worth £300 by John Smith*. Two bills, concerning colleges and chantries in the reign of Edward VI, and the fry and spawn of fish, were committed to him on 8 Apr. and 15 Apr. 1559. During the first session of the 1563 Parliament he was put in charge of bills concerning tanners (29 Jan.), the increase of woodlands (13 Mar.) and bankrupts (20 Mar.), and in 1566 he was appointed to the succession committees on 31 Oct., and put in charge of a committee concerning chantry lands (13 Nov.). In 1571 he was appointed to the subsidy committee (7 Apr.) and to committees concerning griefs and petitions (7 Apr.) and fraudulent conveyances (14 May).

His opinion on Arthur Hall's famous speech in 1572 was that the Commons' right to freedom of speech did not extend to treasonable words, Hall having in effect accused the peers of unjustly condemning the Duke of Norfolk (17 May). On 31 May, after Peter Wentworth had urged the execution of the Duke, Marshe spoke in support of a motion to set up a committee that would peruse any written arguments prepared by Members. Something of Marshe's philosophy as a merchant may be gained from two other speeches made in the session of 1572. The first was made during the debate on the bill dealing with the export of leather (3 June). In Marshe's opinion the export of leather was the cause of the dearth at home. 'No merchant', he urged, 'should seek his living to the spoil of his country … Licences cannot do so much hurt as the carrying of everybody. The licences although they be hurtful cannot be denied to the Prince; but he wisheth it were well looked to, such persons as have licences did not so deceive the Queen and the realm.' The second debate (24 June) was on the bill to assure the true dyeing of cloth, which restricted it in all places except cities, boroughs and corporate market towns, and also aimed at restraining the carriage of undyed cloth out of the realm. Marshe was completely opposed to this precursor of Cokayne's project:

The whole bill to be overthrown, the innovation so great and so perilous to the state. The commodities of England now distributed through Christendom; trial sufficient that we want no vent as they be now used. Besides, we have not that wherewith we should dye in our own realm, but must be holpen by others: of our woad from France, with whom we have not assurance of peace. It is very doubtful being dyed how they shall be liked in other countries. Not like we shall make colour to please all nations, and then they will be unbought and clothiers and kersey men driven to give over their occupations and wool will wax cheap which is not for the commodity of England. For good dyeing there is already a good act in force. There is also other towns more fit for clothing than either borough towns or market towns. They must needs be dyed where there is plenty of wood. The procuring of licences to carry clothes over sea undressed hath cost a marvellous mass of money. It would not cost much more when they must also be dyed. Such monopoly to the undoing of the whole state he cannot allow.

He spoke against Mary Queen of Scots on 9 June 1572. He was appointed to the committee concerned with vagabonds (29 May) and spoke the next day in favour of including minstrels within the provisions of the bill. He was named to two committees on the continuance of statutes (25, 26 June). In 1576 he was appointed to the committee to examine Peter Wentworth* on 8 Feb., and the next day was instructed to 'confer touching the number of burgesses and knights in the Parliament'. He argued to the bill about lands without covin on 18 Feb. and was appointed to the committee the same day. Other committee work included such topics as bastardy (15 Feb.), the making of woollen cloths (16 Feb.), the dangerous abusing of dags and pistolets (17 Feb.), tanned leather (18 Feb., 13 Mar.), the treatment of aliens (24 Feb.), dilapidations (24 Feb.), artificers (5 Mar.), the double searching of cloths (9 Mar.), excess of apparel (10 Mar.), benefit of clergy (12 Mar.), Lord Stourton's bill (12 Mar.), wharves and quays (13 Mar.), and London goldsmiths (13 Mar.).[3]

Marshe had wide trading interests; he was behind the foundation of the Spanish Company. Anthony Jenkinson, his son-in-law, was employed by the Muscovy Company, of which Marshe was also a member, in the opening up of trade with Persia. Wool was his principal export, and he was naturally a leading member of the Merchant Adventurers' Company, attending to its affairs in the Low Countries in 1568 and 1570. Most of his correspondence was with Cecil, to whom he sent information from abroad. He had land in Northamptonshire, and an office unconnected with his activities as a merchant, that of augmentations surveyor for the county. He settled his own landed estate in the county before his death. His eldest son was to inherit Bozeat, and his son-in-law Sywell. Marshe made his nuncupative will on 7 Jan. 1579, leaving a third of his goods 'to his children unadvanced', and the rest to his wife, the executrix. The will was proved on 28 Jan. 1579. Marshe was buried in the church of St. Michael, Wood Street, the advowson of which he had bought in 1565.[4]

[1] C142/62/98; E150/494/3; *LP Hen. VIII*, xviii(1), p. 281; C2Eliz./ P10/23; PCC 2 Bakon, 2 Alenger; *Vis. London* (Harl. Soc. cix, cx), 67. [2] *LP Hen. VIII*, xviii(1), p. 125; City of London RO, Guildhall, rep. 10, f. 345v; 11, ff. 226, 344; 15, ff. 194, 201v, 315; Stowe 571, f. 11v; O. de Smedt, *De Engelse Natie te Antwerpen*, ii. 90; Mercers' Co. court acts, 1527–60, f. 297a; 1560–95, f. 81b; *CPR*, 1558–60, p. 40; 1560–3, p. 29; 1569–72, p. 440. [3] Bodl. e Museo 17; Guildford Mus. Loseley 1331/2; *Cam. Misc.* ix(3), p. 60; D'Ewes, 48, 53, 60, 88, 127, 128, 159, 183, 220, 224, 241, 244, 247, 249, 259, 260, 262; *CJ*, i. 59, 60, 64, 69, 70, 77, 83, 87, 99, 102, 103, 104, 105, 106, 108, 110, 113, 114, 115; *HMC Lords*, n.s. xi. 8; Neale, *Parlts*. i. 278; Trinity, Dublin, Thos. Cromwell's jnl. ff. 22, 48, 57, 63–4. [4] P. Croft, *Spanish Co.* (London Rec. Soc. ix), p. xi; T. S. Willan, *Muscovy Merchants of 1555*, p. 112; *CSP For.* 1569–71, passim; *CSP Dom.* 1547–80, p. 236 et passim; Add. 1566–79, p. 502; *APC*, vii. 378; viii. 186–7; *VCH Northants.* iv. 4, 133; PCC 2 Bakon; Stow, *Survey London*, ed. Kingsford, i. 298.

A.M.M.

MARTIN, Nicholas (*d.* 1599), of Exeter, Devon.

BERE ALSTON   1586

2nd s. of Richard Martin, mayor of Exeter, by his 2nd w. Julian, da. of William Hurst†, merchant of Exeter; bro. of William*. *m.* (1) 1561, Mary (*d.* 1576), da. of Leonard Yeo*, 4s. 3da.; (2) Mary (*d.* 1579), da. of William Strode I*, of Newnham, wid. of Thomas Prestwood†, *s.p.*; (3) Elizabeth, da. of Anthony Rous, 4s.
  Bailiff, Exeter 1571, mayor 1574–5, 1585–6, sheriff 1582; j.p. Dorset from 1579.

Martin's grandfather, Sir William Martin of Athelhampton, Dorset, married into the Paulet family, and no doubt it was the Marquess of Winchester (who shared the patronage at Bere Alston equally with Lord Mountjoy) who brought Martin into Parliament for the borough in 1586. No activity has been recorded in his name for the 1586 Parliament, but a 'Mr. Martin' was the victim of an arrest by one William White. This episode may refer to Nicholas Martin, or to Henry Martyn*. Named in the 1560 charter of the Exeter merchant adventurers, Martin and his brothers traded in fruit, soap and wine, with the Netherlands and France. He died in March 1599, and was buried at St. Petrock's, Exeter.

Vivian, *Vis. Devon*, 553–4; J. J. Alexander, *Exeter MPs*; *HMC Exeter*, 57, 402; St. Ch. 5/E2/9; W. Cotton, *Eliz. Guild, Exeter*, 118; *Trans. Dev. Assoc.* xliv. 269.

P.W.H.

MARTIN, Richard (1570–1618), of the Middle Temple, London.

BARNSTAPLE   1601
CHRISTCHURCH   1604, 1614

b. 1570, s. of William Martin* of Exeter by his 1st w. Anne, da. of Richard Parker of Suss. *educ.* Broadgates Hall, Oxf. 1585; New Inn; M. Temple 1587, called 1602. *unm.*
  Lent reader, M. Temple 1615, bencher by 1616; recorder, London 1618.

Whether born at Exeter, as he stated in his maiden speech in Parliament, or at Otterton, as he wrote in his will, Martin had a riotous student career at the Middle Temple, and had still not been called to the bar when, aged just over 30, he was nominated by Robert Chichester to one of the Barnstaple seats in Elizabeth's last Parliament. 'Mr. Martin of the Temple' took to the House as a duck to water. His first speech, 10 Nov. 1601, was in favour of a bill for uniting several small churches in Exeter, and 'against such a man as he that last spake [the bishop's servant of Exeter, as the journal puts it] who spake more for his master's benefit than for God's honour'. Martin next took a swipe at 'Serjeant Heale [John Hele I*] that had yesterday so much flattered his prince' in the subsidy debate, and went on to urge the committal of the bill. This wish to get the discussion off the floor of the House and into committee is interesting at this stage of the evolution of the House of Commons. It recurred on 2 Dec. when he thought discussion on the bill for church attendance was a 'matter more fit to be decided at a committee than here'. Martin disliked the 'extravagant speeches' some Members were making on the depredations of the Dunkirk pirates, 3 Dec.,

like to men whose houses being on fire ... run out into the streets like madmen ... I wish that those who first propounded this matter to the House had also laid down some project, though never so small, of remedy.

He spoke against fining recusants £20 a month (under the 1581 Act) and 1*s.* a week, 'the law will not tolerate two remedies for one inconvenience ... I can never agree in conscience to consent to a double remedy for one offence'. He was outspoken against monopolies, 20 Nov.:

I speak for a town that grieves and pines, and for a country that groans under the burden of monstrous and unconscionable substitutes, the monopolitans of starch, tin, fish, cloth, oil, vinegar, salt, and I know not what. Nay, what not? The principal commodities both of my town and country are ingrossed into the hands of these bloodsuckers of the commonwealth ... If these bloodsuckers be still let alone, to suck up the best ... commodities which the earth ... has given us, what shall become of us, from whom the fruits of our own soil and the commodities of our own labour, which, with the sweat of our brows (even up to the knees in mire and dirt) we have laboured for, shall be taken from us by warrant of supreme authority, which the poor subject dares not gainsay?

And the next day he persuaded the House not to allow 'the old officers' of the Exchequer to have counsel to represent them before the committal of the Exchequer reform bill. 'I am utterly against that they should have counsel ... I hold it best to proceed to the question.' Martin was himself appointed to the committee. The bill passed both Houses and was vetoed by the Queen.

On 23 Nov., on the adjourned monopolies debate, it was Martin who seconded Henry Montagu's* motion 'that the patentees shall have no other remedies than by the laws of the realm'. That afternoon, at the committee, Martin spoke after the same John Davies* who had broken a cudgel over Martin's head at dinner in Middle Temple Hall 9 Feb. 1598. Davies wished to proceed to rectify the grievances by bill. His zeal, said Martin, had masked his reason – a petition would be better. This was something of a *volte face* on Martin's part, and it may be significant that he was one of those selected, 28 Nov., to thank the Queen for her concessionary message about monopolies. By this time Martin had obviously acquired something of a reputation in Parliament. On 8 Dec. he was appointed to a privilege committee, and the following day he humiliated Secretary Cecil. The business was trivial enough: whether a proviso in favour of a Mr. Dormer should be inserted in a land bill. The Speaker put it to the question, pronounced for the ayes, the noes demanded a division, 'so the door being set open, no man offered to go forth'. At this point Martin intervened:

> Mr. Speaker I have observed it that ever this Parliament the noes upon the division of the House have carried it. The reason whereof, as I conceive it, is because divers are loth to go forth for fear of losing their places. And many that cry aye aye aye will sit still with the noes. I therefore do but move this unto the House, that all those that have given their aye aye aye would, according to their consciences, go forth. And for my part I'll begin.

Martin and the rest of the ayes had 178, the noes, including Cecil, 134. Cecil was furious, saying that Martin 'spake persuadingly to draw those out of the House who perhaps meant it not', that he had 'laid an imputation upon the House' which he should answer 'at the bar'. But Knollys, comptroller of the Household, backed Martin: 'Surely for not removing out of places, I have heard fault found before this time'. Martin asked the Speaker if he might answer. 'The House cried aye, aye, aye. "No", quoth the Secretary, "you must stand at the bar". And the House cried no, no, no.'

> Then Mr. Secretary desired it might be put to the question, whether he should speak or no, and so it was, and not twenty said No. Then it was put to the question whether he should speak at the bar or no? And Mr. Brown the lawyer [probably John Browne] stood up and said 'Mr. Speaker, *par in parem non habet imperium*, we are all members of one body and one cannot judge of another'. So, being put to the question, there were not above twelve aye, aye, aye that he should stand at the bar.

Martin could now rub it in. 'Standing in his seat [he] showed the cause of his speech to have been only for the order of the House, and not out of any persuasive meaning that he had, for ... he neither knew the man nor the matter.'

Martin's last intervention in this Parliament was typical both of his wit and his liking for pressing on with the business. During a straggling debate on alehouses, Martin justified an intervention by another Member, then went on 'But that hath led us out of the ale house ... I wish that we might make a quick return by putting it, without further disputation, to the question'. He continued to sit in the next period, making an interesting suggestion for reforming the committee system 16 Apr. 1604, was sworn recorder of London 1 Oct. 1618, and died on the 31st, according to Aubrey, of drink. He appointed as executor his brother Thomas, mayor of Exeter at the time the will was made, and left £5 to Otterton 'where I was born'.

DNB; Townshend, *Hist. Colls.* 206, 219, 228, 234, 237, 243, 244, 276, 278, 281–2, 301–3, 306; D'Ewes, 640, 645–6, 649, 650, 651, 657, 664, 666, 673, 675; Inner Temple Petyt ms 501/1, f. 319; PCC 111 Meade.

P.W.H.

MARTIN, Thomas (c.1530–83), of Park Pale, Tolpuddle, Dorset.

DORCHESTER 1563

b. c.1530, 2nd s. of Robert Martin of Athelhampton by Elizabeth, da. of Sir John Keilway of Rockbourne, Hants. *m.* Elizabeth, da. of William Gerard (*d.*1568) of Trent, Dorset, at least 5s. 3da.[1]

There is some doubt about the identity of the senior Member for Dorchester in the 1563 Parliament. Several authorities have assumed that Thomas Martin, the civil lawyer and strong supporter of Mary's religious policies, was the Member in question. He was after all an experienced Commons man, having sat in four Marian Parliaments, and came from Cerne, quite close to Dorchester. Nor would his Catholicism bar him from the House in 1563. But other factors make the identity less likely. Though a Dorset man, Martin seems to have severed his connexions with the county many years earlier and was living in Cambridgeshire. Because of this he would have needed a patron to secure his return. The only outsider who enjoyed any regular parliamentary patronage at Dorchester was the 2nd Earl of Bedford, a leading puritan. It is unlikely, therefore, though not impossible, that Thomas Martin, the civilian, occupied the seat.[2]

Another Martin family had lived in the Dorchester area since the reign of Edward I or even earlier. By the Tudor period, their principal seat was Athelhampton, enlarged by Sir William Martin into a splendid manor house towards the end of the fifteenth century. Besides this, they owned several manors in Puddletown, Tolpuddle and adjoining parishes. When Robert Martin, the head of the family, died in 1548 he left the bulk of his property to the eldest son Nicholas, but he also remembered his younger children. One of these, the second son Thomas, may have been the Dorchester MP. As well as being among the principal landholders in the district, the Martins owned property in the town itself, and it would be natural for the lord of Athelhampton's brother to be elected by its burgesses as one of their Members.[3]

Judging by his will, Robert Martin had been a prosperous sheep farmer, for several thousand animals are mentioned. He left Thomas, who was still a minor, a small income from the estate at Faringdon in Shroton, Dorset, but it was also arranged that he should succeed his uncle, Henry, in the possession of all the Martin lands in the parish of Tolpuddle. As a result the manor house of Park Pale became the home of his branch of the family, and there they remained for nearly a century. Next to nothing is known about Thomas's life after he settled there. Probably, like his father, he was a sheep farmer. The families into which his own relatives married – the Wallops and Keilways of Hampshire, the Wadhams of Somerset, the Tregonwells – show that he was known to a wide social circle in the west country, and one of his brothers-in-law was Sir George Bingham, killed by the Irish after a stormy career as governor of Sligo. As a younger son, Martin had little to do with local government, though the Privy Council are known to have called on his services on one occasion, in 1581, when he and several other Dorset gentlemen were commissioned to examine two men, Hugh Cheverell and George Martin – perhaps a relative – accused of making slanderous statements about Viscount Bindon. In the will of his brother-in-law, Thomas Gerard, Martin was asked to help supervise his property during the minority of the heir. This was in July 1583, but Martin died in the same year. His burial, in Puddletown church close to many of his relatives, is recorded in the parish register. His brother Nicholas was the last of the Martins to occupy Athelhampton, being succeeded by four daughters, but his own family survived at Park Pale until the estate was seized in 1645 following a charge of recusancy.[4]

[1] Hutchins, *Dorset*, ii. 582; *Genealogist*, n.s. iii. 163–4; *Vis. Dorset* (Harl. Soc. xx), 66; *Vis. Dorset, Add.* ed. Colby and Rylands, 32–3. [2] *DNB* (Martyn or Martin, Thomas, civilian). [3] W. G. W. Watson, *House of Martin*, 21; Hutchins, i. 447; ii. 586, 589, 615, 617, 627, 632; C142/88/15; PCC 18 Populwell; *CPR*, 1549–51, p. 190; 1550–3, p. 45; *Dorchester Recs.* 320, 326, 332, 334, 338, 358. [4] PCC 18 Populwell, 27 Butts; Hutchins, ii. 623, 632; *APC*, xiii. 150–1.

M.R.P.

MARTIN, William (d. c.1609), of Exeter, Devon.

EXETER 1597

s. of Richard Martin of Exeter by his 2nd w. and bro. of Nicholas*. m. (1) Anne, da. of Richard Parker of Suss., at least 2s. inc. Richard*; (2) 1576, Katherine, da. of William Buggin of Totnes, at least 1s.; in all, at least 5s. 2da.

Bailiff, Exeter 1571, receiver 1583, sheriff 1585, mayor 1590, 1600, part of 1602; gov. merchant adventurers 1578, 1599.

Martin was an Exeter merchant active in public work. He lent money for repairing the harbour, supplied powder to the city, and organized the city's corn supply, in 1597 combining his visit to London for this purpose with attendance at Parliament. He is recorded as sitting on a committee, 10 Nov., concerned with weavers' and spinners' wages. He invested in Sir Humphrey Gilbert's* last voyage. In 1596 he was brought before the Privy Council on a charge of infringing a starch patent, and although, as far as is known, he took no part in the debates on monopolies in the 1597 Parliament, his son Richard spoke out strongly against them in the next.

Martin's will was made 20 Aug. 1609, and proved the following 5 Jan. In a religious preamble containing some nice passages

> like a tale that is told, and as a bird in the air, or a ship on the sea which suddenly parteth away and not seen where they went,

Martin called upon the 'good and gracious presence of Almighty God' to 'bless all these my children that they may be profitable members in His Church and in His Commonwealth'. To each of his younger sons he left land and money, and his daughters received personal possessions and bequests for their children. Two grandsons, sons of his eldest son Thomas, received sums of money. The Exeter Chamber was left £20 to be lent out to tradesmen or artificers. His heir and executor Thomas received 'all that I have, at home or abroad', and 'so', Martin concluded, 'the living God bless him and his'.

Vivian, *Vis. Devon*, 98, 553; *Trans. Dev. Assoc.* xlv. 416; lxi. 209; Roberts thesis; R. Izacke, *Exeter*, 134–43; W. Cotton, *Eliz. Guild of Exeter*, 42, 54; *HMC Exeter*, 30–1, 312; D'Ewes, 555; *Voyages of Gilbert*, ed. Quinn (Hak. Soc. lxxxiv), ii. 333; *APC*, xxv. 373–5; PCC 8 Wingfield, 10 Lyon.

P.W.H.

MARTYN, Henry (c.1564–1626), of Nethercote, Wilts.

WILTON	1586
WOOTTON BASSETT	1604

b. c. 1564, s. of William Martyn of Burderop, by Dorothy, da. of Anthony Fetiplace of Wanborough. educ. Camb. matric. pens. St. John's 1579, BA Christ's 1582–3; G. Inn 9 Feb. 1581. m., 3s.[1]

Servant of 2nd Earl of Pembroke c.1585–1601.
?J.p. Wilts. from c.1592.

The identification of Henry Martyn poses a two-fold problem: was the Member for Wilton in 1586 the same man as the Member for Wootton Bassett in 1604, and is this man – or, if there were two, is either of them – also to be identified with Sir Henry Martyn, the eminent civilian who sat in Parliament for St. Germans in 1625 and for Oxford University in 1628?

Of the Member for Wilton, as of all those returned for that borough during the reign of Elizabeth, it can be said without hesitation that he was a Pembroke nominee; and his identification with the 2nd Earl's servant of that name follows naturally enough. By his will of January 1595 Pembroke directed Matthew Ewens, baron of the Exchequer, and Henry Martyn esquire, whom he had enfeoffed with Devizes park 'upon confidence and trust reposed in them by me', to convey it to his countess for life and afterwards to his heir William; but by a codicil, apparently added in January 1601, he charged the same two feoffees to secure the property first to the countess and then to his second son Philip. Since Martyn was also one of the seven witnesses to the will, although not a beneficiary by it, he was clearly a trusted servant of the Earl's in his declining years. From his style of 'esquire', and from his association with Ewens, it may be inferred that he, too, was a lawyer.[2]

Of the only two men whose early careers entitle them to consideration, it has been usual to identify the civilian with the Henry Martyn of these transactions and with the Member for Wilton. But in September 1586, when 'Henry Martyn esq.' was returned for that borough, the civilian was but 24 years old and a fellow of New College, from which he was to take his BCL in the following June; and the unlikelihood of his either having wanted, or been able, to interrupt his academic career in this way is hardly offset by the consideration that he was probably already known to Pembroke and may have helped to attract the Earl's sons to his college, which they entered a few years later. Moreover, by 1595 he had taken his doctorate, and he can thus almost certainly not have been the 'Henry Martyn esquire' who figures in the Earl's will. As will be shown, however, he was probably a relative of this namesake.[3]

No such difficulties attach to the Henry Martyn who had gone to Gray's Inn in 1581, perhaps after two years at Cambridge and before taking his degree there early in 1583. For him a place in Pembroke's household, and a seat for the family borough, would have been a natural, if gratifyingly swift, sequel to his studies. On this showing the Member for Wilton would have been born about 1564. That he was of a local family, although perhaps of a branch of the Berkshire house which had migrated to Wiltshire, is likely enough; but no discussion of his origin can be usefully entered upon before his identity or relationship with the Member of 1604 is at least surmised.

With this 'Henry Martyn esq.' we reach slightly surer ground. Nothing, and least of all the style used in the return, suggests that he was Dr. Henry Martyn; whereas it is highly probable that he was the Henry Martyn who in 1600–1 had 'lately' purchased from John Pleydell* the manor of Nethercote, near Swindon, and whose acquisition of it gave him standing in the neighbourhood of Wootton Bassett. Since this Henry Martyn was to retain the manor until his death in 1626, something is known for certain about him, and although it does not prove his identity with the Member of 1586 it creates a presumption that they were the same. His son and heir Edward was aged 40 years and more at his death, a fact which suggests that the father had married in the early 1580s, which the Member of 1586 could well have done. Again, the coincidence in time of his acquisition of Nethercote with the death of the 2nd Earl of Pembroke could reflect his withdrawal from Wilton and establishment of an independent position, as it did with others similarly placed. There is thus a case for regarding the Members of 1586 and 1604 as identical, and for distinguishing this Henry Martyn from the civilian; and it is the solution of the problem posed which is adopted here.[4]

There remains the further problem of Henry Martyn's pedigree. If we accept the customary identification of the civilian with Henry, son of Anthony Martyn, citizen and grocer of London (and his entry to Winchester in 1577 certainly supports it), his namesake's parentage has to be sought elsewhere. We may not, however, have to look far. For Anthony Martyn, one of the Berkshire family, had a younger brother William, who married Dorothy Fetiplace of Wanborough, Wiltshire, and himself settled at Burderop, near Swindon. It was William Martyn's son Stephen who was to be called 'cousin' in his uncle Edward's will of 1592, as were the testator's two nieces, his brother Anthony's daughters Anne and Jane; and the 'cousin Henry Martyn' also named in the will could thus have been another son of William's, and brother to Stephen. This relationship would accord with Henry Martyn's decision to settle at Nethercote, hard by his father's home at Burderop; his witnessing of the will of a Burderop man in 1595 suggests a continuing interest in the locality. It would also provide an explanation of his entry into Pembroke's service. For Anthony Martyn, father to one Henry and uncle to the other, appears to have possessed, among the 'lands and tenements … wheresoever they be within the realm of England' which he bequeathed by his will, a property at Downton which was assessed, in his name, at £3 for the subsidy of 1576. Downton was Pembroke territory, and a number of the Earl's servants had holdings there. It is also to be observed that Anthony Martyn's daughter Anne married William Cooke, and that a man of that name was, with Henry Martyn, a witness of Pembroke's will.[5]

To place Henry Martyn in this setting is certainly more rewarding than to attempt to connect him with other families of that name like those of Steeple Ashton,

Wiltshire, and of Hinton, Somerset, or with assorted Martyns who held land of Pembroke either in Wiltshire or in Devon. It does not, however, yield the name of his wife nor add much of detail to his career. A further ambiguity arises in connexion with his Membership in 1586. The proceedings of that Parliament included the episode of the arrest of a Member named Martin by one William White, but since the victim's christian name does not appear he may equally well have been Nicholas Martin, MP for Bere Alston, as Henry. Happily, less doubt attaches to the identity of the 'Mr. Martin' who figures so prominently in the Parliament of 1604; this was clearly not Henry Martyn, but the loquacious Richard who had already made his mark in the House of 1601.[6]

Henry Martyn's will, if he made one, has not been traced. At his death which occurred on 13 July 1626, he possessed, besides the manor of Nethercote, a house and land at Upham and property in Snappe and Aldbourne. In 1605 he and Gabriel Cox junior had suffered a recovery of the manor of Westbury St. Maur; but what Martyn's interest in this property had been, and how he had acquired it, are not known. The Aldbourne land was sold by his sons Edward and Anthony in 1634 to the Goddards. Three years earlier Edward, the heir, described as of Uphaven, had paid £17 10s. as his composition for knighthood.[7]

[1] Vis. Berks. (Harl. Soc. lvi), 43–4, 316; Wilts. IPMs (Brit. Rec. Soc. Index Lib. xxiii), 395–6. [2] Dugdale, Originales, 218; PCC 39 Woodhall. [3] Wood, Athenae, ed. Bliss, iii. 17; Al. Ox. i. 977; CP. [4] Wilts. Arch. Mag. xlix. 483; Wilts. IPMs, loc. cit. [5] Athenae, iii. 17; Al. Ox. i. 977; Winchester Scholars, 147; PCC 3 Arundel, 61 Harte; Wilts. Arch. Mag. xxx. 136; Two Taxation Lists (Wilts. Arch. Soc. recs. br. x), 117; PCC 30 Woodhall. [6] Wilts. N. and Q. vi, vii. passim; PCC 22 Carew; Wilts. Vis. Peds. (Harl. Soc. cv, cvi), 123–4; M.T. Adm. Reg. i. 63; Al. Ox. i. 977; PCC 21 Lewyn, 8 Fenner; Pembroke Survey (Roxburghe Club), index sub Martin; D'Ewes, 410, 412, 414; Neale, Parlts. ii. 379–80, 382–3, 398, 402, 418–19. [7] Wilts. IPMs, loc. cit.; recovery roll, Trin. 3 Jas. I, r. 76; Wilts. N. and Q. i. 107; iii. 270–5.

S.T.B.

MARVYN, Edmund (c.1555–1604), of Petersfield, Hants.

PETERSFIELD   1584, 1586, 1589

b. c.1555, 1st s. of Henry Marvyn (d.1614), of Durford by Edith, da. of Sir Anthony Windsor of Harting. educ. Clement's Inn; M. Temple 1572, called 1581. m. by 1583, Anne, da. of William Jephson of Froyle, 1s. and other ch.[1]

J.p.q. Hants by 1601.

Marvyn was the grandson of Sir Edmund Marvyn (a younger son of the Marvyns of Fonthill Gifford, Wiltshire) who was a judge in the reigns of Henry VIII, Edward VI and Queen Mary. Marrying into the Pakenham family, Sir Edmund acquired the Hampshire manor of Bramshott, and he was later granted the site of Durford abbey, Sussex, and a manor at Petersfield. Marvyn himself married into a good Hampshire family, and lived at Petersfield, being returned for the borough at the first election after his marriage, and for the two succeeding Parliaments. He did not sit after 1589, for in 1593 the junior seat was taken by a member of the Weston family, the absentee owners of the borough, and by the election of 1597 the Westons had given way to a new and active resident owner who wanted both seats.[2]

Marvyn was in chambers at the Middle Temple at intervals throughout his life. In 1596 his reading was deferred because of his sickness, and in 1599 he was heavily fined for not reading. Among other Hampshire men admitted to his chambers was Richard Norton, son of Richard Norton II of Rotherfield, who had sat for Petersfield in 1572. The Nortons were inclined to puritanism, as was Sir Henry Wallop*, who in 1585 asked that Marvyn be allowed to act as his deputy in the stewardships of Somerford and Lymington, Hampshire; and Marvyn's father and father-in-law had both been listed as 'favourers' of true religion in the bishop's report on the j.p.s of 1564. Possibly Marvyn himself had puritan sympathies; his will expresses his confidence in his election as a 'citizen of [Christ's] celestial court in heaven'.[3]

Marvyn died v.p. 9 Sept. 1604. Henry, his son and heir, was then betrothed to Christine Audley, the granddaughter of (Sir) James Marvyn* of Fonthill, who had arranged the match in order to keep Fonthill in the ownership of Marvyns, for Lucy, Christine Audley's mother, the wife of George, Lord Audley, later 1st Earl of Castlehaven, was his only child. Sir James, having settled Fonthill on the young couple, complained in his will that Edmund Marvyn had not made them the equivalent gift which had been agreed upon. The marriage took place, however, and Henry Marvyn's son, who rose to be vice-admiral of the narrow seas, inherited Fonthill.[4]

[1] Vis. Suss. (Harl. Soc. liii), 76–7; Wilts. Peds. (Harl. Soc. cv, cvi), 124; C142/683/187; Mousley thesis, 605–7. [2] VCH Hants, ii. 492; iii, 117; VCH Suss. iv. 15, 25; Lansd. 49, f. 144; PCC 11 Hayes; CSP Dom. 1591–4, p. 510. [3] M.T. Recs. i. 234, 247, 258, 368, 380, 395, 398, 412, 421; ii. 448; CSP Ire. 1574–85, p. 546; Cam. Misc. ix(3), pp. 9, 55; PCC 11 Hayes. [4] C142/683/187; CP, iii. 86; PCC 89 Wood.

A.H.

MARVYN, James (1529–1611), of Fonthill Gifford, Wilts.

WILTSHIRE   1572
HINDON   1597

b. 1529, 1st s. of Sir John Marvyn† by Jane, da. of Philip Baskerville of Sherborne, Dorset, wid. of William Peverell of Bradford Peverell, Som. educ. M. Temple 1553. m. (1) by 1566, Amy, da. of Valentine Clark by Elizabeth, da. and h. of Roland Bridges, wid. of one Horne of Sarsden, Oxon., 1da.; (2) bet. 1590 and 1601, Deborah, da. and coh. of James Pilkington, bp. of Durham, wid. of Walter Dunch*, s.p. suc. fa. 18 June 1566. Kntd. 1574.[1]

J.p. Wilts. from 1573, commr. recusancy; sheriff, Wilts. 1597–8; dep. lt. from 1601; col. of Wilts. trained bands sent to I.o.W. 1590, 1596; collector of customs and subsidies, Exeter and Dartmouth 1585, 1592.

Esquire of the body 1558 or 1559–1603; master of the swans 1561–?1611; bailiff of Wittelsmere 1561–?1611; duchy of Lancaster steward for Dorset regranted 1573, surrendered ?1583.[2]

Among the families that were gathering together a complex of holdings in Wiltshire during the fifteenth century were the Marvyns. This family had made its home at Fonthill for five generations before Sir John Marvyn[1] purchased the adjoining manor of Compton Bassett in 1553. His heir, despite the four younger brothers and six surviving sisters also to be provided for, could look forward to an assured position in the county.[3]

Although his brothers John and Philip are claimed by Eton as *alumni*, no evidence has been found to connect James Marvyn with any school nor, apart from a reference in his will to his 'college jugg', to either university. James was about 24 when he was admitted generally to the clerks' commons of the Middle Temple, too old to regard the inn as a finishing school, but young enough to spend such time there during the next six years as to qualify him four times for inclusion among the officers of the inn's Christmas revels. He had the opportunity therefore, to acquire some grounding during his young manhood in what in the sixteenth century was the most important aspect of business.[4]

His appointment to an office at court so early in Elizabeth's reign suggests that his loyalty to her was assured from the outset. The office yielded £40 a year in fees and gave him a vantage point from which to pick up rewards and further offices. Thus he was able to acquire, for his services and a fine of £176, the lease for 21 years of the parish church of Chester-le-Street, county Durham, in 1564, and had become a pluralist in offices even earlier. As a collector of customs and subsidies he was still owing £400 from his first term of office two years after its expiry, and during his second complained to Burghley that the commissioners were hampering him by their refusal to acquaint him with their proceedings. The extent to which Marvyn had launched himself independently of his family expectations is reflected perhaps in his father's will. Sir John concerned himself exclusively with his younger sons, made the two youngest his executors and, by settling his purchased lands (Compton Bassett) on his eldest grandson, John Marvyn*, cut James down to the entail. When he had to defend Compton Bassett against a claim of assart in 1607, James included papers drawn up while he was contesting his father's deposition of it. He had challenged the will as forged by his stepmother and the parson, asserted that the purchased lands had been rented by the family for 200 years and were intermingled with 'his old inheritors round about his house even to his door', and

maintained that his father, far from wishing to visit his dislikes upon his heir, had held him in great affection.[5]

As a corollary to his employment in offices of profit Marvyn was called upon to serve in offices for which the only reward was a sense of duty done or of the prestige accruing to them. He bore more than his bare share of duty with the county militia; his friendship with (Sir) Henry Knyvet*, whose burial certificate he signed, may suggest a shared interest in military affairs. His own experience as colonel of the shire's forces may, however, have made him the readier to sympathize with his grandson by marriage, (Sir) Thomas Thynne II*, when this irksome duty fell to the younger man's lot in 1608; certainly Hertford, then lord lieutenant, regarded Marvyn as guilty of connivance in Thynne's efforts to evade it. Marvyn's name appears on two lists jotted upon the dorse of letters to Sir Robert Cecil of 1597 and 1599, probably in connexion with the militia. It was a name which occurred frequently also to members of the Council when they had inquiries to make and disputes to settle in the shire; its appearances on a list of persons to be examined, presumably concerning the proposed marriage between the Queen of Scots and the Duke of Norfolk in 1569, is harder to explain, since its owner appears to have been anti-Catholic and loyal. He was one of those chosen to confer with the recusants of his shire and send particulars of their answers to the Council in April 1586.[6]

Considering his prominence in the affairs of the county it is hard to explain why Marvyn was content to sit in only two Parliaments. His one appearance as knight of the shire was certainly no more than he was entitled to expect as a leading gentleman there; and we know that he was one of the spokesmen who urged on the Earl of Pembroke the desire of the Wiltshire gentry 'to have their due reserved unto them' in the matter of county representation. But while many of his fellow gentlemen were anxious to represent a borough *faute de mieux*, Marvyn appears to have found one experience of this sufficient also. He had property within the borough of Hindon and his seat at Fonthill Gifford was only two miles away from that borough. It is easier to see why he sat for it once than why he did not sit for it more often. He used his influence there on behalf of his nephew John and almost certainly exerted himself to get his grand-daughter's husband, Thomas Thynne, elected there in 1601; apparently he valued the power to sway elections more than the election itself. He does not appear to have made much of his own parliamentary experience, being named only once on a committee, concerning the subsidy (25 Jan. 1581), and is not known to have spoken in debate.[7]

Perhaps he found it more gratifying to see himself as Marvyn of 'Marvyn's division', as his administrative section of the shire was called, than to find himself a little-known Member amongst strangers. Certainly there were many demands on his attention both in connexion with his offices and in the shire itself. His feud with Sir John Thynne* which lasted for 15 years and culminated in an armed affray between their followers and an action in the Star Chamber may have had its origin in the failure of a marriage projected between Thynne and Marvyn's daughter in 1574. If so, its bitterness was a measure of his disappointment in failing to effect an alliance with a family which, though newer in the county than his own, was even more markedly prosperous. Marvyn achieved this connexion in the end, when his grand-daughter Maria Audley married Sir Thomas Thynne.[8]

A marriage alliance which appears to have brought Marvyn little but trouble was that of his stepdaughter Elizabeth Horne of Sarsden, Oxfordshire with Anthony Bourne. Bourne's disputes with Sir John Conway, who held part of the manor of Cutteslowe in trust for him and his wife and their two daughters and had charge of one of the girls, brought Bourne to the Tower in 1579 and his father-in-law the burden of managing his affairs. When he had laboured to reduce these to order and had made what appears to have been a sincere attempt to reach an equitable arrangement, Marvyn was exasperated to find that Bourne was preparing to set aside one of his decisions and that Elizabeth regarded him as a 'mercenary man' who was favouring her husband at her expense. When the Bournes and the Conways reached a settlement nine years later Marvyn was bound in £2,000 for Bourne's performance of his part of it.[9]

He was substantial enough to have paid it had the need arisen. To his patrimony of the manors of Fonthill Gifford, Fernchull, Fonthill Charterhouse, Hatche, Swallowcliffe, Compton Bassett, and Widcombe he had added the dowries of two widows, the second bringing him a life interest in Avebury Manor, where his initials on the south porch testify to his responsibility for the building of this side of the house. He was alleged to possess concealed lands in 1583 and appears as the farmer of recusant lands in East Meon, Hampshire, and in Laverstock, Wiltshire, in 1592–3. He had a London residence in Farringdon-Without, probably in Fetter Lane; he was one of those in that ward who had refused to pay towards the setting out of ships for the Queen's service in August 1596 on the grounds that they had paid elsewhere, the sum in question being £30.[10]

Proud of his name and of his family's standing in Wiltshire, he sought to perpetuate both after his death. His only daughter, Lucy, wife of George, Lord Audley, predeceased her father and her heir, Sir Mervyn Audley, was his grandfather's heir also. But Marvyn was not satisfied with so tenuous a projection of the family name. He arranged a marriage between Henry†, eldest son and heir of a remote cousin Edmund Marvyn* (of the Durford Abbey branch of the family), and Christian Audley, one of Lucy's daughters, settling Fonthill upon them and their heirs to perpetuate the name and line there, and

demanded from Henry assurances that he would similarly settle his own inheritance of Durford and Bramshill upon himself, Lucy and their heirs. These assurances had not been given when Marvyn drew up his will in 1610, and after his death, which occurred on 1 May 1611, Henry sold Fonthill to Sir Mervyn, on whose attainder in 1631 it passed out of the family for ever.[11]

James Marvyn showed many of the virtues of his type. He tried in his will to remember his nephews and nieces, to fulfil the obligations of his position in gifts to the parish churches connected with the family at Fonthill, Tisbury, East Knoyle, Bishop's Fonthill and Barwick St. Leonards; to reward family servants and safeguard the security of tenants, to provide, though belatedly, for a tomb to be erected for his parents in Fonthill church and to ensure that his brother Ambrose should continue to find a home at the manor house after his death as he had done during his life.

[1] *Vis. Herefs. 1569*, p. 7, gives Marvyn's fa.-in-law as 'of Eardisley', Herefs.; *Misc. Gen. et Her.* n.s. i. 358–9; W. R. Drake, *Fasciculus Mervinensis* (privately 1873), pp. 10–14, app. 1. [2] *VCH Wilts.* v. 82; Lansd. 3, f. 193; 63, f. 70; 70, ff. 157, 171; *CPR, 1560–3*, p. 212; 1563–6, p. 151; LC2/4/4; *CSP Dom.* 1603–10, p. 81; Somerville, *Duchy*, i. 630; Harl. 474; *HMC Hatfield*, vi. 506; Add. 22115, f. 12. [3] *Wilts. Arch. Mag.* xlix. 505. [4] *Eton Coll. Reg.* 1441–1698, p. 225; *M.T. Recs.* i. 94, 98, 113, 118. [5] *CPR, 1563–6*, p. 151; Lansd. 70, f. 171; Add. 22115, f. 12; *Misc. Gen. et Her.* n.s. i. 362; SP14/192/8. [6] Sir H. Knyvet, *Defence of the Realm*, p. xxii; *Wilts. Arch. Mag.* i. 223; ii. 174–5; *HMC Hatfield*, i. 456; vii. 341; ix. 252; *APC*, x. 28–9; xiv. 173, 319; xv. 112; xvii. 183, 301–2; xviii. 399; xix. 19; xx. 130–1; xxii. 501–2; xxvi. 488–9; xxvii. 112–13; *CSP Dom.* 1581–90, p. 319. [7] *CJ*, i. 119. [8] *VCH Wilts.* v. 125. [9] *APC*, xi. 34, 124, 128, 340; xiii. 438–9; xiv. 30; xv. 195; xvi. 51, 118, 139–41, 380, 383; xviii. 418, 445–6; *CSP Dom.* Add. 1566–79, pp. 559–60; Drake, 20–1. [10] *Wilts. Arch. Mag.* 440–1; *Remembrancia City of London*, 114–15; *Recusant Roll* (Cath. Rec. Soc. xviii), 275, 352; *HMC Hatfield*, xii. 487; Lansd. 78, f. 166; 81, f. 81. [11] *Misc. Gen. et Her.* n.s. i. 358–9, 362–5.

M.B.

MARVYN, John (*b.*1559), of the Middle Temple, London.

HINDON   1584*, 1586, 1589

b. 1559, 1st s. of Edmund Marvyn by Jane, da. of Sir Richard Catesby of Warws., wid. of Robert Gaynesford of Carshalton, Surr. *educ.* Trinity, Oxf. 1581; M. Temple, from New Inn 1583.[1]

A John Marvyn was returned for Hindon at a by-election in February 1585, following Dr. Dale's preference for the seat at Chichester to which he had also been elected. In the two subsequent Parliaments of 1586 and 1589 a John Marvyn was again chosen at Hindon. The problem is whether on each occasion the Member was the same person or whether two relatives of the same name are involved. The Member for 1586 is described in the return as 'esq. of the Middle Temple', and this fixes his identity as the eldest grandson of Sir John Marvyn† and nephew of (Sir) James Marvyn* of Fonthill Gifford, near

Hindon, who more or less controlled one of the Hindon nominations from 1585 on. The by-election return in 1585 gives no status or description for the Member, but as the official stress in 1586 was on returning Members of the previous Parliament, we can probably accept the same identity.

In 1589 the return gives no status or description, but in the Crown Office list both Members for Hindon are described as gentlemen. If this is to be taken seriously, a plausible case could be made for identifying the 1589 Member as John Marvyn of Pertwood, Wiltshire, eldest son of John Marvyn of Pertwood and husband of Melior Goldsborough. He was older than his cousin John and belonged to a younger branch of the family. He owned property in Hindon. But the description on the Crown Office list is not conclusive. In fact the second Member for Hindon in 1589, John Lyly, is bracketed with Marvyn as 'gentleman', but when returned for Aylesbury in 1593 is described as 'esq.'. It would be stranger for John Marvyn of Pertwood to develop parliamentary leanings in mature life than for the other John, young and educated at the university and inns of court, to prevail on his uncle to return him thrice to Parliament.

John Marvyn of the Middle Temple was the eldest grandson of Sir John Marvynǂ, but his father was the second son of a family of 13. Although Edmund, the father, had married in February 1559 the daughter of a Warwickshire knight and the widow of a substantial landowner in Surrey, she does not appear to have brought property into the marriage, for later she was said to have 'nothing to live on'; while the description of John's father as 'of Founten' at his entry to the Middle Temple suggests that Edmund had been obliged to find a home with or on the estate of his elder brother. The omission of Edmund's name from his father's will might argue that he was otherwise provided for, yet the fact that Sir John appointed a guardian, his son-in-law John Ryve, as trustee for John and his brothers and for the property he left them seems rather to imply that he regarded Edmund as incompetent.[2]

John Marvyn was thus eldest grandson of one owner of Fonthill Gifford and eldest nephew of another. In the first capacity he was the object, at the age of six, of a considerable benefaction. On his deathbed his grand-father made a will which benefited John and his two brothers at the expense of James, the heir, who had and was to have no son himself. Sir John left the three boys his lease of Boynton and to John, with remainder to his brothers, all his purchased lands, that is to say, the manor of Compton Bassett which he had acquired in 1553. However, as James, in contesting the will, pointed out, these lands had been rented by the family for generations; they lay intermingled with the old inheritance even to the door of the house, and they furnished the 'dairy, ponds, woods, heronsewers, orchard, hopyard' and pastures for beef and mutton for the household at Fonthill. There is reason to think that James was able to upset the will; he was certainly defending Compton Bassett as his own inherited property against claims for assart in 1607.[3]

John Marvyn made his first appearance in public at his grandfather's funeral; and the conspicuous absence of his uncle James from the ceremony might have seemed to augur ill for hopes of patronage from the new owner of Fonthill Gifford. Yet Sir James, although a violent man, was also a forgiving one; and lacking a boy of his own he was driven, in his desire to perpetuate the family name, to favour young male relations, of whom John was the nearest. John must have made his home at Fonthill and have been sent from there, first for not more than two years to Oxford, and then, again briefly, under the aegis of his uncle Ryve, to the Middle Temple. When the parliamentary vacancy occurred at Hindon, John Marvyn at 25 was a not unsuitable candidate for Sir James to put forward.[4]

Marvyn is not known to have made any mark in Parliament, or in public life. The course of his private affairs rests equally obscure. Fonthill church was pulled down and no record survives even of the year of his death. But when his uncle James came to make his will in 1610 he mentioned that John and his brothers were already dead and included their debts to him among his bequests; from which it may be inferred that John Marvyn remained a protégé of Fonthill Manor till the end.[5]

[1] W. R. Drake, *Fasciculus Mervinensis* (privately 1873), p. 9 and app. 1; *Misc. Gen. et Her.* n.s. i. 358. [2] SP14/192/8; Drake, app. 1, p. ix. [3] SP14/192/8. [4] Drake, app. 1, p. xiii; *M.T. Recs.* i. 265. [5] Drake, 19 and app. 1, pp. ix–xii.

M.B.

MASON, Sir John (1503–66), of Abingdon, Berks. and Hartley Wintney, Hants.

READING	1547*
HAMPSHIRE	1554 (Apr.), 1558, 1559, 1563*

b. 1503, ?illegit. s. of a sis. of Thomas, last abbot of Abingdon. *educ.* Abingdon g.s.; All Souls, Oxf., fellow, BA 1521, MA 1525; Paris (King's scholar). *m.* Elizabeth, da. of Thomas Isley of Sundridge, Kent, and wid. of Richard Hill (*d.*1539) of Hartley Wintney, serjeant of the cellar to Henry VIII, 1s. *d.v.p.* Kntd. 22 Feb. 1547.[1]

Sec. to Sir Thomas Wyattǂ (envoy to Emperor 1537–41); envoy to Emperor 1546, 1553–6; French sec. 1542; acting clerk of PC 1541; clerk of PC 1543–5; jt. (with (Sir) William Pagetǂ) master of the posts 1545; j.p. Hants by 1547, q. by 1564; steward of lands and keeper of site of late abbey of Abingdon 1549; dean of Winchester 1549–53; PC 1550–*d.*; ambassador to France 1550–1; (dep. from Jan. 1542) clerk of Parliaments 1550–1, jt. clerk of Parliaments 1551–*d.*; master of requests *c.*1551–8; j.p. Berks. by 1552, q. by 1564; chancellor of Oxf. Univ. Nov. 1552–Oct. 1556, June 1559–Dec. 1564; a founder and 1st master of Christ's hospital, Abingdon 1553; treasurer of the chamber 1559–d.; chief subsidy commr. Mdx. 1559; visitor, Oxf. Univ. 1559.[2]

A diplomat by profession and a 'trimmer' by nature. Sir John Mason retained at the beginning of Elizabeth's reign the high position he had enjoyed under the Queen's three predecessors. Through his marriage he was related to the Dudleys; and through his step-daughter's marriage to Sir John Cheke[†], he was distantly connected with Sir William Cecil*. It was his diplomatic experience, however, which made him indispensable: he was remembered as having 'the quickness of the Italians, the staidness of the Spaniards, the air of the French, the resolution of the Germans and the industry of the Dutch'.[3]

Mason was in London at the time of Queen Mary's death and was instructed, along with Archbishop Heath and Sir William Petre*, to transact necessary business, till Elizabeth and her council should arrive from Hatfield. Thenceforward, until his death in 1566, he played a leading part in framing foreign policy and frequently advised the government on economic affairs. In the first week of the reign he wrote to Cecil urging a speedy peace with France, which should not be allowed to 'stick upon Calais'. The following March he was sent to Cateau-Cambrésis, with instructions to the English commissioners there to be less friendly to the Spanish viewpoint. This was his last mission abroad, but he continued to have frequent interviews with the foreign ambassadors in London and carried on an extensive correspondence with English agents, especially Sir Thomas Chaloner in Spain. He soon veered towards support of an alliance with Spain, to counter French activity in Scotland.[4]

His new friendship to Spain, coupled with his conservatism in religion, made him an object of suspicion to the extreme protestants. In the spring of 1560, John, Lord Grey of Pyrgo, warned Cecil against the 'Philippians', Mason, Arundel and Petre, who 'because they may not have things go after their will and device … had rather bring in a foreign prince'; and Henry Killigrew* told Sir Nicholas Throckmorton*, the English ambassador in Paris, 'our councillors are honest men all, Mason excepted'. Mason complained to Cecil of the 'undeserved vexation' he was receiving from such critics and claimed that his conscience was 'unaccused'. In fact his religious standpoint is obscure. On his death, he was described by the Spanish ambassador as 'a man of importance and apparently a Catholic', and he was the friend and relative of Sir Richard Shelley, a notable Catholic exile. During his education under the patronage of the last abbot of Abingdon, possibly his uncle, Mason had taken acolyte's orders (thus, incidentally, he may not have been strictly speaking a 'lay dean' of Winchester). There is no evidence that his Catholic sympathies affected his official advice, and he was certainly not unfriendly to the Elizabethan settlement. In August 1559 he

recommended to Cecil a 'book of common service in Latin' and a 'little book of private prayers for children and servants', asking that they might be authorised for printing. He took part in the visitation of Oxford University and accepted re-election as chancellor, when the Earl of Arundel resigned, probably for religious reasons; he was scandalized to find that some of the heads of colleges were married. He praised the Queen's care for the state of the church, and in the 1564 bishops' reports was classified by the protestant bishop of Winchester as 'favourable' to true religion. His will gives no indication of his religious beliefs.[5]

The first of his considerable estates in Hampshire had come to Mason through his marriage. He had subsequently been granted some of the temporalities of the bishop of Winchester, and this property, restored to the bishopric by Queen Mary, was returned to Mason and his fellow patentees by the first Parliament of Elizabeth. At his birthplace, the town of Abingdon, Berkshire, he acquired much of the land of the dissolved abbey, and he styled himself high steward of the borough. On the flight of the Catholic, Sir Francis Englefield[†], he was made keeper of Whitley park, near Reading. When the subsidy assessment was made in the first year of Elizabeth's reign, Mason, with lands worth £200 a year, was listed as the richest of the officials in the Queen's household; Cecil, who came second, was assessed at £133. On more than one occasion Mason was asked to deal with threats to the Queen's life or sovereignty. The reign was only a few days old when he was ordered to take action against Sir Anthony Fortescue. Edward Grimston* was in his custody until he was cleared of responsibility for the loss of Calais. Mason was also employed in the Queen's efforts to invalidate the marriage of the Earl of Hertford to Catherine Grey, who had a claim to the succession. In May 1564 Hertford was committed to his charge, which explains his tenure, at the time of his death, of the Earl's house and manor at Elvetham, Hampshire.

Mason's property in Abingdon gave him the parliamentary patronage of the borough but he did not need to sit himself, as he was of sufficient status in Hampshire to be returned as knight of the shire. Though he was knighted in 1547, and there can be no doubt of the identity, on all but one of the occasions, in accordance with contemporary usage, he appears in the journals as plain Mr. As a Privy Councillor Mason was appointed to important committees such as that drafting the petition to the Queen to marry (6 Feb. 1559). He read the Queen's reply to the House on 10 Feb., an appropriate task for the old diplomat, who must have recognised the advantages of leaving the marriage and succession questions undecided. Writing of Parliament's next attempt, in 1563, to get the Queen to name her successor, he thought:

she will not bite at that bait, wherein, in my opinion, she

hath a better judgment than many have of them that be so earnest in the matter.

Nevertheless, as a Privy Councillor, he would have had a hand in drawing up the petition for the Queen's marriage and succession on 19 Jan. 1563. On 25 Jan. the Privy Councillors were appointed to the subsidy committee and on 24 Feb. Mason conducted the inquiry into the alleged frauds of John Smith* (see MARSHE, John). On 3 Mar. Mason spoke about the bishop of Winchester's lands, and on 8 Feb. he reported to the House the results of an inquiry into an affray caused by the servants of Sir Henry Jones*.

In December 1564, Mason resigned the chancellorship of Oxford University in favour of Sir Robert Dudley*, just created Earl of Leicester. Mason last attended a Privy Council meeting on 4 June 1565 and died in the following April; he was buried in St. Paul's cathedral. His will was proved 25 Jan. 1567. He left his books to be shared between All Souls and Winchester colleges and his half-brother's son, Anthony Wyckes. As overseers of his will he appointed Cecil and Sir William Cordell*. His lands he had already settled on Anthony Wyckes, who adopted the name of Mason. Leicester succeeded to his influence at Abingdon, and Sir Francis Knollys* to the treasurership of the chamber. The Hampshire by-election caused by Mason's death was the occasion of a contest between the conservative and the puritan factions in the county.[6]

[1] A. E. Preston, *Christ's Hosp. Abingdon*, 40; Dugdale, *St. Paul's Cath.* (1818), 65; *DNB*; *Vis. Hants* (Harl. Soc. lxiv), 20; Hasted, *Kent*, (1778–9), i. 368. [2] *DNB*; Preston, 42; *Winchester Cath. Statutes*, ed. Goodman and Hutton, 100–1; *LP Hen. VIII*, xvi(2), p. 884; xviii(1), p. 365; xx(2), p. 449; *VCH Hants*, ii. 115; Lansd. 1218, f. 5; *VCH Oxon.* iii. 39, 100, 105; *CPR*, 1553 and App. Edw. VI, pp. 142–3; 1557–8, p. 429; *EHR*, lxxiii. 79, 82. [3] *N. and Q.* (ser. 4), iii. 460; Read, *Cecil*, i. 69. [4] Strype, *Annals*, i(2), p. 390; *CSP For.* 1558–9, pp. 6, 166, 175, 179; 1559–60, pp. 224, 382; 1561–2, pp. 191, 241; 1562, p. 136; *CSP Span.* 1558–67, pp. 34, 39, 48, 50, 59, 232, 366, 380; *CSP Ven.* 1558–80, pp. 40, 81; Read, *Cecil*, i. 242. [5] Read, *Cecil*, i. 168, 174; *CSP Scot.* i. 415; *CSP Span.* 1558–67, p. 544; *Vis. Hants* (Harl. Soc. lxiv), 20; Wright, *Eliz.* i. 137; *Winchester Cath. Statutes*, 100–1; *Liturgical Services of Queen Elizabeth*, ed. Clay (Parker Soc. 1847), 516; if these prayers are indeed by Mason, the date (1568) must be wrong; *CSP For.* 1558–9, p. 468; 1560–1, p. 87; *CSP Dom.* 1547–80, pp. 183, 488; *Cam. Misc.* ix(3), p. 55. [6] *VCH Hants*, iv. 79–80; *VCH Berks.* iii. 207, 373–4, 393, 442; Strype, *Annals*, i(1), 10, 90; i(2), 118, 121; *CPR*, 1560–3, pp. 211–12; Lansd. 3, f. 193; F. Little, *A Monument of Christian Munificence* (ed. Cobham), 34–50; *CJ*, i. 54, 56, 65; D'Ewes, 45, 46, 48, 49, 79, 80, 84; Wright, i. 137; *APC*, vii. 5; *CSP For.* 1559–60, p. 137; 1563, p. 378; *HMC Hatfield*, i. 272, 295; PCC 2 Stonard.

A.H.

MASON, Robert I (by 1527–91), of Ludlow, Salop.

LUDLOW   1558, 1559, 1571

b. by 1527, 1st s. of William Mason by Joyce, da. of George Langford, registrar of Hereford diocese. *m.* (1) Alice Cox; (2) Jane.[1]

Churchwarden, Ludlow by 1551, bailiff 1555–6,

1563–4, 1571–2, alnager in 1558; ?steward of household in council in the marches of Wales 1567–9.[2]

It is uncertain whether Mason, a burgess of Ludlow, probably a cloth merchant, was also the steward in the council in the marches. Ludlow bailiffs – for example William Poughmill, Mason's co-Member in 1572 – sometimes filled council offices, but the junior Member for the borough (and Mason never achieved the senior seat) was often a local merchant unconnected with the council. The known genealogical facts are equally inconclusive. The relevant section of the pedigree of Mason of Minton and of Diddlebury, near Ludlow, gives their recent descent from a London merchant, while their relatives by marriage, the Langfords, were prominent Ludlow burgesses. The steward of the household was styled 'esquire' or 'servant to Sir Henry Sidney', whereas the Ludlow bailiff and MP was described as 'gentleman' or simply as 'of this town'. On the whole it is likely that there were two men. If so, the steward was probably son of William, and husband of Alice Cox only: no Jane appears in the *Visitation* pedigree of Mason of Minton. The bailiff is known to have married Jane, whose maiden name is not given in his will.[3]

There is no reasonable doubt that the Ludlow bailiff was the MP in 1558, 1559 and 1571, but a namesake of his, a tanner, was returned in 1572. Mason's will, made 12 Oct. 1591, was proved 25 Nov., nearly a fortnight after his burial, according to his wish, in Ludlow parish church. Personal property and two houses in Broad Street were bequeathed to the widow. No children were mentioned, but Mason left small legacies to nephews John and William Mason, and to his sister Ancaret Cooke. One of the overseers and witnesses was William Croft.[4]

[1] NLW, will of Robert Mason; *Vis. Salop* (Harl. Soc. xxix), 353–5. [2] *Ludlow Churchwardens' Accts.* (Cam. Soc. cii), 45; *Trans. Salop Arch. Soc.* (ser. 2), vii. 15; C219/28/99; Bodl. Gough Salop ms, i. f. 277v; Salop RO, Ludlow bailiffs' accts. 1558; *HMC De L'Isle and Dudley*, i. 357–9; P. H. Williams, *Council in the Marches of Wales*, 128; T. Wright, *Hist. Ludlow*, 493–4, gives the bailiff for 1571–2 in error as Richard Mason. [3] *Vis. Salop*; Williams, 128; *HMC De L'Isle and Dudley*, i. 359; C219/25/89, 26/78; de Tabley list of 1571 MPs. [4] *CJ*, i. 49; *Trans. Salop Arch. Soc.* (ser. 2), vii. 15; NLW, probate recs. Hereford diocese.

N.M.F.

MASON, Robert II (*d.* by 1581), of Ludlow, Salop.

LUDLOW   1572*

This Member, who on the return is styled 'one Robert Mason, tanner', and who, appropriately, served on the committee of a leather bill in the Commons, 18 Feb. 1576, was clearly not the same man as his namesake, who, after sitting thrice for Ludlow, acted as bailiff and returning officer in 1572, and signed at the head of the election indenture. No further references to the tanner have been found, but as there was a by-election at Ludlow before the

1581 session of this Parliament, and Poughmill, the other Member, lived until 1583, it must be inferred that Mason had died by the time the third session began.

C219/28/99; CJ, i. 106; Salop RO, 356/2/15; Trans. Salop Arch. Soc. (ser. 4), iii.

N.M.F.

MASSEY, William (c.1515–79), of Puddington, Cheshire.

CHESHIRE   1563

b. c.1515, 1st s. of Sir John Massey by Katherine, da. of Thomas Venables, Baron of Kinderton, and aunt of Sir Thomas Venables*. m. (1) Anne (d.1568), da. of George Booth of Dunham, 6s. 2da.; (2) Margaret, wid. of Richard Forsett* and of Roger Amyce*. suc. fa. 1551.

J.p. Cheshire from c.1559, sheriff 1563–4.

Massey owned considerable land in Cheshire, as well as an estate over the Welsh border in Flintshire. He was probably the 'Mr. Massie of Puddington' described in 1568 as 'steward to the [3rd] Earl of Derby': this may refer to the stewardship of Derby's manors rather than to an office in the Earl's household. With the support of the greatest magnate in the district, a relationship with the Venables family, and his own social position in Cheshire, Massey was able to attain the dignity of a county seat. Little is known of his career. Like many other Lancashire and Cheshire gentlemen he favoured Catholicism, remaining however an active official in his county until at least August 1577, when he was one of the commissioners who examined abuses in the collection of customs at Chester, where he owned property in Watergate Street.

He died on 4 June 1579. His will, made 24 Apr. and proved 23 July that year, suggests that he was not a wealthy man. He left £13 6s. 8d. for the building of a monument, and a further £6 6s. 8d. to make a new window and to improve the lighting in the north chapel of St. Nicholas, Burton, where he wished to be buried. The monument, now destroyed, was an alabaster altar tomb, with recumbent figures, inlaid in black marble, of him and his wife.

PRO Chester, 3/70/6; 3/79/6; Vis. Cheshire (Harl. Soc. lix), 173; St. Ch. 5/M7/1; Ormerod, Cheshire, ii. 557, 560–1; T. S. Leatherbarrow, Lancs. Eliz. Recusants (Chetham Soc. n.s. cx), 32; Cam. Misc. ix(3), p. 76; Lansd. 25, f. 10; Lancs. and Cheshire Wills, ed. Irvine (Lancs. and Cheshire Rec. Soc. xxx), 195–8.

N.M.F.

MASSINGER, Arthur (c.1547–1603), of Salisbury, Wilts. and St. Dunstan-in-the-West, London.

WEYMOUTH AND MELCOMBE
    REGIS   1589, 1593
SHAFTESBURY   1601

b. c.1547, s. of William Massinger* of Gloucester by his w. Elizabeth; bro. of Richard*. educ. St. Alban Hall, Oxf.

1571, fellow of Merton 1572, MA 1577, incorp. Camb. 1578. m. by 1582, Anne, da. of William Crompton of Stafford and London, sis. of Thomas Crompton I*, 1s. 1da., three other ch.

Servant of the 2nd and 3rd Earls of Pembroke from c.1583; examiner, council in the marches of Wales 1598.

It has been assumed that Massinger was a native of Salisbury, where there was a family of that name, and where his son Philip, the dramatist, was born in 1583. Massinger himself was born in Gloucester, and his widow and daughter were buried in Gloucester cathedral. After sailing with Sir Humphrey Gilbert in 1578, he entered the service of the 2nd Earl of Pembroke, probably settling in Salisbury at this point in his career. His master, who was president of the council in the marches, obtained for him in 1589 the reversion of the office of examiner against strong competition, and Massinger succeeded Thomas Sherer in that office in 1598. Because he was the Earl's personal representative, and was present during the president's absences, Massinger became a powerful figure in the marches and the object of attack from Pembroke's enemies. Pembroke had Massinger returned for Weymouth to two Elizabethan Parliaments, where, judging from the known records of the House, he made no mark. Massinger recovered from 'a burning fever' in 1600, witnessed the 2nd Earl's will and received an annuity of £20 on his death in 1601. The election for the 1601 Parliament took place nine months after Pembroke's death and, as happened after the death of the 1st Earl, the servants took the opportunity to return themselves for his boroughs. Massinger came in for Shaftesbury again without making any known contribution to the business of the House, afterwards continuing in the service of the 3rd Earl. On one occasion in 1601, he was trying to moderate the wrath of the Queen at his master's protracted absence from court. He died at his house in Shere Lane, London, in 1603 and was buried 4 June in the church of St. Dunstan-in-the-West. His nuncupative will, made in the presence of his brother Richard 2 June 1603 and proved 7 Jan. following, appointed his wife sole executrix and legatee. She is stated to have been a Catholic.

DNB (Massinger, Philip); Hoare, Wilts. Salisbury, 619–20; Glos. RO. D326; Rudder, Glos. 173, 174; Gilbert Voyages, ed. Quinn (Hak. Soc. ser. 2, lxxxiv), 212; P. H. Williams, Council in the Marches of Wales, 167, 294; Som. and Dorset N. and Q. viii. 20–1; Wilts. Arch. Mag. iv. 216; Lansd. 56, f. 98; 62, f. 80; 63, ff. 187, 193; 67, f. 17; 71, f. 197; Cal. Salisbury Corresp. 35, 85; HMC De L'Isle and Dudley, ii. 200, 328, 479; HMC Hatfield, viii. 264, 439; xi. 361; Coll. Topog. iv. 123; PCC 5 Harte, 31 Tirwhite, 39 Woodhall; N. and Q. ccxiii. 256–8.

I.C.

MASSINGER, Richard, of Gloucester and Lambeth and Battersea, Surr.

PENRYN   1601

s. of William Massinger* of Gloucester, and bro. of Arthur*.

Jt. (with Anthony Calton ?1581–8, with George Paule* 1588–1600) registrar of diocese of Ely ?1581–1600.

Massinger was the godson of Richard Pate*, recorder of Gloucester, who left him a silver angel in his will. Both he and his brother left Gloucester to seek their fortunes; Arthur in the service of the earls of Pembroke and Richard as an ecclesiastical official. In 1600 Paule and Massinger sold their registrarship at Ely to John Lambe, later dean of the arches, in return for an annuity of £32 out of its profits. In may be inferred from this that Massinger was, like Paule, in the service of Whitgift or an official in the archbishop's courts. It is not known how Massinger came to be returned for Penryn in 1601. Possibly his brother Arthur arranged it, but he had another link with the borough. John Osborne, who sat in 1593, was the brother of Richard Osborne, who, like Massinger, was a godson of Richard Pate. Their father, Peter Osborne*, was an executor of Pate's will. Massinger spoke at least twice during this Parliament. On 3 Dec. 1601 he moved that anyone who had had, or should have in the future, any private bill passed by the House, should make a contribution toward the relief of ex-soldiers and mariners. A week later he proposed that the House should choose collectors for 'the ten pound and five pound upon every private bill', and that no such bill should be sent to the Lords before the fee had been paid.

The date of Massinger's death is unknown. He was alive in June 1603, when he recorded Arthur's nuncupative will, and in 1606, when he was described in a deed as of Battersea, Surrey. It is possible that he finally retired to his birthplace as a Richard Massinger's will was proved in the consistory court of Gloucester in 1608.

Rudder, *Glos.* 115, 116, 117; *Bristol and Glos. Arch. Soc. Trans.* xxiv. 318; lvi. 223; *CSP Dom.* 1598–1601, pp. 388, 389; Townshend, *Hist. Colls.* 280, 309; PCC 5 Harte, 8 Leicester; Glos. RO, D.326; *Glos. Wills 1541–1650* (Brit. Rec. Soc. Index Lib. xii), 121.

I.C.

MASSINGER, William (c.1515–c.94), of Gloucester.

GLOUCESTER   1554 (Nov.), 1555, 1571

b. c.1515, 1st s. of Thomas Massinger, mayor and sheriff of Gloucester, by his w. Alice. *educ.* L. Inn 1537. *m.* bef. Dec. 1545, Elizabeth, 3s. inc. Arthur* and Richard* 1da. *suc.* fa. 1534.

Sheriff, Gloucester 1562–3, 1566–7, mayor 1569–70, 1585–6.

At his father's death, Massinger inherited small properties at Newent, Swindon and Trynley in Gloucestershire, Barton Regis, near Gloucester, and a house within the city. He had a long career as a member of Gloucester corporation. In Elizabeth's reign his activity is seen in February 1565 as a member of a commission to survey and repair the banks of the river Leddon and in January 1584 he was acting as a justice of the peace for the city in the examination of the seminary priest Robert Alfield. By 1579 he was one of the two senior aldermen and had already followed his father in holding the highest offices in the city. By the time of his second term as mayor in 1585, his son William was also a member of the city council and Massinger himself was thenceforth styled 'senior'.

His re-election to Parliament in 1571 after a long interval was perhaps the by-product of faction within the common council resulting in the exclusion of Richard Pate*, the recorder, from the junior seat. It is difficult to see Massinger in opposition to Pate, who was a close friend and the godfather of his son Richard*, but it is possible that the contesting of the junior seat exposed the senior one also to popular influences. Massinger had just completed his first term as mayor and may well have been a strong candidate with the commoners who were always an important factor in Gloucester elections. His career in the 1571 Parliament was uneventful. It was dissolved before the end of May and on 15 Sept. the common council of Gloucester empowered the mayor and aldermen to assess the burgesses for the Members' wages. £14 13s. 8d. was collected and Massinger and his colleague were paid for 68 days at 2s. *per diem.* Massinger's will was made in June 1593 and proved at Gloucester in the following year. It mentions property in and near the city and contains legacies to the widow, to Massinger's daughter Anne, and to his sons Arthur and Richard who were appointed executors.

E150/367/2; C3/105/20; C142/56/22; *LP Hen. VIII,* xx(2), p. 546; Rudder, *Glos.* 116, 117; *CPR,* 1548–9, p. 265; 1558–60, p. 216; *Gloucester Recs.* ed. Stevenson, 65–6; J. N. Langston, 'Robert Alfield, Schoolmaster of Gloucester', *Bristol and Glos. Arch. Soc. Trans.* lvi. 156; *Gloucester Guild Hall mss* 1451, f. 31; 1500, ff. 105, 136, 138, 198, 229, 236; Neale, *Commons,* 274–5; *Gloucester consist. ct. wills* 1594.

I.C.

MASTER, George (c.1556–1604), of Cirencester Abbey, Glos.

CIRENCESTER   1586, 1589

b. c.1556, 1st s. of Richard Master, MD, physician to Queen Elizabeth, by Elizabeth, da. of John Fultnetby of Fultnetby, Lincs.; bro. of Robert*. *educ.* Trinity Coll. Camb. Mich. 1573; St. John's, Oxf. 1575; L. Inn 6 May 1575. *m.* Bridget, da. of John Cornwall of Marlborough, Wilts., 2s. 3da. *suc.* fa. 1588.

J.p. Glos. from 1592.

Master's father had enjoyed a high reputation as a physician, and had been granted in 1565 by Queen Elizabeth the site and lands of Cirencester abbey. It was here that Master spent most of his life. In 1594 he was one of those who recommended Jasper Stone as comptroller of the port of Gloucester. Eight years later he was mentioned as 'fit to be sheriff' of Gloucestershire but the appointment was not made. In his will, dated 9 Aug. 1604, he trusted 'by the merit of Christ's death and passion' that he would 'be gathered to the Saints in Heaven, and enjoy the blessed communion of God and His Saints in eternal glory'. His wife received an annuity of £200, and 'all her apparel, jewels and rings, and the furniture in her chamber'. To his four younger children he bequeathed £1,000 each, and provision was also made for their 'breeding up ... in virtuous education'. The will was proved on 5 Dec.

Vis. Glos. (Harl. Soc. xxi), iii; W. R. Williams, *Parl. Hist. Glos.* 152; *DNB* (Master, Richard); *Bristol and Glos. Arch. Soc. Trans.* xx. 184; *CSP Dom.* 1591–4, p. 555; *HMC Hatfield*, xii. 497; PCC 94 Harte.

J.J.C.

MASTER, Robert (1565–1625), of London and Alrewas, Staffs.

CRICKLADE 1601

b. 1565, 3rd s. of Richard Master, MD, of London and Cirencester, and bro. of George*. *educ.* Trinity Coll. Oxf. 1578–9; BCL 1590; DCL 1594. *m.* Catherine, da. of Thomas Pagitt of Northants. and of the Middle Temple, London, *s.p.*[1]

A 'carrier' of Oxf. Univ. 1594–8; principal, St. Alban Hall 1599–1603; adv. Doctors' Commons 1599; chancellor of dioceses of Rochester and of Lichfield and judge of the PCC; master in chancery extraordinary 1622; j.p. Staffs.[2]

As the third of seven sons of a royal physician (who also attended Burghley) Robert Master could expect to augment a modest patrimony with the aid of powerful patronage. He had yet to graduate in law when in 1588 he was bequeathed his share of his father's estate: he received, in addition to a piece of plate, a feather bed and some books, an annuity of £10 a year for life charged on lands and the use, rent free, of the family house in Silver Street, St. Olave's, whenever he was in London. During the next two years he made his own way at Oxford, and not until after 1603 did he obtain the official appointments elsewhere which were to be the setting of his later career.[3]

Robert Master's sole appearance in Parliament may reflect either his family's local standing or its influential connexions. His father, a native of Kent, had bought the reversion of Cirencester monastery in 1565, and it was there that his eldest brother George had established himself, sitting for the borough of Cirencester in 1586 and 1589. Cricklade, lying hard by the Gloucestershire border, was often represented by men of that shire, especially while the Lords Chandos held its stewardship. Robert Master may have owed his opportunity to sit for the

borough in 1601 to the involvement of Gray Brydges*, heir to the barony of Chandos, in the Essex rebellion. Brydges had sat for Cricklade in the previous Parliament with (Sir) George Gifford*, who in 1601 was Master's fellow-Member. If Gifford was related to Roger Gifford*, Richard Master's successor as a physician-in-ordinary to the Queen, he may himself have had something to do with Robert Master's claim to the second seat. Master could also perhaps have looked for support from Sir Robert Cecil, who was an overseer of Richard Master's will. However procured, Master's single Membership is unremarked in the known records of Elizabeth's last Parliament.[4]

Master's career after 1603 was divided between his two chancellorships and his work as a Chancery and probate lawyer. In 1616 he bought a property at Alrewas, Staffordshire (his brother had become a canon of Lichfield cathedral in 1613) and his inclusion in the Staffordshire commission of the peace suggests that he made it his residence when not at Westminster. He died 10 July 1625, and was buried in Lichfield cathedral, where an epitaph commemorates him and his wife, who afterwards married Charles Twisden, another civilian and Master's successor as chancellor of Lichfield.[5]

[1] *DNB* (Master, Richard); W. B. Crouch, *Hist. Cricklade*, 143; Shaw, *Staffs.* i. 248. [2] *Reg. Univ. Oxf.* ii(1), pp. 317–20; PCC 43 Wingfield; PRO ms index to petty bag recs. [3] *CPR*, 1558–60, p. 94; Lansd. 121, f. 49; *CSP Dom.* 1547–80, p. 672; PCC 34 Rutland. [4] *CPR*, 1563–6, pp. 201–2; *HMC Hatfield*, xii. 497; PCC 34 Rutland. [5] *Wm. Salt. Arch. Soc.* n.s. iv. 85–6; *Wm. Salt Arch. Soc.* 1934(2), p. 24; *Fasti*, i. 267, 382; Shaw, *Staffs.* i. 248; C. H. Dudley Ward, *Fam. of Twysden and Twisden*, 130–1.

S.T.B.

MATHEW, Charles

CORFE CASTLE 1572*

?s. of Robert Mathew of Bradden, Northants., who *m.* (1) Edith, da. of Richard Turberville of Bere Regis, Dorset, and (2) the niece of Bp. Fisher of Rochester, Kent.

Under 18 Mar. 1581 the parliamentary diary of Thomas Cromwell states that John Leweston was returned in place of Charles Mathew who had been 'made a minister' and 'should attend his cure'. Nothing else is known about Mathew, and the above identification is suggested only because of the standing of the Turberville family in Dorset. Nicholas Turberville served as sheriff of the county (1577–8), while another member of the family, James, was bishop of Exeter. One other (minor) Mathew family with Dorset connexions has been found, with no known member of it named Charles.

Trinity, Dublin, Thos. Cromwell's jnl. f. 114; Roberts thesis; Bridges, *Northants.* i. 237; *DNB* (Turberville, George); PCC 39 Carew.

P.W.H.

MATHEW, Tristram (*b.* bef.1538), of Downton, Wilts.

DOWNTON 1563

b. bef. 1538. ?s. of Edmund Mathew, merchant, of Salisbury and Downton by his w. Joan. *m.* bef. 1569 Elizabeth, apparently *s.p.*[1]

Bailiff and keeper of the warren of Downton 1581–3; reeve of Hindon 1581–3; clerk of the bailiwick of Downton 1585–7; alderman (i.e. mayor) Downton 1586.[2]

Tristram Mathew's parentage is not easy to establish. His identification with a younger son of Edward and Cecily Mathew of Dodbrook, Devon, would leave unexplained both his move from that county to Wiltshire and his connexion with the many persons of his name found in the neighbourhood of Downton during his lifetime. Thus the high collector of the benevolence of 1545 in the hundreds of Downton, Downton South, Cawdon, Cadworth and Chalk was Richard Mathew, 'gentleman', who was himself assessed in East Downton at 23s. 4d. Since in 1576 Tristram Mathew was to be described as of 'Este End, Downton', when assessed for the subsidy of that year, he was domiciled in the same place, and perhaps in the same house, as Richard a generation before. But Richard is less likely to have been Tristram's father than that Edmund Mathew, 'gentleman', who was assessed in Downton in 1576 at the high figure of £18. This Edmund may have been the Salisbury merchant who was in business in the city between 1556 and 1562, was a pew-holder in St. Edmund's church from 1550, and was acquiring property in Salisbury in 1564 and in Wilton in the following year. By 1576 Edmund Mathew could have established himself as a landed gentleman at Downton, having perhaps left one of his sons in Salisbury, where an Andrew Mathew, of New Street, was assessed at £3 in that year.[3]

Of Tristram Mathew the first known fact is that he sued out a pardon as 'of Downton' in 1559. Hoare's statement that he was 'a considerable copyholder' there, coupled with the later evidence of the subsidy assessment and of land transactions, support the view that he was a small squire who derived his main income from the land. But in the course of his life he also acquired official standing. Downton belonged to the bishop of Winchester, and the borough officers were also the manorial officials. From 1581 to 1583 Tristram Mathew was bailiff and from 1585 to 1587 clerk of the bailiwick; and on the election return of 1586 he is named 'alderman' (or mayor) of the borough. (He was also reeve of Hindon, the bishop's other Wiltshire borough, in 1581–3.) He may well have filled one or other of these offices at an earlier period. But if he was thus a bishop's 'man', Mathew also owed allegiance to the lessee of Downton, the Earl of Pembroke. He may indeed have been one of the Earl's household officers, as was the Miles Mathew who was a bearer at the 1st Earl's funeral in 1570.[4]

Mathew's return for Downton in 1563 may thus reflect the patronage of the bishop, or of the Earl, or of both. The bishop concerned was Horne, who was responsible for the return of Mathew's fellow-Member, Henry Kingsmill, and who may have claimed the traditional patronage over both seats. This appears the more likely in that Mathew was not to sit again, as he might have been expected to do if he enjoyed the Earl's backing. As is usually the case with such birds of passage, we know nothing of any part played by Mathew in the 1563 Parliament.

His further career is illuminated only by occasional references. In 1568–9 he and his wife made a fine of lands in East Downton. In 1577 he took certain deeds as security for a debt of £160 1s., a transaction which was to give rise to a Chancery suit in 1591, after which year no trace of him has been found. Among various other bearers of his name at this time in his part of Wiltshire were Tobias Mathew, precentor of Salisbury and father of a celebrated son, and John Mathew, attorney of the common pleas and under-sheriff of the county in 1588.[5]

[1] *Wilts. N. and Q.* iii. 326–7; vi. 354. [2] Winchester bishopric accts. Downton bailiwick, 1581–7. [3] *Vis. Devon 1531, 1564 and 1620*, p. 156; Westcote, *View of Devonshire in 1630*, ed. Oliver and Jones, 599; *Two Taxation Lists* (Wilts. Arch. Soc. recs. br. x), 41, 43, 44, 63, 114, 115, 118, 120; *Wilts. N. and Q.* iii. 326–7; v. 178, 319; *Churchwardens' accts. of St. Edmund and St. Thomas, Sarum* (Wilts. Rec. Soc.), 91, 98, 102; Bishop Jewel bequeathed a gold ring to his 'very loving friend Edmond Mathew' in 1571; PCC 43 Holney. [4] *CPR*, 1558–60, 171; Hoare, *Wilts. Downton*, 19; *EHR*, xxiii. 471 n; *Wilts. Arch. Mag.* xviii. 129. [5] *Wilts. N. and Q.* vi. 354; C3/269/21; *APC*, xvi. 62, 76, 101, 110.

S.T.B.

MATHEW, William (1531–87), of Radyr, Cardiff, Glam. and Drury Lane, London.

GLAMORGANSHIRE 1572*

b. 1531, 1st s. of (Sir) George Mathew† of Radyr by Barbara, da. of Robert Brent of Cossington, Som. *m.* 1550, Margaret, da. of (Sir) George Herbert† of Swansea and Cogan Pill, Glam., 1s. *d.v.p.* 7da. At least 2s. illegit. *suc.* fa. 1558.

J.p. Glam., sheriff 1567–8, 1579–80, commr. piracy 1576.[1]

The Mathews of Radyr were a junior branch of an ancient Welsh family which had adopted the English form of surname and entered the service of the English Crown in the later middle ages. In addition to the capital messuage of Radyr Mathew owned lands leased from the Crown, from the bishop of Llandaff and from the Mansells of Margam, estates scattered over an area extending up to 15 miles west and north-west of Cardiff. Llandaff castle and its appurtenances he leased to a kinsman of the senior branch who married one of his daughters, and he fought a Chancery action to resist encroachments on this property. His inheritance placed him among the dozen leading landlords of the shire: at the musters of 1570 he was one of the ten Glamorganshire gentry charged with the provision of one light horseman. His status was further enhanced by his marriage connexions with the Herberts. It was to fill a vacancy caused by the death of his brother-in-law William Herbert II that Mathew was elected to Parliament on 7 Jan. 1577. He was named to the supply committee (25 Jan. 1581) but was unwise enough to support a measure saddling the shire with more than the fair share of the cost of rebuilding a bridge over the Taf at Cardiff which the county had claimed, since its collapse six years earlier, to be the town's responsibility. Mathew's fellow-gentry were naturally incensed at this move on the part of a man to whom they were paying 5s. a day, 1s. more than the going rate for Welsh county MPs, to represent their interests at Westminster. Next, in 1585, when there was famine in Cardiff, Mathew upset the county by speculating in grain. The next year he incurred, in his capacity of piracy commissioner, the more dangerous wrath of the 2nd Earl of Pembroke by citing his protégés, the borough officials of Cardiff, before the Privy Council on charges of collusion with pirates. Pembroke's reaction was to charge Mathew with collusion in a murder. He evaded summons before the council in the marches of Wales (of which Pembroke had recently become president) on the plea of illness, and denounced to Burghley Pembroke's whole administration of the land; but the Privy Council supported Pembroke and imprisoned Mathew, who died in the summer of 1587 before the matter came to trial. His only legitimate son having predeceased him, the estate passed successively to his brothers Henry and Edmund.[2]

[1] C142/123/79; *Cardiff Recs.* iii. 108–9; iv. 82–6; Clark, *Limbus*, 10–11; E. A. Lewis, *Welsh Port Bks.* 319; Flenley, *Cal. Reg. Council, Marches of Wales*, 91, 142, 173–4, 213; *CSP Dom.* 1547–80, p. 599; *APC*, ix. 269; xii. 118. [2] Clark, *Limbus*, 7–11; *Cardiff Recs.* iii. 83, 108–9; iv. 82; *S. Wales and Mon. Rec. Soc.* iii. 129; D'Ewes. 288; *CJ*, i. 120; *OR* (1878) app. xxxv; *Morgannwg*, iv. 38–46; *Stradling Corresp.* ed. Traherne, 78–83, 126, 259, 291–6; *APC*, xiv. 143, 203; xv. 88, 232; *HMC Hatfield*, iii. 214; SP12/148/8, 9; 200/24, 32, 43, 51; 204/7; 211/161.

A.H.D.

MATTHEW, Tobias (1577–1655), of London.

Newport iuxta Launceston 1601
St. Albans 1604

b. 3 Oct. 1577, 1st s. of Tobias Matthew, dean of Christ Church, bp. of Durham 1595, abp. of York 1606, by Frances, da. of William Barlow, bp. of Chichester, wid. of Matthew Parker (s. of Matthew Parker, abp. of Canterbury). *educ.* Christ Church Oxf. 1590, BA 1594, MA 1597; G. Inn 1599. *unm.* Kntd. 1623.
Envoy to Spain with the Duke of Buckingham 1623.

'Little pretty Tobie Matthew' was a colourful personality, assessments of whom ranged from 'a trifling courtier, too insignificant to serve any cause', to 'a polished gentleman, distinguished for learning, memory, sharpness of wit and sweetness of behaviour'. He spent his youth in diversions at court, suits in law and in frequenting plays and 'worse places', taking no pains but 'to give myself pleasure enough', but of his ability and learning there can be no doubt. His translation of *The Confessions of St. Augustine* first appeared in 1620 and remains in use to the present day.

At Oxford he won a high reputation as an orator and disputant. He made his début at court at the age of 18 when he appeared as the squire in a 'device', the dialogue of which was written by (Sir) Francis Bacon*, whose subsequent friendship was one of the abiding influences in his life. It was for him that Bacon wrote his celebrated essay on *Friendship*, and once in a letter wrote of the 'intireness' between them, a quality of friendship which happily survived disagreements and long separations. Bacon, who on one occasion referred to Matthew as 'to me another myself', had the highest opinion of Matthew's literary ability and Matthew, for his part, said of Bacon: 'I passed my time with him in much gust, for there was not such company in the whole world'.

About 1596 Matthew began to suffer both from sickness and from bad relations with his father. In 1598 he went to France where he stayed with a Catholic friend, named Throckmorton. When he returned he experienced a serious illness, probably mental, caused or aggravated by the continuing quarrel with his father, who called him 'a reprobate, a castaway, an example above example of an irreverent and disobedient child', and who dismissed the disorder as 'hypocritical shows and melancholy illness'. Matthew was in Oxford at the time, attended by his good friend Dudley Carleton†, who was anxious about the 'violence of his disease' and his being 'broken with inward vexations'. Carleton tried to intercede with the father, but the 'barbarous bishop' sent only 'unnatural replies'. Though the parental displeasure had abated by the summer of 1598, father and son were never again on easy terms for long, and Matthew was eventually disinherited.

At Gray's Inn Matthew displayed an interest in politics and public affairs, and the court opponents of the Cecils frequented his father's London house. It is not clear how he came to be returned to Parliament for a Cornish borough in 1601. In 1604 it would have been with Bacon's help. But it was not his ambition to become a Parliament man. He had begun to look across the channel, in particular to Italy.

Despite, or in reaction to his parents' position in regard to the established church, Matthew always had a bias towards Rome, a fact his parents may have grasped when they forbade him to go to Italy. They wanted him to stay at home and marry, so he promised he would only go to France. But once across the channel in 1604 he went straight to Florence, where, moved by the warmth of Catholic devotion and the beauty of the liturgical singing, he began to follow a 'more virtuous and recollected way of life', and finally, after a period of 'frights and sweats and agonies of perplexity and desolation', he became a Catholic and was, though this remained secret, ordained to the priesthood on 20 May 1614 by Cardinal Bellarmine. In spite of bad health – by 1640 he spoke of himself as a dying man – Matthew lived to be nearly 80. He made a number of wills, by the last of which, dated 1647, he bequeathed his written works and manuscripts to his overseer, Walter Montague, son of the 2nd Earl of Manchester. The executors were Henry Taylor, Francis Plowden and Lionel Wake. He died 13 Oct. 1655 in the house of the English tertians of the Society of Jesus at Ghent, where he was buried.

This biography is based on A. H. Mathew, *The Life of Sir Tobie Matthew, The Conversion of Sir Tobie Matthew;* D. Mathew, *Sir Tobie Mathew,* from which the quotations are taken. See also A. G. Petti in *Recusant Hist.* ix. 123–58.

N.M.S.

MAURICE, William (1542–1622), of Clenennau, Caern.

CAERNARVONSHIRE	1593
BEAUMARIS	1601
CAERNARVONSHIRE	1604

b. 1542, 1st s. of Maurice ap Eliza of Clenennau by Elin, da. of (Sir) John Puleston† of Bersham and Caernarvon. *m.* (1) Sept. 1556, Margaret (*d.*1572), da. and h. of John Wynn Lacon of Llangollen, 10ch. inc. 3s. 2da.; (2) 1576, Elin, da. of Hugh ap Llywelyn ap Meredydd, wid. of John Lewis of Chwaen Wen, *s.p.*; (3) 1605, Jane, da. and h. of Rowland Puleston of Caernarvon, wid. of Sir Thomas Jones* of Abermarlais, Carm., *s.p. suc.* fa. 1575. Kntd. 1603.

J.p. Caern. from c.1575, Anglesey, Merion. by 1592; escheator, Caern. 1583–4, sheriff 1581–2, 1595–6; sheriff, Merion. 1590–1, 1605–6; dep. lt. Caern. 1587, custos rot. by 1593; dep. v.-adm. N. Wales prob. by 1590; prob. constable Harlech castle.[1]

By the time Maurice succeeded his father the consolidation of the Clenennau estates was complete and the family surpassed in landed property every house in Lleyn and Eifionydd. Subsequently, most additions to their income came from tithes. From about 1580 Maurice drew over £100 p.a. from Holyhead rectory, while the annuity of £320 that he received with his third wife was mainly a charge on the rectories of Llanbeblig, Caernarvonshire and Llanbadarn Fawr, Cardiganshire. His subsidy assessment of 1597–8 (£10 in lands), was one of the three highest in the county. He kept detailed accounts (which have survived) of the expenditure of the Clenennau household. As befitted his position, he was from an early age actively involved in county administration, holding office in all three Gwynedd shires. His most onerous duties in the later part of the reign were perhaps his responsibilities, as deputy lieutenant, for the military

defence of Caernarvonshire, though his zeal, it appears, did not always fulfil the expectations of the lord lieutenant, the 2nd Earl of Pembroke. His colleague as deputy lieutenant was for many years John Wynn* of Gwydir, to whose support he doubtless owed his election to the 1593 Parliament. As knight for Caernarvonshire he was entitled to attend the subsidy committee and a legal committee appointed on 24 Feb. and 9 Mar. 1593. A temporary estrangement over the musters divisions occurred in 1596, and Maurice did not sit in the next Parliament. In 1601 he turned to the borough of Beaumaris, in which Wynn sometimes showed an interest. On 20 Nov. he informed the House that

as he was coming up to London, on his way his man was arrested at Shrewsbury: whereupon he told the serjeant that he was of the Parliament house, and therefore wished him to discharge his servant. The serjeant said, he could not discharge him, but he would go to the bailiff with him. To whom, when he came, he likewise declared, he was of the Parliament house, and therefore required his servant. To whom the bailiff answered, he could not discharge him without the consent of him that procured the arrest. To whom he also went, and he answered the serjeant and him, keep him fast, I will not release him until I be satisfied. Then he told the creditor that he was of the Parliament house, and therefore his servant was privileged. Whereunto the creditor made this answer: I care not for that, keep him fast, I will be your warrant. I thought good to move the House herein, referring it to your consideration. And because I am willing that the privileges of the House may be known as well afar off as here at hand, I thought good to move the same.

The House was indignant at this breach of privilege crying 'To the Tower, to the Tower with them! Send for them! Send for them!' It was decided that the serjeant-at-arms should go to Shrewsbury and fetch the offenders back to London. However, seven days later the matter was raised again by Thomas Holcroft II who claimed that 'nothing was done therein'. Maurice also claimed that he did not know of any further developments. When questioned, the serjeant reported

that he was with Mr. Maurice and that he offered him to send one of his men, but because he was in doubt of finding him, he desired some part of his fees, or money for his charges or horses, or else he would find horses, and get one of his fellow serjeants to go because he could not well be spared from his service. If not, he would for his more expedition procure a pursuivant to go with a warrant under Mr. Speaker's hand, and some of the honourable of the council in this House for the more speedy passage. All which causes Mr. Maurice rejected. And I hope the House meant not I should go or send on my own purse, or hazard the charge myself. And therefore I hope this will be sufficient for my discharge.

The House sympathized with the serjeant, and the matter was 'shuffled up'. Maurice is not known to have taken any further part in the 1601 proceedings.[2]

For over 30 years Maurice was engaged in a disastrous struggle for control of lands at Gest, Eifionydd, from Owen Ellis of Ystumllyn; he had a long legal duel with his stepson Sir Harry Jones (or Johnes) over Rowland Puleston's property; and to some of his neighbours he was known as a 'turbulent and contentious man ... carrying a greedy mind unlawfully to enrich himself'. Forced entry, unlawful assembly, forcible ouster and assault lay to his charge in the Star Chamber. Still, another contemporary spoke of 'the more than vulgar affection which always you have borne unto learning and the professions thereof', and he is reported as giving strong encouragement to native culture at a time when old bardic traditions were beginning to decline for want of patronage. He was quick to expostulate with one he suspected of 'detraction of your own country and countrymen. Foul is fowl that [de]files his own nest'. Again, he was careful to keep on good terms with the Earl of Leicester's agents. He died 10 Aug. 1622.[3]

[1] E. N. Williams, 'Sir William Maurice of Clenennau', *Trans Caern. Hist. Soc.* xxiv. 78–97; *Clenennau Letters and Pprs.* pp. xviii, xix; Griffith, *Peds.* 218; Flenley, *Cal. Reg. Council, Marches of Wales*, 133; *APC*, xxiii. 261; *Cal. Wynn Pprs.* 112; St. Ch. 5/G21/7; *HMC Hatfield*, vii. 486; W. R. Williams, *Parl. Hist. Wales*, 59. [2] *Clenennau Pprs.* pp. xvii–xviii, 4, 31; *Bull. Bd. Celtic Studies* 1937, p. 336; *Trans. Caern. Hist. Soc.* xxiv. 79, 89; *Cal. Wynn Pprs.* 33; Townshend, *Hist. Colls.* 229, 255–6; D'Ewes, 474, 496, 643–4, 655. [3] *Clenennau Pprs.* 61–2; *Trans. Caern. Hist. Soc.* xxiv. passim.

H.G.O.

MAWDLEY, John (by 1501–72), of the Middle Temple, London, and Wells, Som.

WELLS   1529, 1539, 1545, 1554 (Apr.), 1558, 1559

b. by 1501, s. of John Mawdley[†] of Wells by his w. Joan. *educ.* M. Temple 1517. *m.* (1) Joyce (?Ashe), 1da.; (2) Eleanor, da. of Thomas Popwell, 2s. 1da. *suc.* fa. 1540.[1]

Master of the revels, M. Temple 1519, reader 1533, 1543, bencher 1533, treasurer 1551–2; freeman, Wells 1529, jurat 1534; j.p. Som. Jan. 1543–4, from c.1559; steward, sheriff's ct. of Bristol c.1554; escheator, Dorset, Som. 1552–3.[2]

The outline of Mawdley's life is clear, the details obscured by the activities of various namesakes, including his father. The son of a wealthy clothier, probably of a junior branch of the Mawdleys of Nunney, Somerset, he became a lawyer, his admission as a freeman of Wells excusing him the usual duties and offices on condition that he acted as counsel to the city. During the next 30 years he held a number of offices there and from 1543 was on the commission of the peace and other commissions in Somerset. He may also have carried on his father's cloth-making business.[3]

In January 1558 Mawdley and John Aylworth were returned to Parliament on promising to serve without wages. The same condition was probably made in December of that year when Wells returned the same two men to Elizabeth's first Parliament. Though he did not sit again, Mawdley continued to be active as a local magistrate, and in January 1570 was appointed one of the revived inner council of the city. He had inherited some lands from his father and held at his death considerable property in Wells, with the manor of Ford and other lands in Somerset. His will, made 31 Mar. 1570, and proved 27 Nov. 1573, included charitable bequests. His wife and two sons were executors, and William Bowerman* an overseer. He died 6 Apr. 1572.[4]

[1] C142/83/160; Harl. 1559, f. 19; PCC 17 Alenger. [2] *M.T. Recs.* i. 60, 83; *M.T. Bench Bk.* 61; Wells corp. act bk. passim; *APC*, iv. 67. [3] Wells corp. act bk.; *LP Hen. VIII*, xviii(1), p. 68; *CPR*, 1547–8, p. 89; 1553–4, p. 36; Leland, *Itinerary*, i. 145. [4] Wells corp. act bk.; *CPR*, 1558–60, p. 423; C142/83/160, 172/132; PCC 36 Peter.

R.V.

MAWDLEY, Roger (*d.*1630), of Poole, Dorset.

POOLE   1597

s. of Richard Mawdley of Nunney by Anne, da. of William Thynne of Erith, Kent. *m.* Margery, wid. of Sir Walter Hungerford of Farleigh Castle, Som., 3da.

Mayor, Poole 1588–9, 1594–5, 1600–1, 1609–10; collector of revenues 1592.

The only reference found to Mawdley in the records of his one Parliament is his being licensed to depart, 29 Nov. 1597, leaving 5s. for the poor and the minister. Thenceforward all that is known about him shows him dispensing hospitality: a dinner for Judge Edward Fenner*, one of the justices of assize, when he visited Poole in 1598, for which the town was to repay him £3; a dinner for the deputy lieutenants who were dealing with the recusancy of a local gentleman's son, when once again the town reimbursed him; and, in 1601, a Sunday supper for the prisoners in Poole gaol. He died 22 Sept. 1630, when his son-in-law Arthur Radford was granted administration of his property.

This biography is based upon the Roberts thesis and information from J. P. Ferris. Other sources include the following: Harl. 1559, f. 128v; *HMC Egmont*, i. 85; *Vis. Dorset* (Harl. Soc. xx), 78; Hutchins, *Dorset*, i. 9, 33, 34; Poole recs. audit bk. ff. 3, 10; *Vis. Som.* (Harl. Soc. xi), 73; St. Ch. 5/B48/16; *Spanish Armada*, ed. Laughton (Navy Recs. Soc. i), 129; D'Ewes, 565; *HMC Hatfield*, xii. 229, 245, 535; *Som. and Dorset N. and Q.* iii. 166; C142/762/155, 260/141; PCC admon. act bk. 1629, f. 129.

P.W.H.

MAYE, George, of Canterbury, Kent.

CANTERBURY   1559

m. ?(1) by 1545, a da. of Simon Hoigges; (2) 1559, the wid. of one Nevell.[1]

Sheriff, Canterbury 1549, alderman by 1557, mayor 1557–8, 1565–6; city auditor 1564–5.[2]

The name 'Maye' was common in the Canterbury area in the sixteenth century. It seems likely that at least three men called George Maye lived in the city in the period from about 1525 to 1600, and with no pedigrees, wills or inquisitions post mortem it is difficult to separate them. One or two points are clear, however. It is evident that the Member was the 'Mr. Maye, alderman', who married the widowed Mrs. Nevell in 1559. But she may not have been his first wife. In 1545 an apothecary of this name acquired his freedom because he was married to the daughter of Simon Hoigges, another freeman.[3] In documents of 1543 a George Maye is mentioned who was evidently quite well known in the city by that date. In that year Archbishop Cranmer was investigating the conduct of several priests in Kent who were opposed to the reformation in the Church. Three of the most conservative of them claimed that several Canterbury citizens, including Maye, had brought false charges against them. One of them, Robert Serles, said their accusers were 'men of evil fame noted in the city', and another, Edmund Shether, singled out George Maye of St. John's house, as a person 'suspect of evil opinions'. This Maye, probably, was churchwarden of St. Andrew's from about 1550 to 1552 and, more important, was one of the commissioners appointed very early in Edward VI's reign to survey and sell church goods in Canterbury. It seems reasonable to suppose, therefore, that a man of this name was a strong supporter of the new religion from the early 1540s onwards, and was of sufficient standing by 1559 to be returned to Parliament. There is some evidence that the majority of the freemen felt that the Elizabethan Church settlement was not radical enough, and it is quite possible they chose as Member a man with left-wing religious views.[4]

While the 1559 Parliament was sitting, Maye and his fellow-Member, Sir Thomas Finch*, were instructed by the Privy Council to investigate the rumours that Dr. Harpsfield, archdeacon of Canterbury, was resisting changes in the established religion. They were to question him and other suspects and discover what arms were to be found in the cathedral buildings.[5]

At least two factions appeared in local politics in Canterbury in the first few years of the reign, and Maye seems to have become involved in their quarrels. In the records of the city burmote, or council, occurs a letter, probably dated October 1562,[6] which refers to the matter. Hearing that Maye, a man 'very well commended by sundry means unto us', had withdrawn from the body of aldermen, the Privy Council ordered the authorities to re-admit him. Presumably the order was obeyed, for Maye became mayor for the second time in 1565.[7]

Other references which can be ascribed with confidence to Maye are few. He was probably the 'Mr. Maye' who

held the lease of St. Gregory's priory, just outside the city walls, in 1560. He enclosed part of the churchyard of the parish of Northgate, claiming that this was property belonging to the holders of the priory, the archbishops and their successors. Interestingly, the property was leased later by another Canterbury Member, John Boys*, who built a new house on the site. The Member may also have leased a messuage called the White House in the parish of St. Mary Magdalen in 1550, and received a rent or fee-farm from Canterbury, worth £7 10s. a year, in 1557. This was paid twice yearly by the mayor and sheriff: he sold the right to Simon Brome* three years later.[8]

Nothing is known of Maye's life after 1565. Another George Maye, of St. Dunstan's parish, perhaps his son, was married in 1575 and died in 1611.[9]

[1] *Reg. St. Alphage, Canterbury*, ed. Cowper, 105; J. M. Cowper, *Freemen Canterbury*, 138. [2] *Arch. Cant.* xiv. 316; *CPR, 1555–7*, p. 344; Hasted, *Hist. Kent*, xii. 606. [3] Cowper, *Freemen*, 138. [4] *LP Hen. VIII*, xviii(2), pp. 334, 345–6, 357, 365–6; J. Ridley, *Thomas Cranmer*, 229 seq.; *Arch. Cant.* viii. 86; xiv. 316, 318; *CPR, 1550–3*, p. 396. [5] *APC*, vii. 53. [6] The letter copied into the burmote bk. has 'Oct. 1561', but it occurs after other letters dated 1562. Burmote bk. 1542–78, f. 151. [7] Hasted, xii. 606. [8] *CPR, 1549–51*, p. 183; *1555–7*, p. 344; *1558–60*, p. 262. [9] *Kent Mar. Licences (ser. 1), 1568–1618*, p. 281; *Reg. St. Dunstan, Canterbury*, ed. Cowper, 116.

M.R.P.

MAYLARD, Rowland (d. 1596), of Hampton Court, Mdx.

BLETCHINGLEY	1571
GATTON	1572

m. Mary, 4s. 1da.
    Keeper of gardens at Hampton Court by 1573; clerk of peace, Surr.; master of swans on Thames by 1593.

A servant of the Howards of Effingham, Maylard acquired a variety of local offices. He was a mourner at the funeral in 1569 of Edward, third son of William Howard, the lord chamberlain, and was no doubt brought into Parliament for both his borough seats through Howard patronage. In his will he asked to be buried in Hampton parish church, 'and my funeral to be done in decent sort without any great charges'. He died between the date of a codicil 25 Oct. and the proof of the will, 30 Oct. 1596.

PCC 71 Drake, 31 Harte; E351/541/152, 176; *HMC 7th Rep.* 641, 651–2; *Surr. Arch. Colls.* ix. 425; Add. 48018; Kempe, *Loseley Mss.* 306.

H.G.O./A.D.K.H.

MAYNARD, Henry (aft. 1547–1610), of St. Albans, Herts., later of Little Easton, Essex.

ST. ALBANS	1584, 1586, 1589, 1593, 1597
ESSEX	1601

b. aft. 1547, 2nd s. of John Maynard† of St. Albans, being 1st s. by his 2nd w. Dorothy, da. of Robert Parrott of

Oxford, wid. of John Bridges. *m.* Susan, 2nd da. of William or Thomas Pierson, 8s. 2da. Kntd. 1603.[1]

Sec. to Sir Nicholas Bacon†; to Lord Burghley by 1582; j.p. Essex from c.1592, commr. musters from 1599, sheriff 1603–4, dep. lt. 1603, surveyor crown lands by 1606, custos rot. from 1608; surveyor musters, Ireland Oct. 1598, muster master gen. for life Dec. 1604.[2]

Maynard's father became steward of his home town of St. Albans when it was first granted a charter in 1553, retaining the office until his death in 1556. He possessed a good deal of ex-monastic land in St. Albans. He left Henry next to nothing in his will. Maynard himself, when still a young man, entered the service of his kinsman by marriage, Sir Nicholas Bacon, and at the time of Bacon's death in 1579 had risen to be his confidential secretary. By 1582 he was employed by Bacon's friend and colleague Lord Burghley and thenceforth Maynard sat in every Elizabethan Parliament. He was five times returned for his local borough of St. Albans until by 1601 he had achieved sufficient status to obtain one of the Essex county seats. As with others members of the secretariat he played no prominent part in the business of the Commons. No intervention in debate has been recorded, and his first recorded committee concerned recusancy (4 Apr. 1593). In 1597 he was appointed to committees concerning horse-stealing (16 Nov.), double payments on shop books (2 Dec.), a private bill (9 Dec.) and Great Yarmouth (23 Jan. 1598). Those in 1601 included privileges and returns (31 Oct.), the penal laws (2 Nov.), the main business committee (3 Nov.), procedure (11 Nov.), painters and stainers (24 Nov.), fustians (4 Dec.), charitable uses (12 Dec.) and cattle stealing (12 Dec.). As knight for Essex in 1601 he was eligible to attend committees on the clothworkers (18 Nov.) and monopolies (23 Nov.). He has a place in history as the chairman of the subsidy committee of 7 Nov. 1601, when, 'by the consent of the whole House' he put on his hat to register the committee's orders. Maynard was mistakenly referred to as Anthony on this occasion.[3]

During the last years of Burghley's life Maynard was one of his two leading secretaries. Michael Hickes* acted as patronage secretary, while Maynard concerned himself with 'matters of state'. Thus contemporaries regarded him as the more important of the two, sometimes referring to him as 'principal' or 'chief' secretary. He masterminded the activities of Sir Horatio Palavicino, as envoy to France and Germany in 1590 and 1591, ensured that Palavicino received letters to the French king and German princes, drew up detailed instructions and drafted Burghley's letters to the envoy. Between 1590 and 1594 he was immersed in the business of the Netherlands, seeing to the supply of ordnance and corresponding with Sir Edmund Uvedale*, marshal of Flushing, and with Thomas Bodley*, the English ambassador. He also dealt with Irish and Scottish business, making arrangements for transporting money to Ireland in 1582 and assisting

Burghley to draw up the proclamation against Tyrone in 1595. Letters, information and messages dealing with Ireland passed frequently between Maynard and Robert Cecil during the last years of Burghley's life, and the Scottish ambassador, Archibald Douglas, frequently wrote to Maynard on matters of common concern. Many notes and drafts relating to the English armed forces are in his hand, and he was in the habit of endorsing documents addressed to Burghley on naval and military affairs.[4]

Though Burghley became increasingly dependent on Maynard and Hickes during the last years of his life, he reacted vigorously to any suggestion that he could be controlled by his subordinates. Maynard wrote him a long letter in July 1593, expressing 'exceeding grief' at his master's 'hard opinion' of him. For two or three years past he had found Burghley's former favour withdrawn, he believed, because of reports which had come to Burghley's ears that he had boasted that he could 'rule or govern' his master. Clearly this was related to payments suitors were prepared to make to Maynard to secure his or Burghley's favour. On one occasion in 1597 Maynard was offered £100 for his help in a comparatively minor suit about the reversion of land in Ireland. In 1593 it was alleged that Thomas Shirley I*, treasurer at war, had 'infinitely bribed' Maynard to conceal his misappropria-tion of funds for the Netherlands. Shirley admitted making at least one payment to Maynard:

> I do swear by the living God that to my remembrance I have not given to Mr. Maynard above ten pounds in one year for all his pains, being ashamed to make it known that I have used so small gratuity for so great pains as I have continually put him to.

In view of the wide range of functions and duties which Maynard performed, his yearly profits from gratuities must have been considerable.[5]

In August 1598, shortly after Burghley's death, John Chamberlain reported that Maynard had 'become the Queen's man' and that he was so highly favoured that he was thought 'nearest in election to be secretary'. Instead he became surveyor of the musters in Ireland. Similarly, a rumour that he was to be appointed ambassador to France in 1604 was succeeded by another Irish appointment, that of muster master general. He died on 11 May 1610, leaving a considerable estate. Besides lands of the dissolved monastery of Tilty in Essex, which he purchased in 1588 for £5,000, and the manor of Little Easton, which he obtained in 1589 and which became his Essex seat, he held nine manors in possession and reversion, eight in Essex and one in Surrey; some of this property had been entailed on him by his father. He also had land in Westminster and London. He left £2,000 each to his daughters Elizabeth and Mary, and 400 ozs. of plate to his widow.[6]

[1] *Vis. Essex* (Harl. Soc. xiii), 76; (xiv), 595; F. Chancellor, *Ancient Sep. Mons. of Essex*, 83; *Essex Rev.* xliv. 76–8. On Maynard generally,

see A. G. R. Smith, 'Sir Michael Hickes and the Secretariat of the Cecils, circa 1580–1612' (London Univ. PhD thesis, 1962) chs. 2, 3, 10. [2] Essex RO, Q/SR passim; CSP Ire. 1600–1, p. 249; APC, xxix. 701; xxxii. 501; SP14/60; Lansd. 171, f. 397; Colvin, Lieutenants and Keepers of Rolls of Essex, 80. [3] Clutterbuck, Herts. iii. 497; account of expenses of funeral of Sir Nicholas Bacon, Raynham mss; Gen. Mag. vi. 635–41; HMC Hatfield, ii. 532, 533; D'Ewes, 517, 558, 566, 571, 586, 622–3, 624, 631, 635, 642, 649, 650, 668, 680, 681; Townshend, Hist. Colls. 106, 111, 114, 200. [4] SP12/204–14, 262–5; 63/179/20, 21; 81/6/48, 86–91, 112; 81/7/1; 84/48/76; 84/50/3–8, 43, 95, 108–10; Hatfield mss 49/113; Lansd. 79, f. 186; HMC Hatfield, ii. 532, 533; iv. 72; v. 100; vi. 58, 249–50; viii. 162, 254; CSP Ire. 1596–7, p. 238; CSP Scot. xi. 37. [5] SP12/244/69; 245/51; HMC Hatfield, iv. 323, 606; v. 360, 511; vi. 191, 425–6, 448; vii. 231, 266, 293, 378, 393; viii. 205; xiii. 577; Hatfield mss 28/71, 75; 32/30; 53/20; Lansd. 87, f. 71; CSP Dom. 1591–4, p. 370; CSP Ire. 1592–6, p. 229. [6] Chamberlain Letters ed. McClure, i. 42, 198; CSP Ire. 1600–1, p. 249; Egerton 2644, f. 145; HMC Hatfield, xvi. 205–6, 350; Essex Rev. v. 99; vii. 249; C142/107/58; 319/195; PCC 43 Wingfield.

A.G.R.S.

MELLES, Arthur, ?of Ipswich and Cockfield Hall, Suff.

DUNWICH   1586

In the fourteenth century Sir Peter de Melles owned a manor about five miles from Dunwich, and although the property descended through his daughter to another family, the name Melles or Myles remained in that district until the sixteenth century and later. A Thomas Melles was one of the puritan ministers who in the early 1580s drew up objections to Bishop Freake's demands for subscription to the complete prayer book. All this said, the 1586 MP was almost certainly 'Arthur Mills of Ipswich', godson of Anthony Wingfield*, the other Member for Dunwich in 1586. In 1593 Wingfield conveyed to him the manor house of Cockfield Hall, Suffolk. This man or his father may have been the Arthur Mylles to whom one of the Hoptons, probably Sir Owen, owed the large sum of £2,000 in 1576. This might suggest that the family was engaged in trade, but further information is lacking.

Suckling, Antiqs. of Suff. ii. 184; W. A. Copinger, Suff. Manors, ii. 120, 184; Collinson thesis, 419 n. 3; Ipswich RO, Blois mss 312/78, 155; HMC Var. vii. 87.

N.M.F.

MERE, Henry (d. 1608), of the Inner Temple, London, and of Sherborne, Dorset.

CHRISTCHURCH   1601

3rd s. of Hugh Mere of Sherborne by Alice, da. of Thomas Alombridge or Alanbridge of Dorset; bro. of William*. educ. Sherborne c.1560; I. Temple 1576, called 1587. m. 1582, Magdalen, da. of Bartholomew Lyte of Tucks Cary, Som., 1s. 6da.

Escheator, Som. and Dorset 1591–2; collector for the bailiwick of Fineshade, Northants.; gov. Sherborne sch. 1592, warden 1599.[1]

In the 1601 return for Christchurch this Member was

said to be of the Middle Temple, but there is no record of such a person entering this inn of court. A Henry Mere or Meres was a barrister of the Inner Temple, and it is assumed that he became the Member for Christchurch in 1601, even though he was again described as of the Middle Temple when accused, in the Star Chamber, of antedating a writ in order to invalidate a sentence of outlawry against his brother John. As the third son of a minor country gentleman he was lucky to inherit property in Grimstone, Stratton and Wootton Glanville in Dorset. A professional lawyer, in 1589 he was disbarred for not pursuing the required exercises, being re-admitted on paying £3 6s. 8d.[2]

In 1592 his younger brother John became Sir Walter Ralegh's bailiff at Sherborne. Ralegh granted him considerable copyhold land there, and the probability is that John Mere began swindling him. He was dismissed and initiated proceedings against Ralegh in the Star Chamber, with the support of Henry and the protection of Thomas Howard*, 3rd Viscount Howard of Bindon. It was probably Bindon who had Henry Mere returned to Parliament for Christchurch, perhaps in connexion with this episode. Writing from Sherborne to Henry Brooke II*, 11th Lord Cobham in August 1601, Ralegh promised to be with him as soon as he had settled his business with the justices 'about those rogues the Meres'. But the accession of James I was the opportunity the two brothers had been waiting for. John Mere gained a place on the commission to view Ralegh's lands in Sherborne, while Henry continued to prosecute him in the Star Chamber. In 1605 some sort of deal was suggested, whereby the Earl of Northumberland would cease a prosecution for debt against Henry Mere in return for Mere dropping his suit against Ralegh. There were other complaints about Mere, Henry Lyte writing A record of the villainy and knavery wrought by Henry Meere and The tyrannical dealings of Henry Meer against his uncle Henry Lyte, esquire, copies of which cannot now be traced. Mere died in 1608, apparently intestate, and was buried in the parish church of Sherborne.[3]

[1] Vis. Dorset 1623 (Harl. Soc. xx), 68–9; CSP Dom. 1604–10, p. 472. [2] St. Ch. 5/A22/38; PCC 33 Tirwhite; Cal. I. T. Recs. i. 358–9, 362. [3] Neale, Commons, 243; St. Ch. 5/M3/25; Edwards, Life of Ralegh, i. 470–1; ii. 228, 238, 308; HMC Hatfield, xvii. 505–6; CSP Dom. 1603–10, p. 472; PCC 77 Skinner.

A.M.M.

MERE, William (d by 1582), of Sherborne, Dorset.

MELCOMBE REGIS   1563

1st s. of Hugh Mere of Sherborne, and bro. of Henry*. educ. I. Temple 1556. unm.

The Meres were tenants of the Dorset manor of Chaldon Bois, owned by the Russell family, and it was presumably the 2nd Earl of Bedford who supplied Mere with his seat at Melcombe in 1563. He may have been as much of a rogue as his brothers. He was dead by 1582.

Vis. Dorset (Harl. Soc. xx), 68–9; *Vis. Wilts.* (Harl. Soc. cv, cvi), 231–5; St. Ch. 5/B15/39; Roberts thesis.

P.W.H.

MEREDITH, William (d. c.1604), of Blackfriars, London, and Stansty, Denb.

WOOTTON BASSETT   1593

2nd s. of Richard Meredith of Stansty by Jane, da. of Morgan ap David ap Robert. *m.* (1) bef. 12 Feb. 1566, Martha, da. and coh. of Robert Long, mercer of London, 2s. 2da.; (2) Jane, da. of Sir Thomas Palmer of Wingham, Kent. Kntd. 1603.[1]

Bailiff and collector of lordship of Swinfield; collector and bailiff of manor of Newington, Kent 1598; dep. treasurer at war in the Netherlands 1587–97; acting treasurer at war Apr. 1597; paymaster of the forces there from May 1597; dep. treasurer at war 1599.[2]

Meredith came of an old Denbighshire family. In 1558 he was a merchant in Antwerp and in October of that year, while abroad, was elected a master bachelor of the Mercers' Company. One Robert Meredith, who may have been a relative, was a mercer in March 1541. In 1565 William purchased land in Kent from Bartholomew Page, a London mercer.[3]

From May 1587 to May 1597 he was the deputy of Thomas Shirley I*, treasurer at war in the Netherlands. On 12 Mar. 1597 when Shirley was about to be superseded, Rowland Whyte wrote to Sir Robert Sidney that 'the Lords offered Mr. Meredith the paymaster's place, with £200 fee. He refuses, not willing to meddle in the affairs of princes, nor content with so small means'. However, on 30 Apr. 1597 Meredith wrote to Burghley:

If the Queen shall think me fit for the office of paymaster of the forces in the Low Countries, I will do my uttermost to perform the best service I can, and give security for £3,000, being almost a month's pay there. Whereas Sir Thomas Fludd [*] has £2 1s. 8d. per diem, for the entertainment of himself and his under officers, I will serve the place for 30s. a day ... By this means the Queen shall be well secured of the charge committed to me, and shall save £200 odd yearly.

On the following 14 May he was granted the office of paymaster, thus virtually replacing Fludd as treasurer. Meredith's fee was 10s. a day and 5s. for each of four clerks. On 15 June 1597 Thomas Fanshawe I* wrote to Burghley that 19 persons had entered into bonds worth £4,000 altogether as security for Meredith, and that Meredith himself was bound in £4,000 for the office. About September of that year Meredith wrote to Burghley, 'I have undertaken the service of the Low Countries at a less rate than any other has done, and beg consideration'. He kept the office till his death, between 6 July 1603 and 8 Feb. 1604. In January 1598 his brother, John Meredith, was his deputy in the west country, and he also acted as his deputy

at Middelburg in the Netherlands in May 1601. On 12 Aug. 1599 William was appointed deputy to Sir John Stanhope, treasurer at war for the armies. He was knighted at the coronation of James I.[4]

By his will, dated 6 July 1603, Meredith left his wife 1,000 marks in ready money and the parsonage of Bassingbourn, Cambridgeshire, for 45 years, with remainder after her death to his son William, his executor. To his daughter Anne he left £1,000 and to his daughter Jane 1,000 marks. To Sir Thomas Palmer and Lady Palmer, Lady Shirley, Lady Tracy, and 21 others he gave each a gold ring with an engraved death's-head and the inscription *Memento mori*. He bequeathed £5 to the parson of St. Alban's in Woodstreet and the same amount to the poor of the parish, £5 to the poor of Blackfriars, £10 to the poor of Stansty, and 7 nobles to a cannoneer. He left £30 for the yearly wage of a preacher at Wrexham, expressing the hope that the people of the parish would thereafter maintain a learned and godly minister there, as had not been done in any of the parishes of Bromfield and Yale within his memory. He expressed a desire for the King to reform the lamentable state of all the churches of North Wales. Other money bequests in the will amounted to £205.[5] His wife married secondly Sir John Vaughan*, 1st Earl of Carbery, of Golden Grove, Carmarthenshire.[6]

Meredith may have been a nominee of (Sir) Henry Knyvet* at Wootton Bassett in 1593, since John Hungerford, the other Member for the borough that year, was not. No connexion between Knyvet and Meredith has been established. They may have become acquainted through both being engaged in military service. Also, Knyvet as sheriff and receiver of Wiltshire, may have known Meredith as a considerable landowner in Wiltshire, for in 1574 the latter bought a third part of the manors of Comberford, Stokeleigh, Calston, Westbury, Bowars, Chapmanslade, Goddesfeld, Calne, Pollesholte, Ashton, and Hilperton, and a third part of the hundred of Calne. Meredith was not named to any committee, but as burgess for Wootton Bassett he could have attended a cloth committee on 15 Mar. 1593.[7]

[1] Lloyd, *Powys Fadog*, iii. 82; Palmer, *Wrexham*, 195; *Vis. Kent* (Harl. Soc. liv), 114; *GEC Baronetage*, i. 209; *CPR*, 1547–8, pp. 11, 280, 360; 1553 and App. Edw. VI, 388; 1563–6, pp. 524–5; *Arch. Camb.* lxxxvii. 243. [2] E315/309/116; *HMC Ancaster*, 81, 119, 229; *HMC De L'Isle and Dudley*, ii. 267, 269, 271–2, 277, 278, 281, 317, 321, 487–8; *HMC 5th Rep.* 287; *HMC Hatfield*, vii. 178, 196, 200, 248, 305, 426; viii. 19; ix. 93, 97–8; xvi. 415; *CSP Dom.* 1595–7, pp. 405–13; Add. 1580–1625, p. 205; *APC*, xxvii. 16, 130, 134, 135, 143, 333, 334–5; xxviii. 310; xxix. 12–13, 25, 130, 136–7, 139, 419–20, 595, 644–5, 712; xxx, xxxi, xxxii, passim. [3] *Arch. Camb.* lxxxvii. 240–1; *HMC Sackville*, i. 5; Sir J. Watney, *Hosp. St. Thos. of Acon*, 128–9, 183, 184–5; *CPR*, 1563–6, p. 304. [4] *HMC De L'Isle and Dudley*, ii. 249; *CSP Dom.* 1595–7, pp. 401, 415, 442, 507; 1598–1601, p. 290; 1603–10, p. 217; PCC 14 Hayes; *APC*, xxviii. 263; *HMC Hodgkins*, 273; *HMC Foljambe*, 101–2. [5] PCC 14 Hayes. [6] *DNB* (Vaughan, Richard); Lloyd, loc. cit.; Palmer, 196. [7] *Wilts. N. and Q.* viii. 133; D'Ewes, 501.

S.T.B.

MEREDITH, *see* AMEREDITH

MEREDYDD, Rowland ap (by 1529–1600 or later), of Bodowyr, Anglesey.

ANGLESEY   1558, 1559

b. by 1529, 1st s. of Meredydd ap Rhys ap Hywel of Bodowyr by Catherine, da. of Owen ap Meurig of Bodowen. *m.* Agnes, da. of Rhydderch ap David of Myfyrian in Llanidan, 4s. 1da. *suc.* fa. ?1555 or later.[1]

Bailiff, commote of Twrcelyn 1550; j.p. Anglesey from 1555; collector of relief 1558, subsidy 1563; commr. defence 1569; escheator 1570–1; commr. inquiry into concealed lands in manor of Aberffraw, Anglesey 1590.[2]

Rowland ap Meredydd, or Rowland Meredith as he tended to call himself in official documents from 1558 (though the surname was never stabilised), stood in direct descent from the clan which, led by Owain Gwynedd's brother-in-law Llywarch ap Brân, effected the settlement of south-western Anglesey in the twelfth century. Reduced by frequent sub-division, the estate of Bodowyr was by Tudor times among the smallest of those of surviving members of the clan in the commote of Menai, being rated for subsidy at only £2; but the shell of the house as it stood in 1846 showed it to have been a place of some consequence. Meredydd's maternal uncle, Lewis Owen ap Meurig*, represented Anglesey in March 1553 and 1572, and was sheriff when Meredydd was returned to the 1559 Parliament. Both Owen and Meredydd opposed the growing domination of the island by the Bulkeleys and it may be significant that neither was returned to Parliament once the Bulkeleys had consolidated their pre-eminence in the county.[3]

Meredydd was an assiduous builder of mills. He erected two on his own estate at Bodowyr, and about 1587–8 helped his grandson Jasper Price to erect two tide mills on the Menai Straits near Porthaethwy. These in 1593 became the subject of a petition to the Exchequer by the lessee of the ferry across the Straits, who claimed, apparently unsuccessfully, that his rights were infringed and his tolls injured thereby. The date of Meredydd's death has not been established. He remained an active local official until at least 1600. Two of his sons evidently predeceased him, and the estate passed to his grandson Jasper, son of his second son Rhys.[4]

[1] Griffith, *Peds.* 51; *Arch. Camb.* 1848, pp. 241–3; Dwnn, *Vis. Wales,* ii. 137. [2] *Augmentations,* ed. Lewis and Davies (Univ. Wales Bd. of Celtic Studies, Hist. and Law ser. xiii), 177; *Star Chamber,* ed. Edwards (same ser. i), 16; E179/219/7, 12, 13; Flenley, *Cal. Reg. Council, Marches of Wales,* 56–7; *Trans. Anglesey Antiq. Soc.* 1939, p. 67. [3] *Arch. Camb.* 1846, p. 202; 1848, pp. 241–2; 1863, p. 260; *Trans. Anglesey Antiq. Soc.* 1939, pp. 62–3; 1951, p. 13; E179/219/3–17; St. Ch. 4/8/6; 4/57. [4] *Star Chamber,* ed. Edwards, loc. cit.; St. Ch. 5/ L40/2; *Arch. Camb.* 1848, p. 243; *Exchequer,* ed. E. G. Jones (Univ. Wales Bd. of Celtic Studies, Hist. and Law ser. iv), 22; *Conway and*

Menai Ferries, ed. H. R. Davies (same ser. viii), 132–3, 137–8; UCNW Plas Coch ms 137; Harl. 1974, f. 23.

A.H.D./P.S.E.

MERES, Lawrence (*d.* c.1593), of Lincs., Later Yorks.; ? Suff.

ORFORD   1563

s. of Sir John Meres of Kirton, Lincs. by his 2nd w. Jane, da. of William Bleasby of Bleasby. *educ.* G. Inn 1540, called bef. 1552. *m.* (1) Constance Stegle, 2da.; (2) Faith, da. of Sir William Tyrwhitt of Scotter, Lincs., wid. of Ambrose Sutton† of Wellingore, Lincs., *s.p.*[1]

J.p. Suff. from c.1561, Lincs. (Lindsey, Holland) from 1564–87; recorder, Grimsby 1565; member, council in the north by 1568; j.p. Cumb. Northumb. Westmld. and all three ridings of Yorks. by 1574; escheator, Yorks. Jan.–Oct. 1579, Lincs. (Lindsey) 1582.[2]

Meres probably owed his Orford seat to his family's connexions with the Duchess of Suffolk and her relatives. One of his brothers, Roger, had been lawyer to her first husband, while another, Anthony, went abroad in Mary's reign with the Duchess and her second husband Richard Bertie*, knight of the shire for Lincolnshire in 1563. By a settlement with the Duchess's relative Lord Willoughby in 1562, the Berties were confirmed in their possession of the manor of Orford, with Willoughby as their tenant.

It seems possible that by the time he entered Parliament Meres was living in Suffolk. The previous year his name had appeared on the commission of the peace for that county, very near the end of the list, his membership of the quorum presumably depending on his knowledge of the law rather than on social prominence. In 1564 the bishop of Lincoln, commenting on Lincolnshire justices, described him as 'earnest in religion' – an attitude likely to have commended him to the Duchess, an ardent puritan, and to her family.[3]

Most of our information about Meres concerns his period as a member of the council in the north. His salary rose from £40 until by about 1586 it had reached £100, half of which came from fines and forfeitures: one reference, presumably later, describes it as 200 marks. The Earl of Sussex wrote to Cecil in March 1569:

> I have no cause to mislike any of her Majesty's council here, but must recommend the great care and upright dealing of Sir Thomas Gargrave [*] and Mr. Meres; in all causes in the court they proceed learnedly to the matter, without respect of the person.

In the following summer, when Meres came to London to renew a suit which Sussex had been 'moving' for him at court, the Earl wrote to Cecil that 'in his desire to her Majesty's service, [Meres] has determined to leave his habitation in Lincolnshire, and settle in Yorkshire'.[4]

Apart from the fact that a list of lawyers, drawn up about 1576, described him as 'of good living', almost nothing is known of Meres's private or domestic life. His will, drawn up in 1591, was proved on 27 May 1593. He was buried in York minster, and his property divided between his two daughters.[5]

[1] *Lincs. Peds.* (Harl. Soc. li), 664–5; *Genealogist*, iv. 257–8; *Pens. Bk. G. Inn*, i. 499. [2] *HMC 14th Rep. VIII*, 296; *CSP Dom.* Add. 1566–79, p. 61; Lansd. 35, f. 134; 121, f. 69; *CPR*, 1563–6, p. 24. [3] W. A. Copinger, *Suff. Manors*, v. 149; Lincs. AO, Anc. v/b/4; 3 Anc./8/3, p. 72; *Cam. Misc.* ix(3), p. 27. [4] *CSP Dom.* Add. 1566–79, pp. 61, 74, 309; Lansd. 10, ff. 2–10; 49, ff. 194–5. [5] Lansd. 683, f. 64; *Lincs. Peds.*; York prob. reg. 25, f. 1362.

N.M.F.

MEWES (MEUX), William (c.1530–89), of Kingston, I.o.W.

NEWTOWN I.o.W.   1584

b. c.1530, 1st s. of Richard Mewes of Kingston by Dorothy, da. of Thomas Cooke of Fordingbridge, Hants. *m.* Elinor, da. of Sir Henry Strangeways, 1s. 2da. *suc.* fa. bef. 1568, uncle 1568.

Of the senior branch of his family, Mewes inherited most of his lands from his uncle John, the last male representative of a cadet branch. The principal manor, Kingston, was situated between Chillerton Down and St. Catherine Down, on the south coast of the Isle of Wight. It was here that Mewes lived, becoming, as his will indicates, a considerable sheep farmer. Newtown first sent Members to Parliament in Elizabeth's reign in 1584, at the suit of Sir George Carey*, who subsequently controlled the patronage, and Mewes must have been acceptable to him in 1584. However, he was ready to oppose Carey some four years later, as he signed the letter demanding the release of Robert Dillington*. Mewes died 5 Mar. 1589, having made his will the previous 24 Sept. It was proved 17 June 1589 by his son and heir John.

C142/152/143, 222/47; *Vis. Hants* (Harl. Soc. lxiv), 135; *Hist. Isle of Wight*, ed. Worsley, 103; PCC 56 Leicester.

A.M.M.

MEYRICK (MERRICK), Gelly (c.1556–1601), of Gellyswick, Hascard, Pemb.; Wigmore Castle, Herefs.; Gladestry, Rad.; and Essex House, London.

CARMARTHEN BOROUGHS   1589
PEMBROKESHIRE   1597[1]

b. c.1556, 1st s. of Rowland Meyrick, bp. of Bangor, by Catherine, da. of Owen Barret of Gellyswick. *m.* 1584, Elizabeth or Margaret, da. of Ieuan Lewis* of Gladestry, wid. of John Gwynne of Llanelwedd, Rad., 2s. 1da. *suc.* fa. 1566. Kntd. 1596.

Steward of Welsh lands of Robert, 2nd Earl of Essex c.1587, his receiver gen. for wine impost 1598; j.p. Rad. from c.1591, custos rot. 1598, dep. lt. 1598; lt.-col. under Essex at Cadiz 1596, Azores 1597, marshal of forces under Essex in Ulster 1599.[2]

Although Meyrick's immediate antecedents were clerical, his remoter – and perhaps more significant – background was military. The family, of ancient Powys stock, came into prominence when Llywelyn ap Heilyn fought for Henry of Richmond at Bosworth, and his son Meurig ap Llywelyn for Henry VIII in France, receiving as reward a lease of the royal manor of Aberffraw in Anglesey. This dwindled under litigation into the small estate of Bodorgan, and the Anglesey Meyricks remained until the eighteenth century among the smaller gentry of the island. Gelly Meyrick's father, Rowland, second son of Meurig ap Llywelyn, entered the church, received preferment in the diocese of St. David's, married into the Pembrokeshire gentry, and, after losing his offices during the reign of Queen Mary, became bishop of Bangor under Elizabeth. On his death his children, still under age, were taken to their mother's Pembrokeshire estate, and Meyrick became a page in the neighbouring house of Lamphey, then in the occupation of George Devereux*, brother of the 1st Earl of Essex. There, from about 1579, Meyrick entered the service of the 2nd Earl, who was brought up at Lamphey. He looked after Essex's estates in south-west Wales and served him in the field, in the Netherlands, in Portugal, Normandy, Cadiz (where he was lieutenant-colonel and commissioner of stores, receiving his knighthood from Essex at the capture of the city), the Azores and Ireland.

By 1592 Meyrick was the Earl's principal man of business, and had acquired the reputation of being completely devoted to his patron. His service was well rewarded. In 1595 Essex persuaded the Queen to grant him a joint lease of the honour, manor and castle of Wigmore (which became his principal residence), together with other manors and forests in the counties of Hereford and Radnor, to which he added the castle of Manorbier in Pembrokeshire. After Meyrick's death, detractors claimed that these were granted only in trust, for the payment of his master's debts. Meanwhile Meyrick had consolidated his own position and influence in south Wales by marrying into a leading Radnorshire family, thereby acquiring estates and connexions in that county. The marriage which he arranged for his daughter Margaret, with Sir John Vaughan* of Golden Grove, also provided him with an entry into Carmarthenshire society. His personal fortune was swollen by the spoils of Cadiz, which caused envious comment.[3]

Meyrick owed his first parliamentary seat in 1589 to Devereux influence. The 1st Earl of Essex had shown considerable friendliness to the authorities at Carmarthen, in whose parish church he had asked to be buried. By 1593, however, the 2nd Earl of Essex was relying on Meyrick to secure the return of his followers at the Welsh elections. Half the borough seats of the principality – Brecon, Cardigan, Carmarthen, Haverfordwest, Pembroke and New Radnor – returned candidates connected with the

Earl's faction that year. At the 1597 elections both the Earl and his steward were abroad on the Islands voyage but Meyrick was apparently elected for Pembrokeshire in his absence – a striking illustration of the strength of their party in south Wales. Possibly James Perrot*, owner of Haroldston and a follower of Essex, who himself represented Haverfordwest in this Parliament, organised local support at the county election. Elsewhere in Wales, however, Essex's election successes were less striking than in the previous Parliament. Perhaps it was Meyrick's absence during the weeks before the elections which accounted for the loss of Brecon Boroughs to a local man, and possibly also for a defection at New Radnor. In this Parliament Meyrick sat on two committees, 20 Dec. and 26 Jan., both concerned with soldiers and mariners. If he was back in time he could as knight of the shire for Pembrokeshire have attended committees on enclosures (5 Nov.), poor law (5, 22 Nov.), armour and weapons (8 Nov.), penal laws (8 Nov.), monopolies (10 Nov.), the subsidy (15 Nov.) and Newport bridge (29 Nov.).[4]

Meyrick was equally assiduous over forming an Essex faction in local government. His attempt in 1598 to control, on his patron's behalf, nominations for the commission of lieutenancy in Radnorshire was denounced as a challenge to his authority by the 2nd Earl of Pembroke, the president of the council in the marches of Wales, who also opposed Meyrick's own inclusion on the ground that he held no land in the shire in his own right. Meyrick even traded on his north Wales connexions by pressing the claims of a cousin of his as under-sheriff of Caernarvonshire. Towards the end of Essex's disastrous campaign in Ireland, Meyrick was sent home with letters, arriving in August 1599, a few weeks before his master. In the following year some of Essex's friends, who considered Meyrick a dangerous counsellor, brought about his temporary dismissal from the stewardship, but he soon regained his position, and before the rising of 1601 was active in bringing Essex's supporters to London and providing arms for them. It was he who is said to have given 40s. to the Globe actors to perform the play *Richard II* on the night before the day fixed for the rising. When Essex rode into London, Meyrick took charge of the barricading of Essex House against the government forces. His execution for treason on 13 Mar. 1601 necessarily meant the dispersion of his estates. His brother, Sir Francis Meyrick, though under suspicion, was never brought to trial, but his daughter Lady Vaughan of Golden Grove, to whom he was said to have conveyed some of his treasure before the collapse, was involved in her father's attainder. Both she and her surviving brother were restored in blood and name in 1606, and the Meyricks continued to play a part in Pembrokeshire politics till the eighteenth century.[5]

[1] Folger V. b. 298. [2] *DWB*; Dwnn, *Vis. Wales*, i. 70, 136–7, 185, 214; *HMC Hatfield*, viii. 368; *APC*, xxviii. 500; D. Mathew, *Celtic Peoples and Renaissance Europe*, 348; PRO Index 4208. [3] *DWB*; Lansd.

69, f. 177; *HMC Hatfield*, vi. 422; vii. 306; ix. 147; xi. 413; xiii. 195; *Arch. Camb.* (ser. 3), x. 20 seq. [4] Mathew, 340–58; A. H. Dodd, *Studies in Stuart Wales*, 36, 183–4; Neale, *Commons*, 80–2, 238; D'Ewes, 552, 553, 555, 557, 561, 565, 575, 588. [5] *HMC Hatfield*, viii. 233–4; xi. 81–2, 113–14, 135; xiv. 195; NLW *Cal. Clenennau Letters and Pprs.* 121–2; *HMC Rutland*, i. 367–70; *CSP Dom.* 1598–1601, pp. 549, 565, 572–3, 582; *Arch. Camb.* (ser. 3), x. 23–7; *CJ*, i. 291–2, 300–1; 3 Jac. I, c.28.

N.M.F.

MICHELBORNE, Edward (c.1562–1609), of Hammonds Place in Clayton, Suss.

BRAMBER 1593

b. c.1562, 1st s. of Edward Michelborne of Clayton, by his 1st w. Jane, da. of Thomas Parsons of Steyning. *educ.* ?G. Inn 1580. *m.* Anne, da. and h. of Richard Shelley of Patcham, 2s. *suc.* fa. 1587. Kntd. 1599.

Capt. in the Netherlands 1591; served under 2nd Earl of Essex Azores expedition 1597, in Ireland 1597, gent. pens. to James I.[1]

Michelborne was a soldier and adventurer, in whose life a seat in Parliament played only an incidental rôle. He became one of Bramber's representatives in 1593, presumably having enough influence as a local landowner to secure his own return. He had inherited land there from his mother. He may have taken up a military career before 1591, in which year he was a captain in the Queen's pay in the Netherlands; he was still in command of a company of foot, stationed in Ostend, in 1598. In that year Michelborne's company was removed from the Queen's pay, entering that of the Dutch estates. He had not spent all the intervening years abroad. In 1593 he was presumably in England for the Parliament, and two years later was reported to be living in Queenhithe in London. It was probably during this period that he became a follower of the Earl of Essex. He commanded the *Moon* in the Islands voyage in 1597, and in 1599 accompanied the Earl to Ireland, where he served under him in the field that summer. At the end of the campaign he was knighted by Essex in Dublin. Michelborne was implicated in the Essex revolt, being lucky to get away with a fine of £200. He had, so he said, gone to Essex's house to hear a sermon, had met the Earl and his followers, and had then accompanied them to Sheriff Smith's house, but, hearing that the Queen had given orders for the Earl's arrest, he had returned to his lodgings.[2]

Michelborne next found a protector in Lord Treasurer Buckhurst, who in 1601 attempted to gain him the command of the East India Company's first trading venture to the east. The promoters, however, refused to employ 'gentlemen' in any place of charge or command, desiring to 'sort their business with men of their own quality'. When Michelborne failed to pay the amount he had promised for the first voyage, the governors took the opportunity of 'disfranchising' him 'out of the freedom and privileges of this fellowship'. But Michelborne got his own back under James I, obtaining a licence to 'discover' and trade with Japan and China, notwithstanding any previous grant. He thus became the first interloper in the East India trade. He sailed with John Davis as navigator from Plymouth on 1 Dec. 1604, in the *Tiger* (240 tons) and the *Tiger's Whelp*. He returned on 9 July 1606.[3]

Michelborne made his will on 22 Mar. 1609. After a conventional religious preamble, he left a total of £55 to the poor of the three Sussex parishes of Clayton, Penshurst and Lickfold, and a further £20 to the poor of the parish in which he happened to be buried. His other bequests were to his servants and family. The will mentioned a debt of £400 which the 2nd Earl of Dorset owed him. Edward, his executor and eldest son and heir, proved the will on the day that his father died, 27 Apr. 1609. The overseers were Sir Thomas Leeds and Thomas Rooth. Michelborne was buried at Hackney, where he owned a house and lands.[4]

[1] C142/212/1; 314/111; J. Comber, *Suss. Genealogies, Lewes Centre*, 248–9; *Vis. Suss.* (Harl. Soc. liii), 88; *Voyages and Works of John Davis* (Hakluyt Soc. lix), p. lxxi. [2] *DNB*; *HMC De L'Isle and Dudley*, p. lxxvi; Lansd. 78, f. 165; *HMC Hatfield*, ix. 145; xi. 87, 214; *CSP Dom.* 1601–3, p. 13. [3] *Voyages of Sir James Lancaster* (Hakluyt Soc. lvi), pp. ii, v–vi; H. Stevens, *Dawn of Brit. Trade to East Indies*, 28, 178; *Purchas His Pilgrimes* (1905 ed.), ii. 347, 365, 366. [4] PCC 33 Dorset; C142/314/111; *Vis. Suss.* (Harl. Soc. liii), 88.

A.M.M.

MICHELBORNE, Thomas (d. 1582), of Gray's Inn, London, afterwards Winchester, Hants.

WINCHESTER   1563, 1571, 1572*

3rd s. of John Michelborne of Westmeston, Suss. by Joan, da. of Richard Hother of Ditchling, Suss. *educ.* Christ's, Camb. 1550; G. Inn 1551, called. *m.* c.1560, Alice, da. and h. of William Lawrence* of Winchester, wid. of one Warren, 4s. 4da.

Of counsel to Winchester; ancient, G. Inn 1570; escheator, Hants and Wilts. 1570–1; j.p. Hants from 1579.

Though he received land in Hampshire, Sussex, Wiltshire and Yorkshire at the time of his marriage, for some years afterwards Michelborne evidently lived in London, practising as a barrister. He was not resident in Winchester when he first represented the city in 1563, probably being introduced by his father-in-law, his fellow-Member. However, he moved there in 1571, leasing some property from the city, including a large house in Parchment Street. Soon after his arrival he was made a freeman, without payment and on the understanding that he would not be called upon to hold municipal office. He was also granted the lease of some property in Buck Street, on condition that he would serve as MP throughout the next Parliament for only 1s. 4d. a day. During the 1572 Parliament he sat on a committee concerning the engrossing of wool (1 Mar. 1576). Finally, in 1574 it was

agreed that Michelborne should rank as though he had been mayor, though without precedence over ex-mayors. Towards the end of his life Michelborne and his heirs were given a perpetual lease of his house in Parchment Street for £2 a year.

Michelborne died at Otterbourne, just outside Winchester, 29 Dec. 1582, being buried at St. Maurice's, Winchester. He had made his will earlier that month, having already settled most of his lands on his eldest son, Lawrence. His house in Parchment Street and lands in New Alresford and Petersfield went to his wife for life with remainder to his second son Edward, the Latin poet, who also received the Wiltshire manor of Manton, subject to the provision of £200 apiece for his three unmarried sisters. To his youngest sons, John and Thomas, Michelborne bequeathed lands in Yorkshire and Sussex, and provided for his married daughter from his lands in Holderness. His wife was sole executrix unless she remarried, in which event, Michelborne's brother was to be the executor. The overseer was John Fisher of Chilton Candover, Hampshire. The probate, originally granted in May 1583, was annulled, a new grant being made on 10 Feb. 1584.

Suss. Arch. Colls. l. 97–9; *Vis. Hants* (Harl. Soc. lxiv), 113; *Yorks. Arch. Soc. Rec. Ser.* ii, 231; *VCH Suss.* ix. 55; *VCH Hants*, iii. 98; *CJ*, i. 109; D'Ewes, 251; *DNB* (Michelborne, Edward); PCC 24 Rowe.

P.H.

MICHELL, Gilbert (c.1557–1614), of Bodmin, Cornw.

BODMIN   1584

b. c.1557, 1st s. of Ralph Michell[†], mayor of Bodmin. *educ.* Gloucester Hall, Oxf. 1575; L. Inn 1576, called 1584. *m.* 21 Nov. 1589, Frances, da. of Anthony Roscarrock of Crowan, 4s. 2da. *suc.* fa. 1578.

Mayor, Bodmin 1604–5.

There were various branches of the Michell family in Cornwall. The Bodmin Michells became prominent about the middle of the sixteenth century, maintaining their local importance for at least three generations. The family was described as having 'an hereditary mildness of disposition and universal benevolence', and as being 'genteel without ambition'. Michell himself was presumably a practising lawyer. At the time of his death he held four acres of land in Bodmin and over 40 acres in other places, as well as various gardens, orchards, and a share in the ownership of at least six houses. He died 28 Mar. 1614, being succeeded by his son Philip. His will has not been found.

Vivian, *Vis. Cornw.* 321; J. Maclean, *Trigg Minor*, i. 192, 236, 292; C. S. Gilbert, *Hist. Surv. Cornw.* ii. 199; C142/340/198.

N.M.S.

MICHELL, Humphrey (1526–98), of Dunton, Beds. and Old Windsor, Berks.

POOLE	1559, 1563
NEW WINDSOR	1571, 1572*
CAMELFORD	1593

b. 1 Apr. 1526, 1st s. of William Michell, yeoman, of Dunton by his w. Katherine. *m.* (1) Katherine Hobbs, 1s.; (2) Frances, da. of Francis Waller, ?of Surr., 1s. 4da. *suc.* fa. Dec. 1536.[1]

Bailiff to Edward Courtenay, Earl of Devon 1555; dep. receiver for south parts, duchy of Lancaster 1560; servant of 2nd Earl of Bedford by 1561; clerk of the works at Windsor castle c.1569–79; water bailiff, river Severn 1578–92; j.p. Isle of Ely from 1582.[2]

Michell was apparently in government employ soon after receiving livery of his lands in May 1547, for he is recorded in 1549 as taking wages to mercenaries employed against Kett. He served Sir Thomas Smith* during Edward VI's reign, and was entrusted by him with the financial affairs of Eton College. It may be that he had family connexions in the south-west of England, where Michell was a common name, for he entered the service of the Earl of Devon, to whom he later became deputy receiver of the duchy of Lancaster. By 1555 he was the bailiff of a Courtenay manor in Somerset, and in 1556 he 'thought it his duty', like Edmund Tremayne*, to follow the Earl to Italy.[3]

After Courtenay's death at Venice in September 1556, Michell, again like Tremayne, passed into the service of the 2nd Earl of Bedford. Bedford was clearly his patron when he was elected to Parliament in 1559 (the return describing him as of Dunton, Bedfordshire) though he is not recorded as in the Earl's service till 1561. Michell's puritan leanings are apparent in a remark of his eldest son Francis† (himself secretary to (Sir) William Russell*, Bedford's son), who wrote of his father after his death that he had been 'too much seduced' by 'brain-sick sectaries'.[4]

As clerk of the works at Windsor, where he may have settled when Sir Thomas Smith was provost of Eton, Michell must have enjoyed the patronage of the Earl of Leicester, constable of the castle and steward of the borough, and another patron favourable to puritan views. He was returned for Windsor in 1571, and again at a by-election in the next Parliament in the place of Richard Gallys, who died on 30 Nov. 1574. Perhaps Leicester's failure to nominate him in 1572 is to be explained by one of the disputes arising from the great building activity which marked Michell's time as clerk. Michell was assiduous in recommending new projects to Burghley. In November 1575 he summarized for him the work of the previous six years, during which £6,651 had been spent, complained of delays in obtaining funds and passing accounts, and asked to be relieved of his duties. The complaint achieved its purpose, and Leicester made regulations giving Michell control of expenditure, though excluding him from the supervision of the works. Michell concluded one of his letters to Burghley: 'praying the living lord ... to increase daily your zeal to the furtherance of the building-up of the church of God'.[5]

When the repairs at Windsor were completed, Michell was not returned again for the borough, though he continued to reside nearby in Old Windsor. Despite his powerful connexions – along with Francis Walsingham and others he was party to the indenture by which Sir Thomas Smith settled his property just before his death in 1577 – he did not secure another seat till 1593, and his patron on that occasion is not obvious, though the name of (Sir) William Peryam*, the judge, suggests itself.[6]

In 1578 Michell was appointed water bailiff of the Severn: later in the reign the justices in the counties along the river were chided by the Privy Council for failing to assist him in keeping his official courts. Michell's heir became Burghley's secretary as well as Sir William Russell's, and it was perhaps on this account that in 1579 Tremayne thanked Burghley for his kindness to Michell. On the other side of England from the Severn, Michell acquired a manor in the Isle of Ely, where he was sent with George Carleton* in 1580 to prepare Wisbech castle for the arrival of the first recusants confined there; and with Carleton he embarked upon a project for draining the fens. He was granted arms in 1581 as being descended from 'the Michells of Yorkshire'. In 1588 he was one of the officials in the mineral and battery works who were accused of taking profits for their own use. He was closely associated with Sir Richard Martyn in a number of the company's transactions, including the Tintern wire works and the attempted manufacture of brass at Isleworth.[7]

Michell died 10 Oct. 1598 and was buried in Old Windsor church. In his will he expressed assurance of the pardon of all his sins and stipulated that there should be 'no blacks or funeral pomp, neither ringing of bells, after my decease'. He left money for stock to provide work for the poor of Old Windsor, and to one of his daughters bequeathed the bed he lay in when in London. His 'very good and honourable friend' Sir William Peryam, and Robert Clayton were to decide any disputes over the will, and the latter was to have a gilt bowl given to Michell by the Countess of Warwick, Bedford's daughter and the widow of Leicester's brother.[8]

[1] C142/60/57; *Mdx. Peds.* (Harl. Soc. lxv), 38. [2] *CSP Dom.* 1547–80. pp. 72–3, 85; 1591–4, p. 201; Somerville, *Duchy*, i. 624; Add. 37999, f. 2; *CPR*, 1566–8, p. 399; 1569–72, p. 154; Flenley, *Cal. Reg. Council, Marches of Wales*, 181. [3] *CPR*, 1553 and App. Edw. VI, p. 310; *APC*, ii. 316; M. Dewar, *Sir Thomas Smith*, 69; *CSP Dom.* 1547–80, pp. 72, 73, 85; *DNB* (Tremayne, Edmund). [4] *DNB* (Michell, Sir Francis); *N. and Q.* (ser. 9), vii. 144–5; Camb. Univ. Lib. Bb 10/18/3 (preface). [5] W. H. St. John Hope, *Windsor Castle*, 266–74, 276, 278–80, 283–5. [6] *CSP Dom.* 1581–90, p. 668; Strype, *Smith*, 158. [7] Flenley, 181–3, 211, 221; *APC*, xii. 69, 157; xiii. 153; xxi. 123; *HMC Hatfield*, ix. 112; *CSP*

Dom. 1547–80, pp. 638, 681; *VCH Cambs. and Ely,* iv. 182; *N. and Q.* (ser. 9), vii. 145; Lansd. 56, f. 163; M. B. Donald, *Elizabethan Monopolies,* 21, 73–6, 119, 123, 181–2. [8] E. Ashmole, *Berks.* iii. 43–5; PCC 58 Kidd.

A.H.

MICHELL, John (*d.* c.1588), of Truro, Cornw.

TRURO   1563

1st s. of John Michell of St. Columb by Alice, da. of Pole Beauchamp of Som. *m.* Jane, da. of John Killigrew, sis. of Henry*, John I* and William Killigrew*, 7s. 3da.[1]
   Mayor, Truro 1584.[2]

Michell, who came of an old Cornish family, with branches at Truro, Liskeard, Harlyn, St. Neot and Bodmin, was a merchant who combined trade with piracy, like his relatives the Killigrews. The first known reference found to him is as captain of the *Maudlyn* of Truro in May 1537. The deputy searcher of the port reported to the Council that he had boarded the ship, which was bound for Lantregar in Brittany with 'a company of riotous persons feigning a pope holy pilgrimage'. Michell and his crew first knocked him overboard and then carried him off to Brittany, where he was shouldered and buffeted by the inhabitants, egged on by his captors, 'as though he had been a Turk or a Saracen'. It took him three weeks to find a ship to carry him back to England.[3]

By the early part of Elizabeth's reign Michell was wealthy enough to have obtained the manor of Killigrew, in St. Erme, the ancestral estate of the Killigrews, but about 1568 he suffered heavy losses at sea. In 1587 several members of his family were involved in a lawsuit brought by Stephen Nicholas or Nantsmere, who alleged that he had been wrongfully evicted from his farm, imprisoned and put in the stocks at Truro by 'Hugh and John Michell, gentlemen', probably the MP's sons, and one William Roberts. The Council asked Peter Edgecombe* to inquire into the matter. This younger John was the capital burgess and first steward of the town appointed by the charter of 1589. Another son, Peter, was a sea captain who sailed round the world with Drake.[4]

Michell died intestate before 21 June 1588, when letters of administration were granted to his son Hugh. On the following day Hugh received a similar grant for a brother, Thomas.[5]

[1] Vivian, *Vis. Cornw.* 268, 322. [2] C219/29/31. [3] J. Allen, *Hist. Liskeard,* 486–7; *LP Hen. VIII,* xii(2), pp. 476–7. [4] *Jnl. R. Inst. Cornw.* xiv. 211–12; SP12/47, f. 155; *APC,* xv. 206–7; Vivian, 322. [5] PCC admon. act bk. 1588, f. 65v.

N.M.F.

MICHELL, Robert (*d.* 1563), of Norwich, Norf.

NORWICH   1563*

m., at least 1s.
   Freeman, Norwich 1532, sheriff 1546–7, alderman 1552, mayor 1560–1.

The only known character sketch of Michell, a scrivener, is provided by one Thomas Eton, a skinner, in 1563:

> never poor man's friend but always a mortal foe to all poor men and hath the goodwill of no poor men within Norwich ... if there were no man alive but Mr. Mychells I could find it in my heart to be his hangman.

Returned for the city in 1563, he was given leave of absence 'for his affairs' on 16 Mar. He received wages of 2s. a day. He died later in 1563, his will being proved in the Norwich consistory court.

Reg. Norwich Freemen, ed. Millican, 117; H. Le Strange, *Norf. Official Lists,* 107–8; Norwich min. bk. 1551–68, f. 113, 128; *Cal. Norwich Freemen,* 96; *Recs. Gild of St. George, Norwich* (Norf. Rec. Soc. ix), 147 etc.; *Depositions before the Mayor and Aldermen of Norwich,* ed. Rye, 77; *CJ,* i. 69; Norwich corp. ct. bk. 1562–9, p. 122; Norwich consist. ct. 248 Knighton.

R.V.

MIDDLETON, Robert (*d.* 1610), of Colchester, Essex.

COLCHESTER   1572*

s. of Robert Middleton, bailiff and alderman of Colchester. *educ.* ?St. John's, Camb., matric. pens. 1558; I. Temple 1568, called. *m.* Jane, wid. of Ambrose Gilbert, 1s.
   ?J.p. Harwich 1603.

As Middleton is described in the election return as 'Robert Middleton, junior esq.' it seems likely that his father, who lived in St. Runwald's parish, was still alive in 1579 and that it was he, not the son, who held many offices in Colchester between 1568 and 1579, as well as before that period. In 1579, however, Robert Middleton the younger was granted an annuity for life as counsel for the town. He was returned in May 1579 to fill the vacancy in Parliament caused by the death of Nicholas Clere. Clere himself had replaced Henry Golding I, who had been returned in 1572 and died in 1576. All three were local men. In 1602 Middleton's heir was admitted to the Inner Temple because his father was 'an ancient utter barrister, and near for antiquity unto the degree of the bench'.

In his will, dated 27 Aug. and proved 30 Nov. 1610, Middleton left most of his land and chattels to his son Robert, the executor. He also bequeathed legacies to various friends, relatives and servants, and £3 to the poor of St. James's parish.

Essex Rev. i. 154; iv. 241; *Cal. Harwich Borough Muniments,* 21; *Cal. Colchester Ct. Rolls,* ed. Harrod, 75; Colchester recs. assembly bk. 1576–99; *Trans. Essex Arch. Soc.* n.s. xvii. 37; *Cal. I.T. Recs.* i. 451; PCC 94 Wingfield.

J.H.

MIDDLETON, *see also* **MYDDELTON**

MIDWINTER, Edmund

WESTBURY   1584

In the fifteenth century the west-country Midwinters had ranked among the richest woolmen of the Cotswolds, and though by the Elizabethan period they had sunk into obscurity, their descendants were still living at Marlborough and Malmesbury in Wiltshire, as well as in Devon and Somerset. The christian name Edmund does not seem to have been common in the family, and it has not proved possible to identify this Member. The general pattern of Westbury representation in the second half of Elizabeth's reign would suggest that he was either a Wiltshire gentleman or a Londoner connected with one of the local families. In May 1560 an Edmund (son of John) Midwinter of the city of London – possibly the Westbury MP – bought land in Somerset near the Wiltshire border.

G. D. Ramsay, *Wilts. Woollen Industry*, 7; *Wilts. Vis. Peds.* (Harl. Soc. cv, cvi), 231–2; *Som. Enrolled Deeds* (Som. Rec. Soc. li), 55.

N.M.F.

MILDMAY, Anthony (c.1549–1617), of Apethorpe, Northants. and London.

NEWTON   1571
WILTSHIRE   1584
WESTMINSTER   1597*

b. c.1549, 1st s. of Sir Walter Mildmay* of Apethorpe by Mary, da. of William Walsingham of Footscray, Kent, sis. of (Sir) Francis Walsingham*; bro. of Humphrey*. *educ.* Peterhouse, Camb. 1562. *m.* 1567, Grace, 1st surv. da. and coh. of Henry Sharington* of Lacock, Wilts., 1da. *suc.* fa. 1589. Kntd. 1596.[1]

Auditor, north parts duchy of Lancaster 1589–94 (reversion to fa. 1568); j.p. Northants. from 1579, Wilts. from 1583; sheriff, Northants. 1580–1, 1592–3, dep. lt. from 1607; ambassador to France 1596–7; commr. charitable uses 1603, for goods of gunpowder conspirators 1606; dep. steward Yaxley, Northants.[2]

Mildmay was born, as it appears from his widow's provision for a memorial sermon to him, on the Nativity of Our Lady (8 Sept.), but in what year has not been ascertained. To judge from the date of his entry to Peterhouse, it may have been 1549. By the time he was ready for Cambridge his father had survived partial eclipse under Mary and had recovered his official position at Elizabeth's accession, while his uncle Walsingham had returned from exile to attach himself to William Cecil. It was, perhaps, as much a tribute to his parents as to himself that Mildmay was chosen to greet the Queen with an ode when she visited Peterhouse in August 1564. He did so with credit, and probably met her again two summers later when she hunted and dined at Apethorpe. Like his father, he appears to have left Cambridge without taking a degree.[3]

Mildmay's failure to make a public career is a measure of his shortcomings. 'I always knew him', John Chamberlain wrote in 1597, 'to be *paucorum hominem*'; and there must have been few who found Mildmay worth cultivating. The memorial which his father wrote for him in 1570 – presumably on his coming of age – abounds in moral precepts, but it was beyond Walter Mildmay to inculcate what he had failed to transmit, the ingredients of success. He certainly pushed both Anthony and his brother Humphrey forward. Anthony could not have been much above 18 when he married a co-heir of Lacock, an alliance which, if its material rewards were to accrue only after his father-in-law's death in 1580, and then at the cost of bitter squabbling with his relatives, gave Mildmay a footing in Wiltshire soon to be advanced by the marriage of his sister Martha to the influential William Brouncker* of Melksham. Mildmay's brief experience of military service at the time of the northern rebellion was followed by his return to the Parliament of 1571 for Newton, perhaps through the influence of the chancellor of the duchy of Lancaster, of which his father was auditor. Not surprisingly, the senior burgess for Newton, one of the youngest men in the House, left no mark on its proceedings.[4]

Mildmay accompanied Walsingham and Lord Cobham to Antwerp in July 1578,[5] when he was sent on a special mission to Duke Casimir of the Palatinate, but at home he was not employed. His late admission to Gray's Inn – in which he again followed paternal precedent – was presumably honorific. Not having been returned to Parliament in 1572, he had to wait until 1584 for his next chance to sit, when he was returned as junior knight of the shire for Wiltshire in right of his wife, and as such he could have attended the subsidy committee 24 Feb. 1585. His standing in the House could not compare with that of several natives, including his brothers-in-law, William* and Henry Brouncker*, who on this occasion sat for boroughs. The suggestion that Mildmay was a 'compromise candidate', who with powerful backing from outside carried the day, derives some colour from the fact that, unlike his fellow-knight Carew Ralegh (and his own brother Humphrey at Higham Ferrers), he was not to profit from the Crown's directive by being re-elected in 1586. In 1584–5 Sir Walter Mildmay's leadership of the House may have put his sons as firmly in the shade as before; and in the record of the session Anthony figures only as a member of the subsidy committee appointed on 24 Feb. after the chancellor of the Exchequer had made one of his speeches on supply.[6]

His embassy to France was Mildmay's one public employment of consequence. Since it coincided with the mission of the Earl of Shrewsbury (Gilbert Talbot*) to invest Henry IV with the Garter, the choice of so inexperienced and, as it proved, so unsuitable an envoy may have owed something to Shrewsbury, whom

Mildmay had come to know when his father, the old Earl, had guarded Mary Queen of Scots. Mildmay himself was reluctant to go, but his pleas of weak health, poverty and unsuitability were ignored; solaced with a knighthood, in September 1596 he crossed to Dieppe. Early in October he was presented to the King by Shrewsbury at Rouen, where he was to remain until, early in 1597, he accompanied Henry to Paris. Although Mildmay's behaviour was certainly maladroit, he was not to blame for the fiasco of the embassy. Its two purposes, the general one of keeping France in the war and the particular one of persuading Henry to recapture Calais, were difficult, perhaps impossible, of achievement, as Mildmay was quick to realise, and the gulf which soon came to separate King and ambassador was not of either's sole making. Mildmay probably had too much of his father's puritanism ever to condone Henry's calculated conversion, while the King's condemnation of his trafficking with 'those of the religion' made no allowance for the ambassador's affinity with the Huguenots. Even the celebrated episode of Henry's all but striking Mildmay, and then ordering him out, was not provoked, if Anthony Bacon* had the rights of it, by the ambassador himself, but by his delivery of a note from his sovereign. Mildmay was soon finding the negotiations 'too troublesome and unfit for my poor capacity' and asking the Earl of Essex to solicit his recall. Although the King accused Mildmay of ill-will towards Essex, the regularity and frankness with which the ambassador reported to the Earl seem to reflect more than prudence. With Essex's aid, Mildmay was back in England by August 1597. Within a month he obeyed a Privy Council summons, provoked by an invasion scare, to bring a force of servants from Northamptonshire. This he did again in August 1599, this time perhaps in anticipation of Essex's rumoured *coup de main* from Ireland; but when 18 months later the Earl did strike, Mildmay was ill and could only send Cecil his congratulations. It was, however, less a quickened interest in state affairs than the complexities of his own which had prompted him in January 1598 to seize the opportunity of the death of Thomas Cole, Member for Westminster, to get himself returned to Parliament at the ensuing by-election, presumably on Lord Burghley's nomination. His finances, confused by years of delay in the execution of his father's will, had been further damaged during his embassy, and he evidently saw no alternative to parting with land. Apart from serving on the committee 'to inform themselves' on relations with the Lords (14 Jan. 1598) and that discussing the bill to make receivers' lands liable for their debts (31 Jan.), it was the bill to break his father's entail which absorbed him in the House. It was committed on 16 Jan., after a second reading, to the secretary and the chancellor of the Exchequer (Cecil and John Fortescue I*) and several others; presumably this committee killed the bill, for it did not reach the Lords. He may also have been the 'Mr. Anthony Wildman'

appointed to a committee concerning the continuation of statutes (14 Jan. 1598). Mildmay was not returned to the Commons in 1601. However, he 'was called before their Lordships' on 7 Dec. to give evidence about a matter of copyhold lands belonging to Edward Neville I* and Sir Henry Neville II*. From 1593 by virtue of his wife's family status Mildmay was regularly nominating the Members at Chippenham. Mildmay canvassed for a Northamptonshire seat in April 1603, but failed to obtain one.[7]

Mildmay made an advantageous marriage for his daughter and sole heiress, Mary, which was to make her in turn a baroness and a countess and to establish the Earls of Westmorland at Apethorpe for close on three centuries. He had an early opportunity of commending himself to James I, who visited Apethorpe on his way south in April 1603, and became a regular guest, much taken, it was said, with Lady Mildmay's confectionery. Mildmay made his will 14 Feb. 1615, declaring his hope of salvation through Christ's death and passion, 'and by no other help or means whatever'. He named his 'well beloved wife' executrix bequeathing her his 'caroche' and coach horses, plate, jewels and household goods, the cattle, nags and geldings at Apethorpe and Leistrop, Leicestershire, and the residue of his goods. His other horses were to pass to Sir Francis Fane. Every servant received a year's wages, and one of them, William Bellamy, £40 for his pains in proving the will, of which the overseers were Sir George Manners† and Sir Francis Fane. An 'old friend', Sir Augustine Neville the judge, was to have plate, as were Francis Harvey II* serjeant at law, William Haske and William Downhall; but, to John Chamberlain's surprise, Edward Wymarke received 'not so much as a rush-ring for remembrance'. The provision destined, as it was designed, to have most lasting effect was that which assigned £1,000 to the testator's tomb in Apethorpe church; this large sum, with the cost of the funeral and of debt-redemption, was to be defrayed from the sale of Great Leistrop manor. Mildmay had raised 25 years earlier the impressive monument in St. Batholomew-the-Great which still proclaims his father's virtues; but this was to be far outstripped by his own, 'one of the most sumptuous of its time in England'. Its erection, after Mildmay's death 2 Sept. 1617, served to commemorate with egregious splendour a life singularly devoid of distinction.[8]

[1] *DNB* (Mildmay, Sir Walter); *Peterhouse Biog. Reg.* i. 227. [2] Somerville, *Duchy*, i. 437; W. R. Williams, *Official Lists of the Duchy and County Palatine of Lancaster*, 53; *CSP Dom.* 1591-4, p. 524; *APC*, xxx. 677-9; 1613-14, p. 299-300; *Peterborough Feoffees' Accounts* 1614-74 (Northants. Rec. Soc. x), 207-8; *HMC Hatfield*, xviii. 39; *Elizabethan Peterborough* (Northants. Rec. Soc. xviii), 33-4; *Montagu Musters Bk.* (Northants. Rec. Soc. vii), 221. [3] *Peterhouse Biog. Reg.* i. 227; Wards 7/64/48; Nichols, *Progresses Eliz.* i. 173. [4] *Chamberlain Letters* ed. McClure, i. 29; *CSP Dom.* 1595-7, p. 35; 1547-80, p. 251. [5] Instructions given to Mr. Anthony Mildmay (Antwerp, 1578) ex inf. T. M. Hofmann. [6] Lansd. 33, anon. jnl. f. 171; *HMC Hatfield*, vi. 260; Wards 7/64/48; *Wilts. Arch. Mag.* xxxvii. 615; D'Ewes, 356; Neale, *Parlts.* ii. 54-6. D'Ewes's reference (p. 263) to Sir Anthony

Mildmay, 14 Mar. 1576, is a slip for Sir Walter. [7] Lansd. 49, f. 171; 85, f. 53; APC, xiv. 235; HMC Hatfield, vi. 260, 281, 368, 394, 401, 430, 433, 451, 541–2; vii. 64, 99, 143–4, 145, 182, 209, 357, 500–1, 507; ix. 176, 378–9; x. 314; xi. 41–2; xii. 435; Birch, Mems. ii. 244, 270, 271–2, 281, 292, 305, 312–13, 340; Chamberlain Letters, i. 85; CSP Dom. 1598–1601, p. 546; D'Ewes, 580, 581, 591, 610; HMC Buccleuch, v(3), p. 74. [8] Nichols, Progresses Jas. I, i. 96, 523–4; ii. 457; iii. 18, 185, 258, 559; iv. 1104; PCC 100 Weldon; Chamberlain Letters, ii. 99; N. Pevsner, Buildings Northants. 50, 75–6; C142/376/94.

S.T.B.

MILDMAY, Humphrey (c.1555–1613), of Danbury, Essex.

| PETERBOROUGH | 1572* |
| HIGHAM FERRERS | 1584, 1586 |

b. c.1555, 2nd s. of Sir Walter Mildmay*, and bro. of Anthony*. *educ.* Peterhouse, Camb. 1569; G. Inn 1573. *m.* 10 July 1586, Mary (*d.*1633), da. of Henry Capell I* of Hadham, Herts., 5s. 1da.

J.p. Essex from 1591, sheriff 1594–5.

Mildmay was returned to Parliament for Peterborough at a by-election in 1576, probably about the time he attained his majority. His father was the North-amptonshire county Member, and no doubt arranged matters with their relation Sir William Fitzwilliam II*. Sir Walter Mildmay no doubt also arranged the two subsequent returns at Higham Ferrers. Mildmay's own few appearances in the records suggest that he had little enthusiasm for public service. In 1592 he upset the Privy Council by attempting to evade the command of 200 men in Essex. He promised to mend his ways, and in consideration of his father's position, he was let off. But he continued to reside in London during his shrievalty, and when he was due to hand over to his successor, he was late arriving. He frequently defaulted in paying his taxes. No doubt he spent his days in the social and business engagements so well reflected for the following generation in the diary of his eldest son and namesake. He died a little in debt on 9 Aug. 1613 and was buried at Danbury.

Morant, Essex, ii. 29; P. L. Ralph, Sir Humphrey Mildmay, 5–6; APC, xxiii. 262–3; xxx. 131, 248, 349; CSP Dom. 1595–7, p. 116; Lansd. 78, f. 166; 81, f. 79; 113, f. 190; VCH Essex, ii. 222; HMC Hatfield, viii. 261; PCC 96 Capell; C142/335/4.

S.M.T.

MILDMAY, Thomas I (bef. 1515–66), of Moulsham, Essex, and of London.

HELSTON	1547, 1553 (Mar.)
BODMIN	1553 (Oct.)
HELSTON	1555, 1558
LOSTWITHIEL	1559

b. bef. 1515, 1st s. of Thomas Mildmay of Chelmsford, Essex by his w. Agnes Read; bro. of Sir Walter*. *m.* Avis, da. of William Gonson of London, 8s. inc. Thomas II* 7da.[1]

Auditor ct. of augmentations 1536–c.54; jt. auditor, duchy of Cornw. 1537, sole 1556; auditor ct. of gen. surveyors by 1545; j.p. Essex 1541, q. 1554, commr. subsidy by 1550; sheriff, Essex and Herts. 1558–9; 'ass. man.' commr. duchy of Cornw. 1563.[2]

Mildmay, brother of Queen Elizabeth's chancellor of the Exchequer, was born into an Essex family of humble origin which had risen to some prosperity by the efforts of his father. Mildmay himself married the daughter of a. treasurer of marine causes who was a colleague of Thomas Cromwell†.[3]

It was Mildmay's position as auditor of the duchy of Cornwall which gained him a parliamentary seat on six occasions. He had visited Lostwithiel, which he represented in 1559, in almost every autumn since 1537 to audit the duchy accounts. He was sufficiently prominent to secure his own return in 1559 and that of his son in the next Parliament. At the time of the return in January 1559, Mildmay was sheriff of his native county.[4]

In 1564 Mildmay was described by the bishop of London as 'indifferent in religion', an estimate confirmed by his earlier career. He retained his offices during Mary's reign and was active as a justice in prosecuting protestants in Essex. Still, he was on intimate terms with Sir Philip Hoby who, when inviting Sir William Cecil to spend the Christmas of 1557 with him at Bisham, used Mildmay's intended presence as an inducement. During the disturbed months following Queen Elizabeth's accession, Mildmay was one of those to whom the Privy Council entrusted the task of suppressing (and sometimes arresting) unlicensed preachers in Essex.[5]

In November 1565 Mildmay's name was deleted from a commission for piracy in Essex, probably because of ill-health, for two months later he made his will and within a year he was dead. He made provision for the education and maintenance of his younger sons, but left the bulk of his lands in Essex and property in London to his eldest son Thomas. Among several charitable bequests was an annuity of twenty marks to Chelmsford school, of which he and his brother Sir Walter were governors, and property at Moulsham out of which the bishop of London was to maintain six poor people of the parish. Mildmay died 21 Sept. 1566, was buried at Chelmsford beside his wife, and the will was proved in January 1567 by the heir and his uncle Sir Walter Mildmay.[6]

[1] Vis. Essex (Harl. Soc. xiii), 250–1. [2] LP Hen. VIII, xii(1), pp. 602–3; xiii(1), p. 573; xvi. p. 280; xx(2), p. 554; CPR, 1553, p. 353; 1553–4, p. 19; 1554–5, p. 107; Duchy Cornw. roll 123, m. 3d; 235, m. 5; 501, m. 1. [3] Trans. Essex Arch. Soc. n.s. xv. 7–9, 12; LP Hen. VIII, xi, pp. 114–15, 140, 253, 367; xii(1), pp. 113, 218, 239, 265; (2), p. 282; xiii(1), p. 573; xv. p. 478; xix(1), p. 637; CPR, 1560–3, pp. 563, 613–14. [4] Duchy Cornw. roll 123, m. 6v; 225, m. 13; LP Hen. VIII, xix(2), p. 271. [5] Cam. Misc. ix (3), p. 62; Strype, Eccles. Memorials, iii(1), p. 440; APC, v. 172; CSP Dom. 1547–80, p. 95; APC, vii. 87–8, 92. [6] HMC Hatfield, i. 266; APC, vii. 109, 285; PCC 3 Stonard; C142/147/142; T. Wright, Hist. Essex, i. 79.

I.C.

MILDMAY, Thomas II (c.1540–1608), of Moulsham, Essex.

LOSTWITHIEL	1563
ESSEX	1571

b. c.1540, 1st s. of Thomas Mildmay I* by Avis, da. of William Gonson of London. *educ.* Christ's, Camb. May 1555; L. Inn 1559. *m.* (1) Frances, da. of Henry Radcliffe, 2nd Earl of Sussex, 3s. inc. Thomas III* 1da.; (2) 2 Dec. 1605, Margaret Whettle (or Whitwell), *s.p. suc.* fa. 25 Sept. 1566. Kntd. 23 June 1567.[1]

J.p. Essex by 1571, q. by 1574, sheriff 1572–3, custos rot. c.1576, commr. piracy 1577, dep. lt. from 1584, commr. grain 1586; high steward, Maldon by 1603.[2]

Mildmay owed his return at Lostwithiel to his father, auditor of the duchy of Cornwall, who had himself sat for the borough in the previous Parliament. In 1571, having succeeded to the family estates, he obtained an Essex county seat, but he never again sat in Parliament despite an active local career extending over the remainder of the reign, including membership of piracy and grain commissions, the apprehension of coiners, conjurers and other felons and in 1576 an inquiry into complaints by the inhabitants of Colchester against their bailiff. As a deputy lieutenant he supervised the equipment and training of the levies, quarrelled (June 1584) with Lord Darcy over the command of the half hundred of Witham, and (after 1588, when Lord Burghley became lord lieutenant) with the central authorities over such matters as the muster-master's wages. In February 1596 the Privy Council were surprised that Essex could not provide the number of cattle required for the royal service, and complained of excessive grain prices in the county. During the vacancy in the lieutenancy, 1598–9, the Council refused to agree to a reduction in the numbers of horsemen from Essex, and censured the commissioners for musters for allowing the justices of the peace to make an insufficient assessment. Soon afterwards the question of local taxation arose again over a petition from the townsmen of Upminster against new rates, and Mildmay and his fellow commissioners were reminded that the Privy Council expected them to prevent the wealthier sort from unburdening themselves at the expense of the poor.[3]

A few letters survive about more personal matters. In February 1591 Mildmay was trying to enlist the support of Michael Hickes* for his suit for 'registering strangers'. He was prepared to pay £40 annually for the grant, and asked Hickes to remind Burghley that his 22 years' service for the Crown deserved some consideration. He had not been successful by January 1595, when he pressed Hickes to expedite matters. Nothing more is known of this project, but his name occurs on a 1597 list of suits for the sole refining of sugar in England. His petition described him as having served 'painfully and chargeably' for 13 years under Leicester and Burghley as deputy lieutenant of Essex.[4]

Towards the end of his life Mildmay divided his time between Moulsham and his town house in Aldgate. His will, drawn up in 1606, and proved 30 Nov. 1608, mentions extensive property in Essex, and contains charitable legacies to the poor of various parishes in the county, as well as to those of St. Botolph's, Bishopsgate. The document sheds some light on his domestic circumstances. At the age of 65 he married Margaret Whettle, settling the manors of Chelmsford and Moulsham on her for life. The will quotes this conveyance, and details the property which was to descend to Mildmay's eldest son Thomas. The widow, the sole executrix and residuary legatee, was to see that her husband was buried in the Mildmay chapel at Chelmsford 'in honest and decent sort without any unnecessary pomp or ceremony', at an expense of not more than £200. Mildmay asked six relatives and friends, including Sir Anthony Mildmay* and Sir John Petre* to act as overseers. He died 21 July 1608, and was buried, as he had asked, at Chelmsford.[5]

[1] C142/147/142; Wards 7/25/66; *Vis. Essex* (Harl. Soc. xiii), 251; *CP*, xii(1), p. 522; Morant, *Essex*, ii. 5. [2] Lansd. 48, f. 136; 83, f. 29; 146, f. 18; 683, f. 28; *APC*, xiv. 195; xxxii. 500–1; Essex RO, DB 3/3/205/1, 272. [3] *APC*, ix. 153, 271, 391–2; x. 62–3; *APC*, xxi. 374–5; xxv. 195–6; xxix. 484–5, 588–9; *CSP Dom.* 1581–90, pp. 180–3. [4] Lansd. 66, f. 156; 78, ff. 62, 64; 83, ff. 29 seq., 213–14. [5] Lansd. 78, f. 166; PCC 108 Windebanck; Wards 7/25/66; C142/309/194.

N.M.F.

MILDMAY, Thomas III (c.1573–1626), of Moulsham, Essex.

MALDON	1593

b. c.1573, 1st s. of (Sir) Thomas Mildmay II* of Moulsham by his 1st w. Frances, da. of Henry Radcliffe, 2nd Earl of Sussex. *educ.* Queens', Camb. 1589, Corpus Christi 1590. *m.* (1) Elizabeth, da. of (Sir) John Puckering*, *s.p.*; (2) Ann, da. of Sir John Savile or Savill. Kntd. 1603; *suc.* fa. 1608; *cr.* Bt. 1611.

J.p. Essex from 1591, sheriff 1608–9.

Mildmay was returned unopposed to Parliament for Maldon through his father's influence. The chamberlain's accounts for 1593 show the charges 'about the eating of the buck given to the town by the right worshipful Sir Thomas Mildmay … in the entertaining of Mr. Thomas Mildmay'. It was apparently intended to put him up again in February 1604, but in the event he was not returned. He appears not to have enjoyed the confidence of his father, who, in his will dated 1606, adjured his second son Henry 'not to follow or incline to his elder brother Thomas and his vain and unthrifty courses'.

He died on 13 Feb. 1626 and was succeeded by his brother Henry. The 1593 Maldon Member is not to be confused with a namesake of Springfield, Essex, who died in 1613.

W. Berry, *Essex Genealogies*, 150; C142/309/194; 733/3; Essex RO, DB, 3/3/270; PCC 108 Windebanck; PCC admon. act bk. 1626, f. 68.

J.H.

MILDMAY, Sir Walter (bef. 1523–89), of Apethorpe, Northants and St. Bartholomew-the-Great, London.

LOSTWITHIEL	1545
LEWES	1547
MALDON	1553 (Mar.)
PETERBOROUGH	1553 (Oct.)
NORTHAMPTONSHIRE	1558, 1559, 1563, 1571, 1572, 1584, 1586, 1589

b. bef. 1523, 4th s. of Thomas Mildmay of Chelmsford, Essex by his w. Agnes Read; bro. of Thomas I*. *educ.* Christ's, Camb. c.1537. *m.* 25 May 1546, Mary, da. of William Walsingham of Footscray, Kent, 2s. Anthony* and Humphrey* 3da. Kntd. 1547.[1]

Dep. receiver, ct. of augmentations by 1540, jt. auditor (with bro. Thomas), Norf., Suff., Cambs., Hunts., Essex, Herts., Mdx., London 1545–50, gen. surveyor 1547–54; jt. auditor, the King's works 1543 (with bro. Thomas) duchy of Cornw. 1546–54; assistant treasurer, French war 1544; auditor, ct. of gen. surveyors of the King's lands by 1545–7, duchy of Lancaster, north parts 1546–86; j.p. Essex 1547–53, Mdx. 1559–*d.*, Northants. 1559–*d.* Hunts. c.1564–*d.*; treasurer, expedition to Calais 1558–9; chancellor of the Exchequer 5 Feb. 1559–*d.*; PC from July/August 1566; under-treasurer 1567–*d.*; jt. ld. lt. Hunts. 1569, ld. lt. 1587–*d.*[2]

By November 1558 Mildmay was an experienced administrator with many years' service in various financial courts. Though as a convinced protestant he voted against the government's religious measures in the Parliament of October 1553, and was to some extent out of favour in Mary's reign, he did not join his brother-in-law, Francis Walsingham*, in voluntary exile. In fact he retained his chief offices and served on a number of Marian financial commissions.[3] In Mary's last House of Commons he represented Northamptonshire for the first time, continuing as knight of the shire in all the Elizabethan Parliaments until his death. In 1563, when Sir William Cecil sat for Northamptonshire, and in 1584 and 1586, when the senior Member was Sir Christopher Hatton, Mildmay had to be content with the second seat, but in his other Parliaments he took precedence of local men. Having begun as a borough Member in Henry VIII's reign, he sat in the House of Commons 12 times – an impressive record, leading to a valuable knowledge of parliamentary procedure.

Though he attended a university and inn of court, Mildmay apparently neither graduated nor was called to the bar. His late admission to Gray's Inn, when he was already in government service, may have been to gain such knowledge of the common law as would be useful in his auditor's work. It is therefore the more interesting that in November 1583 he paid £550 for the site of the Black Friars at Cambridge, where, in the following January, he obtained the Queen's licence to found Emmanuel College. The story of Elizabeth's conversation with him in which she described Emmanuel as a 'puritan foundation' may be apocryphal, but the choice of Laurence Chaderton as first master of the college reflects Mildmay's religious sympathies, and in the early years of Emmanuel many puritans sent their sons there. Mildmay also founded scholarships, a Greek lecture and a preachership at his old college of Christ's. His collected parliamentary speeches show considerable literary ability, and he is said to have written Latin verses as well as a book called *A Note to know a Good Man*. His *Memorial* of precepts for his son Anthony was printed by a Victorian descendant.[4]

As befitted a brother-in-law of Francis Walsingham and Peter Wentworth, Mildmay in general supported puritanism, but more cautiously than they. William Fuller, a London gentleman who returned from Geneva at the beginning of Elizabeth's reign, visited him as one 'whom of long time I had known to be so well affected to true religion that I had made him privy of my purpose of going to Geneva, and provoked him also to go (that said he fain would but could not)'. Mildmay's sympathy with puritanism combined with his reverence for the monarchy, his financial and administrative ability, and his quality as an orator, made him a leading Privy Councillor in the House of Commons. The recurrent themes of his speeches were the 'preservation of the cause of religion' and the Queen's safety, and his Elizabethan career was devoted to strengthening these 'twin pillars' of state security. His fellow puritan Sir Nicholas Throckmorton* thought highly enough of him to recommend him to Elizabeth on her accession, as Cecil's colleague in the secretaryship. No notice was taken of Throckmorton's advice.[5]

During the early years of the reign Mildmay's work was financial. On the death of Sir John Baker† in December 1558, the lord treasurer, the Marquess of Winchester, advised Cecil to have Mildmay appointed as chancellor of the Exchequer. However, it is unlikely that Cecil, a former contemporary of Mildmay at Cambridge and his colleague in Edward VI's government, needed the recommendation. The chancellor's duties were mainly to deputise for the lord treasurer in the day-to-day business of the Exchequer, and these duties Mildmay shared with another ex-colleague from his period in the augmentations, Sir Richard Sackville*. They heard accounts, assigned debts, paid allowances and surveyed land. The chancellor's office was not sufficiently senior to carry automatic membership of the Privy Council, and there is no evidence that Mildmay had any hand in deciding overall financial policy, but as an acknowledged expert he sat on all the important commissions, including those to consider the recoinage and the repayment of crown debts; the sale of crown lands; and the financial affairs of Ireland. It looks as if much of the preparation of information for such commissions fell to Mildmay, who must thus have had considerable indirect influence on their decisions.

He sympathized with the policy of retrenchment and reform which he was instructed to carry out, but he needed tact to avoid offending either the Queen or courtiers. For example, in 1566 the Earl of Leicester was negotiating an exchange of lands with Elizabeth who, after approving the project, took exception to the property which he chose. As the official through whom the matter was settled, Mildmay had a difficult task. In July of the same year the Queen showed her appreciation of his services by hunting and dining with him on her progress through the Midlands. Later in the month he was sworn a member of the Privy Council, his first recorded attendance being in October. Soon after Sackville's death, Mildmay was allowed to combine the under-treasurer's duties with his own – useful, since it provided a link between the upper and lower Exchequer. Winchester's growing infirmity left control increasingly in his hands. When Cecil became lord treasurer he and Mildmay worked together amicably, being agreed on the necessity for economy, and of avoiding two dangerous methods of acquiring ready money – the sale of crown lands and the raising of short-term loans at high interest. At least temporarily, Mildmay was able to achieve the results he desired. He died just early enough to avoid seeing his system crumble before the demands of war on the treasury: late in 1589 land sales were resumed on a large scale.[6]

Gradually Mildmay was drawn into wider discussions of Council policy, and many of his letters survive on Scottish affairs. In 1568 he was mentioned as a probable commissioner to treat between the Queen of Scots and her subjects, but Sir Ralph Sadler* was chosen. In all, Mildmay was appointed a commissioner for Scotland four times, but he was never allowed to go there, though the Scottish government would have welcomed him. He met Mary Stuart more than once, visiting her at Chatsworth with Cecil when she claimed to have important information for Elizabeth. After the northern rising, during which Mildmay was temporarily appointed lord lieutenant of Huntingdonshire, he was one of those who examined Sir Nicholas Throckmorton, and in 1571, at the time of the Norfolk marriage plot, he interviewed Mary's agent, the bishop of Ross, and Lord Lumley. He also helped to prepare the evidence against Norfolk himself and was present at his trial. This must have been an unpleasant duty; he was on friendly terms with the Duke, who asked that after the execution Mildmay should have some of his fine glass and gold spoons with pearl handles. When in

1586 Elizabeth finally agreed to have Mary tried, Mildmay went to Fotheringay and informed her of the decision: he was appointed one of the commissioners for the trial. He played a leading part in Council discussions on such topics as the negotiations for Elizabeth's marriage and English policy in the Netherlands: on both these matters he supported the Leicester–Walsingham section of the Council.[7]

No activity is recorded for Mildmay in Elizabethan Parliaments until his appearance on the succession and subsidy committees in October/November 1566, some three months after he had become a Privy Councillor. Thenceforth he was active in all his parliaments, including all three sessions of that of 1572. He is recorded as serving on 10 committees in 1571; 11 in 1572; 14 in 1576; 23 in 1581; 22 in 1584–5; 6 in 1586–7; 2 in 1589. His first recorded speech came in the last minutes of the 1571 Parliament when he suggested that as Members

> were met together in peace and love, [he] did wish they should so depart; and that no advantage should be taken of any words there passed, but all to the best.

In 1572 he took part in the debates on Mary Queen of Scots, and on financial matters, but he is not recorded as speaking during the radical efforts to establish the legality of puritan rites. Though later, when faced with Whitgift's rigidity, he clearly showed his puritan sympathies in the House, he was evidently not prepared to support the measures advocated by his brother-in-law Peter Wentworth. Like Walsingham, Mildmay saw the religious problem against a European background, and was aware of the danger of protestant divisions when the Catholics threatened.

From 1576 he began to act as one of the government spokesmen in the House, four speeches being recorded in this session, and seven in 1581. At the beginning of the 1584–5 Parliament (on 28 Nov.) he 'used a speech for the space of one hour and more', which, in Recorder Fleetwood's words, 'tended to a generality' on the subject of the Queen's safety. Altogether in this Parliament he spoke at least 15 times, in 1586–7 five times, and in 1589 three. His opening speech in the debate on supply, 10 Feb. 1576, set a pattern of orderly presentation which he often afterwards followed: how the Queen had found the realm, 'how she hath restored and conserved it', and 'how we stand now'. In contrast to the 'wretched time and wretched ministers' of Mary's reign, he pointed to the financial re-organization of the early years of Elizabeth, reminding the House that the Crown's debts to London merchants and others had been met, and that in spite of all the efforts of the Pope, 'the most principal and malicious enemy of this State', England now stood 'in wealth and in all prosperity ... and, that which is the greatest, we enjoy the freedom of our consciences, delivered from the bondage of Rome'. He had the gift of imparting details to Members to bring home the seriousness of the financial position: in a similar speech in 1585 he told them that Ireland alone, since the last Parliament, had consumed the whole grant then made for defence, and more. He worked on the anti-Catholic feeling of the House, and its devotion to the Queen, and he was a master of peroration:

> for such a Queen and such a country, and for the defence of the honour and surety of them both, nothing ought to be so dear unto us that with most willing hearts we should not spend and adventure freely.

Over religion, he steered a course between an official position as Privy Councillor and support for puritan objections to the Elizabethan religious settlement. Outside Parliament he gave his personal beliefs freer expression – as when he secured Chaderton's appointment at Emmanuel, or in 1574 signed a letter to Bishop Parkhurst of Norwich asking him to allow 'prophesyings' to continue. He supported the puritan petitions in the 1576 House of Commons, joining Hatton*, Walsingham* and Thomas Wilson* in approaching the bishops about them before the next meeting of Parliament early in 1581; and when that session also failed to achieve any results, he gave Walsingham a series of 'reform articles' to bring privately before the Queen. During the 1581 debates on the petitions he intervened to blame the 'negligence and slackness' of leading bishops for the failure to redress puritan grievances, refusing to admit that the Queen herself was one of the main obstructions to the measure. When tempers rose high and the more ardent Members wanted a delegation, or the whole House, to go to Elizabeth about the matter, Mildmay persuaded them instead to ask the Speaker, in his closing oration, to give the Queen their humble and dutiful thanks, and put her 'in remembrance for the execution and accomplishment of her promise at her good pleasure'. In 1584 he was responsible for having a committee appointed to study the puritan petitions from the localities and to approach the House of Lords. When, however, a revolutionary measure – Cope's bill and book – was introduced into the Commons early in 1587, Mildmay joined Hatton and the solicitor-general in attacking it. He stressed the poor judgment and inexperience shown in the bill, and the danger in its proposal to sweep away old laws 'made so many years past, even from the statute of Magna Carta'. He doubted whether a 'mere popular election' of ministers would produce more worthy men. However, he was a strong advocate of a learned ministry: in an earlier Parliament, following a point made by Francis Alford* that 2,000 parishes had livings worth only £8 à year, he interjected, 'There is none of £8 in the Queen's books, but is worth £20. Besides, who will not contribute to a learned minister?'.

During the 1586–7 Parliament, Mildmay was still junior to Sir Christopher Hatton, but in 1589, when Hatton sat in the Lords, Mildmay made the main government speech on supply, 11 Feb. His son-in-law William Fitzwilliam jotted down its main points, headed 'Notes touching the Spanish enterprise against England'.

> The fire kindled long and carefully nourished by the Pope and his ministers ... broke forth into a terrible and dangerous flame [causing] rebellion in the north, rebellion in Ireland, invasion there, the great king, as they call him, of Spain, his last great navy sent hither this summer with forces from the Duke of Parma out of Flanders, aid from the Duke of Guise out of France. [But] the mighty hand of God, the providence of the Queen's Majesty; her invincible courage; the magnanimity and constancy of the nobility, the fidelity and readiness of the people; the Queen's forces by sea; her forces by land; the goodness of the quarrel; the defence of the gospel and the realm; the prayers of good people; the honourable and good dealing of the King and realm of Scotland, tied unto us with bond of religion [had caused] their whole enterprise [to be] disappointed, and that so soon as her Majesty may say, as Caesar did, veni, vidi, vici. [But] this storm is over ... the clouds nevertheless remain still ... wise mariners after a dangerous storm provide to resist another that may follow, doubting the second may be worse than the former ... so we, having overcome this first attempt of our enemies ... we are to think upon a second from enemies ... so proud ... they will seek to repair the credit they have lost ... and therefore provision is to be made [for] a great mass of treasure ... the last contribution not [being] able to bear out half the charge.

Before the next House of Commons met, Mildmay was dead. Perhaps some of the troubles of the last three Parliaments of the reign might have been mitigated if the Councillors in the Commons had been as experienced and respected as Mildmay and Hatton. One reason why Members were prepared to follow his lead was his sense of the dignity of the Commons. He was the perfect spokesman for delegations to the Lords:

> They would yield unto their Lordships all dutiful reverence so far as the same were not prejudicial to the liberties of their House, which it behoved them to leave to their posterity in the same freedom they received them.

Again, his respect for Elizabeth did not make him blind to the danger of royal power. In 1576, during discussions on the Lords bill allowing the Queen to settle by proclamation the kind of apparel to be worn, he warned Members that 'it is seen by daily experience that of precedents great hold is taken, especially in the case of Princes'.[8]

Mildmay's work in the Exchequer left him little time to live as a country gentleman. On various occasions he received extensive land grants in the home counties and the west of England, but this was property speculation.

Little information survives about his private life. His will indicates that he managed his own affairs with the same efficiency that he showed over the nation's finances. His last illness must have been short, for he was active in Parliament and on Council business up to the end of March 1589, and died on 31 May. He was buried in St. Bartholomew-the-Great, Smithfield. His will, drawn up at the beginning of April, left in cash bequests nearly £4,600, and plate valued at little short of £2,000. He bequeathed his soul to God, 'being most certainly persuaded that my sins, which be grievous and heavy, are forgiven and my election sealed up in the only blood and merit of my Lord and Saviour'. His executors were 'to avoid such vain funeral pomp as the world by custom in the time of darkness hath long used, a thing most unfit for us Christians that do profess sincerely the gospel'. The masters and fellows of Emmanuel received £200, as well as the £30 additional bequest of plate made to the college: his own old college, Christ's, was bequeathed £20. There were many legacies to the poor of London and other places where Mildmay owned property. The 'poor preachers' of Northamptonshire received £20, two ministers, White and Clarke, being remembered by name. Specific bequests to servants amounted to £345. The list of court personalities in the will was headed by the Queen, who was to have a jewel worth £100, and included Lord Burghley, the Earl of Huntingdon, Lord Buckhurst and, among Members of the House of Commons, Sir Francis Walsingham, Sir Francis Knollys, Henry Killigrew and Thomas Randolph. The executors were Walsingham, Edward Carey* and William Dodington*.[9]

[1] Vis. Essex (Harl. Soc. xiii), 452–4; Marriage Licences in Faculty Office (Harl. Soc. xxiv), 7; PCC 51 Leicester; J. H. Round, Family Origins, 62–3. [2] LP Hen. VIII, xviii(1), p. 365; xx(2), pp. 554–5; xxi(1), p. 774; xxi(2), p. 409; Somerville, Duchy, i. 437; CSP Dom. 1547–80, p. 97; Northants. RO, Westmorland (Apethorpe), box 1, bdle. 1, no. 16; CPR, 1558–60, p. 57; 1566–9, p. 274; cal. patent rolls 1–16 Eliz. PRO 9(11), 218. [3] Bodl. e Museo 17; CPR, 1553–4, pp. 196, 300–2; 1555–7, pp. 23, 304–5; 1557–8, p. 73. [4] DNB; J. Peile, Biog. Reg. Christ's Coll. i. 24–5; Shuckburgh, Hist. Emmanuel, 26. [5] A. Peel, Second Parte of a Reg. ii. 58; Sloane 326 passim; EHR, lxv. 96. [6] CPR, 1558–60, 1560–3, 1563–6 passim; CSP Dom. 1547–80 and Add. 1547–65 passim; Add. 1566–79, pp. 2–4; HMC 10th Rep. IV, 3; Lansd. 171, f. 408; Read, Cecil, 353; W. C. Richardson, Ct. of Augmentations, 453, 456–65. [7] DNB; Sir H. Nicolas, Hatton; CSP Dom. 1547–80, pp. 295–7 et passim; 1581–90, pp. 20–139 passim; N. Williams, Duke of Norfolk, 233, 248. [8] The following are the journals' references to Mildmay's Commons activities, whether these are entered under his own name, under his office, or are those in which he took part as a Privy Councillor. D'Ewes, 103, 124, 126, 155, 157, 159, 160, 165, 168, 176, 178, 179, 181, 182, 183, 184, 186, 188, 189, 190, 205, 206, 212, 213, 219, 220, 221, 222, 241, 247, 248, 249, 250, 251, 252, 253, 255–7, 258, 259, 260, 262, 263–4, 267, 279, 284, 285–8, 289, 290, 291, 292, 293, 294, 295, 299, 300, 301, 302, 303, 306, 307, 309, 333–4, 335, 336, 337, 340, 343, 345, 347, 349, 350, 351, 352, 353, 354, 355, 356, 361, 362, 363, 364, 365, 366, 369, 370, 371, 372, 373, 393, 394, 395, 399, 403, 405, 407, 409, 410, 412, 413, 414, 415, 416, 417, 430, 431, 432, 433, 434, 437, 438, 440, 442, 443, 448, 453, 454; CJ, i. 85, 86, 87, 89, 90, 92, 93, 94, 95, 98, 99, 100, 101, 102, 104, 105, 106, 107, 108, 110, 112, 113, 114, 115, 116, 119, 120, 121, 122, 123, 125, 128, 129,

130, 131, 132, 135, 136; Trinity, Dublin, Thos. Cromwell's jnl., passim; Lansd. 41, Wm. Fleetwood's jnl., f. 45; Lansd. 43, anon. jnl. f. 171; Camb. Univ. Lib. Gg. iii. 34, p. 209; Northants. RO, Fitzwilliam of Melton pprs. 147; Sloane, 326; W, Pierce, Hist. Intro. Martin Marprelate Tracts, 61. [9] CSP Dom. Add. 1547–65, p. 407; CPR, 1560–3, p. 261; PCC 51 Leicester.

S.M.T.

MILL, Richard (1557–1613), of Nursling, Hants.

b. Jan. 1557, 1st s. of Thomas Mill[†], town clerk and recorder of Southampton, by Alice, da. of Robert or Thomas Coker of Mappowder, Dorset. m. c.1585, Mary, da. of Sir John Savage of Rocksavage, Cheshire, by Elizabeth, da. of Thomas Manners, 1st Earl of Rutland, s.p. suc. fa. 1560, uncle 1568. Kntd. 1601.

Freeman, Southampton 1581; j.p. Hants from 1591, commr. recusants, by 1592, sheriff 1593–4, commr. piracy 1603.

John Mill, recorder of Southampton and MP for the borough during the Reformation Parliament, purchased extensive property in Hampshire, which passed on his death to his eldest son George, who died s.p. 19 Feb. 1568. The lands then descended to his nephew Richard, who succeeded aged 11, when his wardship was sold to Henry, Earl of Arundel. Mill enlarged his interest in the Nursling property by leasing the Old Manor House and Grove Place from the dean and chapter of Windsor. His fortunate marriage may itself have been a result of Sir John Savage's marriage to the widow of the Hampshire landowner Sir Richard Pexall, and it may even have encouraged Mill to serve in his only Parliament at the age of 40. His wife's brothers, John and Edward Savage, and her sisters' husbands, Sir William Brereton II, Thomas Langton, Thomas Wilkes and Sir Henry Bagnall were all Members of the House of Commons. Mill was named to only one committee, on the poor law, 22 Nov. 1597, though, as a knight of the shire, he was entitled to attend the committees on enclosures (5 Nov.), the poor law (5, 22 Nov.), armour and weapons (8 Nov.), the penal laws (8 Nov.), monopolies (10 Nov.) and the subsidy (15 Nov.). He was knighted by the Queen on her visit to the 4th Marquess of Winchester at Basing.

Mill died 20 Oct. 1613, and was buried in Nursling church, where his monument survives. In his will, dated 2 May 1610, he recalled the promise of God 'to His elect'. He bequeathed plate and money to various relations and left £10 and the use of Nursling mills to his steward, Andrew Munday, who was formerly employed by the Countess of Southampton and who later married into the Mill family. He appointed his 'very loving friend and cousin' Sir Thomas West, his brother-in-law Edward Savage, his friend William Brocke of Longwood, and his steward, Andrew Munday, as overseers. The will was proved 24 Nov. by his widow, the executrix and residuary legatee.

Wards 9/140/42–5; *Assembly Bks.* (Soton Rec. Soc.), passim; *Vis. Hants* (Harl. Soc. lxiv), 160; B. B. Woodward, et al. *Hist. Hants*, i. 394; *Vis. Cheshire* (Harl. Soc. lix), 206; *Recusant Roll* (Cath. Rec. Soc. xviii), 334; Lansd. 142, f. 204; *CPR*, 1566–7, p. 395; *VCH Hants*, iii. 435–6; iv. 617–19, 622, 628; v. 143, 150–1, 230; Harl. 75, f. 123v; D'Ewes, 552, 553, 555, 557, 561; PCC 98 Capell.

R.C.G.

MILL, William (*d.*1608), of Charterhouse Churchyard, London, and Harscombe, Glos.

WEYMOUTH AND MELCOMBE
    REGIS   1589

2nd s. of William Mill, attorney in the Star Chamber, of Croydon, Surr. (*d.* Jan. 1564), by his 2nd w. Hawisa Harwell of Worcester. *educ.* G. Inn 1574. *m.* Margaret, wid. of William Butler, *s.p.*

Clerk of the Star Chamber in reversion 22 Aug. 1583, succeeded 1 Oct. 1587; j.p. Surr. from c.1592.

Mill was a moneylender with a useful job in the Star Chamber, where his tenure of office was challenged in 1591 and subsequently. In 1601 he was cleared of various charges and confirmed in office. An unknown compiler (probably a subordinate Star Chamber official) of a list of 'exceptions' against Mill wrote:

I am credibly informed that when there was a matter in question between a great personage and him, he said he had the Earl of Shrewsbury as assured to him as the skin on his face, and also the Earl owes him a great sum of money.

Others who owed him money included Lord Burgh, the ward of Lord Cobham, and the Earl of Essex. With all these contacts the name of his parliamentary patron at Weymouth and Melcombe Regis cannot be guessed.

Mill died 16 July 1608. His will mentions some personalities of the period and property in the city and county of Gloucester. He desired a funeral 'that may be thought fit for a man of my condition and place wherein I have served and lived in this commonwealth'. He mentioned six godchildren, to one of whom he left £500. His 'loving wife', for whom he had a 'resolute opinion', for 'her tender love and care of her children' (by her former marriage), was to be executrix and residuary legatee. He appointed as overseers (Sir) John Brograve* and Thomas Cooke of Gray's Inn: the latter was to receive £300.

He left bequests to the poor, to relatives and to personal servants, but

for my other servants which I have employed in my office I think I need not bestow anything on them because I hope that God has well blessed their labours with sufficient profit.

An inquisition post mortem held 20 Jan. 1609 named as heir his sister Margaret, wife of Richard Michell†.

Upon Mill's death Francis Bacon* obtained the lucrative appointment in the Star Chamber for which he had been waiting for 19 years and which he reckoned to be worth £2,000 p.a.

This biography is based upon the following: Bodl. Rawl. B. 429, ff. 6–8 and C142/316/42, ex inf. T. G. Barnes, Univ. California, Berkeley; E. Skelton, 'Ct. of Star Chamber, Reign of Eliz.' (London Univ. MA thesis 1930); *Egerton Pprs.* (Cam. Soc. xii), pp. 316–7; Lansd. 66, f. 254; Harl. 6853, f. 70; *CSP Dom.* 1598–1601, p. 33; 1601–3, p. 121; *HMC Hatfield*, ix. 425; x. 164, 348; St. Ch. 5/ C1/8/23; Bodl. Tanner 283, ff. 31, 41; PCC 69 Windebanck; J. Spedding, *Francis Bacon*, iv. 21.

P.W.H.

MILLER, Robert (c.1564–1624), of Winterbourne Came and Upcerne, Dorset.[1]

POOLE   1601
BRIDPORT   1604

b. c.1564, 1st. s. of John Miller of Winterbourne Came by Anne, da. of Giles Winterhay of Chetnole. *educ.* I. Temple 1578. *m.* (1) Dorothy (*d.* 15 Oct. 1591), da. and h. of Henry Bailey of I.o.W., 1s.; (2) Margaret, da. of Robert Freke of Iwerne Courtenay, sis. of Thomas Freke*, 1s. 1da. *suc.* fa. 1595. Kntd. 1603.

Receiver of the revenue in the Exchequer for Som. and Dorset 1589; j.p. Dorset from c.1601, sheriff 1599–1600.

Miller was related to John Wolley*, the Latin secretary (after whom he named one of his sons); Richard Swayne*, recorder of Poole; and Edward Yarde*, the 2nd Earl of Bedford's west country agent. It was presumably Swayne who arranged his return for Poole in 1601. Apart from a few land transactions, and records connected with the performance of his county offices, very little has been discovered about Miller in the Elizabethan period. He was fined 40s. by the Star Chamber for an irregularity committed when sheriff. He died between 30 Apr. and 24 Sept. 1624, aged 60, leaving bequests to his family, and appointing Thomas Freke and Swayne his executors.[2]

[1] This biography is based upon the Roberts thesis. [2] Hutchins, *Dorset*, i. 296; ii. 186, 290; *Vis. Hants* (Harl. Soc. lxiv), 10; *Vis. Dorset* (Harl. Soc. xx), 70; *Som. Wills* vi. 48; *Som. and Dorset N. and Q.* vi. 254–5, 258; Dorset Co. Mus. 6267/97; Lansd. 106, f. 1; *Cam. Misc.* iv(2), pp. 40, 42; Harl. 3324, f. 20; E101/123/25; PCC 81 Byrde.

P.W.H.

MILLS, see MYLLES

MITFORD, Henry (c.1543–96), of Newcastle-upon-Tyne, Northumb.

NEWCASTLE-UPON-TYNE   1589, 1593

b. c.1543, 1st s. of Christopher Mitford of Newcastle by Jane, da. of Henry Anderson of Newcastle. *m.* Barbara (*d.* 1596), da. and coh. of Edmund Perkinson of Hulam, co. Dur., 7s. 6da. *suc.* fa. 1581.

Alderman, sheriff, Newcastle 1582–3, mayor 1584–5, comptroller of the port.

Mitford's family had traded as citizens of Newcastle in the fourteenth century. His grandfather, Christopher Mitford, a junior member of the Mitfords of Seghill, was apprenticed to Bertram Anderson in 1532 and subsequently became a freeman, merchant and boothman of Newcastle. His business further prospered under his son, and the family acquired estates at Heaton, Tynemouth and Deanham, as well as property and coal mines in Newcastle itself. Most of these possessions came to Mitford who also acquired Hulam through his marriage.

Though allied to the Andersons and Chapmans, and one of the Newcastle grand lessees, Mitford was never prominent in the controversy which dominated Newcastle politics during the last decades of the century (see CHAPMAN, Henry). He purchased his comptrollership of the port from Charles Smythe* for £10 p.a. Although not mentioned by name in the parliamentary journals, Mitford may have attended a committee concerning Hartlepool pier (28 Feb. 1589) to which burgesses for Newcastle were appointed. He died in May 1596 and was buried on the 16th at St. Nicholas, Newcastle. His widow survived him by only a few days and was buried beside her husband. Their eldest son Christopher, who married a daughter of Sir John Conyers of Sockburn Hall, succeeded him.

Gen. Mag. vi. 491–4; J. U. Nef, *British Coal Industry*, passim; *Surtees Soc.* xxxviii. 30–2; R. Welford, *Hist. Newcastle and Gateshead*, ii. 401–2; D'Ewes, 440; *Hist. Northumb.* (Northumb. Co. Hist. Comm.), xiii. 411; PCC 62 Spencer.

B.D.

MOCKET, John, of Melcombe Regis, Dorset.

WEYMOUTH AND MELCOMBE
    REGIS   1597

m. 15 Sept. 1574, Eleanor, da. of Peter Mounsell of Weymouth, 2s. 1da.
Mayor, Weymouth 1585–6, 1598–9.

Mocket's name first appears in the records in connexion with his earlier mayoralty. He was necessarily involved in the disputes between Weymouth and Melcombe, which continued even after their amalgamation. He sent Walsingham a petition requesting ordnance and munitions for defence, and in 1588 was one of the burgesses who signed the town's letter pleading poverty when charged for preparations against the Armada. He was brought into Parliament for the combined boroughs after a double return in 1597, the accounts showing an item of £4 10s. 6d. for 'the establishing of the burgesses in

the Parliament house'; the MPs themselves were paid for 113 days' attendance at the rate of 5s. 8d. per day. The date of Mocket's death has not been found. The new charter Weymouth obtained in 1616 mentioned him as one of the first aldermen and he was still alderman in the following year, but not in 1625. His elder son was Dr. Richard Mocket, warden of All Souls.

Hutchins, *Dorset*, ii. 431, 480, 482; *Proc. Dorset Nat. Hist. and Antiq. Field Club*, xvi. 65; *HMC 5th Rep.* 581; *HMC Hatfield*, viii. 408; C219/72, 73; *CSP Dom.* 1581–90, p. 449; J. K. Laughton, *Span. Armada*, i. 151–3; *Weymouth Charters*, 134, 135; *DNB*.

P.W.H.

MOFFETT, Thomas (1553–1604), of London, later of Bulbridge, near Wilton, Wilts.

WILTON   1597

b. 1553, 2nd s. of Thomas Moffett, haberdasher of London, by his w. Alice Ashley of Kent. *educ.* Merchant Taylors'; Trinity Coll. Camb. 1569, Caius 1572, BA 1573, MA 1576; Basle MD 1578; travelled Italy and Spain 1579, Germany 1580–2; MD Camb. 1582. *m.* (1) 23 Dec. 1580, Jane (*d.* 1600), da. of Richard Wheeler of St. Ethelburga's, London; (2) Catherine (*d.* 1626), da. of Robert Sadler of Salthorpe, Wilts., wid. of Richard Brown, 1da.

Candidate, coll. of physicians 1585, fellow and censor 1588; physician to the forces in Normandy 1591–2; physician to the 2nd Earl of Pembroke.

Moffett was a fashionable physician who was taken up by Mary Herbert, wife of the 2nd Earl of Pembroke. She induced her husband to give him a pension and quarters first at Wilton House then at Bulbridge close by. Pembroke returned him for his borough of Wilton to the 1597 Parliament, from which Moffett obtained leave of absence 5 Dec. He died 5 June 1604.

DNB; Harl. 75, f. 132; D'Ewes, 568; Townshend, *Hist. Colls,* 112.

R.C.G.

MOHUN, Reginald I (1507/8–67), of Hall and Boconnoc, Cornw.

NEWPORT IUXTA LAUNCESTON 1547
PLYMPTON ERLE   1553 (Oct.)
HELSTON   1554 (Nov.)
RYE   1555
LISKEARD   ?1559,[1] 1563

b. 1507/8, yr. s. of John Mohun of Hall (*d.* 1508) by Anne, da. of Richard Coode of Morval, *m.* Joan or Jane, da. of Sir William Trevanion of Carhayes by Anne, da. of Sir Richard Edgecombe†, 4s. inc. William* 4da. *suc.* bro. 1516.[2]

Esquire of body by Sept. 1552–3; j.p. Cornw. 1547–53, 1559–c.61, sheriff 1552–3, 1559–60, commr. piracy 1565.[3]

Mohun's elder brothers predeceasing him, he succeeded to large estates in the south-west. His maternal grandmother was a daughter of Sir Hugh Courtenay, and on the death of Edward Courtenay, Earl of Devon, in 1556, Mohun shared the large inheritance with the three other co-heirs – Margaret Buller, John Vivian and John Trelawny*. Though his name does not appear among those who 'stood for the true religion' in the Parliament of October 1553, he was probably the 'Mr. Mone' who voted against a government measure in 1555. He did not sit in Mary's last House of Commons, and was removed from the commission of the peace during her reign. His son possibly went to Padua at this period, but there is no evidence that Mohun himself was a Marian exile: he presumably lived in retirement on his estates after giving up the court office he had held under John Dudley†, Duke of Northumberland.

On Elizabeth's accession he was restored to the commission of the peace, but after his term as sheriff he apparently did not serve again as a justice, his only known public office after 1560 being that of piracy commissioner. He may have been ill, but judging from Star Chamber cases of 1565 he was as factious and lawless as others of the Cornish gentry. In 1565 Sir William Godolphin accused him of forcibly evicting tenants from the Godolphin manor of Lelant and carrying off corn and other crops. Mohun denied violence, but his servants who had carted the corn deposed that he had promised to 'bear them out'. In the same year a feud between him and John Killigrew I* came to a head. It is an indication of Mohun's standing in the county that he dared to bring before the Council a long list of charges against Killigrew, who in general relied on his relatives at court to protect him from trouble. If so prominent a Cornishman required a parliamentary patron, one need look no further than the 2nd Earl of Bedford, from whom Mohun leased Boconnoc. There is no record of any parliamentary activity by Mohun. He died 22 Apr. 1567 and his inquisition post mortem was taken at Bodmin the following 17 Jan.[4]

¹ E371/402(1). This, the only known record of the election, gives no christian name. ² C142/78/116; Vis. Cornw. (Harl. Soc. ix), 145, 239–40; Vivian, Vis. Cornw. 324–5, 501 (Vivian has confused the generations); CPR, 1557–8, pp. 6–7; Maxwell Lyte, Hist. Dunster, ii. 481–2. ³ J. Maclean, Trigg Minor, iii. 139 n; APC, vii. 283. ⁴ Guildford Mus. Loseley 1331/2; C. H. Garrett, Marian Exiles, 228–9; CPR, 1553–4, p. 411; 1557–8, pp. 6–7; 1560–3, p. 603; 1563–6, pp. 497–8; St. Ch. 5/G1/25, G6/37; APC, vii. 225, 230, 292, 294; C142/150/186.

N.M.F.

MOHUN, Reginald II (c.1564–1639), of Hall and Boconnoc, Cornw.

FOWEY	1584, 1586
EAST LOOE	1614

b. c.1564, 1st s. of William Mohun* of Hall and Boconnoc by his 1st w. Elizabeth, da. of Sir John Horsey†. m. (1) 7 Sept. 1589, Mary, da. of Henry Killigrew*, 1s. d.v.p.; (2) bef. 1593, Philippa, da. of John Hele I*, 1s. 1da.; (3) bef. 1604, Dorothy, da. of John Chudleigh*, 3s. 4da. suc. fa. 6 Apr. 1588. Kntd. 1599; cr. Bt. 26 Nov. 1611.

J.p. Cornw. from c.1591, q. 1593, sheriff 1592–3, dep. lt. 1600; portreeve, Fowey 1595; recorder, East Looe prob. from 1588, Lostwithiel 1608.

Though Mohun succeeded his father as recorder of East Looe, no record of any legal education has been found for him. His family's local influence was twice sufficient to secure his return to Parliament for Fowey, near his seat at Hall. He was very likely the 'Mr. Mohun' who was 'portreeve', or mayor, there in 1595. Mohun is not mentioned in the known surviving records of his Parliaments. His life was that of a country gentleman. He was made a deputy lieutenant upon the death of Sir William Bevill*, because he 'doth dwell in a convenient place … and is a gentleman of good sufficiency and credit to supply that place'. According to Richard Carew* of Antony, Mohun, 'by his courteous, just and liberal course of life' maintained his reputation and increased the love borne to his ancestors. From his father, he received Boconnoc and a good number of other 'fair possessions'. Hall was a place of 'diversified pleasings', of 'present fruitfulness', which Carew described with the love of an old familiar, tracing 'a shadow thereof', so that his readers might 'guess at the substance'.

In his brief will, dated 14 Jan. 1639, Mohun wished to be buried in the chancel of the church at Boconnoc. He left 20s. to the poor of that parish, a similar sum to the poor of two other parishes, and small bequests to two sons and four daughters. Otherwise all went to his third wife, the sole executrix. (Sir) George Chudleigh* and Sir Henry Carew were overseers. Mohun died 26 Dec. 1639.

Vivian, Vis. Cornw. 325; J. Keast, Fowey, 49; F. M. Hext, Lostwithiel, 35; SP14/36/29; T. Bond, E. and W. Looe, 236; APC, xxx. 544; Carew's Surv. Cornw. ed. Halliday, 136, 206; PCC 50 Rutland; H. C. Maxwell Lyte, Hist. Dunster, ii. 483–5.

N.M.S.

MOHUN, William (c.1540–88), of Hall and Boconnoc, Cornw.

ST. GERMANS	1563
CORNWALL	1571, 1584, 1586

b. c.1540, 1st s. of Reginald Mohun I* by Joan, da. of Sir William Trevanion. educ. ?Padua 1556–7; L. Inn 1559. m. (1) Elizabeth, da. of Sir John Horsey†, 2s. inc. Reginald II* 1da.; (2) Anne, da. and coh. of William Reskimer, wid. of John Trelawny of Menheniot, 3s. 2da. suc. fa. 22 Apr. 1567. Kntd. 1583.[1]

Sheriff, Cornw. 1571–2, 1577–8; customer, Falmouth 1572; j.p. Cornw. from c.1569, Devon from c.1579; commr. piracy, Cornw. 1577, dep. lt. and commr. musters by 1585, commr. grain 1586; recorder, East Looe 1587.[2]

Though there is no evidence that Mohun's father was a Marian exile, it may be that he sent his son abroad. A 'William Mono', who may or may not be the Elizabethan MP, was at Padua during Mary's reign.[3]

Mohun was related to many of the leading county families, and, as demonstrated by his three elections as knight of the shire, was himself of considerable standing. His first return, for the local borough of St. Germans, was no doubt pleasing to the 2nd Earl of Bedford, whose religious views Mohun probably shared and who leased him Boconnoc. Mohun was named to committees on grievances and petitions (7 Apr. 1571), the navigation bill (8 May 1571), observing the Sabbath (27 Nov. 1584), confirming Ralegh's letters patent (14 Dec. 1584), the subsidy (24 Feb. 1585), Devonshire kerseys (15 Mar. 1585) and the Norfolk privilege case (11 Nov. 1586). As a justice of the peace, sheriff and deputy lieutenant, he was in constant touch with the Privy Council, mostly over shipping and defence.[4]

Mohun made a brief will on the day of his death, 6 Apr. 1588. The executor was his son and heir Reginald, aged about 23. To another son, William, he left three manors, to his third son, Thomas, an annuity of £40, and £500 each to his two daughters. His widow received household goods and his steward an annuity of £5.[5]

[1] Vivian, *Vis. Cornw.* 325, 396; H. C. Maxwell Lyte, *Hist. Dunster*, ii. 483. [2] Lansd. 14, f. 108; 48, f. 136; 56, f. 168; 146, f. 19; A. L. Rowse, *Tudor Cornw.* 393; T. Bond, *E. and W. Looe*, 236. [3] C. H. Garrett, *Marian Exiles*, 228–9. [4] *CPR*, 1560–3, p. 603; *HMC Foljambe*, 17; *CSP Dom.* 1581–90, p. 304; *CJ*, i. 83, 88; D'Ewes, 333, 339, 356, 368, 399, 409. [5] PCC 39 Rutland; C142/218/43.

N.M.S.

MOLYNEUX, Edmund (*d.*1605), of Thorpe nr. Newark, Notts. and Ludlow, Salop.

BRIDGNORTH   1572*

Yr. s. of Sir Edmund Molyneux of Thorpe by Jane, da. of John Cheyney of Chesham Bois, Bucks.; bro. of John I*. *unm.*

Sec. to Sir Henry Sidney; clerk to council in Ireland by 1569–71; clerk in signet office, council in the marches of Wales 1581.

A 'gentleman of worshipful patronage', 'honest, diligent, and circumspect', Molyneux was brought into Parliament for Bridgnorth by his master at a by-election (13 Feb. 1579) to replace Thomas Seckford II. He left no trace upon the known surviving records of the House of Commons, indeed most of what is known about him concerns the Sidneys. In 1574 he neglected to send a promised message to Lady Mary Sidney. On another occasion Philip Sidney accused him of opening his letters to his father, and Molyneux admitted having taken 'great delight and profit in reading some of them'. Under threat of a dagger-thrust, he promised to desist. As a general

factotum he found accommodation for various members of the Sidney family at Hampton Court, transacted their private business in London, and drew up petitions. In the account of the family which he furnished for Holinshed's *Chronicles*, Molyneux complained that his master failed to obtain him a comfortable office or reward. An explanation might be that he was the 'one Mollineux' who was employed by Cecil and 'misused' him, before seeking employment as secretary to Sir Henry Norris in 1567. Perhaps, too, he was 'Mollineux ... an inventor of odd devices', who was offering his services in The Hague in 1598, for it was Sir Robert Sidney who was asked to supply information about him.

Molyneux died in September or October 1605. As he lay 'very sick and weak in body', on 29 Sept., his brother Thomas Molyneux, having promised to bestow 'some portion' on the poor on his behalf, asked him in the presence of the parson if he wished to give his goods to his nephew, Edward Molyneux. He could only answer 'yea, yea', and must have died shortly after, as the nuncupative will was proved on 23 Oct.

DNB; G. Molineux, *Memoir Molyneux Fam.* 30–1; A. Collins, *Letters and Memorials*, 256, 296; *CSP Ire.* 1509–73, pp. 443, 462; 1574–85, p. 142; Flenley, *Cal. Reg. Council, Marches of Wales*, 211; *HMC De Lisle and Dudley*, i. 355; ii. 20, 87, 99, 310–11; *Scrinia Ceciliana* (1663), 116; PCC 70 Hayes.

J.J.C.

MOLYNEUX, John I (*d.*1588), of Thorpe, Notts.

NOTTINGHAMSHIRE   1563

1st s. of Sir Edmund Molyneux of Thorpe and bro. of Edmund*. *educ.* ?G. Inn.[1] *m.* Anne, da. of George or John Lascelles of Gateford and Sturton, 6s. 4da. *suc.* fa. 1552.[2]

Escheator, Notts. and Derbys. 1563–4; j.p. Yorks. (N. Riding) from c.1569, Notts. from c.1579.

By Elizabeth's reign the Molyneux family of Lancashire and Nottinghamshire was declining in importance. The Nottinghamshire branch was descended from Sir Richard Molyneux of Sefton, one of the heroes of Agincourt. The 1563 MP's grandfather was a counsellor of Yorkist and Tudor kings, and his father, a follower of Protector Somerset, was a judge. With John Molyneux and the generations which followed him, however, the family horizon rarely extended beyond Nottinghamshire.[3]

Molyneux himself inherited property along the river Trent between Newark and Nottingham, together with lands in Lincolnshire, in Swaledale, Yorkshire, and in Chesham, Buckinghamshire. He added the manors of Carlton Kingston and Carlton Baron, received from the Queen, together with other lands formerly held by Thomas, Lord Dacre; Gonerby manor, Lincolnshire, bought from Thomas Stanhope* in 1561; and, probably, Shipton manor, Shropshire, acquired from a London goldsmith. He was thus able to secure election as knight of the shire in Elizabeth's second Parliament, but it was not until the eighteenth century that the Nottinghamshire branches of the family won a county seat again.[4]

A Member named Molyneux made a significant contribution to a debate on the succession question on 18 Oct. 1566. John Molyneux's cousin Richard Molyneux I* is known to have been present, but the likelihood is that the Nottinghamshire Member is meant. The clerk of the House recorded: 'A motion, made by Mr. Molyneux, for the reviving of the suit for succession and to proceed with the subsidy, was very well allowed of the House'. This early example of the linking of the two topics, which was clearly part of an organized attempt to withhold the grant of money until the Queen could be induced to name a successor – and a protestant successor at that – earned Molyneux a place, as 'Molyneux the mover', in a contemporary lampoon styling forty-three of the more vociferous Members as a rebellious 'choir'. However, it would be dangerous to assume from this that, like the majority of these men, he was inclined to puritanism, for the evidence on his religious views points, if anywhere, in the other direction. Several branches of the Molyneux family, particularly those in Lancashire, adhered to the old faith, and at some date in the mid-1580s a Catholic, Henry Slater, revealed on examination that a priest named Robinson had been sheltered by John Molyneux at Thorpe. Furthermore, at least two of Molyneux's children were recusants. Nor does his appointment to the commission of the peace necessarily contradict the view that he was conservative in religion: many gentlemen with similar views were so employed in the northern counties, especially in the first half of the reign. His name disappears from the commission lists by the mid-1580s. It seems likely, therefore, that his anxiety over the succession was the only point of contact he had with the puritan opposition in Parliament. If he had been of more use to them, a seat would surely have been found for him in later Parliaments.[5]

Private letters, Privy Council and other government records, and above all Star Chamber proceedings, confirm that Molyneux was argumentative and litigious, not averse from disturbing the peace of the county by the use of force in settling quarrels with his neighbours. Some of these disputes seem to have been family feuds lasting for many years, particularly with the Markhams and the Stanhopes. The fact that the Markhams could count on the support of the powerful earls of Rutland and other leading local families did not deter Molyneux from openly demonstrating his hostility. The bitterness usually expressed itself in skirmishes between servants, seizure of livestock, breaking down of fences and other minor incidents. Several times Molyneux brought Star Chamber cases for redress of his grievances. On the whole, however, the Markham feud was not as serious as that with Sir

Thomas Stanhope, a contest which was brought to the notice of the Privy Council. In December 1578, for example, Molyneux complained to the Council that Stanhope had defaced the parish church, enclosed the common and committed other offences in the parish of Saxondale, where Molyneux was lord of the manor and owner of the advowson. The Council's investigation made it clear that both parties had shown equal disregard for the law, and they were ordered to put up £200 as surety for future good behaviour. Later, Molyneux asserted that Stanhope, having broken the peace between them at the county assizes, should forfeit his surety. The Council, who were not convinced that Molyneux's charges were of 'sufficient validity', re-imposed the surety on both men. Other neighbours, including Robert Fletcher, Molyneux's brother-in-law; Anthony Forster, steward of the manor of Newark; John Arnold, Lawrence Wright, Richard Peele and Sir Gervase Clifton* are known to have been involved in quarrels with him, usually involving the seizure of land or livestock. Altogether, Molyneux had to find the money for at least sixteen Star Chamber cases on disputes of this nature.[6]

The paucity of local records makes it difficult to judge the extent of Molyneux's political and military duties in his own county. He certainly played a leading part in the organisation of the local musters in 1570, when he led three hundred soldiers from the county to fight against the northern rebels. Soon after the expedition, he was charged with detaining 'in his hands certain armour belonging to the county and the money due for wages to the soldiers'. The matter was investigated by the Earl of Shrewsbury, who sent complete details of the money and armour collected in Nottinghamshire to the Privy Council. Molyneux strenuously denied the charge, claiming that some of the signatures of local gentlemen on the document which contained the accusation were forged. The Earl of Rutland also became involved in the inquiry, and as a result of his report Molyneux was ordered by the Council to 'answer to the soldiers and the country for wages and armour'. This dispute may have further exacerbated the hostility between him and some of his neighbours.

Because of his extensive land holdings in the remote area around Upper Swaledale, Molyneux was also a justice of the peace for the North Riding of Yorkshire, though it is not clear how active he was in that county. In 1574 the Earl of Huntingdon wrote to him and another Yorkshire justice to search out 'fugitive traitors' who were bringing messages to the Queen of Scots under the guise of horse trading. 'Let diligent regard be had for their apprehension', the letter ends.[7]

Molyneux died on 15 July 1588. In the York registry are to be found 'certain notes and remembrances of the speeches of Mr. John Molyneux, esq., deceased, spoken upon his deathbed'. His eldest son, Edmund, reminded him that he had provided for all his children except 'my brother John'. He answered that John should have 1,000 marks, but then altered it to £500 and told Simon Buck to put it into writing. The executors were Simon Buck and 'my brother Fretchwell'. The inquisition post mortem contains long indentures by which he had settled lands on all his other children.[8]

[1] His name does not appear in the *G. Inn Adm. Reg.*, but he is called 'of Gray's Inn, Middlesex' in 1559, *CPR* 1558–60, p. 204. [2] *Vis. Notts.* (Harl. Soc. iv), 73–4; *DNB* (Molyneux, Sir Edmund). [3] *CPR* 1563–6, p. 38; Egerton 2345, f. 15. [4] *PCC* 31 Powell, printed in G. Molineux, *Hist. Fam. of Molyneux*, 41, 103–12; *CPR*, 1553 & App. Ed. VI, p. 4; 1560–3, pp. 203, 204; J. T. Godfrey, *Notes on Churches of Notts, Bingham Hundred*, 280. [5] *CJ*, i. 74; D'Ewes, 124, 127; Neale, *Parlts.* i. 137–8; SP12/185/70; C. Brown, *Newark*, ii. 20. [6] St. Ch. 4/M1/32, M2/1, 2, 3; St. Ch. 5/M6/35, M28/3, M44/17; *HMC Rutland*, i. 92, 217; *APC*, x. 412; xi. 97, 291; xii. 6–7; Thoroton, *Notts.* ed. Throsby, i. 352; Brown, ii. 156. [7] SP12/70/1; *APC*, vii. 379; *HMC 12th Rep. IV*, p. 90; *HMC Rutland*, i. 90; Molineux, 41; Coll. of Arms, Talbot mss, transcribed by G. R. Batho, E. f. 249; *VCH Yorks. N. Riding*, i. 241; *F. of Fines, Tudor Period*, pt. ii (Yorks. Arch. and Top. Soc. rec. ser. v), 134. [8] York prob. reg. 24, f. 304; C142/273/103.

M.R.P.

MOLYNEUX, John II, of Croxteth and New Hall, Lancs.

LIVERPOOL   1584

3rd s. of Sir Richard Molyneux of Sefton by his 1st w. Eleanor, da. of Sir Alexander Ratcliffe* of Ordsall; bro. of Richard Molyneux I*. *m.* Anne, da. of Richard Ratcliffe of Langley, at least 1s.
?J.p. Lancs.; burgess, Liverpool 1589.

Curiously little is known about Molyneux, returned to Parliament in 1584 by the chancellor of the duchy of Lancaster. He has been confused with three namesakes, one of Melling Wood, another his nephew, and a third the distant relation who sat for Nottinghamshire in 1563. The Liverpool Member was a Catholic alleged to have taken an oath in 1568, together with his father and three sisters, declaring the Pope supreme head of the church. He was therefore presumably the John Molyneux, justice of the peace, of whom it was said in 1591 that his wife and family were 'very evilly disposed', and that he retained 'the most notorious papists' in his service. However, this could have referred to the nephew, younger son of his elder brother William.

Vis. Lancs. (Chetham Soc. lxxxi), 104; Foster, *Lancs. Peds.*; J. A. Twemlow, *Liverpool Town Bks.* ii. 119, 839; *CSP Dom.* 1547–80, p. 321; J. S. Leatherbarrow, *Lancs. Eliz. Recusants* (Chetham Soc. n.s. cx), 109.

N.M.S.

MOLYNEUX, Richard I, of Sefton, Lancs.

LIVERPOOL   1563

2nd s. of Sir Richard Molyneux of Sefton and bro. of

John II*. *educ.* M. Temple 1556, called. *m.* Anne, da. of John Molyneux of Melling, nr. Maghull.
J.p. Lancs. bef. 1587.

Little is known about Molyneux, a lawyer, who was returned for Liverpool after a contest through the influence of his father, crown lessee of the lordship. It is likely that the Mr. Molyneux referred to in the journals in October 1566 was John Molyneux I, in which case no parliamentary activity is known for the Liverpool man. He lost his room in the Middle Temple by discontinuance in 1573, was fined £5 for not acting as Autumn reader in 1575, and again for failing to read at Lent 1576. Like other members of his family, he was a Catholic, described as 'very evil' in 1591. His will has not been found and it is not known when he died.

Vis. Lancs. (Chetham Soc. lxxxi), 104; Foster, *Lancs. Peds.*; Lansd. 53, f. 179; J. S. Leatherbarrow, *Lancs. Eliz. Recusants* (Chetham Soc. n.s. cx), 109; J. A. Twemlow, *Liverpool Town Bks.* i. 216 n. 3; Picton, *Memorials of Liverpool*, i. 53; D'Ewes, 124, 127; *M.T. Recs.* i. 105, 196, 207, 210; *HMC Hatfield*, iv. 242.

N.M.S.

MOLYNEUX, Richard II (c.1559–1623), of Croxteth, and Sefton, Lancs.

WIGAN   1572*
LANCASHIRE   1584, 1593, 1604

b. c.1559, 1st s. of William Molyneux by Brigitta, da. of John Caryll† of Warnham, Suss. *educ.* Univ. Coll. Oxf. 1577. *m.* (1) by 1567, a da. of Lord Strange; (2) Frances (*d.* 1621), da. of Sir Gilbert Gerard*, 6s. 7da. *suc.* fa. 1567, gd.-fa. 1569. Kntd. 1586; *cr.* Bt. 1611.[1]
Hereditary constable, Liverpool castle; steward of Blackburn hundred, duchy of Lancaster 1581; j.p. from c.1583; mayor, Liverpool 1588–9; sheriff, Lancs. 1588–9, 1596–7; collector royal loans 1590, 1597; commr. subsidy 1594, 1599, musters 1596, 1599; receiver-gen. duchy of Lancaster 1607; butler in Lancashire bef. 1611.[2]

Molyneux inherited from his grandfather the lordship of Liverpool and other hereditary offices which opened up the prospect of a distinguished local career as soon as he attained his majority. In the meantime he was a ward of his future father-in-law, Sir Gilbert Gerard, who returned him to Parliament for Wigan in place of Edward Fitton, who pleaded employment on the Queen's business. But, on 18 Mar. 1581, the last day of the session, the House changed its mind about allowing replacements for living Members, and ordered Fitton to 'stand and continue'. In 1584 and 1593 Molyneux obtained election for the county. It was probably he, rather than John Molyneux II, who was named to the subsidy committee, 24 Feb. 1585, and he was named to a committee on 4 Apr. 1593 concerned with measures against recusants. As knight for Lancashire he was entitled to attend the subsidy committee (26 Feb. 1593) and a legal committee (9 Mar. 1593).[3]

Like his grandfather before him, Molyneux had disagreements with the corporation of Liverpool. In 1592 he also contrived to quarrel with the 4th Earl of Derby, lord lieutenant of the county, canvassed successfully for one of the county seats at the forthcoming election in the face of Derby's opposition, and, presumably after the 1593 session of Parliament, which ended on 10 Apr., was committed to the Fleet, making his submission to the Privy Council in May. By the time of the next election he was sheriff, and seized the opportunity of taking a small revenge by sending back to London the election writ on a technicality.[4]

No doubt because of his Catholic relations, the question of Molyneux's religion was closely watched. An anonymous letter to Walsingham dated 29 Dec. 1586 accused him of Catholic sympathies, but in 1587 'he hath lately showed himself very well affected and there is great hope of him, being courteously used'. Three years later he was said to make 'show of good conformity, but many of his company are in evil note'. Perhaps this was the reason why he received the sinister cross against his name on Lord Burghley's map of Lancashire that same year, 1590, indicating that he required careful watching. It was alleged that Mass was regularly said in the private chapels at Croxteth and Sefton, but there does not seem to have been any evidence against Molyneux himself. In 1592 he was described as being 'of the better sort'. The preamble to his will suggests that he ended his life by conforming, but this does not necessarily indicate his religious opinions during the Elizabethan period. Still, as justice of the peace and sheriff of the county, he appears to have displayed sufficient zeal in the persecution of priests and recusants to win him the favour of Sir Robert Cecil. In August 1598 he claimed of late to have brought in many 'to be comers to the church and to hear divine service, which were before recusant'. He played the normal part of a leading gentleman in the military affairs of the county. In 1600 and again in 1601 he was required to furnish one light horse for Ireland.[5]

He made his will 1 Apr. 1618, hoping to be buried without pomp or unnecessary charge, in 'my chancel' in the parish church of Sefton. He wanted a 'fair tomb made over us [himself and his wife] with two alabaster pictures laid thereupon'. With the exception of one manor in Leicestershire, which was to be sold to pay his debts, he left all his property to his eldest son Richard, his sole executor, who was to pay an annuity of £100 to three younger brothers, and to receive a large jewel set with diamonds, 18 diamond buttons and a necklace of pearls at a total value of £1,400. The rest of the jewels, plate, goods and chattels were divided between Richard and his mother. Molyneux was buried on 8 Feb. 1623 in Sefton church.[6]

[1] Vis. Lancs. (Chetham Soc. lxxxi), 104; Foster, Lancs. Peds. [2] Somerville, Duchy i. 501; Lansd. 53, f. 178; J. A. Twemlow, Liverpool Town Bks. ii. 531, 1069, 1070; APC, xx. 186–7; xxvi. 460; CSP Dom. 1603–10, p. 364; 1611–18, p. 38. [3] Foster, Lancs. Peds.; PCC 30 Neville; D'Ewes, 308, 356, 517. [4] APC, xxiv. 256–7; see also LANCASHIRE. [5] Harl. 286, art. 60, f. 97; Lansd. 53, f. 178; Gillow, Burghley's Map of Lancs. 40; HMC Hatfield, iv. 241; v. 486–7; vii. 496; viii. 293; xiv. 179; xv. 200; APC, xxx. 440; xxxii. 283. [6] PCC 128 Swann.

N.M.S.

MOLYNS, Michael (d. 1615), of Mackney and Clapcot, Berks.

WALLINGFORD 1589

3rd s. of William Molyns of Sandall or Sandhills, Hants, and Mackney by his 3rd w. Ann, da. of Sir Alexander Culpepper of Bedgebury, Kent; half-bro. of Robert*. educ. I. Temple 1561. m. (1) by 1574, Frances, da. of Sir Anthony Huddleston of Millom, Cumb., 1s. 1da.; ?(2) aft. 1588, Elizabeth, da. and h. of Edward Gilbert, alderman of London, wid. of Thomas Colby I* of Sherfield-upon-Loddon, Hants, ?s.p. Kntd. ?1592.[1]

J.p.q. Oxon. from c.1573, Berks. from c.1575, Hants c.1592; commr. musters Oxon. 1580, Berks. 1586; sheriff, Oxon. 1575–6, Berks. 1583–4; collector of loan, Oxon. 1590.[2]

As the youngest son of a man of small fortune, Molyns's rise to the position of a leading official in Oxfordshire and Berkshire must be attributed to his finding the right patrons, holding the right opinions (while his elder brothers were probably hampered by recusancy), and to his marriage to Frances Huddleston, whose mother came from one of the leading families in that county, the Barantynes of Little Haseley. His first estates were probably the manors in Oxfordshire which he held from Sir Henry Norris I*, later 1st Lord Norris of Rycote and joint lord lieutenant of both Oxfordshire and Berkshire. In 1576 he bought from (Sir) Thomas Bromley*, the solicitor-general, the manor of Clapcot, Berkshire, neighbour to the family estate at Mackney, of which he was probably already in possession. Much of his property in both counties lay within the honour of Wallingford and, combined with Norris's patronage, obtained his return for the borough. In 1589 his daughter may already have been married to Michael Stampe, presumably one of the family of his fellow-burgess, Thomas Stampe.[3]

In later years Molyns's ambition met some disappointments, in which he looked for help to the highest places. In June 1592 he sent Burghley the draft of a speech, which, as justice 'in sundry counties', he proposed to deliver at sessions of the peace: the speech praised the 'singular virtues' of the Queen's minister, who apparently replied favourably, suggesting emendations. Four months later Molyns wrote again with a sad tale: he had been summoned to be knighted by the Queen, but the event 'was (at the very instant) crossed by the envious and malicious device of his enemies', and he was 'rejected as a man unworthy and of no desert'. Asking Burghley for redress, he once more called attention to his 'public speeches', in which he had always been wont to extol her Majesty. He seems to have obtained his knighthood soon afterwards, but he had to go to Ireland for it, if he was the Michael Molyns knighted about 1592 by the lord deputy.[4]

Molyns was probably married twice. If so, with his second wife he acquired a step-daughter, Dorothy, who soon became the second wife of the rich Sir Francis Willoughby of Wollaton, Nottinghamshire. Willoughby died in 1596, leaving his wife pregnant and Molyns in charge of his estates. The husband of a daughter of Sir Francis by his first marriage told Burghley that Molyns was conspiring to pass off a countrywoman's son as the posthumous child, and thus as Sir Francis's heir. It was at length admitted that the child was a daughter, but there was still strong competition for the wardship, at first given to Sir Robert Cecil, in which Molyns acted for his step-daughter's new husband Philip, 3rd Baron Wharton. He was further accused of procuring an absolute conveyance of all Willoughby's estates.[5]

Molyns died 14 May 1615, seised only of his Oxfordshire and Berkshire manors and some lands in Hampshire. Francis Englefield, head of the great Berkshire family, was one of his executors, and the heir was his son, Sir Barantyne Molyns, who was almost blind from injuries received in the Queen's service.[6]

[1] PCC 19 Tashe, 9 Leicester; *Vis. Berks.* (Harl. Soc. lvi), 112; *Vis. Hants* (Harl. Soc. lxiv), 122; *Vis. Notts.* (Harl. Soc. iv), 149; *Bristol and Glos. Arch. Soc. Trans.* xxviii. 52; Foster, *Al. Ox.* early ser. 1018. [2] *APC*, xii. 17; xiv. 56; xx. 187. [3] *HMC Hatfield*, iii. 106–7; *VCH Berks.* iii. 468, 509–10, 531, 536, 539, 548; C142/378/130. [4] Lansd. 72, ff. 199–201; Shaw, *Knights*, ii. 89. [5] *HMC Middleton*, 573, 580, 583, 618, 620; *CSP Dom.* 1595–7, p. 557; *HMC Hatfield*, vii. 146, 233; viii. 179; *APC*, xxvi. 524. [6] C142/378/130; *CSP Dom.* 1611–18, p. 401.

A.H.

MOLYNS, Robert (c.1516–74), of Bridgwater, Som.

BRIDGWATER   1554 (Apr.), 1558, 1559

b. c.1516, s. of William Molyns of Sandall or Sandhills, Hants by his ?1st w. Evelyn, da. of William Walrond of Bovey House, near Seaton, Devon; half-bro. of Michael*. *m.* Ellen, da. of Thomas Halworthie, *s.p.*

Bailiff, Bridgwater 1544–5, 1550–1; mayor 1555–6, 1566–7; controller of customs, Bridgwater 1554–aft. July 1572.

Though of a minor gentry family, references to Robert Molyns are connected with his activities in Bridgwater. Described as 'gentleman', there is no evidence of his engaging in trade. No record has been found of his owning land except in the town and he lived there some years before becoming a customs official. He was paid for unspecified 'charges' under Edward VI and in 1555. His receipt for his wages for 64 days at the 1559 Parliament and for the expenses incurred during the passing of an act concerning Bridgwater cloth, is in the borough archives.

Molyns made his will 22 Aug. 1574. The 'son' mentioned is presumably his son-in-law Robert Cuffe. He left £60 to the poor, made bequests to his servants and bequeathed the residue to his wife, the sole executrix. The will was proved 8 Oct. 1574.

Bridgwater archives, nos. 393, 804, 1456, 1698, 1916; *Vis. Som.* ed. Weaver, 51; S. Jarman, *Hist. Bridgwater*, 269; E122/28/16, 29/2, 8; Lansd. 14, f. 107; PCC 36 Martyn.

R.V.

MOMPESSON, Richard (*d.* 1627), of Salisbury, Wilts.

DEVIZES   1593

4th s. of William Mompesson of Maiden Bradley by Bridget, da. of Robert Browne of Walcot, Northants. *m.* (1) ?1587, Mary, da. of William Lord Howard of Effingham, wid. of Edward Lord Dudley, *s.p.*; (2) by Feb. 1601, Elizabeth, da. of John Oglethorpe of Newington, Oxon, wid. of John Alford* of Holt Castle, Denb. and Fawley, Bucks., *s.p.*; (3) aft. 1610, Katherine, da. of Sir Thomas Pakington of Aylesbury, Bucks., wid. of (Sir) Jasper Moore*, *s.p.* Kntd. 22 Apr. 1603.[1]

Esquire of the royal stables from ?1574.

When, in 1594, Richard Mompesson and Robert Alexander were granted a licence to bring in aniseed and sumach, they were described as having been esquires of the stables for 20 years; and the lack of any information about Mompesson before 1574 suggests that he had embraced this career from an early age. He came of a family of minor gentry in Wiltshire whose main seat was at Bathampton; but his own branch was settled at Maiden Bradley, where in 1576 his father was assessed for subsidy on goods worth £10 and was called upon to pay 16s. 8d.[2]

Mompesson figures in the records of the period chiefly as a recipient of crown grants. In 1581 a Spaniard captured at Smerwick and committed by Mompesson, 'unto whom the said prisoner was given', escaped from the Counter; the episode was still under investigation four years later. In 1586 he was granted the proceeds of a prosecution in Wiltshire for coining, and early in the following year charged an alehouse keeper at Salisbury with perjury in defence of the convicted men. The licence to import aniseed and sumach granted to Mompesson and Alexander in 1594 was a reward of greater value and one which reflects Mompesson's advance at court. It appears, too, that after Burghley's death in 1598 the Queen promised Mompesson a park which Burghley's heir wanted for himself, and that to pacify the offended peer she 'recalled her promise, preserved my Lord's honour, and graciously satisfied her servant another way'. By October 1601 he was a favoured candidate for a place in the privy chamber, which appears, however, to have eluded him.[3]

Mompesson's career doubtless owed a good deal to the first of his three marriages: Lady Dudley was the daughter of one lord high admiral and the sister of another, whose wife was the Queen's cousin and intimate friend. A seat in Parliament was thus a natural and legitimate aspiration, and in 1593 he was returned at Devizes as a man with local affiliations and powerful backing. He seems, however, to have been one of the numerous company who were content with a single return to the Commons. Though not mentioned by name in the parliamentary journals, he may have attended a cloth committee to which the burgesses for Devizes were appointed (15 Mar.). On his wife's death in 1600 he married another widow, Elizabeth Alford, thus acquiring both the domicile in Buckinghamshire which he was to cite at his knighthood and a stepson, Henry Alford, who was to prove a disappointment. It was about this time that Sir John Davies, who had become a Catholic, asked 'Mr. Mompesson', whom he took to be of that faith, to procure him a priest; if it was Richard Mompesson who was thus approached he must have been confused with his recusant namesake.[4]

In April 1603 Mompesson rendered his first professional service to James I by taking six geldings and a coach and four to help equip the King on his way south. He encountered the new monarch at Newark, and was rewarded with a knighthood. The new reign was, however, to bring him no further advance in honour or office, and it is likely that he soon retired, first to West Harnham and then to the house in Salisbury Close which, when rebuilt by a successor towards the close of the century, was to link his name with its dignified beauty. His last marriage, to yet another widow, again combined Wiltshire with Buckinghamshire in its connexions;[5] she died in 1622, having left a strange will made much to her husband's prejudice.

Mompesson prefaced his own will, which he made 4 Sept. 1627 with a mind 'settled to die in peace', by an expression of his hope of salvation through Christ's passion. He asked to be buried in Salisbury cathedral, stipulated that blacks were to be provided only for his family and for the poor, and gave £50 to the corporation for loan to needy tradesmen and £5 to the poor. Among the relatives who received legacies were his sister Dorothy Thorpe (£500 and his own bed), his nephew Henry Poole, and his cousin Thomas Mompesson of Little Bathampton, whom he appointed executor and who received £750, as well as hangings and plate. Mompesson's bequest of household goods and remission of debt to his stepson Henry Alford was made conditional on him proving 'a quiet man' towards the executor; he would himself have been named such if the testator had not found him 'failing my expectation' in his behaviour.[6]

[1] *Wilts. Vis. Peds.* (Harl. Soc. cv, cvi), 135; *Genealogist*, n.s. xii. 168–9; *CP*, iv. 482. The Richard Mompesson whose son Jasper matriculated at Hart Hall, Oxf. 24 Oct. 1600 was his kinsman of Codford St. Mary. [2] *CSP Dom.* 1594, p. 483; *Two Taxation Lists* (Wilts.

Arch. Soc. rec. br. x), 158. [3] *APC*, xiii. 229–30; xiv. 169; *CSP Dom.* 1581–90, pp. 225, 391; 1601–3, p. 115; *HMC Hatfield*, viii. 71; xi. 375. [4] B. H. Cunnington, *Annals Devizes*, i. 23, 62; D'Ewes, 501; *CSP Dom.* 1591–4, pp. 258, 262, 490; 1598–1601, 548; *HMC Hatfield*, xiii. 117–18; xv. 35. [5] *Chamberlain Letters* ed. McClure, i. 192; *Wilts. Arch. Mag.* ii. 183–4, 430–1; *CSP Dom.* 1611–18, p. 392. [6] PCC 116 Skynner.

S.T.B.

MONCKTON, Christopher (by 1517–1600), of Cavell and Londesborough, Yorks.

APPLEBY 1559, 1563

b. by 1517, s. of William Monckton of Cavell by Anne, da. of Robert Aske of Aughton. *m.* Frances, da. of George Hussey of Duffield by his w. Anne, da. of Sir Robert Constable of Flamborough, 1s. *d.v.p. suc.* fa. 1557.[1]

Christopher Monckton was one of those to whom the Earl of Cumberland was licensed in 1555 to make a nominal conveyance of all his possessions, 'the office of sheriff of Westmorland only excepted'. Among other parties to the arrangement were Sir Thomas Dacre and James Bankes, Members for Cumberland and Appleby respectively in 1553 (Oct.), and Leonard Dacre*.[2] It may be inferred that it was through the Earl's influence – he owned the castle at Appleby and another residence at Londesborough – that Monckton was returned to the first two Elizabethan Parliaments. A third Parliament, if his ambition lay in that direction, was denied him after the religious legislation of 1563, for the Moncktons were Catholics, closely linked a generation earlier with the Pilgrimage of Grace, and displaying throughout Elizabeth's reign the religious conservatism characteristic of many families in the northern counties.

In May 1560 Monckton granted all his property to Gerard Lowther*, Lawrence Banester* and Thomas Bates†, reserving to himself and his heirs the full use of the property, with unrestricted power to lease or otherwise dispose of it. This agreement, or 'use', was still in force at his death. Transactions involving parts of the property – in all it comprised the manors of Cavell and Burlande, 20 messuages, eight cottages, and a windmill – were negotiated in 1566, 1567 and 1573.[3]

The return of Catholics in York diocese in 1577 lists Monckton as worth £40 in goods and £20 in lands. The following January he was summoned to appear before the High Commission at York as an excommunicate who refused to receive communion. Apparently he did not attend, whereupon the court ordered his attachment. This he evaded, with the result that a fresh order was fixed to the door of his house demanding his appearance before the court on pain of £100. On 26 May 1578 he appeared, admitted that he did not attend church and did not take communion, and was committed to custody. After several further appearances he was persuaded to conform, only to retract his statement the following day and again be taken into custody. In October 1580 he was imprisoned at Hull; in April 1582, being bound in £300 to go to church, he certified that he had dutifully done so, and was ordered to take communion. Periodically thereafter until April 1586 and possibly later he appeared before the commissioners, submitted to conferences with learned preachers, but adamantly refused the further conformity demanded of him. In 1592, with other recusants, he was again committed to prison at Hull.[4]

Monckton died 3 Feb. 1600, being then more than 83 years old. His grandson Philip was his heir.[5]

[1] *Vis. Yorks.* ed. Foster, 92, 134; C142/116/29. [2] *CPR*, 1554–5, ii. 247. [3] C142/259/55; *Yorks. Arch. Soc. rec. ser.* ii. 241, 337; *Ancient Deeds, Kingston-upon-Hull*, deeds 645, 646, 649a. [4] *Cath. Rec. Soc.* xviii. 52; xxii. 16; York, Borthwick Institute, act bk. of High Commission (ex inf. F. X. Walker, SJ); *HMC Hatfield*, iv. 273. [5] C142/259/55.

E.L.C.M.

MONSON, Robert (*d.* 1583), of Lincoln and South Carlton, Lincs.

DUNHEVED (LAUNCESTON)	1553 (Oct.)
WEST LOOE	1554 (Apr.)
NEWPORT IUXTA LAUNCESTON	1554 (Nov.), 1555
DUNHEVED (LAUNCESTON)	1558
LINCOLN	1563, 1571
TOTNES	1572*

3rd s. of William Monson of South Carlton by Elizabeth, da. of Sir Robert Tyrwhitt of Kettleby. *educ.* Camb.; L. Inn 1546, called 1552. *m.* 12 Sept. 1559, Elizabeth, da. and h. of John Dyon of Tathwell, *s.p.*

J.p. Lincs. (Lindsey) from c.1561, (Kesteven) from c.1564, (Holland) from c.1573; reader, Thavies Inn 1557; bencher, L. Inn 1562, Autumn reader 1565, keeper of black bk. 1565–6, treasurer 1567–8, governor 1569–72, Lent reader 1570; legal counsel to Lincoln by 1559, recorder 1570–2; eccles commr., dioceses of Lincoln and Peterborough 1571; serjeant-at-law 1572; j.c.p. (and j.p. many S.E. counties) 1572–80; c.j. Lancaster (and j.p. many northern counties) 1577–9.

In 1559 the mayor and aldermen of Lincoln intended to choose Monson both as recorder and MP for the city, until the 2nd Earl of Rutland forced them to give both positions to Anthony Thorold*. Monson was, however, retained as legal counsel, at 26s. 8d., later 40s. p.a., and in 1564 – the year in which he was classified as a justice of the peace 'earnest in religion' – a bye-law permitted the mayor to invite him to any council meeting, or informal sitting of members of the corporation, thus making him a sort of *de facto* recorder. At first Thorold resented Monson, but by 1570 the two were reconciled, and Thorold, apparently on his own initiative, gave up the recordership to his former rival. After twice representing Lincoln in Parliament, Monson, for some unascertained reason, came in for

Totnes, where his relative the 2nd Earl of Bedford had influence. There was no quarrel with the Lincoln authorities who expressed their gratitude for Monson's arbitrating between them and the Earl of Rutland over a fee-farm, by granting him a renewal, on more favourable terms, of his existing lease of Hanslope parsonage and other town property. As late as 1580 he was still a musters commissioner for Lincoln and he was a generous benefactor to the city in his will.

No activity has been found for Monson during the first session of the 1563 Parliament, but on 19 Oct. 1566 he spoke 'very boldly and judiciously' in favour of renewing the succession question, and on 23 Oct. he, Robert Bell* and Richard Kingsmill* spoke before the Lords on behalf of the Commons. Monson was appointed to the succession committee on 31 Oct., and was one of the leaders of the agitation to mention the succession question in the preamble to the subsidy bill. On 29 Nov. Sir William Cordell*, master of the rolls, wrote to Cecil to report that Monson's objections to the subsidy bill had been overcome.

On 6 Apr. 1571 Monson was appointed to a committee on returns and spoke the next day to arrange the time and the place for the committee to meet. He was named to a committee concerning the reform of canon law (6 Apr.), and reported from the bishops (10 Apr.) about a proposed conference with the Lords on the subject. He spoke on the treasons bill on 12 Apr. and was appointed to two committees on the bill (12 Apr., 11 May). Other committee work included topics such as griefs and petitions (7 Apr.), fraudulent conveyances (11 Apr.), church attendance (21 Apr., 19 May), order of business (21, 28 Apr.), vagabonds (23 Apr.), tellers and receivers (23 Apr.), fugitives (24 Apr., 25 May), priests disguised as servants (1, 2 May), respite of homage (2, 17 May), sheriffs (11 May), and counsellors' fees (28 May). He was also appointed to a committee to investigate allegations of corruption in the House (28 May).

In the first session of the 1572 Parliament, Monson spoke in the debates on Mary Queen of Scots and the Duke of Norfolk (19 May, 9 June) and was appointed to the committees (12, 28 May, 6 June). On 11 June he spoke against the tale-tellers – he was 'fully resolved they be papists' – who misrepresented outside the Commons some of the speeches made there. He spoke on the fraudulent conveyances bill (16 May) and was appointed to two committees on the bill (16 May, 3 June); and he was named to a committee on recoveries (31 May). Appointed to the committee on the vagabonds bill on 29 May, he spoke the next day in favour of including minstrels within the provisions of the bill. Monson was made a judge soon after the end of the session and in the next session served in the House of Lords. However, by 1576 he had 'suffered discomfort and discredit by her Majesty's displeasure', and his standing up to the Queen over the sentence on John Stubbe* in October 1579 ruined him. He resigned his

Lancaster office and from November 1579 to the following February was in the Fleet. After retiring formally from the common pleas in the middle of the Easter term 1580 he retreated to his Lincolnshire property. He died 23 Sept. 1583, and was buried in Lincoln cathedral.

DNB; *Lincs. Peds.* (Harl. Soc. li), 527–8, 681; *HMC 14th Rep. VIII*, 56, 62, 64, 66; J. W. F. Hill, *Tudor and Stuart Lincoln*, passim; Foss, *Judges*, v. 524–9; Somerville, *Duchy*, i. 474; *Cam. Misc.* ix(3), p. 27; Lansd. 20, f. 53; 23, f. 85; 27, f. 29; St. Ch. 5/M26/20; *HMC Rutland*, i. 110; *CSP Dom. 1547–80*, p. 530; Rymer, *Foedera*, xv. 470; Lodge, *Illus.* ii. 224; *CPR*, 1558–60, pp. 151, 265; *M.T. Bench Bk.* 80; D'Ewes, 124, 125, 127, 156, 157, 159, 160, 164, 165, 176, 178, 179, 180, 181, 183, 184, 186, 188, 189, 190, 206, 207, 220, 221, 222, 228, 229, 262; *CJ*, i. 75, 83, 84, 85, 86, 87, 89, 90, 91, 92, 93, 95, 99, 100, 101, 115; Trinity, Dublin, anon. jnl. f. 18; Thos. Cromwell's jnl. ff. 20, 27, 58, 63; *HMC Lords*, n.s. xi. 8; Neale, *Parlts.* i. 162; *HMC Hatfield*, i. 341.

N.M.F.

MONSON, Sir Thomas (1564–1641), of South Carlton, Lincs.

LINCOLNSHIRE	1597
CASTLE RISING	1604
CRICKLADE	1614

b. 1564, 1st s. of Sir John Monson of South Carlton by Jane, da. of Robert Dighton of Little Sturton; bro. of Sir William*. *educ.* Magdalen Coll. Oxf. 1579. *m.* July 1590, Margaret (*d.*1630), da. of Sir Edmund Anderson, l.c.j. common pleas, 4s. 5da. *suc.* fa. 1593. Kntd. c.1597; *cr.* Bt. 1611.[1]

J.p. Lincs. (Lindsey) from c.1592, (Kesteven, Holland) from c.1601, sheriff 1597–8, col. of horse 1599; surveyor of royal lands, Lincs. and Lincoln Feb. 1599; master falconer to James I; chancellor to Queen Anne of Denmark 1603; keeper of the armoury at Greenwich; master of the armoury at the Tower June 1611; rem. from all offices 1615; jt. gent. usher of privy chamber; steward of duchy of Lancaster 1618; clerk of the King's letters bef. the council in the north 1625.[2]

The Monson family, resident in Lincolnshire since the fourteenth century, became established at South Carlton during the lifetime of John Monson, who died in 1542. Three succeeding generations increased the family property and in 1593 Monson himself succeeded. A justice for the Lindsey division of the shire within a year of his father's death, he was 'sufficient' and impartial, and in October 1596 was recommended to Robert Cecil for the office of sheriff of Lincolnshire by Lord Sheffield, who had some lawsuits awaiting trial in the county. Though neither his father nor his grandfather had sat in Parliament, Monson was of sufficient standing to take a turn as knight of the shire. He was named to a committee concerning corn on 3 Feb. 1598, and as knight for Lincolnshire he was entitled to attend the following committees: on enclosures (5 Nov.), the poor law (5, 22 Nov.), armour and weapons (8 Nov.), the penal laws (8 Nov.), monopolies (10 Nov.), the subsidy (15 Nov.) and land reclamation (3 Dec.). His later

career he owed to the patronage of Henry Howard, Earl of Northampton, whose cousin was Charles Howard, Earl of Nottingham, the lord admiral, under whom Monson's brother had served at sea. With Northampton's spectacular rise to favour at the court of James I, Monson obtained a number of court offices. His close attachment to the Howards implicated him in 1615 in the murder of Thomas Overbury, and he was imprisoned in the Tower for nearly a year. He died in May 1641 and was buried at South Carlton 29 June.[3]

[1] *Lincs. Peds.* (Harl. Soc. li), 682; Collins, *Peerage*, vii. 228–32; *DNB*. [2] PRO Index 4208; *APC*, xxx. 74; E315/309/122; Lodge, *Illus.* iii. 64–5. [3] *APC*, xxv. 132; *HMC Hatfield*, vi. 458; D'Ewes, 552, 553, 555, 557, 561, 592; Townshend, *Hist. Colls.* 124; *Naval Tracts of Sir William Monson*, ed. Oppenheim (Navy Recs. Soc. xxii), pp. vii–xxxiii; *DNB* (Howard, Henry); *HMC Hatfield*, xvi. 449; xvii. 594; *Letters of George Lord Carew* (Cam. Soc. lxxvi), 17, 20, 37, 44; *HMC 1st Rep.* 47.

R.C.G.

MONSON, Sir William (c.1567–1643), of South Carlton, Lincs., Charterhouse, London and Kinnersley, Surr.[1]

MALMESBURY	1601

b. c.1567, 3rd but 2nd surv. s. of Sir John Monson of South Carlton by Jane, da. of Robert Dighton of Little Sturton; bro. of Sir Thomas*. *educ.* Balliol, Oxf. May 1581, aged 14; MA 9 July 1594; G. Inn 8 Aug. 1594. *m.* 1595, Dorothy, e. da. of Richard Wallop of Bugbrooke, Northants., wid. of Richard Smith of Shelford, Cambs., 3s. 9da. Kntd. at Cadiz by Earl of Essex ?22 June 1596.

Privateer capt. 1587; on pinnace *Charles* 1588; sailed with Earl of Cumberland 1589–95; in command *Rainbow* Apr. 1596; flag-capt. Cadiz expedition 1596; Islands voyage 1597; in command *Defiance* 1599; v.-adm. to Richard Leveson* 1602–3; adm. Narrow Seas July 1604–Jan. 1616; v.-adm. of fleet 1635; member, council of war May 1637; commr. to investigate Dutch naval activities 1639.

J.p.q. Lincs. (Lindsey) 1601.

From Balliol Monson ran away to sea, 'led thereunto', he later wrote, 'by the wildness of my youth'. Between 1585 and 1587 he engaged in privateering, but from 1588, when he first served in a Queen's ship, he was to interrupt his service in the Royal Navy only by voyaging with the Earl of Cumberland. On his second voyage with Cumberland in 1591 Monson was captured, and he remained a prisoner, first in the galleys and then in Lisbon castle, until July 1592. He was at sea again with Cumberland in 1593, but his father's death towards the close of that year, which brought him some property in Lincolnshire, and a return of the ill-health which had troubled him in 1590 appear to have inclined him for a time to life ashore. In the summer of 1594 he took his MA at Oxford and entered Gray's Inn, and early in the following year he married a widow who brought him a stepson and perhaps some property. A possibility of his succeeding (Sir) John Hawkins* as treasurer of the navy did not materialize, and after a final voyage with Cumberland in 1595, leading to a quarrel which put an end to their association, Monson's appointment to the command of the *Rainbow* in the spring of 1596 marked the beginning of 20 years' almost continuous service with the Royal Navy.[2]

It also marked the beginning of Monson's attachment to the Earl of Essex. He was to be the Earl's flag-captain on the Cadiz expedition, and he received his knighthood from Essex probably on the morrow of the city's capture. He sailed again with Essex on the Islands voyage of 1597, and it was Cumberland's hostile comments on his conduct during that expedition which led Monson to challenge Cumberland to a duel, apparently without result. Although Monson was not to be implicated in the decline and fall of Essex, he seems to have suffered some interruption of employment in 1600–1; and his return to the Parliament of 1601 signalled a fresh allegiance. His new patrons were the Howards. For his professional prospects he looked chiefly to Charles Howard I*, Earl of Nottingham, the admiral, and his son-in-law Sir Richard Leveson, with both of whom he had served at Cadiz; it was they who were to bring him fresh activity, as Leveson's vice-admiral in 1602–3, and to occasion the greatest of his naval exploits, the capture of the carrack *St. Valentine*, which earned him and Leveson 'great commendation both for courage and advice'. His return to Parliament he owed to Thomas, Lord Howard de Walden, whose marriage to Catherine, eldest daughter of (Sir) Henry Knyvet*, had given him, on Knyvet's death in 1598, control of the borough of Malmesbury. Neither Monson nor his fellow-Member, Sidney Montagu, had any personal connexion with that borough, and apart from Sir Robert Cecil, to whom both could have looked for support, no one was in a position to procure their return save Thomas Howard. There was to be much discussion of sea affairs in that Parliament, but Monson is not known to have contributed to it.[3]

With the accession of James I Monson's prospects must have appeared bright. Even if he had not been, as one source claims, in touch with James beforehand, Robert Cecil was his friend, and he might hope to advance in step with his elder brother Thomas, who, under the patronage of Henry Howard, Earl of Northampton, was rising at court. In fact Monson did obtain the command of the Channel squadron, which he retained for 11 years; but in the years 1613–15 Sir John Digby†, the ambassador in Spain, obtained and transmitted evidence that Monson was among those who had been since 1604 in receipt of Spanish pensions. Damaging as it was, this revelation might have had less consequence but for the circumstance that in January 1616, when the final proof was received, Cecil and Northampton were both dead, the remaining Howards were in disgrace in consequence of the Overbury

affair, and Monson's brother Thomas was in the Tower as a suspected accomplice in that murder. Monson's imprisonment in the Tower, which lasted from January to July 1616, was generally believed to be connected with the same episode. His own explanation of it, that he had incurred enmity by his advocacy of naval reforms, his arrest of Arbella Stuart, and his hostility to the Dutch, is unconvincing; a set of questions put to him relate only to the pension and to subversive activities into which it might have drawn him. Whatever Monson's culpability, it was James's devotion to the Spanish alliance which saved him from worse disaster. His only punishment was the loss of his command.[4]

Nearly 20 years were to pass before Monson, then in his late sixties, was given his next and last command; in 1635 he sailed as vice-admiral in the fleet under Lindsey. After that he retired to the estate at Kinnersley near Reigate which he had had since at least 1624 and where his neighbours included his patrons the Howards. Although he was appointed to the council of war established in May 1637, the preoccupation of his closing years was the compilation of the 'Tracts' which he had begun about 1624. It is upon these, in which he combined naval history with an exposition of policy, strategy and administration, that his fame rests.

Monson died intestate in February 1643 and was buried at St. Martin-in-the-Fields on the 13th of that month. Administration was granted to his second son William. Besides Kinnersley, he possessed land in Kent and the manors of Croft and Skegness in Lincolnshire. The bulk of his property went to his eldest son John, a Catholic who died in 1645 and whose daughter Anne, the wife of Sir Francis Throckmorton, sold Kinnersley in 1666. The second son, William†, went to court and gained an Irish viscounty of which he was deprived, together with his freedom, as one of the surviving regicides at the Restoration. Since this William's son was childless, and the admiral's third son Francis died young and unmarried, the male line failed.

[1] Except where stated otherwise, this biography is based upon *Naval Tracts of Sir William Monson* (Navy Recs. Soc. xxii, xxiii, xliii, xlv, xlvii). [2] *DNB*; Collins, *Peerage*, vii.241. [3] *CSP Dom.* 1595–7, pp. 275, 283, 285–6, 484; 1598–1601, p. 463; 1601–3, pp. 102, 152, 208, 210, 220, 298; *HMC Hatfield*, vi. 355; ix. 427; xii. passim; *HMC Sackville*, i. 49–52; *HMC De L'Isle and Dudley*, ii. 328. [4] *HMC Hatfield*, xvi. 329, 331–2, 346; xvii. 146–8, 297–8, 306–7, 411–12, 415–16, 417, 517–18, 522; xviii. 148–50, 150–2; *HMC Downshire*, ii. 113; iv. 223–47; *HMC De L'Isle and Dudley*, iii. 150, 190; iv. 276; Lansd. 139, f. 94.

S.T.B.

MONTAGU, Edward I (c.1530–1602), of Boughton, Northants.

NORTHAMPTONSHIRE   1559

b. c.1530, 1st surv. s. of Sir Edward Montagu of Boughton by his 3rd w. Helen, da. of John Roper. *m.* 1557, Elizabeth, da. of James Harington I* of Exton, Rutland, 8s. inc. Henry*, Sidney* and Edward Montagu II* 4da. *suc.* fa. 1556. Kntd. bet. 1568 and 1570.

J.p. Northants, from c.1559, sheriff 1559–60, 1570–1, 1588–9, 1600–1, dep. lt. 1570; commr. to regulate 'export' of corn 1572, Peterborough cathedral lands 1574, religious 'disorders' Northampton 1579, recusancy 1590s.

Montagu's father was a judge who speculated in monastic lands, acquiring in Northamptonshire alone 'eleven manors, one castle (presumably Barnwell), one baronial residence' and the patronage of eight livings. After receiving livery of his lands in June 1557 Montagu himself, who represented his shire once only, in the ill-reported 1559 Parliament, added to his Northamptonshire estates by a grant of concealed lands in the county, and bought the manor of Trafford and woods near Brigstock. He also purchased Bedfordshire property at Newton, Overdean and Woodhall. He was rich enough to give two of his daughters marriage portions of £3,000. The bishops' letters to the Council in 1564 described him as an 'earnest furtherer' of religion; locally he was known as 'the friend of Kettering', and many of his contemporaries remarked on his piety and justice, his wisdom and service to the county. In August 1570, when the Earl of Sussex sent him his patent as deputy lieutenant, he added a note that he bestowed it 'with as good a will as I would upon any man in England'. Montagu was one of those who attended the funeral of Mary Queen of Scots on 1 Aug. 1587. He died on 26 Jan. 1602.

C142/109/4, 269/91; *Vis. Northants.* (Harl. Soc. lxxxvii), 136; *HMC Montagu*, 6, 11; Bridges, *Northants.* ii. passim; C. Wise, *Montagus of Boughton*, 17–18; *CPR*, 1555–7, p. 321; *Cam. Misc.* ix(3), p. 35; *APC*, viii. 143, 323, 341; xi. 133, 159; xiii. 153; xiv. 140; xxi. passim; xxii. 52; *CSP Dom.* 1581–90, p. 330; *HMC Bath*, v. 83; PCC 1 Montagu.

N.M.F.

MONTAGU, Edward II (1562–1644), of Boughton, Northants.

BERE ALSTON	1584
TAVISTOCK	1597[1]
BRACKLEY	1601
NORTHAMPTONSHIRE	1604, 1614, 1621*

b. 1562, 1st surv. s. of Edward Montagu I* and bro. of Henry* and Sidney* *educ.* Christ Church, Oxf. c.1574, BA Mar. 1579; M. Temple 1581. *m.* (1) 21 Sept. 1585, Elizabeth (*d.*1611), da. and h. of (Sir) John Jeffrey* of Chiddingly, Suss., 1da.; (2) 24 Feb. 1612, Frances (*d.*1620), da. of Thomas Cotton† of Conington, Hunts., 3s. (1 *d.v.p.*) 1da.; (3) 16 Feb. 1625, Anne, da. of John Crouch of Corneybury, Herts., wid. of Robert Wynchell, painter-stainer, of Richard Chamberlain, and of (Sir) Ralph

Hare* of Stow Bardolph, Norf., *s.p. suc.* fa. 1602; KB 1603; *cr.* Baron Montagu 1621.[2]

J.p. Northants. from c.1595, sheriff 1595–6, commr. musters 1596, dep. lt. from 1602, ld. lt. from 1642; dep. keeper, Rockingham forest by 1593.[3]

The heir to one of the principal estates in Northamptonshire, Montagu, once his formal education was over, divided his time between London and Boughton. As deputy keeper of Rockingham forest Montagu left a musters book that has survived containing letters directed to him, and copies of those he despatched. After his marriage Montagu abandoned attempts to find a suitable residence in the county on the grounds that his wife's health necessitated her staying in London. In a letter to his mother announcing his intention of residing at Boughton when in Northamptonshire, he wrote:

And I may be set so to work that I may at my father's hands earn my victuals, for which I may keep him company at chess, and if need be I may take his part at double-handed Irish, and if there be occasion of weightier matters, as punishing rogues and such like, if it please him to employ me, [it] may ease him. And to do you some service I may in summer time [gather aprico]ts and peaches, or some such like work … And if [none of] all these pains do deserve my meat and drink, yet truly they would be well bestowed of me, because they will be well seen by me especially if I may have froment y and cheesecakes.[4]

In 1584 a seat was found for Montagu at the new parliamentary borough of Bere Alston. The patron was presumably Lord Mountjoy, perhaps acting through his relative Edward Lane*, who was Montagu's cousin. In 1597 he represented Tavistock, where his fellow-Member was Valentine Knightley. Knightley had earlier represented the borough under Russell patronage, and may by 1597 have had enough influence to secure Montagu's return. During this Parliament he sat on a committee considering a bill for the town of Northampton, 16 Nov., and another concerning a bill for tellers and receivers, 12 Dec. His return for Brackley in 1601 was probably procured by his friend Robert Spencer*. On 3 Dec. 1601 Montagu made a charitable motion

which I hope will tend to a charitable end, and briefly it is this: that no private bill may pass this House but the procurers to give something to the poor … Because I offered to the consideration of this House this motion first, I will presume also more particularly to deliver my opinion. I think for every private bill for sale of lands, ten pounds a reasonable benevolence; and for every estate for life or for jointure, five pounds.

The bills against drunkenness and for the proper observing of the Sabbath day were committed to him on 4 Nov., and he spoke in the subsidy debate on 7 Nov. His name appears in a list of Members served with subpoenas in the course of the 1601 Parliament.

In James's reign Montagu successfully claimed a county seat in all the elections before his elevation to the peerage. It is just possible that his reference, in a letter to Robert Spencer, Lord Spencer, during 1625 'I have not a son fit to join with yours, as your lordship and I once did, for the service of the country' – implies that they unsuccessfully contested the county seat in Elizabeth's reign, but it is more probable that it is concerned with their preparations to fight the county seat against Anthony Mildmay*, at the election they expected early in 1603, before Spencer's elevation to the peerage.[5]

James I thought Montagu 'smelt a little of puritanism', and he certainly supported the 1605 petition in favour of puritan ministers. In 1642 he was arrested by Parliament because they feared his influence on the county, where he was popular as a hospitable neighbour and a good landlord. He died in captivity in 1644 and was buried in Weekley church 26 June.[6]

[1] Folger V. b. 298. [2] Vis. Northants. (Harl. Soc. lxxxvii), 137; Vis. Northants. ed. Metcalfe, 114–15; CP; DNB. [3] Musters, Beacons and Subsidies in Northants. ed. Wake (Northants. Rec. Soc. iii), p. cxvi; HMC Buccleuch, i. xix. [4] Lansd. 78, f. 166; 81, f. 79; HMC Buccleuch, i. pp. xix, xx, 224, 225, 228, 231, 233, 234, 235; iii. 41, 52, 55, 65, 66; HMC Montagu, 26, 28. [5] D'Ewes, 557, 572, 626, 637, 665; Townshend, Hist. Colls. 279, 280; HMC Buccleuch, iii. 74–5, 172–3, 257; HMC Hatfield, xi. 485. [6] HMC Buccleuch, i. p. xx; DNB; CP.

S.M.T.

MONTAGU, Henry (c.1563–1642), of the Middle Temple, London.

HIGHAM FERRERS	1593, 1597,[1] 1601
LONDON	1604, 1614

b. c.1563, 3rd s. of Edward Montagu I* and bro. of Sidney* and Edward Montagu II*. educ. Christ's, Camb. 1583; M. Temple 1585, called 1592. m. (1) 1 June 1601, Catherine (d.1612), da. of Sir William Spencer of Yarnton, Oxon. 4s. 3da.; (2) 1613, Anne, da. of William Wincot of Langham, Suff., wid. of Sir Leonard Halliday, ld. mayor of London, s.p.; (3) 26 Apr. 1620, Margaret, da. of John Crouch of Corneybury, Herts., wid. of Allen Elvine, leatherseller, and of John Hare*, 2s. 2da. Kntd. 1603; cr. Baron Kimbolton and Visct. Mandeville 1620; Earl of Manchester 1626.

Recorder, London 1603–16; reader, M. Temple 1606; KC 1607; serjeant-at-law 1611; King's sergeant 1611; l.c.j. King's bench 1616–20; PC 1620; ld. high treasurer 1620–1; 1st commr. of gt. seal May–July 1621; pres. of council 1621–8; master of ct. of wards 1624; chief commr. for Virginia inquiry 1624; ld. lt. Hunts. 1624; ld. privy seal 1628–d.; council for colonies 1634; high steward Camb. Univ. 1634–d.; commr. Treasury 1635–d.; commr. regency Sept. 1640, Aug.–Nov. 1641.[2]

Montagu was a lawyer who had a distinguished career under James I and Charles I. His return for Higham

Ferrers may be explained by his family's standing and connexions in Northamptonshire. In 1597 he was named to two committees concerning private transactions (25 Nov., 9 Dec.). He was probably the 'Mr. Montague' who was appointed to committees concerning defence (8 Dec.), tillage (13 Dec.) and soldiers and mariners (20 Dec.), although his brother Edward's presence in this Parliament makes complete certainty impossible. The same problem of identity exists in 1601, but is complicated still further by the presence in the Commons of the younger brother Sidney. However, Henry was named to the following committees: private business (9 Dec.), letters patent (11 Dec.) and the Belgrave privilege case (17 Dec.). He reported a committee on Exchequer reform on 25 Nov. (a 'Mr. Montague' – presumably Henry – was appointed to a committee on Exchequer reform on the same day), and he also reported the committee concerning soldiers and mariners (11 Dec.). He spoke on the subsidy on 7 Nov., and two days later 'Mr. Montague of the Middle Temple' argued against Serjeant Hele* in the subsidy debate. It is highly likely that it was Henry:

> ... if all the preambles of the subsidies were looked upon, he [Hele] should find that [the subsidy] was of free gift. And although her Majesty requireth this at our hands, yet it is in us to give, not in her to exact of duty ...

On 19 Nov. he spoke in support of a bill to prevent the export of bullion. Two committees concerning the order of business (3 Nov.) and a private bill (28 Nov.) may have been attended by Henry, and he was also probably responsible for two speeches on monopolies – the first on 20 Nov.:

> The matter is good and honest and I like this manner of proceeding by bill well enough in this matter. The grievances are great, and I would only note but thus much unto you, that the last Parliament we proceeded by way of petition, which had no successful effect.

The second on 23 Nov.:

> Mr. Speaker I am loth to speak what I know lest perhaps I should displease. The prerogative royal is that which is now in question and which the laws of the land have ever showed and maintained. My motion then shall be but this: that we may be suitors unto her Majesty, that the patentees shall have no other remedies than by the laws of the realm they may have – and that our Act may be drawn accordingly.

Under James he received promotion, and died in 1642 with a moderate fortune. His eldest son was prominent on the parliamentary side in the civil war.[3]

[1] Folger V. b. 298. [2] CP; DNB; Vis. Northants. ed. Metcalfe, 114–15; A. B. Beaven, Aldermen of London, i. 278; Foss, Judges, vi. 167–72. [3] D'Ewes, 563, 570, 571, 572, 624, 633, 645, 649, 651, 657, 673, 679, 680, 688; Townshend, Hist. Colls. 205, 227, 233, 243, 313; HMC Hatfield, xi. 485; DNB.

S.M.T./M.A.P.

MONTAGU, Sidney (d.1644), of the Middle Temple, London.

BRACKLEY	1593
MALMESBURY	1601
WELLS	1614
HUNTINGDONSHIRE	1640 (Nov.)*

6th s. of Edward Montagu I*, and bro. of Henry* and Edward Montagu II*. *educ.* Christ's, Camb. 1588; M. Temple 1593, called 1601. *m.* (1) 1619, Pauline (d.1638), da. of John Pepys of Cottenham, Cambs., 2s. 1da.; (2) Anne (d.1676), da. of Gregory Isham of Barby, Northants., *s.p.* Kntd. 1616.[1]

Bencher, M. Temple 1615, reader 1620; master of requests 1618–*d.*

Brackley made no difficulty about providing a seat for one of his family in 1593, though 'the townsmen would be glad if [Montagu] would come among them and bestow some courtesies of them'. When Montagu entered the Middle Temple his brother Henry was already an established lawyer. He soon took over from his brother some of the family legal business, and various letters on this subject survive, one of which describes his kind reception at Lord Burghley's Wimbledon house, and the affability of Lord and Lady Zouche. A seat in the 1601 Parliament was found for him at Malmesbury, through the influence of Thomas, Lord Howard de Walden. It is not possible to be explicit about any committee activity in 1601 owing to the presence of his brothers in the House and the failure, for the most part, of the journals to distinguish between them. However, on 2 Dec. 1601 the Townshend journals mention 'Mr. Montague Jr.' – presumably Sidney – as speaking on a legal matter. In 1604 Montagu was hoping for a post at court, and he ultimately became with 'much ado to get in', master of requests. He was described by his brother, Charles, as 'so reserved as none shall be of his counsel'. He lived to sit in the 1640 Parliament, from which he was expelled, and died in 1644.[2]

[1] *Vis. Northants.* (Harl. Soc. lxxxvii), 136–8; *Christ's Coll. Biog. Reg.* ed. Peile, i. 193. [2] *HMC Buccleuch*, i. 234, 236, 250, 252; iii. 31; *HMC Montagu*, 27, 28, 29; Townshend, *Hist. Colls.* 277; *HMC Hatfield*, xvi. 99.

S.M.T.

MONTGOMERY, Lewis (d.1568), of Ecton, Northants.

NORTHAMPTON	1563

s. of Michael Montgomery of Ecton by Elizabeth Lewis. *educ.* G. Inn 1550, ancient 1557. *m.* Jane, da. of Sir Ralph Lane of Horton, *s.p.*

J.p.q. Northants. by 1564.

Montgomery was a puritan lawyer and land speculator, whose connexions in Northamptonshire included the Lanes of Horton, the Yelvertons, Catesbys and Spencers.

He was also known to the 2nd Earl of Bedford who had him returned for Dorchester to the 1563 Parliament. However, his own contacts and standing had been sufficient to gain him one of the Northampton seats (his brother-in-law had the other) and he exercised his option to retain this, a new writ being ordered for Dorchester 25 Jan. The only record found of any activity in the Commons is his membership of the succession committee, 31 Oct. 1566. Montgomery was classified in the 1564 bishops' reports as an 'earnest furtherer of religion'. He died, probably in his early 30s, his will, made when he was 'sick in body', being proved 13 Nov. 1568. One Mr. Foxe – just possibly the famous martyrologist – was to preach his funeral oration and Foxe, or 'some other virtuous and learned preacher', was to preach quarterly in Ecton church for four years. His wife received a life interest in his property, and his youngest brothers (one was only seven) were left annuities while they trained for the law and a residual interest in some property. The rest was to pass to their elder brother William, provided he renounced any claim to his brothers' portion and left Montgomery's wife undisturbed in her tenure of part of Ecton manor. His three sisters were to receive £100 between them.

Bridges, *Northants.* ii. 142; *G. Inn Pens. Bk.* i. 499; *CPR*, 1563–6, p. 25; 1566–9, p. 316; *Northants. Rec. Soc.* xiii. p. lxii; C142/262/129; *Cam. Misc.* ix(3), p. 35; *CJ*, i. 63; D'Ewes, 127; PCC 23 Babington.

S.M.T.

MOONE, Morgan (c.1549–c.1611), of Bridport, Dorset.

BRIDPORT	1584, 1586

b. c.1549, s. of Walter Moone of Bridport by his w. Edith. *educ.* St. Alban Hall, Oxf. 1576, BA 1578. *m.* (1) Alice; (2) 26 Dec. 1611, Dionisia (d.1621), da. of Richard Tyggins, of Bridport, 1s.

Overseer of rope making, Bridport 1580s, cofferer by 1589, sub-bailiff 1590; dep. (to Walter Ralegh*) for subsidy and customs on overlengths of cloth, Devon and Dorset, and (with Henry Wade) for licensing of wines, Cornwall and Devon.

Moone's father was bailiff and cofferer of Bridport and searcher of Poole, where he was succeeded by his brother, Robert*, Morgan Moone's uncle. Robert, who had already paid Walter's debts and provided for the education of his children, made himself responsible for Morgan Moone's education at Oxford. After Walter's death Morgan Moone's mother married one Richard Tyggins, her late husband's partner as cofferer of Bridport, and father of Morgan Moone's second wife.

Upon Robert Moone's death in 1580, his widow took Morgan into her business, and he soon afterwards acquired local offices in Bridport and under Ralegh. The Richard Moone who sailed to the Azores in one of Ralegh's ships in 1586 may have been Morgan's youngest brother. He was killed, or died, on the voyage, and administration of his goods was granted to Morgan as next of kin. Another brother, Anthony, wrote in 1592 to the captain of the *Roebuck*, one of Ralegh's ships, referring to 'our lord and master'. The association between Moone and Ralegh affected the patronage at Bridport, for, though Moone twice represented the town in his own right, because he was also an associate and servant of Ralegh, he paved the way for some Ralegh nominees, such as Gregory Sprint*, John Fortescue II* and Adrian Gilbert*.

Moone borrowed 'a great sum' of money from his co-deputy Wade, with whom he soon quarrelled over the lease of a parsonage formerly belonging to Moone's grandfather. Robert Moone's son Maximilian brought a case against Morgan Moone in the Exchequer court, alleging conspiracy to defraud him of the lease, which he claimed as part of his inheritance. Robert Moone's widow, supporting her son, suggested that the document had been embezzled by Morgan when he first became her business partner after her husband's death. The dispute was still in being in 1600, when both Moone and Wade were sued by Maximilian, this time in Chancery.

Moone died about 1611, when administration of his estate was granted to his widow.

This biography is based upon *New Eng. Hist. and Gen. Reg.* lxxx. 356 and lxxxi. 91–4, 178–85, and E134/42/Eliz./Trin. 2/Dorset and Mdx. Other sources: PCC 43 Daper; Hutchins, *Dorset*, ii. 10; *Som. and Dorset N. and Q.* iii. 93; Bridport dome bk. ff. 330–2; *Bridport Recs.* 48; PCC admon. act bk. 1586–7, f. 5; *HMC Hatfield*, iv. 232.

P.W.H.

MOONE, Robert (c.1519–80), of Bridport, later of Loders and Fleet, Dorset.

BRIDPORT   1559

b. c.1519, yr. s. of Richard Moone† of Ottery, Devon, bailiff of Bridport. *m.* Margaret (*d.*1603), da. and coh. of Stephen Hyde of Hyde, Dorset, 9s. 8da.
Searcher, Poole c.1571.

Moone's father and brother both held offices at Bridport, where he was returned to the 1559 Parliament. The only mention of him to be found in the journals of the House is to leave of absence granted on 18 Mar. 1559. He bought Loders from the Earl of Arundel in 1560 and purchased Fleet about seven years later. He was rated for the subsidy of 1576 on £50 in goods, and continued to buy land for many years, over some of which, probably Chaldon in Purbeck, he fought a Chancery case against the relatives of John Clavell* and John Lovell*. In 1567 he gave evidence on behalf of John Hassard* in a Star Chamber suit concerning a dispute at Lyme Regis. He became searcher of Poole on the death of his brother Walter in 1571. He died on 14 Nov. 1580, and was buried in West Fleet church, where there is a brass to him and his wife. His will, drawn up 1 Sept. 1578, appointed the widow sole executrix, with his son-in-law Richard Sydway and a

kinsman, Serjeant Edmund Anderson, as overseers. Five years after the will was proved in 1581 its validity was challenged unsuccessfully. Moone's descendants became country gentlemen, severing their connexion with Bridport. One branch of the family went to America and founded the family of Derby, merchants of Salem, New England.

This biography is based upon *New Eng. Hist. and Gen. Reg.* lxxxi. 91–4, 181–3, 314, 356. Other sources: *Vis. Dorset* (Harl. Soc. xx), 72; *CJ*, i. 58; Hutchins, *Dorset*, ii. 16; *Dorset Nat. Hist. Antiq. Field Club Procs.* xxvi. 111; liii. 94; *Som. and Dorset N. and Q.* vi. 118; lay subsidy, 18 Eliz. (T/S at PRO); St. Ch. 5/H32/4; PCC 43 Daper, 38 Darcy, 26 Brudenell; C142/193/45.

N.M.F.

MOORE, Francis (1559–1621), of East Ilsley and South Fawley, Berks.

BOROUGHBRIDGE   1589
READING   1597, 1601, 1604, 1614

b. 1559, o. and posth. s. of Edward Moore, yeoman, by Elizabeth, da. and coh. of Hall of Tilehurst. *educ.* Reading g.s.; St. John's, Oxf. 1574; New Inn; M. Temple 1580, called 1587. *m.* Anne, da. of William Twitty of Boreham, Essex, 3s. 2da. *suc.* fa. at birth. Kntd. 1617.[1]
Counsel and under-steward to Oxf. Univ.; counsel to city of London by 1593; Autumn reader, M. Temple 1607; serjeant-at-law 1614.[2]
J.p.q. Berks. from c.1592, custos rot. from 1615.

As Moore made his way in the law, the sons of several of the leading Berkshire gentry entered his chambers at the Middle Temple, and Robert Knollys, son of Francis Knollys* of Reading and grandson of Sir Francis Knollys*, treasurer of the Household, was admitted to the inn at his special request. Amongst those for whom he acted as counsel were Anne, Lady Dacre, sister to Lord Buckhurst, lord treasurer and chancellor of Oxford university, and Sir John Smith, the soldier committed to the Tower in 1596 for attempting to start a rebellion in Essex. Though Moore supported a bill for the stricter enforcement of church attendance in 1601, he had associations with Catholic sympathizers including the great Berkshire family of Englefield, and his daughter Elizabeth became a recusant. Perhaps the Englefield connexion played some part in securing Moore his seat at Boroughbridge, for Sir Edward Fitton, the senior burgess, was the uncle of Francis Englefield. At Reading, where his mother had been born and he himself had been at school, he may have needed no help, though he perhaps enjoyed the patronage of the high steward, the 2nd Earl of Essex, nephew of Francis Knollys of Reading.[3]

Moore was not conspicuously active in his first Parliament of 1589. He was appointed to committees concerning returns (10 Feb.), a private bill (21 Feb.), Exchequer reform (20 Mar.), almshouses in Lambourn, Berkshire (22 Mar.) and a declaration of war with Spain (29

Mar.). In 1593 he was not an MP, but he appeared at the bar of the House on 21 Mar. as counsel for the city of London supporting the exclusion of aliens from the English retail trade.

D'Ewes represents Moore as being one of the first to launch the great attack on monopolies on 7 Nov. 1597. He was appointed to the committee on 10 Nov. and reported the proceedings of a committee considering the form of the reply to the Queen's message on monopolies on 14 Dec. On 8 Nov. he moved to repeal the statute concerning unnecessary armour and weapons, and was named to the committee appointed the same day. The bill for the town of Wantage was committed to him on 10 Nov. and on 12 Nov. he urged the punishment of Ludlow for an irregular return. After reporting one committee concerned with forestallers and regrators on 14 Nov., he was put in charge of a further committee on the subject on 16 Nov. which he reported on 18 Nov. His committee work during the 1597-8 Parliament comprised a high proportion of legal and private bills but also included topics such as ecclesiastical grievances (14 Nov.), abuses in Oxford and Cambridge colleges (19 Nov.), the export of sheepskins (26 Nov.) and the suppression of 'lewd and wandering persons pretending to be soldiers and mariners' (20 Dec.). On 16 Jan. 1598 he was one of those appointed to consider the 31 objections raised by the Lords to the Commons' bill concerning the increase of people for the defence of the realm.

His first speech in the 1601 Parliament contained some controversial ideas on the subsidy (9 Nov.). He moved that

> that which was done might be completely done and the subsidy gathered by commission and not by the old roll – for peradventure some were dead, others fallen to poverty, others richer and so ought to be enhanced etc. And withal he said the granting of this subsidy seemed to be the *alpha* and *omega* of this Parliament.

On 20 Nov. he renewed his agitation over monopolies:

> Mr. Speaker, I know the Queen's prerogative is a thing curious to be dealt withal, yet all grievances are not comparable. I cannot utter with my tongue or conceive with my heart, the great grievances that the town and country for which I served, suffereth by some of these monopolies: it bringeth the general profit into a private hand, and the end of all is beggary and bondage to the subjects ... there is no act of hers that hath been or is more derogatory to her own Majesty, more odious to the subject, more dangerous to the commonwealth than the granting of these monopolies.

However, Moore seems to have lacked the courage necessary to defend his views under pressure, for on 25 Nov. he addressed the House in very different terms:

> I must confess, Mr. Speaker, I moved the House both the last Parliament and this touching this point [monopolies]; but I never meant (and I hope this House

thinketh so) to set limits and bounds to the prerogative royal.

He proposed a motion to thank the Queen for her promise to deal with monopolies, and to crave pardon for 'divers speeches ... made extravagantly in this House, which doubtless have been told her Majesty, and perhaps all ill-conceived of by her'. He was appointed to the conference with the Lords on monopolies on 11 Dec. He was an active speaker on the topic of Members' liberties and privileges during this Parliament. On 19 Nov. he questioned whether a Member's servant was entitled to privilege if his master had not yet attended the Parliament or taken the oaths, owing to illness or some other mishap. In general, however, he was a keen defender of parliamentary privilege, urging strong disciplinary measures to be taken against offenders (20 Nov.) and describing an incident when his own servant was 'well beaten' (28 Nov.). Moore spoke on the subject of church attendance on 20 Nov.:

> ... I think the bill intendeth ... only to punish those with the penalty of one shilling which though they be well addicted yet they be negligent. For my own part I do so much desire the furtherance and good success of this bill or any of the like nature, that he that doth not the like, I would he had neither heart to think nor tongue to speak.

He considered the bill for the abolition of gavelkind in Kent 'a very idle and frivolous bill, and injurious', giving as one of his reasons on 10 Dec.:

> ... if the father commit a felony and be hanged, the son shall not lose his inheritance because the custom is, 'the father to the bough, the son to the plough' ...

Moore introduced two bills into the House, the first confirming grants of land to and by the Queen (11 Nov.), the second concerning hospitals (2 Dec.). He asked that the bill concerning the continuation of certain statutes be read on 7 Dec., and reported the subsequent committee on 14 Dec. As counsel to the London corporation of vintners he proposed a proviso (10 Dec.) to the bill for the abolition of alehouses. His committee work included the following topics: the order of business (3 Nov.), alehouses (7 Nov.), the town of Rochdale, Lancashire (11 Nov.), the abbreviation of the Michaelmas law term (11 Nov.), the confirmation of grants and letters patent (12 Nov., reported by him 18 Nov.); reported Lords conference (15 Dec.), clothworkers (18 Nov.), Exchequer reform (21 Nov.) and the abuses of the clerk of the market (2 Dec.). On the last day of the 1601 Parliament (19 Dec.), as the House 'sat quietly one talking with another', the question arose of the plight of serving women with illegitimate children. The view was put forward that no relief should be offered to the mother, but that penury should be the reward of 'her own sin and her own impiety'. Francis Moore disagreed:

both in charity and by law they both [mother and child] ought to be relieved, by the express words of the statutes.[4]

Although he had not then been a reader, he was admitted as an associate to the bench of the Middle Temple in November 1603 at the desire of the lord chancellor, (Sir) Thomas Egerton I*, who in 1589 sat for Reading, and of (Sir) John Popham*, lord chief justice. On his death on 21 Sept. 1621, he left £1,500 to each of his two daughters as marriage portions. His law reports (King's bench, 1512–1621) and readings on the statute of charitable uses have enjoyed a high reputation; the former were edited by Sir Geoffrey Palmer, Moore's son-in-law, and commended in a preface by Sir Matthew Hale†, who married Moore's grand-daughter.[5]

[1] DNB; Bodl. Wills Berks. 8, f. 134; Vis. Berks. (Harl. Soc. lvi), 246; VCH Berks. iii. 127; iv. 119, 176. [2] D'Ewes, 505–6; M.T. Recs. ii. 586. [3] Bodl. Wills Berks. 8, f. 134; PCC 98 Dale; M.T. Recs. i. 325, 375; ii. 482, 550; Lansd. 77, f. 71; 86, f. 164; APC, xxvi. 207; Townshend, Hist. Colls. 228; VCH Berks. iii. 330; see also BLOUNT, Richard I. [4] D'Ewes, 430, 436, 450, 451, 454, 505, 506, 553, 554, 555, 556, 557, 558, 559, 562, 563, 564, 571, 572, 573, 575, 581, 583, 592, 624, 629, 632, 634, 635, 642, 644, 645, 647, 650, 653–4, 662, 663, 665, 670, 676, 679, 684, 686, 687; Bull. IHR, xii. 11; Townshend, 19, 103, 104, 109, 114, 115, 121, 203, 207, 222, 225, 228, 229, 233, 252, 260, 290, 303, 304, 308, 313, 323, 334. [5] M.T. Recs. ii. 441; C142/392/111; PCC 98 Dale.

A.H./M.A.P.

MOORE, Jasper (c.1550–1610), of Heytesbury, Wilts.

HEYTESBURY   1572*[1]

b. c.1550, 4th s. of Thomas Moore of Taunton, Som., being 1st s. by his 2nd w. Elizabeth, da. of William Stukley. educ. G. Inn 1565. m. c.1583, Katherine, da. of Sir Thomas Pakington of Aylesbury, Bucks., wid. of John Davy of West Harnham, s.p. Kntd. 23 July 1603.[2]

J.p. Wilts. 1577, q. 1592, sheriff 1583–4, 1602–3, keeper of Mere park 1592.[3]

Moore had already established himself in Wiltshire by 1576, when he was assessed for subsidy on lands worth £32 in the east tithing of Heytesbury and was called upon to pay £4 5s. 4d. No explanation has been found for his migration from Somerset to Wiltshire or of how he acquired considerable property there. From his father he received the Somerset manor of Withies and a remainder in the priory of Taunton, but it was at Heytesbury that he settled and in Wiltshire that he pursued his public career. There is no trace of him at either university, nor evidence of his legal training beyond his entry to Gray's Inn. It may have been his practice of the law which led him to his new county and yielded the wherewithal to set himself up there. His marriage to the widowed sister of Mary Pakington, second wife of Sir Walter Long*, both connected him with a number of Wiltshire families and brought him the lease of West Harnham, near Salisbury,

left to his wife by her first husband. He was also to make friends elsewhere in the county, for when Jeffery Whitaker the clothier of Tinhead, whose brother Henry sat for Westbury in 1586, came to make his will in March 1600 he left Moore £160 in trust for his daughter Penelope, appointed him an overseer and gave him his choice of a gelding.[4]

Moore is first heard of in an official capacity when in February 1578 he and others were directed by the Privy Council to investigate abuses in clothmaking in assocation with the notorious Peter Blackborough. He was appointed to the Wiltshire commission of the peace and in 1583 served the first of his two terms as sheriff. By then he had already made his brief and solitary appearance in the House of Commons; the death of Sir John Thynne in 1580 created a vacancy at Heytesbury which Moore filled for the ensuing session. The local standing which secured his election on that occasion might be expected to have done so on at least one other. But so far as Heytesbury was concerned he probably forfeited that prospect by the activities which some years later were to sting the townsmen into an appeal to the Privy Council. In 1589 they charged him and others whose names do not appear, 'lords of the said town', with damage to its hospital and free school by their surcharging of commons, illegal erection of tenements, enclosure and breach of customs. The hostility thus glimpsed may explain why half a century was to pass before a Moore again sat for Heytesbury.[5]

It does not seem, however, to have impaired Moore's wider reputation. He was to be sheriff again in 1602–3, and his knighthood, even though he received it at one of James I's mass creations, marked his social advance. In 1605 he was one of the 20 knights who accompanied the Earl of Hertford on his embassy to Brussels. Three years later he was listed as a principal landowner in the parish of Brook, Wiltshire. The Jasper Moore who was escheator of Shropshire in 1600 was presumably another man, perhaps his half-brother.[6]

Moore had made his will on 1 June 1597. He prefaced it with an affirmation of the Christian man's duty to do so in good time, so that in his last illness he should not be distracted by worldly preoccupation. To his widow he left clothing and household goods, including those given to her by her former husband and chiefly remaining in West Harnham parsonage, grain in the barns there, and a coach and two horses. He left £5 to the parish church of Heytesbury and made other bequests to his servants and carters. The residue was to pass to his executors, his 'nephew' William Guyes and his wife Elizabeth; this was Elizabeth, his sister Florence Walrond's daughter. She and her husband were to inherit his rights in the manor and hundred of Heytesbury. During the 13 years which elapsed between the making of the will and his death Moore added two codicils; by the first, of 1606, he left his wife all money in the house at his death, and a further £200 in cash, and by the second, of 1609, he increased that sum to £400 and added to it the lease of West Harnham. At the time of his death Moore was evidently administering the estate of Sir Edward Estcourt, the residue of whose goods he left to his own executors. Moore died at West Harnham on 7 Mar. 1610. At the inquisition held on 27 Sept. 1613 his heirs were declared to be his niece Elizabeth Guyes and his great-nephew Shilston Cadmadie.[7]

[1] C219/283/22, 23. [2] *Wilts. Vis. Peds.* (Harl. Soc. cv, cvi), 137. [3] *Wilts. Arch. Mag.* xxix. 242. [4] *Two Taxation Lists* (Wilts. Arch. Soc. rec. br. x), 141; C142/172/118; Wards 7/16/42; PCC 25 Woodhall; *Wilts. N. and Q.* iv. 109–110. [5] *APC,* x. 157–8; xvii. 303–4. [6] *HMC Bath,* iv. 200; *Wilts. Arch. Mag.* i. 298; *HMC Hatfield,* x. 94–5. [7] PCC 35 Wingfield; C142/411/154.

S.T.B.

MOORE, John I (1536–97), of Blake Street, York and Bewick, Yorks.

HEDON   1572

b. 1536, 1st s. of Robert Moore of Bewick by Elizabeth, sis. of Sir Edward Darell. *educ.* Christ Church, Oxf. 1555, BA 1556; L. Inn 1560, called 1569. *m.* 1569 Katherine (*d.*1634), da. of John Holme of Paull Holme, wid. of Marmaduke Constable of Wassand, *s.p. suc.* fa. 1581.[1]

J.p. Yorks (E. Riding) from c.1577, q. 1579; commr. oyer and terminer, north parts 1577.[2]

Although the eldest son of a landowner of some substance in Holderness, John Moore was an active lawyer and remained so even after succeeding to the family estates in 1581. After being called to the bar he practised in York, where he was closely connected with the council in the north. His loyalty was beyond question and in 1592 he was one of the East Riding magistrates deputed to impose the oath of supremacy in the county. Not long before his death, in December 1597, he was one of three lawyers recommended by the council at York as fit to succeed William Paler*, the Queen's attorney in the north – and a previous Member of Parliament for Hedon – who had just died.[3]

Details of Moore's life remain obscure, partly because of the confusion which has arisen between him and a namesake also living in York, a serjeant-at-arms in attendance upon the council in the north. Both apparently had married ladies named Katherine. The serjeant-at-arms, however, was buried in St. Michael-le-Belfry in 1595, while the lawyer, who died on 21 Dec. 1597, was buried in the Lady Chapel of the minster. Here his wife joined him in 1634 after, as her monumental inscription tells us, having lived a widow for 36 years. It seems likely that it was the lawyer, a native of Holderness, who married the widow of Marmaduke Constable, herself a native of that district. If so, his return to Parliament for Hedon in 1572 becomes intelligible. Constable's widow remarried within

the year and she and her second husband remained closely associated with the Wassand estates during the minority of her children. Thus, as a neighbour in Holderness, as a servant of the council in the north, and as a family connexion, Moore would be recommended to Sir John Constable*, a patron of the borough.

Little further is known of Moore, except what can be learnt from his conventional epitaph, which describes him as learned in the law and of upright life; distinguished by agreeableness and integrity, willingly sharing his resources with the poor; devoid of vice, and placing his reliance upon faith in Christ.[4]

[1] *Yorks. Peds.* (Harl. Soc. xcv), ii. 288–9; Dugdale, *Vis. Yorks.* iii. 48; Foster, *Yorks. Peds.* ii. [2] SP12/121. [3] *Black Bk. L. Inn,* i. 366, 458; *APC,* xxiii. 257; *HMC Hatfield,* vii. 493, 506. [4] *York Wills* (Yorks. Arch. Soc. rec. ser. xxiv), 72; *Notices of Scoreby and Fam. of Blake* (Yorks. Arch. Jnl. x), 101–2; *Wills and Inventories* (Surtees Soc. xxxviii), 142; *Monumental Brasses in York* (Yorks. Arch. Jnl. xviii), 33; Drake, *Eboracum,* 514.

I.C.

MOORE, John II, of Dover, Kent.

DOVER   1584, 1586

2nd s. and h. of William Moore of Haddon, Oxon. by Margaret, da. and h. of one Henham, of Cambs. *m.* Margery, da. and h. of William Hayward of Harty, Isle of Sheppey, 3da.[1]

Freeman, Dover Jan. 1584, common councilman July 1584, jurat at least in the years 1584–91, 1594–5,[2] mayor 1595–6.[3]

The Moores of Haddon were a recusant family. Moore himself moved to Kent where his advance in Dover civic affairs was rapid. In January 1584 he was 'admitted and sworn a freeman of Dover by the purchase of a house of the yearly rent of 50s.', and by the following November he had been returned to Parliament for the port. Both on this occasion and in the 1586 Parliament his fellow-Member for Dover was the lord warden's nominee, Richard Barrey. Shortly after his first Parliament Moore presented an account of his expenses for travelling and subsistence to the Dover common assembly; the amount was not entered in the council minutes. Both Members were paid 2s. 6d. a day in 1586. In the new year sittings of the 1584–5 Parliament, on 15 Feb., Moore presented a petition 'touching the abuses in the ministry' on behalf of the inhabitants of Folkestone. This was one of a group of puritan petitions offered to Parliament on the same day, and it suggests that he may have sympathized with their cause. As burgess for Dover he may have attended a committee concerning the import of fish on 6 Mar. 1587.[4]

Moore was active in local politics in Dover for a period of just over ten years. Between 1591 and 1594, however, his name disappears from the council records, and in other years he is mentioned as being absent from the ceremonies in which local officials were elected and sworn.

Perhaps his occupation, which has not been traced, entailed frequent absences from the town. In 1586 and 1587 he was one of those who represented Dover at the brodhull meetings of the Cinque Ports, and in the latter year helped to organize the local watch in case of an impending invasion. One of the features of Dover local history in the sixteenth century was its fierce civic discord, and Moore did not remain aloof from the struggles. In August 1582, for example, he was fined £10 and imprisoned for a short time for 'breaking the Queen's Majesty's peace against John Harries, deputy bailiff of Dover, in the presence of the mayor, and shedding of blood'. On another occasion he was charged with contempt for not answering a summons to appear before the town council.[5]

In addition to his house in Dover Moore owned land in Sheppey, possibly acquired through his wife, worth (in 1585) £18 13s. 4d. a year. It is quite likely that he was the 'John Moore' who, in 1592, was leasing some of the land formerly belonging to Dover priory. That he was a man of some substance is suggested by a local 'cess' or levy, taken in 1587: here his assessment was twice that of most of the other jurats.[6]

At the end of his mayoralty, in 1596, Moore told the assembly that he would decline re-election as a jurat because he was 'presently to depart the town and to sojourn in Dover castle'. The castle records having been destroyed, it is not known what this implies. No later references to him have been found, unless he was 'my cousin John More dwelling with me in my house at Haddon' mentioned in the 1608 will of William Moore of Haddon. It is possible that it was the lord warden's service that brought him from Haddon to Dover in the first place, but he was clearly not nominated by Lord Cobham for Parliament.[7]

[1] *Vis. Kent* (Harl. Soc. lxxv), 138. [2] Egerton 2095, ff. 289, 299, 303, 411. [3] Several printed lists of mayors of Dover, e.g. J. B. Jones, *Dover Annals*, 301, state that George Byng was mayor in 1595–6, but the common council minutes show that Moore held the office in that year. [4] *HMC Hatfield*, iv. 270; Egerton 2095, ff. 306–7, 313, 337; D'Ewes, 349, 412. [5] Cinque Ports black bk. f. 53; Egerton 2095, ff. 115, 255, 348. [6] Add. 38823, f. 41; C. Haines, *Dover Priory*, 134. [7] Egerton 2095, f. 418; PCC 13 Dorset.

M.R.P.

MOORE, John III (c.1562–1620), of Lincoln's Inn, London, and North Baddesley, Hants.

WINCHESTER	1597
PORTSMOUTH	1601
WINCHESTER	1604

b. c.1562, ?s. of William More, recorder of Winchester 1548. *educ.* Furnival's Inn; L. Inn 1581, called 1589. *m.* Dowsabelle, da. of James Pagett, wid. of William Pawlet, at least 1s. 2da.

Under-steward, Portsmouth 1590, freeman 1591,

recorder 1600–15; recorder, Winchester 1595; bencher, L. Inn 1603, Autumn reader 1608, keeper of the black bk. 1613–14; serjeant-at-law 1614; j.p.q. Hants by 1601.

Moore was a lawyer who sat in Parliament for the two Hampshire towns where he was recorder. It is not possible to distinguish him with any certainty from other Members of the same name, but he may have been the Mr. Moore who was on the committee of a bill about printers and printing 17 Dec. 1597, and as burgess for Winchester he would have been entitled to attend a committee on bread on 13 Jan. 1598. He had been associated with the city since 1582. Shortly before his death he acquired property in Hampshire, including the manor and rectory of North Baddesley (which he bought from Thomas Fleming I*, his predecessor as reader), two manors in Romsey, and the manor and advowson of Chilworth. He died 15 Aug. 1620, and was buried at Baddesley.

C142/382/30, 389/121; *Black Bk. of Winchester*, 196; PCC 91 Soame; R. East, *Portsmouth Recs.* 139, 346, 420; *OR*, i. 434; *L. Inn Black Bk.* ii. 79, 108, 158, 167; SP13/Case F/11, ff. 29b–30b; D'Ewes, 579, 687; *Hants Field Club Procs.* iii. 115–26; information from Dr. Adrienne Batchelor Rosen.

A.M.M.

MORDAUNT, Lewis (1538–1601), of Turvey, Beds., and Drayton, Northants.

BEDFORDSHIRE	1563

b. 1538, 1st s. of Sir John Mordaunt†, 2nd Baron Mordaunt, by his 1st w. Ela, da. of John Fitzlewis, s. and h. app. of Sir Richard Fitzlewis† of West Horndon, Essex, h. to her gd.-mother Alice, da. and coh. of John Harleston of Shrimpling, Norf. *m.* Elizabeth, da. of Sir Arthur Darcy, sis. of Thomas Lord Darcy, 1s. 3da. Kntd. 1568; *suc.* fa. as 3rd Baron 1571.[1]

J.p.q. Beds. from c.1564; Northants. from c.1583; sheriff, Beds. and Bucks. 1570–1; commr. musters, Beds. 1569, Northants. 1577, trial of Mary Stuart 1586, to search for Jesuits, Northants. 1591, to suppress recusancy, Beds. Aug. 1592.[2]

The Mordaunts married heiresses of the Latimer, Vere and Fitzlewis families, and the 1563 Member inherited land in Bedfordshire, Buckinghamshire, Dorset, Essex, Hertfordshire, Northamptonshire and Somerset. He was for some time on bad terms with his father, owing to his refusal to marry a daughter of his stepmother Joan, daughter of Richard Fermor† of Northamptonshire and widow of Robert Wilford, merchant tailor of London. An undated Chancery case shows father and son quarrelling over land in Stagsden, Bedfordshire, and the elder Mordaunt carried out a recovery of the Fitzlewis lands to his own use for life, after his death to be transferred for 92 years to 'such as it pleased him to appoint'. This attempt to deprive the heir of the profits of a large part of his estates was countered by old Lord Mordaunt, father of

John and grandfather of Lewis, who made another conveyance, ensuring his own lands to Lewis on the latter's marriage to someone more suitable in rank. After succeeding to the estates in 1571, Mordaunt lived mainly at Turvey and on his grandmother's property at Drayton, Northamptonshire, where he carried out extensive building, some of it financed by sales of land in Essex and the west country.[3]

He was an active official in Bedfordshire and later in Northamptonshire. In April 1565 he was one of those asked by the Council to 'take care in the good assessing of the [Bedfordshire] subsidy'; in 1580 he served on the Northamptonshire commission for breeding horses, and he was among the 'principal nobles' who in September 1586 advised the Queen 'on the present state of the realm', owing to the growing danger from Spain. On 23 July 1588, with the Armada excitement at its height, the Council instructed him to come to London, bringing such lances and light horsemen as he could raise. There is another reference to his attending the Queen with troops in 1599, when another attack by Spain was expected.[4]

The family historian describes Mordaunt as

a person of great justice, nobleness and affability, very well parted, and ingenious. He was the idol of the province where he lived, and one that drew unto him more respect and love than all the great men of those parts. Though he was no courtier, yet he was much honoured by them all, and he had a near friendship with the Earl of Leicester and the Lord Chancellor Hatton,

a portrait not borne out by the scattered references to his private life. He was several times asked by the Privy Council to explain affrays resulting from quarrels between his servants and those of Adrian Stokes* about unlawful hunting in Brigstock park, Northamptonshire, where Stokes was keeper; the justices of assize were suspected of partiality towards Mordaunt's followers. On another occasion the Council advised him to show more generosity to a poor tenant over a disputed title to land.[5]

Several members of his family were suspected of Catholicism, and, though described by his bishop as 'earnest' in religion in 1564, his name appears on a Catholic list of 1582 as one favourable to Mary Stuart. According to Camden, Mordaunt agreed most unwillingly to the sentence on Mary Stuart, whose funeral on 1 Aug. 1587 the government ordered him to attend. About November 1586 one of Walsingham's spies reported that Mordaunt and the 4th Earl of Worcester had taken a wherry down the river to Ratcliff, where the *Red Lion* was a favourite haunt of the recusant Francis Brown. He was friendly with the Catholic (presumably 3rd) Lord Vaux, and stood surety for some debts of Sir Thomas Tresham, who defaulted, since his recusancy adversely affected his credit worthiness. Still, he must have conformed, and the

government continued to trust him on religious matters, as in the 1590s he served on commissions to take oaths of supremacy, to prosecute recusants and to search out Jesuits and seminary priests. He died at Drayton 16 June 1601, and was buried 20 July at Turvey. By his will, dated October 1593, £80 was to be spent on an alabaster tomb with 'pictures' of himself and his wife, and £70 distributed to the poor at his burial. He left £2,000 each to his two unmarried daughters Katherine and Elizabeth, appointing two executors to administer lands for this purpose. The residuary legatee, and the sole executor for all other parts of the will, was his only son Henry, aged 33, the Lord Mordaunt arrested after the Gunpowder Plot.[6]

[1] *CP*; Wards 7/1/70; Halstead, *Genealogies Mordaunt of Turvey* (1685), p. 627; *Vis. Beds.* (Harl. Soc. xix), 42. [2] *Cam. Misc.* ix(3), p. 28; *CSP Dom.* 1547–80, p. 341; *APC*, ix. 322; xxiii. 111–12; *HMC Var.* iii. 61; *HMC Bath*, v. 74. [3] Wards 7/26/28; C3/123/29; Halstead, 402–3, 605–7; PCC 39 Holney; Harl. 6767, f. 21v. [4] Lansd. 8, f. 77; Halstead, 607, 613; *HMC Buccleuch*, iii. 18; *APC*, xvi. 169–70; *HMC Foljambe*, 44, 85. [5] Harl. 6767, f. 21v; *APC*, ix. 220; xi. 51, 63; xxii. 190, 249; Halstead, 403, 614. [6] *APC*, xv. 153; xxiii. 111–12; Halstead, 402–3, 613, 619–25; *Cam. Misc.* ix(3), p. 28; *HMC Var.* iii. 33–4, 46, 61; *HMC Bath*, v. 83; *CSP Dom.* 1581–90, p. 370; Wards 7/26/28; *CP*.

N.M.F.

MORDAUNT, Robert (*d.* 1602), of Westbury, Bucks., Little Massingham, Norf. and Hempstead, Essex.

NEWPORT IUXTA LAUNCESTON 1584[1]

3rd s. of Robert Mordaunt of Hempstead by Barbara, da. and h. of John Lestrange of Little Massingham. *m.* after 1550, Jane, da. and h. of Henry Pyne‡, of Ham in Morwenstow, Cornw., wid. of Walter Porter of Launcells, Cornw., *s.p.* suc. bro. 1574.
    Escheator, Beds. and Bucks. 1583–4.[2]

The Mordaunts had accumulated extensive lands through marriages with heiresses. Mordaunt's grandfather was a younger son of the Mordaunts of Turvey, Bedfordshire, from whom descended the Lords Mordaunt and the earls of Peterborough: Lewis Mordaunt* was thus a distant cousin. The younger branch of the family had settled at Hempstead, and Mordaunt's father had made a fortunate marriage with Barbara Lestrange, who brought him land at Little Massingham in Norfolk and Westbury in Buckinghamshire, which was added to the Essex property at Great Sampford, Roding Berners, Wood Hall and Hempstead. Though a younger son, Mordaunt inherited all this. His father was succeeded at his death in 1572 by a grandson, but the boy died less than two years later and was succeeded by his uncle James, Mordaunt's elder brother. A few months later he too was dead.[3]

However, though the list of Mordaunt's manors is impressive, he never attained a place on the commission of the peace, perhaps because of Catholic religious views. His Cornish borough seat in Parliament came to him through his wife's family connexions, the Grenvilles of Penheale, patrons of the borough of Newport. Mordaunt himself was described in the 1559 pardon roll as 'late of Morwenstow, Cornwall' where he had apparently been living on his wife's property, situated in that north-eastern portion of Cornwall which also contained the Grenvilles' seat at Penheale and Newport itself.[4]

Mordaunt died apparently intestate 29 May 1602. His wife made her will a few months after his death;

> renouncing all sects, schisms and heresies, I do firmly and without all doubt hold and believe the Christian faith and every part and point thereof, as our mother the Holy Catholic Church, instructed by the promised spirit of truth, hath taught and declared.[5]

[1] Add. 38823, f. 17. [2] *Vis. Essex* (Harl. Soc. xiii), 253–4, 456–7; Vivian, *Vis. Cornw.* 83. [3] *CP*, ix. 193–7; T. Wright, *Essex*, ii. 79, 279; P. Morant, *Essex*, ii. 365, 475, 529; *VCH Beds.* iv. 251, 264; Blomefield, *Norf.* ix. 17; C142/153/31, 163/53, 170/47. [4] Vivian, *Vis. Cornw.* 84, 383; *Vis. Cornw.* (Harl. Soc. ix), 40, 84–5; *CPR*, 1558–60, p. 180. [5] C142/268/159; PCC 98 Harte; *Al. Ox.* (early ser.), 1224.

I.C.

MORE, Edward (c.1555–1623), of Crabbet, Worth, Suss., Canon Row, Westminster and Odiham, Hants.

MIDHURST	1584
HAMPSHIRE	1601

b. c.1555, o.s. of John More† of Crabbet by Anne or Agnes, da. of John Moulton of Lancs. and Westminster. *educ.* ?Hart Hall, Oxf. by 1568; M. Temple 1 May 1571. *m.* (1) Mary (*d.* 29 Oct. 1591), da. and coh. of Adrian Poynings* of Wherwell, Hants, 5s. 1da.; (2) Lady Frances Brooke *alias* Cobham†, 10th Lord Cobham, wid. of John, 9th Lord Stourton, 1da. Several ch. illegit. *suc.* fa. 1581. Kntd. 1600.[1]

Gent. pens. by 1577–*d.*; j.p. Surr., Suss. from c.1582–c.87, Hants from c.1584.

When More entered the Middle Temple he was bound with his father and Richard Inkpen*, a close associate of Edward Banester*, one of More's predecessors as Member of Parliament for Midhurst, but after a fine for absence from readings, and pardon for another on grounds of ill-health, his name disappears from the Temple records, and within a short time re-appears among the gentlemen pensioners at court. From the late 1570s until at least the end of the reign, when he was an official attendant at the Queen's funeral, he divided his time between the court and his country estates in Sussex and, later, Hampshire. He had a long correspondence with Robert Cecil* over the will of Lady Dacre, widow of the 10th Lord Dacre of the South, who died in 1595 leaving a large part of her estates in Sussex and London to the Cecil family. More was one of the executors of the will and may indeed have been in her service in some capacity. The fact that Lord Buckhurst was also interested in some of the property delayed a final

settlement for several years; More was one of the principal figures involved in the negotiations.

In 1598 he passed on a message of loyalty to Cecil from the new Lord Cobham, who was brother-in-law to both of them, and in 1602 he wrote to the Secretary asking him to find a military appointment in Ireland for his son Edward, who might 'in time, by his care and travail, recover some part of the credit he has lost' (through a marriage of which the father disapproved). Most interesting of all the letters, however, is one dated March 1594 in which More, hearing of the death of George Goring I*, offered Cecil and his father £1,000 for the office of receiver of the court of wards, if they could obtain it for him without further expense. He would withdraw his request if the post was likely to go to George Goring II*.[2]

More was first returned to Parliament in 1584 for Viscount Montagu's borough of Midhurst. It is possible that he owed this to Montagu, who as a fellow-landowner in western Sussex no doubt knew him personally. It has been suggested that More shared the Viscount's Catholicism,[3] and indeed he had many Catholic contacts, including Lady Dacre, the Stourtons (into which family his second wife had previously been married), and members of several leading Sussex families, but as he was on the commission of the peace for three counties, he probably conformed outwardly to the Elizabethan church. In any case he may have owed his return at Midhurst not to Montagu himself but to Richard Lewknor*, who secured the election of several relatives and friends at Midhurst about this time. Nothing is known of any activity by More in his first Parliament.

A case brought in the Star Chamber by James Colbrand* provides evidence of More's connexion with Lewknor, and suggests that More stood unsuccessfully for one of the Sussex county seats in 1586. During the election campaign at Chichester, when More was supporting Lewknor, he became involved in a dispute with Colbrand over their respective social standing and the number of tenants' votes at their command. Colbrand made the disobliging assertion that More's father cut bread in the pantry at court. The entry in D'Ewes's *Journal* for the 1597 Parliament recording that 'Mr. Edward Moore' brought into the House a bill concerning armour and weapons must refer to George More, who did sit on this committee – there is no evidence that Edward was in the Parliament.[4]

At some time in the 1580s More moved to Odiham in Hampshire, where his social position and work as a local administrator enabled him to acquire a county seat in the last Parliament of the reign. During this Parliament he was named to a committee concerning London hospitals on 23 Nov. (which he reported on 8 Dec.), to a private committee on 28 Nov. and to a committee concerning kerseys on 14 Dec. He was probably the 'Mr. Moore' who reported the committee on Cree church on 9 Dec. As knight for Hampshire he was entitled to attend the main business committee (3 Nov.), and committees on clothworkers (18 Nov.) and monopolies (23 Nov.). Though no surviving parliamentary returns of a later date bear his name, this may not have been the end of his career in the Commons. In February 1606, while Parliament was sitting, the Earl of Mar, owner of the manor of Odiham where More lived, reported to Robert Cecil that More intended to seek satisfaction with regard to some leases he held from the Earl 'in a bill which he has brought into Parliament'.[5]

After the turn of the century More spent more time on his country estates and less at court. By that date his possessions were extensive. He enlarged the family holdings at Crabbet, Sussex, building a new house there, and also held the adjoining manor of Worth, with land in seven other parishes. In Surrey he had sold Kinnersley manor, Horley, but still owned some smaller properties. To these he later added Hurtmore, near Godalming, bought in 1606, and Drockenfield manor in Frensham, purchased, with two other men, from Viscount Montagu in 1614. George More* of Loseley, a relative by marriage, sold him Witley Park and leased him iron works at Thursley and Witley for ten years at £95 a year. The lease included equipment and workers' houses. In London he owned land at St. Margaret's and two houses in Canon Row, Westminster, one of which was occupied by Sir Thomas Waller†. In Wales he owned monastic property in Anglesey. An indenture which More drew up in 1602 estimated his lands as being then worth £790 p.a. and that their value would run into four figures within seven years. This indenture throws more light on the quarrel in the More family to which reference has already been made, for it was drawn up to disinherit Edward, the eldest son:

> Whereas Edward More ... notwithstanding the tender love and care that ... Sir Edward has always had over him and the education he [has] given him in schools of learning, universities and travel in foreign countries, to his great charge, hath of late married himself without the ... consent of the said Sir Edward and upon small acquaintance with the woman, which the said Sir Edward for many respects utterly misliketh, [he] is thereby grown out of hope of his well doing and resolved not to trust him with any immediate estate or remainder of his lands and inheritance.

The reasons for his hostility to the lady, who was Dutch, are not clear. Now, surprisingly, he declared his heirs not to be his other children by Mary Poynings, but illegitimate children by three other ladies including Dorothy, daughter of Francis Moore* of the Middle Temple, and Amy, daughter of William Gibbs, also of the Middle Temple. Francis Moore was a witness to the arrangement together with Sir George More of Loseley and Sir Thomas Drewe of Broadhembury, Devon, Sir Edward's son-in-law. The document was drawn up after he had married Lady Stourton as his second wife, but before their daughter was born.[6]

Later in his life More rescinded part of this settlement, giving property to his second legitimate son Adrian on the occasion of his marriage, but he does not seem to have forgiven Edward. Ironically, Sir Edward outlived all his sons, and the eventual heir, when he died in the spring of 1623, was a grandson, the son of the disinherited Edward and his Dutch wife. In his will, More hoped 'to be saved by that bitter death and bloody passion which I believe that Jesus Christ suffered for me, and not by any other works or means', and a letter which he wrote in 1614 provides further evidence about his religious beliefs in the last years of his life. Robert Johnson, vicar of Odiham, accompanied his supplication for a divinity degree at Oxford with the following letter from More:

> Mr. Johnson has been careful in his study and diligent in his preaching, which has been appreciated by his auditory of the best understanding. On account of the smallness of the living, he accepted a lectureship at Great Allhallows, London, for a year and put in a curate here who, in his absence, joining with a faction of troublesome spirits (that profess preciseness of life but practise for the most part malice and dissension) went about to supplant him and to leave no course unattempted that might give them hope of getting his living from him. In this they failed. They had an old quarrel with him because he had, at his first coming, to oppose another troublesome minister of their profession who made some pretence to the vicarage. On this occasion they preferred articles to the High Commission against him. I am one of these commissioners and I have never heard that he was ever censured ... for any matter contained in these articles.

More's will, drawn up 24 Apr. 1623, was proved on 19 May; he asked to be buried in the chancel of Odiham church, 'near unto my two wives'. The executors were given a lease of all his property, in the hope that they could buy the grandson's wardship. More had founded almshouses at Odiham, modelled on Lady Dacre's Emmanuel hospital, Westminster, and he left money for their maintenance. The lease of the manor of Odiham, which may not have had long to run, he left to his daughter, Lady Drewe, on payment of £800. Other relatives were left small annuities. In a codicil, he bequeathed his second wife's clothes to their daughter, now Lady Stourton, and to a grandson a gilt basin bearing the Poynings arms. To his friend Sir Robert Heath, the King's 'solicitor', he left 'my salt which standeth upon pillars of crystal', and to Sir William Pitt 'a ring which my Lord of Salisbury gave me'. There is no mention of his illegitimate children.[7]

[1] *Suss. Rec. Soc.* xxxiii. 1, 16; *Vis. Hants* (Harl. Soc. lxiv), 172–3; Manning and Bray, *Hist. Surr.* i. 626, 628; *CPR*, 1553 and App. Ed. VI, 310; *VCH Hants*, iv. 97. [2] *M.T. Recs.* i. 177, 182, 190; LC2/4/4; *HMC Hatfield*, ii. 218; iv. 497; v. 205–6, 241, 293; vi. 440; viii. 38, 222; x. 309, 311, 313; xii. 199; Lansd. 77, ff. 71 seq.; 86, ff. 164 seq. [3] W. S. Blunt, *Hist. Crabbet*, i. 7. [4] Neale, *Commons*, 266–8; D'Ewes, 624, 642, 648, 649, 658, 670, 674, 684. [5] *APC*, xxii. 222; xxiii. 161–3;

xxiv. 78–9; D'Ewes, 648, 658, 684; *CSP Dom.* 1603–10, p. 286. [6] *VCH Suss.* vii. 195; *Suss. Rec. Soc.* xix. 218, 219; xx. 505; xxxiii. 110; Blunt, i. 2, 6, 11–14, 15–17, 25–6; *VCH Surr.* ii. 273–4, 614; iii. 34, 64, 65, 203; *Surr. Arch. Colls.* xviii. 27, 78; *CPR*, 1563–6, p. 94. [7] Blunt, i. 18–24; W. H. Mildon, 'Puritanism in Hampshire and the Isle of Wight' (Univ. London PhD thesis, 1934), pp. 91–2; PCC 53 Swann.

M.R.P.

MORE, George (1553–1632), of Loseley, Surr.

GUILDFORD	1584, 1586, 1589, 1593
SURREY	1597, 1601
GUILDFORD	1604
SURREY	1614, 1621
GUILDFORD	1624
SURREY	1625, 1626

b. 28 Nov. 1553, o.s. of William More I* by his 2nd w. Margaret, da. and h. of Ralph Daniell of Swaffham, Norf. *educ.* Corpus, Oxf. c.1570–4; I. Temple 1574. *m.* (1) Anne (*d.* 1590), da. and coh. of Adrian Poynings*, 4s. inc. Robert* 5da.; (2) Constance, ?da. of John Michell of Stammerham, Suss., wid. of Richard Knight of St. Denys, Hants, *s.p.* Kntd. c.1598; *suc.* fa. 1600.[1]

Member of Earl of Leicester's household by 1579; commr. musters, Surr. 1580; j.p. Surr. from c.1582, sheriff, Surr. and Suss. 1597–8, Suss. from 1601; commr. recusants, Surr., collector of the loan 1598, dep. lt. 1600; chamberlain of receipt in the Exchequer 1601; treasurer and receiver-gen. to Henry, Prince of Wales ?1603; chancellor of order of the Garter 1611–30; lt. of the Tower 1615–17.[2]

After Oxford and the Inner Temple, More entered the service of the Earl of Leicester, who wrote to More's father:

> I must thank you for him, and do think myself more and more beholding to you, that hath bestowed such a one as not only was dearest to yourself, but I assure you upon my truth is as much to my own liking and contentation every way as my heart can wish ... And as before I knew him he was very welcome to me for your sake, as any of yours must be, so now I must confess he is dear to me for his own sake: so the fruit of his good bringing up doth sufficiently and plainly enough appear in his daily behaviour.[3]

More entered Parliament at the age of about 30, and would no doubt have done so earlier had there been a general election between 1572 and 1584. He represented either his county or Guildford, adjoining the family seat at Loseley, in 12 consecutive Parliaments. His father was a leading Surrey gentleman, in high favour with the Queen; his sister Elizabeth held a court position, and married as her second and third husbands John Wolley* and Thomas Egerton*; while two leading courtiers, Leicester and Lord Howard of Effingham (the latter the leading magnate in Surrey), were friendly with his family. More was an assiduous Commons committeeman and a more prominent speaker than his father in the House. His

committee work covered some of the most important measures of the second half of Elizabeth's reign. In 1584 he was appointed to two committees concerning the better observing of the Sabbath day (27 Nov., 10 Dec.). He made a motion concerning libellers on 19 Feb. 1585, and was put in charge of the ensuing committee. During his second Parliament (1586) he was named to the committee concerning the Queen of Scots (4 Nov.) and the following day he made a speech on the subject, concluding 'after sundry great and weighty reasons first showed' that

> only Popery is the chief and principal root of all the late horrible and wicked treacheries and practices, and the Queen of Scots a principal branch issuing from the same root, and the most perilous and full of poison of all the other branches thereof ... [Catholics] either wish or could easily bear the death of our sovereign lady, the Queen's Majesty, though perhaps they would not show themselves to be actors or dealers therein.

He asked that the existing laws against Catholics should be enforced and that the Queen should be petitioned to retain near her person 'such only as may be well known both to profess the true and sincere religion, and also to be every way true and faithful subjects'. On 8 Nov. he was one of those who made 'sundry speeches' concerning the Queen's safety. He was appointed to the subsidy committee on 18 Mar. 1587.

More spoke on the subject of the reform of purveyors' practices on 15 Feb. 1589 and was appointed to the ensuing committee on the same day. He also attended a conference with the Lords on 27 Feb. concerning the Queen's dislike of the purveyors bill and was appointed to a second committee that day to discuss the Commons' course of action over the bill. Other committee work in this Parliament concerned topics such as the subsidy (11 Feb.), Exchequer reform (18 Feb.), forestallers (5 Mar.), a private bill (15 Mar.) and glass factories (19 Mar.). In 1593 More was appointed to two committees concerning the subsidy (26 Feb., 1 Mar.), and spoke on the subject on 7 Mar.

> ... I speak it with grief, how perilous our estate is and how dangerous a cause we be in. We are not sick of one disease but we labour with a plurality of diseases. To meet therefore with our threefold diseases we ought like good physicians to apply a threefold remedy, a treble subsidy. And as the physic is lost which is not taken in time, so we must seek to minister the medicine in good time. And our disease being a pleurisy it is fit we did so. For a skilful physician though he see in a pleurisy there is no remedy without letting blood, yet he will then choose the time of letting blood when the sign is furthest from the heart. Let us let the people blood, and so prevent the danger.

He spoke twice on matters of privilege and returns (26 Feb., 2 Mar.), and was named to the first standing committee on these subjects (26 Feb.) as well as to committees concerning recusants (28 Feb., 4 Apr.), forgery (10 Mar.), the punishment of rogues (12 Mar.), kerseys (2 Apr.) and timber (5 Apr.).

On 8 Nov. 1597 he proposed a motion concerning the keeping of armour and weapons and was appointed to the committee, which he reported on 14 Nov. On 2 Dec. he brought the bill into the House. He also spoke on a disputed election at Ludlow on 12 Nov. His committees included privileges and returns (5 Nov.), penal laws (8 Nov.), ecclesiastical grievances (14 Nov.), the poor law (19, 22 Nov.), Staines bridge (1 Dec., reported by him 3 Dec.), the double payment on shop books (2 Dec.), tellers and receivers (5 Dec., 23 Jan. 1598), lewd wandering persons (7 Dec.), the export of corn (8 Dec.), painters and stainers (12 Dec.), tillage (13 Dec.), wine casks (3 Feb. 1598) and pawnbrokers (7 Feb.). As knight for Surrey in 1597 he was also entitled to attend committees concerning enclosures (5 Nov.), monopolies (10 Nov.), the subsidy (15 Nov.) and the repair of the Queen's highways in Sussex, Surrey and Kent (27 Jan. 1598).

At the beginning of the 1601 Parliament More moved that a committee be set up to consider the order of business for the session (3 Nov.), to which he was appointed as knight of the shire. He was active in debate during this session: on the same day he made a second motion on the subject of horse stealing, and spoke against drunkenness during a debate on alehouses:

> For although there were laws already against it, yet they did not reach grievous enough to the offence in that kind now committed. And therefore we must not be like spiders that always keep their old and the same webs, so allowing the same laws which must alter with the times. And touching the authority that is given to the justices of assize and justices of the peace by this bill, that they shall assign inns and innkeepers, I think that inconvenient: for an inn is a man's inheritance, and they are set at great rates, and therefore not to be taken away from any particular man.

He spoke again on the subject of alehouses on 10 Dec. wishing that a controversial bill advocating their suppression be committed. He gave the same advice concerning the bill for the setting of watchmen (6 Nov.):

> ... those that be night walkers offend God, do the commonwealth no good and sin in both. In my opinion therefore it were good to limit the continuance of this law, and that the defects therein may be the better examined, that it be committed.

The bill was committed the next day and he was named to the committee. He spoke on the subsidy on 7 Nov. On 10 Nov. More spoke against the bill 'to restrain the multitude of idle people which flock from all parts of the realm to London and the suburbs thereof', on the grounds that no 'mechanical' person would be able to trade in London. He spoke on three major religious bills during 1601, the first

being the bill against plurality of benefices. He supported the commitment of the bill on 16 Nov. considering it

> in the general scope, a good law and tending to a good and religious end. But such is the iniquity of this age that for want of a good law of this nature, many souls do not only languish but perish everlastingly for want of spiritual food.

On 20 Nov. he supported the church attendance bill against Sir Edward Hoby's allegations that there was 'some matter of secret in this statute', and on 2 Dec. he made a long speech in favour of the commitment of the bill.

> Without going to church or doing Christian duties, we cannot be religious; and by religion we learn both our duties to God and the Queen. In doing our duty to God, we shall be the better able to do our duty to our Prince; and the Word biddeth us that we should give unto God, that which is due unto God. *Et Caesari quae sunt Caesaris.* Amongst many laws which we have, we have none for constraint of God's service: I say none though one were made *primo Reginae*, because that law is no law which takes no force, for *executio legis vita legis.* Then let us not give such cause of comfort to our adversaries, that having drawn a bill in question for the service of our God we should stand so much in questioning the same. Once a month coming to church excuses us from the danger of the law, but not from the commandment of God who saith: Thou shalt sanctify the Sabbath day – that is every Sabbath.

On the subject of monopolies More took a moderate line. He spoke for the first time on 20 Nov.:

> I make no question but that this bill offereth good matter ... many grievances have been laid open, touching the monopoly of salt, but if you had added thereunto petre, then you had hit the grief aright with which my country is perplexed.

However he opposed the idea of proceeding by bill on the grounds that 'we know the power of her Majesty cannot be restrained by any act'. He thought it more fitting 'the wisdom and gravity of this House to proceed with all humbleness, rather by petition than bill'. He was appointed to a committee on monopolies on 23 Nov. He spoke twice on the subject of the Queen's message about monopolies, the first time on 25 Nov. expressing his joy and gratitude; the second time, two days later, in opposition to the suggestion that the Queen's message should be recorded in the journals.

> This eating and filthy disease of monopolies I have ever detested with my heart, and the greater the grievance is and hath been, the more inestimable is the grace of her Majesty in repealing them. And therefore to think we can sufficiently record the same, it were to hold a candle before the sun to dim the light. And seeing that she in her clemency and care to us, hath taken the matter into

her own hands, I wish the matter may be no more spoken of, much less proceeded in.

During the debate on iron ordnance on 8 Dec. More again opposed the idea of proceeding by bill. The Queen's recent 'clemency' over monopolies led him to hope that a petition delivered with suitable humility would meet with more success. He was appointed to the committee concerning iron ordnance the same day.

More spoke several times on matters of privilege (14 Nov., 8 Dec.) and was appointed to two committees on the Belgrave privilege case (8, 9 Dec.). He also spoke on the procedural question of the issuing of writs for a by-election on 13 and 14 Nov. He opposed the imposition of 'too infamous a punishment' for abuses in cloth manufacture (18 Nov.). His committee work included such topics as privileges and returns (31 Oct.), the penal laws (2 Nov.), church attendance (4 Nov., committed to him), the poor law (5 Nov.), blasphemous swearing (10 Nov.), the abbreviation of the Michaelmas term (11 Nov.), private bills (19, 23 Nov., 3 Dec.), letters patent (20 Nov.), London hospitals (23 Nov.), painters and stainers (24 Nov., reported by him 12 Dec.), felt makers (26 Nov.), abuses of the clerk of the market (2 Dec.), the local government of London (4 Dec.), London watermen (8 Dec.) and kerseys (14 Dec.). On 19 Dec. the last day of the Parliament, More joined in the discussion on illegitimate children, recommending that any relief given to the mother should also be given to the child.[4]

Most of More's court career lies outside the Tudor period, but there is no doubt that Elizabeth favoured him. When in the summer of 1586 his brother-in-law John Wolley was sent to James of Scotland to explain the English government's attitude to Mary Stuart, he reported to Sir William More that the Queen had personally suggested that George More should accompany him. As Sir William grew older and more infirm, More began to take over some of his father's local duties, and in 1596 a letter from Lord Howard of Effingham told him that the Queen valued his work in Surrey too highly to allow him to go to sea with Howard. From this time until his appointment, presumably on his father's death, as deputy lieutenant, More acted as a special assistant to the deputies. He was given a knighthood, probably early in 1598, as his sister put it, 'for his better countenance in her Majesty's service in the country where he dwelleth, and the comfort of my aged father'. More was still styled 'Mr. George More' on 7 Feb. 1598. The only George More found among the knighthoods for this period (described puzzlingly as 'of the West'), was dubbed on Shrove Tuesday 1598 at Whitehall. More received a further mark of the Queen's favour in November 1601 – a grant of the lordship and hundred of Godalming. He also succeeded, probably early in the same year, to his father's office in the Exchequer. Lord Buckhurst and Lady Warwick supported

his application, the latter assuring More that the Queen thought so well of him that he had 'reason to be hopeful'.[5]

Elizabeth had visited Sir William More's newly built house at Loseley several times during her reign, and James I was entertained there in August 1603 and later. The house may not have been big enough for Sir George More's growing family: at any rate he built a new east wing, with a gallery and chapel. During his period as treasurer to Prince Henry he was apparently a very wealthy man, but the statement that at the prince's death 'then fell all his fortunes', has a measure of truth. In 1613 his subsidy assessment was among the highest in England, and four years later he was able to sell his lieutenancy of the Tower for about £2,500. But he failed to gain a higher office which he coveted (probably that of treasurer or comptroller of the Household), and later claimed that James I had not sufficiently rewarded his services. He had always spent lavishly on hospitality, and in his later years may have had to meet a number of debts contracted by his grandson, Poynings More†. By the time of his death the fortunes of the More family were waning.[6]

Four of his five daughters made good, if not spectacular, marriages, but Anne's to John Donne* was 'immeasurably unwelcome' to More, who had Donne discharged from Egerton's household and imprisoned. After a few months he allowed his relative Francis Wolley* of Pyford to effect a reconciliation.[7]

More died intestate 16 Oct. 1632, and was buried in the chapel at Loseley. Administration of his property was granted to a creditor, and an inventory of goods taken at More's death survives among the Loseley manuscripts. Though he owned lands in Kent and Sussex as well as Surrey, no inquisition post mortem has been found. A 'bequest' of manuscripts and £40 in money to Oxford University was in fact a gift made in 1604, the year before he received an honorary MA. His eldest son Sir Robert having died some years before 1632, the heir was his grandson Poynings More, who represented Haslemere in the Long Parliament.[8]

[1] *Vis. Surr.* (Harl. Soc. xliii), 2; *Vis. Hants* (Harl. Soc. lxiv), 88; Manning and Bray, *Surr.* i. 95; A. J. Kempe, *Loseley Mss*, xvi–xvii n; *HMC 7th Rep.* 625a; *DNB*; Lansd. 84, f. 147; M.I. at St. Nicholas's church, Guildford; PCC admon. act bk. 1631–3, f. 147. [2] Wright, *Eliz.* ii. 102; *APC*, xii. 14; xxi. 12; xxxviii. 559; Harl. 474; PRO Index 4208; p. 196; SP14/33; *CSP Dom.* 1601–3, p. 54; 1611–18, p. 56; 1629–31, p. 164; *DNB*. [3] Kempe, xvi. [4] D'Ewes, 333, 337, 353, 394, 395, 416, 431, 432, 433, 434, 438, 440, 443, 446, 448, 471, 474, 477, 481, 486, 494, 497, 499, 513, 517, 518, 552, 553, 555, 556, 557, 559, 561, 566, 567, 569, 571, 572, 586, 589, 592, 594, 622, 624, 626, 629, 633, 635, 636, 637, 638, 640, 642, 646, 647, 648, 649, 650, 654, 656, 657, 663, 665, 667, 670, 672, 673, 680, 684; Townshend, 23, 27, 75, 76, 103, 105, 106, 110, 111, 112, 113, 115, 181, 185, 193, 206, 211, 213, 215, 218, 222, 228, 234, 252, 258, 274–5, 294, 295, 305, 313, 333; Neale, *Parlts.* ii. 314, 398; *HMC Hatfield*, iv. 292, 295; xi. 484; Kempe, 358–9. [5] Kempe, 492–3; *HMC 7th Rep.* 654a, 658b, 659a; Lansd. 84, f. 147; D'Ewes, 594; *DNB*. [6] Nichols, *Progresses Eliz.* ii. 7; iii. 81; *Progresses Jas. I*, i. 250–1; Kempe, xiv; M. F. Keeler, *Long Parlt.* 277–8;

Chamberlain Letters ed. McClure, ii. 50, 58. [7] Manning and Bray, i. 99; Kempe, 322–40. [8] DNB; Manning and Bray, i. 66, 95, 99; CPR, 1547–8, pp. 280 seq.; CSP Dom. 1547–80, p. 694; Foster, Al. Ox. i(3), 1023; HMC 7th Rep. 677a; PCC admon. act bk. 1631–3, f. 147.

J.C.H./M.A.P.

MORE, John I (d. 1583), of Worcester.

WORCESTER   1563

m., 3s. 1da.

Member of the 48, Worcester 1553, auditor 1554–5, 1570–1, 1572–3, clerk to auditor 1558–9, member of the 24, 1559, chamberlain 1565–6, bailiff 1566–7, 1568–9.

As well as serving in the usual city offices, More was sent on special missions for the city, visiting London in 1555–6 to present a supplication to the Privy Council concerning the weight of cloths. In 1564–5 he was the city's agent in its suit against Tewkesbury before the council in the marches. More was probably a clothier, for in his will he left 'ten sticks of coarse cloth of my own making for the clothing of my brother's children'. Though a reasonably prosperous man, who confidently expected burial in the cathedral church where his wife already lay, More was not rich. He left his youngest son Thomas £100, and his son-in-law, Richard Dawkes, £40. His second son, Edward, received leases of houses in the city and half the residue of the property, while his heir, John, received plate, 'all my books', and the other half of the residue.

Nash, Worcs. ii. p. cxii; Worcester Guildhall, chamber order bk. 1540–1601, f. 100 d; audit bk. 1540–1600; PCC 39 Rowe.

S.M.T.

MORE, John II (d. c.1588), of Ipswich and Little Brisset, Suff.

IPSWICH   1571

s. of Edward More of Burston Haugh, Suff. m. Joan, 6da. suc. fa. 1558.

Chamberlain, Ipswich 1559–60, bailiff 1566–7, 1572–3, 1577–8, 1584–5.

More was an Ipswich cloth merchant, who inherited from his father the manor of Burston Haugh. By the time he made his will in October 1587 he also owned the manor of Little Brisset, near Ipswich, and houses and lands in Oston, Willesham, Waldingfield, Peasenhall, Heveningham, Badingham and elsewhere in Suffolk. In addition to his large house in Ipswich, and various leases from the corporation in and near the town, he possessed Topfield Hall in Hadley, although there is no evidence that he ever lived there. He rented more land from the Earl of Arundel (who in 1585 owed him £100) and from Lord Wentworth, the county magnate asked by the Privy Council in 1571 to supervise the elections in Suffolk boroughs.

Despite all this, More remained pre-eminently a citizen of Ipswich, serving the corporation in various offices for almost 30 years, though for some reason his name does not appear on the lists for September 1580 to September 1582.

There are several references, in the town books and elsewhere, to his trading activities, especially the export of Suffolk cloth. At Antwerp he employed as factor his brother-in-law Robert Barker, presumably a relative of the 1593 Ipswich MP of the same name. In 1572 Barker, who also worked in partnership with William Cardinall of East Bergholt, deposed before the Ipswich bailiffs about his transactions for More in Antwerp before the prohibition of trade with the Spanish Netherlands. The prices quoted for the 'short fine coloured cloths', the 'short whites' and 'long Suffolk cloths' show that More was an exporter on a large scale. In December 1568 the Spanish authorities seized cloth from his Antwerp packhouse, and confiscated sacks of hops which Barker had shipped to him in a Flemish hoy. Some years later, More was one of the 12 merchants asked, on oath before the Ipswich bailiffs, whether they had infringed the Act in Restraint of Trade with the Spanish Netherlands: this he denied. The subsidy return for 1568 assessed him at £20 in goods, higher than others in his ward. For some time he served as 'rentwarden' of Henry Tooley's charitable foundation in Ipswich, and in his will made arrangements for two poor children from Christ's hospital there to be given their indentures of apprenticeship in order to 'get their living and so become necessary members in the commonwealth in time to come'.

More was a puritan who, having the advowson of a local church, referred the choice of a pastor to serve it to the famous Dedham classis. His connexion with Dedham was probably through his business associate William Cardinall II*, who founded Edmund Chapman's lecture there. In Ipswich More and his brother-in-law Barker were constantly active in the puritan interest. The town treasurer's accounts for 1578–9, the year after More's third period as bailiff, show 30s. paid to him for 'arrears of preachers' wages the last year'. This may mean that he had paid the money out of his own pocket.

He left no son, and the greater part of his long and detailed will, proved in 1588, is concerned with the division of his property among his six daughters, one of whom, Mary, married George Waldegrave*; two others married London merchants, Richard Walter and Roger Ofield. More left money to six puritan preachers. His cousin Robert Derehaugh (also associated with the Dedham classis), and his brothers-in-law Robert Barker and Samuel Smith, were appointed supervisors to help the widow, the sole executrix. After her husband's death Joan More remained a leading patron of puritans, providing for a sermon on liberality to preachers and showing 'motherly affection ... towards many' of her fellow radicals in religion.

N. Bacon, *Ipswich Annals*, passim; *CPR*, 1558–60, p. 454; Lansd. 45, f. 208; Add. 48018, f. 294v; Ipswich ass. bk. 6–19 Eliz. pp. 83, 115; Ipswich treasurers accts.; G. Unwin, *Studies in Econ. Hist.* ed. Tawney, 275–6; *Suff. Green Bks.* xii. 164; PCC 36 Rutland; *Presbyterian Movement*, ed. Usher (Cam. Soc. ser. 3, viii), 64 et passim; Collinson thesis, 821, 864–5.

N.M.F.

MORE, Sir John (c.1520–c.76), of Morehayes, Devon.

WEST LOOE	1559
DARTMOUTH	1563

b. c.1520, 1st s. of Humphrey More of Morehayes by Anne or Agnes, da. of Sir Lewis Pollard. *m.* Katherine, da. of Sir Thomas Pomeroy of Berry Pomeroy by Jane, da. of Sir Peter Edgecombe, 8s. 6da. *suc.* fa. 1537. Kntd. 1549.[1]

J.p. Devon from c.1559, dep. lt. 1569.[2]

Though a well-known figure in the west country, More had no known personal connexion with either of the boroughs he represented in Parliament, presumably owing his seats to the 2nd Earl of Bedford, with whom he had fought at St. Quentin in 1557. His strong protestant convictions – in 1564 he was chosen to advise the bishop of Exeter on the religion of Devon justices – were in line with Bedford's own, and his brother James was in the Earl's service. In the second session of the 1563 Parliament More was appointed to the succession committee, 31 Oct. 1566, and to hear the Queen's message on the succession on 5 Nov. 1566. This was his only recorded parliamentary activity.[3]

Still a minor when his father died, More became involved in complex lawsuits over his inheritance. Under Mary he was cited at least once before Star Chamber (on no more serious charge than that of rabbit stealing) and sued out a general pardon at Elizabeth's accession. For the rest of his life he acted as a trusted servant of the Crown in Devon. In 1574 he and his friend Sir Gawain Carew* were thanked by the Privy Council for their help to the Earl of Bedford, who in turn praised their diligence in local affairs. At about the same time More was acting with Arthur Bassett* on a Privy Council assignment to investigate an affray at Dartmouth.[4]

He died intestate, probably early in 1576: in October that year his widow was granted administration of his property. The heir, his son Humphrey, who married a sister of Amias Bampfield*, was a wastrel who was dismissed from the bench of justices for misconduct.[5]

[1] Vivian, *Vis. Devon*, 573; *Vis. Devon 1564*, ed. Colby, 161–2. [2] Lansd. 56, f. 168 seq. [3] *HMC Foljambe*, 7; *Cam. Misc.* ix(3), pp. 68–9; D'Ewes, 126; Camb. Univ. Lib. Gg. iii. 34, p. 209. [4] *PRO Lists and Indexes*, li. 157; vii. 384; liv. 253; xiii. 277, 281, 323; xxi. 153; PRO cal. enrolled deeds 1547–55, p. 10; *CPR*, 1558–60, pp. 214, 228; *APC*, viii. 187, 304; *HMC Hatfield*, ii. 100. [5] PCC admon. act bk. 1576, f. 108v; Vivian, loc. cit.; Hooker, *Carew*, 166; Lansd. 53, f. 170 seq.

N.M.F.

MORE, Richard I (d.1595), of Grantham, Lincs.

PLYMPTON ERLE	1586
GRANTHAM	1589

s. of William More of Lichfield, Staffs. *educ.* ?G. Inn 1557. *m.* (1) a da. of Gabriel Armstrong of Notts., 1s.; (2) Godetha or Goodeth Green (*d.*1608), 4s. 2 or 3da.

Receiver-gen. Lincs. and Lincoln 1569; j.p. Lincs. (Kesteven) from c.1573.

So far as can be discovered, Richard More of Grantham had no direct connexion with Plympton, but if he was the man of this name who entered Gray's Inn during the same year as Francis, 2nd Earl of Bedford, he presumably knew the Earl, who until his death in 1585 sometimes nominated at Plympton, less than 20 miles from his manor at Tavistock. Bedford's widow, who was still living in 1586, had earlier been married to the 2nd Earl of Rutland, and More, as a Grantham man, must have known Rutland's family. A letter survives from him to the 3rd Earl, written in January 1584, asking to be allowed to change the position of his pew in Grantham church as it was 'most unfriendly placed ... amongst boys and apprentices'.

Since no Richard More of Devon of suitable date and status to be the Plympton Member has been found, it has been assumed that More of Grantham represented both Plympton and, in the following Parliament, his home town. His 1586 colleague, Jasper Cholmley, was legal adviser to the widowed Countess of Bedford and her son, and it looks as if she, or Bedford's son-in-law the Earl of Warwick on her behalf, exercised patronage at Plympton in the first election after her husband's death. At Grantham in 1589 the position was somewhat similar, since the young Earl of Rutland was a minor and the Rutland patronage of the borough was in abeyance. In this case More's local prominence was presumably sufficient to gain him a seat. He owned property in and around Grantham, including the manor of Earl's Fields, which he bought in 1571 from Arthur Hall*.

Late in 1579 he accused Hall of slandering the bishop of Lincoln, and himself. In November More was ordered to bring before Privy Councillors his witnesses to Hall's statements, but since he and Hall were known to be at loggerheads and Hall could not produce witnesses, the Council would not accept his charges as proven. After more than ten years the disputes were still continuing. Early in 1591 Hall complained to Burghley that More 'a beggar's brat, a mere upstart' had written defamatory letters about him. If, as is likely, the Catholic recusant Hugh More of Lincolnshire who was executed in Lincoln's Inn Fields in August 1588 was his son, it appears that it was More who denounced him to the authorities.

More's will, drawn up in March 1595 and proved that October, describes him as 'a miserable and wretched sinner, having God before mine eyes'. He bequeathed his soul to God, 'fully hoping that He will receive the same to

His mercy in the merits of His Son Jesus Christ, my Redeemer and most merciful Saviour', and his body to the earth, whence he hoped it would rise and be joined to his soul to appear before 'the tribunal seat of Christ my Judge', and hear that his portion was to be 'everlasting joy and felicity ... amongst the elect vessels of God. Amen'. A long section of the will concerned legacies to four sons and three daughters. One, Mary, (possibly a step-daughter, or illegitimate, as she does not appear in the pedigrees), had evidently shown too much independence. She was to have only 40s. for her wedding if she married Raphael Wiseman, a silkman of London, to whom she might 'have contracted herself' without her father's permission. However, the executor, her brother Alexander, was to pay Wiseman £200, provided he made reasonable provision for his wife. If Mary married anyone else considered suitable – presumably by More's widow and the executor – she herself could have the £200 as a dowry. The other unmarried daughter, Susan, was to have the same amount, and her sister Ursula, wife of John Fisher, £100 if her husband predeceased her. The younger sons were provided for: Thomas was to be apprenticed, and Gabriel to go to a university. The widow, 'Goodeth More, now my wife', received a life interest in various lands and in the family house at Grantham. The only significant charitable bequest was £10 to the poor of the town.

More died 10 Aug. 1595, and was buried at Grantham next day.

Lincs. Peds. (Harl. Soc. li), 687; CPR, 1566–9, p. 335; Lansd. 14, f. 9; 29, f. 179; SP12/145; HMC Rutland, iv. 207; E. M. Unsworth, 'Hugh More of Grantham and the More Fam.', Lincs. Historian, ii. no. 12; Maryat, Hist. Desc. Grantham, 46; Cath. Rec. Soc. v. 10, 154, 158, 159, 289; APC, xi. 313, 326–7; xvii. 326; xxii. 93; CSP Dom. 1591–4, p. 12; PCC 64 Scott.

J.C.H.

MORE, Richard II (d. 1635), of the Middle Temple, London and Cuddington, Bucks.

AYLESBURY 1601

s. and h. of William More of Totternhoe, Beds. educ. New Inn; M. Temple 1586, called 1594. m., 2s. Kntd. 1619.

Master in Chancery extraordinary 1616; assoc. bencher, M. Temple 1616.

More was a London lawyer whose return for Aylesbury probably resulted from some connexion with the lord of the manor, Sir John Pakington. Perhaps this was professional, or perhaps More was related to the Sir Jasper More who married (as her second husband) Sir John Pakington's sister Katherine. By 1605 More himself is described as 'of Aylesbury'. He died in or shortly before June 1635, when the benchers of the Middle Temple arranged for the disposal of goods left in his chamber at his death, and assigned the chamber to a new occupant.

Vis. Bucks. (Harl. Soc. lviii), 192–3; VCH Beds. iii. 449; Cal. Bucks. Recs. (Bucks. Arch. Soc. recs. br. v), 68; M.T. Bench Bk. (2nd ed.), 99; M.T. Recs. i. 286.

I.C.

MORE, Robert (1581–1626), of Loseley and Catshall, Surr.

GUILDFORD	1601
SURREY	1604
GUILDFORD	1614, 1621
SURREY	1624
GUILDFORD	1625

b. 21 May 1581, 1st s. of (Sir) George More* of Loseley by his 1st w. Anne, da. and coh. of (Sir) Adrian Poynings*. educ. Corpus, Oxf. 1595, BA 1598; M. Temple 1600. m. Frances, da. of Sampson Lennard* by Margaret Fiennes, Baroness Dacre, 6s. 5da. Kntd. bet. 17 Oct. 1601 and 28 Feb. 1604.

Jt. keeper with fa. and gd.-fa. of Farnham little park 1600; jt. constable with fa. of Farnham castle ?1603–8; j.p. Surr. temp. Jas. I–d.; dep. lt. by 1619; gent. pens. to Jas. and Chas. I.

More entered Parliament while still a minor, and was elected knight of the shire before he was 25. Guildford was for Elizabethan and Jacobean Parliaments virtually a More family borough. It provided Robert with his first membership of the House of Commons, and a reserve when a county seat was not available. His father lived to be nearly 80, and he did not succeed either to the family estates or to his father's and grandfather's prominent position at court or in Surrey. In the Loseley manuscripts there are few references to him, and the state papers and acts of the Privy Council scarcely mention his name. Even after he became a deputy lieutenant he was inactive in county affairs. Perhaps the intention was to make him a courtier rather than a local gentleman. Probably the 'grandson of Sir William More' at whose christening the sponsors were Anne, Countess of Warwick, and the Earls of Lincoln and Leicester, he was given an excellent education, and probably entered the band of gentlemen pensioners early in James I's reign. When he died, after 'many years' service' in the place, £150 was owing to him in wages. His wife was a daughter of Margaret, Baroness Dacre, and an undated letter from Robert to his father refers to his being in attendance on Lady Dacre, who lived until 1612, and presumably used her influence to further her son-in-law's prospects. If he was the Robert More who wrote to Sir Robert Cecil in August 1599 that he had been 'at court on Friday last, but could not have the opportunity to speak with' him, it suggests that he was not at that time in regular attendance at court. Nothing is known of him in the 1601 House of Commons, to which he was returned styled 'esquire'. By the time of the 1604 return he was a knight.

More died either 2 or 10 Feb. 1626, and was buried in the Loseley chapel at St. Nicholas's, Guildford. His epitaph, which describes him as a gentleman pensioner to James and Charles I, states that he died 'aged forty-four years and a half, ten weeks and one day'. No will is known. His inquisition post mortem gives him as seised of lands in Catshall, Surrey, presumably settled on him by his father.

Vis. Surr. (Harl. Soc. xliii), 3; (lx), 84; Manning and Bray, *Surr.* i. 67; iii. 137; *CSP Dom.* 1603–10, p. 437; *Surr. Arch. Colls.* xxiv. 180; *HMC 7th Rep.* 674b, 675b, 676a, 678b.

N.M.F.

MORE, William I (1520–1600), of Loseley, Surr.[1]

CONSTITUENCY UNKNOWN	1539
REIGATE	1547
GUILDFORD	1553 (Oct.), 1554 (Nov.), 1555
GRANTHAM	1559
SURREY	1563, 1571
GUILDFORD	1572
SURREY	1584, 1586
GUILDFORD	1589
SURREY	1593
GUILDFORD	1597

b. 30 Jan. 1520, 5th but o. surv. s. of (Sir) Christopher More[†], of Loseley, remembrancer of the Exchequer, by his 1st w. Margaret, da. of Walter Mudge or Mugge of Guildford. *m.* (1) settlement 12 June 1545, Mabel (*d.* by 1549), da. of Marchion Digneley of Wolverton, I.o.W., *s.p.*; (2) settlement 1551, Margaret, da. and h. of Ralph Daniell of Swaffham, Norf., 1s. George* 2da. *suc.* fa. 16 Aug. 1549. Kntd. 14 May 1576.[2]

Provost marshal, Surr. 1552, commr. church gds. 1553, musters by 1558, j.p. from 1559; sheriff, Surr. and Suss. 1558–9, 1579–80; v.-adm. Suss. 1559–94; constable, Farnham castle 1565; verderer, Windsor forest by 1561; dep. lt. Surr. 1569, 1580, 1588; eccles. commr. 1572; chamberlain of the Exchequer at *d.*; farmer of alnage in Surr. and Suss. from 1549; collector of loan, Surr. 1589, dep. custos rot. by 1594.[3]

Sir William More of Loseley was the perfect Elizabethan country gentleman. He was absorbed in the local administration of Surrey, and by his impeccable character no less than his efficiency acquired a prestige that was scarcely dimmed by the location in that county of eminent peers, including the Lords Howard of Effingham. He numbered such great men as Lord Burghley, the Earl of Leicester and the 1st Earl of Lincoln among his friends; and through his daughter Elizabeth, who became one of the Queen's ladies at court, there developed an intimacy between More and his sovereign which has preserved for us some charming royal episodes. In Parliament he gave the same assiduous service as in local administration, entering the House of Commons before attaining his majority and sitting in every Elizabethan Parliament (assuming he was there in 1559) until his death.

While it is difficult to determine how radical More's early religious views were, there can be no doubt that he

was a reformer before Elizabeth came to the throne. His close friendship with Sir Thomas Cawarden*, who was involved in Wyatt's rebellion, suggests this; and indeed it is conceivable that through him he became acquainted with Elizabeth before her accession. When Cawarden died in August 1559, More was his executor. More was among those MPs who in 1553 and 1555 resisted the religious legislation of Mary's government, and he did not sit in Mary's last Parliament. At the time of the elections to Elizabeth's first Parliament, when such reformers tended to flock back, More was sheriff of Surrey and unable to return himself for a Surrey constituency. But a William More was elected for Grantham, where Sir William Cecil* was able to nominate Members; and it would accord with what we know of Cecil's activities on this occasion if he took steps to place William More of Loseley in that crucial Parliament. A postscript in a letter dated 27 Feb. 1559 from More's Surrey friend, Richard Byron, has been taken to imply that More was then an MP; and if so, he must have sat for Grantham. The postscript reads: 'Sir, you have the closest Parliament that ever I did know. I heartily desire that I may be bold to have some intelligence from you how things goeth with you'. If this was so, More no doubt acted with the large section of the House of Commons which did its utmost to extract a thoroughgoing protestant settlement from the Queen. In later Parliaments More sat either for Surrey, where for social reasons he took the junior seat, or, when a county seat was not available, for the borough of Guildford about two miles from Loseley.[4]

In the last decade or two of his life, More worked in harmony with the Howards; but this may not always have been so. In 1559 the then Lord Howard, who was the Queen's lord chamberlain, wanted a county seat for his heir Charles and wrote to More as sheriff for his support. More, however, was already pledged to his friend Sir Thomas Cawarden and evidently supported Cawarden in his determination not to give way. Either Howard's candidature was withdrawn or he was defeated at the election. Again, in 1584, when More himself was standing for the county, the Earl of Lincoln and Charles Lord Howard wrote belatedly recommending Howard's heir for election. More must have stood firm on this occasion also, and the Howard candidature was withdrawn. Though the episode may not have caused ill will, it says much for More's resolution and influence that he could withstand two such noblemen, who were also his friends. Otherwise his electoral relations with the Howards were a matter of give and take, when sharing was not feasible. For his last Parliament in 1597, (Sir) William evidently withdrew to the borough seat of Guildford in order that his son and heir George might graduate as a county Member after ten years' apprenticeship in the family's borough seat.

Despite his long experience in Parliament, More spoke

rarely in debate, though he was an active committeeman. For the record, here are his contributions to the business of Elizabethan Parliaments, from 31 Oct. 1566 when he is first mentioned in the journals as a member of the succession committee. He was one of 30 MPs summoned on 5 Nov. 1566 to hear the Queen's message on the succession. He was named to the committee on uniformity of religion (6 Apr. 1571) and was presumably the 'Mr. Moore' who was appointed to committees in 1571 concerning church attendance (21 Apr., 19 May), the preservation of woods (10 May), juries (14 May), great hosen (14 May), the river Lea (26 May) and dividing the bailiwicks of Surrey and Sussex (28 May). During the first session of the 1572 Parliament he was appointed to two committees concerning Mary Queen of Scots (12, 28 May) and also to committees on private matters (20, 22 May) and the ill-treatment of foreign artisans by London corporations (24 May). He was one of those appointed to draw up a petition for the reformation of church discipline on 29 Feb. 1576, and other committee work during the session included the subsidy (10 Feb.), the poor laws (11 Feb.), the manufacture of woollen cloth (16 Feb.), sheriffs (18 Feb.), leather (18 Feb.), assize of wood in the city of London (3 Mar.) and trials by jury (5 Mar.). At the end of the session he was one of those appointed to collect money for the poor (14 Mar.). He was very active in the 1581 session, being named to committees concerning the subsidy (25 Jan.), the preservation of woods (28 Jan.), wrecks (30 Jan.), slanderous words and practices (1 Feb.), cloth (4 Feb.), coneys (9 Feb.), wool and yarn (13 Feb.), the Family of Love (16, 27 Feb.), the preservation of game (18 Feb.), a private bill (20 Feb.), returns (24 Feb.), land reclamation (8 Mar.), the preservation of her Majesty's safety (14 Mar.) and iron mills (18 Mar.). The bill against sowing linseed and hempseed in Hertfordshire was committed to him on 23 Feb. 1581.

More felt so strongly about the wretched Dr. William Parry*, that on 23 Feb. 1585 he made one of his rare interventions in debate, to second a motion urging that a more hideous means of executing him be devised than the usual traitor's death. The proposal was rejected by the Queen. On 11 Mar. that year he was appointed to examine one John Bland concerning a matter of privilege, and he reported the findings of the examination on 13 Mar. On 16 Mar. a bill concerning apprentices was committed to him. Other committee work in this Parliament included topics such as the better observing of the Sabbath day (27 Nov. 1584, 10, 19 Dec.), informers (9 Dec.), tanners and shoemakers (9 Dec.), griefs and petitions (16 Dec.), the Queen's safety (15 Feb. 1585), Jesuits (18 Feb., 9 Mar.), the subsidy (24 Feb.), procedure (3 Mar.), malt (16 Mar.), pheasants and partridges (17 Mar.), and the continuation of a statute concerning the Wednesday fish day (19 Mar.). He reported the committee concerning curriers on 19 Mar. 1585. In 1586 he was appointed to the committee concerning Mary Queen of Scots on 4 Nov., and three days

later was one of those summoned to attend the Lords to arrange a conference on the subject. A bill concerned with horse stealing was committed to him on 10 Mar. 1587, and he was among those appointed to have audience with the Queen concerning the subsidy for the Netherlands on 18 Mar. Other committee work during this session concerned the Norfolk election dispute (9 Nov.), purveyors (3 Mar. 1587), the continuation of statutes (6 Mar., 20 Mar.), a learned ministry (8 Mar.), the puritan MPs sequestered in the Tower (13 Mar.), recusants (16 Mar.) and Suffolk cloth (16 Mar.). On 7 Feb. 1589 More was appointed to the committee to consider all cases of privilege that should arise during the session, and the following day he was appointed to the committee to investigate the returns for that Parliament. His committee work included topics such as informers (8 Feb.), the Aylmer privilege case (12 Feb.), mortmain (22 Feb.), captains and soldiers (26 Feb.), forestallers and regrators (5 Mar.), curriers (6 Mar.), alien retailers (12 Mar.), hue and cry (17 Mar.) and glass factories (19 Mar.). On 15 Feb. 1589 he spoke on the purveyors bill and was appointed to the committee. He was appointed to two committees to consider the Queen's dislike of the bill on 27 Feb., and was one of those appointed on 6 Mar. to attend the Queen with a petition concerning the purveyors bill. In 1593 he was appointed to the first standing committee on privileges and returns (26 Feb.). The House was under pressure to yield an abnormal money grant of three subsidies in 1593, and More was named to three committees considering this, 26 Feb., 1, 3 Mar., and opened the discussion in committee on 2 Mar. He was 'entirely for yielding three subsidies':

> Her Majesty had more cause to have the subsidy than had Henry VIII, Edward VI or Queen Mary; for Henry VIII his wars continued not, though they were violent for the time. His wars were impulsive and not defensive. He had the suppression of all the abbeys, a matter of great riches unto him. He had a benevolence and then a subsidy paid within three months. Edward VI had chantries and all the church plate for relief paid him. Queen Mary had a relief paid her, which she never repaid. But her Majesty that now is, hath been a continual defence of her own realm and her neighbours' kingdoms, England, Ireland, France and the Low Countries; yet hath she repaid the loans, and had not such helps.

He was also appointed to committees concerning recusancy (28 Feb.), rogues (12 Mar.) and petty larceny (16 Mar.). A letter from the court, probably from Brian Ansley*, dated 20 Apr. 1593, refers to More's early departure from this Parliament. He must have been in the House on 23 Mar. however, for a bill concerning Devonshire kerseys was committed to him that day.

Despite being 77 years of age at the beginning of his last Parliament, More was as active as ever in 1597, being appointed to committees concerned with tillage and enclosures (5 Nov., 20 Jan. 1598), privileges and returns (5 Nov.), penal laws (8 Nov.), armour and weapons (8 Nov.), monopolies (10 Nov.), weavers' and spinners' wages (10 Nov.), the continuation of statutes (11 Nov.), ecclesiastical causes (14 Nov.), rogues and sturdy beggars (19 Nov.), the poor law (22 Nov.), confirmation of the deprivation of certain bishops (3 Dec.), lewd wandering persons (7 Dec.), defence (12 Jan. 1598) and the possessions of the bishop of Norwich (16 Jan.). A private bill was committed to him on 16 Dec.[5]

More built himself a new house at Loseley between 1562 and 1568, and the Queen may have visited him there in 1567. She certainly went to Loseley in 1569, and included it in her progresses in 1576, 1583 and 1591; and it was in 1576, when staying at the Earl of Lincoln's house at Pyrford, that she knighted him, employing the Earl of Leicester to give the accolade. Elizabeth apparently sent him frequent messages through his daughter and her husband, John Wolley*, the Latin secretary, both resident at court. In 1579 Wolley told his father-in-law how the Queen

> fell in speech of you, with great good liking and commendation, willing me to send you word that she did perceive that where the young sort of men, wanting experience and trust, did forget their duties, such old servants as you are would remember themselves.

She 'durst commit her life' to his trust, she added. Wolley also reported that the Earl of Leicester had previously been talking to him of 'the very good opinion' which the Queen had of Sir William, 'which he [Leicester] did ever seek to increase'. In 1595 there was a letter from Elizabeth Wolley telling her father of the Queen's concern at his 'troublesome' night-journey home from court – evidently during a progress in Surrey when accommodation with the court was unavailable. 'If her Majesty had known ... she would have had a lodging provided, being likewise sorry that she had no longer time to entertain you'. The Queen sent him three partridges, 'desiring you to eat them for her sake'; but as Sir Robert Cecil, whose hawk had killed the birds, intercepted the gift, Elizabeth Wolley was constrained to ask her father to pretend to the Queen that he had received them. This letter also reported that the Queen had commanded Mistress Wolley to send for her son – whose godmother the Queen was – to come to court, where 'she will pose him in his learning'. Advising her father to forget the command, as she herself intended to do, Mistress Wolley told Sir William to see that the boy's tutor practised him in his French, lest the command be renewed.

Another letter – undated and probably earlier – arose out of More's gift of a gown to the Queen. When she wore it, she

> took thereby occasion to speak to you, saying, ere long I should find a mother-in-law, which was herself; but she

was afraid of the two widows that are there with you, that they would be angry with her for it, and that she would give ten thousand pounds you were twenty years younger, for she had but few such servants as you are.[6]

The rich collection of Loseley manuscripts furnishes an excellent conspectus of his duties and activities as a justice, a deputy lieutenant, a commissioner for many local tasks, and vice-admiral in his shire. Many of the leading men in Elizabethan England were among his correspondents, and the friendly note in their letters is impressive. There is little in the collection about his office of chamberlain of the Exchequer, which he probably discharged by deputy.[7]

More seems to have enjoyed good health until late in life, but a sudden and severe illness in 1594, which drew his daughter temporarily from her duties at court and caused concern to the Queen, appears to have sapped his strength. A few years later he was handing over much of his work to his son George. He died in July 1600 and was buried in the Loseley chapel at St. Nicholas's church, Guildford, where an epitaph describes him as 'evermore a zealous professor of true religion, and a favourer of all those ... truly ... religious, spending his days in the service of our late sovereign of blessed memory, Queen Elizabeth, in whose favour he lived and died ...'.[8]

The will, drawn up in January 1597 and proved by the executor, More's son George, in November 1600, has a devout preamble:

> Having assured hope, through the death, merits and passion of my only Saviour and Redeemer Jesus Christ, not only to have free pardon and remission of all my sins, but also to enjoy with Him His everlasting kingdom, utterly rejecting all other ways and means to attain thereunto than only by my said Saviour Jesus Christ ...

The will enjoins that 'all pomp and vain glory' were to be avoided at the funeral, and ends: 'and thus our Lord God have mercy upon me and receive my soul into His hands'. The provisions were simple, almost everything being left to George and his heirs. (Sir) William's younger daughter Anne, wife of George Mainwaring*, was to have a cup worth £6 13s. 4d., and a cousin, Gillian Cowper, a coach. There were generous bequests to servants, and the executor was asked to 'consider' the poor of Guildford, Godalming, Compton and Shalford. The overseers were More's 'cousin' Laurence Stoughton*, several times MP for Guildford, and his friends Francis Aungier* and George Austen*, both of whom probably owed their Haslemere seats in 1597 to him. Besides property in Kent, Surrey and Sussex, More owned houses in Blackfriars, one of which he leased to James Burbage in 1596 to become the Blackfriars theatre.[9]

[1] This biography owes much to an early version drafted by Sir John Neale. [2] Manning and Bray, *Surr.* i. 95 seq.; W. Berry, *Co. Genealogies, Surr.* 87; *Vis. Surr.* (Harl. Soc. xliii), 2; *CPR,* 1549–51, p. 167; C142/89/134; Loseley mss 346/30/1–2. [3] *HMC 7th Rep.* 607b,

608b, 614a, 615a, 616, 617b, 620a, 622a, 646b, 652, 653a; *Surr. Arch. Coll.* xxxix. 55; Lansd. 106, ff. 1 seq.; 114, ff. 121 seqq.; *CPR*, 1569–72, pp. 440–2; *CSP Dom.* 1601–3, p. 54; PCC 9 Coode. [4] A. J. Kempe, *Loseley Mss*, 175 seq.; Bodl. e Museo 17; Guildford Mus., Loseley mss 1081/5, 1331/2; Loseley mss, Letter Box 1, no. 7; *HMC 7th Rep.* 613a–635b passim. [5] Neale, *Commons*, 43–7; Camb. Univ. Lib. Gg. iii. 34, p. 209; D'Ewes, 127, 157, 176, 181, 182, 183, 186, 189, 206, 212, 213, 214, 220, 244, 247, 288, 289, 291, 294, 295, 298, 299, 300, 303, 306, 308, 333, 337, 340, 343, 349, 351, 352, 355, 356, 362, 365, 366, 368, 369, 370, 371, 394, 395, 396, 412, 413, 414, 415, 416, 417, 429, 430, 432, 433, 437, 439, 440, 443, 445, 446, 448, 471, 474, 477, 481, 484, 486, 499, 502, 507, 517, 552, 553, 555, 557, 559, 561, 567, 569, 574, 578, 581, 584; *CJ*, i. 83, 85, 88, 89, 91, 93, 95, 96, 97, 99, 104, 105, 106, 109, 110, 111, 119, 120, 121, 122, 124, 125, 127, 128, 129, 130, 132, 134, 136; Trinity, Dublin, Thos. Cromwell's jnl. f. 132; Townshend, *Hist. Colls.* 16, 17, 20, 23, 25, 26, 27, 64, 71, 73, 103, 104, 106, 112, 116; Loseley mss, Box 2. [6] E. K. Chambers, *Eliz. Stage*, iv. 84, 93, 100, 106; N. Williams, *4th Duke of Norf.* 157; Kempe, xii–xiii, 265 seq., 313, 317–21; *HMC 7th Rep.* 654b–655a. [7] Kempe, passim; *HMC 7th Rep.* 607–58. [8] *HMC 7th Rep.* 653a, 654a, 658b; Manning and Bray, i. 66. [9] PCC 70 Wallop; C142/264/179; *APC*, xxvi. 448–9; *HMC 7th Rep.* 653b.

M.A.P.

MORE, William II (by 1511–68 or later), of Derby.

DERBY 1554 (Nov.), 1563

b. by 1511, prob. s. of Roger More. *m.*, at least 1s.[1]
Bailiff, Derby 1554–5, 1562–3.[2]

This man may have been a draper and vintner – trades combined by an earlier William More of Derby, perhaps the Member's grandfather, in 1519. In 1543 the 1st Earl of Rutland's executors bought black cloth from 'William Moor of Derby': two years earlier the comptroller of Rutland's household had bought seven gallons of ale from one of the same name.[3]

More owned corn and fulling mills in Derby and the surrounding district, some of them jointly with William Bainbridge* and Humphrey Buxton. In 1568 he and William More junior, presumably his son, took over the lease of certain mills from Bainbridge in exchange for the mortuaries and other profits of All Saints' and St. Alkmund's parishes in Derby. It may have been the Member of Parliament who, with his widowed mother Joan, was granted leases at Spondon and Chaddesden, Derbyshire. In the following year a William More rented land in Fiskerton, Nottinghamshire, formerly belonging to Thurgarton priory.[4]

More was almost certainly senior bailiff of Derby at the time of each of his elections to Parliament. In January 1555 he had been prosecuted, together with Bainbridge, for leaving the House without permission before the end of the session. There are no further parliamentary references to him: the 'Mr. William Moor' who in October 1566 sat on the succession committee was no doubt of Loseley.[5]

No will or inquisition post mortem has been found.

[1] C1/1139/47–8; *CPR*, 1560–3, p. 316. [2] W. Hutton, *Hist. Derby*, 80–1. [3] *LP Hen. VIII*; *HMC Rutland*, iv. 311, 342. [4] St. Ch. 4/9/47;

I. H. Jeayes, *Cal. Recs. Derby*, 31, 35; *CPR*, 1560–3, pp. 264, 316. [5] E. Coke, *Institutes* (1671), iv. 18–19; D'Ewes, 127.

N.M.F.

MORGAN, Sir Edmund (*d.* bef. 3 Feb. 1655), of Penhow, Mon.

WILTON 1601
MONMOUTHSHIRE 1621

2nd s. of Henry Morgan of Penllwyn Sarth, Mynddislwyn, Mon. by Elinor, da. of John Morgan of Pencraig, Mon.; bro. of Henry Morgan II*. *m.* (1) Frances, 2s. *d.v.p.* 3da.; (2) bet. 29 Jan. 1599 and 17 Apr. 1600, Margaret, da. of John Francis of Combe Florey, Som., wid. of William Fortescue of Preston, Som., *s.p.s.* Kntd. ?at Dublin, Aug. 1599.

Capt. in Netherlands 1585, in Normandy 1591, in Jersey 1593, in Netherlands 1594; sergeant-major on Islands voyage 1597–8.

The Morgans of Penllwyn Sarth were a junior branch of the Monmouthshire family of Morgan of Machen, and were related by blood or marriage to several other members of this widespread Glamorgan and Monmouthshire clan, as well as to the Stradlings, Carnes, Mathews and other eminent local families. Edmund Morgan's place in the lineage is confirmed by his will, for he made his nephew Edmund Morgan of Penllwyn Sarth one of his executors.[1]

As a younger son of a cadet branch Edmund Morgan doubtless needed to seek his fortune, and it was as a professional soldier that he did so. His own claim, in a letter of July 1601 to Robert Cecil, to have served for 16 years suggests that he began his career in the expeditionary force sent to the Netherlands in 1585. If so, he was probably already a follower of Robert Sidney* whose steward Thomas Morgan may have been his kinsman; and he is perhaps to be identified with the Edward Morgan who took a company over in August 1585 and was sharing its command four months later with David Powell. How long Morgan remained in the Netherlands is uncertain, but he was in England by the summer of 1591, when he took a company of 150 men from Lincoln to Normandy as part of Essex's expedition against the Spaniards in Brittany. From this mission Morgan had returned by late September, and in an account compiled two months later he is shown as having earned payment at the standard rate of 6s. 8d. a day for ten weeks. In the autumn of 1593 he was commanding 150 foot-soldiers in Jersey. By September 1594 he was back in the Netherlands, this time as a captain in the Flushing garrison under the governorship of Sir Robert Sidney; and he was to serve there (with an absence in the spring of 1596 and another in 1597 when, following an appeal to Essex for advancement, he went as sergeant-major of the Earl's regiment on the Islands voyage) until the close of 1598. He was more than once charged with the governor's letters, and in the spring of 1597 he escorted Lady Sidney from England to Flushing.[2]

Morgan's experience of fighting with Essex made him eager to accompany the Earl to Ireland, and after another mission in charge of reinforcements to Normandy in May 1599 he joined the Irish expedition. If, as is probable, Essex knighted him at Dublin in August, he must have stood well with the lord deputy, and he may have been one of those who returned with Essex in September. He was certainly in England in April 1600, and the marriage with Margaret Fortescue of which he then wrote to Cecil is likely to have taken place after his return. This union may help to explain why Morgan escaped being caught up in the Essex rebellion. It was to Cecil that he had looked for assistance over the disputed wardship of the eight year-old boy to whom, with four sisters, his marriage made him stepfather, and it was to the same source that he was to turn, in July 1601, with a request to be sent back to the Netherlands. It had earlier been reported that Morgan and others would give £300 each to be employed there.[3]

The application was not immediately successful, and in the autumn of 1601 Morgan made the first of his two appearances in the House of Commons. He was at this time living at Kensington, and proximity to Westminster may have strengthened his desire to sit. He owed his return for Wilton to the 3rd Earl of Pembroke, who was in disgrace during 1601 and did not himself attend the Parliament, though his control of Wilton was not affected. Morgan was presumably commended to Pembroke by Sir Robert Sidney, the Earl's uncle.[4]

Morgan occupies a niche in the history of this Parliament by reason of his part in a privilege case. Midway in the session he and Goddard Pemberton, one of the citizens for Peterborough, were each served with a subpoena out of Chancery at the suit of the brothers Sir Walter and Sir Carew Ralegh. When on 24 Nov. Morgan reported this in the Commons, an order for privilege was made, and the two officers who had served the writs were taken into custody by the serjeant-at-arms. Three days later, with the prisoners waiting at the door of the House, the Speaker asked for direction as to what should be done with them. After some discussion, in the course of which a recent case of arrest was also ventilated, the two were brought to the bar. One of them, Christopher Kennall, who had served the writ on Morgan, declared that he had not then known Morgan to be a Member; he had himself, he said, sat in the House and had also served for 18 years in the wars, and he would not have wittingly offended. The other, William Mackerells, 'a poor simple fellow', could only stammer a similar plea in extenuation. As soon as the two had been removed, what might have swelled into an angry insistence upon exemplary punishment was quickly halted by Morgan himself. In a short speech which was 'marvellous well liked of by the House', and which could

indeed serve as a model for all such occasions, he accepted Kennall's plea and urged that 'in regard of his person and good service done to her Majesty' his offence might be 'as freely remitted by the House as it is by me; and that it would please you all to reserve your justice to matters of greater importance'. This example of magnanimity prevailed over a 'churlish' demand by Pemberton for justice on Mackerells, and the two offenders escaped with the pains (and cost) of three days' imprisonment by the serjeant. The episode could not but have further damaged the reputations of the Raleghs.[5]

The remainder of Edmund Morgan's long career, which included more active service and Membership of another Parliament, lies outside the purview of this biography. He is first heard of as established in the neighbourhood of Penhow, between Newport and Chepstow, in 1613, and it was as of that place that he made his will on 18 June 1651. The absence of any reference to his wife and children suggests that he had outlived them, as he had his stepson, Francis Fortescue, who died in 1649. The will was proved 3 Feb. 1655, so that Morgan may well have been a nonagenarian.[6]

[1] Clark, *Limbus*, 317; Vivian, *Vis. Devon*, 357; *HMC Hatfield*, x. 112; Shaw, *Knights*, ii. 97, giving the name 'Richard (Edward) Morgan'. [2] *HMC Hatfield*, iv. 377; vi. 494; xi. 296; *HMC De L'Isle and Dudley*, ii. 155, 176, 214, 237, 269, 284, 286, 312, 323; iii. passim; iv. 161–3, 175, 265; *APC*, xxi. 233, 243, 467; Lansd. 149/49/263; *CSP Dom.* 1595–7, p. 221. [3] *HMC De L'Isle and Dudley*, ii. 359–60, 487–8; *HMC Hatfield*, ix. 165; x. 112; xi. 296. [4] *HMC Hatfield*, xi. 296, 375–6. [5] D'Ewes, 651, 655–6. [6] Bradney, *Mon.* iv. 113; PCC 259 Aylett, 21 Pembroke.

A.H.D./P.W.H.

MORGAN, Edward I (1560–1634), of Llantarnam and Pentrebach, Mon.

MONMOUTHSHIRE 1584, 1586

b. 1560, 1st s. of William Morgan II* of Llantarnam by Elizabeth, da. of Sir Rhys Mansell of Margam, Glam. *m.* (1) Elizabeth, da. of Hugh Smith† of Long Ashton, Som., 4s.; (2) Margery, da. of Hugh Hassel, 3s. 2da. *suc.* fa. 1582. J.p. Mon. from c.1582, sheriff 1582–3, 1601–2.

Connected through his mother with the wealthy Mansells of Margam, and brother-in-law to Sir William Herbert of St. Julian's (his fellow MP for Monmouthshire 1584), Edward aimed still higher and married his son into the princely house of Raglan. Though of suspect religion and with recusant connexions, Morgan served as j.p., sheriff and knight of the shire, in which latter capacity he could have served on the subsidy committee 24 Feb. 1585. He contributed his quota (with three other Monmouthshire gentry), towards resisting the Spanish landing at Kinsale in 1601. In the second year of the next reign he was convicted of recusancy, and after the Gunpowder Plot refused the new oath of allegiance. The penalty was the loss of two-thirds of his revenues; but in 1607 he compounded at £20 a month, and five years later, when pressure was off, he was pardoned and told that the oath would not be tendered to him again.

The protection of the Earl of Worcester relieved him of some of the other penalties of recusancy. In 1613–16 he was exempt for three periods of six months each from the ban on travel imposed on his co-religionists. This enabled him to take steps in the Exchequer against tenants and neighbours who since his first conviction had been taking advantage of his legal insecurity to encroach on his manors and challenge his manorial rights. It also made possible periodic visits to Bath for his health. Morgan seems to have been left in peace for the rest of his life, nor did his descendants sit in Parliament again till 1680, though the estate remained, despite all pains and penalties, a rich and important one, capable of sustaining a baronetcy in 1642 and fines for 'delinquency' amounting to over £900 a year after the war. Allegiance to the ancestral faith was maintained till his great-grandson's time; the family died out in the early eighteenth century.

Bradney, *Mon.* iii. 230–1; *Cath. Rec. Soc.* xiii. 111; xxii. 95; *S. Wales and Mon. Rec. Soc.* iv. 108; *APC*, xxxii. 280; Lansd. 43, anon. jnl. f. 171; *Exchequer*, ed. T. I. J. Jones (Univ. Wales Bd. of Celtic Studies, Hist. and Law ser. xv), 244, 257; *CSP Dom.* 1603–10, p. 352; 1611–18, p. 137; 1628–9, p. 527; *APC*, 1613–14, pp. 44, 484; 1615–16, p. 438.

A.H.D.

MORGAN, Edward II (1576–c.1640), of Golden Grove and Weppre, Flints.

FLINT BOROUGHS 1597

b. 1576, 1st s. of Edward Morgan of Golden Grove by Catherine, da. of John Davies of Gwysaney, Mold. *educ.* prob. Christ Church, Oxf. 1593–6; I. Temple 1594. *m.* Ann, da. of John Conway II*, *s.p.* ?2da. illegit. *suc.* fa. 1612.
Sheriff, Flints. 1620–1.

The family of Morgan of Gwylgre, Goldgreave or Golden Grove was descended, like so many of the leading gentry of North Wales (including the Tudors of Penmynydd), from Ednyfed Fychan, seneschal to Llywelyn the Great. Morgan's father made a fortunate marriage which brought him additional lands in Flintshire, and had a successful law practice among North Wales families like the Wynns of Gwydir. Thus he was able to build or rebuild the family mansion about 1578. Parts of his work survive in the modernised structure of today. In assessments for subsidy the estate ranked second in the hundred of Prestatyn, ranging from £4 in 1581 to £7 in 1601.[1]

Edward Morgan junior, the 1597 MP, was thus both well-to-do and connected with the chief established families of the shire. His mother was a Davies of Gwysaney, and he was doubly linked with the powerful Conways of Bodrhyddan – through his wife (who belonged on her mother's side to the Mostyns of Talacre, the wealthiest landowners of Prestatyn hundred) and through his sister, who married into the next generation of Conways. His Membership for the Boroughs, when he was barely of age, was his first taste of public affairs. As a Welsh constituency MP he could have served on a committee concerning Newport bridge on 29 Nov. 1597. An anonymous Welsh narrative 'carol' written in his honour in 1627 traces his later career. He travelled widely in Europe and Ireland, acquiring a competent knowledge of French and Italian, but a promising career was cut short when, in 1608, he killed John Egerton of Egerton, Cheshire, in a duel. His childless marriage was dissolved, and some time before 1627, and probably after his turn as sheriff he made over the bulk of his estates – including the capital messuage of Golden Grove – to his brother Robert, and retired to live at Weppre, in Northop parish.[2]

In retirement he invested some of his fortune in attempts to develop the neighbouring coal mines of Bagillt, but the work was still in the speculative stage when he died. In his will, dated 12 May 1638 and proved on 31 Mar. 1641, he appointed Captain William Morgan as executor; the 'two loving girls', whom he commends to the executor for legacies should the coal venture succeed, were probably illegitimate daughters. The line was carried on through the children of his brother Robert, who died in the same year; some of them fought for Charles I.[3]

[1] Dwnn, *Vis. Wales*, ii. 297; *NLW Jnl.* vi. 237; *Y Cutta Cyfarwydd*, ed. Thomas (1883), pp. 32, 194, 199; UCNW, Gwysaney ms 7; *Cal. Wynn Pprs.* pp. 23, 29; *RCAM Flints.* 51; *Proc. Llandudno Field Club*, xxvi. 28–9; E179/221/217; 221/225. [2] *NLW Jnl.* vi. 236–9; D'Ewes, 565; Ormerod, *Cheshire*, ii. 629; NLW Peniarth ms 287, p. 164; E179/221/228. [3] *Y Cutta Cyfarwydd*, 194; *NLW Jnl.* vi. 238–9; *Proc. Llandudno Field Club*, xxvi. 36–41.

A.H.D.

MORGAN, Henry I, of Bassaleg, Mon. and Cardiff.

CARDIFF BOROUGHS 1571

5th s. of John Morgan of Bassaleg by either his 1st w. Anne, da. of Lewis ap John of Baglan or his 2nd w. Maud, da. of Richard Jenkins of Llanowen. *m.* Mary, da. and h. of William Robin, at least 2s.[1]
Customer and collector of Cardiff to at least 1597; ?commr. piracy by 1577.[2]

There can be no certainty as to which of the numerous Henry Morgans of south-eastern Wales was the 1571 MP. It seems likely, however, that he was the man who held the position of customer of the port of Cardiff for many years. Research into the origins of the customer's brother, Thomas Morgan, the Catholic conspirator and secretary to Mary Queen of Scots, has shown that they almost certainly came from the Bassaleg branch of the Morgan family of Machen. This being so, Thomas and Henry were first cousins of Thomas Morgan II*, MP for Monmouthshire in 1589. Henry probably owed his position at Cardiff, as well as his return to Parliament, to the earls of Pembroke.[3]

The activities of Thomas Morgan, and of another brother Rowland, who had been converted to Catholicism and sent on the English mission from Rheims in 1582, brought Henry under suspicion at about the time of the Parry and Babington plots. One of his neighbours in south Wales told the authorities that he had harboured Rowland, now a priest, and had conveyed 'moneys yearly beyond the seas'. As a result of this and other accusations, Henry was examined by Edward Flowerdew*. He maintained that he had received no letters from Thomas 'tending either to the hurt of her Majesty or danger of the state'. He agreed that he had sent £40 or £50 overseas for Rowland's education, but had refused to pass on letters from Thomas seeking financial help from a number of prominent Welshmen. On this occasion, he must have cleared himself, but he may have spent a short time in the Gatehouse prison in the summer of 1586. Thomas, in recommending Henry to Mary Queen of Scots, claimed that he 'hath lovingly remembered me in this banishment', and he was still trying to communicate with him in 1590. Still, there is no evidence that Henry was himself a Catholic: indeed he regretted that Rowland had been 'perverted to popery'. One of his accusers claimed to be acting for 'the good and quiet preservation of the state', but he was in fact trying to acquire a lease of the manor of 'Rompney', Glamorganshire, which Thomas, fearing the forfeiture of his property, had conveyed to his brother. Henry, evidently, was allowed to retain the estate, for he renewed the lease for the lives of himself and two sons in 1591. He still held his position at Cardiff in 1597, after which year nothing is known of him.[4]

[1] Clark, *Limbus*, 316; *Trans. Cymmrod. Soc.* 1900–1, pp. 124–7; *Augmentations*, ed. Lewis and Davies (Univ. Wales Bd. of Celtic Studies, Hist. and Law ser. xiii), 455–6. [2] J. Dawson, *Commerce and Customs of Newport*, 14; *CSP Dom.* 1547–80, p. 580; 1595–7, p. 371. [3] Clark, *Limbus*, 316; *Trans. Cymmrod Soc.* loc. cit.; L. Hicks, *An Elizabethan Problem*, 5 and n. 5; *Exchequer*, ed. E. G. Jones (Univ. Wales Bd. of Celtic Studies, Hist. and Law ser. iv), 139. [4] SP12/178/64, 65, 66; *Cath. Rec. Soc.* ii. 267; *CSP Scot.* 1584–5, p. 608; *HMC Hatfield*, iv. 6–10; *CSP Span.* 1587–1603, pp. 565–9; H. Foley, *Recs. of Eng. Prov. of Society of Jesus*, vi. 14–15; L. Hicks, *An Elizabethan Problem*, 5, 91; *Augmentations*, 455–6; *CSP Dom.* 1595–7, p. 371.

M.R.P.

MORGAN, Henry II (*d.*1632), of Penllwyn Sarth, Mynyddislwyn, Mon.

MONMOUTHSHIRE 1601

1st s. of Henry Morgan of Penllwyn Sarth by Elinor, da. of John Morgan of Pencraig; bro. of Sir Edmund*. *m.* Cecily, da. of Arnold Welsh of Llanwern, 5s.

J.p. Mon. from 1583, sheriff 1602–3.

Other than the above, nothing of interest has been ascertained about Morgan in the Elizabethan period. As knight for Monmouthshire he may have attended two committees concerning the order of parliamentary business (3 Nov.) and monopolies (23 Nov.).

Clark, *Limbus*, 317; D'Ewes, 624, 649.

A.H.D.

MORGAN, John I (*?d.* by 28 Jan. 1572), prob. of Arkeston in Kingston, Herefs. and Carmarthen.

LEOMINSTER 1563

?m. Agnes.[1]

There were Morgans living at Arkeston in the sixteenth century, but the pedigrees give no John of a possible date. However, it is likely that the MP was related to this branch of the family: Ann Morgan, almost certainly daughter of Sir Thomas of Arkeston, married Henry Carey†, 1st Baron Hunsdon, who in July 1559 became steward of Leominster.[2]

Morgan of Arkeston, the presumed MP, may be the man of this name who early in 1562 prosecuted James Scudamore of Llanthony, Monmouthshire for a £10 debt, causing him to be outlawed and later imprisoned in the Fleet. In May 1572 Agnes, widow of John Morgan (no seat is given), received a lease of former church property in several counties, including Herefordshire, where some of the land in question had belonged to Leominster priory. The grant is said to have been made for her former husband's service to the Crown. There was a sewer of the chamber of this name in Elizabeth's reign, but the dates known for his career seem too late for the Leominster Member. However, since both Lord Hunsdon and his wife had positions in the royal Household, it is quite conceivable that a relative of Lady Hunsdon held a minor post there. The grantee of ex-monastic lands was presumably the John Morgan of Carmarthen who died intestate before 28 Jan. 1572, when his widow, Agnes, received administration of the property.[3]

Another, though less likely, identification for the Leominster Member is John Morgan of Bassaleg, Monmouthshire, son of Thomas Morgan of Machen, esquire of the body, by Elizabeth, daughter of Roger Vaughan of Porthaml, Breconshire. He married (1) Anne, daughter of Lewis ap John of Baglan, Glamorgan; (2) Maud, daughter of Richard Jenkins of Llanowen (?Llanoethin, Glam.), and had five sons including Henry Morgan I*, customer of Cardiff, and four daughters.[4]

[1] *CPR*, 1569–72, pp. 468–9; PCC admon. act bk. 1572, f. 2. [2] Clark, *Limbus*, 258–9; *CP*, vi. 628–9; *CPR*, 1558–60, p. 90. [3] *CPR*, 1560–3, p. 386; 1569–72, pp. 468–9; G. Owen, 'Desc. Wales', *Desc. Pemb.* ed. H. Owen, ii. 390; PCC admon. act bk. 1572, f. 2. [4] Clark, 311, 316.

N.M.F.

MORGAN, John II, of Carmarthen.

CARMARTHEN BOROUGHS   1563

Burgess, Carmarthen by 1563.[1]

There were several Morgan families in Carmarthenshire from which this MP may have come, but his name does not occur at the appropriate time in any of their pedigrees. The 1563 election return shows that he was a burgess of Carmarthen.

One, and one only, source for names of Members of the 1571 Parliament has a John Morgan sitting for Carmarthen Boroughs. This is the list Browne Willis printed from a manuscript formerly in the collection of Le Neve;[2] the name does not appear on his ms list (Bodl. Willis 9) nor on the other list for the 1571 Parliament (the de Tabley ms), both of which fail to name the Member for this constituency. Browne Willis gives John Vaughan as the county MP, whereas it seems conclusive that this must have been Sir Henry Jones. If Browne Willis supplied the name of the county man by the guesswork for which he is notorious, it is possible that he also guessed at the name of the borough man. A better guess might be John Vaughan II*, whom Willis gives for the county. In any case it is unlikely that the 1563 Carmarthen Boroughs man was re-elected in 1571, if he was the 'John Morgan of Carmarthen' sent with two vessels to cruise off Ireland and Spain to report on any hostile preparations, because this man did not report on his mission until a week after Parliament opened.[3]

The indications are that the John Morgan who sat for Carmarthen in 1563 was not the sewer of the Queen's chamber who began to acquire land in Carmarthenshire and Cardiganshire from 1586.[4]

[1] C219/27/54. [2] See *Interim Report*, 25. [3] *CSP Dom.* 1547-80, pp. 408-9. [4] G. Owen, 'Desc. Wales', *Desc. Pemb.* ed. H. Owen, ii. 390. See under MORGAN, John I.

A.H.D.

MORGAN, Sir Matthew (*b.* c.1563), of Pencarn, Mon.

BRECON BOROUGHS   1593

b. c.1563, 3rd s. of Edward Morgan of Pencarn by Frances, da. of Ralph Leigh of London.[1] prob. *unm.* Kntd. 1591.

Morgan came of fighting stock, a branch of the Morgans of Tredegar: his relative Thomas Morgan I* – 'the warrior', and governor of Bergen op Zoom – left him by will his suit of gilt armour; his younger brother Charles was 'brought up to arms since ten years old', and spent most of his life fighting abroad until his death in 1643. Morgan himself fought under Norris in the Low Countries before 1589, but he was recalled in that year to serve as a captain of horse in the Portuguese expedition. He was dangerously wounded (and knighted by the Earl of Essex)

at the siege of Rouen in 1591, and continued to serve under Essex in the Normandy campaign of the following year until he was sent back to the Netherlands in 1593, and returned home in time for the Parliament.[2]

He had by this time become one of Essex's most devoted henchmen, and his return for Brecon Boroughs in 1593 was part of the campaign of Essex's Welsh steward Gelly Meyrick* to build up an Essex 'interest' in Parliament from those South Wales constituencies where the name of Devereux and Meyrick's own family influence counted. Meyrick's fellow-steward Thomas Crompton II and four of Essex's captains (Sir Conyers and Sir Nicholas Clifford, Sir Ferdinando Gorges and Thomas Baskerville) were all fellow-Members with Morgan for South Wales boroughs in this Parliament. For Morgan, a soldier of fortune, it was evidently something of a financial strain, but through the good offices of Meyrick he was able to borrow £300 from Thomas Myddelton*, the London merchant, to see him through. In the House he sat – along with the county Member, Robert Knollys* – on the committee concerning the recusancy laws (4 Apr.), but it would be rash to make from this any inferences as to his political or religious principles.[3]

In 1596 Morgan went with Essex on the Cadiz expedition, and he was called to account for his booty. If it was as modest as he alleged, he was certainly out-distanced by many of his fellow-captains. In 1597-8 he was campaigning in Flanders again in company with his 'good friend' Sir Robert Sidney* (the future Earl of Leicester), who undertook his defence against the Queen's unexplained displeasure. But his company was depleted for the Irish service, and eventually, after obtaining a minor commission at sea in 1598, he was given a colonelcy of foot under Essex in Ireland. He remained there till the end of 1599, apparently avoiding involvement in his patron's treasons. Essex's death, however, left him without employment and in desperate financial straits. Since 1598 he had been demanding arrears of pay running back several years. A Lincolnshire estate he had bought with his earnings was long since mortgaged to the hilt, and the £300 he borrowed in 1593 had grown by 1595 to more than £1,500. By 1602 he was hopelessly insolvent, and after this date nothing is heard of him.[4]

[1] Clark, *Limbus*, 326. [2] Clark, loc. cit.; *HMC Hatfield*, ix. 18; *DWB*, 640; *HMC Ancaster*, 246; *APC*, xvii. 116, 377, 392-3, 401; xviii. 63, 140; xix. 15, 72, 185; *CSP Dom.* 1591-4, pp. 200, 211, 283-4, 331-2; Lansd. 78, f. 138. [3] Neale, *Commons*, 238; *Parlts.* ii. 280-97; D'Ewes, 517; NLW, Chirk castle mss F. 12540, 122. [4] Lansd. 81, f. 184; 149, f. 31; *CSP Dom.* 1595-7, pp. 273-4; *HMC Hatfield*, vii. 245, 335; viii. 26-7, 312, 340, 501; ix. 18, 145, 147, 331; NLW mss cit., 163, 164, 165, 185, 192, 193, 233; *Eliz. Govt. and Soc.* 277.

A.H.D.

MORGAN, Rice (Rees, Rhys) (*d.* 1577), of Nevern, Pemb.

HAVERFORDWEST   1563

s. of Owen Morgan of Iscoed, St. Ishmael's, Carm. by Anne, da. of Thomas Phillips, wid. of Lewis Sutton of Haverfordwest. *m.* (1) Eva, da. of David ap Ieuan, 1da. *d.v.p.*; (2) 1576, Mary, da. of ?Ludovic Phillipps, 1da.[1]

J.p. Pemb. and Haverfordwest from c.1559; escheator, Pemb. and Carm. 1576–7.[2]

Morgan came of the Morgans of Muddlescombe, Kidwelly, a collateral branch of the Monmouthshire Morgans. His Pembrokeshire lands may have come from his mother, a grand-daughter of the redoubtable Sir Rhys ap Thomas, or from her first husband, and Morgan himself bought property in the county. He also owned property in various towns of Pembrokeshire and in Cardigan. He held the rectory of the Pembrokeshire St. Ishmael's (part of the estate of the dissolved priory of Haverfordwest) from 1561, but it was granted to another in 1575. At the musters of 1570 Rice Morgan was one of the Pembrokeshire gentlemen assessed at 'one light horseman furnished'.[3]

Returned to Parliament through the influence of Sir John Perrot*, and paid £1 18s. by the borough for his services, Morgan had, by 1569 gone over to the anti-Perrot faction. In consequence he was deprived of a seat on the town council, and a contemporary account believed him to have been impoverished by Perrot to the tune of £500. At the time of the 1571 election a supporter of the Perrot group 'railed upon Rhys ap Morgan esq. [saying] that if the Lord had right he should have been hanged 20 years ago'. Still, Morgan's vote was not challenged and he remained a justice of the peace.[4]

Morgan died 3 Oct. 1577, leaving a three month-old daughter.[5]

[1] Dwnn, *Vis. Wales*, i. 198; C142/182/46(1). [2] *CPR*, 1560–3, p. 447; 1563–6, pp. 30, 31; Lansd. 1218, f. 98. [3] Dwnn, loc. cit.; C142/182/46(1); *Augmentations*, ed. Lewis and Davies (Univ. Wales. Bd. of Celtic Studies, Hist. and Law ser. xiii), 476; Flenley, *Cal. Reg. Council, Marches of Wales*, 73–4. [4] Haverfordwest corp. recs. 2139, f. 1; *Star Chamber*, ed. Edwards (Univ. Wales Bd. of Celtic Studies, Hist. and Law ser. i), 135; *EHR*, lxi. 25; Lansd. 72, f. 4. [5] Wards 7/19/66.

A.H.D.

MORGAN, Richard (*d.* c.1630), of Fronfraith (Llandyssil), Mont.

MONTGOMERY BOROUGHS   1593

m. Margaret, da. of Thomas Lloyd of Gwern y buarth, Llandyssil, wid. of Charles Powell of Llandyssil, 3s.[1]

Dep. sheriff, Mont. 1600; bailiff, Montgomery 1610–12.[2]

Nothing is known of the parentage of this Member, whose family cannot have been of any local importance; it appears in none of the contemporary pedigrees and none of its members qualified for local office before Richard Morgan's return to Parliament. The estate was not even assessed to subsidy until Morgan appeared on the roll in

1598 – probably after his marriage, to which he seems to have owed his position in county society. His wife's family, owners of the adjacent estate of Gwern y buarth, had been substantial taxpayers in the parish since 1571, and they had important connexions by marriage. During his term of office as deputy sheriff Morgan was accused by a neighbouring yeoman in Star Chamber of illegal entry into his lands, wrongful imprisonment, corruption and illegal exactions. He had many other disputes about land between 1595 and 1615, but these were settled more peaceably by the process of fine and recovery: they show his territorial interests as extending from his own parish to Montgomery town, Manafon, Castle Caereinion, Llandinam and Kerry, all in the south-eastern section of the shire. He was by now of sufficient standing to send his third son Robert (born in 1608) to Cambridge in 1624; this son became bishop of Bangor after the Restoration (1666–73).[3]

He died intestate before 12 Sept. 1630, when letters of administration were granted to his widow.[4]

[1] Wood, *Ath. Ox.* ed. Bliss, ii. 889–90; Dwnn, *Vis. Wales*, i. 300. [2] *Star Chamber*, ed. Edwards (Univ. Wales Bd. of Celtic Studies, Hist. and Law ser. i), 130; *Mont. Colls.* xliv. 104. [3] E179/222/379, 222/274, 265/266; Dwnn, loc. cit.; *Star Chamber*, loc. cit.; *Mont. Recs.* (Mont. Colls. Supp.) 435, 497, 513, 555, 565; *DWB*, 651. [4] PCC admon. act bk. 1630, f. 189.

A.H.D.

MORGAN, Thomas I (c.1542–95)

SHAFTESBURY	1571
WILTON	1593

b. c.1542, s. of William Morgan of St. George's and Pencarn, Glam. by Anne, da. of Robert Fortescue of Wood, Devon. *m.* 1589, Anna, 4th ch. of Jan Baron van Merode, 2s. 2da. Kntd. 1587.

Capt. in Netherlands Apr. 1572, in Ireland 1574, in Wales 1575, in Netherlands 1578–84; commanded regiment in Netherlands 1584–5; gov. Flushing and other towns 1585–7, of Bergen-op-Zoom and lt.-col. English forces 1588–93.

This Member was the well-known professional soldier, whose distinguished service in the Low Countries earned him rewards both from Elizabeth and the States General. He presumably emerged from obscurity as one of the 1st Earl of Pembroke's many Welsh protégés. A Henry Morgan, presumably a relative, was gentleman usher at the funeral of the 1st Earl in 1570. On the first occasion that Morgan sat in Parliament for a Pembroke borough, it must have been as a young man during an interval in his military service. Pembroke again found a seat for him after the close of his military career. He was named to committees on 12 and 30 Mar. 1593, dealing respectively with the punishment of rogues and with distributing the contributions of both Houses of Parliament towards the relief of poor maimed soldiers. The burgesses of Wilton were appointed to a cloth committee, which he may have attended on 15 Mar. A brave soldier and a modest man, in the will he made a few days before his death on 22 Dec. 1595, he left token bequests to the Earl of Pembroke and his son, and to the Earl of Essex. The lord chamberlain, Lord Hunsdon (Henry Carey†, 1st Baron Hunsdon), was appointed overseer. Through his wife, Morgan was related to the Knollys family.

DNB; DWB; HMC Foljambe, 9; D'Ewes, 499, 501, 512; PCC 18 Drake; Cath. Rec. Soc. xxiv. 17, ex inf. Dr. A. Davidson.

P.W.H.

MORGAN, Thomas II (d. 1603), of Machen and Tredegar, Mon.

1st s. of Rowland Morgan of Machen by Blanche, da. of John Thomas of Llanarth. educ. M. Temple 1567. m. Elizabeth, da. of Roger Bodenham, 4s. 4da. suc. fa. 1577, cos. 1578.[1]
J.p. Mon. from c.1570, sheriff 1580–1, dep. lt. 1587; ?member, council in the marches of Wales 1590.[2]

Morgan belonged to a junior branch of a leading Monmouthshire family. The death of his cousin William Morgan I* in 1569 without legitimate children led eventually to his inheriting Tredegar, long the seat of the senior line of the family. Even before his father's death Morgan was active as a local magistrate, and as holder of Machen his position in the county was far from negligible. But his inheritance of Tredegar gave him recognized county standing. With the Herberts and the Somersets, his kinsmen, he could wield great influence not only in local government, but in the return of Members of Parliament. Thus he was able to secure his own election for the county in 1588. His parliamentary career was uneventful: he was appointed to one committee (12 Feb. 1589) concerning the privilege of Roger Puleston II*, Member for Flintshire, and as first knight for the shire he would have been able to attend the subsidy committee on 11 Feb. He did not sit again himself, but his influence may have been helpful in securing the election of Henry Morgan II* in 1601.[3]

Apart from his one appearance in Parliament, Morgan appears to have been occupied exclusively in local government, serving as a justice of the peace and deputy lieutenant until his death in 1603, when he was succeeded by his son Sir William Morgan†.[4]

[1] Clark, Limbus, 310, 311, 320; A. Morgan, Hist. Morgan Fam. 13–14, 14–15. [2] CPR, 1569–72, p. 77; W. J. Smith, Herbert Corresp. (Univ. Wales Bd. of Celtic Studies, Hist. and Law ser. xxi), 60–1; APC, xxv. 18. Lansd. 63, f. 95 suggests he became a member of the council in the marches in 1590, but he does not appear in P. H. Williams's list of members, Council in the Marches of Wales, app. iv. An undated entry in the Lansdowne mss (111, f. 43) has a Thomas Morgan of Tredegar as member of the council. [3] Clark, 311; G. B.

Morgan, Mems. Morgan Fam. i. 112–21; ii. 65–7; D'Ewes, 431, 432. [4] APC, xxxi. 403; xxxii. 280; Herbert Corresp. 60–1.

I.C.

MORGAN, William I (d. 1569), of Tredegar, Mon.

1st s. of John Morgan of Tredegar by Lettice, da. of George Herbert of St. Julian's. m. Catherine, da. of Sir Thomas Bodenham of Rotherwas, Herefs., s.p.; at least 1s. illegit.[1]
J.p. Mon. from c.1543–4, sheriff 1549–50, 1564–5.

Morgan's ancestors had been territorial magnates in south-eastern Wales since before the Norman penetration. Nearly all the many Morgan families of this area were offshoots of Tredegar stock, the equally important Machen branch being founded by William Morgan's great-uncle Thomas Morgan. William Morgan may have been one of several of that name (not all identifiable) who entered the personal service of the first two Tudors. His father was alive in 1520, but had evidently died by about 1545, when a dispute arose with the Caerleon branch of the clan over the tithes of a group of parishes lying west and north-west of Tredegar, which had been leased by the bishop of Llandaff in 1492 to William Morgan's father, but were counter-claimed by virtue of a lease from the abbots of Llantarnam, in whom (it was alleged) they had long been vested; the case was fought, and apparently won, not by Morgan, but by his widow.[2]

In an Exchequer case of 1559, the sheriff of Monmouthshire was accused by the attorney-general of making a false return in respect of William Morgan's fellow-Member Thomas Herbert. Lacking legitimate heirs, Morgan, in his will (dated 8 Aug. 1568, and proved 27 June following) bequeathed the estate to Miles Morgan, son of his illegitimate child John. Miles perished at sea in the service of Sir Humphrey Gilbert* in 1578, leaving Tredegar to his cousin Thomas Morgan II*.[3]

[1] Clark, Limbus, 311. [2] Augmentations, ed. Lewis and Davies (Univ. Wales Bd. of Celtic Studies, Hist. and Law ser. xiii), 134–5; Exchequer, ed. E. G. Jones (same ser. iv), 212–13, 246–7. [3] E159/340/8; Clark, Limbus, 311; G. B. Morgan, Mems. Morgan Fam. i. 112–21; ii. 65–7; W. Coxe, Hist. Tour Mon. i. 66–7; DWB, 635–6.

A.H.D.

MORGAN, William II (by 1525–82), of Llantarnam, Mon.

b. by 1525, s. of John Morgan (d. 1524/5) of Caerleon. m. 1549, Elizabeth, da. of Sir Rhys Mansell of Margam, Glam., 2s. inc. Edward Morgan I* 1da.[1]
?Collector of subsidy, Newport 1544; commr. relief, Mon. 1550, piracy 1565, 1577, musters 1570, victuals 1574, tanneries 1574; j.p. 1555–d.; sheriff 1567–8, 1572–3.[2]

Morgan made a fortunate marriage and subsequently thrice represented his county in Parliament. He voted against a government measure in 1555, was nevertheless elected to Mary's last Parliament, missed the first two Elizabethan Parliaments, was elected to that of 1571 without leaving any trace in its records, and was defeated in 1572 through the partiality of the sheriff.[3]

He was famous for the hospitality he dispensed at his mansion near Caerleon, built largely of material from Llantarnam abbey. In 1566 he completed the purchase of large neighbouring estates by buying Caerleon park from the 1st Earl of Pembroke. He and his family built and endowed Caerleon free school, and Morgan's widow founded an almshouse.

Morgan had a long career as a local official, but he appears not to have been an entirely satisfactory piracy commissioner. In December 1576 he and a relative, Rowland Morgan, failed to seize a pirate ship at Newport, and according to Dr. Lewis, judge of the Admiralty court, refused to help those officials who were trying to take action against the pirates. Both Morgans had to appear before the Council in London to answer these charges.[4]

Morgan's religious position is not clear. He could hardly have avoided taking the oath of supremacy if it had been tendered to him, but his name was on a list of Catholics drawn up by Bishop Blethyn in 1577, and his son and heir was an open recusant. He made his will in November 1581, and died 29 Mar. 1582. The widow was to have a £100 annuity as well as a house and lands, and the sole executor, Morgan's son Edward, was to have the help of three overseers, including Sir Edward Mansell. The will was proved in April 1582 and the inquisition post mortem valued the landed property at over £155 p.a.[5]

[1] Clark, *Limbus*, 322; *Cal. Penrice and Margam Abbey Mss*, ed. Birch, iv. 5. [2] Lansd. 35, f. 79; 146, f. 20. [3] Guildford Mus. Loseley 1331/2; St. Ch. 5/M13/5, M31/39. [4] T. Churchyard, *Worthiness of Wales*, passim; Birch, loc. cit.; Bradney, *Mon.* iii(2), pp.227–8, 264; *CPR*, 1557–8, pp. 218, 415; 1558–60, p. 188; 1563–6, p. 362; G. B. Morgan, *Mems. Morgan Fam.* ii. 112–18; Flenley, *Cal. Reg. Council, Marches of Wales*, 108–9, 124–6; *APC*, vii. 285; ix. 268, 333, 339; xiii. 115; Lansd. 145, f. 20; *CSP Dom.* 1547–80, pp. 532, 543. [5] J. H. Canning, 'Mon. in Penal Days' (Newport Lib. ms); E. E. Havill, 'Parl. Rep. Mon.' (Univ. Coll. Cardiff MA thesis, 1949), pp. 18 seq.; PCC 14 Tirwhite; C142/196/16; G. B. Morgan, i. 23–4, 27.

A.H.D.

MORGAN, William III (c.1525–1602), of Chilworth, Surr.

HASLEMERE   1586

b. c.1525, o.s. of Richard Morgan of Chilworth by Joan, or Jane, da. of Robert Wintershall of Wintershall, nr. Bramley. *m.* (1)[1] Elizabeth, da. of John Thetcher of Presthawes, Westham, Suss., 1s. 4da.; (2)[1] Katherine, da. of Sir Roger Lewknor, wid. of John Mills of Grentham. Suss., 1da.; (3) by 1585 Julian(a).[2]

Commr. musters, Surr. by 1573, j.p. from c.1582–7, rest. by 1592; commr. recusancy 1590s.

Morgan's grandfather, Henry Morgan of Pencoed, moved to Surrey on his marriage to a Gunter heiress. Their main property was the manor of Chilworth, near Guildford, and they also held Tyting manor in the same parish, Utworth manor at Cranleigh, and Puttenham manor, near Loseley. Morgan's return for Haslemere in 1586 may have been at least approved of and perhaps arranged by (Sir) William More I*. His prominence as a commander of the local musters suggests that Morgan may have had some experience as a professional soldier in his youth. Many of the surviving references to him are concerned with land transactions. In about 1578, for example, he and Richard Hill acquired the manor of Abinger. He bought a share in Paddington Bray, another manor in Abinger parish, at about the same date, and also, at one time, owned a part of Westbrook, near Godalming. These and other properties resulted in a high subsidy assessment of £36 in 1593. Among many routine duties as a local justice, two or three of some interest can be found. On one occasion he and several of his colleagues were ordered by the Privy Council to restrain an Italian from building near Guildford a 'glass house' or factory for producing glass, the inhabitants of Guildford and Godalming being afraid that the woods were 'like to be consumed to the hurt of those towns and the whole country thereabouts'. Why he was dropped from the commission of the peace in 1587 is not known, but he was soon restored and was thenceforth also active as a recusancy commissioner. Once he was asked to search the house of old Lady Montagu, widow of the first Viscount, the investigation to be conducted 'with regard to the quality of the lady'.[3]

Morgan died intestate 10 Dec. 1602. He was buried in St. Martha's church, high on the North Downs above his home. A monument, with 24 lines of bad verse carved upon it, was erected to his memory. His inquisition post mortem, taken at Dorking in August 1603, shows that he had made precise provision for the disposal of his property at the time of his only son's marriage in 1585. The son, John, who was knighted by Lord Admiral Howard at Cadiz in 1596, received some lands as a marriage settlement and was to inherit the rest on the death of his father's third wife. Letters of administration were granted in 1603.[4]

[1] The first two marriages may have been in the reverse order. [2] *Vis. Surr.* (Harl. Soc. xliii), 33–4; Manning and Bray, *Surr.* ii. 118, where the first wife is given as Elizabeth Hager, not Thetcher. [3] Lansd. 35, f. 135; 121, f. 68; E163/14/8; Hatfield ms 278; *VCH Surr.* iii. 36, 88, 104, 105, 131, 133; Manning and Bray, ii. 19, 117, 137–8, 142; *Surr. Arch. Colls.* xix. 82; *HMC 7th Rep.* 642b; *APC*, xxiv. 328–9; *HMC Hatfield*, xi. 170; *Surr. Musters* (Surr. Rec. Soc.), 174, 179, 180, 211, 215, 218, 299, 311, 314, 321, 323; *HMC Foljambe*, 82. [4] *Surr. Arch. Colls.* xlvi. 31 n; Manning and Bray, ii. 120; Wards 7/28/165.

M.R.P.

MORGAN, Sir William (c.1542–83), of Langstone and Pencoed, Llanmartin, Mon.

MONMOUTH BOROUGHS   1572*

b. c.1542, 1st s. of Sir Thomas Morgan[†] of Pencoed by Cicely, da. of Sir George Herbert[†] of Swansea, Glam. *m.* Elizabeth, da. of Sir Andrew Judd, alderman of London, *s.p. suc.* fa. 1565. Kntd. 1574.[1]

J.p. Mon. from c.1570; marshal, Munster 1573; commr. musters, Mon. 1574; v.-adm. S. Wales 1574–8; constable, Dungarvan castle, co. Waterford 1579–82; chief commr. Munster 1580; gov. Youghal 1580.[2]

The Morgans of Langstone and Pencoed were a branch of the Morgans of Tredegar, founded in the fourteenth century when Morgan ap Llywelyn of Tredegar bought the manor of Langstone. In 1566 William Morgan succeeded to a cluster of estates and manors lying between the Usk and the Bristol Channel, encumbered, however, to the point where he was unwilling or unable to live on them. Either from family tradition, or from protestant zeal or simply in the hope of balancing his budget, he spent most of his life in the religious wars of the age. Three years after coming into his inheritance he fought in the Huguenot wars in France, returning to England in 1570, if, as seems likely (for he sometimes acted for the Earl in land transactions) he was the William Morgan who was standard bearer at the 1st Earl of Pembroke's funeral. In France he met Louis of Nassau, who persuaded him to fight in the Netherlands wars. He saw service at Valenciennes and Mons in 1572, and accompanied William the Silent into the northern provinces. Returning home in 1573, he volunteered in the expedition of the 1st Earl of Essex for the conquest and resettlement of Antrim, where he was appointed marshal on the retirement of Sir Peter Carew*, and was allotted a castle and lands as an 'adventurer'. It was no doubt Essex's warm commendation that won Morgan a knighthood on his return in 1574.[3]

The death of Moore Powell* earlier that year left a vacancy in the representation of Monmouth Boroughs, and the newly dubbed knight was elected in his place, but Parliament did not meet again till 1576. In that session of Parliament Morgan sat on the subsidy committee, 10 Feb. In the meantime he had been appointed vice-admiral for South Wales, discharging the duties by deputy – his kinsman and namesake of Llantarnam – while he himself lived at Abergavenny. He did not, however, escape aspersions of at least indirect collusion with the pirates who were infesting the coasts under his vice-admiralty about the years 1576–7, and there were Privy Council investigations. In the summer of 1577 he was reported to be preparing ships at Newport to go to sea 'in a warlike manner', and was forbidden to leave port; but on his promise to desist from any voyage 'which might have bred offences to neighbouring states' the ban was lifted, the

Council placing on record that Morgan was well thought of by the Queen, and denouncing any who should spread abroad 'lewd bruits' of his having been lodged in the Tower.[4]

In the end he did not sail, but a month later instructions from Ireland were sent by Sir Henry Sidney* (combining the offices of lord deputy of Ireland and lord president of Wales) for mobilising 1,000 Welsh levies in readiness for the Irish service, Morgan being put in charge of 200 from south-east Wales. The Queen, however, was now anxious to divert some of the treasure Sidney was lavishing on Ireland to the more urgent theatre of the Netherlands, and the orders were countermanded. Another mysterious episode in Morgan's life followed in 1578, when he was accused of intriguing with the French ambassador in London, on which Burghley interrogated the watermen who conveyed them.[5]

By 1579 Morgan was again in Ireland. Soon after the landing of the papal force at Smerwick, he was put in charge of 100 light horsemen raised in the north of England. After the usual vacillations he was in action in Munster by the end of the year, with a much increased company of both horse and foot. The next year he was sent home to review 800 recruits for Ireland levied in Wales, of whom he took 100 across. His repeated pleas for recall, on the ground of shattered health, from early in 1581, fell on deaf ears: he was still soldiering during the next parliamentary session, and when at last his request was granted in 1582, he had only a short time to live, dying 9 Oct. 1583.[6]

Having no children, Morgan made his younger brother Henry his heir, but to a much diminished estate. Only five years after inheriting, he had begun, but never completed, negotiations for the sale of his manor of St. Brides. Langstone, which had been in the family for 200 years, was disposed of in 1577, and there was small hope of repairing his fortunes in the Ireland of that day. From 1579 onwards there was constant bickering and cheese-paring over his pay. In the end, the Exchequer declared that he had died in debt to the government to the extent of 2,000 marks, and seized his estate, allowing Sir Walter Montagu of Boughton, who had married Anne, his brother's daughter and heiress, to farm the demesne lands of Pencoed until the debt had been cleared. The estate eventually passed to the kindred house of Morgan of Llantarnam.[7]

[1] G. B. Morgan, *Mems. Morgan Fam.* ii. 217–38; Clark, *Limbus*, 320. [2] *CPR*, 1569–72, p. 77; *CSP Ire.* 1509–73, pp. 526–7; 1574–85, pp. 210, 370; *EHR*, xxiii. 757; *APC*, xi. 280–1; xii. 101–2. [3] *DNB*; *Wilts. Mag.* xviii. 128; *Star Chamber*, ed. Edwards (Univ. Wales Bd. of Celtic Studies, Hist. and Law ser. i), 97; Bagwell, *Ireland under the Tudors*, ii. 243; Lansd. 56, f. 168; *CSP Ire.* 1509–73, pp. 526–7. [4] D'Ewes, 247; *Arch. Camb.* (ser. 5), xiv. 318; xv. 310; *CSP Dom.* 1547–80, p. 532; *APC*, ix. 269, 383–4, 389; x. 5, 19. [5] *Sidney Letters*, ed. Collins, i. 213; *APC*, x. 3, 30; Bagwell, ii. 346; *CSP Dom.* 1547–80, p. 595. [6] *APC*, xi. 595; xii. 66, 78, 86, 93; *CSP Ire.* 1574–85, p. 288; G. B. Morgan, loc. cit. [7] *Exchequer*, ed. E. G. Jones (Univ. Wales Bd. of

Celtic Studies, Hist. and Law ser. iv), 258–9, 261, 264; Clark, *Limbus*, 320; *APC*, xi. 280–1; xii. 101–2, 122, 223.

A.H.D.

MORICE, James (1539–97), of Chipping Ongar, Essex.

WAREHAM	1563
COLCHESTER	1584, 1586, 1589, 1593

b. 1539, 1st s. of William Morice† of Chipping Ongar by Anne Isaac of Kent. *educ.* M. Temple 1558, called. *m.* by 1560, Elizabeth (*d.* 1603), da. of George Medley of Tilty Abbey, Essex and 'Whitnes' (?Whitnash), Warws., 4s. inc. John* 3da. *suc.* fa. 1554.[1]

J.p. Essex from c.1573, q. by 1586, commr. piracy 1577; town clerk, Colchester by 1578; bencher and Autumn reader, M. Temple 1578; treasurer 1596; commr. musters, Essex 1583; recorder, Maldon from c.1586 (though, by 1593, called dep. recorder to Earl of Essex there); attorney of ct. of wards 16 Oct. 1589.[2]

Morice's importance as a Parliament man dates from the 1584 House of Commons, but it is likely that he was the James Morice who sat as a young man for Wareham, where his patron was almost certainly the 2nd Earl of Bedford, to whom (it would appear from Lady Elizabeth Russell's later remarks) he may have been related. Morice's father, who came from 'Roydon, Hertfordshire', bought in 1543 the site of a castle at Chipping Ongar, and there built the house which became the family seat. He died in 1554, when James was still a minor, and the son was not granted livery of his lands until July 1560, by which time he was a student at the Middle Temple.

As well as being an active local official, in Essex, Morice was a natural choice as a legal official in the strongly puritan towns of Colchester and Maldon. When Bishop Aylmer suspended George Northey, the popular town preacher of Colchester, Morice exerted himself to get him restored. In 1579, when the Queen visited Colchester, he delivered, as town clerk, the oration of welcome: he was unable to entertain her, as his children had measles. His first return as Member of Parliament for the borough he owed to the recorder, (Sir) Francis Walsingham*, who was granted both nominations by the borough authorities. Before the following election, in the autumn of 1586, the Council sent a circular letter to the sheriffs advocating the return of the same Members as in 1584–5, a recommendation which in this case Walsingham ignored. Morice and his 1584 colleague, Francis Harvey, had already been elected, and Walsingham readily accepted this arrangement, on the ground of the Queen's wish, 'as also in respect of their sufficiency for that place'. Walsingham was still recorder at the election of 1589, and in 1593 his successor (Sir) Thomas Heneage* seems not to have attempted to replace Morice by a nominee of his own. If Morice had lived to see another parliamentary election, his activities in the 1593 session would almost certainly have lost him Heneage's support.[3]

In the Commons, Morice became known as a foremost supporter of the cause of liberty as he saw it, to be secured through reliance on the common law. His interpretation of the constitution was historically inaccurate, but at a time when Whitgift was using his disciplinary powers harshly to enforce uniformity in the church, Morice's speeches were invaluable and highly effective. On 8 Dec. 1584 he was ordered to draft a bill concerning recusants and in this Parliament he was appointed to committees on the continuation of statutes (1 Dec., 19 Mar.), private bills (7, 15 Dec., 13 Feb.), informers (9 Dec.), the puritan petitions from the counties concerning a learned ministry (16 Dec.), penal laws (21 Dec.), hue and cry (4 Feb.), a privilege case (11 Feb.), procedure (13 Feb.), fraudulent conveyances (15, 18 Feb., 2, 17 Mar.), Jesuits (18 Feb.), Canterbury hospital (20 Feb.), the order of business (3 Mar.), the punishment of rogues (5 Mar.), the better government of the city of Westminster (22 Mar.) and excessive fines in ecclesiastical courts (22 Mar.). A legal bill was committed to him on 5 Mar. and he was appointed to another legal committee the same day.

In the following Parliament he was again appointed to numerous committees, including those concerning Mary Queen of Scots (4 Nov.), Norfolk returns (9 Nov.), legal matters (24 Feb. 1587), the bill for attainder (25 Feb.), a privilege case (6 Mar.), a learned ministry (8 Mar.), fish (9 Mar.), a private bill (15 Mar.) and the continuation of statutes (20 Mar.). A bill concerning horse stealing was committed to him on 7 Mar. 1587. He spoke twice concerning the subsidy to be levied for the expedition in the Low Countries (6 Mar.), arguing that the prelates, who were exempt from the burden of musters, were better able to bear the expense of a benevolence in addition to the subsidy than were the lay taxpayers. In December 1588 he was one of 16 lawyers asked by the Privy Council to prepare bills on the reform of justice for the forthcoming Parliament and to consider the revision of existing statutes. During the 1589 Parliament he was appointed to the main privilege committee (7 Feb.), and also to committees concerning the subsidy (11 Feb.), the Puleston privilege case (12 Feb.), legal committees (14, 25 Feb.), purveyors (27 Feb., 6 Mar.), the continuation of statutes (20 Mar.), Exchequer reform (20 Mar.), excess of apparel (21 Mar.), almshouses in Lambourn, Berkshire (22 Mar.) and forcible entries (24 Mar.). He was appointed to the committee concerning pluralities and non-residents on 1 Mar. 1589. He reported the bill concerning benefit of clergy on 3 Mar. 1589, spoke on the subject of Tonbridge school on 8 Mar., and reported the committee on presentations to benefices on 22 Mar.

By 1593 Morice had gained the lucrative office of attorney of the court of wards, doubtless by Lord Burghley's influence: some years later, in a letter to the lord treasurer, he wrote that he believed, 'besides your lordship and that honourable person your son, I have never an honourable friend'. Burghley appreciated his ability, as he showed by using him to defend Robert Cawdrey, a Rutland clergyman deprived for refusing to accept Whitgift's articles. Morice certainly found the lord treasurer's friendship valuable when in 1593 his parliamentary opposition to Whitgift led him into trouble. He had apparently made up his mind some time before Parliament began that he would attack the legality of the court of High Commission's proceedings, and was dismayed to find that Peter Wentworth* was planning the introduction of a bill on the succession question, which would be bound to rouse the Queen's anger against the puritans. Morice utterly disliked both the matter and form of Wentworth's speech and refused to confer with Wentworth's supporters, since 'never a wise man in the House will like of your motion'. However, though against meddling over the succession, Morice was ready to launch his own attack on the royal prerogative on the second full day of business in the session, 27 Feb., when he asked the House to consider three 'matters of very great weight and importance' – the *ex officio* oath, an 'ungodly and intolerable inquisition'; Whitgift's articles, 'a lawless subscription'; and the oath of ecclesiastical obedience required of excommunicated persons before absolution. He claimed that all three were against the law and common justice, violating Magna Carta, and challenged the bishops to 'declare to the world by what authority they do these things'. 'We ... the subjects of this kingdom, are born and brought up in due obedience, but far from servitude and bondage; subject to lawful authority and commandment, but freed from licentious will and tyranny.' This heritage, 'dearly purchased ... by our ancestors, yea, even with the effusion of their blood', it was the sacred duty of the present generation to hand on undefiled to posterity. He therefore presented two bills couched as petitions, against unlawful oaths and illegal imprisonment, asking the House to read the first immediately. A stormy debate followed, James Dalton, Sir John Wolley and Dr. William Lewin opposing Morice, and Sir Francis Knollys, the senior Privy Councillor present, upholding his 'good zeal and meaning'. Finally Robert Cecil tried to ease the tension. Describing Morice as learned and wise, and one whom he loved, he recommended that the Queen should be consulted. He could not carry the House, nor could Speaker Coke, who maintained that the bill was too long to proceed with immediately. Only the length of the debate, which had made it too late to do anything more that morning, prevented Morice from getting his bill read. He was given no further chance to raise the matter. The next day he was examined by five Privy Councillors, and showed himself so impenitent that even Burghley, who intervened several times in his favour, reprimanded him: 'Some little submission, Mr. Morice, would do well'. He was finally committed to the indulgent custody of (Sir) John Fortescue

I* at whose London house he remained for two months, until after the end of the session. About a fortnight after the start of his house arrest, Robert Wroth I* pleaded in the Commons for his release, but Privy Councillors managed to stifle the motion. When eventually he was set at liberty, the lord keeper and Burghley told him that, in spite of his recent activities, Elizabeth thought him 'both an honest man and a good subject'; but they reminded him that, since he was of counsel to the Queen, he should complain, if he believed 'aught were amiss in the church or commonwealth', to her rather than to the House of Commons. It is doubtful whether Morice would have acted on this advice if he had lived to see another Parliament. During the first few days of the 1593 Parliament he was appointed to several committees as attorney of the court of wards: privileges and returns (26 Feb.), the subsidy (26, 28 Feb.), and a legal committee (27 Feb.). In view of his sequestration on 28 Feb., it is not known how many of these committees he was able to attend.[4]

It may have been true that Elizabeth had no personal antipathy towards him. Later in 1593 the Earl of Essex (recently appointed recorder of Maldon, with Morice, the former recorder, serving as his deputy), tried to get him appointed attorney-general. Anyone but Essex might have hesitated to suggest him, considering his recent record. Elizabeth's reaction seems to have been surprisingly mild: she 'acknowledged his gifts, but said his speaking against her in such a manner as he had done should be a bar against any preferment at her hands'. Another person who tried to help him was Lady Elizabeth Russell, who wrote to Robert Cecil soon after Morice's release from confinement: 'My cousin, Morice, has been with me this afternoon, poor man ... Oh, good nephew! the gravity, wisdom, care of maintaining law of the land, learning and piety of the man' ought to be rewarded by membership of the Council. The mastership of the rolls was the office Lady Russell had in mind for her protégé, whom she described as Burghley's 'kinsman and friend'. She reported Morice's own opinion of his recent treatment:

> Himself wished no better, he said, but that he might have been called to answer and to have been chidden of her Majesty than of the Council, for he thinketh it hard measure to be committed two months only upon her Majesty's displeasure and not to answer it to her Majesty's self what he had done.[5]

Despite his temporary disgrace, Morice retained his court of wards office, but he became dissatisfied at receiving no further promotion. In June 1596 he wrote to Burghley describing himself as aged nearly 60, rich only in children and grandchildren, and having not 'added one foot of land to the little patrimony left me by my father'. He assured his correspondent that his 'Brief Treatise' against unlawful oaths had not been intended for publication, but that Dr. Richard Cosin* had got hold of a copy, and 'in the beginning of the last Parliament' published a confutation of it, 'perverting it and abusing the author'. Nothing daunted Morice's spirit for long. 'By God's grace', he had earlier told Burghley, 'while life doth last, which I hope now after so many cracks and crazes will not be long, I will not be ashamed in good and lawful sort to strive for the freedom of conscience, public justice, and the liberties of my country'.[6]

He died 2 Feb. 1597, leaving unaccounted for £200 which had passed through his hands as treasurer of the Middle Temple. As late as 1604 the Temple authorities were still trying to obtain the money. The Morice lands, mainly at Chipping Ongar, Sutton and surrounding districts in Essex, descended to John, the eldest son, who was in his mid-twenties. Morice's will, drawn up on 7 Mar. 1596, was proved in July 1598. His puritanism is evident from the preamble, which speaks of his being called 'out of this wretched and transitory life', being in full hope to inherit 'the blessing of the children of God, even life and joy everlasting'. He asked the executors, his widow and son John, to pay various debts and to supervise legacies to his other children (including £200 to an unmarried daughter). In addition to the lands, John was to have all his father's 'books of the laws of England ... Latin, Greek and French books'. Morice besought God 'so to bless him [John] and the rest of my children that they may spend and pass the time of this their short and miserable life in all virtuous and godly conversation and behaviour, studying and endeavouring (by the grace of God) to be profitable members of Christ's church and good subjects in the commonwealth'. There were surprisingly few bequests to friends and servants, and the only charitable legacy was £10 to the poor of Chipping Ongar.[7]

[1] Burke, *Landed Gentry* (1871), ii. 947; *Vis. Essex* (Harl. Soc. xiii), 256, 457–8; Morant, *Essex*, i. 129; *CPR*, 1558–60, p. 447; will at Essex RO, 231/ER/17. [2] Essex RO Assize File 35/15/3; Lansd. 146, f. 18; Essex Arch. Soc., Morant mss; *M. T. Recs.* i. 221, 224, 284, 367; Morant, i. 51; Essex RO, Maldon borough recs. DB 3/3/256, 264, 265, 270, 272; *CSP Dom.* 1547–80, p. 635, where date of attorneyship is given in error as 1579; pat. roll 31 Eliz. pt. 10. [3] Collinson thesis, 398; Morant mss; Colchester ass. bk. 1576–99 (Nov. 1584); Neale, *Commons*, 299–300. [4] Trinity, Dublin, Thos. Cromwell's jnl. f. 82; Harl. 7188, anon. jnl. ff. 100–2; D'Ewes, 334, 336, 337, 339, 340, 345, 346, 348, 349, 351, 352, 353, 362, 363, 369, 371, 394, 396, 410, 412, 413, 415, 417, 429, 431, 432, 439, 440, 441, 443, 444, 447, 449, 450, 451, 452, 471, 474, 476, 478; Townshend, *Hist. Colls.* 17, 22, 27, 60, 61; Neale, *Parlts.* ii. 257–9, 267–79; *APC*, xvi. 416; Lodge, *Illus.* ii. 444; W. Pierce, *Hist. Intro. to Martin Marprelate Tracts*, 79; Lansd. 68, ff. 104, 106; 73, f. 109. [5] Lodge, ii. 446; *HMC Hatfield*, iv. 460. [6] *CSP Dom.* Add. 1580–1625, p. 376; Lansd. 82, ff. 148, 150–1; Lodge, ii. 445. [7] *M. T. Recs.* ii. 443; C142/258/74; will at Essex RO, 231/ER/17.

J.H.

MORICE (afterwards **POYNTZ**), **John** (1568–1618), of Chipping Ongar, Essex, and Heneage House, London.

APPLEBY   1601, 1604

bap. 17 Oct. 1568, 1st s. of James Morice*. *educ.* ?Camb.; M. Temple 1586. *m.* (1) 24 Oct. 1593, Katherine, da. and h. of Sir Gabriel Poyntz of North Ockendon, at least 3s. 2da.; (2) 27 Feb. 1606, Lettice, da. of Edward Fitzgerald, wid. of (Sir) Ambrose Coppinger*, *s.p. suc.* fa. Feb. 1597. Kntd. 22 May 1603.[1]

Gent. pens. by 1602–1610/13; j.p. and dep. lt. Essex 1613; chamberlain of the Exchequer by 1615.[2]

Admitted to the Middle Temple without fine because his father was a bencher, Morice may have been educated at Cambridge, where there were two of his name in the early 1580s. He remained at the Middle Temple, in his father's chambers, for some years, being joined there in 1589 by Anthony Luther, an associate of his future father-in-law, and in 1597, after his father's death, by his younger brother Henry, who was bound with Luther and an Edward Turner who married the Morices' sister Anne.[3]

Before May 1600 Morice left the Middle Temple; he does not appear to have been called to the bar or to have practised as a lawyer. Having inherited most of his father's property – the manor of Chipping Ongar had been settled on him at his marriage – and with the sure expectation of the manor of North Ockendon which his father-in-law Poyntz (whose family name Morice took) had settled on him and his wife upon the same occasion, it seems that he lived as a country gentleman, emerging to sit in two Parliaments for Appleby, a borough whose Members not infrequently were lawyers and connected, if only tenuously, with the Cliffords, earls of Cumberland. In the case of Morice the link may well have been Lady Elizabeth Russell, the Countess of Cumberland's sister-in-law. To Lady Elizabeth, Morice's father was 'my cousin', and as she was Lady Burghley's sister the relationship embraced the Cecils as well: the elder Morice was Burghley's 'kinsman and friend'. A request for a parliamentary seat, addressed to Cumberland from such a source, was unlikely to be refused, and the supposition that Lady Elizabeth Russell played a key role in the business is strengthened by the fact that it was also as Member for Appleby that Thomas Posthumous Hoby, her son by a previous marriage, made his parliamentary début. Morice is not known to have played any part in the proceedings of the 1601 Parliament. However, he may have attended a committee concerning the strengthening of the north parts to which the burgesses for Appleby were appointed on 3 Dec.[4]

The picture of Morice (or Poyntz) which emerges from his undated will, written before he set off for 'the Spa' to recover his health, is of a contented, God-fearing man, happy in his possessions and in the affection and fortune of his second wife. Through God's grace, and by the sale of Dame Lettice's 'fair jointure' and other goods of hers for 'a great sum of money', he had acquired lands and goods 'beyond expectation or any probability in the judgment of man' and been enabled to meet the expenses of his eldest son's suits at law and the cost of building at Heneage House (Bevis Marks) in London and at Ockendon. There was £1,000 to his credit in the hands of his 'brother' Sir Nicholas Carew, but even so he expected his debts to amount to £1,600, more than his goods and chattels might realise. The deficiency, if any, he charged his eldest son, Sir James Poyntz, to make good, 'for the honour of his dear father that he be not said to have lived with the reputation of an honest man and died with the report of an unconscionable deceiver'. As he and their grandfather Poyntz had already made provision for the younger sons and daughters, Morice left the bulk of his property to Sir James, together with all his armour and a library – presumably those 'books of the laws of England' and other works in Latin, Greek and French bequeathed to him by his own father – which he enjoined Sir James not to sell but to preserve for his posterity. His 'dear and worthy wife' he made his sole executrix, hoping it might please God to bless his journey and continue his life so that in short time he would be able to ease her of the burden. He died 31 Jan. 1618.[5]

[1] Vis. Essex (Harl. Soc. xiii), 92, 256; Morant, Essex, i. 103, 129; Crisp, Ongar Par. Reg.; VCH Essex, iv. 161; Lodge, Peerage of Ireland (1789), i. 199; Lysons, Mdx. Parishes, 133. [2] LC2/4/4; APC, 1613–14, pp. 278–9; information from Mr. F. G. Emmison, citing calendar of assize files 1615–17 in Essex RO. [3] M. T. Recs. i. 284, 309, 371, 404. [4] C142/258/74; Jas. Morice's will, Essex RO, D/AER17, f. 231; and see MORICE, James. [5] PCC 25 Meade and 3 Windebanck; C142/369/148; Morant, Essex, i. 103 and cf. Chamberlain Letters ed. McClure, ii.136

E.L.C.M.

MORISON, Charles (1549–99), of Cassiobury, Herts.

TAVISTOCK   1572*

b. 1549, o.s. of (Sir) Richard Morison[†] of Cassiobury by Bridget, da. of John, Lord Hussey. She afterwards married Henry Manners, 2nd Earl of Rutland and Francis Russell[†], 2nd Earl of Bedford. educ. Trinity Coll. Camb. 1564, G. Inn 1566. m. aft. Apr. 1573, Dorothy, da. of Nicholas Clerke of North Weston, Oxon., wid. of Henry Long*, 1s. 3da. suc. fa. 1557.

J.p. Herts. from c.1577, sheriff 1579–80; keeper of Rockingham forest to 1583.[1]

Morison's father, while secretary to Thomas Cromwell[†], acquired monastic lands formerly belonging to the abbey of St. Albans. The manor of Cassiobury, which became the family seat, was a residence of the abbots. Sir Richard Morison passed from the service of Cromwell to that of Henry VIII and Edward VI, who sent him as ambassador to the emperor. In Mary's reign he retired to Strasbourg, where he died, leaving the family influence in Hertfordshire to be developed by his son. Charles Morison was probably with his parents in Strasbourg as a child, but he had presumably returned to England with his mother by July 1557, when his wardship was granted to John

Throckmorton I*, despite his father's expressed wish that his wardship should be granted to Katherine, Duchess of Suffolk, whose religious views coincided with his own. Morison was soon incorporated in the circle of the 2nd Earl of Bedford, who became his mother's third husband, his sister Jane marrying Bedford's son by a previous marriage. It was Bedford who gained for Morison a seat in Parliament in 1576, when he was returned for Tavistock in place of Robert Farrar, who had died. His one recorded occurrence in the proceedings of this Parliament comes in the session of 1581 when he was appointed to the subsidy committee on 25 Jan.[2]

In Hertfordshire Morison was a patron of one of 'the spiritual brethren', Thomas Wilcox (who dedicated some of his works to him), and encouraged preachers in neighbouring churches. As a leading Hertfordshire magistrate, Morison was careful of the material as well as the spiritual welfare of the county, and in 1596 he received a Privy Council letter commending 'the care you have taken for the relief of the poor, by remedying as much as you could the causes of the great dearth of grain in your markets.'[3]

Morison was appealed to by both sides in the 1584 contested county election. In 1588 Burghley asked him to support the candidacy of his son Robert Cecil*, and in the 1590s Morison wrote on several occasions to thank Sir Robert Cecil for the continuance of his favours. Morison wrote again in December 1598 apologizing for his inability to do Cecil service because of ill-health, and thanked him for his 'honourable remembrance of a dead man to this world'. Morison's son married a niece of Michael Hickes*, Burghley's secretary and Robert Cecil's friend. Morison was also on friendly terms with Walsingham, who sent him a remedy for gout in March 1590.[4]

Morison died 31 Mar. 1599, leaving an heir Charles, aged 12. His will named Bridget, dowager Countess of Bedford; Henry, 6th Earl of Kent; and Thomas, Lord Grey of Wilton, as possible guardians. It recommended that the boy be left in the care of his mother while she remained unmarried and that 200 marks should be paid to her annually for his diet until he was 14 years old. He was to go to Cambridge, to stay with Mr. Sutton his schoolmaster until he was 17, there to learn Greek and Latin. Trustees were appointed for the extensive property in Bedfordshire, Hertfordshire and London. The overseers of the will were the Earl of Kent, (Sir) Dru Drury* and Sir William Clerke. The elaborate arrangements made for the trusteeship of the land, and Morison's belief that they would be honoured, suggest that he had used his connexion with the Cecils to make a private arrangement with the master of the wards about the heir. Morison's inquisition post mortem was taken 25 July 1599.[5]

[1] Vis. Herts. (Harl. Soc. xxii), 116; C142/110/170; R. Clutterbuck, Herts. i. 238; Al. Cant. iii. 216; PCC 28 Wrastley; SP12/121/15; CSP Dom. 1581–90, p. 114. [2] Clutterbuck, i. 236–8; C. H. Garrett, Marian

Exiles, 229–30; *CPR*, 1557–8, p. 192; D'Ewes, 288. [3] Collinson, 58, 947; *APC*, xxvi. 258. [4] Neale, *Commons*, 28–9, 330; *HMC Var.* vii. 340, 341; *HMC Hatfield*, vii. 468; viii. 476; *CSP Dom.* 1595–7, pp. 86, 90; *HMC Rutland*, i. 281. [5] PCC 64 Kidd; C142/257/45.

I.C.

MORLEY, Herbert (1562–1610), of Glynde, Suss.

| WINCHELSEA | 1589 |
| NEW SHOREHAM | 1593 |

b. 1562, 1st s. of William Morley* of Glynde by his 1st w. Ann, da. of Anthony Pelham of Bucksteep in Warbleton. *educ.* Clare, Camb. 1577; Furnival's Inn; M. Temple 1579. *m.* (1) c.1586, Dorothy, da. of Edmund Downing* of London, *s.p.*; (2) c.1592, Ann (*d.*1624), da. of Sampson Lennard* of Chevening, Kent, 2da. *suc.* fa. 1597.

J.p.q. Suss. from c.1601; sheriff, Surr. and Suss. 1607–8.

Though Morley was on good terms with Thomas Sackville*, Lord Buckhurst, lord lieutenant of Sussex, his own standing was sufficient to ensure his being returned to Parliament for both Winchelsea (where his uncle Herbert Pelham* and his father were jurats) and for New Shoreham, some dozen miles from Glynde. So far as is known he took no part in the business of the Parliaments. He died 15 Oct. 1610. His will, leaving £100 to Lewes for the benefit of 'poor new married folks and young beginners', was proved in the same month, and confirmed by sentence in November 1611.

W. Berry, *Co. Genealogies, Suss.* (Comber's copy at Chichester), 173–5; *Glynde Place Archives*, ed. Dell, 25, 26; C66/1549; Harl. 703, ff. 16, 49; C142/253/98, 325/184; PCC 3 Lewyn, 83 Wingfield, 93 Wood; *Suss. Arch. Colls.* ii. 214.

J.E.M.

MORLEY, John I (*d.*1587), of Halnaker, Suss. and St. Botolph-without-Aldersgate, London.

| CHIPPING WYCOMBE | 1584 |
| ST. IVES | 1586 |

m. Elizabeth, da. of Edward Wotton, MD, 3s. inc. John II* 3da.[1]

?An official in the Star Chamber from 7 July 1565; jt. surveyor of customs on cloth and wines by 1568; engrosser of the great roll and clerk of the pipe July 1579.[2]

Morley, of 'Saxham', Suffolk, who purchased lands at Halnaker, Sussex, was an Exchequer official turned country gentleman. He evidently had some connexion with the Earl of Leicester, who in 1585 described him as 'my friend' when petitioning Burghley on his behalf, but his return to Parliament for Wycombe in 1584 was presumably due to the dean of Windsor. Morley had property in Old Windsor, but either Leicester or Burghley

may have acted as an intermediary on his behalf. Burghley, to whom he must have been known through his work in the Exchequer, was presumably responsible for his return for St. Ives. Morley was recorded as serving on one committee in each of his two Parliaments, concerning the true payment of tithes (6 Mar. 1585), and a proviso to the bill for the continuation of statutes (17 Mar. 1587).[3]

He died 14 Nov. 1587. In his will, made 10 Nov., proved 22 June in the following year, he remembered a number of friends and the poor of St. Botolph's, Old Windsor and Boxgrove. The widow and his son and heir John were the executors, and Morley's brother-in-law John Sotherton, baron of the Exchequer, who also lived in St. Botolph's, and Sir Walter Mildmay* were appointed overseers.[4]

[1] J. Dallaway, *W. Suss.* ii. 182; *Vis. Suss.* (Harl. Soc. liii), 140; PCC 42 Rutland. [2] The Star Chamber office may have been a reversion: Inner Temple, Petyt mss, 39; *CSP Dom.* 1547–80, p. 310; PRO Index 16774, f. 18. [3] Mousley thesis, 620; *VCH Berks.* iii. 82; C142/218/20; PCC 42 Rutland; Lansd. 45, f. 84; D'Ewes, 364, 416. [4] PCC 42 Rutland.

W.J.J.

MORLEY, John II (c.1572–1622), of Halnaker, Suss. and St. Botolph-without-Aldersgate, London.

NEW SHOREHAM	1601
CHICHESTER	1604*,[1] 1614
NEW SHOREHAM	1621

b. c.1572, 1st s. of John Morley I* of Halnaker and London. *educ.* Christ Church, Oxf. 1586; I. Temple 1587. *m.* Cicely, da. of Sir Edward Caryll of Harting, 2s. 2da. *suc.* fa. 1587. Kntd. 23 July 1603.[2]

Morley added by purchase to the estates his father had acquired as a government official, so that within two generations the family had established itself as one of the most prominent in western Sussex. Thus Morley would have had no difficulty in being returned to the 1601 Parliament for New Shoreham. He left no trace upon the known surviving records of this Parliament, and the remainder of his career belongs to the Stuart period. At one time he found himself in difficulties with the authorities because of his Catholicism, and some of his property was confiscated. His father-in-law, who was also a Catholic, had paid for Morley's training at the Inner Temple, and his association with the Carylls remained close. Morley died rich between 21 and 27 Dec. 1622.[3]

[1] By-election in Apr. 1610. [2] *Vis. Suss.* (Harl. Soc. liii), 140–1; *Vis. Suss.* (Harl. Soc. lxxxix), 77; PCC 42 Rutland; J. Dallaway, *W. Suss.* i. 132. [3] *Suss. Rec. Soc.* xix. 3, 58, 147; xx. 289, 482; xxxiii. 32; *VCH Suss.* iv. 101, 102, 143, 149, 177, 238; Dallaway, i. 9; D. G. C. Elwes and C. J. Robinson, *Castles and Manor Houses of W. Suss.* 41, 70 n, 231; *Suss. Arch. Colls.* xliii. 201–13; lxxxii. 60–4; *CSP Dom.* 1611–18, p. 120; *Cal. I.T. Recs.* i. 353; PCC 115 Savile; Add. 38133, f. 27; C142/399/156; *Chamberlain letters* ed. McClure, ii. 15.

M.R.P.

MORLEY, William (c.1531–97), of Glynde, Suss.

LEWES 1571

b. c.1531, 1st s. of Thomas Morley[†] by Elizabeth, da. of Anthony Maycott of Reculver, Kent. *educ.* ?Queens', Camb. 1545, BA 1548–9, fellow 1548–50. *m.* (1) settlement 14 Oct. 1560, Ann, da. of Anthony Pelham of Warbleton, Suss., 1 or 2s. inc. Herbert Morley* 3da.; (2) Sept. 1570, Margaret (*d.*1632), da. of William Roberts of Warbleton, 2 or 3s. 1da. *suc.* fa. 1559.[1]

J.p. Suss. from c.1570, commr. piracy 1577, capt. of musters by 1584; sheriff, Surr. and Suss. 1580–1; jurat, Winchelsea 1582, mayor and brodhull rep. 1583–4.[2]

Morley was 'consiliarius' of the English at Padua university in 1556. He afterwards left Padua in the company of his cousin John Pelham* and travelled to Geneva, where they were received into the congregation of John Knox on 26 Nov. 1557. He and Pelham were both in the 1571 Parliament, where Morley spoke on usury (19 Apr.) and was appointed to a conference on 28 May to discuss whether Surrey and Sussex should have separate or joint sheriffs. He bought the manor of Combe, Sussex, with land in several parishes, from Lord Windsor in January 1563, but otherwise is not known to have added to the estates he inherited from his father, which included eight manors besides Glynde, and an interest in an iron mill and furnaces in Hawkesden Mayfield. His subsidy assessment, £20 in 1560, had by 1572 risen to £30, still a comparatively small amount. However, he carried out extensive rebuilding at Glynde, where his coat of arms in the inner quadrangle is dated 1569.[3]

Morley was classified by his bishop in 1564 as a 'favourer of godly proceedings'. A number of letters were sent to him from the Privy Council on such matters as using his influence to end quarrels between local gentlemen, putting down highway robbery in Sussex, or regulating fishing at Rye. In June 1584 he and George Goring I* asked permission to resign their offices of captains of musters for the rape of Pevensey, pointing out that they already had to attend in their respective divisions of Lewes and the Cinque Ports. Sussex often experienced trouble in distributing officials over the county. A list of justices drawn up in October 1587 says that although Morley was a 'good justice as well in respect of religion as of the common wealth', he was unsuitable for service in the rape of 'Levefsey' (?Pevensey) as he lived near Lewes. He made one of the largest contributions from his county – £60 – to the Armada fund of 1588–9. In his will, drawn up in October 1573, Morley made arrangements for his widow, and for his first wife's children, but much of this was out of date by his death on 24 Nov. 1597. The executor was the heir, Herbert, and the overseers were three relatives, Herbert Pelham*, Anthony Morley and Anthony Staple or Stapley. The will was proved in January 1598.[4]

[1] *Suss. Rec. Soc.* xiv. 165; W. Berry, *Co. Genealogies, Suss.* (Comber's

copy at Chichester); *Glynde Place Archives*, ed. Dell, 23–7; Lansd. 146, ff. 19–20. [2] *CPR*, 1563–6, p. 405; E. Suss. RO, Winchelsea hundred bk. iv. 165, 171, 194; Cinque Ports black bk. f. 45; *CSP Dom.* 1581–90, p. 181. [3] C. H. Garrett, *Marian Exiles*, 231; D'Ewes, 171–2; *CJ*, i. 93; *Suss. Rec. Soc.* xiv. 165; *Suss. Arch. Colls.* iii. 214; xviii. 13–14; xx. 73; *CPR*, 1560–3, pp. 614–15; Berry, loc. cit. [4] *Cam. Misc.* ix(3), p. 11; *APC*, x. 100, 190; xiii. 417; xviii. 355–6; *CSP Dom.* 1581–90, p. 181; Lansd. 53, ff. 160–1; T. C. Noble, *Names of Those who Subscribed*, 64; PCC 3 Lewyn; C142/253/98; *Suss. Rec. Soc.* xiv. 165.

N.M.F./K.B.

MORRANTE, Edmund (?*d.*1593), ?of Rye, Suss. and/or St. Sepulchre's, London.

NEW ROMNEY 1571

This Member has not been identified. He may have belonged to the Kent family of that name, seated at Morants Court at Chevening: they owned one of the manors in Romney Marsh, and four times in the mid-fourteenth century represented the county in Parliament. The family does not appear in the heralds' visitations of the Elizabethan period. The 1571 MP may have been the man who was paid, in 1572, a 40s. fee owing to him for unspecified services to the Cinque Ports. The fee was paid through Rye, and may indicate that he lived there. This was a usual fee for sixteenth century boroughs to pay their legal counsel, and it may, therefore, indicate Morrante's occupation, though his name has not been traced in the inns of court registers. One of this name, of the parish of St. Sepulchre, was about 1589 assessed on £30 in fees for a London subsidy. Administration of this man's property was granted to his son Thomas, with the consent of Jane, the widow, on 13 May 1593.

Since William Eppes, his co-Member in 1571, was a local man, Morrante, whoever he was, may have been nominated by the lord warden.

M. T. Derville, *Level and Liberty of Romney Marsh*, 110; *Arch. Cant.* xxi. 208–9; Cinque Ports black bk. f. 3; *Vis. London* (Harl. Soc. cix, cx), 160; PCC admon. act bk. 1593, f. 58.

N.M.F.

MORRISON, Thomas (*d.*1592), of Cadeby, Lincs. and St. Botolph-without-Aldersgate, London.

GREAT GRIMSBY 1572, 1584, 1586, 1589

1st s. of George Morrison of Waltham, Lincs. *m.* c.1559, Elizabeth, da. and coh. of Thomas Moigne of North Willingham, Lincs., 5s. 2da.

Commr. sewers for Cambs., Hunts., Isle of Ely, Lincs., Northants. and Notts. 1555; j.p. Lincs. (Lindsey) from c.1564; dep. to Christopher Smith* in the Exchequer by July 1569; mayor, Great Grimsby 1576; clerk of pipe in the Exchequer by Jan. 1579.

Morrison was an Exchequer official who came into Parliament for Grimsby, near his Lincoln estates. He left no mark on the records of the House. The family's interest in the affairs of the town is attested by his own service as mayor, and that of his son Edward as recorder. His father-in-law Thomas Moigne, before his attainder for his part in the Pilgrimage of Grace, had also held lands close to Grimsby: in 1559 Morrison was granted a crown lease of these lands for 21 years. In 1561 he purchased the manor of Bestby, which also lay close to the town. He was friendly with Thomas St. Poll* the 1571 Member for Great Grimsby, who appointed him one of the trustees of his estate, and Morrison's choice of the christian name Fynes for one of his sons suggests a connexion with the earls of Lincoln.

In 1564 Morrison was classified by his bishop as 'earnest in religion and fit to be trusted'. His Exchequer job must often have kept him in London, where he had a house and a chamber in Gray's Inn. He was thus in all probability the Thomas Morrison who was admitted to the Inn on 28 Feb. 1584 at Lord Burghley's request. He died 19 Feb. 1592, having made his will a month before. It was proved on 24 Apr. The preamble stated his belief that only through the 'merits of the most bitter death and passion' of Jesus Christ would he have 'clear and free forgiveness and pardon' of his sins, which protestant sentiments suggest that he was the Thomas Morrison to whom the puritan Thomas Farnham* left his books and 'great desk'. Morrison bequeathed £5 to the poor of St. Botolph's, £5 to those of four Lincolnshire parishes, and £1 to those of another parish in the same county where he held land. He left the manor of Daniels in Sandon, Hertfordshire, which he had purchased in 1573, to a younger son, Thomas. He appointed his 'very good lord', the lord chief justice (Sir) Christopher Wray*, Sir Dru Drury*, and his 'very loving and assured friends' Hugh Allington and Thomas Tailor to be overseers, while his executors were his eldest son and heir Edward, and his sons-in-law George Allington (also an official in the pipe office), and Francis Mussenden.

C142/234/70; *Vis. Lincs. 1592*, ed. Metcalfe, 52; *Cam. Misc.* ix(3), p. 27; *CPR*, 1558–60, p. 86; 1560–3, p. 374; 1566–9, pp. 26, 182, 362; Egerton 2345, f. 22; *HMC 14th Rep. VIII*, 262, 290; PRO Index 16774, 21 Eliz. f. 11; A. R. Maddison, *Lincs. Wills*, i. 98–100; M. H. Dodd, *Pilgrimage of Grace 1536–7*, passim; *Lincs. Historian*, ii(2), p. 18; PCC 28 Harrington; *VCH Herts.* iii. 272.

A.M.M.

MORTON, George (b. c.1540), of East Stour, Chilham, Kent.

HYTHE   1572*, 1584*

b. c.1540, 1st s. of Robert Morton (d.1559), of Molesworth, Hunts. and Holborn, Mdx. by Eleanor, da. of Sir Richard Finch of the Mote, Maidstone, Kent. m. Mary, da. of Robert Honywood of Charing, Kent, 4s. 2da.[1]

J.p. Kent from c.1561–c.87; capt. of cavalry, Low Countries by 1589; capt. in Brittany by 1591.

Morton belonged to a family of Milborne St. Andrew, Dorset, of which Cardinal John ('Morton's Fork') Morton, was the most famous. Morton's father inherited property in Somerset and also owned the manor of Molesworth, Huntingdonshire, but lived mainly in Holborn. His marriage to Eleanor Finch must have ended in some form of divorce or annulment, and when she re-married the young George Morton went to live at Boughton Malherbe, near Maidstone, Kent, the seat of her second husband, Thomas Wotton. Robert Morton left his property to his second wife Dorothy, and made no mention of his first, Eleanor, or of the son George whose wardship was nevertheless granted jointly to the two ladies. There was no love lost between them and legal proceedings took place, the exact nature of which is now obscure, and, whether as a result of these, or because of Dorothy's death, which occurred in 1565, George Morton came into possession of Molesworth and his father's other estates. This, together with his mother's second marriage and his own into a Kent county family, should have assured his quiet future as a country gentleman.

Perhaps the litigation had been a drain on the estate; perhaps Morton regarded the Huntingdonshire property as expendable; or perhaps, as his stepfather thought, he was a spendthrift. At any rate, in 1571 he conveyed Molesworth to two Huntingdonshire men, one of whom had been his father's servant, in circumstances suggesting that this was as security for a loan. Three years later he mortgaged the property for £2,000, and the mortgagee died possessed of it in 1585. Letters addressed to Morton from his stepfather in the early 1580s are of interest, though inconclusive evidence on the reasons for Morton's financial difficulties. After complaining that Morton was enjoying himself in London while his wife and children remained in the country, Wotton went on:

Smally do you regard or esteem me, when to my great grief I may plainly see that you spend so precious a thing as time idly (which is ill), or in lewd play (which is worse) and that play many times accompanied with wicked oaths (which is worst of all). From the eyes of me alone, being but one and often from you, you may sometime hold these things: from the eyes of all men, and from the eyes of Almighty God ... you can never hide ... any of these things. I do in this place, in this time, hereupon straightly charge you that I may not hereafter with my eyes see, or by true report hear, that you do with any of my servants play at dice, tables or cards, or upon any occasion use any wicked oath ... And if yet, against that that I have already often said, and do now say unto you, you will still from your book spend your time idly, or with ... rascal boys accompany yourself basely, the grief is now mine: the shame already is, and the loss will hereafter be, yours.

The threat was carried out: Wotton excluded Morton from his will.

It must have been in the midst of these other diversions that Morton found time to attend Parliament, having been returned at a by-election for Hythe in 1581 in place of Thomas Honywood, deceased. No direct evidence of such a by-election has been found, but as a 'Mr. Moreton' was appointed to a committee on Dover harbour on 4 Mar. that year, it is a fair assumption that this was the same man who certainly was returned in 1584 after Thomas Bodley had preferred Portsmouth. By this time Morton had been able to buy (how does not appear) the East Stour estate, near Canterbury, and it was presumably because of his own and his in-laws' local standing and connexions that he was selected. For, though Bodley had been nominated by the warden of the Cinque Ports, there is no evidence that this official had anything to do with Morton.

Like so much of Morton's life the dates of his service as a j.p. are conjectural. His name is in two lists, but is crossed out on the first and has 'deleted' written next to it on the other, referring to the period 1584–7. However, he was active in local affairs, signing a protest against the ejection of a Kent puritan minister, and was a member of the deputation from the county to Archbishop Whitgift in 1584, urging greater toleration of dissident clergy.

By 1586 Morton was acting as a diplomatic messenger between Utrecht and London and by 1589 was a captain of cavalry in the Low Countries. Two years later, when he was stationed at Bergen-op-Zoom, he was commissioned by the Privy Council to join the Brittany expedition led by Sir John Norris* and Sir John Wingfield*. For the next two or three years he spent much of his time raising troops in England and transporting them to Brittany, together with fresh supplies. By 1595 he was back in the Low Countries, at Flushing, with Sir Robert Sidney*. No further references to this restless man have been found and no will. He may have died in 1613, when his heir was given special leave to return home from Flushing to attend to 'some business concerning his private estate'. Three of his sons were knighted for services to the Crown. Sir Robert and Sir Thomas both followed their father into the army, while the youngest son, Sir Albertus, sat in Parliament for Kent in 1625 and became secretary of state to Charles I.[2]

[1] *Vis. Kent* (Harl. Soc. lxxv), ii. 79, 105; *Fam. Min. Gent.* (Harl. Soc. xl), 1298. [2] *HMC 4th Rep.* 430–1; Hythe ass. bk. f. 116; *CJ*, i. 131; Hutchins, *Dorset*, ii. 594–5 table; iv. 34; PCC 54 Chaynay, 4 Spencer; L. P. Smith, *Life and Letters Sir Henry Wotton*, i. 3; *CPR*, 1558–60, p. 328; 1563–6, p. 318; *Cal. Feet of Fines, Hunts.* (Camb. Antiq. Soc. xxxvii), 164; *Lincoln Episcopal Regs.* ed. Foster (Cant. and York Soc. xi), 65, 272; *VCH Hunts.* iii. 94; *Kentish Wills*, ed. Clarke, 79; Collinson, *Somerset*, iii. 130; *Thos. Wotton's Letter Bk.* ed. Eland, 41, 47, 48–9; Hasted, *Hist. Kent*, vii. 279–80; Peel, *Second Parte of a Register*, i. 115; Collinson thesis, 444 n. 5; *CSP For.* 1586–7, p. 48; 1589 (Jan.–July), p. 377; *APC*, xxi. 21, 25; xxii. 361–2; *CSP Dom.* 1591–4, p. 542; *HMC Hatfield*, v. 507; *APC*, 1613–14, p. 448; *DNB*.

M.R.P./P.W.H.

MORTON, Gilbert, of Whalley, Lancs.

PRESTON 1563

Exchequer feodary, Lancs. by Sept. 1560, particular surveyor 1565.[1]

Though the will of John Morton, who died in 1609, refers to 'my brother Gilbert, deceased', his name does not appear in the Lancashire Visitations, and no details of his marriage or children have been found. He was related to a number of parliamentary families in Lancashire, including the Fleetwoods and Nowells, but he almost certainly owed his seat at Preston, not to his local connexions, but to the 3rd Earl of Derby, lord lieutenant of the county. A list of the Earl's servants, drawn up in 1562, contains the entry under 'wages, annuities, etc. Gilbert Moreton 53s. 4d.', but gives no information about his actual status in Derby's household.[2]

As feodary he found it almost impossible to find out how much land was held of the Crown, owing to the complicated conveyances devised by landowners. In September 1560 he made a determined (though apparently unsuccessful) attempt to collect all 'men of worship, gentlemen and freeholders' at key points in Lancashire to show proof of tenure. In July 1565 he received his patent for the surveyorship of Lancashire, with an annuity of 20 marks. Late in 1566 he was granted two crown leases of lands in Lancashire, on condition that he kept them in repair. The last reference found to him is to his sitting on an inquisition post mortem commission at Whalley in 1579.[3]

[1] J. Hurstfield, *Queen's Wards*, 34; *CPR*, 1563–6, p. 319; 1566–9, p. 311. [2] W. D. Pink and A. B. Beaven, *Parl. Rep. Lancs.* 144; *VCH Lancs.* vi. 387, n. 51; *Lancs. and Cheshire Wills* (Chetham Soc. n.s. iii), 223–4; *Vis. Lancs. 1613*, ed. Raines (Chetham Soc. lxxxii), 66; Lancs. RO, Stanley pprs. DDK/6/3, p. 17. [3] *CPR*, 1563–6, pp. 319, 397, 482; *Abstracts of IPMs* (Chetham Soc. xcix), 159.

N.M.F.

MORTON, William, of Berwick-upon-Tweed, Northumb.

BERWICK-UPON-TWEED 1584, 1589, 1593

s. of Thomas Morton, alderman and mayor of Berwick. *m.*, at least 1da.
Alderman, Berwick, mayor 1574, 1581, 1588, 1592.

The Mortons appear as merchants at Berwick in the mid-fifteenth century. Morton himself, as mayor, led a campaign for the extension of the civil authorities' power, at the expense of the military officials, under the governor of Berwick, Lord Hunsdon. During his last term as mayor, when he was also MP for Berwick, he presented a list of complaints to the Queen, charging Hunsdon and his subordinates with infringements of his authority and the town's ancient privileges. Though he claimed to be in terror of the governor's 'indignation', this did not cause him to moderate his criticisms either of Lord Hunsdon, whom he condemned as an absentee official, or his subordinates, whom he accused of corruption, inefficiency and nepotism.

Morton continued, as alderman, to support the next mayor in the struggle with the governor, but he is less in evidence after his final term of office in 1593. He last appears in the records four years later, when his aunt, Phyllis Clavering, appointed him executor of her will.

The Berwick guild book shows payments to Morton as MP in 1584, when he and his colleague had 7s. 6d. a day between them 'from the time of their setting forth from the town to their returning again', and in 1593 when he was paid, but his colleague, an official, was not. He is not mentioned by name in the journals of the House of Commons, but he may have attended two committees concerning salted fish and the town of Berwick, to which the Members for Berwick were appointed on 11 Mar. and 14 Mar. 1589.

Surtees Soc. xxxviii. 70, 71; J. Scott, *Hist. Berwick*, 286–7, 456–61, 479; *Bronnen tot de Geschiedenis van den Handel met Engeland, Schotland en Ierland*, ed. Smit, ii (R.G.P.91), p. 1317, n. 2; Raine, *North Durham*, 254; D'Ewes, 445, 446; *Border Pprs.* i. 433–9 et passim.

B.D.

MOSELEY, Humphrey (by 1526–92), of St. Nicholas Coleabbey, London.

MARLBOROUGH	1547
MITCHELL	1553 (Mar.)
AYLESBURY	1554 (Apr.)
GATTON	1555
WOOTTON BASSETT	1558, 1559

b. by 1526, 2nd or 3rd s. of Nicholas Moseley of Staffs. *educ.* M. Temple, called. *m.* by 1561, Margaret (*d.*1607), da. of (Sir) Clement Heigham† of Barrow, Suff., 4s. 1, 2 or 3da.[1]

Under-treasurer, M. Temple 1551–6; secondary of Wood Street Compter 1557; under-sheriff, Mdx. 1560–1.[2]

Moseley was a carpet-bagging lawyer who found a parliamentary seat where he could. At Wootton Bassett this would have been through Sir John Thynne*, whom he had served as solicitor. By 1562 Moseley was an 'ancient of the utter bar' at the Middle Temple. Two years later he was fined for not acting as Autumn reader. Another fine recorded against him was for refusing to take up the office of steward. As secondary, one of the clerks who worked under the sheriff in the city of London, Moseley was involved in the case of Arthur Hall* during the second session of the 1572 Parliament, being one of the officers responsible for the arrest of Hall's servant.[3]

Moseley was evidently a wealthy man by the time he died in July 1592. His inquisition post mortem lists estates in Staffordshire and Suffolk, with Middlesex property in

Harefield, Ruislip and elsewhere, and other lands in Shropshire. Some of this property came to him through inheritance and his marriage, but it is likely that he bought much of it. His will mentions other lands and tenements in Surrey, which were bequeathed to his eldest son Richard, aged about 28. A daughter, Anne, was to have £600 at her marriage or on her 24th birthday, and all his 'books of the civil and common law' were left to his second son, William. The widow was sole executrix and residuary legatee.[4]

[1] PCC 67 Harrington, 11 Huddleston; S. Shaw, *Hist. Staffs.* ii. 276; C142/241/106; *Vis. Suff.* ed. Metcalfe, 41. [2] *M.T. Mins.* i. 83, 85, 105; A. B. Beaven, *Aldermen of London*, i. 299; *APC*, xxiv. 115; London, Rep. 13, ii, f. 538d; 14, f. 384. [3] Bath mss, Thynne pprs. ii, f. 176, ex. inf. J. Cooper; *M.T. Bench Bk.* (1937) ed. Williamson, p. 315; *M.T. Recs.* i. 140, 144; Neale, *Parlts.* i. 340. [4] C142/241/106; PCC 67 Harrington.

N.M.F.

MOSELEY, Thomas (c.1539–1624), of York.

YORK 1597

b. c.1539, 2nd s. of John Moseley of North Castle Grange, Cawthorne, Yorks. by his w. née Simpkinson. *m.* 9 Sept. 1578, Jane (*d.* Oct.1632), da. of John Wormeley of Hatfield, Yorks., 1s. *d.v.p.*

Freeman, York 1574–5, chamberlain 1578–9, sheriff 1583–4, alderman Mar. 1589, ld. mayor 1590–1, 1602–3; gov. York merchant adventurers 1589, 1595–7, 1608–10.

Moseley was left only a few pounds under his father's will and was placed in the care of a kinsman, Alderman John Beane† of York. Apprenticed to his uncle, Ralph Micklethwaite, he became first a member of the merchants' company and then, by 1584, one of its agents in Hamburg. He served in every rank of the York corporation, and performed a varied range of duties for his city. In 1587 he was sent to London to obtain royal assistance for the York merchants against the Dunkirk pirates. Next year he was committed to ward for refusing to pay the poor rate, and was fined 13s. 4d. for contempt of the mayor. This did not prevent his being elected alderman in March 1589, following which he became warden of Walmegat Ward, and an overseer of John Cheseman's trade school for pauper children. He was put down for a £50 loan to the Queen in 1590, and was assessed to the subsidy at £26 in goods in 1598. During times of dearth he was head collector of poor relief.

Moseley made an unsuccessful attempt to get into Parliament in 1593, when he polled second place among the freemen or commons, with 29 voices, but was rejected by the city assembly. When the system of voting was changed in 1597, the votes of assembly and commons then being added together, he obtained second place out of nine candidates, defeating two former Members, Robert

Brooke and Andrew Trewe. In 1601 he was beaten into third place but when one of the successful candidates withdrew, Moseley again failed to be elected. So far as is known he did not speak in the House, but he was appointed to a number of committees by virtue of his position as citizen for York – forestallers etc. (7 Nov. 1597), maltsters (9 Nov., 7 Dec., 12 Jan. 1598), monopolies (10 Nov. 1597), navigation (12 Nov.), cloth (18 Nov.), mariners (9 Dec.), the Exeter merchant guild (12 Dec.) and wine casks (3 Feb. 1598). He died in 1624.

York City Lib., Skaife mss; Foster, *Vis. Yorks.* 1584–1612, p. 555; York house bks. passim; *York Freemen* (Surtees Soc. cii); *York Mercers* (Surtees Soc. cxxix), passim; *York Civic Recs.* passim; J. J. Cartwright, *Chapters in Yorks. Hist.* 372–4; E179/218/167; York chamberlain's accts. 60, ff. 51, 119; D'Ewes, 552, 554, 555, 556, 558, 569, 570, 571, 578, 592; *Yorks. Fines* (Yorks. Arch. Soc. rec. ser. v), 68, 178; (vii), 33, 50, 178; (viii), 104, 113, 116, 123, 149; (liii), 197; (lviii), 87, 155; Jordan, *Charities of Rural England*, 378.

R.C.G.

MOSTYN, Thomas (by 1543–1618), of Mostyn, Flints. and Gloddaeth, Caern.[1]

FLINTSHIRE 1572*

b. by 1543, 1st s. of William Mostyn* by Margaret, da. of Robert ap Hywel of Whittington, Salop. *m.* (1) Ursula, da. of William Goodman, mayor of Chester, 3s. 2da.; (2) Catherine, da. of Peter Mostyn* of Talacre, wid. of Sir Rhys Gruffydd[†] (*d.*1580), of Penrhyn, Caern., *s.p. suc.* fa. 1576. Kntd. 1599.[2]

Sheriff, Anglesey 1574–5, 1587–8, Flints. 1577–8, 1586–7, Caern. 1583–4; j.p. Flints. from c.1577, Caern. from c.1582; dep. lt. and muster master, Flints. from c.1576; custos rot. Caern. from 1596; member, council in the marches of Wales 1602.[3]

The wide estates and ancient lineage of the Mostyns marked the heir for public service. He was put on the commissions of the peace in his father's lifetime, and his five periods as sheriff were distributed between three different shires. But parliamentary honours do not appear to have attracted him: he was returned at a by-election for Flintshire in February 1577 to replace his deceased father, but he never stood again, living as a country gentleman, except for a period of military service with Essex in Ireland. It was Essex who knighted Mostyn in Ireland in 1599, but he escaped involvement in the rebellion of 1601. He was on good terms with Lord Burghley, the earls of Pembroke, the Welsh judges, and other leading men of the day. However, he quarrelled with his eldest son Roger, whose marriage in 1597 to a daughter of John Wynn* involved the house of Gwydir in the dispute. The estrangement lasted (with temporary reconciliations), till Mostyn's death.[4]

In 1584 Mostyn secured a lease for 30 years, on behalf of himself, his son and grandson, of the lordship of Mostyn; but the outright grant of the lordship for which he had

engaged John Wynn's good offices as part of his daughter's marriage settlement, was withheld until in 1614 it was secured by Wynn's son Richard, through his influence at court, for Roger Mostyn, passing over the father. It was this family quarrel that involved Sir Thomas in his only important litigation.[5]

Mostyn died 21 Feb. 1618. His will, dated 10 Dec. 1617, was not proved until 13 June 1625, owing to the heir's share of the personalty being willed to trustees.[6]

[1] Except where otherwise stated, this biography is based upon L. N. V. Lloyd-Mostyn and T. A. Glenn, *Mostyns of Mostyn*. [2] Date of birth estimated from age at father's i.p.m., Wards 7/18/113; Lansd. 87, f. 138. [3] *Cal. Wynn Pprs.* 86; Flenley, *Cal. Reg. Council, Marches of Wales*, 212, 213; Harl. 1974, f. 23; E. Breese, *Kal. of Gwynedd*, 26; G. Owen, *Taylors Cussion*, ed. Pritchard (1906), ff. 36, 37; *CSP Dom.* 1598–1601, p. 403; *HMC 13th Rep.* IV, 249. [4] *Cal. Wynn Pprs.* 86; Flenley, 212; Pennant, *Tours*, ed. Rhys (1883), i. 14; Lansd. 63, f. 95. [5] *Augmentations*, ed. Lewis and Davies (Univ. Wales Bd. of Celtic Studies, Hist. and Law ser. xiii), 403–4. [6] PCC 65 Clark.

A.H.D.

MOSTYN, William (by 1518–76), of Mostyn, Flints. and Gloddaeth, Caern.[1]

FLINTSHIRE 1554 (Apr.), 1554 (Nov.), 1572*

b. by 1518, 1st s. of Thomas Mostyn of Mostyn and Gloddaeth by Jane (or Siân), da. of Sir William Gruffydd of Penrhyn, Caern. *m.* (1) by 1543, Margaret, da. of Robert ap Hywel of Whittington, Salop, 3s. inc. Thomas* 2da.; (2) Margaret, da. of Sir William Brereton[†] of Brereton, Cheshire. *suc.* fa. 1558.

J.p. Flints., sheriff 1560–1, 1565–6, 1570–1, Caern. 1567–8; commr. piracy, Flints. 1565, militia 1570, victuals 1574, tanneries 1574.[2]

The Mostyns were among the most ancient and influential of Welsh families, related by blood to Owain Glyn Dwr and also to the Tudors, whom they consistently supported, in arms and otherwise, both before and after they succeeded to the throne. They were also great patrons and collectors. The manuscript library of Welsh literature they built up over the ages remains one of the basic collections in that field. Originating in Denbighshire, they had in the course of the middle ages acquired through fortunate marriages wide estates in three other counties. One of these, the manor house and lands of Mostyn in Flintshire, became the principal seat of the family from the time of William Mostyn's great-grandfather, and from the next generation the name of the seat was adopted as a family surname. In 1570 William Mostyn began extensive additions to the house.

Mostyn served Queen Mary against Wyatt's rebel forces in January 1554, and represented Flintshire in both the Parliaments of that year. Thereafter he did not sit again until 1572, and it was in the course of this Parliament that he died, 19 Sept. 1576, lamented by bards of Denbighshire,

Flintshire and Caernarvonshire, 'hand and eyelid for the whole of Wales, and a strong hand in England'. His will, dated 20 Feb. 1566, and proved 17 Nov. 1576, named his 'well-beloved wife' executrix.[3] He was succeeded in the representation of Flintshire by his son Thomas.

William Mostyn the elder, the subject of this biography, is sometimes confused with two relatives and namesakes: his own younger brother (usually referred to as William Mostyn the younger), and his cousin of Basingwerk and Cornish, Holywell, son of the founder of the Talacre branch of the family.

[1] Except where otherwise stated, this biography is based upon L. N. V. Lloyd-Mostyn and T. A. Glenn, *Mostyns of Mostyn.* [2] *CPR*, 1563–6, p. 36; *APC*, vii. 286; *HMC Welsh*, i. 291–5; Flenley, *Cal. Reg. Council, Marches of Wales*, 60, 69, 109. [3] PCC 37 Carew.

A.H.D.

MOYLE, Adam, of Winchelsea, Suss.

WINCHELSEA   1586, 1589

Jurat, Winchelsea by 1581, mayor 1585–6, 1586–7. 1587–8.

This man's background is obscure. He may have been a member of the Moyle family of Eastwell, Kent, who does not appear in their pedigrees. John Moyle of West Twyford, Middlesex, who was serjeant of the Queen's livery, had a brother called Adam, but there is nothing to connect him with Winchelsea.

In the 1570s Moyle was in difficulties with the Winchelsea authorities. A decree had been passed stating that only seamen or those prepared to 'adventure £10 at sea' would have the right to be freemen in future, and on 21 June 1577 Moyle was disfranchised for failing to meet the requirement. Three years later, the decree having been repealed, he was re-admitted on payment of 20s. When he was returned to Parliament in 1586 the corporation agreed to pay £1 'towards his charges'. It is possible that relations between the Winchelsea authorities and the Privy Council were strained at that time. Earlier in the year the Council had suggested two men as suitable mayors but Moyle was chosen instead. Now, the Council's wish that the 1584 Members of Parliament should be re-elected in as many places as possible was not acted upon at Winchelsea. He is not mentioned by name in the journals but he may have attended a committee concerning the import of fish to which the burgesses for Winchelsea were appointed on 6 Mar. 1587.

When the Queen granted to Winchelsea in 1586 part of the land formerly owned by the Black Friars, Moyle received a messuage and a garden in the town. He may, perhaps, have been the Mr. Moyle who was a servant of (Sir) Roger Manwood*.

E. Suss. RO, Winchelsea mss; *Misc. Gen. et Her.* (ser. 5), iv. 233; *APC*, xiv. 51; D'Ewes, 412; W. Cooper, *Hist. Winchelsea*, 109; Lansd. 40, f. 148.

M.R.P.

MOYNES, John, of Bridport, Dorset.

BRIDPORT   1554 (Nov.)
MELCOMBE REGIS   1559

Cofferer of Bridport 1555–7, bailiff 1561–2.[1]

Moynes – a leading member of Bridport corporation – was returned to Elizabeth's first Parliament for Melcombe at the instance of the 2nd Earl of Bedford, who in January 1559 wrote thanking the mayor and corporation of Melcombe Regis for letting him have the nomination. The borough was excused payment of his wages. Nothing is known of Moynes's family. He may have come originally from Somerset, but was settled in Dorset by the reign of Edward VI. He owned tenements in Weymouth and other property in the county.

For the subsidy of 1560 he was rated at Bridport on £10 in goods: the heralds' visitation of 1565 mentions him as one of the principal burgesses. No later reference to him has been found.[2]

[1] *Bridport Recs.* 64; ms list at Town Hall, Bridport. [2] *HMC 5th Rep.* 582; *Cal. Proc. Chanc. Q. Eliz.* ii. 185, 222, 267; PRO, cal. of enrolled deeds, Easter 7 Edw. VI; E179/104/216; *Genealogist*, ii. 224.

N.M.F.

MULCASTER, Richard (1532–1611), of London.

CARLISLE   1559

b. 1532, 1st s. of William Mulcaster* of Carlisle, Cumb., and ?bro. of Robert*. *educ.* Eton; King's, Camb. 1548–50, Peterhouse BA 1554; Christ Church, Oxf. 1555, MA 1557. *m.* c.1559, Katherine, 1s.

Headmaster, Merchant Taylors' 1561–86; vicar of Cranbrook, Kent 1590–1; prebendary of Yatesbury 1594; high master, St. Paul's 1596–1608; rector of Stanford Rivers, Essex 1598–*d.*

Richard Mulcaster, 'by ancient parentage and lineal descent an esquire born', was a native of Carlisle and presumably owed his return to the influence there of his father, though his own distinction and the fact that he was living in London at the time must have been additional recommendations. After leaving Oxford, where he had gained a reputation for his knowledge of Greek, Latin and Hebrew, he had established himself as a teacher in the capital and been commissioned to write 'the book containing and declaring the histories set forth in and by the City's pageants' when the Queen passed through London before her coronation, 'which book was given unto the Queen's grace'. His membership of the first Parliament of the reign was but an interlude in a scholastic career. Chosen in 1561 to be the first headmaster of the Merchant Taylors' new school, he was found 'worthy of great commendation' when the school's visitors reported in the following year. They did, however, criticize the children's indistinct pronunciation, ascribing it to the ushers, most of whom being 'northern men born' did not speak as clearly as men brought up in the schools of the south. Apparently the fault, such as it was, was corrected, for the boys of the school on a number of occasions performed plays at court.[1]

The First Part of the Elementarie, published in 1582, Mulcaster dedicated to his 'very good lord' the Earl of Leicester. 'I do not see', he wrote,

> that there is any one about her Majesty (without offence be it spoken, either to your honour, if you desire not to hear it, or to any other person which deserves well that way) which either justly can or unjustly will compare with your honour, either for the encouraging of students to the attainment of learning, or for helping the learned to advancement of living. Which two points I take to be most evident proofs of general patronage to all learning, to nourish it being green, to cherish it being grown ... I do find myself exceedingly indebted unto your honour for your special goodness and most favourable countenance these many years, whereby I am bound to declare the vow of my service unto your honour.

Mulcaster's association with Leicester makes it likely that he was, as has been suggested, responsible for part of the entertainment at Kenilworth in 1575, and suggests also that he shared his patron's sympathy with radical religious attitudes. Indeed it may have been for this reason, as well as for his learning, that he first commended himself to Richard Hills*, the moving spirit in the foundation of the Merchant Taylors' school, who had kept in close contact throughout Mary's reign with the religious émigrés on the Continent.[2]

Disputes with the Merchant Taylors, in which his dissatisfaction with his salary was a recurring theme, led Mulcaster eventually to resign the headmastership that he had held for 25 years. Taking a house in the country, he attempted to set up a school for the sons of noblemen and borrowed money from London merchants for its furnishings, in one instance pledging plate worth £300. The venture failed. In June 1589 the Privy Council asked the lord mayor to obtain for him some respite from his creditors. His debts had grown, wrote the Council, by 'casualty and mishap' to one who deserved well of the city because of his 'travail and pains' as a schoolmaster. Receiving the vicarage of Cranbrook in the following year he resigned shortly afterwards and, after applying to Puckering*, received the modest Salisbury prebend of Yatesbury. In 1591 he was appointed high master of St. Paul's – apparently he had for a time kept a school in Milk Street attended by some of Paul's boys during the dispute between the governors and his predecessor – and two years later became rector of Stanford Rivers, a substantial living in the Queen's gift, retiring there when he resigned from St. Paul's at the age of 76. The Mercers, who managed the school, allowed him a generous yearly pension of £66 13s. 4d., but his financial difficulties seem to

have increased. His request to the Merchant Taylors for similar recognition of his services was rejected on the ground that their school was less well endowed. He died intestate 15 Apr. 1611.[3]

[1] *Al. Cant.* iii. 226; Walker, *Peterhouse Biog. Reg.* i. 181; H. B. Wilson, *Hist. Merchant Taylors' School,* i. 21–5, 65; F. W. M. Draper, *Four Centuries of Merchant Taylors' School,* 13, 252–3. [2] *Mulcaster's Elementarie,* ed. Campagnac, dedication; Draper, 5–7, 30. [3] Wilson, i. 34, 57, 74–5, 89–91; C3/227/48; Req.2/149/53; *APC,* xvii. 258; Harl. 6996, ff. 33, 35; M. F. J. McDonnell, *Hist. St. Paul's School,* 143, 147; J. Oliphant, *Educational Writings of Richard Mulcaster,* p. xvii.

A.M.M.

MULCASTER, Robert (*d.* by Feb. 1576), of Carlisle, Cumb.

CARLISLE	1572*

?yr. s. of William Mulcaster*, and ?bro. of Richard*. *educ.* ?Clare, Camb. 1554.

Common councilman, Carlisle by 1569.

Described as 'gentleman', Mulcaster's name has been deleted and the comment 'mort' added beside it on a first session Crown Office list partially corrected for the interim period before the second session of the 1572 Parliament. Thomas Tallentyre's name was substituted.

CSP Scot. ii. 633; C193/32/8.

N.M.F.

MULCASTER, William, of Carlisle, Cumb.

CARLISLE	1563

1st s. of Richard Mulcaster of Brackenhill Castle, Cumb. *m.* poss. a da. of one Tilliol of Scaleby, 2s. Richard* and ?Robert*.

Alderman, Carlisle by 1561.

Mulcaster, whose family claimed to have been established on the border from the time of the Conquest, was by Elizabethan standards an elderly man when returned to Parliament. The earliest reference found to him is for October 1537, when he sat on a special jury at Carlisle following a riot in Gilsland, and the latest in 1566, when he joined with Thomas Barne*, Thomas Pattenson* and others in a complaint against the then mayor.

Vis. Surr. (Harl. Soc. xliii), 131; Burke, *Landed Gentry* (1855), 833; *Carlisle Recs.* (Cumb. and Westmld. Antiq. and Arch. Soc. extra ser. iv), 86; *LP Hen. VIII,* xii (2), p. 294; Carlisle mss CA/2/210–17.

N.M.F.

MUNCK, Levinus (c.1568–1623), of London and Mortlake, Surr.

GREAT BEDWYN	1601

b. c.1568. *m.* Elizabeth, da. of Peter Tryon, London merchant, 1s. 2da.

Sec. to Sir Robert Cecil c.1596–1612; clerk of the signet in reversion 1603; keeper of state papers 1610–14; commr. to accompany Princess Elizabeth to Germany 1613.[1]

Munck was born in Ghent, coming to England before 1592 and entering Robert Cecil's service by 1596. He was returned for Great Bedwyn in 1601 by the Earl of Hertford, to whom he had lent money. A passage in the *Commons Journals* (i. 732), makes it clear that he sat in the 1601 Parliament as a denizen – that is before his formal naturalization, which took place in 1610.[2]

As secretary to Cecil, Munck bore a heavy load of work and carried much responsibility. He was employed in a variety of tasks, such as transmitting messages from Cecil and drawing up memoranda for him, but his main duties lay in the field of foreign affairs. He was the most important of Cecil's secretaries, probably a reflection of the fact that he was so intimately concerned with matters of state. In November 1608 (Sir) Walter Cope* extolled his 'honesty and sufficiency' and a few months later it was rumoured, without foundation, that he was to be appointed ambassador to the United Provinces. In the year before the Queen's death Cecil maintained contacts with Scotland through George Nicholson, English agent at the Scottish court, and also through the sinister Master of Gray, James VI's favourite and confidant, exchanging information with them about foreign as well as Scottish affairs. Munck played an important part in these exchanges, drafting many of Cecil's letters to both Nicholson and the Master. He also concerned himself with Irish affairs. In 1598, when the government was considering asking for a 'voluntary' contribution because of the Irish troubles, it was Munck who drew up reasons which could be put forward to justify the demand, and he who conducted Cecil's correspondence with the lord deputy.[3]

Munck played an important part in the transaction of business with the United Provinces. In 1602 Gilpin, English agent at The Hague, died and Sir William Browne, anxious to obtain the vacant post, successfully approached Cecil through Munck. When, in 1605, Caron, the agent in England of the States General, had bad news to give to Salisbury, he did not present it in person but sought out Munck who, equipped with the papers, was expected to present things in the best possible light. From 1603 Sir Ralph Winwood was England's representative at The Hague and letters to him from John More, his agent in London, and from Munck himself contain proof of Munck's interest in Dutch business between 1603 and 1611.[4]

Munck was also concerned with the other half of the divided Netherlands. In September 1601 the Archduke sent a private representative, Coamans, to England, to engage in tentative and unofficial peace negotiations.

Unable to approach Cecil, Coamans went to Munck, in whose presence he spoke to Thomas Edmondes*, clerk of the Privy Council, a man who had already engaged in peace negotiations with the Archduke. In 1604, on the conclusion of peace with Spain, Edmondes became ambassador to the Archduke. Munck continued to communicate with him and kept him informed of diplomatic developments elsewhere. Some indication of the relatively free hand which he possessed can be gained by noticing that he sometimes passed such news on to Edmondes without prior reference to Cecil himself.[5]

Munck concerned himself too with Spanish affairs, and indeed at one time or another with almost every area in Europe which was significant in the conduct of English foreign policy: France, Lorraine, German principalities, Florence and the Ottoman Empire. It is uncertain whether or not his work took him frequently to the Continent. He certainly went abroad at times, as when he visited Brussels in 1600.[6]

After his master's death in 1612, Munck continued for a time to deal with foreign affairs, acting as assistant to James I, who temporarily assumed the duties of secretary of state. In 1613 he was one of the commissioners who accompanied Princess Elizabeth to Germany after her marriage to see that she was well settled in her new home. He was little concerned with the business of the state paper office, soon surrendering the keepership, and devoting the rest of his life to his duties as clerk of the signet, except in 1618, when he was licensed to spend a year in Spain with his wife, son and servants. He died 27 May 1623, John Chamberlain reporting that he was 'very rich for a clerk of the signet, his state falling out they say toward forty thousand pounds'. He left considerable property, and bequeathed £12,000 in cash to his children, £6,000 to his son Robert and £3,000 to each of his daughters. The residue of his personal estate went to his wife. He had, in addition, houses in London and at Mortlake in Surrey and considerable landed property in Buckinghamshire, which he held by free socage as of the manor of East Greenwich – a tenure that brought considerable practical advantages, notably freedom from wardship if the heir was under age, as he was in this case. Munck is an interesting and unusual figure in this period, the foreign adventurer whose acumen enabled him to accumulate vast wealth through successful service in an official position.

In the pious preamble to his will, in which he stated that he was aged 'about 55 years', he expressed his personal conviction that he was one of the elect. He made bequests of money to the French and Dutch churches in London and asked his wife and friends not to permit his children to marry other than persons of 'honest and godly behaviour, such as are not infected with popish superstition and irreligious atheism'.[7]

[1] *Vis. Essex*, (Harl. Soc. xiii), 303; *EHR*, lxviii. 236; *Chamberlain Letters* ed. McClure, i. 429, 433; SP84/69/60; *CSP Dom.* 1603–10,

p. 14; 1611–18, p. 248; F. S. Thomas. *Hist. State Paper Office*, 7. [2] *EHR*, lxviii. 234; PCC 36 Swann; *Statutes of the Realm*, iv. p. lxviii. [3] *CSP Dom.* 1598–1601, p. 241; 1603–10, 512; *CSP Ire.* 1600–1, p. 201; *HMC Hatfield*, xi. 509; SP14/26/27; *Chamberlain Letters*, i. 268; Hatfield mss 78/26(2), 79/73, 97/3(2), 213/114, 116, 118, 120; 24/66. [4] *HMC De L'Isle and Dudley*, ii. 602, 613; Hatfield mss 191/6; *HMC Buccleuch*, i. 44, 49–50, 59, 85, 87, 98, 104. [5] SP12/281/79; *HMC Hatfield*, xi. 393; *DNB* (Edmondes, Thomas); Hatfield mss 227/8. [6] SP78/54/130–1; 94/10/97; 94/11/152–6, 192–4; 94/12 passim; 97/5/72; Hatfield mss 100/142, 113/122, 116/66; *HMC Hatfield*, xv. pp. xxviii, 152, 154–5; xviii. 187; *HMC Buccleuch*, i. 93; *CSP Dom.* 1598–1601, p. 392. [7] *Chamberlain Letters*, i. 359; ii. 502; PRO Index 6805; PCC 36 Swann; C142/406/27.

A.G.R.S.

MUSGRAVE, Christopher (*b.* c.1553), of Hartley Castle, Westmld.

CARLISLE 1571

b. c.1553, 1st s. of Sir Simon Musgrave*. *educ.* ?Jesus, Camb. 1567. *m.* Jane or Joan, da. of Henry Curwen* of Workington, Cumb., 1s. Richard† 3da.

Capt. Bewcastle by 1585–May 1586.

Musgrave's return for Carlisle, while probably still in his teens, may be attributed to Henry, Lord Scrope, warden of the west march. Musgrave made no mark on the surviving records of the 1571 Parliament. In fact the only references to him are either to his participation with his father in various land transactions or to his martial exploits on the borders. In 1568 he appeared before Lord Scrope to answer for his part with Francis Dacre* in a riot in Carlisle. In January 1583 Scrope reported to Walsingham that the execution of three 'notable thieves' taken by Musgrave had been followed by forays in the Liddesdale-Bewcastle section of the border, the defence of which was becoming increasingly difficult. Another letter from Scrope, dated 23 July 1585, reported that Musgrave and a Captain Case, acting contrary to treaties and his own strict orders, had led a punitive expedition across the frontier, rescuing some English prisoners and capturing nearly 40 Scots. Scrope asked how he should proceed against the offenders who, while acknowledging their 'great oversight', pleaded that they had thought only of safeguarding the frontier. For example's sake, some action was called for, but as both gentlemen had done good service the warden hoped 'their former good deeds' might not be 'cast into oblivion, to their disgrace and discouragement hereafter'. It is not known whether any action was taken. Musgrave probably died or was killed soon afterwards, as in May 1586 his brother Richard, and in 1589 another brother, Thomas, became deputy to Sir Simon at Bewcastle.

Vis. Westmld. 1615 ed. Bridger, 8–9; Nicolson and Burn, *Hist. Cumb. and Westmld.* i. 596; *Yorks. Fines, Tudor period* (Yorks. Arch. Soc. rec. ser.), ii. 25, 61, 103; *Later Records relating to N. Westmld.* (Cumb. and Westmld. Antiq. and Arch. Soc. rec. ser. viii), 350–1; *CSP Dom.* Add. 1566–79, pp. 54–6; *Border Pprs.* i. 93–4, 188, 224; H. Pease, *Lord Wardens of the Marches*, 54.

N.M.F.

MUSGRAVE, Sir Simon (*d.*1597), of Eden Hall, Cumb., and Hartley Castle, Westmld.

CUMBERLAND 1571, 1572

3rd s. of Sir Edward Musgrave of Hartley Castle by his 2nd w. Joan, da. and coh. of Sir Christopher Ward of Givendale, Yorks. *m.* Julian, da. of William Ellerker of Ellerker, Yorks., 4s. (inc. Christopher* *d.v.p.*) 1da. Kntd. 28 Aug. 1570.[1]

Constable, Bewcastle from 1555; dep. receiver, Pickering forest bef. 1566; j.p. Cumb. from c.1569, sheriff 1569–70; j.p.q. Westmld. from c.1574, sheriff 1575; border commr. 1581; master of ordnance in the north from 1583.[2]

The Musgraves were among the oldest and most numerous of the west border families, with estates in Cumberland and Westmorland, and connexions with such prominent north country families as the Cliffords and Whartons. To these estates, and others in Northumberland and Yorkshire, Simon Musgrave succeeded when the male line failed in 1565. Next year he even tried to usurp the rights of his great-niece Eleanor (who about this time married Robert Bowes I*) on the grounds of her bastardy. Sir Thomas Gargrave*, in 1572, listed him as a protestant and one of the principal gentlemen of the West Riding; but it was in the border counties that he had his roots.[3]

As constable of Bewcastle, where he had succeeded another Musgrave, his patent being re-issued in December 1558, his income was estimated in 1594 at not less than £400, derived from lands, rents and fees, but it was an onerous and at times dangerous appointment. The castle, where the constable was required to reside, faced across the 'wastes' into Liddesdale, home of the unruly Grahams and Armstrongs, between whom and the Musgraves there was a violent personal feud. In one raid, the constable's own mill and barns were burnt down, and in another he narrowly escaped with his life. So intense became the raids, which drove away the tenants on whom the castle depended for its defence, that reinforcements were brought in from Berwick, but they quickly departed, leaving the area again open to attack. The ultimate cause of these disorders, in Musgrave's view, was the instability of government in Scotland and the frequent changes among Scottish border officials. He advised more rigorous punishment of offenders and the prohibition, except on licence, of marriages between English and Scottish borderers, 'the greatest occasion of the spoils and robberies'.[4]

In 1569 Musgrave commanded 400 horse against the northern rebels and in the following year again served under Lord Scrope, warden of the west march, and the Earl of Sussex in their punitive expedition into Scotland. 'Very forward', in the opinion of Sir George Bowes, though less satisfactory in the view of his bishop, his ability in the field won him Scrope's commendation and from Sussex a knighthood, at Carlisle, both valuable preliminaries to his election to Parliament for his county in 1571 (when his son Christopher also became an MP) and 1572. How often he attended the House is not known; during his known visits to London Parliament was not sitting. In 1577 he was evidently thought suitable for appointment to the council in the north but Huntingdon, the president, did not press for his inclusion and he was never appointed.[5]

Deputing one of his sons, first Christopher, then Richard, then Thomas, to take command at Bewcastle, Musgrave from 1583 discharged the physically less exacting duties of master of the ordnance, being responsible for its receipt, storage and distribution at Berwick, Newcastle and elsewhere. As his years advanced, complaints of his absences and neglect of duty changed to accusations of mismanagement and peculation. In 1593, after entertaining the Earl of Bothwell at Eden Hall in March, 'very pleasant and merry', he was again in the county 'at his ease' in April. The following month, Burghley's busy correspondent at Berwick, its captain and chamberlain John Carey*, reporting on Musgrave's excessive demands for munition, likened him to 'an old Parliament man who goes about to overthrow a bill by clogging it with more devotion'.[6]

After 40 years of service on the borders, Musgrave died on 30 Jan. 1597. Eden Hall and other property in Cumberland and Westmorland passed to his grandson Richard, Christopher's son.[7]

[1] Nicolson and Burn, *Hist. Cumb. and Westmld.* i. 594–6. [2] *CPR*, 1555–7, pp. 21, 167; Somerville, *Duchy* i, 535; *Border Pprs.* i. 35; AO 1/1832/5. [3] *CPR*, 1563–6, pp. 105–6; 1565–6, pp. 487–8; *Yorks. Fines, Tudor period* (Yorks. Arch. Soc. rec. ser.), i. 334, 350, 360; *VCH Yorks. N. Riding*, i. 393; J. J. Cartwright, *Chapters in Yorks. Hist.* 68. [4] *CPR*, 1555–7, pp. 21, 167; 1558–60, pp. 59–60; *HMC Hatfield*, v. 65; *APC*, xiii. 263–4; *Border Pprs.* passim. [5] Sharp, *Memorials of the Rebellion*, pp. 86, 102; *Miscellanea xii* (Cath. Rec. Soc. xx), 117; *CSP Dom.* Add. 1566–79, p. 516 et passim. [6] *Border Pprs.* [7] C142/248/14.

B.D.

MUSGRAVE, William (*d.* 1597), of Hayton, Cumb.

CUMBERLAND 1559

1st s. of Thomas Musgrave of Hayton, marshal of Berwick, by Elizabeth, da. of William Lord Dacre of Gilsland. *m.* bef. 1546, Isabel, da. and coh. of James Martindale of Newton, wid. of Humphrey Dacre, at least 2s. 1da. *suc.* fa. 1542.[1]

J.p. Cumb. 1559, 1571–87, sheriff 1562–3, 1573–4, 1592–3; commr. to survey forts and castles on borders 1580–1.[2]

Musgrave was granted livery of his father's lands in February 1542 and took advantage of the general pardon at the beginning of Mary's reign, but he is not known to have played any part in the affairs of his county before 1559 when he became a justice of the peace and one of its representatives in Parliament. The explanation of this sudden emergence into public life can be found in his connexion with the Dacre family. William Lord Dacre, the warden of the west march and head of one of the oldest and most powerful families in the north-west, was his maternal grandfather; his wife was a Dacre by her previous marriage, and his fellow-Member for the county was Leonard Dacre, the lord warden's second son. In 1562 Musgrave became sheriff and for some years thereafter served infrequently on commissions of lunacy and of inquiry post mortem, but it is noticeable that he was dropped from the commission of the peace soon after 1559, not to reappear as a justice until 1571. Possibly his connexion with the Dacres, once an asset, became a liability. Because of his part, with two other Musgraves, in a riot led by Francis Dacre* in Carlisle in 1568, he was arrested and ordered by Lord Scrope, Lord Dacre's successor as warden, to appear before the Council in London. John Aglionby of Carlisle, one of the two friends who stood surety for his appearance in the sum of £200 each, had earlier been described as 'not staid' in religion and several of the Dacre family were known to be similarly unreliable. Possibly Musgrave shared their conservative religious views. He did, however, keep clear of the northern rebellion and the treasonable activities of Leonard Dacre*, though in 1571 Cuthbert Musgrave alleged that he had had 'much and often conference' with the traitor and been a 'daily practiser' with him.[3]

In a border county the gentry, whatever their views, were required to take part in its defence. Musgrave participated in a reprisal raid into Scotland in 1570, and ten years later was a commissioner to survey the border forts and castles. However, in a report on the musters of light horsemen made on Walsingham's orders in 1583, Musgrave and a neighbour were said to have defaulted in the number of horsemen they should have produced, pleading a recent raid against them as their excuse. A note in the margin – in Burghley's hand – urged that they should be 'treated withal'.[4]

The Star Chamber suits brought by Musgrave and Cuthbert Musgrave in 1571 seem to have been the culmination of a long-standing quarrel that had been given new life by the indictment of Cuthbert Musgrave's son for a minor offence at quarter sessions when William Musgrave was on the bench. To the charges and counter-charges the parties laid against one another, Cuthbert Musgrave added the complaint that, as part of the quarrel, he and his tenants had been subjected to raids by unknown Scots. This had an echo in 1588 when a widow, Jane Briscoe, alleged that her house had been attacked and plundered by a band of Scots procured and guided by certain of Musgrave's tenants. A further petition from her in 1591 claimed that nothing had been done to restore her possessions and that she was still pursued by threats and open violence.[5]

Musgrave died 18 Aug. 1597, his heir being his second son, Edward. Some of his property was to go to Isabella, daughter and heiress of his deceased first son Thomas.[6]

[1] Hutchinson, *Hist. Cumb.* ii. 289; *LP Hen. VIII*, xvi. 267; Req. 2/265/69. [2] St. Ch. 5/M18/29; *Border Pprs.* i. 35. [3] *LP Hen. VIII*, xvii. 57; *CPR*, 1553-4, p. 411; 1563-6, pp. 35, 489; 1566-9, p. 133, 155; *CSP Dom.* Add. 1568-79, pp. 55, 57; SP 15/14/22(1); *Cam. Misc.* ix(3), 50; C. Sharp, *Memorials of the Rebellion*, 231; St. Ch. 5/M18/29 and M30/34. [4] *CSP Scot.* iii. 130; *Border Pprs.* i. 99. [5] *APC*, xvi. 360; xx. 347. [6] C142/253/75.

A.M.M.

MYDDELTON, Thomas (c.1556–1631), of Galch Hill, Denb., Tower Street, London and later of Stansted Mountfichet, Essex.[1]

MERIONETH	1597
LONDON	1624, 1625, 1626

b. c.1556, 4th s. of Richard Myddelton[†] by Jane, da. of Hugh Dryhurst, alderman of Denbigh. *m.* (1) bef. Oct. 1585, Hester, da. of (Sir) Richard Saltonstall*, 2s. inc. Thomas[†]; (2) c.1587, Elizabeth, wid. of John Olmstead of Ingatestone, Essex, 2s. 2da.; (3) Elizabeth, wid. of Miles Hobart, clothworker, of London; (4) Anne, wid. of Jacob Wittewronge, brewer, of London. Kntd. 1603.

J.p. Denb. from c.1592; constable, Denbigh castle and chief forester, Denbigh Sept. 1596; j.p. and custos rot. Merioneth 1599.

Freeman, Grocers' Co. 1582, liveryman 1592, assistant 1611; jt. surveyor of the outports 17 Feb. 1592; member E.I. Co. 1600; alderman, London 1603, sheriff June 1603, ld. mayor 1613–14; pres. Bridewell and Bethlehem hospitals; col. city militia.

The Myddelton family traced its origin to a Welsh clan which settled in the neighbourhood of Oswestry in the twelfth century, married into the Shropshire family in the fifteenth, and thereafter acquired official positions under the Crown in North Wales and estates in Denbighshire. Myddelton's father was governor of Denbigh castle and lieutenant to the Earl of Leicester in his lordship of Denbigh. By 1578 Myddelton himself was factor to Ferdinando Poyntz at Flushing, dealing mainly in sugar; four years later he set up on his own account, with a succession of partners, and by 1595 he owned (in Mincing Lane) one of the seven sugar refineries in England. From 1588 he had his own depot at Stade on the Elbe, where he dealt wholesale in cloth and mercery as well as in sugar and spices.[2]

A few years earlier Sir Francis Walsingham had appointed him his deputy in collecting the customs he had farmed since 1585. This led to his appointment in 1592 as one of the four surveyors of the outports, an office which not only brought him an annual fee of £425, but provided valuable contacts with the leading seamen of the day and temporary control of substantial capital. By these means he was able to make large and profitable investments (in

partnership with Drake, Hawkins and Ralegh as well as his own business associates) in the voyages of reprisal against Spain which followed the defeat of the Armada. The profits of these voyages were invested in loans (at ten per cent) to a wide range of clients, until by the middle '90s Myddelton had become virtually a sleeping partner in his wholesale business and operated in the main as financier. Loans on mortgage, especially to his needy neighbours in Wales, brought him increasing blocks of land in the counties of Denbigh, Montgomery and Merioneth. These were supplemented by outright purchases, culminating in his acquisition in 1595 (for £4,800) of the lordship and castle of Chirk, Denbighshire, where in 1612 he settled his eldest son Thomas. His capital played an important part in the Elizabethan land settlement in North Wales; he was also frequently called in by the government as financial assessor and to take care of prizes, and served as treasurer to many of the expeditions of the reign.[3]

His entry into Merioneth rather than Denbighshire politics may have owed something to a family tradition (probably incorrect) that the distant founder of the clan had been lord of Penllyn, which formed part of the shire. A more practical consideration was his close association (chiefly financial) with the families of (Sir) Robert Salesbury* of Rûg and Griffith Nanney* of Nannau in Merioneth. (Sir) Robert Salesbury's father-in-law was Sir Henry Bagnall*, whose Irish expedition of 1595 Myddelton helped to victual. Myddelton stood for the county seat in 1597 with the backing of the Salesburys and the Nanneys, but met with opposition from a rival faction led by John Lewis Owen and Cadwaladr Price, who had represented the shire in 1572 and 1584 respectively and were now deputy lieutenants. This led to a contested election.[4]

Owen at first canvassed for Price's return, but the latter decided to back the candidature of John Vaughan of Caer Gai, a young member of a family yet to make its mark on Merioneth politics but related to Price on the maternal side. Despite the corrupt influences alleged in Star Chamber to have been exerted by the deputy lieutenants (resulting in their removal from the commission soon afterwards), and the supposed introduction of outside freeholders to vote for Vaughan, Myddelton won the election. As knight of the shire for Merioneth in 1597 Myddelton could have served on committees concerned with enclosures (5 Nov.), poor law (5, 22 Nov.), armour and weapons (8 Nov.), penal laws (8 Nov.), monopolies (10 Nov.), the subsidy (15 Nov.) and Newport bridge (29 Nov.). The settlement of a business man as lord of Chirk aroused resentment in the local community, resulting in another Star Chamber action the same year, in which Myddelton was accused of unlawful enclosure. The opposition, which flared up afresh when he settled his son there in 1612, was sharpened by religious differences, led as it was by the recusant family of Edwards of Chirkland, who had snatched the Denbighshire seat in 1589, while Myddelton belonged both by marriage and by business association to a strongly puritan circle. Myddelton financed the publication of a Welsh metrical psalter by his cousin William Myddelton and the translation of other works of a puritan complexion, and his last and most enduring service to Wales was his joint responsibility in 1630 for the publication of the first popular edition of the Bible in Welsh.[5]

After 1603 Myddelton's activities were concentrated mainly on London, where he played an increasingly prominent part in civic administration. He was elected lord mayor on Michaelmas day 1613, the day chosen by his brother Hugh to open the New River Head. In 1615 he purchased the estate of Stansted Mountfichet in Essex, which was inherited by the elder son of his second marriage. Chirk castle and lordship, with his other North Wales properties, were inherited under his will (dated 20 Nov. 1630) by Thomas, the second son of his first wife (the elder brother having died in infancy); this was the future Roundhead general and MP for Weymouth in 1624 and for Denbighshire in 1625 and November 1640. Myddelton died 12 Aug. 1631.[6]

[1] This biography is largely based upon A. H. Dodd 'Mr. Myddelton, the Merchant of Tower Street', *Eliz. Govt. and Soc.* 249–81. [2] *DNB*; *DWB*; *Arch. Camb.* cviii. 108–13; *CSP Dom.* 1595–7, p. 91. [3] E403/1693/114; Lansd. 69, f. 50; 70, ff. 64, 98, 173; 142, f. 61 et passim. [4] *HMC Hatfield*, v. 369; xii. 482–3; UCNW, Nannau-Hengwrt mss 189, 207, 229, 240, 276, 287, 329–40, 357; *Star Chamber*, ed. Edwards (Univ. Wales Bd. of Celtic Studies, Hist. and Law ser. i), 90. [5] Griffith, *Peds.* 3; D'Ewes, 552, 553, 555, 557, 561, 565; *APC*, xxviii. 448, 457, 463, 557; xxx. 80–1; *Star Chamber*, 61; NLW, Edw. Owen deeds 31, 38. [6] PCC 94 St. John.

A.H.D.

MYLES, John (*d.*1597), of Coventry, Warws.

COVENTRY   1593

    m. (?1) c.1560, Margery Tryckett; (?2) aft. 1574, Bridget, da. of Henry Over†, wid. of John Nethermill* and of Stephen Hales*; 2s. 4da.
    Sheriff, Coventry 1571–2, mayor 1580–1, alderman from 1588.

Myles was probably related to the family which lived at Berkswell, six miles from Coventry, and which was trading in the city in 1540. Perhaps he was the John, son of Thomas Myles, who between 1562 and 1579 sued Samuel Marrow, owner of Berkswell, about the seizure of his copyhold, and was described in Marrow's reply as a 'villein regardaunt'.

Myles, the 1593 MP, is not known to have taken an active part in the affairs of the House beyond his appointment to a committee concerning cloth on 14 Mar. He was a draper entrusted with the supervision of part of the corporation's estates, and naturally profited from his position to obtain leases of property from the city. The general recession in the city's business, however, is

reflected in the modest size of the fortune he bequeathed his children, in comparison with that left by his father-in-law, Henry Over. Though he was sometimes sent on messages to the Earl of Leicester, it is unlikely that Myles's interests extended much beyond Coventry. He is not to be confused with a namesake of Chester who was concerned in several suits over the recovery of loans. John Myles of Coventry died in 1597, leaving his estates to his eldest son and modest endowments to his younger children.

Vis. Warws. (Harl. Soc. xii), 253; *EHR*, lxi. 237; C3/119/87; 130/3, 119; D'Ewes, 501; *Coventry Leet Bk.* 821, 831; Coventry council bk. ff. 189, 191, 197, 205, 219; Coventry bk. of payments, ff. 60, 68; *Trans. R. Hist. Soc.* (ser. vi), 1–19; *CSP Dom.* 1581–90, pp. 52, 76; PCC 61 Cobham.

S.M.T.

MYLLES, Francis (*d.*1618), of God's House, Southampton, of Bitterne, Hants and of London.

POOLE   1584, 1586
WINCHESTER   1589

    educ. Queen's, Oxf., All Souls, BA 1559, fellow, MA Dec. 1562. *m.* Alice, da. of Richard James* (or John James) of Newport, I.o.W., 4s. 2da.[1]
    Sub-warden, All Souls by 1564; sec. to Francis Walsingham* c.1566–90; bailiff of liberty of bp. of Winchester 1581–2; clerk of the peace, Hants 1581–1606; burgess, Southampton 1582, commr. subsidy 1599; freeman, Winchester 1585; clerk of privy seal, clerk of ct. of requests, clerk of the signet by 1606, clerk for loans 1611; ?member, Spanish Co. 1605–6.[2]

Mylles's life is typical of that of many government officials in the Elizabethan and Jacobean periods. Having embarked originally on an academic career, he entered Walsingham's service and later became a clerk of the privy seal. Edward Reynolds* had a similar career. Both men were educated at the same Oxford college; both attached themselves to powerful men; and both were able, as a result of their experience and influential acquaintances, to acquire lucrative posts for life.

Little is known about Mylles's origin. A family of that name, give or take variant spellings, was prominent in Southampton affairs and owned estates on the Hampshire-Sussex border, but it has not proved possible to connect Francis Mylles with them. A Richard Mills or Mylles of Ashford, Kent, married Joan, daughter or Thomas Glover of Ashford and sister of Robert Glover, Somerset herald, who once mentions Mylles as his nephew, but the only sons shown on the pedigree are William, John and Thomas. This may, however, be because Francis was omitted as dead by 1619, and on the whole this Richard Mylles, is most likely to have been Francis's father.[3]

Having taken his degree at Oxford, Mylles became a fellow of All Souls and, by 1565, sub-warden on the nomination of Archbishop Parker. One of his colleagues was Andrew Kingsmill, the civilian whose early death in 1569 ended a promising career. Mylles may have been attracted by Kingsmill's puritan fervour and Christian life – 'a rare example of godliness among gentlemen', was his estimate of him. At any rate Mylles was drawn to puritanism at an early age, and his religious beliefs remained the dominating influence in his life. The exact date of his appointment to Walsingham's service is not known, but in a letter of October 1586 he says he had been with Walsingham for 20 years. In the middle 1560s Walsingham was concerned with the government's secret service organization and Mylles, no doubt, joined in the work of keeping in touch with agents on the Continent and reporting the movements of Catholics at home.[4]

Mylles stayed in Walsingham's service until the latter's death in 1590. By the 1580s he was one of his most important servants and, judging by a notebook now in the British Library, was closely informed of many of the secretary's activities. His first concern, however, was the Catholic threat to the stability of the throne. Mylles spent much time interviewing suspects and searching private houses, while spies and informers supplied him with information about the arrival of priests or other Catholic subversives from Europe. During the time that the Babington plotters were under observation in 1586, Mylles wrote many letters to Walsingham, reporting on each new development in the game of cat and mouse then being played. Mylles had nothing but contempt for those who still adhered to Rome, and deplored those who did not share his zeal. London prison governors were nearly all 'not worthy to be trusted', and the searchers at the ports were too corrupt to be reliable. When the city authorities of London released a Catholic priest, Mylles complained to Walsingham that 'many that take great pains to find out these miscreants are discouraged to see many of them receive so much favour'. For some time during August 1586 Nau and Curle, secretaries to Mary Queen of Scots, were in Mylles's custody in his London house.[5]

Mylles was naturally in close contact with the leading puritans, such as Leicester, Thomas Randolph* (to whom he reported with delight the new measures taken against Catholics in the 1581 session of Parliament), and William Davison*. In October 1586 following Davison's appointment as secretary he wrote:

I trust sir, as it hath pleased God and her Majesty to change your estate by calling you to a place of honour, so it shall not be offensive to you sometimes upon honest occasions to be troubled with suits and letters of the godly and poor men, in which sort I do account myself, for choosing sincerely as you have long done the gospel of Christ, I hope He hath advanced you now for the furtherance thereof and for the comfort of all the charges of the same. And in this hope, rejoicing [at] your preferment to honour, so I most heartily pray God to increase all His good graces and gifts in you, especially

His spirit of wisdom and zeal, whereby His Church, her Majesty and her realm may reap profit of the place you now hold.

A few days later he wrote again to Davison, rejoicing (belatedly, for Babington was in prison in August) in their capture of Babington and his fellow conspirators, and in the preservation of the Queen from harm. To Mylles, as to Walsingham, the most important aspect of the plot was the opportunity it provided for bringing the Scottish Queen to the block. No doubt Mylles witnessed the execution, for he was at Fotheringay at the time.[6]

Mylles's powerful puritan friends at court were probably responsible for his return to three successive Parliaments. In 1584 his patron was probably Leicester. He was chosen again in 1586, perhaps with the help of Leicester's brother, the Earl of Warwick, but more likely on his own account in return for favours he did for Poole in the meantime. In October 1585, for example, the borough authorities wrote asking him to further a suit for them with Walsingham:

We have thought good to use some boldness with your worship in this behalf, wherein you shall bind us to do you any pleasure that may lie in us at any time.

Mylles was returned for Winchester in 1588, the document describing him 'of Winchester', though he is not known to have lived there. Walsingham, the high steward, must have been responsible. Mylles had been made a freeman in 1585 and on at least one occasion the corporation sent him a New Year's gift. He was not active in the House, serving on a committee concerned with Queen's College, 5 Feb. 1585, having no reported activity in 1586, and being named twice in 1589, once to a committee on Dover harbour (5 Mar.) and later urging the government to declare war with Spain (29 Mar.).[7]

In the autumn of 1586 Mylles acquired, with the help of Walsingham and Davison, a reversion to one of the privy seal clerkships, but the office did not fall vacant until some time afterwards. At about the turn of the century he added to it the closely related duties of clerk of the court of requests. By 1606 he was also a clerk of the signet. Judging by the many letters which Edward Reynolds wrote to him during James I's reign, Mylles was by then rarely present in London himself, and his son acted for him. Reynolds kept him informed of changes in the office and of any other gossip, and sent him his money as it became due.[8]

After Walsingham's death in 1590, Mylles may have entered Burghley's service, for in a letter to Robert Cecil in 1599, he referred to Cecil's father as 'my late master'. By the end of the century, however, he had retired to his home in Hampshire and journeyed to London only infrequently. He had a house in Southampton, the former hospital of St. Julian or God's House, which he modernised, and another at Bitterne nearby, called Pear Tree House. William Camden visited his friend there and was shown round the ruins of the Roman fort which once occupied the site. Mylles pulled down earlier buildings to erect his new home and private chapel.[9]

In his retirement Mylles took some part in local affairs. He had already been made a burgess of Southampton in 1582 and in 1599 was appointed one of its subsidy commissioners. He was present at a number of meetings of the Southampton assembly, including that which proclaimed the new sovereign in 1603. He assisted trading ventures, becoming a member of the society of merchants of Spain and Portugal in 1605. Shortly after his accession, James wrote to All Souls asking the college to lease to Mylles some of its land in Northamptonshire, 'in consideration of his long service to the late Queen'.[10]

The last surviving letter to Mylles from Reynolds is dated July 1618,[11] and he must have died shortly afterwards. He left no will; administration of his property was granted the following October.

[1] *Vis. Hants* (Harl. Soc. lxiv), 170. [2] *Reg. Univ. Oxf.* ed. Boase, i. 238; ii(2), ed. Clark, xv. 10; *Al. Ox.* 1015; *London Mar. Lic.* 1005; Collinson, *Som.* ii. 377; SP12/194/42; PRO Index 16774; 22 Eliz., f. 14; *CSP Dom.* 1581–90, pp. 360, 362; 1603–10, p. 336; 1611–18, pp. 83, 102, 103; Speed, *Hist. Southampton*, 132; Stephens, *Clerks of the Counties*, 947; Cott. Vesp. F. ix. [3] *Vis. Hants*, 170; *Chamberlain Letters* ed. McClure, ii. 37 n 2; *Southampton Ass. Bks.* i. 11 n; A. Merson, *Third Bk. of Remembrance of Southampton*, i. p.xiii; *Vis. Kent 1615* (Harl. Soc. xlii), 150. [4] *Cat. of Archives at All Souls*, ed. Martin, 303; *Southampton Ass. Bks.* iv. p. xxxv; *DNB* (Kingsmill, Andrew); SP12/194/42. [5] F. Evans, *Principal Sec. of State*, 157; Harl. 6035; *CSP Dom.* 1547–80, pp. 483–7; 1581–90, pp. 110, 160, 284, 354; *Jnl. of Sir Francis Walsingham* (Cam. Misc. vi), passim; Strype, *Annals*, iii(2), 466–8; SP12/172/113; *CSP Scot.* 1585–6, passim; 1586–8, pp. 22–4; Read, *Walsingham*, ii. 319 n 4, 336 n; iii. 45; Read, *Burghley*, ii. 345. [6] Lansd. 31, f. 112; *CSP Scot.* 1574–81, p. 664; 1586–8, p. 304; *CSP Dom.* 1581–90, pp. 360, 362, 364; SP12/194/18, 23, 42. [7] Hutchins, *Dorset*, i. 25, 26; Roberts thesis, 84; Poole recs. nos. 38, 52; B. Woodward, *Hist. Hants*, ii. 112 n; J. Milner, *Hist. Winchester*, 3rd ed. i. 285–6; D'Ewes, 346, 442, 454. [8] PRO Index 6800; SP12/194/23; SP14/34/1, 15; SP14/66/101, 80/21, 86/68; *Eliz. Govt. and Soc.* 235–6 and n; W. Allsebrook, 'Court of Requests in Reign of Elizabeth' (London Univ. MA thesis, 1936), pp. 37–42; *CSP Dom.* 1603–10, 1611–18 passim; *Southampton Ass. Bks.* iv. pp. xxxvi–xxxvii. [9] *HMC Hatfield*, ix. 85; J. S. Davies, *Hist. Southampton*, 462; Speed, *Hist. Southampton*, 132, 142; Camden, *Britannia* (1806), i. 166. [10] *Southampton Ass. Bks.* i. 24 n, 31; ii. pp. xxviii, 25; Lansd. 142, f. 204; *APC*, xxix. 193, 211; *CSP Dom.* 1603–10, p. 82; Add. 1580–1625, pp. 428, 432. [11] *CSP Dom.* 1611–18, p. 554.

M.R.P.

MYND, Thomas (1510–77), of Wallingford, Berks., later of London.

WALLINGFORD   1555, 1558, 1559

b. 8 July 1510, 2nd s. of Richard Mynd of Myndtown, Salop by his 2nd w. Ankeret, da. of John Leighton of Church Stretton, Salop. *m.* Anne, ?da. of Martin Dockwra and sis. of Edmund Dockwra* of Chamberhouse, Berks., *s.p.*[1]

Mynd had left Shropshire for Berkshire by April 1550, probably on his marriage. By 1559 he owned property in

Wallingford, which returned him to Elizabeth's first Parliament. On 21 Feb. 1559 he was licensed to be absent from the Commons, 'for his special business at the assizes'. Moving to London, he probably practised as a civil lawyer. He died 7 Feb. 1577, and was buried at St. Faith's under St. Paul's, next to Thomas Dockwra, presumably a member of his wife's family, who was a notary and proctor of the arches. His will has a long preamble asking the Trinity to assist him 'in the bitter conflict of death against the assaults of my ghostly enemy'. He hoped to be among 'the elect children of salvation'.[2]

[1] H. Owen and J. B. Blakeway, *Hist. Shrewsbury*, ii. 123; *Vis. Salop* (Harl. Soc. xxix), 370; PCC 6 Daughtry; S. Barfield, *Thatcham, Berks.* ii. 250–1. [2] *CPR*, 1549–51, p. 201; 1555–7, p. 214; PCC 6 Daughtry; *CJ*, i. 55; *I.T. Recs.* i. 169; Dugdale, *Old St. Paul's* (1818), p. 79.

A.H.

MYNGAYE, Francis (c.1574–1632), of Ilkestall St. Margaret, Suff., later of The Bridge House, Southwark, Surr.

DUNWICH   1601

b. c.1574, 1st s. of William Myngaye of Amringale, Norf. by Winifred, da. of Robert Coke and sis. of (Sir) Edward*. *educ.* I. Temple 1591, called 1600. *m.* Frances, da. and h. of Edmund Richers of Swannington, Norf., at least 2s. 2da.

Bencher, I. Temple 1617; j.p. Surr. by 1623.

Myngaye was a lawyer and moneylender who owed his education at the Inner Temple to his uncle the solicitor-general, who used on his nephew's behalf the special admission accorded to him in January 1593 by virtue of his first reading. Coke also saw to Myngaye's return at Dunwich. Myngaye is not named in the proceedings of the House, and it is not clear where he was residing at the time. He was living at Ilkestall St. Margaret in 1592, and his will mentions property also at South Clincham and elsewhere in Suffolk, but his main residence by the time of his death was at Southwark. He died in 1632, and his will, dated 28 Apr. in that year, was proved 28 June. He had 'put out' sums of money in the names of his daughters, Anne and Martha, and his many clients included Sir George Vernon and Sir Richard More. His partner in these moneylending activities was one Peter Bramble, who was asked to look after the interests of Myngaye's family as he had 'given him board for 20 years together, and done him many extraordinary kindnesses'.

Vis. Surr. (Harl. Soc. xliii), 133; *Cal. I.T. Recs.* i. 386, 434; ii. 102; *HMC Var.* vii. 87; Dunwich min. bk. 1595–1619, f. 84; *Norf. Arch.* xxvii. 43; PCC 64 Audley.

N.M.F.

MYNGE, John (*d.* c.1605), of New Romney, Kent.

NEW ROMNEY   1593, 1601

?s. of Daniel Mynge of Rye, Suss. by Ann Rybaulte. *m.* 1593, Judith Hamon of Acrise.

Jurat, New Romney, town clerk by 1582, mayor 1598, 1604; brodhull rep. in at least the years 1582, 1583, 1593, 1594, 1597; bailiff to Yarmouth 1594.

As town clerk, Mynge was involved in the disputes which disrupted New Romney in the middle years of Elizabeth's reign. At first associated with William Southland*, he afterwards identified himself with the lord warden, Lord Cobham, who was increasingly hostile to Southland. By 1588 Mynge was described by the Southland faction as 'a pernicious enemy to the good government, state, quiet and commonwealth of this corporation'. After Southland's fall in 1590, Mynge remained on good terms with Lord Cobham, and was chosen as senior Member of Parliament for Romney in 1593, perhaps with Cobham's support. It was necessary for the Cinque Ports as a whole to encourage Cobham's friendship at this date, in view of their lawsuit with the City of London. Mynge, as one of those appointed by the brodhull meeting in 1593 to further their case, provided an important link with Cobham, especially as the proceedings kept him in London for much of the time. The case had still not been resolved when in 1597 Lord Cobham's son Henry (equally well disposed to Mynge) succeeded to the office of lord warden. In a long letter, dated October 1597, Mynge sent the mayor and jurats of Romney a report on Cobham's position:

He is very desirous to be in person in the common pleas when our matter of withernam shall be heard, and because his health would not serve him to be there this day, which should have been the day of argument, he hath wrought the means to have it deferred until the week after All-Hallowtide. In the mean season he purposeth to solicit the judges himself, one after another, and to move her Majesty also, for he saith [that] if he may not keep us in as good state of our liberties as he found us, he will pray her Majesty to take back her patent again.

At the same time the question of Romney's representation in the forthcoming Parliament was under discussion. Cobham wished to nominate Mynge for one of the seats, but Mynge

told his lordship nay, for I had entreated my friends to spare me this Parliament. 'Nay, by my faith', said my lord, 'you shall not be spared now. I will rather write specially to the mayor and jurats that you should be chosen'. I told his lordship he should not need to do so, for they were too forward that way already, but rather entreated his lordship to write that I might be spared by reason of my business in the country.

Mynge went on to warn his fellow townsmen that attempts would be made in Parliament to remove some of the Ports' legal privileges, and also to impose fifteenths on

them. This made it doubly important that they retain Cobham's friendship. Mynge sat for Romney for the second time in the last Parliament of the reign. He was paid 2s. a day, the same amount as in 1593, and 4s. for the five day's travel to and from London. He may have attended three committees, to which the burgesses for New Romney were appointed, concerning the explanation of statutes (28 Nov. 1593), the order of business (3 Nov. 1601) and the Severn harbour (21 Nov. 1601).

Mynge was involved in other lawsuits during his long membership of the brodhull and he may have had some legal training, no trace of which has been found. In 1582 he was censured for his behaviour at one of their meetings. He acted as bailiff to Yarmouth in 1594, and a diary which he and his colleague kept during the visit has been preserved. In 1596 he was commissioned to collect money from Romney to help finance the navy. The date of his death is not known. Administration of his property was granted 23 Jan. 1606. His widow, a sister of Sir Thomas Hamon, or Hamond, lived until 1616. Vice-admiral Sir Christopher Mings, whose funeral Pepys attended 13 June 1666 was a descendant.

J. Cowper, *Canterbury Mar. Lic. 1568–1618*, p. 297; Cinque Ports black bk. ff. 43, 45, 60, 61, 68, 73, 81, 107; *Arch. Cant.* xx. 3; xxxvii. 52; xlii. 22; *HMC 13th Rep. IV*, pp. 36, 60; *CSP Dom.* 1547–80, p. 611; 1581–90, pp. 167–8; 1603–10, p. 302; New Romney assembly bk. 1577–1622, ff. 47, 65, 119; New Romney recs. bundle 54; D'Ewes, 511, 624, 647; K. M. E. Murray, *Const. Hist. of the Cinque Ports*, 114; *APC*, xxv. 374; information from C. S. Fry of Hove.

M.R.P.

MYNN, Nicholas, of Little Walsingham, Norf.

BRAMBER	1558
HORSHAM	1559
NEW SHOREHAM	1563
MORPETH	1571
CASTLE RISING	1572

2nd s. of John Mynn of Woodcote, Surr. *m.* Elizabeth, da. of Robert Drury†, wid. of Thomas Grey of Merton, 3s. 3da.

Servant of 4th Duke of Norfolk by 1558–72.

The Mynns, whose tangled pedigree contains several Nicholases, appear mainly in Norfolk and Suffolk. Mynn himself, however, was from the Surrey branch of the family, and he later (certainly by 1560) moved to Little Walsingham. He was in the service of the Duke of Norfolk by 1558, when he was in Rome negotiating the dispensation for Norfolk's second marriage. All the boroughs for which Mynn sat belonged to the Duke. By the time of the 1572 elections Norfolk was in disgrace, but Mynn's connexion with him, and perhaps his own residence nearby was still enough to secure his election. Nothing has been ascertained about him after 1572.

Vis. Rutland (Harl. Soc. iii), 5; *Vis. Surr.* (Harl. Soc. lxiii), 18; *East Anglia Peds.* (Harl. Soc. xcvii), 74; *Vis. Norf.* (Norf. Arch.), ii. 218; C. A. Carthew, *Hundred of Launditch*, ii. 481–91; *CSP For.* 1553–8, p. 389; *APC*, viii. 51.

B.D.

NANNEY, Griffith (1568–1609), of Nannau, Llangach-reth, and Maelan, Dolgelly, Merion.

MERIONETH   1593

 b. 1568, 1st s. of Hugh Nanney of Nannau by Anne, da. of Rhys Vaughan of Cors y gedol. *educ.* Shrewsbury; Jesus, Oxf. July 1585. *m.* Ellen, da. of John Wyn ap Cadwaladr* of Rhiwlas, 3s. 2da.
 Commr. subsidy Merion. 1595, j.p. from c.1599.

Unlike the Salesburys of Rûg, the Prices of Rhiwlas and the Owens of Llwyn, all of recent standing, the Nanney family had been seated in Merioneth since the thirteenth century. Head of the family between 1580 and 1623, and first of his stock to use the surname consistently, was Hugh Nanney, who rebuilt the family mansion and increased his patrimony by acquisitions from the dissolved abbey of Cymmer. Apart from their inter-marriages with the neighbouring houses of Vaughan of Hengwrt, of Caer Gai and of Cors y gedol, the Nanneys had many friends in the shire, as appeared when Hugh Nanney was in prison in 1606.

Griffith Nanney predeceased his father and did not inherit the family estate, but he appears to have been endowed with lands on reaching his majority and these he increased by purchases and leases; he also had by 1597 his own separate establishment at Maelan, in the township of Garth Maelan, a mile or so south of Rûg. He thus became involved in the family hereditary feuds. His election to Parliament in 1593 was intended to forestall the aspirations of John Lewis Owen*, the principal rival of the Nanneys, who had represented the shire in 1572, and it inaugurated a period of bloody strife between the rival factions. A Star Chamber suit about the wrongful conversion of money levied to pay the MP indicates that Nanney received £15 or £16 for his services as knight of the shire. The under-sheriff was alleged to have collected £50 in the county and embezzled the balance. As knight of the shire for Merioneth, Nanney could have attended committees on the subsidy (26 Feb.) and a legal matter (9 Mar.).

The year after the election Griffith Nanney sued John Lewis Owen in Star Chamber for illegal intrusion and violent breaking down of enclosures (alleged to have been themselves encroachments on common land) at Tyddyn Bach in Garth y Maelan. An accusation against Nanney of unlawful enclosure came before the same court in 1606–7. He was also associated with his father in 1604 in charges brought by the Crown before the court of Exchequer (but attributed to the malice of the Owens of Llwyn) of sales of

timber from 1588–94 from Penrhos woods, north of Nannau, which were claimed as crown commons and part of the forest of Snowdon. A heavy fine was imposed, and the father suffered a term of imprisonment for non-payment, but in a later action a crown witness was proved to be perjured. A compromise was reached the year after Griffith's death, not, however, before the feud had issued in gross disorders in the town of Dolgelly and in charges and counter-charges before the Star Chamber and the council of Wales of mutual forays on the proprietary pews of the respective families in Dolgelly church. Griffith was further accused of unlawful detention of a commissioner in the Penrhos wood case and of other misdemeanours as a magistrate; and he accepted a challenge from one of the Llwyn faction to a duel, which apparently never took place. All this cost money, and Nanney was soon borrowing from Thomas Myddelton*. In 1606 a writ of attachment was out against him for £200; but the London merchant's regard for his 'cousins' of Nannau made some accommodation possible, and Nanney was still borrowing money on mortgage to within a couple of years of his death. He died in 1609, letters of administration being granted 28 July. He was lamented in an elegy by the Nannau household bard, Richard Phylip.

This biography is based upon E. D. Jones, 'Fam. of Nannau', *Jnl. Merion. Hist. Soc.* ii. 15; B. R. Parry, 'Hist. Nannau Fam. to 1623', UCNW MA thesis 1958. Other sources include: Griffith, *Peds.* 200; UCNW Nannau-Hengwrt mss; *Star Chamber*, ed. Edwards (Univ. Wales Bd. of Celtic Studies, Hist. and Law ser. i), 91, 94, 185; D'Ewes, 474, 496; St. Ch. 5/N10/34; 8/221/24, 223/17, 225/15; 5/W28/23; *Arch. Camb.* (ser.iii), x. 104; NLW Peniarth mss 327, pt.1; *HMC Welsh*, i. 269.

H.G.O.

NAPIER (NAPPER), Robert (c.1543–1615), of Middle-marsh Hall, Minterne Magna, Dorset.

DORCHESTER   1586
BRIDPORT   1601
WAREHAM   1604

 b. c.1543, 3rd s. of James Napier of Puncknoll by his w., the da. of one Hilliard of Dorset. *educ.* Exeter Coll. Oxf. 1559, BA 1562; M. Temple 1566. *m.* (1) Katherine, da. of John Wareham of Dorset, 1da.; (2) Magdalyn or Margaret, da. of William Denton of Tonbridge, Kent, 1s. Kntd. 1593.
 Bencher, M. Temple by 1588; chief baron of the Exchequer [I] 1593–1602; j.p. Dorset from c.1591, rem. 1595, rest. 1602; sheriff, Dorset 1606.

Napier, or Napper as the name was frequently spelled, was involved (1574–5) in land transactions with the 2nd Earl of Bedford, to whom he may have been related through his grandmother Anne Russell. There was a Bedfordshire branch of Napier's family. As a lawyer, his name occurs in numerous connexions: witnessing the marriage settlement of John Browne of Frampton in 1579;

being overseer to the will of Browne's father in 1583; giving an arbitration award against Anthony Paulet in 1592; acting as trustee for Dorchester School and purchasing land for the school. He was retained by Melcombe Regis in 1579, by Dorchester in 1583 and 1585, and by Lyme Regis in 1593. In March 1591 he and Dr. Tertullian Pyne were sent to Jersey to investigate complaints against the Paulets, and they produced a code of ordinances for the island. Two years later Napier was made an Irish judge. He was dismissed in 1602 for frequent absences in England.

At Bridport and possibly Dorchester Napier was of sufficient local importance to procure his own return to Parliament. However, on the Dorchester election return his name was inserted in such a way as to suggest that he may have been nominated by a patron, perhaps the Earl of Warwick, guardian of the 3rd Earl of Bedford. Unusually for a lawyer in the later Elizabethan House of Commons, Napier is not mentioned in its records in either 1586 or 1601. He is stated to have died on 20 Sept. 1615. In his will, made that August and proved in November, he describes himself as 'about the age of threescore years and twelve'. A long preamble expressed the hope that his sins 'will be made white and clean by the blood and passion of the Lord', but his religious position is obscure. He may have had Catholic connexions, and his second wife almost certainly did. She received a life interest in most of his property, while his eldest son, Nathaniel, received £500 and goods. Two married daughters, grandchildren and other relations and servants are mentioned. A large section of the will is devoted to charitable bequests and to a scheme for establishing almshouses at Dorchester. Napier desired that a monument to the value of £50 should be erected to his memory, carrying the inscription 'I believe in the Resurrection of the Dead'.

Vis. Dorset (Harl. Soc. xx), 74; *Vis. Beds.* (Harl. Soc. xix), 183; G. Scott Thomson, *Two Cents. Fam. Hist.* 56, 119, 120, 122; Hutchins, *Dorset*, ii. 367–8; *Weymouth Charters*, ed. Moule, 131; *Dorchester Recs.* ed. Mayo, 480; *Dorset Nat. Hist. and Arch. Soc. Procs.* lix. 69, 77, 83–4; A. J. Eagleston, *Channel Is. under Tudor Govt.* 95; PCC 21 Brudenell, 108 Rudd; *VCH Oxon.*; *DNB*.

P.W.H.

NAPPER, *see* NAPIER

NASH, Richard (*d.* 1605), of Worcester.

WORCESTER   1584

s. of John Nash of Tapenhall in Ombersley, Worcs. by his w. Dorothy. *m.* Margaret, da. of Thomas Walsgrove *alias* Fleet*, 3s. 5da.
   Bailiff, Worcester 1581–2.

Nash was the son of a local farmer who became a clothier, prospered, and married into a leading Worcester family. He was not himself active in city life, serving once only as a bailiff without proceeding through the usual hierarchy of appointments; neither did he take any part in the 1584 parliamentary proceedings. He bought one or two small estates in the vicinity of Worcester, and houses in the city, some from George Wild*, and acquired leases from local gentlemen such as William Lygon*, the bulk of which he entailed upon his heirs male. The two younger sons were given one or two messuages which were then specially entailed. His eldest daughter was given a house and meadow, his younger daughters £100 dowries, and most of the household stuff, wool, cloth and yarn was equally divided between the daughters. He died 3 Oct. 1605.

PCC 38 Arundel, 60 Lewyn, 24 Lawe, 70 Hayes; Nash, *Worcs.* ii. p. cxii; Worcester Guildhall, chamber order bk. 1540–1601, f. 159; C142/311/95.

S.M.T.

NEALE, Francis, of St. Dunstan-in-the-West, London, and East Meon, Hants.

GRANTHAM   1593, 1597

Prob. s. of William Neale of Warnford, Hants, auditor of the Exchequer, by his 1st w. Agnes, da. of Robert Bowyer[†]. *m.* 10 July 1605, Florence, da. of Sir William Uvedale of Wickham, Hants, at least 2s. *d.v.p.* 1da. Kntd. 2 Jan. 1609.
   Auditor of the Exchequer from c.1593 to at least 1625; j.p. Hants 1625, commr. martial law 1627.

Neale's grandfather, father and elder brother Thomas were all auditors of the Exchequer, and the family must have been well known to Lord Burghley, who twice brought Neale into Parliament for Grantham. In 1590 he or a namesake received a small grant of land in Cambridgeshire. During his first Parliament he was arrested for debt at the suit of a brewer. He paid up and was released, but, 'in regard of the preservation of the liberties and privileges' of the Commons, he brought the matter before the House on 5 Apr. 1593. The arresting officer and the brewer were summoned before the House next day and put in the Tower. Neale probably retired from his Exchequer post to his Hampshire estates about 1625. The date of his death has not been ascertained.

Vis. Hants (Harl. Soc. lxiv), 149; *Misc. Gen. et Her.* (ser. 2), v. 297; *Coll. Top. et Gen.* iv. 124; v. 372; *Hants Mar. Lic.* 1607–40, p. 53; *APC*, xxiv. 46; *HMC Hatfield*, vii. 22; xi. 340; *Vis. Leics.* (Harl. Soc. ii), 46; *CSP Dom.* 1581–90, p. 676; 1625–6, p. 536; 1627–8, p. 440; Rymer, *Foedera*, viii. pt. 2, p. 15; D'Ewes, 518, 519.

N.M.F./J.P.F.

NECTON, William, of London.

NEW SHOREHAM   1584, 1586, 1589, 1593, 1597

   m. Elizabeth.[1]

Ct. of wards feodary, London and Mdx. c.1565–c.1601; surveyor of works; receiver to Philip, Earl of Arundel.

Next to nothing has been ascertained about Necton's background. He may have been related to the family of that name who lived in Norwich in the reign of Henry VIII, and/or have been the William Necton of that city who in 1553 was speculating with the advowsons of several Norfolk parishes, and/or the man who bought the rectory and advowson of Newendon, in Kent, from Lord North in 1557.

Whatever his origins, during the time he served as Member of Parliament, always for New Shoreham, Necton was a feodary of the court of wards, though whether this employment preceded his receivership to Philip, Earl of Arundel, or was perhaps a consequence of it, is again obscure. Necton undoubtedly put his knowledge of the management of land and revenues to the use of private individuals, including Sir Walter Mildmay*, and his return to Parliament for New Shoreham was due to Arundel, who owned the borough, but the fact that he continued to occupy the seat after Arundel's attainder in 1589 suggests that he had other friends at court, possibly including Lord Burghley. Necton's name has not been found in the journals of any of his Parliaments, but he was probably the man who was appointed to a committee about Paris Garden on 19 Jan. 1598. After Arundel's attainder Necton and William Dix* corresponded with and visited him in prison. Indeed, their correspondence may have been the means whereby Arundel kept in touch with Catholic sympathizers. Necton presumably died about the turn of the century when a new appointment was made to his court of wards position. Perhaps the James Necton who studied at Gray's Inn and was deputy surveyor for Middlesex in 1611 was his son.[2]

[1] Her christian name only has been found, in the 1588 inquisition post mortem (C142/218/20) of John Morley I.* [2] J. Hurstfield, Queen's Wards, 81; Lansd. 30, ff. 217 seq.; 52, ff. 68–9; 62, f. 153; 66, ff. 120 seq.; 86, ff. 151 seq.; CPR, 1553 and App. Ed. VI, pp. 231–2; 1555–7, p. 377; 1563–6, pp. 403, 508; CSP Dom. 1547–80, p. 666; 1581–90, p. 382; 1598–1601, p. 168; 1611–18, p. 6; APC, xxvi. 448; Strype, Parker, ii. 432; Cath. Rec. Soc. xxi. 304, 305, 312–13, 314, 320–1, 381; Townshend, Hist. Colls. 121; D'Ewes, 583.

M.R.P.

NEEDHAM, Robert (c.1565–1631), of Shavington, Salop.

SHROPSHIRE 1593, 1604

b. c.1565, 1st s. of Robert Needham of Shavington by Frances, da. of Sir Edward Aston of Tixall. educ. Shrewsbury 1577; St. John's, Camb. 1582; I. Temple 1583. m. (1) Jane (d. 1591), da. of John Lacy of Borston, Som., 1s.; (2) Anne Doyley, wid. of one Wilmott; (3) aft. 1627, Catherine (d.1628), da. of John Robinson of London, wid. of George Huxley; (4) Dorothy, da. of Humphrey Smith of London, wid. of Sir John

Pakington. Kntd. 1594; suc. fa. 1603. cr. Visct. Kilmorey [I] 1625.

J.p. Salop by 1596, dep. lt. 1600, sheriff 1606–7; member, council in marches of Wales 1609, vice-pres. 1614.

As a young man, Needham held several commands in Ireland, where he was knighted by the lord deputy. If he was back in time for the 1593 Parliament Needham would, as a knight of the shire, have been entitled to attend committees on the subsidy (26 Feb.) and springing uses and perpetuities (9 Mar.). He was certainly in England in 1596, claiming a reimbursement of £75 from the government: he received £30 two years later. In Shropshire he was employed in such matters as endeavouring to prevent excessive brewing and 'tippling and disorderly drinking' in two alehouses in Market Drayton, and in searching for Jesuits and seminary priests. He remained active in local affairs all his life, and obtained an Irish peerage from Charles I. He died in 1631, and was buried at Adderley.

Vis. Salop (Harl. Soc. xxix), 372; Trans. Salop Arch. Soc. (ser. 4), xi. 156; CP, vii. 260; APC, xxvi. 335; xxx. 399; H. O. Harrod, Hist. Shavington, 22–49; D'Ewes, 474, 496.

J.J.C.

NETHERMILL, John (by 1515–59), of Coventry, Warws.

COVENTRY 1553 (Oct.), 1559

b. by 1515, 1st s. of Julian Nethermill of Coventry by his w. Joan. m. settlement 18 Nov. 1550, Bridget, da. of Henry Over alias Waver† of Coventry, 1s. suc. fa. 11 Apr. 1539.

Sheriff or bailiff, Coventry 1547–8, mayor 1557–8.

Nethermill was a draper, some of whose wealth derived from speculations in chantry lands during Edward VI's reign. Thus he had some interest in the establishment of protestantism and by October 1553 he was radical enough to be classified as one of those who 'stood for the true religion' in the House of Commons. Perhaps it was his religious views that encouraged his fellow burgesses to return him again in 1559 when, in the first Parliament of Queen Elizabeth, radical religious changes were expected. It would also have recommended his candidature to Lord Ambrose Dudley and his brother Lord Robert, who exercised some influence in the city. His name does not occur in the defective journals of that Parliament, and he did not long survive its dissolution, dying 31 Oct. 1559 and being buried in the drapers' chapel in St. Michael's church 'with such order of funerals as for such men is there accustomed'. He had made his will little more than a month earlier. To his wife he left a life interest in a house at Exhall. Other property in Warwickshire and Staffordshire was to be held by Coventry corporation until his son's majority, and the revenue arising was to be used in loans to drapers, clothiers and cappers of the town.

Nethermill's executors were his widow, his son John, and his brother-in-law Sir William Garrard†, alderman of London. One of the overseers was Thomas Dudley*. Bridget Nethermill later married Stephen Hales* and their heir's wardship was obtained by the Coventry corporation.

C142/65/16, 170/14; Dugdale, *Warws.* i. 167; *Vis. Warws.* (Harl. Soc. xii), 253; *Coventry Leet Bk.* ii. 783, 788; Coventry council bk. f. 17; Coventry mayors' accts. 1542–61, p. 19; *CPR*, 1549–51, p. 21; *VCH Warws.* iii. 144; v. 25, 83, 175; Bodl. e Museo 17; PCC 24 Mellershe; Coventry bk. of payments, f. 25.

I.C.

NEVILLE, Alexander (1544–1614), of Canterbury and St. Mary-without-Bishopsgate, Mdx.

CHRISTCHURCH	1584
PETERBOROUGH	1597[1]
SALTASH	1601

b. 1544, 1st s. of Richard Neville of South Leverton, Notts. and of Canterbury, by Anne, da. of Sir Walter Mantell of Heyford, Northants. *educ.* St. John's, Camb. 1559, hon. MA 1581. *m.* Jane, da. of Richard Duncombe of Morton, Bucks., wid. of Sir Gilbert Dethick, *s.p.*[2] Sec. to Archbishops Parker, Grindal and Whitgift.

Born in Nottinghamshire, Neville moved with his parents to Canterbury at an early age. After spending some time in Cambridge, he apparently studied law in London (though his name is not in the printed inns of court registers) possibly at Gray's Inn, with George Gascoigne*, among whose close friends he was soon numbered. In 1560 he published a verse translation of the *Oedipus* of Seneca, which was well enough received to be reissued in 1581 as part of a collected edition of Seneca's plays. In 1563 his cousin Barnaby Googe*, another of Gascoigne's literary group, published a volume of *Eclogs, Epytaphes and Sonnetes*, which contained poems addressed to Neville.

It was probably soon after this that Neville entered the service of Archbishop Parker, who appears to have employed him particularly as a collaborator in his historical works. He was much attracted by the studious life followed in Parker's household and himself embarked upon an account of Ket's rebellion, which was published in 1575, together with a description of Norwich. He acknowledged his master's help in the composition of the work, which he dedicated to him. Government pressure caused it to be withdrawn almost at once, however, until passages reflecting upon the laziness and cowardice of the Welsh levies employed in the suppression of the rebellion were deleted. A revised edition soon appeared, with an additional dedication to Archbishop Grindal, whose service the author entered after Parker's death. Neville expiated his offence further by publishing an apology to the Welsh.[3]

Neville spent much of his life in the service of Archbishop Parker and his two successors, but he was not without other influential connexions, as for example the Earl of Leicester, who in July 1585 was relying upon him and his brother Thomas to impress upon Archbishop Whitgift the necessity of encouraging the Queen to help the Netherlands. Two years later, Neville dedicated to Leicester his *Academiae Cantabrigiensis lacrimae tumulo Philippi Sidnei sacratae*.[4]

It was presumably through Leicester that he returned to Parliament in 1584. The immediate patron at Christchurch was probably the 3rd Earl of Huntingdon, Leicester's brother-in-law. Upon this occasion, the mayor refused a nomination to Walsingham on the ground that one Member had already been elected and that the other seat belonged to Huntingdon 'of ancient right'. At Peterborough Neville presumably owed his seat to the Cecils, but how he obtained election at Saltash in 1601 is obscure. He had no apparent connexion with any of the local families, but may have been nominated through the intervention of Sir Robert Cecil or Archbishop Whitgift. He is not known to have contributed to the proceedings of his three Parliaments.[5]

Neville died on 4 Oct. 1614 in London. He had made his will less than two months earlier, 'being by age and sickness somewhat enfeebled'. He left no children and his wife had predeceased him, but other relatives received substantial tokens of his affection. His brother Thomas, now dean of Canterbury, was to have an annuity of £120, to which a bequest of £100 was added in a codicil. Anthony Neville, son of George Neville, 'my nearest kinsman', was to receive £200, as was Barnaby Googe, 'my wellbeloved cousin' – the son of the poet – who was now Master of Magdalene College, Cambridge and was soon to become chancellor of the diocese of Exeter. He was also generous to his servants; one received £200, another £10 and another an annuity of £6. There were also legacies to the poor of Canterbury and to the parish where he should die. The executor and residuary legatee was Tobias Worthington, 'my servant for twenty-five years', who had long managed Neville's affairs. The will directed burial in Neville's chapel in Canterbury cathedral, where his brother, the dean, had prepared a tomb for both of them, adding that

> wheresoever my body lies, right sure I am my redeemer lives; and though worms devour my flesh, yet I myself shall see him and none other for me, at that day when he shall appear in His majesty to judge both quick and dead.[6]

[1] Folger V. b. 298. [2] *Vis. Kent* (Harl. Soc. xlii), 87; *DNB*. [3] *DNB* (Gascoigne, George; Googe, Barnabe); Strype, *Parker*, ii. 432, 436–7, 441–2; iii. 346–50; *Grindal*, 292; *Annals*, iii(1), p. 744; Pollard and Redgrave, *Short Title Catalogue*, 421. [4] Lansd. 45, f. 98; Strype, *Whitgift*, i. 435. [5] *CSP Dom.* 1581–90, p. 208. [6] PCC 102 Lawe; Hasted, *Kent*, xi. 347, 392–3.

I.C.

NEVILLE, Edward I (c.1550–1622), of Birling, Kent.

NEW WINDSOR   1589*

> b. c.1550, 1st s. of Edward Neville of Newton St. Loe, Som. by his 1st w. Katherine, da. of Sir John Brome of Holton, Oxon. *educ.* G. Inn 1563. *m.* c.1574, Rachel, da. of John Lennard of Chevening and Knole, 6s. inc. Sir Henry II* 5da. *suc.* fa. 1589; recognised as Lord Bergavenny 1604.[1]
>
> Burgess, New Windsor 1588, j.p.q. Mon., Kent and Suss. by 1595.

On 10 Oct. 1588, Henry Neville*, Edward's cousin, was chosen burgess for New Windsor, where his father was high steward; on 24 Oct. Edward Neville was sworn 'brother assistant' of Windsor, and the following day was returned to Parliament for the borough, 'because Henry Neville, esquire, was chosen a knight for Sussex'. This record of the election on 24 Oct., quoted from Ashmole's transcripts of the borough manuscripts (the originals are now lost), continues: 'but he [Edward Neville] served not, for that the Lord Bergavenny died before the Parliament'. Clearly, the remark 'but he served not', cannot have been a part of the original entry in the borough minutes for 24 or 25 October, and may well be Ashmole's own comment. In fact, Neville's father did not die until 10 Feb. 1589, when the Parliament was a week old, and it was another 16 years before Neville was summoned to Parliament as a peer. Therefore, it is quite likely that he did sit in the Commons in 1589, although he is not reported to have taken part in its proceedings. It is improbable – since, like his father, he called himself Lord Bergavenny – that he sought to be returned to another Parliament as a Member of the Commons; the 'Edward Neville, gentleman' who sat for New Windsor in 1593 was probably another of his cousins.[2]

The protests of Lady Fane against Neville's assumption of the title led to a hearing of the dispute in 1598, before the Earl of Essex and other commissioners for the office of earl marshal. Despite Neville's vigorous advancement of precedents for the descent of titles by entail, the matter was left in suspense until an arrangement between the parties was reached at the beginning of James I's reign, as a result of which Neville was summoned to Parliament in May 1604. Lady Fane carried her feud with Neville into the 1601 Parliament, endeavouring unsuccessfully to prevent him disposing of certain copyhold lands.[3]

At the hearing before the Earl of Essex, Neville had as ally his brother-in-law, Sampson Lennard*, who was himself claiming the barony of Dacre of the South. Endowed with great estates, Neville was able to arrange good matches for his children. His eldest son, Sir Henry Neville, married the daughter of his Kent neighbour, Thomas Sackville*, Lord Treasurer Buckhurst; at the election of 1601 Sir Henry was supported by (Sir) Robert Sidney* as a candidate for the senior seat in Kent, for

which he competed with Lady Fane's son. One of Neville's daughters married Sir John Grey*; another George Goring, later 1st Earl of Norwich. Neville himself held no great offices and had little influence of his own: he and his sons were returned to Parliament in Elizabeth's reign through the influence of their Berkshire relatives or Kent friends. Neville lost three of his younger sons, drowned off Gravesend, in March 1616, and was himself, according to John Chamberlain, killed by the cold of December 1622.[4]

[1] *CP*; D. Rowland, *Fam. of Neville*, 150–1, 162; *Vis. Berks.* (Harl. Soc. lvii), 181. [2] Bodl. Ashmole 1126, f. 50; *CP*. [3] Rowland, 154; *CSP Dom.* 1598–1601, pp. 122–3, 130–1; *HMC Hatfield*, xiv. 83; D'Ewes, 610, 611. [4] *CSP Dom.* 1581–90, p. 639; *Chamberlain Letters* ed. McClure, i. 56, 616; ii. 466; PCC 106 Savile.

A.H.

NEVILLE, Edward II (b.1567), of Wargrave and Windsor, Berks.

NEW WINDSOR   1593

> b. 1567, 2nd s. of Sir Henry Neville I* of Billingbear by his 2nd w. Elizabeth, da. of Sir John Gresham of Titsey, Surr.; bro. of Henry*. *educ.* L. Inn 1586. *m.* by 1604, 5s.
>
> Burgess, New Windsor 1593.

The Edward Neville returned for Windsor in 1593 is unlikely to have been Edward Neville I*, who at this time was claiming the barony of Bergavenny. The Member of 1589 is designated 'esquire' in the return, and the Member of 1593, 'gentleman'. Both were admitted to the freedom of the borough immediately before return, and to complete the confusion over status the 1593 Member appears as 'esquire' in the borough's record of admission. If Edward Neville I be ruled out, the 1593 MP was in all probability his cousin and namesake the second son of Sir Henry Neville, high steward of Windsor, and younger brother of Henry Neville, the other 1593 burgess. There might easily have been doubts as to whether he should be styled 'gentleman', as in the return, or 'esquire', as in the borough records, when he had just been left the manor of Culham, in the parish of Wargrave, and other property in Berkshire, and all his father's 'household stuff' at the Savoy in London. He was presumably the Edward Neville of Culham, Sunninghill and Windsor, whose fourth son, Charles, was born in 1608 and educated at Eton and Oxford. Charles Neville took his BA in 1626 as *equitis aurati filius*; there is no other evidence that Edward Neville was knighted, and the date of his death is unknown.

Misc. Gen. et Her. ii. 318; *Vis. Berks.* (Harl. Soc. lvi), 250; PCC 1 Nevell; *Eton Reg.*; *Al. Ox.* 1057; Bodl. Ashmole 1126, f. 38v.

A.H.

NEVILLE, Henry (1562–1615), of Billingbear, Berks. and Mayfield, Suss.

NEW WINDSOR   1584, 1586
SUSSEX   1589

NEW WINDSOR   1593
LISKEARD   1597
BERKSHIRE   1604, 1614

b. 1562, 1st s. of Sir Henry Neville I* by his 2nd w., and
bro. of Edward Neville II*. *educ.* Merton, Oxf. 1577. *m.*
by 1588, Anne, da. of Henry Killigrew*, 5s. 6da. *suc.* fa.
1593. Kntd. c.1597.[1]
Burgess, New Windsor 1584; j.p., commr. recusancy
and dep. lt. Suss. from c.1591; j.p. Berks from c.1583,
sheriff 1594–5, custos rot. 1596; steward of royal manors
of Donnington and Sonning, bailiff of crown lands in
Newbury 1593; high steward of Wokingham; ambassador to France and jt. teller of the Exchequer
1599–1601.[2]

Neville's father was a leading figure in Berkshire and
steward of royal lands around Windsor. He had influence
in the borough during the absence in the Netherlands of
the high steward, the Earl of Leicester; and, on Leicester's
death in 1588, succeeded to the high stewardship itself. On
25 Oct. 1584, his son, the subject of this biography, was
sworn a burgess of the town and 'brother assistant of the
company of the guildhall', and just one month later was
returned as burgess for the Parliament.[3]

By 1588 Neville's standing had been increased by his
marriage to a niece of Lord Burghley. For the Parliament
of 1589 he was able to secure election as a knight for
Sussex, where he often resided during his father's lifetime,
on property left to his father in 1579 by his mother's
cousin, the celebrated Sir Thomas Gresham. He was next
chosen, on 10 Oct. 1588, as burgess for New Windsor, but
the town book records that on 24 Oct. his cousin Edward
Neville I* was chosen burgess 'because Henry Neville is
chosen knight of Sussex'. In 1593 Neville sat again for
Windsor, but his father's death in that year ended the
family representation of the borough, the high
stewardship being one of his father's offices to which
Neville did not succeed.[4]

In 1597 Neville gave up the last of his Sussex lands, sold
to consolidate his Berkshire estates. He was not, however,
strong enough to challenge a Norris or a Knollys for a
Berkshire seat in the 1597 Parliament, and had to turn to
the Cornish borough of Liskeard, of which his brother-in-
law Jonathan Trelawny*, in that year knight for Cornwall, was the steward: the two men were friendly,
Trelawny appointing Neville a trustee of his lands in his
will. As far as it is possible to tell, Neville did not speak in
Parliament and served on committees only in the 1597
Parliament, considering the repeal of statutes imposing
irksome and outdated military obligations (8 Nov.),
monopolies (10 Nov.), poor relief (10 Nov.), horse stealing
(16 Nov.), and abuses committed by the rude and licentious
soldiery (27 Jan. 1598). He was presumably the Mr. 'Nevill'
who was appointed to a committee concerning John
Sharpe's debts on 20 Jan. 1598.[5]

In 1598 the government decided to use Neville as a
diplomat, a sphere in which his father-in-law had done
good service. He tried to excuse himself, telling Cecil that
he had sold his lands in Sussex to buy the Berkshire estates
of (Sir) Henry Unton* (who had just died), and was bound
to pay £12,000 within three months, 'impossible of
accomplishment if he was employed'. At last, in the spring
of 1599, he set out for France, where an observer described
him as 'a puritan and entirely Scottish … he confers much
with the Scottish ambassador'. He tried to arrange the
return to England of the anti-Jesuit faction among the
Catholic exiles; and he was commissioned to negotiate for
a peace with Spain in the Netherlands, his attempt to this
end resulting in little more than a wrangle with the
Spanish ambassador over precedence.[6]

Perhaps he was too much a follower of Essex to be
enthusiastic for peace with Spain. In January 1600, he
hoped that the Queen would not 'deprive herself of a
servant so necessary [as Essex, though] I have little interest
in his standing or falling except that I hold him a
profitable instrument'. At the same time, he complained
of the burden of hospitality he was bearing in Paris, and
the lack of courtesy shown him there. His motto, he said,
should soon be 'fie upon honour that brings no profit': he
would return and live a hermit in Windsor forest, doing
penance for his faults as ambassador. A plea of increasing
deafness (a family weakness) secured him leave to come
home in August 1600, and he showed 'resolute resistance'
to attempts to send him back to his post.[7]

On his return to England, according to his own account,
he was approached by Essex's agent, Henry Cuffe, with
the information that he would indeed be made to do
penance for his faults as ambassador, particularly the
fiasco of the Spanish negotiations: only through Essex,
Cuffe suggested, would he obtain justice, and he might
even become secretary of state under a new régime.
Neville maintained that he resisted these overtures, and
that, unwillingly drawn into the conference of Essex's
supporters on Candlemas day, he said that he would never
be party to an attack on Cecil. He was certainly not at
Essex House on the day of the rising.[8]

On 20 Feb., the day after his condemnation, Essex,
resentful that Neville had not been more active in his
behalf, named him as one privy to the plotting of the
rebellion. Presumably anticipating this, Neville at last set
off for France, only to be turned back at Dover, and placed
in the custody of the lord admiral at Chelsea, and, from 1
May, in the Tower. For the next two years he sent appeal
after appeal to Cecil, who seems to have been genuinely
'grieved for him', as one drawn to him both by 'friendship
and nature'. At the beginning of July he was sentenced to
lose all his offices and pay a fine of £10,000. He thanked
Cecil for saving his life, and bent his energies to getting his
fine reduced. But none of the many arrangements he
proposed was accepted, and he was released only on the
accession of James I. He died in July 1615.[9]

[1] *DNB*; C142/240/95; *Vis. Berks.* (Harl. Soc. lvii), 181; *Misc. Gen. et Her.* (n.s.), ii. 317. [2] *APC*, xii. 93; xxv. 424; *CSP Dom.* 1595–7, p. 297; *Cath. Rec. Soc.* xvii. 329, 331; PRO Index 16674, f. 34; *VCH Berks.* iii. 227; *HMC Hatfield*, xi. 274; xiv. 279. [3] PCC 1 Nevell; *VCH Berks.* iii. 178–80; Berks. RO, Neville ms O. 15; Bodl. Ashmole 1126, f. 50. [4] Horsfield, *Suss.* ii. 417; *CP*; Bodl. Ashmole 1126, f. 50. [5] *Suss. Arch. Colls.* ii. 245; xxi. 8; *DNB* (Killigrew, Sir Henry); PCC 101 Harte; D'Ewes, 553, 555, 558, 589; Townshend, *Hist. Colls.* 103, 121. [6] *HMC 1st Rep.* 32; *HMC Hatfield*, viii. 158; ix. 72; x. 145–6, 166; *CSP Dom.* 1597–1601, pp. 221, 356; *Chamberlain Letters* ed. McClure, i. 51, 65. [7] *CSP Dom.* 1597–1601, pp. 152, 379; *HMC Hatfield*, x. 261, 371; *Chamberlain Letters*, i. 110–11. [8] *CSP Dom.* 1601–3, pp. 2, 6, 15; *HMC Rutland*, i. 370. [9] *CSP Dom.* 1597–1601, p. 59; 1601–3, pp. 16, 91; Birch, *Mems.* ii. 479, 494–5; *HMC Hatfield*, xi. 76, 110, 145, 176, 193, 273, 300, 321, 526, 570; xii. 6, 43, 72, 80, 113, 152, 268, 589; *HMC Buccleuch*, i. 31; *Chamberlain Letters*, i. 145, 192.

A.H.

NEVILLE, Sir Henry I (*d.* 1593), of Billingbear, Berks.

BERKSHIRE   1553 (Mar.), 1559, 1563, 1571, 1584

s. of Sir Edward Neville (executed 1539), by Eleanor, da. of Andrew Windsor†, 1st Baron Windsor, wid. of Ralph, 9th Lord Scrope of Upsall. *m.* (1) c.1551, Winifred, da. of Hugh Loss of Whitchurch, Mdx., ?*s.p.*; (2) bef. 1561, Elizabeth (*d.*1573), da. of Sir John Gresham of Titsey, Surr., 4s. inc. Henry*and Edward Neville II*, 2da.; (3) c.May 1578, Elizabeth, da. of Sir Nicholas Bacon†, wid. of Robert Doyley*, *s.p.*[1] Kntd. 1551.

Groom of privy chamber by 1546, gent. by Oct. 1550–?1553; master of the harriers 1552–5; j.p.q. and jt. (with Sir William Fitzwilliam I*) ld. lt. Berks from 1559, sheriff 1572–3, custos rot. from c.1584, dep. lt. from c.1587; j.p. Wilts. from c.1574; steward of Mote park in Windsor 1557, of Donnington and bailiff of crown lands in Newbury, Berks. 1562; guardian of Duke of Norfolk in the Tower 1569–70; high steward, Reading 1588, New Windsor 1588.[2]

Neville's career was not seriously affected by the attainder of his father. As Henry VIII's godson he received a £20 annuity, which during the reign of Edward VI was raised to £50, and he continued as an official of the privy chamber until at least 1553. Since he had signed the letters patent for Lady Jane Grey's succession, he was unlikely to find great favour with Queen Mary: however, he kept his office of master of the harriers for the first part of her reign. The details of his career between 1553 and 1558 are obscure. He was in Padua in August 1554 and was reported to have returned to England by 1556.[3]

After Elizabeth's accession almost all the references to him, except for a short period when he was guarding the Duke of Norfolk in the Tower, are concerned with Berkshire. He already owned considerable property there in Billingbear, Waltham St. Lawrence, Culham, Warfield and Wargrave, most of it included in a royal grant of September 1551. Outside Berkshire he was keeper of Addington park, Kent, and owned a number of rectories and tithes in Yorkshire. Presumably he also had property

in Wiltshire, as he was a justice of the peace there.[4]

His position as a leading landowner in Berkshire gained him the county seat on five occasions. It seems unlikely that his candidature was ever seriously challenged: the Star Chamber suit about the 1571 election almost certainly concerned the junior seat. In Parliament he served on committees considering the succession (31 Oct. 1566), uniformity of religion (6 Apr. 1571), treason (12 Apr. 1571), Sabbath observance (27 Nov. 1584), cloth (10 Dec.), the maintenance of the navy (19 Dec.), ecclesiastical livings (19 Dec.), grain (19 Dec., 4 Mar. 1585), Jesuits (18 Feb.), the subsidy (24 Feb.), hats and caps (10 Mar.), a legal procedure (10 Mar.), water bailiffs (12 Mar.), the preservation of woods in Kent (18 Mar.) and London curriers (18 Mar.). He was probably the 'Mr. Nevell' to whom a family bill concerning Lord Bergavenny's lands was committed on 22 Mar. 1563.[5]

Neville carried out the usual tasks of an Elizabethan local official. The bishops' letters to the Privy Council in 1564 commended him as an earnest furtherer of religion, and from time to time he was ordered to suppress recusancy in Berkshire or to examine religious fanatics. In August 1581 he arrested some printers of Latin books who had set up a secret press in the lodge at Lady Stonor's house in the county: for some time after this he was required to prevent her from communicating with Catholic priests. At various times he appears as dealing with witches suspected of making wax figures of the Queen; arranging for grain barges to move down the river to supply London; trying to settle a dispute between clothiers and dyers at Reading; and examining a keeper of Windsor park accused of harbouring a robber. Unlawful hunting in Windsor forest was a recurrent trouble to him. In the town of Windsor he had considerable influence, which he used as a parliamentary patron. In 1563 his brother-in-law John Gresham was elected, and in each Parliament from 1584 to 1593 members of the Neville family were returned for the borough. In 1562 and again in 1586 he was active in raising troops from Berkshire. In general his loyalty and hard work went unrewarded: however, in March 1573 he was granted for his 'good and faithful service', a licence to ship cloth overseas.[6]

About 1586 he became involved in complicated legal issues over non-payment of legacies to several members of his family from the estate of Sir Thomas Gresham. Although the Privy Council intervened, settlement had still not been reached by May 1588. He also had a sharp quarrel with Ambrose Dudley, the Earl of Warwick over the right to cast and sell ordnance.[7]

He died 13 Jan. 1593, and was buried in the church of Waltham St. Lawrence. On the wall of the north chapel there is an elaborate marble monument to him and to his second wife Elizabeth Gresham, with figures of the couple, their eldest daughter Elizabeth and Sir Henry's mother-in-law, Lady Frances Gresham. His will, made in April 1592, was proved 6 Feb. 1593. Among the property mentioned is 'my late house or lodging called the Savoy by the Strand in London'. The lord admiral, Charles Howard I*, 2nd Baron Howard of Effingham, was to have 'my falcon hawk with my man Buller who now keepeth her'.[7]

[1] C142/240/95; PCC 1 Nevell; VCH Berks. iii. 183; CPR, 1550–3, pp. 151–2; PCC 29 More; Vis. Berks. (Harl. Soc. lvii), 181; Misc. Gen. et Her. (ser. 1), ii. 317–18; CP, i. 35. [2] LP Hen. VIII, xxi(2), p. 322; CPR, 1549–51, p. 222; 1550–3, p. 381; 1555–7, pp. 184, 252; 1560–3, p. 234; NRA, D/DBy/1; E163/14/8; HMC Hatfield, i. 429, 443, 474 seq.; CSP Dom. Add. 1566–79, p. 313; HMC Foljambe, 26; J. H. Guilding, Recs. Reading, i. 416; Ashmole 1126, f. 50. [3] LP Hen. VIII, xiv(2), p. 158; xvii. p. 152; CPR, 1549–51, p. 222; 1553–4, pp. 61–2; Chron. Q. Jane and Q. Mary (Cam. Soc. xlviii), 100; Cam. Misc. x(2), p. 116; C. H. Garrett, Marian Exiles, 235–6; Trans. R. Hist. Soc. n.s. xi. 129. [4] C142/240/95; Lansd. 83, f. 217; CPR, 1550–3, pp. 151–2, 406; 1553–4, pp. 353–4. [5] St. Ch. 5/N10/11, N16/38; D'Ewes, 126, 157, 165, 333, 338, 343, 352, 356, 363, 365, 366, 370; CJ, i. 70, 83, 84. [6] Cam. Misc. ix(3), p. 38; APC, vii. 128; viii. 217; x. 270; xi. 22, 165; xiii. 154, 186, 189–90, 264, 396–7; xiv. 56; xviii. 260; Lansd. 16, ff. 130–1. [7] APC, xiv. 164; xv. 360, 378–9; xvi. 46, 56; Lansd. 65, f. 82; Misc. Gen. et Her. n.s. i. 436; PCC 1 Nevell.

N.M.F.

NEVILLE, Sir Henry II (c.1575–1641), of Birling, Kent.

KENT	1601
LEWES	1604
WILTON	1621*

b. c.1575, 1st s. of Edward Neville I* by Rachel, da. of John Lennard. educ. Queens', Camb. 1586, BA 1589, incorp. MA Oxf. 1594; travelled abroad. m. (1) by c.1596, Mary (d.1612), da. of Thomas Sackville*, 2s. 5da.; (2) bef. 1616, Catherine, da. of George Vaux (d.1594), s. of William, 3rd Lord Vaux of Harrowden, 2s. 3da. Kntd. 1596. suc. fa. as 9th Lord Bergavenny 1622.[1]

During Sir Henry Neville's early manhood, his father was engaged in asserting his rights to the barony of Bergavenny. Edward Neville's possession of the extensive lands of the barony was secure, since they had been entailed to heirs male, but his claim to the title was disputed by his cousin's daughter, Lady Fane, and was not successful till 1604. Neville's own marriage to the daughter of Lord Buckhurst no doubt assisted his father's efforts. Neville may already have been connected with Buckhurst (who was chancellor of Oxford University) when he was incorporated as MA at Oxford in the summer of 1594. The next few years he spent travelling in Europe. He was at Venice in July 1594, being approached there by English Catholics. In 1596 he served under Essex at Cadiz. In June 1597 he was licensed to travel abroad for two years with Thomas Sackville, Buckhurst's son. The alliance with Buckhurst had a commercial aspect: the Nevilles and the Sackvilles each owned several iron foundries, and by December 1596 Henry Neville and Thomas Sackville had a patent giving them a monopoly in the production of ordnance. This patent was mentioned during the attack on monopolies in the Parliament of 1601. The only other mention of Neville by name in this Parliament is of his sitting on a committee considering penal laws, 2 Nov., but as knight for Kent he was entitled to attend the main business committee (3 Nov.), the clothworkers committee (18 Nov.) and the monopolies committee (23 Nov.).[2]

After his service at Cadiz, Neville may have been in the following of the Earl of Essex, though he did not become as deeply involved in the Earl's enterprises as his cousin and namesake of Billingbear, Berkshire. Four days after Essex's rising in February 1601, Neville was approached by Captain Thomas Lee with a proposal to put the Queen under duress till she signed a warrant for the Earl's release. This scheme he revealed to the government.[3]

Perhaps it was through Essex that Neville gained the friendship of (Sir) Robert Sidney*, with whose support he was chosen knight of the shire for Kent in 1601. There were more than two candidates for the county seats on that occasion, Neville's chief rival being Francis Fane*, son of the Lady Fane who was claiming the barony of Bergavenny against Neville's father. Fane was supported by Lord Cobham, Sidney's great rival in Kent. There was consequently some thorough canvassing, Sidney directing his agent by letter from Flushing. Neville and Fane were both returned. According to a servant of Fane, his master had the 'first voice' in the election, and this statement is supported by Manningham, the diarist, but in the Crown Office list Neville's name stands first.[4]

The Nevilles' great estates seem to have given them no parliamentary patronage, except possibly at Lewes, where Neville himself was returned in 1604. Neville sat for Wilton at a by-election in 1621, presumably on the nomination of the Earl of Pembroke, Sir Robert Sidney's nephew. He succeeded as Baron Bergavenny in the following year. In 1626 he was named in a Commons petition as a suspected Catholic. He died in 1641.[5]

[1] CP; Al. Ox. (Neville, Thomas); Chamberlain Letters ed. McClure, i. 429; Hasted, Kent, ii. 240, 486. [2] CSP Dom. 1591–4, p. 536; 1595–7, p. 442; HMC Hatfield, vi. 505; ix. 131; xvi. 299; EHR, xlviii. 91 seq.; D'Ewes, 623, 624, 642, 649, 650. [3] CSP Ire. 1600–1, p. 201 (both Sir Henry Nevilles are mentioned in the letter); CSP Dom. 1598–1601, p. 598; Chamberlain Letters, i. 119. [4] Neale, Commons, 72–4; Collins, Sidney State Pprs. ii. 231–2; HMC 10th Rep. IV, 16; Manningham Diary (Cam. Soc. xcix), 13. [5] Harl. 160, art. 15, f. 91v.

A.H.

NEWDIGATE, Francis (1519–82), of Hanworth, Mdx.

GREAT BEDWYN	1559
CHIPPENHAM	1563
MIDDLESEX	1571

b. 25 Oct. 1519, 5th s. of John Newdigate of Moor Hall, Harefield, Mdx. and Arbury, Warws. by Anne, da. of Nicholas Hilton† of Cambridge; bro. of John†, Nicholas† and Robert I*. m. 1558, Anne, da. of Sir Edward Stanhope, wid. of Edward, Duke of Somerset, s.p.[1]

Gent. of household of Edward, Duke of Somerset to

1552; servant of Duchess of Somerset 1552–8; j.p. Mdx. from c.1573.[2]

The Newdigate family was well represented in the Tudor House of Commons. Francis Newdigate's father is not known to have sat there, but his uncle William had represented Bedwyn in the early sessions of the Reformation Parliament, his eldest brother John was knight of the shire for Middlesex four times between 1547 and 1558, and another brother, Nicholas, had sat in Mary's last Parliament for Westminster.

The turning point in Francis Newdigate's life was his marriage to the Duchess of Somerset. Until then his career had been that of a servant to nobility. His uncle Nicholas and brother John were both at Eton and King's, but his own name is not to be found in the register of either college, and it is probable that his education took the form of service with a leading family. It is not known how soon he entered the Seymour household, but he seems to have risen with his master, and he was sufficiently close to the Protector to be implicated in his fall, when he suffered the confiscation of his property. Nine months after Somerset's execution Newdigate was pardoned and had his lands and goods restored. During the Duchess's imprisonment in the Tower, which seems to have lasted until the accession of Mary, he was doubtless active in salvaging the family fortunes, and his knowledge of what went on was later to be drawn upon by the commission set up in 1555 to trace the disposal of the dead Duke's property. His devotion to her service was presumably a principal reason for the Duchess's acceptance of him as her second husband in a marriage which could have appeared a disparagement. Whether he suffered from her 'haughty stomach' does not appear, and there is no suggestion of any marital discord.[3]

Shortly before the marriage, and perhaps in preparation for it, the Duchess obtained from the Crown a grant of the manor of Hanworth, Middlesex, and it was as 'of Hanworth' that a few months later Newdigate sued out his general pardon. The manor, a royal property, had formerly been held and occupied by Catherine Parr, and it was in the manor house that the Princess Elizabeth had passed some of her early years. Of that house, which was to remain the couple's principal residence for the remainder of their lives, parts of the walls and two large fireplaces alone survived a fire in 1797; but it must have been an imposing one and have reflected Newdigate's dignity as a leading gentleman of the shire. He also had some property of his own in Middlesex, including the waste called Ashford Marsh which was the scene of a depredation in 1562.[4]

Within a few months of his marriage Newdigate made his first appearance in the House of Commons, having been returned for Great Bedwyn to the first Parliament of the new reign. Both the choice of borough, which was a Seymour preserve, and the fact that he was the only

Newdigate to sit in this Parliament bespeak the Duchess's influence. Even before the next crisis in the Seymour fortunes, it would clearly be advantageous as well as honorific for the young Earl of Hertford to have a henchman in the Lower House. Of any part played by Newdigate in the important transactions of this Parliament there is, however, no trace.

It is otherwise with the next Parliament, that of 1563. On this occasion Francis Newdigate sat for Chippenham, a borough also amenable to the Duchess's influence, since she had a lease of the manor of Monkton Farleigh there; and he was joined by his brother Robert, who was returned for Buckingham. Two episodes were to bring Francis Newdigate into prominence during the lifetime of this House. The first was the affair of Gabriel Pleydell*, whom Newdigate accused during the session of 1563 of forgery in connexion with a lawsuit. Since the suit itself concerned the Duchess's lease of Monkton Farleigh, the matter was of keen personal interest to both her and Newdigate, as well as to the borough which had returned him.[5]

The second episode was a much weightier one: it was the secret marriage between Hertford and Catherine Grey. This union, with its grave implications for the succession to the Crown, had come to light before Parliament sat, and throughout the session the offending pair were incarcerated in the Tower. That their friends in Parliament were exercised about their misfortune is known, and that there may have been some campaigning done for them is probable: and we may be sure that the Earl's stepfather would have been in the centre of the picture. Not until the following year, however, is evidence forthcoming of his involvement. Then, after the revelation of John Hales I's* tract on the succession, the government began to investigate, and Francis Newdigate was one of those questioned. In late April and early May 1564 he was twice interrogated about the marriage, and also had to defend himself against the misreporting by Sir Thomas Smith* of his part in an alleged plan of Somerset's to ally himself with the Swedish royal house. Whether Newdigate came near to sharing the imprisonment which befell Hales, or even the 'house arrest' imposed on Hertford himself, we cannot say: but he evidently got off scot-free, and unlike Hales was in the Commons for the session of 1566, during which he was named to the succession committee (31 Oct.). When, in the course of that session, the Queen condemned public discussion of the succession on the ground that kinsfolk, servants and tenants of the various claimants would support their masters and mistresses, she might well have had in mind such Members as Newdigate. For him, however, the question was soon to lose its family interest, since the death of Catherine Grey in 1568 put an end to Hertford's dynastic importance, and with it his kinsman's obligations to support his claim.[6]

Newdigate's parliamentary career reached its apogee in 1571, when he and his nephew John were returned as knights of the shire for Middlesex, Francis taking the senior place. But it was his brother Robert, sitting again for Buckingham, who left his mark on the records of this Parliament, as he was to do again in the next. Whether Francis sought election we do not know, but his absence from the long-lived Parliament of 1572 was to mean that he would not sit again. In any case, his place in the history of the Commons owed more to his having been caught up in affairs of moment than to any gifts of his own.

His declining years seem to have been occupied with domestic and local affairs. The Duchess, now a septuagenarian, may well have absorbed the greater part of them; but if so she was still in return his resolute protectrix, as when in 1574 she complained to Cecil of an affront given to him, apparently by the lord chamberlain, the 3rd Earl of Sussex. His own family also gave him some trouble; in 1581 he was instructed by the Privy Council to compose a dispute between his brothers Robert and Thomas. He continued to engage in land transactions almost up to his death.[7]

Francis Newdigate made his will 31 May 1580. Declaring that he had received all his preferment by his marriage to the Duchess, he bequeathed to her all his property, real and personal. The former consisted of a house in Canon Row, Westminster, which he had bought of Henry Carey, 1st Baron Hunsdon; the *Bull* inn at Isleworth; and the manors of Littleton, Middlesex, and Little Ashtead, Surrey. He made his wife sole executrix. During the 18 months which were to separate this will from the testator's death on 26 Jan. 1582 he bought the manor of Great Ashtead, Surrey, from Philip, Earl of Arundel, and since this was not covered by the will it had to be made the subject of a codicil to which Newdigate gave his assent an hour before his death on 26 Jan. This codicil his nephew John challenged on the ground that it had been contrived by those around the dying man, he being then no longer 'in perfect memory'. The dispute was referred to arbitrators, including the 3rd Earl of Huntingdon, but its issue does not appear. A valuation of Newdigate's lands made by the nephew in connexion with the dispute gave a yearly total of £370.[8]

The Duchess survived her second husband by five years, dying at an advanced age (although hardly the 90 which has been claimed) on 16 Apr. 1587. She was buried in Westminster abbey, where she has a monument.[9]

[1] *Mdx. Peds.* (Harl. Soc. lxv), 67; *Wilts. Arch. Mag.* vi. 296; A. E. Newdigate-Newdegate, *Gossip from a Muniment Room*, 4. [2] C3/17/9. [3] A. F. Pollard, *Somerset*, 293, 302; *CPR, 1550–3*, p. 262; 1554–5, p. 342; 1555–7, p. 356; R. Baker, *Chron.* (1653), p. 439. [4] *CPR, 1557–8*, p. 298; 1558–60, p. 195; *Lond. Mdx. Arch. Soc.* xix. 168–9; N. Pevsner, *Buildings, Mdx.* 87; *Mdx. Co. Recs.* i. 40. [5] C3/132/16; *CJ*, i. 70–2; D'Ewes, 127. [6] *HMC Hatfield*, i. 294–5, 454; *CSP Dom. 1547–80*, p. 241; Neale, *Parlts.* i. 149. [7] *Gent. Mag.* n.s. xxiii. 374; *APC*, x.

385–6; xiii. 114–15, 127; *HMC Bath*, iv. 190. [8] PCC 29 Rowe; Strype, *Annals*, iii(1), pp. 89–91; *HMC Bath*, iv. 190. [9] *Gent. Mag.* n.s. xiii. 380.

M.B.

NEWDIGATE, John (c.1542–92), of Harefield, Mdx. and Arbury, Warws.

MIDDLESEX 1571

b. c.1542, 1st s. of John Newdigate[†] of Moor Hall, Harefield by his 1st w. Mary, da. of Robert Cheyney of Chesham Bois, Bucks. *educ.* Eton c.1554–9; King's, Camb. 1559, BA 1564, fellow c.1564; began MA at Prague 1564 or 1565. *m.* (1) Martha (*d.*1575), da. and coh. of Anthony Cave of Chicheley, Bucks., by Elizabeth, da. of Thomas Lovett, 8s. 3da.; (2) c.1575, Mary Smith, 1s.; (3) c.1577, Winifred Wells, *s.p. suc.* fa. 1565.[1]

J.p.q. Mdx. from c.1573.

Newdigate received a varied education, including a period of European travel, but contrary to some authorities he did not attend Lincoln's Inn, the only man of this name given in the contemporary registers being admitted in 1557, when John of Harefield was still a boy at Eton. Near the beginning of Elizabeth's reign Newdigate went up to Cambridge, where he contributed some stanzas to the university collection of poems on the 'Life, Death and Restoration of Bucer and Fagius', produced in 1560, and gained a high enough reputation as a scholar for his college to award him a fellowship. He was studying abroad when his father died in August 1565, and as the new head of the family, he returned to administer his considerable property in Middlesex, Buckinghamshire and Surrey. On the death of his uncle Francis* John gained more Middlesex land. With these large estates to administer, and his increasing family to provide for, it is not surprising that he did not fulfil his early promise as a scholar.[2]

The scarcity of references to Newdigate in official documents is probably explained by the fact that, although he was the head of the elder branch of the family, his uncle Francis, the second husband of the widowed Duchess of Somerset, had a higher social status. Francis took the senior seat when in 1571 uncle and nephew were elected knights of the shire for Middlesex. John Newdigate had been suggested for Clitheroe in the previous Parliament by his relation Sir Ambrose Cave*, chancellor of the duchy of Lancaster, but a local man, protégé of the 3rd Earl of Derby, got the seat. In 1571 neither Francis nor John was active in the House.[3]

Towards the end of his life Newdigate was in low water financially, and there is evidence to suggest that he was in the Fleet prison, presumably for debt, when he died. He may have been a spendthrift, or his troubles may have been due to litigation. He was a defendant in at least three Chancery cases concerned with his Middlesex and Buckinghamshire property, and his name also appears in several Star Chamber suits. In July 1577 the Privy Council ordered him to come before them following a dispute between a serjeant-at-arms and two of the Ashby family of Harefield. On this occasion he unsuccessfully pleaded illness. In November 1584 he was outlawed for debt: according to him, a Buckinghamshire jury had committed perjury over the value of his goods.[4]

A year later he gave up his property at Moor Hall in part exchange for Sir Edmund Anderson's manor of Arbury, Warwickshire. But his debts were still serious, and he sailed too close to the wind in attempting to lighten the burden. (Sir) Edward Fitton*, whose daughter Anne married Newdigate's eldest son, also John, had leased 'the chief house of old Newdigate to his great charge' for the use of the young couple, but in December 1591 the Privy Council ordered an inquiry into the conduct of John Newdigate and John Croke II* for trying to deprive the younger John Newdigate, aged about 20, of land which had been assigned for his maintenance, presumably by the marriage settlement.[5]

The Privy Council order of December 1591 does not state whether Newdigate was in prison at the time. He died intestate between 21 and 27 Feb. 1592, and was buried in the London church of St. Mildred, Poultry. His inquisition post mortem, taken in May 1592, lists lands in Harefield and Ickenham, and a house in Brackenbury, Middlesex.[6]

[1] C142/145/61; 232/15; E150/51/31; A. E. Newdigate-Newdigate, *Gossip from a Muniment Room*; *Mdx. Peds.* (Harl. Soc. lxv), 67; Kimber and Johnson, *Baronetage*, ii. 417; W. Sterry, *Eton Coll. Reg. 1441–1698*, p. 244; *Vis. Eng. and Wales*, ed. Howard and Crisp, *Notes*, vii. 35. [2] *Al. Cant.*, i(3), p. 248; E150/51/31; C142/232/15; PCC 29 Rowe. [3] C193/32/4 and 5; *OR*, i. 404. [4] Newdigate-Newdigate, 4; Sterry; Crisp; C3/39/12, 92/4, 188/54; St. Ch. 5/L9/16, N9/27; *APC*, ix. 376, 387. [5] *APC*, xxii. 108–9. [6] Sterry; C142/232/58; T. Milbourn, *Hist. St. Mildred*, 34.

N.M.F.

NEWDIGATE, Robert I (1528–84), of Hawnes, Beds.

BUCKINGHAM	1563, 1571
BERWICK-UPON-TWEED	1572

b. 14 Sept. 1528, 7th s. of John Newdigate of Moor Hall, Harefield, Mdx. and Arbury, Warws. by Anne, da. and h. of Nicholas Hilton[†] of Cambridge; bro. of Francis*, John[†] and Nicholas[†]. *educ.* L. Inn 1550. *m.* Anne, da. of Edmund Conquest[†] of Houghton Conquest, at least 1s. Robert II*.[1]

Escheator, Beds. and Bucks. 1560–1; j.p. Beds. from c.1561; feodary, Bucks. by Apr. 1562.[2]

Newdigate owned a considerable amount of property in Bedfordshire. The first mention of him there is in June 1554, when he was leasing land in Wilhamstead. In April 1563 he sold this manor, with other property formerly belonging to Elstow priory, and soon afterwards bought the larger part of the manor of Hawnes (now Haynes)

from Sir Edward Bray*. The bishop of Lincoln described Newdigate as 'esquire', 'earnest' in religion in Bedfordshire and as 'gent.', 'indifferent' in Buckinghamshire. He was an active official in both counties and so may have been in a position to have himself returned for Buckingham even without the influence of Henry Carey[†], 1st Baron Hunsdon, who was, however, in the position of parliamentary patron both there and at Berwick. Hunsdon took his side in an incident in September 1570, when he wrote to Cecil, saying that he thought the Queen's anger with Newdigate, apparently after complaints from the Duchess of Suffolk, unjustified. The question at issue seems to have been the stewardship of Ampthill, Bedfordshire, which Lady Suffolk had wanted her son to buy from Hunsdon. She was 'greatly offended' with Newdigate, whom she blamed (according to Hunsdon, unjustly) for the failure of the scheme.[3]

Newdigate was an active committeeman in all his Parliaments – he was named to 15 or 16 in the three sessions of that of 1572. Several of his speeches were thought worth reporting by the diarists. There is no record of his speaking in 1563 or 1566, but he probably did so: 'Newdigate the crier' appears in the lampoon on the Members of the 1566–7 session. He was named to the succession committee on 31 Oct. 1566. On 7 Apr. 1571 he caused a storm by proposing a subsidy before any of the Privy Councillors had raised the matter. The motion was not liked by the House but he was appointed to the committee the same day. In the 1572 Parliament he became really prominent. On 17 May, evidently fearing that the question of Mary Stuart and the Duke of Norfolk might be sidetracked by Members' reactions to an ill-timed speech of Arthur Hall, he asked that the House should give 'a full resolution' of its opinion on the execution of Norfolk. The Speaker put the question, and it was 'passed without any negative voice'. The following week on 23 May Newdigate spoke on Elizabeth's rejection of the proposed bill of attainder against Mary.

> He sorroweth to see so small care in the Queen's Majesty of herself. He feareth she depend too much upon God's providence, … though she [Mary] pretend a title for the present, if she may prevail she will claim by conquest and then all our lands be lost, all our goods forfeit. This most gainful to her and fittest for her honour. Therefore now not only to be deposed, but her head cut off whilst she is in our hands, that we may seem to embrace so great a benefit offered us. Since the Queen in respect of her own safety is not to be induced hereunto, let us make petition she will do it in respect of our safety. I have heard she delighteth to be called our mother. Let us desire her to be pitiful over us her children who have not deserved death.

However, he does not appear to have favoured forcing the Queen's hand. On 31 May he supported Sir Francis Knollys and Sir James Croft in an appeal to the House not to send an urgent petition asking her to execute Norfolk at once. He was appointed to two committees concerning the jurors of Middlesex on 19 May and 22 May, and spoke against a bill concerning the freeholders in Middlesex. Newdigate spoke on 5 June 1572 on the third reading of the bill concerning Worcester's water supply from the River Severn. He did not think that

> any men's inheritance should be taken from them against the wills of the owners, especially for so small a commodity as increase of water ... and although some means be appointed for recompense, he liketh not that commissioners should set price of other men's lands.

During the 1576 session Newdigate spoke several times in support of Arthur Hall, whose servant was involved in a privilege case. He was also named to committees concerning the avoidance of idleness (11 Feb.), legal matters (13, 18 Feb., 7 Mar.) and the treatment of aliens (24 Feb.). During the last session of 1581 he does not appear to have spoken, but to have concentrated on his committee activity, which included the punishment of bigamy (31 Jan.), slanderous libelling (3 Feb.), private bills (6 Feb.), the unlawful hunting of coneys (9 Feb.), pheasants and partridges (18 Feb.), attorneys (20 Feb.), hats and caps (22 Feb.), the sowing of hemp in the county of Hertford (23 Feb.), the city of Carlisle (27 Feb.) and mariners (15 Mar.).[4]

The few references to Newdigate's private character show him as a quarrelsome member of that faction in Bedfordshire opposed to the 6th Earl of Kent. No will has been found; his inquisition post mortem, taken in January 1586, gives the date of his death, 4 May 1584, and describes his Bedfordshire lands as in the custody of the widow on behalf of her son Robert.[5]

[1] Kimber and Johnson, *Baronetage*, ii. 416; C142/209/16; *Vis. Beds.* (Harl. Soc. xix), 20, 185. [2] *CPR*, 1560-3, p. 448. [3] *CPR*, 1553-4, p. 344; 1560-3, p. 602; *Cam. Misc.* ix(3), pp. 28, 32; C142/209/16; *VCH Beds.* ii. 340-1; *CSP Dom.* Add. 1566-79, p. 320. [4] D'Ewes, 127, 158, 159, 212, 213, 247, 290, 292, 294, 299; *CJ*, i. 83, 96, 97, 105, 106, 108, 111, 121, 122, 124, 128, 129, 130, 134; Trinity, Dublin, Thos. Cromwell's jnl. ff. 13, 22, 36, 39, 51; Neale, *Parlts.* i. 92, 218, 280, 336-9. [5] Beds. RO, L24/647, 654 ex inf. Miss J. Godber; C142/209/16.

N.M.F.

NEWDIGATE, Robert II (c.1565-1613), of Hawnes, Beds.

GRAMPOUND 1597
BUCKINGHAM 1601

b. c.1565. 1st s. of Robert Newdigate I*. *educ.* G. Inn 18 Mar. 1590. *m.* Elizabeth, da. of Thomas Stutteville of Dalham, Suff., 2s. 4da. *suc.* fa. 1584. Kntd. 11 May 1603.
Esquire of the body to Queen Elizabeth in or bef. 1603.

It is not known how Newdigate obtained a seat for Grampound in 1597: he had no obvious patron who could have obtained it for him. He presumably owed his

Buckingham seat in 1601 to Lord Hunsdon's son, Sir George Carey*. In this Parliament Newdigate was a member of the committee appointed on 3 Nov. to consider the order of business for the session. This is the only time he is mentioned in the proceedings of the House.

James I was a regular visitor at Hawnes. Newdigate died in debt in 1613, having conveyed lands to Alderman Cockaine, one of his creditors, and goods to another creditor, Dr. Newcome, as security. His indebtedness was possibly the result of standing surety for Sir Gervase Clifton*, Lord Clifton. Nevertheless, he left his daughter Anne a marriage portion of £1,500. He must have remained on good terms with his brother-in-law (Sir) Martin Stutteville*, whom he appointed one of the executors of his will. The family was, in 1668, included in a list of those who had left the county 'within less than the space of fifty years'.

Vis. Beds. (Harl. Soc. xix), 20, 185, 207; C142/209/16; LC2/4/4; *VCH Beds.* ii. 339-41; iii. 326; D'Ewes, 624; Nichols, *Progresses Jas. I*; PCC 94 Capell; *CSP Dom.* 1611-12, p. 66.

A.M.M.

NEWMAN, George (c.1562-1627), of Canterbury, Kent.

DOVER 1601
CANTERBURY 1614, 1621

b. c.1562, s. of Richard Newman. *educ.* Trinity Hall, Camb. 1581, LLB. 1584, LLD. 1589. *m.* (1) Elizabeth, da. of Peter Wycliffe of Wycliffe, Yorks., 1s. 1da.; (2) Mary Gough, 1da.; (3) Sybilla, da. of George Wenland of Allensmore, Herefs., 4s. 4da. Kntd. 12 Nov. 1616.[1]
Commissary, diocese of Canterbury by 1587; judge of the Admiralty of the Cinque Ports Mar. 1602; master in Chancery extraordinary 1603; member, Coll. of Advocates 30 Jan. 1604; judge, ct. of audience 1617.[2]

Newman's background is obscure. By 1587, after spending several years at Cambridge as a student of the civil law, he was Archbishop Whitgift's commissary for the diocese of Canterbury, retaining the office under Bancroft and Abbot, and exercising the jurisdiction of his principals as ordinaries of the diocese of Canterbury. While he was commissary he obtained the reversion of the office of dean of the arches, but when (Sir) Daniel Dunne* died in the autumn of 1617, Newman was passed over, although he did obtain, as consolation, the position of judge of the court of audience.

In March 1602 Henry Brooke *alias* Cobham II*, 11th Lord Cobham, warden of the Cinque Ports, appointed Newman judge of the Admiralty court of the Ports, granting him as his deputy full powers. These were considerable, as by the sixteenth century the warden, by virtue of his office of admiral, possessed in the Ports all the jurisdiction which the lord high admiral exercised in the rest of the country. Cobham's successors continued

Newman in office until his death, and the state papers and Privy Council registers contain much information about his activities. He dealt with a great variety of business, doing justice in cases involving wreck, fishing rights, and the possession of disputed goods.[3]

On 16 Oct. 1601, before Newman became judge of the Ports, a common assembly was held at Dover to choose MPs. Newman presented himself, craving

> to be admitted a freeman of this town and tendered the sum of five pounds in gold for the redeeming of the same, which, in respect of the good which hereafter he may do for this town … is repaid unto him again.

He was then elected 'by general assent and consent of the whole house'. The other Member was nominated by the lord warden. Newman made at least one speech in the 1601 Parliament. On 9 Dec., at the second reading and commitment of a bill for the true making of cloth, he offered a proviso safeguarding the rights of alnagers to seize any cloth sold contrary to law. The House instructed him to place it before the committee. They must have received it favourably, as it was included in the final Act. The barons of the Cinque Ports were appointed to two committees in 1601: the main business committee (3 Nov.) and one on the Severn harbour (21 Nov.).[4]

Newman died 7 June 1627, leaving property in Kent to his wife and children. In his brief will he bequeathed £10 to Doctors' Commons. The widow was executrix.[5]

[1] P. Parsons, *Monuments and Painted Glass in Kent*, 259–60; *Vis. Kent.* (Harl. Soc. liv), 119. [2] *Arch. Cant.* lvi. 1; *HMC 5th Rep.* 139; PRO ms index Petty Bag Office: C. Coote, *Civilians*, 68; *Chamberlain Letters* ed. McClure, ii. 105. [3] Parsons, 259; Holdsworth, *Eng. Law*, i (7th ed.), 599; *Arch. Cant.* xxii. 103; xxv. 14; xxvi. 22, 36; xlix. 183; lvi. 1; *Chamberlain Letters*, ii. 99, 105; *HMC 5th Rep.* 139, 140; *HMC 13th Rep.* IV, 124, 143; *CSP Dom.* 1598–1601, p. 117; 1601–3, pp. 233–4; 1603–10, p. 377; 1611–18, pp. 352, 414, 481; 1619–23, pp. 225, 357, 376, 411, 555; 1623–5, pp. 162, 194, 200, 222, 376, 484, 489, 491, 493; 1625–6, pp. 22, 47, 192, 255, 358, 363, 367; Add. 1580–1625, p. 660; *APC*, 1625–6, pp. 95, 123, 194, 316, 368, 390, 394; 1626 (June–Dec.), 44, 261; 1627 (Jan.–Aug.), 393; K. M. E. Murray, *Const. Hist. Cinque Ports*, 128–9. [4] Egerton 2095, f. 446; Townshend, *Hist. Colls.* 298; D'Ewes, 624, 647; *Statutes of the Realm*, iv. 977. [5] C142/435/122; PCC 65 Skynner.

A.G.R.S.

NEWMAN, John, of St. Ives, Cornw.

ST. IVES   1571

m., at least 1da.
  Dep. customer of Mounts Bay, Cornw.

John Newman of St. Ives, whose lands there were valued at £4 in 1571, has been preferred as the 1571 MP to a number of contemporary namesakes because his connexions can explain his return. His customer's job brought him into touch with the Exchequer, and therefore with the treasurer, the Marquess of Winchester, father of John Paulet, Lord St. John, who, together with

James Blount, 6th Lord Mountjoy, was lord of the borough.

J. H. Matthews, *Hist. St. Ives*, 139; Vivian, *Vis. Cornw.* 78; Lansd. 143, f. 65.

w.j.j.

NEWMAN, William (bef. 1517–c.89), of Poole, Dorset.

POOLE   1553 (Mar.), 1571

b. bef. 1517, 1st s. of John Newman of Salisbury, Wilts. by his w. Dorothy. *m.* Alice, da. of Richard Haviland of Poole. *suc.* fa. 1519.
  Bailiff, Poole 1548, mayor 1554–5, 1568–9, 1575–6; commr. piracy 1583.

Newman was one of the three leading merchants of Poole who, in 1568, gave Lord Mountjoy a bond of £50 that the town's new charter would not infringe his local rights. He was empowered to spend up to £500 on this new charter, the total cost of which, in the event, amounted to rather more than £370. He seems to have been generous to the borough both with his money and his time: he and the mayor received £12 5s. 6d. expenses for going to London in 1561. Poole owed him £80 in 1569, and he spent another £42 5s. 6d. when in London on the town's business in 1571. He also visited Southampton, and with other leading citizens in 1574 went to see the 1st Viscount Bindon for advice about a piracy commission.

Newman made his will 25 June 1583, by which time any children he may have had were dead. He asked to be buried either at Poole or at Salisbury. After charitable bequests to hospitals at Salisbury, and to the poor of Poole, he left the bulk of his fortune, including property at Corfe Castle and Poole, and the lease of Poole parsonage, to the four daughters of John and Ursula Newman. Administration was granted to the overseers 21 Apr. 1589.

PCC 10 Stokton, 21 Ayloffe, 38 Leicester; Hutchins, *Dorset*, i. 8, 20, 21, 22, 34; H. P. Smith, *Hist. Poole*, ii. 16, 93, 98; C219/23, m 51; Poole recs., 'Greate Boke', ff. 7, 33; J. Sydenham, *Hist. Poole*, 167.

P.W.H.

NEWPORT, Andrew (1563–1611), of High Ercall, Salop.

SHREWSBURY   1589

b. 1563, 4th but 2nd surv. s. of (Sir) Richard Newport[†] of High Ercall by Margaret, da. and h. of Sir Thomas Bromley[†]. *educ.* Shrewsbury 1574, I. Temple 1581, called. *unm.*
  Member, council in the marches of Wales 1601.

On his tomb at Wroxeter, Newport describes himself as the second son of Sir Richard, but on his parents' monument in the same church two other sons are shown, both bearing the crescent on their shield of arms; one of these must have died an infant, and the other predeceased his father, leaving Andrew as the second surviving son. He was thus the younger brother of the 'worthy and valiant' Francis Newport who was sheriff of Shropshire in 1586, and whose influence probably secured his brother's return to Parliament two years later. His sister Magdalene married Richard Herbert of Lysmawr and became the mother of Lord Herbert of Chirbury and the poet, George Herbert. Another sister married Thomas Lawley* of Wenlock. Little is known of Newport's career. He composed his own epitaph when 'nearly at the hour of death' in 1611, stating that he

> lived and died in the faith of Jesus Christ [a] true professor of the doctrine according to the best reformed churches in the time wherein he lived, ever hating and detesting the imposture and abominations of the Church of Rome as now it standeth.

Vis. Salop (Harl. Soc. xxix), 372–4; *Trans. Salop Arch. Soc.* (ser. 2), i. 18–20; (ser. 4), xi. 155; xii. 195–6; *Arch. Camb.* (1915), p. 122; *Early Chrons. Shrewsbury* ed. Leighton, 108.

J.J.C.

NEWPORT, Francis I, of Droitwich, Worcs.

DROITWICH   1559

This Member came of a well-known Droitwich family, and was presumably related to the George Newport who represented the borough in two Marian Parliaments. Their Droitwich residence was classified by the seventeenth-century antiquary Habington among the 'fair houses' of the town, 'most eminent, mounted apart on the south, and overlooking all the rest', and by Elizabeth's reign they owned also the Worcestershire manor of Hanley William. Their position seems to have come directly from the salt industry. During Edward VI's reign John Newport, a former bailiff of Droitwich, leased the tithe of salt for the town at an annual payment of £7 and 32 bushels of white salt. The only reference to Newport himself in the local records is in the salt tax accounts for 1566–7, which describe him as owning a 'phate', a measure containing over 216 vessels of salt water. This was the burgess qualification at Droitwich. No will has been found either at Worcester or London.

Vis. Worcs. (Harl. Soc. xxvii), 156; *Habington's Worcs.* (Worcs. Hist. Soc.) ii. 64, 295; J. Noake, *Monastery and Cath. of Worcester*, 504; Worcs. RO, bulk accession 1006, bdle. 32, no. 433.

N.M.F.

NEWPORT, Francis II (c.1555–1623), of High Ercall, Salop.

SHROPSHIRE   1593

b. c.1555, 1st s. of (Sir) Richard Newport†, and bro. of Andrew*. *educ.* Shrewsbury 1569–71; Magdalen Coll. Oxf. 1574; I. Temple 1577. *m.* Beatrice, da. of Roland Lacon* of Willey, 3s. 4da. *suc.* fa. 1570. Kntd. 21 Apr. 1603.[1]

J.p. Salop from c.1582, sheriff 1586–7, 1601–2, dep. lt. 1590, commr. for poor 1598; member, council in the marches of Wales 1601.[2]

Sir Richard Newport, a member of the council in the marches, and thrice sheriff of Shropshire, bequeathed an important position in the county to his son, who became a ward of the Queen. During his own second shrievalty, Francis Newport was described as a 'worthy and valiant man'. He must have been wealthy, for in 1588 he contributed £50 for the defence of the realm. The Privy Council entrusted him with several difficult commissions, such as the apprehension, in 1593, of three servants of (Sir) Walter Leveson*. In 1600, as a man 'of good discretion, and well affected in religion' he was charged to arrest seminary priests, supposed to be hiding in the district. As knight for Shropshire in 1593 he was entitled to attend the subsidy committee on 26 Feb., and a legal committee 9 Mar.[3]

One of his chief interests, and the focus of much of his energy, was the rebuilding of his two houses, Eyton-on-Severn, and High Ercall Hall: the former was completed by 1595, the latter in 1608. At Eyton he employed as his master mason one Walter Hancocks, 'a very skilful man in the art of masonry, in setting of plots for buildings and performing the same' but before High Ercall was completed, Hancocks had died, which may explain the peculiar structure of the house, the two lower storeys being of massive stonework, and the top of diapered brick.[4]

Newport was a kindly man and a benefactor to the poor like his mother, 'a virtuous lady all her life, and very good to the poor in town and country'. In 1582 he wrote to the bailiffs of Shrewsbury, asking them to give the scholars 'leave to play', while in 1594 he commended a poor widow to their charity. In his will he left over £80 to be divided between the poor of Shrewsbury, Wellington, Newport, High Ercall, Wroxeter, Atcham, Upton Magna and Waters Upton. The will, dated 18 Feb. 1621, made provision for his children, and left legacies to several servants. It directed that he was to be buried in the church of the parish where his death occurred. He died 6 Mar. 1623, and an inquisition post mortem was held the same year.[5]

[1] *Vis. Salop* (Harl. Soc. xxix), 374; *Trans. Salop Arch. Soc.* (ser. 4), xi. 155; *Early Chrons. Shrewsbury*, ed. Leighton, 31. [2] J. B. Blakeway, *Sheriffs of Salop; APC*, xx. 12; *Trans. Salop Arch. Soc.* (ser. 3), i. 410; P. H. Williams, *Council in the Marches of Wales*, 352–3. [3] *Shrewsbury Chrons.* 108; *Trans. Salop Arch. Soc.* (ser. 1), iii. 378; D'Ewes, 474, 496; *APC*, xxiv. 444; xxx. 559. [4] *Trans. Salop Arch. Soc.* (ser. 4), vii. 138; *HMC 15th Rep. X*, 60; *Salop N. and Q.* 1894, p. 88. [5] *Shrewsbury Chrons.* 101; *Salop N. and Q.* loc. cit.; PCC 48 Swann; C142/402/146.

J.J.C.

NEWPORT, *see also* **HATTON** (formerly **NEWPORT**)

NEWTON, Henry (c.1531–99), of East Harptree, Som., Barr's Court and Hanham, Glos.

WELLS   1571

b. c.1531, 1st s. of Sir John Newton of East Harptree by his 1st w. Margaret, da. of Sir Anthony Poyntz of Alderley, Glos. *educ.* ?Christ's, Camb. 1549. *m.* Katherine, da. of Sir Thomas Paston† of Norf. 1s. 4da. *suc.* fa. 1568. Kntd. 1592.

   Freeman, Wells 1571; j.p. Som. from c.1573, sheriff 1581–2.[1]

When he was two years old Newton's parents took him to France and Flanders. No other references to his boyhood or youth have been found. His career was that of a country gentleman. He inherited large estates in Gloucestershire and Somerset, and the corporation of Bath paid him rent for property held of his manor of Hanham. The chamberlains' accounts record a number of presents of wine made to him. In 1577, when he visited St. John's hospital, Bath, 'to review the new church', the authorities paid 13s. 4d. for a dinner in his honour.[2]

Some time after his father's death, Newton began a series of quarrels with his stepmother, Lady Jane Newton, and her son Thomas Buckland. Lady Jane, who had a life interest in the manor of Netherbadgworth, Somerset, claimed the right to make arrangements about tenancies of the property, but Newton refused to recognize these conveyances, and a Chancery case resulted. By 1580 the Star Chamber, Chancery and the common law courts were trying to settle the family disputes, which now centred mainly on Thomas Buckland's claims to dig for iron ore in the Mendips, at East Harptree and elsewhere. Newton insisted that the district concerned was under the control of his 'mynarye' court, and that Buckland and his accomplices had not only illegally carried off lead ore worth £400, but had caused serious disturbances of the peace by their violence. No judgment in these cases is known.[3]

Newton's father had left money to the dean and chapter of Wells to supply a preacher, and the son repeated the terms of the endowment in his own will. He kept up a connexion with the city, and was made a freeman at the time of his election to Parliament. His one mention in the journals shows him sitting, 12 Apr., on the committee for a bill concerned with Bristol.[4]

In 1577 he again went to London on behalf of the city of Wells, this time as one of the three agents chosen to negotiate for a new charter. A year later he was acting as feoffee for a mansion house in Wells belonging to Thomas Leigh.[5]

Newton's daughter Frances was married to Giles Strangways, upon whose death in 1596 the Queen, who had shown favour to Newton some years before this by setting aside a prior agreement so that he should have a coveted wardship, sent him a sympathetic note. Newton

wrote to Robert Cecil that he would keep the Queen's 'most gracious comfort sent me down by you' as the most 'precious thing which I shall ever have, and so leave it to my son'. Daily in his prayers he asked God to 'increase those most excellent and royal graces in her which never any historians have recorded in any Queen as in our most excellent paragon'. But in a letter sent to the lord treasurer in June 1598, old Lady Young complained of Newton's behaviour as executor of the will of John Strangways, who was Giles's father and her son; 'My son Strangways his daughter's poor distressed orphans ... are detained from their whole portions by Sir Henry Newton'.[6]

Newton died at East Harptree on 2 May 1599, leaving as heir his son Theodore, aged 15. A large part of his will, made in January and proved in June the same year is given up to the quotation of English and Latin texts concerned with justification and salvation by faith in Christ alone. Newton declared his steadfast hope of 'life everlasting through the bitter death and passion of Christ', and his wish to be buried without 'blacks' or any unnecessary expense. Among relatives mentioned were his brother John, his 'base brother' Theodore and 'Mary his sister'. The wedding portions of his two unmarried daughters, Anne and Elizabeth, were to be provided by his brother-in-law Edward Paston and others as feoffees of two parts of his lands. Details of these are given in the inquisition taken at Taunton.[7]

[1] E150/952/4; *Vis. Som.* ed. Weaver, 105; Wells corp. act bk. 1553–1623, f. 80. [2] *LP Hen. VIII*, vi, p. 262; *Bath Chamberlains' Accts.* (Som. Rec. Soc. xxxviii), 3, 30, 63, 122, 194. [3] C3/42/25, 146/3; St. Ch. 5/N2/14, N7/35. [4] PCC 49 Kidd; *Wells Charters* (Som. Rec. Soc. xlvi), 184; *CJ*, i. 84. [5] *Wells Charters*, p. xx; *Som. Enrolled Deeds* (Som. Rec. Soc. li), 120. [6] *HMC Hatfield*, iii. 303; vi. 416; viii. 220. For Young-Strangways relationship see YOUNG, John I. [7] PCC 49 Kidd; Wards 7/24/219.

N.M.F.

NICHOLAS, Reginald (d. 1613), of Prestbury, Glos.

PLYMOUTH   1589
LISKEARD   1604

s. of Humphrey Nicholas. *m.* Winifred, da. of William Person of London, 3s. 3da.
   ?Servant of Sir Thomas Chamberlain* (d. 1580), of Earl of Essex by 1599.

This Member may or may not be connected with the Cornish family of Nicholls, to which belonged Philip Nicholls, Sir Francis Drake's puritan chaplain. Nicholas had no apparent connexion with Plymouth and presumably owed his parliamentary seat there to a patron at court, possibly Sir Francis Drake, Lord Burghley, or Burghley's secretary Henry Maynard*, who was Nicholas's brother-in-law. In 1599 he was a follower of the Earl of Essex, entrusted with the task of acquiring horses for service in Ireland, but even if he was already in Essex's service ten years earlier, this would not help to explain his return for Plymouth.

Nicholas acquired the reversion of his land at Prestbury during the lifetime of Sir Thomas Chamberlain. After succeeding to the property he got into debt to the Crown. By the time of his death 7 June 1613 he had sold Prestbury, but was buried there, as he had directed in his will. His son Thomas[t] continued to live in Gloucestershire, becoming sheriff in 1627.

Vis. Glos. (Harl. Soc. xxi), 78, 106, 117; *Vis. Cornw.* (Harl. Soc. ix), 139 140, 156, 157; *HMC Hatfield*, ix. 125; *Vis. Essex* (Harl. Soc. xiv), 595; Vivian, *Vis. Devon*, 561; R. Atkyns, *Ancient and Present State of Glos.* 317; T. D. Fosbrooke, *Glos.* ii. 366–7; E178/947; *Bristol and Glos. Arch. Soc. Trans.* xvii. 235; W. B. Willcox, *Glos. 1590–1640*, 119; C142/335/27; PCC 87 Capell, 77 Lewyn.

I.C.

NOBLE, William (d. 1592), of Oxford.

OXFORD   1584

m., 6ch.

Freeman, Oxford c.1553, common councilman 1559, chamberlain 1571–2, bailiff 1573–4, alderman 1579, coroner 1579–80, mayor 1581–2, member of the 'associates' or mayor's council 1583.

Noble was landlord of the Swindlestock tavern, on the south west corner of Carfax, in which had begun the battle of St. Scholastica's day. He was of an ideal temperament to lead the townsmen in their perennial disputes with the university. As bailiff of the city in 1574, he shut the doors of the guildhall against the vice-chancellor, Dr. Humfrey, thus preventing the university from holding its court leet. A special convocation promptly committed him to the castle prison, from which he was released 12 days later when Sir Francis Knollys*, high steward of Oxford, guaranteed his appearance to answer for his contempt before the Privy Council. To the lords of the council Noble himself submitted a long remonstrance, alleging that the university was trying to ruin his business by making him out to be a 'bankrupt knave'; the university's wider purpose was to cow the citizens by fear of imprisonment and 'discommoning' (excommunication), penalties which it inflicted, Noble hinted, on authority originally conferred by the Pope. In October 1574 the attorney-general, solicitor-general and two judges were commissioned to mediate between town and university. Knollys wrote to them on behalf of the town, the Earl of Leicester supporting the university, of which he was chancellor. In the following April Noble submitted a new list of outrages by the scholars, together with a complaint that the mayor and aldermen were not fulfilling their duties as justices of the peace. On 17 May 1575 the Privy Council upheld the university's privileges on many points, but in the matter of the court leet spared the town, 'for this time only', the forfeit laid down some

years before, on the occasion of a similar incident. Noble remained unreconciled. Humfrey assured Burghley that convocation earnestly desired his restoration, but he refused to submit, and in March 1576 the attorney-general and the solicitor-general were again instructed to attempt a settlement. According to Anthony Wood, Noble did at length submit during a serious illness in November 1576. One night in January 1580, however, the townsmen, summoned by a cry of 'Murder, murder, light, light, for the passion of God', found Noble being assaulted in his own house by a group of Christ Church graduates, and in vain pressed the vice-chancellor to intervene.

Though a difficult colleague on the corporation (Noble had been a common councilman only three years when he was gaoled for insulting the mayor), he was popular with the citizens generally, and his election to Parliament in 1584 reflects this. It is interesting to see that his punishment for a contempt was remitted in February 1584 because Noble was serving as an MP. The university was still complaining about him in December 1585, 'one Mr. Noble, who ever delighted in raising contentions', but by March 1592 he was in the Fleet prison, at the suit of the creditor of a bankrupt for whom he was surety. On the eighth of that month, the Privy Council appointed a commission to investigate the matter, but Noble was still there when he made his nuncupative will 6 Oct. and there he died a few days later. He left his possessions to his daughter Marion, 'and concerning the rest of his children he said that they had been but bad and comfortless children unto him and he prayed God to deal better with them than they had done with him in his misery'. His wife having died on 2 Apr., and Noble having named no executors, letters of administration were issued to Marion. On 13 Oct. the corporation of Oxford licensed a man to sell wine in the place of 'Mr. Alderman Noble, deceased', and soon afterwards granted 30s. to Noble's son Edward, 'in consideration of his poverty'.

W. H. Turner, *Oxford Recs.* passim; H. E. Salter, *Oxf. Council Acts* (Oxf. Hist. Soc. lxxxvii), passim; H. E. Salter, *Oxford City Properties* (Oxf. Hist. Soc. lxxxiii), 155–8; A. Wood, *Univ. of Oxford*, ii. 185–6; *City of Oxford* (Oxf. Hist. Soc. xxxvii), 231; *CSP Dom.* 1547–80, p. 498; 1581–90, pp. 294, 308; *APC*, ix. 97, 106; xxii. 319; C. Monro, *Acta Canc.* 541–2; PCC 90 Harrington.

A.H.

NOEL (NOWELL), Andrew (c.1552–1607), of Dalby, Leics. and Brooke, Rutland.

RUTLAND   1584, 1586, 1589, 1593, 1601*

b. c.1552, 2nd s. of Sir Andrew Noel (Nowell)[t] of Dalby being 1st by his 2nd w. Elizabeth, da. and h. of John Hopton of Glos., wid. of Sir John Perient; bro. of Henry*. *educ.* Peterhouse, Camb. 1565. *m.* Mabel (d.1603), da. of (Sir) James Harington I* of Exton, Rutland, 4s. inc. Edward* 3da. *suc.* fa. 1563. Kntd. 1586.

J.p. Leics. from c.1579, sheriff 1583–4, dep. lt. or commr. musters from 1587; j.p. Rutland from c.1582, dep. lt. or commr. musters from 1587, sheriff 1587–8, 1595–6, 1600–1.

Noel's father, the founder of the family fortunes, left instructions that his cousin, the lawyer Robert Nowell*, was to explain to the Queen the special reasons why his property was to go to Andrew Noel, the second son, instead of the eldest son John. Presumably all parties accepted the situation as the settlement was not challenged. Thus Noel became a substantial landowner in both Leicestershire and Rutland, enhancing his position in Rutland by his marriage into the best county family. Noel was rated at £50 for the 1589 loan. From 1584 to 1593 Noel shared the Rutland county seats with his in-laws. He was probably the Sir Andrew 'Nevill' appointed to attend the Queen to submit the petition about Mary Queen of Scots, 11 Nov. 1586. Otherwise he made little impact on the journals, though as a knight of the shire he would have been able to attend the subsidy committees of 24 Feb. 1585 and 26 Feb. 1593 and a legal committee on 9 Mar. 1593.

In 1597 Noel conceded his Rutland seat to William Cecil*, who was elected with James Harington II. Perhaps Noel saw this as the thin end of the wedge, for at the time of the 1601 election when, through bad luck, he was sheriff, he made frantic efforts to retain his grip on a county seat. Hesitating to return himself, which was illegal, though it sometimes happened, Noel tried to promote the candidature of his 19 year-old son Edward, which was opposed by his brother-in-law (Sir) John Harington II*. In the event he returned himself, the House declared the election void and Edward Noel was returned at the ensuing by-election, his father declaring he would rather 'lie in the dust' that fail to have his son elected. Harington now pursued Noel in Star Chamber and humiliated him and his servants in the county. The animosity must have abated by the time Noel made his will, for he named Harington one of the supervisors. Noel died 19 Oct. 1607 at Brooke, and was buried at Dalby with great pomp on 8 Dec. He could bequeath another seat, Stonesby, to his second son Charles, and leave £100 annuities to his younger sons, without embarrassing his heir's position. To a daughter, Elizabeth, he left a dowry of £3,000, and to various trusted servants generous annuities. Noel's daughter Theodosia married a Cecil.

DNB; C142/137/29, 33; 303/145; Vis. Leics. (Harl. Soc. ii), 3–4; VCH Rutland, i. 180, 182, 261, 270; ii. 34, 35, 38, 40, 49; APC, xv. 152; xviii. 105; xx. 187; xxi. 249; xxv. 307; CSP Dom. 1591–4, pp. 124, 180; HMC Hatfield, xiv. 148; xvii. 603; Neale, Commons, 129–39; EHR, lxi. 32 seq.; D'Ewes, 474, 496, 624–5; Lansd. 43, anon. jnl. f. 171; PCC 6 Chayre, 44 Windebanck.

S.M.T.

NOEL, Edward (1582–1643), of Brooke, Rutland.

RUTLAND 1601*

b. 1582, 1st s. of Andrew Noel* by Mabel, da. of James Harington I*. educ. Sidney Sussex, Camb. 1598, BA 1599/1600; I. Temple 1600. m. 20 Dec. 1605, Julianna, da. and coh. of Sir Baptist Hickes, 2s. 3da. Kntd. 1602; suc. fa. 1607; cr. Bt. 1611, 1st Baron Noel 1617; suc. fa.-in-law as 2nd Visct. Campden 1629.

J.p. Rutland, dep. lt. or commr. musters from c.1607, sheriff 1608–9, 1615–16, custos rot. 1628; master of game in Lyfield forest by 1614, bailiff 1623.

Noel's candidature for the county seat in 1601, when he was 19, was promoted by his father, who was sheriff at the time, in the face of opposition from (Sir) John Harington II*. He finally came in at a by-election, the date of which has not been ascertained. No activity has been found for him in the 1601 Parliament. Noel was knighted by Lord Mountjoy in 1602 and served in the Irish wars as a knight banneret. In 1603 his father wrote to Cecil asking him to take his son, who was about to enter court, under his protection, and Noel soon made a fortunate marriage to the daughter of Baptist Hickes, brother of Michael Hickes*. Though he succeeded to his father's position in Rutland, and entertained James I at Brooke, he spent much time at court. In his later years he supported the royalist cause, he and his eldest son following Charles I into the north in 1639. He died 8 Mar. 1643 in camp at Oxford and was buried four days later at Campden, without the 'ripping or bowelling' of his body, which he had feared. The 'convenient tomb', for which he left £200 to the minister, was not erected until the Restoration. His own and his wife's estates had long been divided by settlement between their two sons.

CP; DNB; HMC Hastings, iv. 192, 204; CSP Dom. 1610–18, p. 266; PRO Index 4211; HMC Hatfield, xv. 187; VCH Rutland, i. 184; ii. 17, 35, 37, 38, 40, 49, 92, 93, 199; Chamberlain Letters ed. McClure, ii. 65–6.

S.M.T.

NOEL, Henry (d. 1597), of Dalby, Leics.

| MORPETH | 1589 |
| CRICKLADE | 1593 |

Yr. s. of Sir Andrew Noel (Nowell)[†] of Dalby, by his 2nd w. and bro. of Andrew*. unm.[1]

With Leicester in the Netherlands 1587; ?gent. pens. 1590s.

Noel was a courtier from about 1583, though his name has not been found on the lists of office holders. According to an unsupported statement in the heralds' visitation of 1619, he was a gentleman pensioner. That he was the Queen's servant, however, is amply confirmed by references in a succession of royal grants in the '80s and '90s.

For person, parentage, grace, gesture, valour and many excellent parts (amongst which skill in music), [he] was of the first rank in the court.

He was also a persistent and generally successful suitor for royal rewards, including a grant of concealed lands in 1584, and a free gift of £668 in 1592. He was created MA during the Queen's visit to Oxford in September of that year. Among his patrons were the Earl of Leicester, who praised Noel's services in the Low Countries, and Sir Robert Cecil, who secured him a monopoly of the import of pottery and stoneware in 1593. In thanking Cecil, Noel begged for further favours:

> That bounty is admired which, with a present gift offers an after hope, like to the Indian tree which beareth ripe fruit and young blossoms.

A few weeks later, when illness and creditors drove him to the Spa, Noel again petitioned Cecil for help. He died in February 1597 and was buried, on the Queen's direction, in Westminster abbey in St. Andrew's chapel. His monument has not survived. Madrigals lamenting his death are in Thomas Morley's *Canzonets or Little Short Airs* (1597) and Thomas Weelkes's *Madrigals of Six Parts* (1600).[2]

Noel had no personal connexion with either Morpeth or Cricklade. Presumably he owed his return at the former to another courtier, Henry Carey, 1st Baron Hunsdon, captain of the band of gentlemen pensioners, and at the latter to Giles Brydges* 3rd Baron Chandos. The burgesses for Cricklade were appointed to a committee on 15 Mar. 1593 concerning cloth.

[1] *Vis. Leics. 1619*, 3, 114; *DNB* (Noel, Sir Andrew). [2] Lansd. 38, f. 32; 47, f. 31; Fuller, *Worthies* (1840), ii. 243–4; PRO Index 6800, ff. 341, 416; C66/1398/38–40; *HMC Hatfield*, iii. 424; iv. 323, 342, 346–7; *CSP For.* 1587, pp. 335, 373, 385; D'Ewes, 501; J. Dart, *Westmonasterium*, ii. 7; information from Mr. David Greer.

B.D.

NOEL, *see also* **NOWELL**

NORRIS, Edward (c.1550–1603), of Rycote, Oxon. and Englefield, Berks.

| OXFORD | 1572* |
| ABINGDON | 1584, 1589 |

b. c.1550, 3rd s. of Sir Henry Norris I*, 1st Lord Norris of Rycote, by Margery or Margaret, da. and coh. of John Williams†, Lord Williams of Thame; bro. of Sir Henry II*, Sir John* and William*. *m.* 1600, Elizabeth, da. and h. of John Norris* of Fyfield, Berks., wid. of one Webb of Salisbury, *s.p.* Kntd. 1586.[1]

Capt. in the Netherlands 1578, in Ireland c.1584; lt. to (Sir) Philip Sidney* as gov. of Flushing; capt. on the Portugal expedition 1589; sewer of the Household by 1590; gov. Ostend 1590–9; j.p. Berks. 1598, custos rot. 1601, j.p.q. Berks. and Oxon. 1601; clerk of the petty bag by May 1600.[2]

Though the Norris and Knollys families were rivals in Oxfordshire, Edward Norris was returned for Oxford at a by-election in January 1581, while Sir Francis Knollys* was high steward and one of his sons the senior burgess for the town; it was Knollys, indeed, who had recently broken the corporation's opposition to the return of 'outsiders'. Possibly Norris's election for Oxford, like his return for Abingdon in 1584, was the result of his father's purchase in 1574 of the Earl of Leicester's estate on Cumnor hill, which overlooks both towns. Some time after this purchase Lord Norris may have succeeded Leicester as high steward of Abingdon, of which Edward Norris was sworn a secondary burgess on 18 Nov. 1584 and immediately chosen MP.[3]

Leicester had no good opinion of Norris, whom he blamed for his brother John's insubordination. Defending John's honour, Edward was involved in August 1586 in a drunken brawl with a Count Hohenloe, whom he tried to provoke to a duel, Sir Philip Sidney bearing the cartel; in May 1588 Norris was still pleading with Walsingham that he might be allowed to fight Hohenloe, which Leicester had forbidden. As the Armada approached he asked to be allowed to return home, and both Edward and John Norris were in England, personally attending upon the Queen, in the autumn of 1588, and able to secure return to Parliament. In July 1590 Burghley secured the governorship of Ostend for Norris, who had recovered from a head wound received on the Portugal expedition. The Queen, displeased at his impending departure from court, forbade him to go till his office of sewer had been filled. Norris was clearly something of a favourite. As governor, facing several attacks upon Ostend and an attempt on his life with a poisoned dagger by an agent of the Cardinal Archduke, he received personal letters of exhortation from the Queen, who addressed him as 'Ned'. He had harsher treatment from Elizabeth than from the Privy Council, however, in the matter of the continual complaints about his conduct made by the Dutch estates, which he was told to answer in person. In 1599 his last two surviving brothers died in Ireland, and in September he was recalled to comfort his aged parents.[4]

On his return, Norris settled at Englefield in the house, which he bought for £1,500, forfeited by the attainted Catholic exile, Sir Francis Englefield†; the Queen visited him there in 1601. Despite rumours in 1600 that he would become president of Munster, and in 1602 that he was to be appointed deputy of Ireland, and although he kept himself informed of events in Ireland and the Netherlands through his servants, Captain George Whitton and Dudley Carleton†, he was thenceforward less interested in resuming his military activities than in building up his property and influence in Oxfordshire and Berkshire. Excluded from succession to Lord Norris's wealth by the son of the eldest of his dead brothers, he hoped to found a new line by marrying the daughter and only child of John Norris* of Fyfield. He enlarged his house and made a new park for the sake of his wife, already a rich widow, and in

October 1600 went to court 'well attended with martial followers ... to present himself a married man'. But no heir was born, and it was reported that his wife 'feigned a miscarriage'.[5]

It appears that Norris took advantage of the age of his father and the youth of his father's heir. He 'gave it out' that no one was to communicate with his father except through him. When Lord Norris died in the summer of 1601, Edward was executor with his mother, and in this capacity engaged in litigation with the new Lord Norris 'even to the making of him[self] ridiculous'. But his nephew's wife was the niece of Sir Robert Cecil, with whom Norris himself was at odds. Perhaps in consequence he acted in a compromising fashion towards Essex, whom he sped to Ireland with hopes that he would return in glory. When he took his wife to court, he effected some reconciliation with Cecil, and 'had his face washed with court holy water', but 'he speedily returned to his climacterical talk, and in the way homeward, marred all again by his visitation of my Lord of Essex, with many caresses and kind greetings'. Friendship with Essex did not mean any lessening in the traditional rivalry with the Earl's uncle, (Sir) William Knollys*, however, and here Norris had no success. The two men quarrelled scandalously over the stewardship of Sonning, at the funeral of Lord Norris, to whose lieutenancies Knollys succeeded, though Norris had asked them of Cecil. Norris was not 'of the Parliament' in 1601, as John Chamberlain remarked, though he was much in town.[6]

In London he feasted, was 'much visited by cavaliers' and attended the gaming tables, comforting himself with the reflection that losses there were less dangerous than in competition at court, a 'base kind of business ... wherein we give matter to all men to speak, but none to our good'. In an isolated revelation of religious conviction, he remarked that 'God has made in our family patterns for men to judge what the world is worth, and how vain all is, save only the contemplation of God'. He died 8 Sept. 1603, and was buried in Englefield church. His nephew, Lord Norris, succeeded to his estates. His will, which has not survived, was the subject of a suit between his heir and his widow's third husband; Lord Norris offered to settle by paying 'the pretended executors' £2,000 for Norris's debts and £1,000 for his servants.[7]

[1] DNB; Vis. Berks. (Harl. Soc. lvii), 185; CP. [2] Lansd. 64, ff. 155, 157; CSP Dom. 1598–1601, p. 435; HMC De L'Isle and Dudley, iii. 270. [3] Sir R. Naunton, Fragmenta Regalia, ed. Arber, 39–41; VCH Berks. iv. 400; A. E. Preston, St. Nicholas, Abingdon, 425–7; Abingdon bor. recs. minutes, 1, f. 52v. [4] Leycester Corresp. (Cam. Soc. xxvii), 301, 391–2, 394, 473; CSP For. 1586–7, p. 173; 1587, pp. 205–7; Jan.–June 1588(1), pp. 346, 531; July–Dec. 1588, pp. 18, 175, 366; Lansd. 64, ff. 149, 155, 157; 100, f. 100 seq.; HMC Hatfield, v. 500; viii. 133–5; APC, xxi. 273; xxii. 109–11, 362, 392; xxv. 172; CSP Dom. 1595–7, p. 362; 1598–1601, p. 319; J. L. Motley, United Netherlands, iii. 268. [5] CSP Dom. 1598–1601, pp. 34, 392, 444, 478, 481; 1601–3, p. 65; HMC De L'Isle and Dudley, ii. 40; Chamberlain Letters ed. McClure, i. 131, 142, 149. [6] HMC Hatfield, viii. 281, 404, 506; x. 15, 251, 296; xi.

324, 584; xv. 177–8, 184; PCC 51 Woodhall; CSP Dom. 1598–1601, pp. 197–8, 456, 478; Chamberlain Letters, i. 128, 134. [7] Chamberlain Letters, i. 182; CSP Dom. 1598–1601, pp. 433, 458; Add. 1580–1625, p. 431; C142/314/127; HMC Hatfield, xvi. 247, 344; A. C. Baker, Historic Abingdon, 35.

A.H.

NORRIS, Sir Henry I (c.1525–1601), of Rycote, Oxon. and Bray, Berks.

BERKSHIRE	1547
OXFORDSHIRE	1571

b. c.1525, 1st s. of Henry Norris of Bray by Mary, da. of Thomas Fiennes, Lord Dacre of the South. m. by 1544, Margery or Margaret (d.1599), yr. da. and coh. of John Williams†, Lord Williams of Thame, 6s. inc. Edward*, Sir Henry II*, Sir John* and William* 1da. suc. fa. 1536. Kntd. 1566; cr. Lord Norris 1572.

In King's service by Aug. 1544; official of royal stables by 1546; gent. of privy chamber to Edw. VI by 1547; butler of Poole 1553; j.p. Berks. from 1559, Oxon. from c.1561, sheriff, Oxon. and Berks. 1562–3; ambassador to France 1566–70; keeper of the armoury and porter of the outer gate, Windsor castle 1578; high steward, Abingdon c.1580, Wallingford from 1588; jt. ld. lt. Oxon. and Berks. from c.1585–99, first with Sir Francis*, then with (Sir) William Knollys*; capt. of light horse, the Queen's bodyguard July 1588.[1]

Norris moved about 1559 from Berkshire to Rycote, his main seat for the rest of his life. In 1565 the death of his uncle Sir John Norris added to his original inheritance in Berkshire. He had a town house at Charing Cross, where as an old man he received the governor of Dunkirk into custody.

At Elizabeth's accession he and his wife became firm favourites at court, Sir Robert Dudley*, Earl of Leicester, describing them as 'a hearty noble couple ... as ever I saw towards her Highness'. Lady Norris became an intimate friend of Elizabeth, who gave her the nickname of her 'Crow'.[2]

In September 1562, during a change of ambassadors, Norris was for a short time in Paris, where he tried to explain Elizabeth's anger at recent developments in French policy. After his return he spent much of his time at court, and was a competitor in the tournament held in November 1565 to celebrate the Earl of Warwick's marriage. The Queen knighted him on her visit to Rycote in 1566. During his period as ambassador to France, Cecil several times urged him to economize. By February 1569 he was asking to be recalled, and his successor was sent out in December 1570.[3]

By the time of the election for the 1571 Parliament, Norris was an obvious choice for an Oxfordshire seat, and he was instrumental in getting Richard Ward* elected for Berkshire. There is evidence that Norris was able to exercise influence at Abingdon during the 1580s. Norris was active in the Parliament of 1571. He made a 'short, mild and plain speech' on the bill to preserve the Queen's safety, 9 Apr. and two days later spoke on the Bristol merchants' bill. He served on committees considering the subsidy, 7 Apr.; religion, 10 Apr.; the treasons bill, 11 May and fugitives, 25 May. He received a writ of summons to the Lords in May 1572 and in 1576 Parliament passed an Act restoring him in blood. A statute in 1585 settled a land dispute Norris and his wife had with Lord and Lady Dacre.[4]

Norris and Sir Francis Knollys were the two leading magnates in Berkshire and Oxfordshire. Each had a large family of sons:

> No county in England can present such a brace of families contemporaries, with such a bunch of brethren ... for eminent achievements. So great their states and stomachs that they often jostled together; and no wonder if Oxfordshire wanted room for them, when all England could not hold them together.

However, the two fathers seem usually to have worked amicably with each other, perhaps because both had puritan sympathies. Jointly in 1579 they petitioned Leicester, as chancellor of Oxford university, to obtain a licence for the puritan preacher John Field, as they wished to 'place him in a lecture at Henley'. All but one of Norris's sons died as soldiers, his heir, William, in 1579, and between 1593 and the autumn of 1599 four younger sons. In August 1599 two sons died within a week, both in Ireland. Elizabeth wrote a personal letter of sympathy to the bereaved parents, promising to recall their one remaining son, Sir Edward, to England, 'as we know that it would stay your sorrow to see him that is in foreign parts'. Before the end of the year Lady Norris was also dead, leaving her husband with considerable financial complications. He was a wealthy man, but most of his land was entailed or 'engaged in the Queen's hands', and several of his sons had died in debt. Elizabeth wrote off £2,000 owing to her from one of them, Sir John, in the Netherlands, but Lord Norris, now an old man, found the amount of work involved in the settlement of so many different estates a severe strain. In addition there was a court of wards commission to inquire into his wife's property. In July 1600 he wrote to Sir Robert Cecil with a sharpness unusual for him:

> I perceive by your letters there is a great looking into my proceedings. My course of life has been such that I may hope to obtain the privilege ... to do with my own as seems to me best.

His health had begun to fail, but he refused to give up his old manner of life. Dudley Carleton† wrote in October:

> Our old Lord draws every day downward, and yet retains his old stirring spirits, being every morning on horseback before any man else be on foot.

He died on 27 June 1601, and in August was buried at Rycote. His will, made in September 1599, was proved in July 1601. His wife was still named as an executrix. Her co-executor was their son Edward, and the supervisor (Sir) Thomas Egerton*, the lord keeper, to whom Norris left £100.[5]

[1] CP; LJ, i. 704; LP Hen. VIII, xvii. p. 564; xxi(2), p. 401; CPR, 1553-4, p. 276; OR, i. 375; Bull. IHR, v. 20-1; APC, xv. 118; xvi. 196; CSP Dom. 1595-7, p. 296; LP Hen. VIII, ix(2) g 166(64). [2] LP Hen. VIII, xvii. p. 564; xix(2), p. 82; CPR, 1553-4, p. 276; 1558-60, p. 448; 1560-3, pp. 383-4; 1563-6, p. 196; C142/141/1; HMC Hatfield, vii. 434-5; Chron. Q. Jane and Q. Mary (Cam. Soc. xlviii), 100; H. Nicolas, Sir Christopher Hatton, 270. [3] CSP For. 1562, p. 296; 1569-71, pp. 32, 378; Strype, Cheke, 134; Read, Cecil, 391-2. [4] St. Ch. 5/N10/11, N16/38; D'Ewes, 159, 160, 161, 178, 183, 188; CJ, i. 83, 84, 85, 89, 92; Trinity, Dublin, anon. jnl. ff. 8-9; Private Act 18 Eliz. 27; CSP Dom. 1547-80, p. 516; LJ, ii. 87. [5] Fuller, Worthies, iii. 15; Reg. Oxf. Univ. (Oxf. Hist. Soc. x), ii(1), p. 149; SP40/1, p. 126; CSP Dom. 1547-80, p. 703; 1598-1601, pp. 11, 319, 481; CSP For. 1584-5, pp. 676-7; 1585-6, p. 33; HMC Hatfield, iv. 377; vi. 469; x. 111, 251; APC, xxx. 138-9; PCC 51 Woodhall.

N.M.F.

NORRIS, Sir Henry II (c.1554–99), of Rycote, Oxon.

BERKSHIRE   1589, 1597

b. c.1554, 4th s. of Sir Henry Norris I* and bro. of Edward*, Sir John* and William*. educ. Magdalen Coll. Oxf. 1571. unm. Kntd. Sept. 1586; KG Apr. 1592.[1]

Capt. English volunteers at Antwerp June 1583; capt. Berks. contingent for defence of England 1588, on Portugal expedition 1589, in Brittany 1591; col.-gen. of infantry in Ireland 1595.[2]

Norris and his five brothers were all soldiers, and comprised the most distinguished military family of their time. Norris followed the second-born, 'General' Sir John Norris, to the Netherlands, Portugal, Brittany and Ireland. He was knighted by Sir Robert Dudley*, Earl of Leicester at Zutphen in 1586, and returned to England a year later to help in the preparation of defences against the Armada and lead the Berkshire contingent in Leicester's army at Tilbury. In April 1588 Norris received an honorary MA at Oxford. That autumn he was chosen knight of the shire for Berkshire and Sir John was elected for Oxfordshire. Although he was not mentioned by name in the journals of the 1589 Parliament he may have attended the subsidy committee to which the first knights of the shires were appointed on 11 Feb. 1589. Soon after the end of the Parliament he took part in the Portugal venture, and he was not, in fact, in England for any length of time until 1596. In December of that year he was ordered by the Privy Council to bring to London the ringleaders of the recent insurrection against enclosures in Oxfordshire, whom his father had examined. In 1597 he was again elected for Berkshire and was appointed to committees on bills concerned with the gentry's obligation to maintain armour and weapons (8 Nov.), the punishment of rogues disguised as soldiers and mariners (20 Dec.), maltsters (12 Jan. 1598) and the relief of mariners and soldiers (26 Jan. 1598). As knight for Berkshire he was entitled to attend the committees concerning enclosures (5 Nov.), the poor law (5, 22 Nov.), the penal laws (8 Nov.), monopolies (10 Nov.), the town of Wantage (10 Nov.) and the subsidy (15 Nov.). He was apparently served with a subpoena while in Parliament, a breach of privilege which Sir Edward Hoby* brought to the attention of the House on 16 Jan. 1598. He was sent to Deptford in December 1597 to receive and escort to London the governor of Dunkirk, captured by Sir Edward Norris.[3]

By the summer of 1599 he was back in Ireland. Serving under Essex in Munster, he and his brother, Sir Thomas Norris, who had become president of Munster on Sir John Norris's death two years before, both received mortal wounds. The deaths of Sir Thomas on 16 Aug. and of Sir Henry, after the amputation of his leg, on 21 Aug. were reported as an 'infinite disaster'. The Queen wrote to console Lord and Lady Norris 'in this bitter accident', in which she proposed herself as an example of fortitude, 'our loss being no less than yours'; and promised to recall from the Netherlands Sir Edward, the last survivor of the six martial brothers. No will or inquisition post mortem survives for Norris.[4]

[1] DNB (Sir Henry, Baron Norris); Lansd. 94, f. 110. [2] HMC 2nd Rep. 73; HMC Foljambe, 47, 49, 51; CSP For. 1589 (Jan.–July), 119; APC, xxi. 25; CSP Dom. 1591–4, p. 397; Cal. Carew Pprs. iii. 113. [3] VCH Berks. iii. 105; HMC Hatfield, iv. 202; CSP Dom. 1595–7, pp. 13, 318; D'Ewes, 431, 552, 553, 555, 557, 561, 575, 578, 581, 588; APC, xxviii. 11, 165. [4] CSP Ire. 1599–1600, pp. 66, 128; Chamberlain Letters ed. McClure, i. 82, 84; CSP Dom. 1598–1601, p. 319.

A.H.

NORRIS, John (c.1550–Dec.1612 or Jan.1613), of Fifield and Bray, Berks. and Woodwicks, Herts.

NEW WINDSOR   1597, 1601

b. c.1550, 1st s. of William Norris† by Mary, da. of Sir Adrian Fortescue of Shirburn, Oxon. m. Mary, da. of George Basford of Rickmansworth, Herts., wid. of Roger Colte (d.1575), 1s. d.v.p. 1da. suc. fa. 1591. Kntd. 1601.[1]

Comptroller of works, Windsor castle 16 Apr. 1591; woodward of Cookham and Bray, keeper of Cranborne lodge in Windsor forest, ?1596; j.p.q. Berks. from c.1592, sheriff 1601–2.[2]

John Norris of Fifield (not to be confused with 'General' Sir John Norris of the Rycote branch of the family) was the son of an official of the Household and burgess for Windsor in three Marian Parliaments. He inherited his father's job as comptroller of the works at Windsor and was returned to Parliament for the borough, leaving no trace on the known surviving records of his two Parliaments.[3]

In July 1600 Norris's daughter and sole surviving child,

already a rich widow, married (Sir) Edward Norris*, then aged about 50, the only surviving son of Lord Norris of Rycote. Sir Edward evidently hoped to found a new line upon the reunion of two branches of the family, but he died childless in October 1603. The scheme had its advantages for John Norris. He was knighted at Englefield when the Queen dined there in September 1601, and some did 'much marvel' that Sir Edward Norris 'would be the means to make such a Sir John Norris'. He attempted to arbitrate in the disputes between Sir Edward and the now Lord Norris.[4]

His daughter married, as her third husband, Thomas Erskine, 1st Viscount of Fentoun. Norris's nuncupative will, registered in 1616, declares that in December 1612, in his last illness, he called his daughter to him and said "All is thine, Bess ... be good to your tenants that they may bid you good morrow with a cheerful heart'; no executors are mentioned, and Lady Fentoun was granted letters of administration. According to John Chamberlain, writing in January 1613, however, Norris had appointed Sir Henry Neville II* and Sir William Bowyer his executors, but 'his daughter ... hath put herself in possession and means to carry it away by strong hand'. The matter caused a dispute between Neville and Lord Fentoun, in which the latter, 'very violent', complained to the King.[5]

[1] C142/228/30; Vis. Berks. (Harl. Soc. lvii), 185; VCH Berks. iii. 128, 173; VCH Herts. ii. 383. [2] CSP Dom. 1594–7, p. 327; 1611–18, p. 58; Hope, Windsor Castle, i. 287, 289; The King's Works, iii. 416. [3] DNB (Norris, Sir Henry); E. Ashmole, Hist. Berks. iii. 11–12. [4] Though the Visitation credits him with a son, John Norris seems to have left no male heir, VCH Berks. iii. 128, 173; Chamberlain Letters ed. McClure, i. 131; HMC Hatfield, xii. 265. [5] CP, vii. 101, incorrectly identifies Lady Fentoun as the widow of Edward, John Norris's brother, who was still alive in 1612: cf. Norris's will and Vis. Berks. (Harl. Soc. lvii), 185; PCC 19–20 Weldon; Chamberlain Letters, i. 405, 409, 414.

A.H.

NORRIS, Sir John (c.1547–97), of Rycote, Oxon. and Yattendon and Notley, Berks.

OXFORDSHIRE   1589

b. c.1547, 2nd s. of Sir Henry Norris I* and bro. of Edward*, Sir Henry II* and William*. unm. Kntd. 1586. MP [I] 1585.

Volunteer under Coligny 1571; capt. in Ulster 1573–5, in the Netherlands 1577–84; ld. pres. of Munster from 1584; gen. in the Netherlands Aug.–Dec. 1585; capt. under Leicester ?1585–8; commr. to inspect defences of channel coast Apr. 1588; gen. of the Portugal expedition 1589, of the army in Brittany 1591–2, 1593–4; j.p. Oxon. 1596.[1]

Sir John Norris, commonly known as 'general' or 'black Jack' Norris, was the most distinguished of Lord Norris's six martial sons, and probably the ablest English soldier of his time. As a young man he seems to have spent some time in the care of Sir William Cecil*, while his father was ambassador in France. It was while visiting his father during the clashes between the Catholics and the Huguenots, that he had his first experience of fighting, and he became an enthusiastic partisan of the protestant cause. He was the obvious choice for command of the first English troops in the Netherlands, where his early victories brought him a sudden rise to fame, showing that the Spaniards were 'no devils' and persuading Elizabeth to become more deeply involved in the struggle. For the rest of his life he remained a professional soldier, to whom Ireland presented opportunities for action when he was not needed elsewhere; from his first acquaintance with Ireland, he maintained that it could not 'be brought to obedience but by force'. He had a streak of ruthlessness, which caused him to massacre the population of Carrickfergus which he captured in 1575, and a professional's contempt for noble amateurs such as Leicester and the 2nd Earl of Essex.[2]

His relationship with the two Earls is the aspect of his military career which most concerns his return to Parliament. He was a valued captain in Ulster under the 1st Earl of Essex, and was recommended by both Knollys and Leicester for the captaincy in the Netherlands, Leicester describing him as the fittest 'for birth, skill, courage, wisdom, modesty ... faithfulness to the Prince ... religion' and, considering his youth, 'good experience'. Yet, according to Sir Robert Naunton[1], the Knollyses competed with the Norrises for leadership in Oxfordshire and favour with the Queen, and Leicester, married to Sir Francis Knollys's daughter Lettice, was the 'pillar' of that family; while Leicester lived, 'none of the other side took deep rooting in court', and thus, the Norrises were forced to live by the sword. Perhaps some such rivalry did grow up as Norris's fame increased. After Leicester's arrival in the Netherlands in December 1585, the English cause was undermined by a series of quarrels between the Earl and Norris, who returned to England early in 1588, proclaiming that he would never serve under Leicester again.[3]

If the Knollyses had hoped for this rift, they presumably did not intend the outcome: that in the autumn of 1588 Norris was in England and able to secure return to Parliament as knight for Oxfordshire along with Sir Francis Knollys. Norris's service during the Armada threat perhaps increased his eligibility. He was used by the Privy Council to inspect the defences of the south coast and advise the lord lieutenants and the lord mayor of London. He was also the marshal of Leicester's camp at Tilbury, where he escorted the Queen on her famous visit, but he was rarely at his post, and Leicester complained once more of his conduct.[4]

The Armada was barely past when Norris put forward a grandiose plan 'to invade and destroy all who have attempted to invade England'. It may have been in connexion with this venture, for which Norris offered to

find half of the £40,000 at which he estimated the cost, that the mayor of Oxford went to London in January 1589 'to talk with Sir John Norris touching provision of armour and powder'. Later that year the Portugal expedition set out with Norris and Drake in command, and for the rest of his life Norris had no opportunity to sit in Parliament. He is not mentioned by name in the records of the House, although he may have attended one committee as knight of the shire concerning the possessions of the bishop of Oxford, which was appointed on 13 Mar. 1589.[5]

Naunton considered that the Earl of Essex, Lettice Knollys's son by her first marriage, inherited Leicester's role as the agent of the Knollys family against Norris, who returned to Ireland in 1594, complaining to Sir Robert Cecil as he went, that 'encouragement is given to my enemies to disgrace me when absent'. In Norris's remaining years, wrote Naunton, Essex 'not only crushed and upon all occasions quelled the growth of this brave man and his famous brethren; but therewith drew on his own fatal end, by undertaking the Irish action'. In August 1595, when denying that he had said that Essex neglected better captains than he rewarded, Norris was provoked to write to the Earl: 'this often manner of expostulating with me makes me doubt that, because I have earnestly sought your good opinion, you do the more condemn me'.[6]

Incurable differences between Norris and the lord deputy, (Sir) William Russell*, at length decided the Privy Council to recall both men. Norris, convinced that the Queen herself had at last turned against him, and suffering from a lame thigh and a 'falling of rheum in the lungs', asked for his recall to be hastened. Before relief came, he died at Mallow of gangrene, apparently on 3 July 1597 (though his inquisition post mortem states 28 Sept.) in the arms of his brother Thomas. The Queen wrote to his mother, advising her against 'immoderate grief'. 'Nature can have stirred no more dolorous affection in you as a mother for a dear son, than gratefulness and memory of his service past have wrought in us, his sovereign, apprehension of our miss of so worthy a servant'. She promised, perhaps with a slight sense of guilt, to show her 'estimation of him that was, in our gracious care of you and yours that are left, in valuing rightly all their faithful and honest endeavours'. Norris is said to have been buried at Yattendon, Berkshire, a manor given to him by his father. He is commemorated in a monument in Westminster abbey. Administration of Norris's estates was granted first in October 1597 to his brother, Sir Henry, then, upon his death, to Sir Edward Norris. When Sir Edward died it passed to Sir Francis Norris (October 1603) who renounced it.[7]

[1] *DNB*; *CP*. [2] G. Mattingly, *Defeat of Spanish Armada*, 59, 291; *CSP For.* 1566–8, p. 374; 1569–71, p. 96; 1575–7, p. 223; 1577–8, pp. 193, 201, 589; 1578–9, pp. 130–1. [3] *CSP Ire.* 1509–73, p. 526; *CSP For.* 1577–8, p. 716; 1578–9, pp. 130–1; Birch, *Mems.* i. 37; Naunton, *Fragmenta Regalia*, ed. Arber, 39–40; *HMC Hatfield*, iii. 168–9; *APC*,

xv. 176; *Leycester Corresp.* (Cam. Soc. xxvii), 222, 264, 301, 306, 379, 385; Mattingly, 59. [4] *CSP Dom.* 1581–90, pp. 473, 511–12; *APC*, xv. 414; xvi. 20, 145; Mattingly, 294. [5] *CSP Dom.* 1581–90, pp. 545, 551; *Oxf. Council Acts*, ed. Salter (Oxf. Hist. Soc. lxxxvii), 53; D'Ewes, 445. [6] Naunton, 41; *CSP Dom.* 1595–7, p. 32; *HMC Hatfield*, v. 413–14; vi. 290–1. [7] Birch, *Mems.* ii. 225; *APC*, xxvi. 421; xxvii. 89; *CSP Ire.* 1596–7, passim; C142/293/13; Nichols, *Progresses Eliz.* iii. 420; *VCH Berks.* iv. 127; *PCC Admons.* iv (Brit. Rec. Soc. Index Lib. lxxxi), 94.

A.H.

NORRIS, Thomas (d.1607), of Congham, Norf.

CASTLE RISING	1586

1st s. of John Norris of Congham by Alice, da. of Robert Might of Flitcham. *educ.* I. Temple 1572, ancient 1601. *m.* 30 Dec. 1583, Elizabeth, da. of Humphrey Guybon of Castle Acre, 2s. 1da. *suc.* fa. 1572.

Norris never achieved the status of a Norfolk j.p. though his marriage to the sister of a fellow-member of the Inner Temple, Thomas Guybon*, must have brought him connexions with the gentry in the neighbourhood of Lynn and Castle Rising. His return for the latter borough in 1586 was probably due to his friendship with Edward Coke*, his near-contemporary at the Inner Temple, whom he made overseer of his will. Norris died 4 Nov. 1607, leaving his lands to his elder son and his goods to his daughter Alice. Two of his executors were his brother Cuthbert and his 'loving uncle' William Guybon. Norris was not the man who was deputy to the vice-chancellor of the duchy of Lancaster in 1574.

Vis. Norf. 1664 (Harl. Soc. lxxxvi), 147; *Vis. Norf.* (Norf. and Norwich Arch. Soc.), i. 180; *Cal. I.T. Recs.* i. 441; PCC 95 Windebanck; C142/304/70; Somerville, *Duchy*, i. 481.

R.V.

NORRIS, William (c.1545–79), of Rycote, Oxon. and Yattendon, Berks.

BERKSHIRE	1572*

b. c.1545, 1st s. of Sir Henry Norris I* and bro. of Edward*, Sir Henry II* and Sir John*. *educ.* Eton c.1557. *m.* c.1577, Elizabeth, da. of (Sir) Richard Morison† of Cassiobury, Herts., 1s.[1]

Capt. in Ulster 1573; temp. marshal of Berwick 1576; receiver of the Exchequer, Essex, Herts., London, Mdx. Apr. 1579.[2]

As a young man Norris spent some time in France, where his father was ambassador, and on his own account reported to Cecil about the activities of the Huguenots. At the end of 1569 his father sent him home to serve the Queen during the northern rebellion. By October 1573 he was serving in Ireland, he and his brother John being commended by Essex, in whose favour they clearly were. On 3 Feb. 1576 he was returned to Parliament for Berkshire at a by-election but it is doubtful whether in fact

he took his seat in the Commons, for in May 1576, two months after the session of that year had ended, he was paid 100 marks for the extra expense of his voyage home from Ireland, which had taken seven weeks through bad weather. He was dead before the next session of the Parliament. On his marriage Norris became a Berkshire landlord in his own right, for an indenture between his father and Elizabeth Morison's stepfather, the 2nd Earl of Bedford, settled on the couple a score of manors in the county. In the autumn of 1579, a year after the birth of his son, to whom the Queen was godmother, he was busy mustering troops for Ireland and dealing with complaints by the corporation of Stamford of the unruly conduct of his men. He sailed from Chester in October or November and died at Newry on the morning of Christmas day, of 'a violent fever' by which 'his heart was utterly consumed' and 'his spleen corrupted'.

The lord justice of Ireland was ordered to estimate, but not pay, the sums due to Norris for his service, since he owed 'a round sum' for the post as receiver which he had held for barely nine months. He was succeeded by his son Francis, who was also heir to old Lord Norris in 1601, and was later created Earl of Berkshire. The widow married Sir Henry Clinton*, 2nd Earl of Lincoln.[3]

[1] *CP*; Wards 7/20/190. [2] *CSP Ire.* 1509–73, p. 526; Camden, *Annals* (1635), 563; *HMC Hatfield*, ii. 247. [3] *CSP For.* 1566–8, pp. 374, 565, 586; 1569–71, pp 96, 143, 153; *CSP Ire.* 1509–73, p. 525; 1574–85, pp. 5, 188, 201; R. Naunton, *Fragmenta Regalia*, ed. Arber, 39–41; N. J. O'Conor, *Godes Peace and the Queenes*, 36–7; Wards 7/20/190; *APC*, ix. 117; xi. 23, 186, 235, 259–60, 264, 340, 426; *Genealogist* n.s. ii. 295; *Cal. Carew Pprs.* ii. 183, 191, 193; SP12/131/81.

A.H.

NORTH, Henry (1556–1620), of Wickhambrook and Mildenhall, Suff.

CAMBRIDGE	1584
CAMBRIDGESHIRE	1597

b. 28 Dec. 1556, 3rd s. of Sir Roger North*, 2nd Lord North, by Winifred, da. of Richard Rich†, 1st Baron Rich, wid. of Sir Henry Dudley; bro. of John*. *educ.* ?Jesus, Camb. 1569–74;[1] L. Inn 1575. *m.* 1574, Mary, da. and coh. of Richard Knyvet of Norf., 3s. 3da. Kntd. 1586.[2]

Capt. in Ireland 1579; with Leicester in the Netherlands 1586; j.p. Suff. from c.1591, Isle of Ely from c.1592; dep. lt. Cambs. 1598; commr. musters, Suff. by 1596, sheriff 1619–20.[3]

North was born at his father's London home, the Charterhouse, and 'was christened by the Earl of Arundel, the Lord Lumley being his deputy, and by the Lord Darcy of Essex, the Countess of Worcester being his godmother'. The son of a peer who remained high in the Queen's favour for the whole of his life, North does not seem to have been attracted to the life of a courtier, and, after a comparatively short period of travel and military service, was content to retire to the Suffolk estates his father had given him and live the life of a country gentleman.[4]

Unfortunately several contemporary sources speak of a Captain North without being more specific. As well as Henry, these could refer to his brother John, heir to the barony, his uncle Thomas (the translator of Plutarch), and his nephew Edward, all of whom are known to have been active soldiers in the last 20 years of the century. It is clear, however, that it was Henry who served in Ireland in 1579 under Sir Humphrey Gilbert*. At his departure his father gave him £27 'besides all furniture', and £1 each for his two servants. It has also been suggested that Henry accompanied Gilbert on his first abortive attempt to reach the New World. In March 1583 'Mr. North' returned from an expedition to Poland: he had seen service under Alaski, the Palatine of Poland, and according to Dr. Dee's *Diary* reported his experiences to the Queen. The most important period of North's military career was, however, in the service of the Earl of Leicester in the Low Countries. He distinguished himself with the cavalry at Zutphen, where George Whetstone, an eye-witness, reported, in a poem on the encounter, 'the younger North did forward courage show'. His reward was a knighthood at Leicester's hands. He next appears in action in the Armada campaign – at least, the North who was in Poland does. He was aboard one of the ships opposed to the Spanish fleet. He may have been the Captain North in the Earl of Essex's expedition to Brittany in 1591, and may also have been in Portugal in 1598 – the man concerned had served in Ireland – but this is only conjecture: his active career could have ended much earlier.[5]

Although North was to move to Suffolk, his family's country seat was at Kirtling in Cambridgeshire, a county where Lord North enjoyed great authority. North himself was first returned to Parliament by the town of Cambridge, of which his father was high steward. According to the borough's bye-laws, Henry, as a 'foreigner', was not eligible for the seat, but such was Lord North's influence that two of his sons were returned in succession. Henry made no mark on the surviving records of the 1584 Parliament. After a long interval, he acquired the county seat in Parliament, even though he was almost certainly not resident in Cambridgeshire at the time: he was presumably the 'Sir Henry Worth' appointed to receive information about illegal marriages on 14 Nov. 1597, and he was named to a committee on maltsters, 12 Jan. 1598. As knight for Cambridgeshire he was also appointed to committees concerning enclosures (5 Nov.), the poor law (5, 22 Nov.), armour and weapons (8 Nov.), the penal laws (8 Nov.), monopolies (10 Nov.), the subsidy (15 Nov.) and draining the fens (3 Dec.). In 1598 a commission was issued appointing him a deputy lieutenant to his father, with special supervision of the Isle of Ely.[6]

When Lord North died in 1600 Sir Henry North must have taken on some of the duties of head of the family, for the new Lord North was still a minor. By this date he had been living for some time in Suffolk, firstly at Wickhambrook and then at Mildenhall, where he built a fine mansion. His duties in the county followed a similar pattern to those in Cambridgeshire, but in 1598 he was censured by the Privy Council for his tardiness in sending Suffolk's £300 contribution towards the maintenance of troops in Ireland. Little is heard of him in James's reign. He died 20 Nov. 1620. A handsome monument marks his burial place in Mildenhall church. Apart from small bequests to the poor of Mildenhall and Wickhambrook, he left all his property to his immediate family. His three daughters, two of whom were married, were left substantial sums of money. The single daughter, Dorothy, was to have £1,500 at her marriage, 'provided that she do not marry herself to her notorious and manifest disparagement'. The widow received the lease of the parsonage of Moulton, Suffolk, with the bulk of the household goods and farm stock and equipment; she was also to have the best coach, with two horses. The second son, Henry, received an annuity of £50 and a small estate in Cambridgeshire, while the heir, Roger[†], was to have the principal estates and be executor. Roger sat in seven Stuart Parliaments, and the branch of the family which Sir Henry had established in Suffolk was to play a major part in the county's affairs for well over 100 years.[7]

[1] The surname only appears in the university records, but the admission date is suitable, and several other members of the family were educated at Cambridge. [2] *EHR*, xxxvii. 566; *Vis. Notts.* (Harl. Soc. iv), 83; W. A. Copinger, *Suff. Manors*, iv. 178; *DNB* (Roger, 2nd Baron North); *CP*; Lansd. 94, f. 94. [3] *CSP Dom.* Add. 1580–1625, p. 419; *APC*, xxvi. 388; xxviii. 630; Hatfield ms 278. [4] *EHR*, xxxvii. 566. [5] Nichols, *Progresses Eliz.* ii. 246, 247; Lady Frances Bushby, *Three Men of the Tudor Time*, 107; *Diary of John Dee* (Cam. Soc. xix), 19; E. M. Tenison, *Eliz. England*, vi. 191; *CSP For.* 1586–7, p. 214; P. J. Blok, *Corresp. inédite de Robert Dudley, comte de Leycester, et de François et Jean Hotman*, 100 n; Laughton, *Defeat of Spanish Armada* (Navy Recs. Soc. i and ii), ii. 144; *HMC Hatfield*, iv. 169; *CSP Dom.* 1598–1601, p. 75. [6] Neale, *Commons*, 166; D'Ewes, 552, 553, 555, 557, 561, 567, 578; *APC*, xxviii. 630. [7] PCC 6 Woodhall, printed *Coll. Top et Gen.* vi. 99; Copinger, iv. 177–8, 183; v. 302; vii. 363; *CSP Dom.* 1611–18, p. 247; *APC*, xxix. 343; Add. 32484; PCC 99 Soame; C142/387/111.

M.R.P.

NORTH, John (c.1551–97), of Cambridgeshire.

CAMBRIDGE	1572*
CAMBRIDGESHIRE	1584, 1586, 1589
ORFORD	1593

b. c.1551, 1st s. of Sir Roger North*, 2nd Lord North, and bro. of Henry*. educ. Peterhouse, Camb. 1562, Trinity Coll. 1567, MA 1572; G. Inn 1572; travelled (Italy) 1576–8. m. Dorothy, da. and h. of Dr. Valentine Dale*, 4s. 2da. Kntd. 1596.[1]

Free burgess and alderman, Cambridge 1572; commander in Netherlands 1582, in Ireland c.1596; j.p. Suff. from c.1591.[2]

As a boy, North was put under John Whitgift at Cambridge for instruction in 'good learning and christian manners', and moved to Trinity College when Whitgift became master there – a strange upbringing for the heir of a puritan like Lord North. About the time of his 21st birthday he was created an MA of his university (perhaps the degree was honorary), and made an honorary alderman of Cambridge. After a period on the continent he went to the Netherlands, serving under Sir John Norris*. In May 1582 he was in England, with a commission from the Duke of Anjou to raise eight companies of 150 men for the defence of the Netherlands. His regiment fought at Ghent in September the same year. North was a brave and efficient soldier, but his relations with Sir John Norris were bad. His movements during the period 1579 to 1588 are not easy to trace. Presumably he spent time in England between campaigns in the Low Countries. In 1581 he was returned to Parliament at a by-election for Cambridge, where his father was high steward, leaving no trace upon the records of that session. In the following Parliament he took his seat for the first time as knight of the shire for Cambridgeshire, and was named to committees for revising statutes (23, 24, Feb. 1585), considering ropes (23, 24, Feb.), the subsidy (24 Feb.), and draining the fens (22 Mar.). His name is again absent from the journals of the 1586 Parliament, but as senior knight for Cambridgeshire in both 1586 and 1589 he was entitled to attend the subsidy committees appointed on 22 Feb. 1587 and 11 Feb. 1589. On 26 Feb. 1589 he served on a committee for the bill concerning captains and soldiers, and spoke on the first reading. He was appointed to a second committee on the subject on 19 Mar. North was a member of the committee for the final conference with the Lords at the end of this Parliament (29 Mar.) urging a declaration of war with Spain. For one reason or another – perhaps because of his frequent absences abroad – he was not elected for the county in 1593, but it is surprising that he should have had to go outside Cambridgeshire. Lord North had written to Cambridge corporation asking for a nomination before the 1593 election, but the town returned two local men, and John North found a seat at Orford – perhaps again through his father's influence, although a local patron (probably one of the Wingfields) may have been directly responsible for his return. He does not appear to have contributed to the proceedings of the House in this Parliament.[3]

His military career had taken on a new phase after Lord North's appointment as governor of Flushing in 1586. He had his own troop of 150 men in the town by September 1587, but before the end of the year he was writing to the Earl of Essex from a civil prison at Dordrecht explaining that he had been imprisoned for taking the Earl's part in a dispute against one Webbe, a follower of the Earl of Sussex, who had cast aspersions on Essex's reputation. After his release he may have come back to England, but

the 'Mr. North' referred to in Dr. Dee's diary as having visited Poland, and returned home in time for the Armada fighting, was probably his younger brother Henry. By 1596 John North was in Ireland, where on Easter day he was knighted at Christ Church, Dublin. In the May he returned to England, and in July was claiming the patronage of a benefice in Wales. He died in London 5 June 1597, and was buried the following day at St. Gregory's by St. Paul's. His widow, described by Dudley Carleton† as 'like a star among the fairest ladies', remarried in 1604.[4]

[1] *CP*, ix. 654–5. [2] *DNB*; Neale, *Commons*, 165–6; *CSP For.* 1581–2, p. 618 et passim; *Cal. Carew Pprs.* iii. 244–5. [3] Strype, *Whitgift*, i. 14; *CSP For.* 1581–2, passim; 1582, pp. 33–4; 1583, pp. 299–300; 1583–4, pp. 124, 204; Neale, *Commons*, 165–6; D'Ewes, 355, 356, 371, 409, 431, 439, 448, 454. [4] *Cam. Soc.* xix. 19; *CSP For.* 1587 (Apr.–Dec.), pp. 104, 335; *Chamberlain Letters* ed. McClure, i. 31; *Cal. Carew Pprs.* iii. 244–5; *HMC Hatfield*, vi. 257–8, 270–1; PCC 58 Cobham.

N.M.F.

NORTH, Sir Roger (1531–1600), of Kirtling, Cambs. and Mildenhall, Suff.

CAMBRIDGESHIRE   1555, 1559, 1563*

b. 27 Feb. 1531, 1st s. of Edward North†, 1st Lord North, by his 1st w. Alice, da. of Oliver Squire of Southby, Hants, wid. of Edward Murfyn of London and of John Brigandine of Southampton. *educ.* ?Peterhouse, Camb. *m.* c.1547, Winifred, da. of Richard Rich†, 1st Baron Rich, wid. of Sir Henry Dudley, 3s. inc. Henry* and John* 1da. KB Jan. 1559; *suc.* fa. as 2nd Lord North 1564. Kt. banneret at Zutphen 1586.[1]

J.p. Cambs. from c.1559, Suff. and Isle of Ely from c.1579, Mdx. 1591; ld. lt. Cambs. 1569, custos rot. c.1573; alderman, Cambridge 1568, high steward 1572; steward, duchy of Lancaster lands in Cambs., Norf., Suff. 1572; ambassador to Vienna 1568, France 1574; gov. Flushing June 1586, Utrecht and Harlingen July 1586; PC and treasurer of the Household Aug. 1596.[2]

North succeeded to large estates in Cambridgeshire and Suffolk, with property in Harrow, Pinner and other parts of Middlesex, and a London mansion built on the site of the Charterhouse. At about the time he received livery of his estates in June 1565, he sold a house and chapel at Clerkenwell to the Duke of Norfolk and lands in Huntingdonshire to (Sir) Henry Cromwell *alias* Williams*. Later he increased his Suffolk property by buying an estate at Mildenhall, and in 1597 he was granted the reversion to the keepership of Eltham and Horne parks in Kent. By the accession of Elizabeth he was spending much time at court. In May 1559 he received a licence for the export of 2,000 woollen cloths and kerseys, and in July 1559 he was one of the challengers at the grand tournament held in Greenwich park. The first household subsidy of the reign assessed him at £30. In religion North was a radical. He had voted against a government bill in the 1555 Parliament, and the bishops' letters of 1564 reported favourably on his attitude to Elizabeth's church settlement. In Suffolk he showed himself a supporter of the group of puritan justices of the peace who quarrelled with successive bishops of Norwich, and he was accused of leading his friend the Earl of Leicester into the radical protestant camp.[3]

The only reference found to his activities in the 1563 session of Parliament is the committal to him of a bill concerning the fens, 5 Feb. On the first day of the second session he took his seat in the Lords, where he served as a trier of petitions in the Parliaments of 1571, 1572, 1584 and 1597. Between his two foreign embassies he was one of the peers who condemned the Duke of Norfolk at his trial for treason in January 1572.[4]

North was an energetic local official, organizing county musters, supervising schemes for draining the fens, and inquiring into the activities of the religious sect known as the Family of Love. Cambridge found in him an ally in disputes with the university. In May 1569 he had his first clash with the university authorities, over the liability of students' servants to be called to the musters. That December he forced a student who had used 'evil and foul words' to the mayor to apologise on his knees and to stand for three hours in the pillory. In 1591 he complained to the Privy Council that a group of undergraduates had attacked the inn where he was eating after holding sessions at the castle, and released a prisoner, whom they took to the vice-chancellor's house. The corporation frequently gave him presents, varying from plate to oxen and foodstuffs.[5]

In September 1578 North entertained the Queen for two days at Kirtling, an honour which according to his household books cost him £762, including a gift of jewellery worth £120. During this progress he had a 'sudden and passionate' quarrel with the Earl of Sussex – a dispute which Elizabeth personally intervened to settle. He had already had a dispute with Lord Zouche, for which the two were called before the Privy Council, and with the bishop of Ely, who was refusing to grant a lease at Somersham, a matter in which North had the Queen's support.[6]

North accompanied Leicester to the Netherlands in 1585, and at once began writing the usual complaints to Burghley about his 'intolerable charge'. In the following February it was reported to Leicester that 'the Lord North seemeth to be a malcontent, and hath so written to her Majesty', and information was sent to Walsingham that at Utrecht he had supported a seditious preacher. Still, he fought with gallantry at Zutphen, where he was wounded, and proved an energetic administrator at Flushing and Utrecht. Leicester was unstinting in his praise. At the end of 1586 North returned to England, but was again in the Netherlands from June to September 1587, when he came home 'scant well-pleased ... having stood in hope either of (the post of) general of the horse or governor of Flushing'. During the Armada attack he commanded part of the

Queen's bodyguard at Tilbury, and later in the year failed to persuade Burghley to secure for him the governorship of Berwick.[7]

Promotion came to North during the last few years of his life. On the death of Sir Francis Knollys* in 1596, he was made a Privy Councillor and treasurer of the Household – according to his own claim achieving great economies in the latter office. He was one of the signatories to the treaty with the Netherlands in August 1598. By this time he was suffering from deafness, and the Queen wrote out a homely remedy for him. He died at the Charterhouse 3 Dec. 1600, leaving as heir his grandson Dudley North, aged about 18, whom he had tried unsuccessfully to marry to a relative of Burghley's. The funeral service was on 22 Dec. at St. Paul's, and he was buried at Kirtling on 12 Feb. following. His will, made on 22 Oct. 1600, was proved 23 Jan. 1601. It made detailed arrangements for financial provision based on rent charges from lands for his elder surviving son Sir Henry, and for annuities and bequests totalling £1,300 to a number of grandchildren. North left £100 to the Queen, 'from whom I have received advancements to honour and many and continual favours'; plate went to his overseer (Sir) John Popham*; 'my fairest cup' and £20 to the Countess of Warwick, 'whose house I have always loved and honoured'; and £10 and a gilt cup to Sir Robert Cecil.[8]

[1] *EHR*, xxxvii. 566; *CP*, ix. 652–3; *DNB*; The generally accepted date for his marriage, 1557, is an error based on the wrong identification of Sir Henry Dudley, his wife's former husband. [2] *CP*; Somerville, *Duchy*, i. 595; SP12/59/190, SP12/93; *Cambridge Charters*, 103; *CSP For.* 1572–4, pp. 560–2; *CSP Ven.* 1558–80, pp. 520–1. [3] C142/265/75; Wards 7/10/126; *CPR*, 1558–60, p. 110; 1563–6, pp. 274, 306–8; *DNB*; *CSP Dom.* 1595–7, p. 450; Add. 1580–1625, p. 404; Lansd. 3, ff. 193 seq.; Guildford Mus., Loseley 1331/2; *Cam. Misc.* ix(3), p. 24; P. Collinson, 'Puritan Classical Movement in the Reign of Eliz. I' (London Univ. PhD thesis 1957), 657, 870, 886, 898–9, 905, 916–17, 934 n. 1, 949. [4] *CJ*, i. 64; D'Ewes, 84; *LJ*, i. 667, 703; ii. 62, 191; *CSP For.* 1572–4, pp. 560–4, 569; *CSP Ven.* 1558–60, pp. 520–2; Howell, *State Trials*, i. col. 957. [5] *APC*, xii. 233; xvii. 112; A. Gray, *Town of Cambridge*, 103–5. [6] *Archaeologia*, xix. 287–90; *DNB*; *APC*, ix. 86; *HMC Hatfield*, ii. 121; *CSP Dom.* 1547–80, p. 507. [7] *CSP For.* 1585–6, p. 328; Apr.–Dec. 1587, p. 268 et passim; *Leycester Corresp.* (Cam. Soc. xxvii), 114, 192, 411, 417; Lansd. 57, f. 112; *HMC Foljambe*, 40, 56. [8] *APC*, xxvi. 135; *CP*; Lady Frances Bushby, *Three Men of the Tudor Time*, 162; Rymer, *Foedera*, xvi. 343; *HMC Hatfield*, ii. 523; vi. 510; ix. 90; C142/265/75; Lansd. 84, f. 129; *CSP Dom.* 1598–1601, p. 501; PCC 6 Woodhall, abstracted in *Coll. Top. et Gen.* vi. 99–101.

N.M.F.

NORTON, Richard I (c.1530–92), of Rotherfield in East Tisted, Hants.

HAMPSHIRE   1571, 1572

b. c.1530, 1st s. of John Norton† of East Tisted by Anne, da. of Sir George Puttenham of Sherfield. m. (1) by 1564, Elizabeth, da. and h. of William Wayte of Wymering, Hants, 2s. inc. Richard Norton II*; (2) Catherine, da. of

Sir John Kingsmill of Sydmonton, 2s. 1da. *suc.* fa. 1561. Kntd. by 1577.[1]

J.p. Hants from c.1561, sheriff 1564–5, 1588–9; 'officer' of bp. of Winchester by July 1587.[2]

In the course of the sixteenth century the Nortons became one of the leading families in Hampshire, buying a number of estates in the vicinity of East Tisted, where they had been settled since 1308. Norton's father was twice knight of the shire during Mary's reign, and Norton himself twice represented Hampshire in Elizabeth's. So far as is known he took no noteworthy part in the business of the House, but the great activity of Thomas Norton who was also a Member in 1571 and 1572 makes it impossible to be certain.

On the death of his father, Norton entered into possession of lands his father had bequeathed to his mother over and above her jointure. These, she complained, Norton had persuaded her to assign to him when she was 'in great heaviness and sorrow for the death of her late husband' and unaware of what she was doing. Through his second wife, Norton was related to the Giffords of Kings Somborne and the Kingsmills of Sydmonton, with whom he was involved in suits and counter-suits brought in the Star Chamber about the county by-election held at Winchester in 1566, following the death of Sir John Mason*. Norton was classified in 1564 as a favourer of religion, and ten years later was one of a commission appointed to search places where it was thought the mass was still celebrated.[3]

His father had at one time been a servant of the bishop of Winchester and Norton himself held an office in the bishopric, possibly throughout his career, although there is no evidence of this before 1587. Bishop Horne appointed him an executor of his will. After the bishop's death in 1580, Norton sent two certificates to Walsingham about lands belonging to the bishopric in Hampshire and Surrey. Horne's successor, John Weston, died in January 1584 and was followed by Thomas Cooper, who wrote to Lord Burghley asking for greater authority against papists and suggesting that Norton, among others, should be included in any commission appointed for that purpose. The two men, however, did not remain on good terms. On 3 July 1587, Cooper complained to Burghley that Norton was 'of a great stomach and useth broad speech, thinking belike to make me afraid as he doth some others'. He had apparently alleged that Cooper was 'hard and covetous'. During these years, Norton also served on a large number of commissions, including those to view St. Andrews and other castles in the county, to control grain supplies and to muster trained men for service in Ireland. In 1586 he was ordered to alert soldiers for the defence of Portsmouth following rumours of a French landing in Sussex, and in 1588 he served on a commission of musters.[4]

In his will, made 3 Aug. 1586, he asked to be buried at East Tisted without any pomp. To three sons he left amounts of money, dividing between them the manors of Overton and Old Alresford, granted to him by the Queen after they had been devised to her by the bishop of Winchester. Another son, Henry, received £100, but no land. To his daughter Constance he bequeathed 1,000 marks as well as the manor of Rotherfield, which she was to enjoy until her elder half-brother, Richard, agreed to pay her a further £500 on her marriage or at the age of twenty. His wife Catherine was the sole executrix. He died a year later, 11 Mar. 1592, and was succeeded by his eldest son, Richard.[5]

[1] C142/131/184; *CPR*, 1560–3, p. 365; 1563–6, p. 274; *Vis. Hants* (Harl. Soc. lxiv), 2, 14, 17; *APC*, x. 16. [2] Lansd. 52, f. 177. [3] *VCH Hants*, iii. 9, 28, 31, 34, 39, 99, 264, 459; iv. 16, 85, 424, 630; C3/132/17; St. Ch. 4/P7/18, P30/32, W36/33, W45/38; *Cam. Misc.* ix(3), p. 55; *APC*, viii. 257–8. [4] *LP Hen. VIII*, xiv(1), p. 332; *CSP Dom.* 1547–80, p. 662; Strype, *Annals*, ii(2), 378; Lansd. 42, f. 101; 48, f. 136 seq.; 52, f. 177; *APC*, x. 16, 342, 417; xii. 223, 255; xiv. 212. [5] PCC 22 Harrington; C142/233/118.

P.H.

NORTON, Richard II (c.1552–1611), of Rotherfield in East Tisted, Hants.

PETERSFIELD   1572

b. c.1552, 1st s. of Richard Norton I* of East Tisted by his 1st w. *m.* (1) c.1576, Mabel, da. of Henry Beecher, alderman and haberdasher of London, 3s. 2da.; (2) Elizabeth, da. of Richard Capell, wid. of Humphrey Adderley of Weddington, Warws. *suc.* fa. 1592. Kntd. 1601.

J.p. Hants from c.1592, sheriff 1596–7.

Norton was the son of a well-connected country gentleman with estates in the eastern half of Hampshire, who twice represented the county in Parliament, and may have been responsible for finding his son a seat at Petersfield, where the family had a little property. Little more is known about Norton's career. On his first marriage, the manor of Nutley and lands in Preston Candover were settled on him, but the family home at East Tisted was at the same time secured to his stepmother, who lived until the year of his own death, 1611. In his undated will, Norton bequeathed his soul to Almighty God, hoping to be accepted 'among the holy company of the elect' and to be saved 'through the only merits of His dear son Jesus Christ'. He asked to be buried at East Tisted and left some lands at Alton to his second son, £700 to his youngest son, £10 to his married daughter and £2,000 to his unmarried daughter. He left £300, his livestock and half his household goods at Rotherfield to his wife and the residue to his son, Sir Richard Norton†, whom he appointed the sole executor. He died 31 Aug. 1611.

Vis. Hants (Harl. Soc. lxiv), 15; *Vis. Warws.* (Harl. Soc. xii), 263; C142/131/184, 233/118, 322/170; PCC 22 Harrington, 90 Wood.

P.H.

NORTON, Thomas (by 1532-84), of London and Sharpenhoe, Beds.

GATTON	1558
BERWICK-UPON-TWEED	1563
LONDON	1571, 1572

b. by 1532, 1st s. of Thomas Norton, grocer of London, by Elizabeth, da. of Robert Merry of Northaw, Herts. *educ.* Michaelhouse, Camb. matric. c. 1544, MA 1570; I. Temple 1555. *m.* (1) Margaret, da. of Thomas Cranmer, abp. of Canterbury, *s.p.*; (2) by 1568, Alice, da. of Edmund Cranmer, bro. of Thomas, 4s. 2da. *suc.* fa. 10 Mar. 1583.[1]

Servant of Protector Somerset by 1550; freeman, Grocers' Co. 1558; counsel to Stationers' Co. 1562; remembrancer, London 6 Feb. 1571, ?garbler of spices Mar. 1583-*d.*; commr. to examine Catholic prisoners 1578-83, for Guernsey 1579, for Sark 1583; censor for bp. of London by 1581; solicitor to Merchant Taylors' Co. 1581.[2]

Of a Bedfordshire yeoman family,[3] Norton was returned to Mary's last Parliament through the good offices of his Inner Temple friend Thomas Copley*, to whom, however, he may by 1563 have become unwilling to be indebted because of Copley's by then open Catholicism. Norton appears to have found a new patron in William, 13th Lord Grey of Wilton, warden of the east march and governor of Berwick. Grey, like Norton, had been associated with Protector Somerset. Norton's office as remembrancer of London, granted him in February 1571, accounts for his election for the city to the Parliament which met two months later.

Norton soon acquired a reputation for 'his sundry excellent speeches in Parliament, wherein he expressed himself in such sort to be a true and zealous philopater'. Contemporaries knew him as 'Master Norton, the Parliament man'. The author of an anonymous lampoon on the puritans in the 1566 session of Parliament epitomized him as 'the scold', saying that he would 'act, insist, speak, read, write, in session and out'. As early as 26 Jan. 1563 he was in action, reading to the House the committee's version of the petition to the Queen on the succession. Since the bill had been given to the comptroller of the Household, it is strange that it was Norton who reported it to the House. Perhaps his skill as a draftsman was the reason, or perhaps he and his fellow radicals were dominating the committee. Norton was also a member of the conference with the Lords on the subject, 31 Oct. 1566. The defective journals for this Parliament also record him on an unnamed committee (22 Mar. 1563), and in charge of two others on cloth (5 Apr. 1563) and benefit of clergy (24 Oct. 1566).

During the Parliament of 1571, Norton was one of the leaders of the puritan attack on the 1559 religious settlement. On 6 Apr. William Strickland* moved that Norton, 'a man neither ill-disposed to religion nor a negligent keeper of such matters of charge' should be asked to produce and explain to the House the Edwardian *Reformatio Legum Ecclesiasticarum*. As Cranmer's son-in-law, Norton owned the archbishop's original manuscript, which he had recently allowed his friend John Foxe to publish, with the permission of Archbishop Parker. Norton, 'a man wise, bold and eloquent' in the eyes of the anonymous diarist of this Parliament, expounded the provisions of the *Reformatio* to the House, and offered a copy for the consideration of Members. He was one of 25 Members immediately appointed to confer with the bishops on these matters. The following day (7 Apr.), Strickland again proposed that Norton 'might be required to deliver such books as he had' to the House. These were the six religious bills which had been debated in the previous Parliament: perhaps the fact that they were now in his possession indicates that he was the original draftsman. On 11 Apr. it was decided to confer once again with the Lords 'for the cause of religion'. Norton supported the idea of the conference, but warned the lay members 'not to stand at the direction of the bishops further than their consciences should be satisfied'. On 14 Apr. during a debate concerning licences and dispensations granted by the archbishop of Canterbury, Norton moved for the abolition of benefit of clergy.

He proved it might not be said a liberty of the church except they will claim a liberty to sin, wherein indeed their principal liberty hath stood, and for the which they have not spared to hazard, nay give their bodies and souls to become traitors to God and man. Thus did that rebel bishop, Becket, whose principal quarrel and cause of all his stir was that the King would have punished one of his mark, a priest, for an abominable incest committed by him, which trifling fault forsooth, this holy saint could not brook to be rebuked by a temporal judge ... He showed it could not be said a privilege or encouragement to learning, since it was no other but a cloak for their naughtiness, and for such as might be of the Pope's suite, as well appeared in that it was allowed to none but to such as might enter their holy orders ...

He was given authority by the House to draft a bill against benefit of clergy, which was eventually rejected by the Lords. On 20 Apr. he spoke in favour of the bill concerning church attendance, although he warned that

not only the external and outward show is to be sought but the very secrets of the heart in God's cause ... must come to a reckoning, and the good seed so sifted from the cockle that the one may be known from the other.

He wanted a proviso concerning irregularly conducted services to be added to the bill, and attended a conference with the Lords on the subject on 19 May. He was also appointed to committees concerning the bill against papal bulls (23 Apr.), a religious bill (28 Apr.), priests disguised as servants (1 May), licences and dispensations granted by the archbishop of Canterbury (4 May), and he was one of a large delegation named to take religious bills to the Lords on 5 May.

Norton's initiative over the treasons bill proved without doubt to be his major contribution to the 1571 Parliament. On 9 Apr. the bill drafted by the Queen's learned counsel had its first reading. Norton immediately voiced his opinion that the bill did not go far enough, and proposed an addition to it in the form of a bill he had already drafted himself. He declared that

> her Majesty was and is the only pillar and stay of all safety, as well for our politic quiet as for the state of religion, and for religion the very base and pillar throughout Christendom ... therefore that for preservation of her estate, our care, prayer and chief endeavour must be.

The additions he had in mind were firstly that

> whosoever in her [the Queen's] life hath done or shall make claim to the imperial crown of this realm, that he, or they, or their heirs, to be forbarred of any claim, challenge or title to be made to that crown at any time hereafter; and that every person who shall maintain that title to be accounted a traitor.

This proposal was to cause considerable embarrassment to the Queen and government, bringing, as was no doubt the intention, Mary Queen of Scots within its scope. The second proposal was that 'whosoever shall say the court of Parliament hath not authority to enact and bind the title of the Crown to be adjudged a traitor'. Norton's bill was strenuously opposed by Henry Goodere*, a follower of Mary, on 12 Apr. He made allegations of partiality clearly directed at Norton, which the latter refuted, 'in his accustomed manner of natural eloquence'.

> He protested that he neither thought nor meant any other title than the sole preservation of her Majesty, and to that end was he and the whole House (as he supposed) settled and bent ...

He defended the retrospective nature of his bill claiming that 'where ambition hath once entered, such is the nature of the same that it never will be satisfied, and the thirst for a kingdom is unquenchable'. Besides, retrospective legislation was not an innovation of his, as he showed by quoting a precedent from Mary Tudor's reign:

> And surely if in the case of a private man, as was this Bennet Smythes, such consideration and so good discretion was, who can imagine it to be odious? No, who is it that would not the like or greater care should be had for a prince and of so good a prince as she for whom our conference now is?

On the theme of partiality, he turned the tables on Goodere:

> But yet we are charged with partial affection, unsettled minds, doubleness. Whether this speech now be an offence to the House he earnestly craved the judgment of the House. For that it might seem by the gentleman's earnestness who spake that some one his friend, whom he was bent to serve, would be touched.

After this speech of 12 Apr. nothing more is known about Norton in the context of the treasons bill, until his appointment to two committees on 11 May. In the end, despite his spirited defence of his bill, the first proviso, concerning retrospective legislation, disappeared and the second was heavily amended. Perhaps Goodere was not the only Member to doubt Norton's impartiality. On 29 May the committee for examination of fees or rewards taken for voices in the House was reported, and Norton felt impelled to declare that

> he heard that some had him in suspicion, justified himself and was upon the question purged by the voice of the whole House, and their good opinion of him, and of his honest and dutiful dealing and great pains taking in the service of this House were in very good and acceptable part declared and affirmed by the like voice of the whole House.

His other activity during the 1571 Parliament included a 'somewhat long' speech on usury (19 Apr.) and his intervention in (possibly initiation of) the debate on non-resident burgesses (19 Apr.). He 'argued that the whole body of the realm and the good service of the same was rather to be respected than the private regard of place, privilege or degree of any person'. On 9 May he moved that on the remaining Mondays, Wednesdays and Fridays until the end of the session, the House should sit from 3 p.m. until 5 p.m. in order to read private bills. His committee work during this Parliament included such topics as the Bristol merchants (12 Apr.), order of business (21 Apr., 23, 26 Apr.), tellers and receivers (23 Apr., 26 May), the maintenance of navigation (8 May), conveyances (14 May), fugitives (25 May) and the river Lea (26 May).

In the 1572 Parliament Norton followed a uniquely consistent line in pressing for the execution, first of the Duke of Norfolk and secondly of Mary Queen of Scots, believing the one to be a necessary prelude to the other. On 12 May 1572 he was appointed to a conference with the Lords to consider steps to be taken in 'the great cause'. Three days later he discouraged any talk of the succession, believing that the Queen 'in good time will provide for the same'. The Commons' task was 'in the meantime to strike down the bushes which lie in the way'.

> Execution is the thing he specially moveth [reported Thomas Cromwell*] ... when he considereth the peril which is to come in sparing of execution, he is driven to put all fear aside and to utter his conscience, and since

he cannot devise how the Queen's Majesty may be assured in his [the Duke of Norfolk's] life, he thinketh it necessary she be assured in his death. All ways and means have been attempted, none left to be tried, whereby any hope may be he should ever be a good subject ... Besides the examples of immunity in this case will encourage others to new rebellions and treasons. It will also discourage the revealers if it be more perilous to disclose than to do treason ... The Scot hard to be removed without this execution. They are knit together so as while the one liveth, the faction is strong. Take the one away and weaken the other by all his friends. Mercy is good in some cases but woe worth that mercy which bringeth misery.

He was constantly urging the Commons to petition the Queen in the strongest terms for the execution of the Duke, speaking twice on the subject on 16 May and 19 May. Not surprisingly, on 17 May he wished Arthur Hall* to be brought to the bar of the House to justify his speech on Norfolk's behalf. On 21 May, fearing that Parliament's bill of attainder against Mary would come to nought, he moved that

Sithence time is to be used in trial of the Queen of Scots, and that it is determined she shall come to her trial, it will occasion her to attempt what she may, for desperate necessity dareth the uttermost mischief that can be devised: therefore necessary the Duke be executed in the mean season, which will be half the execution of the Queen of Scots.

On 23 May, news reached the Commons that the Queen had rejected the bill of attainder. Norton saw 'now no remedy but to make humble suit for execution of the Duke':

... though heretofore we did agree the resolution of the House should come to the Queen's Majesty by way of opinion that was *pro re et tempore*. Now ... execution of necessity is to be urged during the session. No hope to be had of him [the Duke]. He hath lately received communion with protestations of his faith, and yet most feigned. And therefore we to urge this importunately either jointly with the Lords or by our Speaker without them.

The extant journals give no indication of Norton's reaction to the Duke's execution on 2 June 1572. He would have seen it as but a step towards the execution of Mary, and to this he immediately turned his attention. On 6 June he complained that the Commons' current bill against Mary was not forceful enough. 'This Parliament called for matters of great necessity, and therefore not good to do nothing, much worse to do stark nought'. He recalled the fate of the treasons bill in the previous Parliament and his own additions to it. His disappointment at the failure of parliamentary legislation against Mary and a sense of resentment at the Queen's interference in the management of the House may be guessed at. He spoke

again against Mary on 7 June, 9 June and 25 June, calling always for the strongest measures to be taken against her, and was included in conferences with the Lords on the subject on 28 May and 6 June.

Other references to him during the 1572 session of the Parliament concern speeches on tellers and receivers (12 May, appointed to the committee 14 May), the vagabonds bill (20 May), the preservation of wood within 20 miles of London (21 May), the Queen's castles and ships (4 June), a privilege case (27 June) and a private bill (30 June). His committee work included topics such as a private lands bill (20 May), Tonbridge school (23 May), the continuation of statutes (26 June) and the length of kerseys (28 June).

No speeches are recorded in his name in the 1576 journals. He was, however, active in committee. He was appointed to committees concerning the avoiding of idleness (11 Feb.), recoveries (13 Feb.), ports (13 Feb.), private bills (14 Feb., 12 Mar.), coins of the realm (15 Feb.), bastardy (15 Feb.), cloth (16 Feb., 9 Mar.), leather (18 Feb.), the reciprocal treatment of aliens (24 Feb.), the county palatine of Chester (25 Feb.), letters patent (25 Feb., 3 Mar.), fraudulent conveyances made by the northern rebels (25 Feb.), haberdashers (28 Feb.), broggers and drovers (28 Feb.), the Arthur Hall privilege case (28 Feb.), church discipline (2 Mar.), aliens' children (3 Mar.), assize of wood in the city of London (3 Mar.), excess of apparel (10 Mar.), the Queen's marriage (12 Mar.), wharves and quays (13 Mar.) and London goldsmiths (13 Mar.).

Throughout his parliamentary career Norton had been actively employed in the drafting of bills. In 1581 a fellow guest at a supper party at William Grice's* house said to him, 'You have taken great pains this Parliament, and there be few of the acts which either you have not drawn, or travailed about penning them at committees'. In reply, Norton insisted that, 'all that I have done I did by commandment of the House, and specially of the Queen's Council there', but he agreed that he had also 'written many a bill of articles that the House did not see'. Norton's leading role in the drafting of the subsidy bill corroborates this story. On 25 Jan. 1581 Sir Walter Mildmay* made the customary government speech introducing the subsidy. He was followed by Norton, who proposed the setting up of a committee of the Privy Councillors, and 'certain other fit persons ... to consult of bills conveniently to be framed according to the said motion'. The committee, to which Norton was named, met that afternoon in the Exchequer chamber where 'Mr. Norton spake very well ... and did hereupon exhibit certain articles ... which were by the committees considered'. He and four lawyers were then appointed by the committee to 'set down the matters which they had there agreed, and, having digested them into articles, should exhibit them at the next meeting of the committees'. On 28 Jan. the journals report that 'the articles which were exhibited by Mr. Norton concerning the bill of subsidy were allowed by the committees, and he appointed to draw the bill accordingly'.

His other activity during this Parliament included speeches on returns (19 Jan. 1581), a public fast (21 Jan.), the clergy (27 Jan.), a legal matter (27 Jan.) and procedure (7 Feb.). He also lodged a complaint on 1 Feb. that 'two porters of Serjeant's Inn in Fleet Street have much misused him in his attending the service of this House'. Later that day the two offenders were brought before the bar of the House for breach of parliamentary privilege where Norton testified against them. He spoke in favour of the bill that aliens' children should not be counted as English on 25 Jan., and was appointed to two committees on the subject (25 Jan., 7 Feb.). He wished Arthur Hall to be brought to the bar to answer for one of his numerous breaches of privilege (4 Feb.), and was appointed to two committees concerning Hall on 6 Feb. and 8 Mar. He was also named to committees concerning the preservation of woods (28 Jan.), defeasances of the statute staple (28 Jan.), cloth (4 Feb.), seals of corporations (11 Feb.), private bills (14, 20 Feb., 9 Mar.), defence (25 Feb.), the city of Carlisle (27 Feb.), heretics (27 Feb.), the corporation of merchant adventurers (2 Mar.), fines and recoveries (10 Mar.), the Queen's safety (14 Mar.), maintenance of mariners (15, 17 Mar.) and iron mills (18 Mar.).[4]

The topics of the religious settlement and the succession dominated Norton's personal writings as they had his parliamentary speeches. He collaborated with Thomas Sackville* in the tragedy of Gorboduc, produced by the Inner Temple students before the Queen in January 1562. The plot of the play turns on the uncertainty of the succession to the Crown in default of issue of the reigning monarch and the last act is a scarcely veiled attack on Mary Stuart's title to the English throne. As the translator of Calvin's Institutes, he was thoroughly grounded in his theology, and his pamphlets against the Catholics added to his reputation as a puritan leader, within and without Parliament. He found himself in the uncomfortable position of other radicals, pleased that the Queen upheld protestantism in face of the growing Catholic danger, but opposed to much of the Elizabethan church settlement. An original prayer included in his 'Devices' to restrain popish recusants asked for a blessing upon

> me and my poor hod upon my back among the mortar bearers in the work of God, or rather among the carriers away of dung and rubbish to make room for workmen and builders, in cleansing and reparation of the house of Jesus Christ, the church of England, committed to His Solomon, our gracious Queen.[5]

There is no need to doubt Norton's sincerity in stating that he fled from 'innovations and alterations', but this was not authority's view of him. After the supper party at Grice's house already referred to, he was denounced to the Privy Council by a fellow guest for slandering the bishops.

Norton agreed that he had blamed the bishops for not reforming the ministry, and for tolerating abuses in the church, but maintained that his purpose had been to defend Elizabeth herself from slander.

> The Queen was most honourable, and did not use to dissemble with her subjects, to make to them openly a show of granting her people's petition, and under-hand to overthrow it by contrary commandments to bishops.

He admitted that he 'grew offended', and might have gone too far in the heat of argument. An opponent 'said he would complain to the bishops of me, and I bade him not to spare; and so he hath done, contra Jovem hospitalem'. No sequel to this incident is known, but it no doubt entered into the reckoning when some further indiscretions over the projected Anjou marriage (an issue on which the Queen was particularly sensitive) came up towards the end of 1581. Norton was put in the Tower, whence he bombarded his wife and his puritan friends with plans to achieve his release. His wife (15 Dec.) was to keep a note of those who visited him so that Norton might pray for them. If Sir Walter Mildmay* understood his case he would intervene with Burghley, who 'hath a gracious memory of the Cranmers to which race you and our children appertain'. 'There can no papist feel the grief for offending the Queen that I feel' (29 Dec.). His wife was to 'lay up fair' the book of martyrs for 'my good daughter Ann'. She was to lobby Mr. Vice-Chamberlain (Christopher Hatton*), (Sir) Thomas Heneage* 'and the Speaker himself ... to put my case ... at court'. The poor lady was at this time on the brink of the mental breakdown that was to end in complete insanity in 1582. To another correspondent (28 Dec.),

> When all is said and done this is true; that God sent us our Queen in His blessing. It is God that preserveth and blesseth her. It is the only religion of God that knitteth true subjects unto her ... Woe is to me wretch, that in offending her have wounded the profession of that religion.

On 6 Jan. Burghley

> knoweth what burdens of labour in the last Parliament I did bear at his and Mr. Vice-Chamberlain's commandment in hope and zeal to please her Majesty.

To Recorder [William] Fleetwood* two days later:

> Lord, how I wonder at myself that I should offend my Queen Elizabeth! And therefore no marvel though all the world wonder at me, that wonder at myself.

He was released to house arrest the next month, and in April freed altogether. He did not sit in Parliament again.[6]

An aspect of Norton's career that must be mentioned is his work as a government agent against the Catholics. For some months in 1579 and 1580 he was in Rome gathering intelligence, and between 1578 and 1583 there are numerous references to his examining Catholic prisoners in England, among them Campion and Francis Throckmorton. His frequent recommendations to the Privy Council that torture should be used earned him the harsh soubriquet of 'rackmaster-general', and on his own admission he threatened to stretch a Catholic prisoner a foot longer than God had made him. As licenser of printing in London he censored or suppressed books and pamphlets the Privy Council thought subversive. In 1582 he became involved in the disputes arising from complaints made by the workmen printers of London against printing monopolies, and he was accused in a petition to Burghley, signed by over 200 London stationers and others, of letting his position as counsel to the company prejudice his advice as city remembrancer. In fact much of Norton's time and energy was devoted to the corporation of London, and the city companies. In 1574 he wrote

> I am born a citizen and here brought up: according to my right, I have accepted my freedom, and bound myself to this city by the oath of a freeman

and many are the city officials mentioned in his correspondence from the Tower in 1581/2, Mr. Recorder, Mr. Whitacre, Mr. Sheriff Martin, Mr. [Thomas] Aldersey*, the town clerk, Mr. Wilkes, the dean of St. Paul's among them.[7]

Norton died at Sharpenhoe on 10 Mar. 1584. In a nuncupative death-bed will, he asked his brother-in-law, Thomas Cranmer, to care for the widow and their children. He was buried at Streatley. His heir, Henry, was 13.[8]

[1] DNB; C142/203/12; N. and Q. (ser. 3), iv. 480; Harl. 1234, f. 113; 1547, f. 45v; Her. and Gen. iii. 276. [2] Archaeologia, xxxvi(1), pp. 106, 115; Lansd. 33, f. 150; 48, f. 188; APC, viii. 319; xi. passim; xii. 62, 88–9, 264–5; xiii. 37, 144, 164–5; CSP Dom. 1581–90, p. 48. [3] Beds. RO, A BP/R 15, f. 52, ex inf. Miss J. Godber. [4] Archaeologia, xxxvi(1), 109–14; D'Ewes, 80, 89, 90, 127, 157, 158, 159, 162–3, 165, 167, 168, 174, 177, 178, 179, 180, 181, 182, 183, 186, 188, 189, 190, 206, 212, 214, 220, 222, 224, 244, 247, 248, 250, 251, 252, 260, 281, 282, 285, 288, 289, 290, 291, 292, 293, 294, 295, 304, 306, 307, 308; CJ, i. 63, 72, 75, 83, 84, 85, 86, 87, 88, 89, 91, 92, 93, 95, 96, 97, 99, 100, 101, 103, 104, 105, 106, 108, 109, 110, 113, 114, 115, 119, 120, 121, 122, 123, 124, 128, 129, 130, 132, 133, 134, 135, 136; Trinity, Dublin, anon. jnl. ff. 6, 8, 12, 15–16, 23, 24, 25, 33, and additions from Cott. Titus, F. 1; Trinity, Dublin, Thos. Cromwell's jnl. ff. 5, 13, 14, 15, 19, 20, 21, 25, 27, 29, 33, 36–7, 50, 53, 54, 58, 65, 67, 69. [5] E. St. John Brooks, Hatton, 36–40; Lansd. 155, ff. 87–113. [6] Lansd. 155, ff. 87–113; Archaeologia, xxxvi(1), 105–14; Neale, Parlts. i. 404–6; H. Nicolas, Hatton, 234–5, 242–3; Add. 48023. [7] HMC 2nd Rep. 40–1; APC, viii. 319; xi. xii and xiii passim; CSP Dom. 1581–90, p. 48; C. Blagden, Stationers' Co. 67–8; W. W. Greg and E. Boswell, Recs. Stationers' Co: 1576–1602, p. 14; Archaeologia, xxxvi(1), pp. 101–4. [8] C142/203/38; VCH Beds. ii. 382–3.

P.W.H.

NOWELL, Laurence (d. ?by 1583)

KNARESBOROUGH	1559

2nd s. of Alexander Nowell of Read Hall, Whalley, Lancs. by Grace, da. of Ralph Catherall of Mitton, Lancs.

Nowell's cousins, the two Elizabethan churchmen, Alexander Nowell, dean of St. Paul's, and Laurence Nowell, dean of Lichfield, were both Marian exiles, and the branch of the family to which Nowell belonged may have shared their religious beliefs. A radical alignment is further suggested by the marriage of Thomas, one of Laurence's younger brothers, to Joan, the daughter of Thomas Bowyer of London. Francis Bowyer, another member of this family, helped Dean Alexander Nowell to escape abroad in 1555. Little is known about Nowell himself during Elizabeth's reign. It is probable that he owed his seat at Knaresborough to Sir Ambrose Cave*, the chancellor of the duchy of Lancaster. His cousin Robert Nowell*, an attorney in the court of wards, mentioned him in his will, drawn up in 1563, bequeathing him an annuity of £5, as well as 'so much satin as will make him a coat and doublet'. However, early in 1568 – before the will was proved – Laurence left the country. In a court of requests case of 1572 brought against William Lambarde*, the antiquary and executor of Nowell's will, the beneficiaries under it claimed that, as Laurence had not been heard of for two years and inquiry for him had proved fruitless, the will should be proved. Lambarde's answer provides the history of Laurence's travels. Nowell had left the country early in 1568, 'endeavouring to make himself through knowledge of language and good learning abroad the more serviceable subject' to the Queen. After spending some time at the University of Paris he went to Venice and Padua, Vienna, Basle and finally Leipzig, where he arrived about August 1570, sending a letter to Lambarde that month from the house of a Leipzig burgess. Lambarde thought Nowell had not been missed for so long 'but that there remaineth hope that in time he may be revealed', but when Nowell's brother, Thomas, made his will in 1583 he did not mention him, so presumably he had died abroad.

Vis. Suss. (Harl. Soc. liii), 70; DNB (Nowell, Alexander; Nowell, Laurence); A. B. Grosart, The Spending of the Money of Robert Nowell, p. xxxi; Guildford Mus., Loseley mss 1331/2; PCC 13 Sheffelde, 44 Rowe; Req. 2/45/13.

A.M.M.

NOWELL, Robert (c.1520–69), of Gray's Inn and Hendon, Mdx.

WESTMINSTER	1547*
SALTASH	1555
WESTMINSTER	1563

b. c.1520, 4th s. of John Nowell of Read, Lancs. by his 2nd w. Elizabeth, da. of Robert Kay of Rochdale, Lancs. educ. Middleton g.s. Lancs.; Brasenose, Oxf.; G. Inn 1544. prob. unm.[1]

Eccles. commr. Canterbury, Chichester, Rochester and Winchester dioceses 1559; Autumn reader, G. Inn 1561; attorney of ct. of wards from 1561; steward to dean and chapter of St. Paul's; commr. to audit accounts in the Queen's household 1565;[2] j.p. Mdx. from 1564.

Kinsman of Andrew Noel* and his father, to whom he acted as legal adviser, Robert Nowell belonged to the senior branch of the family, which retained the older spelling of the name. A convinced protestant, like his cousins Alexander and Laurence, he had been out of favour in Mary's reign, but soon after Elizabeth's accession was found a profitable post in the court of wards by his close friend and patron, Sir William Cecil.* It was doubtless also Cecil who, as high steward of Westminster, promoted Nowell's candidature at Westminster in 1563. Nowell was described as a 'favourer' of religion in the 1564 bishops' reports.[3]

By 1563, when he made his will during an outbreak of plague, Nowell held leases of property in Hertfordshire and Cardiganshire. He made numerous bequests to various relatives and friends, including 100 marks to Cecil, (advising him, 'neither to trust too much to himself, nor to this deceitful world'), but devoted most of his fortune to charity. He died 6 Feb. 1569. Many years later his brother and executor, Dean Nowell, recounted to Burghley how Robert as he lay dying in his chamber at Gray's Inn, charged him to deal faithfully in the matter of these charities, showing particular anxiety that their own school and college should be remembered, adding 'If you would procure anything to continue with my money, you shall do it best and most surely in the Queen's Majesty's name, whose poor officer I have been'. Nowell was buried in St. Paul's, 'in the place called *sancta sanctor*', after an elaborate funeral attended by heralds, all the canons of the cathedral, and many poor men to whom gowns were distributed.[4]

[1] A. B. Grosart, *The Spending of the Money of Robert Nowell*, pp. xxxi, xxxv, xxxvi. [2] *HMC 11th Rep. III*, 94; *CPR*, 1560–3, p. 6; Grosart, xxxvi. [3] *DNB* (Nowell, Alexander); *CPR*, 1563–6, p. 342; J. Hurstfield, *Ct. of Wards*, 225; Westminster Abbey, Reg. 5, f. 18b; *Cam. Misc.* ix(3), p. 60. [4] Grosart, xxxvi, xxxvii, xliv–lii; *CSP Dom.* 1547–80, p. 431.

S.M.T.

NOWELL, see also NOEL

NUTALL, John (d. 1586), of Caton Hall, Cheshire.

TAMWORTH 1572

1st s. of Richard Nutall of Caton Hall by Alice, da. of Thomas Harleston. *educ.* I. Temple, called bef. 1572. *m.* Jane, da. of Robert Newport of Sandon, Staffs., 1s.

Nothing has been ascertained about Nutall beyond the fact that he received a grant of arms in 1581, and in 1585 wrote to Burghley about a proposed Act of Parliament 'for repealing of letters patent granted to Peter Gray', concerning concealed lands in the deanery of Chester. He died 8 Feb. 1586, being buried at Frodsham five days later.

Vis. Cheshire (Harl. Soc. xviii), 186–7; J. C. Wedgwood, *Staffs. Parl. Hist.* (Wm. Salt Arch. Soc.), i. 375; *CSP Dom.* 1581–90, p. 231.

J.J.C.

OGLE, Nicholas (c.1539–82), of Bolingbroke, Lincs.

PLYMPTON ERLE 1563

b. c.1539, 2nd s. of Richard Ogle of Pinchbeck by Beatrix, da. of John Cooke* of Gidea Hall, Essex. *educ.* Trinity Coll. Camb. 1552; I. Temple 1557. *m.* Anne, da. and coh. of John Freeman of Hagnaby, Lincs. and Collier Row, Essex.

Steward of manor of Spalding; duchy of Lancaster feodary, Lincs. from 1569.

Ogle's uncle, Sir Anthony Cooke*, was a strong protestant, one of whose daughters married Sir William Cecil*, another Sir Nicholas Bacon, and a third John Russell*, heir of the 2nd Earl of Bedford, through whose influence Ogle presumably obtained his seat at Plympton in 1563, though the marriage itself was a decade later. Ogle's sister married first John Man*, his predecessor as duchy of Lancaster feodary, and secondly Vincent Skinner*, his successor in the office. Ogle died in September 1582, his will, dated 1 Sept., being proved on the 20th. Ogle left 1s. to 'the mother church' of Lincoln, 10s. to Bolingbroke church 'for my burial', and 10s. and coal to the poor at his funeral.

Lincs. Peds. (Harl. Soc. li), 731; (lii), 992; Somerville, *Duchy*, i. 582; *Lincoln Episc. Recs.* (Cant. and York Soc. xi), 315; *DNB* (Throckmorton, Francis); H. Ogle, *Fam. Ogle and Bothal*; PCC 36 Tirwhite.

P.W.H.

OGLETHORPE, Owen (c.1542–1616), of Newington, Oxon., later Chalfont St. Giles, Bucks.

CHIPPING WYCOMBE 1589
WALLINGFORD 1597

b. c.1542, 1st s. of John Oglethorpe of Newington by Alice, da. of John Goodwin of Upper Winchendon, Bucks. *educ.* L. Inn 1562. *m.* by 1577, Jane (d. 1608), da. of Francis Conyers of Wakerley, Northants., 1s. 2da. *suc.* fa. 1579. Kntd. July 1603.

J.p. Oxon. from c.1582, sheriff 1584–5, 1595–6, commr. recusancy 1592.

Oglethorpe was the kinsman and namesake of Bishop Oglethorpe of Carlisle, whose appointment to the rectory of Newington in Henry VIII's reign had introduced his family to Oxfordshire. Soon after he had crowned Queen Elizabeth, the bishop was deprived for his Catholic views.

Oglethorpe's father remained a Catholic, was listed as a recusant and asked in his will that tapers should be carried at his funeral. Oglethorpe himself was listed as a recusant in the diocesan return for Oxford, 1577, but within three years of his father's death he conformed, and was put on the commission of the peace. In 1592 he was associated with Ralph Warcoppe*, a servant of the Knollyses with puritan sympathies, in a commission to decide a dispute between Lady Stonor, Edmund Campion's protector, and her son and guardian Francis Stonor*.

Oglethorpe resided at Chalfont St. Giles during the second half of his life, and in 1588 he and (Sir) James Marvyn* stood surety in the sum of £2,000 for one of the Catholic Dormer family. Oglethorpe's move to Buckinghamshire may have been due to his connexion with the Goodwins, who were perhaps also responsible for his return at Chipping Wycombe. Francis Goodwin was returned with him as junior burgess. At Wallingford in 1597 Oglethorpe presumably needed no patron, for Newington was only four miles away, and much of his property was part of the honour of Wallingford. His return may have been assisted, however, by the high steward of the borough, Sir Henry Norris I*, Lord Norris of Rycote, for whose favour he strove in the last years of Elizabeth's reign. In seeking Norris's attentions Oglethorpe co-operated with Dudley Carleton†, son of another of Francis Goodwin's relatives. In the Parliament of 1589 Oglethorpe was named to one committee to consider lands in the diocese of Oxford, 13 Mar. In that of 1597-8 he served on committees dealing with private arrangements relating to jointures and lands (8 Nov., 24 Jan., 7 Feb.). On 8 Nov. 1597, he was named to the committee of the bill considering obsolete obligations to provide armour and weapons; on 10 Nov. to that of a bill to regulate the government of Wantage; on 12 Jan. 1598 to the committee of the bill considering the excessive making of malt; and on 27 Jan. to the committee of a bill considering the wear and tear on highways caused by the transport of iron.

Oglethorpe's knighthood at James's coronation was the reward for his service in county offices and his cultivation of influential connexions. He spent his last illness at the London house of Thomas Cecil*, 1st Earl of Exeter, who had married the widow of Oglethorpe's friend Thomas Smith*, master of requests. Oglethorpe died there on 2 June 1616, 'leaving little or nothing … behind him, scant so much as a good name'.

Vis. Oxon. (Harl. Soc. v), 123, 125; C142/186/51; Chamberlain Letters ed. McClure, i. 276; ii. 7; Cath. Rec. Soc. xviii. 255; xxii. 111, 114; DNB (Oglethorpe, Owen); CSP Dom. 1581-90, p. 275; 1598-1601, pp. 34, 52, 409; 1603-10, p. 563; 1611-18, p. 185; HMC Hatfield, iii. 106-7; Lansd. 71, f. 170; Vis. Bucks. (Harl. Soc. lviii), 64; APC, xvi. 141; D'Ewes, 445, 553, 555, 578, 587, 589, 594; PCC 16 Bakon, 81 Cope.

A.H.

OLDSWORTH, Arnold (b. c.1561), of St. Martin's Lane, London, and Bradley in Wotton, Glos.

TREGONY	1593
CIRENCESTER	1604

b. c.1561, 1st s. of Edward Oldsworth* by Tacy, da. of Arthur Porter*. educ. under Alexander Nowell, dean of St. Paul's; Magdalen Hall, Oxf. 1578; Thavies Inn; L. Inn 1580, called, assoc. bencher 1612. m. Lucy, da. of Francis Barty of Antwerp, at least 2s. suc. fa. bef. March 1574.
Member, Antiq. Soc. by 1604; clerk of hanaper prob. by 1604, certainly by 1614; receiver of fines, King's bench 1607.

Oldsworth was a London lawyer. He was a shareholder in the Mines Royal, and in 1585 petitioned, with what success does not appear, to be made steward of the stannary court of Blackmore. About a year after Elizabeth's death, his first son, Edward, was granted the reversion of his office of clerk of the hanaper. In 1604 he acted as executor of the will of Anne, Countess of Warwick, daughter of the 2nd Earl of Bedford. This suggests that he may have been the Mr. Oldsworth mentioned as in her service from about 1595. This goes some way to explaining his return at Tregony even as late as 1593. Oldsworth died abroad, administration of the estate being granted to his son Michael 19 June 1633.

DNB (Oldisworth, Michael); Vis. Glos. (Harl. Soc. xxi), 256; PCC 38 Carew; A. Collins, Lives of the Sidneys, 44; Sidney State Pprs. i. 364, 369; ii. 64; Bristol and Glos. Arch. Soc. Trans. vi. 135; M. B. Donald, Eliz. Monopolies, 57; CSP Dom. 1581-90, p. 264; 1603-10, pp. 116, 381; PCC admon. act bk. 1633, f. 175.

N.M.F.

OLDSWORTH, Edward (d. by Mar. 1574), of Poulton, Glos.

AYLESBURY	1559*

s. of one Oldsworth of Poulton m. Tacy, da. of Arthur Porter*, at least 2s. inc. Arnold* 2da.
Escheator, Glos. 1566-7.

In the election of 1559 Aylesbury returned Arthur Porter and Thomas Crawley. Crawley died during this Parliament and Edward Oldsworth, probably already Porter's son-in-law, was returned at a by-election, presumably through Porter's influence with Sir Thomas Pakington, lord of the borough. The only reference to him in the journals is to his being granted leave of absence on 23 Feb. 1559.

Little is known of Oldsworth. He seems to have held no county offices, other than the escheatorship. He received a confirmation of his arms in 1569, and may have died soon afterwards. No will or inquisition post mortem is known. He may have shared Porter's protestant outlook: one member of the family was a Marian exile, and

Oldsworth's widow's will, made in 1573 or early 1574, proved in 1576, suggests puritanism. Arnold, the future clerk of the hanaper, was 'bequeathed' to the radical dean of St. Paul's, Alexander Nowell; Archdeacon Eaton of Gloucester was to supervise the upbringing of another son, Thomas; while the two daughters, Dorothy and Margaret, were to be brought up by Giles Codrington and Lady Arnold respectively.

CJ, i. 55; *Vis. Glos.* (Harl. Soc. xxi), 256; PCC 38 Carew; *Bristol and Glos Arch. Soc. Trans.* vi. 184.

N.M.F.

OLDSWORTH, Joseph (*b.* aft. 1561), of London and Poulton, Glos.

LICHFIELD   1597

b. aft. 1561 when his fa. Thomas Oldsworth of Poulton *m.* Margaret, da. of Richard Hardkin of Essex.
Auditor to Earl of Essex July 1597.

Oldsworth owed his return for Lichfield to his master the Earl of Essex. In July 1597 he took Burghley the accounts of Essex's fleet, and in the following month he was acting for Essex over the lease of sweet wines. In the conspiracy of February 1601 a witness reported his presence in a room at Essex House where musketeers were ready to fire. No later reference to him has been found. It has been assumed that the 'Mr. Oldsworth' who sat on committees in the 1597 Parliament was William*.

Vis. Glos. (Harl. Soc. xxi), 256; *CSP Dom.* 1595–7, p. 476; 1598–1601, p. 549; *HMC Hatfield*, vii. 350.

R.C.G.

OLDSWORTH, William (*d.* 1603), of Gloucester.

GLOUCESTER   1597, 1601

educ. L. Inn 1564, called 1573. *m.*, at least 1s.[1]
Bencher, L. Inn 1584, Autumn reader 1586, Lent reader 1596; recorder, Gloucester from Nov. 1587; justice of Carm. circuit 1592; j.p. Glos. from 1577, q. by 1583; j.p. Carm., Card., Pemb. from 1592; member, council in the marches of Wales and justice of great sessions in Pemb. 1601.[2]

Richard Pate*, from whom Oldsworth had presumably bought the office, wished Oldsworth to succeed him as recorder in 1586, but in spite of pressure from the Privy Council (acting through Giles Brydges*, 3rd Baron Chandos, the justices of assize and the two chief justices), the mayor of Gloucester, Luke Garnons*, refused to allow an election to be held and Oldsworth had to wait for the office until the end of Garnons' term of office as mayor in November 1587. Even after Oldsworth had been appointed, he was not returned to Parliament until 1597, and then his election was unsuccessfully challenged by Thomas Atkins*, the town clerk, on the ground that it had

been rigged by the mayor. Oldsworth was named to committees considering the local government of Wantage (10 Nov. 1597), monopolies (10 Nov.), bridges in Monmouthshire (29 Nov.) and Herefordshire (13 Jan. 1598), tillage (13 Dec.), herrings (20 Jan.), law reform (3 Feb.), privileges and returns (31 Oct. 1601) and the penal laws (2 Nov. 1601). In 1597 the burgesses for Gloucester were appointed to committees concerning forestallers (7 Nov., 8 Dec.), maltsters (9 Nov., 12 Jan. 1598) and the city of Bristol (28 Nov.).[3]

In 1575 Oldsworth is mentioned as one of the two patrons of the rectory of Brockworth, Gloucestershire. He was one of the witnesses to Richard Pate's will, and with two others was to make an inventory of his goods. The will remitted half of £20 which Oldsworth owed to Pate. Oldsworth died intestate in April 1603, and administration was granted to his son Robert.[4]

[1] *L. Inn Black Bk.* i. 434, 458; PCC admon. act bk. 1603, f. 156. [2] *APC*, xv. 291–2; xvi. 75; T. D. Fosbrooke, *Glos.* 211; C181/1; Cardiff Lib. ms 4/609, ex inf. P. H. Williams; P. H. Williams, *Council in the Marches of Wales*, 353. [3] *L. Inn Black Bk.* i. 386, 434, 440; ii. 17, 22, 28, 30, 38, 42, 50, 52, 57; Neale, *Commons*, 276–81; St. Ch. 5/A1/5, 10/6, 20/11, 49/5; *APC*, xiv. 321–2; xv. 17, 136, 291, 292; xvi. 75; D'Ewes, 552, 554, 555, 565, 569, 572, 578, 579, 584, 592, 622. [4] *Bristol and Glos. Arch. Soc. Trans.* vii. 169; lvi. 219–225; W. R. Williams, *Welsh Judges*, 165; PCC admon. act bk. 1603, f. 156.

N.M.F.

ONLEY, Edward (1522–82), of Catesby, Northants.

BRACKLEY   1563*[1]

b. 1522, 3rd but 1st surv. s. of John Onley† of London and Catesby by his 1st w. Jane, da. of (?Henry) Smith of Sherborne, Warws.; bro. of Thomas*. *m.* Catherine, da. of Thomas Catesby of Whiston, 3s. 3da. *suc.* fa. 22 Nov. 1537.
Escheator, Northants. Jan-Dec. 1565, sheriff 1574–5, j.p. from c.1573.

Onley and his younger brother Thomas were brought up in the household of their uncle George Cotton, whose nephew Richard† married their sister. In 1561 the 3rd Earl of Derby allied himself to the two families by marrying as his third wife Mary (or Margaret) Cotton, Edward Onley's cousin. The union was not a success. A dispute over the marriage settlement developed, Mary turned to her relatives for aid, and for the next 12 years Edward Onley supported his cousin. By 1574, when an agreement between the Countess and her stepson, the new Earl, was reached through the mediation of the Earl of Leicester, Edward and Thomas Onley acting as 'especial dealers' on her behalf, Edward claimed that he had incurred debts of £3,000 for his cousin. With this dispute dividing the two families, it cannot be assumed that it was the Earl of Derby who supported Edward Onley's candidature at Brackley at the by-election for the 1566 session. It is likely, however, that at this time Lady Derby had influence in the borough, which formed part of the dower that the Earl had intended to settle on her. She no doubt supported her cousin, and this combined with his own local influence was enough to secure his return.

The settlement of 1574 only heralded a further period of litigation. The Countess had promised to compensate Onley when she had reached an agreement with her husband's family, and in fact refused to come to terms with her stepson until he agreed to grant a 40-year lease of the manors of Brackley and Holborn to Edward Onley. Shortly afterwards, however – possibly at the time she married the Earl of Kent – she changed her mind. The leases had already been made out, but in order to prevent Onley taking possession, she procrastinated and the suit was still in being at Onley's death on 15 June 1582, after which it was continued by his executors to the financial hardship of the family.

Onley's will, made on 4 June 1582 and proved on 6 Aug. following, contains a long religious preamble. His heir was still a minor, and the widow was to receive the household goods, most of the livestock, and was to regulate the daughters' portions, each receiving at least £400. The servants were bequeathed small sums, and the poor of Northampton, and three other Northamptonshire parishes were left a total of £2 10s.[2]

[1] Folger V. b. 298. [2] Cat. Lib. Maj. J. R. Abbey (Sotheby and Co., 1 Dec. 1970), 30–2; Vis. Northants. ed. Metcalfe, 38–9, 121–2; PCC 17 Dyngeley, 33 Tirwhite; CP; Northants. RO, Ellesmere mss; C142/196/30.

A.M.M.

ONLEY, Thomas (1523–89), of London and Charwelton, Northants.

BRACKLEY   1554 (Apr.), 1554 (Nov.), 1572

b. 24 Nov. 1523, 4th but 2nd surv. s. of John Onley† of London and Catesby by his 1st w.; bro. of Edward*. educ. I. Temple 1550. m. by 15 Jan. 1559, Jane, da. and coh. of one Rigges of Cumberworth, Lincs., wid. of Julian Morgan of Ilford, Essex, 1s. 3da.[1]

Onley, who held a lease of pastures in Catesby from his brother Edward, married an heiress and secured the wardship of his stepson. Through their close relatives the Cottons of Combermere he and his brother were probably already acquainted with the 3rd Earl of Derby before 1561 when Derby married their cousin as his third wife. When the marriage broke down the Countess turned for help to the Onleys, to whom the wardship of her brother George had recently been committed. Thomas Onley travelled north to bring the lady home, and during the next 12 years he and his brother supported the Countess (whose husband died in 1572), claiming to have incurred debts of over £3,000 on her behalf. Thus it is curious to find Onley in 1572 returned for the third time for the Earl of Derby's borough of Brackley. The Earl,

however, was neglecting his patronage in the borough at this period, while the Countess was endeavouring to acquire it as part of her dower. In any case local influence would probably have sufficed to obtain Onley's election. He was named to committees on wool (13 Feb. 1581) and navigation (15 Mar. 1581). He acted as collector of part of the subsidy granted by that Parliament.[2]

The Derby settlement of 1574 was to be the cause of a further 15 years' litigation, carried on by Edward Onley, on whose death Thomas Onley, as executor and the guardian of his children, revived the suit and, with the advice of men such as Yelverton and Pickering, pressed it with vigour. It was apparently nearing a favourable conclusion when he addressed his last surviving letter on the subject in 1588. Onley evidently died early in 1589. A letter of condolence from a nephew to his son, dated 27 Feb. 1589, ends, 'I am very well contented, for that it was also my father's desire as well as his own, that he should lie by him in Catesby church'.[3]

[1] Cat. Lib. Maj. J. R. Abbey (Sotheby and Co., 1 Dec. 1970), 30–2; Baker, Northants. i. 287; Vis. Northants. ed. Metcalfe, 38–9, 121; Bridges, Northants. i. 35. [2] C142/196/30; CPR, 1558–60, pp. 175, 347; 1560–3, p. 333; Wards Pleadings, 14; PCC 17 Dyngeley; Vis. Northants. ed. Metcalfe; CP, iv. 210; Add. Ch. 89968(6); CJ, i. 125, 134. [3] Northants. RO, Ellesmere mss; SP15/34/58, f. 196.

S.M.T.

ONSLOW, Richard (1527/28–71), of Blackfriars, London.

STEYNING	1558
ALDBOROUGH	1559
STEYNING	1563

b. 1527/28, yr. s. of Roger Onslow of Shrewsbury, Salop by his 1st w. Margaret, da. of Thomas Poyner of Salop. educ. I. Temple, adm. 1545. m. 7 Aug. 1559, Catherine, da. and coh. of William Harding of Knowle in Cranleigh, Surr., 2s. 5da.[1]

Bencher, I. Temple 1559, Autumn reader 1562, gov. 1564–6.

Member, council in the marches of Wales by 1560–d.; clerk of council, duchy of Lancaster 1561–d.; eccles. commr. 1562; j.p.q. Salop from 1562, Mdx. 1564; recorder, London by 13 June 1563–June 1566; solicitor-gen. 27 June 1566–Mar. 1569; attorney, ct. of wards from 12 Mar. 1569.[2]

Speaker of House of Commons 1566.

The Onslows had been in Shropshire since the thirteenth century and were connected with the Corbets, Devereux and Dudleys. As the younger son of a younger son Onslow had to make his own way, and an admission was arranged for him at the Inner Temple, from which body he was expelled, with seven others, for making an affray in 1556. After a period in the Fleet and an apology, the malefactors were pardoned and re-admitted. Onslow was 'lord chancellor' at the Inner Temple Christmas festivities of 1562–3, presided over by Sir Robert Dudley*, and it may have been on this occasion that he was first noticed by the Queen. By this time he had already given one reading (a second was excused in 1566 as he was Speaker) and had begun to practise in the duchy of Lancaster court. He had also sat twice in Parliament, once for Steyning at the end of Mary's reign, and in 1559 for Aldborough, presumably on the nomination of Sir Ambrose Cave*, chancellor of the duchy of Lancaster, who appointed him an overseer of his will.[3]

In 1563 he was again returned to Parliament for Steyning, no doubt through one of his Inner Temple connexions. Surprisingly for an up and coming lawyer, Onslow, as far as is known, made no speeches and was appointed to no committees in the 1563 session. Though the journals are defective, the complete absence of his name creates a doubt as to whether he was present, but there is no evidence that he was not. Onslow was made recorder of London after the end of the session, and was expected to represent the City in Parliament, in accordance with custom. Two of the later Crown Office lists for this Parliament actually give his name as one of the London Members. However, Onslow resigned the recordership, on becoming solicitor-general, before the 1566 session of Parliament began. As solicitor-general his proper place was in the Lords, with a writ of assistance. Such a writ was issued (possibly the fact that he was MP for Steyning was overlooked), but when Speaker Williams died and the government wished Onslow to succeed him he reappeared in the Lower House, still MP for Steyning. On the motion of the comptroller of the Household, the Commons went through the form of asking the Lords to restore Onslow to their House, and he was duly nominated Speaker. Normally the disabling speech made by a Speaker-elect on his nomination was purely formal, but Onslow himself raised the substantial objection that his oath as solicitor-general was incompatible with the office of Speaker and his election was agreed to only after a division 82 for, 70 against. A division on the election of a Speaker was rare, so rare that the Spanish ambassador mistakenly took it to mean that two candidates had been nominated. When on the next day Onslow was formally presented to the Queen as Speaker-elect, he again mentioned the difficulty arising from his office.

Much ink has been expended in describing the difficult session of 1566 over which Onslow presided, with the Queen and Commons at odds over the marriage and the succession, and a vocal element insisting on debating religion instead of government business. Though his own inclinations may have been towards the puritans, Onslow kept control, warning James Dalton*, for example, not to offend the Queen by raising the matter of James VI's title to the English crown, and preventing extremists getting control of the delegation which saw Elizabeth about her marriage and the succession. At the closing of Parliament on 2 Jan. 1567 he made 'an excellent oration of two hours long', deriding the Pope while eulogising hereditary as opposed to elective monarchy, and supporting the puritans by declaring that a sovereign's duty towards the church was to put away 'all hurtful or unprofitable ceremonies in any wise contrary to God's word'. The common law of England was 'grounded on God's laws and nature'. The sovereign's prerogative was limited:

> Although thereby for the Prince is provided many princely prerogatives and royalties, yet is it not such as the Prince can take money or other things or do as he will at his own pleasure without order.

The Queen's promise to marry was noted:

> God grant, as your Majesty hath defended the faith of Abraham, you may have the like desire of issue with him, and for that purpose that you would most shortly embrace the holy state of matrimony.

All in all not a subservient speech for a man whose future depended on government patronage. The Queen replied, in the words of the journal, 'in a most excellent phrase of speech and sentence that she seemed not pleased with the doings of the Commons, for busying themselves, in this session, with matters which did not appertain at this time'. For all that, Onslow's outspokenness did him no damage. He was given the lucrative attorneyship of the court of wards a year or two later and sat on many *ad hoc* commissions, from inquiring into crimes committed within the 'verge of the Household' to mustering and viewing horses in Middlesex. It is unlikely that he had much time for his duties as a Shropshire justice of the peace, or as a member of the council in the marches of Wales, but it was while visiting his uncle Humphrey at Shrewsbury, perhaps after a visit to the council headquarters at Ludlow, that he caught a 'pestilential fever' and died within a week, on 2 Apr. 1571, aged only 43 or 44. Perhaps he knew of an outbreak of plague. At any rate he had made his long and complex will, when in good health, on 20 Mar., wishing to settle his affairs so that if he should be visited by mortal sickness

> my whole heart and mind may be occupied and employed in godly and heavenly things touching mine earnest repentance of my former sinful life and my spiritual comfort and consolation in my God by His merciful promises of forgiveness of my sins and free gift unto me of everlasting inheritance in heaven through the precious death and bloodshedding of Jesus Christ, mine only Saviour and Redeemer.

He appointed his 'entirely beloved wife' executrix (she afterwards married Richard Browne I*), as the elder son Robert was only ten. Kinsmen and servants were to receive black gowns, and all who had been in his employment for a year, a year's wages. The Earl of Leicester (to whom he was 'most bounden') and Lord Burghley (his 'especial good lord') were respectively to have 'my best standing cup with a cover' and a gilt bowl. Peter Osborne*, John Marshe* and William Leighton were the overseers. Probate was granted on 25 Apr. 1571. Onslow was buried at St. Chad's, Shrewsbury on 7 Apr., his body being brought from Harnage, some miles outside the town, where he had been lying ill. An inscription on his 'fair raised tomb' gives the dates of his life and offices, and describes him as of good stature, agreeable mien, and grave voice. In 1742 Arthur Onslow, one of the two later Speakers of the House of Commons in the Onslow family, had the monument repaired.

Only scattered references to Onslow's private and domestic life survive. His wife's father had died in 1549, when she was only a child, and Onslow presumably came into possession of her property in 1561, at which date she and her elder sister, already a widow, received livery of their lands. He also managed his sister-in-law's share of the estates, and he was one of the feoffees appointed in 1562 for assurance of the jointure of Lady Mary Sidney, Sir Robert Dudley's sister. Onslow's own landed property was not extensive. In addition to his Blackfriars house he owned a little land in Buckinghamshire, and a year before his death leased the chapel of St. Nicholas, Shrewsbury. Some years earlier he had received a royal grant, in fee simple, of the 'site of the late castle of Shrewsbury', and he bought property at Much Wenlock and elsewhere in Shropshire from John Dudley. Onslow's heir, Robert, died unmarried, and the family was continued by the other son, Sir Edward, who married Isabel, daughter of (Sir) Thomas Shirley I*, of Wiston, Sussex, and was the ancestor of the earls of Onslow.[4]

[1] *Vis. Salop* (Harl. Soc. xxix), 379 and *Vis. Surr.* (Harl. Soc. xliii), 154, where he is given as 1st s. of Roger, and his father-in-law is called Richard Harding; Manning and Bray, *Surr.* i. 537 seq.; *CPR, 1560-3*, pp. 52, 117. [2] *CJ*, i. 50, 73; *Trans. Salop Arch. Soc.* (ser. 1), iii. 269-70; *Masters of Bench of I. Temple*, 10; *Cal. I.T. Recs.* i. 139, 201, 221, 233, 236 et passim; *HMC De L'Isle and Dudley*, i. 323; Somerville, *Duchy*, i. 320 n. 3, 333, 414-15; *CPR, 1560-3*, pp. 279, 523; *1563-6*, p. 474; *1566-9*, pp. 395, 396; *Cam. Misc.* ix(3), p. 60; H. E. Bell, *Ct. of Wards and Liveries*, 22-3. [3] *Surr. Arch. Colls.* xxxix. 65-7; *Cal. I.T. Recs.* i. 139, 186-7; J. A. Manning, *Lives of the Speakers*, 230; PCC 9 Daper. [4] C193/32/6, 7; *HMC 7th Rep.* 621b; *CSP Span.* 1558-67, p. 583; A. B. Beaven, *Aldermen*, i. 275, 289; *CJ*, i. 72, 73, 76, 78, 81; D'Ewes, 96-8, 121, 135; Neale, *Parlts.* i. 145, 153, 157, 159, 171; P. Laundy, *Office of Speaker*, 169-71, 454; *HMC 14th Rep.* IX, 473-6; *CSP Dom.* 1547-80, p. 255; H. Owen and J. B. Blakeway, *Hist. Shrewsbury*, ii. 167; *Trans. Salop Arch. Soc.* iii. 269-70; Wards 7/5/16, 42; 7/13/131; *CPR, 1558-60*, p. 406; *1560-3*, pp. 52, 117, 224, 404, 417; *1563-6*, p. 274; *1566-9*, p. 392; PCC 14 Holney; *HMC 15th Rep.* X, 16, 17; C. E. Vulliamy, *Onslow Fam.* 3-7; *Suss. N. and Q.* ix. 104; Manning, 234-5.

P.W.H.

ONSLOW, William (d. c.1612), of St. Bartholomew's by the Exchange, London.

ST. MAWES	1584
PENRYN	1586

4th s. of Edward Onslow of Onslow, Salop by Anne, da.

and h. of Richard Houghton. *m.* (1) a da. of one Kynaston; (2) Elizabeth, da. of Thomas Saunders of Uxbridge, Mdx., sis. of Nicholas Saunders*, ?2s.

Attorney in common pleas by 1600.

Onslow established himself in London as a minor legal official. He was presumably returned at both St. Mawes and Penryn through the influence of his brother-in-law and London neighbour, William Killigrew*. On 15 Feb. 1587 he was appointed to deputize as clerk of the Commons during the illness of Fulk Onslow, who, on another occasion complained that William Onslow had attempted to withhold a lease assigned to him in trust. Late in 1598 William Onslow was called before the Privy Council for not paying £200 required of him for a government loan, and two years later a contribution from him was again overdue.

He probably died in 1612. His will, dated 19 Jan. 1609, and confirmed by him on 24 July of the following year, was proved 5 Jan. 1613.

Vis. Salop (Harl. Soc. xxix), 379; J. Maclean, *Trigg Minor*, iii. 398; *Vis. London* (Harl. Soc. i), 153; D'Ewes, 407; *APC*, xxix. 367; xxx. 30, 308, 605; PCC 56 Montague, 6 Capell.

W.J.J.

ORENGE, James (d. 1626), of Marston Bigott, Som.[1]

POOLE	1593, 1597

2nd s. of William Orenge of Mells by his w., the da. of one Cleeve. *educ.* M. Temple 1567. *m.* Joan Somerfield of Shaftesbury, wid. of William Hunton of Wilts., at least 1s.

Sec. to the ld. chancellor Thomas Bromley* (1580s) and the ld. keeper John Puckering* (1590s).

Orenge probably came to be returned for Poole through the influence of his uncle Thomas Hannam*. His job close to the fountain head of patronage brought him a vast correspondence from people asking for their suits to be favoured. Even the Middle Temple thought it wise 'in consequence of his kindness' to excuse him from 'all pensions and vacations'.

Only one mention of Orenge in Somerset has been found during the Elizabethan period: his witnessing of a document in 1595. He had a house at Marston Bigott, and bought the manor of Forscote from (Sir) Henry Berkeley II* in 1601. He had a nephew who wrote from Salisbury to thank him for obtaining him a post as schoolmaster, and a cousin who was a clothier of Mells. Orenge died 7 Aug. 1626, leaving a son Edward aged over 30.[2]

[1] This biography is based upon the Roberts thesis. [2] *Vis. Som.* (Harl. Soc. xi), 81; J. Collinson, *Som.* iii. 350; *M.T. Mins.* i. 163, 235, 268, 293, 367; *Cal. Proc. Chanc. Q. Eliz.* iii. 90; Harl. 286, ff. 230, 234, 236, 241; *Dorset Nat. Hist. and Arch. Soc. Procs.* lxix. 78; *Som. Wills*, i. 32, 94-5; C142/422/7.

P.W.H.

OSBALDESTON, Geoffrey (1558–aft. 1628), of London and Ireland.

NEWTON 1597[1]

b. 1558, 3rd s. of Edward Osbaldeston of Osbaldeston, Lancs. by Maud, da. of Sir Thomas Halsall; bro. of John*. *educ.* St. Mary Hall, Oxf. 1575; G. Inn 1577, called 1595. *m.* Louisa or Lucy, da. of John Warren of Poynton, Cheshire, 2s. 1da.

Justice of King's bench [I] 1605–7, c.j. of Connaught 1607 – at least 1628.

Osbaldeston was a lawyer from an old Lancashire family, related to the Stanleys, earls of Derby. He presumably owed his return at Newton to Thomas Langton*, who was himself related to the Stanleys through his second marriage. Twice in 1601 Lady Derby canvassed Robert Cecil* on Osbaldeston's behalf, first asking for a general recommendation to the lord deputy in Ireland. Then, the office of Queen's serjeant-at-law in Ireland, which Cecil had suggested for him, having gone to another, she asked for him to be given the chief justiceship in Connaught. Six years later, when he was appointed to this office, it came as a demotion, Osbaldeston having been found inefficient as a judge of the King's bench in Ireland.[2]

[1] Folger, V. b. 298. [2] *Al. Ox.* i(3), 1093; Baines, *Lancs.* iv. facing p. 56; F. Elrington Ball, *Judges in Ireland*, i. 241, 315; *CSP Ire.* 1625–32, p. 89; *HMC Hatfield*, xi. 247, 354.

A.M.M.

OSBALDESTON, John (c.1555–1603), of Osbaldeston, Lancs.

CLITHEROE 1601

b. c.1555, 1st s. of Edward Osbaldeston and bro. of Geoffrey*. *m.* bef. 1573, Ellen, da. and coh. of John Bradley of Bradley Hall, Chipping. 5s. 3da. *suc.* fa. 7 Sept. 1590.

Osbaldeston was one of the few Clitheroe MPs to owe his return to his own local standing. What little is known about him suggests that he was a country gentleman, farming the land he inherited from his father, whose will bequeathed him farming equipment, armour, weapons, plate, and the glass casements and wainscoting of Osbaldeston Hall. Both father and son carried out additions and improvements to the house, and the wainscoting mentioned in Edward's will is still considered a fine example of its kind. There is no mention of Osbaldeston's own religion, but his father was one of the most obstinate recusants in the county, and the private chapel at Osbaldeston Hall was served by a priest. Other members of the family were also Catholics, including a cousin Edward, who was a priest executed in 1594. Osbaldeston died in 1603 and was buried on 30 Nov. in Blackburn church.

Vis. Lancs. (Chetham Soc. lxxxii), 84; Abram, *Blackburn*, 603, 604; *Lancs. and Cheshire Wills* (Chetham Soc. li), 74–7; Baines, *Lancs* ed. Croston, iv. 56; *VCH Lancs.* iv. 322; Gillow, *Burghley's Map of Lancs.* 20; G. Anstruther, *Seminary Priests*, i. 261.

N.M.S.

OSBORNE, Christopher (*d.* 1600), of Grey Friars, London, and North Fambridge, Essex.

HELSTON 1589

2nd s. of Peter Osborne* and bro. of John*. *educ.* Eton c.1571; King's, Camb. 1575, fellow 1578. *m.* 1590, Joan, da. of Humphrey Moseley*, 1s.

Clerk in the office of the ld. treasurer's remembrancer in the Exchequer; attorney of duchy of Lancaster in the Exchequer 1579–93.

Osborne inherited two offices in the Exchequer, which must have provided him with the greater part of his income until 1591, when the Queen granted him the manor of North Fambridge, adjacent to his father's property in South Fambridge, part of which had been settled upon him at his marriage the year before. He no doubt owed his seat at Helston to his own and his father's patron, Lord Burghley. In 1589 all three Osbornes were in the House, and it is therefore impossible to apportion their activity with any confidence. What there is appears under Peter Osborne.

Osborne died in 1600, in 'strong hope of a joyful resurrection'. He left money and tokens of remembrance to his brothers and sisters, and a piece of gilt plate 'in fashion like a cluster of grapes' to his mother. His only child, John, was to have £100 at 20 and £200 at 21; by a codicil this was increased by a further £100. John was also to receive a Bible, 'printed at Antwerp at the King of Spain's charge', and other books. The issues and revenues of all his lands were left to his wife. Osborne made his brother Henry his heir in several lawsuits, to prosecute them and receive the profits he expected from them, and he asked his clerks to bring his Exchequer accounts up to date, for which they would receive double their usual fees.

Lansd. 106, f. 1; Somerville, *Duchy*, i. 459; *DNB* (Osborne, Peter); T. Wright, *Essex*, ii. 672; C142/249/59, 262/124; *London IPMs* (Brit. Rec. Soc., Index Lib. xxxvi), 245–9, 272–5; PCC 18 Wallop; *HMC Hatfield*, x. 112.

I.C.

OSBORNE, Sir Edward (?1530–92), of St. Dionis Backchurch, London.

LONDON 1586

b. ?1530, 1st s. of Richard Osborne of Ashford, Kent by Jane, da. of John or Richard Broughton of Broughton, Cumb. *educ.* travelled abroad 1554–62. *m.* (1) 1562, Anne (*d.* 1585), da. and h. of Sir William Hewett of London, 2s. 3da.; (2) 15 Sept. 1588, Margaret Chapman of St. Olave's, Southwark, *s.p. suc.* fa. 1584. Kntd. 2 Feb. 1584.

Alderman, London 1573, sheriff 1575–6, ld. mayor 1583–4; gov. Levant Co. 1581; treasurer, St. Thomas's hosp. 1571–3, pres. 1586–*d.*; surveyor gen. of London hospitals 1590–2.

The son of a minor country gentleman, Osborne was apprenticed to a leading London merchant whose only child he rescued from drowning when a careless nurse allowed her to fall into the Thames from her father's house on London Bridge. When she was of marriageable age her father contracted her to Osborne, although she had many suitors of superior status, and at Hewett's death in 1567, Osborne came into possession of his estates in Yorkshire and London. At the end of his apprenticeship in 1554, Osborne was made free of the Clothworkers' Company, travelled abroad, and became a merchant and financial agent. He was assessed for the 1589 subsidy at £250 and was himself one of the subsidy commissioners. His principal export was cloth, and in the early part of his life his main trading interests were with Spain and Portugal, though he also exported cloth to the Baltic and was concerned in re-establishing English trade with the Levant. In 1575 he and Richard Staper despatched agents to Turkey at their own expense, as a preliminary to the signing of a treaty, granting trading privileges to English merchants. The charter of the Levant Company – granted in 1581 – recognised their pioneering work, and Osborne, 'as the principal setter forth and doer in the opening and putting to use' of the Levant trade, was made governor of the Company then and when it was granted a second charter in 1592. Another example of his enterprise may be found in the expedition of Ralph Fitch to India in 1583, which he and Staper helped to finance.

Osborne was frequently appointed by the Privy Council to act as arbitrator in commercial disputes. In 1576, for example, he had to deal with an insurance matter, 'the case so strange as requireth the advice and consultation of such as be experienced in these kind of dealings'. Three years later he was among those instructed to investigate the closure of a mineral works recently started by a German in the north of England, and the possibility of raising the capital to re-open it. Later in 1579 he arbitrated between the clothiers, and the artificers and weavers of Taunton.

Osborne's own commercial career was not without blemish. In 1576 William Villiers, a London merchant, complained to the Privy Council that he had paid insurance of 100 nobles due on a cargo belonging to Osborne and Staper that had been taken by the Portuguese. To indemnify themselves they had subsequently impounded the goods of certain Portuguese merchants in England, but had refused to repay the money. In a dispute with two poor men, John and Thomas Castlyn, Osborne and Staper were believed by the Council to have lengthened the suit unnecessarily. In a letter to the Admiralty judges in 1592 the Council wrote,

'We do understand that the said Sir Edward Osborne and Staper have gone about to weary the said poor men' and ordered the judges to settle the dispute arbitrarily. Sir Edward sat in only one Parliament, as the senior Member for London, and the only known record of his activities in the House is the addition of his name, at the last minute, to the large committee to attend the Queen, 11 Nov. 1586, to present reasons for executing Mary Queen of Scots. He died intestate on 4 Feb. 1592, and was buried on 15 Feb. in St. Dionis Backchurch in London. His heir was Hewett Osborne, his son by his first wife. His widow soon after his death married Robert Clarke of Pleshey, Essex, a baron of the Exchequer.

DNB; *Vis. London* (Harl. Soc. cix, cx), 82, 161; R. E. C. Waters, *Gen. Mems. Chester of Chicheley*, i. 237; *Reg. St. Dionis Backchurch* (Harl. Soc. Regs. iii), 6, 11, 198, 201; A. B. Beaven, *Aldermen of London*, i. 82; ii. 39; A. C. Wood, *Hist. Levant Co.* 7, 8, 17; Lansd. 29, f. 125; Hakluyt, *Voyages* (1903–5), v. 192, 195, 465; vi. 73 seq.; *CSP Dom.* 1591–4, p. 59; *APC*, ix. 90, 118; xi. 58, 168; xxiii. 33–4; D'Ewes, 399.

A.M.M.

OSBORNE, John (?1549–1628), of Ivy Lane, London and Chicksands, Beds.

WESTMINSTER	1572*
NEWPORT IUXTA LAUNCESTON	1586
BRAMBER	1589
PENRYN	1593
DARTMOUTH	1597[1]
ST. GERMANS	1601

b. ?1549,[2] 1st s. of Peter Osborne* and bro. of Christopher*. *educ.* Eton, King's scholar 1565; King's, Camb. 1568, BA 1573, fellow 1571–4; L. Inn 1574. *m.* Dorothy, da. of Richard Barlee of Easingham Hall, Essex, lady of privy chamber to Anne of Denmark, 5s. 1da. *suc.* fa. 1592. Kntd. 1619.

Auditor of the Exchequer by 15 Mar. 1571, ld. treasurer's remembrancer from 1592; commr. for the navy and household 1618.

J.p. Beds. from c.1591.[3]

Osborne inherited his father's Bedfordshire lands and his Exchequer office, the reversion of which had been obtained for him in December 1577 or January 1578 by Lord Burghley. This office remained in the possession of the Osbornes until 1698.[4]

It was probably through Burghley that Osborne obtained his earlier parliamentary seats. Burghley was high steward of Westminster, for which Osborne sat in 1576, and would have been able to bring him in for Newport in 1586 and for Penryn in 1593. Seats had been obtained for Exchequer officials there in 1571 and 1572, perhaps through Burghley's relatives, the Killigrews. It is not clear how Osborne secured a seat at Bramber in 1588. Presumably Burghley was again responsible, perhaps through Lord Buckhurst. At Dartmouth and St. Germans, Osborne probably owed his returns to Robert Cecil, to whom, after Burghley's death, he transferred his allegiance. It is assumed that the Mr. Osborne who sat on committees in the 1572, 1586 and 1589 Parliaments was Peter. No record has been found of any activity that can certainly be attributed to John. In July 1598 the Earl of Essex referred to Osborne as 'my good friend', but Osborne avoided compromising himself with that rash nobleman. In the debate on the Exchequer bill (21 Nov. 1601), the question arose whether the clerks of Mr. Osborne's office should be heard before the commitment. It was decided that the bill should be committed first, and that the clerk's counsel should be heard later.[5]

One of Osborne's duties as an Exchequer official was the collection of debts. In 1593 he was responsible for distraining the manor of Wanstead in satisfaction of the Earl of Leicester's debts to the Crown, and the debts of (Sir) Thomas Shirley I* occupied him intermittently between 1597 and 1624 when final payments were completed. In 1598 he wrote for the Queen a 'book' of some dozen folios on the 'state of the revenue' and 'what means I could think of to make any mass of money for your highness'. During James I's reign his duties included managing the sequestrated lands of recusants and it was to him that Salisbury wrote in 1608 to implement a grant of 'the benefit of four recusants' to one of his servants.[6]

In 1618 Osborne was appointed to a commission to investigate the state of the navy, under the chairmanship of his relative by marriage, Lionel Cranfield†. Osborne's experience in dealing with recusants' lands may have suggested the proposal that part of the money for the new ships be raised by greater severity in exacting recusancy fines north of the Trent. His work on the commission was rewarded with a knighthood in 1619. By the beginning of 1627 he was in poor health, being excused from acting as a commissioner for the loan in Bedfordshire because he 'has lately been visited with gout and cannot travel'. He had already made his will in the belief that at the age of 77 he must be prepared for imminent death. He died 2 Nov. 1628, and was buried in Campton church, Bedfordshire.[7]

[1] Folger V. b. 298. [2] Osborne's will, PCC 25 Ridley, suggests he was born in 1549; Venn, *Al. Cant.* iii. 285, gives 1551 and Peter Osborne's i.p.m., C142/249/59, suggests 1559, which is much too late. For other facts in this paragraph see *DNB* (Osborne, Peter). [3] *CPR,* 1569–72, p. 290; *CSP Dom.* 1590–4, p. 234; Hatfield ms 278; C66/1549; *APC,* 1618–19, 174, 179. [4] *HMC Hatfield,* ii. 171; *DNB*; *VCH Beds.* ii. 271. [5] *HMC Hatfield,* viii. 284; xi. 5, 513; Townshend, *Hist. Colls.* 237. [6] *CSP Dom.* 1591–4, p. 386; 1595–7, p. 413; 1623–5, pp. 353–4; Add. 1580–1625, p. 509; Egerton 3369; Lansd. 153, ff. 161, 163. [7] *APC,* 1618–19, 174, 179; 1627 (Jan.–Aug.), 283–4; SP14/100/2; 101/2–3; S. R. Gardiner, *Hist. England 1603–42,* ii. 187; iii. 203; *Chamberlain Letters* ed. McClure, ii. 210; *CSP Dom.* 1627–8, p. 30; PCC 25 Ridley; C142/451/106; *DNB.*

I.C./P.W.H.

OSBORNE, Peter (1521–92), of South Fambridge, Essex, Chicksands, Beds. and Ivy Lane, London.

TREGONY	1559
HORSHAM	1563
GUILDFORD	1571
PLYMPTON ERLE	1572
ALDEBURGH	1584, 1586
WESTMINSTER	1589

b. 1521, 2nd *s.* of Richard Osborne of Tyld Hall, Lockingdon, Essex by Elizabeth Coke or Cooke. *educ.* ?Camb.; L. Inn 1543. *m.* Anne (*d.*1615), da. of Dr. John Blyth, regius professor of physic at Camb. and niece of Sir John Cheke†, 11s. inc. Christopher* and John* 11da.

Clerk of the faculties 1551; keeper of privy purse to Edward VI 1551; ld. treasurer's remembrancer in the Exchequer 1552–3, from 1559; eccles. commr. 1562; assoc. bencher, L. Inn 1566; dep. gov. mineral and battery works 1568; commr. on disputes with Portugal 1573, piracy 1580; j.p.q. Mdx. from c.1562.

Osborne rose to prominence during the Northumberland régime, then fell out of favour under Mary, when his sympathies were with his relative Sir John Cheke and the protestant reforming group. He may have been imprisoned. He is not known to have been a Marian exile. At Elizabeth's accession he was reinstated at the Exchequer, where he was employed in 1560 in connexion with the new coinage. A number of letters to his master and marriage relation Sir William Cecil survive, mainly on the subjects of general foreign trade, customs duties and commercial treaties. On 9 Oct. 1572 Osborne sent him a resumé of the personnel of the Exchequer and their responsibilities, and in the same year he was making a collection of statutes, letters patent and charters relating to English trade since the reign of Henry III. The friendship between the two men outlasted Osborne's death, for Burghley looked after Osborne's son John, for whom he had already secured the reversion of the remembrancer's office, 'the stay of his house, his wife and children after him', until 1698 in fact. Though Osborne bought a small amount of landed property, unusually for the period he refrained from speculating with public money, and his estates were not extensive. He bought South Fambridge in 1561 and Chicksands priory, Bedfordshire in 1576. The family remained at Chicksands, and were in the royal service at least until 1812, and MPs until 1824.[1]

Osborne owed all his parliamentary seats to Cecil. A letter is extant[2] of January 1553 signed by Christopher Smythe* of the Exchequer and Thomas Hyde, recommending Osborne for election at Bridport. It described him as 'towards the privy chamber and a great officer in the Exchequer', and promised that if he were returned he would not ask for wages. It is not known whether or not he was successful. His immediate patron at Tregony, as later at Plympton Erle, was presumably the 2nd Earl of Bedford. Horsham was controlled during the first part of Elizabeth's reign by the Duke of Norfolk, to whom, again presumably, Cecil applied for a nomination. The inference is that he did also to William More I*, himself a former Exchequer official, at Guildford in 1571. The Cecil connexion may also have secured Osborne's return for Aldeburgh; alternatively this may have been due to his mother's family. There is no doubt about Westminster, where Burghley was high steward. In turn Osborne had his own relatives returned to Parliament, for example George Blyth at Maldon in 1571 and, probably, Edmund Bell for Aldeburgh in 1586. It is likely that it was Peter Osborne who was the 'Mr. Osborne' appointed to committees concerning the clerk of the market (27 Jan. 1581), the reformation of disorders of sheriffs (committed to him 4 Feb. 1581), Mary Queen of Scots (4 Nov. 1586) and the debts of Thomas Hanford (18 Mar. 1589). It was certainly he who spoke, 18 Feb. 1589, to the effect that he had no objections to an Exchequer reform suggested by (Sir) Edward Hoby*.[3]

By 1587 Osborne was suffering from the stone, and in the spring of 1591 he was 'at more leisure from Westminster and going abroad, by reason of my lameness and sickliness, than heretofore'. He died 7 June 1592, and was buried at St. Faith's under St. Paul's. No will has been found.[4]

[1] *DNB*; Lansd. 14, 18, 24, 26, 52, 56, 146 passim; *L. Inn Black Bks.* passim; Egerton 3369; *HMC Hatfield*, ii. 171; Hatfield mss 223/7, 278; Cooper, *Ath. Cant.* ii. 126; *Eliz. Govt. and Soc.* 115–16; *Vis. Essex* (Harl. Soc. xiii), 177; *CPR*, 1560–3, pp. 42, 279. The matriculation date of 1548 in Venn, *Al. Cant.* i(3), p. 285 is too late. Osborne was not called to the bar, his associate benchership was 'for board only'. [2] *HMC 6th Rep.* 497. [3] *CJ*, i. 120, 122; D'Ewes, 291, 394, 434, 447. [4] Lansd. 52, f. 90; 66, f. 217; C142/249/59.

N.M.F.

OTLEY, Thomas (d. 1603), of Pitchford, Salop.

BRIDGNORTH   1571

2nd s. of Adam Otley of Pitchford by Mary, da. of Richard Mainwaring of Ightfield, sis. of Sir Arthur Mainwaring*. *educ.* Shrewsbury 1562; I. Temple 1565. *m.* Christabel, da. of Richard Lister of Rowton, ?wid. of Thomas Welles or Welkes, 3da.[1]

Otley's family owned property at Bridgnorth, for which he was returned to the 1571 Parliament, no doubt with the approval of Sir Andrew Corbet*, to whom the Privy Council wrote before the election, urging him to see that suitable burgesses were chosen in Shropshire. Otley's maternal grandmother was a Corbet, and the two families remained on friendly terms throughout Elizabeth's reign. Otley's niece Martha, daughter of his elder brother Richard, married Richard Corbet, a young relative of Sir Andrew.

Otley also owned at least three houses in Shrewsbury, probably acquired after his father's death in 1578. The elder Otley had connexions with the town. Otley himself may have practised as a lawyer. There is no record of his having been called to the bar, but he, or a namesake from

Suffolk admitted a year earlier, held minor offices at the Inner Temple, acting as steward for the reader's dinner as late as 1587, when he was described as 'Mr. Otley the elder': by this time the Bridgnorth Member's nephew and namesake was also in residence at the Inn. The last mention of the name in the Inner Temple records which may possibly refer to the MP is dated 3 Nov. 1590. Soon after the end of the 1571 Parliament Otley's cousin John Hall, a former servant of the (probably the 6th) Earl of Shrewsbury, confessed to having communicated with Mary Stuart's agent, the bishop of Ross, at the time of the Norfolk conspiracy. He had spent some time at the end of the previous year in Shropshire at the house of 'one Thomas Oteley, my cousin german, with whom I had before appointed to be all that winter'. His host had warned him that Shrewsbury's servants had been searching for him and offering large sums for his capture. Otley's own loyalty does not seem to have been in doubt – at least there is no record of his being questioned.[2]

Some time before his death Otley was in financial difficulty. His will, made 12 May and proved 11 July 1603, lists property in Shrewsbury, plate, law books and other goods, all to be sold to pay debts. (Sir) Francis Newport II* and Otley's brother Richard were appointed overseers, and the widow joint executrix with her youngest daughter. Two other daughters, Elizabeth and Mary, are also mentioned. In a preamble, Otley claimed 'full assurance of my salvation through the merits of Christ Jesus my Saviour'.[3]

[1] *Vis. Salop* (Harl. Soc. xxix), 329, 348–9, 381–2. [2] NLW, Pitchford mss, ex inf. Dr. J. F. A. Mason; Add. 48018, f. 294v; *Vis. Salop* (Harl. Soc. xxviii), 136; (xxix), 381, 382; *HMC 15th Rep.* X, 49, 52; *HMC Hatfield*, i. 500, 507. [3] PCC 58 Bolein.

N.M.F.

OVERSALL, John (b. c.1517), of Hull, Yorks.

KINGSTON-UPON-HULL   1559

b. c.1517, 1st s. of Hugh Oversall, sheriff of Hull 1534–5. *suc.* fa. 1538.
Chamberlain, Hull 1538–9, sheriff 1546–7, mayor 1550–1.

In addition to being a prominent member of the Hull corporation, Oversall was a local landowner, inheriting the manor of Elstanwyk, a mansion at Winestead in Holderness, and land in Southsomercotes and Fulstowmarsh, Lincolnshire. In July 1548 he was one of the 'aldermen and burgesses' who agreed to grant Sir William Knollys a tenement in High Gate, Hull, and in October 1557, as an alderman, he accompanied the mayor to London in answer to a Privy Council summons.

He was granted leave of absence by the House on grounds of sickness 28 Feb. 1559. No later references to him have been found, and no will or inquisition post mortem.

C142/60/110, 136; *LP Hen. VIII*, xiv(2), p. 160; *Hull Deeds*, ed. Stanewell, 376; T. Gent, *Annales Regioduni Hullini*, 117–18; W. Brown, *Yorks. Deeds* (Yorks. Arch. Soc. rec. ser. lxiii), 56; *APC*, vi. 182; *CJ*, i. 56.

N.M.F.

OWEN, Hugh, of Cae'rberllan, Llanfihangel y pennant, Merion.

BOSSINEY	1563
MERIONETH	1571

2nd s. of Lewis Owen† by Margaret, da. of Robert Puleston of Hafod y wern, nr. Wrexham, Denb. and of Gresford, Denb.; bro. of John Lewis Owen*. *educ.* Christ Church, Oxf. 1550, BA 1553; ?L. Inn 1556. *m.* Catherine, da. of John ap Hugh ap Ieuan of Mathafarn, Llanwrin, Mont., 4s. 2da.

    J.p. Merion. from c.1569, escheator 1570–1, 1574–5.

Owen's father, the baron of the Caernarvon Exchequer who was slain by bandits in the course of his duties in 1555, came of ancient and distinguished local stock, represented the shire on a number of occasions, and accumulated a sufficient estate (partly from the lands of the dissolved abbey of Cymmer) to provide for eight sons, several of whom founded families of local eminence. Hugh's second cousin Robert Puleston*, who belonged to a family with three centuries of influence in three shires, went with him, as Member for Denbighshire, to the Parliament of 1571. His sister Elizabeth married into the rising Merioneth Nanneys, and his eldest son John into the Prices of Plas Iolyn, Denbighshire and Rhiwlas, Merioneth, firmly established through the services of its founder to Henry VII at Bosworth and the consequent favours of Wolsey and Cromwell. Rowland Pugh, who represented Montgomery Boroughs in the Parliament of 1572, was his wife's relative.

    Owen himself, as a younger son, was trained to the law, and practised at Ludlow, as well as arbitrating from time to time in the many disputes between his neighbours. A court connexion, probably Sir Robert Dudley*, afterwards Earl of Leicester, gained him the nomination at Bossiney. There was a contest for the Merioneth seat in 1571 between Owen and John Salesbury* of Rûg, the deciding factor being the support of Owen's relative Ellis Price*. No record has been found of any activity in Parliament on Owen's part.[1]

    The Salesburys were at this time opposing the Earl of Leicester in Merioneth under the powers granted him for searching out encroachments into the forest of Snowdon, an opposition under cover of which recusants and partisans of the Queen of Scots were liable to shelter. In 1574 one of the latter claimed Hugh Owen 'and all his brethren' as sympathizers, despite the declaration of Hugh and his elder brother John Lewis Owen as justices, only five years earlier, of loyalty to the Act of Uniformity. In

November 1577 Hugh was summoned with five Caernarvonshire gentlemen (some of them conspicuous in their opposition to Leicester) to appear before the Privy Council; the five were committed to the Fleet, but Owen appears to have cleared himself after interrogation.[2]

    Owen's estate lay some eight miles south-east of the family seat, and in another commote, but in 1568 he extended it northwards by leasing over 600 acres of crown land (nearly a third of them old Cymmer lands). It was, however, largely 'void barren ground' awaiting development. At the 1570 musters he was one of ten Merioneth gentry assessed at the standard 'one light horseman furnished', and by the end of the reign he was one of the thirteen £3 subsidy men of his commote, with only one rated higher. Though less litigious than his elder brother, he had his share of territorial disputes. He joined with a number of the principal gentry of Merioneth and Caernarvonshire to resist the claims of the Anwyl family of Llanfrothen (in the north of the county) to certain sheepwalks; and a more violent dispute with his relative by marriage Richard Nanney of Cefndeuddwr led to a commission from Ludlow and a Star Chamber action in 1601, involving a wide section of Merioneth society.[3]

    As deputy sheriff in the next reign he initiated another Star Chamber action against three defendants, alleged to have attempted a forcible rescue of a debtor from arrest. He was dead before the end of James I's reign, his elegy being sung by one of the leading contemporary bards of Gwynedd.[4]

[1] Griffith, *Peds.* 204, 274, 275, 363; T. P. Ellis, *Dolgelly and Llanelltyd*, 85; Lloyd, *Powys Fadog*, vi. 37–8; Add. 14874, no. 131; UCNW Nannau, 94, 96, 170; and see MERIONETH. [2] P. H. Williams, *Council in the Marches of Wales*, 237–9; *EHR*, lix. 353; Lansd. 27, ff. 187–206; 737, f. 174; *Cath. Rec. Soc.* xiii. 110; SP12/66/19; *APC*, x. 99, 122, 124; *Cal. Wynn Pprs.* pp. 8–9; *Salusbury Corresp.* ed. Smith (Univ. Wales Bd. of Celtic Studies, Hist. and Law ser. xiv), 6–7. [3] *Augmentations*, ed. Lewis and Davies (Univ. Wales Bd. of Celtic Studies, Hist. and Law ser. i), 91; *Star Chamber*, ed. Edwards (same ser. xiii), 437; *Star Chamber*, ed. Edwards (same ser. i), 91; *Exchequer*, ed. E. G. Jones (same ser. iv), 239; *Arch. Camb.* (ser. 4), x. 125; E179/222/325–7. [4] Flenley, *Cal. Reg. Council, Marches of Wales*, 74; *Star Chamber*, ed. Edwards, 186; Add. 14874, no. 131; Griffith, 274.

A.H.D.

OWEN, John (*d.* 1613), of Bodsilin, Anglesey; Clenennau, Caern., and Porkington, Salop.

CAERNARVON BOROUGHS	1597

4th s. of Owen ap Robert of Bodsilin, Llanfeirian, Caern. by Angharad, da. and coh. of David ap William ap Griffith of Cochurllan. *educ.* ?Shrewsbury 1577. *m.* bef. 1596, Elin (*d.* 1626), da. or gd.-da. of William Maurice* of Clenennau, 3s. 5da.

    Servant of (Sir) Francis Walsingham*, of (Sir) Robert Sidney* by 1607; muster master, Caern. 1595; dep. mayor and constable of Caernarvon castle by 1597.

Owen's return as the representative for Caernarvon Boroughs in 1597 is no doubt accounted for by his offices of deputy mayor and constable. The earlier part of his career was spent in the service of Sir Francis Walsingham. After Walsingham's death he had hoped to enter the service of Robert Cecil but was in fact employed in France in the following years, though he must have been in England for his marriage and, presumably, (though he made no mark there) to attend the 1597 Parliament. The burgesses of Caernarvon Boroughs were appointed to committees concerning navigation (12 Nov.) and Newport bridge (29 Nov.). Writing to Cecil in August 1601 he again expressed his desire to enter his service, but by October 1607 he was serving Sir Robert Sidney, then Viscount Lisle, who refers to him as John Owen, son of Robert of Bodsilin. Owen's subsequent career is obscure. He died on 16 Mar. 1613, leaving his eldest son, the future royalist officer in the civil war, little more than 12 years old. The widow married Sir Francis Eure.

DNB (Owen, Sir John); DWB, 624, 709; Griffith, Peds. 136, 218; Dwnn, Vis. Wales, ii. 157, 164; T. Jones Pierce, Clenennau Letters, 33; HMC Hatfield, xi. 371; D'Ewes, 556, 565; Cal. Wynn Pprs. nos. 155, 1034; C142/339/101.

A.M.M.

OWEN, John Lewis (d. 1606), of Llwyn, Dolgelly, Merion.

MERIONETH　　　　　　　　　　1572

1st s. of Lewis Owen[†] and bro. of Hugh*. m. Ursula, da. of Richard Mytton[†] of Shrewsbury and Halston, Salop, and Dinas Mawddy, Merion., 3s. 6da. suc. fa. 1555.[1]

Escheator, Merion. 1562–3, 1568–9, j.p. from 1563, sheriff 1565–6, 1572–3, 1589–90, dep. lt. by 1597; custodian of armour and commr. musters, Merion. 1569; commr. of victualling for Ireland and for tanneries 1574, for discovery and arrest of felons, Merion. and Mont. 1575; commr. subsidy Penllyn 1585 and Tal y bont 1600.[2]

Owen succeeded his younger brother Hugh as county Member. He was granted leave of absence on 11 June 1572 'for his great sickness'. His inherited fortune was not impressive: during the Privy Council investigations of 1598 it was reported that he owed his wealth partly to exploitation of public office (in which there appears to be some truth), partly to his wife, mistakenly alleged (through confusion with his mother) to be a Puleston. His assessment for subsidy rose from £2 at the beginning of the reign (well below the average for his commote) to £6 at the end, a sum equalled only by the Nanneys of Nannau. At the musters of 1570 he was assessed at the normal rating of 'one light horseman furnished'. Still, his ancient descent and the repute of his father were enough to assure his position in the county.[3]

His residence at Llwyn placed him in proximity to the rising family of Nanney. At first the two families were on excellent terms. But the election for Merioneth in 1593 of Griffith Nanney*, who was not even head of a household, when the seat was coveted by the older and more experienced John Lewis Owen, started a feud between the families in which Owen and his three sons, many of his remoter connexions and neighbours, and even a junior branch of Nanney itself, fought an unremitting war for the rest of his life against a family now threatening to dominate the shire and the shire town of Dolgelly. In the year after this election, trouble arose over alleged common land outside Dolgelly which Hugh Nanney was enclosing: according to depositions in Star Chamber, John Lewis Owen led an armed band, including his three sons and a nephew, which tore down Nanney's six-foot walls and threatened all who resisted. The issue is unknown, but the same lands were in dispute again before the council of Wales eight years later.[4]

The Salesburys of Rûg were also rivals. In 1571 John Salesbury attempted to seize the reversion of a grant of the township of Dolgelly held by Owen. In the same year Salesbury unsuccessfully challenged John's brother, Hugh, for one of the Merioneth parliamentary seats. In the contested election of 1597 Salesbury and Owen backed opposing candidates, and this time Owen's faction was defeated. The following year, Pyers Lloyd of Dol Edeyrn, Corwen, a close neighbour and probably an ally of the Salesburys, brought a Star Chamber action against Owen and his co-deputy lieutenant and relation, Cadwaladr Price* of Rhiwlas, accusing them of embezzlement, false imprisonment, bribery, extortion and intimidation and fraudulent promotion of their candidate at the last election. The Privy Council instituted inquiries, and, on a petition from Pyers Lloyd, instructed the council in the marches to stay vexatious suits which Owen was said to be promoting there as impediments to the Star Chamber action. The upshot was that at the Council's instance the 2nd Earl of Pembroke, who as lord president of the council in the marches of Wales had been responsible for the appointment of the two deputy lieutenants, had them removed in 1600 from both the commission of lieutenancy and the commission of the peace.[5]

The quarrel with the Nanneys flared up again at the first Christmas of the next reign, when (according to allegations made in Star Chamber by one of John Lewis Owen's sons) a Nanney gang assembled outside Llwyn to hurl abuse at the Owens, and wreaked their wrath on the Owen pew in Dolgelly church. For a short time relations became easier; but in 1606, the last year of his life, John Lewis Owen made a final bid for mastery in Dolgelly (a source of rivalry with both Nanneys and Salesburys), alleging in the Exchequer that divers townsmen were violating his crown grant of the farm of the town and its waste lands during markets and fairs (with the right to levy dues on the merchants' standings) by building cottages, enclosing patches of waste, and encroaching on Dolgelly's narrow streets. This was his last fling; but the feud with the Nanney family was maintained by his children for another nine years.

Owen's elegy was sung by a Merioneth bard of repute, parson of a neighbouring parish. At least five other eulogies from bards of other shires have survived, including one which competed at the Caerwys eisteddfod of 1567 and one apparently inspired by his election to Parliament.[6]

[1] Griffith, *Peds.* 362; *Mont. Colls.* xxiv. 283. [2] *CPR*, 1563–6, p. 31; *APC*, xxviii. 448; Flenley, *Cal. Reg. Council, Marches of Wales*, 60, 69, 109, 127, 135, 146, 212; Harl. E. 15; E179/222/326. [3] *CJ*, i. 102; P. H. Williams, *Council in the Marches of Wales*, 125–6; E179/222/323, 325–6; Flenley, 73–4. [4] UCNW, Nannau 85–6, 220; B. R. Parry, 'Hist. Nannau Fam.' (UCNW thesis), 237–85; *Star Chamber*, ed. Edwards (Univ. Wales Bd. of Celtic Studies, Hist. and Law ser. i), 91. [5] *HMC Bath*, v. 188–9; E179/222/326; *Star Chamber*, 90; *APC*, xxviii. 448, 457, 463, 551; xxx. 180. [6] Parry, 237, 266–8; *Star Chamber*, 186; *Exchequer*, ed. T. I. J. Jones (Univ. Wales Bd. of Celtic Studies, Hist. and Law ser. xv), 224–5; UCNW, Nannau 233, 238; *HMC Welsh*, i. 154; ii. 184, 987.

A.H.D.

OWEN ap MEURIG, Lewis ab (by 1524–90), of Brondeg, nr. Newborough, Anglesey.

ANGLESEY   1553 (Mar.), 1572

b. by 1524, 6th s. of Owen ap Meurig of Bodeon, Llangadwaladr by his 2nd w. Ellen, da. of Robert ap Meredydd of Glynllifon, Caern. *m.* (1) Alice, da. of Dafydd ap Evan ap Matto, 1da.; (2) Ellen, da. of William ap William of Vaynol, Caern., 2s. 2da.

Under-steward to William Herbert[†], 1st Earl of Pembroke, and to bp. of Bangor, Anglesey and Caern. c.1553; commr. goods of churches and fraternities, Anglesey 1553, defence 1569, musters 1574; j.p. from 1555, custos rot. temp. Mary, sheriff 1558–9, steward, lordship of Rhosfair c.1565; escheator, Anglesey 1568–9.

Until the emergence of Sir Hugh Owen in the closing years of the century, the Brondeg branch of the Bodeon family, vigorously led by Lewis Owen, tended to overshadow the parent stock. Owen otherwise had few useful connexions in the island, but he had links with two important Caernarvonshire houses – Glynllifon and Vaynol – and indirectly with the still more important Puleston and Griffith families.[1]

Typical of that generation of Gwynedd gentry, Owen was recurrently involved in litigation in Star Chamber and Exchequer over questions of encroachment in Anglesey townships. On one occasion he was also sued for misdemeanours at quarter sessions. His most serious conflict, however, occurred towards the end of his life when he pitted himself against Richard Bulkeley I* and found his lands and goods seized and his wife ejected from her dwelling house, 'to her great discomfort and the trouble and vexation of the old man'. The Privy Council, taking into account his public services and his zeal in 'the advancement of true religion', appealed on his behalf to the Earl of Pembroke as president of the council in the marches of Wales, but an undated reference to Bulkeley's

success against 'that old viper Lewis ap Owen' suggests that little came of this.[2]

His death in 1590 was lamented by Huw Pennant, a bard who qualified at the Caerwys eisteddfod of 1568. He was succeeded by his son William, to whom (according to the antiquary Henry Rowlands, with his inside knowledge of the local families) he left 'most richly-stocked possessions'. This is confirmed by taxation returns, which show Lewis Owen, from Henry VIII's time, among the chief taxpayers in a hundred including families like the Griffiths and Bulkeleys of Porthamel and the Woods of Rhosmor; by 1586 he headed the list with £5, and his son William after him stood second of some 30 subsidy men of Menai.[3]

[1] Griffith, *Peds.* 58–9, 172, 190, 275; *Star Chamber*, ed. Edwards (Univ. Wales Bd. of Celtic Studies, Hist. and Law ser. i), 16; *CPR*, 1553, p. 419; 1560–3, p. 446; Flenley, *Cal. Reg. Council, Marches of Wales*, 56; *Trans. Anglesey Antiq. Soc.* 1946, p. 27. [2] *Star Chamber*, 18; *Exchequer*, ed. E. G. Jones (Univ. Wales Bd. of Celtic Studies, Hist. and Law ser. iv), 17; *Trans. Anglesey Antiq. Soc.* 1934, pp. 57–8; *APC*, xv. 375, 383–4; NLW, *Cal. Wynn Pprs.* 66. [3] NLW Peniarth, 71, f. 56; *DWB*, 401; *Arch. Camb.* 1846, p. 309; E179/219/3–18; *CPR*, 1566–9, p. 202.

H.G.O.

OWEN, Roger (1573–1617), of Condover, Salop.

SHREWSBURY   1597
SHROPSHIRE   1601, 1604*, 1614

b. 1573, 1st s. of Thomas Owen* of Condover by his 1st w. Sarah, da. of Humphrey Baskerville. *educ.* Shrewsbury 1583; Christ Church, Oxf. B.A. 1592; L. Inn 1589, called 1597. *m.* Ursula, da. of William Elkin, alderman of London, 2da. *suc.* fa. 1598. Kntd. 1604.

J.p.q. Salop by 1601–14, sheriff 1603–4; member, council in the marches of Wales 1602–7; bencher, L. Inn 1611, treasurer 1612–13.

Owen's father procured his return to Parliament in 1597, and built Condover Hall for him. In Shropshire Owen enjoyed a reputation for 'all manner of learning, care of the good of the commonwealth, for composing of controversies, buying peace with his own purse, maintaining of amity, and love to his neighbours'. Camden considered him to be 'worthy of so excellent a father', but he was the lesser man. His appointment as sheriff was challenged on the grounds that he was partial to the Vernon family, and his factiousness led to his dismissal from the council in the marches of Wales.[1]

Returned for the county after coming into his estate, Owen took an active part in the proceedings of the 1601 Parliament, and narrowly missed landing himself in deep trouble on account of his speeches, which were not always favourably received. He spoke against the pluralities bill on 16 Nov., and on 27 Nov. answered allegations that a privilege case concerning an MP's servant had not been properly looked into. The breach of privilege had been committed in Shrewsbury and the House had ordered the serjeant-at-arms to go to Shrewsbury to fetch the culprits back to London.

> May it please you, Mr. Speaker, myself being chosen for the shire, I think it my part to speak something, seeing the burgesses for the town neglect their duties, in not speaking. True it is that such order was given by the House; but Mr. Morrice and some others being willing to let me have the examination of the matter, they came before me. And upon examination (a wise examination no doubt, said Mr. Secretary Cecil), I found he was no menial servant, but only a servant that brought him part of the way and was to go no further with him towards the Parliament: whereupon I think, the serjeant having some notice, stayed.

Owen spoke against the bill concerning church attendance on 2 Dec. objecting on the grounds that it would over-burden the justices of the peace who were already 'laden with a number of penal statutes' and 'therefore for my part away with the bill'. This infuriated the Privy Councillors in the House, still smarting from Glascock's speeches the previous day. Sir George Moore referred to 'the corruption of his heart' and Sir Francis Knollys wondered 'that any voice durst be so bold or desperate to cry "Away with this Bill".' Owen was significantly appointed to the committee that day, but he spoke again on 5 Dec., refusing to modify his views:

> ... he was of the same opinion he before had been of, for amendment of the said bill ... and so he proceeded, and made a brief repetition with some arguments for confirmation of the same speech he first made.

At this point Humphrey Winch stepped in with a well-timed testimonial for Owen:

> I much marvel that the gentleman which last spake would speak against this bill, allowing so well the matter. I know him well, and his bringing up and both his sufficiency and zeal which I very well know, and am well persuaded of.

Owen's last speech in this Parliament, 12 Dec., requested a proviso to exempt Shropshire from contributing to the relief for maimed soldiers, owing to 'the poor estate' of the county. 'But it was replied to him that he went about to deck up his particular cabin when the ship was on fire'. He was named to a committee on a private bill on 24 Nov., and as knight for Shropshire was appointed to the main business committee (3 Nov.) and the monopolies committee (23 Nov.).

Owen took a prominent part in the Parliaments of James I's reign. He died intestate in London 29 May 1617 and was buried at Condover.[2]

[1] *DNB*; *Vis. Salop* (Harl. Soc. xxix), 388; *Trans. Salop Arch. Soc.* (ser. 4), xii. 197–9; Egerton 2882, f. 20; *HMC 5th Rep.* 342; H. Owen and J. B. Blakeway, *Shrewsbury*, i. 392; *HMC Hatfield*, xii. 496–7; P. H.

[2] Williams, *Council in the Marches of Wales*, 305. [2] D'Ewes, 624, 641, 649, 650, 655, 663, 664; Townshend, *Hist. Colls.* 220, 255, 273, 287, 317; *CSP Dom.* 1611–18, p. 471–2.

J.J.C.

OWEN, Thomas (*d.* 1598), of Lincoln's Inn, London, later of Condover, Salop.

SHREWSBURY   1584

1st s. of Richard Owen, merchant and bailiff of Shrewsbury by Mary, da. of Thomas Otley of Salop. *educ.* Christ Church or Broadgates Hall, Oxf., BA 1559; L. Inn 1562, called 1570. *m.* (1) Sarah, da. of Humphrey Baskerville, 5s. inc. Roger Owen* 5da.; (2) Alice, da. of Thomas Wilkes of London, wid. of William Elkin, alderman of London and possibly of Henry Robinson, brewer of London.

Bencher, L. Inn 1579, marshal 1582–3, keeper of the Black Book 1586–7, treasurer 1588–9; recorder, Shrewsbury 1588–92; serjeant 1589, Queen's serjeant 1593; member, council in the marches of Wales 1590; justice of the common pleas 1595.[1]

J.p. Salop from c.1583, many other counties from c.1595.

Owen was a lawyer who retained his connexions with Shrewsbury, his counsel often being sought by the bailiffs on such matters as the holding of a weekly court, and the payment of a public preacher. In 1589 he told the burgesses that they were not obliged to return a resident to Parliament, and in 1591 he was consulted about the 'Shearmen's Tree', a maypole whose appearance had enraged the puritans in the town. His own views on the matter were liberal: he ruled that the tree 'should be used as heretofore, so it be done civilly and in loving order, without contention'. The borough made him occasional presents, and at his request, returned his eldest son to Parliament in 1597. At his own election in 1584 he received 366 votes, as against the 299 and 176 polled by his opponents. Presumably he did not wish to sit again – it is inconceivable that, as recorder, he could not have obtained a seat if he had wished for one.[2]

Although Owen bought Condover, near Shrewsbury, in 1586, and built a fine red sandstone house there, he does not seem to have lived in it himself, nor did he spend much time in attendance on the council in the marches of Wales. No doubt this can be explained by the frequent demands made by the Privy Council on his services. From 1577 onwards he received numerous charges: he was instructed to examine the petition of a seaman's wife, the causes of a riot in London, and several traitors, under torture. He examined charges of corruption, coining and rape. It was his task in 1591 to deport a 'lewd and unreverent' Walloon, and in December 1588 he was one of 16 lawyers instructed to consider repealing or reforming certain statutes for the coming Parliament.[3]

In the Parliament of 1584 he sat on committees

concerning common informers (9 Dec.), the preservation of grain (19 Dec.), ecclesiastical livings (19 Dec.), the maintenance of the navy (19 Dec.), fraudulent conveyances (18 Feb. 1585), delays of executions (5 Mar.), assurances (22 Mar.) and the good government of the city of Westminster (22 Mar.). After he became Queen's serjeant he was often employed to carry bills and messages between the Commons and the Lords. As a judge, he was attached to various committees of the Lords in 1597 and 1598.[4]

As well as Condover, he owned or leased considerable property in Essex and Montgomery. He must have stood high in Burghley's estimation, for he was employed in the abortive marriage negotiations between Bridget Vere and William, Lord Herbert. In fact, he was mentioned as a possible successor to Burghley as master of the court of wards, but he died on 21 Dec. 1598. On 9 Dec. he had made his will, 'considering the uncertainty of this transitory life, that it passeth away as a shadow, and fadeth as the grass of the field'. He left the bulk of his property to his eldest son, and made substantial bequests to his younger children, servants and clerks. The bailiffs of Shrewsbury received money for the relief of 'decayed householders' and 'poor impotent persons' in the parish of St. Chad, where he was born. There were also bequests to the poor of Condover and Westminster, and the deans of St. Paul's and Westminster each received a small legacy. His 'faithful and kind' wife, although already provided for, was left the wainscot, glass, tables, stools and bedsteads in his house. His funeral was to be 'without any pomp, or great charge, or any blacks for mourning apparel'. He was buried in Westminster abbey.[5]

[1] *Vis. Salop* (Harl. Soc. xxix), 126; *Trans. Salop Arch. Soc.* (ser. 4), xii. 191–3; H. Owen and J. B. Blakeway, *Shrewsbury*, i. 392, 538; *CSP Dom.* 1581–90, p. 703. [2] Owen and Blakeway, i. 394, 531–2; *HMC 5th Rep.* 342; *HMC 15th Rep. X*, 18; *Early Chrons. of Shrewsbury*, ed. Leighton, 62, 322. [3] *Condover Par. Reg.* (Salop Par. Reg. Lichfield vi); Harl. 4293, f. 37v; 6995, f. 12; *APC*, xiii. 135; xv. 334–5, 365; xvi. 417; xx. 45; xxi. 297, 299; xxii. 126; xxv. 355. [4] D'Ewes, 337, 343, 353, 363, 371, 502, 504, 509, 510, 511, 514, 517, 518, 520, 521, 530, 537, 539, 543; Townshend, *Hist. Colls.* 76, 78. [5] *CSP Dom.* 1595–7, p. 497; 1598–1601, p. 147; PCC 15 Kidd.

J.J.C.

OWEN, William (c.1540–80), of Oxford.

OXFORD   1572*

b., c.1540, 2nd s. of George Owen[1] (d.1558) of Godstow, Oxon. prob. by his 1st w. Lettice of Suff. educ. L. Inn Feb. 1557. m. (1) c.1557, Ursula, da. of Alexander Fettiplace of Swinbrook, Oxon., ?s.p.; (2) by May 1562, Anne, da. of John Rawley of Billesby, Northants., 2s. 3da.
    Freeman, Oxford 1570.[1]

Owen's father, receiver general of the duchy of Lancaster and physician to Henry VIII, Edward VI and Mary, acquired property in Berkshire and to the west of Oxford, including Godstow nunnery. He died in debt to the duchy, leaving his widow, the eldest son Richard and Owen himself to pay off what they could by instalments. Owen sold much of the Berkshire property. He leased Cumnor Place, once the house of the abbots of Abingdon, to Anthony Forster*, steward to Sir Robert Dudley*. 'Mrs. Owen', probably Owen's second wife, dined there with Amy Robsart just before her death in Sept. 1560. In 1561 Owen sold Cumnor Place to Forster.[2]

The corporation of Oxford made frequent use of Owen's legal training and connexions in London, and four months before his election as burgess for Parliament on 14 Apr. 1572, granted him a lease of a tenement and garden on the south side of the east gate. It was probably William Owen rather than John Lewis Owen or Lewis Owen ap Meurig who served on Commons committees dealing with weights and measures (23 May 1572), the poor (11 Feb. 1576), excessive drinking (17 Feb.) and cloth (9 Mar.). In the account for the year ending in September 1573, he is recorded as receiving £2 'for his pains in the town's business'. He accompanied the mayor on a visit to the Earl of Leicester and the high steward in January 1577, 'to retain such learned counsel as they shall appoint', and in May was one of the deputation sent to explain to the Privy Council the city's refusal to take the annual oath to respect the privileges of the university. Fifty years before, Owen's father had been in the university camp in similar disputes. Their descendants were freemen of the city.[3]

Owen was dead by 23 Nov. 1580, when a new election writ was issued. In August 1582 letters of administration were granted to a creditor. There is no indication that Owen shared his elder brother's Catholicism.[4]

[1] C142/116/5; *Vis. Oxon.* (Harl. Soc. v), 127; *CPR*, 1557–8, p. 234; 1560–3, p. 389; *Oxford Recs.* 331; *DNB* (Owen, George). [2] DL 41/34/2, f. 70; *CPR*, 1558–60, p. 81; 1560–3, p. 389; *VCH Berks.* iv. 400; *DNB* (Robert Dudley); Foster, *Al. Ox.* i. 1102; see FORSTER, Anthony. [3] *CPR*, 1558–60, p. 234; *Oxford Recs.* 331, 339, 341, 350, 357, 388; H. E. Salter, *Oxford Council Acts* (Oxford Hist. Soc. lxxxvii), 69, 253; *CJ*, i. 97, 105, 106, 113. [4] C219/283/35–6; PCC admon. act bk. 1582, f. 44; A. Davidson, 'Catholicism in Oxon. 1580–1640 (Bristol Univ. PhD thesis 1970), 116–24.

A.H.

OXBOROUGH, Thomas (d.1623), of King's Lynn, Norf.

KING'S LYNN   1586, 1597, 1601, 1604, 1614

s. of Thomas Oxborough of Beckham Well. educ. L. Inn 1572, called 1581. m. (1) Thomasine, da. of Thomas Heward of Oxborough, 4s. 3da.; (2) Margaret, da. of Richard Slyford of Slyford, Lincs., wid. of Patrick Cartwright of King's Lynn.
    Town clerk of King's Lynn 1584–97, recorder from 1597; j.p. Norf. from c.1596; commr. sewers for Ely ?1594, Lincs. and Norf. by 1597.

Most of our information about Oxborough comes from the records of King's Lynn. He received a number of payments for his work on the town's behalf. In April 1585 he was given £5, 'towards such charges as he shall be at for the town this next term for such matters and causes as he is appointed to have to do for the town'. In July 1590 he was paid £10 for his 'great pains' about the borough's business, and in September 1592 received £3 6s. 8d. for his part in discussion between Lynn and the 'Cambridge-men'. The town also showed its appreciation in other ways. In 1594 and 1599 he was granted leases of lands and houses in Lynn, and in January 1601 was given part of a hogshead of wine.[1]

Oxborough received burgess money on each of the occasions, during the Elizabethan period, on which he represented Lynn in Parliament. He was paid £13 6s. 8d. for the 1586 Parliament and £6 for the Parliament of 1601. The amount for the 1597 Parliament is unknown, as he received his burgess money and a debt which the town owed him in a lump sum of £25. On 3 Dec. 1597 he was named to a committee for a bill for the draining of the fens. The burgesses for King's Lynn were appointed to committees in 1597 concerning the bishop of Norwich's possessions on 30 Nov. and the Exeter merchants on 12 Dec. He was also a commissioner for sewers, interested in land reclamation, as the Privy Council registers show.[2]

Oxborough died on 30 Dec. 1623. He left his lands in King's Lynn, Tilney, Middleton, Terrington St. Johns, and Islington to his children and grandchildren. His second wife, Margaret, received land in Lynn and a life interest in her husband's mansion house in the town.[3]

[1] *Vis. Norf.* (Norf. and Norwich Arch. Soc.), i. 150; *Vis. Norf.* (Harl. Soc. xxxii), 211; *Vis. Norf. 1664* (Norf. Rec. Soc. v), 152; PCC 3 Byrde; SP12/Case F/11; *APC*, xxvii. f. 274; Lansd. 76, f. 130; King's Lynn congregation bks. 1569–91, ff. 289, 297, 409; 1591–1611, ff. 17, 42, 130, 183, 216. [2] King's Lynn congregation bks. 1569–91, f. 368; 1591–1611, ff. 223, 254; Townshend, *Hist. Colls.* 111; D'Ewes, 565, 567, 571; *APC*, xxvii. 274–6; 1613–14, 265–7. [3] C142/406/26; PCC 3 Byrde.

A.G.R.S.

PAGE, William (d. aft. 1584)

BRIDPORT	1559
OXFORD	1563
SALTASH	1571, 1572

Page first appears as a servant of Peter Vannes, the English agent in Venice, who asked for his arrest in June 1554 for expressing a desire to kill Queen Mary. The council of ten refused because in Venice 'everybody discourses, even of princes, according to their opinions'. In any case Vannes was a 'very timid' man, in great 'fear about religious matters', and it was not 'becoming to imprison men for light causes, such as the words of a base menial who was either mad or drunk'. Next, in December of that year, Vannes wrote to Sir Philip Hoby† in Padua recommending his servant to him as being young, and with good Italian and English, even though Page 'with

lewd and presumptuous words offended the Queen's Majesty'. Page had requested this letter of reference because he had 'a great fancy to serve' in Hoby's household, probably thinking that his religious and political views would be better tolerated by him than by Vannes. When Mary died Page returned to England to become a secretary to the 2nd Earl of Bedford, to whom he had probably been introduced by the Hobys, the widow of Thomas Hoby having married Lord John Russell, the son of Francis, Earl of Bedford.[1]

It is Page's service with the 2nd Earl of Bedford that explains his return to the first four Parliaments of Elizabeth. Bridport was near one of Bedford's estates. That nobleman was high steward of Oxford and an Oxford council minute for 7 Dec. 1562 records that

> William Page, gentleman, was admitted into the liberties of the city at the request of the Lord the Earl of Bedford and the same day elected one of the burgesses for Parliament.

In 1571 and 1572 Bedford was instructed to supervise the elections in Cornwall, where he was warden of the stannaries. At Saltash in 1572, the burgesses of 1571 were re-elected.

Page probably accompanied Bedford on his duties in the north. In July 1565 Thomas Randolph*, Bedford's fellow commissioner in the business of the marriage of the Queen of Scots, wrote to the Earl, regretting his inability to meet him and suggesting that Bedford send a messenger 'of some appearance ... if any of your own, either Mr. Page or Mr. Lilgrave'. Doubtless equipped in the marches with a practical knowledge of military problems, Page spoke in the Commons on 3 June 1572, at the second reading of a bill 'for the well-making of calivers', to assert that the lieutenant of the ordnance was a fitter person than the armourers to decide on the size of bullets. Page was still alive, though possibly retired, when Bedford made his will in April 1584. Described as 'sometime' the Earl's servant, he was left £10. He may well have retired to Plymouth, across the river from his 1571 and 1572 constituency, for letters of administration were issued in February 1591 for the possessions of a man of his name.[2]

[1] *CSP Ven.* v. 515–16; Harl. 5009, letter bk. 1553–6, f. 74. [2] A. Wood, *City of Oxford*, ed. Clark (Oxf. Hist. Soc. xxxvii), 57; G. Scott Thomson, *Fam. Background*, 202; Add. 48018, ff. 282, 283, 294; W. H. Turner, *Oxford Recs.* 277, 302, 306; *CSP Scot.* ii. 184; Trinity Dublin, Thos. Cromwell's jnl. f. 48; PCC 45 Windsor; PCC admon. act bk. 1591, f. 167.

K.B./A.H.

PAGET, Sir Henry (1536/7–68), of Beaudesert Park, Staffs., West Drayton, Mdx. and London.

ARUNDEL	1555
LICHFIELD	1559, 1563*

b. 1536/7, 1st s. of William Paget†, 1st Lord Paget of Beaudesert by Anne, da. of Henry Preston of Preston, Lancs. *educ.* travelled, France, Italy. *m.* 20 May 1567, Catherine (*d.* 1622), da. of Sir Henry Knyvet of East Horsley, Surr., 1da. KB 29 Sept. 1553; *suc.* fa. as 2nd Lord Paget 9 June 1563.

J.p.q. Staffs. from 1563.

Paget was twice returned for Lichfield by his father, to whom the borough owed its re-enfranchisement in 1547. He took his seat in the Lords on the opening day of the 1566 session, 30 Sept., but no record has been found of a by-election at Lichfield. He died 28 Dec. 1568, having made his will, 'diseased in body', on 27 Nov.

PALER, William (c.1532–97), of Nun Monkton, near York.

HEDON 1571

b. c.1532, *educ.* Trinity Coll., Camb. 1550; L. Inn 1556, called 1563. *m.* Anne, 5s. 7da.[1]

J.p. Yorks. (E. Riding) 1575, q. 1576; recorder, Beverley 1576–97; legal member of council in the north by 1581; j.p.q. Yorks. (all ridings) by 1594; Queen's attorney in the north 1589–97.[2]

Paler presumably owed his return at Hedon to his connexion with the Constable family. A practising lawyer, he was presumably in residence at Lincoln's Inn when the 1571 Parliament met; in February 1569 he had been granted a chamber in the new buildings. He was chosen to act as steward for the reader's dinner in the autumn of 1571, but was discharged on condition of paying £10, £5 of which was still outstanding some 14 years later. The only other record of him at the inn is his appointment as butler in November 1572. By 1575 he had evidently settled in Yorkshire. His house at Nun Monkton was about seven miles from York. He had another in the city itself, and must also have spent part of his time at Beverley, where he was recorder from about 1576; in that year he helped the corporation to draw up new ordinances for the government of the town. Several official letters signed by him survive among the York archives. In June 1579 he was one of the ecclesiastical commissioners who wrote from Bishopthorpe to the corporation about the poor rate, and 18 months later his signature appears on a council of the north order for the city to raise 20 foot soldiers. He also served on commissions for oyer and terminer, and to put down piracy on the Yorkshire coast.[3]

His attorneyship in the north was a profitable office which Sir Anthony Thorold had in 1566 refused to surrender for a place as a member of the council in the north. However, the duties were arduous, and by April 1597 Paler was 'old and indisposed'. During the summer he was still at work, but on 7 Dec. the council at York told Burghley, 'This morning Mr. Payler, the Queen's attorney

in these parts, departed this life' and urged the appointment of a young and healthy man as his successor. 'It is sometimes requisite for the attorney to accompany some of this council to the furthest northern parts, which journeys require able and strong bodies.'[4]

Paler was buried in St. Martin's church, Coney Street, York, where an inscription reads:

> Here lieth the body of William Paler esquire, the Queen's Majesty's attorney in the north parts, who had by Anne his wife twelve children, viz. five sons and seven daughters, who lived till the age of sixty-five years.

His will, made in August 1596, was proved at York 17 Dec. 1597. The preamble mentions 'that part [of St. Martin's church] where divers of my children are buried'. Anne, the testator's 'most faithful and loving wife', was bequeathed the parsonage and manor of Waghen in Holderness and the manor and prebend of Oswaldwick, together with 'the house in which I now dwell in Coney Street', with 'the houses and gardens thereunto belonging'. The will contains details of legacies, usually in money or plate, to children and relatives – 'to my daughter Jane Watkinson ... whom I loved always dearly, half an ounce of angel gold'. Books were to go to a son John, co-executor with the widow and another son, Edward. One of the four overseers was William Palmer, 'chancellor of York'; another was Robert Waterhouse*.[5]

[1] Dugdale, *Vis. Yorks.* iii. 15; *L. Inn Black Bks.* i. 339; Drake, *Eboracum*, 328. [2] *HMC Beverley*, 58; T. Gent. *Rippon*, 99; *York Civic Recs.* (Yorks. Arch. Soc. rec. ser. cxix), 42; Reid, *Council of the North*, 489. [3] York wills 23, ff. 539, 1000; *L. Inn Black Bks.* i. 364, 375, 377–8, 385, 439; Dugdale, loc. cit.; Surtees Soc. xxxviii. 142 n; G. Poulson, *Beverlac*, i. 322; *York Civic Recs.* 13, 42; SP12/121, f. 3; Lansd. 146, f. 20. [4] Reid, 378–9; *HMC Hatfield*, vii. 162, 252, 506; *Border Pprs.* ii. 386. [5] *HMC Hatfield*, vii. 506; Drake, 328; York wills 26, ff. 417–18.

N.M.F.

PALLADY, Richard (1515/16–59/63), of St. Bride's, London, Ruscombe, Berks. and Buckland, Glos.

PETERBOROUGH 1547
HEYTESBURY 1559

b. 1515/16, ?of Pallady fam. of Irthlingborough, Northants., yeoman farmers. *educ.* Eton c.1529–33; King's, Camb. 1533, fellow 1536–7. *m.* (1) by 1544, Catherine, da. of Guy Armston of Armston, Northants.; (2) Anne, da. of William Kirkby of Upper Rawcliffe, Lancs., ?s.p.

Attorney, sheriff's ct. London 1540; servant of Protector Somerset by 1548.

J.p. Berks. 1559.

Pallady was employed by Protector Somerset as clerk of the works for the building of Somerset House. The first certain reference to his being in this service is 1548, though the work began in 1546. On Somerset's fall, Pallady suffered a period of imprisonment in the Tower. During his period as a servant of the Duke he must have known Sir John Thynne*, who presumably obtained his return at Heytesbury to Elizabeth's first Parliament.

Pallady's name appears in lawsuits over Northamptonshire land which descended to his first wife, but was claimed by her male relatives. His speculation in chantry lands was presumably on behalf of a wealthy client, as there is no evidence that he was a considerable landowner. The 1559 pardon roll described him as late of Ruscombe, Berkshire, and letters of administration granted to his widow on 27 Mar. 1563 give Buckland, Gloucestershire, as his residence.

Northampton Wills Bk. G, f. 41; Y, f. 176; C3/139/9; Peterborough Cath. Lib. no. 28, p. 37; *Eton College Reg.* ed. Sterry, 255; *Al. Cant.* i(3), 298; J. Bridges, *Northants.* ii. 418; *Vis. Lancs.* (Chetham Soc. lxxxi), 41; London Guildhall rep. 10, f. 168b; Egerton 2815; *APC*, ii. 273, 322, 372; C1/1020/52; Req. 2/6/133, 7/120; *CPR*, 1548–9, p. 25; 1558–60, p. 150; PCC admon. act bk. 1563, f. 59.

N.M.F.

PALMER, Andrew (c.1544–99), of Cheapside and St. Peter-le-Poor, London.

LONDON   1589, 1593

b. c.1544, ?s. of Simon Palmer, goldsmith of London. *m.* (1), at least 4ch.; (2) 1581, Elizabeth Bannister, 4ch. Auditor, London 1579–81; dep. comptroller of the mint by c.1576, comptroller from 1582; chamberlain of London c.1582; sec. of mineral and battery works 1568–85.[1]

After being apprenticed in 1558 to Richard Trappes, Palmer practised as a goldsmith in Cheapside, later becoming a mint official. When the corporation of London elected him chamberlain, Burghley asked them, 1 Jan. 1583, to choose someone else, as Palmer 'should give all his time to the mint'. His fee was at first £66 13s. 4d. per annum, reduced by 1594 as an economy measure. As comptroller he checked that the coins issued tallied with the bullion received, and, with the warden of the mint, presented occasional reports to the Council, meeting in the Star Chamber.[2]

On 15 Feb. 1589 Palmer spoke on the purveyors bill and was appointed to the committee on the same day. He was named to a committee concerning glass factories on 21 Mar., and reported the committee on the measuring of casks on 22 Mar. In 1593 he was appointed to a committee concerning the punishment of rogues (12 Mar.), and reported (23 Mar.) that the committee dealing with the retailers bill could not reach an agreement, although D'Ewes points out that he was never appointed to that committee. The London Members were also appointed to committees concerning maimed soldiers (2 Apr.), brewers (3 Apr.) and town planning permission (6 Apr.).

Palmer was often consulted by the government on currency matters. In 1575, for example, in a letter to Francis Walsingham*, he recommended that the proposed loan from Germany should be received only in dollars (thalers), and later he urged Walsingham and Burghley to set up a committee of inquiry into the standard weights for gold. He investigated the export of gold currency from the realm, and interrogated Thomas Parry, a fellow goldsmith, who was accused of receiving stolen plate. He suggested a new issue of farthings made of copper rather than silver, and was one of those commissioned to examine 'the account of trying of the ore, and for all other things belonging to the late voyage of Martin Frobisher', recently returned from Muscovy. The Council also employed him to investigate disputes between London merchants, considering him a person 'of good understanding in matters of merchandise'.[3]

Palmer invested some of his money in land and property, and also in industrial enterprises. In 1563 he acquired a house called the *White Hart* in Holy Trinity parish, London, though he did not live there, and he was probably the Andrew Palmer who, with John Herbert, received small land grants from the Crown in 1575. These were as far apart as Stoke Bliss, Worcestershire, Burnham in Buckinghamshire, and Royston, Hertfordshire. He acquired part of the manor of Southam, Gloucestershire, but on this occasion appears to have been acting for Sir Francis Walsingham.[4]

The most important industrial concern with which he became associated was the mineral and battery works, whose mining and manufacturing operations in several parts of the country attracted many leading political figures as investors. At its formation in 1568 Palmer, a shareholder, became the first secretary and held that office until 1585, when his apprentices took over. In 1587 Palmer, together with his son-in-law John Brode, Richard Martin and Humphrey Michell*, took out a licence at £50 per annum, and each of the partners invested about £800 in the Isleworth Copper and Brass Works. Shortly after William Laborer became a partner, difficulties arose and Palmer tried to withdraw his investment, was unable to do so, and alleged inefficiency and dishonesty in his partners, particularly Brode. The legal dispute lasted into the following reign.[5]

Palmer was a witness to the will of John Field, the puritan. His own will was made and proved in August 1599. He made provision for his family, except for his children by his first wife, who had already received their share of his goods. One of them, Richard, had qualified as a doctor. His son Andrew, whose wife Elizabeth was named as executrix, was assay master of the mint to the first two Stuart kings. The two overseers were each given a book from his library.[6]

[1] PCC 67 Kidd; A. B. Beaven, *Aldermen of London*, i. 289; *Analytical Index to the Remembrancia of the City of London*, 278; M. P. Donald, *Elizabethan Monopolies*, 36, 58; information on the mint from Dr. C.

E. Challis. [2] A. Heal, *London Goldsmiths*, 215; *Vis. London*, (Harl. Soc. xvii), 140, 141; W. Chaffers, *Gilda Aurifabrorum*, 230–1; Donald, 58; *Remembrancia*, 278; J. Craig, *The Mint*, 124; Lansd. 37, f. 137; 47, ff. 170, 172, 174; E101/304/14. [3] D'Ewes, 432, 433, 450, 451, 499, 508, 513, 514, 519; City of London Recs. R 22, ff. 36, 216; *APC*, x. 148; xi. 86, 89, 392–3; xii. 116, 238; xiii. 20–1; xv. 211–12; xviii. 384–5; *CSP Dom.* 1547–80, pp. 506, 605, 617; 1581–90, p. 86; Lansd. 31, f. 168; 37, ff. 125, 139. [4] *VCH Worcs.* iv. 353; *VCH Bucks.* iii. 182; *VCH Herts.* iii. 257; *CPR*, 1560–3, p. 585; *Bristol and Glos. Arch. Soc. Trans.* l. 303. [5] *CPR*, 1566–9, p. 274; Donald, 36, 58, 61, 71–2, 76, 97–8, 106–7, 158–60, 181–4; Lansd. 76, ff. 72 seq.; *VCH Mdx.* ii. 128–9. [6] PCC 38 Rutland, 67 Kidd, 47 Clarke.

M.R.P.

PALMER, Thomas I (1542–by 1616), of Angmering, Suss. and Blackwall, Mdx.

SUSSEX   1571, 1589

b. Oct. 1542, 2nd but 1st surv. s. of John Palmer† of Angmering, being o.s. by his 2nd w. Mary, da. of William, 1st Baron Sandys. *educ.* ?G. Inn 1562. *m.* (1) Mary, da. of Sir Thomas Palmer* of Parham, 7s. 1da.; (2) Alice. *suc.* fa.. 1563. Kntd. 1573.[1]

J.p. Suss. 1572; sheriff, Surr. and Suss. 1572–3; dep. lt. Suss. June 1585 – at least 1591.[2]

The Palmers had been established in Sussex from at least the beginning of the fourteenth century, and towards its end a fortunate marriage brought them lands in Angmering. It was there that the senior line resided under Elizabeth. Collateral branches of considerable influence also appeared, after the dissolution of the monasteries, at Parham, Sussex, and Wingham, Kent.[3]

Palmer was elected to Parliament for the county at a time when there was little competition. He served on committees dealing with the maintenance of the navy and the increase of tillage (21 May 1571), and the sheriffs of Surrey and Sussex (28 May). On 12 July 1574 he was sent to the Fleet for slandering the 12th Earl of Arundel. He was released 27 July. During the 1580s, he became deputy lieutenant of Sussex in partnership with Thomas Shirley I* and Walter Covert*, and was given a variety of local duties, including the disarming of Sussex recusants and the regulation of grain. In 1585 he took charge of the armour of William Shelley, a Sussex gentleman indicted for treason, and was granted some of his land. He was responsible for a survey of the Sussex coast in preparation against invasion in 1587. He was senior knight of the shire in the 1589 Parliament and thus entitled to serve on the subsidy committee appointed on 11 Feb. He was granted leave of absence 'to repair home ... for his special occasions of business', 22 Feb., but had evidently returned by 27 Feb. when he was nominated to attend the Lords over the purveyors bill. However, it may be that the clerk confused Sir Thomas with Andrew Palmer, who is also noted as being concerned with the purveyors bill. In May 1591 he was still a deputy lieutenant of Sussex, described as residing mainly at Blackwall, near London.

He built a new house at Angmering, known as 'New Place', which descended to his third son, Thomas, his eldest having died an infant and his second having become a gipsy. A fourth son, William, became a captain in the Netherlands, perhaps through the influence of Sir Thomas Shirley. Palmer was nominated to the Stepney Vestry in 1612 and marked 'dead' in or before 1616.[4]

[1] W. Berry, *Co. Genealogies, Suss.* (Comber's copy at Chichester), 46; *Vis. Suss.* (Harl. Soc. liii), 24; *Suss. Rec. Soc.* xiv. 175. [2] PRO Assizes 35 S.E. Circuit Suss. 14; *HMC Hatfield*, iii. 297; *APC*, xxi. 91. [3] Mousley thesis, 621 seq.; *DNB*. [4] D'Ewes, 187, 189, 431, 432–3, 440; Townshend, *Hist. Colls.* 20; *APC*, viii. 261–2, 267, 275; xxi. 91; Harl. 474, ff. 80v, 90v, 92; *Suss. Arch. Colls.* lv. 298; lviii. 161; *Suss. Rec. Soc.* xx. 289, 490; Lansd. l, f. 39; D. G. C. Elwes and C. J. Robinson, *Hist. West Suss.* 11; Lysons, *Environs*, iii. 449; *Mems. Stepney Par.* ed. Hill and Frere, 61, 73.

J.E.M.

PALMER, Thomas II (c.1541–1625), of Wingham, Kent.

ARUNDEL   1586, 1601

b. c.1541, s. of Sir Henry Palmer† of Wingham by Jane, da. of Sir Richard Windebank of Guisnes. *educ.* ?G. Inn 1562. *m.* c.1562, Margaret, da. of John Poley of Badley, Suff., 6s. 5da. *suc.* fa. 15 Jan. 1559. Kntd. 1603; *cr.* Bt. 1621.

J.p. Kent from 1577, sheriff 1595–6; gent. of privy chamber to James I.[1]

The identification of Thomas Palmer of Wingham as the MP for Arundel rests upon his being the only one of the Sussex family and its branches then living who was both an 'esquire' and of a suitable age to sit. He farmed one of the Earl of Arundel's manors, and was first cousin to Thomas Palmer I* of Angmering, Sussex, who lived only four miles from Arundel and may have helped to place him in Parliament. He was only 17 years old when his father died a year after being captured by the French at Guisnes, and became the ward of one John Muschamp, until 1562, when he entered on his property, including Wingham, a dissolved religious house.[2]

Possibly he was the Thomas Palmer appointed in or about November 1564 by Lord Cobham, on instructions from the Privy Council, to keep the moats and bulwarks of Kent at 6d. a day, and to have charge of munitions there. At any rate, in 1589 he and two others were called on by the Privy Council to sort out a local dispute concerned with the alleged smuggling of munitions to the enemy. In 1591 he was among those charged by the Council to investigate the 'great disorders and factious divisions' at New Romney, dating from the parliamentary election of 1588. He and his lady are said to have kept 60 'open Christmases' at Wingham without intermission. He died 7 Jan. 1625 and was succeeded by his grandson Thomas, his eldest son having died in 1608. Neither will nor inquisition post mortem has been found.[3]

[1] C142/123/93; W. Berry, *Co. Genealogies, Suss.* (Comber's copy at Chichester), 206; Lansd. 35, f. 133v; R. Jenyns, *Palmer Fam. of Suss.* (1672), 31–2. [2] SC 6 Eliz. 2213; *CSP Dom.* 1547–80, p. 105; *CPR*, 1558–60, p. 43. [3] *APC*, vii. 275; xviii. 396; xxi. 287–8; Jenyns, 6, 31–2; Wards 7/42/142.

J.E.M.

PALMER, Sir Thomas (by 1520–82), of Parham, Suss.

ARUNDEL	1553 (Mar.), 1553 (Oct.)
SUSSEX	1554 (Apr.)
GUILDFORD	1559

b. by 1520, 1st s. of Robert Palmer, citizen and merchant of London and Parham by his 1st w. Bridget or Beatrice, da. and coh. of John Wesse or West of Millington Yorks., alderman of London. *m.* (1) Griselda or Bridget, da. of John Caryll, serjeant-at-law of Warnham, 3da.; (2) by 1557, Katherine, da. of Sir Edward Stradling of St. Donats, Glam., 1 or 2s. *suc.* fa. May 1544. Kntd. 2 Oct. 1553.[1]

J.p. Suss. from 1547, q. by 1562; sheriff, Surr. and Suss. 1559–60; commr. piracy, Suss. 1565, dep. lt. 1569.[2]

Palmer held extensive lands in Sussex and built Parham House, which his family retained until the last years of Elizabeth's reign, when it was first leased then sold to (Sir) Thomas Bishopp*. Among a large number of land transactions in which Palmer took part was the purchase from the Crown, in July 1557, of £300 worth of Sussex property, much of it formerly belonging to Tortington priory. In April 1561 he was one of those to whom Laurence Stoughton apparently enfeoffed the manor of Stoughton near Guildford, though this may have been simply an arrangement under the statute of uses. However, Palmer's return to Elizabeth's first Parliament for Guildford was presumably due to his connexion with Henry, Earl of Arundel, high steward of the borough, who knighted him in October 1553, and whose servant he became.[3]

Palmer held office under Edward VI, Mary and Elizabeth, and was described by the bishop of Chichester in 1564 as a 'faint furtherer' of religion. The archbishop's visitation of the diocese during the vacancy of the see in 1569 included him among the gentlemen who 'at Easter receive communion at home in their chapels, and choose priests from a distance'. With a later bishop, Richard Curteys, he was on bad terms. In December 1573 Curteys brought unspecified charges against Palmer, and the Council appointed a commission to investigate them. The matter dragged on for some years, with Curteys citing Palmer for popery, and Sir Thomas and his friends complaining that the bishop was over-zealous in prosecuting the gentlemen of the shire. At the same time Palmer was involved in the affairs of his son-in-law John Leeds, who had gone abroad for religious reasons. When Leeds' wife Elizabeth returned to England in 1577, Palmer wrote to the Council that he would refuse to deal with his

daughter's matters unless their lordships approved. The government evidently discounted the charges against Sir Thomas himself: in 1579 he was asked to inquire into the activities of John Apsley's schoolmaster, Bywater, suspected of being a 'massing priest'.[4]

Palmer's name appeared regularly on Elizabethan commissions, from those dealing with important business such as musters, grain supplies and the suppression of piracy, to inquiries into such matters as 'lewd words' spoken by the sexton of Chichester cathedral. The last reference found to his official activities concerns the Sussex musters in May 1580.[5]

He died on or about 14 Apr. 1582 and was buried at Parham. His will, made in February 1580, left bequests to his children and sons-in-law, and £100 to a grand-daughter, Grizeld Roberts. After making arrangements for payments to the Queen out of his lands at Lyminster, he directed that the residue of his goods should be equally divided between his widow, Dame Katherine, and his son and heir William, aged 28 at the inquisition post mortem.[6]

[1] C142/70/46; 197/60; D. G. C. Elwes and C. J. Robinson, *Castles, Mansions and Manors of W. Suss.* 253; *Vis. Suss.* (Harl. Soc. liii), 24–5; PCC 12 Pynnyng, 18 Tirwhite; Add. 14311, f. 14; *LP Hen. VIII*, xix(2), p. 413; Mousley thesis, 641. [2] *CPR*, 1547–8, p. 90; *APC*, vii. 283; SP12/59/61. [3] C142/70/46; 197/60; *Suss. N. and Q.* xii. 46; Add. 6174, p. 59; *Surr. Feet of Fines* (Surr. Rec. Soc. xix), 144, 166; *CPR*, 1554–5, p. 305; 1555–7, pp. 251, 325; *Suss. Arch. Colls.* ix. 224; lxxvii. 256; Dallaway, *Hist. W. Suss.* ii(1), p. 26; PCC 18 Tirwhite. [4] *Cam. Misc.* ix(3), p. 9; R. B. Manning, *Religion and Soc. in Eliz. Suss.* 82; *VCH Suss.* ii. 25, 26; *Suss. Arch. Colls.* xvii. 81; *APC*, viii. 166; x. 50; xi. 77, 95; *CSP Dom.* 1547–80, p. 542 seq.; E. Heron-Allen, *Selsey Bill*, 165. [5] *APC*, vii. 19, 126, 283, 309; xii. 8; *CPR*, 1560–3, p. 443. [6] Dallaway, ii(1), p. 208; PCC 18 Tirwhite; *Suss. N. and Q.* ii. 62–3; C142/197/60.

N.M.F.

PALMES, Francis (c.1554–1613), of Lindley, Yorks. and Lancelevy, Hants.

KNARESBOROUGH	1586

b. c.1554, s. and h. of Sir Francis Palmes of Lindley by Margaret, da. of Roger Corbet of Moreton, Salop. *educ.* Magdalen Coll. Oxf. 1571; I. Temple 1573. *m.* Mary (*d.* 21 Mar. 1595), da. and coh. of Stephen Hadnall of Lancelevy, 6s. 5da. *suc.* fa. 1567. Kntd. 1601.

J.p. Yorks. (W. Riding) by 1582–1608, Hants 1600–8; member high commission, province of York 1599; sheriff, Hants 1600–1.

The Palmes family came from Naburn in Yorkshire, where they had been seated for several centuries. In 1516 they acquired the manor of Ashwell in Rutland, which Palmes's grandfather made the principal family seat. Having succeeded his father at the age of about 13, Palmes entered Oxford as of Ashwell, Rutland, and Lindley, Yorkshire, and the Inner Temple as of Lindley. Through his marriage he acquired lands in Hampshire, and appears to have settled at Lancelevy, near Sherfield, where his wife was buried in 1595. At the time of his return for Knaresborough, however, he held lands at Harrogate, Killinghall and Beckwith, all within the forest of Knaresborough. On 4 Nov. 1586 he was named to a Commons committee dealing with Mary Queen of Scots.

Palmes evidently prospered, perhaps as a lawyer. In 1601, as sheriff of Hampshire, he received the Queen at Silchester and escorted her to Basingstoke, where she knighted him. He made his will in June 1612, commending his spirit into the hands of Almighty God, hoping, through the mercy of Jesus Christ, to be purged of those great offences committed against Him as a result of 'carnal and wordly affections'. He was succeeded by his son Guy Palmes[†], who inherited his estates in Hampshire, Rutland and Yorkshire, as well as all his plate, armour and books. He left £800 each to two daughters for their marriage, as well as money for their maintenance, £10 per annum to a grandson, a similar sum to a godson, and 40s. each, plus one year's wages, to all his servants. His – unnamed – executors were to help the servants to find other jobs or lodgings, and none was to be left wanting a dwelling place.

Palmes died on 30 Mar. 1613.

Foster, *Vis. Yorks. N. Riding*; Woodward, *Hants.* iii. 192–3; *VCH Rutland*, i. 182; ii. 109; Lansd. 53, f. 195; PRO, pat. roll 42 Eliz.; *HMC Hatfield*, ix. 397; *VCH Hants*, iv. 104, 107; D'Ewes, 394; PCC 45 Capell; C142/333/43.

N.M.S.

PANTON, John (*d.* 1619), of Henllan, Denb. and Westminster, Mdx.

DENBIGH BOROUGHS	1597, 1601
HARWICH	1604*

s. of John Panton of Henllan. *m.* Eleanor, 3da.

Sec. and adviser on Welsh affairs to Thomas Egerton I* from c.1593–1617; to surv. crown lands in N. Wales in reversion c.1593; recorder, Denbigh from 1597.

Of an ancient Welsh family, Panton's immediate ancestors lived in the parish of Henllan, adjoining Denbigh, where Panton himself was assessed for taxes at 30s. in Elizabeth's reign. From about 1593, however, his life revolved around his work for Egerton, who, it must have been, arranged Panton's honorary admission to Lincoln's Inn without the obligation to 'continue in commons' while in attendance on his master.[1]

Panton's father had left him lands in Henllan, Llanynys and Llannefydd and a house in Denbigh. To these Panton was able to add further lands in Henllan which his 'cousin' Thomas Myddelton* had acquired for £200 in 1592. Other purchases extended his estate northwards into Llandulas and Abergele, Denbighshire and eastwards to Nannerch in Flintshire. Four years before his death Panton bought from the Crown the estate of Ystrad in Henllan. His one outstanding failure was his bid for a moiety of the crown

manor of Dinorwic, Caernarvonshire: it was granted him in 1597, but the title was challenged in the Exchequer by William Williams of Vaynol and others, and evidently proved defective. He also over-reached himself in his plan for a house in Henllan which should outshine those of his neighbours: only one wing was completed, which still lies in ruins.[2]

Returned to Parliament twice for Denbigh Boroughs through his local standing, Panton was eligible to attend a committee on Newport bridge appointed 29 Nov. 1597. He can hardly have taken his seat in the Commons in 1601, as the postponed election took place only three days before the end of the Parliament. He died at Westminster on 12 Mar. 1619. His will, dated 27 May 1618 and proved 27 Mar. following, divided his estates, subject to a life interest for the widow, between his three daughters, all under age. Though his brother Foulke, who deputized for him as recorder of Denbigh, and others of his family retained some standing there, it was not until the eighteenth century that a Panton again achieved any sort of eminence, in the person of Paul Panton, agricultural pioneer and patron of Welsh literature.[3]

[1] C142/378/120; PCC 12 Parker; J. Williams, *Denbigh Recs.* 64–5; *Surv. Denbigh*, ed. Vinogradoff and Morgan, i. 28, 65; Williams, *Eminent Welshmen* (1852), p. 244; *Arch. Camb.* (ser. 2), iv. 211; Williams, *Ancient and Mod. Denbigh* (1856) ch. xxii; E179/220/166–9, 186–7; Williams, *Parl. Hist. Wales*, 80; PRO ms cal. pat. 35 Eliz.; *CSP Dom.* 1598–1601, p. 388; *L. Inn Black Bk.* ii. 39 [2] Chirk Castle mss F12450, 177, 204; C142/378/120; *Denbigh Recs.* 167–8; *Cal. Wynn Pprs.* pp. 101, 109–10; PRO ms cal. pat. 39 Eliz.; *Augmentations*, ed. Lewis and Davies (Univ. Wales Bd. of Celtic Studies, Hist. and Law ser. xiii), 281; *Exchequer*, ed. E. G. Jones (same ser. iv), 64, 78; Pennant, *Tours* (1833), ii. 142. [3] D'Ewes, 565; C142/378/120; PCC 12 Parker; *Denbigh Recs.* 126–7, 144.

A.H.D.

PAPWORTH, Roger (*d.* c.1620), of Hoxton, Mdx.

DARTMOUTH	1589

Servant of the Earl of Bath from at least Nov. 1587 to at least 1609.

Little has been ascertained about Papworth, who was a servant of the lord lieutenant of Devon, the Earl of Bath. When in 1591 Thomas Hinson* was attacked in the county for exercising undue influence over his master, it was stated that Papworth was 'a man that dareth do nothing' without Hinson's backing. References to Papworth concern a deed between various Devon men and Lyme Regis in 1582; a payment in 1586 for his charges at Barnstaple in connexion with impressing soldiers for Ireland; a payment of 40s. from Exeter corporation, and, in 1590, an estimate of the value of some French prizes then at Ilfracombe. In 1602 Totnes corporation, which had been involved in lawsuits for several years, paid 10s. to him in Exeter for the town's 'former causes'. His name appears in the new company incorporated in 1612 to search for the North West passage. Papworth made his will at his home at Hoxton 1 Jan. 1613, and it was proved 19 Apr. 1620.

Roberts thesis; *Vis. London* (Harl. Soc. xvii), 303; *Lond. Mar. Lic.* (Harl. Soc. xxv), 11; Bodl. Rawl. D406; *Cambs. Par. Regs.* ii. 169; *PRO Lists and Indexes*, vii. 312; Harl. 5827, f. 158; *HMC 15th Rep. VII*, 5; Lansd. 62, f. 20; 68, f. 101; All Souls mss Whadborough 343; *CSP Dom.* 1603–10, p. 488; *Dorset Proc.* 1947, p. 82; *Barnstaple Recs.* ii. 107, 122; Exeter act bk. 4, f. 548; Totnes recs.; *CSP Col.* 1513–1613, p. 240; PCC 31 Soame.

P.W.H.

PARKER, Calthrop (d. 1618), of Erwarton, Suff.

SUFFOLK   1601

1st s. of Sir Philip Parker by Catherine, da. of Sir John Goodwin of Bucks. *educ.* Trinity Coll. Camb. c.1592; L. Inn 1596. *m.* Mercy, da. of Sir Stephen Soame*, at least 5s. 1da. Kntd. 1603; *suc.* fa. c.1605.

J.p. Suff. bef. 1611, sheriff 1611–12.[1]

Parker, a relative of Lord Morley, owned considerable property in Suffolk, and also had lands in Norfolk. Erwarton, the family's chief residence, had come to them in Edward VI's reign through the marriage of Sir Henry Parker to Elizabeth, daughter and heir of Sir Philip Calthrope. The son of this marriage, Sir Philip Parker, was knighted by the Queen when she went on progress through Suffolk in 1578.[2]

Parker himself was brought up against a puritan background, which he shared with a number of the other Suffolk knights of the shire for Elizabeth's reign. Nothing has been ascertained about his religious views, but his father was a close associate of Sir Robert Jermyn and (Sir) John Heigham*, and was included by Bishop Freake of Norwich in the list of his 'adversaries' which he sent to the Privy Council in 1578. A prominent member of the Dedham classis, Anthony Morse, was employed by Sir Philip at Erwarton as a tutor or domestic chaplain; he was a layman, but had received some kind of calling under which he claimed to act as a minister. Sir Philip would no doubt have had the support of his powerful puritan friends had he wished to stand for the county himself, but he clearly had no ambitions in that direction. In the event Calthrop Parker had the support of his father and Sir Robert Jermyn* and there 'suddenly' arose 'a new knight', as Henry Warner* reported to (Sir) Nicholas Bacon*, with little enthusiasm. Although his name does not appear in the records of the 1601 Parliament, Parker could have attended committees on procedure (3 Nov.), cloth-workers (18 Nov.) and monopolies (23 Nov.).[3]

Since Parker did not succeed to his estates until James I's reign, most of his active career lies outside the Elizabethan period. His marriage brought him into close contact with London trading interests, and his will mentions £3,000 which his father-in-law, Sir Stephen Soame, had been commissioned to invest for him in the East India Company. In July 1618 a warrant was issued to pay Parker and others 2,178 crowns, as a bounty on the tonnage of seven newly-built ships.

Some years after the death of his father, as the head of the family, Parker was forced to take steps to protect the interests of his sister Catherine, wife of Sir William Cornwallis. When her husband died in 1614 she was left in financial difficulties, as her father-in-law Sir Charles Cornwallis had not made adequate arrangements for settling lands as her jointure. In July of that year Parker was given permission to visit Sir Charles in the Tower to get the matter settled.

He died on 5 Sept. 1618, still a comparatively young man, leaving a large family, of which the eldest son, Philip, was about seventeen. In his will, drawn up in August 1618 and proved the following January, he spoke of himself as in middle-age and full health. This suggests that he may have died suddenly, but no details are known. He must have been a wealthy man, as in addition to his lands he was able to leave bequests from his 'cattle, wool, shipping and vessels as well in Suffolk as in Norfolk'.

His heir, Sir Philip, and his son-in-law, John Gurdon, represented Suffolk and Ipswich respectively at the beginning of the Long Parliament.[4]

[1] *Vis. Suff.* ed. Metcalfe, 156; C142/288/137; Wards 7/27/226. [2] C142/369/134; Wards 7/59/171; Copinger, *Suff.* vi. 36. [3] Collinson thesis, 359, 883; Univ. Chicago, Bacon mss; D'Ewes, 624, 642, 649. [4] PCC 1 Parker; *CSP Dom.* 1611–18, p. 560; *APC*, 1613–1614, p. 484; Wards 7/59/171.

N.M.F.

PARKER, John I (1548–1619), of Lambeth, Surr., Bekesbourne, Kent, and Cambridge.

QUEENBOROUGH   1571

b. 5 May 1548, 1st s. of Matthew Parker, abp. of Canterbury, by Margaret (d. 1570), da. of Robert Harlestone. *educ.* Peterhouse, Camb. 1562. *m.* Joanna, da. of Richard Cox, bp. of Ely, 4 or 5s. 3da. *suc.* fa. 1575. Kntd. 1603.

Jt. keeper of PCC 1570–1; actuary of ct. of audience 1572–c.74; jt. registrar of PCC 1573, sole 1574; keeper of Archbishop's palace at Canterbury 1573; j.p.q. Kent 1583–93; j.p. Surr. from c.1583; commr. for eccles. causes, Surr. c.1586; steward of Archbishop Whitgift's household 1588; j.p. Isle of Ely 1591.

Until his marriage Parker lived mainly with his father at Canterbury or at Lambeth, where the archbishop bought Lambeth House, formerly the property of the Duke of Norfolk, for his wife Margaret. In 1570 it descended to her son Matthew, and on his death in 1574 to John's son, also Matthew. Joanna Cox brought her husband lands in Leicestershire and Norfolk, and he also had an estate, probably in right of his wife, at Bassingbourn, Essex (now

Cambridgeshire). In 1568 Bishop Cox made him joint master of the game at Somersham park, Huntingdonshire. Between 1572 and 1576 he paid nearly £2,000 to the Marquess of Winchester and his heir for the manor of Nunney Castle, Somerset, but there is no record of his having ever lived there. His favourite property was at Bekesbourne near Canterbury, leased to him about 1586 by Whitgift, who also confirmed him in his lease of the manor of Boughton, Kent. In May 1594 Parker sold Bekesbourne House for over £350, subsequently dividing his time between his chamber in Doctors' Commons, his house at Lambeth, and property called St. Mary Ostle, Cambridge, left him by his father.

Strype quotes a contemporary estimate of Parker and his brother as 'very hopeful young men, and adorned with all their father's and mother's manners', their 'carriage – so obliging, pleasant and humane, that they had the love and esteem of all'. Though he later gained the reputation of a shrewd not to say unscrupulous businessman, Parker was certainly generous to his close relatives. He went much further in providing for his brother's widow than his position as executor for Matthew required, continuing to pay her a £44 annuity from lands in Bexley, Kent, even after they had been sold, buying her late husband's jewels for her and giving her presents of money and plate – 'a large recompense', according to his own notes, 'for that my brother was advanced unto by her'. He was equally generous to his daughter Margaret on her marriage, and it may have been through kindness that he kept as his housekeeper at Cambridge the widow of one of his relatives there, having bought furniture and pictures from her (including portraits of Erasmus and Sir Thomas More†).

Archbishop Parker obtained appointments for his sons in the ecclesiastical courts, and no doubt it was he who had Parker returned as one of Queenborough's first MPs, a letter from the Privy Council asking that suitable burgesses should be returned for the Kent boroughs having been sent to the archbishop and Lord Cobham.

The lands of the archbishopric, which were considerable, needed efficient administration, and from about 1573 Parker acted as surveyor for his father and keeper of the Archbishop's palace at Canterbury, possibly continuing to do much of this work during the sequestration of Grindal and under Whitgift. Among his other duties was that of executor to his father in 1575. The archbishop left books, manuscripts, money and plate, and the administration of the will seems to have been difficult, Parker drawing up memoranda about it as late as 1593. Some books supposed to go to Corpus Christi, Cambridge 'were not found by me in my father's library, but either lent or embezzled, whereby I could not deliver them to the college'.

The last 16 years of Parker's life are not as fully documented as his Elizabethan career. In February 1597

he was granted an honorary admission to Gray's Inn, and he was knighted by James I at Westminster in July 1603. After this date no more references to him in London have been found, and he seems to have retired to Cambridge some years before his death, spending much of his time there in drawing up an illustrated manuscript of heraldry. Though at one time he had been able to pay over £1,900 for an estate, by August 1618 he was in serious financial difficulties (whether through the extravagance of his son Richard, or through his own generosity or for some other reason is not known), and Corpus Christi College made him a grant and paid the expenses of his funeral, which took place at Great St. Mary's, Cambridge, on 29 Jan. 1619.

Parker Corresp. (Parker Soc.), pp. x–xi, 379–81; Strype, *Parker*, passim; *HMC 7th Rep.* 630, 642; Strype, *Whitgift*, i. 46; *CSP Dom.* 1598–1601, p. 527; C3/284/39; PCC 39 Pyckering; Add. 48018, f. 294v; *DNB* (Parker, Matthew); Lansd. 97, f. 177; R. Masters, *Corpus Christi*, ed. Lamb, 337.

N.M.F.

PARKER, John II (c.1548–1617), of Willingdon, Suss. and Charing Cross, London.

HASTINGS	1589
TRURO	1593
DUNHEVED (LAUNCESTON)	1601
EAST LOOE	1604

b. c.1548, 2nd. s. of Thomas Parker† of Willingdon by Eleanor, da. of William Waller of Groomsbridge, Kent; bro. of Sir Nicholas*. *unm.* Kntd. 1603.[1]

Gent. pens. by 1587–1603; constable, Leominster castle 1589; bailiff of Longney manor, Yorks. 1589; keeper of Falmouth castle 1603–*d.*; capt. of Pendennis castle 1603–*d.*[2]

Parker, who came from a Sussex gentry family, spent much of his life in Ireland. Although wounded when storming a castle in Clanricarde, he seems to have attracted little notice until the defeat at Armagh in 1598, when he and his company fought bravely with the rearguard. Some time after this he was transferred to the garrison at Berwick, but evidently finding the place irksome, he wrote to Cecil in 1601, asking to return to Ireland. It is not clear how he obtained his parliamentary seats. His cousin Lord Buckhurst may have promoted his return at Hastings, and Cecil his return for Truro, but Parker was related to, and was to succeed, the captain of Pendennis castle in Cornwall, Sir Nicholas Parker (not to be confused with Sir Nicholas Parker*) who may have contrived his Cornish borough seats in 1593 and 1601.[3]

Parker's years of service, in his own estimation, brought few rewards, though he obtained various small grants, and after the Essex uprising he was assigned a fine of £400 imposed on one of the persons implicated. One grant, however, might have brought in a reasonable income. This was the office to file bills and other pleadings in Chancery, granted to him on 9 Apr. 1594, one day before Egerton became master of the rolls, and during a vacancy in that office. The filing had previously been done by the six clerks, whose appointment lay with the master of the rolls, and no patent would have been granted if the office had not been vacant. Indeed, Parker's letters patent stipulated that before he or his deputies commenced work, they were to take an oath before this dignitary. Naturally Egerton was opposed to the grant and frustrated it by the simple means of refusing to administer the oath. Parker's supplications had no effect, despite support from Buckhurst, though Egerton allowed Parker's office to be listed in the return made by the Chancery commissioners in 1598, and even approved the choice of a deputy. Furthermore the six clerks agreed to let Parker collect his fee of 12d., from some suitors, though they were careful not to allow him to do any filing. Most of the suitors resisted what appeared to them as extortion, and after the accession of James I Parker was able to collect nothing. It was later stated that he 'had never the possession of any one pleading by virtue of his grant, nor could be, for he was not to execute his office before he was sworn'. As Bruce, master of the rolls in the new reign, continued Egerton's policy, Parker submitted the matter to the consideration of three judges. They found against him, stating that the grant was void in law, and affirming that the custody of bills and pleadings belonged to the master of the rolls, under whom the six clerks were subordinate officers for that service. Parker informed Salisbury in June 1606 that he intended to petition the King, and failing satisfaction would retire to Cornwall, which he did. He died 15 Oct. 1617.[4]

[1] Berry, Co. Genealogies, Suss. 12; H. R. Mosse, Mon. Effigies Suss. 161. [2] CSP Ire. 1586–8, p. 41; Mort thesis, 236; CSP Dom. 1603–10, p. 10; Add. 3378, f. 88; PCC 107 Weldon. [3] Egerton Pprs. ed. Collier (Cam. Soc. xii), 198; CSP Ire. 1574–85, pp. 140, 366, 547; 1592–8, passim; 1589, pp. 279, 320; Cal. Carew Pprs. ii. 464; iii. 332; HMC Hatfield, xi. 450. [4] Jones thesis, 156–9; Egerton Pprs. 198–200, 201–2, 203–4, 208–9; PCC 107 Weldon; HMC Hatfield, xviii. 184.

w.j.j.

PARKER, Sir Nicholas (1547–1620), of Ratton and Willingdon, Suss.

SUSSEX   1597

b. 1547, 1st s. of Thomas Parker[†] and bro. of John II*. m. (1) c.Jan. 1573, Jane (d.1557), da. of Sir William Courtenay[†] of Powderham, Devon, wid. of Francis Browne, bro. of Anthony Browne[†], 1st Visct. Montagu, s.p.; (2) Elizabeth, da. of John Baker[†] of London, sis. of Richard Baker*, s.p.; (3) Katherine, da. of Sir John Temple (d.1603), of Stowe, Bucks., 6s. 2da.; (?4) Avis, wid. of one Erisey, ?s.p. suc. fa. 1580. Kntd. 1591.[1]

J.p. Suss. from 1580, sheriff 1586–7, 1593–4, dep. lt. 1587, commr. recusancy July 1592.[2]

Parker was a cousin of Robert Sackville, his fellow knight of the shire in 1597. He was named to a Commons committee on 16 Nov. 1597 dealing with forestallers, regrators and engrossers. His position as knight for Sussex entitled him to attend committees concerning enclosures (5 Nov.), the poor law (5, 22 Nov.), armour and weapons (8 Nov.), penal laws (8 Nov.), monopolies (10 Nov.), the subsidy (15 Nov.), land reclamation (3 Dec.) and the repair of the Queen's highways (27 Jan. 1598). Though presumably conforming to the Elizabethan church, he had Catholic relations, and in 1583 was described as 'suspect or weak, and follows only those noblemen who are dangerous in the county'. Three years later, when he was sheriff, his mother-in-law, a recusant, was living with him at Lewes. However, he had already demonstrated his loyalty in 1584 when he arrested and sent to Walsingham a recusant fleeing to France, and in 1592 he was appointed a recusancy commissioner. Parker was more prominent in the military affairs than in the civil government of Sussex. He became a deputy lieutenant in 1587 and was knighted by Lord Admiral Howard, at Cowdray, Viscount Montagu's mansion. In 1596 he provided 100 Sussex men for Cadiz, and the following May raised 400 for an expedition to be led by the lord admiral and Lord Buckhurst. In October 1597 it was planned that he should take charge of the defence of Sussex in the event of an invasion.[3]

In October 1601 he offered his help at court to the port of Rye, which was seeking government aid to repair its decaying harbour, and he was one of the port's commissioners for sewers in 1604. He remained a deputy lieutenant to his death, and despite his age was engaged on military duties in 1619 when he wrote to Matthew Parker, son of the archbishop, whom he styled his kinsman.[4]

He died 9 Mar. 1620, aged 73, and was buried in the family chapel in Willingdon church. He had made his will in 1615, appointing his wife executrix and his brother Sir John Parker overseer, but both predeceased him. He provided for his younger children, leaving estates in Eastbourne, Hailsham, Jevington and Willingdon to his eldest son Thomas, who was granted administration of the will. Thomas, who became a deputy lieutenant, supported Parliament in the civil war. Henry Parker, younger son of Sir Nicholas, was a writer and scholar.[5]

[1] Mousley thesis, 646–8; Vis. Suss. (Harl. Soc. liii), 22; Lond. Mar. Lic. (Harl. Soc. xxv), 55; Vis. Devon ed. Vivian, 247; Berry, Co. Genealogies, Kent, 216. [2] Harl. 703, ff. 49, 67; Add. 5702, f. 196. [3] D'Ewes, 552, 553, 555, 557, 558, 561, 567, 589; E179/190/298; Vis. Suss.; PCC 1 Dorset; SP12/165/22; Lansd. 53, ff. 164–5; CSP Dom. 1581–90, p. 192; 1595–7, p. 526; HMC Hatfield, vi. 65; vii. 206; APC, xxvii. 105. [4] E. Suss. RO, Rye hundreds 1599–1606, ff. 387, 388; HMC 13th Rep. IV, 131; Suss. Arch. Colls. lix. 118. [5] PCC 25 Soame; Suss. Arch. Colls. v. 35, 102–3; xiv. 101; xvi. 189; xl. 2, 5, 7, 22; lix. 118, 122; DNB.

R.C.G.

PARKER, Thomas (c.1510–70), of Norwich, Norf.

NORWICH   1563

b. c.1510, 5th s. of William Parker, worsted weaver of Norwich by Alice Monings of Suff.; bro. of Matthew Parker, abp. of Canterbury. *m.* Joan Agas, 1s. 5da.

Freeman, Norwich 1538, sheriff and alderman 1559, mayor 1568–9.

Parker was a Norwich haberdasher, not among the wealthiest of the city's merchants. With his brother Matthew, he went into the rebels' camp outside Norwich in 1549 in an unsuccessful attempt to persuade Ket's followers to disperse, He did not reach the higher civic offices until his brother – with whom he always remained friendly – had become powerful. There is no record of any activity by Parker in his one Parliament, for which the city paid him the regulation wages of 2s. a day. During his mayoralty he served on a commission, led by the bishop of Norwich, to survey the state of the cathedral. During this period also, against local opposition, the rules governing the conduct of the immigrants from the Netherlands in Norwich were confirmed. Archbishop Parker's friendly feelings towards the 'strangers' were probably shared by his brother. Parker died in 1570, leaving 'unto my Lord my brother for a remembrance' a gold ring, and small bequests to the archbishop's children and other kinsmen. He bequeathed money for six sermons by 'a godly preacher', and requested that his 'great bible' should be given to a Walsingham church. Most of his goods he left to his wife, the sole executrix; his 'old acquainted and worshipful friend Mr. John Aldrich'* was overseer. The will, dated 6 Apr. 1570, was proved 24 Apr.

Strype, *Parker*, i. 3–6, 52–3; iii. 49; *Cal. Norwich Freemen*, 106; H. Le Strange, *Norf. Official Lists*, 108; Norwich corp. ct. bk. 1562–9, p. 122; *CPR*, 1566–9, pp. 205–6; *The Walloons and their Church at Norwich* (Hug. Soc. i), pt. 1, pp. 19, 38; PCC 13 Lyon.

R.V.

PARKINS (PERKINS), Christopher (c.1543–1622), of London.

RIPON   1597, 1601
MORPETH   1604

b. c.1543. *educ.* Winchester 1555; Oxf. BA 1565; DCL presumably abroad. *m.* 1617, Anne, da. of Anthony Beaumont of Glenmore, Leics., wid. of James Brett of Hoby, Leics., *s.p.* Kntd. 1603.[1]

Intelligence agent in Poland 1588/9; envoy to Poland, Prussia, and the princes of Eastland 1590, to Denmark 1591, 1592, to the Empire 1593, to Denmark 1598 and 1600.[2]

Dean, Carlisle 1596; master of requests extraordinary 1598; member of two commissions for piracy 1599; Latin sec. 1601; commr. suppressing unauthorised books 1603; member, Doctors' Commons ?1605; master of requests 1617; member, Clothworkers' Company.[3]

The career of Christopher Parkins was unusual enough to arouse comment in his own time. It was summed up by the letter writer John Chamberlain, who in 1622 recorded the death of 'Sir Christopher Parkins, Jesuit, doctor, dean, master of requests and what not'.[4]

Though usually said to have belonged to the family of Parkins of Bunny, Nottinghamshire, Christopher was clearly one of another branch of the family, the Parkins or Perkins of Ufton Court, Berkshire, a well-known place of concealment for priests. The only precise information we have about his family background is that he was, in his own words, a 'near kinsman' of the recusant Francis Parkins, who succeeded his childless uncle Richard to the manor of Ufton in 1560. In 1599 Christopher petitioned Sir Robert Cecil for the proceeds of Francis's recusancy fines.[5]

When Parkins went as a scholar to Winchester in 1555, he was said to be 12 years old and to have come from Reading. This was only six miles away from the family seat at Ufton. He went on to Oxford – probably New College – graduated in 1565, and then went abroad for over 20 years. He is said to have become a Jesuit in Rome in 1566 at the age of 19, but he himself stated that he was over 20 when he left England. This is borne out by another statement relating to his age, namely that he was 50 in 1594. It is clear that he must have continued his studies abroad, and his doctorate was presumably obtained at a foreign university, for he was certainly described as doctor when he returned to England, and was said, in 1597, to have held the degree for 30 years. Parkins acquired an excellent reputation for learning, particularly as a Latin scholar, and is supposed to have written some plays in Latin. Bishop Goodman wrote of him in his *Court of James I*: 'Truly he had a great understanding and I have sometimes sat by him when he hath read his petitions and epitomized them, as master of requests, and therein he had an excellent faculty'. Little is known for certain about Parkins's long period abroad: the evidence is confused. However, it is definite that he went to Rome and Venice and that he became both a priest and a Jesuit. He is also believed to have lived in Germany and, according to Strype, was working as a Jesuit in Prague in 1587. About 1585 he had met William Cecil, grandson of Lord Burghley, in Italy. Unknown to Parkins, young William Cecil took home a copy of a pamphlet which Parkins had composed in Venice. Writing to Sir Robert Cecil some years later, the author said that the pamphlet was about the Jesuits and 'written with the respect of the Pope and his church, necessary for my own safety ... though I had for some years before been resolved in those points, and was then working some good means to extricate myself from them'.[6]

Parkins and William Cecil are said to have returned to England together, Cecil repaying help which Parkins had given him on the continent by smoothing the way for his friend in England. However, the little evidence we have suggests rather that Parkins entered Walsingham's service without having first returned to England. They were evidently in touch not later than 1588, since on 16 May 1589 Parkins wrote to Walsingham acknowledging his letter of the previous October, which had only just arrived. He said that he was engaged in business 'in behalf of the Queen's subjects', and was about to go to the court of Poland to confer with the King and nobles, who were favourable to him. He claimed to have been well received – presumably at Elbing – 'as coming from the Queen of England', and said that the citizens there had asked him to deliver certain letters to the King of Poland.[7]

Like other agents of Walsingham, Parkins moved on from intelligence work to the direct service of the Queen. It is difficult to say when the change took place. He was granted an annuity of 100 marks in or before December 1591, but in May of the previous year he had received £300 when he was 'sent on her Majesty's necessary affairs to Poland, Prussia and other parts of the East Country'. At this time he was given an official safe conduct, and as many as ten government letters to deliver to rulers, influential statesmen and local officials in eastern Europe. But he was still not in regular employment. As late as August 1594 he asked Sir Robert Cecil that 'now after five years' proof I may be admitted to her Majesty's service ... These four years I have been used extraordinarily for Latin dispatches ... My suit is that I may do with order what I do already extraordinarily, with some ability for my convenient maintenance'.[8]

It was evidently his religious position which was at first a hindrance to finding government employment. In May 1589 he wrote to Walsingham that he could not approve the religious laws in his home country, though he admired English political institutions and 'would enjoy them'. Among his other troubles at this time, the notorious Edward Kelley, whom he had met in Prague, accused him of being implicated in a plot to murder the Queen. It is not clear by what date he had definitely renounced Catholicism, but he was back in England by the end of 1589. It may have been at this time that he sustained 'undeserved imprisonment and suspicion'. Robert Beale* later referred to having had Parkins a prisoner in his house 'on no small charges'. Apparently it was Beale himself who 'showed Mr. Secretary Walsingham the contrarieties and unlikelihoods' of the accusations against Parkins, 'and so was some means that he got the more favour'. Once accepted as an official agent of the government, Parkins was used on a number of foreign missions, in the course of which he sent home valuable accounts of the places he visited. He acquired some notoriety on the continent, and in March 1596 stated that during his last voyage to Poland the Pope offered 'near £2,000 for his life', because, he alleged, he had 'boldly resisted the insolent proceedings' of the clergy and the Pope's legate against the dignity of

her Majesty. In 1598, before being sent on a mission to Denmark in the company of Lord Zouche, he was appointed an honorary master of requests. He twice wrote to Cecil in this year defending his reputation abroad.[9]

Though the annuity granted him in 1591 kept him from sinking, Parkins was disappointed of being 'settled in her Majesty's service', and he now began to write regularly to Burghley and Cecil asking for preferment. During these years, he also served the government as economic adviser on commercial affairs concerned with Denmark, the Empire, the Hanse towns, Muscovy, Turkey and Poland. Letters to the Queen were sent to him for translation and comment, and were frequently returned by him together with draft replies. This was why, in 1594, he complained to Robert Cecil that for four years he had been used 'extraordinarily', pointing out that there had formerly been two Latin secretaries, 'one for countenance and one for labour'. When the office actually fell vacant in 1596, Parkins became more insistent, pleading that for years he had written 'some good part of the Queen's Latin letters', and that the office should rather be given to 'such as have long laboured in the same, than to interlopers'. He felt that there was prejudice against him for having been a Catholic, and it was 'no small disgrace' that he was rejected. Unable to live on his annuity, which he bestowed upon his servants 'for occasions of her Majesty's service', he could not afford suitable lodgings at court, and had to rely on the hospitality of Alderman Ratcliffe, who had a house in London and another at Harrow. Furthermore, upon at least one of his foreign missions, he had had 'to ground the means of his provision' upon Alderman Ratcliffe's credit. He wanted some 'spiritual living', such as the deanery of York or Eton, Durham or Carlisle, because he had renounced the chance of employment in other parts of the world, had spent his time in 'books and politics', and had given up everything for the Queen's service. But there were some who 'urged' her that it was not honourable to employ him on account of his foreign education, an imputation he refuted with a scholar's care, claiming that he had studied at Winchester and Oxford, and had received no education abroad but 'what might stand with good English duty'. In the end he was given his deanery, and the next year 1597 marked his entry – presumably honorary – into Gray's Inn, and his first appearance in Parliament, for Ripon, a seat presumably made available to Cecil by the archbishop of York. He was named to committees on the penal laws (8 Nov.), the deprivation of bishops at the beginning of the reign (3 Dec.), the double payment of debts on shop books (which he reported to the House 5 Dec.), a legal matter (11 Jan. 1598) and the pawnbrokers bill (7 Feb.). In September and October 1601, he wrote to Cecil asking to be nominated 'a burgess for the coming Parliament', and was again returned for Ripon. This time he served on committees concerned with the penal laws (a hardy perennial in this period), 2 Nov.; the painter-stainers, 24 Nov.; and on either 26 or 27 Nov. he reported to the House a bill concerned with merchants and customs, recommending that it should not 'be any more dealt in by this House'. In this year he quarrelled – apparently over precedence – with his friend and associate Robert Beale.[10]

Parkins eventually obtained the official appointments he sought, and he was no longer poor at the time of his death, having acquired a London house of his own in Cannon Row, perhaps through his late and curious marriage to a widowed sister of the Countess of Buckingham. It is possible that she was his second wife as a 'Lady Parkins' is mentioned in the State Papers for 1612 about whom nothing is known. In his will, dated 30 Aug. 1620, he said that he was 'confident to be saved by Jesus Christ, our only Saviour'. He commended his soul to God, and his body to be buried 'without solemnity in private manner' at Westminster, if he should die there, in some decent place in the collegiate church of St. Peter, to which he left £50, with £20 to the poor of the parish. To the University of Oxford he left an annuity of £25 to increase the salary of the lecturer in divinity. He also left £10 each to Gray's Inn, Doctors' Commons and the Clothworkers' Company. He mentioned no relatives except his wife, and the children of his sister – all unnamed – to whom he left £10 each. He referred to a sum of £1,000 due to him from the Merchant Adventurers, which he divided among three men for their good services. Also in consideration of long service, he constituted Anthony Bright his heir and sole executor, leaving him a small estate. The archbishop of Canterbury was made supervisor, and received a 'great gilt cup with the cover shutting thereunto'. Parkins died at the end of August 1622, and was buried in Westminster abbey.[11]

[1] HMC Hatfield, vi. 122; Chester, Reg. Westminster Abbey, 119. [2] CSP Ven. 1592–1603, pp. 78 n, 83, 99, 116, 410 n; HMC Hatfield, iii. 411; iv. 324; v. 90–1; viii. 187, 235; x. 129; CSP Dom. 1581–90, p. 664; 1591–4, pp. 138, 232; 1595–7, p. 64; 1598–1601, pp. 54–5, 57, 130, 134, 135, 415. [3] Chester, 119; W. B. J. Allsebrook, 'Court of Requests in reign of Eliz.' (London MA thesis 1936), pp. 28–30, 34; CSP Dom. 1598–1601, pp. 147, 271; APC, xxxii. 179, 499; Chamberlain Letters ed. McClure, i. 323; PCC 84 Savile; DNB. [4] CSP Dom. 1619–23, p. 449. [5] Wood, Fasti, i. 166–7; DNB; VCH Berks. iii. 441; HMC Hatfield, ix. 76. [6] Kirby, Winchester Scholars, 133; Wood, Fasti, i. 166–7; Al. Ox. iii. 1117; HMC Hatfield, vi. 122; vii. 404; A. M. Sharp, Hist. Ufton Court, 235; Strype, Annals, pt. ii. 599; CSP Dom. 1591–4, p. 547; 1595–7, p. 126. [7] DNB; Wood, Fasti, i. 166–7; HMC Hatfield, iii. 411. [8] E403/1693, f. 9d; PRO Index 6800, ff. 400–4; HMC Hatfield, iv. 576. [9] HMC Hatfield, iii. 411; vi. 122; vii. 405, 516–17; CSP Dom. 1598–1601, pp. 49, 53, 54–5, 57. [10] CSP Dom. 1591–4, pp. 138, 232, 547; 1595–7, pp. 115, 117–18; HMC Hatfield, iv. 239, 324, 576; v. 369; vi. 92, 122, 248, 432–3; vii. 404–5, 516–17; xi. 390, 444; Kirby, 133; D'Ewes, 567, 568, 578, 594, 622, 650, 654, 657; Townshend, Hist. Colls. 254. [11] CSP Dom. 1611–18, p. 107; PCC 84 Savile; Chester, 119.

N.M.S.

PARKINS, George (c.1576–1626), of Bunny, Notts.

LEICESTER   1597

b. c.1576, 1st s. of Richard Parkins* of Bunny by Elizabeth, da. of Adam or Aden Beresford of Fenney Bentley, Derbys., wid. of Humphrey Barlowe of Stoke, Derbys. educ. I. Temple 1587, called 1598. m. by 1598, Mary, da. and h. of Edward Isham of Walmer Castle, Kent, 4s. 3da. suc. fa. 1603. Kntd. 22 July 1603.[1]

Capt. Walmer castle 1601–9; sheriff, Notts. 1613–14.

Parkins's father was recorder of Leicester and Parkins himself acted as London agent for the town. He was made a freeman in 1598. Long letters from him about the town's petition for a new charter and the attempt to promote Leicester to county status, survive among the borough records. After succeeding to his estates, Parkins probably retired, appearing in the borough records only as the recipient of small gifts. He was never a bencher of his inn of court, and although the visitation of Nottinghamshire, taken in 1614, describes him as recorder of Nottingham, the borough records do not confirm this.[2]

In 1600 the Privy Council issued a warrant for Parkins's apprehension, but the cause cannot have been serious, for the following year he was granted the captaincy of Walmer castle, which his father-in-law had previously held. He evidently resided there for part of the time, undertaking repairs and attending to garrison duties. He also bought an estate called Berry Court, in nearby Old Romney, which he later resold. He died intestate on 23 Aug. 1626 and was buried at Bunny. Two years before his death he had settled his wife's Kent estate upon his daughter Mary. His paternal estates descended to his son Isham, to whom administration of the property was granted.[3]

[1] C142/280/79; Vis. Notts. (Harl. Soc. iv), 159–60; Thoresby, Notts. i. 93–4; Annals Nottingham, ed. Barley, ii. 549. [2] Ms cal. and index pat. rolls 37–43 Eliz. PRO 43 (16), p. 26; Walmer Recs. ed. Elvin, 229; Leicester Recs. iii. passim; Nottingham Recs. iv. 426, 429. [3] APC, xxx. 322; Walmer Recs. 169, 179; C142/483/108; Thoresby, i. 94; PCC admon. act bk. 1627, f. 185.

S.M.T.

PARKINS (PERKINS), Richard (?bef. 1539–1603), of Bunny, Notts.

NOTTINGHAM   1584, 1586, 1589, 1593

?b. bef. 1539, ?2nd s. of Richard Parkins of Ashby in Bottesford, Lincs. by his w. née Atkinson. educ. I. Temple, called 1568. m. Elizabeth (d. June 1570), da. of Adam or Aden Beresford of Fenney Bentley, Derbys., wid. of Humphrey Barlowe of Stoke, Derbys., 4s. inc. George* 4da.[1]

Recorder, Leicester from 1575, Nottingham from c.1582; master of Plumptre's hospital, Nottingham; sheriff, Nottingham 1599–1600.

Parkins is said to have been descended from Thomas Parkins of Ufton Court, Berkshire, and if so was probably related to Christopher Parkins*, the diplomat and dean of Carlisle, who appears in an indenture concerning the disposal of Richard's property and is also thought to have originated in Berkshire. Richard, however, had no other connexion with that county, and in a letter to the Earl of Shrewsbury claimed descent from 'divers of the ancient houses' of Staffordshire, Derbyshire, Nottinghamshire, Leicestershire and elsewhere. He was brought up in the household of a 'Mr. Mountsexens' of Peterborough, who was probably John Mountsteven[†], registrar of the bishop of Peterborough. Mountsteven may have been responsible for launching Parkins on his legal career. At any rate, while still at the Inner Temple, 'Mountsexens' introduced Parkins to Mrs. Frideswide Strelley, a wealthy widow of Ulverscroft in Leicestershire, and gentlewoman of the privy chamber under Mary. His entry into Mrs. Strelley's household was of considerable importance in Parkins's career, for it brought him to the notice of the 3rd Earl of Huntingdon. On the lady's death in 1565, Parkins became one of the executors of her will, a position he was accused of abusing, in conspiracy with the Earl, who was said to have favoured the lawyer 'for his protestannical [sic] religion'. How much truth lay in these charges is uncertain, but Parkins's religious beliefs and the Earl's patronage afford an explanation for his appointment as recorder of Leicester in 1575.[2]

The strength of Parkins's position at both Leicester and Nottingham was shown in the parliamentary election in 1584. When news of the issue of the writs reached Leicester, the mayor urged him to accept nomination there rather than at Nottingham, even in the face of a request for nomination of both Members from Sir Ralph Sadler*, chancellor of the duchy of Lancaster. The intervention of another candidate supported by Sir George Hastings, representing the Earl of Huntingdon's interests, further complicated the election, and it was possibly to extricate the mayor from an embarrassing position that Parkins decided to sit for Nottingham, near his estate at Bunny, which he had acquired through his marriage.[3]

Parkins continued to sit for Nottingham but his son George was returned for Leicester in 1597. Despite ill health, and a vague threat to resign his office at Leicester in 1592, Parkins remained in office in both towns right up to his death. His last important duty at Nottingham was performed on 21 Apr. 1603, when he gave an address of welcome to the new King's wife and son. On Thursday, 23 June that year he welcomed them at Leicester. He fell ill on the same day, rode home to Bunny on the Sunday and died there 3 July, being buried in the chancel of the parish church. By his will, drawn up in June 1602, he made provision for his three younger sons, John, Adam and Adrian and his daughters Margaret, Frances, Anne and Elizabeth. His wife Elizabeth was sole executrix. Bunny passed to the eldest son.[4]

[1] Lincs. Peds. (Harl. Soc. lii), 759; Vis. Notts. (Thoroton Soc. rec. ser. xiii), 3; Vis. Notts. (Harl. Soc. iv), 159–60; J. T. Godfrey, Notes on Churches of Notts. Hundred of Rushcliffe, 31. [2] Leicester Recs. iii. 160; J. Blackner, Hist. Nottingham, 137; Nottingham Recs. iv. 422 and n; Coll. of Arms, Talbot mss, transcribed by G. R. Batho, H, f. 507; Thoroton, Notts. ed. Throsby, i. 95; C142/280/79; HMC Rutland, i. 308–9; PCC 34 Morrison. [3] Leicester Recs. iii. 208–10; J. Thompson, Hist. Leicester, 273–6; Neale, Commons, 171–2; Annals Nottingham, ed. Barley, ii. 549. [4] Leicester Recs. iii. 276, 278–9; iv. 3–4; Nottingham Recs. iv. 411; York prob. reg. 29/121; C142/280/79.

B.D.

PARKINSON, Thomas, of Berwick-upon-Tweed, Northumb.

BERWICK-UPON-TWEED   1584, 1586, 1597

Alderman, Berwick, mayor 1583–4, 1589, 1594–7, 1600, 1604, 1614, 1618.

Although Parkinson was a leading citizen of Berwick, the name does not appear in connexion with the town until Parkinson himself first became mayor, by which time he was already a well established local figure. He continued the campaign begun by William Morton* on behalf of the townsmen against the governor, Lord Hunsdon, making several journeys to London in 1603 and 1604 to present a case to the King. A new charter in 1604 conceded many of Berwick's demands.

Parkinson thrice sat for Berwick in the Commons. In 1597 the burgesses for Berwick were appointed to a committee concerning the export of sheepskins on 26 Nov. In 1584 he shared 7s. 6d. a day expenses with his colleague Morton. A prosperous and active citizen, Parkinson, with three others, lent the guild of freemen the money needed to purchase a licence to sell wines; and in his will, dated 13 Dec. 1619, he donated £20 for the erection of a free school or a parsonage, on condition that other members of the gild also contributed. The date of his death has not been found.

J. Scott, Hist. Berwick, 257, 268, 394, 456–61, 479; Border Pprs. passim; D'Ewes, 564; Berwick guild bk. 1585–95.

B.D.

PARRY (ap HARRY), John (1517/18–84 or later), of Carmarthen, Carm.

CARMARTHEN BOROUGHS   1554 (Nov.), 1559

b. 1517/18. m. Cecily, da. of Hugh Vaughan of Kidwelly, 1s.[1]

Comptroller of customs, Milford Haven, Pemb. 10 May 1559–84 or later; collector of subsidy, Carmarthen 1562; bailiff, Carmarthen 1563–4.[2]

Parry was first returned for Carmarthen Boroughs where his brother-in-law John Vaughan II* was mayor, and again to Elizabeth's first Parliament. He acquired lands in Gloucestershire in 1553, and nine years later in partnership with a London goldsmith, rents and reversions forfeited to the Crown on the attainder of Sir Rhys ap Gruffydd, not only in the south of his own shire but in five adjacent Welsh counties and the border shires of Hereford and Shropshire. Further ecclesiastical property in New Carmarthen came his way in 1571, and at the same time he took a not very profitable lease of certain crown dues in Cardiganshire. The last reference found to Parry is in 1584.[3]

[1] E178/3345, m. 9v. [2] E159/340, recognizances Easter 45; 179/264/10; *Welsh Port Bks.* (Cymmrodorion Rec. Ser. xii), 329; NLW ms 5586B, p. 10. [3] *CPR*, 1553–4, p. 367; 1560–3, p. 284; *Augmentations*, ed. Lewis and Davies (Univ. Wales Bd. of Celtic Studies, Hist. and Law ser. xiii), 230, 236, 260, 269; *Welsh Port Bks.* 329.

A.H.D.

PARRY, Thomas (1544–1616), of Hampstead Marshall, Berks.

BRIDPORT	1571
BERKSHIRE	1586
ST. ALBANS	1604*
BERKSHIRE	1614*

b. 1544, 1st s. of Sir Thomas Parry* by Anne, da. of Sir William Reade of Boarstall, Bucks., wid. of Sir Giles Greville and of Sir Adrian Fortescue of Shirburn and Stonor Place, Oxon. *educ.* Winchester 1558 (scholar, aged 14); abroad. *m.* Dorothy Brooke of Bristol, maid of honour to the Queen, *s.p. suc.* fa. 1560. Kntd. 1601.

J.p. Berks. from c.1573, commr. musters 1573, sheriff 1575–6, 1587–8, dep. lt. 1593, collector of loans 1590, 1598; ambassador to France 1601–5; PC and chancellor of the duchy of Lancaster Dec. 1607; commr. to regulate King's income 1612.[1]

In June 1560 Thomas Gresham reported from Antwerp to Parry's father that Parry was 'well given to virtue and his studies', was 'well beloved of all men', and needed an increase in his allowance. In February 1561, 'young Mr. Parry and one of his half-brothers' were in Italy, still ignorant that their father had died in the previous December. Though his return to Parliament for Bridport, presumably on the nomination of the 2nd Earl of Bedford, suggests that he maintained his court connexions, Parry, for most of the reign, performed the ordinary duties of a landed gentleman. He purchased new estates in Berkshire, which brought him into debt, but also gained him a turn as knight of the shire, in the Parliament of 1586. He made no known contribution to the business of the House in either of his Parliaments. Presumably on account of his early experience abroad, he was kept in mind by the government as a possible ambassador. In the spring of 1601 he was nominated to succeed Henry Neville* as ambassador to France, and given a knighthood. He did his best to avoid going – in May 1602 he had still not appeared in London to receive his instructions, which 'raised a

conceit of his ineptness for his charge'. Eventually his creditors were dealt with by his half-brother, (Sir) John Fortescue I*, and he went 'over with great power' and 'a flush of secretaries'. Soon after his return he was appointed, in 1607, to succeed Sir John Fortescue as chancellor of the duchy of Lancaster, and he was later given charge of Arbella Stuart. His vigorous interference in the 1614 election for Stockbridge, where the duchy had customarily nominated one Member, caused a notable scandal and his temporary suspension from office. He died, childless and intestate, on 30 May 1616 and was buried, like his father, in Westminster abbey. His heirs were Thomas Knyvet and John Abrahall.[2]

[1] *DNB*; *Vis. Berks.* (Harl. Soc. lvii), 191; *APC*, vii. 98; xx. 187; xxiv. 254; xxviii. 559. [2] *CSP For.* 1560–1, pp. 114, 530; *APC*, xi. 165; xiv. 215; xv. 82; xxiii. 256; *VCH Berks.* iv. 45, 107, 170, 208, 544; *CSP Dom.* 1581–90, p. 667; 1601–3, pp. 222, 267; *Chamberlain Letters* ed. McClure, i. 49, 122, 145, 156, 339; *HMC Hatfield*, xi. 427; Neale, *Commons*, 232; C142/356/129; PCC admon. act bk. 1616, f. 73.

A.H.

PARRY, Sir Thomas (c.1510–60), of Welford, Berks. and Oakley Park, Glos.

WALLINGFORD	1547, 1553 (Mar.), 1555
HERTFORDSHIRE	1559

b. c.1510, 1st s. of Henry Vaughan of Brec. by Gwenllian, da. of William ap Grene or Grono of Brecon. *m.* c.1540, Anne, da. of Sir William Reade of Boarstall, Bucks., wid. of Sir Giles Greville and of Sir Adrian Fortescue of Shirburn and Stonor Place, Oxon., 2s. inc. Thomas* 3da. Kntd. 1558.[1]

Servant of Thomas Cromwell by 1536–40; clerk of the Crown and peace in Glos. 1537–43; cofferer to Princess Elizabeth by 1548; PC and comptroller of the Household 20 Nov. 1558; treasurer of the Household Jan. 1559; steward of the possessions of Westminster abbey Feb. 1559; master of the ct. of wards Jan. or Apr. 1559; j.p. Bucks., Herts. from 1554, Berks., Glos. from 1559; ld. lt. jt. (with Sir Henry Neville I*) Berks. Apr. 1560.[2]

Sir Thomas Parry, properly Sir Thomas ap Harry Vaughan, of an illegitimate branch of the Vaughans of Tretower, Breconshire, was one of the two most influential commoners in the realm between Elizabeth's accession and his death in December 1560, only Sir William Cecil challenging him for the position of the Queen's chief adviser. Parry's rise has sometimes been regarded as dependent on that of Cecil, whose great-grandfather married a Vaughan; and it has been said that Cecil introduced Parry to court. In fact, the family relationship of the two men was distant and obscure, and there is no evidence of a connexion between them before Cecil's earliest contacts with Elizabeth in 1549, which took place through Parry, her cofferer: it may have been Parry who introduced Cecil to the future Queen.[3]

It is certain that Parry was one of a number of

gentlemen of Welsh descent who became prominent servants of the Tudors, a group which included John, Lord Williams of Thame, Oxfordshire, and William Cecil. As Princess Elizabeth's cofferer (1548), Parry became keeper of Hatfield House, and of her property at Cholsey, near Wallingford, Berkshire, in which county he acquired considerable property of his own.[4]

In Mary's reign, Parry, like Cecil, did not go into exile; during his mistress's imprisonment at Woodstock he insisted, to the annoyance of the government, on staying at the *Bull* to look after Elizabeth's affairs. There is evidence that he was instrumental in enlisting promises of military support to ensure Elizabeth's succession when Mary should die. Thus, when his mistress became Queen, Parry was certain of a leading position in the government: the first entry among the *Acts of the Privy Council*, after Elizabeth's proclamation, records that, at Hatfield, three days after Mary's death, 'Sir Thomas Parry was by the Queen's Majesty's commandment and in her presence appointed by her Highness comptroller of the Household and sworn of her Highness's Privy Council'. On the same day, Cecil was appointed principal secretary.[5]

The relative influence of Parry and Cecil in the next two years is difficult to gauge. Having risen through service in Elizabeth's private household, rather than in offices of state, Parry seems to have been the least known of the new Privy Councillors. When listing them for his master, Feria, the Spanish ambassador, does not give Parry's name, but describes him as the Queen's 'late cofferer, a fat man, whom your Majesty will have seen at Hampton Court'. A few weeks afterwards, the ambassador reported that the Queen's 'present comptroller, and secretary Cecil, govern the kingdom'; soon adding, however, that Cecil 'is the man who does everything'. Feria thought he detected hostility between the Queen's two chief advisers. In March 1559 he wrote that Cecil, 'clever, mischievous and a heretic … governs the Queen in spite of the treasurer, for they are not at all good friends and I have done what I can to make them worse'. Parry appeared to Feria to be the most moderate of the Council on religious questions: 'although he is not so good a Catholic as he should be, he is the most reasonable of those near the Queen'. Lady Parry had been on good terms with Queen Mary, and a son by her first marriage, Anthony Fortescue, later became a Catholic exile. The Spanish ambassador naturally paid special attention to Parry and seems to have elicited from him an assurance that the Queen would not take the title: 'Head of the Church'.[6]

Evidence more objective than Feria's gossip suggests that Parry had a large part in the direction of financial business and advice on foreign policy; but there is no indication that he took a lead in the religious settlement. He was appointed master of the wards on the enforced surrender of that office by the Catholic Sir Francis Englefield†, much as Englefield had been appointed to

that crucial office at the beginning of Mary's reign; and he was one of the very few in the secret of Elizabeth's negotiations with the Scottish rebels. In the Parliament of 1559 to which he was returned as senior knight for Hertfordshire, presumably because of his position at Hatfield, he headed the committee on the subsidy (30 Jan. 1559), which was also commissioned to decide on the validity of the Parliament, summoned by a writ in which *supremum caput* was omitted from the Queen's titles. He took a prominent part in procedural matters in this Parliament, sending at least 15 bills to the Lords, arranging for the Speaker to be presented to the Queen and being named to at least two committees, for allowances to sheriffs (1 Mar. 1559) and about the bishop of Winchester's lands (6 Mar.). As Privy Councillor he was also appointed to the committee concerning the petition to the Queen to marry (6 Feb.). He is not recorded as speaking in this Parliament.[7]

There is some evidence that Parry was − or was thought to be − the chief advocate of a plan to marry Elizabeth to Robert Dudley. Late in November 1560, an agent of Sir Nicholas Throckmorton*, the English ambassador in Paris, who was a vigorous critic of Elizabeth's relations with Dudley, reported:

Mr. Treasurer received your lordship's letter very thankfully, but when I went from him, and he had read it over, he was clean changed and not over-courteous. He fell sick the next day, so as I could not speak unto him, and I do well know that letter and the matter of the other were the occasion of his evil. He is half ashamed of his doings for the Lord Robert.

Soon afterwards Parry died, unexpectedly and intestate, on 15 Dec., the Spanish ambassador attributing his death to grief at the course of the affair between Elizabeth and Dudley. Cecil had recently returned from his mission to Scotland − during which Parry had been dealing with the correspondence − and his opposition to the Dudley match was beginning to be felt; the Queen was less decided than ever, and in November was reported to have torn up a patent of peerage drafted for Dudley. It may be true that Parry was losing ground to Cecil before his death.[8]

Parry's lands, augmented by new grants from Elizabeth in Gloucestershire and Berkshire, descended to his son Thomas, aged 19, who became ambassador to France at the end of Elizabeth's reign and a Privy Councillor under James I. Some of Parry's influence was probably inherited by his stepson, John Fortescue I*, who was made keeper of the great wardrobe on Elizabeth's accession, sat twice as burgess for Wallingford, and became one of the Queen's most trusted servants. Parry was buried in Westminster abbey.[9]

[1] *DNB*; *DWB*; *Vis. Berks.* (Harl. Soc. lvii), 191; *LP Hen. VIII*, xv. 510; C142/129/95. [2] *LP Hen. VIII*, xii(2), p. 82; *APC*, ii. 240; vii. 3; *CPR*, 1553–4, pp. 17, 20; 1558–60, pp. 12, 27, 60, 102; *HMC Hatfield*, xiii. 40; *CSP Dom.* 1547–80, pp. 128, 152; NRA, D/DBy/1.

³ T. Jones, *Brec.* iii. 174–5; Lansd. 102, f. 205; *HMC Hatfield*, i. 101, 114; Read, *Cecil*, 64, 118. ⁴ *LP Hen. VIII*, xi. 152; xiii(1), pp. 100, 342; xiii(2), p. 409; xiv(2), pp. 321, 330; *CSP Dom.* 1547–80, p. 28; *VCH Berks.* ii. 105; iii. 297; iv. 59, 117–18, 122, 170. ⁵ *Norf. Arch. Soc.* iv. 155, 161, 171, 177, 187; Bath mss, Thynne Pprs. 3, ff. 21, 23, 24; Neale, *Essays*, 49; *APC*, vii. 3. ⁶ *CSP Span.* 1558–67, pp. 2, 7, 10, 37, 38, 96. ⁷ J. Hurstfield, *Queen's Wards*, 244–6; *APC*, vii. 27, 38; *CSP Dom.* 1547–80, p. 162; *HMC Hatfield*, i. 151, 232; ii. 185; Read, i. 148, 156; D'Ewes, 45; *CJ*, i. 53, 54, 55, 56, 58. ⁸ *Hardwicke State Pprs.* i. 168; *CSP For.* 1560–1, p. 96; PCC admon. act bk. 1559–71, f. 22; *CSP Span.* 1558–67, p. 180; Read, i. 221. ⁹ C142/129/95; *VCH Berks.* iv. 56–7, 181; *Westminster Abbey Reg.* (Harl. Soc. x), 113.

A.H.

PARRY (ap HARRY), William (*d.* 1585), of London.[1]

QUEENBOROUGH 1584*

s. of Harry ap David of Northop, Flints. by Margaret, da. of Peter Conway, archdeacon of St. Asaph and rector of Northop. *educ.* ?King's sch. Chester; DCL Paris 1583.[2] *m.* (1) da. of Sir William Thomas of Carm., wid. of one Powell; (2) Catherine, wid. of Richard Heywood† of London.

Parry has a special, if unenviable, place in the parliamentary history of this period as the only serving Member of the House of Commons to be arrested for high treason. So heinous was his treachery considered to be, that his former colleagues petitioned the Queen on 23 Feb. 1585 that

for as much as that villainous traitor Parry was a Member of this House in the time of some of his most horrible and traitorous conspiracies … her Majesty would vouchsafe to give licence to this House … to proceed to the devising and making of some law for his execution after his conviction, as may be thought fittest for his so extraordinary and most horrible kind of treason.

Parry's early career is difficult to reconstruct as the two main sources of information, his own autobiographical letter to Burghley, and government propaganda after his execution, are equally unreliable. According to Parry his father was 'a gentleman of good family' who was in royal service for a long time, brought up 30 children by his two wives, and lived to be 108. He also claimed that his mother was descended from the ancient and distinguished Conway family of Flintshire, a claim supported by Sir John Conway's offer, later, of £1,000 as surety for his good behaviour. Parry was apprenticed early to a Chester lawyer, combining his legal training with attendance at a local grammar school. After several attempts, he ran away to London about 1560. He married a Carmarthenshire widow, whose money 'was soon consumed with his dissolute and wasteful manner of life', and then entered the household of William Herbert†, 1st Earl of Pembroke, serving him until the Earl's death in 1570.

It was at this time that Parry entered the Queen's employment. At first he occupied a minor post (unascertained) which no doubt furnished him with the opportunity to meet his second wife, the wealthy widow of Richard Heywood, a King's bench official. Government propaganda later asserted that the woman was old enough to be his mother and that he slept with her daughter, but whatever the truth of that accusation, it is certain that he persuaded his wife to make over to him her lands in Lincolnshire and Kent, worth £80 a year. In the early 1570s Parry went abroad for the first time, and it was during this journey that he began his career as a government spy. He sent home regular reports about English Catholics from Paris, Rome and Siena. One aspect of these early despatches merits attention in the light of his controversial speech to the 1584 Parliament on the bill against Jesuits. On several occasions in his letters to Burghley Parry took it upon himself to urge clemency for religious exiles such as Sir Thomas Copley*, the Ropers and the Earl of Westmorland. This was an unexpected attitude to find in the letters of a government spy, which Parry justified on grounds of political expediency, arguing that enforced exile and confiscation of their lands merely served to make these men more dangerous. Later, during his trial, much was made of these letters as evidence that he had always had sympathy for the Catholics and was already working for them. Nevertheless, at the time of receiving Parry's reports Burghley does not appear to have been alarmed. In 1579 for example, when Anthony Bacon*, Burghley's nephew by marriage, was going abroad, the lord treasurer recommended Parry to him, assuring the Queen that Bacon 'should not be shaken either in religion or loyalty by his conversation with Parry'.

Throughout this period Parry lived beyond his means and in 1577 he was back in London petitioning Burghley for money to meet his expenses. Not long afterwards he fled to France to escape his English creditors. It was his financial difficulties which, in the autumn of 1580, brought him for the first time within the shadow of the scaffold. Parry owed Hugh Hare* £600 and in desperation had recourse to violence. Exactly what happened is not clear but Parry was charged with breaking into Hare's lodgings in the Inner Temple on the night of 2 Nov. 1580, and attempting to rob and murder the usurer. He was found guilty, sentenced to death and then pardoned by the Queen. In his account of the trial given later in his confessions, Parry said: 'I can prove that the recorder spoke with the jury, and that the foreman did drink'. He also stated that he had been so oppressed by two great men to whom he had of late been beholden that he had never had a contented mind since. However the reprieve was contrived, he appears to have spent a year or more in the Poultry prison. On 2 Jan. 1581 several leading courtiers offered bonds of £100 each on his behalf as surety against the payment of his debt to Hare, and later he was bound over to keep the peace with Hare in two sureties of £1,000 each.

When he was released, Parry obtained a licence to travel abroad for three years and left the country in August 1582 'with doubtful mind to return'. Once abroad, he returned to his old occupation as agent for Burghley and also, increasingly, for Walsingham. The latter gave him impressive references in a letter to (Sir) Henry Brooke *alias* Cobham I*, the English ambassador in Paris until 1583. The Catholic community in Paris, into which Parry attempted to re-integrate himself, obviously and naturally distrusted him, so 'to put all men out of doubt with me', Parry left for Italy where he 'justified' himself 'before the inquisition' in Milan. He made a great show of his adherence to Catholicism and hinted widely that he had news from Catholics in England which he wished to impart to the Pope himself. Soon Parry was in negotiation with the papal nuncio to arrange a journey to Rome and an audience with the Pope, but sufficient guarantees of safe conduct were not forthcoming and so he returned to France. Throughout this period there is evidence to show that he was sounding out the attitude of leading Jesuits and Catholic exiles to the idea of assassinating Elizabeth. He spoke to Father Crighton, a Scottish Jesuit at Lyons, asking him in general terms whether assassination was justifiable in the eyes of the Church. He discussed a definite scheme to murder Elizabeth with Thomas Morgan, an agent of Mary Queen of Scots. He broached the idea to the papal nuncio, who forwarded his letter to Cardinal Como in Rome.

Meanwhile, however, Parry was in constant touch with Burghley, Walsingham and (Sir) Edward Stafford II*, the new ambassador in Paris. It is significant that despite all Parry's efforts the papal nuncio attached to his letter to Como a warning that he had received bad reports of Parry and that he was not to be trusted. At the same time as Parry wrote the following in a letter to the Pope (1 Jan. 1584)

Most Holy Father,
I have in mind to undertake an enterprise which, with the grace of God, I shall ere long carry through for the public good, the peace of the whole of Christendom, the restoration of England to its ancient obedience to the Apostolic See, and the liberation from her long and weary sufferings of the Queen of Scotland, that only true and undoubted heiress of the crown of England ...

Stafford wrote two letters on Parry's behalf, one to Walsingham and the second to the Queen herself, in which he warmly recommended Parry and stated:

Besides that I think he hath some matter of importance that he hath kept to deliver to yourself for the good will he hath to do your service.

Parry himself took both Stafford's letters to England in January 1584 and obtained an audience with the Queen at Whitehall. He revealed to her at this audience all his dealings on the Continent and specifically that he had been sent back to England by Morgan and other friends of the Queen of Scots in order to assassinate Elizabeth. He claimed that he would shortly receive a letter from Rome which would convey the Pope's blessing and approval of the deed. The promised letter came from Como, cardinal secretary of state, reached Parry in England in March, and ran in part as follows:

His Holiness hath seen your letter of the first with the certificate [of confession] included and cannot but commend the good disposition and resolution which you write you have towards the public service and benefit: wherein his Holiness does exhort you to persevere and to bring to effect that which you have promised.

Parry showed this letter to the Queen at court as proof of his earlier statements and his story appears to have been accepted. Parry himself was jubilant at his success and in May 1584 wrote to Burghley asking for the mastership of St. Katharine's hospital in London. This was not forthcoming, but Parry was given a generous pension and was received at court on several occasions with marked favour by the Queen. Apparently he expected more, for in September 1584 he was writing to Burghley again: 'In the meantime, if it please you to commend me as a fit man for a deanery, provostship or mastership of requests, it is all I crave'. Parry's activities during the summer after his return to England are almost undocumented. To all appearances he had abandoned his role as government agent. A letter from him to his erstwhile fellow conspirator, Morgan, (dated 22 Feb. 1584) which, unknown to Parry, was intercepted by the government, confirms this:

I have not been careless of the debt undertaken, but being meanly satisfied before my departure from Paris, I laboured for conference with a singular man on this side to be fully informed what might be done in conscience in that case for the common good. I was very learnedly ... assured that it might not fall into the thought of a good Christian. The difficulties besides are so many and in this vigilant time, full of despair. The service you know did never pass your hand and mine: and may therefore with more ease and less offence be concealed and suppressed.

He was evidently in the service of Sir Edward Hoby*, Burghley's nephew, who, being at Berwick, appointed Parry his 'solicitor' at court and begged Burghley to give him as much credit as he would himself. It was no doubt through Hoby's influence that Parry was returned to Parliament for Queenborough in November 1584.

Another man might have been satisfied with a stable, even promising situation. Parry, however, sometime in the summer of 1584, entered into secret negotiations with one Edward Neville, and attempted to persuade him to join a conspiracy to assassinate the Queen. Neville was an agent for the English government recently returned from Rouen, but he was distrusted both by the government and by Parry, who had himself denounced Neville to the Queen as disaffected. Neville had a grudge against Burghley, whose eldest son, Thomas Cecil*, had acquired by marriage the lands of the 4th Lord Latimer to which Neville considered himself the rightful heir. The reasons Parry had for contacting such a man and making such proposals can only be guessed, but the similarity between Parry's dealings with Neville and those earlier meetings with Thomas Morgan makes it probable that Parry was once more playing the role of *agent provocateur*, this time on his own account. Certainly Walsingham and Burghley were both ignorant of what was happening and it is at least possible, in view of later events, that Parry hoped to take any information he might procure straight to the Queen to his own maximum advantage. Whatever his exact intentions, he was playing with fire. It would seem, however, that Parry was both too confident of his own abilities and too arrogant about his past successes to realize that his activities might be ill-construed.

Rash as these secret meetings with Neville no doubt were, Parry's behaviour in the House of Commons on Thursday 17 Dec. 1584 was the purest folly. If his aim was to draw the royal attention to himself, his success was spectacular, but instead of impressing the Queen and Privy Council he was from this time on merely a source of embarrassment to them. The events of 17 Dec. 1584 are recorded in the journal of William Fitzwilliam*:

the bill of Jesuits being engrossed received its last reading in the Nether House, one burgess among the rest named Parry, a doctor of the civil law, stood up and inveighed against it not in any orderly sort considering the parts by themselves but *ex abrupto*, saying that it carried nothing with it but blood, danger, terror, despair, confiscation and that not to the Queen's commodity but to other men's. And that he doubted not though it passed this House and the Lords, yet it should come to such a blessed hand as would use it thereafter, naming her Majesty, to whom only and to nobody else he said that he would give the reasons of his speech.

The House with this found themselves greatly grieved and that for two respects:
1. The first for that one only member thereof should charge the whole body of that grave assembly with so horrible matters as the seeking of blood, danger, terror, despair and confiscation of the subject and that not so much for the Queen's safety which they would seem to pretend, as for the satisfying of their own greedy desires after such matters.
2. The second that he would give no reason to the House why he used those words against the bill, a thing contrary to the orders of the House, but as it were in contempt of the whole Council, which had given their

consents to so odious a matter as that was, he disdained to yield to them, as men unworthy, the reasons which he conceived against it.

Whereupon it was moved that to the end he should neither see the particular men that inveighed against him nor hear their proper invectives, he might, according to the ancient custom of the House in such cases, be delivered to the Serjeant to be conveyed forth until the House's pleasure were further known.

But this was gainsaid by one that thought it not agreeable to the liberties and freedom of the House that any member thereof, for showing his opinion in a bill read among themselves should be taken from his seat and sequestered from the society: for both as he said it would touch the majesty of the House if men should not therein have *libera suffragia* and also it would be most perilous to such matters as should be propounded among them: for that the only way to have matters perfectly understood and rightly digested was to suffer men freely to utter their conceits of both sides. Besides he thought it was injustice that seeing all men in that place had like authority, one as much as another, any Member there should be punished by his fellow Member.

For all this Parry was delivered to the Serjeant by a general consent to be conveyed out. Which done one of the House in answer to the former speech, said that the liberty and freedom of the House suffered every man freely to deliver his opinion of the bill read, either with it or against it, for therein consisted both the majesty of the House, and the perfection of such matters as passed from them. But if any man would speak impertinently to the cause neither fortifying nor confuting the parts thereof, but abruptly would utter a speech to the offence of the whole company (for he that speaks must speak to the matter of the bill either with it or against it) that was by ancient precedents severely to be punished ...

Presently ... Parry was by the Serjeant brought to the bar within the House, where kneeling, being demanded by the Speaker, first whether he would stand to words which he had before uttered, and secondly if he would, then whether he would give any reason why he used the same: he answered that the words which he had spoken, he would avow, and thereupon repeated them over as before. And the reasons why he spake them, he would reserve to show to her Majesty and none other.

D'Ewes adds that Parry here entered 'into some declaration of his own estate, tending altogether to his own credit, as of his sundry good services done to her Majesty, his reputation with persons of good sort, and other suchlike speeches in his own commendation ...'

Hereupon, as a prisoner, was he delivered to the Serjeant, to remain with him, until order were given for his further committing.

The next day, (Sir) Christopher Hatton I*, vice-chamberlain of the Household, informed the Commons that, on the Queen's orders, Parry had been questioned by 'some of the Lords of the Council' – his plan to gain a private audience with the Queen had thus misfired – and had given his reasons for his speech 'and that partly to the satisfaction of her Highness'. At the Queen's suggestion Parry was brought to the bar of the House where 'kneeling upon his knee in very humble manner [he] affirmed directly that he had very undutifully misbehaved himself and had rashly and unadvisedly uttered those speeches he used and was with all his heart very sorry for it'. Pleading ignorance of the customs of the House as an MP for the first time, Parry was allowed to remain a member of the Commons after much discussion, a second 'humble submission' and a promise that 'if ever after he should give any just cause of offence again to this House or any Member thereof, he would then never after crave any more favour of them'. There the matter ended for the time being.[2]

It is not known what explanation of his behaviour Parry gave to the Privy Council, but it is tempting to think that he laid before them new information of a Catholic plot, Neville being his source. But however important his information, Parry had done himself irreparable damage. Firstly, he had been pursuing his career as *agent provocateur* unknown to Walsingham, who prided himself on the tight control he had over his secret service. Secondly, the melodramatic and high-handed manner he had used in the House was hardly calculated to appeal to the cautious, restrained Privy Councillors. Thirdly, he had greatly offended the House of Commons and caused a debate on the liberties of the House and the freedom of speech – topics which the Privy Council discouraged as often as possible. Fourthly, he had, in the most spectacular way imaginable, raised an issue the Privy Council least wanted to hear about – that of religious toleration. Fifthly, he had unambiguously accused those behind the bill against Jesuits of self-interest. Whatever he might have thought, Parry had little to set off on the credit side. His long career as *agent provocateur* left him exposed and his recent activities open to any interpretation the government cared to place upon them. Government agents were expendable.

The only sources for the events leading from this point up to Parry's execution are his own confessions and the government's tract, published after his death, *A True and Plain Declaration of the Horrible Treasons practised by William Parry, the Traitor, against the Queen's Majesty* (1585). From these accounts it appears that, sometime during the parliamentary recess (21 Dec.–4 Feb. 1585), Parry contacted Neville on two occasions, again putting forward a plan to assassinate the Queen. On 8 Feb. Neville made a deposition against Parry. Walsingham, who had been watching Parry closely since his intervention in the House, was instructed by the Queen to give Parry a private interview and a chance to clear himself. Walsingham informed Parry that

the Queen had been advertised that there was somewhat intended against her own person, wherewith she thought he could not but be acquainted, considering the great trust that some of her most affected subjects reposed in him; and that her pleasure was that he should declare ... his knowledge therein, and whether the said Parry himself had let fall any speech unto any person (though with an intent only to discover his disposition) that might draw him into suspicion as though he himself had any such wicked intent.

According to the text of the same government pamphlet, Parry denied all knowledge of assassination plots or conversations about them. The following day, when he was confronted with Neville, he merely said that, unless the government could produce a witness, it was only Neville's word against his and that was not enough to convict a man of treason. He was put in the Tower and a few days later made a full confession. At his trial, which began on 25 Feb., he maintained at first that the confession was made 'freely and without constraint' and seemed convinced that he would be pardoned. As it became apparent that he was doomed, however, he changed his story, and declared that the confession was extorted. At the last minute he realized that the confession had been his undoing, saying 'I see that I must die because I have not been consistent with myself'.

Meanwhile Parliament had been informed of the charges against Parry, and on 18 Feb. on the motion of Thomas Digges he was expelled the House. Even before the trial began, the House was petitioning for 'some more severe punishment than ordinary' to be meted out to Parry. On 24 Feb., the day before Parry's trial began, Sir Christopher Hatton made a lengthy speech to the House in which he set out the government's version of Parry's career. With a few minor discrepancies, the details of Parry's activities abroad were recounted accurately, the facts being only too open to the interpretation that he had been all along in the pay of the Catholics. The letter from Cardinal Como (cited above) was produced as evidence of Parry's intentions to assassinate the Queen with the Pope's approval. His letter to Morgan (cited above, 22 Feb. 1584) was suppressed. His revelation of the plots of Morgan and others to the Queen on his return to England was explained away as a piece of devilish cunning designed to gain the Queen's confidence. Then followed an unconvincing account of Parry's attempts on the Queen's life. On the first occasion at Oatlands he failed 'having in haste left his girdle and dagger behind him in a tent'. On two other occasions 'when he meant to execute the fact, he was driven to turn about and weep'.

Parry's confession and government propaganda before the trial, like Hatton's speech to the Commons, made the verdict of guilty inevitable. Parry's reaction to the verdict – 'I here summon Queen Elizabeth to answer for my blood' – stands in marked contrast to that of the Catholic conspirator, Anthony Babington, a year later. On 2 Mar. 1585, from the scaffold, Parry once again asserted his innocence:

> I die a true servant to Queen Elizabeth; from any evil thought that ever I had to harm her, it never came into my mind; she knoweth it and her conscience can tell her so ... I die guiltless and free in mind from ever thinking hurt to her Majesty.

Parry was hanged, drawn and quartered, according to 'the ordinary course of law' for traitors.

[1] This account is based upon L. Hicks, 'The Strange Case of Dr. William Parry', *Studies*, xxxvi. 343–62. [2] Trinity, Dublin, Thos. Cromwell's jnl. ff. 83–6; D'Ewes, 340–2, 352, 355; Fitzwilliam mss, Wm. Fitzwilliam's jnl. ff. 17–18.

M.A.P.

PARTRIDGE, William (d. 1598), of Bridge, Kent.

CAMELFORD	1563
ROCHESTER	1572

1st s. of Thomas Partridge of Lenham by Elizabeth Sibbell of Kent. m. (1) Alice Duffield of London, *s.p.*; (2) Katherine, da. of John Wilde of Terbury (?Canterbury), 1s.; (3) Affra.[1]

Feodary, Kent by 1562, j.p. from c.1573, piracy commr. 1577; commr. Dover haven 1580; sewers, Kent 1583–96, musters 1584; surveyor of ordnance by 1595.[2]

This Member, presumably related to the Nicholas Partridge of Lenham who was well known in Continental reforming circles in the 1530s, was a minor Kent land-owner, holding the manors of Patricksbourne, Kingston and Bridge in the Bekesbourne area, near Canterbury. Outside the county he owned a large house with other property in East Smithfield, valued at £10 a year. He must have owed his return to Parliament for Camelford to court patronage – perhaps to his 'singular good master' Sir William Cecil, who may have approached the 2nd Earl of Bedford on his behalf. Alternatively it is possible that Partridge, who had at one time been a servant of Sir Thomas Parry*, may have known Bedford well enough to ask him directly for a seat. By 1572 he had been an official in Kent for some years, but again court rather than local influence probably accounts for his return. He sat on a legal committee 24 Feb. 1576. For the 1581 session he was, owing to his illness, replaced by Samuel Coxe, but at the end of the session (18 Mar.) the House reversed an earlier decision and ruled this substitution to have been out of order.[3]

Partridge was concerned with local administration in Kent for over 35 years, his duties including the supervision of grain supplies and the project for rebuilding Dover haven. He was also concerned with Kent boroughs, in June 1580 investigating the complaints made by foreigners living in Canterbury that the corporation was taxing them too heavily, and some years later joining the dean of Canterbury and others on a commission to inquire into the mayor's action in imprisoning 'certain gentlemen ... bringing treasure from Sir Thomas Shirley [I*]'. Following a threatened riot at Sandwich in June 1587, he went to the town to uphold the mayor's authority and to send the ringleaders under guard to Canterbury. Four years later, when the Privy Council had lost patience with the factiousness and corruption of the New Romney corporation, he and other justices were ordered to inspect the town accounts and report generally.[4]

Some of his surviving letters on other topics are of interest. In December 1568 he petitioned (apparently unsuccessfully) to be allowed to farm the customs and impost on beer. Like other Kent gentlemen, he detested (Sir) Roger Manwood*, writing to Burghley in April 1592 that Manwood was a 'snake', 'as proud a man as ever I knew', hardly able to abide equals, much less superiors, and given to revenge. As surveyor of ordnance – the office carried a salary of 2s. a day – Partridge was an official of the Tower, and as such he sat on commissions to deal with unruly warders and to see that the inhabitants of the Tower precincts provided the salary of a minister and paid their poor rate. In July 1595 he requested the appointment of a keeper of the stores there. The supply of munitions 'rusts and cankers' and the powder was kept in the ordnance office instead of in the vaults – a dangerous arrangement 'if any chimney within the Tower should take fire, and sparks fly, or a flint stone strike fire'. 'Her Majesty may better spare any officer in England, than lack a keeper of so weighty a charge'. In March 1596 he began a tour of inspection of all the castles and forts in the Cinque Ports: an undated report, sent to 'Mr. Clapham at Court' (presumably John Clapham*) and enclosing the plan of a sea-coast fortification, probably refers to this journey.[5]

His will, made on 21 June 1598, the day of his death, was proved a fortnight later by his widow, the executrix and residuary legatee. To his son Edward, aged about 23, he left £200, in addition to money from timber sales and some non-entailed lands in Kent. A nephew, also Edward, received the London property and £100.[6]

[1] *Vis. Kent* (Harl. Soc. lxxv), 18. The order of wives is not made clear. Probate of will granted to widow Affra (PCC 62 Lewyn). 'Afra' also in i.p.m. (C142/253/82); i.e. probably a third w. not a shortened form of name of his second wife. [2] *CPR*, 1560–3, p. 547; Lansd. 146, f. 18; *CSP Dom*. 1547–80, p. 671; 1595–7, pp. 81, 223–4; *Twysden Lieutenancy Pprs*. ed. Scott Thomson (Kent Arch. Soc. recs. br. x), 67. [3] *Zurich Letters* (Parker Soc.), ii, iii passim; C142/253/82; PCC 62 Lewyn; Lansd. 81, f. 83; SP12/48/52; C24/103; *CJ*, i. 108, 135. [4] Lansd. 48, f. 136 seq.; 66, f. 27 seq.; *CSP Dom*. 1581–90, p. 170; *APC*, xii. 73–4, 161, 192; xiv. 383–4; xv. 123, 154; xxi. 84, 287–8. [5] Lansd. 71, f. 2; 80, f. 97; *CSP Dom*. 1547–80, p. 323; 1595–7, pp. 81, 331; 1598–1601, p. 156; *APC*, xxv. 102–3, 372. [6] PCC 62 Lewyn; C142/253/82.

N.M.F.

PASTON, Clement (by 1523–98), of Oxnead, Norf.

NORFOLK	1563*[1]

b. by 1523, 5th but 4th surv. s. of Sir William Paston of Caister and Oxnead, by Bridget, da. of Sir Henry Heydon† of Baconsthorpe; bro. of Erasmus†, John† and Sir Thomas†. *m.* aft. 1567, Alice, da. of Humphrey Pakington of London, wid. of Richard Lambert of London, *s.p.*

Gent. pens. by 1544–*d.*; j.p. Norf. from c.1577, commr. musters by 1579.[2]

Mentioned in 1544 as 'one of the pensioners' and as a fitting person to command one of the King's ships, Clement Paston was given a command in 1545 and, with the accession of Elizabeth, he was active both in the navy and the army. Though still described as the 'Queen's servant' in 1559, he then retired to his Norfolk estates and lived as a country gentleman. At the by-election of 1566 the 4th Duke of Norfolk told the sheriff to nominate 'those I talked with you of', i.e. Roger Townshend* and Clement Paston, with the proviso that should Sir Richard Fulmerston* – then a burgess for Thetford – ask for the second county seat, his request should be granted, and Paston would then be accommodated at Thetford. Fulmerston, however, retained the seat at Thetford.[3]

Though Paston's name was on a list drawn up in the interests of Mary Stuart in 1574, and though his attitude to the Elizabethan settlement was reported lukewarm as late as 1587, he kept clear of a plot discovered in July 1570 to free the Duke of Norfolk from the Tower and commit other 'horrible treason', and was appointed a commissioner to deal with those involved. He also avoided the disputes which occupied the Norfolk justices after the fall of the Duke in 1572.[4]

Paston was bequeathed by his father the family property at Oxnead, and having married a rich widow, he built a new house there. There 'he spent his old age honourably, quietly and in good-housekeeping', and there he died on 18 Feb. 1598. His will, made on 5 Sept. 1594, was proved on 14 Mar. 1598. He asked to be buried at Oxnead church, bequeathed the household goods and £1,000 to his wife, and remembered relatives and friends. The prisoners of Norwich were left £28.[5]

[1] Folger V. b. 298. [2] *Vis. Norf.* (Harl. Soc. xxxii), 216–17; PCC 26 Stonard; Mill Stephenson, *Mon. Brasses*, 359; A. H. Smith thesis, App. I.; *LP Hen. VIII*, xix; LC2/4/2. [3] *DNB*; *CPR*, 1558–60, p. 66; A. H. Smith thesis, 113, 226, 235; SP12/133/14. [4] *Trans. Norf. Arch. Soc.* v. 75–6; *CSP Dom.* 1547–80, p. 390; *APC*, ix. 344; xiii. 310; xxii. 87–8, 93; *Cath. Rec. Soc. Misc.* viii. 95; Strype, *Annals*, iii(2), 460. [5] Mason, *Hist. Norf.* 153; Fuller, *Worthies*, ii. 456; *The Pastons: the Story of a Norf. Fam.* (Norwich Castle Mus. 1953), 17; PCC 27, 28 Lewyn.

A.M.M.

PATE, Richard (1516–88), of Minsterworth, Glos.

GLOUCESTER   1558, 1559, 1563, 1586

b. 24 Sept. 1516, ?s. of Walter Pate of Cheltenham. *educ.* Corpus, Oxf. 1532; L. Inn Aug. 1541, called 1558. *m.* Matilda, da. of John Rastell of Gloucester, wid. of Henry

Marmion, mayor of Gloucester 1533, 1541, and of Thomas Lane† of Gloucester, 1s. 3da.

Steward of reader's dinner, L. Inn 1562, Lent reader 1563, assoc. bencher 1571; commr. chantries, Glos. 1547, escheator 1548–9; recorder, Gloucester 1556–87; j.p. Glos. from 1547, Cheshire, Herefs., Salop, some Welsh counties 1564; dep. justice, Glam., Brec., and Rad. 1559; member, council in marches of Wales 1560; commr. grain, Glos. 1573, piracy 1577, sheriff 1580–1.

Pate was the nephew and namesake of the Marian bishop of Worcester deprived in 1559. He was himself, despite his Marian offices, 'an ancient professor of the gospel', and a speculator in ex-monastic lands. On the accession of Elizabeth he received a general pardon as 'of Minsterworth *alias* of Lincoln's Inn' and was appointed to the council in the marches, regularly attending its meetings and being otherwise active in local affairs. As recorder he might have expected to be returned to Parliament for Gloucester as a matter of course, but after sitting in the first two Elizabethan Parliaments and being one of four Members appointed to draw up the subsidy (31 Jan. 1559), Pate was at least twice defeated by his deputy Thomas Atkins*. In 1571 Sir William Cordell* protested to Burghley that Pate, 'a good Parliament man, and very diligent and painful there', had been 'unkindly used', and supplied, by way of a precedent, a writ directed to London in the time of Henry VIII, ordering a new election to be held, on the grounds that the recorder had not been returned. It is unlikely that Burghley would have sanctioned the extension of this precedent to Gloucester, and, as Pate himself wrote, there was insufficient time to take any action before Parliament met. In any event Pate was anxious lest 'the doing thereof might breed more unquietness' in the city. 'Unquietness' arose next year, when Atkins defeated Pate 'by gathering together of a multitude by great labour, and by some threatening words, contrary to the law'. This time Pate appealed direct to Burghley, who again refrained from interfering. Atkins was returned in 1584, but in 1586 Pate, now in his seventies, regained his seat, taking Atkins with him to Westminster as his junior colleague. On 4 Nov. 1586 Pate was appointed to the committee on Mary Queen of Scots. Shortly afterwards, being 'aged and weak in body', he sought to resign his recordership to his 'friend' William Oldsworth*, which caused more trouble in Gloucester.

Pate died 27 Oct. 1588, aged 73. In his will, made 30 Aug. that year 'not without some heaviness of heart' for his sins, he directed that his body was to be buried in Gloucester cathedral and divided his property between his widow and his orphaned grand-daughter Susan Brooke, the executrix, with remainder to his nephews. He left small bequests to Magdalen and Corpus, Oxford. The will was proved 2 Nov.

Emden, *Biog. Reg. Oxf.* 1501–40, p. 436; *DNB*; W. R. Williams, *Parl. Hist. Glos.* 190; *Bristol and Glos. Arch. Soc. Trans.* xlvi. 329–35; lvi.

201–25; *Gloucester Recs.* ed. Stevenson, 33, 444; *CPR*, 1547–8, p. 84; 1558–60, pp. 92, 184, 394; 1560–3, p. 490; P. H. Williams, *Council in the Marches of Wales*, 274–5; *APC*, viii. 159; x. 133; xi. 266–7, 455; xiv. 321; *CSP Dom.* 1548–80, pp. 408, 441; 1581–90, p. 320; *CJ*, i. 53; D'Ewes, 394; PCC 4 Leicester.

J.J.C.

PATRICK, Richard (d.1566), of Huntingdon.

HUNTINGDON   1559

> *educ.* St. John's, Camb. BA 1543, MA c.1547, senior fellow 1549, MD 1553. *?m.* Alice (d. c.1583).
> Bailiff, Huntingdon 1554, 1559.

Among possible ancestors and relations of this man, whose parentage has not been traced, were 'Patrick the surgeon', mentioned in a 1524 account of the royal ships as serving in the *Christopher Arundel*, and the mayor of Calais in 1529. Two namesakes were the comptroller of tonnage and poundage at London before the Tudor period, and a citizen and haberdasher of London at the beginning of Elizabeth's reign. Patrick himself is a shadowy figure after 1554. In June 1556 the Privy Council sent a letter to the 'bailiff, constable and post of Huntingdon', instructing them 'not to molest or trouble henceforth Doctor Patrick, physician' by taking his horses 'for such as ride in post that way'. His one appearance in Parliament left no trace upon the records of its proceedings. He received a royal grant of lands in Kent about 1560, but it is not known whether he resided there. Administration of the goods of a Richard Patrick, surely the doctor, was granted at Huntingdon in 1566. An Alice Patrick, of Huntingdon St. Mary, possibly his wife, had her will proved in 1583.

Al. Cant. i(3), p. 318; C219/26/37; E. Griffith, *Huntingdon Recs.* 96–7; *LP Hen. VIII*, iv(1), p. 105; (3), p. 2655; *CPR*, 1558–60, p. 228; 1553 and App. Edw. VI, 392; *APC*, v. 290; Cooper, *Ath. Cant.* i. 213; *Hunts. Wills* (Brit. Rec. Soc. Index Lib. xlii), 87, 144.

N.M.F.

PATTENSON, Thomas, of Carlisle, Cumb.

CARLISLE   1572

Mayor, Carlisle 1561, 1569.[1]

Described as 'alderman and merchant' in 1566, when with Thomas Barne*, William Mulcaster* and others he was a plaintiff in a case against the then mayor, and as 'gentleman' on the return, Pattenson belonged to a family whose name recurs frequently in the records of Carlisle and its vicinity. A Thomas Patynson 'of Sedbourne' (possibly Sebergham, 10 miles from Carlisle) occurs on the pardon roll, 7 Nov. 1553.[2]

On 27 Feb. 1581 Pattenson was appointed to the committee for the second reading of the bill for Carlisle.[3]

[1] *Carlisle Recs.* (Cumb. and Westmld. Antiq. and Arch. Soc. extra ser. iv), 86; *CSP Scot.* ii.633. [2] Carlisle mss CA/2/210–17; *CPR*, 1553–4, p. 465. [3] *CJ*, i. 130.

E.L.C.M.

PATTESON, Matthew

WEST LOOE   1589
HEDON   1601

This Member has proved difficult to identify. On grounds of dating, it seems possible that he was the Matthew Patteson who matriculated from Peterhouse in 1575, though this person has been identified with the Catholic controversialist who was physician to Charles I.[1] With more assurance he may be identified as the chamber official in 1603,[2] whose superior was Sir John Stanhope, treasurer of the chamber and an intimate of the Cecils. The Cecil connexion would explain his election at West Looe, where Burghley was a likely patron. It was evidently this Matthew Patteson who was on friendly terms with (Sir) Henry Constable* in 1593[3] and was commissioned by him to find a gelding suitable for presentation to Sir Robert Cecil. The Constables shared control of Hedon and in this way his return there in 1601 can be explained. Probably Robert Cecil arranged it through Constable.[4] The known facts about this man indicate that he was a dependant of the Cecils.[5]

[1] *Al. Cant.* i(3), p. 319; *Peterhouse Biog. Reg.* ii. 5. [2] LC2/4/4. [3] *HMC Hatfield*, iv. 362–3. [4] By 1609 the mayor of Hedon was offering the nomination of a burgess to Cecil direct; *CSP Dom.* 1603–10, p. 558. [5] *HMC Hatfield*, xv. 54.

J.E.N.

PAULE, George (c.1563–1635), of Lambeth, Surr.

DOWNTON   1597
HINDON   1601
BRIDGNORTH   1625, 1628

> *b.* c.1563, 2nd s. of Richard Paule of Norf. and Bridgnorth, Salop by Dorothy, da. of Fulk Lee of Langley, Salop. *m.* (1) Joan, da. of Nicholas Oldman of Berks., 3s. 1da.; (2) Rachel. Kntd. 1607.[1]
> Servant of Abp. Whitgift 1584, comptroller of his household by 1599; jt. (with Richard Massinger*) registrar of the diocese of Ely 1588–1600; jt. registrar and clerk of the acts 1603; j.p. Surr. by 1610; jt. chief clerk for enrolling pleas in King's bench 1621–9; principal registrar to the high commrs. for eccles. causes by 1625.[2]

Paule's career lies for the most part outside the Elizabethan period, but its pattern was set in 1584, when as a young man, barely of age, he entered Whitgift's household. Henceforward he was to hold one ecclesiastical or legal office after another, mainly as registrar or clerk for enrolments. No doubt Whitgift had Paule returned for both Downton and Hindon, boroughs where the bishops of Winchester had considerable power. There is no record of Paule in the 1597 journals, but he sat on two committees in the 1601 Parliament, one on 23 Nov. for the confirmation of a grant to three London hospitals and the other on 9 Dec. for the assurances of certain manors.[3]

Domestic details about Paule are sparse. It seems unlikely that he had no formal higher education, but his name has not been found on university or inns of court registers. In addition to his house at Lambeth, he leased in March 1586 the parsonage of Graveney, Kent, part of the possessions of the archbishop of Canterbury. The lease was renewed in 1590, Paule's annual rent being £7 6s. 8d. In 1600 he and Richard Massinger sold their joint interest as registrars of Ely diocese to John Lamb.[4]

Paule is now remembered for his adulatory life of Whitgift, published in 1612 with a dedication to Archbishop Abbott. As a member of Whitgift's household for over 20 years, and comptroller for the last eight years of his master's life, he was better placed to collect valuable material than to appreciate the opposition aroused by Whitgift's tactless methods. In the latter part of James I's reign Paule became a follower of Buckingham, who obtained for him his King's bench office. While principal registrar of the high commission court he died 16 Apr. 1635.[5]

[1] CSP Dom. 1629–31, p. 540; Vis. Salop (Harl. Soc. xxix), 393; Vis. Surr. (Harl. Soc. xliii), 205; J. C. Weyman, Bridgnorth MPs, 55–6; HMC 6th Rep. 79b. [2] Strype, Whitgift, i. 414; ii. 418, 507; CSP Dom. 1598–1601, pp. 388–9; 1603–10, p. 8; SP14/33. [3] Harl. 75, ff. 143, 154; D'Ewes, 648, 674. [4] CSP Dom. 1598–1601, pp. 388–9, 527. [5] Strype, Whitgift, ii. 418, 507, 518; DNB.

R.C.G.

PAULET, Amias (c.1533–88), of Hinton St. George, Som. and Sampford Peverell, Devon.[1]

SOMERSET   1571

b. c.1533, 1st s. of Sir Hugh Paulet* by his 1st w. Philippa, da. of Sir Lewis Pollard† of King's Nympton, Devon. m. Margaret, da. and h. of Anthony Harvey of Columbjohn, Devon, 3s. 3da. suc. fa. 1573. Kntd. Oct. 1575.
Lt. gov. Jersey Apr. 1559, jt. (with his fa.) gov. Nov. 1571, sole 1572; j.p. Devon from 1569, Som. from c.1573; custos rot. Som. c.1577; ambassador to France Sept. 1576–Nov. 1579; PC 1585; guardian of Mary Queen of Scots 1585; chancellor of the order of the Garter Feb. 1587–early 1588; commr. in the Netherlands Feb. 1588.[2]

Paulet was a considerable landowner in south-west England. In spite of his frequent absences in the Channel Islands and elsewhere, he was regularly included in the commission of the peace for Devon and Somerset from 1573 until his death, although the Devon list for 1575 adds the comment 'abiding in Jersey' beside his name. When in England he was active in local affairs. He served under his father in Jersey for some time before being officially appointed lieutenant governor, and he resided there regularly until 1571, except for a period early in 1567. Protestantism was strong among the islanders, and until 1587 the Paulets found little trouble in governing them.

During his first period of active control (1559–71) he appointed a Huguenot minister from Anjou to the most important benefice in Jersey. He also obtained the Queen's permission for the form of service used by the French protestants in London to be introduced at St. Helier, afterwards extending it unofficially to the other churches on the island. He welcomed Huguenot refugees to the Channel Islands in 1568, although his father (whose religious views were less pronounced than his own) advised him to limit their numbers, and he took care to see that Jersey was fortified against a possible French attack.[3]

Paulet returned to England in time to head the poll in a contested election for Somerset in 1571. His father was one of those who had been instructed by the Privy Council to see that suitable men were chosen, and it is interesting to see that he waited until 1572 before standing himself. Paulet's fellow knight of the shire, George Rogers*, was a personal friend. Paulet's only known activity in the 1571 Commons was his appointment to the subsidy committee 7 Apr.[4]

Paulet's copy-book illuminates his embassy to France. He saw no hope for the Huguenots unless they received help from abroad, yet in the face of his own puritanism he tried to forward the Alençon marriage scheme. Always the courtier, in November 1577 he sent the Queen satin for two gowns, writing that although the silk was not 'of so good price as I would wish', the French Queen had very recently worn a gown of similar material. In November 1579, after many appeals to be recalled, Paulet left France, having written to Walsingham:

I am Jack out of office, I thank God for it; yet I cannot forbear my wonted course, to write somewhat to Sir Francis Walsingham.

He told Burghley that he did not regret his period in France, saddened though he was by the death of his eldest son and another child. To friends who commiserated with him about his expenses he replied that he had lived 'as good cheap' in France as in England, and 'could live here long time before it should pinch me'.[5]

For the next few years Paulet divided his time between England and Jersey. He intended to spend the winter of 1582–3 in London, but finding 'the sickness' there returned to Devon. Later in 1583 he was in Jersey, where at the beginning of 1585 he received a summons to become guardian of Mary Stuart at Tutbury. Several months before this the Queen had been intending to make him a Privy Councillor, and he was sworn on his return to England, which was delayed by his ill-health. His letters from 1576 onwards refer frequently to bouts of sickness, and to his fear of developing gall-stones. He arrived at Tutbury in April 1585, remaining as Mary's custodian there, and later at Chartley and Fotheringay, until her death. A harsh gaoler, he was congratulated by Elizabeth on his vigilance, but to William Davison's* suggestion that he should connive at Mary's murder, Paulet replied:

> My goods and my life are at her Majesty's disposition, but God forbid I should make so foul a shipwreck of my conscience, or leave so great a blot on my poor posterity.

He was rewarded after Mary's execution with the chancellorship of the Garter.[6]

Some months before his death he was included among the commissioners to treat for peace in the Netherlands, against opposition from the Catholics that the 'gaoler to the Holy Queen and Martyress' was a bad choice. In a list drawn up by Burghley in this year, headed 'knights of great possessions suitable to be created barons', Paulet's name was included. He died on 26 Sept. 1588, and was buried at St. Martin-in-the-Fields. His will, which had been made nearly three years earlier, has a puritan preamble followed by a number of charitable bequests. His daughter Sara, who was under 15, was to have £2,000 on her marriage, or two years after her father's death. Paulet's other children also received large legacies. The overseers to help his son Anthony, the sole executor, were the attorney-general, John Popham*, and 'my trusty and well-beloved friend John Col(l)es*'. His inquisition post mortem, taken in January 1589, lists 14 manors in Somerset, four in Devon, and a large house with an acre of land in Clerkenwell.[7]

[1] This biography is largely based upon *Copy-book of letters written during [Paulet's] embassy to France* (Roxburghe Club, 1866) and *Letter-books of Sir Amias Paulet*, ed. Morris. [2] Collinson, *Som.* ii. 167; *Vis. Devon*, ed. Colby, 168; *CSP Dom.* 1581–90, p. 200; Add. 1547–65, p. 490; Add. 1580–1625, p. 242; G. R. Balleine, *Biog. Dict. Jersey*, 652 seq.; SP12/121, f. 29; *CSP For.* 1575–7, p. 385; 1579–80, p. 98; 1587, p. 473; *CSP Scot.* 1585–6; 1586–8, passim; Ashmole, *Order of the Garter*, 1672, p. 521. [3] Wards 7/23/56, 40/82; *CPR*, 1563–6, p. 196; *Trans. Devon Assoc.* lix. 260; *CSP Dom.* 1547–80, p. 515; Add. 1547–65, p. 490; Add. 1566–79, p. 29 et passim; St. Ch. 5/P1/27; A. J. Eagleston, *Channel Islands under Tudor Govt.* 90; *HMC Hatfield*, i. 274, 342. [4] Add. 48018, f. 294; PCC 40 Tirwhite; Som. RO Phelips mss; *CJ*, i. 83. [5] *CSP For.* 1577–80, pp. 93, 403; 1578–9, p. 485; 1579–80, p. 96. [6] *CSP Dom.* 1581–90, pp. 73, 200; *CSP For.* 1577–8, p. 621; *CSP Scot.* 1584–5, p. 558 et passim; 1585–6, p. 657; 1586–8, pp. 288, 292. [7] *CSP Dom.* Add. 1580–1625, p. 242; Lansd. 104, ff. 51 seq.; *Som. Arch. Soc. Proc.* lxxiv (plate vi); PCC 27 Leicester; C142/167/78.

N.M.F.

PAULET, George (1553–1608), of Crondall, Hants.

BRIDPORT	1589

b. 1553, s. of Sir George Paulet of Crondall, bro. of 1st Mq. of Winchester by his 3rd w. Elizabeth, da. of William Windsor†, 2nd Lord Windsor; half-bro. of Hampden Paulet*. *educ.* Eton 1564–72, KS 1564; King's, Camb. 1572–5. *m.* bef. 1586, Joan, da. and coh. of Richard Kyme of Lewes, Suss., 1s. 1da. *suc.* fa. 1558. Kntd. 1607.

J.p. Hants 1593–1602, capt. musters 1600; gov. Derry 1606.

The identification of this 1589 MP is conjectural. Sir

George Paulet may have had two sons named George, by different wives, and there were two other namesakes, a son of Lord Thomas Paulet of Melplash, Dorset, and a George Paulet who worked in Jersey, brother of Amias Paulet*. Whoever he was, the 1589 Member may be assumed to have owed his return at Bridport to the 3rd Marquess of Winchester, to whom he was servant. The man whose particulars are given above went to Ireland in about 1602, became governor of Derry, was knighted by the lord deputy at Slane, and died in action in 1608, administration of his estate being granted to his widow on 27 Aug.

VCH Hants, iv. 13; *Suss. Arch. Coll.* c. 120–1; *CSP Ire.* 1603–6, p. 259; 1606–8, passim; *Dorset Nat. Hist. Antiq. Field Club Procs. 1934*, p. 127 et passim; A. J. Eagleston, *Channel Islands under Tudor Govt.* passim; Bodl. Tanner 115, ff. 3, 31; 283, ff. 15, 172; Rawl. D754, f. 54; *APC*, xxxi. 153–4; PCC admon. act bk. 1608, f. 126.

P.W.H.

PAULET, Hampden (b. by 1550), of Nether Wallop and Buckland, Hants.

STOCKBRIDGE	1584
LYME REGIS	1589

b. by 1550, 1st s. of Sir George Paulet of Crondall by his 2nd w. Barbara, da. of Sir John Hampden, wid. of Henry Smith; half-bro. of George Paulet*. *educ.* L. Inn 1569. *m.* (1) Anne, da. and coh. of Stephen Hadnall; (2) Margaret, da. of William More I*, 1da. *suc.* fa. 1558. Kntd. 1601.

Served under Leicester in the Netherlands Jan. 1586, lt. of ordnance at Portsmouth 1597; j.p. Hants from c.1591, dep. lt. by 1599.

Paulet was returned at Stockbridge through his own local influence and at Lyme through that of his cousin Sir William Paulet*, 3rd Marquess of Winchester. In neither Parliament did he make any mark in the House. He was a soldier, serving at The Hague, and, later in 1586 levying foot soldiers in Berkshire and Hampshire. He held a military appointment at Southampton in 1588 and in the following year took reinforcements of Hampshire levies to France. Twice he avoided being pricked as sheriff of Hampshire: in 1598 he approached the Earl of Essex through Mountjoy, and in 1601 the 2nd Baron Hunsdon wrote to Sir Robert Cecil on his behalf. On a number of occasions Paulet can be seen acting for the 4th Marquess of Winchester, to whom he lent £400. A curious incident occurred in 1602 when the Marchioness complained to her uncle, Sir Robert Cecil, that Paulet had been slandered by William St. John in 'most unfitting terms by him in public delivered'. Paulet himself frequently wrote business letters to Cecil, in 1601 complaining that Portsmouth was short of necessities, and the next year sending him items of shipping news. The last record found of him is a letter to Cecil in 1603, signed by 18 other knights, refusing to surrender his post at Portsmouth to Sir Henry Danvers.

VCH Hants, iv. 13, 345, 494; Mill Stephenson, *Mon. Brasses*, 94, 165; *HMC 7th Rep.* 655a; *APC*, xxvii. 201; xxix. 681; Collins, *Peerage*, ii. 370; E. M. Tenison, *Eliz. England*, vi. 45; *APC*, xiv. 55; xvii. 96; *HMC Foljambe*, 42; *HMC Hatfield*, viii. 464, 465; xi. 322, 498; xii. 34, 378, 701; Harl. 4713, ff. 93, 94, 272.

P.W.H.

PAULET, Sir Hugh (c.1510–73), of Hinton St. George, Som.

SOMERSET	?1529*, ?1536, 1539, 1572*

b. c.1510, 1st s. of Sir Amias Paulet† by his 2nd w. Laura, da. of William Kellaway of Rockbourne, Hants. *educ.* M. Temple. *m.* (1) 1530, Philippa, da. of Sir Lewis Pollard† of King's Nympton, Devon, 3s. inc. Amias* 2da.; (2) 1560, Elizabeth Blount, da. of Walter Blount† of Blount's Hall, Burton-on-Trent, Staffs., wid. of (Sir) Thomas Pope†, founder of Trinity Coll. Oxf. Kntd. 1536; *suc.* fa. 1538.[1]

J.p. Devon, Dorset, Som. from 1532; sheriff, Dorset, Som. 1536–7, 1542–3, 1547–8, Devon 1541–2; commr. church lands 1535; member, council in the west 1539; v.-adm. Som. 1539; administrator, Glastonbury abbey 1539; treasurer, Boulogne 1544–6; gov. Jersey 1550–*d.*; vice-president, council in the marches of Wales 1559; custos rot. Som. from c.1562, commr. musters 1569.[2]

Paulet's family had been prominent in Somerset since the mid-fifteenth century. A soldier, he accompanied Henry VIII to Flanders, and served Edward VI during the western rebellion, before being appointed first to investigate the affairs of Jersey (November 1549) then governor of the island. Concerned by the proximity of his command to a potentially hostile France, he made the improvement of the fortifications his chief priority, often advancing his own money and using building material from the island's churches. The initial impact of the Reformation on Jersey had already occurred by the time of Paulet's appointment, and few repressive acts were necessary, though a priest was fined for 'obstructing the word of God and upholding the superstitions of Rome' and the elders of one parish were instructed to report mockeries, disturbances and popish acts. Though his appointment must have been influenced by his protestant predilections, there was no attempt to replace him under Mary. Indeed it was with the accession of Elizabeth that his personal connexion with Jersey came to an end, as his son Amias assumed his responsibilities on the island, while Paulet himself became vice-president of the council in the marches of Wales. Here his job was to prepare the ground for the new lord president, Lord Williams, who took the place of the Marian Bishop Bourne of Bath and Wells. Paulet's vigorous activities during his short stay paralleled those of his first visit to Jersey in 1549. He investigated all branches of the council's administration and on his return to London presented a memorandum on Welsh government, which favoured wide powers for the lord president over his officials and recommended severe repression of theft and disorder.[3]

By this time Paulet had acquired a reputation as a trouble shooter. He was one of the commissioners appointed in June 1562 to deal with law and revenue in Ireland (though in the event he did not go) and in October 1562, when the Le Havre Huguenots surrendered the town to Elizabeth, Paulet, 'a man of wisdom and long experience', was sent to advise the captain-general of the expeditionary force. He remained at Le Havre until August 1563, when he returned to Portsmouth to discharge his men. The aftermath of the expedition continued to occupy him for some time; he tried to secure some of the discharged men for service in Jersey, and in November 1563 served on the commission appointed to satisfy the debts of the expedition and pay off the soldiers who had taken part in it.[4]

In 1571 he and Sir Maurice Berkeley were instructed by the Council to see that suitable MPs were returned for Somerset. Among these was his son Amias, who successfully contested the county, and Richard Blount, a connexion of his second wife, who sat for Taunton. Paulet himself sat as knight of the shire in 1572, and was named to committees on Mary Queen of Scots (12, 28 May 1572), fraudulent conveyances (3 June), hospitals (28 June) and the bill for Sir W. Harper (30 May).[5]

With this Parliament Paulet's public career came to an end. He was still active in Somerset in June 1573, made his will at the beginning of that December and died on the 6th of the same month. His widow revealed herself as an open Catholic, was presented as a recusant and accused of harbouring Jesuits in her house in Clerkenwell.[6]

[1] *DNB*; C142/61/14; *Vis. Som.* ed. Weaver; Balleine, *Biog. Dict Jersey*, 662ff; Harbin, *Som. MPs*, 127; Collins, *Peerage*, iv. 3; *Som. Rec. Soc.* xxi. 40; PCC 18 Dyngeley. [2] *CPR*, 1553–4, pp. 18, 23, 28; 1560–3, pp. 435, 436, 443; 1563–6, p. 327; C66/985; *CSP Dom.* 1547–80, pp. 37, 340, 462; *Som. Rec. Soc.* xx. 15, 25; *LP Hen. VIII*, xii(2), p. 320; xiv(1), p. 360, (2), p. 130; Cotton Titus B I, 161. [3] *LP Hen. VIII*, xix(1), pp. 155, 161–2, 175, 240, 245, 296, 468; Rose-Troup, *Western Rebellion 1549*, p. 305; A. J. Eagleston, *Channel Islands under Tudor Govt.* 38, 90–1; Stowe 571, f.47v; *CPR*, 1550–3, p. 12; 1553–4, p. 266; 1560–3, pp. 277, 425; 1563–6, p. 181; *APC*, vii. 81–2, 203, 223–4, 250; *HMC Hatfield*, i. 76, 271, 278, 282, 293; PCC 8 Martyn; *CSP Dom.* 1547–80, pp. 85, 123, 132, 140, 340, 372, 462; Add. 1547–65, p. 566; *Som. Rec. Soc.* xx. 15, 25; SP12/7/3; 12/107/4; 15/9/20; P. H. Williams, *Council in the Marches of Wales*, 250. [4] *HMC Hatfield*, i. 266, 273, 277, 282, 284; *Cecil State Pprs.* ed. Haynes, 387, 388; *APC*, vii. 139; *CSP Dom.* 1547–80, p. 213. [5] *APC*, viii. 15; D'Ewes, 206, 219, 220, 221, 224–5; *CJ*, i. 94, 98, 99, 100, 103. [6] *CSP Dom.* 1547–80, p. 462; 1581–90, p. 287; Add. 1556–79, p. 551; PCC 8 Martyn.

I.C.

PAULET, Sir William (c.1532–98), of Hooke Court, Dorset.

DORSET	1571

b. c.1532, 1st s. of John, 2nd Mq. of Winchester by his 1st

w. Elizabeth, da. and coh. of Robert, 2nd Lord Willoughby de Broke. *educ.* I. Temple 1546. *m.* by 1548, Agnes or Anne (*d.*1601), 1st da. of William, 1st Baron Howard of Effingham, 1s. 3da. At least 4s. illegit. KB 1553; *summ.* to Lords in his fa.'s barony as Lord St. John 5 May 1572; *suc.* fa. as 3rd Mq. of Winchester 4 Nov. 1576.

J.p. Hants from c.1559, Dorset from 1564; sheriff, Hants 1560–1; commr. musters, Dorset 1569; high steward, Dorchester by 1570; jt. ld. lt. Dorset 1569, Hants 1585; commr. trial of Mary Queen of Scots 1586; ld. high steward 1589, 1597; ld. lt. Dorset 1586; commr. eccles. causes, diocese of Winchester 1597.[1]

After an unsuccessful attempt at a by-election for Hampshire in 1566, when the sheriff declared him ineligible to sit by reason of his non-residence in the county, Paulet sat once as knight of the shire for Dorset before being called to the Lords. He was one of those asked by the Privy Council in 1571 to ensure the return of well-affected MPs. His Commons committees in 1571 concerned the subsidy (7 Apr.), church attendance (5 May) and corrupt presentations (25 May).[2]

Paulet was involved in a long series of public and private disputes. Already in 1570 he had been reprimanded for failing to appear before the Privy Council in connexion with a quarrel with John Young I*. It was on this occasion that his relative, the 2nd Earl of Bedford, recognising that the Earl of Leicester would be unfriendly towards Paulet, wrote a letter in his favour to Burghley. Bedford later supported Paulet when, after his succession to the title, his marriage broke down. (Sir) Amias Paulet*, however, another courtier, took Lady Winchester's part. Her fault 'consisted only in some points of wilfulness and disobedience', and Sir Amias advised a reconciliation:

> that you shall hereby purchase the profit and assured friendship of many great personages, and I cannot tell how the greatest in the world can live in credit without the favour of the court.

There was also a reference to 'your Lordship's continued abode in the country', meaning Jane Lambert, by whom he had at least four illegitimate sons. Despite the scandal of his private life, and a growing list of lawsuits and other quarrels, including one with the bishop of Winchester, the Marquess did not suffer the eclipse predicted by Sir Amias, and, as high steward, bore the sword before Elizabeth at her entry into London for the Armada thanksgiving.[3]

In the later years of his life, Paulet was involved in a series of Star Chamber suits, and a number of cases in the common pleas – eventually settled by Act of Parliament – relating to lands he owned jointly with Lord Mountjoy. His death, on 24 Nov. 1598, was the signal for his family to close in on Jane Lambert. Their Chancery action listed her misdeeds, making him 'a stranger and enemy to gentlemen of account and his nearest kinsmen'; 'procuring a preacher to write a book justifying the said

lord marquess' in leaving his wife and marrying Mistress Lambert; opposing the marriage of Paulet's son to the daughter of Thomas Cecil*; 'planting her own brothers and her friends in all principal places about him that might fill his ears full of their conceits'; 'not suffering his own kinsmen or well willers to have access' and so on. The family believed that 'when he grew near his death he lay in extreme torment', and that he accused himself of being 'the notablest beast that ever lived'. He repented, they thought, of his sins, declared that he had left his heir a poor house, 'and in these passions died', 24 Nov. 1598, appointing three of the Lamberts executors and principal beneficiaries of his will, which his own family then successfully contested.[4]

[1] Hutchins, *Dorset*, ii. 651; St. Ch. 5/7/9; 2/5; E. K. Chambers, *Eliz. Stage*, i. 35; E. M. Tenison, *Eliz. Eng.* vii. 391; J. Coker, *Surv. Dorset*, 60, 61. [2] St. Ch. 4/7/18; Add. 48018, f. 294; *Cath. Rec. Soc.* xiii. 89; xxii. 59; *Cam. Misc.* ix(3), pp. 55, 56; *CJ*, i. 83, 88, 92, 93; D'Ewes, 159, 181, 188, 189. [3] *APC*, vii. 404–5; viii. 12; xv. 40–2, 273; xvi. 174–5; xvii. 169; *HMC Hatfield*, i. 477; D'Ewes, 272; Bodl. Add. C82, ff. 85, 137; Dugdale, *Baronetage*, ii. 375; SP12/148/18; Lansd. 72, ff. 1, 5; *CSP Dom.* 1581–90, pp. 406, 458, 497–8, 567. Some of these and the succeeding references are taken from the Roberts thesis. [4] St. Ch. 5/W11/35, W19/19, W20/34, P10/2; C. Monro, *Acta Canc.* 717; *HMC Hatfield*, xi. 410–11; Bodl. Rawl. D1346, Tanner 115, f. 3; PCC 46 Hayes; Harl. 4713, f. 272.

P.W.H.

PAYCOCK, Gregory (*d.* aft.1584), of York.

YORK	1572*

m. a sis. of William Watson*, wid. of William Pennington, merchant, at least 1da.

Freeman, York c.1547, chamberlain 1548–9, sheriff 1566–7, alderman 1567–77, ld. mayor 1571–2; constable, merchant adventurers 1549–51, gov. 1568–71.

Paycock was a lead and cloth merchant. During the 1569 rebellion he relayed to the Earl of Sussex information obtained from three captured fishermen to the effect that there were 200 foot soldiers in Hartlepool, and he gave evidence against a gaoler of York castle who had been sympathetic towards the rebels. Returned MP for the city in 1572, Paycock took an active part in parliamentary business. On 12 May he attended the conference with the Lords to discuss Mary Queen of Scots, and he served on committees on cloth (1 Mar. 1576), to remove the benefit of clergy from rapists and burglars (7 Mar.) and on wharves and quays (13 May). By March 1577 Paycock was requesting the city council to relieve him of the office of alderman, 'for that he is not of ability, neither of body, nor yet of goods nor living to maintain the part and room of an alderman, and also is not meet nor able to come and assist the lord mayor', and he received an annuity of £6 13s. 4d. The city sued for a new writ in October 1579, and the seat was filled 1 Feb. 1581, Paycock being put down in the Commons journals as 'incurably sick and diseased'. His successor's election was allowed on 18 Mar. 1581. Paycock was still receiving a reduced annuity in 1584.

York City Lib., Skaife mss; *York Freemen* (Surtees Soc. xcvi), 266–7; (cii), 12; *York Mercers* (Surtees Soc. cxxix), 324; *York Civic Recs.* passim; Cott. Calig. B. 9, p. 79; *CSP Dom.* Add. 1566–79, p. 223; D'Ewes, 206, 251, 308; *CJ*, i. 95, 109, 111, 114, 135; York chamberlain's accts. 5, f. 56.

A.M.M.

PEAKE, Edward (c.1545–?1607), of Sandwich and Ash, Kent.

SANDWICH	1572*, 1584, 1586, 1589, 1593, 1597, 1601, 1604*

b. c.1545, yr. s. of Nicholas Peake† of Sandwich by Joan, da. of Roger Manwood† of Sandwich. *educ.* I. Temple 1560. *m.* (1) Elizabeth, da. and h. of Thomas Norton of Faversham, at least 6s. 5da.; (2) 22 July 1586, Mary, da. of Thomas Cox of Berks., wid. of one Tysar of Sandwich, at least 1s. 2da.[1]

Jurat, Sandwich from Dec. 1571, mayor 1575–6, 1576–7, 1586–7, 1592–3, 1597–8;[2] brodhull rep. many times aft. 1572.[3]

As a younger son Peake did not inherit the family's main residence in Sandwich, but his father left him a house and quay there, together with the nearby manor of Ash. Either Edward or his son made Ash the principal seat, turning the family from townsmen into country gentlemen. Peake was returned to Parliament in 1576, during his first mayoralty, at a by-election caused by the elevation of his relative Roger Manwood* to the bench. From that date onwards he sat in every Parliament until his death. In 1584 he and Edward Wood* were successsful when four candidates took part in the election. There was a contest in 1586 also, but a letter from the lord warden, passing on the Privy Council's request that the 1584 Members should be returned again, carried the day. Where details survive, Peake was paid 4s. a day parliamentary wages.[4]

Peake is not mentioned by name in the journals of the Commons before 1593, but, as a Member for a port town, he could have sat on committees concerning fish (6 Mar. 1587 and 5 Mar. 1593), statutes (28 Mar. 1593) and brewers (3 Apr. 1593). He was put on the committees for privileges and returns (5 Nov. 1597), forestallers (8 Nov.) and maltsters (12 Jan. 1598). As a burgess of a port town he could have attended the committees on monopolies (10 Nov. 1597), the navigation bill (12 Nov.), the Great Yarmouth charter (23 Nov.), mariners (9 Dec.) and corn (3 Feb. 1598). In 1601 he was again of the committee for privileges and returns (31 Oct.) and that on alehouses (5 Nov.). He could also have attended the main business committee (3 Nov.) and committees considering cloth workers (15 Nov.), monopolies (23 Nov.) and ships and seamen (9 Dec.). On 3 Dec. 1601 he made his only recorded speech, urging greater protection for coastal towns and their ships against the Dunkirk pirates:

> Every day men come home, their goods and all they have taken away, yea their very apparel; and if the ships might also be carried away they would do it ... We had need to cherish this subject, I think him to be the best and most necessary member of the commonwealth, I mean the navigator.

Peake was one of the committee appointed to consider the matter.[5]

In addition to his activities in Sandwich, Peake was a representative at the Cinque Ports brodhull and one of the Ports' 'solicitors' in a legal action against the city of London in 1593. In 1598 he was given the honour of administering the oath to the new lord warden, and was one of the canopy bearers at James I's coronation, a traditional duty for barons of the Ports. Earlier he had been prominent in the preparations for the Queen's visit in 1573, and was an officer in the local musters.[6]

His standing in eastern Kent is shown by his appearance in a number of local commissions appointed by the Privy Council. With Sir Thomas Scott*, the dean of Rochester, and others, he was ordered to investigate the disturbances in Hythe connected with the mayoralty of Christopher Honeywood*, and in 1587 he and other Sandwich men were instructed to send under guard to Canterbury the ringleaders in the 'late intended commotion in those parts'. He also carried out commissions from the lord warden, especially with regard to the restraint of suspected persons from going overseas. In 1599 he interrogated ten Sandwich men suspected of carrying ashore goods from a Dutch ship which had run aground on the Goodwin sands.[7]

The date of Peake's death has not been found. A parliamentary by-election to choose his successor took place on 11 Jan. 1608.

[1] *Vis. Kent* (Harl. Soc. lxxv), 135, 141; J. Cowper, *Cant. Mar. Lic. 1568–1618*, p. 320. [2] There are discrepancies as to the mayors, 1591–3, between *Vis. Kent*, p. 144 and W. Boys, *Sandwich*, i. 419. [3] Sandwich, new red bk. 1568–81, f. 56; Boys, i. 419 seq.; Cinque Ports black bk. passim. [4] PCC 10 Loftes; Sandwich year bks. 1582–1608, ff. 26, 59, 101, 179, 234, 295. [5] D'Ewes, 412, 487, 511, 514, 552, 555, 556, 562, 570, 592, 622, 624, 626, 642, 649, 666, 674; Townshend, *Hist. Colls.* 103, 281. [6] Cinque Ports black bk. ff. 60, 67, 79 et passim; Boys, i. 213, 692; Add. 33511, ff. 150 seq. [7] *CSP Dom.* 1581–90, p. 87; 1591–4, p. 394; 1598–1601, p. 162; *APC*, xv. 154.

M.R.P.

PEARD, George (1548–1621), of Barnstaple, Devon.

BARNSTAPLE	1597, 1604

bap. 3 Mar. 1548, s. of John Peard, chamberlain of Barnstaple. *educ.* L. Inn 1573, called. *m.* 24 Sept. 1576, Agnes, da. of John Jewel of East Down, at least 1da.

Three members of Peard's family were goldsmiths, and his brother Edward was a judge of the Admiralty court in

Devon. A Richard Peard was mayor of Barnstaple in 1587, and Peard himself was of counsel to the borough. His wife was a niece of Bishop Jewel. At the parliamentary election of 1597 the townsmen, who were quarrelling with the lord lieutenant, the Earl of Bath, first elected their former bailiff and mayor, Bartholomew Harris, but Bath disapproving of their choice, the townsmen turned to Peard, who was returned along with the Earl's servant Thomas Hinson. Peard died 31 Jan. 1621.

Barnstaple Recs. i. 46, 200; ii. 77, 103, 113, 166; Vivian, *Vis. Devon,* 505, 531, 808; *Trans. Dev. Assoc.* lxxii. 257; Devon RO, Tingey 1662; St. Ch. 5/A51/19; Roberts thesis; PCC 30 Dale; C142/766/77.

P.W.H.

PEARMAN, George (*d.* 1604), of Bath, Som.

BATH   1571, 1572

    m. Anne.
      Mayor, Bath 1572–3, 1577–8, 1578–9, 1583–4, alderman from 1573.

The municipal records show the payment of Pearman's stipend as mayor and a few routine matters connected with his mayoralty, but he appeared prominently in local affairs only once. In 1585 concealed chantry lands in Bath were granted by the Crown to William Shareston* and John Sachfield. It was claimed that a part of the land in question was not chantry land but belonged to the parishes of St. Mary de Stalles and St. Michael extra muros. Pearman, acting on behalf of the parishes, brought a Chancery action against Shareston and Sachfield, who were both defended at the expense of the city chamber. According to the registers of Bath abbey, Pearman died in April 1604, being survived by his wife Anne, who lived until November 1612.

Bath Chamberlains' Accts. (Som. Rec. Soc. xxxviii), passim; *Bath Recs.* p. xiii. 40, 47; BM Cartae Antiquae 83 H.4; *Regs. Bath Abbey,* 339, 344.

I.C.

PECKE, Ashburnham, of Winchelsea, Suss.

WINCHELSEA   1593

    1st s. of John Pecke, jurat and mayor of Winchelsea, by Mary, da. of James Blechendon of Aldington, Kent. *m.,* at least 10s. *suc.* fa. c.1581.[1]
    Jurat, Winchelsea 1590.

When, in 1586, the Queen granted Winchelsea part of the estates formerly belonging to the Black Friars there, Pecke secured 12 acres of arable land near Catsfield, a windmill near King's Green for 12*d.* and a messuage and two gardens in the town for 6*d.* Pecke, as his christian name suggests, was connected with his neighbour and fellow-member for Winchelsea, Adam Ashburnham, some of whose marshland at Pevensey he occupied and

who was an overseer of his father's will. He also held some property of Adam Ashburnham's half-brother, Lawrence Levett of Hollington, who was another neighbour. Among his relatives was John Pecke of Winchelsea who, in his will dated March 1602, gave to Ashburnham Pecke and his ten sons reversionary interests in his estate. Pecke was the 'Member named Peck' to whom 'Black' Oliver St. John spoke when he was trying to whip up support for Wentworth's proposed speech on the succession in 1593, but no certain evidence remains of Pecke's one membership of Parliament. As a burgess of a Cinque Port he would have been entitled to attend committees concerned with fish (5 Mar. 1593) and statutes (28 Mar.).[2]

[1] *Vis. Suss.* (Harl. Soc. liii), 134; PCC 77 Montague; Lewes Archdeaconry, wills register, A7, f. 186; E. Suss. RO, Winchelsea mss; *HMC 9th Rep.* pt. 1, 306. [2] *Suss. Arch. Colls.* xxviii. 95; W. D. Cooper, *Winchelsea,* 107–110; PCC 18 Lewyn, 5 Windsor, 77 Montague; *EHR,* xxxix. 187–8; Harl. 6846, f. 88; D'Ewes, 487, 511.

J.E.M.

PELHAM, Edmund[1] (*d.* 1606), of Catsfield, Suss.

HASTINGS   1597

    5th s. of Sir William Pelham of Laughton, being 3rd s. by his 2nd w. Mary, da. of William, 1st Baron Sandys, ld. chamberlain to Henry VIII; half-bro. of Sir Nicholas Pelham†. *educ.* G. Inn 1563, called 1574. *m.* Ellen or Helen, da. of Thomas Darrell of Scotney, 5s. 3da. Kntd. 1604.
    Of counsel to Winchelsea 1579, to Cinque Ports 1582, Hastings prob. by 1583, Rye by 1584; brodhull rep. for Hastings 1583; j.p. Suss. from c.1583; pens. G. Inn 1586, Autumn reader 1588, Lent 1601; serjeant-at-law 1601; chief baron of the Exchequer and PC [I] 1602.[2]

Though Pelham was a close kinsman of the leading Sussex magnate, Lord Buckhurst, they were not on good terms. Pelham's own family standing and legal career in the Cinque Ports, however, freed him from the necessity of relying on Buckhurst's favour. In the Commons Pelham spoke on an election return (12 Nov.), and was appointed to committees on the lands of Lord Mountjoy (24 Nov.), defence (8 Dec.) and corporations (12 Jan. 1598). As a burgess of a port town he could also have sat on committees dealing with monopolies (10 Nov. 1597), navigation (12 Nov.), the Great Yarmouth charter (23 Nov.), mariners (9 Dec.) and corn (3 Feb. 1598).[3]

Pelham had been put on the Sussex commission of the peace despite his wife's recusancy and his own reputation as 'a cold professor in religion and a lawyer much in London'. The deputy lieutenants described him towards the end of Elizabeth's reign as the chief justice of the peace in his district, but 'very backward in religion and cometh to church but slackly', not having taken communion for a year. Nevertheless, he was appointed an Irish judge and made serjeant. Buckhurst wrote to Cecil, 19 Oct. 1601, 'the arrival of the Spaniards hath daunted him extremely ... and if he could tell how to go back, he would', and, next May, John Chamberlain: 'Now he hath got the coif he makes no haste, but had rather tarry by it here'. He arrived in Ireland during the summer of 1602. There was a dispute with his predecessor, (Sir) Robert Napier*, and it was agreed to pay Pelham from 20 Apr. In the summer of 1603, Pelham went on circuit through Ulster, the first English judge to do so, and reported

> that the multitude that had been subject to oppression and misery did reverence him as if he had been a good angel sent from heaven, and prayed him upon their knees to return again to minister justice unto them.

Described as a 'very learned and worthy judge' his patent was renewed by James I, and he was knighted at Greenwich. He returned to Ireland soon afterwards and in the following spring was on circuit in Neath.[4]

While living at Drogheda, he made his will, dated 5 July 1604. He left a life interest in Catsfield to his wife and £200 each to his daughters, annuities of £15 to his younger sons, and lands and law books to the heir Herbert. The widow was executrix and residuary legatee, and his brothers-in-law, Henry Darrell and Thomas Tinkell, overseers. Pelham died at Chester on his way home from Ireland, on 4 July 1606. On 30 Nov. 1609 his will was proved for his widow, who was still in trouble over her religion.[5]

[1] Sometimes Edward in contemporary documents. [2] *DNB*; *Suss. Arch. Colls.* xiv. 107; *Suss. Genealogies, Lewes Centre*, 206–7; Mousley thesis, 659–60; PCC 103 Dorset; *HMC 13th Rep. IV*, 357; Rye hundreds accts. 1573–93, f. 228; Winchelsea hundreds, no. 4, f. 130; Cinque Ports black bk. f. 45. [3] Mousley thesis, 264–70; *G. Inn Pens. Bk.* i. 38, 73, 79, 88, 89; Cinque Ports black bk. f. 45; Rye hundreds accts. 1593–1606, ff. 65, 70; D'Ewes, 555, 556, 562, 570, 592; Townshend, *Hist. Colls.* 113, 119; Harl. 75, ff. 125, 127, 134, 142–3. [4] *HMC Hatfield*, ii. 502; Lansd. 82, f. 103; *Suss. Arch. Colls.* lix. 30, 56; *APC*, xxx. 30, 308. [5] *HMC Hatfield*, xi. 437; *Chamberlain Letters* ed. McClure, i. 144; *CSP Ire.* 1601–3, pp. 485–6; 1603–6, pp. 111, 282, 522; PCC 103 Dorset; *Suss. Arch. Colls.* xlix. 56.

R.C.G.

PELHAM, Herbert (c.1546–1620), of Michelham Priory, nr. Hailsham, Suss. and Compton Valence, Dorset.

| WINCHELSEA | 1584 |
| REIGATE | 1604 |

b. c.1546, o.s. of Anthony Pelham of Hendall manor in Bucksteep, Warbleton, Suss. by Margaret Hall, wid. of Percy de Buckthorpe of Suss. *educ.* Queens', Camb. 1562. *m.* (1) Katherine (*d.* by 1612), da. of John Thatcher, of Priesthawes, Westham, Suss., 3s. 1da.; (2) Elizabeth (*d.* 15 Jan. 1639), da. of Thomas West, 2nd Baron de la Warr, 1s. 1da. *suc.* fa. 1566.[1]

Sheriff, Surr. and Suss. Apr.–Nov. 1576, 1590–1; j.p. Suss. 1582–7; brodhull rep. 1583; bailiff to Yarmouth 1583; freeman, Winchelsea 22 Jan. 1583, jurat 7 Apr. 1583.[2]

In the sixteenth century Bucksteep was the seat of a cadet branch of the Sussex Pelhams. When Pelham became head of this branch, he inherited lands in Sussex, Dorset, Kent, Lincolnshire, Northumberland, Surrey, Yorkshire and 'elsewhere within the realm of England'. Through a fortunate second marriage, he gained the manor of Compton Valance in Dorset.[3]

An active member of the Winchelsea corporation, Pelham would naturally have found a borough seat there when he was unsuccessful for the county in 1584. He had already served once as sheriff of Surrey and Sussex, and had been imprisoned by the lord treasurer for refusing to do so a second time. When summoned before the Privy Council for this refusal in April 1582, he gave as excuse his residence within the liberty of the Cinque Ports. He was on the commission of the peace for only three years. A 1587 report on Sussex justices explained that he was dropped because his judgment was unreliable.[4]

Pelham's purchase, in October 1587, of the site of Michelham priory, was followed by financial troubles, though these may have derived from the failing business of his brother-in-law Anthony Morley, a Sussex ironmaster. In 1590 he borrowed £400 from John Michell of Cuckfield, Sussex, and in 1599 his entire interest in Michelham was made over to his relative, Thomas Pelham* of Laughton and two others, as trustees for sale, to provide an annuity of £400 a year and to discharge the debts. On 6 Apr. 1601 the trustees sold Michelham to Lord Buckhurst for £4,700. Pelham also disposed of estates at Whatlington and Peplesham. He died intestate 12 Apr. 1620.[5]

[1] Hutchins, *Dorset*, ii. 294; C142/145/12; J. Comber, *Suss. Genealogies, Lewes Centre*, 211, 287; Collins, *Peerage* (1812), v. 19; *CPR*, 1566–9, p. 12. [2] PRO Assizes, 35, S.E. Circuit, Suss. 24–7; E. Suss. RO, Winchelsea mss. [3] *Suss. Arch. Colls.* ix. 220–1; Hutchins, loc. cit. [4] Cinque Ports black bk. f. 45v; Winchelsea mss; Harl. 703, ff. 18v, 19v; *HMC Hatfield*, ii. 502; Lansd. 53, ff. 160–1; *Suss. Arch. Colls.* ii. 60; xlix. 30; PRO Assizes, 35, S.E. Circuit, Suss. passim. [5] *Suss. Arch. Colls.* vi. 160–1; ix. 220–1; xxxvii. 47; liii. 59; lxii. 152; *Suss. Rec. Soc.* xx. 404; Horsfield, *Suss.* i. 527; Mousley thesis, 621; Wards 7/64/33; C142/417/8; Lincoln consistory ct. admon. 1624. no. 132.

J.E.M.

PELHAM, John (1537–80), of Laughton, nr. Lewes, Suss.

| SUSSEX | 1571 |

b. 1537, 1st s. of Sir Nicholas Pelham† of Laughton by Anne, da. of John Sackville† of Withyham, sis. of Sir Richard Sackville*, and aunt of Thomas Sackville*, Baron Buckhurst; bro. of Thomas*. *educ.* ?Queens', Camb. 1549. *m.* Judith (*d.*1607), da. of Oliver St.John†, 1st Baron St. John, of Bletsoe, Beds., 1s. *suc.* fa. 1560. Kntd. 1573.

Commr. sewers, Suss. 1564, j.p. from c. Mar. 1565; sheriff, Surr. and Suss. 1571–2; commr. musters, Suss.; commr piracy, Suss. and Cinque Ports.

Pelham was a Marian exile with his cousin William Morley* at Padua and Geneva. Soon after the accession of Elizabeth his father left him the manors of Bevilham, Burwash, Crowhurst and Laughton, with other Sussex property. His subsidy assessment at £40 in lands was only half that of his father, and he had difficulties about the title to some of his estates. A suit, which involved a crown tenant at Laughton, was begun about 1569 in the duchy of Lancaster court, was later brought before the Star Chamber, and was still unsettled at Pelham's death, by which time he had been sent to the Fleet prison at least twice and possibly four times. Pelham owned two forges and an iron furnace in Sussex.[1]

Classified by the bishop of Chichester as a 'favourer of godly proceedings', he was on the Sussex commission of the peace by March 1565. Both he and Morley were in the 1571 Parliament, when, as senior knight of the shire for a maritime county, Pelham was appointed to the committee for the navigation bill, 8 May, his only recorded activity.

While still in office as sheriff in 1572, Pelham took the part of George Goring I* against Lord Buckhurst in a dispute over excessive felling of timber at Balneath, near Lewes. In 1579 he joined Henry Bowyer* and others in attacking Edmund Curteys, vicar of Cuckfield and brother of the bishop of Chichester. On another occasion he was ordered by the Privy Council to help to settle a local dispute between Lord Dacre and Herbert Pelham*. He investigated seditious speeches at Winchelsea in November 1574. He died 12 Oct. 1580, and was buried 'by torchlight' in Holy Trinity church in the Minories, London. His will, dated July 1580, was proved 15 Nov. following.[2]

[1] Suss. Rec. Soc. xiv. 181–2; W. Berry, Co. Genealogies, Suss. 314; CPR, 1563–6, p. 40; APC, vii. 203; PRO Assizes, 35 S. E. Circuit, Suss. 7–23; Lansd. 56, ff. 168 seq.; Mousley thesis, 649 seq.; E179/190/225, 283, 298; C3/1/105; 195/11; Add. 33187, ff. 134 seq.; Suss. Arch. Colls. xiv. 234–5; Stowe 570, f. 104. [2] Cam. Misc. ix(3), pp. 10–11; CJ, i. 88; Add. 33084, ff. 12, 14, 17 seq.; Suss. Arch. Colls. xliv. 16; APC, viii. 316; x. 190, 293, 330; Lansd. 146, f. 19; C142/195/119; Rylands Eng. ms 315; PCC 46 Arundel.

N.M.F.

PELHAM, Thomas (d.1624), of Laughton, later of Halland Place, Suss.

LEWES	1584
SUSSEX	1586

2nd s. of Sir Nicholas Pelham†, and bro. of John*. educ. Lewes g.s. 1557; Queens', Camb. 1561; ?G. Inn 1566. m. Mary, da. of Sir Thomas Walsingham* of Chislehurst, Kent, 1s. 1da. suc. nephew Oliver Pelham 1585. cr. Bt. 1611.[1]

J.p.q. Suss. from c.1583; sheriff, Surr. and Suss. 1589–90; dep. lt. Suss. from 1601.[2]

Pelham succeeded to the lordship of the hundred of Shiplake in Sussex, the manors of Laughton and Colbrands and other lands in Laughton and Ripe. He also inherited the reversion of Hawksborough, Shoyswell and Baldslow hundreds in the same county, of Burwash, Bevilham and Crowhurst manors and of the messuage called 'Halland' in East Hoathly, in all of which Oliver's mother, Judith Pelham, had an interest until her death in 1607.[3]

He was returned through his local standing for Lewes in 1584, his estate at Laughton being less than five miles distant. In 1586 he was elected for the county seat when his rival, Sir Thomas Shirley I*, was in the Netherlands.[4]

He held his full share of local offices and was regularly a justice of the quorum. When the list of justices was overhauled in 1587 he was reported to be a good justice 'as well in respect of religion as of the commonwealth' but since he was 'full of infirmity', a fresh appointment was recommended. If in fact his name was removed it was replaced by 1591. Pelham successfully concluded the long struggle (begun in the lifetime of John Pelham) between his family and Anthony Smyth, the Crown's lessee, for possession of the Dicker common, comprising some 450 acres in Hellingly, near Laughton. This went on in the duchy of Lancaster court, the Star Chamber and Queen's bench and, during the minority of Oliver Pelham, in the court of wards. After 1585, Thomas Pelham defended his family's cause both in the duchy court and in Queen's bench, where a special jury of Sussex men found for him and against the Crown. There is much evidence of Pelham's prosperity in the later years of Elizabeth. For the Armada loan he was assessed at £100, the highest rate known in Sussex; in 1589 he bought the manor of Foxhunt for £780 and both built and endowed Cuckfield school; and two years later he bought the castle, lordship and rape of Hastings from Henry, 3rd Earl of Huntingdon. Meanwhile he was building a new residence, Halland Place, in East Hoathly, to which he moved from Laughton in 1595. A principal source of his wealth may have been his ironworks at Waldron. In 1610 the Earl of Sussex had asked Salisbury for the wardship of Pelham's son, in the event of the father's early death, thinking him a suitable match for his younger daughter, and in the following year Pelham was one of the first to buy himself a baronetcy.[5]

Pelham died 2 Dec. 1624. In his will, made in April 1620, he asked to be buried in St. Michael's, Lewes. His lands, he said, had been divided into three parts in 1615, at the time of his son's marriage: the first, including the manors of Laughton and Colbrands, was then settled on his son and daughter-in-law; the second, including the mansion house of Halland, the manors of Bishopstone, Foxhunt and Cowden, and property in Lewes, was reserved to the use of his 'loving wife'; and the third, including three manors and hundreds in the rape of Hastings as well as sundry ironworks and woods for their maintenace, was to enable his son, the executor, to pay debts and legacies.[6]

[1] J. Comber, *Suss. Genealogies, Lewes Centre*, 207–8; Add. 33142, f. 1; *VCH Suss.* vii. 16; *DNB*, (Walsingham, Sir Francis, Walsingham, Sir Edmund); C142/206/24; *GEC Baronetage*, i. 8. [2] PRO Assizes, 35 S.E. Circuit, Suss. 27–32, 37–44; *APC*, xxxii. 400; PRO Index 4208, f. 220; *CSP Dom.* 1603–10, p. 78. [3] *GEC Baronetage*, loc. cit.; *Suss. Rec. Soc.* xiv. 182; *VCH Suss.* ix. 79. [4] Add. 33142, ff. 79, 85v; *Suss. Rec. Soc.* xxxiv. 10, 11; PCC 27 Clarke; C142/311/110. [5] *APC*, 1615–16, p. 145; C66/1435, 1468, 1482, 1493, 1523, 1549, 1594; *Suss. Arch. Colls.* i. 32, 37 et passim; ii. 59; iii. 228; xiii. 89; xiv. 234–5; xxxvii. 44; xlii. 44; xliii. 7; Add. 33084, f. 5; 33187, ff. 134–48, 168 seq.; 33188, ff. 1–59; 33058 passim; PCC 27 Clarke, 46 Arundel; Stowe 570, f. 104; Lansd. 152, f. 16; *CSP Dom.* 1603–10, p. 609. [6] *Suss. Rec. Soc.* xiv. 182; PCC 27 Clarke.

J.E.M.

PELHAM, William (1567–1629), of Brocklesby, Lincs.

LINCOLNSHIRE 1597

b. 10 Apr. 1567, 1st s. of Sir William Pelham (marshal of Leicester's army in the Netherlands) of Brocklesby by Eleanor, da. of Henry, 5th Earl of Westmorland. *educ.* New Coll. Oxf. 1582; G. Inn 1588. *m.* by 1593, Katherine (or Anne), da. of Charles, 2nd Baron Willoughby of Parham, 8s. 1da. *suc.* fa. 1587. Kntd. 1603.

J.p. Lincs. (Lindsey) from 1584, (Holland, Kesteven) 1584–7; commr. musters, Lincs. 17 May 1601, sheriff 1602–3, dep. lt. 1624.[1]

Pelham's father had died in debt to the Crown, and in 1590 Pelham had to surrender the lease of Killingholme rectory, worth £100 a year, in part payment, the Queen allowing him to lease it again at £50 p.a. As the debt was apparently over £9,000, there must presumably have been other payments, but the details are lacking. Many years later, referring to some of his obligations (probably including those inherited from his father) Pelham said it would doubtless be discovered that they had been paid 'if the records could be found', and described them as the prey of some 'caterpillar of the community'. Still, he was of standing enough to be returned as knight of the shire, possibly helped by the influence of the 5th Earl of Rutland, to whom he sometimes sent gifts. The Mr. Pelham in the journals of the 1597 Parliament is probably Edmund, but as a knight of the shire in that year William Pelham could have attended the committees on enclosures (5 Nov.), the poor law (5, 22 Nov.), armour and weapons (8 Nov.), penal laws (8 Nov.), monopolies (10 Nov.), the subsidy (15 Nov.) and draining the fens (3 Dec.). He was required to contribute a light horse for service in Ireland. While serving as sheriff in 1603 he escorted James I from Newark to Belvoir, where he was knighted. He died in 1629, his will, dated 10 Dec. 1628, being proved on 13 July 1629. His son and successor William was a royalist commander, and a younger son, Henry, a supporter of Parliament.[2]

[1] C142/217/120; *DNB* (Pelham, Sir William); *Lincs. Peds.* (Harl. Soc. lii), 765–6; *APC*, xxxi. 358; *CSP Dom.* 1623–5, p. 396. [2] Collins, *Peerage*, viii. 387; C142/217/120; PRO Index 6800; *HMC Rutland*, i., iv. passim; *APC*. xxxii. 280; Nichols, *Progresses Jas. I*, i. 90–1; D'Ewes, 552, 553, 555, 557, 561, 567; Maddison, *Lincs. Wills*, 167–8;

CSP Dom. 1619–23, p. 463; 1623–5, pp. 170, 214; 1625–6, p. 291; *Cal. Lincoln Wills* (Brit. Rec. Soc. Index Lib. lvii), iv. 141; *HMC Bath*, i. 12, 13, 16.

R.C.G.

PELL, John (c.1527–1608), of King's Lynn and Dersingham, Norf.

KING'S LYNN 1572

b. c.1527, 1st or o.s. of John Pell of Dersingham by Margaret, da. of James Cletheroe of Dersingham. *m.* by 1548, Mary (*d.*1593), da. of William Overend, alderman of King's Lynn, 6s. 3da.

Freeman, King's Lynn c.1547, alderman 1560–78, mayor 1560–1.

Pell was a King's Lynn merchant whose parents lived at Dersingham, nearby. His son Jeffrey, when he became a freeman in 1578, was described as his 'son and apprentice', but the exact nature of his trade is not known. He served on the governing body of King's Lynn for nearly 20 years, until he was discharged as an alderman for 'reasonable cause' and at his own request in July 1578. He often rode to London on the borough's business, and, during his period as MP he was instructed to consult his colleague Robert Bell*, recorder of King's Lynn, as to whether the Earl of Leicester or Lord Burghley should be offered the high stewardship. When Leicester was chosen, Pell was one of the two townsmen appointed to give Burghley the £5 fee which Lynn had paid to the previous lord treasurer. Between 1572 and 1581 he also acted for the town on matters such as admiralty jurisdiction, customs duties, and a suit about the 'liberty of clothes and corn', for which he tried to secure Burghley's support. On various occasions during Elizabeth's reign he was given special instructions to interview local magnates on borough business. His name also appears on the commission of 1568 to make a survey of all houses and land belonging to the corporation, and in 1576 he was a collector for a special tax in Lynn.

Little is known of Pell's membership of the House of Commons. The borough paid him wages and travelling expenses in August 1572, and again in March 1576 – the latter an interim payment of £10. On 23 May 1572 he sat on a Commons committee concerned with weights and measures, and on 13 Feb. 1576 as one of the Lynn burgesses he could have been on a committee about ports. How he came to be put in the Fleet prison in May of this year is not clear, but it was not the only time he was in trouble. In March 1562 the Lynn congregation book recorded that if he and Richard Spence continued to quarrel, they were to pay £5 to the use of the 'commons'; then, in 1581, the Privy Council inquired into his 'slanderous libel and rhymes' against two 'pious and godly ministers'.

He died on 5 Feb. 1608, and was buried at St. Nicholas,

Dersingham. A marble tomb, as he asked in his will, was inscribed with his name and his wife's, together with the dates of birth of their nine children. The will, drawn up on 15 Jan. and proved on 1 Mar., has a short religious preamble. Pell made provision for his widow, leaving her dwelling rooms in his 'head house' at Dersingham, and requiring three of his sons to pay her annuities.

Vis. Norf. (Norf. Rec. Soc. v), 162–3; Blomefield, *Norf.* viii. 401; *Lynn Freemen*, 94, 102, 114; King's Lynn congregation bk. 1544–69, passim; *Vis. Norf.* i. (Norf and Norwich Arch. Soc.), 188; H. J. Hillen, *Hist. King's Lynn*, i. 300–17 passim; *CSP Dom.* 1581–90, p. 34; *APC*, ix. 130; *CJ*, i. 97; D'Ewes, 247; PCC 18 Windebanck.

N.M.F.

PELLATT, Richard (*d.* 1587), of Charlton Court, Steyning, Suss.

STEYNING 1572

1st s. of William Pellatt†. *educ.* Corpus, Camb. 1548; G. Inn 1551. *m.* Mary, 2s. 1da. *suc.* fa. 1558.

The Pellatts were an old Sussex family, paying tax at Steyning as early as 1296, and though they did not achieve county status until the time of Richard Pellatt's son Benjamin, it may be assumed that Richard Pellatt was of sufficient standing to secure his own return to Parliament in the election of 1572, when, in any case, all three local magnates – Henry, Earl of Arundel and his sons-in-law the Duke of Norfolk and Lord Lumley – were in the Tower. In February 1581, on the marriage of his son Benjamin to Dorothy Lewknor, he enfeoffed his manors of Charlton and Ashurst for their benefit. He added to his Sussex property in 1584 by buying Bignor park, near Petworth, and (unless this is a namesake) in his later years he married an Essex heiress and moved to that county, dying, according to the inquisition post mortem, 21 Jan. 1587. There is a discrepancy in the dates of the contemporary documents, as administration of his estate, describing him as 'late of Maldon', Essex, is stated to have been granted to his widow, Mary, on 16 Jan. that year.

Vis. Suss. (Harl. Soc. liii), 153; D. G. C. Elwes and C. J. Robinson, *Castles, Mansions, Manors of W. Sussex*, 32, 34; *Suss. Arch. Colls.* xxxviii. 101–22; *Vis. Essex* (Harl. Soc. xiii), 229, 427, 430; *CPR*, 1555–7, pp. 227, 285; 1558–60, p. 447; Add. 5685, ff. 42, 91; C142/214/222; PCC admon. act bk. 1587, f. 1.

N.M.F.

PEMBERTON, Goddard (*d.* 1616), of Hertingfordbury and St. Albans, Herts.

PETERBOROUGH 1601
HIGHAM FERRERS 1604

18th child of Robert Pemberton of Pemberton, Lancs. and Rushden, Northants. by Margaret, da. of Richard Throckmorton of Higham Park, Northants. *m.* Susan, da. and coh. of Henry Macwilliam* of Stambourne,

Essex, wid. of Edward Saunders of Harrington, Northants., *s.p.* Kntd. 1603.

Sheriff, Herts. 1615–d.

It may have been his elder brother, Robert, gentleman usher to the Queen, who introduced Pemberton to court circles. Next, he made a fortunate marriage, and it was his wife's brother-in-law, (Sir) John Stanhope*, who had him returned to the 1601 Parliament both for Lewes (through Stanhope's friend Lord Buckhurst) and Peterborough (where Stanhope was high steward of the cathedral). Pemberton chose Peterborough. On 14 and 24 Nov. 1601 it was reported to the House that Pemberton had been subpoenaed to appear in Chancery 'at the suit of Sir Walter Ralegh and Carew Ralegh' (the substance of the matter is not known) and he asked for privilege. The man who served the writ was described by the clerk as 'a poor simple fellow' but by Pemberton as 'a very knave', and Pemberton 'would not entreat the favour of the House' on his behalf, but rather wished to 'let him have the justice of the House'. 'Which speech', noted the clerk, 'was generally misliked as churlish'.

Pemberton, whose house at Hertingfordbury was granted to him by Sir John Stanhope's brother Michael*, died suddenly of an ague on 1 Aug. 1616. He left his estate to his nephew Lewis Pemberton, who was appointed sole executor of the will he had made 27 May 1614. Lady Stanhope received velvet for a gown, and small bequests were made to the poor of Hertingfordbury and elsewhere. The will was proved 2 Aug. 1616.

Bridges, *Northants.* i. 193; ii. 191, 192, 193; J. Cole, *Higham Ferrers*, 212; *Vis. Northants.* ed. Metcalfe, 41; D'Ewes, 622, 637, 651, 655–6; Townshend, *Hist. Colls.* 246, 257; *Chamberlain Letters* ed. McClure, ii. 20; Chauncy, *Herts.* ii. 324; *St. Albans and Herts. Arch. Soc.* n.s. i. 20–2; iv. 196–7; *Le Neve's Knights* (Harl. Soc. viii), 301; PCC 86 Cope.

S.M.T./P.W.H.

PEMBRIDGE, Anthony (*d.* 1610), of Wotton, Herefs.

HEREFORD 1597, 1604*

4th s. of Thomas Pembridge of Mansell Gamage by Jane, da. of William Baskerville. *educ.* I. Temple 1585, called 11 May 1595. *m.* Anne, da. of John Breynton of Stretton, at least 4s. 2da.

Servant to the Earl of Essex by 1593; commr. recusancy Herefs. 1592–3, j.p. from c.1601.[1]

Pembridge was a lawyer on the Oxford circuit, who came into possession of the manor of Wotton through his maternal uncle Thomas Baskerville, and settled in the county. From about 1593 he was in receipt of an annuity from the Earl of Essex who no doubt returned him for Hereford in 1597 after he had asked the town for the nominations. In 1590, one Henry Scudamore had accused Pembridge and his wife of recusancy, and Essex had joined with Thomas Coningsby II*, Gregory Price* and Thomas Pembridge, one of the Queen's chaplains, to assure the

Council that the accusation was unfounded. The matter was dismissed as seeming 'to proceed of evil will from the said Scudamore', who had, in the same year, made 'an outrage and riot' against Pembridge. There may, however, have been some substance in the accusation, for in 1605 the bishop of Hereford included his name in a list of 'justices unfit' because his wife was 'a recusant indicted'. In the 1597 Parliament he sat on committees concerned with benefit of clergy (7 Nov.), monopolies (10 Nov.), repairing bridges in Monmouthshire (29 Nov.), maltsters (12 Jan.), and the relief of soldiers and mariners, which he reported to the House, on 28 Jan. The printed D'Ewes makes more than usually heavy weather over his name, which apppears as 'Bembridge' and even 'Peutridge'.[2]

In his will, dated 15 July and proved 10 Oct. 1610, Pembridge bequeathed his soul to God, praying that he might die a 'true and faithful member of His Holy Catholic Church', and, on the day of judgment, appear as 'one of His elect'. He had previously made a settlement of his property in favour of his 'dearly beloved wife' Anne and his children, and he charged his eldest son to see to its administration. He left 20s. for the repair of the parish church of Willington, 40s. to the poor of Willington and 10s. to the vicar of the parish. His brother-in-law John Breynton, and his nephew Walter Pembridge, received 40s. each, and were appointed executors.[3]

[1] W. R. Williams, *Parl. Hist. Herefs.* 87; *Vis. Herefs.* ed. Weaver, 55–6; *Vis. Glos.* ed. Fenwick and Metcalfe, 133; *HMC Bath*, v. 255, 269; PCC 86 Wingfield. [2] J. Duncumb, *Herefs.* iii. 176; *HMC 13th Rep.* IV, 339; D'Ewes, 552, 555, 565, 578, 590; Townshend, *Hist. Colls.* 110; *HMC Hatfield*, vii. 477; xvii. 235; Neale, *Commons*, 239; *APC*, xx. 115, 116. [3] PCC 86 Wingfield.

J.J.C.

PENISTON, Thomas (c.1542–c.1603), of Hawridge, Bucks., Dean, Oxon. and Brilley Michaelchurch, Herefs.

NEW WOODSTOCK   1571

b. c.1542, 1st s. of Anthony Peniston of Hawridge by his w. Jane Newport of Rushock, Worcs. *educ.* I. Temple 1559. *m.* by 1568, Elizabeth, da. of Humphrey Ashfield of Heythrop, Oxon., 2s. 1da. *suc.* fa. 1560[1].

Lt. of Woodstock 1571 (for a short time); j.p. Bucks. from c.1569, Oxon. from c.1573–94, temp. rem. c.1587; j.p. Herefs. and Rad. from c.1592.

Peniston's great-aunt, Lettice Peniston, was the mother of Sir Francis Knollys*, from whom Peniston's father held the manor of Hawridge. Thus in 1563 he was described by an opponent in a lawsuit as 'a man well friended and greatly kinned and allied'. Though the Penistons had for some time been tenants in the manor of Dean, near Woodstock, it was probably through Knollys that Peniston himself secured the lieutenancy of Woodstock in 1571. In the same year he was returned to Parliament for the

borough with Martin Johnson, a servant of Knollys. He sold Hawridge in 1574, and in 1575 it was noted, on a Buckinghamshire list of j.p.s, that he was 'seldom or never resident to do service' in that shire.

The reason for his speedily surrendering the lieutenancy of Woodstock, which passed to a relative of himself and Knollys, Sir Henry Lee*, is not clear, but it may have been connected with his propensity to quarrel with his family and friends. In 1563 he carried on a long and undignified suit for the return of jewels given by him to a Norfolk lady. He sued his mother's second husband and his own wife's family over property, and involved himself in disputes with servants of the locally powerful Earl of Leicester and, after 1578, Knollys's son-in-law. He used his position as j.p. to persecute the recusant Edward Sheldon, for whose father Leicester had secured a reversionary lease of Dean, and in 1586 the Privy Council warned him not to seize the goods of his wife's brother and Leicester's servant, John Ashfield, during Ashfield's absence in the Netherlands. The Council had cause on several other occasions to complain of Peniston's behaviour as a justice; in 1592 it received a petition from the inhabitants of Eynsham against his 'very foul abuses, misdemeanours and oppressions'.[2]

Peniston's conduct was the more imprudent if, as is likely, he himself continued to rely on the patronage of Leicester and the Knollys family. The continuance of this connexion would explain the fact that, when Oxfordshire became too uncomfortable for him, he retired, not to Buckinghamshire, but to the borders of Herefordshire and Radnorshire, where he is described as residing in the records of another Star Chamber suit concerning Eynsham in 1594. The Earl of Essex, Lettice Knollys's son, owned property in Herefordshire and was at that time building up his influence in the marches. As soon as Peniston's name disappears from the Oxfordshire commission of the peace, it appears in 1597 in the commissions for Radnorshire and Herefordshire. The same commissions included Robert Knollys*, Sir Francis's son; he had married into the marcher family of Vaughan, with whom the Penistons were soon at law.[3]

Peniston died before 1604, when letters of administration were granted to his daughter, Anne Hanslapp. His eldest son, a second Thomas Peniston, who predeceased him, made his will in August 1601 from the preamble of which it appears that he may have been a puritan. Peniston's second son had been slain on the Portugal expedition in 1589.[4]

[1] C142/134/191; *Vis. Bucks.* (Harl. Soc. lviii), 98–9; PCC 58 Woodhall; C3/1/61, 3/99; *VCH Bucks.* iii. 368. [2] E. K. Chambers, *Sir Henry Lee*, 16, 82; C142/129/5; C3/1/61; Stowe 570, f. 13; *CSP Dom.* 1547–80, p. 491; C3/1/46, 61, 3/99, 144/106, 168/6; St. Ch. 5/A13/38, P6/37; *APC*, xiii. 97; xiv. 128; xv. 239–40; xxii. 515–16; *Hist. Dean and Chalford* (Oxon. Rec. Soc. xvii), 72, 76; *The Archdeacon's Court* (same ser. xxiii), 109. [3] St. Ch. 5/P4/18; *Star Chamber*, ed.

Edwards (Univ. Wales Bd. of Celtic Studies, Hist. and Law ser. i), 138, 218. [4] PCC admon. act bk. 1604, f. 199; PCC 58 Woodhall; *Vis. Bucks.* (Harl. Soc. lviii), 99; *VCH Bucks.* iv. 237.

N.M.F.

PENKEVELL, Richard (*d.*1616), of Roserrow in St. Minver, Cornw.

TREGONY   1589

1st s. of Francis Penkevell (*d.*1622), of Roserrow by Katherine (*d.*1621), da. of Richard Roscarrock[†] of Roscarrock in St. Endellion. *m.* aft. 1590, Jane (*d.*1623), da. and h. of ?Hugh Pomeroy of Tregony, 8s. 3 or 4da.[1]

The Penkevells had been established at St. Michael Penkivel, near Truro, since at least the time of Edward II, intermarrying with many of the leading Cornish families. Penkevell himself appears seldom in the records of local affairs as he died before succeeding to his estates. Interested in voyages of exploration, he was in 1607 granted a licence for seven years to discover the passage to China, Cathay, the Moluccas and other regions of the East Indies. He was a member of the 'Colleagues of the fellowship for the discovery of the North West passage', who promoted Henry Hudson's last voyage in 1610, and in July 1612 he is mentioned with Peter, Benjamin, Nicholas and Digory Penkevell among members of a company for the discovery of the North West passage. His return to Parliament for Tregony may be attributed to his family's local influence and, no doubt, friendship with the Pomeroy family, into which he married shortly afterwards. Penkevell died *v.p.* in 1616. The estates passed to his son in 1622, but were lost before the end of the century.[2]

[1] Vivian, *Vis. Cornw.* 414–16; J. Maclean *Trigg Minor*, iii. 70–4. [2] Carew, *Surv. Cornw.* (1811 ed.), 338; C. S. Gilbert, *Hist. Surv. Cornw.* ii. 225; Anon. *Paroch. Hist. Cornw.* i. 284, 381; iii. 353; D. Gilbert, *Paroch. Hist. Cornw.* i. 297, 420; ii. 336; iii. 214; *CSP Dom.* 1603–10, p. 344; *CSP Col.* ii. 146, 240.

I.C.

PENNINGTON, Joseph (1564–c.1640), of Muncaster, Cumb.

CUMBERLAND   1597

b. 7 June 1564, 1st s. of William Pennington of Muncaster by Bridget, da. of John Hudleston of Farington, Lancs., wid. of Sir Hugh Ayscough (Askew) of Seaton. *educ.* L. Inn 1582. *m.* Isabel, da. of Alvery or William Copley, wid. of Sir Robert Savile, 1s. 1da. *suc.* fa. 1573.
     Steward of lands of former priory of Calder 1589 (fee 10*s.* p.a.); j.p. Cumb. from c.1591, sheriff 1599–1600, 1610–11; border commr. 1605.

Of a family settled at Muncaster from the twelfth century, Pennington succeeded as well to other substantial estates in Cumberland, Westmorland and Lancashire.

Elected for Cumberland in 1597, he could have attended committees on enclosures (5 Nov.), the poor law (5, 22 Nov.), armour and weapons (8 Nov.), penal laws (8 Nov.), monopolies (10 Nov.), the subsidy (15 Nov.) and horse theft (16 Nov.). He died about 1640.

C142/168/16; *Vis. Cumb.* (Harl. Soc. vii), 22–4; E315/309, f. 69; *HMC 10th Rep. IV*, 229, 236–72; *VCH Lancs.* viii. 338–40, 355; *Border Pprs.* i. 106; D'Ewes, 552, 553, 555, 557, 558, 561; Townshend, *Hist. Colls.* 106; *CSP Dom.* 1603–10, p. 193.

R.C.G.

PENRUDDOCK, Edward (*d.*1613), of Compton Chamberlayne, Wilts.

WEYMOUTH AND MELCOMBE
      REGIS   1584
WILTON   1586

1st s. of Sir George Penruddock* by his 1st w. Elizabeth, da. and h. of William Apryce of Faulstone; bro. of Robert*. *m.* (1) Anne, da. and h. of Thomas Crawley* of Elmdon and Wenden Loftes, Essex, *s.p.*; (2) by 1598, Mary, da. and h. of George Massie of Puddington, Cheshire, 7s. 4da. *suc.* fa. 1581. Kntd. 1603.
     J.p. Wilts. from c.1583, sheriff 1598–9.

Penruddock's father, a soldier in the service of the 1st Earl of Pembroke, purchased the reversion of a moiety of the manor of Compton Chamberlayne, and began to establish his family as country gentlemen. The son continued the process, purchasing the other half of the estates and receiving his father's share by way of marriage settlement in 1575–6. It was presumably the 2nd Earl of Pembroke who obtained his seats at Weymouth and Wilton. The only certain reference found to him in the journals of the House is permission for him to depart, 16 Mar. 1587. In fact, little is known about any of his activities. He attended the Wiltshire quarter sessions at Devizes, Salisbury and Warminster; he and his second wife were defendants in a lawsuit in 1598 concerning a house in Clerkenwell, presumably the one he inherited from his father; Pembroke wrote in that year to thank Sir Robert Cecil for his 'good furtherance' of a request made on Penruddock's behalf. He died 1 Feb. 1613, and administration of his estate was granted to his 4th but 1st surviving son John in March of that year.

Hoare, *Wilts.* Dunworth, 81; *Mins. Proc. Sess. 1563* (Wilts. Arch. and Nat. Hist. Soc. rec. br. iv), 99 et passim; D'Ewes, 416; Coke, *Reports*, v. 100; *HMC Hatfield*, viii. 264; Wards 7/47/116; PCC admon. act bk. 1613, f. 94. See also PENRUDDOCK, Sir George.

P.W.H.

PENRUDDOCK, Sir George (*d.*1581), of Ivy Church and Compton Chamberlayne, Wilts., Broxbourne, Herts., and Clerkenwell, Mdx.

SALISBURY   1553 (Mar.)
WILTSHIRE   1558

DOWNTON   1571
WILTSHIRE   1572

3rd s. of Edward Penruddock of Arkleby, Cumb. by
Elizabeth, da. of Robert Highmore of Armathwaite,
Cumb. *m.* (1) Elizabeth (*d.* c.1557), da. and h. of William
Apryce of Faulstone, Wilts., 2s. Edward* and Robert*;
(2) (bef. 1 Apr. 1560), Anne, da. of Thomas Goodyer or
Goodere of Hadley, Herts., wid. of John Cocke† of
Broxbourne, *s.p.* Kntd. 7 Aug. 1568.[1]

Steward to 1st Earl of Pembroke by 1559; provost
marshal 1559; esquire of the body by 1565; j.p. Wilts.
from 1554, Herts. from 1561; sheriff, Wilts 1562–3,
Herts. 1567–8; dep. lt. Wilts.; commr. subsidy Wilts. and
Salisbury 1576.[2]

Penruddock attached himself to the 1st Earl of
Pembroke, lived in Wiltshire, and married an heiress. By
disposition, if not profession, a soldier, he did some
campaigning, in the course of which he is said to have
earned a jewelled chain from Catherine Parr. He was
certainly one of those so rewarded by the Imperial
ambassador in March 1554, but this was for following the
lead of his master Pembroke in his *rapprochement* with the
Marian régime. The Earl's intimacy with Philip also
identified Penruddock with the King's enterprises and led
to the best-known episode in his career, his part in
Pembroke's victory at St. Quentin in August 1557. As
standard-bearer on that field Penruddock won great
honour by overcoming a French nobleman in single
combat.[3]

With the laurels of this exploit fresh upon him
Penruddock sat in Mary's last Parliament as senior knight
for Wiltshire; and when within three weeks of its
dissolution by the Queen's death, her successor called a
new one, Pembroke doubtless expected him to be
returned again, although this time he was allotted the
second place. Penruddock was, however, opposed by Sir
John Thynne of Longleat, and although he received a
large majority of the votes, was declared elected and held a
festive dinner at Wilton, he was cheated of membership of
the Parliament by the sheriff's collusive return of Thynne;
and the ensuing Star Chamber case, although it went
against the sheriff, who was fined and imprisoned, did not
upset that result.[4]

Among the doubts cast by his opponents on
Penruddock's eligibility for the seat were allegations that
he was of insufficient status and that he had no freehold in
the shire. Although neither could well be pressed against a
former first knight, they were not wholly specious.
Penruddock was no Wiltshireman, his grant of arms in
Cumberland dated only from 1548, he was not yet a j.p.,
and in both his military and civilian capacities he could be
looked on as the creature of a nobleman. In particular, the
charge that he possessed no freehold in the county may
well have been true, and it may explain a transaction into
which he entered immediately afterwards. Although it was

in 1558 that he had acquired from Andrew Baynton the
reversion of a moiety of Compton Chamberlayne on the
death of Isabella Baynton, only in Easter term 1559 did
Isabella and her new husband Sir James Stumpe†
quitclaim this life-interest to Penruddock at a rent of £25 a
year. Possession of this half-manor, to which his son
Edward would later add the other moiety by purchase
from the Nicholas family, gave Penruddock a 'stake in the
country' and began his family's long association with
Compton Chamberlayne. Sheriff in 1562–3 (and hence
disabled from sitting in the Parliament which met in 1563
and again in 1566), justice of the peace and deputy
lieutenant, he built a position in the county which would
survive the death of his master, at whose funeral in 1570
he bore the standard.[5]

After his first wife's death about 1557 Penruddock
married a Hertfordshire widow whose late husband had
held the manor of Broxbourne, and, fortified by his own
acquisition (perhaps a studied one) of a freehold in
Broxbourne, he was qualified to be pricked sheriff of that
county in 1567. It was during his year of office – and
presumably of residence – that he was knighted at Hatfield
by the Earl of Leicester. In the same year he and his wife
exercised their patronage by presenting Christopher
Allanby to the rectory of Anstie.[6]

It was nevertheless to Wiltshire that Penruddock turned
for the remainder of his parliamentary career; and to
which he brought his stepson Henry Cocke, with whom he
was returned for Downton in 1571; their election marked
the ascendancy of the new Earl of Pembroke in that
borough at the expense of its traditional patron, the
bishop of Winchester, although Penruddock's domicile at
neighbouring Ivy Church and his lease of the Winchester
manor of Bishopstone gave him a personal claim, perhaps
reflected in his gaining both Downton seats. In the
following year Penruddock repeated his success of 1558 by
becoming first knight of the shire and at the same time
sweetly avenged the defeat of '59. For his old enemy
Thynne, who had obtained the senior seat in 1571,
evidently meant – as Penruddock himself had once made
the mistake of doing – to have it again; and it needed all
Pembroke's support, given on grounds which the Earl
explained in his well-known letter to Thynne, to carry
Penruddock's cause to victory. Penruddock can scarcely be
said to have justified this effort by his contribution to the
business of the Parliament, for the silence which shrouds
his earlier sojourns there is but rarely broken on this, his
last and longest. In the session of 1572 he belonged to a
committee on a private bill, 21 May, and in that of 1576 he
was named to committees dealing with wool (16 Feb.),
juries (5 Mar.) land reclaimed from the sea (6 Mar.), private
bills (8 Mar.), and the bill against excess of apparel (10
Mar.). The omission of his name from the proceedings of
the final session, which was held within six months of his
death, may imply his absence. He appears to have

attended his last quarter-sessions in Wiltshire in January 1579.[7]

Among Penruddock's transactions in property had been his purchase of a reversion to the manor of Gussage All Saints, Dorset, in 1560 for just over £400. In 1575–6 he made a marriage settlement of the property at Compton Chamberlayne (which he had recently increased by purchase) in favour of his son and daughter-in-law, and thereafter he lived at Ivy Church, where his father also passed his last years, Broxbourne and London. On Ivy Church he was assessed at £40 for the subsidy of 1576, of which he was a Wiltshire commissioner. Described as of London when, about 1566, he was exempted from impost upon one tun of wine, Penruddock owned a house in St. John's Street, Clerkenwell, which was evidently of recent erection. In January 1572, he was prosecuted for its encroachment by two feet on the public way.[8]

Penruddock died, apparently intestate, on 8 July 1581. His heir Edward, although then described as aged 20 years and more, must have attained his majority several years before. Both he and his brother Robert sat in Elizabethan Parliaments, as did their cousin John Penruddock and his son Thomas; and Edward, Robert and Thomas were all to be knighted at the coronation of James I.[9]

[1] Wilts. Vis. Peds. (Harl. Soc. cv, cvi), 148–9; CPR, 1558–60, p. 455. [2] EHR, xxiii, 470–6; CSP Dom. 1547–80, p. 140; CPR, 1553–4, p. 25; Req. 2/30/78; Two Taxation Lists (Wilts. Arch. Soc. rec. br. x), 63, 109. [3] ·Pembroke Survey (Roxburghe Club), 68, 184, 202; Wilts. Arch. Mag. xliv. 256; CSP Span. xii. 159; Wilts. Vis. Peds. 150. [4] EHR, xxiii. 470–6; Neale, Commons, 97–8. [5] Wilts. Vis. Peds. 148; feet of fines, Wilts. Trin. 4 and 5 Ph. and M., Easter I Eliz.; C142/340/205; CSP Dom. 1547–80, p. 377; CPR, 1566–9, p. 205; Wilts. Arch. Mag. xviii. 128–30. [6] VCH Herts. ii. 399; iv. 13; Lansd. 106, ff. 146, seq.; Trans. E. Herts. Arch. Soc. viii. 129–30; Clutterbuck, Herts. iii. 344; Cussans, Herts. Edwinstree, 63; CSP Dom. 1547–80, p. 435. [7] Pembroke Survey, 299–300; VCH Wilts. v. 124 (wrongly dated 1580); CJ, i. 96, 106, 111, 112, 113; D'Ewes, 212, 253, 255; Wilts. Sess. Minutes (Wilts. Arch. Soc. recs. br. iv), 45; APC, xi. 125–6. [8] CPR, 1558–60, 455; C142/340/205; Two Taxation Lists, 127; Lansd. 9, f. 34; Mdx. County Recs. i. 73. [9] C142/197/82.

S.T.B.

PENRUDDOCK, John (bef. 1542–1601), of Hale, Hants.

WILTON	1584
SOUTHAMPTON	1586

b. bef. 1542, 1st s. of Anthony Penruddock of Arkleby, Cumb. by a da. of William English of Oughterside, Cumb. educ. Christ's, Camb. 1560; G. Inn 1562, called 1564. m. Jane, da. of (?John) Lamplugh of Lamplugh, Cumb., 4s. inc. Thomas* 5da.[1]

Recorder, Southampton from c.1571, burgess 31 May 1572; pens. G. Inn 9 May 1572, reader 29 May 1574, receiver of admission money 28 Oct. 1588, double reader 16 Nov. 1592; of counsel to Salisbury from 1587.[2]

J.p. Wilts from 1563, Cumb. 1569–c.74, Hants from c.1592; commr. Admiralty, Southampton 13 May 1583.[3]

Penruddock followed his uncles Robert[t] and Sir George* from their native Cumberland to Wiltshire and Hampshire. If his own qualities were to yield him a distinguished career at his inn, they were doubtless assisted by Sir George Penruddock's standing with the 1st Earl of Pembroke, in procuring John's early advancement both in Wiltshire, where he appeared on the commission of the peace before his call to the bar, and at Southampton, where he became recorder at about the age of 30. Thenceforward John Penruddock's career alternated between his local engagements and his chambers at Gray's Inn, with occasional excursions further afield. It was a condition of the recordership that he should reside at Southampton during vacations. From at least the late seventies he also had a house in Salisbury, and some time after the death in 1583 of his uncle Robert, who had settled at Hale, John Penruddock made this manor house, conveniently situated on the border of his two adopted counties, his principal residence for the rest of his life. He was much employed by the Privy Council for local inquiries, and was assiduous in his attendance at sessions; he also rarely missed the annual 'pensions' of his inn.[4]

For some reason Penruddock was returned to Parliament in 1584 not for Southampton but for the 2nd Earl of Pembroke's borough of Wilton. It is likely that it was he rather than Edward Penruddock who was named to a legal committee, 19 Dec. 1584, and one concerning privilege on the following 13 Feb. At the next election, in 1586, Penruddock was returned by Southampton, leaving no mark on the surviving journals of Parliament. Neither his advancement at his inn nor service in local government was to lead, as he might have expected and hoped, to the coif or the bench. In November 1593 he asked Sir Robert Cecil to secure him priority in the call of serjeants: it was, he complained, almost too late for him to practise among 'children', especially those whom he had taught. As it was, he had to content himself with his municipal appointments and local standing, and with the domestic and material comforts which they had yielded. When he came to make his will, in May 1600, he thanked God that he had already been able to provide for them in some measure. Of his four sons, two, Thomas and Manwood (a name eloquent of professional pride) had followed him through Gray's Inn, and two of his daughters were already married. The will opens with a pious preamble. His 'sweet, true and dearly beloved' wife was to have the house at Hale for life, while two houses in Salisbury, one by the Close Gate, the other, called the Dolphin, in New Street, were to go to his youngest son William. The second of these houses appears, however, to have been sold before the testator's death. Among his other bequests was one to his daughter Mary of a debt owed him by the Earl of Pembroke: this consisted of one sum of upwards of £200, and another of 100 marks which he had incurred in expenses in procuring a bond for

Pembroke in London, 'whereof his Lordship has had profit ever since and I promise of recompense'. Penruddock died 8 Mar. 1601.[5]

[1] *Wilts. Vis. Peds.* (Harl. Soc. cv, cvi), 148–9; W. Hutchinson, *Hist. Cumb.*. ii. 94–5. [2] J. S. Davies, *Hist. Soton*, 184–5; *G. Inn Pens. Bk.* 1569–1669, pp. 54, 63, 81, 96; Salisbury corpn. ledger C. ff. 99, 167. [3] *Wilts. Sess. Bk.* (Wilts. Arch. Soc. recs. br. iv), 20–153; *Letters Patent* (Soton Rec. Soc.), 126 et seq. [4] Davies, 184; PCC 17 Rowe; *APC*, x. 157–8; xv. 217; xvii. 297, 301–2; xix. 351; xx. 126–7, 147–8; xxi. 42; xxii. 308–9; xxiv. 161; xxviii. 449–50. [5] D'Ewes, 343, 349; *Letters of the 15th and 16th cents.* (Soton Rec. Soc.), 134, 137 n. 2; *HMC Hatfield*, iv. 419; PCC 26 Woodhall; C142/267/18.

S.T.B.

PENRUDDOCK, Robert (c.1559–1615), of Compton Chamberlayne, Wilts.

WILTON	1589, 1593, 1597
LUDGERSHALL	1601

b. c.1559, 2nd s. of Sir George Penruddock* by his 1st w. and bro. of Edward.* *educ.* Oxf. BA 1575, MA 1578; ?Barnard's Inn. prob. *unm.* Kntd. 23 July 1603.
Feodary, Wilts. 1591.

This Member must be distinguished from two namesakes: his uncle, the Marian MP, of Hale, Hampshire, a j.p. for Wiltshire who died in 1583, and his nephew the sixth son of his brother Sir Edward. Penruddock's mother may have died giving birth to him, for his father married again before April 1560, after which he divided his time between Wiltshire and his wife's county of Hertfordshire, but it is likely that Robert and his elder brother Edward passed their boyhood in Wiltshire, where they were to spend most of their lives. Unlike his brother, Robert went to Oxford, where his gaining of a BA and MA might have seemed to presage a learned profession. After leaving Oxford he may, indeed, have entered Barnard's Inn, but it is as a soldier that he is next heard of. This had been his father's *métier*, and it was perhaps before Sir George's death in 1581 that Robert went to serve with Rowland York in the Netherlands. York eventually defected to the Spaniards, but Penruddock evidently had no part in that act of treachery; on the contrary, in April 1587 his evidence of a rumour implicating Leicester in it was included in a list of such slanders drawn up as a state paper.[1]

Penruddock was probably back in England by the early summer of 1588, when his name appears on a list of gentlemen who had seen active service, compiled by or for the 2nd Earl of Pembroke against the threat of invasion. When Parliament was summoned in the following September Penruddock was returned for Pembroke's borough of Wilton. By 1601 the 2nd Earl was dead, and Penruddock was returned for another borough open to Pembroke influence. Despite the regularity of his appearances in the Commons Penruddock made little mark there. On 28 Mar. 1593 he was named to a legal

committee, and as burgess for Wilton, he could have sat on the committee for cloth, 15 Mar. Soon afterwards (31 Mar.) he was given leave to depart on the Queen's and his own business, and his name does not appear again in the proceedings.[2]

Although we are not told the nature of the public business which helped to excuse Penruddock in March 1593, it may well have been his duties as feodary of the court of wards in Wiltshire. His service in it doubtless attached him to Burghley and Robert Cecil, his official chiefs; either he or Thomas gave Cecil a salt weighing 28 ounces at Christmas 1602 and Cecil for his part perhaps lent his support to Penruddock's election at Ludgershall in 1601. The, probably honorary, admission of Penruddock to Gray's Inn in 1591 may have been connected with this appointment. Penruddock also assisted in the administration of the family estate; it was he who with William Bower compiled a field-book of the manor of Compton Chamberlayne in 1597. He also acquired landed interests of his own; in July 1590 he took a lease from the Crown, at £13 6s. 8d. a year, of the sequestrated property of a recusant at Compton Chamberlayne.[3]

In the early 1590s Penruddock was involved in a feud lasting several years between his brother Edward and the family of Errington of Great Woodford. This was largely fought out in Salisbury, where the Penruddock and Errington houses stood in hostile propinquity, and for Robert it culminated in an affray in 1592 in which Thomas Errington was forced into a water-course and drowned. Penruddock's claim that he killed Errington in self-defence was evidently accepted.[4]

Both Edward and Robert Penruddock were knighted at the coronation of James I, as their cousin Thomas*, but the new reign brought them no further advancement. Robert died in 1615; he had no issue, and he may not have married.

[1] *Wilts. Vis. Peds.* (Harl. Soc. cv, cvi), 148–9; *Al. Ox.* 1143; Lansd. 47/118, f. 94v; *Mins. Proc. Sess.* (Wilts. Arch. Soc. rec. br. iv), 17, 24, 41; *HMC Var.* iv. 134; *CSP For.* 1587, p. 43. [2] *CSP For.* 1587, p. 43; D'Ewes, 501, 511, 513. [3] *HMC Hatfield*, xii. 528; Wilts. RO, 332 no. 252; *Recusant Roll no. 1* (Cath. Rec. Soc. xviii), 353. [4] St. Ch. 5/P6/19, P11/8, 33, P13/23, P33/36, P39/12.

S.T.B.

PENRUDDOCK, Thomas (c.1578–1637), of Arkleby, Cumb. and Hale, Hants.

DOWNTON	1601
CUMBERLAND	1614

b. c.1578, 1st s. of John Penruddock* of Hale by his w. Jane. *educ.* G. Inn 11 Feb. 1590. Queen's, Oxf. 22 Feb. 1594 aged 16. *m.* Susan, da. of John Polden of Durweston, Dorset, wid. of Robert Freke of Faringdon in Ewern Courtney, Dorset, at least 1s. *suc.* fa. 8 Mar. 1601. Kntd. 23 July 1603.[1]

King's sewer 1604; capt. of militia, Wilts. bef. 1608;

commr. to inquire into the state of Ireland 20 Mar. 1622–26 Feb. 1623.[2]

As recorder of Southampton and counsellor of Salisbury John Penruddock maintained houses at both places; and after the death of his uncle Robert in 1583 he made the manor house of Hale, situated between them, his country residence. His eldest son Thomas probably passed much of his boyhood in one or other of these homes, although the description 'of Arkelby' given him when he matriculated at Oxford suggests that he may have been sent for schooling to this, the original home of the family, which had come to his father by gift from Robert and which lay within a few miles of his mother's home at Lamplugh. He was enrolled very young at Gray's Inn, where his father was reader, and where his brother Manwood followed him eight years later. No doubt his father wished his sons to be given the benefit of a legal education under his own eye.[3]

Penruddock was only 23 when his father died early in 1601, and from then on he had the dual responsibility of administering his own estate and of helping his mother, who survived her husband 13 years, in launching the younger of her nine children, whose ages ranged down to nine. Within a few months of his father's death Penruddock was returned to Parliament for Downton. As the new master of Hale, some two miles south of Downton, Penruddock had a good local claim, but this would scarcely have prevailed without the reinforcement of influence. Such influence the 3rd Earl of Pembroke, who like Penruddock had recently succeeded his father, may have furnished, for the Penruddocks had a long record of service to and favours from Wilton. There is also the possibility that Sir Robert Cecil lent Penruddock his support; Cecil was to receive a New Year's gift from 'Mr. Penruddock' (either Robert or Thomas) at Christmas 1602.[4]

Penruddock was to sit in Parliament once again. His knighthood, at James I's coronation, he received in the presence of his brother Manwood and his cousins Edward and Robert, as well as of over 400 other persons. He died in 1637, being succeeded at Hale by his son John.[5]

[1] Wilts. Vis. Peds. (Harl. Soc. cv, cvi), 149; W. Hutchinson, Hist. Cumb. ii. 94; Wilts. Arch. Mag. xxxvi. 634–5; Hutchins, Dorset, iv. 86; C142/267/18. [2] CSP Dom. 1603–10, p. 126; Wilts. Arch. Mag. i. 230; CSP Ire. 1615–25, pp. 345–7; APC, 1621–3, p. 421–2. [3] PCC 17 Rowe. [4] C142/267/18; Wilts. N. and Q. vi. 547; HMC Hatfield, xii. 528. [5] Wilts. Vis. Peds. 149; CSP Dom. 1603–10, p. 126; 1633–4, p. 318; Add. 35906, f. 12; Nichols, Progresses Jas. I., iii. 540; iv. 1047. VCH Hants, iv. 578.

S.T.B.

PEPPER, Cuthbert (d.1608), of East Cowton, near Richmond, Yorks.

RICHMOND 1597, 1601

s. of Robert Pepper and his w. Marjorie. educ. G. Inn 1570, called 1578. m. Margaret, da. of Robert Wild of East Cowton, 3s. 3da. Kntd. 1604.[1]

J.p. Yorks (N. Riding) from c.1582; Summer reader, G. Inn 1595, treasurer 1604; recorder, Richmond 1596–1603; attorney in the north 1598–1603; member, council in the north 1599; member, high commission, province of York 1599, 1603; surveyor of court of wards 1600–7, attorney from 1607; judge in the northern court from 1603.[2]

Pepper, who sat twice for Richmond during his recordership, was a lawyer from a minor Yorkshire family. His appointment as attorney in the north following the death of William Paler*, who had been ailing for some time, was as much 'in respect of his years and strength of body', as of his legal qualifications. He died 11 Aug. 1608, having made his will 24 Sept. 1606. He expressed the hope, through Christ, to be 'adopted a co-heir in the Kingdom where the Holy and Blessed Trinity shall be praised eternally'. His daughter Dorothy received £500, his younger sons annuities of £50 each, and his mother an annuity of £15. He was succeeded by his eldest son Robert, the sole executor, who lost no time in writing to inform Lord Salisbury that his father, on his deathbed, 'earnestly prayed his Lordship's favour for his children'.[3]

[1] Whitaker, Richmondshire, i. 246. [2] Lansd. 53, f. 195; G. Inn Pens. Bk. i. 109, 500; Clarkson, Richmond, app. xlvii; CSP Dom. 1598–1601, p. 5; Add. 1580–1625, p. 428; 1603–10, pp. 363, 380; Reid, Council of the North, 245; J. Hurstfield, Queen's Wards, 224; HMC Hatfield, ix. 396; x. 369; xv. 394. [3] Al. Cant. iii. 343; Richmond Wills and Inventories (Surtees Soc. xxvi), 180; HMC Hatfield, vii. 506; York wills 31/72; C142/310/64; CSP Dom. 1603–10, p. 451.

N.M.S.

PEPPER, John (c.1537–1603), of St. Martins, Richmond, Yorks.

RICHMOND 1584, 1593

b. c.1537, s. and h. of William Pepper of St. Martins by his w. Margaret. m. Anne, da. of Michael Hall of Leventhorpe, at least 1s. suc. fa. 1572.

Alderman (i.e. mayor), Richmond 1586–7, 1594–5.

Pepper's father bought the manor, site and precinct of the late cell of St. Martins in 1551, he and two others paying Lord Clinton £800 for the property. On dividing the estate with his partners, he retained the manor, which thus descended to John Pepper, giving him sufficient status to secure his return for the borough in two Parliaments, and to have his son Christopher appointed recorder in succession to Cuthbert Pepper*, who was probably John's cousin. As the representative of a Yorkshire borough Pepper may have served on committees concerned with cloth (23 Mar. 1593) and weirs (28 Mar. 1593). Pepper died 14 June 1603, leaving the estate to Christopher.

C142/160/50, 280/73; C219/30/66; Foster, Vis. Yorks. 298; Yorks. Fines (Yorks. Arch. Soc. rec. ser. ii), 380; Clarkson, Richmond, 173, 329, 341–3; D'Ewes, 507, 512.

B.D.

PERCY, Sir Henry (c.1532–85), of Tynemouth and Norham Castles, Northumb. and Petworth, Suss.

MORPETH	1554 (Nov.)
NORTHUMBERLAND	1571

b. c.1532, 2nd s. of Sir Thomas Percy of Prudhoe, Northumb. (exec. 1537) by Eleanor, da. and event. coh. of Sir Guischard Harbottle of Beamish, co. Dur.; bro. of Thomas†. *m.* by 25 Jan. 1562, Catherine, da. and coh. of John (Neville), 4th Lord Latimer, 8s. 3da. Kntd. 30 Apr. 1557; *suc.* bro. as 2nd Earl of Northumberland 22 Aug. 1572.[1]

Capt. Norham castle by Jan. 1558; constable, Tynemouth castle 1559, gov. 1560–83; steward of crown property at Tynemouth 1570–83; member, council in the north Dec. 1558–Apr. 1571; j.p. co. Dur., Northumb. from 1559, Cumb., Yorks. (N. and E. Ridings) from 1569; sheriff, Northumb. 1562–3.

Commr. to treat with Scottish congregation 1559, with French 1560; capt. in Scottish campaign 1560; commr. piracy 1565, to enforce Acts of Uniformity and Supremacy in province of York 1568.[2]

Percy first became well-known as a soldier on the Scottish border. In 1557 and 1558 he was warmly commended for his activity in the fighting against the Scots at Norham and elsewhere. In September 1558 he was wounded and 'driven to lie at Berwick for recovery of his hurt', and he further enhanced his reputation in the campaign of 1560. On 10 Apr. Thomas Randolph* wrote, 'How worthily Sir Henry Percy behaved himself the first day against the enemy; I would be loth to write more than truth, but never saw man do better since I was born'. Proud and quarrelsome, and, except when the Scottish danger was threatening, on bad terms with his neighbours, Percy disputed with them the smallest matters, such as the right to the custody of prisoners and trivial amounts of money. One of these, over a plea of trespass, for £16 10s., dragged on for years.[3]

If the northern rebellion of 1569 placed him in a dilemma this was not apparent, though opinions differed as to whether his loyalty was disinterested, or arose from a desire to succeed to his brother's peerages. There was no doubt that his decision, which ensured that Tynemouth castle was held by loyal troops, was of the greatest value to the government. The Queen wrote to him on 17 Nov. 1569,

> We are very glad to understand ... of your constancy and forwardness in our service, although ... against your brother of Northumberland ... Continuing your service and duty, we will have regard to ... the continuance of such a house in the person and blood of so faithful a servant.

The Act for Confirmation of Attainders, May 1571, contained a special clause saving Percy's rights; it was possibly with this in mind that he stood for election to the Parliament of that year. Northumberland and Cumber-land both returned him as senior knight of the shire; he chose Northumberland, and a new writ for Cumberland was issued on 9 Apr. He and his legal advisers were heard on the attainder bill before it was passed. Why, at this moment when he was in high favour with the authorities, Percy should have become involved in the plot to free Mary Stuart and to marry her to the Duke of Norfolk, is not clear. His Catholic sympathies hardly furnish an explanation in the light of his previous conduct. The Duke of Norfolk distrusted him and by 15 Nov. he was in the Tower. He admitted discussing the matter of Mary's escape with one of Norfolk's friends 'last Lent, in the parliament time', Mary to be freed 'by six or seven tall men on horseback in the night', but maintained that he himself 'would be no doer in anything to offend the Queen's Majesty'. His trial, at which he was sentenced to a fine of 5,000 marks, took place in the Queen's bench the following Easter. When his brother was executed over the northern rebellion, Percy was still in the Tower. To appeals on his behalf Elizabeth replied that 'his fault was as great as any man's, though it be no high treason'. He was let out in May 1573 but for some months longer was not allowed to leave London. By January 1575, when he was specially admitted to Gray's Inn, he had apparently been restored to favour: at the beginning of the second session of Parliament, on 8 Feb. 1576, he took his seat in the House of Lords, as Earl of Northumberland, and in November was one of the commissioners for the prorogation.[4]

For the next few years he lived comparatively quietly. In addition to extensive lands in the north he had property to administer in Burton Latimer, Northamptonshire and elsewhere, which came to him in right of his wife on the death of Lord Latimer in April 1577, and about 1576 he began to rebuild Petworth, where he lived frequently during the last ten years of his life, acting as a commissioner for breeding warhorses in the county and helping the local justices to suppress unlawful hunting in Lord Montagu's park at Cowdray. The Queen was expected to come to Petworth during the progress of July 1583, but whether she did is not known. Had she arrived in the September she would have found strange company in the person of Francis Throckmorton's accomplice Charles Paget, who thought that Northumberland's Sussex estates would make a good base for the proposed invasion of England. There had been some communication between the conspirators and the Earl, but Paget's arrival 'much appalled' Northumberland, who reportedly said, 'Well! he is come, I cannot help it now'. Paget stayed hidden in a lodge in the park for about a week, and drew the Earl into the plot, though he had 'not much living or many followers in Sussex'. Northumberland was arrested in December, released, re-arrested on 9 Jan. 1584 and sent to the Tower. Walsingham seems to have been well disposed, writing to the ambassador in Paris who had to make arrangements for three of the Earl's young sons who were living there: 'Charles Paget is a most dangerous instrument, and I wish for the Earl of Northumberland's sake he had never been born'.

No preparations were made for his trial, but some 18 months later a servant of Sir Christopher Hatton, who was known to be on bad terms with Northumberland, was appointed his gaoler, and the next day, about midnight 20/21 June 1585, Northumberland was found dead in bed, shot by a bullet from his own pistol. He was buried at St. Peter ad Vincula in the Tower some days later. The government tried to prove suicide, but, as Sir Francis Russell* wrote to Walsingham from Tynemouth on 26 June, 'The Lord of Northumberland's death will hardly be believed in this country to be as you have written'.[5]

[1] Lansd. 874, f. 118; CSP Dom. Add. 1580–1625, p. 131. [2] CSP Dom. Add. 1547–65, pp. 468–9; C. Sharp, Memorials of the Rebellion, p. 351; Northumb. Co. Hist. viii. 165; W. S. Gibson, Monastery of Tynemouth, i. 239–41; ii. 115–19; CSP Scot. 1547–63, p. 391; Reid, Council of the North, 186, 210, 493; CPR, 1560–3, pp. 11–12, 187; 1566–9, p. 172; 1569–72, pp. 151–2, 223–4; Camden, Annals, i. 57; CSP For. 1560–1, p. 78; Lansd. 4, ff. 126 seq.; APC, vii. 284. [3] APC, vi. 143, 221, 374, 396, 399; vii. 233; CSP Scot. 1547–63, p. 355; CSP For. 1560–1, p. 553; 1562, p. 34; 1564–5, p. 117; St. Ch. 5/N6/21; Border Pprs. 1560–94, p. 81. [4] Haynes, State Pprs. 555; HMC Hatfield, i. 535–72 passim; Murdin, State Pprs. 229; Cobbett, State Trials, i. col. 1115; APC, viii. 102, 130; LJ, i. 729, 753; D'Ewes, 159. [5] D. G. C. Elwes and C. J. Robinson, Western Suss. 171; CSP Dom. 1547–80, p. 688; 1581–90, p. 113; APC, xiii. 414; HMC Hatfield, xiii. 270–81 passim; CSP For. 1583–4, pp. 272, 301, 351; N. St. John Brooks, Sir Christopher Hatton, 244 seq.; CSP Dom. Add. 1580–1625, p. 145; C142/208/167.

N.M.F.

PERCY, Thomas, of Islington and Stanwell, Mdx.

PLYMPTON ERLE   1563*

Prob. of Percy fam. of Shaftesbury, Dorset, poss. s. of George Percye of Rushton by Elizabeth, da. of Henry Ashley.* educ. ?G. Inn 1544. m. Joan, da. of Richard Patten alias Wainfleet, wid. of William Streete.
Escheator, Kent and Mdx. 1551–2.

If the above parentage is correct, this man was the grandson of John Percy† who sat for Shaftesbury in 1491, and was admitted to Gray's Inn in 1544 at the same time as his brother Edward Percy. But he is a shadowy figure, not the only one of his name; and it is not known how he came to sit for Plympton. Some connexion can be traced with the 2nd Earl of Bedford, who had influence at Plympton. On the other hand Percy also had connexions with the 1st Earl of Pembroke, who owned lands in Islington where Percy was living in 1563.

Percy was dead by 1566, being replaced by Edmund Wiseman in that session of the 1563 Parliament.

Hutchins, Dorset, iv. 74; PCC 10 Wrastley; Mdx. Peds. (Harl. Soc. lxv), 66; C142/135/72; Roberts thesis; Mdx. County Recs. ed. Jeaffreson, i.46.

P.W.H.

PERKINS, see PARKINS

PERNE, Christopher (b. by 1530), of London.

? BOSSINEY	1555
? PLYMPTON ERLE	1558
ST. IVES	1559
GRAMPOUND	1563*

b. by 1530, prob. yr. s. of John Perne of East Bilney, Norf. educ. Queens', Camb. 1544. ?m., at least 3s.

The sixteenth-century pedigree of the Perne family gives two names only – Andrew Perne, who was a fellow of Queens', Cambridge and afterwards master of Peterhouse, and John Perne of Bilney, Norfolk, Andrew's father. This was probably the John whose widow Cecily and sons Gregory, William and John are mentioned in the Betely court rolls (1557–8). There seem to have been several branches of the family in East Anglia: a Christopher Perne of Little Walsingham, Norfolk, died about 1535, and Bridget, daughter of Christopher Perne of West Barsham, Norfolk, married into a Pensthorpe family in the same county. The Christopher Perne who matriculated at Queens' soon after Andrew became a fellow there, was presumably a relative, probably a younger brother rather than a nephew, as his nephews were much younger and attended Peterhouse after he had become master. Perne's parliamentary constituencies suggest a connexion with the 2nd Earl of Bedford, who would have been his contemporary at Cambridge. It is likely that he is to be identified with the Mr. Perne who opposed a government bill in the Parliament of 1555, as, two days after the dissolution, he was committed to the Fleet. Otherwise only scattered references to Perne have been found, all concerned with the period 1553–66. The pardon roll at the beginning of Mary's reign described him simply as 'of London, gent.' As well as the episode already mentioned, he was implicated in the Henry Dudley plot, being committed to ward on 30 May 1556. His membership of the 1558 Parliament was challenged on the ground that he had no warrant for his return, and he was put in the custody of the serjeant-at-arms. Obviously the authorities wanted him out of the way. The Privy Council banished him seven miles from the court ten days after the end of the first session of that Parliament.[1]

Things were no better after Elizabeth's accession. On 26 Feb. 1563 a correspondent wrote to Sir Thomas Smith* 'your old scholar Perne hath lit into a great mishap, taken with a lewd manner in picking of gold buttons, and ... other briberies found in his chamber; it shall be hard to recover his name'. A parliamentary precedent book, founded on the treatise by William Lambarde*, provides a sequel: 'Perne was committed to the Marshalsea for pickery, without any notice given to the House'. A new writ was issued for Grampound 29 Oct. 1566, Perne being 'reported to be lunatic'.[2]

[1] *Vis. Cambs.* (Harl. Soc. xli), 93; G. A. Carthew, *Hundred of Launditch*, ii. 639–40; Norwich consistory ct. wills 1535, 40, 41 Puntyng; *Vis. Norf.* (Harl. Soc. xxxii), 149; Guildford Mus. Loseley 1331/2; *CPR*, 1555–7, p. 453; *APC*, v. 203, 275; vi. 287; *CJ*, i. 51. [2] *N. and Q.* (ser.. 6), ii. 185. No reference is given for this letter, which is ascribed in error to Robert Cecil; Add. 5123, f. 16v; *CJ*, i. 75; D'Ewes, 126.

N.M.F.

PERROT, James (c.1571–1637), of Westmede, Carm. and Haroldston, Pemb.

HAVERFORDWEST	1597, 1604, 1614, 1621
PEMBROKESHIRE	1624
CONSTITUENCY UNKNOWN	1626
HAVERFORDWEST	1628

b. c.1571, illegit. *s.* of Sir John Perrot* by Sybil Jones of Radnorshire. *educ.* Jesus, Oxf. 8 July 1586, aged 14 or 15; I. Temple 9 Jan. 1591. *m.* Mary, da. of Robert Ashfield of Chesham, Bucks., *s.p.* Kntd. 1603.

J.p. and custos rot. Pemb. from c.1601; alderman, Haverfordwest 1603, mayor 1605; dep. v.-adm. S. Wales 1611; v.-adm. Pemb. 1626; dep. lt. and commr. piracy Pemb. by 1634.[1]

In the settlement of his estate which he devised in 1575, Sir John Perrot made his four year-old illegitimate son heir in succession to his two legitimate sons Thomas and William. The contingency then seemed so remote that he prepared him for a profession by sending him to Oxford and the Inner Temple. But soon after James came of age his father died, predeceased by his childless younger son and survived for little over two years by an elder son, who left only daughters. Thus James Perrot was able to invoke the settlement of 1575, and came into Haroldston, the ancestral home, where he resided for the rest of his life. He also secured a 21-year lease of the priory lands in Haverfordwest, which gave him a position in the borough, and a natural claim to represent it in Parliament and to head the list of aldermen when James I conferred a new charter. There is no record of any parliamentary activity by Perrot, except for his membership of the Newport bridge committee (29 Nov. 1597) to which all the Welsh constituency Members were appointed.[2]

Perrot's learning brought him considerable prestige in the House of Commons under the Stuarts, to which period his parliamentary biography properly belongs. Setting out under the patronage of the Earl of Essex, he afterwards attached himself to the Earl of Pembroke, whose deputy he became in south-west Wales. To these two patrons he dedicated two of his radically puritan religious works – an attack on the popish emigrés for the Earl of Essex in 1596 and a book of puritan devotions inscribed to Pembroke in 1630. Ruthless in his own constituency in pursuit of stray recusants (though his wife was one), Perrot compiled reports on recusants by counties, was instrumental in the imposition, from 1614, of the sacramental test on

Members of Parliament, and supported a preaching and catechising ministry, sabbatarian legislation and measures against drunkenness. As an expert on procedure he was one of the committee of five called on to straighten out the business of the House in May 1628 when it was fumbling its way towards the Petition of Right, but on other occasions, as in the resumed session after Buckingham's murder, he was one of those who called for moderation.[3]

Perrot died 4 Feb. 1637, bequeathing Haroldston and his Haverfordwest lands to a distant connexion, Herbert Perrot of Moortown, Herefordshire.[4]

[1] *DNB*; *Al. Ox.* i(2), p. 1149; PRO Index 4208; G. Owen, *Pemb.* i. 159; *Arch. Camb.* (ser. 3), xi. 127; Warren, *Hist. St. Mary's Haverfordwest*, 41–2; *CSP Dom.* 1629–31, p. 93; 1634–5, pp. 169–70. [2] *Arch. Camb.* (ser. 3), xii. 478–81; Warren, loc. cit., *HMC Hatfield*, vii. 233; E315/309/137; *Exchequer*, ed. E. G. Jones (Univ. Wales Bd. of Celtic Studies, Hist. and Law ser. iv), 308; *CSP Dom.* 1603–10, p. 201; D'Ewes, 565. [3] *Ath. Ox.* ii. 605–7; *CSP Dom.* 1611–18, p. 123; 1619–23, p. 213; 1627–8, p. 487; A. H. Dodd, 'Wales's Parl. Apprenticeship', *Trans. Cymmrod Soc.* 1942, pp. 29–30, 39–40, 43–6, 49–53; 1945, pp. 33–4, 39–42, 46. [4] *DNB*; Leach, *Civil War in Pemb.* 41, 58–9, 89, 129, 140, 220.

A.H.D./P.W.H.

PERROT, Sir John (1528/9–92), of Haroldston and Carew Castle, Pemb.

CARMARTHENSHIRE	1547*
SANDWICH	1553 (Oct.), 1555
WAREHAM	1559
PEMBROKESHIRE	1563
HAVERFORDWEST	1589

b. 1528/9, reputed illegit. *s.* of Henry VIII by Mary, da. of James Berkeley of Thornbury, Glos., w. of Thomas Perrot of Islington, Mdx. and Haroldston; half-bro. of Sir Henry* and Richard Jones*. *educ.* St. Davids. *m.* (1) Anne (*d.* Sept. 1553), da. of Sir Thomas Cheyne(y)† of Shurland, Kent, 1s. Sir Thomas*; (2) by 1566, Jane, da. of Hugh Prust of Hartland, Devon, wid. of Sir Lewis Pollard of Oakford, Devon, 1s. 2da.; at least 1s. illegit. James* 2da. illegit. *suc.* Thomas Perrot 1531. Kntd. 17 Nov. 1549.[1]

Sheriff, Pemb. 1551–2; commr. goods of churches and fraternities, Pemb. 1553, concealed lands 1561, armour 1569; commr. musters Pemb. 1570, Denb. 1580, Haverfordwest 1581, piracy Card., Carm. 1575, Pemb. 1577; j.p. Pemb. 1555–8, q. Card., Carm., Pemb. 1559–*d.*, q. all Welsh counties 1579–*d.*, marcher counties 1582; steward, manors of Carew, Coedraeth and Narberth, Pemb., and St. Clears, Carm. 1559, lordship of Cilgerran, Pemb. 1570; constable, Narberth and Tenby castles, Pemb. 1559; gaoler, Haverfordwest 1559; mayor, Haverfordwest 1560–1, 1570–1, 1575–6; custos rot. Pemb. by 1562; pres. of Munster 1570–3; member, council in the marches of Wales by 1574; ld. dep. Ireland 1584–8; dep. lt. Pemb. in 1587; PC 10 Feb. 1589.[2]

In both the Marian Parliaments in which he sat, Perrot opposed government measures, and he was one of the 'right protestants' who met at 'Harondayles home' to discuss parliamentary tactics in 1555. He sheltered protestants at Haroldston, and served under the 1st Earl of Pembroke at St. Quentin in 1557. Upon Elizabeth's accession he became a favoured courtier. Freed from a sentence of outlawry for non-appearance at court on an attachment for debt (which he expiated in the Marshalsea), Perrot rapidly became a key man in the administration of his own shire and the recipient of profitable crown offices there, as well as grants of land and advowsons both there and in England. His commissionership for concealed lands brought into his net some of the former lands of the dissolved priory of Haverfordwest – not without violent quarrels, carried into Star Chamber in 1561, with those whose titles were challenged. He also made a successful bid for some of the lands forfeited to the Crown 30 years earlier by the attainder of his stepfather's great kinsman Sir Rhys ap Gruffydd. The grant made on his petition in 1554 (for his 'service heretofore and hereafter to be done') of Rhys's old lordship and castle of Carew does not seem to have become effective, since it was only in 1559 that he received the stewardship and not until 1562–6 that a succession of crown leases rounded off his control of the lordship. The castle he largely rebuilt, and eventually made his principal seat.[3]

Perrot was returned to the 1559 Parliament for Wareham, presumably through pressure exerted on the Rogers family by the 2nd Earl of Bedford, his former commander. In the next Parliament he came in for Pembrokeshire, and was appointed to the succession committee, 31 Oct. 1566. He was one of 30 MPs summoned on 5 Nov. to hear the Queen's message on the succession. His mayoralty of Haverfordwest in 1570 gave him control of the borough machinery, and although his departure for Ireland enabled an anti-Perrot faction to put up a candidate for the borough in the 1571 parliamentary election, the pro-Perrot sheriff fraudulently returned his patron's man, John Garnons*. By 1572 the opposing faction controlled the borough and was able to return its man, Alban Stepneth*, but Perrot's partisans (Wogans and Bowens) kept up a running faction fight with Stepneth's family group (Philipps of Picton, Owen of Henllys and Barlow of Slebech) in the streets of Haverfordwest for most of the year, with soldiers recruited for Perrot's bodyguard in Ireland, or returning thence as deserters, to add to the turmoil. Perrot came home from Ireland in 1573, and settled in Pembrokeshire. He had been replaced as vice-admiral by Sir William Morgan* of Pencoed with Richard Vaughan of Whitland as his deputy in the west. But Perrot was himself one of the Pembrokeshire commissioners for piracy, and there were conflicts of jurisdiction and mutual accusations of trafficking with the pirates. In 1579 Perrot was entrusted with a squadron of ships to clear the seas not only of pirates, but of Spanish vessels making for Ireland. In this,

to the glee of his enemies, he had no great success, nor did he make much progress in his allotted task of fortifying Milford Haven. In a different sphere, he was one of a commission appointed in 1581 by the Privy Council to inquire into irregularities in the diocese of St. David's, with whose bishops he was on chronically bad terms.[4]

During the years 1583–4 he was consolidating his influence round Haverfordwest by obtaining the lease of further rectories and granges in the former priory lands, extending it eastwards by acquisitions across the Carmarthenshire border, and exploiting what he already possessed by rack-renting and encroachments, all in face of a deteriorating financial situation. Several disputes arising out of these transactions came before Star Chamber in 1583. Now that he was a member of the council in the marches of Wales, the Privy Council would not allow his suits to be heard there, but referred them to the local assizes. In one quarrel (with Griffith Rice of Newton in 1581) the Council itself intervened. In general, however, it protected this 'inward favourite of the Earl of Leicester' from his many detractors, two of whom served sentences of imprisonment for slander before Perrot's return to Ireland in 1584.[5]

His lord deputyship proved as stormy as his presidency of Munster, and included a spectacular brawl (before members of the Irish Council) with old Sir Nicholas Bagnall* the marshal. In 1588 Perrot returned to Pembrokeshire, living in the renovated Carew castle. In this critical Armada year the Earl of Pembroke as president of the council in the marches of Wales chose him as his deputy while he was busy elsewhere. Bent on reasserting himself in his old sphere of influence, he put up successfully for Haverfordwest at the 1588 election, receiving wages for the ensuing Parliament. Early in 1589 he became a Privy Councillor, and with this added prestige took a more active part than hitherto in the business of the House. On 18 Feb. 1589 he was given charge of the bill for reforming abuses in the Exchequer. Two days later he asked for more time in committee, and on 25 Feb. he took the bill to the Lords, asking them to expedite its passage. On 6 Mar. he was summoned to discuss it with the Queen. He was added to the committee of the Hartlepool harbour bill (1 Mar.), and reported this to the House (12 Mar.) He served on a committee about fish (11 Mar.), on another concerned with Lincoln (15 Mar.), took a bill about forestallers to the Lords (28 Mar.), and spoke on an unrecorded subject (29 Mar). A bill to amend the law relating to the hue and cry was committed to him (18 Mar.), and the next day he reported that the committee recommended no change. On 26 Mar. he reported that the Queen had told him that she needed a bill against the embezzling of her armour and weapons; this was read three times and he took it to the Lords. As a Privy Councillor Perrot was appointed to committees on the subsidy (11 Feb.), purveyors (15, 27 Feb.), Dover harbour (5

Mar.), forestallers (5 Mar.), captains and soldiers (19 Mar.), husbandry and tillage (25 Mar.) and a declaration of war with Spain (29 Mar.).[6]

By this time, Perrot's star was falling. Leicester was dead; Essex, though his sister had married Perrot's son, lent his weight in west Wales to the anti-Perrot faction; and Hatton, whose daughter Perrot was reported to have seduced, bore him a personal grudge. A concerted attack by his enemies resulted in charges of treason which may have had no more solid basis than his own intemperate speeches. In 1591 he was imprisoned in the Tower. Sending home for money for his defence, he raised without difficulty £1,500 from current rents alone, without resort to the iron chest in which he kept his (possibly less legitimate) reserves at Carew.[7]

Volume 72 of the Lansdowne manuscripts in the British Library is largely concerned with Perrot, his lands, quarrels with the Welsh gentry, demands for his trial, and a long account of it. Attainted on 17 Apr. 1592, he died in the Tower, an inquisition post mortem being taken on 26 Sept. His estates included 15 or more well stocked manors. The town of Haverfordwest still benefits from the 'Perrot Trust' he endowed in 1579 for municipal improvement. His son Sir Thomas Perrot was restored in blood within six months of the father's death, and was thus able to inherit Haroldston; Carew was granted by the Queen for a term of years to Sir John's widow. Both Sir Thomas and his father's illegitimate son James Perrot represented the shire in Parliament, but with the latter's death the family came to an end.[8]

[1] DNB; Arch. Camb. (ser. 3), xi. 108–29; xii. 312–25, 337–9, 478–81, 484–7; Wards 9/129, f. 164; Dwnn, Vis. Wales, i. 89, 134; C142/119/114; Lit. Rem. Edw. VI, i. p. ccvii. [2] DNB; DWB; CPR, 1553, p. 418; 1558–60, p. 45; 1560–3, pp. 445, 447; 1563–6, pp. 30, 317; 1569–72, p. 252; St. Ch. 5/P8/32; Flenley, Cal. Reg. Council, Marches of Wales, 60–9, 216; APC, ix. 267–8; xii. 364; xvii. 76; Arch. Camb. loc. cit. and (ser. 5), xiii. 195; P. H. Williams, Council in the Marches of Wales, 60–9, 354–7; CSP Dom. 1547–80, pp. 537–41, 615; HMC Foljambe, 26; Haverfordwest Recs. 30, 184. [3] SP11/4 nos. 22–3; 11/8 no. 35; CPR, 1558–60, pp. 45, 136, 239, 305; 1560–3, pp. 222, 608; CSP Dom. 1547–80, pp. 266, 615; Augmentations, ed. E. A. Lewis and J. C. Davies (Univ. Wales Bd. of Celtic Studies, Hist. and Law ser. xiii), 477, 479, 481–3, 488, 502–3; St. Ch. 5/P8/32; Arch. Camb. (ser. 5), iii. 27–41; xiv. 309–18; Spurrell, Hist. Carew, 9–11, 36–42. [4] D'Ewes, 126–7; Camb. Univ. Lib. Gg. iii. 34, p. 209; EHR, lxi. 18–27; Arch. Camb. (ser. 5), xiii. 193–211; xiv. 318–23; xv. 298–311; CSP Dom. 1547–80, pp. 398, 406, 414, 517–19, 541, 590–1, 629, 631, 636–7, 695; St. Ch. 5/G12/25; APC, ix. 267–8; x. 231, 262; xiii. 142. [5] Augmentations, 245, 257, 487, 499; CSP Dom. 1547–80, pp. 454, 522; St. Ch. 5/P50/21, P53/14, W69/30; APC, x. 283, 297; xii. 24; xiii. 88; J. Wynn, Gwydir Fam. ed. Ballinger, 64; Arch. Camb. (ser. 3), xi. 112–13. [6] Cal. Wynn Pprs. 115; NLW Jnl. ix. 170; D'Ewes, 430, 431, 432, 434, 436, 437, 439, 440, 441, 442, 443, 445, 446, 448, 453, 454; CSP Dom. 1591–4, p. 21. [7] P. H. Williams, 239, 282; Arch. Camb. (ser. 3), xi. 124–5. [8] Arch. Camb. (ser. 3), xi. 116–25; D'Ewes, 510–11; LJ, ii. 182–3; DWB, 749; Exchequer, ed. T. I. J. Jones (Univ. Wales Bd. of Celtic Studies, Hist. and Law ser. xv), 303–4, 306, 308–9.

A.H.D.

PERROT, Rice, of Sandwich, Kent.

SANDWICH	1563

Bailiff and verger, Sandwich by 1557–at least 6 Nov. 1570, jurat by 1560, mayor 1565–6.

Though a branch of the Perrot family possessed several manors in the Sandwich area from as early as the late Norman period, Perrot does not appear to have been directly descended from them. He was distantly related to Sir John Perrot*, and, presumably, to Stephen Perot who was buried in Sandwich church in 1570. He appears to have been the only member of the family to take an active part in Sandwich affairs.

His ancient offices were no longer important, involving such duties as empanelling local juries, safeguarding the prison, and attending at local courts. He was returned to Parliament in 1563 and was given sick leave on 8 Mar. He was one of the first governors of the new school founded at Sandwich by Roger Manwood*, his contribution amounting to £6 13s. 4d. In January 1565 he and others, including the lieutenant of Dover castle and the mayor of Dover, were ordered by the Privy Council to investigate the disappearance at sea of some goods belonging to a Scottish merchant. Perrot was still alive on 6 Nov. 1570; the date of his death has not been ascertained.

W. Boys, Hist. Sandwich, 207–11, 404, 419, 424; E. L. Barnwell, Perrot Notes, 3–4; Hasted, Kent, x. 88–9, 442; Sandwich little black bk. 1552–67, ff. 136, 148, 219; CJ, i. 68; CPR, 1555–7, p. 303; 1558–60, pp. 33, 339; 1560–3, p. 613; 1569–72, p. 81; APC, vii. 185.

M.R.P.

PERROT, Sir Thomas (1553–94), of Haroldston and Narberth, Pemb.

?PEMBROKESHIRE	1572*
CARDIGANSHIRE	1586*[1]
PEMBROKESHIRE	1593

b. Aug./Sept. 1553, 1st s. of Sir John Perrot* by his 1st w. Anne, da. of Sir Thomas Cheyne(y)† of Shurland, Kent. m. 1583, Dorothy, da. of Walter Devereux, 1st Earl of Essex, 1s. 1da. Kntd. 1579; suc. fa. 1593.

J.p. Pemb. from c.1575, dep. lt. 1586–90; commr. musters, Haverfordwest 1581, mayor 1586.[2]

Capt. under Leicester in the Netherlands 1586.

Perrot was a soldier, first employed on his father's voyage of 1579, for which he was knighted on landing at Waterford. Back from Ireland, he was put in the Fleet for a week to restrain him from fighting a duel with Walter Ralegh*. In 1581 Perrot was one of 20 'defendants' of the Castle of Beauty at a pageant staged in the Tilt Yard before the Queen and the French ambassadors. Before long he was back in the Fleet for secretly marrying one of the Queen's ladies in waiting.[3]

Next Perrot campaigned in the Netherlands, taking part in the battle of Zutphen. In the following year his father, now lord deputy of Ireland, tried to have him appointed master of the ordnance, in competition with Sir George Carew*, who, with the support of Burghley and Leicester, gained his point, and Perrot was left to his local duties in Pembrokeshire.[4]

These, at the time of the Armada, soon acquired a more than local importance. Already in April 1588 he had joined with his fellow deputy lieutenant George Owen of Henllys, and other local gentry, in reporting on measures to be taken to defend Milford Haven against a Spanish landing, and in October he was detailed to review there 1,500 to 2,000 levies from all Wales, and to supervise their equipment as musketeers instead of bowmen to meet a Spanish landing in Ireland. The original intention that he should command them in person with the rank of colonel was abandoned as the crisis abated, and the suggestion that he should instead lead a company of 200 was apparently declined. Letters from Perrot in 1587-9 to the Privy Council and to Julius Caesar*, the Admiralty judge, show a concern with piracy which suggests that he may have combined with his deputy lieutenancy the duties of deputy vice-admiral. Another preoccupation of the same period was an attempt to upset in Chancery the will of his maternal grandfather, Sir Thomas Cheyne(y), whose heir died without male heirs in 1587. The case dragged on until Perrot became involved in his father's disgrace, but it was renewed by his daughter in 1619.[5]

In 1590 Sir Christopher Hatton, Perrot's unremitting foe, had him removed from the commission of lieutenancy, and he was in prison (without charges being preferred against him) before the end of 1591. Within a few months of his father's attainder and death in 1592, Egerton, the attorney-general, was reporting on Perrot's claims to the estate. The matter was settled by an Act of March 1593 (rushed through both Houses in four days) restoring him in blood, though not in name. He owed his restoration to the efforts of his brother-in-law the 2nd Earl of Essex. He thus inherited Haroldston and much of the rest of the paternal estate, but not Carew castle, which reverted to the Crown. His right as steward of Cilgerran to appoint town officials was disputed in the Exchequer by his father's old ally John Garnons*, who claimed that the town was incorporate and could appoint its own officials.[6]

In the 1581 session of the 1572 Parliament, the journals record Perrot as sitting on two committees, for supply (25 Jan.) and for the preservation of game (18 Feb.). His constituency remains uncertain; but, John Wogan having died 4 May 1580, Pembrokeshire suggests itself as offering a suitable vacancy at a by-election for that session. He entered the 1586 Parliament as knight for Cardiganshire at a by-election on the death of Griffith Lloyd and so would have been entitled to attend the subsidy committee to which all the knights of shires were appointed on 22 Feb. 1587. His election for Pembrokeshire in February 1593 while still under the cloud of his father's attainder no

doubt reflects the strength of the Earl of Essex at that time. Perrot is not mentioned by name in the journals but he could have attended the subsidy committee 26 Feb. and a legal committee 9 Mar. 1593. By this time, however, Perrot was ill. His will, dated 12 Feb. 1594, dividing his estates (in default of male heirs) between his wife and daughter, was proved three days later.[7]

[1] Hatfield CP 244/4. [2] C142/119/114, 121/102; *Arch. Camb.* (ser. 3), xi. 129-32; (ser. 5), xiii. 195; *LJ,* ii. 182-3; Flenley, *Cal. Reg. Council, Marches of Wales,* 140, 213; *CSP Dom.* 1581-90, p. 251; G. Owen, *Taylors Cussion,* f. 36; *APC,* xii. 364. [3] *Arch. Camb.* (ser. 3), xi. 112; *APC,* xi. 384, 388-9; Wallace, *Raleigh,* 14; Nichols, *Progresses Eliz.,* ii. 132-5; *CSP Dom.* 1581-90, p. 114; Lansd. 72, f. 4; Strype, *Aylmer* (1821), 130, 217-19. [4] *CSP For.* 1585-6, p. 333; 1586-7, p. 165, 244; *Cal. Carew Pprs.* ii. 456-7; iii. 21, 42, 44-5, 52-3. [5] *Arch. Camb.* (ser. 3), viii. 18; *Cal. Wynn Pprs.* 37; *CSP Dom.* 1581-90, pp. 554-5, 558, 648; *APC,* xv. 166; xvi. 319-20; *HMC Ancaster,* 199-200; Add. 12507, ff. 124, 188, 221; Lansd. 55, f. 31; 62, f. 5; *CP,* iii. 192-3; *Chamberlain Letters* ed. McClure, ii. 272. [6] Lansd. 72, ff. 6, 15; 73, f. 21; D'Ewes, 510-11; Spurrell, *Carew,* 40; *Exchequer,* ed. E. G. Jones (Univ. Wales Bd. of Celtic Studies, Hist. and Law ser. iv), 124, 304. [7] Hatfield ms 244/4; Lansd. 76, f. 9; D'Ewes 288, 409, 474, 496; *CJ,* i. 119, 128; PCC 14 Dixy.

A.H.D.

PERYAM, John (1541-c.1618), of Exeter, Devon.

BARNSTAPLE	1584
BOSSINEY	1586
EXETER	1589, 1593

b. 1541, yr. s. of John Peryam, merchant of Exeter by Elizabeth, da. of Robert Hone of Ottery St. Mary; bro. of William*. *educ.* ?New Inn Hall, Oxf.; M. Temple 1562. *m.* (1) Elizabeth, da. of Roger Prideaux†, 3da.; (2) Margaret Peck of Buckarel; (3) wid. of one Hayes of Lyme Regis, Dorset.[1]

Bailiff, Exeter 1574, alderman, receiver 1581-2, sheriff 1582-3, mayor 1587-8; vice-collector of tenths and clergy subsidies, Exeter diocese.

As early as 1572 Peryam was transacting business for Exeter in London, consulting the 2nd Earl of Bedford, Burghley and Sir Peter Carew on the repair of Exeter castle. By 1585 he was living in London, and some two years later the Exeter corporation threatened to expel him unless he came back to take a turn as mayor, which he did. It is likely that his return to Parliament for Barnstaple was due to an arrangement between Bedford and Arthur Bassett*, Peryam's relative by marriage. His brother William probably brought him in at Bossiney in 1586. In the Parliaments of 1589 and 1593 he sat for his native city, being paid wages of 5s. per day. The Exeter MPs were appointed to two committees on kerseys (23 Mar. and 2 Apr. 1593), and Peryam was named to committees on recusants (28 Feb., 4 Apr. 1593) and the poor law (12 Mar. 1593).

By 1595 Peryam was anxious to be relieved of his position as alderman because he could not attend meetings of the corporation, but he was still active in the following year when, with William Martin*, he arranged Exeter's grain supply on advantageous terms. He was generous in his lifetime to young merchants of Exeter, and left bequests to Exeter College. In 1600 he subscribed two-fifths of the annual cost of a puritan preacher for Exeter, Edmund Snape. With another merchant, he gave a bond of £100 for the payment of the stipend. Peryam, who invested in a number of voyages of discovery, died between 10 Aug. 1617 when he added a codicil to his will, and 15 Oct. 1618 when it was proved.[2]

[1] *DNB* (Peryam, Sir William); *Hooker's Common Place Bk.* ed. Harte, 21; *Trans. Dev. Assoc.* lxxii. 255; T. Westcote, *Devon*, 585; Vivian, *Vis. Devon*, 603. [2] Roberts thesis; W. T. MacCaffrey, *Exeter 1540–1640*, passim; Exeter dioc. reg., Bp. Wolton's act bk. 436; *HMC Exeter*, 40, 85, 277; *Trans. Dev. Assoc.* xlv. 413; lxiv. 478–9; lxxii. 255; *Gilbert Voyages*, ed. Quinn (Hak. Soc. ser. 2, lxxxiv), 333; W. Cotton, *Eliz. Guild City Exeter*, 155; D'Ewes, 477, 499, 507, 513, 517; Exeter city mun. act bk. 4, p. 520; 5, p. 309; *Notes and Gleanings* (Exeter 1888), i. 65–6; *Som. N. and Q.* vi. 325; *First Letter Bk. East India Co.* 144; PCC 95 Meade.

P.W.H.

PERYAM, William (1534–1604), of Crediton, Devon.

PLYMOUTH 1563

b. 1534, 1st s. of John Peryam, and bro. of John*. *educ.* Exeter Coll. Oxf. 1551; Clifford's Inn; M. Temple 1553, called 1565. *m.* (1) Margery, da. of John Holcot of Berks.; (2) Anne or Agnes, da. of John Parker of North Molton, Devon, 4da.; (3) Elizabeth, da. of Sir Nicholas Bacon†, lord keeper, wid. of Robert Doyley* and of Sir Henry Neville I*. *suc.* fa. c.1573. Kntd. 1593.

J.p. Devon from c.1569, many other counties from c.1583; bencher, M. Temple 1577, serjeant-at-law 1580; justice of common pleas 1581; chief baron of the Exchequer from 1593; commr. trials of Mary Stuart 1586, Earl of Essex 1601.[1]

The son of a Marian exile, Peryam became a London lawyer. By the time of the 1563 parliamentary election his services were no doubt already retained by the Plymouth corporation, which paid him for drawing up a bill about an almshouse during this Parliament. Peryam was a supporter of the 2nd Earl of Bedford as his father had been of the 1st. He was an overseer of the 2nd Earl's will, and succeeded to his borough patronage at Bossiney and Camelford. Early in 1568 Peryam was called to Ireland by Sir Peter Carew*, then prosecuting his claims to an Irish barony, and he was instrumental in winning Carew's case. This may have led to his suggested appointment as judge under the president of Munster, Sir John Pollard*. Though 'scarcely known' to Sir William Cecil, Peryam wrote to him to try to get out of it, then petitioned the Privy Council against it, mentioning his wife and children, losses previously incurred in Ireland, and his delicate state of health. The Privy Council agreed that he should serve for two years only and in the end he does not seem to have gone at all.

Peryam's name has not been found in the journals of the 1563 Parliament. After distinguished service on the bench he was discharged of his circuit in 1603 'by reason of his weakness', and he died 9 Oct. 1604 at his home near Crediton. Peryam was described by Ralegh as 'my lord puritan Peryam', and Thomas Wilcox, dedicating a work to John Popham* and Peryam wrote 'you both profess the holy gospel of Christ, and may ... be received amongst them that mourn for your own sins'. Peryam's daughter Elizabeth married Robert*, heir of Arthur Bassett* and his daughter Mary married William Pole II*.[2]

[1] Vivian, *Vis. Devon*, 603; Roberts thesis; *HMC Bath*, v. 74, 269. [2] *Plymouth Recs.* 195; PCC 45 Windsor; J. Hooker, *Life of Carew*, ed. Maclean, 80–2; SP63/26/25; 27/28; *CSP Ire.* 1509–73, p. 402; *Trevelyan Pprs.* (Cam. Soc. cv), 50; E. Edwards, *Life of Raleigh*, ii. 250; Stowe 130, f. 110; MacCaffrey thesis, 42; Collinson thesis, 59, 811, n. 1; Harl. 6996, f. 27.

P.W.H.

PETRE, Sir John (1549–1613), of Ingatestone, Essex.

ESSEX 1584, 1586

b. 20 Dec. 1549, 3rd but 1st surv. s. of Sir William Petre* by his 2nd w. *educ.* M. Temple 1567. *m.* 1570, Mary, da. of Sir Edward Waldegrave†, of Borley, 3 surv. s. inc. William*. *suc.* fa. 1572. Kntd. 1576; *cr.* Baron Petre 1603.

J.p. Essex from 1573, sheriff 1575–6, dep. lt. 1590–8, commr. musters 1599–1603.[1]

Petre inherited considerable estates in Essex, and in 1574 completed his father's purchase of Thorndon Hall. In 1588 he was listed by Lord Burghley among 'knights of great possessions'; and in 1595 out of an income of £4,280 from rents, £2,900 came from his Essex properties. He was an active county official, a member of the victualling commission in 1573, the piracy commission in 1577, the grain commission in 1586, a commissioner for the subsidy of 1587, and a collector of loans in 1590, 1591 and 1596–8.[2]

He was acquainted with the Heneage, Mildmay and Radcliffe families, and in 1575 Lord Burghley was godfather to his heir William. Twice knight of the shire, Petre served on committees concerned with tithes (3 Dec. 1584), grain (19 Dec.) and cloth (13 Feb. 1585). Of particular interest, in view of the inclusion of his name in a list drawn up in her interests in 1574, is his membership of the committee which asked for the execution of Mary Queen of Scots (4 Nov. 1586). He was one of those appointed by the House to attend the Queen about the subsidy, 18 Mar. following. In fact Petre is an example of an Elizabethan who resolved conflicting loyalties to Church and State. Though its fortunes had been founded upon the proceeds of the dissolution of the monasteries, the family was, and remained, Catholic. Both Petre's wife and his mother were presented for recusancy in 1581. Petre himself conformed to the extent of attending Anglican services (though not taking communion), and as an MP he must be presumed to have taken the oath of supremacy. In 1591 he served on a commission against seminaries and Jesuits. Clearly he would have nothing to do with 'traitorous priests' or any attempt to subvert the constitution. Still, he was evidently aware of the delicacy of his position: there is a draft and copy of a letter of apology, written in 1605, to be made by a Mr. Bernarde 'for accusing Lord Petre of being a Papist'.[3]

Given a peerage by James I, Petre was henceforth less active in local affairs. Perhaps he was already suffering from the 'long languishing consumption' of which he died. He was present in 1610 at the creation of Prince Henry as Prince of Wales, and at his funeral in 1612. In 1613 Petre made settlements providing portions of £5,000 each to his grandchildren and settling properties on his eldest son William and his heirs. He died 11 Oct. that year at Thorndon and was buried at Ingatestone 29 Oct. His will, drawn up 10 Jan. 1612, and signed 1 Sept. 1613, was proved 18 Nov. He left money to the poor of local parishes, and to prisoners in London, Southwark and Colchester, to London hospitals and to old retainers. He bequeathed £20 to Exeter College, Oxford, £10 for repairs to Ingatestone church, and £5 for repairs to Thorndon church. He also made other monetary bequests to his surviving children.[4]

[1] CP; APC, xxix. 643, 701; R. B. Colvin, Lts. and Keepers of Rolls of Essex. [2] C. T. Kuypers, Thorndon, 17; Lansd. 33, f. 146; 66, f. 208; 104, f. 51 seq.; 146, f. 18; Essex RO, D/DP, E6, D/DP 04; APC, viii. 144; xix. 186; xxviii. 559. [3] Lansd. 33, f. 146; 103, f. 266; F. Chancellor, Ancient Sepulchral Mons. Essex, 316; PCC 108 Windebanck, 82 Leicester; D'Ewes 335, 343, 349, 394, 416; Cath. Rec. Soc. Misc. viii. 96; Collinson thesis 504; H. Foley, Recs. Soc. of Jesus, ii. 580 seq.; Essex RO, 2/SR 78/46, 79/100; D/DP 060; D/DP, Z 30/7, 7A; CSP Dom. 1581-90, p. 88. [4] Chamberlain Letters ed. McClure, i. 479; Nichols, Progresses Jas. I, ii. 335, 497; Essex RO, D/DP, F 14, 22, 23, 24, 29; 17 D/DP, F 18; PCC 105 Capell.

J.H.

PETRE, Robert (d.1593), of St. Stephen's, Westminster and St. Botolph-without-Aldersgate, London.

FOWEY	1571
PENRYN	1572
DARTMOUTH	1586

4th or 6th s. of John Petre of Tor Newton, Devon by Alice, da. of John Collinge of Woodland, Devon; bro. of John[t] and Sir William*. m. Margaret, ?s.p.

Receiver-gen. Berks., Oxon., city of Oxford 1567-80; writer of tallies and auditor of the receipt of the Exchequer from 1569.

Petre owed his advancement not to his family's standing in Devon, but to his brother, the secretary of state and Privy Councillor. There is no trace of Robert Petre before 1569, his religious views possibly preventing him from obtaining any official position under Mary Tudor, in spite of his brother's influence. He presumably owed his offices

in the Exchequer to Sir Walter Mildmay*, who became its chancellor early in Elizabeth's reign. Petre was a full-time government official, acquiring little landed property, and living in one of the three houses in the parish of St. Botolph-without-Aldersgate which he leased from his brother.

During most of his period at the Exchequer, Petre was occupied in a quarrel with Chidiock Wardour*, clerk of the pells, each accusing the other of encroachment, corruption and malpractice. A series of commissions sat to determine the rights of the contestants, while the two rivals continued to issue statement and counter statement. In 1588 Wardour appealed to the Queen and in 1591 Petre petitioned Burghley. Neither received more than nominal satisfaction, but Petre evaded Wardour's attacks, until his death in 1593 left Wardour with a new opponent in Vincent Skinner*.

Petre remained on the closest terms with his brother until Sir William's death in 1572, when he was a mourner at the funeral and an overseer of the will. His relations with Mildmay in the Exchequer were cordial, Mildmay being described in Petre's will as his 'especial good master'. The will, drawn up before Mildmay's death, contains a bequest to him of a silver-gilt cup valued at £10. In all probability Petre owed his parliamentary seat at Fowey to the 2nd Earl of Bedford. At Penryn the immediate patrons were the Killigrews, Petre probably being nominated at Mildmay's or at Burghley's request. The Robert Petre who sat for Dartmouth in 1586 may have been a namesake, of Bowhay and Torbryan, Devon, but it is more likely that the Member for Fowey, Penryn and Dartmouth was one and the same, returned for Dartmouth on his family's local interest.

Petre died on 20 Sept. 1593 at the house of his nephew Sir John Petre*, at Thorndon in Essex. He was buried at Ingatestone, where his monument describes him as one 'who lived and died a faithful officer to the most famous Queen Elizabeth in the receipt of her Majesty's Exchequer'. He left £1,000, along with his plate and household goods, to his wife Margaret, as well as a £20 annuity for her life. His property in Essex and London was bequeathed to his nephew Sir John and £500 to another nephew, William Petre of Torbryan. A jewel worth 20 marks went to Sir John's wife and more jewels valued at £10 each to her sisters-in-law, Robert's nieces. To Lord Burghley he left, 'as a poor remembrance of my good will and duty that I bear and owe unto his lordship', a silver-gilt cup valued at £10, similar to the one he had intended for Mildmay. Unlike others of his family, Petre was a puritan. In the preamble to his will he describes himself as 'a most vile and wicked sinner', but trusted that through Christ's passion he would come 'pure, clean, and by His blood-shedding, unspotted of sin, with His elect to receive with them that most joyful sentence that then shall be pronounced, "Come, you well-beloved of my Father, and receive the kingdom prepared for you before the beginning of the world" '.

Vivian, *Vis. Devon*, 592; E407/71/51; F. G. Emmison, *Tudor Sec.* 83, 290, 292; *CPR, 1566–9*, p. 36; *Eliz. Govt. and Soc.* 213–48; Lansd. 67, f. 25; *Vis. Cornw.* (Harl. Soc. ix), 81; Prince, *Worthies of Devon* (1810), p. 634; PCC 69 Nevell.

I.C.

PETRE, William (1575–1637), of Ingatestone, Essex.

ESSEX   1597

b. 24 June 1575, 1st s. of Sir John Petre*, 1st Baron Petre, by Mary, da. of Sir Edward Waldegrave† of Borley. *educ.* Exeter Coll. Oxf. 1588, BA 1591; M. Temple 1593. *m.* 8 Nov. 1596, Katherine (*d.*1624), 2nd da. of Edward Somerset, 4th Earl of Worcester, 7 surv. s., 3 surv. da. Kntd. 1603; *suc.* fa. as 2nd Baron 1613.

J.p. Essex 1623–5.

Elected knight of the shire at the age of 22, Petre could have attended committees on enclosures (5 Nov.), the poor law (5, 22 Nov.), armour and weapons (8 Nov.), penal laws (8 Nov.), monopolies (10 Nov.), the subsidy (15 Nov.) and draining the fens (3 Dec.). He was less successful than his father in walking the tightrope between the demands of the state and his family religion. Though Lord Burghley was his godfather, he was brought up by a Catholic tutor and eventually, in 1625, 'disarmed' and removed from the commission of the peace. In 1626 he was presented for non-attendance at church; and in 1628–9 he was saved from being tried for recusancy only by the intervention of Charles I. He died 5 May 1637, and was buried at Ingatestone a week later. In his will, dated January 1633 and proved 23 June 1637, he left bequests to the poor of local parishes, to prisoners in Colchester gaol and to his ten surviving children. He hoped he would go 'where I can no more offend God'.

CP; Essex RO, D/DP, F.35; 2/SR 242/124, 250/28, 252/37, 266/117; D'Ewes, 552, 553, 555, 557, 561, 567; *APC, 1625–6*, p. 228; C. T. Kuypers, *Thorndon*; *HMC 10th Rep. IV*, 412; PCC 92 Goare.

J.H.

PETRE, Sir William (1505/6–72), of Ingatestone, Essex and Aldersgate Street, London.[1]

?DOWNTON	1536
ESSEX	1547
?ESSEX	1553 (Mar.)
ESSEX	1553 (Oct.), 1554 (Apr.), 1554 (Nov.), 1555, 1558, 1559, 1563

b. 1505/6, s. of John Petre of Tor Newton, Devon, by Alice, da. of John Collinge of Woodland, Devon;[2] bro. of John† and Robert*. *educ.* Oxf. by 1519; fellow, All Souls 1523; BCL and BCnL 1526; DCL and adv. Doctors' Commons 1533. *m.* (1) ?Feb. 1534, Gertrude (*d.*1541), da. of Sir John Tyrell of Warley, Essex, 1s. *d.v.p.* 2da.; (2) by Mar. 1542, Ann (*d.*1582), da. of William Browne, ld.

mayor of London, wid. of John Tyrell of Heron in East Thorndon, Essex, 4s. inc. Sir John* 2da. Kntd. 1544.

Proctor, ct. of chancellor, Oxf. Univ. by 1527–8; principal, Peckwater Inn, Oxf. Jan. 1530–Feb. 1534; clerk in Chancery by 1533, master 1536–41; official principal and commissary to Cromwell as vicegerent 13 Jan. 1536–40; canon of Lincoln and prebendary of Langford Ecclesia Nov. 1536–Apr. 1537; receiver of petitions in the Lords, Parlts. of 1539, 1542; King's councillor 5 Oct. 1540; principal sec. 21 Jan. 1544–Mar. 1557; j.p. Essex by 1544–*d.*; PC by 1545; custos rot. Essex 1547–*d.*; keeper, seal 'ad causas ecclesiasticus' 18 Aug. 1548; treasurer, ct. of first fruits and tenths 22 Oct. 1549–25 Jan. 1553; commr. relief, Essex 1550, chantries 1553; gov. Chelmsford g.s. 1551; chancellor, order of the Garter 1553.[3]

By the accession of Elizabeth, Petre's political career was nearing its close. 'A man of approved wisdom and exquisite learning', his ability and lack of religious zeal had enabled him to secure and retain high office during the reigns of Henry VIII, Edward VI and Mary. He was, as a contemporary put it in Mary's reign, 'as good as a Council register', and 'behaved as if it were not in the power of fortune to jostle him out of position'. Elizabeth retained him on the Privy Council, but she appointed Cecil to the post of principal secretary which Petre had resigned in 1557. The two men remained on good terms, and for a few months in 1560 when Cecil was in Scotland, Petre was his deputy. No doubt Cecil valued his support in the early years of the new reign, and particularly his knowledge of foreign affairs and diplomacy, gained during Mary's reign when Cecil himself was out of office. His colleagues on the Privy Council acted swiftly when his county seat was threatened in November 1562 by Richard Rich†, 1st Baron Rich, who wanted the seat for his heir. They wrote to Rich:

> Although nature may move you to prefer your son, yet seeing he hath a place as your heir apparent in the higher House, and may also, if you would, by other good means be in the lower house

an attempt to secure the Essex county seat was neither dignified nor necessary. So Petre came in again, for the ninth consecutive time as knight of the shire, to what proved to be his last Parliament. His election expenses were £6 13s. 4d. for dinners in January 1559, and £4 8s. 3d. for provisions in December 1562. Whether because of his old age and deafness or because of the defective records, the only references found to him in his two Elizabethan Parliaments are his membership of the succession committee (31 Oct. 1566) and of the delegation of 30 from the Lower House summoned to hear the Queen's message on the succession (5 Nov. 1566). However, as a Privy Councillor he was appointed to committees concerned with the petition to the Queen to marry (6 Feb. 1559), the petition for the Queen's marriage and the succession (19 Jan., 12 Feb. 1563) and the subsidy (25 Jan. 1563 and 17 Oct. 1566). Until this year, with a break of some months owing to a serious illness in 1559, Petre still attended the Council regularly, and sat on a variety of commissions, from those dealing with vitally important matters such as the newly established English church or the civil wars in France, to minor bodies like the one set up in May 1564 to raise money for the rebuilding of St. Paul's, recently destroyed by fire. From November 1564 to May 1566 Lady Catherine Grey was in his custody at Ingatestone. One of his last known appearances at the Privy Council was in October 1566, when two of his Henrician colleagues, Sir Walter Mildmay* and Sir Ralph Sadler*, were also present, Mildmay for the first time and Sadler after three years' absence. Petre attended a meeting in February 1567 – possibly his last. Beginning three months later, there is a long gap in the Council register.[4]

Petre lived his last years in retirement at Ingatestone. As cautious and farsighted over money as politics, Petre was that rare phenomenon, a statesman who lived within his means. His household accounts show an average annual surplus of over £600, invested almost entirely in land. He acquired considerable property around his ancestral house in Devon, though there is no evidence that he ever lived in that county after his boyhood days. It was in Essex that he mainly increased and developed his estates, with Ingatestone, acquired at the dissolution of the monasteries, as a nucleus, and where he began to build a new house in about 1540. When Elizabeth spent three days there in July 1561, Petre estimated the cost of her food only at over £136. Much of his wealth went to charities, such as his almshouses at Ingatestone, and All Souls and Exeter, Oxford, Exeter College considering him a second founder. In 1566 he was granted letters patent to found seven fellowships, and two years later he endowed an eighth. Altogether he gave £5,000 to charity. Petre made his will in April 1571 and died at Ingatestone on 13 Jan. 1572, and was buried on 1 Feb. in the parish church, where there is a monument. He had suffered for many years from a 'humour' in the leg, probably a varicose ulcer, which forced him to travel in a specially constructed litter. As an elderly man he suffered also from the stone. Though he conformed to the Elizabethan church settlement, taking the oath of supremacy as late as 1569, his wife remained a Catholic, and his family chaplain was the Catholic priest John Woodward, to whom he left a legacy of £40.[5]

[1] This biography is largely based upon F. G. Emmison, *Tudor Secretary*. [2] Vivian, *Vis. Devon*, 592. [3] *LP Hen. VIII*, xx(1), pp. 314, 322; *CPR*, 1547-8, p. 83; 1553-4, p. 160; Emden, *Biog. Reg. Univ. Oxf. 1501-4*, pp. 445-6. [4] Camden, *Britannia* (1610), p. 445; SP12/25/64; Strype, *Annals*, i(1), p. 9; D'Ewes, 45, 79, 80, 84, 103, 124, 126; Read, *Cecil*, 77, 160-77; Camb. Univ. Lib. Gg. iii. 34, p. 209; *CPR*, 1558-60, p. 118; 1560-3, pp. 279, 623; 1563-6, pp. 122-3; *APC*, vii. 147, 314, 326; Essex RO, D/DP/214/1. [5] *CPR*, 1555-7, pp. 542-3; 1563-6, pp. 430-1; C. W. Boase, *Exeter Coll. Reg.* xciv. 74-5; PCC 1 Peter; SP12/3/8, 39/75.

N.M.F.

PETTUS, John (1550–1614), of Norwich, Norf.

NORWICH	1601, 1604

b. 1550, s. of Thomas Pettus, tailor and mayor of Norwich by Christine, da. of Simon Dethick of North Elmingham. *m.* Bridget, da. of Augustine Curteys of Honnington, Suff. and Lincs., 2s. 3da. *suc.* fa. 1598. Kntd. 29 June 1607.

Sheriff, Norwich 1598-9, alderman by 1600, mayor 1608-9.

Pettus came of an old Norwich family. Though no record of his admission as a freeman has been found, he presumably carried on his father's business, and was certainly one of Norwich's richest and most influential citizens during the first decade of the seventeenth century. As MP for the borough in 1601, he was appointed to the committee on penal laws (2 Nov.), the main business committee (3 Nov.) and the committee on tithes at Norwich (23 Nov.). He also obtained from Cecil a concession that Norwich should not pay the subsidy and alnage upon the new draperies. He was the first Norwich citizen to be returned to two consecutive Parliaments since 1558-9, and one of the first to be knighted.

He died in 1614. His lengthy will showed that he had substantial property in Norwich as well as a country estate at Rackheath. Most of this went to his son and grandchildren, but for 'the love, zeal and religious mind' that he bore 'unto the preaching of the word of God', he left some land to endow sermons at Norwich, as well as money to other charities. He was buried near his father in the church of St. Simon and St. Jude, Norwich.

Blomefield, *Norf.* iv. 231, 359; *Vis. Norf.* (Harl. Soc. xxxii), 221; H. Le Strange, *Norf. Official Lists*, 110; P. Millican, *Reg. Norwich Freemen*, 124; *HMC Hatfield*, xi. 532; D'Ewes, 622, 624, 654; PCC 51 Lawe.

R.V.

PEYTON, John I (1544–1630), of Beaupré Hall, Norf., later of Doddington, Ely, Cambs.

KING'S LYNN	1572*, 1584, 1593
MIDDLESEX	1597[1]
WEYMOUTH AND MELCOMBE REGIS	1601

b. 1544, 2nd s. of John Peyton† of Knowlton, Kent (*d.* 1558), by Dorothy, da. of Sir John Tyndale of Hockwold, Norf. *m.* 8 June 1578, Dorothy, da. and coh. of Edmund Beaupré of Beaupré Hall, wid. of (Sir) Robert Bell*, 1s. John III* 1da. Kntd. 24 Nov. 1586.[2]

In household of Sir Henry Sidney* in Ireland c.1564-76; with Leicester in the Netherlands 1586; j.p. Norf. from c.1581, sheriff 1588-9, dep. lt. 1588-96, commr. sewers by 1590; j.p. Isle of Ely from c.1579, commr. sewers by 1594; j.p. Mdx. from c.1597, commr. musters 1598; dep. gov. of Bergen-op-Zoom 1586; receiver, Norf. Hunts. and Norwich 1593; lt. of the Tower 1597; gov. of Jersey 1603-28.[3]

As a young man, Peyton went to Ireland to serve under Sir Henry Sidney, a friend and near neighbour of his father. In 1568 there are references to his bringing despatches from Sidney to England, but few details of his life at this period have been found. He seems to have returned to England finally in 1576.

As a younger son, Peyton had little land of his own, though he inherited leasehold property in Ely and in Cambridgeshire, where another branch of the Peytons had long been settled. However, when the sitting Member for King's Lynn died, Peyton married the widow and on 6 Nov. 1579 was elected to Parliament by the 'congregation' of the borough 'in the lieu and place of Sir Robert Bell', and in the following month was made a freeman and member of the merchants' company. In 1584 he again represented King's Lynn, but was in the Netherlands during the 1586 election, and did not re-enter the House of Commons until 1593. In the 1581 session of the 1572 Parliament Peyton sat on committees concerning the recusancy laws (25 Jan.) and wool (13 Feb.). His name has not been found in the journals of the 1584 Parliament, and in that of 1593 he served only on the subsidy committees (26 Feb. and 1 Mar.) and a cloth committee (23 Mar.). The King's Lynn corporation presented him with a hogshead of claret in June 1593, 'in respect of his service the last Parliament'. At least once he wrote to the Privy Council protesting against monopolies which harmed the town's trade. After he ceased to be Member for King's Lynn there is only one reference to him in the local records, when he acted as a pledge for Sir Robert Southwell* on his becoming a free burgess.[4]

In the ten years succeeding his marriage, Peyton became one of the most active local officials in Norfolk, serving on numerous commissions in addition to carrying out his regular work as a justice of the peace, commissioner for musters or deputy lieutenant. In 1596 he drew up a scheme for the improvement of the county levies, reducing the size of companies and appointing captains with military experience. The Privy Council approving his suggestions, Hunsdon, the lord lieutenant, ordered the Norfolk companies to be reduced in size, and the appointment of new captains. Soon after Peyton moved away the former large companies were restored.

Peyton's court affiliations were with the Sidney-Leicester group, and he counted among his friends influential men like (Sir) Philip Sidney* – who wrote in 1585 that Peyton was 'one whom from my childhood I have had great cause to love' – and Peregrine Bertie, Lord Willoughby de Eresby. It is not surprising, therefore, to find him among those who followed Leicester to the Netherlands, where he was knighted, and in spite of supply difficulties gained some repute as deputy governor of Bergen. Back in England by July 1588, he was appointed a colonel of the Queen's bodyguard at the time of the Armada. When the troops were disbanded he returned to his Norfolk estates, but continued to take an active interest in national affairs. Early in 1596 he sent up to London a detailed report of rumours locally current about the imminent arrival of another Armada, said to have sailed from Lisbon 'more than three weeks since'.[5]

A new period in his career began in 1597 with his appointment as lieutenant of the Tower. Here he had charge of such eminent prisoners as the Earl of Essex and, for a short time, Sir Walter Ralegh, who sent for him five or six times a day 'in such passions as I see his fortitude is [not] competent to support his grief'. Peyton seems to have been a humane and considerate lieutenant: Henry Cuffe, one of the Essex conspirators, in a will presumably declared invalid, bequeathed him £100, since he had 'found all kind favours and christian comforts' at his hands. During his period at the Tower, Peyton served as a justice of the peace for Middlesex, and in 1597 represented the county in Parliament. As a knight of the shire he could have attended committees on enclosures (5 Nov.), the poor law (5, 22 Nov.), armour and weapons (8 Nov.), penal laws (8 Nov.), monopolies (10 Nov.) and the subsidy (15 Nov.). As lieutenant of the Tower he was named to the armour and weapons committee (8 Nov.), and to committees on defeasances (26 Nov.), the provision of a preacher in the Tower (12 Dec.) and the possessions of the bishop of Norwich (16 Jan. 1598). He did not attain a county seat in 1601, returning to the House for Weymouth and Melcombe Regis, where his patron was almost certainly Sir Robert Cecil, perhaps acting through Viscount Bindon. This time he served on committees dealing with the clothworkers bill (18 Nov.), monopolies (23 Nov.), Dunkirk pirates (3 Dec.), the relief of the poor (10 Dec.), the Exchequer bill (16 Dec.) and a bill concerning printers (17 Dec.).

By this time Peyton was complaining of the expenses of his office, which had caused him to sell '£180 a year' of his estate. In September 1601 he asked permission to go into the country for five or six weeks, on the grounds that former lieutenants had been allowed to be absent for most of the summer, until (Sir) Owen Hopton* 'came to the place, who having wasted his estate, necessity enforced him to mortify himself with the privilege of his office'.

Early in 1603, when James VI was intent on securing his succession, he wrote to Peyton, possibly overestimating the importance of his office. Peyton avoided committing himself but, when James had been proclaimed King, sent his son John to Edinburgh with professions of loyalty. As lieutenant, Peyton served as one of the knights of the canopy at Elizabeth's funeral, but he wished to exchange his Tower office for the governorship of Jersey, 'a place', he told Robert Cecil, 'of all others best agreeing with my desires'. He left England in September 1603. In the following month and again in January 1604 his loyalty was suspect owing to the indiscreet activities of his son John, who had been his assistant at the Tower; but nothing came of the rumours that father or son was to be disgraced, and Peyton kept the privilege, granted to him at the beginning of James's reign, of having access to the privy chamber at all times.[6]

Peyton's period as governor of Jersey proved a stormy one. A convinced supporter of the English church settlement, he was soon at odds with the presbyterian party there. In addition he fell foul of the bailiff, John Herault, and the Privy Council received the usual complaints from both sides. In 1616 a special commission was appointed to 'go thither and set all straight between them'. In February 1617 an order in Council stated that 'the charge of the military forces' should be wholly in the governor, and the care of justice and civil affairs in the bailiff.[7]

'Pardon the misguiding of my pen', Peyton wrote to Secretary Conway in December 1624, 'being led by a hand of 80 years'. He was then living on his Doddington estate in the Isle of Ely, where he seems to have spent most of his time when in England after the death of his wife early in 1603. He was lame and his sight was failing. In another letter to Conway he asked the secretary to consider his 'trouble and charges':

> I have had six voyages between England and Jersey on church discipline; my salary is £400 ... less than former governors; I have sold land worth £400 a year and am still £4,000 in debt. I have nine grandchildren to provide for.

He resigned his Jersey office in 1628 and died intestate on 4 Nov. 1630, being buried at Doddington. Administration of the estate was granted to the heir, John, in May 1631. Peyton's complaints about his debts need not be taken at their face value. Judging from the marriage portions he had recently given to his granddaughters, he was a very wealthy man.[8]

[1] C219/33/124, 125. [2] DNB; Vis. Camb. (Harl. Soc. xli), 5; R. E. Chester Waters, Chester of Chicheley Mems. i. 247, 289-98. [3] APC, xv. 385; xxviii. 359; A. H. Smith thesis, passim; Lansd. 63, f. 51; 76, f. 130; CSP Dom. 1595-7, p. 438; Add. 1580-1625, p. 419. [4] CSP Ire. 1509-74, p. 388; Lansd. 34, f. 148; Chester Mems. 289 seq.; King's Lynn congregation bks. 1569-91, ff. 186, 188, 189, 215, 291, 388, 395; 1591-1611, ff. 23, 28, 97; HMC Hatfield, iii. 395; CJ, i. 120, 125; D'Ewes, 288, 474, 481, 507. [5] Lansd. 63, f. 51; 81, f. 37; 88, f. 21; DNB; Chester Mems. 289 seq.; A. H. Smith thesis, passim; APC, xxii. 87; HMC Hatfield, vi. 222-3; CSP Dom. 1581-90, pp. 267, 519; 1591-4, p. 400; 1595-7, p. 179; Cath. Rec. Soc. xviii. 225. [6] D'Ewes, 552, 553, 555, 557, 561, 563, 571, 581, 642, 649, 666, 677, 686, 687; HMC Hatfield, xi. 169, 394; xv. 208-10; Corresp. of King James (Cam. Soc. lxxviii), 80, 81, 92; Chester Mems. 293-6; LC2/4/4; CSP Dom. 1603-10, p. 68; Edwards, Ralegh, i. 373; Harl. 1616, p. 132. [7] Chamberlain Letters ed. McClure, ii. 63, 88; CSP Dom. Add. 1580-1625, pp. 540-1, 550-65 passim. [8] CSP Dom. Add. 1580-1625, pp. 662, 673; Chester Mems. 298.

N.M.F.

PEYTON, John II (c.1561-1616), of Isleham, Cambs.

CAMBRIDGESHIRE   1593, 1604

b. c.1561, 2nd but 1st surv. s. of Robert Peyton* of Isleham by Elizabeth, da. of (Sir) Richard Rich†, 1st Baron Rich of Rochford Hall and Leigh's Priory, Essex. m. 1580, Alice, da. of Sir Edward Osborne* of St. Dionis Backchurch, London, 6s. 5da. suc. fa. 1590. Kntd. 1596; cr. Bt. 1611.

J.p. Isle of Ely from c.1584, Cambs. from c.1591, dep. lt. 1596; sheriff, Cambs. and Hunts. 1593-4.

Peyton, Sir John Cutts* and John Cotton* ran Cambridgeshire at this period, and there is no sign that Peyton's interests ever took him outside the county except for his appearance as knight of the shire, when he could have attended the subsidy committee (26 Feb.) and a legal committee (9 Mar.). It was probably he rather than John Peyton I who was named to the committee on disloyal subjects (4 Apr.), as John Peyton I was knighted by then, but D'Ewes's form of address is not conclusive one way or the other. The Cambridgeshire Peyton may have shared the puritan views of his cousin Lord Rich. In the preamble to his will he wrote that he hoped to be saved by the Lord Jesus Christ,

> the immaculate lamb of God who[m] the lord of Glory, of his endless and everlasting favour towards mankind, did ordain and appoint ... before the world was made that he should be the slain sacrifice for the whole world, but especially for God's elect of whom, and through whom, I hope by the precious blood of Jesus Christ His passion to be saved.

Peyton died 19 Dec. 1616. His daughter Susan, executrix, proved the will 14 May 1617.

C142/228/76, 376/114; Vis. Cambs. (Harl. Soc. xli), 4-5; Hatfield ms 278; APC, xxvi. 192; D'Ewes, 474, 496, 517; PCC 46 Weldon.

A.M.M.

PEYTON, John III (1579-1635), of Wells, Norf.

CASTLE RISING   1601

b. 1579, o.s. of John Peyton I* by his w. Dorothy. educ. Queens', Camb. 1594; travelled abroad (Italy, Eastern Europe) 1598, 1601. m. 25 Nov. 1602, Alice, da. of John II* of Isleham, Cambs., 3s. 6da. Kntd. 1603; suc. fa. 1630.

Gent. of privy chamber c.1603; lt.-gov. Jersey 1628-33.

Peyton no doubt owed his return at Castle Rising to his father's local influence. He left no mark on the records of the 1601 Parliament, and there is nothing of interest to say about him before he rode north to meet James I in March 1603. He was in high favour during the first months of the reign before he became too friendly with his father's prisoners, Cobham and Ralegh. In his later years he served in the Netherlands and with his father in Jersey, and in 1628 became lieutenant governor of that island on his father's retirement to England. In 1630 he succeeded to his father's estates, but died four years later, burdened by lawsuits and illness, in March or April 1635. Administration of his estate was granted on 24 Apr. to his widow.

He wrote an account, now in Cambridge University Library, of his travels as a young man, and had other literary interests. He was a friend of his neighbour, Sir Robert Cotton.

DNB; *Vis. Suff.* ed. Howard, ii. 119 seq.; R. E. Chester Waters, *Chester of Chicheley Mems.* ii. passim; *Al. Cant.* iii. 354; *HMC Hatfield*, viii. 166; x. 434; *CSP Dom.* 1598–1601, p. 419; *Chamberlain Letters* ed. McClure, i. 189, 194; Norwich Cent. Lib. N.R.S. 18407, 33, B.7; Camb. Univ. Lib. 2044 K.K. v.2.

R.V.

PEYTON, Robert (c.1523–90), of Isleham, Cambs.

CAMBRIDGESHIRE 1558, 1563*

b. c.1523, 1st s. of (Sir) Robert Peyton† by Frances, da. and h. of Francis Haselden of Guilden Morden, Cambs. and Chesterford, Essex. *educ.* Jesus, Camb. 1535–6. *m.* by 1550, Elizabeth, da. of (Sir) Richard Rich†, 1st Baron Rich, 3s. inc. John II* 3da. *suc.* fa. Aug. 1550.

Commr. to collect relief, Cambs. 1550, for church goods 1553; j.p. from c.1559, Isle of Ely from c.1564; sheriff, Cambs. and Hunts. 1553–4, 1567–8, 1586–7; dep. lt. Cambs. 1569.

Peyton was a considerable landowner in Cambridgeshire, Suffolk and Essex. As the son-in-law of Lord Rich and brother-in-law of Sir Roger North*, he was of sufficient standing to take a turn as knight of the shire for Cambridgeshire. The bishops' letters to the Privy Council in 1564 described him as 'conformable' in religion. In October 1559 he sat on the commission to inquire into lands taken by the Crown from the bishopric of Ely. In addition to his duties at sessions and in general administration, he was called upon to report to the Council on various private disputes, for example in November 1578 about the complaints made against the bishop of Ely by his tenants at Somersham and elsewhere; some years later he inquired into a case of debt between two of the local gentry. In November 1588 he was given custody of his brother William, who had been arrested for unspecified 'suspicious behaviour'. As a commissioner for musters or deputy lieutenant, he was responsible for training and equipping the Cambridgeshire and Isle of Ely levies.

He died at Isleham 19 Oct. 1590, leaving as heir his second but elder surviving son John, aged nearly 30. His will, made a week before he died and proved 9 Nov. 1590, has a long religious preamble. He asked to be buried in the tomb which he had already prepared in the south chapel of Isleham parish church, 'until it shall please my Saviour to glorify the same at His second coming and to join together my soul and body again, all corruption being taken away'. Apart from bequests of plate to his three

married daughters and a daughter-in-law, and legacies to servants, the whole of the non-landed property was to be divided equally between the two executors, the heir John and the widow. There were no bequests to churches, to the poor, or to friends, and his servants received only the wages due to them.

E150/98/2; *Vis. Cambs.* (Harl. Soc. xli), 4; SP12/59/ff. 200v, 206; *CPR*, 1549–51, p. 189; 1550–3, p. 395; 1553 and App. Edw. VI, pp. 351, 417; 1558–60, pp. 30–1; 1563–6, p. 20; *Cam. Misc.* ix(3), p. 24; *APC*, x. 389; xiv. 296; *HMC Montagu*, 21; Lansd. 56, f. 168 seq.; C142/228/76; PCC 74 Drury.

N.M.F.

PHAER (FAYRE), Thomas (c.1510–c.61), of Forest, Cilgerran, Pemb.

CARMARTHEN 1547
CARDIGAN BOROUGHS 1555, 1558, 1559

b. c.1510, s. of Thomas Phaer of Norwich, Norf. by Elery, da. of Sir Richard Godier or Goodere, prob. of Herts. *educ.* ?L. Inn; Oxf. MB and MD 1559. *m.* (1) at least 1da.; (2) by 1553, Agnes or Anne, da. of Thomas Walter, alderman of Carmarthen (*d.*1547), wid. of John Revell of Forest, 2da.

Steward, Cilgerran 1549, constable of castle from c.1552; crown researcher, Milford Haven by May 1556–*d.*, collector, tonnage and poundage from 1559; solicitor, council in the marches of Wales by 1558; j.p. Card., Carm., Pemb. from 1559; custos rot. Pemb.[1]

Phaer was brought up in the household of William Paulet, 1st Marquess of Winchester, to whom he probably owed his appointment as solicitor in the council in the marches. His introduction to the Revell family, and so to a fortunate second marriage, was probably through their neighbour Sir John Perrot*. But where Phaer acquired his learning in the law, medicine and classics is not known. Anthony Wood's conjecture that he went early to Oxford and then to Lincoln's Inn is not confirmed by the records of either, nor does his name appear in those of Cambridge or of any of the inns of court. Yet apart from his appointment as solicitor, he was writing legal treatises from 1535, and some ten years later he translated a French medical work, with added chapters of his own. It was on the score of this work, and his claim that he had been studying medicine for 20 years, that his Oxford medical degrees were conferred in 1559. His greatest achievement was his pioneer translation of the *Aeneid*. He had completed nine books and commenced the tenth when death overtook him; the first seven were published under the protection of a royal patent, with a dedication to Queen Mary, in 1558. He was also the author of many pieces of occasional verse, including a derogatory poem on Owain Glyndŵr which he contributed to the *Mirrour for Magistrates* in 1559.[2]

Phaer's stewardship of Cilgerran – perhaps acquired as a result of his second marriage – carried with it a 40-year lease of the demesne lands and of the herbage of the royal forest; he also held shorter leases of sundry rectories in the area. Cilgerran lies just beyond the border of Cardiganshire, into which the demesne land no doubt extended. This would account for his nomination as sheriff of Cardiganshire in 1552 (though in the event another name was pricked) and for his parliamentary seat at Cardigan Boroughs. Phaer was a loyal Marian, but this does not mean that a cryptic clause in his will, that his widow should 'pay £5 where she doth know by an appointment between her and me', refers to his burial with Roman rites. In any case, the minimum of conformity required at the beginning of Elizabeth's reign was no bar to his inclusion, by virtue of his office, in the court of the marches, on the commission of the peace for the three shires of west Wales and of the quorum for those in which he held land.[3]

Phaer's will, dated August 1560, was proved the following 30 June. He left legacies to his daughters, and the will provided that if his widow and sole executrix should remarry, she was not to alienate the lands Phaer bequeathed to them. Phaer's estate at Forest, as well as lands he had enjoyed during his stepson's minority, passed eventually to Thomas Revell*. George Owen of Henllys described Phaer as 'a man honoured for his learning, commended for his government, and beloved for his pleasant natural conceits', and in 1563 Barnaby Googe* published a flattering epitaph on him in his *Eclogues*.[4]

[1] Dwnn, *Vis. Wales*, i. 148, 150; *Ath. Ox.* i. 316–20; *Reg. Univ. Oxf.* ed. Boase, i. 239; *CPR*, 1555–7, p. 74; 1558–60, p. 146; PCC 23 Loftes; *Augmentations*, ed. Lewis and Davies (Univ. Wales Bd. of Celtic Studies, Hist. and Law ser. xiii), 471; Phaer, *Seven first bookes of the Eneidos* (1558), dedication; *Welsh Port Bks.* (Cymmrodorion Rec. Ser. xii), 329–30; E159/336 Trin. 23; Lansd. 1218, ff. 94–5; Stowe 571, f. 74. [2] *CPR*, 1555–7, p. 74; 1557–8, p. 309; *Arch. Camb.* (ser. 2), iv. 134–8. [3] *Exchequer*, ed. E. G. Jones (Univ. Wales Bd. of Celtic Studies, Hist. and Law ser. iv), 297; *CPR*, 1553 and App. Edw. VI, p. 387; 1557–8, p. 363; 1560–3, p. 570; *DNB*. [4] PCC 23 Loftes; J. R. Phillips, *Cilgerran*, 102–3; *Desc. Pemb.* (Cymmrodorion Rec. Ser. i), 239.

A.H.D.

PHELIPS, Edward (c.1560–1614), of Chancery Lane, London, and Montacute, Som.

BERE ALSTON	1584
WEYMOUTH AND MELCOMBE	
REGIS	1586
PENRYN	1593
ANDOVER	1597
SOMERSET	1601, 1604

b. c.1560, 4th s. of Thomas Phelips† of Montacute by Elizabeth, da. of Matthew Smith of Bristol. *educ.* New Inn; M. Temple 1572, called 1578. *m.* (1) Margaret (*d.*1590), da. of Robert Newdigate of Newdigate, Surr., 2s.; (2) Elizabeth (*d.*1638), da. of Thomas Pigott of Doddershall, Bucks. Kntd. May 1603.

J.p. Som. from c.1591, custos rot. from c.1608.

Bencher and Autumn reader, M. Temple 1596; King's serjeant 1603; justice of common pleas, Lancs. 1604; master of the rolls 1611; ranger of royal forests 1613.
Speaker of House of Commons 1604–11.

Phelips, the builder of Montacute, was a lawyer related to the Horseys of Dorset, and friendly with Thomas Gorges* and (Sir) Walter Ralegh*, though appearing for the government at the latter's trial. He was first returned for Bere Alston, no doubt through the influence of the dowager Marchioness of Winchester, who in her will of 1586, left him £10, 'for the good counsel he hath given me'. Another of his clients was the 2nd Earl of Pembroke, who was high steward of Weymouth, where Phelips was returned in 1586. His relative (Sir) John Horsey* was sheriff of the county at the time and his uncle had represented the borough in 1554. Phelips's return for Penryn in 1593 is difficult to explain. The patronage there was in the hands of the Killigrew family, who had some influence at court, and Phelips may have obtained the seat through a common acquaintance there, perhaps Sir Walter Ralegh, lord lieutenant of Cornwall and warden of the stannaries. After sitting for Andover in 1597, presumably through the influence of the Sandys family, Phelips achieved a county seat in 1601.

So far as is known Phelips was inactive in the Parliament of 1584. On 17 Mar. 1586 he was named to two committees, one concerned with the continuation of statutes, one with sheriffs. On 28 Feb. 1593 he spoke in favour of the bill against recusants and was appointed to its committee, and to that considering the subsidy. On 1 Mar. he was one of those chosen to discuss the subsidy with the Lords. In the 1597–8 Parliament he was named to committees concerned with rebuilding Langport Eastover (10 Nov.), the poor (22 Nov.), Arthur Hatch (22 Nov.), lewd wandering persons (20 Dec.), corporations (12 Jan.), defence (12, 16 Jan.), Sir A. Mildmay's lands (16 Jan.) and Lady Mary Verney's jointure (24 Jan.). In Elizabeth's last Parliament he was named to the committee on the penal laws (2 Nov.), the main business committee (3 Nov.), and committees on the poor, law reform and alehouses (all 5 Nov.), the reform of the Exchequer (9 Nov.), clothworkers (18 Nov.), Severn harbour (21 Nov.), monopolies (23 Nov. and 11 Dec.), and prisoners in Ludgate (12 Dec.). On 7 Nov. he spoke in the subsidy debate, urging that the £3 men should be spared, and four subsidies be taken from the rich, to be termed a 'contribution' to avoid making a precedent. On 24 Nov. 'he thought it a duty in conscience to offer to the consideration of the House' a bill to explain the Act passed in 1597 concerning charitable uses. After the matter had been referred to a committee, Phelips drew up a bill to repeal the Act, which was opposed by Francis Bacon* in the ensuing debate on 7 Dec. Phelips answered with 'many persuasions for the bill and bitter answers to Mr. Bacon', and desired that it should be put to the question whether the Act should be repealed by public act or private bill. Edward Glascock* also spoke against Phelips,

> so after long dispute till almost one of the clock, it was put to the question, whether it shall be repealed by the general law of repeal and continuance of statutes. And the most voices were ay, ay, ay, and so it was agreed.

Philips was re-elected for Somerset in the first Parliament of the next reign, and became Speaker, when he earned the reputation of being too closely aligned with the court. He died 11 Sept. 1614.

DNB; *Vis. Som.* (Harl. Soc. xi), 85; SP14/33; St. Ch. 5/C21/26; E. Edwards, *Life of Raleigh*, i. 428–9; PCC 32 Windsor; Townshend, *Hist. Colls.* 103, 107, 119, 122, 198, 246, 285, 291; D'Ewes, 416, 476, 477, 478, 481, 561, 575, 578, 581, 587, 622, 624, 626, 631, 642, 647, 649, 679, 681, 685.

P.W.H.

PHILIPPS, John (*d.*1629), of Picton, Pemb. and Clog y fran, Carm.

PEMBROKESHIRE   1601

1st s. of Morgan Philipps of Picton by Elizabeth, da. of Richard Fletcher of Bangor, Caern., registrar of diocese of Bangor. *m.* (1) Ann, da. of Sir John Perrot*, 3s. 8da.; (2) Margaret, da. of Sir Robert Denys* of Bigton, Devon, *s.p. suc.* fa. 1585; *cr.* Bt. 1621.
    J.p. Pemb. 1591, sheriff 1594–5, 1610–11; sheriff, Carm. 1622–3.[1]

Philipps (to adopt the spelling of the name preferred by his descendants) was a nephew of William Philipps*, who had represented the shire in 1559 and 1572 and who bequeathed Picton to his brother, John's father. Other parts of the estate, however, were left to William's daughters Elizabeth and Mary, wives of George Owen of Henllys and Alban Stepneth* of Prendergast respectively; and much of John Philipps's life was spent in territorial disputes, of which the first was over lands in Rhoscrowther, in the extreme west of the shire, south of Milford Haven. In 1583 John Gwyn of Carew accused him and Griffith White of Henllan before the Star Chamber of violent proceedings with regard to these lands, proceedings in which Philipps's father-in-law Sir John Perrot was also concerned. It may have been the costs involved in these disputes that caused Philipps ten years later to borrow £100 from Sir Thomas Myddelton*; the debt was not repaid for eight years.[2]

In the Parliament of 1601 Philipps unsuccessfully promoted a bill to establish the boundaries of Carmarthenshire and Pembrokeshire, which had been left in some confusion by the Acts of Union; but Townshend, the parliamentary journalist who sat for Bishop's Castle in this Parliament, suspected that Philipps's real motive was to 'strengthen his estate' and to overthrow the claims of his cousin's husband, George Owen. As knight for

Pembrokeshire Philipps was entitled to attend the main business committee (3 Nov.) and the monopolies committee (23 Nov.). Two years later Philipps was a defendant in an Exchequer suit brought by the surveyor of crown woods against himself and eight others, on a charge of felling 2,000 oak trees valued at nearly £1,000 in Narberth forest and the neighbouring wood of Canyston, where the deputy woodward – Alban Stepneth, the husband of Philipps's other cousin – was himself one of the accused.[3]

Stepneth succeeded Philipps in the representation of the shire, followed by a Wogan of Wiston, a hereditary foe of the owners of Picton. Soon after Wogan's second term of membership in 1621, when Philipps (now a baronet) was living on his Carmarthenshire property of Clog y fran and serving as sheriff of the county there, a violent quarrel broke out between the families, leading to two Star Chamber suits which involved also the Wogans of Boulston on one side, and Alban Stepneth and Philipps's numerous brothers on the other.[4]

Philipps made his will on 10 Jan. and died 27 Mar. 1629. He was buried at Slebech as he had requested. The Clog y fran lands with the 'growing grain, oxen, kine, bulls and pigs' were left to the widow, while the Pembrokeshire properties passed to the eldest son and executor, Richard, who proved the will 11 June 1629. Two unmarried daughters received £500 each and provision for their wedding clothes, and another daughter, Elizabeth, who was already married 'and I am given to understand in Ireland' – in fact she was married to Edward Medhope, clerk of the House of Commons in Ireland – received £250. Philipps left £12 to St. David's cathedral, and small bequests to his servants. The overseers of the will included his sons-in-law, Sir James Hamilton, and Sir Francis Annesley.[5]

[1] Dwnn, *Vis. Wales*, i. 114–15; *DWB*. [2] PCC 10 Peter; *Star Chamber*, ed. Edwards (Univ. Wales Bd. of Celtic Studies, Hist. and Law ser. i), 131; NLW, Chirk Castle mss. [3] Townshend, *Hist. Colls.* 245, 267; D'Ewes, 624, 649; *Exchequer*, ed. E. G. Jones (Univ. Wales Bd. of Celtic Studies, Hist. and Law ser. iv), 309–10. [4] *Star Chamber*, ed. Edwards, 210, 212. [5] PCC 63 Ridley.

A.H.D.

PHILIPPS, William (c.1530–73), of Picton, Pemb.

PEMBROKESHIRE   1559, 1572*

b. c.1530, 1st s. of John Philipps of Picton by Elizabeth, da. of Sir W. Griffith of Penrhyn, Caern. *m.* Jane, da. of Sir Thomas Perrot of Haroldston, 2da.; 1s. 1da. illegit.[1]
    Sheriff, Carm. 1553–4, Pemb. 1562–3; j.p. Carm., Pemb. from c.1559; commr. musters, Pemb. 1570.[2]

The family of Philipps stood in direct descent from the twelfth-century lords of Cilsant in western Carmarthenshire, which remained the centre of their territorial interest until William Philipps's grandfather Sir Thomas acquired the lordship and castle of Picton in

Pembrokeshire by marriage, and with it manors and lands scattered northwards from Milford Haven and eastwards into Carmarthenshire. Henceforth the family influence lay chiefly in Pembrokeshire, where William was assessed at the musters of 1570 at 'one light horseman furnished'. He was allied by marriage with most of the principal county families: his sisters were married into those of Wyriott of Orielton and Laugharne of St. Bride's, his daughters into those of Owen of Henllys and Stepneth of Prendergast. All these were sworn enemies of Sir John Perrot*, and the fact that Philipps was married to Perrot's half-sister did not prevent him from taking their side.[3]

In February 1559 while Philipps was in London for the Parliament, he and Perrot (with their respective servants) were involved in an affray in London, and bound over by the Council; this may be the context in which Philipps appears on the pardon roll for 1 Eliz. In the election at Haverfordwest in 1571, when Perrot's recent departure for Ireland enabled the opposing faction to muster forces, Philipps (who had rights in the borough) promoted the candidature of Alban Stepneth* against John Garnons*, Perrot's man. To discredit Perrot he sent information to the council about 'disorders' committed by Perrot's servants 'in his late setting forth into Ireland'; but the efforts of Stepneth and Philipps were nullified by the partiality of the mayor and sheriff, nominees of Perrot.[4]

Philipps's election for the shire in the following year was a triumph for the anti-Perrot faction, but his membership lasted less than a year. Vexed – according to a contemporary – by Perrot until he died, in March 1573, Philipps was buried, according to the wish he expressed in his will, in Slebech church. Presumably because she predeceased him there is no mention of his wife in the will Philipps made, 27 Feb. 1573, and which was proved by his brother Morgan, 28 Mar. following. The principal legatees were his mother, his daughters Mary and Elizabeth, and his brother and executor Morgan Philipps. Alban Stepneth and another son-in-law received sums of money, and provision was made for his illegitimate children and his servants. 'The right honourable and my singular good lord the Earl of Essex' received a gold chain and was appointed an overseer, along with Lady Gamage, and two local gentlemen. Philipps's outlying estates were divided between his two daughters, but Picton itself, after his mother's death, passed to his brother Morgan, whose descendants continued the line.[5]

[1] Dwnn, *Vis. Wales*, i. 114–15; PCC 10 Peter. [2] Lansd. 1218, f. 37; *CPR*, 1557–8, p. 364; 1560–3, p. 445; 1563–6, p. 364; Flenley, *Cal. Reg. Council, Marches of Wales*, 69. [3] Nicholas, *Annals of County Fams.* ii. 908; Dwnn, loc. cit.; Wards 7/14/99; Flenley, 74. [4] *APC*, vii. 55–6, 62; viii. 18; *CPR*, 1558–60, p. 197; *EHR*, lxi. 18–27; Neale, *Commons*, 255–60. [5] Lansd. 72, f. 4; Wards 7/14/99; C219/282/25–6; PCC 10 Peter.

A.H.D.

PHILLIPS, Fabian (c.1540–97), of Orlton, Herefs.

LEOMINSTER   1572

b. c.1540, 2nd s. of Robert Phillips of Yarpole and Leominster by Elizabeth, da. of John Price. *educ.* M. Temple 1560, called 1579. *m.* Margaret, da. of William Walter of Wimbledon, 1s.[1]

Member, council in the marches of Wales from 1575; assoc. justice of Chester, 2nd justice of assize, Anglesey circuit 1579–94; justice of assize, S. Wales by 1588; recorder, Carmarthen 9 Feb. 1578 to at least 1585; j.p. many Welsh and border counties from c.1580.[2]

Phillips was brought into Parliament for Leominster by his great-uncle, Sir James Croft*, high steward of the borough, whose faction he naturally supported in local politics. The opposition was thus ready to denigrate him as 'a young man, an utter barrister of small experience at the bar or bench, of no known living, saving a bailiwick or stewardship'. His activities in enforcing the government's religious policy gained him further enemies, notably the bishops of Hereford and St. David's, who complained that he undermined the administration of their dioceses. Still, he did not lack supporters. Whitgift wrote:

> For my own part I know not anything whereupon he can justly be charged, unless it be because he is stout and upright in judgment and not appliable to satisfy other men's affections and pleasures, as peradventure it is looked for. Truly, my lord, I find him one and the same man; but I see how hard it is for such to follow the rules of equity and justice without respect to please all men: and I would to God it were not altogether contrary.

And the bishop of Worcester said that he knew none better than Phillips 'in painfulness, in courage, in faithful and upright dealing'.[3]

No record has been found of any activities by Phillips in the first or second sessions of his one Parliament. On 25 Jan. 1581 he was put on the large committee handling both the subsidy bill and the bill for religion which became the Act to retain the Queen's Majesty's subjects in their due obedience. He was also named to committees dealing with slanderous words and practices (1 Feb. 1581), the reform of sheriffs (4 Feb.), a hospital at Ledbury, Herefordshire (4 Mar. 1581) and the reformation of fines and common recoveries (10 Mar.).[4]

In his career generally, his patron was Sir Francis Walsingham. A judicial member of the council in the marches of Wales, he was present at discussions on reform of abuses in 1576 and 1590, and acted as intermediary between Croft and Burghley when this matter was broached in 1589. He was a frequent member of commissions, including those for piracy in Glamorgan and Monmouthshire and for musters in Denbighshire. In 1590, Thomas Atkins*, the attorney in the marches, unsuccessfully accused him before the Privy Council of associating with recusants. Phillips instituted a suit for slander in the Star Chamber. The case lasted until at least 1594 and while it was in progress both men were suspended from their attendance at the council in the marches.[5]

Phillips bought Orlton in 1580. He also possessed the manor of Bovington and other lands in Worcestershire. He died 15 Feb. 1597, and was succeeded by his son Andrew. No will has been found.[6]

[1] *Vis. Herefs.* ed. Weaver, 57. [2] Flenley, *Cal. Reg. Council, Marches of Wales,* 145–6; PRO, add. misc. roll to patent roll 39 Eliz.; *HMC Hatfield,* ii. 203; P. H. Williams, *Council in the Marches,* 270–1; *APC,* xvi. 106; W. R. Williams, *Welsh Judges,* 89. [3] St. Ch. 5 Eliz.P17/31, P55/17, P59/23; SP12/107/11, 110/13, 131/42, 148/31; Skeel, *Council in the Marches,* 110, 112; Strype, *Annals,* iii(1), 171–2; *Whitgift,* i. 178–9; Lansd. 29, f. 99; 36, f. 68; *APC,* xii. 286; *HMC Hatfield,* ii. 203–4. [4] *CJ,* i. 120, 121, 122, 131, 133; D'Ewes, 288, 302. [5] *Egerton Pprs.* (Cam. Soc. xii), 104–5; *Bull. Bd. Celtic Studies,* xvi. 291–2; *APC,* ix. 165, 298, 317, 339, 341, 379; xi. 48, 116, 190; xvii. 267, 292, 293; xviii. 108, 357; xix. 429; P. H. Williams, 83, 152; Lansd. 60, f. 112, 63, f. 93; *CSP Dom.* 1547–80, pp. 540, 543, 597, 627; 1581–90, pp. 69, 106; E351/541, f. 223; Flenley, 200; Add. 37045, f. 5; Harl. 6995, f. 161; 7004, f. 274. [6] St. Ch. 5 Eliz./P59/23; C142/254/1.

w.j.j.

PHILLIPS, Thomas (c.1556–?1626), of London.

HASTINGS   1584, 1586

b. c.1556, 1st s. of William Phillips of London by Joan, da. of Thomas Houghton. *educ.* ?Trinity, Camb. 1569, BA 1574, MA 1577. *m.* Mary, *s.p. suc.* fa. 1590.[1]

Servant to (Sir) Francis Walsingham* prob. by 1578, to Earl of Essex c.1592; customs official by 1591, collector of petty customs and tonnage and poundage on exports, London by 1594; servant to (Sir) Robert Cecil* by 1600.[2]

The identity of this Member is a matter of inference. No local man of the name connected with Hastings has been found, and it is therefore conceivable that the MP may have been nominated in 1584 by the lord warden of the Cinque Ports, Lord Cobham. His re-election in 1586 would have followed the government advice that the same Members should be chosen as in the previous Parliament. To suggest that the Member was Sir Francis Walsingham's servant, the decipherer Thomas Phillips, may at first seem unlikely, if only because Lord Cobham belonged to Burghley's political group whereas Walsingham – who must have asked Cobham for the seat – belonged to the Leicester group. However, when Lord Cobham's brother, Sir Henry Cobham *alias* Brooke* was ambassador in France from 1579 to 1583 – having Walsingham as a colleague on a special mission in 1581 – Phillips was evidently used by him in deciphering and seems to have been allotted to his service. Consequently the assumption that Phillips was a Cobham nominee in the Parliaments of 1584 and 1586 is reasonable. Though the presence of Edward Phelips in both 1584 and 1586 Parliaments makes

certainty impossible, the likelihood is that the Hastings burgess took no part in the affairs of either Parliament.

Phillips the decipherer first comes to notice in June 1578 when, as 'young Phillips', a servant of Sir Francis Walsingham, he attended Sir Amias Paulet at the Paris embassy as, already, a skilled decipherer and code breaker. Presumably Walsingham was using him as an agent in foreign intelligence work. A letter of March 1583 suggests that he was then travelling on the Continent as a private agent of Walsingham.[3]

Few details of his family background and private life have survived. His father, who died in 1590, was a cloth merchant of modest wealth, and at the time of the heralds' visitation of London in 1568 was one of the customers for wool in the port. The design of the signet ring which Thomas used to seal documents – probably the one mentioned in his father's will – may indicate some relationship to the Phelips family of Montacute. At different times Phillips owned land in Suffolk, Yorkshire and Staffordshire, but his home was London. He inherited a house in Leadenhall Street, and also owned property at Holborn, Chiswick and elsewhere. Because his mother lived until 1613, part of the inheritance did not come to him until after he needed it most. As partial compensation for the paucity of information about Phillips there is a description of him in 1586 by Mary Queen of Scots: 'of low stature, slender every way, dark yellow haired on the head, and clear yellow bearded, eaten in the face with smallpox [and] of short sight'.[4]

It may have been Phillips's puritan views which first brought him to Walsingham's notice. By the mid-1580s he was one of Walsingham's most important confidential servants. The major part of his work, until the secretary's death in 1590, was concerned with the detection of Catholic threats from home and abroad. Walsingham employed many 'intelligencers' or agents on the Continent. Sometimes they reported directly to him, but it was more usual for letters to be sent to Phillips. Under such names as 'John Morice' and 'Peter Halins, merchant', Phillips received despatches from Europe and Scotland and from agents at home. Writers to 'John Morice' had to pretend to be Catholics and one despatch even referred to 'Phillips, that enemy to the cause'. Occasionally he went abroad himself to investigate matters of particular importance. Several times during the 1580s and 1590s he returned to Paris and to other places in France and the Netherlands. Some of the devices used to ensure secrecy can be studied in the State Papers. 'Harry Jobson and his brokers', for example, was the cipher for 'the Queen and her Council'. Occasionally communications had secret messages added in onion juice.

As well as deciphering despatches sent to Walsingham, Phillips handled letters intercepted by the government. He claimed that it took him 20 days to break a cipher about a Spanish invasion plan, probably that of 1593. Sometimes he was not so successful, as a letter to Walsingham, dated 1582, suggests:

> According to your Lordship's order, I have travailed to my uttermost in the cipher which you sent me, wherein I have had such success as appears by what accompanies this; if not so good as was wished, yet I hope sufficient to satisfy her Majesty, who shall thereby find the substance of the letter ... Truly I have had to do, as your Lordship knows, with many ciphers, but I never lit upon any wherewith I was more cumbered.

Of necessity Phillips had a wide command of languages – French, Spanish, Italian, Latin and German at least – and, according to an acquaintance, the ability to 'write any man's hand if he had once seen it as the man himself that writ it'. Naturally his contemporaries were wary of him. One called him a 'notable knave', another 'a severe Huguenot ... greedy of honour and profit'. In any case, after the death of Walsingham in 1590 his affairs took a turn for the worse. In 1592 he was deciphering letters for the Earl of Essex, through the recommendation of Francis Bacon*, and he tried to gain the notice of the Cecils. But he tried to milk too much and too soon a lucrative little job in the customs, perhaps obtained on his father's death, and by the end of 1594 he was heavily in debt to the Crown. Allowed a year's respite, he failed to meet his commitments, and early in 1596 was in prison owing more than £11,500 and facing the Queen's 'tempestuous displeasure'. In June 1597 he was released, 'in consideration of his faithful service', but soon recommitted. As late as 1609 the debt was still considerable – indeed there is no evidence that it was ever repaid.[5]

Even in prison he continued his deciphering, but

> as Samson's strength lay in his hair, so my cunning depended upon the Queen's favour, which, being lost, my spirits became dull.

Gradually, from about 1600, his reputation recovered sufficiently for Cecil to employ him again, at first as an agent in Europe and then as a decipherer. But James I never forgave him for his part in bringing Mary to the block (for which he was still enjoying a pension of 100 marks a year), his contemporaries distrusted him, and his correspondence with the Catholic Hugh Owen proved his undoing. In January 1605 he was 'apprehended and committed, and all his papers seized'. Released in April, he complained that his correspondence with Owen had been solely in the line of business and expressed annoyance at the 'vexatious' manner in which his private papers had been searched and his servants and relatives cross-examined. He resumed his duties and took part in the seizure of the Gunpowder conspirators. But when Owen was found to be involved in the plot, Phillips was put in the Tower, confidence in his integrity gone for ever.[6]

Little is known of his last years. His debt to the Crown was still a burden and in 1618 he was involved in a costly lawsuit. In 1622 he was again in prison, but optimistic enough to petition for an ecclesiastical post 'of the inferior sort'. The last references to him show him in prison in 1625. Accused of revealing the contents of a letter he had deciphered, he wrote a pathetic note describing his career in Elizabeth's reign to a government which was obviously ignorant of his past services. He claimed that he had remained loyal, despite the offer of £1,000 and an annuity of 1,000 marks from a foreign agent. Some months later he was still in prison when called upon to decipher a letter in Spanish. An old man now, confined to prison, deep in debt, his lands seized, he had little to hope for. By March 1626 he was dead.[7]

[1] J. Morris, *Sir Amias Paulet's Letter Bk.* 114–19; *Vis. London* (Harl. Soc. xvii), 161; PCC 13 Sainberbe. [2] *CSP For.* 1578–9, p. 37; Spedding, *Bacon,* i. 117–19; *Cal. Carew Pprs.* iii. 231; F. Dietz, *Eng. Public Finance 1558–1641,* p. 328; *CSP Dom.* 1598–1601, pp. 420, 442–3. [3] *CSP For.* 1578–9, p. 37; *CSP Dom.* Add. 1580–1625, p. 86; *HMC Hatfield,* ii. 410. [4] PCC 13 Sainberbe, 23 Capell; W. A. Copinger, *Suff. Manors,* v. 172; *VCH Yorks. N. Riding,* ii. 445; Morris, 119. [5] C. Read, *Walsingham,* ii. 336; iii. passim; Spedding, i. 117–19, 251, 252; SP12/275/78; *HMC Hatfield,* v.40, 101; vi. 118, 351, 391, 511, 513; vii. 84, 150; Lansd. 31, f. 62; 82, f. 180; 83, ff. 220, 233 seq., 241; 84, f. 58. [6] *HMC Hatfield,* vi. 511, 513; vii. 96–7; *CSP Dom.* 1601–10, passim, esp. 1603–10, pp. 13, 90, 189; *Chamberlain Letters* ed. McClure, i. 202; H. Foley, *Recs. Eng. Prov. Soc. of Jesus,* iii. 513. [7] *CSP Dom.* Add. 1580–1625, pp. 595–6, 630; 1623–5, p. 482; 1625–6, p. 169; 1627–8, p. 81.

M.R.P.

PICKERING, Christopher (c.1556–1621), of Threlkeld, Cumb., later of Ormside *alias* Prinshead, Westmld.

CUMBERLAND 1597

b. c.1556, o.s. of William Pickering by Winifred, da. of Sir Lancelot Threlkeld of Threlkeld. *unm.*, 1da. *suc.* fa. 1587. Kntd. 1607.

J.p. Cumb. from c.1590; sheriff 1590–1, 1605–6, 1607–8, 1611–12; dep. warden of the west march 1601; commr. for the borders 1608.

The senior line of the Pickering family died with Sir Christopher Pickering in 1516. His only daughter, Anne, was married first to Sir Francis Weston, the reputed lover of Anne Boleyn, and secondly to Sir Henry Knyvet. She was thus the mother of three Elizabethan parliamentary figures: Sir Richard Weston, Sir Henry Knyvet and his brother, Thomas. The family name of Pickering was preserved in Cumberland by Sir Christopher's brothers, the youngest of whom, William, married Winifred, coheir of Sir Lancelot Threlkeld, and thereby acquired the manor of Threlkeld, to which Christopher Pickering succeeded in 1587.[1]

Pickering enjoyed the favour of Lord Scrope, warden of the west march, whose influence may have helped Pickering's election in 1597. As knight of the shire in 1597 he could have attended committees on enclosures (5 Nov.), the poor law (5, 22 Nov.), armour and weapons (8 Nov.), the penal laws (8 Nov.), monopolies (10 Nov.) and the subsidy (15 Nov.). About this time Pickering signed a report, drawn up by Scrope and other Cumberland justices, deploring the unwillingness of some inhabitants to pay for arms for the defence of the border. In October 1598 he was declared by Lancelot Carleton, brother of Thomas Carleton*, to be 'affected to Francis Dacres and to have entered into a most dangerous combination by oath and league' with other gentlemen of the march, but these accusations, made in a letter to Robert Cecil, had no effect. Scrope appointed Pickering to be his deputy when he went to court in March 1601.[2]

The problems of the border were not solved by the accession of James I, and the lawlessness of the Graham family continued to disturb the peace of the locality. In September 1605 Pickering was sworn in by the Earl of Cumberland as one of eight constables of the forest of Nichol and the parish of Arthuret, near the border. On 25 Apr. in the following year he and six other gentlemen complained to the border commissioners that 'fore-bearance used towards any that were border malefactors' merely 'bred greater hurt to the country and greater insolence in them', for they were so rooted in a 'desolate' kind of life that it was impossible to reform them. Later in the year, when it was decided to transport the Grahams to Ireland, Pickering, as sheriff, offered to contribute £5 towards the project, but his example was followed by few of the gentry. In 1608 he became a border commissioner with an annual fee of 100 marks, and in November 1609 he and (Sir) John Dalston* were instructed by Salisbury to survey Carlisle castle.[3]

Some time before his death he acquired the manor of Ormside in Westmorland with extensive adjacent property. He died 15 Jan. 1621 and was succeeded by his two sisters, Winifred, formerly wife of Christopher Crackenthorpe, and Mary, wife of Thomas Dalston.[4]

[1] C142/222/31; Vis. Yorks. (Harl. Soc. xvi), 250–1; Border Pprs. ii. 736; CSP Dom. 1603–10, p. 440; Nicolson and Burn, Hist. Cumb. and Westmld. i. 261, 499. [2] D'Ewes, 552, 553, 555, 557, 561; Border Pprs. ii. passim. [3] HMC 10th Rep. IV, 237, 252, 260; CSP Dom. 1603–10, pp. 440, 576. [4] Nicolson and Burn, i. 413; C142/389/112.

R.C.G.

PICKESSE, Drew (b.1564), of Brambletye, nr. East Grinstead, Suss.

EAST GRINSTEAD 1586

b. 1564, s. of James Pickesse of Brambletye. m. Anne, da. of William Muschamp of Unsted and Godalming, Surr. suc. fa. 1590.

Hardly anything is known of Pickesse, whose father's name appears at the head of the list of burgesses on the election return, and who was related to both John Agmondeshams.*

Suss. Rec. Soc. xiv. 185; Vis. Surr. (Harl. Soc. xliii), 22, 54; C219/30/101; PCC 71 Lewyn.

J.E.M.

PIERREPONT, Henry (1546–1616), of Holme Pierrepont, Notts.

NOTTINGHAMSHIRE 1572

b. 18 Sept. 1546, 1st s. of Sir George Pierrepont[†] of Holme Pierrepont by his 2nd w. Winifred, da. and h. of Sir William Thwaites of ?Manningtree, Essex. educ. Trinity Hall, Camb. 1561; G. Inn 1564. m. Frances, da. of Sir William Cavendish[†] of Chatsworth, Derbys., 1s., Robert* at least 1da., Grace, w. of George Manners*. suc. fa. 1564. Kntd. 21 Apr. 1603.

J.p. Notts. from c.1573, temp. rem. c.1587, j.p.q. by 1593, sheriff 1575–6, 1601–2; recorder, Nottingham from 1603.

Aged 17 when his father died, Pierrepont became a ward of Roger Manners I*, esquire of the body to the Queen and uncle of the 5th Earl of Rutland. His mother soon remarried and his wardship was granted to his stepfather, Sir Gervase Clifton[†] of Clifton, Nottinghamshire, in May 1565. Pierrepont's estate, lying mostly in Nottinghamshire, with one manor, Scarcliffe, in Derbyshire, was valued at a little under £300 a year.[1]

The Elizabethan Pierreponts were recusants, Henry's younger brother Gervase being particularly 'obstinate'. Henry, though more discreet, fell foul of the government more than once. It was probably he who was arrested in 1567 for attending mass 'at the ambassador's.' In 1581 he was again detained, this time on the more serious charge of entertaining Edmund Campion and other priests over the previous Christmas. When Campion confessed, Pierrepont's house was searched and he and Gervase were summoned before the Council. They later made a full confession in the Star Chamber and were pardoned. Henry avoided further trouble until November 1592, when Sir Thomas Stanhope* and other j.p.s ordered him to relinquish for the second time his office of justice of the peace, on grounds of recusancy. Pierrepont strongly denied the charge in a protest to the 7th Earl of Shrewsbury, his brother-in-law and Stanhope's enemy, and the Earl was probably successful in quashing the order. In return for the Earl's patronage, and no doubt as an expression of his resentment towards Stanhope, Pierrepont was a prominent supporter of Shrewsbury's candidate, Sir Charles Cavendish*, against the rival Stanhope faction in the county election of 1593. His canvassing for Cavendish was at first misunderstood by Stanhope, who apparently suspected that Pierrepont (who had sat for the county in 1572) intended to stand again himself. He did not, however, enter Parliament again, although his son Robert did, no doubt with Shrewsbury's backing. Pierrepont's ties with Shrewsbury were further strengthened in 1601 when his son married the Earl's niece, Gertrude. Two years later the Earl ranked him with Sir John Byron as 'the best and principal gentleman' in the county, and it was his influence which largely explains Pierrepont's election as recorder of Nottingham in succession to Richard Parkins*. Pierrepont died in March 1616, aged 69. He was buried at Holme Pierrepont, where his wife had a monument erected. In his will, dated 8 July 1615, he made bequests totalling £100 to his servants. His wife was appointed sole executrix of the estate, which descended to Robert.[2]

[1] *Vis. Notts.* (Harl. Soc. iv), 50–1; Wards 9/138/466–9; *HMC 9th Rep.* pt. 2, p. 375; *Nottingham Recs.* iv. 426; C142/140/153; *CPR*, 1563–6, p. 328. [2] *Cath. Rec. Soc. Misc.* i. 49; ii. 231 et passim; *APC*, xiii. 170–1, 247–8, 260–1; Coll. of Arms, Talbot mss, transcribed by G. R. Batho, H. f. 463; Lodge, *Illus.* iii(2), pp. 71, 72; Neale, *Commons*, 65–6; Add. 12506, f. 189; Thoroton, *Notts.* ed. Throsby, i. 180; York prob. reg. 34/76; C142/362/171.

B.D.

PIERREPONT, Robert (1584–1643), of Holme Pierrepont, Notts.

NOTTINGHAMSHIRE 1601

b. 6 Aug. 1584, o.s. of Henry Pierrepont* by his w. Frances. *educ.* Oriel, Oxf. 1596; G. Inn 1600. *m.* 8 Jan. 1601, Gertrude, da. and coh. of Henry Talbot, bro. of Gilbert, 7th Earl of Shrewsbury, 5s. 3da. *suc.* fa. 1616; *cr.* Visct. Newark 1627; Earl of Kingston-upon-Hull 1628.

J.p. Notts., sheriff 1615–16; lt.-gen. King's forces Cambs., Hunts., Lincs., Norf. and Rutland 1643.

In view of the family's Catholic sympathies it is likely that Pierrepont owed his election for the county at 17 to the influence of his in-laws. He could have attended the main business committee (3 Nov.), and the committee on monopolies (23 Nov.). Until the outbreak of the civil war he devoted himself to the improvement of his estates. The war divided his family and resulted in his own death. Two younger sons were Parliamentarians, while Pierrepont and his heir were Royalists. Pierrepont established his headquarters at Gainsborough, was attacked and surprised by Lord Willoughby of Parham, and taken prisoner. While being escorted by pinnace to Hull, he was fired upon by Royalist troops and killed, 1643, and was buried at Cuckney, Nottinghamshire.

CP; DNB (Pierrepont, Robert); D'Ewes, 624, 649; *Proc. Soc. Antiqs.* (ser. 2), ix. 286 seq.

B.D.

PIGOTT, John (c.1550–by 1627), of Gray's Inn, London and Edlesborough, Bucks.

BEDFORD	1589, 1593
BODMIN	1601

b. c.1550, 5th s. of Francis Pigott of Stratton, Beds. by his 2nd w. Margery, da. of Sir John St. John of Bletsoe, wid. of Henry Grey (*d.*1545) of Towcester, Northants.; half-bro. of Thomas I*. *educ.* St. John's, Camb. 1566; G. Inn 1570, called 1581, pensioner 1584. *m.* (1) Winifred, da. and h. of Thomas Sankey of Edlesborough, Bucks., 2s. 3da.; (2) 1592, Winifred, da. of Ambrose Dormer of Ascot and Milton, Oxon., wid. of Sir William Hawtrey of Chequers, Bucks., 3da.

Pigott was a London lawyer, still described as of Gray's Inn as late as 1591. In a Chancery suit two years later, however, he was described as of Edlesborough, where the death of his first wife had left him in sole possession of a manor. Pigott's returns for Bedford doubtless resulted from his local connexions. At Bodmin it was probably Sir Robert Cecil who brought him in, for no ascertained reason unless perhaps to reinforce the lawyers in the House. The lawyers in the 1601 Parliament were collectively appointed to over a score of committees dealing with the main issues of the day (monopolies, 23 Nov.; Dunkirk pirates, 3 Dec.; and the export of ordnance, 8 Dec.), legal matters, and a variety of other topics.

Pigott's second marriage, which followed speedily upon his first wife's death, was to a wealthy widow. Her first husband's father claimed that he had settled the manor of Tetchwick in Ludgershall, Buckinghamshire (worth more than £200 a year) on her for life, instead of a sum of £500 previously agreed. By an oversight, the recognizance which had bound him to pay the £500 had not been discharged but remained 'in extremity of law in full force', and Pigott pressed for its enforcement. Pigott had probably been dead for some time by 1627, when his son was selling off the Edlesborough estate.

VCH Bucks. iii. 352; *Vis. Beds.* (Harl. Soc. xix), 46, 53, 132; *G. Inn Pension Bk.* i. 49, 63; *Vis. Oxon.* (Harl. Soc. v), 142; *APC*, xxii. 162; D'Ewes, 634, 635, 641, 642, 647, 649, 651, 657, 658, 662, 666, 668, 672, 674, 677, 681; C3/247/64; C2 Eliz/H11/51.

A.M.M.

PIGOTT, Thomas I (c.1526–79), of Stratton and Edworth, Beds.

BEDFORDSHIRE 1559

b. c.1526, 1st s. of Francis Pigott of Stratton by his 1st w. Elinor, da. and h. of John Enderby of Stratton; half-bro. of John*. *m.* (1) Anne, da. of Sir Richard Rich†, 1st Baron Rich, 3s. 5da.; (2) Elizabeth, da. of William Thynne of Erith, Kent, 2s. 3da. *suc.* fa. c.1552.

J.p. Beds. from c.1552; sheriff, Beds. and Bucks. 1552–3, 1557–8, Mich. to Nov. 1572; escheator, Beds. 1554–5.

Pigott's father's second wife was a St. John, and no doubt this helped Pigott to be elected for the county in 1559. Still, he had excellent estates at Stratton and

Edworth, the manor of Kingworth, Hertfordshire, and also lands in Northamptonshire which he sold off in the 1560s, partly to the Cave family. Despite his having held a local office in the previous reign, Pigott was classified in 1564 as 'earnest in religion'. His will was dated 15 Mar. 1579 and proved on 31 Mar.

C142/95/1, 160/11, 193/90; *Vis. Beds.* (Harl. Soc. xix), 47; *CSP Dom.* 1547–80, p. 374; Feet of fines, Beds., Trinity, 2 and 3 P. and M.; Wards 7/20/294; *CPR*, 1558–60, pp. 364–5; 1563–6, p. 128; *Cam. Misc.* ix(3), p. 28; PCC 13 Bakon.

N.M.F.

PIGOTT, Thomas II, of Doddershall, Bucks.

AYLESBURY 1589

1st s. of Thomas Pigott (*d.* 1606), of Doddershall by Mary, da. and coh. of Sir Ralph Lane of Hogshaw, Bucks. and Norton, Northants. *m.* (1) Dorothy, da. and coh. of Henry Cottenham of Norf., 1s. 1da.; (2) a da. of Sir John Allott, alderman and ld. mayor of London, *s.p.*

The Pigotts of Doddershall were descended from Thomas, the third son of Thomas Pigott of Whaddon, a serjeant-at-law under Henry VIII. Pigott himself was overshadowed by his father, a j.p. and sheriff in 1593–4, and only one certain reference to him in connexion with local government has been found, his signing an agreement on purveyance for the county in April 1593. He must have been brought into Parliament for Aylesbury by his neighbours, the Pakingtons. No record has been found of any parliamentary activity and the date of his death is unknown.

Vis. Beds. (Harl. Soc. xix), 46; G. Lipscomb, *Bucks.* i. 406; *Verney Pprs.* (Cam. Soc. lvi), 86–7.

A.M.M.

PILKINGTON, Robert (c.1560–1605), of Rivington, Lancs. and Gray's Inn, London.

CLITHEROE 1589

b. c.1560, 2nd but 1st surv. s. of George Pilkington of Rivington by Anne, da. of Geoffrey Shakerley of Holme, Cheshire. *educ.* Rivington g.s. 1575; Staple Inn; G. Inn 1586. *m.* Elizabeth, *s.p. suc.* fa. 1597.
Feodary, Lancs. from 1592; farmer of the Queen's mills at Earl Shilton, Leics. by 1592.

The Pilkingtons of Rivington were a younger branch of an old established Lancashire family. Pilkington himself, after spending Mary's reign in protestant circles on the Continent, had a legal practice in London, maintaining chambers in Gray's Inn at least until 1596, though there is no record of his call to the bar. He may have been engaged in legal work for the duchy of Lancaster, which would explain his return at the duchy borough of Clitheroe in 1589 and his later becoming farmer of the mills at the

duchy manor of Earl Shilton. But as he was a Member for Clitheroe in the only Parliament held while Walsingham was chancellor of the duchy, and as he was a nephew of James Pilkington, the puritan bishop of Durham who died in 1575, it is possible that Walsingham saw him as a favourite candidate. No record has been found of any activities in Parliament.

Pilkington inherited debts arising from his father's litigation, and his financial situation deteriorated still further in consequence of his attempts to enclose the waste at Rivington, and to buy up the leases of 22 tenants at a cost of £4,000. A London grocer who foreclosed on a debt of £250 received the profits from 1602, but Pilkington continued to reside there until his death, which occurred in 1605. His will directed the executors to sell the property outright to pay his debts and legacies. It was not until 1611 that a sale was arranged. His brother James received an annuity secured on the estate. His widow subsequently married Thomas Brocket of Essendon, Hertfordshire.

Pilkington, *Hist. Fam. of Pilkington*, 115–18, 247, 249–50; M. M. Kay, *Hist. Rivington and Blackrod G.S.* 194; Surtees, *Durham*, i. p. lxxii.

A.M.M.

PINCHON, John (aft.1510–73), of Writtle, Essex.

DOVER 1571

b. aft. 1510,[1] 4th s. of Nicholas Pinchon of Writtle and London, by his 2nd w. Agnes. *educ.* New Coll. Oxf. *m.* Jane, da. of Sir Richard Empson, 4s. 2da.[2]
J.p.q. Essex from c.1569.

The John Pinchon resident in Writtle in 1571 is the only man identified who is likely to have been MP for Dover in 1571, but no connexion between him and the constituency has been traced. There is no corroboration for the statement[3] that a John Pinchnee (sic) was an official of Dover castle, but the inference must be that it was the warden of the Cinque Ports who nominated Pinchon at the request of someone at court. Who this might have been is another problem. Sir William Petre* owned the manor of Writtle but was surely too old and sick to concern himself with the matter. Either Sir Thomas Smith* or Lord Burghley might have been behind it, Burghley being the better guess because of his connexion with the Exchequer, on the staff of which were at least three members of the Essex family of Osborne, to whom Pinchon was related by marriage.

Though the Pinchon family had been settled at Writtle since 1328, Pinchon's father was a London butcher, sheriff of the city shortly before his death in 1533. He bequeathed his property in London and Writtle to his wife, and left 50 marks for each of his four sons, who were still all under age when the will was made in February 1529. How John, the youngest of them (judging from the order in the will), came to own the entire Essex property by the time of his death in 1573 is unknown. As early as 1553 'John Pinchon, gentleman' is to be found, on the pardon roll, in possession of the family mansion at Writtle. Perhaps Nicholas's other sons, if they were still alive, continued to live in London, though no trace of them has been found.[4]

Pinchon was not put on the commission of the peace until shortly before his death. His name is on the lists of justices for the assizes held on 8 Mar. and 12 July 1571, but there is no indication that he attended or was excused. He certainly attended quarter sessions on 10 Jan. 1572. Some of his land purchases were made very late in life, as he reveals in his will, and these may have increased his social standing sufficiently to ensure his appointment. There are almost no references to him in the *State Papers* or *Acts of the Privy Council*, apart from his signature on a certificate of August 1571 recording the punishment of rogues and vagabonds in the hundred of Chelmsford. He married the youngest daughter of Sir Richard Empson, formerly chancellor of the duchy of Lancaster, who was executed in 1510.[5]

Pinchon's will, made 10 Nov., proved 11 Dec. 1573, is that of a comparatively wealthy man. He left 500 marks for his daughter Elizabeth at her marriage, and settled land and annuities on his three surviving sons. His estates, which included land in Writtle, Roxwell and Bradwell, were left to his wife. Among the legatees was 'my singular good master, Master Doctor White, warden of the new college of Winchester in Oxford'. The widow, who later married Thomas Wilson*, the secretary of state, and died in 1577, was appointed sole executrix, with Pinchon's 'special good brother-in-law Mr. Peter Osborne' as supervisor. He left 20s. for the repair of Writtle church and £3 6s. 8d. for the poor of the parish. A brass in the church records his marriage and the date of his death – 29 Nov. 1573. On another mutilated tablet effigies of his four sons can still be seen. One of his grandsons, William, founded the town of Springfield, Massachusetts.[6]

[1] His e. bro. was not yet 21 in Feb. 1529. [2] *Essex Rev.* xvi. 175; *Vis. Essex* (Harl. Soc. xiii), 266, 470; *LP Hen. VIII*, xxi(2), p. 420. [3] *Dover Annals*, 378. [4] Essex RO, D/DP M540, ex inf. Dr. F. G. Emmison; PCC 2 Hogen; C142/173/41; *CPR*, 1553–4, p. 457; *LP Hen. VIII*, xii(2), p. 355. [5] Essex RO, Q/SR 38/34; *CSP Dom.* 1547–80, p. 418. [6] PCC 38 Peter; *Essex Arch. Soc. Trans.* n.s. ix. 58–9; S. E. Morrison, *Mass. Hist. Soc. Proc.* (1931), pp. 67–107.

M.R.P.

PINDAR, *see* PYNDER

PISTOR *alias* BAKER,[1] John (*d.* 1574), of Sherborne, Dorset.

WAREHAM 1571

?s. of William Pistor *alias* Baker by Rebecca, da. of William Skilling of Wilts. *m.* Emmeline, 2da.[2]

Gent. pens. 1549–64; regarder, Gillingham forest, Dorset 1568.[3]

In 1564 Pistor disposed of his appointment as a gentleman pensioner to Richard Zouche of Somerset, brother-in-law of the 3rd Lord Monteagle, in return for an annuity of 40 marks. In 1571 the Privy Council began to press Monteagle to pay up, and perhaps Pistor's return for Wareham to the Parliament of that year had something to do with this. In any event Pistor was in all probability returned through the influence of the 2nd Earl of Bedford. One of Pistor's relations was a deputy in the ordnance department to Bedford's son-in-law the Earl of Warwick,[4] and another was the puritan Tristram Pistor who sat for Stockbridge in 1571. Except for a reference to the fraudulent conveyances committee (11 Apr. 1571),[5] which could be to either Tristram or John, the entries in the journals for 1571 refer to Tristram Pistor.

Pistor died in 1574, his will being proved 3 Aug. Despite repeated applications, Monteagle had still not paid the annuity, and on 6 Dec. the Privy Council wrote to him again, telling him to pay the arrears to Pistor's daughter Grace, the executrix and residuary legatee. On 4 Jan. 1575 they warned Monteagle to pay the money 'without delay' or he would be brought before them. Pistor left bequests to the poor and to his daughters said 'I wish you both your heart's desires'.[6]

[1] Browne Willis, *Notitia Parliamentaria* (1715–50), ii. 493 has *Baker*; the ms *Pistor*. [2] W. Berry, *Co. Genealogies, Hants*, 262–3; Hutchins, *Dorset*, iv. 180; *Som. Wills*. iii. 118; PCC 32 Martyn. [3] LC2/4/1, f. 23; Hutchins, iii. 621. [4] *CSP Dom*. 1581–90, p. 283. [5] *CJ*, i. 84. [6] *APC*, viii. 9, 137, 320, 331; PCC 32 Martyn.

P.W.H.

PISTOR, Tristram, of Upper Eldon, nr. Stockbridge, Hants.

STOCKBRIDGE 1571, 1572

1st s. of Robert Pistor of Upper Eldon by Dorothy, da. of John Fauntleroy of Folke, Dorset. *m.* (1) Alice, da. of Richard Waller of Stoke Charity, 2s.; (2) Anne, da. of John Wadham of Catherstone, Dorset, *s.p.*

The Pistors had long held the manor of Upper Eldon, four miles from Stockbridge. Pistor himself claimed to be woodward of nearby property belonging to the duchy of Lancaster, in the face of opposition from William, 3rd Lord Sandys, and Henry Gifford*, his fellow-MP for Stockbridge in 1572, who together sued him in the duchy court for interference with their rights of common. Possibly a connexion with the duchy was responsible for Pistor's return for Stockbridge, possibly he was recommended by one of his influential relatives, Sir William Paulet*, or Richard Kingsmill*, who was first cousin to Alice Waller, Pistor's wife. Pistor evidently sympathized with the large puritan faction in Hampshire, of which Kingsmill was a leader, for he was distinguished in the Commons by a single-minded advocacy of puritan ends. Except for the mention of a Mr. Baker on the fraudulent conveyances committee (11 Apr. 1571), which could as well mean John Baker, all his parliamentary activities were to do with puritanism. On 14 Apr. 1571, described as 'a gentleman betwixt the age of 50 and 60 years ... with a grave and seemly countenance and a good natural eloquence', he spoke on William Strickland's bill for the reformation of the Prayer Book. He was sorry, he said, that the Commons neglected measures for the salvation of souls in favour of bills which were 'terrene, yea trifles in comparison', such as subsidies, crowns, kingdoms; they should seek first the Kingdom of Heaven. The anonymous diarist of that Parliament considered that Pistor presented his arguments 'with vehemency that there lacked no modesty, and with such eloquence that it neither seemed studied nor overmuch affected.' Pistor returned to the charge on 19 May 1572. 'It grieveth him to hear any mislike so good a bill' as that for the reformation of rites and ceremonies, which would have exempted puritan, but not Catholic, dissenters from the Act of Uniformity. Somewhat naively he had 'no doubt of the Queen's Majesty's or bishops' good inclination to the furtherance of this bill'. He was put on the committee of the bill the next day. On the third reading of the same bill (20 May) he was 'sorry to see how as well the last Parliament as this we are slow to further religion' and feared that 'the rod which hath yet but shaken us will shortly destroy us.' He still wished 'the bill to have furtherance and we to give life to the bishops. It shall come to their consideration. He doubteth not that which we have well begun, they will give perfection.' He spoke again in the debate on the unlearned ministry, 29 Feb. 1576, to move 'with great zeal' the drafting of a petition to the Queen against 'the unlearnedness of the ministry, abuse of excommunication, want of discipline, dispensations, and tolerations for non-residency and such like', and was put on the ensuing committee. His only recorded activity in the third session is his membership of the committee on the Queen's safety, 14 Mar. 1581.[1]

Nothing further has been ascertained about Pistor. The namesake who married the sister of John Fitzjames* and died in 1601, leaving an eldest child born about 1579, was probably his son.[2]

[1] Vis. Hants (Harl. Soc. lxiv), 3, 140, 148; Lincs. Peds. (Harl. Soc. lii), 786; Hutchins, Dorset, ii. 216; iv. 180; VCH Hants iv. 470, 477; CJ, i. 84, 96, 109, 134. [2] Som. N. and Q. xvi. 180; C142/268/131.

A.H.

PLEYDELL, Gabriel (by 1519–90/1), of Midgehall in Lydiard Tregoze, Wilts.

WOOTTON BASSETT	1553 (Mar.)
MARLBOROUGH	1555
WOOTTON BASSETT	1563

b. by 1519, 4th s. of William Pleydell of Midgehall, Wilts. and Coleshill, Berks. by Agnes, da. and coh. of John or Robert Reason of Corfe Castle, Dorset; bro. of John*. m. (1) Anne, da. and coh. of Henry Stockes (Stokes) of Sussex, 1s. d.v.p. 1da.; (2) by 17 Nov. 1563, Elizabeth, s.p.; (3) Jane, s.p.[1]

Chief ranger and keeper of Savernake forest, Wilts. by ?1554; receiver-gen. for Anne, Duchess of Somerset in 1554.[2]

Pleydell supported Sir John Thynne* in the disputed shire election of 1559, and four years later could doubtless count on Thynne's influence to augment his own claim to one of the Wootton Bassett seats. He had represented the borough once before; his manor of Midgehall was only a mile to the south, and he had bought houses and land in the borough in 1561 and 1562. He also had property at Chippenham and at Preshute, near Marlborough, the latter doubtless in connexion with his rangership of Savernake.[3]

Under Mary, Pleydell seems to have been a religious and political radical. After the dissolution of the 1555 Parliament, during which he had voted against a government bill, he had been imprisoned in the Fleet, ostensibly because of a riot though later he asserted before the Privy Council that the real reason had been his 'speaking his conscience ... in a bill concerning the commonwealth'. As plaintiff or defendant he had appeared more than once in the Star Chamber; the Privy Council had several times put him under recognizance, and he had experienced imprisonment in the Tower. This record he took the opportunity to expunge by suing out a pardon on Elizabeth's accession.

The record did not remain clean for long. In 1561 or 1562 he acquired from Andrew Baynton* properties in Chippenham and also, in partnership with Henry Sharington*, the manors of Bremhill and Bromham. The actions in Chancery occasioned by these and others of his property deals were numerous and involved. One such action, concerning the manor of Monkton in Chippenham, was pending when Pleydell again became a Member of Parliament in 1563. It had been brought by Francis Newdigate, into whose possession the manor had passed upon his marriage to the widow of Protector Somerset. How and when the matter came before the Commons is not known, but as the nub of the charge against Pleydell was forgery it is conceiveable that Newdigate, himself a Member, introduced it on some date between 11 and 27 Feb. 1563 while the House was concerned with the bill (later the Act 5 Eliz. c. 14) against the forging of title-deeds. The first reference to the affair in the Journal is dated 22 Mar., by which time the House had appointed a committee of inquiry, consisting of the master of the rolls, the recorder of London, Sir Nicholas Arnold, Walter Haddon and Thomas Norton. The inclusion on the committee of the master of the rolls suggests that the initiative could have been Pleydell's asking for privilege, since he was being proceeded against in Chancery while he was a sitting Member. This aspect of the matter remains obscure. On 30 Mar. the committee reported that it found 'great and vehement suspicion' in Pleydell, and complained that he had disregarded its own order to him. The Commons thereupon instructed the committee to lay its report before them that afternoon, the report to be read to Pleydell who should reply either verbally or in writing, as he preferred. The Journal makes no further reference to the subject until 10 Apr., the last day of the session, when the House ordered that both Pleydell and Newdigate should be supplied with copies of the committee's documents, and that Pleydell's own written evidence should be kept in the Rolls office under seal. So far as Parliament was concerned this was the end of the matter; the Journal for the following session does not mention it.[4]

Between sessions, in November 1564, Pleydell found himself again close prisoner in the Fleet, charged with illegal hunting in Selwood forest, apparently in company with Sir John Thynne and others. Bound to appear in Star Chamber on the first day of the approaching law term, he was allowed out under escort so that he might attend to certain 'great suits', a reference perhaps to the litigation resulting from his attempt, again in association with Henry Sharington, to secure yet more of Andrew Baynton's lands. Some years later he was cited in another forgery case, he and his co-defendants then being described as 'persons of long time acquainted with such lewd devices and practices'.[5]

Towards the end of his life Pleydell was again or perhaps still at odds with authority. In some of these proceedings he was described as of Towcester, Northamptonshire, a domicile which he may have acquired from the marriage of one of his kin with a Saunders of Syresham, a manor five miles from Towcester. In 1587 he appeared before the Privy Council, involved in some unexplained way in a dispute composed by the mediation of Sir Henry Knyvet*, and in July 1590, described this time as of Midgehall, he was sent for by warrant, presented himself before a clerk of the Council, and had his appearance registered, but again no reason is given.[6]

On 19 Dec. 1590, when 'sick in body', he made his will, leaving his wife Jane ten kine or £20 in money, 100 sheep or £40 in money, and half of all his household goods at Midgehall. The profits of certain lands he left in trust to Sir Edward Baynton*, Sir John Danvers*, Sir Charles Danvers* and John St. John for the benefit of his grandson Charles Pleydell, a minor. Each of his servants was to receive 10s., the parish church of Lydiard Tregoze 10s., and the poor of that parish 20s. The residue was to go to Agnes, wife of William Bayliffe*, his only daughter and sole executrix. Richard Danvers* and Robert Wells, Pleydell's nephew by his sister Elizabeth, were appointed overseers,

with 20s. each for their pains. Letters of administration were issued to Oliver Frye, a creditor, on 3 Feb. 1591.[7]

[1] Wilts. Vis. Peds. (Harl. Soc. cv), 153; Wilts. N. and Q. v. 175; PCC 12 Sainberbe. [2] St. Ch. 4/1/33, 5/13, 8/48. [3] Wilts. N. and Q. iv. 503, 561–2; CPR, 1558–60, p. 149. [4] Wilts. N. and Q. iv. 559; CPR, 1560–3, p. 381; C3/17/19, 30/9, 132/16, 136/1, 137/60, 138/17, 97, 140/4, 142/3, 144/130, 228/6; CJ, i. 65, 66, 67, 70, 71, 72. [5] APC, vii. 162, 165, 170, 173–4, 176; St. Ch. 7/2/13. [6] Vis. Northants. 1564, 1618–19, p. 132; APC, xiv. 318, 335; xix. 314–15. [7] PCC 12 Sainberbe.

M.B.

PLEYDELL, John (by 1535–1608), of Frampton, Glos.

CRICKLADE   1593

b. by 1535, 7th s. of William Pleydell of Midgehall, Wilts. and Coleshill, Berks. by his w. Agnes; bro. of Gabriel*. *m.* Katherine (?Hawkins).[1]

The description of John Pleydell, on the return for Cricklade in 1593, as 'of Frampton' distinguishes him from four of his nephews and namesakes. They were John Pleydell of the Middle Temple, eldest son of the MP's brother Toby, who died in 1614;[2] the two John Pleydells, sons of his brother Virgil, of whom one died in 1590 and the other may have died young;[3] and John Pleydell, eldest son of his brother Thomas, of the Shrivenham branch of the family.[4] It was probably one of these nephews who was listed in 1582 as a member of the Earl of Hertford's household at Tottenham.[5]

As the 7th son of a squire of moderate fortune John Pleydell of Frampton grew up with no great prospects; but the early deaths of his brothers Anthony and Virgil may have helped to improve them. William Pleydell, who died in 1555 or 1556, showed his regard for his youngest son by making him co-executor with his mother, and Agnes Pleydell did the same when she named him sole executor and residuary legatee in 1567. It does not appear that John was involved in the misadventures of his brother Gabriel during the reign of Mary, although both were then living at Midgehall, the manor near Wootton Bassett of which their father had taken a 95-year lease from the abbot of Stanley in 1534 and which he had sub-leased to Gabriel in September 1553. John Pleydell continued to describe himself as 'of Midgehall' during the first years of Elizabeth's reign, but it is likely that strained relations with his wayward brother (who was unsuccessfully to challenge their mother's will) made him desirous of living elsewhere. In January 1562 he bought the manor and rectory of Ampney Crucis, and the reversion of leases on them for upwards of £1,100, and he probably made his residence there for the next 30 years. He also had a house at Marridge, near Ramsbury, but this he sold in 1575.[6]

It was not until 1592 that John Pleydell began to acquire an estate at some distance from his family's native territory. Since these are the first transactions in which his wife Katherine is found joined with him they perhaps followed a late marriage, and if, as is possible, Katherine was a Hawkins of Winchcomb the location of the properties would also be explained. In 1592 the couple bought the manor of Frampton; in 1593 they added the neighbouring Alderton, and two years later rounded off their purchase with the manor of Prescott. The properties cost them in all £1,620. Situated to the north-west of Winchcomb, on the eastern edge of the Vale of Avon, the new estate was separated by the Cotswolds from the older Pleydell lands at the head of the Thames Valley. It seems likely that at the same time as he bought Frampton John Pleydell parted with Ampney Crucis.[7]

But if it was Frampton which gave John Pleydell the standing for membership of the Commons, it was the borough of Cricklade, in the older Pleydell country, which provided him with a seat there. He had been preceded to Westminster by a number of his relatives: besides his brother Gabriel, his nephew and great-nephew by marriage, William and Henry Bayliffe, had both sat, as had Charles Danvers, a connexion of Henry Bayliffe's wife. In emulating them John Pleydell would naturally have sought the favour of the Brydges family, which controlled the representation of Cricklade, for Frampton lay within three miles of the Brydges residence at Sudeley. It is indeed likely that Pleydell paid court to the Queen when she passed through Alderton on her way to Sudeley in September 1592. As one of the Cricklade MPs he may have served on a committee concerned with cloth, 15 Mar. 1593.[8]

There are occasional glimpses of John Pleydell's position in the county during the closing years of Elizabeth's reign. In the winter of 1597-8 he was one of the sureties, in a sum of £100, for William Lane as receiver-general of four western counties; and towards 1603 – the document in question is undated – his name appears in a list of Gloucestershire knights and gentlemen who were probably being considered for appointment as sheriffs. His advancing years make it unlikely that he was the John Pleydell who was ordered in October 1601 to embark at Bristol for Ireland to help meet the Spanish invasion: this was probably one of his nephews.[9]

In Trinity term 1607 Pleydell arranged for three of his manors to go to his nephews Charles and William Pleydell, from whom he received £1,640, slightly more than he had himself paid 12 years before. That August he entered into an obligation of £1,000 to pay his wife an allowance of £4 a month. But by the following March he had defaulted upon this arrangement, and the forfeiture of the obligation was then granted to Richard Andrews and William Hawkins, the latter perhaps his wife's father or brother. Within a few months, when the £1,000 itself was not forthcoming, Pleydell's lands, which had been 'extended' for the debt, were granted to a groom of the chamber: they were specified as lying in Frampton, Alderton and Prescott, and were stated to be worth £230 a year clear. Pleydell died in 1608.[10]

[1] Wilts. Vis. Peds. (Harl. Soc. cv, cvi), 152-3; Genealogist, n.s. xii. 236; Harl. 888, f. 9; CSP Dom. 1603-10, p. 418; Wilts. Arch. Mag. xlix. 483. [2] M.T. Adm. Reg. i. 27; PCC 126 Lawe. [3] PCC 35 Stonard; Chanc. II/228/52. [4] Vis. Berks. 1566, i. 48. [5] HMC Bath, iv. 194. [6] PCC 5 Ketchyn, 35 Stonard; Wilts. RO, 212A, BRA 247 bdle. 3; CPR, 1560-3, pp. 317-18; Wilts. N. and Q. viii. 317. [7] Bristol and Glos. Arch. Soc. Trans. xvii. 142-3, 150-1, 157-9. [8] Nichols, Progresses Eliz. iii. 129; D'Ewes, 501. [9] HMC Hatfield, vii. 508; xv. 397; Lansd. 86/30; APC, xxxii. 280. [10] Bristol and Glos. Arch. Soc. Trans. xvii 235-6; xlii. 31; SP14/37/601; CSP Dom. 1603-10, pp. 418, 466.

M.B.

POLE (POLEY), William I (1515-87), of Colyford and Shute, Devon.

LYME REGIS	1545
BRIDPORT	1553 (Oct.)
WEST LOOE	1559

b. 9 Aug. 1515, o.s. of William Pole by his 2nd w. Agnes, da. of John Drake of Ash. educ. I. Temple, called. m. (1) 1548, Thomasine (d.1556), da. of John Tudoll of Lyme Regis, wid. of John Strowbridge (d.1539) of Streathayne and of William Beaumont (d.1547), s.p.; (2) by 1559, Katherine, da. of Alexander Popham[†] of Huntworth, Som., 5s. inc. William Pole II* 2da.

Fellow, I. Temple by 1547, bencher 1556, Autumn reader 1557, Lent reader 1562, treasurer 1564; j.p. Devon and Dorset from c.1559; of counsel to Lyme Regis from c.1564.

The name entered on the Exchequer list of 1559 MPs is Poley. No likely William Poley has been traced, so it has been assumed that Poley was a variant spelling of Pole, and that the 1559 MP was William Pole, a wealthy lawyer and speculator in church lands who had already represented two Dorset boroughs in previous Parliaments. His cousin John Saintclere had sat for West Looe in 1555, but Pole's own return there in 1559 may well have been due to the 2nd Earl of Bedford, who knew Pole's mother's family. Whether Pole shared Bedford's protestant religious opinions is another matter. His not sitting after 1559 and his not attaining any higher legal office than that of counsel to Lyme Regis suggests at best a lukewarm acceptance of the new religion, as does his retirement to his country seat of Shute, which he had acquired from the Catholic Petre family, Sir William Petre* having received it after the attainder of Henry Grey, Duke of Suffolk. Still, Pole remained on the commission of the peace and he was employed by the Privy Council in September 1580 to inquire into disturbances at Exeter. His will gives no indication of any religious beliefs. In it he bequeathed 20s. each to the vicars of Colyton and Seaton, remembered the poor of several Devon parishes, and left his widow an annuity and a life interest in the house and park at Shute. The remainder to this property, and the residue of his lands, went to his eldest son, William. John Popham*, attorney-general and the testator's brother-in-law, was one of the executors, another being Thomas Hannam*. Pole died 15 Aug. 1587, and was buried at Colyton.

R. Polwhele, *Devonshire*, iii. 311; Vivian, *Vis. Devon*, 603; *Colyton Par. Regs.* (Devon and Cornw. Rec. Soc. 1928), 20, 21, 459, 570–82; St. Ch. 4/3/10; Lyme Regis mss, Finance, i. 60; *CPR*, 1563–6, p. 81; 1569–72, p. 143; Hutchins, *Dorset*, ii. 223; W. Pole, *Desc. Devon*, 137–8; *APC*, xii. 186; PCC 62 Spencer; C142/213/72.

                                                    H.M./P.W.H.

POLE, William II (1561–1636), of Shute, Devon.

BOSSINEY   1586

bap. 27 Aug. 1561, 1st s. of William Pole I* of Shute by his 2nd w. *educ.* ?Exeter Coll. Oxf.; I. Temple Feb. 1579. *m.* (1) 23 July 1583, Mary (*d.* 1606), da. and coh. of William Peryam* of Crediton, 6s. 5da.; (2) Jane (*d.* 1654), da. of William Sims of Chard, Som., wid. of Roger How of London. *suc.* fa. 1587. Kntd. 1606.

J.p. Devon from 1591, sheriff 1602–3.

Pole, the Devon antiquary, was brought into Parliament for Bossiney by his father-in-law, William Peryam. His pursuits in later life suggest the likelihood of a university education, and some credence may be given to the story, otherwise unsubstantiated, that he went to Exeter College, Oxford, where Peryam had been a fellow. On the death of his father he inherited his Devon property, including Colcombe Castle which he subsequently rebuilt. In later years he subscribed £37 10s. to the Virginia Company and was one of those who sponsored the third Virginia charter. Although not inactive in county affairs, he increasingly devoted himself to the study of antiquities and had, by the time of his death, 9 Feb. 1636, large miscellaneous collections which were later published.

In his will, dated 3 Dec. 1635, he renounced 'this filthy flesh', and announced his sole adherence to Christ. His second wife received all the plate which she had brought at her marriage, 'as well the fashion not altered, as since by her appointment altered and changed into new fashion'. By a nuncupative codicil, made about 30 Dec. 1635, he nominated his eldest son, Sir John, as sole executor. The will was proved in October the following year.

Devonshire Studies, ed. Hoskins, 374, 476; Vivian, *Vis. Devon*, 603; *Trans. Dev. Assoc.* xvii. 256; xviii. 262–8; xxv. 105; *CSP Dom.* 1601–3, p. 193; PCC 38 Goare.

                                                    W.J.J.

POLE, *see also* **POOLE**

POLEY, Edmund[1] (1544–1613), of Badley, Suff.

BODMIN   1572
KNARESBOROUGH   1584
CLITHEROE   1586

b. 1544, s. of John Poley of Badley by Anne, da. of Thomas Wentworth†, 1st Lord Wentworth of Net-

tlestead. *educ.* G. Inn 1563, called 1574. *m.* (1) 1572, Catherine, da. of Francis Seckford and sis. of Charles Seckford* of Great Bealings, 1da.; (2) Alice, da. of Philip Cockran of Hampstead, Mdx., wid. of Richard Kemp, *s.p. suc.* fa. 1590.

J.p.q. Suff. from 1584; recorder, Thetford from 1586; Lent reader, G. Inn from 1586, treasurer 1591, dean of chapel 1595, double reader 1595.

Of a family seated at Badley since the time of Henry VII, Poley was a country gentleman and a lawyer, active in the county even before succeeding his father. The Suffolk manors of Badley, Barking, Stoke Ash and Woodhall were settled on him at the time of his first marriage, a fortunate match that brought him into the circle of such prominent Suffolk families as the Seckfords and the Wingfields. However, it was through his maternal relations' influence with Lord Burghley that Poley came to sit for three boroughs outside Suffolk. At Bodmin Burghley's influence must have been direct; in the other two cases it would have been exerted through the duchy of Lancaster. Poley's parliamentary career was not spectacular, even if all the following references are to him, rather than to Thomas Poole I*. The variant spellings of the names and unknown identity of the latter make confusion all too likely. The only recorded speech (Pooley) was a brief intervention on a matter of privilege, 11 June 1572. The committees were on fines and recoveries, 13 Feb. 1576 (Pooley); grants by the dean and chapter of Norwich, 2 Mar. 1576 (Pooley); questionable returns, 24 Feb. 1581 (Powle, Poole); and Ledbury (Herefordshire) hospital, 4 Mar. 1581 (Pooley, Powley).[2]

Poley died in 1613, leaving a daughter. The estates were to be managed by trustees for 15 years to pay off debts, but the widow had a life interest in Badley. There were legacies to nephews and nieces, to the servants and to the poor, and the eventual heir was a nephew Edmund whose wardship Poley had bought, and which he bequeathed to the boy himself.[3]

[1] *OR* gives the first name of the Bodmin MP as Edward, but the Crown Office lists C193/32/8–10 have Edmund. For Knaresborough in 1584, Add. 38823 has William Poley of Gray's Inn. No real life William Poley of Gray's Inn has been found, and the William is assumed to be an error for Edmund. Clitheroe in 1586 has Edmund Poley of Gray's Inn. [2] *Vis. Suff. 1561*, ed. Metcalfe, 58; *Vis. Suff.* ed. Howard, i. 30; E163/14/8; C142/225/107; *G. Inn Pens. Bk.* i. 74, 89, 101, 112, 128; Thetford hall bk. 1568–1622, p. 129; *CSP Dom.* 1581–90, pp. 21, 74; *HMC Hatfield*, xii. 577; Trinity, Dublin, Thos. Cromwell's jnl. f. 63; *CJ*, i. 105, 110, 129, 131; D'Ewes, 300, 302. [3] PCC 107 Capell.

                                                    P.W.H.

POLEY, Thomas I (c.1527–c.84), of Icklingham and Little Saxham, Suff.

THETFORD   1559

b. c.1527, o.s. of William Poley of Icklingham by his w. Katherine Larke of Thetford, Norf. *m.* aft. Jan. 1557,

Juliana, da. and h. of John Fayre of London, wid. of Thomas Spring of Pakenham. *suc.* fa. 1557.[1]

J.p. Suff. from c.1573, q.1583; keeper of Framlingham castle 1580.[2]

The identification of the 1559 Thetford MP with Thomas Poley of Icklingham rather than with any of a number of namesakes, is based upon no more than the fact that his mother came from Thetford. He was included in the general pardon of 1553, but less than two years later Sir William Drury* and Sir Clement Heigham† were ordered by the Privy Council to arrest him and search his house for writings and other suspicious matter. His wife brought him a life interest in her first husband's estates, and in February 1560 he was licensed to enter into his own lands. Poley was in fact mentioned in Thomas Spring's will, where he was called Spring's cousin, and left £40 to buy a ring.[3]

Thomas Poley of Little Saxham, some seven miles from Icklingham, who was a Suffolk j.p. between 1573 and 1584, was almost certainly the same man. He was active in the puritan interest with Sir Robert Jermyn*, Clement Heigham and William Spring, a connexion of Poley's wife, attempting to install godly ministers in several Norfolk and Suffolk churches and protecting preachers against the bishop of Norwich. On one occasion these activities involved him again in the affairs of Thetford. He was one of the justices who claimed that at Thetford the ruling factions were:

very cold in the cause of religion ... They have been greatly laboured, yet would never consent to entertain a preacher. Such as affect the gospel, they remove from being either burgess or commoner and put in others which be either suspected or enemies.

Another example of his zeal is provided by the case of one Walter Norton who had been hearing Mass privately in his house and had tried to prevent the demolition of the roodloft in Halesworth parish church. When examined by Poley, Norton offered him £10 to 'advertise favourably on his behalf'. The response must have been unfavourable, as the facts were reported to the Privy Council. The last references to Poley are found in 1584; he probably died that year.[4]

[1] *Vis. Suff. 1561*, ed. Metcalfe, 58; *Vis. Suff.* ed. Howard, i. 301; Coppinger, *Suff. Recs. and mss*, ii. 181. [2] Egerton 2345, f. 32v; Royal 18.D.111; *APC*, xii. 143. [3] *CPR*, 1553–4, p. 436; 1558–60, p. 361; *APC*, v. 106; PCC 4 Wrastley. [4] *APC*, ix. 305; x. 100; xiii. 46–8, 50; Collinson thesis, 868, 877–8, 879.

I.C.

POLEY, Thomas II (aft. 1544–bef. 1607), ?of Badley, Suff.

THETFORD 1586

b. aft. 1544, ?3rd s. of John Poley of Badley and bro. of Edmund*. *m.*, 1s. 1da.

As with the Thetford 1559 Member, there is an identity problem, and the identification of the 1586 man with Thomas Poley of Badley is no more than a reasonable inference from his family being well-established in Suffolk and related to Lord Wentworth, one of the leading magnates of East Anglia. If this identification is correct, it would make him the younger brother of Edmund Poley, the recorder of Thetford, who was himself returned for Clitheroe in 1586. Next to nothing is known of Thomas Poley of Badley. It appears from the will of Edmund Poley, made in June 1607, that Thomas left money in trust to his son and daughter. Edmund became their guardian and on his death, without direct male heirs, in 1613, his nephew and ward succeeded to the family estates.

Vis. Suff. 1561, ed. Metcalfe, 58; *Vis. Suff.* ed. Howard, i. 301; Thetford hall bk. 1568–1622, p. 129; Gawdy letter bk. in custody of Norf. Arch. Soc. Lib.; PCC 107 Capell.

I.C.

POLEY, *see also* **POLE (POLEY), William I**

POLLARD, Sir John (c.1528–75), of Trelawne, Cornw. and of Bishopsgate, London.

PLYMPTON ERLE	1553 (Mar.)
BARNSTAPLE	1554 (Apr.)
EXETER	1555, 1559
GRAMPOUND	1563

b. c.1528, 1st s. of (Sir) Richard Pollard† of Forde Abbey, Dorset by Jacquetta, da. of John Bury of Colliton, Devon. *m.* Catherine, at least 3da.; at least 1s. illegit. *suc.* fa. 10 Nov. 1542. Kntd. 10 Nov. 1549.

Eccles. commr. 1559; j.p. Devon from c.1559, q. by 1569, Som. from June 1569; visitor, diocese of Exeter 1559; president, council of Munster 1568.[1]

A distant relation of his namesake the Speaker of 1555, Pollard was one of the 'right protestants' who met at 'Harondayles house' to discuss parliamentary tactics in that Parliament. A ward of the 1st Earl of Bedford, he was from the time he came of age associated with the group of Devon protestants who formed the 2nd Earl of Bedford's closest supporters. He served in the St. Quentin expedition under the earls of Pembroke and Bedford. His association with Exeter was of some years' standing by the time he first represented the city in the Parliament of 1555, during which he voted against a government bill. In 1559 his candidature may have been the result of a compromise between contending city factions. It was an opportune time for Exeter to elect a man in favour with the new government, who had done good service in the city in previous years. In 1563 Pollard was returned for Grampound, being appointed to the succession committee, 31 Oct. 1566. He was obviously on good terms with Sir William Cecil, to whom he wrote, 'In all my doings hitherto I have been still assisted by your honour', and through whom, no doubt, he obtained his appointment in Munster. Described by Cecil as 'a forward gentleman if his gout stay him not backward', he was unable to take up the appointment, 'according to [his] heart's desire'; and was superseded by Sir Humphrey Gilbert*.[2]

Pollard died at his London house between 22 Nov. when he made his will and 29 Dec. 1575, when it was proved. He appointed his brother Matthew executor, leaving him £2,000. Amias Paulet*, Sir Arthur Champernown* and Bernard Drake were the overseers. He left money to the poor of Combe Martin, where he owned the manor, and bequests to his daughters. His wife received the lease of his town house.[3]

[1] *Trans. Dev. Assoc.* lxi. 209; Roberts thesis; *CPR*, 1566–9, p. 350. [2] *LP Hen. VIII*, xxi(2), p. 1; PCC 17 Streat; St. Ch. 7/16/6; SP11/8/35; SP63/25/75, 28/52, 29/12; *HMC Foljambe*, 7; Devon RO, Tingey 553; Vivian, *Vis. Devon*, 579; *HMC Exeter*, 362; Guildford Mus., Loseley 1331/2; D'Ewes, 126; *Cal. Proc. Chancery Q. Eliz.* iii. 133; *CSP Ire.* 1509–73, pp. 5, 392. [3] PCC 47 Pyckering.

P.W.H.

POLSTED (POLSTEAD), Richard (1545–76), of Albury, Surr.

HINDON   1571, 1572*

b. 24 June 1545, o.s. of Henry Polstead[†] of Albury. *m.* 3 Nov. 1567, Elizabeth, da. of William More I* of Loseley. *suc.* fa. 1555.

J.p. Surr. from c.1573; sheriff, Surr. and Suss. from 1575.

Polsted's marriage to Elizabeth More of Loseley was an event of the year, the festivities taking place at Blackfriars from 3 to 17 Nov. Among the guests was the man to whom Polsted must later have owed his return to Parliament for Hindon, Bishop Horne of Winchester. Polsted died 31 Mar. 1576. His nuncupative will left £20 towards his sister-in-law's marriage, and the residue to his wife who was appointed executor, together with Robert Cresswell, William More, Henry Knollys and Alexander Nowell, dean of St. Paul's.

Vis. Surr. (Harl. Soc. xliii) 3; *VCH Surr.* ii. 617; iii. 21, 105, 439, 569; *CPR*, 1555–7, p. 515; C142/109/85, 106/56; *Archaeologia*, xxxvi. 36–9; PCC 6 Carew.

W.J.J.

POOLE, Edward (c.1530–78), of Cirencester, Glos. and Oaksey, Wilts.

MALMESBURY   1563

b. c.1530, 2nd s. of Henry Poole of Poole by Anne, 1st da. of Sir Edward Baynton[†] of Bromham, Wilts. *m.* Margaret (*d.*1597), o. da. and coh. of Thomas Walton of Kemble, Glos. and Crudwell, Wilts. by Margaret, da. of John Earl of Wilts., 3s. inc. Henry* 3da. *suc.* bro. 1556.

The Pooles of Oaksey were a younger branch of the family seated at Sapperton, Gloucestershire. Poole himself resided in the hundred in which the borough of Malmesbury was situated and his wife was the daughter of a local landowner actively concerned in property transactions in the shire. Poole's own property was not extensive; what appear to be the same lands consisted in 1591 of 776 acres, paying a crown rent of £21 6s. 3d., and he himself paid 26s. 8d. on an assessment of £10 towards the subsidy of 1576. Yet even a modest estate situated so near the borough would have recommended its owner, who was moreover allied with many local families. Poole's grandmother was a Danvers, and he was to appoint John Danvers overseer of his will; his mother was a Baynton; and although his sister Anne married 'a man of small wealth', the other sister Cecily allied herself with George Fettiplace of Gloucestershire, who was acquiring land in Wiltshire in the year of Poole's election. Most germane to Poole's return for Malmesbury, however, was his relationship to Sir James Stumpe[†], who had married Bridget Baynton. That Stumpe was a friend as well as a kinsman is shown by his having made Poole one of his two feoffees to uses in September 1559; and although he died in April 1563, the writs for the Parliament of that year had gone out in the previous November, when his influence could still have been exerted in Poole's favour. There is no evidence of any activity by Poole in the two sessions of the 1563 Parliament, and he was not to sit again during his remaining 15 years of life. As the reign advanced, Malmesbury could find more important people to return.

Poole's eldest son and heir, Henry, a boy of 13 at his father's death, was to be an assiduous parliamentarian, as was the grandson Nevill. By the time that Henry and Nevill came to represent Malmesbury the family was rising in the world; in the course of the seventeenth century it was to acquire the manors of Oaksey, Poole and Kemble. In his will, made 16 Mar. 1578, Edward Poole, although 'now of Cirencester', asked to be buried by the side of his good father in Poole parish church, where a rough freestone monument in the north wall recorded his death at the age of 48 on 28 Apr. 1577. That the year should have been given as 1578 appears both from his will and from the inquisition post mortem on his manor of Chelworth.

Wilts. Vis. Peds. (Harl. Soc. cv, cvi), 7; *Vis. Glos.* (Harl. Soc. xxi), 125–6; St. Ch. 4/5/4, 4/7/21; *Wilts. N. and Q.* i. 330–1; iii. 166; iv. 264; v. 27, 176; vii. 211, 553; viii. 447, 522; Aubrey and Jackson, *Wilts. Topog. Colls.* 276 n. 1, 278, 279; *Two Taxation Lists* (Wilts. Arch. Soc. recs. br. x), 49; Req. 75/48 Eliz.; Williams, *Parl. Hist. Glos.* 153; C142/183/85.

S.T.B.

POOLE, Sir Giles (c.1518–89), of Sapperton, Glos.

GLOUCESTERSHIRE   1554 (Apr.), 1559, 1571

b. c.1518, 1st s. of Leonard Poole of Sapperton by Catherine, da. of Sir Giles Brydges of Coberley; bro. of

Henry†. m. (1) Elizabeth (d.1543), da. and coh. of Thomas Whittington of Pauntley, at least 1s. Sir Henry*; (2) Eleanor, da. of Edward Lewknor of Kingston-on-Sea, Suss., wid. of Sir William Wroughton (d.1559), of Broad Hinton, Wilts., s.p. suc. fa. 1538. Kntd. 1547.[1]

Gent. pens. 1540–c.51; j.p. Glos. from 1547; provost marshal [I] 1558; sheriff, Glos. 1565–6, commr. grain 1573; commr. eccles. causes, diocese of Gloucester 1574.

Poole no doubt owed his appointment as one of the original gentlemen pensioners to his maternal uncle, Sir John Brydges†. His cousin Edmund Brydges† was appointed a gentleman pensioner at the same time. As Henry VIII's 'beloved servant' Poole obtained a number of grants of land and money, but his appointment may not have extended into the reigns of Edward VI and Mary. Regarded as a safe Catholic in Mary's reign, nothing is known of his religious views under Elizabeth, though his return for the county to the 1571 Parliament points to his having conformed. Under Elizabeth he was employed only on the usual local duties. He subscribed £25 to the Armada defence fund, just before his death, which took place on 24 or 25 Feb. 1589. His will, drawn up in June 1580, was proved only a week later. Some of his considerable lands had already been enfeoffed to his 'very good lord' Sir Robert Dudley*, Earl of Leicester, and others. Among the bequests were rings to the feoffees and overseers, engraved with the motto, 'Be mindful of thy friend'.[2]

[1] Vis. Glos. (Harl. Soc. xxi), 125; Bristol and Glos. Arch. Soc. Trans. xxxi. 11; LP Hen. VIII, xiv(1), p. 534; Misc. Gen. et Her. (ser. 5), iii. 206–9; Nichols, Lit. Rems. Edw. VI, 216; Stephenson, Mon. Brasses, 154. [2] LP Hen. VIII, iv(1), p. 871; xvii. 567; Bristol and Glos. Arch. Soc. Trans. l. 207–8, lix. 67; CPR, 1547–8, p. 84; 1549–51, p. 310; 1553, p. 354; 1553–4, pp. 19, 27, 37; APC, vi. 370; viii. 132, 158, 356; CP, iii. 126; C142/222/45; Flenley, Cal. Reg. Council, Marches of Wales, 120–1; T. C. Noble, Names of Those who Subscribed, 22; PCC 31 Leicester.

A.D.K.H./N.M.F.

POOLE, Henry (1564–1632), of Kemble, Glos. and Oaksey, Wilts.

CIRENCESTER	1597
CRICKLADE	1604
WILTSHIRE	1614
MALMESBURY	1621
OXFORDSHIRE	1624
WILTSHIRE	1626

b. 1564, 1st s. of Edward Poole* of Cirencester, Glos. and Oaksey, Wilts. educ. Trinity Coll. Oxf. 1580. m. (1) Griselda, da. of Edward Neville, 7th Lord Abergavenny, of Newton St. Loe, Som., 2s. 1da.; (2) c.1614, Anne Barnarde, wid. of Sir James Harrington of Ridlington, Rutland. suc. fa. 1577. Kntd. 1603.

J.p. Wilts. from c.1590, q. by 1601, sheriff 1619–20.

Poole's father had lived in Cirencester, and he himself probably still owned property there when he was returned for the borough in 1597. No doubt his standing met with the approval of Sir Henry Poole* of Sapperton. Charles Danvers*, the lord of the borough, who had fled abroad after a duel in 1594, was still on the Continent in 1597.[1]

Poole's chief estates lay in Wiltshire, but in 1597 his quarrel – then in its fourth year – with (Sir) Henry Knyvet* may have prevented his seeking to be returned there. The quarrel originated in a dispute over the ownership of the manor of Kemble. Poole had inherited a lease of the property, granted by the Crown in 1564, from his grandfather Thomas Walton, and claimed in a Star Chamber suit of 1593 that he had also acquired all other leases relating to the property, of which he had been in quiet possession for 11 years before 1593. However, his grandmother, Margaret Walton, had a life-interest in part of the property which she was persuaded to grant to Knyvet. Immediately thereafter Knyvet, accompanied by armed servants, forced his way into Kemble manor house ostensibly to show Poole the lease, frightening in the process Poole's pregnant wife. Knyvet also took possession of a close where Poole's men were harvesting, making it known in Malmesbury that whoever came to cut corn at Kemble could carry it away without payment, whereupon a large number of poor people came to Kemble, and remained there several days cutting corn. How the dispute ended is not known, but Poole continued to hold property at Kemble. Whoever was in the right it was an unseemly quarrel to occupy two justices. Possibly as a result of this dispute Poole was summoned before the Council in 1596 to answer allegations that he had been neglecting the Queen's service.[2]

One lease of property in Kemble had been in the possession of the Wye family, and it was probably as a further consequence of the dispute with Knyvet that Poole and William Combe, while Members of the Commons, were subpoenaed to give evidence in the Star Chamber by Anne, wife of Thomas Wye. Both successfully pleaded privilege, 28 Nov. 1597, the House ordering that Mistress Wye should be called to answer her contempt.[3]

Under James I Poole became a leading figure in Wiltshire affairs, and a regular Parliament man. He made his will on 17 Mar. 1631. The sole executor and residuary legatee was his eldest son Sir Neville, who, Sir Henry hoped, would not be 'carried away with idle sports and vain delights of the world', but would chiefly apply himself to the service of God, and next to the good of his country. Sir Henry ended his will by beseeching

the most glorious Trinity to vouchsafe me in these my latter days the true spirit of regeneration that ever hereafter I may spend my time in true holiness and righteousness all the days of my life.

The will was proved on 14 Nov. 1632, 11 days after Sir Henry's death.[4]

[1] C142/183/85, 489/144; J. R. Dunlop, Fam. of Poole, 9–10; E163/14/8, f. 39; Hatfield mss 278; C66/1549; PCC 35 Langley.

[2] St. Ch. 5/P20/3, P24/31, P54/25; C2 Eliz./P1/56; *APC*, xxvi. 256.
[3] St. Ch. 5/P54/25; C2 Eliz./P1/56; D'Ewes, 564; Townshend, *Hist. Colls.* 109. [4] PCC 110 Audley; C142/489/144.

A.M.M.

POOLE, Sir Henry (c.1541–1616), of Sapperton, Glos.

GLOUCESTERSHIRE   1593

b. c.1541, 1st s. of Sir Giles Poole* by his 1st w. *educ.* I. Temple 1562. *m.* Anne, da. of Sir William Wroughton of Broad Hinton, Wilts., 3s. 4da. Kntd. 1587; *suc.* fa. 1589.
J.p. Glos. from c.1573, eccles. commr. 1574, sheriff 1588, 1603, subsidy commr. 1593, commr. for restraint of grain; member, council in marches of Wales (and j.p. many border counties) 1594.

Poole increased his inherited estates by judicious purchases of land and advowsons. Before 1585 he had bought the manor of Pinbury, in 1601 he paid £1,320 to the Berkeleys for the manor and advowson of Daglingworth, and the same year he bought the manor of Edgworth. Shortly before his death he paid the Danvers family £2,600 for the manors of Cirencester Oakley, Siddington Peter and Siddington Mary.[1]

Throughout his life Poole was active in local affairs. In 1578 he was one of those who brought to the notice of the Privy Council 'a sect of disordered persons, using to assemble together in a desolate place … appointing unto themselves a minister and a private order of service, according to their own fantasies', and, with his father, was ordered to round them up and send them before the Council. In 1589 he was again occupied with religious matters when he was ordered to search out the publishers of 'divers shameful and infamous letters, libels and other scandalous and shameful devices', which had been circulating in the county, and which tended to discredit the ministry. He received many other commissions from the Council. In 1592, for instance, he was instructed to enforce the use of standard measures in Salisbury, and in 1596 he supervised the Gloucestershire levies for Ireland. On two occasions, in 1600 and 1601, he was himself ordered to send a horse for service there.[2]

Poole was 50 when he made his only appearance in Parliament. There is no record of his speaking, but he was on all three committees concerned with the subsidy negotiations (26 Feb., 1, 3 Mar.); on a committee dealing with rogues (12 Mar.); and, as a knight of the shire in 1593 he could have attended committees on land inheritance (9 Mar.) and cloth (15 Mar.).

On 10 Aug. 1616, being 'sick in body', Poole made his will. After directing that his body should be buried in Sapperton church, and setting aside £5 for 'the reparations and beautifying of the same church', and a further sum of money toward the erection of 'a comely and convenient tomb' for himself and his wife, he left the bulk of his property to his only surviving son, and sole executor, Henry Poole. Poole died on 31 Aug. that year and the will was proved 10 Nov. An inquisition post mortem was held in 1617.[3]

[1] W. R. Williams, *Parl. Hist. Glos.* 48; *Vis. Glos.* (Harl. Soc. xxi), 125–6; J. R. Dunlop, *Fam. of Poole*, 4–5; C142/222/45; *Bristol and Glos. Arch. Soc. Trans.* xii. 55; l. 210–13; lix. 66; *APC*, xxiv. 474; Lansd. 48, f. 137; P. H. Williams, *Council in the Marches of Wales*, 354–5. [2] *APC*, x. 426–7; xi. 37; xviii. 287; xxii. 501; xxvi. 277; xxx. 439. [3] D'Ewes, 474, 481, 486, 496, 499, 501; PCC 116 Cope; C142/365/153.

J.J.C.

POOLE, John (*d.* 1601), of Capenhurst, Cheshire.

LIVERPOOL   1586

1st s. of John Poole of Poole Hall, Wirral by his 2nd w. Katherine, da. of John Minshull of Minshull. *m.* bef. 1561, Mary, da. of Sir Rowland Stanley of Hooton, 6s. 2da.
Burgess, Liverpool 1589.

The Pooles had been seated in Cheshire for several centuries. Poole received from his father certain lands in the county at the time of his marriage, but, dying *v.p.*, the main inheritance passed to his eldest son, also called John, about whom little is known. His return for Liverpool was probably due to his father-in-law, a kinsman of the Earl of Derby. His own religious views, if any, are unknown, but in 1580 his father was one of the justices of Cheshire 'not known to be of any religion, and therefore suspected to be papist'. Poole died 28 July 1601 and was buried two days later.

Lancs. and Cheshire Hist. Soc. n.s. xvi. 176 seq.; Ormerod, *Cheshire*, ii. 424; J. A. Twemlow, *Liverpool Town Bks.* ii. 839; *CSP Dom.* Add. 1580–1625, p. 35.

N.M.S.

POOLE, Sir John.[1]

MUCH WENLOCK   1593

This Member has not been identified. Two knights bear a similar name, but Sir John Poley, who was knighted in the Netherlands in 1588, and killed there in 1594, was almost certainly out of England at the time of the Parliament, while Sir John Poley of Wrongey was not knighted until 1599. Two local families, the Powells of All Stretton, and the Powells of Edenhope, have been considered but neither has recorded in its pedigree a knight of this name.[2]

[1] C193/32/List 12. [2] *Trans. Salop Arch. Soc.* (ser. 3), ii. 318–19; *APC*, xxi. 45; xxii. 432; xxiii. 243; xxiv. 101; *Vis. Salop* (Harl. Soc. xxix), 405–7.

J.J.C.

POOLE (POWLE), Thomas I

CIRENCESTER   1571, 1572

This Member remains unidentified, though he may have belonged to the Pooles of Sapperton, Sir Giles Poole* and the Earl of Leicester uniting to secure his and Gabriel Blike's* return in 1571. But he could hardly have been the Thomas Poole mentioned in the family pedigrees, the son of Sir Giles Poole's brother Mathew, who was married by 1575, for, in his will, Sir Giles bequeathed him a bare 5 marks 'except he shall be provided of some other living or commodity as much in value or better'.

On 4 Mar. 1581 Mr. Powley or Pooley (either the Cirencester MP or Edmund Poley*) was appointed to the committee for the bill for the hospital at Ledbury. The Gabriel Blike already mentioned possessed an estate at Massington, near Ledbury, and perhaps Poole had interests in the area.

PCC 31 Leicester; W. R. Williams, *Parl. Hist. Glos.* 151; J. R. Dunlop, *Fam. of Poole*, 2–4; *Vis. Yorks.* ed. Foster, 351; *OR*, 414; D'Ewes, 302; *CJ*, i. 131.

A.M.M.

POOLE (POWLE), Thomas II

CIRENCESTER 1584

Described as 'junior' in the return, this Member was possibly the son of the Thomas Poole* who sat for Cirencester in 1571 and 1572, though there is no one in the pedigrees with whom he can be identified.[1] The only reference to the Member in Parliament is his request for privilege to be extended to one of his servants who had been arrested upon a *capias utlagatum*. It transpired that the man had entered Poole's service since the beginning of the Parliament expressly to escape imprisonment for debt, and 'it was also suspected that Mr. Poole himself entertained the man but for that purpose', privilege having been solicited on two previous occasions for his servants. It was also noted that 'Mr. Poole had given small attendance during the session'. Upon the vote privilege was denied.[2]

[1] J. R. Dunlop, *Fam. of Poole*, 1–11. [2] Trinity, Dublin, Thos. Cromwell's jnl. f. 93; Lansd. 43, anon. jnl. f. 164.

A.M.M.

POPHAM, Alexander (c.1555–1602), of Huntworth, Som.

BRIDGWATER 1589, 1597, 1601

b. c.1555, 1st s. of Edward Popham* by Jane, da. of Richard Norton of Abbot's Leigh, Bristol. *educ.* M. Temple 1568. *m.* Dorabella, da. of John Bayley, 4s. 8da. *suc.* fa. 1586.

Recorder, Bridgwater 1586; j.p.q. Som. from c.1591.

Popham inherited his father's estate, his influence in Bridgwater, and his office of recorder. This usually carried with it a seat in Parliament, but in 1593 Popham was not returned, perhaps standing down for the mayor, who was. Popham's name has not been found among the surviving records of the Parliament of 1589. On 10 Nov. 1597 he was

appointed to the committee of a bill concerning Langport Eastover, Somerset, and on 14 Dec. 1601 he was one of the committee for the bill repealing a statute regulating the length of kerseys. For his attendance at this Parliament he was paid £6, as well as £2 for his fee as recorder. He died a rich man in 1602, six months before his son Edward came of age.

Vis. Som. (Harl. Soc. xi), 87–8, 125; C142/211/156, 271/149; PCC 19 Montague; Hatfield ms 278; Jarman, *Hist. Bridgwater*, 274; D'Ewes, 684; Townshend, *Hist. Colls.* 103; Bridgwater archives, no. 1586.

I.C.

POPHAM, Edward (by 1530–86), of Huntworth, Som.

GUILDFORD	1558
HYTHE	1563
BRIDGWATER	1571, 1572, 1584

b. by 1530, 1st s. of Alexander Popham† of Huntworth by Joan, da. of Sir Edward Stradling of St. Donat's, Glam.; bro. of John*. *m.* settlement 1 July 1551, Jane, da. of Richard Norton of Abbots Leigh, Bristol, 7s. inc. Alexander* 9da. *suc.* fa. 11 June 1556.

Collector, subsidy, Som. 1553; escheator, Dorset, Som. 1560–1; recorder, Bridgwater from 20 Apr. 1572; j.p.q. Som. from c.1573, commr. piracy 1577, musters by 1583.[1]

Popham's family had been settled in Somerset since the reign of Edward I, and his father acquired lands at the dissolution of the monasteries. His own position as recorder implies some sort of legal education and this may have been at the Middle Temple, though no record has been found of his admission. Three of his sons and his brother John were there.

Popham was presumably returned to Parliament for Hythe as a nominee of the warden of the Cinque Ports. The jurats wrote in 1571: 'We have great cause by a foreign burgess to be careful what burgesses we take for our ports, for at the last parliament we had not a worse enemy than one of our own burgesses [i.e. Popham], being no portman'. Next he sat for Bridgwater, near the family estate of Huntworth. His brother John was then, in 1571, recorder of both Bristol and Bridgwater and sat for Bristol, leaving Bridgwater for Edward, who, by the time of the 1572 return, was himself recorder of Bridgwater. As both brothers were in the Parliaments of 1571 and 1572, it is difficult to apportion their activities, and only those specifically attributed to Edward Popham by the clerk are here allocated to him. This leaves no activities for Edward in 1571; no speeches at all; and appointment to committees on the following: cloth (with his brother), 16 Feb. 1576; ale, 17 Feb. 1576; innholders and tipplers, 17 Feb. 1576; wine, 21 Feb. 1576; the clerk of the market, 27 Jan. 1581; cloth, 4 Feb. 1581; and, his only activity in the 1584 Parliament (of which his brother was not a Member) the committee for the bill for the better observing of the Sabbath Day, 27 Nov. 1584.[2]

Popham died in January 1586. He left bequests to his brother, then attorney-general, to other relatives, and to the poor of North Petherton. The executor and residuary legatee was his son Alexander.[3]

[1] C142/108/104; E179/169/140; *OR*, i. 410; Lansd. 56, f. 168 seq.; 146, f. 17 seq. [2] Collinson, *Som*. iii. 71; *Vis. Som*. (Harl. Soc. xi), 87–8, 125; C142/108/104; PCC 10 Ketchyn; *CPR*, 1555–7, p. 242; G. Wilks, *Barons of the Cinque Ports and the Parl. Rep. Hythe*, 51, 52, 58; D'Ewes, 248, 333; *CJ*, i. 106, 107, 120, 122. [3] C142/211/156; PCC 20 Windsor.

I.C.

POPHAM, Sir Francis (c.1570–1644), of Wellington, Som. and Littlecote, Wilts.

SOMERSET	1597
WILTSHIRE	1604
MARLBOROUGH	1614
GREAT BEDWYN	1621
CHIPPENHAM	1624, 1625, 1626, 1628
MINEHEAD	1640 (Nov.)*

b. c.1570, o.s. of John Popham* by Amy, da. and h. of Hugh Adams of Castleton, Glam. *educ.* Balliol, Oxf. 1588; M. Temple 1589. *m.* Anne, da. and h. of John Dudley I* of Stoke Newington, Mdx., 4s. (2 *d.v.p.*) 7da. Kntd. 1596; KB 1603; *suc.* fa. 1607.

J.p. Wilts. from 1597, Som. by 1602; dep. lt. Wilts., Som. from 1597; constable, Taunton castle 1613; member, Virginia and New England Cos.; member, mines royal.

Popham was elected for the county while still in his twenties, and just after he received his knighthood at Cadiz. His father was chief justice at the time. In the 1597 Parliament Popham was named to two committees: on a private bill, 22 Nov. 1597, and for the relief of soldiers and mariners, 26 Jan. 1598. As a knight of the shire he might also have attended committees on enclosures and the poor law (5 Nov.), armour and weapons and the penal laws (8 Nov.), monopolies (10 Nov.), rebuilding Langport Eastover (10 Nov.), the subsidy (15 Nov.) and the poor law (22 Nov.). Nothing more need here be said about him in the Elizabethan period. He died 28 July 1644, aged 74.

Vis. Som. (Harl. Soc. xi), 87, 125; *Al. Ox.* iii. 1181; Lansd. 94, f. 137; PRO Index 4208, pp. 110, 251; *APC*, xxviii. 91; Harbin, *Som. MPs*, 133; D'Ewes, 552, 553, 555, 557, 561, 588; SP16/502/72.

R.C.G./J.P.F.

POPHAM, John (c.1532–1607), of Wellington, Som.

| LYME REGIS | 1558 |
| BRISTOL | 1571, 1572 |

b. c.1532, 2nd s. of Alexander Popham† of Huntworth by Joan, da. of Sir Edward Stradling of St. Donat's, Glam.; bro. of Edward*. *educ.* Balliol, Oxf. and M.

Temple, Autumn reader 1568, Lent reader 1573, treasurer 1580. *m.* Amy, da. and h. of Hugh Adams of Castleton, Glam., 1s. Sir Francis* 6da. Kntd. 1592.

J.p.q. Som. from c.1573, Mdx. 1583, Wilts., Bucks., Norf. 1594, Beds., Hunts., Suff., Isle of Ely, Cambs. 1600; custos rot. Som. from c.1594; recorder, Bridgwater 1571–2, Bristol 1571–c.77; serjeant-at-law 1579; solicitor-gen. 1579–81, attorney-gen. 1581–9; 2nd justice of Lancaster 1581–9; j.c.p. 1589–92; c.j. Queen's bench 1592–1607; eccles. commr. Sarum diocese 1599; P.C. 1599; commr. chancellorship, duchy of Lancaster 1601; high steward, Dunwich 1602.[1]

Speaker of House of Commons 1581.

Popham came of a family settled in Somerset since the thirteenth century. He inherited from his father property in Bridgwater, of which borough both he and his brother became recorder, and which his brother represented in the Parliaments of 1571 and 1572. Popham himself sat for Bristol, where, as recorder, he had a lien on the senior seat. There is obviously room for confusion over the parliamentary activities of the two brothers in the two Parliaments, and it has therefore been assumed that where the clerk has put plain Mr. Popham, John is meant. On this basis it was John Popham who seconded Bell in the debate on the subsidy bill, 7 Apr. 1571, drawing attention to abuses in collection, practised by

> treasurers of the Crown, as many having in their hands great masses of money, with which either they themselves or some others their friends do purchase lands to their own use, and after become bankrupts, and so cause or practise an instalment of their debts ... which occasioned the lack in the prince's coffers.

On 11 Apr. he spoke in favour of repealing the Act of 1566 restricting Bristol's trade to the merchant venturers. Thinking of 'the common commodity of the city', he described 'the covin used in the last Parliament in penning of the Act', for the statute omitted a vital proviso 'that the guild should not have continuance except it were to the commodity of the city'. The letters patent should have 'their validity according to the law'. He added 'a long discourse of the decay of the navy [and] the hindrance of the mariners'. His committees in 1571 were concerned with grievances (7 Apr.), the Bristol Act (12 Apr.), treasons (12 Apr.), promoters (23 Apr.), respite of homage (27 Apr., 2, 17 May), navigation (8 May), attainders and the bill against papal bulls (10 May).

Popham made four reported speeches in 1572, all on narrow legal points: the expenses of the Middlesex freeholders (22 May); bringing minstrels within the meaning of an Act against vagabonds (30 May); and two interventions on the main issue of that session, Mary Queen of Scots (both 9 June). His committees in 1572 were on Mary Queen of Scots (12, 28 May, 6 June), rites and ceremonies (20 May), the Earl of Kent (21 May), the explanation of statutes and recoveries (28 May), grants by corporations (30 May), fraudulent conveyances (3 June), and delays in judgment (24 June). In the 1576 session, he spoke on lands without covin (18 Feb.); and was appointed to committees on the subsidy (10 Feb.), promoters (10 Feb.), the poor (11 Feb.), fines and recoveries (13 Feb.), William Isley's debts (14, 27 Feb.), the coinage (15 Feb.), jeofails (15 Feb.), cloth (16 Feb.), sheriffs (18 Feb.), dilapidations (24 Feb.), Middlesex jurors (24 Feb.), letters patent (25 Feb.), Arthur Hall (28 Feb.), church discipline (29 Feb.), jurors (5 Mar.), land reclamation (6 Mar.), collateral warranties (7 Mar), the order of business (8 Mar.), dress (10 Mar.), the Queen's marriage (12 Mar.), Lord Stourton's bill (12 Mar.) and wharves and quays (13 Mar.).[2]

Before the next session of Parliament Popham was made first serjeant, then solicitor-general, which caused his appointment as serjeant to be revoked in accordance with the custom of the time, the serjeants regarding the solicitorship as beneath the dignity of their order. As solicitor Popham was made an assistant in the Lords at the beginning of the 1581 session. Whether the Commons would have taken any action about this in other circumstances cannot be known; their concern at the moment was to elect a new Speaker in place of Bell, and Popham was quickly proposed, Mr. Treasurer (Sir Francis Knollys) informing the House

> before their proceeding to election, that he and others had erst seen in the Higher House one that is a member of this House, to wit Mr. John Popham, her Majesty's solicitor-general, being one of the citizens of Bristol.

The Commons thereupon successfully requested Popham's restoration to them, and made him Speaker, 18 Jan. 1581. Three days later, on Saturday 21 Jan. Paul Wentworth's motion for a public fast was agreed to, 115 to 100, the time and place were settled, and Popham was immediately in trouble. On the Monday morning, 23 Jan., 'the House being assembled did sit till eleven of the clock without the Speaker, for that he was, all that time at the Court'. When he arrived he 'declared unto the House that the time was then so far spent, as leisure could not well serve them to proceed unto the reading of any bill' and adjourned the sitting. Next day

> Mr. Speaker declareth himself for his own part, to be very sorry for the error that happened here, in this House upon Saturday last, in resolving to have a public fast, and showeth her Majesty's great misliking of the proceeding of this House therein.

In the end it was

> agreed that Mr. Vicechamberlain [Hatton] should in our names deliver to her Majesty how sorry we were for her conceived offence…

and though 'Mr. Carleton [George*, Wentworth's fellow traveller] was desirous to speak', Mr. Speaker did 'rise and would not tarry'. Anthony Cope charged him with

partiality on 16 Mar. 'that is to say … in some such matters as he hath favoured, he hath … spoken to the bill, and in some other cases, which he did not favour and like of, he would prejudice the speeches, of the Members of this House, with the question', but on the whole Popham did quite well for an Elizabethan Speaker, especially in view of the drubbing he had received at the Queen's hands over the public fast incident. The Queen's view on the reform of abuses in the church was that any action by the House was unnecessary as the bishops were already considering the grievances. The Commons, anxious to avoid another confrontation, adopted the ingenious device of resolving

> that Mr. Speaker, in the name of this whole House, do, in his oration to her Majesty upon the last day of this present session of Parliament … put her Majesty in remembrance for the execution and accomplishment thereof at her highness' good pleasure, in such sort as to Mr. Speaker, without receiving instructions or direction of any of this House, shall seem most meet and convenient.

Unlike Speaker Croke, who, in similar circumstances in 1601, omitted mention of the ordnance matter, Popham discharged his trust. On 18 Mar.

> he remembered a petition made by the common house the last session of Parliament to the Queen's majesty for redress to be had of certain enormities to the church, which he noted to be these. The admitting of unlearned and insufficient ministers. Next the abuse of excommunication used in things of small moment. Thirdly the commutation of penance into money even in the greatest offences. And lastly the great inconveniences given by reason of pluralities and dispensations. Whereunto her Majesty [had] made them a most gracious answer, that she had and would give order therein, for the which he rendered to her most humble and dutiful thanks. He remembered likewise that because those things for lack of time were not fully reformed, the House had eftsoons this session presumed to put her Majesty in mind thereof again, whereunto also as to the former they received a gracious answer, that those matters belonging to her as incident to that supreme authority which she hath over the clergy and state ecclesiastical, she would give such direction therein as all the disorders should be reformed so far as should be necessary. For the which answer also be rendered the like most humble thanks, beseeching her Majesty in the name of the whole Commons that it might please her to command that to be done without delay which the necessity of the things did require.

A good speech, illustrating, if illustration were necessary, that Elizabeth's tactics of procrastination were perfectly apparent to her contemporaries. But Popham's resilience was no doubt exaggerated. Francis Bacon* relates that when the Queen asked 'Well, Mr. Speaker, what hath passed in the Lower House?', he replied 'If it please your Majesty, seven weeks'. His career in the law certainly did not suffer as a result of his having been Speaker, but he may well have been relieved that his part in the next Parliament was limited to attendance in the Upper House as attorney-general, for which he was paid £50.[3]

As a judge, Popham had a mixed reputation. He was considered harsh towards recusants and seminary priests, took part in proceedings against Campion, Tresham, Throckmorton, Parry, Babington and Lopez, and as chief justice, presided at several state trials. Sent to examine Essex in February 1601, he was shut up in Essex House by the conspirators. During Ralegh's trial he apologized for excesses in the attacks made by (Sir) Edward Coke* upon the prisoner: 'Mr. Attorney speaketh out of the zeal of his duty for the service of the King, and you for your life; be valiant on both sides'. Lord Ellesmere [Thomas Egerton I*] called Popham 'a man of great wisdom, and of singular learning and judgment in the law', and Coke described him as

a most revered judge, of a ready apprehension, profound judgment, most excellent understanding and admirable experience of all business which concerned the commonwealth; accompanied with a rare memory, with perpetual industry and labour for the maintenance of the tranquillity and public good of the realm, and in all things with great constancy, integrity and patience.

But his integrity did not go unchallenged. There is extant a letter of 1594 from the Earl of Essex, attempting to influence his judgment in a suit which was to be heard before him; and Aubrey maintained that Popham acquired Littlecote as the price for obtaining a *nolle prosequi* in favour of the murderer William 'Black' Darrell*. Littlecote did in fact pass to Popham on Darrell's death.[4]

Popham was interested in several commercial ventures, including fen drainage and the mines royal, and in colonial settlement. In 1586, together with his sons-in-law Edward Rogers* and Roger Warre, he was made a commissioner for the population of Munster and was granted land there. He tried to interest his west country neighbours in the project and is said to have put £12,000 of his own money into the venture. Together with Sir Ferdinando Gorges* he obtained a patent to exploit the territory in America later known as Maine, by which they were granted authority to levy taxes and coin money and to maintain government for 21 years. Popham sent out two expeditions, one in 1606, the other in the following year. His interest in colonial settlement and in vagrancy gave rise to the myth that he was responsible for the introduction of the deportation of vagabonds.[5]

Popham died 10 June 1607, having amassed the largest fortune of any member of the bar of his day. He left bequests to his wife, son, daughters and sons-in-law, and the poor of Wellington, Taunton, Bridgwater, North Petherton and Ramsbury. He provided for a hospital for six men and six women to be erected at Wellington,

where he had built a house only slightly smaller than Montacute. It was destroyed in the civil war. Popham's magnificent tomb is in Wellington church.[6]

[1] *Vis. Som.* (Harl. Soc. xi), 125; C66/1421; Foss, *Judges*, vi. 179–81; *DNB*; Williams, *Glos. MPs*, 110; W. Barrett, *Hist. Bristol*, 115; *CSP Dom.* 1598–1601, pp. 97, 195; Somerville, *Duchy*, i. 396–7, 474; Dunwich minute bk. 1595–1619, f. 94. [2] PCC 10 Ketchyn; *CJ*, i. 83, 84, 86, 87, 88, 90, 95, 96, 98, 99, 100, 101, 102, 104, 105, 106, 108, 109, 111, 112, 113, 114; D'Ewes, 158, 159, 162, 165, 178, 179, 181, 182, 184, 206, 213, 219, 220, 221, 222, 223, 247, 248, 249, 250, 251, 255, 260, 261; Trinity, Dublin, anon. jnl. ff. 7, 13, 14; Trinity, Dublin, Thos. Cromwell's jnl. ff. 36, 58, 60; *HMC Lords*, xi. 8. [3] D'Ewes, 268–9, 273, 280, 281, 282–3, 302, 303, 310; *CJ*, i. 117, 118, 132, 134; Trinity, Dublin, Thos. Cromwell's jnl. ff. 96, 99; Northants. RO, Fitzwilliam mss 148; Bacon, *Apophthegms* (1626), p. 79; *CSP Dom.* 1581–90, p. 225; *HMC Hatfield*, iii. 100. [4] Fuller, *Worthies* (1840), iii. 98; Dugdale, *Origines*, 127; *State Trials*, i. 1095, 1127, 1229, 1250, 1333, 1340, 1344–7, 1409; ii. 1, 10, 159, 217, 669; *CSP Dom.* 1547–80, p. 569; 1581–90, pp. 30, 187; 1591–4, p. 448; 1598–1601, pp. 227, 421; *APC*, xii. 271, 294; xiii. 249, 253, 267, 290, 400, 433; xvii. 338; xxi. 470; *Wilts. Mag.* xviii. 270; *N. and Q.* (ser. 2), x. 111–15; *Coke 6th Rep.* 75. [5] *CSP Dom.* 1581–90, pp. 320, 323, 325, 403; 1603–10, 300, 326; Add. 1580–1625, p. 457; *CSP Ire.* 1586–8, pp. 77, 449, 508; *APC*, xiv. 8; xv. 76; J. Winsor, *Hist. America*, iii. 175–6, 209; Strachey, *Virginia*, 35, 158; L. B. Wright, *Atlantic Frontier*, 101–2. [6] *DNB*; PCC 58 Windebanck; information from Mr. F. W. Popham, of Kemsing, Kent.

P.W.H.

PORTER, Arthur (*d.* 1559), of Newent and Alvington, Glos.

GLOUCESTERSHIRE	1554 (Nov.)
GLOUCESTER	1555
AYLESBURY	1559

1st or o.s. of Roger Porter by his 1st w. Margaret, da. of John Arthur. *educ.* L. Inn 1523. *m.* (1) Alice, da. of John Arnold, sis. of Sir Nicholas Arnold*, at least 12ch. inc. Sir Thomas*; (2) Isabel, da. of Sir William Denys, wid. of Sir John Berkeley, *s.p. suc.* fa. 1523.[1]

?Escheator, Glos. and marches of Wales 1526–7; esquire at arrival of Anne of Cleves 1539; j.p. Glos. from 1537, j.p.q. 1554, sheriff 1548–9, chantry commr. 1548.[2]

Porter obtained property at the dissolution of the monasteries. A grant of about 1540 included the site of Lanthony priory and the manor house and demesne of Alvington, which he made one of his two chief residences: in 1558 he and several members of the Denys family bought the remainder of the manor. Elsewhere in the county he owned land at Newent, Lydney and Haggafield, and there are records of his buying property at Pitchcombe, Painswick and in the city of Gloucester, where by the end of Mary's reign he had a joint share in over 25 houses. He married well, and was related to influential local families.

As Member for Gloucester in the 1555 Parliament he had joined the two knights of the shire, Sir Anthony Kingston and Sir Nicholas Arnold, and his fellow-Member for Gloucester, William Massinger, in voting against a government bill. It seems strange, therefore, that in 1559 he should have had to go outside his own county for a seat. The reason was probably that Sir John St. Loe, powerful enough in both Somerset and Gloucestershire to gain county membership, decided to sit for Gloucestershire, leaving a Somerset seat available for his son Sir William. Since the second Gloucestershire seat went to Sir Giles Poole, and the city of Gloucester elected Sir Nicholas Arnold and the recorder, Richard Pate, Porter himself was left without a Gloucestershire constituency. He sat for Aylesbury, where the patron was Sir Thomas Pakington, lord of the borough. Since Porter's son-in-law, Edward Oldsworth, was elected for the same borough at a by-election early in February 1559, the odds are that there was some close connexion with the Pakingtons, of which no trace has been found.

Porter did not long survive this Parliament, dying on 31 May 1559. He and his first wife had produced a large family, a number of whom died in infancy. Six were buried at Hempstead, Gloucestershire, before 1549, and two had died earlier at or near Quedgeley, on his Lanthony property. No will has been found.[3]

[1] Harl. 1041, f. 65; *Vis. Glos.* (Harl. Soc. xxi), 127; *Bristol and Glos. Arch. Soc. Trans.* xiii. 148–9; PCC 7 Bodfelde. [2] *LP Hen. VIII,* xii(2), p. 407; xv, p. 6; xvi, p. 53; *CPR,* 1553–4, p. 19; E. Williams, *The Chantries of William Canynges in St. Mary Redcliffe, Bristol,* 31. [3] *LP Hen. VIII,* xv, p. 539; xvi, pp. 383–4; xvii, pp. 695, 703; xix(1), p. 45; (2), p. 419; *CPR,* 1555–7, pp. 211–12; 1558–60, p. 135; C142/118/56; 122/74; Wards 7/102/157, 187; Guildford Mus., Loseley mss 1331/2; *Bristol and Glos. Arch. Soc. Trans.* xiii. 148–9.

N.M.F.

PORTER, John (d.1599), of Cuckfield, Suss.

BRAMBER   1586

Yr. s. of John Porter of Battle and Bayham by Anne, da. of Richard Isted of Mayfield; bro. of Richard*. educ. ?Clifford's Inn; L. Inn 1576, called 1584. m. (1) Winifred, da. and coh. of John Sackville of Chiddingly Park, 3s. 1da.; (2) Judith née Wood, wid. of one Bland, 1da.
J.p. Suss. from c.1592.

The assumption has been made that the John Porter who sat for Bramber in 1586 was one of the five younger brothers of Richard Porter of Bayham who were under 21 in 1574 at the date of their father's will. By that will, John Porter inherited lands, waters and watermills in the parish of Marden, Kent. He also benefited to varying degrees under the wills of his brothers, Richard, Stephen and George, all of whom predeceased him. He married into a cadet branch of the Sackville family, through whom he probably acquired Cuckfield. This marriage may also explain his return to Parliament for Bramber, presumably on the nomination or through the influence of Lord Buckhurst.

Porter died in August 1599. His will affirms that 'by sundry testimonies of the Holy Ghost in me' he knew 'that

God … hath chosen me, unworthy creature, to be one of his peculiar people whom he hath preordained to salvation'. His second wife was to have a life interest in his Cuckfield and Pevensey estates, which would afterwards pass to the heir, Sackville Porter; his other sons, John and Henry, and his unborn child were to have rent charges of £8 each on the Cuckfield property. A daughter was to have £200. The executors were his two surviving brothers, Robert and Thomas Porter, and his brother-in-law Thomas Aynscombe.

W. Berry, *Co. Genealogies, Suss.* (Comber's copy at Chichester), 200, 300; *L. Inn Black Bk.* i. 435; *Suss. Arch. Colls.* vii. 130; PCC 38 Windebanck, 26 Martin, 24 Watson, 17 Darcy, 7 Windsor, 33 Nevell, 63 Dorset; *VCH Suss.* vii. 158; Cuckfield par. reg.

J.E.M.

PORTER, Richard (d.1584), of Bayham, Suss.

MIDHURST   1571

1st s. of John Porter of Battle and Bayham, and bro. of John*. m. Jane, da. of Robert Whitfield of Worth, at least 3s. 4da. suc. fa. 1574.

Porter was descended from a cadet branch of a Nottinghamshire family which had migrated to Sussex in Henry VI's reign, and which, for the past three generations had been settled in the Pevensey and Battle areas. Their father was an ironmaster, who at his death owned a forge in Bayham and managed another in Frant for Viscount Montagu. Richard, whose five younger brothers were then all under 21, inherited from his father certain lands, woodlands and watermills in the parishes of Brenchley and Lamberhurst, including Bayham on the Kent-Sussex boundary, as well as the residue of his goods, leases and debts due. He was no doubt returned to Parliament in 1571 through the influence of Viscount Montagu, whose estate of Battle Abbey was close to some of the Porter lands.

Porter died between 22 Aug. 1584, when he made his will, and 5 Sept. He left his wife Jane, each of his four daughters and two of his sons £200 apiece, and to his unborn child the same, or £300 if a boy. His property included the lease of the parsonage at Goudhurst, Kent, and his ironworks which he asked his brother Thomas to manage. He made bequests to his servants and to the poor of Frant and Lamberhurst. As executors he appointed his brother John Porter and his brother-in-law Thomas Aynscombe, and as overseers his 'Uncle Isted' and his brother-in-law Thomas Whitfield.

W. Berry, *Co. Genealogies, Suss.* (Comber's copy at Chichester), 200; PCC 26 Martin, 24 Watson, 26 Vox; *Suss. Arch. Colls.* iii. 241; v. 192–3; vii. 130; ix. 36 n; Stowe, 570, f. 104; *LP Hen. VIII,* xiii(2), p. 98.

J.E.M.

PORTER, Sir Thomas (1537–98), of Newent and Alvington, Glos.

GLOUCESTERSHIRE   1572*

b. 1537, 2nd but 1st surv. s. of Arthur Porter* by his 1st w. *m.* c.1558, Anne, da. of Richard Denys* of Cold Ashton, Glos., 2s. 2da. *suc.* fa. 1559. Kntd. 1574.
     Sheriff, Glos. 1581–2, collector of loan 1589.

Considering his status as knight of the shire, his knighthood and his serving as sheriff, the question that has to be asked about Porter is why his name is not to be found on the lists of members of the commission of the peace. Perhaps the answer lies in his religion, though he was appointed to a number of other commissions, and he would have been required to take the oaths before being admitted to the House of Commons. His presence in the 1581 session of the 1572 Parliament is known from his membership of the subsidy committee, 25 Jan. 1581. As his uncle Sir Nicholas Arnold had died in 1580, Porter was presumably returned at a by-election to fill the vacancy in the county representation. He died on 2 July 1598, and no will has been found.

C142/122/74, 153/97; *Vis. Glos.* (Harl. Soc. xxi), 127; *CPR*, 1558–60, p. 446; *APC*, viii. 287–9; xii. 193; xiii. 13, 60, 260, 278; xvi. 143; xvii. 72–3; D'Ewes, 288; *CJ*, i. 119.

A.M.M.

PORTER, William (by 1526–?93), of Grantham and Belton, Lincs.

GRANTHAM	1555
BLETCHINGLEY	1559
HELSTON	1563

b. by 1526, 2nd s. of Augustine Porter of Belton by Ellen, da. of one Smith of Withcote, Leics. *educ.* G. Inn 1540. *m.* by 1569, Jane, da. of John Butler of Aston-le-Walls, Northants. by Margaret, da. of John Dudley of Aston-le-Walls, 8s. 2da. *suc.* bro. John 23 Oct. 1575.
     Commr. sewers, Cambs., Isle of Ely, Hunts., Lincs., Northants., Notts. 1555; alderman, Grantham 1559.[1]

Porter, who entered Gray's Inn in the same year as William Cecil, was apparently a practising lawyer. In 1555, when he voted against a government bill, he was described as 'of Gray's Inn', and it was presumably in London that he met Sir Thomas Cawarden*, owner of Bletchingley, who returned him for the borough in 1559. Both Porter and Cawarden were protestants, Porter being described as 'earnest in religion and to be trusted' in the bishops' reports of 1564. In 1563 his fellow-Member for Helston was his relative by marriage John Dudley, who was himself a distant relative and servant of Sir Robert Dudley*, created Earl of Leicester 1564. It may be noted that Sir Thomas Cawarden was associated with the Dudleys, being nominated by Jane Dudley, Duchess of Northumberland, as one of the overseers of her will in 1554. It looks as

though Porter and Dudley had the same patron in 1563, Sir Robert Dudley.[2]

In Lincolnshire Porter was closely connected with the Thorold family. Porter's mother made William Thorold and his son Anthony* supervisors of her will, while Porter himself was allied with Anthony Thorold against the troublesome Lincolnshire landowner, Arthur Hall*. Porter and Hall had originally been on good terms, and their hostility dates from 1574, when the Privy Council instructed Hall not to execute a statute staple against Porter until the Council had discussed the matter with him. Subsequently, affairs in Grantham were the cause of dispute.[3]

Porter is said to have been buried at Grantham on 7 Dec. 1592 but his inquisition post mortem gives the date of his death as January 1593. Letters of administration were granted by the consistory court of Lincoln in that year.[4]

[1] *Lincs. Peds.* (Harl. Soc. lii), 791–2; *Vis. Northants.* ed. Metcalfe, 8; Bridges, *Northants.* 101; *Cam. Misc.* ix(3), p. 27; *CPR*, 1554–5, p. 109; *Royal Charters of Grantham*, ed. Martin, 90–1. [2] Guildford Mus., Loseley mss 1331/2; *Wm. Salt Arch. Soc.* ix(2), pp. 79, 80. [3] H. G. Wright, *Life and Works of Arthur Hall of Grantham*, 94–6, 202. [4] *Lincs. Peds.* 791–2; C142/236/106; *Lincs. Admons.* (Brit. Rec. Soc. Index Lib. lii), 110.

A.M.M.

PORTINGTON, Roger (1544–1605), of Thorpe Salvin, Yorks.

EAST RETFORD   1593, 1597

b. 1544, 1st s. of Lionel Portington of Barnby-upon-Don by Isabel, da. of Roger Wentworth of South Kirby. *educ.* M. Temple 1565. *m.* Mary, da. and h. of Henry Sandford of Thorpe Salvin, *s.p. suc.* fa. 1559. Kntd. 25 July 1603.
     J.p. Yorks. (W. Riding) 1584–7; j.p.q. Notts. 1590–3.

The Portingtons had held land in the parish of Barnby-upon-Don since the latter half of the fifteenth century, and their main estates still lay in the same parish in the sixteenth century. Portington also owned land in Everton, Nottinghamshire, and burgage land in the parish of Leeds, but he preferred to reside at his wife's estate of Thorpe Salvin, close to the Nottinghamshire border and to East Retford, for which he was twice returned during the long minority that followed the death of the 4th Earl of Rutland in 1588. In 1597 he served on committees concerned with monopolies (10 Nov.), and horse stealing (16 Nov.).

He made his will 12 Apr. 1605 at Thorpe Salvin, where he was subsequently buried, and it was proved at York 22 May the same year. He believed that he would be saved, but not by any 'deserving of my own, for that I am conceived and born in sin and sinful do remain during this my miserable pilgrimage'. He multiplied his sins daily and deserved to go to the place of 'utter darkness'. Nevertheless he committed his sinful soul to God when it left his 'vile person'. He provided for his sisters Margaret and Elizabeth, two poor gentlewomen, and appointed his wife Mary, who lived until 1635, his sole executrix.

C142/125/56; 289/96; *Dugdale's Vis. Yorks.* ed. Clay, ii. 422; E163/14/8; Lansd. 121, f. 70; Hatfield ms 278; *Yorks. Wills,* 5/346; D'Ewes, 555, 558; Townshend, *Hist. Colls.* 106; York prob. reg. 29/606.

A.M.M.

PORTMAN, Sir Hugh (c.1562–1604), of Orchard Portman, Som.

SOMERSET 1597

b. c.1562, 1st s. of Sir Henry Portman by Joan, da. of Thomas Mitchell of Cannington. *educ.* M. Temple 1586. *suc.* fa. Jan. 1591. Kntd. by 1597.

J.p. Som. from c.1592, sheriff 1590–1, 1600–1, dep. lt. Nov. 1597.[1]

Portman owned ten manors and over 100 houses in Somerset, where his family had lived as minor gentry since Edward I's reign. (Sir) William Portman† became chief justice of the Queen's bench in Mary's reign and it was he and his son Sir Henry who extended the Somerset estates and acquired land in Devon, Dorset, Hampshire and St. Marylebone, Middlesex.[2]

As knight of the shire for Somerset in the Parliament of 1597, Portman could have served on committees concerned with enclosures (5 Nov.), the poor law (5, 22 Nov.), armour and weapons (8 Nov.), the penal laws (8 Nov.), monopolies (10 Nov.), rebuilding Langport Eastover (10 Nov.) and the subsidy (15 Nov.). He was given leave to depart on 6 Dec. There are a number of references to his activities in Somerset: investigating complaints about the recruitment of soldiers; controlling grain supplies and seeing to the county musters. In 1600 and in the following year he contributed a light horse for service in Ireland. He also had friends in London, among them Sir John Harington, who wrote in 1598 of hoping to see 'your lady' before Christmas next. Who she was is not known; the herald's visitations mention no wife and Portman's will, proved 16 Mar. 1604, does not show him to be married. He asked to be buried at Orchard Portman, and left £100 to the poor, to be distributed by his brother John, his executor and heir. His unmarried sister Rachel received £500, and his 'aunt Stowell' £100. Three brothers-in-law and a number of nephews and nieces were mentioned, as well as his married sisters. Two of the overseers were Edward Phelips* and Edward Hext*.[3]

[1] C142/229/101; *Vis. Som.* (Harl. Soc. xi), 127; *APC,* xxviii. 92. [2] Collinson, *Som.* i. 56–7; ii. 277, 327–8, 333, 346; iii. 73, 103, 274; Foss, *Judges,* v. 387–8; C142/229/101; *VCH Hants,* iv. 456. [3] D'Ewes, 552, 553, 555, 557, 561, 568; *APC,* xxvi. 498; xxvii. 167–8; xxviii. 92, 559; xxx. 439; xxxii. 279; *HMC Hatfield,* vii. 72; J. Harington, *Nugae Antiquae,* ed. Park (1804), i. 236, 317; PCC 31 Harte.

R.C.G.

POTTS, John (*d.*1597), of Lincoln's Inn, London and Mannington, Norf.

ST. MAWES 1589

s. of Roger Potts of L. Inn. *educ.* L. Inn 1578. *m.* (?1587) Anne, da. of John Dodge of Mannington, at least 3s. 1da.

The suggested identification for the 1589 St. Mawes MP rests upon the Lincoln's Inn lawyer being known to have been the cousin of William Buggin, who sat for Helston in the same Parliament. Buggin had a good reason to be returned for Helston, for his father was the mayor; probably it was he who arranged that Potts should be returned at St. Mawes. No other explanation for Potts's return offers itself, and Cornish boroughs frequently elected London lawyers. Potts and Buggin were at Lincoln's Inn together, and it was as of Lincoln's Inn that Potts received his grant of arms in 1583. Some four years or so later he made a fortunate marriage into the Dodge family of Norfolk. Neither Potts nor Buggin is known to have contributed to the business of the Commons. Potts made his will on 4 Nov. 1593, and added a codicil when sick, 7 Dec. 1597, describing himself as 'John Pott of Mannington, Norfolk, esq.'. He died at his mother's house at Eltham, Kent on 20th of that month, leaving a bequest to his cousin William Buggin. Potts's i.p.m. mentions property at Holborn, St. Pancras, Bishopsgate, Hampton Court, Hitchin, Hertfordshire, and estates at Mannington and Wolterton, Norfolk, including some held of Sir Christopher Heydon as lord of Woodhall manor. Potts's widow married Heydon, and his son John Potts, aged 7, became Heydon's ward. Potts's widow died in 1642, aged 75.

Blomefield, *Norf.* vi. 464–5; *Vis. Norf.* (Harl. Soc. lxxvi) 169–70; *Norf. Arch.* ii. 58; *Grantees of Arms* (Harl. Soc. lxvi), 203; PCC 48 Lewyn; C142/40/256.

P.W.H.

POTTS, Nicholas (1546–1623), of Chalgrave, Beds.

BEDFORD 1584

bap. 20 Apr. 1546, s. of Ralph Potts of Chalgrave. *educ.* Christ Church, Oxf. 1560, MA 1565; G. Inn 1567, called by 1577, Autumn reader 1593, bencher 1594. *m.* Elizabeth, at least 8s. 3da.

J.p. Beds. from c.1591, q. by 1593.

Few details about Potts have survived. To be returned for Bedford he must presumably have been on good terms with the St. Johns of Bletsoe, but no connexion has been found. Chalgrave, where Potts lived and in 1579 bought the advowson, was some distance from Bedford, but perhaps he did legal work for the borough. The only office in the county which he is known to have held was that of 'seneschal' (?steward) to Sir Christopher Hoddesdon, lord of the manor of Leighton Buzzard. He died in Jan. or Feb. 1623, and was buried at Chalgrave, 'a member of the true ancient apostolic and Catholic church', hoping to live with 'all the holy company of angels and archangels and blessed saints of heaven'.[1]

There is one reference to his activity in the Parliament of 1584, when he spoke on the bill for woods destroyed by iron mills, saying that while Marcus Crassus would never speak after Hortensius, he himself was speaking after many Crassi and Hortensii.[2]

[1] F. A. Blaydes, *Gen. Bed.* 71, 73, 363; *G. Inn Pens. Bk.* i. 28, 100, 101, 104, 106, 193; *VCH Beds.* iii. 348; PCC 20 Swann. [2] Lansd. 43, anon. jnl, f. 172.

N.M.F.

POUGHMILL, William (*d.* 1583), of Ludlow, Salop.

LUDLOW   1559, 1563, 1571, 1572

m. Elizabeth, wid. of Richard Rogers of Ludlow; 1s. illegit. 1da. illegit.

Bailiff, Ludlow 1561, 1570, 1575, 1582; clerk in signet office, council in the marches of Wales bef. 1581.

Poughmill may have belonged to the Cheshire family of Pownall, or his name may be derived from the Shropshire village of Sponhill. As well as property in Ludlow he owned lands at Llanwennry in Radnorshire. Much of his prosperity he owed to his wife, who brought him 'money, goods and leases, a great substance'. The only reference found to him in the proceedings of his four Parliaments is to leave of absence 'for his great affairs in the marches', 22 Feb. 1563. He died in 1583. His will, dated 18 Jan., directed that he should be buried in Ludlow parish church 'in such decent sort as to my calling doth appertain'. His wife, executrix and sole legatee, was to provide for his bastard children.

Trans. Salop Arch. Soc. (ser. 2), i. 258; vii. 15; Flenley, *Cal. Reg. Council, Marches of Wales*, 210–11; *CJ*, i. 66; PCC 2 Rowe.

J.J.C.

POWELL, Hugh (*d.* 1587), of Sherborne House, Cathedral Close, Salisbury, Wilts., and of Talyllyn, Brec.

DEVIZES   1563
OLD SARUM   1572

?s. of John or Howell Powell of Brec. *educ.* ?BA Oxf. 1559. *m.* aft. 1558, Eleanor, da. of John Corriatt of Salisbury, *d.s.p.*

Registrar, Salisbury diocese 1562–84; sheriff, Brec. 1582–3.[1]

A branch of Powell's family, originally from Breconshire, came into Wiltshire early in the sixteenth century, and the John Powell who in 1550 received a joint grant with 'Jeronimo' Barnaby of the registrarship was probably his brother: Hugh's will refers to land in Fisherton Anger, inherited in 1560 from his brother John. On the authority of pedigrees accepted by Hoare and Berry, Powell's wife has been described as a daughter of Thomas St. Barbe, but the Wiltshire visitations state that her father was John Corriatt of Salisbury, who died in 1558: his will refers to an unmarried daughter Eleanor, and Powell's mentions 'my mother-in-law Anne Corriatt'. The confusion may have arisen from the inscription on Eleanor's tomb in the south aisle of Salisbury cathedral, describing her as 'lineally descended' from the 'ancient and worshipful family of the Saintbarbes of Ashington, Somerset, and cousin-german to that thrice worthy Lady Walsingham, who was mother to the noble countess of Essex'. This descent is likely to have been through Eleanor's mother, but, as no Corriatts except John appear in the visitations, this cannot be substantiated. However, there was a close connexion between the two families, John Corriatt acting as procurator in 1543 when William St. Barbe was made provost of St. Edmund, Salisbury.[2]

Soon after Powell became registrar the dean and chapter gave him a lease of the former prebendal mansion of Sherborne monastery known as Sherborne House, Salisbury, the document describing him as 'of Great Dorneford [?Durnford], Wiltshire, gent.'. There was trouble over his title, as the augmentations office of the Exchequer, claiming it as concealed lands, challenged the right of the ecclesiastical authorities to dispose of it and granted counter leases, but Powell presumably fought off the opposition as his widow was still there some time after his death. On the 1576 subsidy list for New Street ward, Salisbury, he was assessed on £10 in lands.[3]

Powell may have owed his return to Parliament for Devizes to William Herbert, 1st Earl of Pembroke, to whom he was related through 'my cousin William Herbert of London', and another kinsman of the Herberts, Dr. William Aubrey* of Cantreff, Breconshire. However, Bishop Jewel of Salisbury is just as likely to have been behind his return, alone, or by arrangement with Pembroke or the local gentry. Jewel left Powell 40s. in his will which also mentions a 'servant' William Powell, probably one of the two brothers with this christian name styled in Powell's own will 'the elder' and 'the younger'. Jewel's successor as bishop in 1571, Edmund Geste, continued to employ Powell, but his election patron at Old Sarum in the following year was no doubt the 2nd Earl of Pembroke. The 1572 election indenture indicates that the names were inserted after the rest of the document had been made out.[4]

Unlikely though it might appear, the description on the sheriff's list and Powell's own will make it clear that the registrar and the sheriff of Brecon were one and the same. In 1586 a disagreement with Robert Knollys* about 'the keeping of the possession of the pool of Brecknock' led to 'misdemeanours' and the Privy Council ordered the president of the council in the marches to investigate.

Powell died between 1 Aug. and 2 Dec. 1587. His will has the type of religious preamble to be expected from a servant of Bishop Jewel, beseeching God to blot out his sins for Christ's sake, and to bring him to 'that place of all joy and felicity obtained … by the only death and passion of my only lord and saviour Christ Jesus'. He asked to be buried in Salisbury cathedral near his father, and gave instructions for the family arms to be commemorated in a window. He bequeathed £5 to the cathedral and £20 to the poor of the city, together with money to be invested by the mayor and chamberlains to set up young men in merchandise. Several other Wiltshire parishes, including 'Dornford' (where he leased the prebend) received money for their poor, as did Talyllyn, Breconshire. Bequests went to members of his family – including William Herbert and William Aubrey already mentioned. There were two brothers William and their children, sisters Eleanor and Jane, and seven 'brothers-in-law', including George and John Corriatt. The widow was to have a yearly rent from the parsonage of Fisherton Anger and the furnishings of Sherborne House. The executor and residuary legatee was a nephew Thomas. The widow married Thomas Sadler – probably the one styled 'my servant' in Powell's will – who himself became a registrar of Salisbury.[5]

[1] T. Jones, *Hist. Brec.* iii. 217–18; iv. 286; PCC 56 Noodes, 78 Spencer; *Wilts. Vis. Peds.* (Harl. Soc. cv, cvi), 164; *Wilts. Arch. Mag.* xlvii. 382–3; *Wilts. N. and Q.* v. 231–3. [2] *Wilts. Arch. Mag.* xlvii. 382–3, 388–9; PCC 56 Noodes, 78 Spencer; Hoare, *Wilts. Salisbury,* 243; W. Berry, *Co. Genealogies, Hants,* 4; *Wilts. Vis. Peds.* 164; *Wilts. N. and Q.* v. 233, 379–80. [3] *VCH Wilts.* vi. 76; *Wilts. Arch. Mag.* xlvii. 382–3, 387–8, 401. [4] PCC 43 Holney, 78 Spencer, 12 Daughtry; Dwnn, *Vis. Wales,* ii. 37, 40; C219/28/147. [5] *APC,* xiv. 10, 121–2; PCC 78 Spencer.

N.M.F.

POWELL, Moore (d. c.1573), of Monmouth.

MONMOUTH BOROUGHS 1559, 1563, 1572*

1st s. of Thomas Powell of Whitchurch, Herefs. by his w. a da. of Gwllym Moore, vicar of Newland, Glos. *m.* Blanche, da. of Thomas Morgan of Arkeston, *s.p.*
Recorder, Monmouth from c.1564.

Powell was descended from the Powells of Whitchurch, Herefordshire, some four miles from Monmouth. Moore Gwillim* was his sister's son. Despite the fact that his mother was the daughter of a priest, Powell did not share the partiality towards the changes of religion of others in the same position. He was reported to the Privy Council in 1564 as not favourable to the existing religion, and in his will dated 22 Apr. 1573, proved 7 Feb. 1575, he left his soul 'to Almighty God, our Lady Saint Mary, and to all the holy and blessed company of heaven'. He provided for tithes unpaid and left his widow and executrix Blanche Morgan the profit from the parsonage of Dixton and other life interests. After her death Powell's property was

bequeathed to members of the Gwillim family, especially George Gwillim of Tredgett Hall, who received his 'great house' at Monmouth. £5 went to the poor and £2 p.a. to the upkeep of the Wye bridge. No children are mentioned.

Clark, *Limbus,* 265–6 (where a first marriage is incorrectly attributed to Powell); Williams, *Parl. Hist. Wales,* 134; *Cam. Misc.* ix(3), p. 17; PCC 7 Pyckering.

A.H.D.

POWLE, *see* **POOLE**

POYNINGS, Adrian (c.1515–71), of Wherwell, Hants.

TREGONY 1559

b. c.1515, illegit. s. of Sir Edward Poynings[†], treasurer of the household to Henry VIII, of Westenhanger, Kent. *educ.* G. Inn 1533. *m.* Mary, da. and coh. of Sir Owen West of Wherwell, 1s. *d.v.p.* 3da. Kntd. by Aug. 1562.

In household of Thomas Cromwell by 1538; lt. Boulogne citadel Feb. 1546; capt. June 1546–Apr. 1547; lt. Boulogne base town Mar. 1546; lt. Calais castle 1552; capt. Portsmouth from 1559; second in command expedition to France under Ambrose Dudley 1562; marshal, Le Havre Oct.–Nov. 1562.

J.p. Hants from c.1559, Dorset 1561; duchy of Lancaster steward, Dorset 1566; commr. musters, Hants 1569; v.-adm. Hants by 1570.[1]

Poynings was born in Ghent when his father was in the Netherlands as ambassador to the Emperor. He became a soldier, succeeding Thomas Wyatt[†] to commands at Boulogne, and gaining large sums from the ransoms of prisoners. On several occasions in 1551 and 1552 he is referred to as a knight, but thereafter until 1562 as 'esquire' or 'gentleman', perhaps because a first knighthood was foreign and he thought it inexpedient to use the title in view of his alien status after he returned from Calais. Poynings was not employed during Mary's reign. He was present at the battle of St. Quentin in 1557, with 48 foot soldiers, and returned to England soon afterwards. In June 1558 he was appointed lieutenant to Lord Talbot in the army which was being sent northwards, but a month later the commission was cancelled because he was unwilling to serve. He was still an alien when he was returned to Elizabeth's first Parliament for Tregony, no doubt through a court connexion, perhaps the 2nd Earl of Bedford, who would have approved of his puritanism and of his service at St. Quentin. Other possible patrons are his nephew Lord Clinton, later 1st Earl of Lincoln, and his 'cousin' the Marquess of Winchester. His name is not to be found in the records of the 1559 Parliament, such as they are.[2]

After further military service, on the expedition to France in 1562, Poynings received a patent of denization, and his title to his Dorset manors was confirmed. His last years were spent at Portsmouth, quarrelling with the mayor and burgesses, who accused him of high-handedness and violence as captain of the town. In 1567 he unsuccessfully claimed the barony of la Warr in right of his wife. He died intestate at Portsmouth on 15 Feb. 1571, administration being granted to the widow 22 Feb. Poynings's heirs were his three daughters, one of whom married George More* of Loseley and another Edward More* of Sussex. His widow married Richard Rogers*.[3]

[1] *DNB* (Poynings, Sir Edward); *Vis. Hants* (Harl. Soc. lxiv), 173; *LP Hen. VIII*, xxi(1), pp. 118, 200–1, 541; *CPR*, 1550–3, p. 396; 1558–60, p. 415; 1560–3, p. 253; 1569–72, p. 168; *CSP For.* 1562, pp. 321, 349, 351, 417, 425; Lansd. 1218, ff. 27, 63; Somerville, *Duchy*, i. 628, 630; *CSP Dom.* 1547–80, pp. 345, 385. [2] *CPR*, 1550–3, pp. 177, 218, 396; 1563–6, p. 113; *LP Hen. VIII*, xiii(2), p. 497; xx(2), p. 466; xxi(2), p. 89; *APC*, i. 351; ii. 155–6; iv. 103; vi. 346, 349, 351; *CSP For.* 1547–53, pp. 294, 299, 325; *CP*, iv. 157; Hutchins, *Dorset*, i. 369–90; *HMC Foljambe*, 6; SP12/19/36. [3] *CSP Dom.* 1547–80, pp. 142, 163, 206, 207, 208, 212, 221, 226, 227, 272, 413; Add. 1547–65, p. 540; *CSP For.* 1562, pp. 323, 336, 337, 342–3, 347, 349, 351, 359, 365, 409, 411, 417, 425; *HMC Hatfield*, i. 277–82; *Portsmouth Recs.* 422–8; *APC*, vii. 115, 139–40, 168, 176, 190, 207, 234, 238; *CPR*, 1569–72, p. 267; C142/156/29; PCC admon. act bk. 1571, f. 176.

I.C.

POYNTZ, Sir John (c.1560–1633), of Iron Acton, Glos.

GLOUCESTERSHIRE   1593

b. c.1560, 1st s. of Sir Nicholas Poyntz* of Iron Acton by his 1st w. Anne, da. of Sir Ralph Verney of Penley, Herts. *m.* (1) 1578, Ursula, da. of Sir John Sydenham of Brimpton, Som., *s.p.*; (2) 1582, Elizabeth (*d.*1595), da. of Alexander Sydenham of Luxborough, Som., 4s. 3da; (3) Frances (*d.*1599), da. of John Newton, *s.p.*; (4) June 1600, Grissell (*d.*1648), da. of Walter Roberts of Glassenbury, Kent, wid. of Gregory Price* of Hereford, Herefs., 2s. 3da. *suc.* fa. 1585. Kntd. by Nov. 1588.

J.p. Glos. from c.1582, sheriff 1591–2, custos rot. from 1602; j.p. Som. from c.1584; surveyor, south parts, duchy of Lancaster 1591; member, council in marches of Wales 1603; chamberlain of the Exchequer 1613.

From his father, a man 'greatly friended and allied' in Gloucestershire, Poyntz inherited considerable estates and in 1588 he obtained a grant of the forest of Exmoor, at an annual rent of £46 13s. 4d. In 1593 he was elected knight of the shire, as his father had been before him. He was appointed to the subsidy committee (26 Feb.) and to take the Commons' answer to the Lords on this matter (3 Mar.). His other committees were on a legal matter (9 Mar.), the poor law (12 Mar.) and cloth (15 Mar.). In 1597 he bought Beverstone from the Berkeleys, but his financial affairs were deteriorating, and he was forced to sell the estate almost at once. On three separate occasions, in 1601, 1609 and 1619, he was outlawed or imprisoned for debt. In 1609 he sold the manor of Tockington, part of his patrimony, for £2,700, but only three years later he was said to owe more than £10,000, an immense sum at the time, and too

large, one would think, to have been caused by his father's suspect religious views or the Chancery case resulting from his father's will. Whatever the cause, Poyntz died insolvent and intestate in 1633, and was buried at Iron Acton on 29 Nov.

Vis. Glos. (Harl. Soc. xxi), 135; J. Maclean, *Hist. Fam. Poyntz*, 81 seq.; *Bristol and Glos. Arch Soc. Trans.* xi. 206; xii. 136–56; *CSP Dom.* 1591–4, pp. 124, 203, 397; Somerville, *Duchy*, i. 448; PRO Index 4208; *HMC Hatfield*, iv. 295; xv. 392; D'Ewes, 474, 486, 496, 499, 501; *APC*, xix. 350; xxxii. 367.

J.J.C.

POYNTZ, Matthew (aft. 1528–1605), of Alderley, Glos.

WOOTTON BASSETT   1563*

b. aft. 1528, 2nd s. of John Poyntz of Alderley by Elizabeth, da. of Sir Matthew Brown of Betchworth Castle, Surr. *m.* (1) 1554, Winifred (*d.*1578), da. and coh. of William Wild of Camberwell, Surr., 6s. 7da.; (2) Elizabeth Ingler, prob. wid. of one Culpepper *alias* Crew. *suc.* fa. 1544.

J.p. Glos. from c.1573, commr. musters 1577.

Poyntz was a descendant of the barons of that name who lived in Gloucestershire for many years and took part in the Welsh and Scottish wars of Edward I. His elder brother Henry, an imbecile, was 16 years old in 1544. His younger brother, Robert, was born about 1535. In a letter written to Burghley between 1572 and 1598, Poyntz was included in a list of gentlemen of good standing in Gloucestershire. How he obtained his seat in Parliament for Wootton Bassett has not been ascertained. He was returned there at a by-election in 1563 to replace John Hippisley*, who had preferred to sit for Wells. About the year 1591 he seems to have possessed a considerable amount of land in the neighbourhood of Calne. One John Poyntz[1], perhaps his father, had sat for Devizes in the Parliament of 1529. Poyntz died between 12 Aug. and 19 Nov. 1605. In his will, dated 15 June, he asked to be buried in the churchyard of Alderley near the grave of Mr. John Stanton, who, after having been exiled for his religion, had preached in the parish from 1558 till his death in 1579. He left all his instruments and books to Edward Norris, a student of Magdalen Hall, Oxford, except Foxe's *Acts and Monuments*, which he bequeathed to the parish of Alderley. He charged Sir Nicholas Poyntz, his eldest son and heir, and his sons-in-law to uphold the preaching of the Gospel. He left 20s. to the poor of the parishes of Hawksbury, Wootton and Kingswood, and 10s. to the poor of Alderley. He appears to have been an adviser on the property of recusants in Gloucestershire in 1577. His younger brother, Robert Poyntz (*fl.* 1566), was a well-known Catholic divine.

J. Maclean, *Hist. Fam. Poyntz*, i. passim; *Vis. Glos.* (Harl. Soc. xxi), 100, 134–6; *Vis. Surr.* (Harl. Soc. xliii), 169; *Bristol and Glos. Arch. Soc. Trans.* v. 232; *DNB* (Poyntz, Sir Francis, *d.*1528); Lansd. 104, ff. 100 seq.; *CSP Dom.* Add. 1580–1625, p. 331.

S.T.B.

POYNTZ, Sir Nicholas (c.1528–85), of Iron Acton, Glos.

TOTNES   1559
GLOUCESTERSHIRE   1571

b. c.1528, 1st s. of Sir Nicholas Poyntz† by Joan, da. of Thomas, 5th Lord Berkeley. *m.* (1) 1555, Anne, da. of Sir Ralph Verney of Penley, Herts., 1s. Sir John* 2da.; (2) Margaret (*d.*1586), da. of Edward Stanley, 3rd Earl of Derby, wid. of John Jermyn of Rushbrooke, Suff., 3s. *suc.* fa. 1556. KB Jan. 1559.

Esquire of the body by 1560; j.p. Glos. 1559–c.80, sheriff 1569–70; commr. survey river Leddon 1565, piracy 1577, musters; commr. eccles. causes, diocese of Bristol and Gloucester 1574.

Poyntz's grandmother was a daughter and coheiress of Sir William Huddsfield of Dittisham, some few miles from Totnes, where Poyntz was returned in 1559. He was related to the Devon Carews, and, through his sister's marriage, to Sir Thomas Heneage*, and at the time of his return Poyntz was at the height of his own brief court career. At Elizabeth's coronation he was made KB and soon afterwards an esquire of the body. Why, or even if, he resigned this office has not been ascertained, but some time during 1560 he retired to his Gloucestershire estates and thenceforward is referred to as a local official. He was elected to Parliament for Gloucestershire in 1571, and was appointed to the committee of a bill about Bristol, 12 Apr. His servant was granted privilege 3 May.[1]

Poyntz was a considerable landowner in the county, having in 1557 been granted livery of estates including the manors of Iron Acton, Acton Ilger, Tockington and Hill. In June 1560 he obtained a crown lease of 'the disparked park' of Pucklechurch at a rent of £40. Some of his land was held of the dean and chapter of Bristol, who early in Elizabeth's reign brought a Chancery case against him, a man 'greatly friended and allied', for non-payment of £68 rent. In 1565 he sold some property in Ozleworth, where his father had built a manor house with materials from the dissolved monastery of Kingswood. The Berkeleys, who owned land at Ozleworth and Tockington, sold him part of their estates there, and for a time in 1584 he was living at Tockington Lodge. Before his death at Iron Acton on 1 Sept. 1585 he enfeoffed Thomas Throckmorton*, Matthew Poyntz* and others of most of his property, to the use of himself and his heirs.[2]

Poyntz's surviving correspondence shows a highly strung and emotional man, one perhaps who after 1564 never recovered from his mother's death following atrocious treatment at the hands of her second husband Sir Thomas Dyer*. In 1575 Poyntz was 'much troubled to think I must speak to any woman one loving word', the Queen had forgotten him, and he would as soon go into hell as to the court. About 1583 he uttered 'un-reverend speeches against the Queen, the Council and all the ladies and gentlemen of the court'. By this time,

too, his religion was suspect, which may explain why he put his lands in trust. His name disappears from the commission of the peace after 1579, and a report by Ralph Betham, 'minister of the word and curate of Shepperton in Middlesex', dated 10 Feb. 1584 states that Poyntz was 'very well acquainted and known' to the Catholic priest John Colleton 'sometime of Lincoln College in Oxford, who afterwards going beyond the seas, was made priest there', returned to England and 'resorted ... to one Sir Nicholas Poyntz's dwelling at Acton within three miles of Sodberry in Gloucestershire'. Poyntz was on a list of Catholics dated 1582, and his sister Frances was the mother of the abbess Joanna Berkeley. All this is not to say that the government distrusted him in local affairs: shortly before he died he was asked to supervise the despatch of 300 soldiers from Cirencester to London. He made his will in June 1585, and it was proved in the following September. The preamble refers to 'the forged complaint of a varlet, my enemy', possibly one of the Throckmortons, with whom he had a serious quarrel. The widow was sole executrix. Litigation among the family over its provisions went on well into the seventeenth century.[3]

[1] C142/107/51; Lansd. 7, ff. 177–8; *Bristol and Glos. Arch. Soc. Trans.* xii. 153–4; *Vis. Glos.* (Harl. Soc. xxi), 129; J. Maclean, *Fam. Poyntz*, 74 seq.; PCC 31 Windsor; *Vis. Suff.* ed. Metcalfe, 199; *CPR*, 1558–60, p. 332; *EHR*, xxv. 553; *CP*, iv. 210 n; *HMC Finch*, i. 21; *CJ*, i. 84, 87. [2] *CPR*, 1555–7, p. 379; 1558–60, p. 332; 1563–6, p. 268; C3/20/20; C142/107/51, 210/81; *Bristol and Glos. Arch. Soc. Trans.* xi. 214; xii. 136, 159. [3] Lansd. 7, ff. 177–8; 63, f. 187; *HMC Finch*, i. 20, 21, 23; PCC 42 Brudenell; *CSP Dom.* 1581–90, p. 147; W. H. Stevenson, *Gloucester Recs.* 65–6; Lansd. 146, f. 19; W. R. Williams, *Parl. Hist. Glos.* 44; *Bristol and Glos. Arch. Soc. Trans.* lix. 66 seq.; lxxxviii. 24–5; Flenley, *Cal. Reg. Council, Marches of Wales*, 120; SP12/168/25; *Cath. Rec. Soc.* xiii. 141.

P.W.H.

POYNTZ, *see also* **MORICE** (afterwards **POYNTZ**)

PRATT, Richard

RIPON   1563

This Member has not been identified. There was a Richard Pratt who went to Queens', Cambridge, in 1549 and (very likely it was the same man) to Gray's Inn in 1556. There was also a Richard Pratt of Lofthouse – possibly one of several similarly named places in Yorkshire, including one some miles west of Ripon – but, to judge from his will, this man is unlikely to have been the MP. It is to be expected that the 1563 MP, whoever he was, was in some way connected with the archbishop of York, Thomas Young. On 31 Oct. 1566 he was appointed to the succession committee.

York wills, 21/350; D'Ewes, 127.

N.M.S.

PRATT, William

SOUTHWARK 1589

It has not proved possible to identify this Member, whose election for Southwark, in the absence of an original return, rests upon the authority of a Crown Office list. The Southwark MP was presumably the Mr. Prat who was put in charge of a bill about taverns, 19 Feb. 1589, which points to his being a local man, as were most of the Southwark Members in this period. There was a family of leathersellers, Charles, Christopher and Ralph Pratt, but their wills disclose no relation named William, and no pedigrees of the family are known.[1]

A number of isolated references to men called William Pratt occur elsewhere in the records, and the possibility that one or more of them allude to the Member cannot be ruled out. In 1586, for example, a William Pratt, presumably a family servant, organized the solemn progress which brought the body of Sir Henry Sidney* from Worcester to Penshurst. In 1589 Walsingham wrote to the deputy lieutenants of Surrey claiming exemption from military service in that county for William Pratt, his auditor. In 1599 someone of this name married Joan Hardinge in London, and the following year a William Pratt was released on bail from the Gatehouse prison. A final possibility is the son of a Londoner, a servant of Sir Gilbert Gerard*, but he may have been too young to have been returned in 1589.[2]

[1] D'Ewes, 435; PCC 19 Martyn, 32 Leicester, 39 Fenner; VCH Surr. ii. 329 seq.; Surr. Musters, pt. ii (Surr. Rec. Soc. x), p. 203. [2] Lansd. 50, ff. 191 seq.; HMC 7th Rep. 646a; Lond. Mar. Lic. (Brit. Rec. Soc. Index Lib.), i. 1597–1648, p. 4; APC, xxx. 501; PCC 49 Spencer.

M.R.P.

PRESTON, John (c.1573–c.1642), of Furness, Lancs. and Preston Patrick, Westmld.

LANCASTER 1593

b. c.1573, o.s. of Thomas Preston* of Preston Patrick by Anne or Margaret, da. of John Westby of Mowbrick, Lancs. educ. Skelsmergh sch. Westmld.; Caius, Camb. 1587; G. Inn 1591. m. Frances, da. of Richard Holland of Denton, Lancs., 2s. 4da. suc. fa. 14 June 1604.

Though from a local family, Preston may have owed his return for Lancaster in 1593 to another Gray's Inn man, very much his senior, Sir Gilbert Gerard*, vice-chancellor of the duchy. Though he may later have practised as a lawyer, virtually nothing is known about Preston except that he became a recusant, and was a benefactor of the poor of three Lancashire parishes. His will has not been found, but in 1638 he settled the manors of Preston Patrick, Nether Levins and Holme, Westmorland, on the children of his second son and heir, John. He died about 1642.

Burke, Extinct Baronetage, 427; Al. Cant. iii. 393; Lansd. 153, f. 52; Hist. Garstang (Chetham Soc. cv), 151; Lancs. Social Institutions (Chetham Soc. ser. 3, xi), 16; Nicolson and Burn, Hist. Cumb. and Westmld. i. 240.

N.M.S.

PRESTON, Thomas (d. 1604), of Levens Hall in Furness, Lancs. and Preston Patrick, Westmld.

KNARESBOROUGH 1589

o.s. of John Preston of Preston Patrick by Helen, da. of Sir Christopher Curwen, sis. of Sir Thomas Curwen of Workington, Cumb. m. by 1573, Anne or Margaret, da. of John Westby of Mowbrick, Lancs., 1s. John*.

J.p. Lancs., Westmld. from c.1583; sheriff, Lancs. 1584–5, commr. musters, Lancs. by 1596.[1]

Preston's family originally came from Westmorland. His father purchased the site of Furness abbey at the dissolution of the monasteries, and settled in Lancashire. Whether Preston was returned for Knaresborough through his local standing or by the duchy of Lancaster has not been ascertained. The only mention of his name in the proceedings of the House is to his membership of the conference, 29 Mar. 1589, asking the Queen to declare war on Spain.[2]

It is impossible to be certain of the dates of Preston's employment in the local administration of Lancashire, as he was suspect on religious grounds. Certainly it is clear that it was only because of the shortage of gentlemen well disposed to protestantism in that part of the country that he was employed at all. When the question of his removal from the commission of the peace for Lancashire and Westmorland came up in 1587, a case was made for his retention in Lancashire:

This gentleman hath lived in very good order, and all his household, and was lately sheriff, and were needful to be restored, for that there is but one justice in Furness, and he but a mean gentleman.

Preston died 14 June 1604, his will being proved at Richmond in that year. His son and heir became a recusant.[3]

[1] Lancs. Wills at Richmond 1457–1680 (Lancs. and Cheshire Soc. x); Vis. Lancs. 1613 (Chetham Soc. lxxxii), 60; Vis. Cumb. 1615 (Harl. Soc. vii), 30; Lansd. 53, f. 179; 121, f. 71; Royal 18 D.111, f. 74; APC, xxvi. 388. [2] Vis. Lancs. 1613, 60; Notitia Cestriensis, ii(3) (Chetham Soc. xxii), 511; Lancs. Lieutenancy, ii. (Chetham Soc. l), 202; D'Ewes, 454. [3] CSP Dom. 1581–90, pp. 280, 286; Lansd. 53, f. 179; 121, f. 71; Lancs. Lieutenancy, ii. 202; Cath. Rec. Soc. liii. 105; Lancs. Wills at Richmond 1457–1680.

A.M.M.

PRESTWOOD, Richard (d. 1566), of Exeter, Devon.

EXETER 1559

s. of Reginald Prestwood of Worcester, and bro. of Thomas Prestwood[†]. *m.* Alice, da. of John Bodley, 2s. 1da.

Bailiff, Exeter 1549, receiver 1558, sheriff 1559.

Prestwood was an Exeter merchant who supported the group that gained the upper hand in the struggle over the new charter of the merchants' company in the early years of Elizabeth's reign. As sheriff of the city in 1559, he was in the thick of things, and his faction may have chosen him as MP knowing that he could be useful in London where the dispute was partly carried on. Prestwood continued to be the subject of controversy: in 1560 he was fined £5 by the city chamber for not keeping his dinners during his time as receiver, and, in the same year, a member of the chamber named Lake was fined for calling him 'a dissembler and knave and a beast'. Prestwood, who retorted with similar abuse, was also fined. In 1561 John Peryam* – as strong an opponent of the new merchants' company as Prestwood was a supporter – was fined for more 'unseemly speeches' against him. Still, by 1563, when Prestwood was granted the keepership of the new cloth hall at Exeter, John Peryam stood surety for him. Prestwood died in 1566.

Trans. Dev. Assoc. xxxv. 715–16, 717; R. Izacke, *Antiqs. Exeter*, 123, 128; Roberts thesis, 115; Exeter City act bk. 3, pp. 44, 102, 365; *HMC Exeter*, 308; J. Hoker, *Desc. Exeter* (Dev. and Cornw. Rec. Soc.), 934.

P.W.H.

PRICE, Arthur (c.1549–97), of Vaynor, Berriew, Mont.

MONTGOMERY BOROUGHS 1571

b. c.1549, 2nd s. of Matthew Price of Newtown by his 2nd w. Joan or Joyce, da. of Evan Gwyn of Mynachdy, Rad.; bro. of John II*. *m.* (1) Bridget, da. of John Bourchier, 2nd Earl of Bath, at least 1s.; (2) c.1587, Jane, da. of Randle Brereton of Malpas, Cheshire, wid. of Dr. Nicholas Robinson, bp. of Bangor, 2s. 2da.[1]

J.p. Mont. from c.1575, sheriff 1577–8.[2]

The Prices of Newtown were among the most ancient Montgomeryshire families. Arthur Price's sister, Elizabeth, married the first gentleman of the county, Edward Herbert I*, who frequently sat for Montgomeryshire. It must have been with Herbert's goodwill that Price was returned for Montgomery Boroughs in 1571. In 1580 Price was arraigned in Star Chamber by Hywel ap David ap Ieuan Vychan or Vaughan on a charge of having abused his position as j.p. and his 'great influence' in the shire to seize houses and lands in the parish of Berriew (to which both litigants belonged) in face of the complainant's clear title and hitherto undisturbed possession.[3]

At the county election of 1588 Price evidently determined to test the extent of this 'great influence'. He was opposed, however, by a faction which at first adopted as candidate Rowland Pugh*, who withdrew and stood for

the Boroughs, and then persuaded the veteran Edward Herbert I* to emerge from retirement. There followed a violent election in which the sheriff, another son-in-law of Herbert, secured Herbert's return. Price subsequently brought a Star Chamber suit against the sheriff, the issue of which is unknown.[4]

Price died between 8 Aug. 1597, when he made his will, and 23 Sept., when it was proved. Some of his lands were already settled on his wife and elder son Edward. His younger son John was to have an annuity of £20 and a daughter, Elizabeth, the profits from lands mortgaged to Price in Llyvior and Doyriwe. The testator kept a 'black book' of debts owing to him; the will gives several entries from it, including £120 due from his son-in-law Griffith Pugh, and £20 from the head of the family, Arthur's brother, John Price II* of Newtown. The latter was to keep the £20 and a 'standing cup' which he had borrowed. The will also includes bequests of money to a number of servants, and of plate to various relatives. Price's widow and son Edward were appointed executors and residuary legatees, and John Price and 'my brother Thomas Brereton' overseers.[5]

[1] Burke, *Extinct Baronetcies*, 1838, p. 429 (but his 2nd w. was not sis. of Sir Randolph Brereton); C3/140/50; PCC 78 Cobham; *Mont. Colls.* iv. 389. [2] St. Ch. 5/V6/29; C3/140/50; Flenley, *Cal. Reg. Council, Marches of Wales*, 212. [3] Dwnn, *Vis. Wales*, i. 312; St. Ch. 5/V6/29; Flenley, loc. cit. [4] *DWB*, 781–3; *EHR*, xlvi. 227 seq.; Neale, *Commons*, 99–110; St. Ch. 5/P25/34, 57/30, 67/2. [5] PCC 78 Cobham; *Mont. Colls.* xxi. 203–6.

A.H.D.

PRICE, Cadwaladr (b. c.1561), of Rhiwlas, Merion.

MERIONETH 1584

b. c.1561, 1st s. of John Wyn ap Cadwaladr* of Rhiwlas by Jane, da. and h. of Thomas ap Robert of Llwyn Dedwydd, Llangwm. *educ.* Hart Hall, Oxf. 1581. *m.* Catherine, da. of Sir John Lloyd of Bodidris, Denb., 2s. 2da. *suc.* fa. by Nov. 1589.[1]

J.p. Merion., sheriff 1592–3, dep. lt. bef. 1592, rem. 1600.[2]

An early Tudor family, the Prices of Rhiwlas were well established in Merioneth by the Elizabethan period. John Wyn ap Cadwaladr represented the county in the 1559 Parliament, and groomed his son for a public careeer. This son, Cadwaladr, with one of his brothers, abandoned his father's soubriquet of Wyn for the cognomen Price. An important influence behind his election for the county was that of his great-uncle, Dr. Ellis Price*. As knight of the shire in 1584 Price could have served on the subsidy committee (24 Feb. 1585).[3]

In 1592 Price was strongly recommended for the office of sheriff by Henry Herbert, 2nd Earl of Pembroke, lord president in the marches of Wales. His nomination was opposed, however, by an old enemy of Price's family,

Robert Salesbury* of Rûg, who got the job. At this, Pembroke wrote to Burghley complaining that his recommendation had been ignored, as a result of which the decision was changed and the office given to Price. However, Salesbury had his revenge at the contested county election in 1597, when he backed the successful candidate, Thomas Myddelton*, an outsider from Denbighshire, against Price's nominee and kinsman, John Vaughan of Caergai. Price's supporters included the Owens of Llwyn and Cae'rberllan. Alleged misdemeanours committed during the election by Price and John Lewis Owen*, both of whom were deputy lieutenants of the shire, led to a prosecution in Star Chamber. A petition complaining of their misappropriation of armour and munition levies in the county was also sent in 1598 to the Privy Council, who instructed the 2nd Earl of Pembroke to examine the matter and meanwhile to suspend both of them from their lieutenancies. Two years later the Council advised Pembroke not to renew their appointments.

Price was again involved in a Star Chamber case in 1600, when the attorney-general prosecuted a number of his followers alleged to have rescued him at Llanfor (another family property) while he was under arrest upon a commission of rebellion.[4]

The Rhiwlas estate was substantial enough to place Price on the highest subsidy rating in the shire (£5 in 1598, £10 in 1600), and to support a family bard, Ieuan Tew Brydydd, who was one of several Gwynedd bards to sing his praise. Price was dead by November 1608, when his eldest son John was chosen sheriff.[5]

[1] Dwnn, *Vis. Wales*, ii. 228–9; Griffith, *Peds.* 247; *APC*, xviii. 206. [2] *HMC Hatfield*, vii. 485–6; Lansd. 71, f. 197. [3] *DWB*; E179/222/315–16, 321a; Lansd. 43, anon. jnl. f. 171. [4] NLW, *Clennenau Letters*, 17; Lansd. 71, f. 197; Harl. 6997; *HMC Hatfield*, vii. 485–6; St. Ch. 5L/45/36, 5A/45/19; *APC*, xxviii. 448, 464; xxx. 180–1. [5] E179/222/325–7; *HMC Welsh*, i. 166; ii. 199, 401, 928.

H.G.O.

PRICE, Ellis (c.1512–94), of Plas Iolyn, and Ysbyty Ifan, Denb.

MERIONETH   1558, 1563

b. c.1512, 2nd s. of Robert ap Rhys of Plas Iolyn by Margaret, da. of Rhys Lloyd of Gydros, Merion. *educ.* St. Nicholas Hostel, Camb., BCL 1533, DCL 1534. *m.* (1) Catherine, da. of Thomas Conway of Bodrhyddan, Flints., 1s.; (2) Ellyw, da. of Owen Poole, rector of Llanderwyn, Merion., 2s. 4da. At least 2s. illegit.

Visitor of rel. houses in Wales 1535; chancellor of St. Asaph diocese c.1537–8, of Bangor diocese 1560; commissary gen. St. Asaph 1538; member, council in the marches of Wales from 1560; Earl of Leicester's steward of lordship of Denbigh from c.1564; master in Chancery extraordinary.

J.p.q. Merion. from 1543, Denb. from 1555, Caern. from 1561, Anglesey, Mont. 1564, most Welsh counties by 1575, all and Mon. by 1579; sheriff, Denb. 1548–9, 1556–7, 1568–9, 1572–3, Merion. 1551–2, 1555–6, 1563–4, 1567–8, 1573–4, 1578–9, 1583–4, Caern. 1558–9, Anglesey 1577–8, 1585–6; custos rot. Merion. from 1559.[1]

By the beginning of Elizabeth's reign Price, the 'Red Doctor' as he was sometimes called, had secured the patronage of Sir Robert Dudley*, Earl of Leicester. He was one of the four chief tenants who acted for the rest in negotiations with Leicester on his acquisition of the barony of Denbigh in 1564, and he was appointed steward of the lordship. As agent to Leicester he was the most powerful, and, by his fellow gentry, the best hated man in North Wales. Though his private life had long been the subject of comment it was all that Archbishop Parker could do to resist pressure from both Leicester and the 1st Earl of Pembroke to have Price appointed to the see of Bangor in 1566. In a neat piece of understatement Parker described him as neither a priest nor possessing any 'priestly disposition'. Price later joined his successful rival, Nicholas Robinson, on a commission against the recusant gentry of Lleyn. In common with many turbulent characters of the period Price was, however, popular with the bards of Gwynedd, the most skilled of whom sang his praises, and his name stands first in the list of gentry to whom Elizabeth addressed her proclamation for the Caerwys eisteddfod of 1567.

Price intervened frequently in Merioneth elections, but he sat in only one Elizabethan Parliament, and the only reference found to him in the proceedings is to his being granted leave of absence on 15 Mar. 1563. With the emergence of Robert Salesbury* of Rûg, whose father was Price's old enemy, and with the death of the Earl of Leicester that same year, Price's influence began to wane. In 1590 he had to defend an Exchequer suit brought against him for unlawful intrusion into Merioneth lands. He died in his eighties 8 Oct. 1594. In his will, proved 24 May 1596, his heir and executor Thomas, himself a bard of repute, is charged to have regard for another son, Edward, 'if he recover his health', and to 'place my base sons in some service, and not to suffer them to go a begging'. He was also to see to the marriage of a daughter, Gaynor, and to pay the marriage portion of her sister Kathleen. No mention was made of two other daughters and a son who were living at the time of Lewis Dwnn's visitation.[2]

[1] *DWB*; Griffith, *Peds.* 204; *LP Hen. VIII*, ix. pp. 205, 283, 291; D. R. Thomas, *St. Asaph*, i. 253; *Cal. Wynn Pprs.* p. 339; A. I. Pryce, *Diocese of Bangor in 16th Cent.* 20; Strype, *Cranmer* (1853), p. 274; *CPR*, 1560–3, pp. 446–7; Flenley, *Cal. Reg. Council, Marches of Wales*, 132; *HMC De L'Isle and Dudley*, i. 323; SP12/231/57; *HMC Welsh*, i. 291–2. [2] *Denbigh Recs.* 109–13; SP12/123/11, 231/57; Collins, *Sidney Pprs.* i. 276–9; *Cal. Wynn Pprs.* pp. 11, 12; P. H. Williams, *Council in the Marches of Wales*, 187–206; Lansd. 8, f. 195; *APC*, x. 203–4; *CJ*, i. 69; *HMC Welsh*, i. 3; ii. 44, 129–30, 166, 315; *Exchequer*, ed. E. G. Jones (Univ. Wales, Bd. of Celtic Studies, Hist. and Law ser. iv), 228–9; PCC 37 Drake; *Arch. Camb.* (ser. 6), xv. 120; Dwnn, *Vis. Wales*, ii. 344.

A.H.D.

PRICE, Gregory (1535–1600), of Hereford, Herefs. and The Priory, Brec.

HEREFORDSHIRE	1558
HEREFORD	1572, 1584, 1586, 1589, 1593, 1597

b. 6 Aug. 1535, 1st s. of Sir John Price† of Hereford by Joan, da. of John Williams *alias* Cromwell of Southwark, Surr.; bro. of Richard Price I*. *m.* (1) by Nov. 1559, Mary, da. of Humphrey Coningsby* of Hampton Court, Herefs., 1s.; (2) by 1598, Grissel, da. of Walter Roberts of Glassenbury, Kent, wid. of Gervase Gebons, 1da.; 2s. 1da. illegit. *suc.* fa. 1555.

J.p. Herefs. from 1564, Brec. from c.1591; sheriff, Herefs. 1566–7, 1575–6, 1595–6, Brec. Feb.–Dec. 1587, 1594–5; commr. musters, Herefs. 1570, tanneries, Hereford 1574, subsidy, Herefs. 1580, 1591–2; mayor, Hereford 1573–4, 1576–7, 1597–8; dep. lt. Brec. by 1587.

From his father, a noted public servant and antiquary, Price inherited considerable estates in Herefordshire and Wales. He was frequently employed by the Privy Council in Herefordshire. In 1574, for instance, he was instructed to survey and report on tanneries in Hereford, and in 1590 the complaint of a 'poor widow' was referred to him. In the same year, he wrote to tell the Council that Anthony Pembridge* was not a recusant. He was himself accused, at various times, of enclosing common land, diverting a water course, withholding rent, and permitting play in a bowling alley in his garden. Perhaps he had enemies who took advantage of his doubtful religious views. He was classed as neutral in religion in 1564 and his name was on a list drawn up in 1574 in the interests of Mary Queen of Scots. In 1590 his house in Hereford was described as 'a receptacle of all murderers and ill-disposed persons, that do commit any offence in the city'. All the same, Hereford returned him to every Parliament between 1572 and his death. He is unlikely to be the Mr. Price referred to in the journals of the 1572 Parliament, but he may have been on a committee for Newport bridge, 29 Nov. 1597.

Price died 19 Mar. 1600. He had made his will on the 13th, 'remembering that death is a thing most certain and common to every living creature'. He directed that his body should be buried in Hereford cathedral, and divided his property between his brother John and his two bastard sons, while his wife and daughter each received certain lands. Beatrice Evesham, the mother of his illegitimate children, was to have £20, and 'Master Thompson, reader of the divinity lecture in Hereford', to have 'two books of divinity, in written hand'. Small legacies were left to his servants, and to the parish church of St. Peter, Hereford. Price's wife, his brother, his nephew Thomas Wallwyne, and his cousin John Commond, were appointed executors of the will, which was proved on 9 Apr. 1600. His widow married Sir John Poyntz*.

DWB; W. R. Williams, *Parl. Hist. Herefs.* 39, 84; *Vis. Herefs.* ed. Weaver, 58; *CPR*, 1560–3, p. 133; J. Maclean, *Hist. Fam. Poyntz*, 88; PCC 28 Wallop, 39 More; Duncumb, *Herefs.* i. 367; J. Price, *Hereford*, 258; Flenley, *Cal. Reg. Council, Marches of Wales*, 69, 125; *APC*, xx. 23, 67, 116, 132; *DNB* (Price, Sir John); *Cath. Rec. Soc. Misc.* viii. 113; D'Ewes, 565; *HMC 13th Rep. IV*, 328; C142/261/24.

J.J.C.

PRICE, James (*b.* c.1572), of Monaughty or Mynachdy, Rad.

RADNORSHIRE	1593, 1597, 1601, 1604, 1614, 1621

b. c.1572, 1st s. of John Price of Monaughty by Elizabeth, da. of Sir Robert Whitney* of Whitney, Herefs. and Iccomb, Glos. *educ.* ?M. Temple 1588; ?Brasenose, Oxf. 1589. *m.* Alice, da. of Edward Croft* of Croft Castle, Herefs., 1s. 2da. *suc.* fa. by 1588.[1]

J.p. Rad. from c.1592, sheriff 1595–6, dep. lt. ?1598.[2]

The numerous Price families of Montgomery and Radnor shires all traced their descent from the clan which had settled in the lands between Wye and Severn before the Normans came. Many of their descendants still retained their territorial importance in the sixteenth century. During the century following the Acts of Union, for example, the various branches of the Price family provided 15 of Radnorshire's sheriffs, its county Members in 12 Parliaments and Members for the Boroughs in seven. James Price's grandfather and namesake had acquired Monaughty, a former grange of Abbey Cwmhir, and made it the seat of this branch of the family. The estate appears second in George Owen's list of Radnorshire seats in 1602 – next after that of Vaughan of Clyro and before that of Bradshaw of Presteign.[3]

The younger James Price was still a minor, with his education ahead of him, when he succeeded to the estate, and he was barely of age on his first election to Parliament, where he remained the county's representative for nearly 30 years. His brother-in-law Herbert Croft* had sat for Carmarthenshire in 1589, and subsequently represented his own county of Hereford; alliance with so important a family doubtless added to Price's prestige. On the other hand he inherited a long-standing feud with the great border house of Vaughan, firmly established in the counties of Hereford and Radnor and looked to by the local gentry as standing for the old religion and for Welsh traditional loyalties. At the 1597 election Roger Vaughan* of Clyro stood unsuccessfully against Price, and in the following year brought a Star Chamber action against him, his brother Clement of Coedwgan, and the sheriff, who was alleged to have procured Price's return fraudulently. As knight of the shire Price could have attended numerous committees: in 1593 on the subsidy (26 Feb.) and a legal committee (9 Mar.); in 1597 on enclosures (5 Nov.), the poor law (5, 22 Nov.), armour and weapons (8 Nov.), the penals laws (8 Nov.), monopolies (10 Nov.), the subsidy (15

Nov.) Newport bridge (29 Nov.); in 1601 the main business committee (3 Nov.) and the committee on monopolies (23 Nov.).[4]

The 2nd Earl of Pembroke, as president of the council in the marches of Wales, put forward the names of Price and Bradshaw of Presteign for commissions of lieutenancy in their shire as men 'well able to bear the charges, by residence likely to perform the service and for long continuance best esteemed of the inhabitants'; but Essex, pressing the claims of his steward, proved obstructive, and the two lords fell out about it, with Cecil as mediator. Whether on this occasion Price got his deputy lieutenancy is not clear; he and Bradshaw were certainly in the commission in the next reign, when their conduct in office was the subject of two Star Chamber actions, one brought by the attorney-general, the other by Hugh Lloyd of Nantmel, alleging that they embezzled the subsidy money.[5]

[1] Dwnn, *Vis. Wales*, i. 252; J. Williams, *Rad.* 244–5, 247. [2] Flenley, *Cal. Reg. Council, Marches of Wales*, 237; *APC*, xxviii. 500. [3] Williams, *Parl. Hist. Wales*, 172–3, 178–9; Williams, *Rad.* 294–6; *Arch. Camb.* (ser. 5), v. 214; *RCAM Rad.* 15; G. Owen, *Desc. Pemb.* ed. Owen (Cymmrod. rec. ser. i), 237. [4] *HMC Hatfield*, vii. 251–2; D. Mathew, *Celtic Peoples and Renaissance Europe*, 351–8; Neale, *Commons*, 80, 238; *Star Chamber*, ed. Edwards (Univ. Wales Bd. of Celtic Studies, Hist. and Law ser. i), 140; D'Ewes, 474, 496, 552, 553, 555, 557, 561, 565, 624, 649. [5] *APC*, xxviii. 500; *HMC Hatfield*, viii. 233–4, 264–5; *Star Chamber*, 212, 216.

A.H.D.

PRICE, John I (by 1532–84), of the Inner Temple, London and Gogerddan, Card.

CARDIGANSHIRE	1553 (Oct.), 1554 (Apr.), 1563, 1571, 1572

b. by 1532, 1st s. of Richard ap Rhys Dafydd Lloyd of Gogerddan by Elliw, da. and coh. of William ap Jenkin ap Iorwerth. *educ.* I. Temple 1550. *m.* (1) Elizabeth, da. of Thomas Perrot of Islington, Mdx. and Haroldston, Pemb., 2s. Thomas* and Richard Price II* 1da.; (2) Bridget, da. of James Price of Monaughty, Rad., 1s. *suc.* fa. Sept. 1553 or later.[1]

Bencher, I. Temple 1568–71.

J.p. Card. 1555, q. from 1559, Merion. 1573–9, many Welsh and marcher counties from 1579; custos rot. Card. 1559–79; commr. piracy, Card. 1565, armour 1569, musters 1570, victuals 1574, tanneries, Aberystwyth 1574; sheriff, Merion. 1579–80, Card. 1580–1; member, council in the marches of Wales by 1579–81.[2]

Price traced his descent directly from the Welsh clan which had established itself in Ceredigion by the eleventh century. His grandfather Rhys (from whom the family eventually took its surname), was the first to settle in northern Cardiganshire, and may have built the mansion of Gogerddan. The grandson at first called himself John ap Rhys Dafydd Llwyd, or more briefly John ap Rice, but by

1563 the surname had been fixed as Price or Pryse. The family estates, swollen by acquisitions from the former lands of Cymer Abbey in Merioneth, extended into that county, with some outlying property in Lleyn, Caernarvonshire; and intermarriage with the Pembrokeshire Perrots and the Radnorshire Prices (both parliamentary families), brought additional prestige, which was enhanced by John Price's standing as a barrister. In 1574 he acquired from the Crown the lease of a water mill in the neighbouring borough of Aberystwyth, claimed by the burgesses as municipal property; Price therefore drew no profit, and the dispute dragged on into the time of his son Richard. At the musters of 1570 he was assessed, comparatively heavily, at 'two light horsemen furnished'.[3]

In his last Parliament he was a member of the committee of the bill against Catholics, 25 Jan. 1581, and almost certainly the 'Mr. Price' who sat on committees considering weights and measures, 23 May 1572; sheriffs, 18 Feb. 1576, and the bill on fines and recoveries, 7 Mar. 1576.[4]

Price made his will when 'sick in body' on 13 May 1584, two days before his death. He asked to be buried in Llanbadarnfawr church, and made arrangements for the heir Richard and his daughter Elizabeth. James, the son of his second marriage, received most of his Merioneth estates, and went on to establish the family of Price of Ynys y maengwyn, Towyn, Merioneth. The will was proved 7 Dec. 1584. The Gogerddan family remained prominent in county politics and society till the present century.[5]

[1] Dwnn, *Vis. Wales*, i. 44; *I.T. Recs.* i. 249, 259; Burke, *Peerage* (Webley – Parry-Pryse). [2] *CPR*, 1560–3, p. 446; Egerton 2345, f. 47; Flenley, *Cal. Reg. Council, Marches of Wales*, 60, 69, 109, 132; P. H. Williams, *Council in the Marches of Wales*, 354–5. [3] *Trans. Card. Antiq. Soc.* i. 25; PCC 41 Watson; *Exchequer*, ed. E. G. Jones (Univ. Wales Bd. of Celtic Studies, Hist. and Law ser. iv), 47; *Augmentations*, ed. Lewis and Davies (Univ. Wales Bd. of Celtic Studies, Hist. and Law ser. xiii), 231; Flenley, 74. [4] *CJ*, i. 97, 106, 111, 120. [5] PCC 41 Watson; C142/208/242; *DWB*.

A.H.D.

PRICE, John II (d. 1602), of Newtown, Mont.

MONTGOMERY BOROUGHS	1563
MONTGOMERYSHIRE	1572

1st s. of Matthew Price of Newtown by his 2nd w. Joan or Joyce and bro. of Arthur*. *m.* Elizabeth, da. of Rhys ap Morris ap Owain, of Aberbechan, nr. Newtown, 4s. 4da. *suc.* fa. c.1556.[1]

J.p. Mont. from c.1564, sheriff 1565–6, 1585–6, custodian of arms 1569, commr. on victualling for Ireland, and for tanneries 1574, dep. lt. Mont. 1588; sheriff, Card. 1569–70; prothonotary of Mont., commr. subsidy 1577, 1582.[2]

Price was great-grandson of Rhys ap David, who had been squire of the body to Edward IV and was slain at

Banbury in 1469, and through him he claimed descent (in common with other Price families of Montgomery and Radnor shires) from the pre-conquest Welsh lords of the land between Wye and Severn. The family position was enhanced by the spoils from the abbey of Strata Florida, and by the marriage of John Price's sister Elizabeth to Edward Herbert I*. Herbert's and Price's names are next to each other on a list of 1574 drawn up in the interests of Mary Queen of Scots. At the musters of 1570 Price was one of a dozen Montgomeryshire gentlemen rated at 'one light horseman furnished', only Herbert being rated higher. On his mother's side he was descended from the important Radnorshire family of Price of Monaughty, and the marriage of his wife's niece into that of Price of Gogerddan extended his influence into Cardiganshire. On the other hand, his eldest son Edward married a daughter of John Owen Vaughan of Llwydiarth, the lifelong foe of the Herberts of Montgomery. This may help to account for the bitter electoral struggle in 1588 between Edward Herbert and John Price's younger brother Arthur (who had married the Earl of Bath's daughter and represented Montgomery Boroughs in 1571), in which John lent all his weight as deputy lieutenant to his brother's cause.[3]

Price made his will 4 May 1602 when 'somewhat sick in body ... knowing nothing to be more certain than death, nor anything more uncertain than the hour thereof'. The will was proved on 8 Jan. following. His widow inherited the livestock and movables, while the lands, mainly in the neighbourhood of Newtown, were divided between the three sons, of whom the second, Matthew, founded the family of Price of Parke, while the third, vicar of Kerry, was allotted the tolls of Newtown fair, leased by the family since 1521. It was this third son who built the family mansion of Newtown Hall, which survives as municipal offices. John Price's eldest grandson John (the future baronet) inherited the profits of the manorial court of Kerry. The Prices retained their importance in Montgomeryshire till the eighteenth century, towards the close of which the family, much reduced in wealth through extravagance, died out.[4]

[1] C3/140/50; Dwnn, *Vis. Wales*, i. 313–15; *Arch. Camb.* 1887, pp. 62–63; *Mont. Colls.* iii. 158, 306, 400–1; *Star Chamber*, ed. Edwards (Univ. Wales Bd. of Celtic Studies, Hist. and Law ser. i), 129. [2] *CPR*, 1563–6, p. 30; Flenley, *Cal. Reg. Council, Marches of Wales*, 60, 109, 127, 141, 212; Neale, *Commons*, 100. [3] Dwnn; *Mont. Colls.* xxxi. 68–70; *Cath. Rec. Soc. Misc.* viii. 110; Neale, 100–10; Flenley, 74. [4] PCC 7 Bolein; *RCAM Mont.* 162 n.; *DWB*, 802.

A.H.D.

PRICE, John III (?1579–1656), ?of Whitford, Flints.

FLINT BOROUGHS   1601

The identity of this Member has not been established.

A John Price of Tre'r, Whitford, was escheator for Flintshire 1565–6, and an i.p.m. commissioner in that

county in 1565. He was very probably the John ap Rhys ap David who was assessed for the subsidy in Whitford at 20s. between 1570 and 1598. As his name last appears on the subsidy roll in 1599, and was replaced by that of his heir, William ap John ap Rhys, in 1601, he presumably cannot have been the Member for the Boroughs in the October 1601 Parliament.[1]

A John Price, possibly his younger son, matriculated at Christ Church, Oxford, aged 17, in 1596 and was buried at Whitford in 1656, but the identification of this John with the 1601 MP rests only upon his appropriate age and the lack of suitable alternatives.

[1] *CPR*, 1563–6, p. 508; E179/221/214, 216/20, 225.

A.H.D.

PRICE (ap RHYS), Morgan (*d. c.*1580), of New Radnor, Rad.

NEW RADNOR BOROUGHS   1563

1st s. of Rhys ap Dafydd ap Maredudd Vychan by Silian, da. of Richard ap Llywelyn ap Hywel. *m.* Dorothy, da. of Richard Blike[†] of New Radnor, 1s.
Capital burgess, New Radnor 1562.

Little has been ascertained about this man or his family. He was one of the chief burgesses of New Radnor named in the charter of 1562, and five years later he took over from Robert Blike (presumably one of his wife's family) a lease of the crown property of Radnor park for 21 years. It was described as unfenced, with no deer and only small shrubs, hazels and briars, 'much after the fashion of a mountain land of that country'. Price presumably died about 1580, when a new lease was made out to his son John. Although Morgan Price's wife is described by Dwnn as 'sole heiress' to her father, she is not in the Blike pedigree in the Shropshire visitation of 1623.

Dwnn, *Vis. Wales*, i. 263; *CPR*, 1560–3, p. 344; *Augmentations*, ed. Lewis and Davies (Univ. Wales Bd. of Celtic Studies, Hist. and Law ser. xiii), 172, 514, 517–18, 524; *Vis. Salop* (Harl. Soc. xxviii), 57–8.

A.H.D.

PRICE, Richard I (c.1538–c.87), of The Priory, Brecon.

BRECON BOROUGHS   1571

b. c.1538, 2nd or 3rd s. of Sir John Price[†] by Joan, da. of John Williams *alias* Cromwell, of Southwark, Surr.; bro. of Gregory*. *educ.* Oxf. BA 1555; G. Inn 1555. *m.* ?Elizabeth, da. and coh. of William Wightman*, *s.p.*[1]
Bailiff, Brecon 1570–1, 1581–2; sheriff, Brec. 1565–6, 1571–2, Nov. 1586–*d.*, custodian of arms 1570, j.p., commr. musters, and for victualling Ireland 1574, custos rot. by 1575.[2]

Price's father was one of the chief Welsh agents of Thomas Cromwell, his relative by marriage, in carrying out the union with England, the dissolution of the Welsh monasteries and the planting of the Reformation there. He was richly rewarded with monastic estates in Breconshire, Herefordshire and elsewhere. The Herefordshire and other estates went to his eldest son Gregory, but Richard, either in his father's lifetime or by arrangement with the heir, received most of those in Breconshire, including houses, lands and tithes in and around the town which had belonged to Brecon priory. The mansion which had arisen on the Priory site itself became his residence, and remained in the family till the male line died out in the eighteenth century. But the tithes proved 'greatly decayed', and could hardly meet the charges of repairing the priory church (used by the parish) and maintaining a curate. Price also had lands in Radnorshire, Herefordshire and Worcestershire, and he made further purchases, some of them from Sir Roger Vaughan*, his parliamentary colleague for the shire. Between 1567 and 1576 he took out crown leases of oak woods and other lands from the former estates of the Duke of Buckingham as well as in the crown lordship of Brecon, and in 1586 secured a joint lease of mining rights for coal in the wastes of the manor of Dinas, embracing Trefecca and Talgarth. At the musters of 1570 he was charged with 'one light horseman furnished'.[3]

Of his father's valuable collection of manuscripts, the volumes of Welsh poetry went to Gregory, while Richard was allotted 'all my written books of history and humanities' including the manuscript of Sir John's learned reply to Polydore Vergil defending traditional accounts of early Welsh history. This he was enjoined to publish, and he received an annuity of £20 a year for five years, with a lump sum of 20 marks, to encourage him in that work and in the care of his younger brother John, who was to be brought up as a scholar if he showed aptitude. The book was published in 1573 under the title *Historiae Britannicae Defensio*; incorporated in Powel's *Historie* of 1584, it remained the basis of Welsh historiography till the nineteenth century. The tradition that Richard Price was himself a man of letters and an associate of Shakespeare lacks foundation.

In his will, dated 10 Nov. 1586 and proved by his widow, the sole executrix, on 4 Feb. following, Price left £40 to provide work for the poor of Brecon and 20s. for repairs to the church. The only book mentioned in the long and detailed will is Fitzherbert's abridgement of the laws. The supervisors of the will were 'my dear friend Mr. Robert Davy*' and 'my dear and loving cousin Mr. David Williams*'. Price was in good health when he made his will, but was dead by 16 Jan. 1587 when the Earl of Leicester asked for the selection of his successor as sheriff to be delayed. His brother Gregory succeeded him as sheriff in February 1587.[4]

[1] *DWB*; T. Jones, *Brec.* ii. 139–40; iv. 306; *Mdx. Peds.* (Harl. Soc. lxv), 34 gives Wm. Wightman's s.-in-law as John Price, 2nd s. of Sir John. [2] Jones, iv. 306; Flenley, *Cal. Reg. Council, Marches of Wales*, 69,

109, 126, 213; SP12/93. [3] *Augmentations*, ed. Lewis and Davies (Univ. Wales Bd. of Celtic Studies, Hist. and Law ser. xiii), 203, 207–8, 210, 211, 216, 220; J. Lloyd, *Hist. Mem. Brec.* ii. 43–5; PCC 39 More, 9 Spencer; Jones, loc. cit.; *Arch. Camb.* (ser. 4), xiii. 275–80; Burke, *Peerage* (sub Camden); Flenley, 75. [4] PCC 9 Spencer; *DWB*; *CSP Dom.* 1581–90, p. 381.

A.H.D.

PRICE, Richard II (c.1562–1623), of Gogerddan, Llanbadarnfawr, Card.

CARDIGANSHIRE   1584, 1589, 1593, 1601, 1614, 1621

b. c.1562, 1st s. of John Price I* by his 1st w., and bro. of Thomas*. *educ.* I. Temple 1582. *m.* Gwen (or Gwenllian), da. and h. of Thomas ap Rhys ap Morus of Aberbechan, Newtown, Mont., 2s. 5da. *suc.* fa. 1584. Kntd. 1602.[1]

J.p. Card. from c.1583, sheriff 1585–6, 1603–4, custos rot. from c.1592, dep. lt. from 1597; sheriff, Mont. 1590–1, j.p. 1596; member, council in the marches of Wales 1601; Exchequer commr. Card. 1611.[2]

George Owen in his *Description of Wales* places Gogerddan first among the mansions of Cardiganshire. Price's father had left him an ample estate, to which he added by lease or purchase until almost the end of Elizabeth's reign. His acquisitions included crown lands and rectories around Aberystwyth (some of them from the escheated estate of Sir Rhys ap Thomas) and the tolls and fisheries of Aberystwyth itself. His Montgomeryshire marriage extended his interests into that shire, and he added to his estate lands and mills near his wife's home at Newtown. In Merioneth, just north of the Montgomeryshire border, he acquired lands and fishing rights in the Dovey valley. Some of the purchases were made in association with his wife and his son John; some were subsequently disposed of; many involved him in litigation, including nearly a score of Exchequer actions.[3]

The mill at Aberystwyth, of which the town had disputed ownership with his father, was wrecked by a mob after the son had procured a favourable verdict in the courts, and had to be rebuilt. His purchases in the township of Pennal, in the Dovey valley, were a source of even more prolonged trouble, for here he was up against powerful Montgomeryshire neighbours like Matthew Herbert II* and Rowland Pugh*, and he had the case removed to the court of Exchequer on the ground that their local influence precluded an impartial verdict at common law; even so, it cost him at least eight Exchequer suits and his wife yet another. He was himself arraigned before the same court with 25 other freeholders of the townships of Talerddig and Carno, Montgomeryshire, for refusing the customary dues to Sir Roger Owen, who had a life grant of the lordships of Arwystli and Cyfelliog and claimed (what the defendants denied) that the townships lay within his jurisdiction.[4]

As knight of the shire for Cardiganshire Price could, in

this period, have attended the following committees: in 1584–5, on the subsidy (24 Feb.); in 1589, on the subsidy (11 Feb.); in 1593, on the subsidy (26 Feb.) and a legal matter (9 Mar.); in 1601, the main business committee (3 Nov.) and the committee on monopolies (23 Nov.). Like so many of the Welsh gentry of his age, Price had widespread industrial interests. Apart from mills, water rights and fisheries, he appears to have had dealings in the local cloth trade: among the debts left to his widow to collect was one of £20 from a Machynlleth gentleman for five pieces of Welsh cloth sold him by Price. He died 7 Feb. 1623.[5]

[1] Dwnn, *Vis. Wales*, i. 44; C142/208/242; *Star Chamber*, ed. Edwards (Univ. Wales Bd. of Celtic Studies, Hist. and Law ser. i), 40; *Exchequer*, ed. E. G. Jones (same ser. iv), 96; G. Owen, 'Desc. Wales' 1602 in *Desc. Pemb.* ed. H. Owen, ii. 461; Mort thesis. [2] G. Owen, *Taylor's Cussion*, ff. 36–7; *CSP Dom.* 1595–7, p. 536; *Star Chamber*, 40; *APC*, xxx. 775; P. H. Williams, *Council in the Marches of Wales*, 354–5; *Exchequer*, ed. T. I. J. Jones (Univ. Wales Bd. of Celtic Studies, Hist. and Law ser. xv), 99–100. [3] *Exchequer*, ed. E. G. Jones, 90, 96; ed. T. I. J. Jones, 76, 90, 93–4, 97, 102, 104, 239, 263, 280, 281; *Augmentations* (same ser. xiii), 129, 433–4. [4] *Augmentations*, 231; *Exchequer*, ed. E. G. Jones, 96; ed. T. I. J. Jones, 104, 113, 225–6, 228, 237, 272, 280–1, 286; *Mont. Coll. Supp.* 1896–1928, p. 137. [5] Lansd. 43, anon. jnl. f. 171; D'Ewes, 431, 474, 496, 624, 649; *Exchequer Jas. I*, ed. T. I. J. Jones, 112; PCC 28 Swann.

A.H.D.

PRICE, Stephen (*b.*1572), of Gray's Inn, London.

NEW RADNOR BOROUGHS 1601

b. 1572, 2nd s. of John Price (*d.*1597), of Pilleth by Catherine, da. of Roger Vaughan* of Clyro. *educ.* Brasenose, Oxf. 1589, aged 17; G. Inn 1594, called 1599.

The Prices of Pilleth were a junior branch of the Prices of Monaughty. Price's grandfather and namesake had sat for the shire in 1555, and his cousin James* did so between 1593 and 1621. Price was a lawyer 'called to the grand company' of ancients of Gray's Inn in 1613, which entitled him to practice in the courts at Westminster. He had no estate in Radnorshire until 1603 when he was granted some lands forfeited by the attainder of John Baskerville of Aberedw.

Dwnn, *Vis. Wales*, i. 252; *Trans. Rad. Soc.* xxi. 42; *G. Inn Pens. Bk.* 142, 202; *CSP Dom.* 1603–10, p. 19; *HMC Hatfield*, xii. 642.

A.H.D.

PRICE, Thomas (*d.*1623), of Glanvraed, Llanfihangel Geneu'r Glyn, Card.

CARDIGANSHIRE 1597[1]

2nd s. of John Price I* by his 1st w., and bro. of Richard II*. *educ.* ?Shrewsbury 1583; I. Temple 1588. *m.* Bridget, da. and h. of John ap Gruffyd ap Jevan ap Siamcyn of Glanvraed, 5s. 7da.

J.p. Card. from c.1595; steward of five royal manors in Card. 1601.

Price represented Cardiganshire on an occasion when his elder brother evidently did not wish to sit. He could have attended the committees on enclosures (5 Nov.), the poor law (5, 22 Nov.), armour and weapons (8 Nov.), penal laws (8 Nov.), monopolies (10 Nov.), the subsidy (15 Nov.) and Newport bridge (29 Nov.). In 1594 it was alleged in the Star Chamber that he and two others had attacked one of the justices during the great sessions at Cardigan in August 1593. The complainant alleged that Price challenged him 'to the field offering unto him his glove and daring him to fight', and when he refused, 'Price then and there with his dagger suddenly and secretly struck your said subject upon the head and same did cruelly cut to the effusion of much blood'.

Price's stewardship of several royal manors in Cardiganshire brought upon him several suits in the Exchequer, alleging illegal acquisition and retention of office. His will, made 11 Sept. 1623, was proved on the following 12 Nov. by his widow Bridget, and his eldest son Thomas, the executors. It was devoted largely to providing bequests for his younger children, servants and friends. A total of £1,500 was bequeathed to his six unmarried daughters, while his three younger sons received £100 each. Among the overseers was Price's younger brother Sir James.[2]

[1] Folger V. b. 298. [2] Dwnn, *Vis. Wales*, i. 44; Burke, *Commoners*, iii. 467; PCC 112 Swann; Flenley, *Cal. Reg. Council, Marches of Wales*, 237; D'Ewes, 552, 553, 555, 557, 561, 565; St. Ch. 5/L20/32; *Exchequer*, ed. T. I. J. Jones (Univ. Wales Bd. of Celtic Studies, Hist. and Law ser. xv), 91, 93–5.

A.M.M.

PRICE, Walter, of Monaughty, Rad.

RADNORSHIRE 1571

3rd s. of James Price (*d.*1574), of Monaughty by his w. Elizabeth Clement. *educ.* I. Temple Nov. 1565. *m.* Margaret, da. of Thomas Watkin ap Rhys, 2s. 2da.

The principal rivals of the Prices were the Vaughans, who contested Radnorshire with them in 1572 and 1597. In 1571, however, the sheriff was another Price, and so far as is known all went peacefully.

Trans. Rad. Soc. xi. 37; Dwnn, *Vis. Wales*, i. 252.

N.M.F.

PRICE (ap RHYS ap HYWEL), William I, of Beaumaris, Anglesey.

BEAUMARIS 1558, 1559,[1] 1563

1st s. of Rhys ap Hywel of Bodowyr by Alice, da. of Dafydd ap Ieuan. *suc.* fa. 1540.
Capital burgess of Beaumaris 1562.

Price came of a younger branch of the family of Bodowyr, Llanidan. He was a supporter of the Bulkeleys and held ten acres of Richard Bulkeley I* in 1574.[2]

[1] C219/284/45. [2] Griffith, *Peds.* 51, 83; PCC 17 Cromwell; *CPR*, 1560–3, p. 347; C. E. M. Evans, 'Med. Beaumaris and commote of Dindaethwy' (Univ. Wales MA thesis, 1949), pt. 3, p. 96.

PCC 85 Harte; *Bath Chamberlains' Accts.* (Som. Rec. Soc. xxxviii), passim; *Regs. Bath Abbey* (Harl. Soc.), 6, 7, 8, 9, 334, 336; BL Cartae Antiquae 83H4; D'Ewes, 501, 507.

P.S.E.

I.C.

PRICE, *see also* **WYN ap CADWALADR**

PRICE, William II (d. 1596), of Bath, Som.

BATH	1593

m. Susan, 3s. 2da.
Town clerk, Bath 1590–*d.*

William Price of Bath was born in north Wales, probably in Denbighshire where he both inherited lands from his father and acquired others by purchase. Conceivably he was the Mr. Price who in 1573 received from the corporation of Bath a gallon of Gascon wine, but the surname (variously rendered) was not unique in the city: an Edward Apprice occurs in the chamberlain's accounts for the selfsame year. Judging from later entries – and assuming that the identification is correct – the service so rewarded was probably of a minor legal nature, for in 1580 he was paid for making a lease, in 1582 for riding to Mr. Ayshe*, the recorder, about the charters, in 1585 for making certain bonds, letters and other writings, and in 1589 again for legal writings. A suit – 'Price's suit' or 'against William Apprice' – is mentioned in 1586 and 1587. Literate, and possessed of some legal knowledge, he was not during these years of sufficient standing to be accorded at all times the respectful prefix to his name. Between 1584 and 1590 four of his children, but not his first-born son, John were christened in Bath abbey. In the new charter of 1590 William Price, gentleman, was named as town clerk.

There had been town clerks in Bath before Price, but he was the first in this period to be returned to Parliament, the most frequent recipient of this honour being its recorder, generally in company with a townsman of aldermanic or mayoral rank. John Court, recorder during Price's early years as clerk, sat as senior burgess in 1589, and possibly it was to ascertain his inclination in 1593 that the city then wrote to him 'about a burgess'. In the event the mayor, not the recorder, was returned for the senior seat, with Price as his fellow-Member, sitting for the first and only time and serving perhaps on two committees concerned with cloth (15, 23 Mar.). His fee as town clerk, normally 40s. per annum, was raised to 60s. for this particular year, and for his wages at the Parliament he received £4 – 20s. less than was paid to the mayor.

His will, naming John as his heir, and two aldermen as executors – his wife being already dead – has a long religious preamble and is dated 2 Oct. 38 Elizabeth, 'whose reign I pray may long continue to the glory of God and the good of the Church and the commonwealth of this land'. He was buried in Bath abbey on 4 Nov. 1596.

PRIDEAUX, Humphrey (d. 1604), of Westwood in Crediton, Devon.

HELSTON	1584

2nd s. of Richard Prideaux of Theuborough by his 2nd w. Katherine, da. of Sir John Arundell of Trerice. *educ.* L. Inn 1572, called 1581. *m.* Joan, da. of John Bevill of Killigarth, Cornw., 2s. 3da.
Butler, L. Inn 1598–9.

Prideaux was a lawyer who presumably owed his return for Helston to his maternal grandfather Sir John Arundell, the recorder. He died in January 1604, leaving his goods and a life interest in his estates to his 'most dear' wife, whom he appointed executrix. Both sons and the eldest daughter received £200 and the two younger daughters £160 each. The will was proved 3 Feb. 1604.

Vivian, *Vis. Devon*, 619; *Black Bk. L. Inn*, i. 422; ii. 57; *HMC Hatfield*, x. 90; PCC 16 Harte.

I.C.

PRIDEAUX, Nicholas (c. 1550–1628), of Soldon, Devon, and Padstow, Cornw.

CAMELFORD	1571

b. c.1550, 1st s. of Roger Prideaux† of Soldon by Philippa, da. of Roger Yorke. *m.* (1) Thomasine (d. 1573), da. and h. of John Henscott of Henscott, Devon, 1s. *d.v.p.*; (2) 1576, Cheston (d. 1610), da. and coh. of William Vyell or Viall of St. Breock, Cornw., 1s.; (3) 1611, Mary (d. 1647), da. of John Castell of Ashbury, Devon, wid. of Dr. Evan Morice, chancellor of Exeter diocese, *s.p. suc.* fa. 1582. Kntd. Nov. 1606.
J.p. Devon from c. 1584, Cornw. from c. 1591; sheriff, Cornw. 1605–6.[1]

Considering his status, Prideaux's parliamentary career was negligible. He represented one Cornish borough as a young man of about 21, made no contribution (as far as is known) to the proceedings of the House and never sat again. At the dissolution of the monasteries his great-uncle Nicholas had bought considerable property belonging to Bodmin priory, including the manor of Padstow, which he later assigned to Roger Prideaux, upon whose death it passed, with the Devon manors of Holsworthy, Chesworthy, and the family seat at Soldon, to Prideaux himself. In 1600 Prideaux settled Soldon on his son Humphrey at the latter's marriage to Honor, daughter of Edmund Fortescue*, and moved to Padstow, where he had already rebuilt the old house of the monastery, known as Prideaux Place or Place House. About 1602, Richard Carew* wrote:

> Mr. Nicholas Prideaux from his new and stately house thereby taketh a full and large prospect of the town, haven and country adjoining, to all which his wisdom is a stay, his authority a direction.

Prideaux's second marriage brought him the manor of Treworder in Cornwall, where he kept up another establishment. Only a Devon inquisition survives for him: it describes Soldon as held of the Queen as of her duchy of Lancaster. For some years before his death in 1628, Prideaux administered the Soldon property for his grandson Nicholas, Humphrey Prideaux having died of smallpox about 1617.[2]

At one time Prideaux may have been under suspicion for religious reasons. An undated Hatfield manuscript giving information against a recusant of St. Breock states that he was much favoured by Prideaux, whose wife's married sisters were suspected of Catholic sympathies. St. Breock was the paternal home of his second wife's family, and one of her sisters married an Arundell of Lanherne. Prideaux's parents, however, were protestants, and his will suggests that he shared their views. His name was removed from a commission of the peace in 1587, but soon restored. In October 1591 he was one of those who provided ships and victuals for troops going to Ireland from Cornwall, and between October 1598 and February 1599 the Council wrote to him several times about soldiers for Ireland. In the following May he sent a letter to London about a threatened Spanish invasion.[3]

He was knighted at the end of his year as sheriff, and continued writing letters on official business as late as 1623. He died 25 Jan. 1628 at West Putford, Devon: there is an inscription to him at Padstow.

His will, made in January 1625, was proved 24 May 1628. He left £50 and the goods at Padstow to his surviving son John, and £250 to his grandchildren. The residue went to the widow, the sole executrix.[4]

[1] C142/198/37; E163/14/8, f. 7; Vivian, *Vis. Cornw.* 549, 611; J. Maclean, *Trigg Minor*, ii. 226; iii. 433. [2] *LP Hen. VIII*, xx(1), p. 129; *CPR*, 1548–9, p. 226; C142/198/37; Wards 7/78/138; Maclean, ii. 207; PCC 74 Weldon; *Carew's Surv. Cornw.* ed. Halliday, 219; S. Drew, *Hist. Cornw.* (1824), ii. 684. [3] Lansd. 121, f. 66; *HMC Hatfield*, iv. 154; ix. 152; xiv. 313; *Vis. Cornw.*; PCC 7 Tirwhite, 2 Lewyn, 45 Barrington; *APC*, xxix. 241, 521. [4] *CSP Dom.* 1603–10, pp. 287, 609; 1619–23, p. 505; *Vis. Cornw.*; Wards 7/78/138; PCC 45 Barrington.

N.M.F.

PRINCE, Richard (c.1523–98), of Whitehall, Abbey Foregate, Shrewsbury, Salop.

LUDLOW	1558
BRIDGNORTH	1559

b. c.1523, 1st s. of John Prince, master of St. Giles's hospital, Shrewsbury, by Alice, da. of John Bradley of

Wenlock. *educ.* I. Temple Nov. 1553. *m.* (1) Margaret (*d.*1584), da. of Geoffrey Manchester of Manchester; (2) Dorothy, da. of William Leighton of Plaish, 4s. 5da. 1da. illegit. *suc.* fa. 20 July 1557.[1]

Burgess, Shrewsbury 1551; feodary, Salop by 1562–73, commr. musters 1577.[2]

In 1551 Prince (or Prynce as it is sometimes spelled) was granted the two chambers over the porch of Shrewsbury abbey as a reward for his 'good service, labour and travail' on behalf of the parishoners. He obtained a considerable portion of the abbey lands, and with the stone from its dismantled buildings constructed the house in Abbey Foregate now known as Whitehall, which took four years to build and was completed in 1582. He was still living there in July 1598 when he made his will, directing that he should be buried in the abbey church.[3]

Throughout this period his name occurs frequently in the town records, the bailiffs and common council often consulting him on their legal problems. In 1578 the bailiffs were instructed to take his advice on the best means for suppressing idleness, drunkenness and disorders. His counsel was sought by the borough on certain letters, sent to the president of the council in the marches, concerning the voyage of Sir Walter Ralegh in 1584, although at this time he was in disfavour with the bailiffs for allowing his men to sow barley on the common land. Two years later he subscribed £25 for the defence of the kingdom, and in 1593 he wrote to the bailiffs, asking that a collection be made at the next sermon at St. Chad's on behalf of a poor man, who was aged 91, and no longer able to work. Prince also had connexions with Ludlow, where as a 'counsellor-at-the-bar' he practised in the council in the marches of Wales. On one occasion he was removed from this position because he was not an utter barrister of five years standing, but no doubt the fact that his father-in-law, William Leighton, was a member of the council led to his reinstatement after an appeal to the Privy Council in 1577. This connexion with the council in the marches probably explains his return to Parliament for Bridgnorth.[4]

His will reveals him as a provident and charitable man. Although he had suffered 'great losses of late, sustained of bankrupts and others', he made meticulous provision for his family and dependants, not omitting a bastard daughter, a debilitated brother-in-law, and four paupers he maintained in St. Giles's hospital. A clue to Prince's religious convictions occurs in a letter he wrote to the bailiffs of Shrewsbury in 1576 at the height of the plague. In it, he compared them to 'Moses and Aaron' leading God's 'peculiar people, the Israelites ... in the wilderness', and admonishes them to 'let not the sheep perish by default of the shepherds'. There are hints of puritanism here, perceptible again in the preamble to his will, where he hoped to 'inherit the kingdom celestial provided for His elect'. Prince died in October 1598, his will, dated July

1598, being proved in 1599. An inquisition post mortem was held in 1599.[5]

[1] *Vis. Salop* (Harl. Soc. xxix), 410; H. Owen and J. B. Blakeway, *Shrewsbury*, ii. 140; *Trans. Salop Arch. Soc.* (ser. 4), v. 47; viii. 122. [2] *CPR*, 1560–3, p. 449; 1572–5, pp. 154, 354; C. A. J. Skeel, *Council in the Marches*, 255. [3] *Trans. Salop Arch. Soc.* (ser. 1), iii. 290; (ser. 4), v. 47; Owen and Blakeway, ii. 351; town chronicle 1582; PCC 20, 21 Kidd. [4] *HMC 15th Rep.* X, 19, 56, 59; P. H. Williams, *Council in the Marches of Wales*, 173, 190; Owen and Blakeway, i. 389, 550, 564; *Trans. Salop Arch. Soc.* (ser. 1), iii. 302, 325. [5] Owen and Blakeway, i. 369; PCC 20, 21 Kidd; C142/252/41.

J.J.C.

PRINTIS, Robert

MORPETH   1597

This Member has not been identified. He may have been a member of the Prentice family of Wiggenhall, Norfolk, a minor county family, connected by marriage to the Lestranges of Hunstanton, Norfolk, who were, in turn, related to Edward Grey of Howick, constable of Morpeth castle and a servant of Lord William Howard, who claimed the barony of Morpeth as part of his wife's share of the disputed Dacre inheritance. There were two Robert Prentices of Wiggenhall: a youger son of William Prentice (still a minor in 1562) and his brother William's eldest son. It was probably the latter who married a grand-daughter of Sir John Oliff and later moved to Barling, Essex.

Vis. Norf. (Harl. Soc. xxxii). 226; *Hist. Northumb.* (Northumb. Co. Hist. Comm.), ii. 347, 348, 351, 360; W. Rye, *Norf. Fams.* 689; *Surtees Soc.* lxviii. 400, 401, 409; *Vis. Norf.* (Norf. Arch. Soc.), i. 261; *Vis. Essex.* (Harl. Soc. xiv), 598.

B.D.

PROBY, Peter (*d.*1625), of Brampton, Hunts. and Swithin's Lane, London.

KINGSTON-UPON-HULL   1593
LIVERPOOL   1597

2nd s. of Ralph Proby by Alice Bernard of Brampton. *m.* c.1595, Elizabeth (*d.*1644), da. of John Thoroughgood of Chivers, Essex, wid. of Edward Henson of London, 5s. 1da. *suc.* bro. Ralph 1605. Kntd. 1623.

Servant to (Sir) Francis Walsingham*; member, Barber Surgeons' Co.1579, master 1615; servant to (Sir) Thomas Heneage* by 1590; post at Chester 1590, confirmed 1599; duchy of Lancaster feodary in Northants. 1591; bailiff of Long Buckby 1591–2; steward of Ormskirk 1594; master forester, Amounderness 1594; 'solicitor by patent' to Hull by Oct. 1596; dep. (to William Lambarde*) keeper of recs. in the Tower 1601, keeper 1601–2; esquire of the body to Q. Elizabeth and James I; bailiff, manor of Elton 1604–24; alderman of London 1614, sheriff 1614–15; gov. of Irish soc. 1616–22; member, Grocers' Co. 1622; ld. mayor of London 1622–3.[1]

Proby had an extraordinary career. He was born in Chester and his parents later moved to his mother's seat at Brampton. Since Proby was considered for the post of clerk of the prentice at Chester, offered to serve as solicitor of Chester, and did serve as solicitor of Hull, it is possible that he received some legal education, the record of which has not survived. According to his own statement, he entered the Queen's service about 1578, which may have been when he was first employed by Walsingham, whose barber (presumably barber surgeon) John Chamberlain the letter writer, said he was, as did the recorder of London when he presented Proby to the lord keeper as lord mayor of London in 1622. Perhaps he was already one of Walsingham's agents. Requesting the mayor of Chester to grant him the office of clerk of the prentice in 1587, the Privy Council described Proby as 'a servant of Mr. Secretary's', and also as 'very honest and used in place of good credit as one well accounted of by Mr. Secretary'.

Next, Proby appears under the protection of Sir Thomas Heneage. As Proby's eldest son was christened Heneage, it seems likely that he was still a young man when they first came together. Heneage and Walsingham were close personal friends, so it is impossible to determine whether Proby worked for Heneage before Walsingham's death, but he was doing so immediately afterwards.

Walsingham died on 6 Apr. 1590 and on 7 May Proby and one James were estimating for Heneage the cost for continuing 'a course of understanding how things pass' in Flanders, France and Spain. They drew up a list of persons engaged on this work, and Heneage sent both documents to Burghley. Shortly after Heneage succeeded Walsingham as chancellor of the duchy of Lancaster, Proby began to receive duchy offices. It was presumably also Heneage who, as high steward of Hull, procured Proby his seat in Parliament in 1593. As one of the Hull burgesses he could have taken part in committee work on fish (5 Mar.), cloth (23 Mar.), and weirs (28 Mar.).

When Proby sat for Liverpool in 1597, it was presumably through the influence of his new master Sir Rober Cecil, to whom he had turned immediately upon the death of Heneage, 17 Oct. 1595.

Within a week he had sent him some of his old master's books and papers and promised to wait on Cecil at court without delay 'with good testimony of sundry employments of importance, largely promised in her Majesty's name', which he had not yet received. He said he had done good services without making it known to any but such as employed him, so that they had 'the credit and commodity', while he, 'poor man', was left to 'be holpen by her Highness whose service it was, and by true report of Cecil', to whom he had not yet rendered any service at all. Proby gave Cecil no chance to forget him and soon recapitulated the list of his services, which were not 'in words or fables but in deeds, with great charge, pains and danger'. He did not desire 'any great matter', but a 'convenient pension'. From Heneage he had been accustomed to receive £20 p.a. paid quarterly by his steward, as well as his diet, lodgings, carriages and riding charges. He had besides '£20 yearly of his honour, sometimes paid by his commandment by the clerks in the Treasury, and sometimes by him out of such fees of towns that he was officer unto'. Furthermore he had 'his honourable speech and letters for himself and friends very readily, and hoped the Queen would think all this worth £100 yearly'. But as God had taken 'this his means' from him, he hoped the Queen would have him to serve in such places as she told him he should shortly know.[2]

Proby did not hope in vain. By 29 Oct. he had already been commanded to wait at court, and by the beginning of November he enjoyed a chamber there with an allowance of three dishes of meat and was paid an income 'till a treasurer of the chamber be chosen'. Early in March the following year he was sent to Chester to arrange for shipping to carry forces to Ireland. Later in the year he corresponded with Cecil about the price of armour in London. Finally, after Cecil's death, Proby turned to the city of London. Commenting on Proby's being made an alderman in 1614, Chamberlain described him as 'a shrewd, nimble-witted fellow'. As governor of the Irish society in 1616, Proby, accompanied by Matthias Springham, went to Ulster with full powers to view, examine and regulate the affairs of the plantation there, and to report upon it. In 1622 Proby transferred from the Barber Surgeons to the Grocers, one of the 12 great city companies, in anticipation of the mayoralty.[3]

Proby was in debt in 1595, but by the time he made his will, during the last two years of his life, he had evidently prospered. He referred to his great age and included a tribute to his wife for nursing him in his recent illnesses. She received a 40 years' interest in his manor of Elton, Huntingdonshire, and his London house. To his son Henry he left the manor of Yaxley, Huntingdonshire, and three other sons received £1,000 each. Other bequests went to the Barber Surgeons, the Grocers, Bridewell hospital, the poor of Elton, Yaxley and Chester. The executors were his sons Heneage† and Henry, and his son-in-law William Downhall. Proby was buried 14 Mar. 1625 at St. Swithin's.[4]

[1] VCH Hunts. ii. 92; iii. 160; Collins, Peerage, ix. 137; Young, Annals of the Barber Surgeons, 532–3; CSP Dom. 1581–90, p. 663; APC, xxix. 590; Somerville, Duchy, i. 507, 509, 590; Cheshire Sheaf (ser. 3), vii. 94; Chambers, Eliz. Stage, i. 65; HMC Hatfield, vi. 350–1, 436; Queen's Coll. Oxf. mss 155, pp. 247–8; Beaven, Aldermen, i. 74, 193; ii. 53. [2] Chester assembly bk. 52, 55, 58, 61, 62–3; Nichols, Progresses Jas. I, iv. 873; Chamberlain Letters ed. McClure, i. 545; ii. 461; HMC Hatfield, v. 427, 525; vi. 444; APC, xv. 42; xvii. 285; Read, Walsingham, i. 135; iii. 430; D'Ewes, 487, 507, 512; CSP Dom. 1581–90, p. 664. [3] Collins, Sidney Pprs. i. 356, 357–8; APC, xxv. 280; CSP Dom. 1595–7, p. 302; Chamberlain Letters, i. 545; Hist. Narr. of the Origin of the Irish Soc. (privately 1916) 45. [4] PCC 28 Clarke.

N.M.S.

PROGER, William John, of Wernddu, Mon.

MONMOUTHSHIRE   1589

1st s. of John ap William Proger of Wernddu by Jane, da. of David ap Morgan of Triley. m. Margaret, da. of Thomas Morgan of Arkeston, Herefs., at least 5s. 2da.

J.p. Mon. from c.1573, under-sheriff 1566–7, sheriff 1577–8.

The family which came to be called Proger in the sixteenth century had been settled in Monmouthshire for some time. In the fourteenth century an heiress of Wernddu had married into the senior branch of the Herberts. In the Elizabethan period they were still of standing in the county, but, according to Bradney, the Progers of Wernddu were the 'least important and the least distinguished' branch of this family. It may have been Proger's investigations, ordered by the Privy Council in 1581, into riots in Abergavenny that led him into a dispute with the Herberts. On this occasion the Herberts were ordered to keep the peace, whereupon they used their influence with the council in the marches to obtain an order binding Proger to keep the peace, an action which the Privy Council soon countermanded. Next, in the autumn of 1588, Proger entered a bill in the Star Chamber alleging that on 1 July 1588 he had been attacked in Abergavenny, when accompanied by only four friends and four servants, by a crowd of about 60 supporters of Matthew and Charles Herbert. The first riot having been quelled by the bailiffs and officers of the town, within two hours he was again set upon by the same people. A total of about 20 of his friends, servants and kinsmen were murdered near the town. Matthew Herbert denied the allegations and adopted delaying tactics, pleading that it was impossible for him to leave Monmouthshire at this time as he had been appointed a temporary deputy lieutenant by the Earl of Pembroke.

Proger's election for Monmouthshire with Thomas Morgan suggests a temporary eclipse of the Herberts, perhaps as the result of action taken over Proger's complaints. Nothing further has been ascertained about him.

DWB, 800; Bradney, Mon. i. 197, 200, 218, 246; St. Ch. 5/P55/9, J8/40, P48/2, R38/30; Egerton 2345, f. 39; E163/14/8; Hatfield ms 278; Autobiog. of Lord Herbert of Chirbury, ed. Lee, 306; APC, xiii. 115–16; xiv. 6–7; SP12/180/9.

A.M.M.

PROWSE, Conrad (d.1613), of Cleeve, Som., later of Southwark, Surr.

MINEHEAD   1597

2nd s. of William Prowse of Cleeve by Joan, da. of John Michell of Cliffe. educ. Staple Inn; G. Inn 1579.

Prowse was an attorney 'of ability and livelihood of no value at all; in every way very mean, generally evil thought of and noted for a common quarreller'.

Among his many lawsuits were one against Sir Walter Mildmay* at Hertford and several connected with Cleeve. In 1581 he and George Luttrell* jointly bought a chamber at Gray's Inn, and thenceforth they were enemies not only in London but in Somerset, where they quarrelled with so much violence that a j.p. declared he had not heard of such disorder for 20 years. Thus it is curious that on the one occasion Prowse sat in Parliament he should have been returned for what is always regarded as a Luttrell pocket borough. The explanation may be that Prowse somehow contrived his return especially to score a point against Luttrell. This base motive would also account for Prowse's intervention in 1601 when he was not, as far as is known, himself a candidate. There is no record of any activities by Prowse in the 1597 Parliament, but, as a burgess for a Somerset borough, he could have attended the committee concerned with rebuilding Langport Eastover (10 Nov.).

When he died intestate in 1613, Prowse was living in St. George's parish, Southwark. Administration of his goods was granted to his next of kin, Robert Prowse.

PRO Index 6800, f. 409v; *Vis. Som.* ed. Weaver, 64; St. Ch. 5/ L12/22, P31/30, P48/17, P60/2, P65/3; *DKR,* xxxviii. 265–7, 522; Townshend, *Hist. Colls.* 103; *Som. Wills,* ed. Brown, iii. 23; see also MINEHEAD.

P.W.H.

PROWSE, Richard (*d.*1607), of Exeter, Devon.

EXETER 1584

s. of Richard Prowse by Joan, wid. of Thomas ?Pole. *m.* (1) da.; of one Vincent of Exeter, 1da.; (2) Anne Vaughan, wid. of Henry Lok, mercer of London, at least 2s.

Bailiff, Exeter 1563, receiver of revenues 1575, sheriff 1576, alderman 1579, mayor 1578, 1589, 1600.

Prowse was a puritan draper or tailor whose second wife was a correspondent of John Knox. In 1565, at the suit of 'divers gentlemen of special honour and credit' in the county, he was granted permission to have a tennis court and bowling alleys at Exeter. On friendly terms with the Carews, Peryams and Strodes, he represented the city once in Parliament, when the MPs attended to matters concerning the salmon from the haven, a grant of the impost of wines, the mustering of horses in Exeter, and a lease of the fee farm of the manor of Ottery. Prowse was given charge of a bill introduced by his relation Richard Carew, imposing conditions for the manufacture of Devon and Cornish cloth, 15 Mar. 1584, and took charge of a bill about apprentices, 23 Mar. 1584, in which it is possible that he made an attempt to have provisos inserted on the city's behalf. On 27 Nov. 1584 he was put on the committee of the bill for the better observing of the Sabbath day. The Exeter merchant adventurers paid Prowse £3 4s. 'which he hath laid out at the said Parliament time about the suit of the Company'.

Apart from property (including a brewhouse) at Exeter, valued at £10 for the subsidy of 1576, Prowse held land at Cullompton, Devon and at Staverton, near Totnes. He died in 1607, leaving bequests to the poor at various places including Broadhempston, possibly his birthplace, where he had already built an almshouse.

Roberts thesis; *HMC 15th Rep. VII,* 145; Vivian, *Vis. Devon,* 628; *Trans. Dev. Assoc.* lxi. 209; *HMC Exeter,* 24; St. Ch. 5/E2/9; W. Cotton, *Eliz. Guild Exeter,* 61, 74; Exeter City act bk. 4, f. 458; 5, ff. 351, 382; D'Ewes, 333, 363, 368, 371, 372; *Devon N. and Q.* xxvi. 179; PCC 83 Huddleston; Devon RO, Tingay 1537.

P.W.H.

PROWSE, Robert (*d.*1592), of Helstead and Barnstaple, Devon.[1]

BARNSTAPLE 1584

s. of John Prowse, clothier, of Tiverton, by his w. the da. and h. of one White of Tiverton. *m.* 5 Oct. 1573, Joan, da. of Nicholas Witchalse or Wichalles of Barnstaple, 2s. 4da.

Receiver, Barnstaple 1583, mayor 1588–9.

Prowse, a Barnstaple merchant, was paid the large sum of £10 12s. 6d. wages on the only occasion he represented his town in Parliament. His export trade involved him in an incident in 1590 when he shipped £250–£400 worth of cloth for 'the Islands', in the *Marlyn,* paying duty at Barnstaple on the cloth and at London on 10 cwt. of wax. Off the Scilly Isles one of the Queen's ships boarded her and took off some of the cargo, no doubt suspecting evasion of duty. An Exchequer case ensued, depositions being taken at Barnstaple in 1591.

Prowse died 29 June 1592, administration of his goods being granted to his widow 17 July following. He had bought the manor of Helstead in 1560.[2]

[1] This biography is based upon the Roberts thesis. [2] Vivian, *Vis. Devon,* 627; *Vis. Devon* (Harl. Soc. vi), 224; *Barnstaple Recs.* i. 45; ii. 168; *Stradling Corresp.* ed. Treherne, 240–1; G. Bushnell, *Sir Richard Grenville,* 203; E134/33 Eliz. Easter 9; *Vis. Som.* (Harl. Soc. xi), 89; PCC admon. act bk. 1592, f. 24; C142/236/44.

P.W.H.

PUCKERING, John (c.1544–96), of Kew, Surr. and Weston, Herts.

BEDFORD 1584
GATTON 1586

b. c.1544, 1st s. of William Puckering of Flamborough, Yorks. by Anne, da. and h. of John Ashton of Great Lever, Lancs. *educ.* L. Inn 1559, called 1567. *m.* Jane, da. of Nicholas Chownet of Fairlawn, nr. Wrotham, Kent, 1s. 4da. Kntd. 1592.

J.p. Herts. from 1575, q. 1583; of counsel to St. Albans 1587; Lent reader, L. Inn 1577; member, council in the marches of Wales and j.p. many Welsh and border counties from 1577; sole justice Carmarthen circuit 1577–8, c.j. 1578–92, serjeant-at-law 1580, Queen's serjeant 1588; justice of assize and j.p. S.E. counties 1590; ld. keeper and PC from 1592; high steward, Salisbury 1595–d.[1]

Speaker of House of Commons 1584, 1586.

Puckering provides a good example of how an Elizabethan of modest origins could accumulate status and fortune from the law, using the speakership of the House of Commons as a stepping stone on the way. He had, of course, powerful friends, including the 2nd Earl of Essex and Lord Burghley, but it was his legal practice upon which his fortune and reputation were founded. This practice he maintained in London even after being made a Welsh judge, securing letters patent to act by deputy in Wales. No doubt it was Burghley who thought him both pliant and ambitious enough to be Speaker in 1584, although, or even because he had no parliamentary experience. He was returned for Carmarthen Boroughs, on his judicial circuit, on 19 Nov. 1584, though he actually chose to represent Bedford, where the government had already had him returned on 2 Nov. Notwithstanding that this was his first Parliament, Puckering was described as 'a very able member of the said House' when he was chosen Speaker on 23 Nov. 1584. Recorder Fleetwood kept a record of the event:

Mr. Treasurer [Sir Francis Knollys*] moved the House to make an election of a Speaker, whereupon he himself named my brother Puckering who sat next me, and there was not one word spoken. And then I said to my companions about me, 'Cry Puckering!' And then they and I beginning, the rest did the same. And then Mr. Speaker made his excuse standing still in his place, and that done, Mr. Treasurer and Mr. Comptroller [Sir James Croft*] being by me called upon, sitting near, they rose and set him to his place, where indeed they should have set him either before his speech or else at the beginning, and his speech should have been before the chair.[2]

The two Parliaments of which Puckering was Speaker were marked by the desire to assure the Queen's safety, which was an aim acceptable to the government, and by a hankering after religious innovation, which was not. No Speaker could remain uncommitted in these circumstances, and Puckering was plainly the servant of the government, frequently leaning on Burghley for assistance. He reported to the Commons with no apparent qualm that Elizabeth had told him plainly that 'she well understood I was your mouth' but 'I was your mouth by her allowance'. Before Christmas 1584 things went well enough, as the House was united in securing the Queen's safety, but on 14 Dec. three county gentlemen, two of them knights of the shire, presented petitions against restrictions on 'so many good preachers' and Dr. Peter Turner introduced a bill to replace the 1559 prayer book by one based on that of Geneva.

In February 1585, after the recess, Burghley and Whitgift, at a meeting of both Houses, made some show of answering criticisms of the church, but a fresh statement of the puritans' position was never read in the House, for on 1 Mar. 1585 the clerk read a message from Puckering that he had taken 'some physic yesterday [and] now at this instant keepeth his bed'. But that day (1 Mar.) at noon he 'received a message from her Majesty to come presently to the court' though he was 'loath to go'. The result was a further royal prohibition on the discussion of religious matters. 'Some thought best to have the Speaker displaced, for that he durst enterprize to go to the Queen without the privity of the House'. Others suggested open defiance of the Queen, but in the end

was drawn a bill under this title 'An Act for the better execution of a statute made in the xiii year of the … reign for reformation of certain disorders touching ministers of the church', which was delivered to the Speaker with a full conclusion among themselves that if the Speaker should refuse the accepting thereof, then that party who first designed this course should with a speech which he had prepared have maintained the liberties of this House to the uttermost.

This Puckering evaded by 'receiving' the bill but postponing having it read, not a heroic episode in the history of the Speakership. Finally gaining their point on this bill, the extremists resurrected another – against excessive fees in the ecclesiastical courts – and there are signs that before the end of the Parliament control of the House was slipping from the hands of Speaker and Privy Councillors. The fulsome language of Puckering's oration at the end of the Parliament, 29 Mar., contrasts grotesquely with the realities of the situation. He had drafted the speech himself and then borrowed a phrase or two from another which Burghley had written for him.

Puckering was returned to the 1586 Parliament for Gatton, Burghley inserting his name in a blank return (C219/30/100) in his own hand. The pattern of Puckering's second speakership was similar to that of 1584. Until Christmas the House was solely concerned with assuring the Queen's safety, and the Speaker was the mouthpiece of the Commons; after Christmas he was the harassed creature of the government. In seeking the death of Mary Queen of Scots the Members were united, and at the two meetings with Elizabeth in November 1586 Puckering could speak for the House. He took the utmost care in composing his speeches, at least once taking a day off the better to prepare himself. After he had reported back to the House on one occasion, Hatton commended him, asking the Members to extend their hearty thanks to him, 'which they so then did in very loving and courteous sort'. But, after Mary's execution, in February 'the wearisome solicitations of those that commonly be called puritans' began again to 'disturb the good people of the church and commonwealth'. Anthony Cope, Peter Wentworth, and some other 'of these new-fangled refiners' (the words are

Puckering's) had met before the beginning of Parliament and were in touch, probably through John Field, with a meeting of puritan clergy, held in London to coincide with the Parliament. On 27 Feb. Cope introduced a bill which, like Dr. Turner's in the previous Parliament, aimed at replacing the authorised prayer book by a revised form of the Genevan book. After Cope's speech Puckering pleaded with the Members to go no further, reminding them that the Queen had expressly forbidden them to meddle with religion. So firm, however, was the determination to have the bill read that Puckering was about to submit to it, when James Dalton intervened in opposition. The ensuing debate lasted so long that no time remained to read the bill on that occasion, and before the next meeting of the House the Queen had sent to Puckering for Cope's bill and book, and for those introduced by Dr. Turner in the previous Parliament. The debate continued on the following days, ending on 1 Mar. with a speech by Peter Wentworth upholding the right of freedom of speech in the House, and containing his points in the form of questions that he desired the Speaker should put to the House. Puckering, D'Ewes reports, first 'required him to spare his motion', but 'Mr. Wentworth would not be so satisfied'. Finally, Puckering adjourned the debate, 'pocketted up' Wentworth's questions, and 'so handled the matter that Mr. Wentworth went to the Tower, and the questions not at all moved'. A surviving copy of a speech prepared for Puckering in this session sheds light on the limits of his education, the marginal references explaining that Pluto, Aeolus, and Neptune were the gods of riches, the winds and the sea. Puckering's closing speech, 23 Mar. 1587, is unremarkable. There are references to 'my most gracious and benign mistress, by the hand of whose helpful favour I have been sundry times relieved from the ground and set on foot', to the 'imperfections' of his 'rude and unpolished action', to 'such domestical enormities as do annoy and grieve us within the realm', and to ' some very few' of the House who 'have fallen and offended ... by infirmity of judgment and through a preposterous zeal'.

Puckering was in more sheltered waters for the Parliament of 1589, when, as an assistant in the Upper House, he did his share of fetching and carrying bills and messages between the two Houses. Eventually he was made a judge and finally lord keeper.[3]

Elizabeth twice visited Puckering's 'poor hermitage' at Kew, where her entertainment in 1595 was 'great and costly'. Puckering gave her a fan (its handle garnished with diamonds), a jewel valued at £400, and a pair of virginals. The Queen 'to grace his lordship the more ... took from him a salt, a spoon, and a fork of fair agate'. In the same year Puckering complained that serving her as lord keeper was costing him £1,000 a year, that the job had no residential accommodation, and that he had never been paid for being Speaker, which had cost him £2,000 in

losses from his law practice. He claimed £400 was due, as each Parliament had lasted two sessions, but the suggestion that he had not been paid was, in fact, false, as his fee had gone to cancel a debt he owed the Crown.

By the end of his life Puckering had estates in Surrey, Hertfordshire, Warwickshire and Lincolnshire. He died 30 Apr. 1596, and was buried in Westminster abbey.[4]

[1] *DNB*; W. R. Williams, *Hist. of the Great Sessions in Wales*, 163; *Vis. Herts.* (Harl. Soc. xxii), 160; Lansd. 737, f. 139v; P. H. Williams, *Council in the Marches of Wales*, 354–5; W. J. Jones, *Eliz. Court of Chancery*, 45; Foss, *Judges*, v. 531; Strype, *Annals*, iv. 28; *St. Albans Recs.* 19; *HMC Var.* iv. 232. [2] Campbell, *Chancellors*, ii. 163; Lansd. 22, f. 122; 41, f. 45; P. H. Williams, 282; Harl. 6993, f. 112; 6994, ff. 15, 23–4, 48; 7042, f. 70v; Add. 40629, f. 37; D'Ewes, 333. [3] D'Ewes, 313–14, 320, 327, 328, 333, 334, 335, 337, 341, 342, 343, 344, 346, 348, 353, 366, 367, 373, 374, 378, 392, 393, 394, 398, 400, 402, 405, 407, 410, 412, 416, 418, 422, 423, 424, 426, 437, 440, 441–2, 447, 450, 454; Lansd. 43, anon jnl. passim; Lansd. 104, 105; Fitzwilliam mss, Wm. Fitzwilliam's jnl. f. 33; Trinity, Dublin, Thos. Cromwell's jnl. passim; Harl. 6845, ff. 40–2; 6853, f. 285; Queen's, Oxford mss, 284, f. 35; Neale, *Parlts.* ii. 26, 61–2, 65–6, 72–6, 78, 82, 95, 114, 122, 144, 152–7, 180. [4] Strype, iv. 160–1; *HMC Hatfield*, v. 40; Nichols, *Progresses Eliz.* iii. 252–3, 370; Neale, *Commons*, 333; Harl. 7024, f. 170v; C142/246/125; *VCH Herts.* ii. 172–3; *VCH Warws.* v. 105–6; vi. 162–4; PCC admon. act bk. 1596, f. 164.

P.W.H.

PUGH (ap HUGH), Robert (*d.*1565), of Plas Cefn y garlleg, Llansantffraid Glan Conway, Denb. and Penlassog, Creuddyn, Caern.

CAERNARVONSHIRE   1559

s. of Hugh ap Robert (*d.*1565), of Cefn y garlleg. *m.* c.1550, Elizabeth, da. of Foulke Salusbury, dean of St. Asaph, of Berain and Lleweni, Denb., wid. of Rheinallt ap Ieuan of Penrhyn Creuddyn, Caern., 2s. 2da.[1]
?Receiver, Denbighland 1547;[2] j.p. Caern. from 1556, sheriff Caern. 1560–1, Denb. 1561–2.

Pugh came of an ancient family long settled in the lower Conway valley, but his importance in Denbighshire derives from his fortunate marriage. His wife's first husband was descended from Ednyfed Fychan, seneschal to Llywelyn the Great and ancestor of the Tudors. After the English conquest Ednyfed's descendants held immediately of the English Crown the land with which Llywelyn had endowed them, and it was on these terms that Rheinallt ap Ieuan held the manor of Penrhyn, in the parish of Llangwstenyn on the Creuddyn peninsula. Rheinallt died in 1535, leaving an infant son (another Hugh) who was a royal ward. Robert ap Hugh, having married the widow about 1550, obtained the wardship from the Crown; this enabled him to enjoy the estate during the minority and then to marry the ward to his own sister Katherine. This is what gave him his footing in Caernarvonshire, where he served as constable for the hundred of Creuddyn from 1550 to his appointment as justice of the peace six years later. His election for the shire in the lifetime of his father (who outlived him by some months), with little or no freehold land to his name, is a tribute to the prestige this connexion brought with it.[3]

He also acquired a lease of the parochial tithe of Llangwstenyn, which he used to support a private chaplain; a share in the profits of a neighbouring fishing weir, probably that of the former abbey of Rhos Mynach, which survived till recent years; and a sub-lease of the crown ferries over the Conway (Aberconway and Tal y cafn), with the farm of the vill of Penlassog in Creuddyn. Inevitably he had often to go to law to defend his title. His rights over the ferries and Penlassog, which always went together, were challenged in a Star Chamber action towards the end of Henry VIII's reign. In 1551–2 he brought several actions in Caernarvonshire quarter sessions against Creuddyn neighbours for trespass and hedge-breaking, thefts of cattle and cash, and another in the Exchequer to resist alleged violent encroachments on lands he claimed in Llangwstenyn. On the 24 Apr. 1559 he was granted leave of absence from Parliament for his 'great business' at the assizes.[4]

His will, made 3 Jan. 1565 and proved 26 Nov. following, shows that he had many irons in the fire besides his principal business of stock farming. Apart from his investments in ferries and fisheries, he had a share in the 30 ton vessel *Katherine* of Conway, which traded with France, and a store of alum and salt which may have formed part of her cargo. Most of his Denbighshire property went to his elder son David – a minor whom he placed under the guardianship of the lad's second cousin Sir John Salusbury[†]. The younger son and the two daughters were executors and residuary legatees, under the supervision of Salusbury (who received a horse and £40) and another. As it turned out, the executors were still under age when Pugh died, and administration had to be carried out – together with that of his father's will – by the supervisors. Most of the Caernarvonshire property, including the weirs and ferries, was left to a namesake, the son of his former ward, with whose identity there has been frequent confusion. This other man, also a minor, was assigned to the guardianship of Sir Richard Bulkeley*, with the condition, eventually fulfilled, that Sir Richard should give him one of his daughters in marriage, with a dowry of £300.

Benefactions were also left for the repair of neighbouring parish churches, including that of Conway, where he desired to be buried, and some 20 legacies to neighbours and friends, sometimes in stock, sometimes in cash ranging from Salusbury's £40 to the chaplain's 6s. 8d., and amounting in all to about £70. The MP's father, as appears clearly in his will, died a Catholic, and, while the son's will does not afford the same evidence, his descendants were active in the cause of that religion throughout the next century, with the result that although the family status remained until the male line died out early in the eighteenth century, it never again provided an

MP or a sheriff. The Cefn y garlleg stock faded back into insignificance after 1559.[5]

[1] *Trans. Caern. Hist. Soc.* 1957, p. 62; *Cal. Caern. Q.S. Recs.* 249; PCC 33 Morrison. [2] *LP Hen. VIII*, xiv(1), p. 533. [3] *Trans. Anglesey Antiq. Soc.* 1951, pp. 34–72; *LP Hen. VIII*, xix(1), pp. 77–8; *CPR*, 1547–8, p. 356; 1553 and App. Edw. VI, p. 370; *Trans. Caern. Hist. Soc.* 1957, p. 56; *Cal. Caern. Q.S. Recs.* 60, 136; PCC 11 Morrison. [4] N. Tucker, *Colwyn Bay*, pp. 248–53; *Conway and Menai Ferries*, ed. H. R. Davies (Univ. Wales Bd. of Celtic Studies, Hist. and Law ser. viii), 4–5, 83–5; *Augmentations* (same ser. xiii), 45–64; St. Ch. 20/190; *Cal. Caern. Q.S. Recs.* 85, 86, 91, 225; *CJ*, i. 60. [5] PCC 33 Morrison; E. A. Lewis, *Welsh Port Bks.* (Cymmrod. rec. ser. xii), 238; *CPR*, 1560–3, p. 446; 1563–6, p. 31; Lansd. 1218, ff. 97–9; A. H. Dodd, *Studies in Stuart Wales*, 227, 231, 234; *DWB*.

A.H.D.

PUGH, Rowland, of Mathafarn, Llanwrin, Mont.

MONTGOMERY BOROUGHS   1572, 1589

1st s. of John ap Hugh ap Ieuan of Mathafarn by Katherine, da. of Sir Richard Herbert[†] of Montgomery. m. Ellena (Eleanor), da. of Nicholas Purcell of Shervey, Salop, 1s.[1]

Commr. Exchequer, Merion. 1567; commr. subsidy Mont. 1573, 1576; j.p. Mont. and Merion. from c.1573; commr. musters, Mont. 1574; sheriff, Merion. 1574.[2]

The family which consolidated its patronymics into the surname Pugh during this period had been landowners in the hundred of Mathrafal continuously since the thirteenth century. Although Pugh's mother was a Herbert and his grandmother a Vaughan of Llwydiarth the Pughs were a county family of the second rank. They several times filled the office of sheriff, but did not attain a county seat in Parliament. Rowland succeeded his father some time between 1562 (when the latter was still paying subsidy) and 1571 (when the son's name appears in his stead); they were rated at £5, half Edward Herbert I's assessment.[3]

Politically Pugh was firmly attached to the Herberts, and in the stormy Montgomeryshire election of 1588, when he was at first proposed for the shire, he stood down when he found that Edward Herbert I, his uncle, proposed to stand, and took his part in the irregular proceedings which secured Herbert's election. This is the last we hear of him. In 1581, at the beginning of the third session of Pugh's first Parliament, a rumour of his death led to his being replaced by his cousin Richard Herbert I, but at the end of the session, 18 Mar., when Pugh was 'known to be in plain life', Herbert was removed. When Pugh died is not known; but by 1602 the estate had passed to his grandson, another Rowland Pugh, who became sheriff six years later.[4]

[1] Dwnn, *Vis. Wales*, i. 295, 312; *Vis. Salop* (Harl. Soc. xxix), 413; *Mont. Colls. Supp.* 1896–1928, p. 408. [2] *Augmentations*, ed. Lewis and Davies (Univ. Wales Bd. of Celtic Studies, Hist. and Law ser. xiii), 436; E179/222/376; Harley rolls E15; Flenley, *Cal. Reg. Council, Marches of Wales*, 142, 212; *Mont. Colls.* xxii. 119 seq. [3] *Mont. Colls.* viii.

49–50; xxii. 119; *Arch. Camb.* (ser. 3), xiii. 132; E179/222/371, 374.
[4] *Mont. Colls. Supp.* loc. cit.; Neale, *Commons*, 101, 105; *CJ*, i. 136;
D'Ewes, 282, 308.

A.H.D.

PULESTON, Robert (by 1526–83), of Plas ym Mers, Denb.

CAERNARVON BOROUGHS	1547
DENBIGHSHIRE	1553 (Mar.), 1571

b. by 1526, 1st surv. s. of (Sir) John Puleston[†] of
Caernarvon and Bersham by his 1st w. Gaynor, da. of
Robert ap Meredydd ap Hwlkin of Glynllifon, Caern. *m.*
Ellen, da. of William Williams of Cochwillan, Caern., 6s.
2da. *suc.* fa. 1551.[1]

Commr. goods of churches and fraternities, Denb.
1553, for the Exchequer, Merion. 1561, piracy, Denb.
1565, for the eisteddfod at Caerwys, Flints. 1568, to
investigate the loss of victuals sent to Ireland 1574,
musters, Denb. 1580; j.p. Denb. 1555–61, q. 1562–*d.*;
sheriff, Denb. 1558–9, 1569–70, Mont. 1571–2; j.p.
Caern. 1573–*d.*[2]

Puleston's second representation of Denbighshire, some
20 years after he succeeded to the substantial family lands
in that county, left no impression upon the records of the
House.

He extended his estates by taking leases of mountain land
in the crown wastes of Bromfield and Yale, in the town of
Wrexham, where his uncle Hugh Puleston was vicar, and
in the demesne lands of the neighbouring borough of
Holt. At the musters of 1570 he was charged with 'one
light horseman furnished'. He was no more free from
litigation than most of his kind. He brought an action
soon after his father's death against a fellow burgess of
Caernarvon whom he accused of diverting the water from
his mill to work another; but the most serious cases he was
involved in were two Star Chamber suits. The first, which
began in 1569 and was later removed to Chancery, was
brought by John Puleston (probably his distant cousin of
Hafod y wern, Wrexham) against Robert Puleston and Sir
John Salusbury[†] of Lleweni, who were accused of
corrupting the jury in a case about lands in Bromfield; in
the second he was joint defendant with the sheriff of
Shropshire, Thomas Fermor[†], on a charge that during
Puleston's shrievalty of Denbighshire he and his fellow
sheriff had blackmailed a man accused of murder as the
price of securing an acquittal, and that they had extorted
further sums when he was in fact acquitted. Puleston died
15 Aug. 1583.[3]

[1] A. N. Palmer, *Country Townships of Wrexham* (1903), opp. p. 63;
Dwnn, *Vis. Wales*, ii. 359; PCC 7 Bucke. [2] *Augmentations*, ed. Lewis
and Davies (Univ. Wales Bd. of Celtic Studies, Hist. and Law ser.
xiii), 433; *CPR*, 1560–3, p. 446; 1563–6, p. 30; Flenley, *Cal. Reg.
Council, Marches of Wales*, 109, 133, 200–5, 212; *APC*, vii. 286. [3] PCC 7
Bucke; *Augmentations*, 56, 275, 302, 320, 336–7, 385; W. O. Williams,
Cal. Caern. Q. Sess. Recs. i. 66, 88, 91, 110, 257; *Exchequer*, ed. E. G.
Jones (Univ. Wales Bd. of Celtic Studies, Hist. and Law ser. iv), 170;
Flenley, 75; St. Ch. 5/L14/39, P14/4, P62/38; 7/27/54.

A.H.D.

PULESTON, Roger I (bef. 1542–87), of Emral,
Worthenbury, Flints.

GREAT BEDWYN	1584, 1586

b. bef. 1542, 1st s. of Roger Puleston of Emral by Anne,
da. of Richard Grosvenor of Eaton, Cheshire. *educ.* I.
Temple Nov. 1555. *m.* (1) by 1562, Magdalene (Maud), da.
of Thos. Hanmer, 2s. inc. Roger II*, 1 da.; (2) c. June
1582, Margaret. *suc.* fa. 1572.[1]

The Pulestons were a family of Shropshire origin who
settled in Wales as English officials immediately after the
Edwardian conquest, with their principal seat at Emral in
Flintshire. Intermarrying with Welsh heiresses and
becoming assimilated into Welsh society, they established
other branches of the parent stock in the counties of
Denbigh and Caernarvon. In Flintshire they enhanced the
family fortune by marrying into neighbouring families of
superior wealth: this MP and his grandfather married
Hanmers; his father married one of the Cheshire
Grosvenors, who already in Henry VIII's day were also
landowners in Worthenbury, paying subsidy at 20 times
the rate of the Pulestons; his son was to marry a niece of
the lord chancellor.[2]

As the son of another Roger Puleston this man was
distinguished from his father during his young manhood
by the designation 'the younger'. The Roger Puleston on
the commissions of the peace in Flint in 1562 and 1564 is
more likely to have been the father, but the son was
beginning to serve the community and himself about this
time. In June 1564 he acquired the lease of lands in
Denbigh with Sir Edward Puleston and another Roger
Puleston (either his father or Sir Edward's son). Described
as 'of the Inner Temple', he was concerned with his
kinsman Anthony Grosvenor in a Chancery case about the
missing deeds of Astbury Rectory, Cheshire of which they
had the lease, in or after 1566. In 1584 he was one of the
signatories to an instrument of association in Flintshire for
the Queen's preservation.[3]

Despite his interests in Flintshire and the neighbouring
counties and, after 1572, his succession to the family estate
at Emral, Puleston's life was largely spent outside Wales.
He entered the service of the Earl of Hertford some time
between 1572, when his name was not included in a list of
Hertford's lawyers, and 1575, when he and Edward
Stanhope concluded a deed with the Earl. Puleston's
service to Hertford is illustrated in a number of letters in
the Seymour papers. In January 1577 he reported from
Oxford, whither the Earl's two sons had recently gone up,
and tried to enlist his master's sympathy with the new
vice-president of Magdalen on behalf of President
Humphrey. In January 1582 he was handling Hertford's
business at court and two months later he was involved in
John Newdigate's challenge to the will of Francis
Newdigate*; in 1582 he was fobbing off James Howson the
saddler with £40 'on part of payment' of Hertford's

account with him. He was evidently intimately concerned with Hertford's affairs. It was probably he whose name appears in a household expense list of the Earl's for the 13 months ending February 1582, at a rate of 20s. a month. A letter from Puleston to Hertford of 30 Jan. 1585 is the evidence that there was some thought of adjourning the parliamentary session.[4]

It is not difficult to see how Puleston came to sit for Great Bedwyn; this was one of the Seymours' boroughs and the Earl was always pleased to put his lawyers into the family seats. Although he appears to have won his most urgent legal battle for his inheritance before 1584, Hertford always had interests to be cared for. At that time the most delicate was probably the question of the legitimacy of his sons and this might be raised in Parliament at any time. The presence of Puleston in the Commons, together with Richard Wheeler,* his fellow-Member for Great Bedwyn, and Edward Stanhope* who sat for Marlborough, in the two Parliaments which followed the majority of the elder boy may have been in the nature of an insurance. Puleston is not recorded as having spoken in either Parliament.[5]

Puleston was described in his father's inquisition post mortem as '30 years and more' in 1572, and he must have been well over 30 as he had entered the Inner Temple in 1555. By 18 Sept. 1562 he had already been married for some time; on that date a commission was issued to the bishop of London and others to hear an appeal by Maud Pilston (alias Hanmer) against the excommunication and other injustices which she had suffered as the result of proceedings taken against her by her husband before the bishop of Chester. His marriage survived these unpleasantnesses, however, and in his will, which he prudently drafted ten years before his death, which occurred 28 Apr. 1587, he mentioned the affection which he bore Maud when he made provision for her. In the codicil, added a day before he died, he referred to his wife and called her his daughter Dorothy's mother, but there is reason to believe that this was a second wife and a stepmother to the children of the first marriage. In June 1582 he told Hertford that he was settled at Highgate (where he was still living in 1585) 'a newly married man', and the widow in his own inquisition post mortem is named Margaret. As befitted his connexion with Hertford, Puleston was a protestant who hoped to be pardoned and washed from all his sins through the merits of the Saviour's blood-shedding and precious blood and 'to be accounted one of the joyful number of his elect in the general resurrection'. But before that prospect could be fulfilled he carried many earthly responsibilities. He had arranged with his executors to dispense large sums of money for the advancement of his sister, Katherine Puleston, and his daughter, Dorothy, and for the preferment of his youger son George, and younger brothers. He must also remember his married sisters,

Dorothy Bostock and Jane Broughton, and numerous cousins and friends, and leave all his servants a year's wages. Despite his sojourn in London, Puleston's executors were predominantly Welsh: Thomas Mostyn, of Mostyn, Flintshire, George Ravenscroft* of Bretton, Flintshire, Thomas Egerton (a cousin) of Lincoln's Inn, Edward Puleston (another cousin) of the Inner Temple, Thomas Puleston (a brother), and Roger Davith of Dungrey, near Worthenbury, Flintshire. His codicil witnessed rising fortunes. He was able to increase his provision for his younger children, making an especial bequest for George's use when he should enter the inns of court, and to leave £20 towards the building of a new bridge at Bangor if raised 'new out of the ground'. He named the bishop of Chester and the chief justice (Sir) George Bromley*, his elder son's father-in-law, as his overseers.[6]

[1] Vis. Cheshire 1613, p. 115; CPR, 1560–3, p. 253; HMC Bath, iv. 153; C142/163/29, 215/272. [2] DWB, 816–17; E179/221/207, 210. [3] CPR, 1560–3, p. 446; 1563–6, pp. 31, 157; C3/143/55; CSP Dom. 1581–90, p. 211. [4] HMC Bath, iv. 142, 147, 148, 180–1, 204; Wilts. N. and Q. viii. 319; Neale, Parlts. ii. 48. [5] HMC Bath, iv. 197. [6] C142/163/29, 215/272; CPR, 1560–3, p. 253; PCC 27 Spencer; Lansd. 53/176/108.

S.T.B.

PULESTON, Roger II (c.1566–1618), of Emral, Worthenbury, Flints.

FLINTSHIRE	1589
DENBIGHSHIRE	1593
FLINTSHIRE	1604

b. c.1566, 1st surv. s. of Roger Puleston I* of Emral by his w. Magdalene (Maud), da. of Thomas Hanmer. educ. Brasenose, Oxf. 1582, aged 16; I. Temple 1585 or 1586. m. Susanna, da. of (Sir) George Bromley* of Hallon in Worfield, Salop, s.p. suc. fa. 1587. Kntd. 28 Aug. 1617.[1]

J.p. Denb. and Flints. from c.1591; dep. lt. Flints. by 1595; commr. Exchequer 1595, sheriff 1597–8; dep. steward, Denbighland and Bromfield-and-Yale by 1601; custos rot. Denb. from 1596; member, council in marches of Wales 1601.[2]

Puleston's marriage with a niece of the lord chancellor secured him not only free admission to the Inner Temple, but a lifelong patronage to which he owed much of his prestige, and which made him an object of jealousy when it was proposed in 1601 to enrol him in the council in the marches of Wales. The anonymous protest sent to Cecil at the time accused him of ignorance of the law, and of desiring the place only to promote his private factions and to 'repair his decayed estate'. There is not much sign of a 'decayed estate' in the princely mansion (later enlarged, demolished in 1926) which he rebuilt at Emral, and he was involved in only one notable lawsuit. The only occasion when he appeared as a 'stirrer of factions' was in the notorious Denbighshire election of 1588, when he countenanced the disorderly proceedings by which his relative John Edwards* triumphed over the numerically superior supporters of Puleston's second cousin William Aylmer*. Aylmer was unfortunate enough to serve a subpoena on Puleston while the House was sitting, 'to answer unto a bill ... containing almost 40 sheets of paper', and Puleston raised the matter in the House, 12 Feb. 1589. Though Aylmer was found to have committed a breach of privilege he was let off, and told to wait until the end of the session before recommencing hostilities. As knight of the shire in this Parliament Puleston would have been eligible to attend the subsidy committee (11 Feb.) and, in his next, the subsidy (26 Feb. 1593) and a legal committee (9 Mar.).[3]

In 1595, during the panic aroused by Spanish raids on Cornwall, Puleston and his fellow deputy lieutenant Thomas Mostyn* were specially commended by the Council for their diligence in raising the Flintshire musters; it was also a sign of his growing influence that five years later a complaint from the Denbighshire borough of Ruthin about unfair distribution of taxes was referred by the Council to Puleston and two Denbighshire gentlemen.[4]

Puleston was active in James I's first Parliament. He died childless in 1618, and was buried at Gresford on 17 Dec. The Emral estate passed to his younger brother, then to a nephew (the Commonwealth judge), under whose descendants the family retained its political importance in the shire to the end of the century.[5]

[1] Dwnn, *Vis. Wales*, ii. 310; G. Owen, 'Desc. Wales' in *Desc. Pemb.* ed. H. Owen, ii. 576; *I.T. Recs.* i. 341. [2] *APC*, xxiii. 260–1; xxv. 75; *Augmentations*, ed. Lewis and Davies (Univ. Wales Bd. of Celtic Studies, Hist. and Law ser. xiii), 361; *Exchequer*, ed. T. I. J. Jones (same ser. xv), 154; Add. Chart 8659; Harl. 2129, f. 84; 2176, f. 15; *HMC Hatfield*, xi. 561; PRO Index 4208. [3] *HMC Hatfield*, xi. 561; *I.T. Recs.* i. 341; *RCAM Flints.* 115–16; *DWB*; *Augmentations*, 401; *Exchequer*, 198: the Roger Puleston appearing in other lawsuits of the period belonged to a different branch of the family; Neale, *Commons*, 113; D'Ewes, 431–2, 434–5, 451, 474, 496. [4] *APC*, xxv. 75; xxx. 256. [5] *Trans. Cymmrod. Soc.* 1942, p. 28; P. H. Williams, *Council in the Marches of Wales*, 354–5.

A.H.D.

PULTENEY, John (c.1581–1617), of Misterton, Leics.

WIGAN 1601, 1604

b. c.1581, 1st s. of Gabriel Pulteney of Misterton by Dorothy, da. and coh. of Thomas Spencer of Everdon, Northants. *m.* 1602, Margery (*d.*1613), da. of (Sir) John Fortescue I*, 1s. 4da. *suc.* fa. 1599. Kntd. 1603.

The family of Pulteney had been established at Misterton since the early fourteenth century. Pulteney was provided with a seat at Wigan as soon as he came of age, through the influence of his future father-in-law, the acting chancellor of the duchy of Lancaster. He died in 1617 leaving considerable property to his young son John,

upon whose early death without issue, involving a division of the estates among his sisters, the family came to an end.

Nichols, *Leics.* iv(1), p. 319; *Vis. Northants.* ed. Metcalfe, 196; *Chamberlain Letters* ed. McClure, i. 153; C142/259/37, 363/189.

S.M.T.

PULTENEY, Michael (*d.*1567), of Misterton, Leics.

LICHFIELD 1563

1st s. of Francis Pulteney of Misterton by Margaret, 2nd da. of Nicholas Vaux†, 1st Baron Vaux of Harrowden. *m.* Catherine, da. of Sir John Fermor† of Easton Neston, Northants., *s.p. suc.* fa. 1550.

As well as Misterton, Pulteney owned lands in Warwickshire, and the manor and advowson of Shenleybury, Hertfordshire. He may also have resided for a time in London, in the parish of St. Martin-in-the-Fields. Apart from this, little is known of his career. His seat at Lichfield in 1563 was presumably due either to Paget or episcopal influence, though in neither case is the connexion obvious. On 17 Mar. that year, he was given leave of absence from Parliament. He died in 1567, and was buried at Misterton.

J. C. Wedgwood, *Staffs. Parl. Hist.* (Wm. Salt Arch. Soc.), i. 391; Nichols, *Leics.* iv. 319; *CSP Dom.* Add. 1547–1565, p. 307; Cussans, *Herts.* iii(1), p. 84, 308; *CJ*, i. 69; C142/146/128.

J.J.C.

PURCELL, Richard (by 1526–86), of Dinthill, Salop.

SHREWSBURY 1563, 1572

b. by 1526, 1st s. of Nicholas Purcell† by Anne, da. of Randulph Beeston. *m.* Dorothy, da. of Thomas Lee of Langley, 2s. 3da. *suc.* fa. 1559.[1]

Common councilman, Shrewsbury 1553, bailiff 1565, alderman 1568.[2]

Purcell received licence to enter upon his father's lands on 1 May 1560. As well as property in Shrewsbury and elsewhere in Shropshire, he inherited the manor of Talerddig, and bought the manors of Overgorther and Tiertreff Issa, all in Montgomeryshire. During his father's life, he divided his time between Shropshire and Wales: he was admitted a com-brother of the Shrewsbury Drapers' Company in 1547, and in 1554 was foreman of the Montgomeryshire grand jury. After 1560, he spent most of his time in Shropshire. His election as bailiff must have caused some controversy, for in 1565 the 25 men 'who went upon the bailiffs ... were in the election house without meat or drink 20 hours before they could agree'.[3]

Purcell was actively engaged in the Welsh cloth trade, and it was probably his connexion with the Shrewsbury drapers that fixed his residence in Shropshire, at a time when they were slowly acquiring a monopoly of the trade. In 1566 they were given a complete monopoly by Act of

Parliament, but this was short-lived, for the drapers were not sufficiently wealthy or numerous to maintain it, and, after an abortive attempt in 1571, the Act was repealed in 1572. The return of Purcell, master of the drapers from 1569 until his death, to the latter Parliament, probably represents an attempt on the drapers' part to retain their privileges, for they provided him with £50 towards 'the saving of the statute'.

The only time he is mentioned in the journals of the House, however, the reference is to his appointment to confer with the Lords on the bills for reformation of errors in fines and common recoveries, 7 Mar. 1576. He died 24 Nov. 1586, 'a worthy gentleman, of a loving and gentle nature, being a liberal reliever of the poor, and at all times the poor man's friend'. The chronicler was possibly partial: in 1581, the bailiffs had ordered Purcell to pay £20 for arrears of a sum of 40s. due from him yearly to the poor, and he agreed to pay at the rate of £5 each half year. An inquisition post mortem was held at Welshpool on 23 Oct. 1587.[4]

[1] *Vis. Salop* (Harl. Soc. xxviii) 413–4; *Trans. Salop Arch. Soc.* (ser. 4), xii. 189. [2] Shrewsbury mss 76, ff. 3, 82. [3] *CPR*, 1558–60, p. 360; Shrewsbury mss, cal. of deeds and charters, 6, no. 6473; *Mont. Colls.* v. 47; *Trans. Salop Arch. Soc.* (ser. 4), ix. 271; xii. 189; *Early Chrons. of Shrewsbury*, ed. Leighton, 29. [4] *Trans. Salop Arch. Soc.* (ser. 4), ix. 211 seq.; xii. 189; T. C. Mendenhall, *Shrewsbury Drapers and Welsh Wool Trade*, 99, 125–8; *CJ*, i. 111; *Shrewsbury Chrons.* 70; C142/215/279.

J.J.C.

PUREFOY, George (*d.*1615), of Caldecote, Warws., later of Wolvershill.

BEVERLEY   1586

5th s. of Michael Purefoy of Caldecote by Joyce, da. of John Hardwick of Lindley, Leics. *educ.* G. Inn 1566. *m.* Jane, da. of Nicholas Davenport of Bulwick, Northants., 1s. 3da.

Described as junior in the Crown Office list, Purefoy should not be confused with his cousin, and namesake, the head of the senior branch of the family at Fenny Drayton, just across the border in Leicestershire. Though he had family connexions with the earls of Shrewsbury, Leicester and Rutland, Purefoy no doubt owed his return at Beverley to his elder brother Humphrey, a law member of the council in the north, and an admirer of the lord president, the 3rd Earl of Huntingdon. He gradually built up a not inconsiderable estate for his son and heir, Gamaliel. All his land purchases, beginning in 1575 with a moiety of the manor of Bramcote, were of parts of the old Zouche estates, mostly in the parish of Bulkington. To Bramcote he added a moiety of Weston-in-Arden manor, and, in 1601, the manor of Wolvershill. He also bought a moiety of Wibtoft manor. He died in October 1615.

Nichols, *Leics.* iv(2), pp. 599–602; *Leics. Arch. Soc.* xiv. 90–104; *VCH Warws.* vi. 51–3, 258; C142/352/136.

B.D.

PUREFOY, Michael (1562–1627), of Caldecote, Warws., later of Nottingham.

CLITHEROE   1584
NOTTINGHAM   1621

b. 1562, 1st s. of Thomas Purefoy of Caldecote by Elizabeth, da. of Robert Bradshaw of Morborne, Hunts. *educ.* Peterhouse, Camb. 1576, Magdalene, BA 1581/2, MA 1585, incorp. Oxf. 1598. *unm.*
Dep. official of archdeaconry of Notts. from 1598.

It is not easy to explain Purefoy's return for Clitheroe, and it is uncertain in any case whether the MP was the man whose particulars appear above, or his cousin and namesake, a younger son of the senior branch of the family, who was a member of the Inner Temple and servant of the Earl of Rutland. Perhaps the former may be preferred because of a tenuous link with the 3rd Earl of Huntingdon, president of the council in the north, who knew his uncles Humphrey and William. Huntingdon could certainly have secured Purefoy's return and it is highly likely that he spent several years in the service of this uncle Humphrey, who was himself a legal member of the council in the north. Purefoy died in 1627 and was buried in Caldecote church, where his cousin and executor, Gamaliel Purefoy, erected a monument.

Vis. Leics. (Harl. Soc. ii), 34, 37; Nichols, *Leics.* iv(2), 601–2; R. A. Marchant, *Puritans and Church Courts in Yorks. 1560–1642*, 148, 156, 158, 162, 167–8, 171–2, 174, 176–8, 181, 184; *HMC Rutland*, i. 161, 228, 229, 230, 231, 238, 239, 249, 261, 269; PCC 94 Skinner; Dugdale, *Warws.* ii. 1098–9.

S.M.T.

PURFREY, Thomas (c.1556–c.91), of Wells and Banwell, Som.

WELLS   1589

b. c.1556, s. of William Purfrey ?of Hollingbourne, Kent or of Shalston, Bucks. *m.* Blandina, da. of Thomas Godwyn, bp. of Bath and Wells.
Freeman, Wells 1588; bailiff of liberty of Wells 1590.

Purfrey owed his parliamentary seat for Wells, and his eventual disgrace, to his connexion with Bishop Godwyn, who had himself married a Purfrey (though perhaps of a different branch of the family). Immediately upon his marriage to the bishop's daughter he identified himself with Thomas Godwyn*, the bishop's eldest son, and they proceeded to milk the old man and the diocese of all they could. In 1590 Purfrey was appointed bailiff of the liberty of Wells, after the bishop had exerted pressure on the dean and chapter. The grant was conditional upon its not being re-assigned to a Wells burgess and upon Purfrey's taking an oath to uphold the liberties of the bishop. Purfrey entered into a bond of £100 to secure the observance of these articles. When on the bishop's death the relations removed his goods, Purfrey's wife took the carpets and clothes, except for something left 'for a colour that the sheriff might find something' when he came to make his inquisition. Purfrey himself had appropriated the box containing 'treasure', finding, however, only three silver crowns, 5s. of white money, one piece of gold and three seals, instead of the £500 he and Godwyn expected and needed to pay the moneylenders. In November 1590 an Exchequer commission was appointed to investigate the estate, and the leases and lands were confiscated. Purfrey, however, had in the meantime joined Sir Walter Ralegh's settlers at Youghal, where he died about 1591.

Browne Willis, *Bucks.* 262–3; Hasted, *Kent*, v. 464; Farnham and Herbert, *Trans. Leics. Arch. Soc.* xiv(1), 88; P. M. Hembry, 'Bishops of Bath and Wells' (London Univ. PhD. thesis 1956); *HMC Wells*, ii. 311, 312, 318–20; *Wells Charters* (Som. Rec. Soc. xlvi), 190; C2/W18/50; C3/262/7; *Proc. Som. Arch. Nat. Hist. Soc.* xcvi. 78–107.

I.C.

PURSLOW, Nicholas (by 1533–63), of the Inner Temple, London.

APPLEBY	1558
MORPETH	1559

b. by 1533, 1st s. of Robert Purslow of Sidbury, Salop by Margaret, da. and h. of William Sparke. *educ.* I. Temple bef. 1547, called. *m.* Margaret, da. of Thomas Williams of Willaston or Wollaston, Salop, *s.p.*

Steward of reader's dinner, I. Temple 1560, bencher by May 1563.

Purslow may have owed his return at Morpeth to his fellow Inner Templar John Eltoftes*, with whom he had represented Appleby in 1558. Purslow made his will 5 July 1563, and died on 8 Aug. His widow resided at Billingsley after his death, near Sidbury, but it is not known whether Purslow himself had a Shropshire seat. His father outlived him by some eight years.

Trans. Salop Arch. Soc. (ser. 4), iii. 111; C142/142/79; *Vis. Salop* (Harl. Soc. xxix), 415, 442, 507; *CPR*, 1558–60, pp. 6, 10; 1560–3, pp. 72, 546, 615; 1569–72, p. 378.

N.M.F./A.D.K.H.

PURSLOW, Thomas (d. 1618), of Hogstowe, Salop.

STAFFORD	1572

3rd but o. surv. s. of John Purslow of Hogstowe by Anne, da. of Thomas Botrell of Aston Botrell. *m.* Ursula (d. 1604), da. of Edward Cholmeley of Copenhall, Staffs., 3s. 3da.

Purslow's daughter Scholastica was baptised in Castle church, Stafford 9 Feb. 1569, so perhaps he was a servant at the castle. In 1576 a cousin, John Purslow, married the daughter of Sir George Blount of Kinlet, which suggests a link with the Devereux family. Little has been ascertained about him, but on 21 Jan. 1581 Richard Broughton* informed the House that his fellow-Member (presumably Purslow, for there is no reason to think he had been supplanted since his election in 1572), had been indicted of a felony. Purslow died in 1618, and was buried on 15 Apr. at Habberley.

Vis. Salop (Harl. Soc. xxix), 415; *Salop Arch. Soc. Trans.* (ser. 4), iii. 111–18; *Castle Church Par. Reg.* 1; *Sidbury Par. Reg.* 2; *Habberley Par. Reg.* 9; D'Ewes, 283.

J.J.C.

PURVEY, John (by 1525–83), of Wormley, Herts., Rushden, Northants., Louth and Mablethorpe, Lincs.

HUNTINGDON	1553 (Oct.)
HORSHAM	1554 (Nov.)
HERTFORDSHIRE	1558
HIGHAM FERRERS	1559, 1563

b. by 1525. *m.* (1) lic. 1547, Anne, da. and coh. of William Woodliff, mercer, of London, 1s.; (2) in or aft. 1562, Magdalen, da. of Peter Cheke of Cambridge, wid. of Lawrence Eresby or Earsby, *s.p.*[1]

Auditor of south parts, duchy of Lancaster from 1546; j.p. Herts. from 1550, q. and feodary from c.1562; j.p.q. Lincs. (Lindsey) from 1569; warden of Louth 1568, 1573, 1582.[2]

By 1558 Purvey was a minor royal official and member of the household of his brother-in-law Sir William Cecil*, being probably principally concerned with financial affairs. He remained friendly with Cecil all his life, and became related to him by his second marriage. It was doubtless Cecil who obtained his appointment as feodary of Hertfordshire, where Purvey had resided since he obtained the manor of Wormley with his first wife.

Purvey probably owed his return for Higham Ferrers to his position in the duchy, of which the borough formed part. He may have lived at times on the manor of Rushden, adjoining Higham Ferrers, a property which he leased in the 1550s. Despite his friendship with Cecil the bishops' letters of 1564 described Purvey as a 'hinderer of religion', and a John Purvey was actually imprisoned in 1578 as a recusant, but this last must have been a namesake, as there is no evidence that Purvey was put off the commission of the peace before his death, which occurred on 21 Apr. 1583. Since most of his property in Hertfordshire and Norfolk had come to him with his first wife and was entailed upon their only son, William (in his turn auditor of the south parts of the duchy of Lancaster and steward of Higham Ferrers), he had been obliged to settle all his own lands as a jointure upon his second wife. To these he added in his will further property purchased since his marriage, and the greater part of his goods and chattels, provided that she left them to his son at her death. He bequeathed 'to my very good lord, the Lord Burghley', his best gelding.[3]

[1] *VCH Herts.* iii. 488; *Vis. Essex* (Harl. Soc. xiii), 177; *CPR, 1553 and App. Edw. VI*, p. 370; PCC 19 Butts; C142/201/71. [2] Somerville, *Duchy*, i. 443; *CPR, 1560–3*, p. 400; *1563–6*, p. 490; *1566–9*, p. 130; *1569–72*, p. 225; *Louth Old Corp. Recs.* ed. Goulding, 19. [3] Somerville, 404, 408; *CSP Dom. 1547–80*, pp. 371, 458, 474; J. E. Cussans, *Herts.* v, vi. 188; ix, x. 259; *APC*, xii. 301; *CPR, 1553* and App. Edw. VI, p. 370; *1563–6*, p. 123; *1566–9*, p. 130; Lansd. 31, f. 76; *VCH Northants.* iv. 45; *Cam. Misc.* ix(3), p. 30; *Cath. Rec. Soc.* i. 64; C142/201/71; PCC 19 Butts, 73 Drury.

S.M.T.

PUXTON, John (d. 1627), of Salisbury, Wilts.

SALISBURY	1601

educ. ?Barnard's Inn 1586. *m.* Jane, da. of one Studley, 1s. 5da.
Alderman and bailiff, Salisbury 23 Sept. 1623.

Puxton was named in 1595 as one of those who were to represent the city before the Privy Council in its dispute with the bishop, and we can infer that by 1601 he was regarded as a man who could be trusted to back up Giles Tooker*, his colleague, in any matter which touched the independence of the city. In the event he is not recorded as taking part in the business of the Parliament of that year. He assisted Tooker in the preparation of a charter in 1606, and supported him in the negotiations which led to the city's incorporation in 1612. The Salisbury records show that, for serving without wages as the city's Member in 1601, Puxton was excused serving as mayor for five years.

In spite of the obscurity of his background, Puxton throve. The properties specified in his inquisition post mortem had all been 'lately purchased', and nothing he owned had become his by the easier way of patrimony. In Salisbury itself he had purchased a tenement and garden and a messuage and garden in Green Croft Street, as well as a cottage and garden in Salt Lane. Outside the city he had also acquired pasture in Foulston and Wilton (from John Shuter of the Inner Temple), burgages in Downton, houses, buildings and lands in Odstock and the site of the manor of Midsomer Norton in Somerset. Two of Puxton's daughters married well, Frances with a son of Ambrose Smith and Jane in 1611 with John Ivye, goldsmith, who was to be mayor of Salisbury in 1626–7 and 1647–8, the author of the *Declaration* concerning the decline of population in the city in 1661, and a fellow-zealot for the city's independence who successfully negotiated the purchase of the bishop's lands for the city in 1647. Puxton's heir, John, was aged 24 at the time of his father's death.

Puxton died 10 Apr. 1627. A good protestant, he was a parishioner of St. Edmund's church; the rectory and college premises were conveyed to him and Giles Tooker in trust for the parish in 1614. He desired to be buried in the church and bequeathed to it 10s.; he also left £1 to the poor of the parish.

Lansd. 47/118/94v; *Wilts. IPMs* (Brit. Rec. Soc. Index Lib. xxiii), 409; *Vis. Wilts. 1623*, ed. Marshall, 15, 214; *HMC Var.* iv. 232, 234; City of Salisbury mss D(34), f. 167; PCC 54 Skynner; *Wilts. N. and Q.* vii. 525; *VCH Wilts.* vi. 72, 119.

S.T.B.

PYE, Walter (1571–1635), of the Mynde, Herefs. and Middle Temple, London.

SCARBOROUGH	1597
BRECON	1621, 1624, 1625
HEREFORDSHIRE	1626, 1628

bap. 1 Oct. 1571, 1st s. of Roger Pye of the Mynde by Bridget, da. of Thomas or Walter Kirle of Walford, Herefs. *educ.* Oxf.; New Inn; M. Temple 1590, called 1597. *m.* (1) 22 July 1602, Joan (*bur.* 10 Sept. 1625), da. of William Rudhall of Rudhall, Herefs., 7s. 7da.; (2) Hester (*d.* c.1643), da. of John Ireland and wid. of Ellis Crispe, alderman of London. *suc.* fa. 31 Mar. 1590. Kntd. 1621.
Assoc. bencher, M. Temple 1616/17, Lent reader 1617, assistant Autumn reader 1618, treasurer 1626–7; Welsh judge from 1617; attorney of court of wards 1621; ?high steward, Leominster 1623–d.; chief justice of session, S. Wales 1631, 1633.

The Pyes were an old Herefordshire family. Pye himself, a lawyer, bought a good deal of local land, and made improvements to his family seat, the Mynde, including the installation of a new water supply. His return for Scarborough in 1597 was probably due to Lord Howard of Effingham – newly created Earl of Nottingham – high steward of the borough, though no connexion between them has been established. In the Stuart period he was favoured by Buckingham, whom he may have served as legal adviser, and Pye became a regular Parliament man. He died on 26 Dec. 1635, being buried at Much Dewchurch on 9 Jan. 1636.

W. R. Williams, *Parl. Hist. Herefs.* 45–6; G. E. Aylmer, *King's Servants*, 308–9; *Her and Gen.* v. 130–8; Weaver, *Vis. Herefs.* 92; *OR*, i. 462; *M.T. Recs.* ii. 613, 621, 629, 675, 711; Hutchinson, *Notable Middle Templars*, 200–1.

N.M.S.

PYM, Alexander (c. 1547–85), of Brymore, Som.

TAUNTON	1584*

b. c.1547, 1st s. of Erasmus Pym of Brymore by Catherine, da. of Edward Bampfield of Poltimore, Devon. *educ.* M. Temple 1565, called. *m.* (1) settlement

1574/5, Elizabeth, da. of John Conyers of London, 1da.; (2) settlement 31 July 1580, Philippa, da. of Humphrey Colles of Barton, 1s. John† 1da. *suc.* fa. 1582/3.

J.p.q. Som. from c.1579, commr. militia 1584.[1]

The Pyms had owned the manor of Brymore since the thirteenth century, and had acquired more land in Somerset, Devon and Dorset, including the manors of Langham, Stoke Pero and Woolavington, and property in Bridgwater. Pym himself was a lawyer, those bound to him at the Temple including Timothy Pym, son of Thomas, a baron of the Exchequer in Henry VIII's reign, and Thomas Conyers, a relative of his first wife. The Conyers family, originally from Durham, had moved to London when John Conyers entered royal service at about the middle of the century.[2]

Pym was one of several local men returned for Taunton during the period when the bishop of Winchester and the local authorities appear to have been content to share the nominations for each Parliament. Through his mother's family, the Bampfields, he was related to several Members in this and other Elizabethan Parliaments. He did not occupy the seat for long, however, if at all: he was returned in November 1584, held a manorial court in the far west of Somerset 10 Dec., and died 7 Jan. 1585, the new writ being issued 13 Jan. His second wife, whose father and brother were both sheriffs of Somerset, later married Anthony Rous*. John Pym was only a few months old at the time of his father's sudden death.[3]

[1] *Vis. Som.* (Harl. Soc. xi), 66; SP12/145/39; E163/14/8; Lansd. 737, f. 157; Som. RO DD/BW no. 82; C142/187/61. [2] Collinson, *Som.* i. 233–4; ii. 25, 43; iii. 82, 438, 529; PCC 7 Rowe; E. Green, *Preps. in Som. against the Armada*, 34, 51; *Som. Enrolled Deeds*, ed. Harbin, 131; *M.T. Recs.* i. passim; Surtees, *Hist. Durham*, iii. 219; *The Topographer*, i. 177. [3] Som. RO, DD/BW Pym mss, no. 112; C142/206/20; *HMC 10th Rep. VI*, 82; Townshend, *Hist. Colls.* 192. The Som. RO references in this biog. have been kindly supplied by Mr. Conrad Russell.

M.R.P.

PYNDER, John (*d.*1608), of Cheapside, London.

LONDON 1601

?s. of John Pynder, merchant, of London (fl. 1546). *m.* (2) Katherine Taylor, 1ch.

Auditor, London 1595–7.

Pynder, a vintner, may have descended from the Wellingborough, Northamptonshire family of that name, and so have been related to Sir Paul Pindar (Pynder) the seventeenth century financier. He owned the *Nag's Head* in Old Jewry, and was assessed at £80 for the 1589 subsidy. Pynder was elected to the 1601 Parliament as one of the commoners' representatives of the city. The London MPs were put on the main business committee (3 Nov.) and on committees dealing with the following in this Parliament: penal laws (2 Nov.), setting of watches (7 Nov.), customs (10

Nov.), abbreviation of the Michaelmas law term (11 Nov.), cloth and clothworkers (18 Nov., 4 Dec.), monopolies (23 Nov.), feltmakers (26 Nov.), assize of fuel (7 Dec.), Thames watermen (8 Dec.), iron ordnance (8 Dec.), the navy (9 Dec.), silk weavers (10 Dec.), printers and printing (17 Dec.). On 24 Nov. he was given charge of the painters and plasterers bill.

Pynder died between 16 Apr. 1608 when he made his will and 29 July when it was proved. He asked to be buried in the chapel of the Mercers' Company, near his 'late wife and child'. He provided for his widow and left legacies for imprisoned debtors, for maimed soldiers, for Bridewell and for the Vintners' Company.

PCC 70 Windebanck; *APC*, i. 360; *Vis. London* (Harl. Soc. xv), 374; (xvii), 166; (cix, cx), 155; W. K. Jordan, *Charities of London*, 419–20; D'Ewes, 622, 624, 629, 634, 635, 642, 649, 650, 654, 657, 668, 669, 670, 674, 676, 687.

N.M.F.

QUARNBY, Humphrey (*d.* c.1566), of Swine Green, Nottingham.

NOTTINGHAM 1553 (Oct.), 1554 (Apr.), 1563*

o.s. of Thomas Quarnby by Elizabeth, da. and coh. of Henry Tickhill. *m.* Elizabeth, da. and h. of Robert Mellors of Nottingham, at least 3s. 3da.

Alderman, Nottingham by 1541, sheriff 1534–5, mayor 1542–3, 1549–50, 1555–6, 1562–3.

Quarnby, whose family may have taken its name from the village of Quarnby in the West Riding of Yorkshire, was a bell-founder, and active in Nottingham civic affairs for over 30 years. His fortunate marriage to a lady whose grandmother, Dame Agnes Mellors, had re-endowed the Free Grammar School, allied him to a family prominent in the town. He became a warden of the school, and, by the accession of Elizabeth, had occupied nearly every civic office at least once. In 1561 he represented the town in a dispute between the town and the warden of the hospital of St. John.

He was returned to Parliament for the last time during his fourth term as mayor. On 22 Mar., however, shortly after the session began, he was granted leave of absence, perhaps because of illness, and died before the next session began in September 1566. In his will, made in May 1565 and proved at York almost a year later, he asked to be buried next to his father-in-law, Robert Mellors, in St. Mary's church. He divided his considerable property into three parts, 'according to the custom of the province', the first part to his wife, the executrix; the second to his surviving children; and the remainder under the heading of general legacies. The preamble to the will, in which he bequeathed his soul to God, the blessed Virgin Mary and 'all the celestial company of heaven', suggests that he was a Catholic. A difficulty may have arisen over the will: it was proved again in the prerogative court of Canterbury as late as February 1572. Quarnby's youngest daughter, Margery, married John Gregory, who was mayor of Nottingham in 1561.

Nottingham Recs. iii. 194, 225, 443, 465; iv. 20, 101, 108, 124–8, 395, 396, 416–18; Thoroton, *Notts.* ed. Throsby, ii. 40–1; T. Bailey, *Notts. Annals,* 394; J. Blackner, *Nottingham Hist.* 115–18; *VCH Notts.* ii. 216 seq.; *CJ*, i. 70; D'Ewes, 89; York prob. reg. 17/545; PCC 3 Daper; J. T. Godfrey, *Notes on St. Mary's Par. Regs. of Nottingham,* 4, n. 9.

M.R.P.

QUIRKE, James (*d.* 1611), of Minehead, Som.

MINEHEAD   1593

?s. of Robert Quirke of Minehead. *m.* Joan, 3s. 3da.

Quirke was the 'poor burgess' who, on 22 Mar. 1593, was unable or unwilling to pay a contribution of 5s. levied on the borough Members for the poor maimed soldiers. He offered only 2s. 6d. and narrowly escaped being committed to the serjeant's custody. His only other possible activity in that Parliament was his membership of a cloth bill committee on the 15th of that month. Returned again in 1601, he stood down in favour of his friend Lewis Lashbrook*, and the two were then prosecuted in the Star Chamber by Conrad Prowse*, whose long list of complaints against them included allegations that they had assaulted him in Dunster and imprisoned him on the authority of a forged warrant. Quirke had 'by way of unlawful maintenance solicited and followed in other men's [lawsuits] he being no way authorized to follow or solicit any cause in any of your highness's courts whatsoever'. On another occasion, it was said, Quirke and Lashbrook had used forged warrants to gain a judgment against John Bennet of Minehead, who had already paid compensation to Quirke for the assault and battery of which he was accused. Quirke may indeed have been poor. He left only household goods and a small house in Minehead, and his three daughters received only £20 each as dowry. Otherwise his only valuable asset was the rectory of Minehead, upon which these sums were secured. Lashbrook was an overseer of Quirke's will, which was proved on 23 May 1611. His family remained in Minehead, several of them, merchants and seamen, being buried in Minehead church in the following century. His son Robert endowed an almshouse there in 1638.

D'Ewes, 499, 501, 503, 507; Cott. Titus F. ii. f. 70v; St. Ch. 5/P1/5, P31/30; Hancock, *Minehead,* 433; PCC 44 Wood; Collinson, *Som.* ii. 31–2; see also MINEHEAD.

P.W.H.

RADCLIFFE, Alexander (*d.* 1617), of Gray's Inn, London.

EAST RETFORD   1589

4th s. of Charles Radcliffe of Todmorden, Lancs. by Margaret, da. of Thomas Savile of Ecclesall, Yorks. *educ.* Staple Inn, G. Inn 1581. *m.* Grace Savile, wid. of William Vernon, *s.p.*

If Radcliffe was the Mr. Radcliffe who acted as counsel to Isabel, Countess of Rutland, in March 1589 in her suit against the young Earl, it would explain the return of a London lawyer for the borough of East Retford, where, after the death of the 4th Earl, the continuance of Rutland influence had been assured by the election of Sir George Chaworth (cousin and namesake of the other 1589 East Retford MP) as high steward. All that is known about the Gray's Inn man, except for his will, relates to an incident which took place in June 1595. Radcliffe leased a house in Holborn in common with another Gray's Inn lawyer, one Stibbin, whom Radcliffe described as 'a common brawler, quarreller, and a sower of sedition'. According to Radcliffe's subsequent Star Chamber case, Stibbin wished to force him out of the house, to which end he 'daily troubled and molested' him, made a woodyard 'in the fairest walks, alleys and arbours' of the garden, pulled up plants, hedges and fences and finally on 11 June, together with his wife and armed servants, pulled down fences that Radcliffe had erected that morning. When Radcliffe came out to take the air they beat him so 'that the strokes and blows so given were heard by neighbours and others walking in [their] gardens', who, 'doubting that he should be murdered amongst them, came over the fence to save him'. The upshot is unknown.

Radcliffe made his will 20 Mar. 1616. It was proved by the executors, Samuel Radcliffe, principal of Brasenose College, and George Radcliffe of Gray's Inn, the testator's cousin, 4 July 1618. After expressing the hope that he would, following his death, live 'in everlasting felicity with the blessed saints in heaven', Radcliffe bequeathed £20 to the poor of Todmorden, and listed those who were to be provided with 'blacks' for the funeral. The principal bequest was £400 to the dean and chapter of St. Paul's. The interest on £200 was to be used towards the payment of such 'gentlemen scholars of Oxford and Cambridge as shall willingly bestow their pains in preaching the gospel at St. Paul's Cross', while the other £200 was to be used to purchase a pension, the yearly product of which should be divided between the gentlemen choristers and ministers of the choir in St. Paul's. Charles Greenwood, vicar of Thornehill (?Lincolnshire), and the supervisor of the will, was bequeathed £20.

Radcliffe was presumably the Alexander Radcliffe buried at St. Dunstan-in-the-West 5 Nov. 1617.

C. P. Hampson, *Book of the Radclyffes,* 268–9; *HMC Rutland,* i. 269; St. Ch. 5/R39/33; PCC 74 Meade; St. Dunstan-in-the-West par. reg. Guildhall 10342, f. 229.

A.M.M.

RADCLIFFE, Edward (*d.* 1643), of Elstow, Beds.

PETERSFIELD	1586
BEDFORDSHIRE	1589
PORTSMOUTH	1593
BEDFORDSHIRE	1597,[1] 1601, 1604

2nd s. of Sir Humphrey Radcliffe* of Elstow by Isabel or Elizabeth, da. and h. of Edmund Harvey of Elstow; bro. of Thomas*. *m.* (1) 1582 or 1583, Elizabeth, da. of Sir William Petre* of Ingatestone, Essex, wid. of John Gostwick of Willington, *s.p.*; (2) 30 May 1594, Jane, da. of Francis Hynde* of Madingley, Cambs., wid. of John Catesby of Newnham in Goldington, *s.p.*; (3) 22 May 1634, Eleanor, da. of Sir Richard Wortley of Wortley, Yorks., wid. of Sir Henry Lee, Bt., of Quarrendon, Bucks., *s.p.* suc. bro. 1586. Kntd. bef. 30 May 1594; *suc.* cos. as 6th Earl of Sussex 1629.

J.p. Beds. from 1584, sheriff 1598–9; freeman, Portsmouth 8 Aug. 1593.

Radcliffe's father was a younger son of the 1st Earl of Sussex, and it was this connexion which accounts for his returns at Petersfield and Portsmouth, as Sir Henry Radcliffe, the 4th Earl, was lord lieutenant of Hampshire and so could bring pressure to bear on the Weston family who were the patrons at Petersfield, and at Portsmouth he was warden, captain and high steward. Edward Radcliffe was obviously of county status in Bedfordshire, where his so frequent elections are nevertheless a little surprising.[2]

His name has not been found in the journals of the Commons. As knight of the shire in 1597 and 1601 he could have attended committees dealing with enclosures (5 Nov. 1597), the poor law (5, 22 Nov.), armour and weapons (8 Nov.), penals laws (8 Nov.), monopolies (10 Nov.), the subsidy (15 Nov.), draining the fens (3 Dec.) and maltsters (12 Jan. 1598); as well as the main business committee (3 Nov. 1601) and other committees on monopolies (10 Nov. 1597 and 23 Nov. 1601).[3]

Radcliffe was at the Tilbury camp during the Armada crisis, writing to the Earl of Sussex that during the Queen's visit she had given

> me many thanks for my forwardness in this service, telling me I showed from what house I descended, with many gracious words ... Assuring me that before it were long, she would make me better able to serve her, which words being spoken before many did well please me, however the performance follow.

This may have been a reference to the Earl's request that Radcliffe should succeed him as captain of Portsmouth castle, about which he wrote to the Earl of Leicester on 24 Aug. 1588. Radcliffe's later life was passed on the edge of bankruptcy. The Bedfordshire estates were disposed of piecemeal, Elstow itself being sold in 1616. He died intestate in 1643.[4]

[1] Folger V. b. 298. [2] *CP*; *Beds. N. and Q.* i. 126 seq.; E163/14/8; PCC admon. act bk. 1586, f. 193; *VCH Beds.* iii. 281, 304, 328; R. East, *Portsmouth Recs.* 346, 420, 637. [3] D'Ewes, 552, 553, 555, 557, 561, 567, 578, 624, 649. [4] *APC*, xxii. 238; H. Ellis, *Orig. Letters* (ser. 2), iii. 142; *CSP Dom.* 1603–10, p. 478; 1611–18, p. 110; *HMC Bath*, v. 215; *Vis. Beds.* (Harl. Soc. xix), 207; *Verney Pprs.* (Cam. Soc. liii), 159–60; *HMC 7th Rep.* 439, 644.

A.M.M.

RADCLIFFE, Sir Henry (by 1533–93), of Portsmouth, Hants.

MALDON	1555
CHICHESTER	1559
HAMPSHIRE	1571
PORTSMOUTH	1572

b. by 1533, 2nd s. of Henry Radcliffe, 2nd Earl of Sussex, by his 1st w. Elizabeth, da. of Thomas Howard, 2nd Duke of Norfolk; bro. of Thomas†. *m.* lic. 6 Feb. 1549, Honor, da. and coh. of Anthony Pound (*d.*1547) of Drayton in Farlington, 1s. Kntd. 2 Oct. 1553; *suc.* bro. as 4th Earl of Sussex 9 June 1583; KG 22 Apr. 1589.

MP [I] 1560.

Sewer to the Queen by 1556; PC [I] 1557; lt. of Leix and Offaly 1557–64; constable of Portchester castle and lt. of Southbere forest 1560; jt. steward, crown possessions in Essex 1561; warden and capt. of Portsmouth from May 1571; burgess, Portsmouth bef. 1575; high steward from 9 Sept. 1590; j.p. Hants from c.1573, commr. musters by 1576, jt. (with William Paulet*, 3rd Mq. of Winchester) ld. lt. from 1585.[1]

Radcliffe went to Ireland when his elder brother was made lord deputy in 1557. He was returned to Parliament for Chichester, perhaps through the influence of his relative the 12th Earl of Arundel, but whether he was in England during the session is not clear. All the information found about him in these years refers to Ireland, until, in 1564, charges of corruption were brought against him by commissioners dealing with the government of Ireland. He was imprisoned in Ireland in January 1565, but the English Privy Council ordered his release on bail, and he left Ireland soon afterwards on leave from which he never returned. He next settled in Hampshire, where his wife had inherited estates giving him sufficient status to be elected for the county to the 1571 Parliament. He became captain of Portsmouth in May that year and was returned there to the Parliament of 1572. There is no record of his speaking in the House, but he was appointed to committees on ports (13 Feb. 1576), small arms (17 Feb.), sheriffs (18 Feb.), wine (21 Feb.), unlawful weapons (2 Mar.), land reclamation (6 Mar.), removing benefit of clergy from rapists and burglars (7 Mar.), justices of the forest (8 Mar.), Lord Stourton's bill (13 Mar.), London goldsmiths (13 Mar.), the subsidy (25 Jan. 1581) and navigation (17 Mar. 1581). After succeeding to the peerage he was appointed a trier of petitions in the Lords in the Parliaments of 1586, 1589 and 1593.[2]

By 1587 he was writing to the Queen about his own and his family's debts, and his deteriorating financial situation was exacerbated by a dispute with the dowager Countess of Sussex. He also had differences with his fellow lord lieutenant about the Hampshire defences. He made his will a few days before his death on 14 Dec. 1593. The son and heir, Robert, was executor and residuary legatee.[3]

[1] C142/210/84; *CPR*, 1553 and App. Edw. VI, p. 6; 1555–7, p. 516; 1558–60, p. 390; *CP*, xii(1), pp. 526–8; Lansd. 4, f. 156; 56,

f. 168 seq. *CSP Carew*, 1515–74 passim; *CSP Ire.* 1509–73 passim; *CSP Dom.* 1547–80, p. 413; 1581–90, pp. 245–6; 1591–4, p. 418; *Portsmouth Recs.* 133, 137. [2] *APC*, iv. 431; vii. 200, 270, 271; Essex RO, Maldon recs. DB/3/3, 256, 257; *CSP Ire.* 1509–73, pp. 252–4, 339, 344; 1586–8, p. 126; R. Bagwell, *Ireland under the Tudors*, ii. 72–5; D'Ewes, 247, 252, 255, 262, 288, 306, 307; *CJ*, i. 105, 106, 107, 110, 111, 112, 115, 119, 134; *LJ*, ii. 113, 145, 169. [3] *VCH Hants*, ii. 150; iii. 189, 331; *N. and Q.* (ser. 10), iv. 184, 268, 472; Lodge, *Illus.* ii. 319; *CSP Dom.* 1581–90, pp. 144, 245, 261, 319, 458, 497–8; Northants. RO, Stopford Sackville mss 239; PCC 19 Dixy; C142/98/58, 241/109.

P.H.

RADCLIFFE, Sir Humphrey (c.1509–66), of Elstow, Beds.

BEDFORDSHIRE	1553 (Mar.), 1554 (Apr.), 1554 (Nov.), 1555, 1558
MALDON	1559

b. c.1509, 3rd s. of Robert Radcliffe, 1st Earl of Sussex, by his 1st w. Elizabeth, da. of Henry Stafford, 2nd Duke of Buckingham; half-bro. of Sir John*. *m.* Isabel or Elizabeth (*d.*1594), da. and h. of Edmund Harvey of Elstow, 2s. Thomas* and Edward* 3da. Kntd. by June 1536.[1]

Gent. pens. by 1540; lt. of pensioners by 1553; j.p. Beds. from 1554, q. by 1562; sheriff, Beds. and Bucks. 1558–9; steward, manor of Elstow 1563.[2]

Radcliffe's father-in-law, Edmund Harvey, acquired the manor of Elstow, with the site of the convent and its demesne lands, at the dissolution of the monasteries, and Radcliffe himself gained possession in July 1553. At Elizabeth's accession his wife, jointly with their younger son Edward, received a grant of the manor of Houghton Grange, Bedfordshire. Having represented Bedfordshire repeatedly before the opening of this period, voting against a government bill in the 1555 Parliament, Radcliffe found himself ineligible for the county in 1559 through being sheriff, and instead was returned for Maldon through the influence of his nephew, the 3rd Earl of Sussex. In 1563 he was considered for both Liverpool and Bossiney, where his name was finally erased from the Crown Office list, and he was left out of the House altogether: a strange parliamentary career. Radcliffe's support of Henry VIII, Edward VI and Mary indicates that he had no strong religious views and he was in fact classified as indifferent in 1564. That the puritan Edward Underhill thought he had 'always favoured the gospel' is interesting but inconclusive. Radcliffe died intestate 13 Aug. 1566, aged 57.[3]

[1] Doyle, *Baronetage*, iii. 481; *Vis. Beds.* (Harl. Soc. xix), 48, 65; *CPR*, 1558–60, p. 2; *LP Hen. VIII*, x. 509; viii. 524. [2] *LP Hen. VIII*, iv(1), p. 871; xv. p. 5; *Chron. Q. Jane and Q. Mary* (Cam. Soc. xlviii), 128; *Narr. Reformation* (ibid. lxxvii), 161, 168; *CPR*, 1553–4, p. 17; 1560–3, p. 518. [3] *LP Hen. VIII*, xvi. p. 728; xix(1), pp. 161–2; *CPR*, 1553 and App. Edw. VI, p. 232; *VCH Beds.* iii. 293; C193/32/4–6; *Liverpool Town Bks.* ed. Twemlow, i. 216 seq.; *Narr. Reformation*, 161; Guildford Mus. Loseley mss 1331/2; *Cam. Misc.* ix(3), p. 28; *Beds. N. and Q.* i. 126 seq.; *Vis. Beds.* 48, 65; PCC admon. act bk. 1567, f. 122.

N.M.F.

RADCLIFFE, Sir John (1539–68), of Old Cleeve, Som.

CASTLE RISING	1558
GRAMPOUND	1559

bap. 31 Dec. 1539, yr. s. of Robert Radcliffe, 1st Earl of Sussex, by his 3rd w. Mary (*d.*1557), da. of Sir John Arundell of Lanherne, Cornw.; half-bro. of Sir Humphrey*. *m.* Anne, *s.p.* Kntd. 22 Feb. 1547.

Radcliffe – the only surviving child of the 1st Earl of Sussex's third and final marriage – was more than 30 years younger than his eldest half-brother, and still a baby when his father died. In 1554 Henry, Earl of Arundel, his stepfather, was licensed to convey to him the manor of Northam, Devon. Radcliffe thus became a landowner in a small way, but until 1564, when he succeeded to his mother's estate, he was probably in the service of one of the great noble families of Arundel, Sussex or Norfolk to whom he was related.

In 1545 his mother married the Earl of Arundel, and ten years later Arundel's daughter married Thomas Howard, 4th Duke of Norfolk, who in 1558 found Radcliffe a parliamentary seat for his newly-enfranchised borough of Castle Rising. He was only 18, not much younger than his patron. Radcliffe was chosen again for the same borough in 1559, and the return was completed to that effect, but Thomas Steyning, Norfolk's stepfather, evidently wished to sit there and Radcliffe, at the last moment, was found a seat at Grampound, presumably by his mother's family. There is little further to record about Radcliffe's short life. He made his will 18 Oct. 1568, leaving his property to his wife Anne, and a ring each, 'in token and remembrance of good will', to the Earls of Arundel and Sussex. He died 9 Nov. 1568 and was buried ten days later in St. Olave's, Hart Street, London.

H. B. Wilson, *Hist. St. Laurence Pountney*, 129; *CP*, xii(1), 519–20; *CPR*, 1553–4, p. 372; 1563–6, pp. 8, 166; PCC 21 Babington; A. Povah, *Annals of St. Olave, Hart St. and Allhallows, Staining, London*, 93, 173; *Reg. St. Olave, Hart St.* (Harl. Soc. xlvi), 108, 120.

R.V.

RADCLIFFE, Thomas (*d.*1586), of Elstow, Beds.

PORTSMOUTH	1584

1st s. of Sir Humphrey Radcliffe* of Elstow by his w. Isabel or Elizabeth, and bro. of Edward*. suc. fa. 1566.

Steward, manor of Elstow 1566; j.p. Beds. from 1577, q. 1583–*d.*; gent. pens. 1573/7–*d.*[1]

After a possible stab at Bedfordshire in 1584, Radcliffe was brought in for Portsmouth by his cousin Sir Henry Radcliffe*. Nothing has been found of any activities by him in this Parliament; indeed there is so little to relate about him that it is perhaps just worth mentioning a dispute in which he was engaged in the same year that he was returned to Parliament. He had borrowed £50 from a London grocer, William Ormeshaw, who complained to the Privy Council that the loan should have been repaid in 1581, but was not. Ormeshaw had judgment for £112 against Radcliffe, who still refused payment. Ormeshaw then appealed to Sir Henry Carey, 1st Lord Hunsdon, whereupon

> Mr. Radcliffe, showing himself to be very much grieved for that I had complained to my Lord, came to my house in very great anger, and there gave me many ill words, threatening me if I durst cause any execution to be served upon him … he would make me repent it so long as I lived, and in the end called me knave in mine own house. Upon which words I said his betters would not have called me so, who, answering again, said he knew no betters.

Radcliffe was actually imprisoned for a few days before a settlement was reached by which Ormeshaw was to receive £60. On his release Radcliffe had Ormeshaw summoned before the Council for extortion.

In September 1586 Radcliffe's name appeared in a list of gentlemen selected to escort Mary Stuart out of Staffordshire; he was to attend her if she passed through Bedfordshire. He died 18 Sept. 1586, as recorded on the pensioners' roll for that quarter. Administration was granted to William Butler I* in November 1586.[2]

[1] *Vis. Beds.* (Harl. Soc. xix), 48; *VCH Beds.* iii. 283; *CPR, 1566–9,* p. 70; SP12/145, f. 5; Royal 18, D. 111, f. 41; E163/14/8, f. 1; E407/ Box 1/16. [2] Northants. RO. Stopford Sackville mss 239; SP12/175/1; Lansd. 49, f. 171 seq.; PCC admon. act bk. 1586, f. 198; information from Mr. W. J. Tighe.

A.M.M.

RAGLAND, Sir Thomas, of Carnllwyd, Glam., Roughton Holme, Norf. and Walworth, Surr.

MALMESBURY 1563

1st s. of Sir John Ragland of Carnllwyd. *m.* by 1551 Ann, da. of Sir Roger Woodhouse of Kimberley, Norf., wid. of Christopher Coningsby of Wallington, Norf., more than one ch. *suc.* fa. bef. 1550.[1]
J.p. Norf. from 1550.[2]

Ragland's father was a soldier who received his knighthood at Tournai in 1513 and was present at the Field of the Cloth of Gold. Although in 1520 he ranked as a knight of Worcestershire, and in 1524 was granted a manor of the Duke of Buckingham near Brecon, Sir John Ragland resided at Carnllwyd in the vale of Glamorgan, and was also constable of Kenvig castle. His appearance, in a list of 1531, as a principal debtor to the late abbot of Glastonbury cannot but appear prophetic.[3]

Of his son Thomas – to be distinguished from an elder Thomas, Sir John's brother, who by marrying Margaret Carne of Cowbridge became brother-in-law to Sir Edward Carne†, the diplomat – nothing has been discovered before the reign of Edward VI, but it is probable that he followed his father's profession and, like him, received a

knighthood, the date and occasion of which are unknown, in the field. Hailing from the Herberts' country, and springing from a family which shared its origin with those magnates, he may have followed William Herbert in campaigns at home or abroad and thus have earned support when he came to enter Parliament. His marriage with Ann Coningsby also perhaps resulted from connexions formed in military service, for her first husband had been killed in action at Musselburgh in 1547, and his uncle Humphrey, a gentleman pensioner, had fought in both France and Scotland. The alliance gave Ragland an affiliation with Norfolk, for his wife was a Woodhouse of Kimberley and her first husband, part of whose property she obtained after his death along with the wardship of her three young daughters, had inherited Wallington in that county from his father, William Coningsby the judge and MP. The marriage presumably took place between July 1548 when Ann, still a widow, secured the wardship, and December 1550 when Ragland was made a j.p. of his new county.[4]

Almost everything we know about Ragland's career from that point reflects discredit upon him. His wife's stipulation, in the will which she made in December 1562, 'that Sir Thomas Ragland shall not by any ways or means take any benefit or advantage of this will' (save only, it may be inferred, the 'ring with an emerald' she bequeathed him), is revealing alike in its content and tone. That her daughters' inheritance needed safeguarding from their stepfather is all too apparent. His many lawsuits appear to be those of a man out to get whatever he could from anybody. Only a year or two before Ann Ragland's death Caius College had begun a Chancery suit against her and her husband for detention of evidence relating to one of its landed endowments; since the college was pursuing the case some ten years later against him alone, it was probably he who was at the bottom of the affair. A case in the court of requests relating to the year 1563 shows that he then had a house at Walworth, Surrey, in addition to his Norfolk home at Roughton.[5]

It was shortly after his wife made her will (proved 18 Feb. 1563) that Ragland got himself returned to Parliament and she was probably dead before he took his seat. Membership was something which, so far as the evidence goes, no other Ragland ever achieved; but the distinction, like the motive behind it, may have been less enviable than it appears. The Parliament in which he sat had two sessions, in 1563 and 1566. Before the second, in November 1565, he obtained from Chancery a protection until the following 10 Feb., and when this expired he had it renewed until 30 Nov. 1566. Both the terminal date of the first protection, which was three days after the date to which, when it was obtained, Parliament stood prorogued, and the issue of the second, which in the event overlapped the second session by two months, suggest that the two timetables were connected, and that the immunity from suits at law, including actions for debt, which the protections conferred was designed to be extended by parliamentary privilege, as in the upshot it was until 2 Jan. 1567, the day of dissolution. If Ragland's Membership was thus to serve his pecuniary turn in 1566, he may well have sought it from the outset, at least in part, for this purpose.[6]

That, whatever his motives, he had achieved their aim he can scarcely have owed to anyone but the 1st Earl of Pembroke. Ragland is not known to have possessed property in Wiltshire, while the John Ragland, perhaps his great-uncle, who had been assessed at Bishopstone for the benevolence of 1545 at 23s. 4d. and whose goods Sir Thomas seized – at the cost of a Star Chamber action – after his death would have represented, even if he had survived, only meagre and distant support. Ragland's fellow-member at Malmesbury in 1563, Edward Poole, could count on the help of the powerful Stumpe family, but no link between Ragland and either Poole or Stumpe has been traced. Ragland's election there in 1563 thus appears to reflect an interest on the part of the 1st Earl of Pembroke similar to that which the 2nd Earl was to show when at the next two elections Nicholas Snell was returned.[7]

Whatever relief Ragland derived from his Membership could not have outlasted the Parliament itself, and the little that is to be learned about his affairs suggests that thereafter they went from bad to worse. In August 1578 he was in the Gatehouse prison, whence he addressed a plea to Burghley for early hearing in the Exchequer Chamber of a suit between him and two men named Wilgoose and Bradbridge, presumably creditors; and in March 1582 the Privy Council intervened in a dispute arising out of his mortgaging of lands for discharge of debts. Whether he died in prison, and what became of his children (whose names and number are unknown), have eluded discovery.[8]

[1] *Cartae de Glamorgancia*, 1843 ii; *CSP Dom.* Add. 1566–79, p. 47; *CPR*, 1547–8, p. 298; 1553, App. I, p. 357; *Vis. Norf.* (Harl. Soc. xxxii), 13, 322; St. Ch. 7/28/1. [2] *CPR*, 1553, App. I, p. 357. [3] *LP Hen. VIII*, iii. pt. 1, nos. 243, 326, 2214(18), 2288(2); iv. pt. 1, g. 895(24), no. 976; Add. i. pt. 1, no. 742. [4] *Cartae de Glam.* 1847–50; *CPR*, 1547–8, p. 298; 1553, App. I, p. 357; 1553–4, p. 84. [5] PCC 10 Chayre; C3/38/59, 41/18, 70/13, 72/5, 149/15, 151/16, 152/5, 152/22, 153/7, 154/51, 155/8, 156/27, 163/70; Req. 2/37/87. [6] *CPR*, 1563–6, pp. 302, 432. [7] *Two Taxation Lists* (Wilts. Arch. Soc. recs. br. x), 44; *CPR*, 1557–8, p. 204; St. Ch. 5/6/26. [8] *HMC Hatfield*, ii. 191–2; *APC*, xiii. 366–7.

S.T.B.

RALEGH, Carew (c.1550–1626), of Downton, Wilts.

WILTSHIRE	1584, 1586
LUDGERSHALL	1589
FOWEY	1601
DOWNTON	1604, 1621

b. c.1550, 3rd s. (1st by 3rd w.) of Walter Ralegh† of Fardel, Devon, by Katherine, da. of Philip Champernown of Modbury, Devon, wid. of Otho Gilbert; bro. of Walter Ralegh* and half-bro. of Adrian* and Sir Humphrey Gilbert*. *m.* aft. 1580, Dorothy (*d.*1616), da. of Sir William Wroughton† of Broad Hinton, wid. of Sir John Thynne* of Longleat, 3s. 1da. Kntd. 1601.

Gent. of the horse to Sir John Thynne bef. 1580; lt. of Portland castle 6 July 1584–1625; keeper (with his bro. Walter) of Mere park, Wilts. 1586, and of Gillingham park, Dorset; dep. warden of the stannaries by 1588; master of St. John's hospital, Wilton 1589 or 1590; dep. lt. Devon in or bef. 1596; v.-adm. Dorset 1597; j.p.q. Dorset, Wilts. from c.1583.[1]

When Carew Ralegh came to submit his pedigree to the heralds in 1623 he described his father, and three earlier progenitors, as of Fardel (or Fardle, the spelling varies), Devon. In this he was legally correct, since his father remained the owner of the family residence until his death in 1581. Long before that, however, Walter Ralegh had ceased to live there, being driven by the family's failing fortunes to settle in Exeter; he leased the 'barton' or farmhouse (which still stands) at Hayes in East Budleigh and it was there that he raised his third family. Of these children Carew, named after his maternal grandmother, was the eldest; but he had two Ralegh and three Gilbert half-brothers as well as an elder sister. Brought up in relative obscurity but conscious of belonging to one of the oldest families in Devon, Carew Ralegh had to make his way by his own ability and exertion. His mother, through whom he was allied with the gentry of the shire, must have had exceptional talents to transmit, since all five of her sons were to distinguish themselves. Carew's three Gilbert half-brothers influenced his young manhood, while his brother Walter remained a life-long friend. It is perhaps a measure of the elderly father's anxiety for the fortunes of his two youngest sons that he caused Carew and Walter, then both children, to be associated with him in the lease of the tithes of fish at Sidmouth in 1560. While much is known of the progress of the younger boy, it can only be surmised that Carew, who unlike Walter did not go to either university or inn of court, sought adventure early, perhaps serving in France under his cousin Henry Champernown* before being taken by Sir Humphrey Gilbert on his first expedition of discovery in 1578, an enterprise which daunted Ralegh so little by its failure that four years later he was one of those who 'adventured' with Gilbert in money or commodities. He continued to serve at sea, and in 1585 his name appears, with those of Walter and his two Ralegh half-brothers, on a list of captains drawn up under the threat of war with Spain. By this time he was beginning to reap the advantage of the Queen's partiality to Walter, sharing with him the keepership of two parks and being made his deputy warden at the stannaries. He commanded Portland castle at the coming of the Armada – when it was grudgingly supplied by the Privy Council with guns out of a Spanish galleon – continued to oversee its armament, and remained its lieutenant until within a year of his death.[2]

The 'nineties offered greater prizes than those accruing from office, and Carew engaged in privateering expeditions, usually with Walter, during these years of opportunity. The Crown co-operated, but on its own conditions. In 1591 the Raleghs' fleet was augmented by four of the Queen's ships, but in the following May the Privy Council ordered Carew to give up prize goods for fear of reprisals from France. No Ralegh gave up winnings easily: by September their lordships were pointing out that, despite 'our often letters to you', he had failed to comply with their demand. Carew was more fortunate in receiving money from the sale of prizes at Bayonne in June 1592, and in September he was one of three to whom the customer of London was ordered to give access to the sugar and other merchandise captured in a French ship by a vessel which he had 'set' to sea. In the following month, however, he and Sir John Gilbert were again in trouble with the Privy Council, this time over ships of Amsterdam and Middelburg taken by two of their subordinates. His largest windfall came in January 1593 when he was awarded £900 of the £1,000 he claimed as his share of the *Madre de Dios*, the carrack brought in by the galleon *Ralegh*. As late as January 1602 he was delivered prize goods by the customer of Weymouth. Like other privateers Carew was not allowed to forget national needs. In September 1596 the Privy Council ordered him to hand over a piece of brass ordnance which he had taken out of a flyboat bringing guns from Calais. In 1594 he was employed in the provisioning of Brest, and three years later he was made vice-admiral of Dorset.[3]

Some time before the death of Sir John Thynne in 1580 Ralegh had become his gentleman of the horse, and within a year or two he married Thynne's widow. It is usually said that on his marriage Ralegh sold his Devon lands and set himself up at Downton House in Wiltshire; but both statements probably antedate the changes in question. Ralegh's father died in 1581, but the eldest son of the first marriage survived until 1597 as the owner of Fardel and Withycombe Raleigh, while the other two family manors had been settled on the widow, who lived until 1594. By the 1580s Carew was certainly in process of transferring his attachment to Wiltshire – in 1582 he was a j.p. in that county, and two years later he was to represent it in Parliament – but not immediately to the exclusion of interests and duties in the west country. His wife's connexions in Wiltshire, both in her own right as a Wroughton and through the Thynnes, could bring him influence there, but the obscure nature of her first husband's will makes it difficult to assess the material inducements Lady Thynne's second husband might have had to offer the electorate. She was left well-dowered with plate and livestock, but there is no mention of a house for her; since the stock was at Corsley, where she also held the tithes, this may have been the house which Ralegh repaired to in the 'eighties. How soon he acquired one of his own is uncertain. Downton rectory had been leased by Winchester College to Thomas Wilkes* in 1581 for 40 years, but with a clause against sub-letting. Wilkes lived until 1598, but as he spent his closing years, when in England, at Rickmansworth, he may have sold the lease to Ralegh or his executor may have done so. By 1598 Ralegh was well placed to make the transfer, and his disposal of his Devon patrimony may thus have coincided with his establishment at Downton. He is found writing from Downton from January 1601; he soon acquired many burgage tenements in the borough; and either he or his son Gilbert was returned for it in 1604, 1614 and 1621.[4]

Ralegh's earlier elections for Ludgershall and Fowey had been equally in keeping with his position in those years, for Ludgershall returned many parliamentary aspirants with slender local claims and Fowey knew him as deputy warden of the stannaries to his brother, the warden. What is less easy to explain is his securing the knighthood of the shire in 1584 (as such he could have attended the subsidy committee 24 Feb. 1585) and 1586. Even allowing for the Longleat connexion and for the fact that his half-brother Adrian Gilbert was a frequent visitor at Wilton, we are tempted to seek some other explanation of Ralegh's achievement and to find it in Sir Walter's credit with the Queen. Conversely, when in the 'nineties the favourite suffered eclipse, Carew missed two consecutive Parliaments for the only time in his career. His name occurs seldom in the journals of the House. When, on 25 Mar. 1585 the Commons discussed as a matter of privilege the arrest of his servant, it was observed that 'his master came not at the Parliament House all the latter session, but was in the country'. The anonymous journal for this Parliament has two other references to him (unless these are to Walter), one; 'we come not hither to make laws after the Lacedaemonians or Romans but to make Christian laws'; the other reporting that he thought that bishops should support any ministers they had made 'until they be in places'. In 1601 he was appointed to the committee discussing the reform of the penal laws (2 Nov.). The man whom D'Ewes notes as speaking on 2 Dec. on the bill for the more diligent resort to church on Sundays was not Ralegh but Carew Reynell.[5]

For all that Carew Ralegh has been described as 'mean and acquisitive', he was not without personal charm. He had 'a delicate clear voice' and could accompany himself 'skilfully on the olpharion'; he may also have tried his hand at verse. He was associated with his brother and his Gilbert half-brothers in those speculative discussions which earned the group the title of 'Rawley's Atheistical Academy' and brought its members before the Privy Council in 1593 to answer for their religious opinions. In speculation, as in their other joint pursuits, Carew was probably less wholehearted than Sir Walter, for his only recorded utterance among these intimates is the laconic inquiry, 'Soul, what is that?' Perhaps Queen Elizabeth's judgment of him, 'Good Mr. Ralegh, who wonders at his own diligence (because diligence and he are not familiars)', holds the clue to Carew Ralegh's career, which reached its peak, in terms of public recognition, by the time he was 50, and that chiefly through the impetus of his brother's larger ambitions and superior driving power. His personal aspirations appear to have been solid rather than splendid, local rather than general; the knighthood conferred at Basing House honoured a country gentleman, not a national hero. Although he did not desert his brother in prison, he survived Sir Walter's fall, to carry on the life that he had chosen, as little concerned by James I as James was concerned with him.[6]

[1] *DNB*; *Wilts. Vis. Peds.* (Harl. Soc. cv, cvi), 160; *Trans. Dev. Assoc.* xxviii. 273–90; Hoare, *Wilts. Downton*, 29, 30; *Wilts. Arch. Mag.* xxix. 242; Lansd. 100, f. 221; *APC*, xvi. 149; xxvii. 38. [2] *Trans. Dev. Assoc.*; A. L. Rowse, *Ralegh and the Throckmortons*, 129–31; *CSP Dom.* 1595–7, p. 192; *APC*, xvi. 204, 259, 309; xxvi. 316. [3] *CSP Dom.* 1591–4, pp. 15, 231; *APC*, xxii. 496–7; xxiii. 165, 170, 210, 238; xxvi. 188; xxvii. 38; Lansd. 72, f. 40; *HMC Hatfield*, iv. 563; xii. 17. [4] M. J. G. Stanford, 'Hist. Ralegh Fam.' (London Univ. MA thesis 1955), 341–2; PCC 44 Arundel; Hoare, loc. cit. 32–5; *HMC Hatfield*, xi. 14. [5] *VCH Wilts.* vi. 6; D'Ewes, 623, 651, 663; Lansd. 43, anon. jnl., f. 171; Trinity, Dublin, Thos. Cromwell's jnl. [6] Rowse, 130, 176–7; *DNB*; *Wilts. N. and Q.* v. 501; Lansd. 85, f. 37; *HMC Hatfield*, xvi. 193; xvii. 601.

M.B.

RALEGH, Walter (1554–1618), of Durham House, London and Sherborne, Dorset.[1]

DEVON	1584, 1586
MITCHELL	1593
DORSET	1597
CORNWALL	1601

b. 1554, yr. s. of Walter Ralegh[†] of Fardel, Devon by his 3rd w. Katherine, da. of Philip Champernown, wid. of Otho Gilbert; bro. of Carew Ralegh* and half-bro. of Adrian* and Sir Humphrey Gilbert*. *educ.* local g.s.; Oriel, Oxf. c.1572; Lyon's Inn; travelled in France c.1573; M. Temple by 1576. *m.* Nov. 1591, Elizabeth, da. of Sir Nicholas Throckmorton*, 3s. Kntd. 1585.

On Henry Champernown's* expedition to aid French Huguenots 1569; on voyage against Spanish shipping Nov. 1578–9; capt. in Ireland 1580–1; esquire of the body by 1581; warden of stannaries, steward, duchy of Cornw., ld. lt. Cornw., v.-adm. Cornw., Devon 1585–1603; capt. of the guard c.1587–1603; keeper of parks at Gillingham, Dorset and Mere, Wilts.; j.p. Dorset from c.1592–1603, custos rot. 1599–1603; j.p. Som. from c.1592–1603; gov. Jersey Sept. 1600–3.

On Orinoco expedition Feb.–Aug. 1595; Cadiz June 1596; Azores Aug. 1597; Orinoco June 1617–June 1618.[2]

Ralegh's father, of an old-established minor gentry family, had been deputy vice-admiral in the south-west under Mary. He retired to Exeter about 1569, and thenceforth took little part in county affairs. He died early in 1581. Through his father's three marriages the future courtier was connected with many of the leading west-country families. After some time in France, he was back in London by 1574 but it is not known when he first went to court, where his mother's relationship to Elizabeth's friend and confidante, Kate Astley, ensured him a welcome. Adrian Gilbert is said to have loaned him the £10 he needed for his first appearance there. Following a 'fray' with Sir Thomas Perrot* in February 1580, both spent a week in the Fleet. Ralegh was again in prison, this time the Marshalsea, for another 'fray' on 17 Mar.[3]

Next, Ralegh spent some time on active service in Ireland before returning to a minor appointment that was nevertheless close to the sovereign. By 1582 Hatton was complaining that there was 'too much water' at court. Ralegh was given most of the local west-country offices made vacant by the death of the 2nd Earl of Bedford in 1585, but his occupation of Hatton's lodging at court that year is said to have earned him the comment from Elizabeth that 'she had rather see him hanged than equal him with [Hatton] or that the world should think she did so'. There is much in this remark, whether or not it was ever made, for Hatton was a statesman of the first rank as well as a royal favourite, whose abilities took him from the captainship of the guard to membership of the Privy Council and the lord chancellorship. Though Ralegh was made captain of the guard after Hatton, further promotion eluded him. He failed to succeed Heneage as vice-chamberlain in 1595, failed to become chancellor of the duchy of Lancaster, even failed, to his great chagrin, to be made of the Privy Council, as he confidently expected to be before the Parliament of 1601. Had he succeeded in this it is at least possible that he might have weathered the storms of the succession despite the damaging neutrality of Robert Cecil, who was fighting for his own survival at this critical juncture.

Meanwhile, in 1587, Ralegh received many lucrative marks of royal favour. As captain of the guard he had constant access to the Queen, which brought him substantial perquisites from suitors who needed his goodwill; he received – despite objections from Burghley – a grant of the farm of the customs for exporting overlength cloth; wine and tin monopolies; Sherborne; estates in Derbyshire, Lincolnshire and Nottinghamshire from the Babington conspirators, and 40,000 acres in Ireland.[4]

In Parliament, Ralegh was unique in this period in representing three counties. He was junior Member for Devon in 1584, and was knighted by the Queen at Greenwich on Twelfth Day, 6 Jan. 1585, during the Christmas recess. By 1586 he was warden of the stannaries and vice-admiral and he occupied the senior Devon seat. He was in Ireland at the time of the 1588 election and remained out of the 1589 Parliament. In 1593 he came in for Mitchell, probably by courtesy of Richard Carew*. It is true that he was in disgrace at court for seducing one of the Queen's maids of honour, but it is difficult to see how this could have prevented his obtaining a county seat if he had wanted one; conversely, if he could not obtain a county seat his return for Mitchell shows a determination to be of the Parliament that might not have been suspected. In 1597 his Sherborne estate and his general standing in the county brought him election for Dorset, and in 1601 he was elected for Cornwall, where he was lord lieutenant and warden of the stannaries.

He had also some interest in borough patronage, though, as always, it is difficult to disentangle the names of his nominees from those of his friends and the dependants who had sufficient local influence to secure their own return. His servant Edward Hancock found a seat at Plympton Erle in 1597. At Bridport he placed through his servant Morgan Moone*, Gregory Sprint, Adrian Gilbert, and perhaps John Fortescue II. In Cornwall Ralegh was respected both by the gentry as an administrator, and by the lower orders as an employer. Between 1586 and the end of this period some 60 Cornish Members were connected with him, his relatives and his close friends, though again it should be stated that this does not mean he brought them into Parliament. However, Ralegh's concern with borough patronage may be seen from a letter he wrote to Sir John Gilbert in 1601: 'I pray you get some burgesses if you can, and desire C[hristopher] Harris* to write in my name for as many as he can procure'.

Ralegh had a vested interest in the 1584 Parliament which was to give a first reading (14 Dec.) to his bill for the discovery of foreign countries. The committee included a number of his friends, Drake, Grenville, Sir William Courtenay and Sir William Mohun, while Hatton and, probably, Walsingham were appointed for the government. Ralegh himself was appointed to committees on Suffolk cloth (7 Dec.), liberty of ministers (16 Dec.), the continuance of statutes (19 Dec.) and the subsidy (24 Feb. 1585). He is not known to have spoken in this or in his next Parliament, when his committees were on the subsidy (22 Feb. 1587) and on a learned ministry (8 Mar.).

Though he was in disgrace at court and sitting for a borough, Ralegh's parliamentary activity increased dramatically in 1593, when he took a leading part in the tortuous negotiations between Queen, Lords and Commons over the subsidy. Clearly he was trying to work his passage back into favour. His first speech on the subsidy, 2 Mar. – indeed his first known speech in the House – is reported by the anonymous diarist:

> Then Sir Walter Ralegh spake of the subsidy, not only as he protested to please the Queen to whom he was infinitely bound above his desert but for the necessity of that he saw and knew, he very well and exactly discovered the great strength of the King of Spain.

On 5 Mar. he suggested that the Commons should compromise with the Lords over their wish to be concerned with the Commons in the subsidy negotiations. He thought the House would not object to a general conference with the Lords 'without naming a subsidy' and this was agreed to *nem. con.* Elaborating on this next day:

> we agreed all to a general conference but not in particular for the subsidy, for this we refused. If we confer generally it must be of our dangers, and of the remedies, which must be ... money and aid. So our conference must be of subsidy or rather aid, but to agree upon this with any resolution either in the matter or substance, it is not our meaning,

as fine a piece of hair splitting, it may be thought, as occurs within these pages, yet valid for all that. The Lords must not be seen to be joined with the Commons in a financial resolution. On the amount of the subsidy, in the House next day (7 Mar.):

> the longer we defer aid the less able shall we be to yield aid, and in the end the greater aid will be required of us ... For ... one hundred thousand pound would have done the last year that which three will not now do, and three will do this year that which six will not do hereafter.

There is a neat contrast, incidentally, in the length and content of Ralegh's speech and that of Drake, who spoke soon after him. At the committee that afternoon Ralegh developed his theme:

> The time is now more dangerous than it was in '88. For then the Spaniard which came from Spain was to pass dangerous seas, and had no place of retreat or relief if he failed. But now he hath in Brittany great store of shipping, a landing place in Scotland, and men and horses there as good as we have any.

On 23 Mar. 1593 Ralegh made a long speech on the bill against aliens retailing foreign wares in this country, of whose committee he was in charge. It was an 'honour to use strangers as we be used amongst strangers' but 'a baseness in a nation to give a liberty to another nation which we cannot receive again'.

> The Dutchman ... hath gotten trading with all the world into his hands, yea he is now entering into the trade of Scarborough fishing and the fishing of the Newfound-Lands which is the stay of the west countries. They are the people that maintain the King of Spain in his greatness. Were it not for them, he were never able to make out such armies and navies by sea. ... to conclude, in the whole cause I see no matter of honour, no matter of charity, no profit in relieving them.

More far-sighted was his attitude towards the Brownists, a group of nonconformists who wished to secede from the Anglican church. Ralegh agreed (4 Apr.) that they should be 'rooted out'. But to enact a law to transport them was bad in principle:

men not guilty will be included·in it. And that law is hard that taketh life and sendeth into banishment when men's intentions shall be judged by a jury.

And also on grounds of expediency:

At whose charge shall they be transported? or whither will you send them? I am sorry for it, I am afraid there are near 20,000 of them in England, and when they be gone who shall maintain their wives and children?

Ralegh was named first in the committee appointed on this bill that day. Also in 1593 he was appointed to all committees on the subsidy as well as to those on privileges and returns (26 Feb.), provisions against recusants (28 Feb.), springing uses (9 Mar.), forgery (10 Mar.), the poor law (12 Mar.), cordage for the navy (6 Apr.) and a legal bill (7 Apr.).

In the 1597 Parliament Ralegh took a leading part in the committees, conferences and discussions on the poor law. On 14 Jan. 1598 he complained that the Lords had received discourteously the members of the Commons appointed to confer with them, 'to the great indignity of this House, and contrary to all former usage of their lordships', and was nominated to the Commons committee to inquire into this. On 20 Jan. the Lords denied that they had given the commoners 'any just distaste'. Ralegh also sat on committees in this Parliament on armour and weapons (8 Nov.), monopolies (10 Nov.), the subsidy (15 Nov.), merchant strangers (13 Jan.), Thomas Knyvet's lands and explanation of statutes (18 Jan.), excess of apparel (19 Jan.) and a bill concerning debts incurred by tellers and receivers of the Exchequer (31 Jan.). He was not named to the privileges and returns committee of 5 Nov. 1597 (perhaps this is not significant) but he was to that appointed at the outset of the 1601 Parliament, 31 Oct. Despite his open disappointment at his failure to receive promotion in court office or appointment to the Privy Council, Ralegh was active in furthering the interests of government at this time. He was appointed to the main business committee (3 Nov.) and took a prominent part in the debates on the subsidy. On the afternoon of 7 Nov. in the committee of the whole House he moved for the subsidy 'and the manner and quality thereof'. Last Parliament three subsidies had been granted 'upon fear that the Spaniards were coming. But now', he went on, with a reference to the recent landing of a Spanish army in Ireland, 'we see they are come, and have set foot even in the Queen's territories already'. During this committee session Ralegh was asked to stand so that he might be heard better – not the first time he had been asked to speak up. He replied that, the House being in committee 'he might speak sitting or standing, and so repeated over again his former speech'. Still on the subsidy (9 Nov.) he liked not 'that the Spaniards our enemies should know of our selling our pots and pans to pay subsidies'. He was against Francis Bacon's proposal not to exclude the £3

men, 'Call you this *par jugum* when a poor man pays as much as a rich?'.

He was much against hasty economic legislation, especially if this was at the expense of the rights of the individual. On 4 Nov., concerning the sowing of hemp:

I do not like this constraining of men to manure or use their grounds at our wills; but rather, let every man use his ground to that which it is most fit for, and therein use his own discretion.

Again, 2 Dec., he criticized a bill to regulate the conduct of ale houses because one of its provisions would debar the offender from ever being an innkeeper again. 'How dangerous to the innkeepers that might, by negligence of a servant, suffer' such a heavy penalty. On 12 Dec., on the clumsy procedure for convicting offenders under the proposed recusancy bill:

All the church wardens of every shire must come to the Sessions to give information to the grand jury. Say then there be 120 parishes in a shire, there must now come extraordinarily 240 churchwardens. And say that but two in a parish offend in a quarter of a year, that makes 480 persons, with the offenders, to appear. What great multitudes this will bring together! What quarrelling and danger may happen, besides giving authority to a mere churchwarden! How prejudicial this may be!

In the event the bill was lost by one vote, and, during the ensuing recriminations Ralegh caused 'a great loud speech and stir' by confessing to having pulled Members by the sleeve to prevent them going out to vote. But on a previous occasion (9 Dec.) when two Privy Councillors rose to lead Members to vote before he had a chance to speak he was quick to protest:

I thought I had deserved of the House to have been heard to speak as well as he that spoke before the division of the House; and in that I offered to speak and was not heard, I had wrong.

His attitude to the great subject of this Parliament, monopolies, was ambivalent. He contrived (20 Nov.) both to defend the underdog – in this case the tinners – and his own tin monopoly:

I am urged to speak in two respects. The one because I find myself touched in particular, the other in that I take some imputation and slander to be offered unto her Majesty. I mean by the gentleman that first mentioned tin (which was Mr. Martin) for that being one of the principal commodities of this kingdom and being in Cornwall it hath ever (so long as there were any) belonged to the Dukes of Cornwall, and they had special patents of privilege. It pleased her Majesty freely to bestow on me that privilege and that patent being word for word the very same the Duke's is. And because by reason of mine office of lord warden of the stannaries I can sufficiently inform this house of the state thereof I will make bold to deliver it unto you. When the tin is taken out of the mine and moulten and refined then is every piece containing a hundredweight sealed with the Duke's seal and by reason of his privilege (which I now have) he ever had the refusal in buying thereof, for the words of the patent are *nisi nos emere volumus*. Now I will tell you that before the granting of my patent whether tin were but at 17s. and so upwards to 50s. a cwt., yet a poor workman never had above 2s. a week, finding himself. But since my patent whosoever will work may, and be tin at what price soever they have 4s. a week truly paid; there is no poor that will work there but may, and have that wages. Notwithstanding if all other [patents] may be repealed I will give my consent as freely to the cancelling of this as any member of this House.

This 'sharp speech' produced 'a great silence' in the House, and must be accounted one of his failures, as was his attempt (1 Dec.) to get a proviso exempting debts under £5 from the provisions of the bill to prevent double payment of debts upon shop books. Ralegh was in charge of the committee on this bill and was outvoted both by his fellow committeemen and by the House at the report stage. Ralegh's committees in 1601 not already mentioned were on the penal laws (2 Nov.), Exeter churches (10 Nov.), customs duties (10 Nov.), insurance (13 Nov.), pluralities (16 Nov.), clothworkers (18 Nov.), monopolies (23 Nov.), the Marquess of Winchester (28 Nov.), the Countess of Sussex (3, 17 Dec.), Dunkirk pirates (3 Dec.), cloth (4 Dec.), export of ordnance (8 Dec.) – he was sure one of her Majesty's ships could beat twenty Spanish; the Belgrave privilege case (8 Dec.), tillage (9 Dec.), Dover harbour (10, 14 Dec.), Questor's denization (14 Dec.) – he supported Cecil on this; Exchequer reform (16 Dec.), captains, soldiers and mariners (16 Dec.) – he 'much excepted' against this 'by reason of the generality of the bill'; fines within ancient demesnes (17 Dec.) and deceits in auditors (17 Dec.).[5]

Reference has already been made to his seduction of the Queen's maid of honour Elizabeth Throckmorton, and his secret marriage to her some five months after the conception of a boy who was to die in infancy. Less than three weeks before the birth of the child, when the news of his wife's condition was becoming known, Ralegh wrote to Cecil from Chatham, 10 Mar. 1592, where he was fitting out for a reprisal raid against Spain for the loss of Grenville's *Revenge*:

> If any such thing were, I would have imparted it unto yourself before any man living; and, therefore, I pray believe it not, and I beseech you to suppress, what you can, any such malicious report. For, I protest before God, there is none of the face of the earth that I would be fastened unto.

Clearly he hoped to be away before the matter came to the ears of the Queen. In the event he was recalled, arrived back in London in June 1592, and was put in the Tower in July. However, his fleet captured off the Azores the great Portuguese carrack, the *Madre de Dios*, and Ralegh was released in September to supervise the distribution of its immensely valuable cargo. He afterwards complained that he who ventured most in the expedition incurred the greatest loss. He finally settled, on 24 Jan. 1593, for a share amounting to £15,900. Neither he nor his wife apologized for their rash behaviour, and neither was forgiven by the Queen. Almost five years were to pass before Ralegh was again allowed to exercise his captaincy of the guard. He never fully regained the royal favour.[6]

Ralegh was executed on 29 October 1618.

[1] Throughout this article recourse has been had to the *DNB* and the lives of Ralegh by E. Edwards (1868) and W. Stebbing (1891, 1899). [2] A. L. Rowse, *Ralegh and the Throckmortons*, 159–162; *Vis. Devon*, ed. Vivian, 405, 639; C66/1255, m 40; Lansd. 47, f. 41; 105, ff. 99, 101; PRO Index 4208. [3] Ralegh, *Hist. World*, bks. iv. and v.; C. Monro, *Acta Canc.* (1847), pp. 176–7; *APC*, xi. 384, 388–9. [4] E. St. John Brooks, *Hatton*, 301–4; Lansd. 41, ff. 81, 99; 49, f. 51; 71, f. 142. [5] D'Ewes, 337, 339, 340, 343, 356, 409, 413, 471, 474, 477, 481, 484, 486, 488, 490, 492, 493, 496, 497, 499, 508, 509, 517, 519, 520, 552, 553, 555, 557, 561, 575, 578, 579, 580, 581, 582, 583, 585, 586, 589, 591, 622, 624, 629, 630, 632, 633, 634, 635, 636, 641, 642, 646, 647, 649, 651, 658, 661, 665, 666, 668, 671, 672, 673, 674, 676, 677, 678, 680, 683, 684, 686, 687; Cott. Titus F.ii anon. jnl., ff. 42–3; Townshend, *Hist. Colls.* 188, 197, 198, 204, 235, 270, 278, 293, 299, 301, 302–3, 309, 320, 321, 322, 327; *HMC Hatfield*, xi. 484. Some variant readings for 1601 from Stowe 362. [6] Rowse, loc. cit.; Lansd. 70, f. 217; 73, ff. 40–1.

P.W.H.

RANDALL, Nicholas (*d.* c.1562), of Truro, Cornw.

TRURO   1547, 1553 (Mar.), 1553 (Oct.), 1555, 1558, 1559

Constable, Trematon castle, Cornw. 1542; havener, duchy of Cornw. 1542, comptroller and coll. customs c.1554; bailiff, Aylewarton and Penzance, Cornw. 1543.

Randall, a duchy of Cornwall official, was one of the west-country contingent, led by (Sir) Anthony Kingston[†], who opposed a government measure in the Parliament of 1555, and it is not surprising to find him re-elected in 1559, when sound protestants were much sought after. Little is known about his background. A William Randall, four times mayor of Plymouth, was of an age to have been his father, but there is no evidence to connect them. Possibly his wife was the Alice Randall, widow, who was living in Truro after 1562. His descendants apparently remained in the town; the son of a Hannibal Randall of Truro went up to Oxford in 1641. The MP died in the 16th year of his tenure of the manor of Tybesta.

LP Hen. VIII, xvii. p. 492; xviii(1), p. 284; xxi(1), p. 483; Duchy Cornw. 228/36; Guildford Mus., Loseley ms 1331/2; A. L. Rowse, *Tudor Cornw.* 304; R. N. Worth, *Plymouth Recs.* 14, 16; Duchy Cornw. roll 134, m. 4v.

I.C.

RANDOLPH, Thomas (1523–90), of St. Peter's Hill, London, and Milton, Kent.[1]

NEW ROMNEY and/or ST. IVES   1558
GRANTHAM   1559

ST. IVES 1572
MAIDSTONE 1584, 1586, 1589

b. 1523, 2nd s. of Avery Randolph of Badlesmere, Kent by Anne, da. of Sir John Gaynsford of Crowhurst, Suss. *educ.* Canterbury sch.; Christ Church, Oxf., BA 1545, BCL 1548, suppl. DCL 1566, 1574. *m.* (1) 1571, Anne, da. of Thomas Walsingham* of Chislehurst, Kent, *s.p.s.*; (2) by 1575, Ursula, da. of Henry Copinger of Buxhall, Suff., 3s. prob. 3da.[2]

Notary public by Apr. 1548; principal, Broadgates Hall, Oxf. 1549–53; envoy to Germany 1558, Scotland 1559–66, Russia 1568–9, Scotland 1570, 1572, France 1573, 1576, Scotland 1578, 1581, 1586; master of the posts from 1567; constable (by assignment from Sir Robert Constable), Queenborough castle from 1567; steward, manors of Milton and Merden, Kent from 1567; chamberlain of the Exchequer from 1572; j.p. Kent from 1573, commr. musters from c.1584.[3]

Randolph wrote from Strasbourg, early in December 1558, to tell Sir Nicholas Throckmorton* that he was returning to England with Sir Thomas Wroth* and Sir Anthony Cooke*. Throckmorton's 'advice' to Elizabeth was that Randolph should be made clerk of the Privy Council, but she had other plans for him. He was to continue the diplomatic career he may already have begun in the reign of her sister, and which was to continue until within four years of his death.

The Elizabethan diplomats provide poor material for parliamentary biographies, as their activity in the Commons, on the comparatively few occasions their duties permitted their attending the House, is rarely commensurate with the interest of their career outside, which has necessarily to be excluded from consideration. Randolph was brought into the 1559 Parliament by Sir William Cecil*. He missed the 1563 and 1571 Parliaments altogether, was returned for St. Ives in 1572 by the 2nd Earl of Bedford, but missed the 1581 session, of whose proceedings, however, two or three of his friends sent him an account at Edinburgh. At Maidstone, Randolph's parliamentary patron was presumably Sir Francis Walsingham*, his first wife's cousin. The sum total of Randolph's recorded parliamentary activity is his membership of committees on Mary Queen of Scots (12 May 1572, 4 Nov. 1586), rites and ceremonies (20 May 1572), Peter Wentworth* (8 Feb. 1576) and ports (13 Feb. 1576).[4]

Randolph was nearly 50 when he married for the first time, asking Burghley to contrive increased provision for him as his wife was 'richer in virtue than great wealth'. Soon afterwards she died in childbirth, and his next marriage was to a lady whose 'power' was 'great over him'. Both wives were from puritan families. Considering the status of his missions to Scotland and France and the length of his diplomatic career, Randolph was meanly treated by Elizabeth. He received no honours (an expected

knighthood eluded him on several occasions), few royal grants, and her promise of a prebend belonging to Trinity College, Cambridge, was frustrated by the governing body of the college. But his complaints of poverty were unjustified. His will was that of a wealthy man. He died on 8 June 1590, and was buried in St. Peter's, Paul's Wharf, near his London house.[5]

[1] Acknowledgments are due to Drs. K. P. Frescoln and N. M. Sutherland for help with this biography. [2] Wood, *Ath. Ox.* i. 563–7; *Vis. Surr.* (Harl. Soc. xliii), 12; *CSP Dom.* 1547–80, pp. 301, 424; *CSP For.* 1569–71, p. 176; *London IPMs* (Brit. Rec. Soc. Index Lib. xxxvi), 146–7; *Vis. Suff.* ed. Metcalfe, 129; PCC 75 Drury. [3] *CSP Dom.* 1547–80, p. 301; 1581–90, p. 672; Add. 1566–79, p. 453; *CSP For.* 1572–4, pp. 433–4; 1575–7, pp. 302–4; *CPR*, 1566–9, p. 144; 1569–72, p. 448; Lansd. 22, f. 51; 106, f. 132; Harl. 474, f. 75. [4] *CSP For.* 1558–9, pp. 5, 21–3; 1561–2, pp. 380 seq.; *Melville Mems.* (3rd ed.), 231; C. H. Garrett, *Marian Exiles*, 266–7; Lansd. 31, f. 112; 106, f. 132; *EHR*, lxv. 91 seq.; *CJ*, i. 95, 96, 104, 105; D'Ewes, 206, 241, 247, 394; PCC 45 Windsor; *CSP Dom.* 1547–80, p. 424; SP52/29/40; *CSP Scot.* v. 639; Wright, *Eliz.* ii. 129–30. [5] *APC*, xiii. 400–1; xv. 51; xvi. 22–3, 53; *CSP Dom.* 1547–80, pp. 286, 301, 306, 310, 424, 671; 1581–90, p. 291; Camb. Univ. Lib., Baker mss; PCC 75 Drury; Lansd. 13, f. 85; 20, f. 103; 43, f. 7; 48, f. 136; 67, ff. 82, 86; 69, f. 19; *CSP For.* 1569–71, p. 529; *London IPMs*, 146–7.

P.W.H.

RASHLEIGH, John (1554–1624), of Fowey and Menabilly, Cornw.

FOWEY 1589, 1597

b. ?1554, o.s. of John Rashleigh, merchant of Fowey by Alice, da. of William Lanyon. *educ.* ?Hart Hall, Oxf. 1576, aged 19.[1] *m.* 10 Feb. 1576, Alice (*d.*1606), da. of Richard Bonithon of Carclew, 2s. 4da. *suc.* fa. 1582.

Dep. lt. Cornw. 1598, sheriff 1608–9; portreeve, Fowey by 1584.[2]

Rashleigh's grandfather had been the first of the family to settle in Fowey, and it was to his and his son's enterprise that Fowey owed its revival as a port during Elizabeth's reign. By 1582 the Rashleighs were established as one of the three leading families in the town, as important as the Treffrys and the Mohuns. Their wealth depended upon their ships – an effigy of one embellished their house at Fowey. Perhaps this was the *Frances* (or *Francis*, the spelling varies), reputed to have earned a fortune as a privateer, an occupation the family had long found profitable. The *Frances* sailed with Frobisher in 1578 on his third voyage to the north-west passage, and with Drake to the West Indies in 1585, and it may have been the same ship of that name that took part in the Armada engagement, captained by Rashleigh himself, and sailing in Drake's squadron from Plymouth. She was a vessel of 140 tons with a complement of 60 men and, together with a pinnace, had cost £600 to equip. The money was to be raised by the towns of Looe and Fowey, but was advanced by Rashleigh himself. Three months after she had been commissioned he was still owed £500, and the Privy Council was forced to order the deputy lieutenants to levy the money from the two towns and their adjoining hundreds. Rashleigh's trading ventures were not always within the letter of the law. In 1588 he was arrested at the request of the Eastland Company, presumably for trading as an interloper in the Baltic. The arrest of one of his ships by the governor of Le Havre in 1598 evoked letters to secretary Villeroy asking for redress for her owner, 'un honneste marchant de notre nation'. Rashleigh appears also to have had an interest in the Plymouth pilchard fishery, and in 1596 he and William Treffry* were accused of inciting the inhabitants of Fowey to refuse payment of the impost on pilchards, levied for the fortification of Plymouth. Two years later Rashleigh was engaged in transporting troops to Ireland, one of the Irish captains telling Sir Robert Cecil that his 'care was wholly employed therein, giving great and most kind entertainment unto the captains, where we lay during the time of our abode in the town at his own cost. I desire you in our behalf to be thankful unto him for it.' His shipping interests remained throughout his life, and in 1611, when he no longer lived in Fowey, he was still engaged in the Guinea trade.[3]

In 1586 Rashleigh was instrumental in obtaining the return to Parliament for Fowey of his brother-in-law John Bonithon, and Rashleigh himself sat in 1589 and 1597. There is no record of his having taken any active part in the proceedings of the Commons. Both Rashleigh's grandfather and father had bought some land, mostly monastic in origin, while continuing to live in Fowey, but Rashleigh built himself a country seat, Menabilly, some two miles away where he was able to combine the life of a merchant with that of country gentleman. Richard Carew* put the matter thus:

> I may not pass in silence the commendable deserts of Master Rashleigh the elder, for his industrious judgment and adventuring in trade and merchandise first opened a light and way to the townsmen's new thriving, and left his son large wealth and possessions, who (together with a daily bettering his estate) converteth the same to hospitality and other actions fitting a gentleman well affected to his God, Prince and Country.

He died 12 May 1624, leaving bequests of money to two daughters, their husbands and their children. All his lands and other property were left to his second son Jonathan†, the sole executor. The elder son was presumably insane, Rashleigh directing that Jonathan should 'keep and maintain his brother John, allowing him a chamber, meat, drink, apparel and all other necessities and a servant continually to attend him.' The responsibility did not lie long upon Jonathan, as his brother died within a month of their father.[4]

[1] *Al. Ox.* iii. 1233 gives matric. Hart Hall, Dec. 1576, aged 19 (i.e. b.c.1557), but date given for baptism (Vivian, *Vis. Cornw.* 391) is 27 Nov. 1554. [2] J. Keast, *Fowey*, 44–50, 52, 56; *Vis. Cornw.* (Harl. Soc. ix), 183–4; Vivian, *Vis. Cornw.* 391; *Reg. Univ. Oxon.* ed. Clark, ii(2), p. 71; *APC*, xxix. 413. [3] A. L. Rowse, *Tudor Cornw.* 70, 76, 110, 205, 398;

Hakluyt, *Principal Navigations*, (1903–5), ed. MacLehose, vii. 236 seq.; Anon. *Paroch. Hist. Cornw.* ii. 21–31; W. Hals, *Compleat Hist. Cornw.* ii. 136–7; *VCH Cornw.* i. 493; E. W. Rashleigh, *Short Hist. Fowey*, 7–9; *APC*, xvi. 159, 268; xxvi. 349; xxviii. 523; xxix. 413; *CSP Dom.* 1581–90, p. 502; *HMC Hatfield*, viii. 449. [4] Rowse, 205, 210; *Carew's Surv. Cornw.* ed. Halliday, 22, 210–11; *Paroch. Hist. Cornw.* iv. 279–81; Keast, 56; PCC 52 Byrd.

I.C.

RATCLIFFE, John (c.1536–90), of Ordsall, Lancs.

WIGAN	1563
LANCASHIRE	1571, 1572

> b. c.1536, 2nd but 1st surv. s. of Sir William Ratcliffe of Ordsall by Margaret, da. of Sir Edmund Trafford* of Trafford. m. Anne, da. of Thomas Asshawe of Hall-on-the-Hill, Chorley, 5s. 4da. suc. fa. 1568. Kntd. 1578.[1]
>
> J.p. Lancs., dep. lt. by 1574; dep. bailiff of Salford hundred, duchy of Lancaster 1580–1; feoffee of Manchester g.s. 1581.[2]

The Ratcliffes were a wealthy Lancashire family, Ratcliffe himself succeeding to the inheritance on the death of his elder brother Alexander, two weeks before that of their father. He came into extensive lands in Lancashire, as well as others in Cheshire, Derbyshire, Lincolnshire, Nottinghamshire and Yorkshire. He was a follower of the 3rd Earl of Derby, his parliamentary patron at Wigan in 1563, and one of eight assistants to the chief mourners at the Earl's funeral in 1572.[3]

Ratcliffe lived in the family mansion, Ordsall Hall, then a moated house surrounded by a park on the river Irwell. He must, presumably, have devoted much of his time to farming his large estates; he owned a considerable amount of livestock and a fulling mill. Although a j.p. and deputy lieutenant, Ratcliffe was said, about 1586, to be a 'dangerous temporiser' in religion. His will began with the Catholic motto, 'Jesus esto mihi Jesu', and in the preamble he trusted 'through the passion and death of Christ to be one of the elect company of heaven with the blessed Virgin Mary and all the Saints'. He wished to be buried in the chancel of the church in Manchester, among his ancestors. To his children, Margaret, Jane, Anne and William he left a life interest in his lands in Derbyshire, Lancashire and Lincolnshire, and to his son John lands in Lancashire and Nottinghamshire. Each of his daughters received 1,000 marks. The boys were to go to Oxford or Cambridge at the age of 14, and he was anxious that one of them should study law and travel abroad 'for his better furtherance in learning'. The executors were Anne his wife, his cousin Ralph Barton*, Edward Tyldesley, and Christopher Anderton, and the overseers Leonard Chorley and Humphrey Warmincham. Ratcliffe was buried in the collegiate church of Manchester on 11 Feb. 1590.[4]

[1] *VCH Lancs.* iv. 212. [2] *Stanley Pprs.* (Chetham Soc. xxxi), 172; Somerville, *Duchy*, i. 503. [3] Collins, *Peerage*, iii. 76; *VCH Lancs.* iv.

212. ⁴ Taylor, *Old Halls in Lancs. and Cheshire*, 47; *VCH Lancs.* iv. 212 seq.; Leatherbarrow, *Lancs. Eliz. Recusants* (Chetham Soc. n.s. cx), 103; *Lancs and Cheshire Wills* (Chetham Soc. li), 68.

N.M.S.

RATCLIFFE, Owen (c.1541–99), of Langley, Lancs., Gamlingay and Swavesey, Cambs.

WIGAN   1571

b. c.1541, 1st s. of Richard Ratcliffe of Langley by Elizabeth, da. of James Gerard of Ince, Lancs., sis. of Sir Gilbert Gerard*. *m.*, 1da. *suc.* fa. 1577.

Ratcliffe owned only a moderate amount of property, consisting of Langley Hall, about 15 miles from Wigan, some houses in Bolton, and an estate near Rochdale settled upon his father and himself in 1564. He was descended from a junior branch of the Ratcliffes of Ordsall, and so related to John Ratcliffe*, a follower of the 3rd Earl of Derby. It is not clear whether Derby obtained Owen Ratcliffe the seat at Wigan in 1571 or whether this was owed to his mother's family.

Knowledge of Ratcliffe is derived mainly from the records of the lawsuits that ruined him, from duchy of Lancaster inquisitions and from pleadings and Star Chamber documents. By the summer of 1589 he was in the Fleet, employing a solicitor who was 'altogether ignorant of the law' to press the suits he was unable to deal with himself. Upon his release he sued the solicitor, one Meade, in the Star Chamber. Another case between the two men in 1591 shows some of Ratcliffe's activities outside London and Lancashire. In the second bill of complaint he is described as bailiff, for Merton College, Oxford, of the manor and lordship of Gamlingay, Cambridgeshire. Meade was a Cambridgeshire man, and Ratcliffe declared that it was he who caused the bailiff's servants to be injured while they were distraining cattle. Meade's demurrer stated that he was not obliged to answer the charges, as Owen Ratcliffe of Gamlingay was the same person who, as Owen Ratcliffe of Langley, had been outlawed for debt by the court of common pleas, and who was therefore disabled from bringing an action. The question why a Lancashire gentleman should have been representing an Oxford college in Cambridgeshire remains unanswered.

Ratcliffe died intestate 30 Sept. 1599, letters of administration being granted to his daughter Mary, aged 18, the wife of Gabriel Tedder.

Vis. Lancs. (Chetham Soc. lxxxi), 81; DL1/133/R6, 137/R7,10, 151/52; DL7/12/19, 17/4; St. Ch. 5/R2/12, R12/20, R14/25; PCC admon. act bk. 1599, f. 33.

N.M.F.

RAVENSCROFT, George (d. by 1592), of Bretton and Hawarden, Flints.

FLINTSHIRE   1563

1st s. of Thomas Ravenscroft of Bretton by Katherine, da. of Richard Grosvenor of Eaton, Cheshire. *m.* Dorothy, da. of John Davies of Broad Lane, Hawarden, 7s. inc. William* 3da. *suc.* fa. c.1553.[1]

J.p.q. Flints. 1564, sheriff 1578–9.[2]

The Ravenscrofts were an ancient Cheshire family who acquired, about 1440, a Flintshire estate through the marriage of this MP's great-great-grandfather to the heiress of Bretton. This branch of the family continued to hold and to acquire lands in Cheshire till the mid-seventeenth century, and they consolidated their position in Flintshire by successive marriages into the chief local families: Stanley of Ewloe; Mostyn of Mostyn and Talacre; Grosvenor of Eaton. A still more influential match was that of Thomas Ravenscroft's eldest daughter (the 1563 MP's sister) to Thomas Egerton I*, whose family had property in Flintshire which formed the basis of several deals between the two houses.[3]

Ravenscroft himself made good use of these connexions. The Stanley connexion enabled him to enter the service of the influential earls of Derby, lords of Hopedale, Mold and Hawarden, and he took up several leases in these lordships from his patron, as well as acquiring lands elsewhere in the shire. He married his eldest son into the family of Brereton of Halghton, a branch of the Cheshire Breretons, his eldest daughter into that of Davies of Gwysaney (Mold), and a younger daughter into that of Salusbury of Bachegraig, an offshoot of the powerful Salusburys of Lleweni in Denbighshire. In 1583 he was joint mediator with a Brereton in a dispute between his Gwysaney son-in-law and Davies's neighbours the Wynnes of Tower over the ever-provocative question of pews and burial-places in Mold church. His name does not occur in the records again until, some 16 years later, he and Thomas Hanmer* drew the attention of the Privy Council to the neglect of the ruling made some years earlier that Flintshire should be assessed for subsidies at half the rate of Denbighshire and Montgomeryshire, and secured a repetition of the order.[4]

Ravenscroft made his will when 'visited with sickness of body' in August 1591, hoping to be saved 'through the blessed passion of Jesus Christ' and to be 'of that most happy number which shall be saved'. His 'good will' to the Earl of Derby was expressed in the bequest of his best grey gelding. Other bequests went to his seven named sons, to members of the Puleston and Egerton families, and to his servants. Appointed joint executors were his 'loving wife' Dorothy and his 'loving brother' Ralph. His 'dear brother-in-law' Thomas Egerton and son-in-law Robert Davies were the overseers. Ravenscroft's will was proved 20 Nov. 1592. He was buried at Hawarden.[5]

[1] Lloyd, *Powys Fadog*, v. 267; Dwnn, *Vis. Wales*, ii. 135; *NLW, Deeds and Documents*, iii. 11, 28–9. [2] *CPR, 1563–6*, pp. 30, 332. [3] Ormerod, *Cheshire*, iii. 208; *Deeds and Documents*, iii. 14, 17, 22, 28–9, 30; NLW, Plymouth mss 1669–70, Plas Gwyn deeds, 182, 214. [4] *Deeds and*

Documents, iii.14, 15, 17, 19, 21, 27–9, 31, 33, 42; *HMC 6th Rep.* 422, 423; *Powys Fadog*, loc. cit.; *APC*, xxix. 597–9. ⁵ PCC 78 Harrington; W. Ravenscroft, *Some Ravenscrofts*, 19.

A.H.D.

RAVENSCROFT, William (1561–1628), of Lincoln's Inn, London.

FLINTSHIRE	1586, 1597, 1601
OLD SARUM	1604, 1614
FLINT BOROUGHS	1621, 1624, 1625, 1626, 1628*

b. 1561, 2nd surv. s. of George Ravenscroft*. *educ.* Brasenose, Oxf. 1578, aged 17, BA 1580; L. Inn 1580, called 1589. *unm.*

Clerk of the petty bag 1598,[1] assoc. bencher and treasurer, L. Inn 1621, master of the library 1624.

Ravenscroft was related, through his aunt, to Thomas Egerton I*, later Lord Chancellor Ellesmere, whose son John*, 1st Earl of Bridgwater, proved a 'real noble friend' to Ravenscroft and his family. Chosen for a county seat while still a young man, and during his father's lifetime, and again after his elder brother had succeeded to the family estate, Ravenscroft made two minor contributions to debate in the 1601 Parliament, on donations to the poor (2 Dec.) and on privilege (17 Dec.). As knight for Flintshire he was on committees for the subsidy (22 Feb. 1587), enclosures (5 Nov. 1597), poor law (5, 22 Nov.), armour and weapons (8 Nov.), penal laws (8 Nov.), monopolies (10 Nov.), the subsidy (15 Nov.), Newport bridge (29 Nov.) and in 1601 the main business committee (3 Nov.) and the committee on monopolies (23 Nov.). The major part of his legal and parliamentary career belongs to the Stuart period.[2]

'In good and perfect health' when he made his will in October 1628, Ravenscroft died on the 27th of that month, leaving his books to Lincoln's Inn, where he had mainly resided. He must often have stayed with his elder brother Thomas, to whom, with a graceful reference to his 'loving and kind entertainment', he left a large monetary bequest. His younger brother Anthony was executor and residuary legatee. He was buried at Hawarden.[3]

[1] Lloyd, *Powys Fadog*, v. 267; *L. Inn Black Bk.* ii. 11, 85, 220, 225, 248; PRO ms index to petty bag office. [2] *HMC 3rd Rep.* 258; NLW, 1595, f. 159; Townshend, *Hist. Colls.* 280, 330; D'Ewes, 409, 552, 553, 555, 557, 561, 565, 624, 649. [3] PCC 99 Barrington, 17 Ridley; *Misc. Gen. et Her.* (ser. 2), v. 313; W. Ravenscroft, *Some Ravenscrofts*, 20.

A.H.D.

RAWLINS, Thomas (*d.* 1605 or 1606), of Little Wakering, Essex.

CARDIGAN BOROUGHS	1597

s. of (?John) Rawlins of Little Wakering by his w. Elizabeth. *m.* Mary, *s.p.*

Servant of 1st and 2nd Earls of Essex; j.p. Essex from c.1599, q. by 1601, sheriff 1604–5.

As on other occasions Cardigan Boroughs looked far afield for their representative in 1597. In the previous Parliament the influence of the Devereux family had procured the return of the 2nd Earl of Essex's comrade in arms, Sir Ferdinando Gorges. The same influence was no doubt behind Rawlins in 1597. He had been in the service of the 1st Earl, and he was one of the five confidential agents chosen, on the eve of the Earl's death in 1576, to carry out his last wishes and to serve as feoffee of his will, with special regard to the infant heir. No mention of Rawlins occurs in the journal of the 1597 Parliament, but he may have attended the committee on Newport bridge appointed 29 Mar. 1597. The Captain Rawlins in the service of the 2nd Earl was probably Thomas Rawlins's brother John, to whom the Earl's secretary Edward Reynolds* wrote 2 Jan. 1602, saying that the death of Essex had dispersed all their friends and admonishing him 'Perform well the business handed to you by your brother'. Again when Captain Rawlins was away, Reynolds wrote 'your brother is in the country playing the good husband. His wife I think has the gift of enchanting'. Both John and Thomas Rawlins borrowed heavily from Reynolds, who wrote to his own brother, 30 June 1605:

> Mr. Thomas Rawlins is extreme sick, and in great danger. You know how much of my poor state rested in their hands, and therefore it behoved me to hearken after them … But you must inquire … as in kindness, not ministering any suspicions of doubtfulness, for they are very apprehensive. If God call him, I pray you to advertise me by the first opportunity, for I must not [let] businesses of such moment to sleep, and be secure in such accidents, not knowing in what sort their state may be enjoyed.

Rawlins's will – proved by his brother John 23 Mar. 1606 – does not mention these debts. All his lands went to John Rawlins; another brother Edward and the poor of Little and Much Wakering were remembered and the widow Mary was to have his plate and his coach. Edward and Mary disputed the will, and sentence was given in favour of John Rawlins 2 Dec. 1606.

PCC 4 Alenger; 1, 28 Sainberbe; 31, 91 Stafforde; *APC*, xxix. 682–3; xxx. 436; *CSP Dom.* 1598–1601, p. 172; 1601–3, pp. 141, 213; 1603–10, passim; D'Ewes, 565; *HMC Hatfield*, viii. 261; xi. 407, 418–19; xiii. 553; *Cam. Misc.* xiii(3), 5; Lansd. 23, f. 152; SP14/14/62.

P.W.H.

RAYNSFORD, Miles (*d.* 1604).

CALLINGTON	1601

?s. of Thomas Raynsford, servant of Lord Lisle, and ?rel. to Sir John Raynsford† of Bradfield, Essex (*d.s.p.* 1559). *m.* Elizabeth, da. of Thomas Norton* of London and Sharpenhoe, Beds., at least 2s.

Groom of privy chamber 1588; servant of Robert Cecil from c.1597; keeper of Cobham Hall and park, Kent 1603.

Raynsford, connected, according to a family tradition, with the Knollys of Reading Abbey through the Lees of Ditchley Park, must have been returned at Callington by his master Cecil, from whom he received several wardships, the keepership of Cobham Hall and other spoils following the attainder of the 11th Lord Cobham. No trace of Raynsford's membership of Parliament has been found in the journals. He was buried at St. Paul's, Covent Garden 26 Jan. 1604.

DNB (Norton, Thomas); Foster, *Al. Ox.* (early ser.), 1239; *G. Inn Adm.* 157; Hasted, *Kent*, v. 122; 432; *CSP Dom.* 1603–10, pp. 57, 64, 163, 204; Add. 1580–1625, pp. 250, 432; *HMC Hatfield*, viii. 195; x. 444; xi. 507; xii. 527; xv. 199; xvi. 12; xvii. 374; *N. and Q.* clxvii. 454.

I.C.

READE, Henry (1566–1647), of the Middle Temple, London and Faccombe, Hants.

ANDOVER   1589

b. 1566, 1st s. of Andrew Reade (*d.* 1623) of Faccombe. *educ.* Lincoln, Oxf. 1584, BA 1588; M. Temple 1589, called 1596. *m.* Anne (*d.* 1624), 1st da. of Sir Thomas Windebank, 2s. 3da.

Reade was a lawyer, granted chambers in the Middle Temple soon after his admission, which he did not relinquish until 1626, three years after his father's death. When he was called on as a reader in 1616 he preferred to pay a fine of £10 for non-performance. Between 1597 and 1599 he was constantly fined for being out of commons during readings; in 1604 his chamber was assigned to another member of the society, as he had ceased to live in it, but this order was later revoked.

Reade's return for Andover in 1589 was probably obtained through the patronage of the Sandys family. Lord Sandys of The Vyne had influence in the borough, and Edwin Sandys I* (Member for Andover in the previous Parliament, and son of the Miles Sandys* who had used his influence to gain Reade a place at the Middle Temple), had married Lord Sandys' daughter.

Reade was an overseer of his father-in-law's will in 1606, and when Sir Thomas Windebank's eldest son Francis entered the Middle Temple in 1603 he was one of the sureties for his good conduct. Sir Thomas purchased lands in Berkshire and Wiltshire in conjunction with Reade, and at his death Anne and her husband inherited a house at St. Martin-in-the-Fields.

On his father's death Reade did not succeed to the family property, receiving only an annuity of £60, though if he were forced to vacate the parsonage house in Faccombe, in which he was then living, either before or within a year of the testator's death, he was to be allowed half of the manor house at Faccombe for a year, provided he did not contest the will. Reade died in 1647, being buried in Faccombe church, where his son Francis erected a monument to him.

C142/426/84; *VCH Hants.* iv. 316, 318; *Mdx. Peds.* (Harl. Soc. lxv), 123; *M. T. Recs.* i. 309, 375, 377, 385, 389, 395, 397, 429; ii. 444, 610, 714; PCC 1 Windebanck, 100 Swann.

A.M.M.

READE, Thomas (*d.* 1595), of Osterley, Mdx.

PETERBOROUGH   1589, 1593

1st s. of Sir William Reade of Osterley by his 1st w. Gertrude, da. of Sir William Paston of Norf. *educ.* St. John's, Camb. 1583, MA 1594. *m.* Mildred, da. of (Sir) Thomas Cecil*, 1st Earl of Exeter, *s.p.* Kntd. 1592.
J.p. Mdx. from c.1592; ?Berks. from c.1583.

Reade's paternal grandmother's second husband was Sir Thomas Gresham*, in whose household the children and grandchildren of her first marriage were brought up. After Gresham's death in 1579 she and her family continued to reside at Osterley, and it was Reade and his mother who assisted her in her attempts to defraud other beneficiaries under her second husband's will. No doubt it was the Cecils who had Reade returned at Peterborough. No record has been found of any parliamentary activity in 1589, but in 1593 he was appointed to a committee on the poor law (12 Mar.), and he was involved in the subsidy negotiations, being on both committees (26 Feb. and 1 Mar.) and on the delegation sent by the Commons to explain matters to the Lords (3 Mar.). He seems to have suffered a cerebral affliction in 1595, (Sir) Thomas Cecil writing to his brother on 9 July:

> the news of my son Read doth not a little touch me in conceit, both for his own sake and my daughter's; for of all worldly things it is hardest to recover a wit lost. It is a great cross to his friends but a much greater to himself, for to lose it is much more unfortunate than never to have had it.

Reade, who had died intestate (and *v.p.*) six days earlier, was buried on 14 July in Gresham's vault at Osterley. Letters of administration were granted to 'Henry Dennying of Isleworth, yeoman'.

Mdx. Peds. (Harl. Soc. lxv), 56; J. W. Burgon, *Life and Times Thos. Gresham*, i. 52; ii. 491; *CSP Dom.* 1595–7, pp. 139, 328, 329; *VCH Mdx.* iii. 109; D'Ewes, 474, 481, 486, 499; *HMC Hatfield*, iv. 292, 295; v. 273; PCC admon. act bk. 1595, f. 142.

S.M.T.

READE *alias* **KYNNERD, Sir William** (*d.* 1604), of Holy Island, Northumb.

NORTHUMBERLAND   1593

?illegit. s. of one Kynnerd, of Worcs. *m.* (1) Elizabeth (*d.* 1585); (2) Mary (*d.* 1595); (3) Elizabeth, wid. of Charles Towers of Holy Island; 1s. 1da. illegit. Kntd. 1586.[1]
Lt. in command of Wark castle 1547; capt. in Berwick garrison 1555; capt. of Holy and Farne Islands 1555–*d.*; sergeant maj. later lt.-col. gen. with Leicester in the Netherlands 1586.[2]

J.p. Northumb. from 1577, q. from 1593; co. Dur. from 1583, q. from 1593.

Of obscure origins, Reade rose to high military rank, seeing active service on the borders under four monarchs, and acquiring a reputation for gallantry and reliability. At the time of the northern rebellion, however, his previous service with such commanders as Sir Henry Percy* and the Duke of Norfolk brought him under suspicion. He was arrested at the height of the rebellion, but released in time to assist in the defeat of Leonard Dacre's followers at Naworth.[3]

Reade accompanied the Earl of Leicester to the Netherlands. During the campaign he received his knighthood, and rose from captain to sergeant major and, finally, to the high rank of 'lieutenant-colonel general', commanding the infantry at the relief of Sluys. As he later boasted to Burghley, whom he acknowledged as his 'best friend' at court, 'I have passed all offices in the field almost that belong to a soldier – and whether I have discharged them with credit or no, let the world judge'. From the Netherlands, as from all his campaigns, Reade returned to Holy Island, where as captain and keeper he occupied Fenham, the old monastic manor house, which he leased from the Crown in 1564. The house, which he extended and improved, was well furnished. Pictures, with religious themes, decorated the rooms, while in his own chamber he kept his small library and his maps of the Low Countries and the world. His copies of Calvin's 'Commentary upon Job' (presumably the *Sermons upon the booke of Job*, which appeared in several English editions) and a 'Table of the Ten Commandments', which may be identified with Bishop Hooper's *Declaration* of 1548, may reflect his religious beliefs, while his two Latin dictionaries and several chronicles, including Holinshed, suggest a man of scholarly interests.[4]

Towards the end of his life Reade was honoured by being returned to Parliament as senior knight of the shire, and as such he could have sat on the subsidy committee (26 Feb.) and a legal committee (9 Mar.). His name appears once in the journals (12 Mar.), when he was put on a committee concerning the relief of the poor and the punishment of rogues. On his progress south, James I honoured the now blind and aged soldier with a visit, and the 'worthy, honourable soldier ... was so comforted with the presence and gracious speeches of the King, that his spirits seemed so powerful within him, as he boasted himself to feel the warmth of youth stir in his frost-nipped blood'. A year later he died, being buried 6 June 1604. On his tomb was inscribed '*contra vim mortis non medicamen in hortis*'.

He was survived by his third wife, Elizabeth Towers, and two illegitimate children, a son, William, who inherited his Berwick and Holy Island property, and was made joint captain of Holy Island in 1594, and a daughter, Charity,

who inherited £50. In his will, Reade asked the bishop of Durham's wife, Frances Matthew, 'a prudent and provident matron', to tutor Charity during her minority.[5]

[1] *Surtees Soc.* clxii. 2–3. [2] *CPR*, 1554–5, p. 119; *Border Pprs.* ii. 275–6, 786–7; *CSP Scot.* i. 40–1. [3] *CSP Scot.* i. 366, 393; *CSP Dom.* Add. 1566–79, pp. 91 et passim; Raine, *North Durham*, 175. [4] *CSP Scot.* ii. 636; iii. 537, 538; *CSP For.* 1586–7, pp. 77, 214, 279; 1587, p. 192; *Border Pprs.* i. 387; *CPR*, 1563–6, p. 200; Raine, 149, 176, 177. [5] D'Ewes, 474, 496, 499; Nichols, *Progresses Jas. I*, 67; *Surtees Soc.* loc. cit.; *CSP Dom.* Add. 1580–1625, p. 441; *DNB* (Matthew, Tobie).

B.D.

REDGE, Robert, of the Middle Temple, London.

BOSSINEY	1572*
NEWTOWN I.o.W.	1584

3rd. s. of John Redge of Redge, Salop by Margaret, da. of Meredith Porter.[1] *educ.* Barnard's or New Inn; M. Temple 1579, called by 1581.[2] *m.* c.1581, Avis, da. of John Vivian*, sis. of Hannibal Vivian*.

Descended from a Shropshire family originally called Bowlder or Bowlden, who several generations earlier had adopted the name of their chief dwelling house, Redge was a practising lawyer. The reason for his return for Bossiney, at a by-election in 1581, is unknown, but he was already connected with Hannibal Vivian – with whom he was bound at the Middle Temple – and with other Cornish gentlemen, and presumably he found an influential patron, perhaps the 2nd Earl of Bedford, acting through the Vivians. At Newtown he was doubtless nominated by Sir George Carey*, captain of the Isle of Wight. Redge may have been Carey's lawyer: at any rate when he wished to marry Avis Vivian, and her mother and brother Hannibal thought him too poor, Carey provided him with 'some reasonable portion for [her] relief'.[3]

Records of the lawsuits in which Redge is known to have taken part suggest that a plaintiff's description of him as a man of 'most troublesome and lewd disposition', who used his knowledge of the law unjustly and for his private profit, may have been at least partly true. He acted for the defendant, Hannibal Vivian, in a notorious case brought by John Cosgarne*, alleging the abduction of Vivian's young relatives Joan and Anne, Cosgarne's wards, their imprisonment in 'dark and obscure caves under the cliffs of the sea', and illegal marriages. In the later stages of this dispute Redge stopped at nothing to gain victory for his client. He helped to procure the arrest, on a charge of rape, of Cosgarne's son, who carried on the quarrel after his father's death, and according to the bill of complaint first forged a recognizance for debt against his opponent, and then refused to answer Cosgarne's suit against him in the Star Chamber, on the ground that the plaintiff, being now technically an outlaw, could not plead. Charges of forgery and wrongful issue of legal documents were commonplace in Elizabethan lawsuits, but the Cosgarne case was not the only example of this kind of accusation against Redge. About 1595 he was before the Star Chamber answering questions about his alleged illegal serving of a subpoena in Montgomeryshire on John Edwards and others, and a threat to 'beggar' his opponents in the case. Another long and complicated Star Chamber suit involved his infant niece Blanche Redge, daughter and heir of his eldest brother John. Her guardian claimed that Robert Redge, 'bearing a most malicious and envious mind' against her prosperity and advancement, had forged a £500 bond in her father's name to Hannibal Vivian. If this money was not paid, the mansion house of Redge and property in Chirbury, Shropshire, was to go to Avis Vivian (who was about to become Robert Redge's wife), for three years after the death of Blanche's parents. Hannibal Vivian, called upon to explain his own part in the transaction, denied being implicated in any fraud, and claimed that Robert Redge, some years earlier, when his plea for Avis's hand was refused on the ground that he 'being a younger brother was not possessed of any inheritance', stated that his 'possibilities were good' since his brother John had at that time no children, and was unlikely to have any; 'he did verily think that his father and brother would deal well with him towards his advancement if [the Vivians] would give their consent to this match'. Redge also denied the charges.[4]

This lawsuit, begun in January 1596, is the last reference found to him. No will or inquisition post mortem is known, so it is impossible to say whether he died in possession of lands which he had claimed in 1578 from his relatives, the Vaughans, who contested his rights.[5]

[1] Harl. 5848, ff. 27–8; *Vis. Salop* (Harl. Soc. xxix), 418. [2] *M. T. Recs.* i. 242, 245, 359. In a Star Chamber case of 1578 or early 1579 he was described as 'of Barnard's Inn', but the Middle Temple admission register says 'late of New Inn'. It seems unlikely that he would have studied at two inns of chancery before an inn of court. [3] *M. T. Recs.* i. 229; St. Ch. 5/R9/13. [4] St. Ch. 5/C6/4, R9/13, R21/21, E41/34; Add. 37045, f. 63. [5] St. Ch. 5/R18/15, R34/23. He may have been the 'Robert Ridg' brought before the Privy Council in September 1588 in connexion with complaints from the company of 'merchants easterlings' (*APC*, xvi. 267–8).

N.M.F.

REVELL, Thomas (b. c.1540), of Forest, Cilgerran, Pemb.

PEMBROKESHIRE   1584, 1586

b. c.1540, 1st s. of John Revell of Forest by Anne (or Agnes), da. of Thomas Walter of Carmarthen; ?bro. of William*. m. (1) Ellen (or Elliw), da. of Rhys Lloyd of Cardiganshire, ?s.p.; (2) Joan, wid. of one Mercer. At least 1s. illegit.

Escheator, Pemb. 1571; commr. musters, Card. 1574; j.p. Pemb., Card. from c.1575; sheriff, Pemb. 1578–9, Card. 1582–3, 1592–3; dep. lt. Pemb. 1594–1600.

The Revells of Forest were a branch of the Derbyshire Revells, founded by this MP's great-great-grandfather John Revell, who migrated to Pembrokeshire in the time

of Edward IV. Thomas's father, another John Revell, held from the Crown extensive lands in Pembrokeshire. He died in 1547 leaving his seven year-old son Thomas a royal ward, whereupon his widow married Thomas Phaer*, who secured the wardship and with it the enjoyment of the Revell estates until the heir attained his majority. Phaer died without male heirs a few years later, and his estates, as well as those descending from John Revell, eventually passed to Thomas Revell, whose wife brought him further lands in Cardiganshire. These possessions, and others he acquired later, involved him in many lawsuits, some of them no doubt occasioned by the long minority.

In 1576 his stepfather's lease of the demesne lands of Cilgerran, with the herbage of the royal forest, was renewed in Revell's favour. This led to innumerable quarrels, culminating in an Exchequer suit of 1602. In 1578 he had been a litigant in the same court over the disputed ownership of a former grange of Talley abbey, Carmarthenshire, with its appurtenant tithes. But his most troublesome dispute was over the weir at Cilgerran and the fisheries of the Teifi. This dragged on for 12 years (1583–95), and involved him in four Exchequer suits, as well as a Star Chamber action in which he accused some of the witnesses in the former court of perjury. In one of his Exchequer suits he challenged 15 alleged infringers of his fishery rights. His most determined opponent was David Price ap William of Rhydodyn, Carmarthenshire. The only mark left by Revell on the records of his two Parliaments is his membership of the committee to receive the Queen's thanks for the granting of the subsidy, 18 Mar. 1587. As a county Member he could have attended this subsidy committee 22 Feb. 1587, and the previous one, 24 Feb. 1585.

Apart from his illegitimate son Edward, Revell left no children, and the family declined after his death. Administration of his estate was granted to his widow, 1 Oct. 1607.

Dwnn, *Vis. Wales*, i. 155–6; Flenley, *Cal. Reg. Council, Marches of Wales*, 126, 140, 213; Lansd. 35, f. 139; *APC*, xxv. 18; xxviii. 287; xxxii. 25; Wards 7/3/90; *CPR*, 1555–7, p. 74; 1557–8, p. 363; *Exchequer*, ed. E. G. Jones (Univ. Wales Bd. of Celtic Studies, Hist. and Law ser. iv), 86, 115–16, 297, 302, 304, 309; *Star Chamber*, ed. Edwards (same ser. i), 134; D'Ewes, 409, 416; Lansd. 43, anon. jnl. f 171; J. R. Phillips, *Hist. Cilgerran* (1867), 102–3; PCC admon. act bk. 1607, f. 90.

A.H.D.

REVELL, William, of Pembroke.

PEMBROKE BOROUGHS   1563

Prob. yr. s. of John Revell (d.1547), of Forest, Cilgerran by Anne (or Agnes), da. of Thomas Walter of Carmarthen. ?Bro. of Thomas.* m. Mary Griffith; 1s. illegit.

The Member for Pembroke Boroughs in 1563 is given in Crown Office lists as 'William Bevell', but this name is unknown in west Wales and it seems likely that Bevell was written in error for the local name of Revell, in which case the obvious candidate for membership of the Commons is Thomas Revell's younger brother William, born in the early 1540s, whose name is among the voters on the 1584 borough election return, which he also signed. When Lewis Dwnn drew up the Cilgerran family pedigree in 1591, William was dead, being survived by an illegitimate son.

Dwnn, *Vis. Wales*, i. 155–6; C219/29/224.

A.H.D.

REYNELL, Carew (c.1563–1624), of St. Martin-in-the-Fields, London.

CALLINGTON	1593
LANCASTER	1601
WALLINGFORD	1614
CRICKLADE	1621

b. c.1563, 5th s. of Richard Reynell I* of East Ogwell, Devon, by Agnes, da. of John Southcote† of Bovey Tracey, Devon. *m.* aft. 1593, Susan, da. of Walter Hungerford,† of Farleigh Castle, Som. and Hungerford, Wilts., wid. of Michael Erneley of Bishops Canning, Wilts., and of Sir John Marvyn, *s.p.* Kntd. 12 July 1599.[1]

Gent. pens. 1591/3–aft. 1606; Queen's printer in Greek and Latin to 1597; capt. of Duncannon castle, Wexford 1599–1601; keeper of mansion house at Dartford, Kent 1603; gent. usher of privy chamber to James I.[2]

Reynell must have obtained his seat at Callington through either the 3rd Marquess of Winchester or the 7th Lord Mountjoy, joint patrons of the borough. Of the two, Winchester is more likely to have effected the young man's sudden emergence as a fully-fledged courtier in the early 1590s. He not only obtained a place as gentleman pensioner, but was in sufficient favour for the Queen to ask the dean and chapter of Exeter to grant him two manors in Devon. Quite possibly at court it was Sir Robert Cecil who asked one of the borough patrons for the Callington seat, as he almost certainly asked the chancellor of the duchy of Lancaster for Reynell to be given a parliamentary seat at Lancaster in 1601. Apart from a procedural committee on which he may have served as one of the Lancaster burgesses, Reynell was named to two committees in 1601: on abuses of pluralism and non-residence (16 Nov.), and for the more diligent resort to church on Sundays (2 Dec. 1601). He (not Carew Ralegh, as in D'Ewes) made his only recorded speech on this latter subject the same day, specifying various disasters that had overtaken Sabbath breakers. He asked that the 'brutish exercise' of bear baiting should 'be used on some other day' and reported the collapse of 'the house of Paris Garden' on a Sunday when 400 were crushed 'yet by God's mercy only eight were slain outright'.

Close to Cecil as Reynell may have been before 1597, in that year he sailed with the Earl of Essex on the Islands voyage, perhaps in command of the *Foresight*. He later accompanied Essex to Ireland, where he led a troop of foot and held the fort of Duncannon, 'a place of great importance'. Knighted by Essex in Ireland, by June 1600 he had sold his company, and six months later had determined to surrender the captaincy of Duncannon.

When Essex was in disgrace early in 1600, Reynell asked to be allowed to attend him, writing, 'I am particularly bound to my Lord of Essex; yet so that I will never betray the trust reposed in me', and his moderation kept him clear of implication in the Essex rebellion itself. Imprisoned for a short time in February 1601, he was exonerated by the evidence of Sir Christopher Blount* and Sir Charles Danvers*. His loyalty to Essex's memory, however, survived for another twenty years, for in his will he left to the Earl's son 'a tablet jewel set with four score and odd diamonds with his father's picture and £30 to be bestowed upon the making of the said jewel, in remembrance and full satisfaction of all the favours and benefits which I received from his most noble father'.[3]

Throughout the period of his attachment to Essex, Reynell continued to cultivate Cecil. In 1594 he tried unsuccessfully to obtain command of the fort of Plymouth through Cecil's agency, and in January 1601 he wrote offering him the gift of 'an Irish hobby, which in my heart I have only devoted unto you. His pace is easy and I hope will prove fit for your saddle. I entreat you to do me the favour to accept of him'. At the time of his arrest, it was to Cecil that he appealed, asking 'if anybody have accused me as privy or an actor in these rebellious actions, that I may be examined and brought face to face to answer the same for the better proof of my innocency'. He attributed even his release from prison to Cecil's good offices, writing on 12 Mar.:

> I cannot but hold myself greatly bound unto you for being a means for my enlargement, albeit I cannot as yet account myself at liberty, being denied her Majesty's presence. I do humbly desire that you will finish that grace which you have begun.[4]

Reynell continued his court and parliamentary career for 20 years after Elizabeth's death, dying 7 Sept. 1624. He was buried at St. Martin-in-the-Fields.[4]

[1] Vivian, *Vis. Devon*, 643; *Vis. Wilts.* (Harl. Soc. cv, cvi), 56, 91; PCC 91 Byrde; Burke, *Commoners*, iv. 448–50. [2] *CSP Dom.* 1595–7, pp. 93, 378; 1603–10, p. 19; *APC*, xxx. 181–4. [3] D'Ewes, 635, 641, 663, 664; Townshend, *Hist. Colls.* 274; J. Prince, *Worthies of Devon* (1701), pp. 520–2; *CSP Dom.* 1595–7, pp. 93, 467; 1598–1601, p. 379; *CSP Ire.* 1600, p. 214–15; 1600–1, pp. 89, 232; *APC*, xxx. 133, 181–4; xxxi. 200; *HMC Hatfield*, iii. 4; viii. 562; ix. 146, 330, 439; x. 43–4; xi. 103; xiv. 173; PCC 91 Byrde. [4] *HMC Hatfield*, v. 52–3; xi. 13, 121; xiv. 173. Information from W. J. Tighe.

I.C.

REYNELL, Richard I (1519–85), of East Ogwell, Devon.

SALTASH   1559

b. 1519, 2nd s. and h. of John Reynell of East Ogwell, by Margaret, da. of William Fortescue of Wood, Devon. *m.* Agnes, da. of John Southcote† of Bovey Tracey, 5s. inc. Carew* 1da.[1]

J.p. Devon from c.1559, q. 1577; justice for maritime affairs, Devon 1578, sheriff 1584–*d.*[2]

Reynell's family, originally from Cambridgeshire, had lived at East Ogwell since the time of Richard II, intermarrying with prominent Devon families and increasing gradually in landed wealth. Reynell spent his youth at the court of Henry VIII, later travelling in France, Flanders, Italy, Greece and Hungary, where he fought against the Turks. He subsequently served Henry VIII in arms during the French wars. The antiquary Prince said of him that

he was ever most virtuously affected, sound in religion, faithful and serviceable to his princes, upright and zealous in justice, beating down vice, preferring the virtuous and a keeper of great hospitality.

Some of these attributes he was able to display in 1549 when he was active in suppressing the Western Rebellion; for his 'special good services', he was granted the manor of Weston Peverell, near Plymouth.[3]

During Mary's reign Reynell no doubt devoted himself to his private affairs, eventually buying West Ogwell from the Courteneys. The only appearance of his name in the national records during this period is in connexion with his standing surety for a debt of his old friend Sir Peter Carew*, to whom he doubtless owed his return to Elizabeth's first Parliament. He died 29 July 1585 and was buried in the family chapel in East Ogwell church. He had united the manors of East and West Ogwell, which passed to his eldest son, who in 1589 rebuilt the manor house of East Ogwell.[4]

[1] Vivian, *Vis. Devon*, 643–4. [2] Lansd. 1218, f. 9; SP12/121/9; *CPR*, 1560–3, pp. 16, 408; 1563–6, p. 42; Hoker, *Desc. Exeter* (Devon Rec. Soc. 1919), 584–97. [3] J. Prince, *Worthies of Devon* (1701), pp. 520, 521; F. Rose-Troup, *Western Rebellion of 1549*, p. 381. [4] *CPR*, 1550–3, p. 399; 1554–5, p. 4; *APC*, v. 375; Burke, *Commoners*, iv. 448; *Trans. Devon Assoc.* xxxii. 233, 241; xxxiii. 695; PCC 42 Brudenell.

I.C.

REYNELL, Richard II (*d.* 1631), of Creedy Wiger, Devon.

MITCHELL   1593

4th s. of George Reynell of Malston by Joan, da. of Lewis Fortescue of Fallowpit or Fulpit, baron of the Exchequer. *educ.* New Inn; M. Temple 1585, called 1594. *m.* 1593, Mary, da. and coh. of John Peryam*, 2s. 7da. Kntd. 1622.[1]

?Clerk in office of ld. treasurer's remembrancer in the Exchequer by 1593; dep. recorder, Totnes by 1600;

autumn reader, M. Temple 1614, bencher 1618; councillor, Exeter 1617; j.p. Devon by 1627.[2]

Reynell came of a family seated at Malston since the time of Richard II. A younger son, he became a lawyer and was possibly the Richard Reynell who was employed in the office of the lord treasurer's remembrancer in the 1590s. He had Exchequer connexions through his mother and through (Sir) William Peryam*, who became chief baron in the year that Reynell married his niece. As his later interests were focused on Devon, it is unlikely that he held this office for long. He presumably owed his return at Mitchell to his fellow Middle Templar Richard Carew* of Antony. Reynell's distant cousin, Richard Reynell I* of East Ogwell, Devon, had been a close friend of Sir Peter Carew*, a relative of the patron.

After his marriage Reynell was brought increasingly into the orbit of his wife's family in Exeter and South Devon. His legal services may have been useful to the city and he established a position there independent of his father-in-law. Reynell was a friend of John Travers, rector of Farringdon from 1588 until 1620, (brother of the puritan Walter Travers), and was associated with Edmund Snape and Melancthon Jewel, leading Devon puritans. Reynell was the executor of Travers's will and in this capacity presented Elias Travers, his son, who was also a puritan, to the living of Farringdon. He was also active in hunting down Jesuit priests. In November 1621 he wrote to the mayor and aldermen on the subject:

the cause concerns God and the King and [it is] therefore fit we should be most careful therein. I acknowledge your example doth much encourage me to do my best endeavour ... The Lord give a blessing unto our endeavours in this behalf: to whose merciful protection I do with my due respect commend you.[3]

On John Peryam's death Reynell's wife inherited his manor of Creedy Wiger near Crediton, where Reynell lived until his own death in 1631. He left an annuity of £100 to a son, and £1,000 each to three of his daughters. His wife, as sole executrix, was enjoined upon the death of William Orforde, rector of Clyst Hydon, Devon, to present 'my good friend Laurence Bodley of Exeter College'. This benefice seems to have been reserved for Peryam cousins of puritan tendencies. William Orforde was connected both with the Bodleys and the Peryams and had for a short time been the incumbent of an Exeter lectureship. He died within a few months of Reynell, whereupon Laurence Bodley was presented, in accordance with the late patron's wishes.[4]

[1] Vivian, *Vis. Devon*, 645. [2] Lansd. 106, f. 1; *APC*, xliii. 10–11; Roberts thesis, 230; *HMC Exeter*, 110–11. [3] W. T. MacCaffery, *Exeter*, 197; G. Oliver, *Catholic Religion in the West*, 8–9; *HMC Exeter*, 40; SP14/10A/81. [4] W. Pole, *Desc. Devon*, 221; PCC 48 St. John; *HMC Exeter*, 93–7.

I.C.

REYNOLDS, Cuthbert, of Watford, Herts. and the Inner Temple, London.

DARTMOUTH	1572*
APPLEBY	1593

educ. I. Temple 1573, called 1590, steward for the readers' dinner 1603.

The parentage and background of this Member have not been traced. The earliest mention of him is in 1573, when he was admitted to the Inner Temple as of Watford. During the unusually long interval before he was called to the bar he seems to have been for some time in the service of the 2nd Earl and Countess of Bedford, who had a house at Watford, a connexion which would explain his return for Dartmouth in 1580. After the death of William Lyster* in the previous year, Bedford had asked the mayor of Dartmouth for a blank indenture, on which Reynolds' name was inserted. A 'Mr. Reinoldes, esquier' was one of four persons appointed in May 1591 to investigate the allegation that the liberties of Dartmouth lay outside the jurisdiction of the court of Admiralty. He did not sit in the House again until 1593, when the marriage tie between the Bedfords and the Earl of Cumberland probably secured his return for Appleby. He was presumably the Mr. 'Reynold' named to a minor committee 19 Mar. 1593.

It is likely that it was also through the Bedfords that Reynolds became involved, perhaps reluctantly, in the Earl of Lincoln's unsuccessful attempts to establish, first by violence in 1588 and subsequently in the Star Chamber, his ownership of the Oxfordshire manor of Weston, then in the tenancy of James Croft*. Lincoln claimed the property in the name of his wife, widow of William, son of Henry Norris*, 1st Lord Norris, and daughter of the Countess of Bedford by her first marriage. Reynolds explained that he had been 'of long time ... much bounden' to the Countess and referred to the 'love and duty' he bore her.

Roberts thesis, 58; *APC*, xxi. 143; D'Ewes, 503; St. Ch. 5/C67/10; N. J. O'Conor, *Godes Peace and the Queenes*, 53–84 passim.

B.D.

REYNOLDS, Edward (*d.* c.1623), of Essex House, London, and Whiteparish, Wilts.

ANDOVER	1597
WEYMOUTH AND MELCOMBE	
REGIS	1601

2nd s. of Lancelot Reynolds of Melcombe Regis. *educ.* All Souls, Oxf. BA 1580, fellow 1581, MA 1584. *m.* (2) Catherine, wid. of John Mills.[1]

Sec. to Earl of Essex c.1588–1601; clerk of privy seal by 1603; registrar, ct. of requests.[2]

Reynolds, like (Sir) Robert Sidney's* servant at court, Roland White, belongs to that small group of men who, by their close attachment to the great figures of the age, provide us with so much of the intimate detail about their masters which would otherwise be lacking and, equally important, keep us informed of the changing fortunes of those contesting for political power. Reynolds himself emerges as a devoted servant of the Earl of Essex, proud of the trust placed in him and intolerant of rivals. Not without a sense of humour, he was subject to periods of depression and even despair. Though ready to burden his family and friends with his troubles, he was always conscious of the need to maintain his reputation and self-respect.

He was born in Melcombe Regis and among his relatives was Owen Reynolds*, his uncle. After leaving Oxford, Reynolds – in his own words –

> served Sir Amias Paulet* during the whole time of his charge of the Scottish Queen, and under him had the special trust of that service committed unto me, the importance whereof is best known to her Majesty. If that honourable knight lived he would witness my painful travails therein.

Paulet had charge of Mary from April 1585 until her death in February 1587. During part of that time the Queen was held at Chartley, Essex's home in Staffordshire: perhaps it was there that the two men met. At any rate, by the end of 1588 Reynolds had become one of the Earl's secretaries and had entered upon the most important phase of his career.[3]

It is apparent from the tone of many of his letters that Reynolds was soon won over by the charm of his new master. For his part, Essex placed considerable trust in 'good Reynolds'. At first his new servant accompanied him on his foreign journeys. He may have gone with him to Portugal in 1589, and was certainly with him in France in 1591, when he was present at the siege of Rouen. Later, however, his experience and knowledge of the Earl's affairs were a greater asset in London. Essex told Robert Cecil* in 1596, for example, that Reynolds was to have full charge of his affairs during the Cadiz expedition. Reynolds reported that the Queen was opposed to Essex's departure, 'using very hard terms of my Lord's usefulness', and he was obviously disturbed at the use made of the Earl's absence by enemies at court. He was glad therefore to tell Essex on his return that one of the archbishop of Canterbury's chaplains, in a sermon at St. Paul's, 'sounded your lordship's worthy fame, your justice, wisdom, valour and noble carriage in this action'. But there were so many criticisms of Essex's part in the voyage that Henry Cuffe, another of his servants, asked Reynolds to help him concoct an account of it, purporting to have been written by an eye-witness, which would concentrate on Essex's contribution.[4]

In the spring of 1599 Reynolds told a correspondent of Essex's intended departure for Ireland. He continued:

As in his other journeys ... I am of opinion he will leave me at court to follow his business there, which will be better for me than to go to so miserable and wretched a country as that is, and will be no discredit but rather a credit to me.

Gelly Meyrick* kept Reynolds informed of the events in Ireland – calling him 'honest Ned' and 'my worthy choleric Ned' – and he was well prepared therefore for the crisis which was bound to follow Essex's return. All the Earl's closest followers were urging moderation and tact as the best way of appeasing the Queen, and Reynolds himself wrote: 'If he speaks in a high style he will plunge himself further and overthrow his fortune forever. The safety of his person is the mark we all aim at'. There is some evidence that Reynolds helped Essex draft letters on this and other difficult occasions. The devotion and loyalty which Essex inspired is revealed in a letter written by Reynolds in 1605, more than four years after his execution, to the Earl's son. He referred to him as 'the perfect pattern of all true bounty, honour and nobility' and urged the new Earl to

> remember that you are the son of that great and renowned Earl of Essex whom all the world admired, and whose memory all England doth and will forever honour and reverence.[5]

An incident in 1596 shows that Reynolds was reluctant to share with another the honour of serving Essex, whose business affairs necessitated the engagement of a fifth secretary. Reynolds wrote:

> I have served your lordship eight whole years, seven with Mr. [Thomas*] Smith, without any other colleague, who – I speak it without envy – had all the credit of the place. At the time of Mr. Smith's preferment your Lordship knoweth how I neglected the opportunity of a clerkship of the signet, having devoted myself wholly to your service, and desiring a third reversion of the privy seal which it pleased your Lordship to promise me to procure.

When Smith left, Essex had appointed four additional secretaries, 'which makes the world to judge that he did all the service, whereas indeed the burden lay upon my shoulders for the most part'. He regarded the new appointment as a personal affront and ended:

> I leave the key of my cabinet sealed up with Sir Gelly Meyrick, where your Lordship shall find all your papers in good order. For myself, I never desire to be seen more of your Lordship, but will spend my time in fighting for my hard fortune, and praying for your honourable estate and the greatest happiness your heart can wish.

Perhaps Anthony Bacon*, whom he consulted, persuaded him to suppress the letter, for it was never sent.[6]

By 1597 Reynolds was evidently hoping to acquire a profitable government post, but Essex over-estimated his powers of patronage and Reynolds tried other channels, unsuccessfully writing directly to the Queen seeking the office of surveyor of the Ordnance. Next he tried Robert Cecil:

> I have served my lord of Essex nine whole years, with what diligence I refer myself to his honourable testimony; for these services my suit is for a reversion of the offices of the privy seal and court of requests, for both which places my Lord a good while since commended me to her Majesty.

And next Bacon, for 'a just care of my poor estate when decrepit age shall overtake me (whereof I bear already the marks in my head and face)'. He persuaded Bacon to write to Cecil at least twice on his behalf; first for the clerkship of the privy seal, then for the office of clerk of the Parliaments. Reynolds finally managed to acquire a privy seal reversion, which did not, however, fall in until 1608. In 1599 he was still hopeful that Essex might find a suitable post for him, especially if the rumour that the Earl was to be made master of the court of wards were to prove true.[7]

Reynolds' secretarial duties included, perhaps in 1593, when Essex attempted unsuccessfully to find Reynolds a seat at Stafford, certainly in 1597, the management of Essex's parliamentary patronage. The period between the issue of writs for elections to a new Parliament on 23 Aug. 1597 and its first meeting on 24 Oct. coincided almost exactly with the Earl's Islands voyage and, as a result, Reynolds and other servants were left to conduct his election campaign. A letter which Essex sent to several boroughs seeking seats ended with the request that their reply should be sent to Reynolds, who was himself returned at Andover, where Essex had recently been made high steward.[8]

Reynolds was with Essex in the final dramatic gathering in Essex House and suffered a surprisingly short period of imprisonment, being released within a fortnight and even escaping a fine. He retired to Whiteparish, near Salisbury, 'resolved to live a monastic life', though still sufficiently interested to have himself returned to the 1601 Parliament as a Member for Weymouth and Melcombe. No activities are recorded for Reynolds in either of his Parliaments. Soon he was asking his brother Owen Reynolds (not Owen Reynolds*), to find him a London house in Aldersgate Street 'or such like open place'.[9]

In February 1604, Reynolds evidently intended standing again, but his uncle's canvass had been discouraging. Edward Reynolds wrote to Owen:

> You write that you have renewed your request to the mayor of Weymouth for my election to a burgess's place. I did take it long since for a matter already granted ... I am sorry it is now made doubtful. I do hold my reputation and credit so dear as I had rather want ten such places than suffer the disgrace and indignity of a public repulse in the town where I was born. And therefore unless my friends there do see manifest

possibility of speeding and the mayor make an absolute promise of his best furtherance, I pray you give charge that my name may not be propounded ... If I suffer disgrace by a repulse in this election, assure yourself I shall be much disquieted in mind for it, and shall hardly digest it.

Six days later he wrote again, declining, and when he heard that the election had taken place, he deplored that his name had been

> used and abused almost this twelvemonth and in the end I am shifted off with scorn ... But the blow of my credit, in respect that I had communicated this matter to so many friends upon the strong assurances you gave me, is that which most disquieteth my mind and puts me into some distemper.[10]

Several years later Reynolds acquired the privy seal clerkship for which he had waited so long and the profits of which he was to enjoy for the rest of his life. He died 10 Dec. 1623, having made his will the previous 18 June. He died rich, his brothers and cousins benefiting handsomely in cash and property. Other beneficiaries included Sir John Rawlins and Sir Marmaduke Darrell, cofferer to King James, and the poor of the parish where he was buried. He left £20 to support a master at the Southampton free school, and a similar sum to All Souls, Oxford 'for books of divinity ... my name to be inserted in each book'. His final request was for a simple funeral

> with such inscription as my cousin Castle shall think meet to be engraven, together with my arms on the gravestone or in the wall near adjoining to my grave, and this with the advice of Mr. Camden if he be living.

William Camden, in fact, died in November 1623, a week or two before Reynolds.[11]

[1] *Vis. Dorset 1623 Add.* ed. Colby and Rylands, 43; *HMC Hatfield*, iv. 153; *CSP Dom.* 1611–18, p. 37. [2] *HMC Hatfield*, vii. 333; *CSP Dom.* 1603–10, pp. 436, 439; LC2/4/4. [3] *Weymouth Charters*, ed. Moule, passim; *HMC Hatfield*, vii. 333, 419. [4] W. Devereux, *Devereux Earls of Essex*, i. 196, 339–40, 342–3; *HMC Hatfield*, iv. 153, 161, 164; Birch, *Mems.* ii. 80–2, 95–100. [5] SP12/270/69, 273/38; SP14/15/98; *HMC Hatfield*, ix. 157, 343. [6] Birch, ii. 105–7, 109. [7] SP12/265/96; *HMC Hatfield*, vii. 333, 419; Birch, ii. 242–3, 349–50, 359; *CSP Dom.* 1598–1601, p. 158. [8] Neale, *Commons*, 238–40; Devereux, i. 280; *HMC 5th Rep.* 342; *HMC 13th Rep. IV*, 338. [9] *CSP Dom.* 1598–1601, p. 548; 1601–3, pp. 139, 141, 166, 171; Add. 1580–1625, p. 439; *HMC Hatfield*, xi. 44, 87; *APC*, xxxi. 485; SP14/6/56. [10] SP14/1/48, 6/74, 6/82, 6/85, 6/96. [11] *Genealogists' Mag.* vi. 334; PCC 1 Byrde.

M.R.P.

REYNOLDS, George I (by 1518–77), of Rye, Suss.

RYE   1547, 1563

b. by 1518, poss. s. of George Reynolds of Rye. *m.* (1) Margaret, da. of John Wytfield of Wadhurst, *s.p.*

Chamberlain, Rye 1539, 1543; jurat from 1546, mayor 1551–2, 1552–3, 1556–7, 1564–5, 1565–6, dep. mayor 1571–3; bailiff to Yarmouth 1554.

Reynolds, who kept a tavern in Rye, was described in 1556 as 'the Queen's Majesty's servant'. He remained in government favour under Mary, and continued an active official of his town until at least 1569. He made his will 17 Sept. 1577, died 1 Oct., and the will was proved on 4 Oct. The will refers to his 'last two wives', near to whose tombs in Rye parish church he wished to be buried. He bequeathed 10s. to the minister who preached the funeral sermon, 12d. each to the four men who carried his body, and £3 6s. 8d. to the poor of Rye, to be distributed on the day of his burial. No children are mentioned, and Reynolds' property was divided among relatives and friends. The will was contested by one John Rolf of Rye.

Vis. Kent (Harl. Soc. lxxv), 119; E. Suss. RO, Rye mss; Cinque Ports white bk. passim; *Suss. Rec. Soc.* lxiv. 13; (A. Vidler, *New Hist. Rye*, 159–60, list of mayors, has the wrong name for 1564); *CPR*, 1554–5, pp. 236–7; *APC*, v. 327; vi. 112; Lewes archdeaconry, wills bk. A7, f. 67.

N.M.F.

REYNOLDS, George II (*d.* 1577), of Devizes, Wilts.

DEVIZES   1572*

?*educ.* Winchester 1545. *m.*
Mayor, Devizes 1571, 1577.

Though his surname was common in sixteenth-century Wiltshire, Reynolds himself had connexions with south-east England, and may well have been related to his namesake who represented Rye in 1547 and 1563. He acted on behalf of Devizes in a lawsuit in 1576, but this does not mean that he was a lawyer. Nor was he a clothier. His only recorded transaction concerned the purchase of timber, which may, however, have been for private purposes, as he owned a house and other property in the town and leased a barn and some land from the corporation. He had several servants and was assessed at £9 for the 1576 subsidy. He represented the borough in Parliament after promising not to take wages. During the second session he was named to three committees, on 16, 17, 18 Feb. 1576, dealing respectively with woollen cloth, 'innholders and tipplers', and leather. He died in 1577, having made his will 29 July. He bequeathed money to a brother, Thomas, of Romney, and to a number of churches, including that of St. John the Baptist, Devizes, where he asked to be buried.

B. H. Cunnington, *Annals Devizes*, p. xviii et passim; *Two Taxation Lists* (Wilts. Arch. Soc. recs. br. x), passim; C2/Eliz./D.6/16; *CJ*, i. 106; PCC 45 Daughtry.

W.J.J.

REYNOLDS, Owen (c.1519–c.77), of St. Thomas's Street, Melcombe Regis, Dorset.

MELCOMBE REGIS   ?1553 (Mar.), 1553 (Oct.), 1571

b. c.1519, s. of John Reynolds, and uncle of Edward*. *m.* Emma, 4s. 4da.
Mayor, Melcombe Regis 1553–4, 1558–9, 1560–1,

1561–2, 1566–7; mayor, Weymouth and Melcombe 1575–6; customer, Weymouth by 1562; chamberlain, Weymouth and Melcombe 1570–1.

Five times mayor of Melcombe, and twice or thrice MP for the town, Reynolds (who described himself as a yeoman) was involved, as early as 1559, in the disputes between Weymouth and Melcombe Regis which occurred before and after their amalgamation in 1570. His nomination for Parliament in 1571 after a long interval was presumably so that he could supervise the passage of the bill to confirm the union by statute. Little is known about his private life. He was dead by September 1577, when his widow was confirmed in her possession of his house in Melcombe, with remainders to their four sons and four daughters.

E134/11 Eliz. Easter 3; *Vis. Dorset 1623 Add.* ed. Colby and Rylands, 43; *Weymouth Charters*, ed. Moule, 22, 24, 26, 93, 94, 97, 128, 129; Weymouth borough recs. doc. misc. ii. 3, 9, and Sherren Pprs. 29–34; St. Ch. 5/M30/14; *Dorset Nat. Hist. Antiq. Field Club. Procs.* 1877, p. 19.

P.W.H.

RICE, John

WOOTTON BASSETT 1601

This Member has not been identified. He may have been the 'John Ryce' who as early as 1567, together with his wife Christiana, carried out a transaction with Giles Estcourt* concerning property at Newnton, near Imber, or he may have been a younger member of the family – perhaps the John Aprice of Imber who made his will on 27 Oct. 1607, asking to be buried in the church of Imber, to which he gave 10s., with a further 10s. to the poor of the parish. Among the larger sums left to his family were £100 to his son William, £200 each to the younger daughters of another son Thomas, who was dead, and £400 to Thomas's younger son Edward; William also received a lease of property in Imber, held of the dean and chapter of Salisbury. John Aprice, Thomas's elder son, was appointed executor, while William Aprice and a 'cousin' Christopher Polden were named overseers. The amounts of money bequeathed suggest that the testator was comfortably off, and the fact that he 'put to' his 'sign' instead of writing his name may have been due to age or weakness (he was ill when he drew up the will) rather than to illiteracy. The will was proved 28 Jan. 1608.

Imber is a considerable distance from Wootton Bassett, and if the man who made the will in 1607 was the MP, he presumably needed a patron. His colleague in 1601, John Wentworth, almost certainly owed his seat to the Earl of Hertford, and it may be that Hertford was given both nominations in that year. However, no connexion between Hertford and any branch of the Rice or Aprice family has been found.

Wilts. N. and Q. v. 569; PCC 110 Windebanck.

N.M.F.

RICE, Walter (c.1560–?1611), of Newton, Llandefaison, Carm.

| CARMARTHENSHIRE | 1584 |
| CARMARTHEN BOROUGHS | 1601, 1604 |

b. c.1560, 1st s. of Griffith Rice of Auckland, co. Dur. and later Newton, by Elinor, da. of Sir Thomas Jones[†] of Abermarlais. *m.* Elizabeth, da. of (Sir) Edward Mansell[†] of Margam, Glam., 4s. 7da. *suc.* fa. 1584. Kntd. 23 July 1603.[1]

J.p. Carm. from c.1583, sheriff 1585–6.[2]

The West Wales family which eventually shortened its patronymic to the surname Rice rose in the fifteenth century through marriage to a descendant of the princes of South Wales and the acquisition, by lease from the Crown, of their ancient manor and castle of Dynevor, overlooking the Tywi. The climax of the family fortunes came when Rhys ap Thomas led Henry of Richmond's Welsh followers to his aid at Bosworth, and was richly rewarded in lands and offices. He consolidated his position by marrying a daughter of the 2nd (Howard) Duke of Norfolk, and either he or his grandson built at Y Dre Newydd, in the precincts of Dynevor castle, the family seat which went by the name of Newton. But on the grandson's attainder for treason in 1531, Newton and the other widespread estates reverted to the Crown, and most of them went to the neighbouring families of Devereux, Jones of Abermarlais and, later, Perrot. Griffith Rice, Walter's father, was restored in blood by Edward VI's first Parliament, and Queen Mary took him into her service and restored some of the forfeited lands still in her hands. But another attainder – this time for murder committed in County Durham, or according to other accounts at Boulogne – left him once more landless.[3]

Queen Elizabeth pardoned Griffith Rice in 1559, and in 1561 restored to him the Pembrokeshire lands and the old family seat at Newton, to which, two years later, she added some of his father's Cardiganshire property. But it was in Carmarthenshire only that he was able to exercise something of the ancestral sway, and that only in competition with other rising houses. His son Walter, the 1584 Carmarthenshire MP, backed by his influential father-in-law Sir Edward Mansell, succeeded to this position, and also received some preferment at court, the nature of which has not been ascertained. 'In consideration of his service' he was given in 1594 a 41-year lease, without fine, of further crown lands in the counties of Carmarthen and Pembroke.[4]

As a knight of the shire for a Welsh county Rice could have attended the subsidy committee appointed 24 Feb. 1585.[5]

When suspicion fell on the Devereux connexion in south-west Wales after the Essex revolt, Rice, described as 'an esquire of fair living both in counties Pembroke and Carmarthen' was one of those named as being able to report on the position in that area. Rice is stated to have died in 1611, though the man of this name whose death was recorded in the archbishop's prerogative court that year was of Salisbury, Wiltshire. The family remained influential in local and parliamentary politics during the three succeeding centuries, and ultimately rose to the peerage with the title Baron Dinevor.[6]

[1] Dwnn, *Vis. Wales*, i. 210–11; *DWB*, 847–8. Shaw, *Knights*, ii. 117 incorrectly describes Rice as of Lincs., perhaps through a misreading at some stage of Llandefaison for Lincoln. Walter Rice of Newton was certainly kntd. before the 1604 Parliament and no other man of this name has been traced. [2] Harl. 6993, f. 64. [3] *RCAM Carm.* 109–10; *West Wales Hist. Rec.* ii (1912), 118–19; *DWB*, 313, 840–1; *Arch. Camb.* (ser. 5), ix. 211–12; xi. 207–8; *LJ*, i. 312–13; *CPR*, 1548–9, p. 95; 1554–5, p. 28; 1557–8, pp. 310, 377. [4] *CPR*, 1558–60, pp. 113, 386; 1560–3, p. 488; *Exchequer*, ed. E. G. Jones (Univ. Wales Bd. of Celtic Studies, Hist. and Law ser. iv), 84–5; *Augmentations*, ed. Lewis and Davies (same ser. xiii), 232, 237; Harl. 6993, f. 64; *CSP Dom.* 1591–4, p. 527. [5] Lansd. 43, anon. jnl. f. 171. [6] *HMC Hatfield*, xi. 93; *DWB*.

A.H.D.

RICH, Robert (c.1560–1619), of Rochford Hall and Leighs Priory, Essex.

ESSEX 1572*

b. c.1560, 2nd but 1st surv. s. of Robert, 2nd Baron Rich by Elizabeth, da. and h. of George Baldry of Hadley, Suff., alderman of London. *educ.* G. Inn 1578. *m.* Penelope (div. 1605), da. of Walter Devereux, 1st Earl of Essex by Lettice, da. of Sir Francis Knollys*, 3s. inc. Robert[†] 4da.; (2) 1616, Frances, da. of Christopher Wray*, wid. of George St. Poll*. *suc.* fa. as 3rd Baron Rich 1581; KB 1603; *cr.* Earl of Warwick 6 Aug. 1618.
J.p. Essex 1608; PC 1608–*d.*[1]

Rich was the most powerful landlord in Essex and a leading political figure in the county, owning over 75 manors, being lord of the hundreds of Ongar, Harlow and Rochford and controlling many advowsons. He was a member of the Commons for less than three weeks, coming in for the county 7 Feb. 1581 at a by-election on the death of Sir Thomas Smith, and succeeding to his father's peerage 27 Feb. As a peer he is mentioned in the journals, 16 Mar. 1585, in connexion with an award made between him and Sir Thomas Barrington*. He took an active part in parliamentary elections, intervening in the 1588 county election (when the sheriff was his cousin, Robert Wroth I*), until forced by the Privy Council to discontinue his activities, and influencing elections at Maldon. He was particularly active in the 1604 election campaign, canvassing in Chelmsford, Colchester, Maldon, Thaxted and Saffron Walden, and assuring himself of the support of his uncle, Baron Darcy of Chiche, and of the 5th Earl of Sussex, who could sway Dengie and other divisions. He himself controlled the divisions between Braintree, Witham and Harwich and thus secured the re-election of Francis Barrington*.[2]

His political activities were no doubt connected with his religious views. At Rochford Hall he had services conducted by Robert Wright, a puritan minister ordained by Cartwright at Antwerp and the brother-in-law of John Butler II*. In 1581, Bishop Aylmer's complaint to Lord Burghley about these practices precipitated a fierce dispute with the Rich family. In 1586, when Rich was attending the House of Lords, he received a puritan petition from the inhabitants of Dunmow in Essex. In 1588 the Earl of Leicester, writing to Sir Francis Walsingham from the Low Countries, asked for Rich's services, 'though he be no man of war'. It seems unlikely that he went, and Burghley restored to William Waldegrave* the command of 50 lances which Leicester had given to Rich. In 1596 Rich accompanied his brother-in-law, the 2nd Earl of Essex, as one of the adventurers with the fleet to Cadiz, left the fleet early, and went to France with the embassy of Gilbert Talbot*, 7th Earl of Shrewsbury.[3]

Hitherto, Rich's relationship with the Earl of Essex had been close. He had lent Essex money (never recovered), including £1,000 before the Cadiz expedition. He was a commissioner for the trial of Doctor Lopez, significantly perhaps, in view of Essex's determination that Lopez should be condemned and destroyed. Rich, however, did not commit himself completely to the Earl, even in October 1597 seizing a favourable opportunity to write to Sir Robert Cecil, 'Give me leave in my Lord of Essex's absence to presume of your good favour as heretofore'. In the decisive months of 1600–1 he managed to remain apart from the Essex faction, an illness, diplomatic or otherwise, keeping him to his bed.[4]

His wife, who had been open in her devotion to her brother Essex, eventually deserted Rich for Charles Blount*, Lord Mountjoy, by whom she had several children. Rich died 24 Mar. 1619. His will, made 15 Sept. 1617, was proved 8 May 1620. Legacies included silver to (Sir) John Croke III*, £50 to Sir John Ross and plate to the two overseers, (Sir) Francis Bacon* and Thomas, 3rd Baron Darcy. He was buried in the chancel of Felsted church.[5]

[1] *CP*; *Vis. Essex* (Harl. Soc. xiii), 277–8; SP14/33. [2] Morant, *Essex*, ii. 102; Essex RO, DB3/3/205 no. 33; D'Ewes 368; *EHR*, lxviii. 398, 402, 404. [3] Collinson thesis, 688–91; T. W. Davids, *Annals of Evangelical Nonconformity in Essex* (1863), pp. 82–3; *Presbyterian Movement 1582–9*, ed. Usher (Cam. Soc. ser. 3, viii), pp. xxv–xxvi; *Second Parte of a Register*, ed. Peel. ii. 191; *CSP Dom.* 1581–90, pp. 511, 573; 1595–7. pp. 203. 438; *Add.* 1580–1625, p. 454; *Armada State Pprs.* ed. Laughton (Navy Recs. Soc. i), 808; *HMC Hatfield*, vi. 415–16, 429–30; *DWB* (Rich, Penelope). [4] PCC 51 Soame; *CSP Dom.* 1591–4, p. 448; *HMC Hatfield*, vii. 429; *DNB* (Rich, Penelope). [5] *CP*; PCC 51 Soame.

W.J.J.

RIDDLESDEN, Stephen (*d.*1607), of St. Katherine Colman, London.

BLETCHINGLEY 1593

educ. St. John's, Camb. 1571, BA 1575, MA 1578. *m.* Elizabeth, da. of John Palgrave of Barningham Norwood, Norf. by Urith, da. of Sir William Saunder of Ewell, Surr., ?1s. 2da. Kntd. 1604.

Clerk of the ordnance by 1595; ld. admiral's deputy 'for the searching and measuring of coal, grain and salt upon the seas'.

Riddlesden was a Yorkshireman, perhaps connected with the West Riding family of that name. His early patron was Thomas Radcliffe, 3rd Earl of Sussex, who left him £6 on his death in 1583. Shortly afterwards, Riddlesden was in the service of Charles Howard I*, the lord admiral, who obtained him a job connected with prize jurisdiction, employment that enabled him to set up as a moneylender on the side. In 1588 there were complaints that he abused his authority, but by 1595 he appears in the records as clerk of the ordnance, an office confirmed to him, jointly with John Riddlesden, for life in 1604 at a fee of 2s. a day. In 1590 he devised a scheme for reforming the coinage that would, he reckoned, yield a profit of £100,000. Nine years later he declined the comptrollership of the mint on the ground that it had 'no other commodity belonging to it but the bare fee of 100 marks yearly'. His one appearance in the Commons was for the Howard borough of Bletchingley, and his sole recorded activity was his membership of the committee to draw up the subsidy bill, 28 Feb. 1593.

'Lying sick upon his deathbed', in 1607 Riddlesden 'would not be troubled with any worldly matters', and left his widow (who later married Sir Edward Fox) to dispose of his goods. His heir, William, was still a minor. As well as his London house Riddlesden had property at Aldeby, Norfolk, and Clavering-cum-Langley, Essex.

Vis. Norf. (Norf. and Norwich Arch. Soc.), ii. 26; *HMC Var.* iv. 304; Lansd. 39, f. 49; 65, f. 17; 144, f. 55; 145, f. 262; *HMC Hatfield*, iv. 226, 239; v. 347; ix. 346–7; Pevsner, *W. Riding*, 400; *Bradford Hist. Soc.* ii. 131–4; pat. rolls 2 Jas. I, f. 11; *APC*, xv. 368; xvi. 385; xxix. 713; *CSP Dom.* 1603–10, p. 81; D'Ewes, 478; PCC 98 Huddleston, 61 Ridley; C142/327/102; Morant, *Essex*, ii. 612.

H.G.O.

RIDGEWAY, Thomas (1543–98), of Torre Abbey, Devon.[1]

DARTMOUTH   1584

b. Apr. or May 1543, o.s. of John Ridgeway† of the Middle Temple, London and Abbotskerswell, by Elizabeth, da. of John Wendford of Newton Abbot. *educ.* I. Temple 1560. *m.* (1) 12 Jan. 1563, Mary, da. of Thomas Southcote* of Bovey Tracey; (2) Alice; 9s. inc. Thomas† 1da. *suc.* fa. 1560.

J.p. Devon, sheriff 1590–1.

Ridgeway was probably returned for Dartmouth through the influence of the 2nd Earl of Bedford, who had intervened on his behalf when Ridgeway was implicated in a charge of piracy in 1578. He was of moderate means –

his assessment for the 1576 subsidy was £30 – and most of the references found to him concern lawsuits over land transactions. He was 'very aged and sick' in 1595 when his son was excused on these grounds from appearing personally at the Exchequer to make his account as comptroller of customs at Exmouth. It was not until 26 June 1598, the day before his death, that Ridgeway made his will, proved 2 Nov. following. The executor and residuary legatee was his eldest son Thomas, and (Sir) William Strode II* was an overseer.[2]

[1] This biography is based upon the Roberts thesis. [2] PCC 97 Lewyn; C142/252/33.

P.W.H.

RIDLEY, Thomas (bef. 1548–1629), of Doctors' Commons, London and Owslebury, Hants.

CHIPPING WYCOMBE   1586
LYMINGTON   1601

b. bef. 1548, prob. s. of Thomas Ridley (*d.*1548) of Bouldon, Salop and Ely, by Alice or Anne, da. of Richard Day of Worfield, Salop. *educ.* Eton 1562–6 (King's scholar 1563); King's, Camb. 1566, BA 1571, MA 1574, LLD 1583; incorp. DCL Oxf. 1598. *m.* (1) Alice, da. of William Day, bp. of Winchester 1596; (2) Margaret, da. of Sir William Boleyn or Bullen, 2da. Kntd. 24 June 1619, at Greenwich.[1]

Fellow, King's Coll. 1569–79; provost, Eton 1579–83; adv. Doctors' Commons 10 Oct. 1590; chancellor, diocese of Winchester 1596; j.p. Hants, Surr. from 1596; commr. piracy Southampton 1603; master in Chancery extraordinary 1598, ordinary 1609; vicar gen. to Abp. Abbot of Canterbury c.1611–*d.*; member, ct. of high commission.[2]

Ridley, a civil lawyer and ecclesiastical official, was descended from an old north of England family and related to Bishop Nicholas Ridley, the Marian martyr. No contemporary pedigrees of his branch of the family have survived and some modern authorities rely too much on an inaccurate nineteenth-century account of the family. It is generally accepted, however, that Ridley was born in Ely. His father was probably one Thomas Ridley of Shropshire origins, who termed himself 'yeoman' in his will, but leased a house and land in Ely from the dean and chapter. This self-styled yeoman's father, Lancelot Ridley, was possibly the divine who was deprived under Mary but held a good Cambridgeshire living under Elizabeth. If so, he may have been helpful to his grandson in his early years. Thomas Ridley, senior, died in 1548, leaving Ridley to be brought up by the Day family, whose fortunes were linked with those of the Ridleys both in Cambridgeshire and in Shropshire. The Days proved to be Ridley's principal benefactors until his career was firmly established. George Day, afterwards bishop of Chichester, may have known the Ridleys when he was provost of

King's College and vice-chancellor of the University, but it was his brother William, considerably his junior, who did most to shape Thomas Ridley's life. He was like a second father to the young man, but had more patronage and influence to offer than Ridley's own father could have had. Apart from finding him a place at Eton, where he was provost, William Day also secured for his protégé the headmastership of his old school when he returned from Cambridge. Furthermore, it was probably Day, as dean of Windsor, who had him returned to Parliament for Chipping Wycombe in 1586. By 1594 Ridley had evidently become well enough known to the Cecils to ask them to obtain for his benefactor the next vacant bishopric, an advancement for which Day had waited a long time. Though efforts to secure Worcester and Durham failed, in 1596, only a few months before he died, Day was consecrated at Winchester. To crown his many earlier favours, the new bishop now appointed Ridley, a fully qualified civil lawyer, his chancellor. By that date the close ties between the two men had been further strengthened by a marriage between Ridley and one of Day's daughters. According to a late pedigree of the Day family at Shrewsbury, Ridley married a daughter of the bishop's elder brother, also William, but no other evidence of this man's existence has been found and Bishop Day's will refers to a daughter as 'Mrs. Ridley'. It therefore appears that Margaret, daughter of Sir William Boleyn, was Ridley's second wife, and it is she who is mentioned in his will.[3]

Ridley remained chancellor of Winchester diocese for many years after Day's death, and surviving records from the consistory court show that he performed most of his duties in person. He carried out the visitation of the diocese in the autumn of 1606 for Bishop Thomas Bilson and the following year began a metropolitan visitation as Bancroft's deputy. He heard some of the cases brought before him in his own house at Owslebury, a few miles from Winchester. It was during this period that he sat in the Commons again, this time for Lymington, within his diocese, although he probably owed his seat to its new lord, the Earl of Nottingham, possibly at the instance of Sir Robert Cecil.[4]

Soon after George Abbot became archbishop of Canterbury he appointed Ridley his vicar general. Like Day, Abbot was a strong puritan, and probably Ridley shared their views. Ridley's years as an ecclesiastical judge and administrator coincided with an attack on the authority of the church courts by the common lawyers. It was to defeat this and to obtain a body of law capable of meeting the administrative needs of the contemporary church, that Bancroft asked Ridley and two other ecclesiastical lawyers to compile the so-called canons or code of 1604. Of the 141 canons, 44 were new and related to procedure in ecclesiastical courts, the others being based on the old canon law. Ridley's principal

contribution was entitled *A View of the Civil and Ecclesiastical Law*, (1607), dedicated to James I.

Ridley died on 23 Jan. 1629 and was buried four days later at St. Benet's, Paul's Wharf, the Doctors' Commons church. One of the supervisors of his will was Archbishop Abbot's brother, Sir Maurice Abbot[†], a governor of the East India Company.[5]

[1] J. Hodgson, *Hist. Northumb.* ii(2), 322 seq.; iii(2), 340, 343; W. Richardson, *Gen. of Ridley; Vis. Salop* (Harl. Soc. xxix), 162, 419–20; *DNB*; Nichols, *Progresses Jas. I*, iii. 554; Ridlon's *Ancient Ryedales* should be used with caution. [2] H. Maxwell Lyte, *Hist. Eton*, 4th ed. 598; *DNB*; Lansd. 142, f. 204. [3] *Cambs. and Hunts. Arch. Soc.* v. 374, 375, 378; *VCH Cambs.* iv. 49; PCC 12 Populwell; *DNB* (Ridley, Lancelot; Day, George; Day, William); *HMC Hatfield*, iv. 616; v. 7, 48–9. [4] A. J. Willis, *A Hants Misc.* i.; *Metropol. Vis. Archdeaconry of Winchester 1607–8*; B. Woodward, *Hist. Hants*, ii. 154, 326; Strype, *Whitgift*, ii. 332. [5] *DNB* (Abbot, George); *CSP Dom.* 1611–18, p. 272; 1627–8, p. 377; *VCH Surr.* ii. 191; Egerton 1584, f. 308; Add. 38170, f. 348; W. Holdsworth, *Hist. Eng. Law*, i. (7th ed.), 605 seq.; v. 12–13; W. Senior, *Doctors' Commons and the Old Court of Admiralty*, 80–7; R. Usher, *Rise and Fall of High Commission*, 149, 156–7, 159; Rymer, *Foedera*, xvii. 200, 648; xviii. 3, 293; PCC 19 Ridley; *VCH Hants*, iii. 334; *VCH Mdx.* iii. 39; *VCH Worcs.* iii. 254; *VCH Berks.* iii. 104.

M.R.P.

RISELEY, William (c.1527–1603), of Chetwode, Bucks.

BUCKINGHAM   1559

b. c.1527, 1st s. of William Riseley of Witlebury by Alice, da. and coh. of John Newman or Newnam of Staverton, Northants. *m.* Joan or Jane (*d.*1584), da. of Fulk Butlery or Buttery *alias* Mautany of Farthinghoe, Northants., 3s. 5da. *suc.* fa. 1552.

Riseley's father acquired much of the land formerly belonging to the monastery of Notley, Buckinghamshire: in June 1540 he paid £183 for the manor of Chetwode and other Buckinghamshire estates together with the rectories and advowsons of the vicarages of Chetwode, Barton and Barton Hartshorn. Soon after the younger William sat in the 1559 parliament, he conveyed this property and lands in 'Godington', Oxfordshire, to William Chauncy[†] and Cressentius Buttery, reserving the profits of the estates to himself.

Riseley was, on at least two occasions, accused of violence; in Mary's reign some of the parishioners of Chetwode brought a Star Chamber case against him, claiming that by his forcible eviction of one of the villagers from a pew, and by his removal of glass and lead from the parish church, he was interfering with freedom of worship. On the second occasion he was accused, also in the Star Chamber, of destroying crops and animals belonging to a Buckinghamshire neighbour.

He was doubtless the William 'Biseley' described by his bishop in 1564 as 'indifferent' in religion, and, as his name does not appear on commissions of the peace, he may have refused to take the oath of supremacy. He died on 9 Jan. 1603. In addition to the Chetwode estates, his inquisition post mortem gives property in Oxfordshire, and houses at Preston, Buckinghamshire. The heir, his eldest son Paul, was over 40 when he succeeded.

C142/95/3; 280/47; Wards 7/6/94, 28/143; *Vis. Bucks.* (Harl. Soc. lviii), 105–6; G. Lipscomb, *Bucks.* iii. 3; *CPR*, 1553 and App. Edw. VI, 4; 1558–60, pp. 8–9; *LP Hen. VIII*, xv. p. 408; *VCH Bucks.* iv. 148; St. Ch. 4/8/42; 5/C1/35; *Cam. Misc.* ix(3), p. 32.

N.M.F.

RITHE, Christopher (*d.* 1606), of Lincoln's Inn, London and Twickenham, Mdx.

PETERSFIELD	1555, 1558
HASLEMERE	1584

Yr. s. of Marlyon Rithe of Totford, Hants, and bro. or half-bro. of George*. *educ.* L. Inn 1556, called 1563. *m.* Catherine, da. of John Gedney of Bag Enderby, Lincs., 3s. inc. Marlyon* 2da.
J.p. Mdx. from 1569, q. by 1574; pensioner, L. Inn 1570.

Though Christopher Rithe and his brother George married sisters, there must have been a considerable difference in their ages, for Christopher was admitted to Lincoln's Inn no less than 19 years after George. He was admitted 'specially', and described as 'the brother of George Rithe'. After his brother's death in 1561 Rithe sat once more, for Haslemere, probably through the influence of Anthony Browne†, 1st Viscount Montagu.

In his will, dated 3 Sept. 1605, Rithe asked to be buried at Twickenham. He left his house at Chiswick to his wife for life, with remainder to his daughter, Sophronia, and apparel to his younger sons, Mysack and Theophilus. He made a number of small bequests to his numerous grandchildren, and appointed as executors his wife and eldest son, Marlyon. He bequeathed an annuity of £5. 2s. that he received from lands at Liss to one John Randoll, and made his 'kinsman', George Rithe of Liss, one of the overseers of the will. He added a codicil on 28 Aug. 1606 and was buried at Twickenham 6 Nov. The will was proved 12 Dec. His widow died three months later.

Mdx. Peds. (Harl. Soc. lxv), 28; *Vis. Surr.* (Harl. Soc. xliii), 197; *Lincs. Peds.* (Harl. Soc. li), 396; E315/309; *VCH Surr.* iii. 47; see also HASLEMERE; PCC 92 Stafforde, 34 Huddleston. Information from A. Colin Cole Esq., Windsor Herald, on this and other members of the family, is gratefully acknowledged.

A.H.

RITHE, George (*d.* 1561), of Liss, nr. Petersfield, Hants.

BRAMBER	1553 (Mar.)
PETERSFIELD	1553 (Oct.), 1559

s. of Marlyon Rithe of Totford, and bro. or half-bro. of Christopher*. *educ.* L. Inn 1537, called. *m.* c.1542, Elizabeth, da. of John Gedney of Bag Enderby, Lincs., wid. of Thomas Rigges of Cumberworth, Lincs., 2s. inc. Robert I*.

J.p. Hants 1547, Wilts. 1559; escheator, Hants and Wilts. 1549–50; Autumn reader, L. Inn 1556, keeper of black bk. 1556–7, treasurer 1558–9.

The Rithes were a Hampshire family, whose rise was probably due to the exertions of a 'Mr. Rythe' who was agent of Sir Thomas Wriothesley†, later 1st Earl of Southampton, during negotiations in 1537–8 over the purchase of Beaulieu abbey and its estates. Later in the century there were three branches of the family, one at Totford, another at Liss and the third at Twickenham in Middlesex. The only family pedigree was drawn up by the descendants of the Twickenham branch, and Rithe's own name does not appear on it. He was a London lawyer and land speculator, one of whose long-term purchases was an estate at Liss. This made him a substantial landowner in the Petersfield neighbourhood and accounts for his finding a parliamentary seat there for himself in October 1553 and 1559 and for his brother in 1555 and 1558. This ex-monastic property had been in the hands of William Fitzwilliam†, Earl of Southampton, from 1537 until his death without direct heirs in 1542, when it reverted to the Crown.

Rithe's will, drawn up in August 1557, has a devout preamble, trusting 'to inherit the kingdom of heaven prepared by God for all true penitent believers in His mercies'. The elder son Robert was to have most of the landed property and goods, and the widow, the sole executrix, land at Liss. A cousin, Thomas Rythe, was to have the custody of Robert, who was still a minor. Lands in Sussex were bequeathed to the younger son, George, at Robert's death. The executrix was asked to give a whole year's wages to all Rithe's servants. One of the three witnesses was Christopher Rithe, who received a ring. George Rithe was buried at St. Dunstan's-in-the-West, London, 17 Feb. 1561.

Lincs. Peds. (Harl. Soc. li), 396; *CPR*, 1547–8, pp. 84, 98, 335, 361; 1548–9, p. 160; 1553 and App. Edw. VI, 338; 1553–4, p. 19; 1554–5, p. 41; *Black Bk. L. Inn*, i. 314, 317, 318, 325, 331–5; *LP Hen. VIII*, xiii(1), pp. 7, 51–2; xx(2), p. 446; xxi(1), p. 243; xxi(2), p. 419; Add. i. p. 427; ii. p. 450; *Hants Field Club*, i. 182; *Vis. Surr.* (Harl. Soc. xliii), 197; *Mdx. Peds.* (Harl. Soc. lxv), 28; *VCH Hants*, iv. 84–85; PCC 35 Loftes; St. Ch. 3/9/35; 4/1/11, 13; 4/3/76.

P.H.

RITHE, Marlyon (*d.* 1627), of Lincoln's Inn and Twickenham, Mdx.

HASLEMERE	1584

1st s. of Christopher Rithe* of Twickenham. *educ.* L. Inn 1570. *m.* (1) Martha (*d.* 1593), da. and coh. of Robert Harris I*, 1s. 4da.; (2) Urytha (*d.* 1595), wid. of William Batte or Battes, of Mitcham, Surr. *suc.* fa. 1606.

Like his father and others of his family, Rithe was a Lincoln's Inn lawyer. His father and he sat together in the

Parliament of 1584 for Haslemere, when he had probably already married Martha Harris and acquired some of her father's property at Woodmansterne, near Croydon in Surrey. Haslemere is a long way from Woodmansterne, though in the same county, and the return of Rithe and his father was probably unconnected with Marlyon's marriage, rather being due to Anthony Browne[†], Viscount Montagu. Rithe was buried at Twickenham 30 May 1627, and was succeeded by his son, Christopher Rithe of Chipstead, Surrey.

Vis. Surr. (Harl. Soc. xliii), 197–8; *Mdx. Peds.* (Harl. Soc. lxv), 28; *VCH Surr.* iv. 248–9; PCC 95 Lewyn, 92 Stafforde.

P.W.H.

RITHE, Robert I (c.1545–c.94), of Liss, Hants, afterwards of Abingdon, Berks.

PETERSFIELD   1571[1]

b. c.1545, 1st s. of George Rithe* of Liss. *educ.* L. Inn, Jan. 1559, called 1567. *?m.*, 1s. Robert II*. *suc.* fa. 1561.
  Bencher, L. Inn 1578, Autumn reader 1579; keeper of black bk. 1583–4, treasurer 1585–6; j.p. Berks. c.1591, rem. c.1592; j.p. Oxon from c.1593.[2]

After following his father in the representation of Petersfield, Rithe sold his main estate at Liss, nearby, apparently on acquiring interests at Abingdon in Berkshire. Like other members of his family, he was a Lincoln's Inn lawyer. He may have gone to Abingdon in a legal capacity, though it is noteworthy that his great-aunt Jane had married a gentleman from Sutton Courteney, two miles from the town. In April 1587, a Robert Rithe was granted a two-year lease of the rectory and vicarage house of St. Nicholas, Abingdon, by the rector Guy Dobbins, a fellow of Winchester College, who held another rectory in Hampshire not far from Liss. Though the lease – the purpose of which seems to have been to test the right of the rector to the vicarage house – was not renewed, Rithe apparently remained in the neighbourhood: by 1593 he was a j.p. for Berkshire.[3]

His name does not appear in commissions after 1594; and the Robert Rithe of Lincoln's Inn last signed the black book in November that year. It seems likely, therefore, that the Berkshire j.p. and lessee of the Abingdon rectory was Robert Rithe of Liss, who presumably died in the winter of 1594–5; and that the Robert Rithe who sat for Abingdon in 1601 was his son, who was probably the man of that name mentioned at Lincoln's Inn in 1620.

[1] The Browne Willis ms, as opposed to the printed work, has 'Robert Roth', the de Tabley list 'Robert Both'. [2] *Lincs. Peds.* (Harl. Soc. li), 396; *Black Bk. L. Inn*, ii. 356, 405, 411, 433, 440; *CPR*, 1548–9, p. 160; PCC 35 Loftes. [3] *VCH Hants*, iv. 85; *Black Bk. L. Inn*, ii. 38, 226; *Mdx. Peds.* (Harl. Soc. lxv), 28; A. E. Preston, *St. Nicholas, Abingdon*, 208–9.

A.H.

RITHE, Robert II, ?of Abingdon, Berks.

ABINGDON   1601

?s. of Robert Rithe I* of Liss, Hants and Abingdon. *?m.* Mary, da. of Leonard Lydcott, gent. pens. of Checkendon, Oxon.[1]

It is possible that the Robert Rithe of Liss who sat for Petersfield in 1571 was also the burgess for Abingdon in 1601, but the fairly frequent references to his activities at Lincoln's Inn cease in 1594, making it likely that he died about then and that the Abingdon burgess was his son, probably the Robert Rithe of Lincoln's Inn mentioned in 1620. The young Robert Rithe was sworn a burgess of Abingdon 3 Oct. 1601, just before being returned to Parliament for the borough.[2]

Since nothing more of his career is known with certainty, and it is also uncertain who was high steward of Abingdon in 1601, the name of Rithe's patron, if he had one, can only be conjectured. A 'Mr. Rythe', agent of Thomas Wriothesley[†], 1st Earl of Southampton, had been partly responsible for the rise of the Liss family; and towards the end of Elizabeth's reign a Robert Rithe or Writhe, possibly the Abingdon burgess, married into the Lydcott family of Berkshire and Oxfordshire, a family already connected with the Wriothesleys through the Cheneys or Cheyneys of Buckinghamshire. Further, the 1st Earl of Southampton's father had been named Wrythe and was the first to adopt the more elaborate form 'Wriothesley'; possibly, therefore, the Abingdon burgess was a member of a less prominent branch of the Wriothesley family. The 3rd Earl of Southampton was a great ally of the 2nd Earl of Essex, high steward of Oxford, to which Abingdon is close, and much of Essex's patronage was inherited by his relative by marriage, (Sir) William Knollys*, later Earl of Banbury, who was high steward of Abingdon in 1630. In 1601 Knollys may already have been high steward, and Rithe may have entered his service through previous connexions with Southampton and Essex.[3]

[1] *Vis. Berks.* (Harl. Soc. lvii), 175; *Vis. Bucks.* (Harl. Soc. lviii), 178. [2] *Mdx. Peds.* (Harl. Soc. lxv), 28; *VCH Hants*, iv. 85; A. E. Preston, *St. Nicholas, Abingdon* (Oxf. Hist. Soc. xcix), 208–9; Abingdon council mins. i. f. 73. [3] *LP Hen. VIII*, xiii(1), pp. 7, 51–2; Add. i. 427; ii. 450; *Vis. Berks.* 175; *Vis. Bucks.* 177, 219; *Hants Field Club*, i. 82; *DNB* (Wriothesley, Sir Thomas, 1st Earl of Southampton); *Abingdon Recs.* ed. Challenor, 141.

A.H.

RIVERS, George (c.1553–1630), of Chafford, Kent.

EAST GRINSTEAD	1597, 1601
SOUTHWARK	1604
EAST GRINSTEAD	1614
LEWES	1625, 1626

b. c.1553, s. of Sir John Rivers of Chafford by Elizabeth, da. of Sir George Barne. *educ.* ?Trinity, Camb. 1571; M.

Temple 1574. *m.* Frances, da. of William Bowyer of Suss., at least 4s. 1da. *suc.* fa. 1584. Kntd. 1605.[1]

J.p. Kent from c.1583, Suss. from c.1594, q.1601.

Rivers's maternal grandfather and his father were lord mayors of London. Rivers himself, however (though he made an unsuccessful application to succeed William Lambarde* at the alienations office in 1601) was a country gentleman and agricultural improver, with estates in Kent and Sussex. Chafford, near Penshurst, had been acquired by his family in Henry VIII's reign, and Withyham was near an early seat of the Sackvilles. Rivers remained on close terms with this family, being an executor both of Robert, 2nd Earl of Dorset (his 'faithful and dear friend') and Richard the 3rd Earl. It was no doubt through the Sackvilles that Rivers came to be returned at East Grinstead to the last two Elizabethan Parliaments, and in 1606 he obtained for himself a share in the borough. Though both Parliaments are comparatively well documented, Rivers left no mark upon the records. He made his will by January 1630, 'feeling age creeping on' and died 20 Feb. that year.[2]

[1] C142/205/200, 468/89; PCC 37 Butts, 52 Scroope; E. Kimber and R. Johnson, *Baronetage*, i. 211; A. B. Beaven, *Aldermen*, ii. 37, 170, 173. [2] *HMC Hatfield*, viii. 172; Hasted, *Kent*, iii. 250–1; *Arch. Cant.* xlvi. 59; *APC*, 1619–21, pp. 92, 203; 1623–5, p. 200; 1626, p. 26; *CSP Dom.* 1595–7, pp. 305–6; 1603–10, p. 338; 1627–8, p. 449; 1628–9, pp. 180, 586, 595; Beaven, ii. 170; PCC 23 Dorset, 52 Scroope; Lansd. 92, ff. 43 seq.; A. Collins, *Sidney State Pprs.* ii. 231; C142/312/128; Neale, *Commons*, 73; *Statutes of the Realm*, iv. p. lxxvii; Wards 7/79/161.

J.E.M.

RIVETT, Thomas (*d.*1610), of Rattlesden, Suff.

| ORFORD | 1597 |
| ALDEBURGH | 1604* |

1st s. of James Rivett by Dorothy, da. of Sir John Sone or Soame of Wantisden. *educ.* I. Temple 1572. *m.* Katherine, da. of William Cotton of Panfield, Essex, 3s. 1da. *suc.* fa. 1587.

J.p. Suff. from c.1579.

Rivett possibly owed his seat at Orford to his relationship with the Sone or Soame family, who intermarried with the Wingfields and provided other Members for Orford and Dunwich in Elizabethan Parliaments. Roger, Lord North, an influential magnate in Suffolk, who was friendly with the Cambridgeshire branch of the Rivett family, may have asked a local patron for a nomination; North's son and heir John had represented Orford in the previous Parliament. The Rivetts were also on good terms with Edward Coke*, recorder of Orford. As one of the Orford burgesses in 1597 Rivett could have sat on the committee considering draining the fens, 3 Dec.

Almost all the information about him is concerned with land. He died in London, and was buried at St. George's,

Southwark. A writ for a by-election at Aldeburgh was issued on 24 Apr. 1610.

Vis. Suff. ed. Metcalfe, 162, 205; *HMC Hatfield*, ii. 523; *CP*; D'Ewes, 567; W. A. Copinger, *Suff. Manors*, i. 219; ii. 359; iii. 232; iv. 224; vi. 148, 319.

N.M.F.

ROANE, Anthony (*d.*1583), of Hounslow, Mdx.

| RIPON | 1571 |

1st s. of Humphrey Roane of Whiston, Yorks. by Marian, da. of one Selby of Yorks. *m.* (1) Alice Dale, *s.p.*; (2) Audrey, da. of Thomas Fernley of Creeting St. Mary, Suff., 3s. 1da.

Under-auditor of Exchequer by 1558; j.p.q. Mdx. by 1569.[1]

Roane had a little land in the West Riding of Yorkshire at Adel, Cottingham and Wooderson; at one time he also owned the site of Middlesbrough priory, which he sold in 1572. Apart from a crown lease in Carmarthenshire, the rest of his estate was in the south of England. At his death he left fee-simple land in Hatton and Heston, Middlesex, as well as his house at Hounslow and the *New Inn* and a 'brewing-house' there. When in London he presumably lived in the parish of St. Botolph-without-Aldersgate, where he was churchwarden from 1568–9.[2]

His early career is obscure, but he may have been a minor Exchequer official before 1558, when he was granted the reversion to an auditorship then held by Francis Southwell[t]. The latter did not die until November 1581, but a 'Mr. Roane' is described as an auditor as early as June 1558, several months before the patent of reversion was enrolled. Unless there were two Roanes serving in the Exchequer, the 1571 Member was thus an under-auditor before the end of Mary's reign. He was often employed in the north. On 23 Nov. 1569 Sir Ralph Sadler* reported a meeting with him at Burton Stathes, near Barton. 'Mr. Rone, one of her Majesty's auditors, who was at York yesterday with my Lord Sussex' (Sir Thomas Radcliffe[t], 3rd Earl) had given him a gloomy picture of the military position, saying that the army of the rebellious earls was much stronger than the loyal forces, and that York was running short of supplies. Three days later, however, Sadler wrote again to the Council, describing Roane as 'a known fearful man', whose depressing information he now found to be exaggerated.[3]

During the 1571 Parliament the corporation of York wrote to 'Mr. Anthony Rowe, esquire, the Queen's Majesty's auditor of Yorkshire', telling him that their parliamentary representatives wished to know particulars of the Queen's lands in Yorkshire and in the city. If he would help them with his counsel, the mayor and his brethren would be very glad to 'pleasure' him 'if that occasion will serve'. Roane evidently complied with the request, but the burgesses for York 'could not perceive' from his books what chantry lands 'were sold or unsold'. These official connexions with Yorkshire as well as his Yorkshire origins, presumably explain his election to Parliament for Ripon in 1571.[4]

By this time Roane's name had begun to appear on Middlesex commissions of the peace, and after 1572 no further references to him in Yorkshire have been found. In January 1576 he was summoned before the Privy Council in London, possibly to give information about the finances of the Savoy, and later in the same year he was asked to investigate complaints of unlawful enclosure of common land by Sir Thomas Gresham in Osterley park. This must have been a delicate task, as he was on very friendly terms with Sir Thomas's family. Lady Anne Gresham, a relative of Roane's second wife, was godmother to his daughter, who was named after her.[5]

Roane died on or about 11 May 1583. The preamble to his will, which was dated 8 Mar. and proved 24 May, quotes Job's statement that man has but a short time to live and is 'replenished with many miseries', and continues with an assurance of escape from death and damnation through Christ's passion. 'I, most wretched sinner', give God hearty thanks for all His gifts 'and therefore I do say Amen'. He wished to be buried at Hounslow 'in decent order without pomp', a learned man being present to 'exhort the audience to amendment of life whilst time is'. An annuity of £2 was provided for the maintenance of a reader in his house, The Friars, at Hounslow 'for the divine service', and any parishioners were welcome to attend the readings. The will included bequests of £200 to Roane's daughter Anne, £100 to his eldest son Edward (who was only nine years old) on his 22nd birthday, and valuable plate to other relatives and friends. His wife, Audrey, was appointed sole executrix, with four overseers, among them John Conyers*. The widow married Sir Edmund Brudenell shortly after Roane's death, and as she herself died soon afterwards, there were further grants of probate in 1584 and 1587, the first to Sir Edmund and the second to Thomas Brudenell.[6]

[1] *Vis. Essex* (Harl. Soc. xiii), 281; *Mdx. Peds.* (Harl. Soc. lxv), 51; *APC*, vi. 335; *CSP Dom.* 1547–80, p. 109; *CPR*, 1569–72, pp. 226, 290. [2] *CPR*, 1563–6, p. 159; PCC 20 Rowe; C142/276/550; *VCH Yorks. N. Riding*, ii. 270; *LP Hen. VIII*, xxi(1), p. 682; *CSP Dom.* Add. 1566–79, pp. 62, 76. [3] *CPR*, 1563–6, p. 303; SP38/1; PCC 9 Tirwhite; *APC*, vi. 335; *CSP Dom.* Add. 1566–79, pp. 115–16, 124. [4] *York Civic Recs.* (Yorks. Arch. Soc. rec. ser. cxv), 24, 28. [5] Lansd. 109, f. 156; *APC*, ix. 75, 167. [6] PCC 29 Rowe; C142/276/550, which gives the date of death a year too early.

N.M.F.

ROBERTS, David, of Penhow, Mon.

CARDIFF BOROUGHS 1572, 1593

Under-sheriff, Glam. 1571; comptroller of the port of Cardiff 1577–86.

Roberts, 'servant to our very good lord the Earl of Pembroke', lived some 17 miles from Cardiff. In the year of his appointment as comptroller he was called before the Privy Council, with others from the neighbourhood, to answer charges of trafficking with pirates. He remained in office another nine years. In 1585 another of Pembroke's servants, Thomas Wiseman, recommended to Sir Edward Stradling 'Davy Roberts', 'whom my lord and master thinketh very well of' 'to be employed under you in some office'.

Roberts introduced into Parliament in 1581 a bill about Cardiff Bridge, which received its first reading 8 Feb., its second 20 Feb. and its third 2 Mar.

W. R. Williams, *Parl. Hist. Wales*, 105; *Cardiff Recs.* i. 350, 351, 356; v. 531; *APC*, ix. 269, 332–3; *CSP Dom.* 1547–80, p. 843; *Stradling Corresp.* ed. Traherne, 262; *CJ*, i. 123, 128, 130; 23 Eliz. c. 11; see also MATHEW, William.

A.H.D.

ROBINS, John (b. c.1511), of Dover, Kent.

DOVER 1559, 1563

Constable, Dover 1554, chamberlain 1554, jurat in 1556, 1558, 1560, 1562, 1574–8, mayor 1562–3,[1] 1575–6.[2]

Robins was a master mariner who owned some of the ships of the Dover passage. Judging from a deposition taken in February 1577, which estimated his age at 'sixty-five or thereabouts', he must have been born about 1511. His name, however, has not been traced in the extensive Dover records before the middle years of Edward VI's reign, when he would have been nearly 40. This, coupled with the absence of any reference to his family prior to that date, suggests that he may not have been a native of the town. Whatever his origins, he played an important and stormy part in the local affairs of Dover for the next quarter of a century, holding at one time or another virtually every civic office.[3]

He was first returned to Parliament in 1559, at a time when a vacancy in the office of lord warden gave the town the chance to elect two local men. While in London he and other barons of the Cinque Ports asserted their traditional right of carrying the Queen's canopy at her coronation. Shortly after his return from Westminster he became involved in the fierce quarrels in the Dover common council which were a feature of this period: he and Thomas Warren, his fellow-Member, were fined £4 each in July 1559 'for their disobedience to the mayor's commandment'. So bad was the situation that the government set up a commission of inquiry in the same year. Robins's first term as mayor also reflected this disquiet. According to one local historian the Privy Council appointed William Hannington[†] as mayor in September 1561 and, on their instructions, he retained the office for a year and a half, but the Dover common council records show that Robins was mayor by 6 Oct. 1562, less than a month after the normal date of election. Unfortunately the council minutes for 1562–3 are badly mutilated. During his mayoralty Robins was returned to Parliament for the second time. He and Warren were paid at least £12 for 'their Parliament wages'.[4]

Robins served as a jurat on a number of occasions, the gaps in his attendance being presumably due to his business affairs. In 1577 he sought the office of mayor for the third time, and again trouble followed. The Privy Council wrote to the lord warden:

> upon some strife among the inhabitants of Dover for the election of a mayor, their lordships directed their letters to the mayor for the time being, the jurats and commons of the same, advising them to make choice of one Thomas Andrews [II*], recommended unto them to be a fit person for that purpose, [but they], contrary thereunto, have proceeded to the election of one John Robins, whereupon hath risen a tumult to the great disquieting of them all.

Robins and some of his supporters, including Thomas Warren, were summoned before the Council to explain their conduct. Eventually a compromise resulted in the election of a third candidate two months later.[5]

Between his periods of political activity at Dover and in Parliament, Robins seems to have pursued an active career at sea. He owned several ships and was concerned principally with the cross-channel trade to Calais. On at least one occasion, however, he must have ventured further afield. In August 1565 he was summoned before the Privy Council to answer a complaint by the King of Denmark. At that time Denmark was at war with Sweden, and presumably Robins was one of the English merchants who risked Danish displeasure by supplying goods to Sweden at lucrative prices. He also served as a naval captain, as a list of the late 1570s reveals, and in September 1580, when he was not far short of 70, he was commanded by the Privy Council to put himself in readiness to take charge of one of the Queen's ships.

Earlier, in 1551, he and Hugh Lloyd had been paid £50 compensation for delivering up two French prisoners without ransom as a result of the peace treaty. It is just possible that he was the John Robins who was a merchant based on Exeter in the later years of Henry VIII's reign. If that is so, he was imprisoned in Spain for two years from 1539 on a charge of trying to export contraband goods.[6]

Robin's long and eventful life also contained at least one important lawsuit in which a group of merchants, trading with Spain, disputed his right to several valuable cargoes. This proved to be yet another matter which brought him to the notice of the Privy Council. A sum of £10 which he owed the Crown was levied from his goods and chattels by the Dover authorities in 1579. The date of his death has not been found.[7]

[1] Egerton 2094, ff. 108, 155, 200, 219, 240, 294; 2095, ff. 4, 50; Dover accts. 1558–81, f. 1; *Vis. Kent* (Harl. Soc. lxxv), 52; *Dover Charters* ed. Statham, 374. [2] Several printed lists of mayors of Dover, e.g. *Dover Charters*, 428, state that Thomas Warren was mayor in 1575–6, but the common council minutes show conclusively that Robins held the office in that year. He may have been jurat in other years in addition to those shown. [3] Egerton 2094, ff. 27, 41, 308–9. [4] J. B. Jones, *Dover Annals*, 244, 297, 298, 378; *Dover Recs.* ed. Jones, 135–6; Egerton 2094, f. 230; Dover accts. ff. 154, 155. [5] *APC*, x. 27–8, 39, 91, 314, 319. [6] J. B. Jones, *Dover Annals*, 378; *APC*, iii. 290; vii. 248; xii. 212; C. Hill, *Danish Sound Dues and the Command of the Baltic*, 64–5; Lansd. 683, f. 50; Add. 34701, ff. 2–4; *LP Hen. VIII*, xv. 103; xvi. 233. [7] *CPR*, 1560–3, p. 34; *APC*, vii. 198; *Arch. Cant.* xxix. 282; Egerton 2095, f. 93.

M.R.P.

ROBINSON, William I, of Bath, Som.

BATH   1559

Alderman, Bath by 1554.

Nothing is known about Robinson. The William Robinson who accounted as chamberlain in 1569 was probably son of the above.

Bath Recs. app. A, p. xxiv; *Bath Chamberlains' Accts.* (Som. Rec. Soc. xxxviii), 1.

A.M.M.

ROBINSON, William II (1534–1616), of York.

YORK   1584, 1589

b. 1534. m. (1) Isabel, da. of John or Richard Redman of Gressingham, Lancs., at least 1s.; (2) da. of Thomas Harrison of York, at least 1s.

Freeman, York c.1558, chamberlain 1563–4, sheriff 1568–9, 1607–8, master, York merchant adventurers 1578–80, 1590–1, alderman by 1579, ld. mayor 1581–2, 1594–5; member, high commission, province of York 1599, 1603.

Robinson was a wealthy merchant who traded through the Sound. As sheriff of York in 1569, he was censured by the mayor and corporation for not wearing a crimson gown. To the request that he obtain the 'said decent apparel' he made dilatory answers 'sounding to a flat denial', and was finally threatened with the closing of his shop and a £20 fine. In Parliament Robinson was appointed to committees on the subsidy (24 Feb. 1585, 11 Feb. 1589), Orford harbour (13 Feb. 1589), Lincoln (11 Mar. 1589) and another the same day on salted fish and herrings, a subject in which York had a special interest. He was put down for £50 towards the Queen's loan in 1590, and his will, dated 17 Dec. 1614, indicates his prosperity. He owned houses and orchards in York, and at least four manors in other parts of the county. He left a number of charitable bequests and small personal legacies. He died on 1 Aug. 1616, and was buried in his parish church of St. Crux.

York City Lib., Skaife mss; Glover, *Vis. Yorks.* 99; *Vis. Yorks.* (Surtees Soc. xxxvi), 207; *York Mercers* (Surtees Soc. cxxix), 193, 195, 201, 324; *York Freemen* (Surtees Soc. xcvi), 278; (cii), 4, 22, 36; *HMC Hatfield*, ix. 397; xv. 395; D'Ewes, 356, 431, 432, 444, 445; York wills 34, f. 170; J. J. Cartwright, *Chapters in Yorks. Hist.* 372–4.

N.M.S.

ROBOTHAM, Robert (by 1522–71), of London and Raskelf, Yorks.

REIGATE	1553 (Mar.)
DORCHESTER	1555[1]
READING	1563

b. by 1522. *m.* Sept. 1551, Grace, da. of one Paget, wid. of Robert Bull of London, 2s. 3da.

Gent., Prince Edward's household by 1543; groom of the wardrobe by Jan. 1548; yeoman of the robes by Sept. 1549; comptroller of customs, Newcastle-upon-Tyne from 1551; keeper of St. John's wood, Mdx. from May 1552, of Berry Pomeroy park, Devon from June 1552.

A household official under Edward VI and Mary, Robotham was confirmed in his offices by Elizabeth, and was assessed at £61 in goods as a member of the Queen's chamber in the household subsidy list of 1558–9. He received a grant of arms in December 1560, and in the same year obtained the wardship of a London goldsmith's daughter, who subsequently married Robotham's son, bringing him £840 cash and a manor near St. Albans. Robotham was returned to one Elizabethan Parliament through the influence of his friend Sir Henry Neville I*, leaving no trace in its records. Neville was an overseer of the will Robotham made 30 Apr. 1570. There was plate amounting to nearly 5,000 ounces. Sir Walter Mildmay was left a cup. The heir, John, who was still under 21, was sole executor and residuary legatee. 'Good debts owing to me', totalled nearly £3,000, and 'ready money in my house £400'. Probate was granted to the widow 1 Dec. 1571.[2]

[1] Guildford Mus. Loseley 1331/2. [2] *Vis. Herts.* (Harl. Soc. xxii), 87; C1/1394/7; *CPR*, 1553 and App. Edw. VI, pp. 185, 374; *CPR*, 1558–60, p. 427; 1560–3, pp. 80, 357, 542; 1569–72, pp. 70–1; DL1/34/R6; 3/79/H.1.j.; *APC*, iv. 383; Lansd. 3, f. 194; 7, ff. 30–6; LC2/4/2; I. Temple, Petyt ms 538, xxxix. f. 134 seq.; *Misc. Gen. et Her.* (ser. 2), i. 269–70; *CSP Dom.* Add. 1566–79, p. 326; PCC 47 Holney; R. Clutterbuck, *Herts.* i. 106.

N.M.F.

ROGERS, Andrew (*d.* c.1599), of Bryanston, Dorset.

CHRISTCHURCH	1571
WAREHAM	1584
DORSET	1586, 1589
CHRISTCHURCH	1597

1st s. of Richard Rogers* of Bryanston by his 1st w. Cecilia, da. of Andrew Luttrell of Dunster Castle, Som.; bro. of John I*. *educ.* Oxf. BA 1567; I. Temple 1568. *m.* (1)

da. and coh. of Adrian Poynings*, *s.p.*; (2) Lady Mary Seymour, da. of Edward, Duke of Somerset, *s.p.*

J.p. Dorset from c.1577, rem. 1587, rest. by 1592/3; duchy of Lancaster steward of Kingston Lacy, Dorset 1579–25 May 1598.[1]

Rogers went to the Inner Temple in the same year that his uncle, Matthew Ewens*, was admitted to the Middle Temple. Ewens became counsel to the 3rd Earl of Huntingdon, the parliamentary patron of Christchurch, which accounts for Rogers's return in 1571. By 1597 the 3rd Earl was dead, but Rogers owned property in the borough and presumably brought about his own return. He succeeded his father-in-law Sir Adrian Poynings as steward at Kingston Lacy, the office being conveyed to him by Lord Mountjoy. The Rogers family controlled parliamentary returns at Wareham, the two seats being taken by Andrew and his brother John in 1584, and his family standing and marriage connexions were sufficient to gain him two elections as knight of the shire. His father was sheriff at the time when the election writ was issued for the 1589 Parliament, 15 Sept. 1588. Rogers was in good odour at this period. The previous month he had been described as 'a gentleman of good account in these parts' when he had been given the command of a contingent of soldiers sent from Dorset to join the forces assembled at Tilbury against a probable Spanish invasion at the time of the Armada.

Apart from a reference to his implication in the 1577 piracy inquiry in Dorset, most of the early references to Rogers show him acting as intermediary in the dispute between his father and the Earl of Hertford, father of Lord Beauchamp, who had married Andrew Rogers's sister Honora against the Earl's strong opposition. At the end of 1581 Rogers visited the Earl's seat at Tottenham, Wiltshire, where he denied that he had favoured the marriage. In 1587, Lady Mary, Rogers's wife, wrote to Burghley from Camberwell, protesting about the removal of her husband from the Dorset commission of the peace, which she ascribed to 'his absence from the county ... greatly against his will', which in turn had been caused by her 'attendance upon her Grace'. Feeling that her own honour and her husband's 'reputation and credit' were at stake, she asked Burghley to write to the lord chancellor. It is plain from a postscript that she feared her father-in-law would hold her responsible for Andrew's removal. Relations between them were probably strained: in 1600, after Andrew's death, Lady Mary and her brother the Earl had a dispute with Sir Richard Rogers about her jointure.[2]

The date of Rogers's death *s.p.* and *v.p.* is not known: it must have occurred soon after February 1599, when the Dowager Lady Russell wrote to her nephew Sir Robert Cecil asking for a knighthood for him. The acrimonious correspondence between Sir Richard Rogers and the Earl of Hertford over Lady Mary Rogers's jointure had clearly been going on for some time in February 1601. This argues against the only recorded date of death so far discovered (1 Dec. 1601).[3]

[1] Roberts thesis; *Vis. Dorset* (Harl. Soc. xx), 79; Somerville, *Duchy*, i. 630; E133/8/1270. [2] R. Lloyd, *Dorset Elizabethans*, 18; *HMC Bath*, iv 191–3; *Vis. Dorset*, loc. cit.; Hutchins, *Dorset*, i. 250; Lansd. 53, f. 112; *HMC Hatfield*, ix. 28. [3] *HMC Hatfield*, ix. 28; *Sales of Wards* (Som. Rec. Soc. lxvii), 197.

P.W.H.

ROGERS, Daniel (c.1538–91), of Silver Street, St. Olave's, London.[1]

NEWPORT IUXTA LAUNCESTON 1589

b. c.1538, at Wittenberg, 1st s. of John Rogers, preacher, by Adrienne van der Weede of Antwerp. *educ.* Wittenberg 1555–9; Oxf. BA July 1561; MA Aug. 1561. *m.* 1587, Susan, da. of Nicasius Yetswiert, 1s. 1da.

Government agent in Paris 1565–75; envoy in Netherlands Mar. 1575–Mar. 1577; sec. to Merchant Adventurers at Antwerp July 1575–8; envoy in Germany and Netherlands June 1577–Jan. 1578, Oct. 1580; clerk of PC May 1587; ambassador extraordinary to Denmark Sept. 1587–Jan. 1588, July–Aug. 1588, Jan. 1590.[2]

The circumstances of his birth and early life made Rogers both a protestant and a European. The death of his father, the Marian protomartyr, and his own subsequent return to Wittenberg to study under Melancthon must have confirmed the teaching of his youth, and it would not have been surprising if he had entered the ministry as his father had intended him to do. This course was several times urged upon him. As late as 1570 his master Sir Henry Norris I* urged Cecil to persuade Rogers to set his hand to the Lord's harvest, and Dr. Thomas Wilson* suggested that he be given a bishopric in 1576. But his concern for 'the Lord's harvest' was expressed in the political rather than the ecclesiastical field.[3]

After returning to England upon the accession of Elizabeth and taking a degree at Oxford, he entered Norris's household in Paris as steward and tutor to his sons. Next he became an agent for his 'especial friend and patron' (as Rogers once described him), Francis Walsingham, who succeeded Norris as ambassador in Paris in 1570. To Rogers's decade in Paris belong a quantity of Latin poetry and historical works, and here he first began his literary friendship with the leading Dutch humanists, with whom he became so closely associated that when a volume of verse was published to celebrate the foundation of the university of Leyden in 1575, Rogers was the only foreigner among the contributors. In that same year he graduated to official employment as an envoy, an appointment he held in conjunction with that of secretary to the Merchant Adventurers, who naturally soon came to feel that Rogers put their interests second to those of the Crown. In the summer of 1577 he accompanied his fellow *litterateur* Philip Sidney* on a number of journeys between Holland and Germany with the object of negotiating a tripartite defensive agreement between England, the Netherlands and the German protestant princes. That September he was active behind the scenes at the Frankfurt convention, which plastered over the cracks between the doctrines of the Lutheran and Calvinist princes.[4]

On a mission to Germany in the autumn of 1580 Rogers was imprisoned at Bucholtz in the bishopric of Munster as a result of pressure exerted by the King of Spain. His fate arousing concern only among his literary friends, it was not until February 1582 that the government made any attempt to secure his release. A ransom of £200 was eventually agreed, Burghley authorizing Rogers to collect it himself through a levy on the English clergy. Not surprisingly, the money was slow in coming in, thus providing Rogers with an excuse to avoid acceding to demands from the Earl of Leicester for his return to the Netherlands in 1585 and 1586. Again, in 1588, he was suggested for an embassy to the German protestant princes, but by this time, wary of Walsingham, and newly married to the daughter of Queen Elizabeth's French secretary, his 'rare zeal for the good and repose of the Christian republic' was flagging, and he applied for posts at home, first for the treasurership at St. Paul's, then for a prebend at Windsor. Finally accepting a clerkship of the Privy Council, he made three ceremonial missions to Denmark, between the last two of which he was returned to Parliament for a Cornish borough without leaving any mark upon the records. In all probability both Rogers's clerkships and his parliamentary seat were arranged by Burghley, who admired his scholarship, and to whom Rogers had turned increasingly since his return from captivity. For his part Burghley had described Rogers in July 1586 as 'so worthy a man and my very good friend'.[5]

Safe in harbour at last, with a secure job, powerful friends and a young wife about to bear his second child, Rogers died suddenly, in his early fifties, on 10 Feb. 1591. He was buried at Sunbury, Middlesex, beside his father-in-law. In his will, made on the day of his death and proved the next day, he appointed his wife executrix and his brother John and colleague William Waad* overseers. An estate in Shropshire went to his son Francis and the unborn child was to have £30 p.a. if a boy and £300 at the age of 16 if a girl. She was baptized Posthuma.[6]

[1] This biography is based upon J. A. Van Dorsten, *Poets, Patrons and Professors: Sir Philip Sidney, Daniel Rogers and the Leiden Humanists.* [2] Lansd. 155, f. 128; *CSP For.* 1575–7, pp. 67, 78, 603, 605; 1587, p. 65; 1586–8, pp. 369–71, 471; 1588 (Jan.–June), pp. 74–5, 113; *APC*, xv. 111; *CSP Dom.* 1547–80, p. 681; 1581–90, pp. 425, 643. [3] Foxe, *Acts and Mons.* vi. 591–612; *CSP For.* 1567–71, pp. 375–6; K. de Lettenhove, *Relations Politiques des Pays Bas et de l'Angleterre*, ix. 111–13. [4] *CSP For.* 1566–8, pp. 489–90; 1569–70, pp. 30, 263; 1575–7, pp. 67, 71, 87, 102, 120, 126, 137, 149–50, 151–2, 153, 158–9, 163, 603, 605; 1577–8, pp. 22–5, 47–9, 95–7, 97–104, 124, 151–3, 153, 214,

237–9, 293–6, 347; A. G. H. Bachrach, *Huygens and Britain*, i. 13; Read, *Walsingham*, i. 299–300, 303, 311–14, 330, 347, 349–50, 365, 366; *Burghley*, 159–60, 188–9. [5] *CSP Span.* 1580–6, p. 296; *CSP Dom.* 1581–90, pp. 30, 157, 300, 417; Lansd. 42, f. 168; 46, f. 150; *Leycester Corresp.* (Cam. Soc. xxvii), 83, 326, 367, 383, 405; *CSP For.* 1588 (Jan.–June), 33. [6] PCC 7 Sainberbe.

I.C.

ROGERS, Edward (*d.*1627), of Cannington, Som.

| MINEHEAD | 1584 |

s. of (Sir) George Rogers* by Jane, da. and h. of Sir Thomas Winter of Clapton. *educ.* ?Magdalen, Oxf. 1571. *m.* Catherine, da. of John Popham*, 4s. 2da. *suc.* fa. 1583.
    Commr. grain Som. 1586; j.p.q. Som. 1601, sheriff 1603–4.

Rogers was allied through his wife's sisters to the Champernowns, Horners, Warres and the Malletts of Enmore. Through his father-in-law, he became involved in the attempt to colonize Munster. Popham had been authorized to interest the gentlemen of the west country in the enterprise and three of his sons-in-law were among the undertakers. In June 1586, 19 seigneuries in Cork were granted to the Somerset undertakers, among whom Rogers was numbered. During the remainder of 1586 and in 1587 he was active in Irish affairs, making arrangements for defence and for the apportionment of land. By the end of 1587, however, he was disillusioned with the Munster project, finally, with many others of the original undertakers, abandoning it by March 1588.[1]

Another documented episode in Rogers's life was his quarrel with his brother-in-law John Harington, Queen Elizabeth's godson. Both men were hoping to secure for their children the estate of Lady Rogers, Edward's mother. In 1594 Harington sought redress against Rogers, who had reviled his wife, 'calling her names not fit to be spoken', while Harington and his servants had been physically attacked by Rogers and members of his household. In the event, when Lady Rogers died in 1598, her manors were divided among her Harington and Rogers grandsons. The sole executrix was her daughter, Mary Harington, and this gave Rogers the pretext he needed for a renewed attack on his brother-in-law. In January 1603, in the Star Chamber, he claimed that Harington had consulted Lady Rogers's physicians just before her death, and, learning that she could not live above ten days, had hurried to Cannington and removed plate valued at £5,000, as well as destroying Rogers's 'evidences' – the title deeds of the property bequeathed by Lady Rogers. He also alleged that, just before her death, Lady Rogers had accused Harington of robbing her and altering her will. Harington denied the charges, saying that he had acted only upon Lady Rogers's instructions, or· in the manner proper to an executor, in right of his wife. He claimed that the charges had been fabricated by Rogers 'with a desire rather than a hope

utterly to disgrace him'. If this was so, the hope was frustrated by the Privy Council, who referred the dispute to arbitration: 'as the parties are so near allied ... the King's will is that the arbitrament shall be speedily proceeded in, with all regard to preserve brotherly love and amity and to no prejudice to Lady Harington and her eldest son'.[2]

In 1584 Rogers took the senior parliamentary seat for Minehead, a borough under the patronage of the Luttrells of Dunster. There was no close connexion between the two families, for, although a daughter of Sir Andrew Luttrell had married a Rogers, he was a member of the family of Bryanston, Dorset, not that of Cannington. Edward Rogers must have known members of the Luttrell family as fellow justices, and there was a slight connexion through the Malletts: Elizabeth Luttrell had married Richard Mallett, and their grandson, Sir John, had married a daughter of Lord Chief Justice Popham, as had Rogers himself. In the next generation there was a Popham-Luttrell marriage and presumably the network of Malletts, Luttrells and Pophams was strong enough to obtain Rogers the seat.[3]

Rogers died in 1627. His lands were divided between the three elder sons, with a life interest to his wife, while monetary provision was made for the youngest son and two daughters. Sir Francis Popham*, his brother-in-law, was appointed overseer and directed 'to preserve the love and good liking between my wife and children, that there be no dissension between them'.[4]

[1] *Vis. Som.* (Harl. Soc. xi), 128; Foster, *Al. Ox.* iii. 1273; C142/197/52; Lansd. 48, f. 136; *APC* xiv. 70; *Vis. Som.* ed. Weaver, 44; PCC 58 Windebanke, 20 Windsor; *CSP Ire.* 1586–8, pp. 77, 113, 249–50, 271, 449, 508; 1588–92, pp. 69, 130. [2] *HMC Hatfield*, iv. 472; xvi. 99, 437; PCC 15 Montague; St. Ch. 5/R27/32; *CSP Dom.* 1623–5, p. 566. [3] Lyte, *Dunster*, 179; *Vis. Som.* 44; *Vis. Dorset* (Harl. Soc. xx), 79. [4] PCC 116 Skynner.

I.C.

ROGERS, Sir Edward (c.1500–68), of Cannington, Som.

| TAVISTOCK | 1547 |
| SOMERSET | 1553 (Mar.), 1553 (Oct.), 1558, 1559, 1563 |

b. c.1500, 1st s. of George Rogers of Langport by his w. Elizabeth. *m.* Mary, da. and coh. of Sir John Lisle of the Isle of Wight, 1s. George* ?3da. *suc.* fa. Sept. 1524. Kntd. 22 Feb. 1547.[1]
    Esquire of the body by Dec. 1534; bailiff of Hammes and Sangatte, Calais Dec. 1534–Oct. 1540; j.p.q. Dorset Mar. 1538–40, Som. Mar. 1538–53, from c.1559; sewer of the chamber by 1540, carver by 1544, gent. of privy chamber 15 Oct. 1549–July 1553, v.-chamberlain Nov. 1558–Jan. 1559, comptroller of the Household by 21 Jan. 1559; PC by 27 Nov. 1558.[2]

The death of Queen Mary saw Rogers already with Elizabeth at Hatfield and he was soon appointed to her

Privy Council, made vice-chamberlain and by January 1559 comptroller of the Household. This last was one of the few recommendations of Sir Nicholas Throckmorton* to be put into effect. The rudimentary journal of the 1559 Parliament does not mention Rogers by name, but as a Privy Councillor he probably played a part in the proceedings. He was active in both sessions of the 1563 Parliament, being explicitly noted as 'a chief member of that assembly and fellowship' and 'the chief Privy Councillor of the House' and it was he who nominated Thomas Williams as Speaker on 12 Jan. 1563. He was appointed to draw up the articles of a petition to the Queen on her marriage and the succession (19 Jan.) and he reported the Queen's answer (16 Feb.). The subsidy bill was committed to him on 27 Jan. As well as sending numerous bills to the Lords, he was put in charge of a bill on poaching (3 Feb.), was appointed to a privilege committee (1 Feb.) and spoke on procedure (27 Jan.). At the beginning of the 1566 session (1 Oct.) he again nominated the Speaker, Onslow, to replace Williams who had died. He was one of those Privy Councillors administering the oaths (4 Oct.) and he proposed the subsidy (17 Oct.). He spoke on the succession (19 Oct.) and headed the delegation from the Commons appointed on 23 Oct. to discuss the subject with the Lords, reporting on the outcome the same day. He was appointed to the conference with the Lords on 31 Oct., and headed the Commons delegation summoned to Whitehall on 5 Nov. to hear the Queen's message on the succession, which he and Sir William Cecil reported to the House the following day. His only other known activity in this session, apart from sending bills to the Lords, was his membership of the committee on apparel (5 Nov.). Rogers attended Privy Council meetings regularly until the end of 1565, then irregularly, and in the last year of his life, not at all, though he retained his court post. He made his last will 21 Apr. 1568. Apart from some small bequests to his sons-in-law and servants, all his property went to his only son, George, who also succeeded to the estates. He died 3 May 1568, the will being proved on the 21st.[3]

[1] DNB; C142/41/1; PCC 24 Bodfelde, 11 Babington; Vis. Som. (Harl. Soc. xi), 128; Lit. Rems. Ed. VI (Roxburghe Club), i. p. cccii. [2] LP Hen. VIII, vii. 598; xiii(1), p. 409; xvi. 98; xvii. 700; xix(1), p. 504; xx(2) p. 117; Genealogist, n.s. xxx. 19; Lansd. 2, f. 34; APC, ii. 345; CSP Span. 1558–67, p. 6; CPR, 1558–60, p. 59; Strype, Annals, i(2), p. 390. [3] CPR, 1558–60, p. 59; 1560–3, pp. 484–5; Strype, i(2), p. 390; EHR, lxv. 93; Camb. Univ. Lib. Gg. iii. 34, p. 209; D'Ewes, 45, 79, 80, 81, 83, 84, 85, 87, 88, 90, 91, 95, 103, 104, 107, 120, 121, 122, 124, 125, 126, 127, 128; CJ, i. 62, 63, 64, 65, 68, 71, 72, 73, 74, 75, 76; PCC 11 Babington; C142/41/1, 56, 148/28.

R.V.

ROGERS, George (c.1528–82), of Cannington, Som.

SOMERSET 1571

b. c.1528, o.s. of Sir Edward Rogers* by Mary, da. and coh. of Sir John Lisle of the Isle of Wight. m. by May 1551, Jane, da. and h. of Sir Thomas Winter of Clapton, 2s. inc. Edward* 1da. suc. fa. 1568. Kntd. 1574.

Commr. piracy Dorset 1565; sheriff, Som. 1571–2; j.p. Dorset from c.1561, Som. from c.1569, q. 1579.

Rogers was second on the poll in the contested Somerset election of 1571. He left no trace on the known surviving records of the House. In addition to the family lands he had estates in Cornwall in right of his wife. In contrast to his father, he lived as a country gentleman and most of the references found to him are concerned with his local official duties. He died on 10 Sept. 1582. In his will, made the previous June, he trusted to be saved 'only by the death and passion of Christ and not by any desert of mine own'. He made charitable legacies – £20 to the poor of the two parishes, Cannington and Pilton, where his largest estates lay, and £5 each to the parish churches there. His daughter Mary was to have £1,000 at her marriage, his younger son William lands in Dorset and Wiltshire and £100 on his 21st birthday, and the widow (the sole executrix) a life interest in the mansion house at Cannington, unless she remarried. Any property unbequeathed was to be equally divided between Lady Jane and the heir, the eldest son Edward, who married a daughter of John Popham*, the attorney-general. Popham himself, Sir Amias Paulet*, and Sir John Horner were the overseers.

Wards 7/11/73; E150/952/11; CPR, 1550–3, p. 44; 1566–9, p. 350; Vis. Som. (Harl. Soc. xi), 128; Som. RO, Phelips pprs.; LP Hen. VIII, xiii(1), p. 581; Hutchins, Dorset, ii. 620; APC, vii. 200, 283; x. 29; xi. 381, 399; xii. 34; Som. Rec. Soc. xx. 312, 315; C142/197/52; PCC 40 Tirwhite.

N.M.F.

ROGERS, John I (c.1555–1613), of Bryanston, Dorset.

WAREHAM 1584, 1586, 1589

b. c.1555, 2nd but e. surv. s. of Richard Rogers* and bro. of Andrew*. educ. New Inn; M. Temple 1575. m. (1) Jane or Joan (d. 1605), da. of Sir John Brown of Frampton, 1s.; (2) 1609, Margaret, da. of (Sir) Arthur Hopton, 1s. Kntd. 1603; suc. fa. 1605.

J.p. Dorset from c.1601.

Rogers presumably practised as a lawyer until he succeeded to the family estates. His last recorded appearance at the Middle Temple was in 1587, though the election return of October 1588, like that of 1586, described him as a gentleman of the Middle Temple. In 1601 he was concerned in land transactions with John Clavell* and with a member of the Strode family. He appears to have been patron of the living of Langton in Dorset. He was knighted after he became his father's heir on the death of his brother Andrew, and he succeeded to the family estates in 1605 when Sir Richard Rogers died aged almost 80. He was head of the family for less than ten years, dying 22 Dec. 1613. In his will, made 1 Dec. in that year, and proved the following 8 Feb., he left bequests to his wife, family and servants, and remembered the poor of Blandford.

Hutchins, *Dorset*, i. 250, 287; PCC 7 Lawe; *M. T. Mins.* i. 220, 236, 292; *Som. and Dorset N. and Q.* vi. 318; Wards 7/49/253; Roberts thesis.

P.W.H.

ROGERS, John II (*d.*1611/12), of Canterbury, Kent.

CANTERBURY   1601

> 1st s. of Richard Rogers, dean of Canterbury and suffragan bishop of Dover (*d.*1597), by Anne, da. of Thomas Digges of Newington. *educ.* ?G. Inn 1579. *m.* Mary Alcock, wid. of one Webbe.
> Freeman, Canterbury 1598.

The identification of the son of the dean as the MP for Canterbury in 1601 is conjectural, but likely, even though the dean was dead before the Parliament was called. The Canterbury MPs were appointed to two committees in the 1601 Parliament – for fustians, 4 Dec., and for silk weavers, 10 Dec. The Rogers family came from Sutton Valence in Kent, but the dean was a younger son and does not appear to have inherited property there. John Rogers may have been the man who entered Gray's Inn in 1579 (a reasonable date), but, apart from his appearance in the Kent visitation in 1594, nothing is known about him. He is not mentioned in his father's will and disappears from the Canterbury civic records after his election as a freeman of the city. Through his sister Sara's marriage to Thomas Boys* he was related to John Boys*, his fellow-Member for Canterbury in 1601. No will has been found. Rogers was buried in Canterbury cathedral 2 Jan. 1612. His wife was also buried there, 10 June the same year, and his mother 23 July 1613.

Vis. Kent (Harl. Soc. lxxv), 25, 143; D'Ewes, 668, 676; J. M. Cowper, *Freemen of Canterbury*, 323; PCC 61 Cobham; *Reg. Canterbury Cathedral* (Harl. Soc. Reg. ii), 113.

M.R.P.

ROGERS, Sir John (bef. 1507–65), of Bryanston, Dorset.[1]

DORSET   1545, 1547, 1555, 1559

> *b.* bef. 1507, 2nd but 1st surv. s. of Sir John Rogers by his 1st w. Elizabeth, da. of Sir William Courtenay of Powderham, Devon. *m.* 1523, Katherine, da. of Sir Richard Weston[†], 16s. (11 *d.v.p.*) inc. Richard* and Thomas* 4da. (2 *d.v.p.*). *suc.* fa. bet. June 1535 and Feb. 1536. Kntd. bet. July 1538 and Jan. 1540.
> J.p. Dorset 1528, q. by 1562; sheriff, Som. and Dorset 1552–3; duchy of Lancaster steward, lands in Dorset from 1531.[2]

Rogers owned extensive estates in Dorset, at Blandford, Bryanston, Hemsworth, Nutford and elsewhere, together with the 'house of the late Black Friars' at Melcombe

Regis, and several advowsons. He also leased mills and other property at Pimperne. He controlled parliamentary elections at Wareham, less than ten miles from land which he owned at Langton Matravers, and on two or three occasions may have used his influence to secure seats for nominees of the 2nd Earl of Bedford, with whom his family had a longstanding association. In 1559 Rogers brought in his collector for the hundred of Pimperne, Richard Shawe, at Melcombe Regis, as he had done in Mary's last Parliament. By this time Rogers was in financial difficulties, exacerbated by a Chancery case brought against him by Dame Margaret Luttrell, whose daughter was married to his heir Richard. Before his death, which occurred on 2 July 1565 at the house of his god-daughter Lady Essex, he executed a conveyance granting the use of his chattels to Sir John Zouche* and others. A further Chancery suit developed over this deed, the widow claiming that the creditors could not touch the property, the creditors that it was a device drawn up to defraud them. Rogers was buried at Blandford Forum, where a monument was erected in the parish church to him and his wife and children.[3]

[1] This biography is based upon the Roberts thesis. [2] Harl. 1539, ff. 78–9; Hutchins, *Dorset*, i. 214, 218, 225; *London Mar. Lic.* (Harl. Soc. xxv), 3; PCC 8 Alen; *LP Hen. VIII*, x. p. 158; xi. p. 85; xiii(1), g. 1519; xiv(2), p. 225; xv. p. 14; xxi(1), p. 486; Somerville, *Duchy*, i. 628–30; *Ducatus Lanc.* iii. 243. [3] C142/144/158; *CPR*, 1560–3, p. 533; 1563–6, p. 335; *PRO Lists and Indexes*, vii. 334; *Vis. Som.* ed. Weaver, 43; Hutchins, i. 225; C33/33, f. 211v.

N.M.F.

ROGERS, Richard (c.1527–1605), of Bryanston, Dorset.

DORSET   1572

> *b.* c.1527, 1st s. of Sir John Rogers* bro. of Thomas*. *m.* (1) Cecilia (*d.*1566), da. of Andrew Luttrell of Dunster Castle, Som., 2s. Andrew* and John I*; (2) Mary, da. of Owen West, bro. and h. of Thomas West, 9th Lord La Warre, wid. of (Sir) Adrian Poynings*, 1s. *suc.* fa. 1565. Kntd. 1576.
> J.p. Dorset from c.1570, sheriff 1573–4, 1587–8, commr. piracy 1581, col. of musters, Blandford division 1587–1600; lt. of the Isle of Purbeck 1588, dep. lt. by 1601.

Rogers took one turn as knight of the shire, for the long-lasting Parliament of 1572. He was put on a committee, 30 Jan. 1581, concerning wrecks. Described by a modern historian as 'a very great landlord ... and a very great pirate promoter', Rogers was deeply involved in the Dorset piracy scandal of 1577, being fined £100 and bound over to return his loot. Four years later, on the Elizabethan principle of setting a thief to catch a thief, he was granted a commission to eradicate piracy. In 1584 he was again in trouble, the Privy Council making him cool his heels at Windsor for 15 weeks before he was allowed to depart to attend the Dorset assizes. Yet the government knew he could be relied upon in time of danger. When the Armada threatened he travelled the county to inspect defence arrangements, submitting a detailed report to the Privy Council on forts and castles. From 1587 to 1600 he commanded one of the five Dorset defence divisions, and his estate near Blandford was used for training the musters and was designated an assembly point in case of invasion.

Rogers's second marriage to the widow of Sir Adrian Poynings probably coincided with the marriage of his eldest son Andrew to Poynings's daughter. Andrew's second marriage – to the daughter of the Duke of Somerset – led to her nephew, Lord Beauchamp, marrying Andrew's notorious sister Honora. The Earl of Hertford, Beauchamp's father, was opposed to the marriage and deputed one George Ludlow to discuss the situation with the Rogers family. According to Ludlow, who called Honora 'a baggage' and Sir Richard 'a fool', Beauchamp had originally intended to have 'but a night's lodging with her'. The Earl's opinion of Sir Richard was that, 'though outwardly he did nothing', either to oppose the marriage or to bring it about, his daughter had 'inwardly his goodwill'. Rogers's stepdaughter married George More*, the match being 'first moved by the good lord of Lincoln', and John Wolley* travelled to Dorset to arrange matters. This marriage led to an action in Chancery brought by Edward More* and his wife Mary against Sir Richard and Lady Rogers.[1]

Bryanston was a regular stopping place for the justices of assize on circuit, and Rogers entertained them until just before he died. In 1598 he was described as being over 80 years of age (an exaggeration), sick and bedridden, and no longer able to do the Queen service. Nevertheless, when his heir Andrew died he entered into a last controversy over his daughter-in-law's jointure, this time with her brother, the Earl of Hertford. The old man died in 1605, leaving a will in which he cut out his son Richard and his servants and said that only his daughter-in-law Jane – married to his second son John – had not displeased him.[2]

[1] R. Lloyd, Dorset Elizabethans, passim; Roberts thesis; Hutchins, Dorset, i. 250, 284; ii. 455; Harl. 3324, ff. 40, 59; 6993, f. 107; HMC Bath, iv. 191–3; HMC 7th Rep. 633, 634, 650; APC, ix. 329; x. 61, 72, 87, 106, 146, 216; xii. 241; D'Ewes, 289. [2] VCH Dorset, ii. 201; SP12/158/73; Cam. Misc. iv(2), pp. 29, 40; HMC Hatfield, ix. 77; xi. 28; APC, xxix. 432; PCC 31 Hayes.

P.W.H.

ROGERS, Thomas

WAREHAM   1593

2nd s. of Sir John Rogers* and bro. of Richard*.

The identity of the 1593 Wareham MP has not been established, but the Thomas Rogers identified above would be a natural choice to keep up the family interest at Wareham. Little information has survived about him. He was, at some time during Elizabeth's reign, a co-defendant

in a case in the court of requests concerning lands in Hascombe, Godalming and Dunsfold, Surrey. He owned property at Benham Valence, Berkshire and Bridgwater in Somerset. It is likely that the Thomas Rogers who married a widow Grizilla Rogers whose will was proved in 1628 was from a junior branch of the family in Gloucestershire.

Roberts thesis; Som. Wills, ii. 74; M. T. Recs. i. 229; PRO Lists and Indexes, xxi. 223; PCC 92 Barrington.

P.W.H.

ROKEBY, Ralph

HUNTINGDON   1571

There were two relatives, namesakes and burgesses, either of whom may have been the MP. Their family had provided benchers of Lincoln's Inn almost continuously from the reign of Henry VI, and, as one of them wrote, 'ever, in effect, from the creation of the council in the north parts, there hath been one or more of our name served in that council'.

The author of this statement was in 1571 probably still studying at Lincoln's Inn. He was

> 2nd s. of Ralph Rokeby, serjeant-at-law (d. c.1556), by Dorothy, da. of Thomas Danby. educ. Queens', Camb. 1562; L. Inn 1567. m. (1) Douglas (d.1586), da. of William Ferne, s.p.; (2) Joan, da. of John Portington, 2da.
>
> Dep. (to Robert Beale*) sec. council in the north and j.p. many northern counties from c.1587; steward, St. Katharine's hospital by the Tower 1589; jt. (with Beale) sec. council in the north by Oct. 1592.

He died on 12 Mar. 1595, and was buried at York.[1] He wrote Œconomia Rokebeiorum, which is the authority for much of the detailed information on his more eminent namesake and relative, who was

> b. c.1527, 2nd s. of Thomas Rokeby of Mortham, Yorks. by Jane, da. of Robert Constable of Everingham, Yorks. educ. ?Camb.; L. Inn 1547, called 1558. unm.[2]
>
> Bencher, L. Inn 1566, treasurer 1571; c.j. Connaught by July 1569–71; member, council in the north and j.p. many northern counties 1572–c.1582; master of St. Katharine's hospital and j.p. Mdx. 1584; master of requests by 1591.[3]

This man was chief justice of Connaught until 1571, but whether he was back in England in time to be appointed to the Commons committee on the treasons bill on 11 May that year has not been ascertained. The problem of identification is therefore no nearer solution. Either man could have been the MP, and either would have owed his return to a friend at court. The chief justice went on to become a member of the council in the north, for which he had been recommended by Sir Thomas Gargrave*. He was to be in continual attendance, with a salary of £50 and other perquisites. After his appointment as master of St. Katharine's, he moved to London, where he took part in the trials of Babington (1586), the Earl of Arundel (1589), Sir John Perrot* (1592) and others. This job and his subsequent appointment as master of requests made Rokeby a very wealthy man. His will, made on 14 June 1594 and proved on 8 July 1596, contains charitable bequests totalling over £1,000. It is an interesting document, bearing out the comment of Rokeby's namesake in the 1593 additions to his family history: 'Truly he hath much good in him, God be thanked for him'. Contemporaries thought that (Sir) Thomas Egerton II* made £10,000 from his position as executor and residuary legatee. Rokeby died on 14 June 1596, and was buried at St. Andrew's, Holborn.[4]

¹ [1] *Al. Cant.* i(3), 481; *Genealogist*, n.s. xv. 258; *DNB*; Add. 24470, ff. 307, 313, 323–4. [2] Stow, *Survey* (1633), 429b; *Fam. Min. Gent.* (Harl. Soc. xxxviii), 587 seq.; *L. Inn Black Bk.* i. 323, 350, 360, 380; *CSP Ire.* 1509–73, pp. 402, 425, 429; *Cal. Fiants Ire.* 1569–70, p. 212; Add. 24470. [3] *CSP Dom. Add.* 1566–79, p. 427; Lansd. 157, f. 8 seq.; C. Jameson, *R. Hosp. St. Katharine*, 79–81; *HMC Hatfield*, vi. 31; *CSP Dom.* 1547–80, p. 658. [4] *CSP Ire.* 1509–73, pp. 402, 422, 425, 429; *HMC Hatfield*, vi. 31; *CJ*, i. 89; D'Ewes, 183; *CSP Dom.* 1581–90, pp. 77, 268, 625; Add. 1566–79, pp. 424, 427; Add. 1580–1625, p. 81; Egerton 2345, ff. 3–35; Lansd. 155, ff. 254, 267; *CSP Scot.* 1574–81, p. 437; Howell, *State Trials*, i. 1127, 1251, 1315; *APC*, xxii. 551; *HMC 11th Rep. VII*, 154; *Egerton Pprs.* (Cam. Soc. xii), 110, 228–9, 308; PCC 53 Drake; *DNB*.

N.M.F.

ROLLE, John (b.1563), of St. Giles, Great Torrington, Devon.

CALLINGTON   1601

bap. 4 Aug. 1563, 7th s. of John Rolle of Stevenstone by Margaret, da. of John Ford of Ashburton. m. 21 Nov. 1603, Philippa, da. of Richard Halse of Kenedon, 2s. 1da.

A George Rolle†, keeper of records for the court of common pleas, purchased estates in Devon at the dissolution of the monasteries, and the senior branch of the family settled at Stevenstone, near Torrington. A junior branch was of Hearton and Petrockstowe. In the absence of any firm evidence it has been assumed that of several namesakes, it was George Rolle's grandson, a younger son of the senior branch, who sat for Callington in 1601, through the influence of the 4th Marquess of Winchester, to whom the Rolles were (or were shortly to be) related by marriage. Eventually the lordship of the manor of Callington came into the family, who represented it in several early seventeenth-century Parliaments. The date of Rolle's death is unknown. It must have been after May 1628, when he was the executor of his brother Robert's will. His own property was limited to a life interest in lands at Torrington and Buckland Brewer, but his son Henry succeeded to Stevenstone later that century.

Vivian, *Vis. Devon*, 279–80, 653, 654; R. Polwhele, *Hist. Devon*, ii. 223; J. Prince, *Worthies of Devon* (1810 ed.), 706, 709; PCC 122 Capell, 37 Barrington, 31 Lyon; *DNB* (Rolle, Henry and Rolle, John).

I.C.

ROOS, John, of Laxton and ?Egmanton, Notts.

EAST RETFORD   1597

2nd s. of Thomas Roos of Laxton by his 2nd w. Anne Pirton or Pinxton of Notts. m. a da. of Roos of Weston-upon-Trent, Staffs., 1s.

The main line of the Roos family, which acquired a barony in 1299, died out in the early sixteenth century. The title passed, through an heiress, to the Manners, earls of Rutland, then in 1591 to the Cecils. Thus Roos was not short of influential relations. Perhaps he was in the service of the 5th Earl of Rutland. However, his uncle Peter Roos was a j.p. and small landowner, well known in East Retford, so his local connexions may have been sufficient to account for his return. Roos was presumably the Mr. Rosse on a poor law committee (22 Nov. 1597) and a committee about soldiers and mariners (20 Dec. 1597). A Mr. Rose moved for privilege and was added to the privilege committee, 8 Dec. 1597. He was probably living at Egmanton, near Laxton, in 1614 – a man of this name acknowledged a debt of £10 to William Trinder of Nottingham – but after that date he disappears completely. His great nephew Thomas Maxfield was executed as a Catholic priest 1 Jul. 1616.

Vis. Notts. (Harl. Soc. iv), 111–12; *Vis. Notts.* 1662–4 (Thoroton Soc. rec. ser. xiii), 31; *CP*; D'Ewes, 561, 570, 575; *Nottingham Recs.* iv. 404; Wards 7/29/65; *Cath. Rec. Soc.* xxii. 90 n.

M.R.P.

ROSE, John (d.1591), of Canterbury, Kent.

CANTERBURY   1584,[1] 1586

m. 28 Oct. 1557, Ursula Stuard, wid., s.p. Alderman, Canterbury 1569, mayor 1574–5, 1583–4.

Rose, a tailor, may have been a member of the large family of that name which had lived for generations in the village of Chislet, north-east of Canterbury. No pedigree has been found, however, and his will provides no help on this point.

He was prominent in Canterbury affairs for many years before being returned twice to Parliament. During his first term as mayor the city acquired the Poor Priests' hospital, or Bridewell, which had just been surrendered to the Crown. According to a note on the back of the royal grant, Rose and Richard Gaunt, the sheriff, negotiated the acquisition of the hospital at a personal cost of £50, which was reimbursed by a tax on the city. A stronger indication of Rose's concern for the welfare of Canterbury was his desire to improve navigation on the river Stour: ships of any size could only come upstream as far as Fordwich, some three miles distant, and a dredging scheme he had tried to organise during his lifetime met with little success. In his will he left £300 to the mayor and commonalty to make the river navigable between Fordwich and Canterbury for ships of at least 10 tons. If the work had not been completed within six years the money was to be forfeited to his executors.

Rose died late in 1591, being buried in the parish church of St. George 4 Dec. His will was proved the following June.[2]

[1] Browne Willis. [2] J. Cowper, *Reg. St. George Canterbury*, 99, 171, 176, 177; Canterbury burmote bks.; Hasted, *Kent*, xi. 140, 141, 189; xii. 607; Lansd. 35, f. 68; F. Haslewood, *Parish of Chislet*, passim; *Reg. Abp. Parker* (Canterbury and York Soc.), 1139; Somner, *Antiqs. Canterbury*, 22–3; PCC 56 Harrington.

J.J.C.

ROTHERAM, George (1541–99), of Someries, nr. Luton, Beds.

BEDFORDSHIRE	1571, 1572, 1584, 1586, 1593
CLITHEROE	1597

b. 1541, 2nd s. of Thomas Rotheram of Someries by Alice, da. of Thomas Wellesford or Wilford, citizen of London. *educ.* G. Inn 1561. *m.* (1) Jane, da. of Christopher Smythe* of Annables, Herts., 2s. 1da.; (2) Elizabeth, da. of Richard Barnes, mercer, of London, at least 1s. *suc.* fa. 1562, gd.-fa. 1565.
J.p. Beds. from c.1569, sheriff 1575–6, 1590–1, commr. musters.[1]

There were two branches of the Rotheram family in Bedfordshire, the senior of Someries, the junior of Farley. The Elizabethan knight of the shire should not be confused with his namesakes of Farley, one of whom, for example, died in 1579, and another in 1593. Rotheram's father died in his own father's lifetime, and while George was under age. The boy's mother remarried, and his wardship was sold (for £26 13s. 4d.) to Christopher Smythe, his future father-in-law. He was licensed 9 Oct. 1564 to enter into his lands as his mother's son and heir from the time of his majority. An elder son, Thomas, was certified lunatic in 1552, and may have died young. The estates that came to Rotheram from his father – the manors of Kempston, Shillington and Houghton Conquest, valued by the court of wards at £39 6s. 8d. – were augmented by those he inherited from his grandfather, who died in 1565, and whose marriage into the St. John family of Bletsoe augmented Rotheram's own status in Bedfordshire. Rotheram was five times knight of the shire. He is not mentioned in the records of the House until 24 Feb. 1585 when he was put on the subsidy committee. He was not elected for the county in 1589, and presumably did not wish to come in for a borough. In 1593 he was on the

subsidy committee (26 Feb.), a legal committee (9 Mar.) and the committee for the continuation of statutes (28 Mar.). In 1597, unable, presumably, to secure election for the county, he went as far afield as the duchy of Lancaster borough of Clitheroe for a seat in Parliament, and then he appears on the return as junior to a young Gray's Inn lawyer. Perhaps his election there was arranged in some haste, as the rather late date of the document itself suggests, but why he should have gone to this trouble to be returned at all is not clear. His committees were on the penal laws (8 Nov. 1597), the poor law (22 Nov.), the lands of Sir John Spencer (25 Nov.) and maltsters (12 Jan.). In the two last committees his name appears juxtaposed with those of the knights of Bedfordshire and the burgesses of Bedford.[2]

In addition to the usual public duties of an Elizabethan country gentleman, the records show Rotheram performing a number of particular functions for the government, as, for instance on 29 Apr. 1586 when he was instructed by the Privy Council to help recruit men for the Low Countries, and when, some two years later, on 12 June 1588, he was one of three gentlemen who arranged with the Earl of Leicester and Sir Francis Knollys (respectively lord steward and treasurer of the Household) to compound for the delivery of certain provisions for the royal household. Rotheram's appointment as sheriff in 1575 marked the end of a centuries-old custom whereby Bedfordshire and Buckinghamshire had one sheriff between them. In 1594 Rotheram, armed with a pedigree supplied by Garter King of Arms, challenged the right of Henry, Earl of Kent, to the barony of Ruthin. The commissioners executing the office of earl marshal announced their findings against Rotheram on 22 June 1597, and this may have had a bearing on his failure to secure a county seat in the Parliament of that year.[3]

Rotheram made his will 18 Nov. 1599. He asked to be buried in his chapel at Luton. Elizabeth, 'my now wife', was, while she remained unmarried, to dwell at Someries with his eldest son John, the executor and residuary legatee, to whose care the younger children were committed. The will, witnessed by Thomas Snagge (probably his fellow MP in 1571 and 1586), was proved 21 Dec. 1599.[4]

[1] *Vis. Beds.* (Harl. Soc. xix), 50; Rylands Eng. ms 319; *CP*, vi. 161; Egerton 2345 Harl. 474. [2] *DNB*; Rylands Eng. ms 311; Wards 9/138, f. 372; *CPR*, 1563–6, p. 5; *VCH Beds.* iii. 300; D'Ewes, 356, 474, 496, 511, 553, 561, 563, 578; Townshend, *Hist. Colls.* 74, 103, 108. [3] *APC*, xiv. 80; *HMC 3rd Rep.* 274–5; *VCH Beds.* ii. 40 n; *CP*, vi. 161; vii. 166. [4] PCC 95 Kidd.

P.W.H.

ROUS, Anthony (bef. 1560–1620), of Halton St. Dominick, Cornw.

EAST LOOE	1584
CORNWALL	1604

b. bef. 1560, 1st s. of Richard Rous of Rogate, Suss. by Elinor, da. of Sir Edmund Marvyn. *m.* (1) Elizabeth, da. of Thomas Southcote* of Bovey Tracey, Devon, 5s. 1da.; (2) aft. Jan. 1585, Philippa (*d.*1620), da. of Humphrey Colles of Barton, Som., wid. of Alexander Pym* of Brymore, Som., 3da.; (3) 13 Sept. 1620, Susan (*d.*1633), da. of Sir Lewis Pollard of King's Nympton, Devon, wid. of John Copleston, *s.p.* suc. to estates of his uncle John soon aft. 1577. Kntd. 23 July 1603.[1]

J.p.q. Cornw. from c.1583, Devon from c.1592; sheriff, Cornw. 1587–8, 1602–3; dep. warden of stannaries; recorder, Launceston.[2]

Rous was the eldest son of a landless younger son. He was not made an executor of his father's will because of 'dwelling far off'. Soon after the death of his uncle in 1577 (whose brother and heir was over 60), he came into an estate on the Tamar, a few miles to the north of Saltash, which gave him some standing. He was one of the few Elizabethan Members to be returned for East Looe on his own local interest. Several of his relatives and friends also sat in 1584: two of his Marvyn cousins for Petersfield, Richard Carew of Antony for Saltash and Sir Francis Drake for Bossiney. Alexander Pym, whose widow Rous was to marry, represented Taunton.

Rous was an active member of the commission of the peace for Cornwall during the last two decades of Elizabeth's reign, being particularly concerned with piracy. When ships were to be arrested and the cargoes of privateers confiscated at Plymouth, he was usually one of those to whom the Privy Council sent its directions. In 1590 he was ordered to confiscate goods brought in by Hawkins and Frobisher, on the grounds that the Eastland ships they had taken were not lawful prize. The Cornish justices were to make plain 'how offensive it was to her Majesty that this licentious kind of dealing should be used'. The task was not easy. On another occasion Hawkins hijacked a cargo of cochineal that the commissioners had taken from him, and Rous and his colleagues were ordered to recover it.[3]

During 1596 he was much occupied with the affairs of Sir Francis Drake, who had recently died. Rous was one of the trustees of his friend's estate and one of the original executors of his will. This was disputed by Thomas, Sir Francis's brother, the question coming to the notice of the Privy Council. A master of requests was appointed to examine the rival claims. He found in favour of Thomas Drake. Rous and his fellow trustees continued to obstruct Drake in his attempts to execute the will, and the Privy Council instructed a serjeant-at-law to arbitrate. A letter to Sir Robert Cecil in August 1596 shows that the Privy Council was interested in goods held by the trustees, which should have gone to the Crown for the payment of £2,000 in sailors' wages owed by Drake, but which they refused to deliver.[4]

Rous was said to have been pricked sheriff in 1587

because of his stalwart protestantism, and when he served again in 1602–3, increasingly firm measures were taken against Cornish recusants. He was the patron and protector of several puritan ministers, but he was also the friend of Matthew Sutcliffe, dean of Exeter, and an active member of the High Commission.[5]

Rous continued to earn the respect of his Cornish neighbours for his charity, equity and piety during James I's reign as he had done under Elizabeth, and in 1604 sat as knight of the shire for the county where he had lived all his life. He died in 1620.

[1] *Vis. Cornw.* (Harl. Soc. ix), 194–5; Vivian, *Vis. Cornw.* 413; Vivian, *Vis. Devon*, 225, 598, 698; G. C. Boase and W. P. Courtney, *Biblio. Cornub.* 595; PCC 8 Daughtry. [2] PCC 38 Spencer; D. Gilbert, *Paroch. Hist. Cornw.* ii. 423; Lansd. 737, f. 133v; *CSP Dom.* 1591–4, p. 205; C. Fitzgeffrey, *Elisha His Lamentation …* (1622), pp. 43–4; R. and O. B. Peter, *Launceston*, 406. [3] *APC*, xix. 384, 399; xx. 4, 34, 82, 139, 141–2, 148, 226; xxi. 230–1, 345, 377; xxii. 37; xxiii 200. [4] *APC*, xxvi. 21, 49, 137–8; *HMC Hatfield*, vi. 347–8, 355. [5] A. L. Rowse, *Tudor Cornw.* 377, 395; Collinson thesis, 496; Devon RO. Bp. of Exeter mss. 21, ff. 25, 78; SP14/10a/81; *DNB* (Rouse, Francis; Fitzgeffrey, Charles; Hieron, Samuel; Sutcliffe, Matthew); S. Hieron, *Works* (1625), preface; *Elisha His Lamentation*, 37–8, 40–1; R. Winwood, *Mems.* iii. 160–1; T. Birch, *Mems. Q. Eliz.* i. 61.

I.C.

ROUS, Sir Edmund (by 1515–aft. June 1569), of Dunwich, Suff.

GREAT BEDWYN	1554 (Apr.)
DUNWICH	1554 (Nov.)
DOVER	1555
DUNWICH	1559

b. by 1515, 2nd s. of Sir William Rous of Dennington by Alice, da. of Sir John Sulyard[†] of Wetherden; bro. of Anthony[†]. *m.* Mary, da. and coh. of one Paynell of Lincs., 1da. Kntd. bet. Dec. 1550 and Sept. 1552.

Servant of Thomas Cromwell; servant of 3rd Duke of Norfolk.

J.p. Suff. 1543–?53; vice-treasurer of Ireland c.1553–5.[1]

Most of Rous's active career was over by the accession of Elizabeth. He was presumably the 'Sir Edward Rousse of Dunwich' who in September 1568 was granted letters of protection from arrest or seizure of his goods for a year: his low financial state may have accounted for his exclusion from the commission of the peace in Elizabeth's reign. It also no doubt accounts for his claiming wages and travelling expenses in respect of his parliamentary service after having promised not to. In June 1569, described as 'late of Dunwich', he was pardoned for the outlawry pronounced against him for non-appearances in the court of common pleas to answer a debt of £26 8s. 8d. When the pardon was enrolled Rous was in the Fleet prison. The date of Rous's death has not been ascertained. He may have been still alive in 1572.[2]

[1] *Vis. Suff.* ed. Metcalfe, 62, 174; *HMC 7th Rep.* 662; A. Suckling, *Hist. Suff.* ii. 366; *CPR*, 1547–8, p. 89; 1550–3, p. 428; 1553 and App. Edw. VI, p. 358; *LP Hen. VIII*, xviii(1), p. 133; xx(1), pp. 318, 322; *APC*, iv. 378. [2] *CSP Dom.* 1547–80, p. 318; C3/56/91; *CPR*, 1566–9, p. 413; Arundel Castle mss G1/7, f. 7v.

N.M.F.

RUGGE, Francis (1535–1607), of Norwich, Norf.

NORWICH   1589

b. 1535, 4th s. of Robert Rugge[t] by Elizabeth, da. of Robert Wood. *m.* Anne, da. of John Aldrich*, ?*s.p.*
    Freeman, Norwich 1563, alderman from c.1570, sheriff 1572–3, mayor 1587–8, 1598–9, 1602–3.

Rugge's elder brothers became landed gentlemen or clerics, while he inherited his father's position as a Norwich mercer. He was also left two manors and some money and plate on his father's death in 1559. As one of the Norwich burgesses in the 1589 Parliament he received wages of 5*s.* a day, and, on 11 Mar., he could have sat on committees considering the city of Lincoln and salted fish. He was named to the subsidy committee, 11 Feb. 1589. He died 18 Oct. 1607 and was buried in St. Andrew's, Norwich. His will was proved in the consistory court there in November 1609.

Vis. Norf. (Harl. Soc. xxxii), 229; Blomefield, *Norf.* iv. 307; H. Le Strange, *Norf. Official Lists*, 109; Norwich consist. ct. 447 Colman, 121 Turner; *Reg. Norwich Freemen*, ed. Millican, 101; PCC 27 Tirwhite; Norwich corp. ct. bk. 1587–95, p. 260; D'Ewes, 431, 444, 445.

R.V.

RUSH, Anthony, of Sudbourne, near Orford, Suff.

ORFORD   1571, 1572

1st s. of Arthur Rush of Sudbourne by Mary, da. of Sir Anthony Wingfield[t]. *m.* Eleanor, da. of Nicholas Cutler[t] of Eye, 2s. 1da. *suc.* fa. 1537.

Rush's estate of Sudbourne was within a mile or two of Orford, and his family had been connected with the Wingfields, who had the main influence there, for three generations. His grandfather (Sir) Thomas Rush[t] who had himself been a burgess of Orford, had represented Ipswich with Henry Wingfield[t], and had served with Sir Anthony Wingfield as a commissioner for the dissolution of the monasteries. His son and heir Arthur (father of Anthony) had married the daughter of Sir Anthony Wingfield. Sir Thomas and Arthur died within a month of each other in the summer of 1537, leaving Anthony to become the ward of Thomas Wriothesley[t]. Nothing further has been ascertained about Rush beyond the mention of an incident considered by the Privy Council in December 1574 when a London merchant complained of his 'disordered dealings about certain goods laden in a ship of Emden called the *Popinjay*, which perished at Orford'.

The sparseness of information, and the absence of life dates, leaves open the possibility that the MP was the third son of (Sir) Thomas Rush, and thus uncle and namesake of the above, or even that he was the son of Anthony Rush and Eleanor Cutler. In either case the same link with the Wingfields would account for the Orford returns to Parliament.

Vis. Suff. ed. Metcalfe, 23–4, 63; *HMC Var.* iv. 274, 275; *APC*, viii. 321, 326; mss at Orford.

N.M.F.

RUSHAM, Geoffrey (d. c.1589), of London and Suff.

SUDBURY   1586

m. Mary Garnett, ?*s.p.*

Rusham was presumably related to Thomas Risham or Rusham *alias* Barbor, mayor of Sudbury in 1559 and 1570. He may have been trained as a lawyer: in his will he bequeathed to his brother-in-law, Jasper Garnett, a number of law and Latin books. However, his name does not appear in the Elizabethan inns of court registers. Perhaps he attended an inn of Chancery. He evidently lived at, or near, Sudbury: at one time he was assessed for the 1585 subsidy there at 40*s.* The account notes him as 'removed'. His will mentions lands at Cornard Magna, Suffolk, a little over a mile from Sudbury, as still in his possession. In any case, he had enough local influence to be returned to Parliament for the town. His sister Elizabeth, married to William Cole, brother of Martin Cole*, was asked to distribute £4 to the poor of Sudbury in the will Rusham made in July 1587, proved on 12 June 1589.

PCC 51 Leicester; *Cal. Sudbury Muns.* ed. Stokes and Redstone, 52; Sudbury ct. bks. 1563–82, f. 107; 1585–99, f. 6.

N.M.F.

RUSSELL, Sir Francis (d.1585), of Alnwick and Berwick, Northumb.

NORTHUMBERLAND   1572, 1584

3rd s. of (Sir) Francis Russell[t], 2nd Earl of Bedford, by his 1st w. Margaret, da. of Sir John St. John[t] of Bletsoe, Beds.; bro. of John I* and William*. *m.* 15 July 1571, Juliana, da. and coh. of Sir John Foster of Bamburgh, 1s. Kntd. 28 Aug. 1570; *styled* Lord Russell from 1584.
    Chamberlain, Berwick-upon-Tweed from 1575; j.p. Northumb. from c.1573, q. 1580, sheriff 1577; border commr. 1581; capt. Tynemouth castle from 1583.[1]

Russell preferred the active, military life of the northern borders to a career at court. His father was at one time warden of the east march and governor of Berwick, and Russell was probably with him, though his name does not appear in the records of these parts until 1570, when he joined the Earl of Sussex's punitive expedition against the

Scots, in Annandale, being knighted by the earl at Carlisle. Three years later he distinguished himself at the siege of Edinburgh castle.

Between campaigns he may have stayed at Alnwick abbey, one of the houses of the warden of the middle marches, his friend Sir John Foster, whose daughter he married. Even to an earl's son, Foster, a formidable politician with great influence along the borders, could offer valuable patronage. In 1575 Russell was an obvious choice as chamberlain of Berwick, and in the following year, no doubt with Foster's backing, he secured the lease of part of the forfeited Neville estate in the barony of Baliol, on Tyneside.[2]

By the '80s, Russell was well established in Northumberland, and in virtually permanent residence either at Berwick, Alnwick, or, after 1583, at Tynemouth castle, which he gained from Sir Henry Percy's* custody in 1583. He visited the court early in 1582 when he was chosen to escort the Duke of Anjou to Antwerp, and he was elected to two Parliaments as knight of the shire for Northumberland, his recorded activity being his membership of the committee considering the bill for 'the better and more reverent observing of the Sabbath Day', 10 Dec. 1584 and the subsidy committee, 24 Feb. 1585. On 15 Feb. 1585 he took part in a conference with the Lords on procedure.[3]

On his return north, at the session's close, Russell occupied himself with Tynemouth castle, which he had found badly decayed. He frequently sent the Privy Council requests for ordnance and for his allowances, which had been stopped. On 27 July 1585, Russell accompanied his father-in-law to a meeting with some Scotch officials at Hexpathgate, on Windy Gail, during which he was shot. He died shortly afterwards, and was buried at Alnwick. The English government, prompted by Foster, claimed that the killing was premeditated and used it as a political lever to overthrow the Earl of Arran. Russell died only a few hours before his father, and the earldom passed to his son Edward, who was then only 13. In commending the young earl to the Queen, Foster wrote of the father:

No doubt but your Majesty lost a jewel of him, and the poor inhabitants of Northumberland had as great a loss of him as of any nobleman that ever came among them; and for his time, the like of his calling is not to be found that shall be so well thought of with poor and rich as he was.[4]

[1] CP; PRO Index 16774, f. 120v; Border Pprs. i. 35; Hist. Northumb. (Northumb. Co. Hist. Comm.), viii. 165–6. [2] DNB (Russell, Francis, 2nd Earl of Bedford); CSP Scot. iv. 568; J. H. Wiffen, House of Russell, i. 484–5; C. Sharpe, Memorials of the Rebellion, p. 26; Hist. Northumb. vi. 94, 150–1, 270. [3] Hist. Northumb. viii. 165–6; Camden, Eliz. (4th ed.), 273; D'Ewes, 337, 349–50, 356. [4] CSP Dom. Add. 1580–1625, pp. 142, 143, 145, 160–1; Border Pprs. i. 188 passim; Arch. Ael. ii. 289 seq.; D. L. W. Tough, Last Years of a Frontier, 238–40; C142/211/182.

B.D.

RUSSELL, John I (d. 1584), of Blackfriars, London.

| CHIPPING WYCOMBE | 1571 |
| BRIDPORT | 1572* |

2nd s. of (Sir) Francis Russell†, 2nd Earl of Bedford, by his 1st w., and bro. of Sir Francis* and William*. m. 23 Dec. 1574, Elizabeth (d. 1609), da. of Sir Anthony Cooke* of Gidea Hall, Romford, Essex, wid. of Sir Thomas Hoby, 2da. summ. to Lords in his fa.'s barony as Lord Russell Jan. 1581.

Russell married a sister-in-law of Lord Burghley, and the Queen and the Earl of Leicester were godparents to the daughter born in 1575. Both Russell's seats in Parliament were obtained through the influence of his father. On the second occasion some doubt arose as to whether he could continue in his seat after the death of his elder brother entitled him to a courtesy title, and his membership of the Commons was confirmed 9 Feb. 1576. He was appointed to committees concerned with ports (13 Feb.), wines (21 Feb.), church discipline (29 Feb.) and the petition urging the Queen to marry (12 Mar.). Later that year he travelled in Germany and Italy. He was raised to the peerage before the next and last session of the Parliament.

Russell died v.p. at Highgate in July 1584. Administration was granted to his widow on 9 Oct. 1584: a further grant was made, 22 Oct. 1618, to their daughter Anne, Lady Herbert.

CP; J. H. Wiffen, House of Russell, i. 501; Genealogist, n.s. iii. 25; Roberts thesis; CJ, i. 104, 105, 107, 109, 114; PCC admon. act bk. 1584, f. 118; 1618, f. 201v.

P.W.H.

RUSSELL, John II (1551–93), of Strensham, Worcs.

| DROITWICH | 1572 |
| WORCESTERSHIRE | 1584, 1586, 1589 |

b. 1551, 1st s. of Sir Thomas Russell* by his 1st w. Frances, da. of Sir Roger Cholmley*. educ. prob. Oxf. m. 1575, Elizabeth, da. of Ralph Sheldon*, 2s. inc. Thomas* 1da. suc. fa. 1574. Kntd. 1587.[1]

J.p. Worcs. from c.1575, sheriff 1577–8, escheator 1586–8, dep. lt. 1587.

Russell was brought up in the household of the 2nd Earl of Bedford, with whom the family claimed kinship. Probably, like the earl's youngest son, William Russell*, whose close friend Russell became, he went to Oxford, but too many John Russells attended the university in the 1560s and early 1570s for identification of his career there to be feasible. His family's hereditary possession of salt-pans in the borough of Droitwich accounts for his return in 1572.[2]

Russell spent some time abroad, even after succeeding to his estates. He probably accompanied his friend William Russell for at least part of his continental tour in the late 1570s, and fought in the Low Countries under Leicester, being knighted there in 1587.[3]

In Worcestershire his quarrels with relatives and neighbours disturbed the county. His character, indeed, was summed up in a note on a j.p. list, which commended him for 'forwardness in religion, but not so for discretion'. The first dispute, which nearly terminated in bloodshed, was with his stepmother's second husband, Henry Berkeley II*, and concerned her dower lands. The parties are supposed to have been reconciled by Bishop Whitgift, acting president of the council in the marches in Sidney's absence. If so, it must have been yet another dispute for which Russell, while sheriff, was summoned before the Privy Council for refusing to obey the council in the marches. In 1582 Whitgift is again said to have intervened, this time to terminate a disagreement between Russell and Thomas Hanford, his neighbour at Strensham, over the waters of the Avon, which both parties were diverting to their own use, to the inconvenience of others. A more protracted quarrel was waged with his wife and her father, both Catholics. However suitable so far as wealth and social standing were involved, a match between one of Russell's protestant upbringing and a Catholic, could scarcely have been expected to run smoothly. Trouble broke out almost at once. By 1578 Russell had decided to exclude the issue of the marriage from succession to his estates, and on 31 Dec. conveyed his property by indenture to the 2nd Earl of Bedford and Gilbert Lyttelton*, to hold to the use of an entail barring his children by Elizabeth Sheldon, subject only to the proviso that he might at any time by a sealed deed alter the entail. Despite this, he appears to have lived with his wife at least at times in the following years, although she later accused him of ill-treatment. In 1583 Russell caught a priest who confessed to saying mass in Sheldon's house and in Russell's own during his absence overseas. Russell appears to have attempted to use this disclosure against his father-in-law, but no corroboration of the priest's statement was forthcoming and there was evidently no prosecution. About 1583 Russell and his wife finally separated. Russell's friends later asserted that Sheldon by his power in the county threatened Russell with ruin, but a fair part of the blame was apparently Russell's own. Sheldon initially complained to the council in the marches, who, after an attempt at reconciliation, frustrated by Russell, reported to the Privy Council. Formal deeds of separation were drawn up by the lord chancellor and master of the rolls, but Russell, after accepting the arbitration, claimed that the income allowed his wife was too great. Probably in March 1584 he made a new and lower offer to his wife, on the grounds that 'he meant to be good to his children, who should be no further burden' to her. Again he changed his mind and threatened to send Sheldon and his sons a challenge. A messenger was sent to Sheldon and, although the latter denied him private speech, a clash took place at Harewell woods. Another was narrowly averted at Worcester quarter sessions. Russell attacked Sheldon's house on the pretext of re-claiming his daughter – presumably he already had custody of his sons – and Sheldon's son attacked Russell's house in London. Thereupon Russell brought a suit in Star Chamber, reviving his old allegations of papistry against Sheldon. It would seem that the court finally settled the dispute: at all events, in July 1585 Russell rescinded the provisions in his earlier indenture and restored his children to their place in the succession.[4]

In the midst of this dispute Russell was elected senior knight of the shire for the first time, apparently without opposition. As such he was put on the subsidy committee 24 Feb. 1585. He was given leave of absence from Parliament, 5 Mar. 1585, 'for his great business'. In 1586 and 1589 he was again senior knight for Worcestershire and as such he could have sat on the subsidy committees, 22 Feb. 1587 and 11 Feb. 1589. He continued throughout to hold county office. The assertion that he was attainted about this time rests on no more than the supposed 'sale' of Strensham, 'late of John Russell attainted', to Walter Copinger and Thomas Butler. The grant refers to a concealment of lands going back to the mid-fifteenth century when an ancestor and namesake was punished for his part in the Wars of the Roses. The grant, for a consideration, removed a possible flaw in Russell's own title.[5]

In August 1590 Russell was recommended by the 2nd Earl of Pembroke for membership of the council in the marches, but was not appointed. In 1592 he obtained licence to travel overseas. It is not known whether he went, but by September 1593 he had returned to Strensham to die. Under his will, made in April 1587 before he set out for the Low Countries, he bequeathed his soul to God, 'most humbly beseeching Him, even for Jesus Christ's sake ... by whose precious death and passion my only hope and trust is to be saved', to receive it. His younger children were suitably provided for, and as his executor he appointed his old friend, (Sir) William Russell. He had been a careful custodian of the family estates inherited from his father, and had added to them, amongst other lands, the manor of Eckington.[6]

[1] *Vis. Worcs.* (Harl. Soc. xxvii), 119; PCC 64 Lewyn; C142/241/126. [2] J. L. Hotson, *I, William Shakespeare*, 21–2; HMC *Hatfield*, ii. [3] St. Ch. 5/R41/32; Hotson, 37; *VCH Worcs.* iv. 204. [4] Strype, *Annals*, iii(2), p. 457; Fuller, *Worthies*, iii. 382; APC, x. 217; Strype, *Whitgift*, i. 217; C142/241/126; St. Ch. 5/R41/32, S15/38, R12/34. [5] Lansd. 43, anon. jnl. f. 171; D'Ewes, 409, 431; VCH Worcs. iv. 204; *CSP Dom.* 1581–90, p. 622; APC, xix. 304; xxi. 404; C66/1328, m. 31; LR2/70–1. [6] Lansd. 63, f. 95; 111, f. 43 seq.; *Signet Office Docquet Bks. 1584–1624* (Brit. Rec. Soc., Index Lib.), 25; PCC 64 Lewyn; C142/239/124; Habington's *Worcs.* (Worcs. Hist. Soc.), i. 32, 132, 188, 199, 201, 268–9, 303, 310, 312, 389–94, 416, 488; ii. 57, 112, 128, 142, 159, 251, 258, 306, 315; *VCH Worcs.* iii. 424; iv. 27, 71, 96, 148, 167, 202, 331.

S.M.T.

RUSSELL, Thomas (1577–1632), of Strensham, Worcs.

WORCESTERSHIRE   1601

b. 1577, 1st s. of John Russell II* of Strensham. *educ.* St. John's, Oxf. 1591. *m.* 1597, Elizabeth, da. of William Spencer of Yarnton, Oxon., 2s. 3da. *suc.* fa. 1593. Kntd. 1603.

    J.p. Worcs. from 1600, dep. lt. 1603, sheriff 1603–4; master of game in Malvern chase from 1610.

His parents having separated, Russell was brought up in his father's household, and succeeded to the estates aged only 16. He was elected junior knight of the shire to the first Parliament after he came of age. His name is not to be found in its journals, but as a county Member he could have attended the main business committee appointed 3 Nov., that on monopolies appointed 23 Nov. and another, on the assurance of certain manors, 9 Dec. He became a j.p., deputy lieutenant and sheriff, but by 1610 he had openly adopted his mother's religion and become a recusant, remaining, however, on the commission of the peace. Russell died 30 Dec. 1632, his estate not noticeably diminished by his recusancy.

Vis. Worcs. (Harl. Soc. xxvii), 119; (xc), 84; *VCH Worcs.* iii. 204; iv. 25, 27, 204–7, 367, 372; C142/239/124, 241/126, 580/97; *Q. Sess. Pprs. 1591–1643* (Worcs. Hist. Soc.), passim; PRO Index 4208; *APC*, xxxii. 251; D'Ewes, 624, 649, 673; *CSP Dom.* 1603–10, pp. 593, 621; J. L. Hotson, *I, William Shakespeare*, 45–8, 266–8, 288; PCC 1 Russell.

S.M.T.

RUSSELL, Sir Thomas (c.1520–74), of Strensham and Witley, Worcs.

WORCESTERSHIRE   1542*, 1547, 1553 (Oct.), 1559, 1571

b. c.1520, o.s. of Sir John Russell† of Strensham by Edith, da. of Sir Thomas Unton† of Wadley, Berks. *educ.* G. Inn 1544. *m.* (1) by 1544, Frances, da. and coh. of Sir Roger Cholmley*, 1s. John II* 1da.; (2) Margaret, da. of William Lygon of Madresfield, Worcs., 1s. Kntd. 17 Nov. 1549; *suc.* fa. 15 Aug. 1556.

    J.p. Worcs. bef. 1555, q. by 1562, sheriff 1551–2, 1559–60, 1569–70, commr. musters, custos rot. by 1573; supervisor or surveyor, lands of bp. of Worcester by 1564; steward, manor of Martley by 1570; of lands late of Pershore and Great Malvern abbeys, Worcs. at *d.*; commr. to enforce Acts of Uniformity and Supremacy 1572, musters, Worcs. 1573.

Of a family established at Strensham by the end of the thirteenth century, Russell was a little over 21 when first elected for the county. References to him for Elizabeth's reign are almost entirely from official sources, such as the description of him as a favourer of true religion in 1564, and his being asked to 'take care in the good assessing' of the Worcestershire subsidy in 1565. The only domestic incident found was his acceptance of an invitation, in December 1561, to be godfather to Edwin Sandys II*, son

of the bishop of Worcester. During the 1571 Parliament he is mentioned once as being put on a committee the business of which does not appear.

A few days before his death on 9 Apr. 1574, Russell made his will. After a lengthy religious preamble, arrangements were made for the disposal of the non-entailed land. Russell's wife, the executrix (who later married Henry Berkeley II*) was to administer a legacy for the marriage of 20 poor maidens which his father-in-law Sir Roger Cholmley had asked him to supervise. Another clause concerned a promise by Ralph Sheldon* to pay £550 on the marriage of his eldest daughter Elizabeth to Russell's elder son John, who had been brought up in the 2nd Earl of Bedford's household. There were generous bequests to retainers, including two years' wages to the 'gentlemen and yeomen servants', and to Martha Sheldon, in consideration of her long service, £20 towards her marriage. 'Old Humphrey' was 'to have his finding with my wife during his life'. The will also contained a schedule of plate, some of it formerly Sir Roger Cholmley's, kept in 'the tower at Strensham'.

C142/108/128, 172/163; *VCH Worcs.* iv. 203–4; *Vis. Worcs.* (Harl. Soc. xxvii), 119; PCC 17 Ketchyn, 8 Pyckering; SP12/93; *Cam. Misc.* ix(3), pp. 1, 4, 5; Lansd. 8, f. 81; 56, f. 168 seq.; *Habington's Worcs.* (Worcs. Hist. Soc.), ii. 196; *CPR*, 1557–8, p. 337; 1560–3, p. 380; 1569–72, pp. 440 seq.; 1572–5, p. 243; *CSP Dom.* 1547–80, p. 460; Nash, *Worcs.* ii. 222; *CJ*, i. 93.

N.M.F.

RUSSELL, William (c.1553–1613), of Thornhaugh, Northants., Northall, Bucks., and Chiswick, Mdx.

FOWEY   1572

b. c.1553, 4th s. of (Sir) Francis Russell†, 2nd Earl of Bedford, by his 1st w. Margaret, da. of Sir John St. John* of Bletsoe, Beds.; bro. of Sir Francis* and John I*. *educ.* Magdalen Coll. Oxf. *m.* 1585, Elizabeth (*d.*1611), da. and h. of Henry Long* of Shingay, Cambs., 1s. Kntd. 1581; *cr.* Baron Russell 1603.[1]

    Gent. pens c. 1572–93/6; lt.-gen. of horse in Netherlands 1585; gov. of Flushing 1587–9; j.p.q. Cambs., Mdx. from c.1592; j.p. Northants. from c.1586; ld. dep. [I] 1594–7; cdr. of forces in western counties 1599.[2]

Various reasons have been advanced against this William Russell having been the Fowey MP. First, that having been born in 1558, he was in 1572 too young to be returned to Parliament. The historian of the Russell family has established, however, a birth date of about 1553, so that Russell would have been 19 in 1572, not at all too young to sit in Parliament at this period. Next, he is known to have spent several years in his youth travelling abroad. This does not mean, however, that he was not in England for at least the first session of the 1572 Parliament, for his licence to go abroad for three years is dated January 1575. In 1572 the 2nd Earl of Bedford would have had no difficulty in returning his son at Fowey. No contribution by Russell to the business of the Commons has been recorded.[3]

While he was still a child his father settled lands, including the manor of Thornhaugh, upon him, and his position as a wealthy country gentleman was further assured by his marriage in 1585 to the sole heiress of Henry Long. Long's father, Sir Richard, had profited from the dissolution of the monasteries, and extensive lands in Cambridgeshire and the manors of Clifton, Pilling Shingay and Eversholt in Bedfordshire as well as property in Hertfordshire, passed to his granddaughter's husband. Russell continued to add to his lands, the principal acquisitions being the lordships of Chenies, Buckinghamshire, and Tuddington in Northamptonshire, which passed to him upon the death of his brother Edward, and the manor of Northaw in Hertfordshire which he acquired from his sister, the Countess of Warwick.[4]

For a younger son of the puritan 2nd Earl of Bedford, and one who later came under the influence of the Calvinist Dr. Humphrey of Magdalen, the life of a country gentleman was inadequate. Russell therefore became a soldier in the two theatres where protestantism was most threatened – the Netherlands and Ireland. His first major appointment came in 1585, when he accompanied the Earl of Leicester to the Netherlands as lieutenant-general of horse. He was not a novice in military matters, for he had already spent a year in Ireland in 1580–1, commanding a troop in County Wicklow. During his stay in the Netherlands, his reputation as a soldier grew and he played a distinguished part in the battle of Zutphen, in which his friend Sir Philip Sidney* lost his life. Russell took over from Sidney not only his best gilt armour, but also the governorship of Flushing, and thereafter his attention was engrossed by the task of maintaining the town and garrison in good order. His difficulties, which were great, all stemmed from the failure of the English government to make adequate payments. In September 1587 the garrison had been unpaid for twelve months, and as late as 1591 Russell and his men were owed £4,046. At times mutiny was prevented only by Russell's contributions out of his own estate to pay the soldiers, so that his plea that he was 'greatly impoverished by [the Queen's] service and not by any foolish humours of my own' was no exaggeration. Further, he was in constant fear lest some of the companies under his command should be transferred elsewhere and the garrison – which was already 'so weak, evil armed and worse paid' – thus seriously weakened. To this was added in the autumn of 1587 the dread that the Queen would make peace. He wrote frankly to Sir Francis Walsingham*: 'I am not a little sorry to see her Majesty run so violent a course for peace, which can in no way be good for her nor these countries', adding that the States hesitated on this account to give the Earl of Leicester

greater authority, fearing that he would be ordered by the Queen to make peace. Nor did Russell's relations with the States make his position any easier. At his arrival he had been popular and remained so in the town of Flushing, but his close adherence to Leicester in his quarrel with the States aroused their hostility, which his own activities after Leicester's departure intensified. Throughout this period he was closely associated with Leicester and Walsingham, the spokesmen of the protestant cause. It was to Walsingham that his despatches – pleas for money, provisions and support – were addressed, and in October 1587 he asked the secretary to be godfather to his son. It was to these two that he directed his increasingly urgent pleas for recall from a post 'wherein I neither reap profit, honour nor content'. At first he hoped to be appointed master of the ordnance, 'that the world might see I parted not with this government in disgrace, the which some of the Estates have already given out', but when he was recalled in June 1589 he received no consoling office. His departure occasioned rejoicing in Antwerp, where the effects of his good government of Flushing had been wryly appreciated.[5]

After his return from the Low Countries, Russell was unemployed for some years, until in 1594 he was sent as lord deputy to Ireland. After an initial blunder, when he allowed Tyrone to escape, Russell's conduct of operations against the Irish leader was exemplary. In Ireland, as in the Netherlands, he put his faith in a vigorous prosecution of the war, rather than in a negotiated peace. This attitude brought him into conflict with Sir John Norris*, lord president of Munster, who hoped that a settlement could be reached. The two policies appear to have been tried alternately, neither with success. Norris managed to secure the home government's approval for a truce with Tyrone, and – what was even more galling for Russell – obtained the recall of Sir Richard Bingham, who was one of the lord deputy's most active lieutenants. Norris and Russell each believed that the other undermined his efforts, and in the spring of 1597 Norris protested openly when Russell mobilised all his forces to suppress a rising in Wicklow and to capture its ringleader, Fiach MacHugh O'Byrne. In this Russell was successful, but his recall soon followed and he returned home 'very fat, they say, both in body and purse'.[6]

Hereafter, Russell's part in active affairs almost ceased. He was appointed commander of the western forces in the summer of 1599, but the anticipated Spanish invasion did not materialise. He appears to have been regarded as an authority on Irish affairs, upon which he was sometimes consulted by the Privy Council, but with the death of Elizabeth even this passive role ceased. He spent the remaining years of his life in retirement at Northall, having left the court, it is said, in disgust at the licentiousness and profligacy reigning there. He emerged from retirement once only, to attend the funeral of Prince

Henry, to whose accession he had looked for the re-establishment of virtue and good government.[7]

Russell died 9 Aug. 1613. His will, made in the previous October, contains his affirmation of faith,

> knowing assuredly that I shall leave this earthly tabernacle and by God's mercy and the only merits of His only Son mine only Saviour, I shall enjoy and inherit the heavenly and eternal kingdom, whereunto I was ordained and elected before the foundation of the world.

Bequests of jewels and plate were made to his sister, the Countess of Cumberland, to his nieces Lady Anne Clifford and Lady Ann Herbert, and to his cousins Oliver, 3rd Baron St. John of Bletsoe, Mr. Dennys and Mr. George Russell. His nephew, the 3rd Earl of Bedford, was to receive his best horse and sword, and bequests of £10 each went to the poor of Thornhaugh, Northall and Chiswick, while his servants were to receive three years' wages. The residue of the estate was to go to his son and executor Francis. 'My loving cousin', Lord St. John of Bletsoe, and 'my loving uncle', Edward Alford, were appointed executors. Russell was buried, as he had directed, in the church at Thornhaugh, where he had already built his tomb.[8]

[1] *DNB*; *CP*, xi. 239–40; J. H. Wiffen, *House of Russell*, i. 506. [2] *CSP For.* 1585–6, p. 277; 1586–7, p. 348; *APC*, xvii. 421–6; Hatfield ms. 278; *CSP Dom.* 1591–4, p. 482; 1595–7, p. 288; *Chamberlain Letters* ed. McClure, i. 80. [3] G. Scott Thomson, *Fam. Background*, 147–8; E157/1. [4] *VCH Northants.* ii. 530–1; Bridges, *Northants.* ii. 395; *VCH Herts.* ii. 358; *VCH Beds.* ii. 277; iii. 332, 376; C142/342/117, 362/164. [5] *CSP For.* 1586–7, pp. 164–5, 312, 348, 364, 432, et passim.; 1587, pp. 76, 79–80, 334–5, 335, 380, 388, 390, 450, 453; 1588 Jan.–June, pp. 25, 28, 53, 290, 398–9, 400, 409–10, 437, 477; July–Dec., pp. 271–2, 281, et passim; 1589 Jan.–July, pp. 12, 55, 169, 190, 210, 225, 243; 1589–90, passim; *APC*, xvii. 421–6; *CSP Dom.* 1591–4, p. 64; Wiffen, ii. 2–5. [6] R. Bagwell, *Ireland under the Tudors*, iii. 242–79; Wiffen, ii. 14, 21–52; *CSP Ire.* 1592–6 and 1596–7, passim; *Cal. Carew Pprs.* iii. 220–60, et passim; *Chamberlain Letters*, i. 30. [7] *Chamberlain Letters*, i. 80–1, 83; *CSP Dom.* 1598–1601, p. 297; Wiffen, ii. 54, 89. [8] C142/342/117; PCC 86 Capell; *VCH Northants.* i. 419–20; ii. 532; Wiffen, ii. 89–93; Walker, *A Sermon preached at the funeral of William, Lord Russell*.

I.C.

RYLEY, Hugh (c.1540–aft. 1603), of Salisbury, Wilts.

WESTBURY 1563

b. c.1540, 3rd s. of Thomas Ryley of Le Grene, Lancs. by Joan, da. and coh. of James Whitaker of Henthorne, Lancs. *educ.* Brasenose, Oxf. 1552, BA 1555, founder's fellow 17 Oct. 1556, junior bursar 1558–9. *m.* Mary, da. of George Ludlow of Hill Deverell, Wilts.[1]

Steward of John Jewel, bp. of Salisbury 1559–71.[2]

It was probably while he was at Oxford that Ryley met John Jewel, whose service he was afterwards to enter. Jewel taught at Oxford until early in 1555, when he fled to the Continent, and remained an exile for four years. During this time Ryley took his degree and became fellow and junior bursar of his college. Jewel was named bishop of Salisbury in July 1559 and consecrated in the following January; and it is likely that Ryley rejoined him as his steward at the outset of his episcopate. Ryley continued in Jewel's service until his death in 1571, and the bishop paid him a notable tribute by making him, and his fellow-servant William Chambers, executors of his will and by bequeathing to them £50 each in money and the residue of his goods after his many other legacies had been discharged.[3]

Ryley may already have had a connexion with Wiltshire through his mother Joan, with whose family the Whitakers of Westbury (one of whom also sat in Parliament), were perhaps related. It was, however, his marriage to Mary Ludlow, which probably took place while he was serving Jewel, that gave him a footing in Wiltshire society. His father-in-law was sheriff in 1559 and again in 1568, and his brother-in-law Edmund was to begin his long parliamentary career as Member for Old Sarum in 1571, a youthful success to which Ryley's influence may have contributed. Ryley's own return for Westbury he probably owed to his Whitaker connexion, doubtless reinforced by the support of the bishop. It would be interesting to know what the servant of so prominent an ecclesiastic made of the religious issues in that Parliament; but Ryley finds no mention in the record of its proceedings.

Little has come to light about Ryley's later career. He evidently made his home in Salisbury, and it was as a gentleman of the city that at an unknown date he received a grant of arms. In 1581 his wife had a legacy of £20 from her father. Ryley himself was still alive in November 1603, when the inquisition post mortem of John Riley, whose relationship if any to Hugh is not known, recorded an obligation to pay him 20 marks a year for life. Ryley's will has not been found nor has the date of his death been established.[4]

[1] Harl. 1408 f. 157v; *Wilts. Arch. Mag.* xxvi. 173; *Wilts. Vis. Peds.* (Harl. Soc. cv, cvi), 240. [2] Harl. 988 f. 2. [3] PCC 43 Holney. [4] *Two Taxation Lists* (Wilts. Arch. Soc. recs. br. x); *Wilts. Vis. Peds.* 240; PCC 4 Darcy; C142/280/85; Wards 38/175.

S.T.B.

RYTHER, James (1536–95), of Harewood, Yorks.

APPLEBY 1586

b. 1536, o.s. of William Ryther of Canterbury, Kent, and Harewood by Mary, da. of Sir James Hales, l.c.j. common pleas. *m.* c.1570, Elizabeth, da. and coh. of William Atherton of Harewood, 2s. 5da. *suc.* fa. 1563.

J.p. Yorks. (W. Riding) by 1587, q. 1595.[1]

By his own account Ryther was born in Kent and brought up in Northamptonshire. In 1563 he succeeded to the moiety of the manor and castle of Harewood which his father had inherited on the death of a distant cousin, and eventually moved back to Yorkshire. He was descended from Thomas, son of Sir Thomas Ryther (or Ryder) of Ryther in the West Riding, and related through the descendants of Thomas's brother Sir Ralph to the Constables of Flamborough and the Ashes of Aughton, who in turn were related to the Cliffords, earls of Cumberland, the nominal patrons of the borough of Appleby. That he owed his election directly to his kinship with the 3rd Earl is not unlikely, but he was also known to several members of the Russell family and to Lord Burghley.[2]

In a short sequence of letters beginning in 1587 when he had lived in Yorkshire for 20 years and was one of its justices of the peace, Ryther described to Burghley the condition of the county and the district around Kendal. York was very badly governed; the poor committed great disorders which might be prevented if gentlemen were forbidden to dismiss their servants; there was too much engrossing of corn; the number of alehouses had increased because the justices' clerks were making money out of licensing them; the justices were inadequate and too few; and the common people, though courteous and tractable, were attached to custom and not readily disposed to accept the high authority of Parliament; the only northern gentleman worthy of his calling was the Earl of Cumberland; the further north one went, 'the less the truth'; the borderers sold horses to our 'back friends' the Scots; Scottish faults were spreading into England, and so on. In one letter, dated 7 Apr. 1588 but endorsed 7 Apr. 1589, he enjoins Burghley to bear with Christian fortitude the death of the 'late weak lady' who had been lent to him by divine providence for longer than human reason could have expected. Though always respectful, these letters from Ryther to Burghley seem to claim a degree of acquaintance bordering on the familiar; they suggest that Burghley had known him for some years, as indeed he would have done if, as has been asserted, Ryther had been an esquire of the body to the Queen as his father had been to Queen Mary.[3]

A very different picture of Ryther was given by Archbishop Sandys in his report of September 1587 on Yorkshire justices. To the archbishop he was 'a sour and subtle papist', who had been put into the commission for that very reason, 'ready to hinder any matter that shall touch any papist', 'a man unprofitable for the commonwealth and full of contention', dependent on Sir Thomas Fairfax* 'to make good his evil causes'. To another he was 'a man profoundly studied in Macchiavelli'. He remained in the commission, but his unpopularity in the county contributed to a curious change in his fortunes. In January 1592 he was petitioning Burghley, 'his singular good lord and patron', to secure his release from Newgate, whither he had been sent by order of the court of wards because of a debt to the Queen which he claimed he had paid. It was being said of him that he

was 'a troublesome man' to the gentlemen of the county, which was untrue, and that 'I will pay no man his due, a thing far from me'. He was 'a gentleman not meanly descended, a poor servant to her Majesty', to whom he had given good service in his county and who had promised to protect him. As for the allegation that he was at variance with the Fairfaxes, the fact was that he was very closely tied to them by blood and friendship. The end of this affair is not known.[4]

By mid-July 1594 he was a prisoner again, this time in the Fleet. The Countess of Cumberland, writing to an unnamed correspondent, begged him to move Sir Robert Cecil on Ryther's behalf; she herself had spoken in his favour to the Queen. He was still confined on 17 Dec., when Stanwardine Passy, servant to the keeper of the Gatehouse, reported in French to Richard Topcliffe* that there was 'no news but a letter from Mr. Ryder in the Fleet'. A later letter, to Archibald Douglas, the Scotch ambassador in England, from 'you know who', tells more: 'Mr. Rydder was loosed out of prison yesternight and is to be troubled with strait watching which hinders all his business'. The writer had given him £80 and had agreed 'to pleasure' him with £65 more.[5]

Ryther died 4 Sept. 1595. Four years after his death his heir was compelled to sell Harewood to pay his debts.[6]

[1] *Vis. Yorks. 1585*, ed. Foster, 303; *Vis. Yorks.* (Harl. Soc. xvi), 367; *Lincs. Peds.* (Harl. Soc. lii), 841; *Dugdale's Vis. Yorks.* ed. Clay, ii. 456; Whittaker, *Leodis and Elmet*, 166, 168; *CPR, 1560–3*, p. 567. [2] Lansd. 57, f. 50; Whittaker, *Hist. Craven*, 335. [3] Lansd. 54, ff. 141, 154, 184; 57, f. 50; 59, f. 20; 61, ff. 116, 182; 119, f. 108; *Dugdale's Vis. Yorks.* ed. Clay, ii. 456. [4] Lansd. 52, f. 184; 69, ff. 105, 109. [5] *HMC Hatfield*, iv. 563; v. 39; xiii. 520. [6] C142/245/81; J. Parker, 'Lords of Harewood Castle', *Yorks. Arch. Jnl.* xxii. 158.

I.C./E.L.C.M.

SACKVILLE, John (d. 1619), of Brede, later of Sedlescombe, Suss.

EAST GRINSTEAD   1563

1st s. of Christopher Sackville†, of Worth by Constance, da. of Thomas Culpeper of Bedgebury, Kent. *educ.* I. Temple 1555. *m.* Joan, da. and coh. of John Downton of Sedlescombe, 3s. 4da. *suc.* fa. c.1559.

Escheator, Surr. and Suss. 1562–3; j.p. Suss. from c.1575.

It is assumed that John Sackville, nephew of Sir Richard Sackville* and first cousin of Thomas Sackville*, later Lord Buckhurst, was the 1563 Member for East Grinstead rather than John Sackville of Chiddingly, Sir Richard's second cousin. He would have been returned through the influence of his powerful relatives. As late as 1607, he was still resident at Brede, but in his will, dated January 1619, he described himself as of Sedlescombe, and he placed Sedlescombe first on his list of six Sussex parishes whose poor he wanted to assist. Among other beneficiaries were his wife, brother and married sister, his sons, Thomas and John, and a married daughter. Most remarkable were the legacies to his two unmarried daughters, Anne and Joan, each of whom was given £1,000. In a final request appended to the will, Sackville asked his son and executor, Thomas, to give Anne a further £200 as well. He died 21 Dec. 1619.

W. Berry, *Co. Genealogies, Suss.* (Comber's copy at Chichester), 301; Horsfield, *Suss.* i. 514, 524-6; PCC 46 Welles, 1 Dorset, 110 Parker; C142/381/140.

J.E.M.

SACKVILLE, Sir Richard (by 1507-66), of Buckhurst, Suss. and Westenhanger, Kent.

CHICHESTER	1547
?SUSSEX	1553 (Mar.)
PORTSMOUTH	1554 (Apr.)
SUSSEX	1559, 1563*

b. by 1507, 1st s. of John Sackville† of Chiddingly, Suss. by his 1st w. Margaret, da. of Sir William Boleyn of Blickling, Norf. *educ.* ?Camb.; I. Temple. *m.* bef. 1536, Winifred, da. of Sir John Brydges† of London, 3s. inc. Thomas* 1da. Kntd. 1549; *suc.* fa. 27 Sept. 1557.[1]

Escheator, Surr. and Suss. 1541-2; steward of Suss. manors of abp. of Canterbury 1544; j.p. Suss. by 1547-53, from 1555, Essex, Kent, Surr. from 1559; chancellor, ct. of augmentations 1548-53, 20-23 Jan. 1554; custos rot. Suss. from 1549, ld. lt. 1550; gov. I. Temple from 1558; PC from 20 Nov. 1558; under-treasurer of the Exchequer from Feb. 1559; steward, duchy of Lancaster lands in Suss. 1559.[2]

'Fillsack' Sackville came from a family already prominent in Sussex, Essex and Oxfordshire, several of whom had sat in Parliament. He was cut out of his father's will, which he successfully contested, receiving administration of the estate in October 1559. He had already acquired, through speculation in monastic lands, and from the Crown, property in Kent, Surrey, Sussex, Oxfordshire and Yorkshire, and 'spacious estates of fabulous worth' in London, stretching 'from Fleet Street to the banks of the Thames, from Blackfriars to Bridewell'.[3]

First taught by 'a fond schoolmaster' who, 'before he was fully fourteen years old, drove him with fear of beating from all love of learning', he may have studied at Cambridge before becoming a member of the Inner Temple. The details of his early career are obscure, because of confusion with his uncle and namesake. In any case, although under Edward VI he held the profitable office of chancellor of augmentations, he was not a prominent figure in the administration. Having signed the 'device' altering the succession in 1553, he was out of favour with Mary, who did not employ him until nearly the end of her reign, and then not as a regular official.

However, he was granted an annuity of £300 in compensation for loss of office, and in 1558 the accession of his cousin Elizabeth restored his fortunes. He was summoned to her first Council meeting, and placed in charge of arrangements for the coronation. Sir Nicholas Throckmorton* suggested him as master of the rolls, but the 'advice' was ignored and Sir William Cordell* retained the office.[4]

Sackville remained a member of the Privy Council; in 1564 the Spanish ambassador reported a rumour that he was to replace Sir Nicholas Bacon† as lord keeper. He also attended numerous functions on behalf of the Queen, for instance the funeral service held at St. Paul's on the death of Henri II of France in 1559 and of the Emperor in 1564. Margaret, Countess of Lennox, was in his custody in 1562 and again in 1566. As an Exchequer official, he supervised the calling in of the old coinage and the issuing of the new, and was a member of various commissions concerning crown lands, the mint, counterfeit money, and the court of Exchequer. Though his wife was a Catholic, he conformed to the established religion, and in 1559 was appointed to administer clerical oaths, and later to arrange the exchange of episcopal lands. He was also active in local affairs, for example playing a leading part, in 1561-2, on a commission concerned with the endowments of Rochester bridge.[5]

In 1559 Sackville was elected for both Kent and Sussex, choosing Sussex. The exiguous 1559 journal shows him to have been concerned with the cutting of timber (3 Feb.) and restoring first fruits and tenths (17 Feb.). He was again elected for Sussex in 1563, taking charge of a bill (20 Jan.) 'for allowance to sheriffs upon their accounts for justices' diets'. On 3 Feb. he was looking after a bill to punish clippers of the coinage; 5 Feb. he was put in charge of the privilege case concerning Sir Henry Jones's* servants, and, 17 Feb. he reported that the Queen was dealing with the matter of justices' diets mentioned above. As Privy Councillor he was appointed to committees dealing with the petition to the Queen to marry (6 Feb. 1559), the petition concerning the succession (19 Jan., 12 Feb. 1563) and the subsidy (25 Jan. 1563).[6]

According to a schedule drawn up after his death and annotated by Cecil, he had an income of £804 a year from fees and annuities alone. He received £180 p.a. as under-treasurer of the Exchequer, £200 for his 'diet' there, and his £300 annuity. The remainder came from offices he had held in abbeys, since dissolved. In addition, he had the large income from his estates, from Sussex iron works and from ventures with the Muscovy company and the Merchant Adventurers. He could well afford the £5,000 he lent the Queen in 1561 to help restore the exchange at Antwerp. On the day that he made his will, 22 Mar. 1566, Sackville granted his goods and chattels to his friends Anthony Stapleton†, William Baynham, Roger Manwood*, Richard Onslow*, John Trevor and Humfrey

Bridges. He left Westenhanger, Ore and other lands to his wife, with remainder to his son, who was also to have Buckhurst, other property and an annuity of 500 marks during his mother's lifetime. On her death, Sir Richard wished his daughter, Lady Anne Dacre, to enjoy this annuity, provided that she would agree to sign any legal documents that her brother required of her. Sir Richard also left to his family much jewellery and plate, livestock, several leases, an iron mill and £400 of debts owed to him. He bequeathed jewellery to the Queen and £20 each to Onslow, Stapleton and Manwood, making provision also for some of his numerous relatives, including John Sackville*. He appointed as his executors his wife (who renounced her rights), his son, and his 'dear beloved friends', Sir William Cecil*, Sir Ambrose Cave*, Sir William Cordell*, Sir Edward Saunders*, Sir Walter Mildmay*, Sir Anthony Brown*, and Roger Manwood*, leaving them each £20. The overseers were the lord treasurer, the lord admiral, the Earl of Pembroke and the Earl of Leicester; they were to have £20 each, and Leicester was let off £50 from a debt of £250.

Sackville became seriously ill at the end of the same month, and his son's plans to go to Vienna to arrange a marriage between Elizabeth and the Archduke Charles of Austria had to be laid aside. After a rally he died in London 21 Apr. His widow later married John Paulet, later 2nd Marquess of Winchester.[7]

[1] C142/115/49; C. J. Phillips, *Hist. Sackville Fam.* i. 126–50; *Vis. Essex* (Harl. Soc. xiii), 29; *Literary Remains of Edw. VI* (Roxburghe Club), 307. [2] SP11/5/f. 50; 12/39/f. 160v; *LP Hen. VIII*, iv(1), p. 124; *CPR*, 1547–8, pp. 90, 123, 297; 1548–9, p. 181; 1553–4, pp. 67, 73, 300, 441; 1558–60, p. 56; 1560–3, pp. 438, 441, 443; *I. T. Recs.* i. 201, 233, 236; *APC*, vii. 50 et passim; *CSP Dom.* 1547–80, p. 123. [3] *LP Hen. VIII*, xix(1), p. 634; xx(1), p. 128; PCC 48 Chayney; *Machyn Diary* (Cam. Soc. xlii), 153; *CPR*, 1550–3, pp. 69, 427; 1553 and App. Edw. VI, pp. 112, 115; 1553–4, p. 441; 1558–60, p. 243; *Studies in Anglo-Dutch Relations*, ed. Van Dorsten, 40. [4] *Ascham's Scholemaster*, ed. Mayor, intro. 17–18; *LP Hen. VIII*, iv(1), p. 124; v. p. 162; xiii(2), p. 83; xvi. p. 878; *VCH Suss.* ii. 79; iv. 176–8; Chichester town clerk's dept. recs. of three city courts, f. 45; *G. Inn Adm. Reg.* 2; *Valor Eccl.* i. 349, 353; C142/145/11; *Cam. Soc.* xlviii. 100; SP 11/5/f. 50, 11/f. 115; Lansd. 156, ff. 108–10; *CPR*, 1558–60; p. 144; *APC*, vii. 3; *CSP Dom.* 1547–80, pp. 118, 128; *EHR*, lxv. 95. [5] *CSP Span.* 1558–67, p. 369; Strype, *Annals*, i(1), p. 188; i(2), p. 119; *CSP For.* 1562, p. 82; *Three 15th Cent. Chrons.* (Cam. Soc. n.s. xxviii), 121, 141; *CPR*, 1558–60, pp. 118, 443; 1560–3, pp. 37, 92, 237, 483, 523, 623; *APC*, vii. 50; *Wriothesley's Chron.* (Cam. Soc. n.s. xx), 145; *Arch. Cant.* 212–40. [6] D'Ewes, 44, 45, 48, 79, 80, 84, 88; *CJ*, i. 53, 54, 63, 64, 69. [7] Naunton, *Fragmenta Regalia*, ed. Arber, 55; SP12/39/ff. 155–165v; *CSP Dom.* Add. 1547–65, p. 439; *CPR*, 1554–5, p. 56; *CSP For.* 1565–6, p. 144; *CSP Span.* 1558–67, p. 527; PCC 14 Crymes; C142/145/11.

N.M.F.

SACKVILLE, Robert (1561–1609), of Bolbrooke and Buckhurst, Suss. and Knole, Kent.

SUSSEX	1584
LEWES	1589
SUSSEX	1593, 1597, 1601, 1604*

b. 1561, 1st s. of Thomas Sackville*, 1st Baron of Buckhurst and 1st Earl of Dorset, by Cicely, da. of Sir John Baker†, of Sissinghurst, Kent. *educ.* prob. Hart Hall, Oxf. 1576, BA and MA 1579; I. Temple 1580. *m.* (1) Feb. 1580, Lady Margaret Howard (*d.* 19 Aug. 1591), o. da. of Thomas, 4th Duke of Norfolk, 3s. 3da.; (2) Dec. 1592, Anne, da. of Sir John Spencer†, of Althorp, Northants., wid. of William Stanley, 3rd Lord Monteagle and of Henry Compton I*, 1st Lord Compton. *Styled* Lord Buckhurst 1604–8. *suc.* fa. as 2nd Earl of Dorset 1608.[1]

J.p. Suss. from c.1591, Kent from c.1592; dep. lt. Suss. 1601, jt. ld. lt. 1608.[2]

Sackville's preliminary education was directed by a tutor chosen by Roger Ascham, whose own son became his fellow-pupil. This arrangement was the result of a suggestion in December 1563 by Sir Richard Sackville*, Robert's grandfather, to the famous pedagogue whose gentleness and learning so impressed him that he offered to bear the entire expense, 'yea, though they three do cost me a couple of hundred pounds by year'.[3]

Sackville was put into the senior county seat for Sussex at the first election after he attained his majority by his father and Viscount Montagu, each of whom wrote to the sheriff on his behalf. He did not stand in 1586, and came in for a local borough at the election of 1588 when his father had scarcely emerged from a period of royal disfavour. From 1593 he continued in a county seat until his death. No record has been found of his speaking in the House, but he was a fairly active committeeman in 1593 and 1597. He could have taken part in the work of the following committees: in 1584–5 the preservation of Sussex timber (8 Dec.) and the subsidy (24 Feb.); in 1589 the subsidy (11 Feb.); in 1593 the subsidy (26 Feb., 1, 3 Mar.), a legal matter concerning country gentlemen (9 Mar.) and the poor law (12 Mar.); in 1597 enclosures (5 Nov.), the poor law (5, 22 Nov.), penal laws (8 Nov.), armour and weapons (8 Nov.), monopolies (10 Nov.), the subsidy (15 Nov.), draining the fens (3 Dec.), and highways in Surrey, Sussex and Kent (27 Jan. 1598); in 1601 the main business committee (3 Nov.) and monopolies (23 Nov.).[4]

In his middle thirties Sackville embarked on a number of speculative financial ventures, such as the export of iron ordnance. His trading ventures led to his becoming a freeman of Southampton in 1596. When he succeeded to the earldom and vast estates he was within a year of his death, which occurred on 27 Feb. 1609. His first wife had been 'a lady ... of as great virtue ... as is possible for any man to wish to be matched withal'; she was evidently a devout Catholic and may have had a lasting influence on her husband and his household. After her death, Robert Southwell published a small volume in her honour. Sackville asked in his will to be buried at Withyham, 'as near to my first dearly beloved wife ... as can be', and that £200–£300 should be spent on a tomb bearing effigies of them both. His second wife, however, was a woman 'whom without great grief and sorrow inconsolable I cannot remember, in regard of her exceeding unkindness and intolerable evil usage towards myself and my late good lord and father deceased'. He prayed that God would forgive her, and left her a life interest in five rings set with diamonds and sapphires which she often wore in her hair. After her death, the rings were to be shared among other relatives, and Sackville charged her 'if she have in her any spark of the grace of God or any remorse of conscience for those horrible abuses that she hath offered to my lord, my father, that she do not make an increase thereof by embezzling away these rings'. In fact his death occurred during negotiations for a separation on the ground of his wife's misconduct. The will forbade 'blacks' or 'great solemnity of funeral' because the usual ceremonies 'such as heralds set down for noblemen are only good for the heralds and drapers and very prejudicial to the children, servants and friends of the deceased'. He left bequests to the poor of ten Sussex parishes and to various relatives, friends and servants, appointing as executors his brother-in-law, Lord William Howard and his friend, Sir George Rivers*. An interesting legacy was that of £1,000 with an annual endowment of £350 for the foundation and maintenance of a hospital or college in East Grinstead for the relief of 31 poor, unmarried persons. The whole was to be, and was, incorporated and named 'Sackville College for the Poor'.⁵

¹ PCC 1 Dorset; *CP*, iv. 423; ix. 623–4; C3/289/8. ² PRO Assizes, 35, S.E. Circuit, Suss. 33–4; C66/1421d; *APC*, xxvii. 56; xxxi. 400; *CP*, iv. 423. ³ R. Ascham, *The Scholemaster*, ed. Whimster, 13–16. ⁴ Harl. 703, ff. 18b, 19b; Neale, *Commons*, 68–9, 317; *CSP Dom.* 1581–90, pp. 420, 422, 456, 462; *APC*, xv. 176–7; *HMC Hatfield*, iii. 280–4; D'Ewes, 337, 431, 474, 481, 486, 496, 499, 552, 553, 555, 557, 561, 567, 589, 624, 649; Lansd. 43, anon. jnl. f. 171. ⁵ Req. 2/34/104 and 72/42; *CSP Dom.* 1595–7, pp. 153, 171; 1598–1601, p. 411; 1601–3, p. 151; 1603–10, pp. 139, 477, 484; *APC*, xxv. 271, 301; *HMC 11th Rep. III*, 22; *HMC Hatfield*, vi. 131; viii. 131; *HMC 11th Rep. III*, 22; C142/312/128; PCC 23 Dorset; *Cath. Rec. Soc.* ii. 239; xxi. *passim*; *HMC 4th Rep.* 120; *HMC 7th Rep.* 43–4; *DNB*.

J.E.M.

SACKVILLE, Thomas (1535/6–1608), of Buckhurst, nr. East Grinstead, Suss. and Sackville House (later Dorset House), Fleet Street, London.

WESTMORLAND	1558
EAST GRINSTEAD	1559
AYLESBURY	1563

b. 1535/6, prob. 1st s. of Sir Richard Sackville* by Winifred, da. of Sir John Brydges† of London. *educ.* Sullington (?Lullington) g.s.; ?Hart Hall, Oxf.; ?St. John's, Camb.; I. Temple 1555, called; Camb. MA 1571; Oxf. incorp. 1592. *m.* Cecily (*d.*1615), da. of Sir John Baker†, of London and Sissinghurst, Kent, 4s. inc. Robert* 3da.; ?1s. illegit. *suc.* fa. Apr. 1566. Kntd. and *cr.* Baron of Buckhurst 8 June 1567; KG 1589; Earl of Dorset 1604.

J.p. Kent, Suss. from 1559; feodary, duchy of Lancaster lands in Suss. 1561; jt. ld. lt. Suss. 1569; commr. trial Duke of Norfolk 1572; ambassador to France 1571–2, 1591, to Netherlands 1587, 1598; trier of petitions in the Lords, Parlts. of 1572, 1584, 1586, 1589, 1593, 1597; custos rot. Suss. c.1573–*d.*; PC 1586; commr. trial Mary Queen of Scots 1586; high steward, Winchester c.1590; chief butler, England 1590; jt. commr. of great seal Nov. 1591–May 1592; chancellor, Oxf. Univ. 1591; ld. treasurer 1599; ld. high steward for trial of the Earl of Essex Feb. 1601; jt. commr. for office of earl marshal 1601.¹

Sackville was returned to Elizabeth's first Parliament for his family's local borough and in 1563 for Aylesbury, probably through the intervention of his relation Thomas Smythe I*. He made no known contribution to the business of the House, and soon after the end of the 1563 session he went to France and Italy. At Rome he was first imprisoned, then received in audience by Pope Pius IV, an obscure episode open to conflicting interpretation. He was back in England early in 1566, when his departure for Vienna on government business was delayed by his father's illness and death. He succeeded to estates in Essex, Kent, Oxfordshire, Sussex and Yorkshire, and was granted the reversion to Knole, though he had to wait nearly 40 years for possession. However, just over a year after his father's death, after being knighted by the Duke of Norfolk in the Queen's presence at Westminster, he was, on the same day, made a peer, the first of only two really new peerages to be granted in the reign, the other being Secretary Cecil's four years later. Thenceforth Buckhurst was frequently a trier of petitions in the Lords, exercised parliamentary patronage at Arundel, Lewes and Steyning, and from his eponymous seat in Sussex he held sway as lord lieutenant, while remaining above all a courtier and diplomat. The most important of his embassies was the so-called 'expostulatory mission' to the Low Countries from March to July 1587, after Leicester's return to England. Though close to Burghley, Buckhurst was not, it appears, against Leicester until, in the Netherlands, he saw the result of Leicester's 'might', 'malice' and 'intolerable errors', as Buckhurst put it to the Queen. But this frankness now resulted in his own recall and banishment from court. He had still not been allowed back in February 1588, but Leicester's death in the following September altered the balance of power: Buckhurst was restored to favour and soon afterwards made KG. It was he who signed the treaty of peace with Henri IV of France in 1591. In 1598 he joined Burghley in an unsuccessful attempt to achieve peace with Spain, and went again to the Netherlands to make a new treaty. There are frequent references of his entertainment of foreign ambassadors in England.

He was made lord treasurer by Elizabeth in May 1599 in succession to Burghley, and re-appointed by James I. The problems that were to ruin his two successors did not come to a head in Buckhurst's time, and, created Earl of Dorset in 1604, his last years were devoted to this office, to the membership of the commission which finally signed the peace with Spain, and to Knole. He died on 19 Apr. 1608, and was buried at Withyham. The large bequests to his wife were

a true token and testimony of my unspeakable love, affection, estimation, and reverence, long since fixed and settled in my heart and soul towards her.

Members of his family were to have the rings he had been given by James I and the King of Spain, and his jewelled portrait of Queen Elizabeth. Provision was made to build a public granary at Lewes, with £2,000 to stock it when grain was scarce.

As a young man Sackville had some reputation as a poet. He received an honorary MA from Cambridge in 1571 and from Oxford 21 years later, after he had been made chancellor of the university in preference to the Earl of Essex.[2]

¹ CP; DNB; C142/145/11; Vis. Suss. (Harl. Soc. lxxxix), 95; Harl. 1776, f. 48; DL41/23; SP12/59, f. 200 seq.; Somerville, Duchy, i. 619; Hants RO, Winchester 1st bk. of ordinances; Leycester Corresp. (Cam. Soc. xxvii), 364, 378; LJ, i. 703; ii. 62, 113, 145, 168, 191; CSP Dom. 1581–90, p. 702; Howell, State Trials, i. col. 1333; Nichols, Progresses Eliz. iii. 149–167. ² LJ, i. 703; ii. 62, 113, 145, 168, 191; CSP Rome, 1558–71, p. 163; CSP Span. 1558–67, p. 390; CPR, 1560–3, pp. 575–6; C142/145/11; Hasted, Kent, iii. 70–1; HMC Foljambe, 25; Leycester Corresp. (Cam. Soc. xxvii); N. M. Sutherland, Massacre of St. Bartholomew, 141, 159, 160; Motley, United Neths. (1860), p. 216 seq.; C. Wilson, Eliz. and the Revolt of the Netherlands; CSP Dom. 1547–80, p. 318; I. Temple, Petyt ms 538/10, ff. 51–77; HMC Hatfield, iii. 136–7, 280, 283; PCC 1 Dorset. This biography was written before the appearance of C. H. Wilson; 'Thomas Sackville; an Elizabethan poet as citizen', Ten Studies in Anglo-Dutch Relations (Pbls. Sir Thomas Browne Inst. Leiden, gen. ser. v), 3–50.

P.W.H.

SADLER, Henry (c.1538–1618), of Everley, Wilts. and Hungerford, Berks.

LANCASTER 1571, 1572, 1584, 1586

b. c.1538, 3rd s. of Sir Ralph Sadler* and bro. of Thomas*. educ. Gonville, Camb. 1558. m. (1) Dorothy, da. of Edward Gilbert of Everley, 2s. 3da.; (2) by 1604, Ursula, da. of John Gill of Widial, Herts., 4s.

Steward, duchy of Lancaster lands in Wilts. 1570–1618; clerk of the hanaper 1572–1604; constable, Leicester castle 1576; j.p.q. Wilts. 1592, sheriff 1595–6.[1]

Sadler was originally intended for a diplomatic career, serving between 1563 and 1565 in the household of the English resident ambassador in France Sir Thomas Smith*. During the autumn of 1563 he maintained communications between Smith and Sir Nicholas Throckmorton*, who was at that time imprisoned at St. Germain-en-Laye. In November 1564 Sadler carried despatches to London, for which he was paid £30, £7 more than he had claimed as expenses. The last mention of him in Smith's correspondence is a year later, when the ambassador sent him to de Laubespine, the French secretary of state.[2]

The appointment of his father to the chancellorship of the duchy of Lancaster presumably encouraged Sadler to exchange diplomacy for some duchy lands and offices. Appointed duchy steward in Wiltshire, he collected a number of jobs there and in Berkshire, such as woodward of Aldbourne and Braden, keeper of woods at Hungerford and lieutenant of Aldbourne chase in 1579. Eventually, on his father's death, he obtained possession of the duchy manors of Everley and Hungerford. Meanwhile he had been granted a profitable office in Chancery and a post at Leicester of sufficient importance for the corporation to think it worthwhile to obtain his favour by means of a gift in 1584.[3]

Sadler's parliamentary career also depended upon and correlates with his father's tenure of the chancellorship of the duchy. In 1572 the other Member for Lancaster was his brother Thomas; two of his brothers-in-law also sat for duchy boroughs in 1571 and 1572 and one of them in 1586. After his father's death Sadler confined his activities to local affairs in Wiltshire where he was an active magistrate. In 1596 he was reprimanded by the Privy Council because his levies for service in the Isle of Wight were 'unable persons, ill armed and apparelled and long a-coming'. Sadler blamed the colonels of the trained bands and the bad weather.[4]

For some time, however, Sadler maintained his family connexions with Hertfordshire, where his elder brother was established. For a few years he held the manors of Hexton and Aspenden, conveyed to him by his brother Edward and one John Philpot. But the Hertfordshire lands he inherited from his father were sold in 1610, and by the end of his life his landed property was concentrated at Everley and Hungerford. He entertained James I at Everley in August 1603.[5]

He died 17 Mar. 1618, ten days after his eldest son, and was buried in Hungerford church. A life interest in the lands at Everley and Hungerford was bequeathed to his 'well-beloved wife' Ursula, the sole executrix, with a reversion to the eldest surviving son of their marriage. His daughter Joan was left a farm and tenement in Middle Everley, three score ewes and their pasture, and £1,000. In a codicil, he arranged the disinheritance of his son Francis if he lived abroad or fell 'into the Romish or Popish religion'.[6]

¹ Vis. Beds. (Harl. Soc. xix), 136; Al. Cant. iv. 2; Hoare, Wilts. Everley, iii. 3, 6; Somerville, Duchy, i. 395, i 565, 632, 633; CSP Dom. 1581–90, p. 708; Murdin, State Pprs. 808; APC, xxii. 501; Hatfield ms 278. ² CSP For. 1563, pp. 537, 552, 555–6; 1564–5, pp. 6, 123, 128, 238, 240, 510–11; APC, vii. 161. ³ Aubrey and Jackson, Wilts. Colls. 365; Somerville, i. 565, 632, 633; CSP Dom. 1581–90, p. 708; Leicester

Recs. iii. 220. [4] HMC Hatfield, vi. 506–7. [5] PCC 23 Spencer; VCH Herts. ii. 353; iii. 425; iv. 19; Clutterbuck, Herts. ii. 26; iii. 7. [6] PCC 34 Parker; Aubrey and Jackson, 365.

I.C.

SADLER, Sir Ralph (1507–87), of Standon, Herts.

?HINDON	1536
MIDDLESEX	1539
HERTFORDSHIRE	1542
PRESTON	1545
HERTFORDSHIRE	1553 (Mar.), 1559, 1563, 1571, 1572, 1584, 1586

b. 1507, 1st s. of Henry Sadler of Hackney, Mdx. m. bigamously by 1535, Ellen, da. of John Mitchell of Much Hadham, w. of Matthew Barr, at least 3s. inc. Henry* and Thomas* 4da. Kntd. 1538; kt. banneret 1547.

Clerk of hanaper from 1535; gent. of privy chamber 1536, ambassador extraordinary to Scotland 1537, 1540, 1542; prothonotary in Chancery from 1537; P.C. 1540–53, from 20 Nov. 1558; principal sec. 1540–3; master of gt. wardrobe 1543–53; treasurer, war against Scotland 1544, 1547, of northern army 1569–70; receiver, ct. of gen. surveyors by 1545; duchy of Lancaster steward of Hertford and constable of Hertford castle 1549–54, 1559–87; warden of east and middle marches 1559–60; chancellor of duchy of Lancaster from 1568; custodian of Mary Queen of Scots 1584–5.

J.p. Herts 1544–53, from 1559, q. and custos rot. from c.1562, ld. lt. 1569; j.p. Glos. 1547–53; eccles. commr. 1572.[1]

Of obscure birth, Sadler entered successively the service of Thomas Cromwell, Henry VIII and Edward VI. These two Kings granted him manors in Berkshire, Cambridgeshire, Essex and Middlesex, and extensive estates in Gloucestershire formerly belonging to the bishops of Worcester. During Mary's reign he was in retirement. With the accession of Queen Elizabeth he resumed his political career under the protection of his old friend Sir William Cecil, their friendship surviving Cecil's becoming the Queen's chief minister. It was to Sadler's care that Cecil committed his son, Thomas, when the young man had his first taste of army life with the Earl of Sussex's army in 1569.[2]

Sadler's position in Hertfordshire gained him a county seat in every Elizabethan Parliament in his lifetime, even when, as in 1584, there could have been little hope of his attending. As a Privy Councillor and a knight of the shire he was automatically a member of all the major Commons committees throughout his parliamentary career.

The only mention of Sadler's name in the 1559 journal refers to his sending five bills to the Lords, 2 May. During that summer Sadler was in Berwick with Sir James Croft*, under a commission to arrange a peace on the borders of Scotland. He was to supply the Scottish rebels with money

'so as the Queen should not be a party thereto'. In September he wrote to Cecil, complaining of Lord Dacre, who was in communication with Mary of Guise:

> What the cause is why he should send to her we know not, but what he is you know; and to say our opinions to you, we think he would be very loth that the Protestants in Scotland, yea, or in England, should prosper, if he might let it.

In return Cecil asked for his advice about replacing the wardens of the marches. His suggested appointments were not made but in October Sadler himself was appointed warden of the east and middle marches during the absence of the Earl of Northumberland, who had been called to court. He continued to act as paymaster to the Scottish protestants, distributing £3,000 in French coin to disguise its origin, and managed a network of agents to infiltrate the organization of the lords of the congregation, and to survey the fortifications of Leith so that the rebels could be advised how to capture it from the French. Sadler's advice that Leith be taken quickly was no doubt what persuaded Cecil to urge open intervention upon the Queen. Eventually Sadler was authorized to supply the Scots with powder and ammunition from Berwick, while the Queen would defray the cost of the campaign. It was another thing actually to get the money. In November he wrote

> long delay of the sending thereof may be a hindrance; and when it is here, in our opinions, it may stand the Queen's Majesty in as good stead as if it were in her highness's coffers.

By December he wanted to leave:

> If I be grieved with it, you cannot blame me ... And if you mean to keep me still in this country, you must have better consideration of my charges, or else I shall beggar myself in this service. For I assure you, my horse-meat will eat up the one half of my entertainment, all things here be so unreasonably dear. Wherefore, sir, I beseech you, have me in remembrance, for I complain not without cause.

The Queen owed £12,000 at Berwick, the soldiers were unpaid, and lack of money would bring all to nought:

> What is £20,000 more or less in a prince's purse, specially to be employed where such an advantage may be taken as is now likely to be had in this case, whereby, in my poor opinion, it must needs follow, either that these two realms shall be conjoined in perpetual unity, or at the least, to breed such an enmity between the French and the Scots, as the French shall never have opportunity greatly to annoy us by the way of Scotland.

With the open intervention of England and the arrival of the Duke of Norfolk's army, Sadler's mission came to an end. He was appointed to the commission which negotiated the treaty of Edinburgh in the summer of 1560, but the actual negotiations were in the hands of Cecil and Edward Wotton.[3]

Sadler had no further public employment for some years. He was active, however, in the 1563 Parliament. He could have attended the subsidy committee; he was named to a committee on the continuation of Acts of Parliament (10 Oct. 1566); he spoke on the Queen's marriage (18 Oct. 1566) – he had heard her say in the presence of divers of her nobility that she was minded to marry – and he attended the conference on marriage and the succession (31 Oct.). He was a member of the Commons delegation summoned on 5 Nov. to hear the Queen's message on the succession. That he took an active part in the succession question at this time in and out of Parliament is beyond question, but it is difficult to be precise about the dates of his speeches. It was probably in the 1563 session that he attacked the title of the Queen of Scots to the throne of England on the ground that, though next in blood, she was an alien:

> Why should we, for any respect, yield to their Scottish superiority, or consent to establish a Scot in succession to the crown of this realm, contrary to the laws of the realm, and thereby to do so great an injury as to disinherit the next heir of our nation?

In the session of 1566 he again spoke on the succession, but this time he was more concerned with the granting of a subsidy:

> No man living would be more loath than I to set forth or to speak in the furtherance of anything in this place, which might seem to be chargeable or burdensome to my country. Great and weighty causes made a subsidy necessary … When we see our neighbours' homes on fire, it is wisdom to provide and foresee how to keep the smoke and sparks of the same as far from our own.

Money was needed so that Ireland could be made 'civil and obedient'.

> I shall not need to use any persuasions to move or persuade you thereunto. Indeed I will not go about to persuade you; the causes of themselves are sufficient to persuade you, being men of wisdom and judgment, men selected and chosen of the best and wisest sort of the whole realm; such as can discern and judge much better than I can, what is fit for good subjects to do in this cause.

It was not fitting to 'mix or mingle' the succession with the subsidy, 'whereby we might seem, as it were, to condition and covenant with her Majesty'. Assuring the Commons that the Queen was not less careful of the matter than they were themselves, he concluded,

> This is my poor advice; and, if all men here knew as much as I do, I think they would the sooner and the more easily, be persuaded to be of my opinion.

But during a Privy Council meeting at which the Queen was present, Sadler spoke of the consequences of delay:

> If your Majesty should now end your Parliament, and leave your people void of hope, and desperate of this matter of succession, which is now so much urged and required at your hands; and so your nobles and commons go home grieved in their hearts and discontented, and, when they come home, their countrymen shall enquire of them what is done – for your highness may be sure that all men hearken to this matter – and some of them percase will advisedly answer, and some others percase, rashly and inadvisedly, will say 'We have done nothing but given away your money: the Queen hath that she looked for, but she hath no care of us' – how your people's hearts will be wounded with this!

On another occasion, perhaps in October 1579, Sadler spoke bluntly, attacking Elizabeth's proposed marriage with Anjou. Sadler disliked the project because marriage to a Catholic would destroy the Queen's credit with foreign protestants and because he was afraid of English subordination to France if Anjou became king.

> There is another cause of inconvenience depending upon this marriage, and that is, that the same is universally misliked of throughout the realm. Which is a matter not to be neglected, for in mine opinion, it is not good to do things to the general discontent of the whole realm.[4]

Sadler captured only one high office during Elizabeth's reign, the lucrative chancellorship of the duchy of Lancaster, about which Cecil remarked 'as fishes are gotten with baits, so are offices caught with seeking'. Sadler did the job conscientiously, though there were the usual charges that he distributed lands and offices to relatives. When he was forced to spend some time at Tutbury in 1585, he used the occasion to overhaul the administration of the honour, and to prevent dilapidation of woods and parks. He also went into the question of the services owed to the honour by the townships and parishes adjacent to it, with the intention of exacting them effectively. Sadler naturally exercised the duchy's influence in parliamentary elections, nominating at Leicester, Liverpool, Higham Ferrers and elsewhere. His eldest son sat for Lancaster in 1572 and the youngest from 1571 until 1587, while his three sons-in-law, George Horsey*, Edward Bashe*, and Edward Elrington* were returned at various times for Clitheroe, Preston, Aldborough and Wigan.[5]

Reverting to Sadler's parliamentary activities: there is no record of his speaking in 1571. He administered the oaths at the commencement of the Parliament (2 Apr.), took bills to the Lords (22, 28 May) and served on committees dealing with church attendance (21 Apr.), promoters (23 Apr.), abuses by receivers and collectors (23 Apr.) and the river Lea (26, 28 May). He again administered the oaths at the beginning of the 1572 Parliament (8 May). He is recorded in the journals as speaking only once during all three sessions of this long Parliament, when he made a minor intervention on tale tellers (11 June 1572). The subjects of his committees were the Queen of Scots (12 May 1572, 28 May, 6 June), fraudulent conveyances (3 June), the Earl of Kent (4 June), Tonbridge grammar school (28 June), coining (15 Feb. 1576), wine (21 Feb.), slanderous libels (3 Feb. 1581), preservation of game (18 Feb.), disputed returns (24 Feb.) and London merchants (2 Mar.). He took part in some of the tidying up at the end of this session, taking bills to the Lords (8 Mar.) and being appointed to the committee to deal with the imprisoned Arthur Hall and report any action taken to the next session of Parliament. No mention of Sadler has been found in the journals of the 1584 Parliament, and it is highly unlikely that he attended at all, for he was at Wingfield guarding Mary Queen of Scots. On 26 Nov. Walsingham wrote to him there, saying, in an aside as informative about the Queen's attitude to Parliament as it is about Sadler's whereabouts, that she had 'no time to resolve herself' over a certain matter 'by reason of the Parliament'. In his last Parliament Sadler's activities were minimal – he was, after all, nearly 80. He was put on the committee to consider Arthur Hall's claim against Grantham (2 Dec.) and, as a senior knight of the shire he was automatically on the subsidy committee (22 Feb. 1587). His last recorded speech, suitably enough, was made on Mary Queen of Scots (3 Nov. 1586). He had, it is said, held her as a baby in his arms, and, apart from his duchy office, his public employment after 1569 had been concerned almost entirely with her. After her flight to England in May 1568, he was appointed to the commission which sat at York to negotiate a settlement between Mary and her subjects. In the following year he had been with the Earl of Sussex to suppress the northern rebellion which Mary's arrival had provoked. His letters to Cecil during this expedition are like those of 1559. There were reports on officials involved in the army and the administration of the northern counties, and assurances of Sussex's integrity in spite of the insinuations of his enemies. About the condition of the north, Sadler had this to say:

Her Majesty will hardly believe that the force and power of her good subjects in this country should not increase and be able to match with the power of the rebels. But … there be not in all this country ten gentlemen that do favour and allow of her Majesty's proceedings in the cause of religion, and the common people be ignorant, full of superstition and altogether blinded with the old Popish doctrine, and therefore do so much favour the cause, which the rebels make the colour of their rebellion, that though their persons be here with us, I assure you their hearts, for the most part, be with the rebels.

He was recalled in January 1570 and able to live quietly at Standon for a few months. That August he assured Cecil that he had no wish to play the courtier. But the next year

he was one of the Privy Councillors appointed to examine the bishop of Ross about Mary's complicity in the Ridolfi plot. That September he reluctantly undertook the arrest of the Duke of Norfolk, with whom he had been friendly since the Scottish campaign of 1560. Finally, in August 1584, Sadler was appointed Mary's custodian. He soon came under her spell, writing to Elizabeth 7 Dec.:

I find her much altered from that she was when I was first acquainted with her. This restraint of liberty, with the grief of mind which she hath had by the same, I think hath wrought some good effect in her. And if she do not greatly dissemble, truly she is much devoted and affected to your Majesty … Thus she sayeth and protesteth afore God; and as it is the part of an honest man to judge the best of all princes, so do I think that she hath an intention and meaning to perform that she sayeth, which upon proof and trial, time will discover and make manifest.

Sadler had to endure the trouble of two moves, from Sheffield to Wingfield, 2 Sept. 1584, and from Wingfield to Tutbury, 13 and 14 Jan. 1585. By March 1585 he had been caught out taking her hawking, 'a sport which I have always delighted in'. He had sent for his hawks and falconers, 'wherewith to pass this miserable life which I lead here', the Queen of Scots had 'earnestly entreated' him that she might go abroad with him 'to see my hawks fly', and he had allowed it three or four times, 'thinking that it could not be ill taken'. He would rather

yield myself to be a prisoner in the Tower all the days of my life, rather than I would attend any longer here upon this charge. And if I had known, when I came from home, I should have tarried here so long, contrary to all promises made unto me, I would have refused, as others do … For a greater punishment cannot be ministered unto me than to force me to remain here in this sort, being more meet now in mine old and later days to rest at home to prepare myself … and to seek the everlasting quietness of the life to come … and if it might light on me tomorrow, I would think myself most happy, for I assure you I am weary of this life; and the rather for that I see that things well meant by me, are not so well taken.

He was given a good conduct discharge within the month: 'you have served us most faithfully, to your credit and our own singular contentment'.

So the 'long and great discourse' the old man made on 3 Nov. 1586, at the beginning of the Parliament specifically called to sanction Mary's death, is of more than usual interest. The baby he had dandled, the erstwhile hawking companion, was 'the root ground of all' conspiracies,

who living, there is no safety for our most gracious sovereign, into whose heart, God for his mercy, put a willingness (yea, even to the performance) to take away this most wicked and filthy woman by justice, who from the beginning hath thirsted for this crown, is a murderer of her husband (for I have seen by her own letter and hand to the Earl of Bothwell, with whom she wrought his death, to that end), and is a most detestable traitor to our sovereign and enemy to us all.

Mary was executed 8 Feb. 1587. Sadler died, aged almost or just 80, 30 Mar. 1587. Within these seven weeks he is said to have performed his last public service – travelling to Scotland to mollify the King of the 'proud beggarly Scots' (as he was used to call them), the son of 'this most wicked and filthy woman', for her having been put to death. But this is a canard, originating, it appears, from the introduction to the *Sadler Pprs*. – the ambassador was Robert Carey*. The will Sadler made 27 Apr. 1584 was proved 26 May 1587.[6]

[1] *LP Hen. VIII*, xx(2), pp. 412–13; Clutterbuck, *Herts*. iii. 28, 226–8; *DNB*; Lansd. 2, f. 34; 13, f. 48; 16, f. 78; *APC*, ii. 70; vii. 3; *CPR*, 1547–8, pp. 83–4; 1550–3, pp. 141, 394; 1553, pp. 354, 361; 1553–4, p. 326; 1558–60, pp. 156–7; 1560–3, p. 438; 1563–6, pp. 226, 497; 1569–72, p. 440; Somerville, *Duchy*, i. 333–4, 395, 604; Read, *Cecil*, 352; *HMC Hatfield*, i. 443; *Bull. IHR*, xxxviii. 31–47. [2] *Sadler Pprs*. i. pp. xxi, xxii; ii. 33–4; *CSP Scot*. i. 248. [3] *Sadler Pprs*. i. pp. vi, xvi, xxiv–xxv, 387, 391–2, 438–9, 451–3, 460, 470–3, 476, 480, 517, 527, 530, 533, 550–5, 596, 645–7, 651–4, 715–16; ii. 577–95; *CPR*, 1558–60, pp. 296, 380; 1560–3, p. 62; 1563–6, pp. 204, 308; Somerville, 395; Read, 154–6, 157, 158, 172, 174; P. Forbes, *A Full View of Public Transactions*, i. 460. [4] Add. 33593, ff. 3–4; 33591; *Sadler Pprs*. ii. 548–52, 553–5, 556–61, 570–4; *Neale, Parlts*. i. 104–5, 137–9, 144–5; D'Ewes, 55, 80, 103, 124, 126; *CJ*, i. 61, 74, 77; Camb. Univ. Lib. Gg. iii. 34, p. 209; Read, 361. [5] Somerville, i. 327, 333–4, 395; *CSP Dom*. 1547–80, p. 309; *Sadler Pprs*. ii. 146, 486–8; *HMC 4th Rep*. 339; Neale, *Commons*, 172–3, 224, 227–30; *HMC Hatfield*, ii. 148. [6] D'Ewes, 124, 126, 155, 157, 159, 160, 165, 168, 176, 178, 183, 186, 187, 189, 205, 206, 212, 213, 219, 221, 222, 224, 225, 241, 247, 248, 249, 250, 251, 253, 254, 260, 262, 288, 290, 291, 292, 294, 299, 300, 301, 302, 303, 306, 343, 345, 353, 355, 356, 365, 368, 371, 393, 394, 395, 399, 407, 409, 410, 412, 413, 414, 415, 416; *CJ*, i. 85, 91, 93, 94, 98, 100, 101, 103, 106, 107, 121, 128, 129, 130, 132, 136; Trinity, Dublin, Thos. Cromwell's jnl., f. 63; Bodl. Tanner 78, f. 16; *Sadler Pprs*. ii. 41–4, 54–6, 57–60, 69, 74–5, 85–6, 88–9, 144, 146, 356–9, 381, 457, 460–2, 486–8, 538–9, 544; Read, *Cecil*, 407–8, 458–9, 460; *Burghley*, 40; *CSP Dom*. 1547–80, pp. 387, 422; *HMC Hatfield*, i. 167–8, 364, 450, 520, 521, 522; ii. 16, 17, 551; Murdin, *State Pprs*. 152; C142/215/259; PCC 23 Spencer; *Trans. E. Herts. Arch. Soc*. iii. 92.

P.W.H.

SADLER, Thomas (c.1536–1607), of Standon, Herts.

LANCASTER   1572

b. c.1536, 1st s. of Sir Ralph Sadler*, and bro. of Henry*. *educ*. Trinity Hall, Camb. 1554; M. Temple 1558. *m*. (1) Ursula, da. and coh. of Henry Sharington* of Lacock, Wilts., *s.p*.; (2) Gertrude, da. of Robert Markham of Cotham, Notts., 1s. 1da. *suc*. fa. 1587. *Kntd*. 1603.

J.p. Herts. from c.1569, q. 1577; constable of Hertford castle, steward of Hertford and Hertingfordbury Mar.–July 1587; sheriff, Herts. June–Nov. 1588 1595–6.[1]

Sadler came in for Lancaster through his father, the chancellor of the duchy of Lancaster. He did not obtain lucrative offices and leases on the same scale as his brother Henry, and his career emerges from obscurity only through his local duties. Perhaps he suffered from chronic

ill-health. On two occasions he was so ill that he sent for Sir Edward Coke*, who was connected to him by ties of friendship and the marriage of their children, to arrange his affairs. During the second illness, Coke wrote, 'my brother Sir Thomas Sadler is fallen very dangerously sick and hath sent for me about the setting of an order in his house; which by the laws of friendship I cannot deny'. This must have been after April 1603, when Sadler entertained James I at Standon and was knighted.[2]

His will, made during his illness of March 1602, contains a preamble which was repeated verbatim in the will of his brother Henry some 15 years later. Thomas left his lands and the residue of his personal property to his only son Ralph, a cup worth £10 to his brother Henry, and £20 each to the three sons of his brother Edward. There was a bequest of £20 to another nephew and one of £40 to a godson. The supervisor of the will was 'my loving brother and faithful friend' Sir Edward Coke, who was asked to take pains to assist the executor, Sadler's son Ralph. Coke was to receive a standing cup of silver gilt valued at 20 marks, 'in remembrance of my love towards him'. Sir Thomas died on 5 Jan. 1607, and was buried at Standon described as one 'who lived in honourable reputation for his religion, justice, bounty, love of his country, favour of learning and all other virtues, and as he lived, he ended his life Christianly'.[3]

[1] *Vis. Beds*. (Harl. Soc. xix), 136; Clutterbuck, *Herts*. iii. 28; *Al. Cant*. iv. 3; Nichols, *Progresses Jas. I*, i. 106; Egerton 2345, f. 18v; SP12/121/15v; Somerville, *Duchy*, i. 395, 603–4, 605. [2] *CSP Dom*. 1581–90, p. 404; *HMC Hatfield*, xi. 289; xii. 90; *VCH Herts*. iii. 354. [3] PCC 9 Huddleston; Clutterbuck, iii. 236.

I.C.

ST. AUBYN, Thomas (c.1578–1637), of Clowance and Helston, Cornw.

ST. IVES   1601
GRAMPOUND   1614

b. c.1578, 2nd s. of Thomas St. Aubyn of Clowance by Zenobie, da. of John Halet*, of Woodleigh, Devon. *educ*. Queen's, Oxf. 1594; M. Temple 1597, called 1605. *m*. 13 Apr. 1615, Katherine, da. of John Bonython* of Carclew, 2s. 1da.

St. Aubyn's father, 'a merry, facetious, delightful character', was over 80 when he died in 1626, so that there is little to say about St. Aubyn himself in this period. His family was related to the Arundells, Carews, Carnsews and Godolphins, and its local standing was quite sufficient to account for St. Aubyn's return for St. Ives, some ten miles from Clowance. St. Aubyn made his will on 4 Feb. 1637 and was dead by the early summer of that year. The will was proved 5 July.

Paroch. Hist. Cornw. i. 265, 272; Vivian, *Vis. Cornw*. 438; A. L. Rowse, *Tudor Cornw*. 244; *Carew's Surv. Cornw*. ed. Halliday, 69, 228; J. H. Matthews, *Hist. St. Ives*, 498.

N.M.S.

ST. JOHN, Henry (c.1568–1621), of Farleigh Chamberlayne, Hants.

STOCKBRIDGE	1589, 1593

b. c.1568, 1st s. of William St. John* by Barbara Gooce or Goore, wid. of Thomas Twyne of Wonston. *educ.* Magdalen Hall, Oxf. 1585; L. Inn Nov. 1588. *m.* (1) Anne, ?1s.; (2) by 1600, Ursula, da. of Hugh Stewkley of 'Marsh' Som., ?4s. 4da.; (3) c.1614, Margaret, ?da. of Peter Fuller of St. Helens, I.o.W., 1da. *suc.* fa. 1609.

St. John's father's estates were near Stockbridge and both father and son sat for the borough. St. John was involved in a celebrated dispute over his return to the Commons in 1614, in defiance of the chancellor of the duchy of Lancaster. He died 7 Apr. 1621.

Vis. Hants (Harl. Soc. lxiv), 127, 193, 210; W. Berry, *Co. Genealogies, Hants*, 148; *VCH Hants*, iii. 458; iv. 444–5; PCC 53 Dale; C142/321/87, 389/104; *Chamberlain Letters* ed. McClure, i. 130 n, 528; *CJ*, i. 477.

A.H.

ST. JOHN, John I (*d.* ?c.1560), of ?Bletsoe, Beds.

BEDFORDSHIRE	1559

2nd s. of Sir John St. John† (*d.*1558), by his 1st w. Margaret, da. of Sir William Waldegrave of Smallbridge, Suff. *educ.* ?St. John's, Camb. 1545; I. Temple 1549. ?*unm.*

J.p. Beds. 1559.

This John St. John is suggested for the 1559 knight of the shire rather than John St. John II, who at 15 would have been a little on the young side, or a namesake who leased part of the honour of Petworth, rather low in status. But the man suggested remains an obscure figure, his name is not on the heralds' visitation, and his election as county Member merely reflects the standing of his family. He was an executor of his father's will, under which he received £40 and a gold chain. His name is on the 1559 commission of the peace but not on the next one, and the implication is that he died about 1560.

PCC 45 Welles; *CP*, xi. 333 seq.; *CPR*, 1549–51, p. 41; 1555–7, p. 1; 1557–8, pp. 182–3; C142/198/1.

N.M.F.

ST. JOHN, John II (1544–96), of Bletsoe, Beds.

BEDFORDSHIRE	1563

b. 1544, 1st s. of Oliver St. John†, 1st Baron St. John of Bletso, by his 1st w. Agnes, da. and h. of Sir John Fisher of Beds.; bro. of Oliver II. *m.* aft. Feb. 1575, Catherine, da. of Sir William Dormer*, 1da. Anne, *m.* William, Lord Howard*. *suc.* fa. as 2nd Baron 1582.

J.p. Beds. from c.1579; ld. lt. Hunts. by 1587; commr. trials of Mary Stuart, 1586, and Philip, Earl of Arundel, 1589; commr. recusancy, Beds. 1592.

The St. Johns of Bletsoe were eminent enough in Bedfordshire for this man, at the age of 19, to take precedence of Lewis Mordaunt*, also the heir to a peerage. In addition to the family seat, about six miles from Bedford, he inherited extensive lands in other parts of the county, with property in Cambridgeshire and presumably in Huntingdonshire, as well as a house in Bethnal Green. St. John was one of four Bedfordshire commissioners instructed in 1586 to raise men for the Low Countries, and between 1587 and 1592 the Council wrote to him about the inadequacy of the Huntingdonshire musters. In July 1592 Sir Henry Cromwell* was asked to levy foot soldiers in the county, as 'the infirmity of the Lord St. John is such as his lordship is not able to attend the service himself in person'. Infirm or not, St. John was appointed a fortnight later as a commissioner to act against recusants in Bedfordshire, and was one of the four who in October the same year supervised the taking of the oath of supremacy by the county officials. St. John died on 12 Oct. 1596, and his will was proved on 18 Oct.

C142/198/1; *CP*, xi. 334–5; *Vis. Beds.* (Harl. Soc. xix), 54; *HMC Foljambe*, 26; Howell, *State Trials*, i. cols. 1172, 1251; *APC*, xiv. 80, 115; xvi. 22, 145–6, 186, 244; xxiii. 70–1, 111, 256; PCC 70 Drake; C142/249/56.

N.M.F.

ST. JOHN, Nicholas (c.1526–89), of Lydiard Tregoze, Wilts.

CAMELFORD	1553 (Mar.)
?SALTASH	1555
CRICKLADE	1563
GREAT BEDWYN	1571
MARLBOROUGH	1572

b. c.1526, 1st s. of John St. John† of Lydiard Tregoze by his 1st w. Margaret, da. of Sir Richard Carew of Beddington, Surr.; half-bro. of William*. *m.* c.1548, Elizabeth, da. of Sir Richard Blount* of Mapledurham, Oxon., 3s. inc. Oliver III* 5da. *suc.* fa. Apr. 1576.

Gent. pens. by 1552–60; porter of Wallingford castle 1552; j.p. Wilts. from c.1574. sheriff 1579–80.[1]

St. John's protestantism served him well during Edward VI's reign. As porter of Wallingford castle he was the subordinate of Sir Francis Knollys*, the leading puritan in Queen Elizabeth's Privy Council. In 1560 his services to Elizabeth and her predecessors were recognized by a grant of his court office, with a pension of £26 13s. 4d. and exemption from daily attendance upon the Queen. He seems in fact to have confined his official duties to his native county of Wiltshire, where he became a justice of the peace and a commissioner to enforce training in archery. He contributed £25 to the Armada fund. In Berkshire, where he sometimes resided on his estate at Purley Magna, near Pangbourne, he was appointed trustee of part of the lands of the Catholic exile, Sir Francis Englefield†.[2]

He was returned for Cricklade to the Parliament of 1563, presumably by arrangement with his neighbour, the 2nd Lord Chandos, who controlled the borough. In 1571 he sat for Great Bedwyn and in 1572 for Marlborough, both slightly further afield, no doubt through the nomination of the Earl of Hertford. As St. John was a country gentleman, he would not have been expected to claim payment for serving in Parliament, but in 1577, after the second session of the 1572 Parliament, he sued Marlborough in Chancery for his wages. The borough replied, falsely, that he had not attended in 1576, but they had to pay him £8 8s. and were reimbursed by Hertford. In fact St. John was quite active in his last two Parliaments. He spoke on the vagabonds bill (13 Apr. 1571), and served on committees concerned with dress (14 May) and corrupt presentations (25 May). In 1572 he spoke on fraudulent gifts (16 May) and again on vagabonds (20 May), the number of whom, he said, was

> increased by building of cottages upon commons, having no grounds belonging unto them. He would therefore from henceforth no cottage to be builded unless it have three or four acres of ground belonging unto it.

Other speeches were on cattle (4 June), Oxford roads and bridges (7 June) and Mary Queen of Scots (7 June). In this same session he was put on a committee about weights and measures (23 May). In 1576 he is not known to have spoken but he was appointed to committees on broggers and drovers (28 Feb.), cloth (1, 9 Mar.), unlawful weapons (2 Mar.), innholders (5 Mar.), juries (5 Mar.), justices of the forest (8 Mar.), vicars and curates (13 Mar.) and Lord Stourton's bill (14 Mar.). Again no recorded speeches in 1581, but several committees: actions upon the case (26 Jan.), the clerk of the market (27 Jan.), the preservation of woods (28 Jan.) and disorders of sheriffs (4 Feb.).[3]

St. John may have been quarrelsome and was certainly litigious. The impression given by his claim against Marlborough is supported by the note in his will that he had won an action for assault and battery against Giles, 3rd Lord Chandos, son of his presumed patron in 1563, and was accordingly owed money by him; he seems also to have had a dispute with the Webbs, the family into which one of his daughters married. The will affirms his belief that, saved by the merits of Christ and 'by no other means whatsoever', he would 'be received into the holy company of [God's] elect', and he thanked God for 'His gracious visitation' in the shape of the disease afflicting him. His executor was his eldest son, John St. John, and he appointed as supervisors his brother-in-law Michael Blount* and William St. John*. He died 8 Nov. 1589. His second son, Oliver, became lord deputy of Ireland, an English baron and an Irish viscount; one of his daughters married Richard St. George, later Clarenceux King of Arms; and Henry St. John, Lord Bolingbroke, was his direct descendant.[4]

[1] C142/175/99; Wilts. Vis. Peds. (Harl. Soc. cv, cvi), 168; CPR, 1547–8, p. 337; 1550–3, p. 294; Lansd. 3, f. 197. [2] CPR, 1558–60, p. 430; Lansd. 110, f. 47; VCH Berks. iii. 419; iv. 281, 525. [3] C. Monro, Acta Canc. 448–50; Neale, Commons, 156; D'Ewes, 165, 183, 188, 251, 253, 255, 262, 264; CJ, i. 89, 92, 97, 108, 109, 110, 111, 112, 113, 115, 120, 122; Trinity, Dublin, Thos. Cromwell's jnl. ff. 19, 28, 49, 54, 55. [4] PCC 3 Drury; APC, viii. 357; C142/227/208; CP, ii. 206; DNB (St. George Richard).

A.H.

ST. JOHN, Oliver I

BEDFORD   1563

EITHER

Oliver St. John of Sharnbrook, 2nd s. of Sir John St. John of Bletsoe by Sybil, da. of Rice ap Morgan ap Jenkyn ap Philip. m. Mary, da. of William Fitzjeffrey of Thurleigh, Beds., 5s. 4da.
?Sheriff, Beds. and Bucks. 1551–2.

OR

Oliver St. John of Thurleigh and Keysoe, Beds., nephew of the above, 1st s. of Alexander St. John by Jane or Joan, da. of George Dalyson of Shingle or Cranesley, Northants. m. Margaret, da. of Thomas Eston or Easton of Holme, Beds., wid. of John Gooderick of Doddington, Ely, ?1da.
J.p. Beds. by 1579; ?auditor of the Exchequer 1583.[1]

Between 1540 and 1558 there were at least three Oliver St. Johns active in Bedfordshire, the two above and their relative Oliver St. John†, who became 1st Baron St. John in January 1559. Thus, unless a seat is mentioned, it is difficult to say which of the three is meant in any particular instance. The Bedfordshire justice of the peace in 1554 and sheriff for Bedfordshire and Buckinghamshire 1551–2 was probably the future Lord St. John.[2]

By 1563 Oliver St. John of Sharnbrook, about seven miles from Bedford, must have been an elderly man, if, indeed, he was still alive. His brother, Sir John†, died 1558. Oliver St. John of Thurleigh and Keysoe – on the whole the most likely person to have been the 1563 Member – was evidently of age by 1553, when he and Robert Thornton paid over £800 for monastic land in several counties. His career, apart from the one reference to him as an auditor of the Exchequer, is obscure. His will, made 27 Sept. 1586, was proved 5 Feb. 1591. It asked that he should be buried at Keysoe, and left 40s. to the poor of the parish, with legacies to his stepson Henry Gooderick and to other relatives. The widow, Margaret St. John, was appointed sole executrix, with John St. John*, 2nd Baron St. John as one of three overseers. There was evidently a query about the value of the property, as a sentence 'per valore' is attached to the will.[3]

[1] Harl. 5186, p. 22; *Vis. Beds.* (Harl. Soc. xix), 53–5; *Vis. Herts.* (Harl. Soc. xxii), 150; *Vis. Cambs.* (Harl. Soc. xli), 48. One of the pedigrees gives Alice (*m.* John Clopton) as sis. (not da.) of this Oliver. [2] *CP*; *LP Hen. VIII*, xiv(2), p. 202; xv. p. 6; *CPR*, 1553 and App. Ed. VI, p. 351; 1553–4, p. 17. [3] *CPR*, 1553 and App. Ed. VI. pp. 82–8; PCC 9 Sainberbe.

N.M.F.

ST. JOHN, Oliver II (c.1545–1618), of Standfordbury and Bletsoe, Beds.

BEDFORDSHIRE	1589, 1593

b. c.1545, 2nd s. of Oliver, 1st Baron St. John, by his 1st w. Agnes, and bro. of John II*. *m.* Dorothy, da. of John Rede† of Boddington, Glos., 6s. inc. Oliver IV* 7da. *suc.* bro. as 3rd Baron 1596.

J.p. Beds. from c.1584, sheriff 1585–6, 1589–90, custos rot. 1596; ld. lt. Hunts. from 1596; recorder, Bedford by 1596; commr. trials of the Earls of Essex and Southampton 1601.[1]

Although St. John's wife brought him four Gloucestershire manors, and his father bequeathed him Nether Turkdean and other lands in Gloucestershire, he made his chief residence Stanfordbury, which he had purchased in 1564; the parish register records the baptism of six of his children between 1588 and 1596.[2]

St. John was a friend of Peter Wentworth* and brought Humphrey Winch* into Parliament for Bedford in 1593 with the idea of introducing a bill to settle the succession, but the Privy Council heard of the scheme and had Wentworth put in the Tower. St. John and Winch were allowed to continue to attend the House, but the St. John who took part in the debates later in the session was Oliver St. John III. As the senior knight for Bedfordshire St. John could have served on the subsidy committees in both the 1589 (11 Feb.) and 1593 (26 Feb.) Parliaments and on a legal committee, 9 Mar. 1593. In 1597 Wentworth, when his release from the Tower was under discussion, said that St. John (who by now had succeeded to the family peerage), would stand surety for him, and find others to do the same, and that as his wife was dead he would rather live with St. John at Bletsoe. Among St. John's other friends was Christopher Yelverton*, who secured his honorary admission to Gray's Inn in 1598.[3]

As the Bedfordshire lord lieutenancy had, since 1585, been in the hands of Henry Grey, Earl of Kent, whose family had been in the county since the thirteenth century, the head of the St. John family was usually lord lieutenant of Huntingdonshire, in which county they owned some estates. St. John's tenure of the office was, in the Elizabethan period, poisoned by complaints from the Council about the poor quality of his levies. In 1598:

> the country shall be driven to the charge to find new armour and furniture and your Lordship receive that imputation we would be loath should amongst all other lieutenants happen unto you ... we wish amends to be

made with more diligence hereafter upon the occasion of her Majesty's service ...

and, in 1600,

> You have ... given such an example of carelessness as we have not known in any man's lieutenancy.

After 1609 he left the administration of his estates to his eldest son Oliver St. John IV so

> that hereafter I may lead a quiet contemplative life, whereby I may be the better prepared for death when it shall please God to finish my course here on earth.

He looked forward to enjoying 'that blessed estate which is prepared in heaven for the elect children of God'. He died 2 Sept. 1618.[4]

[1] *CP*, xi. 334, 336; S. Rudder, *Glos.* 301; PRO Index 4208; PCC 22 Tirwhite; E163/14/8. [2] PCC 22 Tirwhite; *VCH Beds.* iii. 258; *Beds. Par. Reg.* ed. Emmison, xii. 8–10. [3] D'Ewes, 431, 474, 496; *HMC Hatfield*, vii. 286, 303. [4] *CP*, vii. 172; xi. 336; *VCH Beds.* iii. 326; *APC*, xxix. 47, 154; xxx. 169–70; *VCH Hunts.* ii. 23; Nichols, *Progresses Jas. I*, i. 518, 523; ii. 203; iii. 557, 672, 984; *CSP Dom.* 1598–1601, p. 408; *CSP Dom.* Add. 1580–1625, pp. 448–9; 1611–18, p. 255; PCC 110 Meade; C142/376/126.

A.M.M.

ST. JOHN, Oliver III (c.1560–1630), of Battersea, Surr.

CIRENCESTER	1593
PORTSMOUTH	1604
CONSTITUENCY UNKNOWN	1614

b. c.1560, 2nd s. of Nicholas St. John of Lydiard Tregoze, Wilts. by Elizabeth, da. of Sir Richard Blount* of Mapledurham, Oxon. *educ.* Trinity, Oxf. BA 1578; L. Inn 10 Oct. 1580. *m.* c.1592, Joan, da. and h. of Henry Roydon of Battersea, wid. of Thomas Holcroft I*, *s.p.* Kntd. 28 Feb. 1600; *cr.* Visct. Grandison [I] 1621, Baron Tregoz 1626.

J.p. Surr. 1593; gent. pens. 1593/96–1605/6; master gen. of the ordnance [I] 1605–14, PC [I] 1605; MP [I] 1613–15; ld. dep. [I] 1616–22; PC 1622; high treasurer [I] 1625–30.[1]

The St. Johns of Lydiard Tregoze were a cadet branch of the Bletsoe family, descended from the Sir Oliver St. John who had married Margaret, the Beauchamp heiress. As a younger son, St. John himself was expected to make his own way in the world, his father leaving him only £40 a year. Originally intended for the law, he killed George Best, the companion and chronicler of Frobisher, in a duel ('by nature I am the child of wrath', he said in his will), and was forced to flee the country in 1584. So he served in the Netherlands and later in France, and in 1595 he was included in a list of officers with a note that he had commanded a company of horse at the siege of Rouen, where, on the first day, his horse had been killed in the charge. But he was in England for the Parliament of 1593, and again in 1597, when he took the Surrey levies to London. He is last known to have been on the Continent in 1600, at the battle of Nieuport.[2]

St. John was presumably returned for Cirencester through the influence of Charles Danvers*, who had also served in the Netherlands. As one of the Cirencester Members St. John could have served on a cloth committee, 15 Mar. 1593. He was certainly one of those appointed on 30 Mar. to join with the Lords in distributing the contributions of both Houses for the relief of poor maimed soldiers, and a few days later was among those appointed by the Privy Council to make a list of soldiers who had been maimed or disabled in the Queen's service in the four preceding years, submitting a report to the lord keeper, who would then inform both Houses of Parliament of the situation. He was still concerning himself with the plight of ex-servicemen in the 1604 Parliament.[3]

As Oliver St. John II, friend of Peter Wentworth* and Humphrey Winch*, was also in the 1593 Parliament, it is seemingly perverse to suggest attributing a speech made 27 Feb. in support of James Morice's motion on the 'hard courses of the bishops ... towards sundry learned and godly ministers', to the soldier. But the journalist has him saying 'I am but young' and this fits 33 better than 48. Perhaps Oliver St. John II had asked him to speak on his behalf so as to avoid following Wentworth to the Tower, for the sentiments were certainly his; perhaps there is total confusion and the speech was made by someone else, such as Henry Finch (who certainly did support the motion). However, the entry in D'Ewes is explicit: 'Then up stood Mr. Oliver St. John, as may be collected out of the aforesaid original journal book of the House of Commons, where he is said to have spoken next after Mr. Henry Finch'.

> The ancient charter of this realm says *nullus liber homo*, etc., which is flatly violated by bishops jurisdiction. You know what things Thomas Becket stood upon against the King, which things are now also crept in.

It was useless to cite precedents, or 'thieves may prescribe to take purses on Shooters Hill because time out of mind they had done so ... and because it is allowed in Geneva, so to allow it here, that is no reason. For in Geneva there be many things allowed, which the party speaking [probably William Lewin is meant] would, I daresay, be loath to have used here.' Again, it was probably Oliver St. John III who got into a dispute with Heneage, the vice-chamberlain, on 6 Mar. over the terms of reference to be given to the committee which was to discuss the subsidy with the Lords.[4]

St. John's first mission to Ireland was early in 1600, when he took over from England 800 reinforcements and stayed to take part in the campaigns of the summer, in which he distinguished himself. He continued in command of a company, and was present at the siege of Kinsale in 1601, where he was wounded. He made regular journeys to England with messages for the lord deputy,

and in 1601 Mountjoy suggested him to Cecil as muster master general for Ireland. He finally obtained an Irish office in 1605, became lord deputy under Buckingham, and died 29 Dec. 1630.[5]

[1] *CP*, vi. 74; Hatfield ms 278. [2] *Wilts. Vis. Peds.* (Harl. Soc. cv, cvi), 167–8; J. S. Taylor, *Our Lady of Battersea*, 152; *DNB*; Manning and Bray, *Surr.* iii, App. cxx; PCC 1 St. John; Lansd. 78, f. 138; *HMC Hatfield*, vi. 570; *APC*, xxiv. 416; xxvii. 105, 164. [3] D'Ewes, 501, 512; *APC*, xxiv. 160; *HMC Buccleuch*, iii. 82. [4] D'Ewes, 475, 489–90. [5] *CSP Ire.* 1599–60, p. 479; 1600, pp. 4, 336, 501, 503; 1600–1, pp. 53, 59, 173, 175–7; 1601–3, pp. 13, 203; *APC*, xxx. 809; *HMC Hatfield*, xii. 483; *CP*, vi. 74.

A.M.M./P.W.H.

ST. JOHN, Oliver IV (c.1584–1646), of Bletsoe, Beds.

BEDFORDSHIRE   1601, 1604

b. c.1584, 1st s. of Oliver St. John II* by his w. Dorothy, *educ.* Peterhouse, Camb. c.1595, G. Inn 1597. *m.* Apr. 1602, Elizabeth, da. and h. of William Paulet of Ewalden, Som., 4s. 3da. KB 1610; *suc.* fa. as 4th Baron St. John 1618; *cr.* Earl of Bolingbroke 1624.

Jt. ld. lt. Hunts. 1619; ld. lt. (parlt.) Beds. 1643.

As a knight of the shire in 1601 St. John could have served on the main business committee, 3 Nov. and on the monopolies committee, 23 Nov. But he was only 17 or thereabouts, and is unlikely to have played any significant part in the affairs of his first Parliament. Found 'ever dutiful' by his father, there is little to say about him in the Elizabethan period. Like his father he was host to James I at Bletsoe. In September 1619 the King was 'very nobly entertained at the Lord St. John's, which he took in so good part that he professes he will not forget so honourable usage'. But St. John followed his father in failing to ally himself closely with the court, and went over to Parliament in the civil war.[1]

He died in June 1646. Administration of the estate was granted on 3 July 1646 to the widow, and a new grant was made to a creditor in November 1655.[2]

[1] *CP*; *DNB*; D'Ewes, 624, 649; PCC 110 Meade; *Chamberlain Letters* ed. McClure, ii. 263. [2] PCC admon. act bk. 1646, f. 82; 1655, f. 222.

A.M.M.

ST. JOHN, William (1538–1609), of Farley Chamberlayne, Hants.

STOCKBRIDGE   1563, 1571

b. 1538, s. of John St. John† (*d.*1576), of Lydiard Tregoze, Wilts. by his 2nd w. Elizabeth, da. of Sir Richard Whethill† of London; half-bro. of Nicholas St. John*. *educ.* ?Jesus, Camb. 1547. *m.* by 1568, Barbara Gooce or Goore, wid. of Thomas Twyne of Wonston, 2s. inc. Henry* 4da.

J.p. Hants from c.1577, sheriff 1587–8.

St. John was born on his father's estate at Farley and was presumably living there when he was returned for the newly enfranchised borough of Stockbridge in 1563. A few years after his first election, his marriage brought him another manor in the neighbourhood; and before 1576 – when his half-brother Nicholas inherited the main estates in Wiltshire – Farley and Littleton, Hampshire, were settled upon him. St. John was 'a man of great countenance and credit', often serving as a county official, for example inspecting the fortifications of Portsmouth, and providing horse for the Irish campaigns at the end of the century. In January 1602 he quarrelled with (Sir) Hampden Paulet*, on whose behalf the Marchioness of Winchester complained to the Privy Council.

St. John died 8 Apr. 1609, being succeeded by his son Henry*. In his will, he hoped to be saved by Christ's 'merits, death and passion only' and to be 'received into the company of His elect'. He asked to be buried with 'little charge', but gave detailed specifications for the 'memorial for posterity', made of freestone from the Isle of Wight, which was to be raised to him under the supervision of his son-in-law, (Sir) Francis Castilion*.

PCC 114 Dorset, 32 Carew; *Wilts. Colls.* 170; *VCH Hants*, iii. 458; iv. 374, 444; W. Berry, *Co. Genealogies, Hants*, 148; C142/321/87; *APC*, xix. 68; xxiii. 184, 209, 237; xxxii. 279; Lansd. 104, f. 89; *HMC Hatfield*, xii. 34.

A.H.

ST. LEGER (SELLENGER), Sir Anthony (c.1496–1559), of Ulcombe and Leeds Castle, Kent.

KENT　　　　　　　　　　　　　1559*

b. c.1496, 1st s. of Ralph St. Leger of Ulcombe by Elizabeth, da. of Sir Richard Haut of Kent. *educ.* Camb.; travelled France and Italy; G. Inn. *m.* Agnes or Anne, da. of Hugh Warham of Croydon and niece and h. of William Warham, abp. of Canterbury, at least 5s. inc. Nicholas* 2da. *suc.* fa. 1518. Kntd. 1539; KG 1544.[1]

J.p. Kent by 1526, sheriff 1539–40; commr. to survey Calais 1535, 1552, to defend Kent coast 1539, heresy 1552; gent. privy chamber by 1538–c.53; ld. deputy, Ireland July 1540–48, Aug. 1550–May 1551, Oct. 1553–May 1556; PC 7 Aug. 1553–bef. 1558; envoy to France Aug. 1553.[2]

When twelve years of age [St. Leger] was sent for his grammar learning with his tutor into France, for his carriage into Italy, for his philosophy to Cambridge, for his law to Gray's Inn, and for that which completed all, the government of himself, to court, where his debonairness and freedom took with the King, as his solidity and wisdom with the Cardinal.[3]

Though so carefully prepared, St. Leger was never a principal adviser to any of his sovereigns, being required instead to devote himself to the thankless task of trying to impose an alien government on the Irish. Recognizing that Ireland 'is much easier won than kept', as he put it, he concentrated on the area around Dublin, and endeavoured to win over the local leaders by grants of land, 'small gifts' and 'honest persuasion'. At first successful, the end of his first period in office was marred by a quarrel with Ormond, the most powerful Irishman. Reappointed by Protector Somerset, St. Leger was given the impossible task of imposing the new prayer book. Somerset made no allowance for the differences between England and Ireland, and was warned by St. Leger that the Irish 'should be handled with the more humanity lest they, by extremity, should adhere to other foreign powers'. By Mary's reign money was short and St. Leger's own standing had been undermined by accusations of corruption. John Hooker wrote

> This man ruled and governed very justly and uprightly in a good conscience … [yet] many slanderous informations were made and inveighed against him, which is a fatal destiny, and inevitable to every good governor in that land. For the more pains they take in tillage, the worse is their harvest; and the better be their services, the greater is the malice and envy against them, being not unlike to a fruitful apple tree, which the more apples he beareth, the more cudgels be hurled at him.

The truth of the matter will never be ascertained. His own attitude would no doubt have been the same as a statement he had made when similar accusations had been levelled against him in 1538: 'I have too long abstained from bribery to begin now'. There is no doubt that Mary kept him short of money, and he was said to have left debts in Ireland of over £3,000. His return from Ireland in 1556 to face a Privy Council inquiry marked the end of his active career. The investigation was still in progress when Elizabeth succeeded, and, typically enough, far from dropping the charges, she renewed the inquiry into his accounts. Perhaps it was his vulnerability that led St. Leger, now in his sixties, to seek, for the first time, election to Parliament, or perhaps it was simply that he wished to serve at least once as knight of his shire, an honour his absences in Ireland had often denied him, though he could have sat in Mary's last, where he might have been more at home. The vestigial journals of Elizabeth's first Parliament do not mention his name, and St. Leger died during its course, with the Privy Council inquiry still in progress, on 16 Mar. 1559. He was buried at Ulcombe, his family seat for 450 years. His wife died eight days later, and was buried the day before his own elaborate funeral.

St. Leger must be classed as indifferent in religion. He was attached to both Wolsey and Thomas Cromwell, though he should not be confused with a namesake, a Sussex priest, who was wholly committed to Cromwell. He served both Somerset and Mary, moderating as far as he could, the extremes of both regimes. When the protestant archbishop of Dublin chided him for conservatism he retorted, 'Go to, your matters of religion will mar all'. When the Catholic Bishop Gardiner of Winchester was condemning a priest for conducting reformed services he intervened: 'My good lord chancellor, trouble not yourself with this heretic. I think all the world is full of them'.[4]

[1] *DNB*; Lloyd, *State Worthies*, i. 99; C. Wykeham Martin, *Hist. Leeds Castle*, table after p. 156; *Vis. Kent* (Harl. Soc. lxxv), 69; *LP Hen. VIII*, xix(1), p. 252. Material on St. Leger's Irish policy can be found in *LP Hen. VIII*, vols. xiii–xxi; *State Pprs. Hen. VIII*, vols. ii and iii; R. Bagwell, *Ireland under the Tudors*, vol. i; *Cal. Carew Pprs.* 1515–74; *CSP Ire.* 1509–73; R. D. Edwards, *Church and State in Tudor Ireland*, 92, 133–7, 161; W. A. Phillips, *Hist. Church of Ire.* ii. 248. [2] *LP Hen. VIII*, iv(1), p. 901; ix. pp. 59–60; xiii(2), p. 534; xiv. p. 151; *APC*, iv. 313; *CSP For.* 1553–8, pp. 4–6; *CPR*, 1550–3, p. 355; Strype, *Cranmer*, i. 435. The Imperial ambassador in London confused St. Leger with Sir Thomas Chalenor, MP, which has led several subsequent writers to the belief that St. Leger was in France most of the year. [3] Lloyd, i. 99. [4] *LP Hen. VIII*, xiii(1), p. 88; xiv(1), pp. 158, 163; xv, pp. 417, 468, 469, 563; xvi, p. 721; xix(1), p. 619; *CPR*, 1549–51, pp. 366–8, 428–9; 1550–3, p. 326; Hasted, *Kent*, vols. iii, v–ix passim; *HMC 15th Rep.* 5; Strype, *Annals*, i(1), pp. 21, 34; *Machyn Diary* (Cam. Soc. xlii), 192, 372; PCC 25 Chaynay; Strype, *Memorials*, iii(1), pp. 105–6.

M.R.P./P.W.H.

ST. LEGER (SELLENGER), Sir John (by 1516–93/96), of Annery in Monkleigh, Devon.

DARTMOUTH	1555
DEVON	1559
ARUNDEL	1563
DEVON	1571, 1572
TREGONY	1584

b. by 1516, 1st s. of Sir George St. Leger of Annery by Anne, da. of Edmund Knyvet. *m.* by June 1535, Catherine, da. of George Neville, 5th Lord Bergavenny, at least 2s. 4da. *suc.* fa. bet. 1533 and 1537. Kntd. bet. 1544 and 1547.

Commr. relief, Devon 1550, musters 1569; j.p. from 1554, q. from c.1559, sheriff 1560–1; dep. lt. Cornw. and Devon 1558, Devon 1569.[1]

St. Leger inherited considerable west-country estates, and remained an active local official from the reign of Henry VIII to almost the end of Elizabeth's reign. He conformed to the state church, whether Catholic or protestant, but that his sympathies were with the reformers is suggested by the 2nd Earl of Bedford's appointing him a deputy lieutenant and by Elizabeth's making him a visitor for the diocese of Exeter and giving him a rectory and advowson. St. Leger thrice sat as knight of the shire, and came in for Arundel (through his relative the 12th Earl of Arundel) and Tregony (through the Pomeroy family or the 2nd Earl of Bedford). His parliamentary career is of no special interest. He was on the succession committee (31 Oct. 1566), and was one of 30 Commons MPs summoned on 5 Nov. to hear the Queen's message on the succession. He claimed privilege for a servant 9 Apr. 1571, at a time when he was himself up to his ears in debt, and served on committees concerned with navigation (8 May 1571), Devon harbours (11 May), tanners (11 May), and cloth (8 Feb. 1581).

On 10 Mar. 1581 the Lords sent down a bill for the restitution in blood of St. Leger's two sons John and Dudley (probably Dudley was illegitimate) who had disgraced themselves by 'certain lewd practices' including robbery on Hounslow Heath, and had been in the Fleet after a brawl with the sons of Sir John Perrot*. John St. Leger became a soldier, and wrote to Walsingham from the Netherlands asking him to persuade his father not to 'bury himself in so dark a tomb that he leave no light, sign, or mark of his name, house, wife, family and children'. In 1589, when he was commanding troops in Ireland, the Privy Council granted him permission to visit Annery, where his father was ill, and there is a reference to another projected visit in the following year. In 1592 the old man was too infirm to take the oath of allegiance at the Devon sessions, but he was well enough to meet other justices at Barnstaple about the rating for the 1593 subsidy.

By this time many estates had been sold and St. Leger had been involved in lawsuit after lawsuit over his debts, on which he was paying 20% interest. On one occasion Richard Grenville II* brought a case in the stannary courts against one Hilling for saying publicly to one of St. Leger's servants: 'Thy master is an old drunken bankrupt knave, a rogue and a rascally villain – and so go tell him'. The picture is one of general disintegration. Nothing is known of the last years of St. Leger's life, and no inquisition post mortem survives. He died intestate before 7 Nov. 1596, when letters of administration were granted to his daughter Eulalia Arscott *alias* St. Leger – formerly wife of Edmund Tremayne. She renounced the administration in the following year, no doubt because of the insolvency of the estate. John St. Leger wrote to Salisbury in 1605 'if his father had left him that living which his ancestors left him, the world would have more respected him'. He asked that those who had bought Sir John's lands 'at so low a rate' should give him compensation, and this not materializing, the St. Legers disappeared as a landed Devon family.[2]

[1] *LP Hen. VIII*, v. p. 430; xii(1), p. 603; *Trans. Dev. Assoc.* xlix. 213; PCC 21 Thower; *CPR*, 1547–8, p. 52; *CSP Span.* 1554–8, p. 369; *CSP Dom.* Add. 1566–79, p. 130. [2] *Trevelyan Pprs.* (Cam. Soc. lxxxiv), ii. 100; SP11/12/30; 12/133/14; 12/231/40; *HMC Exeter*, 366–7; Hooker, *Life of Sir Peter Carew*, 54–6; Bodl. Rawl. B 285, f. 2; H. Gee, *Eliz. Clergy*, 98–9; *CPR*, 1558–60, p. 320; 1560–3, pp. 72, 551; 1563–6, p. 309; Devon RO, Tingey, mss 840, 850, 852, 865, 885–7; *Trans. Dev. Assoc.* viii. 525; lxxxvi. 133; C33/37, ff. 304–5; *Som. Enrolled Deeds* (Som. Rec. Soc. li), 64; E133/2/238; A. L. Rowse, *Grenville*, 149–50; Strype, *Annals*, ii(2), 616–17; *Mdx. Sessions Rolls*, i. 89; *APC*, ix. 30, 139, 142–3, 202, 211; xviii. 447; D'Ewes, 126, 159, 181, 183, 293, 304; *CJ*, i. 83, 88, 89, 123; Camb. Univ. Lib. Gg. iii. 34, p. 209; *Archaeologia*, xxviii. 18; *CSP For.* 1579–80, p. 450; Chanter, *Barnstaple*, 95; PCC admon. act bk. 1596, f. 183; *Vis. Devon*, ed. Vivian, 20; *HMC Hatfield*, xvii. 499–500; PCC 45 Tirwhite.

N.M.F.

ST. LEGER (SELLENGER), Nicholas (*d.* c.1589), of Ulcombe, Eastwell Place and Beamstone, Kent.

MAIDSTONE	1571, 1572

3rd s. of Sir Anthony St. Leger* by Agnes or Anne, da. of Hugh Warham of Croydon, Surr. and niece and h. of William Warham, abp. of Canterbury. *educ.* I. Temple 1552. *m.* Katherine (*d.* 1587), da. of Sir Thomas Moyle† of Eastwell, wid. of Sir Thomas Finch* of the Moat, nr. Canterbury and of Eastwell, *s.p.*

J.p. Kent from c.1575; commr. eccles. causes Jan. 1583.[1]

As a member of one of the leading local families St. Leger would have found no difficulty in securing a parliamentary seat at Maidstone. Indeed, the St. Legers could claim that they had occupied the same land at Ulcombe since Robert de Sancto Leodegario settled there in the reign of William I. No mention is made of Nicholas St. Leger in his father's will, so it is impossible to say how well he was provided for, but it is clear that his social and financial position was improved by his marriage, through which he became associated with two other Kent families, the Moyles and the Finches. He appears to have lived most of the time at Eastwell Place and at Beamstone, two manors which his wife had inherited from her father, and, in her right, he presented vicars to the livings of Eastling in 1574 and Eastwell in 1580. But she had only a life interest in the manors, which would revert to Moyle Finch*, her son by her first marriage. St. Leger became involved in a legal dispute over Beamstone when his wife refused to accept her son's reversionary interest there. Sir Thomas Heneage*, one of whose daughters had married Moyle Finch, took up his son-in-law's cause and persuaded St. Leger to abandon any claim, and to agree not to take any profits from the manors after his wife's death. Another Finch manor, Packmanston, had earlier passed permanently into St. Leger hands. Nicholas also bought Willingdon, or Wilmington, from the Duke of Norfolk.[2]

St. Leger's religious views are of more than usual interest. The archbishop of Canterbury's report to the Privy Council in 1564 provides the earliest clue to them. At the end of his list of those sound in religion the archbishop mentions three men, including St. Leger, who were not yet justices but appear to have been suggested as suitable for the office. He says of these:

> which persons, though not of like zeal in religion, yet such as I must say that the furthest off in favourable affection towards the state of religion, be outwardly men conformable and not chargeable to my knowledge of any great extremities uttered by them in afflicting the honest and godly, or in maintaining the perverse and ungodly.

It was not until more than a decade later that St. Leger's name first appears on the commission of the peace, suggesting that a very real doubt existed about his reliability, yet it was in that year, 1575, that he was appointed to a commission to examine certain ecclesiastical statutes.[3]

Apart from his appointment to a Privy Council commission to investigate a case of slander in Maidstone, few links can be traced with the borough which returned St. Leger to Parliament. His only recorded activity in 1571 was his membership of the conference to consider the bill against fugitives (25 May), but in the long Parliament of 1572 his religious interests were well represented. His first reported speech, 16 May 1572, raised more issues than it answered. Was Arthur Hall, who had spoken in defence of the Duke of Norfolk, fit to remain in the House? For his part he thought Hall's malady so great and his leprosy so perilous as to be incurable: 'Speech ought to be contained in bounds, cankers not to be suffered'. After St. Leger 'divers men spake diversely' on the question of freedom of speech. St. Leger was put on the rites and ceremonies committee, 20 May, and on the 22nd was the first to react to the Speaker's declaration that the Queen wanted to scrutinize any religious bills. St. Léger moved that 'those which are to deliver the same to the Queen's Majesty' should ensure 'that there be no scanning of words, but the meaning of the bill to be only considered'. He returned to the charge on 30 May:

> Since the Queen's Majesty's will and pleasure is that we should not proceed nor deal with the first bill against the monstrous and huge dragon and mass of the earth, the Queen of Scots, yet my conscience urgeth and pricketh me to speak and move this House to be in hand with her Majesty with the execution of the roaring lion: I mean the Duke of Norfolk. And although her Majesty be lulled asleep and wrapped in the mantle of her own peril, yet for my part I cannot be silent in uttering of my conscience

and on 9 June he was added to the conference to discuss what action should be taken against the Scottish Queen. He was put on the committee for Tonbridge grammar school (28 May), took a message to the Lords on a privilege matter (6 June) and spoke (10 June) on the question of setting up a parish church at Liverpool instead of the existing chapel. He was against calling the church St. Paul's and he wanted proper provision for the incumbent. In 1576 he was on committees concerning the debts of William Isley on 14 and 27 Feb.; and a committee on cloth (9 Mar.) but is not known to have spoken. On 24 Jan. 1581 he made another strong stand against royal influence after the Queen had expressed disapproval of the Commons' suggestion for a public fast. Speaking with 'discretion and moderation' just after the comptroller of the Household, Sir James Croft*, had 'enforced the fault of the House with much violence', he urged 'the great fault and remissness of the bishops' and wished the Queen and her subjects 'would be ready to express their true repentance to God in humbling themselves in sackcloth and ashes'. He was appointed to committees on the subsidy (25 Jan.); slanderous words and practices (1, 3 Feb.); Arthur Hall (6 Feb.), whose blood he had been after nine years before; corporations (11 Feb.); the debts of Sir Thomas Gresham

(20 Feb.); Dover harbour (4 Mar.); fraudulent conveyances (14 Mar.); the Queen's safety (14 Mar.) and Lord Zouche (17 Mar.). It is a little strange that so active a Member did not sit again. However unpopular his views might have been with the authorities it is hard to imagine that he could not have found a borough seat if he had wished. He certainly continued active in the cause of his religion. In 1584 he was one of the 38 Kent gentlemen who petitioned the Council for the reinstatement of local ministers who had been suspended by Whitgift for failing to subscribe to his articles. A delegation came to London and had a stormy interview with the archbishop. When he defended baptism by women, 'divers of them muttered much' and St. Leger said, 'God forgive you'. We are told that all save one departed angrily, threatening Whitgift with social ostracism in Kent. Not long after this, about 1587, St. Leger's name was deleted from the commission of the peace. This might perhaps have been because of his death, the date of which is not known, but, as he is on a list of those to be removed from the commission, another reason is more likely, though this could as well have been his wife's death and the consequent loss of his estates as his religious views. It .is likely that he was the Nicholas St. Leger 'of Faversham', administration of whose property was granted to Anthony St. Leger on 5 June 1589. Presumably he had moved there after his wife's death had forced him to vacate the Finch manors.[4]

[1] C. W. Martin, *Hist. Leeds Castle*, gen. table facing p. 156; *DNB* (St. Leger, Sir Anthony); C142/222/18; *HMC 13th Rep. IV*, 83; SP12/104, 121, 145; E163/14/8; Lansd. 35, f. 134; 737, f. 143; Royal 18 D 111, f. 23. [2] *DNB*; Martin, 155; Hasted, *Kent*, v. 388–91; vi. 436; vii. 403–5, 409, 411, 418; PCC 25 Chaynay; *Arch. Cant.* xviii. 20; xli. 36; *CSP Dom.* 1547–80, p. 695; *CSP Dom.* Add. 1580–1625, p. 31; *CPR*, 1558–60, p. 9; 1563–6, pp. 4, 496. [3] *Cam. Misc.* ix(3), pp. 57–8; Lansd. 683, f. 70. [4] *APC*, ix. 274–5; xiv. 308; D'Ewes, 188, 222, 250, 284, 288, 292, 294, 306, 307; *CJ*, i. 92, 96, 98, 100–1, 101, 105, 108, 113, 119, 121, 123, 124, 128, 131, 133, 134, 135; Bodl. Tanner 393; House of Lords, Braye mss, Fulk Onslow's jnl. f. 1; Trinity, Dublin, Thos. Cromwell's jnl. f. 16; Lansd. 43, f. 7; 121, f. 68; Dr. Williams's Lib. Morrice mss L V 7; Collinson thesis, 443–5; PCC Admons. iii. 135; *Arch. Cant.* xviii. 28; *Kentish Wills*, ed. Clarke, 89; *Vis. Kent* (Harl. Soc. xlii), 142.

M.R.P./P.W.H.

ST. LOE (SEYNTLOWE), Edward (d.1578), of Sutton Court, Som. and Knighton, Wilts.

Bath	1559
Downton	1572*

2nd s. of Sir John St. Loe*, and bro. of Sir William*. *m.* (1) Bridget, da. of John Malte, wid. of John Scutt; (2) Margaret; 2s. 1da.[1]

Capt. in Ireland 1567.

In 1549 and 1553 St. Loe was associated with his father in grants of local office and revenue,[2] but the family's protestant sympathies and affiliations involved them in trouble during Queen Mary's reign, St. Loe himself being imprisoned in the Fleet in May 1556 for complicity in the Dudley plot. After the accession of Elizabeth, his brother Sir William came into favour at court, and in the 1559 Parliament all three St. Loes gained seats, Edward being returned for Bath through the local standing of his family and his own nearby residence. This was the only known election of an outsider by Bath during the Elizabethan period. There is no mention of St. Loe in the defective journals of this Parliament.

The new reign, which had promised better times, in fact brought trouble, mostly of St. Loe's own making. Early in 1561 he and his mother visited Sir William St. Loe and his wife Bess of Hardwick in London, where Edward St. Loe was suspected of administering poison to them both, after 'much unnaturalness and unseemly speeches' concerning Sir William's marriage, which seemed likely to deprive Edward of his inheritance. In the event it did, for Sir William, after the alleged poisoning attempt 'did of very good will toward [his wife] convey [his lands] unto her'. St. Loe was suspected also of having poisoned his first wife's first husband and then the lady herself. In the circumstances it is perhaps not surprising that after unsuccessfully contesting his brother's will Edward undertook a period of service in Ireland, where in 1567 he was in command of the garrison at Derry.[3]

St. Loe's later career was largely shaped by his connexion with successive earls of Pembroke. The 1st Earl had been an associate of his father (who made him an overseer of his will), and Edward remained in the Wilton entourage. His lease of Knighton, a manor in Broad Chalk a few miles from that house, which had come to Herbert from the Darrells, began at some time after 1563, when the Pembroke survey makes no mention of him there, and perhaps after 1572, when he is described as of 'Stoye', Somerset; in 1576 he was assessed at £10 for the subsidy on lands at Knighton. In July 1575 post horses were ordered for him to visit the 2nd Earl and Lady Pembroke at Spa, to whom he was to carry letters and news from Walsingham. It was doubtless as the nominee of Pembroke that St. Loe was returned to the Parliament of 1572 for Downton. He was presumably the Mr. 'Watslowe' who spoke on the Wykes v. Dennis case 7 June 1572.[4]

St. Loe died intestate in 1578; he was buried in the parish church of Broad Chalk 6 May, where a brass plate long commemorated him. On 11 Feb. 1580 the administration of his estate was granted, with his widow's and son's consent, to Henry Galberd, of Pensford, Publow, Somerset. When his widow Margaret died 13 years later, their two children were already married, John to Elizabeth Hyde, of the rising legal family of Hatch, and Ann to Edward Nicholas, to whom she had already borne the future secretary of state. Margaret St. Loe's reference to her son-in-law Richard Stephens as 'my well beloved in Christ' smacks of religious enthusiasm, perhaps of a puritan kind.[5]

[1] *Vis. Wilts.* (Harl. Soc. cv), 170–1; PCC 20 Nevell; *Som. Wills* (ser. 6), 24. The visitations are confused over the marriages, understandably in view of St. Loe's suspected rôle as a poisoner. His first wife was pregnant, no doubt by St. Loe, at their marriage, but it is not known whether the child lived. [2] *LP Hen. VIII*, xviii(2), p. 44; *Wilts. N. and Q.* iv. 118. [3] *APC*, v. 270; C3/159/9, 170/13, 170/58; *HMC Hatfield*, i. 343; D. N. Durant, *Bess of Hardwick*, 38–9. [4] PCC 4 Chaynay; *Som. Wills* (ser. 6), 24; Feet of Fines, Wilts. Easter 1 Edw. VI; *Pembroke Survey* (Roxburghe Club), i. 306; *Wilts. Subsidy Lists* (Wilts. Arch. Soc. recs. br. x), 136; *APC*, ix. 11; Trinity, Dublin, Thos. Cromwell's jnl. f. 56. [5] *Som. Wills* (ser. 6), 24–5; PCC 20 Nevell.

S.T.B.

ST. LOE (SEYNTLOWE), Sir John (c.1501–59), of Tormarton, Glos.

SOMERSET	1545, ?1555
GLOUCESTERSHIRE	1559*

b. c.1501, 1st s. of Nicholas St. Loe of Chew, Som. by Eleanor, da. and coh. of Sir Thomas Arundell. *m.* Margaret, da. of Sir William Kingston[†], 2s., Sir William* and Edward* 1da. *suc.* fa. 1508. Kntd. bef. Nov. 1528.

Steward of Thornbury and constable of Thornbury castle, Glos. 4 Nov. 1528; chief steward of Portbury, Som. 1533; j.p. Som. from 1532, Glos. May 1547–54, 1558–9; sheriff, Glos. 1536–7, Som. and Dorset 1551–2.

St. Loe's protestantism, marriage into the Kingston family, and opposition to a government bill in the Parliament of 1555 put him under a cloud during Mary Tudor's reign. In May 1556 he was placed under house arrest, no reason being stated in the Privy Council letter, and his son Edward was imprisoned. He was elected for Gloucestershire to the first Parliament of the new reign, and his son and heir for Somerset, but St. Loe died during its course, on 20 Mar. No evidence of a by-election for Gloucestershire has been found. He requested burial 'without pomp or pride'. Most of his lands went to William, the sole executor, to whom he bequeathed also his leases at Keynsham and half his plate and household goods, with an injunction to use certain sums due to him to pay for the wardship of Lord Mountjoy, whom he destined, unsuccessfully, as a husband for his daughter. To his wife he left gold, jewels and apparel, together with half his plate and household stuff and a life interest in property at Tormarton. Overseers included Sir William Herbert, later 1st Earl of Pembroke, and Sir Walter Denys*. The will was dated August 1551 and proved 10 Apr. 1559. St. Loe was buried in the church of Great St. Helen, Bishopsgate. His wishes for a sober funeral were obeyed: though two heralds were present, there was 'neither cross nor clerks, but a sermon, and after a psalm of David'.

Cal. IPM Hen. VII, i. 335; *LP Hen. VIII*, iv(2), p. 2168; xii(1), p. 549; xv. p. 466; xvi. p. 98; xvii, p. 565; xxi(1), p. 41; Stowe 571, f. 57; *Cal. Carew Pprs.* i. 79–81; Guildford Mus. Loseley 1331/2; *APC*, iv. 399; v. 270; PCC 4 Chaynay; E150/46/37; Collinson, *Som.* ii. 403, 441; *Machyn Diary* (Cam. Soc. xlii), 191.

R.V.

ST. LOE (SEYNTLOWE), Sir William (c.1518–c.65), of Tormarton, Glos. and Chatsworth, Derbys.

SOMERSET	1559
DERBYSHIRE	1563*

b. c.1518, 1st s. of Sir John St. Loe*, and bro. of Edward*. *m.* (1) by 1538, Jane, da. of Sir Edward Baynton[†], 2da.; (2) 15 Oct. 1559, Elizabeth, da. of John Hardwick of Hardwick, Derbys., wid. of Robert Barley and of Sir William Cavendish[†], *s.p.* Kntd. 1549; *suc.* fa. 1559.

Lt. King's forts in Leinster 1548; constable Waterford castle by 1551; keeper of the horse to Edward VI 1553; gent. attendant to Princess Elizabeth, temp. Mary; capt. of guard by 1558; chief butler, England and Wales 1559; j.p. Glos., Som. from 1559, Derbys. from 1561.[1]

As Princess Elizabeth's servant St. Loe was charged with complicity in Wyatt's rebellion and committed to the Tower 28 Feb. 1554. He was fined £2,200 and released in January 1555. When his mistress became Queen his loyalty to her was recognized by an annuity and the captainship of the guard. St. Loe was elected knight of the shire for Somerset in her first Parliament, and succeeded his father to the Somerset estates of the family during its course. With the income from his estates, his old and new annuities and the perquisites of his court office, he was a rich man. His marriage to Bess of Hardwick, his second, her third, took place when she owed the Crown £5,000 and had heavy family responsibilities, and his continued attendance at court precluded all but the briefest visits to Chatsworth or to his own estates. His position as her husband brought him election for Derbyshire in the second Parliament of the reign. No record has been found of any activity by him in either Parliament.[2]

St. Loe's surviving correspondence to his wife shows the great affection that can have been his only reason for marrying her. 'My own dear wife Chatsworth', 'My honest, sweet Chatsworth' he calls her, lamenting that the Queen's possessiveness precluded more frequent visits to her. While she was engaged upon one of her perennial building projects there he referred to her as chief overseer of works. Not surprisingly St. Loe's second marriage was resented by his younger brother Edward, who was under heavy suspicion of poisoning St. Loe and his wife. St. Loe's old mother wrote to Bess after an abortive attempt in 1561: 'I was sure you were poisoned when I was at London, and if you had not had a present remedy you had died'. To discourage a further attempt St. Loe made an indenture to hold his lands jointly with his wife. It was in August 1561 that Bess of Hardwick was imprisoned for concealing from the Queen her knowledge of Lady Catherine Grey's marriage to Edward Seymour, Earl of Hertford. Though the conditions were good the term was long, and can probably be seen as part of the Queen's possessiveness over St. Loe, for the circumstances of the offence did not warrant so harsh a punishment upon one whom the Queen had regarded and was to regard as a friend, in so far as this was possible between sovereign and subject. Perhaps if the Queen had a conscience at all in these matters she regretted the incident, for shortly after Bess's release on 25 Mar. 1562 the Queen forgave her £4,000 of the £5,000 she still owed from the estate of her second husband, on condition that the remaining £1,000 was paid by her third, which it was. Soon afterwards St. Loe died, before he could receive the promotion to vice-chamberlain of the Household, which he might have expected. His death took place between November 1564 and March 1565, and he was buried beside his father in the church of Great St. Helen, Bishopsgate. All his property went to the sole executrix, his 'most entirely beloved wife', in consideration of the 'natural affection, mature love and assured good will' which he had always felt for her. The will was unsuccessfully contested.[3]

[1] *Wilts. Vis. Ped.* (Harl. Soc. cv, cvi), 7; *Genealogist*, xi. 248; Collinson, *Som.* ii. 96; Bath mss, Thynne pprs. 3, f. 27. [2] D. N. Durant, *Bess of Hardwick*, 33–49. [3] PCC 24 Morrison; *Som. Wills* (ser. 6), 24–5.

P.W.H.

ST. POLL, George (1562–1613), of Melwood and Snarford, Lincs.

LINCOLNSHIRE	1589, 1593
GREAT GRIMSBY	1604

b. 1562, 1st s. of Thomas St. Poll* of Snarford by Faith, da. of Vincent Grantham† of Goltho, wid. of Thomas Moigne. *educ.* Corpus, Oxf. 1578; L. Inn 1580. *m.* Frances, da. of Christopher Wray* of Glentworth, 1da. *d.v.p. suc.* fa. 1582. Kntd. 1593; *cr.* Bt. 1611.

J.p.q. Lincs. (Lindsey) from c.1583, (Holland, Kesteven) from c.1592; sheriff, Lincs. 1588–9, dep. lt. 1595; collector of the loan 1597, 1598; commr. sewers 1599, gaol delivery, Grimsby 1592, 1598.[1]

On 1 Sept. 1598 St. Poll wrote to Sir Robert Cecil saying that it was 'near 20 years' since he began to serve Cecil's father. Whether or not this may be taken as implying that St. Poll was placed in Burghley's household as a boy, there is no indication that he sought a career at court. His life was that of a country gentleman. After being chosen knight of the shire in 1588 he was pricked as sheriff, and a little over a fortnight after the Parliament began he was given leave of absence to attend to his duties in the county, 21 Feb. 1589. Again elected to a county seat in 1593 he was eligible to attend the subsidy committee appointed 26 Feb., and a legal committee appointed 9 Mar. On 4 Apr. he was named to the committee of the bill to explain the statute of 23 Eliz., concerning recusancy.[2]

St. Poll was among those leading county officials appointed to see that all working justices had taken the oath of supremacy, and he was appointed to many other commissions of inquiry. He was closely associated with

Grimsby, where he paid a fine of £40 to avoid the mayoralty in 1597. He complained about his assessments for supplying horsemen for service in Ireland in 1599, 1600 and 1601. Others wealthier than himself had not been called upon; 'not I think that other men's hurt would be my help, but that others should not think that I had no friends to relieve me, or else that I am so senseless of my own estate as not to feel myself pressed when the burden is heavy upon me'.[3]

The quarrel in which St. Poll and his brother-in-law (Sir) William Wray*, were involved with William Hickman, a London merchant who had recently settled in Lincolnshire, is referred to in Wray's biography. St. Poll was described as 'one of the deputy lieutenants of the said county of Lincoln, a man of great power and might by office and alliance there'. He and Wray were accused in Star Chamber of interfering with the coroner's jury, choosing a partial grand jury, and bribing a witness. St. Poll of course denied the charges.[4]

St. Poll made his will on 18 Oct. 1612, proved 2 June 1614 by his widow, the sole executrix. He died at 4 p.m. 28 Oct. 1613, 'when he had lived 51 years, 7 days, and some odd hours; too short a time, if it had pleased God otherwise'. As he had requested in the will, his funeral sermon was preached by Dr. John Chadwick, who described him as:

a man very much employed with the Lord Willoughby as deputy lieutenant under the most worthy lord treasurer and most wise counsellor the Lord Burghley. And when in the days of our late honoured and never to be forgotten Queen Elizabeth there was great employment for men and money to keep under the superstitious and rebellious Irish, besides the extraordinary pains he took, and the great cost he was at to further that service he disbursed payments out of his own purse for the country till sessments could be conveniently made and money collected.

Dr. Chadwick could name six learned preachers who had been educated at the university at St. Poll's charge, and he had also been a benefactor of Magdalen and Corpus Christi colleges at Oxford. His wife was a kindred spirit. She and her sister financed the education at Cambridge of the puritan preacher, Richard Bernard, who subsequently dedicated his *Christian Advertisements* to St. Poll and his wife. Next to the Bible St. Poll's preferred reading matter had been the works of Bishop Jewel. Though 'he had often studied to see if he could draw any comfort out of the popish doctrine ... he could not see anything in that religion but ambition, human policy, and heathenish superstition'. He had once intervened on behalf of one Mr. Allen, preacher of Louth, who was in trouble for not following the service as it was in the prayer book. St. Poll, 'sitting on the other side of the judge [said] softly that Mr. Allen was an honest man of good conversation'. St. Poll bequeathed Allen, then parson of Ladborough, £5.[5]

[1] C142/202/195; *Lincs. Peds.* (Harl. Soc. lii), 845–6; J. Wilford, *Memorials and Characters*, 181; Corpus battels bk.; Royal 18 D. 111, f. 52; Lansd. 60, f. 189; 82, f. 44; 737, f. 145v; *APC*, xxv. 25; xxviii. 132, 559; *HMC 14th Rep.* VIII, 262, 282. [2] *HMC Hatfield*, viii. 325; D'Ewes, 436, 474, 496, 517. [3] *APC*, xxiii. 258; xxv. 132; xxvi. 73; xxx. 437; xxxi. 46; xxxii. 280; *HMC 14th Rep.* VIII, 262, 282. [4] St. Ch. 5/429/16, H71/39, H72/34; *APC*, xxx. 140–1. [5] PCC 61 Lawe; Wilford, 180–3; J. W. F. Hill, *Tudor and Stuart Lincoln*, 112; Collinson thesis, 732; Lansd. 82, f. 112.

A.M.M.

ST. POLL, Thomas (c.1539–82), of Snarford and North Carlton, Lincs.

GREAT GRIMSBY	1571
LINCOLNSHIRE	1572

b. c.1539, 2nd s. of George St. Poll[†] by Jane, da. of Sir William Ayscough[†] of S. Kelsey. *educ.* L. Inn 1555. *m.* Faith, da. of Vincent Grantham[†], wid. of Thomas Moigne, 2s. inc. George* 1 or 2 da. *suc.* bro. 1560. Kntd. 1580.

J.p. Lincs. (Lindsey) from c.1561, (Kesteven and Holland) from c.1564; sheriff, Lincs. 1565–6, 1579–80; commr. sewers from 1564, piracy from 1577.[1]

St. Poll was connected with the Ayscoughs, Wrays, Girlingtons, Foljambes, Thymblebys and Tyrwhitts. Either of the two last named could have assisted him to a seat at Grimsby in 1571 and at the next election he was returned for the county, where he was already established as an active and reliable justice of the peace, and frequently employed by the government. The bishop of Lincoln, who asked his advice on the religious beliefs of justices, described him as earnest in religion and fit to be trusted, and there are numerous references to him enforcing the recusancy laws. During his second period as sheriff he joined the bishop and chancellor of the diocese in an energetic attack on recusants, receiving several letters of thanks from the Privy Council. A list survives which he sent to Burghley in July 1580, giving the names of those indicted in Lincolnshire for hearing mass. Sometimes these activities brought him into conflict with his Catholic relatives and friends, the Tyrwhitts.[2]

St. Poll was active and constructive in both his Parliaments. He first spoke 7 Apr. 1571, within a day or two of the opening of Parliament, on the subsidy, which he 'liked well'. He criticized the subsidy collectors, 'mean men' who retained 'their charge sometimes a year, sometimes more in their own hands ... convert it to their own uses, and are perhaps never able to satisfy the same'. He was appointed the same day to the committee to inquire into this and other abuses, and to the subsidy committee itself. On 11 Apr. on the question of presentation to church livings, he thought it 'injurious and unreasonable' to take away a right that might have been 'given to a schoolmaster for his service'. On 20 Apr. he 'argued to prove that the inconvenience or evil which

groweth by the sheriffs is not so great but the doings of the justices may as well be doubted of'. He was on the committees for church attendance the next day and 2 May, and on the 23rd he was named to the committees on promoters and tellers and receivers. His other committees in the 1571 Parliament were on the preservation of woods, and privilege (10 May), jeofails (12 May), land conveyances (14 May), respite of homage (17 May), tillage and the navy (21 May), and tellers and receivers (26 May).

In 1572 St. Poll was made a member of the conference discussing Mary Queen of Scots (12 May), but his only speech on the subject (25 June) is moderate in tone, though her death was 'very necessary' and there were precedents for judicial execution. St. Poll liked his precedents. On 17 May 'he never knew in any Parliament liberty of speech so freely granted that a man might say what he listed' and referred to Henry VIII's laws against Rome, Edward IV and the Duke of Clarence. On the vagabonds bill (20 May), he thought it unreasonable that rogues should be imprisoned without bail. 'Considering there is diversity in rogues', it would be fair to allow bail to 'small felons' but 'not great'. On the same subject (24 May) 'the execution of law the life of the law. Leave out the punishment and the negligence will take away the severity of others.' He was put on the committee of the bill (29 May). On the third reading of the fraudulent conveyances bill (3 June) – St. Poll was on the committee – his remarks went beyond the usual interests of the country gentlemen, when they were considering what the position would be if the parties to a dispute were father and son. St. Poll thought 'the purchaser ought rather to be holpen than the son' for 'the son would have it for nothing, the purchaser payeth dear for it'. On a question of privilege (27 June), St. Poll quoted a precedent where a debtor was freed after claiming privilege and the debt never paid. The next day he had 'no liking' for a bill concerning fugitives from justice, and less for the proviso. It had not hitherto been necessary to employ a barrister for such actions as debt and trespass: if this were made mandatory, litigants would be 'driven to greater charges than ever before'. He suspected that the bill was brought in so as to get the proviso. St. Poll's interest in law reform is also reflected in his appointment to the committee for the explanation of statutes (14 May).

On 8 Feb. 1576, the first day of the session, St. Poll was named to the large committee appointed to examine Wentworth on his motion about liberty of speech. Given his interests, it is difficult to imagine that St. Poll took no part in the proceedings, but in the only extant account the speakers are not identified. Two interventions by him are recorded in this session, both on the question of privilege concerning Arthur Hall's servant Smalley. On 20 Feb. he quoted a precedent for Henry VII's reign, and on 7 Mar., on the same subject, he reported that his researches had shown that 'the judges being required to declare their opinions ... they answered ... that of the privileges of the

Parliament that they could not judge'. St. Poll was put on the committee to deal with the matter. His other committees this session included the subsidy (10 Feb.), promoters (10 Feb.), the poor law (11 Feb.), ports (13 Feb.), actions upon the case (13 Feb.), wine (21 Feb.), sheriffs (24 Feb.), reciprocal treatment for foreign merchants (24 Feb.), the universities and church discipline (2 Mar.), children of aliens (3 Mar.), juries (5 Mar.), land reclamation (6 Mar.), removal of benefit of clergy from rapists and burglars (7 Mar.), rogues (7 Mar.), wharves and quays (8, 13 Mar.), justices of the forest (8 Mar.), the Queen's marriage (12 Mar.), Lord Stourton (12 Mar.), vicars and curates (13 Mar.) and the London goldsmiths (13 Mar.).

St. Poll, recently knighted, continued to be active in 1581. On the first day of business, 19 Jan., he opposed Thomas Norton's contention that the House of Commons rather than Chancery should take the initiative over by-elections when Members were sick or absent on the Queen's service. This was clearly against an increase in the area of the prerogative of the House, and so was his next speech, 24 Jan., over Peter Wentworth's proposal for a public fast in face of the Queen's prohibition against meddling in affairs of religion. St. Poll was for 'aggravating the fault of the House and urging submission'. He spoke on purveyors, 28 Jan., and was appointed to the ensuing committee. The subjects of his 1581 committees were: the subsidy (25 Jan.); the clerk of the market (27 Jan.); the preservation of woods (28 Jan.); the defeasance of the statute staple (28 Jan.); slanderous words and practices (1 Feb.); cloth (4 Feb.); sheriffs (4 Feb.); corporations (11 Feb.); too many attorneys (11 Feb.); fortifying the frontier with Scotland (25 Feb.); tenants in tail (27 Feb.); the Family of Love (27 Feb.); London merchants (2 Mar.); Sir Thomas Gresham's debts (9 Mar.); fines and recoveries (10 Mar.); fraudulent conveyances (14 Mar.); Lord Zouche's lands (14 Mar., reported by him 16 Mar.); the Queen's safety (14 Mar.); navigation (15, 17 Mar.); seditious rumours against the Queen (17 Mar.); and iron mills (18 Mar.).[3]

This is an extraordinarily active parliamentary career for any Member, let alone a country gentleman who had, so far as is known, no ambition for office and no other axe to grind. What turn, if any, his life might have taken, or what his future parliamentary conduct might have been, cannot be known. A little more than a year after the end of his second Parliament St. Poll died in his early 40s, 29 Aug. 1582. He was buried at Snarford and his estates went to his heir George, who reached his 21st birthday in time to prove his father's will in September 1583.[4]

[1] Lincs. Peds. (Harl. Soc. lii), 845; CPR, 1558–60, p. 446; 1563–6, p. 40; Lansd. 146, f. 19. [2] Lincs. Episc. Recs. 1571–84, p. 241; Lincs. Wills, ed. Maddison, i. 98–100; Cam. Misc. ix(3), pp. 27, 28; Lansd. 27, f. 84; 30, f. 196; E351/540, f. 10; 351/541, f. 167; APC, viii. 250; x. 425; xi. 188; xii. 18, 68, 70–1, 105–6, 130, 155; xiii. 257, 336, 345; HMC 14th Rep. VIII, 240. [3] D'Ewes, 158, 159, 176, 178, 181, 182, 183, 184, 187, 189, 206, 220, 221, 241, 247, 249, 250, 253, 254, 255, 260,

261, 262, 281, 284, 289, 291, 294, 298, 301, 304, 305, 306, 307, 308; CJ, i. 83, 85, 87, 88, 89, 93, 95, 96, 99, 100, 104, 105, 107, 108, 110, 111, 112, 114, 115, 119, 120, 121, 122, 124, 127, 129, 130, 132, 133, 134, 135, 136; Trinity, Dublin, anon. jnl. ff. 12, 33; Trinity, Dublin, Thos. Cromwell's jnl. ff. 21, 28, 29, 43, 65, 67, 68, 122, 129; HMC Lords, xi. 8. [4] C142/202/195; Lincs. N. and Q. vii. 1–4; x. 56; Lincs. Wills, 98–100; HMC Rutland, i. 142.

P.W.H.

SALESBURY, John (1533–80), of Rûg, Corwen, Merion., and of Bachymbyd, Denb.

MERIONETH	1553 (Oct.)
DENBIGH BOROUGHS	1554 (Apr.), 1558
DENBIGHSHIRE	1559

b. 1533, 1st s. of Robert Salesbury of Rûg and Bachymbyd by Catherine, da. of John ap Madog of Bodvel, Llanor, Caern. m. by 1566, Elizabeth, da. of Sir John Salusbury† of Lleweni, Denb., 3s. inc. Robert* 2da. suc. fa. 1551.

Sheriff, Merion. 1558–9, 1577–8; commr. eisteddfod, Caerwys, Flints. 1568, musters, Denb. 1570, 1580, tanneries, Denb. 1574, felons, Merion., Mont. 1575; j.p. Denb., Merion. 1577, q.1579.

The Salesburys of Rûg were a junior branch of the Salusburys of Lleweni. John Salesbury was a minor when his father died, and the cost of his wardship, his father's debts to the Exchequer and various penalties imposed upon him by the court of wards for offences against feudal law, constituted a drain on family finances and delayed him entering upon his lands. When he eventually came into his estates in 1557, Salesbury was in possession of the former royal manors of Rûg and Glyndyfrdwy, Merioneth, and Dinmael and Bachymbyd, Denbighshire. He consolidated his position in the latter county by renewing a lease on the demesne lands of Ruthin and purchasing two parks near Ruthin, Clocaenog and Pool, and he was elected for Denbighshire when his relatives at Lleweni could not put up a candidate from their own ranks. That he did not represent Merioneth in this period was due to his long-standing feud with Ellis Price*, the Earl of Leicester's land agent in north Wales, whose interference in Merioneth Salesbury naturally resented. He unsuccessfully contested the county in 1571.

In 1577 Salesbury considered buying further estates which would have extended his lordship of Glyndyfrdwy to the whole commote of Edeyrnion, but nothing came of it. He made his will on 14 Nov. 1580 and it was proved by his widow the following 6 Feb. He committed his heir to the care of 'my singular good lord and lady the Earl and Countess of Warwick', expressing the wish that he should be educated in the Bromley household and that he should eventually marry the daughter of Sir George Bromley*.

Salusbury Corresp. ed. Smith (Univ. Wales Bd. of Celtic Studies, Hist. and Law ser. xiv), passim; CPR, 1547–8, p. 374; 1553–4, p. 12; 1555–7, p. 243; 1557–8, p. 31; J. Hurstfield, Queen's Wards, 179;

NLW, Chirk castle mss F 12540, 1, 5, 13, 22–3, 219; *HMC Welsh*, i(1), 291; Flenley, *Cal. Reg. Council, Marches of Wales*, 69, 127, 146, 205, 220–1; PCC 5 Darcy.

A.H.D.

SALESBURY, Robert (1567–99), of Rûg, Corwen, Merion.; Bachymbyd, Llanynys, Denb. and Pool Park, Ruthin, Denb.

DENBIGHSHIRE	1586
MERIONETH	1589

b. 20 June 1567, 1st s. of John Salesbury* of Rûg by Elizabeth, da. of Sir John Salusbury† of Lleweni. *educ.* Brasenose, Oxf. 1584; G. Inn 1586. *m.* Elinor, da. of Sir Henry Bagnall*; 1s. 1da. illegit. *suc.* fa. 1580. Kntd. 1593. J.p. Denb., dep. lt. by 1587; j.p. Merion, by 1591, dep. lt. from c.1592, custos rot. by c.1594.

Salesbury was only 13 when his father died in 1580. This second minority in successive generations dealt a further blow to the family fortunes. In accordance with the terms of his father's will, Robert was brought up under the guardianship of Ambrose Dudley, Earl of Warwick. Salesbury was elected for Denbighshire at the age of 19. He was connected through his guardian with the most powerful figure in Denbighshire, the Earl of Leicester, and through his mother, with the Salusburys of Lleweni, who were themselves under a cloud at this time on account of their implication in the Babington plot. At this stage in his career, therefore, Salesbury was firmly associated with the Dudley party in north Wales. When he came of age in 1588, however, Salesbury entered Merioneth politics and inherited his father's feud with Ellis Price*. Although both John Salesbury and Ellis Price were dead by 1588, the quarrel continued, and Salesbury's election for the county can be seen as a revenge for his father's defeat 18 years before. Even in 1592, Salesbury was still opposing the appointment of Cadwaladr Price of Rhiwlas as sheriff. However, by raking up these old scores, Salesbury aligned himself with the anti-Dudley faction in north Wales and alienated himself from his relatives in Lleweni. In both his Parliaments, Salesbury was appointed to the subsidy committee in his capacity as knight of the shire (22 Feb. 1587, 11 Feb. 1589).

By 1593, Salesbury was serving in Ireland under his father-in-law. Returning with a knighthood, his name was put forward in 1596 for membership of the council in the marches of Wales by Sir Richard Shuttleworth, chief justice of the Chester circuit. Shuttleworth described him as 'well affected in religion, loyal and dutiful to her Majesty, wise, discreet and temperate in all his actions', but he added significantly 'I would wish ... to admonish him to hold an even and independent course in the causes of his country, and not to incline more to the one side nor the other'.

By this time, however, Salesbury was heavily in debt to

his 'cousin' Thomas Myddelton*, whose candidature he supported for the 1597 county election in Merioneth. In 1598 he sold £400 worth of his Merioneth lands, but the following year had to resort to Myddelton again and to lease more of his property. In the same month he fell sick in London, and was nursed in the house of his friend Gabriel Goodman, dean of Westminster, who took him back to Wales, where he died 14 July 1599, lamented by two Denbighshire bards. Like his father and grandfather before him, he left an heir under age, who was placed by his will under the guardianship of Lord Keeper Egerton*. He remembered in his will an illegitimate daughter who was probably the child of his steward's daughter, who was known to be his mistress. The executors were a second cousin, Edward Thelwall of Plas-y-ward, Denbighshire and an unidentified member of the Puleston family. They were offered further leases of Salesbury land provided they paid off the debts and allowed annuities to his two brothers; but they declined the charge, and administration of the estate, valued at over £1,000, was granted to the brother John, who had taken over responsibility for the debts to Myddelton when the executors declined to act. This Captain John Salesbury involved himself in the conspiracy of his patron Essex, but he escaped the block, and eventually succeeded to the estate on the death of his nephew in 1608, to die three years later, leaving as his heir the third brother William, who defended Denbigh for the King in the civil war.

Wards 20/173; *Salusbury Corresp.* ed. Smith (Univ. Wales Bd. of Celtic Studies, Hist. and Law ser. xiv), passim; *CSP Ire.* 1592–6, pp. 200, 301, 321; pat. rolls 36 Eliz.; *HMC Foljambe*, 26; Lansd. 71, f. 197; C66/1421; J. Hurstfield, *Queen's Wards*, 179; PCC 5 Darcy, 41 Wallop; P. H. Williams, *Council in the Marches of Wales*, 237–9; *EHR*, lix. 353; D'Ewes, 409, 431; *DWB*, 900–1; *HMC Hatfield*, vi. 149; ix. 181; *Eliz. Govt. and Soc.* 270–1, 276 n; NLW, Chirk Castle mss 12540, 86, 100, 104, 115, 134, 158–9, 165, 173, 178, 212, 217, 235, 252, 257; *HMC Welsh*, ii(2), 484, 648; *Bull. Bd. of Celtic Studies*, xv. 293.

A.H.D.

SALTERN, William (*d.* by Feb. 1589), of Bristol, Glos.

BRISTOL	1589*

m. Elizabeth, da. of George Snigge, merchant and (1574) mayor of Bristol, 3s. 1da.
Sheriff, Bristol 1574; deputy, Bristol branch, Spanish Co. by 1583.

Saltern traded with Spain and Portugal. In August 1577 he and three other Bristol merchants, including Thomas Aldworth II*, were instructed by the Privy Council to require all men of Bristol 'as are retailers and artificers trading with Spain, to forbear any more to traffic in that country'. Saltern was a supporter of a proposed voyage to America in 1583. In 1588 he was elected to serve in the following Parliament, but died before it met, his replacement being elected on 3 Feb. 1589.

Vis. Som. ed. Weaver, 130; *Bristol and Glos. Arch. Soc. Trans.* xix. 135; P. McGrath, *Bristol Merchant Venturers*, 20–1; *APC*, x. 16; R. Hakluyt, *Principal Navigations* (1904), viii. 133–4.

J.C.H.

SALTONSTALL, Richard (*d.*1601), of London and South Ockendon, Essex.

LONDON   1586

2nd s. of Gilbert Saltonstall of Halifax, Yorks. *m.* Susan, da. of Thomas Poyntz of North Ockendon, Essex, sis. of Sir Gabriel Poyntz, 7s. 9da. At least 1da. illegit. Kntd. 1598.

Common councilman, London by 1583, alderman by 1588, sheriff 1588–9, ld. mayor 1597–8; gov. Merchant Adventurers by 1585; auditor of St. Thomas's hospital 1578–80, treasurer 1595–7; master of Skinners Co. 1589, 1593, 1595–6, 1599–1600; customer of London by 1598–*d.*[1]

Saltonstall – the younger son of a small Yorkshire landowner – was presumably apprenticed in London, and must subsequently have become a factor in the Low Countries, for in 1565 he was allowed to become free of the Merchant Adventurers Company, although he had been living in the Netherlands before 1564 with his wife and family, and had purchased lands there. He developed wide trading interests: a member of the Merchant Adventurers, he was the governor of the company by 1585; he was one of the merchants named in the renewal of privileges granted to the Muscovy Company in 1586, and was again mentioned in the second charter of the Levant Company in 1592. His name also appears in the list of original subscribers for the East India Company's first voyage. Saltonstall was assessed on £200 for the 1589 subsidy.[2]

By 1574 Saltonstall was already well enough established to be named by the Privy Council as an arbitrator in a commercial dispute, and in the following years he was frequently called upon to assist in settling such cases. In 1589, when Dr. Julius Caesar* was ordered to hear and deal summarily with cases which had been depending in the Admiralty court since 1 Oct. 1581, Saltonstall was one of the London aldermen and merchants named to advise him. As an MP for London in 1586, Saltonstall spoke in the Commons committee on the affairs of the Netherlands, 24 Feb. 1587, pointing out the dependence of Philip II on the safe arrival of his treasure fleets. On 4 Mar. he was appointed to a committee considering regrators of barley and on the 14th he was put in charge of a bill concerning curriers.[3]

In 1578 Saltonstall was responsible for conveying an English loan of £20,000 in bullion to the Low Countries, and in 1587 he was abroad again, this time with Giles Fletcher*, attempting to arrange the establishment of a staple for the Merchant Adventurers in Hamburg. The representatives of that city were slow to come to terms, desiring in return privileges in England for all the Hanse towns, and Saltonstall wrote to the Company in London that he had little faith in them. He eventually concluded an agreement with the neighbouring town of Stade. In the following year, however, he returned to Hamburg to try again.[4]

As governor of the Merchant Adventurers Saltonstall forwarded requests from English merchants abroad, and in 1593 objected – on the company's behalf – to the enforcement of the Act which stipulated that every tenth coarse cloth exported should be dressed in England. The Merchant Adventurers claimed that cloths dressed in England were of less value on the Continent than undressed cloths. The company also played a part in helping to finance the war in the Low Countries. In 1587 Saltonstall claimed that the Merchant Adventurers had made a substantial loss, not only by undertaking the exchange of money between England and the Low Countries, but also in the payments they had made for the soldiers on garrison duty there.[5]

As the war in the Netherlands progressed it became the practice for groups of merchants to contract yearly with the government to provide the exchange facilities for the large sums of money required to finance the war. Between June 1594 and June 1595 Saltonstall was one of the contractors. In April 1595 he and his ten partners wrote to Burghley arguing that the rate of exchange to which they had agreed was too high now that the Flemish currency had been devalued.[6]

Successful as a merchant on an international scale, Saltonstall was naturally a leading member of his own livery company, the Skinners. He was master on four occasions. On being elected sheriff, he was granted the customary use of the Company's plate for the year, as well as £40 'towards the repairing and trimming of his house'. 'Old and sickly', in December 1598 he was allowed to use his son Samuel as his deputy for collecting the customs, and although he became master of the Skinners' Company for the last time in 1599 it was on condition that he could have a deputy to act for him when he was indisposed.[7]

Saltonstall also invested in land. At his death he had property in Halifax, Yorkshire, his native county, but his principal estate lay in South Ockendon, the neighbouring Essex parish to that in which his wife's parents lived. He had also purchased the Hertfordshire manor of Moorhall in Yardley, settling it on his son Peter, the founder of a cadet branch of the family.[8]

Following the custom of London Saltonstall divided his personal estate into three: a third for his wife, a third for his children as yet unadvanced, and the remainder for his personal disposal. He left £5 to the poor of St. Thomas's hospital, £5 to those of St. Bartholomew's, and a further £5 to the poor children of Christ's hospital. To the

Skinners' Company he bequeathed £10 for a dinner and £100 to be loaned for two years to four honest young men, who had to be Merchant Adventurers and free of the Skinners' Company; in return they were each to pay 3s. 4d. a year to the masters and the wardens of the Company, and 10d. a year to the clerk of the Company. The remainder of this third of his personal estate (excluding a number of bequests to his numerous children) was to be divided equally between his wife and his younger children. The will was proved on 19 Mar. 1601 by the executors, his wife Susan and his son Samuel. In 1602 the will was challenged by Saltonstall's natural daughter Abigail Baker, and subsequently by Saltonstall's sons. The latter case was still unsettled in 1607. Saltonstall died 17 Mar. 1601, and was buried in the church of South Ockendon. The heir was his eldest son, Richard.[9]

¹ DNB; N. and Q. (ser. 2), xi. 513; (ser. 3), i. 350–1; R. Clutterbuck, Herts. iii. 362; A. B. Beaven, Aldermen, i. 11, 201; ii. 43; CSP For. 1585–6, p. 145; Recs. Skinners' Co. ed. Lambert, 230–75 passim; CSP Dom. 1598–1601, p. 138; information from F. F. Foster. ² CPR, 1563–6, p. 210; CSP For. 1585–6, p. 145; Hakluyt, Voyages (1903–5), iii. 348; vi. 75, 78; H. Stevens, Dawn of British Trade to the East Indies, 3; lay subsidy roll 1576, T/S at PRO. ³ APC, viii. 349; xi, xii, xiii, xiv, xvii, xix, xx, xxi, xxii, xxiv, passim; CSP Dom. 1581–90, p. 627; Neale, Parlts. ii. 178–9; D'Ewes 412, 415. ⁴ CSP For. 1577–8, pp. 697–8; 1586–8, pp. 313–15, 406; 1587 (Apr.–Dec.), p. 225; 1588 (July–Dec.), p. 38. ⁵ Lansd. 145, f. 268; 150, f. 170; CSP Dom. 1591–4, p. 321; CSP Dom. Add. 1580–1625, p. 199. ⁶ CSP Dom. 1595–7, p. 26. ⁷ Beaven, ii. 43; Recs. Skinners' Co., 252, 254, 275; CSP Dom. 1598–1601, p. 138. ⁸ C142/269/25; 271/175; Clutterbuck, iii. 601. ⁹ PCC 32 Woodhall, 51 Montague; J. Watson, Hist. Antiqs Halifax, 579; C142/271/175; DNB; CSP Dom. 1603–10, p. 345.

A.M.M.

SALUSBURY, Sir John (c.1565–1612), of Lleweni, Denb.

DENBIGHSHIRE 1601

b. c.1565, 2nd s. of John Salusbury of Lleweni by Catherine, da. and h. of Tudor ap Robert of Berain, Denb. educ. Jesus, Oxf. 1581. m. Ursula, illegit. da. of Henry, 4th Earl of Derby by Jane Halsall, 7s. 3da. suc. bro. 1586. Kntd. 1601.[1]

Esquire of body to Queen Elizabeth 1595.
J.p.q. Denb., commr. musters by 1592; dep. lt. c.1602, collector of royal loan 1605.[2]

Sir John Salusbury was from an English family which had acquired escheated lands in the lordship of Denbigh after the English conquest and had subsequently risen to pre-eminence in local affairs through military prowess and fortunate marriages. When the county of Denbigh was formed in 1536, the family provided its first officials and some of its earliest MPs. However, in Elizabeth's reign, the family suffered a series of misfortunes and disgraces, which precluded a Salusbury from representing the shire until 1601. Salusbury's grandfather and namesake, Sir John Salusbury†, was in trouble at the beginning of this period over his accounts as Exchequer receiver in north Wales. His heir, John Salusbury, predeceased him, after

acquiring the Berain lands in Denbighshire through a fortunate marriage, and left an infant son, Thomas, who was placed by his grandfather in the care of the Earl of Leicester. This public alliance between the Salusburys and Leicester antagonized many of the minor Gwynedd gentry, struggling against Leicester's encroachments as lord of Denbigh and forester of Snowdon. In their eyes Lleweni was thereby transformed into the centre of court opinion and protestantism in the county. Resentment of Leicester's interference in Denbighshire combined with conservative leanings in religion bred an anti-Lleweni faction in the shire which remained active for the rest of the century.

Any hopes that Thomas Salusbury might represent the shire were dashed by his complicity in the Babington plot. His execution in 1586 plunged the family into serious disgrace. John Salusbury, his younger brother and the subject of this biography, succeeded to the estates, but with greatly diminished prestige and fortune in the county. Much of the Lleweni property was in crown leases, and it took seven years for the new head of the family to obtain a renewal of them, at the cost of ruinous fines – in one case, over £1,200. Meanwhile his enemies were able to keep the family out of public office. At the parliamentary election following his brother's execution, and again in some county appointments the next year, John Salusbury was passed over in favour of his junior kinsman, Robert Salesbury*, whose main seat was at Rûg in Merioneth. Another rebuff followed in 1588, when Salusbury failed to secure the county seat for his ally, William Almer*, of Pant Iocyn. Three years later Salusbury was cited in a Star Chamber suit by a servant of the Earl of Warwick, Leicester's brother and successor in the lordship of Denbigh, in a dispute over the municipal privileges of the borough of Denbigh. The renewal of the borough charter in 1597 provoked yet another feud, this time with Thomas Myddelton*, the new purchaser of the crown lordship of Chirk. A document among the Chirk castle papers, drawn up by or for Myddelton, accuses Salusbury of having taken money to protect several Denbighshire murderers from the law between 1591 and 1599. About this time he was engaged in an Exchequer suit with the prebendary of Llannefydd over the prebendal tithes.

By now, however, he was on the way towards rehabilitation, helped by the strenuous efforts of his relatives by marriage, the earls of Derby. In 1593 he had fought and won a duel in Chester with a relative, Captain Owen Salesbury of Holt, who was under suspicion at court for his recent activities as a mercenary in the Low Countries. The 5th Earl of Derby congratulated his brother-in-law on his triumph over 'that bad fellow of your name' and saw in the event an 'advancement of your credit'. In this he was proved right, for two years later Salusbury was in London with a position at court and honorary admission to the Middle Temple. He won further credit, and a knighthood, for his part in suppressing the Essex revolt of 1601.

With these marks of favour, Salusbury returned to Denbighshire, where his enemies were in disarray, many of them having burnt their fingers in the service of their patron, the Earl of Essex. For the first time during Elizabeth's reign, the Salusburys had the upper hand in the county and were in a good position to stand for election as knight of the shire. However, the anti-Lleweni faction, which had monopolized the local government of the shire for the past five years, mustered a candidate themselves, Sir Richard Trevor* of Trevalun. Trevor was a deputy lieutenant and a member of the council in the marches of Wales, whereas Salusbury still had no local office other than that of j.p. A levy for Ireland, coinciding with the election, gave Trevor, as deputy lieutenant, the opportunity to arm his supporters. The sheriff, according to Salusbury, also loaded the dice against him by delaying the election until the county day was at Wrexham, where Trevor's support was strong, rather than at Denbigh in Salusbury's territory. It was the sheriff also who postponed the election to avert bloodshed, as he declared, though Salusbury alleged that this was merely another trick to prevent his election. Eventually, after much delay, three days before the end of that Parliament, Salusbury was elected knight for Denbighshire, a somewhat hollow victory. Immediately after the dissolution of Parliament, the Star Chamber suits began between the two factions, although they appear to have been inconclusive. After much effort, Salusbury was finally included in the commission of lieutenancy and obtained Trevor's exclusion from that office and even from the shrievalty. But the malice of his enemies was not exhausted. He sent repeated complaints to Cecil and to the council in the marches about his failure to obtain justice against them, especially in respect of the alleged murder of a servant and kinsman with the connivance of Fulk Lloyd of Foxhall, Denbigh, a former sheriff denounced by Salusbury as a 'notorious recusant'.

His triumph was indeed shortlived, and his pleas for preferment on the accession of James I (whom he had the honour of proclaiming at Denbigh) fell on deaf ears. He was never pricked as sheriff, nor elected again to Parliament, and increasing financial embarrassment forced him to borrow heavily on his lands from his former opponent (Sir) Thomas Myddelton. He complained to Cecil of the continued immunity of Fulk Lloyd and his accomplices, and instituted Star Chamber proceedings against them, which were countered by charges of violent interference on Salusbury's part with the course of justice in the interests of a tenant, and of misappropriation of funds entrusted to him as collector of the royal loan. The latter charge was echoed in two suits brought against him in the Exchequer in 1610–11. On the more constructive side of local government he was much exercised in 1605 by an outbreak of plague in the neighbourhood of Denbigh, and the consequent need for tax remissions to the infected area. Soon after this he made up his differences and settled his financial obligations with (Sir) Thomas Myddelton by arranging a marriage between his heir, Henry Salusbury, and Myddelton's daughter.

Salusbury died in 1612. Two sentences affecting his will are on record, but the will itself has not been traced. A patron of bards and an object of their eulogies, Salusbury himself wrote some indifferent English verse and enjoyed the acquaintance of Shakespeare and Ben Jonson, both of whom contributed verses to the volume published in 1601 by his chaplain, Robert Chester, in honour of Sir John and his lady.[3]

[1] Y Cymmrodor, xl. 5; EHR, xlvi. 213 n; Salusbury Corresp. ed. Smith (Univ. Wales Bd. of Celtic Studies, Hist. and Law ser. xiv), table 1; NLW, Jnl. v. 247–8, 261. [2] Star Chamber, ed. Edwards (Univ. Wales Bd. of Celtic Studies, Hist. and Law. ser. i), 55; EHR, xlvi. 222; Arch. Camb. (ser. 6), xv. 120; HMC Hatfield, xii. 391; APC, xxxii. 342; Exchequer, ed. E. G. Jones (Univ. Wales Bd. of Celtic Studies, Hist. and Law. ser. iv), 162, 167. [3] Salusbury Corresp. passim; Y. Cymmrodor, xl. 3–5, 15–19; Augmentations, ed. Lewis and Davies (Univ. Wales Bd. of Celtic Studies, Hist. and Law ser. xiii), 359, 365, 374; EHR, xlvi. 212–226; lix. 348–70; HMC Foljambe, 26; G. Owen, Taylor's Cussion, ff. 36–7; Neale, Commons, 111–18, 120–8; Eliz. Govt. and Soc. 268; NLW, Jnl. vii. 235–8; Exchequer, ed. E. G. Jones, 178; HMC 8th Rep. i. 375; NLW, Cal. Wynn Pprs. pp. 37, 47; APC, xxxii. 342, 374, 380; Star Chamber, 54, 55, 59, 67, 69; D'Ewes, 627, 637; Townshend, Hist. Colls. 190–1, 210–12, 214–16; NLW, Brogyntyn Welsh ms 197; HMC Hatfield, xi. 445; xii. 118, 263, 391; xv. 48; Exchequer, ed. T. I. J. Jones (Univ. Wales Bd. of Celtic Studies, Hist. and Law ser. xv), 162, 167; Harl. 2041, f. 100; PCC 111, 116 Parker; Trans. Cymmrod. Soc. 1940, pp. 109–11; 1948, p. 15; Carleton Brown, Poems by Sir J. Salusbury (Pa. 1914).

A.H.D.

SALVEYN, John, of Hemingbrugh, Yorks.

HEDON   1559

4th s. of George Salveyn of Newbiggin, Egton, by Margaret, da. of Sir William Bulmer. m. Elinor, da. of John Thorpe of Thorpe in Howden.

Salveyn's return for Hedon was due to Sir John Constable*, who had the controlling interest there. Sir Francis Salveyn, John's elder brother, had served with Constable on the frontier with Scotland, and the two families were related through the marriage of Constable's sister to Sir Ralph Ellerker, Sir Francis Salveyn's brother-in-law. The Salveyns were well connected generally, to the Bulmers, Conyers, Askes and the 1st Lord Eure, but both branches of the family, the junior of Newbiggin and the senior of Croxdale, Durham, were Catholic, which accounts for their not being on the commission of the peace in this period after Sir Francis Salveyn's death in 1562. Nothing has been ascertained about John Salveyn after his return to Parliament in 1559.

Vis. Yorks. ed. Foster, 367; *Newbiggin in Egton and the Salvin Fam.* (Yorks. Arch. Soc. xxxiii), 87–104; *Vis. Yorks.* (Harl. Soc. xvi), 43, 109, 168, 321; *CPR*, 1558–60, pp. 21, 259, 426; *CSP Dom.* Add. 1547–65, p. 522; Surtees, *Durham*, i(2), pp. 140–1; H. Aveling, *Northern Catholics*, 40, 102, 116, 180, 268–9.

I.C./A.D.

SALVEYN, Thomas (*d.* 1610), of Durham and Thornton House, co. Dur. and of London.

HEDON   1597

3rd s. of Gerard Salveyn of Croxdale, co. Dur. by Eleanor, da. of William Wrenn of Billyhall, co. Dur. *m.* (1) Jane, *s.p.*; (2) aft. 1592, Rebecca, 7th da. of Sir Cuthbert Collingwood of Dalden Tower, co. Dur. and Eglington, Northants., 4s. 2da.

Salveyn, like his distant relation John*, owed his return at Hedon to the Constable family. He was a minor country gentleman, although in a Chancery suit he brought in 1601 over his wife's jointure he described himself as of the city of London. He was a cousin of George Birket (or Birkhead) the second of the Catholic arch priests. There is no evidence that Salveyn himself was a recusant, but his second wife was. When Salveyn made his will on 15 Oct. 1609, he noted that in consequence of her 'being not obedient to the laws' it was not possible for him to provide for her in the customary manner. He therefore desired his friends, during his son's minority, to provide for her 'in as good sort as she hath been maintained in my time', and his son was to do the same when he came of age. He wished to be buried with other members of the family in St. Oswald's, Durham. His daughter Mary was to receive £500, and his other children £400 each, sums which were to be raised from the rents of Thornton under Ryseborough. Although his eldest son John was a minor, Salveyn appointed him executor, while the supervisors were three local gentlemen, William Wycliffe of Wycliffe, Salveyn's nephew Gerard Salveyn, and his brother-in-law Robert Collingwood.

Salveyn died 23 Feb. 1610, and was buried in St. Oswald's as he had requested. His eldest son John was 13 years and 3 months old when the inquisition post mortem was taken in June 1611.

Surtees, *Durham*, iv. 119, 140–1; G. Anstruther, *Seminary Priests*, i. 35; C2 Eliz./S15/32; *Durham Wills and Inventories* (Surtees Soc. cxlii), 41–3; Wards 7/35/74.

A.M.M./A.D.

SANDERS, Edmund (c.1545–1621), of Charlwood, Surr.

REIGATE   1584, 1586

b. c.1545,[1] 1st s. of Sir Thomas Sanders of Charlwood by Alice, da. of Sir Edmund Walsingham of Scadbury, Kent. *educ.* I. Temple 1561, called 1574. *m.* Phillip, da. of Edward Gage of Firle, Suss., 2s. 4da. *suc.* fa. 1566.

J.p.q. Surr. 1575, Suss. 1583–7; commr. subsidy Surr. 1593.

Of a minor gentry. family resident in Surrey since the fourteenth century, Sanders became a lawyer, in accordance with a desire expressed in his father's will. He possibly practised in London after being called to the bar. Through his mother he was related to the elder branch of the Walsingham family. He came nearer than any other Elizabethan to being returned for Reigate through his own local standing, though he was presumably acceptable to the usual borough patrons, the Howards of Effingham. He was on two committees in 1585, dealing with libellers (19 Feb.) and Sussex timber (4 Mar.). On 18 Nov. 1586 he is mentioned as speaking in favour of the execution of Mary Queen of Scots, and he was put on the committee considering this matter. He died intestate 20 Jan. 1621.[2]

[1] Sanders was 21 in 1566 when licensed (as a ward) to enter on his father's lands, *CPR*, iii. 525. [2] *Vis. Surr.* (Harl. Soc. xliii), 18; *Cal. I.T. Recs.* i. 276; PCC 19 Crymes; Lansd. 35, ff. 135, 136, 137, 152, 158; E163/14/8, f. 38; *Surr. Arch. Colls.* xix. 45; Manning and Bray, *Surr.* i. 305; *VCH Surr.* iii. 185; C142/392/129.

A.M.M.

SANDES, *see also* SONDES

SANDFORD, Thomas

CARLISLE   1597

EITHER

b. 6 June 1567, s. and h. of Thomas Sandford of Askham, Westmld. by Anne, da. of Cuthbert Hutton of Hutton John, Cumb. *m.* Martha, da. of Sir John Widdrington of Widdrington, Northumb. by his 2nd w., 3s. 6da. *suc.* fa. 1574.

Thomas Sandford's birth is recorded with special prominence in the parish register of Askham, where his family had been established from the fourteenth century. A minor at his father's death, his wardship in 1581 was held by the Queen, but entries in the Askham register dated in the autumn of 1587 indicate that he had by then come of age. When his first child was christened, in October 1587, one of the godmothers, present by proxy, had been Lady Scrope, wife of the lord warden of the west march, and in November 1592 her son, the 9th Lord Scrope, was godfather by proxy at the christening of Sandford's fifth child, Thomas, his heir presumptive. These links with the Scropes, whose official residence was in Carlisle, tip the balance in favour of his having been the 1597 MP for the city, though no positive identification has been made. This Thomas Sandford was a Catholic sympathizer who conformed sufficiently to attend church, though he refused to take communion. His wife was regularly presented as a recusant and some of his servants were similarly 'obstinate'. He continued the enlarging and rebuilding of Askham Hall, one of the notable pele strongholds in the county. The work had been begun by his father and continued by his mother during his minority. On 10 Mar. 1589 he conveyed part of his property to John Middleton of Carlisle (possibly his stepfather by his mother's remarriage) and Robert Widdrington*, his wife's brother, to the use of himself and his wife, and in April 1597 he mortgaged the manor of Askham and all lands and tenements formerly belonging to his father and grandfather to Ralph Assheton and John Townley of Lancashire for a maximum term of 80 years. He died 18 July 1609 and was succeeded by his last and ninth child, John.[1]

OR

1st s. of Richard Sandford of Howgill, Westmld. by Anne, da. of John Warriner of Helsington, Westmld. *educ.* G. Inn 1586. prob. *unm.* Kntd. 1603.

This man, who died *v.p.* and *s.p.* was first cousin of his namesake of Askham. The theft of his 'running mare' and two other horses by border thieves was one reason for a retaliatory raid into Scotland reported by Scrope in July 1600. To the ensuing petition from the gentlemen of Cumberland and Westmorland to the Privy Council for soldiers to be placed on the border both Thomas Sandfords put their names. The signature of one of them, with the names of three other gentlemen, all probably commissioners of musters, occurs on an order to the alderman of Kendal in March 1601 requiring him to light the beacons, but only the three others signed the countermanding order which immediately followed.[2]

[1] Nicolson and Burn, *Hist. Cumb. and Westmld.* i. 426; Hodgson, *Northumb.* ii(2), 236; C142/310/74; *Askham Registers*; *Border Pprs.* i. 64; *Trans. Cumb. and Westmld. Antiq. and Arch. Soc.* n.s. xxi. 195–8, 209–22; *Cath. Rec. Soc.* liii. 65, 359; *CSP Dom.* 1595–7, p. 354; 1598–1601, p. 362. [2] C142/391/74; Shaw, *Knights* (where 'of Westminster' should read 'of Westmorland'); *Border Pprs.* ii. 668, 671, 677–8, 761; *HMC 10th Rep. IV*, 307–8.

E.L.C.M.

SANDYS, Edwin I (c.1564–1608), of Eaton Bray, Beds.

ANDOVER   1586

b. c.1564, 1st s. of Miles Sandys* of Latimer by his 1st w. Hester, da. of William Clifton of Barrington, Som. *educ.* ?Eton 1574; M. Temple 1579. *m.* 2 June 1586, Elizabeth, da. of William, 3rd Lord Sandys of The Vyne, Hants, 3s. Kntd. 1599; *suc.* fa. 1601.[1]

J.p.q. Beds. and Bucks. by 1601; sheriff, Beds. Feb.–Nov. 1606.

It has been thought that Edwin Sandys II*, the second son of Archbishop Sandys of York and a celebrated leader of the early Stuart House of Commons, began his parliamentary career by sitting for Andover in 1586. It is fairly certain, however, that the burgess for Andover was the eldest son of the archbishop's brother, Miles Sandys*, for Edwin, son of Miles Sandys, married the daughter of William, 3rd Lord Sandys, a great Hampshire landlord with election patronage, less than five months before the opening of the 1586 Parliament. The Hampshire family and the family of the archbishop and Miles Sandys do not seem to have been related before the marriage of 1586.[2]

It was to be expected that Edwin, eldest son of Miles Sandys, would be returned to Parliament at the first opportunity. Yet he seems to have lacked his father's enthusiasm for the affairs of London and the Commons. He spent several years at the Middle Temple, to which he and at least some of the archbishop's seven sons were admitted without fee by favour of Miles Sandys, treasurer of the Inn, but he did not pursue his career in the law after his father's retirement in 1596.[3] Nor, apparently, did he sit in Parliament a second time (the Member for Plympton in 1589 and 1593 was almost certainly the archbishop's son), although it was presumably due to him or his father that Thomas Temple, who later married Hester Sandys, Edwin's sister, sat for Andover in 1589: Lord Sandys's continuing favour is proved by the nomination of Miles Sandys as burgess for Stockbridge in 1597. In 1604 Lord Sandys's attentions were extended to the archbishop's family, and the other Edwin Sandys was returned for Stockbridge, going on to establish the sort of parliamentary reputation which might have seemed more appropriate to the son of Miles.

Perhaps Sandys was more interested in a military career, for it was in Ireland that he was knighted in 1599. At home, he resided at Eaton Bray, since his mother, who outlived him, kept her husband's main estate at Latimer, Buckinghamshire. Sandys died 15 Mar. 1608. In his will, he recorded that Bishop Chadderton of Lincoln had promised him £1,800 for the marriage arranged between his son and Chadderton's granddaughter, Elizabeth Brooke of Buckden, Huntingdonshire. The Vyne, with the barony of Sandys, was inherited by Sandys's widow in 1629, after which it descended in the line of Colonel Henry Sandys, Sandys's youngest son, and the only one to leave children, who was killed fighting for the King in 1643.[4]

[1] C142/271/161; *Vis. Glos.* (Harl. Soc. xxi), 143; *Eton Coll. Reg.*; *M. T. Recs.* i. 230; *CP*, xi. 445–6; Shaw, *Knights*, ii. 98. [2] *Eton Coll. Reg. 1441–1698.* ed. Sterry, 295; *CSP Dom.* 1598–1601, p. 144. [3] *M. T. Recs.* i. 311, 365, 367, 427. [4] *CSP Ire.* 1600 (Mar.–Oct.), 10; PCC 11 Fenner; *VCH Hants*, iv. 161; *CP*.

A.H.

SANDYS, Edwin II (1561–1629), of the Middle Temple, London, and Northbourne, Kent.

PLYMPTON ERLE	1589, 1593
STOCKBRIDGE	1604
ROCHESTER	1614

b. 1561, s. of Edwin Sandys (d. 1588), bp. of Worcester, later abp. of York, by his 2nd w. Cicely, da. of Thomas Wilsford of Hartridge, Kent; bro. of Samuel*. *educ.* Merchant Taylors' 1571; Corpus Christi, Oxf. 1577, BA 1579, fellow 1579–80, MA 1583, BCL 1589; M. Temple 1590. *m.* (1) Margaret, da. of John Evelegh† of Broad Clyst, Devon, 1da.; (2) Anne, da. of Thomas Southcote* of Bovey Tracey, Devon, ?2da.; (3) Elizabeth, da. of Thomas Nevynson of Eastry, Kent, 1da.; (4) by 1606, Catherine, da. of Richard Bulkeley I* of Anglesey and Lewisham, Kent, 7s. 5da. Kntd. May 1603.[1]

Sheriff, Kent 1615–16; treasurer of Virginia Company 1617.

Edwin Sandys was the most distinguished of the numerous sons of Archbishop Sandys, and became a celebrated leader of the early Stuart Commons. The two men who most influenced his early career were probably Richard Hooker, under whom his father had placed him at Oxford, and his uncle, Miles Sandys*, an active Member of eight Elizabethan Parliaments, by whom he was entered at the Middle Temple after his father's death.[2]

While at Oxford, Sandys was involved in the disputes between his father and Sir Robert Stapleton*. Stapleton accused Archbishop Sandys of giving the chancellorship of York to 'a boy of nine'. In fact, wrote the archbishop to Burghley, he had conferred it upon his son Edwin, aged almost twenty-five and a student of law 'well-learned'; it was Edwin, the letter continued, who had reported one of Stapleton's earlier misdemeanours to Burghley, and 'your lordship then liked well of him'. It seems, indeed, that Sandys quickly made a reputation for learning. By his father's will, he was given, with Tobie Matthew, the task of disposing of his father's books; and from being the pupil he became the friend and assistant of Hooker.[3]

It may be that Sandys entered the Middle Temple in 1590, as soon as he had obtained his BCL at Oxford, in order to be again near Hooker, who, with the assistance of Archbishop Sandys, had been appointed Master of the Temple in 1588. It must have been soon after 1590 that Hooker submitted to Sandys the manuscript of the sixth book of the *Ecclesiastical Polity* – answering the presbyterian argument for the administration of ecclesiastical law by lay elders – and that Sandys wrote the pungent but constructive criticisms which still survive.[4]

He seems to have supported the ecclesiastical settlement with fewer reservations than his father – perhaps because he saw it in a political rather than religious light, for he was a remarkably tolerant observer of diversities of doctrine. In 1596 he accompanied his friend, George Cranmer, on a visit to the Earl of Lincoln, then in Germany on embassy, afterwards spending three years travelling in Europe, the fruit of which was *Europae*

Speculum, or a View or Survey of the State of Religion in the Western Parts of the World, completed at Paris on 9 Apr. 1599, but not published until 1605. In this survey he found good points even in Roman Catholicism.[5]

Thus his leadership of the 'opposition' in the Parliaments of James I did not spring from puritan zeal, and is perhaps rather to be traced to a jealousy for the position and privileges of the Commons, learned from that old 'house of Commons man', his uncle, Miles Sandys. His admission to the Middle Temple in 1590 which reunited him with Hooker, may be a sign of increased reliance upon his uncle after his father's death: Miles was the overseer of the archbishop's will and already had three of the archbishop's sons under his charge at the Middle Temple, of which he was treasurer, before Edwin arrived. The provision which Archbishop Sandys had been able to make for his younger son, consisting principally of the prebend of Wetwang, Yorkshire, was a perilous one. Edwin seems to have had several disputes with his father's successors at York, in which he had to call on the support of his friends in London: he apparently accused Archbishop Matthew Hutton of dealings with the Earl of Essex at the time of the 'rebellion' of 1601, and Hutton denounced him to Cecil as a 'sycophant'.[6]

Sandys made his first two marriages into Devon families, both of which had several members at the Middle Temple. He entered Parliament in 1589 – the Edwin Sandys returned for Andover in 1586 was almost certainly Miles Sandys's own son – by sitting for Plympton, at the same time as his uncle sat for Plymouth. The Southcotes, his second wife's family, no doubt used their influence in his favour, and Richard Southcote was his fellow-burgess when he was chosen again for Plympton in 1593. As a burgess for Plympton in this Parliament he would have been entitled to attend two committees on kerseys, 23 Mar. and 2 Apr. There followed a gap in his parliamentary career, caused partly by his travels. He took the lead in the Commons in the first Parliament of James, to which he was returned for Stockbridge, probably by the favour of Lord Sandys, whose daughter had married Miles Sandys's son. After that, his third marriage to Elizabeth Nevynson brought him seats in Kent constituencies and made him independent of his uncle's family.[7]

Sandys made his name in Stuart Parliaments by his speeches on union with Scotland, monopolies and 'the great contract', his enunciation of the principles of the reciprocal rights of King and people and of kingship by election, and his advocacy of regular keeping of Commons' journals. His work for the Virginia Company gave him a reputation as the founder of democratic government in America. He died in October 1629 and was buried in a sumptuous tomb at Northbourne. In his will, of which he named Sir Robert Naunton† overseer, he endowed lecturerships in 'metaphysic philosophy' at Oxford and Cambridge.[8]

[1] *DNB*; *Vis. Kent* (Harl. Soc. xlii), 104, 148; E. S. Sandys, *Fam. of Sandys*, i. 88, 92–102. [2] *N. and Q.* (ser. 2), xi. 221–2; *M. T. Recs.* i. 312. [3] Strype, *Annals*, iv. 597; PCC 30 Drury. [4] *DNB* (Richard Hooker); *Hooker's Works* (7th ed.), ed. Keble, i. p. xxxiii; iii. 130–9. [5] *APC*, xxv. 496–7; *N. and Q.* (ser. 4), vii. 359; Bodl. e. Museo 211. [6] *APC*, xxv. 496–7; *HMC Hatfield*, xi. 208–9. [7] *CP*, xi. 445–6; D'Ewes, 507, 513. [8] *DNB*; E. S. Sandys, 119–20; PCC 84 Ridley.

A.H.

SANDYS, Miles (*d.* 1601), of Fladbury, Worcs. and Latimer, Bucks.

TAUNTON	1563
LANCASTER	1571
BRIDPORT	1572
BUCKINGHAMSHIRE	1584
ABINGDON	1586*
PLYMOUTH	1589
ANDOVER	1593
STOCKBRIDGE	1597

5th s. of William Sandys of Hawkshead, Lancs. and of London by Margaret, da. of John Dixon of London. *educ.* St. John's, Camb. 1544; M. Temple by 1551. *m.* (1) by c.1563, Hester, da. of William Clifton of Barrington, Som., 4s. inc. Edwin I* 3da.; (2) 1586 or later, Bridget Colt, wid. of alderman Woodcock of London, *s.p.*[1]

Clerk of the Crown and attorney of Queen's bench 1559–97; eccles. commr. 1566; member, council in the marches of Wales 1570–4; j.p.q. Worcs. by 1564–c.1587, Bucks. by 1573, Beds. by 1580, other counties by 1601; bencher, M. Temple 1578, treasurer 1588–95; commr. musters, recusancy, Bucks. 1583, 1586.[2]

Of the several brothers of Edwin Sandys, bishop of Worcester from 1559 and archbishop of York from 1576, Miles was the best known. He may have been in exile with Edwin, certainly shared his protestantism, probably owed him his clerkship of the Crown in Queen's bench at the beginning of Elizabeth's reign, and was overseer of his will. During the early part of the reign he resided near his brother's see, and became a j.p. in Worcestershire and a member of the council in the marches, but it was in Somerset that he acquired lands and made his first marriage.[3]

His puritan sympathies, which recommended him to several influential patrons, are the key to his parliamentary constituencies. Sir Francis Knollys*, who had been in exile with Edwin Sandys, and was lord of the borough, probably nominated him at Taunton in 1563. On the other hand, Taunton's former landlord was the bishop of Winchester, to whom the borough soon reverted, and Bishop Horne, another Marian exile, may have nominated Sandys for Taunton in 1563, as he presumably nominated him for Hindon in 1571. Sandys was also returned for Lancaster in 1571, probably through the influence of the duchy of Lancaster, successive members of his family having held the receivership of the duchy liberty of Furness; and it was for Lancaster that he

preferred to sit, Thomas Dabridgecourt* being returned at Hindon in his place. At Bridport in 1572, his patron was the 2nd Earl of Bedford, who left him an annuity of £20 in his will. It may have been Bedford who introduced Sandys into his own county of Buckinghamshire. In 1567 Sandys purchased Latimer from Sir Fulke Greville†. Soon after his move to Buckinghamshire he seems to have become associated with Lord Sandys of The Vyne. No earlier relationship between these two families of Sandys is known, but Lord Sandys evidently saw in Miles Sandys's eldest son, Edwin, a good match for his daughter. Several years before the marriage took place at Eaton Bray, Bedfordshire, on 2 June 1586, Lord Sandys conveyed considerable lands, including Eaton Bray, to Miles Sandys, in connexion with the match. By 1584 Sandys was sufficiently established in Buckinghamshire to take his turn there as knight of the shire. In 1586 he came in for Abingdon at a by-election, probably through the intervention of the Earl of Leicester or Lord Norris of Rycote. In 1589 he sat for Plymouth, though he is not known to have had any connexion with the town. The long list of Sandys's constituencies is completed by Andover and Stockbridge, at both of which Lord Sandys was probably the patron. At Stockbridge the evidence is clear: Sir Robert Cecil, asking too late for a nomination, was informed that Lord Sandys had already written to the borough, instructing that one seat be given to Miles Sandys and the other to the nominee of the duchy of Lancaster. At Andover Lord Sandys's influence is suggested by the return of Edwin Sandys, Miles's son, in 1586, the year of his marriage to Lord Sandys's daughter, and by the return in 1589 of Thomas Temple*, Miles Sandys's son-in-law.[4]

The only reference found to Sandys in his first Parliament is to his membership of the large committee dealing with the Queen's marriage and the succession question (31 Oct. 1566). Thenceforth he was a very active committeeman in all his Parliaments, but not a frequent speaker. His only recorded speech in 1571 was on the vagabonds bill (13 Apr.), which was 'over sharp and bloody': he thought it might be possible 'to relieve every man at his own house and to stay them from wandering'. His committees in 1571 were on church attendance (6 Apr.), the subsidy (7 Apr.), promoters (23 Apr.), papal bulls (23 Apr.), religion (25 Apr.), respite of homage (25 Apr., 17 May) and fugitives (25 May). He was on the committees to consider the question of Mary Queen of Scots and the Duke of Norfolk (12, 28 May 1572), and he was also named to committees in this session on the Earl of Kent (21 May, 9 June), Wykes v. Denys (22 May), vagabonds (29 May) and delays in judgment (24 June). He spoke on the vagabonds bill (30 May) urging that minstrels should not be included within its provisions. In 1576 the subjects of his committees were: parish registers (10, 13 Feb.), the coinage (15 Feb.), juries (24 Feb., 5 Mar.), unlawful weapons (2 Mar.) and rogues (7 Mar.). In the last session of the 1572 Parliament his committees were concerned with the subsidy (25 Jan. 1581), counterfeit seals (26 Jan.), defeasances of statutes (28 Jan.), slanderous words and practices (1, 3 Feb.), encumbrances against purchasers (4 Feb.), Worcestershire copyholders (6 Feb.), the children of aliens (7 Feb.), the excessive number of attorneys (17 Feb.), the frontier with Scotland (25 Feb.), leases of tenants in tail (27 Feb.), Dover harbour (4 Mar.), the debts of Thomas Gresham (9 Mar.) and the Queen's safety (14 Mar.).

In the Parliament of 1584–5 Sandys ('I have spent the better part of 20 years in the study of the law') was heavily involved in law reform and privilege cases. Speaking on a recurring subject of discussion in Elizabethan Parliaments – the depletion of stocks of standing timber caused by iron mills – he pointed out the irrelevance of the fact that the same bill had previously been rejected, 'for we repeal many bills that we have made in former Parliaments'. Another speech was on general demurrers: 'good pleading is the most honourable and praiseworthy in the law, but I would not have the client's purse pay for the counsel's cunning'. He was in charge of this bill, answered all objections made, and declared it 'very necessary' but a bill about wards was 'better advised upon'. Sandys' first privilege case in this Parliament concerned Arthur Hall* (12 Dec.). On 10 Feb. Sandys, with the diarist Thomas Cromwell and the recorder of London, was instructed to attend the chancellor about a subpoena served on Richard Croke II*, and it was Sandys who reported next day that the chancellor denied the claim. On 11 Feb. he was one of those appointed to tax the costs of the successful claimant in the Alban Stepneth* case. Among other committees to which Sandys was appointed in 1584–5 were those concerned with the continuation of statutes (1 Dec., 11 Mar.), delays in administering justice (5 Dec.), recusants' armour (8 Dec.), assurances (16 Dec.), appeals from ecclesiastical courts (18 Dec.), the Sabbath day (19 Dec.), penal laws (21 Dec.), the hue and cry (4 Feb.), Queen's College, Oxford (5 Feb.), juries (10 Feb.), jesuits (18 Feb., 9 Mar.), fraudulent conveyances (18, 20 Feb.), roads and bridges (24 Feb.), the subsidy (24 Feb.), marriage licences (26 Feb.) and apprentices (10 Mar.).

Sandys was noticeably less active in the Parliament of 1586–7. He is not recorded as speaking, but he was named to committees on Mary Queen of Scots (4 Nov.), the Norfolk election (9 Nov.), the import of fish (6 Mar.), cattle theft (10 Mar.), the subsidy (11 Mar.) and fraudulent conveyances (13 Mar.). In December 1588 he was one of the lawyers asked by the Privy Council to consider which statutes needed repeal or amendment in the forthcoming Parliament, but when it came he apparently served only on the subsidy committee (11 Feb. 1589).

Sandys surfaced again in 1593. He was put on the first privileges and returns committee at the outset of the Parliament (26 Feb.), and he was named to the subsidy

committee the same day, and on 28 Feb. and 1 Mar. He spoke on the Fitzherbert privilege case (2 Mar.) and moved for the consideration of the poor law (12 Mar.). He was appointed to a committee on recusancy (28 Feb.) and wished Brownists to be included within the provisions of this bill (13 Mar.). He spoke again on the subject on 4 Apr. His other committees this Parliament were on cattle theft (5 Mar.), the poor law (12 Mar.) and petty larceny (16 Mar.). He was given leave of absence (17 Mar.) for 'some necessary occasions', and had returned by 4 Apr.

No speech is recorded for Sandys in 1597–8. His committees were on privileges and returns (5 Nov.), armour and weapons (8 Nov.), the penal laws (8 Nov.), the explanation of statutes (12 Nov.), sturdy beggars (22 Nov.), tillage (13 Dec.), writs of error (11 Jan.), malt (12 Jan.), charitable uses (14 Jan.), defence (16 Jan.), mariners (26 Jan.) and bail (27 Jan.).[5]

Outside Parliament, Sandys was one of sixteen commissioners instructed by the Privy Council in 1586 to try to persuade seminary priests, imprisoned in London, to conform. In later years his extra-parliamentary activities were confined more and more to the duties of a justice in Buckinghamshire and Bedfordshire, counties in which he purchased further lands, for more than £1,000, in 1590. In 1592 he was a commissioner to take the oath of supremacy from the Buckinghamshire justices. His tenants accused him of curtailing copyhold rights, refusing access to the court rolls, and charging lands with knight service in order to obtain wardships.[6]

Sandys made his will in November 1600. He was confident of his salvation by 'free grace' and the merits of Christ, and trusted that he would be received 'to dwell among the souls of God's elect'. He was to be buried without 'vain pomp, ostentation or chargeable funeral'. He bade his eldest son, Edwin, be kind to the widow and 'travail in her causes', as he had travailed in Edwin's 'most troublesome and tedious causes'; the widow was bidden, in her turn, to be kind to the children, and God, 'the father of the fatherless orphans', would bless her. Sandys died on 22 Oct. 1601, leaving lands in Bedfordshire, Buckinghamshire, Gloucestershire, Hampshire, Northamptonshire, Sussex, Wiltshire and Worcestershire.[7]

[1] Vis. Worcs. (Harl. Soc. xxvii), 123; VCH Lancs. viii. 377; PCC 47 Windsor. [2] CPR, 1558–60, p. 107; CSP Dom. 1595–7, p. 461; Lansd. 683, f. 70; P. H. Williams, Council in the Marches of Wales, 356–7; Strype, Annals, iii(2), 458; Harl. 474; APC, xiv. 80. [3] Strype, ii(2), 246; Borthwick Inst. Hist. Res., Archbishop Sandys's reg. f. 103; Cam. Misc. ix(3), p. 5. [4] Somerville, Duchy, i. 292, 497; PCC 45 Windsor; VCH Bucks. iii. 148, 207, 209, 398; VCH Beds. iii. 371, 391; VCH Berks. iii. 255; Eton Coll. Reg. i. 295; CSP Dom. 1597–1601, p. 144; HMC De L'Isle and Dudley, i. 333; HMC Hatfield, vii. 432, 484. [5] D'Ewes, 127, 158, 159, 165, 178, 179, 184, 188, 206, 213, 220, 222, 223, 247, 248, 250, 253, 288, 289, 291, 292, 293, 298, 301, 302, 304, 306, 334, 336, 337, 339, 340, 341, 343, 345, 346, 347, 348, 351, 352, 353, 355, 356, 361, 362, 364, 365, 394, 396, 412, 414, 431, 471, 474, 477, 478, 481, 487, 499, 500, 502, 517, 552, 553, 556, 561, 572, 577, 578, 580, 581, 587, 588, 589; CJ, i. 83, 85, 86, 90, 92, 95, 96, 99, 101, 102, 105, 106,

108, 110, 111, 120, 121, 122, 123, 127, 129, 131, 132, 134; Trinity, Dublin, anon. jnl. f. 20; Lansd. 43, anon. jnl. ff. 169, 172, 175; Trinity, Dublin, Thos. Cromwell's jnl. f. 82; Townshend, *Hist. Colls.* 71, 76, 104, 107, 120, 122, 123; *HMC Lords*, n.s. xi. 8; *APC*, xvi. 416. [6] *APC*, xiv. 80; xv. 122; xvii. 77; xviii. 288; xix. 61; xxiii. 256; xxvi. 14; *VCH Bucks*. iii. 209. [7] PCC 65 Woodhall; C142/271/162.

A.H./P.W.H.

SANDYS, Samuel (1560–1623), of Ombersley, Worcs.

| RIPON | 1586 |
| WORCESTERSHIRE | 1604*, 1614, 1621 |

b. 28 Dec. 1560, e. surv. s. of Edwin Sandys, abp. of York, by his 2nd w.; bro. of Edwin II*. *educ.* M. Temple 1579. *m.* at Southwell, Notts. 1586, Mercy (*d.* 1629), da. of Martin Culpepper of Worcs., 4s. 7da. *suc.* fa. 1588. Kntd. 1603.

J.p. Worcs. from c.1600; member, council for Virginia 1612; sheriff, Worcs. 1618–19; member, council in the marches of Wales 1623.

Returned for Ripon through the influence of his father, Sandys was, some four years later, living in Essex where he had property, and his eldest son was baptized at Woodham Ferrers. In 1596 he wrote to Michael Hickes* complaining that his enemies were trying to deprive him of some land, and asked him to intercede with Burghley. About this time he acquired considerable property in Worcestershire, where he eventually settled. By the time he made his will, 16 Feb. 1622, he held property in Worcestershire, Nottinghamshire, Gloucestershire, Yorkshire, Lincolnshire and Essex. He provided for his wife and children, making Sir James Pitts, his brother Edwin*, John Baker and John Brace trustees of the property. He mentions holding stock in the East India Company which his executrix was to make up to £4,000, and which he left to his children. His wife was sole executrix, and his brother Edwin, (Sir) Lawrence Tanfield*, Sir John Denham and John Culpepper were overseers, each receiving £20. Sandys left £200 to be distributed among his servants, and made a number of charitable bequests. He died on 18 Aug. 1623, and was buried at Wickhamford in Worcestershire, where a monument was erected to himself and his wife.

Vivian, *Hist. Sandys Fam.* 152; *Vis. Worcs.* (Harl. Soc. xxvii), 123; E. S. Sandys, *Hist. Sandys Fam.* pt. ii. ped. C; pat. roll, 42 Eliz.; Lansd. 82, f. 140; *VCH Worcs.* ii. 427; PCC 93 Swann.

N.M.S.

SANDYS, Walter (c.1540–1609), of Timsbury, Hants.

| STOCKBRIDGE | 1563 |

b. c.1540, yr. s. of Thomas, 2nd Baron Sandys of The Vyne by Elizabeth, da. of George Manners, Lord Ros. *educ.* I. Temple 1555. *m.* Mabel, da. of Thomas Wriothesley†, 1st Earl of Southampton, 1s. Kntd. 1591.[1]

J.p.q. Hants from c.1574, sheriff 1576–7, 1591–2.

On his father's death in the winter of 1559–60, Sandys was left to exercise much of his family's considerable influence in Hampshire, for the 3rd Baron Sandys was his nephew William, still a minor. In Stockbridge, and nearby at Mottisfont and Timsbury, there was property belonging to the barony. Timsbury was conveyed to Sandys by his nephew at an unknown date; in 1587 he was granted the nearby rectory of Sparsholt by the Queen, and he bought one of the Mottisfont manors in 1591. No doubt he already had interests in that part of the Sandys estates in 1563, when he secured election as the senior of the first two Members returned by Stockbridge on its enfranchisement.[2]

Sandys was an active county official and justice of the peace. In 1580 he, the dean of Winchester, (Sir) Richard Norton I* and Sir William Kingsmill were commissioned – as those most interested in the project – to collect money for the endowment of a house of correction in Winchester. He was one of the two Hampshire collectors of funds contributed for defence in 1587, and one of the six gentlemen in the county required to supply horses for Ireland in 1600. In the 1590s he was involved in a long dispute with his nephew, Lord Sandys, over their respective rights in Mottisfont, complaining to the Privy Council in 1596 that Lord Sandys had seized his manor there by force. In the summer of 1597 Francis Moore* reported to Sir Robert Cecil* that Sandys, 'much unsatisfied' with the arbitration of the case, had personally remonstrated with the lord chief justice, and the dispute continued for at least another year. Sandys's case against his nephew was supported by Sir William Cornwallis*.[3]

Sandys died 29 Aug. 1609, at Winchester, where he had leased a tenement in 1587.[4]

[1] *CP*; *DNB* (Wriothesley, Thomas); C142/312/134. [2] *CPR*, 1558–60, p. 330; *VCH Hants*, iii. 447; iv. 487, 506. [3] *APC*, xi. 417; xiv. 388; xxiii. 184, 209; xxiv. 317; xxvi. 278; xxx. 439; xxxii. 279; *CSP Dom.* 1581–90, p. 395; *HMC Hatfield*, vii. 260; viii. 265, 292. [4] C142/312/134; *VCH Hants*, v. 6.

A.H.

SANFORD, Hugh (d. 1607), of Wilton, Wilts.

| LUDLOW | 1597* |
| WILTON | 1601, 1604* |

Servant of 2nd and 3rd Earls of Pembroke.

Sanford's parentage has not been established; he cannot be fitted into the pedigrees of any of the known gentle families of that name. More puzzling, in view of his evident learning, is his absence from the records of both universities and of the inns of court. His career as tutor to William Herbert (3rd Earl of Pembroke 1601), presumably began before 1590, when William Herbert became ten years of age, and may have ceased by March 1593, when his pupil entered New College, Oxford. At this time Wilton House seemed 'like a little University', and among its ornaments was 'the great Hugh Sanford, learned in all arts, sciences, knowledge humane and divine ... from which I never departed without some profit'. Sanford's range of learning seems to have embraced prophecy. His prediction that his pupil would not live beyond the age of 50 was to be fulfilled when the 3rd Earl, after jokingly alluding to it on his 50th birthday, died the next day.[1]

Sanford was one of the witnesses to the will which the 2nd Earl made in January 1595. By it he received an annuity of £30 a year for life according, as the testator put it, 'to my former grant to him thereof made'. Sanford served both earls in a confidential capacity: in 1599 he was an intermediary in the negotiation between the 2nd Earl and his son-in-law Sir Robert Sidney over the succession to the presidency of the marches of Wales, and in 1604 he was involved in a matrimonial discussion between Sidney and the 3rd Earl.[2]

It was to his two noble masters that Sanford owed his parliamentary career. He was returned for Ludlow at the general election of 1597 as part of a campaign by the 2nd Earl, as president of the council in the marches, to weaken the corporation of Ludlow. The return was investigated by the privileges committee of the House and a new election took place on 5 Dec. (several weeks after the beginning of the session) Sanford then being replaced by a Ludlow man. At the next two elections Sanford was returned for the Pembroke borough of Wilton, for which he was sitting at the time of his death, 21 May 1607. Sanford made a will, but it was nullified by the Prerogative Court of Canterbury, and so not enrolled; its provisions are unknown. From the proceedings in that court it is clear that his mother Florence survived him, as did his brother John and his sister Margaret. His widow Elizabeth, against whom they contested the administration of his estate, married as her second husband William Sharpe of Fugglestone. Sanford's property included lands in Glamorgan worth £16 6s. 8d.[3]

[1] Clarendon, *Hist.* ed. Macray, i. 73; *Wilts. N. and Q.* vi. 441–2, 496. [2] PCC 39 Woodhall; *HMC De L'Isle and Dudley*, ii. 383, 424; iii. 127, 128–9; *HMC Hatfield*, xvii. 33. [3] D'Ewes, 556, 593; PCC 65 Windebanck, 55 Capell; C142/310/65.

S.T.B.

SAPCOTE, John (d. 1574), of Therfield, Herts. and of Lincs.

RIPON 1559

1st s. of Henry Sapcote of Lincs. by Jane (d. 1546), da. and h. of Robert Smyth. *educ.* Oxf. supp. BA 1537, BCL 1545. *m.* Mary, da. of William Shelton of Suff., 3s. 2da. *suc.* fa. 1553.

Sapcote was a member of the household of Nicholas Heath, archbishop of York, who nominated him at Ripon. He came of a family closely connected with the church, his father (twice mayor of Lincoln) having been registrar general of Lincoln cathedral, where John's uncle William was a canon. Both Henry Sapcote and his wife were buried there. Sapcote himself may have been in minor orders, and when Heath had been deprived early in Elizabeth's reign, he could have expected no further employment. Instead of living on his property in and around Lincoln, he seems to have retired to the south of England. The preamble to his will, made 29 Apr. 1574, is Catholic: he commended his soul to the Trinity and to Mary, Mother of God. Most of the will is in Latin, but the last section, which includes a list of small debts, is in English. Evidently a punctilious man, he asked his executors, Thomas Turner and Richard Proctor, to pay his grocer for spice and his tailor 8s. owing to him. The executors were to receive annual payments, Turner of £4 and Proctor of £6, for 10 years after Sapcote's death. His widow was to distribute £10 to the poor. The will in general is that of a man in only moderate circumstances. For some reason it was not admitted to probate, and letters of administration were granted in December 1574 to the widow. A new grant was made in June 1588, after her death, to one William Dalton of St. Andrew, Holborn.

Vis. Herts. (Harl. Soc. xx), 162; *Lincs. Peds.* (Harl. Soc. lii), 853; Lansd. 109, ff. 204–5; *CPR*, 1558–60, p. 172; PCC 46 Martyn; PCC admon. act. bk. 1588, f. 66.

N.M.F.

SAUNDER, Thomas (d. ?1582), of Southover, Lewes, Suss.

LEWES 1559

?s. of Thomas Saunder (d. 1535) of Southover. *m.* (2) Anne, a wid.

In 1553 it was agreed that Southover, a parish adjoining Lewes and recognized as a 'member' of the borough, should elect one Member to every second Parliament. Saunder, of merchant or yeoman stock, was no doubt chosen as a result of this understanding. He may have been in the service of Thomas Sackville*, later Lord Buckhurst, whose father, Sir Richard*, owned a half share of the manor there. In his will, made 11 Dec. 1581, and proved the following May, Saunder left a gold ring to 'the right honourable the Lady Buckhurst, my singular good lady'. Buckhurst's steward William Newton, who built the Grange, Southover, was one of the overseers of Saunder's will.

Suss. Rec. Soc. xix. 10; xliii. 106; lvi. 96, 101; *VCH Suss.* vii. 36, 45; PCC 20 Tirwhite.

M.R.P.

SAUNDERS, Nicholas I (d. 1605), of London.

PENRYN	1589
ST. IVES	1593
HELSTON	1597
LOSTWITHIEL	1601

o.s. of Thomas Saunders of Uxbridge, Mdx. by his w. Elizabeth. *educ.* King's, Camb. 1565. *suc.* fa. 1565. *unm.*, 1s.

Govt. messenger in Italy 1581, to the Porte 1584, to the Low Countries 1586, ?in Ireland 1596.

Little is known of Saunders' father, who must, however, have been of some standing in Middlesex as he nominated as one of the overseers of his will John Newdigate†, the head of one of the county families, but his will mentions no estates and no inquisition post mortem has been found. Saunders himself, when he came to make his will in 1604, held no property in Uxbridge, although the family's interest there continued beyond the death of the father, for in 1576 Margaret or Margery, one of Thomas Saunders' daughters, paid for the enclosure of the new cemetery.

Saunders had some connexion with the Killigrew family, through whose good offices he presumably embarked on his diplomatic career, such as it was. In 1572 he was with Henry Killigrew* on the Continent, and was subsequently employed by the government in taking messages overseas. By July 1585 he had returned to England, and in the following year he was again sent to the Low Countries. At this time, hoping to be made ambassador at Constantinople, Saunders sought the favour of the Earl of Leicester, who wrote on his behalf to Sir Francis Walsingham. Saunders also canvassed the support of Sir Thomas Cecil*, but there is nothing to show that he was employed again even as a messenger until after 1590. Towards the end of 1585 he was in prison for debt, and two years later, still insolvent, he was engaged in a complex suit with a London merchant, William Beecher, over debt. He had also another suit, against Edward Wynter*, who was then in captivity.

Saunders probably owed all his parliamentary seats to the Killigrews, unless St. Ives was obtained through Burghley. It is not clear whether the Nicholas Saunders who was appointed to committees dealing with the subsidy on 26 Feb. and 1 Mar., and to the committee to peruse the statutes concerning the relief of the poor and the punishment of rogues (12 Mar.) in the 1593 Parliament was Nicholas Saunders of London or his namesake of Ewell.

Little is known of the remainder of the London man's career. He was probably the Mr. Saunders who was in Ireland in 1596 as a government messenger. Perhaps he was also the Nicholas Saunders mentioned at the trial of the 11th Lord Cobham in 1604. It was then alleged that Cobham had instructed one of his servants to ask a Nicholas Saunders to offer the attorney-general £100 for his opinion on the case. Later a Nicholas Saunders was given permission to visit Cobham in the Tower.

Saunders' will, drawn up in 1604, was revised shortly before his death, which occurred on 7 Apr. 1605. He had never married, and the residuary legatee was his 5-year-

old child Nicholas Councell, who was to be raised so 'that I do hope his virtue by good bringing up will redeem my offence'. In 1604 Saunders thought that the estate might amount to £4,000, but he was less optimistic the next year. The child's mother was bequeathed £500 and a further £500 when her son came of age. Sir William Killigrew and Saunders' nephew, Sir Maurice Berkeley II*, were the executors. The will was contested by Saunders' younger sister Elizabeth, wife of William Onslow*.

PCC 33 Morrison, 26 Bakon, 40 Hayes; S. Lysons, *Acct. of those Parishes in Mdx. not Described in the Environs of London*, 183; *CSP For.* 1578–9, p. 45; 1581–2, p. 153; 1584–5, pp. 167, 181, 186, 268, 605; 1586–7, pp. 92, 98; 1589–90, p. 350; C2Eliz./S26/40; D'Ewes, 474, 481, 499; *HMC Hatfield*, vi. 250; xvi. 193, 197–8; Nichols, *Progresses Jas. I*, i. 298; C142/304/503.

A.M.M.

SAUNDERS, Nicholas II (1563–1649), of Ewell, Surr.[1]

HASLEMERE	1593
GATTON	1604
WINCHELSEA	1626

b. 1563, 1st s. of Nicholas Saunders† of Ewell by his 1st w. Isabel, da. of Sir Nicholas Carew† of Beddington. *educ.* Balliol, Oxf. 1581; I. Temple 1583. *m.* by 1585 Elizabeth, o. da. and h. of Richard Blount I* of Coleman Street, London and Williton, Som., 1s. 1da. *suc.* fa. 1587. Kntd. 1603.[2]

J.p.q. Surr. 1590–c.96.

Saunders' grandfather was cofferer to Queen Mary and his father a Catholic recusant in 1577, 1580 and 1585. He, the father, remained on good terms with Lord Burghley, to whom he bequeathed an emerald ring and to whose 'honourable favour, direction and protection' he commended his son, the 1593 Haslemere MP. The latter, also a Catholic, was presented with his father for non-conformity in 1585, but after his father's death he conformed (though his wife did not) and was even on the 1592 Surrey commission for the suppression of Jesuits. Saunders seems to have had a special relationship with the puritan William More I*, who brought him into Parliament for Haslemere, and to whom Saunders wrote after More had left that Parliament prematurely:

as I am very glad for your own sake that you are quiet now at home, free from the wearisome attendance here, so I am sorry for mine own sake that you are gone in that I am half out of countenance wanting your presence here.

Saunders, who described himself as More's 'dutiful son and assured friend', told More about the Commons proceedings of 6 Apr. The bill against sectaries had a difficult report stage, and while the committee for the bill and the objectors to it met separately, the remainder of the House passed away the time reasonably pleasantly in arguing a merry bill of the brewers, which we have passed, and by Mr. Stevenson's speech to it, who was called up by my means to speak, who of himself meant it not. But the chiefest matter of pleasure to the House was through the bill of Cranbrooke, which I procured to be read.

Eventually the committee returned, having agreed on a number of amendments, and the bill against sectaries passed the House. 'We were content to yield anything so we might rise, for it was past three ere this was concluded and ended'. It is not clear which of the two Nicholas Saunders in the House it was who was appointed to committees on the subsidy on 26 Feb. and 1 Mar. and to one on the poor law, 12 Mar.[3]

In 1596 Saunders took part in the Cadiz expedition, presumably as a follower of Lord Howard of Effingham, a commander of the expedition. Saunders was instructed to wait at Plymouth after the main fleet had left, and to join it 'as soon as certain business was ended'. He was, however, arrested at the suit of a trader to whom he had promised to sell some sugar, having received £400 as an advance payment. The mayor of Plymouth informed Cecil that Saunders had laid up his ship, landed his ordnance and was trying to sell both. He was released at Cecil's request, and wrote on 23 July that he would shortly be sailing. The fact that he had sugar to sell in 1596 suggests that he may have been the Nicholas Saunders who was a privateer in the 1590s.[4]

Saunders' father married as his second wife Margaret, widow of Richard Blount, and Saunders himself made a fortunate marriage to her daughter. Between 1591 and 1601 he sold three estates, including land in Lambeth inherited by his wife, as well as part of the Ewell property. When suggesting himself to the Earl of Salisbury in 1605 as a successor to Sir George Harvey as lieutenant of the Tower, he commented that his estate, though somewhat lessened by others' unjust dealing, was yet worth £500 a year. Saunders died 9 Feb. 1649.

[1] Information from Mr. J. W. Walker is gratefully acknowledged. [2] *Vis. Surr.* (Harl. Soc. xliii), 69; PCC 47 Pyckering, 7 Rutland; *Surr. Arch. Colls.* liv. 96-7. [3] C. H. Dudley Ward, *Fam. of Twysden of Twisden,* 140; *Surr. Arch. Colls.* liv. 94, 96-7; Hyland, *A Century of Persecution,* 202-3, 229, 231-2, 327, 388, 392-3; *APC,* xii. 152; PCC 7 Rutland; *The Times,* 12 Dec. 1929; Neale, *Commons,* 402-3; *Parlts.* ii. 288-92; W. Prynne, *Hidden Workes of Darkenes,* 69; D'Ewes, 474, 481, 499. [4] *APC,* xxv. 399, 460-1; Lansd. 150, f. 186; *HMC Hatfield,* vi. 228-9, 244, 258-9, 280. [5] *Vis. Surr.* loc. cit.; PCC 47 Pyckering; *Surr. Arch. Colls.* liv. 82; *VCH Surr.* iv. 59; *HMC Hatfield,* xvii. 242; *Chamberlain Letters* ed. McClure, i. 150, 152, 165, 167, 173.

A.M.M.

SAUNDERS, Robert (c.1514-59), of Flore, Northants.

BRACKLEY	1553 (Mar.), 1553 (Oct.), 1558, 1559

b. c.1514, 2nd surv. s. of Thomas Saunders of Sibbertoft by Margaret, da. of Richard Cave of Stanford; bro. of

Edward Saunders[†]. *educ.* M. Temple, ?adm. 1518. *m.* (1) Margaret, da. and h. of Thomas Stanton of Stanton, Mon., 2s. 1da.; (2) by Oct. 1558, Joyce, da. of Sir John Goodwin of Upper Winchendon, Bucks., at least 1s.

Jt. (with Francis Saunders[†]) steward, Brackley 1558.

Saunders' life was spent for the most part in and around Brackley, where the records show him buying wool and suing various local merchants for minor debts. Two of his brothers were better known. Edward was a judge under Queen Mary, and Lawrence was martyred at Coventry in the same reign. As Robert himself was one of those who 'stood for the true religion' in the Parliament of October 1553 it is likely that his religious views were closer to those of Lawrence than to those of Edward, who had written to Lawrence urging him to submit. After his stand in 1553 Robert Saunders did not represent his borough again in Parliament until Mary's last, before the second session of which he made his will, 3 Oct. 1558, bequeathing £1 towards the repair of Flore church, and a further £1 to the poor of the parish. By this time he had made a second marriage into the well-known family of Goodwin, and his wife Joyce was residuary legatee. Saunders was sick when he made the will. Nevertheless he was returned to Elizabeth's first Parliament, but died soon afterwards, 13 Nov. 1559. The joint executors were the widow and Saunders' brother Blase, and it was the latter who proved the will on 27 Aug. 1560. The widow married Anthony Carleton*.

PCC 31 Porche, 44 Mellershe; Baker, *Northants.* i. 152, 153, 293, 509; Bridges, *Northants.* i. 508, 509; Northants. RO, Ellesmere mss; Foxe, *Acts and Mons.* vi. 612-36; Bodl. e Museo 17; *Vis. Bucks.* (Harl. Soc. lviii), 64.

A.M.M.

SAUNDERS, Thomas, of Coventry, Warws.

COVENTRY	1586, 1589, 1593, 1597, 1601

?s. of John or Thomas Saunders (both graziers) of Coventry.

Sheriff, Coventry 1570-1, mayor 1579-80, alderman.

The Saunders family had been prosperous and prolific in Coventry since the mid-fifteenth century. Saunders himself was a grazier. He was frequently chosen by the city council for special duties, and served five times as burgess in Parliament. It is likely that he was the Mr. Sanders or Saunders who was put on committees concerning the Norfolk election (9 Nov. 1586), a learned ministry (8 Mar. 1587), merchant strangers (14 Mar.) and the continuation of statutes (20 Mar.). As a burgess of Coventry he may have served on cloth committees (14 Mar. 1593, 18 Nov. 1597 and 9 Dec. 1597), and on committees discussing forestallers and regrators (7 Nov. 1597) and maltsters (12 Jan. 1598). He was assessed highly towards the provision of troops for the musters and light horse for Ireland, and was one of those who complained that the city was unjustly burdened, 'being much decayed and greatly pestered with poor, and daily charged with carts, carriages and posthorses, being the thoroughfare towards Ireland'. No will has been found, and the date of Saunders' death has not been ascertained. In 1604 a croft was leased to a widow, Bridget Saunders.

B. Poole, *Coventry*, 371; T. W. Whitley, *Parl. Rep. Coventry*, 61; Coventry mayors' accts.; Coventry hand bk.; Coventry bk. of payments, ff. 51, 58, 60, 68; Coventry council bk. ff. 189, 225, 226, 250, 279; *HMC Hatfield*, viii. 486; D'Ewes, 396, 413, 415, 417, 501, 552, 558, 570, 578.

S.M.T.

SAUNDERSON, Nicholas (c.1562–1631), of Saxby, Lincs.

| GREAT GRIMSBY | 1593 |
| LINCOLNSHIRE | 1625 |

b. c.1562, 1st s. of Robert Saunderson of Saxby and Fillingham by his 2nd w. Catherine, yst. da. of Vincent Grantham† of St. Katherine's, Lincoln; bro. of Robert*. *educ.* Oxf. BA 1579; L. Inn 1579. *m.* (1) bef. 1593, da. of William Rokeby; (2) bef. 1599, Mildred, da. and h. of John Hiltofte of Boston, 4s. 3da. *suc.* fa. 2 Nov. 1583, aged 21. Kntd. 1603; *cr.* Bt. 1611, Visct. Castleton [I] 1627.

J.p. Lincs. (Lindsey) from 1591; Notts. from c.1592; commr. sewers Lincs. by 1589, sheriff 1592–3, 1613–14, commr. recusancy 1624.

One of the leading landowners – by inheritance, marriage and purchase – in north Lincolnshire, Saunderson owned estates also in south Yorkshire. His influence in the Grimsby neighbourhood in particular may have been derived from the leasehold he held in Tetney, a few miles away, possibly from his uncle, Thomas Grantham I*. Counted among the leading 'depopulators by enclosure' in the county, Saunderson lived in style, employing the musician Giles Farnaby to teach his children, two of whom married into the Rutland and Bertie families. He left no mark upon the surviving records of the 1593 Parliament, purchased a baronetcy in 1611, obtained a peerage in 1627 and died in 1631. His will was proved at Lincoln.

CP; NRA cal. Lumley Castle mss passim; Lincs. AO, LCC 1630/1, 467, Aswarby 2/5/8; Lansd. 60, f. 189; *HMC Rutland*, i. 463, 471; *CSP Dom.* 1591–4, p. 178; *HMC Hatfield*, xiii. 189; xi. 440; *EHR*, lxvii. 392–6; *Music and Letters*, xlii(2), pp. 151–4; *Cal. Lincoln Wills* (Brit. Rec. Soc. Index Lib. xli), 159.

D.O.

SAUNDERSON, Robert (*b.* aft. 1561), ?of Saxby, Lincs.

| WEST LOOE | 1589 |

b. aft. 1561, 2nd s. of Robert Saunderson of Saxby and Fillingham, and bro. of Nicholas*. *educ.* Broadgates Hall, Oxf. 1579; L. Inn 1579. prob. *unm.*

Few details of Saunderson's life are known. In May 1589 he wrote to Michael Hickes*, Lord Burghley's secretary, about a crazy ex-servant of his own, who had undertaken to remove a brood of devils. He was probably the Mr. Saunderson mentioned in a letter written in July 1603 by Vincent Skinner* to Robert Cecil, from which it appears that Saunderson had been instrumental in bringing about the arrest of a fugitive priest. It was presumably his connexion with the Cecils which brought about Saunderson's return to Parliament for West Looe in 1589.

Vis. Lincs. ed. Metcalfe, 62; *CP*, iii. 99–100; *CPR*, 1550–3, pp. 69, 75; 1553–4, p. 349; 1555–7, p. 411; *LP Hen. VIII*, xxi(1), p. 762; Lansd. 99, f. 75; *HMC Hatfield*, xv. 181.

I.C.

SAVAGE, Edward (1560–c.1622), of Beaurepaire, Hants, later of the Savoy, Mdx.

| NEWTON | 1584, 1586 |
| STOCKBRIDGE | 1601 |

b. 1560, yr. s. of Sir John Savage of Clifton and Rock Savage, Cheshire, by his 1st w. Elizabeth, da. of Thomas Manners, 1st Earl of Rutland; bro. of John*. *educ.* Brasenose, Oxf. 1576; I. Temple 1578. *m.* Polyxena, da. of William Grice*, at least 1s.

Constable of Halton castle, duchy of Lancaster 1577; dep. keeper of Hainault walk 1582; j.p.q. Hants from c.1601; freeman, Chester 1607.

Savage's father was one of the principal gentlemen of Cheshire, seven times sheriff of the county, and three times mayor of Chester. His three daughters married Sir William Brereton*, Thomas Langton* and Sir Henry Bagnall*. Little is known about Savage himself; possibly he was a lawyer. He married a niece of his stepmother Eleanor, widow of Sir Richard Pexall of Beaurepaire, Hampshire. Sir John Savage settled at Beaurepaire and intended that Edward should receive the Hampshire property which came to him as the inheritance of his second wife. Unfortunately its ownership was contested by Eleanor's relations, and although Edward Savage grew up in possession of Beaurepaire, where he entertained the Queen in 1601, he appears to have lost it about 1613 or possibly after the death of his stepmother in 1618.

Savage was returned at Newton through his brother-in-law Thomas Langton*, and at Stockbridge through his neighbour William, 3rd Lord Sandys. He made no mark on the records of the House of Commons. In 1598 he went to Ireland with his brother John to inquire into the estates of their late brother-in-law, Sir Henry Bagnall.

Savage died before 29 Nov. 1622, when administration of his property was granted to his son.

Ormerod, *Cheshire*, i. 715–16; G. Armstrong, *Fam. Savages of the Ards*, 33–6; Lansd. 34, f. 97; Somerville, *Duchy*, i. 511; *Chester Freemen Rolls* (Lancs. and Cheshire Rec. Soc. l), 92; *VCH Hants*, iv. 166; M. Burrows, *Fam. Brocas of Beaurepaire*, 211, 218, 222; *APC*, xxix. 168; PCC admon. act bk. 1622, f. 208.

N.M.S.

SAVAGE, John (1554–1615), of Clifton, Cheshire.

CHESHIRE   1586, 1589

b. 1554, 2nd but 1st surv. s. of Sir John Savage by his 1st w. and bro. of Edward*. *educ.* L. Inn 1571. *m.* c.1576, Mary, da. and coh. of Richard Allington, 5s. 2da. *suc.* fa. 1597. Kntd. ?28 June 1599; *cr.* Bt. 29 June 1611.

Bailiff of manor and forest and keeper of the gaol of Macclesfield from 1597; steward, Macclesfield from 1598, of manor of Halton from 1598; j.p.q. and commr. musters, Cheshire from c.1598, sheriff 1606–7, dep. lt. from c.1608; mayor, Chester 1607–8.[1]

Savage's father built a new house at Clifton in 1567, which came to be known as Rock Savage. A number of the family's manors lay between Clifton and Chester, where they also held property, with a secondary group between Middlewich and Nantwich on the river Dane. It was on this considerable landed estate, built up since the fourteenth century, that the family's importance rested during Elizabeth's reign. Savage first comes to notice in 1576 for refusing to make adequate arrangements for his mistress (one of his stepmother's relatives, before his marriage to Mary Allington). After his marriage he lived in or near London, perhaps at court, but, finding the cost too great, in 1579 he accompanied Sir William Norris to Ireland. From Chester he wrote to his cousin the 3rd Earl of Rutland, asking him to provide him with a good horse, as the other gentlemen in the company were well mounted, and he 'would be loath to be inferior'. He was back in England by 30 July 1585, when he was again writing to the Earl of Rutland, this time in an effort to prevent his father from disposing of certain entailed estates, an issue on which father and son had reached agreement within a year. Savage twice sat for the county before becoming head of the family in 1597. He did not gain possession of all the family estates, however, until after the death of his stepmother in 1612, and he appears to have been in financial difficulties, perhaps a result of his father's debts, though the father was listed as of 'great possessions' in 1588. Even after coming into all the Savage lands, the heir complained of poverty, still, however, being among the first to purchase a baronetcy. He died at Rock Savage 7 July 1615, having made his will the previous 20 June. To his overseer, his worthy friend the bishop of Chester, he bequeathed a piece of plate worth £5, and to the city of Chester a pair of silver gilt flagons, valued at £20. His wife received his houses in Holborn and in Chester, and his coach and horses. He was buried at Macclesfield on 14 July 1615, leaving as heir his eldest son Thomas. The will was not proved until 1618.[2]

[1] Ormerod, *Cheshire*, i. 716; C66/1549; *PRO Lists and Indexes*, iii. 18; Gabriel thesis; *APC*, xxviii. 578; J. P. Earwaker, *East Cheshire*, ii. 467; *Cheshire Inquisitions post mortem* (Lancs. and Cheshire Rec. Soc. xci), 40. He inherited these offices from his father. [2] Ormerod, i. 711, 716; *HMC Rutland*, i. 107, 118, 177, 198; *APC*, xxviii. 578;

Cheshire Inquisitions post mortem, 40–4; Lansd. 104, ff. 51 seq.; PCC 40 Montague; *HMC Hatfield*, xvii. 403; *Stanley Pprs.* ii (Chetham Soc. xxxi), 170–1.

A.M.M.

SAVERY, Christopher (*d.*1623), of Totnes and Shilston, Devon.[1]

TOTNES   1584, 1593

s. of Stephen Savery of Totnes by Joan, da. and coh. of John Servington of Tavistock. *m.* Joan, da. of Thomas Carew of Haccombe, 3s. 5da.

Member of Totnes merchant company 1579, governor 1580; freeman, Totnes 1584, mayor 1593; sheriff, Devon 1619.[2]

Savery was twice returned to Parliament for his borough, leaving no trace upon the records of the House, though he may well have served on committees concerning kerseys, 23 Mar. and 2 Apr. 1593. He was the leader of the group of richer Totnes merchants who successfully attempted to exclude the commonalty, led by William Blackall and John Giles*, from participation in the town's affairs, and was naturally one of the 14 councillors named in the charter of 1596. Thenceforward he was attacked with increasing bitterness by the opposing faction, who sent a petition to the Privy Council in 1598 accusing him of various malpractices. In 1602 Blackall was still attacking him but by the following year he had bought the manor of Ford in Broadhempston from Edward Seymour I* and was described as 'esq.' of Little Hempston. His name appears in various connexions, subscribing £25 to the Armada fund, involved in litigation with the Buggin family, selling Totnes castle in 1591, able to lend the King £30 in 1611, and so on. By 1614 he had settled as a country gentleman at Shilston. He died in 1623, and was buried at Ugborough on 8 Oct.[3]

[1] This biography is based upon the Roberts thesis. [2] Vivian, *Vis. Devon*, 670–1; *Vis. Devon* (Harl. Soc. vi), 253–4; *Trans. Dev. Assoc.* xxxii. 439; xl. 152, 156; Devon RO 1579 unclassified f. 5. [3] D'Ewes, 507, 513; *Western Antiq.* ix. 152; W. Cotton, *Antiqs. Totnes*, 28, 34, 94; St. Ch. 5/B21/6; Totnes recs. petition of 1598, letter of 11 Jan. 1601; Devon RO, Tingey 1402; *Devon N. and Q.* xxvi. 124; Vivian, 670.

P.W.H.

SAVILE, George I (1551–1622), of Lupset, Yorks. and Barrowby, Lincs.

BOROUGHBRIDGE   1586
YORKSHIRE   1593

b. 1551, 2nd but 1st surv. s. of Henry Savile I* of Lupset and Barrowby by his 2nd w. Joan, da. and h. of William Vernon of Barrowby. *educ.* St. John's, Oxf. by 1566; L. Inn 1568. *m.* (1) 1583, Lady Mary Talbot, da. of George, 6th Earl of Shrewsbury, 1s. George Savile II*, *d.v.p.*; (2) by 1599, Elizabeth (*bur.* 25 Jan. 1626), da. of Sir Edward

Ayscough of South Kelsey, Lincs., wid. of George Savile of Stanley, Wakefield, Yorks., 3s. 4da. *suc.* fa. 1569. Kntd. June 1587; *cr.* Bt. 1611.

J.p. Yorks (W. Riding) from c.1573; commr. musters 1595, sheriff 1613–14.[1]

Despite his family connexions, little is known about Savile. His first marriage linked him with both the Manners and Talbot families and brought him the Rufford estates in Nottinghamshire. In 1603, upon the death of his unstable cousin Edward Savile, he also succeeded to Thornhill near Wakefield, thereafter living as a country gentleman, not overburdened with local offices. He appears to have been on friendly terms with Sir Robert Cecil*, with whom he sometimes corresponded about dogs and falcons. He was of sufficient standing to get himself returned for Boroughbridge in the Parliament of 1586 and to obtain a county seat in 1593. So far as is known he took no part in the proceedings of the 1586 Parliament, but as a knight of the shire in 1593 he could have served on committees concerning the subsidy (26 Feb. and 1 Mar.), springing uses and perpetuities (9 Mar.), maintaining weirs (28 Mar.) and cloth (14, 15, 23 Mar.). He died 12 Nov. 1622, and was buried at Thornhill.[2]

[1] *GEC Baronetage*, i. 49; Foster, *Yorks. Peds. W. Riding*; *HMC Rutland*, i. 273; Gooder, *Parl. Rep. Yorks.* ii. 36. [2] *Yorks. Arch. Jnl.* xxv. 16–19; *HMC Rutland*, i. passim; J. Hunter, *Antiquarian Notices*, 26; *HMC Hatfield*, v. 382; vii. 171; J. B. Greenwood, *Early Eccles. Hist. Dewsbury*, 210; D'Ewes, 474, 496, 501, 507, 512.

N.M.S.

SAVILE, George II (c.1583–1614), of Barrowby, Lincs.

| MORPETH | 1601 |
| APPLEBY | 1614 |

b. c.1583, 1st s. of George Savile I* by his 1st w. Lady Mary Talbot, da. of George, 6th Earl of Shrewsbury. *educ.* Univ. Coll. Oxf. 1598, BA 1601. *m.* (1) Sarah, da. of John Rede of Colesbrooke, Northants.; (2) 14 Sept. 1607, Anne, da. of Sir William Wentworth of Wentworth Woodhouse, 2s. Kntd. 11 May 1603.

Savile owed his seat in Elizabeth's last Parliament to his uncle, Edward Talbot*, whom he mentions in a letter of thanks to 'the bailiffs, aldermen and the rest of the burgomasters of Morpeth', addressed to them from Doncaster 21 Oct. Only 18 at the time, Savile had just come down from Oxford, where he had studied under the master of University College, George Abbot, afterwards archbishop of Canterbury. Savile later remembered his old tutor in his will, appointing him an executor, and placing a son in his care. In 1601 Savile lived at Barrowby, but he moved to Yorkshire when his father inherited the Savile estates. He died *v.p.* in August 1614.

Yorks. Arch. Jnl. xxv. 22–4; *DNB* (Abbot, George); Morpeth corporation mss Eliz. I, 27, ex inf. Dr. H. S. Reinmuth.

B.D.

SAVILE, Henry I (1517/18–69), of Lupset, Yorks.

| GRANTHAM | 1558 |
| YORKSHIRE | 1559 |

b. 1517/18, 1st s. of John Savile by Anne, da. of William Wyatt. *educ.* ?Oxf. BCL 1535. *m.* (1) 1545, Margaret, da. and coh. of Henry Fowler or Fuller, ?s.p.; (2) by 1551, Joan, da. and h. of William Vernon of Barrowby, Lincs., wid. of Sir Richard Bozom of Long Clawson, Leics., 3s. inc. George Savile I* 2da.; (3) Dorothy, da. of Richard Grosvenor of Eaton, Cheshire, wid. of Richard Wilbraham[†] (*d.*1558), *s.p. suc.* fa. 1530.[1]

J.p. Yorks. (W. Riding) from c.1547, (all ridings) from 1562, Lincs. (Kesteven) from c.1554; commr. chantries, Yorks. (W. Riding) 1548, relief, Lincs. (Kesteven), Yorks. 1550; surveyor, ct. of augmentations, Yorks. (N. Riding) by 1552–4, Exchequer 1554–*d.*; keeper, New park, Wakefield, Yorks. 1554; escheator, Lincs. 1555–6; member, council in the north from Dec. 1558; sheriff, Yorks. 1567–8; commr. to enforce Acts of Uniformity and Supremacy, province of York 1561.[2]

In addition to the extensive family estates to which Savile succeeded, he was heir male of his relative Edward Savile, the idiot son of Sir Henry Savile[†]. In September 1559 Edward Savile made a settlement of his property on the Lupset branch of the family, and by 1567 Henry Savile already held much of it. About 1564 he successfully fought a case in the duchy of Lancaster court concerning his title to Edward's duchy lands. He made two fortunate marriages, his second bringing him considerable Lincolnshire property. As knight of the shire for Yorkshire in 1559 he is not mentioned in the journals.[3]

Savile was an active local official throughout Mary's reign, but he evidently supported the Elizabethan church settlement and was classified as a 'favourer' of sound religion in 1564. He was one of those members of the council in the north 'bounden to continual attendance', which, with his salary of £40, suggests that he was a lawyer. As his name has not been found in any inn of court register he was probably the man of his name who graduated BCL in 1535, though his youth militates against the identification. The last reference found to him in an official capacity is in November 1565 as an arbitrator in a dispute concerning the tenants of the archbishop of York.[4]

Savile's will, made in January 1569, was proved the following May. His heir, George, aged 18 at his father's death, married a daughter of the 6th Earl of Shrewsbury, a union arranged by the parents when the prospective bridegroom was only ten. A younger child had been named after his godfather, Sir William Cordell*, master of the rolls, who was an executor of the will, and who was asked to bring up Bridget, Savile's unmarried daughter. The main charitable bequest was for setting up an almshouse at Wakefield.[5]

[1] C142/51/106; Glover, *Vis. Yorks.* ed. Foster, 341; *Al. Ox.* i(4), p. 1319; Emden, *Biog. Reg. Oxf. 1501–40*, p. 505; PCC 11 Sheffelde;

Yorks. Arch. Jnl. xxv. 16 seq. [2] *Inventories of Church Goods* (Surtees Soc. xcvii), 109; *CPR*, 1547–8, p. 92; 1553–4, pp. 21, 238; 1554–5, p. 109; 1560–3, p. 436; 1566–9, p. 172; Lansd. 1218, f. 12; *CSP For.* 1558–9, p. 55; J. J. Cartwright, *Chapters in Yorks. Hist.* 19 n; Reid, *Council of the North*, 493. [3] *LP Hen. VIII*, v. 237; xx(2), p. 453; *Yorks. Arch. Jnl.* viii. 488 n; xi. 161–2; xxv. 16; *W. Riding Sessions Rolls* (Yorks. Arch. Soc. rec. ser. iii), 216 n; *CSP Dom.* 1547–80, p. 129; J. Watson, *Hist. Antiqs. Halifax*, 86 seq.; C142/155/138; Wards 7/12/52. [4] *Cam. Misc.* ix(3), p. 70; *CPR*, 1560–3, pp. 170, 186–7; *CSP For.* 1558–9, p. 55; *CSP Dom.* Add. 1566–79, p. 61; *APC*, vii. 293. [5] *PCC* 11 Sheffelde; *Yorks. Arch. Jnl.* xxv. 16; *CSP Dom.* 1547–80, p. 151.

N.M.F.

SAVILE, Henry II (1549–1622), of Oxford and Eton, Bucks.

BOSSINEY	1589
DUNWICH	1593

b. 30 Nov. 1549, yr. s. of Henry Savile (*d.*1566) of Bradley, Yorks. by Elizabeth, da. of Robert Ramsden; bro. of John I*. *educ.* Brasenose, Oxf., fellow of Merton 1565, BA 1566, MA 1570; Padua; I. Temple c.1578. *m.* c.1592, Margaret, da. of George Dacres* of Cheshunt, Herts., wid. of George Gerrard of Bucks., 1s. *d.v.p.* 1da. Kntd. 1604.

Junior proctor Oxford Univ. 1575–7; warden, Merton from 1585; Latin sec. and dean of Carlisle 1595 or 1596; provost of Eton and j.p. Bucks. from c.1596.

Savile was one of the leading scholars of the second half of Elizabeth's reign, a friend of Thomas Bodley*, whose library he helped to found, and a translator of the classics. In 1591 his edition of Tacitus was published, and between 1610 and 1613 his translation of the works of St. Chrysostom. He was one of the committee which prepared the Authorised Version of the Bible. In 1620 he gave the first geometry lectures at Oxford, later founding eponymous chairs in that subject and in astronomy. He is said to have taught Greek to Queen Elizabeth, and he entertained her at Merton in 1592. Savile's Inner Temple membership was probably honorary.

Savile's patron at Bossiney could have been John Hender*, who entered the Middle Temple at the same time as Savile's brother John, or even Sir William Peryam*, another of the borough's patrons, whom Savile probably knew through Thomas Bodley. Savile took charge of the bill about Anne Neville's jointure, 24 Feb. 1589. At Dunwich he was no doubt nominated by his friend and one-time pupil, the Earl of Essex, high steward of the borough. The journals do not mention him in 1593. His appointment as Latin secretary necessitated his spending some time at court, where he fell into temporary disfavour at the time of the Essex rebellion. Though committed to private custody he was not deprived of his offices, and by the time of the 1601 Parliament he had recovered the Queen's good opinion, for she gave him a copy of her 'Golden Speech'. James I knighted him at Eton in September 1604. Savile died there on 19 Feb. 1622, and

was buried in the college chapel 'by torchlight to save expense'.

DNB; Clay, *Dugdale's Vis. Yorks.* i. 334; *Al. Ox.* i(4), p. 1319; Neale, *Parlts.* ii. 392–3; D'Ewes, 438; *Chamberlain Letters* ed. McClure, i. 121; PCC 44 Savile.

J.C.H.

SAVILE, John I (1546–1607), of Bradley and Methley, Yorks.[1]

NEWTON	1572

b. 26 Mar. 1546, 1st s. of Henry Savile of Bradley, and bro. of Henry Savile II*. *educ.* Brasenose, Oxf. 1561, ?BA 1563; Clement's Inn 1564; M. Temple 1565, called 1573, bencher and Autumn reader 1586, serjeant-at-law 1594. *m.* (1) 1575, Jane, da. of Richard Garth of Morden, Surr., 1s. 2da.; (2) 1587, Elizabeth, da. of Thomas Wentworth of Elmsall, wid. of Richard Tempest of Bowling, 1s. 2da.; (3) 1594, Dorothy, da. of Thomas Wentworth[†], 1st Baron Wentworth of Nettlestead, wid. of Paul Wythypole of Ipswich, Suff. and of Sir Martin Frobisher; (4) 1603, Margery, da. of Ambrose Peake of London, wid. of Sir Jerome Weston of Essex and of one Thwaites of London. *suc.* fa. 1566. Kntd. 1603.[2]

J.p. co. Dur. and Hexhamshire from c.1576, q. 1583; commr. eccles. causes, diocese of Durham 1576–7; j.p. Yorks. (W. Riding) from c.1580, q. 1583; justice oyer and terminer, N. circuit 1580–1; commr. subsidy, Yorks. (W. Riding) 1582; baron of the Exchequer 1598, justice of assize, N. circuit 1598; c.j. Lancaster 1598; member, northern high commission 1599, council in the north 1599; commr. chancellorship of duchy of Lancaster 1599–1601; j.p.q. Cumb., Northumb., Westmld. 1601.[3]

Member, Antiq. Soc. c.1591.

By the sixteenth century the Savile family had many branches in Yorkshire. Savile himself belonged to a younger branch of the Saviles of Copley. In his autobiography he relates that he received his early education from neighbouring clergymen at Elland and Huddersfield, with whom he read the classics before going up to Oxford in 1561. He remained there for two years. His statement that he graduated BA is unsupported. In the summer of 1563 he returned to Bradley to avoid the plague and there devoted himself to the reading of Littleton's *Tenures*, the statutes, Rastall's *Abbreviamenta*, the year books of Richard III, Henry VII and Henry VIII. Thus prepared, he entered Clement's Inn in October 1564, removing to the Middle Temple four months later. He maintained his connexion with the Middle Temple for the rest of his life and in such a manner that in 1600 his 'great favours to the House' were acknowledged. While still there he was returned to Parliament for Newton, Lancashire, presumably through his friendship with William Fleetwood I*, the recorder of London and steward of the borough, whose wife stood godmother to Savile's eldest daughter in 1577. Another influential friend was Sir Henry Gates*, who called him 'my assured good friend and faithful counsellor' and left him an annuity of £5 'for his great pains on my behalf for my causes in law'. Gates was godparent to Savile's eldest son, together with Sir William Cordell*, master of the rolls, and the wife of Robert Monson*, one of the justices of common pleas. Savile was present during all three sessions of the 1572 Parliament, but his recorded activity covers only 1576 and 1581. On 24 Feb. 1576 he sat on a committee for a bill for the explanation of the statute against dilapidations; on 1 Mar. on committees for four bills about clothiers and cloth; on 12 Mar. he was appointed to the committee for the restitution in blood of Lord Stourton, and the next day to the committee considering the relief of vicars and curates. On 13 Feb. 1581, he was one of those to whom the bill against the inordinate selling of wool and yarn was committed.[4]

In February 1573 Savile was called to the bar and in the summer of 1574 he extended his practice to the northern circuit. Two years later he received his first public appointments, becoming an ecclesiastical commissioner for Durham. His legal practice must already have been prosperous, for soon afterwards he began rebuilding his house at Bradley, which was finished in the summer of 1580. From this time he resided mainly in Yorkshire, still continuing, however, his London practice, and in 1586 he was made a bencher of the Middle Temple upon his appointment as autumn reader. In August he delivered 15 lectures on the statute of 1 Edward VI, cap. 14, on the dissolution of colleges.

Savile's legal practice in Yorkshire soon brought him into conflict with the council in the north, where attempts to enforce the statutes against regrators and wool gatherers, and against frauds in cloth making, which the Yorkshire clothiers found restrictive, aroused the opposition of the West Riding justices of the peace, who were encouraged by Savile to deny the council's authority. Savile was not disinterested. As a common lawyer he resented prerogative jurisdiction and, like John Savile* of Howley, he no doubt had clothing interests himself. He therefore insisted that offences against the penal statutes could only be dealt with by the common law process of inquest and verdict by a jury. It has been suggested that Savile's elevation to the bench was an attempt to buy him off. But the obdurate justice who denied ship money in the West Riding in 1597–8 was in all probability his namesake, Sir John Savile of Howley, and there is no need to see Savile's promotion in 1598 as due to anything but a combination of his own merits and the influence of his extensive legal connexions. In fact, as a justice of assize, Savile continued to imprison or bind over anyone who appealed to the council at York against the assize justices or the justices of the peace. During the summer assizes of 1600 and 1601 he supported his colleague, Christopher Yelverton*, who advanced his own and Savile's authority over the other members of the council.[5]

Savile's attitude toward the execution of penal statutes was maintained into the new reign and in 1604 he was one of the judges who advised James I that their prosecution and execution could not be granted away. However, he was only irrevocably opposed to the prerogative when it involved a conflict of jurisdiction with the common law courts, for in 1606 he was one of the judges who decided that the King could levy import and export duties by prerogative alone, without a parliamentary grant.[6]

Savile's interests were not confined to his profession. In 1593 he finished building his new house at Methley, near Leeds, about 20 miles from Bradley. In religion he inclined toward puritanism and was an active and 'singular patron of preachers of God's word' in Yorkshire. He is said to have endowed a large number of charities there, but only the foundation of chapels at Bradley and Methley, an interest in the rebuilding of a chapel at Rastrick and a gift of £5 to the recently founded Halifax grammar school, have been traced to him. He numbered prominent puritans among his friends: Robert Monson and William Fleetwood, both members of the puritan 'choir' in the House of Commons. Like Fleetwood, Savile was active in seeking out recusants, especially in his capacity as a judge of assize in the north. In 1604 he was alleged to have expressly directed a grand jury at Manchester that persons attending mass celebrated by a Jesuit or seminary priest were guilty of felony. Savile died at Serjeants' Inn 2 Feb. 1607 and was buried at St. Dunstan's-in-the-West, his heart being removed to the church at Methley, where he had lived since 1593.[7]

[1] Except where otherwise stated this biography is based on 'Autobiog. of Sir John Savile', *Yorks. Arch. Jnl.* xv. 420–42. [2] *Vis. Yorks.* (Surtees Soc. xxxvi), 346–7; *Vis. Yorks.* ed. Foster, 57; 'Savile Fam.', *Yorks. Arch. Jnl.* xxv. 4–41; *DNB*; Foss, *Judges*, vi. 186; Reid, *Council of the North*, 496. [3] Lansd. 35, ff. 133v, 138v; 737, f. 179v; Royal 18 D.111; *CSP Dom.* 1598–1601, pp. 71, 154; 1603–10, p. 133; Somerville, *Duchy*, i. 336, 396, 471; C66/1549. [4] *M. T. Recs.* i. 404; *Northern Wills* (Surtees Soc. cxxi), 141; *CJ*, i. 108, 109, 114, 115, 125; D'Ewes 251, 260, 262. [5] Reid, 221, 222, 336, 338, 350–1; Heaton, *Yorks. Woollen and Worsted Industry*, 76–7; *APC*, xxv. 325; *CSP Dom.* 1598–1601, p. 232; 1601–3, p. 155; *HMC Hatfield*, vii. 203. [6] *HMC Hatfield*, xvi. 349–50; xviii. 274–5; Gardiner, *Hist. England 1603–42*, ii. 6. [7] Jordan, *Charities of Rural England*, 325, 395; Neale, *Parlts.* i. 91, 142; *N. and Q.* (ser. 2), x. 81–5; *Notable M. Templars*, 217; Guildhall mss 10342, ff. 2–3; C142/298/99.

I.C.

SAVILE, John II (1556–1630), of Doddington, Lincs. and Howley, Yorks.

LINCOLN	1586
YORKSHIRE	1597, 1604, 1614, 1624, 1626

b. 1556, 1st s. of Sir Robert Savile of Barkston, Lincs. by Anne, da. and coh. of Sir Robert Hussey of Linwood in Blankney, Lincs., wid. of Matthew Thymbleby of Poolam in Edlington, Lincs.; half-bro. of Stephen Thymbleby*. *educ.* Trinity Coll. Camb. 1572; L. Inn

1577. m. (1) Catherine, da. of Charles, 2nd Baron Willoughby of Parham, s.p.; (2) 20 Nov. 1586, Elizabeth, da. of Edward Carey*, 5s. 3da. suc. fa. 1585. Kntd. by 1597; cr. Baron Savile 1628.[1]

Steward, honour of Wakefield 1588, honour of Ponefract; j.p. Lincs. (Lindsey) and Yorks. (W. Riding) from c.1591; custos rot. Yorks. (W. Riding) from c.1594; member, northern high commission 1599, council in the north from 1603, v.-pres. 1626–8; PC 1626; alderman (mayor) of Leeds 1626; commr. navy 1626, loan in Yorks. 1627, fees and offices 1627; receiver of revenues of northern recusants 1627; comptroller of the Household 1627.[2]

Savile is best known for his implacable hostility to Sir Thomas Wentworth†, afterwards Earl of Strafford, with whom he fought for supremacy in the north. But Savile was older than Wentworth and more than half of his active life lay in Elizabeth's reign. His grandfather, Sir Henry Savile† of Thornhill, had provided his illegitimate son Sir Robert – father of the subject of this biography – with lands in Lincolnshire, as well as with the manor of Howley in Yorkshire, of which he deprived his legitimate issue. Sir Robert had extended his property by marriage to a Lincolnshire heiress. He was soon well established in the county, of which he was sheriff in 1573, and was able to arrange an advantageous match for his heir with the daughter of Lord Willoughby of Parham.

Savile was returned for Lincoln in 1586, soon after buying the nearby manor of Doddington. His half-brother, Stephen, had been recorder of the borough since 1572. Savile chose Lincoln instead of Poole, for which he had also been elected, apparently through the good offices of the Earl of Warwick. Savile is noted as sitting on one committee in his first Parliament, for East Retford, 10 Mar. 1586, and he is not known to have spoken.[3]

During the next few years Savile devoted himself to the management of his estates at Barkston and Doddington. But his interests were early transferred to Yorkshire, so that, although a Lincolnshire justice of the peace, he was never sheriff as his father had been. His Yorkshire possessions were concentrated in the West Riding, around the new manufacturing centres of Leeds and Batley. Near the latter he built his house at Howley, described by Camden as sedes elegantissima, which was finished about 1590. Extensive interests in the woollen industry not only enriched Savile, but also gave him control over the local inhabitants, many of whom he employed as weavers; a popularity which contemporary disapproval of democratic appeal did not inhibit him from using.[4] By 1593 he was settled permanently in Yorkshire and so able to put himself forward as a native in the county election of 1597, which he successfully contested against two strangers. No speeches by him are recorded in the 1597 House of Commons, but he was named to a committee on spinners and weavers (21 Nov.) and, as knight of the shire,

he could have attended the committees on enclosures (5 Nov.), the poor law (5, 22 Nov.), armour and weapons (8 Nov.), penal laws (8 Nov.), monopolies (10 Nov.) and the subsidy (15 Nov.).[5]

Since 1593 the West Riding clothiers had been suffering under the attempts of the council in the north to enforce the statute against the stretching of cloths and kindred legislation aimed at controlling the price and quality of West Riding cloths. The attempts were resisted under Savile's leadership, assisted by John Savile I*. By 1597 it scarcely needed Savile's condemnation of T. P. Hoby* as a stranger to arouse feeling against him, for it was widely broadcast that in the previous Parliament Hoby's brother Edward* had promoted a bill against northern cloths. Throughout 1597 Savile was fully occupied in prosecuting the quarrel of the Yorkshire clothiers with the council in the north. This was typified in the West Riding ship money struggle. Unlike John Savile of Methley, and the common lawyers, Sir John and his fellow clothiers were not concerned with the claims of conflicting jurisdictions, but with the desire to avoid payment of the £400 demanded of them. Serjeant Savile's claims for the common law were to them merely a welcome rationalization of their determination not to pay. By 1597, conflict on this question had been imminent for some time. The original demand that Leeds, Wakefield and Halifax should contribute toward the cost of a ship provided by Hull had been waived by the Privy Council upon the plea of the West Riding justices of the peace that they had no traffic with Hull. In 1595, when Hull was required to provide a ship for the Cadiz expedition, this excuse was no longer accepted. But the clothiers, under Savile's leadership, refused to pay. The consequent struggle between them and the council in the north lasted for some years, until in February 1598 five of the ringleaders were summoned to appear before the Privy Council in London. Savile was particularly reprimanded and the five sent back to Yorkshire with orders to further the collection of the levy. The assessment was duly made at the quarter sessions held at Pontefract at Easter. Savile himself, and his cousin and supporter, Serjeant Savile, were to make the assessment in the wapentakes of Askrigg and Morley.[6]

During the remaining years of Elizabeth's reign Savile avoided any overt conflict with authority, although there is no reason to suppose that his hostility toward the council in the north lessened, and he was certainly not averse from using any weapon to discomfit its members. He was to fight the same battles for election to Parliament and over ship money again later, but with weapons sharpened by these earlier experiences and by the need to assert himself against one specific and resourceful adversary, Sir Thomas Wentworth.[7]

[1] 'Savile Fam.' (Yorks. Arch. Jnl. xxv), 1–47; DNB; CP, xi. 459–61.
[2] Somerville, Duchy, i. 523; Hatfield ms 278; Reid, Council of the North, 496; Thoresby, Ducatus Leodensis, 150, 263; HMC Hatfield, ix. 396;

C66/1421; PRO, Index 4211. ³ R. E. G. Cole, *Hist. Doddington*, 53, 56; D'Ewes, 414. ⁴ C. V. Wedgwood, *Strafford: a Revaluation*, 30; Heaton, *Yorks. Woollen and Worsted Industry*, 80. ⁵ D'Ewes, 552, 553, 555, 557, 560, 561. ⁶ *APC*, xxvi. 304, 325; xxviii. 66, 319, 400, 403; Heaton, 81–3; Reid, 221, 222–3; *W. Riding Session Rolls* (Yorks. Arch. Soc. rec. ser. iii), 70–1. ⁷ Lansd. 86, ff. 34–5; Clarendon, *Rebellion*, i. 341.

I.C.

SAYER, Richard (c.1562–1603), of St. Michael Penkivel, Cornw.

| GRAMPOUND | 1589 |
| ST. MAWES | 1597 |

b. c.1562, 1st s. of Hugh Sayer of St. Michael Penkivel by Margaret, da. of Richard Digby of Coleshill, Warws. *educ.* Hart Hall, Oxf. 1577. *m.* Ursula, da. of Hugh Trevelyan of Yarnscombe, Devon, 3s.
    J.p. Cornw. 1603.

Sayer's estate of St. Michael Penkivel was near enough to both Grampound and St. Mawes to account for his return for these boroughs. Through the Trevelyans he was connected with some of the leading Cornish families. He died intestate and was buried 11 Sept. 1603 at St. Michael Penkivel. Administration of his estate was granted to his widow on 5 Nov. 1603. He was survived by two sons, both minors, a third having predeceased him. There is nothing to indicate that the Cornish country gentleman was the Richard Sayer who wrote to Robert Cecil between 1591 and 1603 about the Queen's title to the liberties of St. Albans, applying for a job in their administration.

Vivian, *Vis. Cornw.* 420; *Vis. Cornw.* (Harl. Soc. ix), 197; *Vis. Warws.* (Harl. Soc. xii), 17; Foster, *Al. Ox.* iv. 1322; PRO Index 4208, f. 297; PCC admon. act bk. 1603, f. 175; *HMC Hatfield*, xiv. 272.

I.C.

SCAMBLER, James (d.1633), of Peterborough, Northants, later of Hickling, Norf.

| PETERBOROUGH | 1584 |

s. of Edmund Scambler by Julian, wid. of one Francys of London. *m.* (1) by 1577, Jane, da. of John Freeman of Billing, Northants., *s.p.*; (2) Mary, da. of William Loveday of Norwich, *s.p.*[1]
    Feoffee of town lands, Peterborough from 1572; clerk of the foreign appostes in the Exchequer by 1589; j.p. Norf. 1593, rem. c.1596, rest. c.1598, q. 1601.[2]

After a period spent in the service of his father, the bishop of Peterborough, and in the administration of the town lands, Scambler was returned to Parliament for the borough, at about the time that he obtained his job in the Exchequer, no doubt through the good offices of Lord Burghley, patron of both father and son. Early in 1585 the bishop was translated to Norwich, and the family followed him to Norfolk, where Scambler himself bought property and became, by 1600, a moderately substantial landowner.

In his later years he lived as a country gentleman. He died in 1633.[3]

¹ *Vis. Norf.* (Harl. Soc. xxxii), 241; *Vis. Norf. 1664* (Norf. Rec. Soc. v), 192. ² *Northants. Rec. Soc.* ix. 195; xiii, p. lxxi; Add. 22924, ff. 6, 19; Lansd. 106, f. 1 seq.; A. H. Smith thesis, apps. ii, v; *Stiffkey Pprs.* (Cam. Soc. ser. 3, xxvi), 33–6. ³ *Northants. Rec. Soc.* xviii, pp. xl, 83 n, 86, 169; *DNB* (Scambler, Edmund); Lansd. 37, f. 30; 46, f. 25; *HMC Hatfield*, x. 18; *APC*, xxxi. 405; *Corresp. Lady Catherine Paston* (Norf. Rec. Soc. xiv), 54, 112; Blomefield, *Norf.* ix. 299; PCC 38 Sadler.

P.W.H.

SCORY, Sylvanus (d.1617), of Cordwainer Street, London.

| NEWTOWN I.o.W. | 1597 |

s. of John Scory, bp. of Hereford, by his w. Elizabeth. *m.* Alice, da. of Francis Walshe of Shelsley, Worcs., 2da. *suc.* fa. 1585.
    Servant of the Earl of Leicester by 1584.
    Prebendary of Hinton 1565–9; esquire of the body at Queen Elizabeth's funeral; gent. of privy chamber to James I.

Scory's father, one of the less heroic figures of the Reformation, submitted to Bishop Bonner and renounced his wife at the outset of Mary's reign, then fled abroad. On Elizabeth's accession he returned to England and was given the see of Hereford. Scory himself held the prebend of Hinton for four years during his father's tenure of the bishopric, and leased several ecclesiastical properties, including the manor of Whitbourne and Colwall Park, Herefordshire. How Scory came to be a servant of Robert Dudley, Earl of Leicester, has not been ascertained, but he was sufficiently close to Leicester to be suspected by the Privy Council of being behind the libellous *Leycester's Commonwealth*, published in 1584, and he admitted introducing Leicester to the Spanish ambassador during a dinner held at the house of Thomas Smythe I*, customer of London. Suspected of treason and in disgrace with his father, he persuaded the French ambassador, Mauvissière, to write to Walsingham on 21 June 1585 asking him and Leicester to intervene with the Queen on his behalf, as he wished 'to justify himself and be a faithful subject to her Majesty and a good servant to the Earl' and so prevent his father from disinheriting him. Mauvissière's story was that Scory spoke only of 'matters of state' and had visited him to thank him for hospitality received.[1]

When his father died a short time later, Scory's brother-in-law Giles Allen complained of his 'ungodly, unnatural, blasphemous and unlawful conduct' to the dying bishop, in that he prevented anyone from 'performing the necessary offices to the dead corpse', though he had time enough to write to Leicester asking for a suit to be tried in which he alleged that corrupt practices, presumably connected with the distribution of his father's estate, had deprived him of several thousand pounds. While the case was still pending, he followed Leicester to the Netherlands and through an ill-advised duel aroused Burghley's displeasure, in the meantime being accused by the new bishop of Hereford of wrongfully retaining the manor of Whitbourne. Scory's tenant and kinsman, Mr. Walshe, was ordered by the Privy Council to vacate Whitbourne, 'as there was no other convenient place of residence within his diocese belonging to the bishop', but was allowed to remove Scory's property. At the same time the Council wrote to the Earl of Leicester requesting that Scory might be sent back to England. On 15 July 1587 the case was referred to three arbitrators who awarded the bishop Whitbourne, and Scory Colwall Park, adding that Scory should pay the bishop £275 dilapidations. After further delay the Privy Council confirmed the arbitrators' award but Scory refused to agree and was put in the Marshalsea.[2]

The next few years of his career are once more obscure, but he went abroad again and for an unknown reason his lands were forfeited. He had returned by 1596, when he owned a house in Cordwainer Street, London, valued at £15 p.a. On the 1598 subsidy roll for London he was assessed on £100 in goods. He retained friends at court, being a creditor of several minor officials there, and by the death of Elizabeth had become an esquire of the body. He was probably returned to Parliament, through his court connexions, at the instance of Sir George Carey*, 2nd Baron Hunsdon, the lord chamberlain and captain of the Isle of Wight, who nominated at Newtown.[3]

Under James I, Scory became a gentleman of the privy chamber, and is said to have suggested to the King several money-raising ideas. Chamberlain, who disliked him, reported that 'the wags say he shall be chief churchwarden over all England and have the placing of women'. A Star Chamber case in February 1617 alleged that Scory had tried to remove by force from a private house the corpse of his son. Scory died on 14 Oct. that year of 'apoplexy', and was buried in St. Leonard's, Shoreditch.[4]

[1] *Vis. Worcs.* (Harl. Soc. xxvii), 125; Cooper, *Ath. Cant.* i. 511–13; LC2/4/4; St. Ch. 8/22/11; *DNB* (Scory, John); Le Neve, *Fasti* (1854), i. 508; *APC*, xiv. 101, 136, 138; R. C. Strong and J. A. Van Dorsten, *Leicester's Triumph*, 129; *CSP Dom.* 1581–90, pp. 156, 227, 427; *CSP For.* 1584–5, pp. 547–8, 584, 587. [2] *CSP Dom.* 1581–90, pp. 249, 254, 355, 408; SP84/6/9; *APC*, xiv. 101, 136, 138; xv. 65, 161, 163; xvi. 225–6; xvii. 435; xviii. 413; xix. 138; Strype, *Annals* iii(2), p. 453; *HMC Hatfield*, iii. 355, 406; G. Croke, *Law Reports, Eliz.* 874. [3] Lansd. 69, f. 175; 81, f. 81; E179/146/369; *HMC Hatfield*, ix. 138; LC2/4/4. [4] *CSP Dom.* 1603–10, p. 208; *Chamberlain Letters* ed. McClure, i. 601, 604; ii. 105; St. Ch. 8/22/11; PCC 124 Weldon; C142/367/95.

R.C.G.

SCOTT, Edmund, of the Middle Temple, London.

2nd s. of John Scott of Bromley, Kent. *educ.* Staple Inn; M. Temple 1595.

If the above identity is correct, Scott was presumably returned for the Rogers' family borough of Wareham through the patronage of John Rogers I*, who apparently practised as a Middle Temple lawyer before succeeding to his estates in 1605. Alternatively, Scott may have been one of Robert Cecil's nominees through the influence of Thomas Howard*, 3rd Viscount Howard of Bindon, though no connexion with Cecil has come to light. Little is known about Scott's life, apart from routine references to him in the Middle Temple records, and a case brought in 1600 in the court of requests by his elder brother John Scott of Lincoln's Inn, who complained that an experienced gambler, Thomas Rich of Lincoln's Inn, had drawn Edmund into playing the game called primero, 'wherein he had small skill and less judgment and contrariwise he the said Rich very skilful at it, as also at the dice and other games'. When playing for small sums Rich allowed Edmund and others to win, but when they were playing for 'any round or great sum', Rich usually won; in this way Edmund had lost the allowance provided by his father. In June 1597 Edmund borrowed £25 from Samuel Thornhill*, entering into a bond of £50 for repayment. Rich, however, had kept £20 of the borrowed money in his own hands until John Scott had entered into a bond for £100 to save Rich harmless from the transaction, and by the time John appealed to the court of requests Rich was threatening to have him imprisoned for non-payment. Whether this had any bearing on Scott's wishing to sit in Parliament in 1601 is unknown.

M. T. Adm. 359; *M. T. Recs.* i. 359, 375; ii. 509; Req. 2/268/14.

A.M.M.

SCOTT, John I (bef. 1534–1619), of Chippenham, Wilts.

Burgess, Chippenham 1554, bailiff 1558, 1568, 1610.

Scott, a clothier, was one of the first 12 burgesses of Chippenham named in the 1554 charter of incorporation. He engaged in local affairs and served on a number of local juries. His assessment of £20, for the subsidy of 1576, was the highest in the town and his annual contribution towards provisioning the royal household was raised in the reign of James I from 3s. 4d. to 4s. 2d. He may have been the John Scott who possessed lands in the manor of Amesbury. In 1605 he leased some of the town lands from which, in 1610, he made a gift of 30s. to the corporation. He died before 27 Dec. 1619.

CPR, 1553–4, p. 104; *Chippenham Recs.* 16, 17, 18, 23, 24, 27, 28, 41–2, 44, 47, 297, 315, 327, 342; *Mins. Proc. Sess.* (Wilts. Arch. Soc. recs. br. iv), 3; *Two Taxation Lists* (Wilts. Arch. Soc. recs. br. x), 54; *Cal. Antrobus Deeds* (Wilts. Arch. Soc. recs. br. iii), 93.

W.J.J.

SCOTT, John II

RIPON   1572

> Steward of the household to Abp. Grindal; j.p.
> Hexhamshire by 1575.

Scott was returned for Ripon in 1572 through the
influence of the archbishop of York. His appointment as a
j.p. in the archbishop's liberties of Hexhamshire suggests
that he was a native of these parts, perhaps connected with
the Scotts of Earle. He was in the service of Edmund
Grindal, then bishop of London and himself a native of
Cumberland, by 1562, when he was furnishing John Foxe
with materials out of Grindal's papers for the *Acts and
Monuments*, presumably for the English edition of 1563 in
which Grindal was interested. Scott followed Grindal to
York in 1570, and to Lambeth in 1575, when Grindal was
translated to Canterbury. He was one of the executors of
Grindal's will, by which he received £50 and 'my gelding
called Old Marshall'. The execution of the will occupied
him for some time. In July 1584 he was writing to
Walsingham to secure his support in the question of
dilapidations owed by the estate of the late archbishop, in
composition of which the executors were prepared to pay
£250. It is likely but not certain that Scott remained in the
service of Grindal's successor. Certainly, he was active
under Bancroft in 1604, when he drew up memoranda to
induce James I to grant the temporalities of the see to the
new archbishop from the death of Whitgift. The place and
date of his death are unknown.

PCC 39 Rowe; SP12/104; *Hist. Northumb.* xiv. 173; Strype, *Annals*,
i(1), p. 559; Strype, *Grindal*, 429, 604, 605; *CSP Dom.* 1581–90, p. 190;
HMC Hatfield, xvi. 407–8.

I.C.

SCOTT, Reginald (c.1537–99), of Smeeth and Aldington, Kent.

NEW ROMNEY   1589

> *b.* c.1537, 1st s. of Richard Scott of Scot's Hall by Mary,
> da. of George Whetenall of Hextall's Place, East
> Peckham. *educ.* Hart Hall, Oxf. 1555. *m.* (1) 11 Oct. 1568,
> Jane, da. of Thomas Cobbe of Cobbe's Place, Aldington,
> 1da.; (2) Alice ?Collyer, wid., *s.p.*
> Subsidy collector, lathe of Shepway 1586–7.

Scott's local standing was quite sufficient to secure his
return for New Romney, though his connexions in the
county were excellent, his father being a younger brother
of Sir Reginald Scott of Scot's Hall, the distinguished
soldier. It was at Scot's Hall that Scott spent much of his
time, helping his cousin Sir Thomas with his business
affairs. His name frequently appears as a witness to family
documents, and he may even have been Sir Thomas's
steward. In 1588 he served as a captain of foot-soldiers and
'trench-master' in the local levies which Sir Thomas Scott

encamped near Dover at the time of the Spanish Armada.
Scott's first marriage, to the daughter of a yeoman family
long resident at Cobbe's Place, brought him Aldington. In
1597 he claimed a manor in Romney Marsh in right of his
second wife, his attempt to eject the occupant by force
being frustrated by the Privy Council.

Scott made his will on 15 Sept. and died on 9 Oct. 1599,
probably being buried at Brabourne. The will was proved
on 22 Nov. Apart from small bequests to his only
grandchild, to his cousin Sir John Scott[t], and one or two
other minor legacies, his household goods, lands and
leases went to his second wife, Alice, whom he had
married late in life. The uncertainty of the will on one
point led to a lawsuit between his widow, the executrix,
and his daughter (and only child) by his first marriage.
Scott was the author of the *Discovery of Witchcraft*, an
attempt to enlist 'Christian compassion' towards those
accused of witchcraft. James I ordered it to be burned, but
the book, published in Holland in 1609, had a great vogue
on the Continent. Pepys' *Diary* for 12 Aug. 1667 has the
entry '... to my booksellers, there and did buy Scott's
discourse of Witches'.

DNB; J. R. Scott, *Scott of Scot's Hall*, pp. lxviii, 180, 187–9, 252;
Discovery of Witchcraft, ed. Nicholson, passim; *Arch. Cant.* xi. 388;
APC, ix. 342; PCC 86 Kidd; C142/272/71.

M.R.P.

SCOTT, Thomas (c.1563–1610), of Scot's Hall, Smeeth, Kent.

AYLESBURY   1586

> *b.* c.1563, 1st s. of Sir Thomas Scott* of Scot's Hall by his
> 1st w. Elizabeth, da. of Sir John Baker[t], of Sissinghurst,
> Kent; bro. of Edward Scott[t] and Sir John Scott[t]. *educ.*
> Hart Hall, Oxf. 1580. *m.* (1) Mary, da. of John Knatchbull
> of Mersham, 1s. *d.v.p.*; (2) bef. 1587, Elizabeth, da. and h.
> of Thomas Honywood* of Sene, Newington, *s.p. suc.* fa.
> 30 Dec. 1594.[1]
> Capt. of lancers, Northbourne camp, 1588, 1589;
> j.p.q. Kent from c.1596, sheriff 1601–2; commr. survey
> crown lands in Kent 1608.[2]

Scott was brought into Parliament for Aylesbury by his
father, who was knight of the shire for Kent in 1586. Sir
Thomas had already tried to secure him a parliamentary
seat at Hythe in 1581. That it was the son who sat for
Aylesbury in 1586 is clear from D'Ewes, 8 Mar. 1587: 'Sir
Thomas Scott and his son have leave to depart'. The Scotts
were related by marriage to Thomas Smythe I*, the
customer of London, who himself represented Aylesbury,
as did two of his sons. Thomas Sackville*, the 1563
Aylesbury MP, was also a relative.[3]

For the eldest son of a leading Kent landowner,
surprisingly little is known about Scott, the absence of
whose name from national and local records is all the
more surprising when the active lives of his younger

brothers are comparatively well documented. Several of them married into important families; two were knighted and sat for Kent in Parliament. That Sir John Scott, the second son, was knight of the shire and deputy lieutenant while his elder brother was still alive and head of the family, testifies to the importance of the Scotts in Kent and, at the same time, accentuates Thomas's minor role. He had no military experience, was not knighted, performed few services for the county (though holding the shrievalty once), and neither of his two wives belonged to families which were his social equal or the equal of those into which his brothers married. The reason for this undistinguished obscurity is matter for speculation. Perhaps, as a letter from a Kent neighbour, Thomas Wotton, suggests, efforts had been made to estrange Sir Thomas Scott from his eldest son, though if so they were reconciled by the time of Sir Thomas's death. Thomas, his principal executor and residuary legatee, inherited seven manors, his seat at Scot's Hall and all his goods. In 1599 Thomas leased three manors to Anthony St. Leger and Richard Smythe, and three years later made a similar grant to Thomas Honywood and John Gibbon. The lands were to revert to Thomas's younger brothers, John and Edward, and their families. Scott was one of those appointed, in September 1608, to help the lord lieutenant, Edward, Lord Wotton*, to survey the Crown's lands in Kent. Earlier, he had acted as trustee for the lands of his brother, Sir John Scott, when he was abroad in the army.[4]

Scott's own military service was limited to Kent. In 1588 and in the following year he served as a captain of lancers in the army assembled at Northbourne, near Dover, under his father's command, to resist any Spanish landing. Later, he appears from time to time among the officers for the county musters, and he helped to supply men to watch the coast at Romney Marsh. In 1604 he attended upon the lord lieutenant when he welcomed the constable of Spain.[5]

Scott died on 24 Sept. 1610,[6] leaving his brother John as heir: the last known reference to him appears to be in September 1608. No will has been found, but a reference in an indenture reveals that he made one. This mentions that he left £2,000 to his niece, Elizabeth Scott, and his widow was to be looked after by Sir John; on the latter's death, which occurred in 1616, she was to receive a life annuity of £240. She died in May 1627 and was buried in Brabourne church. By that time the lord of Scot's Hall was Scott's younger brother Sir Edward.

[1] J. R. Scott, *Scott of Scot's Hall*, App. lxix. Elsewhere (p. 213) the author says that Scott's first wife lived until 1600. Except where otherwise stated this biography is based upon this work. [2] SP13/Case F/11. [3] G. Wilks, *Barons of the Cinque Ports and Parl. Rep. Hythe*, 62. [4] *Thomas Wotton's Letter Bk. 1574–86* ed. Eland, p. 65; PCC 1 Scott; *Arch. Cant.* l. 158. [5] *Arch. Cant.* xi. 389; APC, xxx. 436; HMC Foljambe, 37; HMC Hatfield, xiv. 148; xv. 215; Egerton 860, f. 29; Add. 33924, f. 23; M. Teichman Derville, *The Level and Liberty of Romney Marsh*, 125–7. [6] C142/322/178.

                                                                M.R.P.

SCOTT, Sir Thomas (c.1535–94), of Scot's Hall, Smeeth, Kent.

b. c.1535,[1] 1st s. of Sir Reginald Scott of Scot's Hall by Emmeline, da. of Sir William Kempe of Olantigh, Wye. *educ.* I. Temple Nov. 1554. *m.* (1) Elizabeth, da. of Sir John Baker[†] of Sissinghurst, 17 ch. at least 11s. inc. Thomas*; (2) Elizabeth, da. of Ralph Heyman of Somerfield House, Sellinge, *s.p.*; (3) Dorothy, da. of John Bere of Horsman's Place, Dartford, *s.p. suc.* fa. 1554. Kntd. 1570.[2]

J.p. Kent from c.1561, q. by 1571, commr. piracy 1565, grain by 1573, sheriff 1576–7, dep. lt. by 1582; commr. piracy Cinque Ports in Suss. 1578; superintendent of works, Dover harbour 1580; col.-gen. of Kent forces 1588, 1589.[3]

Scott's family had owned estates in Kent since the fourteenth century and had lived in style at Scot's Hall since the reign of Henry VI. Contemporary sources contain many examples of his wealth and hospitality, and describe his life style in terms usually associated with the great medieval barons. He was related to Leicester and corresponded with many leading statesmen. With him his family, perhaps, reached the highest point of their history.[4]

Barely a month after his entry into the Inner Temple he heard of the death of his father, who left him the bulk of his property consisting of 30 manors centred on Brabourne and Smeeth near Ashford. Scott was still under 20, but a marriage had already been arranged with the daughter of one of their wealthiest neighbours, and Sir John Baker, his future father-in-law, may have acquired his wardship as well. In May 1556 he came of age and entered into his inheritance. From that date until his death 38 years later, he is said to have held sway over a part of Kent like a reigning monarch.[5]

Unlike his neighbour Michael Sondes*, Scott did not invest the profits from his estates in the purchase of more land, though he bought a lease of the Great Park at Aldington. The largest single increase in his holdings occurred on the death of Lady Winifred Rainsford in 1575, when much of her land reverted to the main Scott line. For the most part his estates in the south of the county and along the Medway valley had either been owned by his family for many years or had belonged to his mother. He did, however, rebuild much of the magnificent mansion of Scot's Hall, now vanished without trace, as he did also Nettlestead Place, which was to be occupied by his second son, Sir John[†].[6]

It was not long before Scott was actively engaged in the many duties which a man of his social standing was expected to fulfil. Among these was the defence of Kent. In 1569 he was appointed to a commission to organize coastal defence; its main concern was to ensure that the arrangements for firing beacons were co-ordinated and that sufficient light horsemen were available to patrol the coast day and night and give the earliest possible warning of the approach of a hostile fleet. In some coastal areas disputes arose as to who should supply the watch in specified areas. A serious quarrel at Lydd resulted, despite Scott's efforts, in an inadequate watch being kept of that stretch of coastline during the critical moments of 1588 and for several years afterwards. The main outcome of the business, so far as Scott was concerned, was that he provoked the criticism of both sides.[7]

A constant problem was the provision of sufficient able men, with their equipment, to meet the military requirements expected from the various divisions of the county. Scott dealt mainly with the lathe of Shepway, but in Armada year he also became colonel of several thousand infantry and commander of the camp set up at Northbourne, near Dover, to repel any attempted invasion. He was confident that 4,000 men could 'make head against the enemy' when they landed. He held a similar command at Northbourne in 1589, and in 1591 he despatched the Kent contingent to join the Earl of Essex's French expedition. Another aspect of his military organization which interested Scott was the breeding and training of horses, upon which subject he wrote a book now lost.[8]

At Dover in the 1580s Scott supervised the rebuilding of the harbour in co-operation with Richard Barrey*, lieutenant of the castle, as he did also the construction of a new sea wall between Romney, Lydd and Dungeness, and he was a commissioner for draining and improving Romney Marsh. At one time or another he was asked by Lord Cobham the lord lieutenant or by the Privy Council to investigate civic disputes in most of the Ports. In 1584 and 1588 he examined complaints by the poorer citizens of New Romney that they were over-taxed and misgoverned. Lydd had to be coerced into paying its share for the fitting out of a ship for the Queen's service. It is evident that Scott used his reputation in the Cinque Ports to try to influence their parliamentary elections. In 1581 he wrote to the mayor and council of Hythe in an unsuccessful attempt to obtain a seat for a relative on the very day on which the former Member died:

Forasmuch as I am certified that Mr. Bridgman is departed out of this life, I earnestly desire you to grant your favourable and friendly consent that either my brother, Charles Scott, or my eldest son may be chosen by you as burgess for your town in the Parliament house in his place, in doing whereof you give me just cause to be careful that nothing pass in the said Parliament house that may be prejudicial to the estate of your town, or any liberty you have.

On another occasion, in 1588, he probably helped his cousin, Reginald Scott*, acquire a seat at New Romney.[9]
Scott was thrice elected for his county. His name is

recorded on no fewer than 47 committees, in many of which he was in charge, and he played a major part in the debates on Peter Wentworth and Arthur Hall. The following were the subjects of his main committees. In 1571: church attendance (6 Apr., 5 May), griefs and petitions (7 Apr.), religion (28 Apr.), priests disguised as servants (1 May), preservation of woods (10 May), treasons (11 May), fugitives (25 May), privilege (28 May). In 1572: Mary Queen of Scots (12, 28 May, 9 June), rites and ceremonies (20 May), Tonbridge school (28 May, 30 June), fraudulent conveyances (3 June). In 1576: Peter Wentworth (8 Feb.), the subsidy (10 Feb.), ports (13 Feb.), bastards (15 Feb.), dags and pistols (17 Feb.), sheriffs (24 Feb.), church discipline (29 Feb.), cloth (1, 9 Mar.), unlawful weapons (2 Mar.), wharves and quays (8 Mar.), excess of apparel (10 Mar.), the Queen's marriage (12 Mar.). In 1581: the subsidy (25 Jan.), preservation of woods (28 Jan., 4 Feb.), wrecks (30 Jan.), slanderous words and practices (1 Feb.), Arthur Hall (4, 6 Feb., 8 Mar.), rabbits (9 Feb.), corporations (11 Feb.), the Family of Love (16, 20 Feb.), preservation of game (18 Feb.), growing hemp in Hertfordshire (23 Feb.), draining marshes near London (8 Mar.). In 1586–7: Mary Queen of Scots (4 Nov. 1586), Jesuits (24 Feb. 1587), purveyors (3 Mar.).[10]

The best recorded aspect of Scott's parliamentary career concerns the early sittings of the 1572 Parliament, when the Catholic plots associated with the Duke of Norfolk and Ridolfi increased the hostility felt towards Mary Stuart. Scott was in no doubt that Mary should be executed immediately. In a major speech on 15 May he saw

the Queen in danger, the nobility in peril, and the whole state of the realm in a most dreadful estate. The disease therefore is deadly; the more need to have remedy applied in time. A good physician, before he ministereth his medicine, seeketh out the cause of the disease, whose order herein he meaneth to follow. Papistry [is] the principal which hath produced rebellion. He seeth the papists placed in authority in all places, in commission of peace, in seat of judgment, in noblemen's houses, in the court, yea, about the Queen's own person. This encouraged the Queen of Scots to make this attempt, thinking the party to be strong; this encouraged the Pope to send out his bulls, hoping the papists were able and would maintain it; this encouraged the rebels to rise, the King of Spain and the Duke of Alva to join in their assistance. The second cause [is] the uncertainty of our state. This procured the noblemen and gentlemen, seeing her pretended title to the Crown and seeing likelihood she should prevail, to join with the Queen of Scots. This sore hath two heads, both very great, yea such as if they be not cut off will eat up our heads.

He suggested three remedies:

The first in executing the Queen of Scots, the second disabling her title, the third the establishment of the Crown, which is the principal, and giveth assurance to the subject which loveth her Majesty. If the title be disabled and not her head cut off, the wished fruit will not follow ... The Queen's Majesty hath now tarried so long she can tarry no longer. It remaineth only, if she do, [for] her nobility to be spoiled, her realm conquered, and herself deposed.

Again, on 7 June, he pressed for immediate action, reminding the Queen that a combination of the Catholics in England and Scotland, the Pope, the King of Spain, and the Duke of Anjou and the Guise party in France, could be disastrous. Cromwell reports the end of his speech:

He misliketh the place of her imprisonment, and would in the mean season have kept her in safer guard. She [was] now kept in the north near the rebels which would be ready to assist her, near also to her own country where, if she do escape, she shall soon be received. He humbly desireth those which be of the Queen's Majesty's Privy Council, or that have access to her Majesty, earnestly to incite her in this matter. The request being reasonable, he trusteth easy to be obtained.

Scott is reported by a foreign correspondent to have introduced the proposal in the Commons on 6 Mar. that the Queen should be petitioned to accept the sovereignty of the Netherlands. In the same session he favoured petitioning the Queen to marry, and towards the end of the 1586 Parliament he was instructed by the House to search buildings in Westminster suspected of harbouring Jesuits. Twice in the 1586 Parliament he spoke in favour of Mary's execution.[11]

It is not easy to define Scott's religious position. In 1564 he satisfied the archbishop of Canterbury of his suitability as a justice of the peace, and he was a Kent recusancy commissioner for many years. Although he was one of the county commissioners to impose Whitgift's Articles on the clergy in 1584, he constantly pressed for more time for ministers to make their decision regarding conformity to the conditions. In March he wrote to Lord Burghley in an attempt to help the Kent ministers in their predicament, and in May he led a delegation to see Whitgift at Lambeth. They presented the archbishop with a petition, signed by most of the prominent gentlemen in Kent, asking for the release of those ministers who had been suspended already. Whitgift condemned their attitude and they left without achieving their aim. The account of this incident records that all of them left angrily except Scott, who was impressed by Whitgift's case.[12]

Scott died 30 Dec. 1594, aged about 59. His will was proved on 7 Jan. 1595. If his mode of living was as luxurious as writers suggest, it was still within his financial resources. He left part of his household goods and several portions of lands, including the manor of Thevegate, to his wife, who had to surrender her jointure, Nettlestead, to the second son, John. The bulk of the estates went to the eldest son, Thomas, the new lord of Scot's Hall. The other

surviving sons were remembered, either by grants of land or by annuities; even grandchildren find their place in the will. There were no charitable bequests, in contrast with his generosity while still alive, though his wife's maidservant was singled out and given £5 'for the pains she hath taken in the times of my sickness'. The executors were his sons Thomas and Sir John, and his brother Charles. Lord Buckhurst, a relative, acted as overseer, for which he was paid £40. The will ends with a list of the household items at Scot's Hall which the widow could remove, and a request to the executors to complete the buildings at Thevegate, where she was to live.[13]

Scott was buried with his ancestors in Brabourne church, despite a plea by the citizens of Ashford that he might be laid to rest in the chancel of their church, free of all charges. His tomb, according to local tradition, was desecrated by Parliamentarians in the civil war. No trace of it remains in the church, but in what was formerly the chapel of Scot's Hall itself a mural slab was found in the nineteenth century, bearing the words: 'Here lies all that is mortal of Sir Thomas Scott'. Perhaps his body was transferred there after the civil war. Three of his sons succeeded him in the possession of Scot's Hall, but its great days died with him.[14]

[1] He took possession of his lands in May 1556, presumably when he had come of age (CPR, 1555–7, pp. 8–9). [2] Vis. Kent (Harl. Soc. xlii), 128; Berry, County Genealogies: Kent, 170; J. R. Scott, Scott of Scot's Hall, 178, 185, 206–29, 252 table; I. T. Adm. 19; Cal. I. T. Recs. i. 177. [3] Lansd. 1218, f. 69; Egerton 2345, f. 20; APC, vii. 282; viii. 49, 145; x. 293; xii. 161, 316; Harl. 474; SP12/209/106, 212/40; Scott, 213, note 'e'. [4] Hasted, Kent, viii. 4–5; Scott, App. pp. iii–iv passim. [5] Scott, 206; PCC 40 More; CPR, 1555–7, pp. 8–9. [6] Scott, 196, App. pp. lxvii–lxx; CSP Dom. 1591–4, p. 147; 1595–7, p. 539. [7] Scott, 195; Arch. Cant. viii. 293–310. [8] CSP Dom. 1547–80, pp. 451, 685; 1581–90, pp. 478, 501, 502, 514, 527, 530, 542; B. Nicholson's edition of R. Scott's Discovery of Witchcraft, intro. pp. xxiii–xxiv; HMC Foljambe, 37; Arch. Cant. xi. 388–91; APC, xvi. 154; xxiii. 67; Scott, App. pp. vi–xiv. [9] APC, x. 39; xii. 161; xv. 421–2; xvi. 22, 53–4; xxii. 591; xxiii. 17, 24–5; Lansd. 34, f. 161; 66, ff. 27 seq.; CSP Dom. 1547–80, pp. 630, 671–2; 1581–90, pp. 87, 167–8; 1591–4, p. 1; Scott, 194, App. p. iv; SP12/169/39; Strype, Whitgift, i. 516. [10] CJ, i. 83, 86, 87, 88, 89, 92, 93, 94, 96, 98, 99, 100, 101, 104, 106, 108, 109, 110, 112, 113, 114, 119, 120, 121, 122, 123, 124, 127, 128, 129, 132; D'Ewes, 157, 159, 180, 181, 182, 183, 188, 189, 206, 212, 219, 221, 222, 225, 241, 247, 248, 250, 251, 252, 255, 260, 288, 289, 291, 292, 294, 298, 299, 300, 303, 304, 393, 394, 410, 412. [11] Trinity, Dublin, Thos. Cromwell's jnl. ff. 11–12, 54; Scott, App. p. ii; D'Ewes, 393, 394, 403, 410; K. de Lettenhove, Relations Politiques des Pays-Bas, viii. 249, ex inf. Dr. N. M. Sutherland. [12] CSP Dom. 1547–80, p. 560; 1581–90, p. 164; Cam. Misc. ix(3), p. 58; SP12/169/12; Dr. Williams's Lib. ms Morrice L.V. 7; Collinson thesis pp. 443–5; Scott, App. pp. v and note 'k', x, xiii. [13] PCC 1 Scott. [14] Scott, 41–2, 197; Arch. Cant. x. 265–6; F. Peck, Oliver Cromwell (1740), pp. 28–32.

M.R.P./P.W.H.

SCOTT, William (c.1579–aft. 1611), of Godmersham, Kent.

NEW WOODSTOCK 1601

b. c.1579, 2nd s. of Charles Scott (*d.* 1596) by Jane, da. of Sir Thomas Wyatt†, of Allington Castle. *educ.* I. Temple June 1595.

?Clerk in the ordnance office bef. 1601.

Scott was the great-grandson of Sir Thomas Wyatt the elder, whose sister was the mother of Sir Henry Lee*, the high steward of New Woodstock, and probably the grandmother of Elizabeth, first wife of Lawrence Tanfield, the senior burgess for Woodstock in 1601. Scott was admitted to the Inner Temple at 'Mr. Tanfield's request' in June 1595, a few months before the death of his father. Like John Lee*, another of Sir Henry Lee's relations, Scott may have obtained a post in the ordnance office. Either he or a namesake was a servant to the surveyor of the ordnance, Sir John Davis, and was involved with Davis in Essex's rebellion. The burgess for Woodstock may also have been the man alleged in 1605 to have lampooned Sir Robert Cecil. He certainly had literary pretensions, dedicating to Sir Henry Lee a composition called *The Model of Poesy* and translating a religious work by a Huguenot poet. As 'a sharer in his blood as well as in many his honourable favours', he was privileged in 1611 to compose the inscription for the tomb of Sir Henry Lee, whose education he attributed to the Wyatts. Scott witnessed Lee's will and sent a man to the funeral. Nothing is known of his subsequent career.

Vis. Kent. (Harl. Soc. xlii), 127; E. K. Chambers, *Sir Henry Lee,* 20, 248, 268-9, 298, 305; PCC 37 Drake; *HMC Hatfield,* x. 100; xvi. 14-15; *CSP Dom.* 1598-1601, p. 549; *APC,* xxxi. 160.

A.H.

SCRIVEN, John (*d.* 1560), of Poole and Lyme Regis, Dorset.

| POOLE | 1553 (Oct.) |
| WAREHAM | 1559 |

m. Agnes, da. of William Biddlecombe† of Poole, 2s. 3da. Bailiff, Poole 1549-50, mayor 1557-8.

If Scriven was related to Thomas Scriven, paymaster of the privy chamber and clerk to the cofferer of the royal household between 1552 and 1554 (his will included gifts to Thomas's children), he must have come from the Shropshire landed family. Whatever his origins, by 1599 he was one of the ten wealthiest Poole merchants, trading in sugar, oil, fish, wine, canvas and lead. When he sued out a general pardon on Elizabeth's accession he described himself as a merchant of Lyme. He presumably owed his return for Wareham to the Rogers family of Bryanston. Sir John Rogers* was knight of the shire for Dorset in 1559.

Scriven made his will on his deathbed, 8 Dec. 1560, and probate was granted six days later. He asked to be buried in Poole church. There were charitable legacies, totalling £45, to the corporation of Poole, and £5 towards the never-ending job of repairing the cobb at Lyme Regis. Each of his two sons, Robert and John, was to have £200,

and the three daughters £173. 6s. 8d. apiece. His wife Agnes was bequeathed £800. These legacies were to be reduced 'if it should happen any part or portion of my goods be lost by misfortune of the sea or otherwise by evil debtors, as God defend'. The two sons were named executors, but probate was granted, during the minority of all the children, to their five guardians, local men apparently, who were appointed overseers.

Hutchins, *Dorset,* i. 34; J. Sydenham, *Hist. Poole,* 235-6; E122/122/4, 7, 21; 123/2; *CPR,* 1558-60, p. 161; *APC,* iv. 57; PCC 60 Mellershe.

N.M.F.

SCRIVEN, Reginald (1551-1636), of Frodesley, Salop.

SHREWSBURY 1586, 1589, 1593, 1597, 1601

bap. 20 Sept. 1551 at Frodesley, 2nd s. of Thomas Scriven of Frodesley by Elizabeth, da. of John Leighton of Wattlesburgh. *educ.* Shrewsbury 1562; All Souls, Oxf., fellow 1569, BA 1572, MA 1577. *m.* Elizabeth, da. of William Swanne of Branxston, Northumb., wid. of Fulk Onslow of Herts.

Sec. to Thomas Bromley* as ld. chancellor from 1583.

Receiver and surveyor, duchy of Lancaster manor of Tutbury; receiver, duchy of Lancaster manor of Castle Donington.

Scriven's seat at Frodesley was near Shrewsbury, which he represented in five Parliaments. Though he was educated there and his sister Elizabeth married a Shrewsbury man, Robert Ireland*, Scriven himself was not a burgess of the town, and might never have been returned except for Shrewsbury's increasing difficulty in meeting parliamentary expenses, and perhaps a feeling of exhaustion in the corporation following a long duel between the mercers and the drapers. In 1588, the council asked their recorder, Thomas Owen*, whether they were obliged to return a resident burgess; he replied that they were not, and Scriven continued to represent the borough throughout the reign, being preferred, in 1597, to a nominee of the Earl of Essex.

Scriven's name appears on a list of candidates for knighthoods at James I's coronation, marked 'not knighted': it is unlikely that this was because his death intervened, for in 1636 the Condover register records the burial of 'Reinold Scriven, gent.'. If this is the Shrewsbury MP he would have been 85, a good age for the period.

Vis. Salop (Harl. Soc. xxviii), 271; (xxix), 435; *Trans. Salop Arch. Soc.* (ser. 4), xii. 193; SP46/71/64; PRO Index, duchy of Lancaster patents, p. 15; Shrewsbury mss 76.

J.J.C.

SCROPE, Edward (c.1540-80).

CUMBERLAND 1572*

b. c.1540, 4th s. of John Scrope, 8th Lord Scrope of Bolton by Catherine, da. of Henry Clifford, Earl of Cumberland. *educ.* L. Inn 1561. prob. *unm, d.s.p.*

This man has been identified as the 1572 Cumberland knight of the shire because he is the only known Edward Scrope whose election can readily be explained. It would have been obtained through the influence of his brother, the 9th Lord Scrope, who had been appointed warden of the west march in 1562. Scrope's birth date has been estimated from that of his brother and his own admission to Lincoln's Inn, and his death date from the fact that a by-election was held to replace one of the Cumberland MPs in 1580; the other Member is known to have lived until 1597. The latest known appearance of Scrope's name in the records is a reference to his obtaining a lease for Thomas Warcop* in 1574.

CP; Burke, *Extinct Peerage*, 481; *HMC Hatfield*, ii. 78.

B.D./P.W.H.

SCROPE, Henry (c.1570–1625), of Greenwich, Kent.

CARLISLE   1589, 1593, 1597, 1601

b. c.1570, 2nd s. of Henry, 9th Lord Scrope of Bolton, Yorks. by his 2nd w. Lady Margaret Howard da. of Henry, Earl of Surrey; bro. of Thomas*. *educ.* Emmanuel, Camb. 1585, MA 1588; G. Inn 1588. *unm.*

One of the parliamentary seats for Carlisle during the reign of Elizabeth was commonly at the disposal of the warden of the west march, so Henry Scrope, son of one warden and brother of another had an obvious claim. As one of its representatives in 1601 he might have served on committees to strengthen the north parts (3 Dec.) and to regulate the government of the northern counties (14 Dec.). Almost nothing is known about him. From Venice in 1593 he sent to Horatio Palavicino a letter for the Earl of Essex 'to be delivered with all haste'. The purpose of his visit to Italy is as obscure as the circumstances that prompted his brother to observe in 1597 that Henry 'by this course that he takes, I fear me will be a man of no long life'. He died on 5 Oct. 1625, his will being proved on 7 Oct. that year. All his bequests, mainly of money from rents at Easby and Ewcott Grange in Whitby, Yorks., were to servants and godchildren. In a codicil he gave £5 to the poor of East Greenwich. He was buried there on 6 Oct. in the chancel of the parish church, where he had asked to be covered with a stone carved with his arms, 'in all comely and decent manner'.

Genealogist, n.s. xv. 166; D'Ewes, 665, 685; *HMC Hatfield*, iv. 361; *Border Pprs*. ii. 288; PCC 104 Coke.

B.D.

SCROPE, Thomas (c.1567–1609), of Carlisle, Cumb.

CUMBERLAND   1584, 1589

b. c.1567, s. and h. of Henry, 9th Lord Scrope of Bolton by his 2nd w., and bro. of Henry*. *m.* c.1584, Philadelphia, da. of Henry, 1st Baron Hunsdon, 1s.

Kntd. 1585. *suc.* fa. as 10th Lord Scrope 13 June 1592. KG 1599.

Warden of west march and keeper of Carlisle, j.p. and custos rot. Cumb. from Mar. 1593; steward, Inglewood forest; eccles. commr. for province of York 1599; bailiff, Richmond and Middleham castles from Nov. 1603; steward, Richmond and Richmondshire.

Little is known of Scrope's early years. Probably he was with his father at Carlisle, where he was to spend most of his own active public life. First elected senior knight of the shire while still in his teens, and again in 1588, Scrope could have served on the subsidy committees of 24 Feb. 1585 and 11 Feb. 1589. When his father died at Carlisle, where he had been warden of the west march for almost 30 years, Scrope was clearly in line for the office, which he received some eight months later. In the interim he apparently shared the duties with Richard Lowther, who was to become one of his strongest opponents in border affairs. Thus Scrope saw little of his estates – 20 manors in Yorkshire and Hambledon, Buckinghamshire. He was a rich man: his rents amounted to almost £2,000, and jointly with his wife, he inherited property worth over £1,700 a year. The fees of the warden, in his father's time, were over £400 a year.

Apart from occasional brief visits south, for which the Queen gave her permission reluctantly, Scrope stayed at Carlisle from the spring of 1593 to the end of the reign. He began cautiously, as the Queen had advised, but he was soon urging strong action against the Scots. The borders, he complained in July 1593, would 'break' if the English were not allowed to make reprisals. Scrope also adopted an aggressive attitude towards his own borderers, quickly antagonizing such families as the Carletons and Lowthers. During his feud with Thomas Carleton* and Gerard Lowther*, Scrope found little support within the marches. In his correspondence he often lamented his isolation, intensified by his wife's absence at court and his son's at Oxford. The government gave him little encouragement, and the bishop of Durham described him as 'of deep wit, of noble and liberal inclination, but so secret and sole in his intentions as some hold him over jealous'. Scrope, in turn, complained to his father-in-law, Lord Hunsdon, that those who 'crossed' him were better countenanced than he at court. Next, Scrope antagonized James of Scotland, who protested at his impertinence and negligence, and as late as 1602 the Council reprimanded him for the 'undecent or violent terms' of his letters to James. But on the other hand he was criticized for referring too many problems to the Council: 'the fewer questions you ask … the better [the Queen] is pleased'. Refused permission to resign, Scrope was still in office on James's accession, and he attended the new King at Newcastle in April. James withdrew him from the march as part of his general policy of suppressing the wardenries, and in 1605 Scrope complained that all the wardens but he had been finally discharged and rewarded. He was lucky to obtain by way of compensation the bailiwick of Richmond and Middleham castles and the stewardship of Richmond and Richmondshire. He apparently retired to his estates and took no further part in government or politics, dying at Langar, Nottinghamshire, on 2 Sept. 1609.

CP; PRO Indexes 16776, 16779; C66/1421; Lansd. anon. jnl. f. 171; D'Ewes 431; HMC Hatfield, vii. 41; xi. 345; xii. 384–5; xv. 44, 46; xvi. 636; CSP Dom. Add. 1580–1625, pp. 332–3; C142/320/70; Border Pprs. i, ii, passim; J. T. Godfrey, Notes on the Churches of Notts. Hundred of Bingham, 304.

B.D.

SCUDAMORE, John (c.1542–1623), of Holme Lacy, Herefs.

HEREFORDSHIRE   1571, 1572, 1584, 1586, 1589, 1597

b. c.1542, 1st s. of William Scudamore (d. bef. 1560) by Ursula, da. of (Sir) John Pakington† of Hampton Lovett, Worcs. educ. I. Temple, Nov. 1559. m. (1) Eleanor (d.1569), da. of Sir James Croft* of Croft Castle, 3s. 2da.; (2) Mary, da. of Sir John Shelton of Shelton, Norf., 2s. suc. gd.-fa. 1571. Kntd. bef. 1593.

J.p. Herefs. by 1570, sheriff 1581–2, custos rot. and dep. lt. 1581–90; commr. musters, recusants by 1583; steward, Ashperton, Stretton and Yorkhill 1571, Kidwelly 1587, Hereford 1616–17; seneschal of Cradley, Ledbury, Ross and Bishop's Castle; gent. pens. by 1573–1603, standard bearer 1599; gent. usher to Queen Elizabeth; member, council in the marches of Wales 1602.[1]

Scudamore's wardship was sold, in 1561, to Sir James Croft. The yearly value of his property was then rated at £14 13s. 4d. and in 1563 he had licence to enter upon his lands. In 1571, however, he inherited the estates of his grandfather, a gentleman of wealth and consequence in the county, though 'no favourer of religion', and this, together with his marriage to Croft's daughter, gave him a position in Herefordshire surpassed only by that of Croft and the Coningsbys.[2]

In every Parliament between 1571 and 1589 he was returned as junior Member to Sir James Croft. He considered sitting in the 1593 Parliament, but decided to give place to his brother-in-law, Herbert Croft. In 1597, however, he was back. So far as is known he did not speak in the House. He was named to committees on Ledbury hospital (4 Mar. 1581), ecclesiastical matters (14 Nov. 1597) and bridging the river Wye (12 Dec. 1597). As a knight of the shire in 1584–5 he could have served on the subsidy committee (24 Feb.), and the following committees in 1597: enclosures (5 Nov.), the poor law (5, 22 Nov.), armour and weapons (8 Nov.), penal laws (8 Nov.), monopolies (10 Nov.), the subsidy (15 Nov.) and Newport bridge (29 Nov.).[3]

Scudamore's standpoint over religion is not clear. His name appears on a list drawn up in the interests of Mary Queen of Scots in 1574, but in 1576 he wrote to the Council, warning them that the next mayor of Hereford might be 'a hinderer of the godly proceeding of the present state of religion', and in the same year he furnished the names of recusants 'not to be reduced to conformity by any good persuasion'. In any event his loyalty was unquestioned. The Privy Council frequently referred cases to him: in 1589, he was to hear a controversy between an esquire of the Queen's stable and a London merchant, and the next year he was instructed to examine a case of disputed inheritance. His second marriage, to a cousin and lady of the bedchamber to Queen Elizabeth, led to a post at court, and hence to his 'continual absence out of the county', and in 1590 he was replaced as deputy lieutenant of Herefordshire. Scudamore was a patron of the mathematician Thomas Allen, and a benefactor of the Bodleian, whose founder he knew. His sister married a recusant; his eldest surviving son John became a Catholic priest, John Dowland in 1595 reporting to Cecil that he had encountered in Florence an English priest, 'son and heir to Sir John Scudamore of the court'. On 20 July 1619 Scudamore made his will, 'hoping assuredly through the only merits of Jesus Christ', to be received 'into the company of the heavenly angels and blessed saints'. The bulk of his property passed to his grandson, John Scudamore, with legacies to his other grandsons, Barnaby and James, to his brother Rowland, and to several friends. The poor were also remembered. Sir John Pakington and Walter Pye* were overseers and the will was proved 7 May 1623.[4]

[1] W. R. Williams, Parl. Hist. Herefs. 41; Vis. Herefs. ed. Weaver, 64; Early Hist. Scudamore Fam. ed. Collins; Duncomb, Herefs. ii. 174; PCC 44 Holney; Coll. of Arms, Talbot mss vol. H, p. 519; Flenley, Cal. Reg. Council, Marches of Wales, 69; APC, xii. 33; xiii. 293; P. H. Williams, Council in the Marches of Wales, 356–7; Somerville, Duchy, i. 637, 640. [2] CPR, 1558–60, p. 340; 1560–3, pp. 111, 596; PCC 44 Holney; Cam. Misc. ix(3), p. 12. [3] D'Ewes, 302, 552, 553, 555, 557, 561, 565, 572; Lansd. 43, anon. jnl. f. 171. [4] Cath. Rec. Soc. Misc. viii. 112; APC, ix. 197, 225; xviii. 163, 364, 398; xx. 38; CSP Dom. 1581–90, p. 615; Letters by Eminent Persons (ed. Walker), ii. 203; DNB (Scudamore, Sir John); Duncomb, ii. 172; Chamberlain Letters ed. McClure, i. 223; HMC Hatfield, v. 446; PCC 84 Swann.

J.J.C.

SEBRIGHT, William (d.1620), of Wolverley, Worcs. and of London.

DROITWICH   1572

2nd s. of Edward Sebright of Blakeshall, Wolverley by Joyce, da. of William Grosvenor of Bushbury, Staffs. educ. I. Temple 1565. m. (1) da. of one Goldston of London, s.p.; (2) c.1574, Elizabeth, da. of James Morley of London, wid. of Thomas Bourcher, s.p.

Town clerk, London in reversion 1568, succeeded 1574–1613.

It has not been ascertained how Sebright came by the reversion of the town clerkship of London only three years after entering his inn of court. Presumably it was through one of his family ties with the Grocers' Company. In 1572 he was returned to Parliament for Droitwich, a borough not far from his family seat. His only recorded parliamentary activity is his appointment to a committee on sheriffs, 24 Feb. 1576. His purchase of the lease of Blockley Park, Worcestershire from his brother-in-law, John Talbot, for £200 was complicated by his courtship of a wealthy widow. His own resources not being great enough to meet the expense, Sebright persuaded Talbot to provide a release of the debt to show to Mrs. Bourcher. It is by no means clear that Sebright paid the purchase money even after his finances were established by his fortunate marriage and his successsion to the town clerkship, which he held for nearly 40 years. From time to time he was named by the government to commissions concerning London affairs, and in 1596 he was in trouble over the subsidy assessment, but in general he makes only formal appearances in the records. By the end of the century he was investing in lands in his own county, as well as in London, and was, at his death, the owner of a comfortable estate. He had no offspring of his own, but many step-children, and was always much concerned with family affairs, the oversight of his brother's numerous family and the care of his sister's daughters, all of whom made good marriages, especially his brother's daughter, Sarah, who married Thomas Coventry†, the lord keeper, whom Sebright made overseer of his will. All the surviving children received monetary bequests and the residue went to Sebright's nephew Edward Sebright. About £2,245 was bequeathed to charity. He endowed a grammar school at Wolverley. Sebright resigned his office in 1613 and died 27 Oct. 1620, being buried in his parish church of St. Edmund the King, Lombard Street.

Vis. Worcs. (Harl. Soc. xxvii), 126; *Vis. London* (Harl. Soc. i), 121; *Remembrancia, City of London 1579–1664*, p. 31; *CJ*, i. 108; *CSP Dom.* 1595–7, p. 361; 1601–3, pp. 4, 314; *APC*, xxii. 270; xxv. 50; xxvii. 304; Lansd. 78, f. 126 seq.; PCC 97 Soame, 12 Dale, 58 Nevell; *VCH Worcs.* iii. 16 n. 43, 177, 222, 272, 515, 570, 572; iv. 21–3, 155, 473, 529, 530; Nash, *Worcs.* i. 78; Wards 7/64/46; C142/386/85; W. K. Jordan, *Charities of London*, 112, 238, 340.

S.M.T.

SECKFORD, Charles (1551–92), of Great Bealings, Suff.

ALDEBURGH	1572

b. 3 Jan. 1551,[1] s. of Francis Seckford. *educ.* Trinity Coll. Camb. 1562; G. Inn 1567. *m.* 6 Oct. 1575, Mary, da. of Thomas Steyning* by Frances, Countess of Surrey; at least 2s. *suc.* gd.-fa. to Seckford Manor 30 Sept. 1575, and uncle Thomas* to Woodbridge properties 1587.[2]

J.p. Suff. from c.1582.

Seckford was orphaned before he was seven. Little is known about his father, Francis, the eldest of the seven sons of the Thomas Seckford who died in 1575. He seems

to have married into a Berkshire or Staffordshire family and was dead by April 1557. In 1557 the two Thomas Seckfords, Charles' grandfather and his uncle, settled the family estates upon him and his heirs male. The elder Thomas Seckford was to have a life interest, and, in the event of his death before Charles came of age, the younger Thomas was to administer them.[3]

Seckford was presumably returned for Aldeburgh through the influence of his uncle, the master of requests, whose estates were nearby. It is also possible that it was his uncle who arranged his marriage – certainly he made a settlement upon Charles's heirs of all lands belonging to the priory manor of Woodbridge.[4]

Seckford died in 1592, and was buried at Woodbridge on 20 Feb. His will, made 10 Feb. and proved 11 Apr. of that year, provided for the sale of land in order to meet debts. To his wife he bequeathed all his 'apparel, chains, gold borders, goldsmiths' work and jewels'. He appointed his 'cousin' Anthony Wingfield*, his brother-in-law Edmund Poley*- and his 'very well beloved cousin Humphrey Wingfield, of Brantham' executors and guardians for his sons Thomas and Henry. His widow was buried beside him on 24 Aug. 1596.[5]

[1] Wards 7/23/57. [2] PCC 27 Harrington, 3 Adeane; C142/175/69; Norwich consist. ct. 75, 76 Puntyng; will of Margaret Sampson formerly w. of Thomas Seckford, dated 4 Jan. 1542; paper on the Seckfords, read by P. Chandler before the Soc. of Antiquaries 2 June 1923. [3] Loder, *Stats. Ordins. Govt. of Almshouses* (Woodbridge 1792), gives Francis's w. as 'Ellen, da. of Sir Thomas Newbury, of Staffs. quaere Ellen, da. of – Whittington'. Chandler (op. cit) interprets this as 'Ellen, da. of – Whittington, of Newbury, Staffs.'. Venn, *Al. Cant.* has 'Eleanor, da. of Sir Thomas Newbury'. [4] C142/175/69; Chandler, op. cit.; Ipswich and E. Suff. RO., T3/1/2; L. Dow, 'Two 16th cent. marriage settlements', *Procs. Suff. Inst. Archaeol.* xxvi(2). [5] PCC 27 Harrington; Wards 7/23/134; Woodbridge reg.

M.I.R.

SECKFORD, Thomas I (1515 or 1516–87), of Woodbridge and Ipswich, Suff. and Clerkenwell, London.

RIPON	1554 (Nov.)
ORFORD	1555, 1558
IPSWICH	1559,[1] 1563
SUFFOLK	1571
IPSWICH	1572

b. 1515 or 1516, 2nd s. of Thomas Seckford by Margaret, da. of Sir John Wingfield of Letheringham, Suff. by Anne, da. of Lord Audley. *educ.* Camb.; G. Inn 1540, called 1542. *m.* Elizabeth (*d.* 28 Nov. 1586), da. of Thomas Harlowe, wid. of William Billingsley and of Sir Martin Bowes*.[2]

Ancient, G. Inn, Lent reader 1556, treasurer 1565; dep. chief steward, duchy of Lancaster, northern parts 6 Sept. 1558–c.65; master of requests 9 Dec. 1558; steward of Marshalsea ct. by 1559–70; eccles. commr. 1559; j.p. Mdx. and Suff. from c.1559, Essex from c.1569; steward, bp. of Ely's liberty, Suff. 1563; surveyor of ct. of wards 1579.[3]

Seckford, who had been at Gray's Inn with Cecil (a relative of his mother's), voted against a government bill in the Parliament of 1555, and, like Cecil, had to wait until the accession of Elizabeth to obtain a major office. He received £60 for his first year as master of requests, and £50 for the next six months, but the job carried perquisites and huge opportunities for gain from those whose petitions were in his hands awaiting presentation to the Queen. He was bombarded by letters even from the most eminent, seeking to gain his favour for friends and dependants over grants of land, leases, offices and similar suits, but the Queen was often inaccessible. There is a story that she once reproved Seckford for wearing stinking boots. 'Madam', he answered, 'it is not my boots that stink, but the stale bills that I have kept so long'. Attendance on Elizabeth, wherever she might be, and the giving of legal advice, was an important aspect of his job, in respect of which he was granted an annuity of £100 for 1561. He had also formal duties in the court of requests.[4]

The amount of work undertaken by Seckford is impressive. In 1559, during the illness of (Sir) Nicholas Bacon[†], he was on the commission to perform the office of the Great Seal. He appeared regularly as an ecclesiastical commissioner and served on the commissions for felonies and robberies. He was employed in the examination of prisoners in the Tower and elsewhere, notably after the northern rebellion, and was occasionally appointed to hear cases of high treason, for example, that of William Parry*. In addition, he took part in innumerable inquiries, hearings, arbitrations, references and settlements out of court. His appointment in 1579 as surveyor of the court of wards was another source of profit. His work in this court again brought him close to Cecil, now Lord Burghley, and the two men, both keen cartographers, supported Saxton, who was then surveying and engraving his maps of England and Wales, beginning with Norfolk in 1574. The proofs were delivered to Burghley as they came off the plates. Upon the maps appeared the royal arms, the name of the engraver, and Seckford's arms with the motto 'pestis patriae pigricies', later changed to 'industria naturam ornat'. Seckford also assisted William Harrison in 'describing the rivers and streams of Britain', and Harrison dedicated to him his 'Description of Scotland' printed in Holinshed's Chronicles.[5]

In addition to his national appointments, Seckford was steward of the Suffolk liberty of St. Etheldreda, and in that capacity removed the sessions from Melton to Woodbridge, and built a new sessions hall for the liberty above an open hall which he had already built for the market belonging to his manor of Woodbridge Priory. His successors frequently paid for the repair of the building. Seckford had acquired this manor from the Crown in 1564, subject to the life interest of the widow of the former lessee, his grandfather Sir John Wingfield, and he seems to have completed the demolition of the old priory

buildings and built himself a new house – the present 'Abbey' building – nearby. His arms and the date, 1564, are over the south porch. He was granted the rectory of Barnes, Suffolk in 1576, and leased the hundred of Looes, which he subsequently attempted to prove belonged to the dean and chapter of Ely. He built himself the 'Great House' (sometimes called 'Seckford House') at Ipswich and two houses at Clerkenwell, in one of which, named Woodbridge Hall, he detained his cousin, Lady Margaret Clifford, as prisoner on behalf of the Queen. The other house, on the south side of St. Mary's Close, was his private London residence, close to that of his brother Sir Henry Seckford, a groom of the privy chamber.[6]

He was active in Suffolk affairs, was listed as a 'favourer of religion' in 1564, and served on a commission of piracy in 1577. He was returned for Ipswich through his own local standing, having first been made a freeman, and took a turn in the county seat in 1571. As might be expected, Seckford supported the official view in the Commons. Interrogating Wentworth in 1576 he remarked 'Mr. Wentworth will never acknowledge himself to make a fault, nor say that he is sorry for anything that he doth speak. You shall hear none of these things come out of his mouth'. Again, 24 Jan. 1581, Seckford was for submitting to the Queen over Wentworth's suggestion of a public fast. But in fact Seckford was not, so far as can be seen from the defective records of the early Parliaments of this period, a frequent speaker in debate, his only other interventions being as follows: asking for more time to consider a bill on fraudulent gifts and conveyances, 11 Apr. 1571; against changing the poor law, 20 May 1572 ('experience will find out all mischiefs, which then may be remedied'); against confirming the grant of the hospital at Ledbury, Herefordshire (21 May 1572); and in favour of including minstrels within the provisions of the vagabonds bill (30 May 1572).

His committees were as follows: none recorded in 1559; one in 1563, about servants, 24 Feb. In 1566: fines and recoveries (19 Oct.), the Queen's marriage and the succession (31 Oct.), the subsidy (27 Nov.), fraudulent gifts (9 Dec.) and informers (11 Dec.). In 1571: fraudulent gifts and conveyances (11 Apr.) and tellers and receivers (23 Apr.). In 1572: foreign artificers (24 May), corporations (30 May), fraudulent conveyances (3 June). In 1576: privileges and returns (9 Feb.), jeofails (15 Feb.), cloth (9 Mar.). In 1581: the preservation of game (18 Feb.) and errors in fines and recoveries (10 Mar.).[7]

After the death of his wife Seckford intended to retire to Woodbridge to plan the foundation of his almshouses for 13 poor men, but in the event he did not have time to do so. Shortly after his death the charity was given a royal licence, supported by his Clerkenwell estates. It has kept the family name prominent in Suffolk, and the governors of the Seckford trust still base their regulations upon the statutes drawn up by the founder. The governors also support from the Clerkenwell estate Woodbridge School, founded by the widow of the last of the Seckford line, the preparatory school that now occupies the 'Abbey' building, and the local free library. Seckford died at Clerkenwell on 19 Dec. 1587, and after temporary burial in St. James's in that parish, was, in accordance with his instructions, re-interred at Woodbridge in the chapel on the north-east side of the church. He had made his will on 1 Aug. 1587, commending his soul to Almighty God, his creator, and to the Holy Ghost, his 'fortifier and comforter'. Frequent reference is made to the almshouses, and his nephew and heir, Charles*, was charged not to hinder the project in any way. Substantial bequests of property in London and Suffolk were made to Seckford's brothers Henry and Humphrey. Other beneficiaries included a nephew, Henry, 'the son of his late brother Thomas*, and his 'loving friend and late son-in-law' William Bowes, to help him educate Aubrey, 'the son of my late brother John'. The poor of Clerkenwell, Woodbridge and Ipswich received £10 apiece. Apart from the houses at Clerkenwell, whose rents were to support the almshouses, another large house is mentioned for the use of the Seckford family whenever they should come to London, and other property in Clerkenwell, apparently occupied by the Countess of Derby. The will was proved 3 Jan. 1588.[8]

[1] He was also returned for Orford, E371/402(1). [2] Monument at Gt. Bealings Church; C142/175/69; paper on the Seckfords, read by P. Chandler before the Soc. of Antiquaries 2 June 1923; *London Mar Licences*, ed. Chester (Harl. Soc. xxv), 35; Wards 7/23/57; *Vis. Suff.* ed. Metcalfe, 64. [3] *APC*, vii. 17; *CPR*, 1558–60, pp. 19, 28, 118; Lansd. 104, f. 53; Exchequer deposition Mich. 44–5, Eliz. 39 at Woodbridge; J. Hurstfield, *Queen's Wards*, 224. [4] Guildford Mus., Loseley 1331/2; W. J. Allsebrook 'The Ct. of Requests in the reign of Eliz.' (London MA thesis 1936), pp. 13–14; Lansd. 9, f. 30; 24, f. 76; 38, ff. 11, 17; *CSP Dom*. Add. 1566–79, pp. 347–50, 540–1, 552, 668; 1580–1625, pp. 45, 63, 139; *APC*, vii. 226; *HMC Hatfield*, ii. 58, 69, 80, 84, 130, 133, 134, 147, 156, 312, 502; xiii. 63, 120, 138, 144, 153, 154, 176, 193, 202, 231, 268; C. Monro, *Acta Canc*. 378; *Select Cases in Ct. of Requests*, ed. Leadam (Selden Soc. xii), p. xix.; *CPR*, 1560–3, p. 69; Neale, *Essays in Eliz. Hist*. 99. [5] Prothero, *Statutes and Const. Docs*. 227, 233; Strype, *Grindal*, 310; *Annals* ii(1), p. 419; *APC*, vii. 7, 19, 84, 169, 216, 218, 409; viii. 67, 168; ix. 45–6, 84–5, 94; xi. 34, 115, 419–20; xiii. 89; *HMC Hatfield*, i. 544, 548, 551; ii. 76; *4th Rep. D.K.* App. ii. 263, 268; *CSP Dom*. Add. 1566–79, p. 337; 1580–1625, pp. 46, 180; H. E. Bell, *Ct. of Wards and Liveries*, 35; E. Lynham, *Br. Maps and Map Makers*, 17 seq.; *Thoresby Soc*. xxviii.(2), p. i; *DNB*. [6] V. B. Redstone, *Bygone Woodbridge*, 32; Copinger, *Suff. Manors*, passim; Wards 7/23/57; *Index Monasticus* (Dioc. of Norwich 1821 ed.), 99; Tanner, *Not. Mon*. (1787), under Suffolk, Woodbridge; paper on history of present 'Abbey' building read by A. Welford to Ipswich and Dist. Hist. Soc.; *HMC Hatfield*, xiii. 137; Lansd. 56, f. 104; Ipswich borough lib. inset on plan of borough of Ipswich supplied by J. Ogilby 1674; PCC 4 Rutland; W. Pinks, *Hist. Clerkenwell* (2nd ed.), 176. [7] *Cam. Misc*. ix(3), p. 60; Lansd. 166, f. 18; *CJ*, i. 66, 74, 78, 79, 84, 85, 97, 99, 100, 104, 106, 113, 119, 128, 133; *HMC Lords*, n.s. xi. 8; Neale, *Parlts*. i. 329, 381; D'Ewes, 124, 127, 131, 132, 160, 178, 214, 220, 221, 244, 248, 284; Trinity, Dublin, Thos. Cromwell's jnl. ff. 29, 34. [8] *Charity Commrs. Rep*. (1835–9), xxxii. 484; L. J. Redstone, 'Hist. of the Seckford Trust' (T/S at

office of Seckford Governors); Wards 7/23/57; *Reg. St. James Clerkenwell*; Woodbridge Reg. under 1587; J. Dallenger, *Rec. of Woodbridge Parish Church* (Woodbridge 1875); PCC 4 Rutland.

M.I.R.

SECKFORD, Thomas II (d. c.1579), of Ludlow, Salop.

BRIDGNORTH 1572*

7th s. of Thomas Seckford and bro. of Thomas I*. m., at least 1s.

Jt. (with Thomas Somerset‡) porter and keeper of prison, council in the marches of Wales 1563; steward of household, council in the marches of Wales 1569–74; steward of Marshalsea ct. from 1570.

Seckford was a servant of his relative, Sir Henry Sidney*, whom he accompanied to Ireland, and it was as 'receiver and servant to Sir Henry Sidney' that he presented the household accounts of the council in the marches. Seckford was thus well-placed to be returned to the 1572 Parliament for Bridgnorth. He was licensed to depart 24 May 1572. His death must have occurred before 13 Feb. 1579, when a by-election was held to replace him.

Vis. Suff. ed. Metcalfe; PCC 4 Rutland; paper on the Seckfords read by P. Chandler before the Soc. of Antiquaries, 2 June 1923; C142/175/69; *CPR*, 1560–3, p. 611; 1569–72, p. 14; *DNB* (which conflates the two brothers, and confuses them with their father); *HMC De L'Isle and Dudley*, i. 358–61, 381, 385–6; P. H. Williams, *Council in the Marches of Wales*, 128; *CJ*, i. 98.

J.J.C.

SEKERSTON, Ralph (d. c.1575), of Liverpool, Lancs.

LIVERPOOL 1563, 1571, 1572*

m. Alice, 1s. 2da. all *d.v.p.*

Bailiff, Liverpool 1540–1, alderman, mayor 1550–1, 1560–1, freeman 1562.

Sekerston was a Liverpool merchant, probably a draper, whose parliamentary career was of more than usual interest. Elected by his fellow townsmen to the 1559 Parliament, and still assumed to be their Member a week after the election, it was then discovered that the chancellor of the duchy of Lancaster had erased his name from the parliamentary return and inserted that of an outsider. By 1563 the corporation had learned a lesson. The duchy chancellor planned to return Sir Humphrey Ratcliffe* and William Wynter*, while the borough was already committed to return Richard Molyneux I*, son of the crown lessee of the lordship. Determined to have Sekerston for the other seat, the corporation informed the chancellor that they were reserving the second nomination for the 3rd Earl of Derby, whose wishes were as yet unknown. Sekerston now went to London, where he persuaded the Earl to adopt him as his nominee. The chancellor then tried to prevent Sekerston from taking his seat, who not only 'did [stick] to the matter still, and obtained his room' but 'where other town burgesses had and did retain speakers for them in the Parliament house, he retained none, but stood up after the manner there and was speaker himself, to the great grief of master chancellor'.

There is no record of the resourceful Sekerston again speaking in this Parliament, but he made use of his 'politic wit and wisdom' to present a petition to the Queen, requesting her to relieve the decaying town of Liverpool:

> Liverpool is your own town. Your Majesty hath a castle and two chantries ... the fee farms of the town, the ferry boat, two windmills, the custom of the duchy, the new custom of tonnage and poundage, which was never paid in Liverpool before your time; you have a good haven, and all the whole town and the commodity thereof is your Majesty's. For your own sake, suffer us not utterly to be cast away in your Grace's time, but relieve us like a mother.

The petition was successful and Liverpool relieved.

Having obtained the favour of the Earl of Derby, Sekerston was again returned to Parliament under his protection in 1571 and 1572. There is no record of his speaking in 1571, but he was appointed to committees on dress (14 May), navigation (25 May) and tillage (25 May). His only recorded committee in 1572 was about cloth (28 June), but he was an active speaker on social and economic questions. On 20 May 1572 he objected that Liverpool and other small boroughs were not provided for in the vagabonds bill. It was 'a great enormity' that bishops and other lords and gentlemen kept so few servants, 'which breedeth vagabonds'. He spoke 31 May on the bill that Liverpool should be integrated within the parochial system ('the chapel fairer than the church'); on 3 June on the hide trade he wished the gentlemen 'which sell the hides so dear ... might be hanged'. Export licences were 'very hurtful'. 'Under colour of every licence a great many more are carried than the licence will extend to'. As they were 'endorsed in many parts' it was 'hard to know' when the number permitted had been reached. Next day, and again 6 June, Sekerston spoke against special treatment for Hamburg merchants, and, 10 June, he pointed out that it was not always 'beneficial to the commonwealth' to sell commodities cheaply: 'though our leather go forth they have it not for nothing. Good money is returned for the same'. On 25 June he spoke up for Stafford 'the head town of the shire', and two days later, on sea marks and hoys, he made a typical little speech in defence of boroughs such as his own: 'Every man now seeketh all commodities to come to London, as though all the knights and burgesses of the rest of the realm come in vain'.

Before the next session of Parliament Sekerston had died. His will has not been found, and the circumstances of his death (though he was obviously elderly) are unknown. He died between November 1574 and 24 Oct. 1575.

J. A. Twemlow, *Liverpool Town Bks.* passim; Gregson, *Lancs. Fragments*, 161; Picton, *Memorials of Liverpool*, i. 52–3, 57; D'Ewes, 183, 189, 223, 224; *CJ*, i. 89, 93, 103; Trinity, Dublin, Thos. Cromwell's jnl. ff. 28, 47, 48, 49, 52, 61, 65, 66; *Moore Rental* (Chetham Soc. xii), 87.

N.M.S./P.W.H.

SELBY, George (c.1557–1625), of Newcastle-upon-Tyne, Northumb.

NEWCASTLE-UPON-TYNE   1601, 1604

b. c.1557, 1st s. of William Selby I* of Newcastle by Elizabeth, da. and h. of Gerard Fenwick of Newcastle. *m.* Margaret, da. of Sir John Selby of Branxton, Northumb. and Twizell, co. Dur., 5s. 6da. *suc.* fa. 1614. Kntd. 23 July 1603.

Water-bailiff, Newcastle by 1588, freeman by 1589; alderman, sheriff 1594, mayor 1600, 1606, 1611, 1622; gov. Newcastle merchants' co. 1600, 1606, 1611, 1622; sheriff, Northumb. 1607, co. Dur. 1617; j.p. Northumb. by 1620.

Like his father, Selby was one of the grand lessees of Newcastle who monopolized the municipal offices and exploited the controversial lease of the manors of Gateshead and Whickham. The faction on the corporation which was first to curb the power of the grand lessees (see CHAPMAN, Henry) complained that Selby's election as sheriff in 1594 was rigged. He became a member of the hostmen's company when it received official status in the charter of 1600, and at the same time he was confirmed as alderman and appointed sergeant-at-mace. Selby was also a considerable figure in the county palatine and in Northumberland. No mention of him has been found in the journals of his first Parliament, but he may have served on a committee about alehouses, 5 Nov.

He died in 1625, aged 68.

Surtees, *Hist. Dur.* ii. 274; R. Welford, *Men of Mark 'twixt Tyne and Tweed*, iii. 374–6; Req. 2/170/31; *Arch. Ael.* (ser. 4), xxiii. 136; Welford, *Hist. Newcastle and Gateshead*, iii. 120, 138, 142; D'Ewes, 626.

B.D.

SELBY, William I (c.1527–1613), of Newcastle-upon-Tyne, Northumb.

NEWCASTLE-UPON-TYNE   1572

b. c.1527, s. of George Selby of Newcastle by his w. Margaret Anderson. *m.* Elizabeth, da. and h. of Gerard Fenwick of Newcastle, 5s. inc. George* 8da.

Sheriff, Newcastle 1564, alderman, mayor 1573, 1589.

Selby's family had been established in Newcastle from the fourteenth century. Selby himself was a leading member of the hostmen's company, one of the original lessees of the coal-bearing manors of Gateshead and Whickham, granted to him and Henry Anderson as trustees for the town. Other hostmen such as Henry

Chapman* were admitted, and these few 'grand lessees' obtained a virtual monopoly of mining and shipping coal during the last two decades of the century. The other members of the corporation led by the customer, Henry Saunderson, challenged the grand lessees in a series of lawsuits, one specific charge against Selby being that he rigged his son's election as sheriff in 1594. In the end the grand lessees had their way.

During the last two sessions of the 1572 Parliament Selby was appointed to committees on the status of foreigners in England (24 Feb. 1576), border defences (25 Feb. 1581) and the repair of Dover harbour (4 Mar. 1581). Newcastle paid him wages at the rate of 8s. a day. He died a rich man in December 1613, and was buried in the chancel of St. Nicholas church. His funeral in January was attended by over 1,000 people, the bishop of Durham officiating.

Surtees, *Hist. Durham*, ii. 274; R. Welford, *Hist. Newcastle and Gateshead*, iii. 18–19, 78, 120, 199, 211; *Men of Mark 'twixt Tyne and Tweed*, iii. 376–7; *Arch. Ael.* (ser. 4), xxiii. 134; J. U. Nef, *British Coal Industry*, ii. 20, 39, 42, 120 seq.; *CSP Dom.* 1595–7, pp. 428–9; *APC*, xxviii. 317–19; *CJ*, i. 108, 129, 131; Newcastle chamberlains' accts.

B.D.

SELBY, William II (*d.* 1612), of Berwick-upon-Tweed, Northumb., later of Ightham Mote, Kent.

BERWICK-UPON-TWEED 1589, 1593, 1597, 1601, 1604

2nd s. of John Selby of Branxton, Northumb. and Twizell, co. Dur. by his w. Elizabeth. *unm.* Kntd. 10 June 1603.[1]

Served with Leicester in the Netherlands 1586; capt. and pensioner, Berwick for life 1587; gent. porter, Berwick from 1595 (jointly with his nephew William Selby III from Aug. 1599); comptroller of ordnance in north 1596; j.p. Northumb. from c.1591.[2]

Selby was a 'discreet and valiant' soldier, who served under, among others, Leicester and both earls of Essex in France, Ireland, Scotland and the Low Countries. By 1595 he had seen 40 years of service and was recognised as one of the principal captains of his day. On returning from his last campaign, he settled at Berwick, where he had quarters in the garrison and an allowance, as captain and pensioner, of 5s. a day. His reputation as a soldier, his seniority in the garrison, and his brother's influence (before his death in 1595) as gentleman porter, all ensured him considerable status. His employment as paymaster of the garrison, and the usual chaos of the accounts, including some claims for pay in arrear over seven years, prompted his observation that inadequate payments were worse than none at all. This situation must have been particularly vexatious in view of the reputation for efficiency he had acquired when paying off his troops in Ireland in the 70s. On his brother's death in November 1595, he was an obvious choice for the vacant office of gentleman porter, which was now by way of becoming a

family possession. He also had powerful support from another old soldier Sir William Reade*, his friend for the past 40 years, and Burghley, who offered to stand bond for him when the appointment was made. There was local opposition, however, from John Carey*, deputy governor under his father, Lord Hunsdon. Carey had already stood in the way of an earlier application by Selby for an office in the garrison, and he later became one of Selby's most vigorous opponents. Their frequent arguments over the running of the garrison, though usually concerned with trivial points, undermined its efficiency and encouraged the development of faction in the town. Selby, of course, blamed Carey's unreasonable hatred of him, but it was he who was admonished by the Privy Council.[3]

Selby earned respect – and additional duties – by his energetic work at Berwick and along the borders. Ralph Lord Eure*, an influential figure in the marches, recommended his appointment (apparently unsuccessfully) as a border commissioner, considering him one of the three most suitable candidates from all Cumberland and Northumberland. As comptroller of ordnance from 1596 he was required to inspect the ordnance at Carlisle, and consequently antagonised the resident officials, including Lord Scrope. In his own county he also quarrelled with the Grey family, touching off a decade long feud. Selby was clearly not a man of tact, but he made firm friends, including Sir William Bowes, who supported a claim of his for compensation for his custody of Buccleuch, one of the Scottish pledges handed over during the border negotiations in 1597. Selby received Buccleuch in October, intending to escort him to London on his way to Parliament. Buccleuch, however, remained at Berwick under his constant watch, thus Selby was prevented from attending. Perhaps he did not mind. He made no known contribution to the proceedings of the House, unless, as one of the Berwick burgesses, he sat on two committees in March 1589 (salted fish on the 11th and one concerning the town of Berwick on the 14th). He was probably returned as a man acceptable to both factions of the townsmen *versus* garrison power struggle. In contrast to his townsman colleague in 1593 Selby paid his own expenses.[4]

After four years at Berwick, Selby requested leave to attend to private business, and his nephew, William Selby, was appointed joint gentleman porter, sharing the fee of £20. Relieved of his duties, though not of his post, Selby spent most of the remaining years of Elizabeth's reign at his estate at Ightham, which he had bought from Charles Allen in 1591, and which he left to his nephew. He died on New Year's Day 1612.[5]

[1] Raine, *North Durham*, 315; Burke, *Landed Gentry*, 2284. [2] *Border Pprs.* i. 274; PRO Index 6800, f. 568v; *APC*, xxvi. 184–5. [3] *Border Pprs.* passim; Lansd. 78, f. 138; *HMC Hatfield*, vi. 570; *APC*, viii. 361, 362, 366; *CSP Ire.* 1574–85, pp. 50, 82; *Cal. Carew Pprs.* ii. 28, 29; *CSP For.* 1575–7, pp. 377, 380, 381–2; 1586–7, pp. 18, 243–4; *CSP Span.*

iii. 554. ⁴ *Border Pprs.* passim; *HMC Hatfield*, viii. 23–4; D'Ewes 445, 446; Berwick guild bk. 1585–95. ⁵ *APC*, xxx. 241; *Arch. Cant.* xlix. 39–40; *Chamberlain Letters* ed. McClure, 328.

B.D.

SELBY, William III (c.1556–1638), of Branxton, Northumb. and Twizell, co. Dur., later of Ightham Mote, Kent.

NORTHUMBERLAND   1597,¹ 1601

b. c.1556, 1st s. of Sir John Selby, gentleman porter of Berwick, of Branxton and Twizell by his w. Margaret. *educ.* Peterhouse, Camb. 1573; G. Inn 1576. *m.* Dorothy, da. and h. of Charles Bonham of Malling, Kent, *s.p. suc.* fa. 1595, and uncle William Selby II* to Ightham 1612. Kntd. 6 Apr. 1603.²

Jt. (with his uncle) gent. porter, Berwick from 1599; j.p.q. Northumb. from c.1601; sheriff, Northumb. 1604, 1606; border commr. from 1605; capt. Tynemouth castle from 1606; j.p. Kent by 1632.³

Although the Selbys had estates in Northumberland and co. Durham, they are usually associated with Berwick, where they held offices over several generations. Selby's grandfather, father and uncle were gentlemen porters of the town, and others of the family held captaincies in the garrison during the same period. Selby himself was attached to the garrison in 1586, when he led some of his soldiers in an attack on members of two prominent rival families, the Collingwoods and Claverings. The affray led to the death of one of the Claverings, but Selby, apparently through Walsingham's influence, escaped punishment.⁴

In return for Walsingham's help on that occasion, and other favours, the Selbys pledged themselves to his service. The younger Selby was employed by Walsingham, in connexion with Scottish affairs, in 1582, and a few years later he again offered his services to the Secretary, with whom he was in contact throughout the 1580s through his correspondence with Archibald Douglas, the Scottish ambassador in England, and an intimate of Walsingham. Even though Selby had been knighted in the Arne, his friendship with Douglas, an ex-minister as well as a leading figure in the Scottish presbyterian party, and his own father's puritan views, suggest that he was the 'master Selby' of Berwick who was urged to organize puritan ministers and gentry in that area to subscribe to the millenary petition in 1603.⁵

Selby did not take up his share of duties as gentleman porter at Berwick until the spring of 1600, when the warden, Lord Willoughby, was instructed to admit Selby to his office. Almost immediately the two men were at odds, with Selby accusing the warden of attempting, with Sir William Bowes*, to establish absolute rule in Berwick. The struggle was obviously uneven, and in November 1600 Selby asked Cecil to release him from his duties.

Although the reply was unfavourable, Selby ceased to be active at Berwick and apparently absented himself to join his uncle in Kent.⁶

Selby's absence from Berwick, which drew adverse comment from his superiors, was partly explained by his attendance at Parliament, where, on 9 Dec. 1601, he spoke on a bill concerned with the statute of tillage. The statute had placed severe restrictions on enclosures in order to ease economic distress and check depopulation, and the 1601 Parliament saw an attempt by the 'great sheep-masters' to secure its repeal. Selby, in a long but briefly reported speech, submitted that Northumberland should be exempt from the statute,

> because it was so nigh the Scots; and the country was so infested with the plague, that, not only whole families, but whole villages had been swept away with that calamity.

Selby is not mentioned by name as sitting on committees in either of his Parliaments but as a knight of the shire for Northumberland he may have served on committees for enclosures (5 Nov. 1597), the poor law (5, 22 Nov.), armour and weapons (8 Nov.), penal laws (8 Nov.), monopolies (10 Nov.), the subsidy (15 Nov.), the order of business (3 Nov. 1601), monopolies (23 Nov.), strengthening the northern frontier (3 Dec.) and reforming the local government of the northern counties (14 Dec.).⁷

Selby returned to Berwick in time to welcome King James and receive one of the first knighthoods of the new reign,⁸ then retired to his estates. He was pricked sheriff in 1604 but the King gave him special permission to remain in the south. By June 1604, when he was granted an annuity of £184 13s. 4d., he had also retired from his office as gentleman porter. Less than a year later, however, he was once more back in the north, where his knowledge and experience were highly valued. In February 1605 he was appointed a border commissioner, an office which demanded much of his time and attention during the next few years. He was again sheriff in 1606, and, in that capacity, was given custody of Tynemouth castle, which remained in his charge for at least seven years, though he was never in permanent residence. During that time, he received an annual allowance of £231 5s., while, as a border commissioner, he was made a further grant, in 1608, of 100 marks a year.⁹

It is not certain when Selby finally returned to Kent, but he probably did so soon after he inherited Ightham Mote from his uncle in 1612. By the 1620s he was well established in Kent, and despite advancing age and ill health, played a small part in the administration of his new county.¹⁰

Selby died in his eighties at Ightham 14 Feb. 1638 and was buried with his uncle in the chancel of Ightham church. By the time of his death he had become a wealthy man, with his estates in the north alone valued, in 1630, at over £2,000 a year. In his will he made gifts of money, amounting to over £10,000, including £4,000 to his wife, Dorothy. About another £4,000, due from the King in respect of his pension, he bequeathed to Berwick corporation for the construction of a church and the purchase of lands to maintain a schoolmaster and an usher for a grammar school. Having no children, Selby had entailed his northern estates first to his wife, then to his nephew, William Selby, who succeeded Lady Dorothy in 1641. The southern estate passed to a cousin, George Selby of Billingsgate.[11]

[1] Folger V. b. 298. [2] Raine, *North Durham*, 315; *Arch. Cant.* xxvii. 30; C142/245/62. [3] *CSP Dom.* 1598–1601, p. 306; 1631–3, pp. 477–8; *HMC 10th Rep. IV*, 245; *HMC Hatfield*, xviii. 366–7. [4] Raine, 315; *CSP Dom.* Add. 1580–1625, pp. 193–6; *HMC Hatfield*, xiii. 353–7; *Hist. Northumb.* (Northumb. Co. Hist. Comm.), xiv. 516; *Border Pprs.* i. 327. [5] *Border Pprs.* i. 78, 91, 130, 131, 221, 327; *HMC Hatfield*, iii. 100, 105, 176, 416–17, 444; iv. 553; H. Scott, *Fasti Ecclesiae Scoticanae*, iii. 455–6; D. Calderwood, *Hist. Kirk of Scot.* 234–5. [6] C142/245/62; 250/38; *CSP Dom.* 1598–1601, p. 306; *APC*, xxx. 241; *Border Pprs.* ii. 655–6. [7] *Border Pprs.* ii. 809; Townshend, *Hist. Colls.* p. 300; D'Ewes, 552, 553, 555, 557, 561, 624, 649, 657, 665, 685; Lipson, *Econ. Hist. Eng.* ii. 402. [8] That William jun., rather than his uncle, received the knighthood in April, is verified by a letter dated 14 Apr. which refers to Sir William Selby and Captain Selby, *HMC Hatfield*, xv. 46. [9] *Egerton Pprs.* (Cam. Soc. xii), 389–90; *HMC 10th Rep. IV*, 245; *HMC Hatfield*, xvii. 132; xviii. 366–7; *Hist. Northumb.* viii. 176–7; *CSP Dom.* 1603–10, p. 440. [10] *Arch. Cant.* xxvii. 30; *APC*, 1626, pp. 221, 224; *CSP Dom.* 1631–3, pp. 477–8. [11] *Misc. Gen. et Her.* i. 20–3; *Hist. Northumb.* xi. 112–14.

B.D.

SELLENGER, *see* ST. LEGER

SEMYS, Thomas (*d.* 1603), of Gloucester.

GLOUCESTER   1572

?s. of John Semys of Gloucester (*d.* 1540). *m.* 1da.
    Sheriff, Gloucester 1558–9, 1563–4, alderman, mayor 1565, 1578, 1599.

Semys, a clothier, leased a considerable portion of the site of the Greyfriars in Gloucester. He was active in civic affairs, and is frequently mentioned in the city's records. In 1565 he was appointed to survey and repair the 'walls, ditches, banks and weirs ... by the coast of the sea', a subject reflected in his membership of a Commons committee about the 'inning' of salt marshes (6 Mar. 1576). Another of Semys's committees concerned cloth (4 Feb. 1581). That April he was paid £17 6s. 0d. for his service in Parliament.

Semys died in 1603, leaving his property to his daughter Margaret, to her heirs, and to the mayor and burgesses of Gloucester, to be employed in 'charitable uses'.

W. R. Williams, *Parl. Hist. Glos.* 191; *Gloucester Recs.* 66–7, 445, 448, 449–50, ed. Stevenson; *CJ*, i. 111, 122; *HMC 12th Rep. IX*, 454; Gloucester Guild Hall ms 1450, H 73, 154; *Gloucester Wills*, ed. Phillimore and Duncan.

J.J.C.

SERLE, Henry (*d.* 1567), of Cambridge.

CAMBRIDGE   1563

m. (1) bef. 1545, Alice, da. and h. of John Bowyer (who was bro. of Sir William Bowyer[†], ld. mayor of London); (2) by 1561, Joan, wid. of John Lyne, alderman of Cambridge, 5s., at least 1da.[1]
    Mayor, Cambridge 1562–3.[1]

As a member of Cambridge corporation, from whom he rented property in Butter Row and elsewhere, Serle carried on a violent dispute with the University in conjunction with Roger Slegge*, his son-in-law and colleague in the 1563 Parliament. The only reference found to him there is leave of absence granted 12 Mar. 1563. Cited before the vice-chancellor's court, the two were accused of various enormities, such as releasing a prisoner committed by the vice-chancellor to the Tolbooth, resisting arrest ('If we had had weapons, the proctor should never have gone a live man out of that ground'), and so on. Charges and counter-charges finally came before the Privy Council who, on 16 Sept. 1564, put Serle and Slegge in the Fleet. But by 2 Nov. Serle was back in the vice-chancellor's court at Cambridge to answer charges of gambling, drunkenness, adultery (with his maidservant) and 'whether, as mayor ... he did cut out one portion of the records of the town, and insert another, to defraud'. Serle only avoided excommunication by paying the legal costs and swearing to obey the church. As it happened, the bishops' letters to the Privy Council earlier that year had described him as 'conformable' in religion. Next, Serle, 'of a perverse, froward and wilful stomach and mind' sued out writs of error against the vice-chancellor's decisions in private cases affecting him, calling them 'directly contrary to law and equity and therefore reversible in the common law courts'. This time he was stymied by Sir William Cecil, who, as chancellor of the University, persuaded the lord keeper to intervene to uphold his vice-chancellor. But by 1566 the corporation had had enough of Serle and Slegge and on 24 Sept. 1566, just before the new session of Parliament, a letter went off to Cecil asking that they should be replaced as MPs 'for sundry ... causes which do much consume our quiet governing'. Nothing happened, but after the Parliament, on 6 June 1567, Serle was disfranchised as a freeman. He drew up his will on 24 July 1567, asking that at his funeral there should be 'no pride or pomp of this world', and died before 18 Aug. following, when the will was proved.[2]

[1] *LP Hen. VIII*, xx(1), p. 326; *CPR*, 1547–8, p. 204; C3/154/132; 162/36; PCC 24 Stonard, 11 Pynnyng; *Vis. Cambs.* (Harl. Soc. xli), 46; Downing Coll. Camb. Bowtell mss; C142/70/40. [2] *CJ*, i. 69; J. M. Gray, *Notes on Cambridge Mayors*, 28; SP12/34, f. 175; 35, f. 16 seq.; *APC*, vii. 149; *CSP Dom.* Add. 1547–65, pp. 553–4; *Cam. Misc.* ix(3), p. 25; C3/48/53; Lansd. 50, f. 93; SP12/40/65; C193/32, lists 3–7; Cambridge Guildhall, day bk. 1564–77, p. 69; PCC 24 Stonard.

N.M.F.

SERVINGTON, *see* **CERVINGTON**

SEXTON, Edmund (*d.* c.1589), of Westminster and Uxbridge, Mdx.

ST. MAWES	1563

Prob. 3rd s. of Thomas Sexton of Lavenham, Suff. (*d.* c.1529), by Elizabeth, da. and h. of Thomas Mountney, of Mountnessing, Essex. *m.*, ?1da.[1]

Described in a sixteenth century pedigree as 'dwelling in Westminster near unto the Parliament house',[2] Sexton presumably held at some time a minor office, for his will refers to a debt to the Queen which he was responsible for collecting. The will also makes apparent that he was on fairly intimate terms with Sir Walter Mildmay*, who, early in Elizabeth's reign, had some influence in Cornwall, and may have secured his nomination for St. Mawes. It may have been Mildmay who obtained for him, in 1567, a lease of tin tolls from the manor of Treveryn.[3]

Sexton owned land at Ringshall, Suffolk, valued at £3 in the 1566–8 subsidy. Little is known of his early career; in fact almost all the information found about him concerns the period some twenty years after his return for St. Mawes, at which time he was a recusant. He was sent to the Marshalsea in March 1582, and remained there until July 1586, when his transfer to Wisbech was recommended. He was described as a 'gentleman, and of wealth ... brought before the bishop of London, by him examined and so committed, and since his imprisonment unexamined'.[4]

He made his will in October 1586. The preamble is Catholic:

I do most humbly beseech our blessed Lady, the mother of God, that it may please her to be intercessor to her son Jesus Christ for me. And also all the holy company of saints in heaven I beseech to pray for me, that it may please Almighty God the Father to forgive and forget my sins committed.

His 'daughter' Mary Hayers was to have 'all her mother's apparel', but whether this refers to Sexton's own daughter or to a step-daughter is not clear. The printed *Visitation* states that Sexton died *s.p.* There were legacies to the children of his brother Thomas, 'because they be clean left without all manner of furniture', and to a young cousin named Calwell, 'now prisoner in Bridewell in London'. The will mentions Sexton's lease in the palace of Westminster. John Emers and his wife, probably Sexton's servants, were to keep their lodgings at the old rent, and to have their debts cancelled, since they had 'been at great charges' ever since Sexton went to prison. The sole executor, his step-brother Martin Sidley, was asked to try to collect a debt owed to the Queen by a certain Mr. Bayley, now dead. Sexton hoped 'one way or another to have sufficient' for the expenses involved, and trusted that Sir Walter Mildmay would prove helpful. His conscience was troubling him about a debt of 40*s.* to 'Foskewe: he limpeth. I never saw the man since Queen Mary's time'. Sexton died before 28 Apr. 1589, when the will was proved.[5]

[1] *Vis. Norf.* (Harl. Soc. xxxii), 273–4; PCC 15 Jankyn, 40 Leicester. [2] Add. 19148, f. 290v. In the absence of a precise date the possibility of this being another Edmund Sexton cannot be excluded. [3] PCC 40 Leicester; *CPR*, 1566–9, p. 140. [4] *Suff. Green Bks.* xii. 83; *Cath. Rec. Soc.* ii. 233, 235, 240, 242, 244, 251, 254. [5] PCC 40 Leicester.

N.M.F.

SEYMOUR, Edward I (c.1563–1613), of Berry Pomeroy, Devon.

DEVON	1593, 1601, 1604

b. c.1563, 1st s. of Edward Seymour (s. of Protector Somerset) of Berry Pomeroy by Jane, da. of John Walshe*, justice of the common pleas, of Cathanger, Som. *m.* Elizabeth, da. of Sir Arthur Champernown*, of Dartington, 5s. inc. Edward Seymour II* 4da. *suc.* fa. 1593. *cr.* Bt. 1611.

J.p. Devon from c.1583, rem. 1586, rest. 1590, dep. v.-adm. 1586, sheriff 1595–6, dep. lt. 1596.

Seymour was an obvious choice to take his turn as knight of the shire for Devon, and, as such, he may have taken part in the committees on the subsidy (26 Feb. 1593), a legal matter (9 Mar.), kerseys (23 Mar. and 2 Apr.), the order of business (3 Nov. 1601), procedure (11 Nov.), the Severn harbour (21 Nov.) and monopolies (23 Nov.). He had a particular reason for being in the 1601 Parliament as a bill dealing with the Seymour estates that had descended from the Duke of Somerset came into the Commons then; it did not reach the committee stage in 1601, but it did in 1604.

Seymour spent a good deal on his home at Berry Pomeroy. His father had purchased Totnes castle in 1591 but there is no indication that he could exercise parliamentary patronage in the borough during Elizabeth's reign. Seymour sometimes appeared at court in the 1590s and was on good terms with Sir Robert Cecil and with the lord lieutenant of Devon, the Earl of Bath. Seymour died 11 Apr. 1613.

Roberts thesis; D'Ewes, 474, 496, 507, 513, 624, 635, 647, 649, 657; *CJ*, i. 237; PCC admon. act bk. 1613, f. 118.

P.W.H.

SEYMOUR, Edward II (c.1580–1659), of Berry Pomeroy, Devon.

PENRYN	1601
NEWPORT IUXTA LAUNCESTON	1604
LYME REGIS	1614
DEVON	1621
CALLINGTON	1624
TOTNES	1625

b. c.1580, 1st s. of Edward Seymour I*. *educ.* M. Temple 1598. *m.* 15 Dec. 1600, Dorothy (*d.*1643), da. of (Sir) Henry Killigrew* by his 1st w. Catherine, da. of Sir Anthony Cooke* of Gidea Hall, Essex, 6s. 6da. Kntd. 1603; *suc.* fa. as 2nd Bt. 1613.

Ambassador to Denmark 1603; gov. Dartmouth 1613; j.p. Devon, dep. lt. 1617, v.-adm. 1617.

Seymour was returned through the influence of his father-in-law, leaving no trace upon the records of his first Parliament. Early in 1601 he was brought to the notice of Sir Robert Cecil*. He became an Admiralty official and privateer and was a Royalist in the civil war, when he was captured and Berry Pomeroy destroyed. He died on 5 Oct. 1659.

GEC Baronetage, i. 34; T. Westcote, *View of Devonshire* (1845), p. 480; *Chamberlain Letters* ed. McClure, i. 113; E. B. Powley, *House of de la Pomerai*, 114–15; H. St. Maur, *Annals of the Seymours*, 273–4; *HMC Hatfield*, xi. 175; xv. 9.

W.J.J.

SEYMOUR, John (1560–1618), of Merwell, Hants.

GREAT BEDWYN   1589

b. 25 Jan. 1560, 1st s. of Sir Henry Seymour† of Merwell by Barbara, da. of Morgan Wolfe. *m.* c.1581, Susan, da. of Chideock Paulet† of Wade, 3s. *suc.* fa. 1579. Kntd. 1591.

J.p. Hants from 1587, q. by 1593, sheriff 1592–3.[1]

In his will Sir Henry Seymour appointed his nephews Edward, Earl of Hertford, and Henry Ughtred* executors, giving them permission to administer the lands until Seymour's majority. Hertford and Ughtred secured his wardship, the court of wards survey giving the yearly income of the estates as £245 14s. 2½d. or £208 1s. 8d. excluding the income from the manor of Hurn, in Hampshire, which was to be sold under the terms of Sir Henry's will to pay his debts and legacies. In Hampshire, besides the residence at Merwell, Sir Henry possessed the manor and advowson of Twyford, and a lease of the parsonage there, as well as the manor of Temple Gothington. He owned one tenement in Southampton itself, a number of houses in Winchester, and, in the neighbouring county of Buckingham, the manor of West Wycombe. At his death Seymour himself was still in possession of most of this property. The manor of West Wycombe had been sold in 1598, but Hurn – apparently not sold as Sir Henry had requested – was still in his possession.[2]

Seymour gained his seat at Great Bedwyn through the influence of the Earl of Hertford. No record of any parliamentary activity has been found.

Seymour was added to the commission of the peace for Hampshire in 1587 on the recommendation of the 4th Earl of Sussex, who had been asked by Burghley and the lord chancellor to present the names of gentlemen who

would strengthen the commission, 'especially at this time'. In 1586 he was involved with a number of other gentlemen – including Henry Ughtred and William Paulet – in settling the counties of Connello and Kerry, a total of 8,000 acres, in Munster. For that purpose they were licensed to take money, gold, or silver out of the realm. In 1589 he was involved in a dispute with Dr. Bennett, master of the hospital of St. Cross, Winchester, over the possession of the manor of Twyford, which Seymour attempted to gain by force. In 1597 the Privy Council became concerned with a dispute between him and Edward Darcy*, groom of the privy chamber, over the possession of Waltham Park, Seymour again having attempted forcible entry. For this he was called before the Council, Darcy's rights were confirmed, and Seymour was ordered to pay costs. Another reprehensible affair was his attempt in 1601 to deprive the copyholders of Twyford and Merwell of their rights of common grazing and wood cutting.[3]

Seymour died at Merwell on 10 Aug. 1618, and was buried at Winchester cathedral. His wife survived him; his heir was his eldest son Edward, then 27 years old.[4]

[1] C142/183/64, 373/49; Hoare, *Wilts.* Mere 117; SP12/205/59; E163/14/8; Hatfield ms 178. [2] PCC 20 Langley; Wards 9/140, ff. 635–6; *VCH Bucks.* iii. 137; C142/373/49. [3] *VCH Wilts.* v. 115; Hoare, *Wilts.* Mere 117; SP12/205/59; *CSP Ire.* 1586–88, p. 51; *APC*, xiv. 191; xvii. 265–6; xxvi. 533, 551–2, 555–6; xxvii. 318. [4] C2.Eliz./T11/59; C142/373/49.

A.M.M.

SEYNTLOWE, *see* ST. LOE

SHARESTON, William (*d.*1621), of Bath, Som.

BATH   1584, 1586, 1593, 1597, 1601, 1604

m., 1s. 3da.

Chamberlain, Bath 1579, 1580, mayor 1581–2, 1583–4, 1585–6, 1590–1, 1593–4, 1599–?1600, 1607–8.

Shareston's ties with the other members of the Bath chamber were close. Alice Walley, the wife of the younger John Walley, chamberlain of Bath, was probably his sister, since William and John Shareston were both referred to as brothers in Walley's will. John Sachfield, also sometime chamberlain of Bath, was associated with Shareston in several business dealings, while both of them were appointed overseers of the wills of John Walley* senior and William Price*, members of the same group. The names of his parents and wife have eluded discovery, and his children are known only through his will.[1]

In 1584 a commission was issued to inquire into concealed church lands, and 56 tenements were discovered in Bath belonging to the Crown. In March 1585, at the request of Sir James Croft*, these were granted to Shareston and Sachfield. Some of this property was apparently not monastic land at all, but belonged to the parish churches of St. Mary de Stalles and St. Michael extra muros. When an action was brought against Shareston and Sachfield by George Pearman* on behalf of the two parishes, the defendants' costs were met by the city chamber. A conveyance to transfer the property to the city was prepared in 1598, and again in 1601, but was not in fact completed until 1618. Until this date Shareston and Sachfield enjoyed the profits.[2]

Shareston acted as the city's agent on several occasions. Payments to him are recorded for going to London and for seeing Lord Pembroke on the city's business, and in 1590 he was defended at the city's expense in another Chancery suit. In 1590 he was named as the first mayor in Bath's new charter, and reputedly was responsible for extending the city's boundaries as defined in this charter. Previously the limits had been the city walls, but Shareston contrived to have included within the city certain land at Barton, of which he was the tenant. The new jurisdiction was not at once exercised, probably to allow local memory to fade before the legality of the city's claim was asserted. It was not until 1619 that the city, represented by Shareston, brought a Chancery action against William Snigge, a farmer of Barton, to ascertain the rights of the citizens. The case was referred to the arbitration of Nicholas Hyde†, recorder of Bath, who, in June 1619, found that the citizens ought to have rights of common in Barton, but that this would be to the great prejudice of the farmer of Barton. It was therefore decided to allot some of the land to the citizens, and to grant the rest to William Snigge and his heirs.[3]

Another indication of Shareston's eminence in Bath was his parliamentary career. He sat more often than any other alderman of Bath during this period, six times in all, taking the junior seat in 1584 and 1586 and the senior thereafter. In 1593 he was paid £5 for his wages in Parliament, in 1598 he and the other burgess, Heath, received £20 for 14 weeks' service and Shareston received £6 6s. in 1602. As MP for a Somerset borough he could have attended the committee on rebuilding Langport Eastover (10 Nov. 1597), and as one of the Bath MPs two committees on cloth (15, 23 Mar. 1593) and the committee of the bill about Bristol, 28 Nov. 1597. He died in 1621, making bequests to several grandchildren, including Arthur Shareston, a future mayor of Bath, and William Prynne the pamphleteer. Shareston did not share Prynne's aversion to bishops, and left £100 for the repair of Bath abbey, inspired perhaps by the example of Bishop Montagu who had spent £1,000 on the fabric.[4]

[1] BL Cartae Antiquae 83 H 4; PCC 71 Nevell; PCC 85 Harte. [2] *Bath Chamberlains' Accts.* (Som. Rec. Soc. xxxviii), 205; *Bath Recs.* p. xiv–xv, 39–40. [3] *Chamberlains' Accts.* 73, 92, 112, 118; Warner, *Hist. Bath,* 186–92. [4] *D'Ewes,* 501, 507, 564; *Bath Recs.* p. xxx; *Chamberlains' Accts.* 130–1, 164, 187, 207; Collinson, *Som.* i. 163; *DNB* (Montagu, James); PCC 91 Dale; *Vis. Som.* (Harl. Soc. xi), 20.

I.C.

SHARINGTON, Henry (c.1518–81), of Lacock, Wilts.

LUDGERSHALL 1559

b. c.1518, 3rd s. of Thomas Sharington of Sharrington, Norf. by Katherine (or Elizabeth), da. of William Pyrton of Little Bentley, Essex. Bro. and h. of Sir William Sharington†, of Lacock. *m.* Ann (*d.*1607), da. of Robert Paget, alderman of London, 1s. *d.v.p.* 3da. *suc.* bro. 1553. Kntd. 1574.[1]

Cdr. of troops in France 1557; j.p. Wilts. 1561, q. by 1574, sheriff 1567–8; commr. musters by 1573.[2]

Sharington's brother, a man of his time, was both a speculator in monastic lands and a debaser of the coinage. He used the profits of one sale to finance another, and his admitted depredations as a mint official caused him to be condemned to death. He survived, however, and lived to buy back the property forfeited by his attainder. Thus the manors of Lacock, Charlton, Liddington, Walcot, Woodrow and Winterbourne, with other valuable Wiltshire lands, passed to Henry Sharington, any doubts being settled by an Exchequer judgment about 1560. It was because of his local standing that Sharington was returned for Ludgershall to Elizabeth's first Parliament, leaving no trace upon the vestigial journals of 1559. The local records, however, contain many references to his buying and selling property. In particular, with Gabriel Pleydell* he entered into numerous deals to the disadvantage of the simple-minded Andrew Baynton*, the two finally contriving to have themselves appointed executors of Baynton's will, though in the event they were forced to compromise so that some of the 'overplus' after paying legacies went, not to them, as they intended, but to Baynton's brother Edward.[3]

Classified in 1564 as a 'furtherer earnest' of sound religion, Sharington was a friend of Bishop Jewell, who in 1571 preached his last sermon at Lacock. Sharington was one of the commissioners appointed in 1574 to inquire at Chippenham into property bequeathed for the maintenance of 'obits, lights and anniversaries', and to find out what had happened to it since Edward VI's reign. It was in the September of that year that Queen Elizabeth stopped at Lacock on her progress between Bristol and Wilton, knighting Sharington on the occasion.[4]

Despite his obvious eminence in the county, Sharington's conduct was on several occasions too much for the Privy Council. In 1567 the inhabitants of Chippenham, where he was lord of the hundred, complained that he had provoked a brawl by ordering his servants to pull down 'shambles and shops' in the town. Later in the same year, when he was sheriff of Wiltshire, he was accused of arresting the 'balie' and constable of Chippenham and refusing bail; he had also taken away the key of 'the church house of Chippenham called the guildhall', claiming the building as his private property. The matter was apparently settled in Sharington's favour, since in 1572 the town was paying him rent for the guildhall.[5]

He also quarrelled with the local authorities of Devizes, whose mayor, in 1574, complained to the Privy Council that Sharington had said 'that the mayor ... hath no more authority to punish than his horse'. Details of the charges are missing, but Sharington was ordered to come to London, having told his accusers the time and place of his summons, so that they could also be present. The Council ordered Sir John Thynne* and others to 'hear and end the matter'. Next, Sharington became involved in the dispute between Peter Blackborowe and the Wiltshire clothiers. In pursuit of their policy to force the cloth industry back into the corporate towns, the Privy Council in 1577 ordered Sharington and others to deal with Blackborowe's grievances. Several Council letters, written between September of that year and the following June, and growing sharper in tone, suggest that the Wiltshire gentry, many of them sheep farmers, had no desire to be embroiled with a wealthy vested interest in the county, where the cloth factories by 1578 were largely outside the towns.[6]

Sharington's propensity for causing trouble followed him beyond the grave. His only son having died in 1563, his property fell to be divided between his three daughters: Grace, who married Anthony Mildmay*, Ursula, wife of Thomas Sadler*, and Olive, married first to John Talbot of Salwarpe, Worcestershire, and secondly to Sir Robert Stapleton*. Sharington drew up a draft will on 17 Nov. 1575, to which was attached a detailed household inventory showing goods valued at over £1,000, and the existence at Lacock of a vast retinue of hangers on. This will was never proved, however, the court accepting a nuncupative will made in January 1581. Probate was delayed until the following December while the widow and sole executrix went to law with Grace Mildmay. Among the State Papers is 'Sir Walter Mildmay's request on behalf of his son against unjust attempts of John Talbot to deprive his son's wife of manors allotted to her by her father, Sir Henry Sharington'.[7]

[1] C142/101/121; Genealogist, n.s. xii. 241; CPR, 1554-5, p. 309. [2] HMC Foljambe, 6; Lansd. 56, ff. 168 seq. [3] C142/101/121; Aubrey, Wilts. Topog. Colls. ed. Jackson, 91 n, 92 n; Wilts. Boro. Recs. (Wilts. Arch. Soc. recs. br. v), 9; Lansd. 56, f. 168 seq.; Wilts. N. and Q. iii. 168; iv. 160, 375, 504-5; v. 26-7. [4] Cam. Misc. ix(3), p. 38; DNB (Jewell, John); Wilts N. and Q. vii. 201; Nichols, Progresses Eliz. i. 408; Wilts. Arch. Mag. xxvi. 46-7; lxiii. 72-82. [5] Wilts. Boro. Recs. 9; F. H. Goldney, Chippenham Recs. 292 seq., 323. [6] B. H. Cunnington, Annals Devizes, i. 60-1; APC, viii. 284, 286; x. 28-9, 157-8, 233-4. [7] Wilts. Arch. Mag. xxvi. 46-47; xxxvii. 615; lxiii. 72-82; Genealogist, n.s. xii. 241; PCC 44 Darcy; CSP Dom. 1581-90, p. 35; C142/276/464; 193/91.

N.M.F.

SHAW, Richard, of Langton Matravers, Dorset.

POOLE	1554 (Apr.)

MELCOMBE REGIS	1558, 1559
WAREHAM	1563

It is known that Shaw was nominated at Melcombe Regis in 1558 by Sir John Rogers*, and probable that the same thing happened in 1559. As the parliamentary return for that year describes Shaw as 'yeoman' it is unlikely that he would have been of sufficient status to come in through his own local standing at Wareham in 1563, despite the proximity of Langton Matravers to that borough, and despite his being by then described as 'gentleman'. Furthermore, Shaw was subsidy collector for the hundred of Pimperne, where Rogers was bailiff. Shaw was licensed to leave the 1563 Parliament for his 'affairs at the assizes', 24 Feb. He may therefore have been a lawyer and so, possibly, the Richard Shaw 'late of Staple Inn', administration of whose goods was granted 10 Nov. 1591.

Vis. Dorset, ed. Colby and Rylands, 21; Roberts thesis; CJ, i. 66; PCC admon. act bk. 1591, f. 193; Dorset Mus. 6267/2.

P.W.H.

SHEFFIELD, John (d. 1614), of Lincs.

LINCOLNSHIRE	1601, 1604

2nd s. of Edmund, 3rd Baron Sheffield of Butterwick, by his 1st w. Ursula, da. of Sir Robert Tyrwhitt of Kettleby. m. c.1610, Grizel, da. of Sir Edmund Anderson, c.j. of common pleas, 1s. Edmund who suc. gd.-fa. as 2nd Earl of Mulgrave 1646. Kntd. 1605.

Sheffield was evidently of age by 1601, when he was a party in a suit for debt. As a knight of the shire in 1601 he could have attended the main business committee (3 Nov.) and the monopolies committee (23 Nov.). After twice sitting for his county in Parliament and receiving a knighthood, he may have travelled abroad for some years, re-entering public life on his marriage. Before the influence of his father, of his mother's relatives and of his wife's powerful family could gain him further distinction, Sheffield was drowned, with two of his brothers, in the passage of the Humber, December 1614. He probably died intestate, but administration was not granted until his son came of age in 1632.

CP; D'Ewes, 624, 649; HMC Hatfield, xii. 16; HMC Rutland, i. 421; Lincoln Rec. Soc. xvi. 330.

D.O.

SHELBERY, John (1557-aft. June 1641), of Holborn and Perivale, Mdx.[1]

WEST LOOE	1593*

bap. 17 Jan. 1557, s. of Thomas Shelbery (d. 7 Aug. 1563), grocer, of St. Michael Bassishaw, London by Mary, afterwards (14 June 1565) w. of Thomas Lodge of Lincoln's Inn. m. (1) 26 Aug. 1579, Mary Poste, spinster, of St. Andrew-in-the-Wardrobe, London; (2) 1600, Joan Pites, wid. of George Millet of Perivale; issue.[2]

John Shelbery was probably a grandson of Dyryck *alias* Richard Shelbery, a native of Flanders who settled in Colchester, prospered there as a haberdasher, obtained a grant of denization in 1527, and founded the English family of his name. If it was the same John Shelbery, of Middlesex and the son of a commoner, who matriculated from Magdalen Hall Oxford in 1575, his age would have been 18 years, not 14 as stated in the register. He is not known to have taken a degree. By 1578, as he 'did well remember' some 45 years later, he was 'a young clerk under Mr. Lodge of Lincoln's Inn', his stepfather. He himself was admitted to the same society in 1590 as of Thavie's Inn, one of those lesser inns of chancery dependent on an inn of court – in this case Lincoln's Inn – and 'mostly inhabited by attorneys, solicitors, and clerks'. That he had then been in practice for some years is suggested by a letter from him to the 3rd Earl of Rutland, dated 1585, apologizing for the state of the Earl's garden at Walthamstow and explaining that he had stopped further spending there until other work was completed. A similar lawyer-client relationship, this time with Sir Walter Ralegh, may explain his brief and only occurrence in the House of Commons, when he filled – presumably as a stop-gap, at short notice and in Ralegh's interest – one of the two seats for which Robert Crosse*, a Ralegh follower, had previously been returned. Manningham's diary for October 1602 records the occasion when 'one Sheborough', Ralegh's solicitor, 'was very malapert and saucy in speech' to Mr. Justice Walmesley in the common pleas, 'so far that, after words passed hotly betwixt them', Walmesley threatened to commit him for contempt – and probably would have done if the other judges had not sat 'mum'.[3]

The connexion with Ralegh is clear from 1596, when Shelbery and Robert Smith, with Richard Dickens as assistant, were appointed to administer Ralegh's wine licences patent, the trio conducting their business from Durham House, where Ralegh had his lodging. The patent, in common with other monopolies, was suspended by proclamation in May 1603, and confiscated upon Ralegh's attainder later in the year, but the wine office continued to function under Shelbery, Smith and Dickens as before, its revenues – as distinct from the arrearages, which Ralegh claimed – going not to Ralegh but to the Crown, and Shelbery in April 1604 being named the King's officer to collect them. Even after the grant of a new patent to the 1st Earl of Nottingham (Charles Howard I*) and his eldest son, and their surrender of effective control of the business to a merchant syndicate, the day to day management of the wine office continued in the hands of the deputies appointed by Ralegh in 1596. Through these arrangements Shelbery remained strategically well-placed to recover the arrearages with which to ease Ralegh's financial plight and preserve his own liberty. In a letter praying (Sir) Michael Hickes*, an

importunate creditor, to 'spare John Shelbury for a little time' Ralegh stated the position:

> He stands bound for me for £1,500, and if he be arrested for my part he must lie in prison for all. God is my witness that if he be restrained, that he cannot recover the wine arrearages, these debts will never be paid. It cannot profit you any way to molest him, but it may be his undoing, and I may thereby lose all those debts of the wine office and then never [be] able to pay mine own.

The danger passed, and in March 1605 Shelbery and Smith, to whom the King had granted all Ralegh's personal estate as trustees for his creditors and for the maintenance of his wife and child, effected with the farmers of the patent a composition which apparently provided some income for Ralegh until 1606 and an annuity of £50 for Shelbery until 1609 and possibly later.[4]

During the early part, at least, of Ralegh's imprisonment, first at Winchester and subsequently in the Tower, Shelbery was allowed access to him. The business they discussed, and Shelbery's discharge of his responsibilities as trustee, can be glimpsed in the documentary records of the time. The cost to himself can be gauged from the statement he made in the course of an action by Lady Ralegh in 1622:

> the unlooked for troubles which fell upon the said Sir Walter both at his attainder and afterwards did so amaze and astonish him as that it did much impair both his health and memory for a long time after.

Five years later, when he was 70, he again testified in support of Lady Ralegh. He was by this time resident in the Holborn parish of St. Giles-in-the-Fields where he 'was very sorry to hear' but could not well remember the absolutist sermon delivered in May 1628 by its rector, the King's chaplain-in-ordinary Dr. Manwaring, and where one of his daughters, Frances, was married to Thomas St. George in May 1630. Still active in 1636, and described as tenant and servant to the earl marshal (Thomas Howard, Earl of Arundel), he petitioned the heralds to allow his coat of arms and his harmlessly mistaken descent from an ancestor who came to England as a servant to Anne of Cleves. The last known reference to him occurs under June 1641 in the diary of Richard Boyle, Earl of Cork: 'Given old Mr. Shelberry that was in wants, having been solicitor to Sir Walter Raleigh, twenty shillings.'[5]

[1] The assistance of Mr. Henry Manisty is gratefully acknowledged. [2] *Lond. Mar. Lic.* (Harl. Soc. xxv), 90; *Hist. Mon. Comm. Mdx.* 101. Unused here is the marriage, undated, of John son of Thomas to the widow of one Carew of Navestock, Essex, in *Lond. Vis. Peds.* (Harl. Soc. xcii), 121, and also the cause of contract of marriage by Anne Hewitt against John Shelbury of London, in *CSP Dom.* 1595-7, p. 349. [3] *LP Hen. VIII*, iv(2), grant 3622(8); *Letters of Denization* (Huguenot Soc. viii), 219; Bodl. Reg. Matric. 1564-1614, f. 577; C24/501/74; Sir R. Roxburgh, *Origins of L.I.* 43; Jacob, *New Law Dict.* (1772); *HMC Rutland*, i. 175; *Manningham Diary* (Cam. Soc. xcix),

58–9. [4] *HMC Sackville*, i. 78–93; *HMC Bath*, ii. 54. [5] *CSP Dom.* 1603–10, pp. 141, 334, 484; *HMC Hatfield*, xv. 305, 307; xvi. 193; xvii. 444, 573; *APC*, 1617–19, p. 254; C24/497/80; C41/4/185; House of Lords RO, Braye mss, i. ff. 67, 72; St. Giles-in-the-Fields mar. reg.; Bodl. Rawl. D.766, f. 59; *Lismore Pprs.* (ser. 1), v. 180.

E.L.C.M.

SHELDON, Ralph (c.1537–1613), of Beoley, Worcs.

| WORCESTERSHIRE | 1563 |

b. c.1537, 1st s. of William Sheldon[†] of Beoley by Mary, da. and coh. of William Willington of Barston, Warws. *educ.* with tutor, Richard Hicks, abroad 1554–5. *m.* (1) Anne, da. of Sir Robert Throckmorton[†] of Coughton, Warws. 1s. 9da.; (2) aft. 1605, Jane, da. of William West, 1st Baron De La Warr, wid. of Thomas Wenman*, James Cressy and Thomas Tasburgh*. *suc.* fa. 24 Dec. 1570.[1]

J.p.q. Worcs. 1574–aft. 1586, sheriff 1576–7, commr. musters.[2]

Sheldon was one of those who found the natural outlet for their gifts increasingly barred to them because of their adherence to Catholicism. His cousin, Sir John Harington of Kelston, commented on his narrow escape from serious trouble over the plot to kill the Queen in 1594; 'not half a year before, I heard one that was a great courtier say that he thought [Sheldon] one of the sufficientest wise men ... fittest to have been made of the Council, but for one matter'. Thomas Habington, the contemporary Worcestershire antiquary, thought Sheldon deserved, 'for his singular parts of mind which flowed from his tongue and pen, a pre-eminent dignity'.[3]

Impressed by the tapestry-weaving which he and his tutor had encountered in Europe, Sheldon persuaded his father to establish a factory at Barcheston, Warwickshire, which, as well as producing exquisite work, gave employment to the poor and was therefore favoured by the government. It was perhaps one reason for the moderation of the authorities over his recusancy.[4]

At first Sheldon's life was not greatly troubled because of his faith. His election as knight of the shire while still in his mid-twenties and before he had succeeded to his estates caused no comment, and soon after his father's death he was placed on the commission of the peace, and served a turn as sheriff. It is therefore unlikely that he was the Sheldon known in 1570 to be an agent of Mary Queen of Scots. In 1580, however, the Privy Council determined on severer measure against Catholics, and Sheldon was summoned to attend, appearing on 21 Aug., and later being imprisoned in the Marshalsea until, falling ill, he was transferred to the custody of the dean of Westminster, who persuaded him to make some show of conformity. Soon afterwards Sheldon quarrelled with his son-in-law, John Russell II*, who brought a Star Chamber case against Sheldon, in the course of which he brought up the matter

of the priest Hall's confession that he had said mass in Sheldon's house. Sheldon protested that since his submission, he had 'in all things to his knowledge dutifully and most faithfully performed his duty and allegiance'.[5]

In June 1587 Sheldon was before the Council on some other matter, but he avoided trouble, and in the 1590s he was even appointed to various commissions. After the discovery of a Catholic conspiracy in 1594, however, he was implicated in the confessions of others, summoned to London and his house searched. Neither the search nor the questioning revealed anything further, and no more serious indictment than a charge of hearing mass could be framed against him. Thenceforward however he paid recusancy fines. In 1603 letters from him to his nephew Francis Plowden were intercepted and found 'somewhat mystical and dark', which they remain. Plowden appeared before (Sir) Richard Lewknor*, but no sequel is known.[6]

Sheldon spent the rest of his life in retirement. The only part he is known to have taken in public affairs concerned the parliamentary election in 1601, when he clearly intended opposing the candidature of Sir Thomas Leighton* as Member for Worcestershire. The Privy Council warned him not to 'do [himself] the wrong to be transported with any such passion'. Sheldon's grandson, Thomas Russell*, himself a Catholic, though not openly so in 1601, was elected in the junior seat. Sheldon was relatively unmolested in his later years, possibly through the favour of Robert Cecil*, whom in 1603 he thanked for assistance. He avoided becoming implicated in the 1605 plot, although several of his friends and relatives were involved, as was the interesting lady who was soon to become his second wife. Born a protestant, she was converted by her second husband (who was her father's servant); conformed to Anglicanism during her third marriage, and was presumably Catholic while married to Sheldon, as she certainly was after fulfilling his hope that she would 'overlive and survive' him.[7]

Probably because of recusancy fines, the protection he was having to buy, and penal interest rates, Sheldon became deeply indebted to a recusant moneylender named Thomas Hoord, whose estate falling into crown hands, left Sheldon the Crown's debtor for between £20,000 and £40,000. Despite the sale of estates his debts were not settled at his death. It is thus something of a tribute to Sheldon's interest in the university of Oxford that he felt able to give £50 towards the extension of the Bodleian Library begun in 1610 as well as to the mathematician Thomas Allen, of Gloucester Hall, and to Anthony Blencowe, provost of Oriel. Sheldon died in March 1613 and was buried in the tomb he had erected for his wife and himself in Beoley church. In his will, he reaffirmed his faith: 'I do protest to live, and by God's grace and assistance, do hope to die in the unity of the Catholic church, and to become a member of His church triumphant forever'.[8]

[1] C142/159/87; *Vis. Worcs.* (Harl. Soc. xxvii), 128. [2] Lansd. 56, f. 168 seq. [3] J. L. Hotson, *I, William Shakespeare*, 152–3; *Habington's Worcs.* (Worcs. Hist. Soc.), i. 70. [4] E. A. B. Barnard, *The Sheldons*, 14–16, 23–4. [5] *CSP Dom.* 1547–80, p. 691; 1581–90, p. 142; Add. 1566–79, p. 236; *APC*, xii. 166, 254, 301; *VCH Worcs.* ii. 214; St. Ch. 5/R12/32, R41/34, S15/38. [6] *APC*, xv. 137; xx. 242, 266; xxi. 187; *CSP Dom.* 1591–4, pp. 531, 540–7, 552, 554–5; *HMC Hatfield*, iv. 618–19; SP14/3/2, 13. [7] *APC*, xxxii. 251; *HMC Hatfield*, xv. 60; A. Davidson, 'The Second Mrs. Sheldon', 'Ralph Sheldon and the Provost of Oriel' (*Worcs. Recusant*, Dec. 1969, June 1973). [8] *CSP Dom.* 1603–10, pp. 360, 479, 591; Add. 1580–1625, p. 527; PCC 28 Capell; C142/334/58; *VCH Worcs.* iii. 226–7, 268–9, 550; iv. 4–5, 14–18, 38–9, 84–5, 339–41; *Bodl. Lib. Rec.* viii. 252–7.

S.M.T./A.D.

SHELLEY, Henry (c.1563–c.1634), of Patcham, Suss.

STEYNING	1586
BRAMBER	1604

b. c.1563, 1st s. of Richard Shelley of Patcham by Dorothy, da. of Richard Hill of Hartley Wintney, Hants, wid. of one Welche. *educ.* I. Temple 1584. *m.* (1) into Walsingham fam.; (2) Jane, da. of Richard Bellingham of Hangleton and Newtimber, 6s. 7da. *suc.* fa. 1594.
J.p. Suss. from c.1583.

The Shelleys had been established in Sussex certainly since the late fourteenth century, though the Patcham branch began in the sixteenth. Shelley and his father, protestants in an otherwise recusant family, were the only two in the Elizabethan period to be active in local administration. Lord Buckhurst emphasized Shelley's adherence to the established church when successfully recommending him as 'a gentleman of so honest sort and honour' to Burghley in 1586 for the lease of a sheep pasture forfeited for treason by William Shelley of Michelgrove. Shelley's uncle Robert Byng* had come into Parliament for Steyning in 1555, and Shelley was presumably returned through his own local standing in 1586. (Sir) Thomas Shirley I* was then in the Netherlands. Shelley stated in 1619 that he had lived in Patcham nearly all his life. His will, dated 28 Aug. 1630, was proved at Lewes 17 Feb. 1634.

J. Comber, *Suss. Genealogies, Lewes Centre*, 248–9; *Vis. Hants* (Harl. Soc. lxiv), 20; Lansd. 50, f. 39; 737, f. 158d; Royal 18 D. 111; Hatfield ms 278; Mousley thesis; PRO Index 6800; *Suss. Arch. Colls.* lvi. 11.

A.M.M.

SHERWIN, John (c.1527–89), of Chichester, Suss.

CHICHESTER	1563

b. c.1527. *m.* ?Agnes, at least 1s.
Alderman, Chichester, mayor 1570.

After he had been chosen as Chichester's Member of Parliament, Sherwin agreed, 'upon the tedious suit' of one George Stoughton, to give up his place to Thomas Lewknor, a local gentleman and no freeman. The mayor vetoed this, but the incident must have rankled, for Sherwin in his turn objected to the return of the outsider Valentine Dale* in 1572. In 1584 Sherwin favoured the popular candidate, James Colbrand*. In June 1577 'divers gentlemen' witnessed a document, stating that the bishop of Chichester 'was not drunk at the dinner at Mr. John Sherwin's house, as by some he was unjustly slandered'. Sherwin died in 1589, his will being proved at Chichester the same year.

Vis. Hants (Harl. Soc. lxiv), 188; *Chichester City Charters* (Chichester City Council, Chichester Pprs. iii), 23; St. Ch. 5/C23/37 (where the election dispute is incorrectly attributed to Elizabeth's first Parliament); Neale, *Commons*, 261–4; *Chichester Wills* (Brit. Rec. Soc. Index Lib. lxiv), 261. The Star Chamber case established Sherwin's age as about 59 in 1586.

J.J.C.

SHIRLEY, Thomas I (c.1542–1612), of Wiston, Suss.

SUSSEX	1572, 1584, 1593
STEYNING	1601, 1604

b. c.1542, 1st s. of William Shirley of Wiston by Mary, da. of Thomas Isley of Sundridge, Kent. *educ.* Oriel, Oxf, 1554, BA 1557; G. Inn 1559. *m.* Ann, da. of Sir Thomas Kempe* of Olantigh, Kent, 3s. inc. Thomas II* 7da. *suc.* fa. 1551.[1] Kntd. 1573.
J.p., dep. lt. Suss. from c.1569–1601; sheriff, Surr. and Suss. 1577–8; treasurer at war in Netherlands from 1587–97, in France 1591.[2]

The Shirleys of Wiston were descended from a Warwickshire family which acquired Sussex property by a late fourteenth-century marriage. In the mid-fifteenth century this was settled on a younger son, from whom derived both the Wiston line and the still younger branch at West Grinstead, a descendant of which was Thomas Shirley III*. By the mid-sixteenth century the Wiston Shirleys had intermarried with such leading Sussex families as the Dawtreys of Petworth and the Shelleys of Michelgrove; they were also connected with the Blounts, Lords Mountjoy, and the Walsinghams.[3]

Shirley himself, who was only nine years old at his father's death, and who became the ward of Cardinal Pole, inherited the manors of Wiston, Heene, Chiltington Slaughter and Eringham in Sussex and of Wedenhill in Buckinghamshire. A protégé of the Earl of Leicester, who may later have secured him his knighthood, he was made a deputy lieutenant at an early age. His name appears frequently on local commissions, such as those for suppressing piracy and recusancy and for the regulation of the grain trade. In 1583–4 the young Countess of Arundel, whose husband was then under house arrest in London, was put in his custody at Wiston.[4]

In 1585 Shirley accompanied Leicester to the Low Countries with a troop he had raised himself. When Leicester incurred the Queen's displeasure by accepting the governorship of the Netherlands contrary to her instructions, he sent Shirley home to plead his cause. Shirley wrote back describing her 'bitter words' against Leicester, and his efforts to reason with her. Probably he returned to the Netherlands later that year when the trouble had subsided, and no doubt it was Leicester who obtained him, in February 1587, the post of treasurer at war to the English forces in the Netherlands, in succession to Richard Huddleston*, who had got into difficulties with the accounts. Shirley himself at once began speculating with the soldiers' pay, sold concessions to the army victuallers and set himself up as a moneylender. Reports of his income varied between £16,000 and £3,000 a year, apart from his stipend of 20s. a day. In 1591 the Queen set up a commission of inquiry, despite which he was made treasurer of the forces in France. His land purchases reached their peak in the early 1590s, and included certain lands of the Pellatt family in Sussex and others belonging to Norwich cathedral. After an unsuccessful attempt to secure the comptrollership of the Household in 1592, his financial position deteriorated and on 4 Apr. 1597 he was superseded as treasurer at war by Sir Thomas Fludd*; in 1601 he was put off the commission of the peace and the deputy lieutenantship of Sussex; and finally, in March 1604, he was arrested and sent to the Fleet. This happened at a particularly inappropriate moment, made 'Shirley's case' a landmark in the history of parliamentary privilege, and ended in the committal of the warden of the Fleet to the 'Little Ease'. Shirley was released and allowed to take his seat, but his debts remained unpaid. He sold his estates (except Wiston, which he settled on his wife), and died intestate in October 1612. The family finances never recovered.[5]

So far as it is possible to disentangle Shirley's committees from those of his namesakes in the House (there was always at least one), he was active in his first three Parliaments. In that of 1572 he was appointed to the committee on the subsidy (10 Feb. 1576), the large committee 'to consult of bills convenient to be framed' (25 Jan. 1581), and committees concerned with the preservation of woods (28 Jan.), returns (24 Feb.), the Queen's safety (14 Mar.) and iron mills (18 Mar.). In the 1584 Parliament he was again on a preservation of timber committee (8 Dec.); served on the conference appointed 15 Feb. 1585 to consider the Lords' complaints about the Commons' attitude to them over the fraudulent conveyances bill, and was on the subsidy committee (24 Feb.). By 1593 his son also had been knighted, and there can thus be no certainty as to which of them was appointed to the following, though the father is more likely: the committee on recusants (28 Feb. 1593); the second subsidy committee (1 Mar.) – he would have been on the first (26 Feb.) by reason of being a knight of the shire – and the committees on salted herrings (5 Mar.), the poor law (12 Mar.) and the relief of wounded soldiers (30

Mar.). On the last day of the session the House refused Shirley permission to bring in a proviso to a bill explaining a statute of Henry VIII for confirmation of letters patent. By 1601 he was no longer able to sit for the county and instead was returned for his local borough of Steyning. He made no recorded contribution to the business of this Parliament.[6]

[1] Berry, Co. Genealogies, Suss. (J. Comber's copy at Chichester), 172; Registrum Orielense, ed. Shadwell, i. 23; PCC 19 Bucke; C142/94/76. [2] SP 12/59, no. 61; 179, nos. 52–3; HMC Hatfield, iii. 297; APC, xxi. 91; xxxi. 400; PRO Assizes 35, S.E. Circuit, Suss. 15–43; Lansd. 737, f. 158; CSP Dom. 1581–90, p. 663; PRO, ms cal. pat. 30 Eliz., f. 13b; PRO Index 6800, f. 113; DNB. [3] Berry, loc. cit.; Suss. Arch. Colls. v. 8 seq.; Mousley thesis, 732 seq. [4] C142/94/76; SP 11/11/57; Suss. Rec. Soc. xiv. 205; PCC 19 Bucke; DNB; Harl. 703, f. 67v; 474 passim; Lansd. 48, f. 136; 146, f. 19; Suss. Arch. Colls. ii. 59; v. 16; DNB (Howard, Philip). [5] R. C. Strong and J. A. Van Dorstan, Leicester's Triumph, 129; DNB; Cotton, Galba C.IX, ff. 120, 128, 136; F. C. Dietz, English Public Finance 1558–1641, pp. 452 seq.; Trans. Leics. Arch. Soc. xxiv. 57; C. G. Cruickshank, Elizabeth's Army, 96; Lansd. 45, f. 156; 50, f. 153; 51, f. 152; 54, f. 78; 58, ff. 2, 62; 64, ff. 2, 4; 75, f. 92; 85, f. 24; 149, f. 49 seq.; CSP Dom. 1595–7, p. 44; Horsfield, Suss. i. 235; Suss. Arch. Colls. v. 22; xxxviii. 111, 116; xlviii. 9 n; lxxii. 230; Devereux mss at Longleat, iii. nos. 126 seq.; SP 12/242/50; APC, xxvii. 16; EHR, viii. 733–40. [6] D'Ewes, 247, 288, 300, 306, 308, 337, 349, 356, 474, 477, 481, 487, 499, 512, 521; CJ, i. 104, 119, 120, 129, 134, 136.

J.E.M.

SHIRLEY, Thomas II (1564–c.1630), of Wiston, Suss., later of the I.o.W.

STEYNING	1584, 1593
HASTINGS	1601
STEYNING	1614, 1621

b. 1564, 1st s. of Thomas Shirley I* of Wiston by Ann, da. of Sir Thomas Kempe* of Olantigh, Kent. educ. Hart Hall, Oxf. 1579; I. Temple 1581. m. (1) 1591, Frances, da. of Henry Vavasour of Copmanthorpe and Hazlewood, Yorks., 3s. 4da.; (2) Dec. 1617, Judith, da. of William Bennett of London, wid. of one Taylor, 6s. 6da. Kntd. 1589; suc. fa. 1612.[1]

Capt. in the Netherlands 1593; commanded the Foresight 1599.

At the age of 21, after an orthodox education, Shirley accompanied his father and brother Anthony to the Low Countries, later serving in Ireland where he was knighted by the lord deputy, Sir William Fitzwilliam II*. On his return to England, he went to court and began an affair with Frances Vavasour (sister of Thomas Vavasour*), one of the Queen's maids of honour. When the Queen learned that they had married, Shirley was put in the Marshalsea, where he remained from September 1591 until the following spring. In 1593 he was again serving in the Low Countries, now with the rank of captain, and while there became entangled in his father's deteriorating financial situation. In debt, he relinquished his company at Flushing to his brother-in-law Thomas Vavasour, and started privateering. His ventures, which included the capture of four Lübeck 'hulks' in the Channel in 1598, with cargoes said to be Spanish, and the pillaging of a township in Portugal in 1602, were evidently financed by such men as Thomas Ridgeway*, Dr. Thomas Crompton I* and Sir Henry Carey*, who received money from him at different times on his return from sea. Sir Robert Cecil, too, may have been involved, for in March 1602 he was reminded by Shirley of a promise to venture £100 with him. Large sums of money were at stake. One ship captured by Shirley on her way from San Domingo with a cargo of sugar, was valued at £4,700: and in April 1600, after bringing two prizes into Plymouth, Shirley offered the Earl of Nottingham, as lord high admiral, £600 for his tenth share in them, saying he had already paid £2,000 for 'the company's thirds'.

The official attitude to his exploits seems to have been tolerant at first; some of his attacks may even have been made with the Queen's ship *Foresight*, which he commanded in 1599. However, in October 1600 Shirley was in trouble with the Admiralty court for seizing a Hamburg ship whose cargo belonged to certain Dutch merchants, and Lord Cobham, a connexion of the Careys, had to intervene on his behalf. His creditors, too, became impatient; among them was Sir Richard Weston*, whose supporters were arraigned by Shirley's father in the Star Chamber for breaking into his house at Blackfriars in July 1600 and threatening him and his son, from whom they demanded payment.[2]

The climax of his career as a privateer was reached when, after sailing with two ships late in 1602 to the Mediterranean and being entertained by the Duke of Tuscany in Florence, he attacked the Turkish-held island of Zea in the Cyclades in January 1603. He was captured and taken prisoner to Constantinople, where he remained until being ransomed in December 1605. He wrote an unpublished 'Discourse of the Turks'. His return to England by way of Naples, whence he sent intelligence to Cecil, took him a year, and was followed by proceedings of the Levant Company against him for infringement of trading rights. In September 1607 he was imprisoned in the Tower on this charge. Four years later, he was declared insolvent in the King's bench, and the death of his bankrupt father in October 1612 increased his problems. His second marriage may have been to relieve his debts, but it also brought him more children. In or about 1624, he sold his house at Wiston, now in poor repair, and retired to the Isle of Wight where he died some six years later. He was succeeded in his estates by his son Thomas, a Royalist, who was last but one of his line; another son, Henry, a dramatist, had predeceased him.

Shirley's representation of Steyning, close to Wiston, in four Parliaments, was natural. Only in 1601 when his father required a borough seat, and Robert Bowyer II*, secretary to Lord Buckhurst, had the other, did Shirley seek election elsewhere. He secured it at Bramber, nearby, but on being returned for Hastings, presumably through the influence of the lord warden of the Cinque Ports, Lord Cobham, who may have made the seat available to Lord Buckhurst, he chose the Cinque Port. As his father was also a member of all Shirley's Elizabethan Parliaments it is possible, but unlikely, that some of the committees attributed to the father could have belonged to the son. As MP for Hastings in 1601, Shirley could have attended committees concerned with the business of the House (3 Nov.) and the Severn harbour project (21 Nov.).[3]

[1] *DNB*; W. Berry, *Co. Genealogies, Suss.* (Comber's annotated copy at Chichester), 172. [2] LC2/4/4; Lansd. 68, f. 236; 142, f. 65; 145, ff. 138, 139; 150, ff. 204 seq.; *HMC Hatfield*, ix. 427; x. 143; xii. 78; St. Ch. 5/S14/4, S67/18, 37. [3] *HMC Hatfield*, xvi. 21; xviii. 147, 177; Mousley thesis, 738–9; D'Ewes, 624, 647.

J.E.M.

SHIRLEY, Thomas III (c.1556–1606), of West Grinstead, Suss.

STEYNING   1597

b. c.1556, 1st s. of Francis Shirley† of West Grinstead by Barbara, da. of Sir Richard Blount* of Mapledurham, Oxon. *m.* (1) Elizabeth, *s.p.*; (2) Philippa, da. of Sir Edward Caryll of Harting, 2da. *suc. fa.* 1578.

Shirley was descended from a younger son of Ralph Shirley, esquire of the body to Henry VII. He was returned at Steyning through the influence of his relative, Thomas Shirley I*. His will, dated 14 May 1606, six days before his death, has a long religious preamble and leaves a £20 annuity for the relief of 'such ministers as have been since the King's reign deprived of their livings within the county of Sussex for not-conformity [sic] to the Church of England', payable for life or until restoration to the living. His leaving an annuity of £2 for 20 years towards the repair of the roads within two miles of his house makes it tempting to assign to him the committee of a bill for the highways of Surrey, Sussex and Kent reported to the House of Commons 31 Jan. 1598. But this seems insufficient for his only parliamentary activity, and has been given to John Shirley I, who regularly reported bills in this Parliament. He divided his main property between his two daughters, the executrices. The elder, Cicely, received the house at West Grinstead and the parish tithes: the younger, Barbara, received four farms in West Grinstead and lands in Lancing. His uncle Richard Blount II* and his cousin Anthony Shirley, were overseers.

Vis. Suss. (Harl. Soc. liii), 7; J. Comber, *Suss. Genealogies, Lewes Centre*, 260–1; Mousley thesis, 749; *Suss. Rec. Soc.* xiv. 205; xx. 475; *Suss. Arch. Colls.* v. 11; D'Ewes, 589, 591; PCC 3 Huddleston.

R.C.G.

SHIRLEY, *see also* SHURLEY

SHOTER, Thomas, of Burge Street, Leominster, Herefs.

LEOMINSTER   1589

Bailiff, Leominster 1574.

Shoter may have belonged to the family which owned the manor of Mere Place, King's Pyon, Herefordshire. William Shoter, possibly Thomas's father, was convicted of murder early in Elizabeth's reign and his property confiscated by the Crown. Shoter himself must have been living in Leominster by 1568 when his name occurs in a case before the local court leet. He and another man complained that when they fetched water from near the door of Richard Powell, who had been Catholic vicar of Leominster in Mary's reign, they were cursed by Powell's wife, 'being a rude person of her tongue, and a disquieter of all her neighbours (as it is well known)'.

Shoter and Humphrey Wall, the two local men returned by Leominster to the 1589 Parliament, were granted leave of absence from the House 'for their special and necessary business' 24 Mar. 1589. The date of Shoter's death has not been ascertained.

CPR, 1558–60, p. 133; 1563–6, p. 12; W. R. Williams, *Parl. Hist. Herefs.* 123; Robinson, *Herefs. Manors*, 160; G. F. Townsend, *Leominster*, 258; D'Ewes, 452; LR2/217, f. 108.

M.R.P.

SHURLEY, John I (*d.*1616), of 'The Friars', Lewes, Suss.

LEWES	1572
LOSTWITHIEL	1584
LEWES	1589, 1597[1], 1604

2nd s. of Edward Shurley of Isfield by Joan, da. of John Fenner of Crawley. *educ.* Queens', Camb. 1562; Clifford's Inn; M. Temple 1565, called by 1575. *m.* (1) aft. Dec. 1570, Elizabeth (*d.* by May 1580), da. and coh. of Richard Kyme of Lewes, 1da.; (2) 14 Sept. 1585, Frances, da. of Henry Capell I* of Hadham, Herts., 1s. 2da.

J.p. Suss. from *c.*1584; bencher, M. Temple 1587, Lent reader 1587, treasurer May 1601; serjeant-at-law 1603.

Shurley was the founder of a cadet branch of the Shurleys of Isfield, some five miles north of Lewes, and uncle to John Shurley II* of the senior line. His house in Lewes, called 'The Friars', was evidently used as their town house by the Isfield Shurleys, since both Shurley's elder brother Thomas and his nephew John died there.[2]

Shurley had to importune Michael Hickes* to ask Cecil for his promotion as serjeant-at-law, on the ground that he was the 'first and ancientest' named of the Middle Temple by the judges. John Rowe, the antiquary, who received his legal training from Shurley, notes that Shurley was of counsel to the constables of Lewes about 1584. In 1605 he was counsel for Hastings, and in 1608 and 1611 for Rye. But Shurley was more a country gentleman than a lawyer. It was probably he who was called upon on 17 Apr. 1600 to provide 100 horses overnight for the governor of Dieppe, who had arrived with a noble retinue

at Newhaven, and needed horses to carry his company to London. Shurley was made responsible for a bequest by his wife's uncle to the borough of Lewes and, in September 1602, was among those entrusted with a fund for the regular relief of the poor of Lewes, Hove and Buckstead.[3]

Shurley's return to Parliament for Lewes requires no explanation, but his return for Lostwithiel does, and one is not forthcoming. No connexion has been established between Shurley and the borough or any possible patron. Thus it must remain uncertain whether it was in fact Shurley who was returned. However, the committee activity of 'Mr. Shirley' in 1584 points to a lawyer, so the assumption has been allowed to stand. With this caveat, and another required by the number of Shirleys in the House – the journals take no account of the different spelling of the surname – Shurley's committees were on collateral warranties (7 Mar. 1576), wrecks (30 Jan. 1581), wool (23 Feb.), lessees in tail (27 Feb.), Erith and Plumstead marshes (8 Mar.), mariners (15 Mar.), tithes and other ecclesiastical law reforms (6 Mar. 1585), highways (9 Mar.), delay in executions (9 Mar.) and assurances (22 Mar.). In the 1589 Parliament he was given leave of absence on 1 Mar. as 'Mr. John Shirley, one of the burgesses for the borough of Lewes' (the journals are often at their most specific when there is no possibility of confusion – there was no other Shirley in 1589), but was back by 17 Mar. for the committee of a bill about the hue and cry. Other committees he was named to in 1589 concerned outlawries (20 Mar.), the Exchequer (20 Mar.), and conferring with the Lords about a declaration of war on Spain (29 Mar.). In the 1597 Parliament his committees, all of which except the last-named he reported to the House, were on the continuation of statutes (11, 18 Nov., 13 Dec., 3 Feb. 1598), John Sharp's debts (23 Jan. 1598), highways in Sussex, Surrey and Kent (27, 31 Jan.), the better execution of judgment (1, 4 Feb.) and corn (3 Feb.).[4]

Shurley died 2 Oct. 1616, apparently intestate, leaving his son a minor. His inquisition post mortem and feodary's survey show that, as well as owning property in Lewes, he died seised of the manor of Broadwater, Sussex, which he had bought in the autumn of 1605.[5]

[1] Folger V. b. 298. [2] *M.T. Recs.* i. 207 et passim; W. Berry, *Co. Genealogies, Suss.* (Comber's copy at Chichester), 204; *Suss. Arch. Colls.* xviii. 129; c. 120–1; *VCH Suss.* vii. 37. [3] Lansd. 108, f. 63; *Suss. Rec. Soc.* xxxiv. pp. vii, 123, 168; xlviii. 31; *HMC 13 Rep. IV*, pp. 137, 140, 148, 360; *Suss. Arch. Colls.* ii. 59; *HMC Hatfield*, x. 113–14. [4] D'Ewes, 290, 301, 364, 371, 441, 446, 449, 450, 454, 559, 572, 586, 589, 591, 592; *CJ*, i. 111, 120, 129, 132, 134; Townshend, *Hist. Colls.* 26, 125. [5] C142/355/63; Wards 5/43, pt. 1, dated 22 Feb. 1617; *Suss. Rec. Soc.* xiv. 206; xix. 66.

J.E.M.

SHURLEY, John II (1568–1631), of Isfield, Suss.

EAST GRINSTEAD	1593
STEYNING	1597

BRAMBER 1604
SUSSEX 1625

b. 1568, 1st s. of Thomas Shurley of Isfield by his 1st w. Ann, da. of (Sir) Nicholas Pelham† of Halland in Laughton. *educ.* Hart Hall, Oxf. 1582; M. Temple 1591. *m.* (1) Jane, da. of Thomas Shirley I* of Wiston, 2s. 7da.; (2) Dorothy, da. of George Goring I* of Ovingdean, wid. of Henry Bowyer*, *s.p. suc.* fa. 1579. Kntd. 1603.[1]

J.p. Suss. from c.1597, dep. lt. from 1624; sheriff, Surr. and Suss. 1616–17.[2]

Shurley inherited the Sussex manors of Crawley, Ifield, Worth in Little Horsted and Isfield itself, the family seat since the late fifteenth century. Both his grandfather and great-grandfather had been cofferers to Henry VIII, and through his mother he was related to the Pelhams of Laughton, and so indirectly to Thomas Sackville*. John Shurley I*, the lawyer, of Lewes, was his uncle, and George Shurley, the future lord chief justice of the King's bench in Ireland, his brother, but he was not connected with the Shirleys of Wiston until his first marriage. In 1593 Shurley was returned for East Grinstead near both Crawley and Ifield manors. In 1597 he may have come in for Steyning through the Wiston Shirleys who lived nearby. Thomas Shirley III* was his fellow-Member. On the other hand, some time later certainly, and perhaps at the time of the election, Shurley himself held the leasehold of Steyning parsonage and the advowson there. He is not known to have taken any active part in either of his first two Parliaments.[3]

The greater part of Shurley's active public life falls outside Elizabeth's reign. In his will, dated 25 Apr. 1631, the day of his death, he asked to be buried 'without pomp and glory' among his ancestors in the chancel of Isfield church. He had already, in December 1625 and April 1631, settled the major part of his lands. His 'dearly beloved wife' was appointed sole executrix. There is a monumental inscription in Isfield church.[4]

[1] W. Berry, *Co. Genealogies, Suss.* (Comber's copy at Chichester), 204; *Suss. Rec. Soc.* xiv. 206; F. E. Ball, *Judges in Ireland,* i. 328; *Suss. Arch. Colls.* xviii. 130–1. [2] *Suss. Arch. Colls.* xviii. 130–1; xl. 2, 5, 7, 32; *CSP Dom.* 1623–5, p. 300. [3] *Suss. Rec. Soc.* xiv. 206; Berry, loc. cit.; J. Comber, *Suss. Genealogies, Lewes Centre,* 252; *Suss. Arch. Colls.* xviii. 124 seq.; PCC 62 St. John. [4] Comber, *Suss. Genealogies,* 253; *Suss. Rec. Soc.* xix. 239, 245; xx. 400; *VCH Suss.* vii. 145; PCC 62 St. John; C142/471/70; *Suss. Arch. Colls.* xviii. 130–1; lxx. 159.

J.E.M.

SHURLEY, *see also* **SHIRLEY**

SHUTE, Richard, of Stamford, Lincs.

STAMFORD 1593

Agent or receiver to Lord Burghley in Stamford region and overseer of work at Burghley House by 1578; commr. sewers in that area 1584; feodary, Lincs. 1588; alderman (i.e. mayor), Stamford 1583, 1591, 1592.[1]

As Lord Burghley's servant and a resident of Stamford Shute was prominent enough in the town to lead the opposition in 1589 to Edward Heron and others who had caused the removal of the town clerk and recorder and deprived Shute himself of his place on the corporation.[2] The Cecil influence evidently soon brought about his restoration, and in 1593 his master secured him a seat in Parliament for the borough. But next year he was Burghley's 'unfaithful servant', accused of stealing building materials. His status at Stamford was soon threatened and in November 1595 the Privy Council ordered him to be examined for 'uttering foul abuses' against the corporation. By 4 Dec. he was a prisoner 'at the Fleet, a place uncomfortable for a heavy heart'. He was, he told Burghley, resigned to his shame, loss and imprisonment, but by 1598 he had convinced himself that he had been wronged, writing to Sir Robert Cecil of his 'long' and 'honest' service to Burghley, and still complaining of his 'great wrongs' in the following year. There is no sign that he was ever restored to favour.[3]

A will of a Richard Shute, 'citizen of London', referring to a family in West Deeping (near Stamford) was proved in 1611.[4] The beneficiaries were the widow, Mary, and the family of Robert Spenser of West Deeping. Provision was made for the wife's children by a previous marriage. The testator is unlikely to have been the 1593 Member, though probably a relative, perhaps his son.

[1] *CSP Dom.* 1547–80, p. 597; *Recs. Commrs. Sewers* (Lincoln Rec. Soc. liv), p. lxxvii; *HMC Rutland,* i. 261, 263; J. Drakard, *Hist. Stamford,* 102. [2] *APC,* xvii. 66, 91, 233; xviii. 193; xxiii. 98. [3] *HMC Ancaster,* 319–20; *APC,* xxv. 76; Lansd. 80, f. 30; *HMC Hatfield,* viii. 296; ix. 223. [4] PCC 104 Wood, 57 Fenner.

D.O.

SHUTE, Robert (c.1528–90), of Oakington, Cambs.

CAMBRIDGE 1571, 1572*

b. c.1528, s. of Christopher Shute of Oakington. *educ.* Camb., ?Peterhouse c.1542; Barnard's Inn; G. Inn 1550, called 1552. *m.* Thomasine, da. of Christopher Burgoyne of Long Stanton, Cambs., at least 6s. 2da.[1]

Recorder, Cambridge from 1558; steward, Peterhouse manorial courts 1568–79; feodary, ct. of wards, Cambs. 1569; Lent reader, G. Inn 1568, treasurer 1577, double reader 1577; prothonotary, Queen's bench c.1572; serjeant-at-law 1577; justice of assize, midland and northern circuits 1579; second baron of the Exchequer 1579; c.j. at Lancaster 1580; judge of the Queen's bench 1586–*d.*

Judge for the liberty of Ely; member, council in the north, council in the marches of Wales.

J.p. Isle of Ely from c.1564, q. by 1574, Cambs. from c.1575, other midland counties from 1579.[2]

By the sixteenth century the Shutes were settled in Leicestershire and Cambridgeshire. Shute became the head of the latter branch, though he was in fact born at

Gargrave, Yorkshire, and raised it to the prominence it enjoyed for generations.[3]

Both Peterhouse and Christ's, Cambridge, claim Shute as an undergraduate, but it is likely that he was the 'Shutte' who entered the former in about 1542, as he later put his legal training at the disposal of Peterhouse as steward of their manorial courts. He remained associated with Gray's Inn, also, for a long time after he had been called to the bar. The pension books show how regular was his attendance at the 'pension' meetings, culminating in his appointment as treasurer for 1577. When more pressing duties compelled him to break his connexion with the Inn, he was awarded a 'benevolence' of £27 10s.[4]

Shute's election in 1558 as recorder of Cambridge by 48 out of its 70 burgesses was the beginning of a long and close connexion with the town. The Queen expressed the wish that George Freville†, though appointed a baron of the Exchequer in that year, should retain the office of recorder, but the corporation, who had already chosen Shute, respectfully begged her to confirm their choice. When the same situation occurred on his own elevation to the bench in 1579, Elizabeth commanded Cambridge to retain him as recorder for life. One of his most difficult tasks in that office was to keep the peace between town and university. When the Queen visited Cambridge in 1564 Shute delivered the welcoming oration. Other tasks which came his way included the organization of the local militia, the introduction of changes in the constitution of the town, and the foundation of a grammar school. The treasurers' accounts note many gifts to him, even after his elevation to the bench made him but an occasional visitor, the occasion marked by a banquet in the mayor's house or by some similar mark of respect. In 1571 an entry in the accounts indicates that Shute was paid 37s. 8d. when the mayor and aldermen went to his house 'to make merry'.[5]

As recorder Shute was twice elected Member for the town, though there was a little fuss in 1571 over the regulation that parliamentary burgesses should be Cambridge residents. This was overcome by an ordinance stating that for election purposes the recorder would be regarded as a local man. Shute was paid almost £6 for his expenses in each session of his two Parliaments. He sat on Commons committees considering vagabonds (23 Apr. 1571), Mary Queen of Scots (12 May 1572), the Earl of Kent's lands (21 May, 9 June 1572), weights and measures (23 May), the continuation of statutes (26 June), sheriffs (24 Feb. 1576), reciprocal treatment for foreigners (24 Feb.) and regulations concerning Eton, Winchester and Oxford and Cambridge colleges (2 Mar.). By the last session of this Parliament, 1581, Shute had become a judge.[6]

Shute's elevation to the bench as second baron of the Exchequer in 1579 was the occasion of an important change in judicial practice. Hitherto barons of the Exchequer had not enjoyed equal status with judges of the other courts; they were not judges of assize, for example,

and did not sit in the Lords as legal assistants but increasing pressure on the courts, particularly in cases connected with revenue and crown debts, necessitated a change, so that in Shute's patent it is for the first time ordered that 'he shall be reputed, and be of the same order, rank, estimation, dignity and pre-eminence, to all intents and purposes, as any puisne judge of either of the two other courts'. In his new office he served on a commission to inquire into certain aspects of Exchequer procedure; the commission's recommendations, which almost advocated a return to medieval practice, were not accepted. Shute's final promotion, to be a judge of the Queen's bench, occurred in 1586. He also frequently served as an assize judge. On the 1587 midland circuit he and his colleague, Thomas Mead, were paid £6 2s. a day for 21 days. Unusually, he was also given a licence to preside at the York assizes, even though this was the county of his birth. Perhaps at the request of Lord North, who wrote to Burghley at least twice on the subject, he was judge for the liberty of Ely while the see was vacant.[7]

He died in April 1590 and was probably buried at Oakington. In a nuncupative will he left all his property to his wife. His eldest son Francis settled at Upton in Leicestershire and was the ancestor of the viscounts Barrington, while his daughter Jane married a cousin of Sir Christopher Hatton*. Another son Robert, after a wild life, associated himself with the Duke of Buckingham in James I's reign and became a Member of Parliament and recorder of London.[8]

[1] Vis. Cambs. (Harl. Soc. xli), 96; Foss, Judges, v. 539–40; DNB. [2] Cooper, Ath. Cant. ii. 92; Cam. Misc. ix(3), p. 25; SP12/104, 12/145; E163/14/8; Royal 18 D 111; Lansd. 737; Somerville, Duchy, i. 471. [3] Morant, Essex, ii. 22–3; Al. Cant. i (4), pp. 71–2. [4] T. A. Walker, Biog. Reg. Peterhouse, i. 137, 138, 144; G. Inn Pens. Bk. i. passim. [5] C. H. Cooper, Cambridge Annals, ii. 146–7, 149–50, 158–9, 225, 231, 278, 310, 347, 371, 380, 426; VCH Cambs. iii. 42, 59; Nichols, Progresses Eliz. iii. 28; APC, vii. 161; CPR, 1560–3, p. 406. [6] Cooper, ii. 269–71; Cambridge Guildhall, Cambridge day bk. 1564–77, pp. 108, 111, 127; Downing Coll. Camb. Bowtell mss.; D'Ewes, 178, 206, 213, 222, 224; CJ, i. 85, 95, 96, 97, 101, 103, 108, 110. [7] Cal. I.T. Recs. i. p. xl; Lansd. 31, f. 140; 53, f. 198; 171, ff. 356–7; Eliz. Govt. and Soc. 228–9; APC, xiv, xv. passim; xvii. 91, 93; CSP For. 1585–6, pp. 563, 687; VCH Cambs. iv. 18. [8] PCC 30 Daughtry; Lodge, Peerage of Ireland, v. 200–1; N. and Q. (ser. 2), x. 95.

M.R.P.

SIDNEY, Sir Henry (1529–86), of Penshurst, Kent.

BRACKLEY	1547
KENT	1553 (Mar.), 1563, 1571, 1572

b. 20 July 1529, 1st s. of Sir William Sidney by Anne, da. of Sir Hugh Pagenham, wid. of Thomas Fitzwilliam. m. 29 Mar. 1551, Mary, da. of Sir John Dudley†, afterwards Duke of Northumberland, 3s. inc. Philip* and Robert* 4da. suc. fa. 1553.[1] Kntd. 1551; KG 1564.[2]

Henchman of Henry VIII c.1538; gent. of privy chamber c.1547; royal cupbearer 1550;[3] keeper, Richmond park from c.1552; high steward of honour of

Otford and of Knole park and master of otterhounds 1553; j.p. Kent from c.1555, many Welsh counties from c.1561; many other English counties from c.1573; vice-treasurer [I] 1556–9; ld. justice 1557–8;[4] president, council in the marches of Wales 1559–86; ld. dep. [I] 1565–71, 1575–8; PC July 1575.[5]

Following the appointment of his father as chamberlain of the household to Prince Edward in 1538, Sidney had become intimate with the prince, and between 1547 and 1553 enjoyed greater royal favour than subsequently. His position was made even stronger by his marriage to Northumberland's daughter; it was during this period that he received large crown grants of land, including Penshurst and a number of other Kent manors, together with property in the counties of Gloucester, Lincoln, Nottingham, Surrey and Sussex, and the profits of monastic lands in Yorkshire.[6]

When Edward died, Sidney lost no time in detaching himself from his father-in-law's party and swearing allegiance to Mary. Although 'neither liking nor liked as [he] had been', he kept most of his court offices, earning the favour of Philip of Spain sufficiently for the King to stand godfather to the future Sir Philip Sidney. Between April 1556 and November 1558 he spent most of his time in Ireland, working under the lord deputy, his brother-in-law Thomas Radcliffe, 3rd Earl of Sussex.[7]

Sidney may have hoped for high office under Elizabeth, for his wife's brother, Sir Robert Dudley*, was the chief favourite at court. But the only new appointment he received was that of lord president of the council in the marches of Wales. There seems no doubt that Cecil was at first hostile to him, probably because of his support for the Dudley marriage scheme, but the two men later became firm friends. In April 1562 Sidney was sent to France to offer mediation in the religious wars, but failed in his mission, and on his return went to Scotland with Elizabeth's letter postponing her projected interview with Mary Queen of Scots, on the ground of the Duke of Guise's cruelty to the French protestants. Between 1561 and his departure for Ireland as lord deputy in 1565 he was made a freeman of London, an honorary member of Gray's Inn, and knight of the shire for Kent. In the 1563 Parliament 'Mr.' Sidney had several matters committed to him: felonies (21 Jan.), Mr. Elrington's Surrey iron mills (30 Jan.) and privilege (5, 8 Feb.).[8]

The best account of Sidney's work in Ireland was written by himself, in a long autobiographical letter sent to Walsingham in March 1583. He found 'everything out of joint' there – the inhabitants of the Pale complaining bitterly of the injustice of taxation by 'cess', Shane O'Neill planning rebellion, and the Irish lords unreliable. In his first six-year period as lord deputy, 1565–71, he campaigned vigorously against O'Neill and the Earl of Desmond, improved communications by building roads and bridges (he found by experience that in many places the only way to cross the Shannon quickly was to swim), and began a number of free schools. He had little time to spare for his private affairs, and later blamed his years in Ireland for his heavy debts. It was probably for financial reasons that arrangements for a marriage between Philip Sidney and Sir William Cecil's daughter Anne came to nothing. Several letters from Sir Henry survive, dated 1569 or early 1570, about the plan. In one he confessed, 'Before God, in these matters I am utterly ignorant, as one that never made a marriage in my life'. While the negotiations were still pending, in September 1569, Cecil stood godfather to one of Sidney's younger sons, whom the father had apparently not yet seen. Writing from Dublin to thank the secretary for 'making a Christian' of the child, Sidney claimed at least to have chosen the name, having 'left order that if it were a boy it should have been a William, if a wench Cycell'.

Elizabeth consistently failed to appreciate Sidney's difficulties in Ireland, and during both his periods as lord deputy sent him 'many a bitter letter' accusing him of extravagance. These, he wrote later, had not only 'tired' him, but had so seriously upset Lady Sidney that 'she fell most grievously sick', and was unconscious for two days. He felt this particularly as his wife – formerly, he told Walsingham, 'a most fair lady, to me the fairest' – had lost all her beauty through smallpox following her devoted nursing of Elizabeth, from whom she deserved better treatment. Disputes about the expenses of the Irish administration led to Sidney's recall in March 1571.[9]

He arrived back in England in time to attend Parliament, passing through Shrewsbury on his way, where he was asked to deal with a petition about the sale of Welsh cloth. He is not recorded on any committees in 1571, but he spoke in support of Mildmay's appeal for money to bring Ireland 'into good order'. Again knight of the shire for Kent in 1572, his only recorded activity was a speech in defence of iron mills, 21 May 1572. He was in Ireland by the time the second session met, and though he was again in England for the third in 1581 his name is not mentioned in the journals. However, if he was present in the House during the session he would, as a Privy Councillor, have been entitled to attend committees on (among other matters) the subsidy (25 Jan. 1581), seditious practices (1 Feb.), encumbrances (4 Feb.), the examination of Arthur Hall (6 Feb.), defence (25 Feb.), Dover harbour (6 Mar.) and the Queen's safety (14 Mar.).[10]

Between 1571 and 1575 he spent some time at Ludlow, as president of the council of Wales, proving as efficient as he had been in Ireland. Perhaps by comparison with his previous post, he enjoyed his work in Wales, reporting that 'a better people to govern than the Welsh ... Europe holdeth not'. In 1572 there was a suggestion of making him a peer, but Lady Sidney told Burghley that her husband was not wealthy enough to maintain the necessary state, and the offer was not made.[11]

Since his departure from Ireland the position there had deteriorated, and in July 1575 he was asked to return, with wider powers and more satisfactory financial arrangements. A few days before he left he was sworn a Privy Councillor. For the next three years he worked tirelessly to restore good government, campaigned in Ulster and the South, and made unsuccessful attempts to commute the hated 'cess' for an annual payment of £2,000. By now the value of his administration was better appreciated at home. The Queen might complain that he was 'ever a costly servant, and had alienated ... her good subjects' hearts', but even his enemies admitted that his firm but moderate policy was much more effective than 'rougher dealing'. During his last term of office he made repeated but largely unsuccessful efforts to improve the protestant church in Ireland, suggesting that Irish-speaking ministers might be persuaded to come from Scotland. He also appealed time and again for a standing army in Ireland.

Financial difficulties were once more responsible for his recall early in 1578. He refused to be 'hounded out' of the country, and remained there for another six months, conducting yet another campaign, this time against Rory Oge O'More. When he finally left Ireland, he was seriously ill at Chester for several weeks.[12]

For the last eight years of his life he remained an active Privy Councillor, continuing the re-organization of the council of Wales he had begun before 1575. In January 1579 he was sent to Canterbury to escort Prince John Casimir to London. A suggestion in 1582 that he should go back to Ireland came to nothing. He was able to spend more time than formerly at Penshurst, and was included on several local commissions.[13]

Sidney was a cultured, attractive and genial man. 'You degenerate from your father', he wrote to Philip, 'if you find not yourself most able in wit and body to do anything, when you be most merry'. His household accounts show considerable payments for books, musical instruments and pictures, side by side with entries of his shares in voyages of discovery, and heavy losses at play. By the time he returned from Ireland, however, he was prematurely aged, 'toothless and trembling', as he told Walsingham, and embittered by the Queen's unjust treatment. He died at Ludlow on 5 May 1586; a large train of mourners accompanied his body to Penshurst, the journey and funeral costing over £700.

His will, made in January 1582, was proved on 25 May 1586. The heavy debts he incurred in Ireland had forced him to sell lands which formed part of his wife's jointure, and he made arrangements to compensate her with property in Kent and Lincolnshire to the value of nearly £170. He asked his brothers-in-law, the Earls of Leicester, Warwick and Huntingdon, and his son-in-law, the Earl of Pembroke, to act as overseers, with Philip, the heir, as executor and residuary legatee.[14]

[1] DNB; W. Berry, Co. Genealogies, Kent, 47; Collins, Sidney State Pprs. i. 96; CPR, 1553 and App. Edw. VI, p. 7. [2] Lansd. 94, f. 34; 102, f. 89. [3] SP12/159/1; CPR, 1549-51, p. 174; DNB. [4] APC, iv. 242-3; CPR, 1553 and App. Edw. VI, pp. 201-2; 1555-7, p. 82; 1557-8, pp. 2, 457; 1558-60, p. 120. [5] Stowe, 571, f. 53; Flenley, Cal. Reg. Council, Marches of Wales, 11, 30 et passim; CSP Ire. 1509-73, pp. 265, 441; 1574-85, pp. 77, 142; APC, ix. 11. [6] CSP Ire. 1509-73, pp. 133-159 passim; LP Hen. VIII, xiii (1), p. 213; APC, iv. 19, 196, 242-3; HMC De L'Isle and Dudley, i. 253; Lansd. 10, ff. 186-7; CPR, 1553 and App. Edw. VI, pp. 60-2, 242; 1553-4, pp. 215-17. [7] SP12/159/1; DNB; Collins, Sidney State Pprs. i. 98; CSP Ire. 1509-73. [8] Read, Cecil, 245 seq.; HMC De L'Isle and Dudley, i. 241; D'Ewes, 80, 83, 84; CJ, i. 63, 64, 65. [9] SP12/159/1; Lansd. 102, f. 132; E. Rosenberg, Leicester, Patron of Letters, passim; HMC Hatfield, i. 404-5; CSP Ire. 1509-73, pp. 411, 430, 441. [10] Trans. Salop Arch. Soc. (ser. 1), iii. 270; Trinity, Dublin, Thos. Cromwell's jnl. f. 33; Neale, Parlts. i. 236; D'Ewes, 288, 290, 291, 292, 294, 301, 302, 306. [11] SP12/159/1; CSP Dom. 1547-80, p. 442; 1581-90, pp. 98-9. [12] CSP Dom. Add. 1566-79, p. 287; CSP Ire. 1574-85, pp. 92-3, 142 et passim. [13] DNB; CSP Dom. 1547-80, p. 685. [14] HMC De L'Isle and Dudley, i. 241, 405 et passim; Sidney State Pprs. i. 8-9; Lansd. 50, f. 191 seq.; PCC 27 Windsor.

N.M.F.

SIDNEY, Philip (1554-86), of Penshurst, Kent.

SHREWSBURY	1572*
KENT	1584[1]

b. 1554, 1st s. of Sir Henry Sidney*, and bro. of Robert*. *educ.* Shrewsbury 1564; Christ Church, Oxf. c.1568-71; G. Inn 1568; travelled abroad 1572-7. *m.* 20 Sept. 1583, Frances, da. of Francis Walsingham*, 1da. Kntd. 13 Jan. 1583; *suc.* fa. 5 May 1586.

Member of Earl of Lincoln's embassy to France May-Aug. 1572; on diplomatic mission in Germany with Edward Wotton* Dec. 1574-June 1575; royal cupbearer c.1575; served in Ireland under his fa. 1575-6; envoy to Germany 1577; steward to bishopric of Winchester 1580; general of horse 1583; envoy to France 1584; jt. master of ordnance with Earl of Warwick 1585; gov. Flushing Nov. 1585-d.[2]

Sidney's godfather was King Philip of Spain, the other sponsors at his baptism being the 1st Earl of Bedford and the Duchess of Northumberland. He was related to a number of leading statesmen of Elizabeth's reign. The Earls of Leicester, Warwick, Huntingdon and Sussex were his uncles, the Earl of Pembroke was his brother-in-law, while his own marriage connected him with the Walsinghams, Mildmays, Wentworths and Killigrews, and through the last family with Sir Anthony Cooke*, the Bacons, and Elizabeth's chief minister, William Cecil. Sir Henry Sidney had been careful not to jeopardize his career by showing too much enthusiasm for any one form of religion, but Philip consistently supported the Earls of Leicester and Warwick in their radical protestant policy, even to the extent of risking the loss of Elizabeth's favour by writing a long letter urging her not to marry the Duke of Anjou. The Walsingham marriage strengthened his radical connexions, and he saw the campaign in the

Netherlands (doubtful as he was of its military wisdom) as a crusade against the Catholic enemies of England. It is significant that more than 20 years after his death a Calvinist in Flushing, urging Robert Sidney, Viscount Lisle, to appoint laymen to help a minister in the town, should have commended the 'order brought into this church by your honour's brother ... and confirmed by the Earl of Leicester'. Leicester's patronage was probably more important than any other influence in Sidney's early life, and his reply to the scurrilous *Leycester's Commonwealth* of 1584 expressed loyalty and gratitude to his patron:

I am a Dudley in blood, that Duke's daughter's son, and do acknowledge, though in all truth I may justly affirm that I am by my father's side of ancient and always well-esteemed and well-matched gentry, yet I do acknowledge, I say, that my chiefest honour is to be a Dudley.[3]

After some years at Shrewsbury, where he began his education on the same day as his friend and biographer Fulke Greville*, and at Christ Church (not New College as in his father's household accounts), Sidney went abroad, meeting the protestant scholar Hubert Languet, who remained one of his closest friends. Sidney was in Paris at the time of the St. Bartholomew massacre. His admission to Gray's Inn involved no study of the law. Between December 1574 and the Netherlands campaign, Sidney was employed on several foreign missions. The almost universal admiration felt for him by his contemporaries was expressed by a number of European statesmen, including the Emperor and William of Orange. 'There hath not been any gentleman, I am sure, these many years', wrote Walsingham to Sir Henry Sidney in 1577, 'that hath gone through so honourable a charge with as great commendation as he.' Time has inevitably obscured the fascination of his personality, but a man who won the respect of such contemporaries as William the Silent, Don John of Austria, Languet and Walsingham, must have been unusual by any standard. Charles IX of France appointed him a gentleman of his bedchamber; a tutor at Oxford, Thomas Thoraton, asked that it should be inscribed on his tombstone that Sidney was his pupil; the epitaph on Fulke Greville described him as 'servant to Queen Elizabeth, counsellor to King James, friend to Sir Philip Sidney'; while even the Spanish ambassador, whose policy Sidney had consistently opposed, reported his death to the King of Spain in a despatch condoling with 'poor widow England' on her loss. King Philip wrote on the letter, 'He was my godson'.[4]

Sidney personified the Renaissance ideal. He was handsome in spite of smallpox marks, and the combination of good looks with fine horsemanship and military skill made him a brilliant performer at court tournaments. In 1581 he was one of the four 'foster children of desire' who besieged Elizabeth in her 'fortress of perfect beauty' during an elaborate entertainment for the French envoys. He shared the Elizabethan enthusiasm for seafaring and exploration, contributing to Frobisher's and Gilbert's voyages, and in 1585 wanting to sail with Drake in his projected attack on Spain. A letter from Ralph Lane* at about the same time suggests that Sidney had been considered as governor or general of the Virginian colonists.[5]

Any discussion of Sidney's contribution to English literature lies outside the scope of this biography; it was typical of his genius that he achieved what he did 'in the space of ten years, in the interstices of a life devoted to many other things, to politics, diplomacy, tournaments, travel, translation, love and war'. The autobiographical element in *Astrophel and Stella* is well known, and that Sidney's love for Penelope Devereux was one of the formative elements in his life. The 1st Earl of Essex, who died in 1576, was anxious that Philip should marry Penelope, then in her early teens, but after his death negotiations for the marriage lapsed. Sidney's eventual marriage to Frances Walsingham was happy. Though the Queen at first opposed the match, she was godmother to the daughter, Elizabeth, born in October 1585.[6]

Sidney was a constant visitor at the house of his sister Mary, Countess of Pembroke (for whom he wrote the *Arcadia*), and a generous friend to his younger brother Robert. Loyalty to his father was one of his cardinal principles. With typical generosity, he risked his position at court by championing Sir Henry's conduct of affairs in Ireland during a period (autumn 1577) when the Queen's favour was temporarily lost. He also wrote a treatise on Irish affairs, listing the charges against Sir Henry's government and answering them, 'the most excellently', wrote Edward Waterhouse, 'that ever I have read in my life ... But let no man compare with Mr. Philip's pen'. Philip himself had apparently spent only a short time in Ireland, over the winter of 1575–6, when he took part in the fighting there, but on several later occasions, both from Ireland and from Ludlow, Sir Henry expressed the wish that his eldest son should join him. At one time there was apparently a suggestion that Philip should join the council in the marches of Wales, and in 1582 the elder Sidney agreed to return to Ireland for a further term of office only in the hope that Philip would be given a post there, and would be allowed to succeed him as lord deputy. This scheme did not materialize, and Sir Henry remained at Ludlow.[7]

Between his service in Germany in 1577, and his departure for the Low Countries, Sidney sat twice in Parliament. It looks as though his father asked both Ludlow and Shrewsbury to return him to the 1581 session of the 1572 Parliament, there being a vacancy at each. Both complied, and Sidney chose Shrewsbury, a by-election being held at Ludlow a few days later to replace him. He sat on two committees in 1581: the subsidy (25

Jan.) and slanderous practices (1 Feb.). In 1584 he was elected knight of the shire for Kent. He served on committees dealing with the preservation of Sussex timber (8 Dec.), Sir Walter Ralegh's letters patent (14 Dec.), Rochester bridge (5 Feb. 1585), Jesuits (18 Feb.), the subsidy (24 Feb.), the preservation of timber in Kent (18 Mar.) and a bill about curriers (18 Mar.). There is no evidence that he ever spoke in the House.[8]

By the summer of 1585 Sidney's finances were in a bad way, despite a grant in 1583 of over £2,000 from recusancy fines ('I think my fortune very hard that my fortune must be built on other men's punishments'), the joint mastership of the Ordnance, and several Welsh prebends. Made governor of Flushing, he died 17 Oct. 1586, some three weeks after being wounded in the leg at Zutphen. He had volunteered to take part in the action, and had stripped off his leg armour so as to fight on equal terms with Sir William Pelham, who had come unprovided. His will, drawn up some days before his death, appointed his wife executrix, and made arrangements for the support of the daughter Elizabeth and an expected child who was still-born in December. The supervisors were the Earls of Leicester, Warwick, Huntingdon and Pembroke, together with Sir Francis Walsingham. Walsingham is said to have had to pay over £6,000 out of his own pocket towards debts, funeral expenses, and other charges. Sidney was buried in St. Paul's on 16 Feb. 1587, many of the leading statesmen and courtiers of the day taking part in the funeral procession.[9]

[1] Add. 38823, ff. 17–21. [2] DNB; Berry, Co. Genealogies, Kent, 47; A. Collins, Mems. Lives and Actions of the Sidneys, 98–113; HMC De L'Isle and Dudley, i. 428, 437; F. S. Boas, Sir Philip Sidney, 28; CSP For. 1577–86, passim; Lansd. 39, f. 148; Collins, Sidney State Pprs. i. 393; Leycester Corresp. (Cam. Soc. xxvii), passim. [3] Sydney State Pprs. i. 287 seq.; HMC De L'Isle and Dudley, iii. 373–4; Boas, 8. [4] DNB; Lansd. 117, ff. 198, 214; Sidney State Pprs. i. 287 seq.; Boas, 35, 189; Fulke Greville, Life of Sir Philip Sidney, passim. [5] A. C. Judson, Sidney's Appearance, 14–16; E. K. Chambers, Eliz. Stage, i. 144; E. St. John Brooks, Sir Christopher Hatton, 136; Collins, Mems. 101–2; Lansd. 24, f. 159; P. Sidney, Sidneys of Penshurst, 101 n.; DNB; Boas, 173. [6] Boas, 104 et passim; D. Daiches, Critical Hist. of Eng. Literature, i. 166–200, 222–3; K. Muir, Sir Philip Sidney, 12–13, 35; Lansd. 102, f. 149; HMC Hatfield, i. 415–16; Sidney State Pprs. i. 147; HMC De L'Isle and Dudley, i. 272–3; Wards 7/22/114; Genealogist, n.s. ii. 295. [7] Daiches, i. 197; Sidney State Pprs. i. passim; Sidneys of Penshurst, 67; HMC De L'Isle and Dudley, i. 428, 437; ii. 97. [8] CJ, i. 120, 121; D'Ewes, 288, 337, 339, 346, 352, 356, 368, 370; Ludlow corp. mss 6046, f. 293. See also LUDLOW and SHREWSBURY. [9] HMC Hatfield, ii. 432; Sidneys of Penshurst, 97–8; Boas, 164; Sidney State Pprs. i. 393; Lansd. 39, f. 148; HMC De L'Isle and Dudley, i. 271; P. H. Williams, Council in the Marches of Wales, 128; Greville, passim; Collins, Mems. passim; CSP For. 1585–6, p. 130 et passim; June 1586–Mar. 1587, pp. 213, 217–18; CSP Dom. Add. 1580–1625, p. 191; CPR, 1560–3, pp. 404–5; Leycester Corresp. 453–4; Wards 7/22/114; DNB.

N.M.F./J.J.C.

SIDNEY, Robert (1563–1626), of Penshurst, Kent.[1]

GLAMORGANSHIRE	1584, 1593
KENT	1597

b. 19 Nov. 1563, 2nd s. of Sir Henry Sidney*, and bro. of Philip*. educ. Christ Church, Oxf. 1575–9; travelled abroad 1579–81. m. (1) 23 Sept. 1584, Barbara (d. 1621), da. and h. of John Gamage of Coity, Glam. by Gwenlleian, wid. of Watkin Thomas, at least 5s. 8da.; (2) 1625, Sarah (d. ?1655), da. and h. of William Blount, wid. of Thomas Smythe II* of Sutton-at-Hone. Kntd. 7 Oct. 1586; suc. bro. 17 Oct. 1586; cr. Baron Sidney 1603; Visct. Lisle 1605; KG 1616; Earl of Leicester 1618.[2]

J.p. Glam. from c.1584, Kent from 1593, Suss. temp. Jas. I; capt. in the Low Countries 1585–8; capt. of the fort at Rammekins; capt. of light horse, Tilbury 1588; special envoy to Scotland Aug.–Sept. 1588, to France Jan.–Apr. 1594, to the Elector 1613; gov. Flushing June 1589[3]–May 1616; ld. chamberlain to Queen Anne 14 July 1603–19, surveyor-gen. of her revenues 10 Nov. 1603; member of the Queen's council 1604, of council in the marches of Wales; commr. eccles. causes 1620; member, council of war for the Palatinate.

While Robert Sidney displayed neither the political acumen and administrative ability of his father, nor the youthful energy and creative genius of his elder brother, it would be unfair to maintain that he owed his position at the court of James I only to birth and influence. Such rewards were just as much due to the many years of loyal service he gave to Elizabeth. During her reign he was able to show that he shared much of his family's military skill, and the diplomatic tasks which came his way he conducted with tact and efficiency. His failure to secure a number of prominent appointments in the 1590s, when he enjoyed the mixed blessing of the Earl of Essex's patronage, seems to have exhausted his ambitions, and though he enjoyed James's favour, he either was not permitted, or, more probably, did not desire to make the move from courtier to statesman. As a result, his later years were passed listening to gossip in the Queen's presence chamber rather than to political discussion round the council table. He lacked political judgment, was unable to communicate easily, was selfish and indolent, but his intellectual ability, his long experience of continental affairs, and his personal bravery should have earned him better treatment than he received, especially at the hands of Elizabeth. In a way, Sidney's birth and parentage proved a handicap. 'Follow your discreet and virtuous brother's rule', his father told him, and throughout his life he had to try to live up to Philip's example. There was nine years' difference in their ages and throughout his childhood – mainly spent at Ludlow castle, from which his father administered the Welsh marches – and his university career at Oxford, he must have been constantly aware of the fame which Philip was achieving. Clearly, he endeavoured to emulate him. His two years on the Continent were important in deciding his future career. He lived extravagantly, in Germany for the most part, but found time to perfect his knowledge of Dutch and to learn the military skills. If there are any good wars, go to them, Philip told him, accompanying his advice with affectionate greetings and financial aid.[4]

Sidney made a fortunate marriage. Barbara Gamage brought him lands and wealth, and proved an affectionate and loyal wife. The marriage took place in dramatic circumstances. When Barbara's father died, Sir Edward Stradling[†], of St. Donat's castle, became her guardian. As one of the wealthiest heiresses in Wales – her estates were worth more than £1,000 a year – she had many suitors, but the Queen ordered that she be brought to court where her future could be decided. Apparently attracted by the young Robert Sidney, however, she persuaded her guardian to arrange an immediate marriage. The story that the ceremony took place in the chapel at St. Donat's, only a few hours before a messenger arrived from the Queen forbidding it, may have become embellished by the passage of time, but there is no doubt that their union antagonized several prominent people. The outcome was that, combined with his father's position in the marches and his sister's marriage to the Earl of Pembroke, Sidney was now one of the most important men on the Welsh border. He was elected to Parliament for Glamorganshire on or near his twenty-first birthday. Sir Henry Sidney asked for Stradling's support, and Pembroke wrote in a similar vein:

> These are to request you that you will give your election, with such friends as you can procure, unto my brother Robert Sidney, that by your means, with the residue of my friends and freeholders there, he may be chosen knight of the shire ... for the which he shall demand no charge of the country at all.

There is no record of any activity by Sidney in this Parliament, although he could have served on the subsidy committee on 24 Feb. 1585, by reason of his being knight of the shire.[5]

In the autumn of 1585 Sidney joined the expedition to the Low Countries led by his uncle, the Earl of Leicester, and with Sir Philip Sidney among its captains. Philip, who was governor of Flushing, appointed his brother as his deputy, in charge of the fort at Rammekins. Robert fought at Zutphen, where his brother was mortally wounded. Philip's death, following shortly after that of his father and mother, meant that Robert came into possession of Penshurst and had to live up to Philip's enhanced and now posthumous reputation.[6]

The Earl of Leicester, his close relative, assumed the task of looking after his nephew's interests. He knighted him shortly after Zutphen and, on Sidney's return to England after two years' successful campaigning, was instrumental in furthering his career. He may have helped him to acquire a command in the camp at Tilbury in the summer of 1588, and almost certainly persuaded the Queen to make him her special envoy to James VI of Scotland after the defeat of the Armada. Burghley suggested a peerage

for him at this time. When Sidney had to hurry back to London on hearing of Leicester's death, James, who had enjoyed his company, was 'marvellously sorry'. At a later date, Sidney was to take advantage of this personal familiarity with the Scottish King.[7]

With the death of his patron, Sidney's chances of advancement at home lessened considerably, so he resumed his military career on the Continent. After taking part in Norris and Drake's expedition to Portugal, he was appointed, in the summer of 1589, to the most important post of his life, the governorship of Flushing, which he was to retain until the town was given up to the Dutch in 1616, though he rarely visited it after the death of Elizabeth. Flushing's strategic importance kept Sidney fully occupied but his view that nothing else mattered as long as Flushing was safe must have irritated those at home. He bombarded ministers with letters bewailing the lack of supplies and money. In 1595, for example, he urged Burghley to take action or the town would be lost:

> Calais is a fresh and grievous example of a place thought invincible and lost within eleven days ... I trust her Majesty's reign shall not be touched for the like mishap.

At that moment strength was added to his words by a Catholic plot to seize the fortress. After Catholic agents had failed to secure a set of keys by bribery, they urged Sidney to join them in overthrowing the Queen, assuring him that they wished him 'to be a greater man than he is'. He may have exaggerated the dangers to Flushing, but he was certainly no traitor, and it is difficult to understand how such well informed Catholic agents as Griffin Jones and Henry Walpole could have seriously considered the possibility of his being one. Perhaps they were misled by his increasing disgust at the course his career was taking.[8]

To begin with, an important governorship had seemed the perfect way to increase his chances of advancement, but when the call home to high or lucrative office never came, he realised that he had been passed over. Refused leave of absence, he asserted 'a horse is more gently used, for yet a bit is sought out ... that may be most pleasing to him'; still, between 1589 and 1603 he spent more time in England than at Flushing. 'I see Flushing must be the grave of my youth, and, I fear, of my fortune also', he bewailed in 1597, and two years later:

> I have been governor there now ten years and have got neither reputation nor profit, but rather lost thereby, seeing that all of my own rank have been preferred, and some that were behind me set on a level with me or before me. And if now I go back without any sign of the Queen's acceptance of my service, the world may well say that the place I had I got by chance, since, after so long continuance of it, I am not thought worthy of any more. I know the Queen thinks she has done much for me in giving me the government, and I thank her for it, and yet, but for her service, I could wish I had never known the place.

What perhaps annoyed him most was the government's apparent indifference towards him after a series of military and diplomatic successes. He was in Brittany, for example, in 1593, and the following year visited Henri IV of France. He saw the French King again in 1596, and, with Sir Francis Vere*, led the armies in the field in 1597. His brilliant cavalry charge shattered the enemy at the battle of Turnhout, but a letter from his aunt, the Countess of Warwick, advised him that the Queen 'will not thank you for being there'. His frustration in such circumstances can be readily understood.[9]

With hope of promotion turning to despair, it was only natural that he should seek out the support of a powerful patron close to the Queen, and here is the reason for his close ties with the Earl of Essex, who had married Philip Sidney's widow. At first the Cecils seemed to offer the best prospects of promotion. In 1591 Roland White, Sidney's indefatigable agent at court, who kept him closely in touch with all the gossip, urged him to stick to Burghley: 'Old Saturnus is a melancholy and wayward planet, but yet predominant here'; and as late as 1594 Sidney told his wife: 'I hope to have my Lord Treasurer and Sir Robert Cecil my friends'. But it was becoming clear by that date that the rift between Essex and the Cecils was too great for any man to have a foot in both camps, and Sidney chose the Earl. From about 1594 the letters between them became more and more friendly. 'More could be done with Essex than by any other means', White told his master, and Sidney soon began to rely almost entirely on Essex's influence to gain him a suitable appointment:

> When my brother and my uncles died, all their offices, great and small, were given away from me. Since that time I have not left to continue the doing her Majesty's service, and if nothing will light upon me, I must think I deserve very ill or have very ill luck.

Between about 1593 and 1598 Essex sought by various means to acquire a succession of posts for his new ally at Flushing. These included the offices of vice-chamberlain and lord chamberlain, the presidency of the council in the Welsh marches, together with a seat on the Privy Council and a peerage, and, perhaps most significant of all, the wardenship of the Cinque Ports. As well as a test of Essex's power at court, this became a battle for supremacy in Kent between Sidney and Lord Cobham. When it appeared that the wardenship might shortly fall vacant, Essex told White that he held 'nobody so fit' for the office as Sidney. 'If my Lord of Essex is able to do anything it will now appear', White reported, but the doubts which he had always held proved to be justified. Essex overplayed his hand and the office remained in the Cobham family. At this news Sidney, forced to follow the contest from Flushing, gave way to another bout of despair and injured pride. What annoyed him most was the suggestion that because he was not a peer he must be inferior to Lord Cobham:

> I am sure I had a grandfather, a duke, and an uncle that in their time bore the greatest sway in England; and my father, though he were no baron, possessed as great places of commandment as her Majesty can give away, and if they were still alive, I durst say I had not done anything why they should be ashamed of me. But her Majesty will have a baron in that place. I would to God that the Spaniards would run away at the title of a baron, or that it would keep our men from running away, otherwise I fear me our country of Kent and Sussex will be honourably left to be spoiled and burnt.

It has sometimes been claimed that Sidney clung to Essex's party while it was to his advantage but, at the critical moment in 1601, abandoned the Earl to his fate. This suggestion is unwarranted. At least two years earlier their friendship was becoming cooler and, in fact, it was Essex who began the process. As early as 1597 White wrote: 'That you shall receive benefit by his love I have some cause to doubt', and in 1599 he warned Sidney that the Earl was not to be trusted. Sidney, for his part, may have realised that his alliance with a falling star was a hindrance. His appearance as spokesman for the government at the time of the Essex rebellion in 1601, to try to persuade Essex to surrender since his cause was lost, was not a sudden treacherous act: it simply suggests that, because of their former relationship, his tongue would probably be the most persuasive. In the same way his renewal of friendly correspondence with Robert Cecil took place a long time before the crisis.[10]

During the 1590s Sidney was elected to Parliament twice more. In 1593 he sat for Glamorganshire for the second time, serving on subsidy committees (26 Feb., 1, 3 Mar.) and others concerning alien merchants (6 Mar.), the poor (12 Mar.), maimed soldiers (30 Mar.) and reducing disloyal subjects to their true obedience (4 Apr.). He was in the Netherlands at the time of the 1597 election and must have been delighted to hear from his agent: 'I understand that my Lord Cobham was much grieved to see that you … had the chief place given you by the voices of the people, which he would not have believed'. But when Sidney had not arrived in England two weeks later, some attempt seems to have been made to arrange a new election. This came to nothing but it is doubtful whether Sidney returned to England during the course of the Parliament. The journals do not mention his name, and it would be unwise to assume that he took part in the work of the important committees to which the knights of the shire were appointed. There was also a contested election in Kent in 1601, which developed into a struggle between Sidney and Lord Cobham. Sidney supported Sir Henry Neville II*, and Cobham Francis Fane*. About a month before the election Sidney received at Flushing a report on Neville's chances of victory.

> Finding your lordship's great desire to advance the party for Sir Henry Neville, I did presently practise in all

places near about Penshurst, and the next day sent farther off. I am in good hope that you shall be very well satisfied, and shall carry with you a very good troop ... If your lordship could be here, it would give great encouragement to many that otherwise will be afraid to show themselves against the other competitors ... I hope, by the next, to send you the names, and number, of all such as will go for your lordship out of every quarter.

Sidney did come over, but Cobham's candidate won the senior seat and Neville the junior. It would be interesting to know how Sidney reacted to Cobham's downfall in 1603. Even then the lord lieutenancy and the wardenship went to other men. Perhaps county supremacy had, by then, lost its importance for Sidney.[11]

With the accession of James I, Sidney's life changed completely. Gone was the frustration, and fear that he was forgotten while rivals gained all the honours. Just as the court gossips predicted, he received immediate tokens of the new sovereign's favour: the peerage which he had sought for so long, numerous lucrative grants, and a place in the Queen's household. Now that he was living in England the flow of letters between Flushing and London, so revealing of his hopes and opinions, dries up, and it is not easy to see whether he was at last content or not. The last 20 years of his life were spent either at court or at his beloved Penshurst. He corresponded with leading men, patronised the arts and new colonial and trading ventures, undertook an occasional diplomatic mission, such as a visit to Germany in 1613, but his life was without dramatic incident. Though he rarely visited Flushing the governorship had become profitable, and when it was at last decided to abandon the town in 1616, he obtained by way of compensation an additional £1,200 a year, the Garter, and a colonelcy for his son. Finally he paid heavily for the earldom of Leicester.[12]

In his last years Sidney suffered from poor health. He died at Penshurst on 13 July 1626, aged 62, and was buried there three days later. He left no will, and administration of his vast estates went to his second wife and to his fourth, but only surviving son, Robert, who succeeded to his titles and possessions.[13]

[1] There is no full biography of Robert Sidney. The main sources used have been: *HMC De L'Isle and Dudley*, vols. i–v; Collins, *Sidney State Pprs.* 2 vols; *CP*; *DNB*; Doyle, *Official Baronetage*. [2] P. Sidney, *Sidneys of Penshurst*, passim. geneal. table at end. [3] Most sources give the date as July 1588, but he received letters of instruction on his appointment 27 June 1589, *CSP For.* 1589 (Jan.–July), pp. 343–4; *APC*, xvii. 421–6. [4] *HMC De L'Isle and Dudley*, ii. 268–71; Collins, i. 271–2, 283–5; *Sidneys of Penshurst*, 126; *CSP For.* 1581–2, p. 336; H. R. F. Bourne, *Sir Philip Sidney*, 176, 213, 225–6, 235–6. [5] P. H. Williams, *Council in the Marches of Wales*, 243–5; *Stradling Corresp.* ed. Traherne, 3, 11, 21–2, 77; J. Cartwright, '*Sacharissa*', 8–9; Lansd. 43, anon. jnl. f. 171. [6] *HMC De L'Isle and Dudley*, ii. 218; *CSP For.* passim; *CSP Span.* 1580–6, p. 554; *Leycester Corresp.* (Cam. Soc. xxvii), 338; Bourne, 323, 340–1, 344; *HMC Ancaster*, 216, 504. [7] *CSP For.* 1586–7, p. 214; *HMC Foljambe*, 45, 52; *HMC Bath*, v. 97; *HMC De L'Isle and Dudley*, ii. 101; *CSP Scot.* 1586–8, passim; Read, *Walsingham*, iii. 340; Camden, *Eliz.*

(1688), pp. 418–19. [8] *HMC Ancaster*, 246, 261–2; Lansd. 77, f. 155; *CSP Dom.* passim; *HMC Hatfield*, iv. 293; v. 409–12; xiii. 509; *APC*, xxviii. 293–5; *Chamberlain Letters* ed. McClure, i. passim; Birch, *Mems.* i. 303–7; ii. 251–2. [9] *HMC Hatfield*, vii. 24–6, 28–32, 133, 211; ix. 141–3; Collins, i. 114; Stowe 166, f. 78; C. Markham, *The Fighting Veres*, 181, 184, 255–6, 261, 304 n.; *CSP Dom.* 1591–4, pp. 444, 482; 1595–7, passim; 1598–1601, p. 445; *HMC De L'Isle and Dudley*, ii. 144–8, 472, 474, 477–8; Wright, *Queen Eliz. and her Times*, ii. 431; Birch, *Mems.* i. 146–7, 151, 158, 170, 465; Sloane 33, f. 2; Add. 15552, f. 5. [10] Collins, i. 331; ii. 87; *HMC De L'Isle and Dudley*, ii. 153, 238, 246, 276, 281, 314, 389, 391, 397, 398, 421, 473, 479; Birch, *Mems.* ii. 176; *HMC Hatfield*, v. 409, 440–2; vii. 12–13, 62–3, 108–9, 115, 132–3, 198, 225; viii. 29; ix. 157, 188; x. 408, 430; E. K. Chambers, *Sir Henry Lee*, 170–2; *CSP Dom.* 1598–1601, p. 550; Neale, *Commons*, 214–15; Sloane 1856, ff. 11–13. [11] D'Ewes, 474, 481, 486, 489, 499, 512, 517; *HMC Hatfield*, iv. 295; Collins, ii. 62, 231; Neale, 71–5; *Manningham Diary* (Cam. Soc. xcix), 13. [12] *HMC De L'Isle and Dudley*, iii. 19, 27; v. 107–113, 340; *HMC Hatfield*, xvi. 163; *HMC Downshire*, ii. 219; iii. passim; Nichols, *Progresses Jas. I*, ii. 612–21; iii. 488–9; Collins, i. 118; *Chamberlain Letters*, i. 542; *APC*, 1615–16, pp. 514, 541–2, 545–8, 551; *Sidneys of Penshurst*, 134.

M.R.P.

SKEFFINGTON, John (1534–1604), of White Ladies, Salop, Fisherwicke Park and Brewood, Staffs.

NEWCASTLE-UNDER-LYME 1559

b. 1534, 1st s. of William Skeffington of White Ladies and Fisherwicke by Joan (Elizabeth), da. of James Leveson of Lilleshall, Salop and Trentham, Staffs. *educ.* Queens', Camb. 1552; I. Temple 1556. *m.* by 1563, Alice, da. of Sir Thomas Cave of Stanford, Northants., 1s. 1da. *suc.* fa. 1551.[1]

Skeffington's grandfather was a merchant of the staple and sheriff of London who invested in land and founded a branch of the family which by 1559 was of almost equal importance with the Skeffingtons of Skeffington, Leicestershire. Skeffington himself was content with the role of country gentleman, and married into one of the leading Staffordshire families, but his brother George, like his grandfather, was a merchant of the staple.

At his father's death John was still under age, and his wardship was sold to John Ryder, cofferer of the King's Household. He was granted livery of his Yorkshire lands – a group of manors in Holderness – in 1555, and presumably of his other lands at the same time. His interests seem to have been primarily bound up in his estates and their augmentation, for he played no part in county affairs in spite of his connexion with the Levesons and, after his mother's third marriage, the Giffords. His lands in Staffordshire were concentrated in the south-western quarter, at Barr, West Bromwich, Goscote, Rushall, Walsall, Bloxwich, Penn and Wombourn, and in 1563 he settled these upon his wife as her jointure, together with lands at Hornsey, Middlesex, and Walpole, Norfolk. His choice of a wife suggests that Skeffington preferred to maintain close relations with his Leicestershire cousins, rather than with the Staffordshire gentry among whom his father had sought alliances. Alice

Cave was the daughter of a neighbour of the Skeffingtons of Skeffington and her sister married William Skeffington†, the contemporary representative of that branch of the family. The connexion was further strengthened when, after Sir Thomas Cave's death, John Skeffington's brother, James, married Alice's mother.[2]

It may be presumed that Skeffington was already well-known to the Caves of Stanford, and particularly to Alice's uncle, Sir Ambrose*, by December 1558, when the election writs for Elizabeth's first Parliament went out. Sir Ambrose was chancellor of the duchy of Lancaster and as such was able to secure a seat for Skeffington at Newcastle-under-Lyme. It is probable that Skeffington was a convinced protestant, which would have made his return to this Parliament particularly welcome. There is no direct evidence on this point, but what the alliance with the Caves suggests is confirmed by the attitude of other members of the family. The Parliament of 1559 was his sole incursion into public life. Thereafter he returned to the cultivation of his estates. He was tenacious of his rights and in 1561 was involved in a lawsuit concerning some manors in Northamptonshire and Warwickshire, which the Queen ordered Lord Keeper Bacon to settle. By 1566 he was increasing his holdings in south-western Staffordshire by purchase, and it may have been this which gave him the excuse of pleading poverty in 1570, when approached for a privy seal loan of £50. His petition to be excused was supported by the justices of Staffordshire, by his mother-in-law, and by his brother-in-law Roger Cave, who wrote to Sir William Cecil on his behalf. Still, he left an unencumbered estate to his son, who was able to buy a baronetcy in 1627.[3]

Skeffington died at Fisherwicke 7 Nov. 1604, and was buried at St. Michael's Lichfield on the following day. His son William had been playing an active part in his father's and the county's affairs for several years. No will or inquisition post mortem has been found.[4]

[1] Shaw, *Staffs.* i. 372–3; *Vis. Leics.* (Harl. Soc. ii), 110–12; *CPR*, 1558–60, p. 231; C142/93/61, 94/66. [2] *Erdeswick's Surv. Staffs.* 461; C142/49/44, 50/95; Wards 9/154; Poulson, *Holderness*, ii. 31–2; Shaw, loc. cit.; *Colls. Hist. Staffs.* (Wm. Salt Arch. Soc.) xvii. 215. [3] PCC 3 Lewyn, 28 Darcy; Pennington and Roots, *Committee at Stafford 1643–5*, 354; Kidson, *Gentry of Staffs. 1662–3*, 28–9; *CSP Dom.* 1547–80, pp. 171, 386; *Colls. Hist. Staffs.* (Wm. Salt Arch. Soc.) xiii. 263, 277; xv. 132,135, 149; xvi. 159. [4] Shaw, *Staffs.* i. 339, 341.

I.C.

SKEFFINGTON, Thomas (1550–1600), of Skeffington, Leics.

LEICESTERSHIRE 1593

b. 1550, 1st s. of William Skeffington† by Mary, da. of Thomas Cave of Stanford, Northants. *educ.* Jesus, Camb., fellow commoner 1564. *m.* Isabella, da. of Sir John Byron of Newstead, Notts., 4s. 9da. *suc.* fa. 1571.[1]
J.p. Leics. from c.1577, sheriff 1576–7, 1588–9, 1599–1600, commr. musters 1580, 1596.[2]

Coming from an established Leicestershire family holding estates estimated in the early seventeenth century to be worth £1,500, Skeffington was obviously of sufficient status to take a turn as knight of the shire. As such he may have attended a subsidy committee, 26 Feb. 1593, and a legal committee, 9 Mar. 1593. He raised 2,000 troops to send to Tilbury at the time of the Armada, and whenever a delicate or difficult matter arose, such as obliging officials to take the oaths imposed upon them by statute, Skeffington was almost automatically included on the commission. His decisions were not always popular in the town of Leicester: his under-sheriff was sued by the Queen's bailiff for infringement of liberties, and he annoyed the town council by fining some of the 24 who failed to appear when summoned to form part of a jury. But when he wrote in favour of Thomas Wurshippe for the post of mace bearer to the mayor, the town council acceded to his wishes.[3]

He maintained, at Skeffington and at Arley in Warwickshire, a considerable household which included various of his relatives and also his wards, such as his cousin Thomas Belgrave. He sent his eldest surviving son to his own Cambridge college, Jesus, placing him in the care of a master, Anthony Cade, who was later to achieve prominence as tutor and chaplain to George, Duke of Buckingham. Cade's moderate religious views evidently found favour with Skeffington, who left him the next presentation to the vicarage of Billesdon.[4]

Skeffington died 11 May 1600 and was buried in the chancel at Skeffington. His purchased property he left in trust for his younger surviving son John, while his daughters received marriage portions of £400 apiece. The next generation, however, was to see the end of the main branch of the family. His son and heir William was involved in a riot with his cousin, Mr. Burrows, within a few weeks of succeeding to the estates, and when he died without issue in 1605, his widow married her groom, Michael Bray. This was so deeply resented by her brother-in-law, John Skeffington, that disputes between the two men ended in a brawl in which both were killed.[5]

[1] *Vis. Leics.* (Harl. Soc. ii), 7–8, 110–12; Nichols, *Leics.* iii(1), p. 448; C142/161/97. [2] *APC*, xii. 37; xxvi. 56. [3] Nichols, iii(1), p. 448; *Chamberlain Letters* ed. McClure, i. 486; D'Ewes, 474, 496; *CSP Dom.* 1581–90, p. 275; 1590–4, p. 125; *APC*, xi. 290; xii. 37; xx. 266; xxi. 187; xxii. 63; xxiii. 258; xxvi. 57; *Leicester Recs.* iii. 173, 182, 220, 271. [4] PCC 35 Wallop; ms cal. and index pat. rolls, 17–30 Eliz. PRO 28(1) p. 1; Leicester Recs. iii. 255; J. Venn, *Gonville and Caius Coll. Biog. Hist.* i. 109. [5] C142/263/89, 261/35; PCC 35 Wallop; ms cal. and index pat. rolls, 17–30 Eliz. PRO 18(11) p. 23, 28(11) p. 21; 37–43 Eliz. PRO 43(21) p. 38; *Leicester Recs.* iii. 427–8; Nichols, ii(2), 434; *Chamberlain Letters*, i. 486.

S.M.T.

SKINNER, John (c.1535–84), of Reigate, Surr.

REIGATE 1559, 1572

b. c.1535, 1st s. of John Skinner† of Reigate by Anne, da. of Thomas or Walter Newdigate. *educ*. M. Temple 1553. *m*. by 1569, Alice, da. of John Poyntz†, of Alderley, Glos., *s.p. suc*. gt.-uncle James Skinner† 1558, fa. c.1571.

J.p. Surr. by 1568, commr. musters 1569.[1]

Between 1350 and 1572 members of the Skinner family represented Reigate at least 25 times, in addition to gaining Surrey county seats on several occasions. Much of Skinner's inherited property was leased from the Howards of Effingham, lords of the manor of Reigate and parliamentary patrons for the borough. The 1559 return styled Skinner, 'junior, of Reigate, gent.', to distinguish him from his father, who was living in the borough, and who eventually left him the rectory manor of Reigate, the manors of Burstow, Hathersham and Horne, and lands in Woodmansterne, Ewell, Horley and elswhere in Surrey. One of his responsibilities was to administer an annuity left to his sister Dorothy, who was not likely to 'come to ... advancement' by marriage, being 'a woman not most quickest in wit'. There is little evidence that Skinner significantly increased his inheritance: about 1569 he bought the manor of Hartswood and other property in the Reigate district, and by 1581 was leasing property at Banstead.[2]

For many years Skinner was an active local official. The bishops' letters to the Council in 1564, praising his father as 'an indifferent minister of justice', recommended that John the younger should be added to the Surrey commission of the peace. This advice had been taken by March 1568, when father and son both signed a letter to William More I* about putting down vagabondage in the county. There are several references to the younger Skinner in connexion with Surrey musters: after he had become head of the family, his assessment was ten lances, to which 'one light horse' was later added, and in 1583 he and William Howard* 'craved longer day' when they were accused of defaulting on their quota. He was one of the commission set up in February 1574 to inquire whether subsidy assessments had been paid. Little information survives about his personal affairs. In April 1569 he was quarrelling with a 'Mr. Harris', and William More and other Surrey gentlemen were appointed to act as 'referees'. In a letter to More, Skinner asked that the arbitrators should either reach some decision and put an end to the dispute, or allow the case to go to law. Though no connexion has been found between the Reigate MP and Guildford, he was probably the John Skinner who about 1580 gave 20*s*. to the free school there.[3]

Some doubt might be thought to exist about his return for Reigate in 1572, as one of the three Crown Office lists has 'mortuus' in the margin against the name. However, as the return has 'John Skinner, esq. of Reigate', and Skinner's father died between August 1570 and 16 Feb. 1572, when his will was proved, it could not have been he who was returned. The only other namesake found was

the serjeant of the woodyard, whose will indicates no connexion with Reigate. It is therefore evident that the marginal entry on only one list, mentioned above, is an error.

Skinner's will, made 8 May 1584 shortly before his death, states that he had no children and was 'not likely to have (God doeth all things for the best)'. His coheirs were two sisters, Margaret Knight and Elizabeth Sands, and a nephew Richard Elliott. The will, proved 27 June the same year, is long and diffuse, ending with a statement of religious belief in which Skinner declared himself assured of remission of sins through Christ, who 'by that one oblation and once sacrificing His immaculate body upon the altar of the cross' had made salvation possible. There were bequests to his widow, the sole executrix, to his brother-in-law William Poyntz, and for the marriage of the latter's daughter Anne. £10 was to be given to the poor of Reigate, and £40 to the repair of the parish church there. The testator's 'especial good friend Sir Thomas Heneage*', one of the overseers, received a horse and a hawk. The widow remarried, and on 12 Aug. 1606 a grant of administration of the estate was made to Richard Elliott, Alice Skinner *alias* Palmer not having carried out her duties.[4]

[1] Manning and Bray, *Surr*. i. 319, 321–5; Harl. 897, f. 40; PCC 6 Daper, 6 Watson; *VCH Surr*. iii. 225, 243; *Surr. Arch. Colls*. xi. 195; *Surr. Rec. Soc*. iii(10), p. 137. [2] C142/204/123(1); *VCH Surr*. iii. 174, 235, 238; PCC 6 Daper, 6 Watson; H. C. M. Lambert, *Banstead*, ii. 107. [3] *Cam. Misc*. ix(3), pp. 56–7; *HMC 7th Rep*. 620–5; *Surr. Rec. Soc*. loc. cit.; *CSP Dom*. 1547–80, p. 440; Manning and Bray, i. 76 n. [4] PCC 17 Daper, 6 Watson; C142/204/123(1).

N.M.F.

SKINNER, Ralph (1513/14–63), of Durham.

LEICESTER	1547
PENRYN	1553 (Oct.)
?PENRYN	1554 (Apr.)
BOSSINEY	1555
WESTBURY	1559

b. 1513/14. *educ*. Winchester 1528; New Coll. Oxf. BA 1536, fellow 1531–8, MA by 1551. ? *m*. c.1538, Elizabeth, da. of one Ellis, *s.p.*

Lay rector of Broughton Astley, Leics. 1550–3; pro-warden New Coll. 1551–3; warden, Sherburn hospital, Durham 1559; dean of Durham 1560; chancellor and receiver gen. palatinate of Durham c.1561; member, council in the north from Jan. 1561; commr. to enforce Acts of Uniformity and Supremacy, province of York 1561; j.p.q. Yorks. (N. Riding), and diocese of Durham from c.1561; rector of Sedgefield, co. Dur. 1562–*d*.

After opposing government measures in Mary's first Parliament, showing himself a courageous speaker in the Commons in April 1554, and voting against a government measure in 1555, Skinner did not sit in 1558. He was returned in 1559 for Westbury, by whose intervention is not clear – perhaps that of the 6th Lord Mountjoy or one of the Seymour family. It was probably he rather than John Skinner (15 Apr. 1559), with John Carnsew*, who had a certain Thrower, servant of the master of the rolls, brought before the bar for 'evil words' against the House. Some six months later, having been taken up by Archbishop Parker, Skinner was ordained (26 Jan. 1560), and made dean of Durham, the installation being in the following March. It was obviously thought necessary to do something to promote the Elizabethan settlement in a conservative part of the country, and his appointment was specifically stated to be 'on account of the scarcity of learned and good ministers of the gospel in the north'. He was himself troubled about his previous views, preaching a sermon in 1561 against a book he had printed (no details of it are given), which he now described as 'very heresy'. Considering his character, he might well have become a bishop in time, but he died in January 1563, being buried on the 21st at Sedgefield. No will or inquisition post mortem has been traced.

G. Burnet, *Hist. Reformation*, ed. Pocock, ii. 447–8; T. F. Kirby, *Winchester Scholars*, 115; Wood, *Fasti Oxon.* ed. Bliss, i. 102; *LP Hen. VIII*, xvii, p. 126; NRA 6229, no. 97; Reid, *Council of the North*, 494; *CPR*, 1558–60, pp. 5, 390; 1560–3, pp. 61, 170–1, 341; Bodl. e Museo 17; Guildford Mus. Loseley 1331/2; *CJ*, i. 59; Strype, *Grindal*, 73; *Parker*, i. 173; *Annals* i(1), p. 402; *CSP Dom.* 1547–80, p. 161; Le Neve, *Fasti*, ed. Hardy, iii. 299; W. Hutchinson, *Hist. Durham*, ii. 142–3.

N.M.F.

SKINNER, Vincent (d.1616), of Thornton College, Lincs. and London.

TRURO	1571
BARNSTAPLE	1572
BOSTON	1584, 1586, 1589
BOROUGHBRIDGE	1593
ST. IVES	1597
PRESTON	1604

o.s. of John Skinner of Thorpe by Wainfleet by Elizabeth, da. of John Fairfax of Swarby and Thorpe by Wainfleet. *educ.* Trinity Coll. Camb. 1557, scholar 1560, BA and fellow 1561, MA 1564; incorp. Oxf. 1566; L. Inn 1565. *m.* (1) Audrey, da. of Richard Ogle of Pinchbeck, wid. of John Man* of Bolingbroke, *s.p.*; (2) Elizabeth, da. of Robert Fowkes, wid. of Edward Middlemore of Enfield, Mdx., 1s. Kntd. 1603.[1]

Sec. to Lord Burghley by 1575/6–93;[2] escheator, Lincs. 1573–4; receiver of duchy of Lancaster lands in Lincs. in reversion 1575, in office by 1581; duchy of Lancaster feodary, Lincs. from Sept. 1582; constable of Bolingbroke castle Apr. 1583, of Lincoln castle May 1583; j.p. Lincs. (Lindsey) from c.1593; writer of tallies and auditor of the receipt of the Exchequer 1593–1609; keeper of Kirkby park, Lincs. 1604.

Thomas Cartwright, the greatest of Elizabethan puritans, was Skinner's colleague at Trinity, obtaining a fellowship a year before Skinner. The two men were in touch as late as 1590. Two of Skinner's other friends at Trinity, Michael Hickes* and John Stubbe* were notable puritans. Skinner, Hickes and Stubbe, after they left Cambridge, were students together at Lincoln's Inn. Skinner expressed the religious views which he shared with his friends when he acted as a sponsor of the puritan bill in the Parliament of 1572.[3]

Skinner's father was receiver of duchy lands in Lincolnshire and he himself, after the completion of his education, became involved in local administration, first of all as escheator of Lincolnshire in 1573–4. By that time he had already sat in two Parliaments. There is no evidence that he was in Burghley's service before 1578, but in his first Parliament, in 1571, he sat for Truro, a borough subject to Cecil influence during the Elizabethan period. It may be that he had already come to Cecil's attention, and it is worth noting that his fellow secretary, Hickes, also first sat in Parliament for Truro in 1584, when Hickes was certainly in Burghley's service. There is no record of any activity by Skinner in the 1571 Parliament. In 1572 Skinner sat for Barnstaple, where he probably owed his seat to the 2nd Earl of Bedford, perhaps acting for Burghley. In 1584, 1586 and 1589 he sat for Boston as the nominee of Burghley, who was recorder of the town. Boroughbridge, his constituency in 1593, was subject to duchy of Lancaster influence, and his earlier preoccupation with duchy administration in Lincolnshire, together with any influence which Burghley was able to exercise with Chancellor Heneage, doubtless explains his return. In 1597 Skinner sat for St. Ives, where Burghley exercised influence either directly or through the Marquess of Winchester.

Skinner is not known to have spoken in the House. He was named to committees concerned with church ceremonies (20 May 1572), weights and measures (23 May), Eton and Winchester (2 Mar. 1576), removing benefit of clergy from rapists and burglars (7 Mar.), the Queen's marriage (12 Mar.), relief for vicars and curates (13 Mar.), sheriffs (4 Feb. 1581), the Queen's safety (14 Mar.), parsonages (1 Dec. 1584), ministers (16 Dec.), fraudulent conveyances (15 Feb. 1585), libellers (19 Feb.), tellers and receivers (10 Mar.), Mary Queen of Scots (4 Nov. 1586), subsidies (11 Feb. 1589 and 26 Feb. 1593), the poor law (12 Mar. 1593) and reducing disloyal subjects to their true obedience (4 Apr. 1593). In addition it is possible that as a Member for a Yorkshire constituency in 1593 Skinner took part in committee work on cloth (23 Mar.) and weirs (28 Mar.). No activity has been found for Skinner in the 1597 Parliament, which is remarkable in view of his previous record, the relatively good journals and the importance of the issues then under consideration.[4]

Michael Hickes* and Henry Maynard*, Skinner's colleagues in Burghley's secretariat, each performed specialised functions, Hickes dealing with patronage and Maynard with foreign affairs. Skinner, in contrast, does not seem to have devoted the greater part of his time to any one field of work. It is true that he was, during his period of service, responsible for dealing with applications for escheatorships, but his duties in that connexion could have occupied only a limited part of his time: escheators were appointed only in the autumn of each year. He seems, in fact, to have fulfilled a variety of tasks. He acted as a messenger for Burghley, concerned himself with legal matters in which his master was interested, dealt with problems relating to foreign affairs generally, including trades, and acted as intermediary in suits to Burghley.[5]

Skinner left Burghley's personal service in 1593, when he became auditor of the receipt, by that time the principal office in the lower Exchequer. His career after this date was an unhappy one, although his accession to important Exchequer office might have been expected to secure his fortunes. The Hatfield manuscripts and State Papers Domestic afford ample evidence of the importance of his work and of his deep involvement in the financial affairs of the country. During his tenure of office he emerged rather the worse from a protracted quarrel with Chidiock Wardour*, clerk of the pells.[6]

Though he shared in the general distribution of spoils at the beginning of James's reign, Skinner's personal financial affairs deteriorated until, by 1610, they had reached a crisis. Between July 1610 and October 1611 he bombarded Hickes and even Salisbury with pleas for help, and in 1612 he was granted protection from arrest for a year. Catastrophe, however, can never have been far away, and Skinner died intestate 28 Feb. 1616, being buried the following day at St. Andrew's, Holborn, 'out of Isaac Bringhurst's house in High Holborn', a debtor's prison. His wife and son declined administration of the estate.[7]

[1] Lincs. Peds. (Harl. Soc. lii), 887–8. [2] Somerville, Duchy, i. 580, 583; Pat. roll 36 Eliz.; Hatfield ms 278; HMC Hatfield, iv. 377; xiii. 156–8; CSP Dom. 1603–10, p. 99. [3] Collinson thesis, 1065 n. 3; Lansd. 13, f. 116; 33, f. 193; 10, f. 73; 12, f. 117; M. M. Knappen, Tudor Puritanism, 233–4. [4] Somerville, i. 579–80; HMC Hatfield, xiii. 156–8; DNB (Cecil, William); Neale, Commons, 225, 229; CJ, i. 96, 97, 110, 111, 114, 115, 122, 134; D'Ewes, 260, 306, 334, 340, 349, 353, 365, 394, 431, 474, 499, 507, 512, 517. [5] Lansd. 75, f. 134; HMC Hatfield, ii. 200; xiii. 156–8, 425, 446; CSP Dom. 1591–4, pp. 3–4, 18–29; 1581–90, p. 683. [6] G. R. Elton, Tudor Rev. in Govt. 253–4; Eliz. Govt. and Soc. 213–48; HMC Hatfield, iv. 377, 399, 401, 401–2; vii. 227–8, 267; viii. 286, 361; ix. 131, 151–2, 229, 257–8, 298–9, 422; x. 29, 83, 292–3, 339; xi. 197, 348, 373; xii. 435; xv. 229; xvii. 436; xviii. 455; CSP Dom. 1595–7, pp. 21, 180–1, 392, 413, 471; 1598–1601, pp. 19, 190, 241; 1601–3, pp. 133, 137, 167; 1603–10, pp. 15, 587. [7] CSP Dom. 1603–10, p. 351; 1611–18, p. 17; PRO Index 6802; Lansd. 13, f. 116; 91, ff. 109, 159, 162, 163, 165, 166, 171, 174, 178–80, 185, 198, 202, 207; 92, ff. 14, 15, 17, 19, 21, 27, 30, 33, 34, 40, 42, 69, 71–3, 77, 85, 86, 95, 97, 100, 121, 123; Hatfield ms 129/52; PRO Index 6804; C142/356/134; Lincs. Peds. (Harl. Soc. lii), 888.

A.G.R.S.

SKIPWITH, Edward (d. c.1620), of Biscathorpe, and Benniworth, Lincs.

Illegit. s. of Sir William Skipwith[†] of South Ormsby by Ann, da. of John Tothby of Tothby. educ. Magdalene, Camb. 1571; Clement's Inn; L. Inn 1575, called 1584. m. (1) ?1586, Mary (d.1601), da. of Richard Hansard of Biscathorpe, 1s. 2da.; (2) 1604, Elizabeth, da. of Roger Death of Gosberton, wid. of one Bayley.

Member of Grimsby commission for gaol delivery 1592; j.p. Lincs. (Lindsey) from c.1601; bencher, L. Inn 1600, keeper of black bk. 1605–6, excused from treasurership 1611 on account of infirmity; escheator, Lincs. 1618–19.

Skipwith was a lawyer who presumably gained the Great Grimsby seat through his family connexions. His services were used by Louth corporation in 1609 in obtaining an *inspeximus* of its charter. He died between 24 Nov. 1619, when he made his will, and 3 Apr. following, when the will was proved in the Lincoln consistory court.

A.R. Maddison, Lincs. Wills. i. 112; A. Gibbons, Notes on Vis. Lincs. (Lincoln, privately 1893), p. 49; W. O. Massingberd, Hist. Ormsby cum Ketsby (Lincoln, privately ?1894), p. 111; HMC 14th Rep. VIII, 262; Black Bk. L. Inn i. 434; ii. 59, 61, 95, 137; R. W. Goulding, Louth Old Corp. Recs. (Louth, 1891), p. 13.

D.O.

SKIPWITH, Henry (d.1588), of Cotes and Keythorpe, Leics.

5th s. of Sir William Skipwith[†] of South Ormsby, Lincs. by his 2nd w. Alice, da. and coh. of Sir Lionel Dymoke of Mareham-on-the-Hill, Lincs.; half-bro. of Sir William Skipwith[†]. m. Jane (d.1598), da. of Francis Hall of Grantham, Lincs., wid. of Francis Nele (d.1559), of Prestwold and Cotes, 4s. inc. William Skipwith II* 9da.[1]

Keeper of Ampthill great park 1565; equerry of royal stables by 1569; j.p. Leics. from c.1569; steward of crown lands 1570, commr. to enforce Acts of Uniformity and Supremacy, dioceses of Lincoln and Peterborough 1571; commr. musters, Leics. 1583.[2]

Skipwith was already described as the Queen's servant in April 1559, when he was granted the reversion to the keepership of Ampthill great park. On 15 Sept. 1569 Elizabeth employed him to carry to the Earls of Huntingdon and Shrewsbury and Viscount Hereford a confidential message about Mary Stuart. Two years later Skipwith was again employed on delicate business: on 30 July he sent to Burghley, at his request, a list of the members of the Duke of Norfolk's household who were in London; four days later he assisted Sir Ralph Sadler* in guarding Norfolk, who was confined to his room; and on 7 Sept. conducted him to the Tower. There Skipwith remained, under the Queen's orders, to act as custodian. He discovered the cipher and channels whereby Norfolk was communicating with the world outside, and secured his admission to receiving £2,000 of Mary's money from the bishop of Ross.[3]

In 1584 Sadler, chancellor of the duchy of Lancaster, asked for the nomination to both Leicester borough seats, suggesting Skipwith, his former associate, as one candidate. After some delay the townsmen elected Skipwith and Thomas Johnson*, the Hastings candidate, both Members agreeing to pay their own expenses. In 1586 the Privy Council wrote to the sheriff recommending the return of the same Members for the next Parliament, and Skipwith and Johnson were re-elected. There is no record of any activity by Skipwith in this Parliament.

He died intestate 14 Aug. 1588. He had received many rewards from the Queen, including the office of steward of crown lands in Leicestershire, granted just after the troubles of 1569, a lease of the woods of Groby manor, and a twice renewed lease of the rectory of Prestwold, which made a useful addition to the lands there that his wife held in dower from her first husband. Around these he built up a freehold estate, purchasing various manors, granges and small-holdings in the parish and nearby. In 1580 he was obliged to sue his brothers-in-law, Edmund and Henry Hall, for the completion of his title to Keythorpe, but by 1586 he was able to settle the estate on feoffees who included his brothers-in-law, his step-daughter's husband Everard Digby, his daughter-in-law's brothers Thomas* and William Cave, and Thomas Skeffington*. His widow's administration of the goods and chattels was disputed, and she had considerable difficulty in obtaining an account of her husband's lands; the matter was eventually settled in her favour.[4]

[1] Nichols, *Leics.* iii. 368; *Lincs. Peds.* (Harl. Soc. lii), 889; C142/126/124. [2] *HMC Hatfield*, i. 419; *CPR*, 1558–60, p. 108; 1566–9, p. 161; 1569–72, p. 277; cal. and index patent rolls 1–16 Eliz. p. 259; *Leicester Recs.* iii. 196. [3] *HMC Hatfield*, i. 419, 522, 526, 532; *HMC Hastings*, ii. 8; iii. 3, 4, 10, 11, 13, 15, 551; *CSP Dom.* 1547–80, pp. 417, 426, 434; N. Williams, *Duke of Norfolk*, passim; SP12/88/2. [4] *Leicester Recs.* iii. 209–11, 227; C142/126/124; 223/66; *CPR*, 1560–3, p. 409; cal. and index patent rolls 1–16 Eliz. 14(6), p. 294; 17–30 Eliz. 20(6), p. 15; 24(12), p. 18; 28(11), p. 21; PCC 45 Nevell; *Trans. Leics. Arch. Soc.* xvii. 54–9.

S.M.T.

SKIPWITH, William I (*d*. c.1595), of St. Peter's Street, St. Albans, Herts.

ST. ALBANS   1571

1st s. of Thomas Skipwith of St. Albans by Joan, da. of Ralph Rowlet, sis. and coh. of Sir Ralph Rowlet. *m.* Frances, da. of William Nicholson of Mdx., 2s. 7da. *suc.* fa. 1558.

There is no record of any activity by Skipwith during his one appearance in the Commons. As well as his father's property in St. Albans, he inherited from his uncle, Sir Ralph Rowlet, in July 1571, the manor of Radwell and land in Newnham and elsewhere in the county, but by 1580 he had sold much of this and several complicated Chancery cases arose between him and his brothers. In 1562

Skipwith released to his sister Alice and her husband, Robert Austin, all his rights in the manor of Somertons, Oxfordshire. Maybe he did some moneylending on the side. About 1566, one Ralph Johnson of Gray's Inn brought a Chancery suit against him for extortion. He had lent Johnson £100 on the security of lands in Kent, and, according to the bill of complaint, demanded that the plaintiff should buy for 20 marks a jewel 'not worth 26*s.* 8*d.*', insisted on a recognizance of £300, found flaws in the mortgage and brought an action for the amount of the bond, though Johnson was ready to repay the original £100. The only other document surviving in the case is Skipwith's demurrer, objecting to the bill on technical grounds. Skipwith died before 27 June 1595, when letters of administration were granted to his son Stephen.

Vis. Herts. (Harl. Soc. xxii), 20–1; J. E. Cussans, *Inventory of Parish Churches of Herts.* 25–6; *Trans. St. Albans Archit. and Arch. Soc.* 1893–4, p. 13; 1898, p. 135; *Vis. Warws.* (Harl. Soc. xii), 13; Newcome, *St. Albans*, 481; *VCH Herts.* ii. 272; iii. 246; PCC 13 Welles, 33 Holney, 30 Martyn; C3/103/70, 160/3–9; 250/21; Requests 2/89/47; *CSP Dom.* Add. 1547–65, pp. 547–8; PCC admon. act bk. 1592–8, f. 137.

N.M.F.

SKIPWITH, William II (c.1564–1610), of Cotes, Leics.

LEICESTERSHIRE	1601
LEICESTER	1604*

b. c.1564, 1st s. of Henry Skipwith* by his w. Jane. *educ.* Jesus, Camb. c.1579/80. *m.* (1) Margaret (*d.*1594), da. of Roger Cave, of Stanford, Northants., 4s. 4da.; (2) Jane (*d.*1630), da. of John Roberts, wid. of John Markham of Sidebrook, *s.p. suc.* fa. 1588. Kntd. 1603.

J.p. Leics. from c.1592, sheriff 1597–8, commr. musters 1608.

Skipwith was elected second knight of the shire in 1601 against opposition from Sir John Grey*, with the support of the 4th Earl of Huntingdon, with whom he was on friendly terms, and with whose religious views he certainly sympathized, since Skipwith was one of those who in James I's reign petitioned the Crown in favour of the puritan ministers of the shire. All the same, when the case of George Belgrave* was argued in the House on 8 Dec. 1601, Skipwith supported Belgrave. There is no record of any other activity by Skipwith in the 1601 Parliament, though, as knight of the shire, he could have attended the main business committee, 3 Nov. and the committee on monopolies, 23 Nov.

Skipwith wrote verses described by Fuller as 'neither so apparent that every rustic might understand them, nor so obscure that they needed an Oedipus to interpret them'. He died on 3 May 1610 and was buried in Prestwold church, where his widow erected a large monument to his memory on the south side of the altar.

C142/223/66, 317/121; Nichols, *Leics.* iii(1), 366, 368; Townshend, *Hist. Colls.* 296; D'Ewes, 624, 649; Fuller, *Worthies*, ii; PCC 42 Wood;

Leicester Recs. iv. 3, 32, 60, 93, 137; *APC.* xxv. 216; xxxii. 160; *HMC Rutland*, i. 380; *HMC Hatfield*, xvii. 8; *Trans. Leics. Arch. Soc.* xvii. 8.

S.M.T.

SLADE, Thomas (*d.*1580), of Huntingdon, and the Middle Temple, London.

HUNTINGDON　　　　　　　　　　1572*

1st s. of Richard Slade of Huntingdon by Elizabeth, da. of John Spencer of Beds. *educ.* M. Temple 1558, called by 1567. *m.* Clayes Bellikin Clampe, ?da. of Philip Clampe (*d.*1559), of Huntingdon and Brampton, Hunts., 2da. *suc.* fa. 1557.

　　Of counsel to Huntingdon by 1572; j.p. Hunts. from c.1573.

Like his father, from whom he inherited land in five Huntingdonshire parishes, Slade was a lawyer. His chamber at the Temple overlooked Temple Lane. In 1576 he helped to provide the reader's feast, but the following year he was fined for not taking his place at 'the cupboard' to assist the reader, a duty all senior barristers were expected to undertake. Shortly afterwards he was fined £5, perhaps for not taking his own turn as reader. As legal adviser to Huntingdon Slade would have been an obvious man for the borough to return to Parliament. He was himself present at the election. No record has been found of any activity by Slade in the first two sessions of the Parliament, and he died before the third, administration of his estate being granted in 1580.

Vis. Hunts. (Cam. Soc. xliii), 20; SP12/145/18; PCC 13 Wrastley; *M.T. Recs.* i. passim; E. Griffith, *Huntingdon Recs.* 94, 100; *VCH Hunts.* ii. 128; iii. 13; S. C. Lomas, *Edwardian Inventories for Hunts.* (Alcuin Club Colls. vii), 52–3; *Feet of Fines Hunts.* ed. Turner (Camb. Antiq. Soc. Pubs. oct. ser. xxxvii), 165, 169; *Hunts. Wills* (Brit. Rec. Soc. Index Lib. xlii), 147.

M.R.P.

SLANNING, Nicholas (1523/4–83), of Plymouth and Bickleigh, Devon.

PLYMOUTH　　　　　　　　　　1558, 1559

b. 1523/4, 1st s. of Nicholas Slanning of Ley in Plympton St. Mary by Elizabeth, da. of Thomas Maynard of Sherford. *m.* by 1564, Margaret, da. of William Amadas, 1da. *suc.* fa. bet. 1560–68.

　　Town clerk, Plymouth by 1546, coroner by 1552, mayor 1564–5.

The Slannings had acquired land in eastern and southern Devon at the dissolution of Buckland abbey and Plympton priory. At the time of the 1559 election Slanning's father had only recently inherited the bulk of this property from his brother John, and Slanning himself was as yet unprovided with landed estates. His father made this good by settling various manors on him in May 1559 and October 1560. Slanning was still living in Plymouth in 1561 when he contributed 13s. 4d. toward the estab-

lishment of the grammar school, and in 1564–5 when he was mayor. In 1568 he settled the manors of Bickleigh and Shaugh and the advowson of Bickleigh upon his wife Margaret for her life, and in 1579 entailed all his estates on his brother John, with remainder to the heirs of his brother William. Slanning died 8 Apr. 1583, leaving one daughter Agnes, to whom he bequeathed £200 and an annuity of £10. To his nephew Nicholas, son of his youngest brother William, he left the mansion house of Marystow. He also made numerous charitable bequests: to the inhabitants of the almshouse of Plymouth and the sick in the Magdalens of Plymouth and Plympton and to the poor of Bickleigh, as well as 20s. for the repair of the parish church of Bickleigh, of which he had been patron and where he was buried. The executor of the will was his brother and heir, John, who proved it a week after his death.

Vivian, *Vis. Devon*, 687; *Vis. Devon 1564*, ed. Colby, 189; *Trans. Dev. Assoc.* xix. 452–5; lxx. 232, 246–50; Plymouth, receiver's accts.; *CPR*, 1550–3, p. 435; 1558–60, pp. 75, 409; *Plymouth Recs.* 50; PCC 63 Noodes, 18 Rowe; C142/200/11(2).

I.C.

SLATER, Henry (*d.* c.1590), of Portsmouth, Hants.

PORTSMOUTH　　　　　　　　　　1571

　　Burgess, Portsmouth 1555, mayor 1558–9.

Slater was one of only two townsmen to represent Portsmouth in Parliament during Elizabeth's reign. Little is known about his family or private life. On 17 June 1556 Agnes Slater, perhaps his wife, was buried in Portsmouth, but he must have died without children, as his next of kin was Henry Atkinson. His will, of which one Katherine Godfrey claimed to be executrix, was pronounced invalid in November 1591.

R. East, *Portsmouth Recs.* 312, 324, 343, 449, 679; PCC 89 Sainberbe.

N.M.F.

SLEGGE, Roger (c.1519–89), of Cambridge.

CAMBRIDGE　　　　　　1559, 1563, 1571, 1572, 1584, 1586, 1589

b. c.1519, 1st s. of Edward Slegge† of Cambridge by Alice Cockerell of Suff. *m.* (1) c.1544, Elizabeth, illegit. da. of Sir William Bowyer; (2) Joyce, da. and sole h. of Thomas Thorne of Shrewsbury, Salop, 1s. 1da.; (3) Margaret, da. of Henry Serle* of Cambridge, 5s. 1da. *suc.* fa. ?1558.

　　Mayor, Cambridge 1560–1, 1568–9, 1575–6, Mar.– Aug. 1585.

Slegge was a burgess of Cambridge, described in the 1564 bishops' reports as 'of godly religion'. He owned property in the town, and leased from the corporation certain booths, and 'a sink running into the King's ditch'. The borough records show frequent payments to him 'for riding to London on the town's business' and sums paid to him as burgess of Parliament. In the Parliament of 1572 he spoke twice, on Stourbridge fair (10 June 1572) and on the vagabonds bill (20 May), urging the punishment only of 'those minstrels ... which wander abroad, not [those] which keep a continual habitation'.

Slegge and his third father-in-law were the main participants in a quarrel between the town and university of Cambridge, which finally resulted in their being committed to the Fleet, pending a Privy Council inquiry. Slegge was accused of wasting the town's money, keeping a gambling den, sowing sedition between the university and the town, and being a companion of lewd persons.

By 24 Sept. 1566 the corporation had had enough of both Slegge and Serle and the mayor wrote to Cecil to ask that they should by replaced as MPs. They were not, and there is no sign that Slegge changed his attitude to the university, for in January 1568 the vice-chancellor was complaining that the differences between town and gown might be settled 'but for the factious conduct of ... the mayor and his adviser, Roger Slegge'. Slegge died in 1589, and was buried 14 Dec. in St. Sepulchre's church.

St. Ch. 4/2/52; C2/Eliz./S13/58; *Vis. Cambs.* (Harl. Soc. xli), 46; Add. 5812, f. 125; F. Blomefield, *Coll. Cant.* 225; *Cam. Misc.* ix(3), p. 25; Downing Coll. Camb. Bowtell mss; Trinity, Dublin, Thos. Cromwell's jnl. ff. 29, 60; *CSP Dom.* 1547–80, pp. 36, 244, 245, 278, 305; Add. 1547–65, pp. 553–4; *APC*, vii. 149; Lansd. 51, f. 144; 54, f. 34 seq.; 84, f. 225; J. M. Gray, *Notes on Cambridge Mayors*, 28.

J.J.C.

SLINGSBY, Francis (c.1522–1600), of Scriven, Yorks.

KNARESBOROUGH 1572, 1584

b. c.1522, s. and h. of Thomas Slingsby by Joan, da. of Sir John Mallory of Studley. *educ.* ?Oxf. or Camb. *m.* (1) Elizabeth, da. of Sir William Ingleby of Ripley; (2) 1556, Mary (*d.*1598), da. of Sir Thomas Percy, sis. of Thomas† and Henry*, earls of Northumberland, 9s. inc. Henry* and William* 3da. *suc.* fa. 1551.[1]

Jt. (with his fa.) keeper of Haia park, Yorks., duchy of Lancaster 1545; dep. warden of middle march bef. 1559; commr. musters, Northumb. 1559, Yorks 1595; j.p. Yorks (N. and W. Ridings) from c.1559; jt. dep. steward and constable of Knaresborough castle bef. 1569; feodary and master forester of Knaresborough, keeper and paler of Bilton park, porter and watchman 1571; commr. border causes 1596.[2]

Slingsby's name does not appear in the printed registers of either Oxford or Cambridge University, but, according to the inscription on his tomb, it was after leaving university that he served as a captain of horse at the siege of Boulogne, 1544, and afterwards at the battle of Musselburgh. He was also said to have commanded a troop of horse in the reign of Queen Mary, and was active in border affairs. From the time of his second marriage, however, he seems to have settled on his estates, and, for the next 20 years his policy was to sell outlying holdings and consolidate them around Scriven. His new relatives by

marriage seem to have thought that he could be drawn into a plot to rescue Mary Queen of Scots, then in custody in England. Instead, he was one of the 'divers honest gentlemen' who, at the time of the 1569 rebellion, gave the alarm by suddenly leaving their houses to man the defences. Slingsby garrisoned Knaresborough castle, together with his former father-in-law Sir William Ingleby, the joint constable, and sent to the Earl of Sussex, president of the council in the north, for orders. Replying to subsequent inquiries of the Privy Council as to the origins of the alarm, Slingsby said that there had been 'doubts and suspicions in men's minds, some on account of zeal to her Majesty, others for zeal in religion, some from suspicious inclinations and others from having knowledge of some matter'.[3]

Slingsby's residence was adjacent to the borough of Knaresborough, which he twice represented in Parliament, and where two of his sons were later returned. His only recorded activity was his appointment to the committee of a bill for fortifying the frontier with Scotland, 25 Feb. 1581. In 1596 the bishop of Durham welcomed his appointment to a commission for border causes as being 'a wise gentleman of good experience'. His service was considered the more valuable since the Scots were reported to be 'both skilful and tough'. Slingsby died 3 Aug. 1600 and was buried in the Slingsby chapel on the north side of the choir in Knaresborough church, where a monument depicts him in armour. His fourth son, Henry, succeeded to the estates.[4]

[1] Foster, *Yorks. Peds. W. Riding*; Parsons, *Diary of Sir Hen. Slingsby*, 395–408. [2] Lansd. 53, f. 176; Somerville, *Duchy*, i. 526; *LP Hen. VIII*, xx(2), p. 445; *CSP For.* 1558–9, pp. 152, 167; 1559–60, p. 108; *CSP Dom.* Add. 1566–79, p. 96; 1595–7, p. 144; Wheater, *Knaresborough and its Rulers*, 213; *Border Pprs.* ii. 199; C142/93/76. [3] Ackrill, *York and Ainsty Tragedy*, 47; J. J. Cartwright, *Chapters in Yorks. Hist.* 69; *CSP For.* 1559–60, p. 151; *CPR*, 1555–7, p. 412; *Yorks. Fines*, passim.; *Yorks. Deeds*, passim; *HMC Hatfield*, i. 553, 571; *CSP Dom.* Add. 1566–79, pp. 93, 96–7; C. Sharp, *Memorials of the Rebellion*, pp. 8–9. [4] *CJ*, i. 129; *Border Pprs.* ii. 209–10 and passim; C142/263/70; Coghill, *Fam. of Coghill*, 167; Parsons, 398–402.

N.M.S.

SLINGSBY, Henry (1560–1634), of Scriven, Yorks.

KNARESBOROUGH 1601, 1604, 1614, 1621, 1624

b. 1560, 4th but 1st surv. s. of Francis Slingsby* by his 2nd w. and bro. of William*. *m.* Frances (*d.* 24 July 1611), da. of William Vavasour† of Weston, 5s. 9da. *suc.* fa. 1600. Kntd. 1602.

Duchy of Lancaster feodary and receiver of Pontefract castle, feodary of Tickhill, receiver surveyor and collector of Knaresborough and Wakefield 1588; janitor and dep. keeper, Knaresborough castle, bailiff and coroner within the liberty of Knaresborough, chief forester of Knaresborough and Wharfdale, custodian of Bilton park ?1600; j.p. Yorks. (W. Riding) 1601; member, council in the north from 1603; sheriff, Yorks. 1611–12.

Slingsby, whose parliamentary career lay mainly in the Stuart period, succeeded to the family influence at Knaresborough, and repeatedly had himself returned there. He died 17 Dec. 1634 at Nun Monckton, Yorkshire, and was buried on the 28th in the family chapel in Knaresborough church.

Calvert, *Hist. Knaresborough*, 59, 136–7; Coghill, *Fam. of Coghill*, 168; *CSP Dom.* 1601–3, p. 190; Somerville, *Duchy*, i. 518; ms index, duchy of Lancaster patents, 137; Reid, *Council of the North*, 496.

N.M.S.

SLINGSBY, William (1563–1634), of Kippax, Yorks. and Gray's Inn, London.

KNARESBOROUGH	1597, 1601, 1604
APPLEBY	1626

b. 29 Jan. 1563, 7th but 3rd surv. s. of Francis Slingsby* by his 2nd w. and bro. of Henry*. *educ.* Barnard's Inn, G. Inn 1582. *m.* 1617, Elizabeth, da. of Sir Stephen Broad of Broadshill, Suss., at least 2s. 1da. Kntd. 1603.

Commissary of munitions 1596; honorary carver to Queen Anne 1603; j.p. Mdx., dep. lt. 1617, commr. to inquire into fees and offices 1627, 1630, for compounding with recusants 1628.

Slingsby was trained as a lawyer, showed an early taste for soldiering and foreign adventures, and, in the Stuart period, was much at court. As a young man he was evidently known to (Sir) Robert Cecil*, and on at least one occasion is known to have been with (Sir) Thomas Cecil* at Bath.

From 1589 until at least 1591 there was a controversy, which came to the notice of the Privy Council, between the brothers William and Guildford Slingsby on the one hand and Edward Beesley on the other about the clerkship of York castle. By 1594 Slingsby was travelling on the Continent when, 'by others' faults', he and his friends were put in 'several vile dungeons and base prisons' of the castle at Como, then under Spanish rule. He managed to obtain his release by persuading the governor that he was 'a Scottish man and a scholar'. He reached England a few weeks later in July 1594, wondering whether to return in search of new adventures, 'or else to come and do my duty in Yorkshire'. Instead he went to court, where he had 'many honourable entertainments' from 'divers of the Council', and where he hoped, with the help of his 'dearest friend' Sir George Carew*, to obtain an office which would take him on the proposed expedition to Brittany. In 1596 Slingsby served on the Cadiz expedition, and again in 1597 in the fleet equipped against Spain. In August or September that year he travelled home overland from La Rochelle, with letters from Carew to Cecil, claiming the distinction of having been 'the sickest of six hundred' in his ship. While waiting at Plymouth that August, delayed by adverse winds, Slingsby wrote to his brother Henry:

We have news here of a Parliament to begin 12 October next; if it be so, good brother, put my father in mind to make me a burgess of the Parliament, for it is [a] thing I do exceedingly desire,

and he was duly returned for the family borough of Knaresborough. He sat again, with Henry as his colleague, in 1601. Very likely one of them was the 'Mr. Singy' who, on 11 Dec. 1601, thought the author of the bill for the maintenance of good and profitable arts and trades 'was a sugar man, for he used the word *refiner* of arts'.

During the Stuart period Slingsby held a patent for furnaces used in the production of glass from sea coal. He died in August 1634 and was buried in the family chapel in the church at Knaresborough.

Foster, *Yorks. Peds. W. Riding*; Calvert, *Hist. Knaresborough*, 58, 133; *Mem. Francis Slingsby*, 204; *CSP Dom.* 1603–10, p. 625; 1611–18, pp. 13, 425; 1619–23, p. 4; 1627–8, pp. 168, 232; 1628–9, p. 205; 1629–31, pp. 179, 236–7; Parsons, *Diary of Sir Henry Slingsby*, 243–7, 249–53; *APC*, xvii. 139; xxi. 162; *HMC Hatfield*, vii. 382; Townshend, *Hist. Colls.* 311.

N.M.S.

SLYFIELD, Edmund (c.1520–91), of Slyfield Place, Great Bookham, Surr.

GATTON	1571
GRAMPOUND	1572

b. c.1520, 1st (or 2nd but 1st surv.) s. of John Slyfield by his w. Jane. *m.* Elizabeth, da. of Walter Lambert of Carshalton, 5s. 11da. *suc.* fa. 1530.

J.p. Surr. from c.1552, sheriff, Surr. and Suss. 1581–2.

Slyfield was a leading Surrey gentleman, related to the Westons and well known to the Mores of Loseley and to Sir Thomas Cawarden*, whose will he witnessed and who left him a bequest of armour. It was probably his connexion with the Howards of Effingham which gained him a parliamentary seat at Gatton in the absence abroad of Thomas Copley*, lord of the borough. For his return at Grampound he may have relied on court patronage, perhaps the Earl of Bedford or his wife's relatives, the Paulets, Sidneys and Arundells. No record has been found of any activity by Slyfield in either Parliament. His name appears on the first Elizabethan commission of the peace, but is omitted, reason unknown, in 1561 and 1564. In addition to his offices as justice of the peace and sheriff, he was employed in various duties, for example, in 1567 as one of three commissioners appointed by the archbishop of Canterbury to arbitrate in a local dispute between Thomas Purdam and his mother, acting through her second husband John Grove. On at least two occasions Slyfield's own activities were investigated: in 1583, when the good people of Send, where he held property, complained that he had stopped up a highway, and three years later when he quarrelled with John Reve, vicar of Great Bookham.

Slyfield died 13 Feb. 1591, having drawn up his will two months earlier. The widow was sole executrix and the eldest son Henry and son-in-law Edward Skeete, husband of the daughter Audrey, overseers.

Surr. Arch. Colls. v. 43–9; xviii. 212; xxv. 88–90; C142/51/10; PCC 4 Mellershe, 18 Sainberbe; *HMC 7th Rep.* 620, 637, 642, 662; *APC*, xix. 38–9.

N.M.F.

SMARTE, William (c.1530–99), of Ipswich, Suff.

IPSWICH	1589

b. c.1530, 1st s. of Richard Smarte of Ipswich by Alice, da. of Robert Daundy of Ipswich. *m.* Alice, *?s.p. suc.* fa. 1560.

Treasurer, Ipswich 1560, coroner 1562, coroner and claviger 1565, one of council of twelve 1567, portman by 1565, justice 1570, bailiff 1569–70, 1575–6.

Smarte was a member of the corporation of Ipswich for almost 40 years, his bequests to drapers' and tailors' halls in the borough suggesting that he may have been connected with the cloth trade. He owned considerable land in Suffolk and Essex, and the Ipswich treasurers' accounts for 1594–5 record a purchase of rye from him to be

> baked in bread at the town's charge and given to the poor of this town the day before the coronation day ... 1594.

For many years he was treasurer of Christ's hospital, Ipswich, and leased property from the corporation, the rents of which were allocated to the hospital. He also carried out a number of commissions for the borough – meeting the lord keeper when he visited Ipswich in September 1578, surveying a passage-way on behalf of Henry Tooley's foundation, and in 1593 conducting a lawsuit against a certain Thomas Bennet, for which the borough treasurer paid him £23 6s. 8d. He was also active in suits brought by individuals against the corporation itself. For his parliamentary service, 'fee and diet', in 1589 he was paid £6.

He died on 23 Sept. 1599 and was buried in the parish church of St. Mary Tower. A monument to him was set up in the church – a framed wooden tablet with an acrostic inscription in rhyme and a view of Ipswich. His will, drawn up in January 1599, was proved in the following November. It shows him as a considerable benefactor to the town. His wife, the sole executrix, was to have a dwelling-house.

N. Bacon, *Annals of Ipswich*, 251–268; Ipswich ass. bks. 6–19 Eliz. pp. 58, 69, 83, 106; 20–30 Eliz. (unpaginated), *passim*, treasurers' accts. 1573–4, 1575, 1589, 1592, 1594, 1595, 1599; PCC 90 Kidd; Wards 7/8/121.

N.M.F.

SMITH, Christopher (bef. 1510–89), of London and Annables, Herts.

SALTASH	1547
BRIDPORT	1553 (Oct.)
ST. ALBANS	1559

b. bef. 1510, yr. s. of Robert Smith of Waltham, Lincs. by Eleanor, da. and coh. of William Lilbourne of Fenby, Lincs. *m.* c.1540, Margaret, da. of John Hyde of Aldbury, Herts., 2s. 4da.

Clerk of the Exchequer from c.1545, of the pipe from 1551; j.p.q. Herts from c.1564.

In 1555 Smith bought the manor of Annables, about eight miles from St. Albans, and in 1564 the Queen granted to him and Thomas Broughton the reversion to the 'prior's lodging', with a number of houses belonging to it, in St. Albans itself. He also leased the rectory at Flamstead, where he held the advowson. There would have been no problem in being returned there in 1559, either through his own local influence or through an acquaintance at the Exchequer such as Sir Nicholas Bacon[†]. He was presumably the Mr. Smith or Smythe to whom was committed the bill for the recognition of the Queen's title to the Crown (11 Feb. 1559); other committees allocated to Mr. Smith in this Parliament were on the bishop of Winchester's lands (18 Feb.) and unlawful assemblies (18 Mar.).

Smith died on 12 Apr. 1589. His will, made in July 1585 and proved in June 1589, refers to leases at South Elkington, Waltham, and elsewhere in Lincolnshire. He also leased land in Nottinghamshire, Surrey and Gloucestershire, and may for some time have had a messuage in the Charterhouse. The executor, Smith's elder son Thomas, who succeeded him as clerk of the pipe, and may recently have been doing much of the work of the office, received among other bequests an annuity of £20.

Smith had a namesake (allowing for the varying spellings of the surname), also from a Lincolnshire family, who became proctor of the arches, and has been assumed to be the keeper of records in the court of augmentations, and the escheator of Lincolnshire 1549–50.

Cussans, *Herts. Dacorum*, 355–6; *Vis Herts.* (Harl. Soc. xxii), 164; *VCH Herts.* ii. 199, 307–8; *CPR*, 1547–8, p. 279; 1548–9 pp. 8–9; 1549–51, p. 356; 1560–3, pp. 221, 438, 468, 611; 1563–6, pp. 114–15; *LP Hen. VIII*, xix(1), p. 499; (2), p. 73; xx(2), p. 449; xxi(2), pp. 431, 432; *CJ*, i. 54, 55, 58; *APC*, vii. 48; E101/336/26, f. 175; PCC 60 Leicester, 64 Sainberbe; *Lincs. Peds.* (Harl. Soc. l), 20.

N.M.F.

SMITH, Humphrey (c.1542–89), of London and Cullompton, Devon.

BODMIN	1571

b. c.1542. *educ.* I. Temple 1556. *m.* 1586, Ursula, da. of ?Thomas Leveson, 1s.[1]

J.p. Devon from c.1573–87, Mdx. from c.1579; bencher, I. Temple 1574, Autumn reader 1576 or 1577, Lent reader 1587.

Smith was probably brought in for Bodmin by the 2nd Earl of Bedford. He spoke 13 Apr. (the clerk called him Henry) suggesting that if a man should come into some land subsequent to its being established that he was in debt to the Crown, this land could be extended. The next day he was put on the committee considering fraudulent conveyances, and on 28 Apr. he was appointed to the committee discussing a religious bill.[2]

Smith owned land at South Charlton, Devon, and elsewhere in the county, most of it in the Honiton district, and an inn, the *George*, at Cullompton. With the exception of the Surrey manor of Send the rest of his property was in London, in the parishes of St. Dunstan-in-the-West; St. Giles, Cripplegate; St. Peter, Cornhill; All Hallows, St. Sepulchre and Whitefriars; he also owned the *White Horse* in West Smithfield. He was a member of various commissions in London and Middlesex, examining recusants, trying to control the plague in Westminster, and investigating fraudulent dealings by the creditors of John Coping, a prisoner in Queen's bench. His legal duties must have kept him fairly constantly in London; his removal from the Devon commission of the peace in 1587 was probably for non-residence.[3]

Smith died 15 Sept. 1589. His will, made on the day of his death, has a devout preamble. The widow, the sole executrix, was to supervise the upbringing of their son Walter, who was only 18 months old. If, as seems probable, she was one of the Levesons of Hornes Place, Kent, she had an influential relative to help her in (Sir) Roger Manwood*. One of her even more important connexions by marriage, Sir Walter Mildmay*, predeceased Smith by a few months.[4]

[1] C142/221/108; *Lond. Mar. Lic.* (Harl. Soc. xxv), 150. [2] *CJ*, i. 84, 86; D'Ewes, 166, 180; Trinity, Dublin, anon. jnl. f. 19. [3] C142/221/108; *APC*, xii. 211; xiv. 264–5; xv. 392; Lansd. 74, f. 85; 121, f. 66. [4] PCC 70 Leicester; C142/221/108; *Vis. Kent* (Harl. Soc. lxxv), 4–5.

N.M.F.

SMITH (SMYTH), James

| ARUNDEL | 1597 |
| MIDHURST | 1597 |

Though there were numerous Smith families in West Sussex in the sixteenth century, no pedigrees have survived and none is known to have been armigerous. Nor do any of the families of this name from other counties who attained some importance in national affairs contain a James Smith at the right date. The description of the 1597 Member for Midhurst as 'James Smyth, Esq.' on the original return suggests he was of some social standing, but no suitable person has been found. It is on the whole

unlikely that the same man was returned for both constituencies as the returns are dated three weeks apart. The Member for Midhurst probably had some connexion, direct or indirect, with Lord Montagu, owner of the borough, and the choice at Arundel may have been due to Lord Buckhurst, though local men also were returned there at the end of the reign.

In the absence of positive identification some possibilities can be suggested. In 1568 a James Smith married Ann, daughter of Richard Pellatt of Steyning, Sussex. The Pellatt family was of some standing there, supplying MPs in 1555 and 1572. James Smith, whose name appears in the wills of at least two Pellatts, had possible connexions through them with both Arundel and Midhurst. Smith's brother-in-law, Christopher (Pellatt), is called 'of Arundel' in his will, and another member of the Pellatt family married into the Lewknors, who had some influence in Midhurst parliamentary elections, Lewis Lewknor* being the other Member in 1597. But this James Smith would have been too old to be returned for the first time in 1597 if, as is likely, he was the man whose will was proved in the consistory court of Chichester in 1600. Another James Smith, but of low social standing, can be found in the wills of the Lintott family of Horsham.[1]

The most important Smith family in West Sussex, probably, was that which owned the manor of Binderton, near Chichester, for most of the sixteenth century, but no James has been found. The family operated ironworks not far from Midhurst, and William Smith was described as an 'old servant' in 1609 in the will of Lord Lumley, one of Montagu's close friends. There may have been a James Smith in this family in the service of either Lumley or Montagu.[2]

One final possibility, outside the county, suggests itself. James Smith, citizen and grocer of London, left money in 1617 to the poor of Horsham and to several people in Sussex, but he came originally from Lincolnshire, and no connexion with Midhurst, Arundel or their patrons has been found.[3]

[1] *Suss. Arch. Colls.* xxxviii. 99 seq.; xxxix. 90; Probate Reg. at Chichester, vol. 15, f. 84; J. Comber, *Suss. Genealogies Horsham Centre*, 206. [2] *VCH Suss.* iv. 89; *Suss. N. and Q.* xiii. 235–6; PCC 34 Dorset. [3] PCC 102 Weldon.

M.R.P.

SMITH, John (d.1620), of Tregonack in Duloe, Cornw.

| CAMELFORD | 1559 |

2nd s. of Robert Smith (d.1569) of Tregonack by his 1st w. Elizabeth (d. c.1566), da. and h. of John Skenock of Trewint. m. aft. Mar. 1572, Anne (d.1592), da. of Richard Coffin of Portledge, Devon, wid. of Roger Tremayne of Collacombe, Devon, s.p.

The above identity for the 1559 Camelford Member is suggested on the grounds that some of his family held duchy of Cornwall offices, and that his own marriage connected him with the Tremayne family, while his brother Robert's connected him with the Killigrews. Edmund Tremayne* was known to the Courtenays and to the 2nd Earl of Bedford, and the Killigrews to Sir William Cecil, with whom Bedford co-operated over west-country patronage, so that, one way or another, a seat at Camelford might easily have been found for Smith. The only references to him in the journals concern a question of privilege. On 24 Feb. 1559 the London merchant John Marshe* stated in the House that Smith had

> deceived divers merchants in London, taking wares of them to the sum of £300, minding to defraud them of the same, under colour of the privilege of this House.

A committee, headed by Sir John Mason, upheld the charge and it was established that a writ of outlawry had been issued against Smith following a suit for debt. As to whether Smith should have privilege, 'by the more number of voices it seemed that he should not have privilege'. However, on a division, 112 Members voted for privilege, 107 against, 'and therefore it was ordered that he should still continue a Member of the House'.

Nothing further has been ascertained about Smith other than that he was involved in a Chancery case of 1595 concerning a settlement of the manor of Rake, and in 1597 deposed that the borough of East Looe 'found burgesses for the Parliament'. He died – if we are still dealing with the same man – on 7 Jan. 1620, and three days later was buried at Duloe. An Ashmolean manuscript has his will being proved by a great-nephew, also John Smith of Tregonack, but no such will is known to have been proved in Bodmin, Exeter or London.

Vivian, *Vis. Cornw.* 215, 427, 617; *Vis. Devon*, 209; PCC 11 Crymes; *CJ*, i. 55; E134/28 Eliz./Hil 8; C2.Eliz. F. f. 4/54.

N.M.F.

SMITH, Sir Lawrence (c.1516–82), of Chester and Hough, Cheshire.

CHESHIRE	1545, 1555
CHESTER	1558, 1559

b. c.1516, 1st s. of Sir Thomas Smith, mayor of Chester, by Katherine, da. of Sir Andrew Brereton of Brereton. *m.* (1) by 1546, Agnes, da. of Sir Thomas Foulshurst of Crewe, 3s.; (2) Jan. 1561, Jane, da. of Sir Peter Warburton of Arley, wid. of Sir William Brereton I*, 1 or 2 da. *suc.* fa. 1538. Kntd. 11 May 1544.[1]

Mayor, Chester 1540–1, 1558–9, 1563–4, 1570–1; commr. musters, Cheshire 1545, j.p. from c.1543, q. 1564, sheriff 1551–2, 1566–7; commr. to survey church ornaments, Chester c.1553; commr. and deputy to council in marches of Wales 1553; commr. piracy, Cheshire 1565.[2]

Smith's father had given valuable services to Chester, and there is a reference in the borough archives to the 'great good liking of the city' for both Sir Thomas and Sir Lawrence – who may have been the 'Lawrence Smith, goldsmith' mentioned in Chester records for 1543–4. Between 1540 and 1545 he served as a soldier and was knighted at Leith. He voted against a government bill in the Parliament of 1555. Early in Elizabeth's reign he again saw active service, leading a company of 200 men in the Scottish campaign of 1560. Seven years later he was one of three local officials chosen to take musters at the port of Chester, and was responsible, jointly with Sir Hugh Cholmley[†], for transporting soldiers to Ireland. Smith had to borrow from the city for the soldiers' charges.[3]

He was a comparatively wealthy landowner, holding property not only at Chester and Hough, but at Chorlton, Blakenhall and elsewhere in the county; and in a district where a number of the leading gentry were crypto-Catholics, his support of the Elizabethan church settlement (he was classified as favourable in 1564) would have made him a valuable county official. In Chester he continued his father's tradition of generosity, offering to pave the Black Friars, and agreeing with two craftsmen for

> the annual painting of the city's four giants, one unicorn, one dromedary, one luce [pike], one camel, one ass, one dragon, six hobby-horses and six naked boys.

He died on 23 Aug. 1582, and was buried at St. Bride's, Chester.

> The funeral sermon was preached by Mr. Goodman, standing in the window of the high house next adjoining to the church, because the church was so little, and the company so great.[4]

[1] PRO, Chester 3/67/13; 80/19; *Vis. Cheshire* (Harl. Soc. xviii), 209; (lix), 212; G. Ormerod, *Cheshire*, iii. 503; *LP Hen. VIII*, xix(1), 328. [2] Ormerod, i. 213; *Cheshire Sheaf* (ser. 1), ii. 184; Chester mayors' bk. 1541–5, f. 3; G. L. Fenwick, *Hist. Chester*, 534; *LP Hen. VIII*, xx(1), pp. 254, 316; *CPR*, 1547–8, p. 81; 1550–3, p. 397; Chester RO, M/L/5/3; *APC*, vii. 284. [3] Chester RO, A/B/1/187; mayors' bk. f. 9; *HMC Montagu*, 7; *CSP Dom.* 1547–80, pp. 288, 291. [4] PRO, Chester 3/80/19; Chetham Soc. li. 21 seq.; *Cam. Misc.* ix(3), pp. 73, 76; Chester RO, A/B/1/185; Fenwick, 370; Ormerod, iii. 503; J. Hemingway, *Hist. Chester*, i. 152.

N.M.F.

SMITH, Richard, ?of Abingdon and Hartley Court, Berks.

CRICKLADE	1584[1]

?s. of Thomas Smith of Abingdon by Joan Jennings; bro. of Thomas*. *educ.* ?Christ Church, Oxf. 1572, BA 1576, MA 1578.

Seven Richard Smiths appear in the Wiltshire taxation lists of 1576, none of sufficient standing to have been the 1584 Cricklade MP. It is also unlikely that the Cricklade Member was Richard Smythe*, the customer's son, for he had no known connexion with the Brydges family, the patrons at Cricklade. A better guess – and the one made here – might be Richard Smith of Abingdon, some 25 miles from Cricklade, the brother of the 1589 Member, Thomas Smith, who much later married the daughter of William Brydges*, 4th Baron Chandos. It is quite likely that both Thomas and Richard were in the service of the Brydges family by 1584. Nothing more can be said of this Richard Smith, except that he was one of his brother's executors and was then renting from him a large house named Hartley court, near Reading.[2]

[1] Add. 38823. [2] Vis. Berks. (Harl. Soc. lvii), 78; PCC 113 Dorset; CSP Dom. 1603–10, p. 563.

A.H.

SMITH, Thomas (c.1556–1609), of Abingdon, Berks. and Parson's Green, Mdx.

| CRICKLADE | 1589 |
| TAMWORTH | 1593 |

b. c.1556, s. of Thomas Smith, ?mayor of Abingdon 1583–4, by Joan Jennings; bro. of Richard.* educ. Abingdon free sch.; Christ Church, Oxf. student 1573, BA 1574, MA 1578. m. by 1604, Frances, da. of William Brydges*, 4th Baron Chandos of Sudeley, Glos., 1s. d.v.p. 1da. Kntd. May 1603.[1]

Public orator, Oxf. Univ. 1582, proctor 1584; sec. to the Earl of Essex prob. by 1587, certainly by 1591–1601; clerk of PC 1587–1605; clerk of the Parliaments from 1597; Latin sec. from June 1603; master of requests from 1608.[2]

Smith came from a Berkshire family, and may have been related to the Richard Smith (d. c.1568) who was gentleman usher to the Queen. He probably entered the Earl of Essex's service before 1587, if, as is likely, he obtained his clerkship of the Council through the Earl. In 1588 he was returned as a Member for Cricklade, no doubt being nominated by Giles Brydges*, 3rd Baron Chandos, whose niece he was to marry later.[3]

In December 1591 Smith wrote to Cecil from Oxford to support his master's claim to the chancellorship of the university in succession to (Sir) Christopher Hatton*. He asserted that Essex had 'many more voices than any other', and appealed to Cecil against those prepared to sacrifice the university's liberty by soliciting a court nomination, in order to keep Essex out. In September 1592 at Oxford he took a leading part in a disputation before the Queen, who thought his speech 'too long'. He was brought into Parliament by Essex for Tamworth in 1593. No activity can be ascribed to Smith in either of his two Parliaments.[4]

In July 1597 Smith petitioned Cecil – having, he said, no-one else to rely on, in Essex's absence abroad – for the clerkship of the Parliaments, left vacant by the death of Anthony Wyckes, another Abingdon man. He assured

Cecil that the office was 'of small commodity, and may well enough be executed by me, notwithstanding the place of service I have already in the court'. He obtained the office against competition from Robert Bowyer II*, and may have helped to raise the standard of the Lords' journals. He continued right up to the winter of 1600–1, to hold both his job with Essex and his clerkship of the Privy Council. He described the Earl in the generosity of his more fortunate days, as 'yielding moisture unto the dried and withered plants' such as himself, but during Essex's eclipse in the autumn of 1599 declared 'the court is the only school of wisdom in the world' and he avoided any implication in the Earl's final downfall: he was not the Thomas Smith imprisoned for several months after the rebellion in February 1601.[5]

In 1605 he seems to have been persuaded by Robert Cecil, then Earl of Salisbury, to resign his clerkship of the Council, possibly in favour of Edward Jones*; but he was still fully employed as Latin secretary. In his later years Smith was a great friend of Dudley Carleton†. William Knollys*, then Lord Knollys, and Salisbury were godfathers to Smith's son, Salisbury sending Sir Michael Hickes* as his proxy at the christening in August 1605. Smith apologized for being absent from his post for an excessive time at his son's birth; and the boy cannot have lived long, for it was Smith's daughter who inherited. She married as her second husband Sir Edward Herbert†, attorney-general 1641–5. The Smith property went to her daughter by her first marriage, who married John, 1st Viscount Mordaunt. This included a lodging in the Savoy, a house at Shinfield, near Reading, lands in Gloucestershire, Cambridgeshire and Wiltshire and a manor at Berwick-on-Tees: the Berwick estate he had recently purchased from his friend Hugh Middleton, perhaps in hope of obtaining the secretaryship of the council in the north, the reversion of which had been granted to him and Sir Thomas Edmonds* in 1603. He bequeathed £13 6s. 8d. to (Sir) Thomas Bodley* for his library, and £100 to the corporation of Abingdon for the poor.

On 28 Nov. 1609 it was reported to Salisbury that Smith was dead and that his registers of Latin letters were available for return to the government. Smith's widow married Thomas Cecil, 1st Earl of Exeter.[6]

[1] DNB; Vis. Berks. (Harl. Soc. lvii), 78; A. E. Preston, St. Nicholas, Abingdon, 468; CSP Dom. 1581–90, p. 177; Shaw, Knights, ii. 109. [2] CSP Dom. 1595–7, p. 505; 1603–10, p. 14; APC, xxxii. 497. [3] Vis. Berks. (Harl. Soc. lvii), 208; PCC 19 Babington; Birch, Mems. i. 112; DNB (Brydges, Grey). [4] HMC Hatfield, iv. 162; Nichols, Progresses Eliz. iii. 152; Neale, Commons, 238. [5] HMC Hatfield, vi. 242; vii. 229, 334, 335; viii. 334, 399, 400; ix. 48, 149, 310; xi. 102, 208, 530; Neale, Parlts. ii. 332; CSP Dom. 1598–1601, p. 360; APC, xxxii. 70. [6] Lansd. 89, f. 92; HMC Hatfield, xvi. 443–4; xvii. 368, 371, 373, 379; CSP Dom. 1603–10, pp. 63, 176, 432, 515, 552, 563; PCC 113 Dorset; DNB; CP.

A.H.

SMITH, Sir Thomas (1513–77), of Theydon Mount, Essex.[1]

MARLBOROUGH	1547
GRAMPOUND	1553 (Oct.)
LIVERPOOL	1559
ESSEX	1571, 1572*

b. 23 Dec. 1513, 2nd s. of John Smith (d. 1557) of Walden by Agnes, da. of one Charnock of Lancs. educ. Queens', Camb. 1526, BA and fellow 1530–47, MA 1532, LlD and DCL 1542; travelled abroad (France, Italy) 1540–2. m. (1) 15 Apr. 1548, Elizabeth (d. 1552), da. of William Carkeke of London, s.p.; (2) 23 July 1554, Philippa (d. 1578), da. of John Wilford of London, wid. of Sir John Hampden of Theydon Mount, s.p.; 1s. illegit. b. 1547, d. 1573. Kntd. 1549.

Reader in nat. philosophy and Greek, Camb. 1533–50, public orator 1533, regius prof. civil law 1540; vice-president, Queens', Camb.; vice-chancellor, Camb. 1543–4; chancellor to bp. of Ely Jan. 1545; rector, Leverington, Cambs. 1545–9; dean of Carlisle 1548–54, from 1559; provost, Eton 1547–54; sec. to Edward Seymour, Duke of Somerset 1547; clerk of PC 1547–8; envoy to Antwerp 1548, France 1550, 1562–6, 1567, 1571–2; principal sec. 1548–9, from 1572; PC from Mar. 1571; chancellor of the Garter 1572; keeper of privy seal 1573.

J.p. Bucks., Essex from c.1559; commr. subsidy, Essex 1570.

During Mary's reign Smith was deprived of his offices, but he was not obliged to flee the country, and retired to his house near Eton. Within a month of Elizabeth's accession he was appointed to the committee to consider 'all things necessary for the Parliament' of 1559, to which he was returned for Liverpool. It would be logical to find Smith in charge of such bills as that for the recognition of the Queen's title, and indeed a Mr. Smyth was appointed to this, 11 Feb. 1559, and to other committees in February and March. The clerk frequently failed to differentiate between a knight and plain Mr., but the fact that he has Sir Thomas Smith as such introducing a bill to improve the quality of woollen cloth, 2 Mar. 1559, points to the Member on these other committees being Christopher Smith. Later in the year Sir Thomas sat on at least two inquiries into the religious settlement, and in October he was asked to attend the King of Sweden's son while he was in England seeking the royal hand. But these were hardly duties suitable for a former secretary of state and Smith's letters made plain the frustration he felt at this time. In 1561 Sir Nicholas Throckmorton*, ambassador to France, urged the Privy Council to send Smith to join him. Smith left in September 1562 and was away for nearly four years. This was a crucial period in his life, and it cannot be said that he came out of it with an enhanced reputation. From the start there were differences between him and Throckmorton, culminating in a dramatic encounter when they drew their daggers against each other and had to be forcibly restrained. After the Treaty of Troyes in

1564 Throckmorton was permitted to return home in triumph, but Smith, to his chagrin, had to remain in attendance on the peripatetic French court for two more years. His despatches and private correspondence were filled with complaints of the hardships and illnesses which he endured until in April 1566, he was allowed to return home, having lost the respect of Elizabeth and the Council.

After a brief visit to France in April 1567 to make the formal request for Calais which had been agreed to in the Treaty, Smith returned to his country house and his books, no doubt imagining that his days in office were over, especially after an abortive attempt to secure the chancellorship of the duchy of Lancaster. Sir William Cecil, however, whom Smith had known since the days of Edward VI, was in 1571 in need of a reliable colleague to whom he could delegate some of his work, and his elevation to the peerage had removed his guiding hand from the Commons. The upshot was that Smith was made a Privy Councillor a month before being returned to Parliament as knight of the shire for Essex.[2] As a government spokesman in the Commons his task was to restrain the religious extremists and secure a subsidy. He helped to administer the oaths to all Members at the opening of the session, and was soon involved in the debates on the bill for coming to church and receiving communion. He urged support for this measure, but his suggestion that the bishops should be consulted was rejected by the House at the instigation of William Fleetwood I*. He spoke on the treasons bill, and, as Privy Councillor, sat on numerous committees. He was specifically named to those dealing with church attendance (6, 21 Apr.), fugitives (24 Apr.), the order of business (26 Apr.), religious bill B (28 Apr.), dispensations granted by the archbishop of Canterbury (4 May), the bill against bulls (10 May), cloth workers (17 May), corrupt presentations (25 May) and barristers' fees (28 May). For much of the summer and autumn of 1571 Smith was concerned in the examination of many connected with the Norfolk plot. Here he seems at last to have been effectively employed and to have earned royal gratitude, though he refused to torture two prisoners.

Shortly before the end of the year Smith was again in France as ambassador, helping Francis Walsingham* in the negotiations for a possible marriage between Elizabeth and Anjou; reporting fully to the French on the Norfolk plot; and concluding a commercial and defensive treaty. Walsingham let Smith take the lead in the negotiations and the reports he sent home were detailed and witty. He soon realised that Anjou's religious views were too rigid to permit of a satisfactory marriage agreement and he began to press the claims of the younger brother, Alençon, 'not as tall perhaps, not so fair as his brother, but on the other hand, not so obstinate or so papistical and, if rumours were true, more apt for the getting of children'. The treaty signed at Blois (19 Apr. 1572) was quite a triumph for

Smith (even though all its provisions were not applied in practice), and marks the peak of Smith's prestige under Elizabeth. The tone of his last letters home is very different from those he wrote towards the end of his 1562–6 embassy. The Queen approved his 'plain and circumspect usage', and the marks of approval which had evaded him for so long at last began to materialize. He was appointed chancellor of the order of the Garter at £100 p.a., and on 13 July 1572 regained the office of secretary he had held 23 years before. He was again returned to Parliament for Essex, having written to Burghley expressing his desire to be elected, even though he was abroad. He asked Burghley to pass on his request to Lord Rich and to the sheriff of the county, even suggesting that a letter from the Queen might help. However, as Smith was still involved in negotiations with Catherine de Medici on 18 June 1572 it is highly unlikely that he attended the session of Parliament that ended on the 30th of the month.

At this time the office of secretary of state was still only as important as the man holding it. An examination of the correspondence of the years from 1572 to 1576 reveals few instances of Smith having any influence on policymaking. He complained constantly of the Queen's delays and refusal to sign documents, even on minor topics, when Burghley was not at hand to be consulted. Until the Queen had signed he durst 'never adventure to affirm anything, for fear of contrary winds, the which is no news in this court'. For much of the time he was mediating between Burghley, the Queen, the Privy Council and foreign ambassadors. He was now in his sixties, in ill health, and demoralized by the death of his only son in Ireland in 1573. Walsingham's appointment as secretary in 1573 no doubt eased his last few years in office. His last attendance at a Privy Council was in March 1576. Before he retired, however, Smith had to get through another session of Parliament, and, though he did not speak, he did a fair share of the fetching and carrying of bills to the Lords and of committee work generally. He was named to committees on the following: bastardy (15 Feb. 1576), the coinage (15 Feb.), dags and pistols (17 Feb.), butlerage and prizage of wines (21 Feb.), schools and colleges (2 Mar.), grants by Norwich dean and chapter (2 Mar.) and cloth (9 Mar.). He sent a number of bills to the Lords on 10 Mar., and more on the 12th. His last recorded task on the afternoon of 13 Mar. was to be one of a large committee of Members to hear the observations of counsel for the goldsmiths on the bill which was to receive its third reading the next day.[3]

Smith suffered for the rest of his life from an increasingly painful disease, probably cancer of the throat. In September 1576 he was at Bath taking the waters, but returned home shortly afterwards, dying 12 Aug. 1577 at Hill Hall, his second wife's house, which he had rebuilt. A fine monument is still to be seen in Theydon Mount church, within the grounds of the estate which his brother's family still occupies. His will, dated 18 Feb. 1577, includes the gift of a gilt cup with the 'seven planets' for the Queen 'as most worthy, having all the good gifts endowed of God which he ascribed to the seven planets'. He left his fine library of some 350 books to Queens' College 'because I see that none of these which shall succeed me of long time are learned'. Smith was a scholar, an author of wide interests, and a conscientious statesman of the second rank.

[1] This biography is largely based upon M. Dewar, *Sir Thomas Smith, a Tudor Intellectual in Office*. See also *Archaeologia*, xxxviii. 98–127. [2] N. M. Sutherland, *Massacre of St. Bartholomew*, 273–4. [3] For Smith's parliamentary activities the sources are Neale, *Commons*, 225; *Parlts.* i. 195–6, 215, 229; Trinity, Dublin, anon. jnl., ff. 6, 15, 36; *CJ*, i. 54, 55, 56, 58, 83, 85, 86, 87, 88, 90, 92, 93, 106, 107, 110, 112, 113, 114, 115; D'Ewes, 155, 157, 159, 160, 165, 168, 176, 178, 179, 180, 181, 182, 183, 184, 186, 188, 189, 190, 241, 247, 248, 250, 251, 252, 253, 254, 257, 258, 260, 262.

M.R.P.

SMITH, William I (*d.* 1591), of Wells, Som.

WELLS   1586

s. of *either* John Smith (*d.* 1558) of Queen Camel[1] *or* Thomas Smith (*d.* 1555) of Wells.[2] m., 1s. 1da.
Freeman, Wells 1555, master of guild of merchants 1567, 1576.

There were two contemporary William Smiths at Wells: one, a capper, became a freeman in 1555 and the other, a tailor, in 1558.[3] The former, who is the 1586 MP, was one of the pledges when the latter became a freeman. Smith twice held an office equivalent to that of mayor at a time when Wells was struggling to free itself from the domination of Bishop Berkeley, and in 1576 the dissension between the bishop and the borough came to the notice of the Privy Council, who held an inquiry. The bishop thereupon required Smith

to lay down and not use and carry abroad before him his maces within the said borough until the matter in question was tried in law or otherwise determined

but Smith refused. It was eventually agreed that the bishop, for a price, would waive his claims and the city be granted a new charter. When the bishop tried to resile from his agreement, the Privy Council ordered him to perform it, 'in consideration that many disorders are grown by means of that controversy within the town of Wells'.[4]

Smith died in 1591. His will[5] contains bequests to the poor of Wells as well as to his children, his nephew and 'Thomas Smith of Lichfield my brother'. He asked to be buried in St. Cuthbert's church beside his late wife, and affirmed his hope of forgiveness through the blood of God, which would bring him to rest with the elect saints for ever.

[1] Brown, *Som. Wills*, iii. 61. [2] *Som. Wills from Exeter* (Som. Rec. Soc. lxii), 123. [3] *Wells Charters* (Som. Rec. Soc. xlvi), 179, 180. [4] T. Serel, *Mayors of Bath*, 11; Gabriel thesis, 603; *APC*, ix. 378–9. [5] PCC 41 Sainberbe.

I.C.

SMITH, William II (c.1550–1626), of Mounthall, Theydon, Essex.

RIPON	1589

b. c.1550, 1st s. of George Smith, mercer of London. *educ.* ?Peterhouse, Camb. 1570. *m.* Bridget, da. of Thomas Fleetwood* of The Vache, Bucks., 3s. 4da. *suc.* uncle 1577. Kntd. 1603.

J.p. Essex 1590; provost marshal 1601; sheriff, Essex 1619–20, dep. lt.; marshal of the Marshalsea 1616.[1]

Smith was a nephew of Sir Thomas Smith*, whose heir he became. Sir Thomas had received a grant of land in Ireland in 1571, his son had been killed trying to colonize it, and Smith himself, his brothers and their father George – the brother of Sir Thomas – were all involved in further unsuccessful attempts up to 1574. The next attempt was in June 1579, when William Smith landed with 40 men, only to be told that the grant was void because no colony had been established by the end of that March. Smith was again in Ireland in 1580, trying to make good his claim, but by this time he seems to have become less hopeful of colonizing the land, for he and his father alienated a sixth of all the estates in Ireland contained in the 1571 patent, at the annual rent of a boar and a hogshead of claret, or 40s. in lieu. William Smith may or may not have retained an interest in the country, for in 1594 he petitioned Burghley for the office of seneschal of Clanneboy, claiming 24 years' experience of the state of Ireland in his favour.[2]

Smith did not enter into all his uncle's estates immediately on the latter's death, for the widow, Philippa, who held some of them in jointure, was concerned with getting as much from the estate as possible, while Smith accused the executors of failing to finish the house at Theydon, which Sir Thomas had begun, and of disposing of the furniture after Philippa's death. Among the executors was Smith's father, who was accused of prejudicing the inheritance by settling his own pressing debts from it. By a deed of November 1581 the matter was settled by William having all the Essex lands and goods in return for taking over his father's debts.[3]

Smith's name and residence were entered on the 1589 Ripon return in a different hand from the remainder, indicating the intervention of a patron, but who this was has not been determined. The archbishops of York usually nominated there, but the election took place shortly after the death of Archbishop Sandys and before a new appointment had been made. Perhaps it was a government nomination, Lord Burghley acting through the influence of the president of the council in the north.

In Essex Smith became a leading member of the county gentry. As his epitaph states: 'All offices there, sorted with a man of his quality, he right worshipfully performed, and died one of the deputy lieutenants of the shire; a place of no small trust and credit'. He apparently never gained any office of national importance although he may have been the William Smith who was trying to become surveyor of the ordnance in the Tower in 1601. At the beginning of James I's reign he accompanied the new English ambassador on his journey to Spain. As a result, according to Strype, he failed to gain James's ratification of his title to the Irish lands granted to Sir Thomas Smith. He had left his suit in the hands of Sir James Hamilton, and while he was away Hamilton and some Scottish nobles gained a grant of the lands for themselves.[4]

Smith died in London in his 77th year on 13 Nov. 1626. His will was made on 29 June 1625 and proved on 18 Dec. 1626 by the widow, Bridget. His principal landed estate had already been settled. Thomas, his second son, was to have an annuity of £100 during his mother's lifetime while she held land that he was to inherit. He was buried, as he had requested, in Theydon church, which he had rebuilt, and where his widow erected a monument 'to allay her languor and longing after so dear a companion of her life'.[5]

[1] Strype, *Sir Thomas Smith*, 174; *Vis Essex* (Harl. Soc. xiv), 710; Hatfield ms 278; *APC*, xxxi. 164, 188; *CSP Dom.* 1611–18, p. 367. [2] D. B. Quinn, 'Sir Thomas Smith (1513–77) and the beginnings of Eng. colonial theory', *Procs. Am. Phil. Soc.* lxxxix(4), pp. 549–50, 558; *CSP Ire.* 1574–85, pp. 246, 271, 272; 1592–6, p. 211; M. Dewar, 'Sir Thomas Smith' (London PhD thesis, 1956), pp. 332, 334. [3] Dewar thesis, 403, 425–6; Dewar, *Sir Thomas Smith*, 206–8. [4] Strype, 137, 174; *HMC Hatfield*, xi. 37. [5] PCC 150 Hele; C142/468/81; Strype, 151.

A.M.M.

SMYTH, James

MIDHURST	1597

The 'James Smyth Esq.' who was returned for Midhurst has not been identified. Some possibilities are suggested under SMITH, James.

P.W.H.

SMYTH, Nicholas (1559–1622), of London.

TRURO	1593
WIGAN	1597
ST. MAWES	1614

b. 1559, s. of Nicholas Smyth of London. *educ.* St. Paul's; Exeter Coll. Oxf. 1575; I. Temple 1580. *m.* by Aug. 1587, Katherine, da. of William Gardiner* of Bermondsey, wid. of John Stephen of Stepkyn, 4s.

Receiver of the revenue in the Exchequer for Mdx., Herts., Essex and London 1595–at least 1606.

Son of the Nicholas Smyth whose accounts as receiver under Edward VI and Mary appear in the Lansdowne manuscripts, Smyth received £50 p.a. and 1% of his receipts when he was appointed receiver in his turn. He presumably obtained the appointment through Michael Hickes or the Cecils. Both his Elizabethan parliamentary seats were obtained through Cecil influence.

Smyth's relations with his notorious father-in-law were not always amicable, but there was apparently no permanent breach, for on Gardiner's death in 1597, Smyth was executor of his will. He died on 4 Nov. 1622.

Vis. London (Harl. Soc. i), 87; *CSP Dom.* 1595-7, p. 10; 1603-10, pp. 326, 345; Lansd. 68, f. 175; 106, f. 1; 118, ff. 56, 60; *APC*, xv. 190; PCC 1 Cobham; *Sales of Wards* (Som. Rec. Soc. lxvii), 201.

I.C.

SMYTHE, Charles (d.1587), of Windsor, Berks.

ST. ALBANS	1572

m. Catherine, da. of Richard Harvey of Porters or Pottrels, Shenley, Herts., 2s. 2da.

Bailiff, manor of Princes Risborough, Bucks. 1559; page of wardrobe of robes by 1563–at least 1570; master of standing wardrobe at Windsor castle from c.1568; keeper of wardrobe of beds and armoury at Windsor castle from 1571.

Smythe's return for St. Albans was almost certainly due to an acquaintance at court, probably Sir Nicholas Bacon†. On the other hand Smythe was probably related by marriage to Humphrey Coningsby II*, steward of St. Albans, and possibly related to Christopher Smith* the 1559 St. Albans MP, variations in spelling of the surname being of no significance.

Smythe was already described as 'Queen's servant' in the letters patent making him bailiff of Princes Risborough. At various times he received further crown grants, several of them in the form of land leases in Yorkshire, and one including a Durham coal mine. He presumably sold or leased this property: none of it is mentioned in the will he made 3 June 1587, proved 26 Oct. He asked to be buried near Walter Fish*, in the London church of St. Anthony, Budge Row.

Vis. Herts. (Harl. Soc. xxii), 45, 146, 149, 164; *CPR*, 1558-60, p. 104; 1560-3, p. 214; 1563-6, pp. 190, 202, 418; 1569-72, p. 75; E351/541, 542; Cussans, *Herts.* xiv. 355-6; R. Clutterbuck, *Herts.* i. 444; *APC*, x. 108; PCC 62 Spencer.

N.M.F.

SMYTHE, John I (1557-1608), of Westenhanger, Kent.

AYLESBURY	1584
HYTHE	1586, 1589, 1604*

bap. 16 Sept. 1557, 2nd but 1st surv. s. of Thomas Smythe I* of Westenhanger by Alice (d.1593), da. of Sir Andrew Judd of London and Tonbridge; bro. of Richard* and

Thomas II*. *educ.* G. Inn 1577. *m.* by Jan. 1577, Elizabeth, da. and h. of John Fyneux* of Herne by Margaret, da. of Thomas Morley† of Glynde, Suss., 2s. 6da. *suc.* fa. 1591. Kntd. 1603.

J.p. Kent from c.1584, q. by 1601, sheriff 1600-1; dep. gov. mines royal by 1605.[1]

Smythe has remained an obscure figure in comparison with his father, the customer of London, his younger brother Thomas, who became governor of the East India Company, and his son, also Thomas, who was given a peerage by Charles I. For the most part he left the family's business interests to his brother, he himself enjoying the life of a country gentleman on the estates which his father had acquired in Kent, either through marriage or financial acumen. Born after his father had moved to London from Wiltshire, he spent the early years of his life in the capital. By the time he entered an inn of court (if we have the right John Smythe here) he had already made a fortunate marriage to a Kent heiress.[2]

Smythe's return at Aylesbury in 1584 was due to the connexion between the family and the Pakingtons, lords of the borough. The Scotts and the Sackvilles, both related by marriage to the Smythes, their Kent neighbours, also supplied MPs for the borough during Elizabeth's reign, and it is evident that the four families knew each other well. During the rest of his parliamentary career Smythe sat for Hythe, always without payment. Though he had some dealings with the lord warden, there is no reason to suppose that he needed Cobham's support to secure the seat. His principal residence was only a few miles away and he clearly took an interest in Hythe politics: when the corporation chose his brother Sir Richard as Member in 1614 they referred to 'the continual love and affection of your good father and brother towards the town'. Smythe left no mark on the records of the House but he could have taken part in the work of the committee on the import of fish, 6 Mar. 1587.[3]

Smythe succeeded to his father's property, apart from provision made for the widow, on Thomas's death in June 1591. The principal manors were at Ostenhanger (now Westenhanger), near Hythe, and Ashford, which Customer Smythe had inherited from his father-in-law, but there were also at least half a dozen more manors and much other property scattered throughout Kent. In addition, Smythe acquired in 1592, through his wife, the manor of Herne in north Kent and other Fyneux lands in the county. With these extensive estates he became one of the richest men in Kent. As well as performing the duties expected of a man in his position, he took an interest in the affairs of the Cinque Ports, such as the reconstruction of Dover harbour, though it hardly seems likely that he was the 'John Smith' who became an associate of William Southland* in his attempt to control the government of New Romney. As successor to the Fyneux family he also had to provide money to repair Herne and Reculver churches and to rebuild the sea wall at Whitstable.[4]

It is not easy to follow Smythe's activities outside Kent, nor to estimate the extent to which he pursued his father's active interest in the commercial life of London. The task is rendered more difficult by the presence, until his death in 1594, of a port of London official of the same name. Certainly Smythe was less occupied with business than was his brother Thomas, but he did not retire permanently to the country. In 1595, for instance, there occurs a reference to the removal of a large quantity of copper from his warehouse, and as late as 1605 he was still involved in claims by the Crown against his father's estate for the period when he was customer. In 1601 'Smith and his brother', presumably of this family, claimed that the customs officials had been negligent in their duties. Richard Camarden complained to Sir Robert Cecil that Smythe 'seeketh to make show of service upon other men's labours and in the end [will] prove nothing, as all his professed services hitherto have done'. The charges, on investigation, were rejected as groundless.[5]

Smythe followed his father as a shareholder in the mines royal, particularly the part of the company concerned with mining operations in Cornwall and Merioneth. He seems to have sold some or all of his shares by 1595, but ten years later he is found as one of the deputy-governors. In this capacity he was asked to collect some papers from the London house of Lord Cobham, then in the Tower for treason. Smythe may have known Cobham quite well, for he was on the list of permitted visitors. Thomas Smythe, John's brother, who was sheriff of London in 1600–1, was accused of being involved in the Earl of Essex's show of force in the city during his shrievalty, and John was closely questioned as to his brother's activities, though he does not appear to have been involved himself.[6]

He died on 29 Nov. 1608 at the age of fifty-one. Although he urged his executors to avoid 'vain funeral pomp as the world by custom in time of darkness has long used' – a phrase found almost *verbatim* in the will of Sir Walter Mildmay* (1589) – and to prevent 'superfluous cost', they erected a magnificent monument to his memory in Ashford parish church. Dressed in armour, he is kneeling on a cushion, facing his wife, with their three surviving children in front of them. The heir, who was to become Viscount Strangford, was only nine years old when his father died and there was considerable competition for his wardship. One of Smythe's executors, Christopher Toldervey*, also sat in Parliament for Hythe.[7]

[1] H. C. Fanshawe, *Hist. Fanshawe Fam.* 92; *Arch. Cant.* xvii. 193 and n., 199, 200–1, 204; xx. 76–7; A. Pearman, *Hist. Ashford*, 20; E163/14/8; C66/1549; *HMC Hatfield*, xvii. 63. [2] E. C. de Fonblanque, *Lives of the Lords Strangford*, 6. [3] Neale, *Commons*, 183–4; Hythe ass. bk. ff. 146, 203; G. Wilks, *Barons of the Cinque Ports and the Parl. Rep. Hythe*, 64, 65, 68; D'Ewes, 412. [4] Hasted, *Kent*, vii. 529; viii. 74, 123, 214, 291, 340, 511; ix. 79, 88; x. 147–8; xii. 239; *Arch. Cant.* xvi. 165; xxv. 26, 44; *CSP Dom.* 1581–90, p. 109; 1595–7, p. 224; 1598–1601, p. 528; *APC*, xix. 5, 9, 206, 208. [5] *HMC Hatfield*, iv. 108,

181; v. 47; xi. 210; *CSP Dom.* 1603–10, p. 197; *APC*, xxv. 126–7; Lansd. 67, f. 148. [6] *HMC Hatfield*, iv. 519; v. 14–15, 198–9; xvii. 63; W. Scott, *Joint Stock Companies to 1720*, ii. 394 seq.; *CSP Dom.* 1598–1601, pp. 558–9; *APC*, xxxi. 162–3. [7] PCC 43 Dorset; C142/306/141; *Arch. Cant.* xx. 76; Pearman, *Ashford*, 18–20; C. Igglesden, *Ashford Church*, 90; de Fonblanque, 7.

M.R.P.

SMYTHE, John II (d. 1599/1600), of King's Lynn, Norf.[1]

RICHMOND   1589

m., issue.
?Freeman, King's Lynn 1570–1, searcher by 1583.[2]

The explanation for a King's Lynn merchant representing a Yorkshire constituency lies in Smythe's connexion with the salt-pans at Sunderland. In 1585 Thomas Wilkes* was granted a 21-year monopoly of producing the white salt imported through Boston and King's Lynn, to which Hull was added in the following year. Wilkes sold the patent to a syndicate headed by Smythe, reserving himself £100 a year. Smythe's partners in the venture were Robert Anderson, a Tyneside mine owner and shipman, and Robert Bowes I*, treasurer at Berwick. Naturally the patent aroused hostility, first at King's Lynn, then in Yorkshire, where in the spring of 1588 the justices refused to enforce it and appealed to the president of the council in the north. Wilkes travelled to Yorkshire, agreed to reduce the price of salt, conceded that its transport should be confined to Yorkshire towns and seaports, and accepted a four-year limit for the life of the patent. The opposition was organized by such independent producers as Robert Delaval of Seton Delaval, Northumberland, who, in a petition to Burghley, complained that he would be ruined, adding 'at the last Parliament [1589] your said suppliant with others then purposed to crave relief at the same court, but through the persuasion of some honourable and worshipful personage they stayed in proceeding'. Perhaps, therefore, it was the suggestion that the matter might be raised in Parliament that caused Smythe to look for a seat in the Commons, and his partner Bowes to find him one. In the event Bowes went bankrupt in 1591, and the salt-pans reverted to the government. In September 1591 Smythe wrote to Burghley asking for a new and stronger lease 'with Mr. Bowes's consent', which was granted at an increased rent. The patent was again renewed after Wilkes's death, Smythe's rapacity increasing with the prospect of the 1601 Parliament putting an end to monopolies.

He died before 14 Jan. 1600, when letters of administration were granted to his widow Martha, who thus acquired the salt patent. She told Cecil in 1601 that she was afraid it might be cancelled by the coming Parliament, and it was the only livelihood of herself and her children.[3]

¹ Except where otherwise stated, this biography is based upon E. Hughes, *Studies in Admin. and Finance*. However, the suggestion that Smythe was the s. of Charles Smythe, MP St. Albans 1572, has not been accepted in the light of *Al. Cant.* i(4), p. 100, which has him a fellow of King's, Camb. to 1577, then retiring to Little Bardfield, Essex. Salt-pan Smythe's parentage remains unascertained. ² *HMC Hatfield*, xi. 505; *Lynn Freemen*, 110; Req. 2/61/7; E190/429/5. ³ Lansd. 52, f. 48; 59, ff. 188–9; 86, f. 187; J. U. Nef, *Rise of the British Coal Industry*, i. 176; *Hist. Northumb.* ix. 352; SP12/240/13; *Border Pprs.* ii. 92; *HMC Hatfield*, v. 526; xi. 505; *CSP Dom.* 1598–1601, p. 310; PCC admon. act bk. 1599–1605, f. 36.

A.M.M.

SMYTHE, Richard (1563–1628), of Leeds Castle, Kent.

| HEYTESBURY | 1601 |
| HYTHE | 1614 |

b. 1563, 5th but 4th surv. s. of Thomas Smythe I* of Westenhanger by Alice, da. and h. of Sir Andrew Judd of London; bro. of John I* and Thomas II*. *educ.* ?Barnard's Inn c.1585; M. Temple 1585. *m.* (1) Sept. 1589, Elizabeth, da. of Sir Thomas Scott* of Scot's Hall and Nettlestead, wid. of John Knatchbull, 2s. 2da.; (2) aft. 1597, Jane (*d.* 13 Oct. 1607), da. and h. of Sir John White* of London, wid. of Samuel Thornhill of Bromley, 1da.; (3) Mary, da. of Roger Boyle of Preston by Faversham, wid., 1da. Kntd. 23 July 1603.¹
Jt. (with bro. Thomas II) receiver gen. of duchy of Cornw. 1604–26, (with s. Thomas) 1626–*d.*; commr. revenues assigned to Prince Charles; j.p. Kent.²

The identification of this Member with the younger son of 'Customer' Thomas Smythe is placed beyond reasonable doubt by the knowledge that this Richard Smythe was a connexion by marriage of the Thynnes of Longleat. When his sister Katherine married Sir Rowland Hayward*, twice lord mayor of London, she gained three stepdaughters, one of whom, Joan, was already the wife of John Thynne* (*d.*1604). Thynne had himself filled the first seat at Heytesbury in every Parliament save one (that of 1589, when he was knight of the shire) since 1584, while the second went to his relatives and friends; his fellow-Member in 1601 could thus be no other than his wife's step-uncle, and other men bearing these names, including the MP for Cricklade in 1584, can be dismissed from consideration.

With his brothers John, Thomas, Henry, Robert and Simon, Richard Smythe had grown up into the world of business mingled with politics. He did not go to either university (the Richard Smith who matriculated at Magdalen 8 Dec. 1578 was a different man), but he was admitted in his early twenties to the Middle Temple, although presumably not for serious professional study. It was in the same year that his father, a native of Wiltshire, where he had built Corsham House, confirmed his adoption of Kent as his new shire by purchasing Westenhanger from the Crown. Of the sons, only Henry was to establish himself in Wiltshire; the others all made

their homes in Kent. On their father's death in 1591, John, the heir, succeeded to Westenhanger, Thomas acquired Bitborough and Sutton-at-Hone, and Robert, who was to die prematurely, settled at Longport. (The youngest, Simon, also died young, being killed on the Cadiz expedition of 1596). Richard, who received Newchurch under his father's will, soon added to it, by purchase from Sir Warham St. Leger, the manor and castle of Leeds, and it was Leeds which he made his residence for the rest of his life.³

Richard Smythe had a number of contemporary namesakes from whom he is not always readily distinguished. Thus the summons to 'Richard Smith, of the Middle Temple, gent.' to appear before the Privy Council in January 1586 may have concerned the Middle Templar who became a barrister and served on the council of Wales; a similar doubt arises over the 'R. Smith, gentleman' who was sent on the Queen's service to Brittany in January 1593, and who was perhaps the Exchequer official. More easily distinguished is Dr. Richard Smith of Christ Church, Oxford, who in 1592 was listed as a recusant and who in December 1598 was in Paris and in January 1604 in Rheims. The slightness of Richard Smythe's connexion with Wiltshire makes it unlikely that he was any of the men to whom references in that county are found. His position in Kent does, however, find illustration: in 1600 he was one of those whose horses supplied for the Irish war were found defective, and his name occurs in a list relating to that country, probably of 1603.⁴

In 1601 Smythe's brother Sir Thomas, then sheriff of London, was seriously compromised in the Essex rebellion, which cost him his office. That Richard was not deeply implicated is likely in view of his return to the Parliament of that year; but he may have wanted a seat as a vantage point in case his brother was attacked there. There is, however, no evidence that he played any part in the business of the House. His career under James I, as official of the duchy of Cornwall, patentee, landed gentleman, and MP for Hythe in 1614 lies outside the scope of this biography. He died in 1628, having made an elaborate will, and has a monument in Ashford church which includes figures of his three wives and five children and testifies to his public and private virtues.⁵

¹ *Arch. Cant.* xx. 76–81; xxi. 126 seq.; xxiii. 113–14; Lansd. 47, f. 118. ² *CSP Dom.* 1603–10, p. 93; 1625–6, p. 559. ³ *Al. Ox. 1500–1714*, p. 1378; *Vis. Glos.* (Harl. Soc. xxi), 147; Hasted, *Kent*, v. 485–6; viii. 340. ⁴ *APC*, xiv. 295; xxiv. 5; *HMC Hatfield*, iv. 267; xiv. 149; xv. 215; xvi. 33; *CSP Dom.* 1598–1601, p. 138. ⁵ *Arch. Cant.* xx. 82–3; xxviii. p. lxxxvi.; PCC 79 Barrington.

M.B.

SMYTHE, Thomas I (1522–91), of London, Ashford and Westenhanger, Kent.¹

| ?TAVISTOCK | 1553 (Oct.) |
| AYLESBURY | 1554 (Apr.) |

RYE	1554 (Nov.)
WINCHELSEA	1555
PORTSMOUTH	1563

b. 1522, 2nd s. of John Smythe of Corsham, Wilts. by Joan, da. of Robert Brouncker of Melksham. *m.* c.1554, Alice, da. and event. h. of Sir Andrew Judd, merchant of London and Tonbridge, by Joan, da. of Sir Thomas Mirfyn, 7s. inc. John I*, Richard* and Thomas II*, 6da.
    Collector, tonnage and poundage, port of London 1558–69; j.p.q. Kent from c.1577; treasurer for repair of Dover harbour 1580; master, Haberdashers' Co. 1583.[2]

Smythe sat in only one Elizabethan Parliament, for Portsmouth, through an unknown connexion with the captain of that port, Adrian Poynings*. Smythe made no known contribution to the business of the House.

In July 1558 Smythe became collector of the subsidy of tonnage and poundage on goods imported into London. This appointment to the second most important fiscal office in England's principal port began that part of his career for which he is best remembered, and which earned him the soubriquet Customer Smythe. Elizabeth confirmed his appointment, which he retained until he became farmer of the same subsidies in 1569. In 1567, however, it was discovered that he had caused a loss of revenue by issuing privy warrants and his disfavour with the Queen cost him a turn as sheriff of London. In fact he escaped imprisonment only through Cecil's good offices, and remained out of favour until his accounts were settled in 1570. Now began the most profitable period of his association with the customs, his lease of the duties on all goods imported into London (except those on wine), and the duties on all goods imported or exported through Sandwich and Chichester, with the same exception. The lease was renewed in 1576, and then on two subsequent occasions until Smythe relinquished it in 1588. During this period because of an increase in revenue brought about by a general expansion in trade, the annual rent rose from £17,659 6s. 5d. between 1570 and 1576, to £30,000 between 1584 and 1588. Through constant vigilance the government tried to keep track of Smythe's activities and hold his profit within reasonable bounds; nevertheless his total profit for the period when he was farmer of the customs has been estimated at £48,000. Part of this was spent on other ventures less immediately successful, such as prospecting for minerals, and trading with Russia. Smythe became a member of the Muscovy Company on its formation in 1569, and of the Levant Company in 1581. He also attempted to corner the alum market, gaining Burghley's agreement to a three-year monopoly of the English market while he disposed of acquired stock at a profit of 25%. It is a measure of Smythe's influence with Burghley that, while the latter had rejected all previous suggestions of monopoly, he agreed to Smythe's, who thus gained a guaranteed market for his alum, besides benefiting from the increased customs duty on imports.[3]

Through a fortunate marriage Smythe came into the Kent manors of Ashford, Estone and Wall, as well as lands in Hertfordshire. In 1575 he bought Westenhanger, and made further additions to his estates in Kent in 1578 and 1579. In Wiltshire he acquired Holme Park, and West Park in Corsham, where he built a new house as a tangible reminder of his wealth.

There is evidence that Smythe could count the Earl of Leicester among his friends as well as Burghley. In 1585 Sylvanus Scory*, when questioned about the publication of *Leycester's Commonwealth*, admitted that he had introduced Leicester to the Spanish ambassador at a dinner in the Customer's house, and in the same year Smythe was amongst those who promised to finance Leicester's expedition to the Low Countries. Leicester himself referred in his will to 'the great love and long friendship' that there had been between himself and Smythe. Smythe in his own will, made 22 May 1591 and proved by his eldest surviving son John on 29 Oct. 1591, asked to be buried in Ashford parish church. His widow received the lease of his London house; his unmarried daughter Elizabeth was left £1,500; and his married daughters a total of £1,990. Four of his sons were left £100 each, and his household servants £5 each. The poor of Ashford in Kent were to receive £40, those of the London parish of St. Gabriel Fenchurch £10, and those of Corsham in Wiltshire £10. The London prisoners were left a further £40. The total money bequests mentioned in the will, excluding those to servants, amounted to £5,050, not a vast sum when all is considered. The executors were his son John, his sons-in-law Sir Rowland Hayward* and Thomas Fanshawe*, and his friend and fellow merchant Thomas Aldersey*. The overseer was Thomas Owen*. Smythe died 7 June 1591 and was buried in Ashford church, where a monument was erected to him. His epitaph described him as a patron of literature, and his name occurs in the dedication of Richard Robinson's translation of John Leland's book on King Arthur (1562).[4]

[1] Except where otherwise indicated this biography is based upon L. L. S. Lowe, 'Mr. Customer Smythe' (Oxf. Univ. BLitt thesis, 1950). [2] SP12/104; 121/17; *CSP Dom.* 1547–80, p. 671. [3] M. B. Donald, *Eliz. Copper*, 67, 240, 251–3; *Eliz. Monopolies*, 71–3; *CSP Dom.* 1581–90, pp. 131, 158, 164, 183, 290; T. S. Willan, *The Muscovy Merchants of 1555*, p. 122; Hakluyt, *Voyages* (1903–5 ed.), iii. 109, 348; v. 193, 201; L. Stone, *Sir Horatio Palavicino*, 52, 55–6. [4] *CSP Dom.* 1581–90, p. 227; *HMC Hatfield*, xiii. 288; PCC 15 Darcy, 78 Sainberbe; C142/229/142; *Arch. Cant.* xvii. 193, 198, 204.

A.M.M.

SMYTHE, Thomas II (c.1558–1625), of Fenchurch Street, London, and Sutton-at-Hone, Kent.

AYLESBURY	1597
DUNWICH	1604*
SANDWICH	1614
SALTASH	1621

b. c.1558, 3rd but 2nd surv. s. of Thomas Smythe I* of Westenhanger, Kent by Alice (*d.* 1593), da. of Sir Andrew Judd; bro. of John I* and Richard*. *educ.* Merchant Taylors' 1571. *m.* (1) Judith, da. and h. of Richard Culverwell, *s.p.*; (2) Joan, da. and h. of William Hobbs, *s.p.*; (3) Sarah, da. and h. of William Blount, 3s. 1da. Kntd. 13 May 1603.[1]

Freeman, Skinners' Co. by 1580, Haberdashers' Co. by 1580, master, Haberdashers' 1599–1600; customer of London, auditor 1597–8, alderman 1599–1601, sheriff Nov. 1600–Feb. 1601; capt. of city trained bands; treasurer, St. Bartholomew's hosp. 1597–1601; trade commr. to negotiate with the Dutch 1596, 1598, 1619, with the Empire 1603; member of Merchant Adventurers; gov. Muscovy Co. by 1600; member of Levant Co., gov. by 1600; gov. E.I. Co. 1600–1, 1603–5, 1607–21; gov. North West Passage Co.; treasurer, Virginia Co. 1609–19; gov. of Somers Is. Co. 1615–*d.*; ambassador to Russia 1604–5; jt. receiver of duchy of Cornwall Apr. 1604; receiver for Dorset and Somerset May 1604; commr. for navy reform 1619.[2]

In the 30 years ending with the death of James I, Smythe was overseer of virtually all the trade which passed through the port of London. He had two outstanding examples: his maternal grandfather, Sir Andrew Judd, was a leading city merchant and lord mayor in the middle of the sixteenth century, and his father, Customer Smythe, whose shrewd judgment and financial acumen brought him a fortune in the city, and a position among the county families of Kent. Still, it is not easy to follow his career in the years before the turn of the century. As well as his father, who died in 1591, there was at least one other London merchant of the same name. It is clear, however, that he was already well established in his own business during his father's lifetime, presumably with the latter's financial backing. By the end of the century he had three strings to his bow. He occupied a prominent position in the city; he took the lead in the new trading and colonizing companies which were becoming such a marked feature of the commercial life of the period; finally, as his list of offices shows, he put his experience to use in the government's service.[3]

In 1597 Smythe had his first experience of the House of Commons when he was returned for Aylesbury, a seat previously occupied by his father and his elder brother, through his family's long-standing friendship with the Pakingtons. He was named to a committee on the poor law, 22 Nov. 1597, and could have served on one about the highways near Aylesbury, 11 Jan. 1598. Others of his committees included those concerned with maltsters (12 Jan.); two alien merchants (13 Jan.); the sale of the lands and goods of one John Sharp – presumably a merchant – to pay his debts (20 Jan.); and the reformation of abuses in wine casks (3 Feb.).[4]

In the midst of his many successes, Smythe's career nearly came to an abrupt and fatal halt: he found himself deprived of the shrievalty of London, after being in office for only three months, and in prison under suspicion of being implicated in Essex's abortive *coup d'état* of February 1601. On the 14th of that month the Privy Council informed the lord mayor that Smythe had 'forgotten his duty to her Majesty' and that the city would have to elect a new sheriff. On the same day he was placed in the custody of the archbishop of Canterbury and a fortnight later, on 2 Mar., he was put in the Tower. The principal evidence against him related to Essex's visit to his house in Fenchurch Street on the morning of Sunday, 8 Feb., the day on which the Earl attempted to seize power. When examined, several of Essex's followers claimed that the Earl expected Smythe, using his position as captain of the trained bands, to raise the city in his support. Sir Christopher Blount*, later executed for his part in the plot, reported that Essex had received sympathetic messages from the city on the previous evening and that he, Essex, had often mentioned that Smythe could bring him 1,000 loyal men when he needed them. It was claimed by other witnesses that Smythe visited Essex House on the evening of the 7th, that he had also reiterated his loyalty to the Earl through Edward Bromley*, and that he knew of the rising by 5 o'clock on the Sunday morning at the latest. A number of people saw Essex's arrival at Smythe's house and observed them talking in the street outside. Some of these claimed that the sheriff urged Essex to go and seize Ludgate and Aldgate, where he would send him arms very shortly. Clearly there was much for Smythe to explain. His defence was a complete denial of the charges against him. He said that he had had no communication with the Earl for nine years until the day in question. He denied the conversation with Bromley and disclaimed prior knowledge of the plot. When pressed about the meeting with Essex at his house – an incident witnessed by many – he told them that he merely passed on a message from the lord mayor and then left home by the back door. It is surprising that he escaped with a period in prison and a heavy fine.[5]

With the new reign his return to favour was rapid. Knighted in May 1603, he was shortly afterwards employed as ambassador to Russia. As well as recovering his position as governor of all the important trading companies, he played a leading part in new trading ventures in Virginia, in Bermuda and in search of the North West Passage, and financed several voyages of exploration. He was also a leading adviser to the government on commercial and naval matters. His activities during these years, both in furthering trade and in encouraging the foundation of colonies, has led one historian to allot to him a 'unique position among the founders of the Empire'. He eventually retired to an estate he had purchased at Sutton-at-Hone, Kent, where he died 4 Sept. 1625.[6]

[1] *Arch. Cant.* xx. 76 seq.; Nichols, *Progresses Jas. I*, i. 120. [2] *DNB*; *Arch. Cant.* xx. 82 seq.; G. E. Cokayne, *Ld. Mayors and Sheriffs of London*, 1601-25, pp. 4-5; Beaven, *Aldermen*, ii. 47; *CSP Dom.* 1598-1601, p. 72; 1603-10, pp. 93, 112, 114; *CSP Col.* ii. 238; W. Scott, *Jt. Stock Cos. to 1720*, ii. 250, 257, 262; *HMC Hatfield*, xvi. 185-6; xvii. 69, 433; *APC*, 1618-19, pp. 174, 434; *Voyages of Wm. Baffin*, ed. Markham (Hakluyt Soc. lxiii), intro. ii-ix. [3] *Camb. Hist. British Empire*, i. 75; *APC*, xxvi. 451-2; *DNB*; *HMC Hatfield*, x. 236, 329; *CSP Col.* ii. 100, 117; *APC*, xxx. 732; *CSP Dom.* 1598-1601, p. 72. [4] D'Ewes, 561, 577, 578, 579, 583, 592. [5] *APC*, xxxi. 155, 157, 158, 196; *CSP Dom.* 1598-1601, 1601-3, passim; SP12/278/57, 58, 59, 60, 68, 75, 83, 93; 279/3, 8, 10, 30, 58; *HMC Hatfield*, xi. 48-9. [6] *Camb. Hist. British Empire*, i. 75.

M.R.P.

SNAGGE, Robert (*d.* 1605), of Hitchin and Letchworth, Herts.

LOSTWITHIEL   1571, 1572

2nd s. of Thomas Snagge of Letchworth by Elizabeth or Ellen, da. of one Calton of Saffron Walden, Essex; bro. of Thomas I*. *educ.* M. Temple 1559, called. *unm.*
    Lent reader, M. Temple 1580, bencher.[1]
    J.p. Herts from c.1575, rem. 1587.

Snagge was an able, hard-working puritan lawyer who achieved no office, and towards the end of his life was even put off the commission of the peace. While still a student at the Middle Temple he was several times excluded from commons for 'contumacy'. One of his offences, in the autumn of 1570, was to plead 'in English', in a suit at the Guildhall against 'Mr. Fleetwood' (probably William Fleetwood I*, recorder of London), who was a fellow-member of the Temple. Some years later Fleetwood wrote to Burghley sympathizing with a young minister, 'one Tasse', whose marriage to a daughter of Sir Robert Drury had been stopped by 'Robert Snagge, coming into the Temple Church'. By 1580 Snagge was qualified by 'anciency and sufficiency' to become a reader, but it required a Privy Council letter to persuade the Middle Temple authorities to appoint him, and then he had to share the readings with another candidate who had 'travelled and been at charges in preparing himself for the reading'.[2]

It is not clear how Snagge came to be returned to the House of Commons for Lostwithiel. He had no known connexions with the borough, with the duchy of Cornwall, or with the 2nd Earl of Bedford, who, in 1571 and 1572 received instructions from the Privy Council to supervise a 'good choice' of Members. Perhaps Snagge's brother Thomas, who sat for Bedfordshire in that Parliament, was responsible. At any rate, once in Parliament Snagge lost no time in aligning himself with the radicals. On 9 Apr. 1571 on the first reading of the bill for coming to church and receiving communion he 'wished great care for the avoiding of the double lash according to the argument of his brother', and on 14 Apr. he followed 'and far after him indeed, either for order,

proof or matter', Tristram Pistor in support of Strickland's bill for the reformation of the prayer book, repeating a favourite puritan quip that if there must be a law about the posture at communion, then instead of kneeling let it be 'to lie prostrate'. He saw 'nothing derogatory or contrary to the prerogative' in the bill's proposals. His committees in 1571 were on religion (10 Apr.), fraudulent conveyances (11 Apr.), the preservation of woods (10 May) and Plymouth harbour (25 May). In the 1572 session of Parliament Snagge's name appears in the journals for 21 of the 43 working days, sometimes twice or thrice in a day. His committees included those on outlawries (12 May), Plymouth almshouses (13 May), explanation of statutes (14, 19 May) and fraudulent conveyances (16 May). Some 20 interventions in debate are recorded, though sometimes there was 'much talk and to no purpose'. On 5 June the bill concerning Worcester's proposed canalization of water from the river Severn was under discussion following its third reading. Snagge made an ingenuous speech on behalf of William Somerset, the 3rd Earl of Worcester:

> The most part of the land through which the cut should go is my Lord of Worcester['s], who for the benefit of the town is contented therewith, and thinketh it would prove beneficial also to the country adjoining. Besides, the eight commissioners being indifferently chosen would indifferently make the price of the land. There is such provision in the bill as they would never attempt the making of the cut if it should be prejudicial to any, else were there great folly in them, since they are bound at their own costs both to stop up the cut and make recompense, which were to lease an infinite charge, and the cut being stopped up, the water must needs come to his old course.

His weightiest contributions to debates during this session were those concerning Mary Queen of Scots. On the first full working day of the session, 12 May, he moved for a petition to the Queen that 'as she had already by ordinary course of law proceeded to judgment against certain malefactors, so likewise she would proceed further to the execution'. This was the first of a number of urgent appeals for the execution of the 4th Duke of Norfolk. Norfolk had powerful friends at court who, 'if they durst, would pluck him out of the Tower', and who were seeking to influence Elizabeth towards leniency. When on 31 May Peter Wentworth again raised the question of the Duke, Snagge intervened to urge that the whole House should go to the Queen to show their solidarity in favour of execution. But his most passionate speeches were against Mary Stuart. 'The axe must give the next warning. ... What have we to do with *ius gentium*, having law of our own? Shall we say our law is not able to provide for this mischief? We might then say it hath defect in the highest degree'. To Elizabeth's objections to keeping Parliament in session, during an unhealthy time of the year, for the purpose of dealing further with the question of Mary, he had a typical puritan answer, 'Refer it to God'. When the Queen decided against the bill for Mary's execution, and declared her preference for the milder one excluding her from the succession, Snagge was in despair. 'To deal with this second bill were not to do nothing, but to do stark nought'. There were dangerous supporters of Mary in the north of England who would take advantage of Elizabeth's inaction, and recent incidents suggested that Elizabeth's own life was in danger. 'Dags [pistols] have already been taken in the court; and that which hath been, may be'. With Norfolk and Mary still living, there could be nothing but insecurity through further plots. He strongly opposed the government bill about Mary, which had been introduced first in the Lords, objecting to one clause on the ground that it might 'seem to help her son to the succession'.

Snagge made, it is tempting to write 'blundered into', an extraordinarily interesting comment on the House of Lords in one of his unreported speeches in this Parliament to the effect that they 'had not to do with the commonwealth, but that we in the Common House had only the care thereof'. He asked for the protection of the House over this (11 June 1572), when he was supported by Peter Wentworth, Recorder Fleetwood, Sir Ralph Sadler and Speaker Bell. Sir Francis Knollys was sent with a message to the Lords, and the lord keeper, Sir Nicholas Bacon†, intervened. The Commons wanted to know the names of the 'tale-tellers' who had informed against Snagge, and would have continued to press the matter had the Lords not risen before a second message from the Lower House reached them. The matter was not raised again, and it may or may not be significant that no speeches have been recorded for Snagge in the 1576 session. Very likely this reflects only the defects in the journals, and Snagge may have been among the few radical speakers who attempted a revival of religious agitation in this session. He was active enough on committees: poor law (10, 11 Feb.), two legal committees (13 Feb.), bastardy (15 Feb.), weapons (17 Feb., 2 Mar.), leather (18 Feb.), privilege (21 Feb.), foreigners (24 Feb.), Chester (25 Feb.), church discipline (29 Feb,), aliens' children (3 Mar.), juries (5 Mar.), land reclamation (6 Mar.), collateral warranties (7 Mar.), justices of the forest (8 Mar.), excess of apparel (10 Mar.), and wharves and quays (13 Mar.).

In 1581 he was a less active committeeman, but he made two recorded speeches: in favour of admitting Members returned at by-elections caused by illness or absence, and on 28 Jan. on purveyors. He served on committees concerning the clerk of the market (27 Jan.), bigamy (31 Jan.), slanderous words and practices (1 Feb.) and Lord Zouche (17 Mar.).[3]

By this time Snagge had collected a number of enemies. In 1578 he complained of charges, brought by the mayor

of St. Albans, that he had spoken against the Earl of Leicester, and he brought counter-charges before the Council; in 1580 he invoked Privy Councillors in his dispute with the Middle Temple authorities over the readership; and some years later he was thanking Lord Burghley for kindness shown to him at the court at Theobalds, and asking for support against enemies who had misrepresented him to the Queen over his 'thankless office' of justice of the peace, from which he was finally removed. He was not, he assured Burghley, a contentious person nor a 'contempner' of his betters.[4]

By the time he made his will in 1599, Snagge had been left behind: even his radicalism had lost its edge. He believed in

the Articles agreed upon in the Parliament the thirteenth year of her Majesty's reign as the public profession of the church of England (whereof I am a member) and consent therewith therein and according to the creed called the Apostles' Creed, likewise professed in this our church.

And among the list of 'friends that I ever found kind and constant', was John Whitgift 'by God's providence Archbishop of Canterbury', the man who had imprisoned Thomas Cartwright for refusing the ex-officio oath, and who, only a few years before, had engineered the banishment of those caught attending unauthorized religious meetings. Still, Whitgift had come down in favour of the Calvinist views of predestination and election in 1595, and the reason that Snagge mentioned these friends, who also included Edward Coke* and George Rotheram*, 'my adopted brother, my familiar from his childhood', was that 'they never changed their affections towards me for any preferments of theirs nor fault of mine'.

The sole executrix, his widowed sister Anne Dallison, was to have his manor house near Hitchin, and his land at Letchworth. She was asked to see that Snagge was buried

in a comely manner without any superstition or solemnity in some church wherein Christ is served ... according to the order of this church of England, for that I hope to rise again among the rest of the Christians and be glorified with Christ Jesus as one of His church in the great day of the Lord.

He died in 1605, and the will was proved 14 May 1606.[5]

[1] Vis. Beds. (Harl. Soc. xix), 140; Beds. N. and Q. ii. 7; PCC 31 Stafford; APC, x. 433; Lansd. 121, f. 68; M. T. Bench Bk. (1937), p. 82. [2] M. T. Recs. i. 151, 154, 173, 175; APC, xii. 328–9; Lansd. 20, f. 20. [3] CJ, i. 84, 88, 92, 94, 95, 96, 99, 101, 102, 105, 106, 107, 108, 109, 110, 111, 112, 113, 114, 120, 121, 135; D'Ewes, 160, 161, 163, 167, 182, 206, 207, 212, 220, 222, 223, 247, 249, 250, 252, 253, 255, 262, 281, 289, 290, 307; Trinity, Dublin, anon. jnl. and Thos. Cromwell's jnl. passim. [4] APC, x. 433; xi. 75, 455; xii. 328–9; CSP Dom. 1581–90, p. 230; Lansd. 51, f. 8; 54, f. 162. [5] PCC 31 Stafford; M. T. Bench Bk. 82.

P.W.H.

SNAGGE, Thomas I (1536–93), of Marston Moretaine, Beds., and Serjeants' Inn, London.

BEDFORDSHIRE	1571, 1586
BEDFORD	1589

b. 1536, 1st s. of Thomas Snagge of Letchworth and bro. of Robert*. *educ.* G. Inn 1552, called 1554. *m.* bef. 1564, Elizabeth, da. and coh. of Thomas Dickons of Marston Moretaine, 5s. inc. Thomas II* 2da. *suc.* fa. 1571.

J.p. Beds. from c.1569; Autumn reader, G. Inn 1563, 1574, bencher by 1574; attorney-gen. [I] 1577–80; serjeant-at-law 1580; Queen's serjeant 1590; recorder, Bedford from ?c.1569.

Speaker of House of Commons 1589.

Though the principal part of his father's estate passed to his younger brother Robert, Snagge's fortunate marriage assured him an ample estate in Bedfordshire, while his father, a wealthy man, had already settled on him the manor of Howell Bury. In 1569 he added to his Bedfordshire estate by the purchase of the barony and castle of Bedford and the manor of Kempston Daubeney. Still, though he was on the Bedfordshire commission of the peace, he was really a London lawyer, and his election as knight of the shire is surprising. He was classified as 'earnest in religion and fit to be trusted' in the bishops' reports of 1564, and he was a less extreme protestant than his brother Robert. His concern in the debate on the bill for coming to church and receiving communion, 9 Apr. 1571, was that it could be turned against protestants as well as Catholics. He 'showed at large the inconvenience of the old law for coming to service, and of this if they both be conjoined', pointing out that as in many places services were not held according to the book of common prayer as the old law prescribed, sermons often replacing prayers, the addition of the new law to the old would mean that 'if he come not he shall lose £12, and if he do come and be present and the service not said to the prescribed title of the Book, he should lose one hundred marks'. On 13 Apr., on the bill for suppressing simony, he averred

> that the cause of the slanders which the Papists have against the Church of England, in that they say cobblers, tinkers, tailors, millers, etc. are of the ministry, groweth thereby, that the livings are detained by the patrons from the spiritual in their own hands, to their own private uses.

Snagge was active in 1571 on committees appointed for the subsidy (7 Apr.), fraudulent conveyances (11 Apr.), church attendance (21 Apr.); fugitives (24 Apr., 25 May), treasons (11 May), jeofails (12 May) and corrupt presentations (25 May).[1]

In September 1577 Walsingham obtained Snagge the attorneyship in Ireland, at £100 above the usual salary. Walsingham wrote to Sir Henry Sidney:

although the discontinuance, by this means, of his study and practice here, doth bring with it many discommodities, and therefore might move him to be slow in consenting to enter into this fruitless journey, if he had chief regard to his own particular; yet the duty that he oweth to her Majesty and his country with the assurance that he conceiveth, by my promise and otherways, or your lordship's good favour, doth make him leave all other respects, and willingly to dedicate himself to that service.

After a difficult crossing Snagge arrived in Ireland to find things there very different from Westminster Hall, and his tenure of office was poisoned by a quarrel with the master of the rolls, Nicholas White. However, there could be no denying Snagge's efficiency, and he was suggested for the chancellorship of Ireland.[2]

In 1586 Snagge again represented Bedfordshire in Parliament, but was less active than in 1571. He sat on committees dealing with Mary Stuart (4 Nov.), Norfolk returns (9 Nov.), errors in fines (9 Mar. 1587), fish (9 Mar.), and, as a knight of the shire, the subsidy committee (22 Feb.). In 1588 when members of two more influential families took the county seats, Snagge was brought in for the borough, and made Speaker of the 1589 Parliament, a position for which his legal experience and ability made him a natural choice. For some reason at the time he was chosen his first name is given repeatedly in the journals as George. During the course of the session he had to put the Commons' point of view on purveyance and reform of the royal Household to the Queen, and, 8 Mar., report her reply to the House, which was that

> the Queen had as much skill, will and power to rule and govern her own household as any subject.

As Speaker he received the conventional sum of £6 13s. 4d. from the city of London for his favour during the Parliament, and after the dissolution he received the usual promotion to Queen's serjeant. The next year, on 7 Apr. 1591, he made his will, leaving his estates to his sons Thomas and Robert, who went to law about the division after the death of their mother, the executrix. Snagge himself died aged 57 in his chamber at Serjeants' Inn on 16 Mar. 1593, and was buried at Marston Moretaine, where a monument was erected to him.[3]

[1] *DNB*; *Vis. Beds.* (Harl. Soc. xix), 140; *Cam. Misc.* ix(3), p. 29; *CSP Dom.* 1547–80, p. 371; PCC 27 Holney; C2 Eliz./S20/58; *VCH Beds.* ii. 296; iii. 13, 298; D'Ewes, 159, 160, 165, 176, 179, 183, 188; *CJ*, i. 83, 84, 85, 86, 89, 92; Trinity, Dublin, anon. jnl. ff. 9, 16, 19–20; Neale, *Parlts.* i. 192, 225–30. [2] Collins, *Sidney State Pprs.* i. 228, 231; *DNB*; *N. and Q.* (ser. 2), xi. 90–9; A. Dasent, *Speakers of the House of Commons*, 144; *CSP Ire.* 1574–85, pp. 123–6, 151, 165, 319, 342; *APC*, xi. 119–20. [3] D'Ewes, 394, 396, 409, 413, 421, 427, 428, 429, 454, 491, et passim; Trinity, Dublin, anon. jnl. f. 9; Townshend, *Hist. Colls.* 4, 15; Neale, *Parlts.* ii. 201, 212–14; Neale, *Commons*, 337; *DNB*; PCC 38 Nevell; C2 Eliz./S22/52; C142/241/111.

A.M.M.

SNAGGE, Thomas II (c.1564–1627), of Marston Moretaine, Beds.

BEDFORD 1586

b. c.1564, 1st s. of Thomas Snagge I* by his w. Elizabeth. *educ.* G. Inn 1582. *m.* Agnes or Anne, da. of George Rotheram*, 2s. *suc.* fa. 1593. Kntd. 1603.
J.p. Beds. temp. Jas. I, sheriff 1607–8.

It was not unusual for a borough to return a young man of local connexions who was already in London. Such a person was Snagge, who was busy leading 'a very bad and loose life' and borrowing from 'divers cozening and wicked persons' on the expectation of his inheritance. But if his father, who was knight of the shire for Bedfordshire in the 1586 Parliament, hoped to inculcate in him a sense of responsibility, he must have been disappointed, for the situation had not changed when the father made his will in 1591, and the son came within an ace of being disinherited. Still, he settled down in the end, enough at least to become a justice of the peace and sheriff of his county, and at his death he was in possession of his inheritance, the larger part of which came from his mother. James I knighted him and he unsuccessfully claimed the right to act as almoner at the coronation. He also attempted to prove his right to a part of the castle and barony of Bedford, which his father had held. He died early in 1627, and was buried at Marston Moretaine on 2 Feb.

Vis. Beds. (Harl. Soc. xix), 140; *VCH Beds.* iii. 13, 298; *Beds. N. and Q.* ii. 2 seq., 12; C142/241/111; PCC 38 Nevell, 70 Skinner.

N.M.F.

SNELL, John (by 1537–87), of Kington St. Michael, Wilts.

DEVIZES 1572*

b. by 1537, 1st s. of Nicholas Snell* of Kington St. Michael by his 1st w. Alice, da. of John Pye of Rowdon. *m.* (1) Katherine (*d.*1566), da. of John Warneford of Sevenhampton, 2s. 3da.; (2) Susanna (*d.*1570). *suc.* fa. 1577.[1]
J.p. Wilts. from c.1579, sheriff 1584–5; escheator, Wilts. and Hants 1582–3.[2]

The Snells were prominent on the Wiltshire-Somerset border. Snell's grandfather was the last steward of the abbey of Glastonbury's lands in Wiltshire and, at the dissolution, acquired the estates before other speculators had a chance to intervene. Kington St. Michael became the family seat and for at least 100 years afterwards each generation was able to add to the property. Following the example of the monks of Glastonbury they were successful farmers. John Snell, because his father lived to be an old man, was head of the family for ten years only, but he had taken over the administration of the estates before his father's death. In 1575 he paid £385 for the manor of Eaton Piercy, also in Kington St. Michael: after this transaction the family owned virtually the whole parish. Earlier he had sold the manor of West Hatch after Nicholas Snell had admitted concealing for about 20 years that he owned it. The Exchequer demanded £500 arrears from the family.[3]

During the last years of his life Snell was actively concerned in county administration, serving his turn as sheriff in 1584–5. A letter he wrote to the Privy Council during his shrievalty survives among the State Papers. He reported that most of the recusants from whom he had been ordered to demand horses for service abroad, were no longer living in the county. In the last year of his life Snell, together with Edward Hungerford*, was ordered to investigate a quarrel between two local men, Sir John Danvers* and John Watts. Quarter sessions records show that he was also an active justice of the peace.[4]

Snell's career as a Member of Parliament was short. Following the death of George Reynolds, he was returned at a by-election in Devizes on 10 Jan. 1580 and served in the last session of the 1572 Parliament. Snell's election may have been due to his own local influence, perhaps with the approval of the 2nd Earl of Pembroke.[5]

Snell died 17 Nov. 1587, and was buried 13 Dec. at Kington. No will has been found, but his inquisition shows that he had already left the bulk of his estates to his elder son Thomas, mainly on the occasion of his marriage to a daughter of Sir Robert Long of Wraxhall. Thomas achieved some fame as an astrologer and was a captain on the Islands voyage of 1597.[6]

[1] *Wilts. Vis. Peds.* (Harl. Soc. cv, cvi), 183–4; *Vis. Wilts. 1623*, pp. 12, 32; *Wilts. Arch. Mag.* iv. table opp. p. 45; Wards 7/18/149. [2] *Mins. Proc. Sess.* (Wilts. Arch. Soc. recs. br. iv), 48 seq. [3] *Wilts. Arch. Mag.* iv. 36 seq.; *J. Aubrey, N. Wilts.* ed. Jackson, 120 n 2, 130–3, 240, 443; *Wilts. N. and Q.* v. 353, 354; PCC 17 Daughtry; *CPR, 1563–6*, pp. 250–1. [4] SP12/183/41; *APC*, xv. 113; *Mins. Proc. Sess.* loc. cit. [5] C219/283/20–1. [6] C142/221/122.

M.R.P.

SNELL, Nicholas (*d.*1577), of Kington St. Michael, Wilts.

CHIPPENHAM	1555
WILTSHIRE	1558
CHIPPENHAM	1559, 1563
MALMESBURY	1571, 1572*

o.s. of Richard Snell of Kington St. Michael by Joan, da. of Nicholas Marsh of Easton. *m.* (1) bef. 1537, Alice, da. of John Pye of Rowdon, 3s. inc. John* 5da.; (2) Mary, da. of William Cleveland of Wilts., *s.p. suc.* fa. 1547.[1]
?Servant to abbot of Glastonbury bef. 1540; servant to earls of Pembroke from c.1555–*d.*; commr. relief, Wilts. 1550, j.p. 1554–*d.*, q. from 1561, sheriff 1566–7.[2]

Said by Aubrey to have been reeve to the abbot of Glastonbury, Snell is not to be found among Wiltshire contributors to the benevolence of 1545, for which his father, who was a yeoman of the Crown, was assessed at £5. Nicholas Snell was, however, already the owner of

Kington St. Michael, a grange of Glastonbury which he had bought from the Crown for £800 in 1544. According to the visitation of 1623 Alice Snell was a daughter of George Pye of Oxford, but no such person has been traced and there is reason to believe that Snell's first father-in-law was John Pye of Rowdon, and that 'Oxford' is a misreading of 'Hereford', the Pyes' native city. John Pye was both a neighbour and, as a yeoman of the Crown, a colleague of Richard Snell, who may indeed have introduced him to Wiltshire; it is also to be noted that Nicholas Snell was to have a daughter named Cicely and granddaughters named Cicely and Alice, which were the names of two of John Pye's daughters.[3]

Between his father's death in 1547 and the accession of Queen Elizabeth, Snell carved out an enviable position for himself in west Wiltshire, adding considerably to his own and to his father's property, and, as steward to the 1st Earl of Pembroke, helping to administer the extensive Herbert lands. In the Elizabethan period he sat in every Parliament until his death, twice for Chippenham and twice for Malmesbury, some eight miles north of his seat at Kington St. Michael. In spite of his regular appearances, he made no mark in the journals of the House.[4]

In the course of his upward progress, Snell survived an episode which could have spelled disaster. One of his earliest investments had been the lease which he took with his father in 1536 of the manor or chantry of West Hatch. When, a quarter of a century later, the Crown came to grant this property to Cicely Pickerell, it relied for the valuation upon an inquisition, purporting to have been taken at Malmesbury on 30 Nov. 1561 before John Stumpe* and Edward Pleydell, which returned the figure of 13s. 4d. a year. It came to light, however, that no such inquisition had been taken and that the certificate in question was a forgery; an inquisition held on 7 Sept. 1564 before the sheriff, John Erneley*, found that the manor was worth £11 11s. and 1 lb. of pepper a year and that Richard, Nicholas and John Snell had concealed this fact throughout their tenancy. Although the lessees' complicity in the fraud could scarcely be doubted, it may have been difficult to prove that either Nicholas or his son John was guilty of the forgery; and this is perhaps why Nicholas escaped with no more than a demand for payment of the arrears under a recognizance of £500. His appointment as sheriff two years later shows that he was not thereafter a marked man.[5]

An indifferent supporter of the Elizabethan church settlement – he was classified 'no hinderer of religion' by his bishop in 1564 – he had no cause to quarrel with state or society. His assessment of £20 in lands, involving a payment of 53s. 4d. for the subsidy of 1576, was perhaps no more unrealistic than most, but it could have made a scarcely perceptible dent in the fortune which, on 20 Dec. of that year, Snell distributed in his will. To his 'special good lord' the 2nd Earl of Pembroke, the son of his first

master, he bequeathed his best gelding, and his next best went to his 'very friend' Sir Edward Baynton*. A debt of over £400 which Snell had lately recovered at law from Henry Baynton* he left to his son-in-law Wallis (or Thomas) Baylie. He appointed as his executors his son John and his grandson Thomas, and as his overseer Richard Gore of Aldrington.[6]

The testator's death on 31 Mar. 1577 was followed by a lawsuit over the will between the two younger sons Henry and Thomas. An inquisition, taken on 2 May following, showed how much there was to quarrel over: lands in Dorset, Gloucestershire, Somerset and Hampshire, as well as at Chisenbury, Uphaven, Box and Chippenham in Wiltshire.[7]

[1] Wilts. Vis. Peds. (Harl. Soc. cv, cvi), 183; Genealogist, n.s. xii. 242; C142/179/99; PCC 27 Alen. [2] CSP Dom. Add. 1566–79, p. 455; CPR, 1553, p. 359; 1553–4, p. 25; 1560–3, p. 443; 1563–6, pp. 28, 38, 39; 1569–72, p. 219; Egerton 2345/36; SP12/121/32. [3] J. Aubrey, North Wilts. ed. Jackson, 133; LP Hen. VIII, vii. g.1601(32); xv. g.282(62); xix(1), g.442(31), 273, p. 155; xix(2), g.690(67); xx(1), g.465(77); xx(2), 1035, f. 28, p. 517; Two Taxation Lists (Wilts. Arch. Soc. recs. br. x), 26, 27; Vis. Berks. (Harl. Soc. lvi), 270; CPR, 1551–3, pp. 396, 415; Wilts. N. and Q. ii. 305, 368; iii. 126; viii. 109–111. [4] Wilts. RO 473/12(58), 15(81), 41(228, 230); CPR, 1547–8, p. 53; 1553–4, pp. 288, 453; Wilts. N. and Q. iii. 373, 461, 558; iv. 120, 157, 213, 264, 266; v. 176. [5] CPR, 1563–6, p. 250; 1566–9, p. 34; C3/136/18, 3/159/43, 3/172/30. [6] Cam. Misc. ix(3), p. 38; Two Taxation Lists, 56; Wilts. N. and Q. vi. 406; PCC 17 Daughtry. [7] Req. 2/90/37; C142/179/99, 221/122; Wilts. N. and Q. vi. 244–6.

S.T.B.

SNIGGE, George (c.1545–1618), of Bristol.

CRICKLADE	1589
BRISTOL	1597,[1] 1601, 1604*

b. c.1545, 1st s. of George Snigge, bencher of the M. Temple and mayor of Bristol 1574–5. educ. Christ Church, Oxf. 1564, BA 25 June 1566; M. Temple 9 Aug. 1567, called 17 June 1575. m. Alice, da. of William Young of Ogbourne, Wilts., at least 3da. Kntd. 1605.

Autumn reader, M. Temple 1590, Lent reader 1599, treasurer 1602, serjeant-at-law 1604; j.p.q. Glos. and Som.; alderman, Bristol, recorder 1593–1605; baron of the Exchequer 28 June 1605; c.j. Glamorgan circuit 14 May 1608–Feb. 1618.[2]

Before he became a judge, Snigge was active in the affairs of the county and the port, and was frequently employed there by the Privy Council. On two occasions he wrote to Lord Burghley – in 1586, recommending a man to be comptroller of the port of Bristol, and in 1597, complaining that the Bristol cloth trade was falling into decay, and that London merchants were acquiring a monopoly of 'the iron of Wales, the lead of Mendips, and the calamine stone, being the commodities of these parts'. In 1599 he reported to Sir Robert Cecil that, as many 'recusants and other dangerous persons' were reaching Ireland from Bristol, he had instructed the officers of the port to prevent any but 'known merchants, undertakers, and others sufficiently licensed' from setting sail. In the same year, the Privy Council made him responsible for victualling the troops for Ireland, who were for some considerable time weatherbound in Bristol. In 1597 a merchant complained that Snigge had taken from him 'a great quantity and provision of butter' to the value of £27, 'with pretence to make sale thereof for the relief of the poor'.[3]

Snigge was presumably returned for Cricklade through the Brydges family, but his exact connexion with them has not been traced. Once he was recorder of Bristol he naturally represented that constituency. He left no mark on the records of the 1589 Parliament. The George Snagge mentioned in the journals of that year is Thomas Snagge I the Speaker, who was dead by 1597. Thus the Mr. 'Snagg' repeatedly mentioned in the journals for 1597–8 can safely be said to be George Snigge, active both as committeeman and in debate. He served on the following committees: forestallers (7 Nov.); cloth (18 Nov.); Bristol (28 Nov.); Newport Bridge (29 Nov.); bread (13 Jan. 1598); relief of mariners and soldiers (26 Jan.); bail (27 Jan.); legal matters (1, 3 Feb.); wine casks (3 Feb.). He reported progress on the cloth bill mentioned above on 24 Nov. and again the next day, but on 30 Nov. recommended that it should not be proceeded with. Other bills he reported were concerned with erecting hospitals and workhouses (30 Nov.), defence (9 Dec.), letters patent for Exeter merchants not fit to pass (13 Dec.), a preacher for the Tower of London (16 Dec.), the continuance of statutes (19 Jan. 1598), benefit of clergy (19 Jan.), Lady Verney's jointure (25 Jan.), bail (30 Jan.), and weights and measures (30 Jan.). On ?17 Dec. 1597 in the course of urging men 'ever to have their wills ready' he told a story

> which I have read of a man in Italy, to whom in extremity of sickness the friars came to confess him, but they seeing he would answer nothing, said 'If you hope to be saved through the death and passion of Jesus Christ, then hold up your finger', which he did. 'Then', quoth the friar, 'if you will give such land, and such land, and such a house to our monastery that we may pray for the health of your soul, then hold up your finger', which he did. The son and heir of this man, seeing his father give away his land so fast that even almost all was gone, said 'Father, if I shall beat these friars out from hence with a bedstaff ... hold up your finger', which he did, so he beat forth the friars, saved his land and gave a good example to others to make their wills [in] time.

Snigge was also active in 1601. His committees were on privileges and returns (31 Oct.), penal laws (2 Nov.), the order of business (3 Nov.), silk weavers (10 Dec.) and Dover harbour (14 Dec.). On 11 Nov. he reported two bills (writs of error and fraudulent administration of intestates' goods). Three cloth workers' bills were committed to him

on 18 Nov. and on 7 Dec. he reported that he had 'reduced and drawn the three said bills into one bill'. He spoke on another bill regulating tradesmen, 11 Dec., and again the next day and on 15 Dec. about cloth. On this Parliament's burning question of monopolies, only one intervention by Snigge is recorded, but that was important. It was Snigge who 'wished a commitment to devise a course' to inquire into the scandal, 20 Nov.[4]

Snigge died in London on 11 Nov. 1618, and lay in state for six weeks in the Merchant Taylors' hall, before being buried in St. Stephen's, Bristol. His will, dated 12 Mar. 1612, was proved 6 Feb. 1619, and an inquisition post mortem was held the next year.[5]

[1] Folger V. b. 298. [2] W. R. Williams, *Parl. Hist. Glos.* 112; W. R. Williams, *Welsh Judges*, 131; *Vis. Glos.* (Harl. Soc. xxi), 57, 95; PCC 11 Meade; *CSP Dom.* 1603–10, pp. 125, 156, 429; 1611–18, p. 85. [3] *CSP Dom.* 1581–90, p. 329; 1598–1601, p. 888; Lansd. 86, f. 26; *APC*, xxvi. 338; xxvii. 217; xxix. 488, 556, 561. [4] D'Ewes, 428, 552, 558, 562, 563, 564, 565, 566, 570, 572, 574, 579, 583, 587, 588, 589, 590, 592, 622, 624, 634, 642, 646, 669, 676, 678, 684; Townshend, *Hist. Colls.* 122, 123, 235, 317, 325; *Bull. IHR*, xii. 19. [5] PCC 11 Meade; C142/377/95.

J.J.C./P.W.H.

SNOW, John

| TREGONY | 1593 |
| YARMOUTH I.o.W. | 1597 |

There were several branches of the Snow family in the west country; at Halberton, Devon; West Anstey, on the Devon-Somerset border; and at Exeter, where Simon Snow, son of Thomas, became Member for the city in the Long Parliament. A Nicholas Snow, possibly from the Devon family, was keeper of the wardrobe at Richmond early in Elizabeth's reign, and John, whose name does not appear in the pedigrees, may have been related to him.[1]

Whatever his origins, the John Snow who sat for Tregony and Yarmouth was secretary to Sir George Carey*, 2nd Baron Hunsdon, who secured the enfranchisement of Yarmouth. The earlier return at Tregony was presumably obtained through Sir George Carey's brother, Sir Robert*, who had married into the Trevanion family.

A John Snow of London died near Paul's Wharf in 1607 or 1608, leaving a nuncupative will:

> Memorandum that Mr. John Snow of London, esquire, being sick in body, but of good and perfect mind, did upon St. Stephen's Day in the house of Mistress Britten in London say that he would give all that ever he had to the said Mrs. Britten.

The will was challenged by Robert Snow, described as nearest kinsman of John, and by another relative, but on 14 Nov. 1608 administration was granted to Frances Britten, widow.[2]

[1] Vivian, *Vis. Devon*, 1, 88, 446, 547, 594, 840; *Trans. Dev. Assoc.* xxxv. 595; lxi. 211; *CPR*, 1563–6, p. 161. [2] *APC*, xxxii. 177; PCC 68 Bolein, 103 Windebanck.

N.M.F.

SOAME, Sir Stephen (c.1544–1619), of London.

LONDON   1601

b. c.1544, 2nd s. of Thomas Soame of Bestley, Norf. by Anne, da. and h. of Francis Knighton of Little Bradley, Suff., wid. of Richard Le Hunt of Little Thurlow. *m.* Anne, da. of William Stone of London and of Segenhoe, Beds., 4s. 5da. Kntd. 25 Apr. 1599.[1]

Master, Girdlers' Co. ?1568; alderman, London 26 June 1589, sheriff 1589–90, ld. mayor 1598–9, president, Bethlehem and Bridewell hospitals 1598–9; surveyor-gen. of London hospitals 1609–10, comptroller-gen. 1610–*d.*[2]

Soame came from a minor Norfolk family, established there since the fifteenth century. He was at first a member of the Girdlers' Company, but, when he was elected lord mayor he transferred to the Grocers' Company, to the chagrin of the Girdlers, who removed his arms from their hall. From his early years in London his main interest was probably the cloth trade. In November 1589 the Privy Council wrote on his behalf to the Merchant Adventurers, asking that he should either be admitted to the Company, or be made at least a temporary member for five years, so that he could regain the losses he had suffered in exporting cloth to the Low Countries. As his wealth increased he began moneylending. He was one of the creditors of Sir Walter Leveson* and in 1590, was instrumental in having him imprisoned for debt.[3]

Soame was named to the committee for the assurance of certain manors, 9 Dec. 1601; to that concerned with policies of assurance used amongst merchants (11 Dec.) and to that about prisoners in Ludgate (12 Dec.). He spoke thrice: on St. Bartholomew's hospital (17 Nov.); on the painters and plasterers of London (12 Dec.) and in support of a bill to give the city power over the liberty of St. Katharine's (14 Dec.):

> Mr. Speaker, I say to you, these privileges are the very sink of sin, the nursery of naughty and lewd people, the harbour of rogues, thieves and beggars, and maintainers of idle persons; for when our shops and houses be robbed, thither they fly for relief and sanctuary, and we cannot help ourselves.

In addition, as one of the London Members, he could have sat on the committees to consider the penal laws (2 Nov.), the order of business (3 Nov.), setting watches (7 Nov.), customs regulations (10 Nov.), procedure (11 Nov.), cloth workers (18 Nov.), monopolies (23 Nov.), felt makers (26 Nov.), the local government of London (4 Dec.), cloth (4 Dec.), the relief of Theophilus Adams (5 Dec.), the assize of fuel (7 Dec.), Thames watermen (8 Dec.), iron ordnance (8 Dec.), the maintenance of the navy (9 Dec.), silk weavers (10 Dec.), and printers and printing (17 Dec.).[4]

By the end of the sixteenth century Soame was principally an Eastland merchant. As lord mayor he was chairman of the first meeting of merchants to discuss the formation of the East India Company; he promised £200 on his own behalf for the first voyage, and a further £400 in conjunction with Richard Carter. With the decline of the Eastland trade in the first decade of the seventeenth century, he transferred his main interests to the Levant. As a cloth exporter looking for new markets he was a leading supporter of Cokayne's project, which was aimed at breaking the monopoly of the Merchant Adventurers. But, although he was an early adherent, he failed to take up his quota of cloths immediately. He had been allotted 300 cloths, but by September 1616 had bought only 80 of them; he made good his default in the following months by exporting 716 cloths, but by then the project was failing.[5]

A large part of the profit Soame gained from trade must have been invested in land. At his death in 1619 he had accumulated enough land in the six counties of Cambridge, Essex, Hertford, Kent, Norfolk and Suffolk to provide each of his four sons with a landed estate. He chose as his own seat Little Thurlow in Suffolk, where he built and endowed nine almshouses, and a free school. The school was to be open to Suffolk children, who were to be taught English, Latin, writing and arithmetic. In his will he also left money to be used for charitable works in London. He bequeathed £100 to enable the Grocers' Company to provide 24 wheaten loaves each Friday for the poor prisoners in the Poultry Counter, and further small sums to provide bread weekly, for a year, for the prisoners in the other London prisons. During his lifetime he 're-edified and newly glazed the great north window of St. Paul's cathedral', and he spent £500, in 1617, on re-roofing the Grocers' hall. 'Sir Stephen Soame, our ancientest alderman' wrote John Chamberlain, 'died on Trinity Sunday [23 May 1619] and left a great estate behind him of better than £6,000 land and £4,000 goods'. This estimate of Soame's landed wealth may be correct, but his personal estate was worth more than Chamberlain believed. Soame thought that if all his ventures abroad were successful, and his debts in London collected, his personal estate would be above £40,000. His will was proved on 26 Jan. 1620. He was buried in Little Thurlow church, where a monument was erected to him. His heir was his son Sir William.[6]

[1] Heath, *Some Account of the Worshipful Company of Grocers*, 254; C142/383/89; *Vis. London* (Harl. Soc. xvii), 250–1; (cix, cx), 130; R. Clutterbuck, *Herts.* iii. 464. [2] A. B. Beaven, *Aldermen*, i. 102; ii. 43. [3] G. A. Carthew, *Hundred of Launditch and Deanery of Brisley*, iii. 61–2; W. D. Smythe, *Girdlers' Co.* 113–14; Beaven, i. 102; *APC*, xviii. 218, 434; xxvi. 338, 508; *HMC Hatfield*, x. 164. [4] D'Ewes, 622, 624, 629,

634, 635, 642, 649, 654, 657, 667, 668, 669, 670, 672, 673, 674, 676, 680, 681, 687; Townshend, *Hist. Colls.* 221, 313, 325. [5] A. Friis, *Cockayne's Project and the Cloth Trade*, 232–3, 242, 310, 326; H. Stevens, *Dawn of British Trade to the East Indies*, 1. [6] PCC 1 Soame; Heath, 15, 254; *Chamberlain Letters* ed. McClure, ii. 241.

A.M.M.

SOMASTER, Henry (b. by 1549–1607), of the Middle Temple, London, and Painsford, Devon.

MITCHELL   1586

b. by 1549, 3rd s. of William Somaster of Painsford by Katherine, da. of Henry Fortescue of Preston, Devon. *educ.* M. Temple 1566, called 1577. *m.* 1583, Alice, da. of John Arundell[†], of Trerice, and coh. of her mother Katherine, da. and h. of Nicholas Cosworth, 2s. 1da. *suc.* fa. 1589.

The Somasters were an old-established Devon family, one of whose members had represented Totnes in the Parliament of 1433. Somaster himself owed his return at Mitchell to his marriage into the Arundells of Trerice. In association with Richard Carew* of Antony, Somaster compiled a survey of the manor of East Luccombe, of which John Arundell was lord. Still, he remains an obscure figure. His eldest brother was disinherited for marrying beneath him, the next was in holy orders, and Henry eventually succeeded to the estates. He did not assume, at least during Elizabeth's reign, any county office in Devon, or in Cornwall, where his wife had property, for he was a London lawyer. The small Cornish boroughs often found it convenient to return such a man with local connexions. Somaster shared with James Hannam and Robert Moyle the cost of building the chambers at the Middle Temple, later known as 'Somaster and Moyle's buildings'. He there supervised young west-country men at the beginning of their inns of court career, including his brother-in-law John Arundell in 1594.

Somaster died on 10 Jan. 1607, when his heir Samuel was 14. His will, drawn up in the previous October and quoted in the inquisition post mortem, has not survived. He asked to be buried near his ancestors in 'our aisle' of Ashprington church, and forbade bell-ringing at the funeral, 'in regard of the superstitious use of the people that say they ring men's souls to heaven'. One 'Thomas Jefferies, minister of God's word and an ancient bachelor of divinity and yet could never obtain a church living' was left a bequest, and the executor was George Somaster, principal of Broadgates Hall, Oxford, who was asked to see that Henry's sons were educated at Oxford. The overseers were John Arundell and an old servant Richard Wolfe.

Vivian, *Vis. Devon*, 695; T. Westcote, *View of Devonshire*, ed. Oliver, Jones and Roberts, 501; C142/220/28, 303/136; NRA, rep. 6310.

N.M.F.

SOMERSET, Charles (by 1534–99), of Chepstow, Mon.

MONMOUTHSHIRE   1571, 1572

b. by 1534, 4th s. of Henry, 2nd Earl of Worcester by his 2nd w. Elizabeth, da. of Sir Anthony Browne, standard bearer to Henry VIII; bro. of Thomas[†] and Francis[†]. *educ.* St. John's, Camb. 1548. *m.* by 1572, Mary (or Emma), da. of Thomas Brayne (or Brague) of Little Dean, Glos., wid. of Giles Morgan[†] (*d.*1570) of Newport, Mon., 1da. At least 1da. illegit. Kntd. 1573.

Gent. pens. 1560, standard bearer c. 1572; j.p. from c.1561, commr. musters 1570, 1588, victuals 1574, tanneries 1574; j.p. Glos. from c.1577; steward, Chepstow c.1572; commr. to inquire into mineral and battery works 1589.

The Somerset earls of Worcester, by virtue of their royal blood, their extensive lands, their strong Welsh connexions and their staunch support for Henry Tudor, held a dominant position in south-eastern Wales from the Act of Union onwards. One of the two Monmouthshire seats in Parliament was always, until after the Restoration, virtually at their disposal, and was frequently held by younger sons, some of whom, like Somerset himself, had little land in the county. Charles Somerset's elder brothers Thomas and Francis had represented the shire in Marian Parliaments; his wife's first husband Giles Morgan had sat for the boroughs under Edward VI.[1]

Somerset's only recorded activity in the House of Commons is his appointment to a committee on Mary Queen of Scots, 11 May 1572. Only two years later his name appears on a list drawn up by one of her more optimistic sympathizers; probably it was included because of the known recusancy of some of Somerset's family. There is no doubt that he conformed. Archbishop Parker himself classified Somerset as 'safe' in 1564, and Somerset's naming the bishop of Llandaff as an overseer of his will underlines the point. Somerset remained in general in favour with Elizabeth and the Privy Council, and it was commonly either to him or to Edward Morgan I* that the Council referred matters concerning Monmouthshire. In 1564, however, he and his elder brother were summoned before the Privy Council for menacing one William James, who was bringing a lawsuit against them. Somerset allowed a servant to assault James, and suffered a period of imprisonment in the Fleet.[2]

Somerset died 3 Mar. 1599. In his will dated 18 Dec. 1598 and proved 6 Oct. 1599, he named his great-nephew the future 5th Earl and 1st Marquess as executor. He asked to be buried next to his wife in St. James's church, Bristol, and left 200 marks for a joint tombstone, 20 nobles for a new bell and 10s. for the church fabric. To the church and the poor of his own parish of Chepstow he left £120, including £40 for a bell and £40 for a house of correction; to Llandaff cathedral a token bequest of 3s. 6d. Cash bequests to family and friends amounted to nearly £6,000.

His daughter Elizabeth inherited the lands that came to him *iure uxoris*: but within three years she was embroiled in a Chancery suit with the families of her two successive husbands over their allocation.[3]

[1] Bradney, *Mon.* ii. 26–7; *CPR*, 1560–3, pp. 249, 444; Flenley, *Cal. Reg. Council, Marches of Wales*, 69, 109, 126; Lansd. 56, f. 168 seq.; *Exchequer*, ed. E. G. Jones (Univ. Wales Bd. of Celtic Studies, Hist. and Law ser. iv), 247. [2] *CJ*, i. 95; *Cath. Rec. Soc. Misc.* viii. 93; *Cam. Misc.* ix(3), p. 81; *S. Wales and Mon. Rec. Soc.* iii. 57–110; *Al. Cant.* i(4), p. 121; *CPR*, 1560–3, p. 249; Add. 12506, f. 419; *APC*, vii. 198, 200–1, 204–7; xiii. 205; xvii. 328–9; xviii. 28, 57, 71; xxv. 317; xxviii. 594–5, 637; Firth and Rait, *Acts and Ordinances*, ii. 58, 1072, 1136. [3] I. Walters, *Chepstow Par. Recs.* 2, 9; PCC 75 Kidd; C142/266/121.

A.H.D.

SOMERSET, Thomas (c.1579–1649), of Troy, nr. Monmouth and Badminton, Glos.

MONMOUTHSHIRE 1601, 1604, 1614

b. c.1579, 3rd s. of Edward Somerset, 4th Earl of Worcester, by Elizabeth, da. of Francis Hastings, 2nd Earl of Huntingdon. *educ.* Magdalen Coll. Oxf. 1593, aged 14; G. Inn 1604. *m.* Aug. 1616, Helena, prob. da. of David Barry, 3rd Visct. Buttevant, wid. of John, s. of Richard, Lord Power [I] and of Thomas Butler, 10th Earl of Ormond, 1da. KB 1605. *cr.* Visct. Somerset [I] 1626.[1]

J.p.q. Mon. 1601; master of the horse to Queen Anne c.1604–19; member, council of Amazon Co. 1620; clerk to treasury of court of common pleas 1621.[2]

The election to one of the two Monmouthshire seats of a junior member of the house of Raglan, when one was available, was almost a matter of routine. Three of Thomas Somerset's great-uncles – Thomas, Francis and Charles – had represented the shire in Marian and early Elizabethan Parliaments. The 4th Earl had no brothers, but his younger son Thomas was returned to the first Parliament after his majority. His name does not appear in the records of the House, but as a knight of the shire in 1601 he could have served on committees concerned with the order of business (3 Nov.) and monopolies (23 Nov.). Along with the Earl of Northumberland's brother Sir Charles Percy, he was sent by the Privy Council to Edinburgh in March 1603 to give official notification to James of Queen Elizabeth's death, returning in time to bear the standard of the lion at the Queen's funeral the following month. He then became master of the horse to James's Queen (as his father had been to Elizabeth), a post which he kept until Queen Anne's death.[3]

Somerset's main parliamentary biography belongs to the following period. He served abroad from 1610 to 1612, played a leading part in forming the Amazon Company for trade and colonization in South America (for which he was reprimanded by James, who forced the surrender of the charter), and was sent with a fleet to Spain to bring home Prince Charles from his wooing of the Infanta in 1623. He died intestate in 1649.[4]

[1] *CP*; *CSP Dom.* 1611–18, p. 426; Add. 1625–49, p. 174. [2] C66/1549; *HMC Hatfield*, xvi. 391–3; *APC*, 1619–21, pp. 204–5; *CSP Dom.* 1619–23, p. 301. [3] D'Ewes, 624, 649; *Reg. P. C. Scot.* vi. 551; *Chamberlain Letters* ed. McClure, i. 189; *CP*. [4] *HMC Downshire*, ii. 348, 400; iii. 161, 286, 356; *HMC De L'Isle and Dudley*, iv. 227; *APC*, 1619–21, pp. 169, 185–6, 193, 204–5; *CSP Dom.* 1619–23, pp. 41, 125, 145, 147; 1623–5, p. 62; *CSP Col.* 1574–1660, pp. 21, 23–4, 77–8; Gardiner, *Hist. England*, 1603–42, v. 119; *CP*.

A.H.D.

SONDES, Michael (*d.*1617), of Throwley, Eastry and Sheldwich, Kent.

MAIDSTONE 1584
QUEENBOROUGH 1586, 1589, 1597, 1601, 1604

2nd s. of Anthony Sondes (*d.*1575) of Throwley by Joan, da. of Sir John Fyneux of Herne. *educ.* L. Inn 1564. *m.* (1) Mary (*d.* 23 Sept. 1603), da. and h. of George Finch of Norton, at least 2s. inc. Richard* 6da.; (2) Ann, wid. of Reginald Parker of Chatham, *s.p.*[1] *suc.* bro. 1593. Kntd. 1598.[2]

J.p.q. Kent by 1579, sheriff 1584–5, 1593–4; j.p.q. Surr. by 1601; commr. surv. Isle of Sheppey 1585; master of ordnance for Kent by 1589.[3]

Sondes's family provides a good example of the rise to wealth and importance of a new class in the sixteenth century. They came originally from Surrey – perhaps from the village of Send – and were living in Dorking in the reign of Henry III, moving later to Lingfield. It was William Sondes's marriage in the 1470s which brought Throwley into the family and transferred their main interest to Kent. Thenceforward the acquisition of landed wealth was steady throughout the Tudor period and beyond. Exactly how the family was able to increase its estates so remarkably is not clear: no fortunate marriage explains it, and no important social connexion or tenure of lucrative office has been traced. Whatever the explanation, Michael Sondes's inquisition post mortem and other sources reveal the extent of the family's wealth: he held land in six counties, including at least 14 manors. As well as his estates in many parts of Kent, with a concentration in the rich lowlands between Ashford and Faversham, he owned land in at least six Surrey and nine Sussex parishes, a house at Clerkenwell, and more lands in Lincolnshire and Nottinghamshire. He himself probably bought more property than any of his ancestors, particularly in his later years, including the manor of Acton in the parish of Charing and three manors at Ashford; in 1596 he was granted a licence to make a park at Throwley. Sondes was naturally prominent in local affairs, and he played a major part in organizing local defence in the part of England probably most liable to attack. He helped to raise horses and men in the county for foreign service in 1596, and for Ireland in the last three years of Elizabeth's reign. As part of his contribution to the latter operation he was to escort 200 men to

Greenwich and Deptford, and put a guard on the ships until they sailed. He was one of those who received a commission from the Privy Council to survey the military preparedness of the Isle of Sheppey in 1585. He also served on Privy Council commissions to examine complaints of mis-government in New Romney and to investigate a charge that Kent soldiers in the Low Countries were not receiving their full wages.[4]

Sondes's return to Parliament for Maidstone was no doubt due to his family's local standing, while at Queenborough his relationship to Lord Cobham is sufficient explanation. However, it is of interest that his son, born in 1585, was christened Hoby, presumably after Sir Edward Hoby*, whose influence at Queenborough increased as the reign progressed. The parliamentary journals consistently have an 'a' as the second letter of Sondes's surname, which makes for confusion with the Sandys family, but it does appear that Sondes was not active in the Commons. In 1584 he was given leave of absence on 12 Dec. to attend to his duties as sheriff, and the remainder of the references likely to apply to him belong to 1601: he was appointed to consider committee procedure on 11 Nov.; a subpoena was served on him on 14 Nov.; and he was a member of committees to consider allowing the breaking of an entail (23 Nov.), land reclamation (1 Dec.) and gavelkind (5 Dec.).[5]

Sondes died 10 Nov. 1617. It is likely that he was buried in Throwley church with the rest of his family.[6]

[1] Manning and Bray, *Surr.* i. 567. [2] *Vis. Kent* (Harl. Soc. xlii), 106; W. Berry, *Co. Genealogies, Kent*, 244; Manning and Bray, i. 567; Hasted, *Kent*, vi. 450–2; *Arch. Cant.* xviii. 295; xxiii. 120; Add. 33920, f. 36. [3] SP12/145; C66/1549; *CSP Dom.* 1581–90, 636. [4] Manning and Bray, i. 563, 565; ii. 348; *VCH Surr.* iii. 144, 146, 148; iv. 268, 307; C142/661/79; Hasted, vi. 403, 441–2, 464, 477; vii. 42, 44, 443, 444, 533; *CSP Dom.* 1581–90, pp. 277, 636; 1595–7, p. 297; *Arch. Cant.* xxiii. 120; *HMC Hatfield*, xiv. 148; xv. 215; *HMC 5th Rep.* 138, 139; *APC*, xv. 301–2, 334; xxx. 434; Add. 33823, ff. 34–44; Lansd. 78, ff. 138 seq. [5] Trinity, Dublin, Thos. Cromwell's jnl., f. 76; D'Ewes, 635, 637, 648, 649, 668. [6] C142/661/79.

M.R.P.

SONDES, Richard (1571–1632), of Throwley and Lees Court, Sheldwich, Kent.

GATTON   1601

b. 1571, 1st s. of Michael Sondes* of Throwley by his 1st w. *educ.* Queens', Camb. 1587. *m.* (1) 1595, Susanna, da. of Edward Montagu I* of Boughton, Northants., at least 3s. 3da.; (2) by 1609, Catherine (*d*.1632), da. of Sir Rowland Hayward*, ld. mayor of London 1571, wid. of Richard Scott, 6s. 2da. *suc.* fa. ?1617. Kntd. 11 May 1603.

J.p.q. Kent from *c*.1601.

Nothing has been found to connect Sondes with Gatton or with Lord Howard of Effingham, who was influential there later in Elizabeth's reign. The possibility that he was living on his father's Surrey estates at Dorking or Lingfield

is ruled out by the fact that those of his children born after 1600 were baptised at Throwley. Perhaps his fellow-Member, Sir Matthew Browne of Betchworth, near the Sondes manor of Bradley, suggested his name to Howard. Sondes's father was also in the 1601 Parliament and Richard Sondes, because of his marriage into the Montagu family, had other close relatives among the Members of this Parliament, his only excursion into affairs of state. His later life was saddened by the insanity of his second wife. He died in 1632 and was buried at Throwley. Administration of his property was granted to his eldest son Sir George (Earl of Faversham 1677) on 9 July, and an inquisition post mortem was held in Kent during the following year.

Vis. Kent (Harl. Soc. xlii), 106; *Vis. Northants.* (Harl. Soc. lxxxvii), 136; Manning and Bray, *Surr.* i. 558, 563, 567; Add. 33920, f. 36; *Arch. Cant.* xviii. 295; *Al. Cant.* i(4), 122; Hasted, *Hist. Kent.* vi. 452; *Chamberlain Letters* ed. McClure, i. 579; ii. 361; C142/488/60, 493/110.

M.R.P.

SONE (SOONE), Francis (c.1518–61), of Wantisden, Suff.

ORFORD   1545, 1558, 1559[1]

b. c.1518, 1st s. of John Sone. *educ.* G. Inn 1537. *m.* (1) Alice, da. of Sir John Spelman of Narborough, Norf.; (2) Margaret, da. of Sir Anthony Wingfield[†]; 3s. 3da., of whom 2s. (Robert and William) were by 2nd w. *suc.* fa. 1552.

J.p. Suff. from *c*.1559.

Sone received livery of his estates in November 1552, and there are several references to his purchases and sales of Suffolk land between that date and his death. His inquisition post mortem lists the manors of Alderton and Wantisden, with property in Orford and 11 other places in the county. By 1559 his local standing was sufficient to secure his return, especially in view of his marriage into the Wingfield family. The preamble to his will, made on the day of his death, 11 Nov. 1561, suggests that by then he was a protestant. The will was not proved until 1575, apparently the date when Sone's heir, his eldest son John, became 21.[2]

[1] E371/402(1). At Orford there is a copy of the return for 1558, which reads 'Francis Sone and Thomas Seckforde, generosi'. This has been altered to serve for 1559, reading 'Thomas Sackforde ar. and Francis Sone, generosus'. [2] Wards 7/6/64; PCC 41 Pyckering; *Vis. Norf.* (Harl. Soc. xxxii), 264–5; *Vis. Suff.* ed. Metcalfe, 81; C142/97/74, 132/43; *APC*, i. passim; ii. 78, 81; *LP Hen. VIII*, xix(1), p. 385; W. A. Copinger, *Suff. Manors*, v. 119, 120, 187; vii. 232–3; *CPR*, 1553 and App. Edw. VI, 117; 1555–7, p. 129.

N.M.F.

SONE (SOONE), Richard (d. c.1597), of Halesworth, Suff.

DUNWICH   1572

m. Prudence, at least 2s. 3da.

Sone was presumably related to the 1559 Orford MP, but his identity has not been established. He may have been the Richard Sone, merchant of Halesworth, about ten miles from Dunwich, who made his will in September 1596, proved 16 Oct. 1597. Two of his executors were his sons-in-law Francis Birkes and John Coppyn, both of whom were known at Dunwich. Whoever he was, the 1572 Dunwich MP served on two Commons committees in 1576, concerning ports (13 Feb.) and innkeepers (5 Mar.).

PCC 89 Cobham; Add. 19149, ff. 248, 252; *Vis. Norf.* (Harl. Soc. xxxii), 264–5; *Vis. Suff.* ed. Metcalfe, 81; *CJ*, i. 105, 111.

N.M.F.

SOTHERTON, George (*d.*1599), of St. Martin Outwich, London.

LONDON 1593, 1597

Yr. s. of Nicholas Sotherton, alderman and grocer of Norwich, by his w. Agnes Wright; bro. of Thomas I*. *m.* Elizabeth, at least 1s. 5da. surv.[1]
 Warden, Merchant Taylors' Co. 1578, 1581, master 1589, auditor of London 1582–4, 1588–90, 1591–3, 1595–7; common councilman, active 1583–99; dep. gov. Merchant Adventurers 1594.
 ?J.p. Essex 1591.

After serving his apprenticeship, Sotherton was admitted a freeman of the Merchant Taylors' Company of London on 24 Oct. 1561, being followed some years later by his cousin Nowell Sotherton*, and later still by George Sotherton junior, his son. Between them, and with the assistance of John Sotherton, Nowell's elder and influential brother at the Exchequer, the Sothertons played a prominent part in the Company's affairs for 50 years. George Sotherton senior prospered quickly. In 1568, while he was still a relatively junior liveryman, the Company honoured him by placing him at the high table at the banquet to the new lord mayor. Two years later, in 1570, he became a freeman of Norwich as a grocer, being then described as of London and son of Nicholas, but though the Sothertons were among the most substantial families in Norwich, related by marriage to other leading citizens, such as Thomas* and Christopher Layer*, it was in London that George, like several more of his family, made a home and career. His house, belonging to the Merchant Taylors, adjoined the new common hall into which, as a special privilege, he was allowed to make a door so that he and his wife might walk in the long gallery. From the Company he had also a garden and tenement in Moorfields, later leased to John Speed, and to the Company when he died went his great silver gilt standing cup and cover.[2]

In 1577 Sotherton was one of 24 admitted to the newly-formed corporation of Spanish merchants; in 1581 he was among those called upon by the Privy Council to investigate the misappropriation of a merchant's goods,

and in 1582 he began the formal association with the corporation which led to his two terms as an MP for London. A list, probably drawn up after 1582, names him among 'the wisest and best merchants in London to deal in the weightiest causes of the city as occasion is offered' – and there is ample evidence that he was so employed.[3]

Only one reference to a 'Mr. Sotherton' in D'Ewes's record of the Commons' business in 1597–8 (concerned with the sale of a debtor's land and goods, 20 Jan. 1598) can reasonably be ascribed to George Sotherton, but it was customary to refer to the London Members as such, rather than by name. Thus Sotherton could have served on committees to consider maimed soldiers and sailors (2 Apr. 1593), brewers (3 Apr.), town planning (6 Apr.), regrators (7 Nov. 1597), penal laws (8 Nov.), monopolies (10 Nov.), Langport Eastover (10 Nov.), navigation (12 Nov.), cloth (18 Nov.), wool (8 Dec.), seamen (9 Dec.), Exeter merchants (12 Dec.), merchant strangers (13 Jan. 1598), bread (13 Jan.), charitable uses (14 Jan.), mariners and soldiers (26 Jan.), wine casks (3 Feb.) and Lady Wentworth's jointure (7 Feb.). Apart from occasional service on commissions appointed by the Privy Council to consider cases of merchants in distress or at variance with authority, Sotherton's life was divided between the city, the Merchant Adventurers, and the Merchant Taylors. He is said to have died 24 May 1599. Administration of his goods was granted to his son and widow 25 Aug. 1599.[4]

[1] *Misc. Gen. et Her.* (ser. 5), ix. 129–31; PCC admon. act bk. 1599, f. 22; PCC 48 Fenner, 56 Meade. [2] A. B. Beaven, *Aldermen*, i. 290; C. M. Clode, *Early Hist. Merchant Taylors*, i. 238, 263, 281; ii. 334, 342, 343, and *Mems.* 31, 93, 117; P. Millican, *Norwich Freemen*, 127. [3] Lansd. 683 (printed *N. and Q.* (ser. 5), vii. 23); *APC*, ix. 330; xiii. 32; xv. 270; xix. 349; xxiii. 248; xxvi. 19; xxvii. 29; xxix. 421–2; Lansd. 76, f. 83; 110, f. 188; 143, f. 96; *HMC Hatfield*, v. 359; viii. 553. [4] D'Ewes, 513, 514, 519, 552, 553, 555, 556, 558, 570, 571, 579, 580, 583, 588, 592; Townshend, *Hist. Colls.* 103, 125; PCC admon. act bk. loc. cit.

E.L.C.M.

SOTHERTON, Nowell (*d.* c.1610), of St. Botolph's-without-Aldersgate, London.

DORCHESTER 1589
ST. IVES 1593, 1597

s. of John Sotherton of Norwich, mercer, by Ellen, da. of Nowell Durgys or Turgys. *m.* Timothea, da. of Anthony Williams, several children, 1 surv. da.[1]
 Warden, Merchant Taylors' Co. 1586, master 1597; clerk of estreats in the Exchequer by 1600, cursitor baron of the Exchequer from July 1606.

Following family custom, Sotherton became a freeman of Norwich as a mercer in 1570; in the same year he was admitted to the London Merchant Taylors' Company by redemption, joining his brother John and cousin George*. He served the Company well until his death, when he – like George – bequeathed it his great gilt standing cup with his arms on the cover, and £25 besides for 'a recreation' in the hall. But whereas George was in business as a London merchant, Nowell was 'bred up' in the Exchequer with his brother John (who became one of its barons in 1579) and he remained an Exchequer official all his life.[2]

Glimpses of Sotherton's activities occur in the printed sources for 1594 and onwards,[3] but that he had made his mark before then may be inferred from his return to Parliament for seats where the 3rd Marquess of Winchester had influence, though no evidence has been found to link him with that nobleman, and it is quite possible that it was Lord Burghley who was responsible for his returns at St. Ives, as he was for other Exchequer officials there at this time. The prolix piety shown in Nowell Sotherton's will suggests that it was he and not George or Thomas whom the House appointed, 1 Dec. 1597, with Sir Robert Wroth, to collect from Members for the relief of the poor and 'for the minister his pains in saying prayers'.[4]

On the death of his aged brother John, and in spite of the efforts of Julius* and Thomas Caesar*, Nowell Sotherton was appointed to succeed him in the Exchequer (though only as baron cursitor), the lord treasurer, Thomas Sackville*, Earl of Dorset, taking particular pains to ensure that the appointment was made.[5] The following year Sotherton was specially admitted to Gray's Inn, and three years later, on 24 May 1610, was mentioned by John Chamberlain, the letter-writer, as 'lately dead' though 'rather of age than any violent sickness'. His will, dated 15 Sept. 1608, provided legacies for a number of the Sotherton family in London and Norwich. To his surviving daughter and her son he gave his lease in reversion of Tracies in Essex, and to Sir Giles Fettiplace* £20 and his silver tankards. The minister of St. Botolph's, in whose church a vault already contained Sotherton's wife and children, was to receive a black gown and 40s. for the funeral sermon. Nearly £100 was to be bestowed on the honest and godly poor of the parish, the poor children of Christ's hospital, the poor in St. Bartholomew's hospital, and the poor prisoners in various prisons in London and Suffolk, the county where the Sotherton family originated. The will was proved 24 May 1610.[6]

[1] Misc. Gen. et Her. (ser. 5), ix. 129–31. [2] Lansd. 106, f. 1 seq.; CSP Dom. 1598–1601, p. 458; Chamberlain Letters ed. McClure, i. 230; P. Millican, Norwich Freemen, 101; C. M. Clode, Early Hist. Merchant Taylors, i. 263–4, 266, 267; ii. 342, 343, and Memorials, 590, 653; Cat. Silver Plate of Merchant Taylors, 148; Foss, Judges, vi. 189–90. [3] Lansd. 76, f. 32; CSP Dom. 1591–4, p. 508; 1598–1601, p. 273. [4] D'Ewes, 566. [5] HMC Hatfield, xviii. 195, 219. [6] PCC 38 Wingfield.

E.L.C.M.

SOTHERTON, Thomas I (c.1520–83), of Norwich, Norf.

NORWICH   1558, 1559

b. c.1520, 1st s. of Nicholas Sotherton, alderman and grocer of Norwich, by his w. Agnes Wright; bro. of George*. m. Elizabeth, da. of Augustine Steward† of Norwich, 4s. 4da. suc. fa. 10 Nov. 1540.

Common councilman, Norwich prob. 1547–54, common speaker 1554, 1555, auditor 1547, 1550, 1555, 1558, 1560, 1569, sheriff 1556–7, alderman 1557–83, mayor 1565–6; commr. to survey Norwich cathedral Oct. 1568.

Under Elizabeth, Sotherton played no outstanding part in civic affairs. He was partly responsible, as mayor, for the acceptance of a number of Flemish immigrants at Norwich against the opposition of the common council. These men, master workmen in the cloth industry, were admitted through the influence of the Duke of Norfolk, and were accommodated in the Strangers' Hall.

In his will dated 13 Oct. 1581 Sotherton bequeathed considerable sums to his children and smaller amounts to brothers and sisters. The residue went to his eldest son Augustine, the sole executor. Sotherton asked to be buried beside his wife in St. Andrew's church, Norwich. He died between April 1583, when he was still an alderman, and 5 Sept. of that year, when his will was proved.

Blomefield, Norf. iv. 291; Misc. Gen. et Her. (ser. 5), ix. 129–31; Norwich consistory ct. 122 Bate; Norwich ass. proc. 2, 3; PCC 21 Alenger; Norwich Recs. i. 313, 318, 415; CPR, 1566–9, pp. 205–6; The Walloons and their Church at Norwich (Hug. Soc. i), pt. 1, p. 18.

R.V.

SOTHERTON, Thomas II (c.1555–1608), of Norwich, Norf.

NORWICH   1597

b. c.1555, s. of John Sotherton, alderman and grocer of Norwich, by Mary, da. of Augustine Steward† of Norwich. m. Frances Fox, wid., da. of Robert Cheke, at least 1s. 3da.

Sheriff, Norwich 1592–3, alderman by 1595, claviour 1596, mayor 1605–6.

Sotherton was the youngest of the three Sothertons in the 1597 House of Commons. Very probably he was the 'Mr. Sotherton' who served on a committee dealing with Norfolk and Norwich worsted yarn, 18 Nov. He may also have served on committees for navigation (12 Nov.), the possessions of the bishop of Norwich (30 Nov.), draining the fens (3 Dec.), cloth (8 Dec.) and maltsters (12 Jan. 1598). His uncle George* and cousin Nowell*, though freemen of Norwich, were virtually Londoners, like others of the family who had newly established themselves in or near the capital, but Thomas was resident in Norwich, a grocer like his father and Thomas I*, his uncle, who had preceded him as the first Sotherton at Westminster. Admitted a freeman in 1576, he rose steadily through the city hierarchy until he became mayor in 1605. A man of considerable wealth, he owned land outside the city, including the manors of Cossey and Aldenham in Weston, Norfolk. He had to contribute £30 towards the forced loan of 1604.

According to his monument in St. John's, Maddermarket, he died in May 1608, aged 53. His will, dated 30 Mar. 1608, contained a number of charitable bequests. His legacies to relatives were large: £6,000 to his son Augustine and dowries of 1,000 marks each to his three daughters.

Misc. Gen. et Her. (ser. 5), ix. 129–31; H. Le Strange, *Norf. Official Lists*, 110; P. Millican, *Norwich Freemen*, 73; Norwich ass. min. bk. 1585–1613, f. 152; D'Ewes, 556, 559, 567, 569, 578; Townshend, *Hist. Colls.* 110; *Norf. Arch.* ii. 341; PCC 49 Windebancke.

R.C.G.

SOUTHCOTE, George (1572–1638), of Shillingford, Devon.

PLYMPTON ERLE 1597

b. 1572, yr. s. of Thomas Southcote* of Bovey Tracey, by his 3rd w. Elizabeth Fitzwilliam; bro. of Richard*. *educ.* I. Temple 1593. *m.* (1) Alice, da. and coh. of John Cole of Buckland Tout Saints, 1s. 1da.; (2) Sarah, da. of Robert Thomas, draper, of London and Spanby, Lincs., 3s. 4da.; (3) lic. 30 June 1635, Martha, da. of Sir John Suckling† of Goodfathers, Twickenham, Surr. *suc.* bro. Richard 1594. Kntd. 1603.

J.p. Devon 1604, sheriff 1616.

Though a younger son Southcote inherited from his father the manors of Shillingford, Stoke Fleming, Townstall and Withycombe, all near Dartmouth, and he was thus able to found a new branch of the family. Both he and his elder brother Richard were returned for Plympton in the lifetime of their father, who had himself sat for the borough. Plympton was a stannary town and no doubt it was the extensive tin workings owned by Thomas Southcote (and his daughter's marriage to William Strode II*) that maintained the connexion between the Southcotes and the borough. Southcote left no mark upon the surviving records of the House of Commons. One of Southcote's half-sisters married the puritan Sir Anthony Rous*, and Southcote himself, as patron of Stoke Fleming, presented Elias Newcomen to the rectory in 1600: an ejected fellow of Magdalene, Newcomen was of radical temper himself and was cousin to one of the authors of *Smectymnus*. Southcote was involved in a scandal in 1591 over a lady named Eleanor Thursby, but a scapegoat in the person of a Stephen Trefulack was found guilty of provoking the affair by witchcraft. Southcote was concerned in Devon defence measures in 1597, mortgaged lands to Sir William Strode in 1604 and in the following year bought a manor in Nottinghamshire. He was certified as able to lend the King £26 in 1612. Southcote committed suicide in 1638, according to one story by cutting his throat after a quarrel with his eldest son. But, according to what purports to be the finding of a coroner's inquest, he hanged himself at Kensington 14 Oct. 1638. His forfeited personal estate was bought back from the Crown for £1,400. Aubrey

commented 'My Lady Southcote, whose husband hanged himself, was Sir John Suckling's sister, to whom he writes a consolatory letter'.

Lincs. Peds. (Harl. Soc. lii), 913; *Norf. Rec. Soc.* v. 209; W. Pole, *Desc. Devon*, 172, 254, 275, 285, 286; PCC 66 Wallop; Devon RO, bps. of Exeter mss, vol. 21, f. 69v; L'Estrange Ewen, *Witchcraft and Demonianism*, 431; HMC *15th Rep.* VII, 32; Devon RO, Tingey mss, 1408, 1422; *Devon N. and Q.* xxvi. 124; *CSP Dom.* 1637–8, p. 98; 1639–40, p. 17; C10/12/116; Aubrey, *Brief Lives*, ii. 244.

I.C./J.P.F.

SOUTHCOTE, Richard (1570–94), of the Inner Temple, London and Shillingford, Devon.

PLYMPTON ERLE 1593

b. 1570, yr. s. of Thomas Southcote* of Bovey Tracey by his 3rd w. and bro. of George*. *educ.* I. Temple c.1588. *unm.*

Southcote was endowed in his father's lifetime with land at Shillingford. His return for Plympton he no doubt owed to his father's interest in tin mining and his connexion with the Strodes. Though he is not named in the journals of the 1593 Parliament he might have sat on two committees concerned with kerseys, 23 Mar. and 2 Apr. Southcote died in December 1594, leaving his brother George his heir. An inquisition post mortem was taken 2 Dec. 1600.

Vivian, *Vis. Devon*, 698, 700–1; D'Ewes, 507, 513; PCC admon. act bk. 1594, f. 100; C142/291/95.

I.C.

SOUTHCOTE, Thomas (by 1528–1600), of Shillingford St. George and Bovey Tracey, Devon.

TAVISTOCK	1555
PLYMPTON ERLE	1558
DARTMOUTH	1559

b. by 1528, 1st s. of John Southcote† by his 1st w. Joanna, da. of Hankford, wid. of one Sydenham; bro. of George Southcote†. *m.* (1) settlement May 1541, Grace (*d.*1547), da. and h. of John Barnhouse of Devon, 1s. 2da.; (2) Susan, da. of Thomas Kirkham of Blagdon in Paignton, 4s. 6da.; (3) Elizabeth, da. of George Fitzwilliam of Mablethorpe, Lincs., 8s. inc. George* and Richard* 4da. *suc.* fa. 14 Sept. 1556.

J.p.q. Devon from 1561; jt. surveyor, Exchequer, Devon and Exeter 1560–98; commr. piracy, Devon 1565, sheriff 1558–9, 1570–1.

Southcote extended the family estates, some of which were derived from the dissolution of the monasteries, buying Hennock and acquiring the manors of Stoke Fleming, Townstall and Clifton upon his second marriage, to a niece of Sir Peter Carew*. Townstall and Clifton were part of the borough of Dartmouth, where Southcote also held other property and this may have encouraged him to seek a parliamentary seat there in 1559, no doubt with the approval of the 2nd Earl of Bedford. Southcote never sat again, though he remained active locally for the rest of the century, dying 10 Aug. 1600. In his will, made in October 1593, he divided his principal lands between his eldest son George, who inherited Hennock and Bovey Tracey, and another George, a son of his third marriage, who was bequeathed Shillingford, Withycombe, Townstall and Stoke Fleming, thus founding the line of Southcote of Dartmouth. A younger son received a farm at Bovey Tracey and a grandson Southcote's Devon tinworks, while two daughters were each left 500 marks. The poor of Bovey Tracey received £20 and £6 13s. 4d. was to be distributed at the funeral.

C142/107/14, 291/95; *Vis. Devon*, ed. Vivian, 697–700; *Lincs. Peds.* (Harl. Soc. l), 357–8; Lansd. 1218, f. 62v; *CPR*, 1558–60, p. 429; *CSP Dom.* 1598–1601, p. 65; *APC*, vii. 283; *Trans. Dev. Assoc.* xxxii. 503; lxix. 466, 467; W. Pole, *Desc. Devon*, 147, 172, 204, 217, 254, 265, 266, 267, 268, 275, 285, 286; P. Russell, *Dartmouth*, 58; *Cam. Misc.* ix(3), p. 69; PCC 66 Wallop.

I.C.

SOUTHLAND, William (d. 1598), of Hope, New Romney and later of St. Andrew's, Holborn, London.

NEW ROMNEY   1584, 1586, 1589

2nd s. of William Southland by a da. of John Byng of Wrotham, Kent. *m.* Bridget Walter, 2s. 3da.

Chamberlain, New Romney 1572, jurat by 1579, mayor 1580, 1581, 1585, 1586; brodhull rep. in at least the years 1572, 1573, 1586; bailiff to Yarmouth 1582.

With a small junta who filled the offices in rotation, Southland was, from about 1584 to 1590, the virtual dictator of New Romney in the face of opposition from the townsmen, the lord warden and even the Privy Council. The way in which he ignored the instructions of successive Privy Council commissions of inquiry, led by some of the leading men of the county, can be traced in national and local records; the local independence which they reveal was extraordinary in a period of strong central government. At last, in March 1590, the Privy Council drew up instructions for the 'reformation of abuses committed in the town of New Romney ... chiefly occasioned by the ambition and corruption of one William Southland and others of his confederacy'. Southland was 'suspended from the franchises of the said town, and from all authority and government in the same'. Some of the land owned by the borough, and the town seal, which Southland and his supporters had seized for their own purposes, were to be returned and a list of prospective mayors, in their order of seniority, was drawn up and imposed on the town. On 3 Apr. Southland and others were summoned to London to explain to the Privy Council why they had still not obeyed 'certain orders set down by their lordships' concerning the government of Romney, and they were put in the Marshalsea. Shortly

afterwards their written submissions were entered in the Council register. Southland's reads:

> I, William Southland of New Romney in the county of Kent, jurat, do acknowledge mine offence in disobeying the lords' orders taken for the election of the mayor and jurats of the said town, and do hereby humbly submit myself to their lordships' orders, craving their honourable favours and pardon for what is past, and do promise in mine own behalf to obey that by their lordships to me shall be appointed.

This was the end of his domination of New Romney. While his power lasted, he had used it as widely as possible. As well as holding numerous offices in the town, he was returned to Parliament several times. There is a possibility that he represented Romney in the 1581 session of Parliament, replacing Edward Wilcocks*, for the vacancy was probably filled during his mayoralty. He was paid wages as an MP at the rate of 4s. a day in 1586 and 1589. On the former occasion he ignored the directive from the Privy Council that the same two Members should be elected as in 1584, and was returned with one of his own supporters. At the 1588 election Cobham ordered New Romney to choose someone else, but the electors refused to abandon their choice, it being 'contrary to their oaths to make a second election'. No recorded activities by Southland appear in the journals, but he could have served on a committee concerned with imports of fish, 6 Mar. 1587.

Southland appointed himself captain of the Romney militia in 1588, and was also overseer of the beacons along the adjoining stretch of coast. When the Privy Council instructed Romney and Lydd to contribute towards the provision of a ship for the navy, also in Armada year, he was the treasurer of the operation. He was discharged from the post of bailiff to Yarmouth, and he antagonized the members of a brodhull meeting in 1583. After his final humiliation over the affairs of New Romney, Southland moved to London, where he made his will, 11 Feb. 1598. There is a short religious preamble, 'all flesh is but as grass and that the beauty thereof soon full fadeth away'. There was a bequest to the poor of St. Andrew's, Holborn, 'where I now do dwell'. The overseer was his brother John, founder of the grammar school at Romney, who was given a gold ring with a blue stone for his services. Southland's heir and executor William established the family's position, being knighted by King James, buying the manor of Lee in the parish of Ickham, Kent, and marrying into a county family.

Vis. Kent, (Harl. Soc. xlii), 27, 158; Cinque Ports black bk. ff. 2, 4, 43, 46, 53; *CSP Dom.* 1581–90, pp. 167–8; Lansd. 67, ff. 209 seq.; K. M. E. Murray, *Const. Hist. Cinque Ports*, 93; *APC*, xii. 339; xiv. 308; xv. 301–2, 421–2; xvi. 22–3, 54; xvii. 101; xviii. 435; xix. 5–8, 9, 206, 208–9; New Romney ass. bk. 1577–1622, ff. 25, 30, 40, 48; D'Ewes, 412; PCC 29 Lewyn; *Arch. Cant.* xiv. 122; xli. 163, 165; li. 188–90; Hasted, *Kent*, ix. 173, 178.

M.R.P.

SOUTHOUSE, Christopher (*d.*1591), ?of St. Benet Fink, London.

St. Mawes 1584

No man of this name appears in the pedigrees of either the Norfolk or Kent families of Southouse. A Christopher Southouse was at Cambridge in 1552, and completed his education abroad. By August 1555 he was a member of William Whittingham's congregation at Frankfurt. He did not follow Whittingham to Geneva, but went to Basle, where he entered the university in December 1557. It is not known whether this man was the St. Mawes MP, though it is tempting to guess that, as a former exile, he might have obtained his return through the favour of the 2nd Earl of Bedford.[1]

A Christopher Southouse, moneylender, and possibly the same man, had a number of transactions with the 3rd Earl of Huntingdon whose manor of Stokenham, Devon, was mortgaged to him in September 1581. Two years later Southouse and one Roger Bromley were buying more lands in Devon from the Earl to satisfy a debt. During 1582 Southouse acted with John Manfield* on behalf of Huntingdon in a quarrel with the 7th Lord Mountjoy over copper and alum mines in Dorset. In May 1584 Huntingdon put one of Lord Lumley's bonds into Southouse's hands in order to cancel a debt, only a few months after a demand for the immediate repayment of £800. Southouse also advanced money to other members of the Hastings family. In 1591 the Earl's brother Walter owed him £525.[2]

Southouse the moneylender died toward the end of 1591. In his will he asked

> all such persons as shall resort unto me in my sickness and shall be present with me at the time of my departure out of this life, to esteem and repute me a good and faithful Christian, notwithstanding any idle or miscreant speeches that may happen to pass from me in mine last end; earnestly requesting them to impute the same unto the infirmity and weakness of the flesh and not unto any want of faith or incredulity in my only Saviour Jesus Christ.

The 'children of the hospital' were to sing Psalm 146 as the body was carried to church and the preacher was to take it as his text for the funeral sermon. No wife or children are mentioned, and his property was bequeathed to his brothers, sister, and their children. The overseers were Richard Braithwaite, a bencher of Lincoln's Inn, and Robert Turner of Westminster, perhaps business associates. A nephew, Martin, was mentioned, who may have been the Martin Southouse of Downham, Norfolk, noticed in the 1664 Visitation.[3]

A Christopher Southouse was a prebendary of Lincoln 1560–79.[4]

[1] *Vis. Norf. 1664*, (Norf. Rec. Soc. v), 203; *Vis. Kent* (Harl. Soc. liv), 153–4; *Al. Cant.* i(4), p. 124; C. H. Garrett, *Marian Exiles*, 290–1. [2] C66/1208, 1233; *CSP Dom.* Add. 1580–1625, p. 65; Huntington Lib. HA 5366, 5369, 5382. [3] PCC 3 Harrington. [4] C. W. Foster, *Lincoln Episcopal Recs. in the time of Bp. Cooper* (Lincoln Rec. Soc. ii), 310.

I.C.

SOUTHWELL, Sir Robert (1563–98), of Wood Rising, Norf.

Guildford 1597

b. 1563, o.s. of Thomas Southwell of Wood Rising by his 2nd w. Mary, da. of Sir Richard Mansell. *educ.* travelled abroad; G. Inn 1580. *m.* 17 Apr. 1583, Elizabeth, da. of Charles Howard I*, 1st Earl of Nottingham, 4s. 4da. *suc.* fa. 1567. Kntd. 1585.[1]

J.p. Norf., Suff. from c.1584; sheriff, Norf. 1589–90; dep. lt. until July 1596, when he became commr. musters; v.-adm. Norf. by 1587–98.[2]

When he was four years old, Southwell succeeded to extensive properties in Norfolk. He was allied to many Norfolk gentry families, and was brought up under Thomas Howard, Duke of Norfolk, an overseer of his father's will. As a youth he travelled in Italy, on his return apparently transferring his allegiance from the Norfolk section of the Howard family to the politically more reputable Effingham branch, marrying Elizabeth Howard, and spending part of his time in Surrey: at least three of his eight children were baptized at Reigate, and he was returned to Parliament for Guildford through the influence of his father-in-law, Charles Howard. Southwell's name is recorded only once in the journals of the 1597 Parliament, for a committee concerned with armour and weapons, 8 Nov. Southwell fought against the Armada, and eight years later distinguished himself at Cadiz.

In Norfolk he was active in county administration, and in 1588 he was listed as a knight of 'great possessions' able to sustain a peerage. He died 12 Oct. 1598 and was buried in the following month at Wood Rising. By his will, dated 2 Oct. 1598, he divided his lands into three parts: one-third to his son Thomas; one-third to his wife; and the remainder to her for the advancement of his daughters. The will was proved by the widow, who in 1604 married Sir John Stewart, Earl of Carrick. Southwell's surviving son, Thomas, aged two at his father's death, sold Wood Rising.[3]

[1] C142/148/58; *Norf. and Norwich Arch. Soc.* i. 125–8; *Surr. Arch. Soc.* i. 413; ix. 425–6. [2] *APC*, xxvi. 53, 351; xxvii. 38, 223; xxviii. 483; xxix. 344. [3] Blomefield, *Norf.* x. 270, 277; C142/148/58; Coll. of Arms, Talbot mss. transcribed by G. Batho, G, f. 128; *CSP Dom.* 1595–7, pp. 190–1; D'Ewes, 553; Lansd. 104, ff. 51 seq.; Devereux, *Earl of Essex*, i. 361; Birch, *Mems.* ii. 54; *HMC Hatfield*, vi. 146; *APC*, xxv. 256; PCC 78 Lewyn; *Surr. Arch. Soc.* ix. 425–6; *Norf. and Norwich Arch. Soc.* i. 128.

R.C.G.

SOUTHWORTH, Sir John (c.1526–95), of Samlesbury, Lancs.

LANCASHIRE 1563

b. c.1526, 1st s. of Sir Thomas Southworth of Samlesbury by Margery, da. of Sir Thomas Butler of Bewsey. *m.* Mary, da. of Sir Richard Assheton of Middleton, 7s. 4da. *suc.* fa. 1546. Kntd. 1547.

J.p. Lancs. by 1561, sheriff 1561–2; commr. eccles. causes, diocese of Chester July 1562–?7.[1]

In early life Southworth fought in the Scottish wars, being knighted in the field. During Mary's reign he was often in London, probably because of a series of land disputes heard in the court of duchy chamber. By the early years of Elizabeth he was back on his Lancashire estates, and represented the county in the Parliament of 1563. There is no record of any activity by him in the Commons until 21 Oct. 1566 when he had a cloth bill committed to him. On 31 Oct. he was put on the committee to consult with the Lords concerning the Queen's marriage and the succession.[2]

In October 1564 Southworth was classified as unfavourable to the newly-established church, and some four years later he was proceeded against by the bishop of Chester for not attending church and for speaking against the prayer book. After examination before the ecclesiastical commission at Lathom, he was sent to London to appear before the Privy Council. In July 1568 he was examined by Archbishop Parker, who failed to persuade him to conform. Next he went to Bath, where he consorted with 'noted hinderers of God's word'. Accused of planning a western rebellion to coincide with the rising in the north, he was put into the custody of Bishop Grindal, who reported to Cecil that

> he was altogether unlearned, carried with a blind zeal without knowledge ... His principal grounds were that he would follow the faith of his fathers; and that he would die in the faith wherein he was baptized.

Dean Nowell's persuasions proving equally fruitless, Southworth remained in prison in London until August 1569, when Grindal petitioned the Privy Council for his release on account of the unhealthy conditions in prison during the summer. Southworth's name appears on a list drawn up in the interest of Mary Queen of Scots in 1574, and he was reported by the bishop of Chester as a recusant in 1576 and 1577. At Easter 1581 he entertained Campion at Samlesbury, where Mass was said before a congregation of his household and neighbours. Campion was arrested in July and Southworth soon afterwards. He spent much of the next three years in the New Fleet at Salford, under the care of Robert Worsley*. He was permitted to exercise and to see his friends only in Worsley's presence. In July 1584 he was removed from Worsley's care and sent first to London, then (by March 1586) to Chester. In that month

the Privy Council let him visit Bath. Southworth next appears in Cheshire, where, in May 1586, he was re-arrested. In July 1587 he was released so that he could make arrangements for the payment of fines, now amounting to more than £900. He may have conformed about this time and part of this sum was remitted. He subscribed £25 to the Armada fund in 1588 and in January 1589 he attended a sermon at the Earl of Derby's house at Lathom. In 1592 he and his son were arrested after a search at Samlesbury had revealed a vault over the dining chamber, containing an altar canopy and candlesticks, 14 images and 11 'books of papistry'. How long Southworth stayed in prison on this occasion is unknown, but he had presumably been released before his death, which occurred on 3 Nov. 1595. His heavily encumbered estate, which had been vested in trustees in 1588, passed to his son Thomas. Much of it was sold early in the seventeenth century.[3]

[1] *Vis. Lancs.* (Chetham Soc. lxxxviii), 277–8; *CPR*, 1560–3, pp. 280–1; *CSP Dom. Add.* 1566–79, p. 47. [2] *Lancs. Lieutenancy Pprs.* (Chetham Soc. xlix), 4, 18–19; Whitaker, *Hist. Whalley* (1818), 539; DL5/9/170v; *VCH Lancs.* vi. 271; *CPR*, 1558–60, p. 226; *CJ*, i. 75; D'Ewes, 125, 126. [3] *Cam. Misc. ix*(3), p. 77; Leatherbarrow, *Lancs. Eliz. Recusants* (Chetham Soc. n.s. cx), 34–5; Strype, *Parker*, i. 525–7; Grindal, 204–5, *Annals*, i(2), 260–1; Lansd. 11, ff. 136, 140; *Cath. Rec. Soc. Misc.* viii. 91; *Lancs. Registers* (Cath. Rec. Soc. xxiii), 2, 308–9; *APC*, xiii. 98, 256–7, 270, 335–6; xiv. 27, 125; xv. 163; *CSP Dom.* 1581–90, p. 50; Peck, *Desiderata Curiosa*, i. bk. iv. 4, 13, 20, 28, 33, 34, 36, 37; *Stanley Pprs.* (Chetham Soc. xxxi), 58; *VCH Lancs.* vi. 306; T. C. Noble, *Names of Those who Subscribed*, 35; *HMC Hatfield*, iv. 242, 266; *Egerton Pprs.* (Cam. Soc. xii), 163–4; DL7/17/3.

I.C.

SOWCHE, *see* ZOUCHE, Richard

SPARRY, Richard (c.1530–1602), of Totnes and Staverton, Devon.

TOTNES 1593

b. c.1530, prob. s. of William Sparry of Worcester, bencher of M. Temple. *m.* (1) aft. Sept. 1563, Elizabeth, da. of Henry Fortescue of Preston, wid. of Simon Worth; (2) aft. Apr. 1591, Prothesia, da. of John Bodley, wid. of Walter Buggin of Totnes, ?s.p.

J.p. Devon from 1582, commr. musters 1583; recorder, Totnes by 1593–8.

As recorder of Totnes, Sparry was faced with the task of trying to keep a balance between the parties to the disputes within the borough which occurred when a group of the richer citizens, led by Christopher Savery*, successfully attempted to oust the lesser citizens from any say in borough affairs. His second marriage made him the stepfather of Christopher Buggin*, the heir of Savery's enemy Walter Buggin. His first wife's niece married Charles Champernown, Ralegh's friend. Probably Sparry came to settle in Devon as a result of his first marriage, to the widow of Simon Worth, who owned land at Tiverton. Alternatively it is possible that there was some relationship with the family of Richard Prestwood*, who also came from Worcester and married another daughter of John Bodley. Sparry's stepbrother continued to live in Worcestershire, and Sparry himself owned some land there in addition to Buckenden, his house at Staverton, for which he was rated for the 1576 subsidy at £10 in lands. He also had houses at Exeter and Totnes. Sparry must presumably have had some legal training, but no record of his attendance at an inn of court has been found. In the earlier years of his public life he served on a number of commissions, investigating concealed lands with Richard Edgecombe I*, serving on an Exchequer commission at Ashburton and on a number of commissions concerning Totnes.

In the Parliament of 1593 Sparry sat on committees considering Devon kerseys, 23 Mar. and 2 Apr. He was accompanied to Westminster by Savery, and in a later petition against Savery's group, it was said that Sparry, as recorder, had often warned them that they were behaving unlawfully in their administration of the borough. His neutrality eventually caused Sparry to be displaced as recorder by George Carey* of Cockington, who was more sympathetic to the machinations of the richer burgesses. Sparry's interest in local affairs continued however to the year of his death, 1602. He had made his will 16 Feb. 1601, leaving to his wife, the sole executrix, a life interest in all his property and lands. No children are mentioned. Sparry's step-son Arthur Worth received household goods. The will was proved 5 Feb. 1603.

Roberts thesis; Vivian, *Vis. Devon*, 357, 806; *Trans. Dev. Assoc.* viii. 522; xxxv. 729, 744; lvi. 221; Totnes recs. grant 16 Apr. 1598, receivers acct. 1602, letter 3 Oct. 1602; St. Ch.5/C9/7, W15/14; *Abstract Som. Wills*, ii. 81; SP12/162/37; *HMC 15th Rep. VII*, 8; Devon q. sess. order bk. 1592–1600, passim; D'Ewes, 507, 513; PCC 17 Bolein.

P.W.H.

SPEAKE (SPEKE), Sir George (c.1530–84), of White Lackington, Som.

SOMERSET 1572*

b. c.1530, s. and h. of Sir Thomas Speke† by his 1st w. Anne, da. of Sir Richard Berkeley of Stoke. *m.* (1) Elizabeth, da. of Sir Andrew Luttrell of Dunster, wid. of Richard Mallet of Currypool, 1s. 2da.; (2) Dorothy, da. of Edward Gilbert of London, 1s. 2da. *suc.* fa. 1551. KB Jan. 1559.[1]

J.p. Som. 1559, q. 1577, sheriff 1562–3; commr. oyer and terminer, Cornw., Devon, Dorset, Hants, Som., Wilts. 1564; commr. piracy, Som. 1577, musters by 1588.

The Speakes had been settled in Somerset since the time of Henry II, acquiring their estates by judicious marriages and benefiting from the dissolution of the monasteries. The earliest reference found to Speake himself is his summons before Lord Chief Justice Portman in 1555 for misdemeanours in Neroche forest, but after this youthful escapade he settled down to the usual administrative and judicial functions of a country gentleman in his shire.[2]

Speake was connected with William, 1st Earl of Pembroke, at whose funeral in 1570 he acted as one of the four assistants of the body. In the previous year, Pembroke had been examined by the Privy Council on suspicion of complicity in the scheme to marry Mary Queen of Scots to the Duke of Norfolk, and Speake was one of those he called as a witness for the defence. Speake's return at a by-election in 1576, occasioned by the death of Sir Hugh Paulet, probably owed nothing to this connexion. Sir Maurice Berkeley I, the other knight of the shire, was Speake's uncle and the two families were sufficiently influential to secure him a turn as knight of the shire. Several of his friends and relations were already sitting: his wife's nephew George Luttrell for Minehead; George Trenchard, his son-in-law, for Dorchester; and John Popham, one of the 'trusty kinsmen and friends' who acted as overseers of his will. Speake sat on the committees which drafted the subsidy bills on 10 Feb. 1576 and 25 Jan. 1581. His other committees concerned ports (13 Feb. 1576), cloth (16 Feb. 1576 and 4 and 13 Feb. 1581) and the referring of legal actions back to the county of origin (26 Jan. 1581).[3]

Speake died in 1584. To his 'well beloved wife Dorothy' he left furniture at White Lackington 'as long as she lives there without absenting herself above 40 weeks in one year, and shall live sole and unmarried'. To Dorothy also he left the tithes of Ilminster, 'the stone jug covered with silver, late the Countess of Pembroke's', wood for her household at White Lackington and 20 kine, a bull and a plough of eight oxen. There were small bequests to his daughters and younger sons, and the residue of the estate went to the eldest son, who was sole executor.[4]

[1] *Vis. Som.* (Harl. Soc. xi), 103; *Vis. Som.* ed. Weaver, 4, 43, 45–6; *Machyn Diary* (Cam. Soc. xlii), 186, 370; *Som. Med. Wills* (Som. Rec. Soc. xxi), 125; *EHR*, xxv. 553. [2] SP12/121/29; Lansd. 61, f. 168; 73, f. 162; 147, f. 19; *CPR*, 1563–4, p. 42; Collinson, *Som.* i. 67–8; Harbin, *Som. MPs*, 128; *APC*, v. 161–2. [3] *HMC Hatfield*, i. 431; *Wilts. Mag.* xviii. 128–30; D'Ewes, 247, 288, 289, 291, 295; *CJ*, i. 104, 105, 106, 119, 120, 122, 125. [4] PCC 19 Watson; C142/205/198.

I.C.

SPELMAN, Henry (c.1564–1641), of Congham and Hunstanton, Norf.

CASTLE RISING 1593, 1597
WORCESTER 1625

b. c.1564, 1st s. of Henry Spelman of Congham by his 2nd w. Frances, da. of William Saunders† of Ewell, Surr. *educ.* Walsingham g.s.; Trinity Coll. Camb. 1580, BA 1583; Furnival's Inn; L. Inn 1586. *m.* 18 Apr. 1590, Eleanor, da. and coh. of John Lestrange of Sedgeford, 4s. 4da. *suc.* fa. 1581. Kntd. 1604.

Member, Antiq. Soc. c.1591; j.p. Norf. from 1598, sheriff Nov. 1604–Feb. 1606.

Henry Spelman, historian and antiquary, obtained the foundations of his education at the local grammar school and at Cambridge where his studies were interrupted by his father's death. After putting his estates in order, he proceeded to the inns of court where he spent three years before returning to Norfolk to marry an heiress, though he did not obtain most of her estates until the death of her mother, who married Richard Stubbe*. He did, however, secure the wardship of Hamon Lestrange on the death of his father, Sir Nicholas, in December 1591, and lived at the Lestrange manor of Hunstanton for the next few years. Spelman was no doubt returned for Castle Rising through his control of the Lestrange influence in this borough, which lay close to the Lestrange estates. As a burgess for Castle Rising he may have been concerned with a committee on kerseys (23 Mar. 1593) and another for draining the fens, 25 Nov. and 3 Dec. 1597.

Until the end of Elizabeth's reign Spelman's life was that of a country gentleman; and his antiquarian and historical work was done in the second half of his life. He died in 1641.

DNB; *Vis. Norf.* (Norf. and Norwich Arch. Soc.), i. 252–3; J. Evans, *Hist. Antiq. Soc.* 12; E. Gibson, *English Works of Sir Henry Spelman*, intro.; G. A. Carthew, *Hundred of Launditch*, i. 145, 216; D'Ewes, 507, 563, 567; Aubrey, *Brief Lives*, ii. 539–40.

R.V.

SPENCER, John (c.1549–1600), of Newnham, Warws. and Althorp, Northants.

NORTHAMPTON   1572

b. c.1549, 1st s. of Sir John Spencer† of Althorp by Katherine, da. of Sir Thomas Kitson of Hengrave, Suff.; bro. of Richard* and William*. *educ.* Trinity Coll. Camb. 1561, M. Temple 1564. *m.* 1566, Mary, da. and h. of Sir Robert Catlin, 1s. Robert*. *suc.* fa. 1586. Kntd. 1588.[1]

J.p. Beds. from c.1577, Northants. from c.1584; sheriff, Northants. 1578–9, 1590–1, commr. musters by 1593–7; steward of Higham Ferrers, Daventry, Long Buckby and Passenham from 1592.[2]

The Spencers' administration of their Northamptonshire and Warwickshire estates was admired and often emulated by gentlemen all over England. Sheep from their pastures were purchased for breeding and it is probable that the family's success as farmers was rarely equalled in the century. Spencer himself, however, in the years before his father's death was frequently in debt, perhaps because he had been over-ambitious in his purchases of land, or because of too lavish hospitality. The estate was not freed from the burdens of his debts and his father's legacies until 1590.[3]

The family was well-known to most of the important men of the day. Three of Spencer's sisters married

noblemen: George Carey, 2nd Baron Hunsdon, the Queen's cousin; Ferdinando Stanley, 5th Earl of Derby; William Stanley, 3rd Baron Monteagle. His father refers to the honourable favour shown to him and his family by Burghley and Sir Walter Mildmay. A man so powerfully connected might come into Parliament for a neighbouring borough more or less when he liked, and the reason for Spencer's having himself returned is probably to be found in the subject of his only recorded participation in the business of the House, when he managed in committee a bill to assure certain lands his father had sold to (Sir) Christopher Hatton I*, 14 Feb. 1576. Spencer did not bother to sit in later Parliaments, though his two younger brothers and his son did. Spencer obtained no court or central government appointments, and in comparison with such men as Sir Richard Knightley* and Sir Edward Montagu* he played a minor role in county life.[4]

Spencer died on 9 Jan. 1600. His main contribution to the expansion of the estates to a size which was to support an earldom in his grandson's time, came through his marriage. Mary Catlin brought him the vast estates in Leicestershire and Northamptonshire which her father had built up from the profits of a successful legal career. Besides these, his own purchase of the manor of Sandys and the rectory of Dunton in Bedfordshire were insignificant. As he had only one child, his will is mainly concerned with small legacies to his servants, to those who had cared for him in his last sickness, which may have been of some length, and to his minister Thomas Campion. He was buried, as he had requested, in Brington church.[5]

[1] C142/215/258; Baker, *Northants.* i. 109; M. Finch, *Five Northants. Fams.* (Northants. Rec. Soc. xix) ped. ii. [2] Harl. 5968, no. 139; *Musters, Beacons and Subsidies* ed. Wake (Northants. Rec. Soc. iii), 34, 35; *HMC Buccleuch*, iii. 33; *HMC Montagu*, 25; Somerville, *Duchy*, i. 587, 591. [3] J. H. Round, *Studies in Peerage and Fam. Hist.* 281; H. R. Trevor Roper, *The Gentry 1540–1640* (Econ. Hist. Rev. Supp. 1), 12; Finch, 38, 51–2 seq. [4] PCC 1 Spencer; *CJ*, i. 105; *CSP Dom.* 1581–90, p. 207; 1595–7, p. 210; *APC*, xxii. 123, 442, 546; xxiii. 258, 286; xxiv. 454; xxv. 157, 392; xxviii. 47; *HMC Montagu*, 24, 25; *HMC Buccleuch*, iii. 33, 36, 39, 48, 49, 50–4. [5] Finch, 50–1, app. iv; C142/262/129; PCC 95 Kidd; Baker, *Northants.* i. 97.

S.M.T.

SPENCER, Richard (1553–1624), of Offley, Herts.

EAST LOOE	1584
BERE ALSTON	1589
BRACKLEY	1604

b. 1553, 4th s. of Sir John Spencer† of Althorp, and bro. of John* and William*. *educ.* Magdalen Coll. Oxf. BA 1572, MA 1575; incorp. Camb. 1575. *m.* 1588, Helen, da. and coh. of John Brocket* of Brocket Hall, 1s. 3da. Kntd. 7 May 1603.[1]

On mission to Duke of Parma 1588; j.p. Herts. from c.1592, sheriff 1597–8, provost marshal 1599; gent. of privy chamber to James I; commr. at The Hague 1607–8.[2]

Although a younger son, Spencer was not unprovided for. By good management and a prudent marriage, his father had improved and extended his estates in Northamptonshire, and was able to provide substantial dowries for his daughters and independence for his younger sons. He did this, not by dividing the family estates and so impoverishing his heirs, but by saving out of income and buying lands outside the county, and settling them upon his sons during his lifetime. Thus in 1554 he bought the manors of Offley and Cockernhoe in Hertfordshire, followed by further lands there in 1571. These were conveyed to Richard Spencer in 1577. On his father's death he inherited a further £500 and a third part of £4,000. His marriage brought him more lands in Hertfordshire, his wife inheriting in 1598 the manors of Almshoe and Symond's Hyde, and land in Sandridge, Stevenage and Ayot St. Peter.[3]

Before the life of a country gentleman was opened to him, Spencer spent some time travelling abroad. In June 1577 he sent a newsletter from Paris to Lord Burghley, whom he acknowledged as his patron, and who had commended him to Sir Amias Paulet*, the English ambassador in France. He was in England again at the end of 1579, but by August 1581 was writing to Burghley from Padua:

> When I think of your kindness, I think myself highly blessed by God, to have betaken myself to your service. What greater patron could I have to look after my interests?

In July 1582 he wrote a newsletter to Burghley from Augsburg, and in the following May he was again in Paris, described by Nicholas Faunt* as 'a gentleman of a good, open and kind disposition and well grounded in all humane learning'. He reached home in August via the Netherlands and Scotland. He remained in touch with Burghley, who brought him into the 1584 Parliament for East Looe. Early in 1588 the Earl of Derby, father-in-law of Spencer's sister, was being sent on a mission to treat for peace with the Duke of Parma, and he asked Burghley to appoint Spencer one of the commissioners to accompany him on his 'painful journey'. Spencer would be useful, he claimed, 'both by his sundry languages and former experience', and it was Spencer who announced the arrival of the commissioners to Alexander of Parma, when they reached Ostend.[4]

Back in England in time for the 1588 election, Spencer was returned to Parliament for Bere Alston, presumably again relying upon the influence of Lord Burghley, exercised through Lord Mountjoy. There is no mention of Spencer in the known records of either of his Elizabethan Parliaments. He declined the post of ambassador to Spain in 1604, and except for a few months spent as commissioner at The Hague in 1607–8, served no more abroad. He built his house at Offley in 1600 and lived there until his death on 7 Mar. 1624.

[1] *Vis. Herts.* (Harl. Soc. xxii), 165; R. Clutterbuck, *Herts.* i. 107; Lansd. 58, f. 94. [2] SP13/Case F/11, f. 16–17; *HMC Hatfield,* ix. 288; Lansd. 57, f. 68; R. Winwood, *Mems.* ii. 328. [3] M. E. Finch, *Five Northants. Fams.* (Northants. Rec. Soc. xix), 57–8, 174–5; *VCH Herts.* ii. 64, 145, 434; iii. 26, 40–2; Clutterbuck, ii. 357, 361; iii. 63, 96, 97. [4] *CSP For.* 1575–7, pp. 576, 600; 1579–80, p. 86; 1581–2, p. 307; 1588 (July–Dec.), p. 71; *HMC Hatfield,* ii. 507; T. Birch, *Mems. of Queen Eliz.* i. 35, 40; Lansd. 55, f. 118; 57, f. 68.

I.C.

SPENCER, Robert (1570–1627), of Wormleighton, Warws. and later of Althorp, Northants.

BRACKLEY	1597

b. 1570, s. of John Spencer* of Althorp by Mary, da. and h. of Sir Robert Catlin. *m.* 15 Feb. 1588 (with £4,000), Margaret (*d.*1597), 3rd da. and coh. of Sir Francis Willoughby of Wollaton, Notts., 4s. 3da. *suc.* fa. 1600. Kntd. 1601; *cr.* Baron Spencer 21 July 1603.[1]

J.p., commr. musters or dep. lt. Northants. from c.1601, sheriff 1601–2.[2]

Heir to one of the greatest fortunes in England, Spencer was married at 18 to an heiress who broke off a long-standing negotiation in favour of the more brilliant match. The marriage is said to have been happy: although he survived her for 30 years, Spencer did not marry again. Sir Francis Willoughby, to perpetuate the family name, intended to bestow the greater part of his estates on his eldest daughter, who had married Sir Percival Willoughby of Bone Place. Spencer's design to secure a large part of the estates for himself miscarried. He was at law for 12 years over the inheritance after his father-in-law's death, but all he could recover was one-sixth of the manor of Lambley, which he sold at once for £900.[3]

In 1597 Spencer was returned to Parliament for Brackley, where his aunt, the widow of the 5th Earl of Derby, had influence. In April 1603 he was a candidate for a county seat in the preparations for an expected election, but by the time it took place, he was a peer.[4]

When the news of the Queen's death reached Northamptonshire, Sir Thomas Tresham was anxious to proclaim James immediately, but 'Sir Robert Spencer … thought it very requisite to stay some four and twenty hours, to know the truth, and that within that time or little more they might send up to the Lords'. His caution did Spencer no harm: he received his barony from James within the year. In county life he was more active than his father. He concerned himself, too, with elections: acting in concert with Edward Montagu II*, he sometimes virtually arranged the county representation, and also wrote to Brackley, in the tone of a patron, recommending candidates. He continued the wise management of the estates which he had inherited, buying and breeding and selling his wool direct to the wholesaler, as his father had been accustomed to do. He also subscribed to the Virginia Company.[5]

Spencer died 25 Oct. 1627. His will was dated 14 Feb. 1625 and proved 21 Nov. 1627. His son Sir William was executor, and Henry Earl of Huntingdon and Thomas Earl of Southampton overseers. Spencer asked to be buried at Brington 'by the monument which I have made for Margaret my late beloved wife'. He was buried there 6 Nov.[6]

[1] M. E. Finch, *Five Northants. Fams.* (Northants. Rec. Soc. xix), ped. App. II; *CP*. [2] *HMC Buccleuch*, i, iii passim; *APC*, xxxii. 249; *CP*. [3] *HMC Middleton*, 455, 456, 457, 458, 566, 568, 571, 608; *CSP Dom.* 1595–7, p. 557; Finch, 55. [4] *HMC Buccleuch*, iii. 74, 75, 172, 173, 257. [5] *HMC Var.* iii. 121–3; *DNB*; *HMC Buccleuch*, passim; *HMC Montagu*, 105, 110; Northants. RO, Ellesmere mss; Finch, 44, 53, 63. [6] PCC 111 Skynner; *CP*.

S.M.T.

SPENCER, William (c.1552–1609), of Yarnton, Oxon.

RIPON   1584, 1586

b. c.1552, 3rd s. of Sir John Spencer† of Althorp, and bro. of John* and Richard*. *m.* bef. 1579, Margaret, da. of Francis Bowyer of London, 2s. 5da. Kntd. 1592.

J.p.q. Oxon. from c.1583, sheriff 1591–2, dep. lt. 1593; collector of the loan 1598; auditor of the Exchequer from 1577.

Spencer received a generous portion from his father, including the manor of Ufton and Beaudesert park in Warwickshire, the reversion, after five years, of Thruptown field in Norton by Daventry, and half his goods. It was, however, at Yarnton that he established a new branch of the family, purchasing the manor between 1579 and 1584, probably with the assistance of his wife's fortune. In the following years he continued to buy land: Radstone in Northamptonshire in 1585, and a manor in Thornburgh, Buckinghamshire in 1591. The Queen granted him a lease of the Oxfordshire hundred of Ploughley in 1594.

It was probably Spencer's Carey relatives who secured his return for Ripon in 1584 and 1586. His sister Elizabeth was married to Sir George Carey*, whose father, Lord Hunsdon, was at this time governor of Berwick and a member of the council in the north. Spencer himself was active in the north at this time in connexion with his duties as auditor of the Exchequer, an appointment he retained until the end of his life, though it is likely that he spent a considerable part of his time in Oxfordshire, where he took his share in local administration. Two of his servants were involved in the abortive rising of Oxfordshire peasants in 1596, and he was hated for enclosing common land. Spencer died 18 Dec. 1609, having made his will on 28 July in that year. It was proved by his eldest son and heir, Thomas, on 3 Feb. 1610. Spencer was buried in Yarnton church. Nothing has been ascertained about Spencer's religious views. The family was Catholic in the seventeenth century.

Le Neve, *Mon. Angl.* i. 22; Clutterbuck, *Herts.* i. 107; M. E. Finch, *Five Northants. Fams.* (Northants. Rec. Soc. xix), 57, 174, 175; Lansd. 47, f. 24; 737, f. 151; *APC*, xxiv. 254; xxviii. 559; *VCH Bucks.* iv. 240; *VCH Oxon.* vi. 5; *CSP Dom.* 1595–7, pp. 316–17, 343; *HMC Hatfield*, vii. 50; PCC 1 Spencer, 13 Wingfield.

A.M.M.

SPICER, William (c.1565–c.1612), of Warwick.

WARWICK   1597, 1601, 1604

b. c.1565, s. of William Spicer, surveyor gen. of works, by his w. Margaret Griffin of London. *educ.* Magdalen Coll. Oxf. 1579, BA 1583, MA 1586. *m.* Philippa, 4s. 3da.

Bailiff, Warwick 1592–3, ?dep. recorder.

Spicer's grandfather died in 1554 seised of lands in Crewkerne, Somerset. His father had some connexion with the Earl of Leicester, who obtained him a job as surveyor of the works at Berwick, from which he rose to be comptroller, and finally surveyor of the Queen's works. He died about 1605.

Spicer himself, after leaving Oxford, may have had some legal training; his parliamentary speeches suggest this, and the heralds' visitation describes him as deputy recorder of Warwick, but no confirmation of this has been found. In his first Parliament Spicer may have served on committees concerned with a hospital at Warwick (18 Nov.), Norwich diocese (30 Nov.) and maltsters (12 Jan. 1598). An unsuccessful application to be joined with his 'aged father' as surveyor of works may perhaps explain his taking a surprisingly prominent part in the debates on monopolies in the 1601 Parliament. On 20 Nov. the Commons were '*libera gens*, and therefore I hope there is both *libera mens* and *libera lingua*'. Monopolists were 'the whirlpool of the prince's profits', who lacked the last of a man's 'three especial friends, his goods, his kinsfolk and his good name'. 'The town wherein I serve' was 'pestered and continually vexed with the substitutes or vice regents of these monopolitans'. Francis Bacon thought little of Spicer's speech saying that he 'coasted so for and against the bill that for my own part not well hearing him, I did not fully understand him'. On 23 Nov. Spicer thought that to attempt to bind the prince's prerogative would be '*nec gratum, nec tutum*' and they should proceed by way of petition, 'for it is to no purpose to offer to tie her Majesty's hands by way of Act of Parliament, when she may loose herself at her pleasure'. Over the painters and plasterers dispute, 1 Dec., he wished 'that no trade should meddle one with another's'. On 10 Dec. he was again in a dilemma about procedure: 'if I should not agree to the substance of the bill I were no good commonwealth man, and if I should agree to the form I should scarce think myself a good Christian'.

Spicer 'of the borough of Warwick, gent.' made his will when sick 3 Aug. 1611, bequeathing his soul 'to the hands of my Creator with full assurance of salvation [through the] merits of my Redeemer Christ Jesus'. He asked to be buried in the parish church (where his wife had in 1595 disputed the seating arrangements). She received his house, and provision was made for the children and Spicer's 'dear aged mother'. Servants and the poor were remembered. The date of Spicer's death has not been found. The will was proved by the widow 31 Jan. 1614.

Vis. Worcs. 1682–3 ed. Metcalfe, 89; *Black Bk. of Warwick*, 401, 426; *Egerton Pprs.* (Cam. Soc. xi), 101; pat. rolls 17–30 Eliz. PRO 27(7) p. 9; 31–7 Eliz. PRO 37(2), p. 3; E351/3234, 3237, 3238, 3239, 3240, 3241; *CSP Dom.* 1595–7, p. 439; *HMC Hatfield*, x. 181; xiii. 534; xiv. 16, 34; Townshend, *Hist. Colls.* 230, 241, 270–1, 304; D'Ewes, 559, 565, 578, 644, 649; PCC 21 More, 122 Capell.

S.M.T.

SPRINT, Gregory, of Templecombe, Som., and Colaton Raleigh, Devon.[1]

SHAFTESBURY	1586
BRIDPORT	1589

Prob. s. of John Sprint (*d.* c.1588), apothecary, of Bristol by Joan, da. of Thomas Hobby or Halby of London; bro. or half-bro. of William*. *m.* Christina, da. and h. of Richard Duke[†], clerk of the augmentations office, wid. of George Brooke *alias* Cobham*, ?s.p.

Treasurer for maimed soldiers, Devon (with Warwick Hele*) by 1600.

Sprint's mother married four times. Richard Duke, her third husband, who had done well out of the dissolution of the monasteries, had a daughter by a previous wife. At his death in 1572, Sprint's mother, by 'subtle drift and device', arranged her stepdaughter's marriage with Sprint himself, who, from 'not being anything worth nor having anything' then became worth £200 per annum in land and held 1,000 marks' worth of goods.[2]

He was a cousin of John Sprint, treasurer of Salisbury cathedral, and of Lord Burghley's secretary, Michael Hickes*, who sat for Shaftesbury in 1589. Shaftesbury was owned by the 2nd Earl of Pembroke, who had links with both Salisbury and Bristol, the Sprints' family home. A Mr. Sprint was given leave to depart from the Commons on 16 Mar. 1587, but whether this was Gregory or William is unknown. Sprint's return for Bridport two years later can be attributed to (Sir) Walter Ralegh*, whose agent and neighbour he became.[3]

Contemporaries maintained that the wealth Sprint obtained by his marriage turned his head: he became involved in a number of lawsuits, including some against members of the Duke family, and against his mother's fourth husband, Roger Gifford. His tenure of the former Sherborne abbey manor of Stalbridge was disputed in 1589, and a riot there led to another Star Chamber case.

1577 saw the beginning of a long series of lawsuits between Sprint and his wife's sons by her former marriage, Duke and Peter Brooke. The two young men, usually supported by their mother, repeatedly attacked their stepfather, sometimes in court and sometimes in person. In 1583 Sprint seems to have granted the Brookes his seat at Templecombe but refused to give them possession, saying that 'he built the same for himself and their mother and had no other convenient house to dwell in'. An investigation was ordered by the Privy Council, and the feud dragged on for another ten years. In 1591 Sprint was outlawed and his goods seized, in face of his protest that he was being punished for Duke Brooke's debts. In 1604, willingly or unwillingly, Sprint sold some land in Otterton to pay these debts, for which he had stood surety. William Martin*, whose son Richard* Sprint described as his nephew, also paid some of Duke Brooke's debts.[4]

By 1608, possibly much earlier, Sprint moved from Templecombe and retired to Devon. He may still have been alive in 1612, but the dates of his birth and death are as obscure as the rest of his life, with the exception of his lawsuits. His wife was said to be pregnant in 1575, but no children are known.[5]

[1] This biography is based on the Roberts thesis. [2] C3/174/42 Eliz.; J. A. Youings, 'Disposal of Devon Monastic Property' (London PhD thesis, 1950), 192 et passim; *Lond. Mar. Lic.* (Harl. Soc. xxv), 16; Vivian, *Vis. Devon*, 311 is misleading. [3] *DNB* (Sprint, John; Herbert, Sir William); *HMC Foljambe*, 25; *Stradling Corresp.* ed. Traherne, 71, 333 seq.; PCC 9 Noodes, 39 Woodhall; Hutchins, *Dorset*, iii. 675; *Trans. Dev. Assoc.* xxi. 319. [4] *PRO Lists and Indexes*, vii. 130, 353, 362, 388–9; C2/W18/49; *Cal. Proc. Chanc. Q. Eliz.* i. 245; ii. 60; *CSP Dom.* 1581–90, pp. 327, 329; *HMC Hatfield*, xii. 616; Devon RO, Clinton box 96; SP12/189/44; St. Ch. 5/A25/8, 38/37, S5/28, 10/17, 59/39, 77/16, 49/20, 31/18, T14/24. [5] Devon RO, order bk. 1600–7, p. 1; PCC 8 Wingfield; Lansd. 92, ff. 191, 209; St. Ch. 5/S59/39.

P.W.H.

SPRINT, William (*d.* 1592), of Bristol.

WEYMOUTH AND MELCOMBE REGIS	1586

Prob. s. of John Sprint (*d.* c.1588), apothecary, of Bristol by Joan, da. of Thomas Hobby or Halby of London; bro. or half-bro. of Gregory*. *m.* Margaret.[1]

Sprint, a cousin of Michael Hickes* and of John Sprint, treasurer of Salisbury cathedral,[2] was a Bristol merchant; his name appears frequently in the local records. In 1586 the Weymouth authorities sent a blank parliamentary election return to the 2nd Earl of Pembroke, in which Sprint's name was later inserted.[3] Sprint was noted in the town records as a friend of Thomas Hannam*, recorder of both Weymouth and Bristol.[4] The Earl of Pembroke had connexions with Bristol, and it seems likely that he and Hannam together agreed upon Sprint's nomination at Weymouth. Gregory Sprint sat for Shaftesbury, another Pembroke borough, in this Parliament.

Towards the end of his life Sprint appears to have been in financial difficulties. He owed the Queen £200, and a writ of extent was issued against him for two bonds. When his inquisition post mortem was held at Bristol 4 June 1599, it was suggested that he had been involved in fraudulent property transactions. His widow married another Bristol merchant.[5]

[1] CPR, 1560–3, p. 87; PCC 28 Leicester; E178/937/Glos. [2] St. Ch. 5/S49/20; DNB (Sprint, John). [3] Roberts thesis, 205. [4] Cat. Charters Weymouth, ed. Moule, 40. [5] E178/937/Glos.

P.W.H.

SPURLING, John (d. 1603), of Serjeants' Inn, London and Edworth, Beds.

DUNHEVED (LAUNCESTON)   1586, 1589

educ. Trinity Coll. Camb. 1560; G. Inn 1563, called 1565. m. Anne, 2s. 5da.

Double reader, G. Inn 1585, treasurer 1588, double reader and serjeant 1594; j.p. Isle of Ely from c.1591, Herts. from 1596, Beds. 1598; duchy of Lancaster c.j. for Isle of Ely 1603–4.[1]

There is some doubt as to when Spurling became a serjeant-at-law. According to the records of Gray's Inn, this occurred in 1594, but there are references to him as a serjeant as early as 1588, and he appears on a list of serjeants retained by the duchy of Lancaster from 1586. In any event, by 1588 he was sufficiently eminent to be investigating Sir Edward Stanley's claim to some estates of the late Earl of Leicester, and to be one of the lawyers asked to consider unnecessary or defective statutes which might be dealt with in the next Parliament.[2]

It is not clear how Spurling came to be returned for Dunheved. Possibly it was through Burghley by whom he was employed later (by 1596), and/or through some connexion with the Killigrew family. After Burghley's death, Spurling wrote to Cecil offering 'the like services he did his father' and reminding Cecil that he had been his patron when he 'went first serjeant'. Three months later he wrote again, promising to serve Cecil as he had his father, and hoping that he would be allowed to answer some objections that had been made against him.[3]

The proceeds of a prosperous legal career were invested in land. His principal estate was at Edworth in Bedfordshire, which he bought at some time between 1586 and 1588. He bought also the nearby manor of Eyworth, but in 1595 this was sold to his friend Sir Edmund Anderson. In Hertfordshire he held the manor of Weston Argentine from 1591 until 1594, when he sold it to Lord Keeper John Puckering*. In 1597, however, he made a more permanent addition to his estates in the county, when he bought the manor of Caldecote, lying some three miles to the south of Edworth, for £1,200. Edworth was sold by Spurling's widow in 1614 for £3,000. If these sums were at the conventional figure of ten years' purchase,

Spurling's income from these two manors alone was not inconsiderable.[4]

He died in September 1603. In his will he directed that lands at Caldecote, Newnham, Radwell and Hinxworth should be sold by his wife and elder son, in accordance with the advice of his 'especial, honourable and worshipful good friends' Sir Edmund Anderson, chief justice of the common pleas, and (Sir) Peter Warburton*. The fund so created was to be used to pay his debts and the residue divided among his five daughters. His elder son Philip was to receive an annuity of £50 out of the manor of Edworth, which was left to Spurling's wife. To the younger son was bequeathed the next vacancy of the parsonage of Edworth. In accordance with his wishes Spurling was buried in the church of Baldock, near which his lands lay.[5]

[1] G. Inn Pens. Bk. i. 64, 81, 101; PCC 20 Harte; Somerville, Duchy, i. 452; Hatfield mss 278; SP13/Case F/11, f. 16v; patent rolls 36, 38, 40 Eliz.; W. R. Williams, Lancaster Official Lists, 81. [2] CSP Dom. 1581–90, p. 549; APC, xvi. 417. [3] HMC Hatfield, viii. 312, 451; xiv. 47; CSP Dom. 1595–7, p. 315. [4] VCH Beds. ii. 224, 232; VCH Herts. iii. 218–19; Clutterbuck, Herts. ii. 521. [5] PCC 20 Harte.

I.C.

STAFFORD, Edward I (1536–1603), of Stafford Castle.

BANBURY   1554 (Nov.)[1]
STAFFORD   1558, 1559

b. 17 Jan. 1536, 4th s. of Henry Stafford, 1st Baron Stafford (d. 1563), by Ursula, da. of Sir Richard Pole, KG, of Ellesborough, Bucks.; bro. of Sir Henry† and Walter*. m. c.1566, Mary (d. 1609), da. of Edward Stanley, 3rd Earl of Derby, 2s. (1 d.v.p.) 2da. suc. bro. as 3rd Baron Stafford 1566; suc. mother to castle and manor of Stafford 1570.[2]

J.p. Salop from c.1582, q. by 1591, Staffs. by 1583, q. by 1591, Glos., Mont. by 1591; v.-adm. Glos. 1587; member, council in marches of Wales 1601.[3]

The first known reference to Stafford in official sources is a council order of May 1557, presumably connected with the arrest of his elder brother Thomas, executed that month, ordering him to 'repair home to his father, and to continue there until he should receive further order': there is no evidence that any action was taken against him. He may have been the 'Mr. Stafford' who served at Dunbar in August 1560, and was still receiving a pension, in January 1562, for work in Scotland.[4]

He was a 'known wasteful man' who squandered his fortune and by 1601 his lands in Staffordshire were reduced to the 'rotten castle of Stafford'. While he had estates he treated his tenants despicably. Those at Caws complained of wrongful imprisonment and of their landlord's contempt for the sheriff's authority. The Privy Council supported them, writing to Stafford that they 'much disliked' his disorderly dealings, warning him that they wished to 'hear no more of it, as he will upon his peril answer to the contrary'. One of his devices was to claim that free or copyhold tenants were villeins or 'bondsmen', and in 1586 the Council ordered him not to molest Richard Cole*, mayor of Bristol, and his relative Thomas Cole, on this pretext. Private cases brought against him alleged violent treatment, eviction and wrongful imprisonment, and refusal to pay debts: the parson of Church Eaton, Staffordshire, stated that he was afraid of violence resulting from his dispute with Lord Stafford about the title to a parsonage. One Ralph Higgons, who apparently could not substantiate his statement, claimed that Stafford had uttered irreverent and treasonable words against the Queen and her parents. His tongue made him many enemies. He wrote to Richard Bagot, who claimed relationship with the Staffords by marriage, and whom he suspected of supporting Higgons against him: 'Surely I will not exchange my name of Stafford for the name of "A bag of oats", for that is your name'. He knew of no ancestor of his who had married a Bagot, unless 'peradventure she married her servant'. 'Your neighbour', he ended his letter, 'I must be'.[5]

When in 1580 his name was put forward for membership of the council in the marches of Wales, he was blackballed by Sir Henry Sidney*. When he tried again in 1600 it was obvious that the other members did not want him: Henry Townshend* warned the government that, if admitted, Stafford would attend continually to draw the diet and allowances for himself and his servants, and so encumber the council's work. However, he secured admission in the following year, immediately asking for a 'convenient chamber' in the council house, near to the dining room. Townshend and John Croke III* demurred, pointing out that as it was vacation time there was no need for his attendance, and that they had no suitable room available.[6]

Despite the bad example he set to other officials, Stafford was expected to carry out the duties suitable to his position. The story that he was removed from the Staffordshire commission of the peace for harbouring a murderer is apocryphal. He was one of the peers who tried Mary Stuart and the Earl of Essex, and at one time he was joined with Edward, 4th Lord Dudley in putting down riots in Staffordshire.

Stafford was a Catholic sympathizer. His name was on a list drawn up in the interest of Mary Stuart in 1574; on another five years later 'specially recorded in the agreement given to the Pope and sent to the King of Spain'; and, in October 1592 he was included among the 'relievers and followers of Jesuits and seminary priests'. No action was taken against him. He died intestate 18 Oct. 1603. Letters of administration were granted to his surviving son and heir, Edward.[7]

[1] Huntington Lib., Hastings mss. [2] CP; Vis. Staffs. (Wm. Salt Arch. Soc. v. pt. 2), 276–7; Staffs. Peds. (Harl. Soc. lxiii), 213; C142/284/33; CPR, 1569–72, pp. 35, 245; VCH Staffs. v. 87. [3] Flenley, Cal. Reg. Council, Marches of Wales, 216; P. H. Williams, Council in the Marches of Wales, 358–9; Staffs. Q. Sess. Rolls (Wm. Salt Arch. Soc.), passim; APC,

xv. 254. [4] APC, vi. 83; CSP For. 1560–1, p. 209; 1561–2, p. 457. [5] CPR, 1569–72, pp. 236, 458, 460, 461; J. C. Wedgwood, Staffs. Parl. Hist. (Wm. Salt Arch. Soc.), i. 350; Wm. Salt Arch. Soc. iv(2), 17, 35; viii(2), 149; n.s. xi. 85–6; xii. 82; xiii–xv, passim; J. A. Longford, Staffs. and Warws. i. 404; C142/284/33; APC, x. 206; xi. 64, 215; xii. 171; xiii. 114; xiv. 48–9, 100, 153, 190–1; xv. 303–4; xix. 291; NLW 14800; Staffs. Rec. Soc. 1938, pp. 93–4; P. H. Williams, 308, 309; Lansd. 70, f. 6. [6] P. H. Williams, 139, 309; HMC Hatfield, xi. 225, 320. [7] Flenley, 151, 169, 216; APC, x. 324; Cath. Rec. Soc. Misc. viii. 90; Cath. Rec. Soc. liii. 125, 230; HMC Hatfield, iv. 242; PCC admon. act bk. 1604, f. 190; CP.

N.M.F.

STAFFORD, Edward II (1552–1605), of London.

MITCHELL	1571
HEYTESBURY	1572
WINCHESTER	1593
STAFFORD	1597, 1601
QUEENBOROUGH	1604*

b. 1552, 1st s. of Sir William Stafford† of Chebsey, Staffs., Rochford, Essex, and London by his 2nd w. Dorothy, mistress of the robes to Queen Elizabeth, da. of Henry, 1st Baron Stafford; bro. of John*. educ. St. John's, Camb. (impubes), Pembroke, Camb. 1564. m. (1) a da. of Alexander Chapman of Norf., 1s. 2da.; (2) 1578, Douglas, da. of William, 1st Baron Howard of Effingham, wid. of John, 2nd Baron Sheffield, and of Sir Robert Dudley*, Earl of Leicester, 2s. suc. fa. 1556. Kntd. 1583.

Gent. pens. by 1573–1603; ambassador to France 1583–91; master of the pipe office in the Exchequer 1591; remembrancer of first fruits and tenths in the Exchequer 1591.[1]

Edward Stafford possessed two qualifications important for success at the Elizabethan court: influential relatives and personal ability. He lacked a third – wealth. His mother, Dorothy, entered the Queen's service about 1563 and, as her epitaph states, attended the Queen for 40 years, 'lying in the bedchamber'. Through her mother, Dorothy Stafford was descended from George, Duke of Clarence, Edward IV's brother, and through her father from Edward, last Duke of Buckingham. Sir William Stafford, Edward's father, had married as his first wife, Mary Boleyn, Elizabeth's aunt. Edward, therefore, had some claim on Elizabeth's patronage, and in his mother he had a suitor always able to gain the Queen's attention. Sir William Stafford was a Marian exile, who left the country in 1555 with his whole household, arriving in Geneva in March, and becoming a member of the English congregation there on its formation in November of that year. Calvin himself was godfather to the Staffords' third son, John, born at the end of 1555. Sir William died in May 1556, and his wife, after a dispute with Calvin over the custody of John, removed to Basle, remaining there until January 1559. As Dorothy Stafford entered the Queen's service soon after her return, Edward Stafford probably spent the remainder of his youth close to the court, and as Burghley seems to have been his patron from the beginning of his career, it is not impossible that he was educated in Burghley's household. On the first two occasions that he sat for Parliament Stafford was still under age. Mitchell provided seats for a number of officials in the first half of Elizabeth's reign. It was no doubt through court influence – perhaps that of Burghley – that Stafford gained his seat there in 1571. At Heytesbury Sir John Thynne* wielded considerable influence, and was presumably Stafford's patron in 1572. Stafford is found on only one committee in his first two Parliaments, 27 Feb. 1581, for a bill dealing with the punishment of the Family of Love.[2]

Stafford's first diplomatic mission came at the end of 1574, when he was only twenty-two. He was despatched to report on the situation in East Friesland, where there was a dispute between two earls, one of whom favoured a Spanish alliance. In May 1578 he was again on the Continent to protest to Catherine de Medici against Alençon's intention of accepting the sovereignty of the Netherlands; and his association with France was continued when, in the following year he was chosen to carry out the negotiations for the marriage between Elizabeth and Alençon. Stafford seems to have been in favour of the match, believing that friendship between France and England would strengthen the position of the French Huguenots, and would present Spain with such a formidable alliance that she would bring the war with the Dutch to an end. On his arrival in London in 1581 Alençon stayed in Stafford's house.[3]

From an early point in his career Stafford was in financial difficulties. In 1574 he sold the manor of Chebsey, part of the estate inherited from his father, thenceforward relying on royal favour for his maintenance. Indeed his marriage to Lady Douglas Sheffield in 1578 was possibly influenced by the fact that, her son being a minor, she was temporarily in control of the Sheffield estates. The Queen provided him with some financial reward for his services in the form of a grant of the revenue from the discovery of concealed benefices in July 1581, but a petition presented by a poor man in 1592 illustrates his continual need for ready money. The petitioner complained that 10 or 12 years previously Stafford and some others had borrowed his ready money and goods in order to wait upon the Queen who was on progress. They had since pretended, he alleged, that they were privileged by their service to use poor men's goods at their pleasure, making repayment when they chose or not at all.[4]

It was probably Stafford's precarious financial position that delayed his being chosen as ambassador to France. Writing to Burghley in June 1583, he stated the position frankly: 'As for mine estate, truly (as her Majesty sayeth) it is poor'. He had served only the Queen, he added:

Yet do I live better contented, being satisfied in my conscience with my poverty, than if, in following of any course else, I had been able to purchase for my children. Yet, my lord, if I do stay any longer, truly I shall be poorer, for where now I have some half dozen of hundred pounds a year by my wife's means to help rub it out in such a service, shortly the increase of my Lord Sheffield's years will abate a round sum of that, and I quite unable to be employed after so well.

In addition he hoped that the Queen might lend him some money interest free. The suggestion that Stafford should succeed Sir Henry Brooke *alias* Cobham I* in France came from Sir Francis Walsingham*, but Stafford, though he was undoubtedly anxious to be appointed, was unwilling to have any patron other than Burghley. He disliked Walsingham's and Leicester's policy of open alliance with protestant against Catholic Europe. Not unnaturally, he thought greater benefit could be won by diplomatic means, by playing off France against Spain. His relations with Walsingham, therefore, throughout his embassy, were not particularly amicable. He had a more personal reason for disliking Leicester, a former lover of his wife.[5]

The details of Stafford's long embassy cannot be related here, though the accusation made by one historian, that he was guilty of treason, must be mentioned. There is now general agreement that Stafford's dealings with the Spanish ambassador, though they involved selling information, sprang from a desire to gain the latter's confidence in the hope of obtaining information useful to England.[6]

By 1590 Stafford's financial affairs were desperate. He returned to England in the summer of that year and was unable to return to France without financial assistance. The Queen complained that she would not be 'dallied with', and that he must return immediately 'or else she would lay him by the heels'. Stafford agreed to go, provided that the French ambassador be asked to dissuade a creditor from pressing for the return of £1,800. With this promise and £500 borrowed from Burghley he returned. After spending the autumn in Henry of Navarre's camp outside Paris, he returned finally to England. A new ambassador was appointed in July 1591, and Stafford was allowed £3 6s. 8d. for each day of his service, and a gratuity of £500. He also received some honorary recognition from Oxford and two of the inns of court, and two offices in the Exchequer. A rumoured secretaryship of state never materialized, nor did the chancellorship of the duchy of Lancaster, though he did obtain a grant of land from James I in compensation, the office, as the grant noted, having been promised to him by Elizabeth.[7]

Stafford sat in each Parliament after his return from France until his death. His patron at Winchester in 1593 was probably the new high steward, Sir Thomas Heneage. In the last two Parliaments of Elizabeth's reign he represented Stafford, where family influence was no doubt strong enough to secure his return. On 26 Feb. 1593 he spoke on the subsidy, and was appointed to the committee the same day. On 3 Mar. he negotiated with the Lords on the subject, and on 7 Mar., after the vice-chamberlain had reported the meeting with the Lords,

> Sir Edward Stafford thought subsidies were not so fit a remedy for the danger we were in, but advised rather, there being 10,000 parishes in England, that it should be imposed on every parish to send so many men for the wars; and the richer parishes to help the poorer. And the allowance for every man yearly to be £12. After this he moved to have the Parliament prorogued.

He urged, 28 Feb., that the guardians for the children of Catholic families should not be chosen by one justice of the peace only, as he might be an enemy of the family in question; the choice should be made by two or three justices. Subjects of his committee work in this Parliament included alien merchants (6 Mar.), the poor law (12 Mar.), and the religious questions of this Parliament (28 Feb., 4 Apr.). In that of 1601 he was named to committees dealing with privileges and returns (31 Oct.), monopolies (20 Nov.), cloth (21 Nov.) and charitable uses (28 Nov.). Privilege matters he was concerned with included the Denbighshire election case and that concerning George Belgrave.[8]

Although he was passed over for the higher government appointments, Stafford took seriously his work in the pipe office. In a letter to Burghley of July 1596 he claimed that he had cut down the fees exacted by his underlings. But his debts in France still bothered him – he was, for example, dunned by a French jeweller, who substantiated a claim before Sir Robert Cecil. In August 1604 Baron Bruce of Kinlosse and Sir John Herbert were instructed to decide a suit of debt between Stafford and Paulo Lardo, the Venetian agent. This debt was still outstanding at his death, as was one to Diana, sister of Lady Burghley. He died early in February 1605, leaving a son William, and on 5 Feb. was buried at St. Margaret's, Westminster.[9]

[1] DNB; C. H. Garrett, *Marian Exiles*, 296; *Huntington Lib. Bull.* ix. 15–26; Lansd. 31, f. 137. [2] Nichols, *Progresses Eliz.* iii. 544; Garrett, 296; *CJ*, i. 130. [3] *CSP For.* 1572–4, pp. 576, 579–80; C. Read, *Burghley*, 211–12, 387; M. Hume, *Courtships of Q. Eliz.* 222, 264. [4] *Al. Ox.* 1404; Harl. 6993, f. 44; Lansd. 31, f. 137; SP12/159/37; *CSP Dom.* 1591–4, p. 269. [5] Harl. 6993, f. 44; *EHR*, xliv. 216; *Am. Hist. Rev.* xx. 293; *HL Bull.* ix. 15–26. [6] *Am. Hist. Rev.* xx. 292 seq.; xxxv. 560–6; *EHR*, xliv. 203 seq. [7] *CSP For.* 1589, pp. 177–8, 209; Lansd. 64, f. 151; *CSP Dom.* 1581–90, p. 680; 1591–4, p. 97; 1597–1601, pp. 222, 481; 1601–3, pp. 63, 201; 1603–10, pp. 14, 139. [8] D'Ewes, 471–2, 474, 477, 486, 489, 492, 499, 517, 622, 637, 647, 657, 686, 688; Townshend, *Hist. Colls.* 212, 327. [9] SP12/259/63; *HMC Hatfield*, vi. 509, 525, 527; xvii. 357, 576; *CSP For.* 1589–90, p. 302; *CSP Dom.* 1603–10, p. 144; *Chamberlain Letters* ed. McClure, i. 204; PCC 107 Byrde.

A.M.M.

STAFFORD, John (1556–1624), of Marlwood, Glos.

STAFFORD	1584, 1586
WAREHAM	1601

bap. Jan. 1556, 3rd s. of Sir William Stafford† by his 2nd w., and bro. of Edward Stafford II*. *educ.* Corpus Christi, Camb. 1569; G. Inn 1572. *m.* wid. of John Whynniard, *s.p.* Kntd. 1596.[1]

J.p. Glos., Mont., Salop, Staffs. from c.1591; constable, Bristol castle 1601; gent. pens. 1597–*d.*[2]

Stafford was the first child to be baptized in the newly-formed English congregation at Geneva, Calvin himself being godfather. After Sir William Stafford's death in May 1556, Calvin forbade the widow to remove the child from Geneva, and it was only through the intervention of her brother-in-law, Robert Stafford, that she secured permission to go to Basle, where the family remained until January 1559, when Lady Stafford and her three sons returned to England. She now became mistress of the robes, and obviously felt it worthwhile to make certain that John Stafford's nationality would not be questioned in view of his birth abroad. At any rate it was enacted in the 1566 session of Parliament that he was to be 'as born in England'. After Cambridge and Gray's Inn, Stafford settled in Gloucestershire. He was presumably returned for Stafford through his uncle, Edward Stafford I*. The 1584 return, oddly enough, spells out that Stafford was the son of Lady Dorothy Stafford. He made no known contribution to the proceedings of any of his Parliaments. Possibly he was the Mr. 'Stoverd' who was given leave of absence 7 Mar. 1587. His return for Wareham in 1601 may have been due to the influence of Thomas Howard*, 3rd Viscount Howard of Bindon, who collected several Dorset borough nominations and offered the package to Sir Robert Cecil. When Stafford first became acquainted with Cecil is unknown, but by November 1601 he felt sufficiently assured of his favour to ask him to secure the reversal of a Star Chamber judgment against Sir Henry Winston, a Gloucestershire neighbour. An earlier association with the Earl of Essex in 1596, when Stafford accompanied him to Cadiz and was there knighted by him, does not appear to have damaged his relations with Cecil. In August 1602, a Captain Wigmore, writing to Cecil from Dort, assumed that he would have received an account of affairs in the Netherlands from Stafford, who had recently returned to England. The duration of his stay in the Low Countries is unknown, but probably it had some military purpose, as he was later to use it as a reason for making him a commissioner for musters.[3]

In Gloucestershire, Stafford was mainly concerned with local administration. After succeeding the 2nd Earl of Pembroke as constable of Bristol castle early in 1601, he asked to be made a commissioner for musters in Bristol: 'I shall be in some sort disgraced if I may not attain to the same pre-eminence [as Pembroke]'. He would be better able to keep Cecil informed on local affairs, and 'the grant of my request will encourage me in her Majesty's service'. He desired 'nothing but grace and credit among my neighbours, whereby I may be better able to serve her

Majesty'. He renewed his suit in 1608, and in 1611 he tried to buy the castle from the Crown. By 1621 his conduct brought complaints to the Privy Council from Bristol corporation, who alleged that he was non-resident, and that his deputy allowed 240 beggars to live in the castle.[4]

Stafford's will makes no mention of wife or children, but a petition of 1611 refers to his marriage to John Whynniard's widow. He died on 28 Sept. 1624 and was buried at Thornbury two days later, 'assuredly expecting to rise justified through the merits, death and passion of my Lord and Saviour Jesus Christ'. Stafford's heir was his nephew, the son of his brother William, upon whom his lands had previously been settled. All his personal property he left to Richard Stafford (grandson of his brother Sir Edward), who was appointed executor. At the time of his great-uncle's death, Richard was still under age and administration was granted to Sir Richard Lovelace, one of the overseers. Richard Stafford proved the will in November 1629.[5]

[1] *Genealogist*, n.s. xxxi. 177–8; J. C. Wedgwood, *Staffs. Parl. Hist.* (Wm. Salt Arch. Soc. 1917), i. 378. [2] Hatfield mss 278; SP13/Case F/11, ff. 15–16; *HMC Hatfield*, xi. 565; *CSP Dom.* 1611–18, p. 33. [3] C. H. Garrett, *Marian Exiles*, 294, 295–6; *DNB* (Stafford, Edward, William); Atkyns, *Ancient and Present State of Glos.* 404; *CJ*, i. 75; D'Ewes, 413; *HMC Hatfield*, xi. 486; xii. 307. [4] *APC*, xxiii. 290; *HMC Hatfield*, xi. 565; xii. 32, 562–3; xiv. 192; *CSP Dom.* 1603–10, p. 436; 1611–18, pp. 79, 107, 277; *APC*, 1619–21, p. 364. [5] *CSP Dom.* 1611–18, p. 106; PCC 107 Byrde.

I.C.

STAFFORD, Reade (c.1542–1605), of Bradfield, Berks.

| EAST GRINSTEAD | 1593 |
| TRURO | 1597 |

b. c.1542, 1st s. of Thomas Stafford of Bradfield by Anne, da. of one Best of London. *m.* aft. 1568, Mabel, da. of Richard Staverton of Warvile, wid. of Francis Waferer of London, and of Nicholas Williams of Burfield, *s.p. suc.* fa. 1584. Kntd. 1601.

Escheator, Oxon. and Berks. 1585–6; j.p. Berks. from c.1583.[1]

A branch of the Stafford family, descended from the Staffords of Chebsey, Staffordshire, had settled in Berkshire in the time of this Member's grandfather. Since then they had prospered, acquiring lands in the vicinity of Reading by purchase and by marriage. Stafford, a country gentleman, was in financial difficulties by the early 1590s, possibly because his father had settled lands on his younger sons. He therefore tried, in 1593, to break the entail on his property so that land could be sold to satisfy his and his father's creditors. It may have been this that caused Stafford to seek election to Parliament for the first time in 1593, when he was already more than 50 years old, for a bill concerning his lands was discussed during this session. He made no known contribution to the business of either of his Parliaments. His return for East Grinstead,

a duchy of Lancaster borough, was possibly due either to Sir Thomas Heneage*, chancellor of the duchy, or to Lord Buckhurst. Stafford had no connexion with Heneage that is readily apparent, but he had at least two relatives at court, Lady Stafford, mistress of the robes, and his father-in-law, a gentleman pensioner of the Queen. His return for Truro was presumably due to Cecil acting through the Killigrews.

Stafford died 16 June 1605 leaving as his heir a 12 year-old nephew. His health had been bad for some time. More than a year before his death, upon hearing that his relative was at the last gasp, Sir Edward Stafford had written to Cecil, asking for the wardship of the heir or a lease of his lands. Some time later Cecil received a similar request from the Countess of Southampton on behalf of a friend. In his will Stafford showed himself more concerned for the welfare of another nephew, Robert, than for that of Edward, his heir. Edward was mentioned once only, when his uncle begged the lord chancellor and the master of the wards to deal justly with him. After making bequests amounting to more than £300 to his sisters and nieces, Stafford concentrated on his main concern. Robert Stafford was to be educated at the charge of the estate until he was of age. The executors, Sir Francis Stafford, the boy's father, and Francis Englefield, were instructed to see

> that due care be had and taken that until that age he be not suffered to lose any time, myself knowing by long experience how precious a thing time well spent is.

When he reached the age of 20 the young man was to be sent to the Middle Temple (with an annual allowance of £30) as his uncle knew 'how honourable and profitable a study of the law is'. Bequests were made to the poor of Aldworth, Ashampstead, Bradfield, Burfield and Englefield, in which parishes the principal Stafford properties lay, and the residue of the unentailed estate was left to young Robert. As he had requested, Stafford was buried beside his wife in Bradfield church. An inquisition post mortem was taken 22 Aug. 1605.[2]

[1] *Vis. Berks.* (Harl. Soc. lvi), 58, 130, 288; (lvii), 215; *CSP Dom.* 1601–3, p. 113. [2] *VCH Berks.* iii. 121, 308, 396, 403, 431; iv. 5, 102; C142/203/21, 290/121; *CSP Dom.* 1581–90, p. 354; 1591–4, p. 334; *APC*, xiv. 215; Cott. Titus F. ii, anon. jnl. f. 59; *HMC Hatfield*, xi. 84; xvi. 204; xvii. 641; PCC 1 Stafford.

I.C.

STAFFORD, Thomas (c.1574–1655).

WEYMOUTH AND MELCOMBE	
REGIS	1593
HELSTON	1621
BODMIN	1624, 1625

b. c.1574, illegit. s. of Sir George Carew†, later Earl of Totness. *m.* aft. 1633, Mary, da. of Sir Henry Woodhouse* of Kimberley, Norf., wid. of Sir Robert Killigrew* of St. Margaret Lothbury, London. Kntd. 1611.

Gent. usher of privy chamber to Queen Anne by 1619, and to Queen Henrietta Maria.

Stafford may have been brought up in Sir George Carew's household, and was possibly associated, from an early date, with his activities in Ireland. In his will Carew bequeathed Stafford his pension of £500 a year payable from the alienations office, as well as all his books and manuscripts. Stafford's return for Weymouth and Melcombe Regis in 1593 was presumably arranged by (Sir) Walter Ralegh*. As 'Sir' Thomas Stafford he was at the conference with the Lords about the subsidy, 1 Mar. 1593. This is the only reference found to him in the 1593 Parliament, and the remainder of his career lies outside the purview of this biography. His will was made 25 Aug. 1653 and proved by his widow 20 Feb. 1655. He was buried in the parish church of Stratford-on-Avon in the same tomb as the Earl of Totness.

Analecta Hibernica, ii. 295; *EHR*, xlii. 263–4; *DNB* (Killigrew, Robert); *G. Inn Adm. Reg.* 153; PCC 36 Ridley, 243 Aylett; Roberts thesis, 210; D'Ewes, 481; *CP*, xii(1), p. 801.

A.M.M.

STAFFORD, Walter (b. aft. 1536).

STAFFORD   1571

b. aft. 1536, 6th s. of Henry, 1st Baron Stafford by Ursula, da. of Sir Richard Pole, KG of Ellesborough, Bucks.; bro. of Edward Stafford I* and Sir Henry Stafford†.

This Member was one of the younger sons of the nobility whose careers in sixteenth-century England are so difficult to trace. He may have died soon after the 1571 Parliament, in which he sat for the family borough. The last reference found to him is dated Easter 1571.

Stafford was associated with his elder brothers Edward and Richard in the custody of Cannock chase; between 1567 and 1571 they sold their rights to herbage and pannage and the keeping of hay in much of the forest to Sir Edward Lyttelton, John Leveson, Thomas Moreton and others. These transactions were probably part of the attempts by Edward Stafford to satisfy his creditors. In September 1567 he granted to Walter rights in Cannock chase, and an undated Chancery case survives in which the new owner prosecuted Walter Whytall and others for putting cattle on land within the forest precincts to 'dispasture' it. The defendants, who claimed common pasture rights on the land in question, brought a counter-petition against John Norrys, 'servant to Walter Stafford, esquire', for impounding animals. An assize jury gave a verdict for the owners of the cattle, but Stafford declared in Chancery that the jury was corrupt. No result of the case has been found.

As a younger member of an impoverished family, Stafford was often in financial difficulties. In October 1564 he was trying to get a lease of meadowland from his widowed mother, apparently for someone to whom he had incurred obligations: in the same year he claimed in Chancery that he had paid, 'soon after' the agreed date, £30 for which in March 1563 he had mortgaged one of his forest offices. Probably only a wealthy marriage could have restored his fortunes, but he is not known to have married.

Burke, *Extinct Peerage*; *Staffs. Peds.* (Harl. Soc. lxiii), 213; *Wm. Salt Arch. Soc.* xiii. 264, 267, 269, 281; *EHR*, lxxviii. 229 seq.; *Staffs. Rec. Soc.* 1938, pp. 65, 81–2; *Wm. Salt Arch. Soc.* 1928, p. 156.

N.M.F.

STALLENGE, William (b. c.1545), of Plymouth, Devon.

PLYMOUTH   1597, 1601

b. c.1545, prob. 1st s. of John Stallenge of Taunton, Som. by his w. Thomasine.

Freeman, Plymouth 1595, sequestrator in customer's office 1602.[1]

Stallenge was a Plymouth merchant, grandson of a Taunton clothier. When he was appointed by Sir Francis Drake* to assist the carrack commissioners at Saltash, he was found 'both honest and discreet', and gave 'great help to understand the Spanish'. In 1588 Drake sent him to court with news about the Armada, and in the following year Stallenge sent the lord admiral a scheme 'for the keeping of the accounts of the prize goods', to be effected by a careful entry, by one person appointed in every port, of all incoming and outgoing pieces of gold, silver and merchandise, so that

> his Lordship may at all times, with an hour's warning, be informed sufficiently how the things do pass ... a far better course than to be troubled in the end with many disordered accounts as in other the like affairs I fear his lordship daily is.

In 1594 Plymouth gave him a silver-gilt basin and ewer in return for his work on behalf of the town over the pilchard tax. He concerned himself with the new Plymouth haven, and collected intelligence for Cecil from Brittany, Spain and Portugal. From time to time he sent Cecil reports about Spanish fleet movements. Though Stallenge twice represented Plymouth in Parliament no record has been found of any activities there, and in 1601 he can have made but a fleeting appearance as his presence there was delayed by the arrival of Sir John Gilbert's prizes (about which he was still writing to Cecil from Plymouth on 6 Nov.) and he was home again by 5 Dec.[2]

Stallenge's letters to Cecil mentioned personal debts he owed in Spain, presumably as a result of his trading activities, and on one occasion he was granted ten years' protection of his person by privy seal against all creditors. On the other hand he once offered to pay the Plymouth garrison himself, to be repaid through a London merchant with a charge of 1% for the exchange. He spent £1,627 1s. 5d. on the fort at Plymouth between 1592 and 1595, presumably not unconnected with the determined efforts he made in 1596 to have Sir Ferdinando Gorges* removed from the captaincy. Sometimes Stallenge reminded Cecil that he had not been paid, adding 'I am a very bad beggar'. The last recorded reference found to him is in 1604, when he was given permission to keep silk worms and a mulberry garden.[3]

[1] Som. Medieval Wills, 1531–58 (Som. Rec. Soc. xxi), 202; Plymouth black bk. f. 301; HMC Hatfield, iv. 240; xi. 457. [2] Copy Bk. of Sir Amias Paulet (Roxburghe Club), 313; Lansd. 115, ff. 253, 263; Armada State Pprs. ed. Laughton (Navy Recs. Soc. i), 165; Plymouth Recs. 141; Trans. Dev. Assoc. xiv. 541; Roberts thesis, 285; HMC Hatfield, xi. 446, 480, 512. [3] HMC Hatfield, vi. 457; viii. 2; ix. 92, 307; xi. 480; xii. 36, 456–7; 469, 471; xvi. 348; PRO Index 6800, f. 477; R. N. Worth, Hist. Plymouth (1890), p. 411; R. A. Preston, Gorges of Plymouth, 87, 93; Add. 33378, f. 74.

P.W.H.

STAMPE, Thomas (c.1546–1613), of Wallingford, Berks. and Lincoln's Inn, London.

WALLINGFORD   1586, 1589

b. c.1546, 2nd s. of John Stampe of Newnham Murren, Oxon. by Elizabeth, da. of John Plotte or Platte of Hanney, Berks. educ. L. Inn 1561, called 1570. unm.

Master of Christ's Hospital and legal counsel to Abingdon by 1578; butler, L. Inn 1583, pensioner 1585; steward (recorder), Wallingford Mar. 1584–Mar. 1607, auditor c.1589; j.p.q. Berks. from c.1593.

Stampe was a younger son from a family of minor gentry, the several branches of which all resided in the vicinity of Wallingford. His father left him a mere £20 in his will, and he and two of his brothers made their way in the law. It was presumably his appointment as steward (recorder) of his native town which brought him his return to Parliament, a position usually reserved at Wallingford for more eminent local gentlemen. The only mention found of Stampe in the journals of the House is to leave of absence granted him 8 Mar. 1587.

Stampe resided mainly at Lincoln's Inn, and any money he acquired he seems to have sunk in trading ventures. When he made his will in August 1612, he had recently invested £300 in a voyage to the Guinea coast; and his whole fortune, indeterminate in size till his ship came in, he left to be administered by his 'best friend', Richard Martin of Tottenham, and his brother, Zachary Stampe. The will was proved on 13 Oct. 1613.

Vis. Berks. (Harl. Soc. lvi), 52–3; Vis. Oxon. (Harl. Soc. v), 121; Berks. RO, Wallingford minute bk. ff. 68, 93; bailiffs' accounts; D'Ewes, 413; PCC 16 Ketchyn, 90 Capell.

A.H.

STANFORD, John I (1537–1603), of Leicester and Elmesthorpe, Leics.

LEICESTER   1572, 1593

b. 1537, 1st s. of Thomas Stanford, mayor of Leicester. m. (2) Elizabeth, da. of John Heyrick, sis. of Robert* and William Heyrick*, 4s. inc. John II* 1da. suc. fa. 1583.

Freeman, Leicester 1558, chamberlain 1565, coroner 1573–4, mayor 1576–7, 1592–3.

Stanford was a butcher who inherited property in the parish of St. Nicholas, Leicester, and the manors of Barkby, Elmesthorpe and Hamilton. He contributed £25 towards the Armada fund and was assessed at £14 14s. in goods for the second payment of the subsidy in 1590. For at least the second and third sessions of the 1572 Parliament he received wages at 2s. a day and his charges. This amounted to £7 14s. in 1576 and £6 6s. in 1581. The common council jibbed at the latter payment because Stanford had promised to take no payment or charges 'except he did good to the town' and this, they said, he had not done. Certainly his name has not been found in the known surviving records of either of his Parliaments. Still, he was instrumental in preserving Leicester's independence during his second mayoralty when Thomas Heneage*, newly made chancellor of the duchy of Lancaster, tried to get both nominations to Parliament 'as heretofore it hath been to my predecessors'. This was a reference to 1584 when Sir Ralph Sadler* had asked for both seats and received one. Stanford and the majority of the common hall 'agreed to have no stranger' and elected two townsmen, including Stanford himself, before presenting Heneage with the fait accompli and telling him that the concession to Sadler in 1584 was unique.

Towards the end of his life, Stanford returned to Elmesthorpe, where he died, 17 Mar. 1603. He was buried three days later in Barkby church. His will, made on 31 Aug. 1600 and proved 18 May 1603, expressed his confidence in redemption 'from sin, hell and death'.

Leicester Mayors, ed. Hartopp, 66, 72, 73; Vis. Leics. (Harl. Soc. ii), 160; DL1/81/24; Leicester Recs. iii. 137, 146–7, 157, 163, 167, 187, 188, 250, 266, 465; Neale, Commons, 173; PCC 37 Bolein.

M.N.

STANFORD, John II (d.1603), of Leicester and Elmesthorpe, Leics.

LEICESTER   1597

1st s. of John Stanford I* of Leicester by his 2nd w. educ. G. Inn 1586, called. m. Elizabeth, da. of William Baynbrigge of Lockington, 1s. 2da. suc. fa. 1603.

Reader, Barnard's Inn 1601; ancient, G. Inn 1603; of counsel to Leicester by 1600, meat taster 1601, recorder July–Dec. 1603.

Stanford no doubt owed his return at Leicester to his family's standing in the town. He served without wages and was made a freeman after the Parliament. He was first employed in 1600 as an assistant to Richard Parkins* and appeared in various actions between Leicester and the duchy of Lancaster. He died intestate 1 Dec. 1603 and was buried at Barkby.

C142/283/197; *Vis. Leics.* (Harl. Soc. ii), 45–6; *Leicester Recs.* iii. 336, 347, 393, 431, 434, 446, 461, 468; iv. 5, 520; PCC admon. act bk. 1603, f. 179.

S.M.T.

STANHOPE, Edward I (c.1543–1603), of Shelford, Notts., Grimston and Edlington, Yorks., and Chigwell, Essex.

| NOTTINGHAMSHIRE | 1571, 1572 |
| YORKSHIRE | 1601 |

b. c.1543, 2nd s. of Sir Michael Stanhope† of Shelford by Anne, da. of Nicholas Rawson of Aveley, Essex; bro. of John*, Michael*, Sir Thomas* and Edward Stanhope II*. *educ.* St. John's, Camb. 1554, MA 1563; pens. G. Inn 1569, treasurer 1587. *m.* Susan, da. and coh. of Thomas Colshill* of Chigwell, Essex, and Hackney, Mdx., 5s. inc. Edward Stanhope III* 3da. Kntd. 1601.[1]

Surveyor of crown lands, Notts. 1575, duchy of Lancaster gen. surveyor of north parts 1576; j.p. Lincs. (Lindsey) from c.1573, Notts. from 1579; member, council in the north 1587, and j.p. many northern counties and Essex, Mdx. from c.1591; commr. sewers for river Lea 1587; recorder, Doncaster by 1596; member, northern high commission 1599.[2]

Stanhope was one of five brothers who sat in Parliament during Elizabeth's reign. Their father was executed in 1552 as a partisan of his brother-in-law Protector Somerset, an event which possibly drew the family closer to Sir William Cecil, with whom they were distantly connected. Stanhope had chambers at Gray's Inn throughout his life, and occupied them whenever he was in London. His building activities there were accepted, even though they were contrary to statute, and when his public duties in the north prevented him from fulfilling the duties of reader in 1579, he was granted seniority as if he had held the office, a privilege which was again allowed him in the following year. Three years later he was appointed to audit the treasurer's accounts, and in 1587 was himself elected treasurer. In that year, however, he was appointed to the council in the north, and thereafter he spent much of his time in York, where he acquired a house in the Minster garth, and another at Grimston, a few miles from the city. He remained an active member of the council until his death, serving under the 3rd Earl of Huntingdon, Archbishop Hutton and Thomas, Lord Burghley as presidents. He was one of the members who carried on the government after Huntingdon's death, and, under his successor, became one of the quorum of councillors. In 1598 he obtained the appointment of Thomas Hesketh*, attorney of the court of wards, to a vacant seat on the council. In 1602 he was one of those who defended the authority of the vice-president against the West Riding justices of the peace led by John Savile I*.[3]

Stanhope sat in Parliament three times. In 1571 and 1572, before his removal to the north, he was elected for his own county, and in 1601 for Yorkshire, no doubt with the support of the council in the north, though he was himself a landowner of standing in the county. He served on the subsidy committee, 7 Apr. 1571, and on committees in 1572 concerned with Plymouth almshouses (13 May), fraudulent conveyances (16 May) and weights and measures (23 May). In the 1576 session his committees included the subsidy (10 Feb.) and keeping parish registers (10 Feb.). He sat again on the subsidy committee of 25 Jan. 1581, and, in this session, on legal committees, 27 Feb. and 4 Mar. He was appointed to the committee to settle the order of business, 3 Nov. 1601, and to one regulating alehouses, 5 Nov. He spoke on alehouses, 5 Nov., but this was not in fact his first intervention in debate as he had reported a little earlier that day on by-election procedure, a subject upon which he was appointed to go to the lord keeper with three other senior Members, 13 Nov. Stanhope made a strong speech against the salt monopoly on the afternoon of 21 Nov., and, as a knight of the shire, was a member of the committee appointed to consider the matter of monopolies in general, 23 Nov. He is last mentioned as a member of a committee concerned with charitable uses, 12 Dec. 1601. All these parliamentary activities can be assigned to Edward Stanhope with some degree of confidence, but in addition, a number of references to Mr. Stanhope, mostly on legal subjects and mostly in 1576, are probably to Edward rather than John Stanhope. These include committees on lands without covin (14 May 1571 and 18 Feb. 1576); tillage and navigation (25 May); actions upon the case (13 Feb. 1576); errors in fines and recoveries (13 Feb.); Mr. Isley's debts (14 Feb.); tanned leather (18 Feb.); reciprocity of treatment for foreigners (24 Feb.); reformation of sheriffs (24 Feb.); fraudulent conveyances (25 Feb.); innkeepers (5 Mar.); justices of the forest (8 Mar.); excess of apparel (10 Mar.); Lord Stourton's bill (12 Mar.); wharves and quays (13 Mar.); vicars and curates (13 Mar.). In 1597 Stanhope actively supported his brother in the disputed Yorkshire election, and was afterwards one of those who examined John Savile II* of Howley on his conduct during it. For this Parliament also he tried to create a new constituency. In August 1596 he wrote to Cecil from York, congratulating him on his appointment as secretary, which gave 'great joy to all our name, who have always depended upon your father and yourself'. But the main purpose of the letter was to inform Cecil that the stewardship of Doncaster was vacant by the death of Lord Hunsdon and that Stanhope, as recorder, had suggested him as successor. Cecil accepted the office, and when a Parliament was summoned in the following year Stanhope obtained for him the nomination of two Members for the borough, assuring him that Doncaster had 'anciently' returned Members of Parliament, and that in 1593 one seat had been offered to him as recorder and the other to Lord Hunsdon by the mayor and burgesses. As Stanhope had been unable to spare time from his duties at York, both Members, he said, had been returned by Hunsdon, and so far as he knew, had been allowed to take their seats. The time had passed, however, when a borough might enfranchise itself or be enfranchised in this manner, and in spite of Stanhope's efforts Cecil's nominees were not admitted.[4]

Stanhope made his will 8 Aug. 1603. He died on 12 Aug. and the will was proved in the following February. He expressed his belief in 'the company of the heavenly angels and blessed saints'. His property was to be divided among his wife and children. His eldest daughter was to receive a dowry of £1,000 and the two younger ones £500 each. Property in Westmorland was left to his second son as well as a rent charge of £20 a year as soon as he became an utter barrister, and property in Yorkshire and Somerset was secured to the third and fourth sons, while the youngest, Thomas, was to have an annuity of £40. Some of the Yorkshire lands were to go to his widow as an addition to her jointure, but most of it descended to his eldest son Sir Edward*, aged about 24, the executor of the will. Stanhope's brothers, Sir John, Sir Edward and Sir Michael, were appointed supervisors, with Sir Percival Hart*, his son-in-law. Stanhope was buried in the church at Kirkby Wharfe, the parish in which Grimston lay.[5]

[1] Vis. Notts. (Harl. Soc. iv.), 7–8; CP; HMC Hatfield, xi. 232. [2] Lansd. 19, f. 95; Somerville, Duchy, i. 446–7; SP12/121, f. 19v; 145, f. 29; Hatfield ms 278; Reid, Council of the North, 227; Lansd. 53, f. 168; Doncaster Recs. i. 230; HMC Hatfield, ix. 396. [3] G. Inn Pens. Bk. i. 5, 32, 38, 42, 53–4, 56, 60, 77; CSP Dom. 1581–90, p. 80; 1601–3, pp. 156, 194; Add. 1580–1625, pp. 80–1; Lansd. 79, f. 128; 82, f. 50; 115, f. 4; HMC Hatfield, v. 505, 506–7; viii. 341, 390. [4] CJ, i. 83, 89, 93, 95, 97, 104, 105, 106, 108, 111, 112, 113, 114, 115, 120, 129, 131; D'Ewes, 159, 183, 189, 206, 207, 214, 247, 253, 255, 261, 288, 301, 302, 624, 626, 637, 649, 681; Townshend, Hist. Colls. 191, 212, 238; HMC Hatfield, vi. 316–17; vii. 28, 412, 437, 442; Neale, Commons, 144–5. [5] PCC 16 Harte.

I.C./P.W.H.

STANHOPE, Edward II (c.1547–1608), of London.

MARLBOROUGH   1584, 1586

b. c.1547, 4th s. of Sir Michael Stanhope†, and bro. of John*, Michael*, Sir Thomas* and Edward Stanhope I*. educ. Trinity Coll. Camb., scholar 1560, BA 1563, minor fellow 1564, MA 1566, major fellow 1569, LlD 1575; incorp. MA Oxon 1566, suppl. DCL 1578. unm. KB 25 July 1603.[1]

Prebendary of Botevant, York 1572–91; adv. Doctors' Commons 1575; master in Chancery 1577; chancellor, diocese of London 1579; eccles. commr. from 1587, commr. fines office 1589; rector of Terrington, Norf. 1589; prebendary of Kentish Town in St. Paul's 1591; receiver of petitions, Parliaments from 1593; commr. 'touching Jesuits and other disguised persons' Mar. 1595, for Chancery 1593, oyer and terminer, London Feb. 1594, to survey eccles. cts., London diocese 1594,

piracy 1601, to try Ralegh and others for treason 1603, to examine books printed without authority 1603; jt. vicar-gen. Canterbury 27 June 1605.[2]

Sir Michael Stanhope, the brother-in-law and partisan of Protector Somerset, named two of his sons Edward, perhaps as a tribute to his patron. As both were lawyers, and both sat in Parliament, there has been, from the time of Strype onwards, a tendency to confuse them; and the confusion has been made worse by the attribution in a heralds' visitation of the elder brother's wife Susan to the younger brother, who did not in fact marry.[3]

Edward Stanhope the younger was born at Hull, probably during the period of Sir Michael's governorship of that town, 1547–9. Early deprived of his father, who was executed in February 1552, the boy went to Trinity College, Cambridge, where, as he was to record gratefully in his will, he studied 'from infancy' and lived for many years at its charge as scholar and fellow. The college, too, was in its infancy, but it already boasted eminent names. During Stanhope's years there it had Robert Beaumont and John Whitgift as masters, and among its fellows, until his expulsion in 1572, was Thomas Cartwright; while its undergraduates included Edward Coke and Robert, Earl of Essex. What part, if any, Stanhope played in the college's struggle with its puritan element is not known; but his later record as a servant of the established church suggests that he was repelled rather than attracted by such radicalism.[4]

The favour of William Cecil, which Stanhope perhaps owed to his parentage, was doubtless strengthened by his membership of the university over which Cecil presided as chancellor; and it was to Cecil that he, and his mother on his behalf, were to look for advancement. It was Cecil who secured his first preferment, to the prebend of Botevant, worth £20 a year, as a means of enabling him to study the civil law. With his appointment in 1577 as a master in Chancery he began a crowded and prosperous career. His steady accumulation of offices was, indeed, remarkable. On Aylmer's appointment as bishop of London, Stanhope became his chancellor, and when in 1579 and 1583 there was a prospect of Aylmer's translation his mother besought Burghley to see to it that her son kept the office; Aylmer was to retain the see until his death in 1594, and Stanhope the chancellorship, under Aylmer's successors, until his own death in 1608. In 1605 he achieved a yet higher office, the vicar generalship of Canterbury, under Archbishop Bancroft. These ecclesiastical appointments Stanhope supplemented in 1589, again through Burghley's favour, by a commissionership in the fines office.[5]

Stanhope's place in episcopal jurisdiction, and his membership from 1587 of the ecclesiastical commission, made him an active and prominent defender of the Elizabethan church against its critics. He shared the odium which attached to Aylmer's, and later Bancroft's, harrying of the puritans in the diocese, and became one of the targets of Martin Marprelate's abuse. Among those against whom he proceeded was his old Trinity colleague Cartwright; he was one of the commissioners before whom Cartwright appeared in May 1591, although on that occasion he remained silent, perhaps for old times' sake. Stanhope also had much to do with recusancy, both as a diocesan official and as royal commissioner, while a variety of other matters fell to his attention at the instance of the Privy Council. In December 1599 he was to incur, with Bancroft, the Queen's displeasure at the sympathy shown for the Earl of Essex in the London pulpit and press; he defended himself and his master in a long letter to his brother Sir John*, treasurer of the chamber, through whom the admonition had reached them.[6]

Stanhope's involvement in secular politics was, however, chiefly due to his family connexion with the Seymours. He certainly owed his two appearances in Parliament to his first cousin the Earl of Hertford. Hertford may have had a particular reason for choosing Stanhope, among his various clients, to sit in 1584 and 1586. In those Parliaments two of the Earl's lawyer-servants, Roger Puleston and Richard Wheeler, sat for Great Bedwyn, another Seymour borough; and this concentration of the family's legal resources in the Commons suggests that the Earl had some private business to promote there. Although there is no evidence that he did so, and thus no clue to what the business might have been, the two most likely preoccupations were the vexed question of his sons' legitimacy and the complications of his landed estate; on the first of these, in particular, the support of a prominent civilian would have been valuable. That Stanhope carried some weight in the House, at least on his re-election in 1586, appears from his inclusion in two important committees, that of 4 Nov. 1586 on the fate of Mary Queen of Scots, and that of 8 Mar. 1587 on ecclesiastical discipline and education. In the last four Parliaments of the reign Stanhope was active in carrying bills between the two Houses.[7]

It was the legitimacy question which was to bring Stanhope a few years later into discomfiture and even danger. In 1592 he and his brother Edward had borne witness to the legitimacy of Hertford's second son Thomas Seymour, who had been born in the Tower after his father and mother, Catherine Grey, had been sent there and their marriage declared invalid. When, late in 1595, this tendentious transaction came to the Queen's notice, it revived memories of that 30 year-old scandal and led to the committal, although for a few days only, of the Earl himself and of his two cousins in the same prison. It is to be presumed that Whitgift, to whom the business was referred, protected his chancellor from more serious consequences. The matter was to crop up once again in Stanhope's lifetime, when in 1604 the descent of the Seymour lands came into question and a bill about them

was brought into the Commons. It was then urged that Stanhope should be allowed no part in the affair in view of his past record in it.[8]

The occasional hazards of Stanhope's career did not extend to its material side. To the combined remuneration of his various offices he was able to add the income from two prebends and a parsonage as well as from some landed investment; and since his outgoings were modest he became a wealthy man. There is some trace of moneylending – as early as 1585 the Earl of Arundel owed him £380, and later Sir William Sandys was bound to him for £800 – but whether he made a practice of it is not known. His refusal, in August 1596, to contribute towards the setting out of ships for the Queen's service on the ground that he had paid subsidy elsewhere was perhaps no more than legitimate carefulness, and his New Year's gift at Christmas 1602 to Sir Robert Cecil was doubtless a prudent outlay. By contrast, the gift during his lifetime of £100 for a library at Trinity bespeaks an affection for the college and a love of learning which, brightly as they were to glow again in his will and in his authorship of a college history, redeem his reputation from the charge of unrelieved material and intellectual self-centredness.[9]

Stanhope's personality and interests reveal themselves most clearly in his will, a document (originally written in his own hand on 23 pages) which combines a profession of the worthlessness of good works with the meticulous exposition of his own testamentary ones. The will was made in 1602, when Stanhope was approaching 55. It directed that, if he died in London, he was to be buried in the north aisle of St. Paul's and that his epitaph should be placed on the same wall as that which bore Linacre's. (This was duly carried out, the inscription being composed by William Camden.) He desired the attendance at the funeral of his particular friends and colleagues Drs. Daniel Dunn, Gibson and Farrand; gave mourning garments to his relatives and, among others, the archbishop, the bishop, George Paule*, 40 poor men, and all his own servants; and made provision for a godly preacher. He left £20 for the relief of the poor, but not of vagrants; £40 each to the prisons of Ludgate, Newgate, and the two Counters, for distribution to their prisoners according to elaborate directions; £200 for the employment of the poor in his native town of Hull, and the same amount towards Whitgift's college at Croydon; and bequests to Terrington, Norfolk, and Kentish Town, Middlesex, where he held a parsonage and a prebend respectively. His largest benefaction was reserved for his old college, to which, after his parents, he owed 'all which I have since been enabled unto'. Of his three bequests to Trinity, one was of £40 for 20 poor sub-sizers having their names in the buttery book; a second of £700 for a librarian and assistant, this being accompanied by detailed instructions on the management of the library; and the third of 15 manuscripts and more than 300 books, including a polyglot bible. The residue of the estate he divided among his numerous kin.[10]

Stanhope died 20 Mar. 1608.[11]

[1] *DNB*; *Vis. Essex*, ii. 562; Lansd. 94, f. 137. [2] Lansd. 22, f. 52; 28, f. 150; *HMC Hatfield*, xv. 224; xvi. 290; *CSP Dom.* 1591-4, p. 311; D'Ewes, 458, 525, 600; Churchill, *Canterbury Administration*, i. 598 n. [3] *Vis. Essex*, ii. 562; C142/300/173. [4] *DNB*; PCC 22 Windebanck; *VCH Cambs.* iii. 466. [5] Lansd. 16, f. 84; 28, f. 150; 39, f. 156; 58, f. 96; Churchill, loc. cit. [6] *DNB*; Lansd. 39, f. 150; 68, ff. 50, 106; *Marprelate Tracts*, ed. Pierce; *CSP Dom.* 1581-90, pp. 219, 589; 1591-4, p. 245; 1593-1601, pp. 361, 365, 396; 1601-3, p. 295; *HMC Rutland*, i. 312, 335; *APC*, xxvi. 378, 425-6, 448-9; *Wilts. Arch. Mag.* xxxix. 45. [7] D'Ewes, 394, 413. [8] *CSP Dom.* 1591-4, p. 282; *HMC De L'Isle and Dudley*, ii. 183-4; *HMC Hatfield*, v. 507; xvi. 440; *VCH Wilts.* v. 127. [9] *CSP Dom.* 1591-4, pp. 524, 527; C142/310/53; Lansd. 45, f. 208; 81, f. 80; *HMC Hatfield*, xii. 527; xviii. 442. [10] PCC 22, 65 Windebanck. [11] C142/310/53.

S.T.B.

STANHOPE, Edward III (c.1579-1646), of Grimston, later of Edlington, Yorks.

SCARBOROUGH	1601

b. c.1579, 1st s. of Edward Stanhope I*. *educ.* G. Inn 1592-3. *m.* Margaret, da. of Sir Henry Constable of Burton Constable, Yorks., 3s. 3da. KB July 1603; *suc.* fa. 12 Aug. 1603.

Sheriff, Yorks. 1615-16.

Stanhope no doubt owed his return for Scarborough to his father, who was elected for the county in the same year. It is not, however, clear through which of three possible patrons this influence was exercised. Either the Eures or Sir Thomas Posthumous Hoby*, contestants for patronage in the borough, might have assisted Stanhope's election. The Stanhopes were related to Hoby, and Sir Edward had supported him in the county election campaign in 1597. On the other hand, he had worked closely and amicably with Lord Eure on the council in the north and on border affairs. A third possibility is the Earl of Nottingham, high steward of Scarborough. Stanhope inherited considerable landed property from his father and made a good marriage. He was living at Edlington, near Doncaster, in the house his father had built, when he gave a silver cup to Doncaster to be competed for in horse races on the moor. But he gradually disposed of his estates, until he was left with property worth only £194 a year. He took little part in county administration, except for his one term as sheriff. He signed the 1640 petition of the Yorkshire gentry against the billeting of soldiers, and was buried at Kirkby Wharfe on 3 Oct. 1646, being succeeded by his eldest son Edward.

Dugdale's Vis. Yorks. ed. Clay, i. 219-21; C142/300/173; PCC 16 Harte; St. Ch. 8/269/4; J. T. Cliffe, 'Yorks. gentry on the eve of the civil war', (London Univ. PhD thesis 1960), p. 459; *CSP Dom.* Apr.-Aug. 1640, p. 524.

B.D.

STANHOPE, John (c.1545-1621), of Harrington, Northants. and St. Martin-in-the-Fields, London.

TOTNES	1571
MARLBOROUGH	1572
BEVERLEY	1584[1]
TRURO	1586
ROCHESTER	1589
PRESTON	1597
NORTHAMPTONSHIRE	1601
NEWTOWN I.o.W.	1604

b. c.1545, 3rd s. of Sir Michael Stanhope† and bro. of Edward Stanhope I*, Edward Stanhope II*, Michael Stanhope* and Sir Thomas Stanhope*. *educ.* Trinity Coll. Camb. 1556; G. Inn (poss. hon.) 1556. *m.* (1) bef. Sept. 1557, Mary (*d.*1568), 1st da. and coh. of Sir William Knowles of Bilton in Holderness, alderman of Kingston-upon-Hull, *s.p.*; (2) 6 May 1589, Margaret, da. of Henry Macwilliam*, 1s. 2da. Kntd. Aug. or Sept. 1596; *cr.* Baron Stanhope 1605.

?Gent of privy chamber by 1578; ?bailiff of church lands, Beverley by 1584; v.-adm. Yorks. by 1587, master of posts 1590; j.p.q. Yorks. (N. Riding), custos rot. by 1593; treasurer of the chamber 1596-1618; treasurer at war 1599; keeper of Colchester castle 1599; steward of Higham Ferrers and other duchy of Lancaster manors in Northants. 1600; high steward, Peterborough cathedral Oct. 1600; vice-chamberlain Jan. 1601-Apr. 1616; PC June 1601; feodary, Northants. 1602; commr. for union with Scotland 1604; steward, manor of Eltham 1604; councillor for colony of Virginia 1609; commr. for surrender of Flushing and Brill 1616; commr. eccles. causes 1620.[2]

Stanhope's aunt, the widowed Duchess of Somerset, obtained a place for him in the household of Sir William Cecil* by 1555, but it was many years before he achieved a regular and lucrative office. He has been described as having been a gentleman of the privy chamber in 1578, but according to a letter he wrote to his patron Sir Christopher Hatton in 1587, he 'enjoyed neither fee, pension nor wage' though he had never been away from court for more than six weeks. It was probably through Hatton that in 1575 Stanhope was assigned the Queen's interest in a 70-year lease made to her by the bishop of Durham, worth about £80 a year, and his property at Harrington, Northamptonshire, was probably held as a sub-tenant of Hatton. In 1577 Stanhope joined the Earl of Leicester in persuading Hatton to make up a quarrel with Burghley over the question of the pirate Callis, with whom Hatton was said to have had dealings. A number of Stanhope's letters to Burghley and Robert Cecil, on court or private matters, survive among the Hatfield manuscripts. It was presumably Burghley who, on the death of Thomas Randolph*, gained Stanhope a lucrative job as master of the posts, the turning-point in his career.[3]

By this time he had sat in five Parliaments, finding a borough seat where he could. At Totnes in 1571 he was probably nominated by the 2nd Earl of Bedford; at Marlborough by his relative the Earl of Hertford; his (or one of his brother's) position as royal bailiff of church lands must have been decisive at Beverley; the Killigrews or Cecil at Truro, and some other court influence at Rochester. The status of knight of the shire eluded him for many years. In 1597 he canvassed Yorkshire with the support of the archbishop and council in the north, but in an election characterized by fraud and violence, he and Sir Thomas Posthumous Hoby* were defeated. As Hoby was relatively new to the county, pairing with him was unwise, for Stanhope, though he was custos rotulorum there and owned lands in Yorkshire, resided in Northamptonshire when he was not at court. In the end Sir Robert Cecil, then chancellor of the duchy of Lancaster, found him a seat at Preston. In fact it is just possible that Stanhope came in for Yorkshire following the death of Sir William Fairfax*, but no evidence survives. In 1601, aged about 56, Stanhope was elected senior knight of the shire for Northamptonshire. As there was at least one other Stanhope in all his Parliaments, it is impossible to be certain about John Stanhope's parliamentary activity but the indications are that this was sparse or non-existent, save for a committee, 13 Mar. 1589, for 'the bill touching Mr. Southwell' and his being appointed to administer the oaths to MPs, 27 Oct. 1601. He may, however, have attended the numerous committees to which all the Privy Councillors were appointed during 1601.[4]

From the time that he became master of the posts, Stanhope appears with increasing frequency as a court official who was worth cultivating. The Queen favoured him, and he played his part in the game of court flattery. 'I long to be near her', he wrote to Robert Cecil in 1593, in a letter doubtless meant for Elizabeth to read, 'whose presence preserveth all those who know her worth'; and in 1597 he was one of those who eulogized the Queen's extemporary Latin tirade against the Polish ambassador. As treasurer of the chamber, and later vice-chamberlain, he had constant access to Elizabeth, and many suitors tried to persuade him to approach her on their behalf. One of his letters to Sir Robert Cecil suggests that even powerful friends made use of him at times in this way.

> I left the Queen at six very quiet, and as I guess will not stir till it be very late, but I will attend the time and present it [i.e. whatever it was Cecil wanted] if she do but breathe a little while afore her going to bed.

When Burghley died in 1598, it was to Stanhope that his sons Thomas and Robert sent a 'memento of their father for the Queen'.[5]

As a thorough-going Cecilian, it was not likely that Stanhope would be closely associated with the Earl of Essex, though, as far as he could, he tried to remain in the Earl's good books. But in the growing friction between Essex and the Cecils, Stanhope wisely remained faithful to

his old friends, his connexion with whom was strengthened by his second marriage to Margaret Macwilliam, whose mother, the widow of Sir John Cheke, was related to Burghley. After the final triumph of the Cecilian party with the fall of Essex, Stanhope became a Privy Councillor. He was assiduous in his attendance at Council meetings, and though he never became a front-rank statesman, he did well enough under the new King. In addition to his barony and the renewal of his offices he received other marks of James's favour, being allowed to associate his son Charles, born about 1598, with himself as master of the posts and keeper of Colchester castle – a valuable way of providing for the boy when he should come of age; and he received a number of lucrative private grants. On at least one occasion James visited him at Eltham. He remained active almost until his death, being appointed an ecclesiastical commissioner as late as 1620.[6]

Stanhope died on 9 Mar. 1621, and was buried at St. Martin-in-the-Fields, 'because', as he stated in his will, made 5 Oct. 1620, 'I have lived there the space of thirty years and above'. The will was proved by the widow in April 1621.[7]

[1] Add. 38823. [2] CP, xxi(1), pp. 239 seq.; Archaeologia, xxxviii(2), pp. 389–404; Eliz. Govt. and Soc. 112–13; APC, xv. 354; CSP Dom. 1581–90, pp. 672, 676; 1595–7, pp. 267, 511; 1598–1601, pp. 357, 388; 1603–10, pp. 15, 160, 354; Add. 1580–1625, p. 426; Somerville, Duchy, i. 588, 591, 603; Northants. Rec. Soc. xviii. 41; APC, xxxii. 485 et passim; Kingsbury, Recs. of Virginia Co. iv. 369; Rymer, Feodera, xvi. 783; xvii. 201. [3] Eliz. Govt. and Soc. 112–13; Lansd. 85, f. 12; 118, f. 36; E. St. J. Brooks, Hatton, 156–7; PRO Index 6800; HMC Hatfield, ii. 156. [4] G. Oliver, Hist. Beverley, 187 et passim; HMC Hatfield, vii. 412, 416–17, 435–6, 484; VCH Yorks. N. Riding, i. 60, 249; CSP Dom. 1566–79, p. 307; CPR, 1569–72, p. 474; Neale, Commons, 83 seq.; Townshend, Hist. Colls. 25, 173; D'Ewes, 445, 620, 622, 624, 631, 634, 635, 636, 641, 647, 649, 658, 664, 665, 666, 668, 678, 685. [5] Eliz. Govt. and Soc. loc. cit.; HMC Hatfield, iv. 425–6; vii. 55, 320; viii. 370. [6] HMC Hatfield, iv. 68–9; CSP Dom. 1595–7, p. 518; APC, xxxii. 485 et passim; CP; DNB; Chamberlain Letters ed. McClure, i. 43, 46; Archaeologia, xxxviii(2), p. 396. [7] PCC 31 Dale; CP.

N.M.F.

STANHOPE, Michael (c.1549–c.1621), of Sudbourne, Suff.

CASTLE RISING	1584
IPSWICH	1597, 1601
ORFORD	1604

b. c.1549, 5th s. of Sir Michael Stanhope† and bro. of Edward Stanhope I*, Edward Stanhope II*, John Stanhope* and Sir Thomas Stanhope*. educ. Trinity Coll. Camb. 1561; G. Inn 1568. m. Anne, da. and h. of Sir William Read, 4da. Kntd. 7 May 1603.

Groom of privy chamber by 1594, gent. of privy chamber by 1603; j.p.q. Suff. from c.1593; freeman, Ipswich 1597; keeper of the game in Sherwood forest by 1599; keeper of Hertingfordbury park, Herts. by 1604.

Stanhope no doubt followed his brother John to court in the 1570s, and, like John, he had to wait some time for an office of profit. There were the usual complaints of poverty, but at last, in 1594, he obtained the monopoly of importing Spanish wool for felt hats and he died wealthy. His return for Castle Rising in 1584 was probably secured through his brother-in-law, Roger Townshend* of Raynham, Norfolk, whose son John represented the borough in 1593. In spite of his position and his connexions with the Cecils, he did not sit in the next three Parliaments. In August 1596 Sir Robert Cecil wrote to Ipswich recommending Stanhope as the next high steward of the borough: the town council rejected the nomination in favour of the Earl of Essex, but in compensation returned him to the following two Parliaments. As one of the Ipswich burgesses in the 1597 Parliament he could have attended the committee on draining the fens, 3 Dec. He was on the privileges and returns committee in both 1597 and 1601, on a committee concerned with malt, 12 Jan. 1598, and on one for abridging the penal laws, 2 Nov. 1601.

Stanhope married, probably late in life, the daughter of another Suffolk landowner. When she died, in April 1616, John Chamberlain thought

it no ill turn for her after her late disgrace of having a daughter (as is said) by Sir Eustace Hart. But the world talks somewhat suspiciously of her end.

Stanhope made his will 6 Nov. 1621, so 'disabled by the gout that he could not write his name'. Among many bequests was £100 to the library of Trinity, Cambridge 'in which college I was once a scholar'. The will was proved 6 Feb. 1622.

Vis. Notts. (Harl. Soc. iv), 7–8; *Sales of Wards* (Som. Rec. Soc. lxvii), 194; *CSP Dom.* 1591–4, p. 556; 1601–4, p. 351; *HMC Hatfield*, iv. 67, 423; v. 104, 475; vi. 49, 287, 332–3, 463; vii. 344, 500; xviii. 161; N. Bacon, *Annals of Ipswich*, 390; D'Ewes, 552, 567, 578, 622, 623; *Chamberlain Letters* ed. McClure, i. 626; PCC 10 Savile.

R.V.

STANHOPE, Sir Thomas (c.1540–96), of Shelford, Notts.

NOTTINGHAMSHIRE   1586

b. c.1540, 1st s. of Sir Michael Stanhope† and bro. of Edward Stanhope I*, Edward Stanhope II*, John Stanhope* and Michael Stanhope*. m. Margaret, 3rd da. and coh. of Sir John Porte† of Etwall, Derbys. by Elizabeth, o. da. of Sir Thomas Gifford of Chillington, Staffs., 3s. 1da. suc. fa. 1552. Kntd. 1575.

J.p.q. Notts. from c.1561, sheriff 1562–3, 1574–5, 1587–8, dep. lt. by 1591, custos rot. from c.1594; j.p.q. Derbys. from c.1561, sheriff 1562–3.[1]

After the execution of Stanhope's father a small portion of his estates was leased to his widow, and in 1555 Queen Mary confirmed the manors in fee to the family. Further large grants in fee of manors in Derbyshire, Lincolnshire and Nottinghamshire were made at the time to Lady Stanhope with remainder to her eldest son Thomas, who

also received an immediate grant of the manors of Gonwardby and Manthorpe in Lincolnshire. When Lady Stanhope died in 1588, Thomas was living at Shelford, the principal seat of the family, his mother probably having given him the control of the property long before her death.

These extensive estates, and the protection of Sir William Cecil, Lord Burghley, would have allowed Stanhope to have indulged himself in a career at court had he wished. He was related to Burghley's second wife, Mildred, the daughter of Sir Anthony Cooke*. Sending Burghley a New Year's gift in December 1579, he acknowledged he had received 'more good and grave counsel and advice from you in my time than from any other man (good Sir Anthony Cooke except), I mean when I was very young. I have had more commodity by your free gift than of all persons now living'. Though he remained a country gentleman Stanhope solicited occasional favours from Burghley, such as the wardship of his nephew Thomas Cooper in 1570. He was appointed to a number of local commissions and was active against suspected Roman Catholics. Sir Gervase Clifton, who had been described as a good subject 'and necessary for service in [his] country but in religion very cold' in the bishops' letters of 1564, wrote in May 1584 to the 3rd Earl of Rutland, complaining that Stanhope had threatened to 'come to Clifton, and he would have me and all my whole house, man, woman and child at the church'.

Though Stanhope could clearly have maintained an independent position in Nottinghamshire, he chose rather to associate himself with the earls of Rutland. He loaned the 4th Earl £200 in June 1587, was among the chief mourners at his funeral in 1588, and invited the young 5th Earl to the wedding of his daughter in April 1591. It is not surprising, therefore, that when he decided to stand for Nottinghamshire in 1586 he should have asked for support from the Earl of Rutland. In the House he is known to have been a member of only one committee, that to decide on the motion to be made to Elizabeth regarding Mary Queen of Scots, 4 Nov. At the time of the 1588 elections Stanhope was sheriff; he stood for the county unsuccessfully in 1593 in the following circumstances.[2]

The death of the 3rd Earl of Rutland in 1587 and of his brother in the following year, left an heir who was only eleven. Into this vacuum moved, in 1590, Gilbert Talbot, 7th Earl of Shrewsbury, an irascible man with several family quarrels already to his discredit. Stanhope had a similar reputation. In 1577, for example, he had been engaged in a quarrel with Sir John Zouche†, who accused Stanhope in Star Chamber of attacking his followers in Derby. At the beginning of Michaelmas term 1577 the two parties were called before the Privy Council, and with their mutual agreement the case was removed from the Star Chamber to be settled by the Council, where Stanhope came off second best. In 1578 Stanhope quarrelled with another local gentleman, Henry Sacheverell, and between 1578 and 1580 with John Molyneux* of Thorpe, Northamptonshire, the two being bound in bonds of £200 in April 1579 to keep the peace. It may have been because of one of these disputes that Stanhope was committed to the Fleet by the Council in June 1578.[3]

Thus it was predictable that Shrewsbury, as the most powerful nobleman in the county, should quarrel with Stanhope, the principal supporter of a family in eclipse. One occasion for recrimination between them was the marriage in 1591 of Stanhope's daughter to John Holles. There had been an understanding between Sir William Holles and George, 6th Earl of Shrewsbury, that John should marry a kinswoman of the Earl, but after Sir William's death Holles chose Stanhope's daughter instead, 'which the Earl took as the greatest affront in the world', and described Stanhope as 'one of the most ambitious, proud, covetous, and subtle persons that ever I was acquainted with'. Things began to heat up in 1592 over a weir Stanhope had built about 15 years earlier on the Trent at Shelford, to provide power for his corn mills. Shrewsbury organized a petition signed by 500 of the villagers living close to the river, which Stanhope countered with a paper signed by Shrewsbury himself, by his father, and other gentry of the county, testifying to the necessity for the weir. The Privy Council decided that the matter should be settled by the commission of sewers, and instructed the lord keeper to have particular care in appointing the commissioners to decide the matter. At this moment the writs were issued for the 1593 parliamentary election. The details of this campaign appear elsewhere, but the upshot was that Shrewsbury won, and determined to finish off Stanhope and his weir in a carefully planned commando operation just before Easter 1593. Twelve of Shrewsbury's henchmen erected on his own ground at one end of the weir a prefabricated 'timber house in manner of a fort', which they manned and equipped with armour and weapons so as to cover the building of a trench 60 yards long to divert the Trent and render the weir useless. Stanhope's faction called a special sessions at Nottingham to punish the offenders, but the sheriff, Shrewsbury's man, refused to attend and convened the other justices at Newark, where Stanhope's weir was presented as a nuisance. The Queen refused to allow Stanhope to prosecute Shrewsbury, but 13 of those who had actually taken part in the weir's destruction were fined. In October of the same year Shrewsbury's forces pulled down the wall of Stanhope's park at Horsley, Derbyshire.[4]

Stanhope died 'after many years worshipfully spent' at his house in East Stoke on 3 Aug. 1596, and was buried at Shelford on 27 Sept. His heir was his eldest son John.[5]

[1] C142/280/90; DNB (Stanhope, Sir Michael); Thoroton, Notts. ed. Throsby, i. 290–2; Lansd. 1218, ff. 616, 636; C66/1421; HMC Hatfield, iv. 212–15. [2] CPR, 1554–5, pp. 16–18, 300–1; Lansd. 29, f. 9;

J. Hurstfield, Queen's Wards, 58–9; APC, xi, xiii, xv, xxii, passim; Cam. Misc. ix (3), p. 72; Archaeologia, xxxi. 214; Nottingham Recs. iv. 236–7; HMC Rutland, i. 166, 208, 219, 244, 290, 301; D'Ewes, 394. [3] St. Ch. 6/9/Z.10; APC, ix. 115, 117, 166, 374, 390; x. 172, 246, 412; xi. 97, 291–2; xii. 7; Lansd. 27, f. 68. [4] Mems. Holles Fam. (Cam. Soc. ser. 3), 90; Coll. of Arms, Talbot mss, transcribed by G. R. Batho, H, f. 151; HMC Hatfield, iv. 113, 312–13, 319; v. 527; APC, xxii. 257; xxiii. 17, 149, 155–6, 191; xxiv. 267; Bull. IHR, xxxiii. 73 seq.; St. Ch. 5/S25/16, S77/36; CSP Dom. 1595–7, p. 48. [5] Thoroton, Notts. i. 292; C142/280/90.

A.M.M.

STANLEY, Thomas (1530–91), of Weaver and Alderley, Cheshire.

CHESHIRE	1571

b. 1530, 1st s. of Thomas Stanley by Joan, da. of Thomas Davenport of Henbury. educ. ?G. Inn 1552. m. Ursula, da. of Richard Cholmondeley of Cholmondeley, 3s. 3da. suc. fa. 1556.[1]

J.p. Cheshire prob. soon aft. 1564, q. by 1583, sheriff 1571–2.

Stanley had extensive lands in Cheshire, mainly in the Macclesfield area: some of his property, at Little Meols, involved him in an expensive lawsuit before the Exchequer court of Chester. In November 1556 his father, who was in bad health, conveyed to him land in Alderley, Weaver and elsewhere, in return for a £30 annuity. By the end of the year Stanley had succeeded to the whole estate, and was soon appointed to the customary local offices for one of his social position. In 1564 the bishop of Chester recommended him as a suitable justice of the peace; and he was no doubt added to the commission before November 1571, when he became sheriff. Earlier in 1571 he had represented Cheshire in Parliament.[2]

Apart from a reference to 'Mr. Stanley of Alderley' as a guest of his distant relative Henry, 4th Earl of Derby at Lathom in July 1587, no references to Stanley's private life have been found. There is an inquisition post mortem, but no will. He died 1 Aug. 1591 and was buried at Alderley. During the renovation of the church in 1878 an alabaster slab was found, with a recumbent figure in armour and an inscription giving his name and details of his family, together with a statement that he built the houses of Alderley and Weaver.[3]

[1] Ormerod, Cheshire, iii. 577–8; Vis. Cheshire (Harl. Soc. xviii), 216; C142/109/9; PRO Chester 3/72/8. [2] PRO Chester 3/82/24, 72/8; C142/109/9; J. Brownbill, West Kirby and Hilbre, 246; Cam. Misc. ix(3), p. 751; APC, viii. 235; xii. 159. [3] Stanley Pprs. (Chetham Soc. xxxi), 30; PRO Chester 3/82/24; Ormerod, iii. 570–1.

N.M.F.

STAPLETON, Sir Robert (c.1547–1606), of Wighill, Yorks.

YORKSHIRE	1572*
WELLS	1604*

b. c.1547, 1st surv. s. of Sir Robert Stapleton of Wighill by Elizabeth, da. of Sir William Mallory of Studley. educ.

L. Inn 1565. *m*. (1) Catherine, da. of Sir Marmaduke Constable of Everingham, 2s. 1da.; (2) c.1584, Olive, da. and coh. of Henry Sharington* of Lacock, Wilts., wid. of John Talbot of Salwarpe, Worcs., *s.p. suc.* fa. 1557. Kntd. 1570.[1]

J.p. Yorks. (W. Riding) from c.1569, q. 1577; j.p.q. Yorks. (E. Riding) from c.1575; rem. from all commissions c.1583; j.p.q. Yorks. (E. and N. ridings) by 1603; commr. musters, Yorks. by 1573, sheriff 1581–2.[2]

At about ten years of age Stapleton became the ward of Susan Tonge, first lady of the bedchamber to Queen Mary, known as Susan Clarencieux or Mrs. Clarentius from her husband having been Clarenceux king of arms. He was sent to Lincoln's Inn, but by 1569 was commanding the garrison at York against the northern rebels. Next he joined in the invasion of Scotland, under the 3rd Earl of Sussex, who knighted him at Carlisle. Sir Thomas Gargrave* classified him in his 1572 list of protestant gentry as of the 'meaner sort' in Yorkshire, but he was of sufficient standing to secure a county seat at the by-election of February 1576, following the death of Thomas Waterton. He was put on the subsidy committee, 25 Jan. 1581 and a committee for a bill about Carlisle, 27 Feb. 1581.[3]

For the next few years Stapleton found favour at court, where Camden noted him as 'a gentleman for person, address, and skill in languages, said to have had no superior in England nor equal, except Sir Philip Sydney'. In January 1579 Elizabeth recommended him to Olive Talbot as a suitable bridegroom. He was wealthy enough to raise 'seven score men in livery', and from about 1577 (before his first wife died) he was buying further lands in Yorkshire. From a second marriage, with a rich heiress, he hoped to gain over £1,200 a year. In the event, the wedding was delayed owing to the crisis in Stapleton's fortunes following a spectacular quarrel with Edwin Sandys, archbishop of York.[4]

Relations between the two men were strained at least as early as 1578, when Stapleton, who was already trying to acquire some of the archbishop's lands, was appointed a commissioner to investigate complaints by Sandys against the dean of Durham. An accidental meeting at the *Bull*, Doncaster, in May 1581 brought matters to a head. Stapleton and Sir Francis Mallory, on their way to London, put up for the night at the inn, owned by one Sysson, whose wife, perhaps significantly, was a former servant of Sandys. The archbishop was staying there, and Sandys and Stapleton renewed their quarrel. During the night the innkeeper forced his way into the archbishop's room and found him 'in naked bed' with Mrs. Sysson. Sandys, whose story was that the event had been contrived by Stapleton to discredit him, now bribed Stapleton and the innkeeper to keep silence. After some months, Sandys found Sysson's increasing demands excessive, and told Burghley the story, alleging that Stapleton ('the Queen's messenger') thought

that he was safe in the royal favour and could 'say what he will'. In the ensuing Star Chamber case the archbishop was vindicated at the expense of Stapleton and his associates. Stapleton was sentenced to three years' imprisonment and fined £300; Sysson fined £500 and to be pilloried with his ears nailed, and his servant 'Alexander the Scot' to be fined £500 and to have his ears cut off. Stapleton was to read a prepared apology 'upon his knees' at York assizes, which he did in a low voice 'as fast as he could'. This piece of defiance earned him a period of confinement in the Tower, whence in December 1583 he expressed his repentance and asked to be allowed to exercise in the fresh air. He was transferred to the Fleet and released some time in 1584, Burghley having unsuccessfully attempted to persuade Sandys to intercede for his former opponent.[5]

In the meantime his second marriage had taken place, the eldest child being baptized in April 1585. His court career in ruins, Stapleton paid a short visit to the Earl of Leicester in the Netherlands. In April 1586 he thought of returning there, perhaps to serve in the English army, only to be told by Leicester that the Queen had been displeased by his first visit. Stapleton now sold some of his Yorkshire estates, either to pay his fine, or to move from the scene of his humiliation. Between 1585 and 1603 he moved between Wiltshire, where his wife had property, to Wales, the Isle of Man, and London. James I remitted part of his debt to the Crown, and Stapleton found a borough seat in the first Parliament of the new reign, but he never retrieved his fortunes at court, and died intestate in the autumn of 1606, being buried at Wighill 3 Oct.[6]

[1] *CPR*, 1566–9, p. 288; Glover, *Vis. Yorks.* ed. Foster, 333; A. Gooder, *Parl. Rep. Yorks.* (Yorks. Arch. Soc. rec. ser. xcvi), 24–6; H. E. C. Stapylton, *The Stapletons of Yorks.* passim. [2] *CPR*, 1569–72, p. 224; *York Civic Recs.* (Yorks. Arch. Soc. rec. ser. cxv), 77, 158; (cxix), 33; Lansd. 56, f. 168. [3] *CPR*, 1557–8, p. 304; *York Civic Recs.* (Yorks. Arch. Soc. rec. ser. cxii), 169; Lansd. 13, f. 127; *CJ*, i. 119, 129. [4] *Camden, Britannia*, ed. Gough, iii. 291; *Yorks. Fines* (Yorks. Arch. Soc. rec. ser. v), 99, 100; Gooder; Stapylton, 224. [5] Gooder; Strype, *Annals*, iii(1), pp. 142–58; Sloane 326, ff. 56–70; Harl. 2143, f. 16; Lansd. 37, ff. 32–3; 38, ff. 156–7; 39, f. 199; 43, f. 9; 115, f. 19 seq.; *CSP Dom.* 1581–90, passim. [6] R. C. Strong and J. A. Van Dorsten, *Leicester's Triumph*, 130; Gooder; *CSP For.* 1585–6, p. 589; *Yorks. Fines*, passim; Stapylton, 231; *York Wills* (Yorks. Arch. Soc. rec. ser. xxvi), 205.

P.W.H.

STAUNTON, William (*d*.1587), of St. Margaret's, Westminster, Mdx.

WESTMINSTER   1571

s. of John Staunton (or Stanton) of Hoo, Beds. by Alice, da. of John Cooper of Northants. *m*. (1) Margaret (*d*. by 1572), da. of Richard Gawen of Chayham, Surr., 1s. *d.v.p.* 1da.; (2) c. 1572, Prudence Gyle.

Clerk in the receipt of the Exchequer 1550–60; yeoman usher of the receipt and keeper of Star Chamber 1556–73; comptroller of the pell 1565–74.

Staunton's return to Parliament for Westminster in 1571 needs no explanation. There is no record of his having made any contribution to the business of the House. He neglected the security of the receipt of the Exchequer at Easter 1573, and was held responsible for the break-in and theft of £380. After a period in the Marshalsea prison he was deprived of his offices, continuing, however, to reside at Westminster. When Westminster was granted its own municipal government in 1585 he became one of the ten assistant burgesses named to assist two chief burgesses under Burghley's high stewardship. He was buried at St. Margaret's 24 Mar. 1587.

Vis. London (Harl. Soc. cix, cx), 92; Burke, *Westminster Memorials,* 287; J. D. Alsop, 'Exchequer of receipt' (Camb. Univ. PhD. thesis, 1978), passim; Hall, *Antiquities,* 96–104; W. H. Manchée, *Memorials St. Margaret's Westminster;* M. E. C. Walcott, *Westminster Memorials,* 125; E. Smith, *Westminster Recs. at Caxton Street,* 89; information from Mr. C. H. D. Coleman.

P.W.H.

STEPHENS, Edward (b. c.1552), of Dover, Kent.

DOVER   1589

Dep. searcher, Dover by 1582, common councilman 1584, chamberlain 1584–5, jurat from 1584, brodhull rep. 1587.

A deputy searcher, responsible for examining goods entering and leaving a port, was a vulnerable man, and depositions in the town records show that many threats were made against Stephens. At least once he applied to the Privy Council for protection. Sometimes he found himself involved in national issues, as in September 1585 when he was commended by the warden of the Cinque Ports for detaining a French ship on which the ambassador Mauvissière was returning home. Several people were brought ashore and interrogated, among them one Dodswell, a Catholic sympathizer, who provided the government with information concerning the whereabouts of Jesuit priests and revealed an attempt to free Mary Queen of Scots. Of only local concern were the occasions when Stephens was fined and bound over for fighting with other borough officials, as, for example, the deputy bailiff in 1582 and, later, for attacking his own superior, the searcher, on a market day. When the Spanish invasion was imminent, in November 1587, Stephens and another jurat were allotted a quarter of the town to patrol with 20 men. In the autumn of 1588 he twice unsuccessfully contested the mayoralty, the second opportunity occurring on the sudden death of the newly-appointed official. Elected to Parliament instead, he was paid wages at 2s. 6d. a day, from three days before its commencement, to three days after its end. Nothing has been found to show that he participated other than passively in its proceedings, nor is it known that he made any contribution towards the rebuilding of Dover

harbour. He did, however, receive payment in 1594 for having carried 'the model of the harbour' to court the year before. No later reference to him is known.

Egerton 2095, passim; 2109, f. 82; *CSP Dom.* 1581–90, pp. 147, 266–8, 295, 383.

M.R.P.

STEPHENS, Richard (d. 1599), of Eastington, Glos. and the Middle Temple, London.

NEWPORT IUXTA LAUNCESTON 1593

1st s. of Edward Stephens of Eastington by Joan, da. of Richard Fowler of Stonehouse; bro. of Thomas*. *educ.* Corpus, Oxf. 1567, BA 1568, fellow 1569; Furnival's Inn; M. Temple 1572, called by 1582. *m.* by 1587, Margaret (d. 1591), da. of Edward St. Loe*, of Knighton, Wilts., 2s. 2da. *suc.* fa. 1587.[1]
J.p.q. Glos. 1592.

Stephens's family – established at Eastington since the twelfth century – were traditionally lawyers. His uncle and namesake, who died in 1577, was a bencher of the Middle Temple and Lent reader in 1574, and Stephens himself continued to occupy chambers in the inn after succeeding to the family estates in 1587. His puritan religious views emerge from a series of letters exchanged between him and his 'sister' (step-sister or sister-in-law), Elizabeth Palmer in 1589. She was contemplating a second marriage, to Sir William Bowes*, and Stephens was concerned not only in the material aspects of the arrangement but with inquiries into Bowes's 'soundness for judgment in religion and sanctification'. The conclusion he reached was adverse, for in conference with a group of puritan preachers – including Cartwright, Travers and Egerton – Bowes had shown himself defective in the doctrine of justification and the question of church government. Consequently, in spite of their shared preference for the preaching of Whitfield, Stephens counselled Mrs. Palmer to reject her suitor.[2]

How Stephens came to be returned to Parliament for Newport in 1593 is not clear. Presumably his legal career was the determining factor, for several of the Newport Members during this period were Middle Temple lawyers. It is also possible that he had connexions at court. He certainly had with the Earl of Essex, though it is not possible to see Essex as a direct patron in a Cornish constituency. In 1590, while Elizabeth Palmer was still pondering her matrimonial future, she was visited at Parham by Essex, who was pressing the suits of both Henry Savile II* and Henry Bromley*. At the beginning of the 1593 Parliament it was Stephens who introduced Bromley and his fellow county-Member Walsh into Peter Wentworth's group of young hotheads who intended to raise the succession question in the House. Stephens was apparently disconcerted by the youth and inexperience of the others, wishing there were 'more ancient gentlemen' present, but his attempt to stiffen them by the addition of two knights of the shire – albeit both in the early thirties – was disastrous for all three. The presentation of Wentworth's bill was forestalled by the Privy Council, Wentworth was sent to the Tower, and Stephens, Bromley and Walsh to the Fleet. By including Stephens among the few to suffer imprisonment the authorities warned that imprudent conspirators were no fit company for men who had reached years of discretion.[3]

After remaining in prison until Parliament was dissolved, Stephens presumably returned to his legal practice and his duties in Gloucestershire. He died 8 Aug. 1599, and his inquisition post mortem was taken at Gloucester castle on the 29th of that month. His heir was his son Nathaniel, then aged just over ten.[4]

[1] Vis. Glos. (Harl. Soc. xxi), 151–2; Vis. Glos. ed. Fenwick and Metcalfe, 174–5; M. T. Mins. i. 251. [2] R. Atkyns, Glos. 218; HMC 6th Rep. 345–6. [3] HMC 6th Rep. 346; D'Ewes, 470, 471; Townshend, Hist. Colls. 54; APC, xxiv. 116; Neale, Parlts. ii. 257–60. [4] C142/256/39.

I.C.

STEPHENS, Thomas (d. 1613), of the Middle Temple, London and Over Lypiatt, Glos.

WEYMOUTH AND MELCOMBE
   REGIS   1593

3rd s. of Edward Stephens of Eastington, Glos. and bro. of Richard*. educ. ?Magdalen Hall, Oxf. 1575, BA 1578; New Inn; M. Temple 1578, called 1585. m. Elizabeth, da. and coh. of John Stone of London, 3s. 2da.

Bencher, M. Temple 1604, Autumn reader 1604, treasurer 1612; attorney to the Princes Henry and Charles.

Stephens was a Middle Temple lawyer, who probably owed his return for Weymouth and Melcombe to another Middle Templar, William Weston, recorder of the combined boroughs. Stephens made a fortunate marriage, and a few years before his death purchased the Gloucestershire manors of Cherington, Over Lypiatt, Chipping, Little and Old Sodbury. He obtained a court appointment under James I, and in 1609 intervened on behalf of two Middle Templars who had killed a royal stag. He left his landed property to be divided between his three sons, all of whom were under age, gave his wife a life interest in Over Lypiatt, and left portions of £2,000 each to his two daughters. The will, dated 8 Mar. 1612, was proved 24 Nov. 1613. Stephens died on 26 Apr. of that year.

Vis. Glos. (Harl. Soc. xxi), 151; Atkyns, Glos. 218; M.T. Bench Bk. 92; M.T. Recs. i. 336, 426; ii. 440, 445, 523, 554, 557, 589; PCC 109 Capell, 70 Spencer; S. Rudder, Glos. 338, 674, 713; C142/335/30.

A.M.M.

STEPHENSON (STEPHENS, STEVENS), John, of Hythe, Kent.

HYTHE   1571

m. ?Margaret, da. of John Martyn of Horton.

Jurat, Hythe by 1567, bailiff 1569, brodhull rep. 1569, 1573, 1580.

In 1571 the Hythe corporation accepted the lord warden's nominee for one seat, but refused him a second and elected Stephenson, a fishmonger. The last reference found to him is dated 1592.

Vis. Kent (Harl. Soc. lxxv), 7, 131; HMC 4th Rep. 430; Hythe ass. bks. passim; G. Wilks, Barons of the Cinque Ports and the Parl. Rep. Hythe, 52–4.

N.M.F.

STEPNETH, Alban (d. 1611), of Prendergast, Pemb.

HAVERFORDWEST	1572, 1584, 1586
CARDIGAN BOROUGHS	1589
PEMBROKESHIRE	1604

3rd s. of Thomas Stepneth of St. Albans, Herts. by Dorothy, da. of John Winde of Ramsay, Lincs. educ. Christ's, Camb. 1552; Clement's Inn. m. (1) 1565, Margaret (or Ann), da. and coh. of Thomas Cathern of Prendergast, s.p.; (2) Mary, da. and coh. of William Philipps* of Picton, 3s. 2da.[1]

Receiver and registrar, St. David's diocese 1561; sheriff, Pemb. 1572–3, 1589–90, 1604–5, Carm. 1596–7; j.p. Haverfordwest; j.p. Pemb. from c.1575, ?Carm. 1585; commr. tanneries Pemb. 1574, goods of Sir John Perrot* 1592, goods of the Earl of Essex 1602; dep. lt. Pemb. 1602.[2]

The family of Stepneth or Stepney (the first form being in more general use till the seventeenth century) rose to local eminence in Hertfordshire in the fifteenth century and profited by the dissolution of St. Albans abbey in the sixteenth. Alban Stepneth moved to Carmarthenshire in 1561, when his relative by marriage, Richard Davies, was translated from the see of St. Asaph to that of St. David's and took up residence at the episcopal palace of Abergwili.[3]

Four years after his arrival in the county Stepneth married one of the four coheirs of Thomas Cathern of Prendergast, who owned extensive estates in Pembrokeshire and Carmarthenshire. Not long after the marriage, his wife died and after arbitration Stepneth received Prendergast in 1573, with much of its surrounding territory and further lands in Abergwili. Stepneth's kinsman, Thomas Woodford, also married into the Cathern family, acquiring thereby the estate of Castell Pigyn near Abergwili, part of which Stepneth purchased from him in 1579 in order to round off his own estate. Stepneth's second marriage, into the Philipps family of Picton, further increased the number of his West Wales connexions: an undated list of kin drawn up by him, and preserved among the papers of one of them (George Owen of Henllys), runs to several pages and includes nearly every family of note in Pembrokeshire and several from adjoining shires. In these circumstances it is not surprising that he should have been chosen for the shrievalty and for Parliament within a dozen years of his arrival.[4]

It was also inevitable that he should have been drawn into the family feuds which went with these connexions. Both families into which Stepneth had married had long-standing feuds with Sir John Perrot. In 1571 a dispute arose over the disappearance of victuals despatched by Stepneth for Perrot's forces in Ireland, but Stepneth was exonerated by the Privy Council when the case came before them in 1573.[5]

Meanwhile Perrot's absence in Ireland emboldened his enemies to put up Stepneth as candidate in the 1571 elections at Haverfordwest, a borough usually under Perrot's control. Stepneth stood against Perrot's protégé, John Garnons*. The borough officials, however, had been appointed during Perrot's mayoralty the preceding year, and the sheriff barefacedly returned Garnons on a minority vote – an offence for which he was fined and imprisoned by the Star Chamber. At the 1572 election, with officials appointed in Perrot's continued absence, Stepneth was returned for Haverfordwest and his father-in-law Philipps for the shire. He kept the seat in the elections of 1584 and 1586, when Perrot was again in Ireland, but for the 1589 Parliament, after the great man's return and resumption of borough control, Stepneth had to look for another seat.

By this time he had come under the patronage of the 2nd Earl of Essex, whose father had been patron to Stepneth's relative, Bishop Davies. It was Essex who recommended Stepneth in 1583 as a j.p. for Carmarthenshire, and to the same patronage may be attributed his election for Cardigan Boroughs (where the return of Ferdinando Gorges* and Thomas Rawlins* at the next two elections can also be traced to the Earl's influence). Stepneth subscribed £50 towards the Cadiz expedition in 1596. After the execution of Essex, Stepneth was appointed as one of the commissioners for the dead man's goods and chattels. He made little mark in Parliament. He was put on a committee concerning vicars and curates, 13 Mar. 1576, and on 11 Feb. 1585 was responsible for having one Anthony Kirk committed to the serjeant's custody for serving a subpoena on him as he was coming to the House. He obtained £3 6s. 8d. compensation for Kirk, who was released on 16 Feb.[6]

Stepneth steadily accumulated property in the three shires of West Wales. In Haverfordwest itself he early acquired enough burgages to qualify as a burgess, and he farmed the tithe of the borough's most ancient church. He also built there a new water mill, the subject of long-drawn-out Exchequer suits with William Morgan, a prosperous tailor and a champion of the Perrot faction in the borough, who claimed that it interfered with the town mills which had come into his possession. Similar charges were preferred by Stepneth himself in the same court against another fellow-burgess in respect of a mill in the crown lordship of Rhosmarket, south of the borough (part of the spoils of the dissolved preceptory of Slebech), the manorial rights of which he had acquired with the rectorial tithe; he further added charges of unlawful enclosure and conversion of arable to pasture.[7]

He was well placed, by his diocesan offices and the complaisance of his relative the bishop, for profitable traffic in tithes, notably of Slebech and of the former college of Abergwili, where Thomas Woodford had been receiver general since 1568. Here complaint was made against Stepneth in 1594 to the Exchequer court by the 22 prebendaries (now attached to Henry VIII's substitute foundation of Christ's College, Brecon) of unlawful detention of tithe. Bishop Davies died in 1581, and there followed the unhappy episcopate of Marmaduke Middleton, who would not have Stepneth as his registrar and receiver. Stepneth took a prominent part in the proceedings against Middleton which began in 1587, and ended in the bishop's suspension in 1590 and deposition in 1592. In 1590 Stepneth was arraigned by the attorney-general before the Exchequer on a charge of tampering with the temporalities of the see during the suspension.[8]

Both his private and public conduct were frequently under fire. In 1589 he was outlawed for non-appearance in court to answer for a small debt. His appointment as j.p. was cavilled at, during the episcopate of Richard Davies, on the ground that he was in the bishop's 'livery'; and in 1598 he was summoned before the Exchequer by two Carmarthenshire litigants who claimed that during his year as sheriff he had impeded the settlement of a private debt by unlawful seizure of the chattels concerned. As deputy woodward he was prosecuted, at the very end of the reign, for spoil of timber in Canyston wood, part of the royal forest of Narbeth. On the other hand, he was assiduous in measures for the safety of the Pembrokeshire coast, and in particular the defence of Milford Haven, against Spanish attack, and later as sheriff in alerting the countryside against the danger of invasion during the panic following the Gunpowder Plot.[9]

The malice of old enemies pursued him into James I's reign. After William Morgan's death his daughter's guardian, William Warren of Trewern (Nevern), brought against Stepneth five Star Chamber suits and one in the Exchequer, reviving the old quarrel about Haverfordwest mills and the settlement of Sir John Perrot's estate, and impugning Stepneth's conduct as sheriff in 1604–5. Stepneth riposted by prosecuting one of Warren's backers for perjury. He was also able to gloat over Warren's discomfiture when at the beginning of the second session of Parliament the latter was reprimanded at the bar of the House for serving a process on Stepneth after his election. Warren's plea that he supposed Stepneth's duties as sheriff would keep him from the House, as they had done in the preceding session, is belied by the fact that in the course of that session he had sat on the committee for the bill on scandalous ministers – a subject on which he spoke again in May 1606.[10]

He did not long survive the dissolution of Parliament. In his will, dated 30 Apr. 1611, proved 19 Nov. the same year, apart from provision for his sons and daughters, he left £5 for charitable uses in each of the parishes of St. Albans, Hertford, Carmarthen and Haverfordwest; £1 for the repair of St. David's cathedral; and £2 to the parish church of Prendergast. The Stepneys (as they came to call themselves) remained a force in the politics of Pembrokeshire until in the eighteenth century they disposed of their estates there, and afterwards in the politics of Carmarthenshire and Monmouthshire until the male line died out in 1825.[11]

[1] West Wales Hist. Recs. vii. 118–20; Dwnn, Vis. Wales, i. 135, 180; DWB, 924. The matriculation date is taken from Biog. Reg. Christ's Coll. ed. Peile, i. 51. [2] West Wales Hist. Recs. loc. cit.; Add. Chart 39994; Lansd. 53, f. 182; 156, f. 366; Exchequer, ed. E. G. Jones (Univ. Wales Bd. of Celtic Studies, Hist. and Law ser. iv), 90; Flenley, Cal. Reg. Council, Marches of Wales, 126, 140, 236; Harl. 6993, f. 116; Arch. Camb. (ser. 3), xi. 123, 130; xii. 324, 481–4; APC, xxxii. 282. [3] Trans. Carm. Antiq. Soc. x. 58, 84. [4] West Wales Hist. Recs. vii. 118–20; PCC 87 Wood; Arch. Camb. (ser. 2) v. 35–8. [5] APC, viii. 51–2, 190–1; Flenley, 63–4. [6] EHR, lxi. 18–27; Neale, Commons, 255–60; HMC Bath, v. 263; Arch. Camb. (ser. 5), xiii. 193–211; CJ, i. 115; D'Ewes, 348, 350. [7] G. Williams, Bywyd ac amserau 'r Esgob Richard Davies, 67; Neale, 256, 257; Add. Chart 32973; Exchequer, ed. T. I. J. Jones (Univ. Wales Bd. of Celtic Studies, Hist. and Law ser. xv), 291; Exchequer, ed. E. G. Jones (same ser. iv), 297–8, 300–1; West Wales Hist. Recs. vii. 122–4. [8] Harl. Chart 83 H16; West Wales Hist. Recs. vii. 122–4; G. Williams, 66; Exchequer, ed. E. G. Jones, 38, 305; HMC Hatfield, iv. 279–84. [9] Add. Chart 1861; Lansd. 53, f. 182; Exchequer, ed. E. G. Jones, 122, 309–10; Arch. Camb. (ser. 2), v. 33–41; CSP Dom. 1598–1601, pp. 267–8, 309; HMC Hatfield, xvii. 485. [10] Star Chamber, ed. Edwards (Univ. Wales Bd. of Celtic Studies, Hist. and Law ser. i), 210–12; Exchequer, ed. T. I. J. Jones, 291, 294; CJ, i. 237, 313; R. Bowyer, Diary, ed. Willson, 37, 45–6. [11] PCC 87 Wood; DWB, 924.

A.H.D.

STEVENSON, Richard (d. 1611), of Boston, Lincs.

| BOSTON | 1586, 1593, 1597 |

m. Sisill, poss. da. of Thomas Thory of Halton Holegate, at least 1s.
Mayor, Boston 1586–7, alderman from 1586.

Stevenson was probably related both to Robert Stevenson, the Queen's farmer at Boston, and to the Stevenson family long established at Wrangle, some eight miles north-east of Boston, but the connexion has not been firmly established. He was prominent in the Boston corporation for 15 years after his mayoralty, and one of the town's wealthiest citizens. When the friction between the town and the port officials came to a head about 1593, it was Stevenson, with Anthony Irby*, who spoke for the town in the ensuing negotiations which took place under the aegis of Burghley, the town's 'head recorder'. In 1596 he was the leading citizen implicated in the trouble over

sheep grazing on the West fen. He also took part as 'a man of great credit in those parts' in the efforts to have the fens drained.

In the 1593 Parliament Stevenson was on committees concerning recusants (28 Feb.) and he spoke on the Fitzherbert privilege case (2 Mar.). On 9 Mar. in the debate on jury service, the anonymous journal reports an intervention by Stevenson: 'I protest I no more meant to speak in this matter than I did to bid you all to breakfast'. At this there was general laughter. He was put on the committee for the 'merry bill of the brewers' (3 Apr.) and, according to Nicholas Saunders II*, he spoke to it on 6 Apr., though he 'meant it not'. Boston agreed to pay his expenses at the 1597 Parliament, when he served on committees concerning penal laws (8 Nov.), the possessions of the bishopric of Norwich (30 Nov.), the deprivation of Marian bishops (3 Dec.), malt (12 Jan. 1598) and wine casks (3 Feb.).

Stevenson died in 1611, asking to be buried in the choir of the church at Boston.

A. R. Maddison, Lincs. Wills, ii. 132, 136, 185; Boston corp. min. bk. passim; C142/216/97, 238/40; P. Thompson, Hist. Antiqs. Boston, 75, 76, 454, 623; HMC Hatfield, iv. 315, 317; viii. 244; Lansd. 73, f. 132; 87, f. 8 seq.; CSP Dom. 1581–90, p. 691; 1591–4, p. 130; 1595–7, p. 70; 1598–1601, p. 19; D'Ewes, 477, 481, 514, 553, 565, 567, 578, 592; Cott. Titus F.ii, anon. jnl. f. 54.

S.M.T.

STEWARD, Mark (1524–1604), of Heckfield, Hants, later of Stuntney, Cambs.

| ST. IVES | 1589 |
| STOCKBRIDGE | 1597 |

b. 1524, 3rd s. of Simeon Steward of Lakenheath, Suff. and Stuntney by Joan, da. and h. of Edward Besteney of Soham, Cambs. *educ.* ?St. John's, Camb. 1544. *m.* Anna, da. of Robert Huicke, physician to Queen Elizabeth, 1s. 1da. *suc.* bro. 1598. Kntd. July 1603.[1]

Officer issuing protections authorizing people to collect alms 1567–92; j.p.q. Hants 1583, capt. of musters, Holdshott hundred c.1587, sheriff 1597–8.

The Stewards had settled in East Anglia in the fifteenth century. One of Steward's uncles was the last prior of Ely and, acquiescing in the religious changes, became the first dean in 1541; another was chancellor (in 1554, dean) of Winchester, and was deprived at the accession of Elizabeth; and a third went into exile under Mary, became pastor of the English congregation at Frankfurt and was associated with William Whittingham and John Knox.[2]

Steward himself, a younger son with only an annuity of £20 left to him by his father, was forced to seek his fortune away from the family estates. He was described as a servant of the Queen in 1567, and afterwards entered the service of Sir William Paulet*, 3rd Marquess of Winchester. By the 1580s he resided at Heckfield, Hampshire, where Winchester had some land, and throughout the decade he supported the Marquess in his struggle with the Earl of Sussex for supremacy in Hampshire. Steward was soon involved in a quarrel on his own account with another of Winchester's servants, Thomas Dabridgecourt*, both men having been appointed to the same captainship of musters. Steward brought a Star Chamber action against Dabridgecourt, and the Privy Council instructed Winchester to settle the matter by dividing Holdshott hundred between the two claimants. Steward sat in the 1589 Parliament for Winchester's borough of St. Ives, but by April 1592, when the dispute with Dabridgecourt was at its height, Winchester was complaining that Steward had not 'carried himself toward [him] in the prosecution of this cause with that regard he ought to have had'. In 1597 Steward's own local influence obtained him a seat at Stockbridge, shortly before he became sheriff of Hampshire. He is recorded as sitting on a committee to reform the poor law, 22 Nov. that year, and is not known to have spoken in the House. Next year he retired to Stuntney, which he had inherited from an elder brother. He retained a London house, where in 1599 an agent, sent by James VI of Scotland to the Pope and the King of Spain, was imprisoned. Steward died in March 1604 and was buried in Ely cathedral. He had made his will when the doctors declared his case hopeless, confessing that he had felt more confidence 'of God's mercy within these seven days' than 'in seven years of his life before'. The executor was his son Simeon[†], who received his estates free of encumbrance. A copyhold of £20 went to a servant, 'whose body and wits in my service I have worn out'. Stuntney passed to his cousin Elizabeth and her son, Oliver Cromwell[†].[3]

[1] *Vis. Cambs.* (Harl. Soc. xli), 11, 128; *Genealogist*, n.s. ii. 37; J. Bentham, *Cathedral Church of Ely*, App. 48–9. [2] *DNB*; *Al. Cant.* iv. 161, 162; C. H. Garrett, *Marian Exiles*, 299. [3] *CPR*, 1566–9, p. 62; *APC*, xxii. 237–8, 394; xxxii. 281; St. Ch. 5/S6/1, S51/19; D'Ewes, 561; *VCH Cambs.* iv. 49, 137; C66/1549; *VCH Hants.* ii. 509; *CSP Dom.* 1598–1601, pp. 251–2; M. Noble, *Protectoral House of Cromwell*, i. 84; PCC 10 Babington, 47 Harte; C142/285/144.

I.C.

STEYNING, Thomas (d. ?c.1582), of Earl Soham, Suff.

CASTLE RISING   1559

2nd s. of Edward Steyning (d.1525) of Holnicote in Selworthy, Som. by Jane Michell of Cannington, Som. m. by 1553, Frances (c.1517–77), da. of John De Vere, 15th Earl of Oxford, wid. of Henry Howard, Earl of Surrey, 1s. 1da.[1]

J.p. Norf. from c.1599, Suff. by 1564; commr. musters, Suff. by 1569.[2]

Steyning was the younger son of a minor west-country gentleman who made a fortunate marriage to the widowed Countess of Surrey, thus becoming the stepfather of the 4th Duke of Norfolk, and the possessor of widespread lands in East Anglia. How he and the Countess, with such different backgrounds, came to marry is not at all clear.

Edward Steyning, Thomas's father, lived in west Somerset and moved in the same circle as the Luttrells and the Pyms. At his death in 1525, he left Thomas the profits from his Devonshire lands. There is nothing in his father's will to suggest that Thomas was still a minor at that date. From then until his marriage to the Countess, nothing is known about him. It is likely, though not certain, that he had moved to East Anglia in the meantime; he may have lived at Woodbridge in Suffolk. Later sources refer to him as of Earl Soham, but this was his wife's property and it is not known whether he owned any East Anglian estates himself.[3]

Frances, Countess of Surrey, was widowed by the execution of Henry Howard, the young Earl, in the last few days of Henry VIII's life. It was during the next reign that Steyning became her second husband. Surrey's property had been forfeited to the Crown, but Edward VI returned the manor of Earl Soham to the Countess and this became Steyning's home. The ageing 3rd Duke of Norfolk gave his daughter-in-law and her new husband nine manors, including Rising, worth in all £353 a year. The couple are found presenting to the living of Earl Soham in 1554 and Steyning soon began to participate in the duties in the county expected of a man in his greatly enhanced social position. He became a justice of the peace in both Norfolk and Suffolk and in 1559 he joined a commission to select quays at King's Lynn and adjoining creeks for the execution of a new statute regulating the loading and unloading of wares. He was also active in organizing the local musters. It seems that he enjoyed a life annuity of £20 from Queen Mary, but the reason for this grant has not been discovered.[4]

Steyning sat in the first Parliament of Queen Elizabeth for Castle Rising, enfranchised a year earlier, when the two Members had been the Duke of Norfolk's kinsman Sir John Radcliffe, and his steward Sir Nicholas Lestrange. The same two names appear on the election return for 1559, but Steyning evidently wished to sit in this Parliament, and for some reason not ascertained he was brought in at Castle Rising, while Radcliffe had to find a seat at Grampound. Steyning was presumably one of the Norfolk justices whom the bishop of Norwich in 1564 described as 'very well affected and given to executing of the orders and laws of this realm established for the ecclesiastical policy'. There is no evidence that Steyning was connected with the activities which led to the Duke of Norfolk's arrest in 1569: indeed, he attempted, though with little success, to raise men to preserve order in Suffolk. Steyning's wife died at Earl Soham in June 1577 and was probably buried at Framlingham, near her first husband. The year before, she had received a valuable lease from Philip, Earl of Arundel, the new head of the Howard family, but this and the other sources of income which Steyning had held through his wife were now lost. He also forfeited the stewardship of the manors of Framlingham and Saxtead which he had enjoyed since 1563. The date of his own death has not been found. His name appears on the Suffolk commission of the peace for 1582 but has been deleted, presumably either because of his advanced years or his death. No will has been found. Steyning left a son, Henry, and a daughter, Mary, who married Charles Seckford* of Seckford Hall, Suffolk.[5]

[1] *Vis. Som.* ed. Weaver, p. 80; *Vis. Som.* (Harl. Soc. xi), 103–4; *Vis. Suff. 1561*, p. 68. [2] Lansd. 1218, f. 22; *CPR*, 1560–3, p. 440; SP12/145, ff. 30, 37; N. Williams, *Duke of Norfolk*, 160. [3] PCC 33 Bodfelde; Copinger, *Suff. Manors*, iv. 251. [4] Williams, 30–1, 160; L.R.1/42, f. 269v; Copinger, iv. 251; *CPR*, 1558–60, p. 32; E407/74, unfoliated documents. [5] *Cam. Misc.* ix(3), p. 58; *HMC Var.* ii. 232, 234 n; *Cath. Rec. Soc.* xxi. 386; Copinger, iv. 251; Lansd. 35, ff. 132 seq.; Harl. 1560, f. 78v.

M.R.P.

STOKES, Adrian (c.1533–85), of Beaumanor, Leics.

LEICESTERSHIRE   1559, 1571

b. c.1533, ?s. of Robert Stokes of Prestwold. *m.* (1) 1 Mar. 1555, Lady Frances Brandon (d. 21 Nov. 1559), da. of Charles, 1st Duke of Suffolk, wid. of Henry, Duke of Suffolk by a new creation, 1da. *d.v.p.*; (2) 20 Apr. 1572, Anne, da. of Sir Nicholas Carew, wid. of Sir Nicholas Throckmorton, *s.p.*[1]

J.p. Leics. from c.1564, commr. subsidy 1565, musters 1573, 1577, 1583, recusants 1577; keeper of Brigstock park by 1577.[2]

Stokes's origins are unknown, the usual suggestion being that he came of yeoman stock. If, as is possible, the William Stokes who was claiming in 1558 the lands of his Staunton ancestors, can be identified with Adrian's known elder brother William (born c.1525), then Adrian's father was Robert Stokes of Prestwold, and his grandmother a member of an established family of minor gentry. This identification is supported by the fact that the Stokes of Prestwold were connected by marriage with a local family named Price (or Aprice), and his 'cousin and heir', Robert Price, benefited considerably from Adrian Stokes's estate.[3]

Stokes became groom, equerry or 'master of the horse' to the Duchess of Suffolk (the mother of Lady Jane Grey), whose husband was executed 23 Feb. 1554. Within a few days (according to some accounts), but more likely, after just over a year (the discrepancy can be accounted for by confusion over old and new style dates), the Duchess, aged about 38, and Stokes, aged about 22, married. This caused comment from contemporaries and provided a fund of stories more or less *ben trovato*; when Cecil told the Queen she exclaimed 'What! Has she married her horse keeper?'. And Cecil replied, 'Yes, and she says you would like to do the same with yours'. In the event the marriage

was happy, but brief, and a daughter was born who died in 1556. The Duchess made her will 7 Nov. 1559, and died on the 21st, leaving Stokes her goods, a life interest in most of her land, and an acknowledged position in society, eventually to be consolidated by a second fortunate, though necessarily less spectacular, marriage. Before this, however, Stokes had received a crown lease of Beaumanor, and twice been elected knight of the shire. There is no mention of any activity by him in the defective journals of the 1559 Parliament, and no record of his speaking in 1571, but he was named to committees on religion and church government (10 Apr. 1571), treasons (12 Apr., 11 May), abuses in conveyancing (14 Apr.), the order of business (21, 26 Apr.), respite of homage and church attendance (5, 19 May), apparel (14 May) and corrupt presentations (25 May). Stokes was classified by his bishop as earnest in religion in 1564, and he served on many local commissions including those to enforce attendance at church and those concerned with discovering recusants.[4]

Stokes's second marriage brought him the administration of the valuable Throckmorton estates, perhaps a mixed blessing as he was obliged to borrow substantially to provide dowries for his new step-daughters. His keepership of Brigstock park also brought its problems in the guise of poaching and affrays by the local people who resented the restrictions Stokes was obliged to impose. In the end the Privy Council gave him permission to use 'lawful means to defend Her Majesty's parks by force'.[5]

In 1582 Stokes settled the remainder of his crown lease of Beaumanor on his brother and Robert Price. His Devon manor of Kanacre was settled on his wife and her children, and other lands had been sold, presumably to pay Stokes's debts, which still amounted to some £4,000 at his death. In his will, dated 15 Apr. 1585, Stokes asked to be buried without any pomp 'as it has been used in the papists' time', and left most of his goods and chattels to his brother, William Stokes, the executor. Attached to the will are detailed inventories of houses in London and Leicester. There were portraits of Catherine Parr, Mary Tudor, Elizabeth and 'the French queen'. Robert Price's widow successfully claimed part of the estate, estimated by the Privy Council at £2,000. The heirs of Simon FitzRichard, Stokes's sister's husband, also claimed £1,000. Stokes died on 3 Nov. 1585 and was buried, as he requested, in the chapel at Beaumanor. An inquisition post mortem taken at Torrington, Devon, 25 May 1586 shows little land in that county.[6]

[1] *CP*, iv. 422; C142/128/91; Nichols, *Leics.* iii. 145; C1/1468/64–7; Harl. 760, f. 203. [2] *Leicester Recs.* iii. 140, 168; *CSP Dom.* 1547–80, pp. 561, 567; Lansd. 8, f. 79; 56, f. 168 seq.; *APC*, ix. 384. [3] C1/1468/64–7; *Trans. Leics. Arch. Soc.* xvii. 54; Nichols, iii. 144ff; *APC*, xx. 200. [4] *N. and Q.* vi. 225; xii. 451–2; *CPR*, 1558–60, pp. 4, 141; 1563–6, pp. 491, 494; C142/128/91; C142/166/6; PCC 59 Chaynay, 53 Brudenell; SC6/Eliz.; Lansd. 8, f. 79; 56, f. 168 seq.; *Leicester Recs.* iii. 140, 168; *APC*, ix. 23, 133; xi. 290; xiii. 164, 187;

CSP Dom. 1547–80, p. 561; *HMC Hastings*, ii. 4; D'Ewes, 160, 165, 166, 178, 179, 181, 183, 186, 188; *CJ*, i. 84, 85, 86, 89, 91, 92; *Cam. Misc.* ix(3), p. 30. ⁵ *APC*, ix. 384; xi. 63, 237; *HMC Buccleuch*, iii. 15–18. ⁶ Ms cal. and index to pat. rolls 1–16 Eliz. PRO 9(4), p. 199; 15(5), p. 309; *CSP Dom.* 1547–80, pp. 426, 441; Nichols, iii. 145; PCC 53 Brudenell; C142/210/62; *APC*, xx. 200, 243, 267; Req.2/164/147; Harl. 760, f. 191.

S.M.T./P.W.H.

STONE, Thomas (*d.*1604), of Trevigo in St. Minver, Cornw.

EAST LOOE 1572

o.s. of John Stone of Trevigo by Jane, da. of John Callard of Callard, Devon. *m.* Elizabeth, da. of William Harris of Hayne, Devon, 2s. 2da. *suc.* fa. 1573.

Stone belonged to a minor Cornish gentry family which held several parcels of land in St. Minver, some of it from John Hender* and John Trelawny*. His return for East Looe was probably due to his relatives the Mohuns of Hall. In 1580 he was brought before the Privy Council for transporting grain out of Cornwall. In his latter years he was in poor health and there were rumours of his imminent death in January 1602. He must have been a man of some substance, for William Stallenge*, a merchant of Plymouth, wrote to Cecil asking for the wardship of his son. When he died in July 1604, Sir George Gifford* wrote to Cecil with the same object, 'which will be a means for my delivery out of this wretched life of imprisonment'. These suitors presumably expected some immediate profit, probably from the marriage of Stone's elder son and heir, William, as he was within five months of his 21st birthday at the time of his father's death. Stone, who was buried 28 July 1604 in the church of St. Minver, appears to have left no will.

Vis. Cornw. (Harl. Soc. ix), 215; Vivian, *Vis. Cornw.* 446; *Paroch. Hist. Cornw.* iii. 367, 370–1; *APC*, xii. 266; *HMC Hatfield*, xii. 36; xvi. 247; C142/282/42.

I.C.

STONELEY, Richard (c.1520–1600), of Itchington, Warws., Doddinghurst, Essex, and London.

NEWTON 1571

b. c.1520. *m.* Anne, 2da.
  Teller of the Exchequer 10 Feb. 1554–c.1597, receiver of first fruits and tenths 31 Mar. 1560–27 Feb. 1578.[1]

Nothing has been ascertained about Stoneley's early life. His family may have come from Stoneley (now Stoneleigh), Warwickshire, near to which he had an estate at Over Itchington. During his period at the Exchequer he speculated heavily in land, buying the manor of Doddinghurst, Essex, from the 17th Earl of Oxford in 1579 and acquiring a considerable amount of other property in London, Berkshire, Kent and Essex. He also held the

manor of Wendlebury, Oxfordshire, the farm of Newark Wood in Sussex and a lease from the Queen, granted in 1570, of the manor of Moulsoe, Buckinghamshire. His town house was at St. Botolph's without Aldersgate, but his inquisition post mortem describes his widow Anne as living at Kensington's, where he may have retired towards the end of his life.[2]

So far as is known, Stoneley had no connexion with Lancashire, and like his fellow-Member for Newton in 1571 he may have owed his seat to Sir Ralph Sadler*, chancellor of the duchy of Lancaster, to whom he must have been known through the Exchequer post he held for over 40 years, and which gave him the usual opportunities for financial adventure. By 1580 he was already seriously embarrassed in consequence of his extensive land speculation. Thomas Lichfield*, who was investigating abuses in the Exchequer, declared in August 1584 that Stoneley had defrauded the Crown by concealing fines and by other means, that his denial of the charges, and demands to be allowed to answer them in a court of law, were subterfuges, and that Lord Burghley should call Stoneley before him to answer the accusations. An account survives, dated 4 Aug. 1585 and endorsed by Burghley 'Stoneley's estate', showing the amount of money in his hands as teller, and giving Stoneley's own reasons for his losses. He described himself as 'being now in case to beg in his old days, being 65 years of age'. In the following summer the crash came. Robert Petre* reported to Burghley (4 Aug. 1586) that 'Mr. Stoneley being unable to make up his accounts by £16,000, he has been forced to lay the burthen on the other three tellers'. In February 1588 Stoneley again gave a long explanation of his failure, claiming that over £2,000 had been stolen while he was unable to go to his house for fear of plague; he had lost over £1,000, being 'overwhelmed with the receipt of such great sums of money', sometimes £300,000 a year; £500 had gone 'in double toll of the Treasury in all this time', and another £200 by 'sundry falls of the coin'; he had 'double charged' himself 'of sundry sums of money', and 'to avoid concealing of anything, I have charged myself with above £40,000 more than any auditor can charge me withal'. He asked to be allowed to remain in office until Michaelmas, by which time he hoped to have put everything in order by selling his lands and recovering debts. 'Howsoever others deal with me', he insisted, 'I will be found a true man in my dealing to her Majesty with all that I have, and my body to prison if need should so require.' The account to which this petition is attached is complicated, but it appears that Stoneley hoped to raise nearly £14,000. The lands mentioned were in East and West Ham, Barking, Dagenham, and other parts of Essex, and in Berkshire and Buckinghamshire. Leases of lands and houses in London and of the *Saracen's Head*, Westminster, should raise £900, and 'annuities' nearly another £400.[3]

Some sort of respite was apparently granted, for on 20 Dec. the same year Stoneley wrote once more to Burghley that a number of people had come to Westminster to pay money to him, 'but Mr. Peter [? Petre] saith I may do nothing there before he hear from your honour'. He was anxious to be allowed to ride into the country to sell land at East and West Ham. It is difficult to follow his movements during the next 10 years, but the government seems to have given him repeated opportunities to retrieve his position. Another letter about his finances survives, dated October 1593, and about December 1596 he paid in £3,000. By May 1597, however, most of his property (which included over 400 books) had been sequestered by the Crown. He died, probably in prison, on 19 Feb. 1600. His inquisition post mortem, drawn up in January 1601 at the London Guildhall, gives details of the dates when he had to surrender houses and lands. His debts, presumably only those to the Crown, are estimated at nearly £13,000. A house and 25 acres at Doddinghurst, which he had conveyed in trust to John Braunche of London and others, remained in his hands. The coheirs were his daughters, Dorothy, aged 40, the widow of William Dawtrey, and Anne, wife of William Heigham. Administration of his estate was granted to a creditor in 1605.[4]

[1] *CSP Dom.* 1547–80, p. 59; 1581–90, p. 257; 1595–7, p. 413; C142/266/81; *CPR*, 1553–4, p. 84; Essex RO, D/DFa 03; E 36/266/90. [2] Morant, *Essex*, i. 191–2; SP12/139/28; G. Lipscomb, *Bucks.* iv. 252–3; *CPR*, 1563–6, p. 85; 1569–72, p. 152. [3] *CSP Dom.* 1547–80, pp. 661, 701; 1581–90, pp. 257, 343; *APC*, xii. 278; Lansd. 40, ff. 86, 130 seq.; *HMC Hatfield*, iii. 310–12. [4] *HMC Hatfield*, iii. 377; iv. 401; *CSP Dom.* 1595–7, pp. 314, 413; *Vis. Suss.* (Harl. Soc. liii), 32; *EHR*, lxxviii. 240; *Studies in Bibliography* (Univ. of Virginia), ii. 49–51; C142/266/81; PCC admon. act bk. 1605, f. 22.

N.M.F.

STONOR, Francis (1551–1625), of Blount's Court and Stonor Park, Oxon., and of London.

NEW WOODSTOCK	1586

b. 1551, 1st s. of Sir Francis Stonor by Cecily, da. of Sir Leonard Chamberlain† of Shirburn, Oxon. *educ.* sp. adm. M. Temple 1572 (bound with John Southcote, the judge's son). *m.* by 1579, Martha, da. of John Southcote†, c.j. Queen's bench, of Witham, Essex, 3s. *suc.* fa. 1566. Kntd. 1601.[1]

Escheator, Oxon. 1584–5, sheriff 1593–4, 1621–2, j.p. by c.1592.

The Stonors were a Catholic family (though Stonor himself escaped indictment for recusancy until 1612) and were consequently declining from their ancient position as one of Oxfordshire's leading families. They neither owned property near Woodstock nor had any close connexion with Sir Henry Lee*, the high steward, and it is not certain exactly how Stonor came to be returned for the borough in 1586. The Chamberlains, his mother's family, held the

lieutenancy till 1570 and retained some interest in Woodstock; John Doyley, once Stonor's guardian, was sheriff at the time of the election; and the influence of Sir Francis Knollys*, neighbour to the Stonors, after whom Stonor himself may have been named, had earlier extended to Woodstock. Perhaps however, a powerful kinsman, John Fortescue I*, ranger of Wychwood, near Woodstock, is the most likely patron.[2]

Shortly after the capture of Edmund Campion in the summer of 1581, an order was given for the searching of Stonor Park, and there was discovered the press on which Campion and Parsons had printed the *Decem Rationes* under the protection of Stonor's mother. Stonor had removed himself to another of his manors, and may or may not have been ignorant of the activities of the Catholics his mother had gathered round her. Lady Stonor and later his brother John were committed to his charge, to see only 'Francis, and such other godly and learned persons as he shall think meet … to reduce [them] to conformity'. Stonor also farmed for some £250 a year the lands taken from Lady Stonor for her recusancy. He was a sympathetic guardian, obtaining leave for his mother to visit Bath for treatment, and defending his brother in lawsuits. In 1603 he transmitted to Cecil a petition from John Stonor, who had been an exile in the Netherlands for 20 years, asserting that his brother had never intended any 'undutiful action'. In fact Stonor devoted assiduous attention to Sir Robert Cecil, whom he thanked for securing his knighthood in December 1601 and plied with congratulations and New Year presents. Though Stonor's wife, sister and daughter were committed to prison and he was on one occasion summoned before the Privy Council and on another actually indicted, he never quite fell out of favour, and even served a term as sheriff. He suffered from gout, and like his mother and son, Francis, paid visits to Bath, where in 1624 he erected a rail about the King's bath in memory of benefits received on a previous visit. He died on 21 Oct. 1625, leaving £1,630 in money, £300 of it to charity. The will was disputed and sentence pronounced in June 1626.[3]

[1] C142/274/150; *Vis. Oxon.* (Harl. Soc. v), 237; Foster, *Al. Ox.* i. 1430. [2] Trinity, Camb. mss R.5.14, art. 6; E. K. Chambers, *Sir Henry Lee*, 81–2; Wards 9/138, f. 680; R. J. Stonor, *Stonor: a Catholic Sanctuary*, 233. [3] *APC*, xiii. 151, 190, 396–7; xv. 84; xx. 291, 310; xxvi. 112–13; xxxiv. 166; *Cath. Rec. Soc.* ii. 29; xviii. 251; xxxix. p. xxxviii; *Egerton Pprs.* (Cam. Soc. xii), 453; *HMC Hatfield*, xi. 510; xv. 199, 291; xvi. 316; xvii. 215; *CSP Dom.* 1603–10, pp. 570–1, 611; 1611–18, p. 145; 1623–5, p. 5; Lansd. 71, f. 170; 78, f. 165; Stonor, 270, 273; C142/423/76; PCC 130 Clarke.

A.H.

STORY, John (1504–71).

SALISBURY	1545
HINDON	1547*
EAST GRINSTEAD	1553 (Oct.)
BRAMBER	1554 (Apr.)

BATH	1554 (Nov.)
LUDGERSHALL	1555
DOWNTON	1559

b. 1504, s. of Nicholas Story of Salisbury by his w. Joan. *educ.* Hinxsey Hall, Oxf., BCL 8 May 1531, DCL 29 July 1538; adv. Doctors' Commons 1539. *m.* bef. 1549, Joan Watts, 1da. and 4 other ch.[1]

Principal, Broadgates Hall, Oxf. 1537–9, 1st Regius lecturer and prof. civil law 1535, re-appointed 1553; vicar-gen. diocese of London Nov. 1539–bef. 16 July 1540, chancellor dioceses of London and Oxf. Jan. 1554–9; j.p.q. Mdx. 18 Feb. 1554–9; Queen's proctor at the trial of Cranmer 1555; commr. against heresy 1557–8; master in Chancery for a few months in 1558.[2]

Of humble birth, Story had a chequered career at Oxford. In the 1540s he was a civil lawyer in the service of both the Crown and the Church. A strong Catholic, his attack on the Prayer Book in Parliament in 1549 led to his imprisonment in the Tower and eventual flight to the Continent. He returned on Mary's accession and, as Bishop Bonner's chancellor ('worse than Bonner' said Foxe), played an active part in the persecution of protestants from 1555 to 1558.[3]

He was returned to the Parliament of 1559 for Downton by the Marian Bishop White of Winchester, and on 23 Mar. 1559 was reprimanded by the Commons for acting as counsel for White before the Lords. Story confessed his fault and was pardoned by the House. In the same Parliament he justified his conduct under Mary, regretting only that the Catholics had then

> laboured about the young and little twigs whereas they should have struck at the root.

'And herein, most traitorously', wrote the author of an anonymous pamphlet, 'he meant the destruction of our dear and sovereign lady, Queen Elizabeth'. 'Story had his wanton words' said William Fleetwood in the Parliament of 1572 'and passed without punishment'. He was in fact sent to the Fleet on 20 May 1560, though soon released. But on 31 May 1562 Bishop Parkhurst wrote to Henry Bullinger at Zurich: 'Story, that little man of law and most impudent papist, has been arrested, as I understand, in the west of England in his barrister's robes'. He was imprisoned until the next year, when the oath of supremacy was put to him and presumably refused. The Spanish ambassador now despaired for his life, but, with the aid of the chaplain at the Spanish embassy, Story escaped to the Netherlands. There he secured a pension from Philip II and the post of inspector of incoming ships at Antwerp and elsewhere – probably with the duty of preventing the entry of heretical books.[4]

The Queen may not have regretted his flight, for she had delayed signing the commission for his trial, and Story himself later claimed that she had given him licence to go abroad, considering him 'an abject and cast away'. In July

1570, however, some English seamen fastened the hatches while he was searching their ship and brought him to England where in due course he was arraigned for treason at Westminster Hall, 26 May 1571. Story refused to plead, claiming to be a subject of Philip II, and the sentence was a foregone conclusion.[5]

On 1 June 1571 he was led to execution, and allowed to make a long speech. He recalled how he had twice lost everything he possessed by exile, and asked charity for 'the faithfullest wife, the lovingest and constantest that ever man had', and for their children. He stated that he died 'in the faith Catholic of my King', and claimed that

> every man is free-born and hath the whole face of the earth before him, to dwell and abide in where he liketh best; and if he cannot live here, he may go elsewhere.

Cut down alive from the scaffold, a near-contemporary account of the execution describes him as attacking the executioner as he began to disembowel him. His trial and death furnished material for the pamphleteers on both sides in the years to come. He was beatified on 29 Dec. 1886.[6]

[1] *Harl. Misc.* (1808), iii. 105, 107; I. Temple Petyt mss 538, vol. 47, f. 66; *CJ,* i. 7. [2] *Ath. Oxon.* i. 386–7; *CPR,* 1553–4, p. 395; 1555–6, p. 281; Guildhall mss, Bonner's register ff. 1b, 3; Strype, *Cranmer,* i. 533; E101/520/17. [3] *DNB; Ath. Oxon.* i. 386–7; C. E. Coote, *English Civilians,* i. 34; *CPR,* 1553–4, p. 395; *CJ,* i. 6–9; Strype, *Annals,* ii. 296–7; *Examinations and Writings of Archdeacon Philpot* (Parker Soc. 1842), 4–13, 47–8. [4] *CJ,* i. 58; *Harl. Misc.* iii. 102; Neale, *Parlts.* i. 62; Strype, *Annals,* i(1), 220; *Parker,* ii. 366–7; *Zurich Letters* 1558–69 (Parker Soc.), 111; *CSP Span.* 1558–67, pp. 322–3. [5] *CSP Span.* 1558–67, p. 323; 1568–79, pp. 267, 272–3, 276–7, 288, 296, 312; *Harl. Misc.* iii. 106; viii. 608–12; *CSP Dom.* 1547–80, pp. 389–415 passim; Strype, *Parker,* ii. 366–7; *APC,* vii. 385; T. B. Howell, *State Trials* (1816), i. 1087–95. [6] *Harl. Misc.* iii. 105–8; *DNB.*

R.V.

STOUGHTON, Adrian (1556–1614), of West Stoke, nr. Chichester, Suss.

| HASLEMERE | 1593 |
| CHICHESTER | 1597, 1601, 1604, 1614 |

b. 7 May 1556, 2nd s. of Thomas Stoughton* by his 2nd w., and bro. of Laurence*. *educ.* I. Temple 1579, called 1587. *m.* c.1583, Mary (*d.* 1635), da. of William Jordyn I* of Chitterne, Wilts., 16 ch. of whom 2s. 6da. living at fa.'s death.[1]

J.p. Suss. from 1591, q. from 1597; recorder, Chichester from 1600.

Like his father, who sat for Chichester four times, Stoughton was a lawyer. His return for Haslemere was probably due to his elder brother Laurence's connexion with the More family. Stoughton then sat for Chichester, first in company with his uncle Richard Lewknor, then recorder of the city, and afterwards during his own recordership. He was appointed to only one reported committee in the Elizabethan period, 12 Jan. 1598, on maltsters.[2]

He died 25 Oct. 1614. His will, made on the previous 2 June, asked that his burial should be without 'needless expense' and that his wife should bestow no 'blacks'. She, or if she re-married, Laurence Stoughton, was to obtain the wardship of their eldest son. A younger son, Adrian, and six daughters are mentioned. Stoughton was buried at West Stoke, where a monument was later erected to him and his wife.[3]

[1] Manning and Bray, *Surr.* i. 171 table; *Vis. Surr.* (Harl. Soc. xliii), 87; *Surr. Arch. Colls.* xii. gen. table; *VCH Suss.* iv. 193; Add. 6174, f. 128; *Cal. I.T. Recs.* i. 346; *Vis. Wilts.* (Harl. Soc. cv, cvi), 104; H. R. Mosse, *Monumental Effigies Suss. 1250–1650*, p. 137; PCC 113 Lawe. [2] PRO Index 4208, p. 177; *VCH Surr.* iii. 371; *CSP Dom.* 1547–80, p. 153; *HMC Hatfield*, i. 436; D'Ewes, 578. [3] *Suss. Rec. Soc.* xiv. 218; PCC 113 Lawe; Horsfield, *Suss.* ii 75; *Suss. Arch. Colls.* lxxiv 204.

J.E.M.

STOUGHTON, Laurence (1554–1615), of Stoughton, Surr.

| GUILDFORD | 1572*, 1584, 1586, 1593 |

b. 12 Nov. 1554, 1st s. of Thomas Stoughton* by his 2nd w., and bro. of Adrian*. *educ.* I. Temple 1572. *m.* 23 Apr. 1575, Rose (*d.*1632), da. of Richard Ive of Kentish Town, Mdx. 11s. 6da. *suc.* fa. 1576. Kntd. 1611.[1]

J.p. Surr. 1577 to at least 1609, q. by 1601; subsidy collector, Surr. 1593–4; capt. local forces 1598; verderer of Windsor forest c.1591; under-steward for crown lands, Suss.[2]

Stoughton succeeded to his father's Surrey estates while still at the Inner Temple. He then married a lady whose stepfather, William Hammond†, was a leading Guildford citizen, and gave them land at East Horsley, Surrey; Rayleigh, Essex; and Billingshurst, Sussex. A seventeenth-century member of the family estimated that Stoughton's marriage brought him between £4,000 and £5,000, and to this was added Hammond's own house on the death of his wife, Rose's mother, in 1592. Stoughton set up as a lawyer, probably in Guildford itself, and acted for the Mores of Loseley both privately (he was an overseer of the will of William More I) and in local government. However, it appears that he owed his first return to Parliament in 1581 to another connexion. When his father, the sitting Member, died, according to a seventeenth-century account, the Earl of Arundel, by this time out of prison, wrote to the corporation suggesting that the son should replace the father in the Guildford seat, and, though that nobleman died before the by-election was held in January 1581, his recommendation may have influenced the corporation. But in any case Stoughton was obviously a strong local candidate, and he was returned for Guildford on three other occasions. In 1589, however, Sir William More had to fall back on the borough seat himself and Stoughton was left out. He was given leave of absence from the 1586 Parliament on 8 Mar. 1587 and in that of 1593 he was put on the first standing committee for

privileges and returns (26 Feb.) and a committee for the poor (12 Mar.).[3]

His father's connexion with the Arundel household enabled Stoughton to succeed him as deputy to Lord Lumley, steward of the Crown's lands in Sussex. Unlike his father, Stoughton was, a letter from Sir William More assured the Council, 'sound and well affected in religion'. He became a Surrey ecclesiastical commissioner 'to inquire diligently of the secret repair into our realm of a number of seminaries, priests and Jesuits, of malicious purpose', and searched Catholic houses, including that of the aged Lady Montagu.[4]

Towards the end of the century Stoughton sold East Horsley, Effingham rectory and his wife's Essex inheritance, and bought the manor of Stoke-next-Guildford. His subsidy assessment in 1594 reflects his wealth. King James visited him at Stoughton, recently enlarged, and knighted him at Bagshot nearby. He was a friend of Archbishop Abbott, a Guildford man, and an active local figure in such matters as education, poor relief, the intended diversion of a river to improve navigation, the cloth trade and local defence. He died 13 Dec. 1615 and was buried in the Stoughton chapel at Stoke church. His will was proved 31 Jan. 1616 in the archdeacon's court. Six of his sons went to Oxford and five of those to the Inner Temple as well.[5]

[1] *Vis. Surr.* 87; Manning and Bray, *Surr.* i. 170; Add. 6174, ff. 129–30; *Surr. Arch. Colls.* xii. gen. table; *VCH Surr.* iii. 372. [2] Add. 6174, f. 132; Lansd. 35, f. 135; 737, f. 152; C66/1549; E163/14/8; *Surr. Arch. Colls.* xix. 59, 101; *Surr. Rec. Soc.* x. 179, 182, 212, 215; xiii. 386; *HMC 7th Rep.* 660b. [3] *Cal. I. T. Recs.* ed. Inderwick, i. 263, 269, 310, 367; Add. 6174, ff. 4–5, 7, 16, 60–1, 129–32; *VCH Surr.* iii. 350; Manning and Bray, i. 77; PCC 19 Pyckering; D'Ewes, 413, 471, 499. [4] *HMC 7th Rep.* 630a, 649b, 664a; *CSP Dom.* 1581–90, p. 151; *APC*, xxiv. 328–9. [5] *Hist. Guildford* (1801), pp. 96, 124–5, 129–30; Add. 6174, ff. 18, 132, 133; *VCH Surr.* ii. 347; iii. 85, 326, 350, 371; Manning and Bray, i. 168, 170; *Surr. Arch. Colls.* xix. 62; xxi. 179; *Surr. Rec. Soc.* xxii. 108–9; Allen, *Hist. Surr.* ii. 155.

M.R.P.

STOUGHTON, Thomas (1521–76), of Stoughton, Surr. and West Stoke, Suss.

GUILDFORD	1547*
CHICHESTER	1553 (Mar.), 1553 (Oct.), 1554 (Apr.)
GUILDFORD	1559
CHICHESTER	1563
GUILDFORD	1572*

b. 25 Mar. 1521, 1st s. of Laurence Stoughton of Stoughton by Anne, ?da. of Thomas Combes of Guildford. *educ.* I. Temple. *m.* (1) Ann, da. of Francis Fleming of London, *s.p.*; (2) 27 Feb. 1553, Elizabeth, da. of Edmund Lewknor of Tangmere, Suss., 2s. Adrian* and Laurence* 2da. *suc.* fa. to Stoughton 1571.

Bencher, I. Temple; comptroller, 12th Earl of Arundel's household; under-steward of crown lands in Suss.; j.p. Surr. from c.1559, Suss. c.1559, from 1573; commr. musters, Surr. 1560.[1]

The Stoughtons had lived in Surrey since the twelfth century, and it was Stoughton's position in the household of the Earl of Arundel that enabled him to establish the Sussex branch of the family. Classified in 1564 as 'a misliker of godly orders' and 'a stout scorner of godliness', the visitation of 1569 noted

> there be schoolmasters who teach without licence and be not of a sound and good religion ... as the schoolmaster in the lodge at Stanstead, who teacheth Mr. Stoughton's children.

Stoughton was privy to Arundel's role in the Duke of Norfolk's plot of that year and he was further compromised in the eyes of the authorities by disputes with other Sussex gentlemen on Arundel's behalf. Clearly it was Arundel who was behind Stoughton's return to Parliament for Guildford and Chichester until 1572, by which time, Arundel being in prison and Stoughton having succeeded to his father's manor nearby, he came in for Guildford through his own local influence. He died intestate 26 Mar. 1576, at Arundel House in the Strand, and was buried at St. Clement Danes. Administration was granted on 31 Mar. to John Browne of Stoke, 'yeoman', on behalf of Thomas's elder son and heir, Laurence.[2]

[1] *VCH Surr.* ii. 167; iii. 371; Add. 6174, ff. 23, 127, 128; Manning and Bray, *Hist. Surr.* i. 171, table; *Vis. Surr.* 86–7; *Surr. Arch. Colls.* xii. gen. table; *HMC Hatfield*, i. 436; Lansd. 1218, ff. 26, 76; *CPR*, 1563–6, pp. 26, 38, 39, 40; SP10/3/14, f. 114; 12/104. [2] Manning and Bray, i. 38; *I.T. Recs.* i. 8, 12, 17, 19, 23, 25, 28; *CPR*, 1558–60, pp. 319–20; Mousley thesis, 777; *CSP Dom.* 1547–80, p. 153; Add. 6174, ff. 127, 128; *Cam. Misc.* ix(3), p. 10; *VCH Suss.* ii. 25; *APC*, vii. 189, 193, 197, 200–1; viii. 261–2, 267, 275; *CP*; *HMC 7th Rep.* 624; PCC admon. act bk. 1576, f. 96v; C142/179/81.

M.R.P.

STOUGHTON, William (?1543–1612), of Worplesdon, Witley and Stoke-next-Guildford, Surr.

GRAMPOUND[1]   1584

> *b.* ?1543, 1st s. of Anthony Stoughton of Warwick by his 1st w. Jane, da. of Thomas Jones of Witley. *m.* Elizabeth, da. of William Muschamp of East Horsley, Surr. and Kensington, Mdx., 7s. 3da. *suc.* fa. 1574.[2]
> Lay commissary of peculiar of Groby, Leics. by 1575.

Stoughton's father began his career in the household of Catherine Howard, and remained a courtier during four reigns. In 1562 Elizabeth confirmed the grant of the hospital of St. John in Warwick, which remained his family's main residence. Stoughton himself, though the eldest son and heir, remained in Surrey. His background is obscure. If he was the William Stoughton who qualified as a civil lawyer, it is odd that he should be described as 'gent.' on the election return. At any rate he became associated in some way (probably as a member of his household) with the puritan 3rd Earl of Huntingdon, whose religious views he shared, and who may have

obtained for him the position at Groby, since, as a peculiar, it was exempt from diocesan jurisdiction. His return to Parliament for Grampound in 1584 may have been due to Huntingdon's friendship with the 2nd Earl of Bedford. Stoughton was added, 16 Dec. 1584, to the committee examining the many religious petitions offered to the House, which, in turn, compiled a petition for the Lords containing a demand for the removal of unqualified ministers. On the following 15 Feb. he 'offered unto this house a certain supplication in parchment of certain abuses in the ministry within the county of Leicester', one of several county reports which the puritans had been compiling for some time. His interests as a country gentleman are reflected in his appointment to a committee for the preservation of game, 17 Mar. 1585, and on 26 Mar. he was in charge of a committee dominated by puritans which, contrary to the Queen's specific order, revived a bill against excessive fees in ecclesiastical courts.[3]

Little is known about Stoughton's later career. He appears as a witness to several wills in Surrey in the 1590s but there is no local evidence to indicate whether he was pursuing any puritan activities there. Early in James I's reign he published abroad *An Assertion for True and Christian Church Policy*, advocating a reformed episcopate and an end to canon law. He thought ministers should be selected by their congregations.[4]

Stoughton's will, made in January and proved in November 1612 suggests that he died in debt, though he made provision for his wife and six surviving sons and daughters. He owned land in Witley, Kingston, Pirbright and Stoke, Surrey, and some of his furniture was in the parsonage at Stoke. A long passage towards the end of the will suggests that his religious beliefs had not changed.[5]

[1] Dugdale, *Warws.* 460. [2] Manning and Bray, *Surr.* i. 171 table; iii. 29; *Vis. Surr.* (Harl. Soc. xliii); *Vis. Warws.* (Harl. Soc. xii), 141, 315; P. Collinson, *Letters of Thomas Wood*, x; *Eliz. Puritan Movement*, 181. [3] *LP Hen. VIII*, xv. 9 and xvi. 175; *CSP Dom.* 1547–80, p. 110; *CPR*, 1555–7, p. 396; *VCH Warws.* ii. 115–16; v. 121; Collinson thesis, 504, 508–11; Nichols, *Leics.* iv. 632–3; D'Ewes, 340, 349, 369, 373. [4] *Surr. Rec. Soc.* iii. 52, 92, 106–7; W. Stoughton, *An Assertion*, 13–14, 36–7, 191, 247. [5] PCC 103 Fenner.

M.R.P.

STRANGE, Thomas (*d.*1594), of Chesterton, Cirencester, Glos.

CIRENCESTER   1572

> ? s. of Robert Strange, bailiff of Cirencester. *m.* Bridgett.

If the identification is correct, Strange was a sheep farmer elected through the influence of his father the bailiff. He was named to committees concerning lands without covin (18 Feb. 1576), and the sale of wool and yarn (13 Feb. 1581). He died in 1594. In his will, made 16 Mar. and proved 10 May of that year, he left his lands to his brother and executor, Anthony. Bequests of sheep were made to a number of servants. He provided a legacy of £40 for his wife on condition that she gave up her obstinate refusal to attend divine service.

PCC 43 Dixy; *Valor Ecclesiasticus*, ii. 469; *Bristol and Glos. Arch. Soc. Trans.* ix. 342; xvii. 182; *CJ*, i. 106, 125.

W.J.J.

STRANGE, *see also* LESTRANGE

STRANGWAYS, Sir Giles (1528–62), of Melbury Sampford, Dorset.[1]

DORSET   1553 (Oct.), 1554 (Apr.), 1555, 1558, 1559

b. 1528, 1st s. of Henry Strangways by Margaret, da. of George Manners, Lord Ros, and sis. of Thomas, 1st Earl of Rutland. *m.* 1546, Joan, da. of John Wadham of Merifield, Som., at least 4s. 2da. *suc.* gd.-fa. Sir Giles Strangways[†] 1546. Kntd. 1549.[2]

Warden, Neroche forest, Som. 1551; commr. church goods, Dorset 1553, j.p. from 1554.[3]

Strangways owned extensive estates in Dorset, including the site of the monastery of Abbotsbury. Through his wife his heirs acquired rights to considerable property in Somerset, which he himself did not live to enjoy. He also owned lands in Yorkshire, whence the family had moved to Dorset in the fifteenth century. He was a protestant during Edward VI's reign, when he served as a commissioner for church goods. After Mary's accession he came up to London to render an account of his proceedings in the latter capacity. He was one of those who 'stood for the true religion' in the October 1553 Parliament, and in 1555 he opposed a government bill, but he must have given the Marian government general support in the county, as he continued to serve on the Dorset commission of the peace and his wardenship of Neroche forest was renewed by a patent of November 1555. In 1557 he commanded 50 men in the 1st Earl of Pembroke's expedition to St. Quentin. Sir William Courtenay[†], who died on the campaign, appointed him an executor.[4]

Strangways lived – and died – extravagantly. In June 1555 he surrendered himself to the Fleet to avoid outlawry for debts that included over £100 to two London tailors. He sold 700 ewes, 600 wethers and 300 hogs, leaving three estates denuded of livestock. When he died in his early thirties on 11 Apr. 1562, he left his widow with at least six children under 21. His will, which he made before going on the St. Quentin campaign and to which he added two codicils, in 1558 and 1562, required his wife, if she married again, to give a bond of £2,000 to carry out her duties as executrix. The 13 overseers to whom she was bound received a total of £72 plus expenses. The executrix was compelled to sell all the household goods to pay debts amounting to over £3,000. Strangways left 1,000 marks to his daughter Anne on her marriage and 600 marks to a younger son. Among numerous charitable bequests were some to poor prisoners at Ilchester and Dorchester, and to the lazar-house of Bridport. There is an effigy of him in plate armour at Melbury Sampford church.[5]

[1] This biography is based upon the Roberts thesis. [2] C142/136/7; Wards 7/9/32; Harl. 1539, f. 104; Hutchins, *Dorset*, ii. 662–4; PCC 17 Streat, 24 Alen. [3] *CPR*, 1550–3, pp. 195, 414; 1553–4, p. 18. [4] C142/136/7; Wards 7/9/32; *LP Hen. VIII*, xxi(2), g.332–91; xxi(2), p. 167; Hutchins, ii. 662; *CSP Dom.* Add. 1566–79, p. 289; *CSP Ven.* 1555–6, p. 400; *CPR*, 1550–3, pp. 142, 394; 1555–7, p. 102; *VCH Dorset*, ii. 28–9; Bodl. e Museo 17; Guildford Mus. Loseley 1331/2; *HMC Foljambe*, 5. [5] *CPR*, 1554–5, p. 259; Hutchins, ii. 678; PCC 17 Streat.

N.M.F.

STREATE, Francis (*d.* 1607), of St. Clement's, Worcester.

WORCESTER   1571

?s. of Henry Streate, bailiff of Worcester. *m.* (1) Ellen; (2) Margaret; at least 2s. One of his wives was da. of Christopher Dighton I*.

Member of the 48, Worcester 1557–8, of the 24 1558, auditor 1563–4, 1564–5, 1571–2, bailiff 1567–8, 1570–1, 1588–9 or 1589–90, alderman 1568–9, 1571–2; gov. Worcester free school and almshouses by 1582.

Streate owned or rented a number of houses in the city and pasture land nearby called the Pool meadow. Under 19 June 1571 the Worcester chamber order book records:

agreed that Mr. High Bailiff Mr. Streate and Mr. Bullingham, citizens for the last Parliament shall receive for their fees for 58 days in the parliament time and six days to and from the same, amounting in the whole to 64 days and 12*d.* a day for their men, £16.

Judging from his will, which made arrangements for the disposal of a malt-house and two kilns, he was probably a brewer. The will, dated 29 Dec. 1606, was proved 20 Apr. following, and refers to a number of people of his surname without mentioning relationships, though presumably the brothers 'Francis and John Streate the younger' were the testator's sons. Streate asked to be buried in the cathedral graveyard near his late wife Ellen, and appointed his second wife Margaret executrix and residuary legatee.

Nash, *Worcs.* ii. app. cxii.; Worcester Guildhall, audit of city accts. 1540–1600; *Early Education in Worcester* (Worcs. Hist. Soc.), 230–6; *Worcester Charters* (Worcs. Hist. Soc.), 107; PCC 32 Huddleston.

N.M.F.

STRELLEY, Philip (c.1557–1607), of Strelley, Notts.

NOTTINGHAMSHIRE   1593

b. c.1557, 1st s. of Sir Anthony Strelley of Strelley by Joan, da. of Sir George Baynham of Clorewall, Glos. *m.*

Elizabeth, da. of Thomas Garneys of Garnishe, Norf., 1s. *suc.* fa. 1591. Kntd. 1603.[1]

J.p. Notts. from c.1593.

Nothing is known of Strelley's upbringing; probably he followed the family tradition and was trained as a soldier. The lands he inherited were only a fraction of the fifteenth-century Strelley estates, which had largely descended to female heirs, and the property was further encumbered by the debt his famous grandfather, Sir Nicholas, had incurred. The debt had in the course of time been transferred to the Crown, and the family manor of Eccleshall forfeited. In 1604 Strelley petitioned Cecil for the return of the property, promising to pay £100 a year until the debt was cleared, a small favour, he considered, after his father's and his grandfather's long years of service in the wars without preferment.[2]

His diminished inheritance explains Strelley's undistinguished role in county affairs, but he did not lack prominent friends, particularly the earls of Rutland and the Willoughbys of Wollaton, at whose houses he was a welcome guest. His family had long been on friendly terms with the Shrewsburys, but he was not involved in the dispute between the 7th Earl and Sir Thomas Stanhope*, which reached a crisis at the election of 1593, and he may, therefore, have been seen as a suitable candidate to lend an air of respectability to the Earl's proceedings in the election. He was paired with the Earl's brother-in-law Sir Charles Cavendish*, against Stanhope and Thomas Markham*, and they were elected by a ruse. As a county Member Strelley could have served on the subsidy committee, 26 Feb. 1593, and a legal committee, 9 Mar.[3]

Strelley did not sit again. The year before he died he arranged a marriage for his only son Nicholas, with Bridget, Sir Percival Willoughby's daughter. Strelley died intestate on 29 Sept. 1607, and as his son had no issue, the lands ultimately passed to Strelley's brothers according to the entail he had established. Administration of the property was granted to a creditor, John Martine.[4]

[1] *Vis. Notts.* (Harl. Soc. iv), 19–22; *Derbys. Arch. Soc.* xiv. 73 seq.; C142/251/171. [2] *HMC Hatfield*, xvi. 128. [3] *APC*, xxvii. 117; *HMC Rutland*, passim; *HMC Middleton*, passim; Lansd. 85, f. 34; Neale, *Commons*, 66; *Bull. IHR*, xxxiii. 73 seq.; D'Ewes, 474, 496. [4] C142/292/166; *HMC Middleton*, 621; *Yorks. Arch. Soc. rec. ser.* xxvi. 206; PCC admon. act bk. 1608, f. 106.

S.M.T.

STRICKLAND, Thomas (c.1564–1612), of Sizergh, Westmld. and Thornton Bridge, Yorks.[1]

b. c.1564, s. and h. of Walter Strickland* by his 2nd w. *educ.* Trinity Coll. Camb. 1580. *m.* (1) Elizabeth Seymour of Bristol, 1da.; (2) Margaret, da. of Nicholas Curwen*, 4s. 3da. *suc.* fa. 1569. KB 1603.

J.p. and custos rot.[2] Westmld. from c.1584, custos rot, 1592; sheriff, Yorks. 1602; member, council in the north 1603.

Aged about five at his father's death, Strickland was brought up by his mother, who purchased his wardship and marriage from William Cooke*, to whom they had been granted in October 1569. He had special livery of his lands in Westmorland and Yorkshire in 1585, his mother next year releasing to him all her interest in them. As a knight of the shire for Westmorland in 1601 Strickland could have served on committees concerned with the order of business (3 Nov.), monopolies (23 Nov.), strengthening the northern counties (3 Dec.), and regulating local government in the north (14 Dec.).[3]

Though concerned in the administration of his two counties and eventually a member of the council in the north, Strickland spent much of his time in London, reducing the 'plentiful fortune' of his family by his extravagance and gambling. In 1593, when he could have been little more than 30, he was one of those, 'the oldest and most experienced gentlemen of the wardenry' whose advice was sought by the warden, the 10th Lord Scrope, and in 1597 Scrope chose him to advise the deputy-warden, Henry Leigh*.[4] He was made KB on the eve of the King's coronation. He died in 1612.

[1] This biography derives from H. Hornyold, *Gen. Mems. of Strickland of Sizergh* (Kendal, 1928) and the authorities therein cited. [2] E163/14/8. [3] D'Ewes, 624, 649, 665, 685. [4] *Border Pprs.* ii. 400.

B.D.

STRICKLAND, Walter (c.1516–69), of Sizergh, Westmld. and Thornton Bridge, Yorks.[1]

b. c.1516, s. and h. of Sir Walter Strickland of Sizergh by his 2nd w. Katherine, da. and coh. of Ralph Neville of Thornton Bridge. *m.* (1) by Apr. 1537, Agnes; (2) 1561, Alice, da. of Nicholas Tempest of Stanley and Holmside, co. Dur., wid. of Christopher Place of Halnaby, Yorks., 1s. 2da. *suc.* fa. 1528.

J.p. Westmld. from c.1547, Yorks. (N. Riding) from c.1564; hereditary dep. steward, Kendal barony.

Aged 14 at the date of his father's inquisition post mortem in April 1530, and head of a family that had been resident at Sizergh, in the barony of Kendal, for several centuries, Strickland became a ward first of Wolsey, subsequently of Sir Arthur Darcy. On 8 Mar. 1535 he was contracted to marry Margaret, daughter of Sir Stephen Hamerton of Wigglesworth in Yorkshire, but the marriage is not known to have taken place. While still under age he became involved, though only slightly, in the northern rebellion of October 1536 and was pardoned. By an indenture dated 28 Apr. 1537 he was granted livery of his lands and in the following May he was named, though in the event he did not serve, as a juror for the trial of the leading rebels, some of them his kinsmen and neighbours. Soon afterwards, when several local gentlemen were appointed to assist Sir Thomas Wharton, the new deputy warden of the west march, in keeping the peace and administering justice, Strickland among others seems to have been overlooked. At Wharton's request the Duke of Norfolk, then commanding in the north, wrote to Cromwell, 12 July 1537, asking for additional appointments to be made and describing Strickland as 'a very toward young man, and a great friend of Wharton's', able to serve 'with more men than any three in the book'. Strickland duly received his patent, apparently antedated to 28 June to accord with the others, and an annual payment of £10. He was with Wharton at Carlisle in 1542 preparing to meet the threatened Scotch invasion, and he commanded 200 Kendal archers at Solway Moss, where the Scots were routed. Describing the fight in a letter to the Earl of Hertford, Wharton referred to Strickland as his 'nigh cousin'. In 1543, when the Westmorland gentlemen were again called out for border service, Strickland's contingent of 200 horse, drawn from among his household servants and tenants, was far larger than any other gentleman could muster. More of his 'exploits done upon the Scots' were reported by Wharton in July 1544.

Subsequent references to Strickland are infrequent and of a different nature. His name follows that of the Earl of Cumberland in the commission of 1552–3 for the seizure of church goods in Westmorland and comes first in the commission for Carlisle; in both he is wrongly described as 'Sir'. In June 1563 he was one of the commissioners who investigated the military preparedness of Carlisle, and in 1564 he was favourably reported on as a justice of Westmorland and the North Riding who was 'of good religion'.[2] In his later years he made many additions and improvements to Sizergh Hall and began the decoration which his widow and son completed. Becoming one of the knights of the shire in 1563, he was licensed to depart on 7 Dec. 1566, 'diseased with the gout'.[3] He died at Sizergh 8 Apr. 1569, leaving legacies to his two daughters and all his property to his wife and after her to his brother-in-law Thomas Tempest and cousin Thomas Strickland in trust for his son Thomas*.

[1] This biography derives from H. Hornyold, *Gen. Mems. of Strickland of Sizergh* (Kendal, 1928) and the authorities therein cited. [2] For other local commissions to which he was appointed see *CPR*, 1560–3, 1563–6, 1566–9. [3] *CJ*, i. 79.

B.D./E.L.C.M.

STRICKLAND, William (*d*.1598), of Boynton, nr. Bridlington, Yorks.

SCARBOROUGH   1559, 1563, 1571, 1584

s. of Roger Strickland of Marske by his w. Mary Appleton. *m.* Elizabeth, da. of Sir Walter Strickland of Sizergh, Westmld., 2s. 3da.

J.p. Yorks (E. Riding) from c.1559, commr. to inquire into offences against the Act of Uniformity, province of York 1559, to appoint soldiers, Yorks. (E. Riding) 1572.[1]

The founder of the Stricklands of Boynton, acquired in 1549, was little in evidence before Elizabeth's reign, his puritanism, the basis of his later fame, explaining his early obscurity. On the new Queen's accession he took his place in the county, and served in four Parliaments for his local borough.

Classified as a favourer of religion in 1564, Strickland made his religious sympathies clear in Parliament. Nothing is reported of him in the 1559 House of Commons, nor in the first session of the next, but it was probably he, rather than his brother-in-law Walter Strickland, who sat on the succession committee, 31 Oct. 1566. That his reputation as a parliamentarian was as great then as it was later is implied in the lampoonist's description of him in 1566 as 'Strickland the stinger'; and his position as a leader of the puritan group in the 1571 Parliament suggests that he may have had a similar reputation in the previous assembly. Described in 1571 by the anonymous diarist as a 'grave and ancient man of great zeal', Strickland had been chosen by the puritans to open their campaign, which he did with a long speech on 6 Apr., in which he linked 'God's goodness' with the Queen's 'gracious disposition' and moved that his fellow-puritan, Thomas Norton*, should be allowed to produce before the House the *Reformatio Legum*. Two days later he and Norton employed the same tactics with the six 'alphabetical' bills of religion. Later Strickland introduced his own bill for the reformation of the Prayer Book, the crux of the puritan programme. For this he was summoned before the Council and sequestered from the House. But he was not arrested, as was carefully explained to the House, and he soon returned, appropriately enough, just at the moment when the committee was being formed to consider the bill for church attendance. By urgent demand of the House he was put on to the committee (21 Apr.). He was also on the conference with the Lords which considered the bill against priests disguising themselves as servants (1 May). Strickland also served on committees concerned with navigation (8, 25 May) and tillage (25 May). He did not sit in 1572. In 1584 he was appointed to committees on the Sabbath Day (27 Nov.), fraudulent conveyances (15 Feb. 1585), marriage licences (26 Feb.), the continuation of statutes (6, 11 Mar.) and the reform of ecclesiastical courts (22 Mar.). He is recorded as speaking only once, on the bill to set a minimum age of 24 for ministers. To the demand 'where will you have sufficient number to supply?', he replied 'You may have a good many out of the inns of court'.[2]

Strickland's last years were occupied with his estates, to which he added several manors, including Wintringham, near Malton. On his death in 1598 he held five manors, and property in Bridlington, Huttons Ambo and Woburn. His eldest son, Walter, who married Peter Wentworth's* daughter Frances, succeeded to the estate.[3]

[1] *Vis. Yorks.* ed. Foster, 166; Lansd. 13, f. 127; *CPR, 1563–6*, p. 21. [2] *Yorks. Fines* (Yorks. Arch. Soc. rec. ser. ii), 145; *CPR, 1560–3*, pp. 171, 321; *CSP Dom.* 1547–80, p. 406; *HMC Rutland*, i. 75, 76; *Cam. Misc.* ix(3), p. 71; Neale, *Commons*, 283; Trinity, Dublin, anon. jnl. ff. 5v–6, 7, 10, 12v, 21, 24v; Strype, *Annals*, ii(1), 93 seq.; D'Ewes, 127, 156, 157, 158, 159, 161, 166, 168, 176, 179, 180, 181, 186, 188, 189, 333, 349, 361, 364, 365, 371; Lansd. 43, anon. jnl. f. 164; *CJ*, i. 83, 85, 86, 87, 88, 91, 92, 93. [3] *Yorks. Fines* (Yorks. Arch. Soc. rec. ser. viii), 12, 112, 204; C142/273/84.

B.D.

STRINGER, Robert (*b.* c.1532), of Derby.

DERBY   1571, 1572, 1593, 1597[1]

b. c.1532, ?s. of George Stringer† or of Richard Stringer, bailiff of Derby.

Bailiff, Derby 1560–1, 1571–2, 1582–3, 1591–2, 1599–1600.

Stringer, a vintner, was descended from a family of tradesmen established in Derby since at least the reign of Edward IV. He was appointed to a committee on leatherworkers, 18 Feb. 1576, and to one on maltsters, 12 Jan. 1598. As one of the Derby burgesses he may have served on the monopolies committee, 10 Nov. 1597, and a committee concerning spinners and weavers appointed the same day. He may have been the Robert Stringer who, 'about December 1592' was one of those employed by the 7th Earl of Shrewsbury, to go to court to complain about Sir Thomas Stanhope's weir. In the same year he was a witness in a court of Exchequer inquiry into a local land dispute. The date of his death has not been found. If he is the man who appears on a list of Derby residents in 1611, he would have been about 80 at that date. Thomas Stringer, probably a relative, was bailiff in 1617.[2]

[1] Folger V. b. 298. [2] J. C. Cox, *Churches of Derbys.* iv. 78; W. Hutton, *Hist. Derby*, 80–2; I. H. Jeayes, *Derbys. Charters*, 122, 123; R. Simpson, *Coll. Fragments Illus. Hist. Derbys.* 94, 378, 379; C2.Eliz. S15/13; *CJ*, i. 106; D'Ewes, 555, 578; St. Ch. 5/S19/34; *Derbys. Arch. Jnl.* xxxvi. 90–6.

M.R.P.

STRODE, George (aft. 1563–1648), of the Middle Temple, London and Wimborne Minster, Dorset.

WAREHAM   1593

b. aft. 1563, 5th but 3rd surv. s. of John Strode* of Parnham, Dorset by his 1st w. Katherine, da. of Gregory Cromwell†, 1st Baron Cromwell. *educ.* New Inn; M. Temple 1585, called 1589. *m.* Mary, da. of William Fleet of Chatham, Kent, 2s. 1da.

Strode was a lawyer who spent most of his adult life at the Middle Temple, where, in 1620 he was 'one of the most ancient masters of the outer bar'. His one

appearance in Parliament must have been owed to his relatives, the Rogers family, patrons at Wareham. Strode was buried at Hampreston 11 Mar. 1648.

Hutchins, *Dorset*, ii. 130–1; I.o.W. RO, Oglander mss; *M.T. Recs.* i. 280, 311, 345; ii. 651; *Dorset Protestation Returns*, ed. Fry, 125; Soc. Gen. Hampreston par. reg.

J.P.F./P.W.H.

STRODE, John (1524–81), of Parnham, Dorset.[1]

DORSET   1572

b. 1524, 1st s. of Robert Strode of Parnham by Elizabeth, da. of Reginald Hody. *m.* (1) Katherine, da. of Gregory Cromwell†, 1st Baron Cromwell, 6s. inc. George*; (2) Margaret, da. and h. of Christopher (or Christian) Hadley of Withycombe, Som., wid. of Thomas Luttrell*, 1s. 5da. *suc.* fa. 1559.

J.p. Dorset from c.1575, capt. of musters by 1560, commr. concealed lands, sheriff 1572–3.

Strode served once as knight of the shire without leaving any mark on the known surviving records. During the later years of his life his name occurs in various connexions: at Lyme Regis investigating taverns and grain supplies; at Bridport entertaining the 2nd Earl of Bedford; staying at Marshwood with Sir Amias Paulet*, the lord of the manor; investigating horse theft; and, in 1578, investigating at the request of the Privy Council the causes of the dispute between Sir Henry Ashley* and Henry Howard. The Privy Council praised him for his 'great travail' in 1580, when he and others had been examining the recusant, Lady Tregonwell. Strode died 2 Sept. 1581, leaving £1,400 in money to his children, and appointing Henry Coker overseer. His eldest son Robert, aged about 22, was executor and residuary legatee.[2]

[1] This biography is based upon the Roberts thesis. [2] Hutchins, *Dorset*, ii. 130–1; *Vis. Dorset* (Harl. Soc. xx), 88–9; H. C. Maxwell-Lyte, *Hist. Dunster*, i. 171–2; *CSP Dom.* 1547–80, p. 67; SP12/13/5; Lyme Regis recs. fugitive pieces 17, 21; 1578 town accts.; St. Ch. 5/H32/4; *Bridport recs.* 64; *Stradling Corresp.* 183–4; *APC*, x. 258; xii. 59, 131; PCC 33 Darcy; C142/193/67.

P.W.H.

STRODE, Richard (1528–81), of Newnham in Plympton St. Mary, Devon.

PLYMPTON ERLE   1553 (Mar.), 1559

b. 22 May 1528, 1st s. of William Strode of Newnham by Elizabeth, da. and h. of Philip Courtenay of Molland; bro. of William Strode I*. *m.* 11 Nov. 1560, Frances (*d.* 7 Feb. 1562), da. of Gregory Cromwell†, 1st Baron Cromwell, 1s. William Strode II*. *suc.* fa. 5 May 1579.

Escheator, Devon and Cornw. 1565–6.

The Strodes were an old-established and wealthy stannary family seated near Plympton Erle, where they were well able to secure their own return to Parliament.

Strode was also connected with the 2nd Earl of Bedford, his sister Agnes having married Bedford's agent Edward Yarde*. In 1596 Strode and his father were rated for the subsidy at £30 in lands. Strode died 5 Aug. 1581, only two years after his father, leaving landed property worth over £60 p.a. to his son and heir William, aged 19. Strode's will was proved 9 Sept. that year.

Burke, *LG* (1939), 2173; *Vis. Eng. and Wales Notes*, xii. 121; Vivian, *Vis. Devon* (Harl. Soc. vi), 278; *Vis. Devon*, ed. Colby, 196; *CPR, Vis. Devon*, 251, 706–7, 718–19, 830; *Vis. Devon* (Harl. Soc. vi), 278; *Vis. Devon*, ed. Colby, 196; *CPR*, 1563–6, p. 492; Roberts thesis; Foxe, *Acts and Mons.* (1838), v. 18; *HMC Hatfield*, xviii. 297; C142/95/20, 192/12; C2 Eliz. 516/20; NRA 4154, p. 128.

N.M.F.

STRODE, William I (*d.*1605), of Carswell, Devon.

PLYMPTON ERLE	1572

3rd s. of William Strode of Newnham and bro. of Richard.* *educ.* prob. I. Temple. *m.* Joan, da. of John Darte* of Barnstaple, 3s. 5da.

  J.p. Devon from c.1559.

Strode's family had a natural parliamentary interest at Plympton. As he was a younger son, little information has survived about Strode himself. He made his will 17 Aug. 1603, and in 1605 administration was granted to his widow during the minority of his heir and residuary legatee, Adam. The will, which was finally proved in 1624, mentions also sons named Philip and Sampson, five daughters, Lewis Darte his brother-in-law, and land he had obtained from George Carey* of Cockington.

Vivian, *Vis. Devon*, 251, 718, 733; *Cal. I.T. Recs.* i. 296 n; PCC 40 Hayes.

P.W.H.

STRODE, William II (1562–1637), of Newnham, nr. Plympton, Devon.[1]

DEVON	1597
PLYMPTON ERLE	1601, 1604
PLYMOUTH	1614
PLYMPTON ERLE	1621
DEVON	1624
PLYMPTON ERLE	1625

b. 1562, 1st s. of Richard Strode* of Newnham by Frances, da. of Gregory Cromwell[†]. *educ.* I. Temple 1580. *m.* (1) 1581, Mary (*d.*1618), da. of Thomas Southcote* of Bovey Tracey, 3s. 7da.; (2) 1624, Dunes (*d.*1635), da. of Stephen Vosper, *s.p. suc.* fa. 1581. Kntd. 1598.

  J.p. Devon from c.1592, q. from 1601, sheriff 1593–4; surveyor of house and castle of Templeton, Devon for life 1598, dep. lt. 1599; surveyor, Devon for life 1606.[2]

Strode, held in 'great honour, wealth and esteem', was 'richly and fairly seated' at Newnham, near the parliamentary borough of Plympton Erle, for which he

was so frequently returned. The family tin-mining interests were at first handled by his uncle, Philip, but as soon as these came into Strode's own hands, in 1593, his desire to enlarge his industrial facilities led to a brush with the Plymouth town planners. Strode's friend Francis Drake* reported that 'Mr. Sparke, the counsel for the town, has done as much [on the town's behalf] as could possibly be done, for he has not only stood in answer of the cause at the Council board, but he also laboured all the chief lords apart'. However, Mr. Sparke laboured in vain, for, 'upon examination of the matter, the lords said they saw no great reason to prohibit him to build upon his own land', and, after inquiry, sanctioned the project, appointing commissioners, including Drake, Richard Champernown*, Edward Seymour I*, George Carey* and Sir John Gilbert to see that Strode was given a free run. Though encouraged by other friends, including Edward Drew*, Michael Hickes* and (Sir) Walter Ralegh*, the last calling Strode his 'especial friend and kinsman', it seems that, in the end, Drake dissuaded him from the project, and instead gardens were laid out on the land in question. Another of Strode's friends was Ralegh's servant, Christopher Harris*, with whom he superintended the works on Plymouth fort in 1595, the two men being executors of Drake's will. At the time of the Armada Strode was appointed a colonel of the stannary of Plympton, commanding 100 men. In 1595 he was to lead his men to the defence of Plymouth in case of necessity. His relations with Plymouth do not seem to have suffered as a result of the tin-mine controversy, for the borough gave him several commissions, and £20 for 'assisting the town withstanding the patent for packing and salting of fish and for other things'.[3]

  Chosen as senior knight of the shire in the Parliament of 1597, Strode is not mentioned by name in the journals of the House, but as a county Member for Devon he may have served on the committees to consider enclosures (5 Nov.), the poor law (5, 22 Nov.), armour and weapons (8 Nov.), penal laws (8 Nov.), monopolies (10 Nov.), the subsidy (15 Nov.) and Devon cloth-making (8 Dec.). In the Parliament of 1601 he was on committees for the penal laws (2 Nov.) and the order of business (3 Nov.). He continued to sit in the Commons throughout the first quarter of the seventeenth century, and died in 1637, believing that all his sins would be washed away by Christ's most precious blood, and asking to be buried 'where my most loving and religious wives are buried'. He was on bad terms with his eldest son Sir Richard[†], and the will was proved 21 Feb. 1638 by his second son William[†], one of the five Members whom Charles I tried to arrest.[4]

[1] This biography is based upon the Roberts thesis. [2] Vivian, *Vis. Devon*, 718–19; *HMC 15th Rep. VII*, 6, 13, 42. [3] Lady Elliot-Drake, *Fam. and Heirs of Sir Francis Drake*, i. 68 n; Plymouth stannary docs.; *Plymouth Recs.* ed. Worth, 80, 151–2, 197–8, 214; Lansd. 76, f. 46; 78, f. 22; E. Edwards, *Life of Ralegh*, ii. 106; *CSP Dom.*

1595-7, pp. 76, 81; *APC*, xxv. 92, 227; PCC 1 Drake; *HMC 15th Rep.*
VII, 6, 13, 42; *HMC 9th Rep.* 265. [4] D'Ewes, 552, 553, 555, 557, 561,
569, 623, 624; PCC 18 Lee.

P.W.H.

STUBBE, John (c.1543–90), of Thelveton, Norf.

GREAT YARMOUTH   1589

b. c.1543, 1st s. of John Stubbe of Buxton, Norf. *educ.*
Trinity Coll. Camb. 1555 (impubes), BA 1561; L. Inn
1562, called 1572. *m.* Anne, wid. of Christopher
Sharnborne of Sharnborne, Norf., 2s. *suc.* fa. 1562.[1]
Under-steward, Great Yarmouth 1585–9.[2]

Stubbe was in residence at Trinity College, Cambridge,
when it was one of the most important centres of
Elizabethan puritanism. A great contemporary was
Thomas Cartwright, who later married his sister; and two
of his closest friends at the college were Michael Hickes*
and Vincent Skinner*, who were both strong protestants.
In fact there is evidence for the existence of a closely knit
puritan circle at Trinity College and later at Lincoln's Inn,
where Stubbe, Hickes and Skinner were students together
after they had completed their university education.[3]

This puritan circle may have produced, as a combined
literary effort, that brilliant lampoon of Archbishop
Parker's *De Antiquitate Britannicae Ecclesiae* which appeared
anonymously in 1574 under the title, *The Life of the 70th
Archbishop of Canterbury ... Englished.* This tract has usually
been attributed to Stubbe alone, but it seems at least as
likely that he wrote it in collaboration with friends. It is
possible too that these friends had a hand in a more
famous literary venture for which Stubbe received the
credit and bore the pain. That was the notorious *Gaping
Gulf*, published in 1579, a bitter attack on the proposed
Alençon marriage. The pamphlet reflected the views of an
influential group of English statesmen headed by the Earl
of Leicester and Walsingham who were almost certainly
behind the publication, in December 1579, of Edmund
Spenser's *Shepheardes Calender*, an allegory containing a
veiled attack on the French marriage. The *Gaping Gulf*
should probably be regarded as part of the propaganda of
the Leicester House circle.

Stubbe wrote of the Queen in terms of the greatest
loyalty and affection, but affirmed that the Duke of
Alençon was rotten with debauchery, 'the old serpent
himself in the form of a man, come a second time to
seduce the English Eve and ruin the English paradise'. He
freely discussed questions of policy and roused the Queen's
special resentment by suggesting that she was too old to
marry and bear children. The pamphlet was widely read.
On 27 Sept. 1579 a royal proclamation was issued
prohibiting its further circulation, and on 13 Oct. Stubbe
was tried at Westminster with his publisher and printer on
a charge of disseminating seditious writings. It is ironic
that the Act under which he was arraigned was one of

1554–5, designed to protect Philip of Spain from libellous
attacks, the court holding that the statute was equally
applicable to the Queen's suitor. He and his two
companions were sentenced to have their right hands cut
off.

Stubbe wrote to the Queen immediately after the trial.
It was a pathetic letter in which he stated that he was the
'sorrowfullest man in the world' to have angered her,
protested that his 'poor heart never conceived malicious
thought or wicked purpose', implored 'some better
conceiving' of his 'single-hearted allegiance', and asked
that his hand might be spared. Elizabeth refused his plea,
although she did pardon Singleton, the printer. The
sentence on Stubbe and his publisher, Page, was carried
out on 3 Nov. They were brought from the Tower to a
scaffold set up in the market-place at Westminster and
from it Stubbe addressed the onlookers. 'Pray with me', he
asked,

> that God will strengthen me to endure and abide the
> pain that I am to suffer and [will] grant me this grace:
> that the loss of my hand do not withdraw any part of my
> duty and affection towards her Majesty.

It was a brave speech. Afterwards his right hand was cut
off 'with a cleaver driven through the wrist by the force of
a mallet'. His agony did not prevent him from taking off
his hat with his left hand and crying in a loud voice, 'God
save the Queen'. He then swooned and had to be carried
back to the Tower. Camden, who was present, affirmed
that the multitude standing about was 'deeply silent'
during the proceedings.[4]

The sentence on Stubbe, who always thereafter signed
himself 'scaeva', produced echoes in Parliament. In 1581
the government introduced in the Lords an 'Act against
seditious words uttered against the Queen's most excellent
Majesty'. It was designed as an anti-Catholic measure, but
was worded as an extension of the 1554–5 Act under
which Stubbe had suffered. This was now declared to be
insufficient in its punishments. The bill passed the Lords,
but the Commons seem to have realised that it might
prove dangerous to puritans as well as recusants and
moderated its terms in such a way as to safeguard
protestant zealots. It is difficult to believe that Stubbe's fate
was not in the forefront of Members' minds during the
proceedings.[5]

The treatment meted out to Stubbe did not deter him
from making use of his literary abilities in the pamphlet
war against the Catholic propagandists. In 1583 Cecil
produced his tract *The Execution of Justice in England*, the
official apology for Elizabeth's treatment of Catholic
missionaries. The following year William Allen replied.
His *Modest Defence of the English Catholics* was generally agreed
to be a most able piece of work and Stubbe was
commisioned to write an answer. He sent his manuscript
to Cecil in 1587. That is the last we hear of it.[6]

While Stubbe was writing his reply to Allen he was also acting as confidential servant to Peregrine Bertie, Lord Willoughby De Eresby. He had entered his service by 1585 and between the winter of that year and the summer of 1588 spent much of his time at Willoughby's house in London. His master was engaged, during these years, in diplomatic and military missions abroad and Stubbe kept him well supplied with news from London. In 1587 and 1588 he was Willoughby's channel of communication with Burghley and Walsingham. In the middle of 1588, when Lady Willoughby decided to visit her husband in Holland, Stubbe accompanied her, returning in the autumn when Willoughby recommended him for the office of auditor and controller of the checks, a post which he failed to obtain.[7]

Stubbe spent some of his time during the 1580s in Norfolk, his home county. In 1585 he was elected under-steward of Great Yarmouth, an office which involved him in judicial duties in the town. On 1 Oct. of the same year he was sworn a freeman of the borough. In 1586 or 1587 the Earl of Leicester, high steward of Great Yarmouth, tried to obtain the under-stewardship for one of his protégés, Jeffrey Whitney. The bailiffs of the town seem, however, to have resented this attempt to interfere with their rights of election, and Stubbe retained the office until 1589, the year he represented the town in Parliament. He was appointed to committees on the subsidy (11 Feb.), Hartlepool pier (28 Feb.) and Lincoln (11 Mar.); and he spoke on a matter of privilege (21 Feb.). During the last days of the session it is clear that he tried to stop the bishops' proceeding against puritan ministers, though the details are obscure. Stubbe may have initiated the discussion in the House and had a 'supplication' to the Queen drawn up in readiness. The House seems to have appointed a committee to consider the matter and, as a result, the petition was modified. There was probably no time to present this second petition before the close of the session.

In Stubbe's original version he spoke with his usual frankness, castigating non-resident and unlearned ministers, and praising puritan pastors, whom he described as being of 'better conscience and more profitable learning'. He then launched into a bitter attack on the ex officio oath and on the bishops, whom he discussed in the most slighting terms. He concluded with a paean of praise for the Queen herself, wishing that she might continue to reign for many years

in health of your person, in honour of your name, in joy of your heart, and in all flourishing happiness ... We shall ... employ the services of our goods, bodies, lives and all our means whatsoever [on your behalf] ... [both] in regard to our natural allegiance and for the infinite graces which we enjoy by you ... [May] God ... bless your Majesty and curse all those that say not thereto 'Amen'.

It was a strange mixture of loyalty and defiance.[8]

Stubbe was clearly a man of striking personality and able to inspire devotion in his friends. Michael Hickes retained affection and respect for him in later years and kept in touch with him until shortly before his death, which took place the year after he sat in Parliament.

On 25 Sept. 1589, when he drew up his will, he stated that he was

driven to do this ... upon my sudden journey into France with [Lord Willoughby De Eresby], the most honourable general of the forces of her Majesty, to aid the most Christian King against his rebels.

He bequeathed to his mother his 'greatest bible' and a ring of gold engraved with the word 'mortal'; left all the rest of his movable possessions to his wife Anne; and appointed Lord Willoughby as a supervisor. He also mentioned his 'good cousin' Sampson Lennard* and his 'dearly beloved and worthily trusted' friend Sir Robert Jermyn*.

The fact that the will was drawn up in haste may explain the absence of a pious preamble, but Stubbe did not neglect to pay a last tribute to the Queen. 'I protest and contest', he stated,

that I lived and do die the true man and most loyal subject of her most excellent Majesty Elizabeth, by God's singular grace our happy Queen, beseeching her most merciful and royal nature that after my death my most true and well-deserving wife, mine executrix, may find that grace and favour in her Majesty's eyes which, though I could not deserve, I yet would have esteemed for a great blessing on earth.

These words serve as an appropriate epitaph to Stubbe's career. Throughout his life he had hoped to retain the Queen's favour while opposing her politics. In the face of death he sought indulgence for his wife, who was one of the most notable of Elizabethan Brownists. His sense of loyalty was matched only by his lack of realism.

He died in France and was buried, with military honours, on the seashore near the town of Havre de Grace. His will was proved 27 June 1590.[9]

[1] PCC 40 Drury; DNB; Al. Cant. i(4), p. 178; Norf. Rec. Soc. Pubs. xxi. 162. [2] C. J. Palmer, Yarmouth, 339; Cal. Yarmouth Freemen, 1429–1800, p. 43. [3] Lansd. 10, f. 73; 12, f. 117. [4] Collinson thesis, 145; Neale, Parlts. i. 373; DNB; C. Read, Burghley, 217; E. M. Tenison, Eliz. England, iii. 176–7; Camden, Elizabeth (4th ed., 1688), p. 270; E. Rosenberg, Leicester, Patron of Letters, 339; P. E. McLane, Spenser's Shepheardes Calender, 19, 22, 24–5, 30, 50, 74, 288. [5] Neale, Parlts. i. 393–7. [6] Tudor Govt. and Soc. 37–8. [7] HMC Ancaster, 16, 18, 21, 25, 31–3, 293, 478; CSP For. 1587, p. 453; 1588 (Jan.–June), p. 165; 1588 (July–Dec.), pp. 68, 89, 134, 148, 150. [8] Lansd. 88, f. 147; Cal. Yarmouth Freemen, 1429–1800, p. 43; Yarmouth ass. bk. 1579–98, 155, 158; Palmer, 105–6, 336, 339; Neale, Commons, 179–80; D'Ewes, 431, 436, 440, 444; Neale, Parlts. ii. 234–8; Add. 48101, ff. 136–7; Rosenberg, 310–11. [9] Lansd. 12, ff. 117, 217; 23, f. 179; 36, ff. 212–13; 61, f. 170; 107, ff. 168, 170; PCC 40 Drury; Cartwrightiana, ed. Peel and Carlson, 58; DNB; A. F. S. Pearson, Thomas Cartwright and Elizabethan Puritanism, 306; Ath. Cant. ii. 112.

A.G.R.S.

STUBBE, Richard (*d*.1619), of Sedgeford, Norf.

CASTLE RISING   1589

> *m.* bef. 1586, Anne, da. and h. of Richard Gooding of Boston, Lincs., wid. of John Lestrange of Sedgeford, 2da.

Nothing has been discovered about the parentage and early life of this Member. Though he may have inherited some property, and certainly acquired Sedgeford and other manors through marriage, it is clear that he obtained the bulk of his considerable estates through his law practice. He acted as attorney for John Peyton I* in 1584, and from about 1580 to 1585 he was general surveyor and solicitor to Sir William Heydon, one of Norfolk's leading gentlemen: it is probable that he acted in similar capacities to members of the Lestrange family. Though Stubbe was on a number of commissions, together with Sir William Heydon, in the period 1558–90, he never attained the commission of the peace, in spite of his wealth and high connexions. His return for Castle Rising in 1589 was perhaps due to the influence of the Lestranges. By a number of settlements and by his will, made on 2 May 1617, Stubbe devised all his land to his two daughters, married respectively to Sir William Yelverton and Sir Hamon Lestrange, and to their children. He made bequests to kinsmen and servants and for the upkeep of almshouses at Sedgeford. He died 24 Nov. 1619.

G. Carthew, *Hundred of Launditch*, i. 217; ii. 438–9, 457, 478; *Vis. Norf.* (Harl. Soc. xxxii), 273–4; W. Rye, *Norf. Fams.* 859; C142/387/114; Blomefield, *Norf.* viii. 455; C.2. Eliz./H10/35; *APC*, xv. 386; xvi. 112; xvii. 244; xix. 178; PCC 3 Soame.

R.V.

STUBBS, William (*d.* aft. 1610), of Latton, Essex, later of Congleton, Cheshire.

YARMOUTH I.o.W.   1584

> Bailiff, Congleton manor 1574–99; mayor, Congleton 1595–6; bailiff of the south parts of the duchy of Lancaster 1588–99, of the Savoy 1588–91.

Stubbs spent the greater part of his life in the service of the duchy of Lancaster. In 1587 he was employed surveying manors in Wiltshire for the then chancellor, Sir Francis Walsingham, and he was one of those employed to search, successfully, for Walsingham's will in 1590. Between 1590 and 1596 he moved from Latton to Congleton, where he was the duchy of Lancaster's bailiff, and he continued to reside there after resigning that office to Bartholomew Stubbs in 1599. He presented to the nearby parish of Gawsworth in 1596 and the last reference found to him shows him still residing at Congleton in March 1610. Stubbs's surname appears frequently in the parish registers of Gawsworth, and it is therefore likely that he originated from this part of Cheshire. His return as one of the first two MPs for Yarmouth in 1584 was no

doubt due to Sir George Carey*, captain of the Isle of Wight, at whose request the borough was enfranchised, but what the connexion was between them is unknown.

Somerville, *Duchy*, i. 448; Harl. 844, f. 28; Earwaker, *East Cheshire*, ii. 589, 593; *CSP Dom.* 1581–90, p. 428; *Wills from Doctors' Commons* (Cam. Soc. lxxxiii), 71.

A.M.M.

STUMPE, John (c.1525–1600), of Malmesbury, Wilts.

MALMESBURY   1584

> *b.* c.1525, 2nd s. of William Stumpe† of Malmesbury by Joyce, da. of James Berkeley of Bradley, Glos. *m.* (1) c.1552, da. of Matthew King† of Malmesbury, 3s.; (2) c.1566, Christian, da. of William Chaffin of Bulford, wid. of Thomas Dowse of Collingbourne Ducis, *s.p.*[1]
> Bailiff and collector of Malmesbury from c.1563.[2]

Stumpe was probably born about the time that his father migrated from Gloucestershire to Malmesbury, and he grew up with the celebrated cloth manufactory there. His elder brother, Sir James†, appears early to have taken the mantle of gentility, whereas John followed his father in the business. William Stumpe died in July 1552, having bequeathed to John, by his will of October 1550, the leases of three houses, ten broad looms and £500 in cash; and when, by a codicil added on the day of his death, he left his remaining looms to the infant son of his second marriage, their employment may well have devolved upon the grown-up brother. It was perhaps upon his father's death that John entered upon his first marriage, to a daughter of Matthew King, who was to succeed William Stumpe as Malmesbury's leading clothier; and the match sounds even more of a business affair than most. Stumpe's wife was to bear him three sons – the second and third of whom were probably twins – between 1555 and 1559 before her death early in Elizabeth's reign.[3]

The new Queen's accession may well have brought relief to John Stumpe by dispelling not only the cloud of royal disfavour which had hung over secularisers of monastic property but also the more serious suspicion of involvement in treasonable activities. In April 1554 a servant of his brother's had been summoned before the Council and he himself mentioned during the examination of a suspect at about the same time. Sir James died in July 1563. Although his daughter Elizabeth and her husband Henry Knyvet* were to inherit the bulk of the patrimony (not surprisingly at the cost of a disputed will), they betook themselves to Charlton and left John as the family's figurehead in Malmesbury. They also conveyed or leased to him some of their property there, and it was the Abbey House, which survives largely as he or his son rebuilt it, that he made his home at least until the early 1590s. To his urban estate Stumpe added some country leases, one of tithes in Corston and Rodbourne formerly belonging to the abbey, another of the ex-priory of Longbridge, near Berkeley, in his father's native county; he also acquired from Matthew King the manor of Througham which had once been his father's, but this he soon parted with.[4]

It was during these years that there came to light a transaction which might have compromised Stumpe. In 1564 it transpired that the Exchequer had been supplied with an inquisition, purporting to have been taken at Malmesbury in November 1561, before him and Edward Pleydell, by which the chantry of West Hatch had been valued at 13s. 4d. a year. The inquisition was a forgery, and since the chantry had been leased since 1545 to the Snells the purpose of its manufacture was doubtless to conceal the under-assessment by which the lessees had long benefited. A fresh inquisition was held in September 1564, before the sheriff, John Erneley*, at which the true value of £11 11s. and 1 lb. of pepper a year was established, and Nicholas Snell* escaped lightly with no more than a demand for payment of arrears, under a recognizance of £500. There is nothing to suggest that Stumpe was other than an innocent victim of the conspiracy.[5]

In September 1566 Stumpe and nine other burgesses of Malmesbury took a lease of all lands in Malmesbury and Westport formerly belonging to the abbey which still remained to the Crown, at an annual rent of £58. At the same time they leased certain other properties, and because the buildings in question stood in need of repairs they offered to make these at their own costs; Stumpe himself further offered to surrender his patent (and fee of £4 a year) as bailiff and to discharge that office voluntarily. It was the first of two public-spirited actions on his part. Fourteen years later he acquired partly by gift and partly by purchase, the former hospital of St. John in the borough, which he conveyed to the corporation for 41 marks.[6]

We hear little of John Stumpe during the last 20 years of his life. He was probably the principal mourner of that name at the funeral of his niece Elizabeth Knyvet in 1585. His own wife died in 1595, and he himself on 3 May 1600; it was as 'John Stumpe, gent., the elder' that he was buried on 6 May in the abbey church. He appears to have made no will, but his inquisition, taken on 22 Apr. 1601, shows him to have owned numerous properties in and around Malmesbury. His son and heir James, who was then upwards of 45 years old, died in September 1602, leaving only the third son, Basil, to reach old age.[7]

John Stumpe's standing in Malmesbury, reinforced by his kinship with Sir Henry Knyvet of Charlton, would sufficiently account for his return in 1584, with Knyvet as his fellow-Member; and it is only the existence of his son John which casts any doubt upon the identification. By 1584 this son was a man of 25 and a member of the Inner Temple, to which he had gone after a spell at Oxford with his two brothers and of which he would become an utter-

barrister in 1587. By his marriage to the heiress of a Devon gentleman who had died in 1566 John Stumpe the younger acquired a stepson, Reuben Crane, and four daughters, of whom the first three were born in London between 1588 and 1592, and the fourth at Malmesbury in September 1593. In November 1591 he had taken a long lease of the Abbey House, and the next month acquired the reversion of it. These were the first of a number of transactions by which he acquired a considerable part of the family property in the town, and which seem to reflect a decision to invest the yield of his legal practice and lucrative marriage in an establishment there.[8]

The closing years of his short life furnish a couple of interesting sidelights on Stumpe. When engaged by Sir Walter Longe* to advise enclosure rioters on how they should pull down Sir John Danvers's fences, he counselled them to work in pairs and thus evade the charge of rioting which could only be committed by three or more persons acting together. It was an argument which cut no ice in the Star Chamber, which adjudged the affair in 1596 and imprisoned and fined Longe for his incitement. Some years earlier Stumpe had been complained of to the Privy Council by the bishop of Exeter and others for his vexation of the old incumbent of Plymtre rectory, of which Stumpe and his wife held the patronage.[9]

Stumpe died 7 Dec. 1598 and was buried, as 'John Stumpe, gent., the younger of the Abbey', in the abbey church on the following day. He had probably foreseen his end for some months, since in the previous August he had enfeoffed two gentlemen, John Warnford and Francis Bradshaw, in all his Wiltshire property to the use of his wife and children after his own. It was Warnford whom his widow was to marry in July 1601. The three surviving daughters married, two in 1607, the third in 1611.[10]

But for his early death John Stumpe the younger might well have cut a notable figure in Malmesbury and have prolonged his family's representation of the borough in Parliament, especially with Sir Henry Knyvet in continuing control. It is, however, unlikely that he was the man to sit in 1584, since unless there was then a call – of which there is no indication – for his legal acumen, his father's claim in both seniority and standing far outweighed his own.

[1] PCC 26 Powell; *Wilts. N. and Q.* viii. 390; C3/107/49, 3/164/17; *Wilts. Vis. Peds.* (Harl. Soc. cv, cvi), 37. [2] *CPR, 1563–6*, p. 463. [3] *CPR, 1555–7*, p. 146; PCC 26 Powell; G. D. Ramsay, *Wilts. Woollen Industry*; Basil and John Stumpe were both aged 16 when they matriculated at Oxford in 1575, *Al. Ox. 1500–1714*, p. 1440. [4] *APC,* v. 14; *CSP Dom. 1547–80*, p. 82; C3/106/11; *CPR, 1550–3*, p. 259; 1560–3, pp. 330, 357; 1563–6, pp. 129–30, 265; 1566–9, P. 305; *Wilts. N. and Q.* vi. 355; vii. 411, 417; viii. 537. [5] *CPR, 1563–6*, p. 250. [6] *CPR, 1563–6*, pp. 463–4; J. M. Moffatt, *Hist. Malmesbury*, 121–2. [7] *Wilts. N. and Q.* viii. 449, 532; C142/264/135, 272/60, 752/215; PCC 10 Bolein [8] *Cal. I.T. Recs.* i. 324–5, 346, 349, 415, 426; *Al. Ox. 1500–1714*, p. 1440; C142/260/151; *Wilts. N. and Q.* viii. 532. [9] *Wilts. Arch. Mag.* i. 447–8; *APC*, xxiii. 301. [10] C142/260/151, 296/98; *Wilts. N. and Q.* viii. 451–4, 532.

S.T.B.

STUTTEVILLE, Martin (c.1569–1631), of Dalham and Southwood Park, Suff.

ALDEBURGH 1601

b. c.1569, 1st s. of Thomas Stutteville of Dalham by Anne, da. of Nicholas Whitney of Walden, Essex. *educ.* King's Camb. 1585; L. Inn 1587. *m.* (1) Katherine, da. of John Holland; (2) Susan, da. of Thomas Isham of Lamport, Northants., 1s. At least 1 other s., several das. Kntd. 1604; *suc.* fa. 1606.

J.p. Suff., sheriff 1612–13.

As a young man Stutteville is said to have sailed with Drake, but almost all the information about him concerns Suffolk, where he lived as a country gentleman at Dalham. He also had rights in Southwood park, near Hargrave. Most of his property was in the extreme west of the county, and it is not clear how he came to be returned for Aldeburgh. He had been at Cambridge and Lincoln's Inn at the same time as his co-Member Francis Corbett.

After his father's death in 1606 he became active in county government, and his will, drawn up in his own hand on 4 Mar. 1626, describes him as still in 'perfect health of mind and body'. During the last few years of his life he had trouble with his younger son John, who went up to Cambridge about the beginning of Charles I's reign, and was described by his tutor as of little industry. As late as December 1630 father and son were still quarrelling, but Stutteville made no alterations in the generous bequests to John in his will. He died on 13 June 1631, aged 62.

Al. Cant. i(4), p. 181; *Vis. Suff.* ed. Metcalfe, 69, 103; J. Gage, *Hist. Suff. Thingoe Hundred*, 344; J. Peile, *Biog. Reg. of Christ's College*, i. 366; PCC 85 St. John; Wards 7/81/200; C142/479/81

N.M.F.

SUCKLING, John (1569–1627), of London.

DUNWICH	1601
REIGATE	1614
MIDDLESEX	1624
YARMOUTH I.o.W.	1625
NORWICH	1626[1]

b. 1569, 3rd s. of Robert Suckling* by Elizabeth, da. of William Barwick. *educ.* G. Inn 1590. *m.* (1) Martha (*d.*1613), da. of Thomas Cranfield, sis. of Lionel Cranfield, 1st Earl of Middlesex, 1s. 4da.; (2) Jane Reve or Reeve, wid. of Charles Hawkins, *?s.p.* Kntd. Jan. 1616.

Sec. to Lord Buckhurst by 1601; receiver of fines and alienations 1604; master of requests 1620; comptroller of the Household 1622; sec. of state 1622; PC 1625.

Almost the whole of Suckling's political career lies outside the Elizabethan period. His father, a wealthy Norwich merchant who died in 1589, left him most of his extensive property in Norwich and neighbouring districts, as his eldest son Edmund was a clergyman (afterwards dean of Norwich) and the next was a Catholic. John sold

much of this, and did not live for any length of time in Norfolk. His election for Dunwich in 1601 is recorded in the town minute book, where he is described as 'secretary to the right honourable the lord high treasurer of England'. He bought land and advowsons in various parts of the country, including (about 1600) Roos Hall, near Beccles, Suffolk, and was reported as 'paying well for the post' of comptroller of the Household. He died on 27 Mar. 1627. His son John was the poet.[2]

[1] In 1624 he was also returned for Lichfield and Kingston-upon-Hull, and in 1626 for Sandwich. [2] *DNB* (Suckling, Sir John); *HMC Var.* vii. 87; *CSP Dom.* 1603–10, pp. 162, 175, 377; 1619–23, pp. 161, 434; Suckling, *Hist. Suff.* i. 29; Dunwich minute bk. 1595–1619, f. 84.

N.M.F.

SUCKLING, Robert (1520–89), of St. Andrew's, Norwich, Norf.

NORWICH 1571, 1586

b. 1520, 1st s. of Richard Suckling, alderman and baker of Norwich. *m.* (1) 1551, Elizabeth, da. of William Barwick (*d.*1569), 5s. inc. John* 5da.; (2) 1569, Margaret Pettingale (*d.*1576), wid. of William Wingfield, William Barrett and Richard Head, *?s.p.*; (3) 1577, Joan, da. of William Cardinall I* of Bromley, Essex, 3s.

Freeman, Norwich 1548, alderman 1559, sheriff 1564–5, mayor 1572–3, 1582–3.

Suckling was a mercer and merchant adventurer. He purchased in 1562 and rebuilt a large house in Norwich, part of which survives, and he had property at Woodeton and elsewhere in the neighbourhood. In 1571 he took part in discussion with the ecclesiastical commissioners about the jurisdiction over the churches of the Flemish immigrants in the city. His parliamentary wages were 2s. a day in 1571, and 5s. in 1586.

He died in November 1589. An inventory of his property taken in 1590 included four Bibles and a copy of Calvin's *Institutes*. As executors he appointed his wife and his son-in-law, Charles Cardinall, who on 24 Oct. 1590 secured a sentence in their favour against the eldest son Edmund, who had received only £100 in the will.

Vis. Norf. (Harl. Soc. xxxii), 274; H. Le Strange, *Norf. Official Lists*, 108–9; Blomefield, *Norf.* iii. 278; iv. 308–10; P. Millican, *Norwich Freemen*, 100; *Bronnen tot de Geschiedenis van den Handel met Engeland, Schotland en Ierland*, ed. Smit, ii. 805, 807, 812, 850; *Norf. Arch.* xix. 197–8, 208; xx. 158–77; Norwich ass. min. bk. 1551–68, f. 171; *The Walloons and their Church at Norwich* (Hug. Soc. i), pt. 1, pp. 19, 39; Norwich corp. ct. bk. 1569–76, p. 177; 1582–7, p. 704; PCC 70 Drury.

R.V.

SULYARD, Edward (?1540–1610), of Flemings, Essex.

MALDON 1572*

b. ?1540, o.s. of Eustace Sulyard of Flemings by Margaret, da. of Robert Forster of Little Birch, wid. of

Gregory Bassett of Bradwell. *educ.* L. Inn 1559. *m.* by 1564, Ann Edon of Suff., 2s. 2da. *suc.* fa. 1547. Kntd. 1603.

J.p. Essex from c.1579, sheriff 1595–6.

Sulyard belonged to a branch of the Suffolk family which had settled in Essex in the fifteenth century. He succeeded to the manors of Claydon, Flemings, Runwell, and lands in Downham, Ramsden Bellhouse, Rawreth, Rettendon, Wickford and the Hanningfields, all in southeast Essex. He also became, presumably by inheritance, landlord of Lincoln's Inn, for which he was paid an annual rent of £6 13s. 4d., and in 1572 made an associate bencher. In 1580 he sold his rights as landlord for £520, retaining the use of the chambers he then occupied, and the right of free admission for his heirs. It may have been at Lincoln's Inn that his friendship with Michael Hickes* originated, and, through Hickes, with Henry Maynard*, to whose house he was invited in 1605. Though no Catholic, Sulyard was close enough to Sir John Petre* to refer to him in his will as 'very honourable good lord and very kind friend'.

Sulyard was returned for Maldon at a by-election in time for the second session of the 1572 Parliament, probably with the support of Thomas Radcliffe†, 3rd Earl of Sussex, from whom he held the manor of Claydon, though there was a family connexion between Sulyard and the man he replaced, Vincent Harris, Sulyard's daughter having married Harris's nephew. Sulyard's name does not appear in the extant journals of his Parliament, unless he was the 'Mr Edward Gerrard' appointed to the committee on dags and pistols, 17 Feb. 1576. There was no Edward Gerard in the House, and William Gerard I was probably in Ireland. Sulyard died 5 June 1610, having made his will four days previously. His widow and heir Edward were the executors.

C142/86/63; *Trans. Essex Arch. Soc.* n.s. iii. 180–3; ix. 35; xvii. 37; Morant, *Essex*, ii. 42; *Black Bk. L. Inn.* i, passim; Lansd. 43, f. 6; 88, f. 179; 89, ff. 130, 175; A. G. R. Smith, 'Michael Hickes' (London Univ. PhD thesis, 1962), p. 272; *CJ*, i. 106; *Vis. Essex* (Harl. Soc. xiii), 59; PCC 72 Wingfield.

J.H.

SUTTON, Richard (d.1634), of Lincoln's Inn, later of Acton, Mdx.

| NEWPORT I.o.W. | 1586 |
| NEWTOWN I.o.W. | 1589 |

o.s. of John Sutton of Henley-on-Thames, Oxon. by Elizabeth, da. of one Tailor of Edial, Staffs. *educ.* L. Inn 1572, called 1579. *m.* Elizabeth, da. of George Fishe, 1da. Kntd. 1619.

Auditor of the Exchequer from c.1600.

Sutton was a lawyer who acted both for the Earl of Leicester and the Earl of Warwick. He was, however, brought into Parliament by Sir George Carey*, the governor of the Isle of Wight. On 18 Feb. 1589 he was appointed to a committee on the Exchequer (of which he

later became an official), and on 20 Mar. that year, when the amendments to the bill for the relief of George Ognell were under discussion, Sutton informed the House that, as the Earl of Warwick was 'not to be in town', it would not be practicable for his counsel to meet the committee in charge of the bill that afternoon.

In 1603 he appealed to Sir Robert Cecil to be excused from going to Ireland a second time on grounds of ill-health and an estate 'in disorder'. During the reign of James I he served on a number of commissions for the reform of various branches of the administration; it was while he was one of the commissioners 'employed about the matters of the Household and navy' that he was knighted. He remained an auditor until his death, instructing his deputy, in the will he made 26 Feb. 1634, to deliver carefully to his successor the records belonging to his office. Sutton died 26 Apr. 1634 in possession of a London house in the parish of St. Botolph without Aldersgate, a house and lands in Acton, the manor of Sapperton in Lincolnshire, and the manors of North Bersted and Shripney in Sussex. The will was proved by the residuary legatee, his only child Elizabeth, on 21 June of the same year. His charitable bequests were £20 to the poor of St. Botolph, £10 to those of Acton, and £4 towards the restoration of St. Paul's. He had previously made a separate will disposing of the property of his relative, Thomas Sutton, the founder of the Charterhouse, one of whose executors he was.

C142/514/45/; *Vis. London 1568* (Harl. Soc. i), 77; *Black Bk.L. Inn* passim; *APC*, xxxii. 19; 1617–19, pp. 174, 179; Lansd. 64, f. 49; D'Ewes, 434, 449; *CSP Ire.* 1599–1600, pp. 379, 382, 443; 1600, pp. 304–5; *HMC Hatfield*, xii. 614; *CPS Dom.* 1581–90, p. 692; 1591–4, p. 9; 1603–10, p. 470; 1619–23, p. 42; *Chamberlain Letters* ed. McClure, ii. 210; PCC 53 Seager.

A.M.M.

SUTTON, see also DUDLEY alias SUTTON

SWALE, Richard (d.1608), of Rotherhithe, Surr. and Askham Richard, Yorks.

| HIGHAM FERRERS | 1589 |

s. of Thomas Swale of Askham Richard. *educ.* Jesus, Camb. 1566, BA 1568–9, MA 1572, LlD Caius 1587. *m.* Susan, da. of James Rolfe of St. Albans, *s.p.* Kntd. 1603.[1]

Fellow, Jesus, Camb. 1571–6; Caius 1576–89, president 1582, bursar 1585; official of the archdeaconry of Ely 1583; master in Chancery from 1587; chancellor and vicar-gen. Ely diocese 1588-1606; lay rector of Ely and Emneth, Norf. 1588–1606; lay preb. Newbald, York from 1589; member, ct. of delegates from 1589; auditor of causes ct. of audience, see of Canterbury from 1598; officer in ct. of arches by 1600; envoy in mission to Emden 1600; commr. eccles. causes from 1602.

J.p. Isle of Ely from c.1591, Cambs. from c.1592.[2]

Swale doubtless owed his election as fellow and tutor of

Caius to the master, Dr. Thomas Legge, who had been a tutor at his old college, Jesus. He soon became well known as a tutor, a class then rising to prominence, and it is significant that he was named as one of those who refused to read lectures. About 1582 his position was threatened by a faction within the college who differed from his conservative religious views. Burghley agreed to a petition from a number of fellows for a visitation and Swale had himself elected proctor with the assistance of Hatton, who described him as of 'great sufficiency, gravity and good government'. Next, Burghley quashed the election, complaining that Swale and Legge had abused 'my courtesy shewn to them' by maintaining 'covertly in the college a faction against the true religion received'. However, the visitation itself cannot have damaged Swale's chances for he was soon elected president and in the autumn wrote to complain that one Gerard had refused to obey the visitors.[3]

Hatton's appointment as lord chancellor in 1587 provided Swale with the prospect of a new career. His patron's inexperience in the law necessitated the presence of an expert to advise him, and Swale, who was about to qualify for a doctorate in civil law, was, as a long-standing friend, an obvious choice. In May he was appointed a master in Chancery, in July he became a doctor of civil law and in October he entered Doctors' Commons.[4]

As a doctor of civil law Swale practised mostly in the Admiralty and ecclesiastical courts. By 1589 he was beginning to appear on the commissions to which disputed matters in the ecclesiastical courts were referred. His return for Higham Ferrers to the Parliament which met in that year was no doubt promoted by Hatton. No record of any activities by Swale in this Parliament has been found, but as a receiver of petitions in that of 1601 he frequently brought messages and bills from the Lords. The Mr. Swale mentioned as speaking on 8 and 10 Dec. 1601 is Richard Swayne.[5]

After Hatton's death Swale continued to prosper, and he was chosen for the mission to Emden in 1600, the sort of diplomatic work for which civil lawyers were still considered peculiarly suitable. Swale was unwilling to go, and a firm letter from the Privy Council was necessary before he resigned himself to the prospect. He attended the Hampton Court conference in 1604, and was afterwards on a commission to regulate books printed without authority.[6]

Swale died on 30 May 1608, seised of lands in Askham Richard and elsewhere in Yorkshire. His heir male was his distant cousin John Swale, but in a brief nuncupative will he left most of his property to his wife, whom he appointed his executrix. When he asked whether he would have any other executor he replied, 'Who should be but she?'.[7]

[1] DNB; Al. Cant. iv. 189; J. Venn, Biog. Hist. Gonville and Caius, i. 85.
[2] DNB; APC, xvii. 71; CSP Dom. 1591-4, pp. 177, 189; Canterbury,

D. and Ch. Archives, Reg. x, f. 103r; I. J. Churchill, Canterbury Administration, i. 598 n.; HMC Hatfield, x. 5; R. G. Usher, Rise and Fall of the High Commission, 358. [3] J. Heywood and Wright, Camb. Univ. Trans. i. 314-69; Lansd. 33, f. 91; 36, ff. 86, 108; HMC Hatfield, xiii. 204; CSP Dom. 1547-80, p. 304; 1581-90, pp. 70, 72; Sir Harris Nicolas, Life and Times Sir C Hatton, 250, 254, 261. [4] C. Coote, Civilians, 60; Nicolas, 467, 468; J. Caius, Annals of Gonville and Caius, ed. Venn (Cambridge Antiq. Soc. xl), 350; Lansd. 69, f. 195; E. St. John Brooks, Hatton, 336-7, 350. [5] W. Senior, Doctors' Commons and the old Court of Admiralty, 78; APC, xvii. 71; CSP Dom. 1581-90, p. 589; 1591-4, pp. 177, 189, 203; D'Ewes, 600, 614, 672, 678, 684. [6] APC, xx. 199; xxi. 398; xxii. 144, 250, 258, 309; xxiv. 208; xxx. 29, 227; CSP Dom. 1601-3, p. 295; 1603-10, p. 216; HMC Hatfield, x. 129; xvi. 440; Senior, 59; Strype, Whitgift, ii. 496, 504. [7] C142/302/115; PCC 49 Windebanck.

S.M.T.

SWAYNE, Richard (c.1556-c.1636), of Blandford Forum, Dorset.

| WEYMOUTH AND MELCOMBE | |
| REGIS | 1597, 1601 |

b. c.1556, 2nd s. of John Swayne, merchant, of Blandford Forum by Agnes, da of Robert Ryves of Damory Court. educ. New Inn; M. Temple 1573, called 1582. m. Mary, da. of William Grove of Ferne, Wilts., 3da.

Bencher, M. Temple 1592, treasurer 1607; j.p. Dorset from c.1592; recorder, Poole by 1592, Weymouth and Melcombe Regis 1594-c.1615, 1628-36; steward of duchy of Lancaster lands in Dorset for life 1603.[1]

Swayne's services as counsel were retained by both Weymouth and Melcombe (possibly as early as 1584, when he made an unsuccessful attempt to be returned to Parliament there) and Poole (by 1589) before he was appointed to his recorderships. He stood again for Weymouth and Melcombe in the first election after he became recorder and was involved in a disputed return, his Membership not being confirmed until 8 Nov. 1597. His name appears on two committees in this Parliament, on maltsters (12 Jan. 1598) and on tellers and receivers (31 Jan.). He was returned without dispute in 1601, and was appointed to the committee discussing the alteration of the Michaelmas law term (11 Nov.). On 8 Dec., as 'Mr. Swale of the Middle Temple', he spoke for the bill to forbid the export of ordnance. Two days later, again as Mr. 'Swale' (this cannot be Dr. Richard Swale who was not in the House, though his name does appear in the journals as a receiver of petitions) he spoke on the Dover harbour bill:

much money hath been levied – it comes to at least 1,000 marks a year – and the haven never the better. Nay, Mr Speaker, it is grown into a proverb 'If a tax can be once on foot, God shield it continues not as Dover haven'.[2]

As a Dorset lawyer, Swayne was involved in a number of land transactions and charitable trusts. He speculated a little on his own account and with Thomas Freke*. In 1590 the two men bought lands worth £64 p.a. from the

Crown, for nearly £2,000. In the same year Swayne, John Ryves and John Turberville were granted some Dorset tenements because of 'sundry chargeable purchases' they had made from the Queen. He was the 'Mr. Swain' who with one Hussey was complained of by Mary Lady Rogers to Robert Cecil in June 1598, for their proceedings under Cecil's authority as chancellor of the duchy of Lancaster in the matter of Holt Lodge in Wimborne chase. When his own town, Blandford Forum, received its first charter in 1606, Swayne was appointed steward for life and possibly also recorder. He certainly spent his last years there.[3]

Swayne had evidently ceased to be recorder of Weymouth by the time of the new charter, 1615, for Hugh Pyne was named as such therein, and held office until his death in 1628. Presumably Swayne then became recorder again, as in September 1636 he resigned in favour of his nephew Ellis. He made his will 'sick of body' on 20 Nov., and must have died by the following 15 Feb. when the will was proved. He asked to be buried 'without pomp', and the poor of Blandford were to receive £10 to be distributed by the vicar, the bailiffs of the town and by Swayne's nephew, Thomas Pitt. Those of Wimborne Minster received a similar amount to be distributed by 'Mr. Lewis, preacher of God's word' there. Swayne had mortgaged some of his Blandford property to Lady Freke (to whom he left a ring 'as a token of my love unto her'), and when the mortgage had been discharged, this was to go to the many grandchildren mentioned in the will, who, between them, received houses, gardens, shops, orchards and outhouses, all at Blandford. The executors – his cousin Thomas and William Pitt – were to sell further lands and tenements there, together with his library and other personal goods, to pay his debts.[4]

[1] Hutchins, *Dorset*, i. 35, 101; ii. 440; iii. 453; iv. 96; *Vis. Dorset* (Harl. Soc. xx), 1, 49; H. J. Moule, *Weymouth Docs.* 112; Somerville, *Duchy of Lancaster Office-holders*, 220. [2] Hutchins, i. 35; iv. 96; *Som. and Dorset N. and Q.* vii. 76; *M.T. Recs.* ii. 481, 511; Poole recs. bk. of the staple; *Weymouth Charters*, ed. Moule, 49, 95, 132, 164; St. Ch. 5/R27/34; D'Ewes, 578, 591, 635, 672,; Townshend, *Hist. Colls.* 294–5, 308. [3] *Som. and Dorset N. and Q.* vi. 168, 170, 216 et passim; *Cal. Dorchester Recs.* ed. Mayo, 552; *New Eng. Hist. Gen. Reg.* lxxxi. 91–94; Hutchins, i. 35, 218; ii. 280, 591; iii. 452, 660; iv. 337; PCC 23 Stafford; PRO Index 6800, pp. 219, 242; *HMC Hatfield*, viii. 241. [4] PCC 17 Goare.

P.W.H.

SWAYNE, William (d.1613), of Hackney, Mdx.[1]

CHIPPENHAM 1589

m. (1) 1da.; (2) c. May 1612, Bridget, wid. of William Newce of Much Hadham, Herts., *s.p.*
Barber-surgeon bef. 1565–*d.*; warden 1575, 1581; steward and collector of manors of Aldworth, St. Leonard Stanley and Bisley, Glos. ?bef. 1589–*d.*; commr. for sale of Hackney parsonage bef. Aug. 1601.[2]

William Swayne's parentage has not been established. The surname was common throughout the country; in

Wiltshire it is found at Salisbury, Wilton and Steeple Ashton, while in Dorset the Swaynes of Blandford and Tarrant Gunville were to provide an Elizabethan MP in Richard Swayne. If, as is likely, William Swayne was a native of Chippenham, he was doubtless related to one or more of its inhabitants who bore his name: to the William Swayne *alias* Bayly whose lease of a tenement in Foghamshere, Chippenham, had occasioned a suit in the court of requests in 1541; to Thomas and William Swane, executors of (perhaps the above-mentioned) William Swayne, who were sued in that court at about the same time; or to John Swayne, weaver or husbandman, who was licensed as a corn badger in 1575 and stood surety for others so licensed. An earlier John Swayne had witnessed the will made in 1533 by the mother of the last abbess of Lacock. The use by this man of the *alias* Bayly suggests a connexion with William Bayliffe or Bayly, MP for Chippenham in 1572; in his will Swayne was to leave a ring to his 'cousin' Richard Bayly. That the Swaynes of Chippenham were modest folk is evident from the absence of any person of that name both from the records as printed by Goldney and from the subsidy list of 1576 for the borough and hundred.[3]

Whatever his origin, there need be little hesitation in identifying the Member with William Swayne, barber-surgeon and twice warden of his company. This individual's career exhibits two distinguishing features. The first, his share in the musical life of his age, was to be reflected most clearly in his will; but it is illustrated by an episode from his early life. In January 1565 one David Ellis was sentenced to death at the Middlesex sessions for robbing William Swayne at Westminster. The majority of the articles stolen, a barber's metal basin and pot, three razors, a pair of shears and two combs, were tools of the owner's trade, but the thief also took two musical instruments, a pair of clarichords and a gittern. It was then the custom of barbers to furnish their clients with such means of diversion, and William Swayne's interest in music was doubtless stimulated by his adoption of the practice in his shop.[4]

It was another connexion which metamorphosed the barber-surgeon into the Member of Parliament and Crown official. How early, or in what way, William Swayne came to the notice of Sir Walter Mildmay* has not been discovered. Their association may have derived from the link between Mildmay and Henry Sharington*, which was strengthened by a marriage alliance in 1567, for Sharington was the leading magnate in the vicinity of Chippenham; but it is tempting to imagine that Swayne numbered Mildmay among the customers of his Westminster establishment and that the barber's chair yielded advancement as well as affluence. Its first fruit is perhaps to be seen in the 21-year lease of two Nottinghamshire chantries granted to William Swayne in May 1569. What is almost certain is that Mildmay procured Swayne's return for Chippenham nearly 20 years later. By that date his son Anthony*, who had married one of Sharington's daughters, was well established in Wiltshire, and Sir Walter's influence could easily have been brought to bear in support of this local boy who had made good. (It was to Mildmay that the borough had drafted a petition in 1578 against Sir Walter Hungerford.) A point of interest is that, in consequence of the decision to postpone the meeting of Parliament until 4 Feb. 1589, the elections in Wiltshire, as in some other shires, took place in two stages: the elections for the shire and for 12 of the boroughs were held between 14 Oct. and 3 Nov. 1588, and those for three other boroughs between 26 Jan. and 1 Feb. 1589 (the dates for the two remaining boroughs being unknown). Chippenham was one of the boroughs to make its return late, doing so on 26 Jan. Whether its belatedness had any effect upon the election we cannot say; but it may be thought to have increased the competition for the seats thus left open and so to have made Swayne's success the more notable.[5]

A seat in Parliament was not to prove, however, the limit of Mildmay's favour. Two months after the session had ended Sir Walter, conscious that his days were numbered, took the pains to write to Burghley asking that Swayne should be allowed to keep the 'little office' which Mildmay had given him and in which he had served very faithfully. The office in question may have been the stewardship of three Gloucestershire manors which Swayne was holding in August 1601; the 'Mr Swain' who had been acting three years earlier with one Hussy for Robert Cecil as chancellor of the duchy of Lancaster was not William but Richard Swayne*. It may have been to Burghley, however, that William owed his appointment as a commissioner for the sale of Hackney parsonage to Ralph Bell, who in 1601 was rendering weekly accounts of his receipts from it to Swayne and his colleagues. This suggests that Swayne had established himself at Hackney already at the turn of the century, although he still had houses in London. Interestingly enough a William Swayne dedicated to Lord Burghley his edition of William Damon's psalms published in 1591, which, if it is our man (and no other candidate presents himself), illustrates the heights he had attained in the two overlapping worlds of music and the court. It needs but a little imagination to see Swayne as an early example of a character to become an eighteenth-century stereotype, a Figaro, who, through skill and discreet behaviour, could progress from shaving the gentry to dealing quietly and without fuss with unwanted pregnancies and other accidents and emergencies at court. In this manner Swayne would have been able to indulge a taste for theory and practice of music and at the same time accumulate the substantial estate evident from the will he made at Hackney on 13 Oct. 1613. He died on the following 1 Nov. He had married for the second time 18 months before, and had

acquired, with their widowed mother, the step-children whom he was to remember in his will; but his revocation, three days after making it, of the generous provision – the use of two houses, a coach and geldings, and £200 in cash – which it contained for his wife appears to reflect some deathbed disharmony between them. The will, whose preamble is that of a devout Anglican, shows Swayne to have died both a wealthy man and a philanthropic one. Among his charitable bequests were sums of £20 each to Christ's hospital for poor children and St. Botolph's without Aldersgate for its poor, and of £10 each to St. Bartholomew's hospital and to the poor in London prisons; he also left £100 with which the parish of Hackney was to buy land for the relief of its poor, a legacy which, under the name of 'Swain's Charity', still survives. To his daughter Ann he left his first wife's rings and jewels, to his nephews Thomas, Arthur and Nathaniel £300, £400 and £20 respectively, to his 'cousins' Thomas Walkeden* and Mirabile Newett £5 and £10, and to his servants amounts ranging from £5 to £30. He appointed his nephew William Swayne, his brother Edward's son and perhaps the Cambridge graduate of 1597, his executor, and Sir John Leveson* and John Newett overseers.[6]

The chief interest of the will, however, lies in its revelation of Swayne's musical interests. His brother Alban was given, besides an annuity of £20 from a lease at Ampthill, Bedfordshire, a chest of viols, a pair of virginals, and 'all my books of music'; while among the 25 recipients of rings were 'Mr. Holborne, Mr. Jones ... and William Bird esquire', that is to say, presumably William Holborne the cittern player and composer, Robert Jones the lutenist, and the great William Byrd. As a resident at Stondon Massey, Essex, Byrd may well have found Swayne's house at Hackney a convenient halting-place on the way to and from Westminster and have caused its parlour to echo to some notable music-making. In another sense, too, the friendship could have been of advantage to Byrd; one of Swayne's circle was his kinsman by marriage Theophilus Elmer or Aylmer, son of the bishop and himself archdeacon of London, and a man whose goodwill would certainly have done Byrd no harm in view of his stubborn recusancy. Elmer was bequeathed a ring, as were three other divines, several prominent Londoners, a leading barber-surgeon, Alexander Baker, and a number of Swayne's relatives.[7]

A final point of interest is yielded by the inquisition into Swayne's property, which was taken at Tewkesbury, Gloucestershire, presumably because he held the ex-monastic manor of Oxendon in that county. Among the properties listed the most notable is the inn called 'the Angils' at Islington, whose galleries – demolished when the old building was pulled down in 1819 – may thus also have resounded to the music of the cittern, as had the barber's shop in Westminster, and the gentleman's residence at Hackney.[8]

[1] We are indebted to the late Thurston Dart for reading and commenting upon a draft of this biography. [2] C142/343/136; S. Young, *Annals of the Barber-Surgeons*, 6; E315/309/138; *CSP Dom. Add. 1580–1625*, p. 410. [3] *VCH Wilts.* vi. 149–52; *Devizes Mus. ms vol. on Swayne fam. of Wilton*; *Wilts. N. and Q.* vi. 371–424 passim, 561; vii, 36, 225, 330; Req. 2/11/43, 76; *Mins. Proc. Sess.* (Wilts. Arch. Soc. recs. br. iv), 2, 5, 6, 12; PCC 99 Capell. [4] Young, *Barber-Surgeons*, 6; *Mdx. County Recs.* i. 52. [5] *CPR, 1566–9*, p. 344; *Chippenham Recs.* 296–7. [6] Lansd. 61/128; E315/309/138; *HMC Hatfield*, viii. 241; *CSP Dom. Add. 1580–1625*, p. 410; *Index of Dedications and Commendatory Verses* (Bibliographical Soc. 1962), ex inf. Professor Thurston Dart; PCC 99 Capell; C142/343/136; W. Robinson, *Hist. Hackney*, 107, 360–1; *Al. Cant.* i(4), p. 191. [7] PCC 99 Capell; Grove, *Dict. Music* (ed. 5), i. 1055 et seq.; iv. 319–20, 660–1; *Vis. Herts.* (Harl. Soc. xxii), 141; Beaven, *Aldermen*, i. 92; ii. 46, 51, 68; Young, *Barber-Surgeons*, 8, 495. [8] C142/343/136; S. Lewis, *Hist. St. Mary, Islington*, 414–5.

S.T.B.

SWINNERTON, John (1564–1616), of St. Mary Aldermanbury, London.

PETERSFIELD	1601
EAST GRINSTEAD	1604

b. 1564, 1st s. of John Swinnerton, merchant, of London by Mary, da. of one Fawnte. *educ.* Merchant Taylors' 1576 . *m.* 22 July 1586, Thomasine, da. of Richard Buckfolde of London, 4s 3da. Kntd. 26 July 1603. *suc.* fa. 1608.[1]

Alderman, London 22 June 1602, sheriff 1602–3, ld. mayor 1612–13; farmer of imposts on French and Rhenish wines 1593–7, 1599–1607, of imposts on sweet wines 1612; gov. Christ's Hospital.[2]

Swinnerton was probably apprenticed to his father upon leaving Merchant Taylors' school. Wright, in his *History of Essex*, suggests that he spent a number of his formative years in Spain, there acquiring the character of an accomplished gentleman. No evidence is adduced for this, but it is quite possible that he did serve abroad as an agent for his father. By 1589, however, when he was made free by patrimony of the Merchant Taylors' Company, he must have been trading on his own behalf.[3]

It was his interest in the Bordeaux trade that led him, no doubt, to put in his successful tender for the farm of the wines in 1593. Apart from two years when the imposts were not farmed out but collected by government agents, Swinnerton was farmer for 14 years, though rarely able to enjoy the grant peacefully. His first year's profit was estimated by a government official at over £3,000 which, despite increases in his rent, had risen in the nine months from Michaelmas 1599 to June 1600, to over £14,000 for London alone. Swinnerton invested part of his profit in land. In 1601 he bought the manors of Belhouse, Dagenham and Stanway in Essex, erecting a 'stately structure' on the ruins of the old house at Stanway. In the following year he purchased an estate in the parish of St. Mary Aldermanbury, from the 4th Marquess of Winchester. Included was a house leased by the Countess of Shrewsbury, to whom Fulke Greville* expressed his

belief that 'your Ladyship would not willingly become a tenant to such a fellow'.[4]

Swinnerton sat in one Parliament during Elizabeth's reign, presumably as the nominee of Thomas Hanbury, who had purchased Petersfield in 1597.

He was amongst the merchants who formed the East India Company in 1599, promising £300 for the first voyage. He died 8 Dec. 1616 'not altogether so great or rich a man as he was held, and made show of'. In his will, drawn up 7 Sept. 1616, proved 13 Dec., he divided his personal estate into three parts, 'after the laudable custom of the city of London': a third for his wife, a third for his five younger children, and a third for his personal bequests. By a codicil made 7 Dec. he attempted to ensure that his daughters would marry. His executors were his wife Thomasine, and his eldest son Henry. The preamble to the will declared that, 'by Jesus Christ and His merits only I faithfully believe to be saved, and that after this mortal life ended my soul shall ascend into heaven and be glorified there forever in the presence of God, and His son Christ, and all the holy angels, saints and martyrs, as it is written'. At his funeral a sermon was to be preached by 'a godly, learned preacher, not that it availeth the departed, since all come unto God by Christ, who ever liveth to make intercession for the believer'. He left a number of charitable bequests: £100 towards the relief of poor children of the hospital of Christ Church, of which he was a governor; £10 each to the three other London hospitals; £5 each to four London prisons, and £10 to the poor of the parish of St. Mary Aldermanbury, in which he lived, with £7 a year to those of St. Alphege where he had been born. He was buried in the church of St. Mary Aldermanbury.[5]

[1] *Merchant Taylors' School Reg.* ed. Hart, 11 (unpaginated); *London Mar. Lic.* (Harl. Soc. xxv), 27, 151; PCC 125 Cope, 8 Dorset. [2] J. J. Baddeley, *Aldermen of Cripplegate Ward*, 58; G. E. Cokayne, *Lord Mayors and Sheriffs of the City of London*, 55; F. C. Dietz, *Eng. Public Finance, 1558–1641*, pp. 74–5, 91; R. H. Tawney, *Business and Politics under James I*, 96 n. 2, 104 n.2; PCC 125 Cope. [3] T. Wright, *Hist. Essex*, i. 401; C. M. Clode, *Early Hist. Merchant Taylors' Co.* i. 263. [4] A. P. Newton, 'Establishment of the Great Farm of the Eng. Custom', *Trans. R. Hist. Soc.* (ser. 4), i. 145; Dietz, 74, 91; C2 Eliz./S24/59; *HMC Hatfield*, xiv. 138–9; Lansd. 81, ff. 64–5; *CSP Dom. 1595–7*, pp. 18, 32, 218; *1598–1601*, pp. 445–6; Wright, i. 401–2, 487; Nichols, *Progresses Eliz.* iii. 598. [5] Baddeley, 58; A. L. Simon, *Hist. Wine Trade*, iii. 3, 6; Cokayne, 55; *Chamberlain Letters* ed. McClure, ii. 44; PCC 125 Cope; *Regs. of St. Mary the Virgin, Aldermanbury* (Harl. Soc. Regs. lxi), 96; Clode, i. 263.

A.M.M.

SYMCOTS, William, of Huntingdon.

HUNTINGDON	1559

Prob. s. of John Symcots, merchant of London, by Elizabeth. *m.* Alice, da. of Barnard Copes of Hunts., 3da., or 1s. 2da.

Symcots was licensed to keep a tavern in Huntingdon in April 1555. He was probably the William Symcots who in 1535 had rented property at Sawtrey, Huntingdonshire, from the abbot of St. Mary Sawtrey, and who later acquired houses and land at Leighton Bromswold and Huntingdon. About 1558 died George Symcots, a justice of the peace for Huntingdonshire, and possibly William's brother, leaving property in Fennystanton in the county. William and another relative, John Symcots of London, became involved in a Chancery case over the lease of some of this land. In 1564 Symcots was described as one of 'the ancient of the corporation', earnest in religion. No later reference to him has been found.

Harl. 890, f. 45; *Cam. Misc.* ix(3), p. 29; C219/26/37; *Huntingdon Recs.* 97; *CPR, 1553–4,* p. 20; 1554–5, p. 130; *LP Hen. VIII,* xii(2), p. 468; xx(1), p. 318; *Cal. Feet of Fines, Hunts.* ed. Turner (Camb. Antiq. Soc. Pubs. oct. ser. xxxvii), 131, 157; PCC 22 Welles; *VCH Hunts.* ii. 283.

N.M.F.

SYMNELL, Richard (d.1608), of Colchester, Essex.

COLCHESTER   1597, 1601

?s. of Thomas Symnell. *educ.* St. John's, Camb., matric. pens. 1558. *m.* (1) Jane; (2) Elizabeth, *s.p.*

Alderman, Colchester 1597, dep. (to James Morice*) town clerk 1578 to at least 1583, bailiff 1598, 1603.

The Symnells were a well-known Colchester family. Thomas, who was probably Richard Symnell's father, lived in the parish of St. Runwald about 1548, while Symnell himself resided in All Saints parish, where he was churchwarden. He owned at least two other houses in the town, and was practising as an attorney in the Colchester courts before 1578. In 1597 he may well have been elected to Parliament as a suitable successor to his master James Morice. In 1601 he and Robert Barker* were re-elected 'with one general consent of voice'. The Colchester burgesses were put on committees for draining the fens, 3 Dec. 1597 and for a cloth bill, 4 Dec. 1601. Symnell himself, by way of scoring a point against Whitgift, raised in the House, 11 Nov. 1597, the question of marriages without banns and was put on the ensuing committee. He reported (14 Nov.) that their terms of reference were not clear, continued on this committee, and was in addition appointed to a new one that hoped to deal with ecclesiastical affairs generally. On 7 Dec. that year he was appointed to the committee dealing with unemployed soldiers and sailors. He reported and recommended an end to a private bill, 23 Nov. 1601, was one of those named to attend the Queen, 28 Nov., served on a committee concerning the clerk of the market, 2 Dec., and spoke on the subsidy, 5 Dec.: asking 'their honours that sit about the chair' to petition the Queen that the terms of the usual general pardon granted at the beginning of a Parliament should be not too narrow. It was he who moved, 8 Dec., that the export of ordnance should be restricted, a motion

which led to one of the great debates of this Parliament. All in all a creditable record for the deputy town clerk of Colchester.

Symnell's will, dated 9 Dec. 1607 and proved 22 July 1608, has a long and pious preamble. He founded a scholarship from the newly established Colchester grammar school to St. John's, Cambridge, and left £20 to the poor of Colchester. He also gave £10 to the town for two silver gilt bowls for the feasts in the Moot Hall, besides numerous and substantial bequests to his brothers, sisters, nephews and nieces.

Al. Cant. iv. 244; G. Rickward, *Bailiffs and Mayors of Colchester,* 16; *Trans. Essex Arch. Soc.* xiii. 166; *Essex Rev.* iv. 244; li. 180, 183; Essex Arch. Soc., Morant mss; D'Ewes, 555, 556, 567, 569, 648, 657, 663, 668, 670; Townshend, *Hist. Colls.* 104, 286–7; PCC 71 Windebanck.

J.H.

TAILBOYES, Anthony (d.1584), of Skirmington, co. Dur.

ALDBOROUGH   1563

?3rd s. of Ralph Tailboyes of Thornton Hall, Conscliffe by Eleanor, da. of Henry Killinghall of Middleton St. George. *educ.* Camb. 1544. *m.* aft. 1569, Elizabeth, da. of Anthony Eshe, of Skirmington, wid. of Thomas Norton.

J.p.q. co. Dur. and other northern counties and commr. in north parts 1577.

Descended from the baronial family, the Tailboys of Kyme, Lincolnshire, Tailboyes himself, like his eldest brother Robert, was an ecclesiastical lawyer and an official of the bishopric of Durham. When the dean of Durham, William Whittingham, died in 1597 he made Tailboyes one of the trustees of his property. These connexions of Anthony and Robert Tailboyes suggest puritan religious views, yet they were closely connected with Thomas Norton, who was executed for his part in the rebellion of 1569: Ralph Tailboyes received a grant of Norton's lands, which he later transferred to Thomas Norton the younger, while Anthony married his widow and probably had charge of the education of his son. Moreover, the William Tailboyes who was a confidential servant of Thomas Percy, the gunpowder conspirator, may well have been the brother of Robert and Anthony.

Tailboyes probably owed his return for Aldborough to the influence of the 2nd Lord Eure, a member of the council in the north, whose son referred to Robert Tailboyes as 'my friend and kinsman'. He died intestate in 1584. Administration was granted to Ralph and William Tailboyes – presumably his father and his brother – in November of that year. His widow was still living in 1606.

Surtees, *Hist. Durham,* iii. 345, 382, 382 n; *Depositions* (Surtees Soc. xxi), 293–5; SP12/121; *APC,* xxvi. 138–9, 231, 318–19; *HMC Hatfield,* vi. 411–13; *Wills and Inventories* (Surtees Soc. xxxviii), 17–18; *CSP Dom.* 1595–7, p. 281; 1603–10, pp. 260, 272, 286; 1611–18, pp. 365, 406; Neale, *Commons,* 228–9; *Border Pprs.* ii. 193, 457, 460.

I.C.

TALBOT, Edward (c.1561–1618), of Bothal Castle, Northumb.

NORTHUMBERLAND   1584, 1586

bap. 25 Feb. 1561, 3rd s. of George, 6th Earl of Shrewsbury, by his 1st w. Lady Gertrude Manners, da. of Thomas, 1st Earl of Rutland; bro. of Gilbert* and Henry*. *educ.* Magdalen Coll. Oxf. 1579; travelled abroad 1582–3. *m.* Dec. 1583, Jane, e. da. and coh. of Cuthbert, 7th Lord Ogle of Ogle, Northumb., 1s. *d.v.p. suc.* bro. as 8th Earl of Shrewsbury 8 May 1616.

J.p. Northumb. from c.1592, sheriff 1601–2, 1609–10, custos rot. 1603; j.p. Yorks. (W. Riding) from 1602; muster commr. of the middle march 1596; member, high commission, province of York 1599, council in the north 1603–d., council in the marches of Wales 1616; jt. border commr. and guardian of peace 1618.[1]

After leaving Oxford, Edward and his younger brother Henry went to court before leaving for a tour abroad early in 1582, in the company of their father's servant Thomas Baldwin. They went to Italy and France, where, under the general care of the ambassador, Sir Henry Cobham, they visited Paris and Orleans, and travelled in Brittany and Poitou. They returned in the summer of 1583, by which time his father had arranged for Edward to marry Lord Ogle's daughter, a previous proposed match with Lord Burghley's daughter Elizabeth having fallen through in 1574. Jane Ogle's younger sister Catherine later married Shrewsbury's stepson, Sir Charles Cavendish*.[2]

Both Talbot brothers were elected to the next two Parliaments summoned after their return to England, Henry for Derbyshire and Edward for Northumberland. Neither is named in the records of the House. Edward could have attended the subsidy committee appointed 24 Feb. 1585.[3]

Edward Talbot was not involved in the estrangement between his father and stepmother, Bess of Hardwick, but on his father's death in 1590 he declined to be an executor and soon quarrelled with his elder brother Gilbert, now 7th Earl, about the inheritance. In 1594 Gilbert challenged Edward to a duel, which was declined in terms of studied moderation. The correspondence was shown to the Queen, and no doubt served Edward well when Gilbert again challenged him, this time in Star Chamber. Gilbert charged Edward with conspiring with one Wood, an apothecary, to poison him; Edward brought an action for slander against the physician. But the Queen's patience had been exhausted by the 6th Earl's behaviour towards Bess of Hardwick, and she was in any case less well disposed to the 7th Earl. After Gilbert's accusation of poison she banished him from court.[4]

In 1597 the brothers were again opposed over the Yorkshire election, when Gilbert supported Sir John Savile and Sir William Fairfax against Sir John Stanhope and Sir Thomas Hoby. Edward was Stanhope's lieutenant, and

took a prominent part in the protests which followed his defeat. Gilbert's hatred of Edward re-emerged when, on his deathbed in 1616, he secured letters from the Privy Council forbidding Edward to enter the estates until he could establish a legal title, though he could not prevent him inheriting the earldom, and it was as 8th Earl of Shrewsbury that Edward Talbot died on 8 Feb. 1618, in London. He was buried in Westminster abbey next day.[5]

[1] *CP*; *HMC Hatfield*, ix. 396; Reid, *Council of the North*, 496. [2] E. Lodge, *Illus.* ii. 52–6, 184, 190, 202; *Les Reportes del Cases in Camera Stellata*, ed. Baildon, 18; *CSP For.* 1583, p. 420; *Border Pprs.* i. 156; *HMC Shrewsbury and Talbot*, ii. 96–7, 118–19. [3] Lansd. 43, anon. jnl. f. 171. [4] Lodge, 463, 472–9; *Camera Stellata*, 13–19; St. Ch. 5/T12/16; D. N. Durant, *Bess of Hardwick*, 119, 151, 190–1. [5] *HMC 10th Rep. I*, 109; *APC*, 1615–16, pp. 526, 566–7; St. Ch. 8/277/6; J. Hunter, *Hist. Sheffield* (ed. Gatty), 125 seq.

B.D.

TALBOT, Gilbert (1552–1616), of Chatsworth, Derbys., Worksop, Notts., and Sheffield, Yorks.[1]

DERBYSHIRE   1572

b. 20 Nov. 1552, 2nd but 1st surv. s. of George, 6th Earl of Shrewsbury, by his 1st w. and bro. of Edward* and Henry*. *educ.* St. John's, Oxf. c.1566; travelled abroad 1568, Hamburg, Padua, Venice. *m.* 9 Feb. 1568, Mary, da. of Sir William Cavendish† of Chatsworth, 2s. *d.v.p.* 3da. *styled* Lord Talbot 1582; *summ.* to Lords in his fa.'s barony as Lord Talbot 1589; *suc.* fa. as 7th Earl of Shrewsbury 1590. KG 1592.

Steward of Pontefract and Tutbury, constable of Pontefract, Radnor, Tutbury and Wigmore castles 1589; j.p. Cumb., Derbys. (1573), Herefs. (1577), Notts., Salop and Yorks. 1590 or earlier; on embassy to Henri IV of France 1596; PC 1601; eccles. commr. province of York 1605; c.j. forests beyond Trent 1603; ld. lt. Derbys. 1605; constable and steward, Newark, forester of Sherwood 1607.[2]

Talbot was elected for Derbyshire with Henry Cavendish, to whom he had become brother-in-law in a double marriage following the match between the 6th Earl of Shrewsbury and Bess of Hardwick. Both knights of the shire were under 21. Talbot was appointed to the subsidy committee, 25 Jan. 1581, and perhaps to two others (unlawful weapons, 2 Mar. 1576, and wharves and quays, 13 Mar.) unless the Mr. Talbot in question was the Worcestershire knight of the shire. Called up to the Lords in 1589, Gilbert Talbot reported to his father 'Divers pure fellows are very hot and earnest' about religious matters in the Commons, and 'Mr. Beale hath made a very sharp speech, which is nothing well liked by the bishops'. During the 1593 election, the first after he succeeded to the earldom, he took advantage of the minority of the Earl of Rutland to intervene in Nottinghamshire, where Charles Cavendish and Philip Strelley were standing against Talbot's enemy Sir Thomas Stanhope*.[3]

Until he succeeded to the earldom, Talbot's life was circumscribed by the quarrel between his father and his stepmother, Bess of Hardwick; by his father's custody of Mary Stuart, which frequently involved his being turned out of his father's house, for the Queen would not allow even the family to remain where Mary was kept; and by his own acute shortage of money. The Talbot and Lansdowne manuscripts contain many of his requests to Michael Hickes* and others to borrow on bonds for him or otherwise help him out financially, and he also raised money from London merchants. His persistent litigation in Star Chamber and elsewhere, perhaps itself the result of so much personal insecurity, worsened his financial position. During the estrangement between his father and the Countess he remained on good terms with his stepmother, but his relations with his father suffered from the frequent efforts he made to prevent things going too far in the early stages, and, later, from his attempts to effect a reconciliation. When, finally, the Privy Council came into the picture, Talbot withdrew, and it was his wife Mary in partnership with the Queen herself who brought about a settlement, whereupon Shrewsbury retired to Sheffield to pass his last few years with one Mrs. Britton. Upon his death Talbot, now 7th Earl, entered upon a long dispute over the will with his mother-in-law, his next brother Edward and his youngest brother Henry. He also quarrelled violently with his mother's relatives the Manners family, and with many of his neighbours in Nottinghamshire and Yorkshire, including the Wortleys and the Stanhopes, with whom he had a particularly unwise dispute about a weir at Shelford. His challenging his brother Edward to a duel in 1594 and the mention of poison being used between them caused Talbot to be banished from court. In the upshot Bess of Hardwick won the legal contest over the will by pre-empting the services of all the available lawyers during her final visit to London in 1591–2, but the matter was still in dispute between them as late as July 1606. The dowager countess made peace with his daughter Mary in January 1608, a month before her death, but Gilbert Talbot received nothing under her will.[4]

In 1596 (it can have been because of his rank only) Talbot was included in an embassy to France, and he was a cupbearer at Elizabeth's funeral in 1603. He entertained James I at Worksop and was a commissioner for claims at the coronation. He was at first high in James's favour, being granted a lucrative office in the royal forests, but he was implicated in the so-called main and bye plots, and possibly in the Gunpowder Plot. His enemies, by now numerous, raked up old accusations that he was a secret Catholic. These dated back to at least 1592, and were given substance when Mary Talbot openly avowed her own Catholicism and advanced the claims of her niece Arbella Stuart. In 1611 Mary Talbot was put in the Tower, and all Shrewsbury's efforts failed to secure her release. The letter writer, John Chamberlain, reported in 1613 that although she had previously had the liberty of the Tower, 'and sometimes leave to attend her lord in his sickness' (gout), she had recently been confined more strictly. Shrewsbury voluntarily absented himself from Privy Council meetings, and continued to press for her pardon. She was released in December 1615, five months before her husband's death on 8 May 1616 at his London house in Broad Street. He was buried that August at St. Peter's, Sheffield, 'with the greatest pomp ever seen in the kingdom'.[5]

[1] This biography is based upon HMC Shrewsbury and Talbot, ii, and D. N. Durant, Bess of Hardwick. [2] Somerville, Duchy, i. 541–2. [3] LJ, ii. 149; CJ, i. 110, 114, 120; D'Ewes, 288. [4] Lansd. 90, f. 112; 91, ff. 49 seq., 141–2; 134, ff. 3–41 passim; CSP Dom. 1591–4, p. 342; Harl. 6995, 6996; Popham, Reports, p. 66; Chamberlain Letters ed. McClure, i. 75. [5] HMC Hatfield, iv. 113; E. K. Chambers, Eliz. Stage, i. 46; iv. 116; Nichols, Progresses Jas. I, i. 84–7; CSP Dom. 1595–7, pp. 14, 26, 52; 1603–10, pp. 19, 24, 522; 1611–18, pp. 80, 426; Chamberlain Letters, i. 410; ii. 2, 139; PCC 51 Cope; CP.

N.M.F.

TALBOT, Henry (1563–96), of Orton Longueville, Hunts. and Burton Abbey, Yorks.

DERBYSHIRE 1584, 1586

b. 1563, 4th s. of George, 6th Earl of Shrewsbury, by his 1st w. and bro. of Edward* and Gilbert*. educ. Magdalen Coll. Oxf. 1579; travelled abroad 1582–3. m. aft. Oct. 1586, Elizabeth, da. and h. of Sir William Reyner of Orton Longueville, 2da.

J.p. Notts. from c.1584, Derbys. from c.1589, commr. recusancy by 1592.

After returning from the Continent in 1583 Talbot was sent 'to occupy himself in the study of the law'. In fact he went to court, where he avoided embroiling himself unnecessarily in the disputes between his father and his stepmother. He remained on good terms with his father, acting as his confidential messenger and intermediary with the Queen, and sending him news from court. In return, Shrewsbury arranged for Talbot's elections as knight of the shire for Derbyshire. His presence is unnoticed in the records of his two Parliaments. As a county Member, however, he could have served on the subsidy committees of 24 Feb. 1585 and 22 Feb. 1587. His marriage to Elizabeth Reyner took place after an earlier arrangement with Sir Henry Darcy's daughter had broken down. His father stayed with Henry at Orton Longueville, some 16 miles from Fotheringay, during the trial of Mary Stuart, and made him a co-executor of his will with Edward, but both brothers renounced this in favour of the Countess, and both younger brothers found themselves in difficulties with their elder brother Gilbert, the 7th Earl, in consequence. Henry extricated himself sufficiently to avoid implication in the Talbot-Stanhope quarrels over Shelford weir. He died early in January 1596, when an investigation into a charge that he was unjustly withholding a poor man's money was pending. Although part of his inheritance from his father passed to Edward as next heir male under the entail, Henry's daughters were nevertheless heirs to a comfortable estate, part of which he had purchased. In his will, where he describes himself as of Burton Abbey, he left two parts of his lands to his wife, the executrix, until his younger daughter should be 18, and, thereafter, one part. His uncle, Roger Manners*, and his wife's second husband, Thomas Holcroft*, went to law with Gilbert over these provisos.

C142/248/15; 250/36; *HMC Shrewsbury and Talbot*, ii. 127, 136, 154, 168, 170, 211; D. N. Durant, *Bess of Hardwick*, 93, 119, 145, 151; Lodge, *Illus.* ii, iii passim; D'Ewes, 356, 409; *HMC Rutland*, i. 181, 302; *APC*, xxiv. 267; xxv. 175, 183; Lansd. 86, ff. 10 seq.; *HMC Hatfield*, iv. 312; v. 75; PCC 4 Drake.

S.M.T.

TALBOT, John (1545–1611), of Grafton, Worcs.

WORCESTERSHIRE   1572

b. 1545, 1st s. of Sir John Talbot of Grafton by Frances, da. of Sir John Giffard† of Chillington, Staffs. *educ.* Oxf.; M. Temple 1560. *m.* 1561, Katherine, da. of Sir William Petre*, 3s. 3da. *suc.* fa. 1555.[1]

The identification of the 1572 Worcestershire knight of the shire is anything but easy. A previous suggestion, that he was John Talbot of Longford, Shropshire, father of the 10th Earl of Shrewsbury, has to be discarded on grounds of his extreme youth, his eldest brother having been born in 1566. Another namesake, of Salwarpe, great-uncle of the 9th Earl, had only a small estate. John Talbot of Grafton would be an unexceptionable choice were it not for his Catholicism, which ought to have disqualified him from the Commons in 1572. In his favour it has to be noted that a number of the Worcestershire county families were undoubtedly Catholic; the sheriff who conducted the 1572 county election was himself classed as 'indifferent' in 1564; and Talbot had not publicly declared his religion at the time of his election.

Talbot was brought up by, and married into the Catholic family of Sir William Petre, though Petre himself conformed, which Talbot never did. He made no mark on the journals of his one Parliament. Indeed, before the third session took place, he and other suspected Worcestershire Catholics were summoned before the Privy Council, when he entered a formal plea for time to think things over. He was committed to the custody of the dean of Westminster by whom, the Council hoped, he might be 'resolved in conscience', but he was not persuaded even to outward conformity, and by the time of the 1581 session of the 1572 Parliament he was in confinement, first in the Tower, then by October in the custody of his brother-in-law, Sir John Petre. On 30 June

1593 he asked permission to reside at his own house instead of in the Isle of Ely, and much of the rest of his life passed in varying degrees of confinement. From time to time he was given permission to visit his home or London on grounds of sickness, for business reasons, or to prosecute lawsuits. Finally in 1597 or 1598 he was freed, though continuing to pay £20 a month until his death, to the great detriment of his estate. Shortly before the 1601 general election the Privy Council ordered him not to oppose the candidature of Sir Thomas Leighton* as knight of the shire. After the election of 1604 he complained that the sheriff had made an 'undue return'. In 1604, when a bill for stricter measures against recusants was before the King, Lord Windsor wrote to Talbot asking him to come to London and join in a petition against it. At this time Talbot was trying to be discharged of his recusancy money – an attempt which was taken amiss by the Council, and obliged Talbot to protest that he 'never intended to seek for any toleration from his Highness, but only to be discharged for my life'.[2]

In the aftermath of the Gunpowder Plot Talbot was examined and his papers searched. Several relatives were implicated including his son-in-law, Robert Winter, but no proof of Talbot's own participation was found. He was one of the few members of his family to remain on good terms with his cousin Gilbert Talbot, 7th Earl of Shrewsbury, who frequently helped him with his estates and visited him at Grafton. Talbot died 28 Jan. 1611 and was buried at Albrighton. His eldest son, George, succeeded to the earldom of Shrewsbury in 1618.[3]

[1] *Vis. Worcs.* (Harl. Soc. xxvii), 135–6; *VCH Worcs.* iii. 126; F. G. Emmison, *Tudor Secretary*, 303–5. [2] W. R. Williams, *Parl. Hist. Worcs.* 34; *CP*, xi. 717; *Cam. Misc.* ix(3), pp. 1–8; *VCH Worcs.* iii. 126, 207; PCC 22 Butts; *CPR*, 1555–7, p. 165; Lansd. 27, f. 72; 153, f. 177; *APC*, xii. 166, 169; xiii. 4, 183, 219; xv. 102; xvi. 389; xvii. 40, 198; xviii. 9, 45, 415; xix. 159; xx. 142; xxi. 307; xxiii. 198; xxiv. 76, 206, 304, 344, 476; xxvi. 523; xxvii. 80; xxviii. 102; xxxii. 251; *CSP Dom.* 1547–80, p. 671; 1581–90, p. 583; 1603–10, pp. 87, 146, 157, 173; Add. 1580–1625, p. 488; *Cath. Rec. Soc. Misc.* i.; Coll. of Arms, Talbot mss, transcribed by G. Batho, I, f. 168; *HMC Hatfield*, iv. 268; xiii. 472; xvi. 25, 49, 187; Lodge, *Illus.* iii. app. 87, 112. [3] *CSP Dom.* 1603–10, pp. 222, 242, 253, 267, 281, 282, 283, 293; *APC*, xxiv. 344; *HMC Hatfield*, xvi. 382–3; xvii. 25, 477, 494, 527; Lodge, *Illus.* iii. app. 85, 87, 90, 91, 92, 98, 100, 101, 112; *VCH Worcs.* iii. 15, 27, 123, 126–7, 272, 565; C142/305/108; *CP*, xi. 717–18.

S.M.T.

TALBOT, Sharington (1577–1642), of Lacock, Wilts., and Salwarpe, Worcs.

CHIPPENHAM   1597

b. 1577, 1st s. of John Talbot of Salwarpe by Olive, da. and coh. of Henry Sharington* of Lacock. *m.* (1) Elizabeth, da. of Sir Thomas Leighton* of Feckenham, Worcs., 5s. 5da.; (2) Mary, da. of John Washbourne of Wichenford, Worcs., wid. of William Kingston (*d.*1614), of Miserden, Glos., 4s. *suc.* fa. 1581.

Jt. master of the game, keeper, and ranger of Feckenham forest, Worcs. 1614; sheriff, Worcs. 1614–15.

When only four years of age, Talbot succeeded his father to Salwarpe, which had come into the family during the reign of Henry VII. He lived, however, at Lacock near Chippenham with his mother who, together with her sister Grace, wife of Anthony Mildmay*, was a coheir of Sir Henry Sharington. She survived her husband, her son Sharington, and her second husband Sir Robert Stapleton*, and lived at Lacock 'in an old-fashioned style', giving hospitality to many travellers including royalty, until 1646.

Talbot was only 20 when returned to Parliament for Chippenham. The bailiffs of the borough had paid an annual rent of £58 to Henry Sharington for the tolls of markets and fairs, and after his death they divided the amount between Mildmay and Stapleton, the husbands of the coheirs, so the family influence is plain. Apart from his one return to Parliament (where the only reference to him is his payment of 10s. for the poor when given leave to depart, 25 Nov. 1597), the whole of Talbot's public career lies outside the Elizabethan period. He was buried 6 Dec. 1642 at Salwarpe, and was succeeded by a son of the same name, a royalist in the civil war.

C142/197/89; Burke, *Landed Gentry*, ii. 2204–5; *CSP Dom.* 1611–18, p. 235; *Shrewsbury Peerage Case*, 189, 326; Rudder, *Glos.* 555; Nash, *Worcs.* 336; *Wilts. Arch. Mag.* xxiv. 63, 325–7; *Chippenham Recs.* 197, 292–3, 301–2, 324; D'Ewes, 565.

R.C.G./J.P.F.

TALLENTYRE, Thomas (d. c.1579), of Carlisle, Cumb.

CARLISLE 1572*

Tallentyre was returned at a by-election for the 1576 session of the 1572 Parliament in place of Robert Mulcaster*. A writ for a by-election occasioned by his own death was issued on 24 Jan. 1579. A Thomas Tallentyre, perhaps his son, was living at Castle Sowerby in 1581.

C193/32/8; C219/283/5, 6; *Border Pprs.* i. 45.

N.M.F.

TAMWORTH, Christopher (1529–71), of Leake, Lincs., and later of Ryall, Rutland.

KNARESBOROUGH 1563

b. 1529, 1st s. of John Tamworth of Leake by Anne, da. of John Meres of Kirton. m. (1) Margaret, da. of John Digby or Driby of Preston, 3s. 2da.; (2) Elinor. suc. fa. 1539.

Tamworth was the cousin of the better-known John Tamworth*. John made Christopher an executor and substantial beneficiary of his will, including his lease of the duchy of Lancaster manor of Sutton in Lincolnshire, and the reversion to his house in St. Botolph's without

Aldersgate, and his other lands in London. Two of Christopher's sons also benefited. They received John's interests in the mines royal and the mineral and battery works. In 1563 Christopher sat in Parliament for Knaresborough, where the duchy of Lancaster had influence, and since John Tamworth nominated as another of his executors Sir Walter Mildmay*, auditor of the duchy, it is likely that Christopher secured his seat at Knaresborough through the duchy. However, John Tamworth also knew the Earl of Leicester, and Christopher too had dealings with him.

In his will of 19 Dec. 1569, Tamworth described himself as of Ryall in Rutland. The poor of Tilton and Hallstead, Leicestershire, and Ryall and Besthorpe, Rutland received £3. 6s. 8d. If his wife, Elinor, accepted £40 a year out of the manor of Hallstead in lieu of thirds, then she was also to receive all the goods, including the corn and cattle, in and about his houses at Ryall and Coswick. His younger daughter, Dorothy, was to have 300 marks as her marriage portion, as well as all the goods, corn and cattle at Tilton and Hallstead. A codicil was made eight or ten days before Tamworth's death when he was lying 'sick in his bed' at the sign of the *Bear* in Smithfield. Asked whether he wished to change anything, Tamworth replied that he did not. Pressed to give his daughter, Dorothy, something more he said that he would not, adding that she should 'get her living with the travail of her body'. Tamworth named Kenelm* and Everard Digby, as well as his eldest son John, executors, but the will was proved on 4 Apr. 1572 by John alone. Tamworth had died the previous 13 Dec.

C142/62/14, 161/98; *Lincs. Peds.* (Harl. Soc. liii), iii. 948; *CSP Dom.* Add. 1547–65, p. 546; *CPR*, 1563–6, p. 132; PCC 8 Lyon, 11 Daper.

A.M.M.

TAMWORTH, John (c.1524–69), of Sandon, Essex; Sutton, Lincs. and St. Botolph, Bishopsgate.

BOSTON 1563*

b. c.1524, o.s. of Thomas Tamworth of Lincs. and Essex by Elizabeth, da. and h. of Philip Denkaring. m. 1562, Christian, da. of William Walsingham, sis. of Sir Francis*, 1da. suc. fa. 1533.[1]

Clerk of Windsor castle and receiver-gen. of Oxon., Berks. and Oxford from 1559; groom of privy chamber and keeper of privy purse from Jan. 1559; master of the toyles from c.1560; freeman, London from 1560; receiver-gen. Lincs. and Lincoln 1559, 1562; j.p.q. Essex from c.1559.[2]

Tamworth's family had lived for some time near Boston, and he was the patron of the living of Fishtoft, but there is no evidence that he himself lived on his Lincolnshire estates, the most important of which was the duchy of Lancaster manor of Sutton. As receiver of the county and with his connexions among the great, he must have been well known at Boston, where he came in at a by-election after Thomas Heneage chose to sit for the county. Tamworth left no mark on the surviving records of his only Parliament.[3]

The earliest references to him are found during Edward VI's reign, when in 1550 a mandate to the Exchequer was issued, ordering the payment of money due to him by his father's will, apparently under a recognizance of statute staple. His name appears on the Marian pardon roll for 1554, where he is described as 'of Sandon, Essex *alias* of London', but by the summer of that year he had gone abroad – assuming that he was the 'Mr. Tamworth' whom Sir Thomas Hoby met in August at Padua. This is likely, as he was a protestant, whose marriage into the Walsingham family linked him with the puritan group at court. He was also related by marriage to Sir Walter Mildmay* and to Peter Wentworth*.[4]

Early in Elizabeth's reign he came into royal favour, receiving several posts at Windsor castle and the mastership of the toyles, the fence for the Queen's hunting. Three years later he was promised the next appointment to a canonry or prebend at Canterbury cathedral, in order to present one William King. However, Archbishop Parker was anxious to have it for his almoner, Thomas Peerson, and Tamworth either waived his right, or was forestalled. A similar grant to him appears on the 1564 patent roll. Tamworth was classified as a 'favourer' of the Elizabethan settlement in 1564.[5] On one occasion he was given £100, 'in reward' for unspecified services, and he was chosen in 1565 to go to Scotland to intercede with Mary Stuart on behalf of the Scottish lords who had opposed the Darnley marriage. His mission failed, and he reported that Mary spoke to him 'some sharp words that biteth the quick'. He accompanied Elizabeth to Oxford during the 1566 progress, receiving an honorary MA from the university.[6]

Some of the money gained from his court offices he invested in commercial ventures. He was certainly connected with the mines royal and mineral and battery works, and was presumably the John Tamworth (styled 'Sir' in one reference in the *State Papers Foreign*) who wrote to Cecil about the Muscovy Company. He also speculated in land, acquiring estates and advowsons in Essex, Hertfordshire, London, Middlesex and Radnorshire. Between 1558 and 1564 he sold property in Bishopsgate Street, London, and his manor of Sandon, Essex. During the last years of his life he lived at his town house, though about 1566 he was a feoffee for Sir Henry Stanley's Lincolnshire lands. He also acted for the Earl of Leicester in land transactions, and was a friend of Sir Francis Knollys* and of Thomas Randolph*. A letter from Randolph, presumably to Walsingham, complaining of the cold in Russia, continues

As for your brother Tamworth, I think him more happy than wise that could so clearly shift himself of this

journey when he saw neither likelihood of honour or profit.

After Tamworth's death, which took place between 18 and 27 Apr. 1569, the Earl of Leicester wrote to Randolph, 'You have lost of late two of your good friends, that is to say my Lady Knollys and Tamworth'. It was Leicester who asked London (7 May 1560) to make Tamworth a freeman.[7]

His will, drawn up in March 1569, has a religious preamble, and arranges for his burial at St. Botolph's 'where now my pew is'. He left £40 for a memorial, made arrangements for his widow's maintenance, and appointed as executors Sir Walter Mildmay, Kenelm Digby*, Edmund Downing*, Christopher Tamworth* and Edmund Danyell. Mildmay was to have 'my best basin and ewer which my Lord of Leicester gave me'. There was only one charitable bequest – 40s. for the repair of the parish church – and that was described as 'for tithes forgotten or negligently withholden'. The will was proved on 2 Mar. 1570.[8]

[1] *Lincs. Peds.* (Harl. Soc. lii), 947–8; C142/55/58; C. H. Garrett, *Marian Exiles*, 302. [2] *CPR*, 1558–60, pp. 108, 431; 1560–3, p. 342; E. K. Chambers, *Eliz. Stage*, i. 62; Nichols, *Progresses Eliz.* i. 264–73; Lansd. 4, ff. 57–61. [3] PCC 8 Lyon; P. Thompson, *Hist. Antiqs. Boston*, 482. [4] *CPR*, 1549–51, p. 195; 1553–4, p. 458; *Cam. Misc.* x(2), p. 116; Garrett, 302. [5] *CPR*, 1558–60, pp. 108, 431; 1560–3, p. 521; 1563–6, p. 371; 1566–9, p. 2; 1569–72, p. 73; Strype, *Parker*, i. 285; *Cam. Misc.* ix(3), p. 62. [6] *HMC Hatfield*, i. 261; Wood, *Fasti*, ed. Bliss, i. 178; Read, *Cecil*, 338–9; Lansd. 102, f. 114; Foster, *Al. Ox.* i(4), p. 1455. [7] M. B. Donald, *Eliz. Monopolies*, 35, 41; *CPR*, 1557–8, p. 329; 1563–6, p. 595; 1566–9, pp. 211, 274; PCC 8 Lyon; *CSP Dom.* 1547–80, p. 316; *CSP For.* 1566–8, p. 556; Lansd. 11, f. 50 seq.; 111, f. 203; NRA, Lumley mss, 689, 695, 697. [8] *CPR*, 1566–9, p. 194; Donald, *Eliz. Copper*, 56; Nichols, i. 264; Lansd. 111, f. 203; 141, f. 278; London Rep. 14, f. 331; PCC 8 Lyon.

N.M.F.

TANFIELD, Lawrence (c.1554–1625), of Burford, Oxon.

NEW WOODSTOCK	1584, 1586, 1589, 1593, 1597, 1601
OXFORDSHIRE	1604*

b. c.1554, 1st s. of Robert Tanfield of Burford by his w. Wilgiford Fitzherbert. *educ.* Eton; I. Temple 1569, called by 1579. *m.* (1) by 1585, Elizabeth, da. of Giles Symonds of Cley, Norf., 1da.; (2) by 1620, Elizabeth Evans of Loddington, Northants. *suc.* fa. c.1557. Kntd. 1604.[1]

?Recorder, New Woodstock; j.p. Oxon. from c.1583; bencher, I. Temple 1591, Lent reader 1595; of counsel to Oxf. Univ. 1597; serjeant-at-law 1603; puisne judge King's bench 1606; chief baron of the Exchequer 1607.[2]

Tanfield inherited little from his father (a younger son) but made a fortunate marriage to the niece of Sir Henry Lee*, high steward of New Woodstock. By Lee's patronage and through his own position as recorder (if he was), he was returned for Woodstock in 1584 and to all subsequent Elizabethan Parliaments, but, for an ambitious lawyer his record in the House is not spectacular. He served on committees concerned with juries, 4 Dec. 1584; the subsidy, 11 Feb. 1589; privileges and returns, 26 Feb. 1593; recusants, 28 Feb. 1593, and made his only recorded speech on 2 Mar. that year on the Fitzherbert privilege case:

> though the common law doth disable [an outlaw], yet the privilege of the House being urged, that prevaileth over the law.

Others of his committees, concerned with legal questions, were appointed on 1 Feb. 1598; 2, 4 and 12 Nov. 1601 and 3 Dec. 1601.

Before 1586 Tanfield acquired Burford priory, on the site of which he built his residence. In 1594 he was a candidate for the post of solicitor-general, when the Earl of Essex listed his demerits in order to promote the candidature of Francis Bacon*. Three years later Thomas Sackville*, Lord Buckhurst, chancellor of Oxford University and himself a member of the Inner Temple, recommended the university to employ Tanfield in one of its perennial disputes with the town: it may have been intended that he should assist in the campaign to institute MPs for the universities to look after their long term interests. The writs for the new serjeants-at-law in February 1603 were abated by the Queen's death, but Tanfield was soon so appointed by James I, who stayed at his house in September that year. Tanfield then bought the lordship of the town of Burford and the manor of Great Tew. His harshness to his tenants caused several petitions to be brought against him in 1620, inspiring his second wife to threaten to 'play the very devil' among the villagers of Great Tew and 'grind them to powder'.[3]

Tanfield died on 30 Apr. 1625. In his will, made to dispose of the worldly goods, 'whereof God has bestowed upon me a plentiful part', he left the estates to his grandson, Lucius Carey, the 2nd Lord Falkland. The overseers were Sir Richard Hutton and the testator's 'nephew' (he had married into Tanfield's second wife's family) William Lenthall, who later bought Burford priory and became Speaker of the Long Parliament. Tanfield's daughter was a writer and Catholic convert.[4]

[1] DNB; Life of Lady Falkland, ed. 'R. S.' (Richard Simpson), London, 1861, pp. 1–7; Vis. Essex (Harl. Soc. xiii), 295–6; N. and Q. (ser. 2), x. 209; R. H. Gretton, Burford Recs. 268. [2] Liber Famelicus of Sir James Whitelocke (Cam. Soc. lxx), 19; I. T. Recs. i. 378, 397; Wood, Oxf. Univ. ii. 264. [3] Gretton, 54–5, 268–72; E. K. Chambers, Sir Henry Lee, 206–8; D'Ewes, 335, 431, 471, 477, 481–2, 592, 622, 626, 635, 665; Birch, Mems. i. 166; Wood, ii. 264; Nichols, Progresses Jas. I, i. 157, 250; HMC 3rd Rep. 31–3. [4] C142/417/44; PCC 45 Clarke; Gretton, 274–5; Life of Lady Falkland, 11; DNB (Lenthall, William); Gent. Mag. (1820), ii 584–7; A. Wood and R. Rawlinson, Parochial Colls. (Oxon. Rec. Soc. ii), 67.

A.H.

TARRETT, see **FITZGERALD**

TASBURGH, John (c.1576–1629), of Beaconsfield and Hawridge, Bucks., later of Flixton Abbey, Suff.

CHIPPING WYCOMBE   1597

b. c.1576, 1st s. of John Tasburgh of Flixton by Elizabeth, da. of John Tracy of Norwich. educ. Balliol, Oxf. Nov. 1594; L. Inn 6 Aug. 1595. m. Lettice, da. of James Cressy, 5s. 7da. suc. uncle 1603, fa. 1607. Kntd. 11 May 1603.[1]

The Tasburghs acquired an estate in the parish of South Elmham St. Peter early in the reign of Edward III. This remained their chief residence until Tasburgh's grandfather acquired Flixton Abbey after the dissolution of the monasteries. Tasburgh himself built a new house there in 1616. His marriage to Lettice Cressy was arranged by his father and his uncle, Thomas Tasburgh* of Beaconsfield, Buckinghamshire, who was Lettice's guardian, no doubt because of her fortune, estimated by a seventeenth-century source to be of £10,000. Thomas Tasburgh appears to have adopted his nephew as his heir, for the election return of 1597 describes Tasburgh himself as of Beaconsfield, where Thomas had his seat, and two years previously, on his admission to Lincoln's Inn, he had also been described as of Buckinghamshire. A Chancery suit followed the marriage, Thomas Tasburgh complaining that while he had fulfilled his part of the marriage bargain by settling the reversion of his manor of Hawridge on John and Lettice, his brother had not honoured his part of the agreement, which was to settle an annuity of £120 on them for their present maintenance.[2]

Tasburgh was presumably returned for Chipping Wycombe through his uncle's local standing, and influence with Henry, 5th Baron Windsor, high steward of the town. It is likely that the 'Mr. Tasburgh' mentioned in the journals for this Parliament was this uncle.

Tasburgh may have left Buckinghamshire on his uncle's death in 1603, and sold Hawridge in 1606, subsequently living in Suffolk on his father's estates. He made his will 9 Sept. 1626, and it was proved on 10 Feb. 1630. In a conventional preamble he commended his soul into the hands of Almighty God, 'hoping assuredly through the merits of Christ Jesus ... to be made a partaker of life everlasting', and he desired to be buried 'without any funeral pomp or glorious vanity, but rather in a very private fashion'. Tasburgh himself was regarded by his religious opponents as 'a hot protestant', 'a most perverse heretic' who threatened his daughter on her conversion to Catholicism that 'he would cut her tongue out of her head if she spoke one word more in defence of her religion'. His wife was also a Catholic and his eldest son, Charles, whose estates were sequestrated for recusancy during the civil war. Tasburgh died 24 Apr. 1629 a wealthy man. It was thought that £2,000 would be offered for the wardship of his son. He left the larger part of his disposable estate in trust for the payment of his debts and legacies, which amounted to £5,200. There were also charitable bequests to the poor of four Suffolk parishes. His executors were three local gentlemen, to whom he bequeathed £20 each.[3]

[1] Foster, *Al. Ox.* early ser. 1456; C142/298/9, 449/38; *Vis. Suff.* ed. Metcalfe, 71. [2] A. I. Suckling, *Hist. Suff.* i. 197, 200; C142/449/38; Harl. 991, p. 75; C2 Eliz./T5/38. [3] *VCH Bucks.* iii. 368; PCC 17 Scroope; *Suff. Recs.* ed. Copinger, ii. 388; *Chron. Eng. Canonesses, St. Monica's, Louvain* (1904), i. 253-6; W. Prynne, *Hidden Workes of Darkenes*, 68; *CSP Dom.* 1628-9, p. 487; C142/449/38.

A.M.M.

TASBURGH, Thomas (c.1554–c.1602), of Hawridge, later of Beaconsfield, Bucks.

AYLESBURY	1584, 1586
BUCKINGHAMSHIRE	1589
CHIPPING WYCOMBE	1593
AYLESBURY	1597

b. c.1554, 4th s. (?posth.)[1] of John Tasburgh of Flixton, Suff. by his 2nd w. Elizabeth, da. of John Davy of Norwich, Norf., wid. of John Tracy of Norwich. *educ.* G. Inn 1573. *m.* (1) aft. 1571, Dorothy (*d.*1577), da. of Sir Thomas Kitson of Hengrave, Suff., wid. of Sir Thomas Pakington of Hampton, Worcs., *s.p.*; (2) Jane, da. of William West, 1st Baron Delaware, wid. of Thomas Wenman* and James Cressy, *s.p.* Kntd. 9 May 1599.
J.p. Bucks. from 1579, q. by 1590; sheriff, Bucks. 1581–2, commr. musters 1595, collector of the loan 1598; teller of the Exchequer 1598–1602.[2]

Tasburgh belonged to an old established Suffolk family, but as a younger son he was left to his own resources. He entered Gray's Inn, and although there is no evidence that he was called to the bar, his name appears on a list of Gray's Inn lawyers dated January 1600 who were required to help towards the payment of levies for Ireland. He purchased Hawridge in 1572, and consolidated his position in the county by his marriage into the family which owned Aylesbury itself and other estates in Buckinghamshire. Though there is no evidence that Tasburgh and his wife were on bad terms – in her will she left him all that the law allowed her to bequeath – he was not in fact returned for the borough until after her death. He remained friendly with Sir John Pakington, Dorothy Pakington's son by her first husband, and joined with him in a number of land transactions.[3]

After twice being returned for Aylesbury, Tasburgh achieved a county seat for the Parliament of 1589. Next time he was returned for Chipping Wycombe, presumably through the patronage of Henry, 5th Lord Windsor, steward of the town, before returning to Aylesbury for his last appearance in Parliament in 1597. He served on committees concerned with highways and bridges (6 Mar. 1585), the poor (12 Mar.), returns (11 Nov. 1586), and a learned ministry (8 Mar. 1587). On 18 Mar. that year he was one of those who attended the Queen on the matter of the subsidy. He was a member of the subsidy committee of 11 Feb. 1589, and on the 15th of that month spoke on the

purveyors. On 24 Mar. he reported the bill concerning jurors and freeholders. Among his committees in 1593 were those on privileges and returns (26 Feb.), recusancy (28 Feb., 4 Apr.), the subsidy (1 Mar.) and jurors (10, 23 Mar.). He spoke on a privilege matter (2 Mar.) and moved the amendments of the jurors bill (7 Apr.). He did not speak in his last Parliament, when his committees included privileges and returns (5 Nov. 1597), armour and weapons (8 Nov.), monopolies and poor relief (10 Nov.), workhouses (18 Nov.), rogues and sturdy beggars (22 Nov.), husbandry and tillage (26 Nov.), tellers and receivers (5 Dec.), and alehouses and wine casks (3 Feb. 1598). As one of the Aylesbury burgesses he could have served on the committee discussing the roads of the district (11 Jan.).[4]

According to a seventeenth-century account, Tasburgh's fortunate second marriage was contrived in the following fashion:

> This person of the Exchequer knowing a lady that became Catholic in Queen Bess time ... found ways to trouble her in the Exchequer about her religion and took her off and troubled her again and took her off, at last she could find no rest and would be advised by him what to do, he advised her there was no way but to marry a protestant and he got her; she had a daughter [Lettice] by Cressy ... worth £10,000 and he married her to his nephew [and heir John*].

Tasburgh's crony Sir John Pakington was one of the few people of quality to attend the marriage, which brought Tasburgh, through her first marriage, the manor of Twyford and part of the manor of Eton Hastings, Berkshire, and, by her second, Wilton manor in Beaconsfield, where she and Tasburgh now resided. But another ambition of Tasburgh's almost ruined him. In June 1595 Penelope Lady Rich wrote on his behalf to Cecil, pleading that Tasburgh had 'long had cause to expect that the Queen would lay the grace of knighthood on him'. Eventually realising that she had no such intention, Tasburgh went without leave to attach himself to Essex in Ireland, where he persuaded that nobleman, always a generous distributor of the honour, to knight him at Dublin. Returning to England he was imprisoned at the end of May 1599, addressing appeal after appeal to Cecil:

> The degree my lord gave me ... I sought not for it, and when I told him I thought her Majesty would be offended, he said he hoped not ...

Five weeks later:

> It is no small heart's grief here thus to dwell in her Majesty's displeasure, therefore give me leave once again to importune you to be a happy suitor to her Majesty for my liberty.

He was lucky not to lose his tellership of the Exchequer.[5]

Tasburgh died between making his will on 20 Aug. 1601 and its proof on 29 Jan. 1603. He appointed his widow executrix, mentioned a debt of £150 owed to his brother John of Flixton, Suffolk, and left some bequests to the poor of Aylesbury and Beaconsfield. Hawridge went to the nephew John already mentioned.[6]

[1] He is not mentioned in his father's will, PCC 26 Tashe. [2] *Chamberlain Letters* ed. McClure, i. 181; *Vis. Suff.* ed. Metcalfe, 71; *DNB* (Pakington, John); *VCH Worcs.* iii. 155; PCC 24 Daughtry; A. I. Suckling, *Hist. Suff.* i. 198; SP12/145, ff. 5–6; *HMC Hatfield*, v. 523; ix. 180; xii. 401. [3] *APC*, xxx. 31; G. Lipscomb, *Bucks.* iii. 4, 375; *VCH Bucks.* iii. 10, 368; PCC 24 Daughtry; *CSP Dom.* 1595–7, p. 16; *Bucks. Arch. Soc.* (recs. br.), v. 2, 10. [4] D'Ewes, 364, 366, 399, 413, 416, 431, 432, 452, 471, 474, 477, 481, 496, 508, 517, 520, 552, 553, 555, 558, 561, 564, 568, 577, 592. [5] Harl. 991, p. 75; *HMC Hatfield*, iv. 534; v. 236, 523; ix. 175, 180, 181, 216; *APC*, xxviii. 298, 559; *VCH Bucks.* iii. 162; iv. 255; *VCH Berks.* iv. 530; C2/Eliz./T6/59. [6] PCC 3 Bolein.

A.M.M./P.W.H.

TATE, Bartholomew (bef. 1532–1601), of Coventry, Warws. and Delapré, Northants.

COVENTRY   1572*

b. bef. 1532, 1st s. of Sir Bartholomew Tate of Laxton, Northants. by Anne (*d.*1564), da. of Laurence Saunders of Harrington, Northants., prob. wid. of one Befford. *m.* (1) by 1550, Elinor or Elizabeth, da. and h. of Richard Pauncefote, prob. 1da.; (2) c.1557, Dorothy, da. of Francis Tanfield of Gayton, Northants., 3s. inc. Francis* and William*, 3 or 4da. *suc.* fa. 1532.[1]
Freeman, Northampton.[2]
Escheator, Northants. 1560–2, j.p. by 1582, q. 1584–*d.*; sheriff 1585–6.

In the fifteenth century the Tates were London merchants. Tate's father became a member of the royal household and held office in Calais, probably as vice-marshal or marshal. Tate himself must have been employed by Elizabeth before her accession, as she gave him a grant 'for his service' in the reign of Queen Mary.

After his father's death his mother married Sir Thomas Longueville, but the latter died without surviving issue in 1536 and Tate was probably brought up either on his father's Coventry manor, Whitley, or by his mother's family, the Saunders. Some time between 1544 and 1548 his mother married Andrew, a younger son of Nicholas Wadham of Merrifield, Somerset, and on 13 Feb. 1548 they bought Delapré from John Mershe with remainder to Bartholomew. The following day Mershe obtained a licence to alienate the property to Tate's two Saunders uncles, probably by way of a settlement. Tate and his mother immediately built a range of rooms on the site of the old nunnery and it may have been to these that he brought his first wife, his cousin Elizabeth Pauncefote, granddaughter of Robert Tate[†], and her father's heir. She evidently died young, for in 1557 Tate enfeoffed his Kent manor of Stokebury to a group of Tanfield feoffees; and his eldest son, William, was baptized in 1559. Elizabeth Pauncefote has been described as dying without issue, but for two reasons it seems probable that she left a daughter:

in the first place Tate retained the Pauncefote estates, and secondly in about 1576 his eldest daughter, Dorothy, married Robert Tanfield, his second wife's brother.[3]

Tate had many relatives who might have assisted him to obtain advancement: his cousin, Richard Tate, the ambassador, who left Tate's brother Anthony a £20 annuity; his second wife's family, the Tanfields, prominent in legal circles; her cousins the Caves, royal officials; and above all his cousin, Sir Christopher Hatton. His friends, and the marriages arranged for his children show him to have been a member of Hatton's circle, yet Tate does not himself appear to have derived any benefit from his relatives. The Tanfields undoubtedly promoted the legal career of his son Francis and the connexion with the Hattons probably helped his son William to a seat in Parliament.

In the late 1550s and the 1560s Tate was occupied in reorganizing his Northamptonshire estates, dividing his time between his Coventry manor of Whitley and Delapré. In 1564 he was recommended by the bishop of his diocese for inclusion on the commission of the peace as 'an earnest furtherer' of religion – a claim which receives no confirmation from the Catholic sympathies of the husbands he chose for his daughters. He does not appear on the commission until the eighties, and then played only a minor role in county affairs. He served the usual term as sheriff and was occasionally called upon to act on special commissions.[4]

In Coventry Tate was a well known figure as the owner of one of the principal manors within the city boundaries, and the descendant of prominent benefactors of the borough. A dispute over commons was settled by arbitration in 1569, and there was no quarrel outstanding in April 1573 when Tate was elected to replace Edmund Brownell, deceased, who had represented Coventry in the first session of this Parliament. In 1581 he was named one of the trustees, under Thomas Dudley's will, of property left for charitable uses. By 1593 there was a further dispute: a reference in the council book to £23 in gold sent to London for Mr. Tate's suits is presumably the prelude to the agreement in 1594 between Tate and the city concerning lands and tithes at Stivichall and Stretton.[5]

In Parliament Tate has only one recorded committee, 11 Feb. 1576, on the poor law. It may have been he who, about this time, wrote a treatise, wrongly ascribed to his son Francis, offering advice on the management of the House of Commons to a Privy Councillor – possibly the comparatively inexperienced Hatton, who is known to have been seeking advice.[6]

Tate died 23 Apr. 1601, and was buried at Hardingstone. He had expanded his estates shortly before his death by the acquisition from the Crown of the manor of Cotton and the purchase of Byfield rectory from Valentine Knightley*. The bulk of his estates descended to his eldest son William, for whom in 1597 he had negotiated a splendid match with the eldest daughter, and presumptive coheir, of Edward, Lord Zouche of Harringworth.[7]

[1] PCC 24 Thower, 29 Tashe; *Vis. Northants.* ed. Metcalfe, 45, 198; *Vis. Notts.* (Harl. Soc. iv), 84; the pedigrees are confused about the numbering and names of his mother's husbands, Wadham being generally given as her second. [2] *Northampton Recs.* ii. 45. [3] W. K. Jordan, *Charities of London*, 137, 271, 299, 300, 352, 405; S. Thrupp, *Merchant Class of Medieval London*, 369; *Chronicle of Calais* (Cam. Soc. xxxv), xxxix. 100, 163; PCC 16 Pynnyng; Baker, *Northants.* i. 27; Lipscomb, *Bucks.* iv. 315; Wards 7/26/44; R. M. Serjeantson, *Hist. Delapré*, 33; J. Wake and W. A. Pantin, *Northants. Past and Present*, ii. no. 5, 230; *CPR*, 1547–8, p. 332; 1555–7, p. 434; 1556–9, p. 321. [4] *CPR*, 1558–60, pp. 12, 405; 1560–3, p. 326; Wards 7/26/44; Bridges, *Northants.* i. 363, 364, 365, 392; ii. 35; E. St. John Brooks, *Sir Christopher Hatton*, 68–70, 159; *Cam. Misc.* ix(3), p. 36; *APC*, xix. 68; xxii. 546; xxiv. 41; Lansd. 49, f. 171. [5] Jordan, loc. cit.; Coventry Bk. of Payments, ff. 17, 44, 69; *Coventry Loans, Benefactions and Charities* (1802), p. 61; T. W. Whitley, *Parl. Rep. Coventry*, 59. [6] *CJ*, i. 105; Harl. 253, ff. 32 et seq.; Neale, *Parlts.* i. 422–4; Sir Harris Nicholas, *Sir C. Hatton*, 216–18, 226. [7] C142/265/58; PRO, cal. and index pat. rolls 31–7 Eliz. 32 (17), p. 24, 37–43 Eliz. 41(11); Baker, ii. 276; *CP*, xii. 951–2.

S.M.T.

TATE, Francis (1560–1616), of Delapré, Northants.

NORTHAMPTON	1601
SHREWSBURY	1604

b. 1560, 2nd s. of Bartholomew Tate* by his 2nd w. and bro. of William*. *educ.* Magdalen Hall, Oxf. 1577; Staple Inn bef. 1579; M. Temple 1579, called 1587. *unm.*

Member, Antiq. Soc. 1591.

Of counsel to Northampton; j.p. Brec., Glam., Rad. 1604; justice of assize Brec. circuit 1604; Lent reader M. Temple 1608, treasurer 1615.[1]

Tate and his brother William entered the Middle Temple together under the auspices of their uncle Robert Tanfield, a prominent member and later treasurer of the inn. William was there to finish a gentleman's education, but Francis was to make the law his career. In subsequent years he acted as surety for his many relatives and friends who entered the inn, and he slowly rose through the hierarchy of offices. He was an original member and sometime secretary of the Society of Antiquaries, corresponding with Sir Robert Cotton* and William Camden. Though a number of his works were published, 'A discourse importing the assembly of Parliament' was not his, for it was written on the eve of the Parliament of 1581, at which time Tate was barely of age, and the author had already sat in Parliament. Perhaps it was written by his father. Tate was, however, interested in the antiquity of Parliament, which he traced back to the ancient Britons. He believed that the 'three parts' of the Parliament – King, Lords and Commons – had always had the same weight and role, and therefore that the exact method of promulgating statutes in the past had little importance: 'words are not much to be regarded, inasmuch as whatsoever the Parliament alloweth it bindeth as a law, though it be set forth only in the King's name, as the statutes of Gloucester and Magna Carta, or in the name of the Commons only', a conclusion which was thought significant in 1621, when this and other tracts on the subject were gathered together.[2]

In 1601 Tate sought election at Northampton, and he was returned as the son of a freeman, resident near the town. He was an active speaker, but sat on only two committees (abbreviation of the Michaelmas law term, 11 Nov. and the Exchequer bill, 25 Nov.). His speeches reflect his antiquarian interests, and his use of precedents anticipates so many speeches in the Parliaments of the 1620s. On 14 Nov. 1601, 'he that presents a precedent without a reason presents a body without a soul'. On 27 Nov. 'heretofore the Houses of Parliament were both one, without division; and that the united body of the Parliament had the same privileges and jurisdictions which we now have'. Next day, on the bill to explain the act touching charitable uses, there 'could be no law which was contrary to the Great Charter'. It was Tate who first brought the dispute between the 4th Earl of Huntingdon* and George Belgrave* to the notice of the House, by producing the information filed by Huntingdon in Star Chamber and requesting that it be referred to the committee on privileges, 3 Dec. When the matter was discussed in the House, Tate prudently suggested (8 Dec.) that rash action might endanger their privileges ('it is not good to utter things suddenly in great matters') and advised that the Lords should be petitioned and, if necessary, a conference held, a course recommended by other speakers and ultimately adopted.[3]

In 1602 Tate was replaced as legal counsel to Northampton, as he was 'shortly ... to remove into Wales, a place so far distant from this town that the corporation upon any opportunity cannot have use of him as heretofore'. The next year he made his will, at a time when he evidently thought he was dying. But he survived until 1616, still an active member of his inn.[4]

[1] *DNB*; *Vis. Northants.* ed. Metcalfe, 199; *Northampton Recs.* ii. 72. [2] *Archaeologia*, i. p. xii; Stowe ms 1045; *CSP Dom.* 1598–1601, p. 553; Harl. 253, f. 32 seq.; 305, f. 248; Neale, *Commons*, 355–8. [3] *Northampton Recs.* ii. 495; D'Ewes, 635, 638, 651, 655, 661, 666, 672–3; Townshend, *Hist. Colls.* 215, 254, 255, 259, 269, 270, 282, 296. [4] *Northampton Recs.* ii. 72; PCC 46 Weldon; *M. T. Bench Bk.* 172.

S.M.T.

TATE, William (1559–1617), of Delapré, Northants.

CORFE CASTLE	1593
NORTHAMPTONSHIRE	1614

b. 1559, 1st s. of Bartholomew Tate* of Delapré by his 2nd w. and bro. of Francis*. *educ.* Magdalen Hall, Oxf. 1576; Staple Inn; I. Temple 1579. *m.* 1597, Elizabeth (*d.*1617), da. and coh. of Edward, 11th Lord Zouche of Harringworth, 4s. 3da. *suc.* fa. 1601. Kntd. 1606.

J.p. Northants. and Warws. from c.1601; dep. lt. or commr. musters, Northants. by 1601, sheriff 1603–4.

His father's longevity prevented Tate from playing a prominent part in county life during Elizabeth's reign. His seat at Corfe Castle was no doubt provided by his father's connexion with the Hattons. He himself continued to act for them in the redemption of the estate from the lord chancellor's debt. His own position was enhanced by his marriage. His father-in-law did all he could to promote Tate's interests, evidently persuading Burghley to forward his career.

Under James I Tate was prominent in county affairs and was evidently an efficient administrator. His outlook on the world was pessimistic. When he made his will two months before his death, he found it a place 'continually inclining to the worst' and was anxious to 'shake hands' with it so that he might dedicate himself 'soul and body to a celestial contemplation of the incomprehensible happiness of that succeeding life promised to all such as by a lively faith in Christ Jesus alone expect a glorification'. He felt assured that he would 'become partaker of those unspeakable joys prepared and reserved for the elect servants and saints of the eternal and everlasting God.' He made careful preparation for the upbringing of his children, hoping that his father-in-law with the assistance of other relatives and servants, would execute the will and obtain his son's wardship. If Zouche could not undertake the office he asked his friends Robert, Baron Spencer*, and Sir Edward Montagu II* to do so. He died 14 Oct. 1617 at Delapré, leaving a considerable estate in North-amptonshire and Warwickshire.

CP; Vis. Northants. ed. Metcalfe, pp. 198–9; HMC Buccleuch, iii. passim; HMC Hatfield, xi. 437; xv. 291; xvii. 490, 496, 563; CSP Dom. 1611–18, p. 386; HMC Montagu, passim; PCC 124 Weldon; C142/365/149.

S.M.T.

TAYLOR, Roger (d. 1578), of Oxford.

OXFORD 1559

m. Elizabeth, at least 3da.
Chamberlain, Oxford 1552–3, bailiff 1553–4, mayor 1563–4, 1569–70, 1574–5.

A member of the Oxford corporation for over 20 years, Taylor's name appears regularly in the town records. There is no definite statement as to his trade or profession, but he owned a brewhouse, and possibly made his living as an inn-keeper. He was evidently wealthy, with a large amount of property in Oxford and the surrounding district: his will mentions his house in the parish of St. Peter's, land in Kidlington near Woodstock and the 'farm and grounds of Walton', which he held from St. John's College. He also owned a number of houses at St. Mary Magdalene in the suburbs of Oxford. Outside Oxfordshire his only known property was at Maidenhead.

The first reference found to Taylor is his assessment –

on £7 in goods – for the 1543 subsidy. Between that date and 1558 he filled various minor offices on the city council; in October 1554 he was in London pursuing a suit about corporation lands. He continued to hold office throughout the religious changes of the period, and soon after Elizabeth's accession was elected one of the eight assistants to the mayor. A new corporation order of September 1562 limited these 'assistants' to four aldermen, with certain other 'ancient persons' including Taylor; but this body soon began to co-opt more 'very sad, discreet and ancient persons' as associates, and the limitation of numbers seems to have been ineffective. Another decree of the same month, in which Taylor is styled 'alderman', nominated him as one of six to represent the city in negotiations with 'Mr. Owen' – probably the Richard Owen who some years later sold lands to St. John's College.

In May 1575, during Taylor's last mayoralty, the long-standing quarrel between city and university became so acute that, following a Star Chamber suit, he and other members of the corporation came before the Privy Council to put their case against Dr. Humfrey, vice-chancellor of the university. The questions discussed ranged from the corporation's obligation to hold a sermon at communion service to commemorate those killed in an earlier riot in Oxford, to the university's exemption from the liability of providing post-horses. Taylor was involved in another local dispute when bailiff William Noble* accused him and other city officials of letting offenders go unconvicted or unpunished, and of allowing dicing and other offences.

Very few later references to Taylor have been found: the last mention of him as an alderman is in July 1577. He died between March and November the following year, leaving a will dividing his property into three parts – to his wife Elizabeth, to his three daughters, and to charitable uses. The only other relatives mentioned were a brother and sister 'in the north country'. Following a dispute about the value of the property, the prerogative court of Canterbury confirmed the will by sentence.

W. H. Turner, Oxford Recs. 212, 221, 222, 277, 294–5, 305, 331, 356, 394; Oriel Coll. Recs. ed. Shadwell and Salter (Oxf. Hist. Soc. lxxxv), 325; Early Hist. St. John's, ed. Stevenson and Salter (Oxf. Hist. Soc. n.s.i), 530; Surveys and Tokens, ed. Salter (Oxf. Hist. Soc. lxxv), 142, 152; APC, viii. 376; CSP Dom. Add. 1566–79, p. 483; PCC 42 Langley.

N.M.F.

TEMPEST, Richard (1534–83), of Bowling and Bracewell, Yorks.

ALDBOROUGH 1572

b. 1534, 1st s. of Nicholas Tempest of Bracewell by his 1st w. Beatrice, da. and h. of John Bradford of Heath, nr. Wakefield. m. (1) by 1567, Helen or Eleanor, da. of John,

8th Lord Scrope, *s.p.*; (2) Elizabeth, da. of Thomas Wentworth of Elmsall, *s.p. suc.* fa. 1571.[1]

J.p.q. Yorks. (W. Riding) from c.1577.

There were several branches of the Tempest family in Elizabethan Yorkshire. Richard was a popular christian name among them, and Richard of Bowling had at least two cousins and namesakes living in 1572 – Richard of Tong, son of Henry Tempest of Tong by Ellen Mirfield, and Richard of Thornton Hall in Bradford Dale. It is easy to confuse the careers of the three, but the parliamentary return is explicit that the Aldborough Member was of Bowling. His sole known contribution to the business of the House is his asking (27 June 1572) for privilege for a servant who had been arrested. He presumably owed his nomination to his local connexions. He came of an old-established family in the West Riding, and was a considerable landowner, described on a list of 1572 as one of the principal protestant gentry in Yorkshire. His brother-in-law, Henry, Lord Scrope, was warden of the west march and a member of the council in the north, and the Tempests were also connected by marriage with Sir Thomas Gargrave* and with other leading Yorkshire families.[2]

The absence of Tempest's name from more than a few lists of Yorkshire officials is probably accounted for by the short time that he was the head of his family, dying in 1583 when still under 50. Most of the references found to him are connected with conveyances. Since he had no children, he may have felt less need to keep his property intact, but the multiplicity of sales and re-sales, many of them involving the Savile family, probably covers a number of marriage settlements or agreements under the Statute of Uses. As usual, these elaborate arrangements led to a good deal of litigation. In his will, dated February and proved in September 1583, Tempest asked his widow, the sole executrix, to arrange for his burial in Bradford church near his ancestors. She was to have most of the non-entailed property, except for the lease of a farm in Waddington, reserved for John Banister (the son of Tempest's sister), described in the will as 'my man and cousin'. The 'household stuff' at Bracewell was bequeathed to the testator's brother and heir Robert. Among lands descending to the executrix was a new 'intake of the common' near Wilsden. The supervisors of the will were her father, and Thomas Wentworth of Woodhouse, styled 'my friend and cousin, now sheriff of York[shire]'. The widow married as her second husband John Savile I*.[3]

[1] R. Glover, *Vis. Yorks.* ed. Foster, 319, 357; *Surtees Soc.* cvi. 60 n; *Yorks. Fines* (Yorks. Arch. Soc. Rec. ser. ii), 342; C142/156/51. [2] J. J. Cartwright, *Chapters in Yorks. Hist.* 68; Trinity, Dublin, Thos. Cromwell's jnl., f. 67. [3] *Yorks. Fines*, passim; *Ducatus Lanc.* iii. 232, 249, 307; iv. 37, 42, 50; *CPR, 1569–72*, p. 353; Cartwright, 83; York prob. reg. 22/447; Foss, *Judges*, vi. 187.

N.M.F.

TEMPLE, Anthony, of Berwick-upon-Tweed, Northumb.

BERWICK-UPON-TWEED 1563

Alderman of Berwick, mayor 1562, 1565, 1571.

Beyond the facts given above, nothing is known of Temple. As one of the Berwick burgesses in 1563 he could have taken part in the committee meetings on the bill about Berwick, 25 Jan.

Arch. Ael. (ser. 4), xxiv. 73; *CJ,* i. 63.

A.M.M.

TEMPLE, Thomas (1567–1637), of Burton Dassett, Warws.

ANDOVER 1589

bap. 9 Jan. 1567, 1st s. of John Temple of Burton Dassett by Susan, da. and h. of Thomas Spencer of Everdon, Northants. *educ.* Univ. Coll. Oxf. 1582; L. Inn 1584. *m.* c.1595, Hester, da. of Miles Sandys* of Latimer, Bucks., 3s. 10da. *suc.* fa. 9 May 1603. Kntd. 1603; *cr.* Bt. 1611.

Sheriff, Oxon. 1606–7, Bucks. 1616–17, Warws. 1620–1.

Of a family established in Warwickshire since the reign of Henry VI, Temple's only appearance in Parliament was owed to the influence of the Sandys family, into which he was to marry a few years later. Temple bought the estate of Stowe, Buckinghamshire, in 1590 and lived as a country gentleman, purchasing a baronetcy in 1611. His will, made on 4 Feb. 1633, was proved by a younger son, Miles, on 13 Mar. 1637. Temple died 10 Feb. 1637; the heir was his son, Sir Peter†.

C142/281/93, 575/142; G. Lipscomb, *Bucks.* iii. 85–6; *VCH Bucks.* iii. 486; iv. 232, 241, 464; *VCH Oxon.* vi. 119, 122; PCC 32 Bolein, 46 Goare.

A.M.M.

TEMPLE, William (c.1555–1627), of London, and later of Trinity College, Dublin.

TAMWORTH 1597

b. c.1555, ?s. of Anthony Temple (*d.*1581), of Coughton, Warws.[1] by Jane, da. of one Bargrave. *educ.* Eton; King's, Camb. 1573, BA 1578, MA 1581, fellow 1576–83. *m.* Martha, da. of Robert Harrison of Derbys., 2s. 3da. Kntd. 4 May 1622.

Schoolmaster, Lincoln g.s. 1583; provost, Trinity, Dublin 1609–*d.*; master in Chancery [I] 1610–*d.*[2]

Temple became known for his publications in support of Peter Ramus, who had attacked the logical system of Aristotle. His first two works were dedicated to the Earl of Arundel, and later Sir Philip Sidney* became his patron. When Sidney was appointed governor of Flushing in 1585, Temple accompanied him as his secretary, and subsequently received an annuity of £30 in his will. In the years after Sidney's death Temple was secretary in turn to William Davison*, secretary of state; Sir Thomas Smith*, clerk of the Council; and in 1594, the Earl of Essex, who was behind his return for Tamworth in 1597. He accompanied the Earl to Ireland in 1599. Temple's admiration for Essex may be seen in a letter he wrote at this time to Edward Reynolds*, another of the Earl's secretaries, describing Essex as the noblest and worthiest lieutenant that Ireland had ever seen.[3]

Temple was under heavy suspicion at the time of the Essex rising. From February to June 1601 he was in the Gatehouse, and he was one of those listed, 26 Feb., as indicted and fit to be arraigned. He was given the liberty of the prison in June 1601, and at the end of that month he was let off with a £100 fine. However, it was some years before he could get another appointment. He asked Cecil in 1602 to write 'a line or two of recommendation to Lord Zouche', whose service he was trying to enter, apparently without success. In an effort to regain favour at court he published *A Logical Analysis of Twenty Select Psalms* in 1605, dedicated to Henry, Prince of Wales. 'Of late', he wrote in the dedication, 'in this time of my idleness, under hope of pardon at the hands of our professed theologians, [I have] attempted by the direction of the said art [logic] an analysis of certain choice psalms'. It was not until 1609 that he obtained employment, and then he had to go to Ireland. As Cecil was chancellor of Trinity College it is possible that he used his influence on Temple's behalf. His salary as provost was, after 1611, £100 a year, but by 1626 he had supplemented this with the annual rent income from lands held on lease in several Irish counties. Temple died in 1627. In his will, made in December 1626, he bequeathed the leases to his wife and his eldest son John and asked that he should be buried without pomp.[4]

[1] Both *DNB* and Temple Prime, *Some Account of the Temple Fam.* (3rd ed. 1896), 24, suggest this parentage, but Anthony Temple does not mention a son William in his will, which names his son Peter, not then 18, as executor. As William must have been older than Peter, it is doubtful whether Anthony Temple was his father. [2] *Al. Cant.* i(4), p. 213; J. C. Wedgwood, *Staffs. Parl. Hist.* (Wm. Salt Arch. Soc.), i. 406–7; *DNB*. [3] *DNB*; Neale, *Commons*, 240 n.; *HMC Hatfield*, ix. 161. [4] *APC*, 1600–1, pp. 160, 434, 483, 488; *CSP Dom.* 1601–3, p. 61; *HMC Hatfield*, xi. 33; xii. 195; J. W. Stubbs, *Hist. Univ. Dublin*, 27; Temple Prime, 109.

A.M.M.

THEAKSTON, Richard (*d.*1609), of the Charterhouse, London, and Theakston, Yorks.

WHITCHURCH	1593
ALDBOROUGH	1601

m. Eleanor, at least 1s. Kntd. 1603.
Clerk in pipe office by 1589; servant of (Sir) John Fortescue I* by 1593–1607; j.p. Yorks. (N. Riding) from c.1601.

Theakston first comes to notice in 1578 when he was involved in a dispute over a 21-year lease of the Nottinghamshire manor of Mansfield, procured from

Thomas Markham* and subsequently sold to the 3rd Earl of Rutland through an agent. Markham had Theakston imprisoned in the Fleet, whence, in the July, he addressed unavailing appeals to Rutland, whose resolution was that he would

> neither purchase Mr. Markham's satisfaction, nor your liberty, with re-delivery of my estate, and this you may assure yourself to be my absolute determination.

Theakston was free by September, still asking the Earl to return the lease. Next Theakston obtained a post in the pipe office, and finally entered the service of the chancellor of the Exchequer, Sir John Fortescue, remaining with Fortescue until the latter's death in 1607, when Theakston was described as his secretary. However, in the meantime Theakston was fluttering around that dangerous flame, the 2nd Earl of Essex. Both Essex and his henchman (Sir) Gelly Meyrick* were trustees in a settlement Theakston made of part of his estate, and Meyrick was Theakston's dining companion on at least one occasion. This leads to speculation as to whether it might have been Essex who intervened with the ecclesiastical authorities to bring about Theakston's return at Whitchurch in 1593. Support for this comes from the fact that the brother of his fellow-Member was later to be deeply implicated in the Essex rising, but against it is the possibility that Theakston secured the seat through his own connexion with the Exchequer. About Aldborough in 1601 there need be no doubt: Fortescue obtained him the seat. There is no evidence of any activity by Theakston in either of his Parliaments.

Theakston's landed estate was in the parish of Theakston in the North Riding of Yorkshire. Towards the end of Elizabeth's reign he purchased from the Crown the manor of Sedbergh, where tenants accused him – 'a man of great living, countenance, kindred and friendship in the county of York' – of trying to deprive them of their customary rights. He was knighted by James I on that monarch's progress south in 1603, made his will on 4 Dec. 1604, and died 6 Sept. 1609, leaving an heir fifteen-and-a-half years old.

Yorks. Arch. Soc. xxvii. 358; Lansd. 27, ff. 4–5; 59, f. 141; *HMC Hatfield*, ii. 202; iv. 334; xiii. 414, 582–4; Add. 12497, f. 143; *HMC 7th Rep.* 528; C142/312/135; C2.Eliz./M13/65; PCC 93 Dorset.

A.M.M.

THELWALL, Simon I (1525/26–86), of Plas-y-ward, Llanynys, Denb.

DENBIGH BOROUGHS	1553 (Mar.), 1553 (Oct.), 1559
DENBIGHSHIRE	1563
DENBIGH BOROUGHS	1571

b. 1525/26, 1st s. of Richard Thelwall of Plas-y-ward by Elizabeth, da. of Thomas Herle of Stanton Harcourt, Oxon. and Aberystwyth, Card. *educ.* I. Temple 1556, called 1568. *m.* (1) Alice, da. of Robert Salesbury of Rûg, Merion. and Bachymbyd, 4s.; (2) Jane, da. of Thomas Massey* of Broxton and Chester, Cheshire, 1s. 2da.; (3) Margaret, da. of Sir William Griffith of Penrhyn, Caern., wid. of Sir Nicholas Dutton, *s.p. suc.* fa. 1568.

Commr. piracy, Denb. 1565, tanneries, Ruthin 1574; seneschal Ruthin manor from 1575; sheriff, Denb. 1571–2, j.p. from 1575, commr. musters 1580; dep. justice, Chester circuit 1576, 1579, vice-justice 1580, 1584; member, council in the marches of Wales c.1577.[1]

The Thelwalls were originally a Cheshire family who migrated to the vale of Clwyd in the fourteenth century. A fortunate marriage brought them Plas-y-ward near Ruthin, and this remained the seat of the main branch of the family. By the beginning of Elizabeth's reign they were established as one of the county's leading families.

Thelwall had an extraordinary career. He entered the Inner Temple at the advanced age of 30, in 1556, and was called in 1568, aged 42. He succeeded to his father's estates in the same year and received the usual local offices in due course. But far from settling down as a country gentleman, he apparently continued his legal career and was deputy justice of the Chester circuit only eight years later, aged 50.

In 1563 Thelwall was elected knight for Denbighshire, while still studying at the Inner Temple and before succeeding to his estates. He also represented Denbigh Boroughs in 1559 and 1571. The only reference to him in the extant Commons journals (22 Mar. 1563) is to his application for leave of absence from Parliament 'for his necessary affairs'.

In west Denbighshire Thelwall's interests were firmly linked to those of the pre-eminent county family, the Salusburys of Lleweni. His first marriage had been into the junior branch of that family, and as a committed protestant he allied himself with the Salusburys in support of the Earl of Leicester and court opinion. It was Thelwall who pronounced the death sentence on Richard Gwyn, the first Welsh Catholic martyr, at Wrexham in 1584. The inclusion of his name in a list of Welsh Catholics drawn up ten years earlier in the interests of Mary Queen of Scots may be dismissed as a piece of wishful thinking.

In the course of his life, Thelwall augmented the family estates by the lease of a moiety of the manor of Dinorben, in north-western Denbighshire; he also farmed from the Crown, jointly with Thomas Pennant of Bychton, mill rights in Dyserth, Flintshire, which involved them both in Exchequer proceedings with the Conways of Bodrhyddan in 1580–2. He held the lease of half the episcopal 'lordship' of Meliden, until he surrendered it to William Hughes, the venal bishop of St. Asaph, in return for a grant of the vicarage of Mold to his son Eubule, who held it from 1576 to 1594.

He died in April 1586 and was buried at Ruthin. In his will, which was made on 16 Apr. and proved 7 Nov. 1586, he aspired to 'enjoy eternal bliss amongst the elect of the

children of God'. His principal heir, his son Edward, was also an executor of his will. His third wife, who survived him by only a few months, inherited a third of his lands.[2]

[1] *DWB*; Griffith, *Peds.* 274; Flenley, *Cal. Reg. Council, Marches of Wales*, 127, 133, 200, 212; W. R. Williams, *Welsh Judges*, 71; Add. Chart 41406; P. H. Williams, *Council in the Marches of Wales*, 358–9; *APC*, vii. 286; SC2/225/14, 23. [2] *DWB*; *HMC Welsh*, i. 291; Harl. 1143, f. 30v; Williams, *Parl. Hist. Wales*, 160; Read, *Burghley*, 39, 45, 157, 315, 550; *CSP Dom.* 1547–80, pp. 685–9, 692; Add. Chart 26069, 51482; J. Y. W. Lloyd, *Powys Fadog*, iii. 128–64; *Cath. Rec. Soc.* xiii. 109; *Trans. Denb. Hist. Soc.* iii. 46–7, 58–9, 87–9; *EHR*, lix. 350; *Augmentations*, ed. Lewis and Davies (Univ. Wales Bd. of Celtic Studies, Hist. and Law ser. xiii), 372; *Exchequer*, ed. E. G. Jones (id. ser. iv), 191–2; *Arch. Camb.* (ser. 5), i. 57; Lansd. 120; f. 24; *CJ*, i. 70; PCC 55 Windsor.

A.H.D.

THELWALL, Simon II (*b.* c.1561), of Bathafarn Park, Llanrhudd, Denb., and later of Woodford, Essex.

DENBIGH BOROUGHS 1593

b. c.1561, 7th s. of John Wyn Thelwall (*d.*1586), of Bathafarn Park by Jane (*d.*1586), da. of Thomas Griffith of Pant y llongdu (or llawndy), Llanasa, Flints. *educ.* Balliol, Oxf. 1581, aged 20; St. Mary Hall, Oxf. BA 1584; L. Inn (from Furnival's) 1591. *m.* Ann Biggs of Woodford, 2s. 2da.

Chief clerk of Sir Daniel Dunne; proctor, ct. of arches; registrar, diocese of Bangor.

The Thelwalls of Bathafarn were founded by this MP's grandfather John Thelwall, a younger son of the parent house of Plas-y-ward and lessee of Bathafarn Park in the crown lordship of Ruthin. This property was later bought by his grandson, the MP's eldest brother, another John Thelwall. The family had no great landed estate, but the ten sons of John Wyn Thelwall (depicted on a monument in Llanrhudd church, kneeling with their four sisters on either side of the parents) brought prominence to this hitherto obscure branch by their prowess in the law and at court, where three of them held positions of trust in three reigns. The most famous was Sir Eubule[†], the eminent civilian who became principal of Jesus College, Oxford, and thrice represented his shire in Parliament. 'There were in our time in that house', wrote Bishop Goodman in 1652, 'many brethren, all of them wise, able, provident men, they did help to raise the house, but they did not share in a foot of the lands'. It was not till 1608 that John, the eldest, obtained a grant of arms.

Simon, like his brother Eubule, followed the law, and from the time of his admission to Lincoln's Inn he lived either in chambers or on his wife's property at Woodford. It was natural that a rising lawyer from the district should be chosen for the Boroughs, but the county seat and the shrievalty called for land. It is likely, therefore, that the sheriff in 1612 and MP in 1614 was his namesake of Plas-y-ward. The date of the death of Simon Thelwall of Bathafarn Park has not been ascertained.

J. Y. W. Lloyd, *Powys Fadog*, iv. 311–16; Griffith, *Peds.* 369; *DWB*, 932–3; *Al. Ox.* i(2), p. 1469; *Exchequer*, ed. E. G. Jones (Univ. Wales Bd. of Celtic Studies, Hist. and Law ser. iv), 158–9; Pennant, *Tours* (1883), ii. 187–90; NLW, Bagot 47; Egerton 2586, f. 124; Add. 14295, f. 69; *Trans. Denb. Hist. Soc.* iii. 87–8.

A.H.D.

THEOBALD, Stephen (*d.* 1619), of the Inner Temple and of Seal, Kent.

YARMOUTH I.o.W.   1601

 1st s. of John Theobald of Seal by Clement, da. of William Linch of Cranbrook. *educ.* St. John's, Camb. 1569, I. Temple 1576, called 1584. *m.* (1) bef. 1576, Katherine (*d.* 1582), da. of Richard Caryll, 4da.; (2) *s.p.*
 J.p. Kent 1601.

Theobald's family had held land at Seal since the early fifteenth century, Theobald himself being the last male representative of the senior branch. Though an eldest son, and continuing to reside at Seal, where his children were born, and where his first wife was buried, Theobald pursued the legal career into which he had been introduced by his sister Dorothy's husband, Roger Manwood*. It may have been Manwood who was responsible for Theobald's being nominated at Yarmouth by Sir George Carey*, patron of the borough. No other connexion between Theobald and Carey has been found.

Theobald's will, drawn up in July 1619, was proved on 27 Aug. of the same year by Edward Mitchell, one of his sons-in-law. A total of £7 was bequeathed to the poor of three parishes in Kent, £10 to the hospital of St. Stephen founded by Sir Roger Manwood, and £5 13s. 4d. each to two other hospitals in London, and one in Southwark. His heirs were the two surviving children of his first marriage, Catherine and Margaret. A monument was erected to him and his two wives in the parish church of Seal.

Vis. Kent (Harl. Soc. lxxv), 36; Hasted, *Kent*, iii. 53, 55, 59; *Arch. Cant.* xxxi. 179–80, 182; *DNB* (Manwood, Sir Roger, and Peter); PCC 78 Parker.

A.M.M.

THOMAS, William I (1551–86), of Caernarvon.

CAERNARVONSHIRE   1572*, 1584

 b. 1551, 1st s. of Rhys Thomas of Aberglasney, Llangathen, Carm., and later of Llanfair Isgaer, Caern. by Jane, da. of Sir John Puleston† of Caernarvon, wid. of Edward Griffith of Penrhyn, Caern. *m.* Ellen, da. of William Griffith of Plas Mawr, Caern., 5s. 4da. *suc.* fa. 1577.[1]
 J.p. Caern. from c.1575, Anglesey from c.1578, Merion. from c.1579; sheriff, Anglesey 1578–9, Caern. 1580–1.

The family which consolidated its patronymics into the surname Thomas in the time of this MP's soldier grandfather Sir William Thomas, and eventually took its place among the leading Caernarvonshire gentry as Thomas of Aber and Coed Alun (or Helen), originated at an early date in Carmarthenshire, where Sir William was the second sheriff to be appointed under the Act of Union. His second son Rhys (the MP's father) made a fortunate marriage and migrated to his wife's lands in Anglesey and Caernarvonshire, where he extended his estates by leases from the Crown, his Puleston relatives, the Earl of Leicester and others. He remained there when his elder brother's death made him heir to Aberglasney, but it was not till after 1594 that the Carmarthenshire lands were disposed of to Bishop Rudd of St. David's, who founded there a new and long influential county family.[2]

Rhys Thomas lived just outside Caernarvon, in the parish of Llanfair Isgaer, and was actively engaged in the county affairs of both Anglesey and Caernarvon, consolidating his position in 1553 by the purchase of the manors of Cemmaes, Anglesey, and Aber, a former Caernarvonshire seat of the princes of Gwynedd. His son William – the subject of this biography – was placed in the household of the Duchess of Somerset, the Protector's widow, where he is said to have learnt Latin, Italian and French. Returning to Wales, he inherited or acquired a house in Caernarvon itself, which his son was to replace by the more ambitious Coed Alun and to supplement by another mansion at Aber – both still standing.[3]

By 1578 he was involved in charges of seizure of land and stock in Llanwnda, Dinas Dinlle and elsewhere and of other extortions. Commissioners appointed to investigate the complaints were discharged through some influence at court (probably Leicester's), and attempts to bring the matter before the council of Wales also broke down; but in 1580 the charges were carried to Star Chamber, with unknown results. This did not prevent him during these years from acting with his father-in-law and the bishop of Bangor as one of the quorum of magistrates to whom the Privy Council addressed its missives on Caernarvonshire and Anglesey affairs – notably one in 1580 summoning before it Rowland Kenrick* of Beaumaris, who had fallen foul of Leicester.[4]

Before this he had been returned to Parliament at a by-election, serving on one recorded committee, on the poor law, 11 Feb. 1576. Re-elected in 1584, there is no sign of any activity in Parliament, although as knight of the shire he was entitled to attend the subsidy committee on 24 Feb. 1585. In fact, like his grandfather, he was primarily a soldier, campaigning in Ireland, and in 1585 taking 200 men from North Wales to serve under Leicester in Flanders, where he fell at Zutphen in 1586. He had already made his will 'by reason I am employed in her Majesty's service in Flanders'. In this he made provision out of his lands in the three shires for five sons and three daughters, all under age, and a child as yet unborn. The younger sons were provided for by annuities out of the Carmarthenshire lands after the death of their mother (to whom these were bequeathed for life) until they had incomes of their own, and she was to pay the daughters' dowries out of the profits of the manor of Aber, which was also hers for life. All other lands went to the heir, another William Thomas, on coming of age; he was joint executor with his mother, and his grandfather, William Griffith, was an overseer, while to protect the legal interests of widow and infant heir, Thomas engaged (for another annuity) the services of the rising lawyer Hugh Hughes* of Plas Coch and Lincoln's Inn, later attorney-general for North Wales. The will was proved 10 Jan. 1587.[5]

[1] DWB, 935–6; Griffiths, Peds. 202. [2] DWB; Augmentations, ed. Lewis and Davies (Univ. Wales Bd. of Celtic Studies, Hist. and Law ser. xiii), 63, 276, 278, 302; Add. Chart 39988; W. L. Bevan, St. David's, 173. [3] CPR, 1554–5, p. 349; 1555–7, pp. 136–7; 1553 and App. Edw. VI, pp. 121, 363, 375, 386, 419; Cal. Q. S. Rec. Caern. ed. Williams, passim; Wynn, Gwydir Fam. 66–7; RCAM Caern. i. 3–4; ii. 158. [4] Lansd. 111, f. 6; St. Ch. 5/J12/23; APC, xi. 418–19. [5] Lansd. 43, f. 171; CSP For. 1585–6; 1586–7 passim; Wynn, Gwydir Fam. 66–7; R. C. Strong and J. A. Van Dorsten, Leicester's Triumph, 131; PCC 2 Spencer; C142/234/83.

A.H.D.

THOMAS, William II (d. 1596), of Bridgwater, Som.

BRIDGWATER 1593

Bailiff, Bridgwater, mayor 1581–2, 1590–1.

Thomas was a Bridgwater merchant and burgess whose family had been established in the town since the middle of the fifteenth century. His seat in Parliament came towards the end of his life when he had already held the chief administrative offices of the town. Thomas and his fellow-Member were appointed to two committees concerned with cloth, 15 and 23 Mar., and received a total of £16 in wages for the session.

Thomas made his will 17 Mar. 1595, proved 19 May 1596. He left 1s. to Wells cathedral, a number of personal bequests, and appointed as overseers Alexander Jones, a Bridgwater merchant, and Alexander Popham*, the recorder, whose son Thomas was bequeathed £40. The executor and residuary legatee was one John Wood.

Bridgwater archives, nos. 1476, 1567; receivers' accts. 1581, f. 11v; E190/1081/3; Bridgwater Borough Archives (Som. Rec. Soc. lx), 97; D'Ewes, 501, 507; PCC 38 Drake.

A.M.M.

THOMSON, John (1521–97), of Husborne Crawley, Beds. and Aldersgate, London.

NEW WINDSOR 1571
BEDFORDSHIRE 1572*

b. 1521, s. of William Thomson, ?of Wellingore, Lincs. by Catherine, da. and coh. of Robert Smyth. m. by 1567, Dorothy, da. of Richard Gilbert of Suff., at least 1s. 2da.[1]
Auditor of the Exchequer by 1553; j.p. Beds. and

Bucks. from c.1563; freeman, New Windsor Nov. 1568; sheriff, Beds. and Bucks. 1581–2; collector of loan, Beds. 1590.[2]

Of a Lincolnshire family – it was the bishop of Lincoln who classified him as earnest in religion in 1564 – Thomson sought and found his fortune in London, obtaining by 1553 a lucrative post in the Exchequer, which he retained after the reforms of 1554. His area comprised Bedford, Berkshire, Buckingham, Kent, Oxford, Surrey and Sussex, and the honour and castle of Windsor. Well placed to acquire estates, Thomson joined with Roger Alford* in January 1560 to purchase property in Bedfordshire and Buckinghamshire worth some £2,000. This brought him to the vicinity of Husborne Crawley, where in 1579 he obtained the manor once belonging to the priory of Dunstable, and in 1591 he purchased the rectory for £492. His return for New Windsor was no doubt connected with his job: in 1572 he audited the accounts of Humphrey Michell*, clerk of the works in the castle. That year Thomson was returned as knight for Bedfordshire, when the original choice, Sir Henry Cheyney*, was summoned to the Lords on the first day of the first session. 'Auditor Thomson' as such is recorded only in the committee of 14 Mar. 1581 on the bill against secret conveyances but it is possible that some of the committees attributed to Laurence Tomson might belong to him.[3]

Thomson died 3 Apr. 1597, leaving to his wife the contents of his house by Charterhouse churchyard. His son and heir, Robert, aged 30, received a gold chain of 1,164 links and all his 'armour, artillery and munition of war'. He 'steadfastly and faithfully' trusted to be saved 'by the merits of the passion and precious death of Jesus Christ', and asked to be 'buried in decent and godly order'. His sumptuous tomb survives in the church at Husborne Crawley.[4]

[1] Beds. N. and Q. ii. 50; Lincs. Peds. (Harl. Soc. lii), 959–60; Vis. Beds. (Harl. Soc. xix), 146, 170; C142/248/34; PCC 24 Cobham. [2] SP10/18/69; Bodl. Ashmole 1126, f. 36; APC, xx. 187. [3] Cam. Misc. ix(3), p. 28; CPR, 1553–4, p. 6; 1558–60, pp. 311–12; VCH Berks. iii. 488; VCH Beds. iii. 286, 307, 395–8; Hope, Windsor Castle, 269; Cath. Rec. Soc. xxii. 164; Neale, Commons, 198; APC, x. 245; CJ, i. 133. [4] C142/248/34; PCC 24 Cobham; Lipscomb, Bucks. iv. 230; VCH Beds. iii. opp. p. 398.

A.H.

THORLEY, William (d. 1611), of Staple Inn, London.

SOUTHAMPTON 1586

Returned at a last minute vacancy for Southampton, Thorley's name was written in over an erasure in the return, the original date of 24 Sept. being left unchanged. He may have been a lawyer, for his will, dated 1 Apr. 1611, was proved 14 days later by his relative and executor, Miles Dodson of Gray's Inn. Thorley's brothers, their children, and a number of other relatives received small bequests. His laundress, and the poor of the parish of St. Andrew Holborn in London and Holme in Yorkshire, where he was born, were among the beneficiaries.

C219/30; PCC 29 Wood.

A.M.M.

THORNBOROUGH, Edward (b. c.1563), of Shoddesden, Hants.

LUDGERSHALL 1593

b. c.1563, 1st s. of John Thornborough of Shoddesden by Margaret, da. of Sir John Kingsmill of Sydmonton. *educ.* Jesus, Oxf. 1575. *m.* Mary, da. of Edward Chester of Royston, Herts.

The Thornboroughs of Shoddesden were a branch of the better-known Yorkshire family, as was also the line at Salisbury from which sprang John Thornborough, bishop of Worcester. Edward Thornborough's father sold Shoddesden to his brother-in-law Richard Kingsmill* between 1556, when he married, and 1561, but he continued to describe himself as of Shoddesden and to reside in Hampshire, of which county he was a j.p. and in 1577–8 sheriff. He was also admitted to the freedom of Southampton in 1569.

Apart from the fact of his matriculation, nothing is certainly known of Edward Thornborough's career until his return to the Parliament of 1593, but if he can be identified with the Edward Thornborough who, at the end of the century, bewailed to Cecil his sickness, poverty and loss of official prospects, he had spent much of his time at court seeking advancement under the Cecils' patronage. Other pointers in the same direction are his marriage to a daughter of Colonel Edward Chester, of the Hertfordshire family, who was much in Burghley's confidence while engaged in the Netherlands, and his brother John's entry into service with Sir Thomas Cecil.

Thornborough's return in 1593 for Ludgershall, which lies just across the Wiltshire border from Shoddesden, doubtless reflected his family's standing and connexions in the area. It is probably significant that his uncle John Kingsmill* had represented the borough in two previous Parliaments. Members of the families of Mompesson and Dyer, into which his brother William and his sisters Constance and Catherine married, also sat in this Parliament. But if Thornborough himself saw it as a move in the game of self-advancement the effort must have proved unrewarding: it was to be his only appearance in the Commons and, not surprisingly, he left no trace on the sessions' proceedings. As one of the burgesses for a town in Wiltshire, however, he could have served on a committee discussing a cloth bill, 15 Mar.

In 1590 he and his father had taken an 80-year crown lease of Chute forest, which stretched north of Shoddesden, for the large sum of £6,200. Twenty years later Thornborough complained that this lease had been ruinous to him and that it was threatening 'the overthrow of an ancient house'. His plea for its revision, which he accompanied with an appeal to Salisbury, was not granted, and the lease presumably continued to aggravate his financial plight. No further trace has been found of either Edward or Mary Thornborough, and it is not known whether they had issue.

Vis. Hants (Harl. Soc. lxiv), 51; Berry, *Hants County Fams.* 86; *VCH Hants*, iv. 374–6; C/3/175/30; *Third Bk. of Remembrance of Southampton* (Soton Rec. Ser.), ii. 118–19; *HMC Hatfield*, ii. 84, 118–19, 137–8, 143; ix. 410; x. 186; *Wilts. Vis. Peds.* (Harl. Soc. cv, cvi), 60; D'Ewes, 501; *CSP Dom.* 1581–90, p. 692; 1591–4, p. 127; 1603–10, p. 653; *VCH Wilts.* iv. 426–7.

S.T.B.

THORNBOROUGH, John (c.1567–1630), of Leckford, Hants.

RIPON 1601

b. c.1567, 2nd s. of John Thornborough of Shoddesden, and bro. of Edward*. *educ.* Magdalen Coll. Oxf. matric. 2 July 1585, aged 17. *m.* (1) Joyce, da. of George Woodnutt of Sherrington, Cheshire, wid. of John Hill of London, 1da.; (2) Elizabeth, *s.p.*; (3) 16 Mar. 1626, Jane Southworth (d. 6 July 1646), *s.p.* Kntd. 23 July 1603.
Constable, Scarborough castle 1603–11.[1]

Thornborough was related to a namesake who was dean of York 1589–93, and subsequently bishop of Limerick, Bristol and Worcester. Doubtless it was this connexion that secured him the seat at Ripon in 1601. No trace has been found of any activities by Thornborough in that Parliament. He had bought the Hampshire manor of Leckford Riches in 1590, and conveyed it to his brother-in-law Thomas Mompesson five years later. His appointment as constable of Scarborough castle was for life, and in 1606 he petitioned Salisbury for the arrears of his wages and for the repayment of £6,000 advanced by him for the levying of troops in Ireland. The arrears of his wages, at least, were paid promptly. In 1608 Thornborough's daughter married into the Gates family of Seamer, Yorkshire. He died 15 Oct. 1630, aged 63.[2]

[1] *Vis. Hants* (Harl. Soc. lxiv), 51; *Vis. Cheshire* (Harl. Soc. xviii), 255; PCC 116 Hele, 8 Essex; Soc. Genealogists, St. Gregory by St. Paul's, London, par. reg., J. B. Whitmore, Hants Church Notes; *CSP Dom.* 1611–18, p. 50. [2] *DNB*; *HMC Hatfield*, xi. 409, 442; *APC*, xxx. 505; *VCH Hants*, iv. 447; *CSP Dom.* 1603–10, p. 21; 1611–18, p. 50; *Hants Mar. Lic.* 1607–40, ed. Willis, 4; Hants Church Notes.

J.J.C./J.P.F.

THORNEFF, Francis (b. c.1515), of Stamford, Lincs.

STAMFORD 1555, 1558, 1563

b. c.1515, 2nd s. of John Thorneff (*d.* 11 Mar. 1521) of Stamford by his w. Edith.[1]

Yeoman of the chamber by Feb. 1555; alderman (i.e. mayor), Stamford 1557-8.[2]

Thorneff held a minor court office under both Mary and Elizabeth, but whether he came into Parliament for Stamford through his own local standing or through some connexion with Sir William Cecil* has not been ascertained. If a connexion with Cecil antedated Queen Mary's reign, both Thorneff's court job and his return for Stamford would be accounted for. At any rate, Thorneff voted against a government bill in 1555, was granted leave of absence on 12 Mar. 1563 for his affairs in the Queen's service, and in that year quarrelled with John Houghton*, his parliamentary colleague, which resulted in Thorneff's being deprived of the freedom of Stamford in 1566. After this date nothing more is known about him.[3]

[1] C1/1272/17-19; E150/1222/8. [2] *CPR*, 1554-5, p. 180; J. Drakard, *Hist. Stamford*, 101. [3] *CPR*, 1553-4, p. 452; E159/333, xci (adhuc com. s. hil. 1 Mary); C3/178/72; Neale, *Commons*, 206; Guildford Mus. Loseley 1331/2; Stamford hall bk. 1566; Lansd. 3, f. 193; *CJ*, i. 69.

P.W.H.

THORNEY, Thomas (*d.*1605), of Portsmouth, Hants.

PORTSMOUTH   1586, 1589, 1593, 1597

m. Mary, at least 1da.
Jurat, Portsmouth 1574, mayor 1578-9, 1585-6.

Nothing is known of Thorney's origins, but it may be assumed that he was a member of the family which had branches in Lincolnshire and Nottinghamshire. His parliamentary wages in 1597 were 2s. a day, and before he departed for London he acknowledged the receipt of £6

for and towards such fees and charges as I shall pay and lay out for the use and benefit of the ... town in the next Parliament, and also in part of my own charges and expenses.

No record has been found of any activities in the Commons. Thorney was one of only two townsmen to represent the borough in the Elizabethan period.

Most of what is known about Thorney relates to his commercial ventures. In 1576 he declared that he had been robbed of a ship and its cargo in the harbour of La Hogue, and between 1578 and 1581 he was involved in a dispute with John Croke I*, a merchant of Southampton. The Privy Council appointed four arbitrators in 1581, urging them – as it was a matter in which Thorney had been gravely prejudiced – 'to have due regard that the poor complainant [Thorney] might be helped and relieved so far as they should find he deserved in equity'.

As one of the principal merchants of Portsmouth, Thorney was appointed a commissioner for assessing the value of the cargoes carried by the vessels taken by Drake

and Norris in their attack on the Spanish coast in 1589. He and some of the other commissioners naturally bought 'great quantities' of wheat and rye 'at base and low prices rated by themselves'. Thorney purchased 380 sacks of wheat and rye, the wheat at 6s. 6d. a quarter, and the rye at 4s. The Privy Council ordered the commissioners to increase the prices to 10s. a quarter for wheat and 5s. 8d. for rye.

Thorney's will, drawn up on 7 Mar. 1603, was proved on 4 July 1605. He left £1 to all the aldermen of Portsmouth in office at the time of his death 'for a memory of my poor good will towards them' and asked them to help gather in his debts. The Queen owed him £480 19s. 2d., Lady Hunsdon £160, the late Earl of Essex £120.

R. East, *Portsmouth Recs.* 149, 313, 326; *Vis. Notts.* (Harl. Soc. iv), 69; *Lincs. Peds.* (Harl. Soc. lii), 969-70; *CSP Dom.* 1547-80, p. 494; *APC*, x. 230, 244; xiii. 42-3; xvii. 370, 429; xviii. 81-2; PCC 57 Hayes.

A.M.M.

THORNHILL, Samuel (*d.*1598), of Bromley, Kent.

BRAMBER   1593

1st s. of Richard Thornhill of London and Bromley. *educ.* G. Inn 1587. *m.* by 1594, Jane, da. and h. of John White of St. Stephen Coleman Street, London, 2s. 1da.

Thornhill's father was a London grocer, who acquired most of his lands in Kent from Henry Cheyney* between 1569 and 1572, probably by foreclosing on mortgages. Thornhill himself attended an inn of court, was returned to Parliament for Bramber through the intervention of a patron whose name has eluded discovery, made a marriage that brought his family more land in Kent, and died 15 Feb. 1598. He had made his will five days before, and it was proved on the following 20 May by his father, the executor. He left his wife some land, £520 he was owed, her jewels, and household goods, which he asked her to accept in lieu of the £700 a year he was bound to give her. There were bequests to servants and to the poor. Thornhill was buried in the church of St. Lawrence Jewry, London.

PCC 34 Lewyn, 18 Woodhall; *Arch. Cant.* xx. 78; Hasted, *Kent*, vi. 7, 95, 128, 281, 509; C142/253/79, 265/76.

A.M.M.

THORNTON, John (*d.*1601), of Hull, Yorks.

KINGSTON-UPON-HULL   1554 (Nov.), 1563, 1571, 1584

Prob. s. of John Thornton (*d.*1540) of Hull by his w. Margaret (*d.*1551). *m.* Joan, da. and coh. of Ralph Constable of St. Sepulchre's in Holderness, at least 1s.

Alderman, Hull by 1550, mayor 1555-6, 1566-7, 1577-8; commr. to inquire into offences against Acts of Uniformity and Supremacy c.1568, of array, Hull 1569; eccles. commr. 1573; gov. Hull fellowship of merchants 1577.

Thornton added to his Hull property in 1562 land purchased in Bilton, Holstwick and Coniston, and, six years later, pasture in the lordship of Gainstede. In 1577 he had a licence from the mayor to buy grain in Yorkshire, Lincolnshire, Norfolk and Hull, for shipment abroad. He played an active part, both in the affairs of the borough and in the Hull fellowship of merchants, of which he was the first governor. Between 1577 and 1580 he was employed in negotiations between the merchants of Hull and those of York, and in 1580 was sent as their joint representative to London, to complain that their trade was being damaged by 'unfreemen and interlopers'. In 1583, with Edward Wakefield*, he again journeyed to London, this time on behalf of the borough, to explain the decay of their 'castles and blockhouses'. Two years later he received a grant of authority to search for concealed lands in Hull. Thornton's overseas contacts occasionally brought useful information such as a report about Alva's troops in January 1570. Thornton was given leave of absence from the Commons 'for his affairs' on 12 Mar. 1563, and appointed to a committee for the maintenance of navigation on 5 Mar. 1571. He died in 1601, and his will was proved that year.

York Wills (Yorks. Arch. Soc. rec. ser. xi), 178, 238; *Vis. Yorks.* ed. Foster, 144, 210; T. Gent, *Kingston-upon-Hull*, 120, 122, 125; *Hull Deeds*, ed. Stanewell, 90, 96, 98, 101, 105, 318; J. J. Sheahan, *Hist. Kingston-upon-Hull*, 92, 95, 96; *CPR*, 1566-9, p. 172; 1572-5, p. 169; *York Merchant Adventurers*, ed. Sellers, 194-5, 212, 213; *CSP Dom.* 1581-90, p. 130; Add. 1566-79, pp. 179-80; *CJ*, i. 69; D'Ewes, 181; *York Wills* (Yorks. Arch. Soc. rec. ser. xxiv), 194.

J.J.C.

THOROLD, Anthony (by 1520-94), of Blankney and Marston, Lincs.

GRANTHAM	1558
LINCOLN	1559

b. by 1520, 1st s. of William Thorold of Hougham and Marston by his 1st w. Dorothy, da. of Thomas Leke of Halloughton, Notts. *educ.* G. Inn 1537. *m.* (1) Margaret, da. of Henry Sutton of Wellingore, 4s. inc. William* 2da.; (2) Anne, da. and coh. of Sir John Constable† of Kinoulton, Notts., wid. of George Babington, 1da. *suc.* fa. 20 Nov. 1569. Kntd. 6 May 1585.

J.p. Notts. c.1559, Lincs. (Kesteven, Holland) from 1554, sheriff 1571-2, dep. lt. from 1587; recorder, Grantham ?1551 to c.1584, of Lincoln 1559-70; Queen's attorney in the north 1561-70; commr. subsidy, Lincs. (Holland) 1563; steward of 1st Earl of Lincoln in 1582.[1]

When the writ for the 1559 parliamentary election reached Lincoln, its recorder and former Member, George St. Poll, was dying, and the city decided first to return the 2nd Earl of Rutland's nominee, Robert Ferrers*, then Robert Monson* whom they probably had in mind as their new recorder. In the event, by 16 Jan. St. Poll had died, and Rutland had intervened to impose on them

Thorold both as recorder and MP, in this way securing both seats for his nominees. In reply the Lincoln corporation snubbed Rutland by appointing Monson and (Sir) Christopher Wray* as their legal advisers, voting Monson 40s. a year for life. Thorold counter-attacked, and 'in consideration he should be diligent' obtained the recordership for life at £4 a year. Thorold was described as 'learned in the law' but the defective records do not show his call to the bar. Any hostility between Monson and Thorold had evaporated by 1570, when Thorold resigned the recordership in favour of Monson.[2]

No evidence survives of any activities by Thorold in the Parliament of 1559. He was classified as 'earnest in religion' in the bishops' reports of 1564, and he was not anxious to have his duties as attorney in the north extended by becoming a full member of the council in the north, as proposed by the archbishop of York in 1566. Thorold objected, to Cecil, that he was 'unworthy' and 'unfit'. Perhaps he was already ill. In February 1570 it was reported that he was too sick to carry out his duties, and now that he had succeeded his father and was able to live as a country gentleman, he decided to resign both as attorney in the north and as recorder of Lincoln.[3]

In the following years, besides fulfilling the usual functions of a justice of the peace, Thorold was appointed by the Privy Council to a number of commissions. Several were concerned with disputed titles to land, one with faction quarrels in Lincoln and the victimisation of a former mayor, and another with an affray in Grantham in 1579. Thorold remained recorder of Grantham, his seat being only a few miles from the town, but his main interest was coursing with the 3rd Earl of Rutland, to whom he wrote, 28 Oct. 1575:

My dogs are all unbreathed. For this fortnight I have kept my house and have not been able to go forth of my house before this day. Neither have I seen any of my dogs run since Michaelmas last; so that they will not be in any good temper so soon ... If I live the day I will wait on you tomorrow at Belvoir. If the day might be deferred a week or two longer, hares would be better and the dogs would be set in breath, so we might see some trial of our dogs.[4]

One of his sons was in the household of the 4th Earl.

A ludicrous episode in 1582 was Thorold's quarrel with his neighbour, Arthur Hall* over the election of a new alderman at Grantham, where Thorold was still recorder. Thorold was too old for Hall to make 'any convenient challenge' to him, but things came to a head at the hiring fair at Billington, close to Marston, when Thorold got together 600 to 1,000 servants under his constable on the pretext that Hall intended to 'pluck' him 'out of his house perforce, or fire it on his head'. This disorder the Council refused to tolerate, and the Earl of Lincoln was instructed to make inquiries. He excused himself, and it fell to the 3rd Earl of Rutland to investigate. Roger Manners* commented, 29 Nov. 1582, 'I am glad to hear that Mr. Thorold in his old age is become so lively that he is charged with making a riot or an unlawful assembly'. Three years after this escapade, Thorold received his knighthood.[5]

Thorold made his will 11 Apr. 1594, arranging for the disposal and running of his farms, and leaving bequests to his daughters. His servants were to receive a year's wages, and the poor of 15 parishes near Marston received small sums. On 17 May Thorold added a codicil giving his 'singular good lord', Lord Burghley, £40 in old angels

as well for a dutiful remembrance of the manifold benefits and favours by his lordship to me in my life time showed, as also in hope that his lordship will stand and be good lord to my executors for the benefit of my children's children, being poor infants, in such suits as they shall hereafter make unto his lordship for the furtherance of my said last will and testament.

Thorold died 26 June and the will was proved on 15 Nov.[6]

[1] C142/155/167; *Lincs. Peds.* (Harl. Soc. lii), 982-3; *HMC Hatfield*, iii. 297; *APC*, xxv. 25; *Recs. Commrs. Sewers* (Lincoln Rec. Soc. liv), p. lxxviii; J. W. F. Hill, *Tudor and Stuart Lincoln*, 69-71; *HMC Ancaster*, 10; Reid, *Council of the North*, 489; H. G. Wright, *Life and Works of Arthur Hall of Grantham*, 101. [2] Hill, 69-71, 98. [3] *Cam. Misc.* ix(3), p. 26; *IIMC 14th Rep. VIII*, 49; *Recs. Commrs. Sewers*, p. lxxviii; Lansd. 8, ff. 77-82; SP15/13/15; *CSP Dom.* Add. 1566-79, pp. 222, 295; Hill, 71; Reid, 489. [4] *APC*, xi. 188, 259; xii. 18, 56; xiii. 345; xix. 172-3, 263-4; *CSP Dom.* 1581-90, p. 322; *HMC Ancaster*, 10; *HMC Rutland*, i. passim. [5] Wright, 99-101; *HMC Rutland*, i. 145. [6] PCC 80 Dixy; C142/239/113.

A.M.M.

THOROLD, William (*d.* by 1594), of Marston, Lincs.

GRANTHAM   1584

2nd s. of Anthony Thorold* of Blankney and Marston by his 1st w. Margaret, da. of Henry Sutton of Wellingore. *educ.* G. Inn ?1577. *m.* Frances, da. of Sir Robert Tyrwhitt of Kettleby, 2s. 4da.
  ?Gent. usher to 4th Earl of Rutland to 1588.
  J.p. Lincs. (Kesteven) from c.1583.

Thorold no doubt came in for Grantham through the influence of his father, the recorder. The 3rd Earl of Rutland, who had asked the borough for a nomination, was told that Arthur Hall and William Thorold 'gentlemen ... such as you may command in any lawful matter', had already been elected. It must have been an uneasy partnership, in view of the uproar in 1582 between Hall and Thorold's father. Thorold died *v.p.* at an unascertained date.

Lincs. Peds. (Harl. Soc. lii), 983; *HMC Ancaster*, 10; *HMC Rutland*, i. 143, 170, 242, 248.

J.J.C.

THROCKMORTON, Anthony (*d.* 1592/3), of London and Box, Wilts.

CRICKLADE   1563

8th s. of Sir George Throckmorton[†] of Coughton, Warws. by Katherine, da. of Nicholas Vaux[†], 1st Baron Vaux; bro. of Clement*, George[†], John I*, Kenelm[†], Sir Nicholas* and Robert[†]. *m.* bef. Apr. 1555, Catherine, da. and coh. of William Willington of Marcheston, Warws., wid. of William Catesby of Ashby Legers, Northants., 5s. 1da.[1]
  Keeper, Haseley park, Warws. 1553.[2]

Throckmorton was a citizen and mercer of London who combined trade with the role of landed proprietor. Of his early life the only hint is that a 'gentleman' of that name was the tenant, and perhaps the occupier, of a tenement in St. Mary-le-Bow, London, in 1548. But from 1553 his career can be traced in some detail. Early in Mary's reign Anthony Throckmorton, described as the Queen's servant, was granted the keepership of Haseley park, Warwickshire, at a fee of 2d. a day, and an additional 20s. a year for the bailiwick of the lordship; he was also given a lease for life of the herbage and pannage of the park. The office had been held by his father, and its grant to Sir George's youngest son was doubtless a mark of royal favour to this prominent family.[3]

In April 1555 Throckmorton's father-in-law, Willington, put lands in trust for himself for life and then for his son-in-law and daughter. The property concerned lay on the borders of Warwickshire, Oxfordshire and Worcestershire. After Willington's death his daughter and her husband went to law with Sir Ambrose Cave* over his personal estate. Throckmorton's purchases of Milbourne Grange, Stoneleigh, Warwickshire in February 1556 (sold in April 1565 to Sir Thomas Leigh*) and, in partnership with Sir Robert Lane, of the crown manors of Addington, Northamptonshire, and Brinklow, Warwickshire, with parcels in other counties, for over £1,000, suggest an ability and disposition to dabble profitably in land speculation. In these transactions Throckmorton was styled 'of Chastleton', Oxfordshire.[4]

Throckmorton's role in public affairs during these years is briefly illuminated by his examination, in March 1556, by Sir John Browne in connexion with the Dudley conspiracy. It does not appear that he was either implicated in, or punished for, this affair, with which his own later career suggests that he would not have been sympathetic.[5]

Towards the end of his life Throckmorton was described by the 2nd Earl of Pembroke as 'her Majesty's sworn man' and no servant of his. It thus appears that he stood in the same relation to Elizabeth as he had to Mary. Although there is no evidence that his service was more than nominal, it may have been of some help to him in finding a seat in the Commons. His return to Elizabeth's second Parliament for Cricklade he doubtless owed, in common with most of that borough's Members during the reign, to his connexion with the Brydges family. Among his fellows in that House were his brother Sir Nicholas, elected for Lyme Regis at a by-election in 1566, and Sir Nicholas's father-in-law, Sir Nicholas Carew, who sat for Castle Rising. As a resolute Catholic, however, he must have found much of the proceedings obnoxious; and even if he had wished to sit again, the imposition of the oath of supremacy would have inhibited him.[6]

The last 15 years of Throckmorton's life were clouded by his sufferings for his faith. In May 1564 he had bought the site of Cheshunt priory from Henry Denny, and in the following May he acquired from Sir John Mason the manor of Charlton, Middlesex. He continued to receive an income from Warwickshire property, but it was as a resident in Hertfordshire that he was presented, with his wife, in October 1577 as having 'obstinately for many years refused to come to their church to hear divine service'. Throckmorton had already spent six weeks in the Fleet during May and June 1577, and he was to undergo at least three further spells of imprisonment, in 1581 in the King's bench prison, in 1582–3 in the Gatehouse, and in 1592 in a prison unnamed. He may also have been the recusant about whose custody Archbishop Whitgift wrote to Sir Thomas Heneage in January 1587. Throckmorton was doubtless the victim, not simply of his own recusancy, but of the treasonable activities associated with his name.[7]

Throckmorton died between 24 July 1592 and 13 Nov. 1593. His will, made on 20 Feb. 1591, opens with an affirmation of his membership of the Catholic Church. The value of his estate shows that his sufferings did not include impoverishment. By the will itself, and two codicils of 20 and 24 July 1592, he left to his wife all the houses and tenements which he had on lease from the Mercers' Company, all his household goods and plate (including certain items formerly belonging to Arnold Everden), £500 and the forfeiture of an outstanding recognizance of £200. She was also to have, if she chose, his mansion house or houses in St. Martin's Lane for 30 years, or her lifetime, at an annual rent of £15. To the four friends whom he named his executors, John Talbot* of Grafton, Worcestershire, Francis Browne of Henley Park, Surrey, Edward Gage of Bentley, Sussex, and John Gage of Wormesley Grange, Herefordshire, he bequeathed the remainder of his goods and lands, including his property in St. Lawrence's Lane, London, and at Box, Wiltshire. Of two debts owing to him by Sir Thomas Throckmorton he forgave one, of £190, and bequeathed the other, of £50, to Sir Thomas's son William: he also left Sir Thomas's three daughters £200 between them. Other bequests to relatives, friends and servants amounted to £343, and there were in addition two annuities of 26s. 8d. each. The testator directed that his clothes should be sold and the proceeds distributed in alms; and he left £10 to 'the poor prisoners Catholics' at Wisbech and £5 to those 'about London'.[8]

[1] *Vis. Warws.* (Harl. Soc. xii), 87–9; *CSP Dom* 1547–80, p. 76; Add. 1547–65, p. 439; *CPR*, 1566–9, p. 412; PCC 79 Nevell. [2] *CPR*, 1553–4,

p. 200. [3] *CPR*, 1547–8, p. 411; 1553–4, p. 200. [4] *CSP Dom.* Add. 1547–65, p. 439; C3/182/24, 25; *CPR*, 1555–7, pp. 63–4; 1557–8, pp. 237, 258; 1563–6, p. 271; *VCH Warws.* vi. 43. [5] *CSP Dom.* 1547–80, p. 76. [6] Lansd. 63, f. 187. [7] *CPR*, 1563–6, pp. 135, 309; *CSP Dom.* Add. 1566–79, pp. 461, 505, 559; *Cath. Rec. Soc.* xxii. 51, 130; *APC*, xiii. 175–6, 217–18; *HMC Hatfield*, iv. 267; *HMC 3rd Rep.* 257. [8] PCC 78, 79, Nevell.

S.T.B.

THROCKMORTON, Arthur (c.1557–1626), of Mile End, nr. London, afterwards of Paulerspury, Northants.

COLCHESTER   1589

b. c.1557, 2nd s. of Sir Nicholas Throckmorton* by Anne, da. of Sir Nicholas Carew[†] of Beddington, Surr.; bro. of Nicholas Throckmorton* (afterwards Carew). *educ.* Magdalen Coll. Oxf. 1571, aged 14; travelled abroad 1580–2. *m.* c.1586, Ann, da. of Sir Thomas Lucas[†] of Colchester, Essex, 4da. *suc.* fa. 1571. Kntd. 1596.

Freeman, Colchester 1589; j.p. Mdx. from c.1591; j.p. and commr. musters, Northants. 1597–1606, capt. of horse, W. division 1601, sheriff Nov. 1604–Feb. 1606, dep. lt. 1613.

Throckmorton (whose elder brother William, born in 1553 was a lunatic), inherited from his parents a high social position, wealth, and estates in Northamptonshire, Buckinghamshire, Oxfordshire, Warwickshire and Worcestershire. After leaving Oxford, where he was a 'careless and negligent student', serving in the Netherlands, and travelling on the Continent, he went to court, and married one of Elizabeth's ladies-in-waiting. A 'hot-headed youth', he suffered the Queen's displeasure on more than one occasion. In Nov. 1588 he was returned to Parliament for Colchester, where his father-in-law, sometime recorder, was a prominent and unpopular figure. Throckmorton had the support of Walsingham, who recommended him to the bailiffs as 'a gentleman of very good credit and ability ... to whom I bear especial good will'. After his election Throckmorton wrote to the bailiffs:

> Your choice of me to be your burgess especially as you write being so generally consented cannot but deserve an especial thankful remembrance from me to you all according to my poor ability and in particular as far as each shall think me worthy. As I [understand] the reasons of your choice are so mingled betwixt such doubtful causes as somewhat I must say you have made them confused, seeking for your own satisfaction to ride as it were by so many anchors as you leave me uncertain where most I am beholden, but like to a man in the dark laying hold upon the first object, so will I now for this pleasure grope no further than to bethink myself how best to thank yourselves, referring my gratitude to others for a greater good turn. Thus resting to you all a loving and a beholding burgess, I pray you to defer mine [freeman] oath until my return [when] I hope in God [I] shall be ... at leisure enough to do all right you

shall think reasonable. From my house at Mile End this 10th of November 1588.

The only mention found of Throckmorton in the journals of the 1589 Parliament is his appointment to the subsidy committee 11 Feb.

In 1596, Throckmorton, as a gentleman volunteer, no doubt, went on the Cadiz expedition through the influence of his brother-in-law, Sir Walter Ralegh, receiving his knighthood during the voyage. Instead of returning to the court he settled at Paulerspury, Northamptonshire, where, in February of that year, he had been granted another 16 acres of land 'for services'. Still, he knew early of the Ralegh marriage and the birth of Bess Ralegh's child, to whom he stood godfather. He was anti-Catholic, in 1599 suggesting it was necessary to restrain and disarm not only recusants, but also those whose wives refused to go to church. In 1605 he took part in searching the houses of Catholic suspects, including Robert Catesby.

Throckmorton was seriously ill in 1606, and again 'in physic' in 1613. He died at Paulerspury 21 July 1626, and was buried there. The will he made 26 Jan. 1625 has a long religious preamble. His wife was executrix and residuary legatee. His respect for his father is implicit in bequests to two of his overseers: to his brother-in-law, Sir Thomas Wotton, he gave a great gilt cup engraved with the Carew and Throckmorton arms, presented to his father by Mary Queen of Scots in France; and to Sir Henry Wotton[†] he bequeathed his father's papers concerning his missions in France and Scotland, asking him to write a book to counter the slanders brought against Sir Nicholas. 'Mr. Serjeant Harvey' (Francis Harvey II*), another friend, was joined with these two as an overseer. He left his library of Italian and French books, which he had purchased abroad, to Magdalen College. To the poor of Tiffield, Northamptonshire, he gave £20, in addition to 6d., a piece of beef and a loaf of bread to each of 71 of his poorest tenants in Northamptonshire. In accordance with his wishes a memorial was erected to him, extolling his piety, character and wealth.

A. L. Rowse, *Ralegh and the Throckmortons*, passim; Bridges, *Northants.* i. 312, 314; *APC*, xxv. 230, 292; xxviii. 359; *Northants. Rec. Soc.* iii. 118–19, 125–6, 174; vii. p. xlii, 232, 238, 247; SP14/33; *Essex Rev.* iv. 242; Essex Arch. Soc., Morant mss; Essex Arch. Soc. library catalogue 52; D'Ewes, 431; Shaw, *Knights*, ii. 92; *CSP Dom.* 1595–7, p. 176; *HMC Hatfield*, ix. 291; PCC 106 Hele; C142/438/126.

J.H.

THROCKMORTON, Clement (by 1515–73), of Haseley and Claverdon, Warws.

WARWICK	1542
DEVIZES	1545
WARWICK	1547, 1553 (Mar.), 1553 (Oct.)
SUDBURY	1559
WARWICKSHIRE	1563
WEST LOOE	1571
WARWICKSHIRE	1572*

b. by 1515, 3rd s. of Sir George Throckmorton[†], and bro. of Anthony*, George[†], John I*, Kenelm[†], Sir Nicholas* and Robert[†]. *m.* by 1545, Katherine, da. of Sir Edward Neville, 6s. inc. Job* 7da.[1]

Receiver, lands formerly of Evesham abbey 15 Dec. 1540; servant of Sir Richard Rich[†] by 1541; surveyor, ct. of augmentations, Warws. by Apr. 1542–53; Exchequer 1553–67; cupbearer, household of Queen Catherine Parr by 1544–8; commr. chantries, Leics. and Warws. 1546, 1548, relief, Warws. 1550, loan, Warws. 1557; particular receiver for Queen Catherine Parr, Leics. and Warws. by 1547–8; j.p. Warws. 1547–72, q. 1573; constable, Kenilworth castle, Warws. from 19 Sept. 1553; member, high commission 1572.[2]

Favoured by powerful relatives, such as his cousin, Queen Catherine Parr, and advanced by his own diligence in crown service, Clement Throckmorton had, by 1558, established himself on a comfortable estate in Warwickshire. This consisted of four or five manors, and the usual amount of property which a reliable royal servant could hope to obtain on lease from the Crown. It centred on Haseley, which he had recently made his principal seat, and where he had rebuilt the old manor house in a style more befitting his new dignity.[3]

Elizabeth's accession to the Crown saw the eclipse of the senior branch of the Throckmorton family, penalized for their adherence to the old religion, and Clement Throckmorton, in consequence, came into greater prominence. The Privy Council occasionally called upon his services in wider matters, but the last 15 years of his life were passed in the usual duties of a country gentleman. In the past he had acted as a friend and arbiter for the cities of Coventry and Warwick, and he still occasionally acted for them, even though Elizabeth's grant of the borough of Warwick to the Earl of Warwick ended a period of at least two decades during which Throckmortons, or their relatives, had been provided with a seat at Warwick in most Parliaments.[4]

Before the grant of Warwick to the earl, Throckmorton himself had turned elsewhere for a seat, representing in 1559 the newly created duchy of Lancaster borough of Sudbury. He presumably owed the seat to Sir Ambrose Cave*. He sat twice for the shire, and in 1571 was found a seat at West Looe by the 2nd Earl of Bedford.

Throckmorton's religious sympathies were puritan. He was a friend of Edward Underhill, the 'hot gospeller', took the education of the children of Thomas Hawkes the protestant martyr upon himself, and had 'stood for the true religion' in the first Parliament of Mary's reign. In 1567 he was one of those incorporated by letters patent as 'governors of the possessions and revenues of the preachers of the gospel in Warwickshire'. His puritanism, however, did not prevent him being appointed to the high commission.[5]

Throckmorton died on 14 Dec. 1573 and was buried in a magnificent tomb in Haseley church. His later years may have seen a decline in his fortunes, for at his death his debts totalled over £3,000, though the money was evidently paid off without undue difficulty. His lands had long since been settled in trust to provide his wife's jointure. As she had also been granted a 20-year lease of other manors, Throckmorton was obliged to ask her assistance to enable him to bequeath Job, his heir, a £20 annuity, and 1,400 marks for the dowries of the three unmarried daughters.[6]

[1] Dugdale, *Warws.* ii. 654; *Vis. Warws.* (Harl. Soc. xii), 88–9. [2] E315/218, f. 60; *Soc. Antiq.* 1790, p. 167; I. Temple Petyt ms 538, ff. 39, 142; Somerville, *Duchy*, i. 561, 563 n; *CPR*, 1566–9, p. 82; *LP Hen. VIII*, xx(2), p. 549; xxi(1), p. 147; R. G. Usher, *Rise and Fall of the High Commission* (1913), p. 359. [3] *VCH Warws.* iii. 73, 104, 106, 117, 143, 151; iv. 223; *CPR*, 1553–4, p. 366; 1554–5, pp. 56, 209; 1555–7, p. 180. [4] *APC*, vii. 34; *CPR*, 1558–60, p. 423; 1560–3, p. 444; *CSP Dom.* 1547–80, p. 95; Coventry corp. accts. receivers, p. 17; chamberlains' accts. 1, 232; *Cal Coventry Recs.* ed. Jeaffreson, 36; Warwick accts. 1546–69, m. 37v. 70v. [5] Harl. 425, p. 94; Bodl. e Museo 17; *CSP Dom.* 1547–80, p. 304; W. Pierce, *Hist. Intro. Marprelate Tracts*, 184–5; *Cam. Misc.* ix(3), pp. 7, 46; Collinson thesis, 678 n 3, 948. [6] C142/172/143; *VCH Warws.* iii. 107, 108; E. W. Badger, *Mon. Brasses Warws.* 27; Lansd. 11, f. 50 seq.; 141, f. 278 seq.; *CPR*, 1554–5, p. 56.

S.M.T.

THROCKMORTON, Job (c.1545–1601), of Haseley, Warws., later of Canons Ashby, Northants.

EAST RETFORD	1572[1]
WARWICK	1586

b. c.1545, 1st s. of Clement Throckmorton* of Haseley by Katherine, da. of Sir Edward Neville. *educ.* Oxf., BA 1566. *m.* by 1580, Dorothy, da. of Thomas Vernon (*d.*1557), of Houndhill in Hanbury, Staffs., 2s. 1da. *suc.* fa. 1573.[2]

A puritan, like his father and his uncle Sir Nicholas*, Throckmorton had none of their reservations about supporting puritan measures in the Commons, nor would he accept the arguments of Walsingham and Mildmay that protestants must wait to set their own house in order until the enemy had been driven from its gates. Brought into the 1572 Parliament for East Retford by the 3rd Earl of Rutland, to whom he was related through his mother, Throckmorton, surprisingly, in view of his later career, left no impression on its records, and his small inheritance meant that he never achieved prominence in the affairs of his county. Throckmorton did not, it appears, stand in 1584, but in 1586 his candidature was sponsored as part of an organized campaign to present the puritan case in Parliament. Other Throckmortons had sat for Warwick, but by 1586 it was customary for the town to return a nominee of the Earl of Warwick together with a townsman. That year Thomas Dudley*, the senior Member for the two preceding Parliaments and the Earl's

nominee, was returned again, but who was to fill the second seat? John Fisher, the town clerk, had represented Warwick in the Parliaments of 1571, 1572, and 1584, and the Earl of Warwick, in his letter recommending Dudley, cited the Privy Council request that the same Members be returned as in 1584. But Throckmorton made a determined and successful bid for the second seat with the support of neighbouring puritan gentry such as (Sir) John Harington II* and Fulke Greville*, combined with like-minded friends within the town led by 'the busy Richard Brook and his complices'. Throckmorton 'made very great labour to many of the inhabitants of this borough for their voices' and won votes for 'good cheer's sake', through a 'solemn dinner' for 60 or 80 at the *Swan*. Alarmed at the thought of an open contest, which would include 'the meanest inhabitants of the borough', the bailiff and principal burgesses first called a meeting with the 12 'assistants' who represented the commoners at elections, and then interviewed Throckmorton, who remained determined 'to put it to the jury by election'. So he was sworn a burgess, and adopted as official candidate.[3]

Throckmorton was quick to let the Commons hear his views. He made his first speech on 4 Nov. 1586, before being placed on the committee 'to confer of some convenient and fit course to be taken' over Mary Queen of Scots. The Jesuits were a 'viperous brood ... the very sink of the stews'; Spain and France were 'already drunk with the lies of that anti-Christian beast'. Was there 'a man that durst once stain his mouth in defence of her whom I protest unto you I know not how to describe?'

> If I should term her the daughter of sedition, the mother of rebellion, the nurse of impiety, the handmaid of iniquity, the sister of unshamefastness; or if I should tell you that which you know already – that she is Scottish of nation, French of education, Papist of profession, a Guisan of blood, a Spaniard in practice, a libertine in life – as all this were not to flatter her, so yet this were nothing near to describe her. [To destroy her would be] one of the fairest riddances that ever the church of God had.

Alluding to Elizabeth's veto of the bill against Mary in 1572, he asked: 'And what got her Majesty, I pray you, by this her lenity? Even as much as commonly one shall get by saving a thief from the gallows: a heap of treasons and conspiracies, huddling one in the neck of the other ...' His remedy was

> that we be all joint suitors to her Majesty that Jezebel may live no longer to persecute the prophets of God nor to attempt still in this manner the vineyard of Naboth by blood; that so the land may be purged, the wrath of God pacified, and her Majesty's days prolonged in peace to the comfort of us and our posterity, which the Lord grant for his Christ's sake.

This was one thing, and the House was with Throckmorton, but his speech on 23 Feb. went too far, for the evolution of the House of Commons had not yet reached the point where the monarch was inclined to be taught lessons in diplomacy by the burgess for Warwick. Throckmorton began with a survey of foreign affairs since the conference at Bayonne, 1565, 'a pestilent conspiracy against the Church of God'. But, an expression Throckmorton uses repeatedly, 'the Lord hath vowed himself to be English', and it was not only the King of Spain (his religion idolatrous, his life licentious, his marriage incestuous, his dominions 'possessed by an incestuous race of bastards') but the rulers of France and Scotland, both enjoying ostensibly friendly relations with England, who were treated with contempt. Catherine de Medici ('I hope I need not describe her') had not 'thanks be to God' many 'left of her loins to pester the earth with … she had brought us into this world such a litter as few women have done … whose principle delight, since they first came out of the shell, hath been in nothing almost but in hypocrisy, filthiness of life and persecuting of the Church of God'. The King of France was 'stricken with a fearful kind of giddiness, as it were a man in a trance or ecstasy, not knowing … which way to wind himself … you will find him occupied when he should do you good; … a Frenchman unreformed is as vile a man as lives'.

> Whither then shall we cast our eye? Northward towards the young imp of Scotland? Alas, it is a cold coast, ye know, and he that should set up his rest upon so young and wavering a head might happen find cold comfort … Ye knew his mother … did ye not? Then I hope ye will all join with me in this prayer, that whatsoever his father was, I beseech the Lord he take not after his mother, for then woe and double woe [to the] Church of God. And how he may degenerate from the humour of his ancestors I know not.

In the event, it was this part of his 'lewd and blasphemous' speech, as Burghley was to call it, made at a time when Elizabeth was trying to propitiate James, that landed Throckmorton in real trouble.

> Well then [Throckmorton went on] we see no hope of Spain, no trust in France, cold comfort in Scotland, whither then shall we direct our course? … is there any man amongst us so dim sighted that doth not here plainly behold the very finger of God directing us … to the low countries?

The offer of the sovereignty of the Netherlands was the only safe policy, 'the people of that nation in all humbleness desiring it, the regard of our own safety … enforcing it [and] the cause of God and religion exacting it at our hands'.

On 25 Feb. Hatton introduced a motion to admonish

> a gentleman of noble blood, zealous in religion [who] spake sharply of princes, and laid indignities on them … We should use great regard of princes in free speech. Hard and intolerable to use ill speeches of the King of

France, continuing in league and friendship with us … The King of Scotland a prince young, of good religion, a friend and in league with her Majesty both offensive and defensive.

A 'sin' to speak ill of him, a 'shame' to detract him. 'This motion may avail to make some repair.' It looks as though Hatton was trying to cover up for Throckmorton here, as he was later to do over Marprelate. But Throckmorton had time to loose off another broadside before nemesis overtook him. On 27 Feb. he spoke, ostensibly in favour of Anthony Cope's proposal for a Genevan prayer book and a presbyterian church, though he was 'half appalled to deal in it'. The speech falls into two parts, his views on freedom of speech in Parliament, and a statement of the high puritan standpoint as it was just after Mary's execution. Throckmorton had to 'begin by way of complaint' that 'when we come first into this house there is laid before us a show of freedom' which turned to 'bondage before we go forth'.

> Ye shall speak in the parliament house freely provided always that ye meddle neither with the reformation of religion nor the establishment of succession, the very pillars and groundworks of all our bliss and happiness.

'If a question were now propounded to the whole house, what is the chief cause of all our meetings and consultations in this honourable assembly', the answer would be the Queen's safety, and 'the surest and safest way' was 'to begin at the house of God'. 'It was, out of all question, a very worthy act that was lately done at Fotheringhay' but 'if I were to give her Majesty advice … I would humbly desire her that after so many and mighty deliverances she would beware she sleep not upon them in peril of her life'. 'It was well done of Henry VIII … to raze … those dens and cloisters of iniquity, but it was better done of King Edward to plant true religion and the gospel here among us.' But

> into what lamentable days and times are we now fallen into? To bewail the distresses of God's children, it is puritanism. To find fault with corruptions of our church, it is puritanism. To reprove a man for swearing, it is puritanism. To banish an adulterer out of the house, it is puritanism. To make humble suit to her Majesty and the High Court of Parliament for a learned ministry, it is puritanism … I fear me we shall shortly come to this, that to do God, and her Majesty good service shall be counted puritanism.

Throckmorton now arrived at 'those things that have been here propounded unto us (I mean the book and the bill)'. Of all 'deformities of our church', said Throckmorton,

> the foulest, the most shameful and unworthiest of all is (as hath been often and notably told you) our dumb, ignorant and unlearned ministry, a thing grown in a manner desperate of all honest defence … if I were

asked what is the bane of the church and commonwealth ... a thousand times, I must say the dumb ministry. I mean our bare reading ministry.

For reformation 'whither should we fly but to this high court? ... Though this Parliament were not summoned to make any new laws ... it were a very honourable course to reform some old laws'.

Is there law to expel out of the ministry a learned man, of life untainted, and is there no law to banish thence an adulterer, an incestuous person, a drunkard, a dumb hireling, a swearer, a blasphemer or such like? Whereof if it come to examination I fear me ye will blush at the number. ... Till,this monster of our unworthy ministry be banished the land there is no remedy ... the church must needs look for heresies, the prince for treasons, the land for hurly-burlys, the people for destruction.

Throckmorton cited a number of grim 'warnings' of political assassinations 'to pull her Majesty by the sleeve, and methinks the remembrance of them should sometimes awaken her out of her sleep ...'

For who doubts but there is a scourge due to us? Long peace, rare quietness, unwonted bliss, happy government, calmness at home, broils abroad, gospel preached, wealth abounding, no awaking out of wickedness, no amendment of manners, religion boldly professed in mouth and badly practised in life, and open resistance of the holy discipline of God: surely he is worse than blind that looks not for a scourge...
Let this be then the issue of the whole ... to waken her Majesty's heart before the day of her account, that she may remember the great weight of her calling, thereby to reform with speed such things as are amiss, especially her ignorant and unlearned ministry. That, as she hath been the beginner, so she may be the finisher of the work; as she hath had the praise to be the planter of the gospel, so she may have the honour to be the reformer of the church ... that so the Lord may be moved to bless us still with her ... that her days may be aged, her reign prosperous, her bliss endless; that [he concluded] the last day of her life may (if so please Him) be the last day of this earth; that when she fleeteth hence to our earthly discomfort, we may then behold His son Jesus, sitting in His throne of judgment, to our endless and everlasting comfort for ever.

Throckmorton might have got away with it all if James VI's London agent had not heard of the relevant passages from the 23rd February speech. Burghley had to do something, and what he did was to write to James's agent on 2 Mar. promising to put Throckmorton in the Tower next day 'as a close prisoner, and shall thereby, for the rashness of his tongue, feel smart in his whole body'. Throckmorton wrote an abject letter to Burghley on 3 Apr. 1587: 'the privilege of the place' had been 'apt enough to bring a young head into a distemperature'.[4]
Throckmorton's parliamentary career was over, but not his propaganda for the puritan cause. In 1588 he and the

Welsh preacher John Penry began the printing of the Martin Marprelate tracts. Although many of the minor actors and ultimately Penry himself were brought to trial, the identity of the author has not been conclusively established. However the style and language of the tracts point to Throckmorton, who is known to have been the kingpin of the organization. Other arguments rule out Penry, and at least one contemporary openly accused Throckmorton of being Martin. It is in any case surprising that he was not punished for his known part in the matter, as were even the most prominent of his supporters, such as Sir Richard Knightley*. In the autumn of 1590 Throckmorton was convicted of participating in the printing, but seems not to have suffered any penalties. The next year he was indicted at the Warwick quarter sessions for supporting the fanatics Coppinger and Hacket, but again he got off. The answer may be that he had the protection of Hatton, the lord chancellor, to whom he wrote at least one submissive letter and who more than once spoke up for him. Throckmorton spent his last years, a sick man, at Canons Ashby receiving spiritual consolation from the puritan John Dod. He is said to have sought in vain, for many years, a 'comfortable assurance' of his salvation, and to have received it within an hour of his death. He died intestate on 23 Feb. 1601 and was buried at Haseley. Administration of the property was granted on 18 May to his widow.[5]

[1] OR, following Crown Office list C193/32/8-10, gives John Throckmorton for East Retford. But a 1st session list brought up to date during the session and a 2nd session list give 'Jobe'. [2] Vis. Warws. (Harl. Soc. xii), 207; Shaw, Staffs. i. 93; C142/263/9(1). [3] C142/172/143; Black Bk. of Warwick, ed. Kemp, 16, 26–7, 56, 104, 367, 387–97. [4] New York, Pierpont Morgan Lib. mss, MA 276; D'Ewes, 393; Harl. 7188, anon. jnl. f. 92; Neale, Parlts. ii. 173–4; Lansd. 53, f. 148. [5] A. L. Rowse, Ralegh and the Throckmortons, 114; W. Pierce, Martin Marprelate Tracts, passim; Collinson thesis; DNB; C142/263/9(1); PCC admon. act bk. 1601, f. 83v.

P.W.H.

THROCKMORTON, John I (c.1520–80), of Feckenham, Worcs.

LEICESTER	1545
CAMELFORD	1547
WARWICK	1553 (Mar.)
OLD SARUM	1553 (Oct.)
COVENTRY	1554 (Nov.), 1555, 1558, 1559

b. c.1520, 7th s. of Sir George Throckmorton† and bro. of Anthony*, Clement*, George†, Kenelm†, Sir Nicholas* and Robert†. educ. M. Temple. m. Margaret, da. of Robert Puttenham of Sherfield-upon-Loddon, Hants, wid. of one Dockray, 4s. 2da. Kntd. 1565.[1]

Attorney, council in the marches of Wales 1550–4; steward, manor of Feckenham 1552; master of requests 1553–9; recorder, Coventry 1553, Worcester from 1559, Ludlow, Shrewsbury by 1560; j.p. Warws. 1554; j.p.q. Chester, Worcs. Denb., Mont., Flints. 1562, Herefs.,

Salop, Warws., Mon., Brec., Glam., Rad., Carm., Pemb., Card., Caern., Anglesey, Merion. 1564; under-steward of Westminster 1557; justice of Chester, Denb. and Mont. 1558–79; member, council in the marches of Wales 1558–80; eccles. commr., diocese of Chester 1562; commr. piracy, Cheshire 1565; justice of Denb. 1566; vice-pres. council in the marches of Wales 1565–9.[2]

John Throckmorton was a younger son of a large though well-connected family. As such, his lack of patrimony could be compensated for by the influence of powerful patrons. His relationship with Catherine Parr introduced John and his elder brothers Clement and Nicholas to court, and during Edward VI's reign his connexion with William Parr, Marquess of Northampton, served him well. But it was under Northumberland that Throckmorton rose rapidly, and it. was he who was credited with drawing up the proclamation which named Lady Jane Grey as Queen, after Sir William Cecil had refused to do so.[3]

Throckmorton, however, was an opportunist of no deep convictions either in religion or politics. Losing faith in Northumberland's success, he soon fled to join Mary at Framlingham and later received an annuity for his services there. As easily as he had accepted the Edwardian prayer books, he now returned to Catholicism and was soon in favour with the Queen, whose will he witnessed. Yet, in spite of the favoured position he occupied at court, Throckmorton did not sever himself completely from his former associates, and his career survived yet another change of ruler and religion. At the beginning of Elizabeth's reign, he was confirmed as justice of Chester, a job given him by Queen Mary just before her death, and soon he became a prominent member of the council in the marches. He sat in Elizabeth's first Parliament for Coventry, of which he had been the active recorder since 1553 and which he had already represented three times in Parliament. It was as recorder of Coventry that he received the Queen in 1565 and was knighted by her.[4]

After the accession of Elizabeth, Throckmorton was principally occupied as a councillor in the marches of Wales. In March 1559 he was granted an annuity of £100 for the good counsel he had already given there and in July 1562 his loyalty and conformity were sufficiently trusted for him to be appointed one of the commissioners to enforce the new religious settlement in the diocese of Chester. In spite of the ambiguous position in which he was placed by the recusancy of his family, Throckmorton himself seems to have accepted the Elizabethan settlement; one of his associates was Whitgift, no friend to recusants or crypto-Catholics. Throckmorton was, however, placed, no doubt optimistically, on a list drawn up in the interests of Mary Stuart in 1574. In the marches Throckmorton had some importance as one of the trusted lieutenants of the president, Sir Henry Sidney*. Besides Sidney, he had as patron the Earl of Leicester, and when Sidney became lord deputy of Ireland in 1565, the two of them secured Throckmorton's appointment as vice-president of the council in the marches, in which position he was not a success. In 1568 he claimed jurisdiction in Cheshire, of which Leicester was chamberlain. When the vice-chamberlain, William Glasier*, pointed out that the county palatine was outside the council's authority, Throckmorton called him a liar, but, upon Leicester's intervening, he retreated, protesting that he had no intention of injuring the Earl's rights. Next, when Sidney's administration was under attack in 1576, Throckmorton was accused of slackness and corruption in that he diverted to his own use fines imposed by the council. Although the charges against him were not proved, his position thereafter deteriorated, the recusancy of his wife and son made his own loyalty suspect, and he finally lost Leicester's favour. A lawsuit brought against his tenants at Feckenham, who had destroyed his enclosures, resulted in his being suspended as justice of Chester. He was accused of partiality towards his brother-in-law John Edwards of Chirk, at whose house Lady Throckmorton and her son were accustomed to hear mass. His final disgrace arose over a judgment he had given in favour of a relation, Edward Grey, concerning the disputed barony of Powys. Throckmorton was fined heavily in the Star Chamber and imprisoned in the Fleet. He may have died there, or in the Counter, for William Herle* wrote to the Earl of Leicester, 24 May 1580, 'God has visited me here in prison with a hectic fever, as he did Sir John Throckmorton'. Neither Throckmorton's will nor his inquisition post mortem is helpful as to the place of his death, which occurred on 22 May 1580, two days after he made his will. Throckmorton instructed his executors to hold his lands, many of which had been mortgaged, to pay his debts. These amounted to more than £4,000, in addition to the unpaid fine of £1,000. He hoped that his executors would be able to find £1,000 for each of his daughters and two of his younger sons. The will was proved 8 Dec. 1580 by the heir Francis, who four years later was executed for treason. Another son, Thomas, was an agent of Mary Queen of Scots, and spent most of his life abroad.[5]

[1] Nash, *Worcs.* i. 453; *Vis. Hants* (Harl. Soc. lxiv), 17–18; PCC 52 Arundel. [2] *CPR*, 1549–50, p. 299; 1550–3, p. 236; 1553–4, p. 269; 1557–8, pp. 461, 462; 1560–3, pp. 280–1; 1563–6, pp. 41–2; *APC*, iv. 324; vii. 284; *Coventry Leet Bk.* ii. 806; B. Poole, *Coventry*, 384; Dugdale, *Warws.* i. 149–50; P. H. Williams, *Council in the Marches of Wales*, 359–60; Westminster Abbey Reg. 4, f. 10v.; Ormerod, *Cheshire*, i. 63. [3] A. L. Rowse, *Ralegh and the Throckmortons*, ch. I; A. L. Browne, 'Sir John Throckmorton of Feckenham' (*Trans. Birmingham Arch. Soc.* lix. 123–42); *CPR*, 1547–8, p. 210; Stowe 57, f. 19v; Strype, *Annals*, iv. 487. [4] Lansd. 156, f. 94; *HMC 5th Rep.* 309; *APC*, iv. 328; *Narratives of the Reformation* (Cam. Soc. lxxvii), 324; Coventry council bk. ff. 2415 seq.; Coventry bk. of payments, ff. 7, 9, receipts, 14; letters, i. 68; mayors' accts. 1542–61, p. 539; Poole, 89–91. [5] *CPR*, 1558–60, p. 06; 1560–63, pp. 280–1; *CSP Dom. Add.* 1547–65, pp. 574–5; *CSP Dom.* 1547–80, pp. 604, 605, 609, 626, 627; P. H. Williams, 198–200, 253, 255, 260, 266–7, 268, 273, 290, 314; *APC*, vii. 246, 372–3; viii. 11–12; x. 363, 375–6, 399–400; xi. 25–6,

69–70, 98, 129–30, 135–6, 168, 188–9, 191–2, 193, 242, 299, 320; *Cath. Rec. Soc. Misc.* viii, 90; PCC 52 Arundel; A. L. Browne, 135–9; *HMC Bath*, v. 202; C142/191/114; *DNB* (Throckmorton, Francis).

I.C.

THROCKMORTON, John II, of Lypiatt, nr. Stroud, Glos.

m. c.1580, Juliana (*d.*1581), wid. of Thomas Wye of Dowdeswell, Glos.
J.p. Glos. from c.1591, q. by 1596.

The above identification is based upon two assumptions – that the 1601 knight of the shire lived in Gloucestershire, and that it was the same John Throckmorton who was elected in 1601 and in 1604. This rules out John Throckmorton of Tortworth, son of Sir Thomas Throckmorton*, and grandson of the Sir Richard Berkeley whose death caused the 1604 by-election, as John Throckmorton of Tortworth was certainly dead by 1607, and probably died, while still a boy, before 1591, whereas the 1604 Gloucestershire MP appears in the proceedings of the Commons as late as 1611. The 1601 MP is not mentioned by name in the journals, but, as a knight of the shire, he could have attended the main business committee (3 Nov.) and the committee on monopolies (23 Nov.).

The court rolls of the manor of Dowdeswell show that John Throckmorton of Lypiatt, and his wife, held the manors of Corse, Pitchcombe, Frampton, Mansell and Rodmarton, and some land at Tetbury. He sold Rodmarton about 1597 to Robert Coxe for £800, but most of the others were still in his possession in 1608 when John Smith of Nibley compiled his muster roll for the county. Throckmorton was assessed at £20 for the subsidy in 1593. In that year, his house, which stands near the church in Lypiatt, was robbed by a gang led by one Thomas King. The Throckmortons of Lypiatt were related to the senior branch of the family at Coughton, Warwickshire. Traditionally they are supposed to have shared the latter's Catholicism and to have lost Lypiatt as a result of their implication in the Gunpowder Plot, but, far from losing Lypiatt in 1605, Throckmorton sold it in 1610 to Thomas Stephens*, attorney to Prince Henry and Prince Charles. Throckmorton was still alive in 1622, when he witnessed a will; his own has not been found.

Bristol and Glos. Arch. Soc. Trans. xvii. 139, 162, 203; xxii. 130; xxxvii. 76–7; lx. 287; lxvii. 131–2, 155, 212; *Vis. Glos.* (Harl. Soc. xxi), 163; Rudder, *Glos.* 391, 603, 713; J. Smith, *Men and Armour for Glos. 1608*, pp. 26, 131; A. L. Rowse, *Ralegh and the Throckmortons*, 190; D'Ewes, 624, 649; *APC*, xxiv. 345; xxvi. 484; PCC 106 Savile.

M.R.P.

THROCKMORTON (afterwards CAREW), Nicholas

(*d.*1644), of ?Paulerspury, Northants. and Beddington, Surr.

5th surv. s. of Sir Nicholas Throckmorton* of Paulerspury by Anne, da. of Sir Nicholas Carew† of Beddington; bro. of Arthur Throckmorton*. *educ.* matric. Padua 1590. *m.* (1) by 1599, Mary, da. of Sir George More* of Loseley, Surr., 5s. 3da.; (2) by 1618, Susan Bright (*d.*1633), of Bury St. Edmunds, Suff., wid. of Henry Butler of London, merchant, 1s. 1da. Kntd. June 1603 at Beddington. *suc.* uncle Francis Carew* of Beddington and changed his name to Carew May 1611.[1]
J.p. Surr. temp. Jas. I; chamberlain of the Exchequer 1613.[2]

Throckmorton, a younger son of the statesman and diplomat, was a minor figure until adopted as his heir by his uncle. Indeed, prior to the discovery of the diary kept by his brother Arthur, his activities before 1600 were almost completely unknown. As it is he is overshadowed by Arthur and by his sister Elizabeth, whose secret marriage to (Sir) Walter Ralegh* caused such uproar at court.

Only a few years old when his father died, Throckmorton was left £500 and a half share (with his younger brother Henry) in the salt monopoly. His mother, who died in 1587, left him a jewel, having two rows of rubies and one of diamonds, and household goods, including satin and velvet hangings 'with falcons and lions embroidered thereon', taffeta curtains, silk and linen quilts and damask towels and napkins. He probably continued to live at the family home at Paulerspury, Northamptonshire. By 1588 he was in Italy, for Arthur recorded in his diary that he had sent his brother some money to continue his continental tour, probably part of a £40 annuity he was looking after for him during this period. Two years later the position was reversed, for Arthur borrowed £300 from Nicholas, at 10%.[3]

Throckmorton was in England again by 1596, for in July of that year he passed on to Sir Francis Carew at Beddington the rumour that Ralegh had been drowned during the expedition to Cadiz. Evidently he was a familiar figure in Surrey by this date, and shortly afterwards he married the daughter of another prominent Surrey gentleman, Sir George More of Loseley. He was returned to Parliament for Lyme Regis in 1601, a seat which his father had once occupied. His patron was presumably his brother-in-law, Sir Walter Ralegh. Others among Throckmorton's relatives, including his father, grandfather, brother, uncle, father-in-law and son, saw service in the House of Commons.[4]

Two letters which Throckmorton wrote to Sir George More have survived among the Loseley papers, the second of which, written shortly after the accession of James I, suggests that the new reign had brought the writer financial difficulties. His credit was strained 'to the uttermost' and he was 'at the last cast'.

My plate is all to pawn, credit I have none, livings or revenues to my company small, or rather none ... Wherefore I pray you do duly consider my case and your daughter's, for whom I am sorry ... No less than £200 at Midsummer next can make me show my face in any company, and a hundred at Michaelmas next, which if I cannot have I must leave my country, and my wife and children to the parish.

Whatever lies behind this – and it is not possible to discover Throckmorton's sources of income at the turn of the century – by 1611 his worries were over. Within the space of a few years he acquired Beddington and other property, a £400 annuity, and a profitable office in the Exchequer. For the rest of his long life Throckmorton was one of the leading gentlemen in Surrey. He died in February 1644, and was buried in Beddington church.[5]

[1] Phillipps mss sold at Sotheby's 14, 15 June 1971. [2] Vis. Surr. (Harl. Soc. xliii), 214; Manning and Bray, Surr. ii. 523 table; Surr. Arch. Colls. i. ped. 1; A. L. Rowse, Ralegh and the Throckmortons, 292. [3] PCC 8 Daper, 74 Spencer; Rowse, 57, 118. [4] HMC Hatfield, vi. 245. [5] A. J. Kempe, Loseley Mss, 359–61; VCH Surr. iii. 255, 317; iv. 170, 173, 174, 221, 231, 232; Add. Ch. 23720; Surr. Arch. Colls. xxxv. 37–9; CSP Dom. 1603–10, p. 581; Lansd. 142, f. 280.

M.R.P.

THROCKMORTON, Sir Nicholas (1515/16–71), of Aldgate, London, and Paulerspury, Northants.

MALDON	1545
DEVIZES	1547
NORTHAMPTONSHIRE	1553 (Mar.)
OLD SARUM	1553 (Oct.)
LYME REGIS	1559
TAVISTOCK	1563

b. 1515/16, 4th s. of Sir George Throckmorton[†], and bro. of Anthony*, Clement*, George[†], John I*, Kenelm[†], and Robert[†]. m. by 1553, Anne, da. of Sir Nicholas Carew[†] of Beddington, Surr., 10s. inc. Arthur* and Nicholas* 3da. Kntd. Jan./May 1551.[1]

Page, household of Henry Fitzroy, Duke of Richmond by 1532–6; servant, household of William, Baron Parr by 1543; sewer, household of Queen Catherine Parr by 1544–7 or 8; gent. privy chamber by 1549–53; under-treasurer of the mint 25 Dec. 1549–24 June 1552; keeper, Brigstock park, Northants. 14 Sept. 1553–d.; j.p. Northants. from c.1559; ambassador to France 1563–4, to Scotland 1565, 1567; chamberlain of the Exchequer from 21 June 1564; chief butler of England and Wales from 28 Nov. 1565.[2]

Though from the Catholic side of the family, Throckmorton believed that a protestant foreign policy was necessary for the defence of England and the recovery of Calais. He remained in England for much of Mary's reign, 'stood for the true religion' in the Parliament of October 1553, and survived implication in Wyatt's rebellion. But the possibility that he might be accused of complicity in the Henry Dudley conspiracy of 1556 decided

him to go abroad. In the event he was pardoned, his property was restored in May 1557, and by early 1558 he was back in England exercising his old office of keeper of Brigstock park. He was thus better placed than most protestants to communicate with Princess Elizabeth at Hatfield.[3]

He was sufficiently in Elizabeth's confidence to believe that at her accession she would appreciate his suggestions for filling a number of appointments. As principal secretary he suggested, safely enough, Sir William Cecil*, but by and large his advice on offices was ignored. His attitude to the Marian Privy Councillors is interesting. He thought that Heath, Catholic archbishop of York, should for the time being be retained as chancellor, along with many of the late Queen's Council. 'For religion and religious proceedings' it was necessary 'to require the Lords to have a good eye that there be no innovations, no tumults or breach of orders'. As a man who had lived through the disorders occasioned by Somerset's religious policy, Throckmorton was anxious that the new reign should not run into trouble through the rash activities of his protestant friends. He suggested 'making you a better party in the Lords House of Parliament [and] for appointing a meet Common House to your proceeding'. Some years earlier, Sir Richard Morison[†] had called him a 'Machiavellist', and the 'advice' to Elizabeth bears out this description.

It shall not be meet that either the old [privy councillors] or the new should wholly understand what you mean, but to use them as instruments to serve yourself with ...

Elizabeth employed Throckmorton, during the critical days just after her accession, in various urgent duties (controlling the ports, examining Cardinal Pole's papers, arranging the state entry into London), but he never attained a major government post.[4]

Throckmorton was returned to Parliament for west-country boroughs in 1559 and 1563 by courtesy of the 2nd Earl of Bedford. There is no mention of him in the defective 1559 journal, or that of 1563. In the 1566 session he was put on committees dealing with law reform (4 Oct.) and the succession (31 Oct.), and was one of the 30 Members of the Commons summoned on 5 Nov. to hear the Queen's message about the succession. His reputation rests, for good or ill, on his work as a diplomat. His knowledge of Elizabethan affairs was unrivalled and he had a flair for intelligence. The defence of England was his preoccupation and he was convinced that the only hope for the survival of protestantism in Europe was support for the Huguenots in France, and for the rebel lords in Scotland. By about 1564, therefore, he became a follower of Sir Robert Dudley* and had begun to think that Cecil was not only opposing the active policy, but trying to keep exponents of it, such as Throckmorton himself, off the Council. Soon Cecil, then the Queen, began to distrust him. He was one of the first to appreciate that Spain, and not France, was England's real enemy. Elizabeth was never fully converted to this view, and, certainly in the 1560s, she was concerned to keep the Spanish door ajar. Here again the Earl of Bedford proved his ally, supporting his request for recall from France in 1563, and four years later, as governor of Berwick, doing all he could to forward the policy of support for the Scottish lords, even against Elizabeth's instructions.[5]

During Throckmorton's first embassy to France, beginning in May 1559, he corresponded regularly and frankly with Cecil. His position was difficult. He refused, for example, to kneel at the elevation of the Host, and was ordered either to conform or to absent himself from religious services. After a visit to England from mid-November 1559 to the following January, he was increasingly suspected by the Guises, especially after the conspiracy of Amboise (March 1560), in which they accused him of being involved. Until the possibility of a marriage between Elizabeth and Dudley was over, Throckmorton's friendship for him did not cause him to hide his conviction that the marriage would be disastrous for Elizabeth's reputation abroad and at home. In October 1560 he wrote to his cousin, the Marquess of Northampton, that there had been speeches at the French court about Elizabeth which 'every hair of my head stareth at' and made his 'ears glow to hear'.[6]

Elizabeth's government thus found him a mixed asset. His position was weak, since Mary Tudor's defeat in France had lowered England's reputation there. Again it was necessary that Condé, Coligny and their friends should be strengthened in their opposition to the Guise Catholic interest, which might otherwise act more effectively against the protestants in Scotland; but Elizabeth shrank from the idea of going to war for the Huguenots. All the time both the Queen and Cecil were aware of the danger of his over-playing his hand, which in the event, happened. He encouraged his government to overestimate the strength of the Huguenots, and in July 1562 urgently advised the Queen to accept their offer of Le Havre. His natural impatience, as well as his growing belief in the danger of Spanish intervention on behalf of the French Catholic interest, caused him to upbraid even Cecil for dilatoriness. In the summer of 1560, on Cecil's departure for Scotland, he had prophesied disaster.

> Who can as well stand fast against the Queen's arguments and doubtful devices? Who will speedily resolve the doubtful delays? Who shall make despatch of anything?[7]

But by 1562 he was becoming convinced that Dudley rather than Cecil was his chief ally with Elizabeth. In June 1562 Lord Robert and Sir Henry Sidney* were godfathers to his son Robert, and early the following year it was to Dudley that he turned for support in his prolonged quarrel with Sir Thomas Smith*. He had originally urged his government to send Smith to France, since he greatly respected his abilities, and even suggested him also as a useful English representative at the Council of Trent. But when Smith arrived, in September 1562, relations between the two men quickly deteriorated. Smith, though anxious to bring about the recovery of Calais (which Throckmorton's experience led him to see was likely to alienate the Huguenots), in general adopted a less aggresive policy than his colleague, and a conflict developed in which Dudley supported Throckmorton while Cecil, though preserving outward impartiality, leaned towards Smith (who was probably carrying out government instructions). Throckmorton persuaded Elizabeth to send troops to help the Huguenots at Le Havre, but this proved an expensive mistake, and Throckmorton's own identification with Condé's army, late in 1562, ostensibly as a captive, prejudiced his position. In December he was taken prisoner by Catholic forces, remaining in custody until February 1563, when he retired to Le Havre and maintained liaison between Condé's forces and the Earl of Warwick. Warwick, however, was unable to hold the town when the Huguenots failed to support him, and, after a short period in England, Throckmorton was sent back to France (June 1563) to negotiate peace terms very different from those he had envisaged. Having no safe-conduct from the French, he was arrested, remaining in prison for some time before Cecil could gain his release. Smith, he complained, did nothing to help him, and although after his release he and Smith officially co-operated in negotiations leading to the Treaty of Troyes (1 Apr. 1564), their personal relations remained bad. At one point during the negotiations both men drew their daggers and were forcibly restrained by the onlookers. After the signing of the treaty, Throckmorton returned to England, where Dudley was making strenuous (and Cecil less strenuous) but unavailing efforts to get him appointed to the Privy Council. Never a wealthy man, he had suffered financially from his period in France, and the two lucrative posts he obtained after his return (chamberlain of the Exchequer and chief butler of England), no doubt eased the burden.

Throckmorton's next assignment was to Scotland, to try to prevent Mary Stuart's marriage to Darnley, and encourage her to marry Leicester. He had little hope of success, and achieved none. Typically, he sent Mary a letter of advice, urging her to show clemency to the banished protestant lords. Whether or not this angered Mary Stuart, the Queen and Cecil both found it infuriating. In May 1566 he and Cecil confronted one another, in the presence of Leicester, and Throckmorton promised to do better next time. But his last mission to Scotland, in the following year, with vague instructions to bring about the release of Mary from captivity and make an agreement between her and the rebel lords, was also a failure. He came to the conclusion that it was the lords 'who must stand her [Elizabeth] in more stead than the Queen of Scots', and believed that they would be prepared, if they were promised support from England, to send young James to be educated there. Otherwise, they would probably turn to France. In spite of his political convictions, he personally sympathized with Mary, who wrote thanking him for the good feeling he had shown her. He tried unsuccessfully to raise a party to support her, and on Elizabeth's instructions refused to attend the coronation of James VI. Having annoyed both sides, his recall in September 1567 followed statements in England that 'he was esteemed to favour too much the lords'.[8]

This was the end of his diplomatic career. His chances with the Queen and Cecil were finally ruined when, in 1569, his implication in the Norfolk marriage plot brought him an examination before the Privy Council and a short period of imprisonment in Windsor castle. He remained under house arrest until the spring of 1570. In February he wrote a *mémoire justificatif* to Cecil asking him to sue for his release, and thenceforward took no further part in politics (though there was a rumour early in 1570 that he would be made vice-chamberlain) until his death in London of 'a peripneumonia' 12 Feb. 1571. Leicester wrote to Walsingham, who was in France, on the 14th:

> We have lost on Monday our good friend Sir Nicholas Throckmorton, who died in my house, being there taken suddenly in great extremity on Tuesday before; his lungs were perished, but a sudden cold he had taken, was the cause of his sudden death; God hath his soul, and we his friends great loss of his body.

He was buried in St. Catherine Cree, Aldgate, the parish where he had his London residence, a large mansion which had belonged to the abbey of Evesham. As a country house he used Beddington, his wife's family home in Surrey.[9]

About his private and domestic life not much is known. His daughter Elizabeth married Sir Walter Ralegh. His books, many of which his son Arthur* bequeathed to Magdalen College, Oxford, are almost exclusively political and religious, and are heavily underlined – essentially the 'library of a practising diplomat'. There are scattered references to hunting and other outdoor amusements in his letters, but no indication of any marked cultural interests. Personally devout, he was opposed to the wilder puritan schemes, or to any kind of pietism. In his criticisms of Mary Tudor's reign he deplored the policy of 'referring all to God, without doing anything ourselves', which he described as tempting God too far. He admitted that there was still some 'popery' in the English church, but wanted as much toleration as was compatible with strong government control, to make a united protestant front against the Spanish Catholic menace abroad. The Earl of Leicester appointed him as a suitable governor of his foundation for the revenues of Warwickshire preachers.[10]

In his will, made four days before his death, he left a life interest in lands in Buckinghamshire, Northamptonshire and Oxfordshire to his widow with reversion to his eldest son. The Worcestershire lands were left to Arthur, the second son, with reversion to his younger brothers. The younger children were also otherwise provided for. Thomas, the fourth son, was to have the London property after the death of his mother, as well as £500. A similar sum and the privileges of the salt monopoly granted to Throckmorton were bequeathed to the two youngest sons and £500 to his only surviving daughter Elizabeth. The supervisors of the will included the Earl of Leicester, Sir Walter Mildmay*, (Sir) John Throckmorton I* and Sir William Cordell*. These were all left tokens, as were the Marquess of Northampton, Sir William Cecil, Lady Warwick and Lady Stafford. Throckmorton's death brought differing comments from various quarters: the Earl of Rutland in Paris told Cecil that the event was no source of regret to the French, but to Lord Buckhurst (Thomas Sackville*), the news brought no small grief, 'not only for his private loss, but the general loss which the Queen and the whole realm thereby suffer'. This sense of Throckmorton's public value was summed up by Walsingham: 'for counsel in peace and for conduct in war he has not left of like sufficiency his successor that I know'.[11] His widow Anne took as her second husband Adrian Stokes*.

[1] *Vis. Northants.* ed. Metcalfe, 200; Camden, *Annals* (1717), 221; Stow, *Survey of London* (1720), i. 63; Nash, *Worcs.* i. 452; PCC 9 Daper. [2] *Soc. Antiq.* 1790, p. 167; *APC*, iv. 76, 77, 84; *CPR*, 1549-51, p. 137; 1553 and App. Edw. VI, p. 9; 1563-6, pp. 118, 234; *CSP Dom. Add.* 1547-65, pp. 503, 561; Lansd. 1218, f. 21v. [3] Bodl. e. Museo 17; *DNB*; Dugdale, *Warws.* ii. 749-52; *EHR*, lxv. 91-8. [4] *EHR*, lxv. 91-8; A. L. Rowse, *Ralegh and the Throckmortons*, 25; C. Read, *Cecil*, 72; *CSP Dom.* 1547-80, p. 115. [5] Lyme Regis archives N23/2/19; *CJ*, i. 73; D'Ewes, 126; Camb. Univ. Lib. Gg. iii. 34, p. 209; *CSP For.* 1561-2, p. 23; 1566-8, pp. 39, 308; *CSP Dom. Add.* 1566-79, p. 19. [6] Neale, *Eliz.* 99; *CSP For.* 1560-1, pp. 342-3, 348; *EHR*, lxxxi. 474-89. [7] Rowse, 38; Read, 174. [8] *CSP For., CSP Span., CSP Scot.*, passim; P. Forbes, *A Full View of Public Transactions*, i. 163-6, 206-12, 216-18, 320-4; ii. 7-14, 36-43, 61-7, 251-9, 342-4; M. Dewar, *Sir Thomas Smith*, passim; *HMC Hatfield*, xii. 255; Lansd. 102, ff. 84, 110; Strype, *Sir Thomas Smith*, 70, 81 et passim; Rowse, 41, 46; T. Wright, *Eliz.* i. 208. [9] Haynes, *State Pprs.* 471, 541-3, 547, 577; *HMC Hatfield*, i. 363, 426, 430, 435, 456, 465; Wright, i. 355; Camden, *Annals* (1717), 221; Stow, *Survey of London*, ed. Kingsford, i. 138, 142-3; ii. 290; Rowse, 46; *CSP Dom.* 1566-79, p. 16; *CPR*, 1560-3, p. 400. [10] *CSP Dom.* 1547-80, p. 304; Rowse, 336-8. [11] PCC 9 Daper; Lansd. 117, ff. 36, 38, 39; *CSP For.* 1569-70, p. 407.

I.C./P.W.H.

THROCKMORTON, Simon (d.1585), of Brampton, Hunts.

Huntingdon	1554 (Apr.)
Huntingdonshire	1559

3rd s. of Richard Throckmorton of Higham Ferrers, Northants. by Joan, da. of Humphrey Beaufoe of Whilton, Northants. *m.* by 1547, 2s.

Throckmorton was one of the family of Coughton, Warwickshire, his father's brother being Sir George Throckmorton, who married Katherine, daughter of Nicholas, 1st Baron Vaux of Harrowden. By 1559 he owned the manor of Fosters in Brampton, which he had bought from Gerard Foster and others in 1550, but Throckmorton never attained the commission of the peace and was not really of knight of the shire status. His election for the county in 1559 he owed to a friend of his father, and his own fellow-Member, Sir Robert Tyrwhitt. Throckmorton alienated the Brampton property in September 1559 to Sir Roger Woodhouse* but this may have been only a conveyance under the Statute of Uses, as his son and heir Robert Throckmorton succeeded to it in 1585. Throckmorton was almost certainly a Catholic (another reason for his not becoming a j.p., at any rate under Elizabeth), and the remainder of his life was passed in comparative obscurity. He died on 27 Mar. 1585.

Harl. 1179, f. 123; Vis. Hunts. (Cam. Soc. xliii), 123–4; Vis. Warws. (Harl. Soc. xii), 203; Baker, Northants. i. 232; CPR, 1549–51, p. 245; C142/210/93.

N.M.F.

THROCKMORTON, Thomas (1534–1615), of Coughton, Warws. and Weston Underwood, Bucks.

| WARWICKSHIRE | 1558 |
| WARWICK | 1559 |

b. by 1534, 1st s. of Sir Robert Throckmorton† of Coughton by his 1st w. Muriel, da. of Thomas, 5th Lord Berkeley. educ. M. Temple 1555. m. by 1556, Margaret, da. and coh. of William Whorwood† of Putney, Surr., 3s. 5da. suc. fa. Feb. 1581.[1]

J.p. Warws. from 1564, rem. 1570.

Heir of the elder branch of a prosperous and prolific family, Throckmorton had three uncles with him in the 1559 Parliament, Clement, John I and Sir Nicholas Throckmorton, and a cousin, Simon. The Throckmortons of Coughton remained Catholic, and for this reason after 1558 Throckmorton could play little part in parliamentary affairs or local government. His reduced position became apparent as early as 1559, for while in Mary's last Parliament he had been knight of the shire, in Elizabeth's first he resorted to the borough, Warwick, where the influence of the Throckmortons was still strong.

The rest of Throckmorton's long life was dogged by the consequences of his recusancy. During the earlier part of the reign he was left alone, though bonds were taken from him to ensure that he did not leave the country, and he was sometimes ordered to stay within five miles of Weston Underwood, the house in Buckinghamshire where he principally resided. In 1570 both he and his father refused to take the oaths and were removed from the commission of the peace. In August 1580 he was summoned to appear before the Privy Council, who committed him to the bishop of London. Thereafter he spent long periods in prison, usually at Banbury castle. In 1586 he offered to pay the Queen £100 in composition of recusancy fines, but this did not save him from further imprisonment. At any time of unrest or danger, particularly in 1588 and during the 1590s, Throckmorton was to be found in Banbury castle.[2]

For many years he was involved in a dispute with (Sir) Moyle Finch*, who had been granted a reversion of the manor of Ravenstone, of which Throckmorton already held a lease. In order to accelerate his possession of the manor, Finch claimed that Throckmorton's lease had been terminated in 1567 when a servant's negligence had caused the rent to remain unpaid for six months. They contested the matter in the court of Exchequer and Finch twice obtained favourable judgments, but Throckmorton continued to fight him, both in common pleas and Queen's bench. In March 1597 he wrote to Sir Robert Cecil from Banbury castle, begging him to secure his release

in regard of the great suits which of late are attempted against me and my tenants by Sir Moyle Finch, for the avoiding of my lease of the manor of Ravenstone; and further, in respect of my own poor estate, which at this instant standeth very dangerously for that by my longer restraint I shall be unable to satisfy my creditors and in worse case to recover that which is my own.

On 24 Nov. 1597 a bill for lessees against patentees was introduced into Parliament which could be turned to Throckmorton's advantage. Not being an MP himself, he asked his friends in the House, particularly (Sir) Walter Ralegh*, to table a special amendment in his favour. On 14 Dec. 1597 he wrote to one of his friends:

Good Sir, I must acknowledge myself most bound unto you for your honourable favour, that you extended towards my cause with many of your good friends in the Parliament house, and it was not a little comfort to me.

On 19 Dec. 'a special proviso for Mr. Throckmorton' was read twice in the House, but rather than include it in the bill, it was agreed by the House, Throckmorton and Finch, both of whom appeared in person, that 'the matter in controversy between them' should be settled by arbitration. The 1597 journals make no mention of Throckmorton's proviso after this point. Eventually the matter was settled by a compromise: Finch was given possession of Ravenstone, but granted Throckmorton a new lease for 14 years at a higher rent.[3]

Throckmorton paid dear for his determined recusancy. In 1584 he was fined £260 and forced to redeem his movables for £600. In 1588 a bond of £5,000 was required of him before he was allowed to remove for seven days from the bishop of London's custody to his own town house in Holborn. In 1596 he was noted as one of the wealthier recusants in the diocese of Worcester, and two years later was forced to contribute £3 to the war in Ireland. Such extraordinary levies in addition to monthly fines of £20 must have depleted his financial reserves. They did not, however, force him to sell any land.[4]

The death of Elizabeth was followed for a time by greater leniency towards Catholics. In November 1604 Throckmorton was among those recusants who were discharged of their unpaid fines by the King, but a year later he was in greater danger than ever. Living principally at Weston Underwood he had lent Coughton to Sir Everard Digby, who arranged the Warwickshire rising which was to coincide with the blowing up of Parliament. Throckmorton's name occurred frequently during the examination of the arrested conspirators and other witnesses, but his own loyalty was not questioned in spite of his relatives being involved in the plot. However, with other recusants, he suffered the consequences. Fines and restrictions were reimposed, and in August 1606, writing to the Earl of Salisbury, he complained that

> of late commissions are come ... for inquiry of the value of my poor living for his Majesty according to the late made statute. And by this late session of Parliament I am restrained not to pass above five miles from my habitation.

He begged to be allowed to travel about his necessary business, adding 'if my poor estate did not urge me to these travels, to satisfy the law and my creditors who stand in danger for me, my old years would desire rest at home'. His efforts to conserve his estates met with some success, for in May 1607, James I agreed to accept £20 monthly for his recusancy instead of the forfeiture of two-thirds of his lands enjoined by the statute.[5]

Throckmorton died in March 1615, aged 81, and was buried at Weston Underwood. By a will made in January that year, he left £150 and his household goods to his daughter Mary and enjoined his grandson and heir, Robert, to maintain all existing leases, even if invalid in law. There were bequests to the poor, to servants and for the maintenance of almshouses at Coughton.[6]

[1] Nash, *Worcs.* i. 453; *Vis. Warws.* (Harl. Soc. xii), 88; C142/193/89. [2] *CSP Dom.* 1547–80, p. 366; 1581–90, p. 321; *APC*, xii. 166; xv. 348; xviii. 415; xx. 6, 7; xxi. 250–1; xxiv. 76, 221, 224, 339; xxvi. 538–9; xxvii. 64; xxviii. 14–15, 102; Coughton Court muniments, boxes 62, 64. [3] Coughton Court muniments, boxes 53, 60, 61, 64; letters file 52; St. Ch. 4/5/52; Lansd. 106, f. 196; C2/W11/62; *VCH Bucks.* iv. 441; D'Ewes, 562, 575. [4] Coughton Court muniments, boxes 60, 62; *APC*, xv. 348; *Cath. Rec. Soc.* xxii. 65; *HMC Hatfield*, vii. 266; *APC*, xxviii. 589; Lansd. 153, f. 177. [5] *CSP Dom.* 1603–10, pp. 171, 248, 260, 263, 295, 356; *HMC Hatfield*, xviii. 240–1. [6] *VCH Bucks.* iv. 499, 501; Coughton Court muniments, wills box 60.

S.M.T./I.C.

THROCKMORTON, Sir Thomas (1538/9–1607), of Tortworth, Glos.

GLOUCESTERSHIRE　　　　　　　　1589

b. 1538/9, 1st s. of Sir Thomas Throckmorton[†] of Coss Court by Margaret, da. and coh. of Thomas

Whittington of Pauntley. *m.* (1) Ellen, da. of Sir Richard Berkeley[†], 2s. 1da.; (2) settlement 6 Nov. 1559, Elizabeth, da. of Sir Edward Rogers* of Cannington, Som., *s.p. suc.* fa. 1568. Kntd. 1587.[1]

Commr. restraint of grain, Glos. 1573, j.p. 1574, sheriff 1587–8, 1600–1601; member, council in the marches of Wales 1590; deprived of all offices 1602.[2]

On succeeding his father to a prominent position in the county, Throckmorton was active in local affairs, and was frequently employed by the Privy Council. In 1579, for example, he was instructed to examine a case of assault on a messenger of the Queen's chamber; the same year he was to inquire into a robbery committed at Gloucester by 'certain disguised persons', and in 1589 he was ordered to search out the publishers of 'infamous letters' which had been circulating in Gloucester, and tended to discredit the ministry. But by this time his overbearing and bellicose nature had begun to assert itself, and soon his reputation was such that a suitor, taking a sugar loaf to appease him, called it 'going to offer my candle to the devil', a phrase which became proverbial in the hundred of Berkeley. In 1580 he was bound over to keep the peace towards Sir Thomas Proctor. In 1589 he was accused of provoking 'a riot, and other outrages', against Nicholas Poyntz, and the next year was summoned before the Privy Council to answer for 'divers misdemeanours and outrages committed by him, his servants and followers', and to explain why he and Sir Richard Berkeley 'had not carried themselves with such indifference ... as was meet for men of their place and calling'. In addition to this, he appears to have used his position as subsidy commissioner to falsify the lists, his captaincy of trained bands to press his enemies and their servants for service in Ireland, and his place on the council in the marches to prosecute his feud with the Poyntz family. In 1602 his quarrel with Sir Henry Winston brought him once more before the Privy Council. He was fined 2,000 marks in Star Chamber, imprisoned and disabled from bearing office 'for divers foul matters, and extortions committed in his country'. He was also mentioned as an example of justices who 'maintain quarrels'.[3]

Little is known of Throckmorton's parliamentary career save that on 5 Mar. 1589 he was licensed to depart. As knight of the shire he may have attended the subsidy committee, 11 Feb. 1589. His private life was as stormy as the rest of his career, complicated by a wife and daughter 'obstinately addicted to Popery'. At one point he appears to have turned his wife out of doors, and refused to provide for her until ordered by the Council to do so.[4]

Throckmorton died on 31 Jan. 1607, 'in happy and peaceable manner', according to his tombstone. In his will, dated 17 Dec. 1600, he commended his soul to God, 'beseeching Him that for His Son Christ Jesu's sake, He will have mercy on the same'. His body was not to be 'opened or bowelled', but buried 'without pomp or unnecessary charges'. The bulk of his property he left to his surviving son, with small annuities to his daughter, and to his 'right honest and loving brother' Anthony Throckmorton, who, with Sir Henry Poole*, was named as overseer of the will. He was buried at Tortworth, his tomb bearing the inscription, 'I have fought a good fight, I have finished my course ... henceforth is laid up for me a crown of righteousness'.[5]

[1] C142/149/130; *Vis. Glos.* (Harl. Soc. xxi), 163; W. R. Williams, *Parl. Hist. Glos.* 47; PCC 8 Babington. [2] *APC*, viii. 116, 288–9; xxiv. 474; P. H. Williams, *Council in the Marches of Wales*, 307; *HMC Hatfield*, xiii. 457. [3] *APC*, xi. 156–7, 272; xii. 284–5; xviii. 200, 287; xix. 48, 400; *Chamberlain Letters* ed. McClure, i. 147; W. B. Willcox, *Glos.* 23–4, 83–4, 94–5, 113–14. [4] D'Ewes, 431, 443; *APC*, xxiv. 279–80, 303, 385. [5] PCC 26 Windebanck; *Bristol and Glos. Arch. Soc. Trans.* xxx. 137–41.

J.J.C.

THURBARNE, James (*d.* 1627), of New Romney, Kent.

NEW ROMNEY   1597

?s. of John Thurbarne of New Romney. *educ.* Clare, Camb. 1580; Barnard's Inn; G. Inn 1585, called. *m.* Mary, da. of Giles Estcourt* of Salisbury, at least 2s. 2da.

Attorney, Barnard's Inn 1585; town clerk, New Romney by 1588; of counsel to Cinque Ports 1594; reader, Staple Inn 1599; ancient, G. Inn 1603; of counsel to Rye 1607; assistant reader of G. Inn 1610, pens. 1611.

The Thurbarnes were prominent in Elizabethan New Romney. John Thurbarne was mayor in 1589; Robert* in 1587, 1594 and 1602; William was a jurat and possibly mayor 1590; all three were supporters of William Southland* and, like him, first defied and later submitted to the Privy Council. It was during this turbulent period in the town's affairs that James Thurbarne became town clerk. While his family was being disciplined by the Privy Council, he was imprisoned for slander at the suit of one Driver of Gray's Inn. Driver, however, had prosecuted without the consent of the benchers of Gray's Inn, and so had to pay Thurbarne's costs.

Thurbarne was paid a 40s. annuity for his counsel to the Cinque Ports, and 2s. a day for his services as MP in the same year that he was employed in a lawsuit against the city of London. John Mynge*, Lord Cobham's ally among the port men, suggested Thurbarne as a suitable adviser on port affairs, but the lord warden, who did not know him, preferred Mynge himself. In 1604 Thurbarne received an extra 20s. from the Ports for his services in connexion with a meeting of the brodhull, and at various times his name appears as a commissioner for the reduction of fifteenths, and as standing counsel for Rye as well as Romney. Although he sat in Parliament once, much of his later work for New Romney was connected with parliamentary matters. He died at Gray's Inn on 6 June 1627, two days after making his will, in which he named his 'well-beloved wife Mary' executrix and

residuary legatee. She was 'to do the best she can' for the younger son James and the eldest daughter Mary.

Vis. Glos. (Harl. Soc. xxi), 56; *CSP Dom.* 1581–90, p. 266; New Romney ass. bk. passim; Cinque Ports black bk. passim; *Pens. Bk. G. Inn* i. 78, 146, 162, 192, 195; *HMC 13th Rep. IV*, 137, 146, 148, 151, 160, 187; *APC*, xix. 5, 7, 9, 208–9; Romney borough recs.; PCC 115 Skinner.

R.C.G.

THURBARNE, Robert, of New Romney, Kent.

NEW ROMNEY   1586

m. 1582, Hannah Stringer of Lydd, wid.

Jurat, New Romney, mayor 1587, 1594, 1602; brodhull rep. in at least the years 1586, 1587, 1594; bailiff to Yarmouth 1597.

Thurbarne first appears in local records in the early 1580s, when he was one of William Southland's faction. The fact that he and Southland were both returned as Romney's representatives to the 1586 Parliament is an indication of their control of the town's affairs during that period. They could have sat on a committee (6 Mar. 1587) concerned with the importing of fish. Thurbarne was paid 4s. daily for his services at Westminster, but both Members 'agreed to compound' with Richard Williams*, who was still pressing for payment for attending the previous Parliament.

Southland's 'confederacy' as the Privy Council called it, came to an end in 1590, and several men, including Thurbarne, had to make written submissions, but his career continued at least up to 1601. His family continued to represent Cinque Ports in Parliament in the seventeenth century.

J. Cowper, *Canterbury Mar. Lic.* i. 414; *Arch. Cant.* xv. 284; xxvii. 52; Cinque Ports black bk. ff. 53, 54, 61, 76–7; D'Ewes, 412; T. Philipott, *Villare Cantianum* (1776), p. 52; New Romney ass. bk. f. 30; *APC*, xix. 5–8, 208.

M.R.P.

THURSTON, Alexander (*d.* c.1621), of Norwich, Norf.

NORWICH   1601

s. of Edmund Thurston, grocer, of Norwich.

Freeman, Norwich 1575, sheriff 1587–8, alderman 1589, mayor 1600–1.

There is little to say about Thurston, who filled the usual corporation offices, and once represented Norwich in Parliament. As one of the Norwich burgesses he could have sat on committees concerned with the penal laws (2 Nov. 1601), the main business (3 Nov.), and the true payment of tithes at Norwich (27 Nov.). His will, made 28 Feb. 1619 and proved by one Thomas Holle on 3 May 1621, mentions no wife or children.

P. Millican, *Norwich Freemen*, 73; H. Le Strange, *Norf. Official Lists*, 109–10; Norwich corp. claviour's bk. 1589; *The Walloons and their Church in Norwich* (Hug. Soc. i), 11, pt. 2, p. 161; D'Ewes, 622, 624, 654; PCC 37 Dale.

R.V.

THYMBLEBY, John (c.1533–1626), of Irnham and Beelsby, Lincs.

GREAT GRIMSBY	1571

b. c.1533, 1st surv. s. and h. of Sir Richard Thymbleby* by his 1st w. Katherine, da. of Sir Robert Tyrwhitt of Kettleby. *m.* (1) bef. Jan. 1559, Mary (*d.*1564), da. of George St. Poll†, sis. of Thomas St. Poll*, 1s. 1da.; (2) Feb. 1567, Magdalen or Maud, da. of Andrew Billesby or Beelsby of Beelsby, 6s. 4da. *suc.* fa. 1590.[1]

Thymbleby was a first cousin of Sir Robert Tyrwhitt, one of Lord Clinton's assistants as lieutenant of Lincolnshire. Most probably he was returned for Grimsby because of his father's position in the county and his family's local connexions. Thymblebys were resident in Grimsby early in the sixteenth century, when a relative of the 1571 Member was mayor six times. At least one of John Thymbleby's children was baptized in the town, and his younger brother Richard is described in the pedigrees as of Grimsby. The court books give details of an angry scene in December 1564, when Richard Thymbleby insulted the mayor in the common hall, saying that his worship was now within his liberties, but that other places would serve to settle the dispute between them. The original quarrel seems to have concerned John, who soon afterwards came in with one Edward Skipwith and spoke threateningly, with 'many unseemly words', to the mayor.[2]

The main family estates at Irnham in Kesteven did not descend to Thymbleby until 1590, though his father had granted him church patronage there by 1584. Before Sir Richard's death, Thymbleby himself no doubt spent much of his time at Beelsby, less than ten miles from Grimsby, where his second wife's family lived and where the manor was in his father's possession. Sir Richard may have conveyed property at East Bridgeford, Nottinghamshire, to him before 1571, as in that year John Thymbleby is mentioned as the patron of the church there. The inquisitions post mortem list other land belonging to the Thymblebys at Poolham in Lindsey and elsewhere in Lincolnshire, but the total value of Thymbleby's property at the beginning of James I's reign was only £133.[3]

Thymbleby presumably took the oath of supremacy in 1571, but by 1579 he and his second wife were being indicted for absence from church. He was 'confined for matters of religion' in October 1580, and at liberty a year later, when he and his wife refused to answer questions as to whether one of their children had been christened 'in popery'. In November 1581 he was sent to the Fleet, and during the next six months was either in prison or out on licence. In November 1582 he was fined £60 for three months' absence from church, and there are many later references to his fines, for which in April 1586 he offered a £20 composition. The Lincolnshire musters list for the furnishing of armour, October 1585, returned him as 'in London'.[4]

By March 1588 he was back in his own county, in the custody of Bartholomew Armyn. The deputy lieutenants reported to Lord Burghley that he refused to undertake not to confer with other recusants. He was 'at liberty upon bonds' in 1592, and in prison at Ely palace in March 1594 and in December 1597.[5]

Thymbleby's finances suffered seriously from the increasing severity of the recusancy laws, especially after the statute of 1586 which allowed the Crown to take the profits of two-thirds of recusants' estates. By 1593 this Act was being applied to his best lands, and his wife was speaking 'bad and unreverend words' of the Queen. In April 1600 his eldest son Richard was examined about a letter in his possession, said to have been written by Robert Persons. At this time both father and son were lodging with a London printer, John East, in Aldersgate Street.[6]

Apart from official valuations of his lands taken at various times during Elizabeth's reign and up to 1606 for purposes of recusancy fines, no later references to Thymbleby have been found. He died intestate on 7 Jan. 1626. His inquisition post mortem, taken at Boston in October, mentions a conveyance of 1602 by which he secured the use of his lands at Irnham and Beelsby to himself – probably an attempt to circumvent the recusancy fines. His heir was his grandson John, aged 22.[7]

[1] C142/228/97; Harl. 1484, f. 8; Lansd. 30, f. 196; *Lincs. Peds.* (Harl. Soc. lii), 845, 957–8, 1019–20. [2] *HMC 14th Rep. VIII*, 280, 289–90. [3] C142/228/97; *Lincs. Episcopal Recs.* 1571–84 (Cant. & York Soc.), p. 249; *Lincs. Peds.* 958; Lansd. 153, f. 159. [4] Lansd. 30, f. 196; 68, f. 112; APC, xii. 234; xiii. 238, 252–409 passim; *HMC Hatfield*, ii. 530; *CSP Dom.* 1581–90, pp. 280, 324. [5] *HMC Cowper*, i. 8; *HMC Hatfield*, iv. 264, 442; APC, xvii. 318; xxi. 142; xxviii. 172; Bodl. Tanner 118, ff. 128 seq. [6] *CSP Dom.* 1598–1601, pp. 254, 423; *Cath. Rec. Soc.* xviii. 148, 150, 153; liii. 14; APC, xxii. 317. [7] Lansd. 153, ff. 129, 159, 166, 220, 253; *Admons. in Consistory Ct. of Lincoln, 1540–1659* (Brit. Rec. Soc. Index Lib.), 349; C142/452/34.

N.M.F.

THYMBLEBY, Sir Richard (c.1507–90), of Irnham, Lincs. and East Bridgeford, Notts.

LINCOLNSHIRE	1559

b. c.1507, 1st s. of Sir John Thymbleby by Margaret, da. of John Boys. *m.* (1) Katherine, da. of Sir Robert Tyrwhitt of Kettleby, Lincs., 3s. inc. John* 4da.; (2) Elizabeth, ?da. of Thomas Moore, 1s. *d.v.p. suc.* fa. 1550. Kntd. bef. Nov. 1551.

Commr. to inquire into church goods, Lincs. 1553; j.p. Lincs. (Kesteven) prob. by 1547, (Lindsey) from c.1559; sheriff, Lincs. 1551–2, 1560–1.

The pardon roll of 1553 described Thymbleby as 'of Irnham ... late of Lynn Regis, Norfolk', but he still had a house at Lynn in July of that year, when (presumably as one of Northumberland's adherents) he was first committed to the custody of the knight marshal, and then licensed to return to Lynn, on condition that he kept away from court until Queen Mary's pleasure was known. A convinced protestant, he was classified as 'earnest in religion'. There are few references to him during the last 20 years of his long life, during which he lived as a country gentleman and sheep-farmer. He died on 25 Sept. 1590, lord of the manor of East Bridgeford, but there seems to be no evidence as to whether he still held any Norfolk property. The heir to his estates at Irnham, Beelsby, Bulby and Hawthorpe, Lincolnshire was his son John, aged 57.

E150/585/15; C142/228/97; *Lincs. Peds.* (Harl. Soc. lii), 957; *Genealogist* (ser. 1), v. 114; vi. 285; *CPR*, 1550–3, p. 45; 1553–4, p. 455; 1553 and App. Edw. VI. pp. 355, 414; 1560–3, p. 439; *APC*, iv. 307, app. 420; *Cam. Misc.* ix(3), p. 27; Lansd. 1218, f. 18; *HMC 14th Rep.* VIII, 240; PCC 17 Coode.

N.M.F.

THYMBLEBY, Stephen (d. 1587), of St. Swithin's, Lincoln.

| BOSTON | 1572 |
| LINCOLN | 1584 |

2nd s. of Matthew Thymbleby of Poolham in Edlington, Lincs. by Anne, da. and coh. of Sir Robert Hussey of Linwood in Blankney; half-bro. of John Savile II*. *educ.* Queens', Camb. 1554, L. Inn 1558, called 1565. *m.* c.1575, Katherine (d. 1587), *s.p.*[1]

Recorder, Lincoln 1572; dep. recorder, Boston 1572; bencher, L. Inn 1573, Autumn reader 1574; j.p. Lincs. (Holland, Lindsey), Isle of Ely from c.1573, (Kesteven) from c.1579.[2]

Through his mother, who married as her second husband Sir Robert Savile, Thymbleby was connected with the local families of Hussey, Savile, Tailor and Monson. Succeeding Robert Monson* as recorder of Lincoln, and obtaining the deputy recordership of Boston,[3] Thymbleby represented both places in Parliament, sitting on the following Commons committees: grants by corporations (30 May 1572), recoveries (31 May), bastardy (15 Feb. 1576), dilapidations (24 Feb.), and, as one 'learned in the laws', that of 1 Dec. 1584 to consider the termination of certain statutes. On 4 Mar. 1585 he was 'licensed to repair home into the country to an assizes'.[4]

Thymbleby had a considerable conveyancing practice in Lincolnshire, for his name appears as attorney in a number of final concords for land there. In 1579 he was involved in a dispute with a servant of the Earl of Leicester over the lease of the parsonage of Belton in Axholme, which was owned by the city; he promised to 'yield up all the interest that he may claim'. During the years 1584–7 he was involved in the disputes about the mayoralty of the

city, which were sufficiently serious for the Privy Council to intervene. His labours were rewarded in January 1587 by a grant from the common council of a hogshead of wine. Thymbleby died before the disputes ended, during an outbreak of plague in Lincoln. Because of the infection no entries were made in the city minute book 20 May–22 Aug. 1587, and the first entry after the interval records Thymbleby's death. He died intestate, as his wife had done the previous April, and administration was granted to William Thymbleby, son of his elder brother Richard. Thymbleby was apparently buried in his parish church of St. Swithin, for, though neither register nor transcripts survive for this period, Gervase Holles recorded his memorial window there.[5]

[1] Lincs. AO, Lincoln minute bk. 1575, city charters 89, final concord. index Easter term 24 Eliz. no. 7; *Lincs. Peds.* (Harl. Soc. lii), 957. [2] J. W. F. Hill, *Tudor and Stuart Lincoln.* 72–3; P. Thompson, *Hist. Antiqs. Boston*, 458. [3] R. E. G. Cole, *Hist. Doddington Pigott* (privately 1897); Hill, loc. cit. [4] *CJ*, i. 99, 106, 108; D'Ewes, 220, 334, 362. [5] Lincs. AO, Foster lib. index of final concords; min. bk. 28 July 1579, Jan. 1587, 22 Aug. 1587; prob. recs. AN, 139, 151; *APC*, xi. 153, 288, 294; *CSP Dom.* 1547–80, p. 618; Hill, op. cit. app. iv. 227–232; G. Holles, *Lincs. Church Notes*, ed. Cole (Linc. Rec. Soc. i), p. 54.

D.O.

THYNNE, John (?1550–1604), of Longleat, Wilts.

HEYTESBURY	1584, 1586
WILTSHIRE	1589
HEYTESBURY	1593, 1597, 1601
WILTSHIRE	1604*

b. ?1550, 1st s. of Sir John Thynne* of Longleat by Christian, da. of Sir Richard Gresham, mercer of London; bro. of Thomas I*. *educ.* Oxf. BA 1573. *m.* 1575/7, Joan (d. 1612), da. of Sir Rowland Hayward, clothworker of London, by Joan, da. of William Tillesworth, goldsmith of London, 2s. inc. Thomas II* 2da. *suc.* fa. 1580. Kntd. 1603.[1]

J.p. Wilts. from c.1583, sheriff 1593–4; j.p. Som. from c.1583, rem. c.1587, rest. 1591; Glos. from c.1583, rem. c.1587; Salop from 1596.

Thynne made no mark in Wiltshire during his father's lifetime. In the mid-1570s, however, he acquired land in Shropshire in right of his wife. Grandson of one lord mayor of London, he became son-in-law to another; and his wife, her mother's coheir, brought by the marriage settlement Caws castle and the manor of All Stretton. Thus John Thynne became lord of the manor next to that on which his forbears had been small freeholders, and he may have lived there before he inherited Longleat. The property was not free from dispute; in March 1579 the Privy Council was exercised about the controversy between Lord Stafford and 'young Thinne' over Caws castle, and although the matter was committed to Justice Gawdy in 1590 for speedy hearing it was still unresolved in 1594. Thynne must have retained this property, as his widow retired to it, but in 1593 Lord Stafford was claiming that, after a long suit of riotous entry in the Star Chamber, he had only been cheated of victory there by the substitution of *et* for *vel* in the indictment. When he came into his patrimony Thynne continued his father's building operations, completing the hall and adding the oak screen and wainscoting. But he leaves the impression of being a less efficient man. He did not resume the detailed building accounts which had lapsed before his father's death; he failed to erect the tomb for which (Sir) John had provided 'a plot thereof made and signed with my own hand' and £100 in his will; and in other respects he appears not to have discharged his duty as executor.[2]

Although he was born into the governing class of the shire, Thynne's wish to be of service did not extend to soldiering; he declined the captaincy of 200 men raised for Ireland in July 1580, pleading the necessity of clearing up his father's affairs. Within the county he carried on a long and bitter feud with Sir James Marvyn*, which, perhaps originating in abortive negotiations for his marriage to Marvyn's daughter in 1574, flared up in 1589 in connexion with a dispute over subsidy assessments, when it spread to partisans and servants and provoked an affray at Hindon. In November 1589 Thynne was called before the Council to answer for his share in the disturbances. It was not his only brush with that body, for in the course of much litigation about his manor of Horningsham, one widow Daniel moved their lordships to order him to give her satisfaction. In February 1597 Burghley received a complaint of his harsh treatment of the Earl of Derby and in the following year another from the Earl of Pembroke that Thynne had commenced a suit against his servant about a weir in the Wye. When early in the following year he offered to make one of a party of gentlemen to accompany (Sir) Robert Cecil* on his French embassy, his offer was evidently declined. Thynne's relations with Marvyn at least improved sufficiently for him to allow Thomas, his heir, to marry Marvyn's grand-daughter, an earl's sister, about the turn of the century. John, Thynne's second boy, settled at Church Stretton, in Shropshire, presumably on his mother's property of Stretton Hall, and both daughters were to connect themselves with families from other parts of the country, Dorothy marrying Charles Roscorrock, of Roscorrock, Cornwall, and Christiana Francis Leigh of Addington in Surrey.[3]

From the time of his succession to Longleat Thynne sat in every Parliament, usually for Heytesbury, the borough nearest to his house and a safe seat for himself or his nominees. Nevertheless the continuity of his representation of this borough was not entirely of his own choosing. In July 1592 he wrote from Caws castle to the bailiffs of Shrewsbury offering himself for election there. He was moved to do so, he said, both by friends in the corporation and by his own inclination, 'for that my ancestors were near inhabitants, and that I conceive a

special good liking of your town and the good government thereof'. Besides gratifying his own ambition, Thynne's acceptance by Shrewsbury would have left him free to nominate at Heytesbury, which his uncle Thomas, who was to sit with him for that borough in the next Parliament, may already have coveted. Any such hope was disappointed by Shrewsbury's failure to adopt him. The greater honour, that of sitting for the shire, he enjoyed on two occasions. On the first, eight years and three Parliaments after his succession to Longleat, Thynne received the Earl of Pembroke's grudging promise of 'neutrality', and reproaches from the Earl's servant, John Penruddock, who had been employed as intermediary, for giving his enemies too early notice of his intentions. True, the moment was not propitious – Thynne's feud with Marvyn was nearing its climax and opinion in the county may well have been divided between them – yet it cannot be said to have been premature. For if the Earl sincerely 'would have all gentlemen to have their due reserved unto them', in the matter of shire representation, as he maintained, then Thynne, well-established in one of the first estates and nearing 40 years of age, could reasonably expect his first taste of that honour. Nevertheless, anxious as Thynne appears to have been to get to Westminster, his service on committees in the Commons was not outstanding. He sat (or could have sat) on the subsidy committees in the Parliaments of 1589 (11 Feb.) and 1593 (26 Feb.), and on committees concerned with Mary Stuart (4 Nov. 1586), poor relief (12 Mar. 1593), cloth (15 Mar.), the order of business (3 Nov. 1601), the Michaelmas law term (11 Nov.) and monopolies (23 Nov.).[4]

This comparatively poor record in the better reported later Parliaments suggests that Thynne was less regarded there than his father had been. He was probably less regarded everywhere. With contacts at court (where his sister Catherine was lady-in-waiting and the John Thynne who was an esquire of the body was probably his younger brother), with many connexions in the shire (for his father's widow had married Carew Raleigh* and the same sister Catherine became the wife of Sir Walter Long*), and possessing in Heytesbury what amounted to a family borough, Thynne enjoyed such honours as were due to the owner of Longleat, but earned no more for himself. He was dropped from the commission of the peace for Somerset and Gloucester about 1587 and the fact that he was not knighted in Elizabeth's reign must have reflected some lack of esteem for him. He may, moreover, have lacked such support as he had reason to expect. Tied to the Seymour, as opposed to the Herbert, interest in the shire, he looked to the Earl of Hertford for favours. But Hertford, who had shown little gratitude to Thynne's father, was not the man to carry over an obligation to a second generation. His letters and papers record three occasions on which Thynne stood surety for his debts but no mention of reciprocal benefits. When in 1601 the death of the Earl of Pembroke left Hertford in the position to exert undisputed influence in an election, he put forward other candidates to represent the shire and solicited Thynne's support for them. What Thynne could not do for himself was unlikely to be done through patronage.[5]

Thynne died 21 Nov. 1604.[6]

[1] *Wilts. Vis. Peds.* (Harl. Soc. cv, cvi), 192–3; Collins, *Peerage*, ii. 499–500; PCC 24 Dixy, 22 Fenner. [2] *APC*, xi. 64; xix. 291; *HMC Hatfield*, iv. 426, 554; Hoare, *Wilts.* Heytesbury, 62, 72; PCC 44 Arundel and *de bonis* n. 1651. [3] *APC*, xii. 105; xxv. 79; *VCH Wilts.* v. 125; Lansd. 83/128/177; *HMC Hatfield*, viii. 16, 220; Hoare, 64; *Wilts. Arch. Mag.* xxxv. 173. [4] *HMC 15th Rep.* X, 56; D'Ewes, 394, 431, 474, 499, 501, 624, 635, 649; *HMC Hatfield*, iv. 295. [5] Collins, 500; LC2/4/4; Lansd. 121/66/246A; 68/246B; *HMC Bath*, iv. 202, 347. [6] C142/195/118.

M.B.

THYNNE, Sir John (1513 or 1515–80), of Longleat, Wilts.

MARLBOROUGH	?1539, ?1542, 1545
SALISBURY	1547*
WILTSHIRE	1559
GREAT BEDWYN	1563
WILTSHIRE	1571
HEYTESBURY	1572*

b. 1513 or 1515, 1st s. of Thomas Thynne of Stretton, Salop by Margaret, da. of Thomas Heynes or Eynes of Stretton. *m.* (1) 1548, Christian or Christiana, da. of Sir Richard Gresham of London, 3s. inc. John* and Thomas I* 3da.; (2) by 1567, Dorothy, da. of William Wroughton of Broadhenton, later wife of Sir Carew Ralegh* of Downton, 5s. Kntd. 1547.[1]

Citizen and mercer of London; high steward, Warminister; surveyor, crown lands, Wilts. 1545, 1580; commr. chantries 1548, musters 1569; sheriff, Som. and Dorset 1548–9, Wilts. 1569–70.

J.p. Wilts. from 1558, Glos. from 1558, Som. from 1573; custos rot. Wilts. from c.1564.[2]

John Thynne, steward to the Earl of Hertford from 1536, had risen with and depended upon his master, created Duke of Somerset in 1547. In 1540 Thynne acquired Longleat priory, and to this added, during the next ten years, wide possessions in Wiltshire and elsewhere from chantry lands and by his first marriage with the only daughter of a lord mayor of London. He fell from power with Protector Somerset, but managed to retire to his Wiltshire estates, where he awaited the return of better days. His known protestant sympathies may have precluded Thynne, who had sat in Parliament as a dependant of Somerset, from membership of the Marian Parliaments, or he may have preferred to avoid any political commitment. He does not appear to have approached Elizabeth until the very eve of her accession, when he wrote to Parry to put troops at her disposal. At home he had already prepared for a change in the political scene. Now that the Seymour influence in the county was crippled by Somerset's attainder, and only represented by

the Protector's son who did not come of age until the year of Elizabeth's accession, Thynne was in a position to aspire to independence in his own western part of the shire; and he felt no need to seek the support of the surviving noble magnate, the 1st Earl of Pembroke, when Elizabeth summoned her first Parliament. Contesting the election of Sir George Penruddock*, Pembroke's steward, as second knight of the shire, Thynne had himself returned in defiance of the poll, and so took precedence at the outset of the new reign.[3]

Such an assumption of supremacy could only succeed when it was unexpected. Thynne's high-handed behaviour in 1559 was an incident in a prolonged feud with Pembroke, and this went to such lengths that in 1564 Thynne was called personally before the Privy Council to account for his part in it. In 1562–3, therefore, Thynne could have had no hope of Pembroke's acquiescence in his candidature for the shire, and must have been glad to fall back on the borough of Great Bedwyn, where the Seymour interest still held, despite the recent disgrace of the young Earl of Hertford. Here, moreover, he must have been well known from the days of his stewardship and had acquired on his own account the tithes of the prebend. By 1571 the 1st Earl of Pembroke was dead and Thynne's relations with his successor had improved sufficiently for Thynne to be elected as first knight of the shire. But that he could expect no monopoly of this honour was demonstrated by his having to seek a seat elsewhere for the next Parliament. He found it at Heytesbury, a borough which was virtually in the hands of his family. Though there is no record of Thynne speaking in debate, he took his share of committee work, serving on one recorded committee (concerning forgers) in 1563, one in 1566 (on the Queen's marriage and succession), nine in 1571, six in 1572 and 12 in 1576. On 5 Nov. 1566 he was one of 30 Commons Members summoned to hear the Queen's message on the succession. In 1571 his committees were on religion (6 Apr., 10 May), the order of business (21, 26 Apr.), treasons (11 May) and legal matters (14, 23 Apr., 14, 28 May). In 1572 his committees concerned Mary Stuart (12, 22, 28 May) and private and privilege matters (20, 22, 30 May). Those of 1576 dealt with the subsidy (10 Feb.), trade (16, 18, 24 Feb.), legal matters (18 Feb., 8, 12, 14 Mar.), the dean and chapter of Norwich (2 Mar.), land reclamation (6 Mar.), apparel (10 Mar.) and the Queen's marriage (12 Mar.). No doubt Thynne valued a seat in Parliament as evidence of his established position in Wiltshire, but he had other connexions with London which made attendance there no hardship. He was provided with a house in Cannon Row and had legal business to pursue. His cousin Francis was at Lincoln's Inn from 1561 and subsequently lived in Poplar and in Bermondsey Street; Sir John's relations by marriage were Londoners.[4]

His position in Wiltshire entailed the customary

demands on his time. As sheriff he was responsible for collecting the privy seal loan of 1570 in the county, and as a leading magistrate he received his share of commands from the Privy Council, but that he did not always allow them to weigh on him too heavily is witnessed by a series of letters of an increasingly apoplectic tone which urged him over a period of eight months to take some action about abuses in the clothing trade. He had much private business on his mind, quarrels to pursue, that with Edward Ludlow* in 1579 again requiring the intervention of the Council. He had also his property to exploit. He had carved his park at Longleat from the woodland and continued to acquire portions of the forest. He used the meadows and pastures to graze cattle and, beginning to keep records of them a year before his death, was able to leave his widow, among other bequests, 30 cows, a bull and 100 sheep at Corseley. But the object which attached his strongest feelings and exacted his most continuous exertions was the great house itself. From 1547 he was building, in a big way, probably as his own architect, calling upon the assistance of contractor or master-mason as each stage was reached. The house was still going up in the last quarter of the century and was visited by the Queen in August 1574.[5]

In addition to his two known marriages, the Shropshire visitation of 1623 attributes to Sir John an intervening one with Anne, widow of one Cole, son of Alexander Cole of London. If this took place, Anne must have been dead by January 1566, when Thynne was being suggested as a husband for Lady St. Loe. By his 11 children he had done his best to ensure that there would always be Thynnes at Longleat. Yet when he came to make his will on 6 May 1580 his anxiety to protect his lands in Wiltshire, Somerset, Gloucestershire, Oxfordshire, Shropshire and Kent, and his houses in London, Bristol and Westminster against all contingencies almost defeated his purpose – a preliminary sentence from the court was necessary to declare him *compos mentis* – and the resulting confusion shows how hard he found it to make an end of the preoccupations of a lifetime. He died on 21 May 1580, and the will was proved on 12 Nov. His memorial stone in Longbridge Deverill church, though only erected in the seventeenth century, was probably after his own design. But his real monument, with his correspondence, accounts and estate papers, and his portrait, painted when he was 51, is Longleat.[6]

[1] *Genealogist*, xi. 193–5; *Wilts. Vis. Peds.* (Harl. Soc. cv, cvi), 192–3; *Vis. Salop* (Harl. Soc. xxviii), 461. [2] Hoare, *Wilts.* Heytesbury, 80; *Wilts. Arch. Mag.* viii. 311–41; Lansd. 19, f. 208; 105, f. 104; *CPR*, 1548–9, p. 135; *CSP Dom.* 1547–80, p. 341; C66/985. [3] Bath mss, Thynne pprs. at Longleat; *VCH Wilts.* v. 124–5; Neale, *Commons*, 97, 98. [4] *Wilts. Arch. Mag.* vi. 26–9; Hugh Hawker to Sir John Thynne, Thynne pprs. 3, f. 252; *VCH Wilts.* v. 124; *CJ*, i. 65, 83, 84, 85, 86, 88, 89, 93, 94, 96, 98, 99, 104, 106, 108, 110, 111, 112, 113, 114, 115; D'Ewes, 126, 166, 178, 179, 181, 182, 183, 190, 206, 212, 213, 219, 220, 247, 248, 249, 255, 259, 260, 262; Camb. Univ. Lib. Gg. iii. 34, p. 209; *DNB* (Thynne, Francis). [5] *Wilts. Arch. Mag.* iii. 284 seq.; xiv.

199 seq.; xv. 195; xlvi. 423; *APC*, vii. 162; viii. 286; ix. 121, 204, 220, 263; xi. 99, 323; E. W. J. Kerridge, 'The Agrarian Development of Wilts. 1540–1640' (London Univ. PhD thesis, 1951), 22, 52; PCC 44 Arundel; J. Lees-Milne, *Tudor Renaissance*, 57–9, 102–4; J. Nichols, *Progresses Eliz.* i. 408. [6] *HMC Hatfield*, i. 325; *Wilts. Arch. Mag.* xv. 194; *HMC Bath*, iv. 135.

M.B.

THYNNE, Thomas I (bef. 1566–1625), of Biddestone St. Nicholas, Wilts.

HEYTESBURY 1593

b. bef. 1566, 3rd s. of Sir John Thynne* by his 1st w. and bro. of John*. *m.* Ann or Dorothy, da. of Thomas Erneley of Brembridge, 2s. 3da., 1s. illegit.[1]

The identity of John Thynne's co-burgess for Heytesbury in 1593 has been established by elimination. He could not have been John's second cousin, Thomas of Deverell, who had died during the previous year; he could not have been John's heir who was only 15; he was unlikely to have been that Thomas Thynne who held meadow in Little Stretton, presumably another kinsman, for this man, a grandfather, was to die during the following summer. But the Thomas Thynne who was John's younger brother was neither too old nor too young and, allowing for fraternal influence, was a suitable candidate for election. The Heytesbury burgesses in this Parliament could have sat on a committee concerned with cloth, 15 Mar. 1593.[2]

In the pedigree printed by Hoare this Thomas Thynne is described as of Bilston, Staffordshire, but this is almost certainly a misreading of Bitston, one of the spellings of Biddestone current in the sixteenth century. The manor of Biddestone St. Nicholas certainly belonged to him, and he made no reference to any lands elsewhere in his will. He did not acquire the manor, with its lands, tenements and a portion of the tithes in Biddestone and Wraxall, until 1602. On the assessment for privy seal loans of 1611 he is rated at £20 (as compared with his brother John's £100). He married, probably about the turn of the century, into a leading Wiltshire family, but not into the most eminent branch of it. Thomas Erneley, who acquired the manor of Brembridge (otherwise Brunbridge or Brembrigge) in 1578, left 13 children when he died in 1595; and one of the two unmarried daughters, Ann and Dorothy, with £100 apiece for a marriage portion, was Thomas Thynne's future wife.[3]

He appears to have outlived her. In his will he made bequests to his heir Henry and his younger son Thomas, and left Tewins parsonage (near Wraxall) to Thomas Glanfield, his natural son. A ruby ring was to go to daughter Fauntleroy, and debts amounting to £600 at least, due from Sir John Chamberlaine, to his daughters Anne and Joan (wife of Edmund Pyke). He named Sir Thomas Thynne, his nephew, among his overseers.[4]

Thynne died 1625.[5]

[1] *Wilts. Vis. Peds.* (Harl. Soc. cv, cvi), 56, 193. [2] Hoare, *Wilts.* Heytesbury, 60; PCC admons. 1592, f. 27; D'Ewes, 501. [3] Bilson in Collins, *Peerage*, vi. 500; feet of fines, East. 44 Eliz.; *Wilts. Arch. Mag.* ii. 185; Hoare, *Wilts.* Westbury 36; PCC 58 Scott. [4] PCC 69 Clarke. [5] C142/245/1.

M.B.

THYNNE, Thomas II (c.1578–1639), of Longleat, Wilts.

HINDON	1601, 1604
HEYTESBURY	1621, 1624
HINDON	1625, 1626, 1628

b. c.1578, 1st s. of John Thynne* by Joan, da. of Sir Rowland Hayward* of London. *educ.* Brasenose, Oxf. *m.* (1) c.1601, Maria, da. of George, Lord Audley; (2) c.1612, Catherine, da. of Charles Howard, 6s. 1da. *suc.* fa. 1604. Kntd. 1604.[1]

Sheriff, Wilts. 1607–8, Glos. 1621–2, Som. 1629–30, Salop 1633–4.

Thynne, the heir to Longleat, allied himself in marriage with a nobleman's daughter who was also grand-daughter to (Sir) James Marvyn*, perhaps the leading man in Wiltshire after the Earl of Pembroke. The borough of Hindon lay within Marvyn's territory and it is thus highly probable that the Thomas Thynne esquire who was returned for it in 1601 was Marvyn's young kinsman, rather than Thomas Thynne I.

Thynne died 1 Aug. 1639.

Wilts. Vis. Peds. (cv, cvi), 193; Ch. Inq. P. M. Misc. 535, 18 Chas. I, pt. 30, no. 47; *Wilts. Arch. Mag.* xxiii. 283.

S.T.B.

TICHBORNE, Benjamin (c.1542–1629), of Tichborne, Hants.

PETERSFIELD	1589
HAMPSHIRE	1593

b. c.1542, 2nd s. of Nicholas Tichborne† of Tichborne by his 2nd w. Elizabeth, sis. and coh. of James Rithe. *m.* (1) a da. of one Shelley of Mapledurham, *s.p.*; (2) 17 May 1571, Amphillis, da. of Richard Weston† of Skreens in Roxwell, Essex, 5s. inc. Richard* 3da. Kntd. 14 Sept. 1601. *cr.* Bt. 8 Mar. 1621.

J.p. Hants from c.1582, sheriff 1579–80, 1602–3; gent. of privy chamber to James I.

The manor of Tichborne in Hampshire had been the residence of the Tichborne family since the twelfth century, but it was not inherited by Tichborne himself until 1571, some years after the death of his half-brother Francis. In that year Tichborne's sister-in-law conveyed her life interest in the manor to him. He was reported to be an 'earnest' or 'strong' Catholic in 1572, and he twice married into families sympathetic to Catholicism. In 1586 one Edward Jones – a government agent – stated that mass was performed daily in the Shelley household at Mapledurham, while Richard Weston*, Earl of Portland, a relation of Tichborne's second wife, and his most 'noble ally and friend', whom he made overseer of his will, was said to have died a Catholic. Members of collateral branches of the Tichborne family were also Catholics. Chidiock Tichborne of Owlsbury was executed in 1586 for his part in the Babington conspiracy, and Nicholas Tichborne of Hartley Mauduit in Hampshire died in 1589 in Winchester gaol, where he was imprisoned for recusancy.

Tichborne, however, presumably conformed sufficiently to take the oath of supremacy on becoming a justice and sheriff, and on entering Parliament. He was returned for Petersfield in 1589, a borough owned by the Westons of Sutton, Surrey, related to the Weston family of Skreenes, into which he had married. In 1593, despite his religious views, he attained a county seat. His only recorded speech was on the bill against recusants, 28 Feb. 1593, to the effect that 'the father should not disinherit the son, nor have power so to do for being made conformable by him that should have the bringing of him up'. As a knight of the shire in the 1593 Parliament Tichborne could have sat on the subsidy committee (26 Feb.) and on a legal committee, 9 Mar.

Tichborne happened to be sheriff of Hampshire when Elizabeth died. Without waiting for a Council directive, he hurried to Winchester, and proclaimed James, receiving by way of reward the fee farm of the castle in perpetuity. Next he was made a gentleman of the privy chamber, but for the most part he remained in Hampshire, where James visited him on four occasions. At the time of the Gunpowder Plot he wrote a few words to Cecil about 'shifting recusants which play at base from county to county'. He died 6 Sept. 1629, having made his will the previous 23 Feb. It was proved 14 Nov. by his eldest son and sole executor, Sir Richard Tichborne.

GEC Baronetage, i. 160; *Vis. Hants* (Harl. Soc. lxiv), 126; E163/14/8; *PRO Lists and Indexes*, iii. 56; *VCH Hants*, ii. 84, 85; iii. 337; v. 12; J. E. Paul, 'Hants Recusants in Reign of Eliz. I' (Soton Univ. PhD thesis 1958); *CSP Dom.* 1581–90, p. 336; *CP*, x. 582–5; E. M. Tenison, *Eliz. England*, vi. 259; D'Ewes, 474, 476–7, 496; *APC*, xxvi. 533; Nichols, *Progresses Jas. I*, i. 116; *HMC Hatfield*, xvii. 492; C142/456/69; PCC 104 Ridley.

A.M.M.

TICHBORNE, Richard (c.1578–1652), of Tichborne, Hants.

LYME REGIS	1597
HAMPSHIRE	1614
WINCHESTER	1621, 1624, 1625, 1626, 1628

b. c.1578, 1st s. of Benjamin Tichborne* of Tichborne by his 2nd w. Amphillis, da. of Richard Weston†, justice of the common pleas. *educ.* M. Temple 1595. *m.* (1) Ellen (*d.*1606), da. and coh. of Robert White of Aldershot, 1da.; (2) c.1616, Susan, da. and coh. of William Waller of

Oldstoke and Stoke Charity, 3s. 3da. Kntd. 11 May 1603. *suc.* fa. to lands and as 2nd Bt. 1629.

Jt. keeper (with his fa.) of Winchester castle 1604; ranger of West Beare forest by 1610; dep. lt. Hants by 1627; gent. of the bedchamber to Charles I; ambassador to the Queen of Bohemia; royalist commander in the civil war.[1]

Tichborne's political career lies outside the Elizabethan period. His election while still a minor for Lyme Regis was due to the 3rd Marquess of Winchester, to whose mistress Jane Lambert he was related. Tichborne was possibly the 'very good friend and neighbour' mentioned by Lucy, wife of the 4th Marquess, in a letter to her uncle Sir Robert Cecil about a quarrel at the assizes in April 1601. Serjeant John Hele* was accused of an offence against Tichborne, whom the Marchioness asked Cecil to favour for 'his many good offices'.[2]

After serving Charles I almost throughout his reign, Tichborne suffered sequestration of his estates in 1650. He died in April 1652.

[1] *CP*; *Vis. Hants* (Harl. Soc. lxiv), 126; *CSP Dom.* 1603–10, pp. 76, 634; 1627–8, p. 106; *GEC Baronetage*, i. 160–1. [2] *HMC Hatfield*, xi. 177, 188.

R.C.G.

TILNEY, Edmund (*d.* 1610), of London and Leatherhead, Surr.

GATTON	1572

o.s. of Philip Tilney, usher of the privy chamber to Henry VIII by his w. Malena Chambre. *m.* 4 May 1583, Mary, wid. of Sir Edmund Bray, ?*s.p. suc.* fa. 1541.[1]

Master of revels 1579–1610; commr. subsidy, Surr. 1593–4.[2]

Tilney's father died in debt and his mother, a member of Catherine Howard's household, was convicted of treason and subsequently pardoned. In 1568 he made a bid for the favour of Queen Elizabeth by dedicating to her his only known publication, *A Brief and Pleasant Discourse of duties in Mariage.* He was returned to Parliament for Gatton through his Howard relations, and was appointed to one committee, concerned with poaching, 9 Feb. 1581.[3]

Tilney was master of the revels during 'the most glorious period in the annals of the English stage'. His preferment at the expense of Thomas Blagrave*, clerk of the revels, was obviously due to his connexion with the Howards. The office was under the control of the lord chamberlain. Tilney had a salary of £100 and a substantial share of the £40 paid yearly as wages to the officers of the revels, as well as fees from licences to companies and theatre owners. There was, after 1586, an official residence in the old hospital of St. John, Clerkenwell. Tilney virtually controlled theatrical productions throughout the country, selecting and revising productions to be performed at court or elsewhere. His power, extended in 1581 and 1606,

caused resentment among the theatrical companies of London. He acquired property in Middlesex and Surrey, and was visited at Leatherhead by the Queen during her progress of 1591. He and his wife were joint patrons of the rectory of Alford, Surrey.[4]

Poor health forced Tilney to surrender some of the functions of the revels office to his kinsman and eventual successor, George Buc*, several years before his death. He was buried near his father's tomb at Streatham, 6 Oct. 1610. His 'apparel wherein I have spent much money very plainly that might have been otherwise better employed' was to be sold for the benefit of the Leatherhead and Streatham poor. £100 was to go towards the repair of the stone bridge at Leatherhead. Thomas Tilney of Shelley, Suffolk, was principal beneficiary and executor of the will, proved 17 Oct. 1610.[5]

[1] F. S. Boas, *Q. Eliz. in Drama*, 39–41; *London Mar. Lic.* (Harl. Soc. xxv), 118. [2] *DNB*; *Surr. Arch. Colls.* xviii. 200. [3] *LP Hen. VIII*, xvi. pp. 617, 618, 664, 680; Boas, 42–7; *Surr. Arch. Colls.* ix. 425; *CJ*, i. 124; D'Ewes, 294. [4] Lansd. 19, f. 206; 27, f. 86; 31, f. 49; 86, f. 151; *CSP Dom.* 1591–4, p. 512; 1595–7, p. 351; 1598–1601, p. 4; 1603–10, pp. 178, 391, 410; E. K. Chambers, *Eliz. Stage*, i. 88, 93–4, 321; iv. 106, 305–9; Boas, 47–51; *Surr. Arch. Colls.* xviii. 210; Manning and Bray, *Surr.* ii. 74. [5] Chambers, i. 96, 99; *Surr. Arch. Colls.* xxiv. 66; PCC 110 Wingfield; Lysons, *Environs of London*, i. 485.

H.G.O.

TIMPERLEY, Thomas (1523/4–94), of Hintlesham, Suff. and Flitcham, Norf.

BRAMBER	1553 (Oct.)
GREAT YARMOUTH	1563

b. 1523/4, 1st s. of William Timperley of Hintlesham by Margaret, (prob. illegit.) da. of Thomas, 3rd Duke of Norfolk; bro. of William*. *m.* (1) by 26 Sept. 1557, Audrey, da. of Sir Nicholas Hare†, 2s. 7da.; ?(2) Catherine. *suc.* fa. 1528.[1]

Freeman, Gt. Yarmouth 1563.

Comptroller of household to Thomas, 4th Duke of Norfolk by 1560; receiver, Suff. for 4th Duke of Norfolk by 1572, for Philip, 13th Earl of Arundel by 1589.[2]

Timperley's father died when he was only four or five years old, and he became the ward of his maternal grandfather, the 3rd Duke of Norfolk. Had the 4th Duke not fallen into disgrace, Timperley might have expected a prosperous career as a courtier, but as it was, it looks as though he retired to his Suffolk estates, remaining there during the reign of Edward VI. He was one of Queen Mary's earliest supporters, but there is little detailed information about him between her accession and the execution of the 4th Duke of Norfolk in 1572. He went on the Scottish campaign with his master in 1560, and in July 1569 he was one of the trustees to whom the Duke enfeoffed his 'liberty' in Norfolk, Suffolk, Cambridgeshire, Essex, Sussex and Surrey. Norfolk's heir, Philip, Earl of Arundel, employed him as his receiver in Suffolk, but there is little evidence of personal association between the two men. After 1572 Timperley seems again to have retired to Hintlesham, where he rebuilt the old house. This was probably completed by the summer of 1579, when Queen Elizabeth, his distant relative, visited Ipswich on progress. She must have passed Hintlesham, which was on the road from the Waldegrave seat at Smallbridge, where she had broken her journey, but there is no evidence that she stopped there. Possibly the family were already in disfavour for their Catholicism: while the court was at Norwich the Privy Council took action against two of Timperley's brothers-in-law as obstinate recusants. Timperley himself apparently conformed until 1577, when he was presented as a recusant in the Norwich diocese. His wife, his son Nicholas, and at least three of Nicholas's sisters, were avowed recusants. Thus it came about that Timperley, a man of wealth and local standing, able to subscribe £25 to the Armada fund, was excluded from the commission of the peace in his county and absent from the Elizabethan Parliaments after his one appearance for a Norfolk borough early in the reign. He owned considerable freehold and copyhold land in East Anglia, and was made a free burgess of Great Yarmouth at the time of his election.[3]

He died, blind, 13 Jan. 1594, and was buried in Hintlesham church, where there is a monumental inscription to him and his wife, joined with one to his son Nicholas, who married Anne Markham. His will, drawn up in October 1592, gave instructions that 10 marks should be given 'by twopenny dole' to the poor who came to his burial, and left £30 for a bell in Hintlesham church, 'to be agreeable for a bass to the other two which be in the steeple there'. His servants were to have six months' wages. The will shows no sign of the financial difficulties caused by recusancy fines which impoverished his heir in later years. In 1577 Timperley's lands and goods had each been valued at £100, and at the time he made his will he was able to leave annuities of £13 and £20 to his brothers William and Henry, with another of £13 to his unmarried daughter Anne if she chose a husband with the consent of her brother Nicholas and the executors, William Timperley, William Hare and her father's old 'servant', Robert Munings. Copinger, *Manors of Suffolk*, vi. 55–7, says that Timperley married a second wife, Catherine, and that she is buried at Hintlesham. Nothing, however, is known of her, and she is not mentioned in Timperley's will.[4]

[1] C142/49/15; G. H. Ryan and L. J. Redstone, *Timperleys of Hintlesham*, passim (individual references not given below); *Vis. Suff.* ed. Metcalfe, 38; Copinger, *Suff. Manors*, vi. 55–7. [2] Gt. Yarmouth ass. bk. 1559–70, f. 39; Add. 19152, f. 53v; Egerton 2074, f. 84. [3] *LP Hen. VIII*, vi(3), p. 2810; *Cath. Rec. Soc.* xxi. 313; xxii. 59; *APC*, iv. 429–32; Add. 19152, f. 53v; Egerton 2074, f. 84; N. Williams, *Duke of Norfolk*, 55, 119; T. C. Noble, *Names of Those who Subscribed*, 61. [4] PCC 60 Dixy.

N.M.F.

TIMPERLEY, William (c.1525–c.1606), of Lincoln's Inn, London and Monewden, Suff.

LICHFIELD   1571

b. c.1525, 2nd s. of William Timperley (*d.*1528) of Hintlesham, and bro. of Thomas*. *educ.* L. Inn 1546, called 1558, assoc. bencher 1568.

Almost everything known about Timperley concerns his career at Lincoln's Inn; how he came to be returned for Lichfield (unless perhaps he had some connexions with the bishop) is not clear. He was originally offered a benchership at Lincoln's Inn in February 1566, but presumably refused, since it was not until November 1568 that he was appointed, on payment of £8, an associate, privileged to sit at the benchers' table, but below 'any person called to the bench for learning'. Among his other duties at the inn, he was butler in 1566, and several times an auditor – in June 1569 for the new buildings, and from 1587–8 for the accounts of Thomas Egerton I* as treasurer. As late as October 1596 he was receiving money for 'apparels' at his inn. In 1571 his work was recognized by the governing body agreeing to discharge his nephew Nicholas of

all offices under the bar ... at the special suit of Mr. William Timperley, his uncle, and in consideration of sundry especial travails and pains which the said Mr. William Timperley hath bestowed in the especial affairs and business of this house.

In April 1583 he was granted the reversion to a chamber at Lincoln's Inn, in gratitude for his work 'touching the building'.

Apart from the Lincoln's Inn references the information found about him concerns financial matters. In September 1577 the bishop of Norwich and others were investigating complaints by John Chetham about the non-payment of £200, the last instalment of the purchase price of £1,200 promised by Timperley, his brother Henry and Robert Bedingfield for houses and lands bought from the plaintiff. On another occasion Timperley asked the Privy Council to help him to collect a £120 debt owed to him since 1590 by Charles Chamberlain, surveyor of clothing to troops in the Netherlands. In spite of a Privy Council order that the amount should be 'defaulted' from Chamberlain's salary, the debt was still partially unpaid in May 1597.

Timperley acted as executor for his brother Thomas, whose will, proved in 1594, left him a £13 annuity from the manor of Monewden, where he apparently already held some property. No mention has been found of a wife or children, and the family history does not give the date of his death. He apparently died intestate, and in February 1606 administration of his property was granted to his brother Henry and his nephew Nicholas.

C142/49/15; PCC admon. act bk. 1606, f. 33; *Vis. Suff.* ed. Metcalfe, 171; G. H. Ryan and L. J. Redstone, *Timperley of Hintlesham*, passim; *Black Bks. L. Inn*, i. 323, 336, 350, 352, 358, 363, 380, 430, 449; ii. 10, 49; *APC*, x. 35; xxvi. 315; xxvii. 135; PCC 60 Dixy.

N.M.F.

TOLDERVEY, Christopher (*d.* 1613), of Allhallows, Lombard Street, London.

HYTHE   1597, 1601, 1604

m. Susan, da. of John Anwick, at least 2s. 2da.

Toldervey was a London merchant who lived at one time in Sandwich. He leased property in Kent, and must have been known to the Hythe corporation, but whether he was known to them prior to his first return for the borough is not clear. Possibly he owed his first election to John Smythe I*, whose seat at Westenhanger, where Toldervey had a third share in the park, was near to the borough. Smythe was the son of 'Customer' Smythe of London, who left Toldervey £200 'for his great care in my affairs'. When Toldervey came to make his own will he appointed Sir John Smythe as overseer, to share the custody of the two sons with Sir John Scott†. Scott, a relative of the Smythes, also had influence in the district, and when, as after the death of William, 10th Lord Cobham, in March 1597, the lord warden of the Cinque Ports appears not to have nominated at Hythe, the Smythe-Scott connexion was probably strong enough to sway the election. By 1601 there was a new lord warden, Cobham's son and heir, the 11th and last Lord Cobham, but Toldervey had connexions with him too, for he is soon found living or working in Cobham's London house, and it was quite possibly Cobham who nominated him to the 1601 Parliament. The only reference to him in the Elizabethan House of Commons is as a member of a committee on the penal laws on 8 Nov. 1597, but as one of the Hythe MPs he could have sat on the main business committee (3 Nov. 1601) and the Severn harbour committee (21 Nov. 1601).

A Londoner, Toldervey was assessed for the 1589 subsidy in Bishopsgate ward on £50 property. In 1598 he paid £10 subsidy. He held shares in the mines royal and the mineral and battery works, and died wealthy. In his will, dated 12 Jan. 1613, he left one daughter £2,000 and the other £1,200. The elder son, Christopher, who became a Kent country gentleman and died only five years after his father, was to have an annuity of £100 until the age of 30, when he would receive the profits of leases at Newington, Faversham and Barksore; while John, the younger son, received Halstowe parsonage and an annuity of £60.

Arch. Cant. xvii. 203; xxv. 130; xl. 126; G. Wilks, *Barons of the Cinque Ports and the Parl. Rep. Hythe*, 65–6; Townshend, *Hist. Colls.* 103; D'Ewes, 624, 647; *Vis. London* (Harl. Soc. xv), 133; (cix and cx), 151;

E179/146/369; *HMC Hatfield*, ix. 425; x. 217, 348; xvii. 63; M. B. Donald, *Eliz. Monopolies*, 54, 64–5, 72, 73, 132, 192; PCC 39 Capell; *Vis. Kent* (Harl. Soc. xlii), 187; C142/367/70.

R.C.G.

TOMLINSON, Richard

WEYMOUTH   1571

This Member has not been identified. The only Richard Tomlinson found was born after 1555 and had no known connexion with Weymouth or any possible patron.

Nichols, *Leics.* iv. 304.

P.W.H.

TOMSON, Laurence (1539–1608), of London, later of Laleham, Mdx.[1]

WEYMOUTH AND MELCOMBE
    REGIS   1572*, 1584, 1586
DOWNTON   1589

b. 1539, of a Northants. family. *educ.* Magdalen Coll. Oxf. 1556, BA 1559, MA 1564, fellow 1559–69; Heidelberg 1568. *m.* Jane, 1da.
    Sec. to Francis Walsingham* 1575–90.

Tomson's parentage is obscure and the details of his later life are not known with certainty, but he stands out as an interesting figure among Elizabethan MPs. His epitaph in the church at Chertsey suggests an imposing list of accomplishments. He could speak 12 languages; had travelled in Sweden, Russia, Denmark, Germany, Italy and France; was versed in theology and 'literaturae politioris scientiae'; and had lectured on the Hebrew tongue in Geneva. Perhaps he first intended to follow an academic career. The only incident in his early life which suggests more worldly interests is his visit to France in the suite of Sir Thomas Hoby, the English ambassador in 1566. In May 1565 his college granted Tomson permission to study on the Continent for a year, his leave later being extended until July 1567. It is possible that he spent part of his time in Geneva, but in March 1568 he and three other Englishmen matriculated at Heidelberg. He was to be a Calvinist for the rest of his life. Already before his travels, he no doubt had puritan sympathies, which he perhaps derived from the master of Magdalen, Laurence Humfrey, for whom Tomson had voted in the election of 1561. In 1569 Tomson resigned his fellowship at Magdalen – it is not known whether he returned to England in that year – and by November 1572 he was living in Leicester, a puritan stronghold under the protection of the 3rd Earl of Huntingdon. Tomson was, at this time, a correspondent of Anthony Gilby, who was protected by Huntingdon when he advocated puritan views at Ashby-de-la-Zouche. Another friend was Huntingdon's brother, Francis Hastings*, whom Tomson later coupled with Walsingham in the dedication of his translation of Beza's *New Testament* (1576). The letters Tomson wrote to Gilby show him to have been writing for the secret puritan printing press, including a reply to Whitgift's *Answer* to the first puritan *Admonition to Parliament*. Tomson's last letter to Gilby from Leicester was written in April 1573. In June 1575 he was said to be 'attendant' on Walsingham, and he was probably appointed one of his secretaries early that year, for in December 1586 he stated that he had held the office for almost 12 years. A matter of interest to both Tomson and Walsingham that occurred soon after the former's appointment was the dissension at Magdalen College, originating in a disagreement between the master and some of the senior members of the college, as a result of which three fellows were expelled. Tomson wrote to the master urging him to take a more lenient course, and Walsingham was asked to write to the bishop of Winchester, the visitor of the college. Their intervention was resented by some of the fellows. Three years later an informant wrote to Tomson that some of them

> speak their pleasure against you after their bitter manner of carping, saying that you go about to seek the ruin of our Church and established religion under the pretence of reformation, the subversion of our colleges, namely of our famous and noble mother Magdalen College, the alienation, sale and spoil of our lands, farms and possessions appertaining to the same, and your reason should be for that as monasteries, so also colleges were erected by Papists.

The writer added that if they dared they would have said the same about Walsingham.

Tomson accompanied Walsingham, and William Brooke†, 10th Lord Cobham, to the Netherlands in 1578, and while staying in Antwerp they worshipped in the Merchant Adventurers' church, for which Tomson and William Davison* had provided a minister, Walter Travers. When the Merchant Adventurers suspended Travers for deviating from the prayer book, both Tomson and Walsingham wrote to Davison to support the minister, and at the same time requested the States to confirm the reformed character of the church.[2]

In 1580 Walsingham sent Tomson to Boulogne to interview a papal agent who had information to sell about Esme Stuart's activities in Scotland. England's trade with the Hanse towns also came within the purview of Tomson's work for Walsingham.[3]

Tomson's parliamentary career coincides exactly with his period of service under Walsingham. Both men came into the 1572 Parliament at a by-election in 1576, and both sat in each subsequent Parliament until Walsingham's death, so it is a fair inference that Walsingham wished Tomson to be of the House, albeit his own interest in the Commons was slight. It was actually the 2nd Earl of Bedford who provided the seat for Tomson, at Weymouth

and Melcombe Regis. He naturally became involved in the dispute over the unification of the two towns. In 1581 Weymouth was attempting to have the 1571 Act repealed, in the face of opposition from Melcombe. It was stated that while Tomson was no enemy to Melcombe he would not venture to displease Bedford. At the next election Tomson was insured against losing the seat by being returned at Poole through the Earl of Leicester. In the event he was returned for Weymouth and Melcombe, and again in 1586. In 1588 Tomson was returned for Downton, probably through the offices of Thomas Wilkes, another of Walsingham's servants.

Tomson's name is recorded on one committee in his first session, 7 Mar. 1576, on a bill to remove the benefit of clergy from rapists. In 1581 his committees were concerned with the subsidy (25 Jan. 1581), the bill against the Family of Love (16, 27 Feb.), the creditors of Sir Thomas Gresham (20 Feb.) and the Queen's safety (14 Mar.). On 16 Dec. 1584 he was appointed to the committee to consider the petitions of unsatisfactory ministers. He described Whitgift's answer to the petition drawn up by this committee as 'rather a discourse than any resolution of a divine', adding that it was not the practice in any church to demand a declaration of belief in all the articles of the religion. On 19 Feb. 1585 he was put on a committee dealing with the law on libel, and on 22 Mar. he was appointed to one concerning the ecclesiastical courts, which topic the Queen had already ordered the Commons to drop. No activity has been recorded for him in the 1589 Parliament.[4]

At Walsingham's death Tomson retired from public life, spending his last 18 years at Laleham, the only surviving record of any dealings with the central government being an inquiry by Cecil in 1599 about some of Walsingham's books and papers. Tomson died there 4 Apr. 1608, having made his will 18 Mar. Until his debts were paid his lands were to be held by his son-in-law Thomas Stapley, Tomson's widow receiving £100 a year. Stapley proved the will on 18 Apr. 1608.[5]

[1] This biography is largely based upon *DNB* and A. F. S. Pearson, *Thomas Cartwright and Elizabethan Puritanism, 1535–1603.* [2] C2Eliz./T10/46; Wood, *Ath. Oxon.* ii. 45; J. R. Bloxham, *Reg. Magdalen Coll.* iv. 113, 118, 138; SP12/103/62, 195/69; *Reg. Magdalen Coll.* ed. Macray, ii. 160; *CSP Dom.* 1547–80, p. 499; Collinson thesis, 128, n. 2, 370. [3] *CSP Dom.* 1547–80, pp. 448, 490; 1584–90, pp. 373, 659; 1595–7, p. 569; Read, *Walsingham*, ii. 372; D. H. Willson, *King James VI and I*, 32. [4] Roberts thesis, 83–4, 191–2, 196, 204; *Weymouth Charters*, ed. Moule, 35; *CJ*, i. 111, 119, 120, 127, 128, 130, 134; D'Ewes, 288, 306, 340, 353, 371. [5] Wood, ii. 45; *HMC Hatfield*, ix. 29–30, 400; PCC 36 Windebanck.

A.M.M.

TOOKER, Giles (c.1565–1623), of Salisbury, Wilts.

SALISBURY   1601, 1604, 1614

b. c.1565, s. of Charles Tooker, yeoman, of Maddingley by Matilda, da. of one Nipperhead. *educ.* Barnard's Inn;

L. Inn 1581, called 1589, treasurer 1617–18. *m.* 9 Sept. 1586, Elizabeth, e. da. of Thomas Eyre* of Salisbury, 2s. 2da. *suc.* fa. 1571.

One of the 24, Salisbury, of counsel to Salisbury 1591, first recorder of the city 1611–23; recorder, Wilton.

Tooker was a natural choice for the burgesses of Salisbury to make to represent them in Elizabeth's last Parliament. Nevertheless, such care as he took of their affairs in the Parliament of 1601 must have been of the nature of a watching brief; there is no record of his having taken part in any parliamentary business. He was a Wiltshire man, the son of a prosperous yeoman, and died possessed not only of a house in Salisbury but also of property in Maydenton, Madington, Burton, Hammington, Charleton, Chesenbury, Bulkington and Eston. His business associates were local men, William Bower, Michael Tidcombe, James Linch, and his brother-in-law William Eyre, and his daughters married into the Chaffyn and Smithers families. In June 1601 the bishop of Salisbury complained to Cecil that Tooker, 'being the mayor's fee'ed man', who has

> ever opposed himself against the lawful rights of the Church in Sarum ... hath of late obtained a new commission of the peace for this city wherein his name is placed ... against my rights ... that any such commission should be granted without my ... allowance.

Ten years later Tooker was to lead the movement for the borough's emancipation. The newly incorporated borough commemorated him by a portrait which is still in its possession, and he remembered the borough in his will by founding a charity for two apprentices to be known as the recorder's apprentices. Tooker died 25 Nov. 1623.

Vis. Wilts. (Harl. Soc. cv, cvi), 196; H. Hatcher, *Old and New Sarum*, i. 306; ii. 711; PCC 4 Byrde; *HMC Hatfield*, xi. 235; *Wilts. Arch. Mag.* xxxv. 147.

S.T.B.

TOOLES, John

BRIDGWATER   1563*[1]

This Member, returned for Bridgwater at a by-election occasioned by the death of Nicholas Halswell, has not been identified. As Bridgwater was throughout this period returning either residents of the borough or local gentlemen, it is probable that he was a Somerset man. In the church of Swell about 15 miles south-east of Bridgwater there is a plate in the chancel floor to one Toole (no christian name is given), who died 10 June 1583. Perhaps he was the Bridgwater MP.[2]

[1] Folger V. b. 298. [2] Collinson, *Som.* i. 66.

A.M.M.

TOPCLIFFE, Richard (1531–1604), of Somerby, Lincs. and Westminster.

BEVERLEY	1572
OLD SARUM	1584, 1586[1]

b. 14 Nov. 1531, 1st s. of Robert Topcliffe of Somerby by Margaret, da. of Thomas Lord Borough. *educ.* G. Inn 1548. *m.* Jane, da. of Sir Edward Willoughby of Wollaton, Notts., 4s. 2da. *suc.* fa. 12 July 1544.

?Entered service of Princess Elizabeth 1557; commr. sewers, Lincs. 1564; j.p. Lincs., Yorks. (W. Riding) from c.1579–c.87; commr. to inquire after Jesuits Mar. 1593; steward of confiscated lands of Richard Norton by 1594.[2]

The name which Richard Topcliffe was to make odious his ancestors had derived from the township so called in the North Riding of Yorkshire, where the family retained property until his own time. It was, however, at Somerby that Richard Topcliffe's grandfather John, a merchant of the staple, was established in the early part of the sixteenth century, and this patrimony, with other lands in Nottinghamshire, descended through John's heir Robert to Richard Topcliffe, Robert's eldest son. Richard was 12 years of age when, his mother being already dead, he was orphaned. His wardship was granted, together with an annuity of 20 marks out of the estate, to his uncle Sir Anthony Neville†, who was thus presumably responsible for his further upbringing. Of this we know only that he was admitted to Grays Inn in 1548. He does not appear to have attended either university, the Richard Topcliffe of Magdalene College, Cambridge, with whom he was formerly identified, being another and seemingly unrelated person. On reaching his majority Topcliffe probably took up the administration of his inheritance, for which he had livery in February 1553. He was soon engaged in litigation with his uncles John and Edmund, and his cousin George, who claimed rights in part of the Somerby property under the will of Richard's grandfather, but with what result is not known.[3]

The time and manner of Topcliffe's entry into public service are alike uncertain. The earliest reference to him as 'her Majesty's servant' dates only from March 1573; but his own claim, made in June 1601, to have done 44 years' service places its beginning much earlier, and indeed hints at a possible entry into Elizabeth's retinue before her accession. His guardian Neville, who died in 1556 or 1557, had been a follower of successive earls of Shrewsbury, and a connexion with that house is a recurrent feature of Topcliffe's career. It was to the earls of Leicester and Warwick, however, that he later avowed his long allegiance (and certainly owed favour), and this connexion he is likely to have formed, or cemented, through his marriage into the family of Willoughby of Wollaton, itself allied to the house of Dudley. The date of Topcliffe's marriage to Jane Willoughby has so far eluded discovery;

but if it took place before 1558 it could have brought him into Princess Elizabeth's entourage, since Jane's niece Margaret, afterwards Lady Arundell, was one of the Princess's attendants at Hatfield. So early an introduction to Elizabeth would help to explain the peculiar position which he was to occupy and the licence allowed to his activities during her reign.[4]

It is, however, only from 1569 that these activities can be traced. The rebellion of that year evidently made an abiding impression on Topcliffe. It may have revived childhood memories of the Lincolnshire rising of 1536 (in which both his father and father-in-law had incurred some suspicion), while the coincidence of its centre with his own Yorkshire property can hardly have failed to move him. In January 1570 Topcliffe reported for service to Leicester at Kenilworth with thirty horses and men at his own cost, and later in the same month carried news of the Queen to the Earl. He had some part in surveying the confiscated lands of Richard Norton, the rebel leader, and his later stewardship of those lands may have been a reward for his services against the rebellion. So also, perhaps, was his return to the Parliament of 1572 for Beverley, although the borough owed its recent enfranchisement to the influence of Leicester, and it may have been he who secured Topcliffe's election. Of his role in the first session of that Parliament nothing is known; but during its second (1576), his committees included the matter of fraudulent conveyances by the rebels of 1569, a subject of personal interest to Topcliffe, who was to return to it in one of his later speeches. Other committees in this session included strictly legal matters (24, 25 Feb., 3, 8, 14 Mar.), the keeping of unlawful weapons (2 Mar.) and land reclamation (6 Mar.).[5]

Before the third and final session of this Parliament, in 1581, Topcliffe had begun his career as an interrogator of suspects. It is likely that he was drawn into this business both through his continuing interest in the northern rebels and by his attachment to the Earl of Shrewsbury, the custodian of Mary Stuart. It was at Shrewsbury's instance that in 1578 Topcliffe helped to investigate the activities of some of the ex-rebels, and it was to the Earl that he reported on these and other matters. But it may well have been the anti-Catholic legislation of the parliamentary session of 1581 which determined that Catholic-hunting should become Topcliffe's life-work. Although we know next to nothing of his part in that session (he was on one minor legal committee, 20 Feb.) his mounting activity in investigation from early in 1582 seems to reflect an accession of zeal as well as an expansion of opportunity. By the time the next Parliament met in the autumn of 1584 Topcliffe could be ranked with the notorious Richard Young as an acknowledged master of this ugly craft.[6]

In that Parliament, and its successor, Topcliffe sat for Old Sarum, a borough whose patron, the 2nd Earl of Pembroke, was son-in-law to Topcliffe's protector Shrewsbury. In 1584-5 we hear little of him, although he was, interestingly enough, one of four Members appointed to examine a skinner found sitting in the House without authority at the end of November. His membership of a committee to confer with the Lords, 18 Feb. 1585, on the bill against Jesuits and Catholic priests must also have been to his liking. He sat on one other recorded committee, 17 Mar., on the preservation of game. But in 1587 he came to the fore. On 24 Feb. he told the Commons of the Romish 'trumpery' discovered in a house near where they were sitting, and he was one of the Members named the same day to search suspected houses in Westminster. A few days later he endorsed Edward Donne Lee's[*] denunciation of the state of the church and called upon all Members to report 'disorders' in their counties, as he offered to do. Topcliffe was on the committee of a bill for East Retford (10 Mar.) and on the subsidy committee (11 Mar.).[7]

The next 15 years of Topcliffe's life were to make his name synonymous with the worst rigours of the Elizabethan struggle against Catholicism. It is clear that in much of what he did Topcliffe was acting under orders – whether under a commission such as that of March 1593 against Jesuits or under one of the numerous Council warrants to him to use torture – and that those who gave him these orders must share the odium of their consequences. Moreover, his superiors made only spasmodic efforts to restrain him. His brutal treatment of Southwell in 1592 cost him a spell in prison; in 1595, following the disclosure of Thomas Fitzherbert's attempt to bribe him into doing two of the Fitzherberts to death, Topcliffe was again committed for a few weeks for maligning Privy Councillors; and early in 1596 he had to answer to the Council for his arbitrary behaviour towards prisoners in the Gatehouse. But every check was followed by a fresh outburst of activity, and only in his last few years did the moderating of official policy, and the failing of his own vigour, bring it to an end.[8]

The gravamen of the indictment of Topcliffe is that he displayed an unmistakable and nauseating relish in the performance of his duties. On this the verdict of contemporaries is amply borne out by the evidence of his many letters and by the marginalia preserved in one of his books. It was, and is, easy to believe any evil of such a man; and to reflect that some of the worst accusations – among them that he reserved his most hideous tortures for infliction in his own house – rest upon fragile evidence is not to excuse him. Nor is there much profit in speculating on the influences which went to his making, although his early loss of both parents, the impact of rebellion upon his infant awareness, and perhaps some marital misfortunes might enter into the reckoning.[9]

Of the general aversion which Topcliffe aroused his disappearance from the House of Commons after 1587 may be a reflection. In commending himself, in December 1590, to the newly-succeeded 7th Earl of Shrewsbury he referred both to his emancipation from dependence upon Leicester and to his 'unkind' treatment by the 6th Earl, which perhaps included, or involved, the withdrawal of the nomination at Old Sarum. The new Earl's quarrelsomeness was likely to make him an unsatisfactory patron, and Topcliffe's own reputation may have stood in his way as a candidate for another seat. But his exclusion from the House did not deter him from meddling in its proceedings: in April 1593 he made 'much stir' in the Commons by spreading it abroad that the sheriff of Derbyshire, William Bassett II*, was a harbourer of Papists. Since the House was then at the climax of its handling of a bill against religious dissidents Topcliffe perhaps hoped to influence that bill's fate.[10]

Less is known of Topcliffe's other activities and interests. He was from time to time employed in miscellaneous investigations, as when, in November 1586, an Admiralty suit was referred to him and a master of requests, or, in August 1597, he and others were instructed to examine Thomas Nash and his fellow-actors in the scandalous play *The Isle of Dogs*. The reference to him of a project for using peat in ironmaking implies an interest in that industry which may have sprung from his Willoughby connexion; he also had a scheme for driving bucks into England from Scotland. Among his lawsuits was a long drawn-out affair concerning a lease of the prebend of Corringham and Stow, Lincolnshire, which he waged first with Sir Christopher Wray*, lord chief justice, and, after Wray's death, with Richard Taylor, the prebendary.[11]

Topcliffe's domestic life was not without its difficulties. His marriage was clouded at least for a time by his alleged failure to pay his wife adequate maintenance. In his later years the criminal escapades of his eldest son, Charles, gave him much anxiety, and in January 1602 Sir Robert Cecil chided him for not having this wayward son 'cleansed'. He also had the humiliation of seeing his nephew Edmund Topcliffe fall under suspicion on his return in May 1600 from a voyage abroad, during which he had assumed another name because of the ill-repute of his own.[12]

Topcliffe had a house in Westminster from at least the end of 1571, when we know that it was burgled, clothes worth over £50 being stolen from the owner, besides other goods probably belonging to Topcliffe's servants: the articles stolen from Topcliffe suggest that he maintained a good wardrobe. It was in this house, or an adjacent successor, that he was accused of torturing prisoners: but its nearness to the Gatehouse prison may have led to confusion between them. In his closing years, during which he suffered from lameness, he appears to have spent more time at Somerby or at Padley Hall, 'a delightful solitary place' as he described it, which he acquired from Thomas Fitzherbert* under circumstances

related in the latter's biography. What property he left at his death is unknown. By his last wishes, expressed in November 1604 and proved as a nuncupative will on 6 Dec. following, he bequeathed the life tenancy of a farm at Heapham to his bailiff there, and all the rest of his goods to his son Charles, apart from trifles – a doublet, a black cloak, a load of wood, and half a doe – to the two witnesses and three other local acquaintances.[13]

[1] *HMC Hatfield*, xv. 386. [2] *HMC Hatfield*, xi. 223–4; *CPR*, 1547–53, p. 373; 1563–6, p. 40; Lansd. 121, f. 70; St. Ch. 7/6/29. [3] P. H. Reaney, *Dict. Brit. Surnames*, 326; PCC 20 Jenkyn, 9 Hogen; C142/51/31; *Abstracts of Inq. Post Mortem Notts.* (Thoroton Soc.), iii. 300–1; *LP Hen. VIII*, xxi(1), pp. 148, 302; *CPR*, 1547–53, p. 373; Req. 2/22/105. [4] *APC*, viii. 213; *HMC Hatfield*, xi. 223–4; C142/112/124; *CPR*, 1553–8, p. 343; C3/178/17; Req. 32/26, 130/16. [5] *LP Hen. VIII*, xii(1), 199; *CSP Dom.* 1547–80, p. 400; Add. 1566–79, pp. 31, 156; Waldman, *Eliz. and Leicester*, 151; *HMC Hatfield*, xiii. 309; *CJ*, i. 108, 110, 111, 112, 115; D'Ewes, 252, 255, 262; Harl. 7188, f. 103. [6] *APC*, xi. 295; *HMC Hatfield*, ii. 176; Lodge, *Illus.* ii. 119, 143, 164–6; *CJ*, i. 128; D'Ewes, 299; *CSP Dom.* 1581–90, passim. [7] D'Ewes, 334, 352, 369, 410, 414; Harl. 7188, ff. 90, 93; Neale, *Parlts.* ii. 176. [8] *CSP Dom.* 1581–90, p. 646; 1595–7, p. 40; *APC*, xvi.273, xx. 100, 175, 204; xxii. 39–40, 41–2; xxv. 237, 254; xxviii. 165, 187; C2/9/63; C24/247; *Recs. Eng. Prov. Soc. Jesus*, iv. 49; Jessopp, *One Generation of a Norfolk House*, 64–9; Harl. 6998, f. 185. [9] Neale, *Parlts.* ii. 153. [10] Lodge, ii. 429–31; *CSP Dom.* 1591–4, p. 342. [11] *APC*, xiv. 242, 248, 301, 303; xv. 231–2; xix. 220–1, 364–5; xxv. 483–4; xxvi. 57–8, 179–80; xxvii. 338; Lansd. 59, f. 200 et seq.; *HMC Hatfield*, xiii. 309; *CSP Dom.* 1581–90, pp. 207, 300. [12] *HMC Middleton*, 530–1; *HMC Hatfield*, vi. 370; x. 150–1; xii. 2–3; *Athenaeum*, 5 Oct. 1878. [13] *Mdx. County Records.* i. 73; *Cath. Rec. Soc.* v. 211–12; P. Hughes, *Reformation in England*, iii. pp. xxvii–xxviii; Lincs. Archives Cttee, D. and C. iv/102; Coll. of Arms, Talbot mss, vol. M. f. 184.

S.T.B.

TOTHILL, Geoffrey (d.1574), of Peamore, near Exeter, Devon.

EXETER   1563, 1571, 1572*

1st s. of William Tothill, mayor of Exeter, by Elizabeth, da. of Geoffrey Matthew of Vorganwg, Pemb. *educ.* M. Temple 1560. *m.* (1) Joan (d.1567), da. of Robert Dillon of Chimwell, 3s.; (2) lic. 24 Nov. 1569, Elizabeth (d.1587), da. of Bartholomew Fortescue of Filleigh, wid. of Lewis Hatch of North Molton, *s.p.*
General attorney, Exeter 1558, recorder from 1563; j.p. Devon from c.1569.

Tothill was a lawyer but the late Middle Temple admission date and the absence of any record of his call to the bar are confusing. The assumption must be that he was qualified by the time he became recorder of Exeter. He received a grant of cranage and wharfage from the city and an annuity of 20 marks for 1564.

The record of Tothill's parliamentary activity is to be found not in the journals of the House but in the Exeter records. In 1563 he and Thomas Williams* were given a 'remembrance of certain articles' the city wished to be dealt with – such matters as the repair of highways, apprentices, and the statute staple. A bill concerning

Exeter churches was also in Tothill's possession. Tothill's handling of the business, together with the good luck of Williams being elected Speaker, resulted in at least three of the six articles being embodied in legislation in this Parliament. Tothill explained his tactics in a letter to John Hooker*:

> The one for the uniting of churches is first in the Lords House, and the other for orphans in the Lower House ... If we should have put both in at one place then peradventure the House would not be best contented with two bills for our private city.

Exeter wanted to share the privileges of London and Norwich regarding apprentices: when a bill (later the Statute of Artificers) dealing with servants came into the Commons, Tothill saw his chance:

> I hope if the bill pass, to get a proviso for all cities in England to take apprentices, and Exeter not named.

Once he asked the mayor to send £10 'as I have retained divers in these causes and must give money about the same'. In the 1566 session 'Trew's matter' had to be considered, that is, the haven which John Trew had contracted to build. Exeter wished to clear the estuary of the river Exe of hindrances to navigation, and Tothill no doubt welcomed a bill to remove fish weirs and other obstructions, lost by three votes on its third reading. Tothill worked for at least four other measures on behalf of the city in this session. In the Parliaments of 1571 and 1572, the burgesses again took with them instructions from the city, but Tothill did not play as prominent a part as in the Parliament of 1563. He was paid wages at the rate of 4s. a day for his attendance at the 1571 Parliament.

Tothill died 15 Sept. 1574, having made his will the previous 29 June. His wife and his son Henry were the executors. The will was proved 10 Nov. 1574.

Misc. Gen. et Her. (ser. 4), iii. 50; Vivian, *Vis. Devon*, 729; Exeter act bk. 2, f. 159; 3, f. 113; receivers roll, pp. 4–5; *Trans. Dev. Assoc.* xliv. 212–13; Roberts thesis; PCC 40 Martyn; and see under EXETER.

P.W.H.

TOWNSEND, John (*d.* aft. 1622), of Warwick.

WARWICK   1597, 1601, 1604, 1614

Yst. s. of Richard Townsend of Warwick by his w. Christian.

Bailiff, Warwick 1589–90, 1603–4, 1621–2.

Townsend was already a prominent Warwick burgess in 1588, when he signed a letter sent by the town to the Earl of Warwick, promising to elect Thomas Dudley* to the next Parliament. His father died soon after this, bequeathing him the house in which he was living and a barn in Brittayne Lane. Though Townsend's name does not appear in the journals of the House of Commons, as one of the burgesses for Warwick in 1597 he could have

attended committees concerned with a hospital or almshouse there (18 Nov.), the possessions of the bishop of Norwich (30 Nov.) and maltsters (12 Jan. 1598). By the time of his last election to Parliament he is described as 'esquire'. In 1620 he was named overseer of his brother Ralph's will, which was proved in the following year. After his third appointment as bailiff, his name disappears from the records.

Black Bk. of Warwick, 399, 426, 427; D'Ewes, 559, 565, 578; PCC 52 Leicester, 9 Savile.

S.M.T.

TOWNSHEND, Hayward (c.1577–c.1603), of Lincoln's Inn, London.

BISHOP'S CASTLE   1597, 1601

b. c.1577, 1st s. of Henry Townshend* of Cound, Salop by his 1st w. Susan, da. of Sir Rowland Hayward*. *educ.* St. Mary Hall, Oxf. BA 1595; L. Inn 1594, called 1601. *m.* Francasina, illegit. da. of Edmund Neville (claimant to earldom of Westmorland) by Francasina or Francelliana, prob. da. of John Townshend of Dereham Abbey, Norf., *s.p.*[1]

Described by A. F. Pollard as 'incomparably the best of the Elizabethan parliamentary journalists', Townshend was returned, while still under age and studying at an inn of court, for Bishop's Castle, where his father was a 'foreign burgess' and its recorder or legal counsel. Two others of his family were in the 1597 Parliament and four in that of 1601. In his first Parliament he was feeling his way, noting precedents and procedural points, but making no contribution of his own. But by 1601 he had not only 'increased in knowledge and confidence', but had also, in all probability, learned shorthand. His journal for that Parliament is excellent, and has been recognized as being so from the early seventeenth century. It provides comprehensive information about proceedings, debates, behaviour and customs of the House, and, unusually for the period, the reactions of Members to speeches, including his own; in sum, 'the personal touch of the participant MP'.

Townshend himself took an active part in the proceedings of the 1601 Parliament. On 9 Nov. he introduced a bill against

> the lewd abuses of prowling solicitors and their great multitude who set dissension between man and man like a snake cut in pieces crawl together to join themselves again...

His steering this through committee was a real achievement for a man of 24 in his second Parliament. On 17 Nov. he asked that a bill against perjury, suggested by 'a gentleman well experienced', should be read, and, 21 Nov., during the monopolies debate, his suggestion that the Speaker should petition the Queen to allow the

Commons to proceed by statute was commended by his relative Francis Bacon* who spoke of the wisdom of 'the young gentleman, even the youngest in the assembly'. Here Bacon exaggerates – there were at least 25 younger.

Townshend was a popular speaker whose legal training enabled him to supply the current demand for precedents. On 12 Dec. he intervened at the last minute to support the painters in their demarcation dispute with the plasterers, as it 'seemed likely to go against the painters'. He quoted precedents from the reigns of Edward III, Henry IV, Edward IV, Henry VI and Henry VIII to the effect that plasterers had intruded themselves so that 'they take not only their own work but painting also, and leave nothing to do for the painters'.

> Workmanship and skill is the gift of God ... if plasterers may be suffered to paint, workmanship in painting will decay, for no workman will keep a prentice four or five years to practise and not able to get a penny ... painters, their wives and children go a begging for want of work ... it is a curious art, and requireth a good eye and steadfast hand, which the infirmity of age decayeth quickly, and then painters beg. Plasterers take money generally from the highest patronage to the lowest, or meanest cottagers whose walls must needs be made. Painters take money but of a few, for their delight ...

'so I think the bill very reasonable and fit to be passed', Townshend concludes, 'and so it did'. He was less successful over a bill concerning silk weaving, offering 'to speak before the question was half asked, but could not be suffered, the "Noes" were so great'. This is the only failure he reports. During a debate on privilege, 15 Dec., he supported a solicitor, one Curwen, a servant of one of the Cumberland Members: 'At length I stood up', he reports, 'and showed the House that he ought to be privileged; for we had given judgment in the like case of the Baron of Walton's solicitor this Parliament. And thereupon it was put to the question, and ordered he should be privileged'. Townshend obviously enjoyed influencing the House. Sometimes he played to the gallery:

> It is not unknown to you that by profession I am a lawyer, and therefore unfit to be a professor of the art of war ... Therefore I pray ... it would please you to admit of a proviso for all lawyers. At which the House laughed heartily, it being done for mirth.

But if for nothing else he deserves the gratitude of posterity for his descriptions. 'They in the rebellious corner in the right hand side of the House' on 27 Jan. 1598 has been seen as the first mention of an opposition, and his accounts of the recurring shambles at the openings and closings of the parliamentary sessions are almost too good to be true. He was unable to get into the House of Lords at the beginning of the 1597 Parliament to hear the lord keeper's speech 'by reason of my late going in and want of knowledge in the fashion of the Parliament', and later

could only take the word of others 'for I could not hear three words together'. At the end of the session, when 'we waited at the Upper House door some half an hour and then were let in [there] was the greatest thrust and most disorder that ever I saw'. In 1601

> the first day of the Parliament ... the knights and burgesses of the lower house being sent for, the door kept so that they went not all in, notwithstanding some were within by some special means before, and heard the lord keeper's speech made unto them ... So that after the burgesses and knights had stayed a good while, it was told them that the lord keeper's speech was done, and thereupon every man went out discontented.

The final entry in his journal, after reporting the close of what was to be the Queen's (and by great misfortune his own) last Parliament is typical:

> Memorandum: as the Queen came out of the parliament house, among the Commons, very few said 'God bless your Majesty' etc. as in all assemblies they were wont: and when she came by the Speaker she only offered her hand to kiss, and went by. And the press being great, and the room she was to pass not above a yard in breadth, she stood still, and with her hand she bade 'Make more room'. And the gentlemen ushers said, 'Make. more room behind'. To which one behind answered aloud 'By God, I can make no more, if you would hang me', which doubtless the Queen might hear, it was so loud spoken, for I stood next her and heard it. But she looked that way from whence it was spoken, very sternly, and said not one word, but went presently through.[2]

It is not known when Townshend died. His name appears in the Lincoln's Inn records until November 1602, when he was appointed to the library committee. As he was not among the members of this committee who reported in April 1605, he had probably died in the meantime. At a guess he died before the elections for the 1604 Parliament, for it is unlikely that so promising and well-connected a Member would not have wished to sit again, and inconceivable that he could not have arranged to be returned if he had wanted to be. Thus it is likely that he died aged only 25 or 26, shortly before or after the Queen herself. He was certainly dead by 2 Apr. 1621, when his father made his will.[3]

[1] *Vis. Salop* (Harl. Soc. xxix), 463–5; *Vis. Norf.* ed. Dashwood (Norf. and Norwich Arch. Soc. 1878), i. 307, 311; *Shrewsbury Burgess Roll*, ed. Forrest, 287; *CSP Dom.* 1629–31, p. 520; J. A. C. Durham, *Townshends of Raynham*, 26. [2] Bp's. Castle minute bk., list of burgesses; H. Townshend, *Hist. Colls.* (1680); *Bull. IHR*, xii. 1–31; xiii. 9–34; xiv. 149–65; xv. 1–18; Stowe 362, ff. 56–261, transcribed by Miss Helen Miller. [3] PCC 107 Dale.

P.W.H.

TOWNSHEND, Henry (?1537–1621), of Cound and Ludlow, Salop.

BRIDGNORTH	1571, 1572
LUDLOW	1614

b. ?1537, s. of Sir Robert Townshend of Ludlow by Alice, da. of John Popey or Poppey of Twyford, Norf. *educ.* L. Inn 1559, called 1569. *m.* (1) Susan (*d.*1592), da. of Sir Rowland Hayward* of London and Cound, 4s. inc. Hayward* 3da.; (2) 1593, Dorothy (*d.*1635), da. of Christopher Heveningham of Aston, Staffs., 1s. Kntd. 1604.[1]

Pens. L. Inn 1578, bencher c.1580, Autumn reader 1581; member, council in the marches of Wales 1576 (j.p. Salop and other neighbouring English and all Welsh counties from c.1579), vice-pres. from 1614; dep. justice, Chester 1577; puisne judge, Chester, Denb., Flints., and Mont. 1578; recorder, Ludlow from 1577; dep. recorder, Bridgnorth 1586–9; recorder, Carmarthen c.1588–90, Leominster from c.1590, Worcester, Oswestry from 1617; judge in sheriff's court, London 1592; steward, Oswestry 1596, Shrewsbury from 1598; vice-chamberlain, Chester from 1604.[2]

Grandson of a Norfolk landowner, and son of a Chester judge, almost all Townshend's connexions were in the west of England and the Welsh marches. When he was one of those that 'desire to be placed justices in Wales' in 1576, he was described as:

> of Lincoln's Inn, an honest gent of good learning and substantial living. He was born in Norfolk, and by reason his father was justice in Chester and of this council he draweth toward these parts and is a counsellor at assizes and sessions in the marches, and well liked of all men, and zealous in religion. I know not a man of better disposition.

Just before this, he had sent to the Privy Council a set of articles about 'sundry things to be reformed in Wales', which the councillors evidently took seriously and considered, with some satisfactory results.[3]

The patron who secured Townshend's parliamentary seat at Bridgnorth, when he had only fairly recently been called to the bar, and apparently before he began his legal career in the west, is not known, but his father (who died in 1557) had friends on the council in the marches, among them no doubt Sir Andrew Corbet*, whom the Privy Council instructed in 1571 to supervise Shropshire elections. A contributory factor in the choice of Townshend may have been that his first wife brought him land in Shropshire. Townshend made no known contribution to the business of the 1571 Parliament. In that of 1572 his committees included those concerned with the explanation of statutes (28 May 1572), recoveries (31 May 1572 and 7 Mar. 1576), innholders and tipplers (17 Feb. 1576), the county palatine of Chester (25 Feb.) and sheriffs (4 Feb. 1581). On 6 Feb. 1581 he and Henry Knollys II were appointed to examine a charge of outlawry brought against Walter Vaughan*. He made two recorded speeches, the first on 5 June 1572 to ask for a bill to be considered concerning lands given to hospitals, 'for that he doubteth it may touch his inheritance', and the second

two days later on a petition by one Robert Wykes for lands which had been illegally withheld from him.[4]

The majority of references to Townshend are concerned with his work as a justice or as a member of the council in the marches, where by 1600 he was one of the three members of the quorum, two being bound to be always in attendance: his salary was by this time £100. In his early years in the marches he was generally allied with the faction of the Earl of Leicester and Sir Henry Sidney*, and opposed to Whitgift and Fabian Phillips*. No clear picture of Townshend as a man emerges, but hints of puritanism may be seen in some of the comments made about him, and in his will, where he asked to buried 'without pomp, feasting or vain glory', and prayed that God would 'of His mere mercy and grace grant unto me that I may be one of His elect children'. He supported the ecclesiastical jurisdiction of the council in the marches, and complained that the 'chancellors and registers' in the 'jurisdiction spiritual' were often at fault themselves in cases which came before the council. With the 2nd Earl of Pembroke, lord president of the council from 1586, Townshend's relations were at first good. But in 1599, when on the death of Sir Richard Shuttleworth, chief justice of Chester, the Privy Council suggested temporarily appointing Townshend in his place, Pembroke 'laboured all that ever he could to the contrary', and a compromise was reached by which the post of justice was put into commission, Townshend being one of the five justices of great sessions appointed. Angry at the loss of his expected promotion, Townshend persuaded Thomas Egerton I*, the lord keeper, to use his influence on his behalf, only to be again blocked by Pembroke, who, while claiming that he had no 'private malice' against Townshend, declared:

> Neither is he for learning (as I think) nor for uprightness (as I know) worthy that place. But so far is he carried either with his own ambition, or by the confidence he reposeth in some men's great favour towards him, that he ceaseth not (as I hear) still to seek it.

Early in 1600 Richard Lewknor* was granted the Chester post, and Townshend now began a campaign against Pembroke, who in turn complained bitterly of statements made by Townshend to Lord Chandos about him. In the end the matter was smoothed over and Townshend kept his place on the quorum. He was presumably consoled by being made vice-chamberlain in 1604.[5]

Townshend's attempt to exercise by deputy his office of judge of the sheriff's court in London was strongly opposed by other lawyers, notably James Dalton*, who declared the proposal to be 'contrary to all law and justice'. References to him in the boroughs where he held office are favourable – 'well learned', 'a most worthy esquire', and (from the town of Shrewsbury) 'so full of pity and mercy that he did what was possible for the life of the prisoners'. Shrewsbury had especial reason to be grateful to him in 1598, when the corporation was sued before the council in the marches for charging excessive market tolls. Townshend gave the borough officials advance notice of the charges, advised them to come prepared with charters and records, and ended 'with my commendations in secret sort'. At Ludlow, where he became a burgess in 1584, he was frequently entertained by the corporation, and his horses regularly provided with hay. In turn, he presented two silver-gilt spoons to the town. The 'fair house' he occupied when in Ludlow is described as 'in St. Austin's, once a friary'.[6]

As his career progressed he became wealthy, through salaries, perquisites, and a profitable grant for concealments. Like other Elizabethan officials he continually complained that he was underpaid. Little information has been found about his domestic life. In August 1610, after a visit to Sir John Wynn* of Gwydir, Townshend's wife and other gentlewomen in the company 'do so sweat from Sir John's good cheer and their ill throwing at dice, that they must needs wash and purify themselves in the Holywell'. Of his children the best-known was Hayward, the parliamentary diarist. Another son, John, is mentioned in his father's will as having died by 1621. Early in 1617 there was a rumour that Townshend himself had died, but he lived until December 1621, and was buried at Cound on the 9th of that month. He 'reckoned himself' to be 84, which would have made him 22 when he entered Lincoln's Inn, a surprisingly late entry. His will, made in April 1621, was proved before the end of the year. He asked the executors, who included his widow and son 'Harry', to see that he was buried at Ludlow or Cound. Various grandchildren were provided for, 100 marks being a usual legacy. An ambiguous clause referring to the stewardship of Whitchurch leaves it doubtful whether Townshend himself had held the office. The executors were reminded that John Vaughan had not paid a £200 debt. Charitable legacies included ten marks to Cound church, and there were individual bequests to several servants, while the others, unnamed, were to have a quarter's wages.[7]

[1] W. R. Williams, *Welsh Judges*, 56–7; *Trans. Salop Arch. Soc.* (ser. 2), x. 332–3; *DNB* (Townshend, Hayward); *Vis. Norf.* (Harl. Soc. xxxii), 291; *Vis. Salop* (Harl. Soc. xxix), 464–5; *Colls. Hist. Staffs.* (Wm. Salt Arch. Soc. v(2)), 173. [2] *Black Bk. L. Inn*, i. 342, 360–1, 395, 397, 416, 418, 422, 457; P. H. Williams, *Council in the Marches of Wales*, 359; *Welsh Judges*; Lansd. 76, f. 22; 79, f. 182; Flenley, *Cal. Reg. Council, Marches of Wales*, 179–237 passim; Bridgnorth leet bk. 3, ff. 2, 16; *Trans. Salop Arch. Soc.* (ser. 1), vii. 259; (ser. 2), x. 332; liv(2), 184; *Cal. Wynn Pprs.* 130. [3] *Black Bk.*; SP12/110/13; *Bull. Celtic Studies*, vi. 70; *CSP Dom.* 1547–80, pp. 404, 514. [4] Add. 48018, f. 294v; *CJ*, i. 96, 98, 99, 106, 108, 111, 122; D'Ewes, 292; Trinity, Dublin, Thos. Cromwell's jnl. ff. 34, 52, 55. [5] P. H. Williams, 104–5, 139, 140, 176, 193, 247–8, 269, 271, 291–3; PCC 107 Dale; *HMC Hatfield*, iv. 554. [6] Lansd. 76, f. 22; 79, f. 182; *Trans. Salop Arch. Soc.* (ser. 2), xi. 318–19; P. H. Williams, 193. [7] Lansd. 47, f. 28; *CSP Dom.* 1581–90, p. 336; 1603–10, pp. 315, 425; 1611–18, p. 425; P. H. Williams, 139; *Cal. Wynn Pprs.* 87; *Trans. Salop Arch. Soc.* (ser. 2), x. 333; PCC 107 Dale.

N.M.F.

TOWNSHEND, John (1568–1603), of Raynham, Norf.

CASTLE RISING	1593
NORFOLK	1597[1]
ORFORD	1601

b. 1568, 1st s. of Roger Townshend* of Raynham by his 2nd w. Jane, da. of Sir Michael Stanhope‡ of Shelford, Notts.; bro. of Robert*. *educ.* Magdalen Hall, Oxf. 1581. *m.* Anne, da. and coh. of Sir Nathaniel Bacon* of Stiffkey, Norf., 2s. *suc.* fa. 1590. Kntd. 1596.[2]

J.p.q. and commr. musters, Norf. from c.1597.

Townshend inherited from his father large estates in Norfolk. He spent some years abroad, including service in the Netherlands, before settling at Raynham and marrying, probably about 1593. His father had been kept away from his home county and the duties of local government by his service with the 4th Duke of Norfolk and the Earl of Arundel, but Townshend soon claimed the place due to him through his wealth and influential connexions. He quickly became involved in the faction struggle inside the county and inevitably took the side of his father-in-law and of his father's friend, Edward Coke*, against the group led by Sir Arthur Heveningham. His return for Castle Rising in 1593 was no doubt due to his personal influence locally, aided by his friendship with the Howard family. His election for the county in 1597, however, suggests the united backing of the Bacon/Coke party. It is possible that wider issues were involved, for Townshend and his friends, especially Coke, were associated with the group hostile to the Earl of Essex, and his return may have been a rebuff for the Earl as well as for Townshend's immediate opponents in the shire. Townshend was returned for Orford to the 1601 Parliament probably through the influence of his cousin, Michael Stanhope* and his friend Coke,[3] who was recorder of the borough. Though his name does not occur in the journals of the House of Commons, Townshend may have attended a committee on kerseys, 23 Mar. 1593, and, as knight of the shire for Norfolk in 1597 he may have served on committees concerned with enclosures (5 Nov.), the poor law (5, 22 Nov.), armour and weapons and the penal laws (8 Nov.), monopolies (10 Nov.), the subsidy (15 Nov.), the export of wool (18 Nov.), the Great Yarmouth charter (23 Nov.) and draining the fens (3 Dec.).[4]

Townshend's aggressive disposition several times inflamed local quarrels and disagreements to the point of breaches of the peace. In 1600 he quarrelled with Theophilus Finch and even more violently with Sir Christopher Heydon*, with whom he was prevented from fighting a duel only by the action of the Privy Council. On this occasion Edward Coke offered to bind himself for Townshend's good behaviour. Heydon's subsequent part in the Essex rising suggests again that the quarrel may have had ramifications outside Norfolk.[5] Townshend accompanied the expedition to Cadiz in

1596 and was knighted there by Lord Howard: as a man 'of good experience in martial affairs' he was appointed to the commission of musters two years later. He died intestate 2 Aug. 1603 from wounds received in a duel with Sir Matthew Browne* on Hounslow Heath. His lands descended to his seven year-old son.[6]

[1] Folger V. b. 298. [2] Vis. Norf. (Norf. and Norwich Arch. Soc.), i. 308 seq.; Al. Oxon. iv. 1500. [3] Carthew, Hundred of Launditch, ii. 781–2; CSP Dom. 1591–4, p. 241; A. H. Smith thesis, 288, 313–15; J. Durham, Townshends of Raynham, 31. [4] D'Ewes, 507, 552, 553, 555, 557, 559, 561, 562, 567. [5] HMC Hatfield, x. 352, 367, 458; APC, xxx. 731. [6] Smith thesis, 305; F. Blomefield, Norf. vii. 134–5.

R.V.

TOWNSHEND, Robert (b.1580), of Raynham, Norf.

CASTLE RISING   1601, 1604

b. 1580, 2nd s. of Roger Townshend* of Raynham by his 2nd w., and bro. of John*. educ. New Coll. Oxf. 1593; G. Inn 1599. ?Kntd. 1603.

Townshend no doubt owed his return for Castle Rising to his family's local standing. Nothing of interest has been ascertained about his life in the Elizabethan period. He was probably dead by 1617, for he is not mentioned in the will of his mother, made in that year, nor in the settlements of her lands.

Vis. Norf. (Norf. and Norwich Arch. Soc.), i. 308; PCC 24 Meade.

R.V.

TOWNSHEND, Roger (c.1544–90), of Raynham, Norf. and Brampton, Suff.

NORFOLK   1563*[1]

b. c.1544, 1st s. of Richard Townshend of Brampton by Catherine, da. and coh. of Sir Humphrey Browne. educ. Trinity Coll. Camb. 1553. m. (1) Ursula, da. of Sir Christopher Heydon*, s.p.; (2) c.1564, Jane, da. of Sir Michael Stanhope†, 2s. John* and Robert*. suc. gt.-gd.-fa. Sir Roger Townshend† 1551. Kntd. 1588.
     Servant of Thomas, 4th Duke of Norfolk and Philip, Earl of Arundel; perhaps member of royal household by 1576.[2]

Townshend's great-grandfather, Sir Roger Townshend, did well out of the dissolution of the monasteries, holding, by his death, over 20 manors in the Raynham district alone. Thus it was a rich inheritance to which Townshend succeeded while still a child. A special commission of February 1565 declared him of age to enter on his lands, and he received the royal licence to do so in the following May. He could have taken his place as one of the leading gentlemen in his county, but, in the same way that his grandfather had been in the service of the 3rd Duke of Norfolk, he entered that of the 4th Duke, as his man of business, for the most part in London, and did not attain even the commission of the peace. He was, however,

elected as knight of the shire at a by-election for the second session of the 1563 Parliament after the 4th Duke had put pressure on the sheriff, William Paston, who received his instructions on 28 Sept. 1566, to nominate 'those I talked with you of'.[3]

In November 1569, when Norfolk was already involved in the Mary Stuart marriage negotiations, Townshend was one of those attendant on the Duke at Kenninghall, and after his master's execution he took charge of the affairs of the heir, the Earl of Arundel, who was still a minor. It was to him, jointly with William Dix*, that Arundel in 1583 made a deed of gift of all his movable goods towards the payment of his outstanding debts. Arundel was sometimes impatient with Townshend, as when, in 1582, Townshend hurried him off by boat to Arundel House, to avoid his becoming embroiled in the affray between the Earl of Oxford and Thomas Knyvet*. Again, Arundel wrote to Burghley in June 1589 complaining that his 'uncle Harry' and a number of poor tenants were suffering through his agent's rigid interpretation of his responsibilities: 'Sir Roger Townshend is so resolute to part with nothing more than he shall be by law enforced'. But his regard for Townshend is apparent in the Earl's will, where he is 'my loving friend', and was bequeathed a 'fair bowl with a cover of 30 oz. double gilt'.[4]

Comparatively little is known of his career after Arundel's imprisonment in 1585. Some notes of Sir Francis Walsingham* in June of that year give his name as one of the Earl's servants 'committed abroad to diverse persons', for whom Richard Topcliffe* may have taken responsibility, but there is no indication that he was in custody for long. The lists of donors of New Year's gifts to the Queen, on which he and his second wife (who perhaps also held a court position) appear between 1576 and 1584, do not contain his name among later entries. Townshend was knighted at sea by Lord Howard of Effingham 26 July 1588. In the following summer he used his bond to get Roger Wyndham of Norfolk released from the Marshalsea.[5]

He died at Stoke Newington, probably in the house bought from Thomas Sutton, on 30 June 1590, and was buried at St. Giles, Cripplegate. Townshend's will, which he had drawn up in December 1587, lists his manors in Norfolk, with outlying property in Suffolk, Oxfordshire and Middlesex, but does not mention an estate which he is known to have acquired in Essex.[6]

[1] Folger V. b. 298. [2] CPR, 1563–6, pp. 198, 199; DNB; Vis. Norf. (Norf. and Norwich Arch. Soc.), i. 308; Vis. Norf. (Harl. Soc. xxxii), 291–2; Wards 7/6/68; J. Durham, Townshends of Raynham, passim; CSP Dom. 1547–80, p. 469; 1581–90, p. 117. [3] Wards 7/6/68; Bodl. Douce 393, f. 94. [4] HMC Hatfield, i. 438; iii. 414–15; Venerable Philip Howard, Earl of Arundel (Cath. Rec. Soc.), 34–6, 38 seq., 368–77. [5] Ven. Philip Howard, 135; Nichols, Progresses Eliz. ii. 1, 76, 87, 259, 270, 420; DNB; APC, xvii. 347. [6] DNB; C142/231/107; PCC 16 Sainberbe.

N.M.F.

TOWSE, William (c.1551–1634), of the Inner Temple, London, and Takeley, Essex.

BRAMBER	1586
BEVERLEY	1614
COLCHESTER	1621, 1624, 1625, 1626

b. c.1551. *educ.* I. Temple 1571, called. *m.* Jean French, 1s. 3da.

J.p.q. Essex from c.1592; bencher, I. Temple 1595, Summer reader 1597, (?Lent) reader 1610, treasurer 1607; serjeant-at-law 1614; town clerk, Colchester by 1620.

In the printed admission register of the Inner Temple Towse is described as of Hingham, Norfolk.[1] Until 1614 he lived in the Inner Temple. Between 1583 and 1600 he five times audited the steward's accounts, and five times those of the treasurer, and was employed on a number of committees to investigate various matters concerning the inn. His return for Bramber was probably brought about by Edward Caryll, the steward of the borough. Towse and Caryll had a mutual friend in Ralph Hare, whose brother Hugh* had sat in 1572. No record has been found of any activity by Towse in the Commons and his subsequent parliamentary career lies outside the purview of this biography. He died 22 Oct. 1634.[2]

[1] An earlier transcript says 'of Henham, Essex, gen., and late of Clifford's Inn': ex inf. William Prest. [2] *Vis. Essex* (Harl. Soc. xiii), 505; E163/114/8; Hatfield ms 278; APC, xxx. 666; xxxi. 244; C142/525/121(2).

A.M.M.

TRACY, Sir John I (*d.*1591), of Toddington, Glos.

GLOUCESTERSHIRE	1584

1st s. of Henry Tracy of Toddington by Elizabeth, da. of Sir John Brydges, 1st Baron Chandos. *educ.* L. Inn 1566. *m.* Anne, da. of Sir Thomas Throckmorton† of Coss Court, 6s. inc. Sir John II* 3da. *suc.* fa. 1557. Kntd. 1574. J.p. Glos. from 1564; eccles commr. 1575; commr. to inquire into decay of cloth trade in Glos. 1577, piracy 1578, recusancy 1580; sheriff 1578–9.

The parliamentary return for Gloucestershire in 1584 is missing. Browne Willis gives the name of this Member as Sir John Darcy, but there was no knight of that name living in Gloucestershire at the time, and the MP was almost certainly Sir John Tracy of Toddington, who was knighted during the Queen's visit to Bristol in 1574. He was on two committees during this Parliament, for the subsidy, 24 Feb. 1585, and for the preservation of game, 4 Mar. Tracy owned considerable estates in Gloucestershire, including Toddington, which had been in the hands of his family since Domesday, and Fairford, which he purchased from Sir Henry Unton* for £1,126. He was active in local affairs, and led the Gloucestershire levies in Armada year. He died 25 Sept. 1591.

Vis. Glos. (Harl. Soc. xxi), 167; PCC 33 Wrastley; *Bristol and Glos. Arch. Soc. Trans.* xv. 37; xvii. 136; lix. 66–70; *CSP Dom.* 1547–80, p. 609; 1581–90, p. 522; D'Ewes, 356, 363; APC, x. 29; xii. 193, 241; C142/232/51.

J.J.C.

TRACY, Sir John II (c.1561–c.1648), of Toddington, Glos.

GLOUCESTERSHIRE	1597

b. c.1561, 1st s. of Sir John Tracy I* of Toddington. *educ.* I. Temple 1580. *m.* c.1590, Anne, 5th da. of Thomas Shirley I* of Wiston, Suss., 2s. 3da. *suc.* fa. 1591. Kntd. 1591; *cr.* Visct. Tracy [I] 1643. J.p. Glos. from c.1591, sheriff 1609–10; commr. to examine waste in forest of Dean caused by ironworks 1618.

Tracy fought in the Netherlands and at the siege of Rouen, where he was knighted by the 2nd Earl of Essex. Soon after his return he succeeded his father to Toddington and other Gloucestershire properties, being granted special livery of his lands on 14 Feb. 1592. During the succeeding decade he sold many properties, including Charlton Abbots, Alderton, Doynton and Great Wormington, for a total of nearly £1,750. In 1608 he bought back Alderton and other lands for £800, and three years afterwards acquired the manor of Frampton for £300.

His social position in Gloucestershire was high enough for him to be elected for the county in 1597. He was named to committees concerning armour and weapons (8 Nov. 1597), maltsters (12 Jan. 1598); and on 22 Nov. 1597 Sir Edward Hoby* successfully moved the House for privilege because Tracy had been put on a jury at the court of common pleas during a session of the House. The serjeant was sent to 'call ... Sir John to his attendance in this House'. As a knight of the shire in this Parliament he could have attended the committees for enclosures (5 Nov.), the poor law (5, 22 Nov.), penal laws (8 Nov.), monopolies (10 Nov.), the subsidy (15 Nov.) and Newport bridge (29 Nov.).

By 1597 it appears that Tracy was holding a minor office at court, as his name appears in the stables section of the household subsidy roll, assessed on £50 lands and fees. He probably owed the post to his connexion with the Earl of Essex, then master of the horse. He is said to have been an active follower of Essex at the rebellion of 1601, but no action was taken against him, and he was not even removed from the commission of the peace. The witness who gave evidence against him may have mistaken him either for his relative Henry Tracy, who had been with the Earl in Ireland, or for Essex's page, also a Tracy, who was killed during the rising.

During the first 15 years of James I's reign Tracy had several business transactions with Michael Hickes*, but the appointment in 1623 of his brother-in-law, Edward Conway†, to be secretary of state did not draw him into political life. Under Charles I he identified himself with the King's party, and gained an Irish peerage. He was presumably too old to take an active part in the civil war. He died between 7 May 1647 and 14 Feb. 1648, administration of his goods being granted to his grandson John in November 1648.

CP; SP Holl. 6/9, ff. 22–4; Rudder, *Glos.* 770–1; *Bristol and Glos. Arch. Soc. Trans.* ix. 353; xvii. 136, 142, 150, 159, 177, 244, 247, 257–8; *CSP Dom.* 1591–4, p. 185; 1595–7, p. 452; 1598–1601, p. 550; 1611–18, p. 155; 1623–5, pp. 161, 190; 1629–31, p. 105; D'Ewes, 552, 553, 555, 557, 560, 561, 565, 578; E179/70/107; *CSP Ire.* 1599–1600, pp. 29, 35, 41, 60; *HMC Hatfield*, ix. 156, 413; xi. 61; xii. 497; Lansd. 90, f. 219; 91, f. 192.

R.C.G.

TRAFFORD, Edmund I (1526–90), of Trafford, Lancs.

LANCASHIRE   1572

b. 23 June 1526, 1st s. of Sir Edmund Trafford by Anne, da. of Sir Alexander Ratcliffe of Ordsall, *m.* (1) Mary, da. of Lord Edmund Howard, sis. of Queen Catherine Howard, *s.p.*; (2) Elizabeth, da. of Sir Ralph Leycester* of Toft, Cheshire, wid. of Sir Randle Mainwairing of Peover, 2s. inc. Edmund II* 2da. Kntd. 1578.

J.p. Lancs. from c.1561; sheriff 1570–1, 1579–80, 1583–4; eccles. commr. province of York 1574; steward of the lands of the collegiate church of Manchester 1575.

The Traffords were related to the Queen through the Howards, and also to many of the leading Lancashire families. Trafford himself was, in the words of Father Campion, 'a most bitter enemy of the Catholics', complaining in May 1580 to the Earl of Leicester that the state of Lancashire was 'lamentable to behold', with masses said in several places. He was commissioned by the Privy Council to question those who had lately harboured Campion, and ordered to search their houses for books and other 'superstitious stuff'. In 1582 Trafford and Robert Worsley informed the Council that the recusants in their custody at the Fleet prison, Salford, continued obstinate for want of instruction, and requested that preachers might be appointed for them. This plea was repeated in April, May and October. That same year Trafford arrested a priest, John Baxter, and in the following year two others, Williamson and Hatton. It was also Trafford who, at the instigation of the bishop of Chester, descended upon Blainscough to arrest a Mr. Worthington. Finding him gone, he went on to Rossall, a house inhabited by Cardinal Allen's widowed sister-in-law. There he is said to have seized £500 on the pretext that it was intended for Allen. These activities did not endear him to the Catholics, and references are found to 'the furious hate of this inhuman wretch … prepared for any nefarious deed'; 'that ferocious man'; 'that utterly barbarous man', and 'the unrighteous sheriff'.

Trafford disputed with Richard Molyneux* the stewardship of Blackburn, Tottington and Clitheroe. He

possessed lands in a large number of parishes in Lancashire, Cheshire and Derbyshire, but his inquisition post mortem reveals a decrease in the Lancashire property. Trafford contributed £100 to the Armada fund in 1588. He is said to have maintained a retinue at Trafford, including huntsmen, a schoolmaster and musicians. He died intestate on 14 May 1590, and was buried in the collegiate church of Manchester on the 21st. The inventory of his property, made on 27 May, shows no great wealth.

S. J. Leatherbarrow, *Lancs. Eliz. Recusants* (Chetham Soc. n.s. cx); Foster, *Lancs. Peds.*; *VCH Lancs.* iv. 332–3; Croston, *Lancs. and Cheshire Fams.* 196; *CSP Dom.* 1547–80, p. 656; 1581–90, pp. 46, 50, 54, 73; *APC*, xiii. 148–9; Gillow, *Haydock Pprs.* 18; *Chetham Soc.* n.s. li. 125, 127, 128, 130; *Derby Household Bk.* (Chetham Soc. xxxi), 63, 99; DL1/122/M.10; *Lancs. and Cheshire Wills* (Chetham Soc. li), 72–4.

N.M.S.

TRAFFORD, Edmund II (c.1560–1620), of Trafford, Lancs.

NEWTON   1589, 1593

b. c.1560, 1st s. of Edmund Trafford I* of Trafford by his 2nd w. *m.* (1) 1573, Margaret, da. of John Booth of Barton, 3s. 1da.; (2) aft. 1595, Mildred (*d.* 23 Dec. 1611), da. of Thomas Cecil, 1st Earl of Exeter, wid of (Sir) Thomas Reade*, 1s. 1da. *suc.* fa. 14 May 1590. Kntd. 1603.[1]

J.p. Lancs. by 1587, dep. lt., sheriff 1601–2, 1608–9, 1616–17; eccles. commr. province of York 1603.[2]

Trafford, brought into Parliament for Newton through a connexion with the Langton family, was, like his father, strongly protestant. In 1564 he was contracted in marriage to Margaret Booth, apparently in order to unite the two family estates and thereby augment the diminishing Trafford properties. The marriage was celebrated when the couple were about 13 and 12 years old respectively. Three years later John Booth died, and Trafford received half the township of Barton. This marriage broke up some time before 1592 and all Margaret's children were later disinherited.[3]

Little is known about Trafford's life, in spite of the eminence of his connexions. He accompanied his uncle, Sir Robert Cecil, to meet King James at York in 1603, and was knighted upon that occasion. He died 8 May 1620 and was buried by torchlight in Manchester collegiate church. He was succeeded by his youngest son, Sir Cecil, who later became a Catholic.[4]

[1] Foster, *Lancs. Peds.*; *VCH Lancs.* iv. 332. [2] Lansd. 53, f. 178; *Stanley Pprs.* (Chetham Soc. xxxi), 99; *VCH Lancs.* iv. 332; *HMC Hatfield*, xv. 394. [3] Crofton, *Stretford* (Chetham Soc. n.s. li), 130–3; *VCH Lancs.* iv. 332–3. [4] Croston, *Lancs. and Cheshire Fams.*, 205.

N.M.S.

TREDENECK, John (*d.* 1566), of Tredinnick, St. Breock, Cornw.

LOSTWITHIEL   1529
HELSTON   1559

1st s. of Christopher Tredeneck of Tredinnick by Joan, da. and coh. of John Gosse. *m.* Frances, da. of one Sutton of Lincoln, 2s. 1da. *suc.* fa. 1532.

Commr. subsidy Cornw. by 1550, j.p. 1547–53, from 1559.

Tredeneck sat in Parliament twice only, first in the Reformation Parliament, and then 30 years later in the first Parliament of Elizabeth. This suggests that he was a man of strongly protestant outlook, a view supported by his exclusion from the commission of the peace during Mary's reign. In this case it is likely that his own claims to a parliamentary seat at Helston would have had the support of the 2nd Earl of Bedford. A fellow-Member in 1559 was Tredeneck's brother-in-law, Nicholas Carminowe*, sitting for Bodmin, who may also have been a protestant partisan who owed his seat to Bedford. Tredeneck was associated for a time with William Carnsewe I* and Thomas Treffry† in exploiting mines discovered by Burchart Cranyce. In 1563 Tredeneck and Carnsewe instituted a Chancery suit against Treffry's heir, who had in his possession large quantities of lead belonging to the syndicate. The sale of this lead would enable them to repay a loan of £600 owing to the duchy of Cornwall, by means of which the venture had originally been financed, and which became due for repayment at midsummer 1563.

Tredeneck died in 1566 and was buried on 20 June that year in the parish church of St. Breock. The heir was his son Charles, who married a daughter of Thomas Marrow†.

Vivian, *Vis. Cornw.* 457–8; PCC 22 Thower; *CPR,* 1547–8, p. 82; 1553 and App. Edw. VI. p. 351; Lansd. 1218, f. 6; *APC,* vi. 118; C3/36/45.

I.C.

TREFFRY, Thomas (1563–1636), of the Middle Temple, London, later of Lostwithiel, Cornw.

FOWEY   1597

bap. 16 June 1563, 3rd s. of John Treffry (d. 1590) of Place, Fowey by his 2nd w. Emlyn, da. of John Tresithny; bro. of William*. *educ.* New Inn; M. Temple 1584, called 1594. *m.* Catherine (d. 1625), da. and coh. of Thomas Hellier *alias* Mayowe of Lostwithiel, 2da.

Mayor, Lostwithiel 1604, 1625, 1631.

The Treffry family, who had risen to a leading position in the borough of Fowey during the fifteenth century, were closely connected with the protestant movement under Edward VI, and some of them were Marian exiles. Treffry himself was a lawyer, who, until he vacated his chamber in the Middle Temple at the end of the century, acted as a London agent for Fowey. In 1595 he was 'emboldened to write' to Sir Robert Cecil, since 'our haven of Fowey being opposed to that part of Brittany

possessed by the enemy, we understand daily the affairs of these parts, and I think sooner than any other part of England, by reason of the shortness of the cut and our common intercourse of merchandise'. Two years later he or his brother William sent intelligence to Cecil about Spanish ships and troops. In December 1598 Treffry was appointed by the Cornish deputy lieutenants to collect £271 from the Exechequer for victualling and transporting 300 soldiers from Fowey to Ireland. Probably before the end of Elizabeth's reign he retired to Lostwithiel, where he became mayor. He died 9 Mar. 1636, leaving two married daughters, Emlyn and Blanche. Treffry had promised his late wife to leave his lands and goods to Blanche, whom he made executrix, and who proved the will 5 July 1636. His 'old true friend', William Leonard, received money for a ring, and his grandson Charles Kendall his law books.

Vis. Cornw. (Harl. Soc. ix), 221 n; Vivian, *Vis. Cornw.* 460; *Burke L G* (1952), p. 2539; J. Maclean, *Trigg Minor,* ii. 252–5; E. W. Rashleigh, *Fowey,* 16, 17; SP46/73/31; A. L. Rowse, *Tudor Cornw.* 350, 381–2; *M.T. Mins.* passim; *CSP Dom.* 1591–4, pp. 463–4; 1595–7, p. 459; *HMC Hatfield,* v. 322; vii. 444; *APC,* xxix. 413; PCC 81 Pike; C142/536/29.

R.C.G.

TREFFRY, William (1559–1603), of Place, Fowey, Cornw.

FOWEY   1584

bap. 18 Feb. 1559, 1st s. of John Treffry of Treffry by his 2nd w. and bro. of Thomas*. *educ.* Oxf. BA 1579. *m.* 3 Apr. 1589, Ursula, da. and coh. of William Tremayne of Upcott, Devon, 1s. 5da. *suc.* fa. 28 Jan. 1591.

Duchy of Cornw. farmer of the manor of Fowey by c.1597; j.p. Cornw. temp. rem. 1596, dep. lt. by 1598; master of the ordnance, Cornw. by 1602.

Treffry, the eldest of 16 children, was returned for Fowey through his family's local standing. He was a follower of (Sir) Walter Ralegh* and a friend of Richard Carew*, who admired his 'rare gifts of learning, wisdom and courage', devoted to the good of his country. He helped Carew with 'judicious corrections' to his *Survey of Cornwall,* where he is described as living in a 'fair and ancient house, castlewise builded', overlooking Fowey harbour. He commanded four companies of troops and paid considerable attention to the fortifications, which were largely the result of his 'providence and direction'.

In 1596 Treffry's name was omitted from the commission of the peace for Cornwall, perhaps because he and John Rashleigh* were accused of fomenting opposition to the tax on pilchards. His relative (Sir) Henry Killigrew* wrote to Cecil complaining of this 'no small disgrace', and asking to have Treffry restored, as a gentleman 'of very sufficient living, of sound religion and of learning and judgment fit to execute such authority', and because there was no other justice in Fowey. As a result, Treffry returned to the commission, perhaps immediately, certainly by 1599.

Treffry made his will 23 Feb. 1603, when he was ill, and died the following day. He wished to be buried at Fowey. After provision for his wife, the sole executrix, two parts of all his property, including more than six manors, went to four daughters until his son John‡, who was a minor, should attain the age of 24. The daughters received £300 each.

Vivian, *Vis. Cornw.* 460; J. Maclean, *Trigg Minor*, ii. 252–3; J. Keast, *Fowey*, 22, 34–43, 51–4; C142/228/59, 280/89; rec. gen. accts. 39–40 Eliz.; *APC*, xxix. 413; *Carew's Surv. Cornw.* ed. Halliday, 154, 155, 209; *CSP Dom.* 1591–4, p. 464; *HMC Hatfield*, vi. 335; ix. 152, 320.

N.M.S.

TREFUSIS, Richard (d. 1611), of Lincoln's Inn, London and Lanleake, Cornw.

CAMELFORD   1584, 1586, 1589

2nd s. of Nicholas Trefusis of Landewe, Cornw. by Grace, da. and coh. of William Millington. *educ.* New Inn. *m.* Anne, da. of Peter Edgecombe*, *s.p.*

L. Inn 1579, called 1587, bencher 1604, marshal and reader 1605–6, keeper of the Black Book 1610–11.

No connexion has been found between the Richard Trefusis who became a parliament man and the borough he represented in three consecutive Parliaments without – as far as is known – contributing to the business of any of them. The Trefusis family had been seated at Trefusis, overlooking Falmouth harbour, 'ever since the Conquest, if not before', yet until 1584 it seems not to have sent a Member to the House of Commons. There is consequently some ground for thinking that the honour on its first occurrence would have fallen to or been claimed by the then head of the family, the Richard who at the age of 17 or more had succeeded his grandfather Thomas Trefusis, and whose will (no longer extant) was possibly the one proved at Exeter on 5 June 1594. However, there was another Richard in the family, Richard of Lanleake, a practising lawyer resident in London and, it may be thought, suitably qualified – as assuredly he was better placed – to represent a small and distant borough.

Somewhat younger than Richard of Trefusis, to whom he was cousin, Richard of Lanleake was descended from their common grandfather Thomas, but by Thomas's second wife. He was already a barrister of New Inn when he was admitted to Lincoln's Inn on 12 Apr. 1579 in company with Thomas Trefusis, possibly his elder brother. Thomas then disappears from the records of the inn, but Richard's career there is clearly outlined: in Nov. 1586 his call to the bar 'next term' was agreed upon; in 1594 he was fined £5 for the stewardship of the reader's dinner; other appointments followed. The will which he himself wrote out in July 1607 and later subjected to some 'interlining, rasure and alteration' because of an

agreement concluded with Sir Richard Edgecombe*, named two members of the inn among his overseers, Giles Tooker* and Richard Waltham: to each he left six of his best printed law books and 40s. to be bestowed in rings, praying them to aid first his dear and well-beloved wife, and next his heirs with their best advice, help and counsel. He died on 30 Aug. 1611. His will was proved on 5 May following, after his nephew Nicholas, Thomas's son, had tried to overturn it.

Vis. Cornw. (Harl. Soc. ix), 64, 135, 223–4; D. Gilbert, *Paroch. Hist. Cornw.* iii. 389; *Devon Wills* (Brit. Rec. Soc. Index Lib. xlvi), 207; PCC 48 Capell; C142/333/13.

E.L.C.M.

TREHERNE, John, ?of Dartmouth, Devon.

DARTMOUTH   1601

Apart from scattered references to him in the Dartmouth records for the period 1578–95,[1] nothing has been ascertained about this MP, who may or may not be connected with the John Trehane of Trehane, Cornwall.[2] He was almost certainly one of the lesser Dartmouth merchants, for his fellow-Member in 1601 and both Members in 1604 were local men.

[1] Exeter city mun. DD61443, 61444, 61460, 61461, 61483, 61503A, 61532, 61533, 61555B, 61567, 61602, cited Roberts thesis. [2] *Vis. Cornw.* (Harl. Soc. ix), 227–8.

P.W.H.

TRELAWNY, Edward (d. 1630), of Bake in Pelynt, Cornw.

EAST LOOE   1586
LISKEARD   1597

1st s. of Robert Trelawny of St. Germans by Agnes, da. of Thomas Spry of Quethiock. *educ.* Lion's Inn; M. Temple 1580. *m.* 29 Apr. 1611, Mary, da. of Tristram Arscott of Annery, Devon, 1s. 7da.

Trelawny belonged to the younger branch of the long-established Cornish family. He inherited lands in Pelynt and around St. Germans, and both his uncle John and his brother Robert were mayors of Plymouth. Trelawny's house at Pelynt was only four miles from East Looe, and his own local standing was sufficient to account for his return there. At Liskeard he was no doubt returned by his cousin Jonathan, the steward of the borough, of whose will he was an executor in 1604. He made his own will 29 Nov. 1625, proved 20 May 1631. He died (or was buried) 7 June 1630, trusting that his soul 'may without spot fly to the place of perpetual rest prepared from all eternity for God's elect'.

Vis. Cornw. (Harl. Soc. ix), 229–30; Keeler, *Long Parlt.* 363; Vivian, *Vis. Cornw.* 480; Vivian, *Vis. Devon*, 20; J. Allen, *Liskeard*, 57–8, 458; Anon. *Paroch. Hist. Cornw.* iv. 33–4; PCC 101 Harte, 63 St. John.

I.C.

TRELAWNY, John (c.1504–63), of Poole in Menheniot, Cornw.

| LISKEARD | 1553 (Mar.) |
| CORNWALL | 1559, 1563* |

b. c.1504, 1st s. of Walter Trelawny of Poole by Isabella, da. of John Toose of Taunton, Som. *m.* (1) Margery, da. and h. of Thomas Lamellyn of Lanteglos by Fowey, 1s.; (2) Lore, da. of Henry Trecarel, 2s. *suc.* fa. 1518; coh. of Edward Courtenay, 11th Earl of Devon 18 Sept. 1556. *Sheriff*, Cornw. 1546–7, 1560–1, j.p. 1555–d.

The identification of the 1553 Liskeard MP rests on the description of him in the return as 'esquire', a style which could hardly apply to his son and namesake, a youth who had not yet attained his majority. That the same return also refers to him as 'the younger' was to distinguish him from an older namesake known to have been alive in 1553. That it was John Trelawny (d.1563), son of Walter Trelawny, who sat for Cornwall in 1563 (and so by implication in 1559) is apparent from the Folger V. b. 298 list, where 'mortuus' is written against his name for the second session. The family had been established in Cornwall since before the Norman Conquest and it maintained its position in subsequent centuries. There is little to say about Trelawny himself, who left no mark in the records of his two Elizabethan Parliaments, and who died in September 1563, being buried at Menheniot. Under a will made in the previous February, he left an annual rent charge of £60 to his wife and annuities of £20 to each of his two younger sons. The remainder of the estate went to the executor of the will, John, his eldest son, who proved the will in June 1564, having been granted livery of his lands the previous month.

Vivian, *Vis. Cornw.* 475–6; *Vis. Som.* (Harl. Soc. xi), 111; *CPR*, 1553 and App. Edw. VI, 351; 1557–8, pp. 6–7; 1560–3, p. 435; 1563–6, p. 1; C. S. Gilbert, *Hist. Surv. Cornw.* i. 546–9; *CSP Dom.* 1547–80, p. 71; PCC 21 Stevenson; C142/138/24.

N.M.F.

TRELAWNY, Jonathan (1568–1604), of Poole in Menheniot, and Trelawne, Cornw.

| LISKEARD | 1586, 1589, 1593 |
| CORNWALL | 1597, 1604* |

b. 17 Dec. 1568, 2nd (posth.) s. of John Trelawny of Menheniot by Anne, da. of William Reskimer. *educ.* Emmanuel, Camb. 1585; M. Temple 1586, *m.* Elizabeth, da. of Henry Killigrew*, 2s. 3da. *suc.* bro. 1569. Kntd. 1598.
    Steward, Liskeard 1587; j.p.q. Cornw. from c.1592, sheriff 1594–5; steward, West Looe 1600; subsidy collector, Cornw.

Trelawny was born two months after the death of his father and within a year had succeeded his brother as head of the family. It was perhaps the Trelawnys' narrow escape from extinction at this time which gave Jonathan that

sense of family which caused him in 1600 to purchase the manor of Trelawne, with which, according to Lysons, the family had no previous connexion. The boy's wardship was acquired by Henry Killigrew in 1572, and he may have received some of his education in Burghley's household as well as with Killigrew's own family, for in November 1582, when he was not yet 14, Killigrew's wife wrote to Burghley, her brother-in-law, thanking him for 'showing favour to young Jonathan'. That he received his university training at Emmanuel was probably due to Killigrew, who was a benefactor of the college, and who would desire to inculcate protestant principles in his ward. The close connexion between the two was cemented by Trelawny's marriage to his guardian's daughter, which probably took place while he was still in wardship.

The extent of Trelawny's estates placed him among the foremost gentlemen of Cornwall. At his death he held land in the Cornish parishes of Altarnun, Southill, St. Ives, Pelynt, Duloe, Antony and St. Teath, as well as his capital manor of Menheniot. He also possessed property in East and West Looe, Launceston, Saltash and Bodmin. In Devon he held land in Plympton, Okehampton, Modbury, and Tiverton; and in Somerset he owned property at Crewkerne. Some of this was acquired by purchase during his lifetime, much was inherited.

It is not surprising, therefore, that Trelawny had assumed a place in local affairs before he was of age, and he was only 17 when first returned to Parliament for Liskeard, which his family had represented in several Parliaments since 1421. In 1597, when he achieved a county seat, his brother-in-law Henry Neville and his relative Edward Trelawny sat for Liskeard, and when in 1601 he wrote to Sir Robert Cecil, offering him two burgess-ships for this Parliament, at least one of them was at Liskeard. Trelawny is not mentioned by name in the journals of the House, but as a knight of the shire in 1597 he could have sat on committees concerned with enclosures (5 Nov.), the poor law (5, 22 Nov.), armour and weapons (8 Nov.), the penal laws (8 Nov.), monopolies (10 Nov.), the subsidy (15 Nov.) and a cloth bill (8 Dec.).

In 1599 Trelawny travelled to France with Neville, the new English ambassador, and he remained there for about six months. During his absence his affairs were left in the hands of his wife, who in October wrote to her cousin Sir Robert Cecil successfully requesting that the sale of the manor of Trelawne might be postponed until her husband could return and buy it. He rebuilt the mansion house there, probably agreeing with Richard Carew* that his house at Poole in Menheniot 'houseth Sir Jonathan Trelawny far beneath his worth and calling'.

Trelawny died 'from a fit of coughing' while serving as knight of the shire in James's first Parliament, 21 June 1604. His will was proved 27 Aug. that year.

Lysons, *Cornw.* 257–8; Vivian, *Vis. Cornw.* 476; *Vis. Cornw.* (Harl. Soc. ix), 229; J. Allen, *Hist. Liskeard*, 58, 458; Hatfield ms 278; G. C.

Boase and W. P. Courtney, *Biblio. Cornub.* 769; *Carew's Surv. Cornw.* ed. Halliday, 135, 185; C. S. Gilbert, *Hist. Surv. Cornw.* ii. 566–7; C142/151/8; 155/97; SP12/155/97; A. C. Miller, *Sir Henry Killigrew*, 231–2; *HMC Hatfield*, ix. 371; xi. 405; D'Ewes, 552, 553, 555, 557, 561, 569; *CSP Dom.* 1598–1601, p. 163; T. Bond, *E. and W. Looe*, 160; *CJ*, i. 244; PCC 100 Harte.

N.M.S.

TREMAYNE, Edmund (c.1525–82), of Collacombe, Devon.

TAVISTOCK	1559
PLYMOUTH	1572

b. c.1525, 2nd s. of Thomas Tremayne of Collacombe by Philippa, da. of Roger Grenville of Stow. *m.* 1576, Eulalia, da. of Sir John St. Leger* of Annery, 1s. 1da. *suc.* e. bro. 13 Mar. 1572.

Duchy of Lancaster receiver in nine counties (inc. Dorset, Som.) 1561–74; dep. (to Sir Nicholas Throckmorton*) butler, Devon 1561; clerk of PC 1571; receiver of the revenues, Devon by 1574; j.p. and piracy commr. Devon from 1577; freeman, Plymouth 1580.

Having served Edward Courtenay, Earl of Devon, and been in the Tower during Mary's reign after Wyatt's rebellion, Tremayne (four of whose brothers were Marian exiles), went to Italy and at some time entered the service of the 2nd Earl of Bedford. With the accession of Elizabeth and Bedford's appointment as lord lieutenant of Devon, he received a number of local offices, then went to court. Next, he was sent (1569) to report on the state of affairs in Ireland. Finally he was made a clerk of the Privy Council, though he made another visit to Ireland (1573) and, certainly from the time he came into the family estates, spent a good deal of his time in the west country. He 'altered and enlarged' Collacombe about 1574.

Bedford returned Tremayne to the first Parliament of the reign for Tavistock, and in 1572 he came in for Plymouth, with John Hawkins, who settled the choice of MPs there in consultation with Bedford. Tremayne and Hawkins were granted leave of absence from the House on 11 Dec. 1576 'for their necessary affairs' but they either had not departed or had returned two days later when they were on a committee concerned with ports. This is Tremayne's only known contribution to the business of the House.

The west-country puritans under Bedford ('our western friends' as (Sir) Amias Paulet* referred to them to Tremayne), were a close-knit group, and none closer than Tremayne and Drake. When Drake returned from his circumnavigation in the autumn of 1580 he was in need of his friends, and, by a happy arrangement on someone's part, probably Walsingham's, it was Tremayne whom the Queen instructed to supervise the registration of the treasure removed that October from the *Golden Hind*, in itself a nice example of Tremayne's mixing central with local affairs, an Elizabethan speciality. Tremayne was careful to take notice only 'of so much as he [Drake] has revealed, and the same I have seen to be weighed, registered and packed'. Entrusted also with the task of investigating charges of cruelty brought against Drake by the Spanish ambassador, Tremayne, to no one's surprise, found these to be 'inferred beyond the truth'.

Tremayne died in September 1582, described by Burghley as 'a man worthy to be beloved for his honesty and virtues'. He appointed Bedford an overseer of his will. Tremayne's only son, named Francis after the Earl, died six weeks later.

DNB; *Trans. Dev. Assoc.* xxxiii. 322; Roberts thesis; *CJ*, i. 105; A. E. W. Mason, *Francis Drake*, 192, 196–8; PCC 54 Tirwhite.

P.W.H.

TRENCHARD, George I (c.1548–1630), of Wolveton, later of Lytchett Matravers, Dorset.[1]

BRIDPORT	1571
DORCHESTER	1572
DORSET	1584

b. c.1548, 1st s. of Thomas Trenchard of Wolveton by Eleanor, da. of Sir John Horsey[†] of Clifton Maybank. *educ.* M. Temple 1570. *m.* (1) Anne (*d.*1588), da. of Sir George Speake* of White Lackington, Som., 4s. inc. George Trenchard II* 3da.; (2) Jane (*d.*1627), da. of Hugh Bampfield of Sturminster Newton, wid. of Thomas Chafin of Folke, 3da. *suc.* fa. 1568. Kntd. 1588.

J.p. Dorset from c.1573, q. 1583, sheriff 1580–1, 1596–7, col. of musters, Dorchester division 1580–at least 1596, commr. piracy 1582, dep. lt. from c.1585; jt. (first with bro.-in-law William Bampfield, then with s. George Trenchard) keeper of Sandsfoot castle from 1591; recorder, Dorchester June 1610–Jan. 1611.[2]

Trenchard – whose grandfather had been an associate of the 1st Earl of Bedford as commissioner for church goods in Dorset – sat for Bridport while still in his twenties: both here and at Dorchester in the following year he was presumably brought into Parliament through the influence of the 2nd Earl of Bedford. Knight of the shire in 1584, Trenchard was named to the subsidy committee, 24 Feb. 1585. He was recommended for appointment as deputy lieutenant by the dying Earl in 1585, and was appointed that year.[3] Discreet and tactful, 'controlling neighbours with velvet-gloved hand', the Privy Council relied upon him at the time of the Armada 'as on no one else in the shire'. He often acted with his friend and relative (Sir) John Horsey* in county affairs, searching for recusants in 1577, submitting recusancy returns in 1580, and three years later, collecting contributions subscribed for the upkeep of the protestant congregation at Geneva. At the time of the Babington plot Trenchard and Horsey submitted a report to the Privy Council on the state of the Dorset gaols 'rented by persons of no credit that live only upon the gain thereof'. Compassion was an element in Trenchard's character. His handling of the search of Chideock castle and his arrest there and subsequent treatment of the Catholic priest John Cornelius was civilized throughout. He and Sir William Paulet*, 3rd Marquess of Winchester, were trustees of Dorchester grammar school and collaborated in other charitable enterprises.[4]

Trenchard concerned himself with several Dorset boroughs, arbitrating in 1577 in a dispute at Weymouth, where he was active at various times until 1590. He intervened in a dispute at Poole in 1586, and in the same year he and Horsey wrote from Wolveton to his 'loving friends the mayor of Poole' and other townsmen, directing them to secure the election to Parliament of the nominee of the Earl of Warwick, 'in consideration of the young Earl of Bedford', his ward. Letters written from Lyme Regis in 1590 were in connexion with his duties as a piracy commissioner.[5] During the Armada crisis Trenchard devoted himself tirelessly to the defence of Dorset, and his knighthood must have been granted in this connexion. He had been reporting on the condition of forts and castles since 1583 (sometimes paying for reparis out of his own pocket), training the junior officers ('more willing than skilled' he reported in 1584), surveying the coast in 1586, and, at the time the invasion was expected, commanding in the field one of the five Dorset defence divisions. Sometimes he slipped up, as over the security arrangements for the stores of the captured *San Salvador*. Writing to the Privy Council, 24 Aug., he apologised for losses of powder and ordnance, at the same time mentioning the 'diseased, naked and chargeable' crew, most of whom subsequently perished, 'the people's charity unto them [being] very cold'.

His friend Sir John Horsey died in 1589 and Trenchard, who was appointed an overseer to his will, received a ring inscribed *vita brevis amicitia longa*. Horsey had made his cousin Ralph* his heir, and thenceforward he and Trenchard frequently acted together in local affairs. In 1593 Trenchard was host to Sir Walter Ralegh, Carew Ralegh and Horsey at the famous dinner party at Wolveton which led to a commission of inquiry into Sir Walter's atheism. Trenchard bought Lytchett Matravers in about 1611, and thereupon resigned the recordership of Dorchester because of his distance from the town. His last years were marred by the extravagance and early death of his heir George and by an illness that confined him to the house. He died 24 Nov. 1630, appointing his second son, Thomas, executor.

[1] R. Lloyd, *Dorset Elizabethans*, has been used throughout this biography. [2] Roberts thesis; F. F. Trenchard, *House of Trenchard*, i(3), pp. 131–4, 137, 141, 142, 143; *Som. and Dorset N. and Q.* ii. 16; *Dorchester Recs.* ed. Mayo, 451. [3] SP12/179/f. 117v; D'Ewes, 356; Bodl. Tanner 241, f. 44v, ex. inf. Dr. Harry Leonard. [4] *VCH Dorset*, ii. 28 n; *Weymouth Charters* ed. Moule, 94; *CSP Dom.* 1547–80, p. 561; APC, xii. 241, 338; *Lyme Regis fugitive pieces* no. 34; Hutchins,

Dorset, ii. 367; Harl. 286, f. 203. [5] *Weymouth Charters*, 27, 32 et passim; APC, x. 249–50, 267; xiv. 230; *CSP Dom.* 1581–90, pp. 644, 647; Sydenham, *Hist. Poole*, 102.

P.W.H.

TRENCHARD, George II (c.1575–1610), of Wolveton, Dorset, and of London.

DORSET 1601

b. c.1575, 1st s. of George Trenchard I* of Wolveton by his 1st w. *educ.* Magdalen Coll. Oxf. 1588; M. Temple 1594. *m.* (1) Elizabeth, da. of John Whitson, alderman of Bristol, *s.p.*; (2) 11 June 1610, Penelope, da. of Thomas Darcy, 3rd Baron Chiche, later Earl Rivers, *s.p.* Kntd. 1603.

Jt. (with his fa.) keeper of Sandsfoot castle 1601.

Trenchard's father wished 'to train up and make serviceable to her Majesty' his eldest son, who thus found himself taking the family's turn as knight of the shire at the age of 26. In this capacity he may have served on the main business committee (3 Nov.) and the committee on monopolies (23 Nov.). But he got into debt in London, confessing in his last illness, 25 June 1610, that his extravagance had almost broken his father's heart: 'and so there is an end of too much because it will wear now very deep (as I know) into your estate'. His widow remarried on 8 July 1611.

Roberts thesis: W. J. Pinks, *Hist. Clerkenwell*, 46; HMC *Hatfield*, xi. 467; D'Ewes, 624, 649; Harl. 1579, f. 132; *Suss. N. and Q.* ix. 8, ex inf. J. P. Ferris.

P.W.H.

TRENTHAM, Thomas I (1538–87), of Rocester, Staffs.

STAFFORDSHIRE 1571

b. 21 Apr. 1538, 1st s. of Richard Trentham[†] of Shrewsbury, Salop and Trentham, Staffs. by Mary, da. of David Ireland of Shrewsbury. *m.* Jane, da. of Sir William Sneyd of Bradwell in Wolstanton and Keele, 2s. Francis[†] and Thomas II* 3da. *suc.* fa. 1 Jan. 1547.

Sheriff, Staffs. 1571–2, 1579–80, j.p.q. from c.1574, custos rot. by 1577, dep. lt. by 1585, prob. by 1570.

Trentham's father acquired the site and demesnes of the monastery of Rocester, near Uttoxeter. Houses and shops in Shrewsbury also came into the family by his marriage, but most of the Shropshire property went to Thomas's younger brothers and sisters, or was sold to pay his father's debts. Thomas Trentham's wardship was granted in November 1547 to Sir Philip Draycott[†], who administered the estates so well that after receiving livery of his lands in June 1559, Trentham was able to add to them by a series of purchases until shortly before his death. Most of the land was put out to pasture. Trentham was content with one appearance as knight of the shire. He left no trace upon the records of the House. A good deal of his local activity consisted of examining suspected recusants and harbourers of Jesuit priests. Sir Ralph Sadler* corresponded with him about Mary Stuart and, as one of the 'principal gentlemen in Staffordshire', he was ordered to attend Mary on her removal in September 1586 to Fotheringay. He was at the March 1587 quarter sessions, and died at Rocester the following May. In his will, made the previous October, he divided the lands not entailed on the elder son Francis (who had just come of age) between the widow and his younger son Thomas. The unmarried daughter, Elizabeth, was left £1,000. She later married Edward de Vere, 17th Earl of Oxford.

Staffs. Peds. (Harl. Soc. lxiii), 224; *Wm. Salt Arch. Soc.* iii(2), pp. 140–1; xiv(1), pp. 168, 180–1, 210; xv. 161; xvii. 233; *Vis. Salop* (Harl. Soc. xxviii), 271; SP12/121; 12/179/52; C142/85/47, 57; *CPR*, 1547–8, p. 65; 1558–60, p. 74; *Staffs. Rec. Soc.* 1938, p. 129; *CSP Dom.* 1547–80, p. 685; *APC*, xi. 208; xiii. 164; Lansd. 102, ff. 62–3; *HMC 4th Rep.* 339; *Staffs. Q. Sess. Rolls*, i. (Wm. Salt Arch. Soc.), 313; PCC 36 Rutland.

N.M.F.

TRENTHAM, Thomas II (1575–1605), of Rocester, Staffs.

NEWCASTLE-UNDER-LYME   1601

b. 1575, 2nd s. of Thomas Trentham I* and bro. of Francis†. *educ.* Balliol, Oxf. 1591. *unm.*

Trentham inherited half the unentailed estate of his father and continued to live at Rocester with his elder brother, Francis. He presumably owed his return for Newcastle-under-Lyme in 1601 to his mother's family, who owned property in the town and supplied the office of mayor in 1593. He died between 8 Apr. and 14 May 1605. He bequeathed £100 each to his mother, his sister Elizabeth, a maid of honour to the Queen, who had married the 17th Earl of Oxford, and to Lady Catherine Stanhope. His brother Francis and the Earl of Oxford received horses, and small mementos, mostly weapons, were left to his cousins. John Stanhope received £5, and the wish that he would 'more measure the assured goodwill of the giver than the meanness of the gift'.

J. C. Wedgwood, *Staffs. Parl. Hist.* (Wm. Salt Arch. Soc., i), 364–5; *Staffs. Peds.* (Harl. Soc. lxiii), 224; *Vis. Staffs.* (Wm. Salt Arch. Soc. v. pt. 2), 289; PCC 36 Rutland, 34 Hayes; T. Pape, *Newcastle-under-Lyme.*

J.J.C.

TREVANION, Charles (d.1601), of St. Michael Caerhayes, Cornw.

GRAMPOUND   1584

4th s. of Sir Hugh Trevanion of Caerhayes by Sybil, da. of Sir Thomas Morgan of ?Arkestone, Herefs. *m.* Joan, da. and h. of Robert Wichalse of Chudleigh, Devon, 2s. 2da. *suc.* bro. 1588.

J.p. Cornw. from c.1592, sheriff 1595–6; v.-adm. Cornw. aft. Oct. 1597–1601.

Trevanion's family had been established in Cornwall since at least the reign of Edward III. His father and grandfather promoted the Reformation in the west during Henry VIII's reign. He was connected by marriage with several neighbours; a sister had married John Trelawny of Fowey, another John Roscarrock (becoming the mother of Nicholas Roscarrock, the recusant historian), and a third John Trevor*. Yet another sister married Robert Carey*, son of Lord Hunsdon, the Queen's cousin.[1]

Trevanion presumably owed his return for Grampound to his family's local standing, Caerhayes being within six miles of the borough. In 1588, Trevanion succeeded unexpectedly to these estates, his three elder brothers having died within twelve years of one another. He became an active justice of the peace, on one occasion sequestering the cargo of the *Flying Hart* of Amsterdam, which had been brought into Fowey by pirates, and on another removing fish-weirs and other obstructions set up in the river Fowey, which were preventing ships sailing up to Lostwithiel. In 1599 he raised five hundred men for the defence of the county and in October 1601, a month before his death, he was recruiting, in his capacity as vice-admiral of Cornwall, two hundred sailors for service in Ireland.

Richard Carew* of Antony wrote of Trevanion:

through his virtue as free from greediness, as through his fair livelihood far from neediness; and by daily experience giving proof, that a mind valuing his reputation at the due price, will easily repute all dishonest gain much inferior thereunto, and that in conversing with the worst sort of people (which his office oftentimes enforceth) he can no more be disgraced than the sunbeams by shining upon a dunghill will be blemished.[2]

He died 11 Nov. 1601. In his will, made the previous August and proved in February 1610, he made exact provision for the disposition of his estate, the heir not being of age. Trevanion's widow was to hold lands in Veryan and Delabole, Cornwall, and Filleigh, Devon, for her son's use until he came of age. But if she married again (in fact she married John Hannam*), refused the charge or died, they were to be held by Sir Reginald Mohun II*, John Trevor, William Treffry*, Hugh Trevanion of Gerrans and John Cardew, who were all appointed overseers of the will. As executrix the widow was bound in £4,000 to the heir for the due performance of her stewardship during the minority.[3]

[1] Vivian, *Vis. Cornw.* 501–2; *APC*, xxxii. 256; D. Gilbert, *Paroch. Hist. Cornw.* iii. 199; A. L. Rowse, *Tudor Cornw.* 223–4, 252, 258, 298. [2] *APC*, xxviii. 68; xxx. 352; xxxii. 256; *Carew's Surv. Cornw.* ed. Halliday, 155, 159, 217. [3] C142/268/141; PCC 16 Wingfield, 91 Wood.

I.C.

TREVANION, Richard (d.1628), of Tregarton in St. Goran, Cornw.

TREGONY   1586

2nd s. of Richard Trevanion of Talvern by Margaret, da. and coh. of Thomas Chamond of Tregarton, wid. of Thomas Arundell of Talvern. *educ.* New Inn; M. Temple 1579, called 1587. *m.* c.1592, Mary, da. of Henry Rolle of Heanton, Devon, wid. of one Prestwood, 1s. 1da.

Trevanion belonged to a younger branch of the family which settled at Talvern during Elizabeth's reign. He was originally intended for a legal career, and had chambers at the Middle Temple from 1581 until about 1587. He was therefore probably resident in London at the time of the 1586 Parliament to which he had been returned at Tregony through his family's local influence. He is not mentioned in the records of his one Parliament, nor was he active in local administration. After the death of his father he settled on his mother's share of the Chamond lands in Launcells and St. Goran. He died 5 June 1628. The heir was his son Nathaniel, aged 27.

Vis. Cornw. (Harl. Soc. ix), 240–1, 302; Vivian, *Vis. Cornw.* 501, 504; *Vis. Devon,* 615; C. S. Gilbert, *Hist. Surv. Cornw.* ii. 304, 305, 306; D. Gilbert, *Paroch. Hist. Cornw.* ii. 414; C142/751/154; *Cornw. Wills* (Brit. Rec. Soc. Index Lib. lvi), 335.

I.C.

TREVOR, John (1563–1630), of Oatlands, Surr.

REIGATE	1593
BLETCHINGLEY	1597
REIGATE	1601
BLETCHINGLEY	1604, 1614
BODMIN	1621
EAST LOOE	1625

b. 1563, 2nd s. of John Trevor of Trevalyn, Denb. by Mary, da. of Sir George Brydges of London; bro. of Sir Richard* and Thomas*. *m.* 24 May 1592, Margaret, da. of Sir Hugh Trevanion of Caerhayes, Cornw., 4s (1 *d.v.p.*) 2da. Kntd. 1603.[1]

Sec. to Charles Howard I* by 1595; surveyor of navy 1599–1611; clerk of Windsor castle and steward and receiver of manor and honour of Windsor 1598; keeper of Chatham castle; keeper of Oatlands park 1603; gent. usher of privy chamber by 1603; gent of privy chamber 1625.[2]

Trevor was a Welshman whose father had been a servant of the Sackville family. Lord Buckhurst referred in 1601 to his 'cousin' Trevor in a letter to Robert Cecil, and it may have been he who brought Trevor to the notice of Charles Howard the lord admiral. Trevor was in close attendance upon Howard by 1593, when he was returned for one of the Surrey boroughs dominated by the family. Until his retirement in 1619 Howard kept a seat for Trevor in every Parliament at either Bletchingley or Reigate. Trevor was on the subsidy committee, 28 Feb. and 1 Mar. 1593, but no mention of him is to be found in the comparatively well reported 1597 Parliament. It is thus uncertain whether it was he or Thomas Trevor who sat on

two committees, 9 Dec. 1601, for ships and seamen (this must surely have been John) and the assurance of certain unspecified manors. It was probably John who was asked to collect the poor money, 17 Dec. 1601.[3]

Trevor augmented his official salaries with the profits of various ventures of his own, and charges of fraud were brought against him in 1608. He resisted a proposed inquiry into naval administration, 1613, and was himself among those appointed to inquire into abuses in the navy in 1626.[4]

He enjoyed a cut from the lord admiral's farm of sweet wines, and another from the farm of the duty on Newcastle coals. His income exposed him to government demands for loans in his later years. By 1621 he had attached himself to the 3rd Earl of Pembroke, who provided him with Cornish borough seats in Parliament. Three of his children were buried in Weybridge church between 1590 and 1605. Trevor died at Plas Teg 2 Feb. 1630, and was buried in Hope church.[5]

[1] *DWB*; SP29/80/59; *Suss. N. and Q.* xv. 339. [2] Lansd. 133, f. 25; *CSP Dom.* 1598–1601, p. 14; 1603–10, pp. 13, 52; *APC*, xxv. 54; SP14/60; pat. rolls 1598; LC 2/4/4 [3] PCC 64 Leicester; *HMC Hatfield*, iv. 292; xi. 572; D'Ewes, 478, 481, 673, 674, 687; *Trans. Cymmrod. Soc.* (1942), 32–3. [4] Lansd. 144, f. 497; 151, f. 151; *HMC Hatfield*, xi. 449; xviii. 40; M. Oppenheim, *Admin. of Royal Navy*, 149, 192; *HMC Cowper*, i. 41; *CSP Dom.* 1603–10, p. 409; 1625–6, p. 494; *Cal. Salusbury Corresp.* ed. Smith, 141; *Trans. Cymmrod. Soc.* (1974/5), 77–102. [5] *CSP Dom.* 1628–9, p. 475; *APC*, 1618–19, p. 222; *Surr. Arch. Colls.* xvii. 80; *HMC Sackville*, i. 90, 175; Manning and Bray, *Surr.* ii. 790.

H.G.O.

TREVOR, Sir Richard (1558–1638), of Trevalyn, Denb.

BLETCHINGLEY	1597*

b. 1558, 1st s. of John Trevor of Trevalyn by Mary, da. of Sir George Brydges of London: bro. of John* and Thomas*. *m.* Katherine, da. of Roger Puleston of Emral, 4da. *suc.* fa. 1589. Kntd. 1597.[1]

Capt. Denb. musters in Ireland 1595–8; dep. lt. Denb. 1595–1601, 1603; v.-adm. N. Wales c.1596–1626; member, council in the marches of Wales 1601; gov. Newry c.1634.[2]

Trevor inherited the substantial estate of Trevalyn and an influential connexion from his father, a servant of the Sackvilles. His marriage linked him with the Pulestons of Emral and together they constituted a powerful interest in east Denbighshire opposed to the Salusburys of Lleweni and their allies. The rivalry between the two factions came to a head in the contested county election of 1588. Trevor wished to stand for election in opposition to William Almer* of Pant Iocyn, who stood with Lleweni backing. However, Trevor's faction had another candidate in John Edwards II* of Chirk, and in the event Trevor, who had not yet succeeded to his estates, stood down in favour of Edwards.

For much of the period 1595–8 Trevor was on active

service in Ireland, where he was knighted by the lord deputy. At home, the 2nd Earl of Pembroke recommended him for the deputy lieutenancy of his county, an appointment which lapsed on the Earl's death. He owed his appointment as vice-admiral of North Wales in 1596 to his brother John's connexions with Charles Howard I*, the lord admiral. In 1597 he was brought in at a by-election for Howard's borough of Bletchingley, where John already had a seat. Meanwhile another brother, Sackville, was serving in Ireland with the Earl of Essex, who had a large following in Denbighshire, including many of the anti-Salusbury faction. It is not known how involved Sir Richard Trevor became with the group of malcontents surrounding Essex – although he had been engaged in pressing men for Essex in Ireland, he was certainly not implicated in the rising of 1601 – but in the contested election of that year in which he was a candidate, he represented Essex's followers against the rising star of Lleweni, Sir John Salusbury*.

In the Star Chamber cases which followed the turbulent 1601 county election at Wrexham, Trevor was charged with rigging the latest musters for Ireland for electioneering purposes, and encouraging his supporters, the Lloyds of Bodidris, the Breretons of Borras, the Salesburys of Rûg, to come to the election with bands of armed men. Owing to the disorder, the election was postponed until three days before Parliament ended, when Salusbury was elected.

With his rival Sir John Salusbury in ascendancy in Denbighshire, Trevor returned to Ireland in 1603 where he commanded a Newry garrison until 1606, retiring with testimonials from Ellesmere, the lord chancellor ('a gentleman whom I love and respect') and an annuity of £50. Although he retained his interest in Ireland – he returned in 1634 to assume his short-lived governorship of Newry and the counties of Down and Armagh – most of his remaining life was taken up with county administration in Denbighshire and the consolidation of his estates there, which involved him in frequent litigation in the Exchequer and Star Chamber courts. His will, drawn up two years before his death, made his nephew, Sir John Trevor†, the heir to Trevalyn and the bulk of his estates. The executrix was Trevor's daughter Magdalene, who had married into the Bagnall family of Plas Newydd, Anglesey.[3]

[1] Dwnn, *Vis. Wales*, ii. 354; *EHR*, lix. 349; PCC 64 Leicester, 8 Coventry. [2] *DWB*; SP14 1/22; Cardiff Lib. ms 4, 609; *CSP Ire.* 1592–6, pp. 313, 318; *Cal. Carew Pprs.* iii. 231, 252, 259; *APC*, xxv. 17. [3] Neale, *Commons*, 119–28; P. H. Williams, *Council in the Marches of Wales*, 122, 285, 288, 297; Lansd. 133, f. 25; *APC*, xxviii. 524, 617; xxx. 216; xxxii. 342, 374; 1613–14, p. 274; *EHR*, lxxv. 708; *HMC Hatfield*, vi. 559; xi. 445, 460, 489; *CSP Ire.* 1603–6, pp. 90, 196, 454, 541; 1606–8, p. 11; 1615–25, p. 12; *CSP Dom.* 1603–10, p. 441; *Exchequer Proc. Jas. I*, ed. T. I. J. Jones (Univ. Wales Bd. of Celtic Studies, Hist. and Law ser. xv), 64, 77, 79, 148, 161; *Cal. Wynn Pprs.* nos. 541, 543, 553, 638; PCC 8 Coventry.

H.G.O.

TREVOR, Thomas (c.1573–1656), of Trevalyn, Denb.; London; Enfield, Mdx.; and Leamington Hastings, Warws.

TREGONY	1601
HARWICH	1604*
NEWPORT IUXTA LAUNCESTON	1614
SALTASH	1621, 1624

b. c.1573, 5th and yst. s. of John Trevor of Trevalyn by Mary, da. of Sir George Brydges of London; bro. of John* and Sir Richard*. *educ.* Shrewsbury 1581; Clifford's Inn; I. Temple 1593, called 1603. *m.* (1) Prudence (*d.*1615), da. of Henry Butler, 1s.; (2) Frances (*d.*1625), da. and h. of Daniel Blennerhasset of Norf., *s.p.*; (3) Ellen (*d.*1654), da. of one Poyntell, wid. of Edward Allen, alderman of London, *s.p.* Kntd. 1619.[1]

Jt. steward of Windsor castle 1605; auditor, I. Temple 1614, 1616, bencher May 1617, summer vacation reader 1620; solicitor-gen. to Prince Charles by 1611; serjeant-at-law 1625; baron of the Exchequer 1625–49; member, ct. of high commission.[2]

Trevor's father made precise provision in his will for his education and he was to be 'ordered' by Robert Sackville*, Lord Buckhurst's heir. While Trevor was at the Inner Temple two of his brothers entered the service of Charles Howard I*, the lord admiral, and Trevor himself followed their example, certainly by October 1604. Meanwhile, in 1601 he had been returned to Parliament for Tregony through the influence of his brother John's wife's family, the Trevanions. It was probably John who was the Mr. Trevor mentioned in the journals of this Parliament.[3]

Though a contemporary held Trevor to be 'no great lawyer', he served as a judge throughout Charles's reign, achieving some notoriety for his defence of ship money and for his condemnation of John Hampden†, a relative, for refusing to pay it. He resigned from the bench after the King's execution and retired to his estate at Leamington Hastings, where he died, aged about 84, 21 Dec. 1656, having outlived his three wives. His only son and heir, Thomas, also represented Tregony in Parliament, and was created a baronet, the title dying with him.[4]

[1] *DNB*; *DWB*; E. Jones, *Trevors of Trevalyn*, 55–63 and ped. at end; *Trans. Cymmrod Soc.* 1937, p. 165n; *Arch. Camb.* (ser. 2), v. 100; PCC 211 Alchin. [2] *I.T. Recs.* ii. passim; Add. 33378, f. 74. [3] J. Whitelocke, *Liber Famelicus* (Cam. Soc. lxx), 103; PCC 64 Leicester; *EHR*, lix. 360; *HMC Hatfield*, xvi. 335; xvii. 347. [4] PCC 8 Ruthen; Dugdale, *Warws.* i. 318–19.

M.R.P.

TREWE, Andrew (*d.*1604), of York.

YORK	1593

s. of Richard Trewe, cordwainer, of York by his w. Jennet. *m.* 15 Nov. 1556, Jane, da. of Oswin Edwyne of York, 1s. 2da.

Freeman, York c.1556, chamberlain 1566–7, sheriff 1568–9, alderman 1581, ld. mayor 1585–6; high commr. prov. of York 1599.

Trewe was a mercer and merchant adventurer who traded through the Sound to the Baltic. His propery was probably all within the city boundaries. He leased the castle mills from the corporation, and in 1589 was granted the lease of another tenement. In 1574 and 1582 he purchased a number of houses in York. When, in 1579, a charter was granted to London's Eastland merchants, he was chosen to go there to resolve disputes. He was of moderate wealth, being put down for £20 in the Queen's loan of 1590. As a draper he was a natural choice to view the city's cloth to determine its selling price. At a council meeting in 1570 the opinion was 'that the cloths made for this city [are appraised] too high in value'. Trewe and another merchant offered to buy them at this price; the offer was accepted, and both failed to pay on the appointed days. In 1593 the York MPs were put on Commons committees concerned with cloth (14 Mar.), kerseys (23 Mar.), weirs (28 Mar.), maimed soldiers (2 Apr.) and spinners and weavers (3 Apr.).

Trewe's was one of the few deaths in All Saints Pavement, York in late 1604 not attributed to plague. He was buried there 29 Nov., the administration of his estate being granted to his widow, Jane, the following 29 Apr. The heir was his son William.

York City Lib., Skaife mss; *HMC Hatfield*, ix. 397; *York Freemen* (Surtees Soc. xcvi), 242, 276; (cii), 7, 26; *York Mercers* (Surtees Soc. cxxix), 195–6, 201–5, 213; J. J. Cartwright, *Chapters in Yorks. Hist.* 372–4; *York Civic Recs.* passim; York house bks. 30, ff. 64, 67–8, 113, 209, 378; 31, ff. 2, 14, 297; 32, f. 106; chamberlain's accts.; D'Ewes, 501, 507, 512, 513, 514; *Yorks. Fines* (Yorks. Arch. Soc. rec. ser. v), 49, 184; *Par. Reg. All Saints Pavement, York* (Yorks. Par. Reg. Soc. c), 111.

A.M.M.

TROTT, Nicholas (*d.*1636), of Gray's Inn, later of Quickswood in Clothill or Clothall, Herts. and Eaton Bray, Beds.

BRAMBER   1597

1st s. of Edward Trott of Yorks. by his w. Elizabeth Parke. *educ.* Peterhouse, Camb. 1567; BA Clare 1571; G. Inn 1573, called 1584. *m.* 1602, Mary, da. of Sir George Perient of Ayot St. Peter, Herts., 3da. Kntd. 1619.
    Sheriff, Herts. 1608–9; master in Chancery by 1619–25.[1]

Electoral patronage at Bramber, after the death of the Duke of Norfolk in 1572, is obscure. One Member – in 1597 Trott's colleague William Comber – was generally a local man, but apart from the fact that the borough often elected a lawyer (between 1572 and 1597 at least two Inner Templars and three from Gray's Inn) it is difficult to find any consistent pattern for the 'outsiders'.

Trott of Quickswood, who had a distinguished career at Gray's Inn, becoming one of the 'great society' there in 1589, seems to have had powerful friends. In 1595 his unsuccessful application for the post of deputy secretary of the council in the north was sponsored by the Earl of Essex, perhaps at the instigation of Francis Bacon*, who was a personal friend of Trott, and borrowed large sums of money from him. In 1594, as the debt was growing uncomfortably large, Bacon had suggested parting with his reversion of the clerkship of the Star Chamber to Trott, but the transaction does not seem to have been carried out, and by 1601 Trott was pressing for a settlement of the debt. Bacon was forced to mortgage Twickenham park to his creditor, promising right of entry if the debt had not been paid by the end of the year. After intervention on Bacon's behalf by Henry Maynard* and Michael Hickes*, the lord treasurer made an award of £1,800 to Trott, who presumably received the money, or most of it, before the mortgage of Twickenham park could become effective. Still, in 1597, however uneasy Trott may have been, the financial position between the two men was not causing open friction, and Bacon may have used his influence to find a parliamentary patron for his friend. At this time Bacon and the Earl of Essex were on terms of intimacy, and although no other connexion between the Earl and the borough of Bramber has been discovered, it seems at least possible that Trott owed his seat to Essex, who in 1597 made a great effort to influence elections in many parts of the country. In any case some court patron, if not Essex, perhaps Lord Buckhurst, was presumably involved.[2]

Only scattered references to Trott's private life survive. His wedding in June 1602 was mentioned by the letter-writer John Chamberlain, who described the bride as 'a lusty tall wench, able to beat two of him'. Since Trott was about 50 at the time, this may have been his second marriage, but no reference to an earlier one has been found. His father-in-law Sir George Perient held property at Clothill (?Clothall), and in 1604, after Bottelea, one of the manors there, had been formally surrendered to the Crown by Perient, it was granted to agents acting for Trott, who sold it in 1617 to William Cecil†, Earl of Salisbury. Trott also acquired property at Eaton Bray, and in 1605 he or a namesake was granted lands in Carmarthenshire.[3]

He died in November 1636, being buried on the 19th at Eaton Bray. An epitaph by one Edmund Cook is on the fly-leaf of an old precedent book said to have belonged to Trott himself:

Hark what the honest lawyer saith; one see
Content with his own lot; no scraping fee.
When will one gownman that's now left alive
Refuse what he resigned in twenty-five?

Lo, here what once was laid: now seemeth not
The body of good old Sir Nicholas Trott,
On's own accord through honesty and grace
That did resign a Chancery's master's place.

A list drawn up in 1668 of 'gentlemen that have sold their estates, and are quite gone out of Bedfordshire within less than the space of 50 years' includes Trott's name.

However, it seems likely that he still held property there at the time of his death, since he was buried at Eaton. He made his will in October 1634 and it was proved by his widow and executrix on 3 Feb. 1637.[4]

[1] *Vis. London* (Harl. Soc. xvii), 297; *G. Inn Pens. Bk.* i. 63; *VCH Herts.* iii. 64, 223, 225; *Misc. Gen. et Her.* n.s. iv. 259; F. A. Blaydes, *Gen. Beds.* 98; PCC 24 Soame; *Beds. N. and Q.* i. 327–8. [2] *G. Inn Pens. Bk.* i. 83; *CSP Dom.* 1595–7, p. 49; Spedding, *Bacon*, i. 248, 259, 300, 323; iii. 40–4; vi. 114–15; Birch, *Mems.* ii. 354–7. [3] *Chamberlain Letters* ed. McClure, i. 154; *VCH Herts.* iii. 223, 225; *CSP Dom.* 1603–10, p. 204. [4] *Gen. Beds.* 98; *Beds. N. and Q.* i. 327–8; *Vis. Mdx. 1663*, ed. Foster, 59; *Vis. Beds.* (Harl. Soc. xix), 207; PCC 34 Goare.

N.M.F.

TROUGHTON, Nicholas, of Great Linford, Bucks.

QUEENBOROUGH   1601

2nd s. of Christopher Troughton of Great Linford by Isabel, da. of Nicholas Bristow of Ayot St. Lawrence, Herts. *m.* (1) Isabel, da. of Thomas Ardes of Sherington, 2s.; (2) Anne, da. of Thomas Belgrave of North Kelworth, Leics., 5s. 3da.; (3) Anne, da. of Simon Bradbury of Wicken Bonhunt, Essex.

The identification of Nicholas Troughton of Great Linford as the 1601 Queenborough MP is based only on the fact that no other likely candidate has been found. Troughton's father, a younger brother of the head of the family, may have been a servant of (Sir) William Cecil* in Edward VI's reign. His mother's father was a clerk of the jewel house to four sovereigns and owned estates in Hertfordshire. None of Troughton's three wives was an heiress. He himself had some sort of clerkship in Chancery. No connexion with Queenborough has been discovered. The blank return was presumably completed according to the instructions of Sir Edward Hoby*, constable of Queenborough castle, on his own behalf or for a friend at court.

Vis. Bucks. (Harl. Soc. lviii), 217–18; *VCH Bucks.* iv. 353, 363, 366, 391; *VCH Herts.* iii. 60 n.44; Clutterbuck, *Herts.* i. 519; Nichols, *Leics.* iv. 201; *CSP Dom.* 1547–80, p. 7; C219/34.

M.R.P.

TRUSLOVE, John (*b.* c.1540), of Beverley, Yorks.

BEVERLEY   1589

b. c.1540.

A 'governor' of Beverley 1575–95, mayor 1586, 1590, 1593, j.p. Jan.–Oct. 1592, Jan.–Sept. 1595.

Truslove's parentage has not been traced. His father, however, was probably of Beverley, where the Trusloves were established from at least the beginning of the sixteenth century. A cadet branch in Wiltshire, described in the heralds' visitation as descended from the Beverley Trusloves, had settled at Avebury before the dissolution.

From 1578, when he was elected one of three new governors or aldermen of the town, Truslove was among its most prominent and active officials. He was deprived of

his municipal offices in 1595, presumably as a result of his quarrel with the corporation over his claims for expenses incurred on behalf of the town. His story was that as a 'governor' he had successfully undertaken several suits for the town at court, resulting in grants to the town of lands and annuities, and that he was out of pocket over lawsuits he had pursued for the corporation. Perhaps he left Beverley. In the Chancery action he brought against the corporation in 1595 he was described as of London.

E134/37–38 Eliz. Mich. 7 York; *Beverley Recs.* (Yorks. Arch. Soc. rec. ser. lxxxiv), passim; G. Oliver, *Hist. Beverley*, 393; *Vis Wilts.* (Harl. Soc. cv, cvi), 198–9; *Wilts. N. and Q.* viii. 215–16; C2 Eliz. T3/46.

B.D.

TUCKER, Hugh (c.1537–c.86), of Salisbury, Wilts.

SALISBURY   1572

b. c.1537, prob. 2nd s. of Robert Tucker of Exeter by Jane, da. of Thomas Palmer of Devon. *m.* bef. 1561, Elizabeth. *educ.* prob. M. Temple bef. 1555.

Tucker's 1576 subsidy assessment for goods in Salisbury was £7. He had also land outside the city. On 21 Apr. 1572 the Salisbury council met and elected Tucker and Giles Estcourt as burgesses for the Parliament. It appears that one of them was chosen on the recommendation of the 2nd Earl of Pembroke, whose interference was resented by the council and it was resolved not to permit it in the future. As Estcourt was a local man, a member of the 24 and an MP on two previous occasions, it follows that it must have been Tucker who received Pembroke's support. The exact date of Tucker's death has not been ascertained, but the churchwardens' accounts for the parish of St. Edmund's, Salisbury, for 1585–6 include the receipt of 6s. 8d. for his grave within the church.

Vis. Wilts. (Harl. Soc. cv, cvi), 195; *CPR*, 1560–3, p. 73; *Churchwardens' Accts. of St. Edmund and St. Thomas, Sarum* (Wilts. Rec. Soc.), passim; *Two Taxation Lists* (Wilts. Arch. Soc. recs. br. x), 65; City of Salisbury mss D(34), f. 22v; Hoare, *Wilts.* Salisbury, 285; *VCH Wilts.* v. 113.

W.J.J.

TUFTON, Nicholas (1578–1631), of Hothfield, Kent.

PETERBOROUGH   1601
KENT   1624

bap. 19 Jan. 1578, 1st s. of Sir John Tufton of Hothfield by his 2nd w. Christian, da. and coh. of Sir Humphrey Browne of Ridley Hall, Terling, Essex. *educ.* Hart Hall, Oxf. 1591; L. Inn 1596. *m.* bef. 3 Sept. 1602, Frances, da. of Thomas Cecil*, 3s. 7da. Kntd. 1603; *suc.* fa. 1624; *cr.* Baron Tufton 1626, Earl of Thanet 1628.
    J.p. Kent temp. James I, dep. lt. 1611.

Tufton's connexion with the Cecils antedated his marriage into the family: a Tufton, probably Nicholas himself, accompanied Robert Cecil* on his mission to France in 1598, and very likely it was Cecil who brought

Tufton into Parliament for Peterborough in 1601. One or two letters from Tufton and his wife to Robert Cecil in subsequent years suggest that they may also have owed him some more material advancement. Tufton represented his own county in the Stuart period, his opponent at the election accusing him of holding Catholic views. His wife's high church sympathies led her to pay for the erection of an altar in Rainham church, Kent, during the period of Laudian influence. There is no evidence that Tufton's personal beliefs were other than moderate.

Tufton, now Earl of Thanet, died 1 July 1631.

CP; *Vis. Kent* (Harl. Soc. xlii), 119; *CSP Dom.* 1598–1601, p. 30; 1619–23, pp. 509, 609; *HMC Hatfield*, xii. 344; xviii. 307; *Arch. Cant.* xliii. 276; PCC 119 St. John.

S.M.T.

TURBRIDGE, John, of Dogfeilyn Llanrhudd, Denb.

DENBIGH BOROUGHS   1589

1st s. of Robert Turbridge, baron of the Exchequer, and particular sureyor of crown lands in North Wales, by Ann (or Jane), da. and coh. of Humphrey Dymock of Lleweni Green. *educ.* Shrewsbury 1577; Furnival's Inn; L. Inn 1582, called 1589. *m.* Margaret, da. and h. of John Lloyd of Llanbedr Dyffryn Clwyd, 2da.

The Turbridges had been settled in Ruthin for some generations before Robert Turbridge, the MP's father, established the family fortune by his appointment in 1562 (jointly with John Gwyn) to the surveyorship of crown lands in recognition of his 'constant diligence about the Queen's affairs in the said counties' – presumably in his capacity of baron of the North Wales Exchequer. Apart from the emoluments of the office, it put him in the way of acquiring during the next few years leases in the town of Ruthin and the crown wastes of Dyffryn Clwyd. He was on good terms with the powerful Wynns of Gwydir until his death, which must have occurred soon after 1607. He was later alleged to have served as 'agent' to the Earl of Leicester and Ellis Price* in their high-handed dealings with the North Wales gentry. Turbridge himself took no known part in public affairs apart from his membership of this one Parliament. He left no son to continue the line, but the succession was maintained through his younger brother Robert, who married into the Conways of Bodrhyddan. His descendants long retained their standing among the minor gentry of the vale of Clwyd, but they never again sat in Parliament.

Harl. 1971, f. 112; Dwnn, *Vis. Wales*, ii. 351; *CPR*, 1560–3, p. 299; *Cal. Wynn Pprs.* pp. 13, 14, 46–7, 66, 69, 71, 72, 284–5, 339; *Augmentations*, ed. Lewis and Davies (Univ. Wales Bd. of Celtic Studies, Hist. and Law ser. xiii), 387, 389; *Al. Ox.* i. 1512; *Trans. Denb. Hist. Soc.* x. 46.

A.H.D.

TURNER, John (d.1607), of Ham, Bletchingley, Surr.

BLETCHINGLEY   1601

s. of John Turner of Ham. *m.*, at least 2s. 4da.

The Turners had settled in Ham during the fourteenth century, and enjoyed a parliamentary link with Bletchingley dating back to Richard II's reign. Their 'considerable Elizabethan house' is thought to have been built by Turner himself in 1583. A decade later, his property in Bletchingley was valued at £6, and his Lingfield lands at £10. He held property from both the Howard and Stoughton families, and was, in 1600, an assistant mourner at the funeral of (Sir) William Howard*. Turner died in 1607, his heir and namesake being then 26.

Surr. Arch. Colls. v. 220; ix. 425; xiv. 46, 49; xxiv. 24; xxxi. 12; *Surr. Rec. Soc.* iii. 142, 272; iv. 79, 254; *Vis. Surr.* (Harl. Soc. xliii), 103, 228; U. Lambert, *Bletchingley*, ii. 429; C142/302/103; *VCH Surr.* iv. 260; Manning and Bray, *Surr.* ii. 273.

H.G.O.

TURNER, Peter (c.1542–1614), of London.

BRIDPORT   1584, 1586

b. c.1542, s. of William Turner† by Jane, da. of George Auder, alderman of Cambridge. She *m.* (2) Richard Cox, bp. of Ely. *educ.* St. John's, Camb. 1564; MD Heidelberg 1571; incorp. Camb. 1575, Oxf 1599; lic. R. Coll. Physicians 1582. *m.* Pascha, da. of Henry Parry, chancellor of Salisbury cathedral, sis. of Henry Parry, bp. of Worcester, at least 4s. 2da. *suc.* fa. 1568.

Physician at St. Bartholomew's hospital 1581–5.[1]

Turner's father was a religious radical, author of anti-Catholic tracts, and a botanist who travelled extensively on the Continent during the last years of Henry VIII's reign. Returning to England on the accession of Edward VI, he became chaplain to the Duke of Somerset, and subsequently dean of Wells, a position lost under Mary, when Turner and his family returned to the Continent. At the beginning of Elizabeth's reign he was influential in the propagation of near-presbyterian principles. The Elizabethan settlement naturally failed to satisfy him, and he circulated tracts against vestments.[2]

Turner himself received tuition in both his father's disciplines, eventually choosing medicine, but it is his religious views that make him of particular interest as an MP. In 1584 he probably gained his seat at Bridport through the influence of the 2nd Earl of Bedford, and in 1586, after the Earl's death, through the Earl of Warwick, both puritan sympathizers. In the 1584 Parliament he was appointed to the committee for the better observing of the Sabbath day, 27 Nov. At this time the moderate puritans were hoping to gain some measure of reform by the presentation of petitions to Parliament from the individual counties. On 14 Dec. 1584 a number of these petitions had been heard and favourably received, when Turner – the representative of a more extreme wing of the party – called for a Bill and Book to be read, which he had previously deposited with the clerk of the House. The bill, which had been 'framed by certain godly and learned ministers', would have had the effect of replacing the prayer book then in use by the Genevan *Form of Prayers*, a new edition of which had only recently been issued in London, and would have set up a presbyterian system of ministers and elders in the church. Turner's motion was received coldly, and after both Sir Francis Knollys and Sir Christopher Hatton had spoken in opposition, and there had been no reply in support of the motion, it was agreed that the Bill and Book should not be read. In the following Parliament the extreme puritans were better organized, although Turner, on this occasion, played only a minor role. The Bill and Book introduced by Cope received a considerable amount of organized support, but Turner, so far as is known, spoke neither in the debate on the Bill and Book, nor in the more general debate on religion that took place on the following day. He showed his solidarity with his fellow puritans, however, when, on 6 Mar. 1587, he moved 'for the liberty of the gentlemen committed to the Tower' for their outspokenness in these debates, 'pleading the liberties of the House'. Earlier in this Parliament Turner had joined the general outcry against Mary Queen of Scots, desiring her execution and stronger laws against papists:

Her Majesty's safety cannot be sufficiently provided for by the speedy cutting off of the Queen of Scots, unless some good means be had withal for the rooting out of Papistry, either by making some good new laws for that purpose, or else by the good and due execution of the laws already in force ... so concluding in his own conscience that no Papist can be a good subject.

He offered a bill to the House to this purpose, asking that it should be read. The Speaker side-stepped the issue by pointing out that as the bill was concerned with the Queen's safety, it should be referred to the committee already discussing the subject. After several speeches this was agreed, and no more was heard of the bill. Later in the same Parliament Turner continued his attack on the papists, desiring 'that by some token they may be known'.[3]

As a physician Turner had a number of important patients, receiving a bequest as 'my physician' under the will of Sir Roger North*, 2nd Lord North, whose family had strong puritan sympathies. He was also physician to Henry Brooke II*, 11th Lord Cobham, and attended Sir Walter Ralegh when he was in the Tower. His list of publications did not equal his father's. He was probably the author of 'A Spiritual Song of Praise' appended to Oliver Pig's *Meditations*, published in 1589, and he also wrote a pamphlet entitled, *The Opinion of Peter Turner Dr. in Physicke, concerning Amulets, or Plague Cakes*, which was published in 1603. His opinion was that they could be valuable in assisting recovery, but 'accursed be he that putteth his whole confidence in secondary means, for it is

neither herb nor salve, nor anything like that healeth, but only the blessing of the head physician'.[4]

Turner died 27 May 1614 and was buried on the following day in St. Olave's, Hart Street, where a monument was erected to him. In his nuncupative will, Turner left the responsibility for raising portions for his younger children to his brother-in-law, Henry Parry, bishop of Worcester, and Thomas Emerson. The widow, Pascha, was granted administration of his estate on 28 July 1614.[5]

[1] A. Povah, *Annals of the Parishes of St. Olave Hart Street and Allhallows Staining*, 80; *DNB* (Turner, Peter; Turner, William); W. Munk, *Roll of Royal Coll. of Physicians*, i. 84; PCC 87 Lawe; N. Moore, *Hist. St. Bartholomew's Hospital*, ii. 427–31. [2] *DNB*; Collinson thesis, 44, n 1, 81; Strype, *Parker*, i. 301. [3] PCC 14 Babington; Roberts thesis, 89; D'Ewes, 333, 339, 395; Collinson, 528–30; Neale, *Parlts*. ii. 61–2, 112, 148–56, 162, 176. [4] Roberts, 89, n. 3; *Coll. Top. et Gen*. vi. 99; *HMC Hatfield*, x. 77; xvii. 444; *DNB*. [5] Povah, 80; PCC 87 Lawe.

A.M.M.

TURNER, Robert

DOWNTON	1597
OLD SARUM	1601

Turner, presumably brought into Parliament in 1597 and 1601 by the 2nd and 3rd Earls of Pembroke respectively, has not been identified. He may have been the Robert Turner who served as steward for Christmas at Lincoln's Inn 1595. No man of this name appears on any inn of court admission register, but one graduated from Trinity Hall, Cambridge, in 1571, became LLB in 1578, and remained a fellow of the college from 1577 to 1634.[1]

Alternatively, he may have been a relative of Dr. Peter Turner*, who married a daughter of Henry Parry, chancellor of Salisbury cathedral. Parry's nephew and executor, Anthony Parry, was one of the five free tenants of Old Sarum who witnessed the return of Robert Turner for the borough in 1601.[2]

[1] *Black Bk. L. Inn*, ii. 44; *Al. Cant*. i(4), p. 276. [2] Le Neve, *Fasti*, ii. 651–2; PCC 12 Daper, 37 Harte; *HMC Hatfield*, xv. 386; xvi. 457–8.

N.M.F.

TURNER, Thomas I, of Reading, Berks.

READING 1559

Jt. constable, Reading (with Thomas Aldworth I*) 1544–5, 1556–7, 1560–1, 1567–8.

Turner leased from Reading corporation a house in Cheese Row, Reading High Street, where he was living by 1540. He may have been the Thomas Turner who in 1547, with his wife Margaret, paid a 6s. 8d. fine in the hanaper for illegally quit-claiming 150 acres of land in Hampstead Norris, Berkshire to William Mathew. He held a minor borough office in 1535, and his career continued through the religious changes of four reigns. He received wages from the town on the only occasion he sat in Parliament. He may have died as late as 1593, when letters of administration were granted to Richard, brother of Thomas Turner of Reading. But probably this was a son or other relative of the MP.

Reading Recs. i. pp. xli–xlv, 187, 257, 258; *CPR*, 1547–8, pp. 3–4; *LP Hen. VIII*, xv. 168; *HMC 11th Rep. VII*, 208; PCC admon. act bk. 1593, f. 71.

N.M.F.

TURNER, Thomas II (*d.* c.1586), of Bath, Som.

BATH   1563

Alderman, Bath, mayor 1575–6.

Nothing has been ascertained about Turner's parentage or domestic life. By the early years of Elizabeth's reign he was a citizen of Bath, sometimes employed to carry out 'writing' for the town. The chamberlains' accounts contain a number of payments to him for this purpose. He may have been a grocer (on at least one occasion the town bought pepper from him), or a builder (he regularly asked for payment for the carriage of earth or other materials for work on new houses or on the baths). In June 1576 he received his mayoral salary of £40. By this time he held considerable property in Bath, and was paying rent to the corporation for houses in Vicars Lane and elsewhere. In 1578 his total bill for leases was £2 6s. 8d. – an amount repeated in the following two years' accounts under the heading 'rents withholden'. Part of his debt was for fishing rights, and like other prominent citizens he had a private door into the King's bath, one of the three large ones in the city: for this privilege he paid 5s. a year. By 1581 he had considerably increased his property, and owed the town, among other obligations, £5 'for the fine of his two houses', and £10 for a 'Bath chamber'.

He died either at the end of 1585, or early the next year, when 'the house which was Mr. Turner's' was leased to another man.

Bath Chamberlains' Accts. (Som. Rec. Soc. xxxviii), passim.

N.M.F.

TURPIN, Anthony

CAMELFORD   1601, 1604

No Anthony has been found among the Turpins of Leicestershire or Huntingdon or amongst those who were merchants of London. The will of an Anthony Turpin of Thorverton in Devon was proved in the archdeaconry court of Exeter in 1647, the only instance of the name that has so far emerged. The man concerned probably belonged to the family of Turpin, settled principally at Ottery St. Mary and Woodbury. No pedigree appears in the heralds' visitation and none of these Turpins was a

justice of the peace. But it is not impossible that a man of such a family – Anthony Turpin of Thorverton or some other – should become an official of the duchy of Cornwall, and so be returned for Camelford. Turpin sat twice for the borough, so his association with the place was evidently more than casual.

Cal. Devon and Cornw. Wills 1540–1799 (Brit. Rec. Soc. Index Lib. xxxv). i. 613; Vivian, *Vis. Devon*, 167, 586, 741, 790, 810; PCC 8 Watson, 37 Huddleston.

I.C.

TURPIN, George (1529–83), of Knaptoft, Leics. and of London.

LEICESTERSHIRE   1554 (Nov.), 1563, 1572

b. 1529, posth. s. of John Turpin of Knaptoft (*d.* 13 Jan. 1529) by Rose, da. of Richard Ruthall of Moulsoe, Bucks. *m.* Frances, da. of Sir Robert Lane* of Horton, Northants., 1s. William* 1da. *suc.* bro. 1551. Kntd. 21 Aug. 1566.
    J.p. Leics. from c.1559, steward, crown lands 1561–9; sheriff, Warws. and Leics. 1565–6, Leics. 1574–5; commr. eccles. causes, dioceses of Lincoln and Peterborough 1571, Lincoln 1575; commr. musters, Leicester 1577, 1580.

The Turpins migrated from Northumberland to Leicestershire during the fifteenth century when they acquired Knaptoft through marriage into the Paynell family. Turpin engaged in a number of land transactions, selling the rectory of Norton in 1559, and acquiring Thornton, Warwickshire from Thomas Nevill in 1562. Two years later he bought the manor of Withybrook, Warwickshire, from Thomas Broome, and sold it to John Grey in 1574. In 1562, together with Nicholas Beaumont*, he leased the manor of Stoughton from Thomas Farnham*, over the supervision of whose will they later quarrelled. Turpin accused Beaumont of breaking the trust reposed in him as overseer, and the matter reached a head in 1570 with a dispute as to which of them might occupy Stoughton.

As it happened Turpin and Beaumont were both in the 1563 and 1572 Parliaments as knights of their shires. Turpin sat on the succession committee, 31 Oct. 1566, and was one of 30 MPs summoned from the Commons on 5 Nov. 1566 to hear the Queen's message on the succession. He also sat on committees concerning private interests (22 May, 2 June 1572), the subsidy (10 Feb. 1576), wool (23 Feb. 1581) and the Queen's safety (14 Mar. 1581). He was put in charge of the Leicester civic lottery in 1570 and undertook a number of duties in the county. He died intestate in 1583.

Vis. Leics. (Harl. Soc. ii), 31; Nichols, *Leics.* iii. 775; iv. 218, 225; *CPR*, 1553, p. 377; 1558–60, pp. 141–2, 278–9; 1563–6, p. 138; *VCH Warws.* v. 80; vi. 265; Somerville, *Duchy*, i. 573; *CSP Dom. Add.* 1566–79, p. 338; G. F. Farnham, *Quorndon Recs.* 225, 238, 353–5;

D'Ewes, 127, 213, 221, 247, 300, 306; Camb. Univ. Lib. Gg.iii. 34, p. 209; *Leicester Recs.* iii. 115, 125, 131, 133, 137, 140, 152, 160; Lansd. 8, ff. 77–8; PCC admon. act bk. 1583, f. 76.

W.J.J.

TURPIN, John (d. ?1591), of Huntingdon.

HUNTINGDON 1572

m. Elizabeth, prob. at least 2s.
Bailiff, Huntingdon 1574.

Little is known about this Member. The town records of Huntingdon and other local sources contain the name from the middle years of the sixteenth century until the reign of Charles I. While this span of time suggests that more than one John Turpin lived there – perhaps father and son – it is impossible to differentiate between them. Unfortunately no pedigrees have survived to clear up the problem, which is further complicated by the abundance of Turpin families in the east Midlands during the years in question.

It is likely that the Member for Huntingdon in 1572 was the John Turpin who died intestate in or just before 1591. He was evidently a prominent man in the town and an active participant in its civic life, serving as bailiff on at least one occasion. If Turpin died in 1591 it is most unlikely that he was the man who entered Lincoln's Inn in 1520, but no doubt he would be the person whom the bishop of Lincoln described as 'earnest in religion' in 1564, when he was an 'ancient' of the borough. This favourable report, however, does not appear to have resulted in a place on the list of local justices. As a bailiff of Huntingdon in 1574 he was sued, with his colleague, in the duchy court over the claim of the adjoining borough of Godmanchester to exemption from tolls imposed by the county town. In 1588 he was one of those summoned to defend the county against Catholic uprising or foreign invasion.

Whatever his profession Turpin's fortunes seem to have prospered, for after 1574 he purchased several small plots of land in Huntingdon, usually with a house or barn attached. The only record of his selling land, in 1589–90, contains a reference to his wife Elizabeth, who died in 1604. Her family background is unknown. There may have been at least two sons of the marriage, the younger John, also prominent in Huntingdon, and Henry, who lived in Bassingbourne, Cambridgeshire. In his will, proved in 1618, the latter refers to his brother, John Turpin of Huntingdon, and leaves him a ring.

Hunts. Wills (Brit. Rec. Soc. Index Lib. xlii), 114, 150; *Cal. Feet of Fines, Hunts.* (Camb. Antiq. Soc. Pubs. oct. ser. xxxvii), 167, 180, 181, 197; E. Griffith, *Huntingdon Recs.* 101; *Cam. Misc.* ix(3), p. 29; DL1/104/K3; W. M. Noble, *Hunts. and the Armada*, 35, 46; Add. 34394, f. 14; PCC 193 Meade, 91 Skinner.

M.R.P.

TURPIN, William (c.1558–1617), of Knaptoft, Leics.

LEICESTERSHIRE 1589

b. c.1558, 1st s. of George Turpin* of Knaptoft by Frances, da. of Sir Robert Lane* of Horton, Northants. *m.* Elizabeth, da. of Sir Richard Fiennes† of Broughton Castle, Oxon., 3s. 4da. *suc.* fa. 1583. Kntd. 1603.
J.p. Leics. from c.1583, sheriff 1585–6, 1593–4, dep. lt. 1608.

On succeeding his father Turpin assumed the usual responsibilities of a country gentleman, including a turn as knight of the shire. His election for the county seat in 1588 may have had the support of the Hastings family. His contemporaries considered Turpin a lettered man well versed in the humanities, but as so often in this period, no trace of any formal education has been found. In 1599 his life was despaired of, but he survived another 18 years, continuing active in county affairs to the last. He died on 20 July 1617 and was buried with his ancestors. His estates had prospered and, with his acquisition of the freehold of Horninghold manor, their annual value reached nearly £1,000. He left his younger sons £400 apiece and his unmarried daughter £1,000.

Nichols, *Leics.* iv. 218, 225; *Leicester Recs.* iii. 227; iv. 76, 98; *APC*, xx. 179, 301; xxv. 216; xxx. 437; 1615–16, p. 281; *HMC Hatfield*, ix. 378; xiv. 148; xvi. 168; *CSP Dom.* 1603–10, p. 251; C142/367/99; *Cal. Pleadings Duchy of Lancaster*, ix. 213, 230, 333; ms cal. pat. rolls, 30–7 Eliz. PRO 34(8), p. 17; 37–43 Eliz. PRO 40(3) p. 6; PCC 106 Weldon.

S.M.T.

TWYNEHO, William (d.1594), of Windsor, Berks.

STAFFORD 1563

The 1563 Stafford MP, whose name is spelled Twynoe on the Crown Office list, was in all probability the William Twyneho who was an overseer of the will of William Paget†, 1st Lord Paget, who died on 18 June 1563, shortly after the end of the parliamentary session. Twyneho was descended from a namesake of Keyford, near Frome, Somerset, and died in 1594, asking to be buried at Windsor, and leaving a ring to Mr. William Paget. The Paget connexion would account for his return to Parliament for Stafford.

It was probably the same man who was ordered to keep a 'very secret' appointment with Thomas, 4th Lord Paget, in 1583.

J. C. Wedgwood, *Staffs. Parl. Hist.* (Wm. Salt Arch. Soc.), i. 355; *CSP Dom.* 1581–90, p. 128; PCC 15 Horne, 15 Blamyr, 27 Chayre, 72 Dixy; Hutchins, *Dorset*, 468, 471.

P.W.H.

TWYSDEN, William (1566–1629), of Roydon Hall, East Peckham, Kent.

CLITHEROE 1593
HELSTON 1601

THETFORD   1604,* 1614
WINCHELSEA   1628*

b. 4 Apr. 1566, 1st s. of Roger Twysden by Anne, da. of Sir Thomas Wyatt†. *educ.* Magdalene, Camb. 1580, BA 1583; G. Inn 1584. *m.* 1591, Anne, aged 16, da. of Moyle Finch* by Elizabeth, da. of Sir Thomas Heneage*, 5s. 2da. *suc.* fa. 1603. Kntd. 1603; *cr.* Bt. 1611.

Capt. of light horse, lathe of Aylesford, Kent 1601; gent. usher of privy chamber to James I.

The Twysdens had been seated in Kent since the thirteenth century, acquiring Roydon by marriage in the reign of Edward VI. Twysden himself was the grandson of Sir Thomas Wyatt, executed after the rising of 1554. It was not until 1601, when his father's health began to fail, that Twysden took any part in local affairs.

Twysden's marriage ceremony was performed by Dean Alexander Nowell of St. Paul's, at Heneage House, the London home of the bride's grandfather, Sir Thomas Heneage, vice-chamberlain and chancellor of the duchy. Thereafter Twysden spent much time at court under Heneage's aegis, and in 1597 he accompanied the 2nd Earl of Essex on the Islands voyage as a volunteer captain. Twysden owed his return to Parliament to his connexion with Heneage, who, in 1593 used his influence as chancellor of the duchy to obtain Twysden a seat at Clitheroe. By 1601 Heneage was dead, and Twysden sat for Helston, a borough where the Cecils sometimes nominated. In both these Parliaments he played the part of an onlooker, and on the latter occasion he kept a diary, of which only fragments remain. His son, Sir Roger†, the antiquary, wrote of the management of an estate, burdened by debt, and Sir William's passion for hunting and hawking, as well as of his life at court and his studies in Hebrew and divinity. But this part of his life belongs to the reigns of the first two Stuarts.

Vis. Kent (Harl. Soc. xlii), 135–6; *GEC Baronetage*, i. 74; J. R. Twisden, *Fam. of Twisden*, 106–7, 110, 117–26; Hasted, *Kent*, v. 96–7; G. S. Thomson, *Twysden Lieutenancy Pprs.* (Kent Arch. Soc. Recs. x), 113; H. S. Toy, *Helston*, 116, 495; Stowe 359, ff. 274–301; R. Twysden, *Govt. of England* (Cam. Soc. xlv), pp. xxviii–xxix.

I.C.

TYNDALE, Francis (1544–1631), of Cambridge, later of Pinner, Mdx.

MORPETH   1593

b. 1544, yr. s. of Sir Thomas Tyndale of Hockwold, Norf. by his 2nd w. Amy, da. of Sir Henry Farmer of Barsham, Norf. *educ.* Caius, Camb. 1561. *unm.*

After spending four years in the Farmer household at East Barsham, Tyndale went up to Cambridge, where he remained for most of his long life. Of his elder brothers, William inherited the Hockwold estates; John, a bencher of Lincoln's Inn, became a Chancery master; and

Humphrey became dean of Ely and president of Queens', Cambridge. In both capacities Humphrey used his influence to obtain Francis leases of estates. It is a little odd that so retiring a man as Francis Tyndale should have wished to attend Parliament. Perhaps there was some special reason, now lost to us, of importance to his family, to Queens' College, or to Henry Carey, 1st Baron Hunsdon who was presumably responsible for bringing him in. Hunsdon was regularly returning Members for Morpeth at this time, and was recorder of Cambridge.

Tyndale became one of two auditors of Queens' in 1611, and later removed to Pinner. He made his will in June 1626, leaving the college £40 to buy a basin and ewer, and £5 for its poor scholars. He died in 1631, aged, if the birth date is correct, 87. An inquisition post mortem shows that he had property in London, at Golding Lane and near Holborn bridge. The heir was his godson, Dean Tyndale, Francis's elder brother John's son.

Vis. Essex (Harl. Soc. xiii, xiv), 511; J. Venn, *Biog. Hist. Gonville and Caius*, i. passim; W. G. Searle, *Queens' College*, 366; C142/517/26.

B.D./P.W.H.

TYRWHITT, Sir Robert (by 1504–72), of Leighton Bromswold, Hunts.

LINCOLNSHIRE   1545
HUNTINGDONSHIRE   1554 (Apr.), 1559

b. by 1504, 2nd s. of Sir Robert Tyrwhitt (*d.*1548) of Kettleby, Lincs. by Maud, da. of Sir Robert Tailboys†, *de jure* 8th Lord Kyme, of Kyme, Lincs.; bro. of Philip†. *m.* (1) Bridget, da. and h. of Sir John Wiltshire of Stone Castle, Kent, wid. of Sir Richard Wingfield of Kimbolton, and Sir Nicholas Harvey† (*d.*1532) of Ickworth, Suff.; (2) by 1540, Elizabeth (*d.*1578), da. of Sir Goddard Oxenbridge of Brede, Suss., at least 1da. *d.v.p.* Kntd. 1543.

Esquire of the body by 1525; chamberlain, Berwick-upon-Tweed, Northumb. 13 Sept. 1525; j.p. Hunts. 1536, 1544, 1554–*d.*, Lincs. (Lindsey) 1538, Northants. 1554, Beds. 1559–*d.*; keeper, manor of Dytton, Bucks. 1536; sheriff, Lincs. 1540–1, Cambs. and Hunts. 1557–8; master of the hunt, Mortlake, Surr. 1540; gent. privy chamber by 1540; subsidy commr. Hunts. 1563, eccles. commr. diocese of Lincoln and Peterborough 1571; servant, household of Queen Catherine Parr July 1543–8, master of the horse by 1544, steward by 1547; constable, Kimbolton castle, Hunts. 1544; steward, duchy of Lancaster, Higham Ferrers, Northants. by 1546; steward, unknown property for Thomas, Baron Seymour of Sudeley by 1548; jt. ld. lt. Hunts. in 1551; numerous other minor offices.

By 1559 Tyrwhitt's active career was over, and he had retired to his estates, where, for the last 14 years of his life he lived as a Huntingdonshire country gentleman, an active justice of the peace, 'earnest in religion'. He died on 10 May 1572, and was buried at Leighton Bromswold, where there is a monument in the parish church to him, his wife and their daughter Katherine. Katherine had married Sir Henry Darcy*, and after her death in 1567 Tyrwhitt, 'being aged and not having nor being like to have' any more children, had demised Leighton Bromswold and other parts of his property to his son-in-law. His will, made in February and proved in June 1572, mentions also a London house. Tyrwhitt stipulated that he was to be buried 'without pomp or pride'. He left bequests to his son-in-law, his nephews Thomas Wingfield, Goddard Tyrwhitt and Robert Monson*, and to his 'especial good friend' Sir Walter Mildmay*, the executor.

LP Hen. VIII, passim; *Harl.* 890, f. 38; *Lincs. Peds.* (Harl. Soc. lii), 1019–10; *VCH Hunts.* iii. 86, 89, 91; *CPR*, 1547–8, p. 172; 1555–7, pp. 69–70; 1569–72, pp. 222, 277–8; R. P. Tyrwhitt, *Fam. Tyrwhitt*, 22; *APC*, iii. 259; iv. 49; *Cal. Feet of Fines, Hunts.* ed. Turner (Cambs. Antiq. Soc. Pubs. oct. ser. xxxvii), 138, 160; *Cam. Misc.* ix(3). p. 29; C142/87/22, 164/113; PCC 21 Daper.

N.M.F.

TYRWHITT, Tristram (c.1530–90), of Grainsby, Lincs.

HUNTINGDON	1571
DERBY	1572*
GREAT GRIMSBY	1586, 1589

b. c.1530, yr. s. of Sir William Tyrwhitt (*d.*1541), of Scotter, Lincs. (sheriff, Lincs. 1537) by Isabel, da. of William Girlington of Normanby, wid. of Christopher Kelke; bro. of Marmaduke† and Sir Robert†. *m.* Alice, da. of Sir William Skipwith† of Ormsby, Lincs., *d.s.p.*[1]

Gent. waiter to 2nd Earl of Rutland 1550; commr. sewers for E. Midland counties 1555; j.p. Lincs. (Lindsey) from c.1559, rem. by 1574, rest. by c.1586; camp-master to the Earl of Sussex's army 1569.[2]

At least six members of this family sat in Parliament during the Tudor period. Three of them, Robert, Tristram and Marmaduke, were the sons of Sir William Tyrwhitt of Scotter, who had held a prominent position in Lincolnshire affairs. Tristram Tyrwhitt was a soldier. He entered the service of Henry Manners, 2nd Earl of Rutland, and was campaigning with him in Scotland and the north in 1549 and 1550. In the latter year he was called 'gentleman waiter' to the Earl. Later, in 1557, he served with the Dudleys in Picardy, taking part in the battle of St. Quentin. By 1569 he had become camp-master in the army which the Earl of Sussex and Lord Clinton led against the northern rebels.[3]

Tyrwhitt owed his return for Huntingdon to his uncle, Sir Robert Tyrwhitt* of Leighton Bromswold, but his return for Derby is not easy to understand. Two explanations suggest themselves. Tyrwhitt's sister married Godfrey Foljambe† of Walton, and Marmaduke Tyrwhitt was an executor of the will of their son Godfrey*. This connexion may have introduced Tyrwhitt to Derby. Alternatively, the 6th Earl of Shrewsbury, who probably enjoyed influence in Derby, was married for many years to

Gertrude Manners, aunt of the 3rd Earl of Rutland at the time of the 1572 election, and may have found a seat there for one of Rutland's followers.[4]

About 1574 Tyrwhitt got into hot water. He was struck off the commission of the peace, forfeited his lands (though his wife was allowed to remain in residence), and possibly imprisoned. Nothing further is heard of him until he appears in Devon in November 1577, dedicating a treatise on the duties and office of a commander-in-chief to the Earl of Leicester, whom he hoped to accompany to the Netherlands.

Though he had some Catholic relations, and was described as 'indifferent in religion' in 1564, he appears in this work a puritan, with a belief in the justness of the Dutch revolt. He exhorted Leicester to

> step forward boldly, go on with what you have begun; the cause is just, it is honest, it is Godly. Be assured that, as the shadow follows the body, so eternal honour shall follow the revengers of the breach of common faith, the rescuers of the church, the saviours of the afflicted ... The Lord is so zealous of his elect, and of those who travail in his vineyard, that he does not only give them grace to perform his good purposes, but also does direct them, always by good means.

Tyrwhitt offered to spend his 'blood and life' at the Earl's feet, but there is no evidence that he saw further active service. Yet he must have re-established himself in order to be attached to Lord Hunsdon's force in the personal defence of the Queen. In October that year he brought home official letters from the English ambassador in Paris. He re-appeared on the Lincolnshire commission of the peace in the mid-1580s and was returned to Parliament again, for Great Grimsby, near his residence at Grainsby. His name does not occur in the known surviving records of any of his Parliaments.[5]

Tyrwhitt was buried at Grainsby 10 May 1590. Administration of his property was granted in the Lincoln consistory court that year.[6]

[1] *Lincs. Peds.* (Harl. Soc. lii), 1020; R. P. Tyrwhitt, *Fam. Tyrwhitt*, 28 seq. [2] *CPR*, 1554–5, p. 109; Lansd. 13, f. 48; 737, f. 145; 1218, f. 18; Egerton 2345, f. 20. [3] *HMC Rutland*, iv. 356, 358–9, 361, 363; Lansd. 13, f. 48; 207c, f. 398. [4] *Lincs. Peds.* 1020; J. C. Cox, *Derby Recs.* 138; *HMC Hatfield*, v. 392. [5] C193/32/9; Egerton 2345, f. 20; *APC*, viii. 286; Harl. 2326; *Cam. Misc.* ix(3), p. 27; Lansd. 53, f. 188; *HMC Foljambe*, 56; *APC*, xvi. 311. [6] *Admons. in Consistory Ct. of Lincoln, 1540–1659*, p. 138.

B.D.

TYSAR, John (by 1516–75), of Sandwich, Kent.

SANDWICH	1554 (Nov.), 1559

b. by 1516. *m.* Margaret, sis. of John Sulyard, at least 2s. 2da.

Constable of the 7th ward, Sandwich 1540–2, member of the common council (St. Peter's parish) 1542–7, (St. Clement's parish) 1547–8, (unknown parish) 1548–9, treasurer 1542–3, jurat 1549–75, mayor 1553–4, 1567–8, bailiff to Yarmouth 1556–7; brodhull rep. 13 times 1549–75; gov Sir Roger Manwood's sch., Sandwich 1563; speaker of the brotherhood 1568.

Tysar, like others of his family, was a grocer trading with the Continent. He was a canopy-bearer at Elizabeth's coronation, and represented Sandwich in her first Parliament. In August 1559 he was chosen to go to the court of Shepway for the installation of the new warden of the Cinque Ports, and during the following two years he went up to London several times over the matter of the harbour.

Tysar died between making his will 15 Apr. 1575 and December the same year, when his name was omitted from the list of jurats. On 6 Mar. 1579 the Privy Council ordered William Cromer* and others to inquire into the allegations of Tysar's widow, who was 'charged with many children', that she was being cheated over the payment of an £18 annuity. She had been appointed sole executrix of her husband's will, which left £20 or £30 legacies to each of the four children. She herself received her husband's shop and half his effects: the will also mentions a claim for compensation for loss of goods against the inhabitants of Newport, Flanders.

Vis. Kent (Harl. Soc. liv), 129; (lxxv), 59, 88; Sandwich old and new red bks., little black bk.; Cinque Ports white and black bks. passim; A. Hussey, *Kent Chantries* (Kent Arch. Soc. rec. br. xii), 260; Coke, *Institutes*, iv. 20; W. Boys, *Hist. Sandwich*, i. 414; *CPR, 1560–3*, p. 613; E122/131/8; PCC 45 Tirwhite; *APC*, xi. 64.

N.M.F.

UGHTRED, Henry (by 1534–aft. Oct. 1598), of Southampton and Ireland.

MARLBOROUGH	1584
GREAT BEDWYN	1589

b. by 1534, presumably s. of Sir Anthony Ughtred (*d.* 1534) by Elizabeth (*d. c.*1562), da. of Sir John Seymour† of Wolf Hall, Wilts., sis. of Edward Seymour, Duke of Somerset. *m.* Elizabeth, da. of Sir John Paulet, 2nd Marquess of Winchester, wid. of Sir William Courtenay†. Kntd. by lord deputy [I] 1593.[1]
    J.p. Hants 1575–*c.*1593, sheriff 1581–2, commr. musters *c.*1585, oyer and terminer and gaol delivery, Soton 1583; member, council of Munster 1587; capt. Netley castle, Hants bef. 1596.[2]

Ughtred pedigrees are confused and contradictory, but assuming that the parentage given above is correct, this Member was related to the Seymours, to Gregory Cromwell†, 1st Baron Cromwell (his mother's second husband) and to the Paulets. In 1554 his mother was married for the third time, to Sir John Paulet, later 2nd Marquess of Winchester, whose daughter married Ughtred himself. He obviously owed his parliamentary seats to the Seymour interest. His first cousin the Earl of

Hertford was lord of Marlborough, and at this period also dominated elections at Great Bedwyn, where Ughtred's co-Member in 1589 was another cousin, John Seymour. Ughtred served on a conference with the Lords concerned ostensibly with fraudulent conveyances but in fact with relations between the Lords and the Commons, 15 Feb. 1585. On 5 Mar. he was named to a Commons committee concerned with the poor law, and on 11 Mar. he was appointed, with his half-brother Thomas Cromwell and Sir William More, to examine a currier accused of making defamatory statements about the House's treatment of a bill concerning tanners. He spoke in the debate on the bill against rogues and vagabonds in this Parliament, maintaining that large sums were being laid out to little purpose on houses of correction. He opposed the return of vagabonds to their own parish, where they had to be supported by the inhabitants of 'poor villages and hamlets' who had 'already more of their own than they have work for'.

> Then if you will have him sent thither what shall he do there? If you have no house, you must build him one. Where? Upon the common. When he is in it, how shall he live? Put his head out at a hole and live like a chameleon off the air or burn him and the house together or else starve.

In the Parliament of 1589 Ughtred served on the subsidy committee, 11 Feb., and on 26 Feb. he spoke on the bill about captains and soldiers, serving also on the committee. The next day he was named to a conference with the Lords on the same lines as that of 15 Feb. 1585. This time the subject was the Queen's dislike of the purveyors bill.[3]

Ughtred was a shipowner, and knew that sailors who had been paid off after a voyage ran a serious risk of becoming unemployed and classed as vagabonds. In the early 1580s Southampton, where he lived for some time, had experience of this problem. Ships were sometimes left to rot in the harbour because the owners could not pay the cost of repairs. This was an old story; a novel twist to it was described in August 1582 when Henry Knollys II* informed Walsingham that a Breton ship he had brought into 'Hampton' had remained there for four years without being claimed. Knollys had then given her to Ughtred, who had no sooner had her repaired than the former owners demanded her back.

The embargo on sending ships to sea, following Philip II's acquisition of Portugal, would have involved Ughtred in serious loss had he not been allowed, 'in consideration of his great charges sustained in building of sundry ships and furnishing of them to the seas', to send out the *Galleon* (500 tons), the *Elizabeth* (140 tons) and the *Joan* (80 tons). A licence he had received to export 500 quarters of wheat to Portugal was cancelled owing to the political situation, but he was permitted to send the same amount to Ireland. In

1582 one of his vessels, the *Ughtred* or *Bear*, valued at £6,035, acted as flagship to Fenton's unsuccessful voyage, and was re-christened the *Leicester*, presumably in compliment to the Earl, the principal shareholder in the adventure. She sailed with Drake in 1585–6, and was one of his west-country squadron against the Armada, later possibly taking part in Cavendish's last voyage. Others of Ughtred's ships were engaged in voyages to the west: in 1582 he petitioned the Privy Council claiming compensation for losses he had sustained in Spain and the West Indies.[4]

Many of the references to Ughtred relate to his lawsuits, some of them incurred as a result of his trading ventures. In November 1582 the Spanish ambassador told Lord Burghley that 'a ship or two', owned by Mr. Ughtred of Southampton, had robbed off Newfoundland more than 20 ships belonging to the King of Spain, and that the Admiralty court had awarded one of these, 'laden with fish and grease', to Ughtred, his ships having brought her into Bristol. Over a year later one Francis Fernando, or Hernandez, was still trying to get compensation for this or another attack on Portuguese ships off Newfoundland.[5]

A further source of litigation was his investment in Irish lands. In 1586 he was granted a licence, with his relative Sir William Courtenay I* and others, to 'undertake the counties of Connoll and Kerry in one consort'. The company was headed by Courtenay, but Ughtred had a considerable stake in it. Unluckily for the 'undertakers', some of the lands in Munster which they were allotted were claimed by Irishmen who were not in rebellion, and the consequent lawsuits were a constant drain on any profits made by the enterprise. In 1591 Ughtred gained a Privy Council decision in his favour over some of the property assigned to him, but two years later it was rescinded, and as late as 1597 the matter was still unsettled.[6]

Nearer home, he became involved in quarrels with his relative by marriage, Sir William Paulet*, 3rd Marquess of Winchester, who accused him, as an executor of the 2nd Marquess's will, of maladministration of the property and refusal to settle the claims of a number of tenants and servants. In June 1582 Ughtred wrote to Lord Burghley, complaining of 'hard words' which Burghley had used to him in the Star Chamber, after which Winchester had intensified his attacks. Maintaining that the Marquess's accusations were unjust, he pointed out that he was now virtually a prisoner in his own house: he had been engaged on the case, which had cost him over £1,000, for seven months, to the great hindrance of his 'private causes', and waste of precious time. In the following year he was imprisoned for some months in the Fleet over the same matter. Winchester pursued the quarrel implacably, as late as 1596 persuading the Privy Council to dismiss Ughtred from the captaincy of Netley castle on the ground that his long absence in Ireland had caused him to neglect

his charge. At one stage the disputes came before the House of Lords, where early in 1585 the question of the jointure of the Dowager Marchioness was examined, and Ughtred gave evidence about his executorship.[7]

Little is known of the later years of his life. He and his wife left their Irish home during the disturbance of 1598, and several of his properties, including the castle of Maine, were burnt by the rebels. No later reference to him has been found. He may have died in Ireland: no will or inquisition post mortem has been found.[8]

[1] *Yorks. Peds.* (Harl. Soc. xcvi), 402, where generations are confused; *CPR*, 1558–60, p. 83; 1560–3, pp. 232, 541; 1566–9, p. 109; *CP*, iii. 557–8; xxi(2), pp. 763–4; Vivian, *Vis. Devon*, 147; *CSP Ire.* 1592–6, p. 200. [2] T. C. Wilks, *Hist. Hants*, iii. 176–7; *Letters Patent Soton*, ii. ed. Gidden (Soton Rec. Soc. x), 127; *APC*, xxv. 193, 465; *CSP Ire.* 1586–8, p. 313. [3] *CP*; Vivian, loc. cit.; D'Ewes, 349, 363, 365, 431, 439, 440; Lansd. 43, anon. jnl. f. 167. [4] K. R. Andrews, 'Economic Aspects of Elizabethan Privateering' (London Univ. PhD thesis 1951), 72; *CSP For.* 1582, p. 272; *APC*, xvii. 5, 320; *CSP Dom.* 1581–90, pp. 34, 50, 56, 146; M. Oppenheim, *Admin. of R. Navy*, 168; *Letters of 15th and 16th Centuries*, ed. Anderson (Soton Rec. Soc. xii), 102–6; *Bk. of Examinations*, 1601–2, ed. Anderson (Soton Rec. Soc. xiv), 67; *Hakluyt's Principal Navigations* (Hakluyt Soc. extra ser.) xi. 172 seq.; *Navy Recs. Soc.* ii. 336; xxii. 124. [5] *CSP For.* 1582, pp. 440–1; *CSP Span.* 1580–6, pp. 357, 410 and n., 432; *CSP Dom.* 1581–90, p. 146; Lansd. 144, f. 40. [6] *CSP Dom.* 1581–90, p. 325; *APC*, xiv. 191; xix. 203–5; xxiv. 138–41; xxvii. 195; *CSP Ire.* 1586–8, pp. 51, 77, 242, 243; 1588–92, pp. 76, 167–8, 257; 1592–6, pp. 2, 45, 48, 278; *HMC Hatfield*, iii. 212. [7] *HMC Hatfield*, ii. 527–8; iii. 212; xiii. 138, 218, 227–40 passim; *CSP Dom.* 1547–80, p. 534; 1581–90, p. 11; Lansd. 36, f. 185; *APC*, xxv. 193, 465; *Soton Rec. Soc.* xii. 105–6; *LJ*, ii. 80, 92, 108. [8] *CSP Ire.* 1598–9, pp. 316–17, 325, 331.

N.M.F.

UNTON, Edward (c.1556–89), of Wadley, Berks. and Langley, Oxon.

BERKSHIRE 1584, 1586

b. c.1556, 1st s. of Sir Edward Unton* by Anne (*d.*1588), da. of Edward Seymour, Duke of Somerset; bro. of Henry*. *educ.* Oriel, Oxf. by 1572, BA 1573. *m.* (1) Dorothy, da. of Sir Richard Knightley* of Fawsley, Northants., *s.p.*; (2) 1579, Catherine, da. of Sir George Hastings*, *s.p. suc.* fa. 1582.[1]

J.p. Berks. and Oxon. from c.1583; member, council of Munster 1587; capt. of Berkshire militia 1588; capt. on Portugal expedition 1589.

Unton was grandson of the Duke of Somerset; his mother was the widow of John Dudley, 2nd Earl of Warwick, the Earl of Leicester's elder brother. With such friends as Leicester and Walsingham, and two fortunate marriages before he was 30, Unton might have seemed set for a brilliant career at court. His mother shared with Leicester the Dudley lands in Oxfordshire and Unton was himself heir to large estates in Berkshire, so that he might well have been a leading figure in both counties. What actually happened was that his father preferred the younger son Henry, his mother went mad, and Unton himself was ruined through a disastrous journey to Italy undertaken just at the time of his father's death. In 1583 he fell into the hands of the Inquisition. On receiving the news that 'Edward Unton, a man of 6,000 crowns income and a kinsman of the Queen', had been arrested in Milan, Leicester threatened reprisals against the Spanish ambassador, and Henry travelled to Lyons to negotiate a ransom. Eventually this was agreed at 10,000 crowns provided Unton remained in Milan, and it was not until the spring of 1584 that he was allowed to return to England. By this time the strands of intrigue surrounding him had become so tangled that he was suspected of returning as a Catholic agent, with 'a most sickly body and melancholy mind'. Nevertheless twice elected knight of the shire for Berkshire, Unton is not named as contributing to the business of either Parliament, though as a county Member he was entitled to serve on the subsidy committees of 24 Feb. 1585 and 22 Feb. 1587. He had to sell land to repay Henry's expenses incurred over the ransom, and in 1587 he went to try his fortunes in the colonization of Munster, from which he was recalled by the threat of the Armada.[2]

Besides giving him responsible military appointments in both Berkshire and Oxfordshire, the Privy Council issued instructions that Unton was not to be arrested for debt, and commended those of his creditors who had granted him respite till 'he should recover his decayed estate'. Next he went on the Portugal expedition led by his Berkshire neighbour, Sir John Norris*. Laid low by wounds or disease, he returned to Plymouth to die intestate on 27 June 1589. Henry Unton was the heir to what was left of the estates. His widow married Sir Walter Chetwynd† of Staffordshire.[3]

[1] C142/203/61; *Vis. Berks.* (Harl. Soc. lvii), 222; J. G. Nichols, *Unton Inventories*, pp. xl–l. [2] *Archaeologia*, xcix. 58–61; Nichols, pp. xlv, lxxxii; *CSP For.* 1582, p. 87; 1583, pp. 145, 161, 213, 261, 280, 382, 385, 388, 390; 1583–4, pp. 75, 340, 476, 481; 1584–5, p. 193; *CSP Span.* 1580–6, pp. 443, 554; Lansd. 43, anon. jnl. f. 171; D'Ewes, 409; *APC*, xiv. 191; *CSP Ire.* 1586–8, pp. 51, 77, 313. [3] *CSP Dom.* 1581–90, pp. 384, 438; *APC*, xv. 344; xvi. 202; Nichols, p. xlix; C142/227/222.

A.H.

UNTON, Sir Edward (1534–82), of Wadley, Berks., and Langley, Oxon.

MALMESBURY	1554 (Nov.)
OXFORDSHIRE	1563*
BERKSHIRE	1572

b. 1534, 1st s. of Sir Alexander Unton of Chequers, Bucks. and Wadley by his 2nd w. Cecily, da. of Edward Bulstrode of Brogborough Park, Beds.; bro. of Henry†. *educ.* I. Temple 1551. *m.* 29 Apr. 1555, Anne, da. of Edward Seymour, Duke of Somerset, wid. of John Dudley, 2nd Earl of Warwick (*d.* 21 Oct. 1554), 5s. inc. Edward* and Henry* 2da. *suc.* fa. 17 Dec. 1547. KB Jan. 1559.[1]

Keeper, Malvern chase, Worcs. and Cornbury park, Oxon.; commr. musters, Berks. 1560, 1569, j.p. from c.1560, sheriff 1567–8; j.p. Oxon. from c.1561, commr. muster of horses 1565, 1580.[2]

Unton's standing in Berkshire was enhanced by his mother's marriage to Robert Keilway*, surveyor of the court of wards, and his own to the Countess of Warwick. Keilway, a Wiltshire man, was probably responsible for securing Anne Seymour as his stepson's bride, the match being made just as Unton ceased to be his mother's ward. Keilway naturally took his profit from the arrangement, by purchasing Warwick's old manor of Minster Lovell, Oxfordshire, from Queen Elizabeth in 1559. The remaining 'Warwick's lands' in Oxfordshire and Gloucestershire, Unton shared with Warwick's brother, the eventual Earl of Leicester; by 1555 he was in possession of the manor of Burford and in 1559 was residing nearby at Langley, where the Queen visited him in 1572, 1574 and 1575.[3]

He seems to have become a servant of Elizabeth soon after her accession, and was made KB at her coronation. He spent much time in London, and in November 1562 he was involved in a 'chance affray' outside Temple Bar with Richard Grenville II* of Stowe, Cornwall. He travelled to Italy in 1564, and went abroad again ten years later, on that occasion accompanied by his eldest son. In Italy he was apparently impressed by the works of Machiavelli. He bought a copy of the *Istorie Fiorentine* in which he wrote: 'Machiavelli maxima: Qui nescit dissimulare nescit vivere'.[4]

In the early years of the reign, Unton looked to Oxfordshire for a seat in Parliament. Sir Richard Blount*, one of the knights for Oxfordshire, died in 1564; on 9 Oct. 1566, records the memorandum book of Burford corporation, 'Sir Edward Unton was chosen knight for the Parliament of Oxfordshire with such a voice of the county the like hath not been seen'. For the Parliament of 1571, the Norris and Knollys families shared Oxfordshire and Unton sought election in Berkshire. There again he was kept out by the Norrises who supported Richard Ward* for election with a Neville. At Abingdon quarter sessions in the autumn following the 1571 Parliament, Unton's servants attacked those of (Sir) John Norris*. During the ensuing Star Chamber case, Unton was reported by Thomas Wenman* to have said that grounds for a 'good and sufficient quarrel' had been provided by the interference of the Norrises in the Berkshire election. Unton himself alleged in the Star Chamber that Sir Henry Norris had sent 'unto certain of his tenants and [had procured] such as had no freehold to appear and give their voice' against him. Perhaps he had, indeed, been kept out by extraordinary means, for in 1572 he was returned for Berkshire as senior knight. His name is mentioned only once in the journals of the House, 25 Jan. 1581, when he was appointed to the committee on the Queen's safety.[5]

Unton's puritan sympathies were enlisted in September 1580, when he and Sir Henry, by then Lord, Norris were commissioned by the Privy Council to search 'with diligence and secrecy' for Jesuits lurking in Oxfordshire. Unton's children married into puritan families: his eldest son, Edward Unton, married first a daughter of Sir Richard Knightley*, and secondly, in 1579, a daughter of Sir George Hastings*; and one of Unton's daughters married one of Knightley's sons, Valentine Knightley*. At the Inner Temple, to which he was introduced by his stepfather, Unton became closely connected with the parliamentary dynasty of Croke; his sister married John Croke II* – son of John Croke, the chancery master, whose will Unton witnessed – and their son, John III* was Speaker of the Commons in 1601. Unton's own sons, Edward and Henry, sat for Berkshire in 1584, 1586 and 1593.[6]

Unton died on 16 Sept. 1582 and was buried in Faringdon church. In his will, made 14 Sept. 1581, and proved 19 Sept. 1582, he looked forward to 'the heavenly life which [God] hath prepared for his elect children before the beginning of the world'. His second son, Henry, and his brother-in-law, John Croke, were his executors. To the eldest son, Edward, was granted the custody of Unton's widow, the Countess of Warwick: since May 1566 she had been 'a lunatic enjoying lucid intervals'. Unton instructed his son Henry 'to govern himself' by the advice of Sir Francis Walsingham.[7]

[1] J. G. Nichols, *Unton Inventories*, pp. xxiv–xlix; *DNB* (Unton, Sir Henry); *CP*; *Vis. Berks.* (Harl. Soc. lvii), 222; *Vis. Bucks.* (Harl. Soc. lviii), 149; Wards 7/4/29; *EHR*, xxv. 553. [2] Nichols, pp. xlii, xliv; *CSP Dom.* 1547–80, pp. 156, 340, 690; *APC*, vii. 251. [3] PRO Index 10217; *CPR*, 1554–5, p. 14; 1558–60, pp. 236, 308; 1560–3; pp. 9–10; R. H. Gretton, *Burford Recs.* 84, 411; E. K. Chambers, *Eliz. Stage*, iv. 88, 90, 92. [4] *CPR*, 1560–3, pp. 9, 509; Nichols, pp. xxxiv, xxxviii; E157/1/1; Brit. Sch. at Rome, *Pprs.* vii. [5] Gretton, 415; Folger V. b. 298; St. Ch. 5/N10/11, N16/38; *CJ*, i. 119. [6] *APC*, xii. 191, 198, 211; Nichols, pp. xxxiv, xlviii; *Vis. Berks.* ii. 222; C142/203/61; A. Croke, *Gen. Hist. Crokes*, 448 seq. [7] C142/203/61; *VCH Berks.* iv. 497; PCC 35 Tirwhite; *CSP Dom.* 1581–90, p. 74; Nichols, p. xliv; *CSP For.* 1582, p. 87.

A.H.

UNTON, Henry (c.1558–96), of Wadley, Berks.[1]

NEW WOODSTOCK	1584
BERKSHIRE	1593

b. c.1558, 2nd s. of Sir Edward Unton* of Wadley by Lady Anne Seymour (*d.*1588), da. of Edward, Duke of Somerset, wid. of John Dudley, 2nd Earl of Warwick; bro. of Edward*. *educ.* Oriel, Oxf. supp. BA Oct. 1573; M. Temple 1575. *m.* 1580, Dorothy (*d.*1634), da. of Thomas Wroughton* of Broad Hinton, Wilts., *s.p. suc.* bro. 1589. Kntd. 1586.

Keeper of Cornbury park, Oxon. 1583, j.p.q. from c.1583, dep. lt. 1587–93, j.p. and dep. lt. Berks. from 1593; capt. under Leicester in Netherlands 1586, of Berkshire horse 1588; ambassador to France July 1591–May 1592, Dec. 1595–*d.*[2]

Unton, a musician, linguist and literary patron, was the son of distinguished parents. His father's favourite son, he enjoyed the favour of three great men, Leicester, Walsingham and Hatton. His father had instructed Henry 'to govern himself' by Walsingham's advice and the advice 'of those of the [puritan] religion', and at the time of his father's death, Unton was looking to Walsingham for an office. He soon had to solicit him for help over the detention of his brother Edward.

It was, however, in the household of Sir Christopher Hatton, whose nephew and heir William Hatton* became his life-long friend, that Unton was educated. He went to the Netherlands with William Hatton in June 1586, carrying a letter from Burghley to Leicester. The friends distinguished themselves at Zutphen, were knighted by Leicester, and returned to England with a dispatch from the Earl to Walsingham. At the funeral of Sir Philip Sidney* in St. Paul's, they walked together amongst the 12 knights of Sidney's 'kindred and friends'. For the next few years Unton performed the normal duties of a country gentleman and consolidated the estates he had been able to acquire through Edward's misfortune. He bought two more manors in Berkshire and, in 1589, succeeded Edward to what remained in his hands of the Unton inheritance. But by now two of Henry's patrons, Leicester and Walsingham, were dead and Unton's expectations were centred upon first Hatton and then Leicester's stepson, the Earl of Essex. In the meantime he had sat in Parliament for Woodstock, presumably by virtue of his office at Cornbury park, and no doubt with the support of Leicester and Sir Henry Lee*, the high steward. He spoke in the debate on a cloth bill in this Parliament,

> of this I am sure, what fault so ever is in our cloth ... the merchant doth answer it to the buyer beyond the sea.[3]

It was presumably either Hatton or Essex who secured Unton's appointment as ambassador to France, where he went 'with great bravery' in July 1591. He became an admirer and intimate of Henri IV, whom he accompanied at the siege of Rouen, and fell into Elizabeth's displeasure for seeming to commit her too far to the King's support against the Catholic League. Hearing that the Duke of Guise had spoken 'impudently, lightly, and overboldly' of Queen Elizabeth, Unton sent the Duke an unanswered challenge to a duel; he claimed that there was no 'inequality of person' between them, 'I being issued of as great a race and house every way as yourself'. But in November 1591 Hatton's death was another blow. He wrote to the Queen:

> It has pleased God to call away my lord chancellor, my honourable good lord chancellor ... with whom I was

first bred up, and to whom (next to your Majesty) I was most bound.

He asked for the Queen's protection 'from the malice and envy of the world, which doth violently burst out since his death against me, by raising untrue reports to defame me'. To Heneage he wrote that he was destitute of friends. The 'untrue reports' were evidently that he wished to stay in France, because there he was safe from his creditors. His return to England, he admitted to Cecil, was necessary for the conservation of his 'poor estate'; he meant 'wholly and only to be directed' by Cecil and would 'never leave to honour and love' him. In particular he denied that he was committed to the service of the Earl of Essex. Yet it was Essex who was his chief friend at court, and who obtained his release from the expensive and now irksome embassy.[4]

Back in England, Unton resumed with more urgency his pursuit of a profitable office, turning further towards Essex and finally breaking with Cecil. His growing estrangement from Cecil may very well have played its part in leading Unton to disaster in the Parliament of 1593, to which he was returned as knight for Berkshire, to which county he had just removed from Oxfordshire. Unton was appointed to the first standing committee on privileges and returns (26 Feb. 1593); to committees concerning recusants (28 Feb., 4 Apr.) and poor maimed soldiers (30 Mar.); and to committees on private matters (6, 8 Mar.). But his main contribution to the business of the House, one which in fact ruined him, was on the subsidy. He was given a prominent place on the committee (26 Feb., 1 Mar.) and he spoke, 6 Mar., in favour of the idea of a triple subsidy, painting a vivid picture of the malice of Spain and the Pope, and pointing to the cost in France of 'preserving a brave and worthy king of our religion'. But, 5 Mar., he protested that the Lords had no right to be joined with the Commons in the matter, and that the names of those who had spoken critically had been reported to the Queen to convey the impression that they were against any grant at all, rather than against reasoned amendments. Cecil denied 'that men's names were given up to the Queen', but in fact Unton's speeches produced an extraordinary reaction from her. As Essex reported to him, she 'startles at your name, chargeth you with popularity and hath every particular of your speeches in Parliament without book'; in particular, 'she stands much upon the bitter speech against Sir Robert Cecil'. Essex told the Queen that it was 'an ill-example ... that, for one displeasure or misconceit, all the merit or service of a man's life should be overthrown', but it was the end of Unton's hopes for a court office.[5]

In disgrace, Unton now begged to be allowed to 'depend on' Cecil 'after the old manner'. It was presumably to Cecil and his friends that Essex referred in the summer of 1595, when he reported to Unton that the courtiers were 'a crew of sycophants, spies and delators', and that he, Essex, was alone to be trusted. But in the

event he could do no more than secure Unton's re-appointment as ambassador in December 1595, with which post Unton was soon 'infinitely discontented'. His own colleagues made it known that he was 'a disgraced man in England' and Essex himself 'ought to have a better feeling of the imminent perils'.[6]

Unton had been ill on his first embassy, and early in 1596 he was afflicted by fever accompanied 'with the purples'. He died at Henri IV's camp before the Spanish-held town of La Fère, 23 Mar. 1596. The King visited him in his last hours, despite the risk of infection. On a baron's hearse, because he died ambassador, he was brought home for burial with great pomp at Faringdon on 8 July. He died intestate and, like his brother, left no children, his heirs being his sister Cicely, wife of John Wentworth*, who was granted letters of administration, and the three daughters of his sister Anne by Valentine Knightley*. Disputes about the debt-encumbered inheritance were settled only by an Act of the Parliament of 1597. A volume of verses in memory of Unton was produced at Oxford, edited by Robert Wright, his chaplain, later bishop of Coventry and Lichfield. Others who enjoyed Unton's patronage were Sir Thomas Edmondes* (his secretary on both his embassies), Matthew Gwinne, the physician, and Robert Ashley*. The picture in the National Portrait Gallery, painted for Unton's widow, shows Unton surrounded by scenes from his life: his birth, travels, service in the Netherlands, the masque performed at his wedding and the funeral procession into Faringdon church.[7]

[1] Unless otherwise stated this biography is based upon J. G. Nichols, *Unton Inventories* and *Unton Corresp.* (Roxburghe Club lxiii). [2] *Vis. Berks.* (Harl. Soc. lvii), 223; C142/227/222; *CSP For.* 1582, p. 87; *Leycester Corresp.* (Cam. Soc. xxvii), 416; *Archaeologia*, xcix. 56, 70, 73; *APC*, xvi. 201; xxiv. 31; *CSP Dom.* 1591–4, pp. 36, 242; Birch, *Mems.* i. 342. [3] Lansd. 43, anon. jnl. f. 174. [4] *CSP For.* 1582, p. 87; 1583, pp. 145, 161, 261, 280, 390; Read, *Walsingham*, ii. 425–6; Lansd. 39, f. 138; 68, f. 216; *CSP Dom.* 1581–90, pp. 74, 91; 1591–4, p. 65; *CSP Span.* 1580–6, p. 554; *Leycester Corresp.* 307, 416; *VCH Berks.* iv. 493, 533; *APC*, xv. 121; xix. 318; xx. 36, 156, xxiii. 259; Nichols, *Progresses Eliz.* iii. 85–89; *State Pprs.* ed. Murdin, 648, 651. [5] *State Pprs.* ed. Murdin, 655; *APC*, xxiv. 31; D'Ewes, 471, 474, 476, 477, 478, 481, 486, 487–8, 489, 490, 492, 495, 512, 517; *CSP Dom.* 1591–4, pp. 333–4; *HMC Hatfield*, iv. 68, 116, 134, 276, 353, 452; Birch, i. 131. [6] *HMC Hatfield*, iv. 362, 499, 506; v. 93, 260, 280; vi. 46, 103; xi. 206; xiii. 537; Birch, i. 353, 374, 392–3, 397, 402, 423; *State Pprs.* ed. Murdin, 701, 706–33. [7] Birch, i. 448–9, 451, 459–60; *State Pprs.* ed. Murdin, 730, 734; C142/253/100; *HMC Hatfield*, vi. 119, 131, 303; *CSP Dom.* 1595–7, p. 315; 1601–3, p. 299; D'Ewes, 558, 560, 562, 568; PCC admon. act bk. 1596, f. 162; *APC*, xxii. 342; *Archaeologia*, xcix. 67–8.

A.H.

UPTON, George (1553–1609), of Warminster, Wilts., later of Wells, Som.

WELLS	1584, 1601
BOSSINEY	1604*

b. 1553, s. of Geoffrey Upton, dep. receiver to bp. of Bath and Wells, of Trelaske, Cornw. and Warminster, Wilts. by Mary, da. and coh. of Thomas Horne of Ottery St. Mary, Devon. *m.* (1) Frances, da. and h. of John Newton of Harptree, Som.; (2) Elizabeth, da. of Thomas Bampfield of Hardington, Som.[1]

Freeman, Wells 1584.

In 1584, when he became a freeman of Wells prior to his first return to Parliament, Upton was described as a stranger. However, he soon acquired property in the city and took up residence. He held no office himself, and was a hanger-on of Thomas Godwyn* the bishop's son, through whom he presumably gained his seat in 1584, at the first election after Bishop Godwyn became bishop, and through whom he certainly gained favourable leases of several tenements and rectories in Wells, including the rectories of St. Cuthbert and Wells. By October 1590 Thomas Godwyn was indebted to Upton to the amount of £210, in part payment of which he surrendered lands valued at £139 13s. 4d., which the bishop had assigned to him, probably for that purpose. Upton's last grant came only five days before Bishop Godwyn's death in November 1590. Naturally the climate soon changed, and in 1594 he was excommunicated for assaulting one of the canons of Wells. In 1600 he was involved in a lawsuit with Bishop Godwyn's successor over the tithes of the rectory of Wells.[2]

It is not clear how Upton came to be returned to Parliament for Wells in 1601. Perhaps his sister's marriage to James Bisse* had something to do with it, perhaps it was just his now established local standing. He sat in James's first Parliament for a Cornish borough until his death, apparently without issue, early in 1609. His heirs were the sons of his sister Elizabeth Bisse, already mentioned, and he made bequests to several nephews and nieces. His nephew Philip Marvyn received £20 'if he shall affect and be obedient to the protestant religion preferred now in England, and if he shall bring a certificate from the bishop of the diocese of his earnest protestation before him, that he abhorreth and detesteth the popish religion'. There were bequests for the fabric of St. Cuthbert's church and of Wells cathedral. Upton also left money to the poor of various parishes where he had property, and five marks and a gown for a funeral sermon. Anyone who challenged the terms of the will was to lose his legacy. Upton's possession of grazing land in the Mendips, which also appears in his will, suggests that he was involved in wool production for the Somerset cloth industry. His commercial activities were varied, however, as he also had an interest in the Mendip lead mines.[3]

[1] *Vis. Som.* ed. Weaver, 82; *Misc. Gen. et Her.* (ser. 2), ii. 320; iv. 22. [2] *HMC 10th Rep. III*, ii. 262, 308, 309, 325, 330, 331, 334, 341, 342, 343, 345; *Wells Charters* (Som. Rec. Soc. xlvi), 189; *Cal. Chanc. Proc.* i. 401; *Proc. Som. Arch. Nat. Hist. Soc.* xcvi. 80, 86. [3] PCC 20 Dorset.

I.C.

UVEDALE, Edmund (*d.* 1621), of Little Crichel, Dorset.

CORFE CASTLE 1572

1st s. of Henry Uvedale by Mabel, da. of Anthony Ernle. *educ.* ?L. Inn 1563.[1] *m.* Elizabeth (div. by 1574), da. of Robert Williams, of Herringston, *s.p. suc.* fa. 1599.

J.p. Dorset from 1582, q. from 1601, sheriff 1609–10.

Edmund Uvedale of Little Crichel has been preferred to his soldier cousin, Sir Edmund Uvedale*, as Member for Corfe Castle both because his family ties are more appropriate, and because the soldier's career hardly suits an appearance for Corfe Castle in 1572. It is true that Uvedale's father was still living in 1572, but this rather explains the son's sitting than weakens the case for the identification, as the father was sheriff at the time and so may have thought it wiser not to stand for a Dorset constituency.

Little has been ascertained about Uvedale's activities in the Elizabethan period. He died 10 Oct. 1621.[2]

[1] Perhaps the Edmund Uvedale admitted to Lincoln's Inn 1563 and/or the Mr. 'Udell' shortlisted for the position of master of the revels two years later. [2] *Misc. Gen. et Her.* (ser. 2), v. 305; Hoare, *Wilts.* Chalk 61.

P.W.H.

UVEDALE, Sir Edmund (*d.* 1606), of Gussage All Saints and Holt Park, Dorset.

DORSET 1601

2nd s. of Sir Francis Uvedale of Horton by Catherine, da. of John, 8th Lord Zouche of Haringworth, Northants. *m.* Mary, da. of Sir William Dormer*, wid. of Anthony Browne, s. and h. of 1st Visct. Montagu, *s.p.* Kntd. 1588; *suc.* fa. 1589.

Capt. in Netherlands by 1587, marshal of Flushing by 1593–7, surveyor gen. of the forces 1598–1604, sergeant major 1599; j.p.q. and dep. lt. Dorset from c.1601, duchy of Lancaster guardian of Holt forest 1598.[1]

As a captain in the Netherlands Uvedale got into difficulties with his accounts, killed the poet George Whetstone in a duel, and returned to England in disgrace. In June 1588 he complained to Sir Francis Walsingham that Sir Thomas Morgan I* had tried, after the duel,

> to take away my life, and gave these judgments: that by law I should be put to death, and both buried in one pit; if pardoned, to have my company taken from me, and banished … it cost me 100 marks, or I had an end.

One of Uvedale's supporters sent Walsingham a testimonial: 'a more honest captain, and one that keepeth his soldiers in better order, is there not in the land', and he was eventually cleared by a council of war. Returning to the Netherlands, he was soon acting as lieutenant governor to Sir Robert Sidney*. He was again in England in 1590, settling his father's estate, but by 1592 he had returned to his post, where he probably remained until 1595 when he came back to attend the christening of

Sidney's child. By this time he was again in trouble over his accounts, and devoted his leave to trying to persuade the Queen to accept them, at the same time assuring Sidney that he was willing to return to the Netherlands as soon as Sidney himself was inconvenienced by his absence. The Queen remaining adamant, Uvedale endeavoured to sweeten Sir Robert Cecil with a gift of a gelding, 200 angels and, later, two choice falcons. These tactics, too, proved fruitless, Rowland Whyte, Sidney's intelligencer, reporting to his master that Uvedale was 'fed but with the ordinary delays of court'. Cecil at length declined to 'meddle in the business for his accounts'. Finally, however, the matter was patched up, and from 1596 Uvedale was again in the Netherlands, whence, in 1597, he sent another present to Cecil 'as a continual remembrance of your favours' shortly before returning to England on sick leave. He now went to Dorset to recover from his illness, and appears not to have returned to his duties abroad, though retaining command of his company in the Netherlands until 1599. An obscure episode in this part of his life concerns a letter he wrote to the Earl of Essex early in 1597, offering to serve him in some capacity. It appears that the Earl declined.[2]

Early in 1598 Uvedale moved to London from Dorset, and was appointed surveyor general of the forces, his cousin, Captain Robert Williams, being appointed his deputy in Dorset. In July 1599, the Queen having 'a good opinion' of his judgment, he was sent to investigate the defences of the Isle of Wight, where he pointed out the greater productivity of 'task men' (piece workers) over pressed men. His promotion to sergeant major of the army soon followed. The commissioners of musters in Dorset were instructed to keep Uvedale informed of their decisions, and he became increasingly identified with the county. By 1601 he was of sufficient status to be elected knight of the shire, his claims to a county seat being no doubt strengthened by the fact that his brother Thomas was sheriff at the time of the election and by the support of his friend the lord lieutenant, Thomas Howard*, Viscount Bindon, who addressed him as 'loving cousin' and 'your very loving friend and kinsman'. No mention of Uvedale by name has been found in the journals of the 1601 Parliament, but as a knight of the shire he could have attended committees concerned with the order of business, 3 Nov., and monopolies, 23 Nov.[3]

Uvedale died 6 Apr. 1606. He left a young horse, 'in token of my true and faithful love', to Charles Blount*, Earl of Devonshire, bequeathed a gilt cup worth £6 to Richard Swayne*, made various other family bequests, and remembered the poor of four or five parishes. His wife, the executrix, received a house and land at Poole, and was residuary legatee. He requested that no ceremony should be used at his funeral and 20s. was paid for his burial fees at Wimborne Minster, where a memorial was erected.[4]

[1] Misc. Gen. et Her. (ser. 2), v. 307; Hutchins, Dorset, iii. 217; CP; Harl. 3324, f. 16. [2] T. C. Izard, George Whetstone, 29–31; 255; Hutchins, iii. 146–7; CSP Dom. 1595–7, p. 493; Add. 1580–1625, p. 282; APC, xviii. 118–19; HMC De L'Isle and Dudley, ii. 179, 184, 186, 210, 369; Lansd. 72, f. 92; HMC Hatfield, vi. 362; vii. 12, 57, 62, 426; xiii. 24; Collins, Sidney State Pprs. i. 362, 372, 377, 381, 384, 385. [3] Harl. 3324, ff. 11, 16, 18, 29, 32, 56; HMC De L'Isle and Dudley, ii. 316; HMC Hatfield, ix. 19–20; xi. 484; D'Ewes, 624, 649. [4] PCC 23 Stafford.

P.W.H.

UVEDALE, William (c.1528–69), of Place House, Wickham, Hants.

HAMPSHIRE	1563

b. c.1528, 1st s. of Arthur Uvedale of Wickham by Agnes or Anne, da. of Edmund Hazelwood of Northants. educ. L. Inn 1546. m. Ellyn (1533–67), 3rd da. of Sir John Gresham of Holt, Norf., ld. mayor of London 1547, 2s. 1da.

J.p. Hants from c.1559, sheriff c.Mar.–Nov. 1560, commr. piracy Nov. 1565.

The Uvedales were already well established among the leading families in Surrey by the reign of Edward I, but a fortunate marriage caused them, in the year of the Peasants' Revolt, to move to Wickham in Hampshire, famous as the birthplace of the contemporary bishop of Winchester. Here they entered into the administrative work of the county. Uvedale himself represented the seventh generation to live at Wickham, but, unlike his father, he died comparatively young, so that there is little information about him. He was one of the members suggested as master of the revels at Lincoln's Inn in 1547, but there is no evidence that he was elected. It is possible, though unlikely, that he was the 'William Uvedall the younger, gent.' who was granted the office of 'clerk of the council of the chamber at Westminster', at £10 p.a. Uvedale himself made a fortunate marriage to the daughter of a rich merchant who had had transactions with his own father during Henry VIII's reign.

The date at which William inherited the family estates is not known. Arthur Uvedale, who, according to the family historian, is thought to have been either mentally retarded or so extravagant that he was not permitted to take charge of his property (or, presumably, both), is said by the same writer to have died in 1537 or 1538. This must be wrong: he was still a Hampshire j.p. in June 1540 and a man of the same name, almost certainly William's father, was alive as late as 1544. No will or inquisition post mortem for Arthur appears to have survived, but William was probably still a minor when he succeeded him. He inherited, in Hampshire, Wickham manor and its appurtenances in several parishes; the manors of Nately Scures, Woodgarston, near Basingstoke, and Widley, held of the Marquess of Winchester; Funtley, held of the Earl of Arundel, and the rectory of Droxford; and, in Surrey, the family's original property, including the manors of Chelsham and Tatsfield, near the Kent border, and two manors in the parish of Titsey. The Surrey property, held of Lord Hunsdon, contained more than 1,700 acres and was worth about £90 a year, but, by an arrangement made in 1562, William paid his uncle, William Uvedale of Himley, Staffordshire, an annuity of £80, so that his own profits from these lands were negligible.

Uvedale was established as a country gentleman and local administrator by the beginning of Elizabeth's reign. In 1564 he was commissioned to examine a controversy between the mayor and governor of Portsmouth, and the following year became a piracy commissioner. Clearly, he knew the leading families in Hampshire, for among the godparents of his son, baptized in 1560, were Sir William Paulet*, grandson of the 1st Marquess of Winchester; Sir William Keilway, father of Francis*; and Lady Jane Wriothesley, widow of Thomas Wriothesley†, 1st Earl of Southampton, whose residence was nearby at Titchfield. Uvedale was elected for the county in 1563, and made no mark in the House before he was granted leave of absence on 25 Feb., halfway through the session. Classified as a 'favourer' of religion in the 1564 bishops' reports on the local justices, Uvedale had in fact been one of those with whom Bishop Horne of Winchester had conferred before sending his reply to the Privy Council, and the bishop put forward his name as a justice to improve the position in Winchester, which was, for the most part, 'addicted to the old superstition'. Horne was one of five men named as executors in Uvedale's will, should his brother Thomas be unable to act. The others, like Horne, were radicals in religion: John Gresham*, Uvedale's brother-in-law; Sir Henry Wallop*, Richard Norton I* and Richard Inkpen*.

Uvedale died on 2 June 1569. In his will, proved 1 July, he asked to be buried in a 'comely and decent manner, as to my degree it shall appertain'. He ordered 'a seemly and decent tomb and monument, the same to be built and set on the south side in my chapel nigh the chancel of the parish church of Wickham', where it still stands, over ten feet high. Such ostentation would have been scorned by the puritans of later years.

This biography is largely based upon H. Leveson Gower 'Notices Fam. of Uvedale', *Surr. Arch. Colls.* iii. The pedigrees in *Vis. Hants* (Harl. Soc. lxiv), 47–8 and Manning and Bray, *Hist. Surr.* ii. 400, are unreliable. Other sources are: *CPR*, 1554–5, p. 268; 1560–3, p. 442; *APC*, v. 262; vi. 29; vii. 207–8, 283; C142/154/103; *VCH Hants*, iii. 171, 234; iv. 153, 232; *CJ*, i. 66; *Cam. Misc.* ix(3), pp. 54, 55; *DNB* (Uvedale, Richard); PCC 17 Sheffelde.

M.R.P.

VAUGHAN, Charles (d. 1597), of Shapwick, Dorset, afterwards Falstone, Wilts.

SHAFTESBURY   1572

4th s. of Richard Vaughan of Bredwardine, Herefs. by Anne, da. of John Butler or Boteler of Dunraven, Glam.

m. (1) Jane, da. of Fulk Prideaux of Threborough, Devon, wid. of Thomas Hussey of Shapwick, *s.p.*; (2) Bridget (*d.* 20 Mar. 1596), *s.p.*

?Burgess, Southampton 1565; servant of 1st and 2nd Earls of Pembroke; j.p. Dorset 1577–82.

Vaugham was treasurer to the 1st Earl of Pembroke, who employed him, along with Robert Grove*, on the well-known survey of his lands. After the death of the Earl, whose funeral he attended on 18 Apr. 1570, Vaughan remained in the service of the family, and came into Parliament for the Pembroke borough of Shaftesbury. It may well have been business of the 2nd Earl that procured him leave of absence from Parliament on 11 June 1572 for his 'great business and affairs' at the next Dorset assizes. He engaged in a number of land transactions, either on behalf of the Earl or on his own account, and, together with Arthur Massinger* and Thomas Hannam*, witnessed the Earl's sale of a park at Cranborne to James Hannam. By 1596 he was living at Falstone. He acted, in 1565, as overseer for the will of his 'loving friend' the vicar of Shapwick, who left Vaughan a personal bequest, and money to distribute to the poor of the district. A touching minor bequest was to Vaughan's wife – she received half the vicar's bees. Vaughan died 22 Mar. 1597. His will, made on 23 Apr. 1596, describes him as of Falstone. He wished to join 'the company of the heavenly and blessed saints' and 'according to the articles of my faith at the great day of general resurrection we shall all appear before the judgment seat of Christ'. He wished to be buried in the north aisle of the parish church of Bishopstone, to which he left £6 13s. 4d. The poor of Salisbury, Wilton and Wimborne Minster received £5, and of Cranborne, Gussage St. Michael and Shapwick £4. The residue went to Vaughan's nephew Walter. An inquisition taken at Shaftesbury on 19 May 1597 shows that Vaughan still held the manor of Gussage Bounde and the advowson of Gussage St. Michael both of which he had bought from Edward Bashe* in 1564.

Hoare, *Wilts.* Downton, 8; *HMC 11th Rep. III*, 20; *Wilts Arch. Mag.* xviii. 128; *Pembroke Survey* (Roxburghe Club), 501; *CJ*, i. 102; *Som. and Dorset N. and Q.* vi. 123, 167; viii. 20–1; xxiv. 169–71; PCC 33 Cobham; C142/249/64; *CPR*, 1563–4, p. 143.

P.W.H.

VAUGHAN, Francis, of Salisbury, Wilts.

WILTON   1572

?*educ.* Trinity Hall, Camb. 1549; G. Inn 1552.
   ?Servant of 1st and/or 2nd Earls of Pembroke; ?coroner, Wilts. 1567.

Vaughan was probably (except that no evidence of a marriage has been found) the father of the 'Francis Vaughan of Sarum, gent.' who was an overseer of the will, made in 1596, of Charles Vaughan*, of Falstone,

Wiltshire, who was himself in the service of the earls of Pembroke. If Francis Vaughan, the 1572 MP, was of Trinity Hall and Gray's Inn (where he would have been a contemporary of Francis Walsingham, afterwards high steward of Salisbury), he was presumably born about 1535 and thus could have been of an age with Charles Vaughan. He was probably the man who bought property in Combe Bissett in 1561 and who, as 'generosus', was assessed for subsidy at £4 in Market ward, Salisbury, in 1576; and he may well have been the coroner who was officiating in Wiltshire in December 1566. On the same supposition, the Francis Vaughan of that county who entered Lincoln's Inn in 1572 was perhaps the son. It was probably this younger Francis Vaughan who in 1593 was to incense the burgesses of Salisbury when, as the bishop's deputy steward, he administered what they regarded as an illegal oath to the mayor-elect. Though the date of the father's death has not been ascertained, on a balance of probability it was the son who made the will proved in February 1614, bequeathing the whole estate to a married daughter, Katherine Small.[1]

Francis Vaughan is specified only twice in the journals of the House of Commons, on 28 June 1572 and 17 Feb. 1581, and on both occasions he was granted leave of absence. The reason given, in the first case 'for his great business' and in the second 'for his necessary business, the assizes', may have been in connexion with the affairs of the 2nd Earl of Pembroke. Interestingly enough Charles Vaughan was given leave of absence from the 1572 session for a similar reason.[2]

[1] Wilts. N. and Q. iv. 455; Two Taxation Lists (Wilts. Arch. Soc. recs. br. x), 65; CPR, 1566-9, p. 13; HMC Var. iv. 231; PCC 15 Lawe. [2] CJ, i. 103, 127.

S.T.B.

VAUGHAN, Henry, of Golden Grove, Carm.

CARMARTHEN BOROUGHS 1597[1]

Yr. s. of John Vaughan II* of Carmarthen by Catherine, da. of Henry Morgan of Muddlescwm; bro. of Walter*. m. Elizabeth, da. of David Ffylibs of Gil y Sant, Carm., at least 1s.

Mayor, Carmarthen 1598.

Vaughan's brother Walter was mayor of Carmarthen at the time of this election. As a nominee of the Earl of Essex had been returned for Carmarthen Boroughs at the previous election, and Walter Vaughan was a follower of the Earl, it is likely that Henry Vaughan gained his seat with the approval of Essex. He was appointed to the maltsters bill committee, 12 Jan. 1598, and as Member for a Welsh constituency he could have served on the Newport bridge committee 29 Nov. 1597.[2]

[1] Folger V. b. 298. [2] Dwnn, Vis. Wales, i. 214; Hist. Carm. ed. Lloyd, ii. 468; D'Ewes, 565, 578.

A.M.M.

VAUGHAN, Hugh (d.1607), of Bedford House, Exeter, and Barton, near Tavistock, Devon.

BRIDPORT	1572*
DARTMOUTH	1584
PLYMOUTH	1586
TAVISTOCK	1593

1st s. of Anthony Vaughan of Littleton, Mdx. by Susan, da. of John Cranmer, wid. of Thomas Brooke (bro. of George, 9th Lord Cobham). m. Elizabeth, da. of John Hals of Kenedon, at least 8s. 4da.

Steward or sec. to 2nd Earl of Bedford by 1577-85; steward of Russell lands in the west country; clerk of peace in Devon from 1596.

Vaughan was related by marriage to (Sir) John Hawkins*, an executor to his will and a trustee of the hospital Hawkins built at Chatham. In 1577 at Exeter, Vaughan was involved in an affray in which Thomas Bruarton* (a distant connexion by marriage) was assaulted. The 2nd Earl of Bedford investigated and 'the more he dealt in the matter ... the worse he found it against his man', and so he handed Vaughan and two others over to the mayor for imprisonment. The mayor later asked the Earl to take Vaughan back into his service.

When in January 1581 Bedford's son John Russell was raised to the peerage, Vaughan came in for Bridport in his place. Perhaps he was the Mr. Vaughan who sat on two legal committees, 26 Jan. and 17 Feb. that year. In 1584 Bedford had him returned for Dartmouth. After Bedford's death in 1585 – Vaughan witnessed his will and received a bequest – he remained in the service of the family as steward of their lands in the west country. In 1586, through the influence of Hawkins, he was returned for Plymouth, where for some time Bedford and Hawkins had amicably divided the patronage, and in 1593, his position as steward of the Russell lands in Devon enabled him to be returned for Tavistock. No parliamentary activity can be certainly ascribed to Vaughan, but he may have served on committees concerned with cloth, 23 Mar. and 2 Apr. 1593. When the 3rd Earl was appointed custos rotulorum in Devon in 1596, he appointed his 'servant and officer' clerk of the peace. Vaughan administered the office by deputy, and his family kept the post certainly until 1615. Vaughan was mentioned in the Countess of Warwick's will made in October 1603, and died 3 Feb. 1607, being buried the same day in St. Lawrence's, Exeter, 'out of the Earl of Bedford's house'. In his will, dated 22 Dec. 1606 and proved 13 Mar. 1607, made 'for the relief and maintenance of my wife and children', Vaughan left leases of a farm called Barton, near Tavistock, and a house in the town to his wife, the executrix and residuary legatee, with remainder to his eldest son Charles, who received immediately a farm called Chillamill, and was given discretion to deal with some of Vaughan's smaller bequests. Concern was shown 'for the better maintenance and education of my five youngest children' and generous marriage portions were provided for his daughters. Several farms and mills are mentioned in the locality and in Cornwall.

Roberts thesis; Gabriel thesis: *Devon N. and Q.* x. 98, 103; *Devon quarter sess. order bk.* 1592–1600, f. 158; PCC 24 Huddleston, 45 Windsor; *Western Antiq.* iv. 120; Vivian, *Vis. Devon*, 439, 729; Exeter freeman's bk. f. 144; D'Ewes, 507, 513; *CJ*, i. 120, 127; A. H. A. Hamilton, *Quarter Sess. Q. Eliz. to Q. Anne* (1878), 51; *Trans. Dev. Assoc.* xlii. 370; C142/295/35.

P.W.H.

VAUGHAN, John I (*d*.1577), of London, Surr. and Sutton-upon-Derwent, Yorks.

?HEREFORDSHIRE	1542
HORSHAM	1547*
SURREY	1547*
PETERSFIELD	1553 (Mar.), 1554 (Apr.), 1554 (Nov.)
BLETCHINGLEY	1555
HEDON	1559
NORTHUMBERLAND	1563
DARTMOUTH	1571
GRANTHAM	1572*

Yr. s. of Thomas Vaughan of Porthaml, Brec. by Elizabeth, da. of Henry Miles *alias* Parry of Newcourt in Bacton, Herefs. *m.* Anne, da. and h. of Sir Christopher Pickering of Killington, Westmld. and Escrick, E. Riding, Yorks., wid. of Sir Francis Weston of Sutton in Woking, Surr. and of Sir Henry Knyvet of East Horsley, Surr., 2s. 2da.[1]

Page of the chamber by 1533, sewer by 1538; steward, Pembridge, Herefs. 1533; member, council in the north and j.p. many northern counties after Dec. 1558; custos rot. Yorks. (E. Riding) 1566; j.p. Surr. from 1559, commr. musters from c.1576; steward, Penrith, Cumb. 1559; sheriff, Yorks. 1559–60; steward, Galtres forest, Yorks. 1564; keeper, Cawood park, Yorks. 1568.[2]

John Vaughan came of a junior branch of the Vaughan family of Porthaml, Breconshire and was a nephew of Blanche Parry, Queen Elizabeth's gentlewoman, and a distant kinsman of Sir Roger Vaughan*, Sir Thomas Parry* and Sir William Cecil*. He served many years in the royal household, and married about 1549 the heiress to great estates in Yorkshire, Middlesex, Cumberland and Westmorland, who was the widow of two former gentlemen of the privy chamber. During the minority of her eldest son, Sir Henry Weston*, she and Vaughan lived at Weston's house at Sutton, Surrey. Vaughan assumed the position due to the owner of one of the largest estates there and was elected to Parliament for the county at a by-election. In his next three Parliaments he sat for Weston's borough of Petersfield, and in 1555 was returned for Bletchingley, which was controlled by Sir Thomas Cawarden*, formerly his fellow-Member for Surrey, and, like Vaughan, one of Princess Elizabeth's circle. In this last

Parliament he opposed a major government bill and did not reappear in the House of Commons under Mary.

After Elizabeth's accession, Vaughan bought the manor of Sutton-upon-Derwent and settled in Yorkshire. He presumably came in for Hedon through his local connexions, and no doubt the government was pleased to have a sound protestant returned for a northern borough. Sir Henry Gates*, another recent arrival in Yorkshire with protestant views, was appointed to the council in the north at the same time as Vaughan. The two new men frequently engaged in disputes with the older nobility, and by 1565 were allied against Sir John Constable*, a man of ancient family and Catholic sympathies. The feud came to a head in 1567 when the president, Archbishop Young of York, admitted Constable to the council, whereupon Vaughan accused the archbishop before the Privy Council of maintaining Constable's party. On 6 Dec. the Privy Council dismissed Constable.[3]

On 11 July 1568, Gates, Vaughan and Sir Thomas Gargrave* warned Cecil of the danger of a rising in favour of Mary Queen of Scots. Gates was ill when the northern rebellion broke out in November 1569 and was therefore unable to take up his appointment as sheriff. When Vaughan heard that the Earl of Sussex planned to appoint him instead, he wrote hastily to Cecil asking to be excused, saying that it would be his undoing, 'as I have written to my aunt [Blanche Parry] more at large'. This appeal to his influential relatives may have led to his plea being successful: at any rate he remained absent from the council, 'sick', until the danger had passed. He was, none the less, chosen as the person to hand over the rebel Earl of Northumberland to the Queen, much to the annoyance of Henry Carey†, Lord Hunsdon, who wrote to Cecil on 7 Apr. 1570:

Her Majesty shall find John Vaughan but an ox, neither able to serve her abroad nor at home, in war nor in peace, but only in words, envying every man that is in authority above himself.

On 2 Sept. 1570 Gargrave suggested to Burghley that Vaughan, Gates and Sir George Bowes* should be made resident councillors, because they were men of weight and 'knew the law'. In 1574 all three were granted freedom from continual attendance unless their presence was required by the president.

Vaughan held little if any land in Northumberland, though his wife's family may have had estates there. He possibly gained a Northumberland county seat in 1563 through the influence of Lord Grey of Wilton, warden of the east march, and a strong protestant. At first sight Vaughan seems an unlikely Member for Dartmouth, in a district far distant from his sphere of activity, but there is no obvious namesake who could have represented the borough, and the 2nd Earl of Bedford, sometimes parliamentary patron there, was a friend of Vaughan's kinsman Lord Burghley. At Grantham, where Vaughan obtained a seat in 1572, Burghley's nominees were returned to several Elizabethan Parliaments. It is likely that Vaughan served on committees concerned with treason (12 Apr. 1571), tillage (21 May 1571), Mary Stuart (12 May 1572) and justices of the forest (8 May 1576). He died on 25 June 1577. In accordance with a settlement made some years before, his property then passed to his eldest son, Francis. A daughter, Frances, married Thomas, 5th Lord Burgh.[4]

[1] *Yorks. Peds.* (Harl. Soc. xcvi), 405–6; T. Jones, *Hist Brec.* iv. 43, 271; *Vis. Yorks.* (Harl. Soc. xvi), 251; *Genealogy Vaughan of Tretower*, ed. C. Vaughan; *Vis. Yorks.* ed. Foster, 120–1; Harl. 2141, f. 200; *Vis. Herefs.* ed. Weaver, 4. [2] *LP Hen. VIII*, vi. p. 552; xiv(2), p. 307; xvi. p. 185; xvii. p. 478; xx(2), pp. 307, 515; *CPR*, 1558–60, p. 36; 1560–3, pp. 170–1, 187, 207; 1563–6, p. 86; Reid, *Council of the North*, 493; Lansd. 10, f. 84; SP13/Case H no. 10; SP12/93. [3] Lansd. 10, f. 4; 56, f. 168; *CPR*, 1553–4, p. 229; 1558–60, p. 207; 1560–3, p. 581; Guildford Mus., Loseley 1331/2; Reid, 187, 196; *Parl. Rep. Yorks.* ed. Gooder, ii. 16, 20–1, 23; *HMC Bath*, ii. 19. [4] *CSP Dom.* Add. 1566–79, p. 515 et passim; *CJ*, i. 84, 95, 112; D'Ewes, 165, 187, 255; C142/177/58.

P.H.

VAUGHAN, John II (by 1525–74), of Kidwelly, Carmarthen and Golden Grove, Carm.

| CARMARTHEN BOROUGHS | 1558, ?1571 |
| CARMARTHENSHIRE | 1572* |

b. by 1525, 1st s. of Hugh Vaughan of Kidwelly by 1st w. Jane, da. of Moris ab Owen of Bryn-y-Beirdd, Llandeilo, Carm. and Upton Castle, Pemb. *m.* Catherine, da. of Henry Morgan of Muddlescwm, 2s. Henry* and Walter* 1da.; at least 6s. 5da. illegit.

Bailiff, Carmarthen in 1553, mayor 1554–5, 1563–4, alderman in 1555; receiver, duchy of Lancaster, Kidwelly 10 Mar. 1554–*d.*; j.p.q. Carm. 1559–*d.*; commr. subsidy 1560, piracy 1565; customer, Milford Haven, Pemb. 1560–*d.*; steward, Cilgerran, Pemb. 1560–*d.*; sheriff, Carm. 1562–3; bailiff, coroner, escheator and town clerk, Kidwelly by 1572.

The Vaughans of Golden Grove (as they came to be known) were of old Powys stock, traditionally of base descent from the princes of Powys. The first to appear in South Wales was Vaughan's father, who made a fortunate marriage into the family of Sir Rhys ap Gruffydd of Dynevor – then the most powerful man in Wales. On Rhys's attainder in 1531, Hugh Vaughan (then a groom of the chamber) was one of those appointed to collect the rents accruing to the Crown from the attainted man's lands in the lordship of Kidwelly.

John Vaughan II added substantially to the lands his father had acquired in the commote of Is-Cennan first by securing a lease of the manor of Dryslwyn, north of the Towy, and then in 1564, by taking leases of Rhys ap Gruffydd's former lands south of the river. It was here that the family mansion of Golden Grove was built, and

tradition makes John Vaughan the builder. However, in all contemporary documents, up to and including his will, he is described as 'of Carmarthen' (or, as in the pardon roll of 1554, 'late of Carmarthen'). On the other hand, his request to be buried in the parish church of Llanfihangel Aberbythych suggests at least an intention to settle in the parish. In 1563 and 1566 he made further acquisitions from the forfeited lands of Rhys ap Gruffydd in and around Llanelly, Pembrey, Llanstephen and St. Clears (east and west of Kidwelly) and in Carmarthen borough. He also accumulated offices both in the lordship of Kidwelly and in Carmarthen borough, where his mayoralty was the subject of a complimentary ode by a bard of Gwynedd, and was followed by return to Parliament for the Boroughs. He became an important figure in the shire, in influence second only to the family of Jones of Abermarlais, the chief beneficiaries by the attainder of their kinsman Rhys ap Gruffydd.

Vaughan had to put up a fight in the court of the duchy of Lancaster in 1570–1 for his duchy lands and offices, and his title was evidently upheld: the offices provided the excuse for a period of leave of absence from Parliament 11 June 1572 and the lands remained in the family. Browne Willis is wrong in giving Vaughan as the Member for Carmarthenshire in 1571 in his printed list, and may also be wrong in giving John Morgan as the Member for Carmarthen Boroughs in 1571. If so, it is at least possible that Vaughan sat for the Boroughs in that Parliament. The John Vaughan who was on two committees in 1571 was presumably John Vaughan I*, but both John Vaughans were on the committee discussing Mary Stuart, 12 May 1572.

Vaughan died in 1574. The parliamentary vacancy was filled by his heir and executor Walter, who also succeeded his father in the mayoralty of Carmarthen, the receivership of Kidwelly, and, later, the shrievalty of Carmarthenshire. In his will, dated 6 Aug. 1568 and proved 19 June 1574, Vaughan bequeathed the Is-Cennan lands centring on Golden Grove to Walter Vaughan, but the outlying estates, including manors, parsonages, townships and house property in and near Carmarthen and Kidwelly and in south Pembrokeshire, to his other son Henry. Those in Llanelly district went to a cousin; and provision was made in cash and stock totalling about £100 for his many illegitimate children. Charitable bequests amounted to no more than ten shillings for the poor, and another £1 for municipal uses, at Carmarthen, and £2 and a black gown to the bishop for a funeral sermon.

F. Jones, 'The Vaughans of Golden Grove', *Trans. Cymmrod. Soc.* 1963, pp. 98–102; *Cal. sheriffs etc. of Carmarthen* (NLW ms 5586B), 9–10; Somerville, *Duchy*, i. 643; J. E. Lloyd, *Carm.* ii. 467; *APC*, vii. 285; E178/3345; *LP Hen. VIII*, xxi(1), p. 248; *CPR*, 1554–5, p. 347; 1558–60, p. 245; 1560–3, p. 445; 1563–6, p. 332; PCC 26 Martyn; *Augmentations*, ed. Lewis and Davies (Univ. Wales Bd. of Celtic Studies, Hist. and Law ser. xiii), 246, 263–4; *Exchequer*, ed. E. G.

Jones (same ser. iv), 114; *Cynfeirdd Lleyn*, 1905, pp. 80–1; Flenley, *Cal. Reg. Council, Marches of Wales*, 75; DL1/80/V2; *CJ*, i. 102; D'Ewes, 206.

A.H.D.

VAUGHAN, John III (by 1553–97 or later), of St. Petrox, Pemb.

PEMBROKE BOROUGHS   1584, 1586

b. by 1553, 5th s. of Robert Vaughan of Castlemartin by Janet, da. of Nicholas Gilbert of Oldcastle, Herefs. *m.* 1561, Catherine, da. of Owain ap John ap Tryhaiarn, 1da.

Customer, Milford Haven, Pemb. 1574–97 or later.

The Vaughans of Castlemartin were a branch of the Vaughans of Tyleglas, Breconshire. Vaughan himself, as a younger son, had to make his way in a profession. The post of customer of Milford Haven (which presumably accounts for his return to Parliament for the county town) covered the coasts from Worms Head in Gower to Barmouth in Merioneth. It was of some importance in view of the brisk trade of this region with France, and Vaughan held it for over 20 years, thanks to the favour of his distant kinsman Lord Burghley. He seems to have executed his duties, consisting chiefly of measures against smuggling, with some vigour; though there were two or three complaints against him, and on one occasion he was summoned before the Privy Council. Vaughan is last heard of in May 1597.

Dwnn, *Vis. Wales*, i. 127; E. Laws, *Little England beyond Wales*, 307; *Welsh Port Bks.* (Cymmrod Soc. rec. ser. xii), pp. xxxi–xxxvi; *CSP Dom.* 1547–80, p. 498; 1581–90, p. 58; *HMC Hatfield*, vi. 449; vii. 228; xiii. 347; *Exchequer*, ed. E. G. Jones (Univ. Wales Bd. of Celtic Studies, Hist. and Law ser. iv), 214; *APC*, xx. 84; *Arch. Camb.* (ser. 5), xiv. 319–20.

A.H.D.

VAUGHAN, Sir John (c.1575–1634), of Golden Grove, Llanfihangel Aberbythych, Carm.

CARMARTHENSHIRE   1601, 1621

b. c.1575, 1st s. of Walter Vaughan* by his 1st w. Mary, da. of Griffith Rice of Newton. *educ.* Jesus, Oxf. 1592, aged 17; I. Temple 1596. *m.* (1) Margaret, da. of Gelly Meyrick*, 1s 1da.; (2) Jane, da. of Sir Thomas Palmer of Wengham, Kent, wid. of Sir William Meredith of Leeds, Kent, *s.p. suc.* fa. 1598. Kntd. 1599; *cr.* Baron Vaughan [I] 1621, Earl of Carbery [I] 1628.[1]

Bailiff, Carmarthen 1598, mayor 1603; j.p. Carm. aft. 1601; commr. oyer and terminer, S. Wales 1601; sheriff, Carm. Nov. 1604–Feb. 1606; bailiff, Kidwelly 1608; comptroller, Prince of Wales's household 1618; commr. on moneys levied for Ireland, Carm. 1627; member, council in the marches of Wales 1633.[2]

Vaughan was heir to an estate estimated in 1601 at £800 a year; in George Owen's list of Carmarthenshire *generosi* a

year or so later he stood second only to Sir Thomas Jones* of Abermarlais, and by the end of his life Golden Grove had outstripped Abermarlais in the Carmarthenshire hierarchy, the primacy of the Vaughans remaining unchallenged through most of the seventeenth century. Within a year of succeeding his father, Vaughan accompanied Essex on his ill-omened Irish campaign, and was knighted by him. The tradition that the Queen 'disallowed' the honour, and that it was again conferred by Lord Deputy St. John in 1617, is contradicted by the consistent use of the title until it was superseded by the peerage; it is likely that the 1617 knight was the 'Captain Vaughan' who spent his life in Ireland, as soldier, planter, privy councillor and Parliament man, until long after the Carmarthenshire Member's peerage and even after his death.[3]

In 1601 Vaughan accused a fellow-magistrate in Star Chamber of 'unlawful affection' for recusants and affrays at the great sessions and Llandeilo market, and complained of the increase of popery in the area. These sound like defensive tactics, for the treason of Essex and his Welsh steward, Meyrick, made the latter's son-in-law vulnerable. In 1601–2 Vaughan was charged, in two other Star Chamber suits, with conspiring with Sir Thomas Jones to cheat a lunatic out of his lands, and with procuring the conveyance of a guest's patrimony by plying him with drink. But in the latter year he quarrelled with Jones over the manors of Hirfryn, Perfedd and Llandovery. These manors, once held by Abermarlais, had been granted by Elizabeth to their ancient lords the Audleys, and Lord Audley had conveyed them to Sir John's father; Sir John now accused Sir Thomas before the Exchequer court of interference with his manorial rights.[4]

More perilous accusations arose out of the Essex conspiracy. The fact that a few weeks before the revolt Vaughan's wife had conveyed her father's plate and chattels to her husband's house naturally aroused suspicion. He was even named among those present at the fateful meeting at Essex House where plans were laid, but a more credible account represents him as having 'turned back' on the way. At all events, before the end of February 1601 he was discharged 'without bonds, indictment, arraignment or fine'. He assured Cecil that the charges against him had been made in revenge for his severity towards recusants. Before autumn he was settled at Golden Grove, acknowledging Cecil's 'favours' and commending to him one of his many brothers, and in October he was entrusted with the raising of horse in Carmarthenshire to meet the Spanish landing in Ireland. In the same month he was elected knight of the shire for Carmarthenshire, which would have entitled him to sit on the main business committee for that Parliament (3 Nov.) and on the monopolies committee (23 Nov.). In the seventeenth century he was to obtain central office, and an Irish peerage. He died 6 May 1634.[5]

[1] *Trans. Cymmrod. Soc.* 1963, pp. 105–12; *Exchequer*, ed. E. G. Jones (Univ. Wales Bd. of Celtic Studies, Hist. and Law ser. iv), 128–9; *HMC Hatfield*, viii. 32, 104. [2] W. R. Williams, *Parl. Hist. Wales*, 44; *Hist. Carm.* ed. Lloyd, iii. 467; *Star Chamber*, ed. Edwards (Univ. Wales Bd. of Celtic Studies, Hist. and Law ser. i), 51; C181/5; *Trans. Cymmrod. Soc.* loc. cit.; *APC*, xxxvi. 333; xli. 114. [3] *HMC Hatfield*, viii. 82, 104; xi. 108; G. Owen, *Desc. Wales*, *Desc. Pemb.* ed. H. Owen, iii. 383; *Hist. Carm.* ii. 33; *DWB*, 995–6; *Exchequer*, ed. E. G. Jones 119; Somerville, *Duchy*, i. 643; *CSP Ire.* 1600–47, passim; *CP*. [4] *Star Chamber*, ed. Edwards, 46, 51; *Exchequer*, ed. E. G. Jones, 128–9; *CSP Dom.* 1591–4, p. 363; *Hist. Carm.* i. 234. [5] *HMC Hatfield*, xi. 82, 87, 107, 113, 126, 135, 160, 329; D'Ewes, 624, 649; *CSP Dom.* 1598–1601, p. 548; *APC*, xxxii. 282.

A.H.D.

VAUGHAN, Robert (by 1524-75 or later), of Presteigne, Rad.

NEW RADNOR BOROUGHS	1554 (Apr.), 1554 (Nov.), 1559

b. by 1524, poss. *s.* of William Vaughan of Glasbury, Rad. ?*m.* at least 1s.

J.p. Rad. 1559–75 or later, sheriff ?1562–3, 1567–8.

Vaughan's one appearance in Parliament in this period left no trace upon the records. He was classified by the bishop of his diocese as indifferent in religion in 1564, but retained his place on the commission of the peace until at least 1575. He was one of 11 Radnorshire gentry assessed at 'one light horseman furnished' at the musters of 1570. The date of his death has not been ascertained.

Trans. Rad. Hist. Soc. xxviii. 15; *Cam. Misc.* ix(3), pp. 16–17; Flenley, *Cal. Reg. Council, Marches of Wales*, 75, 136.

P.S.E./A.D.K.H.

VAUGHAN, Roger (d. by 1615), of Court of Clyro, Rad. and Kynnersley, Herefs.

RADNORSHIRE	1572

1st *s.* of Roger Vaughan by Margaret, da. of Sir William Vaughan of Talgarth, Brec. *m.* Margaret, da. of Richard Monington of Herefs., at least 1s. John.[1]

J.p. Rad. from c.1573, Brec. from c.1591, Herefs. from c.1591; sheriff, Rad. 1576–7, Brec. 1585–6, 1595–6; dep. lt. Rad. by 1601.[2]

The Vaughans of Clyro were a branch of a clan with wide ramifications, through frequent intermarriage and common descent, in Herefordshire, Radnorshire and Breconshire. They owed their position in Radnorshire to judicious purchases and leases from the dissolved abbey of Cwmhir, and Vaughan's own house was former monastic property.[3]

Since 1553 the representation of Radnorshire and its boroughs had, for the most part, been shared between the families of Lewis of Harpton and Price of Mynachdy, with their subordinate branches. It may have been his kinship with the sheriff, Edward Price, that induced Roger Vaughan to challenge this. At any rate in the Star

Chamber action brought against the sheriff in 1573 by the defeated candidate, Thomas Lewis* of Harpton – Vaughan's inveterate foe – it was alleged (with some probability) that the return of Vaughan was contrary to the evidence of the voting. When in 1597 Vaughan challenged again for the county seat one of the arguments used against him was that he lived in Herefordshire. After this, the Vaughans of Clyro fade out of the parliamentary picture, but not out of local politics, where 'the great Vaughan', as he was known, with an estate reckoned at £1,000 a year and key offices in three shires, remained a formidable figure. His 'familiar friend' (Sir) Gelly Meyrick*, who was behind his attempt on the county seat in 1597, was alleged to have 'estated' his lands in trust to Vaughan a month before the Essex rising, 'doubting what might ensue'. Vaughan accompanied him to London, but returned before involving himself irretrievably. He was denounced by neighbours as a 'favourer' of the rising, a crypto-papist and a shelterer of priests (it is true that a 'Vaghan' appears on a list drawn up in the interest of Mary Queen of Scots in 1574 and that his wife and sons were recusants in the reign of James I), with the usual allegations of misuse of his authority, but he appears to have escaped unscathed. He was dead by 1615.[4]

[1] Dwnn, *Vis. Wales*, i. 258; *Exchequer Proc. Jas. I*, ed. T. I. J. Jones (Univ. Wales Bd. of Celtic Studies, Hist. and Law ser. xv), 33–7. [2] *Star Chamber*, ed. Edwards (Univ. Wales Bd. of Celtic Studies, Hist. and Law ser. i), 138–140; Flenley, *Cal. Reg. Council, Marches of Wales*, 237; *HMC Hatfield*, xi. 43; Neale, *Commons*, 80–1. [3] *DWB*, 993; *Arch. Camb.* (ser. 1), iv. 259; D. Mathew, *Celtic Peoples and Renaissance Europe*, 356; *RCAM Rad.* 35. [4] *Star Chamber*, loc. cit.; *HMC Hatfield*, xi. 43, 107, 133; *CSP Dom.* 1603–10, p. 443; *Cath. Rec. Soc. Misc.* viii, 111; *Exchequer*, ed. T. I. J. Jones (Univ. Wales Bd. of Celtic Studies, Hist. and Law ser. xv), 33.

A.H.D.

VAUGHAN, Sir Roger (d.1571), of Porthaml, Talgarth, Brec.

BRECONSHIRE	1553 (Mar.), 1553 (Oct.), 1554 (Apr.), 1559
BRECON BOROUGHS	1563
BRECONSHIRE	1571

1st *s.* of Sir William Vaughan of Porthaml by Catherine, da. of Jenkin Harvard of Brec. *m.* (1) Catherine, da. of (Sir) George Herbert† of Swansea, Glam., 5s. inc. Rowland*; (2) Eleanor, da. of Henry, 2nd Earl of Worcester. *suc. fa.* 1546 or later. Kntd. 1551.[1]

J.p. Brec. from 1543, q. by 1559, sheriff 1551–2, custos rot. by 1559; commr. armour 1569, musters 1570, church goods, Brec. and Herefs. 1553; steward of castles and lordships and keeper of parks, Huntington and Kington, Herefs. from May 1554.[2]

The Vaughans of Porthaml were a junior branch of the Vaughans of Tretower, Breconshire; both, with many other branches, were descended from Roger Vaughan of Bredwardine, Herefordshire, who fell at Agincourt. His son Sir Roger, founder of the Tretower Vaughans, owed his pre-eminence in Breconshire to the favour of William Herbert[t], 1st Earl of Pembroke. Sir Roger's younger son settled at Porthaml and acquired the stewardship of the lordship of Dinas, and his grandson Sir William (the MP's father) further advanced the family fortune and prestige by securing the wardship of the coheiresses of New Court, Herefordshire, and the office of chancellor and receiver of the lordship of Brecknock. He was the first sheriff of the newly-formed shire.[3]

In 1546 Sir William handed over his offices in the lordship of Brecon to his son Roger, and probably died soon afterwards. Roger took up his father's leases of crown land in Breconshire, and as justice of the peace in the 1560s he was involved in the investigation of the 'miraculous apparition' in the grounds of St. Donats, Glamorganshire, and its supposed exploitation in Catholic interests by the owner, Sir Thomas Stradling[t]. Ten years after that he was accused in Star Chamber of 'maintaining' a Herefordshire murderer, and that in association with a priest suspected of popish practices.[4]

He died on 16 June 1571; complications over the inheritance postponed administration of the estate until 31 Mar. 1585. His widow married Sir Henry Jones*.[5]

[1] Wards 7/14/91; *DWB*, 999; T. Jones, *Brec.* iii. 43; Dwnn, *Vis. Wales*, i. 189. [2] *CPR*, 1550–3, p. 394; 1553, App. Edw. VI, pp. 364, 409, 414; 1560–3, p. 445; 1563–6, p. 29; *DWB*; *Exchequer*, ed. E. G. Jones (Univ. Wales Bd. of Celtic Studies, Hist. and Law ser. iv), 34; Flenley, *Cal. Reg. Council, Marches of Wales*, 60, 69. [3] *DWB*, 996–7, 1000–1; *Tretower Court* (Min. of Works), 4. [4] *CPR*, 1555–7, p. 518; 1558–60, p. 207; 1563–6, p. 412; *Augmentations*, ed. Lewis and Davies (Univ. Wales Bd. of Celtic Studies, Hist. and Law ser. xiii), 199, 206, 218–19; *Star Chamber*, ed. Edwards (same ser. i), 27; *CSP Dom.* 1547–80, p. 176; *Welsh Rev.* 1947, pp. 33 seq. [5] Wards 7/14/91; PCC admon. act bk. 1585, f. 134.

A.H.D.

VAUGHAN, Rowland (*d.*1566), of Porthaml, Talgarth, Brec.

BRECON BOROUGHS	1559
BRECONSHIRE	1563*

s. of Sir Roger Vaughan* of Porthaml by Catherine, da. of (Sir) George Herbert[t] of Swansea. *educ.* I. Temple 1556 or 1557. *m.* Elizabeth, da. and coh. of Miles Parry of New Court, Herefs., 1s. 2da.

J.p. Brec. from 1561.

Vaughan's family had dominated Breconshire since the Act of Union. He had his first parliamentary experience, as Member for the Boroughs, soon after he had finished his education at an inn of court. He soon afterwards joined his father on the county bench, and in the next Parliament Sir Roger surrendered to his son the county seat, taking over from him the representation of the Boroughs. It is interesting to see that the 1563 election return styles him Sir Rowland Vaughan. A Rowland

Vaughan was buried at St. Margaret's, Westminster, on 19 Jan. 1566. Whether or not this was the MP, Rowland Vaughan of Porthaml was certainly dead (during the life of his father) by 25 June that year, when administration of his estate was granted to the widow.

T. Jones, *Brec.* iii. 43; *CPR*, 1560–3, p. 445; C219/27/50; PCC admon. act bk. 1566, f. 110.

A.H.D.

VAUGHAN, Walter (*d.*1598), of Golden Grove, Carm.

CARMARTHENSHIRE	1572*, 1593

1st s. of John Vaughan II* of Carmarthen and bro. of Henry*. *educ.* ?G. Inn 1561. *m.* (1) Mary, da. of Griffith Rice of Newton, Llandefaison, 10s. inc. Sir John* 3da.; (2) Lettice, illegit. da. of Sir John Perrot*, wid. of Rowland Laugharne of St. Brides, Pemb., 2da. *suc.* fa. 1574.[1]

Bailiff, Carmarthen 1572–3, mayor 1574, 1580, 1597; receiver, Kidwelly 1574; j.p. Carm. from c.1575, q. by 1579, Pemb. from c.1591; sheriff, Carm. 1584–5, Pemb. 1593–4; commr. Exchequer, Carm. 1581; ragler, Carm. by 1589.[2]

Within three years of his succession to his father's estates Vaughan began to accumulate lands in the neighbourhood of Carmarthen and Llanstephan. In 1581 he leased the manor of Llandeilo from the bishop of St. David's, and ten years later the addition to his holdings of a grist mill on the Llwchwr, near Llanelly, gave him a more southerly foothold. Here he worked 'for the space of half a year ... one vein of coal'. In 1593 he acquired from Lord Audley a life interest in the manors of Hirfryn, Perfedd and Llandovery.[3]

Both Vaughan's offices and his lands brought their tale of litigation. In 1589 he charged before the court of Exchequer 26 tenants of four of the manors of Cantref Mawr (north of the Towy) with defrauding the Crown, and himself as ragler, by withholding customary dues. Two years later he defended before the same court his mill rights on the Llwchwr from tenants who were declining suit of mill. In 1591 he was accused of forging a bond, and the president of the council in the marches of Wales was directed by the Privy Council to look into the matter. In the last year of his life he was arraigned before both Exchequer and Star Chamber on charges of misusing his influence as magistrate to suborn, in the interests of a servant of his under sentence for murder, the jury in an Exchequer commission investigating the title to lands in Llangathen, near Llandeilo; his son John was further accused of assault and battery on the claimant to the lands.[4]

Vaughan was twice elected for his county, where his marriage into the house of Rice of Newton had enhanced his standing. He was elected to the 1576 session of the 1572 Parliament in place of his deceased father. At the beginning of the third session of of that Parliament his membership was challenged because he had been outlawed for debt, but a small and sympathetic committee consisting of the Speaker, Henry Knollys II* and Henry Townshend* excused him on the ground that the debt had been incurred as surety for a friend. Vaughan's brother-in-law Walter Rice* succeeded him in the county representation in 1584. In his second Parliament Vaughan could have attended the subsidy committee appointed 26 Feb. 1593 and a legal committee appointed 9 Mar. His second marriage brought him little advantage, for Sir John Perrot was attainted in 1592. However, Vaughan found a powerful protector in the Earl of Essex, whose livery he wore, and who came to the defence of 'my servant' when in 1585 this 'affectionate follower' was denounced by the judges of the Carmarthen circuit for reprieving, on his patron's directions, a prisoner committed to his custody as sheriff. The Earl's intervention, however, came too late to save him from a Star Chamber fine for interference with the course of justice. In 1592 he was one of those from Carmarthenshire and Pembrokeshire commissioned by the Privy Council to root out recusancy and 'superstitious' practices in West Wales; four months later it came to light that he and several of his colleagues had not yet taken the oath of supremacy.[5]

In 1576 Walter Vaughan joined with others in petitioning for a free school at Carmarthen to replace an earlier one which had decayed. In the instrument granting the petition the Queen named the petitioners among the foundation wardens and governors of what still goes by the name of Queen Elizabeth's Grammar School. Rent charges supporting the endowment were later challenged as an encroachment on common rights, which involved Vaughan's son Sir John in litigation 30 years later. Vaughan died intestate in 1598 and was succeeded by his son and heir John, afterwards Earl of Carbery.[6]

[1] Trans. Cymmrod. Soc. 1963, pp. 103–4; PCC 26 Martyn.
[2] Williams, Parl. Hist. Wales, 43; Hist. Carm. ed. Lloyd, ii. 467; Somerville, Duchy, i. 643; Flenley, Cal. Reg. Council, Marches of Wales, 139, 184, 213; APC, xxii. 122; Augmentations, ed. Lewis and Davies (Univ. Wales Bd. of Celtic Studies, Hist. and Law ser. xiii), 258.
[3] Exchequer, ed. E. G. Jones (Univ. Wales Bd. of Celtic Studies, Hist. and Law ser. iv), 108, 120–1, 128–9; Augmentations (same ser. xiii), 248–9, 254–6; Duchy of Lancaster, ed. Rees (same ser. xii), 262.
[4] Exchequer, 108, 109, 119, 120–1; Star Chamber, ed. Edwards (Univ. Wales Bd. of Celtic Studies, Hist. and Law ser. i), 51; APC, xxii. 122.
[5] CJ, i. 124; D'Ewes, 292, 294, 474, 496; J. M. Lewis, Carreg Cennen Castle (Min. of Works 1960), p. 5; Star Chamber, 45; Lansd. 53, f. 182; Harl. 6994, ff. 3, 15, 48, 62; CSP Dom. 1581–90, p. 335; P. H. Williams, Council in the Marches of Wales, 282–3; APC, xxii. 544; xxiii. 260. [6] Knight, Welsh Grammar Schools to 1600, pp. 16–17; Trans. Cymmrod. Soc. 1963, p. 109; C193/32/9; Exchequer, 128–9; HMC Hatfield, viii. 82, 104; PCC admon. act bk. 1598, f. 240.

A.H.D.

VAUGHAN, Watkin

NEW RADNOR BOROUGHS 1572

The name Watkin appears frequently in the pedigrees of the Vaughans of Herefordshire, Radnorshire and Breconshire and the 1572 MP cannot be identified with certainty. A possibility is a younger (prob. 2nd) s. of Sir William Vaughan of Porthaml, Brec. by his 1st w. Catherine, da. of Jenkin Havard; bro. of Sir Roger Vaughan*. This man, who was j.p. Herefs. by 1574, wrote from Bredwardine to Lord Burghley on 17 Dec. 1584 asking for a bill in Parliament to free the marches from inquiries into crimes committed in adjoining shires, and was presumably dead by 1596, when his name disappears from the commission of the peace.[1]

Another possibility is a common councilman and original burgess of New Radnor named Walter Vaughan, and described as of Presteigne, alias of Harpton, alias of London. He was pardoned in 1559 for offences connected with the clipping of coins. His mother was presumably the Eleanor Vaughan of Harpton, widow, who made her will 30 Dec. 1564, leaving houses and lands to her younger son Walter. Walter Vaughan and his wife 'of Radnor' (presumably the Harpton people) were still alive late in 1601.[2]

[1] T. Jones, Brec. iv. 285; Clarke, Limbus, 242; CSP Dom. 1581–90, p. 215; Harl. 3525, f. 110; C. M. Bradford, Blanche Parry (privately). [2] CPR, 1588–60, p. 289; Trans. Rad. Soc. xxix. 49; Star Chamber, ed. Edwards (Univ. Wales Bd. of Celtic Studies, Hist. and Law ser. i), 140.

M.R.P.

VAUGHAN, see also PARRY, Sir Thomas

VAVASOUR, Thomas (1560–1620), of Skellingthorpe, Lincs., and Ham, Surr.

WOOTTON BASSETT	1584, 1586
MALMESBURY	1589
BOROUGHBRIDGE	1604*
HORSHAM	1614

b. 1560, 1st s. of Henry Vavasour of Copmanthorpe, Yorks. by Margaret, da. of Sir Henry Knyvet of ?Charlton, Wilts. educ. Eton; Caius, Camb., fellow-com. 1576. m. Mary, da. and h. of John Dodge of Copes, Suff., wid. of Peter Houghton, alderman of London, 4s. 2da. Kntd. bef. Aug. 1595.[1]

Capt. in the Netherlands Aug. 1585–May 1591, Feb.–Oct. 1598; gent. pens. 1586–1603; butler of port of London from 1603; knight marshal of Household 1604–18; farmer of alnagership of old draperies, Yorks. 1606; forester, Galtres, Yorks.[2]

Thomas Vavasour came of a family which, long settled in Yorkshire, had also spread into Lincolnshire. Forbears of his had been returned to Parliament from both counties, the most recent of them being his grandfather, Sir William, one of the knights for Yorkshire in Mary's first Parliament. The family was to remain Catholic and some of its members were to be troubled on this score from the time of the northern rebellion onwards.[3]

As nephew to (Sir) Henry Knyvet* of Charlton and his younger brother Thomas Knyvet*, gentleman of the privy chamber, Thomas Vavasour would doubtless have found his way to court even without the example of his sister Anne, who became a gentlewoman of the bedchamber about 1580; but Anne Vavasour's dissolute career was to impinge considerably on her brother's. She began – as she was to end – as the mistress of Sir Henry Lee, the Queen's champion and jouster-in-chief, and it is as a runner against Sir Henry at the tilt of 6 Dec. 1584 that Thomas is first mentioned. By then, however, he was doubtless already involved in the feud between Thomas Knyvet and the Earl of Oxford, by whom Anne had had a child in March 1581; and it was this scandal which led him in January 1585 to challenge Oxford to a duel in a letter beginning: 'If thy body had been as deformed as thy mind is dishonourable, my house had been as yet unspotted and thyself remained with thy cowardice unknown'. Vavasour may have been influenced by the example of Sir Henry Knyvet who five years earlier had fought a duel which nearly cost him his life, but his proposed meeting with Oxford at Newington evidently did not come off.[4]

Vavasour's hostility towards Oxford perhaps owed something to the Earl's conversion to Catholicism and subsequent accusations against leading Catholics. Coming as he did from a Catholic family, Vavasour must have had many ties with members of that Church; there was, for example, his namesake who was imprisoned about 1583 in the Gatehouse and who was later in trouble as a servant of Sir Thomas Tresham. Vavasour's own career, and his connexion with the strongly protestant Knyvets, make it unlikely that he retained his family's religious allegiance, and he died believing in the merits of Christ's Passion.[5]

At the time of his challenge to Oxford, Vavasour was sitting in Parliament for the first time, as senior burgess for Wootton Bassett; he was returned again in that capacity in 1586 and for the neighbouring borough of Malmesbury to the Parliament of 1589. He owed his election on all three occasions to Sir Henry Knyvet, who exercised influence at Wootton Bassett for upwards of 25 years, and at Malmesbury for 15; and it was doubtless a tribute to Knyvet's standing rather than to his own that he was styled 'The Worshipful' in the return of 1584. His name does not appear in the records of any of these Parliaments, and it is possible that he was an absentee Member during at least part of the second, for in August 1585 he went over to the Netherlands as captain of 150 foot from Yorkshire, and he retained this command until 1591. He distinguished himself on two occasions, once in an attack on a sconce near Arnhem in October 1585, and again two years later when he went out with Lord Willoughby to fight the Marques del Guasto. Willoughby declared that he loved Vavasour as himself.[6]

His service in the Netherlands also advanced Vavasour at home. Since December 1585 his company had come under the Earl of Leicester's command and pay, and in the following March he was sent by Leicester with letters and messages to the Queen. His selection for, and discharge of, this delicate duty – for Elizabeth was still angry with Leicester – alike earned the Queen's commendation, and he presumably consolidated his position on subsequent visits. In March 1590 he received a ten-year licence to import 8,000 lasts of cod and ling, and when he resigned his captaincy in May 1591 it was in respect of his attendance on the Queen, probably a reference to his appointment as a gentleman pensioner, a capacity in which he was eventually to attend the monarch's funeral. His services earned for him in July 1591 a respite at the instance of the Privy Council of a lawsuit which was plaguing him. This was a form of protection of which he evidently stood in regular need; in July 1587 he had sought it from Walsingham and ten years later he asked the same favour from Robert Cecil.[7]

Where Vavasour's allegiance lay in the struggle between Cecil and Essex is not wholly clear. The matter is complicated by the obscurity surrounding his knighthood. If he was the Thomas Vavasour who accompanied Essex on the Azores expedition, was knighted in the course of it, and was sent abroad on its return with its news, he may be thought to have attached himself, at least ostensibly and for the time being, to Essex; and this view would not be inconsistent with the phrasing of a letter of August 1595 to Cecil containing the assurance that he 'inwardly' wished most honour to Cecil and styling Cecil 'master'. Since, however, this letter was endorsed as coming from 'Sir Thomas Vavasour', while there exists another letter to Cecil of probably earlier date and similarly endorsed, Vavasour may have obtained his knighthood in the early 1590s and the man so honoured by Essex have been his relative and namesake.[8]

Between February and October 1598 Vavasour again commanded 150 men at Flushing; he took over their captaincy from his brother-in-law (Sir) Thomas Shirley II* and in his turn passed it on to his brother John. This was the close of his active service; the remainder of his career was passed at court. Until the Queen's death he was simply a gentleman pensioner, but with the new reign he was first made butler of the port of London, an appointment whose revocation earned him £1,000 compensation, and then knight marshal of the Household, an office which was confirmed to him for life in 1612 but which he sold – for £3,000, according to John Chamberlain – in 1618, two years before his death. The improvement in his finances was reflected by his erection in 1610 of the fine house at Ham which, added to by later owners, remains his most lasting memorial.[9]

[1] J. Foster, *Yorks. Peds.* i (unpaginated); Glover, *Vis. Yorks. 1584–5,* p. 121; *Al. Cant.* i(4), 297; *Abstr. Wills PCC Reg. Soame,* ed. Lea, 387;

HMC Hatfield, v. 357. [2] *HMC Hatfield*, viii. 313–14; xv. 323–4; *CSP Dom.* 1603–10, p. 164; 1611–18, pp. 159, 586; 1619–23, p. 236; LC 2/4/4; *VCH Yorks.* ii. 414; PRO Index 6800. [3] *CSP Dom.* Add. 1566–79, pp. 277, 406; *HMC Hatfield*, i. 458. [4] *CSP Dom.* 1547–80, p. 703; E. K. Chambers, *Sir Henry Lee*, 135, 151, 158–9, 233–4, 239–40, 292–3; Lansd. 99, f. 252. [5] C. Read, *Burghley*, 274–5; J. T. Cliffe, 'The Yorks. Country on the eve of the Civil War' (London Univ. PhD thesis, 1960), 256; *CSP Dom.* 1581–90, p. 145; *HMC Var.* iii. 43, 46–7, 59–60, 74; *HMC Hatfield*, xvii. 527–8; *APC*, xxii. 18, 52–3; PCC 99 Soame. [6] *HMC De L'Isle and Dudley*, iii. p. xxx; *HMC Ancaster*, 69–70; *HMC De L'Isle and Dudley*, viii. 313–14; *CSP For.* Aug. 1584–Aug. 1585, pp. 635, 691; Sept. 1585–May 1586, p. 85; June 1586–Mar. 1587, pp. 109, 311, 394; Apr.–Dec. 1587, p. 351; July–Dec. 1588, pp. 137–412 passim; Jan.–July 1589, pp. 72, 138, 175–6; *APC*, xxi. 103–4. [7] *HMC De L'Isle and Dudley*, iii. p. xxxiv; *HMC Hatfield*, vii. 279; LC 2/4/4; *CSP Dom.* 1581–90, p. 654; *APC*, xxi. 268–9; *CSP For.* Apr.–Dec. 1587, p. 175. [8] *HMC Hatfield*, iv. 81; v. 357; vi. 214; vii. 279, 443; Shaw, *Knights*, ii. 94. [9] *APC*, xxviii. 301; xxix. 139–40, 258; *HMC Hatfield*, xv. 323–4; *CSP Dom.* 1603–10, p. 66; Chambers, *Lee*, 242; *Chamberlain Letters* ed. McClure, ii. 173.

S.T.B.

VENABLES, Sir Thomas (by 1513–80), of Kinderton, Cheshire.

CHESHIRE	1553 (Mar.), 1563

b. by 1513, 1st s. of Sir William Venables by Eleanor, da. and coh. of Richard Cotton of Ridware, Staffs. *m.* Maud, da. of Sir Robert Needham of Shavington, Salop. 3s. 3da. *suc.* fa. 31 July 1540. Kntd. 11 May 1544.[1]

J.p. Cheshire from 1543, q. by 1561, sheriff 1556–7, commr. musters by 1545, 1548, to collect relief 1550, for church goods 1553; chamberlain, Middlewich from 1540–72.

The Venables family was one of the oldest in Cheshire, and the title baron of Kinderton a relic of the period when Chester had an administration of its own, with a hierarchy of barons of the county palatine. Venables himself succeeded to property at Kinderton, Eccleston, Bradwall and elsewhere in Cheshire, and to the farm of the town of Middlewich and the office of its chamberlain. No one could be made a freeman without his consent and that of the lord treasurer. He owned ten 'salthouses' in Middlewich, and some of his tenants paid him salt as rent.

By Elizabeth's accession he had already served three rulers as a soldier and the first household subsidy of the reign assessed him among the 'old pensioners' at £66 8s. 4d. Although he had been one of the Edwardian commissioners to take inventories of church goods in Cheshire, he disliked the Elizabethan church settlement enough to be classified in the bishops' letters of 1564 as 'unfavourable to sound religion', but not enough to be put off the commission of the peace. Evidence of his participation in at least one local dispute survives: a Chancery writ of *elegit* was issued early in 1575 against him and his son Thomas on behalf of a creditor, William Bromfield, gentleman pensioner.[2]

Venables died on 19 July 1580. His eldest son Thomas, who was 38 when he succeeded to the estates, married as his first wife a daughter of Sir William Brereton I*, and his second son, Anthony, also married into the family. A daughter married another Cheshire gentleman, Peter, son and heir of Sir Piers Legh of Lyme.[3]

[1] PRO Chester 3/67/24; *Vis. Cheshire* (Harl. Soc. xviii), 229; (lix), 241; Ormerod, *Cheshire*, iii. 195. [2] *LP Hen. VIII*, xi, p. 511; xix(1), p. 328; xx(1), pp. 254, 278, 315; xxi(2), p. 223; *CSP Dom.* 1547–80, p. 6; *CPR*, 1553 and App. Edw. VI, pp. 199, 360; 1554–5, pp. 164–5; 1566–9, p. 179; R. H. Morris, *Chester in Plantagenet and Tudor Reigns*, 154; Lansd. 3, f. 196; PRO Chester 3/67/24; *Cam. Misc.* ix(3), p. 76; *APC*, viii. 341–2. [3] Ormerod, iii. 195, 200.

N.M.F.

VENTRIS, Thomas (by 1526–81), of Cambridge.

CAMBRIDGE	1558, 1559

b. by 1526, prob. 2nd s. of Robert Ventris of Cambridge by his w. Agnes. *m.* Joan, 3s.

Treasurer, Cambridge 1547, common councilman 1552, mayor 1559–60, alderman by 1561, j.p. in 1564.

Ventris was an innkeeper, vintner and carrier of grain and other goods between Cambridge and King's Lynn. As MP in 1559 he was paid 1s. a day, 2s. 'for the entry of his name', and had £5 7s. as 'money due for the Parliament'. He may have been a relative of John Ventris the Marian exile, and was himself classified by the bishop of Ely in 1564 as a godly justice in Cambridge. That year he was one of the aldermen ordered by the Privy Council to meet university officials in an attempt to settle the chronic disputes between the two bodies, and in 1580 he was himself at law with St. John's College over landed property. He died intestate later in 1581. Letters of administration were granted to the widow and their sons Daniel, Edward and Thomas.

Cambridge Univ. archives, wills proved in vice-chancellor's court, i. f. 63; PCC admon. act bk. 1581, f. 21; Req. 2/124/16, 288/28; Add. 5812, f. 102; Cooper, *Cambridge Annals*, ii. 22, 66, 205, 268, 311; F. Blomefield, *Coll. Cant.* 225; *CPR*, 1560–3, p. 406; *LP Hen. VIII*, xix(2), p. 473; Downing Coll. Camb., Bowtell mss; C. H. Garrett, *Marian Exiles*, 317–18; *Cam. Misc.* ix(3), p. 25; *APC*, vii. 161; SP12/144/35.

N.M.F.

VERE, Sir Francis (c.1560–1609), of Kirby Hall and Tilbury Lodge, Essex.[1]

LEOMINSTER	1593

b. c.1560,[2] 2nd s. of Geoffrey Vere of Crepping Hall, by Elizabeth, da. of Richard Hardekyn of Wotton House, Castle Hedingham. *m.* 26 Oct. 1607 (with £2,000) Elizabeth (*b.*1591), da. of John Dent of London by his 2nd w. Alice Grant of Manchester. Kntd. 25 Oct. 1588 at Bergen.

Capt. of ft. soldiers in Netherlands 1586; sergeant-major-gen. of English forces Feb. 1589; gen. of English troops in pay of States 1594; high marshal, Cadiz expedition 1596; gen. of Queen's forces in Netherlands and gov. Brill 1598; envoy to States 1598; capt. of Portsmouth June 1606–d.[3]

'Perhaps the most competent English soldier of the time', Vere shattered the myth of Spanish invincibility. From the autumn of 1586, when he received his first independent command in the Netherlands, until after the accession of James I, he rarely saw his own country, and enjoyed, through his professional skill, a record of almost unqualified success. How he first became acquainted with the Earl of Essex is not clear: probably like other young contemporaries Vere was attracted by the Earl's youthful vigour and engaging personality, though they could have had few opportunities to meet. By the early 1590s Vere was probably committed to the Earl's cause, and it was Essex, as high steward of the borough, who secured him a parliamentary seat at Leominster in 1593. This, his only appearance in the House, was squeezed into a hurried visit home. He sat on committees concerned with the subsidy (26 Feb.), recusancy (28 Feb.) and rogues (12 Mar.). No contributions to discussions have been recorded. Though in a letter dated February 1595 Vere wrote

> To your summons no man living shall more willingly give ear than I, who must acknowledge my chief good from you and have vowed myself wholly to your service,

and though he played a conspicuous part in the capture of Cadiz in 1596, Vere's attitude to Essex was becoming cooler, and he may have been surprised to receive an invitation to join the forthcoming expedition to the Netherlands. Before sailing, Vere, hearing that Mountjoy was to command the soldiers, had an interview with Essex and told him that he did not wish to serve with him again when once this voyage had been completed. He had perhaps been asked because his popularity with the Dutch would help secure the release of troops from the Netherlands. The expedition, known as the Islands voyage, was a costly failure, but Vere, though no longer one of Essex's close supporters, was annoyed by the unjustified attacks made on the Earl on their return, and defended him before the Queen, whom he approached as she took her accustomed stroll in the garden, speaking in such a plain manner that her anger towards Essex was temporarily abated.[4]

Vere was loyal to his commander on this occasion and he sought his support to gain the governorship of Brill, but a breach had occurred. In 1599 Essex was annoyed by Vere's reluctance to send his best troops to France. Two strongly worded letters, purporting to come from the Privy Council as a whole but clearly written by Essex, rebuked him for not obeying his instructions.

> All circumstances do prove that you little regarded either the directions given you or the furtherance of the service in any other sort than might best serve ... your own end.

Later, Sir Thomas Knollys, writing from Holland, told Essex that 'he [Vere] is so great and so addicted unto the States that he maketh small account of anything set down by your lordship in England'.[5]

The implication, that Essex had raised Vere to the eminent position he enjoyed by 1600 and that he now regarded himself as sufficiently strong to ignore his benefactor, is absurd. There is nothing to indicate that Vere ever received any material awards or advancement at Essex's hand: his reputation was established before he became attached to Essex. In any case, as a scion of one of the noblest houses in England, he would not have needed to look far for influential friends. His father was a younger brother of John de Vere, 16th Earl of Oxford, and Francis grew up in the shadow of Hedingham castle, the family's Norman stronghold. His mother, who had to bring up a large family after her husband's early death, was the daughter of a prosperous local merchant. According to his own account, written some 30 years later, he spent some time in Paris with friends of his cousin, the 17th Earl, and then saw action in the service of the Guises, for which he was rebuked by the Queen. Next, he served in the Polish army, and joined the Earl of Leicester's expeditionary force to the Netherlands in December 1585. This was the start of 20 years of almost continuous campaigning. Even allowing for the help he received from a relative, Lord Willoughby, who succeeded to Leicester's command in 1587, Vere's promotion was rapid. By 1589 he was already in command of all the English forces outside the garrison towns and from that date, in conjunction with the Dutch leaders, particularly Maurice of Nassau, he played a major part in the conduct of the war.[6]

Opportunities to return home were few, but he corresponded regularly with leading figures at court, especially Walsingham. On a visit to England in 1588, he was introduced by Lord Burghley to the Queen, who appears to have been favourably impressed. Still, Vere never acquired the skills of a courtier. Once, when answering a letter of criticism from Elizabeth, he sent his reply, which took a week to compose, to Burghley asking if it met the situation adequately. If the treasurer approved, he was to deliver it to the Queen. Though annoyed from time to time, as when he was slow to transfer some of his troops to France, she knew his worth. When, towards the end of her life, she was asked to make him a peer, she is said to have replied that he was above a peerage already: it would entomb 'the spirit of a brave soldier in the corpse of a less sightly courtier'. By then, his main advocate at court was Sir Robert Cecil whose nephew, Edward, was one of his junior officers. The only suggestion that Vere had any political ambitions occurs in a letter, dated October 1599, from Roland White to his master, Sir Robert Sidney:

> It was told me that [Vere] did expect a Councillor's place and marvels he goes without it; he hath purchased £400 a year land; he had an opinion he should have grown

great in court, and looked to have had a lodging appointed for him ... He was much respected here, having the happiness of their favour that her Majesty most trusts.[7]

Vere's campaigns refer constantly to his rash disregard for his own safety and he was wounded at least nine times, often seriously. In July 1602, at the siege of Grave, a bullet entered his head beneath his eye and became embedded in his skull. His life was despaired of, but the bullet was removed and by the end of the year he had taken up his command again. The cavalry charge at the battle of Turnhout in 1597 and his defence of the crumbling walls of Ostend provide further instances of his bravery. 'He would rather be killed ten times in a breach than once in a house', a companion wrote. His fine example endeared him to his men, any early promise among whom he was quick to recognise, and to most of his fellow officers. Captain Edward Cecil thought after the victory at Nieuport that he 'hath gotten as much honour as a man can get on earth', and Thomas Bodley* recorded the great reputation he had acquired with 'governors and statesmen' and with the 'common captains and soldiers of both nations'. But he had his enemies, whose voices became stronger as the years went by. He was a cheerless man, spoke little, showed touches of vanity and was tactless. John Chamberlain, the letter writer, reported that Vere was recovering from an injury in 1602, 'but it is said [he] will have an impediment in his tongue, which some think no great harm'. He offended the Earl of Northumberland during the siege of Ostend, probably judging him more on his abilities as a soldier than on his station in life. Northumberland, when they were back in England, challenged him to a duel, but the Queen intervened and the matter went no further. It gave Chamberlain the opportunity for another critical remark: 'For my part, I am very indifferent and respect neither of them greatly'.[8]

The peace treaty which James I signed with Spain in 1604 virtually ended Vere's career, and he retired from the service of the States. For the first time he had the leisure to enjoy the peace of his Essex home, but soon became restive. He offered his services to the government on hearing of the Gunpowder Plot, and took on the office of governor or captain of Portsmouth. In 1605 he returned to the Netherlands, Sir William Browne commenting: 'He is much changed from his melancholic disposition, for now he loves company and mirth; and in truth for two meals which I was with him drunk divers carouses *usque ad hilaritatem*'. But his services were not really needed and after a few months' inactivity he left for home for the last time with a pension of £500 a year from a grateful Dutch nation.[9]

Vere's last few years were spent in Essex or at Portsmouth where he carried out in person the duties of his new command. In 1607 he married a 16 year-old girl, with a good dowry. He also wrote his memoirs. These *Commentaries* provide an account of his campaigns, adding details not to be found in his official reports. He died suddenly and intestate in London 28 Aug. 1609, not yet 50, and was buried next day in Westminster abbey, where his wife erected a black marble monument. He had lived to see the Netherlands conclude the truce with which they virtually gained their independence.[10]

[1] The standard biography of Sir Francis Vere is C. R. Markham's *The Fighting Veres*, upon which this biography is based. See also: *DNB*; *HMC Hatfield*; *HMC De L'Isle and Dudley*, vols. ii–iii; Vere's *Commentaries*, ed. Arber, *English Garner*, vii. [2] His e. bro. was b. 1558 and the next youngest 1562. [3] *CSP Dom.* 1598–1601, pp. 102, 104; *HMC Hatfield*, viii. 222 seq. [4] C. G. Cruickshanks, *Elizabeth's Army*, 256–7; *HMC Hatfield*, v. 287; vi. 60, 67, 70 seq., 86–8, 90, 122, 140; vii. 1–2, 8–9, 75, 171–2; xiii. 455; D'Ewes, 474, 477, 499; *CSP Dom.* 1595–7, pp. 191, 221, 271–3, 360, 437, 452, 477–8; *HMC Bath*, ii. 44–7; *HMC De L'Isle and Dudley*, ii. 244, 281. [5] *HMC Hatfield*, vii. 462; ix. 64, 65, 123, 124; *Commentaries*, 110; *CSP Dom.* 1598–1601, p. 163; *APC*, xxix. 609. [6] *HMC Hatfield*, xvii. 208, 494; *CSP For.* 1588 (Jan.–Jun.), 417. [7] *HMC De L'Isle and Dudley*, ii. 407, 472, 578; *CSP For.* 1588 (Jan.–Jun.), 482–3. [8] *HMC Hatfield*, vii. 24–6; x. 213; xi. passim; xii. 260; *HMC Bath*, ii. 32; *Chamberlain Letters* ed. McClure, i. 151, 161; *CSP Dom.* 1601–3, pp. 202–5. [9] *HMC De L'Isle and Dudley*, iii. 231 seqq., 257; *HMC Hatfield*, xvii. 484. [10] PCC admon. act bk. 1605–10, f. 168; C142/309/182.

M.R.P.

VERNEY, Richard (1563–1630), of Compton, Warws.

WARWICKSHIRE	1589
WEST LOOE	1601
WARWICKSHIRE	?1604,[1] 1614

b. 1563. 1st s. of George Verney by Jane, da. of William Lucy of Charlecote. *educ.* G. Inn 1582. *m.* Margaret, da. of Sir Fulke Greville of Beauchamp Court, 4s. 4da. *suc.* fa. 1574. Kntd. 1603.[2]

J.p. Warws. from c.1584, sheriff 1590–1, 1604–5, commr. musters by 1597.

Verney was only 11 in 1574 when his father died. The Earl of Leicester took an interest in him, writing in July to Lord Burghley about the bad repair of his lands. The wardship passed a year later to Sir John Hibbett, probably at Leicester's instigation. There was talk of marrying Verney to a niece of Burghley, and, although this came to nothing, he was evidently on friendly terms with the Cecils.[3] As soon as he came of age Verney took the place in Warwickshire life to which his status entitled him. During his first shrievalty the escape of an important prisoner made him liable for a penalty of £1,000.[4]

Verney was still in his twenties when he sat for the county with his brother-in-law Fulke Greville. He is recorded as serving on only one committee (about a private estate, 22 Feb.). He did not sit again until a seat was found for him at West Looe in 1601, probably through Cecil influence. He was presumably the Mr. 'Varney' put on a procedural committee, 11 Nov.[5]

A small collection of family letters shows that in private

life Verney was an affectionate family man and a good friend. He evidently spent much of his time in the usual social round of visits and entertainments, and was frequently at Beauchamp Court, the home of the Grevilles. Although his wife was her brother's next of kin, most of the Greville property was settled upon a cousin in order to perpetuate the family name, but this does not seem to have troubled amicable relations between the families. Verney died 7 Aug. 1630 after a short illness and was buried in the church at Compton. In his will, made 30 July 1630, after praising God, who 'now at length so gently and lovingly calls me to enjoy those infinite glories which I am assured to enjoy by His only merit', he made provision for his younger children, servants and the poor. The bulk of his property had previously been settled on his eldest son.[6]

[1] The original return is missing. The name is suggested by Browne Willis and J. Kipling's 'Index'. [2] Dugdale, *Warws.* i. 566–9; *Vis. Warws.* (Harl. Soc. xii), 25; C142/506/160. [3] *APC*, xxvi. 433. [4] Lansd. 18, f. 194; 46, f. 32; *CSP Dom.* 1547–80, p. 498; 1581–90, p. 390; 1591–4, p. 407; Add. 1580–1625, p. 324; *HMC Hatfield*, vii. 244; viii. 483; xi. 233; xv. 179; *APC*, xv. 47; xxii. 132; xxvi. 433; xxvii. 137; xxx. 39. [5] D'Ewes, 437, 635. [6] *HMC Cowper*, i. 44, 47, 59, 63, 67, 68, 69, 70; Dugdale; C142/506/160; PCC 114 St. John.

S.M.T.

VERNON, William (c.1545–1605), of Maldon and Little Beeleigh, Essex.

MALDON   1589*

b. c.1545, 2nd s. of John or Robert Vernon of Notts. *m.* Alice, da. of one Scriven, 1s. 2da.

Coroner, Essex 1567–80; alderman, Maldon 1566–1605, coroner 1571, frequently bailiff and j.p.

Vernon was descended from the Vernons of the Peak in Derbyshire. In 1566 and 1569 he obtained land in St. Peter's parish, Maldon, and at Little Beeleigh, and he soon became a leading figure in Maldon. He served as one of the two town bailiffs at least seven times between 1572 and 1598, and held the position of j.p. for Maldon, an annual appointment, on ten occasions between 1568 and 1590. In 1588 the bailiffs and aldermen decided, 'for some necessary causes for the good of our poor town', to elect 'some fit person of the inhabitants within the said borough' as one of their Members for the forthcoming Parliament, and returned Vernon, together with his son's father-in-law, John Butler II*. It is doubtful whether he took his seat in the Commons, as the session began on 4 Feb. and on the 14th of that month Edward Lewknor was chosen at a by-election in his place, on account of his illness. He continued to be active in Maldon, however, until his death on 2 Aug. 1605. In his will, dated 6 Apr. 1604 and proved on 28 Oct. 1605, he left most of his property to his heir and executor William, then aged about 30. He bequeathed £40 to his daughter Dorothy, a

£10 annuity to his younger daughter Susan, and left a small legacy to 20 of the poor of St. Peter's parish, Maldon. He appointed as overseer William Wiseman*, to one of whose daughters he was godfather. Vernon asked to be buried in the choir in All Saints church there.

Vis Essex (Harl. Soc. xiii), 307; Morant, *Essex*, i. 335; Essex RO, Assize File and sessions bk. D/B passim; D'Ewes, 429; C142/287/96; C219/284/20; PCC 70 Hayes.

J.H.

VINCENT, Henry

ST. MAWES   1593

Yr. s. of David Vincent of Barnack, Northants. and bro. of Thomas*. *m.* aft. 1598, Elizabeth, wid. of Henry Slyfield of Clandon Regis, Surr.

No Henry Vincent having been found among the Vincent families of Cornwall, this Member has been sought outside the county. The most likely person to have been the MP is Henry Vincent of Barnack, whose brother Thomas, the head of the house, held land in Northamptonshire, but had removed to Surrey and become a justice of the peace there by 1582. The land in Northamptonshire was sold, some of it to Thomas Vincent's near neighbour, Lord Burghley, and Barnack itself passed to Burghley's son, Thomas Cecil*, Earl of Exeter, before 1613. Vincent's father had appointed Burghley an overseer of his will, and these connexions with the Cecil family may supply an explanation for Vincent's return at St. Mawes in 1593.

C. S. Gilbert, *Hist. Surv. Cornw.* ii. 316; *Vis. Surr.* (Harl. Soc. xliii), 55–6; Bridges, *Northants.* ii. 492, 495; *VCH Surr.* iii. 347; PCC 29 Crymes.

I.C.

VINCENT, Thomas (1544–1613), of Stoke d'Abernon, Surr.

POOLE   1584

b. 1544, 1st s. of David Vincent, keeper of standing wardrobe at Hampton Court, of Barnack, Northants. by Elizabeth, da. of one Spencer of Berks.; bro. of Henry*. *m.* Jane, o. da. and h. of Thomas Lyfield* of Stoke d'Abernon by Frances, da. of Edmund, 1st Lord Bray and coh. of her bro. John, 2nd Lord Bray, 2s. *suc.* fa. 1565. Kntd. ?1601.

Commr. musters, Surr. 1580, j.p. from c.1582; dep. lt. 1601.[1]

Vincent's father's lands in Northamptonshire lay close to the Cecil estates at Burghley, and he appointed Sir William Cecil an overseer of his will, along with his 'special good lord the Earl of Bedford'. Vincent himself remained closely enough associated with the 2nd Earl of Bedford to carry a bannerol at his funeral, and it can be assumed that it was Bedford who brought him into Parliament for

Poole. Vincent made a fortunate marriage, and had settled in Surrey by 1582, but he did not obtain possession of Stoke d'Abernon until his father-in-law's death in 1596.

The Queen visited him there in 1601 and may have knighted him on that occasion, for he describes himself as a knight in the will he made on 23 Sept. 1613, though his name does not appear in the standard works of reference. The will was prefaced by a 'profession of faith and steadfast belief' in

> one holy Catholic church, that is to say universal, which is the company and fellowship of saints or faithful people out of which there is no salvation.

He bequeathed 40s. to the poor of each of the four Surrey parishes of Fetcham, Great Bookham, Kingston-upon-Thames and Stoke d'Abernon, and 20s. to the poor of Leatherhead. Four preachers of God's word were left 40s. each. He left bequests to his wife Jane, and to his son Sir Francis†, whom he made joint executor with his brother Henry. Vincent died 14 Dec. 1613, and the will was proved on 14 Mar. of the following year. He was buried at Stoke d'Abernon, where a monument was erected to him.[2]

[1] C142/142/131; *GEC Baronetage*, i. 158; *Vis. Surr.* (Harl. Soc. xliii), 56; PCC 20 Lawe; *CPR*, 1563–6, pp. 217–18; SP12/145, f. 34; Lansd. 35, f. 135v; APC, xii. 14; xxxi. 400. [2] Roberts thesis; PCC 29 Crymes, 20 Lawe; *VCH Surr.* iii. 286–7, 290, 458, 461, 463, 518; Nichols, *Progresses Jas. I*, i. 209; Collinson thesis, 1195, n. 4.

A.M.M.

VISER, Robert, of Chippenham, Wilts.

CHIPPENHAM 1571

?rel. to John Viser, bailiff of Chippenham (*d.* c.1586). Burgess, Chippenham by Apr. 1559.

Viser was a haberdasher. In 1560 he was paid 20s. for going to London 'with the supplication', presumably about the confirmation of the borough charter. He went again six years later. In July 1568 he was licensed to turn part of his house into a tavern. A list of householders provisionally dated 1604 is headed by Joan Vizer (sic), widow. The absence of Viser's own name suggests that he died before this date.

Chippenham Recs. 26–8, 307, 327, 336–7, 342; PCC 26 Windsor; *CPR*, 1566–9, p. 319.

N.M.F.

VIVIAN, Hannibal (1554–1610), of Trelowarren, Cornw. and of Blackfriars, London.

PLYMPTON ERLE	1584
HELSTON	1586
TRURO	1589
HELSTON	1601

b. 1554, 1st surv. s. of John Vivian* of Trelowarren by Anne, da. of Baldwin Malet of ?St. Audries, Som. *educ.* Clement's Inn; M. Temple 1573. *m.* 20 Jan. 1574,

Philippa, 2nd da. and coh. of Roger Tremayne of Collacombe, Devon, 7s. inc. Michael* 8da. *suc.* fa. 24 July 1577.

J.p. Cornw. from c.1583; capt. St. Mawes castle Dec. 1587; v.-adm. Cornw. 1592, sheriff 1601–2; attorney-gen. duchy of Cornw. 1601; dep. warden of stannaries 1608–*d.*[1]

In 1582 Vivian bought a one-eighth part of the manor of Plympton, making his first appearance in Parliament for Plympton Erle soon afterwards. In 1586 and 1601 he sat for Helston, near the family seat of Trelowarren, and in 1589 he was returned for Truro, presumably through his family's standing in the county. His sole recorded appearance on a parliamentary committee was that for the subsidy 11 Feb. 1589.[2]

As captain of St. Mawes he wrote several times to the Privy Council about the castle, making the usual complaints about its defences. 'I will not dwell unless I have better supply' he said in 1595. The Spaniards landed and burned Penzance in that year, and Vivian asked Drake to send down good leaders and prepare ships. In 1597 he was again complaining about St. Mawes, this time to Sir Robert Cecil, disclaiming responsibility if enemy action took place there. A memorandum among Cecil's papers in that year contains reasons for not pricking Vivian sheriff of Cornwall; 'because he has a lawsuit of 25 years' continuance [see Cosgarne, John], has many children, and is captain of St. Mawes castle'. Nevertheless he became sheriff in 1601. Vivian's concern over the fortifications at St. Mawes continued, and was the cause of a quarrel with Sir Nicholas Parker, captain of the neighbouring Pendennis castle.[3]

From the time of his appointment as attorney-general of the duchy of Cornwall, any anxiety about provision for his family must have been at an end. He died 4 Feb. 1610 in London, where he had been living at 'Gibson's house', Blackfriars. He was buried 20 Feb. at St. Dunstan-in-the-West. His will was proved in 1610 and an inquisiton post mortem was taken in the following year.[4]

[1] Vivian, *Vis. Devon*, 749; PRO Index 6800; *HMC Hatfield*, iv. 256; Gabriel thesis, 644; *M.T. Recs.* i. 196, 260; Add. 36767, f. 212. [2] J. Brooking-Rowe, *Hist. Plympton Erle*, 24; *Trans. R. Hist. Soc. (1950)*, article on the Vyvyan fam. by Miss M. Coate; Roberts thesis, 170; D'Ewes, 431. [3] *CSP Dom.* 1581–90, p. 46; A. L. Rowse, *Tudor Cornw.* 405, 407; *Tudor and Stuart Proclamations*, i. 99; *HMC Hatfield*, vii. 491, 536; ix. 207, 316; xii. 457. [4] *Coll. Topog.* iv. 123; PCC 83 Wingfield; *Vis. Cornw.* (Harl. Soc. ix), 257; Wards 7/36/173.

P.W.H.

VIVIAN, John (c.1526–77), of Trelowarren, Cornw.

HELSTON 1572*

b. c.1526, 2nd s. of John Vivian of Trelowarren (*d.*1562) by Elizabeth, da. and coh. of Thomas Trethrey or Tretherffe. *m.* Anne, da. and coh. of Baldwin Malet of ?St. Audries, Som., 2s. inc. Hannibal* 5da.

A member of a local gentry family connected with the duchy of Cornwall and the stannary courts, Vivian, who lived about four miles from Helston, can have had little difficulty in gaining a seat there. Nothing is recorded of him in Parliament, and he died before the third session began. Little is known of his life. He may have hoped at one time to succeed his father, the legitimacy of his namesake and elder brother being doubtful, but after a lengthy dispute the elder John was declared his father's lawful heir, and although he died young in 1564 he already had twin daughters, aged 2, who inherited most of the property. However, it seems that Vivian was recognized as *de facto* head of the family from 1564 until his death, 24 July 1577. He was buried 1 Aug. at Mawgan in Meneage, Cornwall.

Vis. Cornw. (Harl. Soc. ix), 252, 257–9; Vivian, *Vis. Cornw* 497, 528–9; *CPR*, 1557–8, pp. 6–7; 1560–3, p. 401; C142/180/22; Wards 7/19/139.

N.M.F.

VIVIAN, Michael (1576–1639), of Trelowarren and Phillack (?Pillick), Cornw.

ST. MAWES   1597

b. 1576, 2nd s. of Hannibal Vivian* by Philippa, da. and coh. of Roger Tremayne of Collacombe, Devon. *educ.* Exeter Coll. Oxf. 1594; M. Temple 1597, called 1605. *m.* 1603, Catherine, da. of James Nanspian of Gurlyn, 1da.

If the date of Vivian's birth given in the heraldic visitation is correct, he went up to Oxford and the inns of court older than was usual at the time. He was returned for St. Mawes through his family influence (his father was captain of St. Mawes castle) while still a law student. The references to him in the Middle Temple records are almost entirely concerned with payments for his chambers, or with fines incurred through absence from vacation readings, or other breaches of the regulations. In November 1611, when he was described as a 'master of the utter bar', he vacated his chamber at the Temple, but as late as 1622 he was once more fined, this time for not reading.

He died and was buried at St. Erth on 19 Oct. 1639. His will, proved at Bodmin less than a fortnight later, styles him 'of Phillack, esquire'. His only daughter Jane married William Williams of Roseworthy, Cornwall.

Vivian, *Vis. Cornw.* 529, 627; *M.T. Recs.* i. 372, 381, 403; ii. 453, 464, 476, 484, 676; *Vis. Cornw.* (Harl. Soc. ix), 259.

R.C.G.

WAAD, Thomas (*d.*1594), of Gray's Inn and St. Michael Basinghall, London.

EAST RETFORD   1584

2nd s. of Armagil Waad† of Belsize, Hampstead, Mdx. by his 1st w. Alice, da. of Richard Patten *alias* Wainfleet

of Newington, London, wid. of Thomas Searle of London; bro. of William*. *educ.* G. Inn 1565, called 1577. *m.* the da. and h. of one Pope.

Reader, G. Inn 1589.

Waad, a lawyer, may have been brought in for East Retford by the 3rd Earl of Rutland, perhaps through the intervention of Waad's brother, the clerk of the Privy Council, who on a number of occasions got him employment on government cases. In 1595 William Waad informed Cecil that the papers relating to the cases on which Thomas had been working had been found amongst his brother's possessions, 'with all his notes and arguments for her Majesty's title' to certain lands that had belonged to the dukes of Norfolk.

Waad's nuncupative will was made on 17 and proved on 31 Dec. 1594. He appointed his wife sole executrix and residuary legatee: 'She shall have all who should have it; I bleed, I bleed that I have no more for her'.

Mdx. Peds. (Harl. Soc. lxv), 33; *G. Inn Pens. Bk.* i. 28, 86; *HMC Rutland*, i. 173, 180; *HMC Hatfield*, v. 492; PCC 20 Alenger, 6 Lyon, 86 Dixy.

A.M.M.

WAAD, William (1546–1623), of Belsize House, Hampstead, Mdx., and Battles Hall, Essex.

ALDBOROUGH	1584
THETFORD	1589
PRESTON	1601
WEST LOOE	1604*

b. 1546, 1st s. of Armagil Waad† by his 1st w.; bro. of Thomas*. *educ.* G. Inn 1571. *m.* (1) 1586, Anne (*d.*1589), da. and h. of Owen Waller of London, 1s. *d.v.p.*; (2) *c.*1599, Anne, da. and coh. of Sir Humphrey Browne, j.c.p., 1s. at least 8da. *suc.* fa. 1568. Kntd. 20 May 1603.[1]

Servant of Burghley by 1576; diplomatic agent in France, Italy, Germany, Spain and the Netherlands between 1576 and 1587; sec. to Walsingham 1581; clerk of PC 1582–1613; j.p. Mdx. from 1591; commr. musters *c.*1595; commissary gen. of England; muster master for troops for Low Countries 1600; inspector of Irish forces; eccles. commr. diocese of Canterbury by 1603; lt. of the Tower 1605–13; member, council of Virginia Co. 1609.[2]

Waad's father was well known to Sir William Cecil, with whom he worked on the Council in Edward VI's time, and Waad's own close relations with Cecil and his circle were doubtless responsible for his return for three duchy of Lancaster boroughs during Elizabeth's reign. He seems to have had no direct connexion with Sir Ralph Sadler*, chancellor of the duchy in 1584, but in 1589 the chancellor was his old master Walsingham, who had tried unsuccessfully to have him returned for Gatton in the previous Parliament. In 1601 Sir Robert Cecil* used a blank return to nominate him at Preston. His name occurs once only in each of his Parliaments; he was on a committee concerning the letters patent of Queen's

College, Oxford, 5 Feb. 1585; on a conference concerned with dress, 29 Mar. 1589; and on 17 Dec. 1601 he was nominated to distribute the collection for the poor.[3]

Waad's usefulness to the government was largely due to his fluency in French and other European languages, and to the experience he gained of continental courts in more than ten years of almost constant service abroad. He seems to have begun his travels, possibly sponsored as a future government agent by Burghley or Walsingham, soon after leaving Gray's Inn, and between September 1574, when he wrote to the lord treasurer from Paris, and June 1587 (the date of his return from a last mission to France), he must have conducted more difficult negotiations than almost any other government official below the rank of ambassador. After some time in France, where Sir Amias Paulet* employed him and in 1576 took him in his train to Blois, he continued his journey to Italy, sending Burghley news of the large numbers of troops being raised there in 1580 for the service of Philip II: he reported that they were almost certainly to be used to further Philip's claims to the throne of Portugal. Instructions survive for Waad as ambassador to Portugal in 1580, but there is no evidence that he went. His letters to the lord treasurer, with their constant expressions of gratitude for favours and fear lest he should have incurred Burghley's displeasure, suggest that he owed his advancement, after the death of both his parents in 1568, to Cecil patronage – an interpretation borne out by contemporary comments. Thomas Digges*, with whom he quarrelled at one time, described him to Burghley as 'a gentleman by your lordship advanced and favoured'. Waad carried out personal commissions for Burghley abroad, or procured for him presents which he knew would suit his tastes – during his Italian journey he sent him over 50 kinds of rare seeds – but, if he is to be believed, he did not try to exploit this relationship with Elizabeth's chief minister for his personal profit. Writing to Sir Robert Cecil in 1593 to further his petition for a relatively unimportant wardship, he claimed that it was the first favour of this kind that he had ever asked from Burghley.[4]

His early work on the Continent evidently convinced the government that he was a vigorous and efficient agent, and after a short time in England as one of Walsingham's secretaries he was sent abroad again – with Lord Willoughby to Denmark and then, within three years, on three exceptionally delicate missions. In January 1584 he went to Madrid in a hopeless attempt to explain the expulsion from England of the Spanish ambassador, Mendoza, and was himself expelled from Spain. In the following year he was sent to Mary Queen of Scots, who was in the Earl of Shrewsbury's charge at Sheffield, to induce her to come to terms with Elizabeth. She objected to his breaking into a conversation which she was carrying on in French, telling him that 'he was not of calling to reason with her'. Waad, according to his own story,

retorted that he was not of calling either 'to hear his own mistress found fault with', and that there were 'few princes in Christendom who would not have made shorter work with her'. Another assignment came his way in March 1585 – a journey to France to persuade the government to surrender the English conspirator, Thomas Morgan. Here again he had to leave without achieving his purpose. On his way back to the coast he became involved in an affray with the Duc d'Aumale and his men, in which he received a severe beating. He was also employed in Germany, Vienna and the Netherlands. He played a prominent part, during the Babington affair, in the seizure of Mary Stuart's papers from Chartley, and the arrest of her secretaries – a task for which he received a reward of £30. His last, and perhaps his most thankless, assignment abroad was in February 1587, when he went once more to France to explain the reason for the execution of Mary, and to demand the recall of the French ambassador in London, who was suspected of complicity in the Stafford plot. With his usual courage and persistence, he at last achieved the audience with the French king which was for some time refused him, and finally returned, in June, to report negotiations over British and French shipping.[5]

Between this date and the end of Elizabeth's reign, he was employed largely in tracking down plots against the state, or in examining recusants and suspected traitors. He was at times as rigorous and brutal as Richard Topcliffe*, who described him to Sir Robert Cecil as a 'good ancient friend'. Waad was prepared to recommend torture, or to carry out examinations with its help, but he showed a trace of humanity in objecting to further proceedings against an old man who was 'surely crazed' and could not be dangerous. He played a large part in the inquiries into the Lopez affair, and assisted Sir Robert Cecil and Edward Coke* to draw up an account of it for publication. He was also active against the Essex conspirators in 1601.[6]

His career during the reign of James I, when he was returned to Parliament at a by-election for a Cornish borough, lies outside the scope of this biography. He was dismissed from his office of lieutenant of the Tower on trumped-up charges in 1613, the Countess of Essex finding his integrity an obstacle to her proposed murder of Sir Thomas Overbury. One set of Waad's letters during this period to the Earl of Salisbury, describes in charming detail the behaviour of a lioness and her cubs he had 'watched a great while' at the Tower.[7]

The majority of references to Waad are concerned with his official work, including the routine duties of his clerkship of the Council – another office which he was forced to resign in 1613, when his great patron, Salisbury, was no longer alive to protect his interests. Comparatively little is known about his private or domestic life. He seems to have lived mainly at Belsize House, Hampstead, which his father had leased from the dean and chapter of St. Paul's, and he also held the manor of Manuden or Battles

Hall, Essex, from the duchy of Lancaster honour of Mandevill. His first wife inherited lands in East Ham, and Waad was involved in complicated lawsuits over the property. He was granted several patents and monopolies, probably the most rewarding being one, jointly with a jeweller Henry Mekins *alias* Pope, to make sulphur, brimstone and oil: he still held this in 1601. With these, and the perquisites of office, he was obviously a very wealthy man.[8]

The picture of Waad which emerges from the official records is that of an energetic, efficient servant of the state, who sometimes regretted that, like (Sir) Christopher Hatton I*, he was unable to spend more time on his estates. Waad wrote to Walter Cope* on 8 Sept. 1602:

I sought you yesterday in the afternoon at London before I went forth of the town 30 miles to a little farm I have in Essex for a sevennight, where I have not been these seven or eight years.

As an ambitious official he obviously came under fire from such men as Lord Cobham at the time of the 'main' and 'bye' plots.[9]

Several of his letters refer to ill health, generally in the form of minor disorders – fits of ague, a 'vehement and grievous indisposition in my stomach', or a face 'so swollen with toothache as I am not fit to come abroad, wherewith of late I have been miserably tormented'. He must, however, had had a strong constitution to endure the strain and discomfort of constant travel and ceaseless activity in public affairs. He lived to be over 75 – by contemporary standards a considerable age – dying at Battles Hall in October 1623. His will, drawn up in 1618, was proved by the heir, his second son, James, still a minor when the will was made. Waad left £100 a year for sending him to a university or inn of court, to be trained as a civilian or common lawyer. He asked the lords of the Council to help his family if there should be trouble over the execution of the will, since he was an 'ancient servitor … at this time the most ancient in the kingdom' who had given 30 years' service as a clerk, and whose father had held the same position. After instructions about the disposal of his goods, and the care of his daughter Anne 'in respect of her infirmity', Waad commended his soul

into the hands and great mercy of my sweet Saviour and Redeemer our Lord and merciful God Christ Jesus, by whose death and passion, through His sufferings and precious blood, I do hope, and leave this world with assured belief to receive pardon of my grievous and manifold sins.

There was to be no 'solemnity of funeral charges'.

He was buried in Manuden church, his epitaph advising servants of the Crown to set their conscience and care

By this true watch of state; whose minutes were

Religious thoughts; whose hours heaven's sacred food;
Whose hand still pointed to the kingdom's good
And sovereign safety; whom ambitious key
Never wound up to guiltiness, bribe or fee.
Zeal only, and a conscience clear and even
Raised him on earth, and wound him up to heaven.[10]

[1] *DNB; Mdx. Peds.* (Harl. Soc. lxv), 33; PCC 20 Alenger, 116 Swann. [2] *DNB; HMC Hatfield*, ii. 254–5, 322; xv. 233; *EHR*, xxxviii. 56; *APC*, xxiii. 258; xxv. 156; xxx. 667; Morant, *Essex*, ii. 620. [3] Neale, *Commons*, 188; D'Ewes, 346, 454, 687. [4] *CSP Ven.* 1581–91, pp. 475–533 passim; Lansd. 23, f. 172; 72, f. 176; *HMC Hatfield*, ii. 254; iv. 488. [5] *CSP Dom.* 1611–18, p. 198; Birch, *Mems.* i. 24, 31, 45, 48; *CSP Span.* 1580–6, pp. 516, 520–1, 625–6; Froude, *Hist.* xi. 448–51; xii. 160 seq.; *APC*, xiv. 211; *CSP Ven.* 1581–91, loc. cit. [6] *HMC Hatfield*, iv. 242; v. 491; vii. 33, 203, 253, 257–8, 260; viii. 414; ix. 209; *CSP Dom.* 1591–1603, passim. [7] *DNB; HMC Hatfield*, xvii. 384–5, 397–8, 402–3; *Chamberlain Letters* ed. McClure, i. 452. [8] *CSP Dom.* 1611–18, p. 198; *DNB* (Waad, Armagil); Morant, *Essex*, ii. 620–1; *APC*, xiv. 235; xviii. 105; xxv. 444–5; Lansd. 22, f. 78; 58, f. 174; 114, ff. 104 seq.; D'Ewes, 650; Neale, *Commons*, 335; King's Lynn congregation bk. 1569–91, f. 389v. [9] *DNB; HMC Hatfield*, xii. 356. [10] *HMC Hatfield*, iv. 424; ix. 209; xvii. 384–5 seq.; PCC 116 Swann; Morant, *Essex*, ii. 620.

N.M.F.

WAKEFIELD, Edward (*d.*1602), of Hull, Yorks.

KINGSTON-UPON-HULL   1586

1st s. of Thomas Wakefield of Pontefract and Hull by Ann, da. of John Eland of Carleton. *m.* (1) Jane, da. of Ronyon Bee of Northumb., 2s.; (2) Janet Johnson of Hull, wid. of one Naylor.
Alderman, Hull, sheriff 1578, mayor 1581, 1592.[1]

Wakefield was one of the principal burgesses of Hull sent to London in 1583 to answer for the decay of Hull's 'castles and blockhouses'. Two years later, with John Thornton* and Leonard Willan*, he received a grant of authority to search for concealed lands in the town. He and his colleague received a long list of instructions when they were the Hull MPs in 1586. In 1591 he was one of those commissioned to apprehend all suspected priests and Jesuits, and the same year carried a letter from Hull to the Council, on the borough's differences with the city of York. He died in 1602, his will being proved at York in April that year.[2]

[1] *Vis. Yorks.* ed. Foster, 139; Clay, *Dugdale's Vis. Yorks.* iii. 368; Tickell, *Hist. Hull*, 676–7. [2] *CSP Dom.* 1581–90, p. 130; *Hull Deeds*, ed. Stanewell, 105, 107, 321; *HMC Hatfield*, iv. 122; *York Wills* (Yorks. Arch. Soc. rec. ser. xxiv), 197.

J.J.C.

WALCOT, Charles (*c.*1542–96), of Walcot, Salop and Builth, Brec.

BISHOP'S CASTLE   1586, 1589

b. c.1542, 1st s. of John Walcot of Walcot by Mary, da. of Sir Peter Newton of Petton. *educ.* ?M. Temple. *m.* (1) 1566, Beatrice, da. of Anthony Girling, 4s. 3da.; (2) Margaret, da. of John Isham, *s.p. suc.* fa. 1562.

Under-porter, council in the marches of Wales bef. 1572; head burgess, Bishop's Castle 1574; j.p. Brec. by 1572–96; sheriff 1572–3, 1580–1; j.p. Salop from c.1575.

Walcot was still a minor when he succeeded his father as head of the senior branch of this prominent Shropshire family, and his wardship was sold to Sir Henry Sidney*. Most of his father's property had been entrusted to his mother for life, and his lands were valued at only £5 p.a. The young man 'denied that he was the Queen's, or any other person's ward', and Sidney was put to 'great charges' in proving his right. No doubt this connexion with Sidney explains his council post at Ludlow, and his being made sheriff of Brecon in 1572, despite his comparative youth and the objection of the 1st Earl of Essex that he was 'a person of no credit'.

Walcot was seated near Bishop's Castle, and in the original charter, granted to the borough in 1574, he was named as one of the 14 head burgesses. Another burgess was Edward Plowden†, the lawyer, who had been overseer of Walcot's father's will, and who doubtless favoured Walcot's return in 1586.

Although occasionally employed by the council in the marches, Walcot received no commissions of importance. In 1596 he was accused of clipping the coinage, and asked that the case might be examined thoroughly, since 'his name had been called in question, to his great discredit'. The outcome of his examination by the master of the mint is unknown, and his death may have intervened, for he was buried at Lydbury North in the same year. No will has been found.

Vis. Salop (Harl. Soc. xxix), 476–8; *Trans. Salop Arch. Soc.* (ser. 2), x. 36–7; J. R. Burton, *Fam. of Walcot*, 20–1; *Ludlow Par. Reg.* ed. Weyman, 4, 62, 64, 66; P. H. Williams, *Council in the Marches of Wales*, 122; Flenley, *Cal. Reg. Council, Marches of Wales*, 125, 138, 213, 216; *HMC Hatfield*, viii. 469; *CSP Dom.* Add. 1547–65. p. 534; *CPR*, 1560–3, p. 620; PCC 41 Welles; *APC*, xxvi. 355.

J.J.C.

WALDEGRAVE, Edward (c.1556–1622), of Lawford, Essex.

SUDBURY   1584

b. c.1556, o.s. of Edward Waldegrave of Lawford by Joan, da. of George Acworth*. *m.* (1) Elizabeth, da. and coh. of Bartholomew Averell of Southminster, Essex, 1da.; (2) Sara, da. of John Heigham*, wid. of Sir Richard Bingham, 1da. *suc.* fa. 1584.

J.p. Essex c.1584.

The Waldegraves had a long-standing connexion with Sudbury, for which Edward Waldegrave was returned soon after he succeeded his father. Lawford was less than 20 miles away, over the Essex border. The mayor's accounts for 26–27 Elizabeth have an entry, 'paid for the hire of a horse to ride to Mr. Edward Waldegrave to come to take his oath to be a free burgess of our town – 8*d.*'

Scattered references in the State Papers and Privy Council documents show Waldegrave as an active country gentleman, carrying out the usual duties of his class. In May 1589 he was one of the commissioners appointed to interview the creditors of a Colchester merchant who was a prisoner in the Fleet. During the spring of the same year Lord Burghley instructed him to resume the captaincy of 50 lances in Essex – a position which he had formerly held, but which the Earl of Leicester had given instead to Lord Rich. James I continued to employ him in local affairs, and in 1616 he was considering the quarrels between Colchester clothiers and the Dutch congregation there, many of whom specialized in the making of baize. He died on 12 Feb. 1622.

Vis. Essex (Harl. Soc. xiii), 120–1; Morant, *Essex*, i. 316, 437; C142/206/23; C. F. D. Sperling, *Hist. Sudbury*, 144–5; Sudbury corp. ct. bk. 1585–99, f. 11; *APC*, xvii. 157; 1615–16, pp. 422–3; *CSP Dom.* 1581–90, pp. 573, 602; PCC 32 Savile; Wards 7/67/85.

N.M.F.

WALDEGRAVE, George (c.1569–1637), of Hitcham, Suff.

SUDBURY   1597

b. c.1569, 1st s. of William Waldegrave of Wetherden Hall, Hitcham by Elizabeth, da. of Richard Poley or Pooley of Boxted. *m.* (1) Mary, da. and coh. of John More* of Ipswich, 2da.; (2) Elizabeth, da. of Sir Thomas Jermy of Metfield, *s.p. suc.* fa. c.1581. Kntd. 1603.

J.p. Suff. by 1601.

Waldegrave presumably came into Parliament for Sudbury through his local standing, Hitcham lying about 12 miles from the town. Supposing that the references in the journals to Mr. Waldegrave are to him rather than to Sir William, Waldegrave spoke on 10 Nov. 1597 'touching the abuses of licences for marriages granted by ecclesiastical persons, and prayeth consideration may be had for reformation thereof by this House'. On 23 Nov., surprisingly for a country gentleman, he submitted a bill against the export of herrings to Leghorn, a practice which he thought caused a scarcity of herrings in this country, and in consequence was 'a great means of spending much butter and cheese to the great enhancing of the prices thereof by reason of the said scarcity of herrings'. The bill was read a second time on 20 Jan. 1598, and committed to Waldegrave and others; on the following day the committee's amendments were accepted by the House, and the bill was engrossed. On 23 Jan. Waldegrave was on the committee to consider the bill 'for the better measuring of seven miles from the town of Great Yarmouth'.

He died on 15 Jan. 1637.

Vis. Essex (Harl. Soc. xiii), 121; Copinger, *Suff. Manors*, iii. 175; Wards 7/20/119; D'Ewes, 555, 562, 584, 585, 586; Townshend, *Hist. Colls.* 104, 122; C142/543/23.

N.M.F.

WALDEGRAVE, William (c.1540–1613), of Smallbridge, Suff. and Wormingford, Essex.

SUFFOLK 1563

b. c.1540, o.s. of Sir William Waldegrave[†] by Juliana, da. of Sir John Raynsford. *educ.* L. Inn 1560. *m.* (1) Elizabeth (*d.*1581), da. of Thomas Mildmay, 6s. inc. Sir William[*] 4da.; (2) Grizelda, da. of William Lord Paget, wid. of Sir Thomas Rivett, *s.p. suc.* fa. 1554. Kntd. 1576.

Master of the revels, L. Inn Nov. 1561; j.p.q. Essex c.1564–87, Suff. from c.1564; sheriff, Norf. and Suff. 1568–9; eccles. commr. diocese of Norwich 1570s; commr. musters, Suff. by 1588; dep. lt. by 1613.

When Waldegrave was granted livery of his lands in November 1561 on coming of age, he was still at Lincoln's Inn. However, he was not called to the bar, instead settling on his considerable East Anglian estates and enjoying the compliment of being elected knight of the shire for Essex to the first Parliament called thereafter. He continued to buy land in east Suffolk, notably at Boxford, where in 1596 he and his heir were governors of the local school, and in 1561 and again in 1579 he entertained the Queen at Smallbridge. Towards the end of the reign he may have been in financial difficulties, as he sold several Suffolk manors to a local clothier. Perhaps this had some connexion with his second wife's recusancy. He was himself classed as a 'favourer' of religion in 1564, and his omission from the Essex commission of the peace from 1587 was almost certainly due to the fact that his main residence was at Smallbridge. Waldegrave led 500 men from Suffolk to join the Earl of Leicester at Tilbury in 1588. He died on 25 Aug. 1613.

CPR, 1560–3, p. 362; *Vis. Essex* (Harl. Soc. xiii), 121–2, 251; *Cam. Misc.* ix(3), p. 62; *HMC 13th Rep. IV,* 435; Collinson thesis, 808, 869; *Recusant Rolls 1592–3* (Cath. Rec. Soc. xviii), 324; *L. Inn Black Bk.* i. 335; Morant, *Essex,* ii. 232 et passim; W. A. Copinger, *Suff. Manors,* passim; PRO Index 6800; Lansd. 48, f. 136 seq.; 56, ff. 168–9; 121, f. 68; 146, f. 18; *APC,* xxv. 96; xxx. 438; C142/335/10.

N.M.F.

WALDEGRAVE, Sir William (c.1573–1613), of Smallbridge, Suff. and Wormingford, Essex.

SUFFOLK 1597

b. c.1573, 1st s. of William Waldegrave[*] by his 1st w. *m.* (1) c.1591, Judith, da. of Sir Robert Jermyn[*], 1da.; (2) Jennemache,or Jemima, da. of (Sir) Nicholas Bacon[*], 3s. 3da. Kntd. 1595; *suc.* fa. Aug. 1613.

On Waldegrave's first marriage, his father settled several manors in Suffolk on him and his wife, and they no doubt had to live on the profits of these. Like other heirs of long-lived fathers, Waldegrave went for some time to Ireland, where he was knighted by the lord deputy. Perhaps in some doubt about gaining the county seat in 1597, he asked the Ipswich corporation to return him, and it was

agreed that Sir William Waldegrave shall have the voices of this town for his election to be one of the burgesses of the Parliament ... according to his request by his letter.

In the event, Waldegrave was elected for the shire. He was named to the armour and weapons committee, 8 Nov. 1597, and as a knight of the shire he could also have sat on committees for enclosures (5 Nov.), the poor law (5, 22 Nov.), penal laws (8 Nov.), monopolies (10 Nov.), the subsidy (15 Nov.), the charter for Great Yarmouth (23 Nov.) and draining the fens (3 Dec.).

He succeeded to his estates at the end of August 1613 and died on 26 Nov., John Chamberlain commenting:

The younger Sir William Waldegrave likewise tarried not long after his father, who died not past three months since, and this within this fortnight.

His heir, William, was ten years old when he succeeded. A second son, Thomas, was MP for Sudbury 1661–77, and a third was hanged for murder in 1649.

Vis. Essex (Harl. Soc. xiii), 121–2; C142/335/10; Bacon, *Ipswich Annals,* 384, 389, 390, 391; D'Ewes, 552, 553, 555, 557, 561, 562, 567; *Chamberlain Letters* ed. McClure, i. 491; Morant, *Essex,* ii. 232; W. A. Copinger, *Suff. Manors,* i. 53 et passim; Add. 19154, ff. 51–2, 67–8.

N.M.F./J.P.F.

WALKEDEN, Thomas, of London.

LUDGERSHALL 1572

b. by 1542, 1st s. of Geoffrey Walkeden, skinner, of London by Margaret, da. of John Loker of Bridgnorth, Salop. *educ.* M. Temple 1564, called 1582. *m.* Anne (*d.*1575), da. of William Goodere of Hadley, Herts., at least 1da. *suc.* fa. Apr. 1599.[1]

Walkeden was descended from a family of minor gentry settled at Stone, Staffordshire. His father was a master of the Skinners' Company, a charter assistant of the Muscovy Company of 1555, a promoter of the Guinea voyage of 1558, and an assistant of the Merchant Adventurers on their re-incorporation in 1564. He was rejected when proposed as alderman of London in January 1567 and never held office in the city.[2]

Since Thomas Walkeden was to be joined with his father in conveyances from the beginning of 1563 he was probably born not later than 1542. His entry to the Middle Temple may thus have followed some other form of training, perhaps in business or an inn of Chancery since there is no trace of him at either university. By then his father had acquired a suburban seat at Tottenham High Cross, and during the next few years the names of father and son are found associated in further property transactions in Edmonton which may represent Edward's introduction to conveyancing practice. His brother Robert, who followed their father into the Skinners' Company, presumably helped in the family business, which centred on the export and import of cloth.[3]

The little that has come to light about Thomas Walkeden's early career contains nothing to account for his return to Parliament in 1572. Ludgershall had recently emerged from its dependence upon the Brydges family and was becoming an asylum for parliamentary vagrants. Walkeden's appearance among them would be most readily explained if he had made a professional link conferring local influence, with the Kingsmills for instance, or even with the 2nd Earl of Pembroke, but no such link has been discovered. His father's connexion with the cloth industry could have been of service: we know that Geoffrey Walkeden acted at aldermanic elections with Edward Jackman, whose son Henry* was later to make some name for himself in the House, sitting for Wiltshire boroughs. However he procured it, Walkeden's membership has left no trace in the proceedings of the House; nor did it inaugurate a parliamentary career. The rest of his life is hardly less obscure than its beginning. He found a wife at Hadley, not far from Tottenham, and when she died he erected a monument to her in Hadley parish church: their only known child married a Londoner and died in 1633. His father lived until April 1599 (and has an epitaph in the parish church at Tottenham), and his brothers Robert and Geoffrey until 1587 and 1603, both leaving wills which reflect material prosperity. It may be that Thomas Walkeden was affluent enough not to need to practise, and that his belated call to the bar, at the age of 40 or thereabouts, was of social rather than professional significance. He is last heard of in 1608 participating in an action over a charitable bequest in his family's parish of St. Giles Cripplegate.[4]

[1] Vis. London (Harl. Soc. i), 18; (Harl. Soc. xvii), 365; 'Vis. Staffs. 1583', Wm. Salt Arch. Soc. iii(2), 135. [2] Wm. Salt Arch. Colls. passim; Grants of Arms, 264; APC, xiii. 256; Recs. of Skinners of London, Edw. I to Jas. I, passim; J. F. Wadmore, Skinners' Co. p. 191; T. S. Willan, Muscovy Merchants, 126; CPR, 1555, pp. 56–7; 1557, p. 419; Beaven, Aldermen, i. 4, 25, 57, 147, 182, 192, 208, 218, 246; PCC 15 Spencer. [3] CPR, 1560–3, p. 547; 1563–6, p. 139; 1566–9, p. 112; Muscovy Merchants, p. 126. [4] Beaven, Aldermen, i. 4, 218; Vis. Mdx. (Harl. Soc. lxv), 24; Lysons, Environs, ii. 521; Vis. London (Harl. Soc. xvii), 365; W. Robinson, Hist. Par. Tottenham, ii. 52; PCC 15 Spencer, 76 Bolein; C2/296/58.

S.T.B.

WALKER, Christopher (d.1590), of Bodmin, Cornw.

TREGONY   1589

m. bef. 1572, Elizabeth (d.1589), da. of one Clickerd, 1s. 1da.

Town clerk, Bodmin from 1568, mayor 1573–4.

Whether this Member was the Christopher Walker of Southwell, Nottinghamshire, who matriculated at King's College in 1552, or whether he was a member of the Walker family of Exeter, his connexion with Bodmin was well established by 1568 when he was paid for his work over an Exchequer suit in which he had succeeded in freeing the mayor and burgesses from the obligation of paying £5 10s. p.a. imposed upon them, as a fee farm rent, by the borough charter of 1563. No record of formal legal education has been found. After 22 years as town clerk of Bodmin, Walker was succeeded by his son-in-law Nicholas Sprey†, and subsequently by his grandson and namesake Christopher Walker. His sole appearance in the Commons was at the end of his life, for Tregony, probably through the influence of the Pomeroys or Trevanions. He left no trace in the proceedings of the Parliament.

Walker's will, made in July 1590, was proved four months later. He wished to be buried at Bodmin, and left 20s. to the poor of the parish and a similar sum to the poor of Egloshayle, five miles to the north. His estate was to be divided among his children and grandchildren.

Vivian, Vis. Cornw. 432; Al. Cant. i(4), 316; J. Maclean, Trigg Minor, i. 39, 160, 213, 236, 239, 254, 293, 294; APC, xviii. 147, 198; PCC 75 Drury.

I.C.

WALL, Humphrey (d.1625), of Leominster and Over Lawton, Herefs.

LEOMINSTER   1589

2nd s. of John Wall (d.1565) of Kingsland by Elizabeth, da. of Miles Cressye of Harpenden, Herts. m. (1) Maud, da. of Richard Perryn of Leominster, 3s. 6da.; (2) Joan.

Wall was related to several Leominster families. His father-in-law was bailiff in 1561, and his brother-in-law in 1594. Nothing is known of his activities in the Commons save that, on 24 Mar. 1589, he and his fellow-Member were granted leave of absence 'for their special and necessary business'. In 1594 Wall received a confirmation of his arms, with the grant of a crest. The rest of his life is obscure until 1625, when, being 'sick in body' he made his will. In it he bequeathed his soul to God, 'trusting that by the merits of Jesus Christ', his body and soul would 'be united together, and glorified at the day of judgment'. He left £20 to each of his grandchildren, and £10 to one Abraham Watts, a prisoner in the Fleet. The rest of his property was left to Joan, his 'now lawful married wife', to pass to her heirs after her death. George Proctor, DD and Thomas Colwell, were appointed overseers of the will, which was proved 19 Sept. that year.

W. R. Williams, Parl. Hist. Glos. 123; Vis. Herefs. ed. Weaver, 98; PCC 90 Clarke; G. F. Townsend, Leominster, 293–4; D'Ewes, 452.

J.J.C.

WALLER, Sir Walter (1544–99), of Groomsbridge, Speldhurst, Kent.

STEYNING   1593

b. 1544, o.s. of William Waller of Groomsbridge by Elizabeth, da. and coh. of Sir Walter Hendley† of

Cranbrook. *educ.* G. Inn 1561. *m.* (1) by 1564, Anne, da. of Philip Choute of Bethersden, 2s. 1da.; (2) Mary, da. of Richard Hardres, *s.p. suc.* gd.-fa. 1556. Kntd. 1572.

J.p. Suss. from c.1573, Kent from 1577.

Waller succeeded his grandfather to the family estates while still a minor. In 1572 he was one of the signatories of a certificate giving details of the able men, armour and weapons in the rape of Pevensey in Sussex. He was knighted in the same year, but the reason has not been ascertained. Perhaps he had already entered upon a military career. In 1585, when he was a captain in the regiment of Thomas Morgan I*, he conducted 150 men from Essex to the Netherlands. His company was at Rheinberg in the following year, and by the beginning of 1588 it was part of the Ostend garrison. Waller was at Ostend in August of the same year when the garrison revolted, he being the only officer who was not imprisoned by the men. In July 1589 his former lieutenant wrote to Walsingham, complaining that Waller had acted 'not like a knight', having sold his company and left his men in want. He was, in fact, in continual financial difficulties, mainly through acting as surety for insolvent friends, but also through his military service. In November 1588 he was reported to owe a total of £283 8s. to two burghers of Flushing and Brill, borrowed two years previously.

Waller was returned to Parliament for Steyning, probably through the influence of Sir Thomas Shirley I*, who had himself served with the Earl of Leicester in the Netherlands. No record has been found of any activity by Waller in the House of Commons. He died intestate 7 July 1599, and was buried in Speldhurst church. In 1602 his widow and his second son Sir Thomas, who succeeded to Groomsbridge, were sued in Chancery for the payment of half the purchase money – which the plaintiff claimed he had never received – for lands in Brenchley, Kent, bought by Waller in 1572.

C142/106/1, 265/70; *Vis. Kent* (Harl. Soc. xlii), 130; *CPR*, 1563–6, p. 143; Hasted, *Kent*, iii. 290–1; *CSP Dom.* 1547–80, p. 451; 1581–90, p. 109; *CSP For.* 1584–5, p. 691; 1585–6, p. 25; 1586–7, p. 110; Jan. to June 1588, p. 3; July to Dec. 1588, pp. 131, 203, 354–5; 1589, p. 382; *APC*, xiii. 141–2; xxi. 337; xxx. 178; Lansd. 72, f. 170; C2 Eliz./S26/47.

A.M.M.

WALLEY, John (*d.* 1615), of Bath, Som.

BATH 1589

s. of William Walley, mayor of Bath 1573, 1582. Mayor, Bath 1585–6.

Walley was concerned, on behalf of the city, in the recovery of chantry lands in 1585. Various payments to him are recorded in the chamberlains' accounts: two stipends of £40 as mayor, £4 for his charges at the musters and £50 which he had spent in the chantry lands business,

as well as £3 paid to him in 1590 as 'burgess money' or parliamentary wages.

Walley's death 'sometime alderman of this city' is recorded in Bath abbey register in April 1615. There was another John Walley, nephew of the 1589 MP, who was mayor in 1589 and died 1593. This man was a marriage connexion of William Shareston*, whom he calls 'my brother' (presumably brother-in-law) in his will.

Bath Chamberlains' Accts. (Som. Rec. Soc. xxxviii), *passim*; *Regs. Bath Abbey*, 345; PCC 71 Nevell.

I.C.

WALLIS, Robert, of Cambridge.

CAMBRIDGE 1597, 1601, 1604

?s. of Edward Wallis, bailiff of Cambridge.
Alderman, Cambridge, mayor 1596–7, 1597–8, 1606; commr. gaol delivery, Cambridge 1597, j.p. 1598.

Though his parentage is uncertain, Wallis certainly came of a Cambridge family, many of whom were christened in the parish of St. Michael. By 1587 he had established his own household, and in that year paid 40s. to the corporation for lead pipes running from Chevin's well to his cistern. Elected mayor in the autumn of 1596, he intensified the friction prevailing between town and university by refusing to take an oath to conserve the privileges of the university. Despite a joint order by Lord Keeper Egerton, the recorder of the borough, and Lord Burghley, chancellor of the university, Wallis refused, denying however in a letter to Burghley that he had made 'malicious speeches' to the lord treasurer's 'prejudice and dishonour'. Re-elected as mayor the following year, he took the oath in a grudging manner, his head covered, 'not so much offering to put hand unto head when he heard the name of Jesus Christ'. In April 1601 the university authorities made further accusations, and a suit against him was brought into the Exchequer. Later in the year, however, to the disgust of the vice-chancellor, who described him as a 'turbulent and factious townsman', he obtained the backing of Sir Robert Cecil over an infringement of regulations concerning Stourbridge fair in the interest of a royal purveyor.

For the Parliament of 1597 Wallis was paid £22 12s. wages at 4s. daily as well as another £23 7s. 6d. for charges. In this Parliament he was appointed to the committee for the bill against the excessive making of malt (12 Jan. 1598). He was appointed to committees for draining the fens (3 Dec. 1597, 28 Nov. 1601) and for bread (13 Jan. 1598). In 1601 his 'parliament fees' amounted to only £10 16s. In addition to his parliamentary wages, several other sums are recorded as paid to him by the borough: £49 15s. 10d. in 1598 for the corporation's suit against King's Lynn, for imposing a duty on coal; £15 10s. to repay a loan in 1601 and £20 in 1605, lent 'about the charter'. In 1606 he became mayor for the third time, after the sudden death of John Edmonds*. In 1611 he fell foul of the majority of the town council, for unseemly speeches against the mayor. By 1612 he was so estranged from the corporation that he was forced to sue out a writ for his parliamentary wages, which were paid him not directly, as on previous occasions, but through the under-sheriff of the county. He took no further part in borough administration, but continued to pay a few trifling rents to the corporation for a number of years.

F. Blomefield, *Coll. Cant.* 225; Lansd. 82, f. 74; 84, ff. 204, 220, 225; PRO Index 4208; C. H. Cooper, *Cambridge Annals*, ii and iii, passim; *Cambridge Bor. Docs.* ed. Palmer, i. 91; *Reg. St. Michael's, Cambridge* ed. Venn (Cambridge Antiq. Soc. xxv), 1–3, 109; Downing Coll. Camb. Bowtell mss; *HMC Hatfield*, xi. 186, 187, 192, 289, 316, 454–5; D'Ewes, 567, 578, 579, 657.

R.C.G.

WALLOP, Henry (1568–1642), of Farleigh Wallop, Hants.

LYMINGTON	1597
HAMPSHIRE	1601
STOCKBRIDGE	1614*
HAMPSHIRE	1621
WHITCHURCH	1624
ANDOVER	1625
HAMPSHIRE	1626, 1628, 1640 (Apr.), 1640 (Nov.)*

b. 18 Oct. 1568, 1st and o. surv. s. of Sir Henry Wallop* by Katherine, da. of Richard Gifford of King's Somborne. *educ.* St. John's, Oxf. 1584, BA from Hart Hall 1588; L. Inn 1590. *m.* by 1597, Elizabeth, da. and coh. of Robert Corbet*, of Moreton Corbet, Salop, 1s. *suc.* fa. 1599. Kntd. 1599.

Jt. steward (with his fa.) of manors of Old and New Lymington and Somerford 1594; dep. (to his fa.) treasurer at war [I] by Apr. 1597; constable, Christchurch castle c.1603; j.p. Hants 1596, sheriff 1603–4, 1629–30, custos rot. 1624; j.p. Salop, sheriff 2 Feb.–17 Nov. 1606; member, council in the marches of Wales 1617.

Wallop owed his return at Lymington, far from the family estates, to his two stewardships, otherwise worth only £4 p.a. In April 1597 he followed his father to Ireland, but presumably returned for the Parliament in the autumn of that year, though no proof that he attended has been found. His father died on 14 Apr. 1599, and his mother just afterwards, John Chamberlain telling Dudley Carleton†:

The world comes very fast upon Master Wallop, who, going into Ireland to bury his father, within five days after his arrival his mother died also, so that he shall put them both into one account.

Wallop returned home after winding up his affairs, and achieved a county seat in 1601. As a knight of the shire in this Parliament, he could have sat on committees for the order of business (3 Nov.), clothworkers (18 Nov.) and monopolies (23 Nov.). He succeeded to ten manors, including Farleigh, Hampshire; Allington, Wiltshire; and Worle, Somerset. Earlier, by his marriage to Elizabeth Corbet, he had obtained lands in Shropshire and the manor of Dallington, Northamptonshire. His first child was baptized at Knebworth, 22 July 1597, when he was staying with his friend, Rowland Lytton*. In the same circle, he was well acquainted with John Chamberlain, the letter writer, who visited him regularly at Farleigh. Under James I he became a leading figure in Shropshire as well as Hampshire, where by 1625 he was the richest man in the county, having succeeded to Wield on the death of his uncle William Wallop* in 1617. He died on 14 Nov. 1642, after many years as a consistent supporter of Parliament against Charles I, and was buried at Farleigh. The heir, his only son Robert†, was a regicide.

R. Warner, *Colls. Hist. Hants* i. 152; iii. 127; *Vis. Hants* (Harl. Soc. xxii), 26; C142/256/16; E316/3/191; *APC*, xxvii. 34; xxviii. 619; xxix. passim; *DNB* (Wallop, Sir Henry and Robert); *Cal. Wynn Pprs.* 130; PRO Index 4211; D'Ewes, 624, 642, 649, 657; PCC 1 Wallop; Baker, *Northants.* i. 131; *Chamberlain Letters* ed. McClure, passim; *CSP Dom.* 1611–18, pp. 233–4; *HMC Cowper*, i. 351; M. F. Keeler, *Long Parl.* 376–8.

R.C.G.

WALLOP, Sir Henry (c.1531–99), of Farleigh Wallop, Hants.

| SOUTHAMPTON | 1572 |

b. c.1531, 1st s. of Sir Oliver Wallop of Farleigh by his 1st w. Bridget Pigott of Beachampton; half-bro. of William Wallop*. *m.* Katherine, da. of Richard Gifford of King's Somborne, 3s. inc. Henry* 3da. *suc.* fa. 1566. Kntd. 1569.
MP [I] 1585.

J.p. Hants from c.1559; freeman, Southampton 1572; commr. musters, Hants by 1573, eccles. commr. 1575, piracy 1577; vice-treasurer [I] 1579–82, ld. justice 1582–9, treasurer at war by 1595–9; steward of manors of Old and New Lymington and Somerford by 1585, jt. steward (with s. Henry) 1594.

Wallop was one of the wealthiest landowners in Hampshire, much of his property having descended to his father as the brother and nearest male heir of Sir John Wallop, who died in 1551. In 1566, a few months after he succeeded to his estates, Wallop unsuccessfully contested a by-election for Hampshire, receiving support from Bishop Horne, who had earlier reported favourably to the Council on his religious views, and the protestant party, led by Richard Norton I* and his relatives the Kingsmills.

In 1572 Wallop was returned at Southampton, where his family was known and where he sometimes resided. The court leet cited him several times, fining him at least once for not having refuse cleared from his back doors in Woolhall and Bugle Street. During his first session in Parliament he was appointed to two legal committees (21,

22 May 1572) and to one on weapons (22 May). In 1576 he was appointed to committees on the ports bill (13 Feb.), a cloth bill (16 Feb.), weapons (17 Feb.), wine (21 Feb.), church discipline (29 Feb.) and wharves and quays (8 Mar.). By the time of the 1581 session he was in Ireland, and the borough returned Fulke Greville* in his place, who remained the sitting Member until, on the last day of the session, the House decided that a Member's absence on the Queen's service did not justify a by-election, and unseated Greville. An efficient administrator in Ireland, Wallop carried out his military duties effectively during the rebellions, and negotiated ably with Tyrone in the truce of 1595. The fact that he quarrelled with Sir John Perrot* is not to his discredit: scarcely a leading English official in Ireland did not. As a Member of the Irish Parliament of 1585, Wallop sponsored an Act about conveyances of land by those attainted of treason, a subject of interest to him as treasurer. It was during his Irish service that the surviving Armada ships straggled along the Irish coast, and a letter from him to Burghley gives details of examinations of Spanish prisoners. He complained, as did other English officials in Ireland, that salary and grants did not cover expenses. By the middle of 1598 he was ill. The Privy Council finally granted his request to be recalled in March 1599, but he died on 14 Apr., the day before his successor arrived. He had made his will on 31 Mar., appointing Henry sole executor. Two servants, Richard Hooper and Philip Hore, received £200 for their 'endeavour to pass' Wallop's accounts as 'vice treasurer and treasurer at war before her Majesty's commission'. Charles Huett received £40, provided that he would 'effectually prosecute my accounts now in his hands'.

DNB; Vis. Hants (Harl. Soc. lxiv), 26; C142/143/26, 256/5; *CSP Ire.* 1574–85, p. 546; 1577–99, passim; Lansd. 24, f. 159; 28, f. 146; 56, f. 168 seq.; 146, f. 18; 683, f. 69; Collins, *Peerage*, iv. 302, 306–17; E316/3/191; *Cam. Misc.* ix(3), p. 55; *VCH Hants*, iii. 365; iv. 35, 253; *CPR*, 1555–7, p. 132; St. Ch. 4/7/18; 5/P30/32, W36/33, 45/38; *HMC 11th Rep. III*, 20; *Ct. Leet Recs.* i (Soton Rec. Soc.), 70; ii. 171; *CJ*, i. 96, 105, 106, 107, 109, 112, 136; D'Ewes, 212, 213, 247, 251, 255, 308; *CSP Dom.* 1547–80, pp. 371, 375, 413, 524; 1581–90, p. 662; *APC*, viii. 146; x. 16, 415; xi. 226, 232–3 et passim; xii. 10, 38, 77 seq.; *HMC Hatfield*, iii. 22; *Eliz. Govt. and Soc.* 46; *CSP Dom.* 1547–80, p. 502; PCC 1 Wallop.

N.M.F.

WALLOP, William (c.1553–1617), of Southampton and Wield, Hants.

| LYMINGTON | 1586 |
| SOUTHAMPTON | 1597 |

b. c.1553, 3rd s. of Sir Oliver Wallop of Farleigh by his 2nd w. Anne, da. of Robert Martin of Athelhampton, Dorset; half-bro. of Sir Henry Wallop*. *educ.* Magdalen Coll. Oxf. 1571. *m.* (1) Margaret, da. of Henry Asheley of Wimborne St. Giles, Dorset, wid. of John Hawles of Monkton Up Wimborne, Dorset, *s.p.*; (2) c.1585, Averine or Averna, da. and coh. of William Knight of Southampton and wid. of William Staveley of Southampton, *s.p.*; (3) c.1614, Margery, da. of John Fisher* of Chilton Candover, *s.p.*

Burgess, Southampton 1584, mayor 1596–7, 1610–11; j.p. Hants 1583–c.1587, q. 1593–6, sheriff 1599–1600.[1]

The younger son of a leading Hampshire family, Wallop became a merchant in Southampton, taking a leading part in the administration of the town after becoming a burgess in 1584. He did, however, own land in the county, and on two occasions was a member of the commission of the peace for Hampshire. A list, probably drawn up in 1587, names him as one of those to be dropped from the commission, the probable reason being that Sir Henry Wallop, another member of the family, was a justice. But between 1593 and 1596 William was again on the commission and a member of the quorum. He first sat in Parliament for Lymington through the influence of his half-brother, Sir Henry Wallop, steward of the manor. Wallop was licensed to depart on 8 Mar. 1589. In 1597 he was returned to Parliament for Southampton, being elected at the end of his first term as mayor. Wallop made his will on 17 Dec. 1616, and it was proved by his executrix, his third wife Margery, on 18 Dec. of the following year. He left £50 to be spent on his tomb and £100 for his funeral expenses, £10 of it to be distributed among the poor. £100 was bequeathed to the town of Southampton as a fund to help poor young men to set up in trade. After his legacies had been paid, the remainder of the personal estate was to go to his wife Margery. Wallop died 15 Nov. 1617, and was buried in the church at Wield.[2]

[1] Hutchins, *Dorset*, iii. 394; *Al. Ox.* 1500–1714, p. 1562; C142/374/84; W. Berry, *Co. Genealogies, Hants*, 43; *Vis. Hants* (Harl. Soc. lxiv), 26; D'Ewes, 413; *Assembly Bks.* (Soton Rec. Soc.), 6, n. 4; iii. 91, n. 1; *Bks. of Examinations 1601–2* (Soton Rec. Soc.), 28, 43, 49; SP12/145, f. 38; Lansd. 121, f. 66. [2] PCC 121 Weldon; *VCH Hants*, iii. 347; C142/374/84.

A.M.M.

WALMESLEY, John (d.1588), of Gray's Inn, London.

| CLITHEROE | 1586 |

yr. (prob. 8th) s. of Thomas Walmesley of Showley, Lancs. by Margaret, da. of James Livesey of Livesey, Lancs.; bro. of Thomas*. *educ.* G. Inn 1578. *unm.*

Walmesley was presumably returned for Clitheroe as a young man of good local family already resident in London and possibly possessed of some training in the law. He was evidently still young when he died, having made his will 2 Jan. 1588. He left some 12 mourning cloaks and gowns to various relatives, bequeathed his law books to a nephew, 40s. to his man Roland Walker, 40s. to the poor of St. Bennet Finck and £4 to the poor of Gray's Inn. His brothers William and Nicholas were the executors.

Foster, *Lancs. Peds.*; PCC 3 Rutland.

N.M.S.

WALMESLEY, Thomas (c.1537–1612), of Dunkenhalgh, Lancs.

LANCASHIRE 1589

b. c.1537, 1st s. of Thomas Walmesley of Showley by Margaret, da. of James Livesey of Livesey. *educ.* L. Inn 1559, called 1567. *m.* Anne (*d.* 19 Apr. 1635), da. and h. of Robert Shuttleworth of Hacking, 1s. *suc.* fa. 16 Apr. 1584. Kntd. 1603.[1]

Gov. L. Inn 1575, Lent reader 1578, autumn reader 1580, serjeant-at-law 1580; commr. musters, Lancs. 1580; j.p. Lancs. by 1587; master forester of Quernmore, duchy of Lancaster 1587, 2nd justice at Lancaster 1589; j.c.p. 1589; freeman, Southampton 1595; commr. eccles. causes 1598 (Chester), 1603, 1604.[2]

Walmesley was a lawyer, already middle aged when elected for Lancashire in 1589. As a knight of the shire he could have sat on the subsidy committee, 11 Feb. He reported the bill about proclamations, 19 Feb., and sat on some minor legal committees, 22, 25 Feb. He also served on committees discussing captains and soldiers, 26 Feb., and the Queen's dislike of the purveyors bill 27 Feb. Made a judge, he served as a receiver of petitions in the Lords in the 1597 and 1601 Parliaments. For all this, Walmesley was the son of a recusant and himself suspect in religion. In 1583 he defended, before the court of common pleas, the validity of papal dispensations issued during Mary's reign, and 23 years later when Lord Sheffield wrote to Lord Salisbury to the effect that if Walmesley came on that (presumably the northern) circuit again 'things standing as they do, it could not but overthrow all, for the Papists have ever borne themselves much upon his favour'.[3]

In 1591 it fell to Walmesley and Mr. Justice Clinch to try Thomas Langton* and his associates for the murder of Mr. Houghton. As the sheriff was not thought to be 'indifferent in that cause', the Privy Council instructed Walmesley to supervise the composition of the jury, but his conduct in the event earned him a sharp reprimand from the Queen for allowing the accused bail contrary to her express command. She wondered 'how he dared presume so far, showing both contempt of her commandment, and little regard for the due administration of justice'. She ordered him 'at his peril' to have the parties immediately returned to prison, to proceed to a speedy trial without bail.[4]

In 1593 or 1594 Walmesley was proposed as vice-chancellor at Lancaster, and may have held the post. As a justice of the common pleas, he rode every circuit in England except that of Norfolk and Suffolk. His account book for the years 1596–1600 has survived and contains an interesting record of the customary presents received while on circuit, and of his expenses. He was a member of the commission before which Essex was arraigned in 1600, and assisted the peers at his trial the following year. He was described by Cecil in 1603 as one of the three 'learnedest judges'. An old man, he suffered at that time from gout and palsy. He was the only dissenter from the judges' decision, in Calvin's case in 1607, that natives of Scotland born since the accession of James I were naturalized Englishmen.[5]

Walmesley acquired property in Lancashire and Yorkshire, rebuilt the mansion on his estate of Dunkenhalgh, and also that of Hacking which came to him in right of his wife. In 1607, by deed of trust, he settled his estates on his only son Thomas, a Catholic. In 1611 he was 'put to his pension', and retired to Dunkenhalgh, where he died on 26 Nov. 1612. He was buried at Blackburn, and his monument – a replica of that of Anne, Duchess of Somerset in Westminster abbey – was destroyed during the civil wars.[6]

[1] Foster, *Lancs. Peds.*; Abram, *Blackburn*, 433. [2] Foss, *Judges*, 698–9; *Lancs. Lieutenancy Pprs.* (Chetham Soc. 1), 109; Lansd. 53, f. 37; Somerville, *Duchy*, i. 474, 509; *CSP Dom.* 1581–90, p. 599; 1598–1601, p. 15; *HMC Hatfield*, xv. 223–4; xvi. 290; *DNB.* [3] *DNB*; *VCH Lancs.* vi. 42; Townshend, *Hist. Colls.* 18–21; D'Ewes, 431, 434, 437, 439, 440, 525, 529, 600, 603; Lansd. 31, f. 12; *HMC Hatfield*, xviii. 36. [4] *APC*, xxi. 385; *CSP Dom.* 1591–4, p. 188. [5] Somerville, i. 481; *CSP Dom.* 1601–3, p. 285; *DNB*; *Cam. Misc.* iv. 3, 13, 44, 55. [6] Abram, 433–4; *VCH Lancs.* vi. 421; Foss, 699.

N.M.S.

WALSGROVE *alias* **FLEET, John** (*d.* 1618), of Worcester and Hallow Park, Worcs.

WORCESTER 1589

2nd s. of Thomas Walsgrove *alias* Fleet* of Worcester. *educ.* I. Temple 1578, called 1585. *m.* (1) Joyce (*d.* 1590); (2) Anne, sis. of Edward Boughton; 2s. 1da. prob. by second w.

Queen's attorney in marches of Wales 1599–1609; j.p. Worcs. from c.1601; ?member, council in the marches of Wales from 1617.

Although Walsgrove's name does not occur in the town books, he resided in Worcester for much of his life, and in his will left his father's picture and his own 'to be set up in the tolsey of the said city amongst the other pictures there'. During his lifetime he supported various city charities. His appointment as attorney in the marches (probably made at the request of the 2nd Earl of Pembroke) enabled him to buy several manors in the county, including Hallow Park and Rydmarley. He also inherited several leases from his father, whose executor he was, and James I asked the dean and chapter of Worcester to grant him a further reversion of one of these. By 1601 he was of standing enough to marry into a county family, be appointed to the commission of the peace, and style himself esquire. He died 19 Jan. 1618.

C142/378/115; PCC 24 Lawe, 18 Parker, 1 Sainberbe; P. H. Williams, *Council in the Marches of Wales*, 330; PRO Index 4208, ff. 138, 242; 6800, f. 473; Nash, *Worcs.* ii. 304.

S.M.T.

WALSGROVE alias FLEET, Thomas (d. c.1613), of Worcester.

WORCESTER 1572

1st s. of John Walsgrove *alias* Fleet of Worcester by Eleanor, da. of Robert Youlet of Worcester. *m.*, 3s. inc. John* 5 or 6da. *suc.* fa. 1567.[1]

Member of the 48, Worcester 1554, chamberlain 1556–7, member of the 24 1558, bailiff 1560–1, 1562–3, 1574–5, auditor 1563–4; gov. Worcester free sch. and almshouses 1561–d., treasurer and receiver 1582, 1592.[2]

Walsgrove, like his father, was a Worcester merchant. Originally a weaver, he had become a clothier by his father's death, and drove a thriving trade, to judge from the large quantities of wool he bought in 1589. He himself may have produced some of the wool he used, since he had pasture land on lease, although as his mother disputed his title he may not have obtained possession until after her death in 1574.[3]

Walsgrove's civic career, probably begun when he was still a relatively young man, followed the customary course. He belonged to the small, frequently inter-married group influential in the city, and obtained election as burgess for the Parliament of 1572 with his friend Christopher Dighton*. He was appointed to several committees in the House, all except one on the poor law (11 Feb. 1576) being concerned with the cloth trade, on which he was evidently considered an expert. These were appointed on 28 June 1572, 16 Feb. and 9 Mar. 1576 and 4, 13 and 23 Feb. 1581.[4]

Walsgrove lived to a great age. He was at least 80 when he died, assuming that he had attained his majority before being appointed to the Worcester corporation in 1554. He maintained to the last an active interest in education in the city, and in the charitable foundations established by his father. In his long and complex will, as well as remembering each of his numerous progeny and other relatives, he made a sizeable contribution to charity, including four recently built almshouses, and he left land for the maintenance of other almshouses in the city. He left the grammar school £10, and an endowment to house poor children, who were 'to be brought up to some laborious course of life'. The greater part of his property, mainly freehold houses in Worcester, went to his grandson and heir Thomas, but he left some of his interests to his younger sons. He bequeathed his soul to God, 'nothing doubting but that for his infinite mercy, set forth in the precious blood of his dearly beloved son, Jesus Christ, my alone Saviour and Redeemer, he will receive my soul into his glory and place it in the company of heavenly angels and blessed saints'.[5]

[1] C3/196/46; PCC 24 Lawe, 18 Parker. [2] Worcester Guildhall, audit of city accts. 1540–1600; Flenley, *Cal. Reg. Council, Marches of Wales*, 126; W. R. Williams, *Worcs. MPs*, 92; CPR, 1560–3, p. 215. [3] C3/196/46; VCH *Worcs.* ii. 290–1. [4] Worcester Guildhall, chamber order bk. 1540–1601, ff. 113–14 seq.; *CJ*, i. 103, 105, 106, 113, 122, 125, 129. [5] *Early Education in Worcester* (Worcs. Hist. Soc.), 230, 231, 232–3, 236, 238; VCH *Worcs.* iv. 414, 416, 417; PCC 24 Lawe.

S.M.T.

WALSH, William (c.1561–1622), of Abberley, Worcs.

WORCESTERSHIRE 1593

b. c.1561, 1st s. of Walter Walsh of Wraysbury, Bucks. by Dorothy, da. of Richard Hill* of London. *m.* Elizabeth, da. of George Board of Cuckfield, Suss., *s.p. suc.* fa. Kntd. 1603.

J.p. Worcs. from c.1591, sheriff 1598–9.

Walsh's grandfather Walter, member of a long established Worcestershire family, had been a favourite courtier of Henry VIII, married an heiress, and established a cadet branch of the family. In 1582 Richard Shelley and his wife Dorothy, probably William's mother and her second husband, transferred the family estates to William, presumably on his coming of age. His father had evidently died some time previously while William was still a minor, for in a suit over copyholds in the manor of Abberley, William was represented by one Edmund Broughton, his '*prochain amy*'. The trouble with tenants at Abberley was recurrent throughout Walsh's life, but evidently did not affect his prosperity. In the 1590s he purchased several further manors, including Upton Snodsbury, Hurcott and Broughton, Worcestershire.

Walsh had relatives in places of influence: his aunts were all married to men with posts at court or in central offices, but he does not appear to have used them to promote his career. Although he served a turn as sheriff and was active as a justice, he played only a minor role in county life. In religion he was a protestant like his maternal grandfather, and his fellow knight of the shire (Sir) Henry Bromley. Their candidature probably had the support of the Lytteltons, who were related to Bromley, and of another strong protestant, John Russell II*. His one experience of Parliament was not happy – in London he and Bromley were recruited by Richard Stephens* to join Wentworth's scheme to raise the succession question in the House, and in consequence they both spent most of the session in the Fleet prison.

He died 8 Apr. 1622 and was buried with his wife in the south aisle of the church at Abberley. His estates descended to his nephew William, who sold some to Thomas Coventry, the lord keeper.

Vis. Worcs. (Harl. Soc. xxvii), 140; Nash, *Worcs.* i. 2–4; Req 2/25/60, 29/105; C3/195/18; VCH *Worcs.* iii. 172; iv. 44, 87, 209, 220–1; *CSP Dom.* 1581–90, p. 682; HMC *Hatfield*, xviii. 34; *Q. Sess. Pprs. 1591–1643* (Worcs. Hist. Soc.), passim; Neale, *Parlts.* ii. 260; *EHR*, xxxix. 192–4; *Habington's Worcs.* (Worcs. Hist. Soc.), i. 244–6.

S.M.T.

WALSHE, John (d.1572), of Cathanger, Som. and Bethnal Green, Mdx.

CRICKLADE	1547
BRISTOL	1553 (Mar.), 1553 (Oct.), 1554 (Apr.), 1554 (Nov.), 1555
SOMERSET	1558
BRISTOL	1559, 1563*

1st s. of John Walshe by his 1st w. Joan, da. of John Broke, serjeant-at-law. *educ.* M. Temple. *m.*, 1da.

Justice Carm., Pemb., Card.; member, council in the marches of Wales 1553.

Recorder, Bristol 1552–?71; j.p. Glos., Herefs., Salop, Som., Worcs. and Welsh counties 1554–9; bencher, M. Temple 1554–9, reader 1555, 1559; serjeant-at-law 1559; j.p. six northern counties 1562; j.c.p. 10 Feb. 1563; c.j. Lancaster 1563.

Apart from his one appearance as knight of the shire for Somerset, Walshe represented Bristol continuously from the last Parliament of Edward VI's reign until 1563, when he became a judge. Bristol gave him a present of wine on his promotion. Next year he advised the bishop of Bath and Wells in the inquiry into the religion of justices of the peace and reported on the charges against Gabriel Pleydell* and others of unlawful hunting in Selwood forest. Soon afterwards he received a Council letter 'to take care in the good assessing of the subsidy' in Somerset. Early in March 1566 he had an audience of the Queen concerning the reprieve of a certain Ralph Swynhoo. Other references show him examining a prisoner in the Tower by 'some touch of the rack', and dealing with abuses in church affairs at Carlisle. He made his will 3 Feb. 1572 and died 12 Feb. He was buried at Fivehead, Somerset. His will was proved in the following June.

Vis. Som. (Harl. Soc. xi), 15; J. Collinson, *Som.* i. 41–2; J. Latimer, *16th Cent. Bristol*, 56–7; *CPR*, 1550–3, p. 54; 1553–4, pp. 19–26; 1557–8, p. 457; 1558–60, p. 245; 1560–3, pp. 435–45, 469; A. B. Beaven, *Bristol Lists*, 403; Bristol recs. mayors' audits, ex inf. Mary Williams, city archivist; Somerville, *Duchy*, i. 471; *Cam. Misc.* ix(3), p. 63; *APC*, vii. 170, 319; Lansd. 8, f. 80; 9, f. 12; *CSP Dom.* Add. 1566–79, p. 62; C142/162/156; PCC 18 Daper.

N.M.F.

WALSHE, Nicholas (c.1534–68), of Little Sodbury and Olveston, Glos.

| GLOUCESTERSHIRE | 1563 |

b. c.1534, yr. s. of Maurice Walshe of Little Sodbury by Bridget, da. of Nicholas, 1st Baron Vaux. *m.* Mary, da. of Sir John Berkeley of Stoke Gifford, 1s. 2da. *suc.* bro. Anthony 1557.

J.p. Glos. by 1559, sheriff 1561–2.

Walshe's prospects as a younger son in a large family were poor until, in the summer of 1556, while the family was at dinner, 'a fiery, sulphurous globe passing from one window to another' killed his father and one of his children, and injured six more so badly that they died within the next few months. Only two sons, Nicholas and

his younger brother Henry, were left alive. So many deaths in a short time made the question of succession complicated, especially as some of the property was held directly of the Crown, and though a jury declared in January 1557 that Nicholas was heir to his elder brother Anthony, it was not until March 1563, when he was sitting in Parliament, that he received livery of his lands. These were extensive, including the manors of Old and Little Sodbury, Olveston, Kingsgrove, Northwick and Radwick. Some of the property was subject to the life interest of his grandmother, Lady Anne Walshe. In May 1565 he increased the value of the Sodbury estate by buying the mansion house of Camers Place from Sir Ralph Sadler*. Walshe took no active part in the affairs of his one Parliament and was granted leave of absence on 12 Mar. 1563. He died in his early thirties 19 Feb. 1568, his will being proved 17 May. As Walshe's heir Henry was only three, the estates were subjected to a long wardship. Then Henry was killed in a duel, whereupon what was left of them went to a cousin.

Vis. Glos. (Harl. Soc. xxi), 8, 265; Wards 7/11/39; PCC 10 Babington; C142/109/71, 77; *Bristol and Glos. Arch. Soc. Trans.* xiii. 4; *CPR*, 1560–3, p. 598; 1563–6, p.308; *CJ*, i. 69.

N.M.F.

WALSINGHAM, Francis (c.1532–90), of Scadbury and Foots Cray, Kent; Barn Elms, Surr.; Seething Lane, London.[1]

BOSSINEY	1559
LYME REGIS	1563
SURREY	1572*, 1584, 1586, 1589

b. c.1532, o.s. of William Walsingham (*d.*1534), of Scadbury, Chislehurst, Kent, by Joyce, da. of Sir Edmund Denny of Cheshunt, Herts. *educ.* King's, Camb. 1548; travelled abroad 1550–2; G. Inn 1552; Padua 1555. *m.* (1) 1562, Anne (*d.*1564), da. of Sir George Barne, lord mayor of London, wid. of Alexander Carleill, *s.p.*; (2) 1566, Ursula, da. of Henry St. Barbe of Som., wid. of Sir Richard Worsley† of Appuldurcombe, I.o.W., 2da. *suc.* fa. Mar. 1534. Kntd. 1 Dec. 1577.

J.p. Herts. 1564, q. by 1574; j.p.q. Hants from c.1573, custos rot. by 1577; j.p.q. Surr. from 1579; recorder, Colchester from 1578; high steward, Salisbury, Ipswich 1581, Winchester 1582, Kingston-upon-Hull by 1583, King's Lynn 1588; ambassador to France 1570–3; principal secretary and PC 21 Dec. 1573; chancellor of the Garter 1578–87; envoy to Netherlands June–Sept. 1578, to France 1581, to Scotland 1583; gov. mines royal 1581; member of commissions to try William Parry* 1585, Babington conspirators Sept. 1586, Mary Stuart Oct. 1586; chancellor, duchy of Lancaster 1587.[2]

Walsingham was born into a family of London vintners who by the early fifteenth century had become wealthy enough to buy a manor in Kent. He was closely related through his mother to one of Henry VIII's ministers, and his father, a lawyer, died when he was a child. His mother at once remarried, and it was in the house of his stepfather, a relation of Henry Carey[†], 1st Baron Hunsdon, and thus connected through the Boleyns with the future Queen Elizabeth, that Walsingham spent his childhood. At the age of 16 he matriculated at the protestant King's College, Cambridge, where Sir John Cheke[†] was provost. Here he must certainly have met Cheke's son-in-law, the future secretary William Cecil. After two years at Cambridge Walsingham, conventionally enough for one of his background, first travelled abroad, then went to an inn of court. Under Queen Mary there was no chance of preferment for a protestant whose close relations were associated both with the attempt to make Lady Jane Grey Queen, and with the Wyatt rebellion. By 1555 he was in Padua, studying civil law, and here he became '*consiliarius* of the English nation', that is spokesman for the English law students in his faculty. Between April 1556 and November 1558 he visited Switzerland and was for a short time at Basle.[3]

On his return to England, soon after Elizabeth's accession, he stayed on his father's estates in Kent until a fortunate marriage led to his renting the manor of Parkbury, Hertfordshire, which was his country residence until he acquired Barn Elms in 1579. All this time, however, he was much at court, assisting Sir William Cecil, who engineered his return to the Commons for Bossiney in 1559 through the 2nd Earl of Bedford. A memorandum by Cecil on forthcoming parliamentary business, written in all probability before the 1563 Parliament, notes 'Mr. Walsingham to be of the House', and Walsingham was returned both at Banbury (through Sir Francis Knollys[*]) and at Lyme Regis (through the 2nd Earl of Bedford). He chose to represent Lyme Regis. Very probably he was already being employed on intelligence work by Cecil, but definite evidence of the connexion is lacking before December 1568, when he proffered Cecil two sibylline opinions on the political situation, opinions which were to be reiterated throughout his career: 'there is less danger in fearing too much than too little', and 'there is nothing more dangerous than security'.[4]

Security was to be the keynote of Walsingham's policy, whether he was trying as ambassador to France to negotiate a treaty binding the French government to help England against a Spanish attack; attempting to persuade Elizabeth to send help to the protestants in Scotland and so counteract French influence there; or unravelling the tangled skeins of plots concerning his chief enemy, 'that devilish woman' the Queen of Scots. Even his protestantism was modified through seeing the dangers of division in the face of the Catholic threat, and he constantly reminded the puritans of their

> great cause to thank God for that we presently enjoy, having God's word sincerely preached and the sacraments truly administered. The rest we lack we are to beg by prayer and attend with patience.

In the summer of 1570 Walsingham went to France on Sir Henry Norris's mission to secure favourable terms for the Huguenots in their negotiations with Charles IX, and later in the year he succeeded Norris as ambassador. At the time of the St. Bartholomew massacre his house became the temporary headquarters of the protestant refugees in Paris, and for a time he favoured a breach of diplomatic relations with France. Shortly after the massacre, he wrote to the Privy Council:

> I leave it to your honours now to judge what account you may make of the amity of this crown. If I may without presumption or offence say my opinion, considering how things presently stand, I think less peril to live with them as enemies than as friends.

Walsingham returned to England in April 1573 with a rooted distrust of Charles IX and Catherine de Medici and a settled conviction that there was little interest there in the fate of Mary Queen of Scots, whom Elizabeth could therefore dispose of without fear of military intervention from France.[5]

As secretary, Walsingham continued to be concerned with European affairs, his own predilections being to support protestant movements everywhere. His justification for the heavy expense this would have entailed was that no support or half-hearted measures were more expensive in the long run, as he wrote to Leicester in 1577, over a subsidy for Duke John Casimir of the Palatinate: 'this our art of saving £20,000 is accomplished with so many mischiefs like to ensue hereby as I fear will not be put off with the expense of a million'.

Unfortunately for Walsingham it was not only Elizabeth's parsimony that stood in his way but her personal antipathy towards him and his 'gloomy prophecies', diluted though this was by her recognition of his ability, honesty and integrity. All this he well understood, and for his part he made no secret of his impatience with her for reserving final decisions for herself: 'I would to God her Majesty would be content to refer these things to them that can best judge of them, as other princes do'.[6] There was not a councillor in her service 'who would not wish himself rather in the furthest part of Ethiopia than to enjoy the fairest palace in England'. Her procrastination he particularly detested:

> For the love of God, madam, let not the cure of your diseased state hang any longer on deliberation. Diseased states are no more cured by consultation, when nothing resolved on is put into execution, than unsound and diseased bodies by only conference with physicians, without receiving remedies by them prescribed.

The Queen might throw her slipper at him, or tell him he was of no use except as 'a protector of heretics';[7] Walsingham might make his genuine ill-health an excuse to absent himself from court; but the fact remains that these two incompatible personalities worked together for nearly 20 years without an open breach. Yet all the time, as he told Leicester, he knew that the Queen would not use his services if she could dispense with them. In what lay Walsingham's strength? In the absence of the personal bond that united the Queen with other leading courtiers, how was Walsingham able to maintain his position? Long before he became secretary he had been given the task of dealing with the early stages of the Ridolfi plot, and thenceforward he built up an intelligence system unmatched in its day through which he was able to turn to advantage conspiracies such as those of Throckmorton and Babington. By combining information from official sources at home and abroad, from merchants, and from undercover agents, many of whom figure (some tragically) in these pages, he was able to make a unique contribution to the stability of Elizabeth's throne. If some of his actions, perhaps those concerning the Babington conspirators, appear to posterity reprehensible, he believed that the end justified the means. As he put it at Mary's trial: 'I call God to witness that as a private person I have done nothing unbeseeming an honest man, nor, as I bear the place of a public man, have I done anything unworthy of my place'.[8] Fortunately for him, he was ill throughout the period when the despatch of Mary's death warrant led to the imprisonment of his colleague, William Davison*, and the temporary disgrace even of Burghley. Elizabeth, of course, was in no doubt of his attitude: she told Davison to call at Walsingham's house to show it to him for 'the grief thereof' would 'go near to kill him outright'.[9] Within a month of the execution he sent Maitland a closely reasoned document illustrating the inadvisability of any retributive action over Mary's death, followed by a private assurance to James VI of his personal support in the question of the English succession. With Burghley out of favour, the Queen could act without restraint in the weeks following Mary's execution, and in March 1587 she alarmed Walsingham by sending a sharp letter to the French King. 'Your Lordship may see', he wrote to Burghley, 'that our courage doth greatly increase, for that we make no difficulty to fall out with all the world.' It was no secret that Philip II of Spain intended to invade England, and at this very time Walsingham was receiving hundreds of intelligence reports on the subject. But all his efforts to persuade Queen and Privy Council to prepare for war were hampered by his lack of personal influence on the Queen and by the pre-eminence of the more cautious and peace-loving Burghley, who, as chief minister, was prepared to support the Queen in her peace overtures to Parma, on the very eve of the Armada's departure. At this time also his relations with Leicester began to deteriorate. Until 1587, Leicester and he had been united by common interests, including a forward protestant policy, but personal and political causes now combined to lead to an estrangement. Walsingham's son-in-law Philip Sidney* had left debts necessitating the sale

of estates, which Leicester was unhelpful in furthering at the same time as he opposed Walsingham's moves to become chancellor of the duchy of Lancaster. Either as cause or effect of these personal disagreements, Walsingham now thought that Leicester, whom he had hitherto supported as governor in the Low Countries, had hopelessly bungled matters. Thus, until the defeat of the Armada, followed immediately by Leicester's death, Walsingham was isolated on the Privy Council, though he had compatible relatives and friends among the ministers and diplomats of the second rank, such as Mildmay, Davison, Henry Killigrew, Beale and Randolph.[10]

Walsingham was not returned at the start of the 1572 Parliament, but on his return from France he took, as befitted his dignity as a Privy Councillor, a Surrey county seat vacated by the succession to a peerage of Charles Howard I*, and Walsingham continued to represent Surrey until his death. In 1576 he was named to three minor committees: on debts (14 Feb.), coins (15 Feb.) and wharves (13 Mar.). He made two interventions in 1581, one on choosing the Speaker at the start of the session (16 Jan.), one on Arthur Hall at the end (18 Mar.). 'Both Mr. Secretaries', Walsingham and Thomas Wilson*, were ordered by the House on 3 Mar. 1581 to confer with the bishops on religion. In 1584 he was appointed to a committee concerning letters patent granted to Sir Walter Ralegh* (14 Dec.), but no further mention of him is made in the journals either in this Parliament or in his last two Parliaments. It is true that as a Privy Councillor and a county Member he could have attended other committees, but he who was at the very centre of affairs made no major speech in the House, and his private papers contain only one reference of any significance to Parliament, a report to the 3rd Earl of Huntingdon in 1581. It is clear that the House of Commons held little appeal for him, but one wonders why the government did not make more use of him in the House where both his puritanism and his sombre manner might have proved assets. That, unlike his brother-in-law Peter Wentworth*, he regarded Parliament as no place to advocate measures for church reform, is clear from a letter he wrote to one of his own religious persuasion who was urging him to take a more positive line:

If you knew with what difficulty we retain what we have and that the seeking of more might hazard (according to man's understanding) that which we already have, you would then deal warily in this time when policy carrieth more sway than zeal.

Similarly Walsingham exercised little parliamentary patronage, despite having almost boundless opportunities to do so. In 1589, the one Parliament when he was chancellor of the duchy of Lancaster, at most a dozen Members for duchy boroughs were his nominees, including Thomas Jermyn (Sudbury), a nephew of his friend Sir Robert Jermyn*; and Francis Harvey (Knaresborough), who had been nominated by Walsingham at Colchester in 1584. The others were lawyers or minor duchy officials. Outside the duchy he could have nominated at boroughs where he was recorder or high steward, but again he did not do so. Colchester's offer of both seats in 1584 may well have been spontaneous, and in 1586 he was so late in applying that the election had already taken place. Far from seeing this as an insult as other patrons did in like circumstances, he at once concurred with their choice.

At Winchester in 1584 and 1586 he presumably nominated John Wolley, the Latin secretary, and in 1589 his own servant Francis Mills, but he made no use of his official position at King's Lynn, Hull or Ipswich to secure seats, though interestingly enough he asked Ipswich to put in his nominee as town preacher. Several of his servants represented boroughs where his friends had influence: in 1584 Lawrence Tomson was returned at Melcombe Regis, with the 2nd Earl of Bedford as his patron; so was Francis Mylles at Poole, probably by the Earl of Leicester. But the total of Walsingham's known nominees remains small.[11]

The last two years of his life were a long struggle against ill-health, with recurring attacks of an internal complaint from which he had suffered since his youth. Ill as he was, he continued with his official work, attending a Council meeting only a fortnight before his death, which occurred at his town house at Seething Lane on 6 Apr. 1590. Because of 'the greatness of my debts, and the mean state I shall leave my wife and heir in', he was buried 'about ten of the clock in the next night following ... in Paul's church without solemnity'.

His will made in December 1589 and found 'in a secret cabinet' on the day after his death, is short. His daughter Frances, Philip Sidney's widow, who later married the Earl of Essex, was to receive £100 p.a. during her mother's lifetime, in addition to £200 a year already settled on her; the sole executrix, 'my most well-beloved wife', a shadowy figure to posterity, was to be residuary legatee. The overseers, Walsingham's 'loving brethren' Edward Carey*, Robert Beale* and William Dodington* were each to have £10 worth of plate.[12]

Walsingham constantly complained about his financial difficulties and there is no doubt that he died heavily in debt to the Queen, but whether this means that his services were not adequately rewarded it is of course impossible to determine. He obtained land, leases of customs in the outposts of north and west England and grants for the export of beer and cloth. Perhaps these were insufficient to cover the expenses of his intelligence operations. The findings of an inquiry some years after his death suggest that his debts to the Crown were offset by those the Crown owed him.[13]

Many theological and philosophical works were

dedicated to Walsingham, but he was himself author of only a few pamphlets. He established a divinity lecture at Oxford, to which he wanted the puritan John Reynolds appointed, and he campaigned for a revival of the study of civil law there. He contributed to the voyages of Drake, Frobisher, the Gilbert brothers and John Davis, and Hakluyt dedicated to him the first edition of his *Voyages*. His friend Dr. Dee interested him in the preparation of Davis's charts of the north-western voyages.[14]

[1] Unless otherwise stated this biography is based upon C. Read, *Mr. Secretary Walsingham and the Policy of Q. Eliz.* [2] *DNB*; E. A. Webb, G. W. Miller and J. Beckwith, *Hist. Chislehurst*, ped. opp. p. 112; SP12/121; *APC*, viii. 169; *HMC Var.* iv. 229; Essex Arch. Soc., Morant mss; N. Bacon, *Ipswich*, 329; J. J. Sheahan, *Hist. Hull*, 255; Neale, *Commons*, 181, 208; *Cam. Misc.* vi(3); Somerville, *Duchy*, i. 395. [3] Ex inf. Dr. Kenneth Bartlett. [4] SP12/40/68, 47/41. [5] *Cam. Misc.* vi(3); D. Digges, *Compleat Ambassador*, 253. [6] Quoted Neale, *Eliz.* 274. [7] *CSP Span.* 1568-79, p. 704. [8] Howell, *State Trials*, i. col. 1182. [9] N. H. Nicolas, *Davison*, app. A, 231 seq. [10] *CSP Ven.* 1581-91, introd. xxix seq.; *CSP Span.* 1580-6, pp. 602, 612, 632; G. Mattingly, *Defeat of Span. Armada*, 123 seq.; C. Read, *Burghley*, 391-409; Lansd. 96, f. 69. [11] SP12/40/68; *HMC Hastings*, ii. 16, 17, 25; *Cam. Misc.* vi(3); *CJ*, i. 105, 106, 114, 116, 130, 136; D'Ewes, 80, 241, 247, 250, 251, 253, 258, 260, 262, 288, 290, 291, 292, 294, 301, 302, 306, 339, 343, 345, 353, 355, 356, 365, 368, 371, 394, 395, 399, 402, 409, 410, 412, 413, 414, 415, 416, 430, 431, 432, 440, 442, 443, 448, 453, 454; [12] Stow, *Survey* (1631), p. 761; *Cam. Misc.* vi(3), pp. 54, 64, 65; *Wills in Doctors' Commons* (Cam. Soc. lxxxiii), 69-71. [13] Lansd. 22, f. 123; 24, f. 159 seq.; 44, f. 176; 49, f. 51; 67, f. 104; 110, f. 103; 141, f. 278. [14] *Diary of John Dee* (Cam. Soc. xix), 4-6, 18, 31-3.

P.W.H.

WALSINGHAM, Thomas (c.1526-84), of Scadbury, Chislehurst, Kent.

MAIDSTONE   1571

b. c.1526, o. surv. s. of Sir Edmund Walsingham† of Scadbury, lt. of the Tower, by his 1st w. Catherine, da. and coh. of John Gunter of Chilworth, Surr. *educ.* L. Inn 1542. *m.* by 1556, Dorothy (*d.*1584), da. of Sir John Guildford† of Benenden, 5s. inc. Sir Thomas* 8da. *suc.* fa. 10 Feb. 1550. Kntd. 1573.
    J.p. Kent from c.1559, q. from c.1569, sheriff 1563-4; gov. Lewisham g.s. 1574.

Though he may have had a minor office under Edward VI, Walsingham, unlike his father, his first cousin Francis* and his son Thomas, preferred the life of a country gentleman. As well as his main estates near Chislehurst he had property in Cambridgeshire, Essex, Surrey and London. He was out of favour under Mary, and after Wyatt's rebellion had to give a £100 bond to be 'continually forthcoming' if the Privy Council wanted him.

From the beginning of Elizabeth's reign his name appears regularly on local commissions, and he carried out various duties, such as attending on the Lady Cecilia of Sweden when she came to England in September 1565, reporting on a dispute between the mayor and town clerk of Rochester in 1579 and supervising the provision of horses in Kent for the royal service. It was while he was taking part in the royal progress through Kent in 1573 that he was knighted by the Queen at Rye. His one appearance in Parliament was not, as his status merited, for his county, but for a local borough, and the timing coincided with an attempt by his puritan friends there to bring about religious changes. He is not known to have taken any active part in the proceedings. Towards the end of his life Walsingham was in financial difficulties.

He died on 15 Jan. 1584, and was buried at Scadbury, where three years previously he had erected an elaborate monument to his father. He signed his will 'Thomas Walsingham on whom the Lord have mercy, and forgive me the misspending of my life in this world in sin'.

Wards 7/5/60; E. A. Webb, G. W. Miller and J. Beckwith, *Hist Chislehurst*, passim; *CPR*, 1549–51, pp. 155, 167; Hasted, *Kent*, ii. 498; *APC*, iv. 400; xi. 341–2; *CSP Dom.* 1547–80, pp. 258, 685; Nichols, *Progresses Eliz.* i. 334; Hasted, *Hist. Kent, Blackheath Hundred*, ed. Drake, 268; PCC 6 Watson.

N.M.F.

WALSINGHAM, Sir Thomas (1561–1630), of Scadbury, Chislehurst, Kent.

ROCHESTER	1597, 1601, 1604
KENT	1614

b. 1561, *s.* of Thomas Walsingham*. *m.* Etheldreda or Audrey (*d.*1631), da. of Sir Ralph Shelton of Norf., 1s. *suc.* bro. Edmund 1589.[1] Kntd. 1597.

J.p. Kent from c.1592, dep. lt. 1595, commr. musters Apr. 1597; keeper, Eltham park 1600; chief keeper of the Queen's wardrobe 1603; warden of Rochester bridge 1615.[2]

By his father's will Walsingham was left an annuity of £24 from Croydon vicarage, to be followed after seven years by another of £50 from Burwell, Cambridgeshire and elsewhere. Five years later he inherited the family estates on the death of his brother Edmund. These, which had been built up by the family from the reign of Edward III, included Scadbury and lands in Chislehurst, St. Paul's Cray, Footscray, St. Mary Cray, North Cray, Eltham, Mottingham, Lee, Orpington, Bromley and Bexley. But they were heavily encumbered both by his father's debts and by the generous provisions of his will.[3]

Walsingham was a patron of literature; the playwright Christopher Marlowe was his servant and was living with him in May 1593 when summoned before the Privy Council for atheism. In 1598 Marlowe's posthumous poem, *Hero and Leander*, was dedicated to Walsingham by his publisher, 'knowing that in his lifetime you bestowed on him many kind favours'. The poem was completed by George Chapman, who also enjoyed Walsingham's patronage.[4]

From about 1594 there are numerous references to

Walsingham as an official in Kent. In November 1596, during the preparations for defence against the second Armada, he and five other captains were ordered to conduct men to Upnor castle, to man boom defence ships across the Medway. In July 1597 the Queen visited him at Scadbury, where she planted oak and fig trees which survived to the present century. Perhaps as a result of her visit, Walsingham obtained a lease of the manor of Dartford, together with lands in Chislehurst, Peckham and Mereworth, known as Richmond's lands, which had previously been held by his father and brother successively. It was also, presumably, at this time that he received his knighthood.[5]

Described in 1603 as one of Rochester's 'principal friends', Walsingham played no prominent part in the proceedings of either of the Elizabethan Parliaments to which he was returned by the borough. However, as a Rochester burgess he was put on the monopolies committee, 10 Nov. 1597. By September 1598, when he was appointed a commissioner in Kent to apprehend rogues, vagabonds and highwaymen marauding in the city of London, he must have been familiar with the problems of vagabondage – an issue dealt with at length in the 1597 Parliament. During the last few years of Elizabeth's reign he became steadily more influential in his county, taking part, for example, in the negotiations for the 1598 Kent by-election, and intriguing for the keepership of Eltham park before (Sir) William Brooke* was cold in his grave. He obtained the reversion to this post in 1599 and the office itself on the death of Lord North in December 1600. In 1599 he exchanged gifts with the Queen. Sir Thomas, who about this time became an honorary member of Gray's Inn, was occasionally employed on ceremonial duties, such as meeting the French ambassador, Biron, when he arrived at Dover in the autumn of 1601; but most of the references to him until 1603 are still concerned with his regular county duties.[6]

In 1603 Walsingham and his wife walked in Elizabeth's funeral procession, and early in the new reign Lady Walsingham accompanied Anne of Denmark from Scotland to London. This led to the joint appointment of husband and wife as keepers of the Queen's wardrobe. Walsingham died in August 1630, between making his will on the 5th and its proof on the 25th. Most of his lands were bequeathed to his son Thomas‡, whom he advised to 'lessen his household'. He left 20 marks to the poor of Chislehurst, money to his servants, and a £1,000 dowry to his grand-daughter Katherine. His funeral expenses amounted to £300 and his debts to over £3,000.[7]

[1] E. A. Webb, G. W. Miller and J. Beckwith, *Hist. Chislehurst*, 112, 137, 420. [2] PRO Index 4208, ff. 78, 246; *APC*, xxvii. 109; *CSP Dom.* 1598–1601, p. 341; 1603–10, p. 79; F. F. Smith, *Rochester in Parl.* 106. [3] PCC 6 Watson; *Hist. Chislehurst*, 111–12, 137, 143; Hasted, *Kent*, ii. 7, 8, 15, 18, 88, 130–8 passim, 393, 498, 499. [4] *APC*, xxii. 244; J. L. Hotson, *Death of Christopher Marlowe*, 10, 48–9; E. K. Chambers, *Eliz.*

Stage, iii. 252, 257. [5] *CSP Dom.* 1595–7, p. 306; *APC*, xxvii. 109, 298, 308; Chambers, iv. 110; *HMC Hatfield*, vii. 331; *Hist. Chislehurst*, 138; Hasted, ii. 6. [6] K. M. E. Murray, *Const. Hist. Cinque Ports*, 98; *HMC Hatfield*, vii. 484; D'Ewes, 555; *APC*, xxix. 142; xxxii. 190, 213, 257, 289; *CSP Dom.* 1598–1601, p. 341; *HMC De L'Isle and Dudley*, ii. 413; Nichols, *Progresses Eliz.* iii. 453, 463, 591. [7] LC 2/4/4; *Hist. Chislehurst*, 137, 140–1, 144–5, 420; *Chamberlain Letters* ed. McClure, i. 516; PCC 70 Scroope; Kent AO, U.119, A.2.

R.C.G.

WALTER, James (c.1563–1625), of Broad Street, Ludlow and Richard's Castle, Salop.

NEW RADNOR BOROUGHS   1589

b. c.1563, 1st s. of Edmund Walter, c.j. of south eastern circuit of great sessions of Wales 1581–94, of Balterley, Staffs. by his 1st w. Mary, da. of Thomas Hakluyt of Eyton, Herefs. *educ.* Brasenose, Oxf. Mar. 1579, aged 15; I. Temple 1581, called c.1586. *unm. suc.* fa. 1594.

Walter probably came in for New Radnor Boroughs through his father, in whose circuit Radnorshire lay. James's younger brother John kept up the legal tradition of the family, becoming chief baron of the Exchequer. Walter himself was a country gentleman, probably the James Walter who in 1595 leased property at Knocklas and elsewhere in Radnorshire, formerly belonging to the Earl of March. He died on 24 June 1625, and was buried in Ludlow church, as he had asked in his will, drawn up in February the same year: he requested his brother John to see that a monument was erected there to their parents. Among the bequests was an annual sum of £20 from Walter's lands at Richard's Castle, Shropshire, of which £10 was to be distributed among the inmates of Hosyer's almshouse, and the rest divided between the rector and preacher of Ludlow.

W. R. Williams, *Welsh Judges*, 128–9; Harl. 1557, f. 29; *Augmentations*, ed. Lewis and Davies (Univ. Wales Bd. of Celtic Studies, Hist. and Law ser. iv) 517 – the name has been transcribed as Walker; *Trans. Salop Arch. Soc.* (ser. 4), iii. 263–8.

J.C.H.

WALTER, Robert (d. c.1594), of Mortlake, Surr.

DROITWICH   1593

2nd s. of William Walter of Wimbledon by Katherine, da. and h. of Humphrey Lawston of Wimbledon. *educ.* Westminster; Christ Church Oxf. 1565, BA 1568. *m.* by 1580, Elizabeth, 2s.

Walter was a stranger to Droitwich, which usually returned local men; presumably he came into Parliament for the borough because of his connexion with Ralph Sheldon*, who owned salt-pans there. His father, of Finedon in Northamptonshire, had settled in Wimbledon on his marriage, maintaining, however, old friendships with the Sheldons, the Lucys and others. He also had influential friends in London, such as Dr. Gabriel Goodman, dean of Westminster, where he sent Robert to school. Robert Walter's mother remembered yet more powerful friends in her will: the Countess of Bedford and the then principal landowner in Wimbledon, Sir Thomas Cecil*. Walter himself was connected with Cecil in land transactions, and all his nearest friends were associates or servants of the Cecils. That he could expect such influential men as Sir Thomas Wilkes*, Sir Thomas Lake*, and Henry Maynard*, all fellow-Members of the 1593 Parliament, to act as his executors, further shows that Walter had greater standing than the scant surviving references to him suggest. Still, though he went to court, he obtained no advancement. Under his father's will, of which he was joint executor, he received the family lands in Wimbledon, after his mother's death – which followed his father's within months – subject to the proviso that he might sell them only to his brother William. His mother further left him half her goods. Nevertheless, he found himself in some difficulties, and when his cousin Nathaniel, only child of his uncle Richard, a wealthy London merchant, died a childless minor, he saw an opportunity to improve his position. Although Richard, who did not mention Robert in his will, had left instructions that if Nathaniel died young, the estate was to be distributed to charity, Robert sought a share in it. He obtained the support of the Privy Council, which directed a strong letter to the archbishop of Canterbury, who had jurisdiction over the will, recommending Robert's suit on the ground that relieving Robert's necessities would 'stand both with charity and good discretion'.

In the late autumn of 1593, Walter felt obliged to draw up his own will, although it was not proved until early in 1595. His estate he left to be equally divided between his two sons when they came of age. To Ralph and Edward Sheldon, whom he made supervisors, he left a book containing 'all the maps of the shires of England in colours'. To Henry Maynard he left a 'harpsichord or great virginals' – one of several bequests which suggest a man of cultivated tastes. Though his will makes no reference to his religious belief, he was doubtless, like the rest of his family, protestant.

Surr. Arch. Colls. x. 152; *Wimbledon Par. Reg.* (Surr. Rec. Soc. xxii), 7, 138; PCC 71 Scott, 6 Rutland, 20 Rutland, 54 Spencer; W. A. Copinger. *Suff. Manors*, ii. 58; *VCH Surr.* iv. 70; cal. and index pat. rolls, 31–7 Eliz., 31(6), p. 9; 36(4), p. 10; 36(8), p. 21; *APC*, xviii. 178.

S.M.T.

WALTON, George (1540–1606), of Great Staughton, Hunts.

HUNTINGDONSHIRE   1586

b. 1540, 1st s. of Thomas Walton of Great Staughton by Elizabeth. *educ.* Trinity Coll. Camb. 1554. *m., s.p.* legit. *suc.* gd.-fa. 1555. Kntd. 1604.

J.p. Hunts. c.1583–7, from c.1601; escheator, Camb. and Hunts. Feb.–Nov. 1594, 1604–5.

The Waltons had been established at Great Staughton since the fourteenth century, frequently representing the county in the Commons. One ancestor did so for 30 years, and was Speaker in 1425. Walton himself came near to losing the estate, for, in his own words, as 'a young man, void of learning and knowledge in the common affairs of the world' he almost sold the fee simple of his birthright to one Thomas Beverley, 'a crafty and subtle man', and when this fell through, Walton perhaps thinking better of it, he gave the same Beverley a 21-year lease of the manor on advantageous terms in 1562. Worse, Beverley contrived for Walton to be bound in the sum of £300 to perform some unreasonable conditions in the lease. Beverley himself re-assigned the lease of the manor to a John Farewell in 1579. In 1582 a Sir Richard Dyer as lessee instituted proceedings against Walton, claiming that he had forcibly entered the rectory manor house and damaged a conduit and water course. In the same year James Farewell sued Sir James Dyer for possession of the rectory. Where Walton resided all this time has not been ascertained, but he continued active in the county, even representing it in the Parliament of 1586, where the only reference to him in the proceedings concerns his complaint against a Mr. Wingfield who had, Walton said, offered 'to draw his weapon upon him and gave evil language'. What a disgrace if this were Edward Wingfield, Walton's fellow knight of the shire! Perhaps it was, for Wingfield's father had lost possession of his estates for leading 'a wasteful course of life' and Edward Wingfield was an aggressive man, reprimanded by the Privy Council both before and after the 1586 incident, at odds with both Cecil and the Queen, and destined to spend some of his last days in the Fleet for debt. Unfortunately D'Ewes's summary of the incident does not make it clear whether or not the Mr. Wingfield was a member of the House. That he 'was brought into this House to answer his misdemeanour' and finally 'discharged' could apply as well to an outsider brought to the bar to answer a charge of breach of privilege as to a Member committed to the custody of the serjeant-at-arms to cool his heels for a day or two. Wingfield claimed that Walton had been an accessory to the murder of his brother, that 'he could not well take it and knew not what might happen'.

Perhaps a factor in Walton's being elected for the shire was his close friendship with Oliver Cromwell*. The two men jointly led the Huntingdonshire levies to the camp at Tilbury at the time of the Armada, and Cromwell erected a monument to Walton in Great Staughton church. Whatever had happened in the interim, when Walton died on 4 June 1606 he was in possession of this rich manor with its 300 acres of arable land, 80 of meadow, 200 of pasture, and 100 of wood, its three mills and a dovecote.

Walton remembered in his will, dated 18 Jan., proved 14 June that year, at least eight household servants, a miller, a shepherd, a brewer, and a herd boy, as well as the poor of Great and Little Staughton, Kimbolton and St. Neots and the prisoners in Huntingdon gaol. Oliver Cromwell, the executor, his 'honourable good friend', received Walton's goods,

> to this end and purpose that hospitality shall be kept in the manor house of Great Staughton, and to give that entertainment he may conveniently to my ancient friends for the space of three years next after my decease.

Walton was succeeded by his cousin Valentine†, who married Oliver Cromwell's niece.

C142/105/82, 337/112; *VCH Hunts.* ii. 14, 26, 357–8, 359–60; Lansd. 53, f. 189; C3/191/80; D'Ewes, 416; Nichols, *Progresses Jas. I*, i. 456; PCC 33 Stafford.

A.M.M.

WARBURTON, Peter (c.1540–1621), of Lincoln's Inn, London; Grey Friars, Watergate Street, Chester; and later of Grafton, Cheshire.

NEWCASTLE-UNDER-LYME	1584
CHESTER	1586, 1589, 1597

b. c.1540, 1st s. of Thomas Warburton of Northwich by Anne, da. of Robert Masterson of Nantwich, Cheshire. *educ.* Staple Inn; L. Inn 1562, called 1572. *m.* (1) Oct. 1574, Margaret, da. of George Barlow of Dronfield Woodhouse, Derbys., 2da.; (2) Elizabeth, da. of Sir Thomas Butler† of Warrington, Lancs., *s.p.*; (3) Alice, da. of Peter Warburton of Arley, Cheshire, *s.p.* Kntd. July 1603.

J.p. Cheshire from c.1573, sheriff 1582–3; bencher, L. Inn 1582, Lent reader 1584; alderman, Chester 1585; Queen's attorney in palatine courts of Chester and Lancaster 1592; vice-chamberlain, Chester 1593; serjeant-at-law 1593; eccles. commr. York 1599, Canterbury 1605; j.c.p. and j.p. many other counties Nov. 1600; member, council in the marches of Wales 1617.[1]

When Warburton was seeking permission to use the family arms in 1597, he described his grandfather as 'a younger son of Sir Geoffrey Warburton by a later wife, and having little to live upon was never married, and so my father [was] illegitimate'. His father was well thought of, Warburton continued, and was sheriff in 1524. Whatever his origins, Warburton made his way as a lawyer, coming to the notice of the Earl of Leicester, chamberlain of the palatinate of Chester, and to that of Henry Stanley, 4th Earl of Derby, who later succeeded Leicester as chamberlain. He was already legal counsel to Chester in 1584, when Leicester and Derby both recommended to the city that he should be made an alderman. Chester took no immediate action and rejected

Leicester's nomination of Warburton there in 1584. Instead Warburton came in for Newcastle-under-Lyme, through his own duchy of Lancaster connexions. By 1586 he was an alderman and resident of the city. He was elected by Chester to the Parliaments of 1586, 1589 and 1597, on the third occasion in the senior place, usually taken by the recorder. In 1593 he declined, being preoccupied by 'great business' for the Queen, for others and for himself, and he considered that his request to be spared was 'the more reasonable, because I have served three sessions already and will hereafter do you the best I can'. Warburton's name occurs in the journals of the House only for his last Parliament, when he was appointed to committees on the poor law (20 Dec. 1597), ordinances made by corporations (12 Jan. 1598), maltsters (12 Jan.), bread (13 Jan.), defence (16 Jan.), Norwich diocese (16 Jan.) and some minor legal matters (11, 14, 16, 18 Jan.). As a serjeant-at-law he could also have attended committees on the penal laws (8 Nov. 1597), the continuation of statutes (11 Nov.), forgery (12 Nov.), the poor law (22 Nov.), monopolies (8 Dec.) and defence (23 Jan. 1598).[2]

After Warburton became a judge he bought the manor of Grafton, built a mansion and attempted to obtain the grant of arms referred to above, asserting that the head of the family – and his eventual father-in-law – Peter Warburton of Arley – supported his claim. His connexion with the earls of Derby was strengthened by the marriage of his only surviving child to Sir Thomas Stanley of Alderley. Trials in which he took part included those of the Earl of Essex, Sir Walter Ralegh and the Gunpowder plotters. He had scarcely become judge when he fell foul of Cecil's aunt, Elizabeth, who felt that Warburton had done her 'an open wrong' by his decision in one of her suits. 'Let him know his duty,' she wrote, 'since he knoweth not honesty nor justice ... For God's sake let me have ... him unjusticed or openly reproved for his insolent breach of justice.' It is doubtful if the complaints of Cecil's 'desolate wronged aunt' much affected Warburton's fortunes. He survived somewhat less easily King James's disfavour in 1616, when he hanged a Scotch falconer at Oxford against the King's command. He died in 1621. In his will he asked to be buried beside his third wife. He made his only surviving child, Dame Elizabeth Stanley, his executrix and left her all his lands, with the exception of his leasehold property in Cheshire, which went, along with £500, to his grandson Thomas Stanley. His three granddaughters were left £266 13s. 4d. each. To John Jeffreys, his 'friend and cousin', Warburton left all his manuscripts and his 'written books of the laws of England', and he bequeathed a small sum of money to his servant Fabian Philipps, possibly the later royalist author.[3]

[1] *DNB*; Foss, *Judges*; *Vis. Cheshire* (Harl. Soc. lix), 245–6; *HMC Bath*, ii. 48; Chester RO, A/B/1/196; *HMC Hatfield*, ix. 396; xvii. 583; *HMC 13th Rep. IV*, 254. [2] *HMC Bath*, ii. 48; Chester RO, assembly bk. ff. 195v–6; Harl. 2173, f. 11; Chester RO, A/B/1/196, 254, 272, 273,

276; M/L/1/31; R. H. Morris, *Chester in the Plantagenet and Tudor Reigns*, 191; C219/29/182; Somerville, *Duchy*, i. 511; *APC*, xxii. 38; Ormerod, *Cheshire*, ii. 704–5; Lansd. 85, ff. 116, 118; *Chetham Soc.* xxxi. 142, 208; D'Ewes, 553, 555, 556, 561, 570, 575, 577, 578, 580, 581, 582, 586. [3] *DNB*; Foss; *HMC Hatfield*, xi. 423; xiv. 192; *Chamberlain Letters* ed. McClure, ii. 26; *HMC Buccleuch*, i. 250.

A.H.

WARBURTON, Richard (*d.*1610), of London.

| BRIDPORT | 1601 |
| PENRYN | 1604* |

3rd s. of Peter Warburton of Hefferston Grange in Weaversham, Cheshire by Alice, da. and coh. of John Cooper of Abbots Bromley, Staffs. *educ.* Clement's Inn; L. Inn 1583. *m.* c.1603, Anne Vavasour, sis. of Thomas Vavasour* lady of the bedchamber to Queen Elizabeth, 1s. Kntd. 1603.

Gent. pens. 1591/3-*d.*1591; constable of Lancaster castle 1600; steward of Lonsdale hundred 1600.

In 1591 Warburton was involved in a dispute with the copyholders of the manor of Over Whitley (Whitley Superior), a duchy of Lancaster manor in Cheshire, recently granted to him by the Queen. Robert Cecil was probably his patron at this time, and he certainly was in 1595, when, in September, Warburton wrote from Plymouth excusing his sudden return from a voyage, the purpose of which is not known. It is likely that it was Cecil who brought Warburton in for Bridport in 1601. Thomas Howard*, 3rd Viscount Bindon, received nominations at several Dorset boroughs for this Parliament, offering them to Cecil. Warburton was named to one committee, concerned with the order of business, 3 Nov. 1601. In 1602 Cecil secured Warburton a command at Brill under Sir Francis Vere, who in 1605 urged Salisbury to allow him to return quickly to the Low Countries. The remainder of Warburton's career lies outside this biography. His widow was granted administration of his estate on 27 Jan. 1610, and the new election return was dated 1 Feb. 1610. The heir was his only child Cecil, so named after the godfather.

Vis. Cheshire (Harl. Soc. xviii), 240; Ormerod, *Cheshire*, i. 573; ii. 175; E. K. Chambers, *Sir Henry Lee*, 162; DL1/159/W8; Somerville, *Duchy*, i. 498; *APC*, xxii. 39; SP12/253/112; Roberts thesis, 296–7; D'Ewes, 624; *Chamberlain Letters* ed. McClure, i. 176; *HMC Hatfield*, xii. 461; xvii. 554; PCC admon. act bk. 1610, f. 183.

A.M.M.

WARCOP, Thomas (*d.* c.1589), of Smardale, Westmld.

WESTMORLAND	1547, 1553 (Oct.), 1554 (Apr.),
	1554 (Nov.), 1559, 1571, 1572,
	1584, 1586, 1589

1st s. of John Warcop of Smardale by Anne, da. of Geoffrey Lancaster of 'Crake Trees'. *m.* Anne, da. of Rowland Thornborough of Hampsfield, Lancs., 2da. *suc.* fa. 1561/2.[1]

Esquire of the body in 1546; gent. pens. 1550/2–d.; gov. Kirkby Stephen g.s. 1565; capt. Carlisle castle from 1568; j.p. Westmld. from c.1573, q. by 1580; commr. pirates' goods Dec. 1588.[2]

Warcop retained his household appointment under Elizabeth, and was classified in 1564 as fit to serve as a justice and 'very good in religion', yet in 1570 he was described as ' *religionis inimicus*', perhaps a mistake, the bishop of Carlisle possibly confusing him with the Thomas Warcop who was executed in 1597 for harbouring priests. At any rate Warcop of Smardale was sent north with cash for the suppression of the rebellion of 1569, and was named by the 9th Lord Scrope of Bolton, whose friendship he enjoyed, as deserving of the Queen's commendation. On 25 Feb. 1581 he was appointed to a committee concerned with the security and fortifications of the borders, and on 27 Feb. he was named to that concerned with a bill for Carlisle. As a shire knight he was appointed to subsidy committees on 24 Feb. 1585, 22 Feb. 1587 and 11 Feb. 1589. His nephew and ward, James Leyburn, was ·executed as a Catholic traitor in 1583.[3]

Warcop extended his property considerably during Elizabeth's reign by obtaining leases from the Crown, chiefly in Yorkshire and Lancashire. He also purchased several wardships, though none was of special value. In 1574 he was granted a lease of lands worth £42, formerly belonging to Leonard Dacre. Two years later he and a Robert Warcop jointly leased crown lands in Yorkshire, Nottinghamshire, Derbyshire and Radnorshire. He also engaged in at least one commercial venture, obtaining in 1571 a licence to export grain for a period of two years. The first shipment, to La Rochelle in 1573, was expected to realise over £1,000, with which he intended to buy salt for resale in England, but the grain was intercepted by the French and confiscated. Faced with an estimated loss of £4,600 (including his expected profits), Warcop went to France to press for compensation, but although successive English ambassadors as well as the French ambassador intervened on his behalf, emphasizing Warcop's position at court and the Queen's interest in the case, it does not appear that he ever received full compensation.[4]

Warcop died 25 Mar. 1589, leaving no male heir. His Westmorland estate, comprising the manors of Smardale, Orton, Sandford, and Cliburn, passed to his daughters Frances, second wife of Sir John Dalston*, and Agnes, wife of Talbot, second son of Sir George Bowes*.[5]

[1] *Vis. Westmld. 1615*, p. 10. [2] Stowe 571, f. 31v; PRO Index 16772, f. 223v; *CPR*, 1563–6, p. 367; 1566–9, p. 200; *CSP Dom.* Add. 1580–1625, p. 290; *APC*, xvi. 385–6; PCC 21 Loftes. [3] *Cam. Misc.* ix(3), p. 51; *Cath. Rec. Soc.* xxii. 117; *HMC Hatfield*, i. 442; *CSP Dom.* Add. 1566–79, pp. 88, 148, 167; *Border Pprs.* i. 155; *CJ*, i. 129, 130; Lansd. 43, anon. jnl. f. 171; D'Ewes, 409, 431; *CPR*, 1560–3, p. 122; J. H. Pollen, *Acts of Eng. Martyrs*, 212–18; Strype, *Annals*, iv. 426. [4] *CPR*, 1558–60, pp. 14, 327; 1560–3, p. 78; 1569–72, p. 177; Wards 9/369/167, 172, 375; PRO Index 16772, f. 338; 16774, f. 2; 6800, f. 116; Req. 2/74/69, 89/9, 166/191; *HMC Hatfield*, ii. 78, 132; HCA

13/20/36–49; *CSP For.* 1572–4, pp. 318, 467, 563; 1575–7, pp. 88 et passim; 1577–8, pp. 495, 509, 520; 1579–80, p. 15; 1581–2, pp. 513, 640; 1582, p. 87; 1585–6, p. 24; *Correspondance Diplomatique de Bertrand de Salignac de la Mothe Fénélon*, vi. 29, 143, 349–50, 374–5. [5] C142/222/8; E407/1/19, ex inf. W. J. Tighe.

B.D.

WARCOPPE, Ralph (1545–1605), of English, Oxon.

OXFORDSHIRE   1601

b. 1545, 1st s. of Cuthbert Warcoppe by Anne Symonds (*d.*1571) of Hatfield, Herts. *educ.* St. Paul's sch.; Peterhouse, Camb. Mich. 1559; Christ Church, Oxf. 1563, BA 1565. *m.* Katherine, da. of William Marsham, alderman of London, *s.p. suc.* fa. 8 Oct. 1557.[1]

Commr. musters, Oxon. 1580, to search for papists 1581; j.p. Oxon. from 1579, dep. lt. 1596.[2]

Warcoppe was christened in the church of St. Antholin, London, his father being a mercer and merchant of the staple as well as an Oxfordshire landowner. Both parents were protestants. His mother befriended John Jewel in his flight from Oxford in 1554 and Laurence Humphrey when sequestered for nonconformity in 1565; his father, probably implicated in the Dudley plot, fled to Frankfurt in the autumn of 1556 with his wife and ten children, and was a leader of the more conservative section of the English community there, until his death in October 1557.[3]

It is likely that the family resettled at English under the protection of Sir Francis Knollys*, a fellow-exile and a near neighbour in Oxfordshire. Warcoppe embarked upon an extensive education, enjoying at Christ Church an exhibition from St. Paul's school which was reserved for mercers' children; but the religious convictions of his family and the experience of foreign countries, which was forced upon him at an early age, remained the main influences in his upbringing. By the time his mother died, Warcoppe had resumed his travels, and in her will she anticipated that he might be unable to act as executor through absence from the realm. In 1571 he published a translation of a work by the French reformer Augustin Marlorat. Anthony Wood had heard that Warcoppe wrote and translated other things and described him as the 'most accomplished gentleman of the age he lived in and master of several languages'. A manuscript which is almost certainly Warcoppe's commonplace book survives in the Bodleian (its attribution to Cuthbert Warcoppe is clearly wrong), containing copies of accounts of the trial and execution of Mary Queen of Scots, of a spy's description of Spain, of notes on the Netherlands written from a protestant viewpoint, and of Lambarde's *Archeion*, written in 1591 but not printed till 1635. From this commonplace book it seems that Warcoppe had access to important state papers. He was probably much employed by Sir Francis and (Sir) William Knollys*, but evidence exists only for his work against papists in Oxfordshire. In 1581 he was instructed with Sir Henry Neville I* to search Lady Stonor's house, where the press used to print Campion's *Decem Rationes* was discovered; he conducted to London the prisoners taken at Stonor and was later employed on several similar tasks.

Warcoppe was not a great landowner, and in 1585 Walsingham gained him exemption from nomination for the shrievalty because of his 'recent losses'. Yet in 1601 he was chosen knight of the shire, clearly at the instance of Sir William Knollys, who had nominated him as deputy lieutenant five years before and was himself returned as senior knight. He was appointed to committees on the penal laws (2 Nov.), the order of business (3 Nov.), monopolies (23 Nov.) and the clerk of the market (2 Dec.). In 1601 John Chamberlain and Dudley Carleton† were hopeful that Warcoppe was about to be appointed ambassador to France, and it may be that he refused such an appointment because of illness.[4]

In July 1605 Warcoppe made his will, so that he could forget worldly things and prepare his heart 'unto the heavenly Jerusalem' to which he was persuaded that his election was 'made sure'. He left a saddle to Knollys in acknowledgement of 'love and favour ever borne' to him; money 'toward a stock for the setting of the poor to work'; and to his nephew, William Kingsmill of New College, all his books 'such as are either Greek or Latin treating either of history, natural or moral philosophy, rhetoric or poetry'. Others who benefited were poor scholars of divinity at Oxford and Warcoppe's 'well-beloved friends', Nicholas Bond, president of Magdalen, and Thomas Holland, regius professor of divinity. His executor was to be Ralph Warcoppe, his nephew and heir, and the overseers included his godson, Edmund Dunch*. The will was proved on 1 Oct. 1605. William Kingsmill and several other scholars of New College printed a book of verses in memory of Warcoppe, 'the most complete esquire of his time', and dedicated it to Knollys.[5]

[1] E150/823/3; *Vis. Oxon.* (Harl. Soc. v), 163; *Misc. Gen. et Her.* (ser. 4), v. 258. [2] *APC*, xii. 17; xiii. 233; *CSP Dom.* 1595–7, p. 297. [3] P. M. Briers, *Hist. Nuffield*, 121–6; *Harl. Soc. Reg.* viii. 5; C. H. Garrett, *Marian Exiles*, 321; PCC 44 Chaynay. [4] M. F. J. McDonnell, *St. Paul's Sch.* 116; PCC 44 Holney; Wood, *Ath. Ox.* (ed. Bliss), i. 754; Bodl. Eng. Hist. b. 117; *APC*, xiii. 154, 177, 264; xvi. 214; xix. 277, 321; *CSP Dom.* 1581–90, p. 152; 1601–3, p. 112; *HMC Bath*, ii. 27; D'Ewes, 623, 624, 649, 663; *Chamberlain Letters* ed. McClure, i. 127; W. Kingsmill, *Encomion R. Warcoppi.* [5] PCC 71 Hayes; *Encomion*.

A.H.

WARD, Richard (c.1514–78), of Hurst, Berks.

NEW WINDSOR	1542, 1547, 1553 (Mar.), 1553 (Oct.), 1554 (Apr.), 1554 (Nov.), 1555
BERKSHIRE	1571

b. c.1514, 1st s. of Thomas Ward† of Winkfield by Maud, da. of Thomas More of Bourton, Bucks. *educ.* Eton c.1520–5; scholar, King's, Camb. 1525. *m.* bef. May 1539, Colubra (*d.*1574), da. of William Flambert or Lambert of Chertsey, Surr., serjeant-at-arms, 8s. 9da. (at least 2s. 4da. *d.v.p.*). *suc.* fa. July 1538.[1]

Clerk of the scullery by 1532, of the poultry by 1537, 2nd clerk of the spicery by 1540, 1st clerk 1549–56, 1550–8; gatekeeper and keeper of the armoury at Windsor castle from 1538; bailiff of liberties of Cookham and Bray, Berks. 1540–64; escheator, Oxon. and Berks. 1542–3; j.p. Berks. from c.1543, Wilts. from c.1564; clerk of the green cloth by 1565; cofferer of the Household from Mar. 1567; duchy of Lancaster receiver, Furness abbey possessions in Lancs., Yorks., Cumb. 1559.[2]

Ward was not an extensive landowner in Berkshire: in 1578 the value of his estates at White Waltham, Winkfield and Hurst was about £70. The Hurst property had been granted to him by Henry VIII in exchange for lands in Surrey, possibly his wife's jointure. At the dissolution he added to his Winkfield estate by buying some of the former property of Abingdon monastery there. Outside Berkshire he had a joint lease with John Norris† of the manor and park of Yate, Gloucestershire, and in addition rented ex-chantry lands in Cambridgeshire and Wiltshire. By 1558 he had already been in the service of three rulers. Much of his work was at Windsor or as a county official in Berkshire but he accompanied Henry VIII to France for the 1544 campaign. Like many other officials of his time, he was prepared to support the religious policy of the day. He carried out a search for heretical books in 1543, was a commissioner for church goods under Edward VI, and in 1560 reported on the lands taken by Elizabeth from the bishop of Salisbury. He presumably took the oath of supremacy, was classified as 'no hinderer' of sound religion in 1564 and in the preamble to his will he bequeathed his 'soul unto Almighty God and to His holy company in heaven', which perhaps indicates that he remained Catholic at heart.[3]

By the beginning of Elizabeth's reign he was a relatively wealthy man. His assessment for the 1559 household subsidy was on £66 13s. 4d. in lands and fees, and he no doubt grew richer after his appointment as cofferer. His duchy of Lancaster duties were carried out by a deputy. His candidature for a county seat in 1571 was supported by the Earl of Leicester, lieutenant of Windsor castle, and by Sir Henry Norris I*, who succeeded to Ward's offices at Windsor castle in the face of opposition from Sir Edward Unton*. The only mention of any activity by Ward in the House of Commons in 1571 is his appointment to a committee considering the liability of the members of the Queen's household to jury service (14 May).[4]

The Queen spent a night at Hurst during her progress of October 1576. Ward died 11 Feb. 1578, and was buried there. His will, which he had made in the previous November, was proved 6 May 1578. He left money and plate to his surviving children and sons-in-law, legacies to the poor of Hurst and of five other parishes, and half a year's wages to his servants. His son Richard was appointed sole executor, with Edmund Plowden†, overseer.[5]

[1] C142/82/85; E150/809/1; Vis. Berks. (Harl. Soc. lvi), 57; E. Ashmole, Berks. iii. 309; W. Sterry, Eton Coll. Reg. 1441–1698, p. 350; Add. 32490, Ll. 11; LP Hen. VIII, xiv(1), p. 483. [2] LP Hen. VIII, xii(2), p. 406; xiii(2), pp. 175, 537; xvi. p. 144; xviii(1), p. 123; xxi(2), p. 429; CPR, 1555–7, p. 404; 1563–6, p. 257; A. Woodworth, Purveyance for the Royal Household (American Philosoph. Soc. xxxv(1), p. 10); Somerville, Duchy, i. 497. [3] C142/82/85; E150/809/1; LP Hen. VIII, xiii(2), pp. 175, 537; xiv(1), p. 483; xv. p. 290; xix(1), pp. 152, 160, 162, 421, 427; Ath. Cant. iii. 3; CPR, 1553 and App. Edw. VI, p. 413; 1558–60, p. 423; Cam. Misc. ix(3), p. 38; PCC 21 Dyngeley, 20 Langley. [4] CSP Dom. 1547–80, p. 703; St. Ch. 5/N10/11, N16/38; D'Ewes, 183; CJ, i. 89. [5] Lansd. 3, f. 199; CPR, 1563–6, p. 184; E. K. Chambers, Eliz. Stage, iv. 93; Add. 32490, Ll. 11; Wards 7/20/76; PCC 20 Langley.

N.M.F.

WARD, William, ? of Morpeth, Northumb.

MORPETH	1553 (Oct.), 1554 (Apr.), 1554 (Nov.)
CARLISLE	1555
MORPETH	1559, 1563

Whether or not Ward was from a family established at Morpeth during the fourteenth century, he certainly owed his returns to Parliament to the lord of the borough, William, 3rd Lord Dacre, whose daughter Dorothy, widow of Sir Thomas Windsor†, left him a grey mare and £3 6s. 8d. Ward was not returned again after the death of Lord Dacre in November 1563. The date of his own death has not been ascertained. There were a number of namesakes.

North Country Wills, ii (Surtees Soc. cxxi), 33–4; J. Hodgson, Northumb. ii(2), 531; CPR, 1563–6, p. 470; 1566–9, p. 380.

B.D.

WARDOUR, Chidiock (1542–1611), of Plaitford, Hants, and St. Martin-in-the-Fields, London.

| STOCKBRIDGE | 1589 |
| LUDGERSHALL | 1593 |

b. 1542, 1st s. of William Wardour of Plaitford by Mary, da. of Edward Bampfield of Poltimore, Devon. m., at least 1s. 1da. suc. fa. 1563.

Clerk of the pells in the Exchequer from 1570; j.p. Mdx. from c.1600.

Most of the surviving information about Wardour is concerned with his disputes with two successive writers of the tallies, Robert Petre* and Vincent Skinner*. As the official responsible for the rolls of receipts and issues, Wardour considered his status superior to that of a tally writer, but recent changes in Exchequer organization had made the latter office more attractive to aspiring officials.

Petre and Skinner were dependants of Sir Walter Mildmay* and Lord Burghley, while Wardour nominally owed his appointment to the aged 1st Marquess of Winchester, the lord treasurer, who had allowed Robert Hare* to sell him the job. Wardour had thus to recoup a heavy outlay at a time when the fees paid by the public for certified copies and other documents were tending to slip out of his hands into those of his rivals. Between 1570 and 1584 Wardour and Petre quarrelled constantly, until a committee of Exchequer officials decided the main questions at issue in Wardour's favour. Burghley, however, took no action on the committee's report and in 1588 Wardour petitioned the Queen. He received only nominal satisfaction, and the dispute was still unsettled when on Petre's death in 1593 he was succeeded by one of Burghley's secretaries, Vincent Skinner, who continued to dispute the spheres of influence of the two offices. Once more Wardour appealed to the Queen, and in 1602 a 'final' decision was taken, by which the two were to share fees. Early in James I's reign Skinner attempted unsuccessfully to re-open the whole matter. Wardour kept his office without further loss of profits until his death, after which it became virtually hereditary in his family for a century: his son Edward† was associated with him in the office as early as 1595.

It may be significant that Wardour's first appearance in Parliament was at a time when a bill to reform the Exchequer was being prepared, and when he was petitioning the Queen for action on behalf of his claims. His family seat at Plaitford was about 15 miles from Stockbridge, and he presumably knew the Kingsmills, a Hampshire family, with offices in the court of wards and other government departments: George Kingsmill* had been appointed steward of the manor of Kings Somborne (in which Stockbridge lay) some years earlier, and had represented the borough in 1584 and 1586. The Kingsmills also owned property near Ludgershall, Wardour's second constituency. They were in general strong puritans, and Wardour himself was apparently of the same faith. In June 1600 he signed, as one of the 'chief parishioners' of St. Martin-in-the-Fields, a letter to Cecil asking that they should be allowed to 'entertain at their own charges a sufficient preacher as a lecturer only'. Their vicar, Mr. Knight, who was Cecil's chaplain, opposed the suggestion, but the signatories assured Sir Robert that the new appointment, if granted, would not prejudice Knight's position.

Wardour's will, drawn up in 1609, was proved on 30 Sept. 1611. He hoped 'to be one of His elected flock that shall inherit the kingdom of heaven to my everlasting salvation'. He wished to be buried near his wife and daughter, the wife of Sir Stephen Lisieur, in a vault at Chiswick church, and asked his son Edward, the executor and residuary legatee, to see that a memorial tablet was placed on the wall of the church. There were numerous bequests to relatives in money, plate and rings: one legacy, to his sister Joyce Gawyne, had the proviso 'that her husband finger not any penny thereof'. The poor of Chiswick benefited from a £10 fund to provide money or bread, as well as from a bequest of 6d. in money and six pennyworth of 'good bread' at Wardour's funeral, and a five mark legacy was left the St. Martin's poor. Sir Stephen Lisieur was appointed overseer.

C142/216/61; Hoare, *Wilts.* Frustfield, 96; *Eliz. Govt. and Soc.* 213–48; PRO Index 4208, f. 196; *HMC Hatfield*, iii. 104; x. 181; xiii. 417; Lansd. 67, ff. 25–6; 137, f. 7; *CSP Dom.* 1547–80, pp. 450, 521; 1595–7, pp. 16, 372; PCC 75 Wood.

J.C.H.

WARNECOMBE, James (c.1522–81), of Ivington, Herefs.

LUDLOW	1554 (Nov.)
LEOMINSTER	1555
HEREFORDSHIRE	1563
HEREFORD	1571, 1572*

b. c.1522, 2nd s. of Richard Warnecombe† of Ivington, Lugwardine and Hereford by his 2nd w. Anne, da. of Richard Bromwich of Hereford; bro. of John Warnecombe†. *educ.* I. Temple 1537, called. *m.* (1), by 1548, Eleanor Hyett, *s.p.*; (2) 24 July 1567, Mary, da. of John Cornwall of Burford, Salop, *s.p.*[1] 1s. illegit.
   Vice-justice of Chester 1545; escheator, Herefs. and marches of Wales 1548–9; recorder, Ludlow 1551–63; standing counsel to Leominster by 1552; j.p. Herefs. from 1554, q. by 1569; mayor, Hereford 1571–2, 1578–9; commr. musters, Herefs. by 1573; dep. justice, Brec. circuit 1575; sheriff, Herefs. 1576–7.[2]

Warnecombe, a lawyer, served as knight of the shire for Herefordshire with his brother-in-law Sir James Croft*. His religious attitude was accommodating. He held office throughout Mary's reign, but in 1564 the bishop of Hereford's list of justices described him as favourable to the protestant religion. In November 1576 he sent a report to the Council on Herefordshire recusants. He served on commissions connected with Herefordshire and the neighbouring shires, surveying the lands taken by the Crown from the bishopric of Hereford in 1559; sending in a report on tanning houses in Hereford and Leominster in 1574; and two years later being appointed to investigate Sir James Croft's complaint that a faction in Hereford intended to elect a mayor unsound in religion. As standing counsel Warnecombe received the same fee (26s. 8d.) as was paid to the recorder in the seventeenth century, and presumably carried out equivalent duties. In 1572 'Mr. Warnecombe's minstrel' was paid 1s. 4d. after the dinner at which the borough welcomed him when he 'came home from the Parliament'.[3]
   About 1574 John Garnons* brought a Star Chamber case against Warnecombe for assault in Hereford cathedral precincts. The bill of complaint listed a number of charges, including assault, inciting his servants to trample

growing crops, abusing his position as a justice by releasing felons at the request of John Scudamore* and others, and insulting the plaintiff at the sessions. Whatever the outcome, this sort of thing cannot have helped him when he came up for promotion to full justice in 1576. Beside his name on the list of nominations is the comment:

> James Warnecombe of Lempster, an ancient gentleman, well learned, honest and of fair living and great wealth, and hath served heretofore as deputy to Sir Robert Townshend with great commendation. He is now grown corpulent and heavy and somewhat given to surfeit with drink in the afternoon.

In fact he was epitomized as 'Warnecombe the weary' by the anonymous writer who lampooned a number of the 1566 MPs, but at this distance of time the description proves nothing beyond the fact that he had made his mark in the House. On 19 Apr. he opposed the repeal of the law making residence in a borough obligatory for election as its representative. If the new bill were passed, he argued, it might 'touch and over-reach' the 'whole liberties' of genuine burgesses. 'Lords' letters shall from henceforth bear all the sway'. Warnecombe spoke again, 21 Apr. in the debate on receiving communion, urging that a certificate from the bishop should be insufficient to obtain a conviction. He served on committees in the House concerning the succession, 31 Oct. 1566; the subsidy, 7 Apr. 1571; four minor committees, 14 May, and the committee of a bill regulating weights and measures, 23 May. By August 1578 he was described as infirm, and only partially recovered from a serious illness, and Whitgift and Fabian Phillips* asked Hereford, apparently unsuccessfully, to choose another man as mayor. Warnecombe lived until 21 Feb. 1581. Letters of administration were granted the next day to his sister, Joan Scudamore, and Edward Croft*. This grant was revoked and a new one made 16 Mar. the same year. There is no evidence of a by-election to replace him as MP.[4]

[1] C142/86/94, 95/93; *Vis. Herefs.* ed. Weaver, 70–1; *I. T. Recs.* i. 116; *Trans. Salop Arch. Soc.* (ser. 2), xi. 313–14. [2] G. Ormerod, *Cheshire*, i. 65; *CPR*, 1553–4, p. 20; G. F. Townsend, *Leominster*, 77–8; J. Duncumb, *Herefs.* i. 367; *Cal. Hereford Docs.* ed. Macray, 31; Lansd. 56, f. 168 seq.; W. R. Williams, *Welsh Judges*, 70. [3] *CPR*, 1558–60, pp. 31, 422; Flenley, *Cal. Reg. Council, Marches of Wales*, 125; *APC*, ix. 197, 225; *Cath. Rec. Soc.* xiii. 134; *Cam. Misc.* ix(3), p. 14; Townsend, 77–8. [4] St. Ch. 5/G9/25, M7/19; SP12/110/13; *Bull. Bd. of Celtic Studies*, vi. 71; Morgan transcripts at Hereford, i. 194; C142/199/90; D'Ewes, 127, 159, 168, 171, 183; *CJ*, i. 97; Trinity, Dublin, anon. jnl. ff. 25, 36; Neale, *Commons*, 158–9; PCC admon. act bk. 1581, ff. 4v, 6.

N.M.F.

WARNECOMBE, John, of Leominster, Herefs.

LEOMINSTER	1601

Escheator, Herefs. Dec. 1601–Jan. 1603.

This Member has not been positively identified, and it is not known whether he was of the family seated at Ivington, and so allied with the Scudamores and the Crofts, and related to James Warnecombe*. He was still alive in 1609, occupying property in Leominster once owned by Thomas Shoter*.

Vis. Herefs. ed. Weaver, 72; C. G. S. Foljambe, *House of Cornewalle*, 214; G. F. Townsend, *Leominster*, 292; LR 2/217/f. 108 seq.

J.J.C.

WARNER, Sir Edward (1511–65), of Plumstead and Polsteadhall, Norf.

GRANTHAM	1545, 1547, 1553 (Mar.), 1553 (Oct.)
GREAT GRIMSBY	1559
NORFOLK	1563*

b. 1511, yr. s. of Henry Warner of Besthorpe by Mary, da. of John Blennerhasset of Frenze; bro. of Robert*. *m.* (1) Elizabeth (*d.* 1560), da. of Thomas Brooke, 8th Lord Cobham, wid. of Sir Thomas Wyatt†, 3s. all *d. inf.*; (2) Audrey, da. and h. of William Hare of Beeston, wid. of Thomas Hobart of Plumstead, *s.p.* Kntd. 18 May 1544.[1]

Member of Henry VIII's household by 1537, sewer by 1545; constable, Clitheroe castle 1542; marshal of the field against Ket's rebellion 1549; esquire of the body by 1552; lt. of the Tower Oct. 1552–July 1553, from Nov. 1558 (jointly with Sir Thomas Cawarden*) to 1563; master of St. Katharine's hospital and steward of East Smithfield 1560; j.p. Mdx. from c.1561, Norf. from c.1564; collector for loan, Mdx. 1562; commr. piracy, Norf. 1565.[2]

By the accession of Elizabeth a large part of Warner's public career was over. He had been a household official and soldier under Henry VIII, earning his knighthood during the Scottish campaign of 1544. Even before the end of Henry's reign there are indications that he had protestant leanings, and he gained his position of lieutenant of the Tower under Northumberland's radically protestant government. His initial support of Lady Jane Grey lost him the post under Mary. In the first Parliament of her reign he was among those who 'stood for the true religion', thereafter interrupting his parliamentary service until the accession of Elizabeth. After a short spell of imprisonment for suspected implication in the Wyatt rebellion of 1554, he was released in the following year, being bound to good behaviour, and presumably lived in retirement until Mary's death.[3]

At the beginning of the new reign he was restored to royal favour and to office, and sat in the first Elizabethan Parliament for Great Grimsby. Lord Clinton, who asked the borough for a nomination, was presumably responsible for his return, but Clinton, not in general an energetic parliamentary patron, may have been acting for Sir William Cecil or some other leading statesman.[4]

The confidence which Elizabeth's government initially had in Warner was shown by his restoration to his former office at the Tower, jointly with Cawarden, presumably as being more dependable in religion than Sir Robert Oxenbridge†, the Marian constable. However, Oxenbridge also remained in office, at least for a time, and during part of November and December 1558 there seem to have been three men in charge of the Tower. From about the end of the year, when Cawarden retired, Warner was the senior official, although Elizabeth never gave him the higher title of constable, as Sir Nicholas Throckmorton* had suggested in his advice on her accession to the throne.

In July 1562 the Privy Council ordered him not to allow the Marian bishops in the Tower to confer freely with one another, and early in the following year his leniency over Lady Catherine Grey and the Earl of Hertford led to his dismissal and imprisonment, when a second child was about to be born to the couple in the Tower. The matter was raised in the House of Commons, since he was a knight of the shire and Parliament was in session. On 1 Feb. 1563 'Mr. Comptroller, with others, was appointed to confer of the privileges of this house, upon motions made for the imprisonment of Sir Edward Warner'. It was apparently decided that privilege could not be extended to him: Sir William Cecil told Members of the judges' advice to the Queen that 'she might commit any of the House during the Parliament for any offence against the Crown and dignity'.[5]

After his release from imprisonment later in the year, Warner seems to have retired to the Norfolk estates which he owned largely in right of his second wife, but he still kept up his London house in Sermon Lane. In September he wrote to Cecil that he was enjoying his leisure from office. However, he was not allowed to remain a plain country gentleman. He was already a justice of the peace for Middlesex (the bishops' letters to the Council describing him as a favourer of sound religion) and in 1564 he was added to the Norfolk commission. In July of that year he served as a commissioner for gaol delivery in the Yarmouth district. Early in 1565 he was one of a general commission appointed to deal with coiners and other felons, and received a Council letter to supervise the 'good assessing' of the subsidy. In the last year of his life he spent some time in the Netherlands, apparently inquiring into the condition of English trade there. It was probably on the same visit to the Continent that he wrote to Cecil from Spa in August 1565. He was worried about a rumour that a secret agent from Elizabeth had been to the Pope to obtain a revocation of the bull declaring her illegitimate.[6]

The last known reference to Warner as an active official is on 3 Nov. 1565, when he was appointed a piracy commissioner for Norfolk. He died four days later at Norwich. The heir was his brother Robert. In his will, drawn up a fortnight before he died, he set aside £40 for his funeral, which was to be 'with as little pomp as may be'. The preamble bequeathed his soul to 'Almighty God our saviour Jesus Christ, by whose death and passion I do verily believe to be received into the everlasting kingdom of heaven'. He asked to have his 'scutcheons' in a number of parish churches, and the executors were to bestow £4 on the poor of Plumstead and other parishes, to be distributed to them ' in their homes'. Warner made detailed arrangements for the support of his widow, her two daughters by her former husband, and her son 'Henry Hobart'*, aged under sixteen. Among bequests in kind were 'the table of my picture in the parlour at Plumstead, and all my books of statutes and chronicles, and all my pedigrees of kings or of any other person'. He was £650 in debt to various relatives and acquaintances, but the Duke of Norfolk and Lord Cobham each owed him £100, and there were other outstanding debts to him which the executors – the widow, his brother Robert and 'cousins' John* and William Blennerhassett – were reminded to collect. He was buried in the chancel of Little Plumstead church, Norfolk, where his monument shows him in armour, his feet resting on a dog. There is a long inscription in English verse.[7]

¹ *DNB*; *Vis. Norf.* (Harl. Soc. xxxii), 308–9; *Vis. Norf. 1563* (Norf. Arch. Soc.), i. 18; *LP Hen. VIII*, xix(1), p. 328. ² *LP Hen. VIII*, xiii(1), p. 579; xx(2), p. 549; Somerville, *Duchy*, i. 499; *DNB*; *CPR, 1550–3*, p. 300; *APC*, iv. 422; vii. 471 n; *CSP Dom. 1547–80*, p. 150; Yale Univ. Lib., Osborn Coll. 71.6.41. ³ *LP Hen. VIII*, xviii(1), pp. 467, 469; xix(1), p. 328; Bodl. e Museo 17; *DNB*; *APC*, i. 411; iv. 422; v. 35, 90. ⁴ *HMC 14th Rep. VIII*, 255. ⁵ *APC*, i. 411; vi. 427; vii. 118–19; J. Bayley, *Hist. Tower*, ii. 663–6; *EHR*, lxv. 94–5; *HMC Hatfield*, i. 261, 264; *CJ*, i. 64; Add. 5123, f. 16. ⁶ *CPR, 1558–60*, p. 141; *1563–6*, pp. 40, 257; Lansd. 7, f. 68; 8, f. 79; *Cam. Misc. ix(3)*, p. 60; *DNB*; *CSP Dom.* Add. 1547–65, p. 571. ⁷ *CSP Dom. 1547–80*, pp. 258, 261; Add. 1547–65, p. 571; *APC*, vii. 285; E150/658/3; PCC 12 Crymes; Mill Stephenson, *Mon. Brasses*, 360.

N.M.F.

WARNER, Henry (?1551–1617), of Mildenhall, Suff.

SUFFOLK	1597
THETFORD	1601

b. ?1551, 1st s. of Robert Warner* of Norwich by his 1st w. Cecily, da. of Walter Marshe of London. *educ.* Peterhouse, Camb. 1567; ?L. Inn 1571, called 1577. *m.* (1) about 1572, Mary (*d.*1601), da. of Robert Wingfield of Letheringham; (2) Frances, da. of Edward Glemham, wid. of Robert Forthe, at least 1s. 2da. *suc.* fa. 1575. Kntd. 1603.

J.p. Suff. from c.1583, sheriff 1598–9, j.p.q. by 1601.[1]

This Member was presumably the Henry Warner who was baptized at Milk Street, London, in January 1551, with Henry, Earl of Rutland and Sir Walter Mildmay* as godfathers. The Duchess of Richmond, daughter of the Duke of Norfolk and widow of Henry VIII's illegitimate son, was godmother. The birth of an heir to Robert was an event of considerable importance in the family, since Sir Edward Warner*, Robert's younger brother, had no

surviving sons. The lands descended to Robert, and then to Henry.[2]

There is no doubt that Warner went to Peterhouse, but the Henry Warner who was admitted to Lincoln's Inn in February 1571 may have been a different man. He is styled in the admission register as 'of London', and it seems unlikely that Sir Edward Warner's nephew, who succeeded to his estates in 1575, would have been described in this way, or that he would have remained at the inns of court to be called to the bar when he had already become the head of his family and assumed the responsibilities of a country gentleman.

Warner's name does not appear among the Suffolk puritans, who so often held at least one of the county seats. In fact he was not at all prominent in the county under Elizabeth – possibly because his position at Mildenhall, where he built, or rebuilt, the manor house, was overshadowed by that of Lord North, who acquired property there about the middle of the reign. It is possible that Warner had in any case interests outside the county. Either he or a namesake was granted, in 1592, a patent for selling and curing fish, which aroused the strong hostility of the justices in Devon and Cornwall.[3]

During the 1597 Parliament he sat on committees concerned with the poor law (22 Nov.) and the possessions of the bishopric of Norwich (30 Nov. 1597 and 16 Jan. 1598). One bill was especially committed to him – a private measure dealing with the affairs of his relative Edward Cotton. In addition, as a knight of the shire he could have sat on committees concerned with enclosures (5 Nov.), the poor law (5, 22 Nov.), armour and weapons (8 Nov.), penal laws (8 Nov.), monopolies (10 Nov.), the subsidy (15 Nov.), Great Yarmouth's charter (23 Nov.) and draining the fens (3 Dec.). There is no reference to him in the journals for 1601, when he sat for Thetford, near his Mildenhall estate. It was from Mildenhall that he wrote to (Sir) Nicholas Bacon* on 10 Oct. 1601 about arrangements for the county election.[4]

Warner's will, made in June 1616, was proved in July the following year. It mentions two daughters (one deceased) and a grandson, but the bulk of the property was to descend to his son Edward. An interesting provision withdrew the use of the property from Edward if he played at cards or dice at the rate of more than 20s. per night. 'Any wife that he [Edward] shall happen to marry' was to have a jointure of £200. Sir John Crofts* and Serjeant Thomas Athowe were the executors, and (Sir) Edward Coke* supervisor.[5]

¹ *Vis. Norf.* (Norf. and Norwich Arch. Soc.), i. 18; *Misc. Gen. et Her.* (ser. 2), iv. 90; Copinger, *Suff. Manors*, iv. 184–7; Nichols, *Top. and Gen.* ii. 388–9; T. A. Walker, *Peterhouse Biog. Reg.* i. 266. The authorities differ as to order of marriages and children. ² *Misc. Gen. et Her.* (ser. 2), iv. 90; *CP*, x. 829–30; *DNB* (Warner, Sir Edward). ³ Lansd. 74, ff. 2–18 passim. ⁴ D'Ewes, 552, 553, 555, 557, 561, 562, 567, 568, 581; Univ. Chicago, Bacon mss. ⁵ PCC 65 Weldon.

N.M.F.

WARNER, Robert (1510–75), of Maiden Lane, London; Cranleigh, Surr. and afterwards Besthorpe and Norwich, Norf.

CHIPPENHAM	1545
WILTON	1547
DOWNTON	1553 (Mar.)
BOSSINEY	1559

b. 1510, 1st s. of Henry Warner of Besthorpe by Mary, da. of John Blennerhasset; bro. of Sir Edward*. *m.* (1) by 1550, Cecily, da. of Walter Marshe of London, wid. of William Harding of Cranleigh, 1s. Henry* 1da.; (2) aft. 1566, Anne, da. of (Sir) Humphrey Wingfield‡, wid. of Alexander Newton. *suc.* fa. 1519, bro. Edward 1565.

Servant of ?Robert, 1st Earl of Sussex by 1538, of Queen Catherine Parr by 1544; receiver of her lands in Hunts. and Northants. 1545–8; first sewer in her household 1546–7; particular receiver of Thomas Seymour‡, Lord Seymour's lands in Hunts. and Northants. by 1548; sewer to Queen Mary by 1556; j.p. Surr. from c.1560–c.64; commr. subsidy, Surr. 1559, Norf. 1569.

Warner's connexions at the Elizabethan court included Sir Robert Dudley*; Walter Devereux, 2nd Viscount Hereford, later 1st Earl of Essex; and the Mores of Loseley, and no doubt it was a simple matter for him to secure a return for a Cornish borough in the first Parliament of the reign. After succeeding his brother, Warner settled as a country gentleman in Norfolk. Next he married into the Suffolk family of Wingfield, and so did his son Henry. Robert Warner made his will in August 1575 and died 7 Oct. that year. His wife had kept up her former establishment at Bresworth, Suffolk: a separate schedule in Warner's will listed household goods 'had from my house at Norwich to Bresworth', including seven 'not very good' curtains. Among bequests to relatives were two of 40s. to nieces, 'for remembrance that I was their poor uncle'. Warner's brother-in-law, John Marshe‡ was supervisor. The widow lived at Bresworth until about 1579.

C219/330/35; *Vis. Norf.* (Harl. Soc. xxxii), 308–9; *Vis. Norf.* (Norf. Arch. Soc.), i. 18; PCC 6 Arundel, 44 Pyckering; C142/34/30; *LP Hen. VIII*, xx(1), p. 448; xx(2), p. 549; xxi(1), p. 281; E115/413/33, 430/94, 433/118; 163/12/17, nos. 30, 38, 51, 54; 315/340, ff. 5v, 52, 68v; *CPR*, 1560–3, p. 441; *Misc. Gen. et Her.* (ser. 2), iv. 90–1; *Surr. Arch. Colls.* iv. 39; xv. 152.

N.M.F.

WARREN, Edward (1563–1609), of Poynton, Cheshire and Woodplumpton, Lancs.

LIVERPOOL	1589

b. 1563, 1st s. of John Warren of Poynton by Margaret, da. of Sir Richard Molyneux of Sefton, Lancs. *educ.* Univ. Coll. Oxf. 1578, BA 1581, MA 1582; G Inn 1589. *m.* (1) 1574, Joan, da. of Sir Edward Fitton of Gawsworth, *s.p.*; (2) 1581, Anne (or Joan), da. of William Davenport of Bramhall, 5s. 9da.; (3) c.1597, Susan, da. of William Booth*, of Dunham Massey, 1s. 1da. *suc.* fa. 1587. Kntd. 1599.

J.p. Cheshire 1593, q.1601, sheriff 1597–8; j.p. Lancs. 1598; dep. steward (to 6th Earl of Derby) of manor and forest of Macclesfield 1603.[1]

Warren was the heir of an old Cheshire family descended in an illegitimate line from the last Warenne earl of Surrey, and established at Poynton since the reign of Edward III. The manors of Poynton and Stockport formed the nucleus of the family estates, which also included property in the neighbouring parishes of Prestbury, Offerton and Woodford. In Poynton itself, as well as the manor and park, Warren owned Lostock House and Stanley House, the former of which was used as a dower house for his mother Margaret. The family also held land at Woodplumpton, Lancashire, but although Warren was on the Lancashire commission of the peace, his interests and influence were concentrated in eastern Cheshire, at Poynton where he lived in some style. Still, he owed an almost feudal allegiance to the 4th Earl of Derby, the great magnate of the north-west. He accompanied him on his embassy to France in 1584 in the capacity of a waiting gentleman, frequently visited him at Lathom and Knowsley and owed him his parliamentary seat for Liverpool in 1589. At the 4th Earl's funeral, in December 1593, Warren bore a standard, and in 1596 the 6th Earl suggested him to Burghley, as a man 'of good sufficiency and account and in religion and due allegiance to her Majesty well affected', for the office of captain of the Isle of Man. Another testimony to Warren's religious conformity was his selection by the Privy Council in October 1592 as one of the gentlemen noted for 'their fidelity and soundness in religion', to arrest recusants in Lancashire. Warred died 12 Nov. 1609 and two days later was buried in the chancel of Stockport church, of which he was the patron.[2]

[1] *Prestbury Reg.* (Lancs. and Cheshire Rec. Soc. v), 10, 45, 70, 183; *Vis. Cheshire* (Harl. Soc. lix), 250; Hatfield ms 278; C66/1549; *Lancs. Q. Sess. Recs.* (Chetham Soc. n.s. lxxvii), i. p. viii; Earwaker, *East Cheshire*, ii. 278–9. [2] Ormerod, *Cheshire*, iii. 680–7; *VCH Lancs.* vii. 285–6; *Shuttleworth Accounts* (Chetham Soc. xxxv), i. 60, 82, 99, 109, 198; *Stanley Pprs.* (Chetham Soc. xxxi), ii. 51, 67, 78, 81, 88, 89, 112; Ormerod, iii. 343–4; *Lancs. Funeral Certs.* (Chetham Soc. lxxv), 26; Lansd. 82, f. 26; *Nathan Walworth's Corresp.* (Chetham Soc. cix), 103–4; *HMC Hatfield*, iv. 241; *Prestbury Reg.* 183; *Notitia Cestrensis* (Chetham Soc. viii), i. 304.

I.C.

WARREN, Richard (c.1545–98), of Claybury, Essex.

ESSEX	1593

b. c.1545, s. of Sir Ralph Warren, mercer, alderman and ld. mayor of London, by his 2nd w. Joan, da. of John Lake of London. *educ.* L. Inn 1564. *m.* Elizabeth, da. of Sir Rowland Hayward*, *s.p.* Kntd.[1]

J.p. Essex from c.1590, sheriff 1591–2.[2]

Warren inherited considerable property in London and Essex from his father, receiving livery of his lands in May 1566. He lived at North Ockendon before moving to Claybury, where his house was of sufficient importance to receive the Queen. He inherited land from his sister Joan or Joanna, probably in trust for her children, and was the principal executor of his father-in-law's will, receiving £500. Warren sat on a number of committees on the one occasion he was a Member of the Commons. Apart from those which all county Members might attend, such as that on the subsidy, 26 Feb., he was named to those dealing with the bill against recusants (28 Feb.) and for the relief of the poor and the punishment of sturdy beggars (12 Mar.). This last was a subject with which he was familiar: he served on a London commission to examine idle and masterless men and women at the Old Bailey, 22 July 1595. Sometime between then and the making of his will Warren received a knighthood. Neither the date of this nor of his death has been ascertained. His will was proved 27 May 1598. After bequests to his widow and to other nephews, he made Oliver Cromwell* his main heir.[3]

[1] Morant, *Essex*, i. 368; *DNB* (Warren, Sir Ralph); A. B. Beaven, *Aldermen*, i. 82; C142/248/42; PCC 49 Lewyn. [2] Essex RO, Q/SR passim; *CSP Dom.* 1591-4, p. 124. [3] *CPR*, 1563-6, p. 525; *Essex Rev.* xxxi. 47; PCC 24 Dixy; D'Ewes, 474, 477, 496, 499, 512; Lansd. 78, f. 126; PCC 49 Lewyn.

J.H.

WARREN, Thomas (*d.* 1591), of Dover and Ripple, Kent.

DOVER   1547, 1555, 1559, 1563, 1572

2nd but o. surv. s. of John Warren† of Dover by Jane, da. of John Monninges of Swanton. *m.* Christian Close of Calais, at least 1s. *suc.* fa. 1547.

Common councilman and chamberlain, Dover 1547-8, jurat for every year for which records survive from Sept. 1551 to 1577, mayor 1548-9, 1549-50, ?1550-Jan. 1551, 1557-8, 1574-5; brodhull rep. several times bef. 1572; bailiff to Yarmouth 1553-4.

Warren's father and grandfather had represented Dover in 11 of the 15 Parliaments held under Henry VII and Henry VIII. His name first appears in the Dover records in 1537. On his father's death he succeeded to his position in the port. His occupation has not been discovered, though the fact that his wife came from Calais suggests that he may have been connected with cross-channel trade. The struggle for power in the town council and the bitter disputes which this engendered did not end with Elizabeth's accession, and Warren suffered a temporary loss of face in 1559 when he was fined £4 for disobeying the mayor. In March 1562 he made peace with a merchant, John Hughson, after a long-standing quarrel between them. In the same year he was appointed one of the arbitrators in the dispute over the will of Alice, widow of Thomas Portway†.

Warren represented Dover in three Elizabethan Parliaments. In 1559 he was paid at least £12 for his services and in 1563 he and John Robins appear to have been paid about the same amount, though in his will Warren complained that he had not received all of his parliamentary wages. As one of the Dover burgesses in 1576 Warren could have sat on the ports bill committee, 13 Feb. He also represented Dover at numerous meetings of the brodhull of the Cinque Ports.

From his father Warren inherited property in Dover, and on his mother's death in 1572 he secured the family mansions there and at Ripple. He probably retired to Ripple in the late 1570s, before the 1581 session of Parliament: the last reference to him in the town books of Dover is on 21 Sept. 1577. In his will, which was made on 11 Apr. and proved on 16 June 1591, he calls himself 'Thomas Warren of Ripple, gent.'. The principal beneficiary was his son John, who was left the main house and lands in Ripple, Sutton, Mongeham, Dover, Hougham, Alkham and Charlton, all in Kent. His wife was to receive an annuity of £30 from these estates and half the household goods. If she was dissatisfied with this arrangement she was to have nothing. John was to be executor, and the overseers were the widow and 'Mr. Crayforde of Mongeham'.

Vis. Kent. (Harl. Soc. lxxv), 45; *Chron. of Calais*, ed. Nichols (Cam. Soc. xxxv), 39; Dover accts. 1547-58, 1558-81; hundred court bk. 1545-88, ff. 88, 116; Cinque Ports white bk. ff. 223, 241, 249; black bk. ff. 13, 16; Egerton 2092, f. 420; 2094 passim; 2095, f. 4; J. B. Jones, *Dover Annals*, 244; D'Ewes, 247; Cant. Prob. Reg. C.21, ff. 57-8; A.48, f. 243; Consistory ct. bk. 32/10.

R.V.

WATERHOUSE, David (1564-aft. 1638), of Ognel Hall, Birstal, Yorks. and the Inner Temple, London.

ALDBOROUGH   1589
BERWICK-UPON-TWEED   1601

b. 1564, 7th s. of John Waterhouse of Shibden, Halifax by Jane or Joan, da. of Thomas Bosvile of Conisborough, Yorks; bro. of Robert*. *educ.* Univ. Coll. Oxf. 1581; I. Temple 1582, called 1593, bencher 1605, serjeant-at-law by 1607. *m.* Elizabeth, da. and coh. of Thomas Craine, 2s. 1da.

Clerk of the Crown, Queen's bench 1596; coroner and attorney, Queen's bench 1597; bencher I. Temple 1605; serjeant-at-law by 1607.[1]

Waterhouse was a younger son of the holder of the manor and lordship of Halifax. He was returned for Aldborough before being called to the bar. His brother Robert had represented the borough in 1584. Both brothers owed their election to their marriage connexion with the Gargrave family. Probably David practised as a lawyer at York, as Robert certainly did. In 1598, upon the death of his brother Robert, he became the guardian of his nephew Edward, and thus temporarily lord of Halifax, where he was holding courts leet in September 1598. In the period of less than four years during which he administered his nephew's lands, he apparently bought property on Edward's behalf at inflated prices, and borrowed money at high interest, which had to be repaid by the heir when he came of age. It appears also that, either from carelessness or fraud, he drew unsatisfactory conveyances so that Edward was threatened with litigation. In 1601 Waterhouse was returned to Parliament for Berwick-upon-Tweed, perhaps because his legal services had at some time been employed by the town. His brother Isaac had been a servant of Lord Willoughby, governor of Berwick, but Willoughby died before the election, and no connexion has been discovered between Waterhouse and his successor.[2]

During this Parliament he spoke twice. On 14 Nov. a point of privilege arose when several Members were subpoenaed to appear in Chancery and Queen's bench to give evidence in suits pending there. There was some discussion as to whether they were bound to obey this summons, and Waterhouse, speaking as a member of the office which had issued it, urged that it should be obeyed on the practical grounds that 'a cause for want of a witness might be lost'. On 16 Nov. he spoke again, this time during the debate on clerical pluralism and non-residence. A previous speaker had claimed that the clergy were like other office holders, who were often non-resident sinecurists. To this Waterhouse retorted:

By the common law, an officer shall forfeit his office for non-attendance: so for a benefice the incumbent shall also forfeit. But after, the statute came, which made this toleration upon eighty days' absence. So that now, if we set this statute at liberty again, this shall be no innovation in us, but a renovation of the common law. I will end, only with this caution to the House, that commonly the most ignorant divines of this land, are double-beneficed.[3]

After the dissolution of this Parliament Waterhouse returned to his legal duties, and his only subsequent association with Parliament was in 1624, when the House of Lords committed him to the Fleet and fined him £500 for writing a scandalous petition. In November 1607, he again acted for a short time as lord of Halifax, but in 1609 financial difficulties forced the family to abandon the lordship to Sir Arthur Ingram†. In 1607 he was the author of an abortive proposal for the more rigorous exaction of first fruits and tenths. During 1608 he was occupied in diverting to his own use part of the capital of Crowther's charity in Halifax, of which he was one of the trustees, and in 1614 he and his nephew were both outlawed for debt. By 1623 he was reduced to appealing to the King for admission to the Charterhouse as a decayed gentleman, and was granted the next vacancy. But 12 years later he was in the Fleet where his evidence before a commission

appointed to examine abuses in the conduct of the prison was ignored as he was 'a man notoriously infamous and of no credit'. In 1638 he brought a Chancery suit against Sir Arthur Ingram. The date of his death is unknown.[4]

[1] Vis. Yorks. 1612, ed. Foster, 353; Halifax Antiq. Soc. Pprs. 1915, pp. 149–50; 1917, p. 60; Hunter, South Yorks. i. 117; Cal. I. T. Recs. i. 387, 421; CSP Dom. 1595–7, pp. 257, 461. [2] Halifax Antiq. Soc. Pprs. 1917, pp. 54–7; North Country Wills (Surtees Soc. cxxi), 191–2; HMC Hatfield, x. 49, 162. [3] Townshend, Hist. Colls. 213, 219. [4] Hunter, South Yorks. i. 117; Halifax Antiq. Soc. Pprs. 1917, pp. 60, 62, 64–5, 75–6, 77, 84, 85, 88; CSP Dom. 1603–10, p. 387; 1611–18, p. 248; 1623–5, pp. 129, 155; 1635, pp. 75–6, 81; 1635–6, pp. 49–50.

I.C.

WATERHOUSE, Robert (1544–98), of Shibden Hall, Halifax, Yorks.

ALDBOROUGH   1584

b. 1544, 1st s. of John Waterhouse, and bro. of David*. educ. I. Temple 1562, called 1570. m. Jane, da. of Thomas Waterton* of Walton and Sandal, 4s. 1da. suc. fa. 1584. J.p.q. Yorks. (W. Riding) from c.1583; bencher, I. Temple 1587; farmer of alnage, Hull and Yorks.[1]

Waterhouse, whose family owned the manor of Halifax, was not content to remain a country gentleman, but was called to the bar and practised as a lawyer at York, maintaining, however, his connexion with the Inner Temple. There are a number of entries in the Inner Temple records relating to his attempts to secure a chamber in which to live whilst in London, the inn objecting on the ground that his visits were infrequent. On two occasions, in 1585 and 1590, the order admitting him to a chamber was revoked, and in 1591 Dr. Caesar was allowed to use the chamber previously granted to Waterhouse, provided the latter was allowed to reside there when in London.[2]

Both Robert and his younger brother David, who represented Aldborough in the Parliament of 1589, owed their election to the influence of the council in the north. Robert had powerful friends in Yorkshire: Cotton Gargrave*, for example was married to his wife's sister and appointed him one of the supervisors of his will. In the 1584–5 Parliament Robert Waterhouse was one of those 'learned in the law' appointed to a committee to compile a list of bills that ought to be renewed.[3]

Perhaps it was through acting as his lawyer that Waterhouse became the 'loving friend' of the great northern magnate, George, 6th Earl of Shrewsbury, of whose will he was both witness and supervisor. At his death Waterhouse left an estate worth about £800 a year. From his cousin, Nicholas Waterhouse, he had purchased a number of properties close to the family estates, including two fulling mills in Southowram, and the old Hall in Halifax, for which he still owed his cousin £400 when he made his will on 10 Feb. 1598. The will, which was proved on 1 Apr. in the same year, stipulated that his lands in Ackworth and a capital messuage in the parish of St. Helen's in York were to be sold to pay his debts. To his eldest son Edward, his heir, he bequeathed all his books, and a chain of gold which the Countess of Shrewsbury had bequeathed to Edward but which was then in the testator's custody. As her marriage portion his daughter Jane was to receive what was left from the sale of lands mentioned above, after his debts had been paid. Among the supervisors was Richard Gargrave*, Sir Cotton Gargrave's son. Waterhouse died on 3 Mar. 1598, and was buried two days later in the church of St. Michael-le-Belfrey, York.[4]

[1] *Halifax Antiq. Soc. Pprs.* 1915, pp. 149–51; 1916, pp. 201, 261; York prob. reg. 27, f. 229; *Vis. Yorks. 1584–5*, ed. Foster, 353; *Cal. I. T. Recs.* i. 344; Royal 18 D 111; SP13/Case F/11, ff. 12–13; C66/1549; Lansd. 114, f. 124. [2] *Halifax Antiq. Soc. Pprs.* 1913, p. 174; 1942, p. 11; Watson, *Hist. and Antiquities Halifax*, 212; *Cal. I. T. Recs.* i. 320, 336, 354, 366, 369, 372. [3] *Vis. Yorks.* 353; York prob. reg. 24, f. 183; *Yorks. Arch. Soc. rec. ser.* xxii. 48; D'Ewes, 334. [4] *North Country Wills* (Surtees Soc. cxxi), 150; *HMC Hatfield*, vi. 252; vii. 506; *Halifax Antiq. Soc. Pprs.* 1916, pp. 278–9; York prob. reg. 27, f. 229; C142/254/11.

A.M.M.

WATERS, Thomas (by 1495–1563/4), of King's Lynn, Norf.

KING'S LYNN	1539, 1542, 1553 (Oct.), 1554 (Apr.), 1554 (Nov.), 1555, 1558, 1559

b. by 1495. *m.* prob. da. of William Coningsby† of King's Lynn, 2s. 1da.

Alderman, Lynn 1525–63, mayor 1535–6, 1551–2, June–Sept. 1558; victualler and purveyor of grain for the armies in the north and in France 1542–50.

There were at least three men called Thomas Waters at Lynn in this period. The references in the Lynn congregation books, however, together with his unbroken record of aldermanic service and the evidence obtained from various wills of the family, make it reasonable to suppose that it was the same man who sat in all these Parliaments and had the career outlined above. In 1559 he was on the commission to ensure the execution in Lynn of the statute 1 Elizabeth c.11 concerning the loading and unloading of goods at wharves. Two years later, he represented Lynn at meetings to settle an old dispute with Cambridge, and through much of 1562 he was in London on the town's business. The will he made 19 Dec. 1563 mentions houses, gardens, orchards and land in Lynn. Apart from one house bequeathed to his daughter, Elizabeth, and her husband, and some small charitable bequests, his property was to be divided between his two sons, William and Edward, whom he named executors. The will was proved 3 May 1564.

HCA 13/10, f. 76v; PCC 13 Alenger, 17 Stevenson, 10 Alen, 19 Burke; Lynn congregation bks. 1554–69, passim; *LP Hen. VIII*, xvii–xx; *APC*, i. passim; E351/130, 198; Norwich consist. ct. 161 Hustinges; *CPR*, 1558–60, p. 32.

R.V.

WATERTON, Thomas (by 1526–75), of Walton and Sandal, Yorks.

THIRSK	1554 (Apr.)
YORKSHIRE	1572*

b. by 1526, 2nd but 1st surv. s. of Sir Thomas Waterton† of Walton and Sandal by Joan, da. of Sir Richard Tempest† of Bracewell and Bowling. *educ.* G. Inn 1544. *m.* by 1552, Beatrice, da. and event. coh. of Edward Restwold of The Vache, Bucks., 2s. 3da. *suc.* fa. 28 July 1558.[1]

J.p.q. Yorks. (W. Riding) from 1561; commr. eccles. causes, province of York 1573.

Waterton was a well-connected country gentleman of middling status. His wife was the daughter by an earlier marriage of his stepmother Agnes, widow of Edward Restwold, who married Sir Thomas Waterton as her second husband. Another family, the Gargraves, were on close terms with the Watertons, Cotton Gargrave* marrying Waterton's daughter Anne.

Most of the references found to Waterton are concerned either with his local offices, or with his many land transactions, some of which led to litigation in the duchy of Lancaster court and in Chancery. Though classed as a favourer of the Elizabethan settlement in the bishops' reports of 1564, Waterton's religious outlook is obscure. A recent historian has described him as a crypto-Catholic. In 1569, the year of the northern rebellion, his estates in and around Sandal and Walton were assessed at £40, and he was required to provide two corselets and a number of arms and weapons for local defence.

He died on 5 Nov. 1575, leaving extensive property in Cawthorne, Heaton, Menstropp and elsewhere in Yorkshire, in addition to his main estates around Sandal. In his will, drawn up two days before he died, he asked to be buried in the church of Sandal Magna. The executors were his widow and their elder son Thomas, aged 23, who was a Catholic on the run in 1582.

Glover, *Vis. Yorks.* ed. Foster, 105; Gooder, *Parl. Rep. Yorks.* ii. 23; Wards 7/16/16; C142/173/55; *Yorks. Fines* (Yorks. Arch. Soc. rec. ser. ii), 162, 164, 232, 243, 280–1, 359, 377; *CPR*, 1558–60, p. 376; 1563–6, p. 68; 1572–5, pp. 168–9; *Ducatus Lanc.* iii. 18; *Yorks. Arch. Jnl.* xxx. 402, 403, 404; *Cam. Misc.* ix(3), p. 70; J. T. Cliffe, *Yorks. Gentry*, 168; J. J. Cartwright, *Chapters in Yorks. Hist.* 69; *CSP Dom. 1580–1625*, p. 71; York wills 19, f. 859.

M.N.

WATKIN, William, of Wells, Som.

WELLS	1597

m., 1da.

Freeman, Wells 1589, constable 1590, mayor 1592.

Described as 'gent, stranger' on being made freeman, Watkin apparently settled in Wells. On 30 Nov. 1591 he was appointed a special commissioner to investigate the circumstances surrounding the disposal of Bishop Godwyn's goods, carried off by his relations on his death in 1590. As one of the Wells burgesses in 1597 Watkin was appointed to the committee considering the bill for Bristol (28 Nov.), and, as burgess for a Somerset borough, he could have attended the committee considering rebuilding Langport Eastover (10 Nov.).

Nothing further has been ascertained about him.

Wells Charters (Som. Rec. Soc. xlvi), 115, 116, 190; D'Ewes, 564; Townshend, *Hist. Colls.* 103; E178/1966, see also GODWYN, Thomas.

R.C.G.

WATSON, Edward (c.1549–1617), of Rockingham, Northants.

STAMFORD   1601

b. c.1549, o.s. of Edward Watson of Rockingham by Dorothy, da. of Edward Montagu I* of Boughton. *educ.* M. Temple 1567. *m.* Apr. 1567, Anne (*d.*1612), da. of Kenelm Digby* of Stoke Dry, Rutland, 2s. 8da. *suc.* fa. 1584. Kntd. 1603.

J.p. Northants. from c.1577, commr. to inquire after seminary priests and Jesuits 1591, sheriff 1591–2, commr. musters 1595, 1596, 1605.

Watson's position in Northamptonshire was assured not only by the wealth he inherited from his grandfather, who was receiver to three successive bishops of Lincoln and married into the family of one of them, William Smith, but also by his father's fortunate marriage, through which the family acquired Rockingham and the oversight of the royal forest. Watson himself added considerably to the estate by purchases from Lord Burghley and his son the Earl of Salisbury.

In August 1587 Watson attended the funeral of Mary Stuart. That October he was noted as suspect in religion, and about 1593 he helped a Northamptonshire recusant, Thomas Colwell, to obtain his release from the Fleet prison, and received a letter from another recusant, Sir Thomas Tresham, thanking him for his services. Clearly he conformed to the law and both Catholics and government were able to use his services. His own status, his connexion with the Digbys and his friendship with the Cecils, all contributed to his return for Stamford in 1601. James I was his guest for three days in 1605. In 1613 he made over his estates to his eldest son, Sir Lewis, later 1st Baron Rockingham. Watson died on 1 Mar. 1617.

C. Wise, *Rockingham Castle and the Watsons*, 19–42; APC, xxiii. 333; xxiv. 41, 354; *HMC Hatfield*, xvi. 38; *M.T. Recs.* 161; *HMC Var.* iii. 33, 61, 75, 77; *HMC Bath*, v. 83; *HMC Buccleuch*, iii. 37, 51, 98; *CSP Dom.* 1591–4, p. 124; 1601–3, p. 131; 1603–10, p. 554; Nichols, *Progresses Jas. I*, i. 524; Lansd. 54, f. 178; *HMC Rutland*, i. 313; *HMC Montagu*, 106.

D.O.

WATSON, Rowland (*d.*1595), of White Webbs, Enfield, Mdx.

DUNHEVED (LAUNCESTON)   1584, 1586, 1589, 1593

3rd s. of William Watson of Newport, Salop by Margaret, da. of John Cooper of Newport. *educ.* L. Inn 1564, called 1574. *m.* 1571, Jane, da. of Hugh Griffith of London, 2s. 5da.

Dep. clerk of the Crown in Chancery from 1574.

Watson probably owed his first return for Dunheved to the influence of the 2nd Earl of Bedford, whose daughter Anne, Countess of Warwick, later described Watson as her 'loving friend'. After Bedford's death in 1585 Watson presumably retained the seat through the influence of the Carew family, George Carew, secretary to Hatton the chancellor and Lord Keeper Puckering, doubtless having become known to him through his office as deputy clerk of the Crown. In practice Watson had complete control of the Crown Office and many of his duties must have been concerned with Parliament. On 9 Nov. 1586, when he was himself an MP, he had, as deputy clerk of the Crown Office, to give evidence to the Commons committee dealing with the Norfolk election. On 8 Feb. 1589 he was appointed to the returns committee. In May of that year, Watson, after lobbying Lord Burghley and Sir Thomas Bromley*, obtained a reversion of Thomas Powle's office of clerk of the Crown. Powle, however, who nominally held the office for almost half a century, outlived Watson, after whose death it transpired that many documents, including letters patent, had never been enrolled. In 1597 these were made up into a roll of supplementary letters patent. Naturally Watson amassed a fortune out of his office, and he had land, leases and properties in London, Middlesex, Leicestershire and Staffordshire. In Middlesex alone his lands were valued at £60 p.a. He had leased property in Chancery Lane and just before his death he bought the manor of Sutton and two rectories in Cheshire. He died 3 July 1595, and was buried at St. Dunstan's-in-the-West. His will, dated 1 Sept. 1592 and proved 28 Oct. 1597, made provision for his widow and children, leaving £250 to his son Rowland, 1,000 marks to his eldest daughter, and 500 marks apiece to his other daughters. Gilt cups were left to Chief Justice Popham and to Watson's 'dear approved good friend', Serjeant Thomas Owen*, who, together with the widow were appointed executors.

Mdx. Peds. (Harl. Soc. lxv), 64; *Vis. Salop* (Harl. Soc. xxix), 491; SP12/190/3; D'Ewes, 396, 430; PRO Index 6800, f. 194v; W. J. Jones, 'The Eliz. Chancery' (London Univ. PhD thesis, 1958), pp. 71, 75–6, 117–18; *CSP Dom.* 1581–90, p. 667; Lysons, *Environs of London*, ii. 305; Guildhall mss 10342, f. 184; PCC 47 Scott.

W.J.J.

WATSON, William (by 1513–68), of York.

YORK   1553 (Mar.), 1559, 1563 *b.* by 1513.

Constable, York merchant adventurers 1536–8, gov. 1547–8, 1566–7; chamberlain, York 1536–7, sheriff 1541–2, alderman Mar. 1543, ld. mayor 1547–8, 1566–7.

Watson was a lead merchant assessed on £50 goods for the 1546 subsidy. Classed as 'a favourer of religion' in 1564, he was a commissioner of inquiry into offences against the Acts of Uniformity and Supremacy in the province of York. On another occasion he was appointed by the council in the north to determine the boundary between York and Yorkshire. Thrice elected MP for York, Watson did not attend the 1566 session, as he was 'presently mayor' of the city, and the corporation regarded his presence there as essential. The city agreed to reimburse him if he should be fined for not attending. Watson made his will on 18 Oct. 1568, proved on 20 Dec. In it, he listed considerable property in York, including houses in North Street, Coppergate and Water Lane. He left legacies to his four nephews, and appointed his brother-in-law, Gregory Paycock*, to be his executor and residuary legatee.

York City Lib., Skaife mss; *York Freemen* (Surtees Soc. xcvi), 252, 255; *York Mercers* (Surtees Soc. cxxix), 135, 140, 324; G. R. Park, *Parl. Rep. Yorks.* 50; *York Civic Recs.* passim; E179/217/110; *CPR,* 1560–3, p. 170; *York Wills* (Yorks. Arch. Soc. rec. ser. xix), 170.

J.J.C.

WATTS, Richard (c.1529–79), of 'Satis', Boley Hill, Rochester, Kent.

ROCHESTER 1563

b. c. 1529, at Peckham. *m.* Marian, *s.p.*
Surveyor of victuals under Edward Bashe* 1551; paymaster, surveyor and clerk of the works at Upnor 1560; treasurer of Rochester bridge estates.

Watts was a government contractor, who took up residence at Rochester early in Elizabeth's reign. The Queen visited him there in September 1573, after which he named his house, still to be seen in the High Street, 'Satis', presumably because she had found it so. Watts died 10 Sept. 1579 and was buried in the cathedral. In his will, made 21 or 22 Aug. 1579, and proved at Rochester a month later, he left the house to his wife for life: afterwards it was to be sold to build and maintain almshouses. Watts failed, however, to make it clear whether the widow and sole executrix was to keep 'Satis' if she remarried. In 1586 the corporation claimed the property from her and her second husband, but agreed to a settlement by which they retained possession. By 1854 the receipts were over £3,250, and the total remaining in Chancery after disbursements was nearly £10,000. In 1736, when another Richard Watts was mayor of Rochester, a tablet was placed in the cathedral to the memory of the earlier man.

DNB; F. F. Smith, *Hist. Rochester*, 85, 145, 495; *Rochester in Parlt.* 98–100; *Arch. Cant.* vi. 51–3; xvii. 212 seq.; *APC*, iii. 263, 266, 287; *CSP Dom.* 1547–80, p. 204; *CPR,* 1548–9, p. 297; *HMC Hatfield*, i. 293; Hasted, *Kent*, iv. 185–7; J. Phippen, *Desc. Rochester*, 39 seq.; *Charity Commission, 30th Rep.* 380; C142/215/267.

N.M.F.

WAY, Thomas (*d.*1596), of St. George's, Southwark, Surr.

SOUTHWARK 1572, 1584

m. (2) Katherine, at least 1s.
Keeper of Marshalsea prison c.1559–*d.*; assessor of Southwark subsidy 1593/4.

Way was keeper of a Southwark prison for the greater part of 40 years, a vestryman of St. George's parish, and owner of a local tavern called the *Queen's Arms*. His Southwark property was valued at £15 in the 1593/4 subsidy.

In the 1572 Parliament, Way sat on committees concerned with the poor (11 Feb. 1576) and with innholders and tipplers, (17 Feb. 1576).

Described as 'yeoman' in the 1559 pardon roll, by the time he made his will on 25 May 1596 he was a 'gentleman'. His wish was to be buried 'in Christian manner without vain pomp or ceremony'. The local poor benefited, likewise his fellow-vestrymen who had £3 'for a drinking', and the Vintners' Company of which he was a member. The only child mentioned was an infirm son, placed in the care of cousins, at an annuity of £20. Way's widow and executrix inherited valuables as well as the *Queen's Arms*. The other principal heir was a nephew, who was instructed to recover sums due from the lord chamberlain and his son, Sir Edward Carey*. The will was proved on 15 June 1596.

CPR, 1558–60, p. 179; *Surr. Arch. Colls.* xviii. 183; *CSP Dom.* 1581–90, p. 243; 1591–4, p. 310; *APC*, xii. 271–2; D'Ewes, 247; *CJ*, i. 105, 106; PCC 50 Drake.

H.G.O.

WEARE *alias* **BROWNE, William** (*d.*1585), of Calne, later of Salisbury, Wilts.

CALNE 1572

?rel. to Robert Weare *alias* Browne†. *m.* Thompson Williamson, wid. of one Hynckley.
Burgess, Calne by 1562, commoner 1564–72, guild steward 1566; gov. Salisbury 1581.

One of the few MPs in this period described as of yeoman status, Weare was active in the local life of his borough. In 1576 he was paid £1 4s. for serving in Parliament. He moved to Salisbury, set up as an innkeeper, and died in 1585. In his will, made 9 May and proved 30 June of that year, he left his property in Salisbury to his wife and provided legacies of £100 apiece to his son John and his stepson. He left 40s. to the chamber of Salisbury, who were asked to distribute a similar amount to the poor at his funeral.

PCC 33 Brudenell; *Wilts. Arch. Soc. recs. br.* vii. passim; Hoare, *Wilts.* Salisbury, 290.

W.J.J.

WEBBE, Anthony (*d.?*1578), of St. Andrew's, Canterbury, and Fordwich, Kent.

CANTERBURY   1572*

s. of George Webbe† of Canterbury by his w. Anne (*d.*1551). *m.* Dorothy (*d.*1594), at least 5s. 1da.
    Freeman, Canterbury 1552, sheriff 1563, alderman 6 Sept. 1569, mayor 1571–2.

Webbe was a mercer like his father, his brother, and probably his eldest son John. Between 1562 and 1574 his name appears frequently among those who read and signed the churchwardens' accounts of St. Andrew's parish. One entry records that he paid 2s. for 'the old communion book'. After being active in civic affairs for a number of years he became mayor, and, while still in office, he was returned to Parliament, being appointed to a committee on alehouses 17 Feb. 1576. He died during the course of the Parliament, having made his will 'much pained in my body' 1 Oct. 1577. His son John, who proved the will on 10 Apr. 1578, later moved to London, though he retained Fordwich as his country estate.

J. M. Cowper, *Freemen of Canterbury*, 89, 308; Somner, *Antiqs. of Canterbury*, 184; *Reg. St. George, Canterbury*, ed. Cowper, 168; burmote bk. 1542–78, ff. 211, 235; C. Bunce, *Charters of Canterbury*, 244; Hasted, *Kent*, xii. 606; J. M. Cowper, *Intrantes of Canterbury*, 193; *Arch. Cant.* xxxv. 53, 54, 58, 66, 69–71, 101; *CJ*, i. 106; PCC 15 Langley; *Reg. St. Alphage, Canterbury*, ed. Cowper, 110.

M.R.P.

WEBBE, John (c.1532–71), of Salisbury and Odstock, Wilts.

SALISBURY   1559

b. c.1532, 1st s. of William Webbe† of Salisbury by Katherine, da. and h. of John Abarough† of Salisbury; bro. of William.* *m.* Anne, da. of Nicholas Wylford† of London 3s. 3da. *suc.* fa. 1554.
    One of the 24, Salisbury by Jan. 1559, mayor 1560–1, auditor for the 24 1564.

On the accession of Elizabeth, Webbe added to his inherited property at Salisbury. He remitted the wages due to him for representing the city in the Parliament of 1559. He died in London 1 Feb. 1571, and was buried in the church of St. Thomas of Canterbury at Salisbury, where he is commemorated by a monumental brass. His will, drawn up a week before his death, left bequests to Christ's hospital, London, as well as to the Salisbury poor and the prisoners in the gaol there. At his burial 20 poor men of Salisbury were to be given gowns and a dinner. The will

provided for the heir John, aged 14, to go to a university and an inn of court. His brother William was an overseer.

C142/274/68; PCC 26 Tashe, 24 Holney; Hoare, *Wilts.* Chalk, 29, Cawden 20, Salisbury, 282, 296, 708; Stephenson, *Mon. Brasses*, 534; City of Salisbury mss leger 1452–1567, ff. 320, 322, 324, 335v; *Wilts. N. and Q,* iii. 124; iv. 309, 322, 374, 456; v. 177; *Wilts. Arch. Mag.* xxxvi. 11; xlviii. 26; Wards 7/13/115; *CPR*, 1569–72, p. 445; *Vis. Surr.* (Harl. Soc. xliii), 141–2.

N.M.F.

WEBBE, Thomas (*d.* by 1566), of Hereford.

HEREFORD   1563*

?rel. to William Webbe, archdeacon of Hereford temp. Henry VIII.
    ?Member of Hereford guild of merchants c.1522, mayor 1559–60.

Though several branches of his family were living in Gloucestershire and Herefordshire during the sixteenth and seventeenth centuries, little information about Webbe himself has survived. He was presumably a member of the city corporation by 1557, when he was asked to provide an above average contribution towards the furnishings needed for the entertainment of the president of the council in the marches. One of many resident burgesses who represented Hereford in Elizabethan Parliaments, he presumably died before the second session of Parliament, beginning 30 Sept. 1566, when he was replaced by John Hyde.

Hereford mss, sack 1, bdle. 1 no. 4; *CPR*, 1560–3, p. 285; *APC*, vi. 199; *HMC 13th Rep. IV*, 325, 328.

N.M.F.

WEBBE, William (*d.*1585), of Salisbury, Wilts., later of Motcombe, Dorset.

SALISBURY   1559

2nd s. of William Webbe† and bro. of John*. *m.* Katherine (*b.*1537), da. and h. of George Tourney or Turney of Motcombe and Gillingham, Dorset, 2s. 3da.
    One of the 24, Salisbury by Apr. 1559, auditor 1559, mayor 1561–2; j.p.q. Dorset from c.1579.

Unlike his elder brother, Webbe asked the chamber of Salisbury to pay him expenses amounting to £10 of the £12 8s. owing to him for representing the city in the Parliament of 1559; he lay 'long sick at London at that time'. He may have left Salisbury soon afterwards to live on his wife's Dorset property. He inherited five Hampshire manors from his father as well as property in Salisbury, to which he added between 1559 and 1574 estates at Wilton and elsewhere in Wiltshire. His own will mentions extensive holdings on the Somerset-Wiltshire border. Despite the status this land might be thought to confer, in 1562 his wife was presented before the Salisbury justices for wearing apparel unsuitable to her social position. Webbe died on 15 Apr. 1585 leaving a number of charitable bequests, but a *de bonis non* grant was made on the estate in July 1587.

Hoare, *Wilts.* Chalk, 29, Cawden, 20; City of Salisbury mss leger 1452–1567, ff. 321, 322, 324; Lansd. 35, f. 132; PCC 26 Tashe, 36 Brudenell; C142/211/189; Wards 7/21/224; *Wilts. N. and Q.* iv. 212; v. 177; vi. 150, 406; vii. 98, 416; *Wilts. Arch. Mag.* xxxii. 308.

N.M.F.

WEDNESTER, Charles (*d*.1597), of Bromyard, Herefs.; Lambeth, Surr., and Farringdon, London.

READING   1593

s. of John Wednester of Bromyard.
    Servant of the Earl of Essex by 1593; auditor of the prests, foreign accounts and first fruits and tenths prob. by 1594.

Wednester's family had probably been in the service of the Devereux family for some time, for their seat lay close to the Devereux estates in Herefordshire, where the 2nd Earl of Essex was born. Wednester received a grant of arms in November 1588. He was returned to Parliament for Reading by the 2nd Earl of Essex, who had been given the nomination of one of the burgesses for the coming Parliament on becoming high steward in January 1593. Wednester's name does not occur in the journals of the 1593 Parliament, but he may have served on the committee discussing a cloth bill, 15 Mar. That July he took a survey of Essex's lands but he was soon afterwards residing at Lambeth, within the archbishop of Canterbury's liberty. Perhaps he had become known to Archbishop Whitgift when that cleric had been bishop of Worcester and vice president in the marches of Wales. At any rate the implication is that by 1594 Wednester had secured the lucrative Exchequer post which he was holding at the time of his death, and to which his successor was appointed on 17 July 1597.

Vis. Herefs. 1569, ed. Weaver, 100; *CSP Dom.* 1595–7, p. 460; 1598–1601, p. 73; *Reading Recs.* i. 416; D'Ewes, 501; *HMC Bath,* v. 256; *Genealogist,* n.s. xxix. 54; *Surr. Arch. Colls.* xviii. 194; Lansd. 78, f. 166.

A.H.

WEEKES, Anthony (*d*.1573), of Crane Street, Salisbury, Wilts.

SALISBURY   1563

m. Margery, da. of John Bartholomew, merchant, of Salisbury, 1s. Christopher*.
    City scavenger 1562, mayor 1565.

Weekes, a brewer, first came to notice in June 1561, endeavouring to recover from the executors a bad debt of £20 for beer consumed by a deceased canon of the cathedral. He was one of six named with the mayor on 3 Feb. 1553 to deliver the account 'of the money for the wheat as also for the money of the gathering against the King's Majesty's coming last past'. In the course of the perennial battle between the city and the bishop, Weekes testified on 27 June 1565 that he had heard the bishop say that the mayor was his mayor and the citizens his subjects.

As well as his Crane Street brewery, Weekes and his wife had two tenements in Winchester Street; a house in the High Street leased from the mayor and commonalty; copyholds at Milford and tenements in Whiteparish. Weekes made his will 15 Feb. 1572, and died in the following year. He provided for his wife, his son Christopher the executor, Christopher's children and the children of his sister Elizabeth. He also bequeathed money for the repair of the cathedral and of his parish church, St. Thomas's, and for the relief of local prisoners.

Wilts. Arch. Mag. xlix. 451, 460; *HMC Var.* iv. 221–5; Hoare, *Wilts.* Salisbury, 696; C3/199/3; PCC 14 Peter; *VCH Wilts.* vi. 126, 127.

S.T.B.

WEEKES, Christopher (*d*.1596), of Salisbury, Wilts.

SALISBURY   1584, 1586, 1589

s. and h. of Anthony Weekes* of Salisbury by Margery, da. of John Bartholomew of Salisbury. *m.* Agnes, wid. of John Kent of Salisbury, 4s. 2da. suc. fa. 1573.[1]
    Clerk of the seal for the recognizance of statute merchant, Salisbury; mayor 1578–9.[2]

Christopher Weekes's father Anthony was a prosperous brewer who sat in the House of Commons in 1563–6. He bequeathed the utensils in his brewhouse to his son, but there is no evidence that Christopher made use of them or that he needed to engage in any other trade. The office which he held of the city yielded a considerable income, and he was highly assessed for taxation. Besides the property which came to him as an only son – several tenements in Salisbury, including the *Crane* which was to remain in the family for 150 years, and copyholds in Milford and Whiteparish – he acquired land for himself, notably in Harnham, where he held of the Earl of Northumberland. The widow whom he married was administering goods valued at £400; but the winding up of this estate led Weekes into litigation with the overseers and later with his stepdaughter's husband about the portion.[3]

As a leading citizen Weekes joined with the mayor and seven others to conclude for the erection of the new council house and to obtain contributions from the citizens towards it in February 1574, and in 1592 was among those named by the Privy Council to make an inquiry in the city. He was active in the city's long drawn out dispute with Bishop Coldwell, being one of eight named in July 1593 to accompany the mayor on a delegation to the bishop and in 1595 among those chosen to represent the city against him before the Privy Council. His is the first signature to a letter of that year to Burghley protesting against the bishop's interference with the city's liberties. He was returned to three successive Parliaments for Salisbury, and was appointed to the subsidy committee, 11 Feb. 1589. On 1 Mar. of that year he was licensed to depart.[4]

In a brief will made three days before his death, which occurred on 13 Jan. 1596, Weekes committed his soul to God trusting that it would be received through his Son's passion, and directed that his body should be buried in the family's parish church of St. Thomas, and gave mourning to 12 aged men and 40s. to the poor. He bequeathed £100 each to his two surviving younger sons, Thomas and John, the profits of his Milford property to his wife, and the residue to his 29 year-old heir Anthony, whom he made his executor.[5]

[1] PCC 14 Peter, 11 Drake; *Wilts. Arch. Mag.* xlix. 478; C3/198/52. [2] *VCH Wilts.* vi. 99 n, 104; *Wilts. Arch. Mag.* xxxvii. 34; xli. 243. [3] *VCH Wilts.* vi. 128; C142/247/66; *Wilts. Arch. Mag.* xlix. 460–5; Req. 2/56/34 Eliz.; C3/24/78, 46/124, 198/52. [4] *HMC Var.* iv. 226, 230–1, 232; *APC*, xxii. 178; Lansd. 78/180/165; D'Ewes, 431. [5] PCC 11 Drake; C142/247/66.

S.T.B.

WELCOME, John (bef. 1523–80), of the High Street, Lincoln.

LINCOLN 1572*

b. bef. 1523, s. of John Welcome, freeman of Lincoln, by his w. Elizabeth. *m.* Anne (*d.*1590), da. of Gregory Ion of Barrow, 2s. 1da.
Alderman, Lincoln 1565–73, mayor 1568.

Described in the early Marian pardon roll as 'yeoman', Welcome advanced his status in city and county through the acquisition of property, some of it ex-monastic. On 27 Mar. 1571 he was appointed by the corporation 'to be solicitor for the affairs of the city at Parliament, at 4s. a day', and again, on 8 Jan. 1572, one of the two 'solicitors' to ride to London 'to advance the city's cause' in a dispute about common rights. At the parliamentary election of May 1572 he was returned as Member for the city, but fell out of favour through disclosing to his fellow-Member the contents of a letter from the corporation to Robert Monson*. Whether or not the affair was connected in some way with the 1572 contest for the succession to Monson as recorder, a contest in which Welcome's father-in-law Gregory Ion unsuccessfully opposed Monson's candidate Stephen Thymbleby*, can only be surmised, but the results for Welcome were calamitous. Because of his 'various offences of opprobrious language and factious proceedings' he was on 16 Mar. 1573 displaced for ever from his aldermanship or from any other civic office.

He died on 26 July 1580, during the course of the 1572 Parliament, and was buried in his parish church of St.

Mary Wigford, to which he bequeathed £10. Two-thirds of his lands 'as well in Lincoln as in Lincolnshire' went to his widow for life, with remainder to his daughter and second son, who were also to receive £500 each; the other third, with £400, he left to his elder son.

Lincs. Peds. (Harl. Soc. lii), 1059; Yorke, *Union of Honour* (1640), p. 51; *CPR*, 1553–4, pp. 122, 461; 1560–3, p. 552; 1563–6, p. 101; Lincoln AO. presentation deed index; *HMC 14th Rep.* VIII, 65; Lincoln min. bk.; J. W. F. Hill, *Tudor and Stuart Lincoln*, 72–3; PCC 38 Arundel.

D.O.

WELDON, Thomas (c.1500–67), of Cookham, Berks.

BERKSHIRE 1542
NEW WINDSOR 1559

b. c.1500, 3rd s. of Hugh Weldon, sewer to Henry VII and Henry VIII. *m.* (1) by 1538, Cecilia; (2) ?by 1551, Anne, 5s. 2da.[1]

Cofferer's clerk 1520; third clerk of kitchen by Mar. 1526, second clerk by 1532, chief clerk by 1538–40; 1st master of Household by 1540; cofferer 1552–3, from 1559; keeper of the leads at Windsor castle from 1540, of the keys by 1553, great wardrobe 1559; j.p. Berks. by 1543, Wilts. from c.1559; capt. in army in France 1544; high steward of New Windsor Apr. 1548–Sept. 1563.[2]

Weldon's rise in the Household was accompanied by the steady acquisition of property. In Berkshire he was granted the manors of White Waltham, which had belonged to Chertsey abbey; Canon Court and the rectory at Cookham, which had belonged to the abbey of Cirencester; the manor of Woolstone, vacant through the attainder of Thomas Seymour†, Lord Seymour of Sudeley; and, in 1563, the manor of Pangbourne.[3]

He was prominent in the Household before Cromwell's fall, and perhaps it was there he acquired the extreme protestant views which took him to the Fleet prison for a time in 1542. His position in the Household brought him the high stewardship of Windsor on the death of Sir Anthony Browne†, master of the horse, but in 1563 the Earl of Leicester was chosen high steward in his place. Described in 1564 as 'a furtherer earnest' of true religion, Weldon may have been largely responsible for the puritan tradition in Windsor, evident in burgesses such as Richard Gallys* returned by the borough to Elizabethan Parliaments.[4]

Weldon died 2 Mar. 1567. In his will he expressed the hope that he would 'rise again and be a partaker of the everlasting life provided for God's elect'. There was to be no pomp or excess at the funeral, and 'a preacher well learned in God's true and holy word' should preach the sermon. Weldon's administration of his offices seems not to have been entirely judicious, for the will records that he had still to repay £800 out of £1,000 of the Queen's money, lent by him to the Earl of Arundel; ten years after his death no goods had come to hand to settle the debt.[5]

[1] *Vis. Berks.* (Harl. Soc. lvi), 139; *VCH Berks.* iii. 172; PCC 5 Babington. [2] *LP Hen. VIII*, xiii(1), p. 457; xiii(2), p. 499; xv. p. 405; xvi. p. 202; xix(1), p. 160; Stowe 571, f. 59; *APC*, iii. 137; A. Woodworth, *Purveyance for the Royal Household* (American Philosoph. Soc.) 10; *CSP Dom.* 1547–80, p. 146; Bodl. Ashmole 1126, f. 41; *CPR*, 1547–8, p. 142; 1550–3, pp. 351, 393; 1553 and App. Edw. VI, pp. 413, 416. [3] *CPR*, 1547–8, pp. 404–5; 1550–3, p. 112; *CSP Dom.* 1547–80, p. 169; *VCH Berks.* iii. 126–8, 132, 151, 166, 172, 304, 463; *LP Hen. VIII*, xvii. p. 632; PCC 5 Babington. [4] Strype, *Mems.* ii(2), p. 53; *APC*, i. 97; *LP Hen. VIII*, xviii(2), p. 140; *CSP Dom.* 1547–80, p. 146; *Cam. Misc.* ix(3), p. 38. [5] E150/824/1; PCC 5 Babington.

A.H.

WELSHE, Arthur

MORPETH   1563

This Member has not been identified. The appearance, at about this time, of others named Welshe at Morpeth suggests that he was a burgess of the town. If so, excluding unidentified Members, he was the only local man to sit for the borough in this period.

Arch. Ael. (ser. 4), xxiv. 94.

B.D.

WENMAN, Sir Richard (1573–1640), of Thame Park, Oxon. and Twyford, Bucks.

OXFORDSHIRE   1597, 1621, 1625

b. 1573, 1st s. of Thomas Wenman* by Jane, da. of William West, 1st Baron Delaware. *educ.* ?Eton 1585; Oxf. Dec. 1587. *m.* (1) c.1595, Agnes (*d.*1617), da. of Sir George Fermor of Easton Neston, Northants., 4s. 5da.; (2) 1618, Anne or Alice, wid. of Thomas Roland and Robert Chamberlain; (3) Elizabeth (*d.* 1629); (4) Mary (*d.*1638), da. and coh. of Thomas Keble of Essex. *suc.* fa. July 1577. Kntd. June 1596. *cr.* Baron Wenman [I] and Visct. Wenman [I] 30 July 1628.[1]

J.p.q. Oxon. by 1621, dep. lt. 1624, sheriff 1627–8.[2]

By marriage to the coheiress of John, Lord Williams of Thame (*d.*1559), Richard Wenman's grandfather had added half Williams's great estate to the already considerable fortune of a Witney clothier. Had they not been hampered by their Catholic sympathies, the Wenmans might have disputed the leadership of the Oxfordshire gentry with the family of Norris (its influence based largely on the other half of Williams's lands) and the parvenu Knollys family. At Oxford, to which he proceeded after a period in the wardship of the Earl of Leicester, Wenman possibly had a tutor of Catholic leanings, and he married a wife who remained faithful to the traditions of a well-known Catholic family.[3]

Wenman was given much trouble by the religion of his first wife, an accomplished woman, who translated John Zonaras's *History of the World*. John Gerard, the Jesuit, was told about Agnes Wenman while sheltering with the Cursons, her mother's family, and went to minister to her

without Wenman's knowledge. It seems to have been at Wenman's house that Gerard had his celebrated encounter with George Abbot. In his autobiography, written in 1609, Gerard describes Wenman himself as a protestant and insinuates that ambition made him so: 'he hoped to be a baron and is still hoping'. When he and his wife were examined separately during the investigations following the Gunpowder Plot, and Agnes was found to have received incriminating letters from Elizabeth Vaux, Wenman protested that he had always strongly disapproved of his wife's friendships.[4]

His knighting by Essex at Cadiz in 1596 and return to Parliament for Oxfordshire in the following year along with Sir William Knollys, Essex's uncle, must have owed something to the support of the Knollys family: it was Sir William Knollys (by this time Viscount Wallingford) who later chose Wenman as deputy lieutenant. Wenman's return was partly, however, a natural result of his position in the county, in a year when the Knollyses could not provide both knights. Wenman's name is not to be found in the journals of the 1597 Parliament, but as a knight of the shire he might have served on the committees for enclosures (5 Nov.), the poor law (5, 22 Nov.), armour and weapons (8 Nov.), penal laws (8 Nov.), monopolies (10 Nov.) and the subsidy (15 Nov.). In 1601 Wenman was named chief overseer of the will of Sir Edward Norris*. After sitting as knight for Oxfordshire in two more Parliaments, he achieved his hoped-for peerage. He died in 1640, and his will, which indicates no strong religious convictions, was proved on 30 Apr. of that year.[5]

[1] *DNB*; *CP*; *Vis. Oxon.* (Harl. Soc. v), 179; F. G. Lee, *Thame Church*, 433–6, 439. [2] *CSP Dom.* 1623–5, p. 407. [3] *CP*; *Cath. Rec. Soc.* xxii. 114 and n; *DNB* (Fermor, Richard). [4] *DNB* (Wenman, Thomas); John Gerard, *Autobiog. of an Elizabethan*, trans. Caraman, 169–70, 265; *CSP Dom.* 1603–10, pp. 240, 259, 266–7. [5] D'Ewes, 552, 553, 555, 557, 561; *CSP Dom.* 1601–3, pp. 65–6; C142/594/49; PCC 47 Coventry.

A.H.

WENMAN, Thomas (c.1548–77), of Twyford, Bucks.

BUCKINGHAM   1571

b. c.1548, 1st s. of (Sir) Richard Wenman† by Isabel, da. and coh. of John Williams†, Lord Williams of Thame. *m.* Jane, da. of William West, 1st Baron Delaware, 3s. inc. Sir Richard* 1da. *suc.* fa. 1573.

Wenman no doubt gained his one parliamentary seat through his family's local influence. His father was a Buckinghamshire country gentleman, his mother an heiress with land in the county, and her sister was married to Sir Henry Norris I*, later Lord Norris. Wenman himself was overshadowed for most of his life by his father, and died after holding his lands for less than five years, apparently a victim of the outbreak of gaol fever at Oxford in 1577. In addition to his estate at Twyford, he had property in Beaconsfield, Amersham, Penn, the

Chalfonts and elsewhere in Buckinghamshire, as well as the manor of Eaton, Berkshire, which Sir Thomas Seymour had sold to his family at the end of Henry VIII's reign. He is not known to have held local office, but his being concerned in the business of the Oxford assizes suggests that he was added to the commission of the peace after his father's death. It is even possible that he held a minor post at court, some of the considerable debts he left at his death being to the Crown; in any case he had borrowed money at high interest on the expectation of his inheritance. On his death, at Twyford on 23 July 1577, much of his property had to be sold, including Eaton to (Sir) John Danvers* for the substantial sum of £7,700. The wardship of his four year-old heir Richard was granted jointly to the widow and to the Earl of Leicester, who sold his interest to James Cressy. Cressy married the widow and defaulted on his agreement to discharge Wenman's debts over a lease of the manor of Hall, Buckinghamshire.

VCH Bucks. iv. 259; Lipscomb, *Bucks.* iii. 131–2; C2/T10/28; C142/ 163/5, 182/42; SP12/143/44; SP15/27A/80, 28/52; Harl. 1110, f. 33; Bodl. Tanner 79, f. 182; Wards 7/22/50.

P.W.H.

WENNESLEY, Richard (d.1594), of Wennesley (now Wensley), Derbys. and of London.

DERBYSHIRE 1563, 1571

1st s. of Thomas Wennesley, prob. by his 1st w. Dorothy, da. of Hugh Teverey of Stampleford, Leics. but perhaps by his 2nd w. Cecily Barrett or Garrett. *educ.* Clement's Inn bef. Sept. 1553. *m.* (1) Lettice (?div. c.1564), da. of Otwell Needham of Snitterton, Derbys., 1 or 2da.; (2) bigamously by Jan. 1565.

J.p. Derbys. c.1573–9.

Of a family settled in Darley Dale, Derbyshire, since the reign of John, Wennesley was the first of its members to attain knight of the shire status. He added to his estates in the early years of Elizabeth's reign by buying from Sir Edward Warner* ex-monastic property, including the demesne lands of Snitterton priory, chantry land in Bonsall, Hognaston and Matlock, and the site of Calke priory. Though the bishop of Coventry and Lichfield recommended Wennesley's inclusion on the commission of the peace in 1564, he was not so appointed until about 1573, and in 1575 it was noted 'he is most resident at London'. Perhaps for this reason, his name does not appear on the commission after the 1570s. His private life also came to the notice of the Privy Council. About 1564 he was involved in a scandalous divorce case, his wife alleging that in order to get rid of her he had suborned witnesses to swear that she had murdered the baby of one Anne Gilbert. He was summoned before the Council in early 1565, but in December the case was still unsettled. Meanwhile, without waiting for his divorce, Wennesley went through a form of marriage with the lady for whom

he had left his wife, and whose name remains undiscovered.

Wennesley was one of the eight nominees of the 6th Earl of Shrewsbury in his 'composition' with the borough of Chesterfield about the town's privileges in January 1568, by which Shrewsbury retained control of the borough despite a recent confirmation of its privileges from the Crown. Another nobleman with whom Wennesley was connected was John, 9th Baron Stourton, who in 1573 was committed to the custody of the archbishop of Canterbury for recusancy. In December Wennesley and Sir John St. Leger* stood surety for him, in the sum of £2,000.

In 1575 Wennesley was also in trouble for illicit lead smelting. William Humfrey, who held a monopoly for certain methods of refining lead, complained to Lord Burghley in 1575, and again in August 1577, that Wennesley had persuaded Sir John Zouche† to put up a 'melting house' at Codnor Castle, thus infringing Humfrey's patent. Wennesley was also 'the first causer of Mr. Cavendish to build his melting-house'. Other charges were that he had 'invited' men from him 'by great wages', and had attempted to monopolize the local supply of lead ore which Wennesley's group in fact succeeded in doing after Humfrey's death in July 1579, helped by the 6th Earl of Shrewsbury and Sir Thomas Fitzherbert.

Wennesley died intestate in 1594, administration of the estate being granted to one William Dudley of London on 24 Feb.

Add. 28113, f. 1; *Genealogist*, n.s. viii. 177; *CPR*, 1553–4, p. 465; 1557–8, p. 214; J. C. Cox, *Notes on Derbys. Churches*, ii. 162, 165, 351, 490; iii. 347; *APC*, vii. 190, 197, 301–2; viii. 169; 'J. T.', *Old Halls, Manors and Fams. of Derbys*. i. 109–10; J. P. Yeatman, *Feudal Hist. Derbys*. ii(3), pp. 118–20; *Cam. Misc*. ix(3), p. 43; Egerton 2345, f. 10; Lansd. 737, f. 134; 24, ff. 123, 125; 31, ff. 162–3; SP12/104; M. B. Donald, *Eliz. Monopolies*, 150–9, 162, 170–3; PCC admon. act bk. 1594, f. 88.

N.M.F.

WENTWORTH, John (1564–1613), of Gosfield Hall, Essex.

ESSEX 1597
WOOTTON BASSETT 1601

b. 1564, o.s. of Sir John Wentworth of Horkesley and Gosfield by his 1st w. Elizabeth, da. of Sir Christopher Heydon*. *m.* Cicely, da. of Sir Edward Unton* by Anne, da. of Edward Seymour, Duke of Somerset, 2s. 4 or 5da. *suc.* fa. 1588.[1]

Sheriff, Essex 1592–3.

Wentworth succeeded to extensive lands in Essex, including Little Horkesley and Gosfield, which his father had inherited from his relative Ann, Lady Maltravers, in 1581. His name does not occur in the journals of the 1597 Parliament, but as a knight of the shire he could have served on committees concerned with enclosures (5 Nov.), the poor law (5, 22 Nov.), armour and weapons (8 Nov.), penal laws (8 Nov.), monopolies (10 Nov.), the subsidy (15 Nov.) and draining the fens (3 Dec.). He is not known to have had any land in Wiltshire or any connexion with Wootton Bassett. His return to Parliament for the borough was presumably due to the influence of his wife's uncle, the Earl of Hertford. The dates make it unlikely that he was the John Wentworth who was a fellow of Lincoln's Inn by 1585, and whose name appears on a list of King's bench lawyers assessed to the loan in 1600. He does not appear to have taken an active part in county affairs. In 1589 the deputy lieutenants wrote to Lord Burghley saying that he was not suitable as a captain of lances. In 1600 he provided one light horse for Ireland. He was apparently either considerate, or over-indulgent, to the poor. In 1590 he gave land at Finchingfield for a poor woman to build a cottage, and in 1601 the villagers at Bocking objected to his allowing a 'lewd, idle and slanderous fellow' to build a 'noisome cott' there. In 1596 he was involved in a dispute over lands bequeathed to his wife by her father, who had also left £23,000 debts. He died in 1613 and was buried at Gosfield, leaving a 'splendid inheritance' to his son, who dissipated it. Wentworth's widow married Sir Edward Hoby*.[2]

[1] *Vis. Essex* (Harl. Soc. xiii), 315–16; *Trans. Essex Arch. Soc.* n.s. iii, ped. opp. p. 221, 224–5. [2] C142/217/132; D'Ewes, 552, 553, 555, 557, 561, 567; *Trans. Essex Arch. Soc.* n.s. iii. 215, 220–7; *L. Inn Black Bk.* i. 438; *APC*, xxx. 29, 438; *CSP Dom.* 1581–90, p. 612; Add. 1580–1625, p. 378; Essex RO, Q/SR 111/51; 159/29, 38.

J.H.

WENTWORTH, Paul (1534–94), of Burnham, Bucks.

CHIPPING WYCOMBE	1559
BUCKINGHAM	1563
LISKEARD	1572

b. 1534, 3rd s. of Sir Nicholas Wentworth of Lillingstone Lovell, Oxon. by Jane, da. of John Josselyn; bro. of Peter*. *m.* 1563, Helen, da. of Richard Agmondesham of Heston, Mdx., wid. of William Tildesley, groom of the chamber, 4s. 4da.

Steward, Burnham manor 1563.

Wentworth entered the House of Commons before his more famous brother, being returned to the first Parliament of the reign for a local borough, and leaving no trace in its surviving records, though he was certainly one of the puritans who tried to impose a radical religious settlement on the Queen. Next time he came in for another borough in the county, which, though more distant from his estates, was still within the sphere of influence of a man with his local and central connexions, among them his relative Sir Walter Mildmay* and Lord Hunsdon, who sometimes nominated at Buckingham. Wentworth made a fortunate marriage to a lady whose first husband left her his lease of the manor of Burnham.

Wentworth held the advowson of the rectory and in 1574 received a crown lease of Abbess park wood there. Yet, despite his standing in the county, he never achieved the commission of the peace, though recommended as earnest in religion and fit to be trusted in a letter from the bishop of Lincoln to the Privy Council in 1564. Perhaps the reason was his being presented, early in 1566, along with his brother Peter, before the Essex justices of the peace 'to answer to transgressions and contempts of which they stand indicted'. As it happened, however, later that year, he became heavily involved in the agitation over the succession in the second session of the 1563 Parliament. The Queen on Saturday 9 Nov. 1566 had ordered an end to any discussion of this subject, and the House then turned to other matters. On the Monday following, Wentworth, who as far as is known had not previously intervened, asked 'whether the Queen's commandment was not against the liberties' of the House. Wentworth posed three questions:

> Whether her Highness' commandment, forbidding the Lower House to speak or treat any more of the succession and of any their excuses in that behalf, be a breach of the liberty of the free speech of the House or not? Whether Mr. Comptroller, the vice chamberlain and Mr. Secretary, pronouncing in the House the said commandment in her Highness' name, are of authority sufficient to bind the House to silence in that behalf, or to bind the House to acknowledge the same to be a direct and sufficient commandment or not? If her Highness' said commandment be no breach of the liberty of the House, or if the commandment pronounced as afore is said [to] be a sufficient commandment to bind the House to take knowledge thereof, then what offence is it for any of the House to err in declaring his opinion to be otherwise?

'Whereupon' as the journal has it, 'arose divers arguments, continuing from nine of the clock till two after noon'. There can be no doubt that this speech of Wentworth's was embarrassing to the government, and it is of the greatest interest in the context of the centuries-long debate on freedom of speech in the Commons, a debate to which Wentworth's brother Peter was to make a significant contribution in 1576. Unlike Peter, Paul is not known to have suffered any punishment.

In October 1569 Wentworth was ordered to lodge the 4th Duke of Norfolk at Burnham until that nobleman was moved to the Tower. At Wentworth's house the Duke was forbidden to confer with anyone without the permission of his host Sir Henry Neville I*, his servants were removed, and no letters were to be delivered to him or sent out. That the last instruction was circumvented is evident from the examination of John, Baron Lumley in 1571 about letters he had received from the Duke 'in the house at Paul Wentworth's'. In 1589, when Wentworth petitioned for a renewal of his lease at Burnham, the Queen granted it, 'calling to mind the long and dutiful service of this suppliant, her Highness's servant, [and] his loyal care, trouble and charge at the committing of the late Duke of Norfolk to his house'.

Wentworth was returned to the 1572 Parliament for a Cornish borough through the intervention of the 2nd Earl of Bedford. On 23 May 1572 he made a brief intervention in the debate on Mary Queen of Scots, urging her execution: the question was 'whether we should call for an axe or an act'. This is the only speech in this session that can be attributed to Paul with certainty; other interventions by 'Mr' Wentworth on the subject of the Duke of Norfolk could as well have been by his brother Peter. Certainly it was Paul who, in an extraordinary speech on behalf of the militant puritans at the beginning of the third session of this Parliament, 21 Jan. 1581, moved

> for a public fast and daily preaching, the fast to be appointed upon some one certain day, but the preaching to be every morning at seven of the clock before the House did sit, that so they, beginning their proceeding with the service and worship of God, He might the better bless them in all their consultations and actions.

This was a plain defiance of the authority of the Queen as head of the Church of England. Two days later the House received her rebuke and the matter was dropped. The end of the session ended Wentworth's parliamentary career, but his anti-Catholic activities continued. In June 1583 some members of Oxford university wrote to him about Catholic undergraduates at Trinity College, especially one who had been sponsored by Lady Paulet. In the following year he conducted a search of Isabel Hampden's house at Stoke Poges, seizing among other goods a 'copy of the pope's letter', an instruction for the singing of mass and a book called *Officium Beatae Mariae*.

Wentworth died on 13 Jan. 1594, and was buried at Burnham, where 'as he lived most Christian-like, so he died most comfortably strong in faith, steadfast in hope, fervent in love, a zealous professor of the truth, and an earnest detester of all superstition'. His will, drawn up on 7 Sept. 1593, was proved in the following February. Not surprisingly it has a puritan preamble, trusting 'by the merits and bitter passion of my Lord and Saviour Jesus Christ to be saved, and to have and enjoy in full measure the joys and comforts of everlasting life, which He hath prepared only for His elect and chosen servants'. Wentworth left £400 to one daughter and £300 to another. The servants were to have a year's wages, and the widow, the sole executrix and residuary legatee, was to supervise the upbringing of the children, with the help of six of Wentworth's friends, among them the 2nd Baron St. John, Lord St. John and Cuthbert Reynolds*. The eldest son, Paul, was of age by August 1594, when the inquisition post mortem was taken.

DNB; Lipscomb, *Bucks*. iii. 206, 220; *VCH Bucks*. i. 315; iii. 173, 179, 181; E316/3/221; *Cam. Misc.* ix(3), p. 32; *HMC 10th Rep.* IV, 472; *HMC Hatfield*, i. 429, 433, 578; iii. 457; D'Ewes, 128, 282; *CJ*, i. 76; Trinity, Dublin, Thos. Cromwell's jnl. ff. 39, 98; *CSP Dom*. 1581–90, pp. 133, 155, 680; C142/240/84; PCC 10 Dixy.

N.M.F.

WENTWORTH, Peter (1524–97), of Lillingstone Lovell, Oxon.[1]

BARNSTAPLE	1571
TREGONY	1572
NORTHAMPTON	1586, 1589, 1593

b. 1524, 1st s. of Sir Nicholas Wentworth of Lillingstone Lovell, chief porter of Calais, by Jane, da. of John Josselyn of Hyde Hall, Sawbridgeworth, Herts.; bro. of Paul*. *educ.* L. Inn 1542. *m.* (1) Lettice, da. of Sir Ralph Lane of Orlingbury, Northants. by Maud, da. and coh. of William, 1st Baron Parr of Horton; (2) Elizabeth (*d*.1596), da. of William Walsingham of Footscray, Kent, sis. of (Sir) Francis Walsingham*4, wid. of Geoffrey Gate(s) of Walton or Waltham, Essex, 4s. inc. Walter* 5da. prob. all by (2). *suc.* fa. 1557.[2]

J.p. Oxon 1559 (rem. bef. 1562).

Wentworth's family setting was both impressive and significant. His grandfather was a younger son of the Wentworths of Nettlestead in Suffolk, a daughter of which house was mother of Jane Seymour and of her brother Protector Somerset, while later Lord Burghley married a daughter into that family. Peter's own first marriage allied him with Queen Katherine Parr. His second marriage, to a sister of Sir Francis Walsingham, made him brother-in-law to Sir Walter Mildmay* as well as Walsingham, and later linked him with Sir Philip Sidney and Robert, Earl of Essex and, more distantly, with the Earl of Leicester. Moreover, through Elizabeth Walsingham's previous marriage to Geoffrey Gates a link was established with another puritan family, while her son by that marriage married a step-daughter of the puritan Thomas Wilson*, secretary to Queen Elizabeth. There can be little doubt that Peter was reared in a radical religious atmosphere. His sister married a prominent Kentish gentleman, Edward Boyes, and in Mary's reign accompanied her husband into exile abroad, while his younger brother Paul was an ardent puritan, who sat in Parliament from 1559 to 1581 and played a notable part as a radical in the proceedings.

The principal seat of Wentworth's father was at Lillingstone Lovell, a few miles north of Buckingham, though then a detached piece of Oxfordshire. He also held lands in Buckinghamshire, Northamptonshire, Essex and Surrey. The Buckinghamshire lands were left to his son Paul and the Northamptonshire lands to younger sons, while Peter inherited Lillingstone Lovell. Little is known about Peter before he entered Parliament in 1571. He appears on the pardon roll of 1553 as late of Lillingstone

Lovell, *alias* late of Epping, in Essex. His name was added to the commission of the peace for Oxfordshire in 1559, but was removed before 1562. Perhaps the need for enthusiastic protestants in the first year of the new reign explains his appearance on the commission; but the isolation of Lillingstone Lovell from the rest of Oxford county hardly warranted locating a justice there, while Wentworth's excessive zeal cannot have appealed to the authorities.[3]

In the light of his own later behaviour in Parliament, and of his younger brother's activities in 1566 (at least), it is curious that Wentworth remained out of the Commons until 1571. In 1593 he told how, 31 years before, he had been stirred to interest himself in politics 'by God's good motion', 'by sundry grave and wise men unknown unto me', and 'by lamentable messages' sent by unknown persons. At any rate he was returned to Parliament in 1571 for Barnstaple, probably through the influence of Arthur Bassett*, or the latter's friend and patron, the 2nd Earl of Bedford. Wentworth almost certainly owed his return at Tregony in the following year to Bedford.

In his first Parliament Wentworth served on the committee of the bill to confirm the Articles of Religion, and was one of a delegation of six whom Archbishop Parker questioned in April 1571 about their exclusion of the non-doctrinal articles from the bill. Asked why they had omitted these, Wentworth answered, 'Because ... we ... had no time to examine ... how they agreed with the word of God'. 'What!', exclaimed Parker, 'surely you mistook the matter. You will refer yourselves wholly to us therein.' 'No, by the faith I bear to God!', answered Wentworth: 'we will pass nothing before we understand what it is, for that were but to make you Popes. Make you Popes who list, for we will make you none.' It was a troublesome session, involving the temporary sequestration from the House of the puritan leader, William Strickland, and a stern, official reprimand for another radical, Robert Bell, who had dared to attack the exercise of the royal prerogative. On the eve of the Easter recess, Sir Humphrey Gilbert made a gratuitous attack on Bell's speech, which provoked Wentworth, 20 Apr., after the recess, to make the first of many speeches in defence of the liberties of the House:

> [Gilbert's speech tended] to no other end than to inculcate fear into those which should be free. He requested care for the credit of the House, and for the maintenance of free speech (the only means of ordinary proceedings), and to preserve the liberties of the House, to reprove liars, inveighing greatly out of the scriptures and otherwise against liars ...

The Parliament of 1572, summoned after the Ridolfi plot, was concerned mainly with the problem of Mary Queen of Scots and with that of her fellow-culprit, the Duke of Norfolk, who stood condemned for treason. On 12

May 1572 Wentworth was placed on the committee which discussed the great cause with a committee of the Lords. He was very active, making several speeches in the House of Commons, calling time and again for the execution of Norfolk and passionately demanding the death of Mary, 'the most notorious whore in all the world'. Thus on 16 May the Lords should join with the Commons in a motion to the Queen for her execution. In an elaborate figure of speech Mary was likened to Abinadab, the Duke to Abinadab's assistant, and Queen Elizabeth to Achab. On 24 May 'It remaineth yet to be considered for our petition to the Queen for execution of the Duke'; on 28th the House should 'forbear to deal in any other matter until this be determined, otherwise ... it will be said unto us justly, "O fool this night shall thy life be taken from thee" '. On 31st he 'moveth for execution of the Duke, that order may be taken for the petition'. When a soothing message from the Queen prompted two Members to move that a delegation should convey their thanks to her, Wentworth opposed the motion, saying that he could give no thanks and urging the House to refuse to do anything more until the Duke of Norfolk was executed, thus cutting off half Mary's head. In the event the Duke was executed on Monday morning 2nd June before the House sat. Wentworth made only two further reported speeches in the session, 9 June on aliens, when he said, with insight, 'that he had rather commit some folly in speech than do injury by silence', and 11 June, on a recurrent complaint of the rank and file in the Commons that 'the freedom of the House [was] taken away by tale tellers'.

Wentworth was not a man who excelled in the cut and thrust of debate. He was of the premeditative, deliberate type. In the interval between 1572 and the second session of that Parliament in 1576, he ruminated on his experience in two Parliaments, especially on the frustration of Members and the disciplinary methods of the government, incorporating these incidents in a draft speech which he realised would probably land him in prison. On the first day of the new session (8 Feb.) he rose to astound and embarrass the House with his indictment, written in his strikingly melodious prose: 'Mr. Speaker, I find written in a little volume these words ... "Sweet indeed is the name of liberty and the thing itself a value beyond all inestimable treasure"'. The speech is deservedly famous among English parliamentary orations. Wentworth claimed for freedom of speech in Parliament a fundamental, entrenched place in the constitution, immune from control by the Crown: a novel and revolutionary conception, without historical justification:

> ... in this House which is termed a place of free speech there is nothing so necessary for the preservation of the prince and state as free speech, and without it it is a scorn and mockery to call it a Parliament house, for in truth it is none, but a very school of flattery and

dissimulation and so a fit place to serve the Devil and his angels in and not to glorify God and benefit the Commonwealth.

Two things did 'very great hurt'.

One is a rumour that runneth about the House, and this it is: take heed what you do, the Queen's majesty liketh not of such a matter. Whosoever preferreth it, she will be much offended with him. Or, the contrary, her Majesty liketh of such a matter, whosoever speaketh against it she will be much offended with him. The other is sometimes a message is brought into the House either of commanding or inhibiting very injurious unto the freedom of speech and consultation. I would to God, Mr. Speaker, that these two were buried in Hell, I mean rumours and messages …

Reviewing the inroads on this freedom that he had witnessed in 1571 and 1572, he was led into explicit criticism of the Queen:

Certain it is, Mr. Speaker that none is without fault, no, not our noble Queen … Her Majesty hath committed great faults, yea dangerous faults to herself and the state … It is a dangerous thing in a prince unkindly to entreat and abuse his or her nobility and people as her Majesty did the last Parliament, and it is a dangerous thing in a prince to oppose or bend herself against her nobility and people … and how could any prince more unkindly entreat, abuse and oppose herself against her nobility and people than her Majesty did the last Parliament? Did she not call it of purpose to prevent traitorous perils to her person and for no other cause? Did not her Majesty send unto us two bills, willing us to make a choice of that we liked best for her safety and thereof to make a law, promising her Majesty's royal consent thereto? And did we not first choose the one and her Majesty refused it, yielding no reason, nay, yielding great reasons why she ought to have yielded to it? Yet did not we nevertheless receive the other and agreeing to make a law thereof did not her Majesty in the end refuse all our travails? And did not we her Majesty's faithful nobility and subjects plainly and openly decipher ourselves unto her Majesty and our hateful enemy? And hath not her Majesty left us all to her open revenge? Is this a just recompense in our Christian Queen for our faithful dealings? The heathen do requite good for good; then how much more is it dutiful in a Christian prince? And will not this her Majesty's handling, think you, Mr. Speaker, make cold dealing in many of her Majesty's subjects toward her? Again I fear it will. And hath it not caused many already, think you, Mr. Speaker, to seek a salve for the head that they have broken? I fear it hath. And many more will do the like if it be not prevented in time. And hath it not marvellously rejoiced and encouraged the hollow hearts of her Majesty's hateful enemies and traitorous subjects? No doubt but it hath.
… It is a great and special part of our duty and office Mr. Speaker to maintain the freedom of consultation and speech for by this are good laws that do set forth God's

glory and are for the preservation of the prince and state made. St. Paul in the same place sayeth, hate that which is evil and cleave unto that which is good; then with St. Paul I do advise you all here present, yea, and heartily and earnestly I desire you from the bottom of your hearts to hate all messengers, tale carriers, or any other thing whatsoever it be that any manner of way infringe the liberties of this honourable council. Yea, hate it or them, I say, as venomous and poison unto our commonwealth, for they are venomous beasts that do use it. Therefore I say again and again, hate that that is evil and cleave to that that is good. And this, loving and faithful hearted, I do wish to be conceived in fear of God, and of love to our prince and state, for we are incorporated into this place to serve God and all England and not to be timeservers and humour feeders.

Wentworth concluded:

I have holden you long with my rude speech, the which since it tendeth wholly with pure consciences to seek the advancement of God's glory, our honourable sovereign's safety and to the sure defence of this noble isle of England, and all by maintaining the liberties of this honourable council, the fountain from whence all these do spring, my humble and hearty suit unto you all is to accept my goodwill and that this that I have here spoken of conscience and great zeal unto my prince and state may not be buried in the pit of oblivion and so no good come thereof.

Wentworth's suit was granted. His speech was widely reported in England and abroad, and copies have survived for posterity. It is the first full statement of the doctrine of freedom of speech in the House. The immediate consequences were that Wentworth was committed to the serjeant's custody and that afternoon examined by a committee of the House. We possess Wentworth's account of the examination. As one of the committee said: 'Mr. Wentworth will never acknowledge himself to make a fault, nor say that he is sorry for anything that he doth speak'. The following day the committee reported back to the House and Wentworth was sent to the Tower. There he remained for just over a month, until, two days before the end of the session, the Queen intervened and returned him to the House, accompanying her action with a gracious and magnanimous message. The episode ended 'to the great contentment of all'.

In 1579 Wentworth was in trouble with the Privy Council on the complaint of his bishop about the great resort of people from Northampton and elsewhere to his house at Lillingstone Lovell, where the sacrament was administered in puritan fashion. Then, in January 1581, came the third and last session of the 1572 Parliament. It started with a *contretemps*, when Paul Wentworth moved and carried a motion for a public fast, in clear breach of the Queen's ecclesiastical rights. His name recalled to Elizabeth Peter's rash action in 1576, and in her withering rebuke to the House she imputed their offence partly to her lenity towards a brother of that man which now made this motion. Thereafter, the session proceeded on a subdued note, and all we hear of Peter Wentworth is his appointment to two committees, 25 Jan. and 17 Mar.

Though the radical puritans with whom Wentworth associated had already established their 'classical' movement and begun their organized campaign against Archbishop Whitgift before the next Parliament met in November 1584, Wentworth did not sit in that Parliament. Nor, indeed, did his friend, neighbour and fellow-enthusiast, Anthony Cope* of Hanwell near Banbury. It is idle to speculate why. Both returned to Westminster in 1586, Wentworth sitting for Northampton, a centre of puritan activity where he was well known and may have owned a house.[4] Called as a result of the Babington plot, the autumn meetings of this Parliament were given over to the clamour for executing Mary Queen of Scots. Congenial as this was to Wentworth, we have no record of him speaking on this subject. Perhaps he reserved himself for the part allotted him in the organized campaign of the puritan classical movement. Their opportunity came in February 1587, after Mary had been executed. Their leaders had determined to presbyterianize the Anglican church by means of a parliamentary bill, and had held meetings in London with Anthony Cope, Wentworth and other Members to plan their campaign. The opening move was made on 27 Feb. when Cope introduced his famous and revolutionary 'bill and book'. The Queen immediately suppressed the bill. Anticipating such action, the zealots had evidently cast Wentworth for the principal role in their next move – the defence of freedom of speech.

On 1 Mar. Wentworth rose to speak, demanding that the Speaker should put a number of questions about the liberties of Parliament to the House. If conceded, they would have stripped the Crown of its prescriptive right of control and discipline and would have left it defenceless except for the royal veto or support in the House of Lords. By implication, if not intent, they were subversive of the constitution. It had been arranged that another Member should support Wentworth, but he 'brake his faith in forsaking the matter' and the Speaker declined to put the questions to the House before he had read them. An opportune summons from the Queen saved the situation, and Cope, Wentworth and three other Members were put in the Tower. Attempts by more moderate puritans to secure their release failed, and, so far as we know, they remained in custody until after the end of the session. This was Wentworth's second experience of the Tower.

Wentworth was elected again for Northampton in the next Parliament of 1589. Patriotic feeling after the defeat of the Armada, the revulsion felt by moderate people against the extravagances of the Marprelate tracts, and the explicit injunction of the Lord Chancellor, Hatton, not to meddle with matters of religion, constituted a strong impediment to all radicals. There was an attempt to secure modification of the Whitgiftian regime and it was evidently organized; but there is no evidence that Wentworth took part in it. His mind was by now set on another subject – the succession to the throne. In 1587, after the death of Mary Queen of Scots, he had drafted *A Pithie Exhortation to her Majestie for establishing her successor to the crowne*, a tract published by a friend after his death. Its language was forthright, his admonitions to the Queen at times needlessly and shockingly frank. In a letter to Burghley he later defended the sharpness of his language by quoting 'the spirit of God in Solomon': 'The wounds of a lover are faithful, and the kisses of an enemy are deceitful'.

Wentworth intended to present his tract in the Parliament of 1589 and launch a campaign for settling the succession; but he evidently found the time unpropitious. He tried to persuade Burghley to approach the Queen on the subject, and again in 1590 came to London to renew this quixotic plan. Next year he turned to the Earl of Essex, hoping that he would present his tract to the Queen. But copies of the tract were leaked to the Privy Council, and in August 1591 they committed him close prisoner, this time to the Gatehouse. He was incorrigible. Instead of seeking pardon, he tried once more to get Burghley to approach the Queen, convinced that this statesman believed as he did: which may, indeed, have been true. Wentworth was released from the Gatehouse in November, confined for a time in a private house, and finally set at liberty in February 1592.

Rightly or wrongly, Wentworth thought that he had the sympathy of several Councillors and even seems to have convinced himself that the Queen had seen his tract and approved of it. In the late summer of 1592 he was talking to friends along these lines, and when a new Parliament was summoned he made his plans on the lines learnt from the puritan classical movement. He was returned again for Northampton and came to Westminster with a bill, speeches and other papers that might be needed. A small group of seven Members, mostly young and inexperienced, met at chambers in Lincoln's Inn on 21 Feb. 1593 to listen to his plans. Some of the group were scared by his intemperate language, and when next morning, at their urging, he went to consult James Morice*, an older and wiser Member, he could evoke nothing but scorn. The group was to have met again that afternoon, but news of Wentworth's intentions had reached the Privy Coucil, and authority descended with heavy hand. The examinations of these men by the Council show Wentworth unrepentant and insisting on his rights as a Member of Parliament.

Wentworth was imprisoned in the Tower, where he remained till his death four-and-a-half years later. It is clear from several surviving petitions and letters that he could have secured his freedom within a reasonable time if he had been prepared to acknowledge his fault and give pledge of future silence, without which he remained a potential focus of unrest and disturber of the Queen's delicately poised policy for the peaceful transition of the crown at her death. Instead of repentance, in every petition he reiterated the argument of his *Pithie Exhortation*: to do otherwise, he declared, would be to 'give her Highness a most detestable Judas-kiss'. In 1594, when Doleman's *Conference about the Next Succession to the Crown of England* was published – a disturbing Catholic tract – he was reckless enough, at the instance of some friends, to write an answer, entitled *A Discourse containing the Author's opinion of the true and lawful successor to her Majesty*. It was published after his death along with his *Pithie Exhortation* and, fortunately for Wentworth, seems to have been kept secret from the authorities. Wentworth pronounced in favour of James VI's title to the succession – a judgment he would have strongly opposed earlier, thus, incidentally, vindicating the Queen in her policy of letting time simplify the problem. Doleman had been led to exalt the rights of Parliament. Thus, ironically enough, Wentworth found himself expounding the limitations of those rights.

To keep Wentworth where he could do no harm to the state was the main concern of Queen and Council. As he put it himself: 'The causes of my long imprisonment ... a truth plainly delivered'. His second wife was permitted to live with him in the Tower, and there she died, July 1596, 'my chiefest comfort in this life, even the best wife that ever poor gentleman enjoyed'. There was a proposal to release him on the pledges of sureties in July 1597, when he asked not to be sent home to Lillingstone Lovell, where memories of his wife would be too much for him. On 10 Nov. that year he died. An inquisition post mortem taken at Oxford in 1599 was concerned with his manor of Lillingstone Lovell and houses, woods, etc. in the parish and in Lillingstone Dayrell.[5] Wentworth's children married into puritan families, and one of his sons, Thomas, emulated his father in Parliament in James I's reign.

Sir John Harington described Wentworth as a man 'of a whet and vehement spirit'. The Queen thought he had a good opinion of his own wit. Though in retrospect he must be acclaimed as one of the immortal pioneering spirits in the history of Parliament, whose extravagant notions about the privileges and powers of Parliament became accepted doctrine with the parliamentary opposition of the next generation, he was an embarrassment to his own generation of Members and would not have been accorded their honorific title of 'great parliament man'. In loyalty, respect and love for his Queen and devotion to his country, he was excelled by none.

[1] For Wentworth's life and references, see Neale, 'Peter Wentworth' *EHR*, xxxix. 36–54, 175–205 and Neale, *Parlts.* vols. i, ii. Wentworth's speech of 8 Feb. 1576 and the subsequent committee proceedings have been dealt with at length in Neale, *Parlts.* i. 318–32. The references for Wentworth's activities in the House of Commons are D'Ewes, 175, 179, 206, 236–44, 260, 288, 307; *CJ*, i. 104, 114; Trinity, Dublin, Thos. Cromwell's jnl. ff. 18, 44, 45, 47, 58, 62; I. Temple, Petyt 538/17. [2] *Vis. Essex* (Harl. Soc. xiii), 225, 229; *Vis. Northants.* ed. Metcalfe, 186; PCC 19 Wrastley; C142/258/142. [3] PCC 19 Wrastley; *CPR*, 1553–4, p. 443. [4] *Northampton Recs.* i. 188. [5] C142/258/142.

J.E.N.

WENTWORTH, Walter (c.1569–1627), of ?Devon and Castle Bytham, Lincs.

TAVISTOCK	1601

b. c.1569, 3rd s. of Peter Wentworth* of Lillingstone Lovell, Oxon. by his 2nd w. *educ.* Univ. Coll. Oxf. Oct. 1584, aged 15. *m.* (1) Mary (*d.*1614), da. of Griffith Hampden* of Great Hampden, Bucks., at least 1s. 1da.; (2) the wid. of one Russell, *s.p.*

?Servant of 3rd Earl of Bedford.

Wentworth's father and uncle Paul were leaders of the puritan opposition in Elizabethan Parliaments; his brother Thomas[†] had a long parliamentary career, suffering imprisonment for a speech he made in the Commons in 1614; and the contribution made to the same cause by his relative by marriage John Hampden[†] is justly famous. Wentworth himself was less significant, appearing in the shadow of others – visiting his father in prison, witnessing his uncle's will, acting as executor for his brother Nicholas.

He entered Oxford on the same day as his elder brother Thomas, but after that his career is lost until his appearance in the last Parliament of the reign. He had probably, meanwhile, entered the service of Edward Russell, 3rd Earl of Bedford, who brought him into Parliament for Tavistock. He is not known to have contributed to the work of the House of Commons in 1601. During James I's reign he is found on several occasions exercising Bedford's patronage of livings in the diocese of Exeter. Towards the end of his life Wentworth moved, for reasons unknown, to Castle Bytham in Lincolnshire, near Lord Willoughby's family seat. He died there in 1627 and was buried in the parish church on 13 Oct. The will, dated the 1st of that month, has a religious preamble:

> I bequeath my soul into the hands of my Redeemer, Christ Jesus, assuredly trusting to be saved by his merits who was put to death for my sins and rose again for my sanctification.

He left £800 and some household goods to his daughter Mary, who was still under age. His widow, who may have been a relative of the Earl of Bedford, is not mentioned, but her sons by an earlier marriage were remembered: Edward Russell received £50 and John £10 a year 'as long as he follows the wars and gets no place of preferment'.

He also left £100 to his brother's children, to be supervised by Sir Peter Wentworth[†], of Lillingstone Lovell, head of the main branch of the family, Sir Edward Boys of Hutton-on-the-Hill, Yorkshire, Thomas Gates of the Inner Temple, and William Strickland of Headingley, Yorkshire, who was made a baronet by Charles I. All these were Walter's relatives. Apart from bequests to servants, to the poor of two parishes, and to another nephew and niece, the residue of the property, the extent of which is not known, went to his only son Samuel, the sole executor. Samuel died without issue in 1637 or 1638.

W. L. Rutton, *Wentworth Fam.* 260, 264, 300–1; J. Wentworth, *Wentworth Gen.* i. 30–1; Devon RO, bps. of Exeter mss. 21, ff. 97, 98, 108; *HMC Exeter*, 93–7; SP14/10a/81; PCC 107 Skinner.

M.R.P.

WEST, Robert (c.1574–94), of the Inner Temple, London.

WHITCHURCH	1593

b. c.1574, 1st s. of Thomas West II* by Anne, da. of Sir Francis Knollys*; bro. of Thomas III*. *educ.* Queen's, Oxf. 1588, BA 1591; I. Temple 1592. *m.* prob. by 1592, Elizabeth, da. of Henry Cocke* of Broxbourne, Herts.[1]

West's father had presumably enough influence in Hampshire to prevail upon the dean and chapter of Winchester, owners of the parliamentary patronage at Whitchurch, to have him returned there, but it is also possible that the Earl of Essex may have intervened. Both West's father and his younger brother Thomas were close to Essex, and it is inconceivable that Robert would not have come under his influence. However it came about, West was an MP while still a student at the Inner Temple, where he had been specially admitted at the request of his father-in-law, and granted permission to build a chamber on White Friars Wall. It was from here that his body was carried on 8 June 1594 to be buried in St. Dunstan-in-the-West.[2]

[1] *Al. Ox.* 1601; *Vis. Hants* (Harl. Soc. lxiv), 59. [2] *I.T. Recs.* i. 381; Guildhall Lib. 10342, f. 182. In the index to vol. i of *I.T. Recs.* two references to a Mr. West in 1595 are assigned to this man instead of to William West.

A.M.M.

WEST, Thomas I (*d.*1622), of Testwood in Eling, Hants.

CHICHESTER	1571
MITCHELL	1572
HAMPSHIRE	1589

2nd s. of Sir George West of Warbleton, Suss. by Elizabeth, 1st da. and coh. of Sir Robert Morton of Lechlade, Glos. *m.* a da. and coh. of one Hotofts of Hants, 1da. Kntd. 1591.

J.p. Hants from c.1573, sheriff 1585–6, collector of the loan 1598, dep. lt. 1599; freeman, Southampton 1585.

West – the younger brother of the 1st Baron Delaware – was granted in 1572 some fugitives' estates in Sussex, where he already held land. His main estate lay in Hampshire, where he was a leading figure. He was active against recusants, being among those appointed to arrest certain Hampshire Catholics in 1580, when the Privy Council urged the commissioners

> to use their best endeavours from time to time to bolt out all such matters as they shall think may by any good means be gotten at their hands, and thereof to advise their lordships forthwith.

West was a superintendent of recusants imprisoned in Portchester castle. He was also concerned with the coastal defences at Southsea, Portsmouth, and at the castles of Hurst, Calshot, St. Andrew's, and Netley. Throughout his life West had close associations with Southampton. Created an honorary burgess in 1585, he was frequently appointed by the Privy Council to join the governors of the town in the investigation of disputes.

It is quite uncertain whether it was West or his nephew and namesake who sat for Chichester in 1571. Either would have been recommended by the recently created Baron Delaware, one of the three joint lords lieutenants for Sussex in 1569 and 1570. It is again uncertain whether it was the uncle or the nephew who sat for Mitchell in 1572, but as East Looe was more likely than Mitchell to return government nominees, and the nephew was the heir apparent of a peer, it is convenient to attribute East Looe to the nephew and Mitchell to the uncle. There may even have been a connexion greater than the coincidence of the surname to account for the return of the uncle to Mitchell – his sister married a Thomas Arundell, and the Arundells of Lanherne owned Mitchell. The identification of the uncle as the knight of the shire in 1589 rests upon his being styled in the return as 'esquire' whereas the nephew had been knighted in 1587. No record of any activities by the uncle in the Commons has been found.

West made his will on 28 Dec. 1621, and it was proved on 14 Nov. 1622. He was buried as he had requested in Eling church.

Vis. Hants (Harl. Soc. lxiv), 59; Egerton 2345, f. 21; SP12/104; *APC*, x. 142, 170; xvi. 392; xviii. 65, 73, 75; xx. 30; xxiv. 193, 211–12, 270; xxv. 193–4, 465; xxvii. 9–10, 299–300; xxviii. 559; xxix. 681, 689; *Soton Ass. Bks.* (Soton Rec. Soc.), ii. 89, n. 2; *CSP Dom.* 1547–80, p. 448; 1595–7, pp. 97, 100; 1601–3, p. 270; Harl. 360, f. 65; Lansd. 104, f. 89; PCC 102 Savile.

A.M.M.

WEST, Thomas II (c.1550–1602), of Offington, Suss. and Wherwell, Hants.

?CHICHESTER	1571
?EAST LOOE	1572
YARMOUTH I.o.W.	1586
AYLESBURY	1593

b. c.1550, 1st s. of William West, 1st Baron Delaware by Elizabeth, da. of Thomas Strange of Chesterton, Glos. *m.* 1571, Anne, da. of Sir Francis Knollys* of Rotherfield Greys, Oxon., 6s. inc. Robert* and Thomas III* 6da. Kntd. 1587; *suc.* fa. as 2nd Baron Delaware 1595.

J.p. Hants from 1582, Suss. from 1596; chamberlain of the Exchequer from 1590; warden of the forests of Woolmer and Alice Holt 1595–d.[1]

The Wests had settled in Sussex during the middle ages, and had acquired by the beginning of the sixteenth century, principally through marriage, a considerable amount of property in the county, including two large houses at Offington and Halnaker. In 1540, with the acquisition of the estates formerly belonging to the monastery of Wherwell, the family interests spread into Hampshire. Offington and Wherwell were henceforth their principal residences and no doubt they resided for part of the year in each; West's father, for example, one of the three lords lieutenants for Sussex in 1569 and 1570, died at Wherwell.

West was in the Low Countries with Leicester and was knighted by him at Flushing, and it was probably through the influence of West's father-in-law Knollys with the 2nd Earl of Bedford that West was returned for East Looe in 1572, the assumption being that this was not his uncle and namesake. Which of the two Thomas Wests was the Chichester MP in 1571 is likewise doubtful. In 1586 it was his relation Sir George Carey*, captain of the Isle of Wight, who secured the nephew's return for Yarmouth; and yet another relation provided him with a seat in 1593. Thomas Tasburgh* the third husband of West's sister, Jane, was by a former marriage the stepfather of the owner of the borough of Aylesbury, Sir John Pakington†, and thus had some influence in the choice of Members. In 1593 West served on committees considering the subsidy (26 Feb., 3 Mar.), recusants (28 Feb.), naturalization bills (5, 6 Mar.), the poor law (12 Mar.) and law reform (4 Apr.).[2]

Richard Blount II*, another of West's brothers-in-law, was also a Member of the 1593 Parliament. He was involved in the preliminary stages of Peter Wentworth's attempt to raise the succession question, but on West's advice refused to meddle in it after a first meeting with Wentworth and others. Blount inclined towards puritanism, but West's other brother-in-law, Thomas Tasburgh, with whom he was on close terms, was, with his wife Jane, West's sister, accused of being a Catholic in 1594. While Jane (like her second husband) was a Catholic both before and after Tasburgh's death, Tasburgh's own protestantism is beyond doubt. When West (now Lord Delaware) and his son Thomas III* set out with Essex in 1599 for Ireland, Tasburgh accompanied them. There is no evidence that West himself went as far as Ireland, nor was he involved in the Essex rising. As a peer he took part in the trials of both Essex and Southampton. West's estates were not extensive enough to support the dignity of a peer, and he suffered financially from his heir's extended travels and involvement in the Essex rebellion. He died intestate 25 Mar. 1602.[3]

[1] C142/245/64; *Feet of Fines* (Suss. Rec. Soc. xx), 369–70, 404: *Vis. Hants* (Harl. Soc. lxiv), 59; Gabriel thesis; SP12/145/53; Lansd. 35, f. 135 v; 52, f. 186; Hatfield ms 278; Mousley thesis, 794; PRO Index 6800 (July 1590); *CSP Dom.* 1581–90, p. 689; *HMC Hatfield*, xii. 84. [2] Mousley, 790–4; *CPR*, 1555–7, pp. 538–9; D'Ewes, 474, 477, 481, 486, 489, 499, 517; *HMC Hatfield*, iv. 292, 295. [3] *HMC Hatfield*, v. 61–2, 198; ix. 175; xii. 84; xvi. 379; *CSP Dom.* 1595–7, pp. 16, 326, 386; C142/273/85.

A.M.M.

WEST, Thomas III (1577–1618), of Wherwell, Hants.

LYMINGTON   1597

b. 9 July 1577, 2nd but 1st surv. s. of Thomas West II*, and bro. of Robert* *educ.* Queen's Oxf. 1592; travelled abroad 1596–7. *m.* 25 Nov. 1602, Cecily, da. of Thomas Shirley I* of Wiston, 9ch. prob. 3s. Kntd. 1599; *suc.* fa. as 3rd Baron Delaware 1602.
Gov. and capt. gen. Virginia 1610.

West's family had been friendly with the Shirleys of Wiston for many years. Sir Thomas Shirley, his father-in-law, had been a sponsor at his baptism and it was with one of Shirley's sons that West travelled to Italy after coming down from Oxford. Their expenses exceeded £1,600. West was back in England in time for the 1597 Parliament, a seat being found for him at Lymington, probably through the good offices of Sir Henry Wallop*. There is nothing to suggest that he was other than a passive Member of the House. In 1599 he followed the Earl of Essex to Ireland, distinguishing himself in action near Arklow, and being knighted by Essex at Dublin. He adhered to Essex even during the revolt of 1601 and was imprisoned in the Wood Street counter. He was lucky to be granted the liberty of the prison before the end of February, and to be sent to his father's house a month later on giving a bond of £2,000. On 28 Apr. and again in the following month he appeared before the Privy Council: he was fined 1,000 marks, but escaped indictment.

Within a year of his release he succeeded to his father's title and to estates in Sussex and Hampshire. There was some difficulty about his entering into possession, and in May 1602 Sir Thomas Shirley petitioned Cecil that the Queen would grant West 'those things which his father enjoyed ... for the young gentleman is left in a most broken estate'. In 1604 he complained that

> through the improvidence of his ancestors he [was] left heir to a bare title, spoiled of all means to maintain the honour of the nobility.

In a letter to Cecil he described himself as 'the poorest baron of this kingdom'. So he went to Virginia. As the first governor of the reconstituted colony he arrived at

Jamestown in July 1609, the expedition being just in time to save the colonists from starvation. It was while on another voyage to Virginia that West died at sea 7 June 1618. Administration of his property was granted on 1 July 1620 to his widow. His eldest son, Henry, aged 14, succeeded.

CP; DNB; W. Berry, Co. Genealogies, Hants, 202–3; HMC Hatfield, v. 227; xvi. 71, 343, 379; PRO Index 6800, f. 527; CSP Dom. 1595–7, p. 326; Cal. Carew Pprs. iii. 311; APC, xxxi. 160, 188, 261, 314, 484; Folger mss 2007 i. p. 7; CSP Col. i. 10, 11, 16, 18, 19.

R.C.G.

WESTON, Sir Henry (1534/5–92), of Sutton Place, Surr.

PETERSFIELD	1554 (Apr.), 1554 (Nov.), 1555, 1558, 1559, 1563.
SURREY	1571
PETERSFIELD	1584

b. 1534/5, s. of Sir Francis Weston by Anne, da. and h. of Sir Christopher Pickering of Killington, Westmld.; half-bro. of Henry Knyvet* and Thomas Knyvet I*. m. (1) 1559, Dorothy, da. of Sir Thomas Arundell† of Wardour castle, Wilts. and Shaftesbury, Dorset, 2s. inc. Richard I* 1da.; (2) Elizabeth, da. of Sir Francis Lovell of Harling, Norf., wid. of Henry Repps (d.1566), of West Walton, Norf., s.p. suc. fa. 17 May 1536, gd.-fa. Sir Richard Weston† 7 Aug. 1541. KB Jan. 1559.[1]

J.P. Surr. from c.1559, Norf. 1557, Isle of Ely from c.1579; sheriff, Surr. 1568–9; commr. musters 1574.[2]

In 1541 Henry Weston was left by the will of his grandfather, Sir Richard Weston, the extensive Weston estates, which, his father having been attainted, he could not at that time inherit. In 1549, when he was restored in blood, he was confirmed in the possession of lands at Clandon, Surrey, which had been leased to Sir Richard, and in 1560 he bought the ajoining manor of Merrow from the Crown for £248. He inherited his mother's estates on her death in 1582, including lands in Surrey which had belonged to her second husband, Sir Henry Knyvet, and to her third husband, John Vaughan I*.

Weston was made KB at Elizabeth's coronation, the Queen perhaps showing him favour as much for his father's fatal attentions to her mother, Anne Boleyn, as for his own recent service in the defence of Calais. His marriage to Dorothy Arundell made him kin both to the Queen and to the Howard family. In a grant of January 1560 he is described as 'the Queen's servant' (though what office he held, if any, is unknown), and Elizabeth stayed at Sutton in August of that year. She had barely left when there was a fire at the house, in consequence of which Weston seems to have lived for the next few years at Clandon, where his sons were born.[3]

In 1564 Weston and Sir Edward Bray* were, for some unascertained reason, imprisoned in the Fleet, being released on bail in November 1564, subject to attending in

the Star Chamber every Friday. In the following month Weston was allowed to return home, providing he saw only his tenants on matters affecting their leases. His influence in Surrey was less than his wealth and connexions might suggest, being overshadowed by that of his neighbour, William More I* of Loseley. At the end of 1558 Weston asked More for his support in the next election of knights of the shire, but the county returned to the Parliament of 1559 the two candidates to whom More was already pledged, rejecting not only Weston but also his kinsman, Charles Howard, son of Lord Howard of Effingham. Charles Howard gained the senior seat in the county in 1563, and More took the junior. In 1571, More took the junior seat once again, and Weston was returned with him, the Howard candidate, Charles Howard, perhaps being at sea. This was the only occasion on which Weston enjoyed the prestige of a county seat. There may have been some antipathy between himself and More: in a letter to More in 1591, Lord Howard recommended Weston, 'his good friend and kinsman', for the post of verderer in Windsor forest, but Howard was soon protesting that he had acted in ignorance of More's preference for Lawrence Stoughton*, whose candidature for the verderership he did not wish to oppose. In any event Weston owned the Hampshire borough of Petersfield, which he represented in Parliament on seven occasions. The only reference found to him in the journals of the House of Commons is to his membership of the subsidy committee, 7 Apr. 1571.[4]

Though Weston ought to have taken the oath of supremacy as a Member of Parliament, and as a county official, he was sympathetic to Catholicism, and his name was on a list prepared in the interests of Mary Queen of Scots in 1574. The letter of 1569 in which Thomas Copley* protested his Catholic faith and begged for neighbourly treatment, was addressed to Weston. In 1584 Weston asked to be relieved of the command of 250 Surrey levies because of the pressing business 'in the north', an excuse plausible enough, in view of his mother's recent death. In any case he had married into a Norfolk family and become a justice in the Isle of Ely, where his second wife may have had estates. He contributed £100 to defence against the Armada. In 1591, the very year that Weston again entertained the Queen at Sutton, the Privy Council ordered a search for one Morgan, 'an obstinate and seditious Papist', who was

> thought to be in Sutton, either in or about Sir Henry Weston's house, or at least, if he be not there now, it is known that at times by starts he useth to come thither in secret sort, and perhaps not called by his right name.

This Morgan may have been a relative of William Morgan III*, whom Weston mentions in the will he made in November 1588. He showed particular concern that his surviving son, Richard Weston, and daughter, Jane, should not disturb his bequests to his second wife, which included 1,600 sheep and the contents of the chamber called 'my lord of Leicester's chamber'. He died 11 Apr. 1592, and was buried near his grandfather, Sir Richard Weston, in Holy Trinity church, Guildford.[5]

[1] F. Harrison, *Annals of an Old Manor House*, 87–96; *DNB* (Weston, Sir Francis); *Vis. Surr.* (Harl. Soc. xliii), 8; *Vis. Norf.* (Harl. Soc. xxxii), 191; *Vis. Norf.* (Norf. Arch. Soc.), i. 195–6; C142/235/90; PCC 100 Cope; *EHR*, xxv. 553. [2] *APC*, xii. 68; *Surr. Rec. Soc.* x. 175. [3] PCC 13 Spert; Manning and Bray, *Surr.* i. 134–5; ii. 640; iii. 122, 669; *CPR*, 1558–60, pp. 358–9; 1566–9, p. 268; *Machyn Diary* (Cam. Soc. xlii), 241. [4] *APC*, vii. 166, 171, 172, 189; *HMC 7th Rep.* 615, 618, 649, 661; Neale, *Commons*, 44; *VCH Hants*, iii. 87, 114, 116, 247; D'Ewes, 159. [5] *Cath. Rec. Soc. Misc.* viii. 91; *Surr. Arch. Colls.* xi. 159; xvi. 249; Manning and Bray, iii. 666; *HMC 7th Rep.* 649; PCC 41 Harrington; C142/235/90.

A.H.

WESTON, James (c.1525–89), of Lichfield, Staffs.

LICHFIELD   1584

b. c.1525, 4th s. of John Weston of Weeford by Cecily, da. of Ralph Neville and sis. of Ralph, 4th Earl of Westmorland; bro. of Robert*. *m.* Margery, da. of Humphrey Lowe of Lichfield, 3s. 4da.

Bailiff, Lichfield 1562–3; registrar and later chancellor, diocese of Coventry and Lichfield by 1562.

Weston was a leading Lichfield figure, one of those to whom a warrant was to be addressed in June 1580 for raising musters in the city. Most of his life was spent in the city or in the diocese, whose bishops he served. He was described by Bishop Bentham in 1564 as a man 'godly and zealous'. He made his will 2 May 1589, and it was proved three weeks later. With sorrowful heart for his transgressions he hoped 'in perfect faith' that 'through the death and resurrection of Jesus Christ' he would have remission of his sins, commending his 'soul into His merciful hands'. He ordered estates to be sold to pay his debts and legacies.

Mathews thesis; *Erdeswick's Surv. Staffs.* 164–5; T Harwood, *Church and City of Lichfield*, 421; *APC*, xii. 45; *HMC Hatfield*, i. 309; PCC 48 Leicester; C142/226/169; *Colls. Hist. Staffs.* (Wm. Salt Arch. Soc. xiii), 270, 297.

A.M.M.

WESTON, Richard I (1564–1613), of Sutton Place, Surr.

PETERSFIELD   1593

b. 1564, 2nd but 1st surv. s. of Sir Henry Weston* of Sutton Place by his 1st w. Dorothy, da. of Sir Thomas Arundell†, of Wardour castle, Wilts. and Shaftesbury, Dorset. *m.* 21 May 1583, Jane, da. and h. of John Dister of Bergholt, Essex, 1s. 1da. *suc.* fa. 1592. Kntd. 1596.

J.p. Surr. from c.1592; keeper of red deer in Windsor park 1604.[1]

Weston inherited the borough of Petersfield and from the family's Surrey lands, Sutton, Headley and lands in Ashtead. His father had settled a life interest in the house and park at West Clandon and the manors of Merrow and Bosgrave on his second wife, who, in the event, outlived her stepson. Weston returned himself for Petersfield to the Parliament of 1593, sold it in 1597, and sold Headley in 1601. He was with the Earl of Essex at Cadiz in 1596, and so was probably the Richard Weston who commanded the *Swan* during the voyage,

> who meeting with a Fleming who refused to vale his foretop, with ... good courage and resolution attempted to bring him in.

As he was described by the letter writer John Chamberlain on his death in 1613 as Sir Richard Weston the hunter, it was evidently he who was a keeper of the King's red deer in Windsor park. By this time he was in financial difficulties, receiving two grants of protection against actions for debt in 1604. In the following year Cecil, then Earl of Salisbury, told the Latin secretary, Lake, to borrow £200 for him if the treasurer had no ready money available. By 1609 Weston was in prison, writing desperate letters to Salisbury. He died intestate 7 Sept. 1613. His heir was his son Richard, the author of books on farming.[2]

[1] Manning and Bray, *Surr.* i. 135; C142/255/90; Hatfield ms 278; *CSP Dom.* 1603–10, p. 79. [2] *Vis. Norf.* (Norf. Arch. Soc.), i. 196; PCC 100 Cope, 41 Harrington; C142/255/90; *VCH Hants*, iii. 114; *VCH Surr.* iii. 292; Hakluyt, *Voyages* (1903–5), iv. 243; *Chamberlain Letters* ed. McClure, i. 476; *CSP Dom.* 1603–10, pp. 81, 108, 115, 237, 503, 551, 553; C142/333/20.

A.M.M.

WESTON, Richard II (1577–1635), of Roxwell Park, Essex, and Nayland, Suff.

MALDON	1601
MIDHURST	1604*
ESSEX	1614
ARUNDEL	1621*
BOSSINEY	1624
CALLINGTON	1625
BODMIN	1626

bap. 1 May 1577, o.s. of Jerome Weston of Roxwell by his 1st w. Mary, da. of Anthony Cave of Chicheley, Bucks. *educ.* Trinity Coll. Camb. BA 1594; M. Temple 1594; travelled abroad. *m.* (1) Elizabeth (*d.*1603), da. of William Pinchon of Writtle, Essex, 1s. 2da.; (2) c.1604, Frances (*d.*1645), da. of Nicholas Walgrave of Borley, Essex, 4s. inc. Jerome Weston† 1da. Kntd. 1603; *suc.* fa. 1603; KG 1630; *cr.* Baron Weston 1628, Earl of Portland 1633.

Collector of petty customs in the port of London 1616; jt. comptroller of the navy 1619; PC 1621; ambassador to Brussels 1622; chancellor and under-treasurer of the Exchequer 1621–8, acting treasurer May–Dec. 1624; commr. Virginia 1624; ld. treasurer 1628; jt. ld. lt. of Essex 1629, Hants 1631–3; 1st commr. of Admiralty 1628, 1632; high steward, Exeter 1630; v.-adm. Hants 1631; capt. I.o.W. 1631–3; bencher, M. Temple by 1633.

Weston was born at Chicheley, his mother's house, of a distinguished Catholic family, whose pedigree has been somewhat obscured by an elaborate seventeenth-century fabrication. Through his local family influence he was returned for Maldon in 1601. He became, under the Stuarts, a national figure concerned with problems of diplomacy and finance. Clarendon described him as a 'man of big looks and of a mean and abject spirit'. He received the last rites from a Catholic priest, died on 13 Mar. 1635 and was buried in Winchester cathedral.

CP; *DNB*; Morant, *Essex*, ii. 71; *Vis. Essex* (Harl. Soc. xiii), 125, 318; C142/286/167.

W.J.J.

WESTON, Robert (by 1522–73), of Lichfield, Staffs. later of Dublin, Ireland.

EXETER	1553 (Mar.)
LICHFIELD	1558, 1559

b. by 1522, 3rd s. of John Weston of Weeford, Staffs. by Cecily, da. of Ralph Neville and sis. of Ralph, 4th Earl of Westmorland; bro. of James*. *educ.* All Souls, Oxf., fellow 1536, law dean 1538, BCL 1538, DCL 1556; Coll. Advocates 1556. *m.* Alice, da. of Richard Jenyns or Jennings of Great Barr, Staffs, 1s. 3da.[1]

Principal, Broadgates Hall, Oxf. 1546–9; vicar-gen. to Richard Sampson, bp. of Lichfield, by 1550; chancellor to Miles Coverdale, bp. of Exeter, 1551–3, to Thomas Bentham, bp. of Lichfield, by 1564; dean of arches 1559–67; commr. to enforce Acts of Uniformity and Supremacy in Ireland 1562, 1568, England 1572; master in Chancery by Feb. 1563; ld. chancellor and ld. justice [I] 1567; dean of St. Patrick's, Dublin 1567, Wells 1570.[2]

Weston began as an 'associate' of Dr. John Story* at Oxford, moved to Exeter in the service of a protestant bishop, was active as a civilian during Mary's reign, and died in office under Elizabeth. It was presumably the bishop of Lichfield who arranged for Weston to serve in the first Parliament of the reign. Sir Nicholas Throckmorton* put his name forward as a possible master of requests, though as usual his recommendation was ignored, and when in February 1560 the Pope was thought to be about to summon a general Council, Throckmorton again suggested Weston, one of the 'canonists and civilians' likely to do credit to the English cause. In May 1561 he wrote again, saying that the French wanted Latin and French translations of the Church of England service book, and suggesting that 'Dr. Weston of the Chancery' should be approached as one of two 'aptest learned men to arm themselves to defend modestly and learnedly their doctrine'. In April 1566 Cecil wrote to the lord deputy of Ireland Sir Henry Sidney* telling him of Weston's forthcoming appointment as chancellor, but the office was not granted until 10 June 1567. The next day he was granted the deanery of St. Patrick's *in commendam*. In

August he wrote to the Queen from Ireland asking her to pardon 100 marks she had lent him, pleading the smallness of his fee and the impoverishment of his deanery. That October he announced he was unsuited to be a lord justice, asked for a younger assistant to be sent over, and was given an additional £100 p.a. But he really wanted to be recalled, pleading 'the gout, the stone and the colic'. In 1570 he was given another deanery, but he was still pleading poverty in 1571, and his complaints of financial difficulties lasted until his death in office in May 1573, ending his life 'as never any more godly'. The lord deputy said he could not 'be corrupted with gifts'; Sir John Perrot* told the Privy Council that 'the very Irishry lament the loss of the late lord chancellor'; the bishop of Meath, Weston's son-in-law, said that his arrival in Ireland was one of the greatest blessings that God had ever bestowed on the 'wretched country'; and John Hooker* declared that 'the whole realm found themselves most happy and blessed to have him serve among them'. He was buried in St. Patrick's, where his grand-daughter's husband, the Earl of Cork, later erected a monument to him. A month after his death the lord deputy and Council in Ireland wrote to the Queen and Privy Council on behalf of his widow, who had 'borne herself as commendably as beseemed the wife of so good a man'. Weston's will appointed her sole executrix and residuary legatee of his modest estate. There was little land to descend to his son and heir, John.[3]

[1] *Erdeswick's Surv. Staffs.* 164–5; PCC 25 Peter; *N. and Q.* iv(4), p. 367. [2] J. Vowell *alias* Hooker, *Bps. of Exeter*, 43; *Cam. Misc.* ix(3), pp. 46–7; *CSP For.* 1558–9, p. 287; 1561–2, p. 127; *CSP Ire.* 1509–73, pp. 294, 335–6; *CSP Dom. Add.* 1566–79, p. 525; *CPR*, 1560–3, pp. 621–2; 1566–9, pp. 173, 328; 1569–72, p. 440. [3] *LP Hen. VIII*, xxi(1), p. 473; Rymer, *Foedera*, xv. 547; *CPR*, 1558–60, p. 28; 1560–3, p. 279; 1566–9, pp. 27, 88; *CSP For.* 1559–60, p. 353; 1561–2, p. 127; *EHR*, lxv. 96; *CSP Dom. Add.* 1566–79, p. 525; *CSP Ire.* 1509–73, pp. 294, 335–6, 347, 367, 384, 420, 434, 447, 455, 464, 504, 510–11; SP63/30/78, 32/29; E. P. Shirley, *Letters and Pprs. Church of Ireland*, 200–300; R. Holinshed, *Chronicles*, ed. Hooker, vi. 336; M. Mason, *St. Patrick's*, 166–7, app. liv; PCC 25 Peter.

N.M.F.

WESTON, William (c.1546–94), of Stalbridge Weston, Dorset.

WEYMOUTH AND MELCOMBE REGIS	1593

b. c.1546, 1st s. of Hugh Weston of Stalbridge Weston. *educ.* Christ Church, Oxf. 1564, BA 1568; M. Temple 1575, called. *m.* Catherine, da. of William Willoughby of Silton, Dorset, at least 2s. Kntd. 1583.

Steward, manor of Gillingham, Dorset by 1588; recorder, Weymouth and Melcombe Regis and j.p. Dorset 1592; l.c.j. [I] 1593.

Weston was one of a group of west-country friends who studied together at the Middle Temple. These included William Fleetwood I*, Richard Swayne* (another recorder of Weymouth and Melcombe), Robert Napper* (who afterwards accompanied Weston to Ireland), Thomas Stephens* and Edward Aylworth*. Aylworth mentions meeting Weston at Mr. James Daccombe's house during his tour of the west country with another law student in the summer of 1573. The four friends went hawking and then Weston left to visit a Mr. Doddington in Wiltshire. Weston was recommended for his post of recorder at Weymouth by his predecessor in the office, another Middle Temple friend, Thomas Hannam*. He represented the joint borough of Weymouth and Melcombe Regis in the first Parliament after his appointment, but two months after the dismissal of the Commons he was in Ireland, where, by September 1594, he was fatally sick. He died on the 23rd of that month at Dublin. James Hannam and Henry Willoughby, his 'good and well-beloved friends' were the overseers of the will he had made before leaving England.

Hutchins, *Dorset*, iii. 622, 675; *Vis Wilts.* (Harl. Soc. cv, cvi), 218; J. Ball, *Judges of Ireland*, i. 152; Lansd. 16, f. 84; *Weymouth Charters*, 95, 101; *Vis. Wilts.* (Harl. Soc. cv, cvi), 218; *Som. and Dorset N. and Q.* vi. 216; *CSP Ire.* 1592–6, pp. 91, 143, 274; *HMC Hatfield*, xiii. 508; PCC 62 Scott.

P.W.H.

WHALLEY, Richard (c.1558–c.1632), of Kirton and Screveton, Notts.

| NOTTINGHAMSHIRE | 1597 |
| BOROUGHBRIDGE | 1601 |

b. c.1558, 1st s. of Thomas Whalley of Kirton by Elizabeth, 1st da. and coh. of Henry Hatfield of Willoughby. *educ.* Trinity Coll. Camb. 1577; Barnard's Inn; G. Inn 1583. *m.* (1) Anne, da. of George Horsey* of Digswell, Herts., 1s., (2) Frances, da. of Sir Henry Cromwell *alias* Williams*, 4s. 3da. *suc.* gd.-fa. 1583.
J.p. Notts. from c.1591, sheriff 1595–6, commr. musters Dec. 1596; steward of manor of Clapton, Leics. 1587.

There were several branches of the Whalley family in Nottinghamshire. Whalley's grandfather had been comptroller of the household to the 1st Earl of Rutland, and about 1581 a Thomas Whalley was styled 'servant of the Earl of Rutland' in a summons to the county musters. This was presumably the same man who wrote on business matters to the 3rd Earl in 1573 and the following year, from Belvoir and Screveton, and so, very likely, Whalley's father. There is no evidence that Whalley himself was a servant of the 5th Earl of Rutland, who, however, may have supported him for the county in 1597. He had two brothers-in-law in this Parliament, Oliver and Richard Cromwell. Whalley was appointed to committees on the poor law (22 Nov. 1597) and on mariners (9 Dec. 1597). As knight of the shire he could also have sat on committees concerned with enclosures (5 Nov.), the poor

law (5, 22 Nov.), armour and weapons (8 Nov.), penal laws (8 Nov.), monopolies (10 Nov.) and the subsidy (15 Nov.). There is no evidence as to how he came to be returned for Boroughbridge: perhaps it was through the council in the north.

Whalley was described by a local historian as 'a man of high character and superior attainments as well as of great wealth and influence'. The Nottingham borough accounts record a gift of 10s. which he made to the poor during the plague of 1592. But 'an unfortunate obstinacy of disposition, the result of pride or ... overwhelming self-esteem', led him into lawsuits which necessitated the sale of a number of manors, partly from his ancestral estates and partly bought in his earlier and more prosperous years. He died, 'much reduced in circumstances', about 1632; no will or inquisition post mortem has been found. One of his sons, Thomas, died before him; another, Edward, was a regicide; a third, Henry, become a judge advocate.

C142/203/39, 275/376; *Vis. Notts.* (Harl. Soc. iv), 116–18; *Vis. Notts.* (Thoroton Soc. rec. ser. xiii), 64; *APC*, xxvi. 389; E315/309/63; *HMC Rutland*, i. 98, 102, 124; iv. 307–8, 320, 326, 334; D'Ewes, 552, 553, 555, 557, 561, 570; T. Bailey, *Notts. Annals*, ii. 524, 559, 589; *Nottingham Recs.* iv. 237.

N.M.F.

WHARTON, George (1583–1609), of Wharton Hall, Westmld.

| WESTMORLAND | 1601 |

b. 1583, 1st s. and h. app. of Philip, 3rd Baron Wharton, by Frances, da. of Henry, 2nd Earl of Cumberland. *educ.* G. Inn 1595; Caius, Camb. 1596, MA 1607. *unm.* KB 1603.
Gent. of privy chamber from 1603.

Wharton was born at Brougham castle, the Cliffords' house on the Cumberland-Westmorland border, south of Penrith. His own family resided at Wharton Hall, in the east of the county, and had been prominent in border affairs for several centuries. The combined influence of the two families – his uncle, the 3rd Earl of Cumberland, was hereditary sheriff of Westmorland – assured Wharton's election, even though he was well under age. As a knight of the shire in this Parliament he could have attended (though, given his age and character it is unlikely that he did) committees concerned with the order of business (3 Nov.), monopolies (23 Nov.), strengthening the northern frontier (3 Dec.) and regulating the local government of the northern counties (14 Dec.).[1]

Made KB on the eve of James's coronation and a gentleman of the privy chamber soon afterwards, Wharton's few adult years were passed mainly at court, hunting, playing cards, and indulging in quarrels with other courtiers. His first, when he was 20, concerned 'a mistress, or some such weighty matter'. His next, with the

Earl of Pembroke, arose over a game of cards and might have ended in a duel if the King had not intervened. There was no intervention on 8 Nov. 1609 when, following another dispute at cards, Wharton and Sir James Stewart, master of Blantyre, fought and killed each other in Islington fields and were united in the same grave.[2]

[1] E. R. Wharton, *Whartons of Wharton Hall*, 28 et passim; D'Ewes, 624, 649, 657, 665, 685. [2] *Chamberlain Letters* ed. McClure, i. 181; Nichols, *Progresses Jas. I*, ii. 207–9; *HMC Downshire*, ii. 182, 184; Lysons, *Environs* (1792–6), iii. 154.

B.D.

WHARTON, Michael (*d.*1590), of Beverley Park, Yorks.

BEVERLEY 1586

o.s. of Lawrence Wharton of Beverley Park and Kingston-upon-Hull by Agnes Radley of Yarborough, Lincs. *educ.* St. John's Camb. 1565, BA 1568; G.Inn 1568. *m.* Joan, da. of John Portington of Portington, 4s. 3da. *suc.* fa. 1572.
A 'governor' of Beverley 1588.

Wharton was of sufficient standing to secure his own return at Beverley. He was presumably related to the 2nd Lord Wharton, who was high steward of the manor of Beverley from October 1553 to his death in 1572, but nothing further has been ascertained about him beyond the will he made on 21 Apr. (proved 28 Sept.) 1590. His considerable lands in and around Beverley went to the heir Michael, the widow received a life annuity of £100, the younger sons maintenance while they were at university and the three daughters marriage portions of 500 marks each. He left his best horse to (Sir) Christopher Hilliard I*, and horses to two other Yorkshire gentlemen, Philip Constable and Ralph Hansby, who was to become the father-in-law of Wharton's eldest son. Wharton died 25 Apr. 1590.

C142/224/31, 226/136; Clay, *Dugdale's Yorks. Peds.* i. 136–8; Yorks. Wills. 24/360; *Beverley Recs.* (Yorks. Arch. Soc. rec. ser. lxxxiv), 95.

A.M.M.

WHELER, Humphrey, of Droitwich, Worcs.

DROITWICH 1601

m., at least 1da.[1]

Wheler's antecedents and connexions have not been ascertained. He was presumably connected with the Droitwich family of that name, which twice provided the borough with bailiffs in the Elizabethan period, but he is not mentioned in any of their available wills, and his own has not been found. It remains possible, therefore, that the MP was Humphrey Wheler, heir to the Ludlow family, a lawyer who married the daughter of Francis Brace*.

Humphrey Wheler of Droitwich was on good terms with Robert Cecil*, later Earl of Salisbury, at whose

command in 1605 Francis Tresham paid Wheler the better part of a debt of £1,000. In 1610 Wheler wrote to Salisbury concerning the apprehension of Richard More*. He must have been moderately prosperous as his daughter married William Savage of Broadway, a county gentleman.[2]

[1] *Vis. Worcs.* (Harl. Soc. xc), 87. [2] *Vis. Worcs.* (Harl. Soc. xxvii), 145; (xc), 101; PCC 32 Drake, 78 Kidd, 2 Darcy, 22 Savile, 34 Dixy, 63 Nevell, 37 Pyckering, 21 Bolein, 58 Hayes; *Worcs. Wills and Admons.* (Brit. Rec. Soc. Index Lib. xxxii), 223; *Genealogist*, xxv. 209; *Vis. Salop* (Harl. Soc. xxix), 497; *Vis. London* (Harl. Soc viii), 341, 342; *HMC Hatfield*, iv. 7; xvii passim; *CSP Dom.* 1591–4, pp. 314, 419; 1603–10, p. 609; *Q. Sess. Pprs. 1549–1643* (Worcs. Hist. Soc.) ii. 47; *Habington's Worcs.* (Worcs. Hist. Soc.), i. 471.

S.M.T.

WHELER, Richard (*d.*1614), of Lincoln's Inn and Thames Ditton, Surr.

GREAT BEDWYN 1584, 1586
MARLBOROUGH 1589, 1593, 1597

1st s. of Sir Edmund Wheler, goldsmith (the business later turned into Child's Bank), of London and Riding Court, Datchet, Bucks., by Elizabeth, da. and coh. of Richard Hanbury, goldsmith, of London. *educ.* Trinity Coll. Camb. matric. pens. 1562, scholar 1563, BA 1565–6, MA 1569; L. Inn, sp. adm. 1566, called 1574, bencher 1586. *m.* Elizabeth, da. of Sir William Pitt of Steepleton Iwerne, Dorset and Hartley Waspade, Hants, *s.p.*[1]
Keeper of Black Bk. L. Inn 1594, treasurer 1596–7, Lent reader 1597; common pleader, London 1587–90, common serjeant from 1601, dep. recorder 1608–*d.*[2]

As a young man, Wheler brought marked ability to his studies. He became a scholar of his college, and a valued member of his inn. From June 1578, when he was named one of a committee to repair the old library, until a few months before his death he was actively concerned with the inn's rebuilding schemes, handling large sums for the purpose – in 1612 more than £3,000 – and usually advancing some of it. A plea of illness excused him from being Summer and Autumn reader in 1588, and he was again discharged in 1589; not until 1597 did he fulfil this obligation by being double reader in Lent.[3]

In 1580 Wheler obtained the reversion of the office of common pleader for the city. He was sworn into the office in 1587 and later rose to be deputy recorder, an appointment he was holding at the time of his death. It is a tribute to his ability that the corporation both retained and advanced him in its service, since by the time he first entered it he already had an exacting private client. Wheler was one of the lawyers concerned with the Earl of Hertford's affairs as early as 1582; he may have owed his introduction to this lavish employer of legal aid to Roger Puleston* a cousin by marriage and himself one of the Earl's counsel. It is likely that Wheler specialized in conveyancing, but his services extended to acting as clerk of the kitchen on Hertford's embassy of 1605 to Brussels and to backing the Earl's frequent borrowings; he repeatedly stood surety for loans, in sums ranging from £200 to £1,000.[4]

It was natural that the Earl should wish to utilise a man so familiar with his affairs in the assembly where those affairs threatened to become public; for in 1582 his elder boy came of age and, if acknowledged as legitimate, would stand in succession to the throne. That acknowledgment was still to seek; in 1594 Wheler was to be one of the witnesses heard by the Privy Council in its consideration of Hertford's 'appeals'. If the matter were to be raised in Parliament, the presence of his principal lawyers might help to direct discussion aright and protect the Earl against any hostile construction of his motives. So far as is known, Hertford's case was not ventilated, and there is no evidence that Wheler spoke in the House. He may, however, have been on a committee concerned with cloth, 15 Mar. 1593. He did not sit in 1601 or later, perhaps because his official position made it undesirable for him to be returned outside London.[5]

Wheler's legal prudence prompted him to draw up his own testament, to keep it brief, and to make it nearly 15 years before his death in March 1614. His father was to survive him, and he had only his wife to provide for, which he did by making her sole legatee and executrix. He described himself as of Lincoln's Inn; the knowledge that he had his private residence at Thames Ditton comes from an entry in the probate act book for 1612–14. The preamble of his will shows that he shared Calvinist principles with his noble client: he thanked God the Father, God the Son and God the Holy Ghost, one in Trinity, 'for calling me from my very childhood to the knowledge and love of His holy and sacred word and for keeping me therein ever since to an assured hope of everlasting life through faith in the righteousness of Jesus Christ mine only Saviour ... redeemed by His precious death and passion ... to be reunited unto my body in the glorious day of Resurrection'.[6]

[1] *Vis. London* (Harl. Soc. xv, xvii), 341; *Vis. Worcs.* (Harl. Soc. xxvii), 145–6; Hilton Price, *Handbook of London Bankers*, 30–1; *Vis. Hants* (Harl. Soc. lxiv), 195. [2] *Remembrancia*, 286 and n. 1. [3] *L. Inn Black Bks.* i. 410, 423, 425, 430; ii. 41, 118, 124, 127, 140, 143, 148, 153, 158. [4] *Remembrancia*, 286 and n. 1; *Vis. Worcs.* 145–6; *Wilts. Arch. Mag.* xxxvi. 244; *IPMs Wilts. Chas. I* (Brit. Rec. Soc. Index Lib. xxxiii), 23–6; *HMC Bath*, iv. 200, 202, 213, 417; Devizes Mus. shelf no. 242, envelope formerly belonging to Canon Jackson. [5] *HMC Hatfield*, xiii. 517; D'Ewes, 501. [6] PCC 25 Lawe.

S.T.B.

WHITAKER, Henry (c.1549–89), of Westbury, Wilts., later of Plymouth, Devon.

WESTBURY 1586

b. c.1549, 1st s. of Stephen Whitaker of Westbury by a da. of Henry Nash of Tinhead, Wilts. *m.* Judith, da. of

William Hawkins of Plymouth, 3s. 1da. *suc.* fa. 9 Nov. 1576.[1]

The Whitakers were one of the most important families in the Wiltshire woollen industry. Although they may have been connected with the Lancashire family of the same name, by the middle of the sixteenth century they were firmly established in and around Westbury. In 1569 Stephen Whitaker took a new lease, for his own life and the lives of his sons Henry and Stephen, of a mill in Westbury which had belonged to Lord Mountjoy, and when he died in 1576 he possessed property in Westbury and Warminster. His son and heir Henry was then rising 28.[2]

Henry Whitaker appears to have led the life of a country gentleman, leaving it to his brother Geoffrey to conduct the clothing business, which Geoffrey did to considerable advantage. Henry's preference may have been strengthened by his marriage to the daughter of William, and niece of Sir John Hawkins, which led him to acquire property in Devon and to settle in Plymouth, whither his younger brother Stephen was to follow him. He kept his lands at Westbury and Bratton, however, being assessed at 20s. for them for the subsidies of 1576 and 1586, and being sued in the Exchequer in 1578 by Francis Martyn in respect of those for which he was a tenant of the Queen. It was his local standing which procured his return, with another local man, Robert Baynard, for Westbury in 1586. Their return constituted a rejection of the Crown's request on that occasion for the return of the Members of 1584–5, and in Whitaker's case may be taken to reflect his social ambitions. There is no trace of his participation in the proceedings of the House, and if he hoped to sit again in the next Parliament he was evidently disappointed. His early death in November 1589 cut short his career and ambitions.[3]

He had made his will on 4 Nov., shortly before he died, and in it he expressed the hope of forgiveness of his sins through Christ's passion. To Robert Whitaker of Westbury, probably a cousin, he left his best bow and 12 shafts. He bequeathed a 21-year reversion of his farm in Westbury to his daughter Elizabeth after his brother Geoffrey's interest in it had expired; this reversion his brother-in-law William Bennett of Norton (perhaps a brother of the Westbury MP in 1588–9) and Richard Joy of Plymouth were to sell to her best advantage, his brother Stephen having an option to buy it and, failing that, being given an interest for his own life and two other lives in it. His wife Judith was given a 60-year, or life, interest in his bargain at Woodford and the reversion of his bargain at Tamerton, both in Devon, and if she surrendered her rights in the Westbury property to the heir she was to have one-half of the personal estate; she was also to enjoy the 'government' of the children and property as long as she remained a widow. The younger sons Anthony and Henry were to have £20 a year, and the heir William all lands in Westbury if his mother remarried. The testator's 'cousin' Richard Joy was appointed overseer, and his sons Anthony and Henry the executors. When Henry Whitaker lay on his deathbed his brother Geoffrey promised to leave Henry's three sons something in his will; and this he did, to the tune of £10 a year each, when he came to make it ten years later. The death, in 1598, of William Hawkins also benefited the three: William received £10 and the others £5 under their grandfather's will, while their mother was given his bargain of Hindwell, Devon. These windfalls did something to supplement their shares of their father's estate, which compared unfavourably with the £1,000 in cash which Geoffrey Whitaker left to his own heir.[4]

¹ C142/179/105. ² Ramsay, *Wilts. Woollen Industry*; Hoare, *Wilts. Westbury*, 42–3; Whitaker, *Hist. Whalley*, 352; land rev. bks. 86/97; C142/179/105. ³ PCC 41 Dixy; *Two Taxation Lists* (Wilts. Arch. Soc. rec. br. x), 72; *Wilts. N. and Q.* iii. 244, 307. ⁴ PCC 78, 84 Leicester, 25 Woodhall.

S.T.B.

WHITE, Goddard (1535–89), of Winchelsea, Suss.

WINCHELSEA   1559

> *b.* 1535, 1st. s. of Nicholas White by Joan, da. and coh. of John Chilton of Wye, Kent. *m.* Ursula, da. of Richard Mockett of Challock, Kent, 3s. 3da. *suc.* fa. c.1540.
> Freeman, Winchelsea 1556, mayor 1558–9, 1565–6, jurat by 1562.

It is not clear how White, a native of Winchelsea, made his living. His father left him property at Fairlight (a few miles from Hastings), Peasmarsh, Playden, Pett and Icklesham: he also owned houses in Winchelsea. One of these, with a garden and a rood of land, formed part of a crown grant to the town early in 1586, covering former monastic and chantry estates. Later in the year it was probably this property which became the focal point of several lawsuits brought before the lord warden of the Cinque Ports between White on the one hand and Francis Bolton, recorder of Winchelsea, and James Thecher of Westham on the other: the town authorities were apparently seeking to substantiate their claims to the land. The Privy Council records have two entries about an unspecified case (probably this one) which, owing to White's illness, was still unsettled by the end of March 1586.

As a local official White had a chequered career. He served as a jurat on a number of occasions, the town court book for May 1573 recording that as he was absent his oath was rescinded. He may have been in London: at about this time he and one John Whitefield were convicted in a riot case before the Star Chamber. In October 1581 he was fined for refusing to serve again as a jurat, the fine being halved at the lord warden's request.

Some time after this he was deprived of his freedom of Winchelsea, but was restored on 19 Apr. 1586 'in pursuance of letters from the Privy Council'.

He was evidently on friendly terms with his relative by marriage, John Frank*, for the latter's will asked him and William White to help the widow to carry out her husband's instructions about selling lands. White's own will, made in January and proved in April 1589, appointed another of his wife's relatives, Christopher Mockett, as overseer. He asked to be buried in the north chancel of St. Thomas's church, Winchelsea, bequeathing 10s. a year for four years after his death to the poor of the town. His eldest son, Adam, the sole executor, was to see that White's three daughters received £100 each at marriage or the age of twenty-one; the three sons, including Adam, were to have the same amount. The widow, the residuary legatee, received a £20 annuity, to be reduced to 20 marks if she remarried.

E. Suss. RO, Winchelsea mss; F. W. T. Attree, *Suss. IPMs* (Suss. Rec. Soc. xiv), 239; C142/62/55; E150/1089/1; PCC 41 Leicester, 15 Chayre, 12 Streat; *Vis. Suss.* (Harl. Soc. liii), 130–1; *Suss. Arch. Colls.* xxiii. 35; *Suss. Rec. Soc.* xlvii. 106, 121, 123–4; W. D. Cooper, *Winchelsea*, 109–10; *APC*, xiv. 9–10, 50.

N.M.F.

WHITE, John (*d.*1597), of the Inner Temple, London.

CLITHEROE   1589

> s. of Thomas White† of Downton, Wilts. by Anne, da. of Stephen Kirton, alderman of London. *educ.* I. Temple 1580. *m.* Mary, da. of George Turberville, of Bere Regis, Dorset, *d.s.p. suc.* fa. 1558¹.

White was still occupying chambers in the Inner Temple at the time of his death, but details of any legal career are lacking. He may have been nominated for a parliamentary seat at Clitheroe in 1589 through acting for the duchy of Lancaster in some legal capacity. If he was the John White who wrote from London to a John Reskymer in May 1585, he was financially involved in the Cornish tin mines, in which case his operations were unremunerative, for at his death in 1597 White left legacies amounting to less than £200. The will mentions neither wife nor children, but his mother had remarried into the Dutton family of Sherborne, Gloucestershire, and White clearly took an interest in his half-brothers and sisters, especially 'my brother William Dutton', who received his best gelding, or £10, for acting as executor of the will. The only member of his own family to whom White made a bequest was 'my aunt Oxenbrigge' – his father's sister Barbara – who was to receive £10. His charitable bequests extended to the poor of the London parish of St. Andrew Undershaft, who were to receive £3, and to the poor of South Warnborough, the parish of his birth, who were to benefit from the investment of £30, as well as receiving £3 at the time of his death. White died between 23 July 1597, when the will was made, and 22 Oct., when it was proved.[2]

[1] *Vis. Hants* (Harl. Soc. lxiv), 81–2; PCC 91 Cobham; *VCH Hants*, v. 93. [2] *VCH Hants*, iii. 379; PCC 4 Stonard, 91 Cobham; *CSP Dom. Add. 1580–1625*, p. 143; Hutchins, *Dorset*, i. 139; *Vis. Glos.* (Harl. Soc. xxi), 54.

I.C.

WHITE, Sir John (d.1573), of London and Aldershot, Hants.

LONDON   1563*,[1] 1571

5th s. of Robert White, merchant, of Farnham, Surr. by Katherine, da. of John Wells. *m.* (1) Sybil, da. of Robert White of South Warnborough, Hants by Elizabeth, da. of Sir Thomas Englefield†, 4s. 3da.; (2) 1558, Catherine, da. of John Soday, apothecary to Queen Mary, and wid. of Ralph Greenway, alderman and grocer of London, 2s. 1da. Kntd. 1564.

Treasurer, St. Bartholomew's hospital 1549; alderman and auditor, London 1554, sheriff 1556–7, ld. mayor 1563–4; master, Grocer's Co. 1555–6, 1560–1; president, Bethlehem and Bridewell hospitals 1568–*d.*; surveyor-gen. of London hospitals 1572–3.[2]

The branches of the White family to be found in Hampshire and Surrey in the sixteenth century were descended from Robert White, a merchant and a mayor of the staple of Calais, who died in 1461/2, having purchased lands in Farnham, Surrey and South Warnborough, Hampshire. White himself had a younger brother, John, who became bishop of Lincoln and subsequently bishop of Winchester during Queen Mary's reign. Bishop White, a resolute pursuer of heretics, voted against the supremacy bill in the House of Lords in Elizabeth's first Parliament. After preaching at Mary's funeral he was imprisoned in the Tower. On his release he retired first to his brother's house in London and then to that of Sir Thomas White*, another Catholic sympathizer, at South Warnborough. White himself, however, appears to have had no strong religious convictions, for his name appears on the pardon roll both at the beginning of Mary's reign, and at the beginning of Elizabeth's. A successful merchant in the Spanish trade, his second wife was of Spanish descent, and her brother, Ralph Soday, had acted in Spain as factor for her first husband, Ralph Greenway, another grocer. A Mr. White, merchant of London, was in Spain in August 1562. In 1570 White was among those appointed to hear the complaints of two English merchants engaged in the Spanish trade. Like most merchants, however, he probably did not confine himself to one market or one class of merchandise. In 1554 he and Sir Henry Hoberthorne were granted a licence to export 100,000 pounds of bell-metal. He also lent money to the Crown, and built up a landed estate. As early as 1548 he and a relative, Stephen Kirton, were granted

Farnham chantry for £407 4s., and he subsequently purchased other lands in Devon, Kent, Surrey, Shropshire and Wiltshire.[3]

White was first returned to Parliament in 1566, when he sat instead of London's new recorder Thomas Bromley*. It was traditional for the recorder to occupy one of London's seats in Parliament, and therefore Bromley seems to have been automatically returned after the death of the former recorder, although he was already representing Guildford in this Parliament. The Commons, however, decided that Bromley should remain Member for Guildford and that there should be a by-election in London. On 31 Oct. 1566 White was present at a conference with the Lords on the Queen's marriage and the succession, and in the Parliament of 1571 he served on four committees: concerning the subsidy (7 Apr.), fraudulent conveyances (11 Apr.), Bristol (19 Apr.) and the river Lea (26 May).[4]

On 29 May 1573 White made his will, proved by his son-in-law Lawrence Hussey, and his sons Robert and William, on 20 Aug. After a short conventional preamble he expressed a desire to be buried in the parish church of Aldershot, where a 'discreet learned man' was to preach a sermon, either at the funeral or on a holiday shortly afterwards. According to London custom his goods were to be divided into three parts: a third for his wife, a third for his children as yet unprovided for, and the remainder for personal bequests. 13s. 4d. was bequeathed to each of his maidservants, 40s. to the poor of Aldershot, £4 to the poor of Cornhill ward, and £4 to the prisoners in Ludgate, Newgate, and the two counters. The overseer was a fellow-grocer, William Townerowe. Sir John died on 9 June 1573 in London, and was buried, as he had requested, at Aldershot.[5]

[1] Folger V. b. 298. [2] PCC 10 Ayloffe; *Vis. Hants* (Harl. Soc. lxiv), 12–13, 82; Manning and Bray, *Surr.* iii. 177; *Vis. London* (Harl. Soc. cix, cx), 7; *Machyn Diary* (Cam. Soc. xlii), 172, 405; T. S. Willan, *Muscovy Merchants*, 99–100; A. B. Beaven, *Aldermen*, i. 74, 131, 412; ii. 34. [3] *DNB* (White, John); *Vis. Hants* (Harl. Soc. lxiv), 12–13, 81–2; *CPR*, 1548–9, pp. 64–7; 1550–3, pp. 44, 117; 1553–4, pp. 408, 419; 1558–60, p. 171; 1560–3, p. 300; 1563–6, p. 431; *HMC Hatfield*, i. 83; Willan, 99–100; *CSP For.* 1562, p. 214; *CSP Dom.* 1547–80, p. 111; *APC*, vii. 406–7. [4] Beaven, i. 275; D'Ewes, 126, 159, 160, 162, 189; *CJ*, i. 83, 84, 93. [5] PCC 40 Peter; C142/165/174; Mill Stephenson, *Mon. Brasses*, 157.

A.M.M.

WHITE, Sir Thomas (1507–66), of South Warnborough, Hants.

HAMPSHIRE   1547, 1553 (Oct.), 1554 (Apr.), 1554 (Nov.), 1555, 1558, 1559

b. 25 Mar. 1507, 1st s. of Robert White of South Warnborough by Elizabeth, da. of Sir Thomas Englefield† of Englefield, Berks. *educ.* I. Temple, called. *m.* bef. 1532, Agnes, da. of Robert White of Farnham, Surr., sis. of Sir John White*, 14s. inc. Henry† and

Thomas[†] 6da. *suc.* fa. 2 Mar. 1521. Kntd. 2 Oct. 1553.

Clerk of the Crown and attorney King's (Queen's) bench 1542–Apr. 1559; treasurer, bishopric of Winchester 1538–*d.*; j.p. Hants 1547, q. by 1554, rem. 1558; keeper of Farnham castle, Surr. 1540–*d.*; master of requests 1553–?58; bencher, I. Temple by 1555, gov. 1557.

Despite his extensive estates acquired at the dissolution of the monasteries, White, a Catholic, was put off the commission of the peace at the accession of Elizabeth. Nevertheless elected knight of the shire he opposed the new prayer book, and stated that Sir Ambrose Cave*, chancellor of the duchy of Lancaster, disliked it. Cave's complaint that White had misrepresented him was upheld by the House on 4 Mar. 1559: 'Therefore Mr. White, standing, asked him forgiveness; which Mr. Chancellor did take thankfully'. Next month White lost his Queen's bench appointment.

White's brother-in-law John White, the Marian bishop of Winchester, spent his last months at White's house after being deprived of the see, and there he died in January 1560. White himself died on 2 Nov. 1566. His will, drawn up in 1564, and proved in February 1567, appointed his wife and Lord Chidiock Paulet[†] executors, and affirmed White's belief in 'all that Holy Church, the very espouse of Christ, holdeth and believeth'. He asked for intercession of 'all the holy company of heaven', 'obsequies, alms and other services' were to be done at his burial and month's mind, and a grandson received £50 to pray for his soul. In December 1567 the vicar of Odiham, an ex-Marian priest, was charged with having buried Sir Thomas White 'with tapers and other papistical ceremonies'. The burial took place at South Warnborough, where a memorial was erected by his descendants, inscribed 'Thomas and Agnes die unto God, and say, "We hope to see the goodness of God in the land of life … Lord Jesu, take our souls into Thy mercy" … God save the Queen'. White's son Henry received livery of his lands on 20 June 1567.

C142/37/82, 127, 148; *Vis. Hants* (Harl. Soc. lxiv), 82, *VCH Hants* ii. 487, 515–16; iii. 380; *Vis. Kent* (Harl. Soc. lxxv), 64; *LP Hen. VIII*, xiii(1), p. 243; xviii(2), pp. 56–7; *CPR*, 1547–8, p. 84; 1553–4, p. 19; 1558–60, p. 107; 1566–9, p. 11; *APC*, iv. 324; PRO Eccl. 2/155881, 155883, 155903; *CJ*, i. 56; Strype, *Annals*, i(1), p. 213; PCC 4 Stonard; J. E. Paul, 'Hants Recusants' *Hants Field Club*, xxi(2), p. 65.

N.M.F.

WHITE, William (1549–94), of Christchurch and Moyles Court, Hants.

LYMINGTON   1589

b. Feb. 1549, o.s. of Robert White[†] of Moyles Court by Katherine, da. of George Barret of Belhus, Essex. *m.* c.1570, Margaret, da. of one Hyde of Berks., 1da.[1] *suc.* fa. 1565.

J.p. Hants from c.1582, q. 1587–*d.*; burgess, Lymington 1588.

White was still a minor on his father's death in 1565, the wardship being granted to Edward Barret, probably his mother's brother. In his will Robert White divided his estate into three portions: a third for his wife, a third for his debts and legacies, and the rest for his heir. By 1579 William had sold the manor of Marchwood Romsey to Richard Beconsawe, another Hampshire gentleman. Four years later a settlement was drawn up arranging for the marriage of White's 13 year-old daughter Alice and Beconsawe's son William. White settled the family estates on his daughter, receiving in return £1,250. The estate did not, however, remain unencumbered, and by the time he came to make his will the manor of Pennington, a mile from Lymington, had been mortgaged to his brother-in-law Edward Passion.

White was presumably well enough known in Lymington to secure his own return to the Parliament of 1589. Shortly after his election he was made a burgess 'for the good by him already done, and in consideration of divers other things'. He would no doubt have been acceptable to the steward, Sir Henry Wallop*. White was named to two committees during the Parliament, one on 20 Mar. 1589 on secret outlawries and the other (29 Mar.) asking for a declaration of war against Spain.

White made his will 19 June 1594, proved by his widow and executrix 15 Nov. White died 8 Aug. 1594, the heir being his only child Alice.[2]

[1] *Vis. Essex* (Harl. Soc. xiii), 145–6; C142/142/88. The White pedigree in *Vis. Hants* (Harl. Soc. lxiv), 81–3, is incorrect: Henry White, the grandfather of this Member, was a son of Robert White of Farnham (PCC 10 Ayloffe, 26 Hogen), not of Robert White of South Warnborough. [2] C. St. Barbe, *Lymington Recs.* 31; *CPR*, 1563–6, p. 236; D'Ewes, 449, 454; C142/142/88, 242/94; *VCH Hants*, iv. 554; PCC 75 Dixy.

A.M.M.

WHITNEY, Robert (c.1536–90), of Thetford, Norf.

THETFORD   1584

b. c.1536, s. of Nicholas Whitney of Saffron Walden, Essex. *educ.* ?Peterhouse, Camb. 1549, aged under 14. *m.* Jane, 2s. 1da.

Servant of Philip, 13th Earl of Arundel by 1580.

The Whitneys of Essex may have been related to the Herefordshire and Gloucestershire landed family of the same name, but the pedigrees are confused and inaccurate. Whitney's will refers to two brothers called Thomas, and it may have been one of these who was a gentleman waiter in the household of Lord Surrey (later Earl of Arundel) in October 1571, and was ordered to leave the Duke of Norfolk's house at Kenninghall, to 'remove to Walden and there to remain in ordinary'. Arundel had land in and around Saffron Walden, and it is therefore likely that the Whitneys were a local family in his service there, perhaps even related to him. In 1580 Whitney was commissioned by Arundel, together with William Necton* and Henry Russell, to take an inventory of the goods in Arundel castle, and his name appears again, as 'my servant', in another of the Earl's commissions three years later, this time a much more far-reaching one dealing with the leases of a large number of tenants. Thus, although Whitney resided at Thetford in 1590, and possibly by 1584, he owed his return for the borough to Arundel, who had a residual interest there, his father having owned the manor. Indeed, the town books noted that Whitney was 'commended by our lord the Earl of Arundel'.

Arundel was imprisoned in 1585 and remained in the Tower until he died 11 years later, and there is little more of interest to say about Whitney. In the later 1580s the Thetford town books record two disputes between him and the corporation, one of them about rights of common at Westwick and possibly connected with a sheep pasture which Arundel had conveyed to Whitney on the understanding that the profits should go to Sir Roger Townshend.

A local subsidy list for 1586 indicates that in the last years of his life Whitney was a man of some substance. He died between 17 Aug. 1590, when he made his will, and 17 Dec. the same year, when it was proved by his widow and executrix. He asked to be buried in St. Peter's church, Thetford, to which he left 40s. The will gives no details about his property. The movable goods were divided into halves, one for the executrix, the other for the two sons, Francis and George, and their sister Anne.

Vis. Suff. ed. Metcalfe, 69, 103; *Vis. Herefs.* ed. Weaver, 75–6; *Vis. Glos.* (Harl. Soc. xxi), 267; Add. 19815, ff. 13, 59; PCC 85 Drury, 16 Sainberbe; *Cath. Rec. Soc.* xxi. 18, 381; Lansd. 30, f. 217 seq.; Thetford hall bk. 1568–1622, pp. 113, 142; loose letter in Gawdy letter bk. Norf. Arch. Soc. lib.; bk. of ancient deeds at Thetford, 267.

N.M.F.

WHITNEY, Sir Robert (c.1525–67), of Whitney, Herefs. and Iccombe, Glos.

HEREFORDSHIRE 1559

b. c.1525, 1st s. of Robert Whitney by Margaret, da. of Robert Wye of Lypiatt Park, Stroud, Glos. *m.* (1) Sybil, da. of Sir James Baskerville of Eardisley, Herefs. 3s.; (2) Mary, 2da.; 1s. illegit. *suc.* fa. 1541 Kntd. Oct. 1553.[1]

Escheator, Herefs. Mar.–Dec. 1548, j.p. by 1555; sheriff, Rad. 1558–9; steward of Clifford, Herefs. and Glasbury, Rad., constable of Clifford castle 1561.[2]

The christian name Robert was a favourite one in the Whitney family, and several namesakes were living in Herefordshire and Gloucestershire between 1540 and 1567. The pedigrees in the heralds' visitations are confused and not to be relied upon, but it is reasonable to suppose that the 1559 MP was the Robert, 'son and heir of Robert Whitney of Whitney', whose wardship was granted in

April 1542 to his uncle James Whitney, a gentleman usher of the chamber; livery of his lands was granted in July 1546. The extensive estates, in Herefordshire and Gloucestershire, included the manor of Pencomb, which was held of the Crown by military service and entitled the holder to a pair of gilt spurs from the family of every manor of Hereford who died in office.[3]

The only reference found to Whitney in Parliament is the licence to return home, 13 Apr. 1559, 'because his wife was lately departed'. There was evidently some trouble over his servants while he was at Westminster: on 21 Apr. the Privy Council wrote ordering him to send before 'the lords at the court' any of his attendants who had been in London during the previous month, or had left the city about his affairs or otherwise within the same period. He remained an active local official throughout the changes of the time, the bishops' letters to the Privy Council in 1564 describing him as a justice 'favourable' to the Elizabethan church settlement, yet he was inexplicably omitted from commissions of the peace in 1561 and 1562. He died intestate at Whitney in August 1567; his widow and the heir, Whitney's son James, were granted letters of administration six months later.[4]

[1] C142/64/114, 146/126; *Trans. Rad. Soc.* xxxviii. 51; Duncumb, *Herefs. Hundred of Huntingdon*, 80 et seq.; Add. 19815, ff. 13, 59; *Vis. Herefs.* ed. Weaver, 8; PCC admon. act bk. 1567, f. 128. [2] *CPR*, 1553 and App. Ed. VI, p. 402; 1560–3, p. 537; 1566–9, p. 320; SP11/5/6. [3] Add. 19815, ff. 13, 59; *Vis. Herefs.* ed. Weaver, 75–6; *Vis. Glos.* (Harl. Soc. xxi), 267; *LP Hen. VIII*, xvii. p. 157; xxi(1), p. 684; Harl. 762, f. 11; Duncumb, op. cit. (1804–12), ii(1), p. 151. [4] *CJ*, i. 59; *APC*, vii. 91; *Cam. Misc.* ix(3), p. 13; C142/146/126; PCC admon. act. bk. 1567, f. 128; *CPR*, 1566–9, p. 291.

N.M.F.

WHITTON, Edward (*d.* by 1593), of Limpsfield, Surr.

GATTON 1571

6th s. of Owen Whitton of Woodstock, Oxon, by Joan, da. of Robert Wyghthyll of Woodstock; bro. of George*. *m.* (1) Lucy Penn of Penn, Bucks., 1da.; (2) by 1569, Ursula, da. of Sir John Gainsford of Crowhurst by his 5th w. Audrey or Etheldreda, da. of Sir John Shaw, ld. mayor of London, 1da.

A younger son with small expectations, Whitton sought his fortune in London, and, presumably, was the Edward Whitton 'late of Woodstock' who was imprisoned in the Fleet on account of a £4 debt to a London haberdasher. Perhaps in London, perhaps through a branch of her family seated near Woodstock, he soon afterwards made a fortunate second marriage and thenceforward resided on his wife's property at Limpsfield, where he was assessed for a corselet and a pike at the musters of 1569. Limpsfield is ten miles from Gatton and, in the absence abroad of the Catholic owner of the borough, Thomas Copley*, Whitton presumably had enough local influence to secure his return to the Parliament of 1571. He was dead by 1593.

Vis. Kent (Harl. Soc. lxxv), 117; *Vis. Surr.* (Harl. Soc. xliii), 12, 93; Harl. 1097, ff. 8, 27; W. D. Gainsford, *House of Gainsford*, 44, 54–5, 62; *CPR*, 1563–6, p. 288; *Surr. Musters* (Surr. Rec. Soc. iii), 141; *Surr. Arch. Colls.* ix. 166.

A.H.

WHITTON, George (d. 1606), of Woodstock, Oxon.[1]

NEW WOODSTOCK	1572
BRACKLEY	1584, 1586

2nd s. of Owen Whitton of Woodstock and bro. of Edward*. *m.* 28 Sept. 1556, Dorothy, da. of Thomas Peniston of Dean, *s.p.* 3ch. illegit. *suc.* bro. 1558.

Yeoman of the chamber by 1550; comptroller of works and surveyor of parks within the manor of Woodstock, keeper of hares and woodward in the lordship of Spelsbury, Oxon. 1550–1600; mayor of Woodstock 1571–3, alderman 1573–81, from 1587, j.p. by Feb. 1587.[2]

Whitton succeeded in 1550 to the comptrollership of the royal park at Woodstock, for which he received, in November 1575, a fee of 1*s.* a day for life. The headship of the family and its estates, consisting principally of the manor of Hensington adjoining Woodstock, was reunited with the comptrollership in March 1558, when Whitton's elder brother died only three years after his father. During Princess Elizabeth's detention at Woodstock, Whitton was able to do, as it was stated some 40 years later, 'many services to the Queen, which in her sister's time procured him disgrace and threatened him danger'. He enjoyed no reward when she ascended the throne. Whitton's return to the Parliament of 1572 was due to his official position at Woodstock and to his connexions with the Penistons, behind whom was the leading figure in Elizabethan Oxfordshire, Sir Francis Knollys*, whose mother, Lettice Peniston, was Dorothy Whitton's aunt. Whitton's fellow-burgess in 1572, Martin Johnson*, was probably already a servant of Knollys's daughter, another Lettice. As mayor, Whitton presumably presided at his own and Johnson's return. At about the time of this election Whitton was confronted with a new lieutenant, Sir Henry Lee*, a more distant connexion of the Penistons with whom he was from the first on bad terms. In December 1580 he complained to the Privy Council that Lee had stolen game from the park, kept him out of his Spelsbury stewardship, and annoyed a London alderman, the husband of his sister-in-law Winifred Peniston. Lee was cleared of the allegations and Whitton committed to the Marshalsea. The affair formed the basis of one of the charges against Lee's friend, the Earl of Leicester, in *Leycester's Commonwealth*.[3]

Whitton was released on 20 June 1581 and immediately found himself at odds with the corporation of Woodstock, where he was senior alderman. In July, 20 of his men occupied by force land claimed by the corporation, which Whitton asserted was part of his manor of Hensington.

Two months later, at elections held according to a procedure which he had himself only recently helped to draft, Whitton was disappointed in his hopes of the mayoralty. In July the corporation had asked Lee, as high steward of the borough, to attend the elections 'to make an oration to the commonalty'. In his disappointment Whitton 'broke out into choleric speeches', demanded a return to the letter of the borough charter and set himself up as a champion of a democratic faction against an alleged attempt of the victuallers to dominate the corporation. Deprived of his place as alderman and disfranchised, he continued his campaign against the borough in Star Chamber and the Exchequer, where he was countered with charges of irregularities in his own term as mayor.[4]

Not surprisingly, Whitton looked elsewhere for a seat in the Parliament of 1584. To that and the succeeding Parliament he was returned by the Northamptonshire borough of Brackley. James Croft*, the senior burgess on each occasion, lived near Woodstock on his wife's manor of Weston-on-the-Green, and presumably asked the 4th Earl of Derby, who nominated at Brackley, to have Whitton returned. But why he was so anxious to be of the House has not been ascertained. He made no known contribution to its business. By 1587 relations between Whitton and Woodstock had been repaired and in 1597 Lee wrote to Cecil asking for Whitton to be released from a privy seal under which he was called to contribute £25 towards a forced loan. On 7 July 1600 Whitton, now an old man, surrendered his comptroller's patent granted him 50 years before, on Lee's writing to Cecil asking that Whitton's nephew be given the office. This would please the 'ancient uncle' and be agreeable to the Earl of Essex, who, as the son of Lettice Knollys, was himself related to Whitton.

Whitton died at Hensington 4 Nov. 1606. His heir was his brother's son, but he left Hensington to his own illegitimate son and £500 to his two illegitimate daughters, all by his servant Alice Darling. In his will Whitton asked that a brass be set up at Woodstock to show that his family had been comptrollers of the park since the time of Henry VII.[5]

[1] This biography is based upon E. K. Chambers, *Sir H. Lee.* [2] Harl. 1110, f. 24; Lansd. 104, f. 35; *Vis. Oxon.* (Harl. Soc. v), 153; *Oxon. Rec. Soc.* xvii. 75; C142/303/131; Bodl. Oxon. wills, ser. 1, vol. 6, f. 117; *CPR*, 1549–51, p. 308; Woodstock borough mss, box 81/1, f. 1. [3] *HMC Hatfield*, x. 75; *Vis. Oxon.* (Harl. Soc. v), 153. [4] Woodstock mss 82, ff. 9, 11, 12; A. Ballard, *Chrons. Woodstock.* [5] *HMC Hatfield*, vii. 310; x. 75, 92; *CPR*, 1549–51, p. 308; C142/303/131; PCC 98 Stafford.

A.H.

WHORWOOD (HORWOOD), Thomas (1544–1616), of Compton Hallows, Staffs.

STAFFORDSHIRE	1572

b. 1544, 1st s. of Edward Whorwood of Compton Hallows by Dorothy, da. of Thomas Bassett of Hintes. *m.* bef. 1563, Magdalene, da. of Rowland Edwards of London, at least 1s. 1da. *suc.* to estate of his fa.'s 1st cos. Lady Ambrose Dudley, da. of William Whorwood†. Kntd. by 1614.

J.p. Staffs. c.1573–c.80, from 1596, sheriff 1574–5, 1596–7.

Whorwood had considerable estates in Shropshire, Staffordshire and Worcestershire, one of which, Tyrley, Staffordshire, he acquired from Thomas Throckmorton, a Catholic, who was often imprisoned and his estate under sequestration. Throckmorton had married Whorwood's sister Margaret, and it is possible that Whorwood himself had Catholic sympathies, which might account for his being left off the commission of the peace between 1580 and 1596.[1]

However this may be, Whorwood was elected knight of the shire for the Parliament of 1572, during which his only recorded intervention was on 25 Jan. 1572 in favour of a bill to keep the assizes at Stafford, his name being entered as 'Lockwoode'. As sheriff at the 1597 election Whorwood behaved 'in very indecent and outrageous manner' to obtain the return of his son-in-law John Dudley *alias* Sutton*. When the defeated candidate brought a Star Chamber case against Whorwood, it is significant that one of the charges against him was that he released recusants, men and women, from Stafford gaol to vote at the election.[2]

Whorwood died 2 Nov. 1616.[3]

[1] J. C. Wedgwood, *Staffs. Parl. Hist.* (Wm. Salt Arch. Soc.) i. 371–2; *CPR*, 1553–4, pp. 53, 259, 284; 1554–5, p. 175; C142/354/104; *Erdeswick's Surv. Staffs.* 377 seq.; Harl. 2143, f. 49; *CSP Dom.* 1611–18, pp. 259, 286; *APC*, xi. 350; *Staffs. Q. Sess. Rolls.* (Wm. Salt Arch. Soc.), ii. 72; *Eliz. Chanc. Proc.* (Staffs. Rec. Soc. n.s. ix), 51–2, 67–8, 72–3, 183–4, 187; *Wm. Salt Arch. Soc.* lxviii. p. 98; xvii. 228. [2] Trinity, Dublin, Thos. Cromwell's jnl. f. 66; St. Ch. 5/L11/24, L11/34, M39/40. [3] C142/354/104.

W.J.J.

WIDDRINGTON, Robert (*d.*1598), of Plessey, Northumb., later of Monkwearmouth, co. Dur.

NORTHUMBERLAND 1589, 1593

3rd s. of Sir John Widdrington of Widdrington, Northumb. by his 2nd w. Agnes, da. of Sir Edward Gower of Stittenham, Yorks. *m.* (1) Margaret, da. of Robert, Lord Ogle, 1s. 1da.; (2) Elizabeth, 1 da.

J.p. Northumb. 1594, sheriff 1595–6.

The Widdringtons were an old and substantial Northumberland family. It was probably on his father's death that Widdrington moved with his mother to Plessey, thence, eventually, to Monkwearmouth, which he purchased shortly before his death. His marriage into the Ogle family no doubt enhanced his position in the county he twice represented as knight of the shire. As such, in

1593, he could have attended the subsidy committee (26 Feb.) and a legal committee (9 Mar.). In November 1595 he was pricked sheriff. 'Honest, religious and wise', he promised to assist the warden, Lord Eure, in restoring order in the county. Illness, however, which prevented him travelling to London at the beginning of his term of office, seems to have interfered with his duties, and in 1596 his neglect of the shrievalty was brought to the Council's attention, and he was summoned to attend in January 1597. He died the next year and, in accordance with the wish expressed in his will, was buried at Monkwearmouth. His house and farm there he bequeathed to his wife, Elizabeth, for life. The remaining lands at Plessey, Chibburn, and Shotton, passed to his son John, then aged 20. The third main beneficiary was a daughter, the wife of Robert Dent. She received the lease of coal mines and £100.

Hodgson, *Hist. Northumb.* ii(2), 235–6, 297, 513; *Surtees Soc.* xxxviii. 286; D'Ewes, 474, 496; *Border Pprs.* ii. 94, 232; *HMC Hatfield*, vii. 71–2; *APC*, xxvi. 426, 507; xxvii. 13.

B.D.

WIGHT, Thomas, of Coventry, Warws.

COVENTRY 1572, 1584

Mayor, Coventry 1572.

Returned to Parliament during his mayoralty, Wight was appointed to a committee on hats and caps, 22 Feb. 1581. He does not appear to have received parliamentary wages or expenses until that year when he and his fellow-Member were paid £20. In 1582 he received £50, and in 1585 £15. In November 1600 he claimed that the corporation still owed him money from the time he was a burgess in Parliament, but as he owed them three years' rent the debts on both sides were cancelled by agreement.

Wight had been on the corporation for more than 20 years when, about 1589 he walked out of the council chamber, refused to submit to the mayor and was expelled. Seven or eight years later, 26 Jan. 1597, he was restored on promising 'never to offend in the like' but to 'do his best endeavour whilst he liveth' for the good of the corporation. He died between 1603 and 1611.

Coventry council bk. passim; bk. of payments, passim; B. Poole, *Coventry*, 371; *Coventry Leet Bk.* ii.57.

R.C.G.

WIGHTMAN, William (bef. 1517–80), of Harrow-on-the-Hill, Mdx.

MIDHURST	1547
WILTON	1553 (Mar.)
POOLE	1554 (Apr.)
CARMARTHEN BOROUGHS	1555
LUDGERSHALL	1559
WILTON	1563, 1571

b. bef. 1517, 1st s. of Richard Wightman, capper, of Coventry, Warws. by Elizabeth, da. of Humphrey Purcell of Wolverhampton, Staffs. *m.* Audrey, da. of [?Thomas] Dering, 5da.[1]

Teller of the change of the coinage and mint in the Tower 31 Jan. 1551–*d.*; jt. receiver, South Wales for ct. of augmentations 1552–4; Exchequer receiver, Wales 1554–*d.*; high treasurer of the army July 1557; j.p.q. Mdx. from c.1569, commr. musters.[2]

After serving Sir Anthony Browne† and Thomas Seymour†, Baron Seymour of Sudeley, Wightman found a new master in the 1st Earl of Pembroke. By the accession of Elizabeth, he had held his crown offices for some years, that in the mint being marked, on an establishment list of December 1560, as 'to cease after him'. His annual fee from the mint was £33 6s. 8d. and from the Exchequer £70, with the usual allowance for porterage. In 1566 he was one of those allowed the free import of a tun of wine. During these years Wightman, helped no doubt by his official position, took leases of various properties, chiefly in Wales; he also acquired further property at Harrow. He sat in three Elizabethan Parliaments, on each occasion for a borough within the patronage of the 1st or 2nd Earl of Pembroke. The only thing recorded of him in the House is his appointment on 10 May 1571 to a committee concerned with the preservation of woods. In 1560 Wightman made an excursion into literary patronage by publishing the eighth and ninth books of the *Aeneid* in the verse translation made by his friend Dr. Thomas Phaer*.[3]

Wightman died in January 1580, and was buried in St. Mary's, Harrow, on 1 Feb. By his will, made 20 Dec. 1578, he bequeathed to his wife a close at Coventry and freeholds at Harrow, and to his wife and eldest daughter his leaseholds at Harrow: this daughter, Frances, was newly married to Robert Streynsham, a former secretary of the 1st Earl of Pembroke, and clerk of the peace for Wiltshire in 1580–1. He also made bequests to two sons-in-law, John Pryce and Humphrey Wynces, and to his 'daughter Vaughan' and 'little niece Ann Vaughan'. The list of debts appended to it yields a total of £614, of which £199 was owing to the Queen, to be paid at a rate of £50 a year, and £20 to 'Mr. Moulton the auditor'; on the other side, Robert Streynsham owed Wightman £800, and Thomas and David Williams over £200. Wightman's widow survived him 16 years.[4]

[1] *Mdx. Peds.* 34; *Coventry Leet Bk.* ii. 728, 735–812; Lysons, *Environs*, ii. 571. [2] *CPR*, 1550–3, p. 108; *APC*, iv. 193; *CSP Dom.* 1547–80, p. 152; *HMC Foljambe*, 4–5. [3] Craig, *The Mint*, 121; Lansd. 4, f. 218; 9, f. 30; 47, f. 176 seq.; *CPR*, 1558–60, p. 433; 1566–9, p. 188; *Augmentations*, ed. Lewis and Davies (Univ. Wales Bd. of Celtic Studies, Hist. and Law ser. xiii), 257, 259, 267, 502; *Exchequer*, ed. E. G. Jones (Univ. Wales Bd. of Celtic Studies, Hist. and Law ser. iv), 84, 87, 99, 115, 309; *HMC Hatfield*, ii. 134–5; PCC 9 Arundel; *CJ*, i. 24. [4] *Reg. St. Mary's, Harrow*, i. 101; PCC 9 Arundel, 59 Lewyn; *Mins. Proc. Sess.* (Wilts. Arch. Soc. recs. br. iv), pp.xix–xx.

S.T.B.

WIGMORE, Thomas (*d.* c.1601), of Shobdon, Herefs.

CARMARTHEN BOROUGHS	1572
LEOMINSTER	1584, 1586

1st s. of William Wigmore of Shobdon by Alice, da. of Richard Warnecombe† of Ivington, Lugwardine and Hereford; half-bro. of Edward* and James Croft*. *educ.* ?G. Inn 1559 or ?Peterhouse, Camb. 6 Oct. 1564. *m.* Mary, da. of Ellis Evans of Northop, Flints., 1s. *suc.* fa. 1540.[1]

J.p. Herefs. from c.1579; j.p. Rad. from c.1579, sheriff 1579–80, 1594–5.[2]

As a member of the younger branch of a family which had seen better days, Wigmore, who was still under age when his father died, owed his social position on the Welsh border and his parliamentary seats to his mother's second marriage to Sir James Croft* of Croft Castle, Herefordshire, comptroller of the Household. As high steward of Leominster, Croft had no trouble in returning his stepson as MP for the borough in two consecutive Parliaments together with his own son, Edward. Croft was no doubt also responsible for Wigmore's return at Carmarthen Boroughs, although it is not clear how this was engineered.

Apart from his parliamentary career, however, Wigmore had little to thank Croft for. A request to Sir Henry Sidney*, president of the council in the marches, to make Wigmore clerk of the fines in the marches met with a refusal, and Croft was unable to obtain Wigmore the recordership of Leominster, which went to Sir Thomas Coningsby*, head of the rival family in Herefordshire. One of Wigmore's servants now attacked one of Coningsby's men and a series of violent affrays ensued in Leominster, Kington and Hereford. Twice Coningsby wrote to Wigmore in 'neighbourly and friendly sort', or so he maintained, asking for an end to the violence, but each time the reply came back 'very sharply' and in abusive language. Finally in 1588, one of Wigmore's servants was slain. Wigmore claimed that Coningsby encouraged violence at the Hereford assizes and that 'sixty or more' of Coningsby's men attacked five or six of his in the square. In the upshot the Privy Council ordered that the matter should go before the Star Chamber, and both parties were ordered to give bonds of £500 for their good behaviour. After Sir James Croft's death in 1590 Wigmore fades into obscurity. He died about 1601, when his son Warnecombe Wigmore was involved in a Chancery case over the inheritance of some of his lands. No will has been found.

There was a Thomas Wigmore at Lucton in the middle years of the century, and, until this man's death in about 1579, it is not easy to separate the careers of the two men.[3]

[1] *Vis. Herefs.* ed. Weaver, 21, 71; Ashmolean mss 831; PCC 8 Alenger. [2] Flenley, *Cal. Reg. Council, Marches of Wales*, 37, 192–3, 213; SP12/145. [3] *Augmentations*, ed. Lewis and Davies (Univ. Wales Bd. of Celtic Studies, Hist. and Law ser. xiii), 232, 260–1; C142/186/7; C. Robinson, *Mansions and Manors of Herefs.* 251; P. H. Williams, *Council*

in the Marches of Wales, 236–7; *CSP Dom.* 1547–80, p. 526; Strype, *Annals*, iii(2), 453–5; SP12/167/45, 46; 213/81; 216/45, 46, 47; *APC*, xvi. 248, 258, 275, 291, 339; xvii. 85; xx. 67; St. Ch. 5/A9/36.

M.R.P.

WILBRAHAM, Thomas (1531–73), of London and Edmonton, Mdx.

| LONDON | 1571 |
| WESTMINSTER | 1572* |

b. 30 Jan. 1531, 3rd s. of Ralph Wilbraham ?of Nantwich, Cheshire by his w. Elizabeth Sandford of Lancs. *educ.* Peterhouse, Camb. 1548; L. Inn 1552, called 1558. *m.* Barbara (*d.*1563), da. of Robert Chudleigh or Chadleigh of Mdx., 3s. 5da.

Bencher, L. Inn 1566; Autumn reader 1569 or 1570; gov. 1571–2, treasurer from 1572; j.p. Mdx. from c.1567, Cheshire from 1582; recorder, London Mar. 1569–Apr. 1571; attorney of ct. of wards from 23 Apr. 1571.

Wilbraham had a distinguished career at Lincoln's Inn, and was still under 40 when appointed recorder of London. As such he was elected MP for the city in the Parliament of 1571, just before being made attorney of the court of wards. He was appointed to committees on the bill against papal bulls (23 Apr.), respite of homage (27 Apr., 2 May), the religious bill B (28 Apr.) and the treasons bill (11 May). In the next Parliament, when he sat for Westminster, probably through the influence of Lord Burghley, he took a prominent part in the debates on Mary Queen of Scots. Although not mentioned as one of the members of the committee of 12 May, Wilbraham reported its proceedings to the House on 14 May, first protesting that he was 'very suddenly taken' and would have to trust to his memory as he had made no notes in writing. If this was true he showed considerable ability in marshalling detailed facts into a lengthy and comprehensive speech. He reminded Members that Mary persisted in claiming the English crown; that she had plotted to marry the Duke of Norfolk, in her own words 'by fair means or else by force'; that her connivance in the northern rebellion, and subsequent relations with the defeated rebels, had been proved; and that she had been implicated in the Ridolfi plot. Wilbraham described a letter of Mary's to Norfolk containing 'great discourses in matters of state (more than woman's wit doth commonly reach unto)', and assured the House that 'six thousand Spaniards were in readiness to have come under the commandment of the Duke of Medina'. He reported a second committee on the Queen of Scots on 19 May where two bills had been drawn 'reciting the truth of the facts, the one varying from the other only in the variety of the punishment'. The first bill attainted Mary for treason, the second merely disabled her from the succession. Wilbraham reported Elizabeth's preference for the second bill, and, like others on the committee, he seems to have

supported the Queen's decision, evidently considering that the death sentence would be postponed only for a short time. On 28 May and 6 June he was appointed to further committees concerning Mary, and he advised on the wording of the bill against her on 7 and 9 June. On 19 May 1572 Wilbraham intervened in a debate concerning Arthur Hall*. He argued against the rogues bill on 25 May and was appointed to a committee on the subject on 29 May. He wished that minstrels might be excluded from the vagabonds bill on 30 May. He was also appointed to committees on tellers and receivers (14 May), recoveries (19, 31 May) and Tonbridge school (29 May).

Wilbraham held his office of attorney of the court of wards for only two years, dying on 10 July 1573, in his early forties. Most of the references to him in the State Papers and Privy Council records are concerned with the routine work of his offices. In November 1569 he was appointed a commissioner to put London in readiness to resist the rebels from the north, and he sat on commissions to try those captured during the rising. He was one of a number of commissioners appointed in July 1572 to help the London magistrates keep the peace during the royal progress. A letter from him to Burghley survives, dated 12 July 1571, setting out precedents from the law books for the 'order of battle', or judicial combat.

In his will, proved 20 Aug. 1573, he divided his property between his widow and their five surviving children, who were still young. He asked his brother Richard to bring up two of them, committing two others to the care of his 'dear and loving friend' Thomas Aldersey*. He was evidently in comfortable circumstances, able to leave £500 to the widow, and another £500 to the children, but some of this, he feared, might have to be raised by the sale of lands at Edmonton. There is no indication of any religious views, the only instruction about his burial being that it should be 'with small expense'.

T. A. Walker, *Peterhouse Biog. Reg.* i. 160–1; Burke, *Commoners*, i. 316; G. Ormerod, *Cheshire*, ii. 137; *CPR*, 1566–9, p. 122; D'Ewes, 178, 179, 180, 181, 183, 206, 207, 220; Trinity, Dublin, Thos. Cromwell's jnl. ff. 7–10, 25, 28; *CJ*, i. 85, 86, 87, 89, 94–5, 96, 99, 101, 102; *HMC Lords*, n.s. xi. 8; *HMC 9th Rep.* pt. 1, 443, 533, 543; *APC*, vii. 400, 407; Lansd. 94, f. 43; *CSP Dom.* 1547–80, p. 414; PCC 27 Peter.

N.M.F.

WILCOCKS, Edward (*d.* 1577), of Jacques Court, Lydd and New Romney, Kent.

| NEW ROMNEY | 1572* |

2nd s. of Ralph Wilcocks of Lydd and Wrotham by his w. Sybil; bro. of William*. *educ.* ?Oxf. 1562. *m.* Susan ?Godfrey, 2da.

Jurat, New Romney by 1572, mayor 1574; brodhull rep. 1572.

Wilcocks shared the representation of New Romney in the 1572 Parliament with his elder brother. Neither of them lived long enough to see its conclusion. Their family played a role in Cinque Ports affairs for many years, and the monuments to several of its members are in the churchyard of St. Nicholas, New Romney.

Under his father's will Edward received property in Lydd, Midley and Old Romney. The executors were to sell household and other goods to the value of £800 and use the money to buy more land. The overseer of the will was Sir John Baker† of Sissinghurst. The lands acquired were to be administered for Edward until he attained his majority. Edward acquired the manor of Jacques Court, Lydd, from the Scotts of Scot's Hall at an unknown date, and it is quite likely that this was the property bought with the £800. He died, in all probability, in January 1577, for his will was proved on the 22nd of that month. After providing for his wife, he divided his property between his daughters Joan and Sybil.

PCC 38 More; Hasted, *Kent*, viii. 429; Foster, *Al. Ox.* 1629; Cinque Ports black bk. f. 1; *Vis. Kent* (Harl. Soc. lxxv), 57; *Kentish Wills*, ed. Clarke, 80; L. Duncan, *Monumental Inscriptions at Lydd*, 46.

M.R.P.

WILCOCKS, William (c.1536–bef. 1576), of Lydd, Kent and the Inner Temple, London.

NEW ROMNEY   1572*

b. c.1536, 1st s. of Ralph Wilcocks of Lydd and of West Park, Wrotham, and bro. of Edward*. *educ.* I. Temple 1556, bencher 1573. *m.* Elizabeth, da. and h. of John Edolph of Romney and Brenzett, Kent, 1s. 2da. *suc.* fa. 1555.

Of counsel to New Romney by 1569.

After being a ward of Thomas Argall, an Exchequer official and registrar to the Prerogative Court at Canterbury, Wilcocks obtained possession of his father's manor of West Park, Wrotham, in February 1557. He sold this in 1562. He also inherited an estate at Lydd, land at Snargate, and the manor of Warehorne. An entry in the New Romney archives of about 1569, records that the town was

to provide and buy for Mr. Wilcocks, counsellor, 4 fat wethers ... to be sent to London for him, towards the preparation of his reading dinner, the charge thereof to arise out of the common purse.

In 1572 Wilcocks and his brother were returned to represent the port in Parliament. He died between January 1574 and February 1576, and was buried in the Temple church, London. He had made a fortunate marriage and died a rich man, able to leave his son John, an infant, at least £2,000. The widow married again before the autumn of 1576.

PCC 38 More, 40 Windsor; L. Duncan, *Monumental Inscriptions at Lydd*, 47; *CPR*, 1555–7, pp. 378, 512; 1560–3, p. 402; *HMC 5th Rep.* 553–4; *Kentish Wills*, ed. Clarke, 79, 85–6; *Vis. Kent* (Harl. Soc. xlii), 70; Hasted, *Kent*, viii. 22–3, 429.

M.R.P.

WILD, George (1550–1616), of Heryots, Droitwich, Worcs.

DROITWICH   1584, 1593, 1604

b. 1550, 2nd s. of Thomas Wild† (*d.*1558) of Worcester by his 2nd w. Eleanor, da. and coh. of George Wall of Droitwich. *educ.* I. Temple 1567, called. *m.* bef. 1589, Frances, da. of Sir Edmund Huddleston of Sawston, Cambs., 2s. 2da.

Bencher, I. Temple 1591, auditor 1593, 1601, reader 1595, 1607, treasurer 1603–5; serjeant-at-law 1614; j.p. Worcs. from c.1594; member, council in the marches of Wales from 1602.

Wild was a Worcester lawyer who inherited from his father, a clothier, a small estate in the city. He had also the prospect of inheriting from his mother the manor of Impney, Worcestershire, and salt-pans and other property in Droitwich. He acquired property in Droitwich on his own behalf and obtained the wardship of his cousin John Buck*, which gave him control of further property there. His return to Parliament for the borough to two Elizabethan parliaments left no trace on the surviving records. Though he may have supported his brother Robert's attempt, in 1574, to exempt Worcester from the jurisdiction of the council in the marches, he was chosen to fill a vacancy in 1602 when the council was being replenished after the death of the 2nd Earl of Pembroke. Wild died 27 Mar. 1616, being buried in the church at Droitwich, where an elaborate monument survives. In his nuncupative will, he assured his wife's jointure and the inheritance of his younger son. The rest of his lands he left to his heir with the words, 'let him take all and pay all'. Wild's own religious views are uncertain. His daughter married into the Catholic Blount family.

Vis. Worcs. (Harl. Soc. xxvii), 151; *Habington's Worcs.* (Worcs. Hist. Soc.), i. 482–3; *CPR*, 1563–6, p. 362; P. H. Williams, *Council in the Marches of Wales*, 360–1; C142/356/104; C2.Eliz./W2/14, W12/51; cal. pat. rolls 17–30 Eliz. 23(2), p. 2; *HMC Hatfield*, xi. 225; xviii. 27, 34; PCC 32 Cope; *VCH Worcs.* iii. 62, 81 n, 210, 433; iv. 194, 287.

S.M.T.

WILFORD, Thomas (c.1530–1610), of Heding, Kent.

WINCHELSEA   1571, 1572

b. c.1530, 3rd s. of Thomas Wilford of Hartridge by his 2nd w. Rose, da. of William Whetenhall of Peckham; half-bro. of Sir James Wilford†. *m.* Mary, da. of Edward Poynings, 3s. inc. Sir Thomas† 1da. Kntd. 1588.[1]

Capt. Camber castle 1566; freeman, Winchelsea 1569, jurat by 1571, mayor 1571–2; capt. of horse with Leicester in the Netherlands 1585; gov. Ostend 1586–9, member of council of war Dec. 1587, sergeant major of the field Feb. 1588, marshal of the expedition to France and col. of the Kent regiment 1589; dep. lt. Kent Oct. 1589; superintendent of harbour works at Dover 1591; j.p. Kent from c.1592; marshal of Berwick 1593.

Wilford joined his brother James in exile during the reign of Mary, signing the 'new discipline' at Frankfurt in

1557. In 1565 he was granted the reversion of various offices at Camber, near Winchelsea, his tenure of which accounts for his election to Parliament for the borough. He was named to a committee concerned with navigation 8 May 1571.

England's intervention in the Netherlands proved to be a turning point in Wilford's life and although he settled himself 'in another course', he resolved to spend his life and fortune 'rather than the action should quail'. He saw it as a crusade: the Netherlands were a testing ground provided by God as 'a school to breed up soldiers to defend the freedom of England'. The consequence of failure would be 'the utter subversion of religion throughout all Christendom', and in correspondence with Walsingham he advocated wholehearted intervention. The candour of his reports alarmed Walsingham and Leicester, who feared their effect on the opponents of intervention in the Netherlands. Towards the close of 1587, with rumours of the Armada growing stronger, and suspicions increasing that the States wished to make a separate peace with the Spaniards, he proposed that a force should march through Brabant, Artois, Flanders, and Guelders. But on becoming a member of Lord Willoughby's council of war, he advised withdrawal to Walcheren, garrisons at Campher and Middleburg and the exaction of a levy on all ships at Flushing, Campher and Brill. By April 1588, Wilford was, in Willoughby's opinion, the only person left in the Netherlands capable of giving good advice, and the Queen contemplated sending him to arrange a settlement of all outstanding differences with Barneveldt. He was wounded at the siege of Bergen-op-Zoom in September 1588. Meanwhile, with support for the campaign diminishing, the suggestion was made that Wilford replace Willoughby. This came to nothing, and Wilford was sent to London to argue the case for continuing the campaign. On his return, early in the next year, he had to levy troops to relieve the siege of Ostend. Six years later he was consulted by the Earl of Essex about the number of soldiers needed to garrison Cadiz, and on 5 Apr. 1596 the Earl appointed him colonel of the English force to invade France. He died intestate at Heding 10 Nov. 1610.[2]

[1] *Vis. Kent* (Harl. Soc. xlii), 104; *Arch. Cant.* xx. 6. [2] *APC*, vii. 406; xviii. 415; PCC 3 Sheffelde; *CPR*, 1563–6, pp. 237, 261; E. Suss. RO, Winchelsea mss; *CSP Dom.* 1591–4, pp. 1, 358, 390; 1595–7, pp. 198, 200; Add. 1580–1625, pp. 202–3; *HMC 5th Rep.* 139; *Border Pprs.* 1560–94, pp. 467–9; C. H. Garrett, *Marian Exiles*, 333; *CJ*, i. 88; Motley, *United Netherlands*, i. 375; *CSP For.* 1585–6, pp. 215, 223, 288, 322, 331; 1587, pp. 451, 463; Jan.–June 1588, pp. 94, 102; July–Dec. 1588, pp. 303, 312, 373, 393, 398; 1589, pp. 8, 187; C. Read, *Walsingham*, iii. 357; *Arch. Cant.* xx. 6; C142/319/190.

W.J.J.

WILKES, Thomas (d. 1598), of Downton, Wilts. and later Rickmansworth, Herts.

DOWNTON	1584, 1586
SOUTHAMPTON	1589, 1593

educ. All Souls, Oxf. 1572, BA and fellow 1573. *m.* (1) bef. 1584, Margaret (*d.* bef. 1597), da. of Ambrose Smith, mercer of London; (2) Frances, da. of Sir John Savage of Rocksavage, Cheshire, 1da. Kntd. 1591.

Sec. to ambassador to France 1573; envoy to Elector Palatine 1575; clerk of PC from 1576; ambassador to Spain 1577–8, to Don John of Austria 1578; freeman, Southampton by 1581; envoy to Netherlands 1578, 1582, 1586; English member of Netherlands council of state 1586–7; envoy to Duke of Parma 1588; ambassador to Netherlands 1590–1, to France 1592, 1593, to the Archduke 1594, to France 1598.[1]

J.p. Wilts. 1583–93, Herts. from c. 1593.

The origin of this prominent public servant is obscure. Against Wood's statement that he was a native of Sussex must be set the possibility of connecting him with one or more of the various individuals and families bearing his name, among them the Thomas Wilkes of Wiltshire, whose will provoked litigation earlier in the century and who was perhaps the Member for Chippenham in the Reformation Parliament. Since, however, a cousin in holy orders, William Wilkes, whom Thomas was to present to the living of Downton in 1587, had been born within the diocese of Lichfield and Coventry, it is likely that both men came of Midland stock, perhaps from that family which produced the Thomas Wilkes, merchant of the staple, who in 1554 purchased the manors of Hodnell and Ascott in Warwickshire, and his brother William, who inherited them from him five years later.[2]

It was, according to his own statement, about the year 1564 that Wilkes began the foreign travels which were to last until his admission to All Souls. What the purpose of this journeying was we do not know, but it was no doubt the experience thus gained which led to Wilkes's appointment, in April 1573, as secretary to Dr. Valentine Dale* in his embassy to France. Dale, himself a fellow of the college, may have chosen Wilkes to accompany him: he certainly took steps to allay the resentment of the fellows at this leave of absence granted to a prob́ationer, an irregularity which was smoothed over by Wilkes's promotion to the fellowship later the same year. But Sir Francis Walsingham*, the ambassador whom Dale replaced, may also have had a hand in the matter. Elizabeth had delayed Dale's appointment on the ground of his inexperience, and the summoning of Wilkes from Oxford to accompany him perhaps argues a confidence in the secretary based on personal knowledge. Wilkes corresponded with Walsingham from Paris even before the latter's appointment as secretary of state, and it was to him that Wilkes looked as his patron and friend for the next eighteen years. After a strenuous apprenticeship to diplomacy in France and the Palatinate, Wilkes was appointed a clerk of the Privy Council. The period of home service which he might have expected in the new post was soon interrupted by two further missions abroad, prompted by the threatening situation in the Netherlands. In December 1577 Wilkes was despatched to Spain to exhort Philip II to recall Don John and to come to terms with the rebels. In Spain he was graciously received (although the King considered the prospect of having him burnt), and in the Netherlands he heard the views of the Prince of Orange on their future. Four months later only his absence from court saved him from being again sent to the Netherlands to check the rebels' tendency to 'go French'.[3]

The early 1580s found Wilkes engaged in domestic administration. Under the arrangement of January 1579 for a six-monthly rotation of duties by the clerks of the Council, Wilkes was to be in attendance from May to August and during November and December, but he was still available at other times for a variety of duties, such as examining Campion on the rack in the Tower in October 1581 and taking charge (in April 1584) of the books and papers of Thomas Norton*, who had been associated with him in that brutality. In November 1583 he stayed at Charlecote with Sir Thomas Lucy* while investigating a local conspiracy. It was to be expected that so active a crown official should find a place in the House of Commons. His first opportunity came in 1584, when he was returned for Downton. As lessee of the rectory and parsonage of Downton, which Winchester College had reluctantly granted him at the Queen's persuasion in March 1582, Wilkes had sufficient local standing to account for his return. In 1586 Southampton offered him a seat: he was a freeman of six years' standing, and the town doubtless judged him a serviceable choice. Wilkes, however, withdrew when he thought that he was shortly to be sent abroad, and had himself re-elected for Downton. There is no record of any activity by Wilkes in his first three Parliaments. Perhaps he was abroad for the duration of that of 1586. In 1593 he was named to the subsidy committee, 26 Feb., and to that concerning some lands sold by the Knightley family, 9 Mar.[4]

In 1587 Lord Buckhurst was to describe Wilkes to the Queen as 'so sufficiently practised in the estate of other countries and so well trained in your affairs at home, with such excellent gifts of utterance, memory, wit, courage and knowledge and with so faithful a heart to serve your Majesty'. It was in recognition of these qualities that in July 1586 the Queen chose him 'to carry my mind and see how all goes' with Leicester and the English forces in the Netherlands. Wilkes discharged this task in August, and in October was sent back to The Hague as Killigrew's successor on the council of state. The objects of this mission, to reduce English expenditure, to promote harmony between Leicester and the states-general, and to prepare the way for the Earl's recall, were as delicate in character as they were difficult of attainment. The high

praise and warm welcome which Leicester at first accorded Wilkes soon gave way to suspicion and jealousy, Wilkes being out of sympathy with Leicester's cultivation of popular support against the regents, upon whom alone, he was convinced, the stability of the new state rested: and although he made sincere efforts to bolster the governor-general's dwindling authority he could scarcely have failed to find himself, with Buckhurst and General Sir John Norris*, the object of Leicester's enmity. During the spring of 1587 Wilkes struggled on in the face of the public disaster of the betrayal of Deventer and the private affliction of a painful illness, but by June 1587 he was driven into the dangerous course of returning home without the Queen's permission and without taking leave of Leicester. He was committed for two or three weeks to the Fleet, where he busied himself with his replies to a questionnaire on his conduct, and was then allowed to move to a friend's house in London: it was, in Leicester's view, inadequate punishment.[5]

There could, however, be no question of Wilkes's rehabilitation while Leicester lived. Thus when in January 1588 he came to London and petitioned for pardon Walsingham warned him that the Earl was still pursuing him and advised him to return to his country house. The first sign of Wilkes's restoration came in August 1588 with his despatch on a mission to the Duke of Parma, one which the choice of so determined an opponent of peace was not calculated to render fruitful. He was returned to the 1589 Parliament for Southampton, but it was not until 4 Aug. 1589 that he reappeared, after a lapse of two years, at the Council board. The remaining years of his life saw Wilkes again continuously in service either at home or abroad, his domestic employment including, besides routine business, the oversight of musters and of the accounts of the troops in the Netherlands. It was during these years that he wrote the treatise of a councillor of state in a monarchy or commonwealth which he dedicated to Sir Robert Cecil. Wilkes's outstanding merits as a servant of the Crown were his devotion to duty and his intelligent performance of it: his work bears the stamp of high-class professionalism. In diplomacy he displayed enterprise and persistence, and he commanded readiness of both tongue and pen. His despatches, and broader surveys of foreign affairs, show a firm grasp of complex situations and problems together with sound judgment in their recommendations. Only under extreme stress, such as he knew at The Hague in 1587, did he allow personal considerations to interfere with public duty, and even then he showed restraint. The lightness of his punishment for that episode, and his rapid recovery of trust and favour on Leicester's death, show that his qualities were valued and his integrity accepted.[6]

So unremitting a public career must have left almost as little leisure for private pursuits as the traces of them which have survived. Twice married, he was trying to secure the residue of his first wife's portion of £1,500 in the midst of his troubles in the Netherlands in 1587. It may have been in connexion with this marriage that Wilkes secured the rectory of Downton, which he used for several years as his country house. During his later years, which were punctuated by illness, Wilkes leased a house and land at Rickmansworth, Hertfordshire, where he lived in the intervals of his public employments.[7]

Wilkes's career provides an interesting case-study of the material rewards of Elizabethan governmental service. His only regular remuneration was the £40 a year and diet attached to the clerkship of the Council and the 40s. a day allowed to him on his missions abroad. It is clear that these would not have yielded him affluence, if indeed they came near to meeting his expenses. Like others in his position, Wilkes looked to his employer for additional rewards. His first was the patent as Queen's printer, which he received in the late 1570s and disposed of to Christopher Barker, whose ill-success in enforcing it Wilkes moved Burghley in July 1578 to remedy. In 1581 he incurred the lord treasurer's rebuke at the Council table for pressing a suit on the Queen through Walsingham. His most notorious achievement was his receipt in 1585 of a 21-year monopoly of the supply of white salt through Boston and Lynn (to which in 1586 Hull was added) at a nominal rent. The exercise – and the profits – of this privilege he straightway disposed of to a consortium which, to judge from the prevalence of the surname Smith in its ranks, may have coalesced round his wife's family. But Wilkes continued to bear the formal responsibility, and the defence of the patent against its critics and victims was to cost him unending anxiety. The worst attacks coincided (perhaps significantly) with his own period of disgrace. Of chief interest in the present context – apart from its contribution to his income – is the bearing of the patent on his parliamentary career. His decision to have himself returned for Downton in October 1586, when on the eve of returning to the Netherlands, may have been designed to hamper criticism of it in the Commons. His Membership of the next two Parliaments, if similarly prompted, may indeed have served his turn. He must have been present in 1589 when the matter was raised by the Members from Yorkshire and Norfolk, only to be dropped 'through the persuasion of some honourable and worshipful personage'; while towards the close of the Parliament of 1593 he had to meet the Members from the shires affected before a committee of the Privy Council.[8]

That Wilkes did not wax fat on the proceeds of this or any other reward is clear from his circumstances on the eve of his death. In January 1598, before leaving for France on his last embassy, Wilkes made his will. After stating that he had assured to his wife £1,000 out of his lands and goods, he instructed his executors, who were his wife and one George Bowne, to find from the residue of his goods £300 for his infant daughter, or if that proved

impossible, at least £200. His only other legacy was one of £13 6s. 8d. to his servant George Bayneham, 'who has long served me without recompense'; the residue he left to his wife. Attached to the will is a list of debts totalling a little over £400, a sum which would be increased by at least £50 raised for the journey. The modesty of Wilkes's estate, with the implication that his goods might not even be equal to raising £300 for his daughter, seems a far from handsome return for the 25 years of service which he had rendered to the state.[9]

Within a few weeks of making his will Thomas Wilkes had died in France, towards the end of February 1598, from the effects of an accident he suffered before his departure.[10]

[1] *DNB*; *Reg. Univ. Oxon.* i. ed. Boase, 274; *Vis. Leics.* (Harl. Soc. ii), 66; *Vis. Cheshire* (Harl. Soc. lix), 205-6; PCC 40 Montague, 14 Watson, 36 Lewyn. [2] Wood, *Fasti Ox.* ed. Bliss, i. 188; Req. 10/208; Wood, *Ath. Ox.* ed. Bliss, ii. 46; *VCH Warws.* vi. 115-16; PCC 40 Welles; *CSP Dom. Add.* 1580-1625, p. 165. [3] *CSP Dom.* 1591-4, p. 398; *APC*, viii. 107; *CSP For.* 1572-4, pp. 318, 349, 395-6, 403-4; 1577-8, pp. 613-16; 1578-9, p. 127; *CSP Span.* 1568-79, p. 553. [4] *APC*, xiii. 249; *HMC Hatfield*, xiii. 251; Add. 22924, f. 50; Neale, *Commons*, 178-9; D'Ewes, 474, 495. [5] Cott. Galba C xi. f. 61, quoted Motley, *United Netherlands* (1901), ii. 265 n; *CSP For.* 1586-7, pp. 94, 122, 143, 168-9, 174; 1587, pp. 149, 163, 181-3, 199-200, 211; *Cabala*, pt. 2, p. 77. [6] *CSP For.* 1577-8, pp. 423, 644-50; 1583-4, p. 109; 1587, pp. 162-6, 433-5; 1588 (Jan.-June), pp. 12-13; *APC*, xviii. 11; xx. 152-3; xxi. 49; xxiii. 44; xxviii. 156, 602; *HMC Hatfield*, vii. 368; Stowe 287. [7] *CSP For.* 1587, p. 68; *HMC Hatfield*, v. 507; vi. 61, 461; *APC*, xxvi. 258-9; C3/253/11. [8] *HMC Hatfield*, ii. 187-8; iii. 107; iv. 315-17; *CSP For.* 1587, pp. 66-8; E. Hughes, *Studies in Admin. and Finance*, 45-65. [9] PCC 36 Lewyn; *HMC Hatfield*, viii. 38. [10] Collins, *Sidney State Pprs.* ii. 94; *HMC Hatfield*, viii. 90.

S.T.B.

WILLAN, Leonard (d. 1599), of Hull, Yorks.

KINGSTON-UPON-HULL   1589, 1593, 1597

m., 1s.

Chamberlain, Hull 1574, mayor 1585, sheriff 1581, alderman 1595; commr. gaol delivery 1599.

A Hull merchant, Willan was appointed to the following Commons committees: salted fish (5 Mar. 1593); cloth (15, 23 Mar. 1593, 18 Nov. 1597); weirs (28 Mar. 1593); maimed soldiers (2 Apr. 1593); spinners and weavers (3 Apr. 1593); maltsters (9, 18 Nov. 1597, 12 Jan. 1598); navigation (12 Nov. 1597) and the poor law (22 Nov. 1597). Otherwise there is little to say about him. His corporation sent him to negotiate with York in 1579, he was to search for concealed lands in Hull in 1584, and in 1596 he signed a letter inviting Cecil to become high steward of Hull. Willan was buried there 20 Feb. 1599.

Vis. Yorks. ed. Foster, 637; *Hull Deeds*, ed. Stanewell, 105, 114; *HMC Hatfield*, v. 439-40; T. Gent, *Annales Regioduni Hullini*, 43, 124, 125; D'Ewes, 487, 507, 512, 513, 514, 554, 556, 558, 559, 561, 578; *York Merchant Adventurers*, ed. M. Sellers, 216; *York Wills* (Yorks. Arch. Soc. rec. ser. xxiv), 203.

P.W.H.

WILLIAMS, David (*d.*1613), of Gwernyfed, Aberllyfni, Brec.; Serjeants' Inn, London; and Kingston House, Kingston Bagpuze, Berks.

Yr. s. of Gwilym ap John Vaughan of Blaen newydd, Ystradfellte, Brec. *educ.* M. Temple 1568, called 1576. *m.* (1) bef. 1579, Margery, da. of John Games of Aberbrân, Brec., 9s. inc. Henry* 2da.; (2) 1597, Dorothy, da. and coh. of Oliver Wellesborne of East Hanney, Berks., wid. of John Latton of Kingston Bagpuze, 1s. 1da. Kntd. 23 July 1603.[1]

J.p. Brec. from c.1577, Carm. from c.1584, Rad. from c.1593; bencher, M. Temple 1590, Lent reader 1591, 1594; attorney-gen. for S. Wales in ct. of great sessions 1581–95; recorder, Brecon 1581–1604; serjeant-at-law 1593; puisne justice of King's bench 1604.[2]

Williams came of an obscure brach of an ancient border family. His father was a 'substantial yeoman' and cousin to Sir John Price† of The Priory. His first wife was sister to Thomas Games, who represented the shire in 1572 and the two succeeding Parliaments, and to Walter Games, who had preceded Williams in the representation of the boroughs; her family was also related to that of Vaughan of Porthaml. But it was to the law that he owed his fortune and standing. Until 1593 his practice was confined to South Wales, but his attainment in that year of the rank of serjeant-at-law ('the youngest of all the serjeants', it was said), enabled him to plead at Westminster and occasionally in Star Chamber and Chancery. He was believed to have owed his preferment to Lord Burghley, who 'much respected him for his honesty, learning and modesty'.

Even before this, about a year after he became a bencher of his inn, the Earl of Pembroke as president had put forward his name in a list of lawyers 'not unworthy appointment' to the council in the marches of Wales, and his name appears again among Cecil's memoranda a decade later on a draft list of councillors, most of whom (but not Williams) were appointed soon afterwards. In 1598 Burghley suggested that Williams should be made a baron of the Exchequer, despite the difficulty of his 'small living' occasioned by his growing family; and in the following year the younger Cecil wished him to succeed Thomas Owen* as puisne judge in the court of common pleas. But Williams had only just been appointed by the dean and chapter of Westminster as their legal adviser (also in succession to Owen), and Dean Gabriel Goodman pleaded that he should be 'spared for the present' from these distracting duties, urging especially his 'charge of children'. In the next reign he was appointed a puisne judge and he never got his seat on the council in the marches of Wales.[3]

Meanwhile he had been steadily increasing his fortune not only by legal fees but by extensive grants and purchases of land, some of them used merely for the profits of re-sale. In his own shire he made early purchases in his ancestral parish, and in 1591 (in association with two of his sons) he leased from the Crown the rectory of Devynock. Queen Elizabeth also granted him the manor of Glasbury, and in 1612 he purchased the great tithes of Gwenddwr – a former monastic property now vested in the Crown and worth about £20 a year. His acquisitions extended also into the parishes of Llandyssul in Cardiganshire, Llandinam in Montgomeryshire, Laugharne in Carmarthenshire, and Upton in Pembrokeshire, and included some of the former possessions of Sir John Perrot*.[4]

He brought a Star Chamber action in 1581 against some of his neighbours alleging perjury at the Brecon sessions and in the council in the marches of Wales concerning lands in Glasbury; and another in the same court two years later, against a Glamorganshire man for theft and subornation of the jury. But in 1585 he himself was accused of having 'instigated' John Games (his father-in-law), Robert Knollys* and others to dispute in a disorderly manner the possession of the demesne lands of Dinas, Breconshire, by Blanche Parry, the Queen's 'chief gentlewoman'; and in 1601 of having, as lessee of the lands of Mary Price, a royal ward (and probably a kinswoman of his), encroached on property in Aylton, Herefordshire.[5]

In 1600 he bought from John Gunter the mansion of Gwernyfed, intending it no doubt as a Breconshire seat for his progeny, who indeed remained prominent in county politics and society until the line died out about a century later. He himself was resident mainly in England, either at Serjeants' Inn or at the Berkshire seat he acquired as a result of his second marriage, which also enabled him to build up substantial estates in Berkshire and Oxfordshire.[6]

In politics and religion Williams naturally stood by the established order. He was careful to dissociate himself from, and ready to denounce, the suspicious activities of some of his border neighbours, notably Roger Vaughan* of Clyro, at the time of the Essex revolt; and the only occasion when the firmness of his religious loyalty was called in question was in 1609, when Eure (then president of the council in the marches of Wales) complained of his laxity at Herefordshire assizes in allowing the local recusants (who had shown their strength a few months before the Gunpowder Plot) to take the new oath of abjuration in a modified form. Yet it was he and his colleague Yelverton who in 1606 had condemned Edward Morgan* of Llantarnam to the forfeiture of a big slice of his estates for recusancy.

Williams was active in his first Parliament, sitting on committees concerning common recoveries in Wales (19 Dec. 1584), perfecting of assurances (22 Mar. 1585) and apprentices (23 Mar.). He was also appointed to a conference with the Lords over the fraudulent conveyances dispute on 15 Feb. 1585. No activity has been found in his name for his next two Parliaments. In 1597, however, he was again active, being named to a committee concerning bridges at Newport and Caerleon on 29 Nov., which he reported to the House on 3 Dec., D'Ewes here confusing him with Yelverton. Williams was also appointed to committees concerning armour and weapons (14 Nov.), a bridge over the river Wye (12 Dec.), defence (16 Jan. 1598), three private bills (18, 20, 30 Jan.) and the manor of Paris Garden (19 Jan.). His son Henry, on coming of age, succeeded him in the borough representation.

Williams died 22 Jan. 1613 at Kingston Bagpuze, where his entrails are buried, his body being taken for burial to Brecon priory, where an elaborate effigy marks the spot. In his will, dated 15 Feb. 1612, proved 27 Jan. 1613, he left plate to the lord chancellor and the vicars choral of Hereford, and he assigned the tithes of Gwenddwr to Breconshire charities including roads and bridges, feast-day sermons in the churches of Glasbury, Ystradfellte and Aberllyfni, and bread for the poor in these parishes and in the vicinity of Gwernyfed. A passage from his will reads:

> Whereas it hath been heretofore agreed between my good and kind brother [Peter] Warburton* and myself that the survivor of us twain should have the other's best scarlet robes, now I do will that my said good brother Warburton shall have the choice of either of my scarlet robes and he to take that shall best like him, praying him that as he hath been a good and kind brother unto me, so he will be a good and kind friend to my children.

Williams's Welsh estates were inherited by his son Henry.[7]

[1] DNB; DWB. [2] M.T. Bench Bk. 86; APC, xii. 350 (the Brecon and Beaumaris names have been transposed); Flenley, Cal. Reg. Council, Marches of Wales, 213, 237. [3] DNB; T. Jones, Brec. iii. 81–3; DWB, 786–7; HMC Hatfield, ix. 45; xi. 567; xiii. 457. [4] Exchequer, ed. E. G. Jones (Univ. Wales Bd. of Celtic Studies, Hist. and Law ser. iv), 97–8; Exchequer Jas. I, ed. T. I. J. Jones (same ser. xv), 89, 91, 97, 123, 138, 276–7, 293, 306; CSP Dom. 1591–4, p. 18; Arch. Camb. (ser. 4), i. 306; Rep. on Charities, 1815–39, xlii. 364. [5] Star Chamber, ed. Edwards (Univ. Wales Bd. of Celtic Studies, Hist. and Law ser. i), 27, 28; Exchequer, ed. E. G. Jones, 31; HMC Hatfield, xi. 575. [6] DWB; DNB. [7] HMC Hatfield, xi. 133; xii. 642; R. Mathias, Whitsun Riot; CSP Dom. 1603–10, p. 378; Exchequer Jas. I, ed. T. I. J. Jones, 257; D'Ewes, 343, 349, 371, 372, 556, 565, 571, 581, 582, 583, 584, 591; N. and Q. (ser. 4), ii. 9, 24; DNB; T. Jones, Brec. loc. cit.

A.H.D.

WILLIAMS, Edward (d. c.1594), of the Inner Temple, London.

| CAMELFORD | 1571 |
| ST. IVES | 1572 |

Surveyor of the stable by 1583–d.; surveyor of Tutbury honour, duchy of Lancaster 1583; ?an official in the ct. of wards.

Williams was admitted to the Inner Temple (1567) at the suit of Edward Anderson, later chief justice of common pleas. During the early years of Elizabeth's reign he was busy as a servant of Sir Ambrose Cave*, chancellor of the duchy of Lancaster, whose books, reckonings and inventories he was responsible for keeping. First in association with Brian Cave, and later with Ralph Browne I*, he purchased extensive lands in Leicestershire and Warwickshire, probably as his master's agent. In 1562, presumably on Cave's initiative, he was granted the stewardship of several manors formerly belonging to the monastery of Basingwerk. Sir Ambrose Cave's will, besides thanking Williams for his excellent book-keeping, left him £20, a gelding and a mare. Henceforth Williams seems to have attached himself to the Knollys family, particularly Henry Knollys II* who, in his will, advised his wife to consult Williams, 'whose counsel I have always used in my business'.

Williams's return for two Cornish boroughs is not easy to explain. The 2nd Earl of Bedford received letters from the Privy Council in 1571 and 1572, asking him to supervise the choice of Members in Cornwall, and it is possible that Bedford secured Williams's return at Camelford just as, in the following year, he probably obtained the return of William Knollys* at Tregony. In that year, 1572, Williams sat for St. Ives, jointly owned by the Marquess of Winchester and Lord Mountjoy. Once again it can only be presumed that some member of the Knollys family acted as intermediary.

Few other facts emerge about Williams's career. In 1580 he was paid £10, on Sir Francis Walsingham's warrant, for taking a letter to Sir William Wynter* in Ireland. In 1583 he acted for a few months as steward of Tutbury honour. By this time he was surveyor of the stable, and it was probably in connexion with this post that he received an annuity of £65 out of the Exchequer.

He died between 6 Dec. 1593, when he made his will, and 13 Aug. 1594, the date of probate. He forbade his friends to wear black at the funeral, 'for my desire is that all my friends shall rejoice and give God thanks for my deliverance out of this miserable world'; he trusted that Alexander Nowell, dean of St. Paul's, might preach the sermon. He left £40 to a cousin, 'if she be not a recusant at the time of my death, or if she do reconcile herself to the Church of England and come to hear divine service according to the Queen's Majesty's proceeding'. Small legacies were made to 'my very good friend' Sir Francis Knollys*, Henry Knollys's widow Margaret, and to Elizabeth and Lettice Knollys. Other bequests included a ring to his 'loving friend' Marmaduke Darrell, and plate to his 'old friend', George Mainwaring*. Part of his wardrobe was left to his 'loving cousin' Anthony Martin, sewer of the chamber and keeper of the Queen's library. Charitable bequests were made to parishes in London and Flintshire, to the prisoners of Ludgate and Newgate, and to the poor of the hospital of the Savoy. As executor he appointed his nephew Thomas Hughes. The overseers were his 'dear and best kinsman' Sir Randall Brereton, Anthony Martin and Richard Johns.

I.T. Recs. i. 241, 375; Somerville, *Duchy*, i. 545; SP12/20/28; PCC 60 Dixy, 9 Daper, 20 Rowe; *CPR*, 1560–3, pp. 43, 290; E315/309, 351/542, f. 10; Lansd. 83, f. 215.

W.J.J.

WILLIAMS, Henry (c.1579–1636), of Gwernyfed, Aberllyfni, Brec.

| BRECON BOROUGHS | 1601, 1604 |
| BRECONSHIRE | 1621, 1624 |

b. c.1579, 1st s. of David Williams* of Gwernyfed by his 1st w. *educ.* ?Shrewsbury 1589; St. John's, Oxf. 16 Apr. 1594, aged 15; M. Temple 1594. *m.* Elinor, da. of Eustace Whitney of Whitney, Herefs., 7s. inc. Henry† 4da. Kntd. 23 July 1603; *suc.* fa. 1613.

Williams inherited the Breconshire estates of his father the judge, while a younger brother came into the English possessions. He had not long come of age when he was returned to his first Parliament, no doubt because his father was recorder of Brecon. He died in 1636. He is sometimes confused with his son and namesake who succeeded to the county representation in 1628 and became a baronet in 1644.

T. Jones, *Brec.* iii. 81–3, 92; *Arch. Camb.* (ser. 4), i. 307–8.

A.H.D.

WILLIAMS, Reginald (d.1612), of Plas y Court, Willaston (now Wollaston), Salop.

| PRESTON | 1571 |
| MONTGOMERYSHIRE | 1593 |

1st s. of Thomas Williams of Willaston by Blanche, da. of Robert Powell. *educ.* I. Temple 1561, called 1571. *m.* (1) Margaret, da. of Gerard Gore of Yorks. and London, 7s. 2da.; (2) Bridget, da. of James Price of Mynachdy, wid. of Walter Baskerville, *s.p.*; (3) Jane, da. of Humphrey Coningsby I* of Hampton Court, Herefs., wid. of William Broughton of Lawford, Warws., *s.p.* Escheator, Salop Feb. 1573–Jan. 1574; jt. prothonotary Flints. and Denb. 1579; j.p. Mont. by 1585, sheriff 1593–4; j.p. Salop 1596.

Williams had no known connexion with the duchy of Lancaster or with its chancellor Sir Ralph Sadler*, and his return for Preston was probably obtained through the patronage of the 3rd Earl of Derby, who was intervening there at that time. Similarly Williams's employment in Flintshire may have been gained through the patronage of the 4th Earl of Derby. We are on surer ground when we come to the 1593 Montgomeryshire return. Both Williams's father and grandfather had been sheriffs of the county, and his seat at Willaston was on the Shropshire border. As a knight of the shire in 1593 he could have attended committees on the subsidy (26 Feb.) and a legal matter (9 Mar.). Williams retained a chamber at the Inner Temple until at least 1599. Some light on his professional

integrity is provided by an incident concerning a relative by marriage, Edward Hussey, who trusted him as his 'kinsman and especial friend'. Hussey's manor of Nethergorth, Shropshire, was at a distance from his other property, so Williams, who lived nearer, agreed to become Hussey's 'tenant', in order that his 'skill and experience in the law' could protect the landlord's rights. Instead, if Hussey is to be believed, Williams drew up the lease in such a form that he became virtual owner. When sued in Chancery for rent arrears, Williams had the case transferred to the common law courts, where he could exert more influence. He died intestate 5 Jan. 1612.

Wards 7/45/1661; *Vis. Salop* (Harl. Soc. xxix), 507; Dwnn, *Vis. Wales*, i. 330; *Mont. Colls.* iii. 378; v. 438–9; D'Ewes, 474, 496; *APC*, xi. 194; xxiii. 261; C2/225/91; PCC admon. act bk. 1611–14, f. 51.

N.M.F.

WILLIAMS, Richard (d.1601), of Blackfriars, London, and Cobham, Kent.

| NEW ROMNEY | 1584 |

Estate manager to the lords Cobham by 1584.

The date of Williams's entry into the service of the Cobham family has not been traced, though it was presumably prior to 1584 when he owed his parliamentary seat to Lord Cobham's nomination. By the late 1590s he exercised overall control of all the family's estates, and most of the surviving references to him relate to this work.

The period from about 1582 until the early years of James I's reign was important in the family's history, for, as a result of the favour shown by Queen Elizabeth to the 10th Lord Cobham, they were able to rebuild Cobham Hall. Williams supervised much of this work, paying the workmen and keeping Cobham informed of progress when he was away from home. Letters exchanged between Williams and his master reveal his activity in connexion with building accounts and household expenses for all Cobham's properties; revenues and timber sales; terms and conditions for tenant farmers; reclamation of marshlands; harvests and re-afforestation; supervision of bailiffs, and dealings with dishonest tenants. The 11th Lord Cobham's sister, who was the widow of Sir Thomas Sondes of Throwley, also seems to have left the management of her estates to Williams and this involved him in disputes with (Sir) Michael Sondes*, who was slow to pay the rent he owed his sister-in-law. Williams urged caution on Lord Cobham regarding the servants' wages, but his own were a different matter:

> My half year's annuity, due last Michaelmas, is not paid me, and if you will give order for its payment, and have consideration of the sum wherewith I over-charged myself, I shall be encouraged to continue to deserve your favour.

His business tactics appear in a letter to Cobham in 1601:

I advise you to sell your woods, but to send down a surveyor, and seem unwilling to sell, so as to gain a larger price ... The trees are eighteen years' growth, but it should not be known that they are under twenty, or people will fear to buy, because the parson can claim tithes of trees under twenty years.[1]

Williams was returned to Parliament for New Romney in 1584 as the nominee of Lord Cobham, who, as lord warden of the Cinque Ports, was asked by the Privy Council to see that suitable Members were chosen. He may have been the Mr. Williams who sat on the committee for a bill concerning apprentices and spoke against a wardship bill. Though Romney, like many other boroughs, usually declined to pay 'foreigners' who represented it in Parliament, Williams pressed hard for his money. Indeed he was still demanding payment when the next Parliament was summoned, and this may have contributed to Romney's refusal to re-elect him, despite pressure from the Privy Council and the lord warden.[2]

That Williams appreciated the patronage of the Cobham family – as well he might, considering the wealth he amassed as estate manager – is clearly demonstrated in his will. He begged Henry, Lord Cobham, that he might be buried

at the feet of the right honourable William, late Lord Cobham, deceased, sometime my most honourable lord and master, in the church or chancel of Cobham in Kent, there to remain in Christian burial till the resurrection of all flesh which I believe and expect.

He had leased lands and tenements in Bedfordshire, Hertfordshire and Kent from Lord Cobham and now returned them to him absolutely, save for a request that the tenants be protected. He estimated that the lands combined yielded £95 a year and could be sold for £600. He may have been the Richard Williams who leased Potton rectory manor, Bedford, from the Queen between 1579 and 1591.

His will, made 27 May 1601 and proved only two days later, provides what clues there are to his family background. It suggests that he came originally from Hereford: he referred to his 'loving cousin' James Smith, mayor of Hereford, and left £1,000 to the corporation to erect a hospital in the city for six poor people. The building, to be called the Williams hospital, was to be governed by Smith and two named aldermen of Hereford and, after their deaths, by the corporation. They were to draw up the rules for the foundation and buy land worth at least £50 a year. The necessary lands were soon purchased and the hospital constructed, but it fell into decay during the civil war and had to be rebuilt in 1675. Several men in Herefordshire and the adjoining Welsh counties were beneficiaries under the will, including Herbert Croft, one of the overseers, who may be the MP for the county, and Roland Vaughan of Breconshire. No immediate family is mentioned in the will. The principal benificiary was Robert Masters, who received £1,000 on condition that he paid his sister Maud a life annuity of £20, and also the residue of the testator's lands and revenues after other bequests had been satisfied. Masters, who is called 'my brother', was the executor. The list of legatees is wide: the wife of Robert Knollys, probably of the prominent Oxfordshire family, who was forgiven a debt of £80, which was to be used to buy 'a basin and ewer of silver, with my arms upon it, to be given as a remembrance of my goodwill to that house'; Robert Johnson, a Buckingham man, who was given £50 to act as overseer and whose wife received £20 to buy a gold chain 'to wear for my sake'; and Henry Best, a Londoner, who also received £50 to serve as overseer. A codicil included legacies to two daughters of Francis Knollys, the mayor of Canterbury, the provost of Queen's College, Oxford, towards the education of poor scholars, two London preachers, the poor of the parish of St. Anne, Blackfriars, in which his London house was situated, and two servants who received all his books and apparel. Nor did he forget Mrs. Frances Dudley, 'who now keepeth me in this sickness', Lord Cobham's maid, or his own laundress. The legacies total nearly £3,500.[3]

[1] *CSP Dom.* 1595-7, pp. 255, 358; 1598-1601, pp. 170, 391, 431-3, 490, 511-15, 531; 1601-3, pp. 46, 121, 139, 274-5; C66/283/62; *Arch. Cant.* xi. p. lxv. seq. [2] New Romney assembly bk. 1577-1622, ff. 25, 30; borough recs. bdle. 115; D'Ewes, 372; Lansd. 43; anon. jnl. f. 166. [3] PCC 33 Woodhall; J. Duncumb, *Herefs.* i. 429; *VCH Beds.* ii. 239.

M.R.P.

WILLIAMS, Thomas (c.1514-66), of Stowford, Devon.

BODMIN	1555
SALTASH	1558
TAVISTOCK	1559
EXETER	1563*

b. c.1514, 1st s. of Adam Williams of Stowford by Alice, da. of Thomas Prideaux of Ashburton. *educ.* I. Temple 1539, called. *m.* Emmeline, da. and coh. of William Cruwys of Chudleigh, at least 2s. 3da.

Attorney, Plymouth from 1546; Lent reader, I. Temple 1558, 1561; feodary, Devon and Exeter in 1559; j.p.q. Devon from c.1559; commr. subsidy 1565.

Speaker of House of Commons 1563.

Williams was a sufficiently committed protestant to oppose a government bill in the Parliament of 1555, to which he was returned through the influence of Sir Richard Edgecombe†. Edgecombe brought him in again in 1558 and 1559. By 1563 Williams had a number of friends at court, including Sir Nicholas Bacon†, the lord keeper, and Thomas Bromley*, the future chancellor, as well as wide connexions in the west country. He submitted a report on the re-coinage of 1560 and was paid a retainer as counsel for both Plymouth and Exeter. He was returned to

Parliament for Exeter in 1563 after the city had twice rejected requests for a nomination by the 2nd Earl of Bedford. In the event the city had made a good choice, for on 12 Jan. 1563 Williams was chosen Speaker.[1]

Described as 'grave, learned and wise' and 'a man excellently learned in the laws of this realm', Williams described himself in his disabling speech

> as one among the Romans, chosen from the plough to a place of estimation, and after went to the plough again; even so, I, a countryman, fit for the same and not for this place ...

For his 'oration' when he presented himself to the Queen on 15 Jan. 1563, he chose as his themes time past, time present and time to come. Time past concerned the benefits the Queen had bestowed upon her people, 'for which your humble subjects most heartily give thanks to God and you by the mouth of me their appointed Speaker'. In the present there were 'three notable monsters: necessity, ignorance and error'. 'Necessity' he said, 'is grown amongst ourselves so that no man is contented with his degree, though he hath never so much'. There was a dearth of schools: 'I dare say a hundred schools want in England ... and if in every school there had been but a hundred scholars, yet that had been ten thousand'. Want of schools, scholars and good schoolmasters brought in its wake the second monster, ignorance. The third was error, 'a serpent with many heads'. 'Pelagians, libertines, papists' left 'God's commandment to follow their own traditions, affections and minds ... Having God's word and His name ever in our mouths, yet we live as infidels'. In time to come the Queen was asked to build a fort for the safety of the realm

> set upon firm ground and steadfast, having two gates, one commonly open, the other as a postern, with two watchmen at either of them, one governor, one lieutenant, four soldiers, and no good thing there wanting. The same to be named the fear of God; the governor thereof to be God, your Majesty the lieutenant, the stones the hearts of faithful people; the two watchmen at the open gate to be called knowledge and virtue, the other two at the postern called mercy and truth; all being spiritual ministers. This fort is invincible if every man will fear God.

Williams was in charge of drawing up the articles for the succession committee, 19 Jan. 1563, and on 28 Jan. in the gallery at Whitehall, he made 'a notable oration' on the subject. At the end of the session, at about 3 p.m. on 10 Apr., Elizabeth came by water from Whitehall to Westminster to prorogue Parliament. After she had taken her place in the Parliament chamber, the Commons appeared at the bar, and Williams opened the proceedings:

> Thus it is, most excellent and virtuous princess, as nature giveth to every reasonable creature to speak, so is

it a grace to be well learned. And I, representing the mouth of such a body as cannot speak for itself, and in the presence of your Majesty's person and nobles, must most humbly desire and crave of your Highness to bear with my imperfection.

After again pressing her to marry, Williams referred to the work of the Parliament, lacing his oration with many historical examples. Finally, with extraordinary persistence, for his future career depended entirely upon retaining the royal favour, Williams thanked the Queen for bearing with his 'unfitting words, uplandish and rude speech' and boldly returned to the charge. The Queen should marry and have children, 'so that you and they may prosperously and as long time reign over us as ever did any kings or princes'.

The Speaker at this time had considerable discretion in deciding when bills were to be introduced and in choosing the order in which they should be read, so that one wonders whether Exeter might have had foreknowledge of the fact that Williams was to be chosen Speaker, or even whether the city helped to arrange this. At any rate he and his colleague took to Westminster a list of six measures the city wished to see adopted, and no less than five of them were embodied in the legislation of the Parliament. Williams was well rewarded. He was paid £20 outright for 'preferring the suit and business of the city', and his annual retainer was doubled. But the wider rewards to which he must have looked forward, promotion to serjeant and the judicial bench, were denied him. He died 'in his young flourishing age' on 1 July 1566, and when Parliament reassembled for the second session on 30 Sept., procedure had to be devised to replace him. In his will he hoped to become

> one of the lively members of the justicial body or temple of God, united to Christ Jesus our head, together with the faithful congregation of believing men and women by perfect and lively working faith.

He left £40 to his daughter Elizabeth if she were to marry the heir of John Trevelyan of Nettlecombe, or else £200. In the former event she got

> no more in consideration of the great charge that I have and must be at about the education and bringing up of the son of the said John Trevelyan.

Williams was depicted on his tomb as an esquire in armour. His epitaph reads:

> Here lieth the corpse of Thomas Williams Esquire
> Twice reader he in court appointed was
> Whose sacred mind to virtue did aspire
> Of Parliament he Speaker hence did pass.
> The common peace he studied to preserve
> And true religion ever to maintain.
> In peace of justice where as he did serve
> And now in heaven with mighty Jove doth reign.[2]

[1] Vivian, *Vis. Devon*, 471–2, 597; *HMC Exeter*, 22; Manning, *Lives of the Speakers*, 223–4; Guildford Mus. Loseley 1331/2; PRO, cal. enrolled deeds 1547–55, pp. 114, 250; Devon RO, Tingey 472 et passim; PCC 23 Crymes, 18 Daper; *APC*, vii. 132; J. Hooker, *Life of Sir Peter Carew*, 185–6; Lansd. 8, f. 8; Plymouth city archives, old audit bk. f. 266; Exeter city act bk. 3, p. 131. [2] Neale, *Commons*, 359; Hooker, 185 n; *CJ*, i. 62, 63, 64; Neale, *Parls.* i. 98–9, 106, 125, 134; Roberts thesis, 130; *Trans. Dev. Assoc.* xlv. 409; A. L. Rowse, *England of Eliz.* 7; A. I. Dasent, *Speakers of the House of Commons*, xxv.

P.W.H.

WILLIAMS, *see also* CROMWELL *alias* WILLIAMS

WILLIS, Simon (*d.*1613), of Milk Street, London.

KNARESBOROUGH	1593
CHRISTCHURCH	1597, 1601

Sec. to Robert Cecil by 1595–1602; clerk of the privy seal in reversion June 1603.[1]

Willis's background is obscure. He was certainly in Cecil's service by 1595 and it is probable that he was his secretary as early as 1593, when he obtained a parliamentary seat for Knaresborough, a borough subject to duchy of Lancaster influence. It seems hardly likely that he could have obtained the seat other than by Cecil's patronage, exercised probably through Sir Thomas Heneage*, chancellor of the duchy. In 1597 and 1601 he sat for Christchurch, where Cecil must again have obtained his nomination, perhaps through Thomas Howard*, 3rd Viscount Howard of Bindon. Though Willis's name has not been found in the journals of the proceedings of any of his Parliaments, as one of the burgesses for Knaresborough he could have sat on any of the following committes in 1593: cloth, 15 Mar., 23 Mar.; weirs, 28 Mar.; maimed soldiers, 2 Apr. and spinners and weavers, 3 Apr.[2]

His principal responsibility in Cecil's secretariat was for intelligence, while Levinus Munck* concentrated on foreign affairs. The gratifications received by such influential officials from their master's clients were considerable, and not necessarily in cash, as appears from Roland Whyte's advice to Sir Robert Sidney* in March 1600:

By the bestowing of a toy your Lordship may make Mr. Willis beholding unto you ... Sir William Brown bestowed upon him a desk, such a one as my Lord Herbert hath, which Sir Walter Ralegh hath taken from him, and he exceedingly desires another.

Against the rewards of office had to be set commensurate or even greater risks. In 1602 Willis was dismissed, John Chamberlain then reporting that Walter Cope* and Hugh Beeston*, two of Cecil's closest friends, had informed him that Willis's removal had followed 'only upon his insolent and harsh behaviour towards his master'. But in 1608 Cecil himself gave a very different explanation (to Sir Henry Wotton†, ambassador to Venice): Willis was removed

because I was loath he should have come to some discovery of that correspondency which I had with the King our sovereign, which, without great difficulty, I could not have avoided, considering his daily and near attendance as my secretary, to whose eyes a packet or paper might have been so visible as he might have raised some such inferences thereof as might have bred some jealousy in the Queen's mind if she had known it or heard any such suspicion to move from him.[3]

When Willis heard that he was dismissed – it was apparently Munck who told him – he begged Cecil for another chance and pressed his three year-old claim to a clerkship of the privy seal in reversion. In December 1602 he wrote again. The tone of the letter was intemperate, very different from what one would expect from a former servant who was addressing the most powerful minister in the country. Nevertheless, in June 1603 he obtained the reversion. In July he was pressing for a lump sum of £300 in return for the surrender of an annuity which Cecil had been paying him. Willis spent a good deal of time abroad in the next few years blackening the character of his former master, who by 29 Mar. 1608, was concerned about his conduct at Rome. Willis, by that time back in England, had already been called before the Council and his account of his actions gave 'just presumptions pregnant enough to suspect him of some such behaviour abroad as sorteth no way with his loyalty to his Majesty nor with his training under me.' Willis, who had already been imprisoned in the Gatehouse for a fortnight, wrote to Salisbury two days later, denying an accusation that he had corresponded with Father Persons, and asking vainly for his release. In February 1609, still from prison, he denied that he had betrayed any of Cecil's secret agents in Italy. Shortly afterwards he secured his liberty, though still forbidden the court. In April he asked for permission to travel abroad again, a request which was no doubt denied.[4]

Willis had been a poor man before he became Cecil's secretary. It is clear that he accumulated capital during his years of service and his misfortunes after 1602 did not render him destitute. Cecil was paying him an annuity as early as 1598 and in 1612 was still paying him £40 p.a. When Willis died in London in October 1613 Chamberlain reported that the value of his estate was 'better than £3,000', and although his will does not confirm this estimate, it does reveal that he had two houses and some money. Willis was unmarried. Two brothers, William and Isaac, are mentioned, and a sister Eleanor. In the preamble he expressed the conviction that if he achieved salvation it would be by Christ's merits alone and not by any of his own.[5]

[1] *HMC Hatfield*, v. 211; Hatfield ms 184/54; *Chamberlain Letters* ed. McClure, i. 163; *CSP Dom.* 1603–10, p. 13; PRO Index 6801.

[2] D'Ewes, 507, 512, 513, 514. [3] HMC Hatfield, vii 8, 95, 358; ix. 76–7, 84–5; xi. 549; xii. 230; xiv. 112; Hatfield ms 178/110; SP94/96, f. 248; CSP Dom. 1598–1601, pp. 168, 245–6; Add. 1580–1625, p. 419; Border Pprs. ii. 721 HMC De L'Isle and Dudley, ii. 449; Chamberlain Letters, i. 163; Sidney State Pprs. ed. Collins, ii. 326. [4] Hatfield ms 184/54; 194/135; 125/79, 80, 90; 127/29; HMC Hatfield, xii. 516; xv. 212–13; CSP Dom. 1603–10, p. 13; PRO Index 6801; Sidney State Pprs. ii. 327; SP14/43/53, 83. [5] Sidney State Pprs. ii. 327; Hatfield House estate pprs., general 11/22; deeds 126/17; Chamberlain Letters. i. 483; PCC 94 Capell.

A.G.R.S.

WILLOUGHBY, Thomas (*d.* bef. 5 July 1596), of Bore Place, Kent.

DOWNTON 1593

1st s. of Robert Willoughby of Bore Place by Dorothy, da. of Sir Edward Willoughby of Wollaton, Notts. *educ.* ?Magdalene, Camb., matric. pens. Easter 1551; L. Inn 30 Apr. 1558. *m.* (1) Catherine, da. of Sir Percival Hart of Lullingstone, Kent, 6s. inc. Percival† 5da.; (2) Mary, 4ch.[1]

J.p. Kent from 1569, sheriff 1573–4, 1590–1; j.p. Suss. from 1592.

The identity of the Member for Downton in 1593 is uncertain. Although it is tempting to connect him with the well-known house of Willoughby of Knoyle and Baverstock, Wiltshire, the only Thomas belonging to that family at this time, a younger son of Henry Willoughby of Knoyle Odierne, was too young (his elder brother was only 16 in November 1591) and probably of too little account to have found a seat in the Parliament of 1593. Nor does Thomas Willoughby of Netherton, Worcestershire, and Stow-on-the-Wold, Gloucestershire, appear to have any connexion which might have led to his return for Downton. Whoever he was, as one of the burgesses for Downton, he could have sat on a committee appointed to consider cloth, 15 Mar. 1593.[2]

The identification adopted here is suggested by the pattern of representation at Downton during these years. Between 1584 and 1589 this pattern is two-fold; whereas one of the seats went on two occasions to a client of the bishop of Winchester, and once to a local squire, the other appears to have been at the disposition of Thomas Wilkes*, clerk of the council, and since 1582 lessee of Downton parsonage. In 1584 and 1586 Wilkes himself sat, but in 1589, when Wilkes was returned for Southampton, he made room at Downton for Lawrence Tomson, secretary to Sir Francis Walsingham, Wilkes's own patron. In 1593 Wilkes again sat for Southampton and he may well have expected to wield some influence at Downton; but by then Walsingham was dead, and the 2nd Earl of Pembroke, who in the 1570s had secured the return of at least two of the Members for Downton, probably took the opportunity of reasserting his influence there, as he was to do in 1597 and his successor the 3rd Earl was to do in 1601. Thomas Willoughby of Kent is likely to have been acceptable both to the Earl and to Wilkes. At Bore Place and Chiddingstone he was a near neighbour of the Sidneys of Penhurst, with whom his relationship was close and friendly. In 1577–8 he sold lands at Penshurst to Sidney for £1,876 10s., and it was at Willoughby's London house that Sir Henry Sidney, who described it to his wife as 'a fine lodging', was to stay when in London in January 1595. Since Sidney was Pembroke's father-in-law and a frequent visitor to Wilton, he could well have commended his neighbour to the Earl. With the Pembroke country and circle Willoughby already had a connexion through the marriage, about 1560, of his cousin Margaret to Sir Matthew Arundell, who had been the 1st Earl's ward and who held Wardour castle by fealty from the second. But Willoughby must also have been well known to Wilkes through their common allegiance to Walsingham. Although there is nothing in the suggestion, which arises from a confusion of pedigrees, that his father was a comrade in exile of Walsingham's, Thomas Willoughby became connected by marriage with Walsingham and he had dealings with the secretary, both officially, as when in September 1585 he was examining suspects in Kent, and privately, as when in August 1582 he was a godfather, with Lady Dorothy Walsingham, at a baptism at Edenbridge.[3]

Grandson of a lord chief justice, grandson-in-law of a chief baron, and himself a member of Lincoln's Inn, Willoughby may have combined legal practice with his interests and duties as a landowner and local official. The town house where Sidney lodged and Willoughby himself, probably on his deathbed, was to add a codicil to his will, stood in Lincoln's Inn Fields (some details of its rooms appear in a lease of its top storey made by Willoughby in July 1595); and his third son, another Thomas, entered the Middle Temple in 1586. The will was proved on 5 July 1596.[4]

Willoughby's first marriage, to Catherine Hart, had been fruitful of children. The firstborn son, named Percival after one of his grandfathers, emulated the other by marrying a Willoughby of Wollaton; he settled in Nottinghamshire, which he represented in the Parliament of 1604, and disposed of his Kentish patrimony.[5]

[1] Vis. Kent (Harl. Soc. lxxv), 48–9; Al. Cant. iv(1), p. 423; L. Inn Adm. Reg. i. 64; PCC 53 Drake. [2] Al. Ox. 1651; CPR, 1566–9, pp. 355, 406; Bristol and Glos. Arch. Soc. Trans. xvii. 133; D'Ewes, 501. [3] HMC De L'Isle and Dudley, i. 14, 250; ii. 157–8; Vis. Kent, loc. cit.; Pembroke Survey (Roxburghe Club), p. xlvii; Chanc. II/237/79; Arch. Cant. xlviii. 256, 287; CSP Dom. 1581–90, pp. 267, 269. [4] Vis. Kent (Harl. Soc. xlii), 144; PCC 53 Drake; MT. Admissions, i. 286. [5] Hasted, Kent, iii. 221.

S.T.B.

WILMOTT, Edward (*d.* 1571), of Southampton.

SOUTHAMPTON 1559

s. of John Wilmott (*d.* 1558) of Merdon, Hants by his w. Joan. *m.* Margaret, 1s. 3da.

Steward, Southampton 1549–50, water bailiff 1551–2, court bailiff 1554–5, sheriff 1555–6, mayor 1559–60.

Wilmott was a well-known figure in Southampton for over 30 years. From 1539 there are references to him, as a stapler engaged in the wool trade with Calais. He also kept an inn, the *Dolphin*, in English Street. He was frequently fined by the court leet, for such matters as not clearing his ditches, selling bottles of hay at short weight, overcharging for wine, forestalling and regrating.

His will, made in 1569, was first proved 27 Nov. 1571, but, following a dispute between Elizabeth Browne and Alicia Smith (presumably two of his daughters), the grant of probate was revoked, and the matter was not settled until 1583.

VCH Hants, iii. 421; PCC 37 Holney, 9 Welles; *Third Remembrance Bk.* ii (Soton Rec. Ser.), 154–5; *Remembrance Bk.* i (Soton Rec. Soc.), 84; J. S. Davies, *Hist. Soton*, 176; *CPR*, 1548–9, p. 48; 1554–5, p. 128; 1557–8, p. 300; 1558–60, p. 215; *LP Hen. VIII*, xiv(2), p. 93; xvii. p. 672 xix(1), p. 600; (2), p. 3; Soton Civic Centre bk. of debts; *Black Bk.* iii (Soton Rec. Soc.), 94; *Ct. Leet Recs.* i. (Soton Rec. Soc.), 7, 9, 23, 27, 34, 44, 52, 60, 165.

N.M.F.

WILSON, Thomas (1523–81), of Washingborough, Lincs. and Edmonton, Mdx.[1]

| MITCHELL | 1563 |
| LINCOLN | 1571, 1572* |

b. 1523, 1st s. of Thomas Wilson of Strubby, Lincs. by Anne, da. and h. of Roger Cumberworth of Cumberworth, Lincs. *educ.* Eton 1537–41; King's Camb. 13 Aug. 1542, fellow 14 Aug. 1545–7, BA 1546 or 1547, MA 1549; Ferrara Univ. DCL 1559. *m.* (1) c.1560, Agnes (*d.* June 1574), da. of John Wynter, of Lydney, Glos., wid. of William Brooke, 1s. 2da. all by 1565; (2) by 1576, Jane (*d.*1577), da. of Richard Empson, of London, wid. of John Pinchon* of Writtle, Essex.[2] Master of St. Katharine's hosp. London 1561–*d.*; adv., ct. of arches 1561; master of requests 1561; j.p.q. Mdx. from c.1564, Essex from c.1577; ambassador to Portugal 1567, to the Netherlands 1574–5, 1576–7; principal sec. and PC 12 Nov. 1577; dean of Durham 1579.[3]

Wilson's ancestors left Yorkshire about the middle of the fifteenth century, settling in Strubby, Lincolnshire. His father made a fortunate marriage, acquired ex-monastic lands and became a friend of Charles Brandon, Duke of Suffolk. Save for the attachment he developed for his master, Nicholas Udall, little record remains of Wilson's career at Eton, where he was a King's scholar. At Cambridge he was taught by such scholars as Cheke, Ascham, Thomas Smith and Haddon: his political and religious preferences at the university can be seen in his associations with the Dudleys, Greys, Brandons and the theologian Martin Bucer. He became tutor to the two sons of his father's friend the Duke of Suffolk, and was devoted to the latter's wife Katherine. Both the young Brandons

and Martin Bucer died in 1551, and thenceforward Wilson spent less time at Cambridge. During the summer of 1552 he had 'a quiet time of vacation with Sir Edward Dymoke*' at Scrivelsby, and, by the following January, he had himself settled in Lincolnshire, at Washingborough.[4]

In view of the opinions expressed in his *Rule of Reason*, and *Art of Rhetorique* (written during his visit to Dymoke), Wilson's eclipse during Mary's reign was predictable. He joined Cheke in Padua in the spring of 1555, where he studied Greek, and, from the funeral oration he delivered for Edward Courtenay, Earl of Devon, in St. Anthony's basilica on 18 Sept. 1556, it seems possible that he may have become the young nobleman's tutor. In the following year he appeared in Rome as a solicitor in the famous Chetwode divorce case, when, in an attempt to obtain a favourable decision for his client, he intrigued against Cardinal Pole. The Pope – Paul IV – at first proved a willing listener. However, in March 1558 Mary ordered Wilson to return to England and appear before the Privy Council, and soon afterwards still, or again, in Rome he was thrown into the papal prison on a charge of heresy. There he suffered torture, escaping only when the mob broke open the prison upon Paul IV's death in August 1559. Wilson took refuge in Ferrara, where in November the university made him a doctor of civil law.[5]

Upon his return to England in 1560 the impoverished scholar received the mastership of St. Katharine's hospital, London, soon being accused of wasting the revenues, destroying the buildings, and selling the fair and the choir. However, the support of Sir Robert Dudley and Sir William Cecil soon brought him further preferment, as a master of requests. Besides the usual cases he frequently dealt with those concerning conspiracy, commercial disputes and diplomacy. He was prominent in the Hales (1564), Creaghe (1565), Cockyn (1575), and Guaras cases, and after the northern rebellion of 1569 he interrogated supporters of Mary Stuart and conducted many of the examinations in connexion with the Ridolfi plot. Frequently employed on missions abroad, his name occurs in connexion with foreign embassies in 1561, 1562 and 1563, but his first important journey was to Portugal in 1567, where he sought redress for damage done to a ship belonging to his brothers-in-law William and George Wynter, made a lengthy Latin oration before the young king Sebastian and was thenceforward frequently employed in negotiations on commercial matters between England and Portugal. By the end of the 1570s he had established himself as an expert in Portuguese affairs, and emerged as the champion of the pretender, Don Antonio, after the latter had fled from the armies of Philip II. As well as leading a mission to Mary Stuart at Sheffield castle, where he interrogated her upon her part in the Ridolfi plot, Wilson served on two separate occasions in the Netherlands. On the first, in late 1574 and early 1575, he negotiated with the Spanish governor on commercial matters and the expulsion of the English Catholics. By the time he went back in 1576 the situation in the Netherlands was chaotic. Mutinous Spanish troops had pillaged Antwerp, while the States, casting in their lot with the Prince of Orange, forced the new Spanish governor, Don John of Austria, to withdraw the Spanish soldiers. Wilson's original idea was to arrange a *modus vivendi* between the protagonists. Gradually, however, he came to fear French intervention and to distrust the intentions of Don John, so that, by the time of his departure in June 1577, he had emerged a partisan of Orange.[6]

Wilson's appointment as principal secretary soon followed his return to England. Although, like others in the Walsingham-Leicester faction of the Council, he deplored the Queen's policy of procrastination over her marriage, and identified England's cause with that of protestantism abroad, he remained subordinate to his colleague Sir Francis Walsingham, and his influence was minimal. He remained a supporter of Orange, of Condé, and of Henry of Navarre. As part of his duties as secretary, he became the first keeper of the state papers.

It was, presumably, court influence that procured Wilson his seat for the Cornish borough of Mitchell in 1563. There is no record of his activities in the first session of that Parliament, but on 31 Oct. 1566, he sat on a conference with the Lords to consider the most important current issues, namely the succession and the Queen's marriage. On 3 Dec. he sat on a committee about the export of sheep. In the next two Parliaments he represented Lincoln, where his friend Robert Monson* was recorder. In 1571 he spoke against vagabonds (13 Apr.) and against usury (19 Apr.). On 21 Apr. he took part in a conference with the Lords where it was decided to afford precedence to public over private bills 'as the season of the year waxed very hot, and dangerous for sickness'. He was named to committees on the river Lea (26 May) and barristers fees (28 May). In 1572 the main topic was Mary Stuart, whose execution Wilson urged:

> No man condemneth the Queen's opinion, nor thinketh her otherwise than wise; yet [he doubts] whether she so fully seeth her own peril. We ought importunately to cry for justice, justice. The case of a king indeed is great, but if they do ill and be wicked, they must be dealt withal. The Scottish Queen shall be heard, and any man besides that will offer to speak for her. It is marvelled at by foreign princes that, her offences being so great and horrible, the Queen's Majesty suffereth her to live. A king, coming hither into England, is no king here. The judges' opinion is that Mary Stuart, called Queen of Scots, is a traitor. The law sayeth that dignity defends not him which liveth unhonestly.

The Queen took exception to the Commons giving a first reading, 21 May 1572, to a bill on religion, and a delegation, including Wilson, waited upon her. He reported back to the Commons on 23 May:

> She had but advised, not debarred us to use any other way, and for the protestants, they should find that, as she hath found them true, so will she be their defence.

In the 1572 session Wilson was appointed to committees concerning Mary Stuart and the Duke of Norfolk, and other, particularly legal, matters. In 1576 he again played a mediating part, this time in the Arthur Hall* affair, and he was of the committee that examined Peter Wentworth after the latter had made his famous speech on the liberties of the House. On the other hand his independence, even as a Privy Councillor, can be seen in 1581, when he spoke for Paul Wentworth's proposal for a public fast. 'Both Mr Secretaries', Wilson and Walsingham, were ordered by the House on 3 Mar. 1581 to confer with the bishops on religion. Throughout the 1572 Parliament, Wilson, as master of requests, was frequently employed fetching and carrying bills and messages to and from the Lords, and on such tasks as drafting bills, examining witnesses and administering oaths. As Privy Councillor he was appointed to several committees including those on the subsidy (25 Jan. 1581), seditious practices (1 Feb.), encumbrances (4 Feb.), the examination of Arthur Hall (6 Feb.), defence (25 Feb.), Dover harbour (6 Mar.) and the Queen's safety (14 Mar.). Wilson died after the end of what proved to be the last session of the 1572 Parliament, but before it was finally dissolved.[7]

Wilson's literary works, like those of More, Crowley and Starkey before him, were concerned with classical studies, and with problems of morality and the commonwealth. At Cambridge in 1551 he contributed Latin verse to Haddon's and Cheke's *De Obitu doctissimi et sanctissimi theologi doctoris Martini Buceri*. A few months later, after the death of his young pupils, he wrote and edited *Epistola de vita et obitu fratrum Suffolciencium Henrici et Caroli Brandon*. The *Rule of Reason*, written in 1551 and dedicated to Edward VI, uses medieval logic to support the doctrines of Geneva, and this was followed by the dedication in Haddon's *Exhortatio ad Literas* to John Dudley, the eldest son of Northumberland, to whom, in 1553, Wilson dedicated his own *Art of Rhetorique*. Like the *Rule of Reason* this dealt with the teachings of the earlier scholars, supplemented by digressions on political, social, religious and moral questions. Similar questions concerned Wilson when he wrote his *Discourse upon Usury* in 1569. Though in close contact with the New Learning, and well informed on current economic problems, Wilson was unable to escape from the limitations of medieval moral precepts. He was especially critical of enclosures and usury, from both of which he feared harm for the commonwealth. In 1570 Wilson translated the *Three Orations of Demosthenes*, to serve as a warning against a new Philip of Macedon, Philip II of Spain.

Apart from his mastership of St. Katharine's hospital, Wilson had several sources of income: his employment as master of requests and secretary brought him £100 p.a. as well as perquisites; he received a life annuity of £100 from the Queen in 1571; and on 28 Jan. 1579 he was appointed lay dean of Durham at £266 with £400 p.a. more from the properties attached to the office. He was installed by proxy and had letters of dispensation for non-residence. With one exception the Durham prebendaries acquiesced in Wilson's appointment. A year before his death he accepted the parsonage of Mansfield, Nottinghamshire. He had of course a substantial income from his Lincolnshire lands, concerning which he remained in close touch with his brothers Humphrey and William who lived in that county, and Godfrey, who was a wealthy London merchant and member of the Drapers' Company. Humphrey, in his will, committed his son Thomas, later a prominent political figure, to his brother's care; but in the event, Humphrey outlived Wilson, who made his own will in May 1581, the day before he died. He had suffered from bouts of sickness – it seems from a kidney complaint – since his return from the Netherlands in 1577, and the Tower Hill water did not provide the cure he hoped for. He was buried 'without charge or pomp' at St. Katharine's hospital, although he had recently been living on his estate, Pymmes, at Edmonton, which he had purchased in 1579 for £340. His son Nicholas, heir and executor, returned to his father's Lincolnshire estates, and his two daughters each received 500 marks.[8]

Wilson belongs to the second rank of Elizabethan statesmen. An able linguist, he had numerous acquaintances among Spanish and Flemish officials in the Netherlands, and, in a wider context, his range of friends included Leicester, Burghley, Hatton, Davison, Sir Francis Knollys, Paulet, Walsingham, William of Orange, Jewel, Parker, Parkhurst, Gresham, Ludovico Guiccardini and Arias Montano.[9]

[1] This biography is based upon a paper by Albert J. Schmidt, Coe College, Cedar Rapids, Iowa, U.S.A. [2] King's Coll. Camb. protocullum bk. 1, p. 104; Harl. 1550, ff. 85–6; Guildhall mss 4546; *Vis. Glos.* (Harl. Soc. xxi) 278; *Vis. Essex* (Harl. Soc. xiii), 470; *Lincs. Historian*, ii(4), pp. 14–24; *DNB.* [3] C. Jamison, *Hosp. St. Katharine*, 69 et passim; *CPR*, 1560–3, p. 102; 1563–6, p. 187; Lansd. 22. f. 52; I. S. Leadam, *Sel. Cases Ct. of Requests* (Selden Soc. 1898), p. xxi.; Cott. Nero B. 1, f. 125; *APC*, x. 85; C66/1188/82. [4] Harl. 1550, ff. 85–6; PRO, Lincs. muster rolls, 1539, Calcewath E36/21, f. 52; PRO town depositions C24, 30; T. Wilson, *Epistola* (London 1551); T. Wilson, *Art of Rhetorique*, ed. Muir. [5] C. H. Garrett, *Marian Exiles*, 339 et passim; *CSP Dom.* 1547–80, p. 100; *CSP Rome*, ii. no. 602; *Art of Rhetorique.* [6] Strype, *Annals*, i(2), pp. 285–6; E. Nuys, *Le Droit Romain, Le Droit Des Gens, et Le College des Docteurs en Droit Civil* (Bruxelles, 1910), p. 144; *HMC Hatfield*, i. 250, 508, 520; *APC*, vii. 205; x. 210; *CSP Ire.* 1509–73, p. 255; *CSP Scot.* 1571–4, nos. 352, 353; 1574–81, nos. 140 seq.; *CSP Span.* 1568–79, passim; 1580–5, passim; Murdin, *State Pprs.* ii. passim; *CSP For.* 1579–80, passim. [7] D'Ewes, 126–7, 157, 206, 219, 220, 222, 241, 249, 251, 252, 255, 282, 288, 290, 291, 292, 293, 294, 301, 302, 306, 309; *CJ*, i. 94, 98, 99, 101, 109, 110, 112, 122, 124, 130, 136; Cott. Titus F. i. ff. 152, 163; Neale, *Parlts.* i. 259, 303–4, 379; Trinity, Dublin, Thos. Cromwell's jnl. f. 42. [8] I. Temple, Petyt 538, ff. 39, 147, 152v; C66/1076/29, 1189/38; C54 close rolls, passim; C142/233/41; C54/1052; Dean and Chapter of Durham treasurer's bk. 1579–80, no. 2; 1580–1, no. 3; reg. 3, ff. 2, 3; Dean and Chapter Acts, 1578–83, ff. 29, 46; Estate House, Old Charlton, Kent, Wilson's household inventory 1581; Lincoln Wills, 2, f. 262; Wards 7/23/112; Harl. 6992, f. 120; Fleet of Fines, CP25(2) 172, 21 Eliz. Trin.; PCC 32 Tirwhite. [9] *CSP For.* 1577–8, no. 820(4); *CSP Dom.* 1575. p. 105; *Corresp. de Philippe II* (Bruxelles 1848–79), iii. 214; Wilson's household inventory.

P.W.H.

WILSON, William (*d.* 1582), of Southwark, Surr.

SOUTHWARK   1571

m. (2) Blith, *s.p.*
    Warden, Clothworkers' Co. 1560; gov. St. Olave's g.s. 1571.

Wilson, of Southwark, was one of the four wardens of the London Clothworkers' Company for the year in which the Queen confirmed its charter. He may have lived at one time in Wandsworth, where a William Wilson, perhaps his father, leased two mills in 1526. The receipts for rents of church lands in Wandsworth, which survive for the years 1546 to 1549, show small amounts paid by a man of this name. In 1569 a William Wilson was assessed there for armour, but was exempted as 'gone out of the parish'.

Wilson's property in Southwark included 12 houses and shops which he had built in Fowl Lane in St. Saviour's parish, and a dwelling-house in 'Long Southwark'. He also had leases of another house, with a wharf; of the Maze, formerly part of the abbot's gardens; and of some meadow-land in 'Peckham marsh'. As a churchwarden at St. Saviour's, he helped to draw up inventories of the church goods in Southwark during Edward VI's reign, returning himself as having bought £27 worth of vestments and altar hangings, some in red damask and others of blue velvet embroidered with flowers. He was one of the six men whom the vestry at St. Olave's appointed in May 1579 to supervise the conveyance of land to the use of the foundation. He died during the first half of 1582: his will, made in March, was proved two months later. His widow was to receive £500 on his death, with a £30 annuity in lieu of her dower. There were £10 legacies to a number of young relatives, with a special grant of £4 a year to 'Richard Wilson, scholar of St. John's, Cambridge'. St. Olave's school received an annuity of 40s. and St. Thomas's hospital the sum of £4. There were also bequests of 'northern dozens' to make gowns for 68 poor people attending the funeral, with gifts of money to the poor in St. Olave's parish, and £5 to the Clothworkers for a funeral feast. A codicil asked the executor, Richard Ward, a London vintner and Wilson's nephew, to pay £190 towards the 'orphanage money' of the two children of 'Thomas Duffilde, draper, deceased, my predecessor'.

There were no surviving children: the house property was to descend to Wilson's nephew Garrett Ward, a fellow clothworker. Among minor legacies were 'six angels to make him a ring' to Thomas King, parson of Clapham, and rings and handkerchiefs of 'blackwork edged with gold lace' to other relatives and friends. Wilson asked to be buried in St. Olave's parish church near his 'late wife'.

PCC 20 Tirwhite; *Charters and Letters Patent granted to the Clothworkers' Co.* 32; W. Rendle, *Old Southwark and its People*, 253; *CPR, 1569–72*, p. 298; *LP Hen. VIII*, iv(1), p. 1026; *Surr. Rec. Soc.* iii(2), p. 12; iii(10), pp. 12, 147; *Surr. Arch. Colls.* i. 168; iv. 81, 85–6.

N.M.F.

WILSTROP, Francis, of Wilstrop, nr. York.

THIRSK   1559

> s. of Sir Oswald Wilstrop (*d.* Apr. 1574) of Wilstrop by Agnes, da. and coh. of Thomas Redman or Redmayne of Bossall, Yorks. *m.* Eleanor, da. and h. of Sir Henry Everingham of Birkin, Yorks, by Anne, da. of Sir William Fairfax, at least 1s.[1]

The Wilstrops, who had been living in the village from which they took their name since the thirteenth century, had become, by the close of the middle ages, one of the leading families in the Ainsty, the area immediately to the west of York. Wilstrop's father, whose career lasted from the later years of Wolsey's ascendancy to the northern rebellion of 1569, was probably the last member of the family to make any contribution to national events. As he outlived his son, the latter's appearances in contemporary records are infrequent.[2]

One reason for the decline of the family during this period was the same as that for many other families in the north of England: inability to accept the new religion. There is no positive evidence that Sir Oswald or Francis Wilstrop were Catholics, but the former's widow, descended from one of the most distinguished families in the north, the lords Scrope, is found as a recusant in 1575 and again two years later. It is probably significant also that Sir Oswald, the owner of great estates, was never a justice of the peace in Elizabeth's reign, and this in a part of the country where moderate Catholics were often selected because there was no one else available. Still, he was loyal to the Queen in 1569.[3]

The extent of Francis Wilstrop's involvement in his father's career is not known. He is first mentioned in 1548 when the Privy Council authorized a payment to him of £5 by the receiver of the court of wards: further details are lacking. In 1555 he was involved in an affray in York. It seems that he took advantage of a shooting contest in the city to renew a feud with another local gentleman, Sir Thomas Metham. Wilstrop 'with sundry his acquaintances', assembled 'intending to have fought with the said ... Metham'. Metham gave the city authorities a pledge of his good behaviour, 'but the said Francis Wilstrop absented himself, notwithstanding the commandment of our officers to repair to us to be bounden for the preservation of the peace'. On another occasion Wilstrop and his father were accused by Lord Latimer of

abusing him while out hunting, pulling down his park fence, and attacking him and his servants.[4]

Sir Oswald's local influence was probably sufficient to secure his son's election at Thirsk for the first Parliament of the reign. The borough was owned by the conservative (if not Catholic) 3rd Earl of Derby but his sphere of influence did not extend to Yorkshire and he took little interest in Thirsk. The date of Wilstrop's death *v.p.* is not known. Land conveyances in which he appears, either as plaintiff or deforciant, come to an end in 1565. Francis's son Charles, born about 1563, succeeded his grandfather to the Wilstrop lands.[5]

[1] *Vis. Yorks.* (Harl Soc. xvi) pp. 116, 355; *Yorks. Peds.* 460. [2] *LP Hen. VIII*, xi and xii, passim; xiii(1), p. 386; *CSP Dom.* Add. 1566–79, p. 412; *Yorks. Arch. Jnl.* xx. 363–4; *York Civic Recs.* (Yorks. Arch. Soc. rec. ser. cx), 127, 172. [3] *Yorks. Arch. Jnl.* xxxv. 166; J. Cartwright, *Chapters in Yorks. Hist.* 149. [4] *APC*, ii. 205; Talbot mss A, f. 399. [5] *Yorks. Fines* (Yorks. Arch. Soc. rec. ser. ii), 201, 272, 286, 314; (v), 18; (vii), 40, 48; C142/169/58.

M.R.P.

WINCH, Humphrey (c.1555–1625), of Everton, Beds.

BEDFORD   1593, 1597, 1601, 1604*

> *b.* c.1555, s. of John Winch (*d.*1582), of Northill. *educ.* St. John's Camb. 1570; L. Inn 1573, called 1581. *m.* Cicely, da. of Richard Onslow*, 2s. 3da. (1s. 2da. *d.v.p.*). Kntd. 1606.
> Dep. recorder, Bedford prob. c.1593, certainly by 1596–1604; j.p. Beds. from c.1601; bencher, L. Inn 1595, Autumn reader 1597, censor 1600, keeper of the black book 1603, treasurer 1605–6; serjeant-at-law, chief baron of Exchequer [I] 1606; c.j. King's bench [I] 1608–11; j.c.p. (England) 1611–*d.*; member, council in the marches of Wales 1623–*d.*[1]

Winch represented Bedford in four successive Parliaments, vacating his seat on his appointment to the Irish judiciary in 1606. He owed his return for the borough to Oliver St. John II*, later 3rd Baron St. John of Bletsoe, who was nominally the recorder of Bedford after the death of Thomas Snagge I* in 1593, but who delegated the performance of the office to Winch. Early in 1593 St. John was supporting Peter Wentworth's scheme for introducing a bill to settle the succession. On 21 Feb. Wentworth and his cronies assembled in Winch's chambers at Lincoln's Inn to discuss the bill and plan their campaign. They intended a second gathering on the following day, after Wentworth had shown his bill to James Morice*, but someone informed on them and Wentworth was put in the Tower. Winch was allowed to continue to attend the Commons, but forbidden to leave London even after the end of the session. For a lawyer he was only moderately active in Parliament. He reported a bill about jurors (15 Mar. 1593), another about horse stealing (21, 22 Nov. 1597), sat on a few legal committees and those considering maltsters (7 Dec. 1597, 12 Jan. 1598).

As one of the Bedford Members he was put on a committee concerned with draining the fens (3 Dec. 1597). He was on the main business committee of the 1601 Parliament (3 Nov.) and on committees concerning the penal laws (2 Nov.), monopolies (23 Nov.), the Exchequer (25 Nov.) and the lands of Lewis Mordaunt* (3 Dec.). On 5 Dec. 1601 he spoke during the debate on church attendance, and on 10 Dec. about the export of ordnance. When the Exchequer bill was received from the Lords, Winch and the solicitor-general were ordered to consider it urgently, as time was running short if the bill were to be completed before Parliament rose. In fact the measure was 'put by', owing to the dissolution several days later.[2]

Winch's later career lies outside the Elizabethan period. In February 1625 he was seized with apoplexy while 'in his robes', and died at Serjeants' Inn on the 4th of the month. His will, drawn up a year earlier, and proved 25 Mar. 1625, mentions property at Everton, part of it over the Huntingdonshire border, and at Potton, Bedfordshire. The widow was sole executrix. An inquisition post mortem was taken at St. Neots 20 Oct. 1625. There is an alabaster effigy of Winch, in judge's robes, at Everton church, with an inscription stating that his embalmed body was brought from London and buried there. Other accounts say that he was buried in the cloisters of Pembroke, Cambridge.[3]

[1] DNB; Foss, Judges, vi. 201–2; Beds. N. and Q. i. 216; F. A. Blaydes, Gen. Bed. 306, 356, 360, 420, 439; OR, i. 442; CSP Dom. 1603–10, p. 334; L. Inn Black Bks. passim. [2] Neale, Parlts. ii. 257–60, 410, 422; T. Birch, Mems. Eliz. i. 96; D'Ewes, 501, 560, 561, 563, 565, 567, 569, 572, 578, 622, 624, 649, 651, 665, 668, 670, 677–8, 685; Townshend, Hist. Colls. 108, 113, 115, 287. [3] Beds. N. and Q. iii. 266–7; VCH Beds. ii. 227, 235; Foss; PCC 29 Clarke; C142/673/28.

N.M.F.

WINCHCOMBE, John (by 1519–74), of Bucklebury, Berks.

READING	1553 (Mar.)
LUDGERSHALL	1554 (Apr.), 1555
WOOTTON BASSETT	1571

b. by 1519, 1st s. of John Winchcombe† of Newbury prob. by his 1st w. Jane (Joan) or Elizabeth. m. bef. 1550, Helen, da. of Thomas St. Loe, 3s. 1da. suc. fa. 2 Dec. 1557.[1]

Commr. or capt. musters, Berks. 1546, commr. church goods Mar. 1553; escheator, Berks. and Oxon. 1552–3, 1560–1; j.p.q. Berks from c.1559, sheriff 1571–2.[2]

Winchcombe's family had been connected with Protector Somerset, whose servant Sir John Thynne* was influential at Wootton Bassett, and Thynne was probably his patron in 1571. In this Parliament Winchcombe sat on committees for griefs and petitions (7 Apr.) and the preservation of woods (10 May).

When he became head of his family in 1557, Winchcombe succeeded to lands bought by his father at the dissolution of the monasteries with money left by the

most famous of the Winchcombes, the great clothier 'Jack of Newbury', who had died in 1520. The 1571 MP was the first of his house to settle at Bucklebury, a few miles north-east of Newbury, centre of a large estate which had formerly belonged to Reading abbey: the property also included the manors of East Lockinge and Thatcham, with many houses and cottages, and over 5,000 acres of land, nearly half of it pasture. The family kept up the clothing business for many years, but the younger John, unlike his father, who supplied the Henrician court with kerseys, does not appear to have played an active part in it. Information about him is largely concerned with county administration, and little has been ascertained about his private life: the presumption is that he lived as a country gentleman on the profits of the family trade. Bishop Jewel in 1564 asked him for information on the religious position of Berkshire justices, and described him as a furtherer of sound religion, and among the returns which Winchcombe sent up to the Council were inventories of a Berkshire recusant's lands. He was also actively interested in the county musters as late as 1560.[3]

He died at the end of February 1574: the entry in the Bucklebury register styled him 'lord of this parish'. Some of the confusion in the family pedigrees may be explained by the death of his eldest son, another John, very soon afterwards. The eventual heir was the second son, Francis, aged about 18. Three months after Winchcombe's death the widow remarried.[4]

[1] E150/822/5; Vis. Berks. (Harl. Soc. lvii), 233; Ashmole, Berks. iii. 300; A. L. Humphreys, Bucklebury, ped. opp. p. 310. [2] LP Hen. VIII, xxi(1), p. 40 seq.; CPR, 1553 and App. Edw. VI, p. 413. [3] CJ, i. 83, 88; LP Hen. VIII, xiv(1), p. 151; xv. p. 109; Humphreys, 311; VCH Berks. iii. 291; E150/822/5; CPR, 1553 and App. Edw. VI, pp. 351, 413; 1563–6, pp. 385–6; Cam. Misc. ix(3), p. 38; CSP Dom. Add. 1547–65, p. 502. [4] Wards 7/15/56; Humphreys, 328; London Mar. Lic. (Harl. Soc. xxv), 60.

N.M.F.

WINGFIELD, Anthony I (c.1554–1605), of Letheringham and Goodwins Hoo, Suff.

ORFORD	1571, 1572
DUNWICH	1584, 1586
SUFFOLK	1589

b. c.1554, 1st s. of Sir Robert Wingfield* by his 1st w. Cecily, da. of Thomas Wentworth†, 1st Baron Wentworth. educ. Peterhouse, Camb. 1566; G. Inn 1572. m. Anne, da. of Thomas Burd of Denston, Suff., s.p. suc. fa. 1596. Kntd. 1597.

J.p. Suff. from c.1583, poss. temp. rem. 1587, dep. lt. and commr. musters c.1596, sheriff 1597–8.

In view of his family's status, Wingfield can have had no difficulty in gaining parliamentary seats in Suffolk, the first (if the dates of his father's inquisition post mortem are correct) when he was aged about 17. His will mentions his relations by marriage, the family of Sone or Soone, who sat for both Orford and Dunwich in this period.

In 1587 a man of his name was removed from the Suffolk commission of the peace. If this was the MP the reason was probably that his father was still on the commission. There was no doubt about Wingfield's protestantism. In 1601 the Privy Council described him as 'well affected in religion', and he was one of those responsible for organizing the removal of recusant prisoners from Wisbech to Framlingham. On several occasions the Council asked him to act as arbitrator in local disputes; and he was joined with other local gentlemen in such varied tasks as inquiring into the complaints of poor debtors in Ipswich gaol, and supervising the collection of timber in Suffolk for shipbuilding. In Parliament the only reference found to him by name is as a member of a committee on the bill for Orford harbour, 13 Feb. 1589. As knight of the shire in 1589 he could have served on the subsidy committee (11 Feb.) and a committee concerning attorneys, 17 Feb.

He died on 29 Dec. 1605, his heir being his brother Sir Thomas. His will, made in October of that year and proved in February 1606, left lands at Staleshoo and Fyttons in Suffolk, from which his widow, the executrix, was to enjoy the revenue. Sir Thomas, to whom he owed £300, was to have the rent from the manor of Dullingham, Cambridgeshire, and armour, a tent and 'implements of war'. There were several legacies to relatives – for example, £200 to Anthony Wingfield of Lincolnshire, and £100 to Robert, son of John Sone or Soone of King's Lynn, 'after he has served his apprenticeship'. Wingfield asked to be buried 'without pomp' in Letheringham church.

Visct. Powerscourt, *Wingfield Muns.* 4, 5, 30; Lansd. 121, f. 65; 737, f. 149; *APC*, xxii. 35; xxvi. 51, 98, 123; xxviii. 121; xxx. 393, 428; xxxi. 327; D'Ewes, 431, 432, 433; PCC 7 Stafford.

J.C.H.

WINGFIELD, Anthony II (c.1550–c.1615), of Wantisden, Suff.

RIPON   1593

b. c.1550, 2nd or 3rd s. of Richard Wingfield* of Wantisden by Mary, da. of John Hardwick of Derbys.; bro. of ? Henry* and Sir John*. *educ.* Trinity Coll. Camb. 1569, BA 1574, fellow 1576, MA 1577; G. Inn 1572. Prob. *unm.*

Reader in Greek to Queen Elizabeth; public orator, Camb. 16 Mar. 1581–25 Sept. 1589; proctor, Camb. 1582.

It is difficult to distinguish Wingfield's career from those of numerous namesakes. He appears not to have been mentioned by name in the journals of the 1593 Parliament, but as one of the burgesses for Ripon he might have served on committees concerned with cloth (15, 23 Mar. and 3 Apr.), weirs (28 Mar.) and maimed soldiers and mariners (2 Apr.). He owed his one appearance in the Commons to his aunt, the well-known

Bess of Hardwick, and a letter survives dated 19 Jan. 1593 from the archbishop of York to the 7th Earl of Shrewsbury promising that the Earl's cousin, Anthony Wingfield, should be 'returned a burgess for one of the towns belonging to the see'. The same influence can be seen in Wingfield's appointment, near the end of Elizabeth's reign, as tutor to the sons of William Cavendish, Bess of Hardwick's stepson.

It may have been this Anthony Wingfield who, in 1595, leased certain prebends of Lincoln cathedral. On 23 May 1599, the Member wrote to Cecil, congratulating him on his appointment as master of the court of wards, though he seems to have had no illusions about Cecil, whom his most famous epigram, 'the peer content', written in 1605, is thought to satirize. About 1608 the philosopher Thomas Hobbes succeeded Wingfield as tutor to the Cavendish children, and after this Wingfield's life is obscure. The date of his death is uncertain, and no will has been found.

DNB; Visct. Powerscourt, *Wingfield Muns.*; *Vis. Suff.* ed. Metcalfe, 175–6; D'Ewes, 507, 512, 513, 514; *APC*, xi. 212; Coll. of Arms, Talbot mss, transcribed by G. Batho; *CSP Dom.* 1595–7, p. 5; *HMC Hatfield*, ix. 179.

J.J.C.

WINGFIELD, Edward (c.1562–1603), of Kimbolton, Hunts.

HUNTINGDONSHIRE   1586, 1589, 1593

b. c.1562, o.s. of Thomas Wingfield of Kimbolton by his 2nd w. Honora, da. of Sir Anthony Denny†, of Cheshunt, Herts. and Waltham Abbey, Essex. *m.* Mary, da. of Sir James Harington* of Exton, Rutland, 5s. 3da.[1] ?Kntd. 1587;[2] *suc.* fa. 1592.

With Leicester in the Netherlands 1587; col. against the Armada 1588; capt. Portugal expedition 1589, at Cadiz 1596; col. in Ireland in 1599, capt. 1602.

J.p. Hunts. from c.1584, temp. rem. 1587, rest. by 1590.[3] Gent. pens. 1591/3–1603.

The Wingfields were one of the three leading families in a county that had no resident peer. Wingfield himself sat as senior knight of the shire for Huntingdonshire in three successive Parliaments, two of them while his father was alive. The county Members as such were appointed to subsidy committees on 22 Feb. 1587, 11 Feb. 1589 and 26 Feb. 1593, and to a legal committee on 9 Mar. 1593.[4]

After the death of his first wife Mary, daughter of Sir Francis Knollys, Wingfield's father 'entered into a wasteful course of life', which was 'likely to have consumed all his living in a very short time'. Control of the family lands was therefore taken out of his hands in February 1574 and vested in trustees: Lord Burghley, the Earl of Sussex, Sir Francis Walsingham, Sir Christopher Hatton, Sir Henry Neville, Henry Knollys and Sir Walter Mildmay. Wingfield himself was soon in trouble with them for contriving the sale of timber from the estate for ready money, without their consent. He was called before the Privy Council and reprimanded.

On his father's death the trustees gave him possession, but he remained always in debt. A loan from Stephen Riddlesden* of £1,000 in 1588 was still unpaid in 1599, when Riddleston told the Privy Council. Wingfield agreed that his lands should be extended to pay the debt, but there were other creditors who had prior claims, including one 'Abbycock Perrye', a seaman on the *Garland* in the Islands voyage on which Wingfield had served. His position declined further over the collection of the 1593 subsidy and over his opposition in 1596 to the tax levied to provide the militia captains' monthly allowance. Three years later he was thought to be using a company he had raised for service in Ireland to pursue a personal vendetta. Failing to obtain the command of Brill in 1598, he went to Ireland, where he was wounded in the following year. At this point he ruined his prospects irretrievably by offending the Queen, though all that is known about the incident is his complaint to Cecil that he had been greatly wronged in false reports to her. He remained in Ireland through the 1601 summer campaign and was wounded at the crossing of the Blackwater, but Cecil, though 'far from wishing him ill' could or would do nothing for him, and Wingfield returned to England in the spring of 1602, his wound making it impossible for him to ride more than ten miles at a stretch. After visiting Kimbolton, and being refused permission to go to court, he went to Bristol to arrange and accompany supplies and reinforcements for Ireland. Towards the end of 1602 the lord deputy put him in command of a company of 200 men. In the meantime Wingfield's wife continued to solicit for preferment until Cecil made it clear that further efforts would 'do him harm rather than good'.[5]

Finally returning from Ireland in 1603 Wingfield was imprisoned in the Fleet for debt. 'Dear lord,' he pleaded with Cecil after three weeks' imprisonment, 'as ever you did love me, now stick unto me, one kind word from your mouth will make me for ever.' He may or may not have been released before his death intestate on 20 Nov. that year. The wardship of his heir was granted to Lady Wingfield but Kimbolton was sold in 1606.[6]

[1] C142/284/35; 310/75; *Vis. Hunts.* (Cam. Soc. xliii), 131. [2] Shaw, *Knights*, ii. 84, gives Edward Wingfield of Kimbolton as knighted in 1586, but in the parliamentary return of that year he is described as esquire, and again in November 1587, Lansd. 53, f. 181. He was probably the Edward Wingfield knighted by the Earl of Leicester at Flushing 7 Dec. 1587, Shaw, *Knights*, ii. 86. [3] C142/310/75; E163/14/8; Lansd. 53, f. 189; Hatfield ms 278. [4] D'Ewes, 409, 431, 474, 496. [5] C2 Eliz./R8/59; *VCH Hunts.* iii. 80; *CSP Ire.* 1586-8, p. 407; 1600-1, pp. 250-1, 403-4, 432; *CSP Dom.* 1547-80, pp. 663-4, 667; 1581-90, pp. 519, 522; 1595-7, pp. 127, 272; 1598-1601, p. 78; 1601-3, p. 175; Hakluyt, *Voyages*, vi. 495; Visct. Powerscourt, *Wingfield Muns.* 26; Lansd. 78, f. 68; *APC*, xii. 93; xxv. 191-2; xxix. 658, 694-5, 713; xxxi. 404; *HMC Hatfield*, ix. 147, 365; x. 292; xi. 569-70; xii. 97, 104-5, 166, 168-9, 171, 191, 209, 372, 565; *Chamberlain Letters* ed. McClure, i. 62; *Cal. Carew Pprs.* 1601-3,

pp. 157, 251, 266, 314, 345, 364; *Letters of Sir Robert Cecil* (Cam. Soc. lxxxviii), 101-2. [6] *HMC Hatfield*, xv. 105, 110, 143; xvi. 296; C142/284/35; *VCH Hunts.* iii. 80.

A.M.M.

WINGFIELD, Edward Maria (c.1550–c.1614), of Stoneley, Hunts.

CHIPPENHAM	1593

b. c.1550, 1st s. of Thomas Maria Wingfield† of Stoneley by Margaret, da. of Edward Kaye of Woodsome, Yorks. *unm. suc.* fa. 15 Aug. 1557.
Capt. in Ireland and Netherlands c.1575–90; patentee of Virginia Co. 10 Apr. 1606; member of council and president, Virginia May–Sept. 1607.[1]

Although Edward Maria Wingfield is well known by reason of his part in the settlement of Virginia, he has not previously been identified with the 'Edward Wingfeild esquire' who sat in the Parliament of 1593. Yet there can be little doubt that they were one and the same: the only contemporary bearing these names, the third son of Edward Wingfield* of Kimbolton, was a child of some seven years at the time of the 1593 election.[2]

There is nothing in the story (dating from 1613) that Edward Wingfield's father acquired the second christian name which he was to transmit to his three sons by being a godson of Queen Mary and Cardinal Pole, for he had been born about 1518; the name was perhaps a mark of respect on the part of his father, the eminent courtier of Henry VIII, for the infant Princess Mary. Thomas Wingfield married a Yorkshire woman, purchased Stoneley priory hard by the family seat of Kimbolton, and sat in four Marian Parliaments before dying prematurely in 1557. His widow soon remarried, and it was to her new husband, James Cruse or Crewes, that the wardship of the young Edward was granted in March 1562. The Cruses were considerable investors in monastic property in the East Midlands, and one of their acquisitions was the suppressed college of Fotheringay, Northamptonshire. It was thus at Stoneley and Fotheringay, which lie about 15 miles apart, that Edward and his younger brothers Thomas and James passed their boyhood.[3]

The Wingfields were a fighting family, and it was to the profession of arms that both Edward and Thomas gravitated. Thomas's career is better documented than Edward's, which is to be inferred rather than followed; it is not clear, for instance, whether he or his cousin of Kimbolton figured in the affray with Walter Ralegh at Westminster in March 1580 which led to imprisonment. Both Edward and Thomas served in Ireland, as did several of their kinsmen, but Thomas may have preceded his brother to the Netherlands when he went over with the expeditionary force in August 1585, for 18 months later the Queen named 'one Wingfield' as ready to murder Mary Queen of Scots, an undertaking for which Edward Wingfield's domicile at Fotheringay would have specially qualified him. When he reached the Netherlands Edward was taken prisoner, and as Thomas was to write in November 1588 of 'my brother's long imprisonment' his capture probably took place soon after his arrival. At least part of his captivity was passed at Lille. Thomas's eagerness to effect Edward's release by taking a valuable prisoner himself was one of the causes of a quarrel between him and General Willoughby which led to his dismissal. Edward was still a prisoner in June 1589 and the date of his release has not been found.[4]

It was perhaps his experiences at Spanish hands which both prompted and commended Wingfield's claim to a seat in Parliament. The one he occupied, in a borough and county with which he had no connexion, he could have owed only to Anthony Mildmay*, whose house at Apethorpe lay next to Fotheringay and whose father had been much involved with the Wingfields of Kimbolton. Through his marriage to Grace Sharington of Lacock, Mildmay acquired patronage at Chippenham which enabled him to nominate to at least one seat there for the last three Elizabethan Parliaments and the first of James's; and Edward Wingfield must be accounted the first beneficiary. His election brought the number of Wingfields in the House to five, although only one of them, Sir Edward of Kimbolton, was his near kinsman. To judge from the lack of reference to him, Edward proved a silent and passive Member, though he may have sat on a committee appointed to consider cloth on 15 Mar. 1593.[5]

A like obscurity surrounds the next 12 years of his life before he emerges, in 1606, as a founder of Virginia. Wingfield's interest in plantation had first been roused in Ireland; in May 1586 he had figured, to the tune of 3,000 or 4,000 acres, in a project for a Wingfield colony in Munster. When, 20 years later, he tried his fortune in Virginia, he met with disaster. Elected first president of the settlement, he fell foul of his colleagues, was deposed and cast in heavy damages for slander. He returned to England in 1608 and spent his closing years at Stoneley which, since he was unmarried, passed at his death (about 1614) to his brother Thomas. Wingfield's diary of the Virginia enterprise was rediscovered and published in 1860.[6]

[1] DNB, which errs in date of birth and name of wife; Vis. Hunts. (Cam. Soc. xliii), 131; VCH Hunts. iii. 81. [2] Sir Edw. Wingfield's s. and h. James was 19 in May 1603, C142/284/35. [3] Vis. Hunts. loc. cit.; Feet of Fines, Hunts. ed. Turner (Camb. Antiq. Soc. oct. ser. xxxvii), 143; Vis. Northants. 1564, ed. Metcalfe, 16; CPR, 1557-8, p. 396; 1560-3, p. 232; 1563-6, p. 74; Bridges, Northants. ii. 458. [4] APC, xi. 421, 429; C. Read, Burghley 368; CSP For. July-Dec. 1588, p. 307; Jan.-July 1589, p. 332; CSP Dom. 1581-90. p. 542. [5] D'Ewes, 501. [6] CSP Ire. 1586-8, pp. 52, 62; DNB; VCH Hunts. loc. cit.

S.T.B.

WINGFIELD, Henry

ORFORD 1584

EITHER

5th s. of Sir Anthony Wingfield[†], vice-chamberlain to Henry VIII, by Elizabeth, da. of Sir George de Vere; bro. of Sir Robert* and Richard*. m. da. of one Bacon, 3s.
J.p. Suff. from c.1592.

OR

1st s. of Richard Wingfield* by Mary, da. of John Hardwick of Derbys.; bro. of Anthony II* and Sir John*. m. Elizabeth, da. of Thomas Revesby of Suff.

The fact that the 1584 Orford MP is styled 'esquire' in the election return makes it marginally more likely that he was the first of the above gentlemen. This branch of the Wingfields was connected with the Sones, several of whom sat for Orford in this period, and Richard Wingfield (brother of the first above-mentioned and father of the second) had sat for Orford, so there would have been no difficulty about securing the return of either. The MP was made a freeman of Orford at his election to Parliament, and gave a signed undertaking not to ask for parliamentary wages. On 12 Mar. 1583 'Mr. Cavendish, Mr. Henry Wingfield and Mr. Sone' figure in the Ipswich assembly book, asking that one Gabriel Dole, tailor, should be made a freeman. Nothing further of interest has been ascertained about either Henry Wingfield, and no will or inquisition post mortem has been found.

Visct. Powerscourt, Wingfield Muns. 5, 30; Orford act bk. p. 16; Ipswich ass. bk. 20-30 Eliz.

N.M.F.

WINGFIELD, John (c.1560-1626), of Tickencote, Rutland.

PETERBOROUGH	1597
STAMFORD	1621
GRANTHAM	1626

b. c.1560, 2nd s. of Robert Wingfield I* of Upton, Northants. by Elizabeth, da. of Richard Cecil[†] of Little Burghley, Northants.; bro. of Robert II*. educ. Westminster; Trinity Coll. Camb. 1578. m. (1) Elizabeth (d.1602), da. and h. of Paul Gresham, at least 3s. 1da.; (2) Margaret (d.1618), da. of Robert Thorold of Haugh, Lincs. and wid. of John Blyth of Denton, 2s. 3da.
?J.p. Lincs. (Kesteven) from c.1583; feodary, Lincs. 1594-1600.

Wingfield's father left the upbringing of his children to his brother-in-law, Lord Burghley. The £120 which his maternal grandmother, Jane Cecil, had given for his advancement Wingfield probably laid out upon the purchase of his marriage to Elizabeth Gresham, which brought him the manor of Tickencote, his principal residence thenceforward. Burghley appointed him to the lucrative post of feodary in Lincolnshire. It was perhaps partly on the profit of this office that Wingfield was able to purchase further lands in Rutland, and to leave his children substantial sums in his will. His return at Peterborough in 1597 was probably promoted by Burghley with the support of Wingfield's elder brother Robert, who was resident within the soke of Peterborough. He was inactive in the House and was licensed to depart on 5 Dec., well before the end of the session. He died in 1626 and was buried, as he requested, in the chapel of Tickencote church with his first wife.

Vis. Rutland (Harl. Soc. iii), 32; Blore, *Rutland*, ii. 70; PCC 104 Hele, 19 Carew; Burke, *Commoners*, ii. 480; *Lincs. Peds.* (Harl. Soc. lii), 979–80; E101/667/43; C142/422/55; *VCH Rutland*, ii. 142, 246, 276–7, 281; D'Ewes, 568.

S.M.T.

WINGFIELD, Sir John (d. 1596), of Withcall, Lincs.

LICHFIELD   1593

2nd or 3rd s. of Richard Wingfield* of Wantisden, Suff. by Mary, da. and coh. of John Hardwick of Derbys.; bro. of Anthony II* and ?Henry* *m.* 30 Sept. 1581, Susan, da. of Richard Bertie* and wid. of Reginald Grey*, *de jure* 5th Earl of Kent, 1s. Kntd. 1586.
    Capt. of ft. under Leicester in Netherlands Dec. 1585; dep. gov. Bergen-op-Zoom June 1587–8; gov. Gertrudenberg July 1588–9; master of the ordnance in Brittany 1591–2; commanded reg. at Cadiz 1596.
    J.p.q. Lincs. (Lindsey) from c.1583.

Wingfield was a soldier, wounded in action before Zutphen in September 1586, and subsequently knighted by Leicester for bravery. He was among the 12 knights 'of his kindred and friends', who walked in the funeral procession of Sir Philip Sidney*.[1]
Wingfield's marriage to the widow of the Earl of Kent aroused the Queen's temporary displeasure, but provided him with a powerful patron in her brother, Peregrine, Lord Willoughby de Eresby, who succeeded Leicester as general of the English forces in the Netherlands. His brother-in-law soon made him his deputy governor, and it was in this capacity that Wingfield wrote to the States in March 1588 asking for more supplies to withstand an attack by Parma. At the end of April he was among those sent to Gertrudenberg to treat with the mutinous garrison, and in July, after the States had agreed to pay the garrison's arrears of pay, Willoughby left him there as governor. It was an appointment satisfactory only to the garrison. The States having opposed the appointment, and desiring a governor who would have made their own control of the town evident, now produced a steady stream of complaints against Wingfield, culminating in the charge that captured supplies were being sold by the garrison to the Spaniards. The Queen urged Willoughby to investigate this charge with 'all partiality of alliance laid aside'. Finally, when the garrison went over to the

Spaniards and Parma allowed Wingfield and his family to leave, they were imprisoned for treason by the States at Breda.[2]
In 1591 Wingfield, as well as commanding a company of 150 footmen, was master of the ordnance under Sir John Norris, in Brittany. He was relieved of his post in 1592. By 1593 he had become associated with the Earl of Essex, who gained him his only seat in Parliament – for Lichfield in that year. He served on the subsidy committee and that for the relief of poor, maimed soldiers and mariners.[3]
Wingfield's last military venture was also undertaken in company with Essex. In the Cadiz expedition of 1596 he was camp master and in command of a regiment, which included his own company of 150 men and seven other companies, each of 100 men. He was the only person of note to be killed in the taking of Cadiz, being struck down by a shot in the market place, at the moment when all resistance was ceasing. He was buried with military honours in the chief church of Cadiz.[4]
Wingfield died intestate. His widow renounced the administration of his estate, which was granted to a creditor, William Browne of London. Lady Wingfield told Cecil in September 1596 that she owed tradesmen £900, as she and her husband had lived on credit for the past seven years, and when she heard the news of her husband's death she had 'not one penny in the house to buy meat … till her Majesty, most like a gracious sovereign, hearing of my misery, sent me £40'. She begged for an annuity, now 'it hath pleased the Lord to lay his heavy cross upon me in taking my husband from me, who hath not only lost all his worldly substance in her Majesty's service, but confirmed his faith and great desire to serve her Majesty with ending his life therein'. She got £100 p.a. for her own life, and that of her son Peregrine.[5]

[1] *DNB*; *CP*, vii. 171; *CSP For.* 1586–7, p. 214; July–Dec. 1588, p. 140; Lansd. 737, f. 145v; *Suff. Green Bks.* xii. 200. [2] *CSP Dom.* 1587–90, p. 95; *HMC Ancaster*, 46, 105–6; *CSP For.* Jan.–July 1588, p. 357; July–Dec. 1588, pp. xiv. 66, 67, 140, 250, 397; Jan.–July 1589, pp. xviii. 169, 187, 194–6, 200, 272. [3] *DNB*; Lansd. 149, f. 49; *APC*, xxii. 329; Neale, *Commons*, 238; D'Ewes, 474; *HMC Hatfield*, iv. 295. [4] *HMC Hatfield*, vi. 361; *DNB*; Strype, *Annals*, iv. 286. [5] PCC admon. act bk. 1596, f. 189; *HMC Hatfield*, vi. 366; *CSP Dom.* 1595–7, p. 454.

A.M.M.

WINGFIELD, Richard (d. c.1591), of Wantisden and Crowfield, Suff.

ORFORD   1559, 1586, 1589

3rd s. of Sir Anthony Wingfield‡, vice-chamberlain to Henry VIII, by Elizabeth, da. of Sir George de Vere; bro. of Sir Robert* and ?Henry*. *m.* (1) Mary, da. and coh. of John Hardwick of Derbys., 3s. Anthony II*, Sir John and ?Henry* 2da.; (2) Johanna or Joan (da. of one Clarke), wid. of John Harbottle of Crowfield, ?s.p.[1]
    J.p. Suff. from c.1559; ?gent. usher c.1578.

Wingfield's first return for Orford followed that of his relative Thomas Seckford for both Orford and Ipswich. Seckford chose Ipswich, and Wingfield came in for Orford. Members of his family continued to represent the borough for some years thereafter. It is not certain that the same man continued to sit in 1586 and 1589, as a namesake, later 1st Viscount Powerscourt, was old enough to have been the Member. But the latter was a soldier in the Netherlands in the autumn of 1586 and on the Portugal expedition in 1589, and the probability is that Richard of Wantisden was the Member on all three occasions. Little is known of his career, which is difficult to distinguish from that of his namesake. There is no evidence as to which of them was the gentleman usher, but Richard of Wantisden, who had family connexions with the Earls of Shrewsbury and Oxford, is quite likely to have held a post at court. In Suffolk he was important enough to be included in the commission of the peace, and in his own part of the country he had considerable influence. In 1582 he supported the petition of puritan justices to the Privy Council, complaining of the activities of assize judges against radical preachers. By 1585, and presumably earlier, he was a free burgess of Orford, where his family had intermarried with the local Sone family.

Wingfield's will, drawn up in May 1588, and proved 14 Aug. 1591, is that of a fairly wealthy country gentleman. It begins with an assertion of his belief that redemption came through Christ, 'by whose only merits, mediation and intercession I look ... to be received into the kingdom of Heaven, there to live in the fellowship of all the chosen saints of God in joy and peace for ever'. Presumably through his first wife, he held lands in Derbyshire, Herefordshire, Staffordshire, Warwickshire and Worcestershire, and the will sets out the arrangements by which these were to descend to his son Henry, who also received a £100 bequest. Another son, John, was bequeathed the manor of Iken, Suffolk, held on lease from Sir Robert Wingfield. John was also to share the profits of manors at Chiselford, where Wingfield apparently bred horses and owned flocks of sheep. There were bequests to several of his relatives, including the Sones, Sir Robert Wingfield and his son Anthony*. A number of servants received 40s. each.[2]

¹ Vis. Suff. ed. Metcalfe, 37, 175–6; Visct. Powerscourt, Wingfield Muns. 5, 30; APC, x. 286, 304. ² HMC Var. iv. 275; DNB (Wingfield, Sir Richard); CP; Orford act bk. 19; CSP For. 1586–7, p. 275; Collinson thesis, 870, 908–10; PCC 62 Sainberbe.

J.C.H.

WINGFIELD, Robert I (d. 1580), of Upton, Northants.

PETERBOROUGH   1559, 1563, 1572*

1st s. of Robert Wingfield of Upton by Margery, da. of George Quarles of Ufford. educ. Pembroke, Camb. 1549; G. Inn 1552. m. Elizabeth, da. of Richard Cecil† of Little

Burghley, 2s. John* and Robert II* 2da. suc. fa. 1576. J.p. Northants. 1559.

Wingfield came from a cadet branch of the Suffolk Wingfields, established as minor gentlemen within the soke of Peterborough. He was no doubt brought into Parliament through the influence of his brother-in-law, Sir William Cecil, referred to in his will as 'my very good lord', and to whom he entrusted the oversight of his children and estates. Like his father, Wingfield was a substantial sheep farmer, and most contemporary references to the family, apart from those relating to a long quarrel with their neighbours the Fitzwilliams, concern the preservation and improvement of their estates. Both father and son were described as 'great furtherers' of religion in the bishops' letters of 1564.

Wingfield died on 31 Mar. 1580. His inquisition post mortem, taken before his cousin, George Quarles, shows that he, like his father, had purchased new lands to consolidate the old. His mother-in-law, Jane Cecil, had given him money to purchase an estate for his younger son John as well, but this he had not accomplished, and he left instructions for the money to be returned so that she could employ it for John's use as she thought fit. His heir was the elder son, Robert, who was to be ruled by Lord Burghley, or 'take no benefit by me of anything herein contained'.

Bridges, Northants. ii. 508; PCC 19 Carew, 25 Arundel; Northants. Rec. Soc. xviii. p. xl; M. Finch, Five Northants. Fams. (Northants. Rec. Soc. xix), 316; HMC Hatfield, i. 253; CPR, 1560–3, p. 320; PRO cal. pat. rolls 1–16 Eliz. 12(10), p. 270; Cam. Misc. ix(3), p. 36; C142/190/52.

S.M.T.

WINGFIELD, Robert II (c. 1558–1609), of Upton, Northants.

STAMFORD   1584, 1586, 1589, 1593, 1597, 1601, 1604*

b. c. 1558, 1st s. of Robert Wingfield I* of Upton by Elizabeth, da. of Richard Cecil† of Little Burghley, Northants.; bro. of John*. educ. G. Inn 1576. m. Prudence, da. of (Sir) John Croke II* of Chilton, Bucks., 3s. 1da. suc. fa. 1580. Kntd. 1603.

J.p. Northants. from c. 1591, q. 1601; keeper of Moorhay walk by 1587; attended funeral of Mary Stuart, 1 Aug. 1587; commr. sewers, Lincs. 1588, Northants. 1600, Hunts., Lincs., Northants. 1601; commr. musters, Northants. 1596; seneschal, manor of Waddington, Lincs. 1598; dep. steward, liberty of Spalding, Lincs. by 1604; surveyor for Northants. in or bef. 1606; subsidy collector, Northants. 1609.[1]

Wingfield's mother was Lord Burghley's sister, and it was to the Cecils that he looked, if not for preferment, then for protection. Thus, after incurring the royal displeasure over monopolies in the 1597 Parliament,

Wingfield wrote to Cecil (28 Dec. 1597), making sure to send a present at the same time: 'Your favour ... towards me this Parliament comforts me as much as if you gave me a great benefit'. And to Burghley early in 1592, asking for a lease, 'I hope your lordship will not forget me for if I have it not by your lordship's means, I look never to have it'.

On Burghley's death Wingfield wrote to Cecil,

Your letters to me, a poor countryman, out of heart since the decease of my honourable lord, brought exceeding comfort, and so much that I am at a strife with myself which way to show myself thankful ... As one confined to the country and vowing to abridge myself of all worldly pleasures, I will ever be devoted to your house in all love.[2]

Evidently Parliament was not among his 'worldly pleasures', for Wingfield sat in every one between 1584 and 1604, as a burgess for Stamford, where he was born, and where the Cecil connexion assured him a place. However, it was not until 18 Dec. 1592 that he became a freeman of the borough in recognition of his willingness 'to do the town any pleasure he can' and 'his sundry travail in the town affairs and specially being often times one of the burgesses for the town at the High Court of Parliament'. Five years later – in October 1597 – he was put on the town council and frequently attended meetings. The Privy Council used him at least twice to settle disputes there.[3]

No parliamentary activity is known for Wingfield before 1597. His committee work in that Parliament included George Durant's will (8 Nov.); marriages without banns (11 Nov.); collecting the clerical subsidy (12 Nov.); enlarging the marriages without banns matter to include other 'grievances touching ecclesiastical causes' (14 Nov.); rogues and sturdy beggars (22 Nov.); (Sir) John Spencer's* lands (25 Nov.); draining the fens (2 Dec.); double payment of debts on shop books (2 Dec.); a bill for the Marquess of Winchester (9 Dec.); ordinances made by corporations (12 Jan. 1598, he reported this 16 Jan.) and a private lands bill (20 Jan.). Wingfield spoke on a procedural matter on 8 Feb., otherwise his only interventions in this Parliament concerned 'sundry enormities growing by patents of privilege and monopolies and the abuses of them', as he put it, 8 Nov. 1597. He was named to the committee dealing with the problem three days later, and, 21 Nov., he 'delivered some particular informations to Mr. Chancellor' about it. But four years later, 9 Nov. 1601, when nothing had been done, and Wingfield felt that the Queen might dissolve Parliament before the great debate could be renewed, he suggested a device that was to become common practice in the seventeenth-century struggles between Crown and Parliament:

that seeing the subsidy was granted, and they yet had

done nothing, it would please her Majesty not to dissolve the Parliament until some Acts were passed.

This was not the sort of blackmail calculated to endear Wingfield to the Queen, and, with this speech, Wingfield must have said goodbye to any hopes of preferment while Elizabeth was on the throne. Perhaps he had already done so. When he returned to the charge on 20 Nov. 1601 his speech reflects his knowledge of the displeasure he had already earned for his interventions on monopolies in 1597:

I would but put the House in mind of the proceedings we had in this matter the last Parliament, in the end whereof Mr. Speaker moved her Majesty by way of petition, that the grief touching the monopolies might be respected, and the grievance coming of them might be redressed. Her Majesty answered by the lord keeper, that she would take care of these monopolies and our griefs should be redressed. If not she would give us free liberty to proceed in making a law the next Parliament. ...
The wound, Mr. Speaker, is still bleeding, and we grieve under the sore and are without remedy. It was my hap the last Parliament to encounter with the word prerogative, but as then, so now, I do it with all humility, and with all happiness, both unto it and her Majesty. I am indifferent touching our proceedings whether by bill or petition ...

When the Queen gave way, Wingfield's reaction (25 Nov.) shows a typically Elizabethan dichotomy – an enthusiastic first part ('My heart is not able to conceive the joy that I feel ... if ever any of her Majesty's words were meritorious before God, I do think these are') to be contrasted with the practical reservations of a second in reply to Francis More's suggestion that the House should 'humbly crave pardon'.

For us to accuse ourselves by excusing a fault with which we are not charged, were a thing, in my opinion, inconvenient and unfitting the wisdom of this House.

Another of Wingfield's preoccupations took place against a local background: land drainage. Already in 1591 or 1592 he had written to Burghley about the completion of an undertaking to drain 400 acres in Northamptonshire, which had cost the county about £100. Next he signed a letter to the Privy Council from 'divers gentlemen and inhabitants' of the counties of Huntingdon, Lincoln, and Northampton, desiring permission to organize further projects of land reclamation. His interest in legislation on the subject in 1597 has already been noted in his committee activity for that Parliament, but the 1597 bill came to nothing, for, after being passed by both Houses it was vetoed by the Queen, whether to pay out Wingfield for his line on monopolies or for some more creditable reason cannot be known. At any rate, after petitioning the Privy Council on the subject in June 1598 Wingfield embarked upon some lobbying in the Parliament of 1601. Hayward Townshend notes (5 Dec.):

> Mr. Wingfield showed me the bill touching fens, which was established the last Parliament, and passed both Houses, but advised upon by her Majesty [and] showed me also the bill for fens in this Parliament.

This was the bill he introduced on 21 Nov. 1601, and supported two days later. It was read a second time on 14 Dec. But he was still concerned with 'the business for the draining of the fens' at Cambridge in 1606, and he had another 'great bill of the fens' in Parliament that year. However, Wingfield's later parliamentary career will be dealt with elsewhere. In the Parliament of 1601 he was appointed to committees on privileges and returns (31 Oct.), penal laws (2 Nov.), the order of business (3 Nov.), the Sabbath day (6 Nov.) and procedure (11 Nov.). His speeches not already noted were on Exchequer reform (21 Nov.) and to suggest a collection for the locum clerk (17 Dec.).[4]

Wingfield could hope for nothing while Elizabeth lived. He thought of going to Ireland with Essex in January 1599 but in July was 'a poor countryman ... no way able to deserve a favourable look ... confined to the country'. Hoping for better things under James, he offered Cecil hospitality when the secretary met the King at Burghley. Wingfield's house was 'within three miles of that place'. More presents to Cecil (a falcon and a 'dainty teg') preceded an application for a job in the privy chamber (12 Feb. 1605). In October 1606 he still hoped 'to deserve the King's favour' but died without it, at Upton, 24 Aug. 1609.[5]

[1] C142/190/52; Hatfield ms 278; C66/1549; *CSP Dom.* 1581–90, p. 397; 1601–3, p. 71; 1603–10, p. 504; Lansd. 57. f. 20; 171, f. 397v; *APC*, xxv. 157; xxx. 677; PRO list duchy patents, f. 17; *HMC Hatfield*, xvi. 343; *HMC Bath*, v. 83. [2] *CSP Dom.* 1595–7, p. 553; Lansd. 67, f. 37; *HMC Hatfield*, ix. 255. [3] Visct. Powerscourt, *Wingfield Muns.* passim; *APC*, xxv. 76; xxx. 73. [4] D'Ewes, 553, 554, 555, 556, 560, 561, 563, 566, 571, 581, 584, 595, 622, 624, 628, 632, 635, 646, 654, 668–9, 685; Townshend, *Hist. Colls.* 102, 104, 108, 111, 114, 119, 204, 234, 236, 237, 240, 252, 331; Lansd. 67, f. 37; *HMC Hatfield*, viii. 244; xviii. 332, 456. [5] *HMC Hatfield*, ix. 53, 255; xv. 41; xvi. 385; xvii. 51; xviii. 332; xxi. 121.

A.M.M./P.W.H.

WINGFIELD, Sir Robert (d. 1596), of Letheringham, Suff.

SUFFOLK   1563, 1572

1st s. of Sir Anthony Wingfield†, vice-chamberlain to Henry VIII, by Elizabeth, da. of Sir George Vere; bro. of Richard* and ?Henry*. *educ.* ?G. Inn 1537. *m.* (1) Cecily, da. of Thomas Wentworth†, 1st Baron Wentworth, 3s. inc. Anthony I* 2da.; (2) aft. 1570, Bridget, da. of Sir John Spring of Lavenham, wid. of Thomas Fleetwood*, ?s.p. suc. fa. 1552, mother 1559. Kntd. ?2 Oct. 1553.

Sheriff, Norf. and Suff. 1560–1; j.p. Suff. from c.1559, commr. piracy by 1578, grain 1580s, dep. lt. 1585.

Wingfield had extensive lands in Suffolk, Buckinghamshire, Cambridgeshire, Leicestershire, Middlesex and Norfolk. He was active in Suffolk affairs, signing a letter to the Privy Council in favour of John Lawrence the puritan preacher in August 1567, and exerting his influence on behalf of the more radical clergy of the district as an ecclesiastical commissioner for the Norwich diocese in the 1570s. His name appears among the signatories to the 1582 petition to the Privy Council from the puritan justices of the peace. With others of his religious group he disliked the extremists known as the Family of Love. In 1581 he was an arbitrator in Sir Robert Drury's tithe dispute with the puritan Oliver Pig.

In April 1565 Wingfield was one of those asked to 'take care in the good assessing of the subsidy'. The only reference found to him during the 1563 session of Parliament is his being granted leave of absence, 'for his affairs at the assizes', 27 Feb. He was a member of the succession committee 31 Oct. 1566 and one of 30 Members summoned from the Commons on 5 Nov. 1566 to hear the Queen's message on the succession. His other committees concerned the lands of the Woodhouse family (20 May 1572) and the subsidies of 10 Feb. 1576 and 25 Jan. 1581. He died on 19 Mar. 1596. His will, made in 1584, was proved 28 June 1596. Apart from several legacies to the poor, he left everything to his eldest son and heir Anthony.

Viscount Powerscourt, *Wingfield Muns.* 4–5; *Vis. Suff.* ed. Metcalfe, 81; *DNB* (Wingfield, Sir Anthony); *CPR*, 1558–60, p. 447; 1560–3, p. 381; Collinson thesis, passim; *Parker Corresp.* (Parker Soc.), 306; *APC*, xi. 138; xiii. 138, 154, 361, 378; A. Peel, *Second Parte of a Register*, i. 31, 48; Lansd. 8, f. 80; 48, f. 136 seq.; 109, f. 210; 146, f. 18; *CJ*, i. 67, 96, 104, 119; D'Ewes, 86, 127, 212, 247, 288; Camb. Univ. Lib. Gg, iii. 34, p. 209; PCC 43 Drake.

N.M.F.

WINTER, *see* **WYNTER**

WISEMAN, Edmund (d. 1605), of London and later of Steventon, Berks.

PLYMPTON ERLE   1563*[1]

Yr. s. of Thomas Wiseman of Thornham, Suff. *m.* Anne (d. 1584), da. and coh. of William Hawkins of London, 4s. (1 d.v.p.) 4da.

Escheator, Oxon. and Berks. 1570–1; j.p. Berks. from c.1577.[2]

Wiseman's early life is obscure. During the 1560s he was granted a number of wardships, and was associated in land transactions with Thomas Andrews I* and Bartholomew Kemp*, both of whom were connected with Sir Nicholas Bacon† and were mentioned in his will. Wiseman was himself known to the lord keeper, as appears from a licence of 20 May 1566 granting Sir

Nicholas Bacon, Andrews and Wiseman permission to alienate the manor of Ingham in Suffolk. Bacon was a member of a small puritan group at court, which included the 2nd Earl of Bedford, and which had sought to have well-disposed Members returned to the first two Elizabethan Parliaments. It seems possible, therefore, that it was Bedford (probably through Sir Nicholas Bacon) who nominated Wiseman for the seat made vacant at Plympton by the death of Thomas Percy.

By 1570, when he was appointed escheator for Oxfordshire and Berkshire, Wiseman presumably resided in Berkshire. He outlived his eldest son William, who died in 1603. Earlier in the same year, on 3 June, Wiseman made his will. After a short religious preamble, in which he stated that he was 'firmly hoping and believing to be saved through the merits and passion of our Lord and Saviour Jesus Christ', he expressed a desire to be buried beside his wife in Steventon church. There were bequests to relatives and friends, as well as a bequest of £5 to form a stock for the poor of Steventon, and £2 as a stock for the poor of Wolston. His son Charles, the executor, proved the will on 13 June 1605, Wiseman having died on 24 Mar.[3]

[1] Folger, V. b. 298. [2] *Vis. Berks.* (Harl. Soc. lvi), 144–5. [3] *CPR,* 1558–60, pp. 304–5; 1560–3, pp. 179, 265, 463, 480–1; 1563–6, pp. 139, 171, 408, 470, 486; 1566–9, pp. 143, 366, 403; PCC 1 Bakon, 46 Hayes; Mill Stephenson, *Mon. Brasses,* 28; C142/290/107.

A.M.M.

WISEMAN, Robert (c.1530–c.99), of Great Canfield, Essex, later of Greenwich, Kent.

BRAMBER 1571

b. c.1530, 2nd s. of John Wiseman† of Canfield by Agnes, da. of (?Ralph) Josselyn of Essex. *educ.* ?Gonville Hall, Camb. 1544. *m.* (?1) Mary. rel. to the Eliotts of Essex; (?2) Anne, da. of Sir Gamaliel Capell of Raynes, Essex, *s.p.*
Gent. pens. by 1564–1602; j.p. Kent from c.1583–c.92.

No coherent story emerges from the few isolated enigmatic incidents known to have occurred in this Member's life. However, there is no doubt that he came into Parliament for Bramber through the unfortunate 4th Duke of Norfolk, who frequently nominated there, and with whom Wiseman is known to have had confidential dealings. It might be guessed therefore that Wiseman would be suspected of Catholicism and that his loyalty might be at issue, were it not for his court office, an office, moreover, especially close to the sovereign, membership of the honourable band of gentlemen pensioners, her bodyguard within the royal palace. Yet such was the case. Sir Ralph Sadler* wrote to Cecil 18 June 1570, a few months after the northern rebellion of Catholics against the Queen:

If her Majesty knew Mr. Wiseman as well as I do, she would not think him worthy of any benefit, for he is one

of the greatest papists I know, and was in the north, in a very suspicious manner, with the Earl of Northumberland, not long before this last rebellion, and brought letters from the Duke of Norfolk. He favours this late rebellion as much as any man in England, and if he were asked whether he was here at the time, and why, you will understand more.

When 'asked', he admitted taking letters from the Duke of Norfolk to the captain of the gentlemen pensioners, the Earl of Sussex, who was then at Cawood, Lancashire. Wiseman took care, however, to be back at Windsor before 'any stir of the northern rebels began', as he put it. There is independent evidence that at least one branch of the Wiseman family in Essex was Catholic.

Then there were two curious and unexplained assaults on his person, the first in about 1564 on an Essex highway when a band of malefactors led by one Leonard Berners cried 'Kill the villain' and almost did, the second sometime before January 1578 when the master of the rolls was trying to settle a dispute between him and 'certain persons in Greenwich touching an assault'. Perhaps for these there is no intentionally concealed explanation, but it is just possible that, in addition to his post at court, which was not full time, he was some sort of government agent. In June 1573 he was provided with post horses for himself, two servants and a guide 'going to Carlisle and returning' on official business. He paid several visits to Ireland between September 1587 and December 1591, clearing the official accounts of a government official named Jacques Wingfield†, who may have been his brother-in-law. Perhaps as a sequel to this the Queen recommended him (about 1594) for the post of clerk of the outlawries, but Edward Coke* scotched the idea, thinking him 'utterly unmeet and insufficient for the place'.

Wiseman and his brother sold Great Canfield soon after coming into the property in 1558. He obtained a 21-year lease of land in Middlesex and Kent in 1568, and, when he was not at court, or otherwise employed, he resided at Greenwich from at least 1578. It was 'from my cabin at Greenwich' that he wrote a begging letter to (Sir) Robert Cecil* in 1599. He was now unable 'by reason of infirmity' to come to court and pleaded his service there 'these 53 years and the Queen's servant 40 years past'. This may be exaggeration, or may refer to a period in his life which, if all accounts of it were not lost, might provide some items of interest to his biographer. Elizabeth was, save with money, generous to her old servants (see for example Thomas Markham*), overlooking Catholicism in their families and even disloyalty, and sheltering them from the jealousy of other courtiers and even from the law itself. Perhaps this is the key to understanding Wiseman's career. At any rate his last plea to Cecil went unheeded, and in all probability he died in want soon after making it, aged about 70.

Vis. Essex (Harl. Soc. xiii), 48, 49, 191–2, 370; PCC 38 Noodes;

C142/118/48; *CPR*, 1558–60, p. 242; 1560–3, p. 201; 1563–6, p. 129; 1566–9, pp. 266–7; W. Berry, *Co. Genealogies, Suss.* 107; Morant, *Essex*, ii. 461; *HMC Hatfield*, i. 435; iv. 511; ix. 241, 244, 248; *CSP Dom.* Add. 1566–79, p. 200; *Cath. Rec. Soc.* ii. 285, 287; iii. 31; St. Ch. 5/W5/5; *APC*, viii. 119; x. 144; xviii. 56; xxiii. 203; *CSP Ire.* 1586–8, p. 407; 1588–92, pp. 293, 442–3; PCC admon. act. bk. 1587, f. 30; A. Vicars, *Index Wills of Ireland*, 501; Lansd. 106, f. 117.

P.W.H.

WISEMAN, William (c.1550–1610), of Mayland, Essex, and of Lincoln's Inn, London.

MALDON 1584, 1597, 1601, 1604*

b. c.1550, 7th s. of John Wiseman (*d.*1559), of Felsted by his w. Joan Lucas of London. *educ.* Peterhouse, Camb. 1564; L. Inn 1567, called c.1578. *m.* Mary, da. of John Cooke of Rochford, Essex 1s. 5da.

J.p. Essex from 1592; of counsel to Maldon 1593, dep. recorder 1597, recorder by 1603.

Wiseman, an interesting minor Commons figure, a little in advance of his time, and not at all the 'rural and country man' he called himself in the House in 1601, was a younger son of an Essex gentry family. His father was an escheator for Essex and Hertfordshire in 1558, and other members of the family held local offices. Wiseman himself was a lawyer who worked for Robert Rich*, 3rd Baron Rich, who may have brought him into Parliament to hold a watching brief for him over 'the bill for the establishment of an award made between the Lord Rich and Sir Thomas Barrington', read 16 Mar. 1585, to the committee of which Wiseman was appointed. He stood unsuccessfully in 1586, and came in again in 1597, the year he became deputy recorder. In that Parliament he was on committees for the poor (24 Nov.), monopolies and draining the fens (3 Dec.), corn (8 Dec.), cloth (10 Dec.), the navy (16 Jan.), the Surrey county boundary (19 Jan.), herrings (20 Jan.), soldiers and mariners (26 Jan.), law reform (1 and 3 Feb.), wine casks (3 Feb.) and pawnbrokers (7 Feb.). Apart from reporting two of these committees he made no speeches in this Parliament. In that of 1601, however, he was an active speaker and committeeman. He was appointed to the committee of privileges and returns (31 Oct.), and spoke (4 Nov.) on the Rutland election case. Sir Andrew Noel, the sheriff, had returned himself. Wiseman spoke of the necessity of having all Members present 'because otherwise the body is but maimed', and it was in any case inadvisable to allow the return of 'great officers' in case freeholders might prefer them to 'men far more sufficient for that place'. On 7 Nov. he spoke in committee on the subsidy, and on 1 Dec. he asked for a call of the House and for a collection for the poor. On 8 Dec. he spoke on a hardy perennial, the misbehaviour of servants on the stairs leading to the Commons chamber ('men dare not go down the stairs without a conductor'). Wiseman's concern for the rights of the ordinary

Members was shown again on 10 Dec. 1601. When the Speaker offered another bill to avoid a discussion on ordnance, Wiseman said, 'I make great difference between the old Roman consuls and [the Speaker] ... we know our own grievances better than Mr. Speaker'. He complained (14 Dec.) that too much time was spent on the affairs of the city of London. Wiseman also spoke on the penal laws (2 Nov.), the composition of committees (11 Nov.), another privilege matter (14 Nov.) and unmarried mothers (twice, 19 Dec.). In the committee of the whole house, 7 Nov., since 'some must break the ice', he proposed the subsidy, but at the low rate of 2s. 8d. in the £. Typically, for this type of Member, he urged leaving 'our orations and speeches, fitter for a Parliament than a committee'. As well as the committee of privileges, already mentioned, Wiseman in 1601 sat on the committees for penal laws (2 Nov.), alehouses (5 Nov.), the better setting of watches (7 Nov.), feltmakers (26 Nov.), the clerk of the market (2 Dec.) and fustians (4 Dec.).[1]

Though others of his family were Catholics, Wiseman himself, as might be expected from his connexions with Lord Rich, was inclined towards puritanism. He was still being referred to as of Lincoln's Inn in 1607. In the preamble to his will, dated 20 July 1608 and proved 15 Feb. 1610, he hoped

> through the death and merit of ... Christ Jesus to have all my sins forgiven and to inherit the kingdom prepared for His elect.

He bequeathed 40s. to a puritan minister of Vange, Essex, who had been twice suspended for not subscribing to the Articles. He left £300 to each of his three unmarried daughters, and made provision for his widow. The ten poorest householders of Southminster, Althorne and Steeple were to have 2s. each, and he gave £10 to his sons-in-law, who, with Lord Rich, were the executors. The bulk of his estate was to go to Robert, his son and heir, aged about 30 when Wiseman died on 19 Jan. 1610.[2]

[1] *Vis. Essex* (Harl. Soc. xiii), 562–7; *CPR*, 1558–60, p. 365; Essex RO, Sessions Bk. DB 1/6; assize file 35/34; DB 3/1/8, DB 3/3/27, DB 3/3/270, 272; *L. Inn Black Bk.* ii. 69; D'Ewes, 368, 369, 562, 567, 569, 571, 581, 583, 584, 588, 592, 594, 622, 624–5, 626, 629, 630, 634, 637, 654, 661, 663, 668, 673, 677; Townshend, *Hist. Colls.* 108, 111, 113, 114, 121, 180, 185–6, 198, 208, 213, 269, 297, 306–7, 325, 333; *HMC Hatfield*, xi. 484. [2] *Trans. Essex Arch. Soc.* xv. 58; PCC 15 Wingfield; *Essex Rev.* xl. 129; C142/323/54.

J.H./P.W.H.

WITHERS, Lawrence (*d.*1574), of London.

LONDON 1563

m., at least 2s., prob. 2da.

Alderman, London 1550–6; president of St. Bartholomew's hospital 1556–7; merchant adventurer by 1564.

Withers was a member of the Salters Company, and was elected to the 1563 Parliament as one of the common council's nominees. In the House he was a member of the succession committee in October 1566.

He was one of a syndicate of London merchants who at the beginning of Elizabeth's reign lent the Queen £30,000 at 10% interest. In 1560, in partnership with Sir William Chester* and others, he was granted reversions and rents of lands in a number of counties. This was presumably another credit transaction with the Crown, since the grantees surrendered their patent early in 1562. Withers owned the manor of Isle Brewers, Somerset, which he settled on his younger son, George. In default of George's heirs the property was to descend to Alice, wife of William Lowes, and Elizabeth, wife of Thomas Davy, salter – presumably George's sisters.

Withers died on 25 Feb. 1574. The heir was his elder son Fabian, aged over 30 when his father died.

Wards 7/15/32, 52; A. B. Beaven, *Aldermen*, i. 182, 246; ii. 33; N. Moore, *Bartholomew's Hospital*, ii. 801; D'Ewes, 127; *CPR*, 1558–60, pp. 353–4, 431 seq.; 1560–3, p. 112; 1563–6, p. 178.

N.M.F.

WITNALL *alias* **ELES, Rowland** (*d.*1595), of Chipping Wycombe, Bucks.

CHIPPING WYCOMBE 1572

?s. of John Witnall of Chipping Wycombe. *m.* Elizabeth, 4da.

Alderman, Chipping Wycombe from 1564, mayor 1561–2, 1562–3, ?1571–2.

This Member called himself 'Rowland Witnall *alias* Eles', the entry in the printed *Return of Members* presumably being a misreading of the second variant as written on the actual election return. In his will, made 20 Mar. and proved 8 Apr. 1595, he mentioned the 'most holy, blessed and undivided Trinity', asked to be buried in the church of Wycombe, and provided small sums towards the repair of the church and the poor of the parish. His brother 'Robert Wytnall *alias* Ellis' was sole executor.

First Wycombe Ledger Bk. ed. Greaves (Bucks. Rec. Soc. xi), passim; PCC 24 Scott.

P.W.H.

WOGAN, John (1538–80), of Wiston, Pemb.

PEMBROKESHIRE 1571, 1572*

b. 1538, 1st s. of Richard Wogan of Wiston by Elizabeth, da. of Sir Thomas Gamage of Coity, Glam., *m.* Cecilia, da. of Sir Edward Carne† of Ewenny priory, Glam., 1s. *suc.* gd.-fa. 24 Aug. 1557.

J.p. Pemb. from 1564, sheriff 1566–7, 1571–2; sheriff, Card. 1563–4.

The Wogans were an old-established family with many branches in Pembrokeshire, the Wogans of Wiston having been prominent in local government since the fifteenth century. Their position in the sixteenth century was assured by this Member's grandfather, (Sir) John Wogan†, who, in return for his services to Henry VIII, received a grant of offices in Cardiganshire and Pembrokeshire. In his will, made shortly before his death in August 1557, Sir John Wogan did not mention his grandson, leaving his personal estate to his widow Alice. But when John was 21 in 1559 (his father having predeceased the grandfather) he must have entered on the major part of his grandfather's landed estate, and his position in the county was soon recognized by his inclusion in the commission of the peace.[1]

In 1564 Wogan was involved in a dispute at court in the company of Edward Vaughan and Francis Langhorne, the other protagonists being apparently nine servants of Lord Cobham. Wogan and his friends were imprisoned in the Fleet, but were released after less than a month's imprisonment, on condition that they entered into bonds for their continued attendance at court. Wogan's principal interests lay in Pembrokeshire, and it is there that he spent the greater part of his short life. In 1570, as one of the wealthier gentry, he was responsible for providing two fully furnished light horsemen at the musters, and in 1572, when he was sheriff, he wrote to Lord Burghley reporting the discovery of some treasure trove, and signed himself 'your Lordship's most assured and poor kinsman at commandment'.[2]

It was only natural that Wogan should play a part in the faction fighting that occupied the Pembrokeshire gentry in the early 1570s. He and his cousin John Wogan of Boulston were supporters of Sir John Perrot*, against the party led by William Philipps* of Picton, Alban Stepneth* and George Owen of Henlys. The story of the 1571 election in Haverfordwest, which was strongly contested by the two groups, has been told elsewhere. It is possible that there was also a contest for the county seat, but no evidence has survived of any objection to Wogan's return. In the following year Wogan was ineligible to stand because he was sheriff, and William Philipps of the opposing party was returned. Wogan regained the seat after Philipps's death in 1573, but only lived long enough to represent the county in the session of 1576, dying 4 May 1580, having previously settled his estate, and leaving a son, William, aged seventeen.[3]

[1] C142/113/3, 114/19; *DWB*, 1090; Dwnn, *Vis. Wales*, i. 108; C66/998; Egerton, 2345, f. 43; SP12/145/51b. [2] *DWB*, 1090; PCC 45 Wrastley; *APC*, vii. 149, 154, 156; Flenley, *Cal. Reg. Council, Marches of Wales*, 73; Lansd, 14, f. 33. [3] *Arch. Camb.* (ser. 5), xiii. 196; Neale, *Commons*, 255–6; *EHR*, lxi. 18–27; C142/191/68.

A.M.M.

WOLLEY, Francis (1583–1609), of Pyrford, Surr.

HASLEMERE 1601

b. 1583, 1st s. of John Wolley* of Pyrford by his 2nd w. Elizabeth, da. of (Sir) William More I* of Loseley, wid. of Richard Polsted* of Albany. *educ.* Merton, Oxf. 1596, BA 1598; L. Inn 1600. *m.* 11 Sept. 1594, Mary, da. of Sir William Hawtry of Pyrford; 1da. illegit. *suc.* fa. 1596. Kntd. 1603.

Clerk of the pipe from 1607.

Wolley, aged 18, was returned to the 1601 Parliament for Haslemere on the nomination of his uncle (Sir) George More*, the lord of the manor. In 1595 his father, the Latin secretary, was trying to provide for his son's future by having him joined with him in his patent as clerk of the pipe, but Francis secured the reversion only in 1605 and the clerkship itself in 1607. He also obtained the reversion of the keepership of Folly park, Windsor forest. On Twelfth Night 1608 he was among those gambling with James I when 'no gamester was admitted that brought not £300', winning over £800. He was named in the second charter of the Virginia Company, and he bought land near his estates in Surrey during these years.

Wolley made his will 11 Aug. 1609, adding a codicil on 1 Nov., six days before his death at Pyrford. It was proved by his executors 12 Dec. He wished to be buried in St. Paul's cathedral, at the feet of his father, and set aside £4,000 for the erection of a 'fair tomb' for his parents and himself. For as long as it remained undefaced, and the bodies undisturbed, the cathedral was to receive £10 a year. He left a total of £1,300 to his servants. His illegitimate daughter, who had been christened by his wife and a Mrs. Bridget Weston 'in Pyrford church and called by the name of Mary Wolley', received the manor of Burgham and other lands in Worplesdon. Sir Arthur Mainwaring inherited most of his estates.

Manning and Bray, *Surr.* i. 155; *HMC 7th Rep.* 652; C142/249/74, 334/60; Add. 35906, f. 2v; *HMC Hatfield*, v. 152–3; *Chamberlain Letters* ed. McClure, i. 204, 253; *CSP Dom.* 1603–10, pp. 236, 369; W. Stith, *Hist. Discovery and Settlement of Virginia*, App, 10; *VCH Surr.* iii. 98, 100; PCC 118 Dorset.

A.M.M.

WOLLEY, John (*d.* 1596), of Thorpe and Pyrford, Surr.

EAST LOOE	1571
WEYMOUTH AND MELCOMBE	
REGIS	1572
WINCHESTER	1584, 1586
DORSET	1589
SURREY	1593

s. of John Wolley of Leigh, Dorset by Edith, da. of John Buckler of Causeway, near Weymouth, Dorset. *educ.* Merton, Oxf. fellow 1553, BA 1553, MA 1557, DCL 1566. *m.* (1) Jane, da. of William Sanderson; (2) by 1583,

Elizabeth, da. of (Sir) William More I* of Loseley, Surr., wid. of Richard Polsted*, at least 1s. Francis*. Kntd. 1592.

In Queen's service by 1563, Latin sec. from c.Dec.1568; prebendary of Compton Dundon, Som. 1569; dean of Carlisle 1577; j.p. Surr. from c.1583; PC 30 Sept. 1586; chancellor of order of the Garter 1589; keeper of recs. ct. of augmentations and clerk of the pipe by 1592; member, ct. of high commission 1590.[1]

From 1571 until his death Wolley sat in every Parliament. Made a Privy Councillor just after the 1586 election, he filled the role of a government spokesman and upholder of the royal prerogative, supporting official policy on all possible occasions. His seats at East Looe and Weymouth were no doubt found for him by the 2nd Earl of Bedford, and at Winchester the name of Walsingham suggests itself. But for so reliable a government servant a vacancy could always be found. His election for Dorset is interesting, for he had not resided in the county for years. The presumption is that, as a Privy Councillor, it was thought he ought to represent a county if possible. Walsingham and William Howard pre-empting the Surrey seats in 1589, someone thought of Wolley's native county. Similarly after his appointment to the Privy Council a change creeps into the style of the references to him in the journals of the House – he is no longer plain Mr. Wolley, but Mr. Secretary Wolley, though his appointment as Latin secretary would in itself have entitled him to the appellation in his first three Parliaments. For his next Parliament he was Sir John Wolley. The earliest recorded mention of him in the journals is a speech on usury, 19 Apr. 1571, when he defended lending money at reasonable interest as against 'the great mischief which doth grow by reason of excessive taking, to the destruction of young gentlemen.' No speech by him has been found in the journals for any session of the long 1572 Parliament, but he sat on committees dealing with church presentations, 19 May 1572; the poor, 11 Feb. 1576; bastardy, 15 Feb. 1576; the subsidy, 25 Jan. 1581; seditious practices, 1 Feb. 1581, and the Queen's safety, 14 Mar. 1581. Again, no speech is recorded for him in the 1584 Parliament, though he was employed in negotiations with the Lords over the fraudulent conveyances bill, 15 and 18 Feb. 1585. He was named to committees on Arthur Hall*, 12 Dec. 1584; the liberty of ministers, 16 Dec.; appeals from ecclesiastical courts, 18 Dec.; ecclesiastical livings, the maintenance of the navy and the preservation of grain, 19 Dec.; and the subsidy, 24 Feb. 1585. On 3 Nov. 1586 he spoke on the subject of Mary Queen of Scots, and he was one of those who presented the petition to the Queen on this subject, 22 Nov. He was on two legal committees, 15 and 17 Mar. 1587. Two speeches by Wolley are recorded in the Parliament of 1589. On 25 Feb. he put the House

in remembrance of her Majesty's express inhibition delivered to this House by the mouth of the lord chancellor at the beginning of this session of Parliament touching any dealing with ecclesiastical causes,

and, 29 Mar., the last day of the session, he urged a declaration of war against Spain. He was named to committees on benefit of clergy, 10 Feb.; the subsidy, 11 Feb.; Richard Southwell, 13 Mar. and church presentations, 20 Mar. At the beginning of his last Parliament Wolley spoke on the subsidy, 26 Feb. 1593. First 'he showed how the princes of the Holy League had conspired the overthrow of this realm', then

> exhorted the House, now the season of the year grows on, which called for many of the knights and burgesses to be in their countries, besides the sickness being in the town, so that many of that House knew not whether he lodged in a house infected or not

to end Parliament as soon as possible. Next, (his only departure from the official line) he urged that a committee be appointed to inquire into the Dunkirk pirates. Finally, after a conventional report for 'a speedy agreeing of a subsidy' he concluded, with a typically Elizabethan appeal to parsimony and patriotism:

> the wars which the King of Spain brought upon this nation had cost her Majesty a million of money [but] where it cost her Majesty one it cost the King of Spain three.

The next day Wolley again warned the House against debating religious matters in the face of the Queen's prohibition. He spoke on a procedural point on 6 Mar. and, 21 Mar., spoke in favour of allowing foreign merchants to trade. His committees during this Parliament included the subsidy, 26 Feb.; alien merchants, 6 Mar.; springing uses, 9 Mar.; a bill about the forgery of counsellors' hands, 10 and 19 Mar. (he reported this the next day, recommending its suppression); kerseys, 23 Mar., and the restraint of new building, 9 Apr. From 1586 onwards he would have attended the many committees to which the Privy Councillors as such were appointed.[2]

On several occasions Wolley described himself as a 'faithful follower' of Lord Burghley. He received a letter of sympathy from Sir Christopher Hatton when endangered by the smallpox, and thanked Sir Francis Walsingham for obtaining an appointment for his father-in-law. Wolley was married to one of the Queen's ladies-in-waiting, a daughter of her old favourite, Sir William More, and she became godmother to Wolley's son in 1583. Eleven years later he sent a letter to Sir Robert Cecil enclosing a petition to her, requesting permission to have his son joined in his grant from the Exchequer. Four months before his death Wolley applied for the chancellorship of the duchy of Lancaster, 20 Oct. 1595. He had served the Queen, in his own words, 'now upon the point of 30 years'.[3]

In 1590 Wolley purchased various parsonages in Surrey for £1,010, and in the subsidy assessment for that county,

taken just before his death, he was rated at over £40. He died at Pyrford on 28 Feb. 1596 and was buried in St. Paul's cathedral. In his will, made three days before his death, and proved on the following 13 Mar., Wolley commended his soul to Almighty God 'whom I humbly thank for my creation'. His body was to be buried 'without any pomp', and his wife, who soon married Lord Keeper Egerton*, was appointed sole executrix and residuary legatee, with his 'very good friends' Sir William* and George More* supervisors. Bequests were made to servants, and debts were to be paid, especial care being taken that no man be defrauded. In a codicil he remembered his sister, Mrs. Eleanor Hardy, and two servants to whom he left £10 each. His widow died before administration of the estate was complete, and on 4 May 1600 his son Francis took over, to be superseded, on his death, by Wolley's brother-in-law, Sir George More.[4]

[1] DNB; APC, xiv. 236; Hutchins, Dorset, ii. 645; CPR, 1566–9, p. 394; CSP Dom. 1591–4, 1595–7. [2] Trinity, Dublin, anon. jnl. f. 29v; CJ, i. 95, 105, 106, 120, 121, 134; D'Ewes, 207, 247, 288, 306, 339, 340, 341, 343, 349, 352, 356, 393, 394, 395, 399, 405, 409, 410, 412, 413, 414, 415, 416, 430, 431, 432, 438, 439, 440, 442, 443, 445, 448, 449, 453, 454, 471, 472, 473, 474, 476, 477, 478, 481, 486, 489, 490, 496, 497, 499, 502, 503, 504, 506, 507, 513, 517, 519, 520, 521; Townshend, Hist. Colls. 16, 25, 58, 59, 78. [3] HMC 7th Rep. 629, 630, 636, 666; HMC Hatfield, v. 152; Lansd. 18, f. 33; 80, f. 16; Genealogist, n.s. ii. 295. [4] PRO Index 6800, f. 223; Surr. Arch. Colls. xix. 88; PCC 21 Drake.

P.W.H.

WOOD, Edward, of Sandwich, Kent.

SANDWICH   1584, 1586

1st s. of Humphrey Wood of Derby by Joan Rogers of Marden. m. Elizabeth, da. of Thomas Bewford of Little Hadham, Herts., 1s.[1]

Freeman, Sandwich 1555, common councilman by 1562, jurat,[2] mayor 1577–8, 1578–9, 1588–9, ?1591–2,[3] brodhull rep. on several occasions.[4]

Wood's family was prominent in the affairs of Sandwich from the middle of the sixteenth to the middle of the seventeenth century, during which time it supplied four mayors. It is not known why Wood's father moved from Derby to Kent, but Wood himself and his younger brother Stephen began to take an active part in the local government of Sandwich in the 1550s. In June 1559, when the silting of the harbour was causing concern, Wood and another local man went over to Flanders to find 'a cunning and expert man in water works for to take in hand the amendment of the haven'. They engaged an engineer called Jacobson, of Amsterdam, who died at Sandwich the following October, having had time only to sketch out a fresh plan at an estimated cost of £10,000. As a common councilman, Wood contributed £3 6s. 8d. in May 1563 to the new school founded by Roger Manwood* and was among its first wardens. By 1573, when the Queen visited Sandwich, he was clearly one of the senior townsmen: he lived next door to the Manwoods, and figured prominently in the ceremonies. During his second mayoralty, the new guildhall was completed and his initials were carved over the door.

Wood was first returned to Parliament in 1584, after a four-cornered contest. A fortnight before the election he and William Crisp, the mayor, had been summoned, with representatives of the other Ports, to the lord warden's house, Cobham Hall, perhaps in connexion with the forthcoming Parliament. He was re-elected in 1586, when the freemen, in another contested election, presumably acted on the Privy Council's request that the 1584 Members would be chosen again. On each occasion he was paid 4s. a day. As one of the Sandwich burgesses in the 1586 Parliament he could have sat on a committee concerned with fish, 6 Mar.[5]

Like most leading townsmen in the Ports, Wood represented his borough at a number of brodhull meetings. Among these was the occasion in 1572 when an attempt was made to restrict the choice of parliamentary burgesses to the freemen of the Ports. Later, in 1580, he was fined £3 'for an injury done against our charters'. The date of Wood's death has not been found, but it probably occurred soon after 1592. His only son, William, was mayor of Sandwich three times between 1596 and 1608.[6]

[1] *Vis. Kent* (Harl. Soc. lxxv), 148. [2] Sandwich little black bk. 1552–67, f. 80; *Vis. Kent* (Harl. Soc. lxxv), 59. [3] There is confusion over the mayors, 1591–3, between *Vis. Kent* and Boys, *Sandwich*, i. 419. [4] Cinque Ports black bk. [5] Little black bk., ff. 80, 140, 147; Gardiner, *Historic Haven*, 202; Boys, *Sandwich*, 207, 208, 213, 692; Hasted, *Hist. Kent*, x. 166; Sandwich year bk., 1582–1608, ff. 26, 59; D'Ewes, 412. [6] Cinque Ports black bk.; *Vis. Kent*, 148; Boys, 419–20.

M.R.P.

WOOD (AWOODE, ATWOODE), Thomas (*d.* aft. 1604), of Cumnor, Berks.

OXFORD   1559, 1563

Though his active life spanned the whole of Elizabeth's reign, Wood is an obscure figure. He was probably the 'Thomas Wood of Woodend in Cumnor *alias* citizen of Oxford, *alias* Thomas Awoode, *alias* Atwoode', who took advantage of the general pardon in 1559. He must be distinguished from the Thomas Atwood who held the office of chamberlain of Oxford in 1583: in the will (dated 1563) of James Atwood, clothier, both Thomas Wood of Cumnor and Thomas Atwood, James's brother, are named as overseers. A Thomas Wood of Cumnor was admitted to Winchester as a scholar in 1540, aged 13.[1]

The Thomas Wood who sat in Parliament was probably a lawyer who was of counsel to the corporation of Oxford: in January 1562 a Mr. Wood was commissioned to accompany the mayor to London 'about the suit of St.

Mary college'. He was probably also a client of John Williams[†], Lord Williams of Thame, a dominant figure in Oxfordshire and high steward of Oxford for several years before his death in October 1559. Williams, who owned much land in the region of Cumnor, in 1557 alienated several manors in Oxfordshire and Berkshire to 'Thomas Woode', and another to the use of himself and his second wife. In January 1559, while Williams was still living, Wood was returned as senior burgess along with an Oxford townsman. Four years later he dropped to second place below a servant of the 2nd Earl of Bedford, Williams's friend and successor as high steward of Oxford.[2]

The loss of his patron, who left no sons, may explain Wood's decline into obscurity. He was still occasionally of use to the Oxford corporation, if he was the Mr. Wood rewarded in 1576 'for his friendship to this city in the commission of sewers' and the Thomas Wood of Cumnor who received 20s. for no stated reason in 1591. Forty years after his second return to Parliament, the council remembered in September 1604 that Thomas Wood had been 'sometime burgess of the Parliament for this city' and gave him £5 'in respect of his great charges then and of his poverty whereunto he is now fallen'.[3]

[1] *CPR*, 1558–60, p. 163; PCC 10 Stevenson; H. E. Salter, *Oxf. Council Acts* (Oxford Hist. Soc. lxxxvii), 3. [2] W. H. Turner, *Oxford Recs.* 277, 287, 299, 302; *CPR*, 1555–7, p. 238; PCC 11 Mellershe. [3] Turner, 387; Salter, 163, 369.

A.H.

WOODHOUSE, Henry (c.1545–1624), of Hickling and Waxham, Norf.

NORFOLK   1572, 1589

b. c.1545, 1st surv. s. and h. of Sir William Woodhouse* of Hickling by his 1st w. Anne, da. of Henry Repps of Thorpe Market. *educ.* Corpus, Camb. 1556; L. Inn 1561. *m.* (1) c.1574, Anne, da. of Sir Nicholas Bacon[†], at least 2s. inc. Sir William[†] 4da.; (2) Cecily, da. of Sir Thomas Gresham, at least 1s.; 11 ch. in all *suc.* fa. to Hickling 1564, uncle Sir Thomas* to Waxham 1572. Kntd. 27 Aug. 1578.

V.-adm. Norf. and Suff. c.1570–8; j.p. Norf. from c.1573 (temp. rem. 1595); commr. survey Great Yarmouth harbour 1571, musters c.1578; sheriff 1584–5; gov. Yarmouth May–Aug. 1588.

Woodhouse continued the close connexion which his father and his uncle had maintained with Admiralty affairs in East Anglia. As vice-admiral of Norfolk and Suffolk he compiled in 1570, jointly with Sir Thomas, a list of ships of over 30 tons in the two counties. From this time there are numerous references to his work on and around the Norfolk coast, and he was included in many commissions concerning such matters as assessment of losses at sea, executing Admiralty judgments, sewers, the control of grain, the trial of coiners, and recusancy. This last was the subject of the only committee to which he was appointed by name in his two Parliaments (25 Jan. 1581). As a first knight of the shire in 1589 he was appointed to the subsidy committee (11 Feb.) and as a Member for Norfolk he was put on the committee discussing the excessive number of attorneys (17 Feb. 1589).

Woodhouse's candidature in 1572 was promoted by the lord keeper who soon afterwards became his father-in-law, but by and large Woodhouse managed to remain outside the county faction fights of this period. In any case despite, or perhaps because of, his extensive estates, he ran into serious financial difficulties, to meet which in 1578 he sold his office of vice-admiral to his father-in-law, who lent him money and gave him good advice. In 1595 he was turned off the commission of the peace, but through the intervention of other county gentlemen he was soon re-appointed. Early in 1597 a schedule of his estates was drawn up in an attempt to regularize the position. In danger of imprisonment for debt, he wrote a desperate letter to the Queen, mentioning his various services, and that August he was granted 12 months' protection. Things were no better by May 1599, when he was again given protection 'till the Queen is satisfied of the debts due to her', probably a reference to his embezzlement of the fifteenths and tenths voted by the 1589 Parliament that he should have collected in Norfolk. As late as 1607 he had not paid up, and was allowed another five years' grace. He died on 8 Oct. 1624. Among his debts still outstanding were £400 to John Dee, a London goldsmith, and £100 to one William Engham. The widow was executrix and residuary legatee.

Vis. Norf. (Harl. Soc. xxxii), 321; *HMC Hatfield*, xi. 110; xiv. 14; E150/658/2; C142/161/116; *CSP Dom.* 1547–80, p. 388; 1581–90, p. 290; 1595–7, pp. 413, 495, 508; 1598–1601, p. 202; 1603–10, p. 377; Yarmouth ass. bk. 1579–98, f. 150; bk. of entries 1538–1635, ff. 204 seq., 320; *APC*, viii. 99, 253; x. 314–15; Lansd. 48, f. 136; 54, f. 134; 56, f. 168; 146, ff. 9, 18; *CPR*, 1569–72, p. 217; *CJ*, i. 119; D'Ewes, 288, 431, 433; A. Simpson, *Wealth of the Gentry*, 13, 15, 57n, 59, 73; Wards 7/86/162; PCC 15 Clarke.

N.M.F.

WOODHOUSE, Philip (d. 1623), of Kimberley, Norf.

CASTLE RISING   1586

1st s. of Roger Woodhouse* of Kimberley by Mary, da. of John Corbet† of Sprowston. *educ.* Trinity Coll. Camb. 1575; L. Inn 1580. *m.* 25 July 1580, Grissell, da. of William Yelverton of Rougham, wid. of Thomas Lestrange of Hunstanton, 6s. 2da. *suc.* fa. 1588. Kntd. 1596; *cr.* Bt. 1611.

J.p. Norf. from c.1591, sheriff 1594–5; commr. musters 1598, custos rot. 1617.

The Woodhouse family of Kimberley was one of the wealthiest in Norfolk, the seventeenth-century family poet writing that he had above £2,000 p.a. in land. Philip

Woodhouse served on a number of commissions without, however, ever becoming one of the leading gentlemen of the shire. He went on the Cadiz expedition in 1596, where he was knighted by the Earl of Essex, thenceforth playing little part in national affairs, though one of his sons was a companion and friend of Prince Henry during the early years of the reign of James I. Woodhouse was protestant but his wife, like many of her family and that of her first husband, was a Catholic. The Jesuit, John Gerard, stated that Woodhouse himself was converted following his wife's severe illness, but conformed again.

His return to Parliament for Castle Rising was no doubt due to his marriage to the widow of Thomas Lestrange and consequent control of her dower lands in north-west Norfolk. There is no trace of him in the records of the House. The fact that he did not sit again may have been because of the county faction fights, in which he supported the unpopular Sir Arthur Heveningham, and this may have cost him the friendship of a number of Norfolk families. In December 1589 he was in trouble for assisting William Downing* to eject Thomas Eden from Marsham parsonage. Woodhouse died 30 Oct. 1623, letters of administration being granted to his widow 2 Oct. 1624.

Vis. Norf. (Norf. and Norwich Arch. Soc. 1878), i. 105; G. A. Carthew, *Hundred of Launditch*, i. 144; C142/408/114; PRO Index 4211; Blomefield, *Norf.* ii. 140, 554; ix. 60–2; *Autobiog. John Gerard*, 19–21; A. H. Smith thesis, 259, 262, 274, 305–6; J. H. Morrison, *Letters of Administration 1620–30*.

R.V.

WOODHOUSE, Roger (c.1541–88), of Kimberley, Norf.

ALDEBURGH	1571
NORFOLK	1572*
THETFORD	1586

b. c.1541, 1st s. of Thomas Woodhouse (killed at Musselburgh 1547) by Margaret, da. of Sir John Shelton† of Shelton. *m.* Mary, da. of John Corbet† of Sprowston, 2s. inc. Philip* 1da. *suc.* gd.-fa. Sir Roger 1560. Kntd. 1578.

J.p. Norf. from c.1573.

Through the Sheltons Woodhouse was related to the Boleyns, and he was therefore a distant kinsman of Queen Elizabeth. He was also a relative of the Duke of Norfolk, and it is not surprising to find him returned as one of the first Members for Aldeburgh (where the Duke was lord of the borough) when it was enfranchised in 1571. After Norfolk's fall the Woodhouse influence can be seen in several later Elizabethan elections at Aldeburgh. At Thetford his patron, if any, is not so obvious. Woodhouse was on friendly terms with Sir Edward Clere* there, but it is quite likely that he did not need to rely on anyone's nomination. Kimberley was 20 miles from Thetford, and at the time of the election the Woodhouse estates were some of the largest in the district. It is surprising that

Woodhouse was not a regular county Member, for he represented Norfolk only once, and then only because of a by-election to fill the place of Francis Wyndham, who had been made a judge.

In 1580, 'by his own earnest suit', Woodhouse avoided being pricked as sheriff. In addition to his mansion at Kimberley he kept up a large house in Norwich, Surrey House, which his grandfather had acquired from an earlier Duke of Norfolk. On a number of occasions the Privy Council used him to arbitrate in local disputes, and in 1586 Woodhouse and Sir Edward Clere were instructed to take recognizances from Nicholas Clover, mayor of Thetford, and two other inhabitants of the borough, who had been summoned to the Council. Woodhouse was knighted by the Queen at Clere's house at Blickling, and during the same progress Elizabeth visited Kimberley, where Woodhouse erected a throne covered with crimson velvet showing the arms of his family and those of his wife. But by this time he had become involved in a number of lawsuits. In 1582 he was retaining Edward Flowerdew* as his lawyer at an annual fee of 40s. Some of his difficulties arose through his position as executor of Sir Thomas Knyvet of Buckenham castle, Norfolk, a relative of Thomas Knyvet*. Since Woodhouse's name appears as plaintiff in over 20 Star Chamber cases, and defendant in a number of others, Flowerdew's position cannot have been a sinecure, but as he too was engaged in the local faction fights, he was probably glad to rely on Woodhouse's support in his quarrel with Sir Arthur Heveningham.

Woodhouse was apparently no more than a conforming member of the Elizabethan church, and certainly no friend to puritans. He may even have been temporarily dropped from the commission of the peace in the 1570s at Bishop Parkhurst's suggestion, and in 1587 Bishop Scambler described him only as an 'observer of law'. He died early in 1588, and was buried on 4 Apr. at Kimberley. His only surviving child was his son Philip. A seventeenth-century poem on his family describes him as 'nobly just and wise in his affairs'; a brave patriot; 'weak men's defence against oppression'; and the 'prop of innocence'.

Vis. Norf. (Norf. and Norwich Arch. Soc. 1878), i. 104–5; Blomefield, *Norf.* passim; A. H. Smith thesis, passim; Lansd. 50, f. 148; *CJ*, i. 82–3, 135; D'Ewes, 156, 159, 307; Add. 36989, f. 5; *APC*, x. 352; xiii. 284, 422; xiv. 42, 71, 202; xv. 13, 100; *Norf. and Norwich Arch. Soc. Trans.* xxiv. 74; St. Ch. 5/R36/26, W4/26, W7/39.

N.M.F.

WOODHOUSE, Sir Thomas (by 1514–72), of Waxham and Great Yarmouth, Norf.

GREAT YARMOUTH 1558, 1559

b. by 1514, 1st s. of John Woodhouse of Waxham by Alice, da. of William Croftes of Wyston; bro. of Sir William*. *educ.* ?L. Inn 1525. *m.* Margaret, da. of William Stubbert, wid. of one Wymer of Scottow, *s.p.*; 1da. illegit. *suc.* fa. prob. by 1533. Kntd. 1549.

Escheator, Norf. and Suff. 1535–6; j.p. Norf. 1542–58, q. 1559–*d.*; jt. v.-adm. Norf. and Suff. 1543–*d.*; commr. relief, Norf. 1550; sheriff, Norf. and Suff. 1553–4, 1563–4.[1]

Woodhouse came of a family of minor gentry, apparently unrelated to the Woodhouses of Kimberley, Norfolk. He improved his status and fortune through his appointment as victualler to the royal armies and garrisons, no doubt having, as the Privy Council put it, 'overmuch regard' for his 'own commodities'. By 1546 he was rich enough to pay £1,500 for Bromholme monastery and its possessions in Norfolk. In September 1548 he paid over £1,000 for chantry estates, the first of many large land purchases, until, at his death, he had a score of manors and numerous other properties. His wealth was constantly supplemented by trade – he was planning, as late as 1565, to export large quantities of grain – and he was a founder-member of the Russia Company. He also indulged in a little piracy on the side. His connexions with Yarmouth were strong though there were the usual disputes over his claims to profits of Admiralty jurisdiction. He sat for the borough in Mary's last Parliament, and again in January 1559, presumably with the consent of the 4th Duke of Norfolk, the high steward. Either Woodhouse or his brother (both of whom were knights) must have been the 'Mr. Woodhouse' to whom a bill about the export of leather was committed in this Parliament, 14 Mar. 1559. In May the same year Woodhouse was asked to give Yarmouth his advice on the new harbour, and 'for his good will and friendship' the assembly granted him a 40s. annuity.[2]

By Elizabeth's accession Woodhouse's career was almost over. He was described by his bishop in 1564 as sound in religion, but he took little further part in public affairs. He died on 21 Jan. 1572, his will, drawn up a year earlier, being proved in June 1572. He left most of his property to his nephews and nieces and his illegitimate daughter Margaret received money and plate. The Duke of Norfolk was appointed an overseer of the will, and was left £10 worth of plate.[3]

[1] *Vis. Norf.* (Harl. Soc. xxxii), 320–1; *LP Hen. VIII*, vi. 530; xvii. pp. 408, 442, 593; xix(1), pp. 147, 247; xx(1) passim; *APC*, i. 123, 325; ii. 73, 207; HCA25/5; *CSP Dom.* 1547–80, p. 388. [2] Blomefield, *Norf.* ii. 540; ix. 353; *APC*, i. 325, 535; vi. 109, 138; vii. 260; *LP Hen. VIII*, xvii. p. 563; xxi(1), p. 570; *CPR*, 1548–9, p. 112; 1549–51, p. 322; 1550–3, p. 29; 1553 and App. Edw. VI, 401; 1554–5, pp. 156, 159 et passim; C142/161/61; *Bronnen tot de Geschiedenis van den Handel met Engeland, Schotland en Ierland*, ed. Smit, ii. 812; H. Manship, *Yarmouth*, i. 259, 325; Yarmouth ass. bks. A, ff. 189, 203, 213; B. ff. 29–32; bk. of entries 1538–1635, f. 320; Lansd. 103, f. 2; F. W. Russell, *Kett's Rebellion*, 46, 151–3; *CJ*, i. 57. [3] *Cam. Misc.* ix(3), p. 58; PCC 18 Daper; C142/161/116.

N.M.F.

WOODHOUSE, Sir William (by 1517–64), of Hickling, Norf.

GREAT YARMOUTH	1545, 1547, 1553 (Mar.)
NORFOLK	1558
NORWICH	1559
NORFOLK	1563*

b. by 1517, 2nd s. of John Woodhouse of Waxham by Alice, da. of William Croftes of Wyston; bro. of Sir Thomas*. *m.* (1) Anne, da. of Henry Repps of Thorpe Market, 2s. inc. Henry* 2da.; (2) settlement 11 Nov. 1552, Elizabeth, da. and h. of Sir Philip Calthrope of Erwarton, Suff., wid. of Sir Henry Parker†, 2s. 2da. Kntd. 13 May 1544.

Escheator, Norf. and Suff. 1538–9; master of naval ordnance 1545–52; lt.-adm. from Dec. 1552; v.-adm. Norf., Suff. 1543–63; keeper of Queenborough castle, Kent c.1546–50; j.p. Norf. from Feb. 1554, custos rot. 1561.

Of a minor gentry family, Woodhouse did well out of the Henrician reconstruction of the navy, and he became a distinguished naval officer. He received his first command by 1542, and served in French and Scottish waters. He became a member of the newly-formed Admiralty Board in 1546 and remained in office under Edward VI and Mary. There is no evidence of his attitude to religion or politics: he was loyal to the government of the day.[1]

Woodhouse obtained considerable, though not extravagant, rewards for his 20 years in the royal service. His post of lieutenant-admiral brought him a salary of £100, together with allowances and, doubtless, perquisites; and he had other gifts and licences. From grants and by judicious dealing after the dissolution of the monasteries, he acquired valuable estates in north-east Norfolk. Also, it is unlikely that his membership of the Russia Company was his only commercial venture.[2]

Woodhouse was returned to Elizabeth's first Parliament for Norwich, where he had some property. He was sworn a citizen on 18 Jan. 1559, a few days before the session began. Either he or his brother must have been the 'Mr. Woodhouse' to whom a leather bill was committed 14 Mar. 1559. In 1563 he secured election as senior knight of the shire, his colleague being Sir Edward Warner, whose ward was married to one of his daughters. Before the second session of Parliament Woodhouse died in London on 22 Nov. 1564. By his will, made a week earlier, he left bequests of money and plate to his children, and his 'best furred black gown' to his brother. He had already settled most of his estates on his second wife, and he now left her, as sole executrix, the lands not previously disposed of. The will was proved 23 Feb. 1565.[3]

[1] *Vis. Norf.* (Harl. Soc. xxxii), 320; *CPR*, 1549–51, p. 308; 1550–3, pp. 272, 329, 403; 1557–8, p. 193; 1558–60, p. 176; 1560–3, p. 440; PCC 6 Morrison; *LP Hen. VIII*, xviii(1), pp. 120–1; (2), pp. 397, 401; xix(1), p. 328; xx(2), p. 2; xxi(1), pp. 52, 275, 296, 305, 356; (2), pp. 448–9; *Norf. Antiq. Misc.* (1906), 160 seq.; *APC*, i. 60; ii. 415; iii. 37, 77; *CSP Scot.* i. 14; *Mariner's Mirror*, xiv. 30, 42–3, 51; *EHR*, xxiii. 747. [2] *APC*, iv. 250; *LP Hen. VIII*, xvii. 260, 699; xx(1), p. 302; *CPR*, 1547–8, p. 373; 1548–9, p. 86; 1550–3, p. 29; 1554–5, p. 56. [3] Norwich ass. procs. 3, f. 47; *CJ*, i. 57; PCC 6 Morrison.

R.V.

WOODROFE, Sir Nicholas (c.1530–98), of London, afterwards of Poyle, Surr.

| LONDON | 1584 |

b. c.1530, 1st s. of David Woodrofe, sheriff and haberdasher of London, by Elizabeth, da. of John Hill, alderman and grocer of London. *m.* Griselda (*d.*1607), da. of Stephen Kyrton of London, 3s. 3da. *suc.* fa. 1563. Kntd. 1580.

Master, Haberdashers' Co. 1585; treasurer, St. Thomas's hospital 1569–71, president 1584–6; alderman, London 1571–88, sheriff 1572–3, ld. mayor 1579–80.

During his membership of the Commons Woodrofe sat on committees dealing with the Sabbath day (27 Nov. 1584), grain, ecclesiastical affairs and the navy (19 Dec.), the subsidy (24 Feb. 1585), London apprentices (2 Mar.), water bailiffs (10 Mar.) and piracy (24 Mar.). At different times he was appointed by the Privy Council to a number of commissions, dealing mainly with disputes between merchants. On one occasion he was himself the subject of a complaint to the Council. In 1580 Thomas Cosgrave of Dublin reported that, though the sheriff's court of London had awarded him £30 in a case of debt, Woodrofe – then lord mayor – would not agree to the verdict, constraining him to take £20.

Woodrofe resigned as alderman in 1588, on grounds of health, and soon afterwards retired to his estate in Surrey, where he made his will on 7 May 1596. 'It hath pleased God', he wrote,

> many ways to diminish my former estate, so that I am not able to remember my wife, children, friends, and servants, with other good uses, as I much desire, and would not omit if ability did serve. I must therefore desire my friends and all others to judge the best, my estate, I protest, being so mean that I cannot accomplish that I owe in good will towards them.

He divided his personal estate according to the custom of London: a third to his wife, a third to his children, and a third for his personal bequests. He left £3 6s. 8d. to a servant, £10 to the poor at his funeral, and £10 to the poor of Farnham, Guildford, and Seale, the parish in which he lived. A further £2 was bequeathed for the repair of Seale church. The remainder of his third he left to his wife and executrix, Griselda, who proved the will on 7 Aug. 1598. He died 18 May 1598, and was buried at Seale. The heir was his son David.

C142/137/31; Manning and Bray, *Surr.* iii. 94, 175, 178; *Surr. Arch.*

Colls. xxxii. 88; *Vis. London* (Harl. Soc. cix, cx), 26; PCC 21 Chayre, 71 Lewyn; A. B. Beaven, *Aldermen,* i. 63, 139; ii. 38; D'Ewes, 333, 343, 356, 362, 365, 372; *APC,* x. 50–1; xi. 223; xii. 279.

A.M.M.

WOODWARD, George (1549–98), of Upton, Bucks.

NEW WINDSOR   1586

b. 1549, 1st s. of John Woodward by Margaret, da. of George Bulstrode of Hedgerley Bulstrode. *educ.* ?Eton 1561. *m.* (1) Katherine, da. of Thomas Woodford of Britwell, 3s.; (2) Elizabeth, da. of Robert Honywood of Charing, Kent, and Markshall, Essex, 3s. *d.v.p.* 9da. *suc.* fa. 1567.

Clerk of the works, Windsor castle and steward of honour of Windsor from July 1579; receiver of the revenue in the Exchequer for the castle and honour by 1587.

Woodward was returned for Windsor by virtue of his office at the castle. His religious sympathies probably lay with the puritans, who were strong at Windsor. On 18 Nov. 1586 he was one of the seven Members of the Commons who urged the necessity of the execution of the Queen of Scots, in reply to Queen Elizabeth's plea that some other solution might be found; and he was added to the committee which was to confer with the Lords on this 'great cause'. In his will, made 3 Jan. 1598, he renounced all other means of salvation save Christ, expressed confidence that he would be received into 'the glory of eternal life', and asked to be buried 'without pomp'. His wealth still lay in the woods which had given his family its name. He instructed three trustees, of whom his brother-in-law Michael Heneage* was one, to have 16 acres of trees felled in each of the 18 years following his death and to allocate the annual profits to his children, each in turn. Woodward was buried at Upton 30 Jan. 1598.

Vis. Bucks. (Harl. Soc. lviii), 131–2; *Eton Coll. Reg.* ed. Sterry, 377; PCC 28 Crymes, 37 Lewyn; *N. and Q.* (ser. 12), iv. 234; PRO Index 16774, f. 6; W. H. St. John Hope, *Windsor Castle,* 275–6; *The King's Works,* iii. 414; Lansd. 55, f. 19; 106, f. 1; *CPR,* 1558–60, p. 108; D'Ewes, 403.

A.H.

WOOLTON, John (c.1564–1614), of Exeter and Pilton, Devon.

TRURO   1589

b. c.1564, 1st s. of John Woolton of Whalley, Lancs. by his 1st w. *educ.* All Souls, Oxf. BA Feb. 1585, MA Jan. 1588, fellow, MB and MD July 1599. *m.* Elizabeth, at least 4s. 2da. *suc.* fa. 1594.[1]

Woolton presumably owed his seat in the Commons to his father, a former Marian exile who occupied the see of Exeter for nearly 15 years, and was a friend of the 2nd Earl of Bedford. The bishop's liberty of Truro adjoined the borough. Woolton's mother, who died about 1581, was the daughter of a priest. The Wooltons were closely related by marriage to the Nowell brothers – Dean Alexander of St. Paul's, Dean Laurence of Lichfield and Robert* – and, through them, with the puritan Bowyer family of London and Sussex, several of whom sat in Elizabethan Parliaments. Woolton himself was licensed to practise medicine in 1593, having already settled in Exeter. He remained in the city at least until 1606, when one of his children was baptized in the cathedral, and then retired to Pillon or Pillard in the parish of Pilton, near Barnstaple, an estate bought by his father. There he died 26 Oct. 1614, aged about 50. His will, dated the previous day, was proved in February 1615. The elder daughter, Elizabeth, was left £100 and the younger, Mary, 100 marks, but they were to receive their legacies only if they married with the approval of the executors. Minor bequests were made to his brother Matthew, to two sisters, including the wife of Thomas Barrett, archdeacon of Exeter, to an 'apprentice' called Katherine, and to the poor of Pilton. An inquisition, held at Barnstaple in September 1616, showed that most of his estates were in and around Pilton and were held of Robert Chichester, the leading figure in that part of Devon. All the children were under age, the heir, Anthony, being 14 years and 4 months.[2]

[1] J. Raach, *Directory of Eng. Country Physicians,* 94; PCC 20 Rudd, 37 Dixy. [2] *DNB* (Woolton or Wolton, John); *The Spending of the Money of Robert Nowell,* ed. Grosart, 267 n; Strype, *Whitgift,* iii. 153–8; *Rectors of Manchester and Wardens of Collegiate Ch.,* ed. F. R. Raines (Chetham Soc. new ser v.) 84–9; *Trans. Dev. Assoc.* lxxxi. 204; *Exeter in 17th Cent.* ed. W. G. Hoskins (Devon and Cornw. Rec. Soc. n.s. ii), 5; PCC 20 Rudd; C142/663/172.

M.R.P.

WORSLEY, Robert (d. 1604/5), of Booths, Lancs.

CALLINGTON   1589

1st s. of Sir Robert Worsley* of Booths by his 1st w. Alice, da. of Thurstan Tyldesley† (the Earl of Derby's receiver) of Wardley. *educ.* St. John's, Camb. 1562. *m.* Elizabeth, da. of Sir Thomas Gerard of Bryn, 3s. 8da. *suc.* fa. 1585.

Keeper of New Fleet prison at Salford c.1579; commr. eccles. causes, diocese of Chester 1580.[1]

Worsley belonged to an old but declining Lancashire family. He was ruined finally by his keepership of Salford gaol, despite having such powerful connexions as the 4th Earl of Derby and the puritan 3rd Earl of Huntingdon. The latter wrote of him in 1581, 'I wish Lancashire and all other counties had many such gentlemen so well affected'. As keeper of Salford gaol he had recusants in his charge, and early in 1582 he was writing to the Privy Council asking that preachers be appointed to attend them, as they 'continue obstinate for want of instruction and conference'. Meanwhile Worsley set up bible readings for the prisoners during meals. In 1581 he was granted a third of recusancy fines in Lancashire and Cheshire, but in August 1582 the justices of Cheshire objected to paying because they were maintaining their own recusants at Chester. By June 1586 Worsley was petitioning the Privy Council, either to be relieved of his post, or to be given a new lease. In December 1589 he appealed again, complaining that his prisoners were unable to pay for their lodgings and diets, and were £800 in debt to him. Even the Privy Councillors reported that Worsley was 'fallen into some decay, which their lordships do in conscience think meet should be repaired'. They recommended the Queen to grant him a 21-year lease of the fines. He also claimed expenses of £6,000 spent 'to the overthrow of his whole estate'. His petition was accepted, but in September 1590 he had still not had his money and the Privy Council again urged his 'painful diligence and care'. In January 1591 the Earl of Derby and the bishop of Chester entered the lists, and a warrant for reimbursing him was issued 30 May 1591, but it was too late. Little by little his lands were sold, including eventually, his manors of Booths and Worsley. Unable to accept his dispossession, in January 1592 he broke into the hall of Booths and re-possessed it, for which he was brought before the next quarter sessions at Wigan. By October 1605 he was dead. Worsley's grandson and heir settled on Yorkshire estates saved from the wreckage at Coulton and Hovingham.[2]

Worsley's return to Parliament for a Cornish borough was an isolated incident in his life. His immediate patron must have been either William, 7th Lord Mountjoy or the 3rd Marquess of Winchester, but as no link with either has been established, it looks as though someone at court – perhaps Derby – interceded for him.

[1] W. Dugdale, *Vis. Lancs.* iii (Chetham Soc. lxxxiii), 339–40; (xcviii), 83; *VCH Lancs.* iv. 383; *CSP Dom.* Add. 1580–1625, p. 25. [2] *HMC Hatfield*, ii. 207, 209; *Stanley Pprs.* (Chetham Soc. xxi), 36, 60; *CSP Dom.* 1547–80, p. 600; 1581–90, pp. 46, 50, 52, 65, 73, 177, 335, 337, 638; *APC*, xviii. 278; xix. 444; xx. 201; xxi. 343; xxii. 468; Lansd. 68, f. 90; 78, f. 42; Peck, *Desiderata Curiosa*, i. bk. 3, pp. 38, 39, 49–50, 51–2; J. S. Leatherbarrow, *Lancs. Eliz. Recusants* (Chetham Soc. n.s. cx), 57, 73–86, 95, 100–1; *VCH Lancs.* iv. 383; *Lancs. Q. Sess. Recs.* (Chetham Soc. n.s. lxxvii), 38, 289–90.

I.C.

WORSLEY, Sir Robert (c.1512–85), of Booths, Lancs.

LANCASHIRE   1553 (Mar.)*, 1559

b. c.1512, 1st s. of Robert Worsley of Booths by Alice, da. and coh. of Hamlet Massy of Rixton. *m.* (1) Alice, (sep. by Sept. 1547), da. of Thurstan Tyldesley[†] of Wardley, 1s. Robert*; ?(2) Margaret Beetham, 3s. *suc.* gd.-fa. 1533. Kntd. at Leith 1544.

J.p. Lancs. from c.1540, sheriff 1548–9, 1559–60; commr. musters 1553; dep. lt.; commr. eccles causes, diocese of Chester 1562.

Worsley had recently come of age when his grand-father died, leaving him considerable estates at Booths, Urmston, Hulme, Ashton-under-Lyne, Rusholme and Farnworth. Later he acquired other land in Lancashire, mainly at Pemberton and Orrell; he also owned property in the Yorkshire manors of Coulton, Holthorpe and Hovingham. But the family was declining. Soon after Elizabeth's accession Worsley began to sell houses and land, and to settle estates on members of his family. His doubtful title to the manor of Orrell, Lancashire caused expensive legal proceedings in the duchy of Lancaster courts, and about 1570 he quarrelled with his son Robert about a conveyance. Nothing is known of him in his one Elizabethan Parliament, and nothing of his religious views. He presumably conformed throughout the ecclesiastical changes of the period; he supported the Elizabethan settlement, and was a member of the commission which in 1562 inquired into the keeping of the Acts of Supremacy and Uniformity in the Chester diocese. The circumstances of his separation from his first wife are obscure. Her father's will reads in part:

> Notwithstanding that my son-in-law Sir Robert Worsley, knight, is married to Margaret Beetham, his wife yet living, yet I remit and pardon to him [a debt of] £7 10s., upon condition that he give yearly unto my daughter Alice his wife £5 or more for her exhibition during her absence from him, or upon condition that he take his said wife into his company and entreat her as he ought to do.

Worsley died in December 1585, and was buried at Eccles. No will or inquisition post mortem has been found.

VCH Lancs. iii. 428; iv. 80, 82, 90, 345, 383; *Chetham Soc.* xxxiii. 100–1; xlix. 2; l. 108–9, 131; lxxviii. 340; pal. Lancaster feet of fines, bdle. 25, m. 1; DL7/7/5; *LP Hen. VIII*, xix(1), p. 238; xxi(2), pp. 422–3; *CPR*, 1560–3, pp. 280–1.

N.M.F.

WOTTON, Edward (1548–1628), of Boughton Malherbe, Kent, and London.

KENT   1584

b. 1548, 2nd but 1st surv. s. of Thomas Wotton[†] of Boughton Malherbe by Elizabeth, da. of Sir John Rudston, ld. mayor of London; half-bro of Sir Henry Wotton.[†] *educ.* abroad. *m.* (1) 1 Sept. 1575, Hester (*d.* 8 May 1592), illegit. da. and h. of Sir William Pickering[†], of London and Yorkshire, at least 3s. 2da.; (2) Sept. 1603, Margaret (*d.*1659), da. of Philip, 3rd Baron Wharton and gd.-da. of Henry Clifford, 2nd Earl of Cumberland. *suc.* fa. 1587. Kntd. 1592; *cr.* Baron Wotton 1603.

Ambassador to Portugal and Spain 1579, Scotland 1585, France 1586, 1610; gent. of privy chamber by 1589; comptroller of the Household 22 Dec. 1602–Nov. 1616; PC Dec. 1602–Apr. 1625; commr. of the Treasury 16 June 1612–14; treasurer of the Household Nov. 1616–Jan. 1618; j.p.q. Kent from c.1593, sheriff 1594–5, ld. lt. 20 Apr. 1604–May 1620; commr. trial of Ralegh

1603, against Jesuits 1603–22, recusant lands 1606, for the surrender of Flushing and Brill 1616, eccles. causes 1620.[1]

Wotton's diplomatic career was in some respects similar to that of his Kent neighbour and friend, Sir Robert Sidney*, though Sidney had advantages derived from the prestige of his father, Sir Henry, and the fame of his elder brother, while Wotton's father was a country gentleman. After a period of study on the Continent learning French, Italian and Spanish, Wotton served as secretary to the embassy at Vienna in the winter of 1574–5. The young Philip Sidney was there also and records in his *Defence of Poesie* that they learned horsemanship together. Later, Sidney was to make Wotton a bequest in his will.[2]

In 1577 'young Mr. Wotton' was appointed to meet the new French ambassador on his arrival in Kent, undertaking a similar task the following year. In 1579 he received his first important mission: to visit Lisbon to congratulate the King of Portugal on his accession, and, in view of the designs Philip of Spain was known to have on Portugal, to assess how secure he was on the throne. Wotton spent 10 days in Lisbon, sending home an appraisal of the chances of success of the three claimants to the throne, and concluding that Philip's strength and resources were likely to prevail. On his way back he visited the King of Spain to convey a friendly greeting from Queen Elizabeth.[3]

In 1585 he went to Scotland to persuade James VI to join Elizabeth's proposed protestant league of defence against the Catholic powers; if he could persuade the King to enter into a suitable marriage as well, so much the better. He was to hint at the prospect of an English pension. At first he made good progress, the King congratulating Elizabeth on her choice of 'so honourable and so wise a gentleman'. But James, still only 19, was influenced by the Earl of Arran, who was hostile to England, and it was not long before one of Wotton's pessimistic despatches produced a characteristic reaction:

> Her Majesty hath written ... to the King, beginning her letter with her own hand in French, in most loving and motherly sort, but, before she had finished it, your advertisements made her forget her French clean and fall to as plain English as ever she wrote in her life, whereof I doubt not but you shall hear soon enough.

After Arran's brother had insulted him in James's presence, Wotton applied for his recall, evidently in fear for his own safety. By the time this was granted he had already fled to Berwick without taking leave of the King.[4]

Within two months Wotton's name was being canvassed as a likely ambassador to France, and in October 1586 he set out. Armed with a dossier showing Mary's approval of the Babington conspiracy, he tried to persuade the French King of Mary's perfidy and

Elizabeth's good faith. Elizabeth later expressed disapproval of Wotton's handling of the embassy, and it was the last he undertook for her, even declining a similar mission in 1601.[5]

After his succession to the family estates he was as much country gentleman as courtier. Already, in 1584, he had represented his county in Parliament, being named to two committees (Rochester bridge 5 Feb. 1585; shoemakers 9 Feb.). As knight of the shire he could have attended the subsidy committee on 24 Feb. 1585. Now he undertook many other duties in Kent, including the shrievalty and the organisation of military defences. The culmination of his work in the county came with the lord lieutenancy, which he received early in James's reign. His patent of appointment was the first one specifically to exclude the Cinque Ports from his jurisdiction. In 1614 his name was suggested to fill the vacancy of lord warden, but his half-brother the diplomat and author, wrote:

> My lord my brother will none of it (as I heard him seriously say) though it were offered him, for reasons which he reserveth in his own breast.[6]

During the last years of Elizabeth's reign no lucrative court appointment came his way. Walsingham helped him to press a claim for a pension (with unknown result), and even his knighthood came late in life. The court was full of rumours of promotion, his name being mentioned as a possible secretary of state – he was confident of this in 1591 – vice-chamberlain, lord warden of the Cinque Ports, and Privy Councillor. He himself sought the treasurership of the chamber from Burghley and was reported to have paid £1,000 to a lady at court to persuade the Earl of Essex to help him acquire a barony. Now that Walsingham was dead, he had to seek a patron elsewhere, and it was fortunate for him that by the time of Essex's disgrace he had established himself as a supporter of Cecil and as a friend of his Kent neighbours, the Brooke-Cobhams. He played an active part in examining witnesses to Essex's behaviour in the streets of London. At last, only a month or two before her death (and perhaps through the influence of Lady Walsingham), Elizabeth gave him the high office which he had sought so long, making him comptroller of her Household, accompanied by admission to the Privy Council.[7]

With James I's accession Wotton became a prominent courtier, with a barony, lucrative offices and grants of land and revenues. So high was he in favour that in 1608 court opinion thought he was about to receive an earldom. On the death of the Earl of Salisbury he was one of the group of commissioners to whom the Treasury was entrusted, and in 1616 received his most profitable office, that of treasurer of the Household. Within two months of his appointment to this position he was negotiating its sale. However, attempts to secure a viscountcy as well as money failed, and opinion turned against him, John Chamberlain writing:

> The world thinks somewhat hardly of the Lord Wotton that he would not rather prefer his brother, Sir Henry, to the place, and withal talk somewhat freely that offices of that nature and especially counsellorships should pass, as it were, by bargain and sale.

In January James summoned him to Theobalds to return his white staff of office. Wotton said he was too ill to come, the King replied that 'his staff was not sick'. At last he obtained his £5,000, but not his promotion in the peerage.[8]

Wotton's religious position is interesting. He was apparently making overtures to Rome from August 1610, the Pope agreeing in February 1612 that he should not be expected to give any public declaration of his renunciation of the established church. He continued to present to the livings under his control, and was even appointed a commissioner for ecclesiastical causes. The truth came out in 1624, when he made a full confession at Maidstone assizes, his widow later inscribing on his tomb the declaration that he 'died a true Catholic of the Roman Church'. By James I's death Wotton was a sick old man, and his dismissal from the Privy Council probably meant little to him. The year before, he had been permitted to absent himself from the House of Lords, and he now retired to his estates in Kent, whence he complained about his subsidy assessment being raised from £200 to £300, writing in his own hand, 7 Nov. 1626, to assert that he had had to become a debtor to pay the smaller amount. His life was saddened by the death of many of his family, including his eldest son Pickering. His own death occurred 4 May 1628, and he was buried at Boughton Malherbe. On his son's death in 1630, the title became extinct.[9]

[1] DNB; CP; Vis. Kent (Harl. Soc. lxxv), 79; G. Inn Adm. Reg. 72; N. and Q. (ser. 7), x. 310; L. P. Smith, Life and Letters of Sir Henry Wotton, i. 284; Add. 33924, f. 16; Hatfield ms 278; Rymer, Foedera, xvi. 489, 597, 691, 783; xvii. 93, 201, 367; HMC Hatfield, xvii. 182. [2] G. Eland, Thomas Wotton's Letter Bk. 1574–86, passim; CSP Span. 1568–79, p. 677; HMC Hatfield, xvi. 244; J. Buxton, Sir Philip Sidney and the Eng. Renaissance, 76, 79. [3] CSP Dom. Add. 1566–79, p. 517; CSP Span. 1568–79, pp. 672, 677, 678, 683–4; CSP For. 1578–9, p. 519; 1579–80, pp. 45–8; APC, x. 437; C. Read, Walsingham, ii. 26. [4] CSP Scot. 1584–5, pp. 611–14, 642–83; 1585–6, intro. pp. ix–xv. pp. 4–129; Border Pprs. i. 191, 198–9; Hamilton Pprs. ii. intro. pp. xxxi–xxxiv. pp. 643–709; Reg. PC of Scot. iii. 748 n; Read, Walsingham, ii. 240–51; Lansd. 45, f. 15; HMC Hatfield, xiii. 268, 269–70. [5] Add. 33256, ff. 172–205; Lansd. 50, f. 189; CSP For. 1585–6, p. 212; 1586–8, pp. 96–8, 105, 119–20, 137, 190; CSP Span. 1587–91, p. 219; CSP Span. 1587–1603, p. 178. [6] Hasted, Kent, vols. iv–viii passim; VCH Yorks. N. Riding, i. 549–50; D'Ewes, 346; Add. 33924, f. 16; Lansd. 43, f. 171; 78, ff. 138 seq.; CSP Dom. 1595–7, p. 525; 1611–18, pp. 316, 328; Egerton 860, ff. 6–39; G. S. Thomson, Twysden Lieutenancy Pprs. 8–9, 113–14; Nichols, Progresses Jas. I, iv. 607; Chamberlain Letters ed. McClure, i. 351; ii. 306; Life of H. Wotton, ii. 41. [7] Lansd. 53, f. 122; 79, f. 62; CSP Span. 1587–1603, p. 215; CSP Dom. 1591–4, p. 97; 1598–1601, pp. 11–18, 282, 407, 580; Life of H. Wotton, i. 295 and n.; 317–18; HMC De L'Isle and Dudley, ii. 286, 293; HMC Hatfield, vi. 192;

viii. 30, 128; ix. 430; xi. 12, 58–9, 66–8; xvi. 186; HMC Downshire, iii. 306; Read, Walsingham, i. 423–43; Strype, Annals, iv. 346–7; Collins, Sidney State Pprs. ii. 25, 27, 30, 54, 85–8, 262; APC, xxxi. 170–1, 187; xxxii. p. 490; Chamberlain Letters, i. 179–80; ii. 609. [8] CSP Dom. 1603–10, p. 221; 1611–18, pp. 407, 418, 446, 512, 519; 1619–23, p. 148; HMC Downshire, ii. 219; Chamberlain Letters, i. 358, 359; ii. 50, 125, 129, 133; HMC Buccleuch, iii. 199; Fortescue Pprs. (Cam. Soc. n.s. i), 38–9, 43. [9] Cantium, ii. 45–7; SP16/39/36 ex inf. J. McGurk; C142/451/99 ex. inf. J. McGurk.

M.R.P.

WRAY, Christopher (c.1522–92), of Glentworth, Lincs.

BOROUGHBRIDGE	1553 (Oct.), 1554 (Apr.), 1554 (Nov.), 1555, 1558
GREAT GRIMSBY	1563
LUDGERSHALL	1571

b. c.1522, 3rd s. of Thomas Wray of Coverham Abbey, Yorks. by Joan, da. of Robert Jackson of Gatenby, Bedale, Yorks. educ. Buckingham (Magdalene), Camb.; L. Inn 1545, called 1550. m. Anne, da. of Nicholas Girlington of Normanby, Yorks., wid. of Robert Brocklesby (d. 3 Apr. 1557), of Glentworth, 1s. William* 4da. Kntd. 6 Nov. 1574.[1]

Steward of Wetherby, Yorks. from Jan. 1559–63; j.p. Lincs (Lindsey) from 1559, (Kesteven) from 1562, (Holland) from 1569; commr. eccles. causes, diocese of Lincoln 1575, to visit Oxf. Univ. 1577; custos rot. Hunts. from 1579; eccles. commr. 1589.[2]

Of counsel to Lincoln c.1559, to Henry Neville, 5th Earl of Westmorland by 1562; Lent reader, L. Inn 1563, 1567, treasurer 1565–6; serjeant-at-law Easter 1567, Queen's serjeant 18 June 1567; justice of assize, Yorks. 31 May 1570; 2nd justice of Lancaster 13 June 1570; j. Queen's bench 14 May 1572 and j.p. many northern counties, Mdx. and Norf.; l.c.j. 8 Nov. 1574.[3]

Speaker of House of Commons 1571.

Wray's career until 1558 was typical of that of a rising lawyer in private practice. A native of Yorkshire, he spent some time at Cambridge, apparently without taking a degree, and then trained at Lincoln's Inn before marrying the widow of the squire of Glentworth, ten miles north of Lincoln. Rising in his profession he soon found himself absorbed into the legal service of the Crown, despite his own Catholic sympathies and his marriage into a Catholic family, which caused him to be classified 'indifferent' in the 1564 bishops' returns. His reliability, however, was never in question: in 1565 he was assigned as counsel to Bonner, and in 1569–70 he dealt with the northern rebels at the York, Carlisle and Durham assizes. Among the submissions he received were those of his brother Thomas and his nephew John Gower. He was also engaged in various legal inquiries, one of them into the privileges of the mineral and battery works.[4]

After repeated elections for Boroughbridge, Wray missed the first Parliament of Elizabeth's reign. In 1563 he was returned for Grimsby (a seat earlier under the control of the earls of Westmorland), following a peremptory demand to the borough from Sir Francis Ayscough, intimating that Wray's election would be pleasing to the Earl. It is during the second session of this Parliament that his name first appears in its proceedings: he had an informers bill committed to him 26 Oct. 1566, and was one of those appointed to confer with the Lords on the Queen's marriage and the succession, 31 Oct. Wray had no known connexion with Wiltshire, unless it was through his fellow of Lincoln's Inn, Richard Kingsmill*, and his return for Ludgershall in 1571 was obviously a case of finding a seat for the Speaker-designate. As a justice of assize he would not normally have been returned to the Commons.[5]

Elected to the Chair on the opening day of the session, Wray was presented to, and confirmed by, the Queen on 4 Apr. His oration included an historical defence of the royal supremacy and a discourse on the administration of justice in the course of which he praised Elizabeth for allowing this to take its proper course. His concluding petition for the customary privileges of the House was answered by the lord keeper, in the Queen's name, with a denial of the Commons' right to 'freedom of speech' save on matters of commonwealth and such matters of state as should be propounded to them. It was an inauspicious beginning to both speakership and Parliament, and the session was to generate much friction and some dangerous moments. With so many eloquent puritans in the House trouble was inevitable, but Wray's chairmanship lacked the astuteness and grasp which might have contained it. He early lost the initiative, and had later to be goaded by Burghley into regaining it. When his closing oration called forth from the lord keeper a denunciation of the dissident minority, Wray must have regarded the whole experience as thankless.[6]

Wray was not to sit in the Commons again. As an assistant in the House of Lords, he is mentioned in the journals of both Houses. In April 1577 he was a member of the committee which investigated the election of John Underhill as rector of Lincoln College, Oxford. In 1587 he and two fellow chief justices were instructed by the Council to postpone the assizes so that they might be free to attend in the Lords. As chief justice for more than 17 years Wray is remembered for the state trials over which he presided, including those of John Stubbe*, Edmund Campion and William Lord Vaux and the conspirators John Somerville and William Parry*. Wray was a member of the commission which attainted William Shelley and condemned Babington and his associates, and he was present as an assessor at the trial of Mary Queen of Scots. He presided at the Star Chamber inquest on the Earl of Northumberland and later in the same court, deputizing for Sir Thomas Bromley*, he censured the zeal of Secretary Davison* before sentencing him. His last state trial was that of Sir John Perrot* in April 1592. His other public duties are reflected in the Privy Council

proceedings and state papers of the period. In 1581 he and the master of the rolls gave a ruling on the rival claims of the merchant adventurers of Chester and the Spanish Company, and about 1590 he arbitrated between the city of London and the dean and chapter about legal jurisdiction over St. Paul's churchyard. In 1577 he reported to the Privy Council on recusants in Serjeants' Inn, and in 1582 to Burghley on similar offenders in various shires. At a conference held in Michaelmas term 1590 he initiated the revision of the form of commissions of the peace.[7]

Wray added considerably to his properties in Lincolnshire, while retaining his patrimony in Yorkshire. He had a fine house at Glentworth, of which part survives in the later mansion, a grant of the profits of the mint, and received many gifts. Both his surviving daughters married well, and remarried better: the elder, Isabel, married successively a gentleman, Godfrey Foljambe*, a knight, Sir William Bowes*, and a peer, John, Baron Darcy of Aston; and the younger, after the death of her first husband, Sir George St. Poll*, who had been knighted at Wray's request, married Robert Rich*, Earl of Warwick.[8]

Wray died on 7 May 1592 and was buried, as he had directed, at Glentworth, where he has a splendid monument in the chancel, with the punning inscription, 're justus, nomine verus'. By his will, made three years earlier, he had provided, in addition to some local benefactions, a bequest for a fellowship at his old college, and one for plate to Serjeants' Inn. He left silver to his daughters and also remembered relatives in the families of Heneage and Tyrwhitt. His wife was given a life interest in much of his property, and his son William, named sole executor, received the remainder and residue. The supervisors were Lord Burghley and the solicitor-general Egerton. By a codicil added on the day of his death Wray remitted a number of debts. His widow survived him for 18 months. Among her bequests were two in favour of Magdalene, the first for scholarships, the second for books.[9]

[1] Lincs. Peds. (Harl. Soc. l), 176; (lv), 1322; Req. 2/42/62; C. Dalton, Wrays of Glentworth, i. 1–64. [2] CPR, 1560–3, pp. 439, 574; 1563–6, pp. 24, 40, 42; 1572–5, pp. 551–2; CSP Dom. 1547–80, p. 543. [3] J. W. F. Hill, Tudor and Stuart Lincoln, 70; Grimsby AO, letter of Francis Ayscough 1562; CPR, 1566–9, p. 70; 1569–72, p. 65; 1572–5, p. 289; Somerville, Duchy, i. 473. [4] CPR, 1558–60, p. 188; Cam. Misc. ix(3), p. 27; CSP Dom. Add. 1566–79, p. 261; VCH Yorks. N. Riding, i. 249; CSP Dom. 1547–80, p. 307; APC, vii. 379. [5] Grimsby AO, ut supra; HMC Hastings, i. 315; CJ, i. 75–6; LJ, i. 640; D'Ewes, 127. [6] Neale, Parlts. i. 187–240. [7] LJ, ii. 61, 113, 145 et passim; D'Ewes, 198, 199, 201; APC, xiv. 314; xvii. 373; xxiii. 16; Lansd. 38, f. 162; 99, f. 92; CSP Dom. 1547–80, p. 567; 1581–90, pp. 19, 32, 606, 645; HMC Hatfield, ii. 509; iv. 460; xiii. 240; G. Elton, Tudor Constitution, 454, 460–2. [8] HMC Rutland, iv. 388; CPR, 1560–3, pp. 208–552; 1563–6, pp. 47, 137, 143, 307; 1566–9, p. 402; C142/233/114; CSP Dom. 1581–90, p. 207; APC, xiv. 242, 301, 303; xv. 231–2; xix. 220–1, 364–5; xxvi. 57–8; Lansd. 69, f. 77. [9] PCC 47 Harrington, 3 Dixy.

S.T.B.

WRAY, George (d. 1594).

LISKEARD	1593

yr. s. of John Wray (d. 1577) of North Russel, Devon, and Trebigh, Cornw. by Blanche, da. of Henry Killigrew of Wolston, Cornw.

With Leicester in the Netherlands 1580s.

Wray was a soldier from a family of sufficient standing to be on the commission of the peace in Devon and Cornwall. A brother was sheriff of Cornwall 1599–1600. Details of Wray's career are lacking until 1589, when he returned to England from the Low Countries to sue for a command. In December of that year the Privy Council allowed him to replace a Captain Champernown in command of a company of 150 footmen, because 'we do have a good report both for his sufficiency for such a charge and also for his care to use the soldiers well'. In 1593 there were the usual difficulties over victualling and pay, the responsible merchants accusing Wray of misappropriation and vice versa. He was in England for the 1593 Parliament, and in May the Privy Council permitted him to extend his stay 'to deal with the merchants for such moneys as are due to him and his company'. In July his company was transferred to garrison Ostend. He was not personally without money during this period, as he was able to lend £50 towards the ransom of one William Ashenden.

In 1593 Wray was returned for Liskeard with Jonathan Trelawny, who lived near his family's residence of Trebigh. Wray's brother, Sir William, became recorder of the borough in James I's reign. His only occurrence in the records of this Parliament is his appointment on 12 Mar. to a committee concerned with the relief of poor maimed soldiers and mariners. In June the next year he was killed at the seige of Groningen, administration being granted 1 July.

Vivian, *Vis. Cornw.* 564; PCC 12 Daughtry; *CSP For.* 1589 (Jan.–Jul.), 51, 396; 1589–90, pp. 114, 135, 136, 137, 144, 171, 178; *CSP Dom.* 1591–4, p. 340; *APC*, xviii. 252, 253; xxiv. 233, 423; *HMC Hatfield*, iv. 293, 295; xiii. 499; D'Ewes, 499; J. Allen, *Hist. Liskeard*, 237; Lansd. 79, f. 37; C. Markham, *The Fighting Veres*, 194; PCC admon. act bk. 1594, f. 104.

I.C.

WRAY, William (c.1555–1617), of Glentworth, Lincs.

GREAT GRIMSBY	1584
LINCOLNSHIRE	1601
GREAT GRIMSBY	1604

b. c.1555, o.s. of Christopher Wray* by Anne, da. of Nicholas Girlington of Normanby, Yorks. *educ.* L. Inn 1576. *m.* (1) 1580, Lucy (d. 1599), e. da. of Sir Edward Montagu of Boughton, Northants., 10s. 5da.; (2) Frances, da. of Sir William Drury*, wid. of Sir Nicholas Clifford*, 3s. 1da.; 3 other da. *suc.* fa. 1592. Kntd. 1596; *cr.* Bt. 1611.[1]

J.p.q. Lincs. (Lindsey) from c.1583; mayor, Grimsby 1588; warden, Louth 1591; sheriff, Lincs. 1594–5; commr. musters 1600, for aid to knight Prince Charles 1603, subsidy 1609.[2]

The son of an eminent father whose considerable estates in the county included property at Ashby cum Fenby, close to Grimsby, Wray was a natural choice to represent the borough in the 1584 Parliament. He inherited Glentworth and his father's other properties in 1592; continued to hold the former monastic properties of Barlings (until selling them in 1614) and Dowood; and continued his father's dispute with Richard Topcliffe* over leases of the episcopal rectories of Stow and Corringham. On this last matter, when Sir William and Topcliffe appeared before the Privy Council in 1596, the Council expressed the hope that the difference 'might be ended without suit in law in some friendly and loving sort between them'.[3]

The development of his estates, and especially of the rich marshlands near Grimsby, seems to have been Wray's chief concern. It involved the enclosure of common lands, and some depopulation, and not surprisingly provoked opposition.[4] But more serious trouble arose nearer home. The Glentworth estate lay close to Gainsborough where the new owner of the manor and market tolls, the London merchant Sir William Hickman, was allegedly levying excessive toll of corn. Wray, his brother-in-law Sir George St. Poll*, and Lord Willoughby of Parham, all justices, were ordered in February 1598 to inquire into the complaints. The whole thing snowballed; the peace of the neighbourhood became disturbed; one of Hickman's servants was killed in a riot; and Wray, his cousin Nicholas Girlington, and St. Poll were accused by Hickman of fomenting the trouble and impeding the course of justice. Again the Privy Council advised 'mediation by some persons of credit', and referred the matter to the good offices of Lords Willoughby and Sheffield. How it all ended is not known.[5] Incidents such as this were commonplace in the life of the Elizabethan country gentleman, and Wray, though a lesser man than his father, was no worse than others of his standing in the county.

Possibly he was better. Gervase Holles, who must have been familiar with his reputation in the Grimsby area, thought him amiable, decent, timid, and somewhat dull. Attaining a county seat for the 1601 Parliament, he could have served on committees considering the order of business (3 Nov.), the better keeping of the Sabbath (4, 6 Nov.), the abbreviation of the Michaelmas law term (11 Nov.), two private bills (19, 23 Nov.), monopolies (23 Nov.) and the drunkenness bill (28 Nov.), which he reported to the House. He intervened (20 Nov.) in the debate on the 1s. fine for recusants, to explain that, when the bill was in committee, it was not the intention that recusants should pay 1s. per week in addition to £20 per month.[6]

In religion Wray was a radical. John Smith, the preacher or lecturer in Lincoln and later minister of a separatist congregation in Gainsborough, dedicated to him an exposition of Psalm xxii

> because I have experienced yourself to be, under the King's Majesty, a principal professor and protector of religion in these quarters (for what a multitude of faithful ministers are debtors to you in the flesh), and for that I, among the rest, have rested under your shadow.[7]

Wray died intestate on 13 Aug. 1617 at Ashby cum Fenby.

[1] *Lincs. Peds.* (Harl. Soc. lv), 1322–3; GEC, *Baronetage*, i. 95; C. Dalton, *Wrays of Glentworth*, i. 65–70. [2] *HMC 14th Rep. VIII*, 290; R. W. Goulding, *Louth Old Corp. Recs.* 19, 58; *APC*, xxx. 190; *NRA Lumley*, no. 946b. [3] *John Rylands Lib. Handlist iii* (1937), nos. 2501–3; *CSP Dom.* 1603–10, p. 499; *APC*, xxvi. 57–8. [4] *NRA Lumley*, nos. 977, 987; J. W. F. Hill, *Tudor and Stuart Lincoln*, 141, citing J. D. Gould, *EHR*, July 1952. [5] *APC*, xxviii. 342; xxix. 202; xxx. 140–1; *HMC Hatfield*, xiv. 93. [6] *Holles' Church Notes* (Lincoln Rec. Soc. i), 64; D'Ewes, 624, 628, 635, 642, 649, 657; Townshend, *Hist. Colls* 228. [7] Hill, 112.

D.O.

WRIGHT, Edmund (*d.* c.1583), of Burnt Bradfield and Sutton, Suff., Little Buckenham, Norf.

STEYNING   1559

1st s. of Robert Wright of Burnt Bradfield by Anne, da. and coh. of one Russell of Bradfield. *m.* ?(1) Anne Salvyn, *s.p.*; (2) Frances, da. of Sir John Spring of Lavenham, Suff., 5 or 6 da.[1]

?Surgeon to Queen Mary 1553 or 1554; escheator, Norf. and Suff. 1553–4, 1560–1.[2]

Wright presumably owed his Steyning seat to the 4th Duke of Norfolk or to the Duke's father-in-law, the 12th Earl of Arundel, steward of the royal honour of Petworth, which included the borough of Steyning. During Henry VIII's reign Wright had been a servant of Thomas Cromwell and was later transferred to the King's service. In 1537, through the influence of the 3rd Duke of Norfolk, he was granted a lease of Lythe parsonage, Yorkshire. In 1545 he added to his property in that county by buying, with a relative, George Wright‡, the manor of Westerdale, together with lands at Castroppe (?Casthorpe), Lincolnshire, and elsewhere. There is no evidence that he lived for long in the north-east, and these estates are not mentioned in his will: he presumably bought them as a speculation. However, he had evidently been in Yorkshire in 1542, when he received coat and conduct money for over 100 soldiers from the county. Another valuable Yorkshire grant to him, of the former priory of 'Grandemonte *alias* Gramonte', mentions his wife Frances Spring. In 1551 he gained the wardship of her brother William, Sir John Spring's heir.[3]

While there need be no doubt that the Norfolk and Suffolk landowner was the Steyning MP, it is not certain that he was the Edmund Wright whose patent as a royal

surgeon, granting him a £40 annuity, was enrolled in July 1554, and who was still holding the position at Elizabeth's coronation, when he was allowed 'five yards of scarlet' for his processional robes. However, in December 1554 Edmund Wright and his wife Frances were granted the reversion of the manor of Bardsall, Yorkshire, 'for his service in the rebellion at Framlingham', and in consideration of his surrendering a patent for a £40 annuity granted in October 1553. This looks very much like the royal surgeon's annuity which, although enrolled in 1554, may have been granted earlier. If a court doctor was escheator of Norfolk and Suffolk, he must have exercised the office by deputy – a not unknown procedure.[4]

After 1559 few references to an Edmund Wright, either as surgeon or landowner, have been found. A man of this name was in 1563 the tenant of a house in the London parish of St. Lawrence Jewry. Wright of 'Buckenham Tofts, Norfolk' made his will in July 1583, proved at Norwich on 4 Feb. 1584. The preamble asked God for Christ's sake 'to receive my soul, and for his sake to put away all my sins and so to bury them in his death and obedience as they may never come up in judgment against me'. Wright wished to be buried 'in honest and comely sort', wherever his widow, Frances, the sole legatee and executrix, thought fit. His daughters and coheiresses had presumably been already provided for. John Heigham*, the husband of one of them, was a witness to the will.[5]

[1] *Vis. Norf.* (Harl. Soc. xxxii), 323; *Vis. Suff.* ed. Metcalfe, 114, 170, 189; *CPR*, 1558–60, p. 172; *LP Hen. VIII*, xii(1), p. 442; xx(2), p. 398. [2] *CPR*, 1553–4, p. 477; *LP Hen. VIII*, xii(2), pp. 264, 291; xiii(2), p. 497; xvii. p. 529; xix(1), p. 81; xx(1), pp. 227, 263; *CPR*, 1550–3, p. 109. [4] *CPR*, 1553–4, p. 477; 1554–5, p. 133; 1557–8, p. 235; E101/429/5. [5] *CPR*, 1560–3, p. 519; Norwich prob. reg., 86 Bate.

N.M.F.

WRIGHT, Richard (c.1568–1639), of Sherborne, Dorset.

DORCHESTER   1597
QUEENBOROUGH   1604*

b. c.1568, 1st s. of Robert Wright of Sturminster Newton. *educ.* Sherborne c.1585; Magdalen Coll. Oxf. Nov. 1588, aged 20; New Coll. BA Feb. 1592; M. Temple 1598. *m.*, issue.[1]

Under sheriff, Dorset 1598; farmer of the import duty on currants 1604; mayor, Lyme Regis 1617–18; customer, Weymouth by 1630/1.[2]

Of a minor family, Wright received an expensive education, and was perhaps destined for the law or church. He began by making himself available for small jobs in the county, and eventually became a customs official. He was employed as a 'clerk' in 1592 when the cargo of the *Madre de Dios*, a captured Spanish carrack, was sold off, and in 1602 his services were especially requested in a similar capacity. His seat in the 1597 Parliament was apparently obtained for him through the influence of the 3rd Marquess of Winchester.[3]

Since Wright was returned for Queenborough as 'Mr. Wright the merchant' he was presumably (there are a number of contemporary namesakes) the 'Mr. Wright, a member of this House' who, it was reported to the Commons on 11 Apr. 1606, was responsible for the celebrated committal to prison of the merchant Bate for not paying duty on a cargo of currants.[4]

'Richard Wright, gent., of Sherborne, Dorset' made his will 7 Mar. 1639, proved 23 May. A sister and several grandchildren are mentioned. The executor and residuary legatee was his son-in-law Charles Lawrence, who was a customs official in Weymouth at the outset of the civil war. The estate included prize ships and goods.[5]

[1] Al. Ox. i(4), p. 1687; M. T. Recs. i. 387; PCC 89 Harvey. [2] St. Ch. 5/R38/3; CSP Dom. 1603–10, pp. 161, 427; G. Roberts, Lyme Regis and Charmouth, 360; E134/9, 10 Chas. I, Hil. 39 [3] HMC Hatfield, iv. 239–40; xii. 202. [4] Bowyer Diary, 119; SP14/18/46, ex inf. Kathleen Sommers. [5] PCC 89 Harvey.

P.W.H.

WRIGHT, Robert (c.1549–1611), of Shrewsbury, Salop and Richmond, Surr.

| TAMWORTH | 1589 |
| SHREWSBURY | 1593 |

b. c.1549, 1st s. of Peter Wright of Shrewsbury. educ. Shrewsbury 1562; Trinity Coll. Camb. BA 1571, MA 1574, BD 1580. m. Dorothy, da. of Sir Richard Walwyn of Much Marcle, Herefs., wid. of John Farnham* of Nether Hall, Leics., s.p. Kntd. 1605.[1]

Tutor to Earl of Essex by 1576, then steward, finally clerk of his stable by 25 Dec. 1596.[2]

Wright was the son of a shoemaker and grandson of a husbandman. His education enabled him to attach himself to the Earl of Essex, and he was described by Sir James Whitelock in his Liber Famelicus as a 'grave and sober man' who had 'attained by his virtue to good estate and quality'. As steward to Essex he had excellent perquisites. He received considerable grants of land on behalf of the Earl, on which his name was usually coupled with those of Thomas Crompton* and Gelly Meyrick*. By 1595 he had twice sat in the Commons, each time in a seat provided by his patron. He was directly nominated at Tamworth after Essex had obtained a new charter for the borough appointing himself high steward. At Shrewsbury, a more delicate approach was necessary. Essex recommended Wright to the bailiffs at a time when the town had recently incurred his displeasure, and they complied with his request 'notwithstanding earnest suit made for others'. Before the election, the bailiffs entertained Wright with 'wine, sugar, biscuits, marmalade, codlings and rosewater'.[3]

It is surprising that Wright's 'unspotted love' for Essex did not involve him in his patron's fall. He apparently even retained his office of clerk of the stable. In his will, dated 21 Nov. 1608, he asked to be buried 'without any solemnity' and, 'again and again in … humblest devotion', commended his soul to the Trinity. The major part of his property he left to his wife, though there were substantial bequests to his brother Richard, his sister Lucy Studley and their children, the boys receiving his books, the girls his bolsters and bedding. £150 was set aside for the almshouses of Richmond. An inquisition post mortem was held in 1611.[4]

[1] Trans. Salop Arch. Soc. (ser. 4), xii. 196–7; H. E. Forrest, Shrewsbury Burgess Roll, 48. [2] HMC Hatfield, ii. 215; CSP Dom. 1595–7, p. 322. [3] CSP Dom. 1581–90, p. 696; 1591–4, pp. 9, 180; 1595–7, p. 61; Neale, Commons, 237–8; HMC 15th Rep. X, 56–7; Owen and Blakeway, Hist. Shrewsbury, i. 550; Early Chrons. Shrewsbury, ed. Leighton, 825–6; Trans. Salop Arch. Soc. (ser. 4), xii. 197. [4] PCC 29 Wingfield; C142/313/93.

J.J.C.

WROTE, Robert (c.1544–89), of Bungay, Suff.; Gunton and Tunstall, Norf.

| BEVERLEY | 1584 |
| DENBIGH BOROUGHS | 1586 |

b. c.1544, s. of John Wrote of Bungay by Bridget, da. of John Harvey of Ickworth, Suff. educ. Jesus, Camb. 'impubes' 1558; I. Temple 1561 or 1562, called. m. Catherine, da. and coh. of Vincent Randall of London, wid. of Thomas Fleet, 2s. 7da.

J.p. Suff. from 1579.

This Member probably owed both his parliamentary seats to Sir Robert Dudley*, Earl of Leicester. His exact connexion with the Earl is difficult to trace, but in 1585 he was acting with Thomas Dudley*, presumably in a legal capacity, over debts owed to Leicester, as lord of Oswestry, by the Earl of Arundel. Though he never rose to any eminence in the law, it is likely that the large sums of money which he bequeathed in his will reflect the gains of a flourishing legal practice. His landed property on the borders of Norfolk and Suffolk was not considerable, and though his wife brought him part of the manor of Sutton at Hone, Kent, he never became a substantial country gentleman in that county or in East Anglia: he was over 30 before his name appeared on the Suffolk commission of the peace. The only reference to his serving on a special commission there is in 1583, when he was instructed to investigate a complaint against Henry Jernegan for attacking one John Thorneton alias Arnold, who had served a subpoena on him.

Wrote died, apparently as a result of violence, on 25 Sept. 1589, though nothing is known of the circumstances beyond the fact that in the following year one Thomas

Wigges was released from the penalty of burning in the hand, to which he had been sentenced 'touching the death of Robert Wrote'. Whatever the story behind this, Wrote had drawn up his will the day before he died. It was proved in November the same year. Among the witnesses was Thomas Crompton, possibly the MP who served Leicester's stepson, the Earl of Essex.

Vis. London (Harl. Soc. xvii), 373; *Vis. Suff.* ed. Metcalfe, 211; *Cal. I.T. Recs.* i. 340; C142/255/174; Lansd. 45, f. 208 seq.; Hasted, *Kent*, ii. 348; *CSP Dom.* 1581–90, pp. 121, 660; PCC 91 Leicester.

N.M.F.

WROTH, John (d. aft. July 1616), of London.

LIVERPOOL   1593

yr. s. of Sir Thomas Wroth* of Durants, Enfield, Mdx. by Mary, da. of Richard Rich‡, 1st Baron Rich; bro. of Richard* and of Robert I*. *m.*

Ambassador to Venice by Nov. 1587–c. July 1589; to Turkey 1598.

This man, one of at least six younger sons, is suggested as the Liverpool MP in preference to two namesakes, his uncle and his nephew, on grounds of age. As his father was a Marian exile, it is possible that he may have spent part of his childhood or adolescence abroad. He received £500 under his father's will, and an equal share with his brothers and sisters of certain properties to be divided between them. His court connexions would have been sufficient to obtain him both his diplomatic appointments and his return for Liverpool, probably through the former chancellor of the duchy of Lancaster, Walsingham, who had been succeeded as chancellor by his friend (Sir) Thomas Heneage*. As it happened, the Wroth family were already connected with the duchy; Wroth's grandfather had been attorney-general, and his brother Robert held duchy lands in Essex and Middlesex. In 1597 Wroth was described by the Privy Council as 'a gentleman of good merit ... lately employed in her Majesty's service to his great charge'. He was in England that summer, went on a mission to Germany, possibly in 1598, and in the autumn of that year was made ambassador to Turkey. In 1602 the letter writer, John Chamberlain, thought he would be a likely candidate to succeed George Gilpin at The Hague, were it not that Wroth, like Thomas Edmondes*, had his 'particular impediments'. Wroth was still alive on 20 July 1616: the date of his death has not been ascertained.

Vis. Essex (Harl. Soc. xiii), 330; *CSP Dom.* 1598–1601, pp. 78, 110; PCC 16 Pyckering; *CSP For.* 1586–8, pp. 409–10, 500–2, 539–40, 649; Jan.–July 1589, pp. 201–2, 302–3, 325–7, 350–1; *Essex Arch. Soc. Trans.* n.s. viii. 145, 150–1; *APC,* xxvi. 409; *Chamberlain Letters* ed. McClure, i. 165; ii. 16.

N.M.S.

WROTH, Richard (d. 1596), of Enfield, Mdx.

APPLEBY   1571
MORPETH   1572

2nd s. of Sir Thomas Wroth*, and bro. of Robert I* and John*. *educ.* St. John's, Camb. 1553. *unm.*

Servant of Thomas Radcliffe, 3rd Earl of Sussex by 1570–83.

In his early teens in 1554, Wroth probably went with his parents into exile at Strasbourg, returning to the family estate at Enfield soon after Elizabeth's accession. He resumed his studies at Cambridge, gaining his LLB in 1562. Next he entered the service of the 3rd Earl of Sussex, who was presumably behind Wroth's return to Parliament for boroughs where Sussex had influence as president of the council in the north. Wroth remained with Sussex until that nobleman's death in 1583, when he was made an executor of his will. He had to account for large sums of money he had handled for the Earl, but his own rewards had been ample, and, with a further £500 inherited from his father in 1573, he bought property in Kent and Essex, and, in 1584, secured the lease of the manor of Highbury. He died in late May or early June 1596, appointing his brother John as his executor.

Vis. London (Harl. Soc. xvii), 374; *CSP Scot.* iii. 156; *CSP Dom. Add.* 1566–79, p. 231; Lansd. 39, f. 96 seq.; PCC 16 Pyckering, 45 Drake; S. Lewis, *Hist. Topog. St. Mary, Islington,* 69.

B.D.

WROTH, Robert I (c.1539–1606), of Durants, Enfield, Mdx. and Loughton, Essex.

ST. ALBANS   1563
BOSSINEY   1571
MIDDLESEX   1572, 1584, 1586, 1589, 1593,
                                             1597, 1601, 1604*

b. c.1539, 1st s. of Sir Thomas Wroth* and bro. of John* and Richard*. *educ.* St. John's Camb. 'impubes' 1552; G. Inn 1559. *m.* Susan, da. and h. of John Stonard of Loughton, 4s. inc. Robert II*. *suc.* fa. 1573, fa.-in-law 1579. Kntd. 1597.[1]

J.p. Mdx. from c.1573, j.p.q. Mdx. and Essex from c.1579; commr. sewers for river Lea Oct. 1587; sheriff, Essex 1587–8; commr. musters, Essex by 1587, Mdx. by 1588; riding forester of Waltham forest 1597, walker 1603.[2]

Wroth accompanied his father into exile in 1554 and remained abroad, in Italy and Germany, until the accession of Elizabeth. He missed her first Parliament but in 1563 he was returned for St. Albans, where Sir Nicholas Bacon‡ was high steward. His next seat, in 1571, was for Bossiney, where the 2nd Earl of Bedford, another zealous protestant, exercised influence: Wroth's brother Thomas was a servant of Bedford. By 1572 Wroth had sufficient standing in Middlesex to gain a county seat, which he held without a break until his death.

Like other significant parliamentary figures, Wroth began slowly. His early committee work in Parliament was chiefly concerned with local matters: no activity in 1563; a bill for the river Lea (26 May 1571), Middlesex jurors (19, 22 May 1572, 24 Feb. 1576), justices of the Queen's forests and parks (8 Mar. 1576), actions upon the case to be brought in proper counties (26 Jan. 1581), the preservation of woods (28 Jan. 1581), the paving of Aldgate Street (9 Feb. 1581), pheasants and partridges (18 Feb. 1581, 26 Mar. 1585), hue and cry (4 Feb. 1585), the maintenance of highways and bridges (24 Feb. 1585) and London apprentices (2 Mar., committed to him 23 Mar. 1585). However, one of his first recorded committees (28 May 1571) concerned the subject for which he was to be remembered, namely, the liberties and privileges of the House. Wroth's first recorded intervention in debate concerned the payment of Middlesex jurors (22 May 1572). As his parliamentary experience increased, so the range of topics covered by his committee work broadened. He was appointed to committees concerning a private bill for Sir Thomas Gresham (20 Feb. 1581), mariners and navigation (17 Mar. 1581), procedure (16 Dec. 1584, 22 Mar. 1585, 8 Mar. 1587), Plymouth harbour (21 Dec. 1584, committed to him 18 Feb. 1585), latitats of the peace in the Queen's bench (5 Mar. 1585), privilege (4 Nov. 1586), Mary Queen of Scots (4 Nov. 1586), a case of privilege brought by Arthur Hall* against the borough of Grantham (2 Dec. 1586), theft of horses and cattle (10 Mar. 1587), fraudulent conveyances (14 Mar. 1587), continuation of statutes (17 Mar. 1587) and extortion by sheriffs (17 Mar. 1587).

Wroth was also named to committees concerning the subsidy on 25 Jan. 1581, 24 Feb. 1585 and 22 Feb. 1587. He was an active supporter of an additional payment to be made towards maintaining the English forces in the Netherlands in 1587, as is clear from the summary report of his speech in the House on 24 Feb.:

Many things well spoken of dangers. Nothing more profitable than to take the Low Countries. If Dunkirk have done us so much harm, what would all the rest do, as Flushing, Brill and Holland etc.? To take the sovereignty of it ... Good to give a large subsidy and that the wills of the good subjects may be tried. That for his own part he would give a hundred pounds by year towards the maintenance of it, these wars.

In the committee that afternoon, Wroth reiterated his view: 'His meaning was that [the Queen] should accept [the] sovereignty'. Again in the committee which met on 6 Mar. he said 'that to take the sovereignty he offered a hundred pounds, and that notwithstanding her Majesty would not take the sovereignty, yet he would mend his subsidy'. He continued to make the suggestion that 'by law', men rated at '£10 upwards, [should] give 2s. in the

pound more' towards the costs in the Netherlands. Not surprisingly, he was one of 20 MPs from the Commons summoned to receive the Queen's thanks for the subsidy on 18 Mar. 1587.

Suitably enough for a future defender of the liberties and privileges of the House, Wroth was named to the first standing committee on privilege ever appointed by the House of Commons on 7 Feb. 1589, and in this connexion he was considering the Puleston privilege case on 12 Feb. 1589. He was put in charge of three bills during this Parliament, concerning benefit of clergy (21 Feb.), Dover pier (10 Mar.) and fish (13 Mar.). On 25 Feb. Wroth moved

for better attendance to be continued and used by the Members of the House ... that none after the House is set do depart before the rising of the same ... unless he do first ask leave of Mr. Speaker, upon pain that everyone hereafter doing the contrary do pay for every time six pence to the use of the poor.

His motion was immediately 'assented unto by the whole House'. Wroth's other committee work in this Parliament concerned the subsidy (11 Feb.), disorders in purveyors (15, 27 Feb., 18 Mar.), writs of covenant (25 Feb.), captains and soldiers (26 Feb.), gauging of casks (4 Mar.), hue and cry (17 Mar.), continuation of statutes (20 Mar.), husbandry and tillage (25 Mar.) and a declaration of war with Spain (29 Mar.).[3]

Wroth's first concern at the beginning of the 1593 Parliament was that a standing committee should be appointed to watch over both privileges and returns (26 Feb.). On three major issues during this Parliament, Wroth spoke out against arbitrary government action. In particular he reminded the House that it was under no obligation to agree to the government device of a conference with the Lords. On 1 Mar. the Lords informed a Commons committee of which Wroth was a member (appointed 26 Feb.), that they would not accept the grant of two subsidies proposed by the Commons, but would insist upon three. They requested a conference on the matter, and were supported in this by Sir Robert Cecil in his report to the Commons on 2 Mar. Francis Bacon, amongst others, took exception to the Lords dictating the terms of the subsidy, and opposed a conference. The question was still being debated the following morning (3 Mar.), when Cecil reiterated his opinion that there should be a conference with the Lords. This time the opposition was led by Wroth, who maintained that it 'would be much prejudicial to the ancient liberties and privileges of this House and the authority of the same'. His side carried the day, and he was one of a delegation appointed to convey the Commons' refusal to the Lords.

On 26 Feb. 1593, the first full day of the Parliament's business, James Morice spoke of the abuses in the court of high commission, in particular the *ex officio* oath, and handed the Speaker two bills to be read. These bills were bound to incur official displeasure, being a direct attack on Whitgift's ecclesiastical hierarchy, and Queen and government had already shown themselves in no mood to brook criticism by imprisoning Peter Wentworth, MP for Northampton, a few days before the Parliament began. There was heated debate in the House that day as to whether Morice's bills should be read, but the Speaker asked for time to peruse them and wished to keep them until the next day, protesting 'I will be faithful and will keep it with all secrecy'. Significantly, the House felt impelled to clarify whether the bills were to be given to the Speaker alone, or to the Privy Councillors and the Speaker, and 'upon a motion made by Mr. Wroth, it was agreed the Speaker only should keep it'.

James Morice was sequestered from the House a few days later and by 10 Mar. a total of seven MPs had been either imprisoned or banned from the House. That day Wroth moved that they might be readmitted

> in respect that some countries might complain of the tax of these many subsidies, their knights and burgesses never consenting unto them nor being present at the grant; and because an instrument, taking away some of its strings, cannot give its pleasant sound.

Wroth's motion was immediately opposed by the Privy Councillors present who suggested that 'for us to press her Majesty with this suit we should but hinder them whose good we seek'. They recommended leaving the matter to the Queen's 'gracious disposition'. Despite the unprecedented gravity of this affront to the liberties of MPs, Wroth received no backing from the rest of the House. As the anonymous diarist put it: 'Hereupon the motion ceased from further speech'.

In the course of this Parliament, the government revived the draconian 1581 anti-Catholic bill, but during the debate on its second reading (28 Feb.) it was objected that the proposed legislation could hit puritans as hard as Catholics. Wroth's contribution to the debate was as usual on the side of moderation.

> The law hath no proviso for leases, no remedy is appointed, as by the distress or otherwise, how the guardian is to come by the money appointed to him for the custody of the child of a recusant ... And the recusant not to forfeit ten pound a month for the keeping of his wife; otherwise for keeping of servants' recusants.

This first bill came to nothing, but the government persisted and before long a new anti-recusant bill was before the Commons. Like the first it was ostensibly directed against the Catholics, but the anonymous diarist called it 'the bill of recusants meant for Brownists', and commented 'the proceeding of this bill was in a strange course, and I think extraordinary, therefore I will note it'. From his description of events the government attempted

to force the bill through the Commons with as little debate as possible. 'Upon Saturday the bill was read the first time. Upon Monday (2 Apr.) very late in the day and after 11 of the clock, the bill was offered to be read.' Wroth, mindful of the danger to the puritans, saw through this manoeuvre and objected.

> Mr. Wroth said, the day was spent, it was a bill of great importance and would require much speaking to, and therefore wished to have it deferred till better leisure and longer time might be spent in it.

His motion produced an outright confrontation:

> The bill was pressed much to be read, many of the House rose and would not hear it read. The Privy Council and many others sat. So a question was made, if it should be read, and it was denied by a No.

When the bill, which had originated in the Lords, eventually reached committee stage in the Commons, it was torn to pieces there. The government, reluctant to let the bill die in the Commons, proposed a conference of the two Houses to discuss the bill, but Wroth argued against a conference, by means of a precedent, and stood by the Commons' right to dash a bill, even if it proceeded from the Lords.

> A precedent was shown by Mr. Wroth that the last Parliament the Lords sent down a bill which being disliked in our House, they demanded for a conference with us. But this House utterly disliking of the bill would not agree thereunto, but, for answer to the Lords, made a collection of all their objections against the bill and sent it up by the hands of two knights, who had only authority to deliver those objections drawn against it and not to reply with any defence for the reason of our so doing.

However, in the face of great pressure from the government, the House failed to avail themselves of Wroth's precedent and agreed to a conference with the Lords.

Several bills were committed to Wroth during this Parliament, among them one against the stealing of oxen. He was put in charge of this bill on 5 Mar. 1593 and reported it on 10 Mar., but the anonymous diarist reports that on 25 Mar. the bill 'being put to the question for engrossing, was dashed, to Mr. Wroth's grief'. Other bills committed to him in 1593 were bills on fish (5 Mar.), the assize of bread (5 Mar., reported by him 15 Mar.), casks (24 Mar., reported 31 Mar.), the continuation of statutes (28 Mar., 4 Apr.), Colchester harbour (29 Mar.), brewers (3 Apr., reported 4 Apr.) and the restraint of enclosures in or near the cities of London and Westminster (6 Apr.). Other 1593 committees concerned cloth (9 Mar.), the deprivation of Bishop Bonner (9 Mar.), jurors (10 Mar.), the poor (12 Mar.), three private bills (16 Mar., 28 Mar.), alien retailers (23 Mar.), the assize of fuel (26 Mar.), weirs (28 Mar.), spinners and weavers (3 Apr.), the assize of timber (5 Apr.), cordage (6 Apr.) and coopers (7 Apr.).

On Saturday 31 Mar. 1593 a proviso concerning the 'punishing of bastard getters' was discussed in the House during the debate on the bill for continuation of statutes. The proviso gave j.p.s the power to have offenders whipped, but this proviso was 'misliked' for the following reasons:

> ... first the punishment thought slavish and not to be inflicted upon a liberal man. Secondly the malice of a justice of peace feared, that upon ill-will might give this correction to one not offending, if he were accused by a whore. Thirdly, the case might chance upon gentlemen, or men of quality, whom it were not fit to put to such a shame.

There was such argument over the proviso that a committee was appointed there and then to 'go up presently to the chamber and agree how to have it', but the committee could not come to a decision either. At this point it was suggested – apparently by Wroth – that the statute should stand as it was 'without addition or alteration'. The anonymous diarist commented: 'Mr. Wroth showed great cunning to reduce it to this, otherwise I fear the Act would have passed shamefully'. Wroth's motion carried the day:

> ... two questions were made. First as many as would have the new proviso, added to the new bill, put out, say aye, and it was affirmed, aye ... the second question, as many as will have the old law to be explained, say, aye, as many as will not have it explained, say, no. The House was divided upon this question, but we of the no got it 28 voices.[4]

Wroth's committee work in the 1597 Parliament was extensive, but, apart from his reporting various bills, only one intervention has been recorded in his name (date unknown) concerning a pardon for those who had alienated their capital lands. A good number of bills were committed to him during this Parliament. His committees covered the following topics: privileges and returns (5 Nov.); maltsters (delivered to him 9 Nov., reported by him 12 Nov.); Langport Eastover (10 Nov.); monopolies (10 Nov.); continuation of statutes (committed to him 11 Nov.); reformation of abuses in marriage licences (14 Nov.); horse stealing (16 Nov.); forestallers (16 Nov.); Warwick hospital (18 Nov.); the relief of the poor and the punishment of rogues (5, 19 Nov., 11 bills on the subject committed to him 22 Nov., one bill committed to him 24 Nov., one bill committed to him 19 Dec., and 12 on 27 Jan. 1598); Arthur Hatch (22 Nov.); a charter for Great Yarmouth (23 Nov.); bills for Sir John Spencer and Robert Cotton (committed to him, 25 Nov.); draining Norfolk fens (committed to him, 25 Nov.); mariners and navigation (26 Nov.); Staines bridge (1 Dec.); lessees and patentees (3, 20 Dec.), cloth (8 Dec.); a bridge over the river Wye (12 Dec.);

tillage (13 Dec.); malt (12 Jan. 1598); the increase of people for the defence of the realm (12 Jan.); charitable uses (14 Jan.); double payment of debts (14 Jan.); the bishopric of Norwich (16 Jan.); benefit of clergy (18 Jan.) and wine casks (3 Feb.).[5]

By 1601 Wroth was one of the most experienced Members of the House of Commons. As he himself said (2 Dec. 1601): 'I have been of this House these 40 years' (actually 38). Nevertheless he was as active as ever, sitting on over 30 committees and speaking on most of the important issues of the session. One of his most notable contributions to the 1601 debates concerned monopolies. On 20 Nov. 'he wished a commitment in which a course might be devised how her Majesty might know our special griefs'. The following day when government spokesmen were attempting to explain away their inaction on monopolies, Wroth would have none of their excuses:

> I would but note, Mr. Solicitor, that you were charged to take care in Hilary term last. Why not before? There was time enough ever since the last Parliament. I speak it, and I speak it boldly: these patentees are worse than ever they were. And I have heard a gentleman affirm in this House, that there is a clause of reversion in these patents. If so, what needed this stir by *quo warranto* and I know not what? when it is but to send for the patents and cause a redelivery.
>
> There have been divers patents granted since the last Parliament. These are now in being, *viz.* the patents for currants, iron, powder, cards, horns, ox shin-bones, train oil, cloth, ashes, bottles, glasses, bags, gloves, aniseed, vinegar, sea-coal, steel, aqua-vitae, brushes, pots, salt, saltpetre, lead, oil, leather, callamint stone, oil of blubber, smoked pilchards, and divers others.

This list prompted Mr. Hakewill's remark, 'is not bread there? ... No, but if order be not taken for these, bread will be there before the next Parliament.'

A considerable number of bills going through the 1601 Parliament were designed to extend the powers of j.p.s, a policy which met with outspoken opposition from Edward Glascock, who thought that this would increase the already prevalent corruption among magistrates. Wroth and he clashed on this subject during debates on the bills concerning blasphemous swearing and church attendance. On 6 Nov. Wroth had been added to a committee considering the bill for the better keeping of the Sabbath, but that bill had been rejected, and on 13 Nov. he introduced a new bill on the subject

> the effect whereof is, for the better gathering of one shilling for every absence ... and the statute is limited to endure the Queen's reign (which was greatly whispered at, and observed in the House).

Wroth was put in charge of a committee on the bill (18 Nov.), but on 20 Nov. it was defeated by 140 votes to 137. However, another puritan, Sir Francis Hastings, determined to get legislation through on this point, introduced his own bill on 27 Nov., which was given its second reading on 2 Dec. As it happened, Glascock had delivered his most stinging attack on j.p.s the day before (1 Dec.), and Wroth, a member of the Middlesex bench for 28 years, availed himself of the debate on church attendance to reply:

> I think the office of a justice of the peace is too good for him that exclaims against it, and I think he will never have the honour to have it. It were good … that he were enjoined to tell who they were he spoke so meanly of: otherwise honest men will be loth to serve the Queen, when they shall be slandered without proof.

He wished Glascock to answer for his speech before the bar of the House, but his motion was rejected. There was much opposition to Hastings' bill on 12 Dec., during the debates on its third reading, but Wroth (a member of the committee appointed 2 Dec.), had a compromise proviso 'ready engrossed' which he hoped might save the bill.

> … that if any man came eight times a year to the church and said the usual divine service twice every Sunday and holy day in his house with his whole family, that should be sufficient dispensation.

However, his proviso was 'utterly misliked' by the House,

> … yet divers which were desirous to overthrow the bill, went forth with the proviso because they would have it joined with the bill to overthrow it.

In the event, despite the joint efforts of Wroth and Hastings, the bill was defeated, 106–105.

On 10 Dec. Wroth himself spoke against extending the functions of j.p.s, but for quite different reasons from those of Glascock. The bill under discussion concerned alehouses, and one of the provisions vested the granting of licences in the local j.p.s. Wroth's objection was the following:

> … what pain and charge this will be to a poor man, to go with some of his neighbours 20 or 30 miles for a licence: and what a monstrous trouble to all the justices, I refer it to your considerations.

In the previous Parliament Wroth had played a vital part in the deliberations leading to the Acts for the relief of the poor and for the punishment of rogues, vagabonds and sturdy beggars. On 5 Nov. 1601 he moved for a committee 'to amend the statute for the relief of the poor and building of houses of correction made the last Parliament'. Nearly a month later (4 Dec.), Wroth introduced a new bill which was read twice and committed, and on 14 Dec. he reported on the committee's amendments and on a proviso which had been added, and the bill was ordered to be engrossed.

He made two contributions to the debates on the subsidy, both characteristic. On 7 Nov. he

moved that £4 lands might pay full subsidy, and £6 goods might pay full subsidy unto her Majesty.

However, notwithstanding his readiness to pay a good subsidy, he was always careful of the privileges of the House. On 9 Nov. he moved that the fourth and exceptional subsidy granted by the House

> might be drawn in a bill by itself, to which should be annexed a preamble of the great necessity, the willingness of the subject and that it might be no precedent.

This motion, however, 'could not be yielded unto'. Several times in this Parliament he drew the attention of MPs to points of procedure (8, 10 Dec.) and on one occasion (1 Dec.) lectured the Speaker himself:

> Mr. Speaker, the use hath been that the general bills should be first read and then the private, and they that carry them to give some brief commendations of them.

Wroth's committee work during this Parliament concerned the following subjects: privileges and returns (31 Oct.), private bills (2, 14, 23, 28 Nov., 3 Dec.), horses (3 Nov.), the suppression of alehouses (5 Nov.), the better setting of watches (7 Nov.), reform of the court of Exchequer (9, 25 Nov.), blasphemous swearing (10 Nov.), the abbreviation of Michaelmas term (11 Nov.), monopolies (17 Nov.), St. Bartholomew's hospital (17 Nov.), clothworkers (18 Nov.), abuses in painting (24 Nov.), draining the fens (1 Dec., reported by him 4 Dec.), Kentish Town high street (committed to him, 2 Dec.), the clerk of the market (2 Dec.), Dunkirk pirates (3 Dec.), the regulation of local government in London (4 Dec.), the assize of fuel (7 Dec.), the Belgrave privilege case (8 Dec.), increase of ships (9 Dec.), and the continuation of statutes (10 Dec.). Wroth spoke on a privilege case on 7 Nov., and also in the debate on the transport of iron ordnance (10 Dec.) when he informed the House that

> a ship is now upon the river ready to go away, laden with thirty-six pieces of ordnance.

In his last three Elizabethan Parliaments (1593, 1597, 1601), Wroth was appointed to make a collection for the poor. In addition to the committees mentioned above, to which he was named, Wroth might also have attended the following committees by virtue of his position as knight of the shire for Middlesex: a legal committee (9 Mar. 1593), enclosures (5 Nov. 1597), armour and weapons (8 Nov.), penal laws (8 Nov.), the subsidy (15 Nov.), the main business committee (3 Nov. 1601), monopolies (23 Nov.) and feltmakers (26 Nov.).[6]

The details of Wroth's work in the 1604 Parliament lie outside the scope of this biography but it is appropriate to notice that it was he who made the first speech in James's first House of Commons, when he moved for immediate discussion of wardship as a 'burden and servitude' to the

King's subjects; suggested consideration of the abuses of purveyance and monopolies; and demanded discussion of dispensations in penal statutes. He was a puritan, though not an extremist of the mould of Wentworth or James Morice; he left the rhetoric to others. He was as sensitive to abuses in the state as to the dangers of recusancy, but his interventions were practical rather than spectacular, and he remained in good odour with the government. His patriotic protestantism made him an obvious choice as a commissioner in Elizabethan and Jacobean treason cases, and he served in that capacity at the trials of William Parry*, Babington and Guy Fawkes. He was a juryman at the trial of (Sir) Walter Ralegh*. He continued to be active in his later years, in both the military and civil aspects of local government. In 1588 he was one of three men in charge of the Middlesex trained bands, and in the years following the defeat of the Armada he continued to be responsible for mustering the militia both there and in Essex.

As a j.p. in these counties, Wroth sometimes received instructions on subjects with which he had become familiar in the Commons, such as securing the peace from the depredations of discharged soldiers, London apprentices, and controlling new building in London, the growth of which was alarming the Privy Council. The despairing tone of an official letter to him of 23 Feb. 1596 on this subject suggests that the government realised the extent of the difficulties.[7]

Wroth's career in Parliament and local government bears witness to the devotion with which he served the state; his contemporaries believed he served God with equal fervour. Roger Morice thought him

a most zealous and excellent person; a great suppressor of vice, and a vigorous promoter of further reformation in the Church [and] of practical godliness,

and he was able to secure the restoration of the puritan Richard Rogers to his priestly functions after he had been suspended by Whitgift.[8]

Wroth was a friend of Michael Hickes*, whom he frequently entertained at Loughton from 1597. Wroth always pressed 'Saint Michael' to bring as many friends and relatives as possible, tempting them with such delicacies as 'very good oysters'. The merry company spent much time at outdoor sports, particularly bowls and hunting.[9]

Wroth died 27 Jan. 1606 and was buried at Enfield the following day. He left estates in five counties, his possessions in the Roding valley alone extended over an unbroken length of three miles. Property in Essex and Wiltshire and £700 went to each of Wroth's three younger sons. The rest of the lands went to the heir and executor, Robert. Money was to be distributed among the poor of Enfield and of three Essex parishes.[10]

[1] C142/171/97; Vis. Essex (Harl. Soc. xiii), 132. [2] Egerton 2345; SP12/145; Lansd. 53, f. 168; 83, f. 216; APC, xv. 11; xvi. 144; CSP Dom. 1603–10, p. 10. [3] D'Ewes, 189, 212, 213, 250, 255, 288, 289, 294, 299, 307, 340, 345, 346, 353, 355, 356, 362, 363, 371, 372, 373, 393, 394, 407, 409, 413, 414, 415, 416, 429, 431, 432, 433, 437, 439, 440, 442, 444, 446, 448, 449, 450, 453, 454; CJ, i. 93, 96, 97, 108, 112, 120, 124, 128, 135; Townshend, Hist. Colls. 26, 27, 28; Trinity, Dublin, Thos. Cromwell's jnl. f. 36; Harl. 7188, anon. jnl. ff. 90–101; Lansd. 43, anon. jnl. f. 173. [4] D'Ewes, 471, 474, 476, 477, 481, 485, 486, 487, 488, 495, 496, 497, 499, 501, 502, 507, 509, 510, 511, 512, 513, 514, 516, 518, 519; Cott. Titus F. ii. anon. jnl. ff. 33, 59, 80, 81, 91, 92; Townshend, 61, 69, 71, 72, 73, 74, 75, 76, 77. [5] D'Ewes, 552, 553, 554, 555, 556, 557, 558, 559, 562, 563, 564, 566, 569, 571, 572, 575, 578, 579, 580, 581, 582, 589, 592; Bull. IHR, xii. 20, 22; Townshend, 103, 104, 105, 106, 107, 108, 110, 111, 115, 117, 119. [6] D'Ewes, 622, 624, 626, 628, 629, 630, 631, 632, 633, 635, 637, 641, 642, 646, 647, 648, 649, 650, 651, 654, 658, 660, 662, 663, 664, 665, 666, 667, 669, 673, 674, 676, 677, 683, 685, 687; Townshend, 190, 196, 198, 203, 210, 235, 236, 238, 270, 276, 279, 284, 286, 296, 304, 305, 307, 333. [7] CJ, i. 150–1; DNB; VCH Mdx. ii. 35; APC, xvi. 144, 202, 219; xviii. 55–6; xix. 189, 350; xx. 63–5, 218–19, 326–7; xxi. 367–8; xxiv. 159–60; xxv. 22, 42–3, 230–1, 437–9; xxvi. 386; xxvii. 313–14; xxviii. 359; xxix. 140–2; xxx. 41, 156; CSP Dom. 1591–4, p. 200. [8] Essex Arch. Soc. Trans. n.s. viii. 151; Two Eliz. Puritan Diaries, ed. Knappen, 29. [9] Lansd. 86, f. 79; 87, ff. 218, 220; 88, ff. 59, 75, 89, 187; 89, f. 36. [10] DNB; C142/294/87, 171/97; Essex. Arch. Soc. Trans. n.s. viii. 148, 150; VCH Essex, iv. 30, 77, 118–19; PRO Index 6800; Morant, Essex, i. 304; PCC 9 Stafford.

A.G.R.S./M.A.P.

WROTH, Robert II (c.1576–1614), of Enfield, Mdx. and Loughton, Essex.

| NEWTOWN I.o.W. | 1601 |
| MIDDLESEX | 1604* |

b. c.1576, 1st s. of Robert Wroth I* of Enfield and Loughton by Susan, da. and h. of John Stonard of Loughton. educ. G. Inn 1594. m. 27 Sept. 1602, Mary, da. of (Sir) Robert Sidney* afterwards Earl of Leicester, 1s. Kntd. 1603; suc. fa. 1606.

Gent. pens. 1601/2–d.; keeper of Walthamstow and Leyton walks, Essex 1603; sheriff, Essex 1613–14.

Wroth owed his return to Parliament for Newtown to the captain of the Isle of Wight, Lord Hunsdon (Sir George Carey*), who had directed the corporation of the borough to send him their writ blank. Wroth did not play any recorded part in the proceedings of the Parliament, and did not sit again until 1607 when he came in for Middlesex at a by-election. His appointment as gentleman pensioner brought him admission to the court, and a fortunate marriage to the beautiful Mary Sidney. James I often hunted with him at Loughton, where he enlarged the house and became famous for his hospitality, described by Ben Jonson in his poem The Forest, dedicated to Wroth.

Wroth's only child was a son, born 'after long longing' in February 1614. Wroth died the following 14 Mar. of gangrene, and estates had to be sold to satisfy the creditors. The executors were an uncle, a brother and a cousin – all named John Wroth – and the overseers were his father-in-law and the 3rd Earl of Pembroke. Wroth's son James died in 1616.

C142/294/87; *Vis. Essex* (Harl. Soc. xiii), 132; Collins, *Sidney State Pprs.* i. 120; LC2/4/4; PRO Index 6801; 16779, f. 94; *Oglander Mems.* pp. xiii–xiv; *Essex Arch. Soc. Trans.* n.s. viii. 156–9; *CSP Dom.* 1611–18, pp. 37, 83, 121, 158; *VCH Essex*, iv. 120; PCC 60 Lawe.

A.G.R.S.

WROTH, Sir Thomas (1518–73), of Durants, Enfield, Mdx. and London.

MIDDLESEX   1545, 1547, 1553 (Mar.), 1559, 1563

b. 1518, o.s. of Robert Wroth† of Durants by Jane, da. of Sir Thomas Hawte. *educ.* St. John's, Camb.; G. Inn 1536. *m.* 1538, Mary, da. of Sir Richard Rich†, 1st Baron Rich, 7s. inc. John*, Richard* and Robert I* 7da. *suc.* fa. 1535. Kntd. 22 Feb. 1547.[1]

Gent. usher of the chamber to Prince Edward 1541–7; gent. of privy chamber 1547–9, principal gent. 1549–53; standard bearer of England Jan.–Nov. 1549; jt. lt. Waltham forest, Essex 1549–58; bailiff, manor of Enfield, Mdx. from 1550, manor of Ware, Herts. 1551–3; jt. ld. lt. Mdx. 1551, 1552, 1553; keeper of Syon House and steward of lordship of Isleworth, Mdx. 1552–3; steward, Elsing and Worcesters manors in Enfield, Mdx. 1553–9; master forester, Enfield chase 1553–9; steward, manor of Edmonton, Mdx. 1553–*d.*; j.p.q. Mdx. from c.1559, Essex from c.1561; keeper, manor of Elsing, Mdx. 1560–*d.*; special commr. to consult with ld. dep. on govt. of Ireland 1562; commr. to raise benevolence in Essex and Mdx. May 1564; woodward, Enfield chase 1564–6; custos rot. Mdx. by 1564.[2]

Wroth was a gentleman of the chamber during the reign of Edward VI, his services being rewarded by numerous marks of royal favour, notably lavish grants of land. He signed the letters patent devising the crown to Lady Jane Grey and was sent to the Tower after Mary's accession. He was soon released, but early in 1554 was suspected of complicity in the Duke of Suffolk's rising. As a result he went into exile, remaining abroad, in Italy and Germany, for the rest of Mary's reign. Just over a month after Elizabeth's accession he set off for England. Edwin Sandys, who reported his departure from Strasbourg (he left 20 Dec. 1558) noted that he travelled with Sir Anthony Cooke* and 'other persons of distinction'. As the Middlesex election return is dated 29 Dec. he was presumably elected knight of the shire *in absentia*, though he would have been in England in time for the opening of the Parliament in 1559. It is likely that Wroth was among those MPs who pressed for a more radical religious settlement than the Queen would allow. On 29 Mar. the bill for the increase of tillage was committed to him, and he was a member of the succession committee 31 Oct. 1566. He was one of 30 Members summoned on 5 Nov.

1566 to hear the Queen's message on the succession. Wroth was also put in charge of a small matter of privilege in this Parliament, his report on 23 Nov. 1566 being the occasion of his only known speech in the House.[3]

The failure of the Marian exiles and their supporters to secure a more complete reformation of the Church than that of 1559 may have weighed heavily on Wroth's spirits. Late in 1559 Peter Martyr, writing from Zurich, complained to John Jewel that neither Wroth nor Sir Anthony Cooke had written to him. Jewel replied:

> ... they are neither in the rank or position you suppose them to be, and in which all [our] Israel hoped they would be ... They have hitherto refrained from writing to you, not from any disinclination or forgetfulness of you, but [because they were really ashamed to write.] Both of them are now suffering most severely under an attack of ague.

Wroth served the government in a variety of capacities during the remaining years of his life. In November 1558 Sir Nicholas Throckmorton* suggested that he should be sent to Germany to negotiate with the protestant princes. Elizabeth seems to have kept this advice in mind as, in July 1562, when there was concern about the course of the French civil war, Wroth was ordered to discuss with the German princes the possibility of raising an army to help the Huguenots. A month before, he had been appointed a special commissioner to consult with the lord deputy on the government of Ireland, though he did not arrive in Dublin until February 1564. In April the lord deputy, the 3rd Earl of Sussex, left for England and Wroth was nominated special assistant to Sir Nicholas Arnold*, who was appointed lord justice during the deputy's absence. But Wroth displeased the Queen:

> We mislike so much of your remissness to satisfy us in this commission that except you can better answer to your doings we shall think it reason to cause you to make account thereof,

and was recalled in October.[4]

Wroth's activities were not confined to the Continent and Ireland. In August 1559 he was one of the commissioners nominated to visit the dioceses of Ely and Norwich. In June 1563 he was appointed to a commission instructed to apprehend, examine and bring to trial persons suspected of murder, felony, counterfeiting or other serious crimes, and in February 1565, when another commission was nominated with the same terms of reference, he was again a member. In April 1565 he was among those Middlesex notables who received instructions to take special care in the 'good assessing' of the subsidy. In July 1569 he helped to muster the county. The Government's confidence in him was reflected in his appointment as a commissioner to examine the circumstances attending the publication in England of the papal bull deposing Elizabeth. On 25 June 1570 the

Council ordered him and the other commissioners to convey to the Tower John Felton, who was charged with having a copy of the printed bull, and with 'speech with the Spanish ambassador'. Felton denying the accusations, the Council ordered him to be 'brought to the place of torture and ... put in fear thereof'. If he still refused to confess he was to be made to 'feel such smart and pains' as the commissioners thought necessary. Wroth was given a rather less dramatic assignment in June 1573, a few months before his death, when he was one of six commissioners appointed to examine a man who was suspected of robbing New College, Oxford.[5]

Wroth, who was assessed at £100 for the subsidy of 1571, was a wealthy man when he died. His father had left him lands in Middlesex and Somerset, but it was his own service to Edward VI that established the family fortunes. Between 1550 and 1553 he obtained grants of ten manors, four in Essex, three in Middlesex, two in Sussex and one in Somerset. When he died, 9 Oct. 1573, he had lands in five counties. In his will dated 5 Oct. 1573, proved 26 Apr. 1575, he bequeathed £400 in cash to each of his four unmarried daughters and £500 to each of his six younger sons. His wife received a life interest in four manors, which were to revert after her death to his heir Robert, who received a direct grant of some of his other lands and the reversion of the remainder. His executors were his brother William, two friends, Peter Osborne* and William Clerke*, and a cousin, James Morice*. The preamble to his will repudiated good works as a means to salvation, and he made no charitable bequests.[6]

[1] C142/57/7, 33; PCC 16 Pyckering; Vis. Essex (Harl. Soc. xiii), 132; D. O. Pam, Protestant Gentlemen: the Wroths of Enfield and Loughton (Edmonton Hundred Hist. Soc. occasional pprs. n.s. xxv), passim. [2] Lansd. 1218; LP Hen. VIII, xvii. p. 688; xxi(2), p. 86; APC, ii. 345; iii. 259; iv. 50, 277; CPR, 1549-51, pp. 329-30; 1553-4, pp. 325-6, 394; 1557-8, p. 211; 1558-60, pp. 299, 351; 1560-3, p. 266; 1563-6, pp. 122-3, 126; Somerville, Duchy, i. 612-13; CSP Dom. 1547-80, p. 40; DNB; Lambeth ms 614, ff. 143, 145, 149; CSP Ire. 1509-73, pp. 230, 246. [3] DNB; C. H. Garrett, Marian Exiles, 344-6; Zurich Letters (ser. 1) (Parker Soc.), 5; CJ, i. 71, 77, 78; D'Ewes, 126-7, 129, 130; Camb. Univ. Lib. Gg. iii. 34, p. 209. [4] Zurich Letters, 53; Read, Cecil, 247; Lambeth ms 614, ff. 143, 145, 149; CSP Ire. 1509-73, pp. 230, 235, 239, 240, 246; EHR, lxv. 95; SP63/11/10. [5] DNB; CPR, 1560-3, pp. 485, 523; 1563-6, p. 257; Lansd. 8, f. 79; APC, vii. 373; viii. 111. [6] DNB; Lansd. 13, ff. 67 seq.; C142/57/7, 33; CPR, 1550-3, pp. 6, 17, 188; 1553 and App. p. 240; PCC 16 Pyckering; C142/171/97.

A.G.R.S.

WROUGHTON, James ?of Broad Hinton, Wilts.

CIRENCESTER   1597

4th s. of Sir William Wroughton† of Broad Hinton by his 2nd w. Eleanor, da. of Edward Lewknor of Kingston Buci, Suss.; bro. of Thomas*.

Wroughton presumably owed his seat at Cirencester to his brother-in-law Sir Henry Poole*, who later bought the manor of Cirencester from the Danvers family. He could have attended a Commons committee appointed to deal with Newport bridge on 29 Nov. 1597. Though of an established, if minor, Wiltshire family, little information survives about Wroughton. In 1579 he was serving in Ireland, and with other officers petitioned the Privy Council about his overdue pay. In March 1582 Sir Henry Sidney* wrote to Sir Francis Walsingham* thanking him for an unspecified favour shown to Wroughton. The latter kept up his connexion with the Sidneys, serving under Sir Philip* in the Low Countries. During the preparations against the Armada, the Earl of Pembroke included his name on the list of those whose help could be relied upon in case of an invasion.

The only reference found to his buying property, in July 1597, shows him joining with a certain John Goad to buy the site of the rectory of Sherston, a few miles west of Malmesbury. The last reference found to him shows that he was living in May 1598, when he received a bequest of £20 under his brother Thomas's will.

Wilts. Vis. Peds. (Harl. Soc. cv, cvi), 219-20; Vis Glos. (Harl. Soc. xxi), 125-6; D'Ewes, 565; Glover's Vis. Yorks. ed. Foster, 351; CSP Ire. 1574-85, pp. 203, 354; HMC Var. iv. 134; pat. roll 39 Eliz. pt. 3; PCC 36 Lewyn.

N.M.F.

WROUGHTON, Thomas (c.1540-97), of Broad Hinton, Wilts.

HEYTESBURY   1571

b. c.1540, 1st s. of Sir William Wroughton† by his 2nd w. Eleanor, and bro. of James*. m. Anne, da. and coh. of John Berwick† of Wilcot, 4s. 3 or 4 da. suc. fa. 1559. Kntd. 1574.[1]

J.p. Wilts. from c.1574, q. by 1576, sheriff 1576-7, capt. of levies 1588, col. by 1596.[2]

Of a family established at Broad Hinton since the mid-fourteenth century, Wroughton's father twice achieved knight of the shire status, but although short-listed thrice for the office, he was never sheriff. Wroughton himself was returned to Parliament only once, for the small borough of Heytesbury, and his brother James was, so far as is known, the last of the family to sit in Parliament.

Before the general election of 1571, Hugh Hawker, the owner of the borough of Heytesbury wrote to Sir John Thynne:[3]

I promised you the nomination of one of the burgesses of Heytesbury ... and when I know whom you will appoint, I then mind to return the same.

In the event Thynne suggested Wroughton, his brother-in-law.

At his father's death, Thomas Wroughton was aged 19, and his wardship was granted to John Berwick, who became his father-in-law. In addition to the manor of

Broad Hinton near Swindon, Wroughton owned property at Beversbrook, a short distance from Calne, and a manor house at Kennett, five miles south-west of Marlborough and close to his wife's lands in Wilcot and Stowell. He also inherited the manor of Bawdrip, Somerset. In 1573 he and Sir Giles Poole* and his wife conveyed Broad Hinton for £700 to Henry Poole† and John Polwell, but the property was entailed, and remained in Wroughton's possession until he died: the transaction was probably a mortgage. The Somerset property caused litigation in the Star Chamber about 1577 over one Humphrey Willis, whom Wroughton had presented to the living at Bawdrip, and who in turn had appointed an 'heretical and idolatrous' curate at a salary of 20 marks. Nevertheless, most of the information about Wroughton shows him going about his official duties in Wiltshire, where from 1574 he attended quarter sessions regularly. In 1576 he was a subsidy commissioner, his own assessment being on £20 in lands. Though in general a satisfactory official, he was censured in 1596 for negligence in connexion with the local levies. Although he was one of the four colonels responsible for sending a detachment to the Isle of Wight, he had remained in London during the preparations, appointing no 'sufficient lieutenant', and his band, instead of reporting with the others at Salisbury, 'went confusedly the nearest way to Southampton'.[4]

Wroughton was fond of hunting, and like other Wiltshire gentlemen was not too particular about the forest boundaries. The Earl of Hertford, warden of Savernake, wrote to Sir John Thynne in 1567 about 'great abuses committed by your brother Wroughton in and about my forest'. William Darrell* complained to the Wiltshire justices (September 1588) that the servants of 'Mr. Wroughton', possibly one of Sir Thomas's sons, had attacked him, and that Wroughton himself was violent. A letter from Sir Francis Walsingham* about the matter advised Darrell to 'stay all proceedings against Sir Thomas Wroughton's men, for that I am in hope to end all controversy between you'. It is unlikely that, considering Darrell's own reputation, authority treated his charges seriously. However, Wroughton may have been partly to blame: at least one of his tenants sued him in Chancery for high-handed and illegal actions.[5]

He died 4 June 1597 and was buried at Broad Hinton, where the parish church contains a monument to him. His will, drawn up in May 1597, was not proved until nearly a year after his death. The bequests, which were mainly to relatives and servants, were in some cases considerable: one daughter, Mary, was to have £900. The will mentioned two married daughters, one of them 'my sweet and well-beloved daughter, the Lady Unton' (Dorothy, wife of Henry Unton*), and four sons. Wroughton asked the executors, his widow and their son Giles, to make arrangements for the disposal of goods, including several satin suits and other clothing which he had left in London.

Sir Henry Knyvet*, Wroughton's brother George and his brother-in-law Sir Henry Poole were to act as overseers. The heir, William, was 36 at his father's death.[6]

[1] Wards 7/102/169; *Wilts. Vis. Peds.* (Harl. Soc. cv, cvi), 219. [2] Harl. 168, ff. 166–9; Lansd. 63, f. 179; *HMC Foljambe*, 38; *HMC Hatfield*, vi. 506. [3] Bath mss, Thynne pprs. 3, f. 252. [4] *CPR*, 1560–3. p. 23; C142/249/81; Wards 7/102/169; *Wilts. N. and Q.* vii. 412; St. Ch. 5/W1/33; *APC*, ix. 157; *Mins. Proc. Sess.* (Wilts. Arch. Soc. recs. br. iv), passim; *Two Taxation Lists* (same ser. x), 78, 87; Lansd. 63, f. 179; *HMC Hatfield*, vi. 506. [5] *Wilts. Arch. Mag.* vi. 209–10; liii. 199; C3/230/18, 252/72. [6] *Aubrey Topog. Colls.* (Wilts. Arch. and Nat. Hist. Soc.), 336; C142/249/81; PCC 36 Lewyn.

N.M.F.

WYAT, Ralph (d. bef. 1594), of Worcester.

WORCESTER	1586

m., at least 1s.

Member of the 48, Worcester by 1555, of the 24, 1560, auditor 1557–8, 1565–6, 1573–4, chamberlain 1567–8, bailiff 1570–1, 1572–3, commr. musters 1574.

Virtually nothing has been discovered about Wyat beyond the bare outline of his civic career, and the evidence of his success as a merchant provided by his purchase of the manor of Lindley in St. Martin, Worcestershire, from Sir John Huband. He also acquired lands by lending money on mortgage.

Wyat was described as 'a worthy magistrate who maintained the honour of his city', probably because he was one of those who, in 1574, successfully resisted the attempt of the Worcestershire commissioners for musters to extend their jurisdiction to the city.

VCH Worcs. iii. 511; C2.Eliz.W6/48; Worcester Guildhall, audit of city accts. 1540–1600; *APC*, viii. 263; W. R. Williams, *Worcs. MPs*, 92.

S.M.T.

WYMARKE, Edward (d. 1634), of London and Luffenham, Rutland.

CHIPPENHAM	1597*, 1601
PETERBOROUGH	1604
PETERBOROUGH	
LIVERPOOL	1614[1]
NEWCASTLE-UNDER-LYME	

o.s. of Edward Wymarke of Luffenham by Margaret, da. of William Dudley of Clopton, Northants. Prob. *unm. suc.* fa. 1599.[2]

Wymarke was one of those fringe Elizabethan officials whose status and occupation defy classification. Holding no specific office, he kept some sort of register of concealed lands, reimbursing himself from the amount recovered for the government. In 1597, for an unascertained reason, this work incurred the Queen's displeasure, and in July he wrote to her asking for the matter to be referred to the lord treasurer, Burghley, and the chancellor of the Exchequer. Whether his wish to be returned for Chippenham in October had anything to do with this episode is not clear. In 1602 he apparently sold his book to Sir Edward Dyer*, payment to be in instalments, which, of course, fell into arrears. Wymarke was presumably nominated for Chippenham by Anthony Mildmay*, son of a former chancellor of the Exchequer, who owned property in the town, and was becoming an active patron there. Wymarke's name was inserted on the return over that of Thomas Edmondes*, the ambassador, who was sent abroad shortly before Parliament met. Wymarke was named to one minor committee 8 Nov. 1597, and, 2 Dec. 1601, to the committee dealing with church attendance.[3]

Wymarke was a friend of and chief source for John Chamberlain, the letter writer, who once noted that he went out only by 'owl light to the *Star* and to the *Windmill*, which course of his is cause of much descanting, and the nearest and dearest friends he hath know not what to guess of this humour'. Wymarke lived in London, in comfortable circumstances. He died 30 Sept. 1634 and was buried in St. Botolph's, Aldersgate. His property went to his sister Frances, wife of John Green of Market Overton, Rutland.[4]

[1] Elected for all three constituencies: preference not known.
[2] *Vis. Rutland* (Harl. Soc. iii), 47. [3] *HMC Hatfield*, vii. 330; x. 231; xii. 16; Lansd. 175, f. 136; E179/146/369; PRO Index 6800, f. 633; C219/33/225; *Chippenham Recs.* 327, 338, 339; D'Ewes, 553, 664.
[4] *Chamberlain Letters* ed. McClure, passim; *Vis. Rutland*, loc. cit.

R.C.G./P.W.H.

WYN ap CADWALADR, John (d. ?1589), of Rhiwlas, Merion.

1st s. of Cadwaladr ap Robert ap Rhys ap Maredudd of Rhiwlas by Jane, da. of Maredudd ap Ieuan ap Robert of Gwydir, Llanrhychwyn, Caern. *m.* Jane, da. and h. of Thomas ap Robert of Llwyn Dedwydd, Llangwm, Merion., 3s. inc. Cadwaladr Price* 6da.

Escheator, Merion. 1564–5, j.p. from c.1573, sheriff 1576–7, 1585–6, dep. lt. 1587.

The family first became prominent through the favour shown by Henry VII towards this Member's great-grandfather, following his support at Bosworth. Wyn's grandfather was a chaplain to Henry VIII, and profited substantially from the dissolution of the religious house at Ysbyty Ifan. Further lands, belonging formerly to the abbey of Strata Marcella in Montgomeryshire, were acquired by Wyn's father.

Although closely connected with three leading county families, Wyn himself is not known to have taken an active part in the political rivalries between the Salesburys, Nanneys and Owens. His social prominence, however, is clear, not only from the public offices he held in the shire,

but from the respect with which he was regarded by the bards of that generation. The precise date of his death is not known, but a reference is made to his 'late' decease in November 1589.

Griffith, *Peds.* 247; *DWB*; Lansd. 35, f. 139; *HMC Foljambe*, 26; NLW, *Cal. Deeds and Docs.* i. 290; PRO, *Cal. Ancient Deeds* C146, C8400, 27 Eliz.; *HMC Welsh*, i. 187; ii. 196, 198, 615; *APC*, xviii. 206.

H.G.O.

WYN ap CADWALADR, *see also* PRICE, Cadwaladr

WYN ap HUGH, John (by 1525–76), of Bodvel in Llannor, Caern.

b. by 1525, 1st s. of Hugh ap John of Bodvel by Catherine, da. of Henry Salusbury of Llanrhaiadr, Denb. *m.* Elizabeth, da. of Sir John Puleston†, 3s. inc. Hugh Gwyn *alias* Bodvel* 1da.; 1s. illegit.[1]

Jt. (with David Lloyd ap Thomas†) bailiff, Pwllheli and high constable, commote of Gafflogion, Caern. in 1546; j.p. Caern. 1550, sheriff 1550–1, 1559–60; commr. relief 1550, goods of churches and fraternities 1553, loan 1557, tanneries 1574.[2]

Wyn's family was of ancient descent and substantial fortune. Why Wyn was returned to Parliament for his county in 1571 after an interval of some 18 years is not clear. Conceivably, as one of the wealthiest among them, he was put up by the group of Caernarvonshire gentlemen opposed to the interference of the Earl of Leicester in the affairs of that county. Wyn acquired lands in Gafflogion and the neighbouring commote of Cymydmaen – some of which he later disposed of to Sir Humphrey Gilbert*, an assiduous collector of Welsh lands and offices – and secured a reversion to his son Hugh of a crown lease he held in the neighbourhood of Dolwyddelan, in the east of the shire. At some unknown date he also secured the farm of the tolls of Pwllheli and of the town fields. His acquisitions brought the usual crop of litigation. One grant was challenged in the court of augmentations by 'upwards of a hundred' persons who alleged he had turned them out of their holdings in Bardsey or Aberdaron, and appealed to a prior lease from Henry VIII. In 1569 he was further charged in Star Chamber with using Bardsey as a depot for pirates, keeping a factor there to despatch the booty to Chester by sea, and involving his less canny neighbours in prosecutions which he himself evaded as 'a man of good countenance, great power, ability and friendship' in the county.[3]

Politically Wyn was one of the leading men of his shire, and his influence was buttressed by his marriage into the Puleston family, which also linked him with the rising house of Gwydir. Though in 1553 Wyn was one of four Caernarvonshire gentlemen associated with the sheriff in a letter from Archbishop Heath, then president of the council of Wales, directing them to choose for Mary's first Parliament 'well-ordered men ... specially of the Catholic religion', it is problematic how far he remained a Catholic. His name appears in a list of Catholics in Wales drawn up by an optimistic supporter of the Queen of Scots in 1574 (with a significant indication that his house lay near the sea); and it was just about this time that he began to take a prominent part in the agitation of the local gentry against the designs on the 'enroached' lands of that protestant champion the Earl of Leicester as forester of Snowdon. The agitation led to many charges and counter-charges of recusancy, in the course of which John's son Hugh Gwyn *alias* Bodvel suffered a term of imprisonment. It is possible that Robert Gwynne, the Catholic missionary and controversialist, was another son, not named in the pedigrees, and that two other missionary priests, Charles Gwynne *alias* Bodvel and Roger Gwynne (a 'seminary' accused of plotting the assassination of James I) were grandsons of his.

Wyn made his nuncupative will 11 Oct. 1576, just before his death. The will was proved 6 Nov. of that year. His son Hugh Gwyn *alias* Bodvel inherited the lands, and with them the money his father had left on mortgage – on condition that he provided for the education of his half-brother William, John Wyn's illegitimate son. There were also legacies to the poor of Llannor and Aberdaron.[4]

¹ Dwnn, *Vis. Wales*, ii. 174. ² *Cal. Caern. Q. Sess. Rec.* ed. W. O. Williams, i. 32, 38, 67, 248 et al.; *CPR* 1553 and App. Edw. VI, 363, 419; *Cal. Wynn Pprs.* 4; Flenley, *Cal. Reg. Council, Marches of Wales*, 127. ³ *Augmentations*, ed. Lewis and Davies (Univ. Wales Bd. of Celtic Studies, Hist. and Law ser. xiii), 60, 298, 302; *Exchequer*, ed. E. G. Jones (same ser. iv), 52, 79; *Star Chamber*, ed. Edwards (same ser. i), 32; *APC*, iv. 209; *CPR*, 1547–8, p. 32. ⁴ *Cal. Wynn Pprs.* 3, 4, 9, 12, 13; Griffith, *Peds.* 181, 275; *CPR*, 1553 and App. Edw. VI, 317; Neale, *Commons*, 286; *Cath. Rec. Soc.* xiii. 108; *EHR*, liii. 635; lix. 353–4; *Trans. Cymmrod. Soc.* 1936, p. 99; *DWB*, 42–3, 332–3; Gardiner, *Hist.* i. 106; PCC 30 Carew.

A.H.D.

WYN, WYNN, *see also* **GWYN, GWYN** *alias* **BODVEL, GWYNNE**

WYNDHAM, Sir Edmund (by 1496–1569), of Felbrigg, Norf.

NORFOLK   1539, 1559[1]

b. by 1496, 1st s. of Sir Thomas Wyndham of Felbrigg by his 1st w. Eleanor, da. of Richard Scrope of Upsall, Yorks. *m.* by Oct. 1521, Susan, da. of Sir Roger Townshend† of Raynham, Norf., 3s. inc. Francis* 3da.; 1da. illegit. *suc.* fa. 29 Apr. 1522. Kntd. 1543.[2]

Commr. subsidy, Norf. 1523, tenths of spiritualities 1535, benevolence 1544/5, relief 1550, goods of churches and fraternities 1553, to enforce Acts of Supremacy and Uniformity 1559, eccles. commr. 1569; servant,

household of Cardinal Wolsey by 1525; j.p. Norf. 1532–58, q. from 1559; sheriff, Norf. and Suff. 1537–8, 1545–6, 1549–50; dep. lt. Norf. 1559, jt. ld. lt. (with Sir Christopher Heydon*, in the absence of the Duke of Norfolk) 1560.[3]

The Wyndhams, having acquired Felbrigg shortly before the Wars of the Roses, rose to a position of wealth and influence in Norfolk second only, by the beginning of this period, to the Duke of Norfolk. Wyndham was therefore a natural choice as knight of the shire in 1559, though he had to take second place to the young Sir Robert Dudley*. A bill about the export of cloth was committed to him, 7 Mar. 1559. Wyndham did not sit again, and for the last decade of his life confined his interests to his native county. He was one of those whom the bishop of Norwich consulted in 1564 before sending his report to the Privy Council on the religious beliefs of Norfolk justices, but there is no reason to suppose that he held any strong views himself. His attitude to the various religious changes of his long life suggests he had none. He died on 23 July 1569 and was buried at Felbrigg. His inquisition post mortem shows that he owned, in Norfolk alone, a dozen manors worth more than £200 a year as well as extensive estates in Yorkshire. He had invested heavily in monastic lands and his principal contribution to the family's lands was the purchase of Beeston priory and most of its estates in 1545.[4]

¹ E371/402(1). This calls the Member 'Sir Edward Wyndham', but no one of his name is known and an abbreviation of 'Edmund' could easily have been misread as 'Edward' when this copy was made. ² H. A. Wyndham, *A Fam. Hist. 1410–1688: the Wyndhams of Norf. and Som.* passim; *Vis. Norf.* (Harl. Soc. xxxvi), 324. ³ *LP Hen. VIII*, iii(2), p. 1366; v. 78; Wyndham, 107; Add. 5752, ff. 254–5; A. H. Smith thesis, 415; *CPR*, 1550–3, p. 396; 1553, pp. 356, 416; 1563–6, p. 25; *CSP Dom.* 1547–80, p. 329. ⁴ *CJ*, i. 57; *Cam. Misc.* ix(3), p. 58; *CPR*, 1558–60, pp. 31–2; *Norf. Arch.* xix. 88; E150/661/13; R. W. K. Cremer, *Felbrigg: the Story of a House*, 26; Blomefield, *Norf.* viii. 113–14; *LP Hen. VIII*, xx(2), p. 216.

M.R.P.

WYNDHAM, Francis (d. 1592), of Norwich, Beeston and Pentney, Norf.

NORFOLK   1572*

2nd s. of Sir Edmund Wyndham* of Felbrigg by Susan, da. of Sir Roger Townshend† of Raynham. *educ.* Camb. prob. Corpus Christi; L. Inn by 1554, called 1560. *m.* 1570, Elizabeth, da. of Sir Nicholas Bacon,† *s.p.*

Of counsel to Norwich 1563–70, steward 1570–5, recorder 1575–80; bencher of L. Inn 1569, Autumn and Lent reader 1571, 1572, treasurer 1575; serjeant-at-law 1577; j.c.p. 1579–d.[1]

J.p. Norf. from c.1573, many other counties from 1577.

Both Wyndham's parents were from Norfolk county families, and his own marriage to the lord keeper's daughter must have raised his prestige still further. As his career shows, he identified himself with the puritan party which was strong in Norfolk.[2]

In the House of Commons he was recorded as serving on committees concerning alehouses, 17 Feb. 1576; dilapidations, 24 Feb.; grants by the dean and chapter of Norwich, 2 Mar.; and taking away the benefit of clergy from rapists, 7 Mar. Before the next session he had been made a judge, and as such was a receiver of petitions in the Lords for the Parliaments of 1584, 1586 and 1589.[3]

Most of the surviving information about Wyndham concerns his legal career. He was a leading member of his inn, holding all the major offices there, and in addition acting as keeper of the 'Black Book' of record for a year from November 1573. His promotion in his profession was relatively fast, and in 1579 he was chosen, against strong competition, to succeed Sir Roger Manwood* as justice of the common pleas. Chief Justice Dyer's list of possible successors for Manwood included, besides Wyndham, Edmund Anderson, Francis Gawdy* and John Popham*.[4]

With the city of Norwich Wyndham had been closely connected since 1563, when he was retained as of counsel to the corporation at an annual fee of 20s. In September 1570, when he was appointed steward, the fee was doubled. From 3 May 1575 until 1580 – when he was succeeded by Edmund Flowerdew* who had already followed him as steward – he was recorder of the city. He seems to have been on intimate terms with Flowerdew: in 1586 they were colleagues on the same circuit, and the writer Geoffrey Whitney addressed two of his *Emblemes* jointly to them both.[5]

Wyndham was an active and conscientious official, whose name appears on a large number of commissions. Some years before his promotion to the bench he was appointed to a special commission of oyer and terminer in Norfolk, and a little later, in 1575, served as arbitrator in a controversy between Yarmouth and the Cinque Ports. With Popham as his colleague, he went on the Oxford circuit in 1578. He officiated at two important treason trials, those of John Somerville in 1583, and William Parry* two years later. Although he was consulted about the trial of Mary Stuart, he was not a commissioner at Fotheringay. In November 1591, after the death of Sir Christopher Hatton, he was one of the commissioners appointed to hear cases in Chancery, continuing to act until the following April, when Sir John Puckering* was appointed lord keeper.[6]

On at least one occasion he ran into serious trouble at court, largely through his puritan convictions. He strongly disapproved of the use by the bishops' courts of examination under the *ex officio* oath, and spoke in open sessions against the procedure. This angered Whitgift, and at about the same time (probably late in 1588) Wyndham made an enemy of Lord Hunsdon, the lord chamberlain and lord lieutenant of Norfolk. Writing to his brother-in-law Nathaniel Bacon* in November 1587, Wyndham had complained of the inadequate preparations made in East Anglia to repel a possible invasion by Parma's army, and in September 1588 he wrote directly to Burghley, asking for an inquiry into the way money raised for defence in Norfolk had been spent, suggesting that people would pay their current subsidy assessment more readily if they were satisfied on this matter. Those who had handled any of the money should not be put in charge of the inquiry, 'for accountants are never fit auditors'.

Not unnaturally, Hunsdon resented what he considered a slight on his administration, and raised the matter with Wyndham when some time later the judges were summoned to a Privy Council meeting at the lord chancellor's house and ordered, among other injunctions, to take strong action against anyone found to be connected with the Martin Marprelate tracts. The Queen believed that some of the judges favoured the Martinists, 'which if she knew she would remove from their places'. Wyndham came under special censure for his opposition to the *ex officio* procedure, being told that his charge had 'bred a scruple to all the bishops in England that they doubt how to proceed' in their jurisdiction. Burghley, who was generally favourably disposed to Wyndham, was absent through illness, and Hunsdon took the opportunity, when the main meeting was over, to make a strong attack on the offender. He referred to attempts Wyndham had made to 'discountenance' him in his lieutenancy, and also raised various minor causes of dispute (some of them concerned with the conduct of Francis's elder brother Roger), as well as other more serious matters. When dinner was announced Hunsdon declared that he had at least twenty further charges to raise, but he apparently let them drop. 'All this while', wrote Wyndham to Nathaniel Bacon, 'the lords let us both alone, and said nothing to us'. However, the two men quarrelled again about the repairing of Norfolk highways – a longstanding dispute which caused serious friction in the county, and in which Hunsdon supported Sir Arthur Heveningham against the puritan group. In 1591 the Privy Council had to intervene to 'restore good feeling and love, friendship and good responding' between them.[7]

Burghley seems to have respected Wyndham's judgment, and at least one letter survives in which Wyndham gave his opinion on suggested legal appointments. His comments emphasise the streak of puritanism which led him to oppose Whitgift and the bishops. Candidates were described as 'backward' or 'not thought forward' in religion, and Wyndham opposed the promotion of Thomas Walmesley* as serjeant, claiming that he was suspected of Catholicism.[8]

With his relatives the Bacons, Wyndham seems to have been on terms of close intimacy. Sir Nicholas, the lord keeper, employed him to negotiate the purchase of Stiffkey from the Banyard family, and the Stiffkey papers have a number of references to him. He himself bought considerable property in Norfolk, including Pentney priory, with the manors of Ashwood, Pentney and West Bilney, which the Mildmay family had acquired at the dissolution of the monasteries. Other branches of the Wyndhams also bought or were granted former monastic estates, and a contemporary rhyme noted that

> Horner, Popham, Wyndham and Thynne,
> When the abbot went out, then they came in.

Wyndham also acquired a large dwelling house near St. Giles gate, Norwich, called the Committee House. It had originally been Lady Morley's, and later had belonged to his maternal grandfather, Sir Roger Townshend.

He died on 18 June 1592, and a monument was set up to him, with an effigy in judge's robes, in St. Peter Mancroft, Norwich. He left to his widow all the Norfolk property, including the site of the dissolved monastery of Pentney, with its manors, mill and lands, which he had bought from Sir Thomas Mildmay*. To ensure payment of a £400 debt to his brother and heir, Dr. Thomas Wyndham, he gave instructions that his house at Norwich was to be offered for sale, first to Nathaniel Bacon for £400, then to Sir Nicholas Bacon* for £500, and finally to Sir Edward Coke* also for £500. If none of the suggested purchasers wished to buy, the house was to go to Dr. Wyndham in settlement of the debt. Plate inscribed with the Wyndham arms was left to the mayor of Norwich in perpetuity. Nathaniel Bacon was an executor, and Justice Gawdy, who received a gilt cup weighing twenty ounces, an overseer. The will was proved on 8 July 1592, but a dispute arose between Elizabeth Wyndham and the executors over the validity of a nuncupative codicil, drawn up on the day Wyndham died, leaving extra property to the widow and adding various small legacies. The codicil was declared valid in November 1594. The widow married as her second husband Sir Robert 'Mansfield' or Mansell*.[9]

[1] DNB; Vis. Norf. (Harl. Soc. xxxii), 324; Black Bk. L. Inn, i. 311, 314, 329, 364, 380, 388, 397, 462; Norwich assembly bk. 1568–85, f. 115; Foss, Judges, v. 551; H. A. Wyndham, Fam. Hist. 1410–1688, pp. 128–40 et passim. [2] Wyndham, loc. cit.; R. W. K. Cremer, Felbrigg: the Story of a House, 27. [3] CJ, i. 106, 108, 110, 111; D'Ewes, 254, 312, 378, 420. [4] Black Bk. i. 388; Lansd. 27, f. 98. [5] Norwich assembly bk. 1568–85, ff. 30, 115, 192; Chamberlain's acct. bk. 1551–67, f. 271; DNB. [6] DNB; APC, x. 291. [7] APC, xxi. 244–6; Wyndham, 134–8; HMC Townshend, 9–10; Stiffkey Pprs. (Cam. Soc. ser. 3, xxvi), 186. The HMC and Cam. Soc. volumes give different dates, both impossible, for Wyndham's letter. It has been dated between 30 Dec. 1590 and 18 Feb. 1591 by P. Collinson, 'The Puritan Classical Movement' (PhD thesis, London, 1957), 1059, n. 1, and A. H. Smith, 'Eliz. Gentry of Norfolk' (PhD thesis, London, 1959), 246–7 and n. The Smith thesis, pp. 159, 160, 220, 222–3, 244, 247, has other references to Wyndham's part in county faction. [8] Lansd. 57, f. 115; Wyndham, 132. [9] Wyndham, 128–30, 139; Blomefield, Norf. viii. 114; C142/234/74; PCC 61 Harrington, 82 Dixy.

N.M.F.

WYNN, Ellis (bef. 1559–1623), of St. Dunstan-in-the-West, London, and Everdon, Northants.

SALTASH   1597

b. bef. 1559, 3rd s. of Maurice Wynn* of Gwydir by his 1st w. Jane (Siân), and bro. of John*. educ. Westminster sch. m. Anne, da. of Alderman Gage, ?s.p.

Gent. harbinger by 1596; clerk of the petty bag in Chancery 1603.

Younger brother of the John Wynn who dominated the life of Caernarvonshire for more than 40 years, Ellis Wynn entered the household of Robert Cecil, who by 1596 had secured for him a lucrative court place as gentleman harbinger, with the duty of allocating lodgings to courtiers. This office, which he seems to have executed both arbitrarily and offensively, enabled him to watch over his brother's interests in London, and much of their correspondence was concerned with John Wynn's lawsuits. But tactlessness and arrogance characterised his actions here, too, as when he told Hatton, the lord chancellor, that he did not consider Lord Grey (which one is not clear) a competent judge of a petition presented on behalf of his brother John.

When the election writs for the 1597 Parliament went out Cecil and lord keeper Thomas Egerton* wrote jointly – and ineffectively – to the electors of Caernarvonshire recommending Wynn as knight of the shire, but instead Wynn came in for Saltash, presumably on Cecil's recommendation. He made another unsuccessful bid for Caernarvonshire in 1604, when his court connexions failed to supply him with another seat, and he appears to have made no further attempt to enter Parliament.

Wynn died 27 Sept. 1623 from an operation for the removal of gall stones. Two days previously he had made his will. He bequeathed his soul

> to Christ with a sure hope, trust and confidence to be saved by the merits of His most bitter death and passion and innocent bloodshedding on the cross for me and all mankind; renouncing all merits and deserts of mine own as a most vile and unworthy sinner who without these manifold mercies of my Saviour deserve nothing but death and damnation.

To his wife he left a life interest in his house and household goods, bequeathing her the linen, jewels and money in her possession absolutely. His lands, including property in Staffordshire and Worcestershire, were to be held by the executors for the payment of debts and legacies. The bishop of Lincoln was to have £100, and tokens of friendship and remembrance were left to several people including the master of the rolls. The will concluded:

> I do give Almighty God most humble thanks upon the knees of my heart for suffering me to live this present hour, for all His blessings and benefits bestowed upon me and for this gentle and fatherly correction

wherewith He hath visited me. Not doubting whensoever His good pleasure shall be to call me hence to enjoy with Him life everlasting. And so I bid this wretched world adieu.

He was buried as he had wished in Westminster abbey.

DNB (Wynn, John); Cal. Wynn Pprs. 18, 24, 25, 36, 39, 41, 45, 49, 71, 76–7, 183; HMC Hatfield, vi. 455; Neale, Commons, 297–8; P. H. Williams, Council in the Marches of Wales, 304; PCC 102 Swann.

I.C.

WYNN, John (1554–1627), of Gwydir, Caern.

CAERNARVONSHIRE 1586

b. 1554, 1st s. of Maurice Wynn* of Gwydir by his 1st w. Jane (Siân), and bro. of Ellis*. educ. All Souls, Oxf. 1570, BA 1578; Furnival's Inn 1572; I. Temple 1576. m. Sydney, da. of William Gerard I*, 10s. 2da. suc. fa. 1580. Kntd. 1606. cr. Bt. 1611.[1]

Clerk of the peace, Caern. 1575; j.p. Caern., Merion. from c.1580, Denb. from 1601; sheriff, Caern. 1587–8, 1602–3, Merion. 1588–9, 1600–1, Denb. Feb.–Nov. 1606; dep. lt. Caern. 1587; member, council in the marches of Wales c.1603; collector of royal loan, Caern. 1606, of aid 1614, farmer of escheat lands by 1615, custos rot. 1618, commr. for moneys raised for Ireland 1626.[2]

After Oxford, Wynn lived in London until the age of 26. He married into a family of lawyers, and retained all his life a passion for litigation. On succeeding to his father's extensive estates in the counties of Caernarvon, Merioneth and Denbigh, he at once became involved in the political storms which centred in the two houses of Gwydir and Lleweni. Indeed, in the struggle between the Earl of Leicester and the gentry of Gwynedd he had already declared himself as the Earl's man before he left London, and his wife's family was heavily committed to the same service, although Leicester himself was by no means convinced that Wynn was not, like his father, a party to the 'stalling' tactics of his neighbours. Leicester, however, died before achieving his ambitions in North Wales, and his heir the Earl of Warwick, after declaring his intention of persisting with his brother's schemes and appointing Wynn in 1590 one of his commissioners, died within the year.[3]

Wynn's professed devotion to Leicester had stopped short of accepting an invitation to serve under him in the Low Countries in 1585, but from 1588 onwards reiterated threats of Spanish invasion and then the recurrent need for levying forces for Ireland and for Essex's foreign adventures, made heavy demands on him as deputy lieutenant, and from time to time involved him in friction with his neighbours. In 1601 he was employed in rounding up local suspects after the Essex revolt. It was only in 1592 that it came to light that he had up to then failed to take the requisite oaths as magistrate; but no doubts were ever cast on his loyalty to the established order in church and state. Among the solemn injunctions he wrote in 1614 to his heir (who died before inheriting) an exhortation never to turn Papist takes pride of place.[4]

Litigation kept him equally busy. Sir Thomas Williams of Vaynol, near Bangor, accused him before the court of Exchequer in 1589 of trying to drive him from a neighbouring property by diverting necessary water supplies, and he declined to mend the quarrel by a match between the families. A more serious quarrel three years later with William Williams of Cochwillan, son-in-law and neighbour of the powerful Sir William Gruffydd of Penrhyn, led to a brawl in Conway church, two Star Chamber actions (in which Williams grossly insulted Wynn's ancestors) and the intervention of the council in the marches of Wales, which censured and fined Wynn. He was again charged in the Exchequer court in 1594 with enclosure, interruption of mill and fishery rights and other high-handed actions in Trefriw, and this was followed four years later by another dispute about mill rights in Caernarvon with Rowland Puleston. Tenants as well as neighbours found him overbearing, especially those former bond tenants whose legal insecurity laid them open to exploitation; accusations of this character were brought against him in the Exchequer court from tenants in the Conway valley and on his Denbighshire escheat lands across the estuary.[5]

His bitterest fights, however, came in the next reign, when he was involved in a ten-year dispute over lands and rectories with Thomas Prys of Plas Iolyn, the bard and buccaneer, which ended in a Star Chamber suit and Prys's imprisonment for debt. From 1611–15 Wynn was at odds with his second cousin, Richard Bulkeley I*, the builder of Baron Hill, over fishery rights and lands in Caernarvonshire. There was a still more prolonged struggle with his Conway cousins, the family of Robert Wynn* of Plas Mawr, over the division in his grandfather's day of the ancestral lands at Dolwyddelan, when John was convinced that two of his uncles had conspired to defraud his ailing and pliable father. A compromise was arranged in 1588, but the dispute flared up again to keep the court of Exchequer busy from 1606 to 1619. There were also disputes about his Merioneth lands, complaints in Star Chamber of tyrannical conduct towards a widowed neighbour, and a wrangle with the Salusburys of Lleweni over 'intermixed' lands in Creuddyn.[6]

It seems to have been this dispute that brought to a head the accumulated grievances against Wynn's harsh dealings both in office and as a litigant. In 1615 he was summoned before the council in the marches of Wales (of which he was now a member), on a multitude of charges. He suffered a term of imprisonment, and but for a reluctant submission and the payment of a heavy fine he would have been stripped of all his dignities. It was a heavy blow to the political ascendancy of Gwydir. He had not himself put up for Parliament since 1586, when he left no trace in the records, though he might have attended the subsidy committee 22 Feb. 1587. He had, however, been untiring at every subsequent election, both in Caernarvonshire and in the neighbouring counties, in his efforts to secure the return of kinsmen and allies, until in 1620 a coalition of smaller squires from western Caernarvonshire procured the defeat of his son Richard† – for which he ineffectively threatened reprisals in Star Chamber, but was overruled; and for 20 years Gwydir abandoned local electioneering.[7]

Like his ancestors, Wynn had few inhibitions about church property. When Bishop William Morgan, the translator of the Bible into Welsh – who had risen from humble beginnings as a protégé of Gwydir – was translated to St. Asaph in 1601, Wynn was incensed at his refusal to lease him the rectory of Llanrwst with the same complaisance as earlier bishops had shown towards his ancestors. The prebend and rectory of Llanfair Dyffryn Clwyd, which had been leased to his uncle Dr. John Gwynne II*, was the occasion of much 'bickering' (as Wynn called it) in 1617–18 with Lewis Bayly, bishop of Bangor, who was determined to have it for his son; but this was too soon after Wynn's humiliation in the council in the marches of Wales for him to show much fight and – fearing for his other rectory of Llandudno – he made it up with the bishop, who indeed became his close ally in the electoral fight of 1620.[8]

Wynn's energy also found more constructive outlets. He had many plans for the economic development of North Wales, including Anglesey copper, Welsh cloth, and (in his closing years), the improvement of his Merioneth estates by the draining of Traeth Mawr – a project not realised till the nineteenth century. None of these came to fruition, nor did he make anything of the extensive leases of coal mines in Anglesey, Caernarvon and Flint which he acquired from the Crown in 1614. But on the Gwydir lands themselves he made trials for copper and had some success with the mining and even smelting of lead, and the fact that one of his sons was a factor at Hamburg helped him to find a continental market.[9]

Another of his varied interests was the fostering of Welsh literature and antiquities. He was one of those who in 1594 petitioned Elizabeth for another eisteddfod like the one held in 1567. He was much concerned with the production of a Welsh metrical psalter in 1610 and of a Latin–Welsh dictionary in 1624–5 – though it was hinted that he was more liberal with unwanted advice than with hard cash. His own *History of the Gwydir Family*, which remained unpublished till 1770, remains, with all its inaccuracies, a valuable source for the history of the period. His genuine care for learning comes out in the trouble he took over the education of his sons, and in his foundation of a grammar school (with almshouses) at Llanrwst – although here again doubts have arisen about how much of Sir John's own fortune actually went into the endowment.[10]

Wynn made his will 28 Feb. and died 1 Mar. 1627. He was buried in Llanrwst church. His eldest son having predeceased him, the will was proved, on 5 Dec., by his second son Richard. The estate afterwards passed to a third son who resumed the parliamentary predominance of Gwydir in Caernarvonshire, but with the death of this man's son in 1674 the direct male line came to an end.[11]

[1] Griffith, *Peds.* 281; *Cal. Wynn Pprs.* pp. 7, 12, 14. [2] Flenley, *Cal. Reg. Council, Marches of Wales*, 135; *Cal. Wynn Pprs.* pp. 69, 113, 115–16, 130; *Clenennau Letters and Pprs.* 5; E179/220/152; APC, xli. 113; PRO Index 4211. [3] *Cal. Wynn Pprs.* pp. 7, 12, 14–15, 16, 17, 19, 20, 22; P. H. Williams, *Council in the Marches of Wales*, 238–9. [4] *Cal. Wynn Pprs.* pp. 19, 21–3, 27–37, 102, 115; *Cal. Salusbury Corresp.* ed. Smith (Univ. Wales Bd. of Celtic Studies, Hist. and Law ser. xiv), 47; APC, xxiii. 261; xxxi. 168, 245. [5] *Exchequer*, ed. E. G. Jones (Univ. Wales Bd. of Celtic Studies, Hist. and Law ser. iv), 52, 59, 65–6, 77–8; *Star Chamber*, ed. Edwards (same ser. i), 37–8; *Exchequer Jas. I*, ed. T. I. J. Jones (same ser. xv), 50; *Cal. Wynn Pprs.* pp. 24–5, 27. [6] *Cal. Wynn Pprs.* pp. 9–11, 47, 49, 50, 72, 97, 107, 108, 109–10, 240; *Star Chamber*, 134; *Exchequer Jas. I*, 46–8, 50–1, 54–5, 57–8, 61–2, 71, 72, 74, 162, 235, 239. [7] *CSP Dom.* 1611–18, pp. 336, 353; *Cal. Wynn Pprs.* pp. 112–16, 716–29; *Trans. Cymmrod. Soc.* 1942, p. 42; A. H. Dodd, *Studies in Stuart Wales*, 179–80; D'Ewes, 409. [8] W. Hughes, *Bp. William Morgan* (1891), p. 72; *Cal. Wynn Pprs.* pp. 36, 39–40, 48–9, 50, 128–9, 133–7; *Trans. Cymmrod. Soc.* loc. cit.; A. I. Pryce, *Diocese of Bangor in 16th Cent.* 38. [9] *Cal. Wynn Pprs.* pp. 76, 77–8, 143, 147, 152, 155, 156, 158–9, 161, 164–202 passim, 219. [10] *HMC Welsh*, i. 291–2; *Cal. Wynn Pprs.* pp. 34, 48, 71–2, 73, 74, 86, 87, 95–6, 101–2, 111, 126, 134–5, 144, 170, 182, 193, 195, 197, 200, 215, 218, 244; *Trans. Denb. Hist. Soc.* ii (1953), 51–63, 66–9. [11] PCC 120 Skinner; *Cal. Wynn Pprs.* pp. 242–3, 431; Pennant, *Tours*, ed. Rhys, ii. 303; *DWB*, 1097–8.

A.H.D.

WYNN, Maurice (by 1526–80), of Gwydir, Caern.

CAERNARVONSHIRE 1553 (Oct.), 1554 (Apr.), 1563

b. by 1526, 1st s. of John Wynn ap Merdydd† of Gwydir by Ellen, da. of Maurice ap John of Clenennau; bro. of Robert*. *m.* (1) Jane (Siân), da. of Sir Richard Bulkeley of Beaumaris, Anglesey (*d.*1547), 3s. inc. Ellis* and John* 5da.; (2) Anne, da. of Edward Greville of Milcote, Warws., 1da.; (3) c.1570, Catherine (*d.* Aug. 1591), da. of Tudor ap Robert of Berain, Denb. and Penmynydd, Anglesey, wid. of John Salusbury of Lleweni, Denb. and of Richard Clough of Bachegraig, Tremeirchion, Flints., 3s. 1da. *suc.* fa. 1559.[1]

Commr. goods of churches and fraternities, Caern. 1553, piracy 1565, subsidy 1570, victuals 1574, tanneries 1574; escheator 1553–4; sheriff 1554–5, 1569–70, 1577–8; j.p. Caern., Merion. 1555–*d.*, Denb. 1575; custos rot. Caern. by 1562–*d.*[2]

Maurice Wynn was the first member of his family to adopt this surname consistently. On his father's death he came into extensive estates in the Conway valley and near Caernarvon, and others in Llanfrothen, Merioneth. Wynn enhanced his family's wealth and prestige by his marriages, notably his third, for in addition to her own considerable lands of Berain, Catherine had been left a handsome fortune by her second husband, the wealthy merchant Richard Clough. However, her first marriage had been into the Salusbury family of Lleweni, and the wardship of her son by that marriage, Thomas Salusbury, caused Maurice Wynn considerable trouble. The child was the ward of the Earl of Leicester, then at the height of his quarrel with the families of Gwynedd, and for the last six years of his life Wynn was at his wits' end to keep on terms with his neighbours without losing the favour of Leicester. He was involved in a number of lawsuits, and the disposition of the ancestral estates at Dolwyddelan was a cause of wrangling which persisted into the next generation. In his own will Maurice bequeathed money for the education of poor children from Beddgelert parish at Friars School, Bangor. He died 18 Aug. 1580.

Wynn's normal assessment for subsidy was between £7 and £12 – rather less than that of his younger brother Robert, who had had to make his own way to fortune, and far less than his father's had been. This may help to explain the determination of his son Sir John to restore the preponderance of the senior branch of the family.

The only record of Wynn in Parliament in the Elizabethan period is for 24 Mar. 1563, when he received permission to depart from the Commons 'for his weighty affairs'.[3]

[1] Griffith, *Peds.* 281. [2] *CPR*, 1553, p. 419; 1560–3, pp. 446–7; 1563–6, p. 31; Flenley, *Cal. Reg. Council, Marches of Wales*, 60, 109, 127, 132; [3] Wynn, *Guydir Fam.* passim; *DWB*, 1097–8; *Augmentations*, ed. Lewis and Davies (Univ. Wales Bd. of Celtic Studies, Hist. and Law ser. xiii), 286, 292; *CPR*, 1563–6, p. 340; *Y Cymmrodor*, xl. 1–42; *Cal. Wynn Pprs.* pp. 6, 7, 8, 11, 12, 13, 15–17, 297; P. H. Williams, *Council in the Marches of Wales*, 238; A. I. Pryce, *Diocese of Bangor in the 16th Cent.* 15; NLW, Wynnstay mss; *Exchequer Jas. I*, ed. T. I. J. Jones (Univ. Wales Bd. of Celtic Studies, Hist. and Law ser. xv), 51, 71, 74; Barker and Lewis, *Hist. Friars Sch.* 172–3; E179/220/133, 135, 141, 144; *CJ*, i. 70.

A.H.D.

WYNN, Robert (1520–98), of Plas Mawr, Conway, Caern.

CAERNARVON BOROUGHS 1589

b. 1520, 3rd s. of John Wynn ap Meredydd of Gwydir by Ellen, da. of Maurice ap John of Clenennau; bro. of Robert.* *m.* (1) by 1576, Dorothy, da. of Sir William Griffith of Penrhyn, wid. of William Williams of Cochwillan, Llandegal, *s.p.*; (2) c.1586, Dorothy, da. of Edward (or Thomas) Dymock of Willington, Flints., 2s. 5da.[1]

J.p. Merion. from c.1573, Caern. from 1575; sheriff, Caern. 1590–1.

As a younger son, Wynn had to make his own way. He served under Sir Philip Hoby at Boulogne in 1544, receiving a gunshot wound 'whereof', said his nephew John Wynn*, 'he was long lame'. He fought again in the expedition against Scotland, 1547, and attended Hoby on several of his European missions.[2]

In 1554 Wynn secured crown leases both in the Conway valley and farther west in Caernarvonshire, including

some of the former lands of the abbey of Maenan. His father arranged that he should share with his brothers part of the ancestral lands in Dolwyddelan and elsewhere, but his nephew John was convinced that Robert in collusion with his brother Dr. John Gwynne had over-reached their elder brother Maurice – Sir John's father – and the legal battle was prolonged into the next generation. Under John Gwynne's will he also claimed a quarter share of the rectory of Eglwys Rhos, near Conway.[3]

His patron, Sir Philip Hoby, had died in 1558, and it was probably about this time that Wynn returned to Wales. He seems to have owed his place on the county bench, alongside his elder brother Maurice, to the influential circles in London in which his brother John moved. From 1566 he was assessed for subsidy at a slightly higher figure than his brother Maurice, and at the musters of 1570 he was charged with 'one light horseman furnished' – the normal complement for the Caernarvonshire gentry except the house of Penrhyn. By 1576 he had married into this pre-eminent house, and between then and 1580 he built at Conway the stately mansion – still surviving – of Plas Mawr. His return to Parliament for Caernarvon was probably due to his marriage into the Griffith family, who dominated borough elections throughout most of the reign.[4]

Wynn's will, dated 12 Oct. 1595, was proved 31 Jan. 1599, the heir being Thomas, son of his second marriage. He was buried at Conway on 30 Nov. 1598.[5]

[1] Griffith, *Peds.* 280, 360. [2] *Cal. Wynn Pprs.* 4, 158; *LP Hen. VIII*, xxi(2), pp. 171, 199; *CPR*, 1553, p. 377; Wynn, *Guydir Fam.* ed. Ballinger, 69–71. [3] *CPR*, 1563–6, pp. 10, 523–4; *Cal. Wynn Pprs.* 6, 9, 235; *Exchequer Jas. I*, ed. T. I. J. Jones (Univ. Wales Bd. of Celtic Studies, Hist. and Law ser. xv), 51, 71, 74; *Exchequer*, ed. E. G. Jones (same ser. iv), 79. [4] *DNB*; *Cal. Wynn Pprs.* 7; E179/220/111, 141, 144; Flenley, *Cal. Reg. Council, Marches of Wales*, 75; *RCHM Caern.* i. 58–64; Griffith, loc. cit.; A. and H. Baker, *Plas Mawr, Conway*, passim. [5] PCC 5, 6 Kidd; *RCHM Caern.* i. 44; R. Williams, *Aberconway*, 105.

A.H.D.

WYNTER, Edward (c.1560–1619), of Lydney, Glos.

NEWPORT IUXTA LAUNCESTON 1586
GLOUCESTERSHIRE 1589, 1601

b. c.1560, 1st s. of William Wynter* by Mary, da. of coh. of Thomas Langton of Glos. *educ.* Brasenose, Oxf. 20 Dec. 1577, aged 17, BA Jan. 1579; M. Temple 1579. *m.* 11 Aug. 1595, Lady Anne Somerset, da. of Edward, 4th Earl of Worcester, 7s. 3da. *suc.* fa. 1589. Kntd. 1595.[1]

Steward and receiver of duchy of Lancaster lands, Glos., Herefs. 1589; j.p. Glos. from c.1592, q. by 1596, sheriff 1598–9, dep. lt. Aug. 1601; dep. constable, forest of Dean; constable, St. Briavel's castle by 1608; v.-adm. Som.; member, council in marches of Wales 1601.[2]

Wynter probably served an apprenticeship on one of his father's ships, perhaps in the expedition to the west coast of Ireland in 1580, but it is not until 1585 that his documented career begins. In September of that year, in command of the *Aid*, he took part in Drake's voyage to the West Indies. The expedition put in at Vigo in Spain on the outward voyage, and Wynter's letter from there to Walsingham was the last that anyone in England heard of the ships until their return in July 1586. Wynter was prominent in the capture of Cartagena, apparently being so anxious to take part personally in the fight that he temporarily exchanged command of his ship for that of a company of soldiers. The expedition later plundered the coast of Florida and returned home with booty worth £60,000.[3]

When it became apparent that there was no immediate prospect of further excitement at home, Wynter determined to seek it on the Continent. In August 1587 he wrote from Bergen-op-Zoom asking Walsingham to secure him the necessary permission:

> Because I despair of any new putting again into the field this year, I am resolved to repair with all speed to the King of Navarre, who, as I hear, useth such gentlemen as come unto him honourably ... I am resolved to live in the wars for a time, or else to travel for a year or two.

He ends by recording that he left his father 'most naturally affected towards me'. Judging by a brief reference in a subsequent letter, Wynter obtained the necessary permission and found the service he had been seeking in the Low Countries. It was quite natural, however, that he should return home the following spring when the threat of a Spanish offensive against England became more real. His role in the naval engagement against the Armada is unrecorded; probably he served on his father's ship. On 17 Aug., some time after the Spanish fleet had been scattered, he dined at Dover with Lord Henry Seymour and Maurice of Nassau, and a week later sent Walsingham the latest information to reach that port. Sailors from Dunkirk had told him that Parma, commander of the Spanish invasion forces in the Netherlands, had fled towards Brussels and had ordered his ships to be unloaded. It was rumoured that the Spanish fleet was somewhere off Orkney. Wynter ended his letter, typically, by telling Walsingham that he was 'resolved to follow the wars' and asked to be remembered 'if there happen any occasion that forces, either of foot or horse, should be employed'.[4]

Between these periods of active service, Wynter passed his time in London and Gloucestershire. His first appearance in Parliament, for the Cornish borough of Newport, was no doubt due to his father's friendship with the Grenvilles, the leading local family. In December 1588, just before he succeeded his father, he was elected to one of the Gloucestershire county seats. Next, he set off 'to pass into France to see the manner of service there', but fell into the hands of the wife of the governor of Eu and Tréport who, 'coming aboard in ye haven, took me away', an obscure episode which cost Wynter four years of

captivity, for her husband sold him to Mendoza, the Spanish ambassador in France.[5] Wynter wrote to Walsingham from Amiens in October 1589, reporting that he had been well treated, but he pressed for the Queen to arrange his release. His idea was that he should be exchanged for Don Pedro de Valdes, a Spanish nobleman who had been captured during the Armada campaign. By the following February he had been transferred to Antwerp castle, and was not so optimistic about his imminent freedom. It had been reported to him that Parma would only exchange him for all Spanish prisoners in England and Holland, an impossible suggestion, as Wynter fully realised. He was also worrying about his relatives and estates at home. Someone had brought a lawsuit against him, and one of his young brothers still needed supervision. Wynter clearly regarded Walsingham as his principal friend in high places, and implored him to look into these matters, but the secretary could only have received these pleas just before his death. The negotiations for Wynter's release dragged on for months, even years, and resignation turned to despair. Eventually the Privy Council agreed in principle to the exchange of Valdes for Wynter. By the summer of 1591 the two men had, by frequent correspondence, become quite well known to each other. Valdes apologised to Mondragon, governor of Antwerp castle, when Wynter tried to escape, promising him he would not do it again, and urged him not to punish his charge as he, Valdes, would suffer also. The negotiations at length failed again because the Queen, in spite of a desperate plea from Wynter to Burghley in 1591, decided that Valdes, who had been one of the principal Armada commanders, was too important to be exchanged for a relatively unknown captain. The Council, in a tactfully worded letter, told Wynter the bad news. At this stage some of his friends, particularly Richard Drake*, intervened and persuaded him to pay for his own ransom. At last, in the spring of 1593, his release was obtained. Wynter's return home did not prove to be a happy one. He discovered that Drake, in order to secure his freedom, had undertaken that Wynter should pay for Valdes's ransom also. His disgust was natural, because Valdes had been living at Drake's house and some of the ransom money would go to Wynter's supposed friend. He refused to meet this payment, much to the annoyance of Cecil and the Queen, who was angry that Drake, one of her equerries, had been spoken of scornfully. One can sympathize with the strongly worded letter which Wynter wrote to Cecil in reply to the charges:

> Judge, I beseech you, whether after almost four years of barbarous imprisonment, after the racking me with infinite devices to pay £4,500 for my ransom and other charges, after the spending the sweetest time of my youth in all melancholy (in all which Mr. Drake hath been the principal meddler), if after all this, out of my justeth griefs I have perchance breathed some words

only of choler, which otherwise might have burst out more violently.[6]

Though still in his early thirties Wynter had now lost his thirst for action. He retired to his home, the White Cross, at Lydney, and busied himself with the management of his estates and other enterprises, such as the establishment of iron furnaces in the Forest of Dean. Though he remained on the commission of the peace, he would undertake no extra local duties, and asked to be excused serving as sheriff in 1595. It may have been his marriage to a daughter of the Earl of Worcester that brought him back to London and the court. He served again as knight of the shire for Gloucestershire in 1601, and as such he could have served on committees dealing with the order of business, 3 Nov., and monopolies, 23 Nov. Wynter was knighted by the Queen at Greenwich, and served as a canopy bearer at her funeral.[7]

He died 3 Mar. 1619. The heir was his son John, who vigorously defended his house against parliamentary soldiers. Nothing is known of Wynter's religious views, but in the next generation the family was Catholic.[8]

[1] *Vis. Worcs.* (Harl. Soc. xxvii), 148–9; *Vis. Glos.* (Harl. Soc. xxi), 273, 278; *DNB* (Winter, Sir William). [2] Somerville, *Duchy*, i. 637, 639; *APC*, xxvii. 37; xxviii. 73; xxxii. 161; *CSP Dom.* 1603–10, p. 395; *HMC Hatfield*, xi. 567. [3] J. S. Corbett, *Navy during the Span. War 1585–7* (Navy Rec. Soc. xi), pp. viii–xvii, 49–51; Corbett, *Drake and Tudor Navy*, ii. 49–50. [4] *CSP For.* 1587, pp. 250–1; J. K. Laughton, *Defeat of Span. Armada* (Navy Rec. Soc. ii), 123, 149–51. [5] SP78/20/112. Some confusion has been caused by the fact that one of the relevant documents, a letter from the Council to Wynter while he was a prisoner (Lansd. 103, f. 105, printed in Strype's *Annals*, iii(2), pp. 38–40), has been wrongly dated 1588 on the manuscript. Another version (SP94/4/125) shows the correct date to be 8 July 1592. It seems likely that Wynter visited France at the end of 1588, but returned in time for the Parliament in Feb. (He was at Dover at the beginning of Feb.) He was still in London when his father's will was proved on 15 Mar. [6] SP77/5/36, 42, 47, 82; SP78/20/112; *CSP Dom.* 1591–4, p. 72; *APC*, xxiii. 300; *HMC Hatfield*, iv. 302–3, 313–14; xiii. 481; Lansd. 76, f. 9. [7] *Bristol and Glos. Arch. Soc. Trans.* xviii. 98; l. 71; *CSP Dom.* 1603–10, p. 160; *HMC Hatfield*, v. 480; xvi. 267; xvii. 315; xviii. 207; *Vis. Worcs.* 149 n; LC2/4/4; *APC*, xxxii. 190; D'Ewes, 624, 649. [8] C142/378/147.

M.R.P.

WYNTER, William (c.1528–89), of Deptford, Kent, and Lydney, Glos.

PORTSMOUTH	1559, 1563
CLITHEROE	1572
GLOUCESTERSHIRE	1586

b. c.1528, 2nd s. of John Wynter (*d.* by 1546) of Bristol and Deptford by Alice, da. and h. of William Tirrey of Cork. *m.* Mary, da. and coh. of Thomas Langton of Glos., 4s. inc. Edward* 4da. Kntd. 12 Aug. 1573.

Served on expeditions against Scotland 1544, 1547, in Channel fleet 1545, keeper of the Deptford storehouse by 1546; surveyor of ships from June 1549; master of naval ordnance from July 1557; adm. in all seagoing expeditions 1557–88; j.p. Glos. from c.1564, commr. sewers, Kent, Surr. and Suss. 1564; on mission to Prince of Orange 1576; steward and receiver, duchy of Lancaster lands in Glos. and Herefs. from 1580.[1]

The Wynters provide an excellent illustration of the strength of family tradition in the English maritime history of the sixteenth century. Originally from Wales, they had been Bristol merchants for several generations when John Wynter moved to London and became the navy's first treasurer after the reorganization of 1545. At least five others of the family in the next two generations were naval administrators or saw service at sea in one capacity or another, but William Wynter was the most prominent, holding senior offices on the navy board for over 40 years and thereby contributing to the success of the fleet which, in the last year of his life, outmanoeuvred and outfought the Spanish Armada. His active career at sea, too, was extraordinary; there was not a naval expedition – as opposed to voyages of exploration or plundering raids – between 1544 and 1588 in which he did not play a prominent part. A man 'to be cherished' as Cecil put it in 1559, Wynter was the key figure in naval administration until the appearance of Hawkins in the 1570s, and the only man knighted personally by the Queen for services to the navy.

Unfortunately a date of birth for Wynter has not been ascertained. He was still being referred to as a 'young gentleman' in 1559, which, in this period, he would hardly have been if he was much over 30, so at a guess he was born about 1528, and made storekeeper at Deptford in his late teens, just possible with his connexions and having served as a boy at sea. His father left him not only a share in a ship called the *George* and the reversion of property at Lydney and Bristol, but, far more important, the official contacts which, with his own ability, enabled him to advance rapidly in his profession and to weather the storms of Queen Mary's reign, particularly his implication in Wyatt's rebellion of January 1554. The role which Wynter played in this, his only venture into politics, is uncertain. Probably he supplied Wyatt with guns and ammunition from his squadron in the Medway and, according to his own 'confession', which was used in the trial of Sir Nicholas Throckmorton*, he acted as a go-between for Throckmorton and Wyatt. He was sentenced to death, put in the Tower, but pardoned in November 1554, probably having been released some time earlier. An odd episode. He retained his surveyorship and even escorted Philip II on his final return to Spain.[2]

The story of Wynter's administration of the navy has still to be written. Until it is, there will remain the temptation to equate Hawkins with efficiency in the dockyards and Wynter with conservative opposition to reform, to write Wynter off (as a modern biographer of Hawkins has it) as a 'masterful man, greedy for wealth and power, careful of his reputation, intolerant of any rival'. Of course the two men were at odds. A contemporary document 'Abuses in the Admiralty touching her Majesty's navy, exhibited by Mr. Hawkins' accuses Wynter of inefficiency, peculation and, of all things, sabotaging England's defences in return for Spanish gold. Wynter for his part called Hawkins a 'dissembling knave'. But the two resolved their differences, and at the end of the day it will no doubt be shown that the navy was not neglected or ill-administered under Wynter, but that most of the credit for the innovations in design of the late 1570s and the 1580s leading to the handier ships that beat the Armada should go to Hawkins. Both men were interested in improving armament.[3]

Wynter sat in the Commons four times. He was elected to the first Parliament of the reign, suitably enough at Portsmouth. In 1563 the chancellor of the duchy of Lancaster tried to bring him in at Liverpool, which resisted the intervention, and Wynter was again returned at Portsmouth. In 1572 he was chosen at another duchy of Lancaster borough, Clitheroe. Finally he was elected knight of the shire for his own county, where, interestingly, he had a duchy of Lancaster appointment. His first known activity in the Commons was to move (6 Feb. 1563) 'that this House would have regard, by some bill, to the navy'. This was agreed to, and Wynter was put in charge. As it finally emerged the object of the bill was to provide a pool of ships and seamen by encouraging fishing, and this was to be effected by increasing the demand for fish by creating a Wednesday fish-day, but by this time the measure had been adopted by Sir William Cecil. Wynter's next intervention in debate was on 3 June 1572 when he spoke on the second reading of a bill on arms, urging that light bullets were preferable to heavy as more could be carried, they would pierce better, and 'fly as far'. He spoke again on the third reading next day, to the same effect. He was appointed to committees on the subsidy (10 Feb. 1576), ports (13 Feb.), arms again (17 Feb.), brokers (28 Feb.), unlawful weapons (2 Mar.), foreign artificers (5 Mar.), salt marshes (6 Mar.) and the Queen's marriage (12 Mar.). But his most dramatic contribution to the business of the House in 1576 was caused by Arthur Hall's claim for privilege for his servant Smalley. Wynter was outraged by Hall's uninhibited behaviour before the committee, and in return Hall accused Wynter of prejudice. Their antipathy continued. On at least two later occasions Wynter attacked Hall in the House, maintaining that on one occasion, when Hall had pleaded illness, he had been gambling at a tavern. In the 1581 session of the 1572 Parliament, after many weary months patrolling off the west of Ireland to prevent a Spanish landing, Wynter's committees concerned the subsidy (25 Jan.), wrecks (30 Jan.), Aldgate (9 Feb.), the Family of Love (27 Feb.), merchant adventurers (2 Mar.) and Dover harbour (4 Mar.). All that is known of him in his last Parliament is his

membership of the committee inquiring into the Norfolk returns (9 Nov. 1586).[4]

Wynter, in his sixties, saw active service against the Armada. In February 1588 he reported on the morale and efficiency of the navy:

I assure you it will do a man's heart good to behold them; and would to God the Prince of Parma were upon the seas with all his forces, and we in the view of them. Then I doubt not but that you should hear that we would make his enterprise very unpleasant to him.

By May he was patrolling the eastern approaches in his flagship, the *Vanguard*, intent on intercepting an invasion from the Netherlands. He realised, however, as no other English commander is known to have done, that Parma's invasion force of 30,000 would need about 300 ships, a quite unmanageable number against the combined English and Dutch fleets. In the same letter to Walsingham in which he put forward this view, he suggested the inconvenience of stationing the lord admiral at Plymouth, where the wind that brought the Spanish fleet up the channel would prevent the admiral leaving harbour. Again, Wynter judged correctly that his own fleet should be near Dover and not off Dunkirk. A report to Walsingham on 1 Aug. gave an account of the battle of Gravelines. In a meeting on Lord Howard's flagship, he suggested the use of the fire-ships and in the close fighting which followed – 'most times within speech one of another' – he was injured in the hip 'by the reversing of one of our demi-cannons'. After the victory, when Howard and other commanders were summoned to London he was left in charge of the fleet. Once again he judged the situation correctly when he thought that the Spanish would circle the British Isles in an attempt to reach home. 'I think the Duke [of Medina Sidonia] would give his dukedom to be in Spain again', he commented. All in all, Wynter's part in the destruction of the Armada was a distinguished one.[5]

He also managed to find time in that momentous year to begin building the White Cross at Lydney in Gloucestershire. He had bought the manor of Lydney in 1561, investing the profits of his career in lands in that area of Gloucestershire beyond the Severn, but he can have had little time to enjoy it. Even after the victory which would have been a suitable climax to his career, he did not retire. At his death, on 20 Feb. 1589, he was still active and his house still building. In his will, made on 1 Feb. and proved on 15 Mar. 1589, he asked to be buried in the chapel he had built in Lydney church. The executor, his heir Edward, had already been provided for. The next son, William, received half the goods in his London house, a fine collection of weapons, and plate. Large sums of money bequeathed to his daughters, together with items of jewellery, are a further reminder of the proceeds of his long career.[6]

[1] *DNB*; *Vis. Worcs.* (Harl. Soc. xxvii), 148–9; *LP Hen. VIII*, xxi(1), p. 660; *CPR*, 1548–9, p. 178; 1563–6, p. 22; *APC*, vi. 136; Somerville, *Duchy*, i. 637, 639. [2] J. K. Laughton, *Defeat of Span. Armada*, i. 213; ii. 266–8; *LP Hen. VIII*, xix(2), p. 379; xx(1), pp. 269, 390; xx(2), p. 145; PCC 3 Alen; *CSP For.* 1547–53, p. 254; *CSP Dom.* 1547–80, pp. 102, 106; Add. 1547–65, p. 455; *APC*, v. 335; vi. 405; *Mariner's Mirror*, xiv. 43; lvi. 5, 15 et passim; *CPR*, 1554–5, p. 202; 1558–60, p. 226; Strype, *Mems.* iii(1), pp. 144, 187; *CSP Span.* 1587–1603, p. 72; *Machyn Diary* (Cam. Soc. xlii), pp. 60–1; Holinshed, *Chron.* (1808), iv. 34–5; J. Corbett, *Drake and Tudor Navy*, i. 69, 136–7, 142–3; *Navy During Span. War.* 207–10, 240, 242–57. [3] Glos. RO, navy ordnance bks.; M. Oppenheim, *Hist. Admin. RN*; J. A. Williamson, *Hawkins* (1927 and 1949 eds.), passim. [4] Neale, *Parlts.* i. 164; *CJ*, i. 65, 104, 105, 106, 108, 109, 110, 111, 114, 119, 120, 124, 130, 131; D'Ewes, 84, 247, 251, 253, 260, 288, 289, 294, 302, 396; Trinity, Dublin, Thos. Cromwell's jnl. ff. 48, 50; *An Account of a Quarrel between Arthur Hall Esq. and Melchisedech Mallorie, Gent.* (In *Misc. Antiqua Anglicana*, i. 1816 ed.), 26, 32–5, 37–8; H. G. Wright, *Arthur Hall of Grantham*, passim. [5] Laughton, i. 80–2, 180–1, 206–7, 212–17, 286, 332–4; ii. 1–3, 7–14, 44–6, 184–5, 309–13; *APC*, xvi. 104–5, 168; Corbett, ii. 145; G. Mattingly, *Defeat of Span. Armada*, 270–1; *CSP Dom.* 1581–90, p. 532. [6] *CPR*, 1558–60, pp. 359–60; 1560–3, p. 205; Atkyns, *Glos.* 282; Rudder, *Glos.* 493, 563; *LP Hen. VIII*, xx(2), pp. 322, 456; xxi(1), p. 77; PCC 32 Leicester; C142/227/204.

M.R.P./P.W.H.

WYTHE, Robert (?1523–86), of Droitwich, Worcs. and the Inner Temple, London.

DROITWICH   1554 (Nov.), 1555, 1558, 1559, 1563

b. ?1523, 2nd s. of John Wythe of Droitwich by Isabel, da. and h. of John More. *educ.* I. Temple 1551. *unm.*

Autumn reader, I. Temple 1565, Lent 1572, treasurer 1576–7; j.p.q. Worcs. from 1574.

Wythe, a lawyer, represented Droitwich from its enfranchisement in 1554 to the end of the 1563 Parliament, although he was absent for most of the session in 1563, being licensed on 20 Feb. to depart 'for his necessary affairs'. By 1577 he had estates as far afield as Wales and Middlesex. He left his property to his brother and executor, with instructions to make their sister an allowance and employ the rest of the income for the advancement of her children and himself. Wythe died 24 Dec. 1586, aged 63, and was buried at Droitwich.

VCH Worcs. iii. 86; *Vis. Worcs.* (Harl. Soc. xxvii), 150; *Cal. I.T. Recs.* i. 159; *Masters of the Bench of the I. Temple*, 12; *CJ*, i. 66; Nash, *Worcs.* i. 328–9; Add. 19816, f. 16; PCC 3 Spencer; Worcs. RO bulk accession 1006, bdle. 32, no. 433.

S.M.T.

WYVELL, Marmaduke (c.1542–1617), of Constable Burton, nr. Richmond, Yorks.

RICHMOND   1584[1], 1597

b. c.1542, 1st s. of Christopher Wyvell of Constable Burton by Margaret, da. of John Scrope of Hambleden, Bucks. *educ.* Pembroke, Camb. 1566; L. Inn 1560. *m.* Magdalen, da. of Sir Christopher Danby of Thorpe Place and Farnley, Yorks. 6s. 4da. *suc.* fa. 1578; *cr.* Bt. 1611.
J.p. Yorks. (N. Riding) from c.1582.

Wyvell's grandfather, Marmaduke†, married a coheiress of Sir Ralph FitzRandall, who had himself married a coheiress of the last Lord Scrope of Masham. Constable Burton, a little over five miles from Richmond, had been part of the old Masham estate. When Wyvell succeeded his father he did not enter immediately into the whole estate, much of the property, including Constable Burton, having been assigned to his mother, Margaret, for life. She was a niece of Henry Lord Scrope of Bolton, and it was no doubt with Scrope's approval that Wyvell was returned for Richmond. He was probably absent from the 1584 session. The journal for 4 Dec. states that he 'is lately fallen very sick and not able to give his attendance on this House till he shall have recovered better health'. Nothing further of interest has been ascertained about him, most of the contemporary references being to his dealings in property. He was living in London in 1595, but spent his last years in Yorkshire, where he died in January 1617. His eldest son, Christopher, having died five years previously, the second son, Marmaduke, inherited the estate. In his will, drawn up in August 1614 and proved in March 1617, Wyvell had made arrangements for £200 to be spent on his funeral. He was buried in the north aisle of Masham church, where he had erected a 'cumbrous and costly' monument.[2]

[1] Add. 38823, ff. 17–21. [2] *GEC Baronetage*, 103; Whitaker, *Richmondshire*, i. 322; C142/180/54. [3] Whitaker, ii. 102–3; *VCH Yorks. N. Riding*, i. 234; C142/180/54; *Richmond Wills and Inventories* (Surtees Soc. xxvi), 270–4; Lansd. 78, f. 166; *Yorks. Fines* (Yorks. Arch. Soc. viii), 185; (liii), 24 passim; York wills 34/398.

B.D.

YARDE, Edward (1531–82), of Churston Ferrers, Devon.

DARTMOUTH   1559

b. 1531, 2nd but 1st surv. s. of Thomas Yarde of Bradley by his 1st w. Elizabeth, da. of John Lewson. *m.* (1) bef. 1557, Agnes, da. of William Strode* of Newnham, 5s. 3da.; (2) Anne, da. of Gregory Huckmore† of Buckyett and Buckland Barton, 1s. 2da. *suc.* fa. 1578.

Agent of the 2nd Earl of Bedford in the west country by 1573; j.p. Devon from 1575.

Yarde was out of the country during at least part of Mary's reign, his father, on making his will in October 1557, wondering 'if he be now alive', and he was friendly with a number of west-country puritans. Though the family owned a little property in Dartmouth and elsewhere, Yarde was added to the commission of the peace only after he had become the Earl of Bedford's west-country agent, and it was no doubt through Bedford that he was returned for the borough. He was responsible for a more intensive exploitation of the Russell estates. Customary tenure was replaced by leasehold, and in the period from about 1565 to 1585, £2,592 13s. 3d. was raised by way of fines. Yarde died towards the end of 1582, being buried at Brixham 4 Jan. 1583. Letters of administration were granted to his second wife, Anne, on 13 June 1583.

C142/122/32; Vivian, *Vis. Devon*, 829–30; PCC 45 Wrastley; Egerton 2345, f. 10; SP 12/104; Royal 18 D 111; Lansd. 737, f. 134v; J. A. Youings, 'Disposal of Devon Monastic Property 1536–58' (London Univ. PhD thesis 1950), p. 254; Roberts thesis, 56; PCC admon. act bk. 1583, f. 71.

A.M.M.

YARDLEY, Robert

EAST LOOE   1601

The name of the junior Member of Parliament for East Looe in 1601 was added to a 'blank' return. There is no reason to suppose that the Member was a Cornishman; the name was probably inserted in London. The East Looe MPs came from all over the country. The only Robert Yardley about whom anything has been discovered was of Chatham in Kent, but there is nothing to connect him either with the borough or with a possible patron. A surviving pedigree shows that he came from Warwickshire. Richard Yardley of Warwick may have been his father, for he left £20 to a second son of this name. Robert's wife, Susan, whom he married in January 1595, was a daughter of Christopher Eaglesfield of Stratford-le-Bow, London. Her father left her £80 and she may also have brought Yardley some property from her first husband, Reginald Barker, who was owner of the manor of Chatham. By the time of his death, Yardley owned lands in Chatham, Gillingham, St. Margaret's and Queenborough. In a deed dated 1615 Susan Yardley is called niece of Dame Ann Sondes, wife of Michael Sondes*. Such a connexion may have proved useful. Yardley's will, dated 8 Jan. 1620, was proved in the consistory court at Rochester on 28 Dec. 1622. He was buried at Chatham. His widow took as her third husband Phineas Pett, the shipbuilder, and Phineas's son John married Yardley's daughter Katherine.

Harl. 4108, f. 70; *Misc. Gen. et Her.* (ser. 2), iv. 232; *Vis. Kent* (Harl. Soc. liv), 186; PCC 37 Wrastley, 53 Harrington; *DNB* (Pett, Phineas).

M.R.P.

YARHAM, Robert (c.1520–95), of Norwich, Norf.

NORWICH   1593

b. c.1520, s. of John Yarham of Cossey. *m.* Amy, da. of Martin Sedley, *s.p.*
    Freeman, Norwich 1565, mayor 1591–2, alderman from 1592.

Yarham was a grocer, apprenticed to John Sotherton, four of whose family sat in Elizabethan Parliaments, two for Norwich. George and Nowell Sotherton were in the

1593 Parliament. No record has been found of any participation by Yarham in the business of the House. In his will of 9 May 1595, proved by his widow, the executrix and residuary legatee, 6 Sept., he left bequests to several members of the Sotherton family, to the poor of Norwich, and to his servants.

Blomefield, *Norf.* iv. 231; Millican, *Norwich Freemen*, 248; Le Strange, *Norf. Official Lists*, 109, 110; PCC 58 Scott.

P.W.H.

YAXLEY, John (d. c.1625), of St. Michael's, Cambridge, later of Waterbeach, Cambs.

CAMBRIDGE   1597, 1601, 1604

educ. prob. G. Inn 1573.
    Alderman, Cambridge by 1597, mayor 1599–1600; steward, manor of Waterbeach-cum-Denny by 1610.

Yaxley was an attorney who acquired an estate at Waterbeach, where he leased the parsonage and tithes in 1595, the manor farm by 1599, and where he resided by 1609. In 1614 he and Edward Aungier of Cambridge purchased the manors of Waterbeach and Causeway from the Crown for £900. The only reference found to Yaxley by name in the journals of the House of Commons is to his being given leave to depart on 11 Dec. 1601. As one of the Cambridge Members, however, he was appointed to committees for draining the fens (3 Dec. 1597, 28 Nov. 1601), maltsters (12 Jan. 1598) and unsized bread (13 Jan. 1598). The Cambridge treasurers' accounts contain a number of references to his parliamentary wages, generally at the rate of 4s. a day, and to extra payments, for example, £5 for his 'charges at Parliament' in 1601, followed later in the year by a payment of £50 5s. 10d. for unspecified expenses, which may have included further parliamentary wages. In 1603–4 he lent Cambridge £20 towards the expenses of having its charter confirmed. His mayoralty was marked by an ordinance whereby common councilmen were to be chosen by the mayor and aldermen, to prevent 'abuses heretofore many times offered ... as well in elections as at other times'. In 1601 he was censured for failing to enforce an order whereby the colleges and the richer Cambridge parishes were to contribute towards poor relief in three other parishes which were overburdened. He died between 20 Sept. 1624, when he made his will, and 22 Nov. 1626, when it was disputed in the prerogative court of Canterbury. There is no mention of wife or children. The executor and principal beneficiary was a 'son-in-law' (possibly a stepson), Robert Spicer of Cambridge. The burial was to be 'without any funeral obsequies', and £900 went to build six almshouses in Waterbeach. An annuity of £12 was to be divided among the six inmates.

F. Blomefield, *Coll. Cant.* 6, 225; PRO Index 4208, p. 103; J. M. Gray, *Biog. Notes on Mayors of Cambridge*, 32; W. K. Clay, *Parish of Waterbeach*

(Camb. Antiq. Soc. Pubs. oct. ser. iv.) 31, 73, 98; CSP Dom. 1603–10, pp. 631–2; D'Ewes, 567, 578, 579, 657, 680; Downing Coll. Camb. Bowtell mss; C. H. Cooper, Cambridge Annals, ii. 594 n, 597; Reg. St. Michael's, Cambridge, ed. Venn, 3, 110; PCC 128 Hele.

R.C.G.

YAXLEY, William

ORFORD   1563

There were two namesakes, uncle and nephew, either of whom might have sat for Orford in 1563. The first named below is the more likely on grounds of age. The family was Catholic, the best known being Francis Yaxley the conspirator, and the nephew became an outright recusant, which, however, would not have prevented him being returned in 1563. So far as is known the MP took no part in the proceedings of the Parliament.

The MP was EITHER

2nd s. of Anthony Yaxley, of Yaxley, Suff. by Elizabeth, da. of John Garneys of Kenton, Suff.

In 1586 he sold the manor of Blowfield, Suffolk, to an Edward Grimston, perhaps the Ipswich and Orford MP of that name whose mother, Anne Garneys, was Yaxley's aunt. It may even have been the Grimstons who had Yaxley (or his nephew) returned in 1563. Yaxley was never a j.p., and it is not known whether he married or when he died.

OR

b. 1546, 1st s. of Richard Yaxley of Mellis, Suff. by Mary, da. of Robert Stokes. educ. G. Inn 1566. m. Eve, da. of Sir Henry Bedingfield.

Yaxley was a ward of Sir Nicholas Bacon† until he came of age in 1567. His will was proved in 1590.

DNB; Vis. Suff. (Harl. Soc. lxi), 35; Vis. Suff. ed. Metcalfe, 83; Cath. Rec. Soc. xxii. 103, 121; W. A. Copinger, Suff. Manors, iii. 105; Rylands Eng. ms 311; Redgrave Hall muniments, Bacon mss (ex inf. E. R. Sandeen); PCC 41 Drury.

N.M.F.

YELVERTON, Christopher (c.1537–1612), of Easton Maudit, Northants. and Cripplegate, London.

BRACKLEY	1563
NORTHAMPTON	1571, 1572
NORTHAMPTONSHIRE	1593
NORTHAMPTON	1597[1]

b. c.1537, 3rd s. of William Yelverton† of Rougham, Norf. by his 1st w. Anne, da. of Sir Henry Farmèr of East Barsham, Norf. educ. Queens', Camb. 1550; G. Inn 1552, called. m. Margaret (d.1611), da. of Thomas Catesby of Whiston, Northants., 4s. inc. Henry* 8da. Kntd. 1603.

Recorder, Northampton 1568–99; j.p. Northants. from c.1573; Lent reader, G. Inn 1574, 1584, treasurer 1579, 1585; serjeant-at-law 1589, Queen's serjeant 1598; 2nd justice at Lancaster 1598; justice of assize, Yorks. and j.p. many northern counties 1599; justice of Queen's bench 1602; commr. eccles. causes 1603.[2]

Speaker of House of Commons 1597.

Yelverton started with few advantages, as he was to recall in his disabling speech when chosen Speaker:

> ... my father dying left me a younger brother, and nothing to me but my bare annuity. Then, growing to man's estate and some small practice of the law, I took a wife by whom I had many children, the keeping of us all being a great impoverishing to my estate, and the daily living of us all nothing but my daily industry.

Which perhaps does less than justice to the part played by his wife's family, for it was not until his marriage that Yelverton began to make real progress in the profession his own family had followed for generations. Further, it was to his father-in-law (sheriff of his adopted county at the time of the election) that he owed his first appearance in the House of Commons. By the 1566 session of this Parliament Yelverton was being lampooned as one of the puritan 'choir' in the 'lewd pasquil', where he appears as Yelverton the poet, a reference, no doubt, to the epilogue he wrote that year to the blank verse tragedy Jocasta, by his Gray's Inn friend George Gascoigne*, and not the only one of the Society's masques and entertainments in which the future judge was prominent at this period of his life. His taste for conviviality was noted later by Sir Roger Wilbraham:

> Serjeant Yelverton said [at dinner], a poor bachelor wishing to be married had no money to pay the priest, only 8d. The priest ... refused to marry him without full pay. He desired he might be married as far as his money would go and promised to pay the rest, and so was. The priest after[wards] asking the debt, 'Nay', said he, 'I will give ten times as much to unmarry us'.[3]

As recorder of Northampton, Yelverton found a ready parliamentary seat in 1571 and 1572. His reputation as a puritan orator was consolidated in the puritan Parliament of 1571, when he spoke (often just before his friend Recorder Fleetwood) on the bill to confirm the articles of religion; against the sequestration of William Strickland* for his activities in the House violating the royal prerogative; on the puritan George Carleton's bill against licences and dispensations; and in favour of the treasons bill, when he commended the provision for excluding James from the succession. The most important of many committees on which he served in this Parliament was that of only four members – all strong puritans – appointed to arrange the religious bills in the best order of precedence. Others of his committees were on the treasons bill (12, 21 Apr., 11 May), church attendance (21 Apr., 19 May), tellers and receivers (23 Apr.), fugitives (24 Apr.), the order of business (26 Apr.), priests disguised as servants (1 May), respite of homage (17 May) and privilege (28 May).[4]

In the first session of the 1572 Parliament, Yelverton was well to the fore in the 'great cause' of Mary Queen of Scots. On 12 May he was one of those chosen by the Commons (Fleetwood and Peter Wentworth were two others) to confer with the Lords, and on Friday 6 June it was he who opened the debate on the second reading of the bill against Mary, objecting to the speed with which the Commons were being forced to deal with the matter, and to many details of the bill itself. Another matter that brought Yelverton to his feet in this session (also Fleetwood and Wentworth) was the question of privilege raised by Robin Snagge, who demanded the names of those who carried tales to the Lords about proceedings in the Commons. Yelverton was concerned lest the reporting of indiscreet speeches should bring disgrace upon the whole Parliament, and went on to suggest an inquiry into talk of bribery in the House. On 26 June he and Fleetwood were the star performers in the debate staged for the benefit of the French diplomatic mission, some of whom were present in the House. Yelverton's committees in this session included those dealing with Mary Queen of Scots (12 May, 6 June), the bill for rites and ceremonies (20 May), the poor (22 May) and various legal matters.[5]

By the time of the 1576 session Yelverton was 'of great wealth', and his behaviour in Parliament became increasingly moderate. After the committal of Peter Wentworth to the Tower, it was by petition rather than by bill that the Commons raised again the subject of religious grievances, and on 29 Feb. Yelverton was appointed a member of the committee to draft this petition, which in the event confined itself to the subject of minor defects in the administration of the Church. He was also a member of the subsidy committee (10 Feb.), various legal and social committees, and the strong committee that met in the afternoon of 12 Mar. to consider the Queen's marriage. In 1581 he again served on the subsidy committee (25 Jan.) and on several legal committees. He also served (with Fleetwood) on a small sub-committee of lawyers to which was delegated the task of drafting a number of bills.[6]

It is interesting that such a man should not have been returned to the Parliaments of 1584, 1586 and 1589 (though Yelverton made at least one appearance at the bar of the House, in the 1584 Parliament in his capacity as legal counsel). But the Northamptonshire knights of the shire in 1584 and 1586 being Privy Councillors of the first rank, even such a great country gentleman as Sir Richard Knightley had to take a borough seat on both occasions. Still, there had been similar competition in 1572, and, in the meantime Yelverton, while remaining recorder of Northampton, had purchased (in 1578, from the Earl of Oxford), a country estate, so that it seems unlikely that he could not have obtained a borough seat if he had wanted one. In 1584 his relative by marriage, Thomas Catesby, sat for Northampton, whether through Yelverton's influence

is not known, but he would hardly have got the seat if Yelverton had wanted it for himself. One wonders, therefore, whether Yelverton perhaps aspired to the county seat to the point where he would rather be out of the Commons than sit for even* such a 'respectable' borough as Northampton. Certainly his pride is obvious in being, in 1593, again, as he put it, 'thrust into the House ... chosen knight of the shire without either my knowledge or my liking'.[7]

By this time Yelverton, a serjeant-at-law and seeking further promotion, came into the category of the 'old, discreet, grave Parliament men', to the disappointment of such as Peter Wentworth, who realized that it would be useless to attempt to recruit him into the small group who were planning to raise the succession question in the House. Appointed to the first standing committee on priveleges and returns, 26 Feb. 1593, he took an active part in the discussion of the Fitzherbert election case, speaking twice on the subject, 1 Mar., and serving on the Commons committee appointed to discuss this with the Lords. His name appears on a number of committees, placed in the journals immediately after the Privy Councillors. As knight of the shire he was included in the subsidy committee, 26 Feb. and another legal committee, 9 Mar.[8]

Elected for one of the Northampton borough seats in 1597, his eldest son Henry taking the other, Yelverton, on 24 Oct., was nominated Speaker by Sir William Knollys, comptroller of the Household. Behind the euphuistic language of his disabling speech, preserved in his own account, can be discerned something of the man:

> ... mean persons can hardly hold the eyes, or enjoy the hearts of a multitude. But yet, neither is the lack of estimation in the face of the world so great disadvantage to this place, or disgrace to myself, as the want of some special favour with her Majesty.

He spoke of his 'timorous and fearful nature' and went on to contrast his 'accustomed pleading in judicial courts' with his new 'cause of so deep and weighty importance':

> There sufficeth plain utterance; here it must be accompanied with exact eloquence; there, sound and naked reason is but sought to be delivered; and here, reason must be clothed with elegant speeches.

Perhaps, in his ornate speeches, over which he took such pains, and of which he was clearly proud, he tried too hard. Despite the beauty of the language, they make difficult reading, and at least one contemporary thought them 'full of elegancies, sweetly delivered, but too full of flattery, too curious and tedious'. Yelverton concluded his disabling speech by expressing his longstanding reluctance to intermeddle with high matters of Parliament.

Then Sir John Fortescue, chancellor of the Exchequer, and one of her Majesty's Privy Council, commending the choice, and not allowing the excuse, the comptroller and he went down to the place where the serjeant sat, and took him, and carried him up, and placed him in the chair.

Three days later, on the occasion of his presentation by the Commons to the Queen, he made, in accordance with custom, a second disabling speech, followed by an elaborate – and masterly – ornamental oration, of which Yelverton again preserved a full text. His account of these proceedings, rather touchingly moving into the first person, ends:

After her Majesty had confirmed me for Speaker, and after that I had ended my oration, her Majesty passing by me, pulled off her glove and gave me her hand to kiss, and said, 'You, sir, you are welcome to the butts, sir', and laid both her hands about my neck, and stayed a good space, and so most graciously departed; and in her privy chamber after, amongst her ladies, said she was sorry she knew me no sooner.[9]

Yelverton's part as Speaker in the debates in the Commons during this Parliament on the vexed question of monopolies; the inclusion in his closing oration on 9 Feb. 1598 of the address of humble thanks for the Queen's most gracious care and favour in the repressing of these abuses; and a detailed consideration of the speech itself appear in print elsewhere. Before the Parliament was dissolved the Queen told him that he had 'so learnedly and so eloquently' defended and 'painfully behaved' himself that his labour deserved 'double hire and thanks', a reference, no doubt, to his getting twice the usual Speaker's fee of £100 per session. This would not have been an extravagant reward for his service in a Parliament sitting from 24 Oct. to 20 Dec. and 11 Jan. to 9 Feb., even though the whole period was one session. His promotion to Queen's serjeant came three months later, but it is a comment on the Queen's frugal policy over honours that he had to wait until the next reign (and the age of 66) for a knighthood.[10]

Though his desire to please the great is obvious: 'I did favour it as much as, with the dignity of my place, I could', he wrote to Cecil about a bill, 'and I am sorry, if you did anything affect it, that it succeeded no better'; though there is no doubt that he did not rise above the standards of his time over such matters as accepting payments for the furtherance of both public and private measures, yet Yelverton must go on record as one of the most able among the Elizabethan lawyer Speakers, whose grasp of procedure at a time when this was becoming settled helped to lead the House of Commons towards its maturity.

As a judge of assize Yelverton served in the 1601 Parliament as an assistant in the Lords, and he is named in the journals a dozen times or so, bringing bills and messages from the Lords. There were one or two complaints about him as a judge, Sir Thomas Posthumous

Hoby* writing to Sir Robert Cecil about 'his very hard dealing', and the president of the council in the north alleging that he twice postponed the York assizes 'for his own private gain in the circuit where he practises'. In June 1600 Yelverton was a commissioner for the trial of the Earl of Essex for his misbehaviour in Ireland, and in the following February his name was put forward by the chief justice to examine some of the less important prisoners taken in the Essex rising in London. Though present at the Earl's arraignment, 19 Feb. 1601, he took no prominent part in the second trial.[11]

Yelverton died 'of very age' 31 Oct. 1612, aged 75, and was buried beside his wife in Easton Maudit church, where there is a monument. Administration was granted to Henry Yelverton 7 Nov. 1612, and £100 was distributed to the poor of the parish. In religion Yelverton was a puritan, described by the preacher Thomas Cartwright as 'the principal wether of the flock, to go before the rest'.[12]

[1] C219/284/27. [2] DNB; Bridges, Northants. ii. 166; Al. Cant. 1(4) p. 489; G. Inn Pens. Bk. 14; Foss, Judges, vi. 203–6; Egerton 2345, f. 25; Somerville, Duchy, i. 475; HMC Hatfield, ix. 390; xv. 223. [3] Cotton, Titus F II, f. 115–16; Neale, Parlts. i. 91–2; Cam. Misc. x. 18–19. [4] D'Ewes, 160–90 passim; CJ, i. 84–93 passim; Trinity, Dublin, anon. jnl. (where the name sometimes appears as Elverton or Ellverton), ff. 9, 12, 24, 35; Parlts. i. 198, 202, 210, 212, 228. [5] D'Ewes, 206, 213, 221, 222; Trinity, Dublin, Thos. Cromwell's jnl., ff. 52–3, 62, 66; CJ, i. 95, 96, 97, 100, 101; Parlts. i. 247, 283–4, 305–6. [6] Lansd. 22, f. 52; CJ, i. 104, 105, 106, 108, 109, 111, 112, 113, 114, 120, 121, 122, 244, 247, 248, 254, 255, 260, 261, 288, 289, 291; Parlts. i. 350, 353, 385–6. [7] D'Ewes, 349; VCH Northants. iv. 13; Add. 48109, f. 16. [8] D'Ewes, 471, 474, 477, 479, 480, 481, 486, 495, 496, 500, 501; Parlts. ii. 258; Townshend, Hist. Colls. 63, 68. [9] Add. 48109, ff. 16, 17, 30; Cam. Misc. x. 11–12. [10] Neale, Commons, 357–62; Parlts. ii. 328–32, 353–4, 364–7; Bull IHR, xii. 25. [11] D'Ewes, 603, 604, 611, 612, 615, 674, 678, 684, 686, 687; Townshend, Hist. Colls. 133, 139, 141, 144, 297–8, 300; HMC Hatfield, ix. 390; xi. 37; CSP Dom. 1601–3, pp. 155–6; Collins, Sidney State Pprs. ii. 199; Lansd. 115, f. 47. [12] PCC admon. act bk. 1612, f. 78; Bridges, Northants. ii. 168; [12]

P.W.H.

YELVERTON, Henry (1566–1630), of Easton Maudit, Northants.

NORTHAMPTON   1597[1], 1604, 1614

b. 29 June 1566, 1st s. of Christopher Yelverton* by Margaret, da. of Thomas Catesby of Whiston. educ. Christ's, Camb. 1581; G. Inn, called. m. Mary, da. of Robert Beale*, 2s. 3da. suc. fa. 1612. Kntd. 1613.

Ancient, G. Inn 1593; Reader, Staple Inn 1595; Autumn reader, G. Inn 1606, Lent 1607; recorder, Northampton 1599, appointed for life 1618; solicitor-gen. 1613–17; attorney-gen. 1617, dismissed 1621; j.c.p. 1625–d.

Yelverton is said to have occupied himself while at Gray's Inn in taking down sermons of Edward Phillips, the puritan preacher, at St. Olave's, Southwark, afterwards printing them, with a dedication to his father, under the title Certain Godly and Learned Sermons. A rising lawyer, he was active in the 1597 Parliament, of which his father was Speaker, sitting on Commons committees concerned with monopolies (10 Nov.), Northampton (16 Nov.), the poor (22 Nov.), draining the fens (25 Nov., 3 Dec.), husbandry and tillage and the export of sheepskins (26 Nov.), maltsters (7 Dec., 12 Jan.), the defence of the realm (16 Jan.), dress (19 Jan.), tellers and receivers (23 Jan.), and the better execution of judgment (25 Jan.).

By the time of the elections to the 1601 Parliament, Yelverton had succeeded his father as recorder of Northampton, but the town chose two other local lawyers. He regained a borough seat in the first Parliament of James I. He died 24 Jan. 1630, having made his will the previous 25 Aug.[2]

[1] C219/284/27. [2] DNB; G. Inn Pens. Bk. i. 100, 111, 138, 178, 208; Northampton Recs. i. 129; ii. 103–5; Collinson thesis; D'Ewes, 555, 557, 561, 563, 564, 567, 569, 578, 581, 583, 586, 587; HMC Hatfield, vii. 477; Townshend, Hist. Colls. 108, 109, 113; PCC 55 Scroope.

P.W.H.

YEO, Leonard (by 1512–86), of Cheapside, London; Totnes, Devon; later of Exeter, Devon.

TOTNES   1555, 1558, 1559

b. by 1512, 2nd s. of Nicholas Yeo of Heanton Satchville, Devon by Joan, da. of Richard Lybbe of Tavistock, Devon. m. (1) ?27 Oct. 1534, Arminell (will dated 8 July 1545), da. of Christopher Beresford of London, wid. of John Broke (d.1533) of London, at least 1s. 2da.; (2) Denise (will dated '1561'), da. of William Dotyn of Harberton, Devon.[1]

Member, Mercers Co. London by 1533; mayor, Totnes 1558–9, 1570–1.

Born in Tavistock, Yeo was apprenticed to a London mercer, whose widow he married and whose business he took over. For some unascertained reason – possibly his stepson wished to continue the London firm – Yeo moved to Totnes, where he served as MP and mayor. In the last year or two of his life when he was, in his own words, 'not only a man of extreme age, but also very weak and feeble of body and remembrance' he had to defend a court of requests case brought by two children of his first wife, who alleged that he was detaining their property to the value of £800. Yeo argued that they 'of long time have held themselves well content therewith until now of late'. By this time he had retired to Exeter, where he had evidently had some property since at least 1542 when one of his daughters was baptized there. In his will, made April 1586, he described himself as of Exeter, and instructed the sole executor, his son George, 'upon my blessing to use my tenants well'. He left 40s. to the poor of Tavistock. Yeo died 30 May 1586, worth over £1,000 and his will was proved that October.[2]

[1] Vis. Devon, ed. Colby, 217; PCC 21 Holgate, 51 Windsor; NRA 5984 (citing Devon RO, S12 M/FY 35, 37–40, 44, 67); Req.2/124/59.

Vis. Devon, ed. Vivian, 834–5 compounds the errors in Vis. Devon (Harl. Soc. vi), 324. [2] Trans. Dev. Assoc. xxxii. 438; Western Antiq. ix. 152; London Rep. 13(2), f. 354a; CPR, 1560–3, p. 389; CSP Dom. 1547–80, p. 638; Req. 2/124/59; Wards 7/21/183; PCC 51 Windsor.

N.M.F./A.D.K.H.

YERWORTH, John (d.1587), of Chester.

CHESTER   1563

m. Elizabeth, da. of Hugh Massey of Denfield, Cheshire by Jane, da. of Sir Thomas Smith of Chester, 1s.

Clerk of the pentice (town clerk), Chester sometime between 1553 and 1562, freeman 1556, sheriff 1558–9, jt. baron of Chester exchequer 1563, auditor 1568; receiver-gen. of Cheshire and Chester by April 1558–c.1562.

Possibly originating from Monmouthshire, and perhaps having had some legal training, Yerworth was an active official of Chester and a leading local personality. His marriage into a county family must have increased his standing but he sat in Parliament only once and left no trace upon the records. He was given a good report by his bishop in 1564, sent to talk to the lord admiral about Chester's privileges on 16 June 1584 and died 29 Apr. 1587.

Vis. Cheshire (Harl. Soc. lix), 171; R. H. Morris, Chester in the Plantagenet and Tudor Reigns, 204–5, 583; Lancs. and Cheshire Rec. Soc. li. 32; APC, vi. 308; Ormerod, Chester, i. 83; Genealogist, n.s. xiii. 91; Chester RO ass. bk. 1, ff. 119, 120, 180, 186v, 191; CPR, 1558–60, p. 112; 1560–3, p. 311; Cam. Misc. ix(3), p. 74; Rylands Eng. ms 311; Cheshire Sheaf, ii. 185.

N.M.F.

YORK, Sir John (d.1569), of York and St. Stephen Walbrook, London.

BOROUGHBRIDGE   1559

3rd s. of John York by Katherine Patterdale. m. Anne, da. of Robert Smyth of London, 11s. inc. Peter* 4da. Kntd. Oct. 1549.[1]

Assay master, Tower I mint 1544–5; under-treasurer, Southwark mint June 1545–51, Tower I mint 1551–2; master of King's woods in southern parts by Aug. 1547–d.; Admiralty official by Feb. 1550–?3; j.p. Mdx. 1547; sheriff, London and Mdx. 1549–50; commr. sewers, Essex and Mdx. 1554.[2]

York's family were merchants of the staple, trading in London and Calais, and maintaining connexions with their native city. By exploiting his position as a merchant trading abroad, York was able to render considerable service to the Crown by raising loans, manipulating the exchange, etc. His post in the mint may have been in recognition of these services, or he may have secured it through the patronage of the Earl of Warwick, with whom he had a common interest in lands belonging to the former abbeys of Byland and Fountains. York undoubtedly supported the Henrician position: in 1535 he condemned 'the malicious intent of the Bishop of Rome' and arrested a 'lewd friar' for delivering slanderous sermons. Certainly one who was a known follower of Warwick, who had been sheriff of London in 1549 and at whose house the Privy Council used to meet in the period preceding the arrest of the Duke of Somerset, would have held religious views acceptable to the protestant temper of the regime.[3]

As a mint official both at Southwark and the Tower, York was allowed to provide bullion at prices higher than those generally in force, and was thus able to make a personal profit. In 1551 he and Sir Nicholas Throckmorton* handled the beginning of the restoration of the coinage and many of the coins then issued were stamped with Y, one of York's mint marks. His conduct in his other offices was of less importance. His zeal in cutting down trees as master of the King's woods earned him more than one rebuke from the Privy Council and his office in the Admiralty is known only because in February 1550 he was ordered to sell a consignment of prize sugar. His public service came to an end with the death of Edward VI, but he had already lost his mint office. His advice on foreign coins was sought in 1553, when the coinage was again being restored, but his association with Northumberland's regime had been too well known for him to be employed again, and in fact he spent some months of 1553 in the Tower, his property sequestrated. Thereafter he confined himself to his trading activities, investing in western exploration, and in the German and Netherlands trade. In 1555 he became one of the 24 assistants of the newly-formed company of merchant adventurers of England for the discovery of unknown lands, under the governorship of Sebastian Cabot.[4]

The reason for York's seeking election to Parliament for the first time in 1559 is unknown. Perhaps it was to lend support to the new protestant regime. Sir Ambrose Cave*, chancellor of the duchy of Lancaster, presumably nominated him at Boroughbridge, perhaps at the instance of Sir Robert Dudley*, in whose service one of his sons was in 1569.[5]

York next appears in Antwerp, in June 1560, buying gunpowder and saltpetre and earning the unfavourable attention of Sir Thomas Gresham, who was trying to monopolize the English trade in these commodities. In October of that year York proffered his advice on the projected re-coinage and on the manipulation of the exchanges to Sir William Cecil, but Cecil presumably felt that with Gresham's services at his command he could ignore York. Concerning the remaining eight years of York's life, little information survives. In January 1566, as a freeman of the Merchant Taylors' Company, he contributed £6 13s. 4d. toward the building of the Royal Exchange.[6]

York made his will in April 1562. He shared his lands, mainly in Yorkshire, among his sons. The East Riding property, at Heslerton, Peddelthorpe, Rudston, Sherburn and Sledmere went to younger sons, but the large estates concentrated in Craven and Nidderdale passed intact to his eldest surviving son Peter. A bequest of 1,000 marks was made to his daughter Jane, and the residue of his movable goods to his wife, the executrix. York died in January or February 1569 and was buried in the church of St. Stephen Walbrook, in which parish he had lived since 1546 when he had bought a house there from Sir Thomas Pope[†].[7]

[1] *Vis. Yorks.* (Harl. Soc. xvi), 357–8; *Vis. London,* (Harl. Soc. i), 81; *DNB.* [2] J. Craig, *The Mint,* 112–13, 115, 116; *LP Hen. VIII,* xix(1), p. 493; xx(1), pp. 301, 529; Richardson, *Ct. of Augmentations,* 154, 155, 220, 305; *APC,* ii. 398–9; Excheq. K.R. Acc. Var. 302(27); Treasury, Misc. Var. 190 nos. 4, 5; *CPR, 1547–8,* p. 86; *1554–5,* p. 108. [3] Clode, *Early Hist. Merchant Taylors Co.* i. 150; *LP Hen. VIII,* ix. p. 88; *CPR, 1547–8,* pp. 209, 234–5; *APC,* i. 551; ii. 337, 383–4, 388; iii. 84, 109, 219, 223, 312, 421; iv. 42. [4] The account of York's mint career is based on information supplied by Dr. C. E. Challis; *APC,* ii, iii, iv, passim; *CPR, 1547–8,* p. 368; *1549–51,* pp. 345, 348; *1550–3,* p. 301; *1553–4,* pp. 316, 411; *1554–5,* pp. 56–7; *CSP Dom. 1547–80,* p. 30; Oman, *Coinage of England,* 259, 263–4, 266–7; Ruding, *Coinage of Gt. Britain,* i. 319. [5] *CSP Dom.* Add. 1566–79, p. 156. [6] *CSP For.* 1560–1, p. 119; Burgon, *Gresham,* i. 325; *CSP Dom. 1547–80,* p. 161; Clode, 228, 251. [7] PCC 4 Sheffelde; *N. Country Wills* (Surtees Soc. cxxi), 38–9; *Reg. St. Stephen Walbrook* (Harl. Soc. xlix), i. 80; J. G. White, *Hist. Walbrook,* 68–9.

I.C.

YORK, Peter (c.1542–89), of Gouthwaite, Yorks.

RIPON   1589

b. c.1542, 2nd but 1st surv. s. of Sir John York*. educ. Peterhouse, Camb. 1555; M. Temple 1557. m. Nov. 1560, Elizabeth, da. of Sir William Ingleby of Ripley, 4s. 1da. suc. fa. 1569.

York inherited, and extended by purchase, extensive estates in Nidderdale and Craven, as well as acquiring his own establishment upon a fortunate marriage. He had town houses in York and London, but made no attempt to establish himself in his father's mercantile and financial circles. He was never put on the commission of the peace, probably because, unlike his father, he was at heart a Catholic. His wife was an open recusant, one younger brother was in arms with the rebels in 1569, and another died a Catholic in the service of Spain. Why, with this background, York should suddenly have wished to be returned to Parliament when in his mid-forties has not been ascertained, though it is perhaps worth noting that his father, too, made but one appearance in Parliament when of mature years. Peter York's patron at Ripon was in all probability his wife's uncle Sir William Mallory*, high steward of the borough. York was appointed to the subsidy committee on 11 Feb. 1589. He was buried on 9 Apr. following at St. Stephen Walbrook, near his parents, and his will was proved that July.

Vis. Yorks. (Harl. Soc. xvi), 172, 195–6, 357; *Vis. London* (Harl. Soc. i), 81; C142/151/45, 221/94; Whittaker, *Deanery of Craven*, 513, 532; *Richmondshire*, ii. 111, 350; *Yorks. Arch. Jnl.* xxxiii. 389; *Recusant Roll 1592–3* (Cath. Rec. Soc. xviii), 78, 108; *Proc. Leeds Philosoph. and Lit. Soc.* x(6), pp. 210, 223; *CSP Dom.* Add. 1566–79, p. 156; D'Ewes, 431; *Reg. St. Stephen Walbrook* (Harl. Soc. xlix), i. 83; *York Wills* (Yorks. Arch. Soc. rec. ser. xxii), 145.

P.W.H.

YOUNG, John I (by 1519–89), of Bristol, Glos.; London, and Melbury Sampford, Dorset.

OLD SARUM	1547
PLYMOUTH	1555
DEVIZES	1559
WEST LOOE	1563
OLD SARUM	1571

b. by 1519, 1st surv. s. of Hugh Young of Bristol and Castle Combe, Wilts. by his w. Alice. *m.* c.1563, Joan, da. of John Wadlam of Merrifield, Som., wid. of Sir Giles Strangways* of Melbury Sampford, 1s. 2da. *suc.* fa. 1534. Kntd. 1574.

Sewer of the chamber by 1546; collector of customs and subsidies, Bristol Mar. 1559; sheriff, Dorset 1569–70; j.p. Dorset, Som. from c.1573, ?Wilts. from c.1583; keeper, Castle Cary park, Som. and Melbury park, Dorset aft. 1563.[1]

There being a number of namesakes it is impossible to be certain that it was the same man who represented all the above constituencies. The matter has been decided on a balance of probabilities.

On this basis John Young appears as a Bristol man who succeeded his father before attaining his majority, and who obtained a post in the royal household by way of his service under Edward Seymour, Earl of Hertford, who was high steward of Bristol. Later Young appears as a servant of Seymour's successor, William Herbert†, 1st Earl of Pembroke, who could have returned him for Devizes in 1559 and have obtained him his appointment as collector of customs at Bristol. Next, Young married the widow of an improvident gentleman, which must, nevertheless, have raised his social status and brought him a country estate. (Both Strangways and Young had voted against a government measure in the 1555 Parliament.) In the Parliament of 1563, Young represented the Cornish borough of West Looe and was appointed to the succession committee 31 Oct. 1566. His remaining recorded parliamentary activities, such as they were, were in the 1571 Parliament, to which he had been returned for the Pembroke borough of Old Sarum, though by this time the 2nd Earl of Pembroke had succeeded to the title. On 11 Apr., described in the journals as 'Mr. Young of Bristol' he spoke up for the lesser merchants against an oligarchy attempting to promote a bill to restrict trading privileges to themselves. He disliked the subtle means whereby the statute was procured without 'the consent of the ...

commons'. He was appointed to the committee for the bill the next day. He intervened again, 21 Apr., this time on the subsidy, but any significance has been lost, for the anonymous journal notes only, at the very end of that vestigial chronicle:

> Mr. John Young offered the house some speech and, licence being obtained, he said to this effect, that the burden of the subsidy and charge by loans oft imposed by the prince upon us, and the charge of the richest and most noblest prince being considered, it were not amiss if it ...

Young died at Bristol 4 Sept. 1589, at the 'Great House' built by him on the site of a Carmelite friary. Queen Elizabeth was received there in 1574.[2]

[1] *Bristol and Glos. Arch. Soc. Trans.* xv. 227–45; *Vis. Dorset* (Harl. Soc. xx), 86; *CPR*, 1558–60, pp. 49, 215; *LP Hen. VIII*, xxi. (1). p. 569; (2), p. 346; St. Ch. 5/Y1/9, 38. [2] Guildford Mus. Loseley 1331/2; *CJ*, i. 84; D'Ewes, 127, 160, 162, 178; Trinity, Dublin, anon. jnl. f. 36; C142/222/51; *Bristol and Glos. Arch. Soc. Trans.* xli. 121, 137.

P.W.H.

YOUNG, John II

MARLBOROUGH	1559

The 'John Younge, gent.' who represented Marlborough in the first Parliament of this period has been assumed to be the John Young, who, by October 1555, was keeping a tavern in Marlborough. Early in Elizabeth's reign he and his wife Margaret sold a house in the borough.

CPR, 1555–7, p. 117; *Wilts. N. and Q.* iv. 404, 455.

N.M.F.

YOUNG, John III

NEW SHOREHAM	1586, 1589, 1597

The identity of the John Young who sat for New Shoreham in three Elizabethan Parliaments has not been established. The name is common in contemporary records: in Sussex alone at least eight John Youngs have left their mark, but not one of them had a known connexion with New Shoreham, or lived in its vicinity. The problem of identification is complicated by the borough's confused parliamentary history in the last two decades of the reign. The Howards, Dukes of Norfolk and later Earls of Arundel, owners of the borough, enjoyed control of elections for a long time, but in 1585 Philip Howard, Earl of Arundel, was sent to the Tower and it is difficult to estimate to what extent the family's local influence survived. Probably it became easier for local gentlemen to be returned, as occurred in 1593 and 1601, and John Young may well be in this category. If so, two possible candidates suggest themselves, one from Petworth, the other from Chichester.

YOUNG, John (*d.* c.1599), of Petworth, Suss.

s. of John Young of Petworth (*d.* c.1558), by Thomasine, da. of John Kymet of Lewes, wid. of John Taylor of Horsham and of John Merlot or Marlott of Horsham.

William Young, who died in 1553, was a Petworth clothier who invested some of his profits in land, including the manor of Ambersham, near Petworth. William Young's son John (*d.*1557/8), married four times and his son by his third wife, also John, may have been the New Shoreham MP. This man seems to have carried on the family business at Petworth, where he died about 1599. Nothing more has been discovered about him, though he may have been a servant of Lady Dacre, mentioned in her will in 1594.[1]

YOUNG, John, of Chichester, Suss.

Customer, Chichester by 1586; ?dep. v.-adm. Suss., commr. sewers 1604.

This man is first heard of in 1581 as proprietor of the former Greyfriars church in Chichester. In August and September 1591 the Privy Council instructed him to prevent the illegal export of ordnance. By 1594 he was in the Gatehouse prison for not furnishing accounts and for imposing his own arbitrary duties. All the same, he retained the office into James I's reign. The award of £4,000 to John Young (if it is the same man), together with George Somers of Chichester, as compensation for the loss of a ship, indicates that he also traded on his own account.[2]

Other John Youngs were a man who sat for Rye in 1604, whose interests were confined to East Sussex, and another who was bailiff of the barony of Lewes in 1560. Still others lived at Wadhurst, Warnham and Malling, all in Sussex.[3]

The possibility that the Member was not a Sussex man, but the nominee of a court patron, cannot be ruled out, but here again no satisfactory candidate has been found. The eminent naval captain who fought against the Armada and later sought favours from the Earl of Essex is hardly likely to have sat, being at Plymouth fitting out his ship for the Drake expedition to Lisbon while the 1589 Parliament was in session. There was also a John Young who was a messenger of the Queen's chamber in 1587 and who was granted the reversion of the office of porter of the great wardrobe in 1608.[4]

[1] J. Comber, *Suss. Genealogies, Lewes Centre*, 144; *Vis. Suss.* (Harl. Soc. liii), 185; PCC 1 Tashe; *VCH Hants*, iii. 78; *Suss. N. and Q.* ii. 182; *Suss. Rec. Soc.* xliii. 246, 248; Chichester consistory ct. wills, vol. 9, f. 17; Dallaway, *Suss.* i. 280. [2] Lansd. 49, f. 38; 60, f. 60; 75, f. 206; 77, f. 184; 115, ff. 196–7; 144, f. 25; *Suss. Arch. Colls.* li. 33; *APC*, xiv. 76; xxi. 417, 431–2; *HMC Hatfield*, ix. 371; *CSP Dom.* 1603–10, p. 164; 1611–18, pp. 19, 108; E. Suss. RO, Rye Recs. 89. [3] *CSP Dom.* 1547–80, p. 159 et passim; 1581–90, p. 27; Add. 1580–1625, p. 135; *CSP For.* 1562, passim; *Suss. Arch. Colls.* xiii. 182 seq.; *APC*, iv. 391, 395; xiii.

417; PCC 10 Parker, 8 Scroope; J. Comber, *Suss. Genealogies, Horsham Centre*, 388–9; *Vis. Hants* (Harl. Soc. lxiv), 112. [4] SP12/259/48; Monson, *Tracts* (Hak. Soc.) i. 182; iv. 202–27; J. K. Laughton, *Defeat of Span. Armada* (Navy Rec. Soc.), i. 158; ii. 287, 337; *CSP Dom.* 1581–90, p. 449; 1591–4, p. 421; 1603–10, p. 396; Add. 1566–79, pp. 387–8; *APC*, xii. 212; xv. 332, 334, 368.

M.R.P.

ZOUCHE, Francis (*d.*1600), of Ansty and later of Shaftesbury, Wilts.

SHAFTESBURY	1586
HEYTESBURY	1589
HINDON	1593

s. of Sir John Zouche* of Ansty. *m.* Philippa, 6th da. of George Ludlow of Hill Deverill, 2s. 1da.
J.p. Wilts. from c.1583; keeper, Mere park 1586.

Zouche may have been a servant of the 1st Earl of Pembroke, who, in his will, asked his son to grant him an annuity; on the other hand Zouche's brother was in Ireland with Ralegh, and it was Ralegh who obtained Zouche the keepership of Mere park in succession to his father. Either way, Zouche was brought in for Shaftesbury by the 2nd Earl of Pembroke. The Ralegh connexion may have helped at Heytesbury, controlled in 1589 by John Thynne*, whose stepson was Carew Ralegh*. Zouche presumably came in at Hindon on his own local standing. He could have sat on a committee concerning cloth, appointed 15 Mar. 1593.

By 1595 Zouche was heavily in debt. He poured out his troubles in a long letter to Cecil about 'some persons in whom I had put great confidence', 'great charge of children' and 'many outlawries and suits pronounced against me'. In February 1594 he had had to sell Ansty for £3,250, and he still owed £1,800 on which he was paying £150 p.a. interest. His wife refused to realise money on her jointure, and had gone to court to petition the Queen about his disposal of Ansty. Zouche 'for my good, her own credit and the better comfort of our children', asked that she be sent home promptly. After being compelled in 1598 to sell to John Hele I* a quarter share in the manor of Wreyland, Devon, Zouche lived in Shaftesbury, where he died in 1600, when his three children were granted administration of his goods.

DNB (Zouche, Richard); Gabriel thesis; Roberts thesis; Harl. 1565, f. 2; *Vis Wilts.* (Harl. Soc. cv, cvi), 223 seq.; C142/209/44; PCC 15 Lyon; *Pembroke Survey* (Roxburghe Club), 558; *CSP Ire.* 1574–85, p. 331; D'Ewes, 501; *HMC Hatfield*, v. 158–9; *CSP Dom.* 1581–90, p. 711; *Wreyland Docs.* ed. Torr, 129–31; PCC admon. act bk. 1600, f. 55; *Som. and Dorset N. and Q.* ii. 271.

P.W.H.

ZOUCHE, John (c.1564–1610), of Codnor, Derbys.

DERBYSHIRE	1589

b. c.1564, s. and h. of Sir John Zouche† of Codnor by

Eleanor, da. of Richard Whalley†. *educ.* G. Inn 1582. *m.* Maria, da. of ?Sir Henry Berkeley of Bruton, Som., 1s. at least 2da. *suc.* fa. 1586. Kntd. 23 Apr. 1603.

J.p. Derbys. by 1594-5.

Zouche was elected knight of the shire to the first Parliament called after he succeeded his father. He left no mark on the surviving records of the House of Commons, and within a year or two he had been outlawed on two counts of debt and was involved in litigation over a third. He was forced to assign his profitable iron works, Laskoe Mill Forge, to Sir Francis Willoughby, subject to £200 a year for his and his wife's maintenance. In 1597, two of his debts, totalling £380, were still outstanding. Probably as a last resort, he entered into an agreement with a Captain Weymouth on the latter's return from a voyage to Virginia in 1605, to found a settlement there, but nothing came of this in his own lifetime. Zouche managed to retain Codnor and estates at Alfreton, Butterly, Heanor and Ripley until his death in April 1610. He was buried in the chancel of Heanor church on 3 Apr. His heir sold up and emigrated to Virginia.

Glover, *Derbys.* (1836), ii(1), pp. 309, 312; PCC 31 Windsor; C2.Eliz. Z1/1, 12; Lansd. 85, f. 76; C. M. Andrews, *Col. Period of American Hist.* i. 80; *CSP Col.* 1574-1660, pp. 130, 201, 217; C142/332/164; *Derbys. Arch. and Nat. Hist. Soc. Jnl.* xxxi. 37.

B.D.

ZOUCHE, Sir John (d. 1585), of Ansty, Wilts.

HINDON	1547*
SHAFTESBURY	1559

s. of John, 8th Lord Zouche of Harringworth, Northants. prob. by 1st w. Dorothy, da. of Sir William Capell† of London. *m.* by c.1545, Catherine, da. of Sir George St. Leger of Annery, Devon, wid. of George Courtenay of Powderham, Devon, 3 or 4s. inc. Francis*. Kntd. 10 Nov. 1549, KB Jan. 1559.[1]

Warden of Gillingham forest and bailiff of town and manor of Gillingham, Dorset 1539; esquire of the body extraordinary 1535/6; keeper of Mere park, Wilts.; steward and bailiff of duchy of Cornwall manor of Mere 1539; j.p. Wilts. from c.1559; sheriff 1559-60.[2]

Zouche presumably gained his Shaftesbury seat through the 1st Earl of Pembroke, to whom he may have been recommended by Sir John Rogers, knight of the shire for Dorset in 1559, and a relative of the Zouches by marriage; Pembroke was later chosen as arbitrator in a lawsuit involving Zouche and Rogers's widow. By Elizabeth's accession Zouche owned considerable property in Wiltshire: an assessment of 1565 charged him on £100 in lands. Early in Elizabeth's reign he was buying land in Devon: his inquisition post mortem mentions the manors of Kingskerswell, Wreyland and Barton.[3]

Under Edward VI Zouche was granted an annuity,

confirmed and increased to £100 by Philip and Mary in consideration of his service to Henry VIII, Edward VI, and themselves. Most of the information about Zouche after 1558 is concerned with Wiltshire, but he was also active in Dorset. The tenants of the manor of Gillingham sued him in the Exchequer for various 'oppressions'; he was acquitted and awarded costs of 100 marks. After a tithes dispute in 1584, he brought an action for slander against the vicar of Gillingham. Dorest also figures in the one reference to him in the journals of the House of Commons: on 16 Feb. 1559 he was put in charge of the bill to tax Frenchmen living in that county, and in Somerset, for the benefit of Melcombe Regis. A few years later he served on the Dorset commission to inquire into breaches of the Act about the keeping of sheep.[4]

In Wiltshire he served as an active official for over 20 years. At the beginning of Elizabeth's reign he was one of those appointed to release prisoners committed to Salisbury gaol by the episcopal officers, and as a 'furtherer earnest' of true religion he advised the bishop of Salisbury on the religious persuasion of local justices of the peace. From 1559 to 1581, and perhaps later, he served regularly on the Wiltshire commission of the peace, his name, from 1575 to 1578, taking precedence in quarter sessions records over everyone but Pembroke himself. His duties included regular attendance at the musters, where his last recorded appearance was as late as 1581. Outside his official career, almost all that is known of him concerns lawsuits. He was personally involved in at least two Star Chamber cases, and in a third strongly supported his distant relative, Arthur, 14th Lord Grey of Wilton, in a dispute with John Fortescue I*. A member of the west-country group of protestants, he was an overseer of the will of his stepson Sir William Courtenay†, and an 'assured friend' of Charles Morison*: it may have been Morison, a stepson of the 2nd Earl of Bedford, who persuaded Bedford to write to Burghley in 1577, asking for the Queen's consent to a renewal of some leases to Zouche. He died on 30 May 1585. The overseers of his will, made in August 1583, were Giles Estcourt* and Lawrence Hyde I*.[5]

[1] Harl. 1565, f. 2; *CP*, xii(2), p. 948; Hoare, *Wilts.* Alderbury, 207; *Vis. Wilts. 1623*, ed. Marshall, 50; *Vis. Wilts.* (Harl. Soc. cv, cvi), 223 seq.; *DNB* (Zouche, Richard); PCC 30 Brudenell; C142/209/44; *EHR*, xxv. 553. [2] *CPR*, 1557-8, p. 312; 1558-60, pp. 86, 103; *LP Hen. VIII*, ii(1), p. 872; xiv(1), p. 74; xvi. p. 727; *Wilts. Arch. Mag.* xxix. 241. [3] C33/33, f. 211v; Harl. 1111, ff. 1-6; *LP Hen. VIII*, xv. p. 341; *CPR*, 1558-60, p. 405; C142/209/44. [4] *LP Hen. VIII*, xvi. p. 727; *CPR*, 1554-5, p. 172; 1557-8, p. 312; 1563-6, p. 260; Hutchins, *Dorset*, iii. 621; *DKR*, xxviii. 205; *CJ*, i. 54. [5] *APC*, vii. 34; x. 28; xiii. 165; *Cam. Misc.* ix(3), p. 38; *DNB* (Zouche, Edward; Zouche, Richard); *Wilts. Arch. Soc. recs. br.* iv passim; *CSP Dom.* 1547-80, pp. 335, 341; St. Ch. 5A27/23; S19/33; T. Fortescue, Lord Clermont, *Fam. of Fortescue*, 314-25; Add. 40629, f. 97; *HMC Hatfield*, ii. 150; C142/209/44; PCC 30 Brudenell; Roberts thesis.

N.M.F.

ZOUCHE, Richard

HINDON   1584

The 'Richard Sowche gent.' who was returned for Hindon in 1584 was, in all probability, one of two cousins and namesakes.

EITHER

yr. s. of Richard, 9th Lord Zouche of Harringworth, prob. by 2nd w. Margaret, da. of John Cheney of West Woodhay, Berks.

    Gent. pens. 1564–73/7

Having inherited some of his father's property at Wincanton, Somerset, Zouche ran through it within the next 12 years, and thenceforth depended upon the Crown. In November 1567, described as a gentleman pensioner, he received, ostensibly for services rendered, a licence to export 1,000 tons of double beer from London for three years. It was probably he who, three years later, acted as a bearer at the funeral of the 1st Earl of Pembroke, whose client he may thus have been. He is next heard of, in July 1578, being sent to Ireland, where he had evidently seen service already and where on this occasion he may have met Colonel John Zouche, of the Derbyshire house, and also perhaps, as we shall see, his namesake from Wiltshire. His spell of soldiering in Ireland lends colour to his identification with the man whose treacherous career was to sully the name of Zouche during the closing years of the reign. A kinsman of Edward, 11th Lord Zouche, who in 1603 denounced him to Robert Cecil, this Richard Zouche went to serve in the Netherlands with Leicester, only to join in Roland Yorke's defection at Zutphen in 1586. After several years' campaigning with the Spaniards, he returned to England in 1598, was imprisoned and then banished to the Netherlands, whence, after killing a man, he came back a year or two later to undergo further spells of imprisonment. His end has not been traced.[1]

OR

b. c.1555, s. of Edward Zouche of Pitton, Wilts. by Christiana, da. of William Chudley of Ashton, Devon. m. aft. 1580, Bridget, da. of Robert Drury of Hawstead, Suff., 4s. 1da. suc. fa. 1 Dec. 1580.[2]

By contrast, the life of this man was brief, respectable and dull. Inheriting a patrimony, the manor of Pitton, near Salisbury, which had been conveyed to his father and mother by Edward's brother Sir John Zouche* of Ansty, and which was hardly greater than that spendthrift had started with (it rated Edward Zouche at only £10 in the subsidy book of 1576), Richard Zouche was to leave it intact to his own heir. He did nothing, however, to augment it and he was to make no mark in local or national affairs; that was left to the Zouches of Ansty. His inconspicuousness makes it the more surprising that Richard Zouche should have allied himself in marriage,

not with a minor local family, but with the house of Drury in Suffolk. This was not, to be sure, a lucrative match, for Bridget, one of the eight children of the Robert Drury who died prematurely in 1558, must have brought a slender dowry; but an alliance at once politically advantageous and geographically remote calls for explanation. With no evidence of a previous connexion between the families, a possible point of contact presents itself in Ireland. In the late 1570s the Drury family was active there: Sir William Drury*, Bridget's great-uncle, was president of Munster and afterwards chief justice at Dublin, and more than one of his relatives served there with him. If Richard Zouche of Pitton, then in his early twenties, had gone over at this time, as both his cousin and his kinsman John Zouche of Codnor did, it might well have been the prelude to his marriage, which took place soon after 1580 and was doubtless helped forward by his father's death at the close of that year. From his marriage until his death, Richard and Bridget Zouche seem to have lived quietly at Pitton. Three sons and a daughter were born to them there, the eldest son on 7 Aug. 1583, but none of the boys can be traced at a university or an inn of court. All the children were under age when their father died on 22 Jan. 1600, ten days after making his will. He commended his soul to God and asked to be buried near his parents' grave in the parish church, to which he bequeathed 5s. for repairs. His sons Walter, John and Robert were to receive £20 each on reaching the age of 24 and his daughter Frances £40 at the 'full age' of 20; the residue was to pass to his widow and his heir William, whom he appointed executors. His trusted friend Robert Bower, the Salisbury lawyer whose daughter Hester was contracted to William, was to oversee the performance of the will and to have the testator's white nag. From the inquest, taken at Hindon on 29 Mar. 1600, we learn that William and Hester Zouche had already been enfeoffed with Pitton.[3]

The matter of who was returned for Hindon in 1584 is complicated by uncertainty as to the patronage involved. Hindon belonged to the bishop of Winchester, who in 1584 was Thomas Cooper, his episcopate having begun that March. The man returned for the senior seat in 1584, Dr. Valentine Dale, was probably of his choosing, and if Cooper also nominated to the second seat, Richard Zouche of Pitton is much the more likely to have filled it; the protestantism of his uncle Sir John, still a power in the shire, would have commended itself to Cooper, while Sir William Drury, who was himself to sit for Suffolk, may have lent his brother-in-law support. But if, as is possible, the 2nd Earl of Pembroke was trying to get a foot in the door at Hindon, the choice is at least as likely to have fallen on Richard Zouche, courtier, pensioner, and perhaps ex-servant of Wilton, as on his younger and obscurer cousin. It is to be observed, however, that when Dale, having got in at Chichester, vacated the Hindon seat, he was replaced in it by young John Marvyn, who clearly owed that privilege to his uncle Sir James Marvyn *; and it is this circumstance which, by seeming to imply that the bishop, with Zouche as his own nominee, was prepared to accept Marvyn for the contingent vacancy, perhaps tips the scale in favour of Richard Zouche of Pitton.

[1] CPR, 1558–60, p. 11; 1560–3, pp. 133, 413; 1563–6, p. 370; 1566–9, p. 40; Lansd. 83, f. 215; Wilts. Arch. Mag. xviii. 128–30; APC, x. 290, 292; xxi. 108; xxix. 224, 234, 506; HMC Hatfield, ii. 416, 432; x. 5; xv. 185–6; HMC Laing, i. 104; HMC De L'Isle and Dudley, iii. 35. [2] Wilts. Vis. Peds. (Harl. Soc. cv, cvi), 225; PCC 17 Wallop. [3] Wilts. N. and Q. v. 175; Two Taxation Lists (Wilts. Arch. Soc. recs. br. x), 128; A. Campling, Hist. Drury Fam. 50; C142/260/155; PCC 17 Wallop.

S.T.B.